Time-Saver Standards for Building Types

Other McGraw-Hill Books of Interest

Time-Saver Standards for Building Types

Third Edition

Edited by

JOSEPH De CHIARA
and
JOHN HANCOCK CALLENDER

MCGRAW-HILL PUBLISHING COMPANY

New York St. Louis San Francisco Auckland Bogotá
Caracas Hamburg Lisbon London Madrid Mexico Milan
Montreal New Delhi Oklahoma City Paris San Juan
São Paulo Singapore Sydney Tokyo Toronto

Library of Congress Cataloging-in-Publication Data

De Chiara, Joseph, date
    Time-saver standards for building types / edited by Joseph
De Chiara and John Hancock Callender.—3rd ed.
        p.   cm.
    ISBN 0-07-016279-4
    1. Modular coordination (Architecture)   2. Building materials—
Standards.   I. Callender, John Hancock.   II. Title.
    NA2760.D42   1990
    729' .2—dc20   89-39819

234567890   HAL/HAL   8954321

ISBN 0-07-016279-4

The editors for this book were Joel Stein and Stephen M. Smith, and the production supervisor
was Suzanne W. Babeuf.

Printed and bound by Arcata Graphics/Halliday.

For more information about other McGraw-Hill materials,
call 1-800-2-MCGRAW in the United States. In other
countries, call your nearest McGraw-Hill office.

Contents

Contributors xiii
Organizations xv
Preface to the Third Edition xvii

1. RESIDENTIAL 1

Dimensions of the Human Figure 3
Basic Activities 5
Living Areas 6
Living Rooms 7
    Furniture 7
    Furniture Sizes 8
    Furniture Arrangements 9
    Furniture Sizes and Clearances 16
Dining Areas 17
Combined Living-Dining Spaces 27
Combined Dining Area-Kitchen 28
Bedrooms 29
Combined Living-Sleeping Areas 41
Home Office or Study 43
Kitchens 44
    Adaptable 53
Laundry Rooms 62
Bathrooms 69
    Handicapped Lavatory/Water Closet 80
    Adaptable 81
Closets 86
Apartments 98
Apartment Buildings 107
    Central Laundry Rooms 119
Housing Densities 121
Housing for the Elderly 126
Housing for the Handicapped 140
Group Homes 159
Senior Citizens' Center 162
Mobile Homes and Parks 169
Youth Hostels 180
Site Planning 186

2. EDUCATIONAL 201

Nursery Schools 203
Children's Center 207
Child Care Centers 208

Contents

Elementary and Secondary Schools 209
  General 209
  Site Selection 213
  Site Planning 213
  Busing 214
  Parking 214
  Recreation Facilities 215
  Drainage 216
  Planting 216
  Safety 216
  Kinds of Schools 218
  Administration Suites 225
  Learning Resource Centers 228
  Classrooms 230
  Multipurpose Rooms 235
  Student Lockers 237
  Language Laboratory 240
  Science Facilities 240
  Arts 245
  Music Facilities 246
  Industrial and Vocational Facilities 250
  Home Arts 251
  Food Service 252
  Physical Education 258
  Auditoriums 269
Guidance Services 271
College and University Facilities 273
  Classrooms 273
  Gymnasiums 276
  Physical Education and Sports
    Facilities 280
  Field House 281
  Dormitories 282
  Handicapped Students 295
  Libraries 297
  Individual Study Carrels 314
  Student Unions 322
  Computation Centers 330
  Communications Centers 333
  Regional Education Center
    (Supplementary) 335
  Resource Facilities (Library) 337
  Large-Group Facilities 340
  Audiovisual 351
  Theater-Arts-Laboratory Teaching
    Station 357
  Programs and Programming 360

3. CULTURAL 363

Museums 365
Small Museums 372
Exhibition Spaces 377
  Visual Arts Facility 378
Libraries 380
  Diagrams of Essential Library
    Elements 380
  Branch Libraries 382
  Space Requirements 383
  Service and Space Relationships 386
  Library Location 387

Accessible to Handicapped	389
Branch Buildings	390
Bookmobiles	390
Bookstack Data	391
Theaters	392
Sight Lines	402
Stage Space	405
Music and Drama Centers	411
House	411
Basic Seating Data	419
Stage	423
Space for Dance	429
Community Theaters	433
Amphitheaters	439
Music Facilities	442
Arts and Crafts Centers	451
Performing Arts Center	463

4. HEALTH **465**

Hospitals	467
Introduction and Flow Charts	467
Bedrooms	467
Nursing Units	474
Surgical Suite	475
Nursery	477
Pediatric Nursing Units	480
Diagnostic X-Ray Suite	484
Pharmacy	490
Teletherapy Units	492
Electroencephalographic Suite	496
Physical Therapy Department	497
Occupational Therapy Department	500
Community Mental Health Center	503
Laboratory	503
Labor-Delivery Suite	509
Radioisotope Facility	511
Outpatient Activity	513
Emergency Activity	528
EDP Unit	530
Rehabilitation Centers	533
Mental Health Centers	548
Nursing Homes	554
Child Health Station	561
Medical Schools	562
Dental Schools	583
Nursing Schools	600
Youth Treatment Centers	616
Multiphasic Health-Screening Centers	622

5. RELIGIOUS **629**

Churches, General	631
Churches, Lutheran	638
Churches, United Methodist	643
Temples and Synagogues	655
Chapels	662
Church Schools	665

Contents

6. GOVERNMENTAL AND PUBLIC **673**

City and Town Halls	675
Courthouses	680
Fire Stations	700
Firehouses	703
Police Stations	708
Police Facility	718
Jails and Prisons	725
YMCA Buildings	741
YWCA Buildings	742
Boy's Clubs	755
Recreation Centers	761
Neighborhood Service Centers	767
Embassies	769
Post Offices	773
Access Ramps for the Handicapped	774
Public Toilet Rooms for the Handicapped	775

7. COMMERCIAL **777**

Regional Shopping Centers	779
Retail Shops	796
General	796
Principles of Retail Shop Design	796
Interiors	796
Layouts and Dimensions	798
Show Windows	807
Women's Wear	808
Men's Wear	811
Bookshops	812
Gift Shops	812
Jewelry Shops	813
Barber Shop	815
Tailor and Cleaner	815
Beauty Shop	816
Shoe-Repair Shop	816
Florist Shops	816
Drugstores	817
Liquor Stores	818
Shoe Stores	820
Supermarkets	823
Banks	825
Restaurants, Eating Places, and Foodservice Facilities	827
Kitchens	843
Offices, General	855
Furniture	857
Work Stations	859
Private and Semiprivate	871
Conference Rooms	873
Layout	874
Space	875
Planning	876
Clearances	887
Washroom Facilities	889
Medical Offices	891
Radiology	896
General Practice	898

Pediatrics	899
Internal Medicine	899
Ophthalmology	900
Plastic Surgery	900
General Surgery	901
Orthopedic Surgery	901
Dental Offices	902
General Dentistry	905
Orthodontics	908
Law Offices	909
Ophthalmological Offices	913
Parking	916
Automobile Dimensions	916
Parking Garages	922
Parking Lots	934
Automobile Service Stations	938
Automotive Shop	942
Gas-Filling and Service Stations	943
Automobile Body Shop	944
Automobile Dealer Centers	947
Truck Dealer and Service Facilities	956
Radio Stations	960
TV Stations	967
Hotels	972
Space Allotments	991
Guestroom Floor	993
Guestroom Design	998
Motels	1004
Computer (EDP) Facilities	1017
Photographic Laboratories	1020
Funeral Homes	1021

8. TRANSPORTATION **1023**

Airports and Terminals	1025
Airport Cargo Facilities	1075
Air Cargo Terminals	1079
Airport Service Equipment Buildings	1081
Aircraft Fire and Rescue Station	1085
Heliports	1087
STOL Ports	1099
Seaplane Terminals	1103
Bus Terminals	1111
Truck Terminals	1117
Truck Types and Dimensions	1123
Docks	1125

9. INDUSTRIAL **1133**

Industrial Parks	1135
Industrial Buildings, General	1141
Industrial Plants	1148
Industrial Railroad Docks	1154
Research Laboratories	1155
Warehouses	1167
Waterfront Warehouses	1170
Airport Industrial Park	1174
Industrial Plants, Parking	1178

Contents

10. RECREATION AND ENTERTAINMENT 1181

Playlots and Playgrounds 1183
Badminton 1192
Basketball (AAU) 1193
Basketball (NCAA) 1194
Biddy Basketball 1195
Goal-Hi Basketball 1196
Boccie Ball 1197
Croquet 1198
One-Wall Handball 1199
Three- and Four-Wall Handball 1200
Hopscotch 1201
Horseshoes 1202
Ice Hockey 1203
Lawn Bowling 1204
Roque 1205
Shuffleboard 1206
Deck Tennis 1207
Platform Tennis 1208
Paddle Tennis 1209
Tennis 1210
Tetherball 1211
Volleyball 1212
Official Baseball 1213
Baseball 1214
  Bronco League (9-12 yr) 1214
  Pony League (13-14 yr) 1215
  Colt League (15-16 yr) 1216
  Little League (9-12 yr) 1217
Field Hockey 1218
Flickerball 1219
Football (NCAA) 1220
Touch and Flag Football 1221
Golf Driving Range 1222
Lacrosse 1223
  Men's 1223
  Women's 1224
Soccer 1225
  Men's and Boys' 1225
  Women's and Girls' 1226
Softball, 12-Inch 1227
Softball, 16-Inch 1228
Speedball 1229
Team Handball 1230
¼-Mile Running Track 1231
Shot Put 1232
Hammer Throw 1233
Discus Throw 1234
Javelin Throw 1235
Long Jump and Triple Jump 1236
Pole Vault 1237
High Jump 1238
Archery 1239
International Shooting Union
  Automatic Trap 1240
Fixed Nets and Posts 1241
Fence Enclosures 1242
Typical Grading and Drainage Details 1243
Typical Playing Surfaces 1244

Baseball and Softball Backstops 1245
Movie Theaters 1246
   Handicapped Seating 1251
   500-Seat Movie Theater 1253
Drive-In Theaters 1255
Bowling Alleys 1257
Swimming Pools 1266
   Public Swimming Pools 1266
   Diving Pools 1269
   Residential Swimming Pools 1271
   50-Meter Recreational Swimming Pool 1273
   25-Meter Recreational Swimming Pool 1274
   25- and 50-Meter Indoor Pools 1275
Health Clubs 1277
Locker Rooms 1278
Bathhouses 1280
Gymnasium 1282
Zoos 1283
Aquariums 1293
Indoor Tennis Building 1300
Sports Arenas 1301
Golf Courses and Clubhouses 1310
Rifle and Pistol Ranges, Indoor 1318
Rifle and Carbine Ranges, Outdoor 1325
Shooting Ranges, Outdoor 1329
   Trapshooting 1329
   Skeet Shooting 1329
   Trap Field 1330
   Skeet Field 1331
   Combination Skeet and Trap Field 1332
Marinas 1333
Camps and Camp Facilities 1343

11. MISCELLANEOUS **1363**

Farmsteads 1365
Farms and Farm Buildings 1367
Animal Facility, Laboratory 1371
Greenhouses 1375
Horse Barns 1376
Horse Stables 1379
Riding Schools 1385
Kennels 1387
Nature Center 1389
Handicapped/Basic Human Dimensions 1392
   Wheelchair Dimensions 1393
   Clearances 1395
Handicapped/Anthropometrics 1398
   Toilets and Urinals 1398
   Drinking Fountains 1399
   Elevators 1400
   Stairs 1401
   Convenience Controls 1402
   Walkway Clearances 1403
   Ramps 1404

Credits 1405
Index 1407

Contributors

Richard M. Adler, AIA

Iris Alex, AIA *Building Consultant YWCA*

Egmont Arens *Industrial Designer*

Leslie Armstrong

James W. Atz *Associate Curator, the American Museum of Natural History*

Geoffrey Baker *Architect*

Vilma Barr

Herbert Behrend, P.E.

Richard M. Bennett, AIA

Frederick Bentel, AIA

Maria Bentel, AIA

Chester Arthur Berry, Ed.D.

Glenn H. Beyer *Housing Research Center, Cornell University*

Charles M. Boldon *Conrad Associates*

William N. Breger, AIA

Charles E. Broudy

Gladys L. Brown *Health, Physical Education, and Recreation Consultant*

C. William Brubaker, AIA *The Perkins & Will Corporation*

Harold Burris-Meyer

Charles A. Chaney

Alonso W. Clark, AIA

Harold Cliffer, AIA

F. G. Cole

Walter L. Cook

William J. Cronin, Jr.

Laurence Curtis

Marvin Cutler, AID

T. P. Deis *Architect*

Clyde H. Dorsett, AIA

Lathrop Douglass, FAIA

Max Fengler *Architect*

W. R. Ferguson

A. Peter Florio *Designer-Consultant*

John J. Fruin, Ph.D.

Bruno Funaro *Architect*

Richard U. Gambrill

Francis W. Gencorelli, AIA

Bryant Putnam Gould

Noyce L. Griffin, E.E.

John J. Grosfeld, AIA

Victor Gruen, AIA

J. L. Gruzen, AIA *Gruzen and Partners*

Don Halamka

Raymond Harrison

Morton Hartman, AIA *The Perkins & Will Corporation*

Ernest J. Hasch

Keith I. Hibner, AIA

August Hoenack *U.S. Public Health Service*

Joseph Horowitz, P.E. *Manager, Facilities Engineering Dept., Columbia Broadcasting System, Inc.*

George A. Hutchinson, AIA *The Perkins & Will Corporation*

Emmet Ingram, AIA *The Perkins & Will Corporation*

David Jones

Edward A Kazarian

Aaron N. Kiff *Architect*

Alexander Kira *Housing Research Center, Cornell University*

Joseph Kleinman *Architect*

Robert L. Knapp, AIA *Charles Luckman Associates*

A. Frederick Kolflat, AIA *The Perkins & Will Corporation*

J. J. Koster *Architect, Gruzen and Partners*

Lendal H. Kotschevar

Alan Lapidus, AIA

Morris Lapidus, AIA

Betsy Laslett

Fred Lawson

Stanton Leggett *Educational Consultant*

Ronald Mace, AIA

Contributors

James Mackenzie

John Macsai

Jain Malkin

Francis Joseph McCarthy, FAIA

William McCoy, AIA *The Perkins & Will Corporation*

Gordon P. McMaster *Architect*

Frank Memoli *Architect*

Emmanuel Mesagna *Architect*

Keyes D. Metcalf

Jo Mielziner *Stage Designer*

William A. Mills *Architectural Consultant*

Maurice Mogulescu

Bruno Molajoli

Roger Morgan

George Muramoto *Architect*

Richard Muther

Clifford E. Nelson, M.D.

Oscar Newman *Architect*

Raymond C. Ovresat, AIA *The Perkins & Will Corporation*

James A. Paddock *Dober, Paddock, Upton and Associates, Inc.*

Julius Panero *Architect and Urban Planning Consultant*

W. Russel Parker *Architect*

Richard H. Penner

Robert Perlman

Frank Harrison Randolph, P.E. *Professor of Hotel Engineering, Cornell University*

Kenneth Ricci *Architect*

Scott Turner Ritenour

Herbert Ross *Industrial Designer*

Richard F. Roti

Walter A. Rutes

Christine F. Salmon, AIA

F. Cuthbert Salmon, AIA

Maurice R. Salo, AIA *Consulting Architect to the Lutheran Church in America*

Ben Schlanger *Architect and Theater Consultant*

Myron E. Schoen, F.T.A. *Director, Commission on Synagogue Administration*

Max B. Schreiber *Architect*

Walter E. Schultz *Architectural Consultant*

Samuel Selden

Peter C. Smith *Associate of the Royal Institute of British Architects*

R. Jackson Smith, AIA

Bernard Spero

William Staniar, M.E.

Wilbur R. Taylor *Architect*

Margaret E. Terrell

James G. Terrill, Jr.

George H. Tryon

Donald B. Tweedy

Howard P. Vermilya, AIA

Joshua H. Vogel, AIA

Mildred C. Widber

Philip Will, Jr., AIA *The Perkins & Will Corporation*

Richard M. Williams *Director, National Building Consultation and Supply Services, Boys' Clubs of America*

Mary Worthen *Architect*

Martin Zelnik, AIA

Organizations

American Association for Health, Physical Education, and Recreation

American Association of Port Authorities

American Association for State and Local History

American Association of Zoological Parks and Aquariums

American Bar Association

American Library Association

American Medical Association

American Psychiatric Association

American Trucking Associations, Inc.

American Youth Hostels, Inc.

Association of College Unions — International

The Athletic Institute

Boy Scouts of America

Boys' Clubs of America

Brunswick Corp.

Canada Mortgage and Housing Corporation

Canadian Museum Association

Center for Architectural Research, Rensselaer Polytechnic Institute

Conference Board of Mathematical Sciences

Civil Aeronautics Administration

The DeVilbiss Company

Educational Facilities Laboratories

Eno Foundation

Federal Aviation Administration

Federal Housing Administration

General Motors Corporation

General Services Administration

Housing and Home Finance Agency

Housing Research Center, Cornell University

Humble Oil & Refining Co.

Institute of Outdoor Drama, University of North Carolina

Institute of Traffic Engineers

International Association of Chiefs of Police

International City Managers' Association

International Youth Hostel Federation

Kelley Company, Inc.

Michigan State Housing Development Authority

Organizations

Mobile Homes Manufacturers Association

Mosler Safe Co.

Motor Vehicle Manufacturers Association of the U.S., Inc.

Music Educators National Conference

National Association of Engine and Boat Manufacturers, Inc.

National Association of Home Builders

National Council of the Young Men's Christian Association of U.S.A.

National Council on the Aging

National Crushed Stone Association

National Education Association

National Fire Protection—International

National Fisheries Center and Aquariums

National Institute of Mental Health

National Golf Association

National Office Products Association

National Recreation and Park Association

National Rifle Association

National Swimming Pool Institute

New York City Housing Authority

New York State University Construction Fund

Philadelphia Housing Association

Rite-Hite Corporation

Texas A & M University, School of Architecture

United Methodist Church, Board of Global Ministries

U.S. Department of Health, Education, and Welfare (now called U.S. Department of Health and Human Services)

U.S. Department of Housing and Urban Development

U.S. Department of the Navy

U.S. Public Health Service

University of California

University of Oregon

University of Washington, Bureau of Government Research and Services

Urban Land Institute

Western States Arts Foundation

Preface

to the Third Edition

TIME-SAVER STANDARDS FOR BUILDING TYPES is a handbook about the architectural planning of buildings. It describes each building type, such as a school, a museum, or a theater, and presents general criteria for, and illustrates the functional relationships between, its component parts. This book does not, as do most architectural books, present the final aesthetic expression of a particular building. The material is intended to be used to assist in the process of designing the building and to ensure that the building functions properly for its particular use.

The third edition of *Time-Saver Standards for Building Types* continues the tradition of a unique and significant publication. The first edition, published in 1973, established for the first time a comprehensive source of reference material dealing with the functional analysis and standards of all major types of buildings. It made available to the architect and designer an extensive amount of essential planning data to analyze and organize, in order to create more successful buildings. The second edition, published in 1980, greatly expanded the scope and depth of the material. It added new building types and updated ones already in the book. This third edition continues to expand and revise the information on those building types that have seen significant changes over the years.

A word of caution on the use of this handbook: The material presents basic or general principles, spatial relationships, and design criteria for each building type. This information should be used only as a reference point from which individual or specific design solutions can be established. This material is not intended to give definitive schematics, rigid formulas, or final designs that will automatically provide the solution to a specific design problem. Rather, these standards and criteria should only be the starting point for further analysis, evaluation, and review of the interrelationships of the elements of each type of building. Primarily, the material in this handbook is intended to be used by the architect, designer, student, or related design professional in the following manner:

1. to assist in developing building programs
2. to establish preliminary space allocations
3. to study general and specific functional relationships
4. to assist in the preparation of preliminary architectural designs
5. to assist in the evaluation of proposals and projects

The future presents many new and exciting challenges to the architect and the entire design profession. Notable are the rapid technological developments that are having strong influences upon the use, functions, and forms of new buildings. Equally important is the search for new aesthetic expressions in architecture and their interrelationships with painting and sculpture. The introduction of new methods, techniques, and materials will significantly influence new construction. Hopefully, this handbook will provide a solid base from which these challenges can be successfully pursued.

Joseph De Chiara

1

Residential

DIMENSIONS OF THE HUMAN FIGURE	3	LAUNDRY ROOMS	62
BASIC ACTIVITIES	5	BATHROOMS	69
LIVING AREAS	6	Handicapped Lavatory/Water Closet	80
LIVING ROOMS	7	Adaptable	81
Furniture	7	CLOSETS	86
Furniture Sizes	8	APARTMENTS	98
Furniture Arrangements	9	APARTMENT BUILDINGS	107
Furniture Sizes and Clearances	16	Central Laundry Rooms	119
DINING AREAS	17	HOUSING DENSITIES	121
COMBINED LIVING-DINING SPACES	27	HOUSING FOR THE ELDERLY	126
COMBINED DINING AREA-KITCHEN	28	HOUSING FOR THE HANDICAPPED	140
BEDROOMS	29	GROUP HOMES	159
COMBINED LIVING-SLEEPING AREAS	41	SENIOR CITIZENS' CENTER	162
HOME OFFICE OR STUDY	43	MOBILE HOMES AND PARKS	169
KITCHENS	44	YOUTH HOSTELS	180
Adaptable	53	SITE PLANNING	186

DIMENSIONS OF ADULTS

The dimensions and clearances shown for the average adult (Fig. 2) represent minimum requirements for use in planning building layouts and furnishings. If possible, clearances should be increased to allow comfortable accommodations for persons larger than average. The height of tabletops shown on the next page is 2 ft 5 in; some authorities prefer 2 ft 6 in, or sometimes 2 ft 6½ in.

Since doorways and passageways must normally be dimensioned to permit the movement of furniture, they should seldom be designed merely on the needs of the average adult. (See section of this book relating to furniture sizes.)

DIMENSIONS OF CHILDREN

Children do not have the same physical proportions as adults, especially during their early years, and their heights vary greatly, but their space requirements can be approximated from the following table and from Fig. 1. (For heights of children's furniture and equipment, see section on "Schools.")

Average Height of Children

Age	Height, in	Age	Height, in
5	44	11	56
6	46	12	58
7	48	13	60
8	50	14	62
9	52	15	64
10	54	16	66

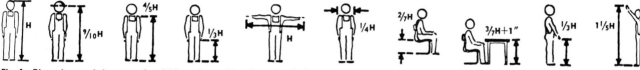

Fig. 1 Dimensions and clearances for children. *Source:* "Time-Saver Standards," 1st ed., F. W. Dodge Corp., New York, 1946.

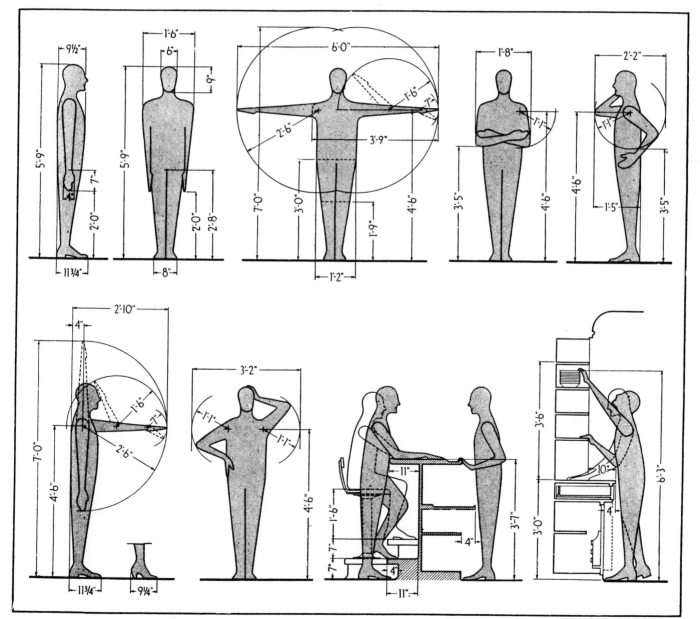

Fig. 2 Dimensions and clearances for adults. *Source:* "Time-Saver Standards," 1st ed., F. W. Dodge Corp., New York, 1946.

DIMENSIONS OF THE HUMAN FIGURE

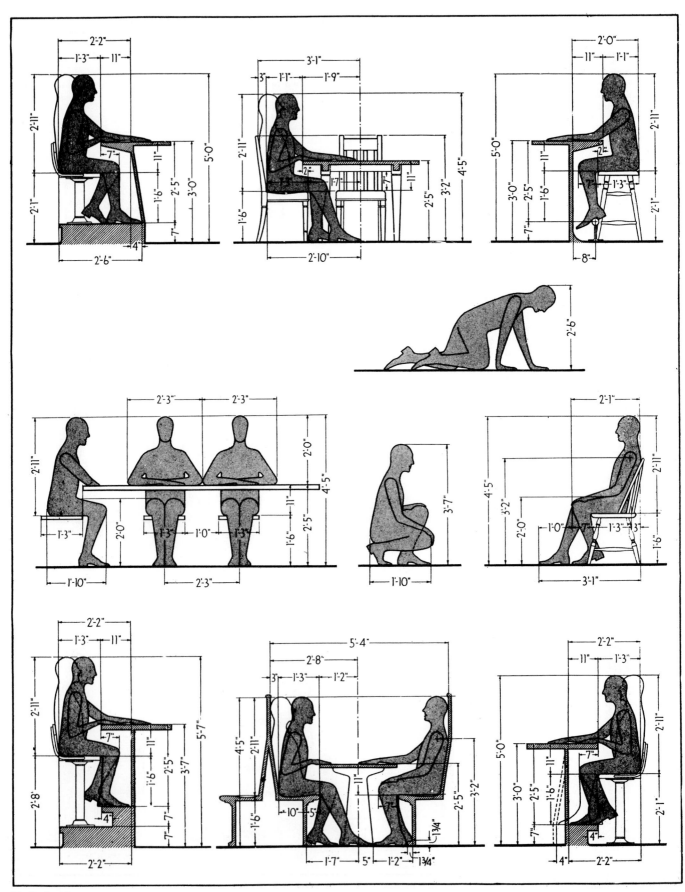

Fig. 2 (cont.)

Walking between
two high walls
(space adequate
for both men
and women)

Two people passing
(figure derived; twice the
space for one person to
walk between two high walls)

Walking between high
wall and 30″ high
table (space adequate
for both men and
women)

Walking with elbows
extended (space ade-
quate for both men
and women)

Kneeling on one
knee (woman only)

Man bending at
a right angle

One person using
coat closet

Two persons using coat closet in foyer
area with space for one person walking

Residential

LIVING AREAS

LIVING AREAS

Planning Considerations

- Through traffic should be separated from activity centers.
- Openings should be located so as to give enough wall space for various furniture arrangements.
- Convenient access should be provided to doors, windows, electric outlets, thermostats, and supply grills.

Furniture Clearances

To assure adequate space for convenient use of furniture in the living area, not less than the following clearances should be observed.

60 in between facing seating
24 in where circulation occurs between furniture
30 in for use of desk
36 in for main traffic
60 in between television set and seating

Seating arranged around a 10-ft diameter circle (Fig. 1) makes a comfortable grouping for conversation. Figure 2 indicates clearances, circulation, and conversation areas.

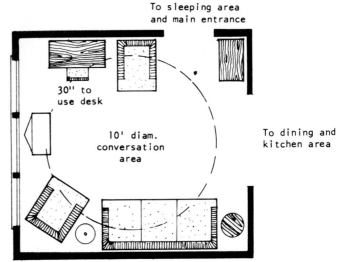

Fig. 1 Plan. *Source:* "Manual of Acceptable Practices," Vol. 4, U.S. Dept. of Housing and Urban Development, 1973.

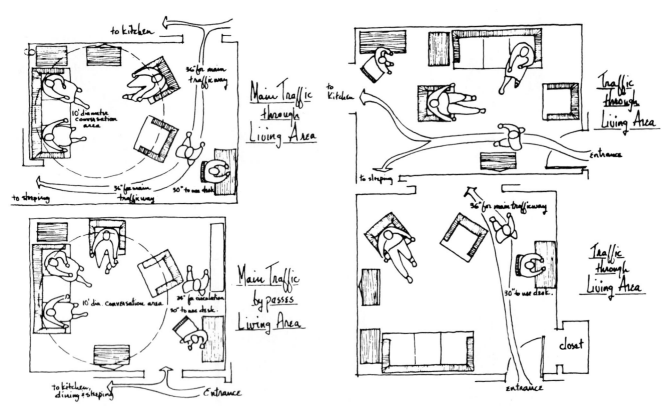

Fig. 2 Minimum clearances, circulation and conversation areas for living rooms.

6

FURNITURE

GENERAL

Typical furniture-group units

While the typical furniture arrangements presented in the following pages by no means cover the entire range of possibilities, they do cover the fundamental uses to which living, dining, and sleeping spaces are put. From the suggested schemes furniture arrangements can be developed to suit any particular problem or set of problems with which a designer may be confronted.

Furniture sizes may vary slightly; those indicated are the averages commonly met with in upper middle-class homes, and are little affected by changes in style or similar matters of individual preference.

Specific space allowances

In studying furniture groupings, it becomes obvious that certain clearances are required. Spaces, lanes, or paths of different types develop naturally between furniture-group units. Minimum distances for comfort have been established by numerous planners. These, and in some cases, maximum distances based upon requirements for human intercourse, have been incorporated in the diagrams. A listing of those generally applicable to all rooms follows:

1. *Single passage* (not a traffic lane) between low objects, such as a sofa and coffee table: 18 in. is the minimum.

2. *Single passage* (not a traffic lane) between tall objects, hip height or over: 2 ft to 2 ft 6 in. is the minimum.

3. *General traffic lane:* 3 ft 4 in. is the practical minimum. As rooms increase in size, this minimum increases, in order to preserve the space scale of the room. The traffic lane between an entrance door and a major group unit is preferably generous in width. It is desirable to place doors so that the central portions of rooms do not become major traffic ways between different parts of the house.

4. *Seating areas, confined* (for instance, between a desk and a wall): 3 ft is a minimum tolerance, which permits one person to pass back of an occupied chair. This minimum does not constitute a major traffic lane.

LIVING ROOM

Typical furniture groups in the living room are as follows:

1. *Primary conversation group:* chairs and sofa normally grouped around the fireplace

2. *Secondary conversation group:* chairs and love seat at end of room or in corner

3. *Reading group or groups:* chair, ottoman, lamp, table

4. *Writing or study group:* desk, lamp, one or two chairs, bookcases

5. *Music group:* piano, bench, storage space

6. *Game group:* game table and four chairs

7. *Television group:* television set and seating for several people

According to the price of a house and the cubage allotted to the living room, two or three or all of the furniture-group units may be included. The fireplace is so closely associated with living room furniture that it has been included in all schemes.

Clearances

Traffic tolerances in living rooms are important, since numbers of people use the room, and narrow lanes between furniture-group units are uncomfortable. An adequate traffic lane between the main entrance and the major seating group is 3 ft 4 in. wide; 4 ft 6 in. is preferred. The minimum clearance between facing pieces of furniture in a fireplace group is 4 ft 8 in. for a fireplace 3 ft wide. For every inch added to the size of the fireplace, 1 in. is added to the minimum clearance space.

If a wide sofa is placed directly opposite the fireplace, this group is often spread. A 6-ft tolerance is usually considered the maximum because it is difficult to carry on a conversation over a greater distance.

A considerable flexibility in location of doors and windows is possible, and all wall pieces can be shifted. Doors flanking a fireplace are to be avoided in order that the furniture group may be concentrated around the fireplace opening.

Residential

LIVING ROOMS
Furniture Sizes

SOFAS

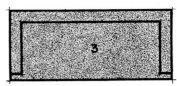

LOVE SEATS

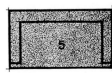

"SHERATON" TYPE
LENGTH 6'-0"
DEPTH 2'-6"
HEIGHT 3'-0"

"CHIPPENDALE" TYPE
L. 6'-6"
D. 2'-6"
H. 3'-0"

PLAIN UPHOLSTERED
L 7'-0"
D 3'-0"
H 3'-0"

SMALL
L 3'-6"
D 2'-0"
H 2'-3"

LARGE
L 4'-6"
D 2'-6"
H 3'-0"

CHAIRS

CLUB
LENGTH 2'-6"
DEPTH 3'-0"
HEIGHT 3'-0"

OCCASIONAL
L 2'-3"
D 2'-6"
H 3'-0"

WING
L 2'-6"
D 2'-6"
H 3'-0"

SIDE OR DESK
L 1'-6"
D 1'-6"
H 2'-6"

UPHOLSTERED ARMLESS
L 2'-0"
D 2'-6"
H 2'-6"

UPHOLSTERED CORNER CHAIR
L 3'-0"
D 3'-0"

BRIDGE ARM
L 2'-0"
D 2'-0"
H 2'-6"

BRIDGE ARMLESS
L 1'-6"
D 1'-6"
H 2'-6"

DESKS

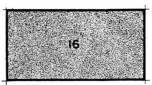

FLAT TOP....SMALL
LENGTH 4'-0"
DEPTH 2'-0"
HEIGHT 2'-6"

FLAT TOP...LARGE
L 5'-0"
D 2'-6"
H 2'-6"

FLAT TOP.....VERY LARGE
L 6'-0"
D 3'-0"
H 2'-6"

GOVERNOR WINTHROP
L 3'-0"
D 2'-0"
H 3'-6"

SECRETARY
L 3'-0"
D 2'-0"
H 7'-0"

BREAKFRONT BOOK CASES

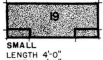
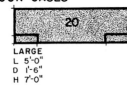

TABLES

SMALL
LENGTH 4'-0"
DEPTH 1'-6"
HEIGHT 6'-6"

LARGE
L 5'-0"
D 1'-6"
H 7'-0"

END
L 2'-0"
D 1'-3"
H 2'-0"

END
L 1'-8"
D 1'-8"
H 2'-0"

COFFEE
L 3'-0"
D 2'-0"
H 1'-6"

BRIDGE
L 3'-0"
D 3'-0"
H 2'-6"

CONSOLE
L 3'-0"
D 1'-6"
H 2'-6"

LOWBOYS

HIGHBOYS

AVERAGE
LENGTH 2'-6"
DEPTH 1'-6"
HEIGHT 2'-6"

LARGE
L 2'-8"
D 1'-8"
H 3'-2"

SWAN TOP
L 3'-0"
D 1'-6"
H 7'-0"

FLAT TOP
L 3'-0"
D 1'-6"
H 5'-0"

CIRCULAR PIECES

LOW COFFEE TABLE
DIAM. 3'-0"
HEIGHT 1'-6"

DRUM TABLE
DIAM. 3'-0"
H 2'-6"

PIECRUST TABLE
DIAM. 3'-0"
H 2'-6"

DUMBWAITER
LARGEST DIAM. 2'-0"
H. 2'-6"

STAND.
DIAM. 1'-0"
H 2'-6"

PIANOS

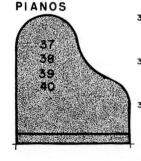
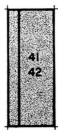

37. **CONCERT GRAND**
L. 9'-0"
D 5'-0"
H 3'-4"

38. **MUSIC ROOM GRAND**
L 7'-0"
D 5'-0"
H 3'-4"

39. **PARLOR GRAND**
L 6'-0"
D 5'-0"
H 3'-4"

40. **BABY GRAND**
L 5'-6"
D 5'-0"
H 3'-4"

41. **CONSOLE**
L 5'-0"
D 2'-0"
H 4'-3"

42. **MINATURE**
L 4'-8"
D 1'-7"
H 3'-0"

LAMP TABLE
DIAM. 2'-0"
H. 2'-6"

ROUNDABOUT SEAT
DEPTH OF SEAT 1'-6"
DIAM. 4'-0"

8

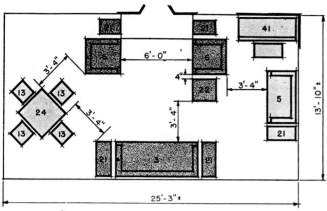

1. In all living rooms shown, main conversation group centered about fireplace is dark gray. Bay or picture windows may be used as focal points, instead of fireplaces.

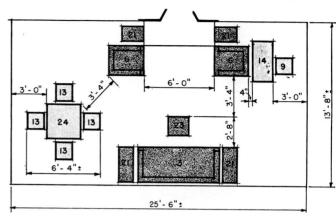

2. Clearance between low coffee table (23) and easy chairs (6) ought to be maintained at 3'-4" even though table is low, because the aisle here constitutes a major traffic way.

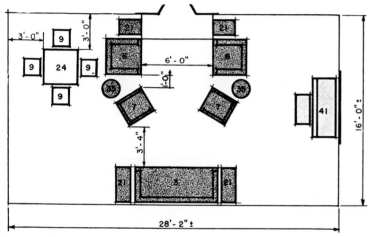

3. For larger families, or for those who entertain often, seating for 7 to 8 persons in the primary group is a reasonable design limitation. Off-center location of game group provides for a corner entrance door.

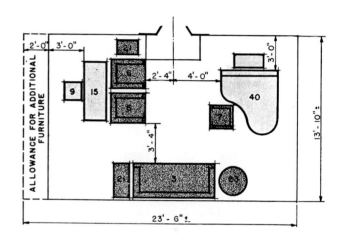

4. Minimum length for a room which must contain a baby grand piano is approximately 20'. If minimum clearances of 1' between piano and wall, and 3' between desk (15) and wall, are to be maintained, room length must be increased.

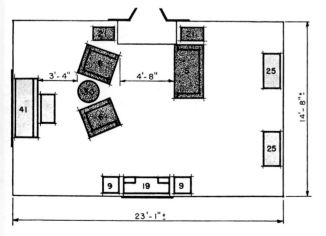

5. If sofa opposite fireplace is omitted, primary group can be brought closer together. In schemes 1 to 4, note that wide groups permit conversation without twisting to see speakers seated on sofa; here this restriction is removed.

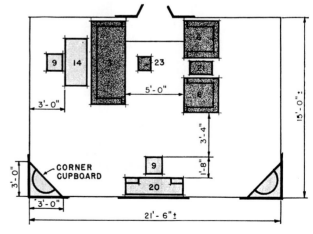

6. Here, presumably, doors at ends of room indicate use of one side of room as a traffic route. Primary furniture is grouped closely about fireplace; wall pieces are all that can be used on opposite side.

LIVING ROOMS
Furniture Arrangements

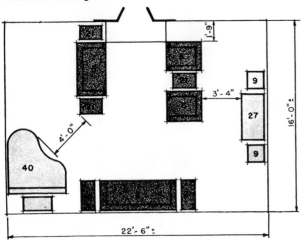

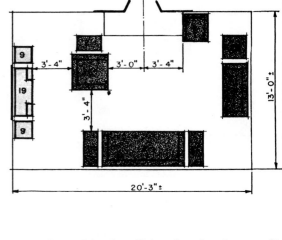

7. Grouping for door locations at both ends of room; ideally, 1-ft clearance is desirable between piano and wall. Chairs (6) are smaller than those previously listed, 2'-6" x 3'-0".

8. If living room has a "dead end" (no doors), primary unit may be spread to include entire end of room. Inclusion of music or game group would demand more area.

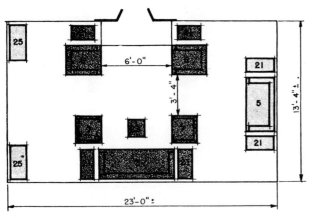

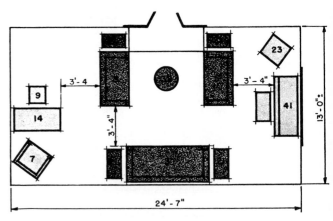

9. Primary group shown is one of most popular arrangements. Unit placing suggests entrance at left end. Secondary conversation unit often becomes music or game group.

10. Writing or study group at left, music or game group at right, and center primary group, need minimum passages only when room is narrow.

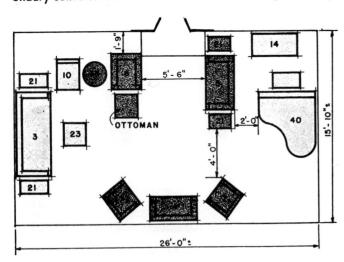

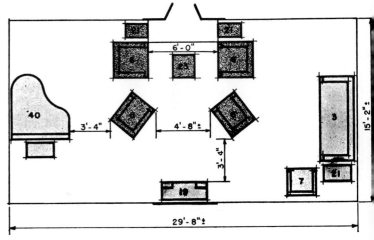

11. Ten persons can be comfortably seated in this type of arrangement, in which primary and secondary conversation groupings almost merge into one.

12. Arrangement designed to permit door locations on side walls rather than ends. Angled chairs (6) are small size noted in Fig. 7, and often used in other arrangements.

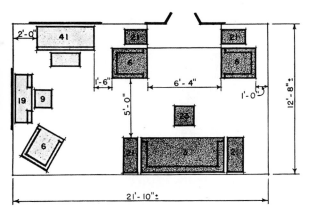

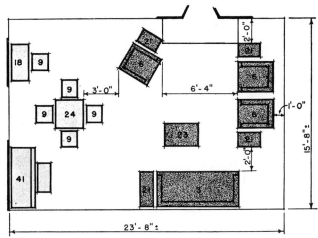

13. Previous diagrams have shown schemes arranged symmetrically about centered fireplaces; on this and the following page are schemes for cases when foci cannot be centered.

14. Off-center rooms often divide naturally into two parts: primary group, and other groups combined. Clearance no greater than 2' will not accommodate a major traffic lane.

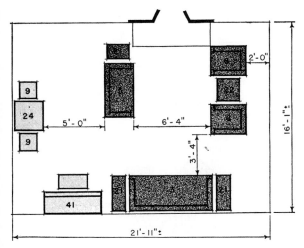

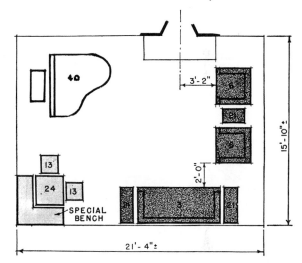

15. If primary, music, and game groups are all to be contained in a small area, one must be curtailed. Here game group consists of table and only two chairs.

16. In this case the primary conversation group is curtailed to permit inclusion of a grand piano; use of corner bench for game group may result in some loss of comfort.

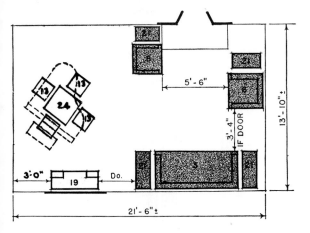

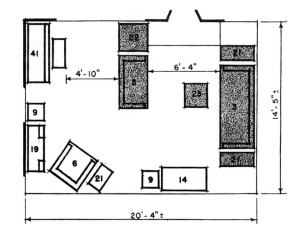

17. Two smaller upholstered chairs (6), each 2'-6" x 3'-0" might be accommodated at the right of the fireplace in this room with only a slight increase in room width.

18. In a room with only one door the minimum traffic lane of 3'-4" needs to be increased to at least 4'-10", which will accommodate two persons side by side, without crowding.

LIVING ROOMS
Furniture Arrangements

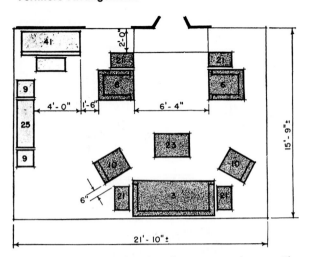

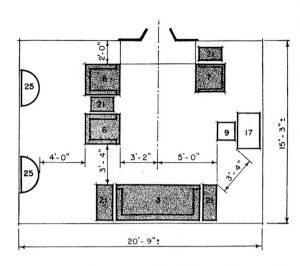

19. Another example of wide entrance lanes. Placement of doors so that at least 10" is allowed between room corners and door trim will permit installation of "built-in" bookcases.

20. Several doors may be accommodated with this type of furniture-group unit arrangement. A traffic lane is assumed to exist at the left end of the room.

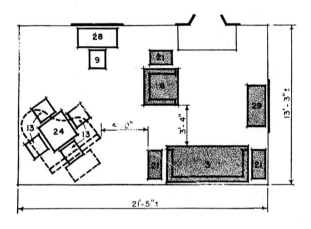

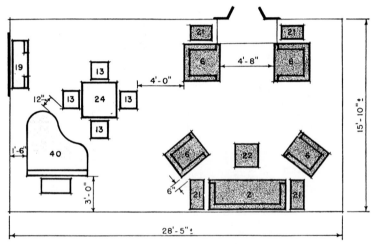

21. Notice that a game-table group occupies almost the same floor area as a baby grand piano. Placement at an angle is intended for informal rooms.

22. Larger rooms may contain four or more furniture-group units; it may be desirable to increase clearances. Use of chairs set at angles requires increased areas.

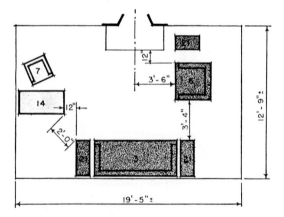

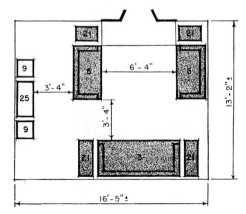

23. Fireplace chairs set 3'-6" back from center line of fireplace permit occupants to gaze at the fire comfortably. General traffic cannot be accommodated in a 2-ft lane.

24. By using love seats instead of pairs of chairs at sides of fireplace, considerable space can be saved even though seats are not placed the minimum distance apart.

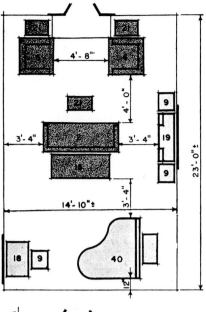

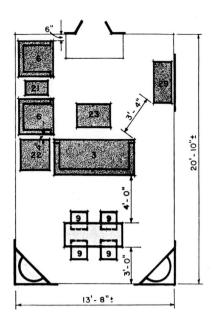

25. In rooms with fire-places in end walls, as in the schemes immediately preceding, furniture arrangements often fall naturally into two distinct groups.

26. One of the two groups may be adapted for dining, eliminating need for a separate dining room. Minimum clearance around dining table should be 3'-0".

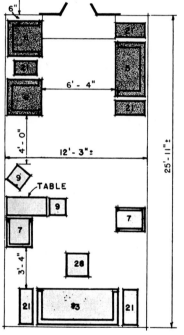

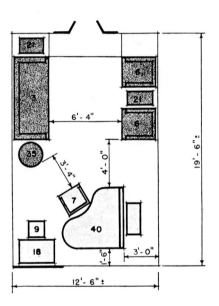

27. In this scheme, by placing the sofa on the long axis opposite the fireplace, furniture is held together as a single unit. There are two obvious positions for an entrance door. It is possible to back the sofa against a group of windows.

28. Backing the primary-group furniture against walls eliminates passage behind them and reduces room width to a minimum.

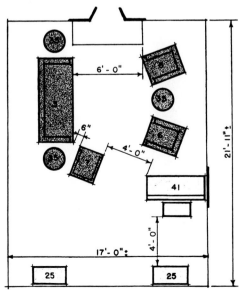

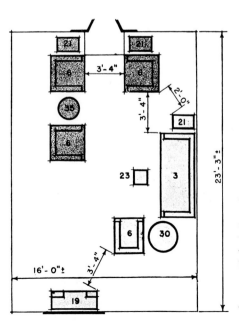

29. Here the left side and end opposite the fireplace are available for doors. Piano should, if possible, be placed against an inside wall.

30. Placing the sofa against one side of the room tends to open up the primary group—in effect, to merge with it the secondary conversation-group furniture.

LIVING ROOMS
Furniture Arrangements

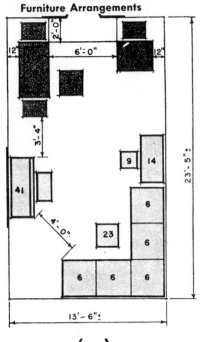

31. The entire area may be treated as a single unit, all furniture being brought into the principal group.

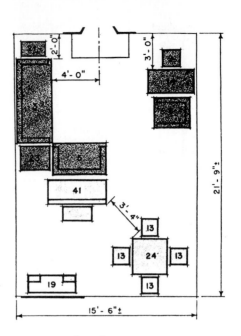

32. Here the placing of the desk group (14) allies it closely with the fireplace unit. Four units are included.

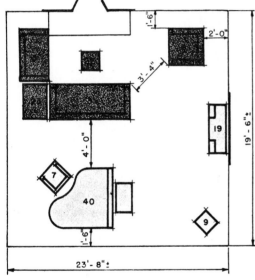

33. By interchanging the positions of the fireplace furniture in Fig. 32, a grand piano can be accommodated.

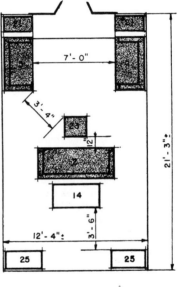

34. Completely symmetrical arrangement in comparatively small space; music group might replace items 14 and 25.

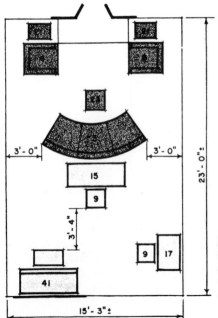

35. Type of sofa shown is becoming increasingly popular. Chairs (6) may be units which can be added to sofa, if desired.

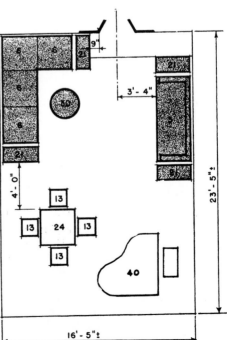

36. "Unit" types of sofas are particularly suited to corner groupings. Scheme shown contains three group units.

SPACE FUNCTION

Primary and secondary activities that usually take place in living rooms or spaces are:

Primary Activities
Entertainment
Watching television
Listening to music
Reading
Writing
Studying
Relaxing
Resting
Children's play

Secondary Activities
Dancing
Hobbies and crafts
Eating
Parlor games
Mending and sewing
Playing music
Giving parties
Projecting slides or films
Operating home computer

FURNITURE REQUIREMENTS

If occupants are to be able to carry out their normal activities in the living room, the size and configuration of the space must accommodate both the furniture and its use. Passive activities, such as listening to music and watching television, will not require as much space for movement in front of furniture as will less sedentary activities like entertaining or playing.

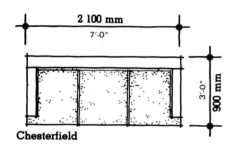

Chesterfield

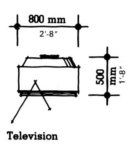

Television

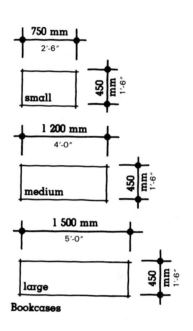

Bookcases

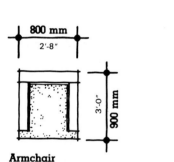

Armchair

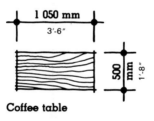

Coffee table

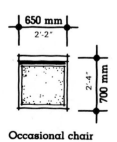

Occasional chair

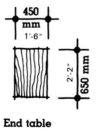

End table

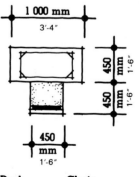

Desk   Chair   Scale 1:50

Fig. 1 Typical living room furniture

LIVING ROOMS
Furniture Sizes and Clearances

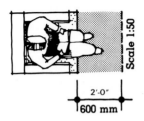

2'-0"
600 mm
Scale 1:50

Fig. 2   Recommended clearance in front of seat: (2'-0')

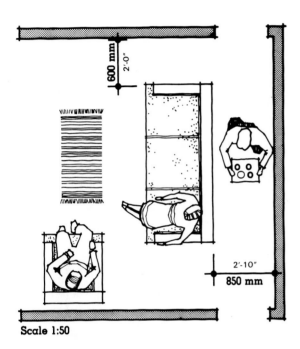

600 mm
2'-0"

2'-10"
850 mm

Scale 1:50

Fig. 3   Recommended clearances for general access: (2'-10') limited access: (2'-0')

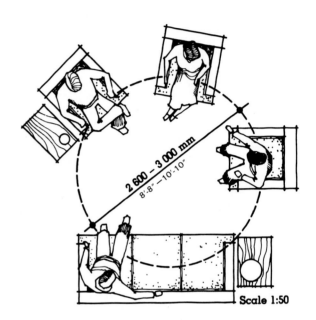

2 600 – 3 000 mm
8'-8" – 10'-10"

Scale 1:50

Fig. 5   Grouping of seats for social interaction: recommended clearance 2 600 - 3 000 mm

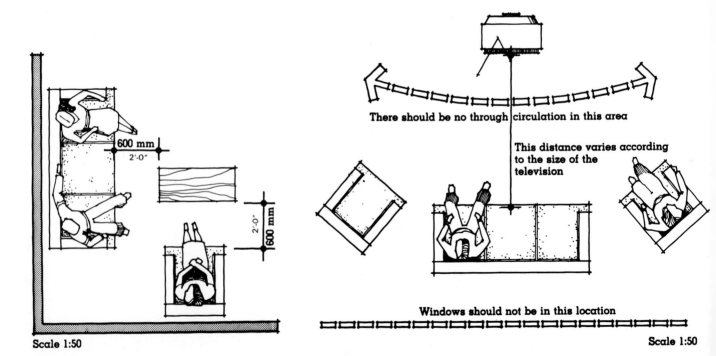

600 mm
2'-0"

2'-0"
600 mm

Scale 1:50

Fig. 4   Limited access between a table and other furniture: recommended clearance (2'-0')

There should be no through circulation in this area

This distance varies according to the size of the television

Windows should not be in this location

Scale 1:50

Fig. 6   Space for television viewing. The television set should be placed where the screen will not reflect light and where it can be seen from the main seating group

16

By GLENN H. BEYER AND ALEXANDER KIRA, *Housing Research Center, Cornell University*

DINING ROOM

The principal factors to be considered in planning the dining area are as follows: (1) Number of persons to be seated; (2) Space used at the table; (3) Space for chairs and for passage behind them; (4) Seating arrangement; (5) Size and type of furniture; and (6) Storage space for china, glassware, silver, and linen.

Recommended space dimensions, based on recent research, are provided below.

SIZE OF PLACE SETTING

The minimum width needed for each place setting is 21 in.; however, a width of up to 29 in. is desirable for greater freedom of movement. A 25-in. width is usually adequate; this permits chairs 19 in. wide to be placed 6 in. apart. The minimum depth for a place setting is $14\frac{1}{2}$ in. These dimensions allow space for china, glassware, silver, and elbow extension (See Fig. 1).

PASSAGE BEHIND CHAIRS

The minimum space recommended for passage behind chairs is 22 in.; a satisfactory range is 22 to 25 in. If passage behind the chairs is not required, a minimum of 5 in. plus the depth of the chair must be provided for pushing back the chair when leaving the table (See Fig. 3).

Size of table

The minimum width recommended is 36 in.; a satisfactory width is 36 to 44 in.

If 25-in.-wide place settings are provided and if one person is seated at each end of the table, then minimum and recommended table lengths are as follows:

Persons	Minimum, in.	Recommended, in.
4	54	60
6	79	84
8	104	108
10	129	132
12	154	156

If no one is seated at either end of the table, the length may be reduced by approximately 4 in.

Space for total dining area

With the same conditions noted above and with an ample 42-in. space for passage on all sides of a 42-in.-wide table, required sizes are as follows:

Persons	$W \times L$	= Area
	ft	sq ft
4	$10\frac{1}{2}$x12	= 126
6	$10\frac{1}{2}$x14	= 147
8	$10\frac{1}{2}$x16	= 168
10	$10\frac{1}{2}$x18	= 189
12	$10\frac{1}{2}$x20	= 210

If no one is to be seated at either end of the table, the length may be reduced by 2 ft (21 sq ft).

Storage space

Linear feet of shelf space required for medium-income families, for both moderate and liberal supplies of dishes and glassware, for everyday and guest use, is as follows:

	12-in. shelves,	20-in. shelves,
	ft-in.	ft
Moderate	21–0	2
Liberal	36–9	2

Drawer space for storage of silver is shown in Table 1. Space for storage of table linens is shown in Table 2.

Table 1. Inside dimensions of drawers for storage of silverware

Adapted from Indoor Dining Areas for Rural Homes in the Western Region, *Report 118, University of Arizona Agricultural Experiment Station, Tucson (June 1955).*

Item	Width, in.	Depth, in.	Height, in.
8 each forks, knives, soupspoons; 12 teaspoons, 6 tablespoons, 4 serving pieces	11	$18\frac{1}{2}$	$2\frac{3}{4}$
12 each forks, knives, salad forks or others, butter spreaders, soupspoons; 18 teaspoons, 6 tablespoons, 3-piece carving set, 3 serving pieces	$14\frac{1}{2}$	20	3
12 each forks, knives, soupspoons, salad forks or butter spreaders; 24 teaspoons, 6 tablespoons, 6 serving pieces	17	$19\frac{3}{4}$	$2\frac{1}{4}$

Table 2. Dimensions of stacks of folded table linens

Adapted from Storage Space Requirements for Household Textiles, A. *Woolrich, M. M. White, and M. A. Richards, Agricultural Research Bulletin 62–2, U.S. Department of Agriculture, Washington, D.C. (1955). Dimensions given are front-to-back, side-to-side, and height.*

Item	Space 16 in. deep		Space 20 in. deep	
	Minimum, in.	Maximum, in.	Minimum, in.	Maximum, in.
2 large tablecloths, guest use	14x19x3	14x36x2	19x14x3	19x28x2
2 medium tablecloths, everyday use	15x19x1	13x28x1	19x10x1	18x28x1
4 small tablecloths, everyday use	14x10x3	14x28x1	10x14x3	15x14x2
3 small tablecloths, guest use	14x10x2	14x28x1	10x14x2	15x14x2
12 small napkins (2 stacks of 6)	7x10x3	7x10x3	10x 5x3	10x 9x2
12 large napkins (2 stacks of 6)	8x10x2	8x10x2	10x 6x2	10x10x1
6 place mats, everyday use	13x19x1	13x19x1	19x13x1	19x13x1
1 table pad	13x21x3	13x21x3	13x21x3	13x21x3

Fig. 1. Size of place setting

Fig. 2. Passage behind chairs

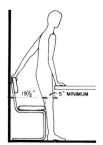

Fig. 3. Leaving the table

Residential
DINING AREAS

SPACE FUNCTION

Primary and secondary activities that usually take place in dining rooms or spaces are:

Primary Activities	Secondary Activities
Setting the table	Children's play
Serving food	Reading
Eating	Writing
Cleaning up after meals	Studying and homework
Storing dishes	Entertainment
	Board games
	Pattern cutting and sewing
	Watching television
	Ironing clothes

FURNITURE REQUIREMENTS

Typical pieces of furniture are listed below, together with their horizontal dimensions. Tables with seating on two sides are generally larger than those specified for seating on four sides. However, seating on two sides will usually require less total room space.

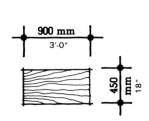

Small buffet

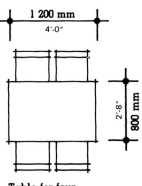

Table for four

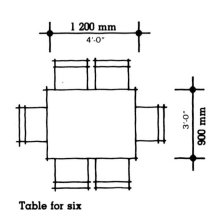

Table for six

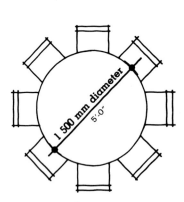

Table for eight

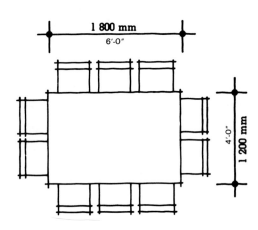

Table for ten

Fig. 4 Typical dining room furniture

Scale 1:150

18

CLEARANCES

Clearances should be provided in front of and sometimes around furniture in the dining room to allow activities to take place efficiently and in comfort. In some cases, greater clearances are required to accommodate the needs of elderly people, wheelchair users and invalids.

Recommendations for clearances around furniture are shown in Figs. 5 to 8.

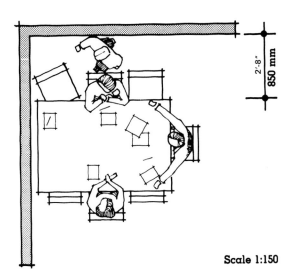

Scale 1:150

Fig. 5   Limited access behind a chair in cul-de-sac circulation space

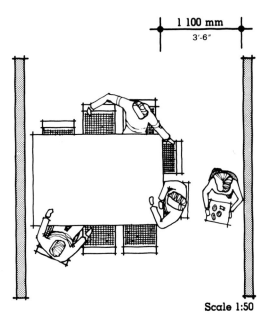

Scale 1:50

Fig. 6   Access behind a chair in through circulation space

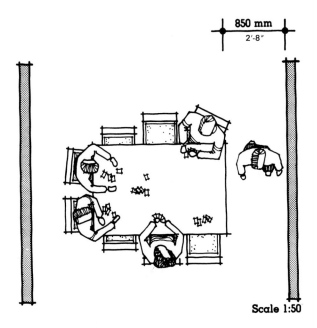

Scale 1:50

Fig. 7   Access behind a table and a wall

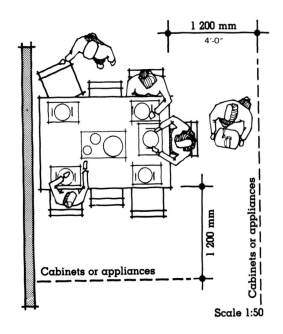

Scale 1:50

Fig. 8   Access behind a chair and cabinets or appliances

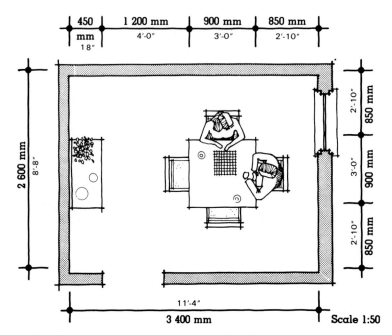

Fig. 9   Two-person household. Recommended net area: 8.84 m²

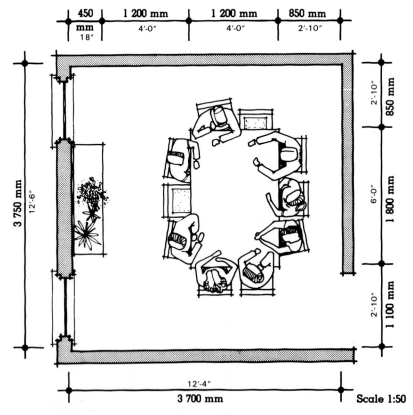

Fig. 10   Eight-person household. Recommended net area: 13.87 m²

DINING AREAS must accommodate furniture—either portable or built-in—for eating, sitting, serving and possible storage. Equipment for these dining functions may also be adapted to meet other possible requirements for this space—as studying, game-playing, etc.

Table space requirements per person are as follows: for crowded seating, 1'-10" on the table's perimeter; for comfort, 2'-0". Adequate clearances for use are indicated on diagrams.

Furniture Sizes:

Portable Tables, round (A):
2'-7" to 5'-10" diam.

Portable Tables, rectangular (C):
2'-6" to 4'-0" by 3'-6" to 8'-0";
or 2'-0" to 4'-0" square

Dining Chairs, portable:
1'-6" to 2'-0" by 1'-6" to 1'-10"

Serving Table (B):
2'-6" to 3'-6" by 1'-2" to 1'-9"

Sideboard or Buffet (B):
4'-0" to 6'-6" by 1'-5" to 2'-1"

China Cabinet (B):
2'-8" to 3'-8" by 1'-2" to 1'-9"

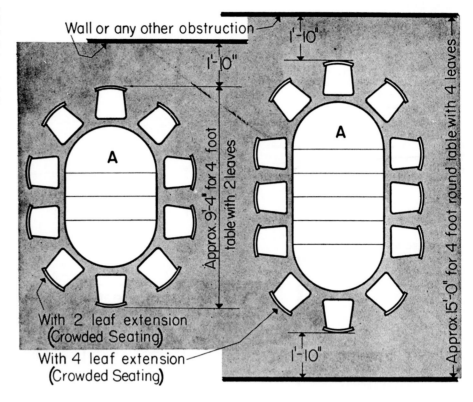

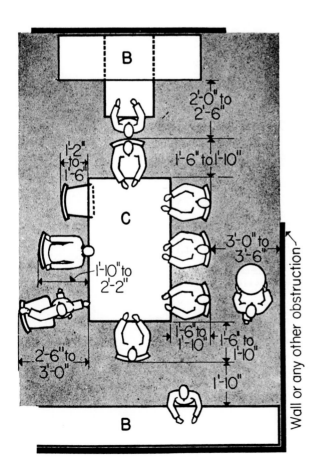

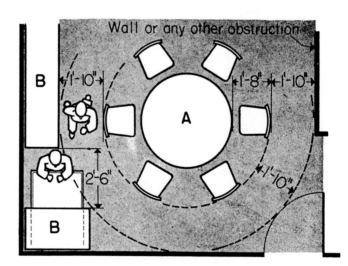

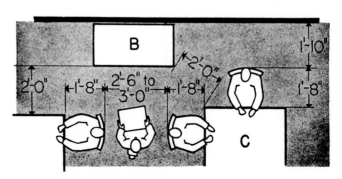

Residential

DINING AREAS

Furniture Clearances

To assure adequate space for convenient use of the dining area, not less than the following clearances from the edge of the dining table should be observed.

32 in for chairs plus access thereto
38 in for chairs plus access and passage
42 in for serving from behind chair
24 in for passage only
48 in from table to base cabinet (in dining-kitchen)

Figures 11, 12, and 13 illustrate proper clearances. Various arrangements appear on the next page.

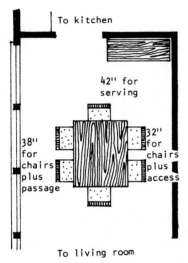

Fig. 11   Dining room for 6-person, 3-bedroom living unit.*

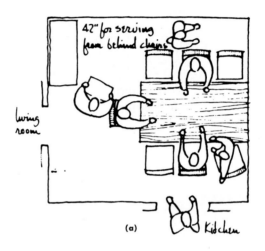

(a)

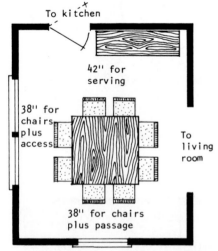

Fig. 12   Dining room for 8-person, 4-bedroom living unit.*

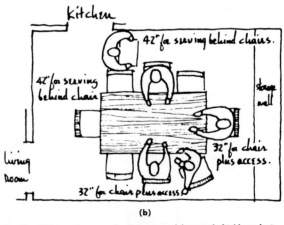

(b)

Fig. 13   Minimum clearances for dining areas. (a) one end of table against wall; (b) serving from one end and one side of table. *Source:* "Housing for the Elderly Development Process," Michigan State Housing Development Authority, 1974.

* From "Manual of Acceptable Practices," Vol. 4, U.S. Department of Housing and Urban Development, 1973.

22

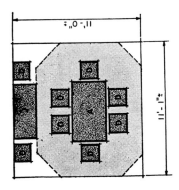
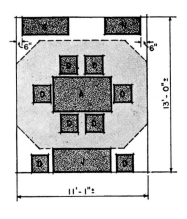
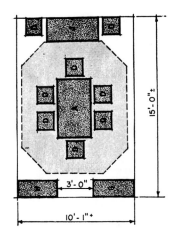

1. Minimum requires 2-ft buffet space on one side only; 3' more length is needed for extension table.

2. Typical dining-room suite, as used in East and on West Coast, requires furniture space on two sides of room.

3. Long narrow area with some waste space results when wall pieces are at ends, and end entrance is needed.

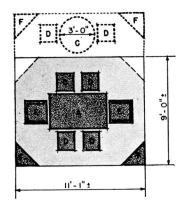
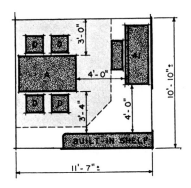
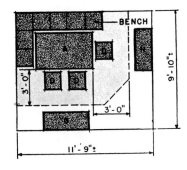

4. Solid lines indicate minimum room with corner cupboards, no wall furniture. Dotted lines indicate added space for 3' breakfast table.

5. Table-and-passage unit in one corner permits use of minimum space for multiple activities; piano may be replaced by desk, love seat, etc.

6. Spaces smaller than the usual minimum can be utilized if built-in seats are included; seating and table-service comfort are sacrificed.

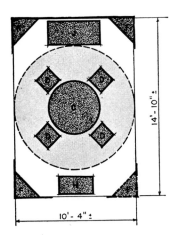
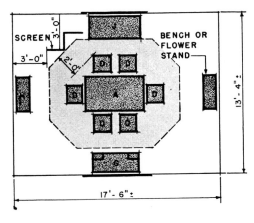
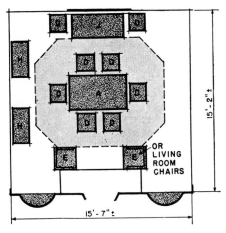

7. The same set of clearances applies to the seldom used round table as to the more popular oblong table.

8. Arrangement of typical suite in larger-than-minimum space, when a screen is used at serving door.

9. Dining rooms with fireplaces have to be larger than minimum for the comfort of those seated at table.

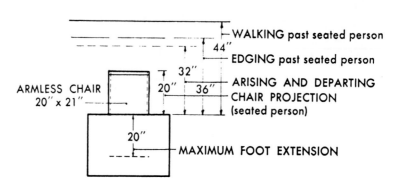

WALKING past seated person

EDGING past seated person

44″

32″

ARMLESS CHAIR
20″ x 21″

20″   36″

ARISING AND DEPARTING
CHAIR PROJECTION
(seated person)

20″

MAXIMUM FOOT EXTENSION

Rising from table, armless
chair (armchair 2″ more)
Fig. 14

Armless chair in place at table

Foot extension, knees crossed,
not at table
Fig. 15

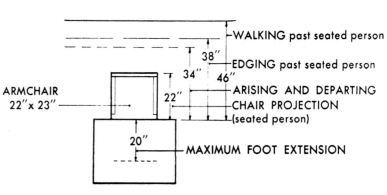

WALKING past seated person

EDGING past seated person

38″

34″   46″

ARMCHAIR
22″ x 23″

22″

ARISING AND DEPARTING
CHAIR PROJECTION
(seated person)

20″

MAXIMUM FOOT EXTENSION

Armchair in place at table

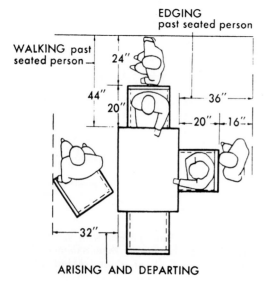

EDGING
past seated person

WALKING past
seated person

24″

44″

20″   36″

20″   16″

32″

ARISING AND DEPARTING

Using tables and chairs in free area

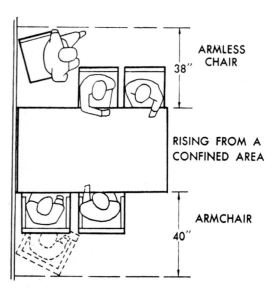

ARMLESS
CHAIR

38″

RISING FROM A
CONFINED AREA

ARMCHAIR

40″

Using tables and chairs in confined area

Walking past
seated person

Edging past
seated person

Arising from
a card table

Fig. 16

Tables and Chairs

Dining areas for eight persons with free-standing table 72 by 40 in, one armchair, and seven armless chairs (calculated on the basis of edging space on sides where there is not serving space, so that all persons can leave their seats without disturbing others).

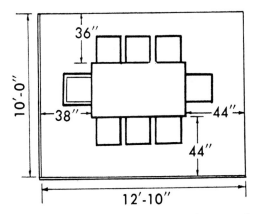

Serving space on one side and one end

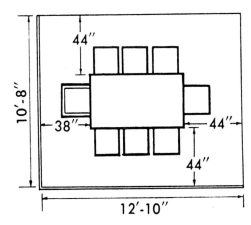

Serving space on two sides and one end

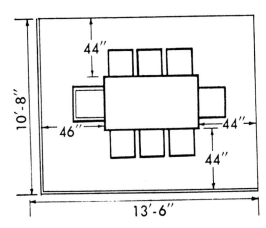

Serving space all around table

Fig. 17

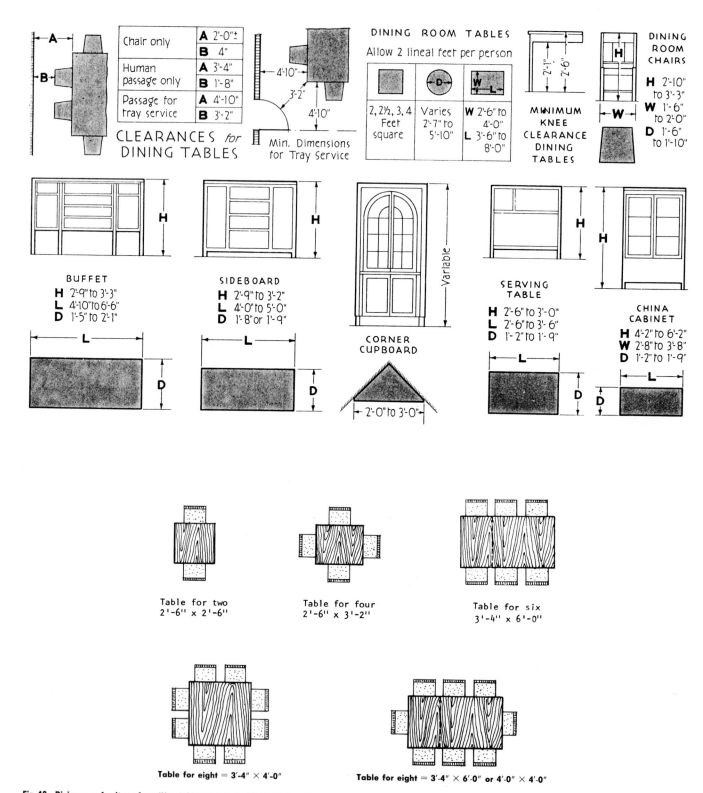

Fig. 18 **Dining room furniture.** *Source:* "Manual of Acceptable Practices," Vol. 4, U.S. Dept. of Housing and Urban Development, 1973.

COMBINED SPACES

Often several compatible living functions can be combined advantageously in a single room. Some of the benefits of such arrangements are that less space is used but it is used more intensively, its functions can be changed making it more flexible and serviceable space, it is adaptable to varied furniture arrangements, while visually it can be made more interesting and seem more generous than if the same functions were dispersed into separate rooms.

For adjacent spaces to be considered a combined room, the clear opening between them should permit common use of the spaces. This usually necessitates an opening of at least 8 ft. Figures 1 and 2 show combined living-dining rooms.

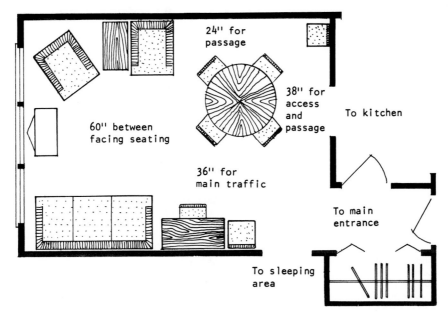

Fig. 1   Combined living-dining room.

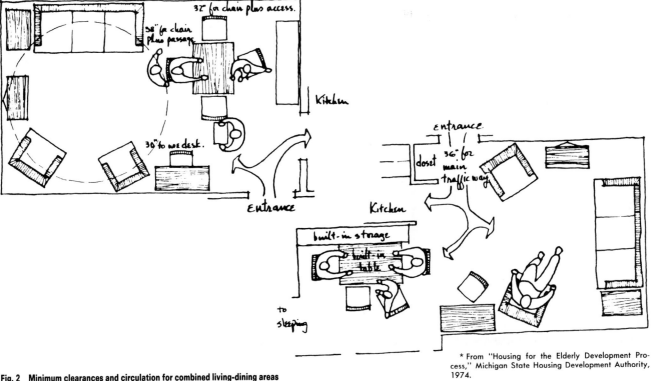

Fig. 2   Minimum clearances and circulation for combined living-dining areas

* From "Housing for the Elderly Development Process," Michigan State Housing Development Authority, 1974.

27

Residential

COMBINED DINING AREA-KITCHEN

A combination dining area–kitchen is preferred by some occupants of small houses and apartments. This arrangement minimizes housekeeping chores and provides space which can be used as the family's day-to-day meeting place.

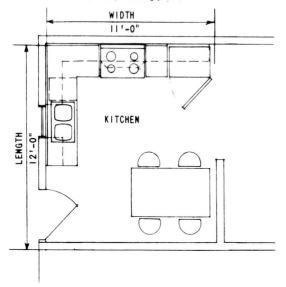

Fig. 1

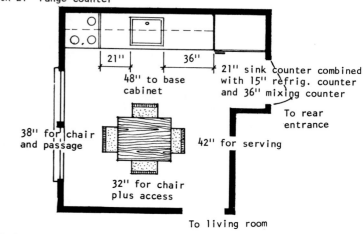

Fig. 2 **Combined dining area-kitchen, 2-bedroom living unit.** Source: "Manual of Acceptable Practices," Vol. 4, U.S. Dept. of Housing and Urban Development, 1973.

One of the primary functions of the kitchen has been to provide a place for informal or family eating. This is different than guest or formal dining in a separate dining room or area. The informal dining generally consists of breakfast, lunch, snacks, or just serving coffee to a neighbor. This eating area should be clearly defined as a separate functional area.

A frequent and desirable arrangement is the **combined kitchen-dining area. Figure 4 shows the** **various possible arrangements. Another arrangement is the kitchen-family room.**

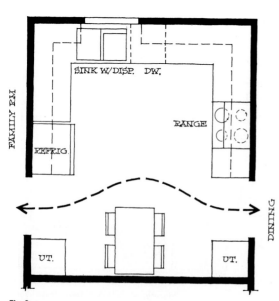

Fig. 3

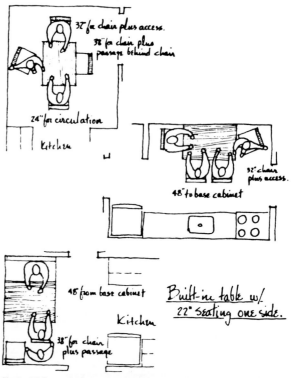

Fig. 4 **Minimum clearances for dining area in kitchen.** Source: "Housing for the Elderly Development Process," Michigan State Housing Development Authority, 1974.

28

SPACE FUNCTION

Primary and secondary activities that usually take place in bedrooms are listed below:

Primary Activities	**Secondary Activities**
Sleeping	Reading
Dressing/undressing	Writing
Storing clothes	Studying
Personal care	Working
	Watching television
	Listening to music
	Children's play
	Caring for infants
	Knitting, mending and sewing
	Ironing
	Telephoning
	Drawing and painting
	Sitting and entertaining
	Doing exercise
	Resting and convalescing
	Hobbies and crafts
	Keeping pets
	Storing bulky items and seasonal clothes

FURNITURE REQUIREMENTS

There are minimum requirements for furniture and space if occupants are to be able to carry out their normal bedroom activities. These are listed below, together with the horizontal dimensions of the recommended furniture.

Two basic types of bedrooms have been identified:

1) the single occupancy bedroom, which will accommodate one single bed;
2) the double occupancy bedroom, which will accommodate one double bed or two single beds.

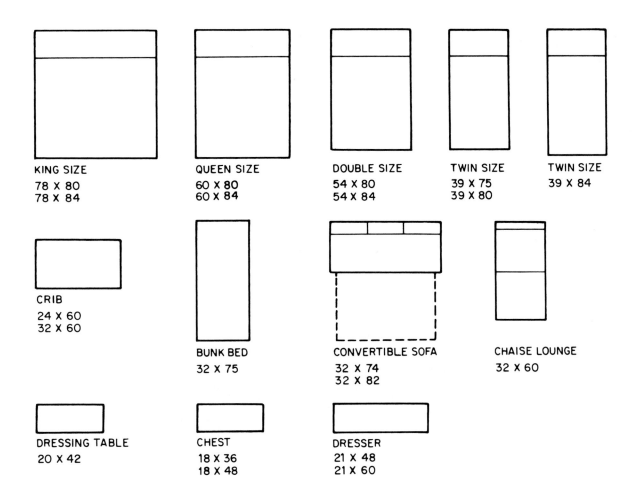

KING SIZE
78 X 80
78 X 84

QUEEN SIZE
60 X 80
60 X 84

DOUBLE SIZE
54 X 80
54 X 84

TWIN SIZE
39 X 75
39 X 80

TWIN SIZE
39 X 84

CRIB
24 X 60
32 X 60

BUNK BED
32 X 75

CONVERTIBLE SOFA
32 X 74
32 X 82

CHAISE LOUNGE
32 X 60

DRESSING TABLE
20 X 42

CHEST
18 X 36
18 X 48

DRESSER
21 X 48
21 X 60

Residential

BEDROOMS

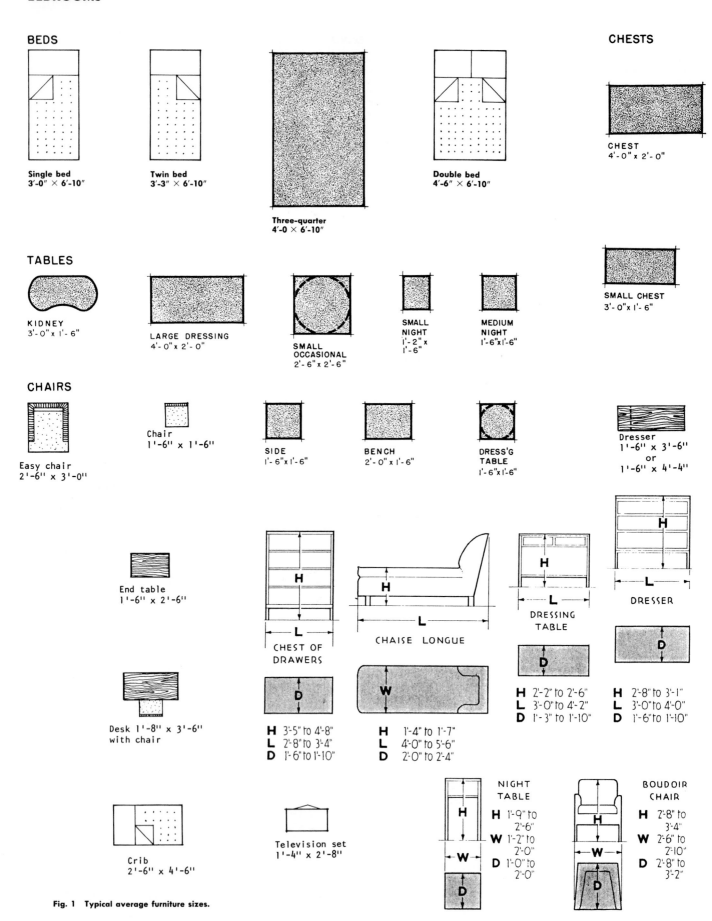

BEDS

Single bed
3'-0" × 6'-10"

Twin bed
3'-3" × 6'-10"

Three-quarter
4'-0 × 6'-10"

Double bed
4'-6" × 6'-10"

CHESTS

CHEST
4'-0" x 2'-0"

TABLES

KIDNEY
3'-0"x 1'-6"

LARGE DRESSING
4'-0"x 2'-0"

SMALL OCCASIONAL
2'-6"x 2'-6"

SMALL NIGHT
1'-2" x 1'-6"

MEDIUM NIGHT
1'-6"x1'-6"

SMALL CHEST
3'-0"x 1'-6"

CHAIRS

Easy chair
2'-6" x 3'-0"

Chair
1'-6" x 1'-6"

SIDE
1'-6"x1'-6"

BENCH
2'-0"x 1'-6"

DRESS'G TABLE
1'-6"x1'-6"

Dresser
1'-6" x 3'-6"
or
1'-6" x 4'-4"

End table
1'-6" x 2'-6"

Desk 1'-8" x 3'-6" with chair

CHEST OF DRAWERS

H 3'-5" to 4'-8"
L 2'-8" to 3'-4"
D 1'-6" to 1'-10"

CHAISE LONGUE

H 1'-4" to 1'-7"
L 4'-0" to 5'-6"
D 2'-0" to 2'-4"

DRESSING TABLE

H 2'-2" to 2'-6"
L 3'-0" to 4'-2"
D 1'-3" to 1'-10"

DRESSER

H 2'-8" to 3'-1"
L 3'-0" to 4'-0"
D 1'-6" to 1'-10"

Crib
2'-6" x 4'-6"

Television set
1'-4" x 2'-8"

NIGHT TABLE

H 1'-9" to 2'-6"
W 1'-2" to 2'-0"
D 1'-0" to 2'-0"

BOUDOIR CHAIR

H 2'-8" to 3'-4"
W 2'-6" to 2'-10"
D 2'-8" to 3'-2"

Fig. 1 Typical average furniture sizes.

30

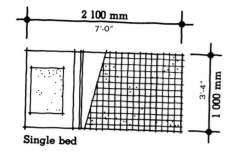

Single bed

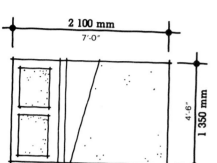

Double bed

Scale 1:50

Fig. 2 Typical bedroom furniture

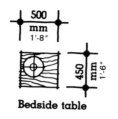

Bedside table

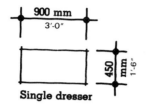

Single dresser

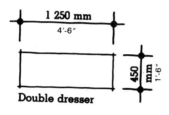

Double dresser

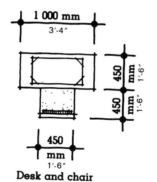

Desk and chair

CLEARANCES

Primary Activities

Clearances should be provided in front of and around furniture in bedrooms so that primary activities can take place efficiently and in comfort. In some cases, greater clearances are required to satisfy the needs of elderly people, wheelchair users and invalids.

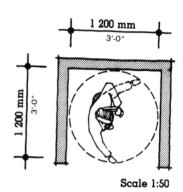

Scale 1:50

Fig. 3   Space for dressing

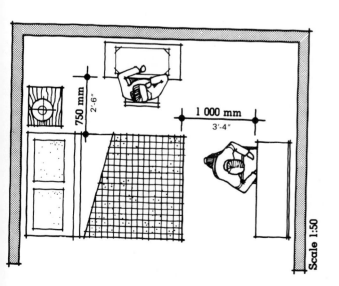

Fig. 4   Access between bed and dresser and between bed and desk

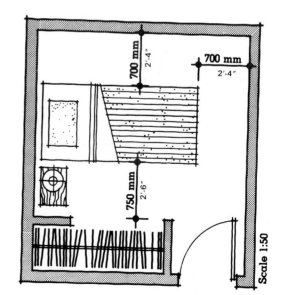

Fig. 5   Access between bed and closet and between bed and wall

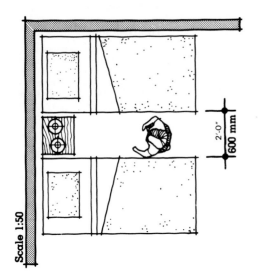

Fig. 6   Access between beds

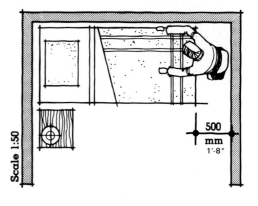

Fig. 7   Space for making beds

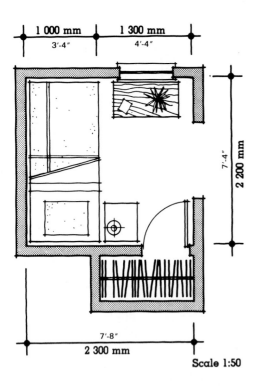

Fig. 8   Single occupancy bedroom in combination with another space. Net area: 5 m². Adults are most likely to be found in this type of bedroom

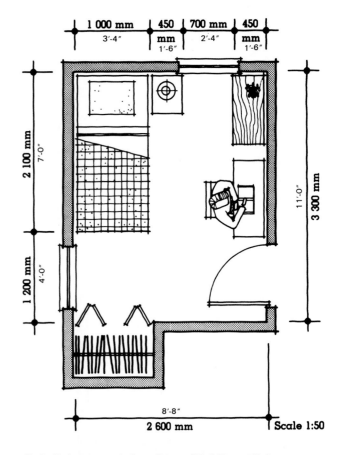

Fig. 9   Single occupancy bedroom. Net area: 8.5 m². The most likely occupants of this bedroom type are: the elderly, adults, teenagers, and the pre-adolescent child (i.e., the school age child, 9 to 12 years old)

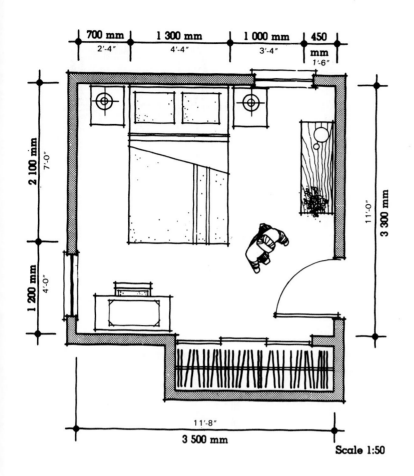

Fig. 10   Double occupancy bedroom. Net area: 11.5 m² (124 SF). Adults are the most likely occupants of this type of bedroom, which is often referred to as the master bedroom

Scale 1:50

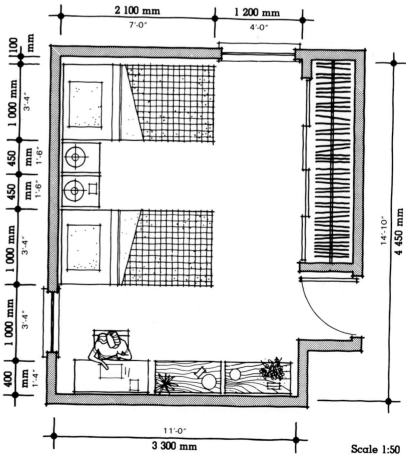

Fig. 11   Double occupancy bedroom. Net area: 14.7 m² (160 SF). The most likely occupants of this type of bedroom are adults, school age children of the same sex, children of different sexes who are less than nine-years old, and preschoolers

Scale 1:50

BEDROOM

DIAGRAMS indicate minimum clearances that should be provided for use of the bedroom furniture shown, dimensions for which are listed below. Many types and sizes of furniture are available; but those listed are most common and can serve as a basis for bedroom design. At least 2 in should be allowed as clearance between walls and furniture; 3 in between furniture units.

Beds:
Single (C), 3'-0" to 3'-3" wide; 6'-10" long.
Twin (F), 3'-3" wide; 6'-10" long.
Three-quarter (E), 4'-0" wide; 6'-10" long
Three-quarter (B), large, 4'-2" to 4'-6" wide; 6'-10" long
Double, 4'-6" wide, 6'-10" long.
Roll-away beds, (A): 2'-0" by 5'-0" on edge, 3" clearance on all sides

Bed Tables (G):
1'-2" to 2'-0" by 1'-0" to 2'-0"

Bedroom Chairs (H):
Small, 1'-8" by 1'-8"; larger, 2'-6" to 2'-10" by 2'-8" to 3'-2"

Dressers (3-drawer) **(D):**
3'-0" to 4'-0" by 1'-6" to 1'-10"

Chest of Drawers (4-drawer) **(D):**
2'-8" to 3'-4" by 1'-6" to 1'-10"

Chaise Longue:
2'-0" to 2'-4" by 4'-0" to 5'-6"

Day Bed:
2'-9" to 3'-3" by 6'-2" to 6'-8"

Dressing Table:
1'-3" to 1'-10" by 3'-0" to 4'-2"

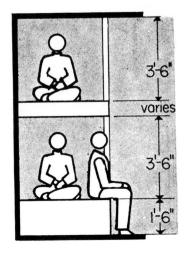

Double-deck bed

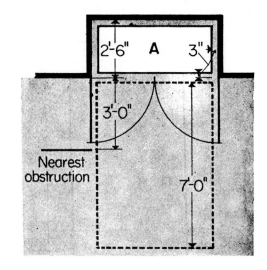

Roll-away bed

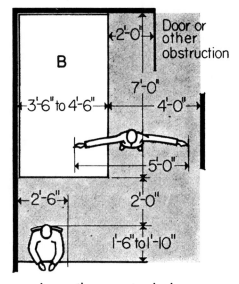

Large three-quarter bed

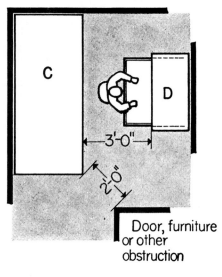

Clearance for dresser

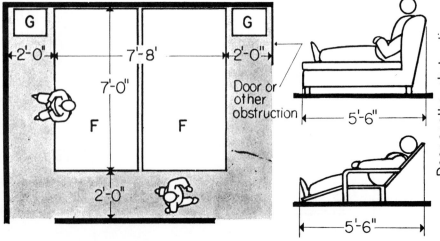

Minimum clearances for twin-bed group

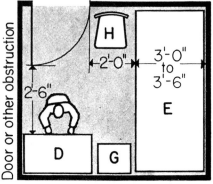

Minimum clearances for single bed and dresser group

STUDIO COUCHES

Making studio couch

Opening and edging-out space
(type tested needed to be
moved out from wall to be
opened; some do not)

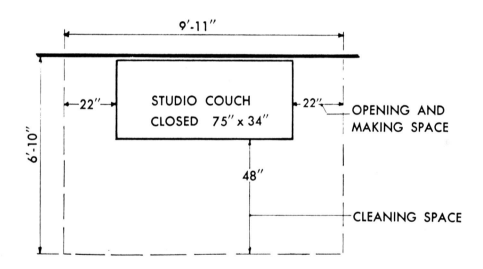

STUDIO COUCH
CLOSED   75" x 34"

9'-11"

6'-10"

22"

22"

48"

OPENING AND
MAKING SPACE

CLEANING SPACE

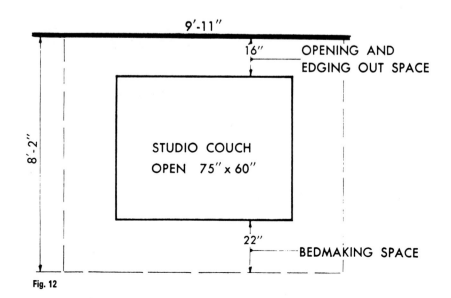

9'-11"

8'-2"

16"

22"

STUDIO COUCH
OPEN   75" x 60"

OPENING AND
EDGING OUT SPACE

BEDMAKING SPACE

Fig. 12

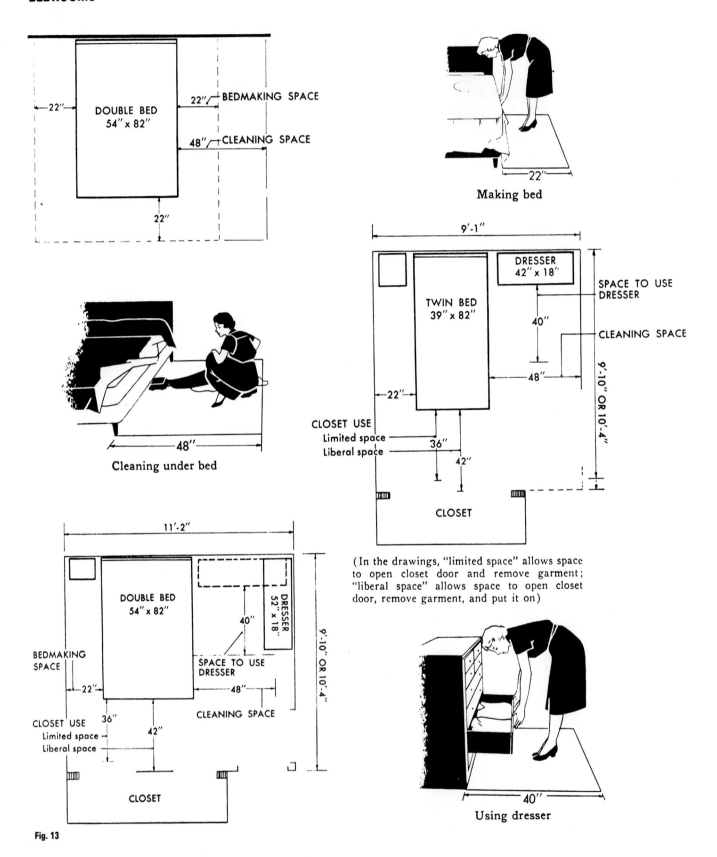

DOUBLE BED 54" x 82" — 22" BEDMAKING SPACE — 48" CLEANING SPACE — 22" — 22"

Making bed — 22"

Cleaning under bed — 48"

TWIN BED 39" x 82" — 9'-1" — DRESSER 42" x 18" — SPACE TO USE DRESSER — CLEANING SPACE — 40" — 48" — 22" — 9'-10" OR 10'-4"

CLOSET USE — Limited space — 36" — Liberal space — 42" — CLOSET

(In the drawings, "limited space" allows space to open closet door and remove garment; "liberal space" allows space to open closet door, remove garment, and put it on)

DOUBLE BED 54" x 82" — 11'-2" — DRESSER 52" x 18" — 40" — SPACE TO USE DRESSER — 48" — 9'-10" OR 10'-4"

BEDMAKING SPACE — 22" — CLEANING SPACE

CLOSET USE — 36" — Limited space — 42" — Liberal space — CLOSET

Fig. 13

Using dresser — 40"

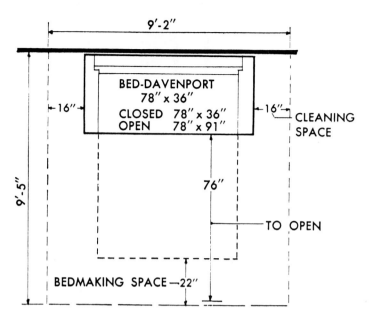

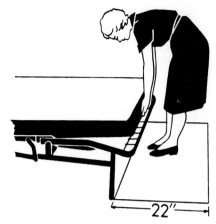

Opening or making bed-davenport

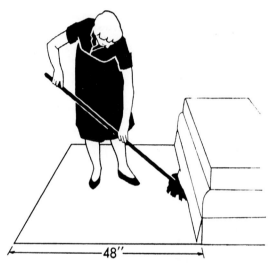

Cleaning under bed-davenport
or studio couch

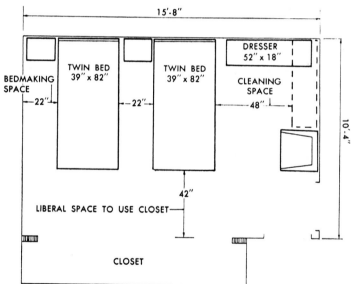

Fig. 14

BOOKCASES

Using bookcase

Cleaning under bookcase

BEDROOMS

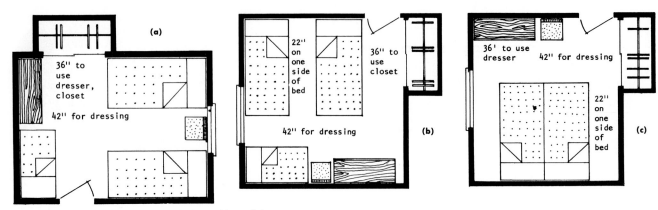

Fig. 15 (a), (c) Primary bedroom, (b) primary bedroom without crib.*

FURNITURE CLEARANCES

To assure adequate space for convenient use of furniture in the bedroom, not less than the following clearances should be observed (Figs. 15 and 16).

42 in at one side or foot of bed for dressing
6 in between side of bed and side of dresser or chest

36 in in front of dresser, closet, and chest of drawers
24 in for major circulation path (door to closet, etc.)
22 in on one side of bed for circulation
12 in on least used side of double bed. The least-used side of a single or twin bed can

be placed against the wall except in bedrooms for the elderly (Fig. 17).

FURNITURE ARRANGEMENTS

The location of doors and windows should permit alternate furniture arrangements.

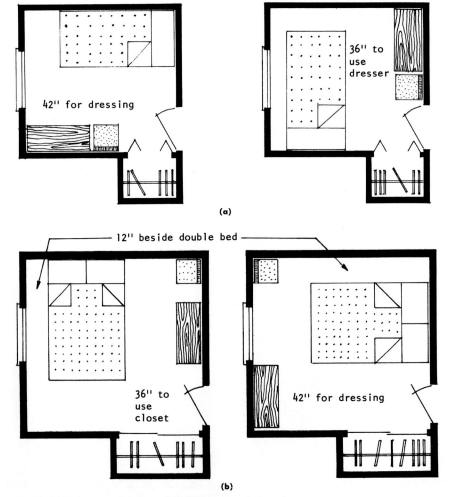

Fig. 16 (a) Single-occupancy bedroom; (b) double-occupancy bedroom.*

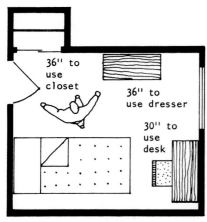

Fig. 17 Single-occupancy bedroom for elderly; there is a 12-in allowance to make the bed.*

Where at least two other sleeping spaces are provided, a dormitory is sometimes preferred by larger families (Fig. 18).*

* From "Manual of Acceptable Practices," Vol. 4, U.S. Department of Housing and Urban Development, 1973.

Fig. 18 Dormitory bedroom.

TYPICAL UNIT ARRANGEMENTS

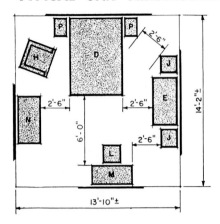

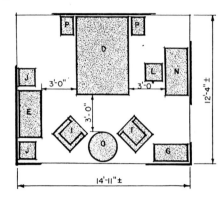

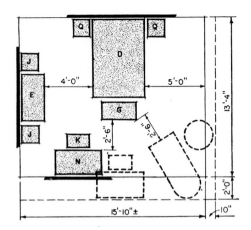

1. For comfort, 2 night tables are desirable with a double bed. A minimum double-bed unit arrangement may be achieved by omitting arm chair and one side chair, and reducing to 3'-6" the traffic lane at foot of bed.

2. Use of small chairs and chest makes possible the addition of conversation or lounging furniture (2 chairs and table) to a typical suite, without increasing square footage. Use of 3-ft passages eliminates crowding.

3. Other types of arrangements beyond the minimum include addition of a chaise longue (shown dotted above), which is usually placed at an angle to walls, requires a table, and necessitates ample passages.

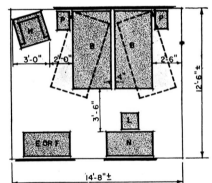

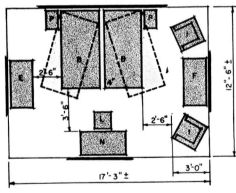

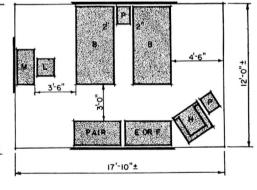

4. Minimum twin-bed group (2 night tables) needs 9'-6" wall.

5. Increased requirements for addition of dressing table and boudoir chair.

6. Twin beds with single night table require 8' of wall space.

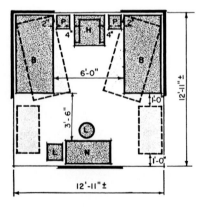

7. Variations on this plan may be developed by replacing the chair between the beds with a dressing table which serves also as a night table. This would free other walls for twin chests, shown dotted.

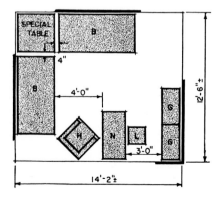

8. Twin beds heading toward a common corner may require less space than is indicated if dressing table and boudoir chair are omitted.

40

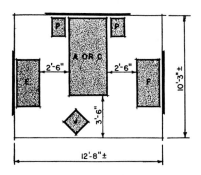

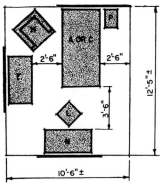

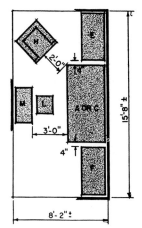

9. Single-bed unit with two night tables requires 6'-6" wall.

10. Minimum dimensions for passage both sides of bed.

11. Unusual but satisfactory arrangement or long, narrow space; if units E and F are reduced 2'-0" in length, room length may be decreased 2'-0".

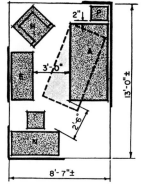

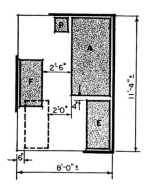

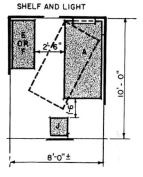

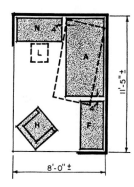

12. Minimum for couch or single bed placed sideways to wall.

13. If position of chest is changed room width may be reduced 6".

14. Door-swings may require increased clearance at foot of bed.

15. Slightly more comfortable than Fig. 14, but bed making is difficult.

COMBINED SPACES

A bed alcove with natural light and ventilation and which can be screened from the living area is desirable in a 0-bedroom living unit (Figs. 1 and 2).

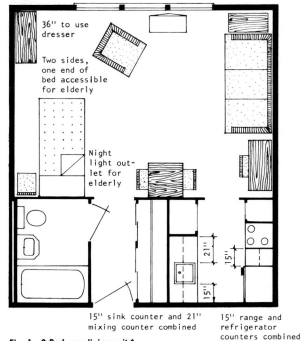

Fig. 1   0-Bedroom living unit.*

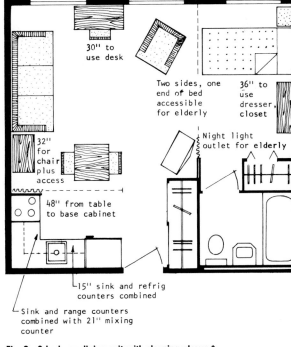

Fig. 2   0-bedroom living unit with sleeping alcove.*

* From "Manual of Acceptable Practices," Vol. 4, U.S. Department of Housing and Urban Development, 1973.

COMBINED LIVING-SLEEPING AREAS

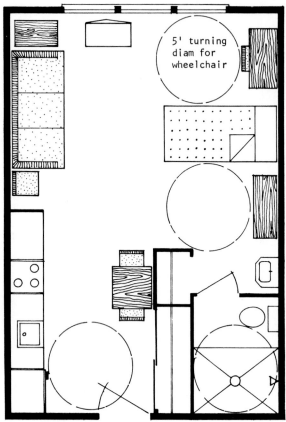

In housing for the elderly and handicapped, the units suitable for wheelchair users often can be placed advantageously on the ground floor (Fig. 3).

Fig. 3 0-Bedroom living unit for wheelchair user.*

Omission of an easy chair is acceptable to give more space for occupant's wheelchair (Fig. 4).

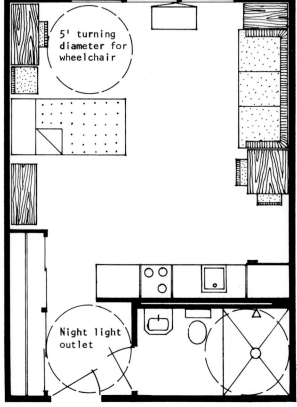

Fig. 4 0-Bedroom living unit for wheelchair user.*

* From "Manual of Acceptable Practices," Vol. 4, U.S. Department of Housing and Urban Development, 1973.

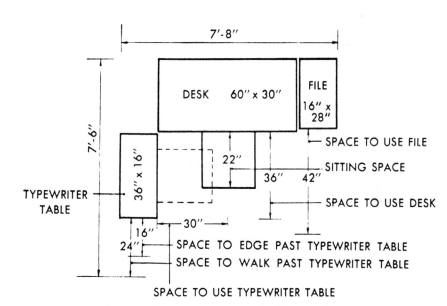

Parallel arrangement of office equipment

Using office desk

Fig. 1

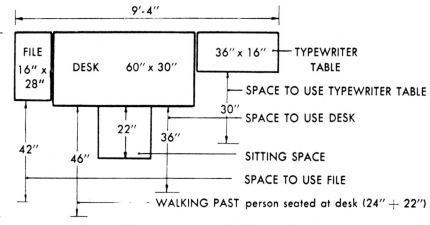

Right-angle arrangement of office equipment

Using file

Fig. 2

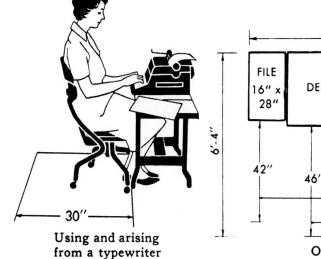

Using and arising
from a typewriter

Fig. 3

One-wall arrangement of office equipment

Residential
KITCHENS

By GLENN H. BEYER AND ALEXANDER KIRA, *Housing Research Center, Cornell University*

KITCHENS

The kitchen is not a specialized workroom, for it has many uses. It is used for preparation of meals, food preservation, storage of food and utensils, and also, in many cases, for eating, laundering, entertaining, and child care. In it a woman uses her own labor and also makes full use of electric power, tap water, and manufactured or bottled gas; she uses refrigerators, stoves, dishwashers, mixers, toasters, and garbage-disposal units, as well as various kinds of storage compartments and work surfaces.

Since more time and effort are frequently spent in the kitchen than in any other area of the house, careful planning is especially important. This requires careful selection of appliances and storage units and convenient arrangement of the area. Some general planning guides are as follows:

FOOD PREPARATION

Arrangement

It is important to keep the basic work area compact, even if the kitchen is of the large "living" type. Consideration should be given, however, to the possibility of more than one person working there. The arrangement will vary according to the size and shape of space available, but we should always keep in mind relationships among functions in different areas of the kitchen.

Traffic lanes

Traffic lanes through work areas should be avoided. Arrange the service entrance and access to the basement so that traffic not essential to food preparation, service, or storage can by-pass the area.

Storage

Kitchen design should be functional in the sense of minimizing reaching and stooping. Storage facilities should be no higher than a woman can reach with both feet flat on the floor. There should be sufficient space to store items so that they may be easily seen, reached, grasped, and taken down and put back without excessive strain. With proper planning, stored items can be located close to where they are first used, and unattractive items can be kept out of sight. Storage space should be sufficiently flexible to permit its adjustment to varying amounts, sizes, and kinds of food, supplies, and utensils. Shelving should be adjustable.

Counters and working surfaces

The height of counters and working surfaces should permit a comfortable working posture. The worker should be able to sit, if she wishes, while doing certain kitchen tasks, such as working at the sink. Continuous lines and surfaces permit ease of movement, and are easier to keep clean.

Servicing and replacement of appliances

Consideration should be given to ease of servicing and replacement of major appliances, especially built-in units.

Materials

Materials and finishes that minimize maintenance and cleaning should be used, and they should be sufficiently light in color to create a pleasant work atmosphere.

Lighting

Good lighting helps to prevent fatigue, as well as promoting safety and a pleasant atmosphere. Comfortable levels of light, with a minimum of shadows, should be planned throughout the kitchen. Adequate daylight or artificial lighting makes the room more agreeable and attractive than a dark or poorly lighted room.

Ventilation

The kitchen should be well ventilated, with an exhaust fan to remove objectionable kitchen odors.

Safety

Burns, scalds, falls, and explosions should be "designed out" of the kitchen. Sharp corners, exposed handles, and control knobs on kitchen equipment should be avoided, and there should be safety catches on doors and drawers to limit the exploratory activities of young children.

Accessibility

There should be easy access to front and back doors, laundry area, telephone, and bathroom.

Decoration

Color, texture, and decoration should be used to create an atmosphere that is attractive, cheerful, and restful.

OTHER KITCHEN ACTIVITIES

Nonworking areas

Nonworking areas should be segregated from working areas. Avoid interruption of work areas by breakfast nooks, general storage closets, rest areas, and other areas not essential to normal food preparation activities.

Eating facilities

Most families want to eat some meals in the kitchen. Provision should be made for this, if possible, even if a separate dining room is also provided.

Child's play

In younger families, especially, there is likely to be one or more children who want to be near their mother. Provision should be made for a play area out from underfoot, but where adequate supervision is possible. Storage space should be provided for toys and games.

Infant care

It is a well-known fact that many kitchens are used for care of infants. If provision is not made in the bathroom for infant care and related supplies, then it should be made in the kitchen.

Grooming

Washing hands and some personal grooming frequently take place in the

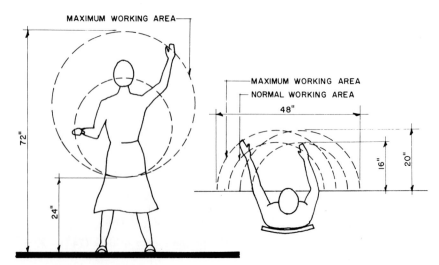

Fig. 1 Vertical and horizontal limits of reach.

kitchen, especially if there is not ready access to the bathroom. A mirror is desirable.

CRITICAL DIMENSIONS

The "critical dimensions" for working space are illustrated in Figs. 1–4. These dimensions are recommended on the basis of research and do not necessarily coincide with either current practice or currently available cabinets and equipment. Width requirements for counter space, in particular, are based on research covering operations at individual work centers. Overlapping is permissible if work at adjacent centers is not being carried on simultaneously.

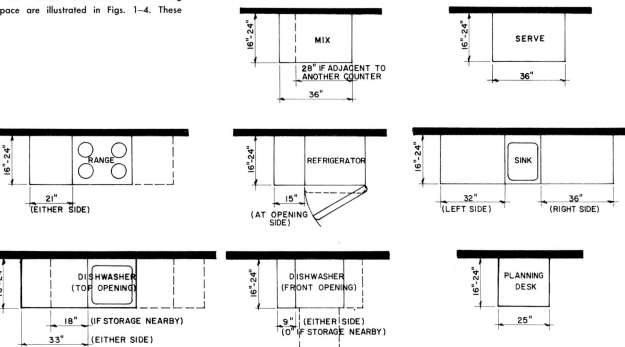

Fig. 2 Minimum counter-width dimensions.

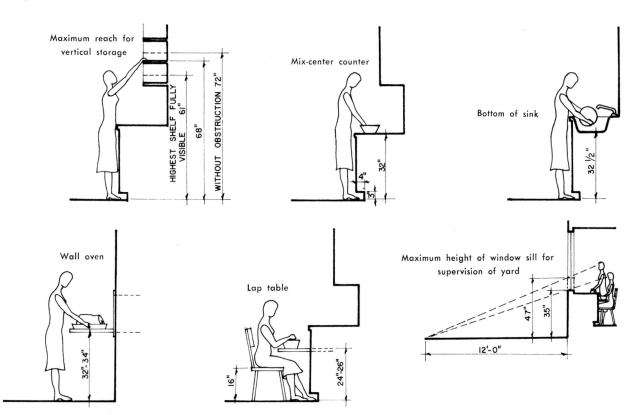

Fig. 3 Comfortable working heights.

Residential
KITCHENS

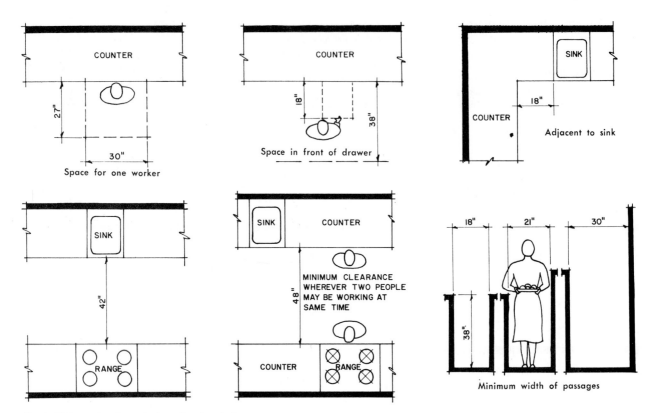

Fig. 4   Minimum clearances—horizontal and vertical.

BASIC WORK AREAS

The work center concept, favorably supported by a great deal of research data from many sources, emphasizes the planning of the kitchen in terms of its major centers of activity. These work centers, in turn, are planned in terms of their constituent parts, their proper functions, and their ideal relationships, one to another. The actual design of the work centers will vary with the size and shape of space available in each project. Four work centers must be considered: sink, range, mix, and serve. In addition, there is the refrigerator (which functions as a closely related *storage* center) and the oven, if it is not an integral part of the range.

Each work center should have three components: (1) Adequate storage space for the various items used there; (2) Adequate counter space for the work to be accomplished; and (3) Necessary utilities and facilities, such as water at the sink, heat at the range, outlet and space for the mixer at the mix center, and adequate lighting at each center.

Equip each work center for the storage of utensils, supplies, and dishes according to their frequency and order of use.

KITCHEN ARRANGEMENT

The relative location of work centers should permit a continuity of kitchen activities as follows: (1) Storage (gathering materials needed for the performance of the task); (2) Cleaning and mixing (or initial preparation); (3) Cooking; (4) Serving, or storing for future use; and (5) Cleaning up. (See Fig. 5.)

In principle, any plan that interrupts this continuity with doors, or with non-working areas or facilities, is faulty because extra steps are required every time the gap is crossed, and, consequently, convenience and working efficiency are reduced.

The actual plan may be U-shaped or L-shaped, or it may be of the corridor type.

The "U" arrangement affords the most compact work area. Frequently, however, this arrangement is impossible to achieve because of the necessity of having a door on one of the three walls. The resulting "Broken U" arrangement still permits compactness, but traffic is allowed through the area. Therefore, special consideration should be given to the arrangement of the work centers in order to minimize the effect of through traffic.

The "L" arrangement is ideally suited where space along two walls is sufficient to accommodate all of the necessary work areas. This arrangement has the advantage of concentrating the work area in one corner, thus minimizing travel, but it has the disadvantage of necessitating longer trips to the extremities of the "L."

The "Corridor" arrangement is satisfactory where doors are necessary at each end of the space. This arrangement frequently has the advantage of the parallel walls being closer together than in the typical "U," but the disadvantage of a greater distance along the corridor.

An important factor in determining the location of specific work areas within any of these over-all arrangements is frequency of use, which in Fig. 6 is expressed as the percentage of trips to and from each area.

Figures 7–9 provide floor plans illustrating some possible arrangements of the basic work centers within each of the plan types. If the space for the kitchen is already established, the number of possible satisfactory arrangements obviously will be limited. If the space is being planned, however, greater choice of arrangements is possible. In either event, the advantage of a shorter distance between some related areas must be balanced against the resulting increase in distance between other related areas. An end-to-end alignment or a right-angle arrangement between areas of close relationship can eliminate trips and reduce the over-all travel distances. Functional relationships between key work centers are, of course, accommodated more ideally in some of the plans than others.

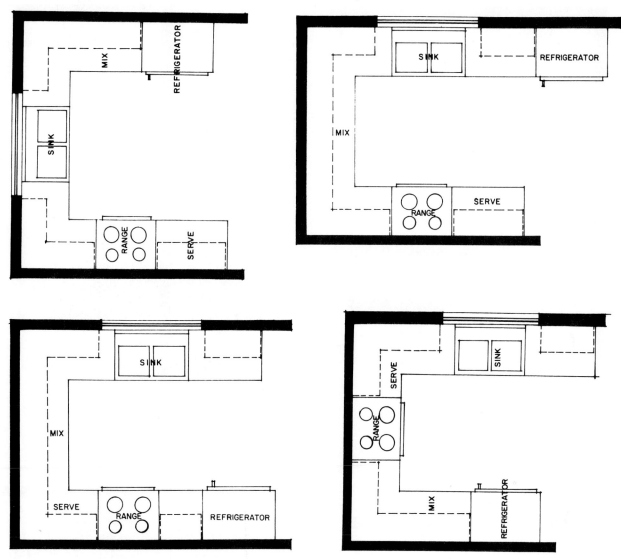

Fig. 5 U-shaped plans. If a dishwasher is desired, it should be located at the sink center.

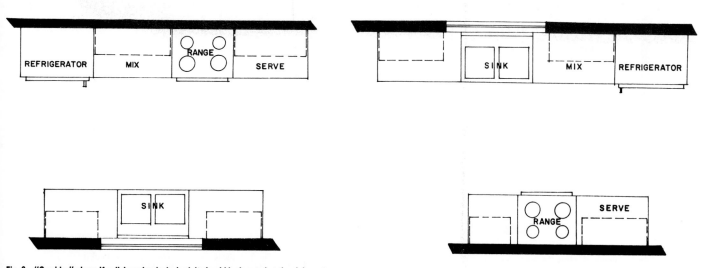

Fig. 6 "Corridor" plans. If a dishwasher is desired, it should be located at the sink center.

Residential

KITCHENS

Fig. 7 "Broken-U" plans. If a dishwasher is desired, it should be located at the sink center.

Fig. 8 L-shaped plans. If a dishwasher is desired, it should be located at the sink center.

48

A work triangle is an efficient kitchen arrangement (Fig. 9). Figures 9–11 and 18–20 are from "Manual of Acceptable Practices," Vol. 4, U.S. Department of Housing and Urban Development, 1973.

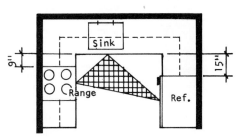

Fig. 9 Minimum distances from appliances to inside corners of base cabinets.

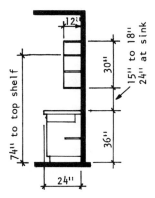

Fig. 10 Typical cabinet dimensions.

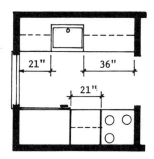

21" sink counter combined with 36" mixing counter

21" range counter combined with 15" refrig counter

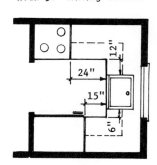

Sink and range counters combined with 36" mixing counter

21" sink counter combined with 15" refrig counter

Fig. 11 Kitchens for 2-bedroom living unit (with minimum storage, counter area, fixtures).

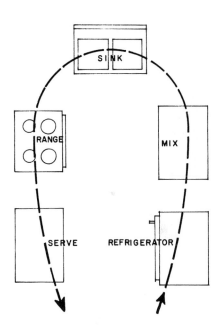

Fig. 12 Flow of work in food preparation

KITCHEN STORAGE

Total shelf area: 50 sq ft minimum; not less than 20 sq ft in either wall or base cabinets.

Total countertop area: 11 sq ft minimum.

Total drawer area: 11 sq ft minimum. (If a 39-in. range is provided, it may be counted as 4 sq ft of base cabinet shelf area and 2 sq ft of countertop area.)

Wall shelving: 74 in. maximum height.

Countertop: 38 in. maximum height, 30 in. minimum height.

Height between wall cabinets and countertop: 24 in. minimum over range and sink, 15 in. minimum elsewhere. (Shelving may be closer if it does not project beyond a line drawn from the front edge of the wall cabinet at an angle of 60 deg to the bottom of the cabinet.)

Depth of shelving: wall shelving—4 in. minimum, 18 in. maximum; base shelving—12 in. minimum, 24 in. maximum; counter-top—15 in. minimum, 24 in. maximum. *Spacing of shelving:* if depth of shelf is 4–6 in., allow 5 in. minimum spacing, if 6–10 in. allow 6 in., if 10–15 in. allow 7 in., if 15–24 in. allow 10 in.

Backsplash (required where countertop abuts walls): 4 in. minimum height.

Steel cabinets: minimum gages—case and drawer slides, 16; gussets and cross rails, 18; bottoms, door and drawer fronts and sides, 20; elsewhere, 22.

Exhaust fan (required in ceiling or wall near range, or in hood over range): minimum capacity—15 air changes per hour.

Using a conventional range

Using a wall oven

Using a refrigerator

Using a base cabinet

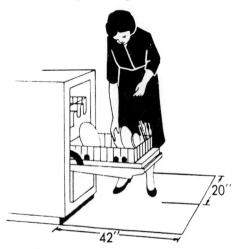

Using a front-opening dishwasher requires 4 inches more space than using other appliances in a kitchen

Fig. 13

Using a cleaning closet

KITCHENS

This section gives recommended minimum counter space dimensions, comments on points to be considered in the layout, and illustrates various shapes of kitchens.

All dimensions given are measured along the front of base cabinets. The dimensions may be angled around a corner, provided that the minimum distances of equipment to base cabinet corners are observed. No dimensions should overlap with each other.

The illustrations show one arrangement of the "handing" of the kitchen—that is, the side of the sink on which the range is located. This may be varied according to design requirements and preferences.

Occupancy of the dwelling is indicated by code—for example, "5 and 6P" means "five and six persons."

All illustrations are diagrammatic; they do not represent detailed room plans.

Fig. 14

TABLE 1 Minimum Width of Sink

1 and 2P	500 mm (1 ft 8 in)
3 and 4P	500 mm (1 ft 8 in)
5 and 6P	500 mm (1 ft 8 in)
7 and 8P	600 mm (2 ft 0 in)

A total clearance of 50 mm (2 in) is allowed (Table **2**).

Fig. 15

TABLE 2 Minimum Space for Range, Including Clearances

1 and 2P	650 mm (2 ft 2 in)
3 and 4P	800 mm (2 ft 8 in)
5 and 6P	800 mm (2 ft 8 in)
7 and 8P	800 mm (2 ft 8 in)

A total clearance of 50 mm (2 in) is allowed. When the refrigerator is located at the end of base cabinets and is open to the room, only 25 mm (1 in) clearance between the refrigerator and cabinets is required (Table **3**).

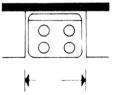

Fig. 16

TABLE 3 Minimum Space for Refrigerator, Including Clearances

1 and 2P	650 mm (2 ft 2 in)
3 and 4P	800 mm (2 ft 8 in)
5 and 6P	800 mm (2 ft 8 in)
7 and 8P	800 mm (2 ft 8 in)

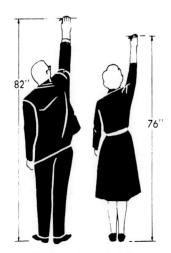

Reaching, maximum height

Reaching over obstruction, 24″ deep and 36″ high

Reaching over obstruction, 12″ deep and 36″ high (women only)

Maximum reach to back of shelf 12″ deep (women only)

Fig. 17

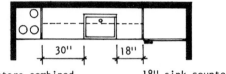

Sink and range counters combined
with 30" mixing counter

18" sink counter combined
with 15" refrig. counter

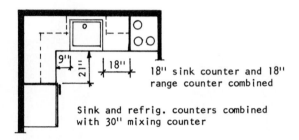

18" sink counter and 18"
range counter combined

Sink and refrig. counters combined
with 30" mixing counter

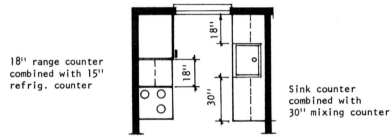

18" range counter
combined with 15"
refrig. counter

Sink counter
combined with
30" mixing counter

Fig. 18   Kitchens for 1-bedroom living units (with minimum storage, counter area, fixtures). For kitchens for 0-bedroom living units, see pp. 27-28.

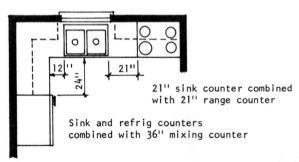

21" sink counter combined
with 21" range counter

Sink and refrig counters
combined with 36" mixing counter

Fig. 19   Kitchen for 3-bedroom living unit (with minimum storage, counter area, fixtures).

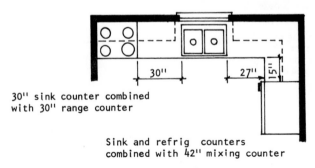

30" sink counter combined
with 30" range counter

Sink and refrig counters
combined with 42" mixing counter

Fig. 20   Kitchen for 4-bedroom living unit (with minimum storage, counter area, fixtures).

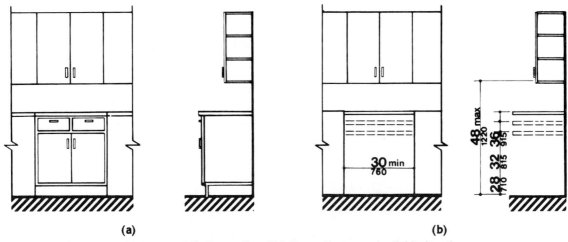

(a)   (b)

Fig. 21   Counter work surface. (a) Before removal of cabinets and base. (b) Cabinets and base removed and height alternatives.

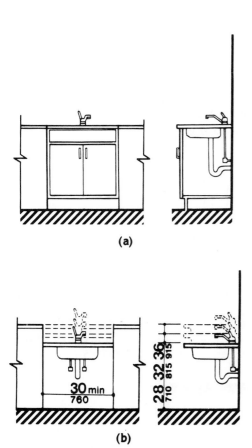

(a)

(b)

Fig. 22   Kitchen sink. (a) Before removal of cabinets and base. (b) Cabinets and base removed and height alternatives.

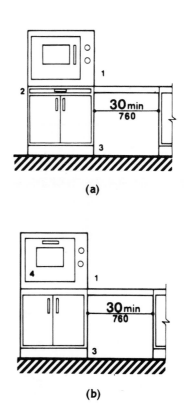

(a)

(b)

SYMBOL KEY:
1. Countertop or wall-mounted oven.
2. Pull-out board preferred with side-opening door.
3. Clear open space.
4. Bottom-hinged door.

Fig. 23   Ovens without self-cleaning feature. (a) Side-hinged door. (b) Bottom-hinged door.

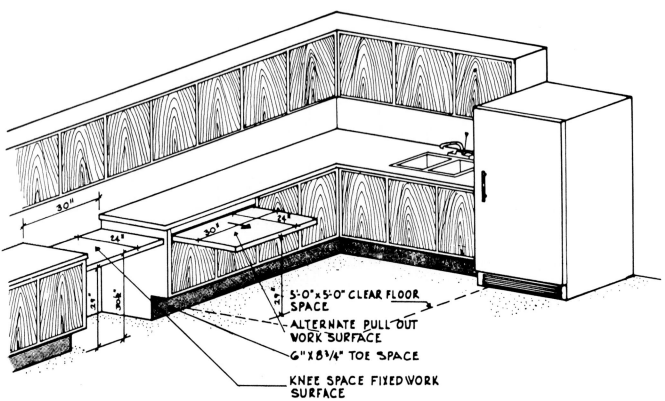

Fig. 24 Adaptable kitchens.

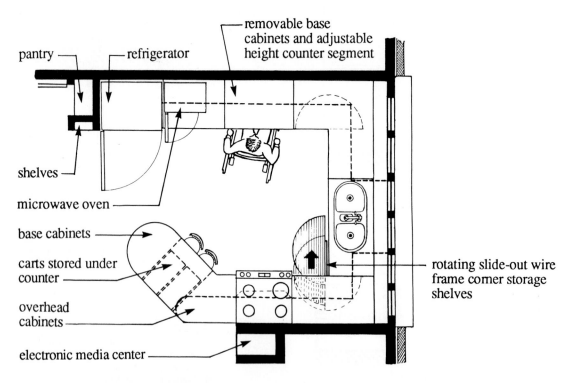

Fig. 25 Plan of elaborate kitchen with adaptable features.

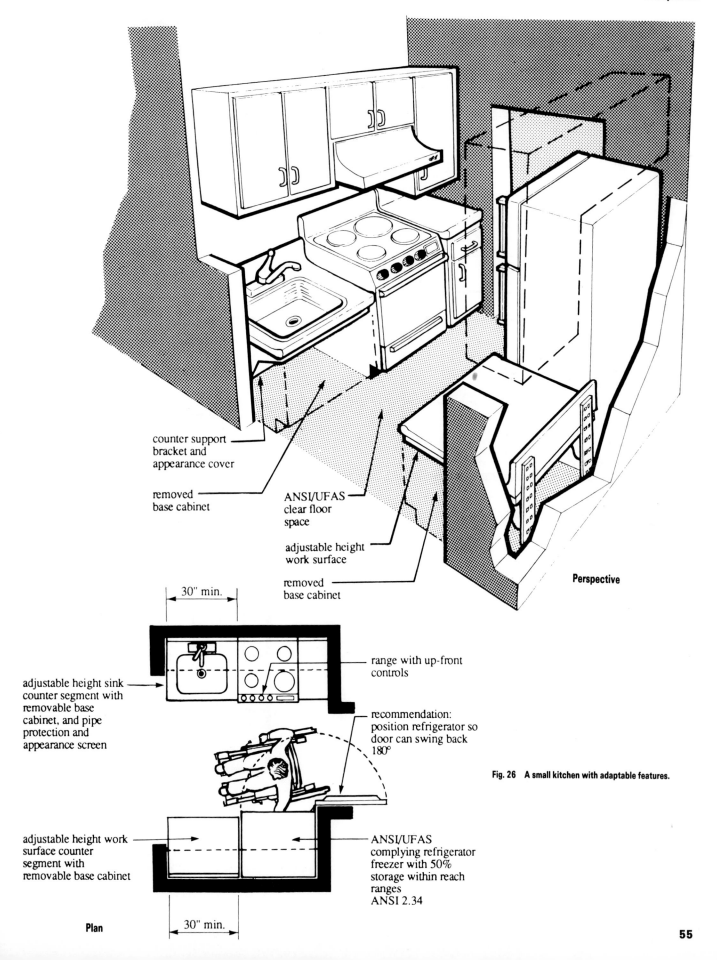

counter support
bracket and
appearance cover

removed
base cabinet

ANSI/UFAS
clear floor
space

adjustable height
work surface

removed
base cabinet

Perspective

30" min.

range with up-front
controls

adjustable height sink
counter segment with
removable base
cabinet, and pipe
protection and
appearance screen

recommendation:
position refrigerator so
door can swing back
180°

Fig. 26 A small kitchen with adaptable features.

adjustable height work
surface counter
segment with
removable base cabinet

ANSI/UFAS
complying refrigerator
freezer with 50%
storage within reach
ranges
ANSI 2.34

Plan   30" min.

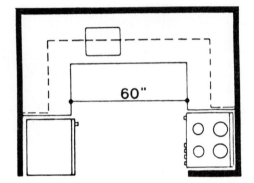

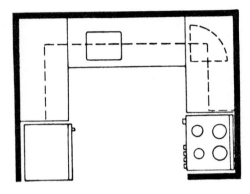

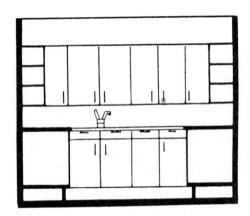

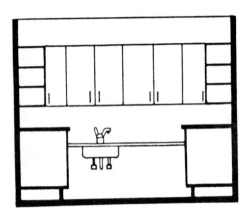

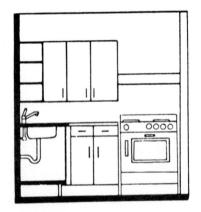

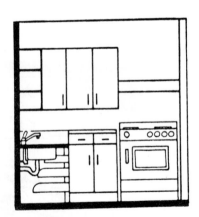

Accessible; before re-
moval of cabinets and
base.

Cabinets and base re-
moved, counter height
lowered.

Fig. 27 Example of adaptable kitchen—U-shaped plan.

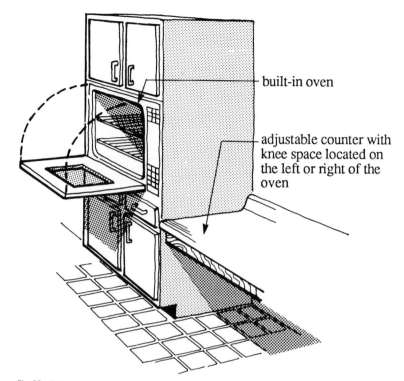

built-in oven

adjustable counter with knee space located on the left or right of the oven

Fig. 28 Work surface at non-self-cleaning oven with drop-front door.

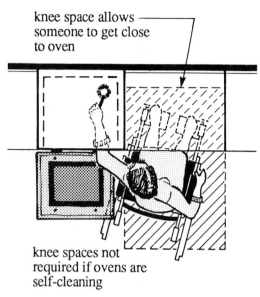

knee space allows someone to get close to oven

knee spaces not required if ovens are self-cleaning

Fig. 29 Use of knee space next to oven.

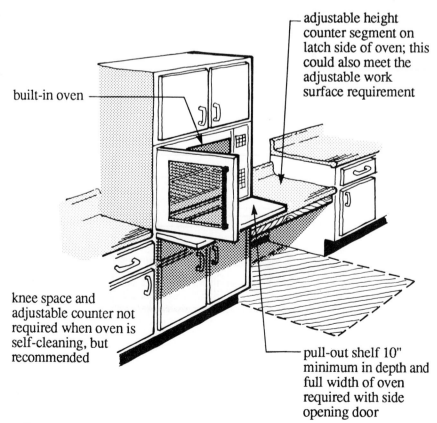

adjustable height counter segment on latch side of oven; this could also meet the adjustable work surface requirement

built-in oven

knee space and adjustable counter not required when oven is self-cleaning, but recommended

pull-out shelf 10" minimum in depth and full width of oven required with side opening door

Fig. 30 Pull-out shelf at non-self-cleaning oven with side-opening door.

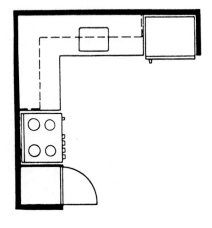

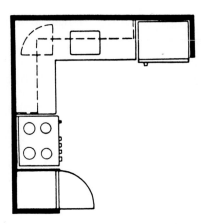

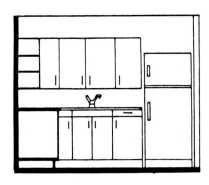

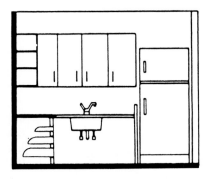

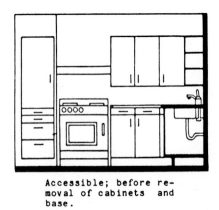

Accessible; before removal of cabinets and base.

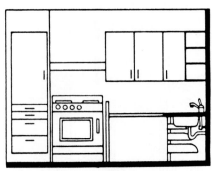

Cabinets and base removed, counter height lowered.

Fig. 31 Example of adaptable kitchen—L-shaped plan.

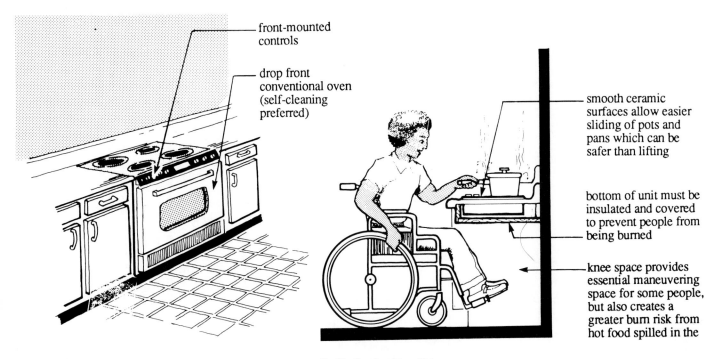

front-mounted controls

drop front conventional oven (self-cleaning preferred)

smooth ceramic surfaces allow easier sliding of pots and pans which can be safer than lifting

bottom of unit must be insulated and covered to prevent people from being burned

knee space provides essential maneuvering space for some people, but also creates a greater burn risk from hot food spilled in the

Fig. 32   Standard range.

Fig. 33   Use of cooktop with knee space.

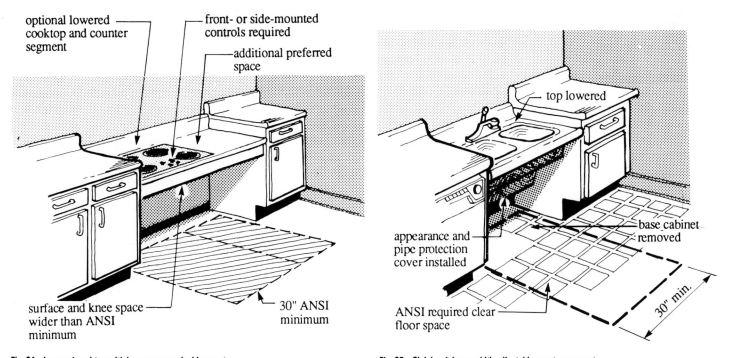

optional lowered cooktop and counter segment

front- or side-mounted controls required

additional preferred space

surface and knee space wider than ANSI minimum

30" ANSI minimum

top lowered

base cabinet removed

appearance and pipe protection cover installed

ANSI required clear floor space

30" min.

Fig. 34   Lowered cooktop with knee space and wide counter.

Fig. 35   Sink in minimum width adjustable counter segment.

EXAMPLES: CLEARANCES OVER COOKING RANGES

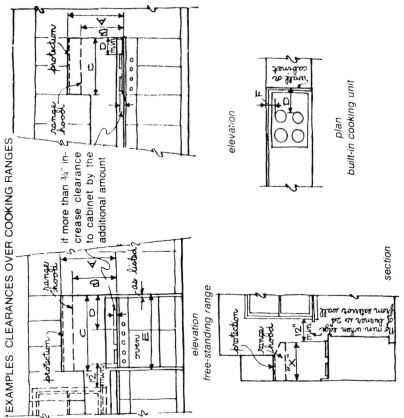

elevation
free-standing range

elevation

plan
built-in cooking unit

section

if more than ¾ in-crease clearance to cabinet by the additional amount

A^1 2'6" min. clearance between top of range and bottom of unprotected wood or metal cabinet,
or—2'0" min. when bottom of wood or metal cabinet is protected.

B   2'0" min. when hood projection "X" is 18" or more,
or—1'10" min. when hood projection "X" is less than 18".

C   Not less than width of range or cooking unit.

D^2 10" min. when vertical side surface extends above countertops.

E^2 When range is not provided by builder, 40" min.

F^2 Min. clearance shall be not less than 3".

[1]cabinet protection shall be at least ¼" asbestos millboard covered with not less than 28 ga. sheet metal (.015 stainless steel, .024 aluminum, or .020 copper).

[2]clearance for D, E, or F shall be not less than listed UL or AGA clearances.

Minimum Kitchen Storage Required

40 to 60 sq. ft. area—Kitchenette (2)

Item	0-BR Liv. Unit (1) (sq. ft.)	1-BR Liv. Unit (sq. ft.)
Total Shelving in Wall and Base Cabinets	24	30
Shelving in Either Wall or Base Cabinets	10	12
Drawer Area	4	5
Countertop Area	5	6

(1) Kitchen unit assemblies serving the kitchen function and occupying less than 40 sq. ft. area in 0-BR Living Units shall not be less than 5 feet in length and shall provide at least 12 sq. ft. of total shelving in wall and base cabinets. Drawer and countertop space shall also be provided. No room count is allowable for this type facility.

60 sq. ft. area and over—Kitchen

Item	1-BR and 2-BR Living Units (sq. ft.)	3-BR and 4-BR Living Units (sq. ft.)
Total Shelving in Wall and Base Cabinets	48	54
Shelving in Either Wall or Base Cabinets	18	20
Drawer Area	8	10
Countertop Area	10	12

a. An area occupied by sink basin(s) and by cooking units shall not be included in countertop area.

b. Usable storage space in or under ranges, or under wall ovens, when provided in the form of shelving or drawers, may be included in the minimum shelf or drawer area.

c. The shelf area of revolving base shelves (lazy susan) may be counted as twice its actual area in determining required shelf area provided the clear width of opening is at least 8-1/2 inches.

d. Drawer area in excess of the required area may be substituted for required base shelf area up to 25 percent of total shelf area.

e. At least 60 percent of required shelf space shall be enclosed by cabinet doors.

Minimum Property Standards, U.S. Department of Housing and Urban Development, Washington, D.C.

Kitchen Storage

Each kitchen or kitchenette shall have: (1) accessible storage space for food and utensils; (2) sufficient space for the average kitchen accessories; (3) sufficient storage space for those items of household equipment normally used and for which storage is not elsewhere provided.

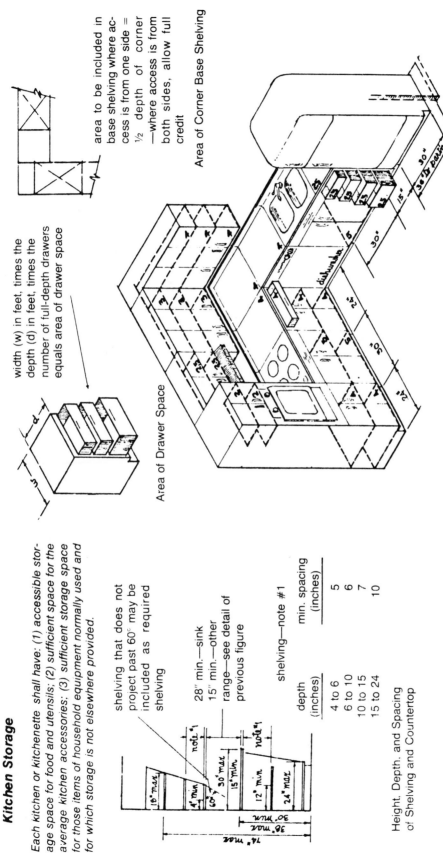

area to be included in base shelving where access is from one side = $\frac{1}{2}$ depth of corner —where access is from both sides, allow full credit

Area of Corner Base Shelving

width (w) in feet, times the depth (d) in feet, times the number of full-depth drawers equals area of drawer space

Area of Drawer Space

shelving that does not project past 60° may be included as required shelving

28" min.—sink
15" min.—other range—see detail of previous figure

shelving—note #1

depth (inches)	min. spacing (inches)
4 to 6	5
6 to 10	6
10 to 15	7
15 to 24	10

Height, Depth, and Spacing of Shelving and Countertop

EXAMPLE: MEASUREMENT OF SHELF AND COUNTERTOP AREAS

wall shelving
2 s. ft.	x 2 =	4 s. ft.	
2.5	x 2 =	5	
3	x 3 =	9	
4	x 3 =	12	
	total	30 s. ft.	

base shelving
4 s. ft.	x 4 =	16 s. ft.	
5	x 3 =	15	
2	x 2 =	4	
	total	35 s. ft.	

countertop
4 s. ft.	x 3 =	12 s. ft.	
2.5	x 1 =	2.5	
	total	14.5 s. ft.	

drawers
4 s. ft.	x 1 =	4 s. ft.	
2.5	x 4 =	10	
	total	14 s. ft.	

Minimum Property Standards, U.S. Department of Housing and Urban Development, Washington, D.C.

Residential
LAUNDRY ROOMS

By GLENN H. BEYER AND ALEXANDER KIRA, *Housing Research Center, Cornell University*
(including material adapted from previously published article by Larch C. Renshaw in 3rd ed. of Time-Saver Standards)

LAUNDRIES

Laundering includes a host of tasks—collecting and sorting dirty clothes, pretreating, washing, drying, sprinkling and ironing—all of which are tiring, for they require a great deal of stooping, lifting, and carrying. To reduce the amount of effort required, a laundry center (either separate or combined with another area) should be carefully planned. Some basic planning considerations are as follows:

Arrangement

The sequence of laundering operations should determine the planning of space and facilities and the placing of equipment.

Traffic lanes

With automatic equipment, many families now wash clothes three or four days a week. Therefore, laundering should not be done in any of the congested areas of the house. Passageways should be at least 4 ft wide. If the laundry area adjoins the kitchen, there should be a barrier of some type, at least a counter, between the two areas.

Equipment and facilities

To reduce the amount of effort required, a laundry center should have a sorting table, a heating surface (such as a hot plate), and storage facilities for soiled clothes, washing supplies, and baskets, as well as a washing machine, dryer, and ironing board; some may also have ironers. A laundry tray (usually a 14-in.-deep porcelain enamel sink) is desirable for prewashing, soaking, or starching some items.

Space

The space should be dry, heated, and well lighted, with sufficient electrical outlets, properly located. The space should be ventilated to remove moisture and odors.

Accessibility

Laundry centers today can be more conveniently located because of the compactness of automatic washers and dryers and the elimination of much of the dampness and disorder formerly associated with household washing. Although many locations are possible (such as the kitchen, bath, separate laundry room, or utility room), the laundry center should be accessible both to the work areas of the house (since frequent trips to and from them may be required during any of the laundering processes) and to outdoor summer drying areas.

FLOW OF WORK

Convenience and efficiency are achieved by placing the equipment in their natural order of use: (1) Clothes chute (with or without bins or hampers), (2) Sorting and pretreating table or counter, (3) Washing machine, (4) Laundry tray (if available), (5) Dryer, (6) Ironing board (and ironer, if available), and (7) Standing or hanging bar and counter for ironed items. In addition, a storage closet or cabinet is necessary for cleaning supplies. In some instances, a hot plate is also needed. Some of these facilities and equipment are described in more detail below.

Clothes chute: In two-story houses, the chute is a handy device for delivering clothes from upstairs. It should empty on or near the sorting table so that the clothes will not have to be carried or handled more than necessary. It should be vertical, because curved sections are likely to cause clothes to clog the chute.

Sorting and pretreating table: Ample space should be allowed on a table or counter for sorting and dampening the clothes, and for a clothes basket, as well as space for the worker using the table. The table size required will depend upon the size of the average wash load. Research at Pennsylvania State University indicates that a table 6x2½ ft is required for a 32-lb, 4-load laundry. For pretreating, an area 20x36 in. is adequate for work and equipment (pan, brush, soap, and kettle).

Washing machine: Automatic washers and dryers permit much more convenient and compact arrangements than were possible with nonautomatic equipment. The total floor area needed is determined by the type of washer, the other equipment needed, and the space for the worker. The old-fashioned, galvanized tubs are not required with automatic equipment, but, as indicated earlier, a laundry tray is desirable. To ensure that a laundry area is both economical in use of space and convenient to work in, the dimensions shown in Fig. 4 should be followed.

Drying: The research at Pennsylvania State University revealed that 124 lin ft of line is required to hang a 4-load laundry of 32 lb.

The space requirements for different styles of dryers, and for operating them, are shown in Fig. 5. The combination washer-dryer or the stacked arrangement of washer and dryer requires less floor area than other arrangements. These dimensions are shown in Fig. 6.

Since some garments must be hung to drip-dry, a pull-out drying rod or similar arrangement should be provided, preferably above a laundry tray (or a floor drain, if the laundry is in the basement).

Ironing: An ironing board adjustable from a height of 23 to 37 in. accommodates most women when sitting or standing to iron. The choice of either a built-in or a freestanding board depends upon personal preference. Freestanding boards should be stored where they are readily accessible. The space needed to use a hand iron at a board is shown in Fig. 2. The space needed to use an ironer, with auxiliary equipment, is shown in Fig. 3.

The *storage closet* should be large enough to accommodate soaps, spoons, sieves, bleaches, bluing, stain remover, starch, clothespins, and the like. If a storage cupboard 8 in. in depth is placed over an automatic washer, it should be at least 20 in. above the washer; and if 12 in. in depth, it should be 24 in. above the washer. This clearance allows for head room when using the water faucets.

SPACE ARRANGEMENTS

Laundering may be done in a room designed especially for this purpose, or in a multiuse room, designed also for food preparation, sewing, child play, and the like.

The best location, of course, is convenient to other work centers, such as the kitchen, and to the drying yard so that there will be a minimum of carrying necessary. Generally, basements are not considered desirable locations because of their inconvenience, dampness, and lack of adequate light.

Figures 7–13 provide floor plans illustrating various arrangements of basic work areas needed for the laundering process. In some of the plans shown, the space needed for laundering is treated as a separate area; in others, possible combinations with other areas are indicated.

EQUIPMENT

Figure 1 and Tables 1 and 2 provide basic dimensions of a typical automatic washer, dryer, combination washer-dryer, and ironer. These dimensions may be used for preliminary planning purposes, but final selection of equipment and detailing of working drawings should always be based on specific manufacturer's data.

Dimensions have been drawn from the current catalogs of leading manufacturers of each type of equipment. Special and nonresidential equipment are not included. Dimensions are generally given only to the nearest half inch since dimensions of new models vary slightly from year to year.

Door swings, location of vents, and the specific requirements for power, waste, and water supply should be checked against the manufacturer's data after units have been tentatively selected.

Table 1. Dimensions for matched automatic washer and dryer

Washer and dryer may be free-standing or built into adjoining base cabinets. Some models are available without tops and splash-boards for undercounter installation (the height is then $34\frac{1}{2}$ in.), with both doors front-opening. Some models have sloped fronts; others may be stacked vertically, built-in.

Depth, in.	Width (W^1), in.	Width (W^2), in.	Height, in.
24	25	25	36
26	24	24	36
26	25	27	36
26	25	30	36
26	29	29	36
27	27	27	36
28	26	31	36
28	31	31	37

Table 2. Dimensions for combination automatic washer-dryer

Some models are available for undercounter installation (the height is then $34\frac{1}{2}$ in.). Some models are also available with sloped fronts.

Depth, in.	Width, in.	Height, in.
25	30	$34\frac{1}{2}$
26	34	45
28	31	36
28	32	37

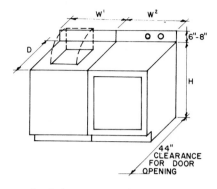

a. Matched automatic washer and dryer

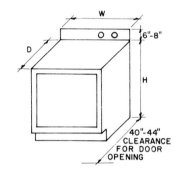

b. Combination automatic washer-dryer

c. Ironer

Fig. 1. Dimensions of household laundry equipment

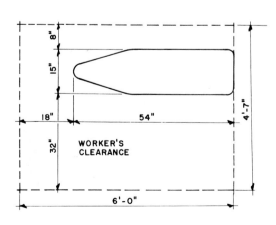

Fig. 2. Space requirements for ironing board

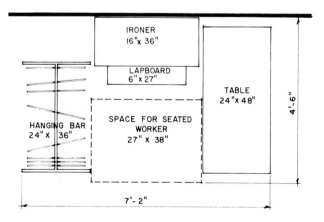

Fig. 3. Space requirements for ironer

Source (Fig. 2 and 3): Cecile P. Sinden and Kathleen A. Johnston, Space for Home Laundering, *Bulletin 658, Pennsylvania State University Agricultural Experiment Station, University Park (July 1959).*

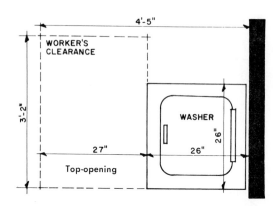 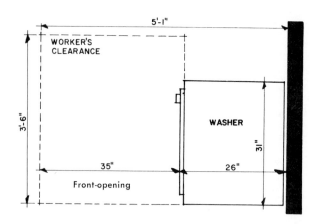

Fig. 4. Space requirements for two types of automatic washers

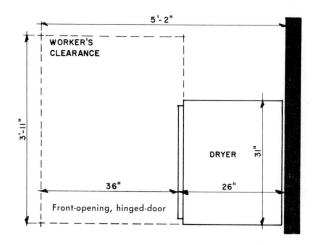 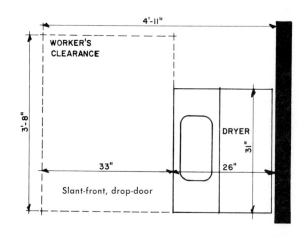

Fig. 5. Space requirements for two types of automatic dryers

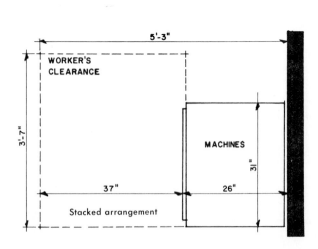 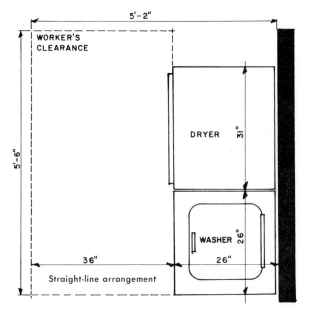

Fig. 6. Space requirements for combination washer-dryer

Worker's clearance (Fig. 4, 5, and 6) can overlap to either left or right of machines. Source (Fig. 4, 5, and 6): Cecile P. Sinden and Kathleen A. Johnston, Space for Home Laundering, *Bulletin 658, Pennsylvania State University Agricultural Experiment Station, University Park (July 1959).*

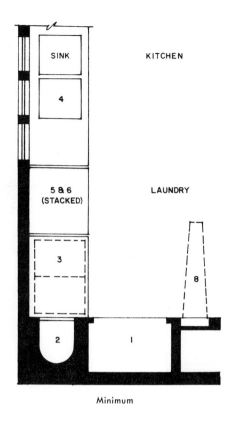

Minimum

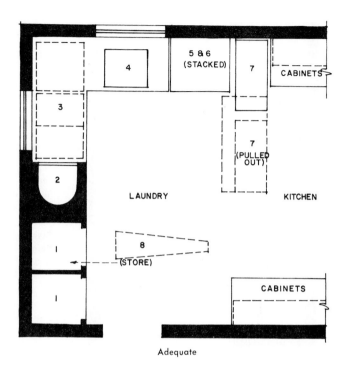

Adequate

Key

1. Storage closet
2. Laundry chute (ventilated)
3. Sorting shelf (ventilated bins below)
4. Laundry tray with mixing faucet and cover
5. Washer
6. Dryer (should be ventilated)
7. Ironer
8. Ironing board

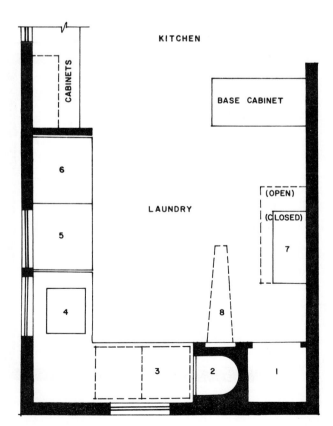

Desirable

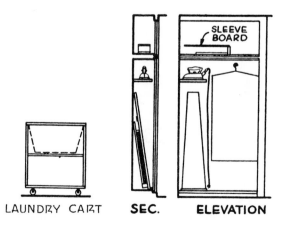

LAUNDRY CART   SEC.   ELEVATION

Fig. 7. Kitchen-laundry plans

Residential

LAUNDRY ROOMS

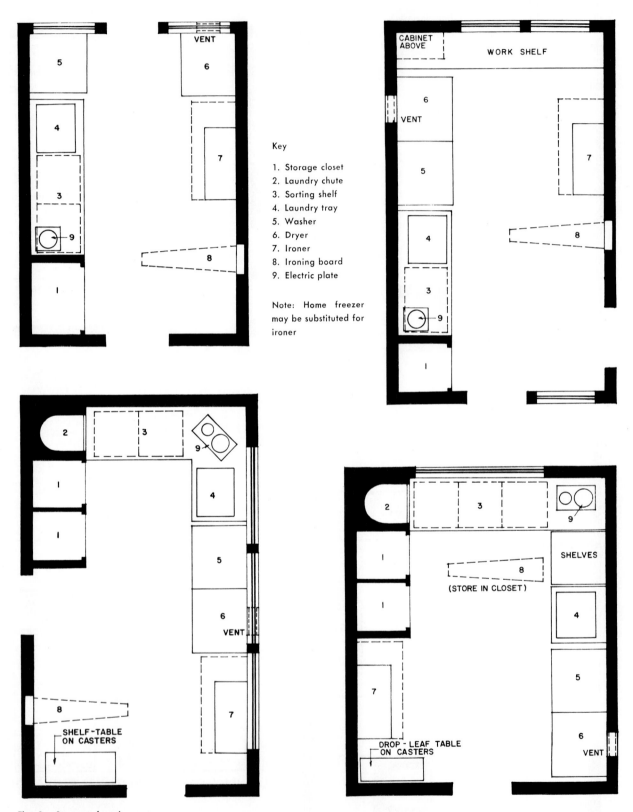

Key

1. Storage closet
2. Laundry chute
3. Sorting shelf
4. Laundry tray
5. Washer
6. Dryer
7. Ironer
8. Ironing board
9. Electric plate

Note: Home freezer may be substituted for ironer

Fig. 8. Separate laundry rooms

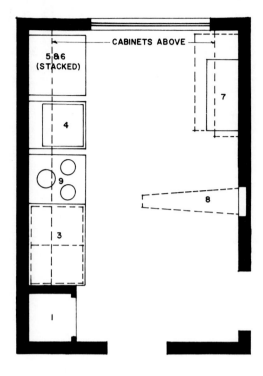

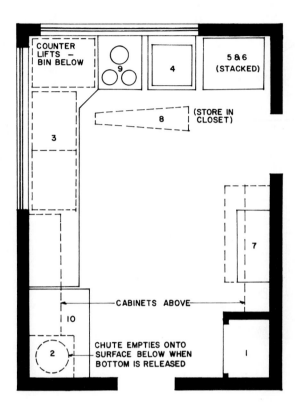

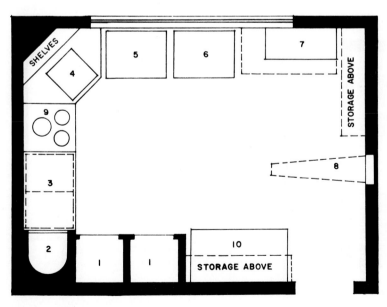

Fig. 9. Separate laundry rooms

Key

1. Storage closet
2. Laundry chute
3. Sorting shelf
4. Laundry tray
5. Washer
6. Dryer
7. Ironer
8. Ironing board
9. Electric plate
10. Home freezer

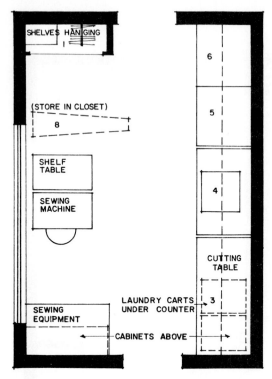

Fig. 10.   Combination laundry-sewing room with storage area

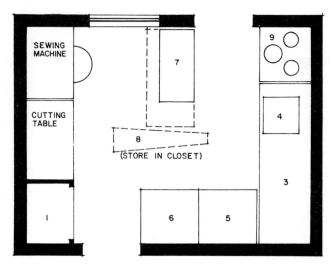

Fig. 11.   Combination laundry-sewing room

Key

1. Storage closet
2. Laundry chute
3. Sorting shelf
4. Laundry tray
5. Washer
6. Dryer
7. Ironer
8. Ironing board
9. Electric plate

Note: Home   freezer
may be substituted for
ironer

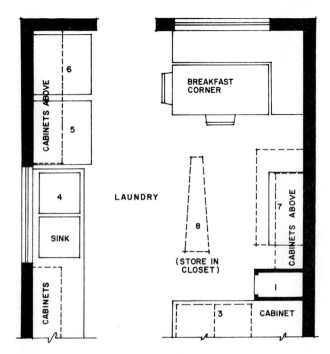

Fig. 12.   Combination laundry-breakfast room

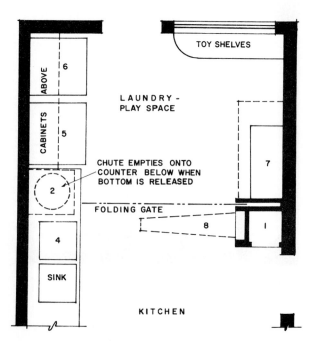

Fig. 13.   Combination laundry-playroom

By GLENN H. BEYER AND ALEXANDER KIRA, *Housing Research Center, Cornell University*

BATHROOMS

Activities commonly performed in the bathroom include washing of hands, face, and hair, bathing, elimination, and grooming, and also such activities as hand laundering and infant care. Often it is also used as a dressing room. Major problems in bathroom design include planning for optimum convenience and privacy of all bathroom functions for all members of the household, adequate provision for storage of supplies and equipment, and ease of cleaning.

Some general planning guides are as follows[1]:

Arrangement

Facilities should be conveniently arranged, with special attention given to clearances. The room arrangement should

[1] *Many of these suggestions are by courtesy of the American Radiator and Standard Sanitary Corporation.*

permit more than one family member to use its facilities at the same time (Fig. 8).

Illumination

Lighting should be adequate for all of the activities performed. For grooming, direct sources of light are essential in order to illuminate the face from all angles. High strip windows, clerestory windows, and skylights provide excellent over-all illumination in the daytime, while still affording privacy. Luminous ceilings are also effective, particularly in interior bathrooms.

Ventilation

Good ventilation is essential in bathrooms, both to reduce humidity and to dispel odors. If a window is relied upon as the sole means of ventilation, care should be taken in its selection and placement to minimize drafts and to permit easy access. Exhaust fans in the wall or ceiling are often used to supplement natural ventilation. In interior bathroom spaces, a mechanical exhaust is, of course, essential.

Sound control

Lack of acoustical privacy is one of the most common complaints with regard to bathrooms. Noise can be reduced by proper placement of the bathroom in relation to other spaces, by the use of closets and storage walls as sound barriers between it and adjacent spaces, as well as by the use of soundproof partitions and tightly fitted doors. Acoustical treatment of the ceiling makes the room more comfortable to use and reduces somewhat the amount of sound transmitted through the walls. Acoustical tiles for use in the bathroom should be moisture resistant and easily cleaned.

Auxiliary heat

A heat lamp or a radiant wall panel can be used to provide quick warmth in the bathroom.

Materials

It is essential that all surface materials used in the bathroom have moisture-resistant finishes.

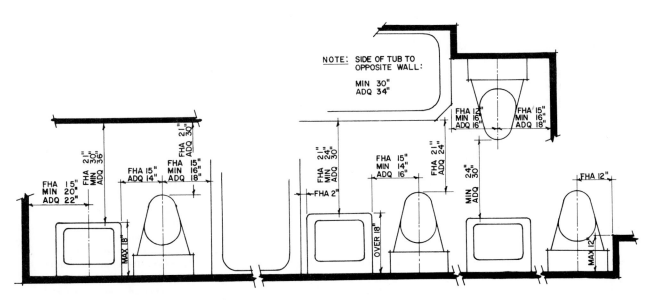

Fig. 1. Fixture clearances (dimensions in inches)

Residential
BATHROOMS

Storage

Adequate storage should be provided for current and reserve supplies. Articles in current use should be located near their place of first use. A closet opening from the bathroom and hallway or laundry is convenient for such items as bathroom linen and cleaning supplies. Medicine cabinets should be as large as possible since increasing numbers of toiletries and medicines are being used by American families. Hamper space is desirable for soiled linen and clothes. Install a cabinet with a self-contained hamper, or, in two-story houses, install a chute from the second floor to the laundry. The minimum requirements for storage of bathroom linens, based on recent research, are shown in Table 3.

Increased countertop space

Larger lavatories and increased countertop surfaces provide excellent facilities for light laundry, hair washing, and bathing and dressing the baby.

Children's convenience

Children's height should be considered in the placement of accessory equipment. A dental lavatory can double as a child's lavatory. If a combination lavatory-dressing table is installed, a step-up retractable stool should be provided for children's use.

Mirrors

An atmosphere of luxury and spaciousness is created by mirrors. A full-length mirror is always desirable. Also recommended is a medicine cabinet with a three-way combination of mirrored doors on either side and a mirror in the center.

Safety features

Grab bars should be used vertically for bathtub and shower and should be located for convenient use. They should be of adequate size and securely fastened to sturdy backing or studs. Use nonskid finishes for flooring. Install a door lock that opens automatically from the inside, and from the outside in case of emergency. Locate light switches out of reach of the bathtub or shower—preferably just outside the bathroom. Electric or radiant heaters should be recessed or protected. Provide a lock for medicine compartments.

Drying facilities and accessories

Add extra racks for drying women's hose and other light laundry. Racks may be concealed in well-ventilated cabinets, which, if desired, may include a receptacle for a low-wattage light bulb to facilitate drying. Sufficient robe hooks, bag hooks,

and toothbrush holders should also be provided.

Accessibility

A bathroom should generally be accessible to each bedroom without requiring passage through another room. A bathroom is desirable near principal indoor living, work, and play areas, and for guest use.

Table 1. Space required at the lavatory and bathtub

See Fig. 1 and 2 for illustration of dimensions.

Dimension	Space required, in.		
	Adequate	Minimum	FHA minimum
Lavatory			
Width:			
Center axis to adjacent wall	22	20	15
Side edge to side of adjacent tub	—	—	2
Depth:			
Front edge to opposite wall	36	34	21
—If not a traffic lane	—	30	—
Front edge to opposite tub	30	24	21
Horizontal clearance from front edge of lavatory to front edge of shelf 9–15 in. above lavatory	17½	—	—
Mirror:			
Height above floor—top	74	69	—
—bottom (5-ft adult)	48	54 (max.)	—
(3½-ft child)	—	36 (max.)	—
Bathtub			
Side of tub to opposite wall	34	30	—

Table 2. Space required at the toilet

Adapted from Bathroom Working Spaces, Monroe, Randall, and Bartlett, Report 82, Maine Agricultural Experiment Station (1959); Minimum Property Standards, Federal Housing Administration, Washington, D.C. (revised, July 1959). See Fig. 1 for illustration of dimensions.

Dimension	Space required, in.			
	Adequate		Minimum	FHA minimum
	1 Person	2 Persons*		
Width:				
Center axis to adjacent wall	18	22	16	15
—If wall projects not more than 12 in.	—	—	—	12
Center axis to side of lavatory 18 in. deep, or less	14	16	—	15
—Lavatory over 18 in. deep	16	18	14	15
Center axis to side of tub	18	18	16	15
Center axis to end of tub	16	18	16	12
Depth:				
Front edge to opposite wall	30	34	—	21
Front edge to opposite tub	24	—	—	21
Front edge to opposite lavatory	30	30	24	—

Space required for one person to assist another at the toilet (dimensions not shown in Fig. 1).

BASIC DIMENSIONS

Space is required not only for the use of particular fixtures but also between fixtures for cleaning purposes and for assisting another person (such as a small child or elderly adult). These last two factors are often completely overlooked. For economy of space, required clearances for each fixture may sometimes overlap (Fig. 8).

Recent research has provided some recommendations for the space required around the three basic fixtures: lavatory, toilet, and bathtub and shower. The basic clearances are given in Tables 1 and 2 and Figs. 1–3.

Miscellaneous activities

In planning the bathroom, the designer should remember that families with infants usually prefer to bathe them in the bathroom. The lack of adequate space has, in the past, caused many families to use the kitchen, which obviously is less appropriate for this activity than the bath. The minimum space needed to bathe and dress an infant is 1 ft $6\frac{1}{2}$ in. deep by 4 ft 11 in. wide by 3 ft high.

In addition, other important activities are often performed in the bathroom. Most women, at least occasionally, launder small items in the bathroom, and provision for this should be made. Many adults, and children, like to use the bathroom for dressing. Since this requires a considerable amount of space, it should be provided only when requested.

ARRANGEMENT

Bathrooms can be classified into four categories: (1) The conventional three-fixture bath; (2) The larger, compartmented bath; (3) The lavatory or "guest" bath; and (4) The "utility" bath.

Three-fixture bath: The conventional three-fixture bath without separate compartments has traditionally been designed for the occupancy and use of one individual at a time. This type of bath, with combination tub-shower, averages about 40 sq ft of floor space (Fig. 5).

Compartmented bath: To avoid the excessive humidity common in the usual three-fixture bath, tub and shower may be located in a separate compartment, with or without an additional lavatory. This plan also affords greater privacy for use of the toilet. Separate doors, possibly with a small entry, are desirable. Connecting doors between compartments are also possible but are not recommended as the only means of access (Figs. 6 and 7).

Another variation is to make the toilet a separate compartment, affording complete privacy. In even the minimum-sized bath of this type there is generally room for an additional lavatory, and the bath proper is often enlarged into a combination bath-dressing room. Dressing tables may be a combination of lavatory and table or individual fixtures. In the latter case, tables should be sufficiently far from lavatories to prevent damage from splashing water.

Table 3. Minimum dimensions for storage of bathroom linens, including allowance for handling

Adapted from Storage Requirements for Household Textiles, *A. Woolrich, M. M. White, and M. A. Richards, Agricultural Research Bulletin 62–2, U.S. Department of Agriculture, Washington, D.C. (1955).*

Item	Number	Minimum dimensions, in.			
		Width	Depth	Height	
				A*	B†
Bath towels:					
Everyday use	12	24	10	12	10
Guest use	6	12	10	12	10
Hand towels:					
Everyday use	10	7	14	12	10
Guest use	8	10	14	7	5
Wash cloths:					
Everyday use	12	16	8	6	4
Guest use	6	8	7	6	4

For storage on fixed shelves.
†*For storage in drawers or on movable shelves.*

Table 4. Sizes of accessories for tiling*

Item	Dimensions, in.						
	12x6	9x6	6x6	3x6	3x3	$8\frac{1}{2}$x$4\frac{1}{4}$	$4\frac{1}{4}$x$4\frac{1}{4}$
Toilet-paper holders			●	●		●	
Combination holders for soap, toothbrush, and tumbler	●	●	●	●		●	●
Separate holders for soap, toothbrush, and tumbler		●	●	●	●	●	●
Bases for towel bars, shelf brackets, door stops, and hooks				●	●		●
Grab bars and soap or sponge holders	●	●					

Some toilet-paper holders are 6×10 in. Radiant heaters are 15×15 in. or larger.

A still greater expansion of this plan provides a separate dressing room and connecting bath, with a compartment for the toilet. The required floor space ranges from 110 to 140 sq ft.

In all plans for baths, showers should be included, either as stalls or over tubs.

Guest bath: The lavatory, or two-fixture "guest" bath, for living portions of residences may vary in size and appointments from a minimum area of about 14 sq ft to rooms of 22 to 25 sq ft or larger when a dressing table is included (Fig. 4).

Utility bath: The "utility" bath provides an area larger than the minimum size required for the three basic fixtures, for other functions, such as laundering.

DOORS AND WINDOWS

Bathroom doors can be as small as 2 ft wide, except for utility bathrooms, for which doors should be not less than 2 ft

4 in. wide to permit passage of equipment as required. In general, bathrooms should contain only one door.

Door swings should be arranged so that: (1) The door cannot strike any person using any fixture; (2) The door will shield or conceal the toilet; and (3) The door may be left fully open for ventilation in warm weather.

Customarily, doors swing into the bathroom. If hall areas are sufficiently large, doors to small bathrooms can sometimes be designed to swing out. In-swinging doors should be set to clear towel-bars or radiators. Sliding doors are frequently desirable, as space savers, between various compartments within the bathroom.

The shape and position of *bathroom windows* is important from the standpoint of light, ventilation, and privacy. Generally, the higher the window, the better. Preferred locations include: clear wall space reserved for portable equipment, space

At lavatory

A. Mirror and medicine cabinet. Size is governed by use of shelf or shelf-topped lavatory; mirror should swing 7 in. over any shelf. (A.1) Fixed mirror is desirable immediately above lavatory for children 7 to 14 years.

B. Shelf. Preferably recessed flush with wall. May be part of medicine cabinet or part of lavatory.

C, D, and E. Soap, toothbrush, and tumbler holders. May be separate units or combined; flush or projecting type.

F. Receptacle for electric razor and hair dryer. Should be above and to right of lavatory; dead front type.

G. Razor blade disposal slot.

H. Towel bars. May be at level of shelf or lavatory top. In congested space provide upper bar for face cloths, lower bar for towels.

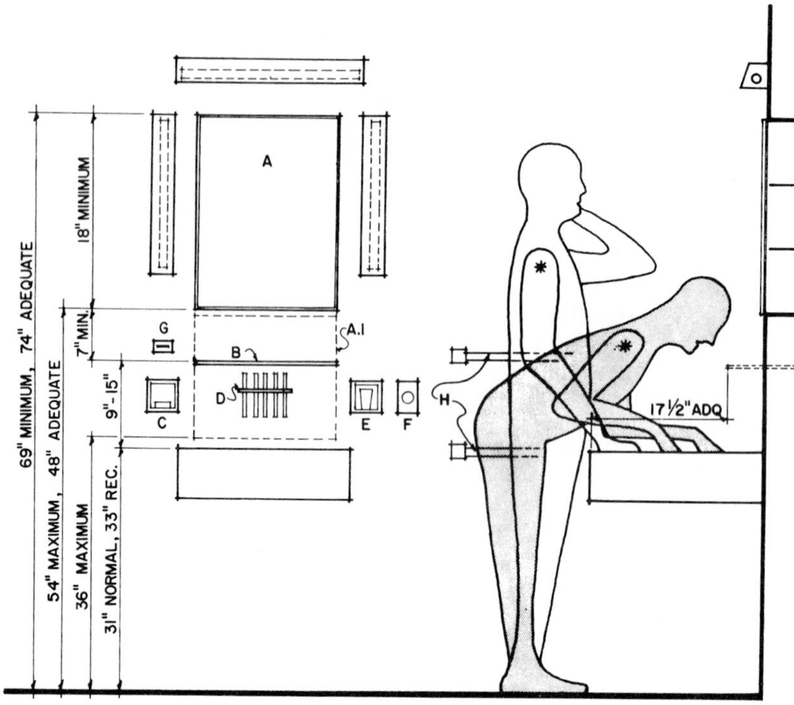

Fig. 2   Dimensions at lavatory, bathtub, and shower.

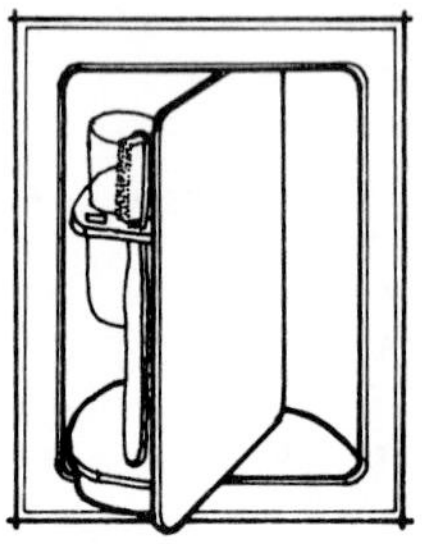

Recessed revolving lavatory unit—holds glass, toothbrush, and soap

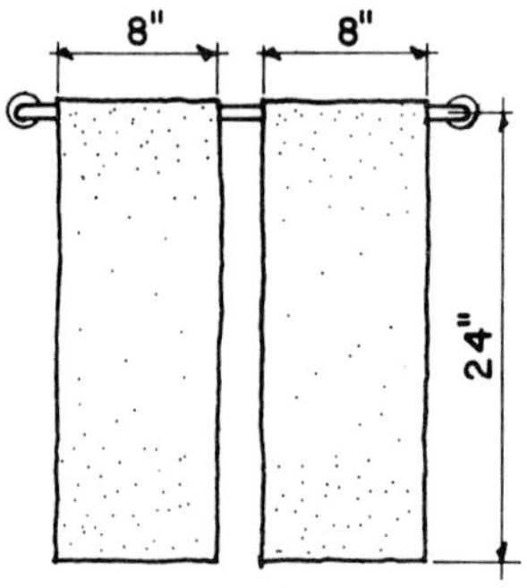

Bath

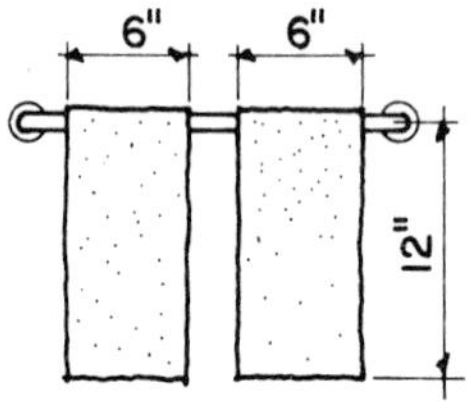

Small face

Towel bars

Stock sizes of bars: 1 ft 6 in., 2 ft, 2 ft 6 in., 3 ft, 3 ft 6 in., 4 ft

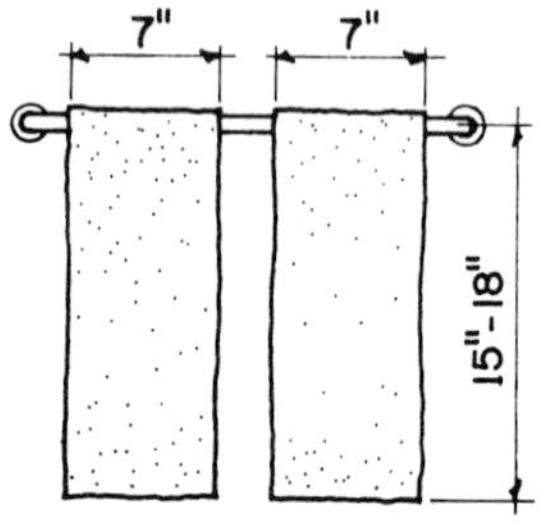

Small bath or large face

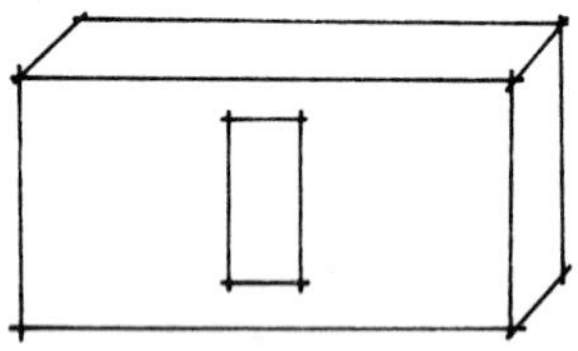

Tissue holder—available surface-mounted or recessed

Towel ring

Soap dish

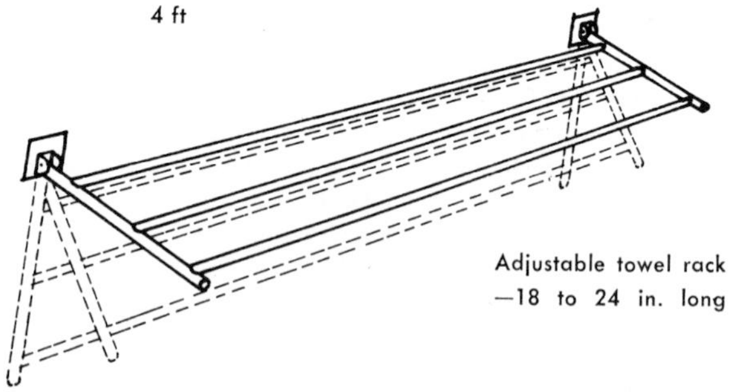

Adjustable towel rack —18 to 24 in. long

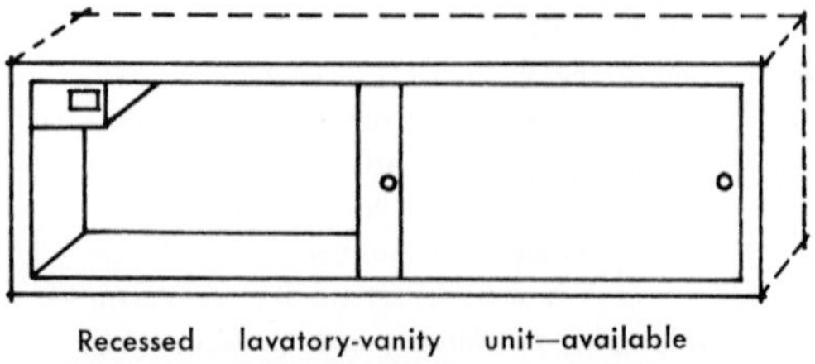

Recessed lavatory-vanity unit—available with electrical outlet and mirrored doors; 30x9x4 in. (nominal)

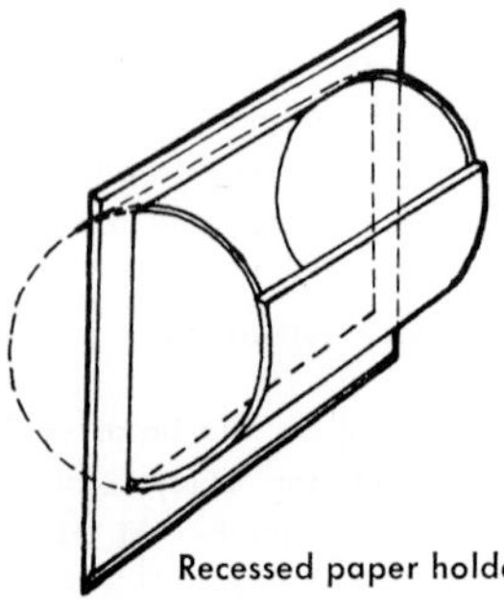

Recessed paper holder

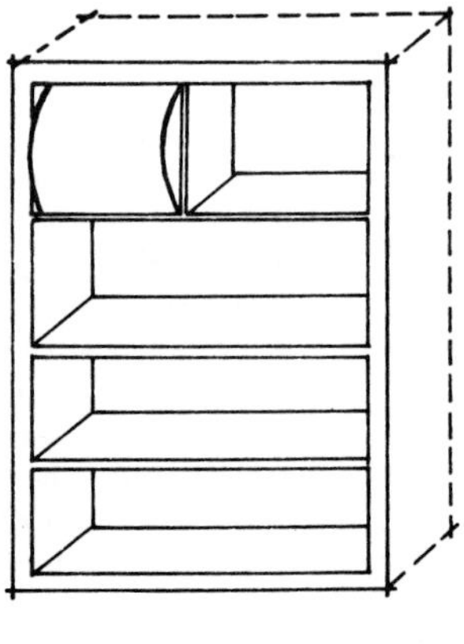

Combination magazine rack, paper holder, and shelf—available surface-mounted or recessed; 12x18x4 in. (nominal)

Fig. 3   Bathroom accessories. The accessories shown are typical. Many other types and styles are available.

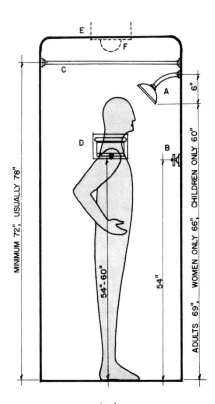

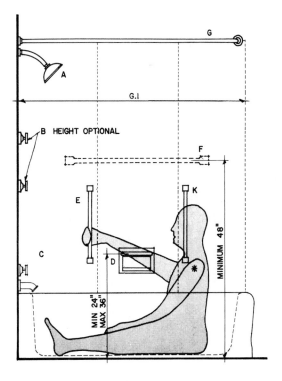

At shower

A. Shower head. Height is governed by client's preferences; may be overhead for men only.

B. Shower valves or mixing valves. Always place near entrance to shower.

C. Shower curtain rod. (C.1) Optional; glass shower enclosure door; place hinges on edge opposite shower control valves.

D. Combination soap and sponge holder and grab bar. Use draining-lip type. May be on rear wall or on side wall opposite shower head.

E. Shower ventilator. Desirable to remove steam; may function as vent for bathroom.

F. Shower stall light. Optional; must be vapor-proof fixture.

At bathtub

A, B, and C. Shower head, shower controls, bath valves and spout. Location is optional with client but must be accessible from outside of tub. See shower stall for recommended heights.

D. Combination soap and sponge holder and grab bar. Draining-lip type preferred.

E. Vertical grab bars. Optional but recommended.

F. Towel bar. Do not use over tub equipped with shower.

G. Curtain rod. Keep within inside face of tub. (G.1) Alternate; glass shower enclosure in place of curtain. Various types, with and without doors, are available.

Not illustrated

Full-length mirror. Usually on door.

Bathroom scale. May be built-in or portable.

Linen hamper. Optional; may be part of cabinet-type lavatory, built-in or portable.

Auxiliary heater. Built-in radiant type desirable; should radiate toward open floor space.

Fig. 2 (cont.).

Telescoping utility rod
—4 to 14 in.

Fig. 3 (cont.).

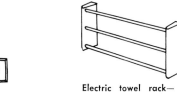

Robe hook

Electric towel rack—
26x13x3 in. (nominal)

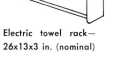

Grab bars

Straight bars—9, 12, 15, 18, 24, and 30 in.

Angle bars—16x32 in.

Residential

BATHROOMS

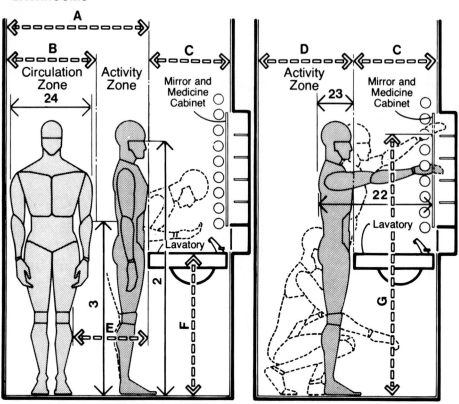

LAVATORY / MALE ANTHROPOMETRIC CONSIDERATIONS

The drawing at the top deals primarily with some of the more critical male anthropometric considerations. A lavatory height above the floor of 37 to 43 in, or 94 to 109.2 cm, is suggested to accommodate the majority of users. In order to establish the location of mirrors above the lavatory, eye height should be taken into consideration.

The two drawings at the bottom of the page explore, in much the same manner, the anthropometric considerations related to women and children, respectively. Given the great variability in body sizes to be accommodated within a single family, a strong case can be presented for the development of a height adjustment capability for the lavatory. Until that is developed, there is no reason, on custom installations, why the architect or interior designer cannot take anthropometric measurements of the client to ensure proper interface between the user and the lavatory.

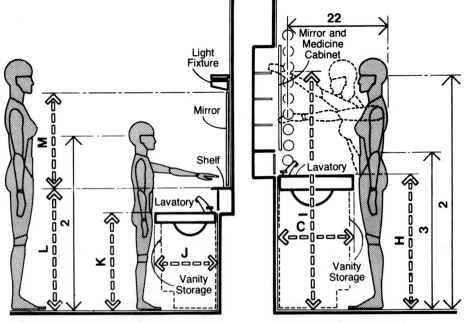

LAVATORY / FEMALE AND CHILD ANTHROPOMETRIC CONSIDERATIONS

	in	cm
A	48	121.9
B	30	76.2
C	19–24	48.3–61.0
D	27 min.	68.6 min.
E	18	45.7
F	37–43	94.0–109.2
G	72 max.	182.9 max.
H	32–36	81.3–91.4
I	69 max.	175.3 max.
J	16–18	40.6–45.7
K	26–32	66.0–81.3
L	32	81.3
M	20–24	50.8–61.0

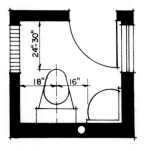 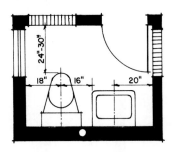

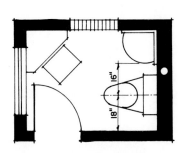 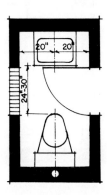

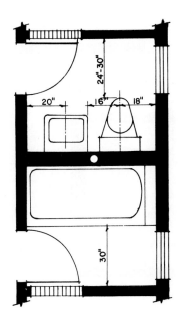 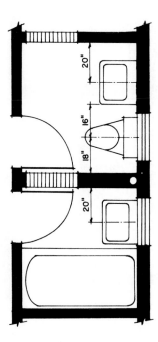

Fig. 4. Two-fixture plans

BATHROOMS

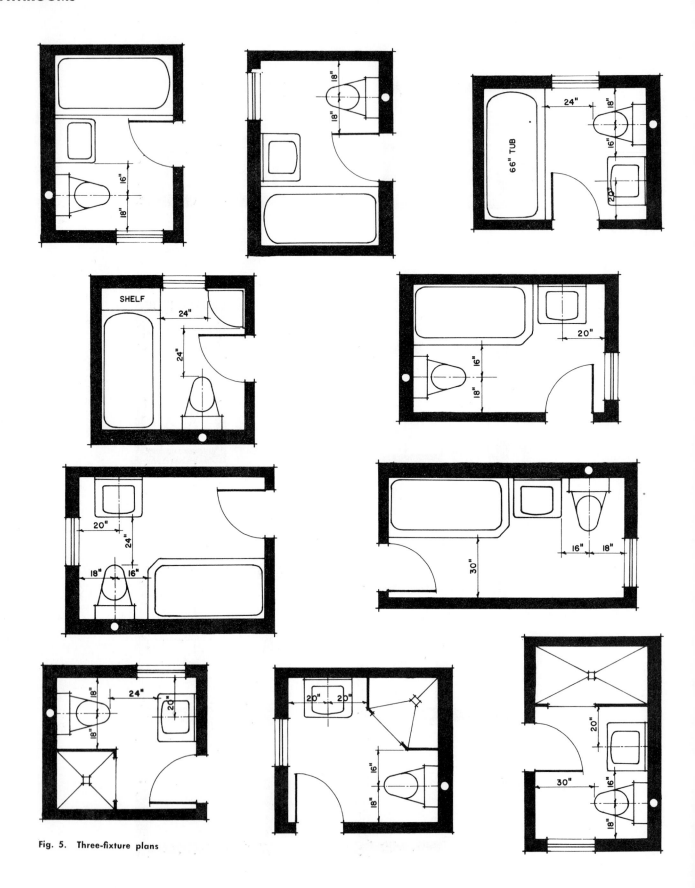

Fig. 5. Three-fixture plans

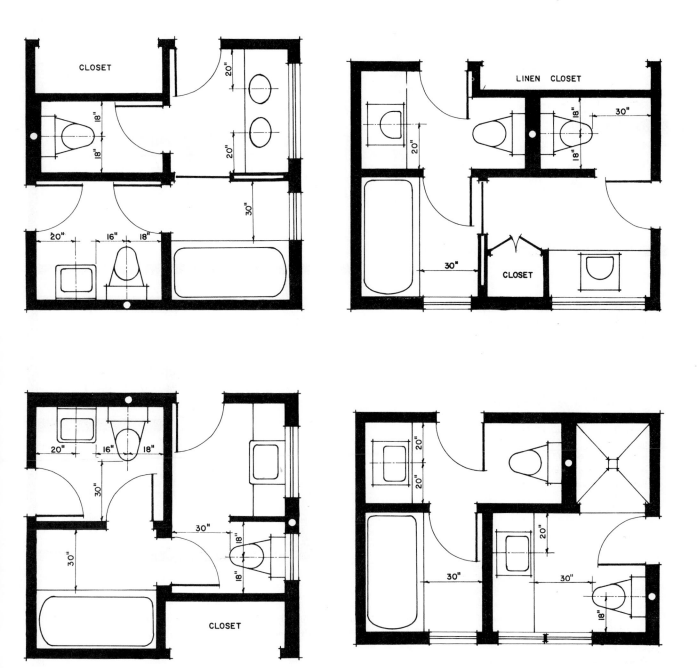

Fig. 6.   Compartmented plans

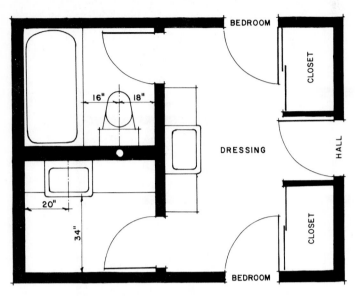

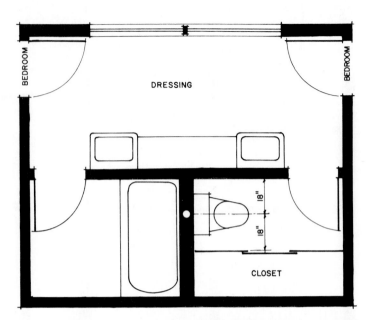

Fig. 7 Compartmented plans.

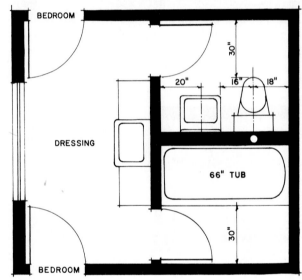

over a dressing table, and space above or on either side of the lavatory. Windows should not be placed over the bathtub unless they are of the casement or awning type opened by a crank. A window behind the toilet is seldom desirable. Skylights may be used to serve top-floor bathrooms if they are large enough to provide adequate light and ventilation. Inside bathrooms without exterior windows are sometimes used but require a dependable system of exhaust ventilation by natural or mechanical means, and greater artificial lighting in lieu of natural light.

ACCESSORIES

The medicine cabinet should be related in size to the type of bathroom or toilet. For guest baths or toilets, space is needed only for dentifrices, shaving accessories, toilet preparations, and a few simple remedies. A bath serving several bedrooms may require a complete supply of medicines in addition to the items mentioned above. Every bathroom should have a storage closet for cleaning utensils and supplies and for reserve stocks of toilet paper, towels, and sundries.

Floor space should be left in every bathroom for portable accessories desired by the owner or needed on occasion for the care of infants or invalids. Also consider allowing space for such items as scales, stool or seat, infant's bath and dressing table (portable type requires about 3 by 4 ft of floor space in use), soiled-linen hamper, exercise devices, dressing table or vanity with bench, and ultra-violet radiation equipment.

Towel bars should be ample in number

and length to serve the needs of each member of the family regularly using the bathroom, or of guests likely to use its facilities, before supplies can be replenished. For each person regularly using the bathroom, there should be separate bar space for bath towel, face towel, and face cloth, as well as an additional rack for guest towels.

Linen storage may consist of towel cabinets recessed in the thickness of plumbing walls (either over fixtures or as full height cabinets) or may be expanded into complete linen closets. Dressing-room baths may include completely fitted wardrobes. (See Table 3.)

Minimum-sized bathrooms and toilets require special planning to ensure ade-

quate wall space for essential accessories (Table 4).

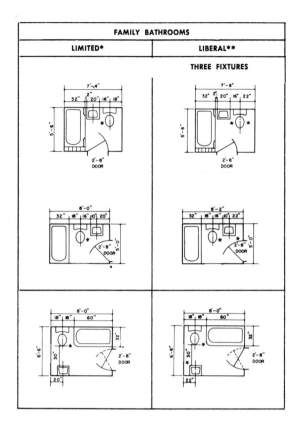

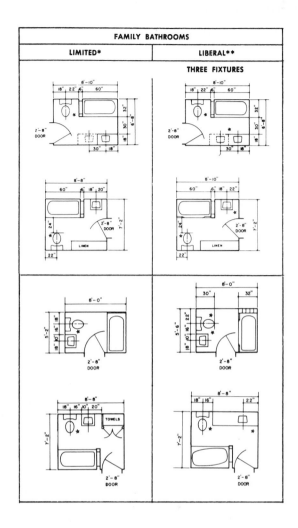

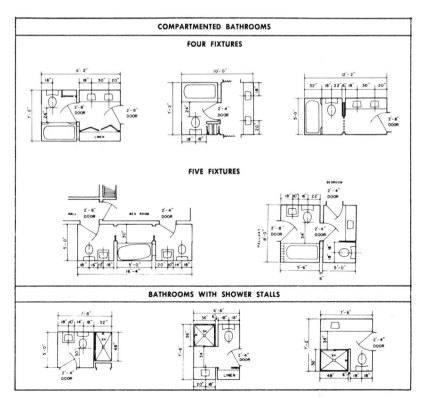

Fig. 8 Bathroom arrangements. *Source:* "Planning Bathrooms for Today's Homes," Home and Garden Bulletin No. 99, U.S. Department of Agriculture, Washington, D.C., 1967.

BATHROOMS
Handicapped Lavatory/Water Closet

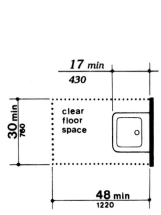

Fig. 9   Clear floor space at lavatories.

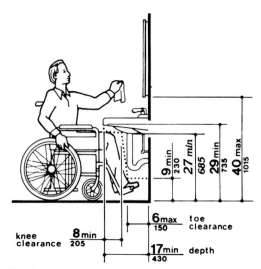

Fig. 10   Lavatory clearances.

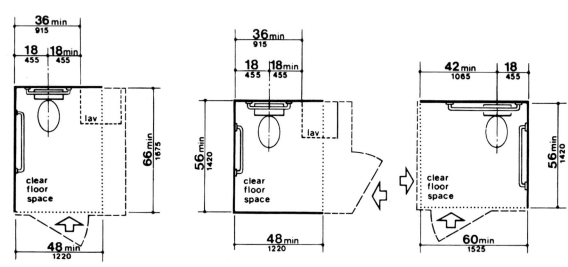

Fig. 11   Clear floor space at water closets.

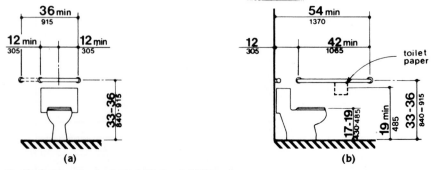

Fig. 12   Grab bars at water closets. (a) Back wall. (b) Side wall.

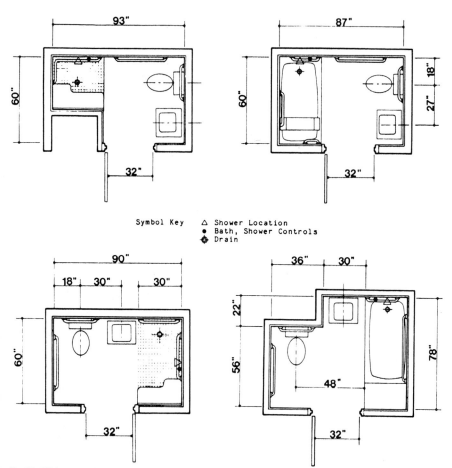

Symbol Key
△ Shower Location
● Bath, Shower Controls
✦ Drain

Fig. 13   Minimum-sized adaptable bathrooms.

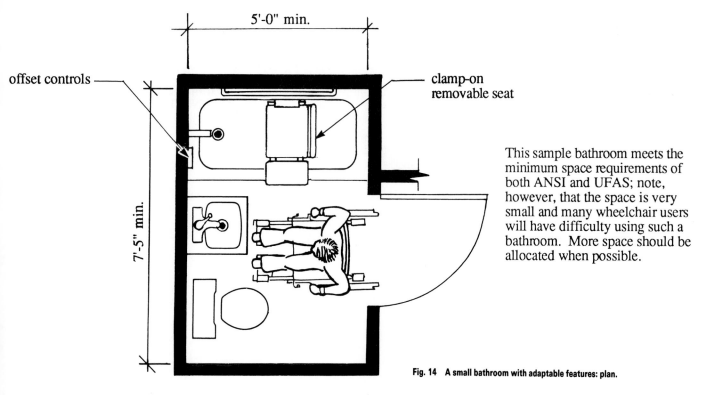

offset controls

clamp-on
removable seat

This sample bathroom meets the minimum space requirements of both ANSI and UFAS; note, however, that the space is very small and many wheelchair users will have difficulty using such a bathroom. More space should be allocated when possible.

Fig. 14   A small bathroom with adaptable features: plan.

81

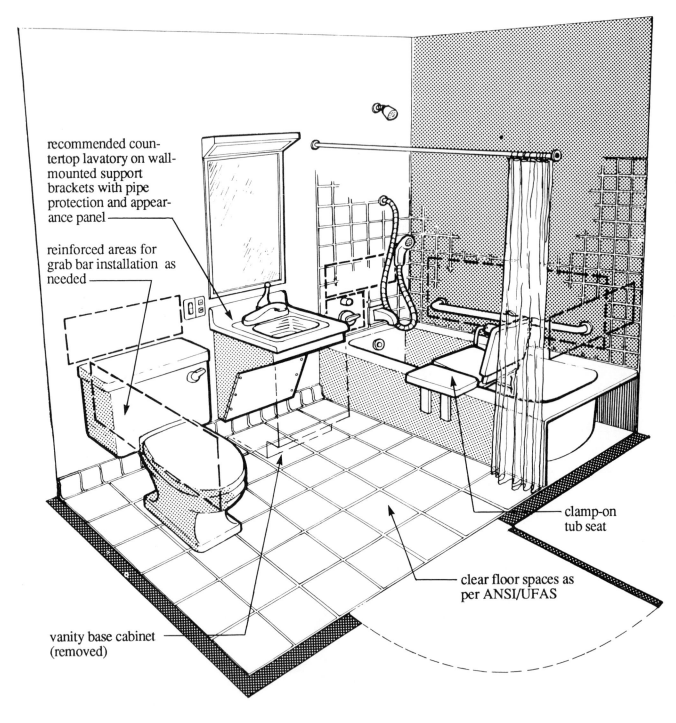

recommended countertop lavatory on wall-mounted support brackets with pipe protection and appearance panel

reinforced areas for grab bar installation as needed

clamp-on tub seat

clear floor spaces as per ANSI/UFAS

vanity base cabinet (removed)

Fig. 15 A small bathroom with adaptable features: perspective.

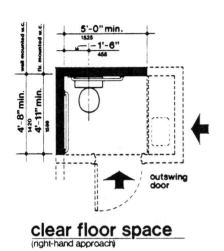

clear floor space
(right-hand approach)

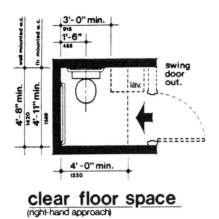

clear floor space
(right-hand approach)

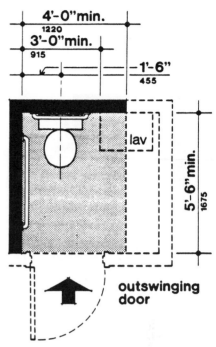

outswinging door

clear floor space
(right-hand approach)

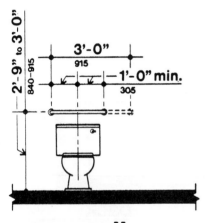

rear wall elevation
without stall
or alternate stalls

Fig. 16

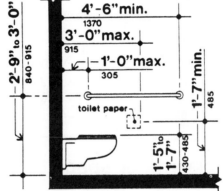

side wall
without stall
or alternate stalls

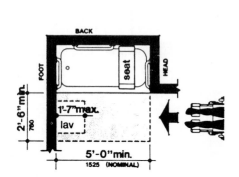

clear floor space
with in-tub seat

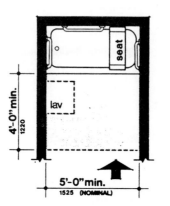

clear floor space
with in-tub seat

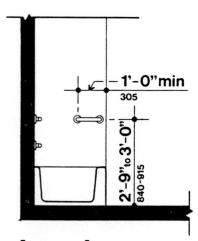

head
with in-tub seat

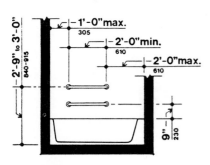

bathtub back
with in-tub seat

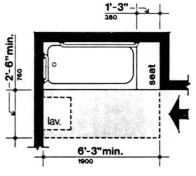

clear floor space
with ledge seat

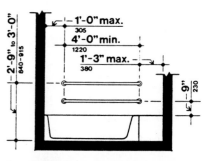

bathtub back
with ledge seat

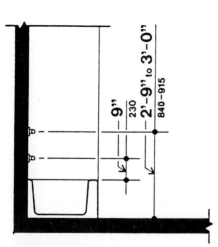

head
with ledge seat

Fig. 17

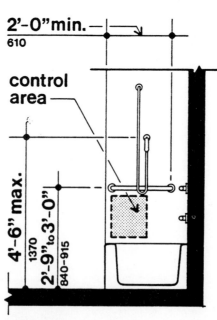

foot

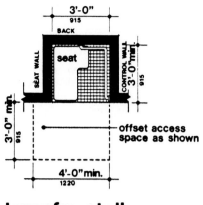

transfer stall

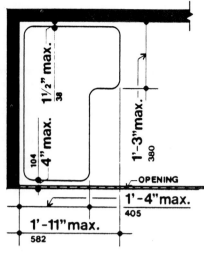

seat
transfer shower

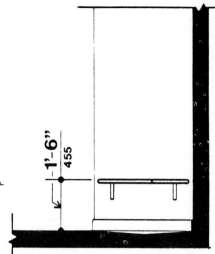

seat wall
transfer shower

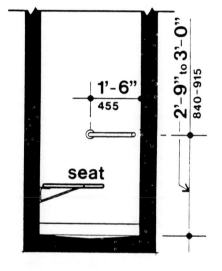

back
transfer shower

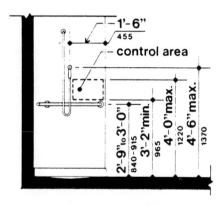

control wall
showers

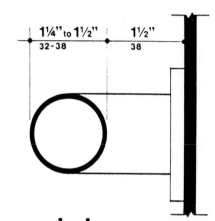

grab bar

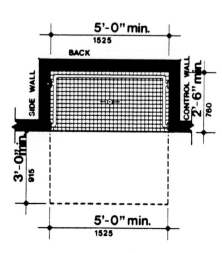

roll-in stall

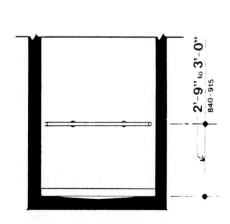

side
roll-in shower

back wall
roll-in shower

Fig. 18

Residential

CLOSETS

By GLENN H. BEYER, and ALEXANDER KIRA, *Housing Research Center, Cornell University*

Drawings by LARCH RENSHAW, AIA

STORAGE

"A place for everything and everything in its place" is the slogan for closet designers as well as housewives. Modern closets should be planned for the storage of the particular clothing or objects of the individual or the group using the space. An accurate list of the objects to be stored is necessary for the scientific allotment and arrangement of space and facilities. A "margin of safety" of some 25 per cent increased capacity should be allowed for the usual accumulation of additional belongings. It is better to have too much space than not enough. Much can be stored in little space if sufficient thought is given to the arrangement of the space and the equipment. Too many closets have unused and unusable space due to poor planning.

Good closet design requires planning, arrangement, and fixtures contributing to:

1. Convenience
   a. Ease of access
   b. Maximum visibility
   c. Orderliness
   d. Maximum accessibility
   e. Maximum of used space
2. Preservation
   a. Of pressed condition
   b. Of freshness (ventilation)
   c. From moths
   d. From dust
   e. From pilfering

The above are not all simultaneously obtainable, and some are mutually exclusive; for instance, eliminating doors gives maximum availability but minimum security from dust, moths, and pilfering; adhering to the principle of maximum accessibility would result in unused space at top and bottom of closet.

Modern closets, by the efficient arrangement of space and fixtures, accommodate much more clothing and material than the inconvenient, space-wasting closets of a few decades ago. The modern closet often replaces pieces of furniture and thus provides a greater amount of free, uncluttered space in the room.

Doors should open the full width of the closet whenever possible. In most cases the most efficient and economical doors are the usual hinged type. Two doors for a 5-ft closet will eliminate dark, inaccessible, hard-to-clean corners. Hooks, racks, and accessories on the backs of swinging doors increase efficiency by using otherwise unoccupied space in the closet.

Alternate closet closing methods may involve more complicated or more expensive construction, though they may obviate the objection that swinging doors form an obstruction in the room. Sliding doors can expose the entire interior of the closet to view and make it immediately accessible. Such doors do not block traffic. Sliding doors, however, do not permit the use of special door fixtures such as tie racks, shoe racks or bags, hat hangers, or mirrors, which are handy and easily reached when attached to a hinged closet door. Banks of wardrobe-type closets with sliding doors are becoming more and more popular. Fitted with drawers or trays, they take the place of bureaus, chests, and chiffoniers and make for more spacious, uncluttered rooms.

Doors which expose the full width of the closet are preferable for both visibility and accessibility. "Walk-in" or "walk-through" closets naturally use more area than others with no "circulation." In some rooms, however, a single door to a large "walk-in" closet may be justified by the need for maximum wall space for furniture.

Some of the various closing methods are shown in Fig. 1.

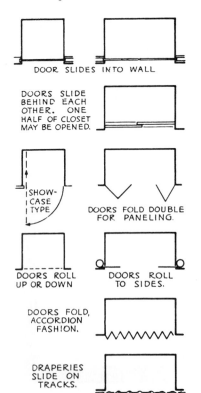

DOOR SLIDES INTO WALL

DOORS SLIDE BEHIND EACH OTHER. ONE HALF OF CLOSET MAY BE OPENED.

SHOW-CASE TYPE

DOORS FOLD DOUBLE FOR PANELING.

DOORS ROLL UP OR DOWN

DOORS ROLL TO SIDES.

DOORS FOLD, ACCORDION FASHION.

DRAPERIES SLIDE ON TRACKS.

Fig. 1. Closet closing methods

Lighting is considered essential and standard in the modern closet unless room lights are located to illuminate fully all portions of the closet. A single tubular or bulb light with a diffusing reflector placed just above the door inside the front of the closet is usually sufficient. Automatic door switches are convenient.

Ventilation is often desirable, particularly in hall closets where damp outer garments or work clothes might be stored. It can be accomplished readily by providing louvers in the closet door or by using louver doors.

Types of closets

Closets are required for various purposes, in different parts of the house. Some have already been mentioned in other sections of this volume: kitchen supplies; dinnerware, glassware, and table linens (discussed under "Kitchens"); and bathroom supplies (discussed under "Bathrooms"). Closets must also be provided for the storage of clothing, bedding, cleaning equipment, books, magazines, and phonograph records, toys and other children's and adults' recreation equipment, and certain items such as luggage that are used only seasonally or infrequently. The discussion here relates only to "active" storage space.

Clothes closet: For clothes closets in bedrooms or dressing rooms, 2 ft is standard depth (2 ft 6 in. if a hook strip is to be used). (See Fig. 2.) This permits clothing to be on hangers on poles, with sufficient clearance. Clothing lengths are shown in Fig. 3. Clothes closet width, parallel to the doors, should be from 3 to 6 ft per person, depending on amounts of clothing and

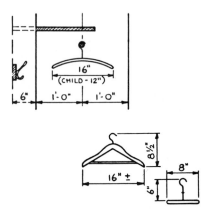

Fig. 2. Closet depth and hanger sizes

86

whether drawers or trays are to be provided in the closet or wardrobe for such items as have in the past been kept in bureaus or other pieces of furniture. Some typical closet plans are illustrated in Fig. 4; suggested layouts for bedroom closets for men, women, and children are shown in Figs. 5–9.

Coat closets, located near the entrance doors, are sometimes made 2 or 3 in. deeper than bedroom closets, to allow for the bulkiness of some overcoats, and to permit better air circulation around the garments which are often damp when hung in the closet. Several designs for coat closets are shown in Figs. 10 and 14.

Closet for cleaning equipment: The dimensions of the storage space needed for cleaning equipment will depend in large part upon the type of vacuum cleaner used: horizontal, upright, or canister; recommended dimensions for each type are shown in Fig. 11. Since families may change from one type of vacuum cleaner to another, the cleaning closet should be made large enough for any type. The closet should be located as near the center of the house as possible, and should be provided with a convenience receptacle so that the vacuum cleaner can be left connected and can reach most areas of the house. A suggested design for a cleaning equipment closet is shown in Fig. 12.

Storage for bedroom linens and bedding: Limited and liberal lists of articles of bedding that require storage, and the minimum dimensions of the space required, are shown in Table 1.

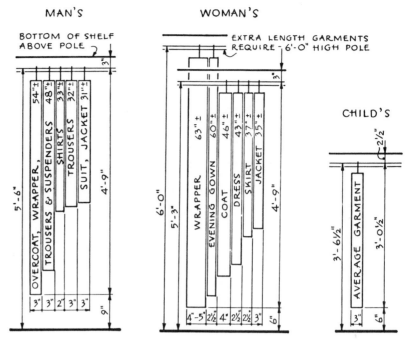

Fig. 3. Sizes of clothes hung in closet

FHA[1] requirements for linen closets are as follows: minimum interior dimensions, 18 in. wide by 14 in. deep (24 in. maximum); shelves spaced approximately 12 in. on center vertically; highest shelf, 74 in. above

[1] Minimum Property Standards for One and Two Living Units, *Federal Housing Administration, Washington, D.C., revised July, 1959.*

the floor; minimum total shelf area for one- and two-bedroom house, 9 sq ft, for three- and four-bedroom house, 12 sq ft; drawers may replace 50 per cent of the shelves. These are minimum dimensions, and about twice this amount is recommended, especially if both bedroom and bathroom linen are to be stored. A suggested layout for such a combined linen closet is shown in Fig. 12.

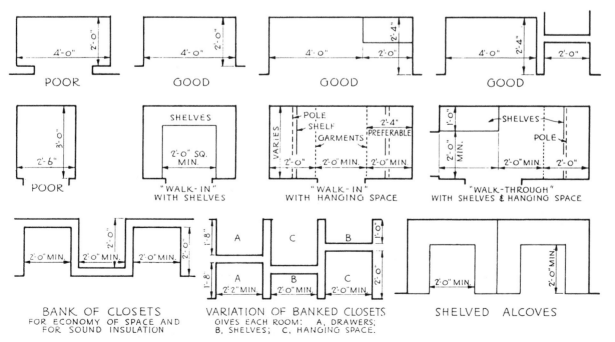

Fig. 4. Typical closet plans

The two drawings at the top of the page show the vertical clearances related to male and female closet and storage facilities. Wherever possible or practical, the closet shelf should be located within human reach. The height shown for the high shelf has been established based on 5th percentile male and female data in order to place it within reach of individuals of smaller body size. Any shelf located at a greater distance above the floor should be used primarily for storage that requires only infrequent access. The location of the shelf just above the rod is essentially a function of rod height. The clearance between the bottom of the shelf and the top of the rod should allow for easy removal of the hanger.

The bottom drawings illustrate two various types of walk-in storage facilities. Undoubtably, it can be argued that the 36-in, or 91.4-cm, clearance shown between the hanging garment and the storage shelf or between opposite garments could be reduced about 50 percent. The authors contend, however, that in order to achieve any degree of comfort in the selection and removal of the desired garment, a minimum of 36 in should be maintained. The degree to which this dimension can be reduced is a question of the level of comfort the user is prepared to tolerate in exchange for the floor space saved. The two drawings of the plan view of the human figure illustrate clearances required for donning a coat or putting on a pair of stockings.

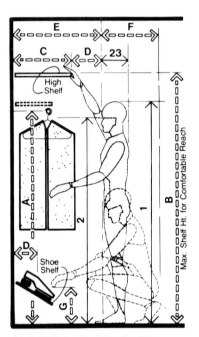

CLOSET AND STORAGE FACILITIES/MALE

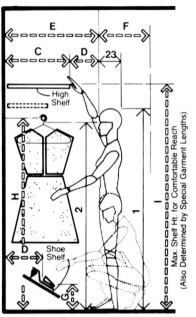

CLOSET AND STORAGE FACILITIES/FEMALE

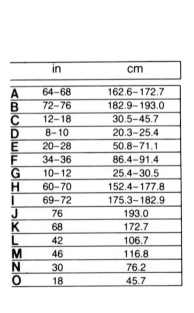

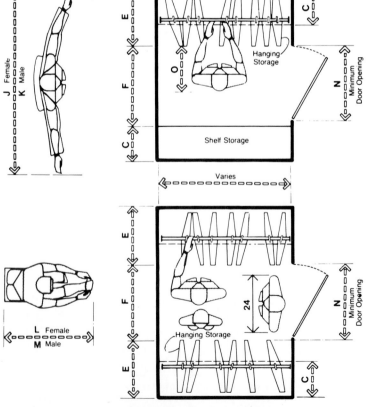

WALK-IN CLOSET AND STORAGE FACILITIES

	in	cm
A	64–68	162.6–172.7
B	72–76	182.9–193.0
C	12–18	30.5–45.7
D	8–10	20.3–25.4
E	20–28	50.8–71.1
F	34–36	86.4–91.4
G	10–12	25.4–30.5
H	60–70	152.4–177.8
I	69–72	175.3–182.9
J	76	193.0
K	68	172.7
L	42	106.7
M	46	116.8
N	30	76.2
O	18	45.7

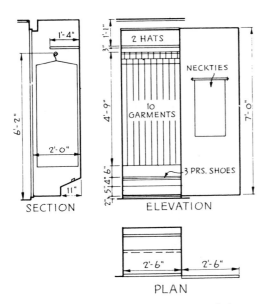

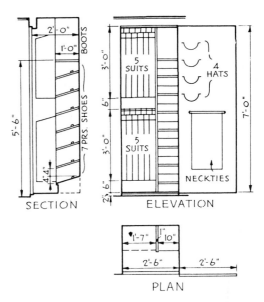

A minimum size closet of a usual type. Shoes can be stored on the raised shelf-rack and three additional pair on the floor in front of the rack. Door could be arranged for hats as shown below, leaving shelf for other storage.

Minimal closet arranged to make shoes more visible and reachable. There is space for hats without crushing or for night clothes hooks if hats are normally stored in a hall closet. Neckties might be in two tiers.

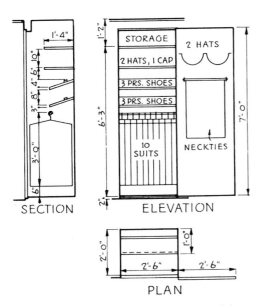

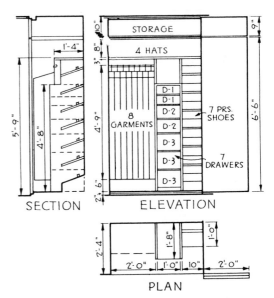

An alternate to the scheme above giving maximum view of shoes and an additional shelf. Trousers would have to be folded over the crossbar of the suit hanger rather than being hung separately from the pole with trouser-hangers.

A four-foot closet with seven drawers for shirts, socks, underwear, etc., and a vertical tier of shoe racks (as above). Night clothes and bathrobe hooks are best on the right hand door, necktie racks flat against the left hand door.

Fig. 5. Bedroom closets for men

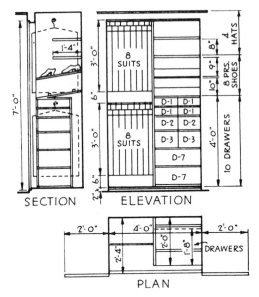

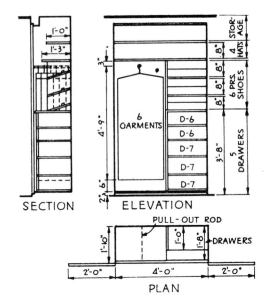

Another four-foot closet with ten standard drawers conveniently arranged. Shoes are placed tandem above the drawers for visibility and reachability. Poles are one above the other, requiring reaching.

A solution to the shallow closet problem. A pull-out rod takes care of the suit, coat and trouser hanging. Five drawers take the place of a small bureau or chest. Shoes are at "no stoop, no squat, no squint" levels.

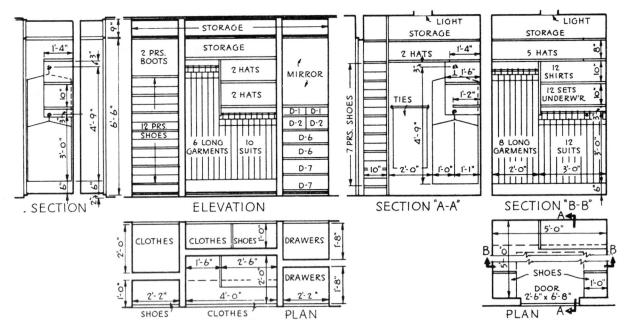

Wide wardrobe closets of more luxurious size planned as part of walls separating two rooms. Four doors, sliding or swinging, can be used. Lower portion of shoe-tiers could be replaced with mothproof "dead-storage" drawers.

A deep walk-in closet. High tiers of shoe racks flank the door jambs. Shelves for live and dead storage on three sides, upper levels. Suit poles range the back wall. Ties are on the left wall, night clothes hooks on right wall.

Fig. 6.   Bedroom closets for men

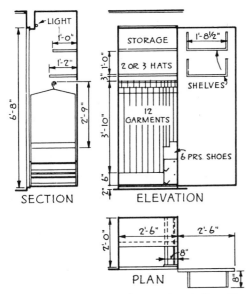

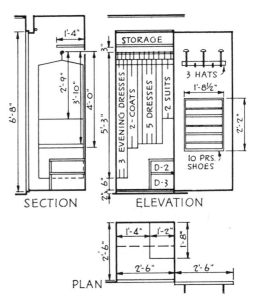

A small closet with shoe racks at the side under short hanging garments. Additional shoe pockets might be placed on the door under the hanging shelves. These handy shelves fold into the space in front of the hat and storage shelves.

An alternate minimum closet arrangment with a high pole for long dresses. Two drawers below the shorter hanging garments. Depth of closet permits a door type shoe rack and a hat rack. Wide hats can go on upper shelf.

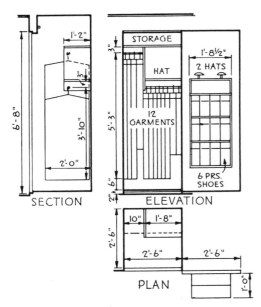

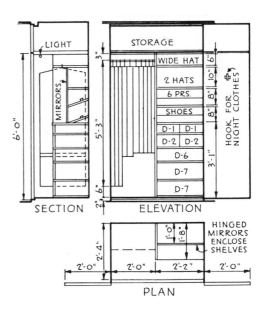

Alternate to closet above. It provides a high pole for hanging evening dresses and a lower pole for other dresses and suits. A large hat shelf is provided above the low pole as well as a hat rack and shoe pockets on the door.

A four-foot closet combining hanging and shelf space with drawers for stockings, underthings, and what-not. Shoes are easily seen and chosen from the almost eye-level cleat rack above the drawers. Hat storage on the shelves.

Fig. 7. Bedroom closets for women

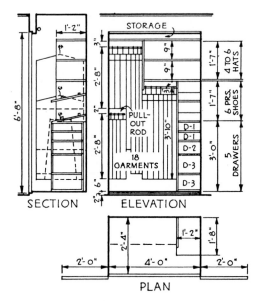

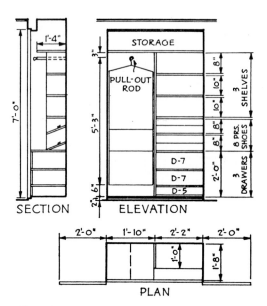

Another four-foot closet with a short canti-lever pole at the left allowing two-decker hanging. Closet drawer space would natur-ally be supplemented by a bureau or other furniture. A shoe rack on the door would increase capacity.

The shallow closet problem solved by the use of a pull-out rod firmly anchored to the back wall. Drawers again at lower right with cleated shoe shelves above, and hat shelves above them. Drawers may have to be shorter than standard.

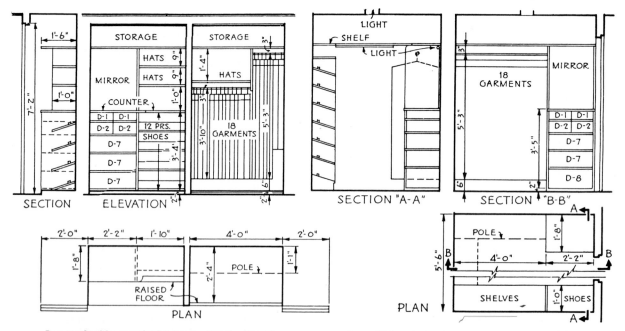

Large double wardrobe type closet, almost half devoted to hanging space. Left half fitted with large and small drawers and wide shelf-counter with mirror above. Sliding doors may be preferred and center par-tition minimized.

A walk-in closet, shoe racks and shallow shelves at one side drawers and hanging pole at the other. Drawers next to door are convenient but hazardous if left open. They could be placed at the back with hanging space near door.

Fig. 8. Bedroom closets for women

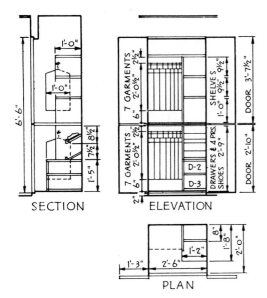

Closet for infants up to about 5 years old. Low hanging pole shelves and drawers permit habits of care and orderliness to be developed at an early age. Upper part would be used by adults. Note two sets of doors.

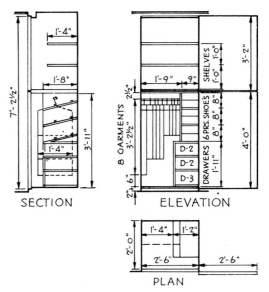

Small closet designed for a child of from 6 to 10 years. Pole at higher but easily reached level. Drawers and shoe racks at convenient heights. Ample shelf room provided above for the storage of possessions.

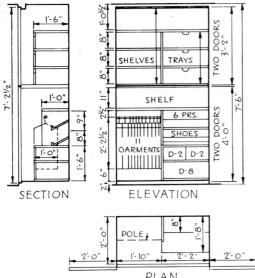

Alternate, and larger, closet for an infant up to 5 years of age. Trays or drawers for folded garments at an upper level for adult use. Hanging space, drawers and shelf available to child using the lower doors.

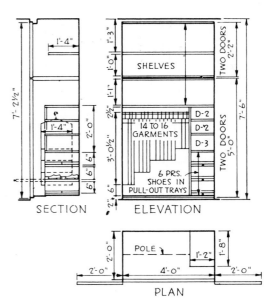

Closet for youngster up to 10 years old, providing greater length of hanging pole and different shoe arrangement, trays instead of cleat racks. A large shelf for hats, toys, or "collections" available to child.

Fig. 9. Bedroom closets for children

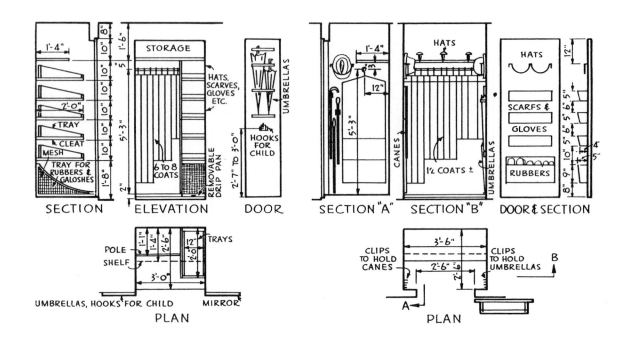

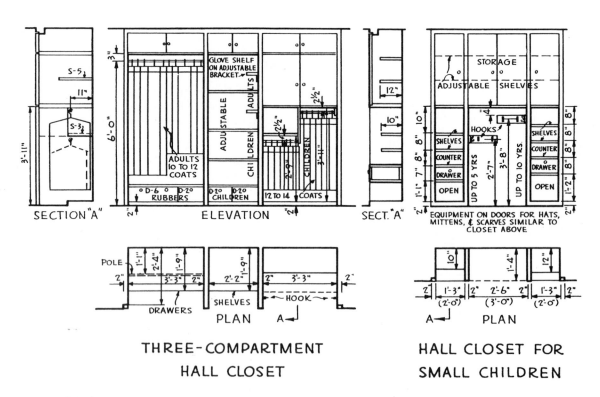

THREE-COMPARTMENT
HALL CLOSET

HALL CLOSET FOR
SMALL CHILDREN

Fig. 10. Coat closets

Miscellaneous storage

A large variety of other articles that are in regular use must be stored somewhere. Included in this category are books, magazines, phonograph records, card tables and chairs, games, movie and slide projectors, screens and film, toys, sports equipment, and tools. If adequate and conveniently located built-in storage is not provided, then portable units (furniture) will have to be used for this purpose.

Book storage is usually required in the living room, study, and each bedroom. Most books (85 per cent) can fit comfortably on shelves 8 in. deep (front to back); some books (10 per cent) need 10-in. shelves, and a few (5 per cent) require 12-in. shelves. Vertical spacing between shelves varies from 8 to 16 in., with the greatest use in the 10 to 12-in. range. Horizontally, books average 7 to 8 volumes per linear foot of shelf.

Phonograph records (12 in.) in albums require shelves with a clear height of 14 in. and a depth of 15 in. (14 in. for long-playing records in cardboard folders).

Card tables are usually 30 in. square but may be as large as 36 in., and are 2 to 3 in. thick when folded. Folded chairs vary widely in dimension, but a fair average is 30 by 16 by 3 in. Space should also be provided for cards, score cards,

rule books, poker chips, chess, etc. (see Fig. 13).

Toy and game storage should be provided in children's bedrooms and wherever the toys are regularly used. Toy storage should be designed for future conversion to other use.

Sports equipment, especially golf bags, skis, and camping equipment, may present a serious storage problem. For some families, a separate closet for this purpose may be justified; a suggested design is shown in Fig. 13. Such a closet should be located near the outside entrance which is most used by the family.

Tools and associated items should, of course, be stored in the workshop, which every house must have. Paints, because of odor and fire hazard, are best stored outside the house.

General storage is required for bulky, seldom-used items, such as trunks, boxes, and extra furniture.

Outdoor storage (i.e., directly accessible from outdoors) is required for lawnmowers, wheelbarrows, sprays, rakes, and other garden tools and equipment; for snow shovels and sleds, ladders, screens, and storm windows; for outdoor furniture, barbecues, hammocks, croquet sets; for bicycles, tricycles, scooters, and perambulators (see Fig. 14).

These last two types of storage (general and outdoor) were provided in the traditional house by the basement, attic, and garage. Modern houses may have none of these spaces, and, in such cases, the architect should take particular care to provide adequate general and outdoor storage space. FHA minimum requirements are 200 cu ft plus 75 cu ft per bedroom, of which at least 25 per cent and not more than 50 per cent should be indoors. Again, it should be emphasized that this is a minimum requirement; more is recommended.

Basic elements

The standard elements of closet storage are shelves, drawers, poles, hooks, and special fixtures. Practically any object can be stored efficiently by one or another of these means. The choice and arrangement of the fixtures depend on the amount and nature of the materials to be stored.

Shelves: Shelves are simple and inexpensive to install, require a minimum of effort to use, and are adaptable to the storage of many types of things, especially those of odd or bulky shape, folded articles, and, of course, books, magazines, etc. However, if open, they are exposed to dust. Also small objects become hidden behind one another if the shelves are deep. A 12-in. shelf is usually adequate for most

Table 1. Storage requirements for bedroom linens and bedding, including allowance for handling

Article	Median number		Minimum dimensions, in.		
	Limited	Liberal	Depth	Width	Height*
Sheets, double bed					
Everyday use	6	6	12	14	12
Guest use	—	4	12	14	9
Pillow cases (pairs)					
Everyday use	5	5	12	8	8
Guest use	3	3	12	8	6
Blankets, comforters, quilts	4†	4†			
Pile of 4			23	19	26
2 piles of 2			23	38	14
Bedspreads, double bed					
Cotton damask	2	2	16	15	9
Chenille	1	1	18	16	8
Pillows		3	18	26	17

For storage on fixed shelves. For storage on sliding shelves or in drawers, deduct 1 to 2 in.

† *Number of warm bed coverings owned is normally larger than this, but balance can be stored in less accessible location than linen closet.*

Source: Avis Woolrich, Mary M. White and Margaret A. Richards, Storage Space Requirements for Household Textiles, *U.S.D.A. Agricultural Research Bulletin 62–2, Washington, 1955.*

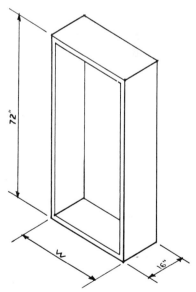

Fig. 11 Cleaning closet sizes for various types of vacuum cleaners.

Upright type   W = 28 in.
Canister type   W = 35 in.
Horizontal type   W = 41 in.

things. Articles of larger dimensions or greater depth should have their special places; linens, for instance, are frequently folded for a 16-in. shelf.

Drawers: Drawers are growing in popularity in closet design because they accommodate numerous articles with a minimum of space and a maximum of convenience. They provide practically dust-free storage and present a neat appearance even when carelessly used. Drawers of different widths and depths make possible classified "filing" of different items, thus providing a great saving in time and an incentive to orderliness. A cabinet made up of a battery of standard drawers, selected for the storage of the known possessions of the user, can easily be made from a comprehensive list, with allowance made for the accumulation of additional items.

Drawer construction is cabinetwork requiring both skillful craftsmanship and the best materials. They must operate freely under all seasonal and climatic conditions.

A recent logical outcome of this situation has been the development of molded plastic drawers in a variety of stock sizes. Fronts of various materials can be attached. All that is required of the builder is the construction of the supporting enclosure.

Poles: Hanging pole length can be estimated roughly at 3 in. per hanger for men's suits (4 in. for heavy coats) and 2 in. per hanger for women's clothing. Height of pole above floor should average 64 in., but should be adjusted to the individual. Clearance between pole and shelf above should be 3 in. Hardwood poles 1 in. in diameter should have intermediate supports if over 4 ft in length. Consult manufacturers for special-purpose hanging rods, extension poles, brackets, etc.

Hooks: A variety of hooks is available.

Special features: Such special features as shoe and hat racks and miscellaneous racks are on the market and greatly increase convenience in storage.

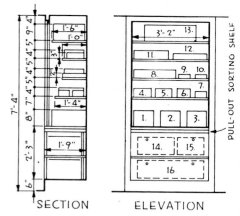

1. 8 SHEETS (10" x 18" x 8" high)
2. " " " " " " "
3. 8 REG. TURKISH TOWELS (10" x 16" x 8" high)
4. 8 REG. PILLOW CASES (9½" x 14" x 4" high)
5. " " " " " " "
6. 12 REG. HAND TOWELS (7" x 14" x 4" high)
7. 12 REG. WASH CLOTHS (2 PILES) (6" x 6" x 3" h.)
8. 4 REG. BATH MATS (22" x 10" x 4" high)
9. 12 SMALL HAND TOWELS (6" x 12" x 2" high)
10. " " " " " " "
11. 4 BLANKET COVERS (18" x 10" x 4" high)
12. 2 SHOWER CURTAINS (18" x 9" x 3" high)
13. 2 PILLOWS (26" x 17" x 9" high)
14. 4 SUMMER BLANKETS (20" x 18" x 8" high)
15. 2 MATTRESS COVERS (14" x 18" x 8" high)
16. 3 WINTER BLANKETS (34" x 18" x 9" high)

BED & BATH LINEN

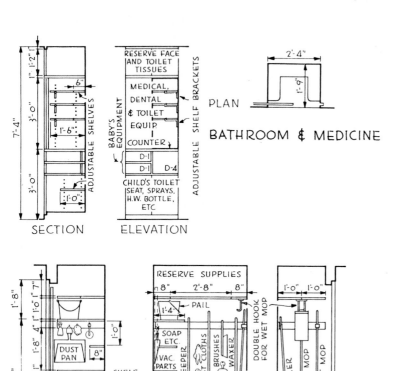

BATHROOM & MEDICINE

CLEANING CLOSET

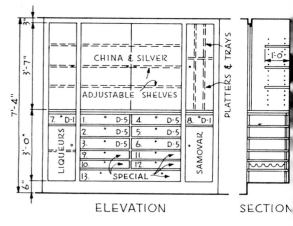

ELEVATION

SECTION

1, 4, 7, 8. FLAT SILVER
2, 3, 5, 6. NAPKINS, TABLE CLOTHS, DOILIES, ETC.
9, 11. PLACE MATS (SHALLOW)
10, 12. SPECIAL LINEN ROLLERS
13. EXTENSION LEAVES.

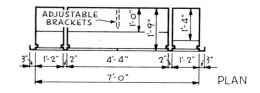

DINING ROOM STORAGE

Fig. 12 Miscellaneous storage

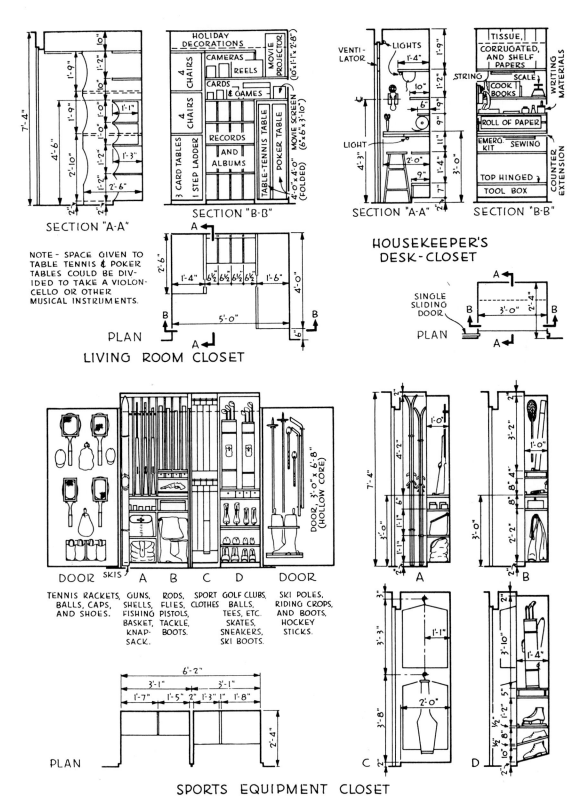

SECTION "A-A"

NOTE - SPACE GIVEN TO TABLE TENNIS & POKER TABLES COULD BE DIVIDED TO TAKE A VIOLONCELLO OR OTHER MUSICAL INSTRUMENTS.

SECTION "B-B"

PLAN

LIVING ROOM CLOSET

HOUSEKEEPER'S DESK-CLOSET

SECTION "A-A"

SECTION "B-B"

PLAN

DOOR SKIS   A   B   C   D   DOOR

TENNIS RACKETS, BALLS, CAPS, AND SHOES.

GUNS, SHELLS, PISTOLS, FISHING BASKET, KNAPSACK.

RODS, FLIES, TACKLE, BOOTS.

SPORT CLOTHES

GOLF CLUBS, BALLS, TEES, ETC. SKATES, SNEAKERS, SKI BOOTS.

SKI POLES, RIDING CROPS, AND BOOTS, HOCKEY STICKS.

PLAN

A   B   C   D

SPORTS EQUIPMENT CLOSET

Fig. 13. Miscellaneous closets

BACKGROUND

In an apartment building the spaces themselves must be simple and universal enough to adapt to a variety of life styles. As far as the movement through the apartment is concerned far more specific criteria can be established relying on basic circulation patterns that are valid for most living conditions.

A well-planned apartment provides maximum privacy for various activities and makes movement to any room possible without crossing another.

Entering the Apartment

In inclement weather outer clothing should be taken off at the entrance and put away; umbrellas and boots should be stored to prevent dirtying the floors of other rooms; space should be provided to accommodate packages.

Entering with Groceries or Leaving with Garbage

Connection between entrance and kitchen should be as direct as possible; preferably through the entry hall and not the living space. A secondary entrance directly into the kitchen solves this problem ideally.

Children Coming in from Play

Children should be able to reach the bathroom or their own rooms without crossing the living space.

Deliveries

Packages should be taken and paid for without having the delivery man enter the living space.

Children Entering While Adult Activity Is Taking Place in the Living Space (or Vice Versa)

Children should be able to get to their bedrooms without crossing the living space.

Passing from Bedroom to Bathroom

It should not be necessary to cross the living space. Ideally, one should not be seen at all.

Passing from Kitchen to Bathroom

This should be done, if possible, without crossing the living space.

Serving from Kitchen to Dining Room

Service should be as direct as possible without crossing any other space (except occasionally the entry hall).

Ideal circulation criteria are achieved by proper planning of the rooms around the core of the apartment, which consists of the entry hall and the bedroom corridor. In fact a well-planned apartment can be divided into two zones, living zone and sleeping zone, separated by the entry hall.

Neither this simple geometric division nor the ideal circulation pattern is always possible. Corner apartments, quadruplex walk-ups, and townhouses often require functional compromise to achieve economy.

Equally important as the relation of each room to the other is the relative position it occupies in relation to daylight and fresh air. Ideally, every room in an apartment should have exterior exposure to ensure light and air. To plan this way, however, would increase the perimeter of the building to an extent that no one could afford to build it. Therefore bathrooms, invariably, kitchens, often, and dining rooms, sometimes, are handled as interior spaces. This is possible because building codes allow bathrooms and kitchens to be mechanically ventilated, because an inside dining alcove is really an extension of the living space, and because the kitchen can be situated to borrow light from the living or dining room. Thus the apartment plan is divided into outer and inner zones. Naturally, units with double exposure—townhouses, duplex walk-ups, and exterior gallery-type buildings—can have kitchens and dining rooms in the outer zone without difficulty.

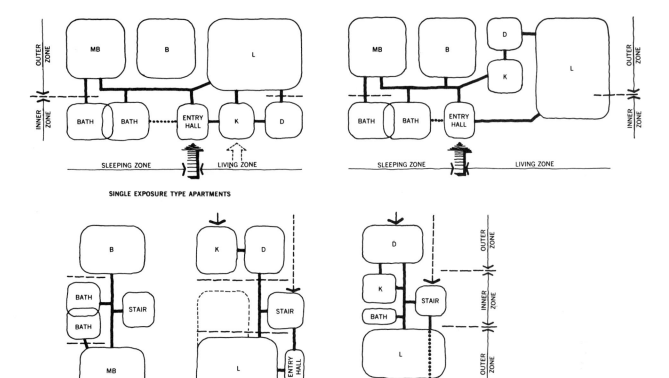

SINGLE EXPOSURE TYPE APARTMENTS

DOUBLE EXPOSURE TYPE (TOWNHOUSE)

The approximate size and proportion of the rooms themselves must be included in the sponsor's program. Extreme care must be taken on public or federally assisted housing jobs because minimum dimensions given as guidelines cannot be accepted without scrutiny.

In the private building sector market conditions and competition are the best gauge of room sizes. Awareness of the local housing market is essential, for market conditions vary considerably not only from city to city but from neighborhood to neighborhood. As an example, the Chicago market demands a separate alcove as a defined din-

ing space; in New York the entry hall is often substituted, thus serving a dual function and increasing the space allotted to the total living area. Considerably larger rooms are called for along Chicago's Lake Shore Drive than in Old Town, just a few blocks away.

The architect's most reliable guide is a thorough analysis of the function, furnishings, and circulation pattern of each space. In this respect HUD guidelines for minimum furniture requirements are quite reliable, assuming naturally that proper circulation space is provided.

TABLE 1 Minimum Room Sizes

Name of Space	Minimum Area (sf)					Least Dimension
	LU with 0-BR	LU with 1-BR	LU with 2-BR	LU with 3-BR	LU with 4-BR	
A. *Minimum Room Sizes for Separate Rooms*						
LR	NA	160	160	170	180	11'-0"
DR	NA	100	100	110	120	8'-4"
BR (primary)	NA	120	120	120	120	9'-4"
BR (secondary)	NA	NA	80	80	80	8'-0"
Total area, BR's	NA	120	200	280	380	—
B. *Minimum Room Sizes for Combined Spaces*						
LR-DA	NA	210	210	230	250	
LR-DA-SL	250	NA	NA	NA	NA	
LR-DA-K	NA	270	270	300	330	
LR-SL	210	NA	NA	NA	NA	
K-DA	100	120	120	140	160	

Abbreviations:
LU = living unit
LR = living room
DR = dining room
DA = dining area

0-BR = LU with no separate bedroom
K = kitchen
NA = not applicable
BR = bedroom
SL = sleeping area

LIVING ROOM (LIVING-DINING ROOM)

The living room should be conducive to general family life and should allow for group activities as well as individual relaxation: "entertaining, reading, writing, listening to music, watching television, and children's play."

The following furniture as a minimum should be accommodated:

One couch, 3'-0" × 6'-10"
Two easy chairs, 2'-6" × 3'-0"
   (one for efficiency apartment)
   (three for four or more bedroom units)
One desk, 1'-8" × 3'-6"
One desk chair, 1'-6" × 1'-6"
One television set, 1'-4" × 2'-8"
One table, 1'-6" × 2'-6"

The living room is the most impressive and largest of all rooms in the apartment, which is why many developers like it to be visible from the entry hall.

To serve as a guide the living room in the average middle income two-bedroom apartment is about 260 to 300 sf; combined living-dining room is about 400 sf. When the living room is also used for dining, its proportions, with minimum waste, become critical. Typical square (20' × 20') living-dining rooms are far less efficient than the oblong (15' × 26') of the same square footage.

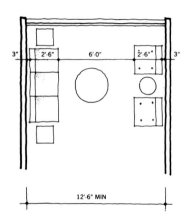

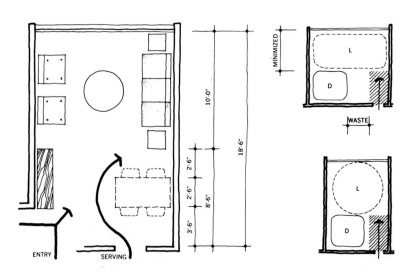

DINING

A truly separate dining room can be afforded only in townhouses or luxury housing. The most common arrangement takes the form of an alcove off the living room. Although this alcove can occupy an inner zone, a windowed area is preferable even though it creates a larger building perimeter and consequently increases costs. When a large group of diners is to be accommodated, the table must be expanded into the living room and space should be provided for it without having to move heavy furniture.

The table and chair requirements listed below should be considered not only with proper circulation space and pattern of food serving in mind but also in relation to space for storage.

Efficiency or one bedroom, two persons: 2'-6" × 2'-6"
Two bedrooms, four persons: 2'-6" × 3'-2"
Three bedrooms, six persons: 3'-4" × 4'-0" or 4'0" round
Four or more bedrooms, eight persons: 3'-4" × 6'-0" or 4'-0" × 4'-0"
Dining chairs: 1'-6" × 1'-6"

In middle-income two-bedroom apartments an average dining alcove is about 100 sf and a separate dining room is about 140 sf.

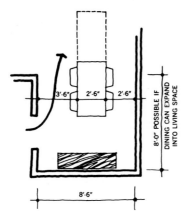

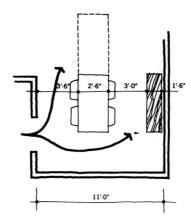

BALCONIES

There is much controversy about the need for balconies, which are costly, and it is questionable in profit-motivated housing whether they will result in increased rent or sales price. Besides the balcony's aesthetic factor (it allows strong articulation) and its symbolic significance (a visible indication of the presence of human beings), its functional role has pros and cons. Those who argue for it stress the delight of sitting outdoors when the weather is pleasant. Its proponents call attention to the visual extension of the living space, to extra storage space, and to the opportunity to grow plants. Those who oppose balconies claim that they cut off daylight, that they are dirt catchers and hard to keep clean, and in many regions can be used only part of the year.

Balconies must be wide enough for proper use (not less than 5 ft) and have adequate privacy.

KITCHEN

To provide for the most efficient food preparation, storage, and service, careful planning is required. Storage space normally provided in cabinets or utility closets can be expanded by the addition of shallow pantries: floor to ceiling shelving behind hinged doors.

Unless space is extremely tight, kitchens should be equipped with a small eating space to augment the regular dining room or alcove. When the kitchen is part of a combined kitchen-dining or kitchen-family room, the food preparation-cooking space should be screened from the dining or family area. When planning kitchens, the basic sequence of refrigerator-sink-stove, starting from the door and progressing toward the serving and eating areas, should be observed. The method of connecting with the dining room or alcove, pass-through or door, needs special attention. Well-planned kitchens in an inner zone should borrow daylight from the living or dining space to make working conditions in the kitchen pleasanter.

In a middle-income two-bedroom apartment an average kitchen with minimum eating space is about 100 sf.

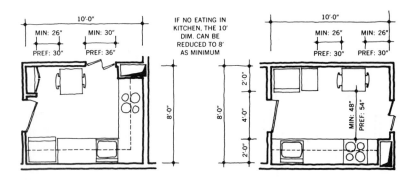

TABLE 2 Countertops and Fixtures

Work Center	Number of Bedrooms				
	0	1	2	3	4
	Minimum Frontages (Lin In.)				
Sink	18	24	24	32^a	32^a
Countertop, each side	15	18	21	24	30
Range or cooktop space	21	21	24	30	30
Countertop, one side	15	18	21	24	30
Refrigerator space	30	30	36	36	36
Countertop, one side	15	15	15	15	18
Mixing countertop	21	30	36	36	42

^{a}When a dishwasher is provided, a 24-in. sink is acceptable.

Storage Area^b

Square Feet	Number of Bedrooms				
	0	1	2	3	4
Minimum shelf area	24	30	38	44	50
Minimum drawer area	4	6	8	10	12

^{b}Wall cabinets over refrigerators and shelves above 74 in. shall not be counted as required storage area.

BEDROOM

Each bedroom should have enough space for double occupancy and provide for the following basic furniture:

Two twin beds, 3'-3" × 6'-10"
One dresser, 1'-6" × 4'-4"
One chair, 1'-6" × 1'-6"
One crib, 2'-6" × 4'-6"

It should be kept in mind that night tables must also be accommodated. Because the bedroom often serves as an extra work area, space for a sewing machine or writing desk is not a luxury.

In middle-income two-bedroom apartments average bedroom sizes (exclusive of closets) are 150 sf for secondary bedrooms and 180 sf for master bedrooms.

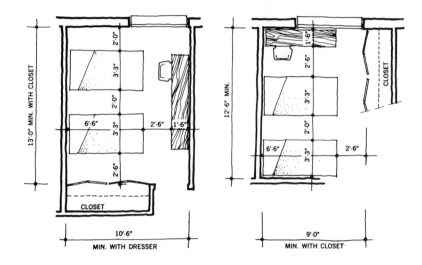

BATHROOMS

For the sake of economy a back-to-back arrangement of bathrooms is preferred either in the same apartment or with one that is adjacent. When there is only one bathroom, a tub and shower combination is standard equipment; when there are two, the second usually contains a stall shower. When an apartment has two or more bathrooms, one is customarily attached to the

master bedroom; the others serve the remaining bedrooms. A powder room or lavatory is sometimes substituted for the second bathroom, although the savings are nominal compared with the convenience of having two baths. In luxury housing compartmentalization is an advantage that allows simultaneous multiple use.

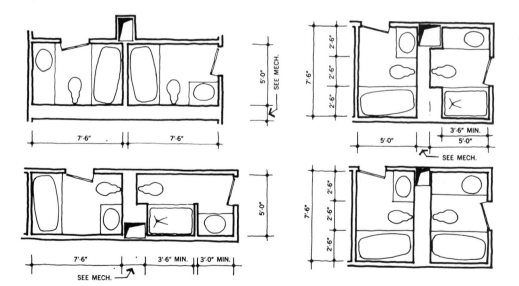

CLOSETS

Although overall apartment size is stated in a client's program, few clients pay attention in the early design stages to the amount and kind of closet space that is provided. It is generally accepted however, that it is never enough for the tenant or buyer. The tabulation that follows is a guide to closet sizes at various rental levels.

	Depth	Length (linear feet)[a]			
		Low Rental	Middle	Luxury	HUD Minimum
Guest closet (in or near entry hall)	2'3"	3'	4'	5'	2'
Utility closet (in or near kitchen)	2'0"	2'	2'	2'	2'
Pantry (in kitchen)	8 to 10"	—	—	4'	—
Linen closet (in bedroom hall)	1'6"	2'	2 to 3'	3 to 4'	1'6"
Master bedroom closet (in bedroom)	2'3"	8'	10'	12'	5'
Second bedroom closet (in bedroom)	2'3"	6'	8'	9'	3'
General storage closet (in entry or bedroom hall)	2'0"	—	—	4'	—

[a]Or equivalent linear feet in a walk-in closet.

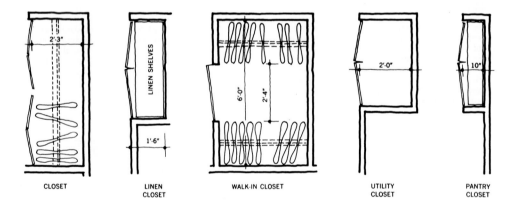

CLOSET   LINEN CLOSET   WALK-IN CLOSET   UTILITY CLOSET   PANTRY CLOSET

ENTRY HALL

The precise function of the entry hall should be stipulated. Is it merely for circulation or for other uses as well? For example, if it is to be used for telephoning, a small desk will be required. It might also become an extension of the living room and made large enough for dining.

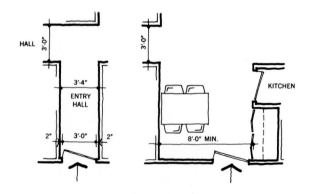

Certain building codes require that large apartments have two exits to the public corridor and that access be made easy to either one without having to pass through the bedrooms. The ideal location for the second exit is in the kitchen (though it may make its planning more difficult).

In this case the connection between the regular entry hall and the kitchen may be eliminated. The second exit, depending on the local code, may also open directly onto the stair landing (with "B" label door), though not when the stair is a smokeproof tower.

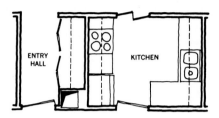

EFFICIENCY APARTMENTS

In efficiency apartments not only room functions but circulation patterns present different problems. Because one space serves for living, dining, and sleeping, precise demarcation is difficult. Still, an attempt must be made to define these

areas. The kitchen is usually considerably smaller than those found in regular apartments, and because there is no bedroom the bedroom-closet should serve as a walk-in dressing room.

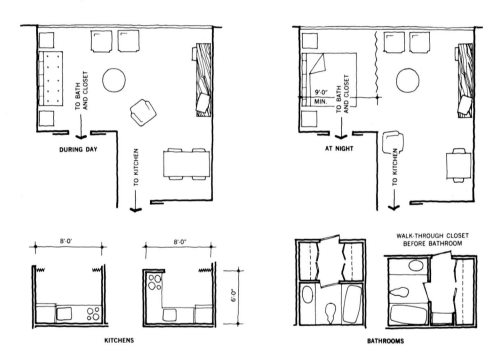

Obviously there is a close relation between room sizes and the total dimensions of the apartment. As a rule of thumb all room areas (living,

dining, bedrooms), kitchen, bathrooms, (but not entry hall), and closet spaces can be added to reach a total that should constitute 80 to 85% of the gross size, leaving 15 to 20% for circulation (entry hall, bedroom corridor), walls, columns, and shafts. Efficiency apartments naturally have less circulation space. In two-story apartments the space occupied on each floor by the stairs should also be taken into consideration as circulation space. It should be kept in mind that the most efficient apartment is not necessarily the largest but one that has the largest rooms within the smallest gross square-foot area and therefore the smallest possible circulation space. Although good, differentiated circulation is important, it

should be handled with a minimum of wasted space.

What one developer considers a small apartment another may find medium; what would be considered medium in a plush suburb may be placed in the luxury class in Greenwich Village. Nevertheless, it is possible within the broadest parameters to propose some guidelines (the HUD minimums in the following table were arrived at by adding up HUD minimum room sizes and closets and adding 20% to them for circulation):

		Gross Size		
Unit	Low	Medium	Luxury	HUD Minimum
Efficiency (1 bath)	450	500 to 550	600+	380
1-bedroom (1 bath)	650	700 to 800	900+	580
2-bedroom (2 baths)	950	1100 to 1200	1250+	750
3-bedroom (2 baths)	1,250	1350 to 1450	1600+	900

It is useful to know how apartment sizes are figured: from the exterior face of the exterior wall (in condominiums) and from the interior face of the exterior wall (in rentals) to the center line of the corridor partition, and from center line to center line of party walls (partitions between the apartments). Balconies are not included in these dimensions.

Apartments for the elderly fall into a special category. These apartments are generally small (550 sf for one bedroom is not unusual) and are mostly one-bedroom units or efficiencies. This limited size de-

mands taut, imaginative planning. Because of the frequent use of wheel chairs, wider doors (2 ft 8 in) are used throughout the apartment, including the bathroom, and bedrooms should be furnished to permit clear passage around each bed. Bathroom layouts are for ease of wheelchair manipulation and kitchen cabinets are built to be reached with minimum bending and stretching. Because many of the elderly are tied to their apartments for long periods, northern orientation—in which no sunlight can reach the interior—should be avoided.

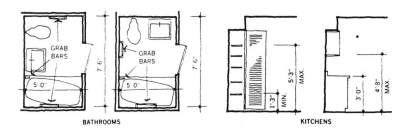

BATHROOMS   KITCHENS

By J. L. GRUZEN and J. J. KOSTER, Gruzen and Partners

INTRODUCTION

At the time of this writing, it is anticipated that within the next 15 years in the United States it will be necessary to construct as many new housing units as have been constructed to date.

This need for new housing, considered against a background of continuing urbanization, clearly indicates that an increasing proportion of an expanding housing market will be devoted to multifamily types of housing or apartments. The inevitability of this trend contains a challenge to the architect to do more than merely meet a statistical demand. He must rather address, identify, and solve the problems of multifamily building types as an attractive alternative to freestanding single-family buildings.

This article will deal with multifamily living in general, with some additional attention to the problems of the medium- and high-rise building type (i.e. building types which require a degree of vertical servicing).

GENERAL

The process of designing an apartment building may be graphically depicted in a general way as in Table 1. This article will be developed in the same sequence as Table 1. It must be borne in mind that, as with any design development, the evolution of an apartment building design is not a sequential process but a process of continuing interaction, feedback, and reevaluation, and that the number and complexity of events will vary according to the program, scope, and funding sources involved. The sequences shown are labeled as *program development*, *site analysis*, *building planning*, and *building design*.

Program development is for the most part evaluation of information over which the architect has relatively little control but which shapes the project in a basic way.

Site analysis involves evaluation of physical data which must be recognized, identified, and weighed by the architect in making basic design decisions dealing with site use, allocation, and development.

PROGRAM

Market Analysis

A market analysis and program formulation may precede the retention of an architect; however, to an increasing degree clients solicit the aid of an architect in these areas. An investigation of the potential market should consider existing market conditions and trends with regard to

1. Type of occupancy
   a. Rental
   b. Cooperative
   c. Condominium
2. Price (rent, maintenance, etc.)
3. Amenities
4. Apartment size (area and number of rooms)

TABLE 1

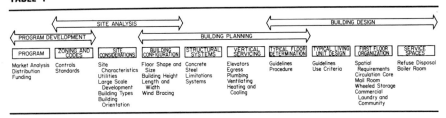

TABLE 2 Comparative Program Elements—Market Range

	Low	Medium	High
		Living unit	
Living	Minimum areas: combined living, dining and entry areas	Larger room sizes: dining alcove, entry alcove	Generous room sizes: separate dining room, separate entry foyer
Kitchen	Minimum counter top and storage; Standard appliances	Additional counter top and storage; snack bar, better appliances, space for dishwasher	Ample workspace, counter top, and storage; built-in appliances, wall oven, dishwasher, eat-in kitchen
Bedrooms. . .	Minimum closets	Walk-in closets	Dressing rooms, storage closets, built-in accessories
Baths	Minimal bath with standard fixtures and accessories; minimum finishes	Higher-quality fixtures, finishes, and accessories; extra half bath at entry or master bedroom	Additional baths and half baths with custom cabinets and fixtures; stall showers, etc. powder room; luxury finishes
		Support facilities	
In apartment.	Few extras limited to security	Intercom, door signal, balconies, unit air conditioners	Doorman and telephone, large balconies, central air conditioning, service entrance, servants' quarters
In building. . . .	Laundry facilities, minimum lobby	Laundry room, commercial space, community room, central storage	Attended parking, convenience shopping, service elevators, doorman, closed-circuit TV security system, valet service, meeting rooms, health club, sheltered swimming facilities
Site	Open parking, drying yard	Secure open or sheltered parking, outdoor play and sitting area, swimming pool	Gardens, recreation areas, country club amenities, swimming pool

5. Building types
6. Vacancy rates
7. Public facilities (transportation, schools, shopping, recreation)

Program items to be resolved include

Price range. What segment of the market is the project to be aimed at?

Amenities. Identified in Table 2 as support facilities and closely interrelated with price range.

Scope. How many units?

Distribution. Percentage of each type of unit.

Building type or types.

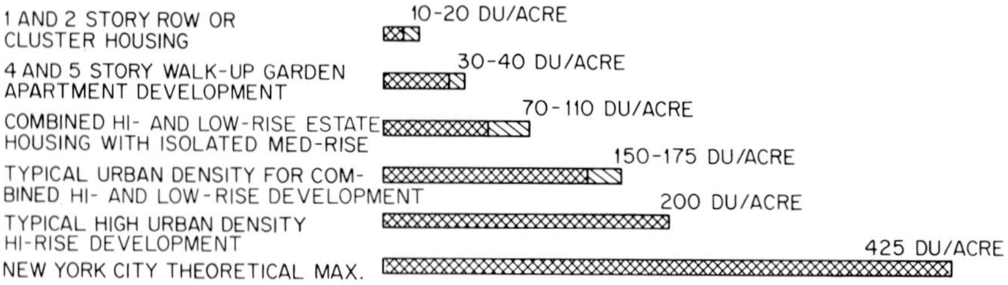

Funding

In many cases a market analysis will conclude that conventional private financing is not economically feasible and that some type of public or semipublic assistance is required if a project is to proceed.

There are a number of sources of such assistance at both federal and state levels. The FHA (Federal Housing Administration) and PHA (Public Housing Administration) are well-known examples of such agencies. As a rule, an agency which provides assistance also requires conformance to agency standards, and frequently such an agency will require approval of or participation in program development.

While the client, local authorities, and funding sources will usually institute basic program direction, it nevertheless remains the responsibility of the architect to catalyze these decisions and formulate the finished program.

Density

Figure 1 compares relative densities of various urban and suburban situations. It is helpful to "have a feel" for the physical reality of density figures as an aid in visualizing possible solutions and to anticipate implications of decisions which are made during program formulation.

ZONING AND CODES
General

Zoning and building codes are of basic importance to any project; and of all types of projects, those which involve housing tend to be regulated to a greater degree by zoning ordinances and codes.

Appropriate local and regional authorities should be contacted in order to determine the type and extent of limitations or controls which may be imposed on a project and, further, to gauge the discretionary powers and flexibility of the governing authorities. To an increasing degree, the philosophy of zoning is changing from one of restrictive limits and controls to an approach which attempts to lead and influence community growth. Many communities and regional authorities have guiding master plans which deal with long-range development and evaluation. The conceptual and planning freedom of the architect is linked with these considerations.

Failure to pursue a thorough investigation of these controls can result in serious problems later on in project development.

Controls

Zoning is concerned principally with questions of use, bulk, density, and location.

Use, bulk, and density are usually controlled

1 AND 2 STORY ROW OR CLUSTER HOUSING — 10-20 DU/ACRE

4 AND 5 STORY WALK-UP GARDEN APARTMENT DEVELOPMENT — 30-40 DU/ACRE

COMBINED HI- AND LOW-RISE ESTATE HOUSING WITH ISOLATED MED-RISE — 70-110 DU/ACRE

TYPICAL URBAN DENSITY FOR COMBINED HI- AND LOW-RISE DEVELOPMENT — 150-175 DU/ACRE

TYPICAL HIGH URBAN DENSITY HI-RISE DEVELOPMENT — 200 DU/ACRE

NEW YORK CITY THEORETICAL MAX. — 425 DU/ACRE

Fig. 1 Comparative densities.

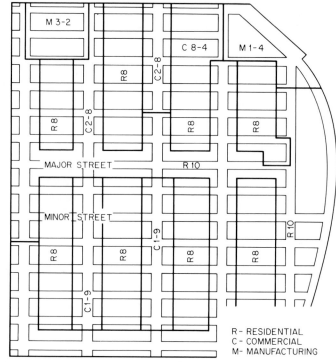

R - RESIDENTIAL
C - COMMERCIAL
M - MANUFACTURING

Fig. 2 Zoning map example.

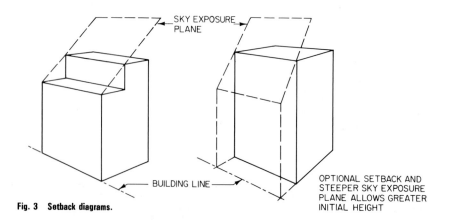

SKY EXPOSURE PLANE

BUILDING LINE

OPTIONAL SETBACK AND STEEPER SKY EXPOSURE PLANE ALLOWS GREATER INITIAL HEIGHT

Fig. 3 Setback diagrams.

on the basis of districts which are generally shown on maps and explained in an accompanying text (Fig. 2).

Uses may be designated as, for example, residential, commercial, manufacturing, and, in some cases, park or recreational. Mixed uses are frequently allowed, and for large housing projects it is considered advantageous to incorporate retail shopping, entertainment, and dining facilities into a program.

Location of buildings is controlled in order to prevent oppressive proximity of building masses. Formulas or diagrams which relate to variables such as building height and density are applied to locate buildings with respect to property lines and/or one another. (See Figs. 3 and 4.)

Density regulations limit the number of people per site-area unit. The basis for density determination will vary from regulation to regulation. Density may range from a low of ten or fewer people per acre in low-density districts to a high of up to 1,500 or more per acre in the highest-density districts.

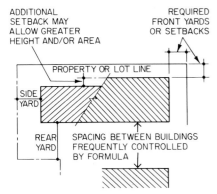

Fig. 4 Building spacing and location diagram.

Bulk is frequently controlled by floor-area ratio, which limits total buildable floor area as a multiple of the site area. In contemporary zoning regulations, floor-area ratio for apartment buildings will range from a low of 1 or less to a high in the range of 14 to 18 in dense metropolitan areas.

Building codes are less regional and vary less than zoning regulations. Many localities adopt national or state building codes as their standard. Such codes are concerned with health and safety requirements such as light and air, access, egress, construction standards, minimum dimensional standards, fire detection and protection, and fire equipment access.[1]

Standards

Similar to zoning and codes and equally important in many cases are governmental agency standards, which apply when public or semi-public funding sources are involved or mortgage standards if private funding is involved.

The need for a thorough initial investigation and continuing review for conformance with controls imposed by zoning, codes and agencies cannot be overemphasized.

[1] *Note:* Local fire departments and fire insurance groups may exert more restrictive controls than the above-mentioned codes.

SITE CONSIDERATIONS

Site Characteristics

Physical characteristics of a site may impose limitations on a building program; therefore an early analysis of site data and conditions should be undertaken by the architect in order to ascertain and evaluate such limitations.

Borings and samples taken at the site will provide information regarding location and extent of rock, bearing capacity of the sub-surface strata at various levels, and the level of a water table.

A survey indicating boundaries, contours, or spot elevations is necessary and, in the case of difficult sites, such a survey may indicate terrain and other conditions which will strongly influence design decisions. Limitations imposed by difficult terrain—in addition to those imposed by local laws or ordinances—may limit such items as location of driveways and parking entrances.

Utilities

Availability, adequacy, and location of site utilities enter into basic decision making. A

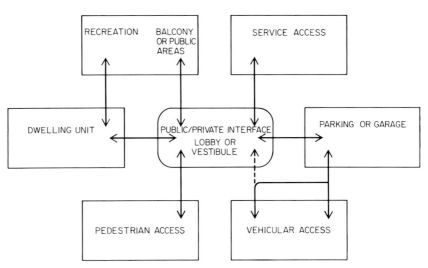

Fig. 5 Site element diagram.

building or buildings may be located so as to minimize expensive service runs. Inadequacy or unavailability of certain services may require on-site generation or disposal facilities.

Large Scale

Large-scale residential developments involve special problems and opportunities. Closing or rerouting of streets wholly within a project is frequently undertaken and can free up area, eliminate restrictions of a street grid pattern, and generally change the scale and feeling of a project. When through streets within a project are closed or otherwise restricted, compensatory widening and improvement of peripheral roads is usually in order not only to offset the effect of the closings but also to accommodate the increased traffic flow generated by the project itself. Similarly, shutting down a utility line and adding to demand generally requires compensatory improvement.

Site Elements

Figure 5 diagrams possible relationships among site layout elements which normally occur in apartment development. As suggested by the diagram, it is desirable to limit cross traffic among circulation elements such as vehicular access and pedestrian access and to maintain proximity or easy access among activity elements such as the dwelling unit, recreation, and parking.

The relationships may be horizontally or vertically arranged, depending on density or tightness of a site. Emphasis on the importance of certain relationships may vary with the program; however, the basic elements and relationships remain. Figure 6 shows examples of different arrangements of the site elements—arrangements which reflect program density relative to site area.

Building Access

Figure 7 diagrams various means of building access and internal circulation, each with different advantages and degrees of suitability to specific design solutions.

Building Orientation

Building orientation may be influenced by a number of factors such as site, view (desirable or undesirable), sun, and prevailing winds. Closely interrelated to building orientation is the question of internal circulation and floor layout of the building. Figure 8 indicates how different layouts lend themselves to solutions of site problems.

BUILDING CONFIGURATION

Floor Shape and Size

The shape and size of an apartment building can have significant influence on the cost and consequently the feasibility of a project.

The shape of the repetitive typical floors influences the cost of constructing and enclosing the floors. For purposes of economy and efficiency, building shape should be such that expensive exterior walls are minimized in

Residential

APARTMENT BUILDINGS

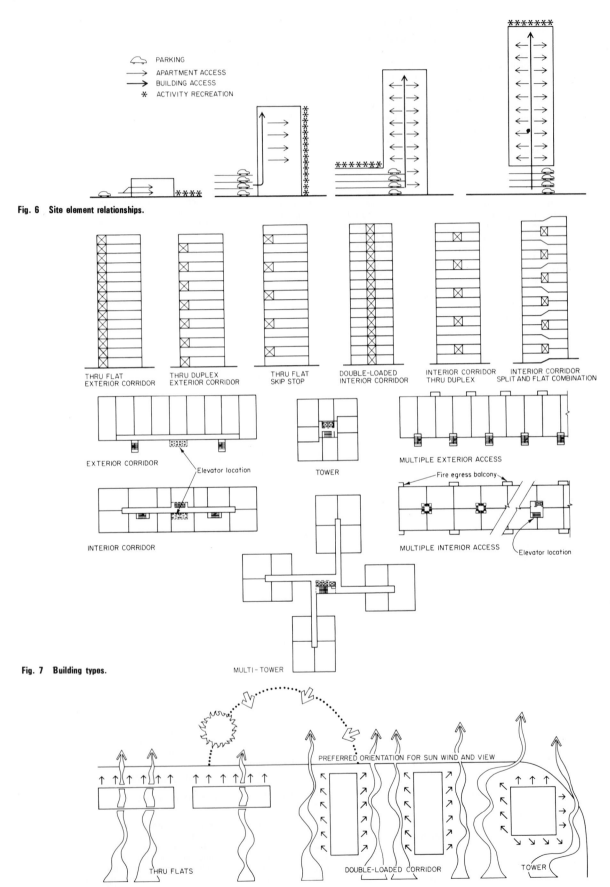

PARKING
APARTMENT ACCESS
BUILDING ACCESS
ACTIVITY RECREATION

Fig. 6 Site element relationships.

THRU FLAT
EXTERIOR CORRIDOR

THRU DUPLEX
EXTERIOR CORRIDOR

THRU FLAT
SKIP STOP

DOUBLE-LOADED
INTERIOR CORRIDOR

INTERIOR CORRIDOR
THRU DUPLEX

INTERIOR CORRIDOR
SPLIT AND FLAT COMBINATION

EXTERIOR CORRIDOR

Elevator location

TOWER

MULTIPLE EXTERIOR ACCESS

INTERIOR CORRIDOR

Fire egress balcony

MULTIPLE INTERIOR ACCESS

Elevator location

MULTI-TOWER

Fig. 7 Building types.

PREFERRED ORIENTATION FOR SUN WIND AND VIEW

THRU FLATS

DOUBLE-LOADED CORRIDOR

TOWER

Fig. 8 Orientation influences.

110

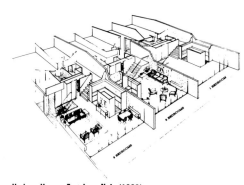

Horizon House, Fort Lee, N.J. (1963)

Court Elevation and Section

Rochester South East Loop (1972)

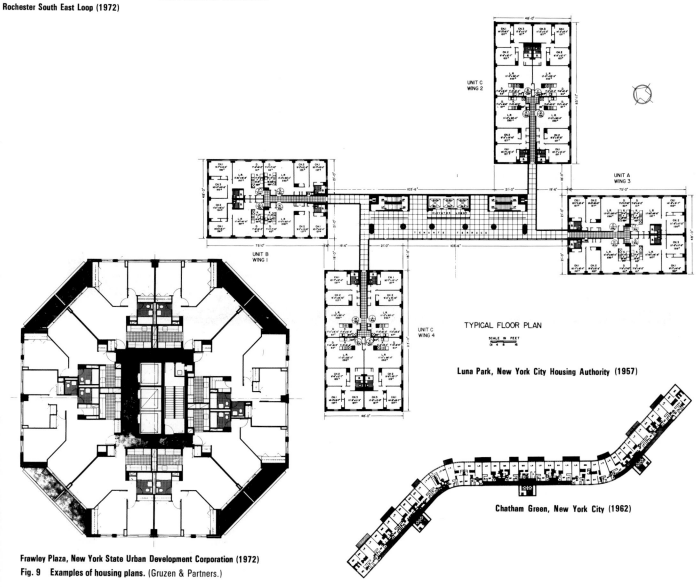

TYPICAL FLOOR PLAN

SCALE IN FEET

Luna Park, New York City Housing Authority (1957)

Chatham Green, New York City (1962)

Frawley Plaza, New York State Urban Development Corporation (1972)

Fig. 9   Examples of housing plans. (Gruzen & Partners.)

ratio to area enclosed and that breaks and direction changes in the perimeter are minimized. (See Fig. 9.)

Area of a typical floor may affect costs. For example, pouring of a typical tier in a cast-in-place concrete building is a continuous process and requires a full concrete crew throughout. The area of a typical floor or part thereof should be such as to efficiently utilize the day's productivity of a concrete crew. Similar analysis and considerations should be applied to other building techniques or systems.

Building Height

The cost of a building may be affected by building height. A building may be of such height that it exceeds prevailing capacities in terms of available construction equipment and contractor experience. In addition to considerations of what is possible, there are considerations of what is practical and efficient from a cost standpoint. Of the various mechanical systems which serve an apartment building, each has various increments and "step-up" points. For example, there is a situation such that the addition of a single extra floor could require a substantial increase in elevator service either through an additional elevator or an expensive increase in elevator speed. Similar situations exist for heating, cooling, plumbing, and ventilating systems, and opinions of the various consultants in these areas should be solicited.

Length and Width

Additional costs resulting from an increase of building length or width are generally proportionate to increase in area, However, as with other such items, there are step-up points at which there are disproportionately large increases in cost for slight dimensional increases.

Wind Bracing

Wind bracing becomes a structural design consideration in buildings beyond the 10- to 12-story range, and one must then consider measures which may be introduced to resist the overturning tendency due to wind loads. Wind bracing may be achieved by introduction of various structural measures. The extent and, therefore, the expense of these measures may be reduced if the building shape itself contributes to wind bracing. As the diagrams (Fig. 10) indicate, certain building shapes obviously have a greater inherent resistance to overturning.

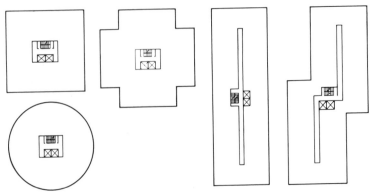

Fig. 10   Building shapes.

STRUCTURAL SYSTEMS

Concrete

The most common structural system presently employed for medium- to high-rise apartment construction is flat-plate cast-in-place reinforced concrete with randomly placed columns. This structural approach has certain advantages which make it particularly adaptable to apartment construction. (See Fig. 11.)

1. The horizontal services normally required in apartment construction may be imbedded

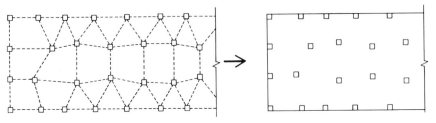

(a) Typical concrete construction

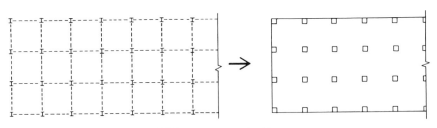

(b) Typical steel construction

Fig. 11   Steel and concrete structural systems.

within the concrete slab, thereby eliminating the need for a hung ceiling and allowing the flat underside of the slab to serve as the finished ceiling of the space below. This reduces floor-to-floor and overall building height and eliminates the separate construction of a hung ceiling.

2. The possibility of placing columns randomly adapts well to the inherently irregular module generated by a typical apartment floor layout. Columns may thus be "buried" in convenient locations within an efficient layout.

3. As a rule, openings for vertical services may be located at will in this type of structure; however, large openings near columns should be handled with care so as to assure continuity of vertical and horizontal reinforcing.

Steel

Although much less common than cast-in-place concrete, steel frame structures are also employed in the construction of apartment buildings.

The advantages of strength and relative simplicity of erection may recommend steel for use in extremely tall structures or for use in locales where there is limited experience in the use of concrete.

Steel structural frames tend to be laid out in a regular grid pattern, and this in turn regularizes the apartment layout. One should bear in mind that in this type of structure mechanical and structural lines may not coincide.

Limitations

As a rule of thumb, spacing between concrete columns may economically be in the range of 12- to 18-ft centers and spacing for steel columns may range from 16 to 24 ft.

Figure 12 may serve as a guide for sizing of concrete columns in preliminary layouts. Three common bay sizes or center-to-center distances have been shown for various building heights. Sizes are for internal columns, expressed in square inches. Peripheral and corner columns will be smaller.

The smallest dimension per side considered acceptable for concrete columns is 10 in., and 4 ft is the limit which normal concrete framework can easily accommodate. Columns with larger dimensions become, in effect, walls and are formed differently.

It is significant to note from the chart that an internal column in a tall building may be on the order of 2 by 3 ft. Such a planning element cannot be overlooked even for preliminary sketching.

Systems Approach

Any discussion of structural considerations in conjunction with housing must recognize that the housing industry appears to be at the beginning of an era of greatly increased prefabrication, which is leading towards full systems building and industrialization of the building process.

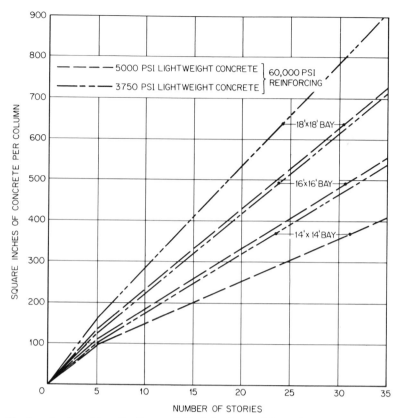

Fig. 12 Concrete-column sizing guide. (Data supplied by Farkas Baron and Partners.)

There are four variables involved in elevator selection:
1. Travel distance
2. Elevator speed
3. Elevator capacity
4. Building population

Travel distance is represented on the graph as "Number of stories" based on the assumption of normal floor-to-floor heights.

Possible speeds for buildings of different heights are shown.

Building population is represented on the graph as "population per floor," with curves shown for typical floor populations. In determining population, two persons per bedroom are assumed.

Egress and Safety

Except in rare circumstances, relatively little in the realm of egress and safety is left to the discretion of the architect. In general, the architect may choose only among accepted and approved procedures as set down in codes.

In most codes, two means of egress must be provided within specified distances from each dwelling unit (Fig. 15a–c) except in the case of duplexes, which frequently require an additional means of egress off the corridors, usually by means of an escape balcony (Fig. 15e).

Figure 15d diagrams a scissor stair which, as shown, is an arrangement which allows for construction of two stairs in one fire enclosure. This is an efficient and cost-saving solution to the two egress requirements. Most codes, however, effectively preclude the use of scissor stairs, in many cases by limiting the allowable length of dead-end corridors. Fire escapes are usually required for construction that is not fireproof; and sprinklers, smoke doors, fire detectors, and alarms are additionally required for various classifications of construction in some codes.

Plumbing

Vertical plumbing risers and waste lines (or "plumbing stacks") are expensive due to both material and labor costs. Reduction in the number of stacks saves money and is, therefore, to a greater or lesser extent advantageous and advisable.

Prefabrication and systems building has been applied widely in European countries for a number of years, and there have been many prototypical developments and limited applications of techniques in this field in the United States.

It is anticipated that, within the foreseeable future, virtually all European housing will be the product of some type of system. It would appear inevitable that progress toward industrialized construction will likewise continue in the United States.

At what precise point the utilization of systems building will become a major consideration in apartment design and what system or systems will survive to become a standard of the future is uncertain; however, it is a significantly growing field which will be watched closely by practitioners in the housing field.

Of the number of systems which are presently available, the following categories may be drawn:

1. Steel or concrete frame with precast planks, self-formed concrete deck or metal deck
2. Poured-in-place concrete tiers utilizing special reusable forms for transverse walls or columns
3. Long-span or short-span precast panel/plank and bearing wall
4. Prefabricated floor-size truss or beam systems with clear span capabilities.
5. Preassembled modules, prepared off site or on site, for stacking or insertion in a structural frame

Figure 13 shows a composite structure including the categories described.

Any proposal to use a building system should be preceded by a thorough investigation as to availability, code and market accepta-bility, union acceptability, adaptability to minor variations, and guarantees regarding erected costs.

VERTICAL SERVICES

Elevators

Figure 14 may serve as a preliminary guide in determining number and type of elevators necessary for an efficient solution.

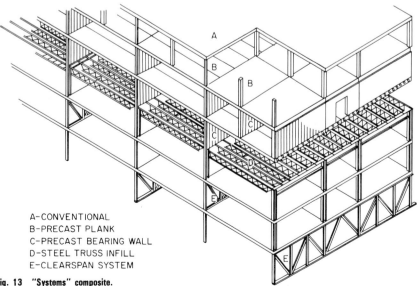

A-CONVENTIONAL
B-PRECAST PLANK
C-PRECAST BEARING WALL
D-STEEL TRUSS INFILL
E-CLEARSPAN SYSTEM

Fig. 13 "Systems" composite.

113

APARTMENT BUILDINGS

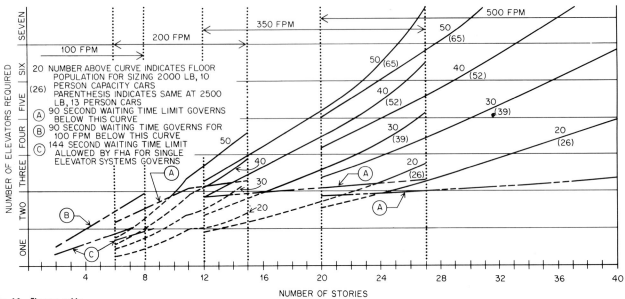

Fig. 14 Elevator guide.

Reduction in the number of plumbing stacks is accomplished by doubling or even tripling up on each stack at each floor. Figure 16 shows common bathroom and/or kitchen layouts with order-of-magnitude dimensions shown.

These dimensions, it should be remembered, are for rough layout purposes only and should be verified by consultants.

Ventilation

Interior spaces such as bathrooms, interior kitchens, and public halls require mechanical exhausting. Figures 17 and 18 may be used as guides, in making preliminary layouts, to determine the floor area to be allocated to exhaust ducts. Figure 18 indicates the area of exhaust and Fig. 17 shows buildup of fireproofing and

finish around the area of exhaust. The ratio of dimensions should be as close to square as possible and should not exceed a ratio of 3:1.

A mechanical engineer should be consulted to determine final data regarding size and location of ducts.

Heating and Cooling

In most cases, planning and spatial layout are not significantly influenced by heating and/or cooling units and their lines of supply. The most common exception is the case in which ducts deliver conditioned air from either a central source or a unit in the apartment. In such a case, ducts may be of such size as to become a planning factor. Otherwise, heating or cooling units are served either by hot and/or chilled

water pipes or electric conduit. Pipe risers as shown in Fig. 19 occupy a space of approximately 3 to 4 sq ft, are located at an outside wall, and generally, if possible, "run out" in two directions to serve two units at each floor. It is desirable to avoid having a common riser between separate apartments.

DETERMINATION OF A TYPICAL FLOOR
General

In discussing determination of a typical floor and specific apartment layouts, the most common structural type—poured-in-place flat-plate concrete construction with repetitive typical floors—is assumed. The principles of the pro-

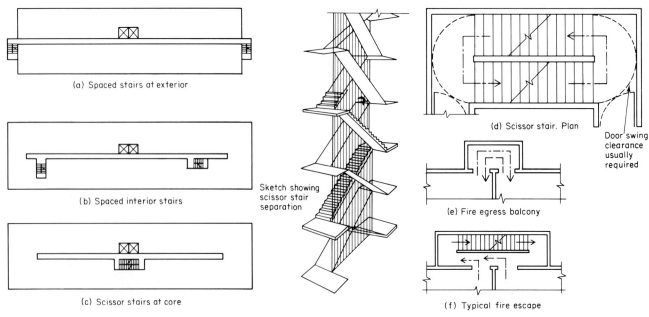

(a) Spaced stairs at exterior

(b) Spaced interior stairs

(c) Scissor stairs at core

Sketch showing scissor stair separation

(d) Scissor stair. Plan

Door swing clearance usually required

(e) Fire egress balcony

(f) Typical fire escape

Fig. 15 Types of stairs.

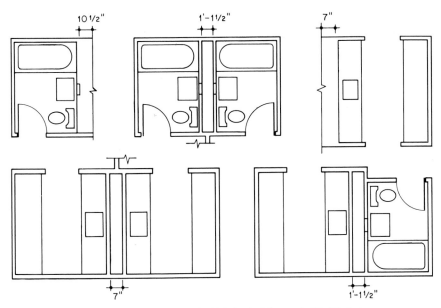

Note: Dimensions shown are clear dimensions for high-rise buildings up to 25–30 stories.

Fig. 16   Plumbing chases.

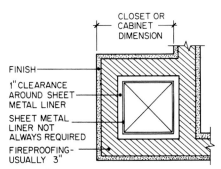

Fig. 17   Exhaust duct.

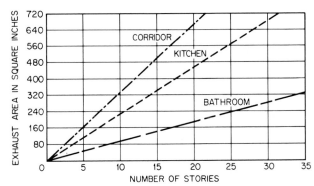

Fig. 18   Exhaust-duct sizing guide.

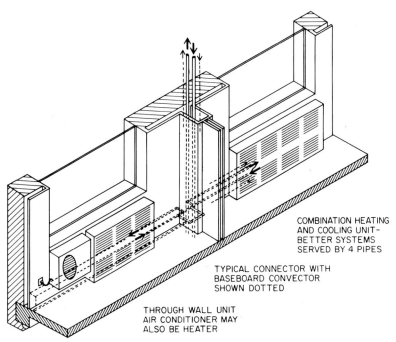

Fig. 19   Heating-cooling composite.

Residential

APARTMENT BUILDINGS

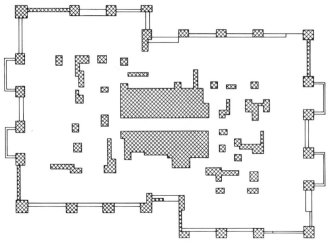

Fig. 20 Plan of 44-story apartment building with hatched areas indicating space devoted to vertical service elements.

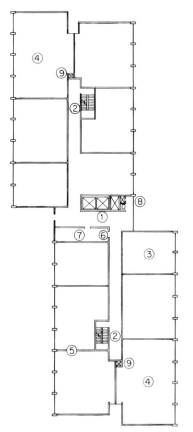

Fig. 21 Typical floor.
(1) It is generally desirable to group vertical services such as the elevator, incinerator or refuse chute, flue, standpipe, and, if possible, stairs so as to minimize above-roof construction. (2) Stairs may be spaced to avoid corridors with lengthy dead ends. (3) Efficiency apartments, probably with higher-than-average late-night traffic, may be best located near the elevator. (4) Multibedroom apartments are best located at corners. Larger multibedroom units lay out more compactly with two exposures. Larger apartments at corners also can cut down on required public corridor. (5) An attempt should be made to back up similar units, such as bedrooms, as well as similar mechanical services. (6) It may be necessary to allow space for electric closets (i.e., electric distribution panels) at every sixth or eighth floor. If electric heat is used, closets may occur more frequently. (7) Community balcony, laundry, vending machines, pram storage, or tenant storage may be provided at each floor or only on certain floors. (8) A janitor's closet is usually located on each floor at the refuse room. (9) If the corridor has no window, mechanical ventilation is indicated. Delivery and exhaust ducts should be planned to be remote from one another.

cedure which will be outlined may, however, be applied to any construction technique or system, bearing in mind the unique characteristics of that technique or system. (See Fig. 20.)

Procedure

Sequentially, the steps in the determination of a typical floor (in an ideal case) could proceed as follows: (See also Fig. 21.)

1. Investigate program with regard to the total number and types of apartments.

2. Identify repetitive groups with each group possibly representing a typical floor.

3. Assign area figures to apartments as determined in program analysis or as required by governmental agency standards. Total up the area of the apartments in a repetitive group and to this total add 10 to 15 percent for corridors and cores. This figure then may represent the area of a typical floor. If the area figure is reasonable and economical, if the size of the building thus generated conforms with various limits of the site, and if the typical floor area is otherwise acceptable, the investigation may proceed.

4. Tentative acceptance of a typical floor fixes a total number of floors. The implications of this number with regard to the potential for efficient utilization of the various mechanical systems, soil-bearing characteristics, zoning limits, etc., should be investigated. If the number of floors checks out acceptably, actual planning and layout may proceed.

5. The typical floor distribution must now be accommodated within the tentatively accepted area and within reasonable dimensions. The elevator core and stairs should be located and apartments laid out around them.

Figure 22 diagrams interrelationships among component elements of a typical living unit.

Although many apartments tend to have much the same layout as the diagram, there are many alternative arrangements which retain the essential component relationships. Apartments may be arranged as corner or floor-through units and—in addition to flats, or apartments on one level—layouts may be on two or three floors or on split levels (see Fig. 23).

As the diagram indicates, it is considered desirable to have ready circulation from the entrance foyer to the activity elements of the kitchen, living room, and sleeping areas and at the same time to maintain degrees of separation among these three elements.

Ideally, each space in an apartment should have access or exposure to the outdoors. However, application of this principle could result in an excessively expensive building type. Therefore baths, foyers, and frequently kitchens and dining areas are usually developed as interior spaces (see Fig. 24).

FIRST-FLOOR ORGANIZATION

General

The first floor of an apartment building fulfills a number of different program requirements. It serves as a connection between the dwelling portion of a building and the outdoors; it relates and interacts with both the outdoor functions and the dwelling units; and, further, it accommodates the physical transition between the dwelling units and the first floor.

Figure 25 illustrates possible interrelationships of first-floor functions with both the outdoors and the dwelling units.

Program requirements for typical first-floor spaces frequently call for larger unobstructed areas than occur at dwelling floors above. Common methods employed to achieve the unobstructed space at the first floor are (1) to "push out" the walls at the ground floor and enclose a larger space with an appropriate structure or, (2) to hang a ceiling in the first floor and "collect" and redirect various vertical services which would otherwise break up space at the ground floor. This is a common method used in the case of plumbing, heating,

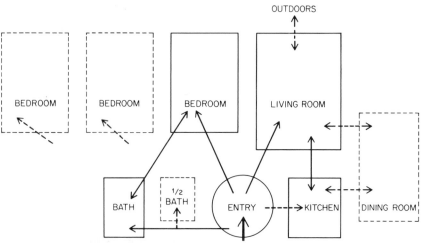

Fig. 22 Apartment element diagram.

116

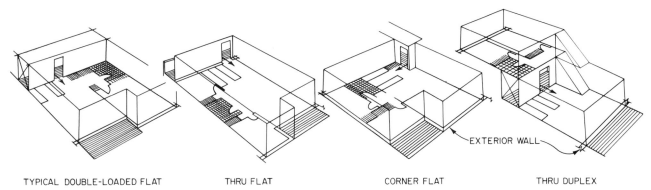

TYPICAL DOUBLE-LOADED FLAT   THRU FLAT   CORNER FLAT   THRU DUPLEX

EXTERIOR WALL

Fig. 23 Typical apartment types.

Fig. 24 Typical apartment layout.
(1) It is advisable to back up similar (kitchen and kitchen, bath and bath) ducts where possible. This allows one fan and fireproof enclosure to serve two ducts but requires measures to avoid excessive sound transmission between backed up spaces. Ducts may be "buried" in closets, kitchen, etc. Kitchen exhausts are best located near the range and close to the ceiling. Bathroom exhausts should, if possible, be placed away from the door in order to pull as much bathroom air as possible. Ducts are not necessary in kitchens or baths with windows (however, baths with windows, like top-floor baths, should be heated). (2) The structure should be spaced as regularly as practicable and within economical center-to-center distances. Columns built into closets or kitchens should assume the dimensions of the closet or cabinet. Column size should be reduced at upper stories of tall buildings. Slab openings along an entire column face should be avoided. (3) Plumbing backup is recommended. Dissimilar uses may be backed up, and it is possible to back up plumbing for more than two spaces. (4) Depth of rooms is sometimes limited by building codes. In any event, room depth relative to window size and location and natural light should be considered.

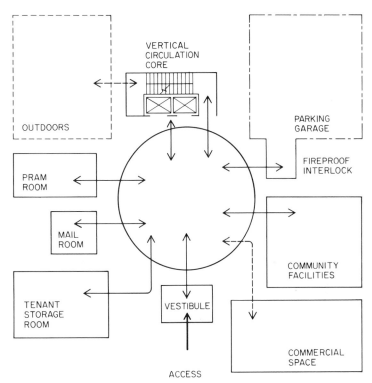

Fig. 25 First-floor diagram.

and electrical lines and not unusual for ventilating ducts. If there is substantial advantage to be gained, structural columns may be picked up and carried on girders concealed by the hung ceiling.

Vertical Circulation Core

For purposes of security and convenience, elevators should be well illuminated and visible from the lobby area. At least one exit stair should lead empty directly to the outside (but not necessarily at the lobby level).

It should be borne in mind that the stair layout in the lobby will frequently differ from a typical floor due to a greater first-floor ceiling height.

Mail Room

Mailboxes as well should be highly visible. If boxes are rear-loading, a locked room behind the boxes should be provided for the mailman's

use. Front-loading boxes require no such room. However, in either case, an additional secure area for packages and deliveries may be advised. Current federal requirements which govern matters such as maximum and minimum height of boxes and size of mail rooms should be consulted.

Wheeled Storage and/or Pram Room

Paths of travel from the main entrance to these areas should be short, direct, and without steps. Layout of the rooms for purposes of security should be such that all parts of the room are visible from the entrance. Lock rails, to which equipment may be secured, should be supplied.

Commercial

Shops and service facilities at the ground floor provide many advantages in terms of activity and convenience. However, much of the advantage to the building may be diminished if

the shops face away from the lobby and provide either no access or poor back-door access from the apartment building itself. On the other hand, easy circulation between a commercial establishment and the lobby may cause security problems which must be considered.

Laundry and Community Room

Laundries and community rooms are frequently found at the first floor for convenient servicing and public access and in order to utilize the additional story height. These facilities should be on a short, direct path from elevators, with as little cross circulation with other activities as possible. (See Figs. 26 to 30.)

Laundries may be located either on typical floors or in a penthouse in conjunction with the community room.

Location of laundry rooms on typical floors has the advantage of convenience which, however, is offset by difficulties of multiple maintenance and problems of odor and noise.

117

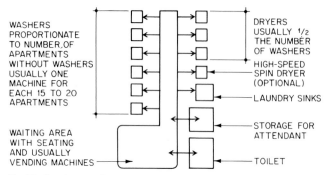

WASHERS PROPORTIONATE TO NUMBER OF APARTMENTS WITHOUT WASHERS USUALLY ONE MACHINE FOR EACH 15 TO 20 APARTMENTS

DRYERS USUALLY 1/2 THE NUMBER OF WASHERS

HIGH-SPEED SPIN DRYER (OPTIONAL)

LAUNDRY SINKS

STORAGE FOR ATTENDANT

TOILET

WAITING AREA WITH SEATING AND USUALLY VENDING MACHINES

Fig. 26   Laundry room diagram.

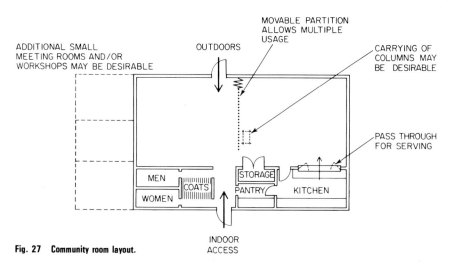

ADDITIONAL SMALL MEETING ROOMS AND/OR WORKSHOPS MAY BE DESIRABLE

MOVABLE PARTITION ALLOWS MULTIPLE USAGE

OUTDOORS

CARRYING OF COLUMNS MAY BE DESIRABLE

PASS THROUGH FOR SERVING

MEN

WOMEN

COATS

STORAGE

PANTRY

KITCHEN

INDOOR ACCESS

Fig. 27   Community room layout.

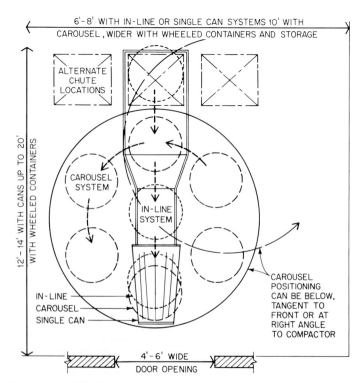

6'-8' WITH IN-LINE OR SINGLE CAN SYSTEMS 10' WITH CAROUSEL, WIDER WITH WHEELED CONTAINERS AND STORAGE

ALTERNATE CHUTE LOCATIONS

12'-14' WITH CANS UP TO 20' WITH WHEELED CONTAINERS

CAROUSEL SYSTEM

IN-LINE SYSTEM

IN-LINE
CAROUSEL
SINGLE CAN

CAROUSEL POSITIONING CAN BE BELOW, TANGENT TO FRONT OR AT RIGHT ANGLE TO COMPACTOR

4'-6' WIDE DOOR OPENING

Fig. 28   Compactor room layout.

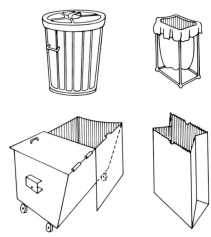

Fig. 29   Typical refuse containers. Consult and co-ordinate with refuse collection agency to assure acceptability of system regarding weight and size of containers, etc.

IT IS GENERALLY RECOMMENDED TO ALLOW RESERVE BOILER CAPACITY IN CASE OF BREAKDOWN

BREECHING FROM BOILERS TO FLUE. AREA AND SHAPE SAME AS NET FLUE AREA.

BOILER FLUE UP TO 60 SQ FT GROSS FLOOR AREA. AS CLOSE TO SQUARE AS POSSIBLE. NO GREATER THAN 2:1 RATIO RECOMMENDED

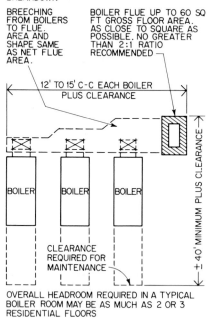

12' TO 15' C-C EACH BOILER PLUS CLEARANCE

± 40' MINIMUM PLUS CLEARANCE

BOILER   BOILER   BOILER

CLEARANCE REQUIRED FOR MAINTENANCE

OVERALL HEADROOM REQUIRED IN A TYPICAL BOILER ROOM MAY BE AS MUCH AS 2 OR 3 RESIDENTIAL FLOORS

Fig. 30   Boiler room layout.

A rooftop location for either of these facilities provides an additional level of amenity; however, it also involves additional expense.

Refuse disposal may be handled in a number of ways. The most widely used methods are by incineration or preferably, by compaction, with the processed refuse hauled away by truck. Both the incinerator and compactor require a storage area for waste containers, which should be nearby and should have easy access to the outdoors. The size of the container storage area will depend upon the type of container employed, frequency of collection, and, in some cases, agency standards. The area required for the refuse chute at typical floors is relatively small, ranging from 4 by 4 ft up to any size desired. The area of the compactor room or incinerator room at a lower level is quite large, and the refuse chute at the typical floor should be located so as to avoid interference problems at the lower levels.

GENERAL ROOM INFORMATION

For most facilities, the central laundry will probably be best from the residents' standpoints. More equipment will be available for their immediate use and large tumbler dryers will undoubtedly be used for faster drying and a higher rate of user turnover. From a design standpoint too, the central room offers some advantages. Foremost would be the central location of utility and venting facilities for dryers.

Where it is not possible to utilize one central room, it might be best to locate a laundry room on every second or every third floor so as to have more equipment in the room than if some equipment were located on every floor. This arrangement would also tend to produce some savings in utilities and venting facilities.

In any case, if at all possible in the laundry room design, make provisions for future expansion. As time passes, more equipment may be required for the same building, and as improvements in equipment occur and new products may be developed, tenants may demand more laundry facilities than originally necessary.

LOW-RISE APARTMENT

Garden apartments with low density can be served well with the typical plan in Fig. 4 for a multibedroom low-rise building. Three washers and three dryers serve a 20-unit apartment.

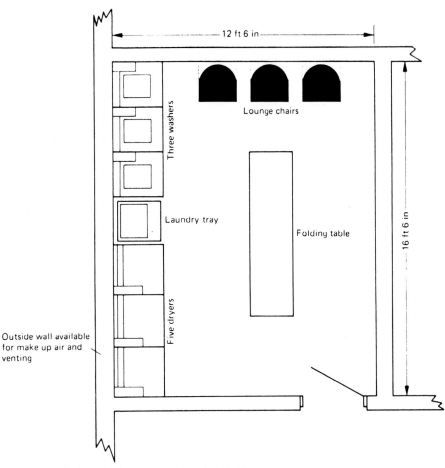

Fig. 1   Typical 20-unit multiple-bedroom, low-rise apartment building.

HIGH-RISE APARTMENT

The plan in Fig. 5 is for a typical 400-unit high-rise apartment building. The plan suggests 20 washers, 10 drying tumblers, and 1 washer extractor. This plan presupposes one central laundry room for the entire building. Some very tall apartment buildings will space smaller laundry rooms throughout the living area of the building.

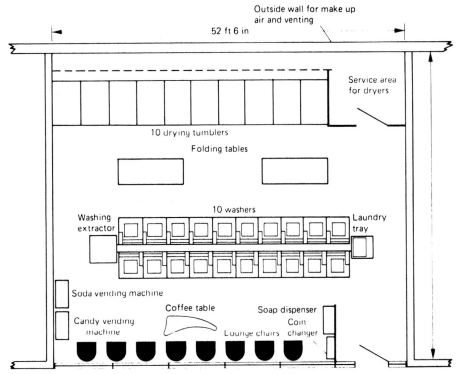

Fig. 2   Typical 400-unit, high-rise apartment building.

Residential

APARTMENT BUILDINGS
Central Laundry Rooms

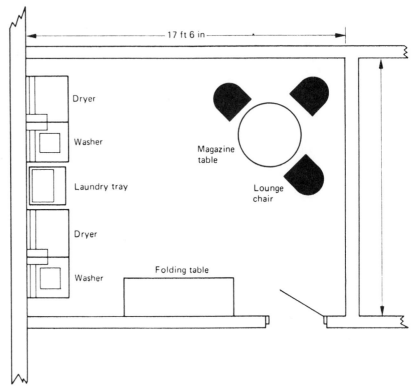

SENIOR CITIZENS RESIDENCE

Convenient laundry facilities are important to senior citizens. The typical plan in Fig. 3 shows two pairs of washers and dryers serving 18 residential units in a multistory home for the elderly. Additional room here is provided for seating and lounge facilities.

Fig. 3   Typical 18-unit-per-floor, high-rise housing for the elderly.

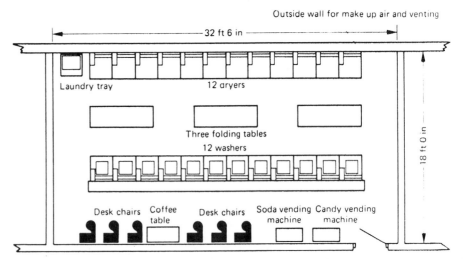

COLLEGE DORMITORY

This typical laundry facility for a large 500-student residence features 12 washers and 12 dryers.

Fig. 4   Typical 500-unit student dormitory.

120

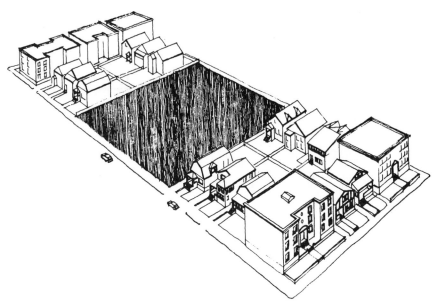

Fig. 1 Typical city block, 200′ x 600′, showing a one-acre (218′ x 200′) vacant site in the center.

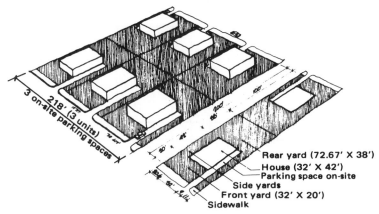

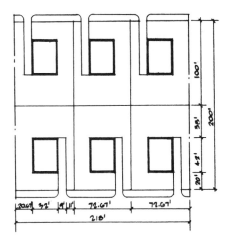

Rear yard (72.67′ X 38′)
House (32′ X 42′)
Parking space on-site
Side yards
Front yard (32′ X 20′)
Sidewalk

Fig. 2 Detached houses, one story, density six units per acre.

- Detached houses on 1-acre site
- Site dimensions: 218′ x 200′ = 43,600 sq ft
- 3 units per side = 6 units per acre
- Typical interior unit dimension 30′ x 40′ = 1,200 sq ft
- 1,200 sq ft = 3-bedroom unit
- Parking: 6 on-site spaces

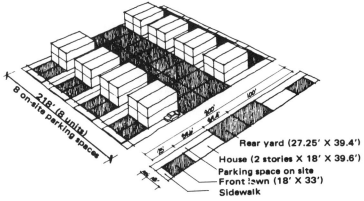

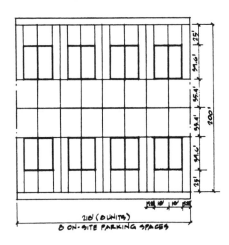

Rear yard (27.25′ X 39.4′)
House (2 stories X 18′ X 39.6′)
Parking space on site
Front lawn (18′ X 33′)
Sidewalk

Fig. 3 Two-story semidetached houses, density 16 units per acre.

- Semidetached on 1-acre site
- Site dimensions: 218′ x 200′ = 43,600 sq ft
- 8 units per side = 16 units per acre
- Typical interior unit dimension: 17′ x 37.6′ x 2 stories = 1280 sq ft
- 1200 sq. ft. = 3-bedroom unit, + 40 sq ft of stairs per floor
- Parking: 16 on-site spaces

Residential

HOUSING DENSITIES

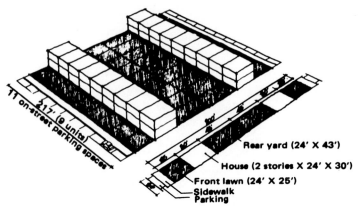

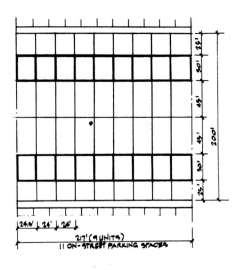

Rear yard (24' X 43')

House (2 stories X 24' X 30')

Front lawn (24' X 25')
Sidewalk
Parking

Fig. 4 Two-story row houses, density 18 units per acre.

- Row houses on 1-acre site
- Site dimensions: 217' x 200' = 43,400 sq ft
- 9 units per side = 18 units per acre
- Typical interior unit dimension: 23' x 28' x 2 stories = 1288 sq ft
- 1,200 sq ft = 3-bedroom unit, + 40 sq ft
- Parking: 22 on street parking spaces

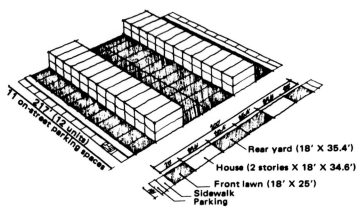

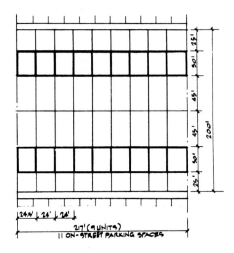

Rear yard (18' X 35.4')

House (2 stories X 18' X 34.6')

Front lawn (18' X 25')
Sidewalk
Parking

Fig. 5 Two-story row houses, density 24 units per acre.

- Row houses on 1-acre site
- Site dimensions: 217' x 200' = 43,400 sq ft
- 12 units per side = 24 units per acre
- Typical interior unit dimensions: 17' x 37.6' x 2 stories = 1280 sq ft
- 1200 sq ft = 3-bedroom unit, + 40 sq ft of stairs per floor
- Parking: 22 on-street parking spaces

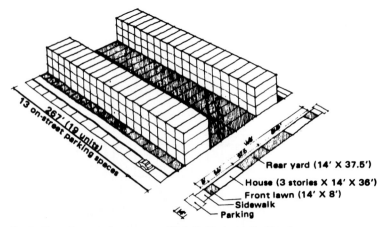

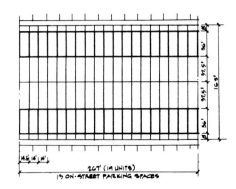

Rear yard (14' X 37.5')

House (3 stories X 14' X 36')

Front lawn (14' X 8')
Sidewalk
Parking

Fig. 6 Three-story row houses on modified city block, density 38 units per acre.

- Row houses on 1-acre site
- Site dimensions: 267' x 163' = 43,321 sq ft
- 19 units per side = 38 units per acre
- Typical interior unit dimensions: 13' x 34' x 3 stories = 1326 sq ft
- 1200 sq ft = 3-bedroom unit, + 40 sq ft of stairs per floor
- Parking: 13 spaces per side (on street), total = 26 spaces

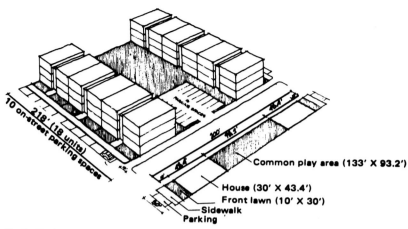

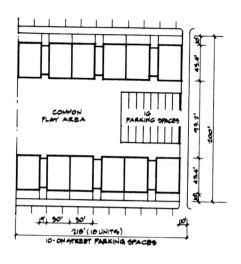

Fig. 7   Garden apartments, density 36 units per acre.

- Garden apartments on 1-acre site, 6 units per entry
- Site dimensions: 218' x 200' = 43,600 sq ft
- 18 units per side = 36 units per acre
- Typical interior unit dimensions: 29' x 41.4' = 1,202 sq ft
- Parking: 10 spaces each side street = 20 spaces, + 16 spaces on interior of site, total = 36 spaces

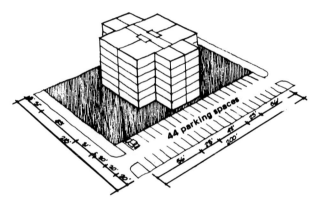

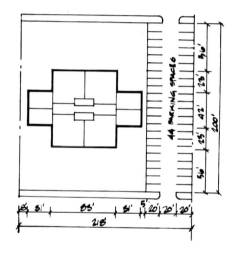

Fig. 8   Medium high-rise apartments, density 35 units per acre.

- Apartments on 1-acre site
- Site dimensions: 218' x 200' = 43,600 sq ft
- Six stories, six apartments per floor = 35–36 units per acre
- Typical interior unit areas (per floor): 2 apartments @ 1,200 sq ft; 4 apartments @ 1,280 sq ft
- 1,200 sq ft = 3-bedroom unit
- Parking: 44 on-site spaces

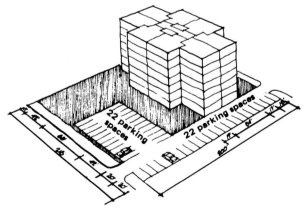

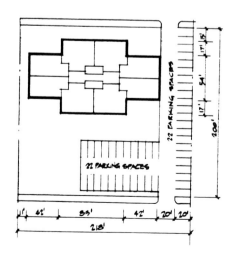

Fig. 9   Medium high-rise apartments, density 55 units per acre.

- Apartments on 1-acre site
- Site dimensions: 218' x 200' = 43,600 sq ft
- Seven stories, eight apartments per floor = 55–56 units per acre
- Typical interior unit areas (per floor): 4 apartments @ 1,202 sq ft; 4 apartments @ 1,227 sq ft
- 1,200 sq ft = 3-bedroom unit
- Parking: 44 on-site spaces

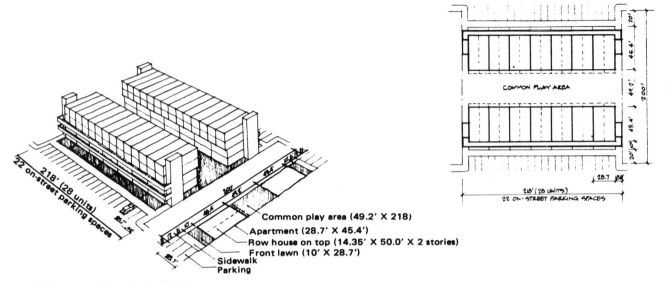

Common play area (49.2' X 218)
Apartment (28.7' X 45.4')
Row house on top (14.35' X 50.0' X 2 stories)
Front lawn (10' X 28.7')
Sidewalk
Parking

Fig. 10 European walk-up, density 56 units per acre.

- Walk-up apartments on 1-acre site
- Site dimensions: 218' x 200' = 43,600 sq ft
- 28 units per side = 56 units per acre
- Typical interior unit dimensions: 27.7' x 43.4' = 1,202 sq ft
- Typical interior unit dimensions, duplex: 13.35' x 48.0' x 2 stories = 1,282 sq ft
- 1,200 sq ft = 3-bedroom unit; + 40 sq ft stairs per floor for duplex
- Parking: 22 spaces per side (on street), total = 44 spaces

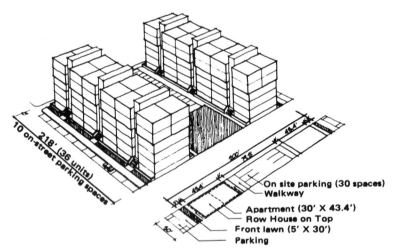
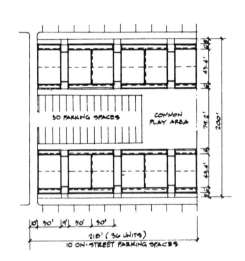

On site parking (30 spaces)
Walkway
Apartment (30' X 43.4')
Row House on Top
Front lawn (5' X 30')
Parking

Fig. 11 High-density walk-up, density 72 units per acre.

- Walk-up apartments on 1-acre site
- Site dimensions: 218' x 200' = 43,600 sq ft
- 36 units per side = 72 units per acre
- Typical interior unit dimensions; 29' x 41.4' = 1,201 sq ft
- Typical interior unit dimensions, duplex: 29' x 22.2' x 2 stories = 1,288 sq ft
- 1,200 = 3-bedroom unit, + 40 sq ft stairs per floor
- Parking: 30 spaces on site + 20 spaces on street, total = 50 spaces

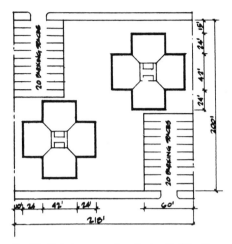

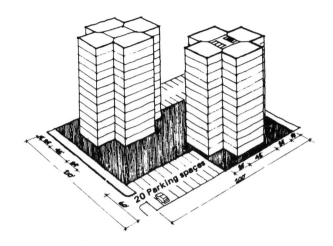

Fig. 12   Twin-tower apartments, density 94 units per acre.

- High-rise apartments on 1-acre site, two 12-story buildings
- Site dimensions: 218' x 200' = 43,600 sq ft
- 47 units per tower = 94 units per acre, 4 units per floor
- Typical interior unit dimensions: approx. 40' x 32' (unit actually 1194 sq ft)
- 1,200 sq ft = 3-bedroom unit
- Parking: 20 on-site spaces per side, total 40 spaces

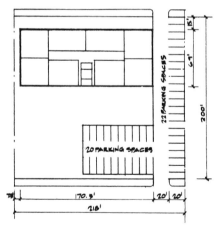

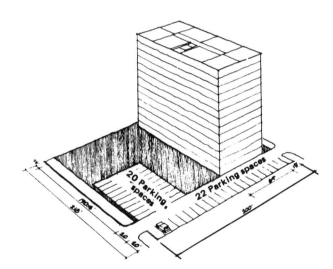

Fig. 13   High-rise apartments, density 103 units per acre.

- Apartments on 1-acre site
- Site dimensions 218' x 200' = 43,600 sq ft
- 13 stories, 8 apartments per floor = 103 units per acre
- Typical interior unit dimensions: 4 apartments @ 33' x 36' = 1,188 sq ft; 2 apartments @ 25.5' x 47.3' = 1,211 sq ft; 2 apartments @ 31.5' x 38' = 1,197 sq ft
- 1,200 sq ft = 3-bedroom unit
- Parking: 42 on-site spaces

Residential

HOUSING FOR THE ELDERLY

By W. RUSSEL PARKER, Architect

BACKGROUND

In the coming years, a greater proportion of houses, apartments, and institutional accommodations will be built for elderly persons than at any previous time in our history. There are several reasons for this. First is the well-known fact that the life-span of mankind has increased through advances in medical science; thus the proportion of older people in the population has increased. Second, with the passing of the three-generation household, more elderly persons are living by themselves and therefore require separate housing accommodations. Third, increased social security benefits and private pension payments have enabled more aged people to pay for suitable accommodations. Finally, many nonprofit groups such as church, labor, and fraternal organizations, charitably supported groups, and tax-supported bodies are, and will continue to be, engaged in the provision of housing specifically for the elderly.

Ordinary design criteria do not always apply to housing for the aged. One of the most striking differences is the high concentration of one- and two-person families as a result of children leaving home or the death of one spouse. Also important are the needs caused by physical deterioration in old age, which requires special design treatments and facilities.

In addition, certain basic psychological and sociological principles should be observed in planning for the elderly. People in this age group usually do not want to break their ties with family and neighborhood and be placed in a new and foreign environment. They need activities, not merely hobbies, and they want to participate in community functions. The objectives, programs, and physical facilities for the housing of the aged should encourage and support the continuance of earlier patterns of living, daily routines, personal care habits, social contacts, and recreational activities. An important objective is to maintain independent living as long as possible.

NEIGHBORHOOD AND SITE

A desirable neighborhood for the elderly should have many of the characteristics of any good neighborhood. It should be basically residential, possess the normal range of community facilities, have convenient public transportation, and be removed from particularly objectionable land uses. In terms of the individual aged person, the ideal neighborhood is often the one in which he has lived most of his life. The development of a broad program and the selection of a particular site should give consideration to old established neighborhoods where many of the aged are likely to be living and to have their roots.

From the point of view of the community

Multi-Unit Retirement Housing for Rural Areas—A Guide to Design Considerations for Architects, Engineers, and Builders, Agricultural Engineering Research Division, Agricultural Research Service, U.S. Department of Agriculture, Washington, D.C., 1965.

itself, there are also many advantages in housing the aged in well-established neighborhoods, where there are more existing facilities and generally better public transportation. Another advantage, which is frequently overlooked, is the sympathy and help that are extended to the aged by friends and neighbors, young and old alike.

The selection of an actual site involves the following considerations:

1. The topography should be as level as possible to minimize the need for steep walks, ramps, or stairs. Relatively level sites encourage walking—a highly desirable exercise.

2. The site should not be bounded on all sides by major traffic arteries. It should be possible to go shopping or to the park without having to cross a major street.

3. Essential commercial facilities should be close at hand and easily accessible—supermarkets, cleaners, laundries, shoe repair shops, drug stores, and the like.

4. Basic community facilities such as churches, libraries, health services, and recreation facilities should also be close at hand. In this connection it should be noted that a half-mile is the maximum walking radius of many aged persons.[1]

5. Public transportation should be immediately available at the site, since many of the services that the aged require, such as specialized medical attention, will in all likelihood be located elsewhere. Transportation is also important for obtaining part-time work, for visiting distant relatives or friends, and generally for maintaining a spirit of self-sufficiency.

6. The site should not be immediately adjacent to a school building or a children's playground, or an active recreation area used by teenagers or adults.

7. The site should be large enough to permit the development of adequate outdoor areas for both active and passive recreation. Ideally,

[1] Most aged persons place great emphasis on the proximity of essential services and facilities such as shops. In one study (Scottish Housing Advisory Committee, Housing of Special Groups, Edinburgh: H.M.S.O. 1952), approximately 90 percent of the aged persons surveyed considered proximity to shops essential. The other facilities desired were, in order: churches, 65 percent; parks, 50 percent; social centers, 37 percent; movies, 30 percent; and active recreation areas, 25 percent.

these areas would be in addition to, and out of the way of, those areas used by other residents, particularly children.

8. Consideration should also be given to possible changes in the over-all land use pattern, in terms of probable trends and projected plans.

These considerations must be taken into account whether the site is to accommodate solely aged persons or whether the aged represent only a portion of a larger "project" population.

DESIGN AND PLANNING PRINCIPLES

In very general terms the criteria for planning housing accommodations for the aged are:

1. Small size and compactness for convenience and economy
2. Fireproof construction planned for maximum safety
3. Minimizing of the problems and effort of housekeeping and daily activities
4. "Livability," pleasantness, and the effect of spaciousness
5. A high degree of privacy
6. Careful avoidance of an institutional look.

Other criteria affecting the different functional areas of the dwelling are discussed briefly in the following paragraphs. Many states have established official standards dealing with minimum areas, design features, etc., for housing for the aged (see Table 1). Before proceeding with specific designs, such local standards, if any, should be consulted.

Leisure Areas

Because the aged are generally retired, a comfortable and pleasant living area is highly important. Particular pains should be taken in the design of these spaces because they are not only intensively used but also tend to be quite small. Some suggested state standards, for example, call for living areas of 80 to 90 sq ft for single-person occupancy. Interesting views and southern exposure should be provided if possible. Extra-wide window stools for plants and built-in shelves and storage spaces are desirable. Privacy from the front door should be provided. If a dining area is included as part of the living area, it should permit location of the table by a window. A light and/or a convenience outlet should be easily accessible to the table.

TABLE 1 Room Areas for Various Types of Housing Accommodations

No. of persons	No. of rooms	Types of rooms	Room area, sq ft					
			Bedroom (B)	Living room (L)	Dining (D)	Kitchen (K)	Bath	Total area
1	4	B,L,D,K	100	80–90	40	50	50	320–330
1	3	B,L-D,K	100–120	120–160		50	35–50	305–380
1	2	B-L,D-K	180		90		50	320
1	2	B-L,D,K	175–200			45–50	35–40	255–290
2	3	B,L,D-K	130–140	150	75–90		40–50	355–430
2	3	B,L-D,K	125–130	155–190		50	40–50	370–420

Data in this table have been compiled from various state regulations and recommendations.

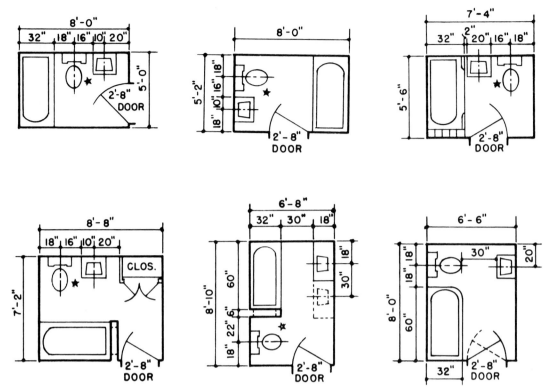

Fig. 1 Bathrooms with tubs. (A star indicates where space has been provided for a helper.)

KITCHEN

Because kitchens are potentially as dangerous as bathrooms, equal care should be given to their layout and design. In locating the kitchen in the plan, provide easy access to the outside and direct access to the dining space, which could be a portion of the living room. In some plans, space can be provided in the kitchens for dining. In these cases, however, an additional 20 to 40 sq ft are necessary. Interior locations are acceptable if mechanical ventilation is provided.

Do not plan extremely compact kitchens for older people; they desire and need ample work space. If the kitchen is too compact, storage space is limited and much of it is either too high or too low to be reached comfortably. Shelves should be no higher than 68 in. from the floor, and no lower than 12 in. Too little counter space leads to crowded work surfaces,

which in turn can create hazardous working conditions.

Clearance between facing equipment and counters should be a minimum of 3 ft for one person. To permit two people to work and pass each other, the between-counter clearance should be 4½ ft.

Equipment should be electric for greatest safety and should be arranged for maximum efficiency. Ranges should be provided with front rather than back controls. Heating elements should visibly glow when hot. In placing the range, consider allowing extra space for ease in making minor repairs and cleaning. A wall oven set at waist height is desirable. Although refrigerators need not be larger than a 6 or 7 cu ft capacity, they should have a large freezing compartment and should be self-defrosting. Do not place the refrigerator too low—as under a counter. In choosing the conventional type of refrigerator, consider the

amount of stooping and reaching that will be necessary.

Double sinks or sink-and-tray combinations should be provided to facilitate hand laundering. Consideration should be given to the provision of complete laundry facilities, particularly in projects. If full laundry facilities are not possible, at least drying racks should be provided.

Storage spaces should be arranged as nearly as possible so that the bulk of the regular-use items can be stored between 27 and 63 in. from the floor. Ideally, stored items should be visible as well as physically accessible. Storage spaces over ranges and refrigerators should be avoided. Sliding cabinet doors are preferable to swinging doors.

Provide adequate lighting over all work surfaces; provide an exhaust fan to assure adequate ventilation and to carry out cooking odors; select floors or floor coverings that will

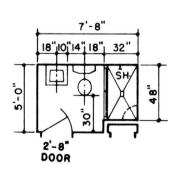

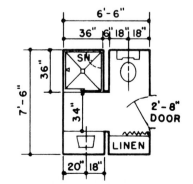

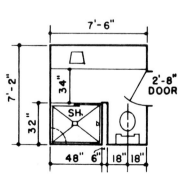

Fig. 2 Bathrooms with showers.

HOUSING FOR THE ELDERLY

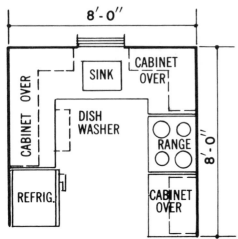

Fig. 3   U-shaped kitchen cabinets.

not absorb grease and become slippery; and provide a fire extinguisher for grease and electric fires. (See Figs. 8 to 11.)

DINING AREAS

The size of the dining space needed is determined by the number of people to be served; furniture including table, chairs, buffet, cabinet, and serving table; and the amount of clearance required for passage and serving.

Allow 21 to 24 in. of table space for each person. The minimum-size table at which eight adults can sit comfortably, three on each side and one at each end, is 40 in. by 72 in. The minimum size for six adults with two on each side and one at each end is 36 in. by 60 in. A round table 42 in. in diameter is minimum for four people, and 48 in. for six people.

Regardless of the size or shape of the dining table, certain minimum clearances around it should be provided. Allow 36 in. between the wall or a piece of furniture and the table in order to edge past a seated person. Serving requires 44 in. from table to wall; 32 in. is needed for rising from a chair at the table. (See Fig. 12.)

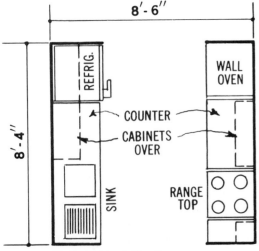

Fig. 4   Parallel wall with wall oven.

General Storage

Ample, lighted closets should be provided for clothes, linens, and miscellaneous household items. Closets should either have sliding doors or be arranged for the use of curtains or screens. Provision must also be made for general storage of bulky items, such as trunks and furniture.

CONSTRUCTION, EQUIPMENT, AND FURNISHINGS

In designing housing for the aged, special consideration must also be given to the selection of materials, hardware, and equipment.

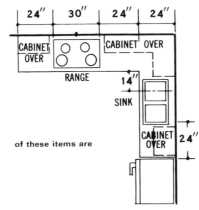

Fig. 5   L-shaped, showing recommended widths and clearances.

Some criteria that should govern the selection of these items are presented below.

Floors

All floor surfaces should be nonslip, outside as well as inside the basic dwelling unit. In this connection, apparent slipperiness is as important, because of the psychological danger, as actual slipperiness. This is particularly pertinent to the design of lobbies and other public spaces which often have large expanses of glossy, although perhaps nonslip, surface. Suitable flooring materials include unglazed tile, cork, vinyl or vinyl-asbestos tile, unwaxed wood, and wall-to-wall carpeting. Throw rugs or deep-pile rugs are generally unsatisfactory because of the danger of tripping. Unwaxed wood floors are particularly satisfactory for the wheelchair user. Floors should be smooth and level, and particular care should be taken with highly jointed materials such as ceramic tile or brick or stone. Door thresholds and minor changes in floor level should be avoided whenever possible.

Doors and Hardware

Door openings should be 3 ft wide to permit easy passage of wheelchairs, stretchers, and persons using crutches. Precautions should be taken to see that doors fit properly and do not stick, and thresholds should be eliminated. Bathroom doors should not have locks; provide easy latches instead. Large, easy-to-grasp doorknobs or lever-type handles should be used. Revolving and double-acting doors and automatic door closers are particularly dangerous and should be avoided. In projects, outside doors should be master-keyed and all devices which cannot be operated from the outside should be prohibited. It is also desirable to

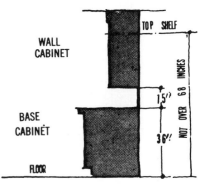

Fig. 6   Cabinet heights.

provide peepholes or vision panels. Sliding doors conserve valuable space in small units and eliminate the danger of walking into half-open doors.

Windows

Whenever possible, windows should look out on an interesting view. In housing for older people, the height of the windows is important, particularly in the living room, dining area, and bedroom. Sitting and looking out of the window is a daily activity for many of the elderly.

The living room windows should be low so that a person sitting in a lounge chair can see out. The bottom of the window should be no higher than 3 ft 2 in. from the floor and can be as low as 1 ft. For window walls, it is desirable to include a guard rail at a height that will not interfere with viewing but that will give a feeling of security. To permit viewing from a standing position, the window should extend to a height of 6 ft. 8 in. (See Fig. 13.)

For *dining areas,* the eye-level zone is determined by the sitting height. The sill of the window can be 2 ft 6 in. from the floor. For the *bathroom* and *kitchen,* the eye-level zone is set by the standing height. The opening of the window should be between 3 ft 6 in. and 6 ft 8 in. from the floor. (See Figs. 14 and 15.)

For *bedrooms,* one window should be low enough to permit a person in bed to look out. In addition to making the room more pleasant, a low window provides an emergency exit. The eye-level zone suggested for the dining area could also apply to bedrooms. Window arrangements that produce a uniform distribution of light are preferable to a spotty placement of openings.

Choose windows that are easily operated. Except for over the bathtub and similar locations, double-hung windows are satisfactory. But in hard-to-reach places, windows that are opened and closed by turning a crank are easier to operate. Many windows have been designed to reverse so that the exterior side of the glass can be turned to be washed from the inside. This is an important safety factor for those who find it difficult to reach or climb. Insect screens, weather stripping, and storm sash should be provided for all windows depending upon the location and climate.

A southerly orientation is most desirable, but provision should be made for shading devices. Roller shades should be avoided because of the danger involved in retrieving a released shade. Venetian blinds or draw-type draperies are preferable.

Lighting

Illumination levels should be approximately double those generally used in residential

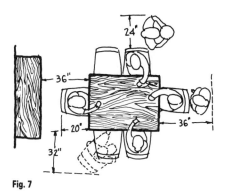

Fig. 7

practice. Light sources should always be shielded. Ceiling-mounted fixtures are not recommended because of the dangers inherent in cleaning the fixtures and changing bulbs. As indicated earlier, it is highly desirable to plan lighting layouts so that lights can always be switched on from a doorway. Wall switches should control all light fixtures. Switched outlets are particularly important in bedrooms or sleeping alcoves so that the elderly person need not stumble around in the dark when looking for the switch or after turning off the light.

Place a convenience outlet for use of a night-light between bed and bath. A night-light in a central location is often useful, as are luminous switch plates. Convenience outlets should never be located less than 18 in. above the floor (30 to 40 in. above the floor is preferable).

Have the entrance well lighted so that steps (if any) can be clearly seen and keyholes can be located.

Heating

The aged generally require a higher temperature level than the standard: approximately $80°F$. The heating system should be quick-acting and arranged to provide a uniform distribution of heat. If the aged are to be housed in structures with younger occupants, consideration should be given to the provision of separate temperature controls or supplementary heat sources. If steam or hot water systems are used, exposed radiators and risers should be avoided. Exposed radiators under operable windows are particularly hazardous. Although cold floors are to be avoided, radiant panel floors seem to be undesirable because they aggravate conditions of impaired blood circulation in the legs.

Sound Control

While a certain degree of acoustical privacy is necessary in any building, it is perhaps more important in housing for the aged than in other residential work. There is a strong desire on the part of the aged to protect their privacy and to be assured of quiet during their rest periods and in the event of illness. Elderly occupants tend to be especially sensitive to the noise of children.

Communications and Alarm Systems

In any building devoted exclusively to housing the aged, an automatic fire alarm system should be provided. Because of the difficulties many elderly persons experience in bedrooms and bathrooms, particularly at night, it is desirable to provide some form of signaling device whereby they can summon help. Usually the device sounds in a neighboring apartment or in a resident manager's or superintendent's

suite. In buildings or projects devoted exclusively to the aged, it may also be desirable to provide a conveniently located public telephone booth, since many aged cannot afford a private telephone. When installed in the dwelling, however, locate a telephone conveniently near the bed. Several outlets would be most helpful.

Vertical Circulation

Whenever possible, accommodations for the aged should be on one level and, unless elevators are used, located on the ground floor. In the case of low buildings where elevators are uneconomical, the aged should not be expected to climb more than one flight. For small unavoidable changes in level, ramps with flat slope not over 5 percent are preferable to stairs. Where stairs must be used, the following precautions should be observed:

1. Risers should not be more than 7 in. high.
2. The proper proportion of run to rise should be scrupulously observed.
3. Fewer than two risers should be avoided.
4. Winders or curved treads should never be used.
5. Nonslip nosings should be used and should be of a contrasting color.

6. Continuous handrails should be provided on both sides of the stairs.
7. Handrails should be of the proper height, of a cross section which is easily grasped, and sturdy in appearance as well as in fact.
8. Stairs should not be less than 3 ft 3 in. in clear width.
9. No doors should open directly onto the stairs.
10. Traffic should not cross the top or bottom of the stairs.
11. The stairs should be well lighted with shielded sources.

Some special considerations should also be observed with respect to elevators:

1. Self-operated elevators should be equipped with automatic doors.
2. A signaling device should be provided to summon assistance.
3. Continuous handrails should be provided, and if the car is sufficiently large, a small bench should be considered.
4. An automatic leveling device is necessary and should be inspected frequently.
5. If there is a possibility of use by a disabled person in a wheelchair, the control panel should be mounted low enough enough to be reached from a sitting position.

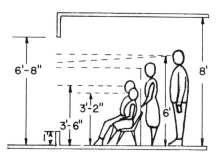

Fig. 8   Eye-level zone for living rooms.

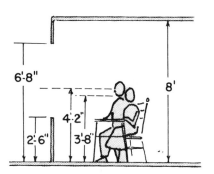

Fig. 9   Eye-level zone for dining areas.

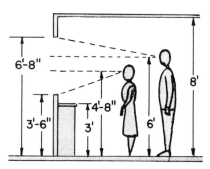

Fig. 10   Eye-level for kitchens and bathrooms.

HOUSING FOR THE ELDERLY

ENTRY/EXIT*

The entry/exit (or front door) is the critical transfer point from the least public area of the development to the least private area of the dwelling unit. If properly designed, it will insure the privacy of unit activities and contribute strongly to the sense of home. It must be a place, not just a door in a wall which opens directly into the living area or other such space. (See Figs. 1 and 2.)

Accessibility The entry/exit area should be directly accessible to the following less private areas of the unit:

- Food preparation
- Living area, with spatial differentiation between the two functions
- Storage/utility

The entry/exit area should be indirectly accessible (minor intermediate activity or a circulation path) to more private areas of the unit:

- Dining
- Private outdoor (optional)
- Personal hygiene
- Sleeping/dressing

The entry/exit area should have both visual and audio contact with visitors outside of the entry door; but visitors should not have visual contact and only controlled audio contact into the entry area of the dwelling unit. This maximizes the ability of the resident to keep out unwanted visitors and allows the resident to control the space just outside the unit.

All of the previously mentioned spaces with direct physical access to the entry/exit area should have visual/audio contact with this area for control and security within the unit. Other areas should have audio but not visual contact to minimize disruption of privacy.

Orientation The orientation of this activity toward view and sunlight is governed by more essential concerns related to building type and the functional organization of other activities.

Furnishability The furnishings and equipment necessary for this area are:

Storage for outer wear, that is, coats, galoshes, umbrellas, etc.; a closet at least 3'-0" by 2'-2" should be provided
A place to sit while putting on outer wear

Spatial Characteristics The space should have sufficient wall area to accommodate a mirror; there should also be a clear dimension area of at least 3'-6" to 4'-0" square for putting on coats as well as greeting guests.

FOOD PREPARATION

The physical characteristics of the aged hamper the normal functions of food preparation, cooking, food and utensil storage, trash disposal, dish washing and drying, and eating. If appropriate physical design adaptation is not made to the food preparation space and facilities, cooking and related activities will become unpleasant, tedious, and possibly dangerous. The net effect will be the creation of a psychological barrier which deters the user from cooking and eating. This situation is particularly unacceptable because dietary problems can become acute for the aged.

Accessibility The food preparation area should be directly accessible to the main entry/exit of the dwelling unit to facilitate carrying of bundles. It should also be directly accessible to the dining area. If the dining area is outside of the kitchen, a small eating surface in the kitchen for breakfast or light meals should be provided. This can be a small table, counter, or pull-out shelf about

24 by 24 inches, set at table height and usable from a wheelchair. The food preparation area should be indirectly accessible to, but visually screened from the living, sleeping, personal hygiene, and private outdoor areas of the dwelling unit. Of these, access should be most direct to the private outdoor space. In all cases, indirect access should be through easily traversed intermediate spaces or corridors.

Visual and audio contact to the entry/exit area should be maintained, while audio contact to the living, sleeping, and personal hygiene areas should be minimized. (See Fig. 3.)

Orientation Often food preparation areas are located at the rear of dwelling units, but, where possible, this should be avoided. The kitchen should be located on an outside wall with an interesting view from a window and it should have morning sunlight if possible.

Furnishability and Equipment The necessary equipment for food preparation and related activities is:

- Ventilation, both mechanical and natural, to eliminate heat and odors
- Sinks and associated work space
- Cooking unit and oven with associated work space
- Refrigerator and freezer with associated loading and unloading counter space
- Storage consisting of wall and base cabinets and pantry
- Dishwasher, optional but should be included where possible
- Dining counter (where formal dining space is outside of the kitchen)
- Clothes washer and dryer; location in the unit is optional, but the kitchen is a good location when this option is exercised

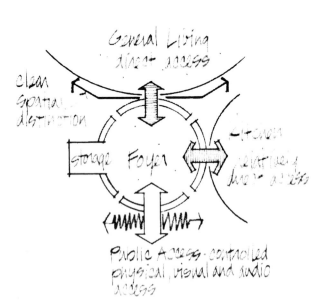

Fig. 2 The foyer.

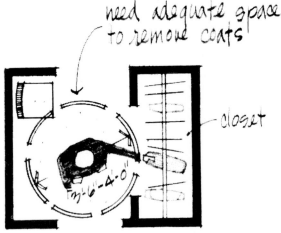

Fig. 1 Unit entry/exit.

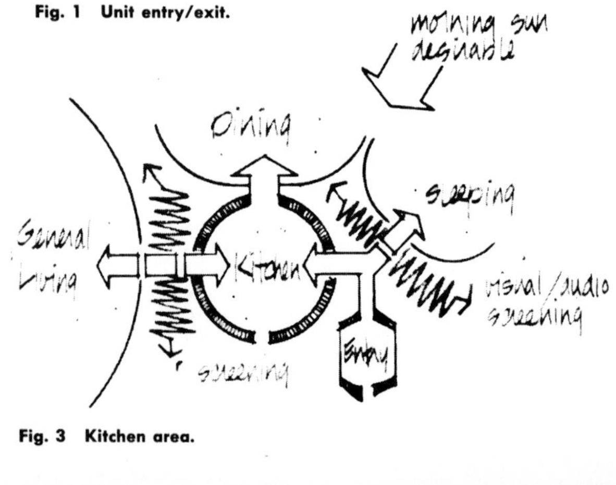

Fig. 3 Kitchen area.

* Pages 92 to 101 from *Housing for the Elderly Development Process,* Michigan State Housing Development Authority, Lansing, Michigan, 1974.

An example of a desirable organization of kitchen activities is shown in Fig. 4.

An L- or U-shaped kitchen is preferable to the pullman or corridor type kitchen. The corridor type is inconvenient for the elderly who, with advancing age and motor/sensory losses, find it difficult to repeatedly turn from one counter to another as they work. The table and Figs. 5–7 give necessary clearances and dimensions.

Equipment should be placed so that there is sufficient operating room between it and any adjacent corner cabinet. At least 12 inches from the edge of the sink and range and 15 inches at the side of the refrigerator are recommended.

A minimum of 42 inches should be provided between base cabinets or appliances opposite each other. This same minimum clearance applies when a wall, storage wall, or work table is opposite a base cabinet.

Desirable kitchen layouts and work area frontages are illustrated in Figs. 5–7. There should be no through circulation in the kitchen work area.

Spatial Characteristics To insure that this space is enjoyable to work in, it is necessary to provide adequate artificial light at all work areas and to create a spatial volume of appropriate scale. These criteria can be translated to mean that the ceiling height should be no lower than 7'-6". Color should be used carefully and be tied to visual identification. It should not create the impression of a closed-in, constricting place. Where ductless range hoods are used, another means of ventilation should be used to carry away cooking heat. Where main dining is combined with food preparation, there should be clear spatial distinction between them, perhaps even a difference in ceiling height.

DINING

There must be a permanent dining place within each dwelling unit for the independent elderly. Depending on the program, the space may be eliminated from units which are part of formal congregate care programs. This place may be within or outside of the food preparation area. Secondary activities will naturally occur within this area such as table games, letter writing and paper work, and hobbies. (See Figs. 8 and 9.)

Accessibility Because of the array of activities that will be carried out, the dining area should have direct accessibility to:

- Food preparation, to facilitate serving of food and cleaning of dishes
- Living area

The dining area may have only indirect (minor intervening activity or circulation path) accessibility to:

- Entry/exit
- Private outdoor

These relationships should be subordinated to the requirements of relationship to the food preparation and living areas. There should be no direct accessibility between the dining activity and:

- Sleeping/dressing
- Personal hygiene

There should be direct visual/audio accessibility between the dining and the food preparation areas. Dependent upon unit organization, there may be direct visual/audio relationship between the dining and living areas; however, in such a case there should be no visual connection between the food preparation and living areas through the dining area. Visual/audio contact between the dining area and the very private areas such as sleeping/dressing and personal hygiene should be minimal or entirely eliminated.

Orientation Wherever possible, the dining area should have views out of the dwelling unit and should also have morning sunlight. Where the orientation is western, it is important to control the harsh effects of the setting sun. Because other

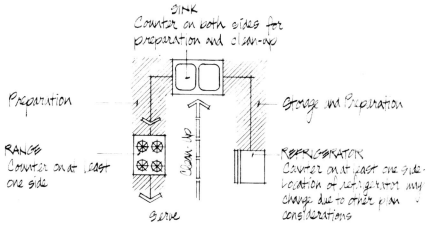

Fig. 4 Kitchen activity pattern—meal preparation and cleanup.

Frontages for Work Centers

Work centers	One bedroom	Two bedrooms
Sink	24"	24"
Counter and base cabinet at each side	18"	21"
Range	24"	24"
Counter and base cabinet at one side	18"	21"
Refrigerator (space)	30"	36"
Counter at latch side	15"	15"
Mixing		
Base and wall cabinet	30"	36"

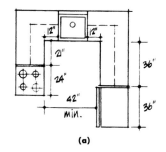

(a)

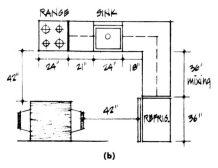

(b)

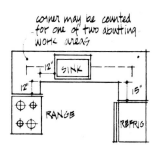

Fig. 5 Minimum corner distances.

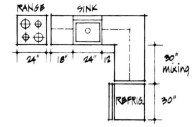

Fig. 6 Minimum frontages and edge distances—one bedroom.

Fig. 7 Minimum frontages and edge distances—two bedrooms.

functional relationships must be achieved (such as entry/exit to the living and food preparation areas, and the food preparation area to the dining area) these orientation criteria must be subordinate and may not be achievable. At the very least, views out should be possible through other activity areas.

Furnishability Each dining space must contain sufficient space to accommodate four people. It is desirable if sufficient space is available to expand this accommodation to six persons for special circumstances. Appropriate space should be provided for the storage of china and large dining articles. There should be space to accommodate the following items of furniture:

- Dining table with a minimum width of 3'-0", and 2'-0" of edge length for each diner (tables should be no less than 3'-0" by 3'-0" square, or 3'-6" in diameter)
- Dining chairs of 1'-6" by 1'-6" sufficient for the number of diners that can be accommodated
- Buffet or storage unit of 1'-6" by 3'-6"

Size of the individual eating space on the table should be based on a frontage of 24 inches and an area of approximately 2 square feet. In addition, table space should be large enough to accommodate serving dishes.

The following minimum clearances from the edge of the table should be provided:

36" for chairs plus access thereto
42" for chairs plus access and passage
42" for serving from behind chair
30" for passage only
48" from table to base cabinet (in kitchen)

In sizing a separate dining room, provision should be made for circulation through the room in addition to space for dining.

Spatial Characteristics As noted above, the dining activity space may be located separately or combined with living or food preparation spaces. Because of economic considerations, a separate dining space seems unlikely but, nevertheless, it is desirable that developments offer both arrangements to provide a variety and choice in responding to the differences between formal or informal lifestyles of various tenants.

The ceiling height of the dining space in a dwelling unit may be raised or lowered for spatial effect; it should, however, be no lower than 7'-6".

The dining table location should be permanent, requiring no rearrangement of furniture at mealtimes, and use of this space should not infringe upon other activities. Wall area should be available for hanging pictures and the like. It should be possible to see the outdoors from the dining table.

Where cabinets are used to separate the food preparation area from the dining area, some of the cabinets should open from both sides to facilitate table setting.

GENERAL LIVING

Each dwelling unit shall have an area or areas which are organized and furnishable for a wide range of activities such as:

- Conversation
- Entertaining
- Reading
- Television viewing
- Radio/record listening
- Contemplation
- Lounging

In most units, more than one of these activities will be provided for in a single space. In larger than standard units or in two-bedroom units, however, it may be desirable to provide more specialized spaces.

Accessibility Direct physical accessibility (no intervening spaces) should be provided to:

- Entry/exit (planning can be too open; therefore, there should be a definite spatial distinction between living area and entry/exit)
- Private outdoor, for the extension of general living activities
- Dining, where these spaces are combined, accessibility should not impair either activity

Indirect physical accessibility (minor intervening activity or circulation path) should exist between:

- Food preparation
- Personal hygiene, for visitor use (this accessibility should not impair the privacy of the sleeping/dressing areas)
- Storage/utility
- Sleeping/dressing

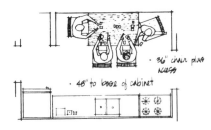

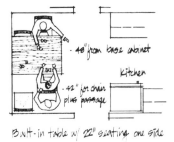

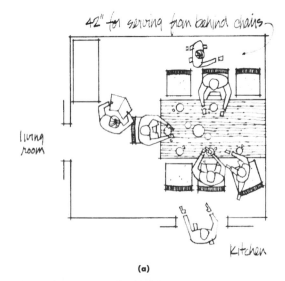

Fig. 8 Minimum clearances for dining areas in kitchens.

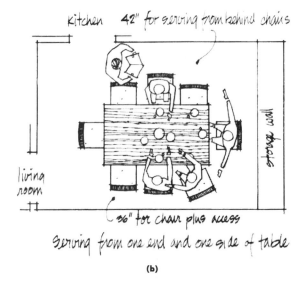

(a) (b)

Fig. 9 Minimum clearances for dining areas: (a) one end of table against wall; (b) serving from one end and one side of table

Visual and audio contact with equally active areas (entry/exit and private outdoor) should be encouraged. Visual and audio contact to the food preparation area should be either minimized or controllable so that it can be minimized or maximized as desired by the resident. The visual/audio relationship between the dining and living areas will vary with the location of the dining area. Visual/audio contact to sleeping/dressing and personal hygiene spaces should be minimized.

Orientation Living spaces will be occupied many hours of the day and should, therefore, be provided with interesting views out of the unit. Windows should be located so that a seated person can see out. In first and second floor units, windows should also be carefully located to avoid loss of internal privacy from outside of the unit. On upper floors, close views from one unit to another should be avoided.

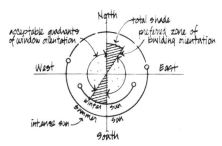

Fig. 10 Sun orientation.

Sunlight is important to both physical and mental conditions and, therefore, planning should insure that living spaces will receive some sunlight during each sunny day (probably no less than 30 percent of the day). Northern orientations should be avoided. Reference should be made to Fig. 10 for acceptable sun orientations.

Furnishability Furniture that should be accommodated in the living area should include the following items (sizes are minimums) for one-bedroom units:

One couch, 3'-0" x 6'-10"
Two easy chairs, 2'-6" x 3'-0"
One television set, 1'-4" x 2'-8"
One table, 1'-6" x 2'-6"

For two-bedroom units one easy chair should be added as well as:

One desk, 1'-8" x 3'-6"
One desk chair, 1'-6" x 1'-6"

Because of the diversity of activities which may occur in this space or spaces, and because provision must be made for a wide variety of lifestyles, special provision should be made in the design process to allow for many alternate furniture types and arrangements. The location of doors, windows, and other openings should be carefully considered so as not to unnecessarily limit furniture arrangement. A substantial amount of uninterrupted wall length is required. It should be remembered that many elderly residents will come from single-family or larger rental housing and many of them can be expected to have much more furniture than described above.

The following specific design criteria shall be used:

- 60" minimum clearance should be provided between facing seating.

- 30" minimum clearance is required for use of a desk.
- 60" minimum distance is necessary between the television set and seating. The designer should make sure that it is possible to locate the set opposite the main seating area.

People gather during social activities in rather small groups and a desirable conversation distance is rather short; an area approximately 10 feet in diameter is workable.

Figures 11–13 illustrate the desired circulation and furnishability requirements.

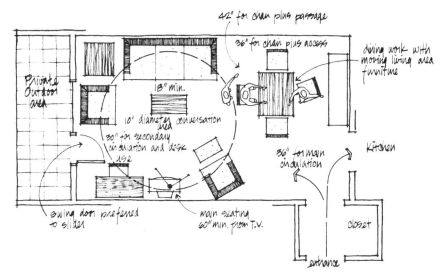

Fig. 11 Minimum clearances, circulation, and conversation areas for living rooms.

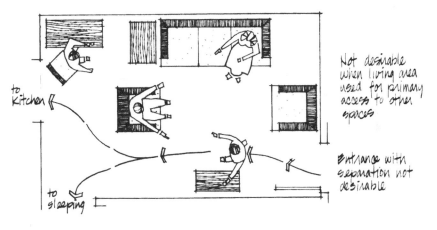

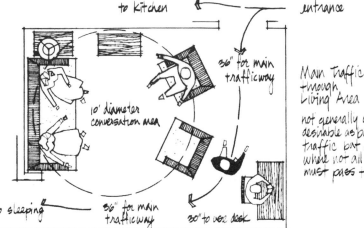

Fig. 12 Living room circulation approaches.

HOUSING FOR THE ELDERLY

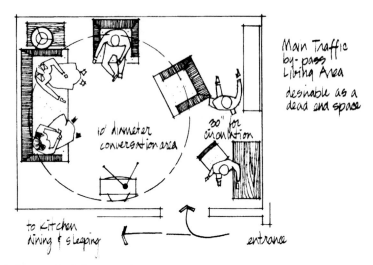

Fig. 13 Living room circulation approaches.

The living area or areas will most probably have to sustain both intra- and interspace circulation. Adequate circulation space which is direct and nondisruptive is important because of the tendency toward infirmity of movement and loss of visual acuity in the elderly. The following criteria pertain:

- 36" minimum clearance should be possible for main traffic paths. This dimension will also accommodate a wheelchair.
- 30" minimum clearance should be allowed where secondary circulation occurs between furniture.

Spatial Characteristics The living area is likely to become the focus of the dwelling unit for many residents. The size of the space, however, is often not as important as good planning which effectively accommodates the living activity while also accounting for circulation, doors, windows, and furniture. This does not mean, however, that a small space is desirable; in fact the living area should be of sufficient size as to allow some excess in floor area for such temporary activities as exercises, ironing in front of the television set, etc. Provision of floor area beyond the minimum space required by the furnishability test will also insure the accommodation of a wider range of lifestyles and activity patterns.

The living activities area may be greatly enhanced in spatial character by a higher than normal ceiling if the building type permits.

As a general rule, it has been found that a width of less than 12 feet is difficult to utilize effectively. It has also been found that rectangular rather than square space is easier to furnish and to zone for different activities.

Consideration should be given in dwelling units of larger than standard size to subdividing the living activities area into two separate areas such as a living room and den/sewing room combination. This can also be accommodated by room configurations (such as L-shape) which are easily subdivided by furniture arrangement. This approach is particularly effective where there are two residents in a unit who wish to carry on different activities simultaneously.

SLEEPING/DRESSING

The elderly make greater use of the bedroom than any other age group except babies. An effi-

cient and commodious bedroom is important for any household but for older people it is absolutely necessary. This is partly because of the need for rest periods but also, as people grow older, many become more susceptible to illness and are bedridden more frequently than younger people.

Accessibility This activity is one of the most private in the dwelling unit. In dwelling units containing two residents it is essential that one resident be able to carry on normal living activities (including entertaining visitors) without serious loss of privacy to the other person in the bedroom. Because of this basic need, direct physical accessibil-

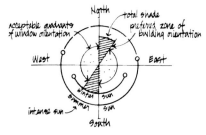

Fig. 14 Sun orientation.

ity (only minor intervening space) should only exist between the sleeping/dressing area and:

- Personal hygiene
- Personal clothing storage

The bathroom may also be accessible through a hall.

In some cases provision for personal living activities may be located within the bedroom. Direct accessibility to private outdoor space may also be acceptable under some circumstances.

Indirect accessibility (through intervening circulation) should exist to:

- Food preparation
- Storage/utility

No direct accessibility should exist between the sleeping/dressing area and:

- Entry/exit, for protection of privacy
- Living
- Dining

Because of the privacy factor and the desire to be able to entertain guests without having to make the whole dwelling unit tidy, the sleeping/dressing area should be isolated from most visual and audio contact with other areas in the dwelling unit. The level of visual/audio contact between the bathroom and the sleeping/dressing area should be controllable to insure bedroom privacy when a guest uses the bathroom. It is desirable that a circulation space serve as a buffer between the sleeping/dressing area and the rest of the dwelling unit.

Like the living area, this area should have excellent views from its windows. Windows should be placed so that a person can easily see out while lying in bed. This space requires direct exposure to the sun for at least 30 percent of the day. Reference should be made to Figs. 14 and 15 for desired sun orientation.

Furnishability In addition to the sleeping and dressing functions, the bedroom should have provisions for such passive living activities as:

Television viewing
Reading
Sewing

The minimum furniture to be provided for is as follows:

Two twin beds (3'-3" x 6'-6") or one double bed (4'-9" x 6'6")
One dresser (1'-6" x 4'-4")
One chair (1'-6" x 1'-6")

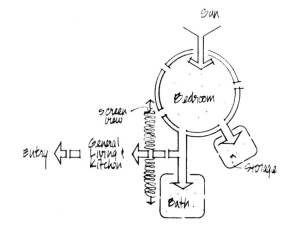

Fig. 15 Space orientation.

One table (1'-6" x 2'-6") for sewing or other work (optional)
Two night stands (1'-6" x 1'-6")
One portable television set

Where both bedrooms of a dwelling unit are primary (as in unrelated occupancy), the above requirements apply to both.

Twin beds should be possible even in the bedroom of a unit programmed for single-person occupancy.

A secondary bedroom for single occupancy should have circulation space and accommodate furniture of the following sizes:

One twin bed (3'-3" x 6'-6")
One dresser (1'-6" x 3'-6")
One chair (1'-6" x 1'-6")
One night stand (1'-6" x 1'-6")

The location of doors, windows, and closets should be planned to allow for the best placement of the bed and other furniture.

The closet should be placed next to the door into the bedroom because the use of available wall space is minimized in this way (Fig. 16).

For reasonable access to and use of bedroom furniture and equipment, the following minimum clearances should be observed:

42" at one side or foot of bed, for dressing
24" clearance for least used side of double bed
6" clearance from side of bed to side of dresser or chest of drawers
36" clearance in front of dresser, closet, or chest of drawers
30" clearance for major circulation path (door to closet, etc.)
24" clearance between twin beds
18" clearance between twin bed and wall for ease of bed making

It should not be necessary to move beds in order to make them up. Bedrooms should be sufficiently large and so designed as to permit alternate arrangements of furniture if at all possible. There should also be space provided for working privately or resting. (See Figs. 17–19.)

PERSONAL HYGIENE

The bathroom is the subject of much public and private research. What is set forth here is not ideal but rather an attempt to synthesize the most current thinking on the subject as it relates to the elderly user. In addition, requirements for adoption of bathroom facilities for use by permanently disabled persons are included. These requirements shall apply to at least 10 percent of the units in developments of 100 units or more. Application to smaller projects will be determined individually for each case.

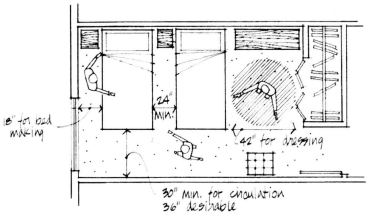

Fig. 17 Typical standard bedroom—with twin beds.

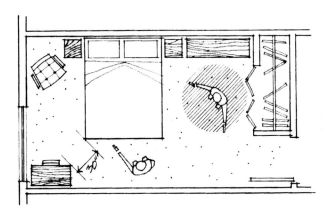

Fig. 18 Typical standard bedroom—with double bed.

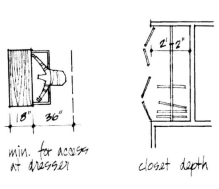

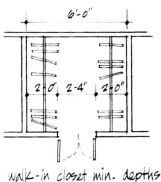

Fig. 16 Closet depths.

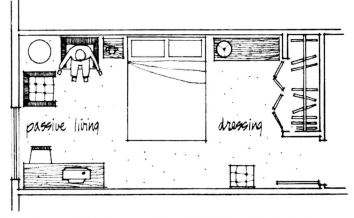

Fig. 19 Larger-than-standard bedroom—may be applicable in larger-than-standard unit or in two-bedroom unrelated occupancy.

HOUSING FOR THE ELDERLY

In general, bathrooms in developments for the elderly should be given great care in design as this space can, if poorly conceived, cause both serious health hazards and, through its inconvenience, great frustration. The general lack of mobility and slow reaction time of the elderly make it mandatory that hygiene spaces be inherently safe from sharp edges and slippery floor surfaces and that they do not require excessive bending, leaning, or twisting to carry out necessary activities.

Accessibility In addition to more frequent than normal use during the day, frequent use of the bathroom at night is common. Therefore, consideration should be given to direct accessibility between the bedroom and the bathroom. Hopefully, this accessibility would not require passage through an intervening circulation space. If it does, the route shall be direct, unobstructed, and of sufficient width for a wheelchair to pass easily. Indirect accessibility should also exist between the bathroom and the more general living areas of the unit for use of the bathroom by guests.

Visual/audio contact between the bathroom and other areas should be minimized. It should not be possible to see into the bathroom from the living, dining, or food preparation areas. (See Fig. 20.)

Orientation Views to the outside and natural light are not necessary to bathroom functions. Where windows are used, the following criteria pertain:

The designer should make sure that no loss of privacy occurs.
Windows should not be located over bathtubs.

Furnishability and Equipment All personal hygiene spaces shall have the following equipment:

Lavatory basin (preferred in a vanity counter top)
Water closet
Bath or shower
Appropriate grab bars
Storage space and mirror
Toilet-paper holder
Towel bars

It is essential for the successful functioning of the bathroom or lavatory that certain minimum clear working areas be provided around fixtures. (See Fig. 21.) These requirements are:

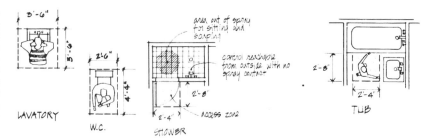

Fig. 21 Minimum clearances—personal hygiene.

- *Lavatory Basins:* 3'-6" x 3'-6"; the sink shall be centered on one dimension and at the extreme of the other.
- *Water Closet:* 2'-6" x 4'-4"; the water closet shall be centered on the 2'-6" dimension and located at the extreme of the 4'-4" dimension.
- *Tub and/or Shower:* 2'-4" clear dimension extending out from access point of fixture and at least 2'-8" along its length; the length dimension shall begin from the central end of the fixture.

An emergency call system shall be included in all developments. An alarm button should be placed in the bathroom in a convenient place, but not where it can be set off accidentally.

All bathrooms and lavatories, whether naturally ventilated or not, shall have air exhaust fans venting to the outside and sized according to the code for an interior bathroom.

Spatial Characteristics All personal hygiene spaces, both bathrooms and lavatories, shall have privacy locks which can be easily unlocked from the outside in case of emergency. The key type of emergency release is not desirable because there may not be sufficient time to locate the key in an emergency. Outward opening doors should be used so that people can get in easily to help someone who is lying on the bathroom floor, perhaps unconscious or helpless.

Non-slip, easily maintained floor surfaces which are free from changes in level shall be provided.

The vertical surfaces of bathrooms should be free from sharp corners and edges, unnecessary projections, and breakable materials. This requirement has particular bearing on room layout and the location of bathroom accessories, such as towel bars, paper holders, etc.

Many bathroom layouts are possible but two are the most common, offering solutions to a wide range of concerns. Each has its own advantages. These layouts (Fig. 22) are described for illustrative purposes below.

Layout 1: In the first layout, the toilet is placed by the wall with the lavatory next to the bathtub. This arrangement allows easy placement of the toilet-paper holder and grab bar on the wall while, at the same time, the edge of the lavatory can be used as a support for getting into and out from the bathtub.

A vertical grab bar mounted on the wall near the bathtub in addition to grab bars on the bathtub wall is recommended. An angled grab bar should also be provided on the wall by the toilet.

Layout 2: In the second layout the bathtub is placed against the wall opposite the lavatory and toilet. As in layout 1, separate grab bars should be provided for the toilet and tub. In

this layout the lavatory can be installed in a vanity counter top with sides. The vanity arrangement can support a toilet-paper holder next to the toilet, a towel rack, and perhaps a small grab bar.

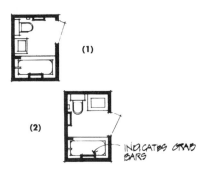

Fig. 22 Illustrative hygiene space layouts—all doors 2'-8".

PRIVATE OUTDOOR

Many older people, either by choice or by limitations of their physical conditions, are largely confined to their dwelling units, and access to a private outdoor space over which they have control is very desirable. It offers a welcome change of atmosphere, a chance to grow flowers, cook out, and enjoy the sun. In the event of fire, a balcony can provide refuge and access to fresh air. Provision for private outdoor activities may take the form of balconies or patios. Requirements for patios are discussed in the *Townhouse Development Process.**

Accessibility The private outdoor space should be directly accessible to the main general living area of the dwelling unit. If possible this area should also be directly accessible to the food preparation area; however, if this is not possible, the indirect accessibility between the outdoor space and the food preparation area should be via a non-circuitous circulation path. Accessibility to all other areas should be indirect and placed as dictated by the functional organization of the dwelling unit, except that there may also be direct accessibility to the sleeping/dressing area.

To protect the privacy of each private outdoor area on the ground floor, direct access from it to the public outdoor area should be avoided by creating an identity for the outdoor private areas. There should be no direct accessibility between the private outdoor areas of separate dwelling units. (See Fig. 23.)

* Michigan State Housing Development Authority, *Townhouse Development Process,* 1970.

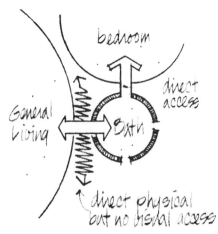

Fig. 20 Accessibility of bathroom.

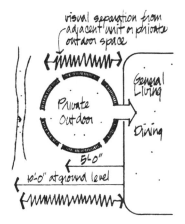

Fig. 23 Privacy at ground level.

Visual accessibility between the private outdoor area and interesting views on and off the site should be maximized, while at the same time loss of privacy from views outside the outdoor area should be minimized. The visual accessibility between the general living area of the unit and the general outdoor area should not be impaired by the design of the private outdoor area.

Orientation The configuration and orientation of the outdoor space should be such that sun falls on the space for at least 30 percent of each day during the prime spring, summer, and fall months.

Furnishability and Spatial Characteristics On-grade patios and/or private areas shall be well defined. Location and design shall provide spatial privacy from other living units and from adjacent walks or drives in public space.

Overhead protection of balconies is very desirable but not required. A shelf for plant pots should be included for all balconies at a height of 24 to 30 inches above the floor.

Access doors to balconies should be fully draft-proof and should not be the only source of natural ventilation to the room. The door sill should be kept as low as possible. Passage doors of the swing type are preferable to sliding glass doors and shall be required when economically feasible to eliminate large sills.

Balconies or terraces above the twelfth floor are generally undesirable and should not be provided except in special or unique circumstances.

Where private balconies are not provided for all the dwelling units on a floor, a common balcony shall be provided at a central location.

All balconies, terraces, and patios shall be provided with artificial lighting which is switched on within the dwelling unit. At least one duplex electric receptacle which is weatherproof shall be provided in each private outdoor space.

The criteria for minimum privacy require that screening walls at the sides of outdoor spaces be provided to protect the space from being overlooked by adjoining dwelling units and their private outdoor spaces. The side of the space opposite the building wall may be partially closed and/or defined by planting.

On-grade private space shall have a least dimension of 12 feet and include a paved patio of at least 100 square feet. The remaining area shall be lawn or planting beds.

Private on-grade outdoor spaces may become a security problem if their design provides the

potential intruder with a space completely free from observance and control. Therefore, completely enclosed patios shall themselves be secure. Partially enclosed patios shall be designed so that they can be controlled visually from public areas.

The paved surface in outdoor spaces shall be smooth and free from unexpected changes in level. All steps required to provide a transition from unit floor level to ground level shall have handrails.

Private outdoor spaces above grade (raised terraces and balconies) should be included in the integral design at the beginning of the design process and not added later as an afterthought. Only in this way can the problems traditionally associated with balconies be overcome. Balconies shall have a least clear dimension of no less than 5 feet and a total clear area of no less than 50 square feet for one-bedroom units and 60 square feet for two-bedroom units. Because the elderly are particularly concerned about security and heights, balconies must not only be safe, but they must also feel safe. The use of solid balustrades is desirable. Where this is not possible, a sturdy railing with a large solid top rail

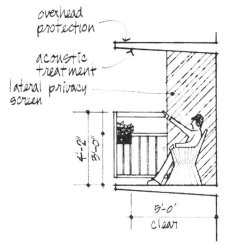

Fig. 24 Example of balcony.

should be used. In either case care should be taken to avoid obscuring views out from the interior of the dwelling unit. For this purpose a solid balustrade to a height of 24 inches with an open handrail above is a good solution. Railings or balustrades shall have a minimum height above the balcony surface of 36 inches and shall extend completely along all open sides of the balcony. (See Fig. 24.)

Whenever possible balconies should be recessed behind the main face of the building because this technique provides a strong sense of enclosure, privacy, and security. Where this is not possible, and where there are adjoining balconies or the balcony is exposed to broad public view, balconies should be provided with screening walls or devices at their sides which achieve privacy and security.

FOOD PREPARATION EQUIPMENT

This section deals with equipment and facilities in the food preparation area of the dwelling unit in terms of quantities, sizes, and detailed location. The question of the functional organization of

the food preparation area and its relationship to other areas of the dwelling unit is discussed earlier. The discussion here is divided into two parts. The first deals directly with the minimum standards against which all proposed developments will be measured and to which all must comply. The second begins with the minimum standards as a base and develops optimum standards for the various components of the food preparation area where appropriate. These optimum standards are not mandatory, and the achievement of some may not be economically feasible within the context of low- and moderate-income housing programs; however, developments which approach or meet some or all of these standards may be given financing priority over those which only satisfy the minimum standards.

Minimum Standards
Refrigerator The refrigerator shall be an upright freestanding model with integral freezing compartment. The minimum acceptable sizes are 10 cubic feet for a one-bedroom unit and 12 cubic feet for a two-bedroom unit. The freezer compartment shall be located at the top or the side of the refrigerator. Refrigerators of the undercounter type are unacceptable because of the excessive stooping required in their use.

The refrigerator shall be of the self-defrosting type. (This is a designated amenity.)

The general storage shelves of the refrigerator should pull out on roller guides and should be removable for ease in cleaning.

Cooking Unit and Oven The cooking unit and oven should be electric; they should be both approved and listed by the Underwriter Laboratories (UL) in their publication, *Electric Appliance and Utilization Equipment List.* Gas cooking devices are not recommended because the elderly often have a poor sense of smell and are forgetful, thus becoming vulnerable to the hazards of fire and explosion.

Cooking devices shall have pilot lights to visually indicate when they are on. A master cutoff switch should be provided if possible. The controls on cooking devices shall be easily read by sight; touch controls should be located at the front of the device to eliminate the necessity of reaching over hot cooking surfaces.

Where an integral cook top and oven unit (stove) are used, the oven should be located below the cook top. Stoves with ovens that are overhead or at eye level are not acceptable because of the reaching required. (See Fig. 25.) The door on

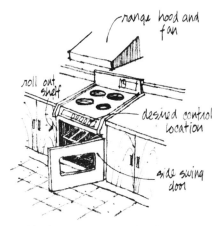

Fig. 25 Oven over stove not desirable.

the oven should be hung on the side and swing out if such units are available. This type of oven door is safer and also allows the oven to be used by someone sitting in a wheelchair.

All cook tops must have a hood and exhaust fan mounted directly above the cooking surface. Ceiling-mounted exhaust fans are unacceptable. The cook top shall have four burners and have a minimum width of 24 inches.

Sink The kitchen sink shall be of stainless steel and mounted on the counter top. The minimum overall dimensions are 24 inches by 21 inches. Where counter top area permits, a sink with a double compartment equal to the capacity of a sink with a single compartment is preferred (Fig. 26).

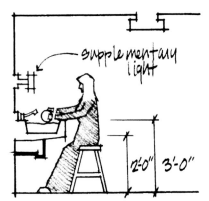

Fig. 26 Desirable knee space at kitchen sink.

Cabinets, Shelves, Counters, and Closets Each kitchen or kitchenette shall have:

1. Accessible storage space for food and cooking and eating utensils
2. Sufficient space for average kitchen accessories
3. Sufficient storage space for those items of household equipment normally used and for which storage is not provided elsewhere such as brooms, mops, soap, etc.
4. Sufficient work surface area for the preparation and serving of food and the cleanup of cooking and eating utensils

Kitchen storage should be provided in the form of wall and base cabinets as follows:

Shelving: 40 sq ft
Drawers: 7 sq ft

Kitchen storage should be designed to satisfy the following requirements (Fig. 27):

1. Usable storage space in or under stoves, or under wall ovens, when provided in the form of shelves or drawers that roll out, may be included in the minimum shelf area.
2. Conventional base cabinets over counter tops shall not be deeper than 12 inches and the highest shelf shall be no more than 66 inches from the floor.
3. No cabinet or shelf space should be located above refrigerators.
4. The minimum clearance between counter tops and wall shelves shall be 24 inches at the sink and 15 inches in other locations.
5. At least 80 percent of all shelving shall be enclosed by cabinetry or a pantry. Cabinet doors shall have rounded edges.

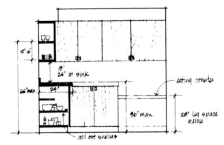

Fig. 27 Kitchen storage and counter space.

No less than 10 square feet of counter top work surface shall be provided in kitchens. Counter tops should be approximately 24 inches deep and no higher than 36 inches above the floor. In calculating the length of the counter top, the length occupied by sinks and cook tops may not be counted. Counter tops should have rounded leading edges. Where possible, supplementary counter top space shall be provided at tabletop height so that a resident can use this space for food preparation and for eating light meals. In apartments designed for the handicapped, half of the required counter space shall be at worktable height.

Storage of household equipment shall be provided by a broom closet at least 3 square feet in floor area. These closets shall have shelves for the storage of cleaning materials and they shall have a clear area of sufficient height to accommodate an upright vacuum cleaner and brooms.

A separate compartment with a door shall be provided in each kitchen for a garbage and trash container.

Garbage Disposal All kitchen sinks shall be equipped with garbage disposals that are fully insulated for sound.

Optimum Standards

The following modifications can be made to optimize kitchen facilities.

Refrigerator A horizontally shaped refrigerator that is hung on the wall and mounted in the range of 34 to 72 inches greatly improves usability by eliminating stooping (Fig. 29).

Cooking Unit and Oven A separate cook top mounted on the counter and an oven mounted

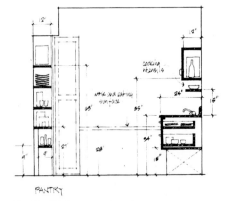

Fig. 28 Kitchen arrangement.

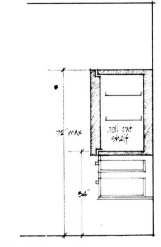

Fig. 29 Wall-hung refrigerator.

on the wall greatly increase flexibility of placement and enhance functional organization and usability. The cook top should be mounted no higher than 34 inches above the floor, while the oven should be mounted at waist level (that is, the bottom of the oven should be 27 inches above the floor).

Sinks Sinks should be mounted 34 inches above the floor.

Cabinets, Shelves, Counters, and Closets Many elderly people tend to develop a stoop and are, consequently, shorter than the average adult. As noted earlier, they also have trouble bending and reaching. Therefore, while maintaining the storage requirement of the minimum standards and increasing the work surface area to 12 square feet, the following changes in location and configuration should be made to optimize storage and work surface facilities.

1. Counter tops should be located 34 inches above the floor. This counter area should be supplemented by some counter area at table height to accommodate light dining and food preparation from a sitting position (4 to 6 square feet). Pull-out counters could provide for this need.
2. Shelves 12 inches or deeper should not be mounted higher than 55 inches above the floor when the shelf is above a counter, or 63 inches above the floor when no counter interferes. Shelves of this depth should not be located lower than 27 inches above the floor.
3. Approximately 50 percent of the kitchen storage space should be provided by pantry cupboards or a closet. Shallow pantry shelves (less than 12 inches) may be mounted as low as 21 inches above the floor (Fig. 28).
4. Storage space under counters should be in the form of deep drawers on roller guides rather than cabinets with shelves.
5. Sliding cabinet doors will be substituted for doors of the swing type in the optimally designed kitchen. Where cabinet doors cannot be avoided on cabinets that are 34 inches or higher above the floor, they should be limited to no more than 15 inches in width.
6. All sharp corners and edges will be rounded off cabinet doors.

7. Wall-mounted hanging devices for cooking utensils such as pots, pans, large spoons, etc., should be provided at convenient locations.

PERSONAL HYGIENE EQUIPMENT

The following requirements are the minimum equipment specifications for elderly developments; they are also applicable for adoption for use by the handicapped. Each requirement is accompanied by locational and size parameters.

The Lavatory Basin Each bathroom or lavatory shall have a lavatory basin firmly supported to withstand pulling or leaning loads of up to 300 pounds. Vanity cabinets are not recommended as they require excessive stooping and leaning to be used. Vanity counter tops are desirable. Provision for storage should be made in wall-hung cabinetry where necessary.

Basins should be of the cantilever type, either wall-mounted on chair hangers or mounted in a vanity top. An installation of this kind is more easily used by someone in a wheelchair. The most desirable mounting height for basins will provide a minimum clear dimension below the basin and/or vanity top of 2 feet and 2 inches and place the top of the basin and/or counter 2 feet and 9 inches above the floor. Water taps on basins should be low profile with cross shaped or lever handles. Round knobs should not be used. (See Fig. 30a.)

The Water Closet Each bathroom or lavatory shall have a water closet with a seat height of 17 inches (the elderly have difficulty with seating and standing motions). If users in wheelchairs are anticipated, the seat height should be 20 inches. Where economically feasible, the water closet should be of the wall-hung type for convenience in floor cleaning. (See Fig. 30b.) The toilet-paper holder should be located in front of or directly at the side of the water closet, in a position where leaning or twisting is not required to use it.

Bath and Shower The question of whether a bathtub or shower is more desirable has been debated at length. It has been fairly well established that showers are both cleaner and safer than bathtubs, and showers seem to better meet the goal of extending the span of independent living for the elderly. Many elderly persons, however, enjoy and need the therapeutic benefits of a sitz bath. The situation could easily be resolved by providing both a shower and a bathtub in separate installations; however, this is not economically feasible. It seems, therefore, that a compromise is required, that is, a specially manufactured tub/shower combination. This compromise is the recommended solution, although showers will be considered where central bathtubs are provided on each occupied floor (one tub for twenty dwelling units).

Bathtubs should have controls that are easily operated from outside of the tub without excessive leaning or stretching and should include an automatic mixing valve with an upper temperature limit of 120 degrees F. Tubs shall have a flat bottom with a non-slip surface. Abrasive tapes and heavy, sharp textures should be avoided. The sides of the bathtub should not be higher than 15 inches and the lengthwise dimension should not be less than 60 inches.

Where showers are provided instead of bathtubs (that is, where centralized bathtubs are available), they shall be of sufficient size to allow the bather to stand or sit outside of the area of the spray while soaping his [her] body. The shower enclosure should be equipped with a folding seat as sitting showers prolong independence for those who either require assistance in standing or who are completely infirm. As mentioned above, the shower head should be variable in height and preferably of the detachable type with a flexible head. The highest shower head position should not exceed 60 inches.

Shower controls should be easily reachable from outside the shower stall and should include both an automatic mixing valve limiting the maximum water temperature at the head to 120 degrees F., and a water temperature testing spout to be used by the bather before entering the shower. The soap dish and grab bar should be conveniently located 51 inches above the floor of the shower. Where technically feasible, the raised entrance curb should be eliminated. If glass is used in the shower enclosure, it shall be tempered for safety.

Soap dishes and similar attachments should be recessed. Water controls should be placed so that they are not a hazard either in normal usage or when the bather slips.

Bathtubs shall be equipped with shower heads. The shower head should be adjustable in height and, preferably, detachable with a flexible head. There should be several wall positions for the head to fix it at various heights. Bathtubs shall be equipped with a detachable seat which allows the bather to shower sitting down. A grab bar and soap dish, placed at a high level about 51 inches from the bottom of the tub will avoid the necessity to bend down for soap or to use the shower curtain for support when taking a shower. Glass enclosures instead of shower curtains are not advisable as they further restrict getting in and out of the tub.

Grab Bars Grab bars are generally overused and sometimes bear little relationship to the anatomy of the human body. If improperly located, they not only fail to serve the user but they can also become a hazard if someone should slip. Grab bars should be used judiciously and wherever possible located to serve more than one bathroom position. Bars should be approximately 1 inch in diameter, be capable of withstanding a pulling or hanging load of 300 pounds, and be fixed to structure members rather than to wall finishes or materials. There should be at least one grab bar at the water closet and another in the bathtub or shower, located and in the configuration shown in Fig. 31.

Storage and Mirror The preferred provision for storage needs is a large mirror behind the lavatory (not a medicine cabinet/mirror combination) and a separate storage unit, built into a wall, large enough to hold both medicine/toiletries and towels. The storage unit should be located so that reaching across counter tops is not required. If towel storage is located externally in a linen closet, the bathroom shall have a mirror behind the lavatory and a separate medicine cabinet which is convenient to the lavatory but placed so that excessive reaching is not required.

Electric Outlets A convenient duplex outlet shall be located adjacent to the mirror and lavatory approximately 6 inches above the height of the lavatory and positioned so that reaching across the lavatory or counter top is not required.

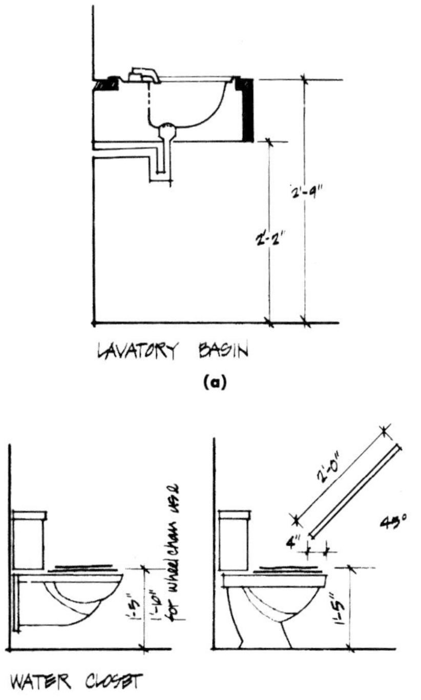

LAVATORY BASIN

(a)

WATER CLOSET

(b)

Fig. 30

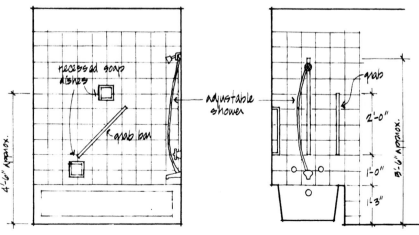

Fig. 31 Bath and shower.

THE NEIGHBORHOOD

Accessibility to community services and facilities is the first factor to consider in site selection.

Primary services and facilities are: employment opportunities; clinics; vocational rehabilitation programs; inexpensive private and public recreation (such as movies, parks "lively" with activities for participation and view, libraries, etc.); churches; stores including drug, grocery and variety; barber and beauty shops; inexpensive restaurants; schools.

Another important factor is accessibility to public transportation. To the employed impaired citizen, as well as to staff and visitors, good public transportation may be a necessity. To the unemployed, good transportation may keep him in touch with the world, participating in meaningful and dignified activities. Economical public transportation with a nearby stop, without intervening hazards, is highly desirable. Such transportation may be either existing or assured by the time the development is first occupied.

A convenient location is so essential for impaired persons that it may outweigh the other standards and criteria for evaluating residential neighborhoods. Neighborhoods close to specialized services, such as sheltered workshops, should be considered if the neighborhood also possesses the other more generally used services and facilities. It is easier and less expensive to arrange transportation for a particular group of tenants using a single facility than to bring the multiple, less specialized, but equally essential public and private facilities and services within reach of all tenants.

Urban renewal areas, which contemplate commercial shopping centers and other adjuncts to housing needs, may furnish desirable sites.

THE SITE

The criteria for selecting residential sites in general should apply. [These criteria cover economy, topography, subsoil conditions, and existing utility services. Sites subject to industrial smoke, traffic hazards, excessive noise, or polluted air should be avoided.]

The site should allow for development so that structures can be oriented to give residents the advantages of local climate.

Odd or irregularly shaped sites should be carefully evaluated based on amount of usable land and cost of its maintenance.

If the community has restrictive ordinances, zoning, or other local controls which would adversely affect the proposed development in a particularly good location and site, waivers should be investigated. In applying for such waivers, it is important to remember that the housing is to be residential, designed for in-

Housing for the Physically Impaired, Department of Housing and Urban Development, Washington, D.C., 1968.

dependent living. It is neither an institution nor a nursing home.

An important special consideration is slope of the site. For the physically impaired, a comparatively flat site is needed. Steeper and more rugged sites may be used but with doubtful success. Such sites should be evaluated in terms of the costs of any special improvements required to serve the limitations and needs of the tenants. Examples of such extra costs would be those for constructing retaining walls to create useful flat outdoor sitting and resting areas or constructing gently sloping pedestrian ramps throughout the site. Extra maintenance costs (upkeep of banks, lawn areas, and in some climates snow removal, etc.) may result in increased rents.

It is important to have outlooks, both natural and created, that provide interest or beauty and contribute to pleasant living. Many tenants will undoubtedly spend more time at home than would a comparable group of nonimpaired individuals. Views of such things as wooded areas, hills, night-lights, and distant traffic; of planes, boats, trains and automobiles are desirable, and count as positive factors in site selection.

Consideration should be given to the existing and proposed approaches to the site (street improvement, widening; surface; sidewalks) and public utilities.

ACCESS, RAMPS, PEDESTRIAN WALKS

Access All building entrances to be used by the tenants should be approached by paved walks, with nonskid surface, sloped for drainage, but not over 1 in 20 (or 5 percent). *Steps should not be used.*

Landing platforms at all building entrance doors should be level, sloped only as required for drainage. The platform width should be at least 1 ft beyond the door jambs. Platforms should be at least 3 ft deep if doors swing in, and 5 ft deep if doors swing out, but never less than 3 ft beyond the edge of the fully open door. (See Fig. 1.)

Ramps Most wheelchair users can negotiate a ramp sloped 5 percent or less without assistance. Steeper ramps limit independent chair use and should never be used. They are hazardous not only to wheelchair users but also to persons with artificial limbs and to the elderly. *Ramp surfaces should be fireproof and nonslip.* (See Fig. 2.)

If the vertical height requires two ramps to achieve the properly graded slope, the ramps should be no longer than 20 ft, separated by a

level platform at least 5 ft–6 in. long, to provide ample rest space. Such two-run ramps may be in a straight line; however, a more desirable and safer arrangement would be a 90 or 180° turn at the platform.

When more than two ramp lengths are required, the descent should be broken by turns to be negotiated on level platforms.

The recommended width for a one-way ramp is 3 ft between handrails. At least 6 ft should be provided for two-way circulation.

Handrails and anchors should support 250 lb for 5 min; they should extend at least 12 in. (24 in. is preferable) beyond the beginning and end of the ramp to assist persons with poor vision, and they should be returned to a wall or an upright post for safety.

Handrails installed specifically for children should be at a height of 24 in. Local codes or special safety objectives might necessitate the installation of additional, higher rails.

Fig. 2 Street-curb ramp for wheelchair.

Pedestrian Walks Pedestrian walks at street curbs should be ramped. The ramp should not protrude onto the street but be indented into the curb; it should have a nonslip surface colored orange, or curb jambs should be colored to assist those with poor vision. Greater slopes than 2 in 12 could hinder wheelchair use.

PARKING

The parking areas should be moderate sized and conveniently located to provide easy and safe access to entrances. (See Fig. 3.)

There should be no steps or curbs from the parking area to the dwelling buildings or to community space. Space should be planned to eliminate pedestrian circulation behind parked vehicles—a particularly hazardous area for the individual with limited mobility.

A desirable plan for multiple parking space would extend the parking surface into the sidewalk, eliminating the need for curbs. Surface drainage would place the sidewalk at the high point and the center of the parking driveway at the low point.

A pipe rail is necessary between the side-

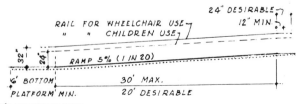

Fig. 1 Single-run entrance ramp.

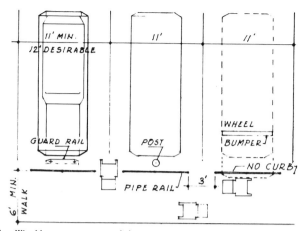

Fig. 3 Parking. Wheel bumper not recommended as car overhangs vary.

walk and parked cars to protect people, particularly those with poor eyesight, from accidents caused by colliding with car bumpers.

For wheelchair users, the minimum width of parking bays is 11 ft (12 ft is desirable). Other orthopedic equipment users will require at least a 9 ft width. The wider bays should be nearest the building entrances. For these tenants, covered parking is desirable.

Parking bays for the nonimpaired may have a minimum width of 8 ft–6 in. under unusual, restricted circumstances. However, the general rule should be 9 ft. Parking areas should not be permitted to obstruct or dominate views from indoor recreation areas or dwellings.

OUTDOOR AREAS, LIGHTING, AND PLANTING

Outdoor facilities and areas (walks, ramps, drives, parking and recreational areas, etc.) should be sloped for drainage and be properly illuminated for safe circulation. Lights should be placed and angled to permit good perception from inside the building.

Existing trees, streams, or rock outcropping of the site should be retained where possible in order to preserve natural beauty. Planting (a few large specimens skillfully located), with emphasis on recreational and sitting areas, contributes to enjoyment and creates a more pleasant environment. Planting around parking area will enhance the site.

The surfaces of concentrated use areas should be paved for maximum safety, use, and interest. For large paved areas, several materials of varied color, design, and texture are recommended to provide a pleasant visual diversity. Nonslip surfaces are desirable — rough surfaces generally present in fieldstone are not recommended.

Rest or sitting areas should be protected from winter winds and excessive summer sun. Some of them should provide a view of the street or of other places where there is animated activity. The best way to provide shade is to use large trees or small, attractive shelters, or both.

Flowering trees and shrubbery can enhance pleasantness and potential enjoyment of the setting.

One-story dwelling buildings and other structures, where appropriate, should have outdoor flower planting areas for the tenants, preferably at or near entrance door.

Every effort should be made to have a sheltered bus stop located at the development. A mail depository box at the same location would be desirable.

Amenities such as a water fountain or a reflecting pool can be included if funds are available. Also, it may be possible to encourage donations of sculpture and other works of art from civic-minded local groups interested in making this housing a visual asset to the residents and the entire community.

Future ease of grounds' maintenance should be kept in mind during the planning and design stage. However, achieving the best possible living environment is the primary objective.

DWELLING STRUCTURES

Entrances

Entrance doors to multifamily structures, community centers, and other public-use space should provide a clear minimum width passage of 3 ft. Entrance doors to individual dwellings should provide a clear minimum width passage of 2 ft–10 in. Thresholds that project above the floor should be avoided when possible. If a projection is unavoidable, it should be no higher than ½ in., featheredged to the floor, and 5 to 6 in. wide.

Hinged entrance doors to dwellings are the most economical and safest. Revolving doors should *never* be installed; they must be collapsed for wheelchair users and are particularly hazardous for users of other orthopedic equipment. For entrance doors to a multifamily building, it is best to have automatic door openers, with floor mat activation, flush with floor. Such mechanisms should fully open the door without restricting the clear 3-ft minimum passage. If the opening mechanism fails to function, the door operation should automatically revert to manual operation. Maintenance

of the automatic door opener can usually be reduced by flanking the automatic doors with hinged doors for use of the physically unimpaired. Safety glass vision panels are recommended for solid panel building entrance doors. (See Fig. 4.)

For those who have poor vision or are blind, the floor directly inside or outside the entrance doors to multifamily buildings should either be slightly ramped or have a finish of a different color, distinguishable from the surrounding floor and of a different texture that will provide more grip for shoe soles, thus suggesting caution. Recessed floor mats meet these requirements.

Exterior doors should be covered by a canopy or hood of ample width. A porte-cochere may be feasible. A canopy or roofed-over service entrance also should be provided for ambulances if the development is for elderly and impaired persons. Other entrances may be made from parking areas and grounds. If a clinic is included, a separate entrance should be provided so that persons outside the project who come to the clinic will not use the main entrance lobby.

The operating hardware of entrance doors should be 2 ft–10 in. to 3 ft above the floor. Door checks or closers should be the adjustable tension type, set for minimum pull to assist persons using wheelchairs and other orthopedic devices. Pull handles, push bars, and panic hardware bars with curved ends are best because they contain no hooks or sharp angles to catch clothing. A lever handle which curves close to the door surface is a most suitable operator for latch or lock. Kickplates 12 in. high help to reduce door maintenance by preventing abrasions caused by footrests and axle hubs on wheelchairs, etc. In multifamily buildings, entrance doors normally used by tenants should be provided with key locks which could be set to operate as latches (no keys needed) for daytime use and as key locks at night. A tenant's key would operate these locks and his apartment door lock. Master keys should be provided for management use.

Public Corridors, Galleries

In mild climates, galleries might be appropriate and desirable for cross ventilation, tenant circulation, relaxation, visiting, etc. Galleries should be at least 7 ft wide to allow enough room both for tenant sitting space and two-way traffic of persons using crutches or wheelchairs. Handrails of a bright color or material in bold contrast to the walls should be provided on corridor walls. Such handrails are especially helpful to people with poor vision and to blind persons.

To avoid hazards, doors should not swing into public corridors. Doors to public corridors

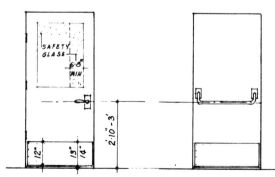

Fig. 4 Building entrance doors and doors to public space should have vision panels.

HOUSING FOR THE HANDICAPPED

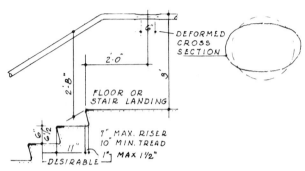

Fig. 5   Interior stair.

should be identified by raised, brightly colored letters to aid the blind and those with poor vision. An important safety precaution is identification of doors not intended for normal use which would expose blind persons to danger if used. Such doors, when key locked, *may* provide sufficient protection.

No columns, radiators, drinking fountains, telephone booths, pipes, or other projections should protrude into public corridors.

Public Stairs or Fire Towers

There should be no stairs or steps in the structure except those contained within fire towers for emergency use. Even such stairs should be especially planned. Single-run stairs between floors are not desirable; at least one landing should be used, two in floor-to-floor height over 9 ft. Straight runs between floors are not advisable; runs with 90 or $180°$ turns at landings are recommended. The most desirable stair would have a 6- to $6\frac{1}{2}$-in. riser and an 11-in. minimum tread. The 11-in. tread places the ball of the descender's foot inside the stair nosing. A safety nosing should be used which *does not project beyond the riser* and which is distinct in color from the rest of the tread, preferably lighter. Risers should slope forward between 1 and $1\frac{1}{2}$ in. to permit the ascender's heel to rest safely on the tread. (See Fig. 5.)

Stair wall handrails should continue around the platform to help anyone using the stair who is blind or has poor vision. The rails should carry a 6-lin-in. marking for hand feel 2 ft before the first down riser at both floor and landing levels. Steel pipes can be marked by deforming, or by a continuous raised welding, ground smooth, or by a smooth welded strip. Wooden rails can be shaved, notched, or marked with domed-end wood dowels.

Open or grating-type fire escapes are not recommended.

Elevators

It should not be necessary to go through the lobby to reach an ambulance. If there is no

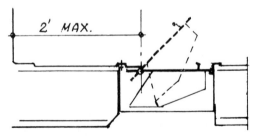

Fig. 6   Incinerator chute hopper doors.

lower-level entrance, the approach should be through a rear or side door in the elevator, thence to the service entrance to the ambulance.

Self-service elevators should level automatically at landings and have automatic sliding cab and hoistway doors with delayed closing, plus two push buttons both overriding the delay timing, one holding doors open, the other to close the doors. An emergency sound alarm system and a cab telephone for emergency use should be installed in each elevator. Cab handrails are required. Cab control panel should be set at a height convenient to persons in wheelchairs, the lowest buttons 3 ft above the floor. The panel location should be on the side cab wall 1 ft back from the front, otherwise a wheelchair will block most of the cab entry.

Back-lighted buttons with raised figures should be used to assist those with poor vision and the blind. These people will need some sounding device which would identify the next floor stop.

Since stairways are of no use to some, consideration should be given to emergency power to operate at least one elevator.

Incinerator Chutes

Incinerator chute hopper doors should be lower than normal. A 2-ft maximum height from floor to hinge is recommended.

Large hopper doors are desirable for convenience and maintenance. For the convenience of persons in wheelchairs, hopper doors should be installed in open corridor or alcove, a location found satisfactory for the elderly. Where codes prohibit this, a waiver should be requested. Anterooms are most inconvenient for many impaired persons—self-closing doors add complications for users of orthopedic equipment and wheelchairs. (See Fig. 6.)

Laundry Facilities

Laundry facilities should be either in one central area or grouped in several areas. Concessionaires who furnish and maintain coin-operated washing and drying machines generally favor, for their convenience, central laundry facilities. Conveniently located group laundries are usually preferred by the impaired and elderly tenants and are recommended.

One automatic washing machine and batch dryer should be installed for each 20 one- and two-person families (one for 17 other families) or fraction thereof. In large central laundries, it is possible to use cabinet-type dryers which can handle more than one batch—useful in projects which include large families. In multifamily buildings, group laundries may be located on each floor or on some floors and not others, whichever is required to meet the demand. In cottage-type developments, laundry facilities

should be located on the basis of walking distance, climate, and convenience.

Laundry rooms must accommodate the necessary equipment: work table, ironing board which is adjustable for standing or sitting, hanging rack, table and chairs for rest and sociability.

Tenant General Storage

Central storage is not recommended for dwellings with one- and two-person occupancy—the general storage provided within the dwellings will suffice.

Mailboxes

In cottage-type developments, where mail is delivered to the individual dwelling unit, a mail receptacle must be provided. The best type is the mail slot with a receiving box inside, the top of which is 2 ft–10 in. to 3 ft above the floor. Impaired persons should not be expected to pick up mail from the floor. A mailbox mounted outside is not desirable. Mail slots should not be located in entrance doors where locked screen doors may make them inaccessible to the mailman or the inside box would interfere with door opening at least $90°$.

Mailboxes in a multistory structure are usually installed in rows stacked above each other. Sometimes, because of limited wall space, the top rows are beyond the reach of wheelchair users; for them the locks to their boxes should not exceed 4 ft–3 in. above the floor. The local post office should be consulted when planning this feature.

Separate mailboxes for community space staff workers are desirable, especially when the management office, where they would otherwise receive their business mail, is located at some distance from the community space.

DWELLING UNITS

General

The major problems in designing most "rental housing" for the physically impaired are how to provide maximum livability and safety for persons with impairments that vary in nature and degree. These problems are somewhat mitigated when the housing is to be designed to aid a specific type of impaired individual, such as the blind or the cardiac. The recommendations that follow, however, are based on the fact that the units will be occupied by people who have varying types of impairment, such as those with little or no vision who may or may not use a guide dog; those using wheelchairs or crutches; and those whose physical condition requires the conservation of energy though they use no orthopedic devices.

For room divisions of the dwelling plan, either fixed or movable partitions are suitable. Divisions may be achieved by movable wood closets that do not reach the ceiling or by fixed or movable baffle walls, which are particularly suitable in warm climates. A desirable feeling of larger space is created when the ceilings of adjoining rooms visibly flow from one to another.

All bathrooms should be enclosed by floor-to-ceiling partitions.

Kitchens may be baffled or shielded. When the open plan is used, the kitchen should be fan-ventilated. View of kitchen equipment from the living room and entrance to the dwelling through the kitchen should be avoided.

Each unit should have sufficient space to

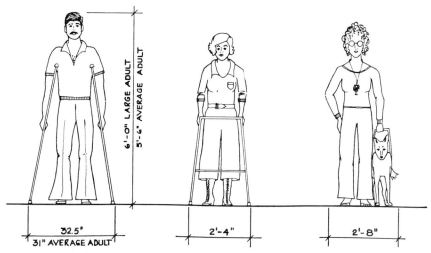

Fig. 7 Average clearances. *Source:* "An Illustrated Handbook of the Handicapped Section of the North Carolina State Building Code," Raleigh, 1977.

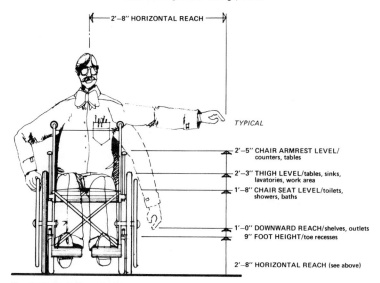

2'-8" HORIZONTAL REACH

TYPICAL

- 2'-5" CHAIR ARMREST LEVEL/ counters, tables
- 2'-3" THIGH LEVEL/tables, sinks, lavatories, work area
- 1'-8" CHAIR SEAT LEVEL/toilets, showers, baths
- 1'-0" DOWNWARD REACH/shelves, outlets
- 9" FOOT HEIGHT/toe recesses
- 2'-8" HORIZONTAL REACH (see above)

Fig. 8 Typical dimensions.*

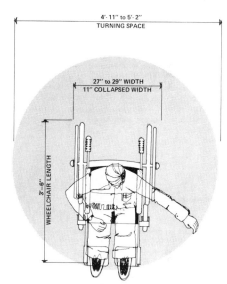

4'-11" to 5'-2"
TURNING SPACE

27" to 29" WIDTH
11" COLLAPSED WIDTH

3'-6" WHEELCHAIR LENGTH

Fig. 9 Wheelchair dimensions.*

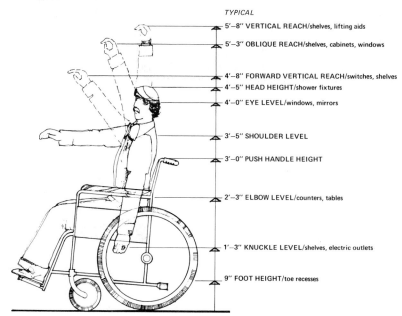

TYPICAL

- 5'-8" VERTICAL REACH/shelves, lifting aids
- 5'-3" OBLIQUE REACH/shelves, cabinets, windows
- 4'-8" FORWARD VERTICAL REACH/switches, shelves
- 4'-5" HEAD HEIGHT/shower fixtures
- 4'-0" EYE LEVEL/windows, mirrors
- 3'-5" SHOULDER LEVEL
- 3'-0" PUSH HANDLE HEIGHT
- 2'-3" ELBOW LEVEL/counters, tables
- 1'-3" KNUCKLE LEVEL/shelves, electric outlets
- 9" FOOT HEIGHT/toe recesses

Fig. 10 Typical dimensions.*

* "Handbook for Design: Specially Adapted Housing," VA Pamphlet 26–13, Veterans Administration, Washington, D.C., 1978.

assure suitable living, sleeping, cooking, and dining accommodations plus adequate storage and sanitary facilities. The space should be planned to permit placement of furniture and essential equipment for circulation by wheelchair users and those on crutches. (See Figs. 7–10.)

Living Room

In general, dwelling entrance should be by way of the living room. Entrance through the kitchen is not desirable. For families without children, a combined living-dining room arrangement is preferable to a kitchen-dining room combination. A wheelchair requires at least 2 ft–6 in. seating space at the dining table. Dining by a window, the stool of which is no higher than the dining table, is pleasant, and particularly desirable for the elderly or impaired persons.

Food service from the kitchen to the living-dining area should be direct, without turning corners, and the distance should be as short as possible. A partition between the living room and kitchen should be provided. A baffle wall, with posts attached to floor and ceiling, the material between the posts not reaching either the floor or ceiling, makes a quite suitable partition and creates a sense of space. Prefabricated wood closets resting on the floor and not quite reaching the ceiling also make suitable living room-bedroom partitions in dwellings for one and perhaps two persons. In these small dwellings, the resulting open plan makes the space look larger than it is.

Kitchen

The kitchen for the physically impaired requires more considered attention than any other room. Unlike the living room, such a kitchen may require more space than one for the nonimpaired.

A 5-ft minimum width should be provided for wheelchair turns between counters on opposite walls or between counter and opposite wall.

Counter tops should be set 2 ft–10 in. above the floor, a workable height from both wheelchair and standing positions.

Base cabinets should have a recessed toe space 6 in. deep and 8¾ in. high to allow the wheelchair homemaker to get close to the counter and to permit maneuverability. A minimum open space 2 ft–4 in. wide should be provided under the sink. Base cabinet storage space involving hinged doors and fixed or adjustable shelves *should not* be used, because many impaired persons cannot bend down enough to use them. Base cabinet storage is most usable when drawers of various depth are provided and revolving units are installed at the reentrant corners. Pull-out vertical units at one or both sides of the work center also are desirable. (See Fig. 11.)

The kitchen sink should be 4 in. deep, single compartment for one- or two-person dwelling and single or double compartment for larger dwellings. The drain should be at the rear of the sink to provide maximum clearance for knees and clearance under the sink for standard wheelchair arms, 29 in. above floor. At this height, the wheelchair homemaker can reach the inside bottom of the sink without undue stress. This height is also suitable for the stand-up user without unnecessary bending. (See Fig. 12.)

When a stainless steel sink is used, undercoating should be applied to prevent condensation, which also acts as insulation. A single-lever-handle water-control mixing faucet should be provided. This type is the easiest to

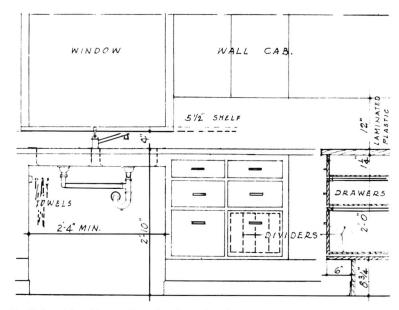

Fig. 11 Kitchen sink and base cabinet elevation and section.

operate for those with hand infirmities. The swing spout should have a built-in aerator to prevent splash, especially in a shallow sink. The sink waste line should have a close-fitting elbow leading to the trap installed near, and parallel to, the back wall.

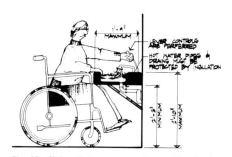

Fig. 12 Sink with knee space. *Source:* "Handbook for Design: Specially Adapted Housing," VA Pamphlet 26–13, Veterans Administration, Washington, D.C., 1978.

Sustained contact with the underside of a sink or trap filled with hot water could burn persons in a sitting position who lack leg or knee sensation. An insulating board under the sink is not a solution, because the hot water at the faucet and in the sink may be between 130 to 140°F, which is a hazard to a person lacking hand sensation. A much safer way is to control all delivered hot water at a maximum of 120°F. Recent tests showed that with 120°F water at the faucet, the water in the undercoated stainless steel sink was 112°F and a safe 95 to 100°F on the sink's undercoating. The maximum hot-water temperature control should be under management supervision only, which may be the control recommended in the bathroom.

One arrangement for the work center would have a kneehole opening, 2 ft wide minimum (2 ft–4 in. is desirable), flanked with vertical pull-out units about 12 in. wide. The vertical units should extend from under the counter to

toe space, with content accessible from the kneehole side when the units are pulled out. One flanker unit could be used for hanging utensils from a peg board. (See Figs. 13-21.)

The other, if installed, could be used for supplies and should have adjustable shelves. Space for the storage of additional supplies should be provided on the counter or in wall cabinets directly in front of the work center.

Another work center arrangement would be the right-hand pedestal 16 to 18 in. wide with drawers, no left pedestal; it is desirable to increase the open space to 28 or 30 in. The storage cabinet above the counter may consist of open adjustable shelves.

A lapboard pull-out shelf beneath the counter at the work center should be installed to provide a working surface for mixing and cutting operations. This shelf should be adjustable in height at 2-in. intervals from about 2 ft–2 in. above the floor to the under-counter posi-

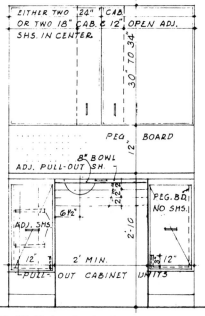

Fig. 13 Work center elevation.

144

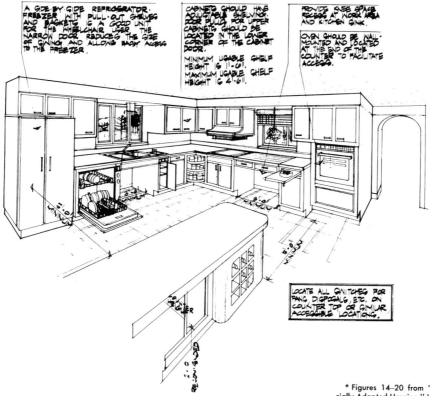

Fig. 14 Kitchen arrangements.*

* Figures 14–20 from "Handbook for Design: Specially Adapted Housing," VA Pamphlet 26–13, Veterans Administration, Washington, D.C., 1978.

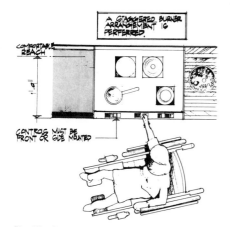

Fig. 15 Counter-mounted cook top.

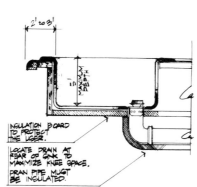

Fig. 17 Sink.

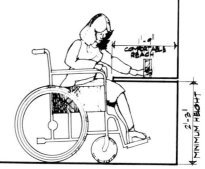

Fig. 19 Knee-space clearance.

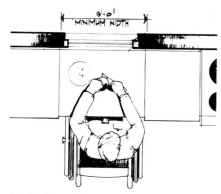

Fig. 16 Knee-recess work area.

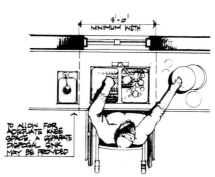

Fig. 18 Disposal sink.

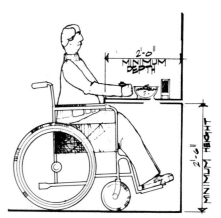

Fig. 20 Armrest clearance.

HOUSING FOR THE HANDICAPPED

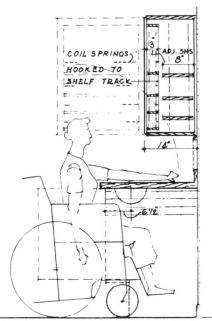

Fig. 21 Work center section. Rear track set ¼ in. lower will cause shelf to slope. Recommended.

tion. The hardwood shelf should be cored to brace firmly an 8-in. diameter mixing bowl. (See Fig. 22.)

Under-counter or wall-storage space should be provided, if possible, for a small (perhaps 18- by 24-in.) tenant-owned wheel table. Such tables are useful for moving several items at one time from the refrigerator to the work center, to the dining table, etc.

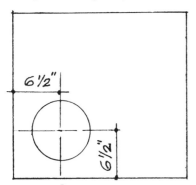

Fig. 22 Pull-out shelf lapboard. A plastic laminated work surface is recommended. The hole is for an 8-in.-diameter stainless steel mixing bowl which should fit snugly when the top rim is about 1 in. above the shelf.

Wall storage cabinets when mounted 12 in. above the counter provide the maximum convenient storage, accessible from a sitting position. The average height (5 ft-4½ in.) female's reach from floor to wrist is 6 ft standing; 4 ft-10 in. sitting in wheelchair, side reach; 4 ft-7 in. sitting in wheelchair under kitchen counter to front of wall cabinet. Standard wall cabinets, 14 in. deep and 30 to 34 in. high with three adjustable shelves, are recommended. The upper shelf of such cabinets is reachable by taller, nonimpaired family members. Cabinet doors should be equipped with 3- to 4-in. drawer-type pulls of simple design and magnetic or nylon roller latches, which are the easiest type to operate. At the work counter, 3-in. adjustable shelves should be installed inside of the cabinet doors to provide convenient storage for numerous small items.

A 5½-in.-wide open shelf placed 7 in. below the wall cabinets may be desirable at some location.

Cabinets should never be installed above counter-top burners or ovens. Such placement creates a fire hazard to the person reaching for stored articles because his clothing might ignite or he might accidentally drop the articles into boiling water or hot grease.

A 14-in.-deep, 18- to 24-in.-wide cabinet, resting on the floor and extending to the same height as the top wall cabinets is also very useful as storage space for the wheelchair user and others. A standard 14-in.-deep cabinet with adjustable 9½-in. shelves and shallow inside-of-door adjustable shelves places within reach from a standing or sitting position many cooking utensils, dishes, and packaged food supplies. The door hinges for such a cabinet should be the continuous piano type. The cabinet bottom can be used for storing serving trays, cookie sheets, muffin pans, etc., when the usual dividers are installed slanting either horizontally or vertically, thus increasing the cabinet's depth and usefulness.

The standard range, with oven below and bottom-hinged door, is unsatisfactory and hazardous for the physically impaired person. Counter-top burners should be provided, preferably with front-of-counter controls. Controls mounted back of the burners are not recommended because of the hazardous reach involved, and controls mounted on the counter to the side of the burners may interfere with the transfer of pots from burners to counter. Easy-to-read large control dials, with safety feature to prevent accidental turn-on of burners, should be provided. To assist the blind and those with poor vision, the control dials, in addition to visual markings, should be marked, shaped, or provided with click stops so that the fingers can feel such marks, shapes, or clicks representing the various heat intensities at the burner. Pushbutton control with indicator light for electrical burners is satisfactory. Burners should not be located below or near a window or near a door. A sep-

arate oven, with a left or right side-hinged door depending on counter-top space and front controls, should be installed so that the height of the pull-out oven shelf at the lowest position is at counter-top level. This permits transfer of hot pans from oven to counter conveniently and safely. Ovens with glide-up doors are also satisfactory.

Electrical top burners are considered by some as safer than gas burners because the gas flame can more easily ignite loose, flimsy garments. Electrical top burners and ovens are generally recommended.

The recommended type of refrigerator-freezer is the standard two-compartment, two-door model with freezer compartment on top and self-defrosting for the food compartment only. Pull-out shelves in the food compartment are desirable. Frequent defrosting of the food compartment is a difficult operation for many impaired persons.

The refrigerator location in the kitchen should never be adjacent to heat-producing equipment such as the oven, top burner, or water heater.

As to garbage grinders, the continuous-feed type of grinder is more convenient to use and costs less to maintain than the batch type and is recommended.

Dishwashers are admittedly desirable, especially those with an electric heat booster.

Whenever possible, natural light and ventilation in kitchens should be provided through windows. Artificial light should be distributed to illuminate all dining and cooking areas effectively. Any required mechanical ventilation should be adequate for removing cooking fumes and odors as well as for summer comfort.

Bedroom

All bedrooms should be partition-enclosed. In one- and perhaps two-person dwellings, one wall may be movable wood closets, a baffle wall, or a sliding or folding partition. Sleeping-living room combinations are *not*

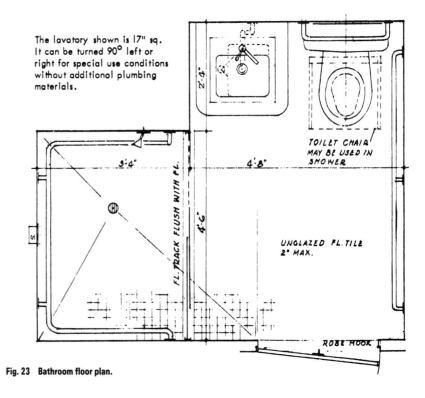

The lavatory shown is 17" sq. It can be turned 90° left or right for special use conditions without additional plumbing materials.

Fig. 23 Bathroom floor plan.

recommended, nor are room layouts which require the bed to be in a corner or the side of the bed to be against a wall.

For two or more persons, at least one bedroom should be planned for twin beds. Bedrooms intended for the impaired will require more floor area than other bedrooms in order to provide for wheelchair circulation. At least 3 ft (preferably 3 ft–4 in.) must be provided for a wheelchair along one side of one bed and in front of clothes closets and furniture.

Bathroom

The bathroom presents more hazards than any other room; therefore, planning for safety is of utmost importance. A bathroom must be larger than standard to permit wheelchair use. The minimal floor area of a carefully planned bathroom is 40 to 45 sq ft. A bathroom that permits a wheelchair to enter but not to turn around is not desirable. For maneuverability, an area 45 to 55 sq ft. is recommended; however, careful planning is more important than increased floor area. (See Fig. 23.)

Grab bars capable of supporting 250 lb should be provided at the water closet, shower, and elsewhere in the bathroom. Grab bars should be devoid of sharp corners, with ends returning to the walls. Towel bars should be of grab bar quality and strength for safety because they may accidentally be used as grab bars.

Bathtub or shower? We are not considering a hospital, or a nursing home, but a dwelling for independent living and self care. The occupants may be physically impaired, single or married, young or elderly. The question therefore is: what will provide a bathing facility which can be used by the most people, over the longest period of time, with the least hazard? The answer is a specially designed shower with these features:

• No curb or step, for ease of access, including wheelchair.

• Internal dimensions of at least 3 ft–4 in. by 4 ft–6 in.

• Unglazed tile floor—the same for the bathroom floor—which drains into shower.

• 4-ft-6-in.-wide opening with sliding nonbreakable doors (not hazardous curtains).

• 120°F maximum temperature delivered hot water under management control; this control would also supply the lavatory and kitchen sink—tenant control for lower temperatures.

• Single lever mixing handle set 3 ft–6 in. above floor, located inside shower compartment, but reachable from outside shower.

• Possibly a flexible metal-covered extension spray head with or without holders at different levels, recommended to be detached for use as hand spray.

• A recessed soap dish—convenient from sitting or standing position.

• Grab bars.

The lavatory should be set 2 ft–10 in. above the floor:

• The maximum depth, 4 in.

• Single-lever water control—aerator spout.

• 120°F maximum-temperature hot water under management control—see shower control.

• Drain opening at the rear of the bowl.

• A close elbow drain, run to the trap, set near and parallel to the wall—so as not to interfere with knee room.

A square lavatory can be installed in a counter top with the faucet at the rear (normal position) or the lavatory can be turned so that the faucet is either to the right or left side. A side arrangement facilitates use by a tenant

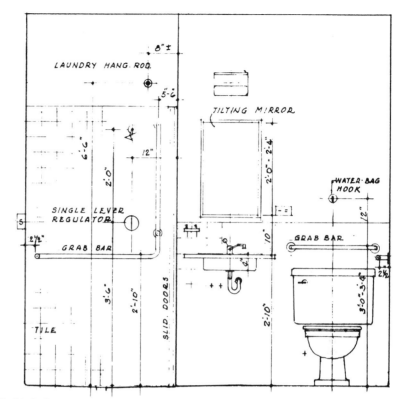

Fig. 24 Bathroom-shower elevation. A grab bar above the toilet assists person making a frontal approach. Shower regulator with temperature control is recommended.

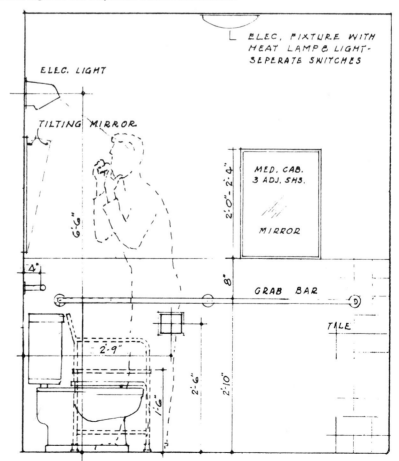

Fig. 25 Bathroom elevation. The standard sanitary toilet chair with seat 18 in. above floor is an aid to impaired persons who have difficulty using the normal toilet.

HOUSING FOR THE HANDICAPPED

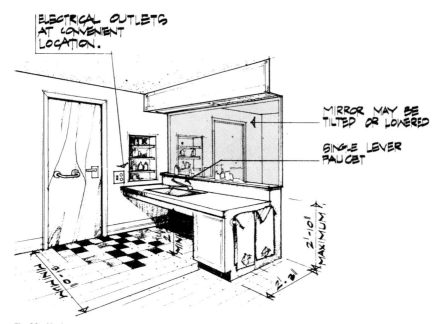

Fig. 26   Vanity.

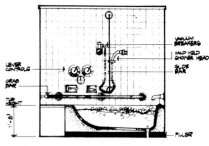

Fig. 31   Combination bathtub/shower.

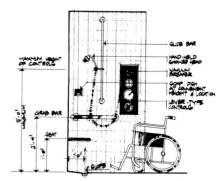

Fig. 32   Shower.

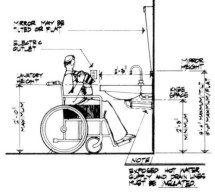

Fig. 27   Floor-mounted water closet.

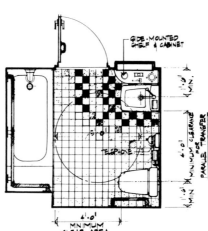

Fig. 29   Typical bathroom arrangement.

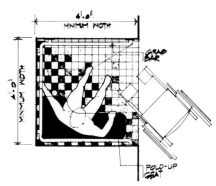

Fig. 33   Shower seat.

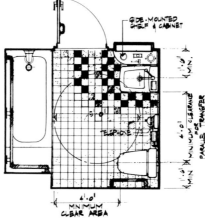

Fig. 28   Lavatory.

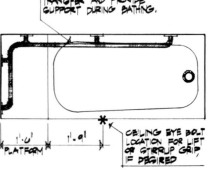

Fig. 30   Bathtub.

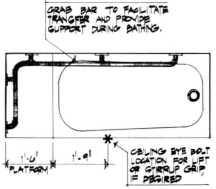

Fig. 34   "Roll-in" shower.

* Figures 26–34 from "Handbook for Design: Specially Adapted Housing," VA Pamphlet 26–13, Veterans Administration, Washington, D.C., 1978.

148

Layout A

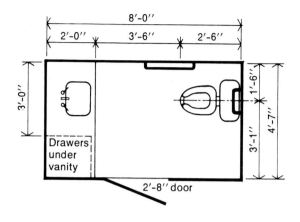

Layout D

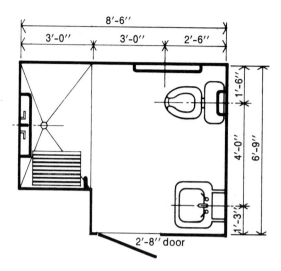

Layout B

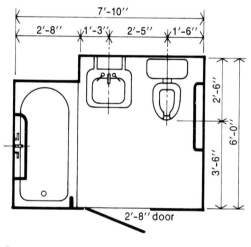

Layout E

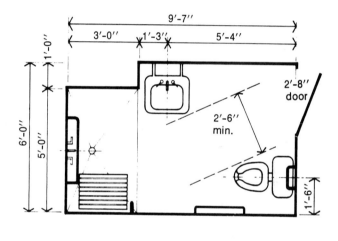

Layout C

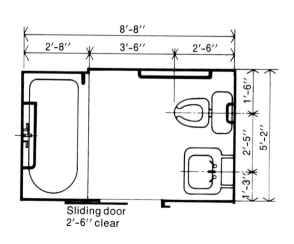

Layout F

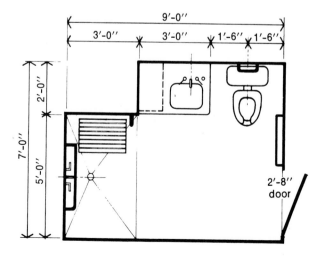

Fig. 34a Layouts of bathrooms for the handicapped.

Residential

HOUSING FOR THE HANDICAPPED

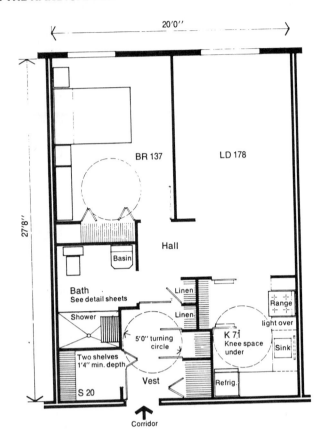

Handicapped 1-bedroom unit
Total net area: 555 sq. feet.

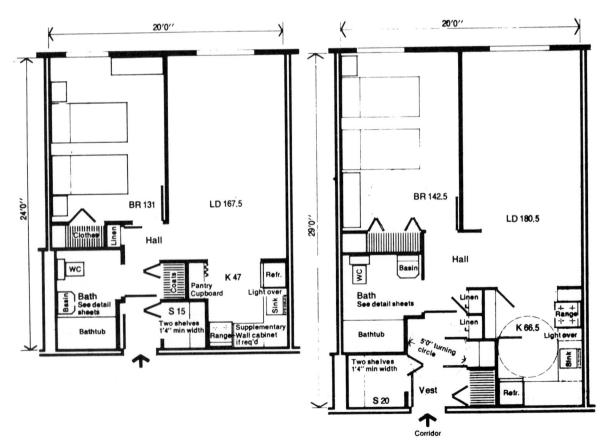

1-bedroom unit
Senior citizens
Total net area: 480 sq. feet.

Handicapped
1-bedroom unit
Total net area: 580 sq. feet.

with limited reach and can easily be converted for convenience of future tenants when it is initially provided with flexible-tube water supplies and ample length slip-joint tailpiece waste line. (See Fig. 24.)

The mirror over the lavatory should be usable from both standing and sitting positions. If fixed to the wall, the mirror should be tilted forward at the top. Bottom-hinged mirror provided with a friction stay arm is available. This mirror permits the top to tilt forward to any distance up to 6 in. and can be installed on the medicine cabinet door.

The medicine cabinet should be mounted so as to be accessible from standing or sitting position, and its location in the bathroom should be carefully considered. (See Fig. 25.)

The water closet seat of standard height, 15 to 16 in., can be used by ambulant impaired persons. For the semiambulant and others who find this height difficult, a standard manufactured sanitary chair with arm rests and seat 18 in. high is recommended. The advantage of the chair is twofold; it can also be used in the shower, and would not be present when not needed by the occupant. Some wheelchairs are equipped to be used as toilet chairs. Grab rails should be provided at the closet. One manufacturer can supply an integral seat, cover, and grab bars. (*Note:* Detachable ring seats that clip on the china bowl or seat are unstable and should be avoided.)

Other recommendations are shown in Figs. 26-34.

Storage

Adequate storage space should be provided within the dwelling. *Separate* units are desirable for hanging coats and for bedroom, linen, and general storage. The storage units may be closets enclosed by partitions or wood cabinets, fixed or movable, to serve as room dividers. Kitchen cabinets are discussed elsewhere.

The cost closet should permit the hanging of clothing from both standing and sitting positions. For the standing position, the fixed shelf height at 5 ft-6 in. with the clothes-hanging pole below is standard. For the wheelchair position, 4 ft to 4 ft-6 in. is most convenient. The lower shelf and pole unit should be adjustable from 4 ft to 5 ft-6 in. (See Fig. 35.)

For one-person dwellings, the coat closet shelves and pole should be made adjustable. For larger dwellings, both the standing position height and the adjustable wheelchair height should be provided by dividing the closet with a wood partition. (See Figs. 36 and 37.)

The bedroom clothes closet should be divided by wood partitions into two sections, one with shelves and pole for the standing position height and the other adjustable for the wheelchair user.

The linen closet shelves should be adjustable in height, from the baseboard up. Persons in a sitting position can easily reach low shelves, but low shelves are difficult for those on crutches. The linen closet often stores items other than linen, such as clothes hamper, bathroom supplies, etc. Adjustable shelves provide the needed flexibility.

A storage unit should be provided for storing supplies and cleaning equipment, ironing board, canned goods, etc. The unit need not be in the kitchen, but it should be easily accessible from the kitchen. It may be a standard prefabricated cabinet resting on the floor or a built-in closet.

A general storage area and kitchen storage space may be combined if located conveniently to the kitchen.

Although the general storage area is not primarily designed for the storage of excess furniture, it should be large enough to store foot lockers, suitcases, vacuum cleaner, large and seldom-used cooking utensils, work clothes and work shoes, and—in large family units, folded baby furniture and unused toys.

Increasing the amount of storage space does not always economically resolve the storage problem. The best use of available space can be made by careful arrangement of varying shelf widths adjustable for height and use of hook strips for hanging such items as brooms, mops, vacuum cleaner hose, etc.

Windows

The following hazards should be avoided when selecting and installing windows: windows that project, outside or inside, beyond the wall line and protrude in the path of persons walking; windows that require climbing or leaning out to clean; windowsills too low to provide adequate safety from falling or high sills which block the view from a sitting or bed position. The recommended windowsill height is 28 to 32 in.; [it can be at floor level if the window opens on a terrace or balcony].

Windows should be easy to operate, lock, and clean. Operating and locking hardware should be located for convenient reach from a sitting or a standing position and be of the type easily grasped by arthritic or otherwise impaired hands.

Window types deserving consideration are:
• The modified double-hung window which, in addition to sliding up and down, permits each sash to pivot and swing inward for cleaning with no interference by insect screens or storm panels when used, or curtains, shades, and venetian blinds.

• The awning type with push bar or rotary gear operator set below the screen (some of these windows require the screen unit to be removed to clean the window, others permit the swing panels to reverse when fully opened for cleaning the outside glass surface). Cleaning of upper glass may be difficult for some.

• The hopper type, somewhat similar to the awning type except that window units open inward and screen is on the outside. This type window may interfere with draperies and shades and may project inward to the point of being a hazard.

• Horizontal sliding windows. Cleaning of upper glass may be difficult for some.

Aluminum windows coated by the manufacturer for protection during shipping and installation have some advantage over windows requiring maintenance painting.

Window items which increase maintenance costs should be avoided. Dissimilar metals that cause galvanic corrosive action in the presence of moisture should not be used. The best rust prevention for steel is hot-dip galvanizing. To prevent condensation and early

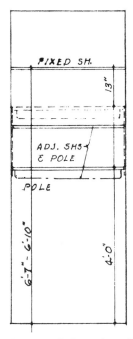

Fig. 36 One-person bedroom closet. Coat closet same but smaller.

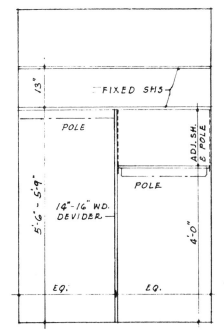

Fig. 35 Two-person bedroom closet. Coat closet same but smaller.

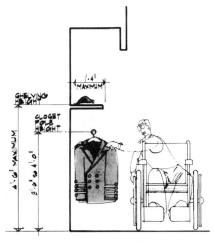

Fig. 37 Closets. *Source:* "Handbook for Design: Specially Adapted Housing," VA Pamphlet 26–13, Veterans Administration, Washington, D.C., 1978.

Residential

HOUSING FOR THE HANDICAPPED

deterioration, a thermal break is advisable between metal windows (steel or aluminum) and butting interior materials, such as plaster or metal jamb liners. Windowsills are subject to hard usage from flower pots and other heavy objects. Glass glazing compounds which harden make glass replacement expensive; vinyl or snap-in beads are recommended.

Two curtain rods or tracks, as well as venetian blinds or shades, should be provided for windows. Ring pull trim on pull-down blinds or shades is convenient for many impaired persons who use a device with a hooked end for many things. Venetian blinds are practical, though difficult to clean. The general tendency toward excessive glass areas makes the cost to the tenant of providing suitable glare-controlling and cold-retarding draperies unreasonably high.

Doors and Hallways

The entrance door to the dwelling should be at least 2 ft-10 in. wide if door opens 180°, otherwise 3 ft. There should be no entrance step or riser. Any threshold should be at least 5 in. wide, featheredged to floor and projecting no more than ½ in. above the floor.

Letters or numbers identifying the dwelling should be visible day and night. Raised numbers are more easily seen by those with poor vision and can be felt by the blind. It is also helpful to have color variation on doors or elsewhere near the entrance. Entrance doors leading directly from the outside should have a protective hood or canopy.

The proper width of pass-through doors within the dwelling depends upon wheelchair dimensions and the ability of the individual to operate the chair. Overall dimensions for the standard wheelchair are 24 to 26 in. wide, 42 in. long and 36 in. high. Special-purpose wheelchairs are larger and require more maneuvering space. The pass-through dimensions that follow, which are identified as minimal, represent what the standard American wheelchair is capable of negotiating; the recommended dimensions represent what *most* wheelchair users can negotiate:

- Hallways in the dwelling: To permit 180° turn, 4-ft minimum width, 4 ft-6 in. *recommended.*
- Pass-through door—straight-line travel: 2-ft-8-in. minimum if door opens 180°; otherwise, 2 ft-10 in. *recommended.*
- Pass-through door—90° wheelchair turn from hallway: 2-ft-10-in. door and 3-ft-4-in. hallway *recommended;* or 3-ft door and 3-ft hallway *recommended.* (See Fig. 38.)

Closet doors and other non-pass-through doors, 2-ft-6-in. minimum width—horizontal sliding or folding doors are easiest to operate from a sitting position, and they eliminate the danger, especially to the blind, of walking into the edge of a partially open door.

Hinged bathroom doors should swing *outward,* to remove collapsed person. If the latch includes a lock feature, it should be the type that can be released from the outside. Sliding or folding doors are satisfactory. Two-way swinging doors are hazardous and should not be used.

Operating hardware on doors should be 2 ft-10 in. to 3 ft above the floor for all doors in the dwelling, including entrance door. Round or oval doorknobs are the most difficult for impaired hands to operate. Lever handles with ends looped back to the door surface to prevent catching of clothing, etc., are best for operating a latch or lock. Pull handles should be of simple design with no hooks to catch clothing and with both ends returned to the

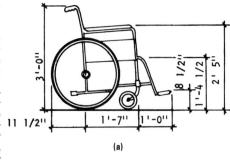

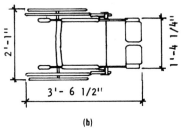

Fig. 38 (a) Side view of standard adult wheelchair. (b) Plan view of standard adult wheelchair.

door. A 5-in. or more door pull handle, mounted on the hinge side, is convenient for pulling the door shut from a wheelchair.

Kickplates on the entrance door are desirable to reduce damage and door maintenance caused by wheelchair foot rests and wheel hubs. (See Fig. 39.)

Thresholds *should not* be installed at interior doors or openings.

Floors

For the physically impaired, floor surface materials should have nonslip properties. Some materials are satisfactory when dry but dangerous when wet and therefore should not be used in the bathroom, kitchen, or near the entrance doors when these doors are in the exterior walls. Slippery floor surfaces are particularly dangerous to users of canes or crutches when

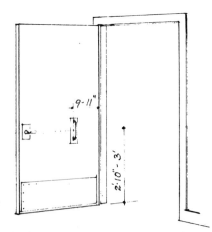

Fig. 39 Dwelling entrance opening out. Door pull assists a wheelchair user to pull door shut on entering. The door pull should be on the outside for an inward opening door.

the rubber ferrules become wet or the floor is wet.

Bare concrete floors are *not* recommended. Carpeted floors, for low-rent housing, cost more initially and in the long run than other suitable floor materials. Carpets need underpads to extend their life and, due to the effort needed to propel a wheelchair, are not desirable for wheelchair users who have arm or hand impediments. Floor materials which require special maintenance equipment or treatment should not be installed inside the dwelling. Floor materials of intermediate colors with a patterned surface should be selected. Very dark or light surfaces, especially solid-colored, show dirt more readily.

For the bathroom and shower, unglazed ceramic floors are recommended. The smaller-sized tiles (2 in. or less) provide some friction at the joints and therefore greater safety. For similar reason, square-edge tiles are more suitable than those with a cushion edge. Coved base makes for easier floor cleaning.

Kitchen floor materials should be grease-resistant. The best materials are those which can be kept clean with warm water and detergent, such as vinyl asbestos.

Floor materials for other dwelling space may be asphalt tile (in the midrange colors), vinyl asbestos, or hardwood. There are numerous wood floor finishes that require little maintenance, such as those formulated with polyurethane (an excellent finish) or epoxy.

Lighting, Telephone, Television, Emergency Signal System

Lighting All light fixtures should be controlled by wall switches. The switches should be uniformly located 2 ft-10 in. to 3 ft above the floor and not over 8 in. from door jamb at latch side of door. A receptacle (not switch controlled) should be combined at some locations with switches, for convenient use of a vacuum cleaner. Tap-type or rocker switches are best for persons with hand impairment. Light fixtures located at a height permitting the tenants to replace light bulbs without using a stepladder are desirable. One way to eliminate this hazard is by the use of a floor or table lamp for room lighting. For this purpose, one receptacle of a wall duplex outlet, conveniently located, should be switch controlled at the room entrance. (See Figs. 40 and 41.)

Adequate light should be provided outside entrance doors so that residents can easily locate their door locks at night. Higher than normal lighting intensity is needed by most elderly and some impaired persons, especially in the kitchen and bathroom.

Wall receptacles should be uniformly placed 18 to 24 in. above the floor to reduce the physical effort of bending. Only those wall receptacles placed above kitchen counters and in dining areas should be mounted higher. Twin wall receptacles are inexpensive and are less hazardous than the cheap substitutes often purchased by tenants.

For safety, the switch(es) controlling electrical outlets in the bathroom should be located outside the bathroom door unless the return wire and the outlet box are grounded.

In low-rent housing, electrical outlets for tenant-owned wall or window air-cooling equipment are permitted subject to approval by HUD-HAA.

The dwelling circuit panel should be located at a height convenient for the wheelchair users. The circuit panel must be of the "dead front" type. Circuit breakers are preferred to plug fuses.

152

Telephone In a one-person dwelling, provision should be made for a telephone outlet near the head of the bed; and in all other dwellings, between the beds of the first bedroom. A second telephone outlet could be placed in the living room of dwellings with one or more bedrooms. Some telephone companies will install one plug-in instrument in a dwelling with more than one plug-in outlet. Most low-income tenants cannot afford the monthly expense of two instruments. (See Fig. 42.)

In developments assisted by HUD-HAA, a

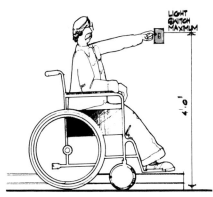

Fig. 40   Wall switches.*

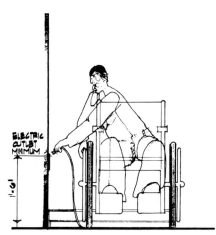

Fig. 41   Electrical outlets.

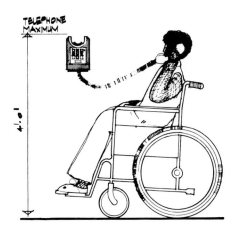

Fig. 42   Telephones.

Figures 40–42 from "Handbook for Design: Specially Adapted Housing," VA Pamphlet 26–13, Veterans Administration, Washington, D.C., 1978.

central telephone switchboard is not recommended because of the manpower operating cost and its resultant effect on rents.

A house emergency telephone and/or other signal device should be installed in each elevator cab. The answering service should be in the management office and the custodial apartment, or other 24-hr service if found to be economical.

Television A television antenna system should be provided when needed for good reception.

Emergency Signal System The system would include one large-diameter pushbutton in the bathroom, another near the head of the bed in a one-person dwelling, and one between the beds of the first bedroom in all other dwellings. Both pushbuttons activate an audio and visual unit located outside the dwelling. A third unit, which can be activated simultaneously, should change the dwelling entrance door from locked to unlocked. The activated unit should be on continuous duty, allowing it to remain in operation until reset. The audio unit tone should be distinct and should differ from the fire alarm. A secondary power supply should be considered for the emergency signal system and the fire alarm.

The audio and visual units may be located outside the entrance door, inside an adjacent dwelling, or in a central location.

Heating

The heating system should be designed to maintain room temperature of $75°F$ for the physically impaired or elderly.

Exposed vertical heating risers and exposed radiators are dangerous. Such equipment can cause severe burns to persons who, in portions of their bodies, have little sensation to heat. All vertical heating pipes should be concealed and radiators covered with cabinets.

In bathrooms, the use of a ceiling-type heat lamp, thermostatically controlled and operated by a manual wall switch, is recommended as safe and economical, providing instant heat day or night. Exposed heaters, radiators, or heat riser pipes are not safe and should not be used.

In multistory structures, a central heating plant is generally most economical. For one-story structures, a central heating plant is costly due to the installation of distribution mains. Either forced warm air or forced hot water as individual units or group plants could be used for one-story structures. The final determination should be based on a detailed utility analysis.

Excessive window glass areas increase heat loss and therefore fuel cost. In summer, rooms with a south or west exposure receive the rays of the hot afternoon sun, which raises the temperature in the unit. Large glass areas exposed to summer sun or winter cold require curtains or draperies, an expensive tenant item.

Whatever form of heat is provided, tenant control is recommended, preferably by thermostat or, in the case of radiators, by shut-off valves.

Domestic Hot Water

In warm climates, individual water heaters installed in a closet with outside entrance makes for ease of maintenance and facilitates management control of water temperature setting.

Custodial Dwelling

The need for a custodial dwelling unit should be considered. Such dwelling should be cen-

trally located and have at least two bedrooms, to suit the housing needs of a couple with children. In a multistory structure, the custodial dwelling should be on the ground floor.

To have the custodian living within the development is desirable and necessary for the physically impaired and the elderly. Therefore, justification for including a custodial dwelling should show the number of tenants who are impaired or elderly.

Although the custodian is an employee with specific work assignments, he should be available for emergencies when off duty. The custodian's wife might be available during the day; however, in most developments there is a management office open during working hours.

COMMUNITY SPACE

General

The following recommendations apply particularly to multiuse community space and to those less specialized community facilities most frequently developed in conjunction with residential housing developments. Local considerations will govern the number and nature of specialized community facilities developed in combination with a residential facility for the physically impaired. Because the range of possibilities in such specialized facilities is so vast—from health clinics to sheltered workshops offering specific types of employment opportunities—anyone undertaking to design them should consult with program directors.

Before the architectural plan and functional layout of the community space can proceed, the local need and available services should be explored in cooperation with local agencies which will finance the staffing and operate the space after it is constructed.

Since the maximum space permitted is determined by the number of families in each development, it is not possible to provide in all developments, especially the smaller ones, space for all activities. The space planning for some areas should provide *for functional use of the maximum number of activities.* Areas or spaces generally considered desirable are a lounge combined with the entrance lobby; group recreational space with kitchen; craft area; library; clinic; facilities such as toilets, public telephones, drinking fountains, and vending machines especially designed or arranged for orthopedic equipment users; and a separate space for the resident children's activities.

Space to be allotted as a health clinic should be planned as a separate functional unit. Health clinic space rarely can be combined with recreational or other space.

Indoor community space should be closely related to outdoor recreational areas with easy access and no intervening stairs or steps. Indoor space should have natural light and ventilation with pleasant outward views. It is not desirable to locate community space in basements or on rooftops detached from outdoor recreational areas.

In general, floor surfacing suitable for the dwelling area is suitable for indoor community space. It may be advisable, however, to install nonstaining flooring in certain special use areas, and more durable flooring—such as nonslip terrazzo, unglazed tile, or quarry tile—in corridors, entrance lobbies, and other concentrated use areas.

General illumination should be of multiple control to allow for varying degrees of intensity. The maximum should be at about 30

HOUSING FOR THE HANDICAPPED

foot-candles at table height. Supplemental movable lights (floor and table lamps in the lounge and library) should be provided at required utilitarian locations for decorative and functional use. Avoid creating hazards by exposed extension cords to floor and table lamps.

There should be no hazards within the community space, such as thresholds, freestanding columns, pilasters, projecting radiators, or drinking fountains.

Air conditioning of all community space used by physically impaired or elderly should be considered.

Lounge

When combined with the entrance lobby of a community building or the elevator lobby of a multistory structure, a lounge provides increased activity and interest. The elderly and the impaired enjoy watching the going and coming tenants and visitors. In cold climates a vestibule entrance is necessary.

Locating the mail delivery room in the elevator lobby near the lounge is recommended.

The décor of the lounge should be coordinated—wall colors, white ceiling, accent colors —in draperies, furniture, lamps, and plastic or cloth upholstery materials. Woven cloth upholstery material used in the lounge must be stainproof.

Selection of chairs and sofas for the physically impaired, especially the semiambulant, deserves special consideration. Seat height 18 in. above floor is best. Sturdy arm rests help the impaired to rise. Chairs should not overbalance when weight is applied on the arm rest. Deep seats (over 20 in.) are undesirable. Semistiff, upholstered furniture is recommended.

Recreation or Multipurpose Room

This space may be subdivided by sliding or folding soundproof dividers or doors—the ceiling should be acoustically treated. The space should be suited for meetings, movies, concerts, plays, lunches, etc. Because of the nature of such activities, convenient storage space for tables and other items should be provided. An inventory of the items is needed to adequately plan an orderly and functional storage—flexibility of use with adjustable shelves is desirable.

Building codes may require emergency exits, but at least one exit door may be desirable for departing guests after evening affairs.

Structural columns or other obstructions within this space should be avoided or eliminated if possible in order that the space may function as one room for certain occasions.

Tables without aprons, which will permit wheelchair arms to fit underneath, are recommended—they also take less space to store.

Kitchen

A kitchen should be provided adjacent to the recreation room. Equipment and arrangement should facilitate efficient and functional food preparation and clean-up. The kitchen may be used by the tenants.

The kitchen should be planned and designed to be useful in demonstrating and instructing on food preparation, in planning balanced diets, and in conducting various consumer education activities. For this purpose, the division between the recreation room and kitchen should be a sliding or folding divider or doors which can be locked or secured.

A two-door refrigerator freezer with auto-matic defrosting food compartment is recommended. In large kitchens, consider how best to provide cold drinking water.

A kitchen service entrance should be planned to accommodate delivery of supplies, catering service, and garbage and trash removal. A garbage grinder may be installed in this kitchen —the continuous-feed type is recommended.

Floor and wall surfaces should be of easily cleaned materials and finishes. Wall cabinets should have adjustable shelves. At least one closet, with lock, for storage of staple supplies should be provided, as well as a cabinet for mops, brooms, and cleaning materials.

Craft Activity Area

The space for craft activities should have maximum flexibility for varied arrangement. Fixed partitioning of cubicles is *not* desirable— no flexibility. It is best to concentrate the craft space in one room, dividing the space with movable (on casters with step-on brakes) wood storage cabinets for materials and supplies. This provides for multiple use of space and permits adapting space size to tenant interest and various activities.

The movable divider cabinets should not extend to the ceiling. A height of about 4 ft provides views [to the person who is] standing and improves ventilation and distribution of light; further, no change in the prearranged distribution of air conditioning is required. The cabinet units should be of sizes easy to move. Standardized units are advisable, but they should be selected or designed for the materials and supplies to be stored. It is also advisable to have cabinets that can be locked and shelves that can be adjusted. Some drawer-type storage space may be desirable. Apronless tables are recommended.

Special consideration should be given to providing outlets for both 110 and 220 volts in craft activity area—consult with operating staff.

Library

The larger community spaces may provide, if need is established, an area for a branch of the city library, which will furnish book stacks. When the book stacks can be locked or otherwise segregated from the rest of the library, then the area generally used for reading could on occasion be used for small gatherings or other uses—again, flexibility. If possible, this space should be large enough for apronless tables and for chairs. Since smaller projects seldom can afford a separate library, the lounge may be provided with adjustable shelves for books and periodicals. This same idea, while less desirable than a separate library, may be considered for large projects.

Health Clinic

A clinic can contribute substantially to the welfare and continued independence of the elderly and physically impaired. Clinic space may be provided when such facilities are not available near the site.

In small developments, the permissible clinic space may consist of an office and examination room for use of doctors and nurses who visit during scheduled periods.

In larger developments, space for a variety

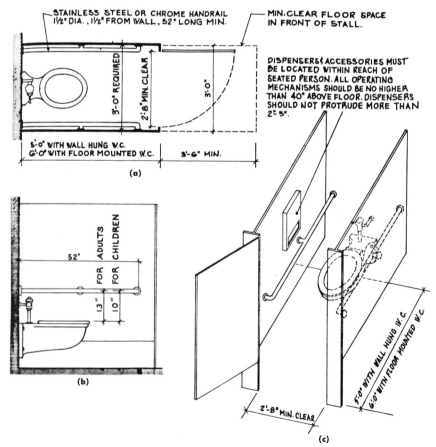

Fig. 43 Toilet stall.

of health services may be provided, including physical therapy and hydrotherapy, a special need of the physically impaired. Occupational therapy may be conducted in the craft activity area. This type of clinic would generally be active each work day and should have a waiting room with a separate outside entrance permitting nontenant patients to come and go without traversing the lobby or lounge.

Washrooms

Separate washrooms for each sex should be provided in community space. At least one water closet compartment for the semiambulant and wheelchair user should be provided in each washroom in addition to other plumbing fixtures.

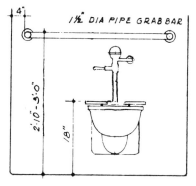

Fig. 44 Wall-hung toilet—desirable.

The washrooms should be located to permit convenient use by outside visitors to the clinic and tenants using the various activity areas.

The toilet stall illustrated in Fig. 43 is a possible solution for persons using wheelchairs.

Maximum maneuverability for persons using crutches or wheelchairs is provided in toilet stalls, with the toilet fixture set toward either side wall.

Horizontal grab bars should be installed on the side and rear wall of the water closet compartment. Such bars ($1\frac{1}{2}$-in. outside diameter) should be at least 4 in. from the wall to prevent pinioning the wrist, hand, or arm in case of a fall. Grab bars should support 250 lb.

The water closet seat should be 18 in. above the floor. A wall-hung closet is most suitable for the semiambulant person—it also makes for ease of floor cleaning and sanitation. (See Fig. 44.)

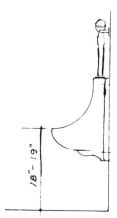

Fig. 45 Wall-hung urinal.

Urinals in the men's room should be of the wall-mounted type, also for sanitary reasons. The front lip of the urinal should be 18 to 19 in. above the floor, which is convenient for persons in wheelchairs as well as others. (See Fig. 45.)

The installation of lavatory and wall mirrors is discussed in the section on "Dwelling Units," under "Bathroom."

A separate staff washroom which can be used by both sexes should be provided in the clinic—two washrooms in the large clinic.

Public Telephones, Drinking Fountains, Vending Machines

Public Telephones The standard public telephone booth is not usable for most physically impaired people.

To assist persons with hearing disabilities, telephone receivers should have adjustable amplifiers.

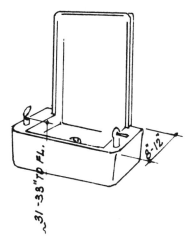

Fig. 46 Semirecessed model with projecting basin is recommended because the wheelchair approach is parallel to the wall. A frontal approach is difficult. Two units may be connected to one water chiller. The second unit should be set 40 to 42 in. above the floor and 5 to 6 ft from the other. The water stream rises about 4 in. above the bubbler orifice.

The pushbutton-dial receiver is more desirable for the impaired than the rotating dial.

The standard coin-box receiver mounted above the table or shelf elevates the coin slot 4 ft above the floor, which is not convenient for some with physical impairments. A desk-type telephone, resting on a table or shelf about 31 in. above the floor, is the most convenient (bottom of shelf must clear wheelchair arm rests). For wheelchair users, the desirable height for coin slots is about 3 ft above the floor or 6 in. above the counter top. The local telephone company should be consulted for advice regarding available special and standard equipment which is especially desirable for the physically impaired.

Drinking Fountains The standard adult drinking fountain is satisfactory to all except wheelchair users. For wheelchair users, the fountain bubbler should be 31 to 33 in. above the floor. Two-level drinking fountains that satisfy both standard and wheelchair height requirements are available, or a low-level unit can be added

on the standard fixture. Persons in wheelchairs can use a children's drinking fountain 31 in. high. Pushbutton control is best for persons with impaired hands. Some drinking fountains are available with both hand and foot control. (See Figs. 46 and 47.)

Drinking fountains with paper cup dispensers should have the dispensing mechanism 30 to 34 in. above the floor. Drinking fountains resting on the floor and projecting into the corridor are a hazard; recessing into wall pockets makes floor cleaning difficult.

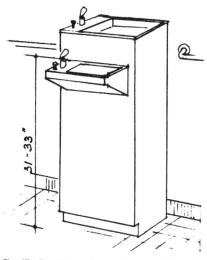

Fig. 47 The floor cabinet model is available with an additive basin; while this two-level unit would serve the dual use, it is not recommended because of the hazard created to persons with poor vision and to blind persons who will be using the wall handrail.

Vending Machines The need for and location (not in prominent view) of vending machines which dispense soft drinks, etc. should be considered.

Other Areas

The minimum corridor width should be 6 ft. Grab rails should be provided on each side wall. (See chapter on dwelling structures for special assistance to those with poor vision.) The minimum door width should be 3 ft. Doors from the corridor to the various rooms, when fully open, should not extend into the corridor. They are a hazard, especially to persons with poor vision.

Consideration should be given to the need for a staff management office. In multistory buildings, such an office should be located to provide an unobtrusive view of the lobby entrance and elevators.

Office space in which tenants may, in privacy, discuss problems with counselors and [which may also serve] for other uses should be considered.

Consideration also should be given to temporary coat and umbrella storage facilities for tenants and visitors using the recreation or multipurpose rooms. This facility is best located where it can be visually supervised. Closed cloakrooms should be avoided.

Certain rooms and storage areas will require locked doors.

HOUSING FOR THE HANDICAPPED

CENTRAL DINING

Seating for wheelchair users should be on at least 2'6" centers. Tables should be 3'-6" wide if chair users are to face each other. Wider tables are not recommended because of chair users' restricted reaching ability. (See Fig. 48.)*

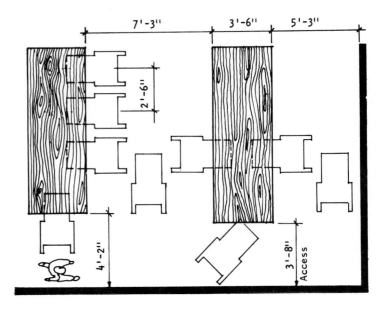

Fig. 48 Clearance for central dining-wheelchair users.

PARKING†

Parking Space Requirements

Parking spaces specifically designed for restricted individuals should be set aside and properly identified through the use of signage so that the spaces are not used indiscriminately by people not needing them. (Fig. 50).

Special elevated platforms, or mechanical lifts attached to vehicles must be provided to facilitate boarding and disembarkment by wheelchair bound people from mass transit vehicles.

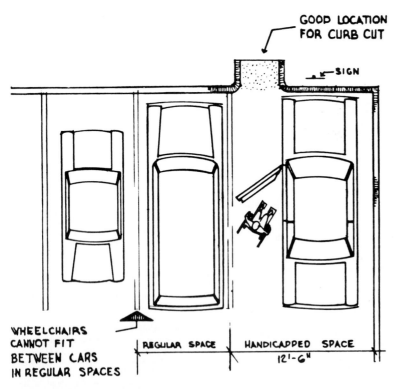

Fig. 49 Clearance for handicapped parking space.

Fig. 50 Suggested signs displaying the international symbol for accessibility.

* Text and Figs. 49–50 from "An Illustrated Handbook of the Handicapped Section of the North Carolina State Building Code," Raleigh, 1977.
† This text and Figs. 51–53 from "Barrier-Free Site Design," The American Society of Landscape Architects Foundation, HUD-PDR-84, Washington, D.C., 1975.

156

1. Parking spaces of greater width than normal are necessary for people who are disabled and use mechanical aids such as wheelchairs, crutches, and walkers. For example, persons who are chairbound must have wider aisles in which to set up their wheelchairs.

2. A minimum of two spaces per parking lot should be designed for use by physically restricted people, or at least one space per 20 cars, whichever is greater.

3. These spaces should be placed as close as possible to a major entrance of a building or function, preferably no more than 100'-0" away.

4. Parking patterns are described in 5 and 6 below (Fig. 51).

5. Parallel Parking:
   Parallel parking spaces should be placed adjacent to a walk system so that access from the car to the destination is over a hard surface. Such spaces should be made 12'-0" wide, 24'-0" long and should either have a 1:6 ramp up to the walk, or should be separated from it by bollards or some other device if the road level is at the same elevation as the walk. These areas should be designated as special parking since they may otherwise appear to be a drop-off zone.

6. 90 Degree and Angled Parking:
   a. Spaces designed for use by disabled people functioning with large mechanical aids as described above, should be 9'-0" wide as a minimum. In addition to the 9'-0", a 3'-6" to 4'-0" wide aisle between cars should be provided for access alongside the vehicle (Figs. 49 and 54). It is important that there be plenty of room to open the car door entirely, and in the case of a dependent chairbound person, that there be room for friends or attendants to assist him [or her] out of the car, into his [or her] chair, and away from the car.

   b. The 9'-0" wide standard space width for a parking stall, with no aisle between spaces, does not drastically hinder semiambulant people with minor impairments, but an 8'-0" width, unless used exclusively for attendant parking, is too narrow and should be avoided.

   c. A 4'-0" minimum clear aisle width should be provided between rows of cars parked end to end. The overhang of the automobile should be taken into account so that the island strip is wide enough to leave a 4'-0" clear aisle when the stalls are filled. A strip 8'-0" wide is a recommended minimum for an on-grade aisle, and 10'-0" is a recommended minimum where the aisle is raised 6" above the parking level.

   d. If the aisle between rows of cars is not at the same grade level as the cars, then ramps must be provided to mount the curbs. A 1:6 (17%) ramp is suitable for such a short distance.

   e. Economically, the installation of an on-grade 4'-0" wide pathway is less expensive than a raised walk. Precast car stops to delineate the passage can be used providing that a 4'-0" wide space between the ends of stops is maintained to allow access to the main passageway.

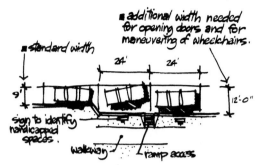

Parallel Parking

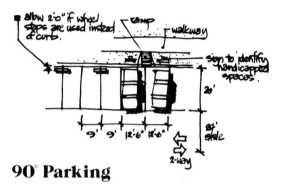

90° Parking

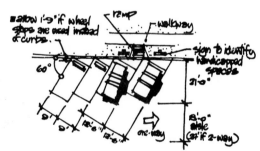

60° Parking

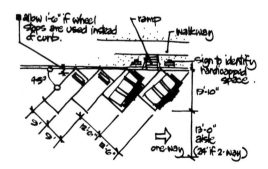

45° Parking

Fig. 51 Parking patterns.

HOUSING FOR THE HANDICAPPED

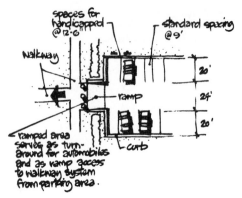

Fig. 52 Parking using end-lot access.

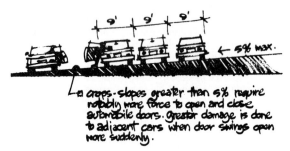

Fig. 53 Cross-slope in parking areas.

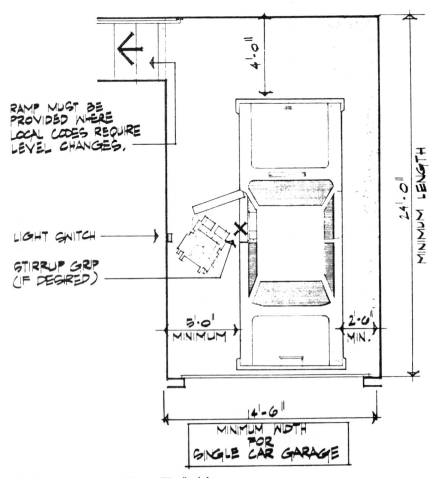

Fig. 54 Garage or carport. *Source:* "Handbook for Design: Specially Adapted Housing," Veterans Administration, Washington, D.C., 1978.

SPATIAL REQUIREMENTS

Building: Approximately 6,650 square feet for a 12-person home and 7,400 square feet for a 16-person home are allotted. This area includes space for the garage and basements. The building can be arranged on one level or on two full or partial levels.

Entry

Major This spatial requirement varies according to the inclusion or exclusion of the vertical circulation element within the space. Normally, an area of approximately 90 square feet should be sufficient. A closet with a minimum of 6 linear feet of hanging space should be adequate.

Minor The size of this space varies; however, it should be adequately sized for ease of circulation through it.

Living Space

This space varies in size. In a typical 16-resident group home it is approximately 400 to 500 square feet.

Recreation Room

This space varies in size. In a typical 16-resident group home it is approximately 400 to 500 square feet and as previously indicated should be sized to seat all residents. It is required that direct access suitable for use by the physically handicapped be provided from the main living area and to the common outdoor activity area.

Kitchen

The area designated for food preparation shall meet all of the requirements of the Michigan Department of Public Health, Michigan Department of Social Services, and the applicable portion of the F.H.A. Minimum Property Standards for Multifamily Housing. The typical kitchen is equipped with the following appliances:

refrigerator
freezer
commercial dishwasher
cooktop range with exhaust hood
double oven
disposal

Dining

The dining space shall have a glazed area of at least 10 percent of the floor area. The following clearances and sizes will be assumed for design purposes:

2'0" for table edge for each diner
3'0" minimum table width for tables seating four to six persons
3'3" for larger tables
4'0" minimum clearance between the table edge and obstruction where seating and circulation occurs
3'0" for circulation clearance
2'6" for seating clearance table to obstruction

Clearances are shown in Fig. 1

Powder Room

This space should be sized to accommodate physically handicapped residents. A water closet and

Special Group Housing for Adults Development Process, Michigan State Housing Development Authority, Lansing, Michigan, 1978.

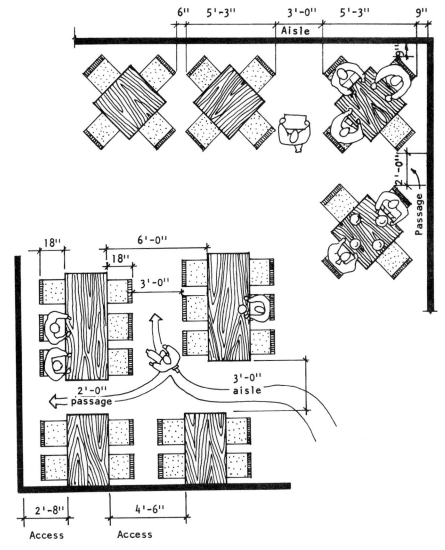

Fig. 1 Clearances for central dining.

a lavatory without vanity base should be provided.

Bedroom

No resident room shall accommodate more than three persons. Each occupant of a room shall be provided with a separate storage closet of at least the following:

- 4'0" x 2'2" clear and an opening width of at least 3' clear.
- The closet shall be equipped with a shelf and hanging rod.
- The bedroom shall be equipped with windows whose glazed area is at least 15 percent of the floor area of the room.
- Windows shall be operable and have a free air ventilation area equal to half the glazed area.
- Resident bedrooms shall accommodate at least the following:

2 beds: 3'3" x 6'6" min.
2 dressers: 3'0" x 1'6" min.
1 lounge chair: 1'10" x 1'10" min.
2 bedside tables: 1'0" x 1'0"

- Specially designed desks/storage units may be used.

Minimum clearance shall be maintained as follows:

1'6" between wall and the side of bed that is least used
3'0" in front of dresser
3'6" diameter area for dressing
2'6" for access to and use of table as a desk
3'0" door opening
2'6" general circulation

The bedroom shall be designed to provide a clearly defined area within the room for each occupant. It is preferable if one occupant does not have to violate the area of another in order to get to or from the room entrance or [*sic*] the bedroom.

If possible, the room should be designed so that there is a visual separation between the sleeping areas. Generally, resident rooms should be grouped together and served from common halls or foyers. These halls shall provide direct access to shared facilities for the residents without the necessity of going out of doors. The room specially adapted for the handicapped shall have such access only via level floors or elevators. The acoustic separation of party walls and floors of a given resident room shall have STC rating of 45 and INR rating of +5. The ceiling height shall be at least 7'6" (8'0" preferred).

BATHROOM

One bathroom shall serve every two resident bedrooms, that is, a total of four residents. The bathroom shall contain a water closet and a vanity base with a pair of lavatories with cabinets mounted on it. The homes specially adapted for the physically handicapped shall have a stall shower of sufficient dimensions to allow soaping out of the spray instead of a tub. Lavatories shall be located in vanity tops without a base. Tubs may be allowed if equipped with appropriate grab bars.

Bathroom shall open directly off the resident's room. All bathrooms will be finished with non-slip materials and will include a storage space for each individual's personal toiletries.

OFFICE

The office shall contain no less than 100 square feet in area. It shall have walls, floors, and ceilings with a rating of 45 STC and +5 INR to insure privacy during counseling.

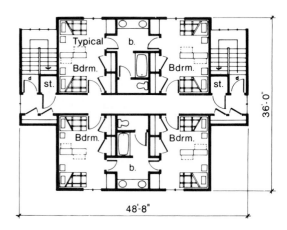

SECOND FLOOR PLAN

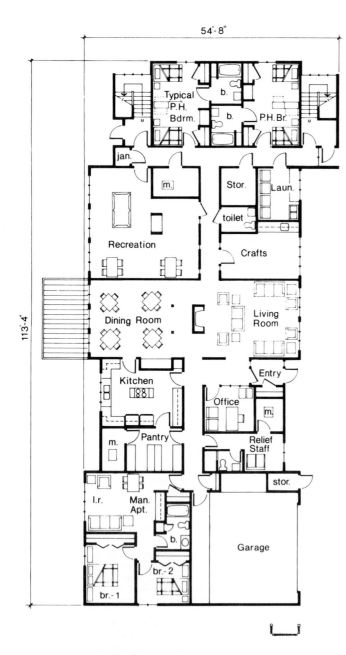

FIRST FLOOR PLAN

Fig. 2 Person group home

Fig. 2 12-Person group home.

OCCUPIED SPACES	2,418
Residents' Bedrooms	
Manager's Apartment	
Relief Staff	
SHARED SPACES	3,112
Recreation	
Living Room	
Dining Room	
Kitchen	
Office	
Corridors	
UTILITY SPACES	510
Storage Room	
Furnace Room	
GARAGE	576
Total Gross Area	6,616 sq ft

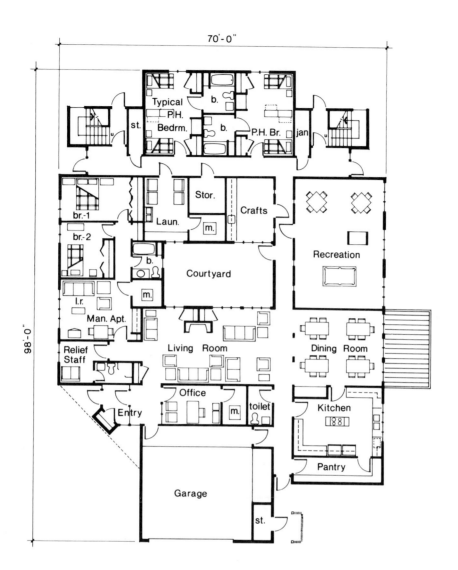

FIRST FLOOR PLAN

Fig. 3 16-Person group home.

OCCUPIED SPACES	2,954
Residents' Bedrooms	
Manager's Apartment	
Relief Staff	
SHARED SPACES	3,416
Recreation	
Living Room	
Dining Room	
Kitchen	
Office	
Corridors	
UTILITY SPACES	600
Storage Room	
Furnace Room	
GARAGE	576
Total Gross Area	7,546 sq ft

SECOND FLOOR PLAN

Residential

SENIOR CITIZENS' CENTER

GENERAL CONSIDERATIONS AND RECOMMENDATIONS

Need	Design recommendations
1. Location	a. Accessible to public transportation.
	b. Centrally located—not remote but with element of privacy. Near other public facilities, if possible, e.g., museums, parks, schools.
2. Site	Level ground is desirable.
3. Layout	a. One level is desirable—elevator for more than two floors.
	b. Window views while seated and physical ease of access to outdoor activities.
	c. Seats at stair landings.
4. Heating and Ventilation	a. Mechanical heating and ventilation throughout.
	b. Separate thermostatic control for selected program areas.
5. Utilities	a. Adequate wiring for electric kitchen appliances, kiln, power machines, audio-visual equipment, etc.
	b. Waist-high electric receptacles in all rooms and convenient outlets as required for power tools, projection equipment, etc.
	c. No loose floor wiring.
	d. Intercommunication system for music, announcements, etc.
	e. Fire alarm.
6. Lighting	a. Intensified but without glare.
	b. Additional lighting in craft areas for depth perception.
7. Acoustics	a. Sound control and acoustical ceilings throughout—special provisions where required.
	b. Investigate problems of hearing aids in large areas. Individual head phones where microphone is used.
8. Equipment	a. Recessed water fountains, fire prevention and control equipment, radiators, pipes, etc.
	b. No projecting parts.
9. Safety	a. All flooring slip-proof.
	b. Elimination of door sills.
	c. Draft control.
	d. Simple circulation between program areas in order to avoid confusion.
	e. Doors wide enough for wheelchairs.
	f. Handrails along hallways.
10. Color	a. Color identification throughout, specifically exits, fire equipment, etc.
	b. Light, bright interior colors.
	c. Avoidance of institutional character.
11. Storage	a. Storage for each area. (See program design recommendations.)

ARRIVAL AND ENTRY

Need	Means and equipment	Design recommendations
1. Pre-arrival	a. Pickup car or bus	a. Storage for car or bus
2. Arrival and Departure		
Members	a. Foot	a. Sheltered approach
	b. Wheelchair	b. Entry without steps
	c. Car	c. Slip-proof pavement
	d. Bus	d. Car and bus turnabout
		e. Accommodation for first high riser for bus
		f. Parking area
Staff, Volunteers, Other Personnel	a. Foot	a. Parking area: Reserved area
	b. Car	b. Separate entry
Visitors	a. Foot	a. Parking area. Same as for members
	b. Car	
Supplies	a. Foot	a. Separate receiving-unloading area
	b. Car	b. Separate receiving-unloading entry
	c. Truck	c. Concealed garbage and refuse storage and pick-up area
3. Entry		
Checking of hats and coats	a. Chair	a. Checkroom with storage space for hats, coats, raingear, parcels
	b. Tables	b. Counter space for 2 attendants
	c. Counter	c. Pocketbook ledge
	d. Clothes racks	d. Good checkroom ventilation
	e. Shelves	

Centers for Older People, The National Council on the Aging, New York, 1962.

162

Need	Means and equipment	Design recommendations
		e. A few tables and chairs to facilitate removal of boots, rubbers, heavy outer clothing
		f. Sufficient space around checkroom for traffic and for checkroom service waiting line.
		g. Toilets
Thrift & Gift Shop	a. Counters b. Tables c. Chairs d. Display case e. Show window f. File	a. Locate near entry with street or lobby show window.
Reception and Daily Registration Desk	a. Desk b. Two chairs c. Bulletin Board	a. Lobby area for daily registration of members at desk and for registration waiting line b. Well-lighted lobby area for bulletin board

SPACE CONSIDERATIONS

Space	Recommended area/person	Recommended minimum areas
1. Entry/Reception	15 sq. ft./person	150 sq. ft.
Coat-room storage	one-lineal foot = 6 garments	50 sq. ft.
2. Quiet Lounge & Library	35 sq. ft./person plus book stack area	
3. Noisy Lounge	35 sq. ft./person	
4. Auditorium and/or Dining	7 sq. ft./person for seated Aud. use 15 sq. ft. for dining and table set-up	
5. Kitchen and Storage	*See footnote	
6. Meeting rooms and/or Classrooms	25 sq. ft./person	
7. Arts and Crafts		
a. Wood working	60 sq. ft./person	600 sq. ft.
b. Painting, ceramics and needlework	25 sq. ft./person	250 sq. ft.
8. Photography Dark Room	80 sq. ft.	80 sq. ft.
9. Arts and Crafts storage	—	80 sq. ft.
10. Administration & Staff Offices		
a. Director and other offices for 1 to 2 persons	—	130 sq. ft.
b. Staff and/or general office	50 sq. ft./person+Files	150 sq. ft.
c. Private Consultation	50 sq. ft./person	600 sq. ft.
d. Staff Rest room	25 sq. ft./person	150 sq. ft.
11. First Aid Room	—	100 sq. ft.
12. Storage (General)	—	100 sq. ft.
13. Toilets	—	(See local or
14. Outdoor Recreation Areas	Varies with site and climate	Nat'l Building Code)
15. Parking	Allow 250 sq. ft./car for parking	

* Note: Size of kitchen would depend on the agency program in respect to serving of meals, snacks, parties, etc.

These rooms may be scheduled for special use. Provision should be made for separate smoking and nonsmoking areas.

LOUNGES AND AUDITORIUM

Need	Means and equipment	Design recommendations
1. Quiet Lounge		
Activities		
Reading	a. Comfortable chairs	a. Self-contained lounge area
Writing	b. Tables, desks	b. Fireplace
Relaxing	c. Books, newspapers,	c. Storage space for:

SENIOR CITIZENS' CENTER

Need	Means and equipment	Design recommendations
Quiet games Meetings	magazines d. Games and cards e. Folding chairs, tables	1. Games (Chess, checkers, dominoes, cards) 2. Extra folding chairs & tables 3. Books, magazines, newspapers

2. Noisy Lounge
Activities
Cards
Active games
Conversation
Parties (small)
Meetings
	a. Chairs and tables
	b. Extra folding chairs and tables
	c. Pool table
	d. Piano
		a. Self-contained lounge area
		b. Storage space for:
		  1. Games (Cards, cues, billiard balls, etc.)
		  2. Folding tables and chairs
		  3. Record player

3. Auditorium
Activities
Parties
Dancing
Movies
Stage Productions
Concerts
 	
Speakers and
Panels
Large meetings
Carnivals; bazaars
Community Service
Projects
Seated dinners
for entire
membership
	a. Chairs—folding and nonfolding
	b. Tables—folding and nonfolding
	c. Audio-visual equipment
	d. Piano
	e. Other musical instruments
	f. Music stands
	g. Public address system
	h. Decoration
	i. Wall exhibits
		a. Area for theater; nonpermanent type seating
		b. Stage
		c. Easy access to stage
		d. Back-stage dressing room
		e. Storage for:
		  1. Folding chairs and tables
		  2. Costumes
		  3. Decorations
		  4. Musical instruments
		  5. Music stands
		  6. Audio-visual equipment (Storage area may be under stage or adjacent to room)
		f. Near kitchen and/or dining room
		g. Near toilets
		h. Wiring for audio-visual equipment must avoid loose floor extension
		i. Wall display space and cabinets
		j. Folding doors

DINING AND REFRESHMENT FACILITIES

Need	Means and equipment	Design recommendations

1. Food Preparation and Service	a. Cooking and baking equipment
	b. Refrigeration
	c. Washing equipment for:
	  1. Dishes, cutlery
	  2. Pots and pans
	  3. Kitchen and dining room cleaning
	d. Cabinets for:
	  1. Dishes, pots, cutlery
	  2. In-use food supplies and staples
	e. Counters for:
	  1. Food preparation
	  2. Food Service
	  3. Return of trays, used dishes
	f. Garbage disposal equipment
	g. Coffee urns
	h. Bulk food supplies
		a. Electrical dishwasher, electric stoves, electric refrigerator
		b. Easy access cabinets—not more than 63 inches high, nor lower than 27 inches for food, dishes, pots, pans, etc.
		c. Exhaust system
		d. Counter space for several serving stations
		e. Counter space for tray returns
		f. Sinks for washing food and cooking utensils and vegetable preparation
		g. Counter space for preparation of food—ample for several kitchen workers
		h. Bulk Storage:
		  1. Adjacent to kitchen for bulk purchased stock
		  2. Direct outside access for deliveries
		i. Area for garbage pails, cleaning equipment, garbage disposal, slop sink for mops
		j. Floor drain wash basin

2. Dining and Snack Service	a. Serving counter and steam tables b. Tray-cutlery-napkin stand	a. Dining area (Cafeteria-style—avoids service of total membership at one time) b. Location—adjacent to large lounge

Need	Means and equipment	Design recommendations
	c. Drinking fountain d. Cashier's table and chair e. Dietician's desk-file f. Program material for groups g. Serving carts—for service other than in cafeteria	or auditorium for seated service of entire membership or other special events c. Counter for sliding trays d. Aisle space to and from counter e. Storage space for trays, cutlery, napkins f. Storage closet for program equipment (Dining room may be used outside of dining hours by special interest groups) g. Storage for serving carts
3. "Portable Home Food Service"*	a. Trays, steam carts b. Car, station wagon, truck	a. Storage for equipment b. Direct access of vehicle to kitchen

* "Portable Home Food Service" is an auxiliary service to home-bound older people, now being offered by some centers, which brings one hot meal and often an additional meal per day into the home of older people in need of such service. It is also alluded to as "Meals on Wheels."

Meetings of groups and classes are a major part of any Center program. These groups may range from classes in creative writing to group discussions on current affairs. They may include a dramatics group or a Great Books course, or any of a wide range of interests. An adequate number of rooms should be provided for these groups, for as the program develops, requirements will increase.

The number of meeting rooms will depend on the size of the Center and the number of individual groups and classes.

Additional meeting space can be provided by using lounge and auditorium space for larger groups.

PROGRAM—GROUP MEETINGS, CLASSES, SPECIAL INTEREST GROUPS

Need	Means and equipment	Design recommendations

1. Music Groups
Choral group
Ensembles
Instrument practice
Listening to music
Music library
TV and hi-fi
	a. Table or desk, file cabinet
	b. Chairs
	c. Piano
	d. TV and adjustable-speed player
	e. Tape recorder
	f. Musical instruments
	g. Music stands
	h. Blackboard
	i. Record albums books
		a. Soundproof room
		b. Storage for:
		  1. Instruments
		  2. Music stands
		  3. Record player and records
		  4. Tape recorder
		c. Built-in blackboard

2. Classes and Meetings	a. Desk or table b. Chairs c. Blackboard d. File cabinet e. Miscellaneous program material	a. Built-in blackboard (Blue or green) b. Storage closet for: Program materials of groups using room (Posters, papers, books) c. Illumination of blackboard area to avoid glare

ARTS AND CRAFTS

Need	Equipment	Design recommendations

Arts and Crafts
Woodworking and metal
	a. Power Tools
	  1. Circular saw
	  2. Jig saw
	  3. Band saw
	  4. Sander
	  5. Grinding wheel
	  6. Wood lathe
	  7. Drill press
	b. Hand tools
		a. Separate room to isolate noise and dirt
		b. Spacious room for free movement around machines
		c. Special wiring for heavy loads with:
		  1. wall and floor outlets
		  2. fuse box switch-off
		d. Storage for:
		  1. Hand tools
		  2. Hardware

Need	Equipment	Design recommendations
	c. Workbenches and chairs	3. Other small equipment and working materials
	d. Heating equipment for metal and jewelry	4. Paints
	e. Lockers	5. Metals and other materials used in metal work
	f. Slop sink	6. Wood:
	g. Wood bins	1. $4' \times 8'$ panels to $2'' \times 4''$ in $8'$ lengths
	h. Paint closet (Metal)	2. Small pieces of wood
	i. Exhaust system	7. Books, patterns, paper
	j. Jewelry bench for two	8. Brooms, dusters
	k. Cleaning equipment	9. First-aid equipment
		e. Wash basin
		f. Slop sink area
Other Arts and Crafts	a. Lockers	g. Fuel area for solder
a. Painting	b. Easels	a. Large room suitable for flexible subdivision into partially separated working areas. (Furniture room dividers not folding walls or panels)
	c. Tables	
	d. Cabinets for supplies	
	e. Chairs	
	f. Slop sinks	b. Occupancy distributed in each working area in changing numbers
b. Ceramics	a. Damp boxes for clay and unfinished work	c. Location—adjacent to all craftsrooms. (Wood-metal, crafts office, craft store room)
	b. Drying shelves	d. Fixed equipment:
	c. Tables and chairs	1. Slop sink, two with special drains and traps
	d. Lockers	2. Ceramics kiln in separate room for safety
	e. Slop sink	3. Closet-like room for drying shelves
	f. Cabinets for glazes, tools and other materials	4. Wash basin
		5. Built-in cabinets with adjustable shelves and upright partitions
	g. Wedging board for two	
	h. Kiln-220 line	
c. Needlework	a. Sewing machines	e. Movable equipment—all equipment other than cabinets should be movable as interests and occupancy vary with changing composition of membership and staff
	b. Tables, chairs	
	c. Cabinets	
		f. Storage for:
d. Weaving and Rug making	a. Floor and table looms	1. Daily supplies—cabinets in rooms
		2. Members' equipment and work lockers
	b. Rug frames	3. Special equipment, supply stock, finished work in separate store room
	c. Tables, chairs	
e. Basketry	a. Slop sink	
	b. Tables, chairs	
	c. Reed lockers	
f. Copper enameling	a. Kiln	4. Books, patterns, files in office
	b. Chairs, tables	
	c. Hand tools	
	d. Glaze cabinets	
g. Other crafts (Paper, leather, shell, etc.)	a. Chairs, tables	
	b. Cabinets	
Photography	a. Sink	a. Small dark room
	b. Rack	b. Sink area plus adequate lighting & ventilation
	c. Chairs, tables	
	d. Developing tanks	
	e. Large trays	
Arts-Crafts Storage	a. Cabinets	a. Central walk-in supply room
	b. Bins	b. Space for:
	c. Shelves	1. Cleaning supplies
	d. Racks	2. Craft materials
		3. Finished articles
Arts-Crafts Office	a. Desks	a. Small area adjacent to crafts rooms with view into them
	b. Files	
	c. Shelves	b. Occupancy: 2–4 part-time workers; 1 full-time worker
	d. Chairs	
	e. Display cabinet	

OUTDOOR ACTIVITIES

Need	Means and equipment	Design recommendations
Relaxing and sunning	a. Chairs b. Tables c. Sun protection (Awnings or umbrellas, trees) d. Fixed trellises, other appropriate baffles	a. Location—accessible only from building b. Level ground with both sun-protected and uncovered areas c. Space for each activity d. Accessible storage space for games and other equipment e. Locate as outdoor extension of lounge
Gardening	a. Ground plots for flowers b. Table top gardens c. Trees and shrubs d. Dwarf fruit trees	
Games a. Quiet games b. Shuffleboard c. Roque d. Boccie e. Croquet	a. Tables b. Chairs c. Benches d. Games equipment and layouts	

ADMINISTRATION AND INDIVIDUAL SERVICES

Need	Means and equipment	Design recommendations
Offices for Administration Counseling, and Other Individual Services		
Director's Office	a. Desk b. Chairs c. Files d. Cabinets	a. Location—adjacent to general office b. Self-contained room—not partitioned c. Coat closet
Program Supervisor's Office	a. Desk b. Chairs c. Files d. Cabinets	a. Location—adjacent to general office b. Self-contained room—not partitioned c. Coat closet

Staff Offices
a. Full-time staff
b. Part-time staff
c. Consultant staff
  1 Medical
  2 Psychiatric
  3 Individual Counseling
  4 Housing
  5 Health & Nutrition
  6 Employment
  7 Others
	a. Desks
	b. Chairs
	c. Files
	d. Bookcases
	e. Cabinets
		All office space which is to be used for individual counseling or consultation must be completely private, not partitioned cubicles. The rooms may be small but comfortable and attractive, and sufficient in number to serve the needs of staff and membership. Office space may be shared by part-time and consultant staff.

Volunteer Office	a. Desks b. Chairs c. Files d. Cabinets	a. Desk space should be allowed for volunteers b. Coat closet
General Office a. Secretarial and clerical staff b. Information Desk	a. Desks b. Chairs c. Files d. Tables e. Safe f. Typewriter	a. Size as required by individual Centers b. Location—adjacent to offices of Director and Supervisor c. Space for members waiting for appointments
Staff Rest Room	a. Chairs b. Couches c. Tables d. Toilets* e. Clothes closet f. Hot plates g. Small refrigerator h. Supply cabinet	a. Space for staff meals b. Plumbing—sinks, toilets c. Location—near offices

* Not opening to staff room if lunches are to be served.

SENIOR CITIZENS' CENTER

Essential Services

Need	Means and equipment	Design recommendations
Toilets	a. Water closets b. Urinals c. Sinks d. Mirrors e. Counters	a. Location—near entry and near activity rooms b. Grab Bars in water closets c. One water closet in each washroom for wheelchair occupant d. Sanitary and slip-proof floors e. Counter space under mirrors for hair-combing, make-up f. Separate staff toilets g. Sanitary wall coverings h. Floor drain i. Self-closing faucets
First-Aid Room*	a. Cot b. Table c. Chairs d. Toilet and sink e. Portable screens f. Stretcher cot	a. Small room for emergency use b. Lavatory
Utility Closets	a. Slop sinks b. Shelves c. Garbage containers d. Broom and mop racks e. Work pails	a. Location—convenient to each area of building b. Size—to hold sink, brooms, brushes, mops, pails and working supply of cleaning materials
Drinking Fountains	Bubble-type, except in dining room	Locate near lounge and craft areas and outdoor areas
Public Telephones	1–2 booths with seats	Locate near entry
General Storage	Extra equipment and miscellaneous supplies	Use space for storage other than specified
Garbage and Refuse	Garbage cans and hand truck	a. Concealed and ventilated b. Floor drain c. Hose bib

* First-Aid Room can be used for individual counseling.

Optional Services

Need	Means and equipment	Design recommendations
Portable Home Food Service	a. Trays, steam carts b. Car, station wagon, truck	a. Storage for equipment b. Direct access of vehicle to kitchen
Vending Machines	a. Candy and cigarettes	a. Locate near lounge-dining area
Thrift-Gift Shop	a. Counters b. Tables c. Chairs d. Display case e. Show window f. File	a. Locate near entry with street or lobby show window
Beauty and Barber Facilities	a. Chairs b. Storage c. Sink facilities d. Mirrors	

SUGGESTED RECOMMENDATIONS FOR PROGRAM FOR 65–100 OCCUPANTS

Space	Building area, sq ft	Occupancy (approx.)
1. Lounge and Game Area	600 Multifunction space	17–60
2. Auditorium Dining-Kitchen		
3. Library		
4. Meeting, class room	500 (Subdivide as per program)	10–50
5. Craft Room		
6. Office for Director	130	
7. First Aid	100	
8. Staff—		
a. Staff or meeting room	150	
b. Staff Lounge	150	
9. a. Dark Room	80	
b. Storage Room	300	
10. Public toilets	200	
	2210	
11. Add 20% walls & circulations	440	
Total Buildings	2650	
12. Outdoor Recreation Areas	Varies with site and climate	
13. Parking 10 cars and pickup	2500	

LOCATION

The location of mobile homes and mobile home developments is usually controlled by zoning. Generally, zoning is based upon a land-use plan for the community, backed up by sound planning principles. However, the basis for mobile home zoning is frequently underlain by emotional considerations, rather than land-use planning.

Mobile homes, and mobile home developments in particular, have the reputation of being visually unattractive and of attracting lower-income housing and people. Communities tend to look at mobile homes as affecting property values and as tax liabilities. For these major reasons, mobile homes are often relegated to parts of the community which are undesirable for other uses or rural

This section is from *Guidelines for Improving the Mobile Home Living Environment,* Office of Policy Development and Research, HUD, Washington, D.C., 1978.

out-of-the-way and out-of-sight places. Most of these areas have neither utilities nor community facilities but are selected to be developed as high-density living environments.

Mobile home developments are rarely allowed or encouraged in areas well suited for residential development. The normally accepted planning principles for residential land-use planning are to locate residential uses:

- in areas of compatible land use and surrounding environments;
- in areas with adequate utility and road support systems;
- in areas with reasonable convenience to community facilities;
- in areas of similar density such as a mobile home density of 4 to 7 dwelling units per acre, much like townhouses and low density apartments; and
- in areas of logical extension or infilling of the existing urban growth pattern.

These principles are often ignored with regard to mobile home zoning.

LAYOUT

The layout of a mobile home subdivision is normally a gridlike arrangement of parallel roads about 200 feet apart linked together by other local or collector roads. This arrangement is used because most development costs are determined by the amount of road frontage required for each lot. Lining the mobile homes up perpendicular to the road requires the least road frontage and is the most economical arrangement of lots.

Common facilities like swimming pools and community buildings, when provided, are usually centrally located within the development and are often located as a focal point along the entrance drive. Facilities are maintained by the developer or homeowners' association and each resident is charged a monthly rate for use and maintenance.

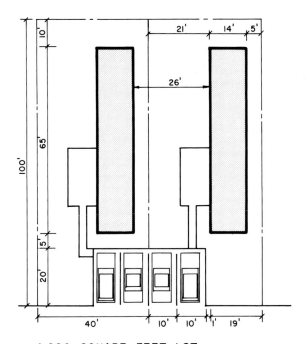

4,000 SQUARE FEET LOT

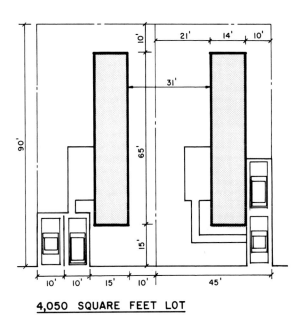

4,050 SQUARE FEET LOT

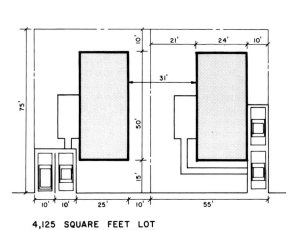

4,125 SQUARE FEET LOT

4,250 SQUARE FEET LOT

Fig. 1

169

MOBILE HOMES AND PARKS

The typical subdivision lot consists of about 4,000–4,500 square feet of land with overall dimensions of 40 by 100 feet or 45 by 90 feet for single and 50 by 85 feet or 55 by 75 feet for double-wide homes. The lot fronts on a road built to local specifications for dedicated roads, but may not actually be dedicated to the municipality. The road right-of-way is usually a minimum of 50 feet wide and contains a 24- to 30-foot paved cartway. (See Fig. 1.)

INDIVIDUAL MOBILE HOME LOT

The mobile home lot is the land area, large or small, upon which the home is placed and which provides space for all of the belongings and activities of its occupant.

Required Functional Areas

The individual mobile home lot consists of six component areas which reflect the basic functions of the mobile home site—pad, parking, entrance, outdoor living, utility corridor and storage. The arrangement of these six functional components of the lot is somewhat variable, but typically looks like Fig. 2.

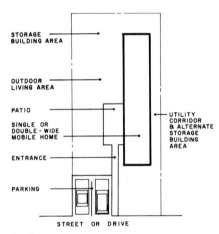

Fig. 2

The only component of this arrangement that is fixed is the utility side of the home which is always on the right side when facing the mobile home hitch. The other areas are variable, depending primarily upon the lot size and unit orientation on the lot.

Each mobile home lot is usually required, by ordinance, to provide the pad, parking area, outdoor living and storage areas. Existing standards vary, but typically define a minimum lot size and minimum yard areas, which does not give the flexibility of lot size required because of the highly variable size of homes. A minimum distance between homes and setbacks allows this lot size flexibility.

Convenience in Relationship of Use Areas

The arrangement of the six functional component areas of the lot should be determined by the floor plan of the home, the characteristics of each site, and the logical and convenient relationship of on-lot space. The sequence in which residents use the component areas should be reflected in the lot arrangement. The occupant arrives at home in a car, makes his way from the car to the door and goes in. He lives in his house and occasionally moves outside of his home into the yard area as an extension of his living space. Logically, the parking area should be between the park entrance and door. The outdoor living area should be adjacent to the home and near one of the two entrances. (See Fig. 3.)

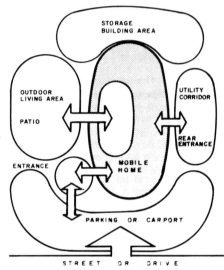

Fig. 3

Circulation—Hierarchy of Streets

Streets within mobile home developments should be grouped into four functional categories: (See Fig. 4).
1. courts, places, culs-de-sac,
2. local streets,
3. subcollectors, and
4. collectors

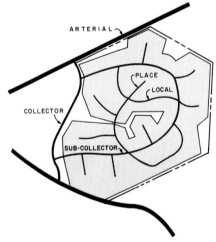

Fig. 4 Street categories.

Courts, places or culs-de-sac are very minor residential streets, the primary purpose of which is to serve individual lots and provide access to local or higher forms of streets. A place may be a dead-end, culs-de-sac street or court with no through traffic and with limited on-street parking. Local streets are generally short and may have culs-de-sac, courts, or occasionally two or three branching places. Usually, no through traffic should exist between two streets of a higher classification. The purpose of a local street is to connect traffic to and from dwelling units to subcollectors.

Subcollectors provide access to local streets and courts, places, or culs-de-sac and conduct this traffic to an activity center or to a collector street. A subcollector may be a loop street connecting one collector or outside arterial street at two points, or conducting traffic between collector streets or arterial streets.

Collectors are the principal traffic arteries within residential areas and carry fairly high traffic volumes. They function to conduct traffic to or between major arterial streets outside the residential areas. A well-planned neighborhood maximizes the number of mobile homes located on either local streets or courts, places, and culs-de-sac where there is no through traffic between streets of higher classification. Homes having direct access to subcollectors and collectors are allowable, but should be minimized. Local streets and courts are safe and desirable places to live; living areas are dominant and traffic movement is subordinate.

Only a single moving traffic lane is necessary on local streets or courts, while subcollectors and collectors should have two moving lanes. Frontage of living areas on entrance roads and collector streets should be minimized.

Street alignments should be based upon sight distance and probable roadway speeds using computation methods endorsed by the Institute of Traffic Engineers. Generally, a minimum practical curve radius in residential areas is 100 feet, with 30 feet acceptable on minor streets. Street alignment at intersections is especially critical. The preferred angle of street intersections is 90 degrees; for safety purposes, streets should never intersect at angles less than 80 degrees. When two streets intersect the same street, they should either form a through intersection or be offset by at least 100 feet.

Street gradients affect the visual character, safety and accessibility of the mobile home development. Generally speaking, grades between 2 and 7 percent are the most desirable; and a minimum of 0.5 percent is necessary on all curbed streets to prevent pooling of water. If gradients must be less than the minimum in very flat areas, special subgrade compaction and street construction controls are necessary. Streets of less than 2 percent grade are visually perceived as flat. Moderate slopes of 2 to 7 percent usually result in a more interesting street-scape and encourage more imagination in the siting of homes.

Streets should generally not exceed 12 percent grade, but on minor streets grades of up to 15 percent are acceptable. Where steep road gradients are unavoidable, care must still be taken to flatten grades at intersection areas; gradients within 100 feet of intersections should not exceed 10 percent, with 4 to 6 percent preferable in snow or ice areas for a distance of 50 feet.

Circulation layout determines the accessibility of the mobile home site within each development. In properly designed residential neighborhoods without through traffic, travel distances from residences to collector streets are short, actual traffic speeds are low, lane capacity is not a controlling design factor, and inconvenience or short delay is a minor consideration.

In conventional single-family residential neighborhoods, traffic speed should be slow: approximately 25 miles per hour. In mobile home areas where density is higher, speed should not exceed 15 miles per hour. Momentary delays to allow other traffic to pass around parked cars is acceptable and it is customary to drive slowly to avoid children and pets.

Pavement widths should be determined by considering probable peak-traffic volume, parking needs, and limitations imposed by sight distance, climate, terrain and maintenance requirements. It is senseless for streets to be wider than absolutely necessary; excessive widths only increase development costs which are passed on to the lot renter or owner. Also, from an ecological point of view, avoiding excessively wide streets means less impervious surface which results in less storm water runoff. The special problem of delivering mobile homes to lots is not a major consideration in determining street widths. Spacing between the mobile homes and the grades from street to lot are of much greater concern. Movement of mobile homes from their original placement on a lot is uncommon. When homes are to be moved through narrow streets, notice may be given to remove parked cars from the street.

Where streets also serve as pedestrian walks, they should be built with a cartway 2 feet wider than otherwise required. All entrance streets and other collector streets with guest parking should be 28 to 30 feet wide; this provides for two moving lanes and a parking lane on one side. Collector streets without parking should be 24 to 26 feet wide. Minor streets with parking on one side should be 26 feet wide; and local streets, courts, plazas and culs-de-sac with no parking should be 20 feet wide. A 20-foot wide pavement is the minimum width which generally offers year-round utility and convenience where snow and ice control is necessary.

One-way streets may be allowed at 11-foot widths in the following situations: (1) adequate off-street parking is assured; (2) the climate is mild, and snow and ice control problems cannot be foreseen; (3) total loop length will not exceed about 500 feet; (4) no more than about 25 dwelling units are served; (5) adequate longitudinal sight distances can be provided; and (6) vehicle speeds may be reasonably expected in the 10- to 15-mile-per-hour range. A 16-foot-wide pavement may be a practical loop street alternative in difficult terrain where cross-pavement ground slopes are severe, where vehicle speeds will not exceed 10 miles per hour, and where other above-outlined considerations can be met. Under the various conditions outlined, the 16-foot-wide pavement can be functionally effective, but will result in a higher level of resident inconvenience than a wider pavement. Sixteen feet cannot be considered a desirable pavement width but must be conceded to be acceptable under certain conditions, where necessary to avoid destruction of natural features.

Street rights-of-way are a consideration unique to the mobile home subdivision development. Streets within rental parks simply aren't dedicated to the municipality since the entire park properly is owned by the park developer-operator. In order to achieve maximum density, a park developer

will usually retain ownership of roads and therefore does not have to meet local standards for roads or reserve a wide right-of-way.

Within the mobile home subdivision, the streets and street rights-of-way are dedicated or retained in the ownership of the homeowners' association.

When roads are to be dedicated, they have to meet the same standards applied to all roads within residential areas. This generally means that a 50-foot right-of-way is required. The resulting arrangement of space, small lots and wide rights-of-way, is comparatively wasteful of space. Space is still lacking where it is most needed (in the outdoor living area of individual homes) because lot sizes are still usually small. On the other hand, an excess of space is provided where it is needed least. The distance between homes on opposite sides of streets is sometimes 70 to 80 feet, a more generous spacing than is needed in a small lot development.

Street rights-of-way must be adequate to provide required street pavements, sidewalks, drainage facilities, and utilities as needed, when they are placed in the rights-of-way. Right-of-way widths are too frequently fixed uniformly by local ordinances, regardless of the actual space required to accommodate necessary improvements. Excessively wide rights-of-way waste land and result in avoidable maintenance costs to the municipality; a community realizes no tax revenue from street rights-of-way. This land would be better devoted to individual building sites rather than public right-of-way.

Sidewalks along the road edge in suburban residential areas are being provided less frequently than in the past, and the amount of pedestrian use varies. Placement of sidewalks immediately adjacent to the road isn't really a safe location unless curbs are provided. More elaborate developments have interior pedestrian paths linking logical origins and destinations such as clusters of individual homes to community facilities or to convenience commercial areas. Paths or sidewalks other than these are not necessary in low-traffic-movement areas.

Drainage facilities may include either grassed swales or curb gutters and subsurface storm drainage structures. Where roadside drainage swales are used, they normally require a right-of-way at least 10 feet wider than the pavement width. Thus if a 28-foot pavement is used and swales are located on both sides, a total right-of-way of 48 feet would be required. If streets are curbed, there may be no justifiable reason for right-of-way widths to be much wider than roadway pavements.

Dead-end streets must be provided with turn-around areas. Turn-arounds in most conventional single family subdivisions are cul-de-sac streets with a 75- to 80-foot-diameter paved area. It is fairly common in mobile home parks to eliminate the turning circle for streets with fewer than twenty-five homes, substituting a "T" or "Y" turn-around incorporated into a parking lot cluster. "T" and "Y" turn-arounds should utilize an 18-foot minimum radius on all turns. The residential dead-end turn-around is basically for automobile use, but larger vehicles must sometimes be accommodated. Residential streets will also be used, in decreasing order of frequency, by refuse collectors, delivery trucks, snowplows, moving vans and fire trucks. Experience has shown that circular paved turning areas 75 to 80 feet in diameter function very well.

Curbs along residential streets are usually justified for three reasons; (1) preventing the roadway pavement from breaking down, (2) controlling traffic from encroaching beyond paved surfaces, and (3) concentrating and channelizing storm-water runoff. Valid arguments have also been made against the use of curbs, making a clearcut answer difficult. Proponents of curbless streets regard curbs as both a needless expense and an ecologically unsound practice which disrupts natural surface drainage and requires expensive storm drainage facilities. Such facilities frequently concentrate storm water and produce water velocities which necessitate the collection of water in pipes and storm water systems. These conditions tend to minimize the amount of water infiltrating the ground and can cause a considerable amount of fast-moving water to leave the site and cause off-site flooding and erosion. Swales, an alternative to curbs, can collect water where velocity is slowed and allow it to be absorbed into the ground. Proponents of curbless streets also question the reliability of curbs as a safety measure, citing how easy it is for a vehicle to strike or go over a curb and out of control.

The decision to use curbs should largely be based on how effectively storm water can be removed from the site without causing harmful on- or off-site impacts. The feasibility of using swales should be explored as a preferred alternative over the use of curbs during the early planning phase. If curbs are used, the rolled curb may be more desirable due to the numerous crossovers required for frequent on-lot parking areas, yet its effectiveness in controlling traffic may be less. If curbs are not used, pavements can be prevented from unraveling by using a thickened-edge pavement, extending the base course beyond the paving surface by 6 to 8 inches, or using anchored steel edging flush with the pavement surface.

COMMUNITY FACILITIES*

The need for community facilities is related to the density of the development. Community facilities are especially important in small lot developments where private outdoor space is limited; they are somewhat less critical where lots are large enough to allow many activities in individual yards. At higher densities, community open space can compensate for small private exterior living space.

Regulations for community facilities and open space systems typically require that at least 8 percent of the gross site area be devoted to recreational facilities and that a community building, storm shelter, laundry and drying facilities, toilets, and a management office be provided. Depending on the size of the development, however, all of these facilities may not be desirable or necessary.

Tot lots and areas for children to play away from the mobile homes are especially necessary to minimize disturbance of the individual residents' outdoor living areas. In developments where lots are greater than 10,000 square feet, there is less dependence upon community space; but playground and park areas for large-scale activities are desirable as in any residential area.

Community areas should have a parklike atmosphere compatible with residential living environments. Community buildings and structures should also be designed in a manner compatible

* SOURCE: *Guidelines for Improving the Mobile Home Living Environment,* Office of Policy Development and Research, HUD, Washington, D.C., 1978.

MOBILE HOMES AND PARKS

with a residential living environment rather than a commercial development.

Public outdoor open space commonly consists of two types: "structured" and "unstructured" facilities. Structured facilities include formal playgrounds, golf courses, shuffleboard courts, tennis courts, swimming pools, and related facilities. Structured facilities are normally developed in a complex with a community building. Equally im-

portant are the unstructured public open spaces which can be as simple as open grass areas for spontaneous team games and other activities. The type of community facilities necessary for any mobile home development is determined by the occupants to be served. A family-oriented development may require more extensive outdoor open space for active recreation, whereas a retirement community may require less space but a greater

variation of activity areas. Community facilities commonly include such things as swimming pools, community buildings, vehicle storage areas, pedestrian paths, tot lots, and court games.

Community Building

A community facility which is common to most new mobile home parks is the community building.

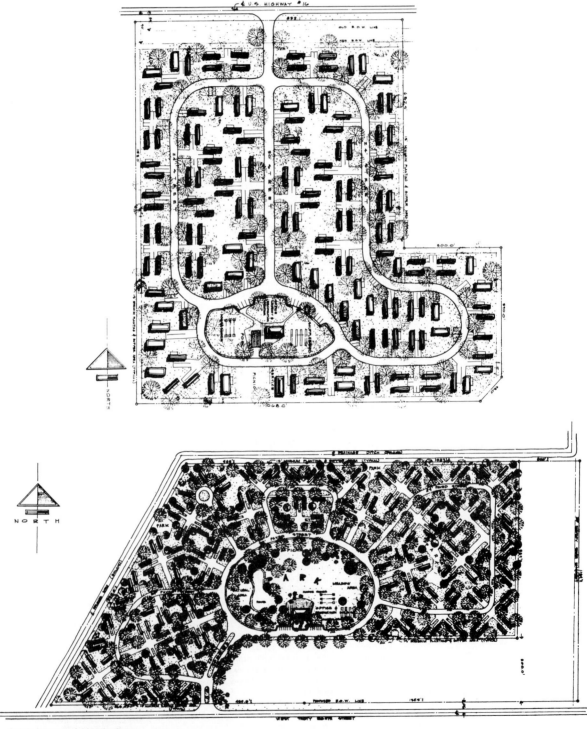

Fig. 5   Mobile home park sketch plans.

It contains more than one activity and serves more than one function. Uses commonly built into a community building include: laundry facilities, meeting rooms, recreation rooms and, in the case of family-oriented parks, day-care centers. The building is normally constructed as part of a complex including structured outdoor recreation facilities, such as swimming pools and limited off-street parking. Community buildings should be designed with a residential character harmonious with the mobile home development. When constructed and managed properly, the community building can be a major asset to the mobile home environment. The key word becomes "management," for after the mobile home development is established and the community building is constructed, it is the responsibility of the homeowners' association in subdivisions, and the operator in parks, to maintain the structure and operate the activity programs.

A secondary, but very important, function of the community building is that of storm shelter for mobile home residents. In areas of the country where dangerous storms might occur, a structurally adequate community building of ample capacity must be provided for the residents' safety.

The Mobile Home Manufacturers Association recommends that approximately 10 to 15 square feet of floor area per mobile home unit should be provided.

Common Vehicular Storage Area

Much of the clutter and disarray in mobile home parks is due to the lack of a defined storage area for seldom-used vehicles or recreational vehicles. Provisions for storage of these vehicles should be included in the mobile home development, especially where lots are small. In many mobile home parks, residents have more leisure time than their conventional housing counterparts; recreational equipment, snowmobiles, boats, and travel trailers are sometimes abundant. Recreational vehicles generally take up too much space to be stored on each individual home site. Common areas accessible to all residents of the development are necessary to store such vehicles or equipment. The storage area should be separated from the living areas of the site and should be a gravel or hard surface area enclosed by a security fence and adequately screened from sight. At least one storage space should be provided for every 19 mobile homes.

Swimming Pools

Swimming pools do much to enhance the image of a mobile home community. In fact, most high-quality mobile home parks include a swimming pool or some equivalent structured recreational facility. The generally isolated location of mobile home developments suggests that such a facility is desirable, especially under certain climatic conditions and for specific segments of the mobile home market. Swimming pools are usually located near a community building and other structured facilities, and should be designed to accommodate the anticipated usership without undue crowding. An estimate of participation rate during typical summer weekends provides the basis for determining an appropriate pool size. This rate of participation varies with the expected population characteristics of the development. Approximately one-quarter of the persons at the pool will be in the water at any one time, and the pool should be designed to provide 10 to 15 square feet of water surface for each wader and 30 square feet for each swimmer. Deck area equal to or larger than the pool surface area should be provided. Most participants also desire a large, fenced-in turf area of equal size for sunbathing.

A general rule of thumb for estimating required pool area is to provide 3 square feet of pool surface for each mobile home lot. (This standard assumes 2 potential participants per home, 20 percent participation rate, 25 percent of actual participants in pool at any one time, and 30 square feet of surface per swimmer.)

Tot Lots and Playgrounds

Tot lots are small playgrounds consisting of several pieces of play apparatus, swings, or climbing equipment provided especially for use by young children. They should be located close to the homes which they serve or within the community recreation area where they can be easily observed and supervised. Ideally, a small tot lot could be established for each grouping of homesites so that children could use them without crossing collector streets in the development. Tot lots also work well when located adjacent to adult recreation areas so that children may be observed by adults using other facilities.

Playgrounds are somewhat larger in scale than tot lots and are normally oriented to elementary-school-age children. They should have safe apparatus which provide opportunities for children to use a variety of motor skills. Such equipment can include: tire or other flexible-seat swings; seesaws with tire safety stops; climbing arches or other apparatus on "soft" surface; and splinter-free climbing blocks.

Court Games

Basketball and tennis courts are popular facilities for adult recreation. They can often be incorporated into a centralized recreation clubhouse complex where they are easily accessible via streets and pedestrian paths. Both facilities require much space, serve a limited number of people at any one time, and can benefit from night lighting which increases the number of people who can be served.

General Court Games

- Provide a variety of facilities to serve various age groups including:

  basketball courts (hard surface)—50 users per half court, daily capacity
  Volleyball (in lawn area)—72 users per court, daily capacity
  shuffleboard (hard surface)—20 users per court, daily capacity

- Lighting for night use of court areas is desirable and will increase daily capacity by 20 to 30 percent.

Tennis Courts

- Provide a fenced, low-maintenance, all-weather (hard-surface) court.
- General capacity is 20 participants per day per court.
- Lighting for night use is desirable and will increase capacity by 40 percent.

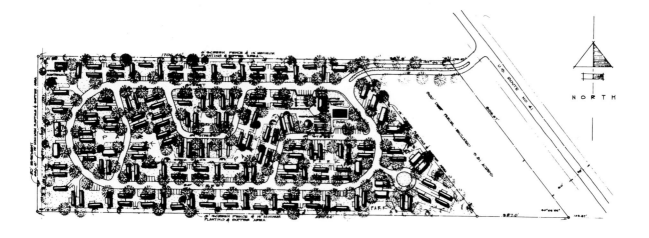

MOBILE HOMES AND PARKS

STANDARD DETAILS – SEWER AND WATER
CONNECTIONS FOR MOBILE HOMES

A	NON-FREEZING WALL HYDRANT
B	MAIN SHUT-OFF VALVE
C	WATER CONNECTION (3/4" COPPER TUBING)
D	WATER RISER PIPE (SEE DETAILS)
E	MOBILE HOME DRAIN OUTLET
F	SEWER CONNECTIONS (SEE DETAIL)
G	SEWER RISER PIPE (SEE DETAIL)

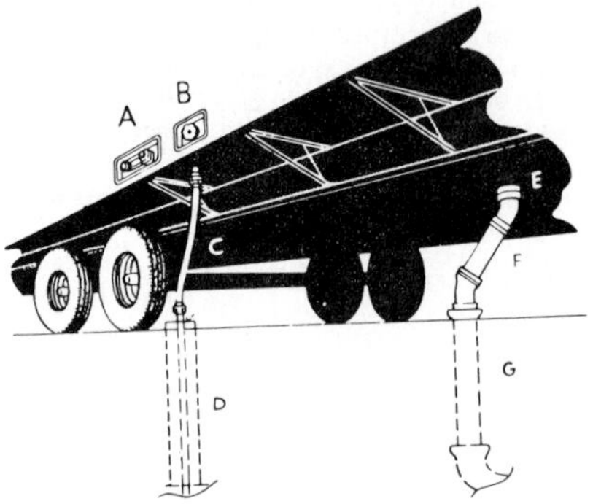

(a)

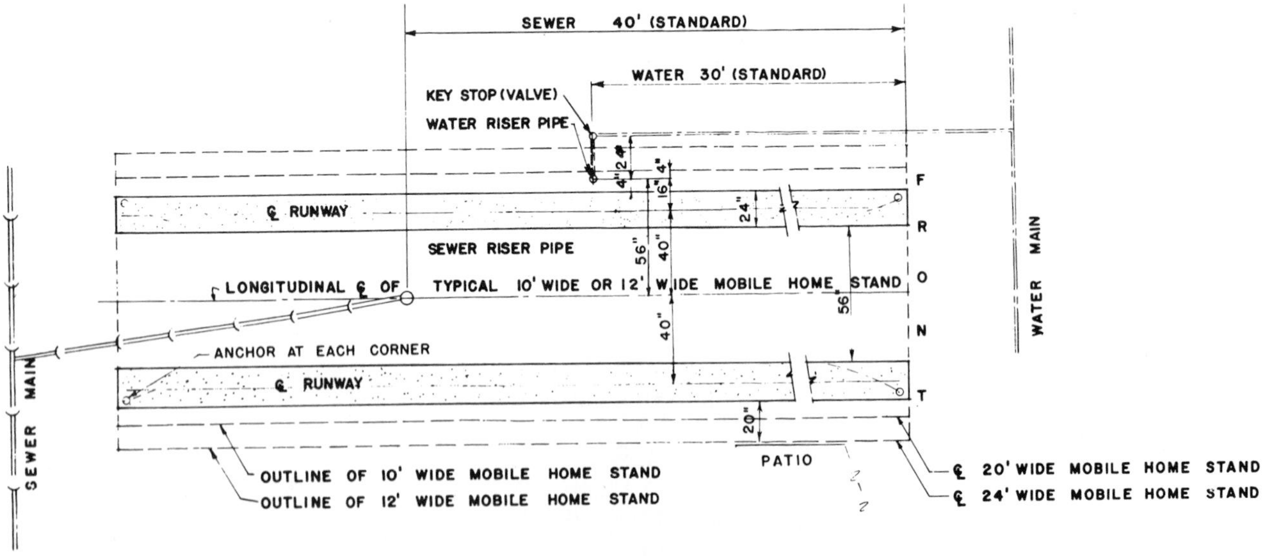

(b)

Fig. 6   (a) Typical pipe connections to mobile homes. (b) Location of water and sewer riser pipes.

SOURCE: Mobile Homes Manufacturers Association.

174

OFFICE, MOBILE HOME PARK

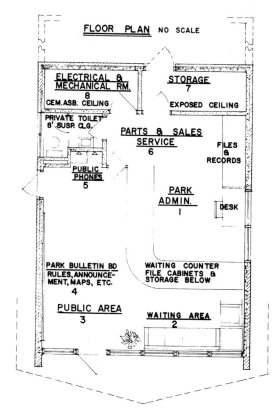

NOTE: SIZE AND FACILITIES SHOWN FOR THIS OFFICE BUILDING IS BASED ON HYPOTHETICAL CONDITIONS AND IS NOT MEANT TO BE AN ILLUSTRATION OF A MODEL OFFICE FOR ANY PARK.

ANY GIVEN PARK HAS CONDITIONS WHICH DICTATE WHAT AN OFFICE BUILDING SHOULD HAVE TO FUNCTION PROPERLY, THE FOLLOWING CONDITIONS SHOULD BE CONSIDERED---

1 PARK ADMINISTRATION AREA

2 WAITING AREA

3 PUBLIC AREA

4 PARK INFORMATION CENTER

5 PUBLIC PHONES

6 PARTS & SALES SERVICE

7 STORAGE

8 ELECTRICAL & MECHANICAL RC

OTHER THAN SIZE OF BUILDING, TYPE OF CONSTRUCTION AND AREA LOCATION, SOME OF THE FACTORS WHICH DICTATE SIZE OF AREA REQUIRED ARE: REQUIREMENTS OF ELECTRIC, PHONE, GAS & WATER COMPANIES & LOCAL CODES FOR INCOMING SERVICES, METERING, PROTECTION & SUPERVISION FOR THE PARK UTILITIES, AS WELL AS VENTILATION, SPACE & WATER HEATING, ELECTRIC PANELS, ETC, FOR THE BUILDING ITSELF.

ADDITIONAL AREA REQUIREMENTS MAY BE: CENTRAL LIGHTING CONTROL STATION AND CENTRAL T.V. ANTENNA RELAY STATION.

NOTE: ALL ABOVE INFORMATION MUST BE DETERMINED LOCALLY BY THE PROSPECTIVE PARK OWNER. THERE ARE NO NATIONAL AVERAGES OR A "TYPICAL" OFFICE BUILDING TO FIT ALL CONDITIONS.

Fig. 7 Park office building. (George Muramoto, Architect)

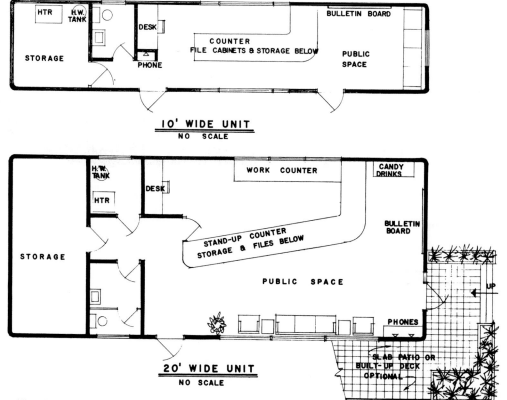

Fig. 8 Park office mobile units. (George Muramoto, Architect)

MOBILE HOMES AND PARKS

LAUNDRY, MOBILE HOME PARK

CHECK OWN PARK DEMANDS BY LOCAL INVESTIGATIONS OF:

1. AVAILABLE COMMUNITY FACILITIES NEARBY.
2. NUMBER OF COACHES WITH OWN LAUNDRY FACILITIES.
   (THE NUMBER OF UNITS MANUFACTURED WITH LAUNDRY FACILITIES IS GROWING EACH YEAR.)
3. SEASONAL AND WEATHER CONDITIONS TO ESTABLISH RATIO OF WASHERS TO DRYERS- AND TENANT PREFERENCES FOR EITHER OR BOTH TYPES OF DRYING.
4. DEMAND FOR ADDITIONAL LAUNDRY SERVICES OR SPACE SUCH AS IRONING, HANDLING, PACKAGING ETC.
5. COMPARE COSTS AND/OR NEED FOR COMMERCIAL-TYPE EXTRACTORS & DRYERS.

INTERIOR ROOM FINISHES

	MINIMUM	GOOD
FLOOR	CONCRETE*	CERAMIC TILE OR TERRAZZO
BASE	COVED CONC.*	COVED CERAMIC TILE, FACING TILE OR TERRAZZO
WALLS	CEMENT ENAMEL OR EPOXY SPRAYED ON CONC. BLOCK.	CERAMIC TILE OR FACING TILE
CEILING	CEM. PLASTER	MINERAL ACOUSTICAL TILE

* WITH HARDENER ADDITIVE

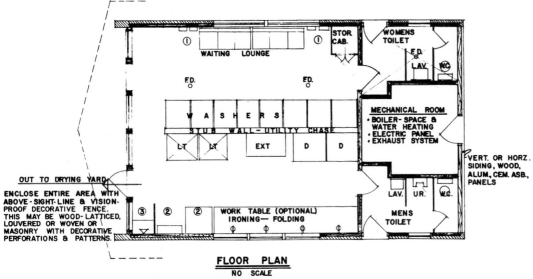

SYMBOLS

W - WASHER
LT- LAUNDRY TRAY, DOUBLE
D - DRYER
EXT- COMMERCIAL EXTRACTOR
SS- SERVICE SINK
⊕ WALL OUTLETS
① DISPENSER-DETERGENT, SOAP, STARCH, BLUING, BLEACH, ETC
② DISPENSER, CANDY, DRINKS, ETC. (OPTIONAL)
③ TELEPHONE

ABBREVIATIONS

W.C. WATER CLOSET
UR. URINAL
LAV. LAVATORY
F.D. FLOOR DRAIN

Fig. 9 Typical minimum laundry building facilities for a mobile home park of about 100 spaces. (George Muramoto, Architect)

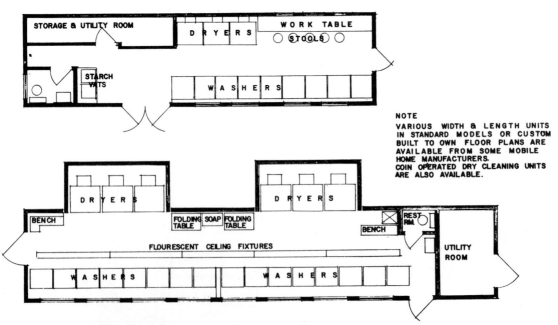

NOTE
VARIOUS WIDTH & LENGTH UNITS IN STANDARD MODELS OR CUSTOM BUILT TO OWN FLOOR PLANS ARE AVAILABLE FROM SOME MOBILE HOME MANUFACTURERS. COIN OPERATED DRY CLEANING UNITS ARE ALSO AVAILABLE.

Fig. 10 Typical mobile laundry units. (George Muramoto, Architect)

MOBILE HOME PARK

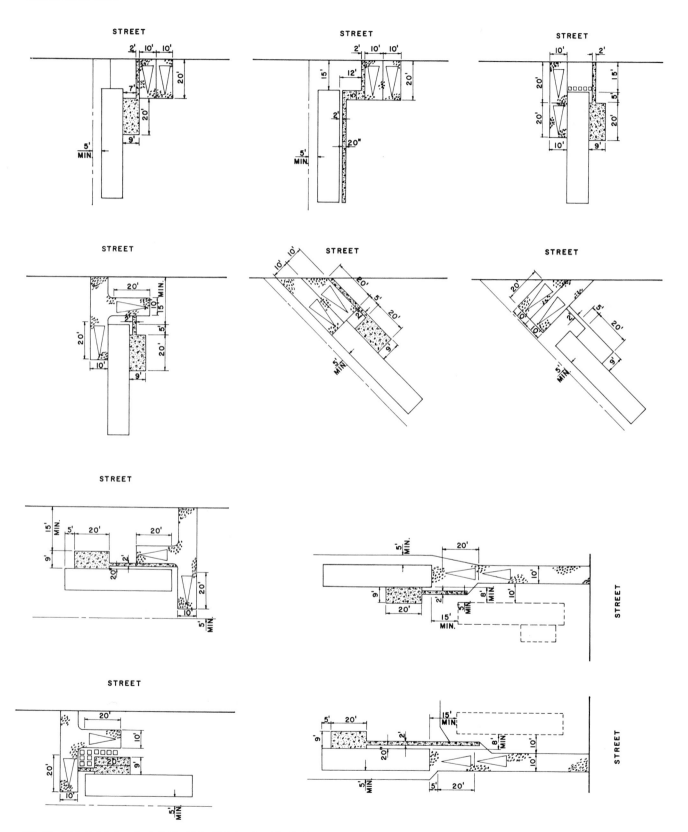

Fig. 11 Typical plot plans for individual lots. (H. Behrend and D. Ghorbani)

MOBILE HOMES AND PARKS

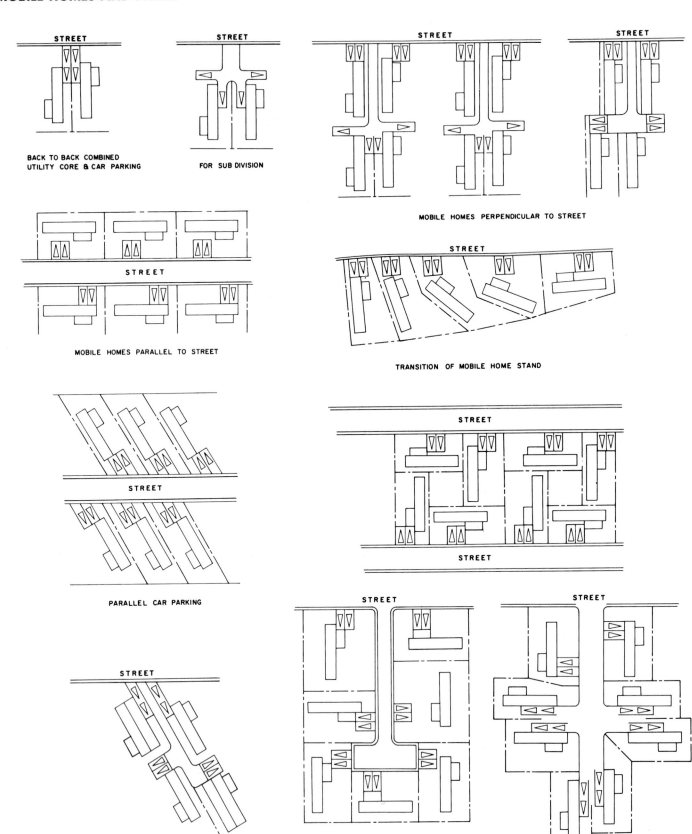

BACK TO BACK COMBINED
UTILITY CORE & CAR PARKING

FOR SUB DIVISION

MOBILE HOMES PERPENDICULAR TO STREET

MOBILE HOMES PARALLEL TO STREET

TRANSITION OF MOBILE HOME STAND

PARALLEL CAR PARKING

TANDEM AND PARALLEL
CAR PARKING

MOBILE HOMES PARALLEL & PERPENDICULAR
TO STREET.

Fig. 12 Mobile home park modules.

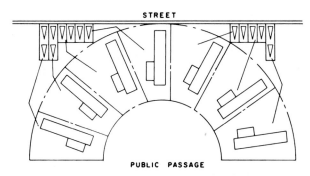

ORIENTATION TOWARD COMMON POINT OF INTEREST.

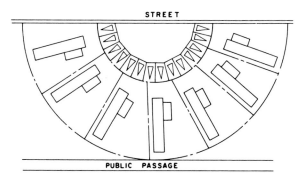

ORIENTATION TOWARD STREET.

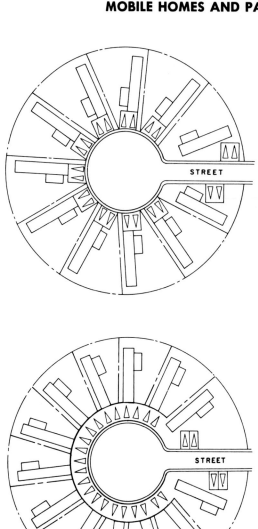

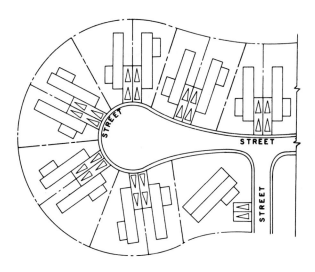

ALL MODULES SHOWN ON THESE SHEETS
HAVE BEEN EXTRACTED FROM WORKING DRAWINGS AND SITE
PLANS PROVIDED BY THE FOLLOWING ARCHITECTS AND LANDSCAPE
ARCHITECTS, CONSULTANTS TO THE LAND DEVELOPMENT
DIVISION OF M.H.M.A.: DAN ABERNATHY, CLAY ADAMSON,
TONY BARNES, JOHN COOPER, ROBERT EBL,JOE GERACI,
EDWARD GEUBTNER, MARTY GILCHRIST, STEVE LUND,TOM MIERZWA,
DONALD MOLNAR, TED POTZNER, ROBERT PHILLIPS, PHILLIPS RUSH,
DOUGLAS RUTH, DONALD WESTPHAL, LARRY WHITLOCK.
THE STAFF OF LAND DEVELOPMENT DIVISION REFINED THESE
MODULES AND COORDINATED THE PROGRAM.

Fig. 12 (cont.)   Mobile home park modules.

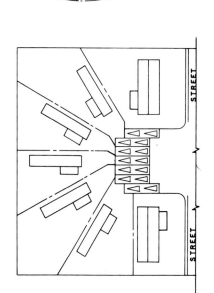

SEVEN UNIT MODULE. SEMI-COMMON
PARKING BAY.

179

Residential

YOUTH HOSTELS

1. INTRODUCTION

A Youth Hostel Described

A youth hostel provides for young people on their travels what a hotel provides for adults: a place to sleep, wash, and eat. But whereas a hotel segregates people—in private rooms and at private tables—a youth hostel brings them together; it is a meeting place at which young people of different nationalities, social backgrounds and opinions can meet and come to know each other.

The simplest youth hostel, in a country district frequented by walkers or climbers, will provide only the basic requirements of dormitories, washrooms, sanitary installation, and a kitchen in which travellers can prepare their own meals. On the other hand, a large modern youth hostel, in a city or main tourist center, will offer comfortable bedrooms with four to eight beds, hot shower baths, recreation rooms, a restaurant or cafeteria, and other facilities. (See Fig. 1.)

Each youth hostel is in the charge of adult houseparents or 'wardens' (generally a married couple) who have an educational as well as an administrative function; their task is to weld the group of young strangers under their roof into a friendly and happy community for the brief period of two or three days. The charge for accommodation is kept to the minimum consistent

SOURCE: *The Design, Construction and Equipment of Youth Hostels,* International Youth Hostel Federation, Welwyn Garden City, England, 1975.

with adequate standards. For this reason simplicity is the rule—there are no servants, and visitors normally take a share of the domestic duties in the hostel; beds are equipped only with mattress and blankets, each visitor bringing his own sheet sleeping bag in place of sheets; furnishing is simple though it may be in good taste.

'Youth' is a word which cannot be rigidly defined, and there are few countries in which a strict age limit is applied. Preference is generally given, however, to visitors aged under 25, while 10 years is considered the minimum age for international usage of hostels.

In order to exercise some control over the use of hostels, admission is restricted to holders of a membership card, but a card can be obtained for a very modest charge (graded according to age) and no discrimination is shown against any applicant on grounds of religion, politics, race, colour, etc. Membership cards issued in any country within the International Youth Hostel Federation are accepted at youth hostels in every other country.

Consequently, hostels should have a certain uniformity, so that, in whatever part of the world it may be, the youth hostel will provide accommodation acceptable to all visitors. Thus for instance, in Japan, western style beds and chairs are to be found alongside the traditional pillows, cushions, and beds placed directly on the floor. At the same time, it is important that each country preserve its individual customs and national char-

acteristics, as these are often the very things which attract visitors. The youth hostel must never be a form of standardized barracks which could be produced in any country and be repeated throughout the world. The converse in fact should be the criteria: no two hostels even in the same country should be identical, in order that each hostel visited will be a new experience. Within this principle, the practical arrangements of spaces and hygiene facilities can, and should, conform to a common minimum standard:

MINIMUM AND NORMAL STANDARDS FOR YOUTH HOSTELS
(adopted at the 28th Conference of the International Youth Hostel Federation, 1970)

Minimum Standards (Obligatory)

Every Youth Hostel must provide:

- Supervision by a warden or other suitable adult person who shall be responsible for the well-being of the person using the hostel.
- Separate dormitories for men and women, with separate entrances (but family rooms may be offered for parents with young children). Dormitories must be equipped with beds, each with a mattress, a pillow, and a sufficient number of blankets according to the climate.
- Separate sanitary installations (toilets and washing facilities) in adequate numbers for men and women, kept in clean and hygienic condition.
- A members' kitchen, equipped with cooking stoves, pots, pans, etc., or some simple facilities for cooking meals. Facilities enabling the hostel staff to provide meals at reasonable prices may also be provided.
- A common room, terrace, or other place (depending on the climate) in which guests can meet and get to know each other.

Additional Facilities (Optional)

Dependent upon the size and function of a youth hostel, other accommodation will be required which may include the following:

(a) A baggage room
(b) Living accommodation for staff
(c) A lockable cycle store
(d) A heated and ventilated drying room for the drying of wet clothing
(e) A kitchen in which the warden and/or staff can prepare meals for supply to the hostellers; also food stores, and facilities for catering staff
(f) A separate small room (or rooms) for leaders or instructors
(g) A sick room (alternatively the leader's room can be used in the case of sickness)
(h) A room in which hostellers can wash, dry, and iron clothes
(i) A room in which the warden (or hostel staff) can launder hostel linen
(j) Additional common rooms which can also be used as dining rooms and as classrooms for school parties
(k) A reception office and store where the warden can receive and book in hostellers
(l) Accommodation for specialist equipment as required depending on the location: ski store, boat sheds, stables, etc.

In the early days of the youth hostel movement many very simple hostels were set up in whatever property was available, such as old cottages, huts, old schools, and farm buildings. This type of simple accommodation is still employed in many parts of the world, especially in those areas where the population is thin and there is a degree of isolation.

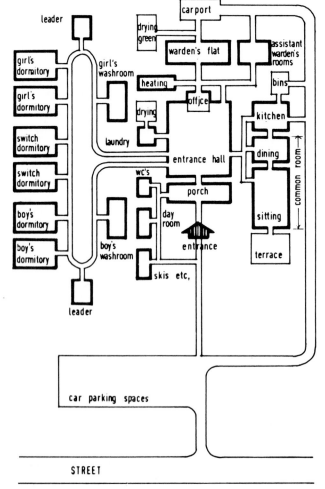

Fig. 1 Diagram showing the relationship between the elements of a modern youth hostel.

INTRODUCTION

This section has been prepared to assist in the designing of a new hostel or in the conversion of an existing building into a hostel.

Each type of room necessary in a hostel is described and all the various features relative to each room are indicated.

The information in this section is based on the physical standards for hostels adopted by the American Youth Hostels in 1962 and on the national building code of National Board of Fire Underwriters.

All the computations are approximate and they must be modified to suit actual conditions. All local or state building codes which are more stringent than the information in this section will take precedence.

Figure 2 illustrates the relationship that should exist among rooms. Entrance through the foyer into the common room; then, access to the boys' and girls' bunk rooms, preferably through a hall. The toilets should be located directly off the bunk rooms, but it is also desirable to have access to them from the hall, so that the bunk room does not become a passageway.

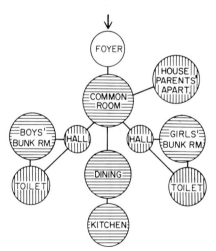

Fig. 2 Flow diagram.

The common room and dining room may be combined in small hostels and provides a big, flexible space for recreation. The kitchen, located off the dining room, should be large enough to handle group cooking activities. If possible, the kitchen should have direct outside access for ease of food and garbage transport.

A Trail Hostel Design Manual, American Youth Hostels, Inc., New York, N.Y.

COMMON ROOM

Room Area

A minimum of 15 sq ft per person is required. For combination dining and common room, 22 sq ft per person should be allowed. (See Table 1 and Fig. 3.)

TABLE 1. Room area chart*

Number of people	Common room, min. sq ft	Dining and common room, min. sq ft
10	150	220
15	225	330
20	300	440
25	375	550
30	450	660
35	525	770
40	600	880

*These are minimum room sizes. More space is always desirable.

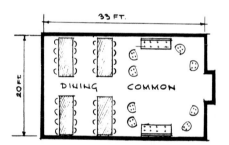

Fig. 3 Dining-common room. Typical layout for 30 people.

DINING ROOM

Room Area

A minimum of 12 sq ft per person for dining room is required. For a combination dining and recreation room, minimum of 20 sq ft per person should be allowed. (See Table 2.)

TABLE 2 Dining room (only) room area chart*

Number of people	Area needed, min. sq ft	Window area, min. sq ft
8	100	8
10	120	10
12	144	12
16	192	16
20	240	20
24	288	23
28	336	27
30	360	29

*These are minimum room sizes. More space is always desirable.

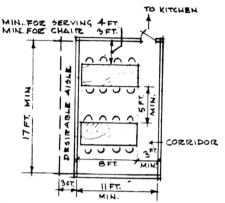

Fig. 4 Typical dining area for 16 people.

KITCHEN

• Add units together to form larger kitchens

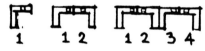

• Should have door to outside handy for garbage or food deliveries
• Should try to line up sinks for economical plumbing
• Should have window or electrical fan for range ventilation

TABLE 3 Schedule of Kitchen Fixtures (Minimum)

Number of people	Sinks	Range burners	Refrig., 9 cu ft	Ovens
10	1	3	1	1
15	2	3	1	1
20	2	4	2	1
25	2	5	2	2
30	3	6	2	2
35	3	7	3	2
40	3	8	3	2

BUNK ROOMS

TABLE 4 Room Area Chart

Number of double bunks	Number of people	Min. area needed, sq ft	Min. window area desired, sq ft
2	4	120	15
4	8	240	30
6	12	360	45
8	16	480	60
10	20	600	75
12	24	720	90
14	28	840	105
16	32	960	120

Must include extra space for blanket and mattress storage in closet.
Minimum ceiling height is to be 8 ft.

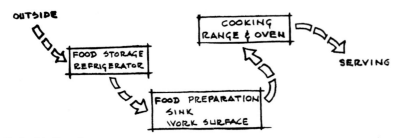

Fig. 5 Food traffic pattern.

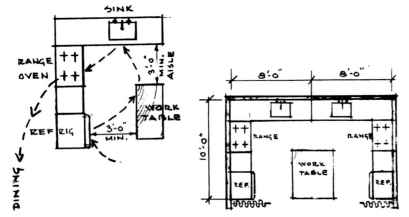

Fig. 6 Typical unit layout (feeds about 15 people). Fig. 7 Typical kitchen (feeds about 30 people).

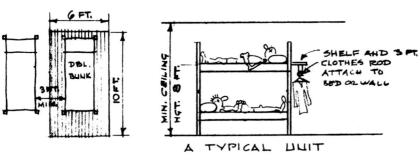

Fig. 8 Minimum area per double bunk, 60 sq ft.

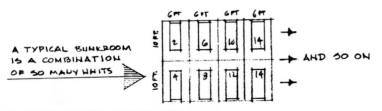

Fig. 9 A typical bunk room is a combination of many units.

TOILETS

TABLE 5 Schedule of Minimum Toilet Requirements

	Boys' toilet			
No. of persons	W.C.	Urinals	Sinks	Showers
4	1	0	1	1
8	1	0	1	1
10	1	1	2	1
12	1	1	2	2
16	2	1	2	2
20	2	1	3	2
24	2	1	3	3
28	2	1	3	3
30	2	2	4	4

	Girls' toilet		
4	1	1	1
8	1	1	1
10	2	2	2
12	2	2	2
16	2	2	2
20	3	3	3
24	3	3	3
28	3	3	3
30	4	4	4

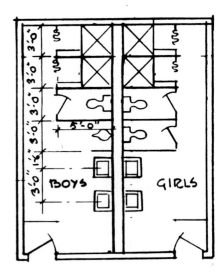

Fig. 10 Typical toilet layout. Note back-to-back placement of plumbing fixtures for economy; common plumbing wall for ease of plumbing access; washroom area separate from toilet area for better usage; water closets in separate compartment for privacy; screen at entrance door to shield interior.

HOUSEPARENTS' APARTMENT

• Houseparents' apartment should be located next to and connected with the hostel common room for control.

• A small office is a good connection to the hostel from the apartment. It should overlook the hostel entrance, if possible.

• A separate outside entrance should be provided.

TABLE 6   Minimum Room Size Schedule

Room	Area, sq ft
Living room	196
Kitchen-dining	90
Bedroom	140
Storage	20
Bathroom	35
Office	80

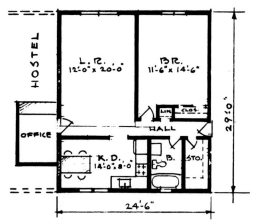

Fig. 11   Typical apartment layout. Note: This is an average-size apartment. More space and room is always desirable. This is one of many possible layouts.

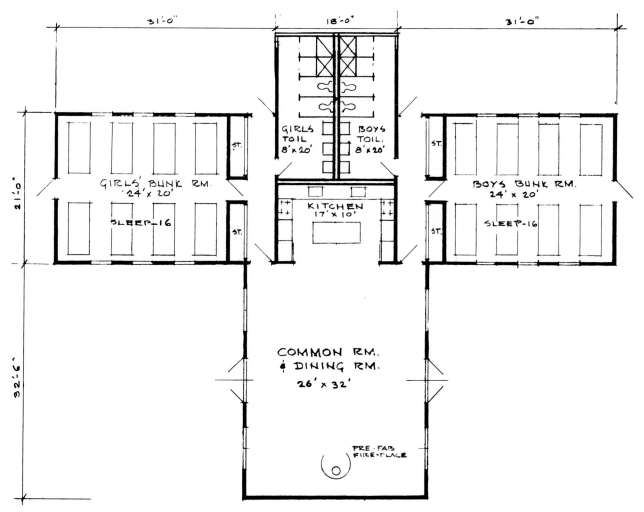

Fig. 12   Trail hostel design 1.

183

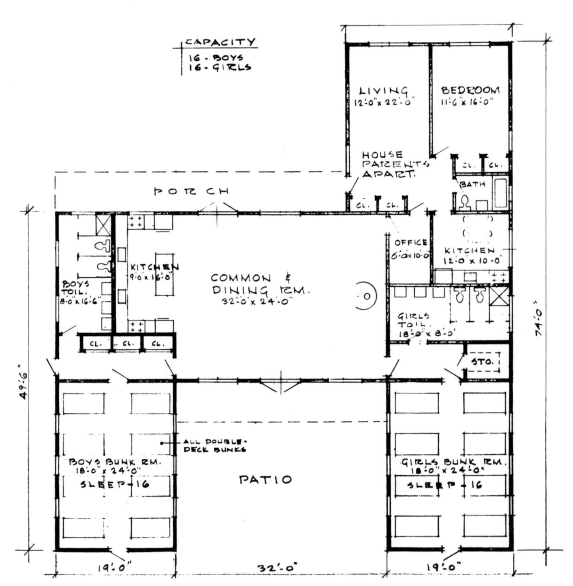

Fig. 13 Trail hostel design 2.

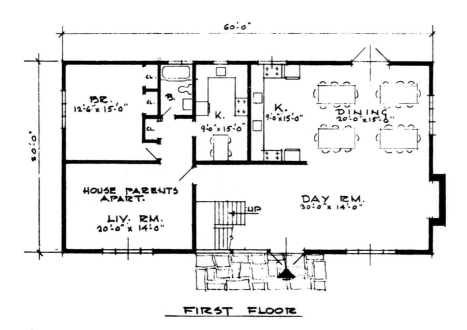

FIRST FLOOR

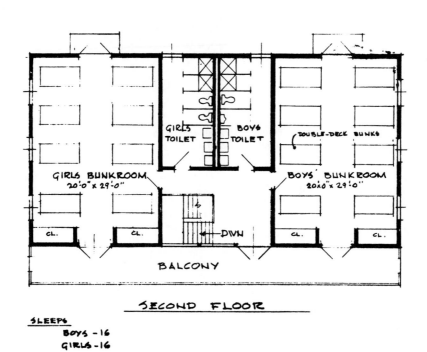

SECOND FLOOR

SLEEPS
BOYS - 16
GIRLS - 16

Fig. 14   Trail hostel design 3, two-story.

Residential
SITE PLANNING

By HOWARD P. VERMILYA, *AIA*

SITE PLANNING AND SUBDIVISION LAYOUT

Site planning in its narrow sense involves the disposition of space for appropriate uses; the positioning of structures to provide effective relationships (well-proportioned masses with attractive outlooks and good orientation); the provision of access to structures in an expeditious, attractive, and safe manner; the design of the services, walks, streets, parking facilities, drainage, and utilities; the preservation of the natural advantage of the site, and its enhancement by landscaping.

In its larger sense, site planning involves consideration of the site in relation to the physical pattern and economic growth trends of the larger area of which it is a part. An analysis of the area should be made based on population growth, family formations, family size, housing inventory, income levels, schools, taxes and assessments, transportation and traffic patterns, and directions of growth. An analysis of site development costs should be made in terms of densities, housing types, construction types, topography and grading, and local requirements with regard to zoning, subdivision regulations, and utility services. This analysis may be made as a basis for site selection or as a basis for determining the most appropriate use of a particular site. For large sites involving several types of housing, commercial or industrial uses, schools, and churches, more extensive analyses may be necessary. For small sites forming parts of neighborhoods already established, the analysis need not be as comprehensive.

A subdivision site plan can be made for a complete community, involving all types of land use found in a typical town or village, or for a neighborhood, usually considered to be a homogeneous area large enough to support an elementary school, or for a segment of a neighborhood. The

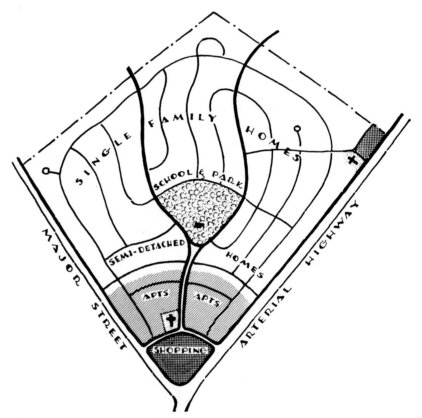

Fig. 1. Principles of neighborhood planning
Courtesy Urban Land Institute

1. *Size.* A residential unit development should provide housing for that population for which one elementary school is ordinarily required, its actual area depending upon its population density.

2. *Boundaries.* The unit should be bounded by arterial streets sufficiently wide to facilitate traffic by-passing the neighborhood instead of passing through it.

3. *Open Spaces.* Small park and recreation space, planned to meet the needs of the particular neighborhood should be provided.

4. *Institution Sites.* Sites for the school and other institutions having service spheres coinciding with the limits of the unit should be suitably grouped about a central point or common, and combined with the neighborhood recreation area, usually.

5. *Local Shopping Center.* If warranted by the population to be served the local convenience shopping facility should be located at the edge preferably at an arterial traffic junction and adjacent to similar commercial districts, if any, of adjoining neighborhoods.

6. *Internal Street System.* The unit should be provided with a special street system, each highway being proportioned to its probable traffic load, and the street net as a whole being designed to facilitate circulation within the unit with good access to main arteries, and to discourage its use by through traffic.

Sites are provided for parks, playing fields and recreational areas.

Church sites are provided in convenient locations.

There is a central shopping area, with off-street parking.

Two school sites are provided, reasonably accessible from all parts of the neighborhood. The Catholic school is off-centre because it also serves adjacent neighborhoods.

"Through" arterial highways, of adequate width, are separated from local service roads by limited access planted strips. Thus both "local" and "through" traffic are safeguarded. There are feeder roads for bus routes. Local residential streets are designed in such a way as to discourage "through" driving, yet remain adequate for local purposes.

At the corners of the area, there are intersections designed to keep "through" traffic moving.

One-family housing is created in an aesthetic as well as a functional setting. Set-backs are arranged to allow for a "rhythmic variation". A buffer strip separates housing from an adjacent industrial zone.

There are also apartments and row housing in a variety of types.

A neighborhood "focus" of larger buildings and open space is included as an essential ingredient of a well-designed residential area.

Fig. 2. Example of well-planned neighborhood
Courtesy Urban Land Institute

principles of neighborhood planning are illustrated in Fig. 1; an example of a well-planned neighborhood is shown in Fig. 2.

Housing types

It is no longer considered good practice to limit housing within a subdivision to one type and price range. For sites of fewer than 100 houses the range of types should be restricted but the range in price should permit some variation, the degree of difference being reduced as the size of the site diminishes. For larger sites not only may the types of single-family houses be varied, but rental housing of either high-rise or garden types may be included where zoning permits. Apartments and town houses (row houses in small groups) often provide a very satisfactory transition between the commercial (shopping) areas and the less dense residential areas.

Single-family housing: Lot sizes for the single-family detached house are wider now than they were 30 years ago; 60 ft is considered the minimum width and 70 to 80 ft is more usual. This has come about because of the popularity of the one-story house

with large glass areas and provisions for outdoor living with a reasonable degree of privacy. Devices such as patios and courts and fenced-in areas are used to provide privacy when lot sizes are small. An example of a typical one-story subdivision house of better than average design is shown in Fig. 3. The split-level house is also popular in subdivision work because it provides the economy of the two-story house but requires less stair climbing.

Row houses or, as they are now called, town houses are finding many advocates because of their economical use of land and low site-development costs. When developed with not more than 8 or 10 units (preferably fewer) in one group and located around a court, cul-de-sac, or loop street, the monotonous appearance usually associated with such housing disappears. Lots should be 20 to 25 ft wide; wider lots with side yards should be provided at the ends of the groups. Garages should be provided either within the house structure itself or as a one-story attached structure, often a carport, at the front of the house. An example of the variety possible within this

housing type is shown in Fig. 4; see also Fig. 16.

Rental housing, for more attractive appearance, is now built at lower densities and with more emphasis on open space; it often includes such club-like features as swimming pools and tennis courts. Densities of 15 to 25 families per acre and coverages of 15 to 25 per cent are standard in well-designed garden apartment developments. Garden apartments are usually two stories high and should not be higher than three stories (Fig. 5). High-rise elevator apartments should restrict land coverage to 10 to 15 per cent. The trend in apartment design is toward larger rooms, more storage, and other facilities in keeping with those of single-family housing.

Lot sizes and development costs

The cost of raw land and the cost of installing streets and utilities has greatly increased in recent years. At the same time, as previously noted, lot widths have markedly increased. In order to keep the cost of the developed lot from rising to prohibi-

Residential

SITE PLANNING

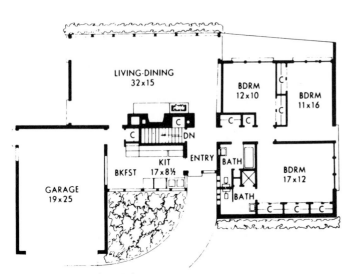

Fig. 3. One-story house plan
Courtesy National Association of Home Builders

tive levels, site planners have resorted to the "superblock." This is typically a long, shallow block (600–800 ft by 200–250 ft) which reduces the number of cross streets and eliminates the need for utilities in them. Typical lot depths are thus likely to be 1½ to 2 times their width. Deep superblocks, penetrated by culs-de-sac or loop streets, are also used. Further economies in development costs result from the use of a functional street system, as described later on, which permits most of the streets to be built to the most economical specifications (see also Fig. 15 and the discussion of the *cluster* plan).

Basic data for estimating lot costs are given in Tables 1 and 2.

Streets

Conformance with the master street plan for the city is usually a requisite for any subdivision plan. As a rule, however, this requirement applies only to major streets. It is a factor which should be given consideration in the initial analysis of the site since it is undesirable to have major streets traverse a residential area. At the boundaries, however, major streets may be an asset if they provide good access to other areas in the community.

Fire protection should be considered in determining the street pattern. Some of the problems to consider are hydrant location, culs-de-sac turn-arounds, access to buildings in multifamily projects and commercial areas, radius of curvature of curbs at intersections, and similar problems.

Streets are necessary evils in a neighborhood or smaller subdivision; they are intended primarily to provide access to and circulation within the area. Streets serving other purposes (arterial streets) should

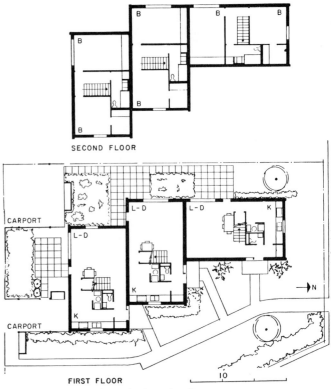

Fig. 4. Row house scheme for irregular site
Yost and Taylor, Architects
George E. Treichel, Landscape Architect

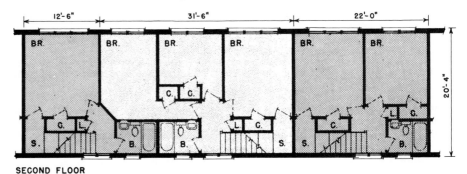

ONE-BEDROOM UNIT
Total Floor Area 753 Sq. Ft.

THREE-BEDROOM UNIT
Total Floor Area 1036 Sq. Ft.

TWO-BEDROOM UNIT
Total Floor Area 896 Sq. Ft.

Fig. 5. Two-story garden apartment plan
Courtesy Federal Housing Administration

Table 1. Lot sizes and dwelling densities

From Community Builders Handbook, *Urban Land Institute.*

Dwelling Unit Type	Lot Dimensions Per Dwelling Unit in Feet	Net Density* Dwelling Units/Acre
Single Family		
Detached houses	100 x 200	2.0
	80 x 160	3.5
	70 x 140	3.3
	60 x 125	4.3
	50 x 100	6.5
Semi-Detached houses	30 x 125	8.7
	26 x 125	10.0
Row houses, two-story	20 x 100	16.3
	16 x 100	20.4
Garden Apartments, two-story		15 – 25
Garden Apartments, three-story		25 – 35
Apartments, multiple story to 12 stories		50 – 85

* Net density represents the number of dwelling units per acre of land within the site, after deducting 25 per cent of the site for allocation to streets, park and recreation areas.

Gross density is computed on the basis of net land area plus area devoted to streets and other nonresidential uses and one-half of bounding streets and one-quarter of bounding street intersections.

Table 2. Lot areas and dwelling densities

Dwelling Unit Type	D.U.'s per Net Acre	Assumed Average Sq. Ft. of Lot per D.U.
Single-family	1	40,000
" "	2	20,000
" "	3	12,500
" "	4	10,000
Two-family	6	6,000
Row house	15	2,600
Garden apartment*	25	1,600
Multi-story apartments*	50	800

* The more intensive the use of land, the greater need there is for recreation space, wider streets and sidewalks, shorter blocks and off-street parking. In multi-family development careful consideration must be given to land coverage and open space needs. High density, multi-family intrusions into single family residential development must be avoided. Apartment buildings must be spaced and located within the project so as to provide transition between residential land uses. The developer of multi-family areas has a responsibility in making such sections of his city fitting, appropriate and serviceable to his community.

bound rather than penetrate the area. The street pattern within the area should be designed to discourage through traffic. The widths of the interior streets should be consistent with their function and the density of housing they serve and should be no greater than necessary, in the interest of safety and economy of installation and maintenance. Subdivision street types are illustrated in Fig. 7. Collector streets, those carrying traffic from minor streets to arterial streets should have a paved width of 36 ft, consisting of two moving lanes and two parking lanes. Minor streets, depending on the off-street parking provisions and the density of the area they serve, should be 26 ft wide for single-family detached houses and 32 ft wide for row houses and apartments. Short access streets, such as culs-de-sac or loop streets, may have mini-

mum paved widths of 20 ft. Culs-de-sac should terminate in a turning circle not less than 80 ft in diameter between curbs. Rights-of-way should be 60 ft wide for collector streets, 50 ft for minor streets, and 40 ft for culs-de-sac and minor access streets. A cul-de-sac should not be in excess of 500 ft in length (see Fig. 8 and Table 3).

The use of the "T" intersection of minor streets and of minor with collector streets, with at least a 125-ft separation between opposing intersections, offers a device to reduce through traffic within a subdivision area and improve the safety conditions (Fig. 9). Slight jogs in the alignment of streets are not desirable.

Where the subdivision borders on arterial highways or streets bearing heavy traffic, houses should not be entered directly

from such streets. Instead, the lots should be backed up to the highway and heavy planting should be provided along the rear-lot lines. Or a local access road should be provided parallel to the highway and screened from it by planting (Fig. 10). Either method serves to reduce the number of street intersections with main traffic ways to a minimum and to keep driveways off the main highway.

Sidewalks

The design of sidewalks is often governed by local regulations. Sometimes they may be omitted in low-density areas of single-family detached homes. Some jurisdictions permit installation on one side of the street only, others require sidewalks within certain distances of schools, usually inside the zones beyond which school busses operate. Higher-density areas (more than 5 families per acre) and streets carrying other than local traffic usually require sidewalks on both sides of the street.

Four feet is the customary design width for sidewalks. When combined with the curb they may sometimes be as narrow as 3 ft 6 in.; in commercial areas they should be much wider. When sidewalks are separated from the curb by a planting strip, the strip should be at least 3 ft wide to provide for snow removal; if trees are included it should be at least 7 ft wide (see Fig. 8 and Table 3).

Curbs

The rolled curb is more economical than the straight curb and does not require cutting at driveways. It is not recommended however on steep grades or in hillside developments. When used, rolled curbs should be molded into straight curbs at intersections to discourage corner cutting. The suggested radius of 15 ft for curbs at right-angle intersections discourages speeding and is intended for intersections of minor streets. Cuts in straight curbs for driveways should provide for 3 to 5 ft radiuses and a 9 or 10-ft wide driveway.

Lot layout

The layout of the lots in a subdivision can make the difference between an attractive and an unattractive development, also the difference between an economical and an uneconomical project. Good and poor lotting practices are illustrated in Fig. 11 and methods of lotting around culs-de-sac are shown in Fig. 12.

Topography

Topography can influence the character of a subdivision. Hilly land, with grades steeper than 10 per cent, may be developed for low-density, higher-priced homes, or for multifamily projects of relatively low density, but it is rarely adaptable to small lots and lower-cost homes. Flat land, because of the difficulty of obtaining good drainage for sewers and storm drains, may also not be suitable for low-priced homes. Gently sloping land without drainage pockets or swampy areas or underlying rock is best for low-cost development. Where public sewerage is not available the character of the soil is an important factor and may even determine the lot sizes. Soil seepage tests are usually required by health departments where septic tanks and disposal fields are installed. If public water service is not available and individual wells must be used, this too may affect lot sizes. Community water and sewerage systems should be provided wherever possible in these cases; wells and septic tanks should be used only as a last resort.

The nature of the topography will affect the street pattern. Streets should be laid out so as to avoid steep grades, excessive cut and fill, and to provide buildable sites with good surface drainage. In general, streets should follow natural drainage lines or ridge locations. On side hill locations, they should cut across the contour lines, in order to avoid cut and fill operations.

Steep grades can be reduced on hilly land by running streets diagonally across the contours.

Surface drainage: Not only must the entire site be graded for proper drainage, but each individual lot and block must be separately and carefully considered. Examples of proper grading for surface drainage of lots and blocks are shown in Figs. 13 and 14.

Off-street parking: For single-family detached houses parking is usually provided in an attached garage or carport. The setback from the street is normally sufficient to permit overflow parking in the driveway. Apartments are usually provided with parking bays or courts located reasonably near the building entrances. Suggested designs for such parking areas are shown in Fig. 15 (see also sections on "Apartments" and "Automobiles: Parking").

For parking areas at neighborhood shopping centers see sections on "Shopping Centers" and "Automobiles: Parking."

Recreation areas are essential and should represent at least 5 per cent of the residential area and more where the lots are small (see sections on "Apartments" and "Recreation.") Playgrounds for small children ("tot lots") may be quite small but they must be widely dispersed throughout the site. Playgrounds for older children are best provided by enlarging the school site and its playground. This provides an adequate recreation area in one place and simplifies supervision and maintenance. Wherever possible, recreation areas should be maintained by the local government. When recreation areas provided by the developer are not taken over by the local government, they must be maintained cooperatively by the residents through a neighborhood association, as discussed farther on.

SUBDIVISION REGULATIONS

Subdivision of the land is a permanent change which determines the use of the land for at least a generation and profoundly affects the surrounding area. The public interest is thus directly concerned and local governments now generally exercize strict controls over this important function. Most municipalities, many counties, and some states now have subdivision regulations. These generally require conformance with established standards of design and construction such as:

Streets: location, types, rights-of-way widths, pavement widths and specifications, grades, intersections, curvatures, alignments, curbs, gutters, sidewalks

Table 3. Design of local residential streets

From Traffic Engineering Handbook *of Institute of Traffic Engineers and* Home Builders Manual for Land Development *of National Association of Home Builders.*

Speed: Based on maximum of 25 m.p.h. in accord with Uniform Vehicle Code recommendation. Recommendations will be reasonably satisfactory if some speeds exceed 25 m.p.h. a little.

	Single-family Units	*Multi-family Units*
Street Width:	50 feet	60 feet
Pavement Width:	26 feet	32 feet
Curbs:	Straight curb recommended	Same
Sidewalks		
Width:	4 feet minimum	Same
Set-Back:	3 feet minimum if no trees, 7 feet minimum with trees	Same
Horizontal Alignment:	200 feet minimum sight distance	Same
Vertical Alignment:	6-8 per cent maximum grade desirable 3-4 per cent per 100 feet maximum rate of change	Same
Cul-de-sac:	400-500 feet maximum length	Same
Turn-arounds:	40 feet minimum curb radius without parking	Same
	50 feet minimum curb radius with parking	Same
Pavement Surface:	Non-skid with strength to carry traffic load	Same

Blocks: length, width, crosswalks, utility easements
Lots: size, shape, minimum dimensions
Open spaces: size, type
Utilities: storm and sanitary sewers, culverts, bridges, water service; monuments
Names: of area and streets; street numbers

PROTECTIVE COVENANTS

Covenants, sometimes called deed restrictions and sometimes protective covenants, are usually drafted by the subdivider of an area to provide land use regulations for the entire area, either supplementing those of the zoning ordinance or in lieu of it. They are, or should be, recorded and made superior to the lien of any mortgage and are intended to preserve

the physical, economic, and esthetic qualities of the subdivision in the interests of the subdivider in aiding his development program and of the purchasers in protecting their investment. Enforcement should be delegated to a home owners or neighborhood association.

Protective covenants, being a contract or agreement between private parties, may include provisions which go well beyond the public health, safety and welfare provisions to which zoning regulations are limited. These may include any or all of the following:

Architectural control—Usually provides procedure for the review of designs for new construction and alterations for approval by a designated individual architect, or committee of the neighborhood

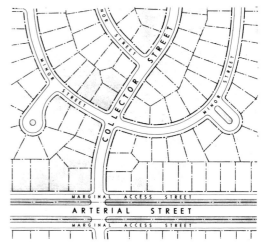

Fig. 6 Subdivision street types
Courtesy Housing and Home Finance Agency

Cross-section A. Provides two-way traffic with parallel parking on both sides. For collector streets in developments of one-family detached houses and for minor streets in apartment developments.

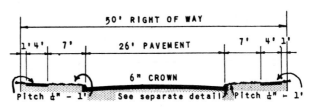

Cross-section B. Provides two-way traffic and one continuous lane of parallel parking on one side or parallel parking alternated on either side of the street. For minor streets in developments of one-family detached houses.

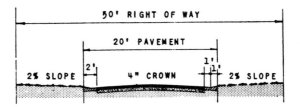

Cross-section C. Provides two-way traffic and drainage with all parking on individual driveways. For streets in country home developments.

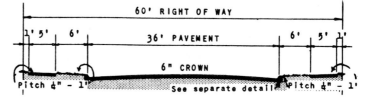

Cross-section D. Marginal access street paralleling an arterial highway. Provides two-way traffic, one lane of parallel parking, safe access to properties and protection from through traffic.

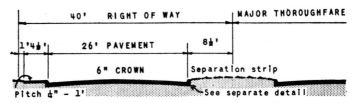

Cross-section E. Provides separated two-way traffic with parallel parking on both sides. For use as collector streets of the boulevard and development entranceway types.

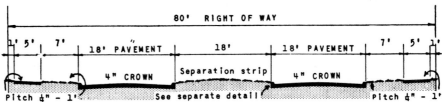

Fig. 7 Typical street cross sections
Courtesy Federal Housing Administration

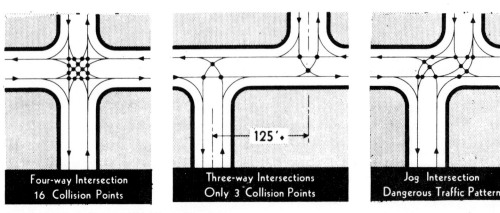

Four-way Intersection
16 Collision Points

Three-way Intersections
Only 3 Collision Points

Jog Intersection
Dangerous Traffic Pattern

Fig. 8   Street intersection types and resulting traffic patterns
Courtesy Housing and Home Finance Agency

association, as to conformity with the esthetic character of the area.

Use and size of the structure may be limited more severely than required by the zoning ordinance. In particular, minimum sizes may be established. Size limitations may refer to height, number of stories, area, volume, or cost; the latter is not an effective device because of fluctuation of building costs.

Lot sizes and setbacks greater than required by the zoning ordinance may be called for.

Landscaping and fences may be con-trolled as to placement and height. This may be desirable for various reasons: to ensure visibility at street intersections, to prevent interference with surface drainage, or to preserve a desired esthetic character for the subdivision as a whole.

Nuisances: Various undesirable usages may be prohibited such as business, farming, mining, signs, outdoor garbage or refuse incineration, tents, trailers, etc.

Covenants usually run with the land for a definite term of years, with provision for renewal unless terminated or modified by agreement of the property owners affected. Restrictive covenants based on race or religion have been declared unconstitutional by the Supreme Court of the United States.

HOME OWNERS ASSOCIATIONS

Home owners associations or neighborhood associations, as they are sometimes called, are usually established by the subdivider to provide a means for carrying out certain community functions, such as the maintenance of recreation areas and the enforcement of protective covenants. The management of the association is usually turned over to the owners of the subdivided land when sales progress to a predetermined ratio. The association is usually established as a corporation with a charter from the state and reference to it is made in the protective covenants or deed restrictions. To be effective it should have the power to assess the property owners to obtain the funds necessary to carry out its functions. It should provide for representation of the owners in the selection of the management in an orderly manner through well-drafted bylaws. The functions of the Association can be any of the following:

Action to enforce the protective covenants in case of violation by any property owner, or where continuing action

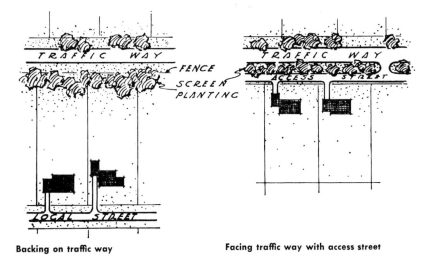

Backing on traffic way

Facing traffic way with access street

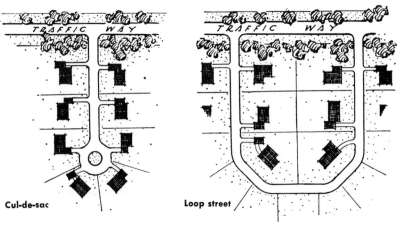

Cul-de-sac

Loop street

Fig. 9   Methods of subdividing along heavy traffic ways
Courtesy Urban Land Institute

is required as in the operation of an architectural control of design.

Operation of community facilities, such as club house or community center and recreational facilities such as playgrounds, swimming pools, tennis courts, or golf courses.

Maintenance of common land such as cul-de-sac turn-arounds and planting strips and unimproved property in absentee ownership (see *cluster* plans).

Maintenance and operation of community sewerage and water systems.

Performance of services such as street repair, snow removal, and garbage collection until taken over by the municipality.

Representation of the owners' needs or opinions to the public authorities.

Development of community programs—social, cultural, or recreational.

NEW APPROACHES

Although the standard subdivision technique of today is a vast improvement over the monotonous grid-iron plots of the past, many planners feel that it still leaves much to be desired. They believe that it is possible to preserve the beauty of the natural land, to relate the houses better to each other and to the site and provide more open space, all at less cost than in today's practice.

An early example of this type of thinking is the Radburn plan (1929) in which the houses are grouped on small lots around culs-de-sac which penetrate the periphery

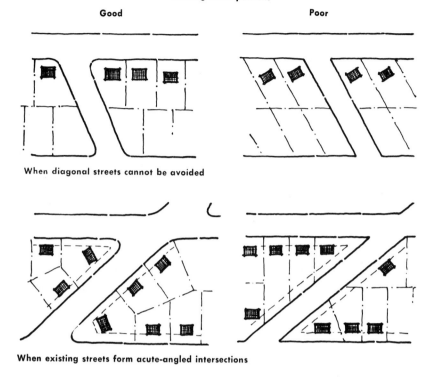

Existing street patterns

Good — Poor

When diagonal streets cannot be avoided

When existing streets form acute-angled intersections

When future street extensions are not required in corners of the property

Economy of utilities

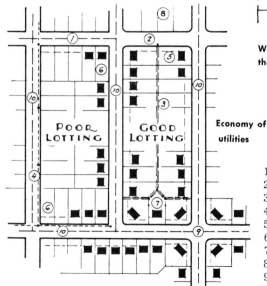

Fig. 10 Good and poor lotting practices
Courtesy Urban Land Institute

EXPLANATION

1. Excess underground utilities at end of block required.
2. No underground utilities at end of block.
3. Rear overhead utility easement.
4. Street overhead utilities.
5. Increased corner lot width.
6. Corner lots too narrow.
7. Good use of butt lot.
8. Butt lots require extra utilities with bad view down rear lot line.
9. Good lotting at street intersection.
10. Required underground utilities.

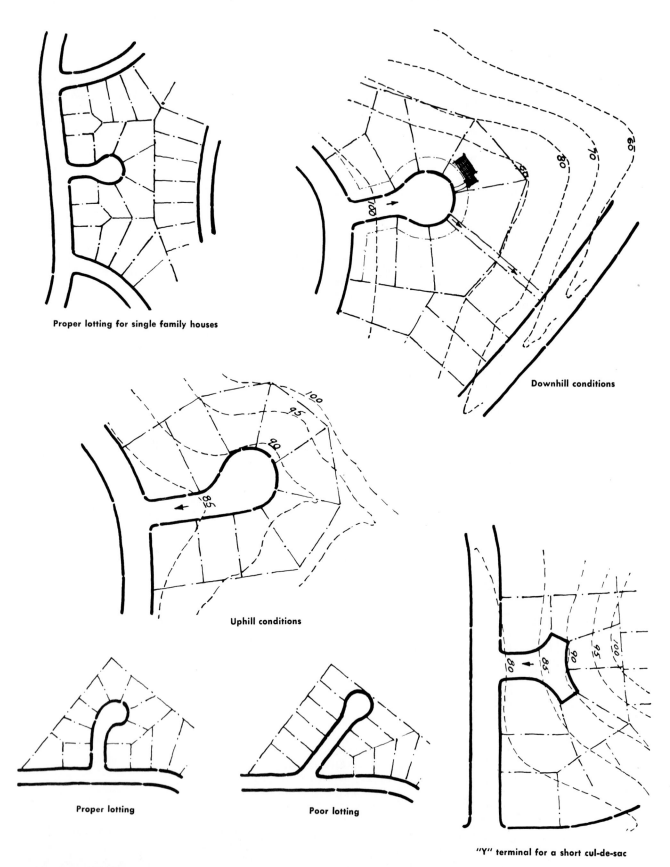

Proper lotting for single family houses

Downhill conditions

Uphill conditions

Proper lotting

Poor lotting

"Y" terminal for a short cul-de-sac

Fig. 11 Lotting around culs-de-sac
Courtesy Urban Land Institute

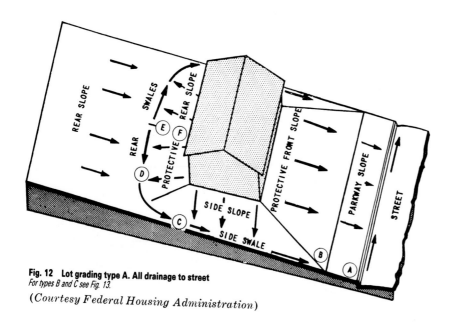

Fig. 12   Lot grading type A. All drainage to street
For types B and C see Fig. 13.

(*Courtesy Federal Housing Administration*)

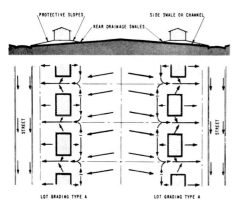

Type 1:   Ridge along rear lot lines

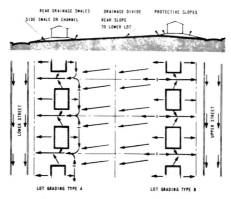

Type 2:   Gentle cross-slope

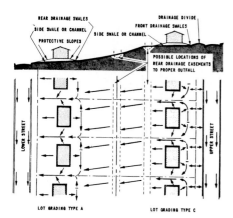

Type 3:   Steep cross-slope

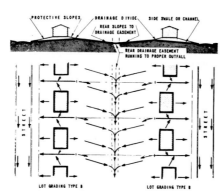

Type 4:   Valley along rear lot lines

Fig. 13   Types of block grading
Courtesy Federal Housing Administration

of huge superblocks. The center of each superblock is a park on which all houses face. Pedestrian walks lead through the parks to schools, shopping, and transportation.

A more recent example of the same general approach is the *cluster* scheme. This plan reduces the cost of streets and utilities by half and leaves approximately half the total site for recreation. Every house abuts on a park or open land. Although normal suburban densities are maintained, the rural character of the land is preserved, there is less monotony in the appearance of the development, and better living qualities are provided, all at less cost than in conventional subdivisions. The common land must be maintained by a neighborhood association; it could be treated as a park or playground or it could be left in its natural state, especially if wooded, rocky, or otherwise attractive in appearance.

Unfortunately, neither the Radburn plan nor the cluster plan is permitted under most existing zoning ordinances and subdivision regulations. The rigidity of these regulations has been a serious handicap to any signficant improvement in subdivision site planning. Further examples of this are illustrated in Fig. 15.

REFERENCES

(all Washington, D.C.)

Home Builder's Manual for Land Development, National Association of Home Builders, 1958.

Community Builder's Handbook, Urban Land Institute, 1956.

New Approaches to Land Development, Technical Bulletin No. 40, Urban Land Institute, 1960.

Neighborhood Standards, Land Planning Bulletin No. 3, Federal Housing Administration, 1956.

Suggested Land Subdivision Regulations, Housing and Home Finance Agency, 1962.

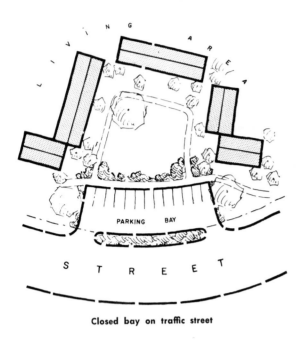

Closed bay on traffic street

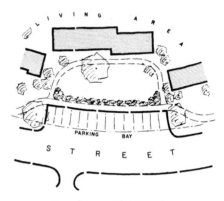

Open bay on minor street

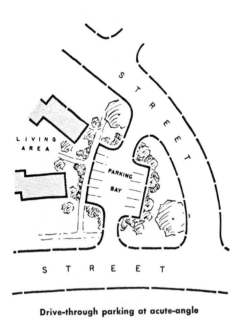

Drive-through parking at acute-angle street intersection

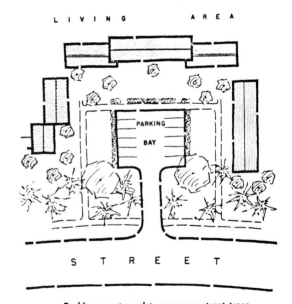

Parking court used to preserve street trees and bring parking closer to buildings

Fig. 14 Parking areas for rental housing
Courtesy National Association of Home Builders

Cluster development

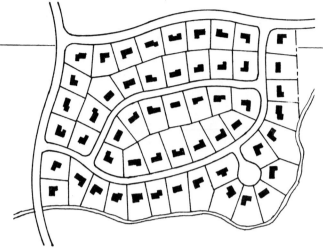

Site: 30 acres; 54-lot subdivision

Conventional subdivision design

In most subdivisions, the entire site is split up into single house lots of ½ acre or more. A large amount of roadway is required for access to the lots, and, since houses are dispersed, utility installation and maintenance costs are high. Lack of open space requires mixing of pedestrian and vehicular traffic, creating safety problems. Privacy is limited, and the landscape is often visually monotonous.

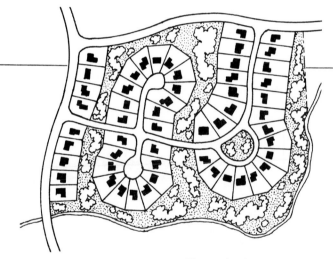

Cluster development: 54 lots

Cluster design

In cluster developments, individual lot size is reduced in favor of common open space areas. Clustering allows for utilization of the best building sites while preserving environmentally sensitive areas. Concentration of buildings lowers installation costs for utilities, and reduces roadbuilding requirements. Pedestrian and vehicular traffic can be separated; safety is increased by locating public recreational areas away from roads. Careful layout of open space can provide increased privacy, and will help maintain the natural character of the site.

Clustering of single-family homes on private lots enables the benefits of private land ownership to be maintained. An alternative which provides larger open space areas and higher housing density is the construction of townhouses or apartments instead of individual homes. This type of development also allows for the most efficient layout of roads and utilities.

The zoning regulations of most Connecticut towns contain no provisions for cluster development; therefore variances would be necessary in most localities. Towns considering the adoption of cluster development ordinances should evaluate road width and surface water drainage standards to allow for narrower cul-de-sacs and drainage systems that, where possible, follow natural drainage patterns.

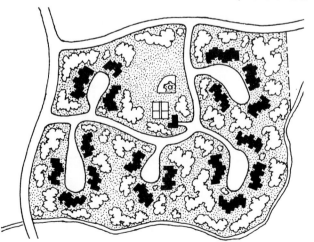

Cluster development: 112 townhouses

Residential
SITE PLANNING

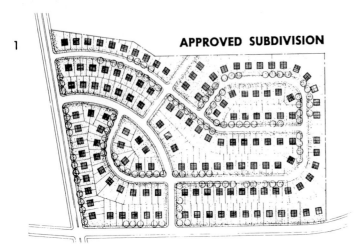

APPROVED SUBDIVISION

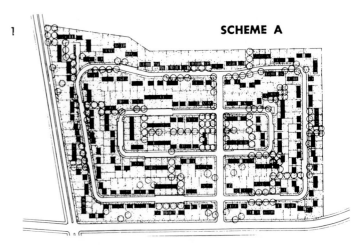

SCHEME A

The approved subdivision represents current development practice fully conforming to most zoning and subdivision ordinances. The subdivision plan (1) provides for 280 families (9.3 families per acre) in twin houses with basement garages. Curving streets are an improvement over the traditional gridiron pattern, but their repetition in numerous subdivisions has created a new monotony. The curving streets only partially obscure another monotony: the uniformly spaced houses. Access from both boundary highways invites through traffic. The similarity of lots, and lack of integrated communal areas, is only too apparent in detail (2). Plan of the typical house, three stories above street level, basement garage, is shown in (3).

Scheme A houses the same 280 families. The new street pattern excludes through traffic. The twin house is replaced by groups of houses of varying lengths and varying setbacks. No houses face on the busy boundary highways. With garages out of the basements, the houses need be only two stories above street level, thus eliminating artificial terraces and giving direct access to private gardens which are supplemented by tot lots, sitting areas, a small common, and parklike walks.

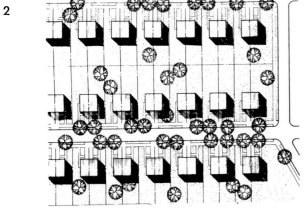

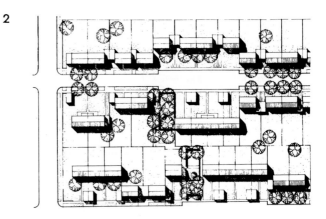

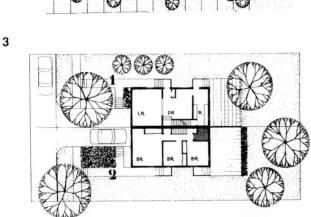

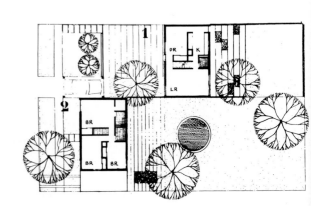

Fig. 15   Existing regulations may block improvements in subdivision design
From a study by the Philadelphia Housing Association, 1961.

198

1

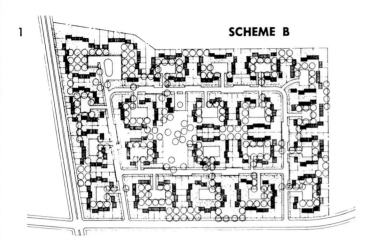

SCHEME B

1

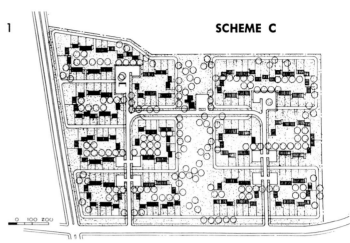

SCHEME C

Scheme B also provides for 280 families. Groups of houses face on courts instead of streets. Parking compounds in each court justify elimination of individual garages. As in Scheme A, tot lots, sitting areas, common areas and interior walks are provided in addition to private yards and gardens.

Scheme C shows the number of families reduced from 280 to 165 (5.7 per acre). Groups of twelve houses front on pedestrian courts. Access for cars and service vehicles is by looping driveways behind the houses. Visitors park in the compounds at the entrances to the courts. The low density results in even more generous open space than in Schemes A and B. Through traffic is excluded from the subdivision and, again, the boundary streets are not used for lot frontages.

Schemes A, B, and C fulfill the basic objectives of zoning: promotion of health and general welfare, provision of adequate light and air, and prevention of overcrowding of the land, of undue congestion. Yet, under most existing zoning ordinances Schemes A, B, and C cannot be built.

2

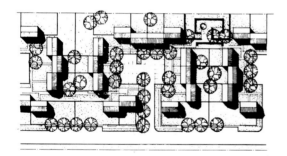

2

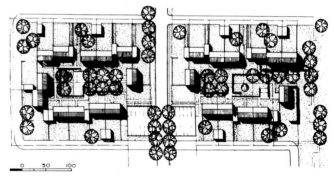

3

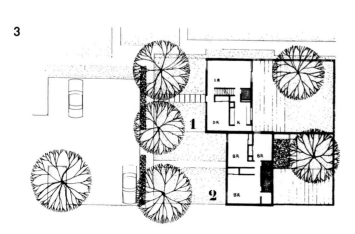

3

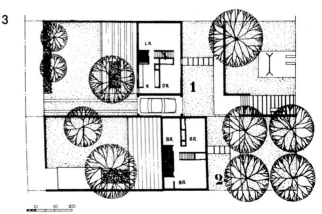

Educational

NURSERY SCHOOLS	203
CHILDREN'S CENTER	207
CHILD CARE CENTERS	208
ELEMENTARY AND SECONDARY SCHOOLS	209
General	209
Site Selection	213
Site Planning	213
Busing	214
Parking	214
Recreation Facilities	215
Drainage	216
Planting	216
Safety	216
Kinds of Schools	218
Administration Suites	225
Learning Resource Centers	228
Classrooms	230
Multipurpose Rooms	235
Student Lockers	237
Language Laboratory	240
Science Facilities	240
Arts	245
Music Facilities	246
Industrial and Vocational Facilities	250
Home Arts	251
Food Service	252
Physical Education	258
Auditoriums	269
GUIDANCE SERVICES	271
COLLEGE AND UNIVERSITY FACILITIES	273
Classrooms	273
Gymnasiums	276
Physical Education and Sports Facilities	280
Field House	281
Dormitories	282
Handicapped Students	295
Libraries	297
Individual Study Carrels	314
Student Unions	322
Computation Centers	330
Communications Centers	333
Regional Education Center (Supplementary)	335
Resource Facilities (Library)	337
Large-Group Facilities	340
Audiovisual	351
Theater-Arts-Laboratory Teaching Station	357
Programs and Programming	360

GENERAL REQUIREMENTS

Typically, the nursery class consists of 15 to 20 children, 1 teacher, and 1 assistant teacher. For this we recommend a minimum of 700 sq ft of instructional space excluding observation and office area. The optimal area would be 1,000 sq ft. This discussion focuses on a classroom for a single group, but, through creative planning, a nursery classroom of unconventional shape could be designed to accommodate two or three nursery class groups (30 to 60 children).

The classroom environment should foster a climate conducive to the educational objectives of the program. For example, children may have difficulty learning to be relatively quiet and attentive in a noisy environment or sitting in uncomfortable positions. Children may be inhibited in the development of self-reliance if the environment forces the teacher to supervise their every move.

The classroom's arrangement should contribute to the child's concepts of order and space. A perceptually clear and distinct room environment, achieved through uncluttered equipment and furniture arranged in an orderly fashion, helps the child focus his attention on the curriculum instead of distracting him with irrelevant stimuli. Daily contact with an uncluttered, structurally simple environment helps to teach time and space organization. Tidiness is a secondary benefit.

The nursery classroom should consist of a series of well-defined, interrelated areas, including a general area for group activities, a reading corner, a doll corner and housekeeping area, an area for blocks and another for manipulative toys, an art corner, and storage cubicles where the children hang their hats and coats and keep their possessions. Rest rooms and storage areas are also essential. A separate tutoring booth is desirable because it provides a special environment for individualization of instruction and for teacher-child interaction. (See Fig. 1.)

The smaller the total space available, the more careful must be the selection of what to include. Regardless of the room's size, it is imperative to maintain neatness, orderliness, and general attractiveness, with adequate space around objects and areas in the room. Empty space around objects is necessary: when a child's attention is directed to a group of rubber animals, for example, he must be able to see them unobscured by adjacent objects.

Teachers who have taught only in square or rectangular rooms seem to prefer large, open spaces which make visual supervision of an entire room possible from any vantage point. If more than one adult is in the room at all times, there is less need for such supervision. Furthermore, a rectangle of 1,000 sq ft has some disadvantages. Such a room appears extremely large to small children. It makes it difficult to create corners for reading and other quiet activities.

Facilities for Early Childhood Education, Educational Facilities Laboratories, New York, N.Y.

And it almost eliminates the possibility for a child to be alone with an adult.

A rectangular room is by no means ideal, and, if it is necessary to use one, it should be broken down into specific areas with freestanding dividers and cabinets.

Acoustical control is a fundamental concern in designing nursery schoolrooms. Children's voices are high-pitched, and many activities, both noisy and quiet, take place at the same time. Because disadvantaged children need special help in discriminating sounds, the classroom itself should be as free as possible of acoustical distractions.

A carpeted floor is recommended for acoustic purposes and for its other advantages. It is attractive, is easy to maintain, and provides a warm, comfortable surface on which the children work and play. Using carpets of different colors and textures helps to define different areas of the school. Only the art corner, because it is cleaned with water, requires a hard surface.

The size of the children must be kept in mind in planning display areas. Any display higher than 4 ft–6 in. is beyond the small child's usual range of awareness. Most children can select their own books or puzzles if the top shelves are not higher than 3 ft–6 in.

In planning the number and placement of windows, consideration ought to be given to the view outside the window. Where the school setting affords a pleasant, changing view, windows might be included as integral parts of the classroom. Windows should be low enough for the children to see through. When windows would expose only the monotony of a brick wall, the space traditionally given them might better be used as space for classroom displays.

In the second case, skylights and translucent wall materials are effective ways of providing natural light in the classroom without losing valuable wall space.

THE GENERAL AREA FOR GROUP ACTIVITIES

As already mentioned, a nursery schoolroom comprises a general area and several specific corners or alcoves for special activities. The general area should be an open space of at least 150 sq ft for group activities like singing, dancing, and listening to a story.

It is frequently advisable to seat all the children and adults around tables. The same tables can be used in the art area, the reading area, or the manipulative toy area as long as they can be pulled together easily in the larger area for group activities.

Music activities can take place in the general area. Carts are needed here for a record player and a tape recorder, and closed shelving for items such as rhythm instruments, autoharp, guitar, and drums.

The general area should have a central place containing shelves for displays that change every few days. The display shelf should be about 4 ft long, with a bulletin board above it and one shelf below. The shelf should be 15 to 20 in. high to accommodate small animal cages, canned vegetables, and the like. A sliding bulletin board over a fixed one would allow various displays to be exposed or covered at the teacher's will.

Where there is no opportunity to grow things out of doors, a planter for raising flowers, plants, or vegetables is essential. Other useful

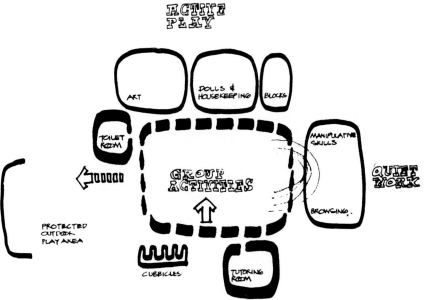

Fig. 1

203

equipment in the general area would include a hot plate and a refrigerator.

THE BLOCK AREA

Blocks provide a wide variety of learning opportunities. These opportunities include development of self-expression, muscular coordination, and cognitive skills. Building structures that are shared with and admired by peers and teachers help the child view himself positively.

The block area could be a little alcove (24 to 30 sq ft) outside of the major traffic area but opening onto the general area. This arrangement creates a protected space where children can build something that won't be inadvertently knocked down by children engaged in other activities, and it also provides the necessary space for several children to play with the blocks simultaneously.

Unpainted, rectangular unit blocks, uniform in height and width but varying in length, are used, along with blocks of various shapes— triangular, curved, and so on. Blocks of the same shape and length are stored in separate stacks with enough space between the stacks to make them easy to arrange. The lengths of the blocks, which vary, are exposed rather than the ends, which do not vary. Silhouettes painted on the shelves help the children to find and replace the blocks by themselves. (See Fig. 2.)

At the beginning of the year, 16 lin ft of shelving, at least 11 in. deep and having at least 10 in. between shelves, is adequate. As the school year progresses, more blocks are added. These may be shelved in movable cabinets that can be rolled into the classroom when needed, and then left in the room. If the storage shelves for the blocks are no higher than 2 ft, small items, such as toy trains, cars, planes, boats, animals, and figures of people, can be displayed on cabinet tops, their places marked by painted silhouettes.

MANIPULATIVE TOY AREA

Play with manipulative toys complements and enhances some of what children learn when playing with the blocks. By playing with colored pegs and pegboards, lockboards, small unit blocks, Cuisenaire rods, puzzles, felt

boards and geometric forms, nuts and bolts, nesting cups, and similar toys, children can learn colors and develop perceptions of size and form as well as of mathematical concepts.

The manipulative toy area is basically a quiet area where children work individually. It can be by itself or part of the area for reading and listening. Two or three two-shelf, open cabinets are sufficient to display the manipulative toys. Puzzles are best displayed on sloping shelves so the children can see them all as they select the ones they want to use. A cabinet above the manipulative toy area is a good place to store toys and puzzles not currently in use; the number and complexity of toys and puzzles are increased as the year progresses. A table that can accommodate at least four or five children should be located near the display cabinets. (See Fig. 3.)

READING AND LISTENING AREA

Children will come, individually or together, to the reading and listening area to look at books, to be read to by the assistant or the teacher, or to listen to a story on a tape recorder. These activities are probably more important for disadvantaged children than for children from more advantaged homes. The typical home of the disadvantaged child might not have available sufficient kinds and quantities of children's reading material, and there will probably not be a quiet, uncrowded place for the child to learn to listen.

The reading and listening area should be a quiet place well away from the block area, art area, and housekeeping corner. The space should be well defined either by walls and dividers, by cabinets, or by a difference in ceiling height, floor elevation, lighting, or color and texture of floor or walls. This area could be elevated two or three steps above the general area, an arrangement that would convey a feeling of its being special, separate, and cozy. If elevated, it can also serve as a platform for dramatic activity, and the children can sit on the steps when they are being read to.

The reading corner requires sufficient display-shelf space for showing the front cover of each of 20 to 25 books. The highest shelf should be no more than 3 ft–6 in. from the floor—preferably 3 ft only. If the shelving

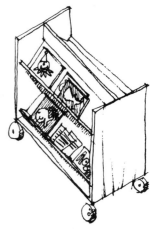

Fig. 3 Sloping shelves for display of books and puzzles.

cannot be adjusted, there should be at least 14 in. between the two shelves. Thirty-two lin ft of shelving provides enough space for books.

There should be a place to display one book and related small objects and pictures. An adjacent bulletin board adds to the display.

In addition to the bookshelves and display area, it is highly desirable to have a low shelf or table, available to as many as six children at a time, on which to place specialized learning equipment such as a cartridge tape recorder.

DOLL AND HOUSEKEEPING AREA

The doll and housekeeping area requires a dress-up area, dolls and necessary accessories, cooking and eating utensils, and general housekeeping equipment. Some authorities feel that as the year progresses, the housekeeping area should be increased, while other authorities would gradually eliminate the area completely.

The doll and housekeeping area is the area most children will first turn to when they come to nursery school. It is a link to the home, and at the same time it provides the opportunity for expanding the child's concept of what a home can be. Some disadvantaged children are unfamiliar with many things that teachers assume are standard equipment or practices in any home. Some families, for instance, may not have organized meals when everyone sits down together to eat. Instead, family members eat at different times, and not necessarily at a table.

The housekeeping area might present a major problem—it can be so attractive to children that some of them will want to spend most of their time there. It is for this reason that some authorities would begin the year with a complete housekeeping corner and gradually eliminate it. Presumably, as the area is decreased, children will either move into other areas of the room, or, if they remain in the housekeeping area, become more creative in their play.

The dress-up area is usually of great interest to the children. It should include a child-size chest of drawers and either hatboxes or open shelves for dress-up clothing (shoes, hats, jewelry, material suitable for belts, trains, capes, veils), a full-length mirror, and a tele-

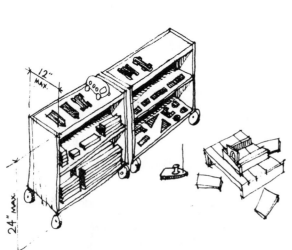

Fig. 2 Block carts. Colored silhouettes indicate storage locations.

phone connected to another telephone elsewhere in the room. One telephone should be placed so that the child can look into the mirror while talking. The second telephone need not be fully enclosed, but neither should the child be able to see or hear (except through the receiver) the one to whom he is talking.

Dolls and the necessary accessories also provide important opportunities for learning. Through their own explorations and through interactions with the teacher, children learn textures, the names and functions of objects, colors, manipulative skills, and the routines of their own daily living—dressing, eating, going to bed, and the like.

The cooking area requires a child's stove and refrigerator, cooking utensils, other equipment such as plastic fruits and vegetables, and a container for juice or milk. There could also be a sink, open shelves, and a pegboard. The shelves would hold table flatware as well as many of the other utensils found in the average kitchen. There should be enough space between objects to present an orderly appearance, and the pegboard should have silhouettes of each object to encourage the children to return each item to its place. A child-size table and chairs complete the cooking area.

Finally, the housekeeping area should include places for a child-size ironing board, iron, clotheslines, mop, dustpan, and broom.

ART AREA

In the art area, a few children at a time paint pictures; make finger paintings, collages, and mobiles; or play with clay, modeling compound, paste, crayons, marking pens, and an assortment of other material such as soda straws and pipe cleaners.

The art area should be away from heavy room traffic and should have limited access. It requires a sink for washing hands and cleaning paintbrushes and sponges. Ideally,

there would be two sinks—one at the appropriate height for the teacher and a lower one for the children. If only one can be provided, it should be at the appropriate height for the children's use.

Two kinds of storage space in the art area are desirable.

In the first, sheets of newsprint (usually 18 by 24 in.) and of colored construction paper should be stored within easy reach of the children. Construction paper should be arranged so that a child can take one color without disturbing the other stacks. The teacher might also store crayons, marking pens, and paintbrushes here.

The second storage space, for such things as scissors and paints, should be closed and out of the reach of the children. The storage cabinets can also serve as room dividers.

The art area should have space enough for two or more children to paint at one time. A regular easel with room for painting on either side is satisfactory; or three or four easels side by side could be provided by sloping a long piece of plywood or masonite out from a wall or room divider. The latter arrangement has the virtue of providing more work area in less space, and it allows the young painters to admire each other's work. Easels should be easy to clean, and the tray that holds the paints and brushes should be removable for cleaning.

A table is important in this area. It should be large enough to accommodate four children playing with clay, using finger paints, or pasting collages. The table should be about 18 in. high and have a work area of 15 sq ft or more.

Art activities provide a feeling of accomplishment and recognition that helps a child feel positive about himself. One of the ways to reinforce this is to display the child's paintings, but to display all the children's paintings simultaneously destroys the clarity and attractiveness of the room. If, somewhere in the room, at child's eye level, a display space is provided for five or six 18- by 24-in. pictures,

and if the pictures are frequently changed, each child can see his work exhibited many times during a year. It is not necessary to display all the children's art work at once.

Provisions should be made for hanging paintings to dry. There should be enough space for at least 12 paintings to dry at one time.

TUTORING BOOTH

It is essential that an enclosed space be provided for teaching one child at a time. The enclosed space, or tutoring booth, enables a child to be free of distractions while working with a teacher or with specialized teaching

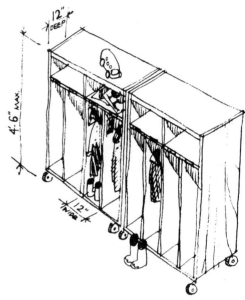

Fig. 4. Individual cubicles.

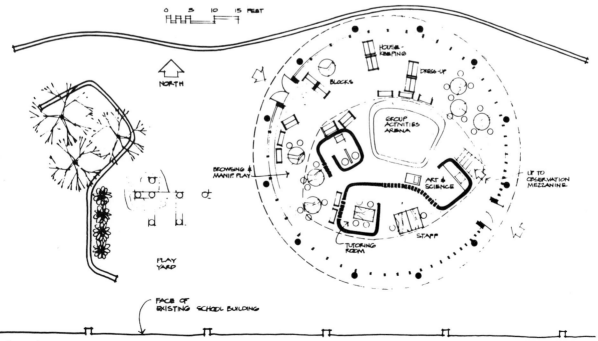

Fig. 5 Proposed nursery.

Educational

NURSERY SCHOOLS

A Summary of Space Requirements

Activity	Space, sq ft Min.	Opt.	Storage	Display	Other
General area	150	200	Carts, closed shelves for music equipment	2 centrally located shelves 4 ft long, 15–20 in. apart; bulletin board	Planter; hot plate and refrigerator (or in additional storage, below); tables (can be tables from other areas if easily movable)
Block alcove	50 (Can be 24–30 if play can expand to general area)	75	Shelving 16 ft long, 11 in. deep, at least 10 in. high, plus supplementary shelving in movable cabinets to be added through school year		
Manipulative toy area	100	150	2 or 3 two-shelf open cabinets; sloping shelves for puzzles; cabinet for toys not in use	Open and sloping shelves (see Storage, left)	Table for 4–5 children; should be quiet area
Reading and listening area	(Combined with manipulative toy area)		Closed case for duplicate books out of children's reach	32 ft of low, open shelving for 20–25 books showing front covers; shelf and bulletin board for special exhibits	Table or low shelf for tape recorder, accommodating up to 6 children
Doll and house-keeping area	100 (Possibly to be increased or decreased progressively)	150	Drawers and open shelving for dress-up clothes; dolls; open shelves and peg-board in cooking area		Full-length mirror; 2 telephones; sink (can be shared with art); table and chairs in cooking area
Art area	100	150	Open shelves for news-print and construction paper; shelves accessible only to teacher for paints, scissors	Sufficient to hang 6 18 x 24 inch paintings	Easels; sinks (one for children — may be shared with housekeeping area; one for teachers — may be in additional storage area); table 18 in. high with area of 15 sq ft; space for paintings to dry
Tutoring booth(s)	45 (each)	50 (each)			Enclosed for privacy; if only one teacher is available, partitions should be glass
Cubicles	60	90	For pupils' clothes and other belongings; should be 4½ ft high, 1 ft wide, 1 ft deep		
Toilets	40	50			
Additional storage	30	100	Refrigerator, hot plate (see General Area, above)		May serve as teacher's utility area
Total	675	1015			
Observation space	Can be combined with additional storage area				
Outdoor play area					

equipment. This space might also serve as a testing area or simply as a place where a child can be alone with an adult. These activities are important and such a space should be provided even if, as a consequence, the size of the main room is reduced.

In some instances, it might be feasible to create a room within a room by enclosing an area large enough to accommodate a small group of five or six who could work away from the distractions of the rest of the class. If only one teacher is to be present in the class, the walls should be transparent to allow the teacher visual control.

INDIVIDUAL CUBICLES FOR STORAGE

Each child should have a place of his own in which to hang his hat and coat, set his rubbers or overshoes, and store things that belong to him. These cubicles, or cubbies, should be about 1 ft deep, 1 ft wide, and 4 ft–6 in. high. The child should be able to sit down in or near his cubicle to put on his shoes. (See Fig. 4.)

TOILETS

Where rest rooms for the children are not adjacent to the classroom, inordinate time is wasted in moving children to and from the rest room. If rest rooms are integral parts of the classroom, children can use them independently and develop self-reliance.

The theory that the fixtures should resemble those in the children's homes has merit, but the overriding considerations are convenience and utility. The wash basin and toilets should be appropriately sized for children.

STORAGE SPACE

To ensure an orderly and neat room and reduce the number of stimuli present at any one time, storage space outside the classroom is important. It can also serve as a utility area for the teacher and should contain a large sink for preparation of paints and for cleaning up.

If a sink is provided here for the teacher, only one sink, placed between the art and housekeeping areas, is necessary in the classroom. The hot plate used in the classroom and a refrigerator for keeping milk and juice belong in the outside storage room if possible.

OUTDOOR PLAY AREA

The outdoor play area could include a planting area, a sandbox, an open area for play with balls, hoops, inner tubes, boxes, and boards. Ideally, some part of this area would be sheltered to allow the children to spend some time outdoors during inclement weather.

A storage space is needed for the outdoor equipment.

OBSERVATION SPACE

An observation area is desirable for programs that encourage parents to observe classes and to become more involved with the school and the education of the child. A combination of one-way glass, microphones, and earphones will ensure separation of pupils and observers; one-way glass with a louvered panel would suffice. (See Fig. 5.)

Ideally, the observation area should be 1 or 2 ft higher than the regular classroom. That would give the observer a good view over the low room dividers and would leave the wall space below the observation windows free for cabinet and display space.

An alternative to an observation room is a closed-circuit television setup that provides viewing at a location removed from the classroom.

Acoustical control in the classroom is essential. Without this control it is virtually impossible to hear or to transmit the speech of the children. Sound-absorbing ceiling and wall tile, draperies, and carpet all merit consideration for inclusion in the classroom.

The observation area should open directly on the corridor or outside, allowing observers to come and go without interfering with the children and the teachers.

CHILDREN'S CENTER

Figure 1 shows one suggested organization for a children's center to accommodate approximately 60 children.

Children's Playrooms

Children's playrooms, one for each age group, shall be provided, as a rule. Playrooms shall be self-contained, without folding partitions. Minimum area of one room (for the youngest children) shall be 550 sq ft; the other rooms shall be at least 750 sq ft each. The minimum area per child is 30 sq ft. Square rooms are preferred. Southern or southeastern exposure is desirable; northern exposure alone is not acceptable.

The rooms shall be protected from public view, either by the playground or by landscaping. Ceilings shall be 10 ft high, and shall have acoustical treatment.

Services for Children's Playrooms

Toilets A toilet for each playroom opening from the room, near the playground door. At least two lavatories and two water closets shall be provided in each toilet room. Water closets shall be 10 in high in toilet for the youngest children, standard height in the other toilets. Lavatories shall be 21 in from floor with strainer in drain.

Play Area Each playroom shall have direct access to an outdoor play area, divided by fencing into two separate unequal sections (the smaller for the youngest group) with gates for access. Minimum area shall be 4,500 sq ft, minimum width, 50 ft. The play area shall be partly shaded by a canopy or overhang from the building.

Toy storage shelter for outdoor toys, with convenient access from both sections of the play area.

Other arrangements are shown in Figs. 2 and 3.

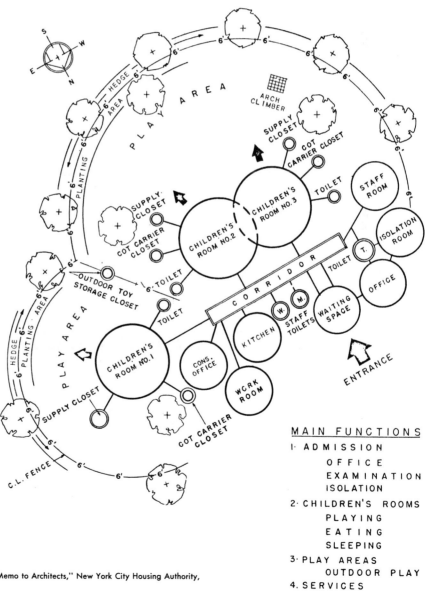

Fig. 1 Children's center space organization. *Source:* "Memo to Architects," New York City Housing Authority, New York.

CHILD CARE CENTERS

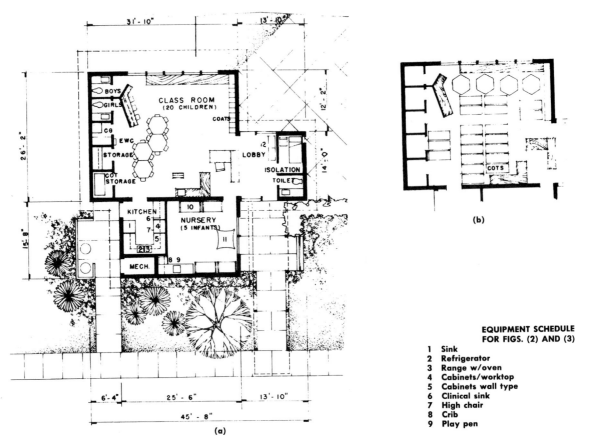

EQUIPMENT SCHEDULE
FOR FIGS. (2) AND (3)

1 Sink
2 Refrigerator
3 Range w/oven
4 Cabinets/worktop
5 Cabinets wall type
6 Clinical sink
7 High chair
8 Crib
9 Play pen

Fig. 2 Care center for 25 children: (a) playtime arrangement; (b) cot arrangement for naptime.

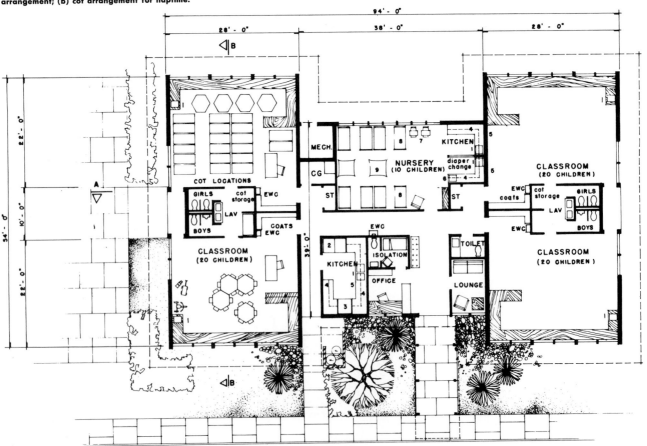

208 **Fig. 3 Care center for a 50-child population.** (From Department of Defense Definitive Designs, Department of the Navy, Washington, 1968.)

By PHILIP WILL, JR., and RAYMOND C. OVRESAT
with the assistance of C. WILLIAM BRUBAKER, MORTON HARTMAN,
GEORGE A. HUTCHINSON, EMMET INGRAM, A. FREDERICK KOLFLAT,
and WILLIAM McCOY, Perkins & Will, Architects

INTRODUCTION

School building has passed through the years and styles of building to finally free itself of the constraints of building in some certain way. The response now is to the *real* needs and reasons for education, to *change* and *flexibility* and an *awareness* that the buildings are simply and primarily for children to learn in, teachers to teach and learn in, and staff and parents to "lend a hand" in.

The log cabin and the one-room little red schoolhouse are a far cry from the prideful community institutions of the early 1900s. But are they indeed so far from ungraded schools, modular scheduling, turf space, magnet schools, and a host of self-initiative plans?

The technological and communication races pace and outpace people's performance and their acquaintance and acceptance of ever-new ideas and increasing information. Learning must be accelerated, horizons broadened, and differences narrowed between urban and rural communities. Still, some communities are doing better and have more innovative programs, more responsive staffs, and more total determination. The facilities alone can only do part of the job.

Education is life and people doing things. The school is both a kind of shelter and a kind of stage. It brings together children and adults on the day-to-day business of contending, learning, working hard, having fun, and growing up. It focuses attention and is a focus of attention. It is its own community and a critical part of the total community.

The process of planning a school which will respond to the real needs of learning, teaching philosophies and community objectives and which will really meet the basic uncommon denominator, its children, is complex and challenging. It demands a nice balance of experience, wisdom, professional skills, and uncommon sense on the part of all involved. Only part of the objective should be a well-conceived, efficient, practical, soundly constructed, quality building. It must, too, be changeable and compatible with its children and its own community of users. Buildings do not die of old age, but of design obsolescence or overindulgence. The architect is and should be regularly challenged to conceive ways in which school facilities may be designed not only to be a practical, efficient response to the needs of today's teaching technologies, but also to anticipate the inevitable changes by which learning will become an entirely different experience.

Environment

The architect's efforts must be put into the creation of a school which actively and attractively suits the functions of the education it serves and which not only *accommodates* but also *contributes* a very special environment

for learning. "Environment for learning" connotes a broad range of special qualities, evidenced by many characteristics of a building's design. The physical aspects of environment—those relating to the bodily senses of temperature, vision, and hearing—may be relatively well controlled by known engineering methods. Those environmental qualities which affect emotions and behavior are far more difficult to accomplish through building design since they are not subject to established formulas or systems. Human scale, homineness, warmth, excitement, and repose are recognizable attributes of a building which engenders real responses from its occupants. The environment of a school should be one which actively stimulates the development of human beings—socially, intellectually, physically, and emotionally. Creating an environment, and not just a space, should not be a bonus, but rather is a minimum essential.

Program Involvement

The architect properly seeks to provide services early in the planning stages prior to the actual design and construction of school facilities. This is so that he can contribute with the best of his experience and technical knowledge in the processes of site selection, preparation for bond issue referenda, time scheduling, programming, and budgeting. During the early planning stages the architect may gain insight into the philosophical attitudes of the school board and administrators and the nature of the community or neighborhood for which new or added school facilities are needed. It is during this time that ideas can be exchanged.

The architect should know the community he serves by considering as parts of his total responsibility the following:

1. The nature of the total community setting and its people

2. The character of the neighborhood surrounding the site, e.g., high-density multi-family, single family, mixed uses, obsolete, declining, stable, or growing, and the presence of significant environmental influences such as air or noise pollution

3. The projected rate of growth, if the community is developing, as an indicator of phased construction of the school

Teaching and learning programs must be formulated and facilities must be planned in response to the anticipated educational, cultural, and social needs not only of the school-age members of the community but of the adult group as well. A predominantly vocational-technical orientation is generally indicated for a school in a largely industrial community. In an area where a high percentage of students go on to college, the school's curriculum must include preparatory liberal arts subjects. The intensified academic programs necessary today are tempting communities to extend the typical

nine-month school year and to lengthen the school day. Summer sessions are becoming conventional both for makeup work and for programs of acceleration and enrichment. Some communities have implemented full twelve-month use of their facilities, some on a basis of 45 days of school, 15 days of vacation. Extracurricular activities, most of which are offshoots of formal scholastic work, such as foreign language and science clubs, school publications, special music groups and dramatic organizations, are carried over into after-school hours and evenings.

In addition to housing the regular school programs, the building will probably also accommodate adult evening classes, PTA meetings, public lectures, concerts, and similar educational-cultural events. Add to these a variety of civic functions, such as town meetings and park recreation projects, and we have the "town hall" school busily serving as its community's educational and cultural center practically around the clock and all year long.

All these considerations influence the broad strokes of decision making for the form of the school. Beyond these are the "educational specifications," which spell out the details of the school program in terms of optimum size of enrollment; teaching loads; scheduling (modular or conventional); organization of the instructional program ("school within a school," "house plan"); learning methods (team teaching, individualized instruction, independent study); and all the mechanical, electronic, and audio-visual aids to the learning process, in addition to the library as "instructional materials center." Additionally, physical education, competitive athletics, recreation, cultural, and social needs must be accounted for.

Space, Quality, Cost

These functions together make up the plan-dictating, form-generating influences that the school board, administration, citizens committees, and architect must consider in establishing the priorities of space, quality, and cost which will govern the design and construction of the new facilities. It is axiomatic that these factors shall be placed in balance, if the results are not somehow to be frustrated. In applying the space $\times$ quality $=$ cost formula, only two factors can be fixed by the client. The architect must be allowed to vary the third; i.e., if space and cost are rigid requirements, the only variable then is *quality* of materials and construction. Obviously, inefficient planning can rob the administration of space urgently needed to carry out the desired programs. Unless appropriate materials, equipment, and finishes are used, the board of education will be forever burdened by excessive maintenance and operation costs; and if, through lack of discipline over these factors of space and quality, the project cost exceeds the funds that have been voted, the community will, assuredly, be most

209

ELEMENTARY AND SECONDARY SCHOOLS
General

articulate in voicing its displeasure. In school design the architect must reject wishful thinking, whether it be his own or that of his client.

It is rarely understood by voters that the overwhelming cost of the school system is for teachers' salaries and related educational expense. Even if schools cost nothing to build, the effect on a citizen's tax bill for education would be relatively trivial. Depending on whether a school district is well established with existing buildings, or newly created with buildings yet to be built, the budget for the building and financing of the physical plant over its lifetime varies from 5 to 15 percent of the cost of educating a child. Of this cost approximately half is chargeable to financing—the interest paid on bonds. Cheap and inadequate educational facilities save little initially and, for the long run, are indeed poor investments and are permanent handicaps to the learning/teaching process. Therefore, those who defend high quality do so on sound economic ground. The benefits of education require no defense.

All of what goes into a school, what must be considered is outlined in the following pages. The task is complex, the options are many, involving the input of people, money, effort, patience, and finally providing a gratifying reward when the job's been done well. Schools can be and should be fun to be in, for everyone.

By STANTON LEGGETT, Educational Consultant

EDUCATIONAL CONSULTING
Purpose

In order to state the needs of an educational institution and to relate a facility more closely to the educational program, communities, schools, and colleges increasingly use an educational consultant as a primary member of the planning team. A school planning project, whether for a new building or for a master plan for an institution, should be used not only to construct a good facility but to provide a setting for effective restudy of educational programs and to allow a time for examining new perspectives of learning. With close personal contact between a consultant with wide experience and a faculty that must search its collective soul before the concrete is poured, a prime time is created for real in-service education. The operative word is *real*.

Procedure

As in education, the name of the game is *process*. While the assessable outcomes of a facility planning procedure are most important, dollars for consulting services can be used twice: once for the building product and once for the process of involving many people in planning and decision making.

Greatest advantage can come by designating a planning cadre who will ultimately take over operation of the new institution. Alternatively, a group of potential operators of the educational system could be involved. Further options include general participation by parallel staff members from other schools or colleges.

When groups to participate and to be involved are identified, one useful device is to select a steering committee. Hopefully, a steering committee will include a cross section of the people who will be involved, people with optimistic but not necessarily similar views.

Also it should be composed so that it will give credibility to the work of the committee. The steering committee should steer. The consultant should become working staff for the committee.

The planning process should involve as many people as possible, and the consultant must be responsive to the direction of the educational institution. The consultant is a temporary employee of the school system. The school system should induct the consultant into the problem, providing wide opportunities for him to get to know *where* the institution is going, *what* the educational aspirations of the community are, and *how* the new facility should help the system achieve its goals.

While the process of induction is going on, where many people tell the consultant about the problem or the purpose, the consultant is making his contribution. This is, essentially, to widen the spectrum of choices or options that are considered by those involved in the planning process. Viewing and discussing ways to meet objectives should go on for some time—long enough so that all the participants feel that they have really explored and participated, but not so long that frustration sets in.

The consultant somewhere along in the process takes on another role—organizer of chaos. It is his task, as temporary staff to a decision-making organization, to develop a first document which states the problems and offers a set of alternatives to consider in decision making about general directions. Such a report should be made widely available to the staff or the involved group for review, critique, revision, deletion, and addition. A program of needs for a building or the base for a master plan evolves from the basic study and evaluation of options, leading through successive revisions to descriptions of spaces in terms of numbers, sizes, and characteristics.

EDUCATIONAL SPECIFICATIONS

The development of a formal document of educational specifications for new educational facilities is now accepted practice in approaching the construction of educational projects of any consequence. The document is designed to formalize and organize the needs of the users of the school so that the design can be developed to house these needs.

Outline of Educational Program Document

1. *Educational concept of the facility.* A brief statement should be made of the educational goals and purposes to be accommodated by the facility. Discussion of the educational philosophy to be followed is necessary. Make a general description of the facility and its basic elements. Draw up a statement of design objectives.
2. *Activity program and space requirements.* Make a general description of the assumed academic curriculum and other activities at the facility. Make a general description of types of space required and teaching methods to be used. Data are to be summarized in four charts:
   a. Activity program chart
   b. Space requirements and utilization chart
   c. Area summary chart
   d. Environmental conditions chart
3. *Detailed area and equipment requirements.* For each activity area, write a *narrative* outline of how the various spaces in it will be used, their relationship to each other, and their relationship to other parts of the facility. For each activity area, provide a detailed list of all spaces, giving areas and equipment for each. Data are to

be summarized on two standard forms:
   a. Space list
   b. Equipment list

Flexibility and Change

All schools must be as flexible as possible in terms of space. The spaces in them must be easily adaptable to new uses and arrangements in the future. The types and division of spaces given in the program should not imply structures that cannot be easily modified for changing needs in the future.

The operative idea in the traditional view of educational specifications is *specific*. The approach assumes that a school or college can be "frozen" at a point and fixed there with all the elements held constant while the architect designs an environment. Change an element and the design process must start over again, for the "program" has changed.

It is not easy to describe a viable alternative to this process, because the human mind cannot deal realistically with an infinite number of variables at the same time and come up with a definite and specific answer, be it a building or educational program. When we have fully learned to supplement the mind of man with the memory of a computer, we will have better success in dealing with the dynamics of a school or college and the creative environment.

The school is a planning process, an envelope for change. The objective is to develop a building that provides the environment for growth and change, not to pin education down.

Process

The educational specifications for a school that emphasizes *process* are as general a set of specifications as it is possible to agree upon while, at the same time, securing an appropriate building. To as large a degree as possible, the arrangement of the space, the staffing of the school, and the deployment of the resources should be left up to the people who will use the school. The educational specifications will be the beginning of the planning process which will continue through the life of the school. The specifications may describe the *first* of any environmental settings for learning experience.

Part of the design process should be to create models of teaching spaces so that the planning group for the school (teachers, students, and parents) could make value judgments about the use of space and try them out. These models serve as bases for simulations. People learn a great deal from simulations, for in this manner the consequences of actions or decisions are seen graphically and realistically.

The educational specifications can help by being constructed on a modular basis and by including examples of the options that exist within the more generalized requirements. The architects can contribute much by graphically representing the wide variety of ways people can organize themselves within the pliable, yet not anonymous, environment the architects have created for them.

The educational consultant is not an architect, nor vice versa. As the planning process moves from words toward lines, the consultant's role changes. The planning organization, of which he is a part, responds to the designs of the architect. For this is a team process. A good team uses all the qualities of the participants as fully as possible and shifts roles unobtrusively, but responsibly.

ARCHITECTURAL PROGRAMMING

Architectural programming is the specific defining and analysis of physical needs. It is also the defining and analysis of constraints, like budget, code, site, and time schedules imposed upon those needs. Architectural programming is not educational programming, but follows and evolves from it.

Objectives

The prime objective is to define the problem: to clearly state the physical spaces required, the uses of these spaces, the functional relationship between them, and the occupancy and equipment needs of each space, all in a format understood and approved by the client.

Procedure

The first step is to determine who will participate in the planning process to follow. Included should be the owner, the educational consultants if involved, the architect, and any others who will have a direct bearing on the end result. These representatives should have the authority to make the day-to-day decisions on the formation of the program. In the case of a larger project, such as an urban high school, additional consultants may be required. They should be brought into the programming process as soon as possible so that the end result benefits best from their expertise when their recommendations of basic philosophy and policy are incorporated.

Secondly, a time schedule should be set with a final target date. It is essential. It should go beyond the programming phase and relate to an overall schedule including completion of construction and occupancy. Adherence to a schedule from the very outset imposes a constructive discipline and a healthy sense of urgency encouraging interaction among the participants. Modification or change of a schedule can then be appraised in light of the overall effect on time of occupancy. The time schedule clearly defines those points in time when approvals and reviews are required or desirable.

Thirdly, there should be a sequence and methodology: establishing the aims, organizing and collecting the facts, seeking out meaningful inherent concepts, and determining the needs (not wants) consistent with realistic constraint. The needs should then be stated in terms of interior and exterior spaces, site, budget, and time schedule.

Fourth, there should be a format and technique that graphically portray the parts. A picture is worth a pile of words. The technique should be consistently followed so that the continuing experiences can be added and their implications made clearly visible.

Finally, meetings should be scheduled in a "neutral" location. Meetings do not have to take place in the school building. In fact, there may be fewer interruptions elsewhere, and new ideas might be generated best in new surroundings where inhibitions are left behind.

Content

A complete architectural program should contain the following information:

1. *Statement of use by owner.* Adult education, community concerts, and other similar activities have a direct bearing on the planning of schools. In some urban schools, for example, specialized instruction in one school serving students throughout the city might require much more ample access into the site, as well as extraordinary circulations and toilet requirements. The complete, intended use of the facility should be made clear, as well as its place in a total educational system since that too may affect its future use.

2. *Basic concepts of teaching/administration.* What the approach to teaching and admin-

istering will be has critical influence on space needs, size, and building type. Team teaching and differentiated staffing would call for large open space and a variety of space sizes. Modular scheduling in a variety of class time periods dramatically affects space utilization. Will it be an open campus with students free to leave the building during "free" periods, or must the entire student body be housed in the building's spaces during all periods? Will there be study halls or free library or lounge access? Will the school be divided into subschools? Particularly in larger schools and school systems the matter of food service can influence decisions on plan organization and program organization. Counseling arrangements can be related to the administration offices or faculty-department grouping. The whole concern of administrative centralization versus decentralization can pull a plan one way or another.

3. *Spaces to be provided.* All details of the space requirements should be recorded, their size, how many of each size, the number of occupants in each space, the number of teaching stations, the equipment demands, their relationship and functions, and other special comments should be noted. With even a minimal experience in school design, a format can be developed to cover all basic types of school facilities as a checklist in developing a particular program. Through experience, certain guidelines and "rules of thumb" have been developed for school planning. Unit areas have gradually increased over the years, with the trend toward more individualized instruction, more specialized and diverse course offerings, and greater reliance on special equipment. Typical basis for calculation includes number of students per teaching station, area per student by types of space, gross square feet per student, and cost per student.

4. *Graphic representation.* It is most useful and makes clear to everyone relative sizes and priorities for consideration if the individual program parts and their numbers are graphically illustrated. All interior spaces and exterior spaces like playfields and parking lots should be shown to give a good overall picture of what the total space needs are in relation to land available and what various parts of the program physically represent in area relation to others. Some initial bulk areas may be additionally included to represent circulation, storage, and service requirements, and to indicate the relationship between net and gross areas.

5. *Limits/constraints.* It is also a prudent reminder to carefully note the various constraints on the programming process, like budget, time schedule, codes, insurance provisions and ratings, zoning and special use requirements, net to gross area limits or projections, and any special considerations (e.g., required review processes by government or other review agencies). Soil borings, site surveys, and information about utility services should be a part of the program data as well.

6. *Architectural statement.* Just as the owner's intended use and teaching-administrative philosophy will significantly guide the formation of the program, so the architect's basic planning approach to the particular problem should be written and recorded as part of the programming process. While this could not or should not be developed until the architect has learned enough about the problem, its incorporation into the programming document can thereafter serve as an important guide for the others who will be involved in making decisions that should relate more clearly to a common philosophy and assure a more consistent and better end result. Also, for reviews by various approval groups, whether they be the school owner or a code official, having all the "whys" stated clarifies understanding and minimizes misinterpretation.

Summary

The architectural program then is the basis for beginning the building, and the more information collected at the outset, and properly evaluated, the more successful the planning process and end result will be. Time and thought carefully spent in programming will bring everyone's ideas together at the outset, give everyone a chance to make his contribution, and advance the project in an orderly manner.

FINANCING

Programming procedures and determinations quickly come to a collision course with financial limitations, and almost invariably the building program has to be adjusted to conform to the hard reality of financial possibilities. The nature of financing school buildings hinges on the type of school and its sponsorship. The job of getting the money is becoming increasingly harder as more complex government funding procedures come into effect, tax allocations are spread across consolidated districts, and the trend to more centralized control and management increases. Campaigns for bond issues and tax increases must become more effective, newspaper publicity, coffee klatches, and public to-dos must be more objectively organized to convince an increasingly well-informed, interested, but demanding public.

Both new communities and old residential-based communities have problems in funding new schools and programs because of the limits of assessed valuation of their total properties. This prompts a search for state and federal support and a concern about the possible loss of local prerogatives. New tax revenues are being sought within the communities by charging for more services and pursuing zoning changes toward a wider mix of community to accomplish a broader tax base.

Types of Financing

A given project will normally be in one of the following categories, requiring a related type of financing:

1. *School districts with taxing power.* Major building projects are financed by a bond issue referendum within the limits established by the differential between existing indebtedness and an allowed percentage of current assessed valuation of taxable property in the district.

2. *School systems under local government.* Project funds are received as appropriations which may or may not represent proceeds from sales of bonds by the governmental taxing authority.

3. *Private schools.* Funding is primarily dependent on bequests, contributions, and mortgage loans. Under special circumstances some facilities may be funded by federal agencies.

These categories, and the traditional methods of financing characteristic of each, generally apply to institutions of higher learning, as well as to secondary and elementary schools. Near exhaustion of traditional financing sources has led in recent years to the development of methods of supplemental aid or procedures for lifting the entire burden of capital investment from the school or institution.

Federal legislation provides grants-in-aid and self-liquidating loans to qualifying institutions through agencies of the Department of Health, Education, and Welfare and to a limited degree through agencies of the Department of Housing and Urban Renewal. State and local govern-

ELEMENTARY AND SECONDARY SCHOOLS
General

ments have assistance programs of their own. A growing trend is toward the establishment of school building authorities or commissions, which will finance and construct buildings for occupancy by a school on a rentlike basis, with costs paid out of operating income.

It has become a routine obligation of school administrators to keep themselves informed about all agencies and assistance programs which may be available to help in financing a project or, in some cases, to make traditional funding unnecessary.

Programming and Budgeting

Financing *patterns* have critical effects on the design and planning of school facilities. If the amount of a bond issue or an appropriation has been established prior to programming or detail planning, the *scope* of the project will be rigidly limited by that amount. The only flexibility then lies in a supplemental bond issue or appropriation, which is usually not feasible. If planning funds are available, programming and preparation of preliminary plans and estimates should be carried out prior to the establishment of a fixed amount of funds available for the project.

If assistance in financing is obtained from outside agencies, these agencies will become reviewing authorities with their own requirements and standards which will directly affect the implementation of the program. Such requirements may include any or all of the following:

1. A maximum allowable cost per square foot
2. A minimum required ratio of net instructional area to gross building area
3. Use of governmental specification standards
4. Specified bidding procedures
5. Designation of construction labor pay scale

In contemplating allowable costs for a proposed project, there must first exist a clear idea of *all* the costs involved. If there is a million dollars to spend, a million-dollar *building* cannot be built. The project budget must cover all costs related to the project which are chargeable to the capital funds available. A typical project budget would contain allowances for the following items:

1. Construction cost of building facilities
2. Site development and utility connections
3. Fixed equipment
4. Architectural and engineering fees
5. Contingency allowance

Additional budget items might include land acquisition, demolition of existing buildings, landscaping, movable equipment and furnishings, legal fees, special consultant fees, and miscellaneous special expenses. As a rule of thumb, in the average building project, construction cost cannot exceed three-quarters of the allowable project cost amount. If the project requires an unusual amount of furnishings and equipment, or if unusual site conditions add heavily to site-related costs, the allowable ratio for building construction cost will be correspondingly reduced.

THE LEARNING ENVIRONMENT

Economics of Comfort Conditioning

Business and industry have amply proved that people perform more efficiently in ideally controlled surroundings, and equally well support-

ed is the fact that financial savings have been made. Translating these arguments to the school situation, it can be said that if students learn and teachers instruct more efficiently in a controlled learning environment, more students can be educated in less time, hence at a lower cost per student. If the building is conditioned for effective 12-month operation and is made attractive for intensive community use, it can certainly be said to be more efficiently and economically used.

Certain characteristics of building designs appropriate to total environment conditioning may, if the educational program permits, facilitate more economical construction, particularly if imagination is used in planning. The compact plan, for example, produces minimum exterior wall area, reduces piping runs, uses corridors and service areas most efficiently, and can be substantially more economical to build, operate, and maintain than other plan arrangements.

More and better use of the school buildings is, in itself, an economy to the community. Add to this the broadened educational and cultural advantages to the community at large, and it becomes apparent that the totally comfort-conditioned school is both practical and necessary.

Architectural Functions

The mechanical elements are the basic, but not the only, considerations for the entire job of climate control. The orientation, the plan arrangement, the design of the building, and the materials used can contribute to the quality of comfort achieved and to the economy (see Fig. 1). Consider the following:

1. *Plan.* Less room and exterior wall exposure in a compact, multistory building will cost less to heat and cool than a sprawling, one-story arrangement of equal area and cubage. A plan consisting of predominantly interior classroom spaces and peripheral corridors provides flexibility of space and economies in heating and cooling.

2. *Orientation.* Classroom windows facing east or west receive excessive heat from the sun. Although this fact assists heating in cold weather, the cooling problem is generally greater. As a general rule, it is preferable to face the majority of rooms north or south.

3. *Fenestration.* "Windowless" buildings are entirely practical: they save on initial cost,

Fig. 1

maintenance, and heat loss and are free of outside dust, smoke, odors, and noise. Some windows should be introduced, however, to avoid that "closed-in" feeling. On the other hand, equally strong arguments can and have been made for the other environmental advantages of large window areas, the benefits of close relationship to the out-of-doors, and the welcome of light and sunshine to one's physical being.

4. *Solar controls.* Wide roof overhangs, solar screens, glass block, and similar devices to control sunlight are no longer as essential. The use of heat-absorbing glass reduces glare and light transmission and produces economies in the HVAC system design. Cleaner, simpler, far less expensive designs are now possible with uniform, high-level electrical illumination.

5. *Insulation.* Adequate insulation of roofs and exterior walls reduces both heat loss and heat gain far more than is generally supposed. Even double glazing adds measurably to more economical climate control.

6. *Space conditioning.* Skillful use of lighting, acoustic materials, and color and form in school design are essential ingredients of conditioning space in the learning environment and, properly applied, act upon our senses of sight and hearing to cause reactions conducive to better learning and teaching.

7. *Lighting.* Good lighting design involves locating illumination sources so that work areas receive adequate light free of glare and excessive contrast or shadow. Both natural and artificial light must be controllable to eliminate glaring shafts of sunlight or to darken the room for projecting pictures. It is desirable to use some incandescent lighting, strategically placed, to create points of variety and accent in the more conventional all-fluorescent systems.

8. *Acoustics.* Acoustical control involves containment, absorption, and reflection or reinforcement of sound. According to the circumstances of the listener, sound should be prevented from leaving a space when it will disturb people in adjacent rooms. Certain amounts of acoustically absorbent material must be used to "soak up" noise in such areas as corridors, toilets, and cafeterias. Accurate and comfortable hearing of music in an auditorium depends on projecting sound from reflection from some surfaces, but absorption in others to prevent distracting echos; a speaker's voice may have to be reinforced by an amplifier in large rooms.

9. *Colors.* Color is a psychological aid to learning. Tastefully used, it can enhance environment, engendering a cheerful, receptive mood. Bright, warm colors stimulate excitement and action in the gymnasium; soft, cool colors create a quiet atmosphere in places of study.

10. *Form.* The physical shapes of our surroundings also have psychological effects which can favorably influence learning. Large rooms, such as the library, cafeteria, or auditorium require higher ceilings, for a sense of airy freedom, than do small offices and conference rooms; corridors should be offset, widened occasionally, and given a view in order to avoid the feeling of interminable constricting length; an atmosphere of spaciousness, or lack of confinement, can be created by making some interior partitions of glass. This is particularly important when the plan design involves large areas of interior spaces, made possible by a climate-conditioned system.

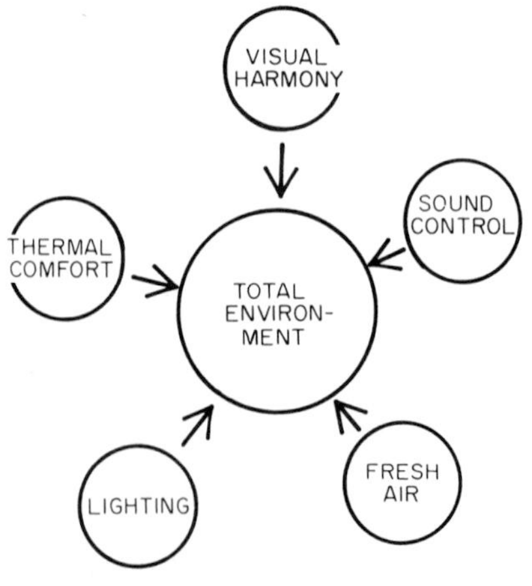

By DON HALAMKA

SITE SELECTION

The farsighted school board will project its needs well into the future and select and acquire sites while land is still available and cheap. Such prudent long-range planning is facilitated by consultation with local county or regional planning agencies that possess knowledge and appreciation of the long-term system needs and growth patterns on community development. Frequently, large-scale development builders can be persuaded to dedicate land to community purposes well in advance of need with consequent savings to taxpayers. The following is a list of basic items for use in the selection of a school site.

I. Present and future environment. Economic, social, and housing makeup of community
II. Integration with community planning. Potential housing expansion relative to size, need, and location
Zoning requirements, limitations or restrictions
III. Role in comprehensive school building plan. Relationship to high schools and other elementary schools in same district (township, county, or community)

IV. Site characteristics. Site location—urban, suburban, or rural (determines demand for minimum and maximum space required); percent of usability of site for building, recreation and playfields, parking, roads, and services; soil conditions—water table, flood plan, adjacent watersheds, and suitable materials for structural applications
V. Utility services. Utilities—availability and cost of electrical service, sanitary service (if none, feasibility of sewage treatment plant or septic tank); initial cost of land versus cost of land versus cost of improvements

SITE PLANNING

Analysis of Site and Surrounding Area

Site analysis, synthesis, and design are best developed by a team including the architect, landscape architect, and engineer working closely with the client. Using the checklist outline below, this analysis should be based on the specifics of the site and surrounding

area, the educational program, and community relationships.

I. Site analysis and evaluation
A. Location
1. Regional
2. Vicinity
B. Description
1. Size and survey locations
2. Existing conditions
a. Soils—classification and uses
b. Topography—contours and grade elevations
c. Hydrography—flood plain, watershed, streams, lakes and swamps
d. Structures—existing types, historic value or landmarks
e. Easements—widths and descriptions
f. Vegetation—type and size of materials
g. Utilities—sanitary, storm, water, gas, and electric
h. Wind and Sun—precipitation and humidity
i. Natural features and present land use
C. Zoning
1. Type and restrictions
D. Environmental conditions
1. Noise, vibration, and interference
a. Aircraft
b. Railroad
c. Auto
d. Commercial
e. Electrical
f. Radar
g. Industrial
2. Smoke and smog
E. Access road characteristics
1. Type—paved, unpaved, etc.
2. Width—paving and right-of-way
3. Volume—daily average and peaks
4. Planned improvements—widening, extensions, expressways
5. Traffic patterns—regional, city and local
II. Site requirements
A. Vehicular
1. Parking requirements
a. Executive
b. Employee
c. Visitor
2. Service
3. Maintenance equipment
4. Public transportation
B. Pedestrian
1. Circulation
2. Recreation

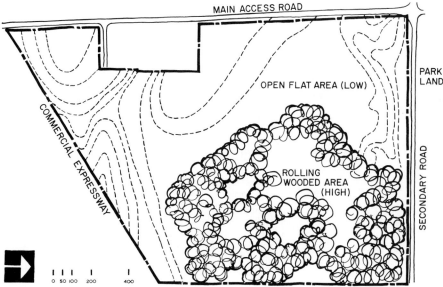

Fig. 1a   Site analysis.

ELEMENTARY AND SECONDARY SCHOOLS
Site Planning; Busing; Parking

C. Utilities
   1. Normal requirement
   2. Special requirement
D. Miscellaneous
   1. Police and fire protection—distance, location, municipality, jurisdiction.
   2. Exhibit areas
   3. Community use

Land Use

Space Allocation Studies should incorporate all the elements and spaces required by the total developed program. In addition, any limitations which may be caused by specific site conditions should be noted.

Relationships The relationships of these proposed site elements and spaces to each other and to the site are best developed visually as diagrammatic studies such as those shown in Figs. 1 to 3.

Circulation

Circulation patterns are continuous from the points of access at property lines to and through the buildings and must be designed as integrated systems. Safety is important, particularly for lower age groups. For safe and efficient movement, separate each different type of circulation. Eliminate or minimize cross traffic between pedestrians and vehicles. Separate drop-off facilities for buses and automobiles. Service vehicles should be excluded from these drop-off areas; if this is not possible, use of service areas should be permitted only at times when pedestrians are not present.

Vehicular/Automobile Differentiate and provide for the three types of automobile traffic normally found on a school site: faculty, student, and visitor or parent.

Vehicular/Bus Give careful consideration to number, loading and unloading areas, site access, and storage of vehicles. Plan so that the backing up of buses is never necessary.

Vehicular/Service Service-vehicle access and loading and unloading areas should permit as short and direct an approach as possible with adequate maneuvering space. Service areas and access should be separate from other circulation systems.

BUSING

Magnet School Busing Study Figures 4 to 7 represent four (4) approaches to developing a system of bus parking and circulation. Presently, 36 buses will be required to provide transportation for 1,800 students to and from the school site (site area required for this service is significant—see land use studies).

Dimensions of buses to be considered are bus length = 36 ft 0 in.; bus width = 8 ft 0 in.; inside turning radius = 45 ft 0 in.; outside turning radius = 60 ft 0 in.; typical stall size = 12 ft 0 in. $\times$ 14 ft 0 in. Buses should not be required to back up. (Tables 1 and 2.)

TABLE 1 Auto Number and Space Requirements*

School	Parking spaces
Elementary	One per classroom + 3
Junior high	One per classroom + 6
High school	One per classroom + 16

* Space requirements average 350 to 400 sq ft per automobile, depending on parking angle. The most efficient is 90° parking.

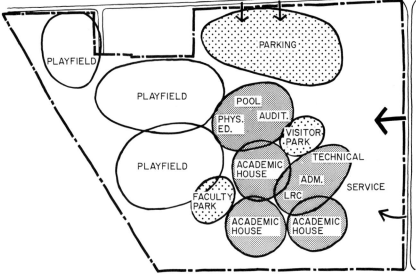

Fig. 2 Land use diagram.

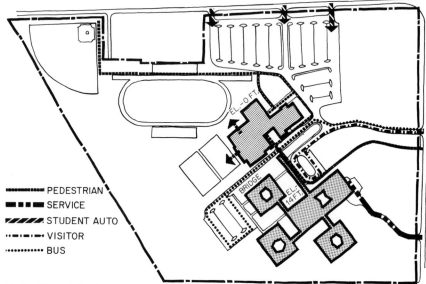

━━━━━ PEDESTRIAN
▬ ▬ ▬ SERVICE
▰▰▰ STUDENT AUTO
▬•▬•▬ VISITOR
•••••••• BUS

Fig. 3 Site circulation plan.

People

Safety is *most important*. Walkways of all-weather, nonskid materials, well delineated and arranged to eliminate or minimize conflict with vehicle circulation can be both safe and pleasant. Where changes in grade are necessary, a ramp is generally preferred to steps and the incline should not exceed 5 percent especially where snow and ice are expected.

PARKING

There is usually merit in separation of the three types of automobile parking, with the daytime visitor taking precedence over faculty and student. Parking facilities should be located to consider all their uses, including daytime uses for visitor, parent, faculty, or student, uses for school-related or community events within the school building, and uses

TABLE 2 Comparison of Busing Study Data

	Minimum width required	Lineal feet required (for 36 buses)	Area required per bus (includes circulation), sq ft*
Parallel single file	12 ft 0 in.	1,584	528
Parallel free access	25 ft 0 in.	2,736	1,900
30° peel-off	55 ft 0 in	860	1,320
30° free access	65 ft 0 in.	860	1,572
45° peel-off	65 ft 0 in.	620	1,100
45° free access	85 ft 0 in.	620	1,440
60° peel-off	85 ft 0 in.	510	1,164
60° free access	115 ft 0 in.	510	1,584

* Data are approximate.

(a) SINGLE-FILE SYSTEM
FIRST BUS IN LINE MUST GO TO END OF SYSTEM AND MUST ALSO LEAVE FIRST. LIMITED.

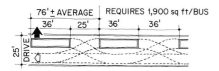

(b) FREE-ACCESS SYSTEM

▲ STUDENT TRAFFIC FLOW

◇ BUS DIRECTION OF TRAVEL

Fig. 4 Parallel bus parking system.

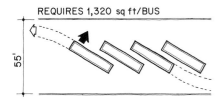

(a) PEEL-OFF SYSTEM
FRONT BUS MUST LEAVE FIRST, THEN NEXT BUS, ETC.

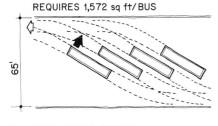

(b) FREE-ACCESS SYSTEM

Fig. 5 30° bus parking system.

relating to various outdoor athletic events. Overflow parking areas may double as paved play areas when properly designed and located.

Access to parking facilities and arrangement of parking lanes should minimize conflict between automobile and pedestrian. Collector walks should be provided and arranged to permit pedestrians to exit vehicle areas as directly as possible (see Fig. 8).

RECREATION FACILITIES

Site Location Considerations

These criteria for recreation areas, such as relation to adjacent property, soil stability and percolation, existing vegetation, existing topography, etc., are important; however, special attention should be given to the need for large open spaces for field games with adjacent existing vegetation to provide shade, oxygen, and windbreak. In dense urban areas, where ordinary open spaces are scarce, such field facilities can be created on air rights, rooftops, and terraced slopes. Informal play areas, especially for the lower grades, can be created in multilevel arrangements conforming to a steep site; this is not possible with field

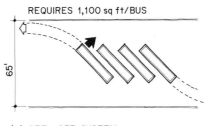

(a) PEEL-OFF SYSTEM
(FIRST BUS MUST LEAVE FIRST).

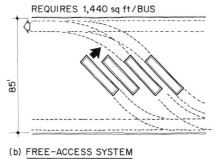

(b) FREE-ACCESS SYSTEM

Fig. 6 45° bus parking system.

recreation facilities for the contact sports enjoyed by upper grades. Superimposition of layouts and multiuse helps conserve space when land is at a premium.

Recreational Facility Layout

One of the best approaches is to construct scale templates (1 in. = 50 ft for most site planning purposes) of all facilities considered in the school program. These can be drawn on tracing vellum, using official court and field dimension layouts as a guide. Cutouts can be used for shifting locations on site plan to determine optimum layout. Construction and funding phasing and types of multiuse can also be developed using these templates.

In creating a unique layout for a site, consider these factors:

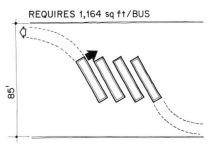

(a) PEEL-OFF SYSTEM
(FIRST BUS MUST LEAVE FIRST).

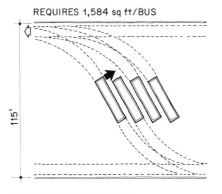

(b) FREE-ACCESS SYSTEM

Fig. 7 60° bus parking system.

1. Optimum orientation for sun and wind control
2. Circulation for players and spectators
3. Buffer zones between action spaces
4. Access from showers, classrooms, student and spectator parking, and buses
5. Access from community where multiuse is possible
6. Flexibility of layout and accommodation of staging or building expansion
7. Programming of play and learning experiences for younger children

TABLE 3 Analysis of Playground Surfacing
From School Sites, *No. 7, U.S. Dept. of Health, Education, and* Welfare.

Type of surface	Year-round utility use	Multiple use	Dustless	Fine-grained, nonabsorbent	Durable	Resilient	All-weather footing	Reasonable cost	Low maintenance	Pleasing appearance
							Qualities			
Earth		●		●	●	●		●		●
Turf		●	●	●		●		●		●
Aggregate	●				●		●	●	●	
Bitumen	●	●	●	●			●	●	●	●
Concrete	●				●		●	●	●	
Masonry	●	●			●		●	●	●	
Miscellaneous*	●	●				●		●	●	

* Tanbark, sawdust, cottonmeal, rubber, plastics and vinyls, asbestos-cement boards, wood.

ELEMENTARY AND SECONDARY SCHOOLS
Parking; Recreation Facilities; Drainage; Planting; Safety

8. Supervision and safety

9. Compatibility of age groups, sexes, and type of activity in contiguous play areas

10. Grading and slope for drainage (or underdrainage)

11. Existing relationship to nearby community facilities

12. Need for balance of action spaces with provision of quiet open spaces

Suggested Facilities According to Age Groups and Grade

• Kindergarten to third grade: Sandboxes, sand trays/cans, slides and tunnels, swings, tree houses, climbers and steppers, trike and bike riding, water features.

• Fourth to seventh grades: Climbers and jungle gyms, shuffleboard, hopscotch, informal group games, little league ball, softball, spider webs and trampolines, adventure playgrounds with junk building materials.

• Eighth to twelfth grades: Softball, baseball, football, touch football, soccer, volleyball, tennis, archery, track and field events, rifle range, physical fitness workout course.

Materials for Recreational Surfaces and Structures

Effect of low-maintenance synthetic surfacing and structural materials is significant. Their increased durability under intensive use makes multiuse and community use feasible. All-weather surfaces maximize use; cleaning by hosing, vacuum, and snow blower minimize maintenance. Durable yet flexible play surfaces allow use in cold or wet weather without injury to surface or players. Regrading, reseeding, fertilizing, aerating, spraying, mowing, and weeding are eliminated.

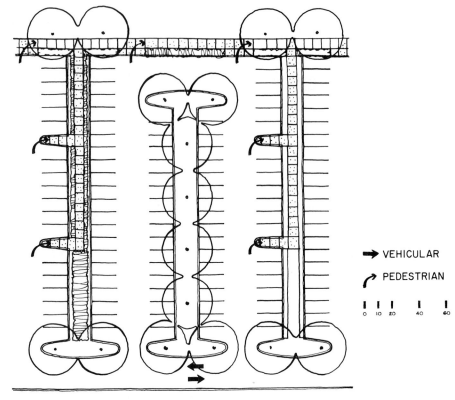

VEHICULAR

PEDESTRIAN

0 10 20 40 60

Fig. 8 Parking area circulation.

DRAINAGE

Proper storm drainage is essential to successful school-site facilities in most areas of the country. Not only do the function and longevity of many facilities and materials depend on good drainage, but in some cases permanent damage may result from water. Surface and subsurface systems or combinations should be designed to adequately handle the needs of buildings and site facilities. Where possible, an overland emergency system should be incorporated, using the relative grade elevations of the site. When circumstances do not permit this, a standby system of pumps or power generators is recommended.

PLANTING

Select materials indigenous to the area where possible, and supplement with ornamental materials that possess characteristics not obtainable with local materials. Plant materials should also have low maintenance requirements and be compatible with existing growing conditions. Plant material for school sites generally consists of shade trees, ornamental trees, evergreen trees and shrubs, deciduous shrubs, vines, and ground covers (see Fig. 9). Though some of the ground-covering material on most school sites functionally is mowed grass, this material remains one of the highest maintenance types. It is recommended that its use be kept to the necessary minimum and the use of meadow and prairie grasses and other types of ground-covering materials be considered. This is particularly important on sites where appropriate ground cover material exists and should be carefully preserved. Select plant material on the basis of its mature size and character to minimize excessive shearing and early replacement. Initial sizes should not be less than a reasonable minimum to ensure survival from injury or damage by students and other causes. In addition to providing an aes-

thetic contribution plant material on the school site can be used to solve many problems such as windbreaks, screens and buffers, sound dampers, sun and light controls, erosion control, and air purification.

SAFETY

Schools, by the nature of their occupancy and use, require higher standards of safety than other types of buildings. Provisions for life safety have the highest priority and affect the entire design in plan, construction, and choice of materials. All phases of health and safety become pervasive program elements that unavoidably add to the complexity and cost of schools and greatly determine their form and plan organization and appearance.

Building codes generally have separate and specific requirements for school construction. Many states and counties have school safety codes established by departments of education,

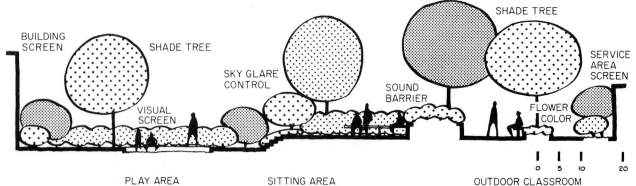

BUILDING SCREEN SHADE TREE SKY GLARE CONTROL SOUND BARRIER SHADE TREE SERVICE AREA SCREEN

VISUAL SCREEN FLOWER COLOR

0 5 10 20

PLAY AREA SITTING AREA OUTDOOR CLASSROOM

Fig. 9

health, and public safety. Architects and engineers are obligated to inform themselves of all reviewing authorities and applicable codes in a given locality. In the absence of adequate local codes, standards of the National Building Code, the National Board of Fire Underwriters, and/or the BOCA (Building Officials Conference of America) Code are good guides. The following are some of the safety considerations of concern:

- Structural safety
  Material strengths and factors of safety
  Fireproof and fire resistive structures
  Windstorm resistance
  Earthquake resistance
- Fire safety
  Provision and protection of exits, corridors, and stairs
  Fire detector and alarm systems
  Sprinkler systems
  Materials and finishes with low flame-spread rating and Nontoxic combustion characteristics
- Health safety
  Ventilation systems and standards
  Lighting standards and electrical code
  Plumbing fixture requirements and plumbing code
  Swimming pool and locker room requirements
- Special emergencies
  Emergency lighting systems
  Air raid shelter and radiation protection
  Tornado protection and shelter
- Accident protection
  Nonslip surfaces (especially stairs, ramps, locker rooms, pool decks)
  Vision panels, door swings and hardware, Hand rails
  Safety glass in doors, sidelights
- Handicapped provisions
  Required accommodations at entrances in circulation provisions, toilets, and other public accommodations for use by handicapped persons.

Sensible corridor planning and location of stairs and exits to handle traffic flow without congestion will usually provide appropriate fire exit facilities. However, codes must be checked to ensure proper corridor widths, corridor lengths, and smoke barriers at suitable intervals. Stair enclosures are required for all stairs connecting more than two levels and are recommended for stairs generally. Most stairs are used for exit purposes and have detailed code requirements which must be met such as width and ratio of tread-to-risers.

School Exits

Exits and emergency exits should be clearly marked so that at no time is there any doubt or

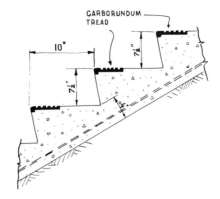

Fig. 11

hesitation as to their purpose. A sign indicating the nearest exit should be visible from every point in the corridor. Two or more exits should be provided from any area within the school. Some states require two exits from each classroom.

It should be possible to open every door from the inside at all times, even after school is closed for the day.

A well-defined exit will include a lighted red exit sign and a white security light connected to an emergency power supply in the event of main power failure.

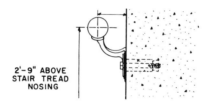

2'-9" ABOVE STAIR TREAD NOSING

Fig. 12

Stairways

One of the most critical parts of school traffic design is the stairway, which should be located in relation to the overall traffic pattern, keeping in mind load distribution, safety, destination of students between periods, and elimination of cross traffic. The stairways should be designed for easy, fast, and safe movement of boys and girls.

Stairways not only provide egress to and from various floor levels, but they are used every period for the vertical circulation of students changing classes. It is important that stairways be designed so that boys and girls with books under their arms may walk side by side to avoid congestion; a width of 4 ft 8 in. to

5 ft between handrails is recommended. Stairways should be of fireproof construction, leading directly to the outdoors. They should be provided with smoke-control facilities, separating the stairwells from the corridors which they serve.

Corridors

A well-designed school has corridors that accommodate the free and informal movement of students. The narrow corridor usually requires formal, regimented, and supervised traffic flow.

The walls of corridors should be free of all projections. Heat units, drinking fountains, fire extinguishers, lockers, doors, and display cases should be recessed in the interest of student safety (Fig. 10).

Acoustical properties are desirable to reduce hall noise. Corridors should be well lighted, with emergency provision in the event of main power failure. Floor covering should be durable, nonskid, and easy to maintain.

The maximum length of unbroken corridors should not exceed 150 to 200 ft. Longer sections give an undesirable perspective.

Stair Treads

Standard dimensions of stair treads and risers should be used in schools. Odd dimensions increase the stair hazards for children as well as adults. Wax used on classroom and corridor floors may be deposited on stair treads by students' shoes. One way to reduce this hazard is to design a tread that will give traction regardless of wax application. Inserted carborundum treads have proved adequate (Fig. 11). Surface-mounted strips are unsatisfactory.

Handrails

Handrails are necessary on both sides of stairways in accordance with the National Building Code. They should be installed with attachment brackets permanently anchored in the masonry wall (Fig. 12). Brackets anchored with lead, wood, or leather expansion bolts often result in unsafe support and considerable maintenance.

Doors

Boys and girls are not expected to use caution in opening and closing doors. The hazard of striking students with doors can be reduced by including a vision panel in the door (Fig. 13) and by recessing the door. The location of this panel should be in proportion to the varying heights of children. Use of tempered or wire glass will provide safety.

Vision panels placed next to doors allow students to see someone approaching the door from the opposite direction. These panels should be designed with opaque sections near the floor and mullions at suitable intervals to clearly identify them as windows, not passageways.

Covered walkways to accommodate interbuilding traffic should be designed to protect students and not for appearance alone. The roof deck should be wide and low. Provision should be made to carry off roof water. Proper outside lighting will be necessary under the roof deck.

Some current trends in school planning such as the open-plan concept depart from traditional room and corridor arrangements and raise new problems in preserving a protected route of exit from all parts of a school building. Attempts to make use of corridor areas for instruction, study, or special purposes must be carefully planned to maintain a clear traffic lane free from obstacles or disruption by movable equipment and furnishings.

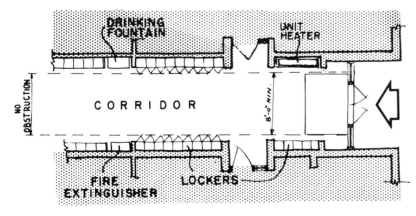

Fig. 10

ELEMENTARY AND SECONDARY SCHOOLS
Safety; Kinds of Schools

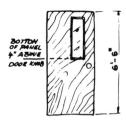  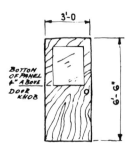

Fig. 13

Efforts to minimize barriers between instructional areas and corridors by glazing with ordinary glass or by eliminating portions of corridor walls run counter to traditional safety requirements, but have been accomplished through special provisions of sprinkler systems, plan organization, and building material use. Open planning for large instructional areas accommodating several groups with no designated corridor areas and with flexible divisions provided by movable partitions and divider units also presents special problems of safety. Since many codes were written before this educational concept became popular, planning of this type will require conferences and cooperation with public safety officials to obtain agreement on acceptable provisions for safety.

Some safety considerations, such as avoidance of risers at entrances, also relate to the needs of the handicapped and the temporarily disabled. Low-pitch ramps instead of stairs at changes in level can be a safety feature as well as a service to the physically handicapped and an aid to the movement of maintenance equipment and supplies. Special additional provisions for the handicapped should be made in toilets and other areas.

Secondary to life-safety considerations, but still a major factor in school design, is the preservation of building integrity and security. Fire insurance bureaus establish requirements of building design and construction which must also be checked for the safety of the occupants and for qualification for reasonable rates of insurance. External security should be provided by night illumination of the area around the building and by other electronic systems. Problems of vandalism are increasing with exterior glass a particular target. Currently, glass areas are being reduced along with the trend to air conditioning, and new types of plastic glazing are being used.

While most responses to the various safety-factor requirements are quite obvious, commonsense planning and aesthetic consideration can make schools more safe in other ways. The particular use of colors and materials can produce an aura of serenity and order in themselves. A plan of sure clarity can minimize confusion and make circulation patterns clearer. Carpeting and other acoustic provisions can reduce noise and distraction. Materials that are attractive but easily maintained will allow a cleaner and safer school. And, lastly, the attitude of those learning and teaching in the school can make it safer. A clean, well-done, well-run, and "happy ship" school is a safe school.

KINDS OF SCHOOLS

There are different kinds of schools, functioning as organizations of students and faculties, that serve various age groups and certain purposes. There are also different kinds of school plans, or ways of organizing the needed space to better respond to the ways of teaching certain age groups and to other requirements such as site and climate conditions, construction and funding phasing, and code restraints.

Organization of Students and Faculties

Time, location, organization, method, and semantics all have had their influence on schools. Sometimes a school's name has little to do with what the school is. There are still grammar schools, but most of this category are now called elementary schools. Secondary schools usually denote grades 9 to 12, but this category now encompasses junior high and middle schools, depending on program and organization. Kindergarten at one time was preschool education. Now almost universally, it has become a part of the elementary school's program. Preschool education can be divided into a number of types: day care, nursery, and Head Start.

There are community, central, neighborhood, regional, vocational, technical, academies, academic, and special schools. All these schools include education before higher education. Even the definition between lower and higher education is now being reconsidered, with the first two years of college and junior college being thought of as the thirteenth and fourteenth years of public education.

Because of the overlapping names, grades, levels, and age groups, the following list of descriptions and Fig. 14 might make this maze somewhat clearer.

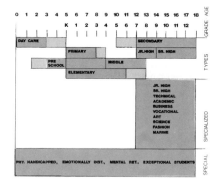

• Day care: Serves the dual function of providing a custodial or care center where working parents can leave their preschool child and providing group learning experience for the child.
• Nursery: May serve the same function as day care, but frequently provides only the group learning experience.
• Head Start: The same function as day care and nursery for socially deprived children, with emphasis on program and experience to remedy or prevent the problems of such deprivation.
• Kindergarten: Usual type of introduction to group learning experience in elementary schools.
• Elementary: Traditionally covers K–8.

However, more frequently in recent years it covers only K–6 with junior high or middle schools experience for the last two years.
• Primary: The earlier years of elementary education, usually K–3, sometimes K–4.
• Middle schools: Usually grades 5–8, sometimes grades 4–8, combining both secondary and elementary pupils. Program is frequently structured as a secondary school.
• Secondary schools: This category includes middle schools, junior high schools, and senior high schools, grades 5-12.
• Junior high schools: The earlier years of secondary education usually grades 7–9, sometimes grades 7 and 8.
• Senior high schools: The latter years of secondary education usually grades 9–12, sometimes grades 10–12.
• Special schools for secondary education: These schools are usually found in large urban areas or in more rural areas as special regional schools. They provide a special curriculum for such studies as vocational training, business, art, drama, science, marine, and fashion and design.
• Special schools: Schools for children who do not fit traditionally into the normal school programs. These schools are for emotionally and physically handicapped, the mentally retarded, or the exceptionally bright.
• Community schools: Community use of the facilities for programs other than the normal school program. This can range from the limited use of a gymnasium for basketball at night to a building that could house social agencies; health agencies; extensive youth programs; and programs for the elderly, social guidance, public assistance, legal aid, etc.
• Neighborhood: Generally means smaller schools identified with a specific neighborhood, where busing is neither necessary nor desirable.
• Central schools and/or regional: Generally found in rural areas where population density does not support adequate school facilities. Children are bused for great distances to allow them to attend facilities that offer them broader program and opportunity.
• Urban: Urban schools can be any of the above, but some new innovations are such things as storefront academies.
• Storefront schools: These schools identify with the people of the street in heavily congested urban areas. Such schools do away with the traditional atmosphere. They relate to the dropout and other youth who are alienated from the traditional institution.
• Schools without walls: In downtown urban areas, schools use the facilities of community space, office space of business organizations, public libraries, etc.

Organization of Spaces

There are many ways to organize the spaces for a school into a plan, and many determinants to consider, beginning with the basic purpose of the specific teaching program and the children to be served. But even this basic premise may have to be considered in the context of how flexible the plan may be made to anticipate the possibility, or rather the probability, that the school could convert to some other organizational structure.

Pupil Capacity

Elementary Schools Before any calculation of school capacity can be made, the school system must have an educational policy establishing the optimum capacity of classrooms. In many schools this figure is set at 27 pupils, which, when used as an average class size, may mean that some rooms will exceed this number.

Kindergartens may be set at 20 pupils in each of the morning and afternoon sessions.

Some schools do not like to exceed 25 pupils per class. It is frequently recommended that when a class goes to 32 pupils it be divided into two sections with two teachers. It is also advisable in determining the capacity of an elementary school to consider each grade separately so that there will be no single classroom housing more than one grade.

High Schools Determining capacity on the secondary school level is considerably more complex than on the elementary school level. Capacity in a good secondary school reflects the kind of educational program and the educational goals of the community. (See Fig. 15.)

The character of the classroom and the subject are determinants of the classroom size. Physical education classes may run to 35 or 40 students; shop classes should not exceed 20 students. Many other areas should not exceed 25 students and might, more likely, hold 20 pupils, including science rooms, homemaking, and fine arts. These class sizes may be adjusted from community to community, but for comparative purposes it would be helpful to maintain a standard formula for determining capacity (Table 4).

Flexibility and the Open Plan

Indeed, flexibility has become a most critical consideration, reflecting the continuing changes in educational thinking *and* building techniques. The open-plan concept derives from a dramatic change from the self-contained classroom to various size spaces to accommodate groups working together and separately, and also from the development of dramatic improvements in lighting and ventilation techniques, acoustic and long-span structural economies, and the total economy of better utilized space.

What is required by users and authorities is a real breakthrough in attitudes toward the *sharing* of a *total space* by a large group of different ages so that the space can be constructed with few or no ceiling-high partitions, without any special concern for being near windows, and with no especially designated bands of space for circulation.

In fact, the open-plan concept responds to a looser, more relaxed society with more confidence in the group, and to the totality of the school's objective of enabling people to get along with each other, and to the step-by-step progress of democracy: an individual into a group, a group into another, into the whole.

As with many ideas in education, the open-plan concept has begun at the elementary school level and has yet to extend appreciably beyond to where concepts of specialization begin, spaces are more especially planned, and innovations are more slowly realized. Such areas of specialization, like science, bring together people of specialized interest and require the use of specialized equipment or teaching techniques that make more difficult the realization of new, combined approaches.

TABLE 4   Classroom Capacity for High Schools

Type of space	No. of units	Capacity of units	Total capacity
Classroom	19	x 27	513
Science laboratory	3	x 25	75
Commercial education	4	x 25	100
Home economics	2	x 25	50
Art	1	x 25	25
Shop	3	x 20	60
Band or chorus	2	x 35	70
Gymnasium, playroom	1	x 35	35
Gymnasium with partition	1	x 70	70
General education laboratory or study hall		x 35	

Maximum capacity: 998
Optimum capacity at 80 per cent utilization: 798

Working Space Relationships

Successful planning puts together the parts in such a way that they work well together. As the open-plan concept responds to a way of teaching and a way of efficiently using space, any good plan stems from and assures efficient function by responding carefully to the educational program and matching it with a logically engineered building expression. Circulation should be as direct and minimal as possible, directed to an efficiency of the total plan to allow for the incorporation of amenities to give the school some special qualities.

The sections following on special areas define their own requirements as part of the total program and further illustrate relationships within their specialties. Circulation to

Variety in Plan Concept

The plans shown have been chosen for the differences they illustrate, simply because many factors other than purpose and function affect and determine the concept of a plan. Some are compact and chunky, containing large amounts of interior, mechanically ventilated spaces for reasons of internal relationships or ultimate use of restricted site. Some are cluster plans using units connected by circulation links to resolve a plan into a series of smaller pieces to give the school better scale, to allow small children to respond better, to relate better to a neighborhood of homes, and to fit better to changing terrain.

Other plans group their parts to resolve a large school into component communities of

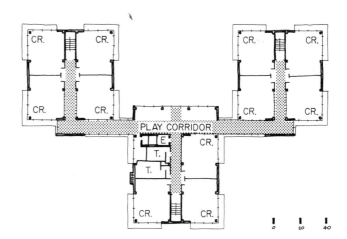

Fig. 16

the school and within the school along with the physical needs of the spaces establishes the plan concept. The plan examples shown vary in total concept yet work as entities in the relationship of their parts.

students. Others especially relate to unusual site conditions, place emphasis on unique circulation requirements, and respond to the need of incremental expansion of classrooms or core elements. Chosen to represent such differences, the examples shown collectively reflect a major trend in school buildings, as in all buildings: a trend away from finger plans or narrow building units dependent on windows toward large plan areas divisible into many combinations, more efficient in usable area, developing less perimeter wall, and generally representing more value for the cost to build, to utilize, and to operate.

Elementary Figure 16 shows a city school of three units, four stories high, dependent on simple stair circulation. Most classrooms get

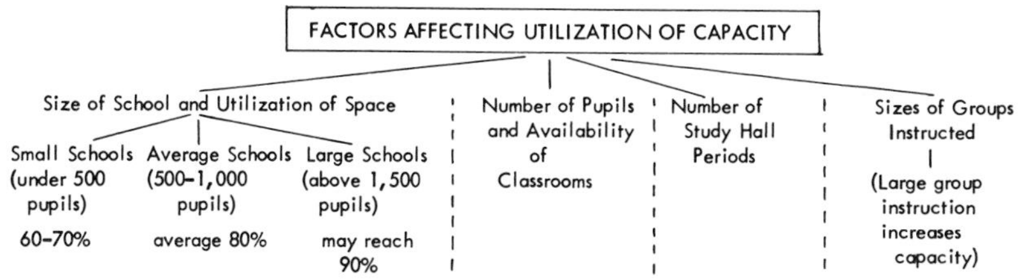

FACTORS AFFECTING UTILIZATION OF CAPACITY

Size of School and Utilization of Space — Number of Pupils and Availability of Classrooms — Number of Study Hall Periods — Sizes of Groups Instructed

Small Schools (under 500 pupils) 60–70% · Average Schools (500–1,000 pupils) average 80% · Large Schools (above 1,500 pupils) may reach 90%

(Large group instruction increases capacity)

Fig. 15

ELEMENTARY AND SECONDARY SCHOOLS
Kinds of Schools

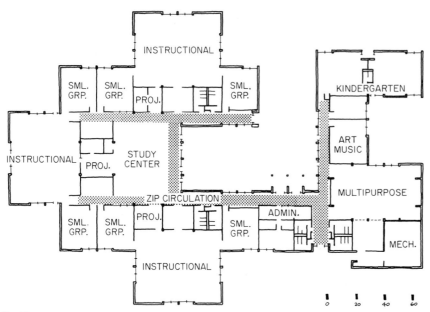

Fig. 17

corner orientation, minimum corridors, simple convertibility to open-plan clusters, efficient site utilization, and repetitive construction.

Figure 17 shows an open-plan concept of spaces for small groups arranged around large group instructional areas for three age groups in turn related to a central study-resource center. Administration and other shared spaces wrap around school court entrance area.

Figure 18 illustrates a cluster plan of divisible classrooms arranged by age groups sharing central entrance areas, relating to shared spaces, and resulting in a plan of residential scale and noninstitutional interiors.

A two-story school, a near square in plan, is shown in Fig. 19. Its lower level accommodates the more fixed elements of special function

requiring special services. The upper floor accommodates the more typical, simpler spaces like classrooms and library and has the potential for complete flexibility around the stair and toilet cores.

In Fig. 20, there is an efficient, one-story plan of alternating classroom clusters opening to private courtyards and connected by a main circulation aisle. Shared facilities are centered in the plan for easy public access through the large entry court.

Figure 21a shows another special city school for ages 3 to 14 on a limited site, three floors, with large corner open-plan spaces for group instruction related to a core space for faculty and seminar use. Rooftops of a related parking area and a communicative arts center are used

to supplement the site's minimal play area.

Figures 21b and c show the communicative arts unit, a centered experimental theater surrounded by art studios of adaptable, divisible space with service utilities on the inner perimeter.

Junior High – Middle Schools The plan shown in Fig. 22 was developed for a narrow city lot, and compactly radiates its parts out from a central activities court. The specialized and public-oriented facilities are all on the ground floor, while stairways at the four corners serve the upper floors of typical classrooms that ring the courtyard.

Figure 23 is a two-story middle school with classroom/laboratory blocks related to a central resource area. All the major units are well articulated, with stair units on the edge of or between flexible units of space. The pool is a later added unit and illustrates the ability to successfully expand such a concept. Figure 23b is the upper floor academic unit, illustrating a classic and basic grouping of classrooms around a large, shared lecture room.

High Schools Figure 24 shows a campus-type plan resolving a relatively large school into smaller elements. Classrooms are grouped around interior laboratory and lecture facilities, and the library is the academic focus; gyms and auditorium are in separate buildings of structures appropriate to their function, as are the academic elements.

Figure 25 demonstrates a basic disposition of functional elements in simple, economic blocks of spaces organizing its public and major entrances to the left, and focusing its emphasis on a pleasant circulation-flanked court to which the learning resource opens.

Again, simple large blocks of space, in Fig.

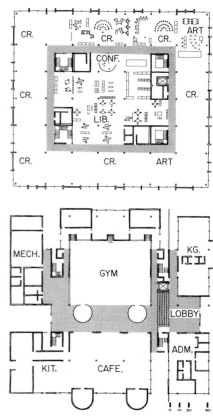

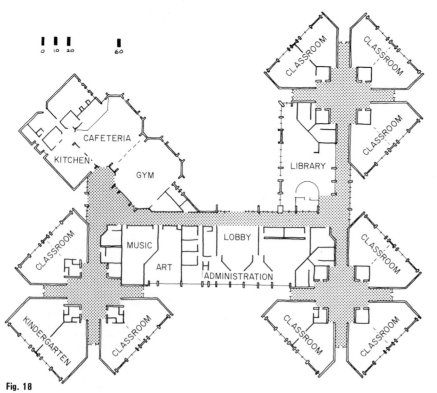

Fig. 18

Fig. 19

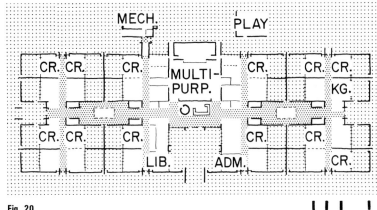

Fig. 20

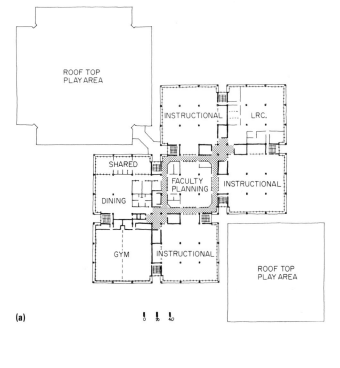

(a)

Fig. 21

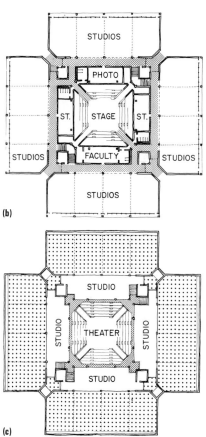

(b)

(c)

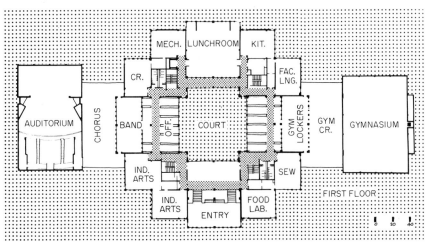

Fig. 22

ELEMENTARY AND SECONDARY SCHOOLS
Kinds of Schools

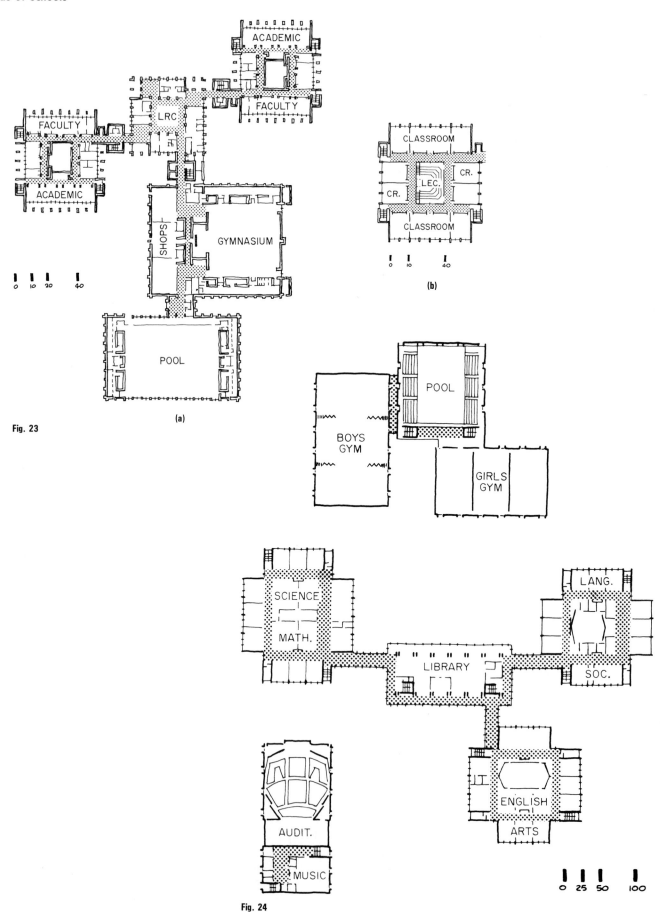

Fig. 23

Fig. 24

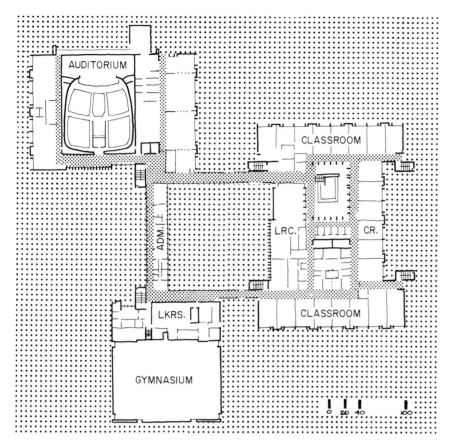

Fig. 25

26, in a compact plan on a restricted city site, connected by a see-through, central, two-story unit of cafeteria, study and lobby and balcony circulation (toned area) and library at the second level. Terrain and grading of site allow academic units to exit without stair units. Form articulation develops a scale compatible to the neighborhood's apartments.

Figure 27 is a school that has been added to many times; its most recent and substantial addition enlarges it from a school for 2,400 students to 6,000 students. The plan expansion develops around courtyards and resolves itself into four subschools, or houses, of 1,500 similar academic facilities, with shared facilities expanded to serve the total. Each "house" of 1,500 has its own resource center, study, and dining facilities, as well as core classrooms giving the students a better sense of identity and scale for learning.

Vocational High Schools A typical floor plan of a high school for business instruction (Fig. 28) is located approximately in a ten-story building in a downtown location. Designed as an office building to expand vertically, it has flexible space around the core of circulation and mechanical requirements. Additional elevators can be accommodated in spaces next to the existing elevators.

Figure 29 proves that vocational schools can indeed be exciting in concept. This plan groups its major shops efficiently in two wings and slashes through a ramping diagonal connecting the changing levels of the site.

The portable or prefabricated classroom (Fig. 30) is a good and useful idea that has developed a somewhat bad reputation. Designed to be temporary, it too seldom has been removed or replaced or refurbished. It remains, however, a good idea to serve temporary peak enrollment loads. Many such facilities are available, and their quality is improving.

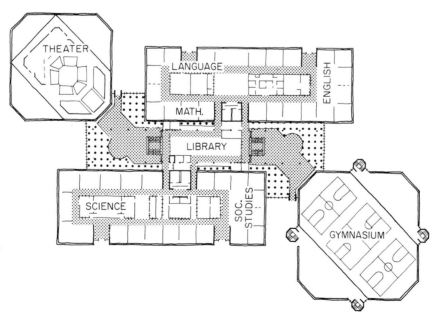

Fig. 26

ELEMENTARY AND SECONDARY SCHOOLS
Kinds of Schools

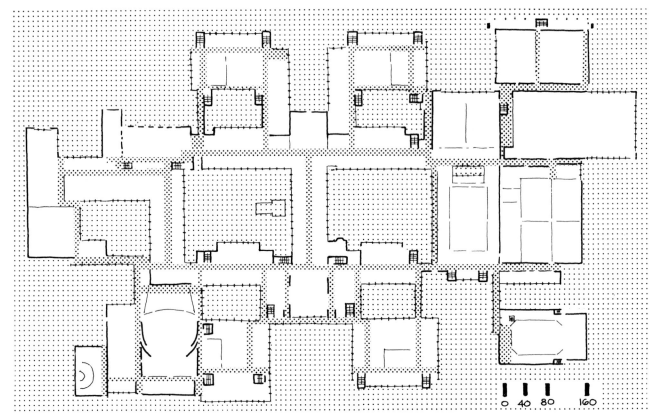

Fig. 27

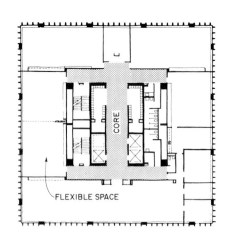

Fig. 28

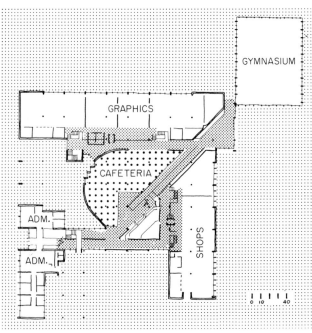

Fig. 29

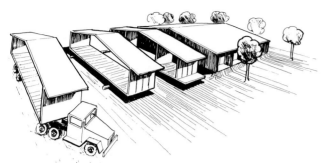

Fig. 30

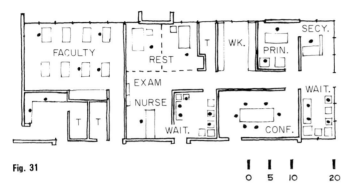

Fig. 31

ADMINISTRATION SUITES

The administrative spaces for a school, whether it's a single office for a teaching principal and a part-time secretary or a battery of offices for a huge high school, are the control center for the school and contact point for parents, students, and faculty alike. Here the school records are kept or reviewed, the ubiquitous public address system originates, budgets are developed, books and records are kept, and counseling and discipline are meted out. It is a first contact point and a crossroads checkpoint and is most always placed near the main entrance, and belongs there.

Essentially it is an office, or a group of offices, conference rooms, work storage rooms, record storage, and money vault. Opening to the entrance lobby, Fig. 31 shows a well-developed suite for an elementary school, containing the basic administrative offices and areas for typical related activities. Figure 32 shows a more extensive development for a junior high school, with added typically related space for counseling offices. Figure 33 shows a high school suite, where counseling occurs elsewhere, but with other facilities and a close relationship to the resource center. Figures 34a and b are details for faculty mail boxes, allowing service from one side and access from the other.

Figure 34c shows another high school office suite including counseling and space for

Fig. 32

Fig. 33

ELEMENTARY AND SECONDARY SCHOOLS
Administration Suites

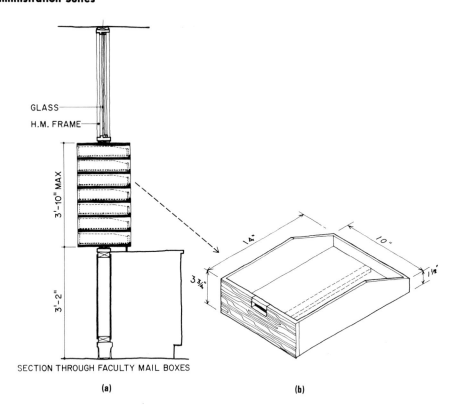

GLASS

H.M. FRAME

3'-10" MAX

3'-2"

SECTION THROUGH FACULTY MAIL BOXES

(a)

14"

10"

1½"

3¾"

(b)

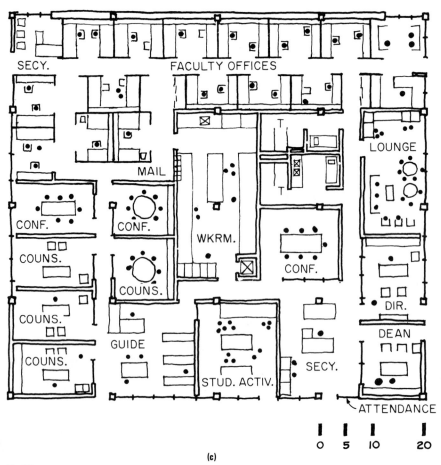

SECY.

FACULTY OFFICES

MAIL

LOUNGE

CONF.

CONF.

WKRM.

CONF.

COUNS.

COUNS.

DIR.

COUNS.

DEAN

GUIDE

COUNS.

STUD. ACTIV.

SECY.

ATTENDANCE

0   5   10   20

(c)

Fig. 34

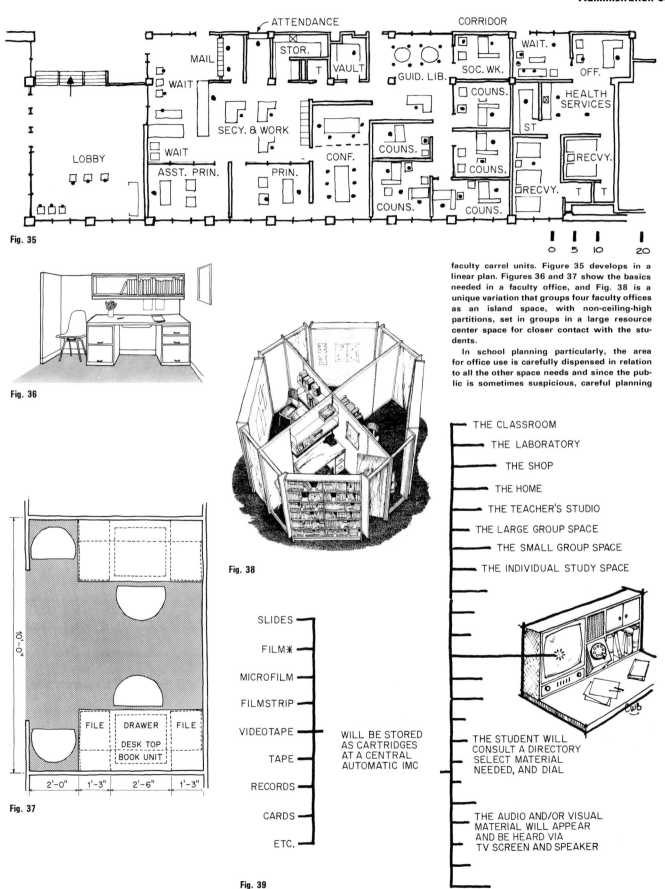

Fig. 35

ATTENDANCE · CORRIDOR · MAIL · STOR. · VAULT · WAIT · SOC. WK. · OFF. · GUID. LIB. · COUNS. · HEALTH SERVICES · SECY. & WORK · ST · WAIT · CONF. · COUNS. · RECVY. · LOBBY · WAIT · ASST. PRIN. · PRIN. · COUNS. · COUNS. · RECVY. · T · T · COUNS. · COUNS.

0 5 10 20

Fig. 36

Fig. 37

10'-0"

FILE · DRAWER · FILE · DESK TOP · BOOK UNIT

2'-0" · 1'-3" · 2'-6" · 1'-3"

Fig. 38

faculty carrel units. Figure 35 develops in a linear plan. Figures 36 and 37 show the basics needed in a faculty office, and Fig. 38 is a unique variation that groups four faculty offices as an island space, with non-ceiling-high partitions, set in groups in a large resource center space for closer contact with the students.

In school planning particularly, the area for office use is carefully dispensed in relation to all the other space needs and since the public is sometimes suspicious, careful planning

THE CLASSROOM
THE LABORATORY
THE SHOP
THE HOME
THE TEACHER'S STUDIO
THE LARGE GROUP SPACE
THE SMALL GROUP SPACE
THE INDIVIDUAL STUDY SPACE

SLIDES
FILM*
MICROFILM
FILMSTRIP
VIDEOTAPE
TAPE
RECORDS
CARDS
ETC.

WILL BE STORED AS CARTRIDGES AT A CENTRAL AUTOMATIC IMC

THE STUDENT WILL CONSULT A DIRECTORY SELECT MATERIAL NEEDED, AND DIAL

THE AUDIO AND/OR VISUAL MATERIAL WILL APPEAR AND BE HEARD VIA TV SCREEN AND SPEAKER

Fig. 39

ELEMENTARY AND SECONDARY SCHOOLS
Learning Resource Centers

and choice of efficient equipment are especially important; minimums are almost invariably exercised, but common sense should be too. A few suggestions: fireproof files for records are less expensive than a fireproof vault; disciplinary offices and waiting rooms should be kept separate from the administrative waiting room for psychological (student) reasons; and teachers' mail should be private but easily accessible.

LEARNING RESOURCE CENTERS

Library may be yesterday's term for yesterday's services, for the school library has become the information and resource center for the school, and is more appropriately and now commonly called learning resource center (LRC), instructional materials center (IMC), or information resource center (IRC). In addition to books and periodicals there are now records, tapes and casettes, closed-circuit TV programming and production, film, cameras, and projection equipment. Alongside the book stacks, chairs, and tables are sight-and-sound-equipped study carrels, listening rooms, earphones and program selectors, film splicers and slide-making equipment, preview rooms, even television studios. It is a supermart of media and a place for its active use, but its ultimate use could be anywhere and everywhere (Fig. 39).

The resource center is now indeed where the action is and should be physically and educationally at the heart-center of the school, as equally accessible as possible to the classrooms, the laboratories, the administrative offices, and the community. It may well be open after school hours and should be located to allow direct access to it.

While the resource center is now a conglomerate of materials and services and successful planning seeks the mixture of these for the convenience of the users, *control* of the materials becomes a greater concern and problem, along with well-related backup preparation and work space. The circulation of the users, the administration of the materials, and the functional accommodation of the materials are the basic planning determinants.

The examples illustrated show various combinations of elements, the constant of the control desk and its more usual relationship to workrooms, reference-periodical areas, and offices. Added required exits are treated as emergency exits with alarm provisions. Areas allocated for books and seating are usually prescribed by state agencies or follow recommendations of the American Library Association. The total program may best be developed with a consultant in the field who is fully aware of equipment needs, current developments, and the proper relation of a program for the resource center to the entire school curriculum.

Though the idea of a quiet reading atmosphere has not been forgotten, the resource center has become a pleasant, busy goldfish-bowl kind of place: glassy, on display itself, extending its welcome to students as a comfortable place they like to learn in. Whether it may be considered a resource center or still a library, whether it is an alcove off the lobby, a room, or a maze of parts, the real goal is to get the students to use the materials and to learn. Carpeting has become very common, and other surfaces are being upgraded, resulting in good looking functional finishes to which everyone responds well.

A resource center for a 1,000- to 2,000-student high school, Fig. 40 well illustrates the many kinds of facilities that can be included,

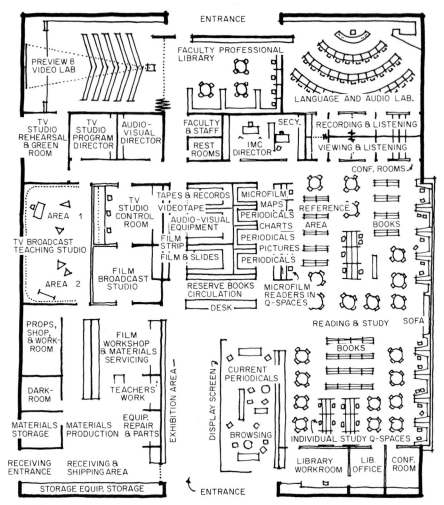

Fig. 40

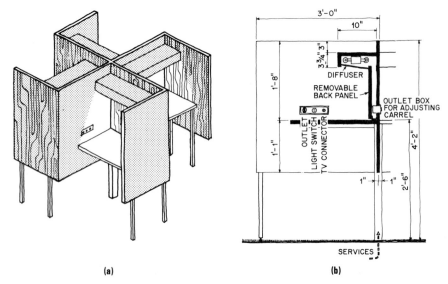

Fig. 41 (a) Study carrel cluster. (b) Section through study carrel cluster.

228

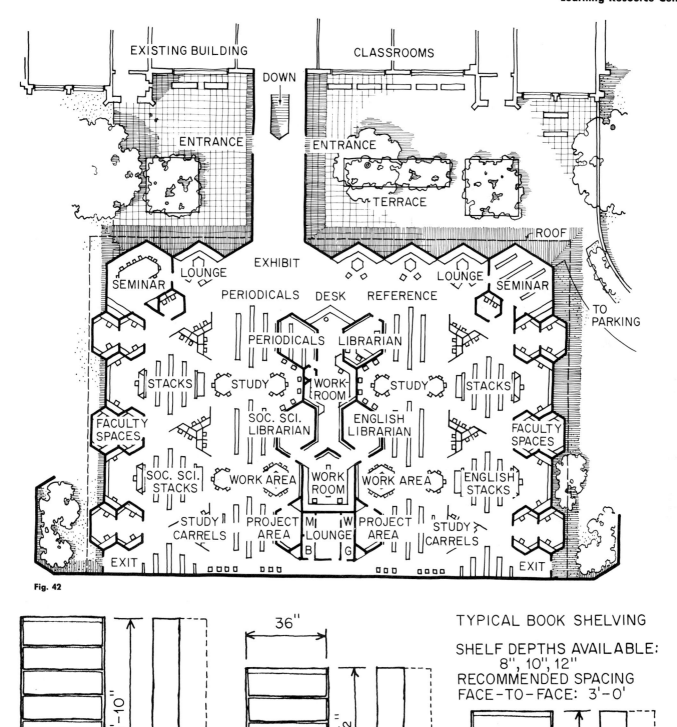

Fig. 42

TYPICAL BOOK SHELVING

SHELF DEPTHS AVAILABLE:
8", 10", 12"
RECOMMENDED SPACING
FACE-TO-FACE: 3'-0'

APPROXIMATE BOOK CAPACITY PER 3' SINGLE-FACE SECTION:
HIGH SHELF UNIT: 150; MEDIUM SHELF UNIT: 105; LOW SHELF UNIT: 65

Fig. 43

ELEMENTARY AND SECONDARY SCHOOLS
Learning Resource Centers; Classrooms

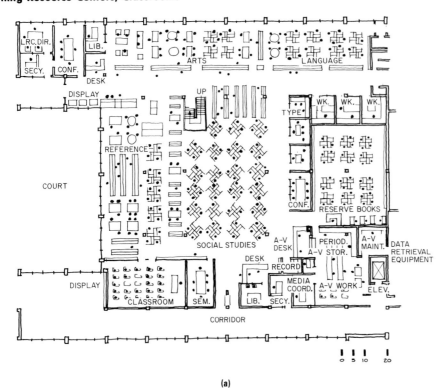

(a)

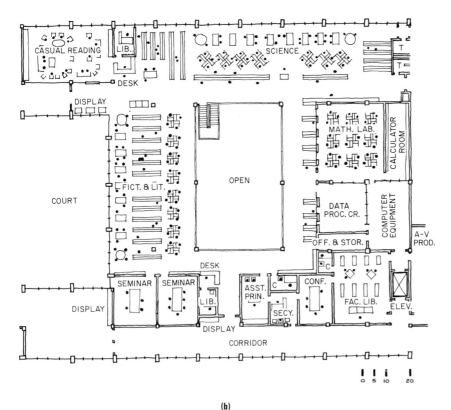

(b)

Fig. 44

the mixing of stacks with group study tables and study carrels, a teacher material preparation area, and a central nerve-control center.

Figure 41 shows a typical carrel unit and detail equipped for audio-visual use. Grouping four together in this manner saves space and is a useful alternative to wall perimeter units.

Responding to the scarcity and high cost of land in certain communities, Fig. 42 shows a center that connects to an existing building, but is air conditioned and all below grade, with its roof developed as landscaped or play space. It also responds 100 percent to the concern by some about windows in the resources center which reduce the wall perimeter for book shelving and other uses.

Accommodating books remains a basic problem in the desire to visually "open up" a resource center; capacities can be gaged from the illustrations in Fig. 43 and Table 5.

A two-level high school resource center is shown in Fig. 49 with entrance (and control) at both levels bringing the center's services closer to more of the school. An opening in the second level and generous stairs between levels unite the spaces that open to an enclosed court.

Figure 45 shows one of four learning resource centers for a high school of 6,000 students that has been organized into four subschools of 1,500 and related groupings of core classrooms. Unique is the accommodating of faculty offices within the study-resource area in group units of non-ceiling-high glass partitions and book shelving units. This develops a close teacher-student relationship and a counseling to the typical resource center by persons expert in specific subject areas.

CLASSROOMS

The classroom layout in Fig. 46 represents a standard size room with a recessed corridor door and a standard seating arrangement.

Figure 47 shows a room designed for ten to fifteen pupils. Rooms of this size can be used for a variety of purposes, such as conference room, student council room, or for small class groups.

The development of the teaching process, extension of classroom activities, and use of group techniques within the classroom have led to new classroom design in recent years. Square classrooms have been proving more satisfactory than rectangular ones. The area of the classroom is increasing with the realization that small classrooms of the past have been the greatest handicap to the improvement of the educational program.

The large group lecture and demonstration room in Fig. 48 is provided with 64 tablet-armed chairs. Proximity to the demonstration table is important for all students. Seats should be tiered for better visibility. In the case of science demonstration, the demonstration table should be immediately adjacent to the preparation room. Natural lighting is generally undesirable but, if required, provision should be made for automatic operation of blinds. The light switch should be near the demonstration table.

Recommended classroom sizes for elementary schools range from 850 to 1,150 sq ft. High school classrooms may range from 750 to 900 sq ft. In some instances where large group teaching or team teaching is taking place, double classrooms may be desirable. In other instances, regular classrooms may be divided by the use of a folding partition which has a satisfactory acoustical separation.

General Requirements for All Classrooms
Design

1. Sufficient space is needed near the front of the room for setting up audiovisual equipment, such as projection screens and charts.

2. Ceilings should be a maximum of $9\frac{1}{2}$ ft high.

3. Light from windows should, if possible, come over a pupil's left shoulder. No teacher should be required to face the windows when addressing the class from the normal teaching position.

4. Ceilings and/or walls should be acoustically treated.

5. Floors should have a cushioning material.

Location The classroom should have as quiet a location as possible, away from noisy outdoor areas. Ease of access to specialized facilities outside the academic unit should be ensured.

Light Control Color films, television, and slides are becoming more and more widely used. Darkening curtains or light-tight blinds should be provided for light control in all teaching areas. The architect should give careful consideration to the problem of darkening clerestories, skylights, and other sources of light. Consideration might be given to the type of venetian blinds that ride in side channels and are easier to operate and to clean than other blinds.

Electrical Services

1. A double electric outlet should be located on each of the three interior walls, and above all counters for use with equipment such as projectors and phonographs. Locations near sinks should be avoided.

2. Eight-inch clocks should be placed in all educational rooms.

3. A fire-alarm system is required.

4. Light switches should be located at the door. It is suggested that switches for corridor lighting be located so that pupils do not have access to them.

5. In planning the building, consideration should be given to ease of wiring a coaxial cable for television, if it will be needed later. Conduit is not recommended, but access to furred ceilings above corridors for this purpose would be desirable. Television reception from broadcast stations may be desirable in large group classrooms. Antennas might be provided here and at other selected points in the building.

6. Telephone service will be required to administrative offices and to other critical points in the school.

Doors

1. Doors should be placed at the front of the classroom and should be recessed so that they do not protrude into the corridor.

2. Thresholds should be avoided so that equipment on wheeled tables, such as mounted movie projectors, can be rolled in and out easily.

3. All doors should have a vision panel of tempered or wire glass.

4. Door hardware snould be such that doors cannot be locked from inside the classroom.

Two large classrooms separated by a movable partition are shown in Fig. 49. When the folding door is open these rooms become an assembly room or an area for large group instruction. Caution should be exercised when selecting a folding door. It should be easy to operate and it should provide suitable acoustical properties. Rooms of this type should have two exits, one for each area.

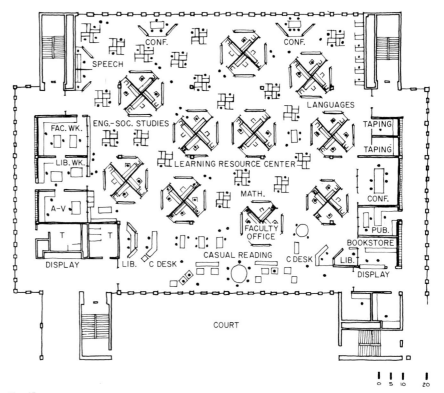

Fig. 45

TABLE 5 Book Shelving Capacity (Approx.)

	Single-face sections			Double-face sections			
No. of 3 ft sections	High — 7 shelves	Medium — 5 shelves	Counter — 3 shelves	High — 7 shelves	Medium — 5 shelves	Counter — 3 shelves	Lineal ft of 3 ft shelving sections
1	150	105	65	300	210	130	3
2	300	210	130	600	420	260	6
3	450	315	195	900	630	390	9
4	600	420	260	1,200	840	520	12
5	750	525	325	1,500	1,050	650	15
6	900	630	390	1,800	1,260	780	18
7	1,050	735	455	2,100	1,470	910	21
8	1,200	840	520	2,400	1,680	1,040	24
9	1,350	945	595	2,700	1,890	1,170	37
10	1,500	1,050	650	3,000	2,100	1,300	30
11	1,650	1,155	715	3,300	2,310	1,430	33
12	1,800	1,260	780	3,600	2,520	1,560	36
13	1,950	1,365	845	3,900	2,730	1,690	39
14	2,100	1,470	910	4,200	2,940	1,820	42
15	2,250	1,575	975	4,500	3,150	1,950	45
16	2,400	1,680	1,040	4,800	3,360	2,080	48
17	2,550	1,785	1,105	5,100	3,570	2,210	51
18	2,700	1,890	1,170	5,400	3,780	2,340	54
19	2,850	1,995	1,235	5,700	3,990	2,470	56
20	3,000	2,100	1,300	6,000	4,200	2,600	59

ELEMENTARY AND SECONDARY SCHOOLS
Classrooms

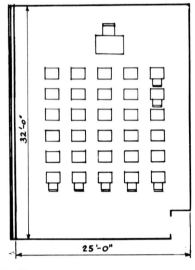

Fig. 46

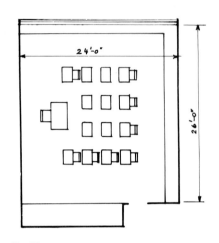

Fig. 47

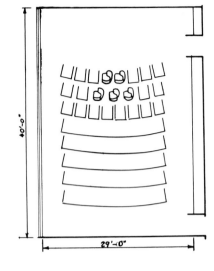

Fig. 48

The split-level plan of the Dundee Elementary School in Greenwich, Conn. (Fig. 50), shows classroom space needed for a team-teaching program. Team teaching, a relatively new technique, is being used in both the elementary and the high school level. The principal requirement for building facilities in team-teaching programs is flexibility—the ability to have space for small, average, and large-size classes, and to be able to shift these spaces from hour to hour. In this type of school the rooms may be constant or variable in size, and in both categories there are small, average, and large-size groups. The illustration indicates how this has been done by the installation of electrically operated folding partitions in many of the rooms. Under this program the movement of pupils is generally much greater than under the homeroom type of elementary program. Ample corridors and stairs are essential. This program also indicates the need for compact design to avoid excessive travel time between rooms. The lower portion of the plan is at ground level; the upper portion is one half story higher. Below the upper level are additional classrooms and the administrative offices.

This plan of the Concord-Carlisle Regional High School, Concord, Mass. (Fig. 51), gives an indication of the variation in sizes of rooms needed to support a modern comprehensive program. Adaptation of room sizes to the needs of the class ensures maximum use of space. Grouping of students within classes is quite common and calls for the availability of small spaces where small groups from classes may meet informally. Likewise, there are many occasions when it is desirable to join two or more classes for a large group experience.

A small platform unit (Fig. 52) is recommended for elementary classrooms. It is portable and designed in four sections. The sections may be used together or separately for a variety of educational activities. This portable unit keeps the floor area flexible, whereas a permanent built-in platform limits the use of a section of the classroom.

Classroom Facilities

Modern teaching procedures require more complex classroom facilities than were considered necessary in the past. Provision should be

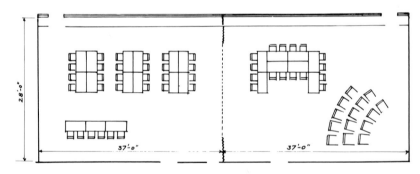

Fig. 49

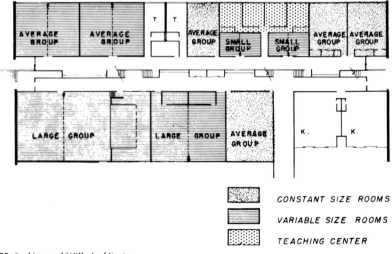

CONSTANT SIZE ROOMS

VARIABLE SIZE ROOMS

TEACHING CENTER

Fig. 50 *Perkins and Will, Architects*

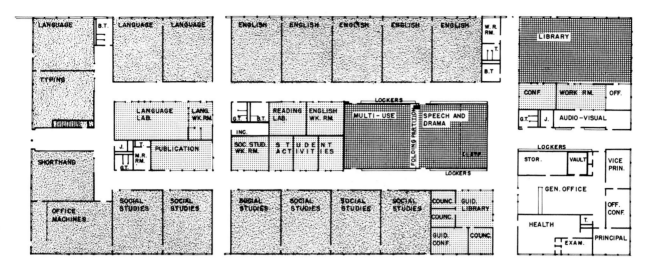

SCALE 10 5 0 10 20 30 40 FEET

LEGEND

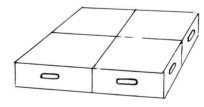

INDIVIDUAL AND SMALL GROUP FACILITIES

MEDIUM SIZE GROUP FACILITIES

LARGE GROUP FACILITIES

Fig. 51 *Warren H. Ashley, Architect*

made for books, audio-visual equipment, recorders, television, tack space, and writing surfaces.

Many communities are building a self-contained classroom in elementary schools. This room requires facilities for teaching various subjects, such as English, mathematics, reading, arts and crafts, music, social studies, and science. This area is used exclusively by one group of pupils. Other schools provide certain facilities in special areas for use by numerous classroom groups. This design, however, may limit the program because it becomes necessary for groups to conform to a time schedule.

The elementary classroom will require storage for such items as science projects and equipment, reference books, paints, paper, posters, maps, globes, coats, boots, audiovisual equipment, records, lunches, and small playground equipment. For kindergarten and primary grades, toilets and coat storage areas located in or adjacent to the classroom are convenient for the teacher to assist the smaller children. Central toilet facilities should be pro-

vided for the intermediate grades and above. Drinking fountains in or adjacent to classrooms are desirable.

Several educational activities require such facilities as sink, counter work area, portable stage, hot and cold water, earth bed, and special furniture. Provision should be made for such items in accordance with the educational program when the building is planned.

Storage Needs in High School

1. Storage space for each group using the classroom should be provided with locks.

2. Storage is needed for the following items: supplies, such as paper and pencils; books and magazines; special equipment for the subject taught in the room (such as blueprints for mechanical drawing, globes and paperback reprints for social studies, and compasses and protractors for mathematics); and the teacher's coat and personal belongings, if not provided for elsewhere.

3. A standard storage closet, either of metal or wood, is recommended for all classrooms.

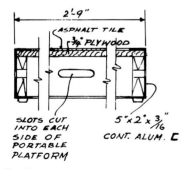

TYPICAL ASSEMBLY: 4-PIECE PLATFORM

2'-9"

ASPHALT TILE

3/4" PLYWOOD

SLOTS CUT INTO EACH SIDE OF PORTABLE PLATFORM

5"x2"x 3/16" CONT. ALUM. ⊏

Fig. 52

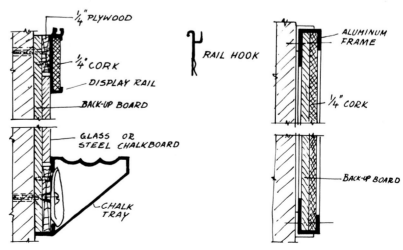

1/4" PLYWOOD

1/4" CORK

DISPLAY RAIL

BACK-UP BOARD

GLASS OR STEEL CHALKBOARD

CHALK TRAY

RAIL HOOK

ALUMINUM FRAME

1/4" CORK

BACK-UP BOARD

Fig. 53

ELEMENTARY AND SECONDARY SCHOOLS
Classrooms

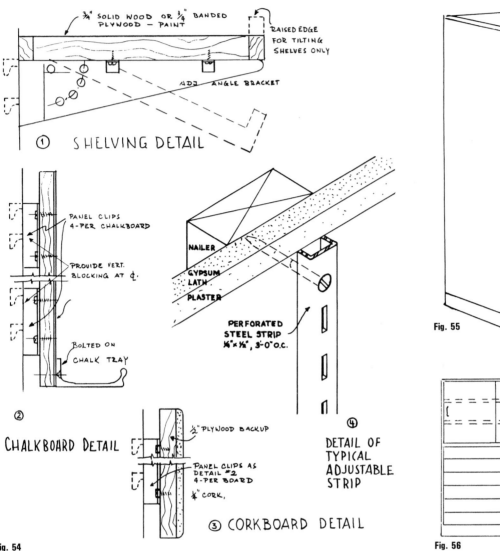

Fig. 54

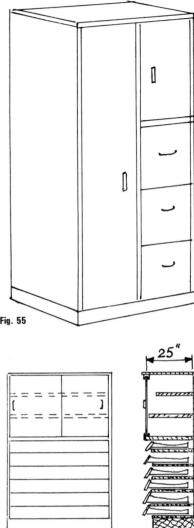

Fig. 55

Fig. 56

Chalkboard and Tackboard

1. The demands for chalkboard and tackboard will vary from subject to subject in the high school. Generally, English and mathematics require more chalkboard than do the social studies, which in turn require more tackboard. The minimum amount of chalkboard in any classroom should be 16 lin ft, and up to 48 lin ft could be used to advantage in many mathematics rooms. Approximately 16 to 32 lin ft of tackboard should be provided.

2. A display rail extending the entire length of the chalkboard is an essential teaching aid. Such a display rail should have hooks with clip fasteners. Provision might also be made for hanging pictures, maps, and charts on other walls of the room. Embedded picture molding should be installed on three walls at a suitable height.

3. Consider installing display cabinets to serve as classroom showcases.

Chalkboard installation is of great importance. For each room, consideration should be given to the type, amount, height, and necessary attachments. The recommended mounting heights can be determined by reviewing the "working heights" chart (Table 6).

Chalkboard may be purchased in several different materials. Glass, slate, and porcelain-enameled steel have proved satisfactory; however, asbestos-cement may be more economical. Avoid hardboard types. If the steel type is used, a three-coat finish will give more lasting results. The chalk tray should be designed for easy cleaning. A map rail is needed, complete with hooks and cork strip (Figs. 53 and 54).

Corkboard should be distributed throughout the school. Display of educational materials will support the educational program. Sixteen-foot sections are recommended for most classrooms and placed for easy viewing by students. The cork should be at least 1/4 in. thick if staples or thumbtacks are used for mounting displays (Fig. 54).

A pegboard may be used to display three-dimensional objects on brackets, hooks, or shelves. The thickness of the board should be no less than 1/4 in.; the tempered grade will give better service.

A high degree of flexibility in the use of wall area can be obtained by building in adjustable hanging strips (Fig. 54).

Steel cabinet (Fig. 55) is a combination of teacher's wardrobe, file drawers, and a small cabinet for personal belongings. This unit should be equipped with a locking device. It can be built into a wall, set in a recess or corner of the classroom. A coat hanger rod and mirror should be included on the wardrobe side.

The unit in Fig. 56 may be used for storing large charts (24 by 48 in.), maps, graphs, large paper, paintings, projects, and audio-visual equipment. The lower half includes long, deep drawers and the top section provides a very flexible space with adjustable shelving. This unit will have its greatest use in elementary schools.

The storage unit in Fig. 57 serves also as a work counter and sink. The height is determined by the size of students. The sliding doors are safer and need less maintenance than swinging doors. The top and splashboard should be a durable plastic.

Figure 58 shows shelving or base cabinets along a window wall. The storage unit makes

TABLE 6 Working Heights in Inches for Elementary and Secondary School Children

| Item | Elementary | | | | | | | | | Junior high | | | Senior high | | |
| | Kindergarten | | | Grades 1–3 | | | Grades 4–6 | | | Grades 7–9 | | | Grades 10–12 | | |
	Min.	Opti-mum	Max.	Min.	Opti-mum	Max.	Min.	Opti-mum	Max.	Min.	Opti-mum	Max.	Min.	Opti-mum	Max.
Cabinet, display (top)		54			56			66			74			77	
Cabinet, display (bottom)		26			29			34			38			39	
Cabinet, pupil use (top)			50			56			65			74			79
Chairs and bench	10	11	11	10	12	13	12	14	16	13	15	17	14	16	18
Chalkboard (top)	68	70	73	72	73	74	76	77	78	79	80	82	80	82	84
Chalkboard (bottom and chalkrail)	20	22	25	24	25	26	28	29	30	31	32	34	32	34	36
Counter, cafeteria	21	27	32	25	31	34	29	36	39	32	40	45	33	42	48
Counter, classroom work (standing)	20	24	26	24	26	29	28	30	34	31	34	38	32	36	39
Counter, general office	20	27	32	24	31	34	28	36	39	31	40	45	32	42	49
Desk and table, classroom	17	18	19	18	20	22	21	23	25	23	26	28	24	27	29
Desk, typing											26			26	
Door knob	19	27	32	24	31	35	28	36	40	30	40	46	31	42	49
Drinking fountain	20	24	27	24	27	29	28	32	34	32	36	40	32	40	44
Fire extinguisher (tank)*															
Hook, coat	32	36	48	38	41	51	47	48	58	53	54	64	54	55	68
Lavatory and sink	20	23	25	24	26	27	28	29	31	32	33	35	32	35	38
Light switch	27	27	46	31	35	49	36	40	56	40	46	64	42	50	68
Mirror, lower edge			35			38			43			48			52
Mirror, upper edge	46			56			65			71			71		
Panic bar	21	27	32	25	31	34	29	36	39	32	40	45	33	42	48
Pencil sharpener	20	27	33	25	31	35	28	36	40	32	40	46	32	42	49
Rail, hand and directional	20	21	32	24	24	34	28	29	39	31	32	45	32	33	48
Shelf, hat and books		41	48		46	51		54	58		60	64		62	68
Soap dispenser	20	27	33	25	31	35	28	36	40	32	40	46	32	42	49
Stool, drawing		19			21			26			28			29	
Table, drawing		26			29			34			38			39	
Table and bench, work (standing)	25	26	28	26	29	32	30	34	38	36	38	41	37	39	42
Tackboard (top)	72	84		72	84		72	84		72	84		72	84	
Tackboard (bottom)	20	22	25	24	25	26	28	29	30	31	32	34	32	34	36
Telephone, wall mounted			35			37			43			48			52
Toilet stall, top of partition	44	44		52	52		61	61		67	67		69	69	
Towel dispenser	23	27	46	28	31	49	33	36	56	37	40	64	37	42	68
Urinal (bottom)				3	3–15	17	3	3–17	20	4	4–18	22	4	4–19	24
Wainscotting	54	54	54	54	54	54	54	54	54	60	60	60	60	60	60
Water closet (seat)	10	10½	12	11	11½	12	13	13½	14	14	14½	15	14½	15	15
Window ledge			29			30			34			38			41

Recessed at baseboard height.

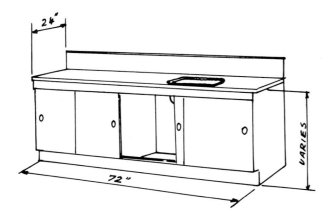

Fig. 57

good use of this area and provides counter space for plants and displays. The units may be prefabricated or custom built.

Working Heights for Students

Table 6 can be used as a general guide to acceptable working heights for elementary and junior and senior high school children. There is a large variation in the size of children within a particular classroom group and in various geographical sections of the country. The architect should obtain the median child height in the particular community and select minimum, optimum, or maximum heights as indicated.

MULTIPURPOSE ROOMS

The layout in Fig. 59 was designed for a small high school. As the student enrollments increase and additional classrooms are built, the stage will be removed and this area converted to dining. The room is located at the main entrance to the building, with a combined corridor and lounge. The chair and table storage is well placed with direct access to the

ELEMENTARY AND SECONDARY SCHOOLS
Multipurpose Rooms

service entrance. The room is opened up to the two wide corridors—an arrangement that permits overflow seating during special assemblies or public performances. The openings can be closed with drapes when desired. The openness reduces traffic congestion and discipline problems.

This cafeteria-assembly room (Fig. 60) is opened up on two sides, with the kitchen at one end. Overflow seating is available on the corridor side. The plan provides space for an adequate program within a limited budget.

The following information and drawings are primarily concerned with large areas in school buildings which are designed and equipped for two or more group activities. The most frequently used room combinations include assembly-cafeteria, assembly-cafeteria-gymnasium, assembly-gymnasium, and a student activity area where many small learning centers may operate at one time.

Assembly-Cafeteria

The assembly-cafeteria combination is popular because the room can be designed with a pleasing environment for both eating and assembly. This type of room is also more adaptable to scheduling without limiting other phases of the educational program.

The room should be furnished with tables that can be quickly moved into a nearby storage area. A large portable folding unit containing table and benches has proved satisfactory for elementary schools. Tables that fold into the wall are also available. Many high schools prefer the smaller folding table and stacking chairs, which permit a more informal and flexible arrangement.

This type of room should have a stage, stage curtain, backdrops, and adequate lighting for dramatic presentations.

Student traffic flow in this area should be planned. Minimum cross traffic is essential during the lunch period when children are carrying food. During student assembly periods good circulation may reduce discipline problems.

Assembly-Cafeteria-Gymnasium

The assembly-cafeteria-gymnasium combination can be found in schools where limited funds are available. This arrangement may seriously curtail the educational program. The time necessary to set up the cafeteria furniture, feed the children, clean the room, and remove the cafeteria furniture will consume a large portion of the school day. The remaining time available for physical and assembly activities may be insufficient for a good program. It is also difficult for the architect to design a room in which the atmosphere is conducive to dining, physical education, and assembly productions.

Assembly-Gymnasium

The assembly-gymnasium combination is a possible solution to seating the total student enrollment when a small or no auditorium is available. This area should be designed with a stage that can also be used for physical activity. Storage space will be needed for chairs, gymnasium equipment, and stage equipment. Acoustics, lighting, ventilation, and traffic flow should be adequate for assembly and physical education. This arrangement is not considered as satisfactory as the assembly-cafeteria combination.

Adequate chair storage is provided in this cafeteria-assembly combination (Fig. 61) for an

Fig. 58

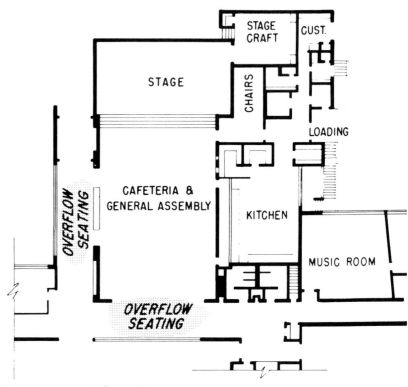

Fig. 59 *Chapman and Leffler, Architects*

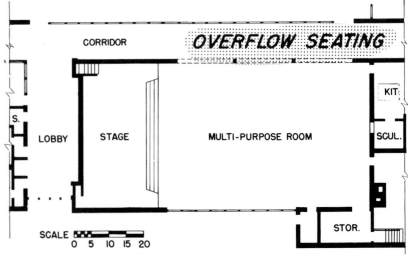

Fig. 60 *Chapman and Leffler, Architects*

236

elementary school. The low display can be moved and overflow seating is available in the lobby corridor. Public toilets are well placed. The stage has outside and inside access independent of the main room. The music room and the stagecraft area provide adequate space for school or public performance preparation.

The gymnasium-assembly combination shown in Fig. 62 provides chair storage, gymnasium storage, stage, and exercise rooms. The large gymnasium has a large folding door which provides two teacher stations. The stage can be divided with a folding door to provide two more stations. Access to shower rooms is on either side of the stage, and the stage can be entered from the corridor on either side. Folding bleachers close the proscenium opening when the stage is used as exercise rooms.

STUDENT LOCKERS

Many different solutions have been developed to solve the problem of storing coats and personal belongings of students. In the elementary school, proximity to the homeroom for ease

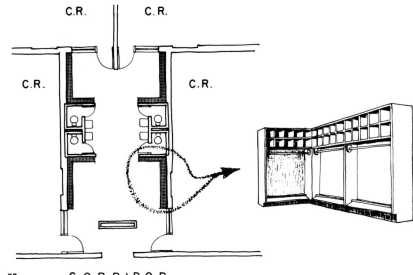

Fig. 63

of teacher supervision is important. Lockers in the high school should be located for easy access between periods. Circulation in the locker areas should be sufficiently adequate to prevent congestion. It is generally necessary to provide arrangements whereby students may lock up personal belongings and books. Most high schools also provide lockers with locks for coats. However, others have been successful in providing small security lockers and open coat racks.

Figure 63 shows one way of storing coats, boots, and small personal articles in a four-classroom unit of an elementary school. Ventilation can be provided economically. This type of open cubicle should have permanently attached coat hangers. The boot rack should be constructed of materials resistant to water and dirt.

Another way of storing coats is within a classroom (Fig. 64), where the storage area serves also for passage of pupils. The area is convenient for teacher supervision. The coat and toilet areas for all four classrooms are located together, permitting economical utilities.

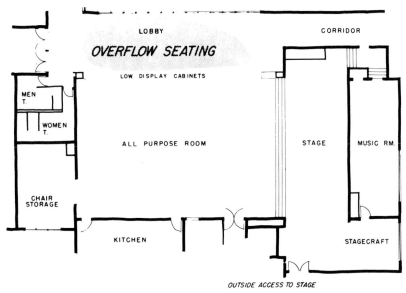

Fig. 61 *Chapman and Leffler, Architects*

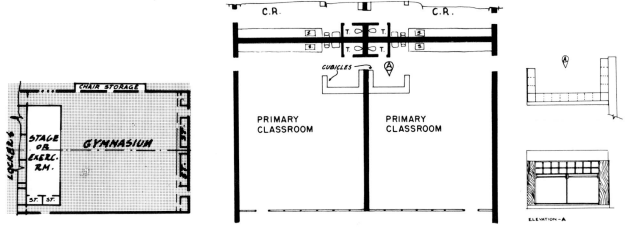

Fig. 62

Fig. 64

ELEMENTARY AND SECONDARY SCHOOLS
Student Lockers

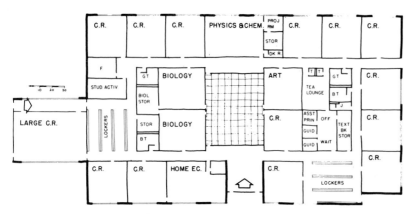

A. G. Odell, Jr. and Associates, Architects

Fig. 65

and circulation. Mechanical ventilation is needed to dry wet clothing and avoid odors. However, this plan uses up wall space that might better be used for educational purposes.

The type of storage shown in Fig. 68 is usually found in elementary schools where open cubicles are desirable. These units are located on the classroom side of a single-loaded corridor for convenient supervision. The walls have been splayed to relieve corridor congestion during the arrival and dismissal of children. The splayed wall also provides a recess for the classroom door.

In Fig. 69, panels fold to provide the doors on the wardrobe. Mechanical ventilation is essential. The large amount of wall area used by this system may introduce serious handi-

Lockers may be concentrated in several conveniently located areas (Fig. 65). These areas are completely open and the wide spaces between rows provide comfortable circulation. This type of locker arrangement eliminates congestion in corridors and frees corridor walls for display and vision panels. As locker alcoves are difficult to supervise, it is essential to provide complete circulation around the entire space.

Another way of treating locker installation in a high school is shown in Fig. 66. The lockers have been concentrated in two areas near the entrance and student center. The areas have been left open with ample space for comfortable circulation. Restrooms are adjacent to the locker area, which may reduce corridor traffic and save student time. Each student is assigned a security locker for books and personal items. Coats and boots are stored in open coat racks.

Coat storage (Fig. 67) in a classroom can be closed off by means of a folding partition. This arrangement gives students easy access to wraps. The area is convenient to supervise and the classroom area provides space for dressing

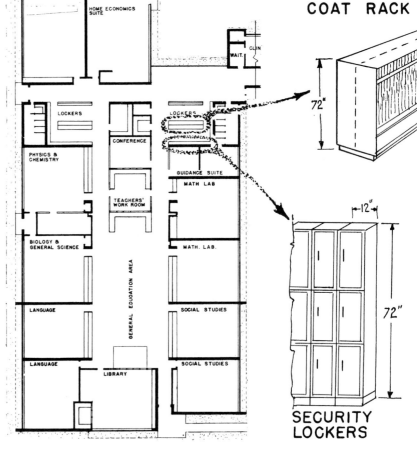

COAT RACK

SECURITY LOCKERS

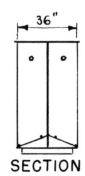

SECTION

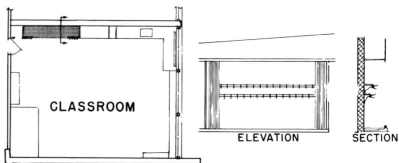

CLASSROOM

ELEVATION   SECTION

Fig. 66 Chapman and Leffler, Architects   **Fig. 67**

caps in the use of the room for teaching purposes.

The locker unit (Fig. 70) is used as a space saver. These units give an economical approach to coat storage. Each student may be assigned a personal locker for books and small personal belongings. The coats are hung on permanently attached hangers. This unit permits natural air circulation for drying coats and is convenient to supervise.

The detail in Fig. 71 shows the recessed corridor lockers, which are seen below in elevation (Fig. 72). The ceramic tile base is used to simplify floor maintenance. The ceiling is furred down to

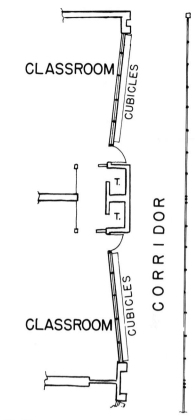

Fig. 70

Fig. 68

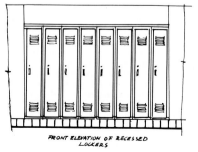

Fig. 71

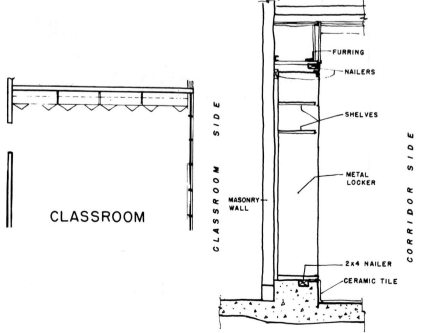

Fig. 69

Fig. 72

ELEMENTARY AND SECONDARY SCHOOLS
Language Laboratory; Science Facilities

eliminate the accumulation of dust and trash on top of the lockers. These units can be ventilated by pulling air through lower front vents and into the plenum above.

LANGUAGE LABORATORY

The language laboratory provides a place where pupils can listen to recordings in a foreign language, make their own recordings, practice speaking a foreign language in private, and carry out drill exercises.

It should have students' booths constructed of sound-absorbent material, approximately 30 or 36 in. wide, 36 in. deep, 54 in. high. These should face the teacher. The top front half should have a see-through glass panel so that the student can see the teacher, and so that the laboratory can easily be adapted for audiovisual aids. The back wall and ceiling should be treated with acoustical or sound-absorbent materials (see Fig. 73).

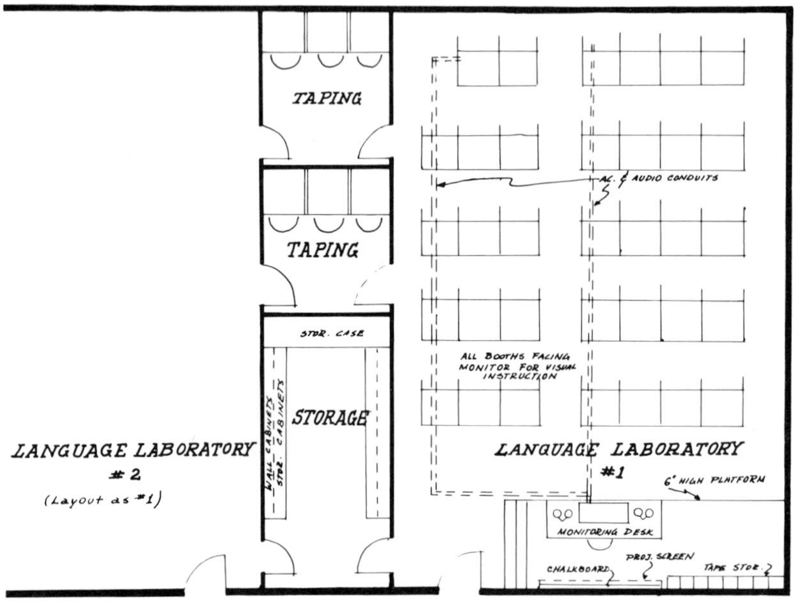

SCIENCE FACILITIES

General Science Rooms and Biology Laboratories

General science rooms and biology laboratories should be located on the first floor, with windows facing south or southwest, a door opening into the preparation room, and a door opening onto the campus so that classes may study outdoors without passing through the building (see Fig. 74).

Activities include lectures, demonstrations, viewing projected materials, individual and group study, writing, and experimentation with animals and plants.

The front wall should be equipped along its entire length with chalkboard, the center section of which should be raisable. There should be a display rail over everything except the raisable section of board. Provision should be made for a projection screen at the front

shelves are desirable. Instructor's demonstration desk should be equipped with hot and cold water, duplex ac receptacle, soapstone sink, upright rods with clamps and wood crossbar, and double gas cock. Also needed are two-student biology desks with one cupboard and two book compartments; chairs, mock-up table; herbarium, aquariums; projection screen; microscopes; models, charts; dissecting trays; specimens; portable germinating bed; terrarium; microprojectors; three sinks with towels and soap dispensers; experiment sheet filing cabinet near tackboard; first-aid cabinet; fire extinguisher.

Electric outlets should be located on each of the walls. If the entire class uses electrically

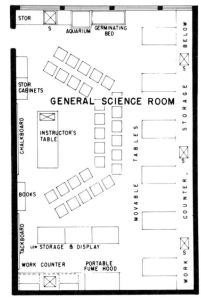

Fig. 74

lighted microscopes, tables will need electric outlets. Sinks and outlets for gas and electricity are needed in counters.

Storage and Preparation Rooms

Storage and preparation rooms should be adjacent to general science and biology. These rooms are used for teacher preparation, storage of bulk supplies, conferences and offices.

This area should be lined with storage spaces for materials and equipment of various sizes. There should be provision for teachers' records and professional books. Room should be outfitted with a sink and gas and electric outlets. Access windows should open into the laboratories.

Storage provision should be made for equipment used in general science and biology. A storage bin, made up of many small drawers, each measuring approximately 4 by 4 in., should be included for efficient storage of small items of equipment. Also needed are desks and chairs; preparation table on wheels; preparation table with drawers; standing storage cabinet for charts; cabinet with slides; bookcase; shelving to ceiling; sink with hot and cold water; gas and electric outlets.

Fig. 73

Booths should be equipped with headphones, microphones attached to a flexible gooseneck stand, magnetic disc or tape recorder, and a control panel with switches for selecting balance and volume. There should be a monitor jack on the same panel.

At the front of the room, the teacher's area should have a platform at least 6 in. high in order to raise the level of vision into the student booths. The master unit should accommodate three channels for simultaneous programs and should also contain two dual-track tape recorders and two phonographs, four-speed. A small soundproof booth will be necessary to enable the teacher to make master tape recordings. A typewriter with international keyboard is needed.

Storage and small recording rooms should be separate.

of the room. Corkboard 4-ft wide should cover the entire width of the back wall above the wainscoting. It is suggested that counters be installed along two sides of the room, one being the window side. Such counters should include several sinks and outlets for gas and electricity.

All laboratory furniture should be acid-resistant and easy to wash and clean. Equipment includes a display case for biological specimens that opens to the corridor from within the room; teacher's combination wardrobe and closet; legal-size file with lock; storage areas for notebooks, aprons, microscopes, instruments, specimens, biologicals, pupil projects, microprojector, and books. A storage cabinet at counter height might be installed along window wall. Locked sliding door extending the entire length of the storage cabinet and metal

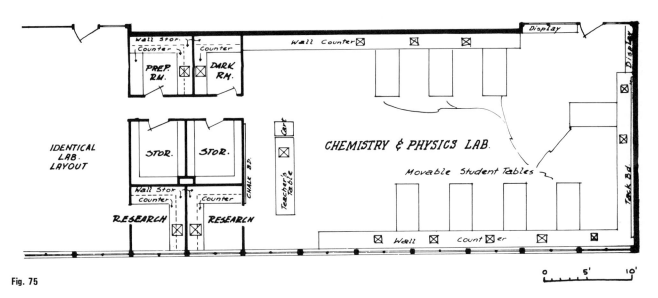

Fig. 75

Plant and Animal Room

The plant and animal room should be located adjacent to the biology laboratory, possibly adjacent to a biology storeroom. Easy access to the outdoors is desirable.

Southern exposure is desirable. This area should be arranged like a greenhouse, with sanitary finishes and a concrete floor with drain so that the room can be hosed down. In addition to sunlight, the plant room will require special ventilation and heating so that it does not get cold overnight. Special heating, thermostatically controlled and separate from other parts of the building, should ensure even heating during weekends and holiday periods.

Equipment includes table and racks for plants; growing beds on wheeled tables; animal cages; feeding trays; storage for food, tools, equipment; sink with hot and cold water; hose; pails; hand garden tools; bins for loam, sand, and peat moss.

Chemistry Laboratories

Chemistry laboratories should be readily accessible from individual research and prepara-

tion rooms (see Fig. 75). Laboratory activities include demonstrations, individual and group study and experimentation, writing, viewing projected materials, and lectures.

At a comfortable height there should be student stations for 24 students, consisting of tables with large free working area and all services available: ac and dc variable voltage should be provided. The front wall should be equipped for its entire length with a chalkboard, the center section of which should be raisable. There should be a display rail over all but the raisable section of board. On the back wall above the wainscoting level, there should be some corkboard and pegboard with hardware. A fume hood, accessible from three sides, should be provided.

One end of the room should contain the teacher's desk and a demonstration area with a 5-in.-high dais for demonstration. Demonstration table should have a stone top, spotlight lighting, and a roll-away extension. All services should be provided for the demonstration, including variable ac and dc voltage. Sound cable should be installed in the floor for projection purposes. Provision should be made for darkening the room.

Special attention should be given to the furniture for this space. As a minimum, it should be acid- and base-resistant and easy to wash and clean. It should include tablet armchairs; teacher's combination wardrobe and closet; acid-proof sinks with dilution tank; storage for chemical supplies; storage space in laboratory tables; normal chemistry laboratory equipment for semi-micro techniques; salt and solution cabinets; three rolling tables to service tables; standard reagent storage area; locked cupboards for delicate instruments and dangerous chemicals; fire extinguishers and first-aid kits; storage for notebooks and aprons; experiment-sheet filing cabinet; charts and models; projection screen.

Physics Laboratories

Physics laboratories are used for lectures, demonstrations, viewing projected material, individual and group study, writing, individual and group experimentation (see Fig. 76).

Around the room on three sides at a comfortable height (higher than the ordinary table) should be a work station for each student,

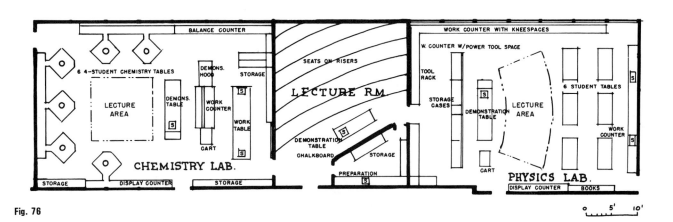

Fig. 76

ELEMENTARY AND SECONDARY SCHOOLS
Science Facilities

consisting of a table with a large free working area and all services available; ac and dc variable voltage should be provided to all stations; voltage should be supplied by several portable voltage-regulating units. Sinks should be available. Some attention should be given to permanent or semipermanent laboratory stands for rigging equipment.

One end of the room should contain the teacher's desk and a demonstration area with a 5-in.-high dais for the demonstration table. The demonstration table should have a stone top, spotlight lighting, and a roll-away extension. All services should be available. Downdraft ventilator is suggested, but it should be positioned so as to give as much unobstructed broad area on table surface as possible. It should not be centrally placed. Tablet armchairs should be placed in front of the demonstration desk.

The room should have as much chalkboard space as possible, since chalkboard work with problems constitutes a considerable part of class time. Ample corkboard space and some pegboard with hardware are needed.

Attention should be given to darkening the room properly. This is important for the projection of movies and slides, as well as for demonstrations that require a darkened room, and for some laboratory work such as photometry. Sound cable should be installed for projection purposes and antenna facilities for television and radio reception. There should be central control of lighting.

Doors should open into the front of the laboratory. An open-joist ceiling has the advantage of permitting hanging of apparatus. A ceiling hook capable of holding a ½-ton load should be provided.

One of the main problems for the physics area will be provision of adequate storage space for a vast amount of demonstration equipment and specialized scientific apparatus. Storage space with glass doors for visibility, bookshelves for a reference library, and a cabinet for notebooks should be provided.

Preparation and Storage Rooms for Chemistry and Physics Laboratories

Preparation and storage rooms should be adjacent to laboratories, with a door leading to corridor and laboratory. They are used for teacher preparation, storage of bulk supplies, and conferences.

The area should be lined with storage spaces for materials and equipment of various sizes (in chemistry, glass tubing, long items, tall items). All shelves should have lips to prevent slippage, and should be built so that the floor supports the weight, unless the storage area is small and specifically designated for light items.

Chemistry Open shelving of cabinets is favored for storage of bulk chemicals. Special transite-lined volatile closets vented to the outside for volatile reagents, acids, and alkalies should be provided, along with provisions for the teacher's records and professional books. The room should be outfitted with sink and gas and electric outlets. It should also have storage provision for all equipment, a preparation table large enough for six analytical balances, adequate work space for preparation, special storage for charts so that they are kept flat, not rolled, desks and chairs, preparation table on wheels, ladders with rail, and a bookcase.

Physics A storage bin made up of many small drawers measuring approximately 4 by 4 in. for efficient storage of small items of equipment is suggested. Electric outlets similar to those provided in demonstration table, as well as plentiful 110-V ac outlets, and adequate lighting should be provided, as well as ladders with rail to reach stored items, and a workbench and sink with drainboard along one side, to repair and set up equipment. The bench should be rugged enough to take considerable hammering.

Individual Research and Project Rooms for Chemistry and Physics

Research and project rooms should be adjacent to chemistry and physics laboratories and separated from them by half-glass partitions. They are used for individual and small group study and experimentation, instruction, and research. (See Fig. 89)

Science Shop

The science shop and the darkroom may be built as a unit and placed back to back between the corridor and the window side. The project room should be located on the window side and have a door opening into a laboratory. A glass wall will enable the teacher to keep the area under observation.

The science shop is used for individual work in making and repairing instruments and equipment.

It should have a workbench and sink along one side of the room. The bench, for repair and setting up of equipment, should be rugged enough for metalworking.

The furniture and equipment should include equipment drawers, work counter, drill press, small metalworking lathe, some storage shelves for reference books, tool storage, sink, and ample space for electrical equipment. Electric outlets similar to those provided in the demonstration desk should be available, as well as 110-V ac outlets.

Darkroom

The darkroom could be placed back to back with the science shop and located on the corridor side with the door opening into the corridor.

It is used for developing film and the storage of darkroom materials and reagents, mounting equipment, and the like.

A vestibule and two-door entrance will prevent light from entering. The area could be divided into a small room near the entrance for weighing and mixing chemicals and a larger room toward the rear for developing and printing.

A counter should be constructed along three sides of the room, 34 to 36 in. high and 24 in. wide. There should be a large chemical-resistant open sink, 24 by 30 in. and 18 in. deep; and a wet bench, attached at either end, draining into the sink. The sink must have both hot and cold water. Stainless-steel surfaces are recommended; finishes must be easily cleaned and stain-resistant.

Shelves 12 in. apart and 10 in. deep should be constructed above the counter. Storage in standard darkroom style should provide tray and chemical storage as well as shelves for dry stock. Since the room will be used for dry work, such as spectroscopy, provision

should be made for sit-down as well as stand-up dry work. Walls should be finished a flat green for eye ease. Serious attention must be given to ensure adequate ventilation of this room.

Furniture and equipment will include retouching table; developing; enlarging, and printing equipment; dryer; print washer; trays; paper cutter; hot plate; safe lights; timer; fire extinguisher; clock.

At least four double electric outlets are needed at the counter. There must be sufficient plugs for all appliances, conveniently placed near all work positions.

AUXILIARY SCIENCE FACILITIES

Special science facilities like animal rooms, greenhouses, vivariums, and planetariums are not exclusively part of large science complexes. Sometimes a given instructor will have

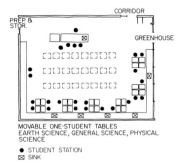

MOVABLE ONE-STUDENT TABLES
EARTH SCIENCE, GENERAL SCIENCE, PHYSICAL SCIENCE

● STUDENT STATION
⊠ SINK

Fig. 77

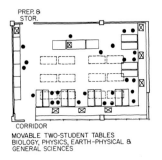

MOVABLE TWO-STUDENT TABLES
BIOLOGY, PHYSICS, EARTH-PHYSICAL & GENERAL SCIENCES

Fig. 78

ELEMENTARY AND SECONDARY SCHOOLS
Science Facilities

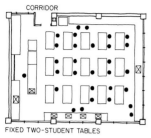

FIXED TWO-STUDENT TABLES

Fig. 79

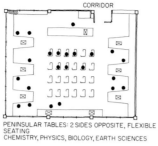

PENINSULAR TABLES: 2 SIDES OPPOSITE, FLEXIBLE SEATING
CHEMISTRY, PHYSICS, BIOLOGY, EARTH SCIENCES

Fig. 84

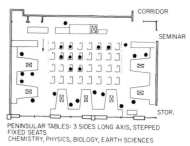

PENINSULAR TABLES: 3 SIDES LONG AXIS, STEPPED FIXED SEATS
CHEMISTRY, PHYSICS, BIOLOGY, EARTH SCIENCES

Fig. 85

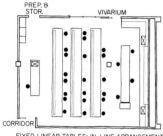

FIXED LINEAR TABLES: IN-LINE ARRANGEMENT
BIOLOGY, CHEMISTRY

Fig. 80

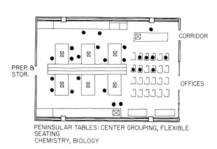

PENINSULAR TABLES: CENTER GROUPING, FLEXIBLE SEATING
CHEMISTRY, BIOLOGY

Fig. 86

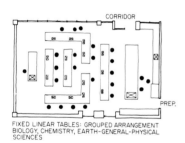

FIXED LINEAR TABLES: GROUPED ARRANGEMENT
BIOLOGY, CHEMISTRY, EARTH-GENERAL-PHYSICAL SCIENCES

Fig. 81

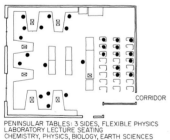

PENINSULAR TABLES: 3 SIDES, FLEXIBLE PHYSICS LABORATORY LECTURE SEATING
CHEMISTRY, PHYSICS, BIOLOGY, EARTH SCIENCES

Fig. 82

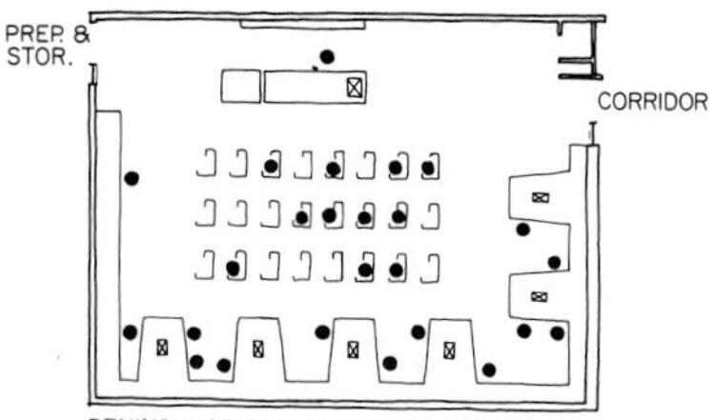

Fig. 87   Combined laboratory and lecture hall.

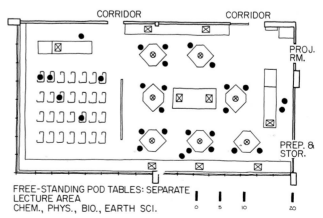

PENINSULAR TABLES: 2 SIDES, ADJUSTABLE, FLEXIBLE LECTURE SEATING
CHEMISTRY, PHYSICS, BIOLOGY, EARTH SCIENCES

Fig. 83

FREE-STANDING POD TABLES: SEPARATE LECTURE AREA
CHEM., PHYS., BIO., EARTH SCI.

0   5   10   20

Fig. 88

ELEMENTARY AND SECONDARY SCHOOLS
Science Facilities

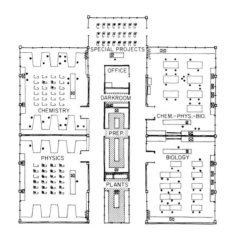

Fig. 89

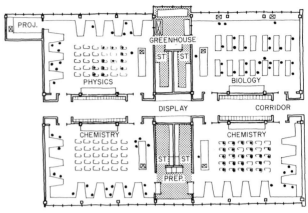

Fig. 92

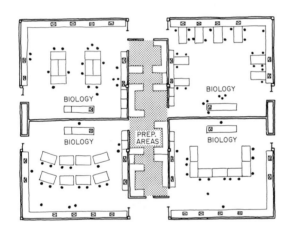

Fig. 90

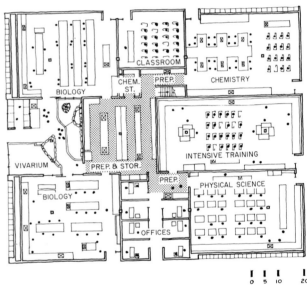

Fig. 93

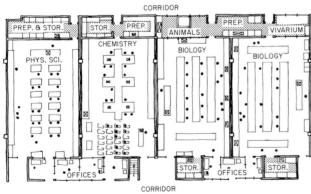

Fig. 91

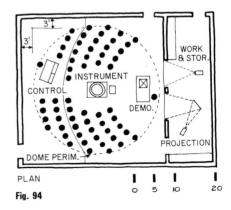

Fig. 94

a special interest, or a local business group or community effort will focus on funding such added programs. As a result, such spaces often get extra special attention in their development

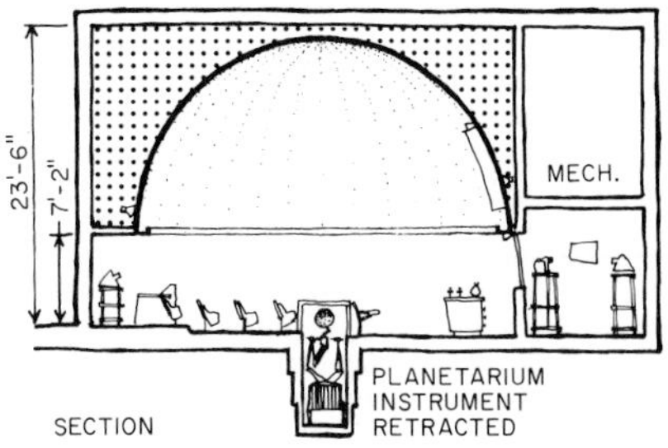

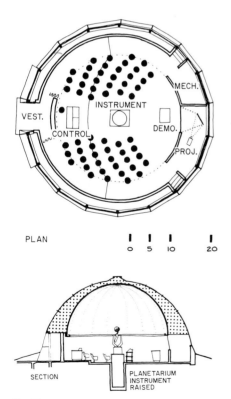

Fig. 95

from everyone, demand research, turn out to be topnotch, and really excite the students.

Figures 95–98 exemplify a vivarium and a planetarium, neither of which requires much area, but both entail special equipment, special care and know-how to construct and operate. The vivarium shown is located in a high school suite between two biology laboratories, backs up to a preparation room, and fronts, through a glass wall, to a main circulation corridor. Skylit, its setting of sun, animals, plants, and water brings nature right into the everyday action of the school.

Fig. 96

Planetariums, as very special spaces, can be accommodated within a building or developed as a satellite facility, as the one example indicates, being built from prefabricated manufactured parts. Many specially motivated students, particular parent and community pride, and unique accomplishment have derived from having such bonus facilities.

ARTS

Working surface, and lots of it, by way of counters and tables is a basic requirement, as is wall space for display and storage cabinetry. Figure 99 shows a well-equipped, typical general art room with sinks (X squares) in the perimeter counterwork, allowing flexibility for various table and desk combinations. Figure 100 shows a larger art suite, with no windows and all kinds of wall space, artificially well lit, with a storage core and peninsula sinks, but otherwise open, flexible space utilizing 7-ft-high storage units as dividers of functions.

Corridors flank the art suite shown in Figure 101 that develops as an interior core unit related to typical classrooms along the corridors. Glass over the work counters allows the creative activities to be seen from the corridors, showcasing an attractive interest center.

Where storage requirements are so unique and stringent, and working techniques so important in the work done, certain special details and ideas develop as useful and practical. Some of these are noted here. Figure 102 shows a room well equipped with all kinds of cabinets and counters, plus one bonus extra, that of wires stretched across to hang prints on to dry. Figure 103 shows a clay wedging board, useful for working in clay. Figure 104 is a common available light track, allowing feature lighting fixtures anywhere. Figure 105 shows a way of storing fabric for use in silk-screen work. A spare roll is kept forward, and the working roll is looped around and then fed under a cutting gate board. Figure 106 shows movable platforms set on lockable casters to serve as a model stand.

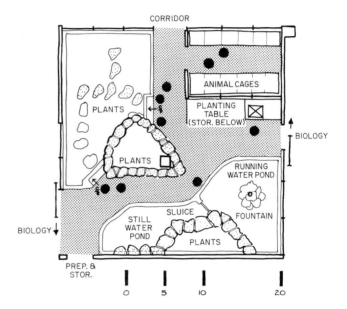

Fig. 97

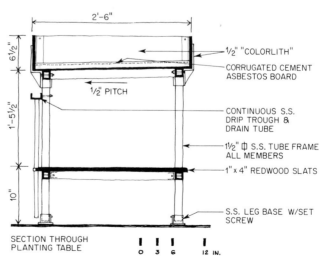

Fig. 98

245

ELEMENTARY AND SECONDARY SCHOOLS
Arts; Music Facilities

Displaying art work itself becomes a creative and practical challenge. Ample tack surface should be available on the wall. Display devices can be hung from the ceiling, developed as free-standing kiosks, or used in other constructions, even in front of windows to set ceramic pieces on. The art room should be an exciting place to be and to work, amid work that has been done to encourage comparison and increasing quality. Finishes should be practical and spartan, for it is a laboratory to work in with freedom to explore and, if necessary, to be messy.

Arts and Crafts Rooms

Arts and crafts rooms should be located near auditorium stage, stagecraft area, homemaking, industrial arts, dramatic, and music rooms. Location should facilitate delivery of supplies. They should have an outside door, for use when holding classes outdoors, and good natural lighting.

The space should be arranged with sufficient imagination so that it is flexible and allows the teacher to vary the curriculum from year to year. The program involves the use of a number of media. Rooms, therefore, should be conceived of as a series of work centers in which activities with different kinds of materials can be carried forward. There is much need for display space for finished work. Walls should be of material that will receive thumbtacks, to eliminate the need for broken-up wall panels and bulletin board. Avoid breaking up wall spaces uneconomically; keep display areas large and simple. Phones, light switches, thermostats, and other necessary electric outlets should be placed where they are accessible but do not interfere with otherwise usable display spaces. Windows should provide adequate light and be high enough for storage and counter space underneath.

Ceilings and/or walls should be acoustically treated. It is preferable to have a vinyl asbestos floor in the general art area; in the ceramics area terrazzo or hardened concrete floor is suggested. Finishes should be easily washed and maintained, and resistant to oils and heat. A chalkboard should be placed where it can be seen easily but where it will not produce reflections or shine. It could be incorporated in a cabinet of vertical sliding balanced sections to include two chalkboards, one corkboard, and one projection screen. A bulletin board and opaque drapes or light-tight venetian blinds for darkening the room are also necessary.

Suitable lighting is needed to ensure effective color rendering on dark days and in the evening. Semi-indirect lighting with daylight bulbs is recommended. If the room is located on the ground floor, it will need protection against ground glare in lower sash of windows. Double sinks with hot and cold water; drinking fountain outlet; gas outlets; enough electric outlets around room for projectors and spotlights; and heating by ceiling or floor radiation to save floor and wall space, or at least a minimum allocation of space to this utility, are also recommended.

Room for bulk storage and storage of papers, illustrative materials, models, cardboard, finished and unfinished projects will have to be supplied. The area will require much protection against fire. Shelving, suspension facilities, and bins should be arranged for great flexibility.

MUSIC FACILITIES

The music program is usually divided into four parts: instrumental activities; choral activities; classes in music theory, music appreciation, and voice; and correlated activities, such as drama and opera projects. Good traffic circulation is essential. Instrument storage area should be planned so that students can circulate easily to collect their instruments, attend class, and return instruments for storage. It should be convenient to move large instruments to buses, stage, and playing field.

The size, shape, and construction material are important factors to consider in planning and designing music facilities for the best sound control possible. The architect should aim for rooms that have optimum reverberation time, even distribution of sound, and freedom from undesirable absorption at certain pitches. Nevertheless, the reverberation period must not be reduced below the point mandatory for correct brilliance of tone. Nonparallel walls or splayed walls and ceilings should be considered; soundproof walls and doors are desirable. Acoustic ceilings and walls should be carefully designed to ensure satisfactory conditions within each room. Storage areas should serve as sound-transmission buffer areas to keep interference between music rooms at a minimum. It is recommended that a competent sound engineer be consulted in preliminary planning stages.

Music Classroom

The music classroom should be part of the music suite and readily accessible to corridor and office (see Fig. 107).

It is used for class instruction, choral work, and as a dressing room for large groups.

It should have sound-tight doors, natural lighting, lavatory, and a dressing table. A chalkboard ruled for music, bulletin board, piano, and tablet armchairs will be needed.

Provision should be made for projection, television, and a high-fidelity sound system.

Choral Room

The choral room should be near the rear of the auditorium stage so that choral groups can move easily onto stage for performances.

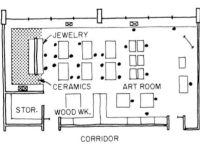

Fig. 99

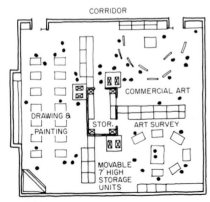

Fig. 100

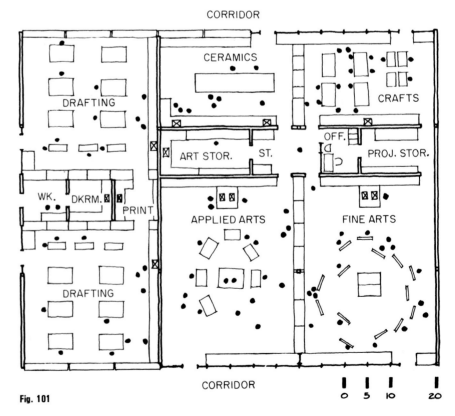

Fig. 101

Fig. 102

It is used for boys' and girls' glee clubs and mixed chorus.

The room should have a flat floor and 6-ft-wide doors so that a piano can be moved in and out. It may be rounded at rear. A chalkboard with music ruling on part of it, a pull-type screen over the chalkboard, and a bulletin board are recommended.

Furniture and equipment include movable seats of the drop-arm type, conductor's platform, record player, tape recorder, storage for records and sheet music, piano, television set, portable risers, and clock.

Room should have natural lighting, ventilation, soundproofing, provisions for music recording and reproduction, two built-in 12-in. speakers with proper connection for either record player or microphone plug-in to serve for broadcasting over school public-address system.

Instrumental Music Room

The instrumental music room should be near the rear of the auditorium so that the band can move instruments easily onto the stage, near an outdoor entrance so that the band can

have access to the field without going through the building, and near practice rooms.

It is used for band, orchestra, brass and woodwind ensemble, chamber music groups, and sectional rehearsals.

The space should have a flat floor and doors 6 ft wide to move piano in and out. Doors should be soundproofed. Storage space in back and sides of room, chalkboard with music ruling on part of it, pull-type screen over chalkboard, and bulletin board are suggested.

Furniture and equipment include movable seats, conductor's platform, record player, tape recorder, piano, television set, music stands, small sink, counters for books with music slots below counters, storage for records and musical scores of various size, portable risers, and clock.

The room should have special soundproofing; natural lighting and ventilation, if possible; provision for music recording and reproduction; two built-in 12-in. speakers with proper connection for either record player or microphone plug-in to serve for broadcasting over school public-address system; outlets for 16-mm sound motion picture projector. Reproduction in music rooms requires high-fidelity equipment.

Practice Rooms

Practice rooms should be near band and orchestra room. They are used for practicing and individual instruction.

They may serve as music listening rooms. Soundproof doors, and soundproof windows into corridor, are necessary for supervision.

Equipment includes music rack, small table, music lamp, chairs, clock, and counter for instruments and books. It may have a piano and phonograph.

Electric outlets and artificial lighting are needed. Special acoustical treatment is necessary to prevent interference between rooms and with other areas and to deaden reverberation. Special attention should be paid to mechanical ventilation.

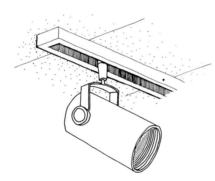

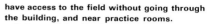

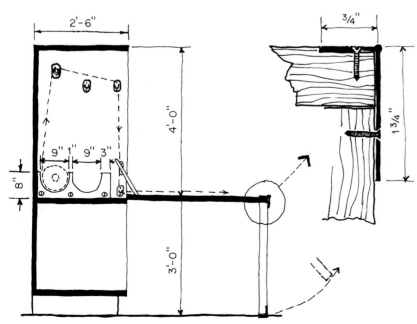

CLAY WEDGING BOARD

Fig. 103

Fig. 104

Fig. 105

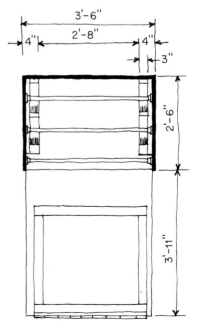

ELEMENTARY AND SECONDARY SCHOOLS
Music Facilities

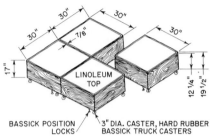

30" 30" 30" 30" 7/8 17" LINOLEUM TOP 12 1/4" 19 1/2"

BASSICK POSITION LOCKS 3" DIA. CASTER, HARD RUBBER BASSICK TRUCK CASTERS

Fig.106

Music Office and Library

The music office and library should be between the choral and instrumental rooms. It should provide good supervision of spaces in music area.

It is used as an office—for teacher conference, teacher preparation, and keeping records—and a library—for research, reading, studying, and storage of music.

Furniture and equipment include teachers' desks and chairs; wardrobe space; conference table; work counter; adjustable shelves on walls; bookcase; cabinet for records; typewriter and stand; phonograph; radio; and playback machines.

Music Storage Room

The music storage room should provide safe, sanitary protection against robe and uniform destruction. Cabinets, 3 ft deep, 30 ft long, equipped with racks and hangers and space above for hats and lockers, for special band equipment such as flags and batons, and with lockable sliding doors are desirable.

Instruments need maximum care and preservation from damage. Adjustable shelving must vary according to instrument sizes. Rollaway racks for bulky instruments are needed. Smaller instruments are best cared for in cabinets. Other provisions include lockers with master-keyed padlocks, student benches, record cabinet, music filing cabinet, piano dolly, and music stands. If possible, a small area for instrument maintenance should be provided: sink with hot and cold water, floor drain, shelves, workbench, gas outlet for Bunsen burner, and counter for instrument repair.

A complete music suite is shown in Fig. 108 accommodating all the functions with related storage. Tiers in the choral and instrumental rooms are often built-up from the flat, main-level structural floor. Figures 109 to 111 show a practice room noted for proper sound isolation and equipped for double duty as a theater dressing room since music facilities are commonly related to the auditorium facilities for instrument storage.

Figure 112 shows in more detail an instrument rehearsal room, with student stations shown as dots, and practice rooms across a typical circulation corridor; a very typical, basic situation allowing free use of the practice rooms and easy access to the small instrument

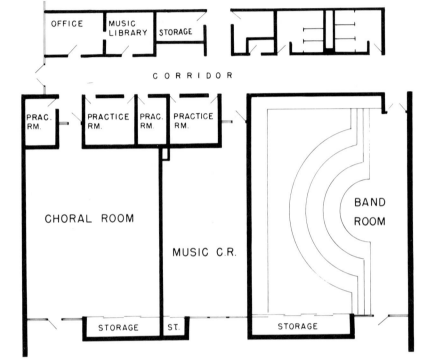

Fig. 107

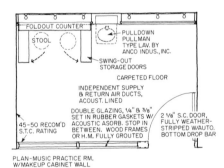

PLAN-MUSIC PRACTICE RM.
W/MAKEUP CABINET WALL

Fig. 109

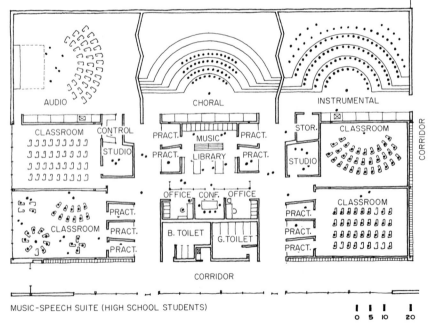

MUSIC-SPEECH SUITE (HIGH SCHOOL STUDENTS)

0 5 10 20

Fig. 108

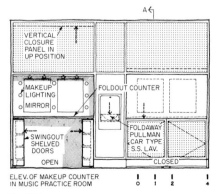

ELEV. OF MAKEUP COUNTER
IN MUSIC PRACTICE ROOM

0 1 2 4

Fig. 110

storage lockers along the corridor (see Fig. 113). Large instruments are stored in the rehearsal room in rolling racks (Fig. 114) to allow for their easy moving for away-from-home performances. In this scheme, the room steps *down* from the corridor, allowing the generation of adequate volume in the room without stepping the roof up. The front wall is made heavily absorbent to sound-simulate playing to an audience: the ceiling is 50 percent reflective and 50 percent absorbent so that one section of the room can hear the other.

Figure 115 shows a related reflected ceiling pattern, and Fig. 116 shows some details for "soft" and "hard" surfaces. Figure 117 is another convenient space saver.

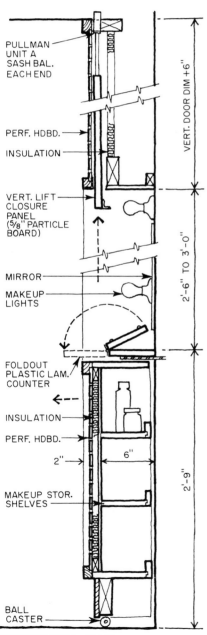

PULLMAN UNIT A SASH BAL. EACH END

PERF. HDBD.

INSULATION

VERT. LIFT CLOSURE PANEL (5/8" PARTICLE BOARD)

MIRROR

MAKEUP LIGHTS

FOLDOUT PLASTIC LAM. COUNTER

INSULATION

PERF. HDBD.

2" 6"

MAKEUP STOR. SHELVES

BALL CASTER

VERT. DOOR DIM +6"

2'-6" TO 3'-0"

2'-9"

SECTION THROUGH PRACTICE ROOM MAKEUP COUNTER

Fig. 111

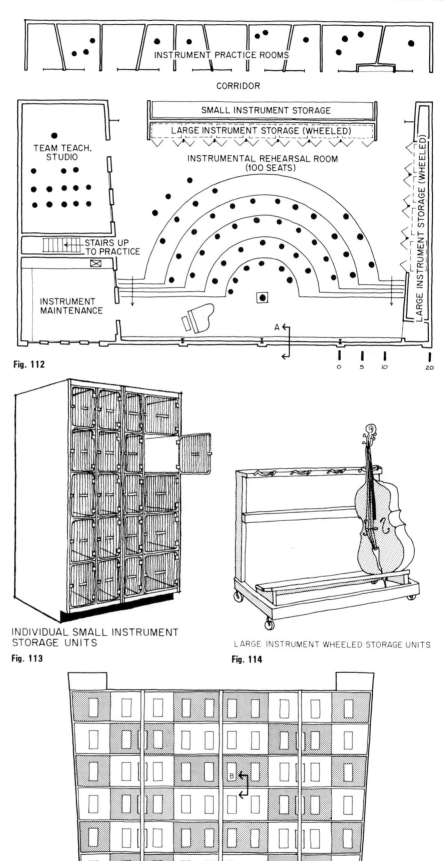

INSTRUMENT PRACTICE ROOMS

CORRIDOR

SMALL INSTRUMENT STORAGE

LARGE INSTRUMENT STORAGE (WHEELED)

TEAM TEACH. STUDIO

INSTRUMENTAL REHEARSAL ROOM (100 SEATS)

LARGE INSTRUMENT STORAGE (WHEELED)

STAIRS UP TO PRACTICE

INSTRUMENT MAINTENANCE

A

0 5 10 20

Fig. 112

INDIVIDUAL SMALL INSTRUMENT STORAGE UNITS

Fig. 113

LARGE INSTRUMENT WHEELED STORAGE UNITS

Fig. 114

B

Fig. 115

249

ELEMENTARY AND SECONDARY SCHOOLS
Industrial and Vocational Facilities

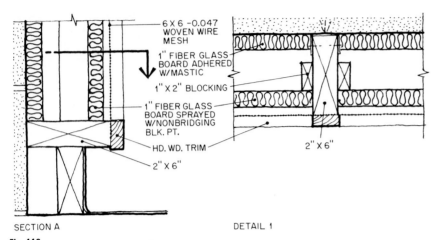

SECTION A

Fig. 116

DETAIL 1

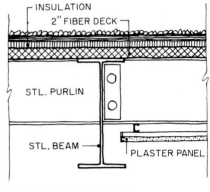

SECTION B THROUGH ROOF

Fig. 117

INDUSTRIAL AND VOCATIONAL FACILITIES

Industrial and vocational education are one and the same, "vocational" being the more current term and implying a more specialized education program designed to train a person for a vocation rather than simply acquainting him with a working knowledge of tools and their uses. Many schools extend their in-school education to cooperative programs with local industries, providing the student with actual on-the-job experience. Additionally, industry representatives counsel and work with the students in the school.

The industrial arts department should be isolated from quieter areas of building, with a service road provided nearby. There should be an outdoor shop area, if possible. Access to shower and locker facilities will be needed. All machines and equipment should be arranged so that a sequence of operations can be carried out with the greatest possible efficiency.

Special servicing requirements of materials, relationship to drives for automotive shops, noise levels, and kinds of functions performed

very realistically determine the relationship of the vocational education area to the total plan. Also, because the school's functions are essentially industrial in nature, related structural and enclosure systems are appropriately different from the more finished elements in the remainder of the school. One-story structures on grade are most common, though mezzanine space is often developed for storage or seminar use.

However, this does not mean that the spaces cannot be attractive in their own way. For it is most important to the student, and the relationship among all students, that no one is being discriminated against. All are being treated equally. And so in relating the vocational education units to the rest of the school, rather than being a separate or tail-end unit as it was so often in the past, it should be made as integral a part of the total school as possible, physically and philosophically.

Basically, the major elements of vocational education are speciality shops like woodworking, electrical, metals, auto, or combined general shops. Additionally, drafting rooms are common as well as supporting classrooms,

offices, and sometimes locker rooms. The layout of any shop should follow the logic of its equipment use and its relationship to electrical and mechanical services. Several things must be considered such as special code and safety concerns, good lighting, sawdust collecting systems, overhead hoist systems, exhaust ducts, and the ability to get large supplies in, out, and stored. It should also be realized that students are learning on the machines, and extra clearances should be allowed for joint teacher-learner use.

Figure 118 shows a layout of typical shop types with related spaces. Typically the class meets first in the classrooms to learn principles, take certain tests, and put these into practice in the shop laboratories. In the diagram the dots represent students, the semicircles group sink-wash units. Figure 119 shows a more comprehensive shop suite. Figure 120 is a section through a not unusual higher-ceiling shop area showing open-structure treatment, rooftop mechanical units, and the development of some double-deck space.

The specific equipment provided in any shop is determined by the client and by the various

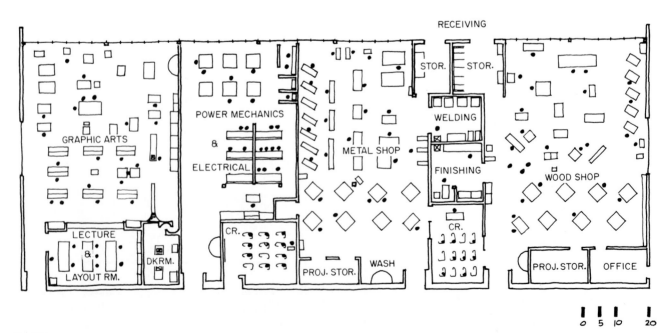

Fig. 118

250

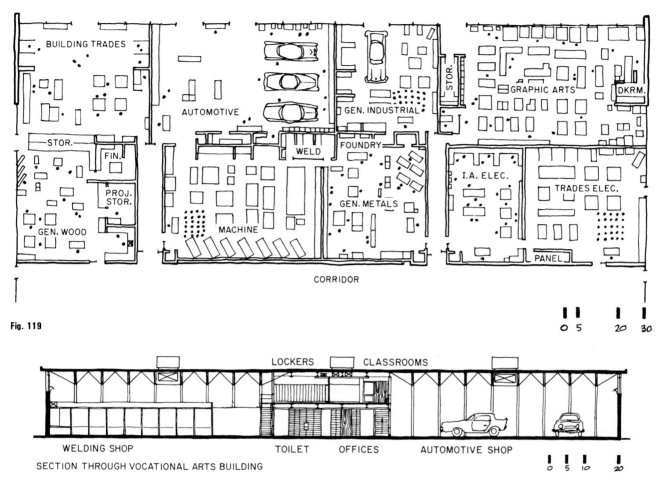

Fig. 119

SECTION THROUGH VOCATIONAL ARTS BUILDING

Fig. 120

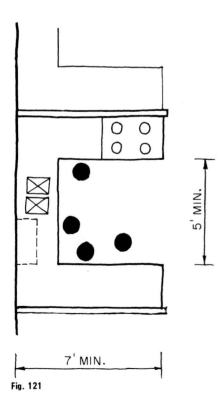

Fig. 121

requirements most states have. Sometimes the equipment itself is leased, another reason for the increasing preference for electrical service being fed down from the ceiling rather than up from the floor, allowing more flexibility. While most surfaces must be hard for maintenance reasons, some acoustic relief can be introduced by acoustic-absorbent mounted blocks in ceiling materials, roof decking, and high wall surfaces.

A sense of order should prevail in considering the equipment needs and the disposition of services to them, for a well-organized shop is itself a deterrent to accidents.

HOME ARTS

Home arts might be better called family-life education, for its purpose is to teach students about everyday living, home life, cooking, sewing, personal care, and caring for a home and family. It would be well if boys could participate more in the curriculum, and this might well be encouraged by a more central location of the facilities in the total plan and merchandising and furbishing it in a less exclusively feminine way. For it should represent the feeling and purpose of the total home in the school; even outdoor patios might be included.

Facilities comprising a home arts program can range from a single laboratory space serving cooking and sewing classes to a full suite of spaces embracing these, and child development, cosmetology, living-dining, and support-

ive classroom areas. The various examples shown here illustrate program emphasis, and the many combinations possible, the relationships of one space to another, and the apparent flow of activity functions. Obviously, the larger the facility, the more difficult to avoid an institutionalized character. But it should be realized that certain of these programs are directed toward institutional vocational education, others toward homemakers.

Food Laboratories

The food laboratories may be divided into cooking area, freezing area, laundry, wall storage (for tote drawers, staples, cleaning supplies, and books), and classroom area large enough to accommodate movable desk chairs for students. Grease-resistant asphalt tile or linoleum flooring is necessary. Folding doors or screens could be used to separate areas.

Unit kitchens should contain equipment for about four students and include stoves, double sinks, counter space, and storage cupboards above and below the counters. Enameled-steel upper and lower cabinets with back splashes which are molded into a curved surface rather than joined together with stainless-steel strips are suggested. Movable supply wagons made of materials similar to those of other kitchen equipment can be built to fit into recessed space under the counter surface. Allowance must be made on the window wall for access to windows. Counters should be made of a durable material with two areas large enough

ELEMENTARY AND SECONDARY SCHOOLS
Home Arts; Food Service

to place two boards 16 by 20 in. next to each other so that two students can work side by side at each area. These should not be located at a corner since this does not allow space for two pupils to stand and work together. Minimum desirable length of counter per pupil is 30 in. If counter width is 24 in., minimum desirable size of one unit kitchen should be 11 by 9 ft, or 99 sq ft. Counter heights should be about 33 to 34 in. To accommodate four students at work, space between counters should be 6 to 8 ft. Just outside each kitchen should be space for a kitchen table and four chairs for serving and eating.

Allowance should be made for adequate ventilation to carry away food odors. Exhaust fan for entire room is suggested. Two duplex electric outlets should be provided in each cooking area. In laundry area, provision should be made for 110/220-V outlet for clothes dryer.

Clothing Laboratory

The clothing laboratory should be equivalent in size to a large classroom. It should include a sewing area (preferably along window wall); grooming area; dressing room area (about 8 feet square), walled off by cabinets on at least one side; storage areas (preferably along walls); and fitting area. Folding doors or screens could be used to separate areas.

Storage should be provided for portable machines, notions, tote boxes (5 in. deep by 14 in. wide by 19 in. long), roll of 36-in. wrapping paper, small articles, textbooks, large fashion magazines, patterns, and teacher's wardrobe, four-drawer, legal-size file with lock. Space is needed for hanging student projects.

Provide adequately keyed electric outlets for machines—suggest one double outlet for each machine—electric outlets for irons and visual-aid machines, one fluorescent light over grooming unit, and adequate light at working surfaces.

Family Living Laboratory

The family living laboratory is used for advanced courses in homemaking: table service, housekeeping, home decoration, selection and arrangement of furniture, entertainment, bed making, home care of sick, leisure time activities, family living, money management, child care, and consumer education.

This is the central core of homemaking facilities. Furniture and equipment should represent advanced solutions of home problems. Space should provide for dining room, living room, and flexible area for home nursing, child care, home furnishing, family living, group discussion, and film viewing. There should be at least one plastered wall for experimentation with wallpapers. Hardwood floors are preferred. Folding doors or screens could be used to separate areas.

Furniture and equipment include upholstered sofa and chairs; side tables and coffee table; lamps and vases; sideboard or hutch; drapes (to be made by class); dining room table and chairs to seat eight; card table and chairs; framed pictures (art project); roll-away bed; built-in storage cabinets for magazines and linens; cleaning supplies; vacuum cleaner; electric drill and attachments for waxing and buffing; samples of home furnishing materials; dishes; silver; table linen; curtain and drapery fixtures; full-length mirrors; home nursing equipment; child-care supplies. Supplies should be stored near area where they will be used.

There should be artificial lighting and switches adapted to house situations; com-

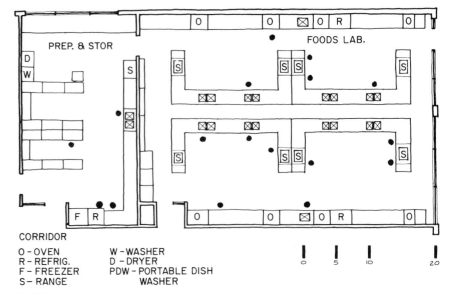

PREP. & STOR

FOODS LAB.

CORRIDOR

O – OVEN	W – WASHER
R – REFRIG.	D – DRYER
F – FREEZER	PDW – PORTABLE DISH
S – RANGE	WASHER

Fig. 122

bination outlet for electric iron, pilot light, switch and outlet; electric clock; special lighting on machines; electric duplex outlet spaced at least every 12 ft of available wall space; sink with hot and cold water.

In laying out the prototype kitchen units it should be remembered that there are both instructors and students using them; hence dimensions between counters should be more ample. Figure 121 indicates some minimum dimensions, while Fig. 122 shows a grouping of U kitchens. Fig. 123 shows perimeter kitchens, allowing for a sit-down class grouping at the tables in the center in a rather typical combined food-and-clothing arrangement.

Typically, various kitchen-plan types as well as various appliance types are incorporated into a layout to allow the student to experience their differences. Counter and cabinet types and finishes, even flooring, might likewise be varied while realizing some discretion toward enough common denominators to give order to the total space.

Like planning any laboratory, equipment functions, clearances, and their electrical and mechanical service requirements should be carefully understood, and most of the needs are larger extensions of home situations, such as extra lengths of counter and space between appliances. Unit kitchen plans should also be designed to allow for periodic appliance replacement with new models, sometimes provided for specific consignment by local utility companies, such as accommodating ranges at counter ends to allow for size changes.

A few miscellaneous planning aids should be provided:
• A minimum of 2 linear feet of counter space per student (wall cabinet storage is underutilized in the prototype kitchen and can be more minimal)
• Tackboard or wall behind sink
• A well-located teacher demonstration kitchen counter (an overhead mirror helps too)
• Pull-out bread boards (they save on counter top wear)
• Spread-out storage for student projects, like sewing
• Portable ironing boards (these are better than built-ins)
• Sewing table unit (for use by four works well)

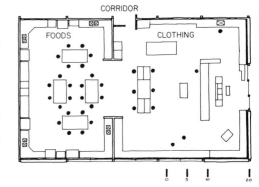

CORRIDOR

FOODS

CLOTHING

Fig. 123

• Corridor exhibit area for display

Summing up, the home arts area is a place for learning about living; make it as easy and pleasant as life can be for the students starting out.

FOOD SERVICE

Lunchtime can and should be break-time, a change of pace in a place different in feeling and fact from the rest of the day. In reality, it is hard to be efficient in the use of space in schools. Most often lunchrooms must serve other purposes. Time for eating is cut too finely between academic periods. Great numbers must be served in a hurry.

All the more reason and need then to try harder while planning to carefully consider the processes of food preparation and serving, together with seating areas and traffic flow, to give the best chance for table manners to survive and a happy shipshape atmosphere to exist amid the hubbub.

There are enough ordinary problems to be solved in planning a dining and kitchen area to allow consideration of a unique design approach. Like anything that is architecture, it grows from those human needs it is serving, asking: Whom are we going to serve? What are we going to serve them? How will we go about it?

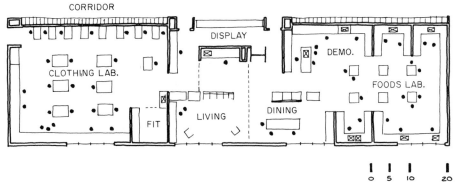

Fig. 124

The program is made up of three factors: patrons, menus, and operation. Particularly in this part of the school, the allocation and arrangement of spaces and the choice of fixtures must develop for specific reasons in order that the total design be functional.

Systems for a School Lunch Program

Each *system* is a kitchen and an arrangement for the distribution of food.

1. Conventional kitchen and adjacent cafeteria.

2. Kitchen, central to site, with adjacent and remote serving stations.

3. Kitchen, central to community, with all serving stations remote. "Satellite" is another term for remote.

The Conventional Kitchen A conventional kitchen and adjacent cafeteria are illustrated in Fig. 129. This particular kitchen produces an a la carte

Fig. 125

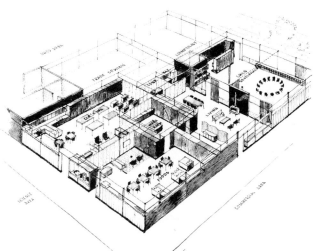

Fig. 126 Home arts, Linton High School, Schenectady, N.Y.

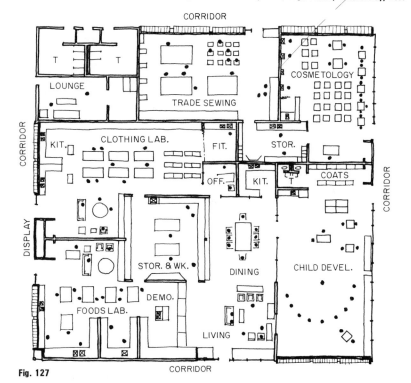

Fig. 127

ELEMENTARY AND SECONDARY SCHOOLS
Food Service

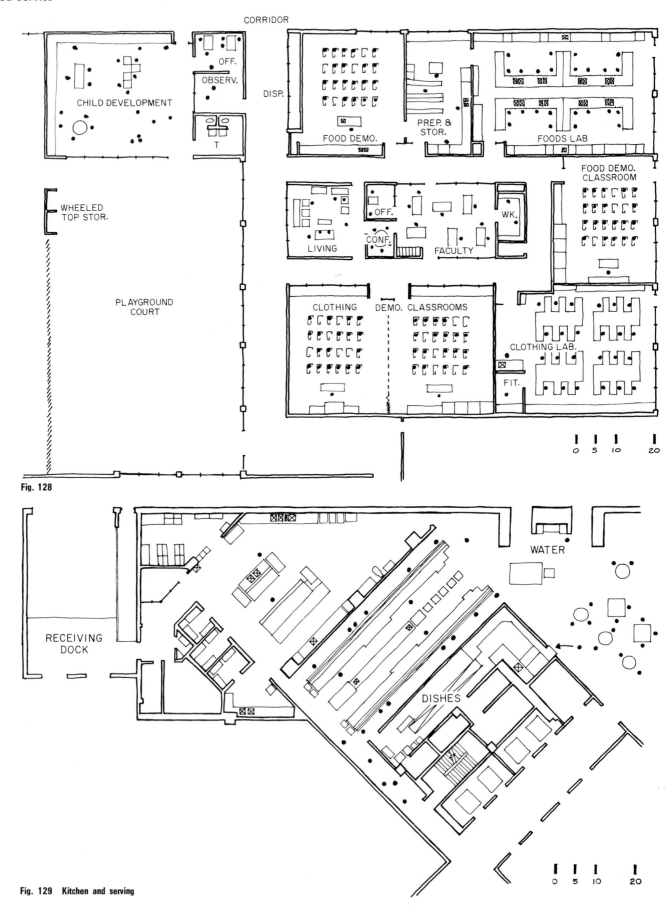

Fig. 128

Fig. 129 Kitchen and serving

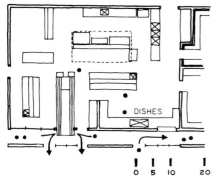

Fig. 130 Kitchen, serving, and dishwashing.

luncheon for approximately 1,100 patrons. Raw foods enter the building at the rear, diagonally opposite the dining room. Food processing follows a straight flow line from receiving to storage to preparation to the counters.

The serving counter adjacent to a conventional kitchen requires little or no cartage of bulk food. In Fig. 130 the distance between prepared food and pickup of trays is but the thickness of a wall. Kitchen personnel assemble trays at both sides of this assembly line. There are no conveyor belts. Trays are set up in advance with napkin-wrapped silver. Output of the line is two trays at a time. Snack bars when they do exist in schools, usually augment cafeteria counter service of a full, hot lunch. Most snack bars serve milk, prepackaged ice cream,

apples, and cookies, as does the small unit in Fig. 131. Some serve soft drinks. The second or third counter in some high schools is an "a la carte" service of prepared sandwiches, packaged snacks, and bakery and soda fountain items (see Fig. 132).

Clean dishes are needed at the serving station; the serving station is adjacent to the cafeteria. Soiled trays and dishes from the cafeteria are usually deposited by student customers at the dishroom. This cycle establishes the location of dishwashing as "adjacent to cafeteria and adjacent to serving," as shown in Figs. 118 and 119.

Large cafeterias utilize conveyor belts because these permit multiple and simultaneous deposit of trays. Figure 133 shows a belt bringing soiled trays from the student and faculty dining rooms to join trays from a third dining room for scraping near the feed end of the dishwasher. The baffle wall between the conveyor and dishroom in Fig. 134 screens that room's activities and sounds from the dining area. Ample dish- and tray-scraping table, disposer, and shelf space can be provided whether or not a conveyor is used.

Flight-type dishwashing machines are commonly employed for patronage numbers as small as 1,000, although conveyor models function efficiently for programs of more than 1,000 people. This choice depends upon many factors, such as the amount of ware to be stored

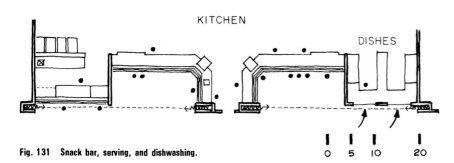

Fig. 131 Snack bar, serving, and dishwashing.

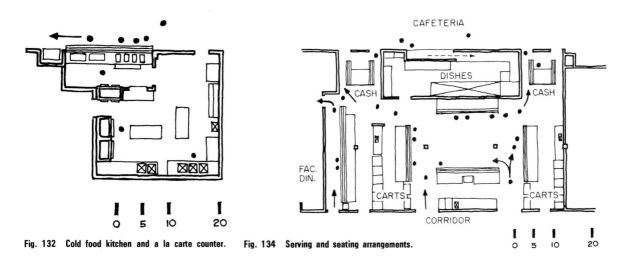

Fig. 132 Cold food kitchen and a la carte counter. Fig. 134 Serving and seating arrangements.

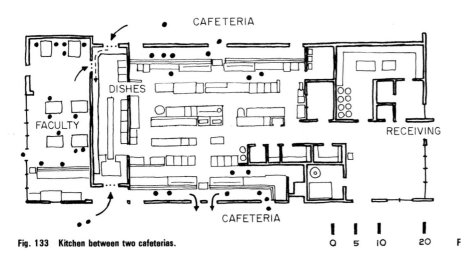

Fig. 133 Kitchen between two cafeterias.

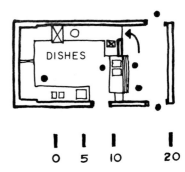

Fig. 135 Remote serving station.

ELEMENTARY AND SECONDARY SCHOOLS
Food Service

and handled in racks, the shape of the room available, and the ratio of trays to dishes, etc.

The dishroom is difficult to ventilate effectively. Provide a steam removal exhaust for dishwasher, ample fresh air supply and exhaust, and keep ceiling high for maximum cubic feet of air in circulation.

Kitchen Central to Site Small bulk-food carts can traverse the corridors or elevators from the kitchen to the remote serving station within a building. The hot food, cold food, and pastry carts shown at the serving station in Fig. 134 have been fitted with tongues and hitches. They are pulled by electric tractor from the existing kitchen in the old school building through the new corridors to this location.

Some remote serving stations have dishwashing facilities. The source of clean dishes must be close to the serving station in any plan. Figure 135 shows a small serving station which includes a counter garaging bulk foods under its top, a back bar with refrigerator and small electric appliances, plus a complete assembly of soiled and clean dish tables with smallest floor-supported dishwasher, a window sill for soiled tray deposit, a disposer, and a silver-soak sink.

Any remote station also requires some dish-scraping facility; it is not practical to transport garbage. Note the location of soiled tray deposit in the remote serving station of Fig.

136. The plan permits the flow of high school student patrons to circulate around this serving station segment of the building without any turning back or crossing of traffic. Pick-up food and entrance to the dining area are at the left of the plan; exit and tray deposit are at the right. Within the segment, dishes are processed in a direction toward the serving station.

Kitchens Central to Community The conventional kitchen differs from the central kitchen in that it does not have to accommodate, wash, garage, and load bulk-food carts. Kitchens central to the community differ from the kitchen central to a building because community bulk-food carts and kitchen cart spaces are large, and these carts are invariably transported by motor vehicle. Each of those shown in Fig. 137 is strapped into place along with a cart of trays inside a truck. The truck is fitted with a hydraulic tailgate to adjust to the various unloading conditions at community schools. Thus, an adjacent, well-appointed loading-dock facility is imperative. If located in a cold climate, the loading dock can be enclosed.

Compartmented trays used in lieu of dishes travel in carts to the remote serving station in the community and are returned to the central kitchen for dishwashing, as shown in Fig. 137. This largest of carts keeping bulk, hot, and cold food has a serving top. It therefore has many applications as a portable counter, for example

for service in the classroom to kindergarten tots and first graders. Figure 136 shows it substituting for a section of built-in counter.

Anatomy of a Kitchen

An efficient kitchen has a straight-through flow of foods being processed from the raw state to finished and ready to serve.

Its Departments	*Their relationship*
Receiving and trash rooms	Near dock
Dry storage	Near the receiving and adjacent to the kitchen
Refrigerated storage	Near the receiving area and adjacent to the kitchen
Pre-preparation sinks, tables	Between refrigerated storage and vegetable prep
Vegetable preparation	Adjacent to the cooking battery
Cooking	Adjacent to the cooking battery
Baking	Can be remote, adjacent to the kitchen
Pot washing	Must be near the cooking area, the baking area or both
Salad making	Near refrigerated storage, can be remote, adjacent to the kitchen

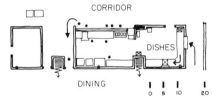

Fig. 136 Remote serving station.

TABLE 7 Kitchen Spaces in Square Feet
(Lunch programs — meals per day)

Department	500	1,000	2,000	3,000
Receiving	50-70	80-100	160-200	240-300
Dry storage*	150-250	300-500	600-1,000	900-1,500
Refrigerated storage	160	180	360	500
Dishwashing†	120-150	240-480	520-720	750-780
Trash room	90-110	130-150	190-240	250-320
Employee lockers and toilets	65-80	100-115	230-250	330-360
Manager's office	80	80	120	140

* Dry storage has direct relationship to quantity of patrons.
† The dishroom shape and size relate to type of machine required.

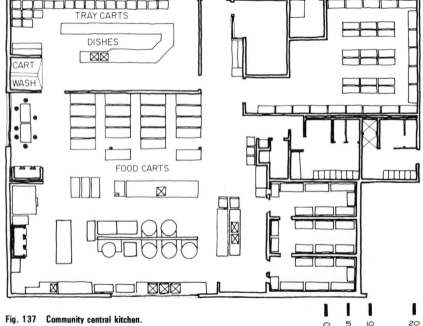

Fig. 137 Community central kitchen.

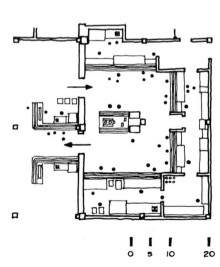

Fig. 138 Serving.

Serving Counters

When the menu is simple and everyone receives the same lunch, tray assembly can be employed for fast service. When food choices are offered, the serving counter is needed to stock and display items. The number of seats in the cafeteria determines the total length of serving counter required (refer to the Food Service Space Requirement Chart). Bottlenecks in student traffic can occur if counters are not of sufficient size, if there are too few cashiers, or if there are not ample seats. As Table 8 illustrates, a counter (35 ft) is required for every 150 to 200 seats. One to two cashiers per counter is recommended. The quantity of seats required is halfway between one-third and one-half of total patrons daily. This formula provides for the peak load in the cafeteria, which will occur during three seating periods.

It is increasingly necessary, with the advent of modular scheduling of classes, to provide for fast pickup of food. For this reason, "scramble" and other configurations should be contemplated as soon as more than one counter is required. This need not increase the quantity of counters. Sections of counters for categories of foods, such as "beverages" or "cold foods"

are arranged separately for direct and quick access.

If the scramble system incorporates parallel units, minimum distance between tray slides is 12 to 13 ft. Duplication of counter sections keeps traffic crisscross at a minimum. The scramble system is most successful in schools or any situations where people eat regularly. The patron who enters the serving area knows

where he is going. The scramble layout in Fig. 138 incorporates a beverage island at the center. Two sides of the island are identical.

The "marketplace" unconnected "sawtooth" arrangement of the counters in Fig. 139 allows the patron to skip certain sections. This layout lends itself to a serving area which is long and narrow. A wide aisle suffices; patron traffic moves quickly.

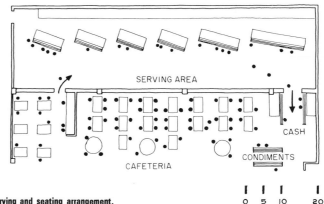

Fig. 139   Serving and seating arrangement.

TABLE 8   Food Service Space Requirement Chart for School, College, and Commercial Lunch Programs

Planned enrollment or patrons	Seats required	Area designation, sq ft		Number of counters†
		Kitchen*	Serving	
400	170	1,500	700	1
500	210	1,650	800	
600	250	1,800	1,540	2
700	290	1,950	1,540	
800	335	2,100	1,920	
900	375	2,250	1,920	
1,000	420	2,400	2,310	3
1,100	460	2,550	2,310	
1,200	500	2,700	2,690	
1,300	540	2,850	2,690	
1,400	585	3,000	2,690	
1,500	625	3,150	3,080	4
1,600	670	3,300	3,080	
1,700	710	3,450	3,460	
1,800	750	3,600	3,460	
1,900	790	3,750	3,460	
2,000	835	3,900	3,850	5
2,100	875	4,050	3,850	
2,200	920	4,200	4,230	
2,300	960	4,350	4,230	
2,400	1,000	4,500	4,620	6
2,500	1,040	4,650	4,620	
2,600	1,085	4,800	5,000	
2,700	1,125	4,950	5,000	
2,800	1,170	5,100	5,000	
2,900	1,210	5,250	5,390	7
3,000	1,250	5,400	5,390	
3,100	1,290	5,550	5,770	
3,200	1,335	5,700	5,770	
3,300	1,375	5,850	5,770	
3,400	1,420	6,000	6,160	8
3,500	1,460	6,150	6,160	
3,600	1,500	6,300	6,540	

* Kitchen space:
    150–650 students = 3 and 4 sq ft per student
    650–2,000 students = 2 and 2¼ sq ft per student
    2,000–6,000 students = 1½ and 1¾ sq ft per student
† Counter = 35 to 40 linear feet of serving equipment.

Dining Rooms, Seating and Plan Arrangements

School dining rooms most often double as study halls and lecture rooms; they are multipurpose and must include functional aspects which are incompatible with a dining atmosphere (see Fig. 140).

While bywords like washable, easily maintained, movable, durable, and economical do and must prevail in selecting furnishings and finishes, the call for character and creativity must then come on stronger. Color, plan arrangement, and the whole "feel" of the room must have a sense of order and sureness, some predominant theme.

Commonsense planning can eliminate a lot of irritations. A partition between the dining and serving area can screen off the clutter, noise, and distractions of the serving lines. The utility aspects of cashier stands, silver and condiment stands, and water stations can be less obstrusively located and "camouflaged" in the room decor. Look at the more attractive commercial cafeterias, their subduing of the "working parts," and the pleasant, sometimes striking, overall look designed with similar criteria. They avoid "namby pamby" colors, too many materials, and disorder; instead, they have an organized theme of color, form, and materials, and acoustical materials too, for noise is a prime chaos contributor.

"Mess-hall"-size spaces, undivided, are unnecessary, as a screen or partition can cut down simply on the vastness and accumulation of noise and visual business. Carpeting with color, texture, and a whole environmental control and order of its own and which is virtually stainproof can be used now to further minimize noise. Or, if the room has to serve for gym or coke dances, all kinds and colors of resilient flooring materials are available.

While air conditioning and new efficient lighting have made windows functionally unnecessary, still a "room with a view" is worth looking into, or out of, and an outward visual release can generate calm with the apparent increase of sensed space. An outlooking view would be all the more appropriate if the school's instructional areas are primarily windowless. Good ventilation is another criti-

ELEMENTARY AND SECONDARY SCHOOLS
Food Service; Physical Education: Gymnasiums

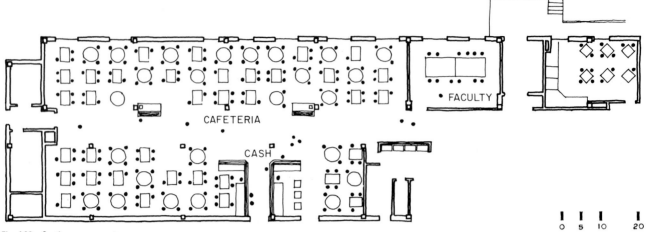

Fig. 140 Seating arrangement.

cal item. Food odors are best controlled by bringing air into the dining room and exhausting it through the kitchen at 30 air changes per hour minimum. In the kitchen itself, 30 to 60 air changes are desirable.

Space and how it's used, though, is the key. A good guide is to allow 12 to 15 sq ft per seat in planning the dining space. Smaller tables will use more space, but will encourage more quiet conversation. The small table for four persons, which makes most of floor space and yields the most elbow space when standard trays are placed on its top is 30×48 in. Four standard 14×18 in. trays will not fit on a 36 in. sq table. Mixing round tables with rectangular ones relieves the monotony of the repetitious, institutional look. Manufacturers provide tables which are 29 in. and 24 in. high for the younger children. All kinds of table and seating types—folding, jackknifing, folding into walls, stacking—allow for countless arrangements and flexibility.

To review briefly, in planning for food service, the simple objectives are getting the food to the student, getting the students to the food, and providing an enjoyable dining atmosphere.

PHYSICAL EDUCATION

Gymnasiums

In this keep-fit, diet-craze, body-bent, sports-minded age, physical education programs have gained a new focus, and top-notch facilities are getting built, from multipurpose 40×60 ft rooms in the elementary grades to multigyms and specialty spaces in the large high schools. The basketball court is the common denominator of the gymnasium plan, overlapped by other court layouts and enlarged for other uses including spectator seating.

Making up the right kind of environment are the factors diagrammed below. Places to play well in should be well designed in all ways, more than super-space boxes. The gymnasium, the whole physical education unit, is most always a place for other performance use, and so its internal planning relationships must serve its everyday use, but its public use sets other demands for its relation in the total plan. Its great volume begs other considerations for separate, special ventilating systems, structural systems, and related massing concerns of its exterior (see Fig. 141).

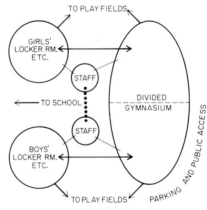

Fig. 141

The gymnasium complex in Fig. 142 shows several relative points: direct relation to parking and playfields, public lobby space and rest rooms, double-decking of locker facilities and auxiliary, or balcony, gym space equating to the height of the main gym, "boys" and "girls" gyms divided by a folding partition

opening to allow the total space for exhibition game use, with bleachers folding out and down from the balcony gyms, and the whole volume given better scale and character inside and out with beams and undulating angular roof/ceiling treatment.

Table 9 gives recommended dimensions for various gymnasium sizes.

The basic relationship of elements and planning fundamentals for a gymnasium are shown in Figs. 143 to 147. In the typical school the staff for boys and girls have a working relationship to each other and a responsibility for instructional supervision to both the gymnasium and locker spaces, as well as a preferred, as-direct-as-possible relationship to the total school, or corridor entry. The staff offices are, in effect, control centers. The locker rooms should be so located and planned to allow direct access to the outdoor playfields as well as to the gym.

Expansion potential should always be considered, and the physical education parts should not be "locked" into other plan elements. As enrollment increases, oft-times added practice gyms or auxiliary spaces like wrestling rooms, a pool, or more locker space may be needed.

The gymnasium itself develops from many functional and prescribed requirements as are noted on Fig. 143.

Figure 148 illustrates a field house complex, with large balcony gyms (above the locker areas) flanking the main exhibition gym. Spectator seating is accommodated by folding/rolling bleachers at both levels. Those at the main floor level can be folded back against the locker room wall to allow more usable space in the main gym and those on the balcony can be rolled and folded back, or could be detailed to fold up to form a wall between the balcony and main gym spaces.

TABLE 9 Recommended Dimensions in feet for Gymnasiums

School	W	L	W_1*	L_1*	Seats
Small elementary	36	52			
Large elementary	52	72			
Junior high school*	65	86	42	74	400
Small senior high school†	79	96	50	84	700
Large senior high school†	100	104	50	84	1,500

W_1 and L_1 are dimensions of basketball court.
†*Use folding partition.*

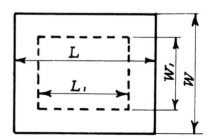

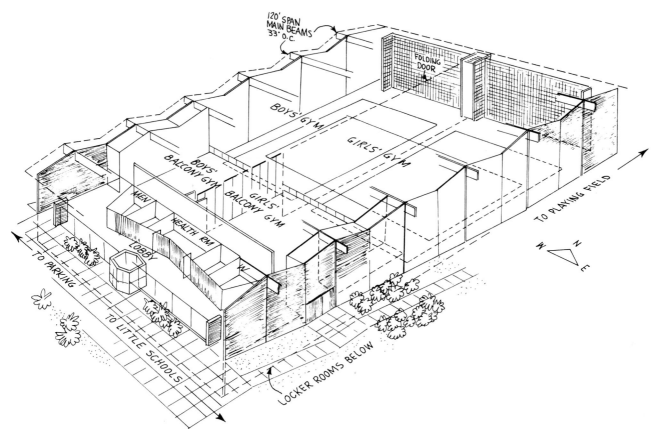

Fig. 142   Physical education unit, Newark High School, Newark, Ohio.

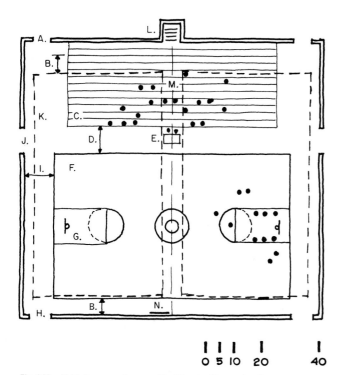

A. ACCESS FROM LOCKER ROOMS
B. 5' MIN. DIMENSIONS RECOMMENDED—FACE OF BLEACHER OR WALL FROM END OR SIDE LINE OF COURT.
C. FOLDING BLEACHERS EXTENDED. VARIES DEPENDING ON REQUIREMENTS. FOR BEST SPECTATOR VIEW, RESTRICT BLEACHER LENGTH TO FACE—TO—FACE DIMENSION OF BACKBOARDS.
D. 6' MIN. —10' RECOMMENDED.
E. SCORERS' TABLE—MAY BE LOCATED IN BLEACHERS. PROVIDE ELECTRICAL OUTLETS, MICROPHONE JACK, AND SCOREBOARD CONTROLS.
F. COURT SIZE: JR. HIGH—42' X 74', HIGH SCHOOL—50' X 84'. SOME HIGH SCHOOLS USE COLLEGE SIZE COURT, 50' X 94', FOR VARSITY TOURNAMENT COURT.
G. HIGH SCHOOL BACKBOARD, GLASS OR METAL, 54'' FAN—SHAPED (PER 1969-1970 N.F.S.H.S.A.A. RULES) KEEP WALLS BEHIND BACKBOARDS FREE OF DOORS AND OBSTRUCTIONS.
H. EGRESS TO PLAYING FIELDS.
I. 10'—RECOMMENDED CLEARANCE FOR TOURNAMENT COURT.
J. ACCESS FOR SPECTATORS. LOCATE TO MIN. TRAFFIC ON GYM FLOOR. (POSSIBLE USE OF CARPET RUNNERS.)
K. PRACTICE COURTS. MAY BE SHORTER AND MORE NARROW THAN STANDARD COURT.
L. STRUCTURE HUNG WD. FOLD. PART. HORIZONTAL PULL OR VERTICAL ROLL NET CURTAIN WITH CANVAS BOTTOM VISUAL BARRIER MAY BE USED.
M. SPAN—ACROSS SEATS (UP TO 6') TO ACCOMMODATE FOLD. PART. OPENING.

Fig. 143   Divided gym, seating one side. (Two teaching stations.)

ELEMENTARY AND SECONDARY SCHOOLS
Physical Education: Gymnasiums

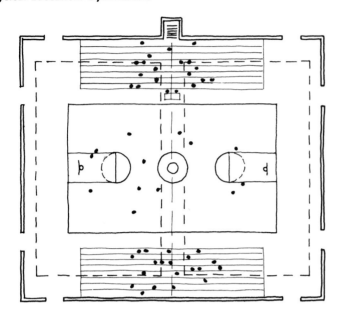

TOURNAMENT COURT: 50' X 84' (50' X 94' POSSIBLE)
TWO CROSS PRACTICE COURTS: 50' X 84' WITH MINIMUM
  END COURT CLEARANCE.
FOLDING BLEACHERS: FOLD. PART. SIDE: 2–16', 2–20',
  SEC. WITH 6' SPAN–ACROSS SEATS AT PART. PACKET.
  11 ROWS = 616 SEATS. OPPOSITE SIDE: 2–8', 4–16' SEC.
  11 ROWS = 660 SEATS.
CAPACITY: 1,276 SEATS AT 16".

Fig. 144   Divided gym, seating two sides. (Two teaching stations.)

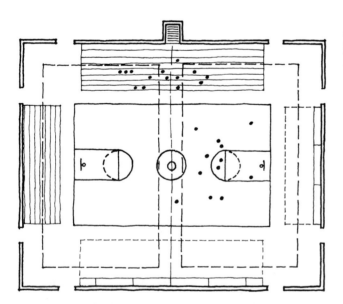

TOURNAMENT COURT: 50' X84' WITH MINIMUM END AND SIDE
  CLEARANCE
TWO CROSS PRACTICE COURTS: 50' X 84' WITH MINIMUM END
  CLEARANCE
FOLDING BLEACHERS: FOLD. PART. SIDE: 2–16', 2–20' SEC.
  WITH 6' SPAN ACROSS–11 ROWS = 616 SEATS. OPPOSITE SIDE:
  4–16', 2–8' SEC., 11 ROWS = 660 SEATS. ENDS: 3–16' SEC.
  EACH, 9 ROWS = 648 SEATS. CAPACITY: 1,924 SEATS AT 16".

Fig. 145   Divided gym, seating four sides. (Two teaching stations.)

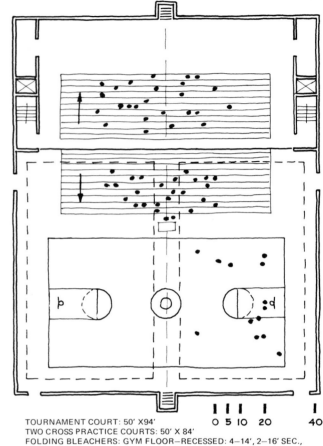

TOURNAMENT COURT: 50' X94'
TWO CROSS PRACTICE COURTS: 50' X 84'
FOLDING BLEACHERS: GYM FLOOR–RECESSED: 4–14', 2–16' SEC.,
  14 ROWS = 846 SEATS. BALCONY–REVERSE FOLD: 4–14', 2–16' SEC.
  15 ROWS = 960 SEATS.
CAPACITY: 1,846 SEATS AT 16".
GYM FLOOR: 94' X 120'.

(a)

PLASTIC "SKY DOMES" PROVIDE EXCELLENT NONGLARE GYM LIGHTING. AREA OF
THE "SKY DOMES" SHOULD EQUAL 4–6% OF THE GYM FLOOR. POWER–GROOVE
FLUORESCENT LAMPED LIGHT FIXTURES, GROUPED ADJUSTABLE TO OR AROUND
THE "SKY DOMES" PROVIDES A GOOD CLEAN LOOKING ELECTRICAL ILLUMINATION
INSTALLATION.

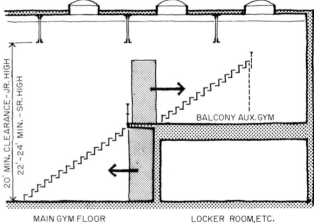

DELAYED ACTION–REVERSE FOLD. BLEACHERS USED ON A BALCONY TEACHING
STATION, PROVIDES NOT ONLY INCREASED SEATING CAPACITY, BUT IN THE
RETRACTED POSITION, CREATES A PHYSICAL AND VISUAL BARRIER BETWEEN
THE BALCONY AND THE MAIN GYM FLOOR. WHEN PLANNING THE USE OF FOLDING
BLEACHERS AS SHOWN ABOVE, CONSULT WITH THE BLEACHER MANUFACTURERS
FOR CORRECT DIMENSIONS, CLEARANCES, MAXIMUM RECOMMENDED ROWS,
OPERATION AND SEAT RISE, FOR OPTIMUM SIGHT LINES.

(b)

**Fig. 146   (a) Divided gym with (b) balcony auxiliary gym, seating one side.
(Four teaching stations.)**

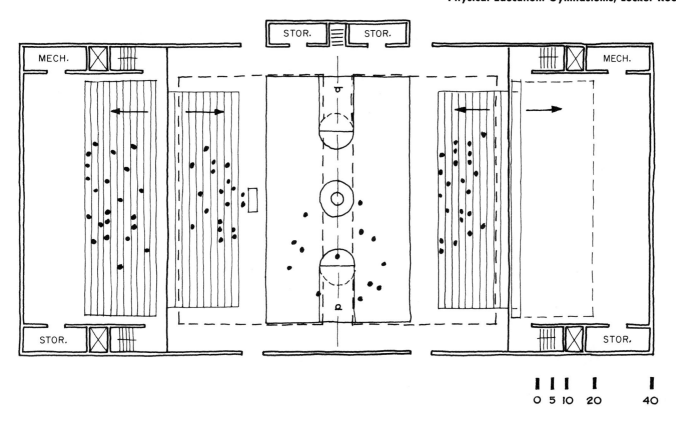

TOURNAMENT COURT: 50' X 84'.
TWO PARALLEL PRACTICE COURTS: 50' X 84'.
FOLDING BLEACHERS: GYM FLOOR – RECESSED: 1–14', 4–16' SEC. –14 ROWS = 812 SEATS ⎱
                            BALCONY – REVERSE FOLD: 5–16' SEC. –15 ROWS = 900 SEATS ⎰ EACH SIDE
                            CAPACITY: 3,424 SEATS AT 16".
GYM FLOOR: 104' X 120'.

Fig. 147   Divided gym with balcony auxiliary gyms, seating two sides. (Four teaching stations.)

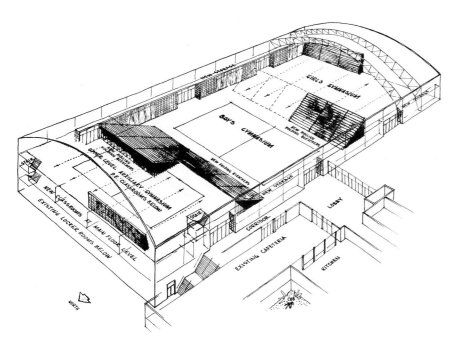

Fig. 148   Field house development, senior high school Englewood, Colo. (Perkins & Will – Wheeler & Lewis, April 15, 1957.)

Figure 149 illustrates a 2,400-student high school physical education complex where the main activity areas develop above a base floor of lockers and auxiliary space. The result is architecturally well articulated, saves on ground coverage for more playfield space on a restricted site, allows for separate student and public access to the pool, provides on-grade access to the playfields, and clearly divides the gyms into usable components (see Fig. 150).

Locker Rooms

Locker rooms need not be the noisy, steamy, smelly, dimly lit spaces too many have been. Because they are very concentrated areas of complex plumbing and ventilation and hard wear requirements, they can be expensive to build and are too often made too minimal to properly function and be maintained.

Locker rooms are busy places for students in a hurry, dressing in never-enough room, with showering humidity, outdoor muck, and emotional pitch and pique as added realities. A very functional plan is a must, one that thoroughly considers traffic flow, the realities of body dressing clearances, locker door swings, clothing storage, systems for towel distribution, uniform drying, and supervision and discipline. Equal concern must be given to good and durable lighting, plumbing, ventilation, and finishes (see Fig. 151).

ELEMENTARY AND SECONDARY SCHOOLS
Physical Education: Gymnasiums, Locker Rooms

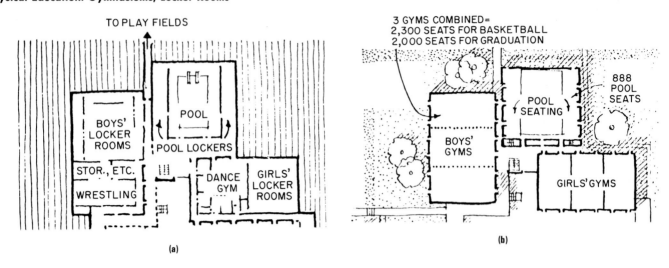

(a)

(b)

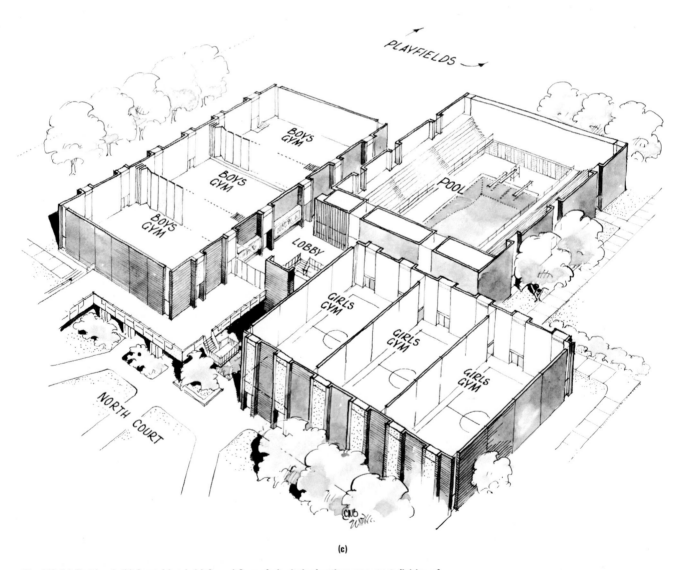

(c)

Fig. 149 (a) First level. (b) Second level. (c) Second floor of physical education area, west division of
New Trier High School. (Used with permission from The Perkins & Will Partnership, Architects, and The Architects
Collaborative, Cambridge, Massachusetts, Associated Architects.)

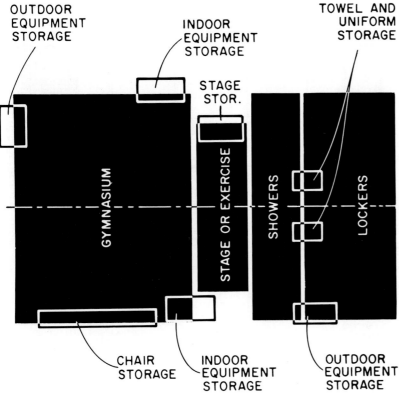

OUTDOOR EQUIPMENT STORAGE

INDOOR EQUIPMENT STORAGE

TOWEL AND UNIFORM STORAGE

STAGE STOR.

GYMNASIUM

STAGE OR EXERCISE

SHOWERS

LOCKERS

CHAIR STORAGE

INDOOR EQUIPMENT STORAGE

OUTDOOR EQUIPMENT STORAGE

Fig. 150

Wire baskets may be used in place of the small lockers for the storage of gym clothes. Although in some cases the baskets have been mounted in a fixed position, it is more desirable to place them on trucks which can be locked in a well-ventilated storage space. The basket system is generally more difficult to manage than the locker system.

A common arrangement is to provide one large dressing locker, together with six storage lockers. This permits the student to have a large locker in which to hang his street clothes and also provides him with a small locker for the storage of gym clothes.

Figures 153 through 157 show various shower arrangements and dimensions for group showering. Additionally, it is still common practice to provide some private showers for special demand usage. As the illustrations indicate, there is a trend to prefabricated plumbing arrangements wherein the plumbing is not built into the walls, reducing its installation and repair costs. It is also quite common to equip the facility with preset temperature valves or graduated settings in walk-through showers. Figure 158 shows the height range for shower heads.

The arrangements shown here are for a 500-student junior high school boys' locker room (Fig. 159) with center benches, a 1,500-student high school girls' locker room (Fig. 160), and the boys' and team locker room (Fig. 161) with benches integral with the locker bases. Note the inclusion of two private showers in the girls' locker room, the supervisory location (and windows) of the office in both areas, the walk-through showers in the one, and showers and drying areas in the other.

Figure 162 shows a very compact, well-organized complex of team locker bays, permitting unused bays to be locked with sliding gates while providing good access from the opened bays to the shower facilities. Figures 163 and 164 show various details and arrangements providing for uniform drying and storage.

Unless the increasingly seldom used system of central basket storage is utilized for clothing storage, the number and ratio of gymsuit to street clothes lockers are determined by the formula

$$T \times N/P = S$$

where T = number of students to be enrolled
N = number of times/week student in course
P = number of periods/week that physical education is given (hours/day $\times$ days/week)

S = number of street clothes (dressing) lockers required

T also then represents the gymsuit lockers needed, and $T/S = R$, or the ratio of gymsuit versus street clothes lockers, varying as shown in Figs. 151 and 152 and determining the total space required for lockers.

The standard type of full-length locker should be set on a masonry base to facilitate cleaning. The unit should be complete with two top shelves, ventilating grilles, and four hooks for hanging clothes. Some type of locking device should be furnished.

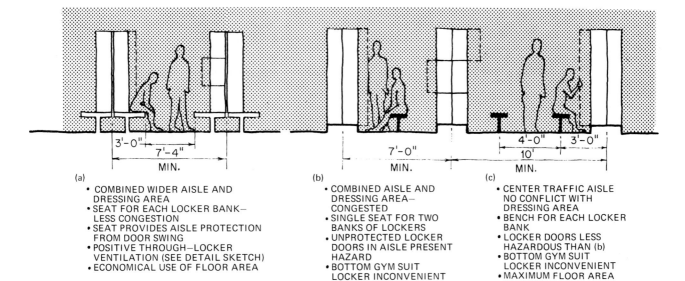

(a)
- COMBINED WIDER AISLE AND DRESSING AREA
- SEAT FOR EACH LOCKER BANK—LESS CONGESTION
- SEAT PROVIDES AISLE PROTECTION FROM DOOR SWING
- POSITIVE THROUGH—LOCKER VENTILATION (SEE DETAIL SKETCH)
- ECONOMICAL USE OF FLOOR AREA

(b)
- COMBINED AISLE AND DRESSING AREA—CONGESTED
- SINGLE SEAT FOR TWO BANKS OF LOCKERS
- UNPROTECTED LOCKER DOORS IN AISLE PRESENT HAZARD
- BOTTOM GYM SUIT LOCKER INCONVENIENT
- ECONOMICAL USE OF FLOOR AREA

(c)
- CENTER TRAFFIC AISLE NO CONFLICT WITH DRESSING AREA
- BENCH FOR EACH LOCKER BANK
- LOCKER DOORS LESS HAZARDOUS THAN (b)
- BOTTOM GYM SUIT LOCKER INCONVENIENT
- MAXIMUM FLOOR AREA REQUIRED

Fig. 151

ELEMENTARY AND SECONDARY SCHOOLS
Physical Education: Locker Rooms

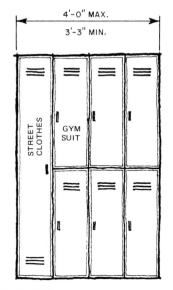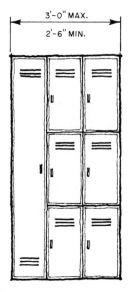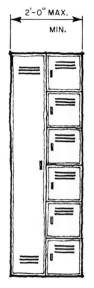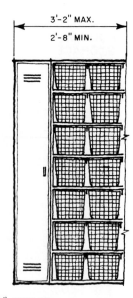

(a) 12" X 12"
X60" .... 12" X 12" X 20"
9" X 12" X 20"

X72" .... 12" X 12" X 24"
9" X 12" X 24"
- RATIO: 6 TO 1

- REQUIRES MOST FLOOR AREA PER RATIO UNIT
- HIGHEST INITIAL COST
- AFFORDS GREATEST HANGING DIMENSION IN GYM SUIT LOCKER FOR GOOD VENTILATION AND DRYING OF GYM SUITS. SEE SKETCH DETAIL OF POSITIVE VENTILATION THROUGH LOCKERS

(b) 12" X 12"
X60" .... 12" X 12" X 30"
9" X 12" X 30"

X72" .... 12" X 12" X 36"
9" X 12" X 36"
- RATIO: 6 TO 1

- ECONOMICAL USE OF FLOOR AREA BETWEEN (a) AND (c)
- GOOD VENTILATION—SINCE HANGING OF GYM SUITS POSSIBLE

(c) 12" X 12"
X60" .... 12" X 12" X 12"
- RATIO: 5 TO 1
X72" .... 12" X 12" X 12"
12" X 12" X 14$^2/_5$"
- RATIO: 6 TO 1
5 TO 1

- REQUIRES LEAST FLOOR SPACE PER RATIO UNIT
- POOR VENTILATION AND DRYING OF GYM SUITS—NO HANGING POSSIBLE

(d) 12" X 12"
X72" .... 12" X 13" X 8"
9" X 13" X 8"
- RATIO: 14 TO 1

- LEAST INITIAL COST
- OPEN BASKET PROVIDES BETTER VENTILATION THAN (c), NOT AS GOOD AS (a) AND (b)
- REMOVABLE BASKETS MORE SUBJECT TO DAMAGE—MAINTENANCE PROBLEM

NOTE: OTHER WIDTHS, DEPTHS AND COMBINATIONS ARE AVAILABLE: THESE SHOWN ARE REPRESENTATIVE.

Fig. 152

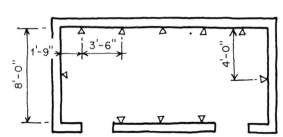

Fig. 153   Conventional shower (in-wall piping); 14 sq ft per head.

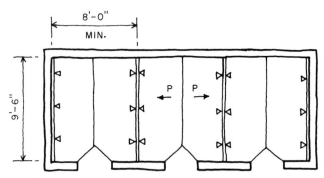

Fig. 155   Prepiped package showers (span-across); 12.2 sq ft per head.

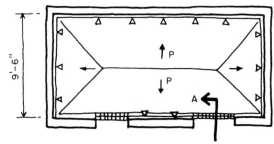

Fig. 154   Prepiped package showers (wall-mounted); 14.6 sq ft per head.

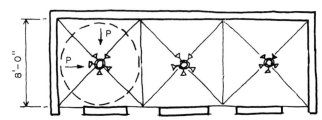

Fig. 156   Column showers. (Available in 4, 5, or 6 heads per column; 12.8 sq ft per head at 5.)

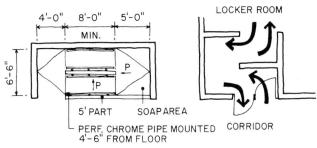

Fig. 157 Walk-through shower.

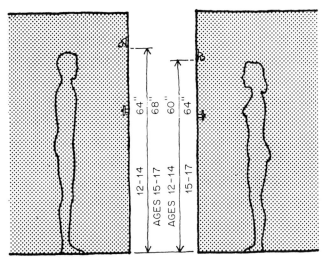

Fig. 158 Recommended shower head heights.
(From "Basic Body Measurement of School Age Children," U.S. Department of Health, Education, and Welfare.)

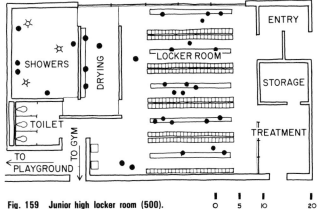

Fig. 159 Junior high locker room (500).

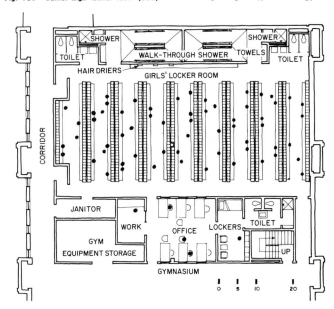

Fig. 160 High school girls' locker room (1500).

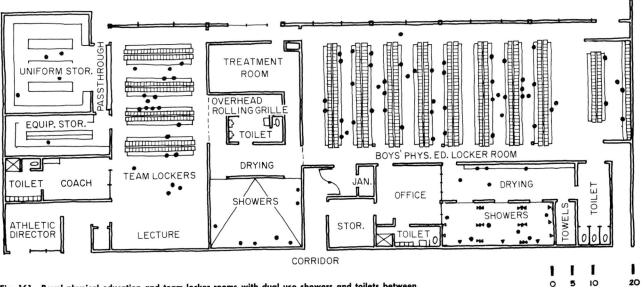

Fig. 161 Boys' physical education and team locker rooms with dual use showers and toilets between.

ELEMENTARY AND SECONDARY SCHOOLS
Physical Education: Locker Rooms

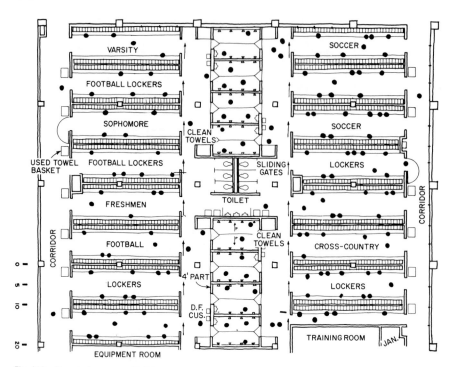

Fig. 162 Team locker rooms with joint showers.

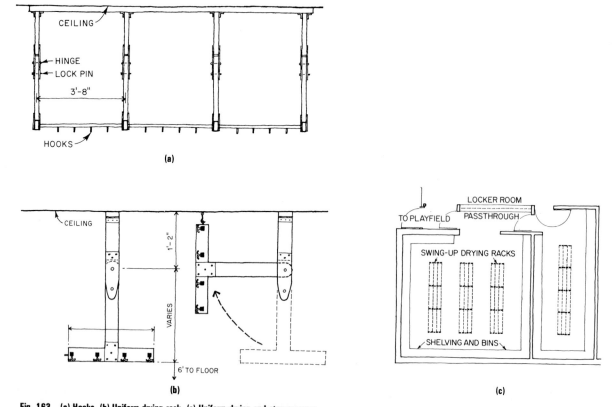

Fig. 163 (a) Hooks. (b) Uniform drying rack. (c) Uniform drying and storage room.

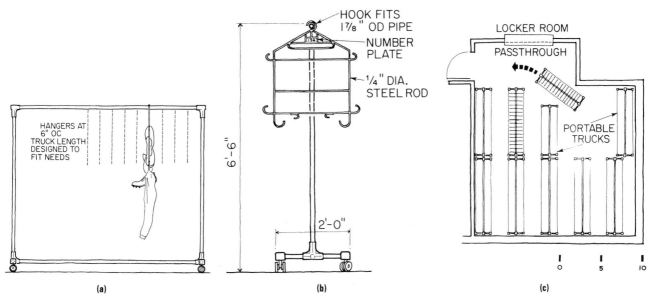

Fig. 164 (a) Uniform drying truck. (b) Truck hanger. (c) Uniform drying and storage room.

Swimming Pools

Swimming pools are a very desirable, but relatively expensive, part of a physical education program. However, with the increasing public interest in participating, more recreational activities are being built as parts of schools or as community facilities.

New finishes like epoxy coatings and prefabricated pool liners of plastic and aluminum are being used more often. Swimming programs divide their activities into diving, swimming instruction, and competitive swimming. The more extensive facilities accommodate these three activities into separate, appropriately designed pools or develop diving "alcove" areas in T- or L-shaped pools.

The basics of pool design are covered in Fig. 165, the various dimensions relating to the age group using the pool. Important also is the amount and location of the surrounding deck area for instructional use, a related advantage of the T- and L-shaped pools (see Fig. 166).

Giving spectators a good and comfortable view involves proper sight lines, plus a careful consideration of acoustic and lighting that takes into account the reflectance of the water. Figure 167 shows one solution where the light source has been screened and the ceiling made nonparallel to the floor to minimize reverberation. Figure 168 illustrates other ideas for user comfort and convenience. A way to accommodate supervision and privacy both is shown in Fig. 169.

Figure 170 illustrates a complete pool and

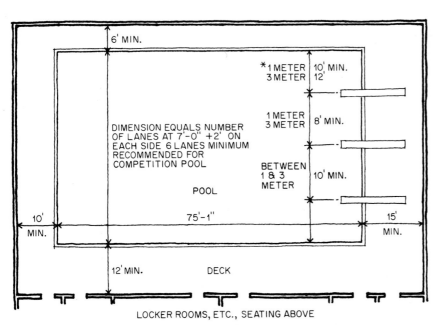

Fig. 165 Recommended minimum pool design dimensions. (*NCAA, 1970; FINA, 1968.)

SIZE RECOMMENDATIONS:

ELEMENTARY SCHOOL

WATER DEPTH: 2' TO 4', 4.5'
MIN. WIDTH: 16'
DESIRABLE WIDTH: 20', 25', 30'
MIN. LENGTH: 36'
DESIRABLE LENGTH: 50', 60', 75'

JR. HIGH SCHOOL

WATER DEPTH: 3'–5'
MIN. WIDTH: 25'
DESIRABLE WIDTH: 30', 36', 42'
MIN. LENGTH: 60'
DESIRABLE LENGTH: 75'

SENIOR HIGH SCHOOL

WATER DEPTH: 3'–6'' TO 9' (1M. BD)*
MIN. WIDTH: 36'   12' (2M. BD)
DESIRABLE WIDTH: 45'–46'
MIN. LENGTH
  DESIRABLE: 75'–1''

*4' SHALLOW DEPTH PERMITS FASTER TURNS.
FASTER SPEEDS ARE POSSIBLE IN 5' OR
DEEPER WATER.

ELEMENTARY AND SECONDARY SCHOOLS
Physical Education: Swimming Pools

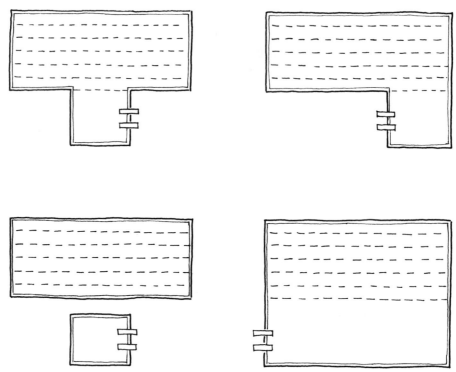

Fig. 166 Additional pool shapes incorporating separated diving pool.

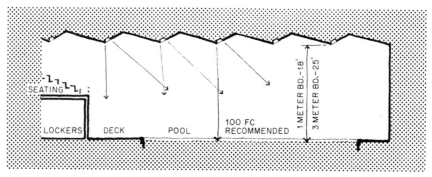

Fig. 167 Light source not visible from spectator area.

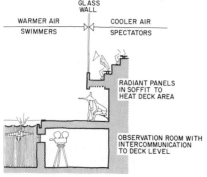

Fig. 168 Comfort control.

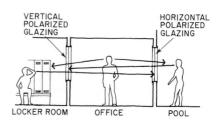

Fig. 169 Visual control for supervision.

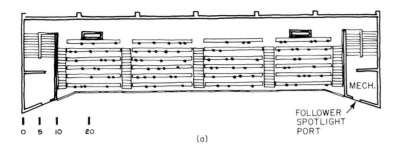

MECH.

FOLLOWER
SPOTLIGHT
PORT

0 5 10 20

(a)

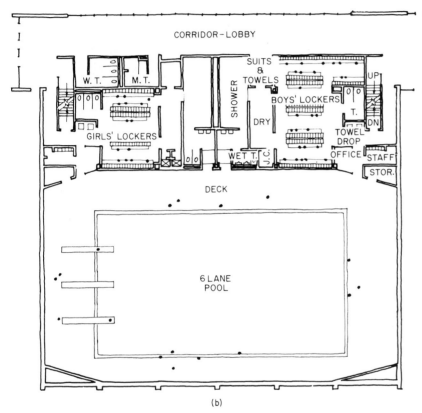

CORRIDOR - LOBBY

W. T.   M. T.

SUITS
&
TOWELS

SHOWER

BOYS' LOCKERS

UP

DRY

T.

DN

GIRLS' LOCKERS

WET T.   J.C.

TOWEL
DROP

OFFICE   STAFF

STOR.

DECK

6 LANE
POOL

(b)

Fig. 170   (a) Balcony seating level. (b) Pool deck level.

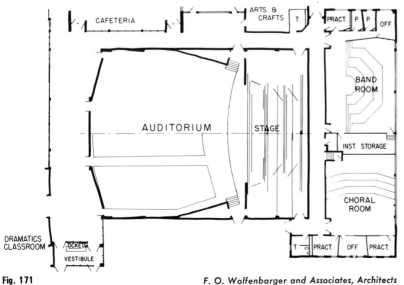

CAFETERIA

ARTS &
CRAFTS   T.

PRACT.   P. P.   OFF.

BAND
ROOM

AUDITORIUM   STAGE

INST. STORAGE

CHORAL
ROOM

DRAMATICS
CLASSROOM

TICKETS

VESTIBULE

T.   PRACT.   OFF.   PRACT.

Fig. 171   *F. O. Wolfenbarger and Associates, Architects*

supporting locker facility. In many states separate locker facilities are required for pool use. Note in the locker room layout, the entry into the pool via the shower room, a basic requirement.

AUDITORIUMS

The school auditorium is frequently used as a center for community affairs. It should be so designed and equipped that it may be used effectively by all groups—amateurs, professionals, youth and adult alike. The use of this facility will extend over a wide range, including concerts, plays, motion pictures, forums, and other forms of presentation.

The stage is the essential educational facility, for it is on the stage that young people have the opportunity to learn to present themselves before large groups. It should be designed for ease of movement of performers and stage sets. Areas that support production, such as stagecraft, band room, choral room, storage, dressing rooms, and restrooms, should be located to give rapid and convenient access to the stage.

Many school officials have expressed a preference for auditoriums without any natural lighting. Absolute light control is essential for a good performance. In some schools, windows can be darkened by automatic controls operated from a central point. Stage lighting should be flexible and simple enough to permit amateurs to operate the equipment effectively.

The seating of the auditorium is not as important from an educational point of view as it may be from the community use standpoint. There is no need for the school auditorium to seat the entire student body. It is best designed when the audience is small enough to make participation possible in group discussions and to ensure a reasonably full assembly area under most types of usage. A capacity of 300 to 800 would normally meet all school requirements. Additional capacity would be dictated largely by community use.

The school auditorium in Figs. 171 and 172 will comfortably seat about 850 students. A ticket booth is located in the foyer of the auditorium lobby. This lobby provides ample circulation space immediately outside the seating area. The placement of seats and aisles gives good traffic circulation. The entire seating area has adequate sight lines giving good view of

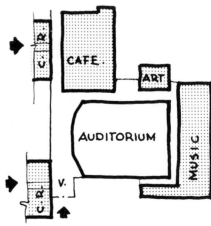

CAFE.

ART

AUDITORIUM

MUSIC

V.

Fig. 172

ELEMENTARY AND SECONDARY SCHOOLS
Auditoriums

the stage from all seats. The front of the stage platform extends beyond the main curtain, providing area for a speaker or discussion panel while the main stage is being set up for a following performance. The stage curtains, teasers, borders, and cyclorama shown on the drawing are adequate to support the various stage activities. The ample corridor space and doors back stage provide rapid circulation of performers, stage crews, and properties. The band and choral rooms are conveniently located with direct access to the stage. Music practice rooms are also used as dressing rooms for performers. This audito-

rium has direct access to a delivery area, which is convenient when delivering or removing stage properties.

This auditorium unit (Fig. 173) is a community art center. Integration of all the arts with the auditorium is highly desirable.

The educational program of the school and the needs of the community resulted in this extensive auditorium center (Fig. 174). Over 1,400 seats are provided on the main floor and balcony area. Adjacent to the stage is a workshop room where scenery and properties may be designed, built, and moved directly to the stage. This room also provides storage

for flats and props. The area in front of the stage is large enough to seat a band or orchestra with adjacent storage for music chairs and stands. Student and adult performers are provided with dressing rooms, make-up room, and toilets.

Figures 175 and 176 illustrate an auditorium unit where considerable emphasis is placed on teaching and preparation for theater, television, and radio productions. This design may be considered more advantageous for student use than for use by community groups. Note the relation in area of the stage and seating space.

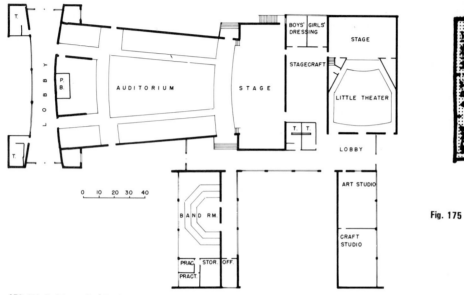

Fig. 173 *W. B. Ittner, Architect*

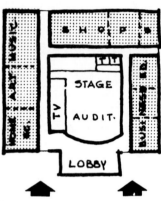

Fig. 175

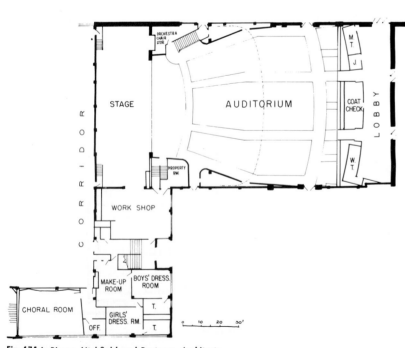

Fig. 174 *LaPierre, Litchfield and Partners, Architects*

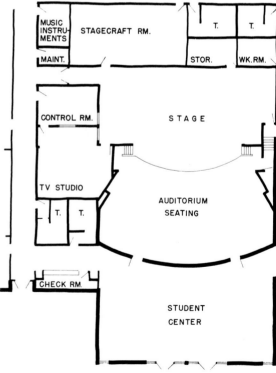

Fig. 176 *M. McDowell Brackett, Architect*

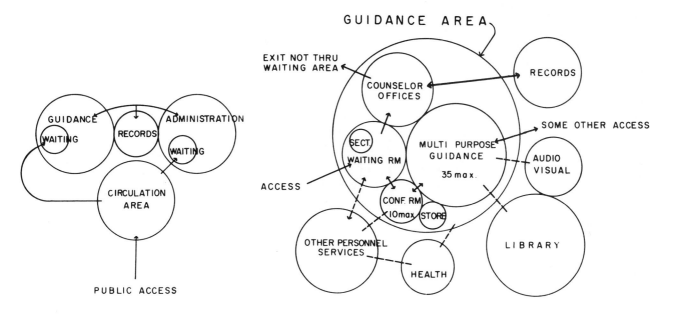

GUIDANCE AREA

EXIT NOT THRU WAITING AREA

COUNSELOR OFFICES

RECORDS

GUIDANCE WAITING

RECORDS

ADMINISTRATION

WAITING

SECT WAITING RM

MULTI PURPOSE GUIDANCE 35 max.

SOME OTHER ACCESS

AUDIO VISUAL

CIRCULATION AREA

ACCESS

CONF. RM 10 max. STORE

OTHER PERSONNEL SERVICES

HEALTH

LIBRARY

PUBLIC ACCESS

DIAGRAMMATIC SCHEME 1   DIAGRAMMATIC SCHEME 2

Fig. 1

Waiting Area

The waiting area is provided as a reception area, as an informational resource area, and as a place for students and others to wait for their appointment with the counselors. This room should be sufficiently large to provide space for a secretary-receptionist and for one student for each counselor available. In addition, there should be space available for three or four additional persons, such as parents or teachers who might be accompanying the student. Thus, for a school which has three counselors, waiting space should be provided for about seven or eight persons.

In order to provide a smoother flow of traffic, and also to minimize possible embarrassment to those students who appear to have experienced an emotional disturbance during the counseling interview, it is desirable that exits other than through the waiting area be provided for students leaving counseling offices. (See Fig. 1.)

Counselors' Offices

The counselor's office is the setting for the interview. There should be an office for each counselor. The interview usually involves only the counselor and the student. However, at times other persons such as a teacher, the child's parents, or another professional worker, such as the visiting teacher, are called into conference. Since the interview

Physical Facilities for School Guidance Services, Office of Education, Dept. of Health, Education, and Welfare, Washington.

is regarded as confidential, the room should offer privacy, and should be reasonably soundproof. The use of partial partitions is not satisfactory.

Small Conference Room

The small conference room will be used for case conferences where as many as 10 persons may be present. It also may be used by such professional persons as the visiting teacher, school psychologist, health and medical services personnel, attendance officer, college admissions personnel, and the school psychometrist or diagnostician for individual testing or for small group (less than 10) testing.

Multipurpose Guidance Room

This room will have many uses. These uses will vary from school to school depending upon the guidance services offered and upon the concept of group procedures in guidance which prevails. The room should be about the same size as a regular classroom. When a multipurpose room as a part of the guidance area is not feasible, some schools make use of a conveniently located classroom. Uses may include group procedures, group testing, and inservice training sessions in guidance. Some schools may use it as a center for information services. (See Fig. 2.)

Storage Room

Storage space is desirable in several of the areas. This could be one area or several smaller areas,

depending on the size of the guidance area and the ingenuity of the architect.

SUMMARY OF LOCATION AND SPACE GUIDELINES

Location

The guidance unit should be:

1. Separate from but near the administrative offices for convenient access to personnel records and certain clerical services. (See Fig. 2.)

2. Accessible by a direct entrance from corridor.

3. Located to provide exits from counseling area separate from entrances, if possible.

4. Readily accessible to students and near the main flow of student traffic to facilitate contact, scheduling, and communication.

5. Readily accessible from a main entrance for the benefit of parents and representatives of community agencies.

6. Reasonably near to related personnel services, such as pupil accounting, health, and psychological services.

7. Reasonably near to the library for convenience in use of display and reference materials.

Space

The guidance unit should provide:

1. Attractive and comfortable reception area with appropriate materials to encourage profitable use of waiting time.

2. Private counseling rooms or offices.

271

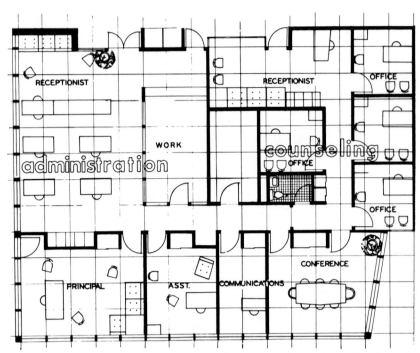

Fig. 2 Location of guidance unit. (Reproduced from "Administrative Facilities in School Buildings," Special Publication No. 6, U.S. Department of Health, Education and Welfare, Office of Education, Washington, 1957.)

3. Conference room for such uses as case conferences; individual testing; special staff personnel such as the school nurse, visiting teacher, speech correctionist; interviewing by prospective employers and representatives of institutions of higher learning.

4. Multipurpose room adjacent to counseling offices for group testing, group procedures, and inservice training activities.

CLASSROOMS

Major factors to be considered in designing a classroom are the following:

1. Seating and writing surfaces
2. Space and furnishings for the lecturer
3. The use of wall space, including chalkboards, screens, size and location of windows, etc.
4. Facilities for projection and television
5. Coat racks, storage, and other conveniences
6. Acoustics and lighting
7. Heating and air conditioning
8. Aesthetic considerations

Classroom Seating The seating arrangement is the most important feature in determining the size and shape of a classroom. Seating arrangements in a mathematics classroom should provide all students with a good view of the front chalkboard, ready access both to the seats and to chalkboards on other walls, an adequate, well-illuminated writing surface at each seat, a place to set books and papers, reasonable comfort, and privacy in taking examinations. In a class of 50 or fewer students, where a long front chalkboard is desirable, it seems better to have the front wall longer than the side walls. This presupposes that there are more students in a row of seats than there are rows; for example, visibility is better in a classroom having five rows of seven seats than in one having seven rows of five seats. In a room measuring 26' × 30' (Fig. 1), with separate tablet armchairs for 35 students, the seven seats in a row might have a spacing of 3'6" between seat centers laterally and 4'6" between the end seat centers and side walls (6 × 3'6" + 9' = 30'). Spacing from front to back in a column might be 3 feet between seat centers with 4 feet behind the back-seat center and 10 feet between the front-seat center and the front chalkboard (4 × 3' + 14' = 26'). This pattern allows for aisles of about 20 inches between columns, a width just under the 22-inch "unit width" used as a standard in estimating the number of persons who can walk abreast in a corridor or stairhall. This arrangement requires about 22 square feet of space per student. Lecture halls whose seats have folding tablet arms may allow 15 square feet or less per student.

Close-packed seating arrangements are not the most desirable, but sometimes are necessary because larger rooms are not available. Laws in some states provide that no person shall have to pass more than six others to reach an aisle; hence 14 persons in a row between aisles is an absolute maximum. If 10 to 14 students sit next to each other in a row behind a long strip table or writing ledge, the ledge should be at least 12 inches wide and should provide at least 2 feet of length per person. An arrangement whereby the nearer half of the writing surface in front of each person can fold up and away from the writer gives more room for students to pass. A spacing between rows of 42 inches be-

J. Sutherland and John W. McLeod, *Buildings and Facilities for the Mathematical Sciences,* Conference Board of the Mathematical Sciences, Washington, 1963.

tween seat centers is adequate for most seating arrangements that use strip tables for writing.

Tablet armchairs are commonly used for seating in college classrooms in the United States and permit rows to be spaced every 3 feet. They are satisfactory for most classes that do not make use of special equipment (such as desk calculators or slide rules), provided they have a large writing surface and a shelf underneath for books and papers. Tablet armchairs may be found either fixed to the floor, fastened together in sets of two to six that can be moved as a group, or individually movable. When chairs are fixed to the floor the arrangement should be one that permits good visibility and ready access. Good visibility may be achieved in three ways: by sloping the floor, by staggering seats in consecutive rows, or by wide spacing.

An arrangement permitting a class of 30 to spread out for examination purposes in a 26' × 26' classroom seating 40 students would be the following (Fig. 2): in each of five rows, spaced 3 feet apart from front to back between seat

centers, let two triples of seats be placed with seat centers 2 feet apart laterally and with a 4-foot central aisle from front to back between triples. In 5-foot aisles at the sides, let movable tablet armchairs be placed next to the fixed seats for lectures and recitations (keeping the 3-foot aisle by the walls), but let these chairs be moved over next to the walls during examinations. If the center chair in each fixed triple were left vacant, there would still be 30 widely spaced chairs available for an examination. Another pattern involves joint activity by two instructors whose adjoining classrooms are separated by a folding partition, and can be combined into a larger room for 60 for appropriate portions of the instruction (Fig. 3).

A Front Platform In front of the students' seating area, there should be enough space for the lecturer to walk back and forth before a long chalkboard. In rooms with more than five rows of seats there is an advantage in having a platform, possibly 8 inches above the floor and extending the

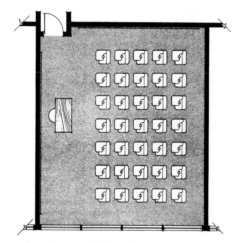

Fig. 1 Seating arrangement in a classroom for 35 students.

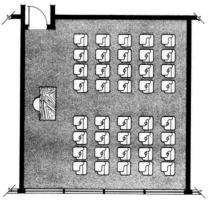

Fig. 2 Classroom for 40, with 10 side seats movable.

COLLEGE AND UNIVERSITY FACILITIES
Classrooms

full width of the room, on which the teacher may walk the length of the board without danger of falling off the end. The chalkboard should then be raised correspondingly higher above the classroom floor for better visibility. The mathematics teacher needs a table on which he [she] can place his [her] lecture notes and papers, but it is better to have this table either movable on casters or fixed at the side of the platform where it does not block the view of the chalkboard from the first two rows of students. If an overhead projector is to be used, there must either be a place where it can be mounted permanently at the front of the room, or there must be provision for rolling it in on a cart and connecting it electrically. In the latter case, the front platform might be slightly lower and be accessible by a ramp. The mathematics teacher seldom sits during a lecture but may wish to sit down during an examination. There should be a chair by his [her] table or desk.

A lecture room should be so placed in a building that it is accessible to students without overcrowding of corridors or stairways. Coat racks, adequate bulletin boards lining the corridors, and ample toilet facilities should be provided nearby. The room itself should be arranged so that the audience can see well, hear well, and be comfortable. In part this depends on temperature, humidity, background of light and sound, and seating space.

Projection Systems The large lecture room should be built to accommodate a variety of projection systems that may be used immediately or in the more distant future. An overhead projector requires an electrical outlet near the lecturer's table, placed so that the lecturer will not trip over the cord, and also a screen properly mounted to assure that the entire class has good visibility with minimum distortion. More screens or a wide screen may be needed to enable the lecturer to use two or more overhead projectors at once. If movies, films, or slides are projected from the rear of the room and reflected from a front screen, the room should have a projection booth, or at least a suitable stand and electrical outlet for the projector. Remote controls for operating the projector are desirable. Shades may be required for darkening a room with windows. If the "rear screen" method of projection is to be used, in which the image is thrown onto a translucent screen mounted in the front wall from a projector in an adjacent room beyond the front wall, the building plans must include adequate provision for this projection room.

A room or space for the preparation of transparencies or other visuals is a corollary of their use. Material can be prepared on ordinary paper and copied quickly onto a transparency by a thermal duplicator or similar equipment. Such copies can be posted after the lecture for inspection by students. Storage for such materials must also be provided, as well as for any materials distributed to students to supplement their lecture notes.

Provision for receiving and transmitting television is also an important consideration in planning a lecture room for large group instruction.

Seating and Visibility Good visibility depends not only on the arrangement of chalkboards and of projection screens and equipment, but also to a large degree upon seating arrangements. Factors to be considered are avoidance of ob-

J. Sutherland and John W. McLeod, *Buildings and Facilities for the Mathematical Sciences*, Conference Board of Mathematical Sciences, Washington, 1963.

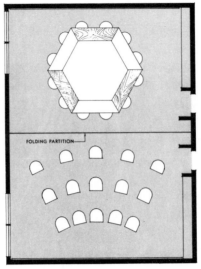
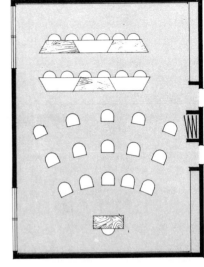

Fig. 3   A classroom divisible into two seminar rooms.

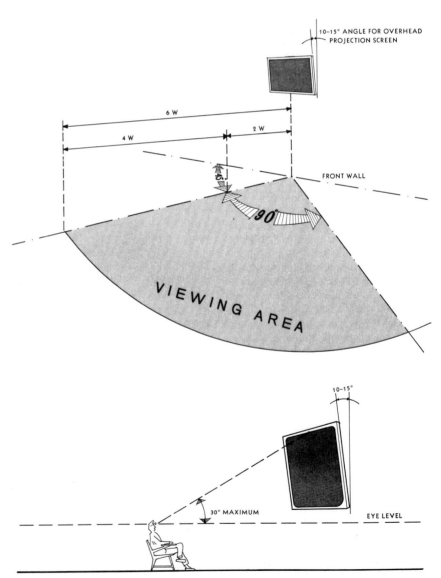

Fig. 4   Optimum viewing angles.

structions, slope of the floor and height of the speaker's platform, viewing distance, and the extreme vertical and horizontal viewing angles. It is clear that a good lecture room will not have columns or supports so placed as to block the front screen and chalkboard from any seat in the room. However, when a large demonstration table stands on a platform between the chalkboard and the audience, the lower 12 to 18 inches of the board often cannot be seen by people in the first few rows. In this case, vertically sliding chalkboards are needed so that the writing may be raised to a level where it can be seen by all. A sloping floor in a lecture room will generally add somewhat to the cost of construction, but in many instances it will be worth the extra cost in providing good visibility for all. The object of a sloping floor is to make it easier for a person

to see over or around the heads of those in front of him and to give the impression of a smaller room. If the seats in successive rows are staggered so that the line of sight from one seat to the lecturer goes directly between the centers of two seats in the next row, the rise required per row may be reduced by half. Closely interdependent are the slope of the floor and the height of the speaker's platform. The use of a raised platform for the teacher has advantages in increased visibility in any room seating more than about 40 persons, provided that the table or other furniture on the platform does not block the chalkboard for those in the front rows. [A possible plan is shown in Fig. 5.]

Studies of distances and angles for satisfactory viewing indicate that seats should be placed at a distance from a screen not less than twice nor

more than six times the width of the screen image to be viewed and that the distance from a person to the chalkboard should not exceed 400 times the size of the smallest letter or digit being written. Thus, if the back row of students is 64 feet away, the lecturer should make his letters and digits at least two inches high. Similar studies indicate that the angle of elevation from the eye to the upper part of an object on the screen or chalkboard should not exceed 30 degrees (see Fig. 4). If lecture rooms are built in a fan shape instead of a rectangular shape, the minimum angle between line of sight and the blackboard should be at least 30 degrees and preferably more than 45 degrees. These limitations of viewing distance and angle impose restrictions on the placement of seats for adequate viewing.

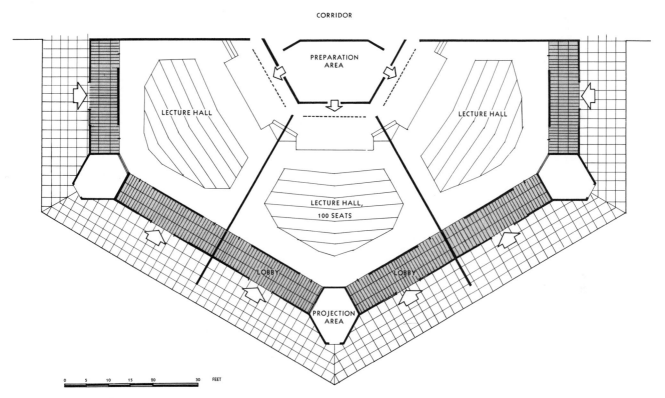

Fig. 5   Three auditoriums with common preparation room.

COLLEGE AND UNIVERSITY FACILITIES
Gymnasiums

GYMNASIUMS

Basic Considerations

The type and size of gymnasium facilities needed for a given college or university will depend upon many factors, one of the most important of which is the anticipated enrollment of the institution. A gymnasium planned to serve 2,000 students will, obviously, be considerably smaller than, and different in design and construction from, a facility planned for a university of 10,000 or more students. In other words, planning must be done with future enrollment in mind, and as part of the master plan for the college or university. If a college or university has a definite enrollment ceiling, the building may be planned for this enrollment. If the enrollment ceiling is indefinite, however, the structure should be planned so that additions to the building are feasible. Most universities or colleges should plan for and build for expansion. Gymnasium space is usually planned to take care of enrollments for at least ten years in advance. Universities of 15,000 or more students may find it desirable to build more than one gymnasium structure, each servicing an area of the campus.

Another factor that will affect the type of building constructed is the philosophy of the administration concerning athletics and physical education. Many questions need to be answered before planning begins. Some of these questions are:

• Will all students be required to take physical education for one, two, three, or four years?

• Is the required program in physical education to be broad in scope; i.e., will a great many opportunities to develop sports skills be extended to students?

• Is teacher education in physical education to be part of the program?

• What responsibility does the college or university take for the physical education, recreation, and fitness of its faculty?

• Is it anticipated that research in physical education, health, and recreation may become an important aspect of the program?

• What is the scope of the varsity athletic program? (The facility requirements are considerably different if varsity teams are to be fielded only in the major sports.)

• What will be done to provide facilities for an expanded program of intramurals and extramurals?

Principles of Gymnasium and Construction

Indoor facilities for sports and athletics should be planned so that all activity areas will be available to both men and women. It is unwise to identify facilities as men's or women's athletic areas. Good planning will permit easy

Planning Areas and Facilities for Health, Physical Education, and Recreation, rev. 1966, The Athletic Institute, Merchandise Mart, Chicago, Ill., American Association for Health, Physical Education, and Recreation, Washington, D.C.

access to all areas from both the men's and women's locker rooms. This type of planning permits the flexibility necessary for efficient utilization and control.

The space used for permanent seating of spectators at athletic events should be kept to a minimum unless space and funds present no problem to be considered. Roll-away or folding bleachers should be used in order to utilize efficiently the space available. Most colleges and universities cannot afford to invest large sums of money nor give large areas of space to permanent seating which is used only a few times each year.

The health and safety of those using the building should be a prime consideration in planning of all activity areas. The disabled and the aging should also be considered.

The construction of the types of facilities and the allocation of adequate square footage to handle a broad athletic and intramural program will provide more than enough gross space for a two-year physical education requirement for all students.

The traffic patterns for a building should be carefully studied. Lockers, showers, and toweling rooms should be centrally located in the building so that they may serve all activity areas. Easy access should be provided from the locker rooms to the playing fields adjacent to the building.

Storage rooms for equipment and supplies should be carefully planned and functionally located. These rooms should be of three types:

• Central receiving storage room, to which all equipment and supplies are delivered. The warehouse storage room should be accessible by truck.

• Utility storage rooms located adjacent to gymnasiums so that bulky equipment may be moved to the floor and back to storage with limited difficulty. Overhead doors or double doors should be large enough to permit free movement of heavy equipment.

• Supply rooms with an attendant's window opening to the locker rooms.

Off-season storage rooms are critically needed. The type of equipment to be moved and stored will define the dimensions of the room and size of the doors needed. Reserve storage should also be provided.

Location of the Gymnasium

If physical education and athletic facilities are used by all of the students at a college or university, the gymnasium facility should be centrally located in order to be easily reached from both the academic buildings and student housing. Physical education facilities, to serve as teaching stations, must be close enough to academic buildings to make it possible for students to move from the classroom into the gymnasium and back within the time provided between classes.

Buildings used only for intramural and intercollegiate activities may be located farther from classrooms and housing than a general-use gymnasium would be. This is especially true if the activities promoted in these build-

ings are scheduled. If the building is to be used for unscheduled participation of students, however, the amount of use will vary inversely with the distance from housing and other campus buildings.

The Main Gymnasium

The criteria for determining the size of the gymnasium are: (1) the nature of the total physical education program; (2) student load as determined by enrollment and attendance requirements per week; (3) spectator interest; and (4) anticipated enrollment growth.

The physical education building should include one main gymnasium to be used for general physical education classwork, intramurals, and intercollegiate athletic activities in basketball and wrestling. Ideally, the size of the main-gymnasium floor for an enrollment of 4,000 students would be approximately 140 by 140 ft. (Use a rectangular dimension if the facility will be heavily used for spectator sports.) This size would provide for one official and three junior-size (35 by 84 ft) basketball courts, with adequate space between the courts and between the courts and walls. If desirable, folding partitions can be used to provide three practice gymnasiums, each 48 by 140 ft. For the basketball courts, backboards that swing up to the ceiling are needed, since nonfolding backboards would interfere with the court usage for volleyball and badminton. In order to increase the number of other instructional units, electrically controlled wooden partitions or nets (nylon or Fiberglas) should be installed.

If the gymnasium is to be used for intercollegiate athletics, seating must be provided for spectators (3 sq ft per person). Portable folding bleachers which can be easily moved are recommended for seating. Portable knock-down bleachers are not recommended because they interfere with classwork while they are being erected, used, and removed. Cost is also an important factor.

The number of seats to be provided will be determined by the size of the student body, the college community, and the degree to which there is public demand for admittance. The seating capacity should be set at a minimum of one-half to two-thirds of the student-faculty population. In larger institutions, it may be necessary to install roll-away bleacher seats in the balcony, which, when combined with the bleachers on the main floor, will provide the required number of seats.

The varsity basketball court should be laid out lengthwise in the center of the gymnasium. If the dimensions of 114 by 145 ft are provided, 25 ft is left on either side for bleachers. A minimum of 5 ft should be left between the first row of seats and the outside boundary line of the court.

Where a permanent balcony is required, it is necessary to plan the line of vision so that the sidelines of the varsity basketball court are plainly visible to the spectators. In this case, the folding bleachers on the floor should be planned to conform to the same line of vision. With the use of roll-away bleachers, added teaching stations can be provided in the balcony area.

If the gymnasium is to be used for intercollegiate sports, the number of entrances and exits equipped with panic hardware should meet fire regulations and be ample in number to control spectator traffic. Spectators should be routed in such a manner that they do not cross the playing courts or other activity areas in the gymnasium.

The height from the floor to the beams in the main gymnasium should be such that in normal use of any of the courts, the balls or badminton birds will not strike the lowest ceiling beam. This height should be a minimum of 22 ft to accommodate the rope climb, basketball, volleyball, and badminton.

Where intercollegiate basketball is played, there should be adequate provision for sportswriters. A press box is recommended if conditions permit. The placing of tables adjacent to playing courts is not a good practice. Provision should be made for telephone and telegraph connections, for reception and transmission lines for television, for timing and scoring devices, and for the operation of a public-address system, including stereophonic music.

When an area is designed for an activity which will require the use of a piano, phonograph, or tape recorder, a space should be provided for storing this equipment. It is preferable to have a space recessed in the side-wall near the place where the instructor will stand to lead the class. Electrical outlets which will provide current at all times will be needed for such equipment as amplifiers. A locking, sliding door should be installed for the protection of the instruments as well as the students. All instructional equipment should be on movable carts.

In addition to the niche described above for the storage of the piano and phonograph, there should be a storage room adjacent to the main gymnasium of sufficient size to accommodate the storage of all types of equipment, such as roll-away standards, mats and gymnastics apparatus, and chairs.

Other audiovisual aids can include still and movie projectors, daylight-projection screens, television sets, a scoreboard, a clock, chalkboards, and an intercommunication system.

Concrete is commonly used as a base in constructing the floor of the main gymnasium. Sleepers of 2 by 2 in. up to 2 by 10 in. are laid on edge. Maple tongue-and-groove is the most popular type of wood finish.

It is suggested that a glazed-tile wainscot be carried up to a height of 7 or 8 ft. From that point to the ceiling, the concrete or cinder block should be painted with a light-colored paint.

Experience has shown that, in general, natural lighting methods have not proved satisfactory. Mercury-vapor or fluorescent lights with diffusion panels have provided satisfactory illumination.

There is some evidence that suspended tracks are no longer favored by physical education directors. However, if there is no balcony in the main gymnasium, a track serves as space for spectator seats and also for additional teaching stations.

If a track is constructed, it should be at least 8 ft wide and 10 ft above the gymnasium floor. The surface should provide good traction, and the curves should be banked.

The Lobby The purpose of the lobby is to furnish an area for the control of admission and distribution of traffic and the provision of information. It should contain well-lighted and locked display cabinets, bulletin boards, and directories. These units should be recessed and flush-mounted. Public telephones should be located in or adjacent to the lobby. Other service facilities needed, as defined by the program, should be provided. Examples of these needs are ticket booths, planters, and special decorations. The lobby should be attractive and of sufficient size to accommodate traffic needs. Vestibules should be included for climate control.

The general administrative offices of the building should be located near the lobby. Corridors should lead from the lobby to locker rooms and spectator areas. Probably the most serviceable and attractive floor for the lobby is terrazzo or a material of similar quality. The walls should be constructed of durable material.

A large checkroom for outer wraps should be placed adjacent to the direct line of traffic, but in an alcove or a side room in order to prevent congestion. The location and arrangement of the checkroom should serve the daily needs of the building as well as the needs of special occasions. The room should have a long, low counter covered with brass or stainless steel, and it should be possible to lock both the room and counter opening when the facility is not in use. Racks permanently numbered for checking coats and hats should be installed. Shelves should also be provided for storing packages and bags.

Toilet and washroom facilities for men and women should be located near the checkroom. Adequate stairways or ramps should lead from the main lobby to balconies or other spectator areas above the first floor.

Offices The central administrative offices serve as the nerve center of the entire physical education plant. They should be located near the entrance of the building, since all who have business with the department will first come to these offices. The office of the director and those of the various faculty members should be adjacent to a large central office which will serve as the workroom for the secretarial and clerical staff, as a repository for all departmental records, and as a reception center and waiting room for persons who have business with the department.

The work area of this central office should be separated from the reception-waiting room area by a counter. The reception-waiting room should open into the main corridor of the building. A large closet should be provided adjacent to the work area for the storage of office supplies and records. The administrative head should have his office in or near the central administrative suite. His office should be of sufficient size to accommodate such things as an executive desk, a number of chairs, a file cabinet, and a small work table. This will require approximately 200 sq ft. The central administrative office unit should include a conference room. This room should be near the office of the administrative head of the department. It should be furnished with a truncated conference table large enough to seat the entire physical education faculty, if possible, or the administrative staff in a larger university.

A small cloakroom and rest rooms should be located near the conference room. The chairs for the conference room should be upholstered in attractive colors of vinyl materials so they can be kept clean. The conference room should be finished in light, attractive colors. It is desirable to have a small, murphy-type kitchen for refreshments.

Each member of the faculty with major re-sponsibilities should be provided a private office. Ideally, each of these offices should occupy a minimum of 120 sq ft and be equipped with necessary office furniture. A workroom with space for a secretarial pool should receive serious consideration.

Classrooms The physical education complex should include sufficient classroom space designed primarily for lectures, discussion, and demonstrations. The number, size, and types of rooms will depend upon the anticipated enrollment and curricular offerings. Institutions offering teacher-training programs in health, physical education, recreation, and safety will have need for more specialized rooms than will those concerned primarily with service and basic instruction courses and varsity athletics.

The sizes of classrooms may well vary to accommodate from 10 to 150 persons. The space per student may vary from approximately 20 sq ft per student in smaller rooms to 12 sq ft per student in rooms for 100 or more persons. Standard classrooms normally seat an average of 40 students. The smaller rooms lend themselves more readily to seminars, conferences and informal discussions, while an assembly room big enough to combine large groups for professional lectures, clinics, and demonstrations is essential.

Where class size warrants, a wall clock visible from all seats should be installed. Acoustical treatment, adequate lighting, and thermostatically controlled mechanical ventilation should be considered for all classrooms. Each classroom should be provided with chalkboards, tackboards, and hook strips. Electrical outlets for audiovisual equipment should be strategically located with due regard for the convenient placement of controls.

Windows should be equipped with effective room-darkening devices which are easily operated. A speakers' platform or podium is frequently desirable in rooms designed for larger groups. Large assembly rooms might well be equipped with a projection booth. A rectangular room is more satisfactory for film projection. Transmission and reception of television, including closed-circuit programs, should be considered when planning modern physical education facilities.

In locating room entrances, due regard should be given to traffic control. The rooms themselves should be placed where they are conveniently accessible yet removed from disturbing noise and distraction.

In smaller classrooms, movable tablet or desk armchairs may be used, or conference tables and straight chairs may be preferred. Large lecture halls and assemblies should be equipped with numbered tablet or desk chairs secured to the floor and so arranged as to provide visual efficiency. It is highly desirable that convenient recessed cabinets and closets be provided for storing instructional materials and personal effects.

Auxiliary Gymnasiums

In addition to the large general gymnasium, or gymnasiums, several other gymnasiums may be required for

- Exercise therapy
- Gymnastics
- Weight exercise
- Wrestling and personal defense
- Street-shoe usage
- Dance studio
- General games

COLLEGE AND UNIVERSITY FACILITIES
Gymnasiums

Exercise-Therapy Facilities Two separate areas should be planned for this specialized program: (1) an exercise-therapy room, which can be used as a clinic, designed for individual ameliorative exercises, is the basic requirement; and (2) a gymnasium for adapted activity is necessary for students assigned to this program.

The exercise-therapy room should be on the ground floor if possible, or accessible to an elevator. It should be well lighted, and the walls and floor attractively finished to lend a cheerful atmosphere. The size of the room is determined by the number of students needing this special attention. Approximately 70 sq ft of floor space is required per student. To accommodate equipment, the minimum size of the room should be 1,600 sq ft. Office space should be located within this area, and the office should be equipped with large glass windows for adequate supervision of the room. The room should be well ventilated, with air conditioning provided where necessary. The dressing and toilet facilities should be close to the exercise-therapy room and should be adjusted to the needs of the handicapped. A sink or washbasin should be provided in this facility. Doors and windows to the room should be designed for privacy. A curtained area should be provided for changes of equipment or appliances when privacy is desired.

Permanent equipment installed in the exercise-therapy room should include stall bars, wall weights (pulley), press bar, weight racks, shoulder wheel, finger ladder, hanging bars, overhead ladder, push-up bars, wall charts and anatomical drawings, mirrors (single), mirrors (triple), and walking rails.

Removable equipment should include: plinths (treatment tables) 26 by 72 by 30½ in.; stall-bar benches; incline boards 7 ft by 30 in. by 3 in.; ankle exercisers; a bicycle (stationary); weights (dumbbells); weights (barbells); exercise mats; iron boots (single); iron boots (double); parallel bars (low); orthopedic stairs; rowing-machine stools; scales; an Elgin table (or improvisation of quadriceps exercise table); wrist rollers; neck-traction halters; cushions or pillows; crutches; a wheelchair; dynamometers (hand, spring cable); goniometers; a chalkboard; and a skeleton.

The equipment in an adapted-activities gymnasium should be the same as in a regular gymnasium, with necessary adaptations. This gymnasium should be in close proximity to the exercise-therapy room so that a student can utilize both facilities.

Gymnastic Facilities With the recent nationwide surge of interest in physical fitness, there has been a renewed support of instruction in gymnastics. Gymnastics make a unique contribution toward overcoming a lack of development of the upper body, which is often neglected in other sports. Gymnastics contribute to building strength, agility, flexibility, coordination, balance, and posture. They also contribute to the mental qualities of alertness, daring, and precision; the character trait of self-discipline; and fun and enjoyment. These values, together with those of preventative and corrective action, place gymnastics in a position of major importance in physical education.

In addition to the main gymnasium where gymnastic meets, exhibitions, and other competitions are held before a viewing public, a separate gymnasium should be provided for the permanent installation and storage of apparatus and equipment and for instruction in gymnastics. The dimensions of this gymnasium should be determined by space requirements needed to accommodate the apparatus and equipment to be installed, by space needs for performance in gymnastics, and by total school enrollment and interest in gymnastics. Ideally, the size of this gymnasium should be 120 by 90 ft, with a minimum ceiling height of 23 ft. This height permits a clearance of 22 ft for the rope climb and is ideal for hanging the various mechanical systems used in gymnastics. Some have found it desirable to install tracks on the ceiling supports to make it possible to use trolleys for moving equipment and for attaching safety belts used in the instruction of trampolining and tumbling.

The safety of performers and instructors should receive major consideration in planning the location and installation of apparatus, equipment, and wall fixtures. Apparatus used in performance should be located so that performers do not interfere with each other when going through their routines. Flying rings should be located so that there is at least 15 ft of free space allowed at each end of the swinging arc. All equipment should be installed according to a plan that will permit, without interference, a full range of movement, including the approach. Mats should be laid completely around the area of performance on horizontal and parallel bars.

Floor plates for attaching equipment should be recessed and flush with the floor. It may be necessary to reinforce the floor to install floor plates adequately where tension is unusually severe. Wall boards should be securely installed to the wall when equipment is attached to it. Apparatus suspended from the ceiling should be securely attached to metal supports.

The ceiling should be acoustically treated. Lights should be shielded and adequate for the program. Doors should be constructed wide enough and without a threshold so as to accommodate the movement of equipment to other areas. Maple has many advantages over other types of flooring. The facility should be air-conditioned in accordance with standard specifications. Wall construction should be of the same materials as recommended for other gymnasiums.

A common failure in planning is to overlook the need for adequate and conveniently placed storage space for gymnastic equipment. If multiple use of this equipment is expected, transportation carts and dollies should be provided. Specifications on size and installation of the various pieces of apparatus and equipment may be obtained from the manufacturers. Ideally, the gymnasium for gymnastics should be equipped with the following types of items: side horses, horizontal bars, long horses, parallel bars, bucks, trampolines, mats, rings, and other special apparatus.

A gymnastic landing pit, 10 ft wide, 20 ft long, and 30 in. deep, filled with sponge rubber—for use with parallel bars, horizontal bars, still rings, and tumbling—is a new development in construction for gymnastics.

Weight-Exercise Room This room should contain a minimum of 2,500 sq ft of floor space. Such space will provide a weight-training area and space for the practice of official events in competitive weight lifting. It is recommended that the floor of this room be covered with a durable, resilient material. A flooring of this type makes it unnecessary to use weight platforms, which are essential to protect a maple or other wood flooring.

The weight-lifting area should be roped off and should be approximately 15 by 15 ft for the practice of official lifts. The rest of the room may be used for exercise with barbells, dumbbells, isometric cables, etc. Several full-length mirrors should be installed on the walls. Barbell and weight racks should be attached to the walls so that the room may be kept tidy.

Wrestling and Personal-Defense Room This room is designed for wrestling, judo, and personal defense activities. The ceiling should be of acoustical material and should be a minimum height of 12 ft. It should be rectangular in shape and should contain two square 40- by 40-ft mats. The floor area not covered by the regulation mats should be covered wall to wall with the same type of mat material. The room should be at least 40 by 80 ft. A satisfactory standard is 40 sq ft per student during peak usage.

The floor of the wrestling room should be constructed of, or covered with, resilient materials to prolong the life of the mats. These materials may be rubberlock products, other newly developed resilient materials, or wood. Concrete is not recommended. The mats should be of plastic-type materials and the walls should be covered with resilient materials up to 5 ft above the floor on all sides. Adequate lighting which is properly screened and forced ventilation are essential in this room.

Street-Shoe Usage Room This room should be of sufficient size—70 by 90 ft—to care for the groups for which it is needed. A floor for street-shoe usage may be needed in any size college or university, or in a program with a variety of offerings. The floor most commonly used for this purpose is hard maple, tongue-and-groove, conventional gymnasium flooring. Square dance, folk dance, social dance, physical education for elementary teachers, marching and band practice, and similar activities can be conducted on such a floor. The demand of special college and community events which need to be served, such as musical and drama production, fairs, and carnivals, may be met. The "make-up" room or "warming room" for department and college outdoor programs can be housed in this area and can be served through a door leading to a corridor and immediately to the out-of-doors.

This street-shoe room, when not scheduled in some manner as indicated above, can serve the purposes of any regular gymnasium if so planned in its equipment and floor markings. The floor will need some extra maintenance for the hard use it will receive, but the desirability of the activities which may be scheduled on it will justify the usage and resultant wear.

Dance Studios Dance areas should be provided to serve the departmental and student needs and to afford opportunity for individual and departmental development. Some of these areas are specific and may be limited to forms of dance activity. Other dance areas are versatile and may serve several purposes. Large colleges and universities with a variety of courses may need to plan for one or more of each of several dance-activity rooms. Classes should be advantageously scheduled for the purposes of floor maintenance or equipment moving. The types of dance areas suggested are discussed in the material which follows.

Main Dance Studio This studio, which should measure no less than 56 by 56 ft, will provide for a class of up to 36 students in modern dance, ballet, or some other dance form performed in bare feet or with soft-sole dance shoes. The floor, which should be of conventional gymnasium construction—tongue-and-groove, select maple—should be free of floor plates, plugs, and other installations. The ceiling height should be 22 ft to be proportional with the room and to give the feeling of height in leaps.

The room should have wall mirrors along one wall—24 ft in length, 6 ft high, and with the bottom being 2 ft from the floor. The mirrors should have a draw drapery controlled by cord pulls. Ballet bars (hand rails) should be installed on two opposite sides of the room at ascending heights of 3, 3½, and 4 ft above the floor.

Audiovisual equipment should include a tackboard, a chalkboard, a hook rail, and a lockable glass-front bulletin board. An amplification system—for a record player and tape recorder—on a roll-away table should be recessed into a lockable cabinet with a sliding door. Other cabinets should provide space for musical instruments, records, music, costumes, and other properties. Some dance studios may have a grand piano in the room. It may be desirable to have an area where a grand piano or an upright piano can be stored when removed from the floor. Storage cabinets for stage equipment, levels, and other items should be provided since floor storage of materials not actively used markedly diminishes the floor space usable for dance activities.

Main-Dance-Studio Balcony Current plans of some major institutions may be considered desirable in the provision for a hanging balcony or a balcony over other class or service areas. This balcony can provide 100 or more seats for viewing activity on the floor of the main dance studio or in the auxiliary dance studio, which can be used as a stage area for the main dance studio. Access to the dance-studio floor through a lockable control door or from the second-floor service hallway. The balcony will provide opportunity for practice-performance viewing from the balcony level by the members of a dance group or will make it possible to seat visitors for an invitation performance.

Auxiliary Dance Studio An auxiliary dance studio of 56 by 40 ft with a ceiling of 22 ft can be located adjacent to the main dance studio on the side opposite from the balcony and can be separated by appropriate folding doors and draperies. This studio can serve as a stage for small concert productions or class projects. Several institutions have successfully constructed such a facility. Traveling draperies suspended from the ceiling can be run on tracks and can be controlled electrically to serve as the traditional "flats" used in staging and in making up a backdrop behind which dancers can cross over. When not used, the draperies can be withdrawn from the staging area and can be stacked along one wall. Stage lighting can be developed to give illumination from the ceiling, from the stage side of the divider, from "projecting" semi-cones in the ceiling of the main dance studio, and from "spots" in the balcony.

This dance studio will need to include those features desirable for the program needs as are included in the main dance studio: ballet bars, mirror, cabinets for classroom materials, and a roll-away table with record player and tape recorder. In addition, there may be a need for piano and equipment storage rooms.

Dance Rehearsal Room One or more dance rehearsal rooms of a minimum of 400 sq ft each will contribute to the development of students in dance who need small-group practices and extra rehearsals. A chalkboard, tackboard, and rolling table for tape recorder player should be provided in such rooms. The table should be housed in a recessed, lockable cabinet. Other lockable cabinets will provide needed storage space for dance practice materials. Ballet bars and mirrors will add to the usefulness of such a room.

Dance Property Construction and Storage Room Flats, levels, and other properties can be made and stored in a room of approximately 25 by 30 ft. This room should be located adjacent to the main dance studio and should have wide double doors with a removable mullion so sets and properties can be moved in and out. The room should have a high ceiling to allow sets to be constructed and moved to a vertical position or to the finished position for painting. Drawers and cabinets, some lockable, a sink with hot and cold water, lumber racks, work counters and tables, and electrical outlets are essential in the planned structure of the room. Tackboards, bulletin boards, and lockable, glass-front display bulletin boards are desirable.

Dance Costume Construction and Storage Room The size of this room will vary according to the program needs for costume construction and the storage needs for costumes made and retained in the department. The room will probably be best used by having cabinets in close-order banks, somewhat as bookcases are placed in the stacks in a library. This will free one end of the room for clothing construction. Costume-storage cabinets should have racks for hanging and bins and drawers for storage. Units can be planned so as to be comprised of several components, which may be used as desired for separate assignment to clubs, groups, or projects.

Cabinets for material and equipment storage, wall-attached ironing boards, an automatic washer-drier, a three-way mirror unit, a washroom basin, a large cutting table of 4 by 8 ft, and a counter sink are additional necessities.

Game Room This is a multiple-purpose room, and its use will determine its dimensions. It should be large enough to accommodate at least six table-tennis tables. A ceiling height of 12 ft is adequate. The room should be equipped with a public-address system and record player for instructional and recreational activities, including social and square dancing. This room should be accessible from the lobby or from a building corridor. It should have some kitchen facilities and a hard-usage type floor. The disabled should be considered in the planning.

Special Instructional and Activity Areas

Handball Courts Handball is a vigorous competitive sport long recognized as an essential activity for a college physical education program. Depending on the size of the institution and the expressed interest in handball, one or more batteries of four-wall handball courts should be provided. The official size of a handball court is 20 ft wide by 40 ft long by 20 ft high. Specifications for handball courts can be found in the official handball rule book.

When more than a single battery of courts is to be constructed, the batteries should be arranged so the back walls of each battery are separated by a corridor approximately 10 ft wide and 8 ft high. A corridor located immediately above, and at least 12 ft high, may serve an instructor or be used as a spectator gallery. Corridors and galleries should be illuminated with indirect light.

The back wall of a single court need not be higher than 12 ft. Shatterproof glass may be used to enclose the remainder of the back wall. The use of wire mesh for this purpose is of questionable value. Many courts are satisfactorily used with an open upper rear wall.

Handball courts may be constructed of hard plaster, concrete, shatterproof glass, or a nonsplintering, durable wood. While plaster is sometimes recommended, it would be wise to consider courts constructed of other materials because of maintenance costs. Glass courts provide maximum spectator participation, but the initial cost may be prohibitive. Hardwood construction is most satisfactory. Courts constructed with a high proportion of glass walls obviously allow for a large number of observers. Open-balcony construction interferes with individual-court air conditioning.

Front walls may be constructed of hard maple laid on diagonal wood sheathing. Studding should be placed close enough to prevent dead spots. A maximum of 16-in. centered studs is recommended. A costly but desirable front-wall construction is to lay maple on edge grain.

Side and back walls may be of nonsplintering, durable wood such as yellow pine or hard maple. Some side and back walls constructed with 1-in. tongue-and-groove marine plywood have been satisfactory and economical. Hardwood floors of standard gymnasium construction are recommended. Plaster ceilings have proved satisfactory. All interior surfaces should be painted with eggshell-white enamel.

Entrance doors should open toward the corridor and be provided with flush-type pulls and hinges. A small shatterproof window installed flush with the interior surface of the door should be located at approximately average-adult-male eye level.

No fixtures, such as heat pipes, ventilating ducts, lights, or any other mechanical equipment, should project into the playing area. Ventilating ducts and lighting fixtures are best located flush with the ceiling surface. Lighting specifications are available for handball courts. Provision for replacement of burnt-out light bulbs from above is a desirable feature.

A single light switch to control all lights in each court should be placed on the corridor side and near the entrance door. Warning lights, located outside each court, should indicate when a court is being used. By use of a sturdy push button, lights can be turned on when an entrance door is closed.

Refrigerated air conditioning, or at least forced ventilation, is essential for individual courts. The ventilation switch can operate in conjunction with the light switch. Climatic conditions may dictate separate switches.

Squash Courts Squash is very popular in some localities and should be provided for in the physical education program. It is recommended that at least one single and one double squash court be included in a physical education complex. A singles court is 18 ft–6 in. wide by 32 ft long by 16 ft high. A doubles court is 25 ft wide by 45 ft long by 20 ft high. The number of courts should be determined by the interest in this activity in a given community.

It is possible to install movable metal "telltales" across the front of handball courts so they can be used for squash. Construction features of squash courts are similar to those of four-wall handball courts relative to floors, walls, ceilings, lighting, heating, and ventilation.

COLLEGE AND UNIVERSITY FACILITIES
Gymnasiums; Physical Education and Sports Facilities

The official rules of the United States Squash Racquets Association and the National Squash Tennis Association should be consulted in planning and constructing squash courts.

Rowing-Practice Facilities In certain colleges and universities, it may be desirable to construct facilities for indoor crew practice. Colleges engaging in competitive rowing will require either fixed rowing machines with accompanying mirrors to reflect the action of the rowers, or a rowing-practice tank. The rowing machines may be installed in a special activity room. If there is space underneath the spectator area in the main gymnasium, they may be installed there. In every case, the area should be well lighted and ventilated.

The rowing tank, when used, should simulate the conditions to be found in open-water rowing. The water should be mechanically circulated in such a manner as to make possible the actual introduction of the oar into the water and the completion of the stroke. The crew should be seated on a rigid platform which spans the pool at actual shell height.

All the specifications for indoor rowing equipment may be obtained from the manufacturers, and the details of the construction of a rowing tank are available through the office of the Intercollegiate Rowing Association.

Indoor Archery Range An indoor archery range is much needed in modern college gymnasiums. The popularity of the Chicago Round has made indoor ranges feasible because of the decreased shooting distances, requiring less space than formerly required for the American and York Rounds. A satisfactory indoor range should be 45 ft in width and 78 ft in length. This will provide space for 15 shooters on the line at the same time, each facing a separate target. The length suggested will provide a distance of 60 ft for the Chicago Round, two feet for backstop material, and 16 ft behind the shooting line for instructors, observers, and those preparing to shoot.

Backstops may be constructed of baled straw treated with fire-resistant materials, or may be purchased from archery equipment manufacturers. The targets may be fastened to the backstop or placed on easels in front of it. The floor in the archery room should be constructed of hard-usage materials to permit street shoes to be worn. The room should be well lighted. The target line should be illuminated by floodlights which shine only on the target area.

Research Laboratory College and university health, physical education, and recreation programs are becoming increasingly involved in research. Graduate studies and faculty research cannot thrive unless space is allocated for this work in the gymnasium building where exercise and sports areas are convenient.

Research in physical education may be of many different types. Some colleges and universities emphasize one or more areas. The research taking place in physical education programs is in the following categories: kinesiologic, tests and measurements, organic (metabolic, cardiovascular, and chemical analysis), and statistical.

A laboratory providing opportunities in the kinds of research mentioned requires a minimum of 2,800 sq ft of space for the basic equipment needed. The maximum space needs will depend upon the number of faculty and students involved and the complexity of the research program. Research laboratory space may be provided in one large room or in several smaller rooms. It is suggested that a separate room of 300 sq ft be used for a statistical laboratory.

Steam Room Some college gymnasium facilities include a steam-bath installation. This may be desirable if supervision is present when the steam room is in use. Unsupervised steam baths or sweat boxes are not recommended.

If a steam room is constructed, a satisfactory size is 8 ft square, with a ceiling 10 ft high. A lockable door containing a window should open outward. The room should be equipped with two or three movable benches of sturdy wood construction. The steam valve used should be a type that can be set to prevent the temperature in the room from exceeding $130°$.

Group Study Rooms If the gymnasium is to serve the needs of students enrolled in a major professional program, the inclusion of small-group study rooms is recommended. Study rooms should occupy approximately 150 sq ft and should be equipped with a large table and sufficient chairs to accommodate a maximum of eight students. These rooms may serve a variety of educational needs in addition to small-group on-campus study.

"In-Uniform" Study-Hour Rooms In gymnasium buildings, there is a need for rooms where men and women students who have one free hour between two activity classes may go in uniform to read or study.

The use of this room will conserve student time, encourage their reading or studying habits, and will clear the dressing rooms. Rooms for in-uniform study should be separate for men and women and should be located near the appropriate dressing rooms.

Workroom Each physical education department may wish to concentrate several work or repair functions in one or more areas according to the program and equipment and dependent upon the secretarial and office needs. Two types of areas are described below. In some colleges, it may be considered practical to combine most of the functions of these two workrooms into one plan.

Secretarial Workroom Secretaries, machines, and typewriters are assigned to some individual offices or to a group of offices, but it may not be practical to have all individual offices so staffed and equipped. Office supplies, typewriters, duplicating machines, and some other needed and desirable office machines can be concentrated in one or more department or college workrooms where services can be performed for faculty members who have limited or irregular need of secretarial help. In such a room, a workroom manager can receive assignments, distribute and allocate this work, receive it from the workers, and return it to the appropriate faculty members.

The room should have area enough to accommodate desks, tables, and cabinets, which must be planned according to the anticipated demands. Acoustical treatment and a generous supply of electrical outlets are essential to the orderly functioning of such a service area. A wall-installed washbasin and a hand-towel cabinet are important to the economy of time in the work area.

Repair and Service Workroom The need for repair and service of equipment will dictate the size of the repair and service workroom. Some departments will perform only minor repairs which can be accomplished in a small, modestly equipped workroom or in a part of some other area already provided. Other faculties will wish to plan to repair archery-target stands, covers, field carts, and other larger pieces which require the use of tools and space. This plan to service and repair large pieces, then, will require space for the equipment to be repaired and tools with which to perform the needed repairs.

A well-equipped workroom will contain such constructional and built-in features as cabinets, a sink, wood and lumber storage racks, shelves, a blower discharge fan, a work shelf, and drawers. Many, or most, of the storage areas should be locked individually or as a group with a master key system.

PHYSICAL EDUCATION AND SPORTS FACILITIES

The following standards are recommended for consideration by those involved in planning college and university facilities for physical education, intramural sports, intercollegiate athletics, and recreation.

Type A—Indoor Teaching Stations

• Space requirements: 8.5 to 9.5 sq ft per student (total undergraduate enrollment)
• Including: Gym floors, mat areas, swimming pools, courts, etc. (adjacent to lockers and showers and within 10-min walking distance of academic classrooms)
• Uses: Physical education class instruction, varsity sports, intramural sports, unorganized informal sports participation, student and faculty recreation, etc.
Breakdown of Type A Space
• A1—Large gymnasium areas with relatively high ceilings (22-ft minimum) for basketball, badminton, gymnastics, apparatus, volleyball, etc. (approximately 55 percent of type A space)
• A2—Activity areas with relatively low ceilings (12-ft minimum) for combatives, therapeutic exercises, dancing, weight lifting, etc. (approximately 30 percent of type A space)
• A3—Swimming and diving pools (approximately 15 percent of type A space)

Type B—Outdoor Teaching Stations

• Space requirements: 70 to 90 sq ft per student (total undergraduate enrollment)
• Including: Sports fields of all types (adjacent to lockers and showers and within 10-min walking distance of academic classrooms)
• Uses: Physical education class instruction, varsity sports, intramural sports participation, student and faculty recreation, etc.
Breakdown of Type B Space
• B1—Sodded areas for soccer, touch football, softball, etc. (approximately 60 percent of Type "B" space)
• B2—Court-type areas for tennis, volleyball, flicker ball, etc. (approximately 15 percent of Type "B" space)
• B3—Specialized athletic areas for track and field, baseball, archery, varsity football, golf, camping demonstrations, etc. (approximately 25 percent of Type "B" space)
• B4—Swimming pools (included in B3 approximation)

Type C – Sports Fields and Buildings; Intramural and General Outdoor Recreation Areas

• Space requirements: 120 to 140 sq ft per student (total undergraduate enrollment)
• Including: Playing fields and athletic buildings of all types; softball diamonds, tennis courts, arenas, field houses, etc. (too far removed from general student lockers, showers, living quarters, and academic buildings for use as teaching stations) (maximum distance from major residence areas — 1 mi)
• Uses: Intramural sports, varsity sports, unorganized informal sports
Breakdown of Type C Space
• C1 — Sodded areas for soccer, touch football, softball, etc. (approximately 40 percent of type C space)
• C2 — Court-type areas for tennis, volleyball, flicker ball, etc. (approximately 10 percent of type C space)
• C3 — Specialized athletic areas for track and field, baseball, archery, varsity football, golf, camping demonstrations, etc. (approximately 45 percent of type C space)
• C4 — Swimming pools (included in C3 approximation)
• C5 — Sports and intramural buildings providing lockers, showers, play space, office space, lounge rooms, etc. (approximately 5 percent of type C space)

Type D – Informal Recreation Areas

• Space requirements: included in C3
• Including: On-campus picnic areas (maximum distance from residence areas — 1½ miles) (approximately 15 percent of total type C space)
• Uses: Picnics, outing activities (including outdoor cookery, evening songfests, storytelling, etc.)

Type E – Off-Campus Outdoor Education, Camping, and Recreation Areas

• Including: Outdoor camping and outdoor education center, off-campus golf course, university country club, etc. (maximum distance from heart of the campus — 25 mi).
• Uses: Overnight camping, picnics, outing activities, camping demonstrations, golf, archery, boating, canoeing, outdoor swimming, formal classes taught outdoors.
• Estimate of space needs of this type area: It is difficult to state these needs on a square-feet-per-student basis. Such areas contribute materially to the outdoor education and outdoor recreation of both men and women students, but the many variables in climate, in topography, in distance from the heart of the campus, and in emphasis on outdoor education make a square-feet-per-student standard difficult to establish.
• It has been estimated by intramural leaders that graduate students participate in physical recreation 25 percent as extensively as undergraduates. Consequently, it is suggested that planners add 25 percent of the graduate enrollment in using the standard.

Ancillary Areas

Investigation indicates that a reasonable standard for determining the space needed for lockers, showers, toweling rooms, equipment storage, supply rooms, and offices associated with type A space is a square footage equaling approximately 40 percent of the play or activity area in a gymnasium facility. As an example of how this figure may be used, assume that a gymnasium is being planned which will provide

100,000 sq ft of activity space. In other words, the square footage in the swimming-pool surface and deck, and all gymnasium floors, including high and low ceiling areas, equals 100,000 sq ft. This would mean that the square footage needed for ancillary areas would be in the neighborhood of 40,000 sq ft. Architects generally speak of the combination of play space and ancillary areas in a gymnasium as "net usable area." Consequently, the net area in the building would be approximately 140,000 sq ft.

All other space in a building, including hallways, stairways, wall thicknesses, lobbies, public toilets, bleachers for public use, custodial space, and space needed for service conduits of all types, is spoken of by many architects as "tare." The space needed for tare varies greatly from building to building, depending upon the function and architectural design. A rough estimate of the area needed for this item is a figure equal to 80 percent of the activity or play area in a gymnasium. By adding tare, ancillary, and play space, a rough estimate of the gross square footage of a gymnasium plan can be computed. This figure is helpful in preliminary discussions of costs involved.

Enrollment Relationships

When standards in terms of square feet per student are used as guides in college or university planning, it is natural to ask where the cut-off begins. At what point, from 10 students up, do the standards become meaningful? Obviously, for a college of 200 students, 9 sq ft per student of indoor area for sports and athletics would be woefully inadequate. It would not even provide one basketball court.

A university or college meeting the space standards for 1,500 students represents the minimum physical-recreation space needs of any collegiate institution. As a college or university increases in size, these standards are applicable regardless of enrollment.

Peak Load After School Hours

Through study of utilization problems at the various universities, it was found that the greatest load on facilities each day occurred between 4 P.M. and 10 P.M. In all the universities studied, either one or two years of physical education was required of all students. As long as the requirement in basic physical education is not greater than 2 years, it seems that the greatest demand for space comes after the usual school hours. This may not be true in universities which require all students to register for physical education each year they are in residence.

A few universities have dropped required physical education in the belief that this will reduce the pressures on facilities for sports and athletics. The futility of this move is obvious. In fact, the elimination of a physical education requirement may increase the demands for this type of space, since all students will then tend to use after-school hours to meet their physical-activity needs. This concentration of student activity will likely make it necessary to provide greater play and exercise space than needed for a balanced program of basic instruction, free-play opportunities, and intramural sports competition.

Application of Standards

Standards are guides for the use of planning committees and administrators. They are not substitutes for creative planning. They help

a great deal in early computations of cost estimates and are also helpful in checking preliminary drawings to determine whether or not enough space has been provided in different categories to meet the program needs of the student enrollment for which the facilities are planned.

FIELD HOUSE

Function

The field house provides enclosed and unobstructed space adaptable to indoor and outdoor sports activities. It is not intended as a substitute for the gymnasium; it is complementary and supplementary to other facilities for indoor and outdoor physical education and recreation activities. The enclosure may also serve purposes other than physical education and recreation.

Typical functions of the field house for a college are as follows: instruction in the service program in physical education; practice for intercollegiate athletics (football, track and field, baseball, basketball, tennis, soccer, lacrosse, and other sports); intramural and intercollegiate competition; informal play; horseback riding; demonstrations and exhibitions which attract large crowds of spectators; commencement exercises; registration; and final examinations. In addition, community uses may include interscholastic games, matches, meets and tournaments; band concerts; school commencement exercises; exhibits; and mass meetings.

The total physical education program, including co-physical education and co-recreation, should be considered when plans are developed, so that facilities for activities such as tennis, volleyball, badminton, and golf practice may be provided. Unless provided in the gymnasium, handball and squash courts should be constructed in the field house. A survey of available facilities for activities common to modern physical education programs will serve to determine the number and kind of activity units to include in the field house.

Location

If needed for class instruction, the preferable location for the field house is adjacent to the main gymnasium building and the natatorium. If space is not available in proximity to the gymnasium, the field house will serve well for intramural activities and intercollegiate sports, even though it is constructed in a peripheral area of the campus. It should, however, be placed in an area contiguous to athletic fields and where parking problems are not critical.

Size

The size of the field house should be determined by careful study of its functions; consideration should be given to the size and number of groups (classes, squads, teams) likely to participate simultaneously in the program. There should be a minimum of interference of groups with each other. The area surrounded by a ⅛-mi track can include the following facilities: a regulation basketball court; a tennis court on each side of the basketball court; broad-jump, high-jump, and pole-vault runways and pits; and a shot-put area.

The minimum length of the field house

COLLEGE AND UNIVERSITY FACILITIES
Field House; Dormitories

should accommodate a 60-yd straightaway for men's track plus sufficient distance for starting and stopping. A wide door at the end of the straightaway to permit competitors to run outside the field house would prevent injuries and eliminate a mental hazard where space is limited. Six regulation lanes are desirable. The track around the portable or permanent basketball floor should be of such size as to be a convenient fraction of a longer standard distance.

Balconies and Bleachers

When permanent balconies are planned, they should be constructed without supporting pillars which would interfere in any way with the playing or visual area. Balconies should be served by ramps which connect directly, or by means of wide corridors, with convenient entrances and exits. Temporary bleachers, when placed in front of and below the permanent balconies, should continue the sight lines of the balconies. Bleachers can be placed inside a $\frac{1}{6}$-mi track on both sides and ends of a basketball court to accommodate approximately 5,000 spectators. Such bleachers should be inspected thoroughly before they are used; their capacity should never be taxed.

The field house should be so designed that normal flow of traffic will not encroach upon the activity areas. It is essential that this be done in order to avoid interference with instruction and participation and to decrease maintenance costs.

Press, Radio, and Scout Accommodations

Accommodations for reporters, sports broadcasters, and scouts should be planned in the original design. Soundproof broadcasting and television booths should be provided for these services when the field house will be used for attractions of considerable public interest.

Entrances

Entrances to the field house should be located with reference to parking facilities and traffic approaches. The main lobby should be large enough to accommodate anticipated crowds seeking tickets and admission. This is particularly important in northern climates. The lobby should be so designed for ticket selling and collecting that the traffic will flow in a straight line, or nearly so, from the entrances to the box offices to the ticket collectors. To avoid congestion, approximately two-thirds of the lobby should be planned for accommodating box offices and ticket purchasers; the remainder should be reserved for ticket holders, who should have direct access to admission gates.

Drinking Fountains

Drinking fountains should be sufficient in number and so located that they do not interfere with the circulation of the crowd.

Service Units

If the field house is adjacent to the main gymnasium building and the natatorium, the requirements for lockers, showers, and toilets can, in some instances, be reduced. An underpass from the gymnasium to the field house may be desirable in order to make the gymnasium service units available to some participants in the field house. If the field house is not adjacent to the gymnasium, consideration

should be given to the erection of a small building or a basement, simple in design, with dressing, shower, and toilet facilities, rather than using space for such purposes which might be utilized more advantageously for activity units.

Convenient and accessible dressing units equipped with chalk and tack boards for the home and visiting teams should be provided. When the field house is to be used for interscholastic basketball tournaments and indoor track meets, consideration should be given to providing separate locker rooms with adjoining shower and toilet facilities. These units could be used regularly throughout the year by intramural participants and intercollegiate squads.

It is desirable to provide passageways from dressing rooms directly to the basketball floor to avoid crowd interference.

A dressing room with adjoining shower and toilet facilities should be provided for staff members. These accommodations can also be used by game officials.

Separate toilet facilities in sufficient number for men and for women spectators should be provided in close proximity to the seating areas. Toilets should be provided near traffic lanes. Where large crowds attend games, it is advisable to place supplementary toilet facilities off the main lobby.

First-Aid and Training Rooms

A room for first-aid treatment should be provided if the field-house program is planned to attract spectators. This room may also serve the purpose of a training room for emergency treatment of participants, and the prevention of injuries.

Lounge and Trophy Room

Provision for a lounge room may be advisable after consideration of such factors as available space and funds, and the functions of such a room for clubs, members of athletic squads, letter men, officials and coaches, and visitors. An adjoining kitchenette is desirable.

Storage Space

Sufficient storage space should be provided to accommodate physical education and maintenance supplies and equipment. Supply rooms, built so that supplies and equipment may be cared for within them and issued from them, should be provided where they are needed.

Concession Booths

When the field house is planned to accommodate large crowds, concession booths should be constructed. They should be equipped with electric or gas stoves, sinks, running water, and sewer connections and should be located where they do not interfere with the normal flow of traffic.

Scoreboards and Timing Devices

Scoreboards and timing devices should be of sufficient number and be so placed that they can be seen readily by players and all spectators. They should be easy to operate and readily accessible for maintenance purposes.

Public-Address System

Provision should be made for the installation of a public-address system. Acoustical treatment of the building is desirable.

Lighting, Heating, and Ventilation

Windows should be equipped with means to prevent the interference of sunlight with player performance at any time during the day. Walls and ceilings should be light in color. Catwalks are necessary for servicing the ceiling lights, spotlights, and net.

Condensation problems should be given major consideration, particularly where there are extremes of temperature, where sprinkling of surface or dirt areas is required, and where large crowds witness events in the field house. As a means whereby some of the excess condensation may be reabsorbed, the building should be heated by the circulation of warm air in addition to fixed radiation. Adequate means should be provided to supply fresh air and to exhaust foul air. The walls inside and outside should be impervious to vapor pressure. Technical heating, ventilating, and lighting problems should be referred to a specialist.

Floors

The floor of the field house should be of an all-weather-resistant construction. Rubber asphalt and several patented rubberlike synthetics should be considered. A portable wood floor for basketball may be used. Dirt floors are not recommended.

DORMITORIES

Area Requirements for Student Room Furniture

1. Furniture sizes and use spaces are the average for existing furnishings.
2. Each furniture layout assumes the item(s) placed along a wall.

Use Space The use space of one item may overlap the use space of another, but no use space should overlap an adjacent item of furniture.

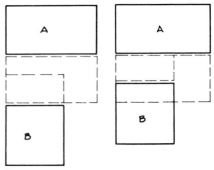

Fig. 1

Designations An item of furniture automatically requires additional space around it to make its use possible. This space should be allowed for in the planning of the room.

User Requirements, URBS Publication 5, University Residential Building System, University of California, Berkeley, Calif., 1969.

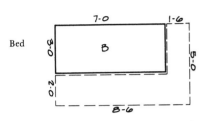

Bed

Desk

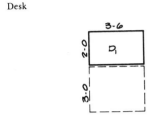

Desk

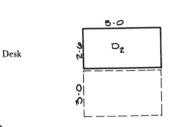

Fig. 2

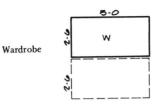

Wardrobe

Door

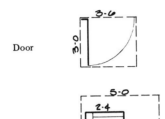

Soft Chair

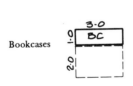

Bookcases

the room. If it is desirable to move the bed from one section to the other, the two sections will be approximately equal in size. If it is not desirable, the interchangeability of other pieces of furniture will control the dimensions and size of each section of the room.

d. An offset room will increase the possibility of space divisibility. In a rectangular room, the items must create the space; in an offset room the walls divide the space.

Student Rooms The student room is the smallest element and the basic space in the housing facility. It is the core environment of the student who spends many of his waking hours here (undergraduate girls, 8 hr; boys, 6 hr). In this space the student studies, sleeps, dresses, and socializes. He stores all of his clothes, books, and personal possessions here except for non-seasonal clothing and larger-size sports equipment. In a very real sense, it is here that his identity within the university is established, since it is the only space on campus which he himself can control in any way.

1. *Study.* Individual study is accomplished within an amazing spectrum of activities. It takes place while standing, walking, sitting, lying, singing, whistling, eating, drinking—alone or with another person. Few participate in group studying.

People study at different rates. Some subject themselves to long periods of monklike concentration; others apply themselves for relatively short periods interspersed with intervals of social or recreational activity. The individual prefers to study in his own room and, for intense study, by himself. For this type of study, the roommate must be elsewhere.

The desk apparently is used for reading only in cases requiring extensive note-taking or use of several reference sources. Otherwise, it is a repository for study and personal equipment including typewriters, calculators, drafting equipment, radios, and phonographs. Yet it does not have the height accommodations or acoustical padding needed to use these materials quietly and effectively. Its length is inadequate for any use—the 42 in. standard desk is overtaxed with books and writing material [as well as] personal paraphernalia. The space requirements for multiple references, collation of materials, or large belongings create overflow onto the bed or floor. Consequently, work is often done on the floor of the room, particularly if it is carpeted, and on the bed.

Sometimes an apparent student idiosyncrasy has a real functional basis. Many students were observed typing on the floor when an adequate table was available. The students then demonstrated the drumlike sound of the unmuffled typewriter which conflicted with their roommate's sleeping. Students often used the corridors and bathrooms as study spaces when typing and study rooms were missing or occupied and roommates were sleeping.

Bookshelves are generally inadequate in size and length. Moreover, the shelves are usually in places of difficult access and are poorly illuminated. There is a need for more shelves, preferably adjustable and flexible as to placement.

Built-in furnishings are resented because their rigidity impedes both individual living and study habits. Students are forced to supplement the university furnishings with such things as orange crates to create an individual study environment. The results may appear cluttered to some, but they accommodate the occupant. Clearly then, a book, pen, reading light, straight back chair, and a 42-in.-long desk

Planning Studies—Single and Double Rooms

General
1. Room dimensions must accommodate:
   a. Furniture sizes and design (wall mounted, freestanding)
   b. Furniture use spaces
   c. Combination of furniture items
2. Room size (and shape) will affect two levels of possible room change:
   a. Adaptability of furniture arrangements
   b. Divisibility of spaces—physical or visual separation of activities

Room Areas
1. Definition of terms used:
   a. *Minimum*—access to furniture items; overlap of items and use space; some restriction in the use of furniture.
   b. *Optimum*—no overlap of items and use space
   c. *Generous*—beginning of space divisibility
2. Single Rooms
   a. Minimum recommended area—90 sq ft
   b. Optimum recommended area—110 sq ft
   c. Generous recommended area—120 sq ft

3. Double rooms with bunked beds
   a. Minimum recommended area—140 sq ft
   b. Optimum recommended area—160 sq ft
   c. Generous recommended area—180 sq ft
4. Double rooms without bunked beds
   a. Minimum recommended area—180 sq ft
   b. Optimum recommended area—220 sq ft
   c. Generous recommended area—240 sq ft

Offset Single Rooms
1. Conclusions
   a. The area of the room with an offset may be comparable to a rectangular room with little or no loss in the adaptability of furniture.
   b. If dimensions of the room and furniture sizes share a common module, an offset room may have a slightly greater amount of furniture adaptability than a rectangular room of equal area.
   c. In an offset room, the controlling object is the bed in determining the proportional areas of the two sections of

COLLEGE AND UNIVERSITY FACILITIES
Dormitories

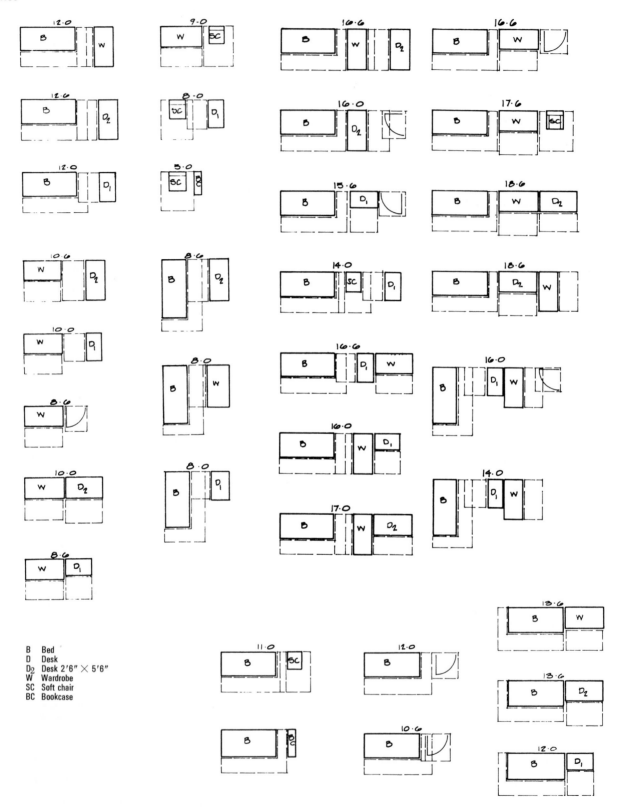

B   Bed
D   Desk
D_2 Desk 2'6" × 5'6"
W   Wardrobe
SC   Soft chair
BC   Bookcase

Fig. 3   Examples of furniture layouts depicting some possible arrangements involved in the planning of the student room.

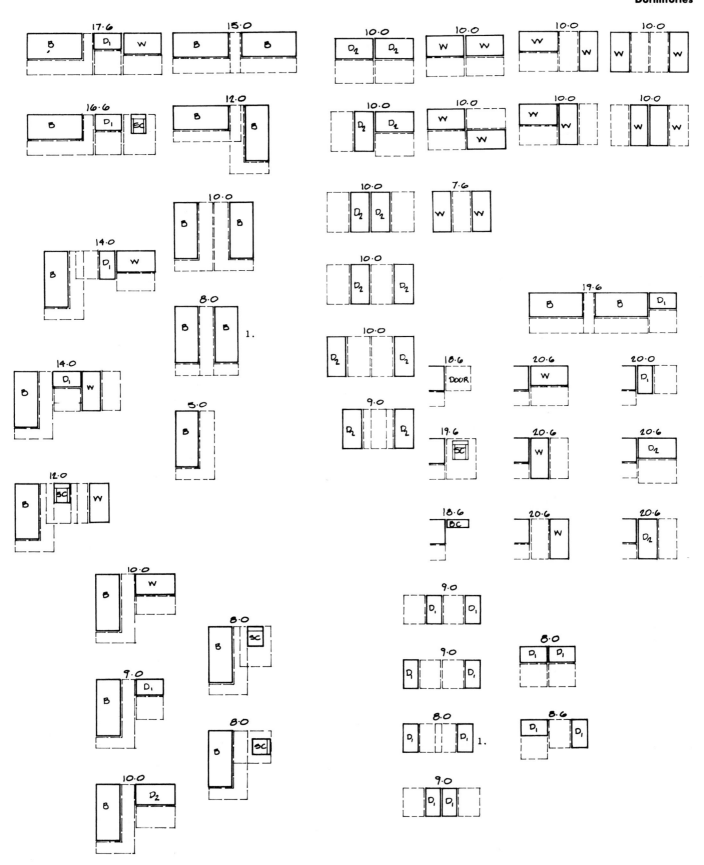

Fig. 3 (cont.) Examples of furniture layouts depicting some possible arrangements involved in the planning of the student room.

COLLEGE AND UNIVERSITY FACILITIES
Dormitories

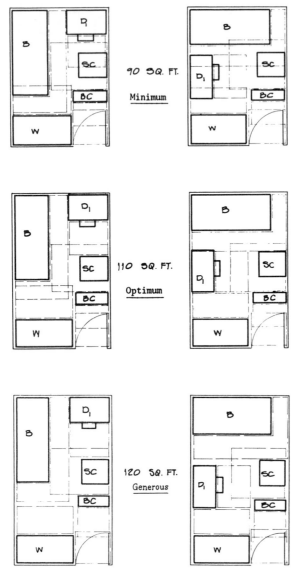

Fig. 4 Diagrammatic arrangements rectangular rooms, single rooms.

constitute less than the optimum answer to the study problem.

The telephone is a most important tool to the student. Its use is restricted only by the university's ability to provide an individual instrument and the student's ability to pay the toll. The telephone is finding increased use—both as a study and a social aid.

The tremendous and continuing advances of the electronics industry are only beginning to be noted in the educational sector. Although the student of today is required to attend unilateral communication lectures in large halls, the student of tomorrow may view the lecture on TV in his room, coming out for seminars or laboratory sessions. Future student housing must accommodate this.

The students of all campuses could simultaneously be able to receive the lecture of one outstanding professor or professional team. Much of this communication will be at the discretion of the student. It is but one indication of the growing importance of the student room as a study aid. Only the provision of conduit access is needed to expand the horizons of the student room beyond imagination.

2. *Sleep.* The student's pattern of activity is rarely consistent; he may sleep at any time of the day or night. Two occupants of a room very rarely follow the same schedule. Exams and social activities modify their patterns even more extensively. It is the varying patterns that present conflicts in multiple-occupancy rooms. Interesting improvisations—hanging blankets, relocated wardrobes and beds, and stacked dressers—were observed in situations where one student wished to study while the other slept. Perhaps beds with suitable acoustical light-separation screens could be one answer; single-occupancy rooms would be better.

Present provisions for sleeping range from the studio bed in single rooms to bunkable beds in multi-occupancy rooms. Beds acquired a decade ago are increasingly limiting to the succeeding generations of taller students. Reading is more often done in the comparatively relaxed attitude of the bed or easy chair. However, the bed is seldom designed to pro-

vide the slight slope for proper sitting; some adjustment therefore is necessary. Beds could be made to resemble couches and have a mechanism allowing a shift from sloping for sitting to level for sleeping position.

3. *Socializing.* The student's room has always attracted social discourse. With more liberal rules, the student's room becomes more of a social center for both sexes. The student room, however, with its split emphasis of study-sleep, presents difficulties as a social environment. The bed is the chief offender. The bed as a bed conjures all sorts of social problems in intervisitation. A bed with cushions or pillows tossed about is not acceptable because of the difficulty of sitting upright comfortably. Its conversion to a sofa, with its contributions as a living room furnishing, is most desirable—not to mention its more comfortable use for multiple seating.

Clothes and storage of personal possessions are also a bedroom symbol. Closets look like closets; dressers look like dressers. Contemporary furniture designers, however, have provided storage units for studio-apartment [which are] quite acceptable as living room pieces. Such pieces have yet to make their appearance in student rooms. It should be possible to have either intimate conversations or sessions with a number of additional individuals within one's own private room. The bed, hard and soft chairs, and even a desk top may be brought into use as sitting surfaces to accommodate a congenial group. The space should be such that furniture can be quickly arranged to make group conversation easy.

4. *Dressing.* The concentration of clothes storage in the student room not only precludes its use as a social environment but also restricts its use for dressing. One study discloses that the normal 4-ft closet and five-drawer dresser just satisfies the male student, and it provides only half the female student's storage requirements. Both sexes require differing volumes and types of storage. Smaller combination-storage units might well accommodate student preference and allow flexibility of room arrangement.

Types of Spaces

1. *Single rooms.* The single room provides controlled privacy for its occupant with respect to all other students. It may open directly to a corridor and thus provide complete privacy coming and going, or it may be part of a suite or apartment. Privacy for sleeping can be controlled if adequate acoustic separation between adjacent spaces is provided.

The single room should be arranged suitably so that it is possible to study effectively with an invited second person. In addition, the student should be able to play the radio, phonograph, tape recorder, or quiet instruments and to indulge in reasonable recreational activity without creating an acoustical problem for his neighbors.

One authority believes the single room is "unlikely to be really humanely satisfactory if it is less than 120 square feet. The furniture should be movable, not fixed, to allow the student to organize his own environment."

2. *Split double rooms.* The split double room provides the social contact obtained by two students sharing a common space but, at the same time, recognizes and solves the problem of conflict of interest in the student's social and study activities. The split double room consists of two spaces with a connecting opening. When connected with a door, there is a degree of acoustic privacy. Without a door, the ar-

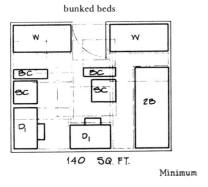

bunked beds

140 SQ. FT.

Minimum

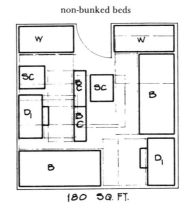

non-bunked beds

180 SQ. FT.

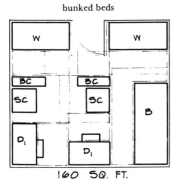

bunked beds

160 SQ. FT.

Optimum

non-bunked beds

220 SQ. FT.

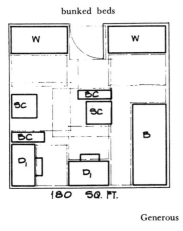

bunked beds

180 SQ. FT.

Generous

non-bunked beds

240 SQ. FT.

Fig. 5 Diagrammatic arrangements rectangular rooms, double rooms.

rangement provides only visual privacy and shielding from illumination sources. The provision of two spaces makes it possible for one student to sleep while the other studies or talks with friends.

The best arrangement would permit the students to treat each of the two spaces as a single room with direct communication between them. Then the spaces may be separated on an activity basis, with the desks, study, and living facilities in one space and sleeping and dressing facilities in the other. When one of the two spaces is large and the other small in size, the students live together much as they would with-

in a traditional double room. Where the habits of two students come into conflict, the second smaller space can relieve the situation. For example, the second room can provide for a late-hour study station. This type of arrangement will not necessarily suffice to provide the appropriate separation between social and sleeping habits, but it may do so if the smaller space has sufficient room for an extra chair.

If two students must share space, the split double represents an optimum arrangement, because easy choice exists for privacy or sociability.

Here again, the space with the two beds should have the atmosphere of a sitting room so that one is not consciously in a bedroom.

3. *Double rooms.* The double room is the present standard in student housing, largely because of the tradition and economies it presumably brings to initial construction costs. This economy is deceptive, however. Since these rooms irritate their inhabitants because of lack of privacy and quiet and because of insufficient study and storage space, it becomes necessary to provide typing rooms, individual study carrels, and large public lounges (furniture showrooms). These factors should be considered when citing the economies of the standard double-room residence hall.

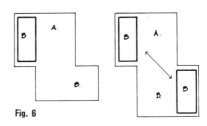

Fig. 6

At present, the area of a double room varies between 145 and 250 sq ft. Within these areas, possibilities for alternative furniture layouts and room shapes are particularly important. Some room configurations make possible the separation of the two students in their study activities; others situate the desks in parallel arrangements for study. The use of movable wardrobes to shield the beds from desks provides the degree of separation between activities within a room but reduces the apparent size of the room. Wardrobes which are grouped to provide dressing alcoves or to line corridors remove valuable space from the room itself. If double rooms are to be provided, there should be sufficient area to convert them into split-double, single, or other types of rooms in the future. *More than enough conventional double facilities already exist on most campuses.*

4. *Triple room.* This form has been popular with some students on a small number of campuses. Where this arrangement has been used with movable furniture, the extra area provided in the single space has made possible a large number of different space arrangements. The resulting individuality of the layout of the room would appear to be a major reason for the popularity of such spaces, since some students do seem to prefer a three-student to a two-student room. The triple room, however, tends to breed more serious interpersonal problems.

5. *Four-student room.* Four students sharing one room have the same problems as the students sharing double- or triple-occupancy rooms. There is a slight advantage in that the space is usually large enough to be subdi-

COLLEGE AND UNIVERSITY FACILITIES
Dormitories

vided by wardrobes, lightweight partitions, and other elements.

Although few students would choose to live in a single space with three other strangers, four friends might choose to be together and succeed at it *if provided* sufficient options for the disposition of the space and for the appropriate screening of different activities.

Large numbers of students may share a space, but more than four require that separate adjacent spaces be provided for conflicting activities. At this point, one must consider the suite plan.

6. *Suites.* A suite is an arrangement in which four or more students share the total space in single and double rooms, with or without a bathroom, and at least one extra common space. In this way, the group of students working and living together have at least one space under their own control which may be used for any of the three major facets of room life: sleep, study, or social activities. "The major value of the suite plan is the opportunity it affords for closer student association and the freedom it gives students using the various spaces as they wish." The common space within a suite (1) reduces some of the pressures felt by two students trying to share a single room; (2) provides for social activities as does a residential living room, and (3) includes in social activities those students who might not have direct or easy association with other students.

The sharing of a fair amount of space by a group of students makes possible a variety of usage patterns and provides considerable flexibility in room rearrangement so the space may be organized in the best possible way.

Typical patterns are a common room also used as a study room; one room used only for sleeping, with separate rooms for study and social purposes; and four single rooms or two double rooms with a common living room.

Suites composed of single rooms rather than double rooms increase the potential for privacy. However, if one desires a separate room for each student, additional square footage above that normally required for four students will be necessary. This space can be regained through a reduction in the large lounge spaces on the ground floor.

Another way to obtain sufficient area for a suite is to incorporate some corridor space in the common room. Corridors may not be necessary for a four-student suite; therefore, this approach works best when perhaps eight or ten students share a suite. A major problem in optimum use of the common room of a suite concerns doors that do not provide sufficient acoustical separation between the common room and the individual's room. In such a case, spaces for study outside the suite become necessary.

Bathroom facilities pose one of the major questions in the design of suites: should these facilities be available just for the suite or for a larger group of students? Although initially it is less expensive to build gang facilities for larger groups, long-term economy can be obtained by providing residential-scale bathrooms for suites wherein students, instead of maids, clean the facility. The reduction in maintenance requirements will more than amortize the increased first cost of smaller bath facilities, while also considerably improving the human quality of the housing environment for the student.

Suites must also be considered for the social impact resulting from them. Students developing a strong social life around the activities of their suite may have less incentive to make friends outside their circle. Objections might be

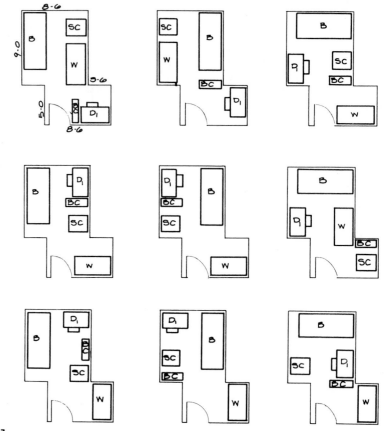

Fig. 7

posed for this reason, especially in regard to freshman students who desire maximum opportunities to meet fellow students.

Another problem in suites composed of four to seven students is the possibility that strong friendship patterns may have a detrimental influence on a student's academic life. The peer group pressure to go out for coffee or a hamburger is quite strong on one out of six. Riesman notes this "encapsulation." One size of an encapsulated group has been equated with the six occupants of an automobile. Therefore, the organization of space into suites must be such that the students in different suites may interrelate. If, for example, three suites of six students share a larger living room so that a group of eighteen have something in common, it is quite unlikely that a small group desiring a coffee break could interrupt the study pattern of the other eleven. More likely, they will find only one or two others willing to go along.

The shared living room also provides a larger base for friends and tends to reduce stress. The value of grouping students into a suite where an ordered pattern of relationships may develop (first with a roommate or perhaps with two or four additional students and then with a larger number) provides some balance in the way outside attachments are formed. Such relationships are not well studied at this time and the patterns of change in the future may be very considerable. *Therefore an approach to the use of suites should leave open the maximum number of options for future living patterns.*

Within the suite it is important to organize the common spaces so that privacy is maintained between the sleeping rooms and the bathroom. Problems occur where the common room(s) in a suite may be open for coed activities and it is necessary to pass through the

common area when going between one's room and bathroom.

With eight or more students in double rooms, more than one common space in a suite is required. At least one separate study as well as a social room should be provided to accommodate privacy for study and typing late at night and the noisy social sessions that inevitably occur within a suite. Obviously, single rooms designed so that privacy may be maintained represent the most ideal solution.

If the suite is entered through a common space, this space is useful only for purposes where quiet and privacy are not essential. Attempts to provide a combined living-study room in the suite are not successful because students soon revert to using their bedrooms for study. The suite telephone must not interfere with study activities.

7. *Apartments.* An apartment differs from the suite in providing a kitchen. It may consist of single or double rooms built around common spaces as in a suite, or it may have a number of students in a sleeping room with the other spaces in common for social, dining, and study purposes.

A consensus of opinion among students indicates that three to five single students form an optimum group for apartment living. This number tends to work well in arranging cooking chores for the week, with weekends left on an individual basis. With more than five students, assignment of cooking chores becomes difficult. Indiana University and Michigan State University have extremely popular facilities accommodating four students.

Some students believe they get better food at less cost if they do their own cooking and shopping. Therefore, the apartment requires adequate food supply capacity to handle a week's supply of groceries. The apartment's dining area must be of a size to permit the occupants to have dinner guests.

Experience indicates that most students living in apartments tire of the responsibility of cooking and cleaning. It would seem appropriate to develop central food service to relieve apartment groups of the cooking chores while still retaining the benefits of apartment-type living.

For example, Indiana University has two living groups of 60 students having common kitchen facilities with another residence hall which provides the food service of the small living unit. Trolleys containing food for 60 students are wheeled from the central kitchen to the serving kitchen within the living units. All services and cleanup are then handled by the living units at a very considerable savings in cost. These two facilities are the most popular ones on the entire campus.

Much of the attraction of the apartment is its comparative freedom from behavioral control, particularly in regard to coeducational activities. This does not mean complete relinquishment of responsibility on the part of the university but rather the more positive recognition of the student's adult qualities.

Students living in apartments tend to develop a very close relationship with those sharing the space. It is a pattern perhaps more appropriate for upper division and graduate students than it is for lower division students. These students have developed a range of acquaintances on a campus and now are interested in cultivating specific friendships. Apartments, like suites, can be grouped to provide activities through combined use of spaces for recreation, study, and social affairs so that a wide range of friendship is possible.

Since the key difference between the suite and the apartment is the kitchen, provision should be included in suites for a plug-in kitchenette so that conversion from suite to apartment may be accomplished quickly. This will enhance flexibility of use during the summer sessions for conferences involving families or for foreign students.

Space Allocation

1. *Dimensions of student rooms.* Rooms of minimum size cause many complaints from students; this was reflected in both the URBS and another recent study. The situation has changed a great deal in the past 25 years. Stern Hall at Berkeley was built in 1940 and allowed 480 gross sq ft per student with 250 sq ft in the student room. Present rooms of 85–95 sq ft per student create serious problems of constriction.

Built-in furnishings compound this problem by preventing an expressive control by students of the layout of their rooms. Movable furniture, in most instances, would not alleviate the problem because the small room size dictates only one possible arrangement. The need for expression is so important to the student that he sometimes resorts to an irrational layout, such as placing the bed across the door opening, in an effort to control his environment.

The allocation of space will be the decision of the campus. Adequate space allocation within the student room must have first priority so that enough space is provided to allow both immediate individual expression by the student and future arrangement by the university.

Several studies have recommended that a single student room of rectangular shape contain 100 to 115 sq ft. The rationale for this recommendation is that a room must contain enough space to provide the student with (1)

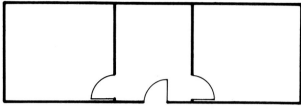

COMMON LIVING ROOM, TWO DOUBLE ROOMS.

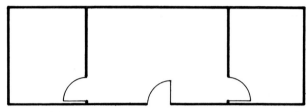

COMBINED SOCIAL AND STUDY ROOMS, SEPARATE SLEEPING.

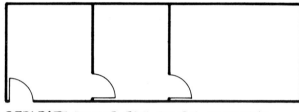

SEPARATE ROOMS FOR STUDY, SLEEPING, AND SOCIAL.

Fig. 8 Suite organization 1.

the furniture he needs, (2) space for the use and service of this furniture (make beds or open drawers), and (3) possibility of a variety of furniture layouts.

Environment

1. *Thermal.* Student rooms require an appropriate thermal environment for the functions carried on within them. The environment is affected by temperature, ventilation, humidity, radiation, and the quality of air produced by filtration.

The thermal system in student housing allows for individual requirements and the wide range of conditions which personal preference may demand. In a mixed community of smokers and nonsmokers, it is important that the air be kept moving and clean, particularly in student rooms, interior spaces, lounges, and study areas. Because of variations in student hygiene,

TABLE 1   Recommended Space Standards per Student from a Group of Recent Studies

University	ASF[a]		OGSF[b]	
	Single	Double	No dining	With dining
University of California[c]	100	100	239	265
California State Colleges[d]	94–110.5	84–91	215.5	230.5
University of Guelph[e]	115	NR	230	
University of Pennsylvania[f]	108	NR	271.5	290
M.I.T.[g]	140		470	486
Aggregate United States[h]				
Men	. . .	96.7	211.1	234.7
Women	. . .	103.5	237.4	261.4

[a] Assignable square feet per student.
[b] Outside gross square feet per student.
[c] University of California. UC Standing Committee on Residence Halls, Meeting of August 29 and 30, 1966, Hilton Inn, San Francisco International Airport.
[d] Development Guide for Campus Housing, California State Colleges, July 1968, Table 1, Summary of Project Norms, p. 13.
[e] University of Guelph Student Housing Study, Evan H. Walker, Student Housing Consultant, November 1965, pp. 56–66.
[f] University of Pennsylvania. Study of Undergraduate Men's Housing System, Geddes, Brecher, Qualls and Cunningham, Architectural Consultants.
[g] Massachusetts Institute of Technology. A Program for Undergraduate Men's Housing, MIT Planning Office, August 1965.
[h] Eugene E. Higgins, M. Louise Steward, and Linda Wright, Residence Hall Planning Aids, Report OE-51004-9A, College and University Physical Facility Series, Department of Health, Education and Welfare, U.S. Office of Education, Washington, D.C.

COLLEGE AND UNIVERSITY FACILITIES
Dormitories

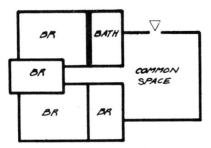

ACCESS TO STUDENT ROOMS
THROUGH COMMON SPACE.

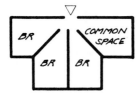

SEPARATE ACCESS TO STUDENT ROOMS
AND COMMON SPACE.

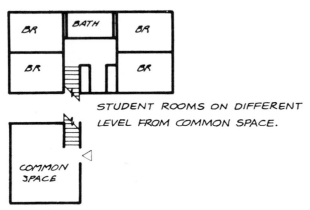

STUDENT ROOMS ON DIFFERENT
LEVEL FROM COMMON SPACE.

Fig. 9 Suite organization 2.

separate ventilation of individual spaces is required, especially in the more athletic men's halls. The odors in many residence halls were found by visitors to be "overpowering."

Although conventional air conditioning is more economical within a sealed space, it is important that students be able to open their windows to enjoy the soft, fresh morning and evening air, and in the lower-height buildings to enjoy communication (but not access) through an open window.

2. *Lighting.* The quality of lighting in student rooms is determined by the quantity and brightness of both the light sources and their general surroundings. High illumination levels are appropriate to study; lower levels to social functions. In the daytime, natural daylight may provide much of the necessary illumination if windows are well placed and the glare eliminated. However, high illumination levels are necessary in areas where concentrated study is to be done, but the brightness contrast between the work and its surroundings must be at a minimum.

Lighting sources in student rooms should be integrated with the movable furnishings. This tends to minimize maintenance and fix the light's proper level. Light for reading in bed, in-

cluding a reading light for a bunk bed, is necessary. Because of the highly individualized nature of activities performed in student rooms, light from a number of well-placed but relocatable point sources is far more useful than light from one central source.

3. *Acoustics.* Quiet is the most desired characteristic of any living arrangement in the opinion of students, so acoustical considerations are of great importance. Fundamental to providing quiet environments are walls, floors, windows, and doors providing adequate reduction of sound from adjacent activities. Doors do not facilitate noise reduction. Since standard doors are poor in acoustic performance and high-performance doors are too expensive for student housing use, a solution isolating noise at low cost will have to be developed. The best inhibitor of noise is good planning of the relationships between rooms. Wherever possible, social areas should be isolated from student rooms by at least two doors.

4. *Color, texture, materials.* Materials presently used are hard, unyielding, and chosen for their durability and ease of maintenance. However, those used invariably lead to a depressing, sterile, institutional appearance.

The student's need for expression and the

university's need for ease of maintenance need not conflict. Walls can be covered with safe, removable wall-covering panels that provide the student with unrestricted freedom of color and decoration. At the same time, these wall coverings can still protect the underlying materials to the university's satisfaction. It should be possible for the student to roll up his wall coverings at the conclusion of use and use them again elsewhere if desired.

Such panels would allow women students to compensate for the universal institutional aspect of student housing by softening the environment through the use of feminine colors, textures, and materials.

It was observed that in rooms with hard walls, pinup materials are often fastened to the softer acoustical tile ceilings. Resawn wood wall panels, however, would permit unrestricted tacking up of decorations.

It was noted that carpeted residence halls are far more quiet and that the behavior of the student was more adult. Since many study and social activities are performed on the floor, the comfort and quiet provided by carpeting are quite desirable.

5. *Appliances.* A revolution in the design, production, and marketing of economical personal appliances has been occurring in recent years. As a result, the number of electrical appliances brought by the student to college invariably exceeds the number anticipated by the designers of present-day residence halls. Consequently, this has precipitated problems of general safety, fire hazards, intolerable odor, noise levels, and frequent interruption of electrical services.

Another significant new trend is in the personalization of entertainment and cultural media; tape recorders, radios, phonographs, and miniature TV sets are within the economic reach of most students. The transistor radio permits the student to listen to the world beyond the campus even as he walks from one class to another. Similarly, the personal, transistorized TV is making the TV room out of date, just when most residence halls are specifically providing such space.

Hot plates, coffee pots, and popcorn poppers are sources of potential fire hazards and odors. At the minimal level of food service, there is need for facilities enabling students to make their own coffee. This requires but an appropriate surface and an outlet, with the student providing the appliance. At the next level is a desire for cold drink storage facilities. Students will sometimes buy old refrigerators—often hazardous and awkward in size and arrangement. The idea of partitioned refrigerators, as in English residence halls where students may keep track of their own belongings, would seem to be a good solution. The minimal cooking done on a hot plate introduces the need for clean-up facilities. The sink becomes necessary; the problem becomes one of the minimal kitchen facility—a project expensive enough to require careful consideration of how many students it is going to serve. Where such kitchens are provided in addition to full food service facilities, they must inevitably be few and far between. Women are far more interested than men in such a facility.

Television, radios, tape recorders, stereos, movie projectors, and phonographs create disturbing noises for others. These require, in most buildings, extensive and expensive noise abatement policing. The better solution to the problem of appliance noise, previously mentioned, is good planning for adequate isolation between rooms.

Most of all, new buildings must recognize the evolution of electrical use by providing initial high capacity with provision for easily adding to that capacity with minimum disruption.

Facilities

1. *Bathing.* The gang bath is one of the most persistent features of residence halls. It has been defended on the basis of economy and its contribution to socialization.

Certainly, the initial construction cost of one central gang bath is less than that of smaller installations in several locations. It is also evident that when a bathroom serves more than a few students, maintenance becomes nobody's business but the university's; the student does not realize that he is paying extra for the university's maintenance of the gang bathroom. The initial extra expense for smaller baths will actually result in long-term cost savings if the students themselves maintain the smaller bathroom, because it eliminates the need for maid service throughout the life of the building.

Another economic factor against the gang bath is its inflexibility. Residence halls with gang baths are far less appropriate for participants in conventions, reunions, and institutes where families or both sexes are involved than are areas with smaller baths serving a few persons.

2. *Dining.* There is universal agreement that the single, large rooms for hundreds of students is not the satisfactory solution to the problem of student dining facilities. Although the large kitchen with its extensive equipment, service line arrangements, and building area is the most economical and efficient method of food preparation, the one large dining room for all students negates a congenial atmosphere for social interaction during mealtime.

Dining facilities that combine the best advantage of the large kitchen—efficiency, economy, and flexibility—while at the same time providing a pleasant and social dining environment can be built. Proper planning permits large central areas to be divided by movable walls into smaller or intimate dining rooms. The walls can be moved when a large scale is needed for social events such as dances, etc.

Food preparation in student rooms presents a safety and sanitary problem, but the need for between-meal snacks can be solved independently of the central dining room. Students can be accommodated by automatic vending machines located at strategic points in the residence hall or by provision of facilities in which they can prepare snacks themselves. Student food preparation problems cannot be solved by unenforceable prohibitions but only by construction of appropriate areas with automatic cooking devices and controlled food storage facilities.

3. *Recreation and social activity.* Assimilation into the student society is the foremost concern of most new students. Recreational spaces and facilities are important in providing environmental support to the personal interaction of students, both new and old, since academic assimilation and involvement are not restricted to the classroom or student room. However, care must be taken in the areas programmed for recreation so that they truly accommodate the intended activities. Otherwise, the spaces will fail to accomplish the intended purposes. Evaluation of the success of social spaces in meeting their intended needs indicates that a variety of smaller spaces are likely to be the most popular and useful.

Student complaints are universal concerning the typical residence hall's main lounge. It has been relatively unpopular with students because of its large size and lack of individualized space. The tendency is for this space to become monopolized by one small group, or even one couple, making other individuals or groups hesitant to intrude. A recent study shows that 32 percent of student residents use the lounges less than once a week and that 36 percent of them use the lounge only one to three times a week. The lounge fails because it cannot simultaneously accommodate incompatible activities. The piano, TV set, and sofa are not appropriate companions. The main lounge, furnished with expensive, hotel-like furnishings, is usually designed, and is mainly suited, for large, quiet groups. It is seldom used by the students for entertaining friends.

The suite living room can accommodate both quiet and active uses, although conflict occurs when the space attempts to serve socializing and study.

Small "date" rooms, as observed on some campuses, are popular when not overly supervised. However, date rooms seem to be an artificial solution to a problem better solved by a wider range of social rooms.

Television rooms are losing their effectiveness as social centers because the diminishing cost of television sets makes it possible for students to have individual sets in floor lounges or in their rooms.

Spaces allowing vigorous activity are important to all students, especially men. At present, such activities (if provided for) are usually located in drab, ill-equipped basements. In those residence halls where suitable spaces are accessible to food sources and open occasionally to both sexes, they are very popular and used continuously.

The comparison of expenses for furnishings between main lounges and recreation spaces shows the latter to be less expensive. Since main lounges are infrequently used, money spent on them is largely wasted. To provide more useful variety than is now available, the question of area allocation to main lounge—recreational spaces should be carefully considered.

One way to provide close at hand recreational space is to equip the rooftops of residence halls for recreational activities. Problems arise in regard to construction, cost, controlling vents, and flues; nevertheless, rooftops are a desirable location for many activities.

Another important form of recreation, but seldom provided for, is student hobbies. The mess and equipment involved in many hobbies suggest that perhaps older utility buildings on campus could provide spaces for these activities. It is more difficult to foresee the needs of hobbyists and expensive to introduce into residence halls the sufficient acoustically isolated spaces for them.

4. *Cultural.* Residence halls can participate in the overall academic environment of the university with the inclusion of facilities for library, music, and discussion. It is part of the

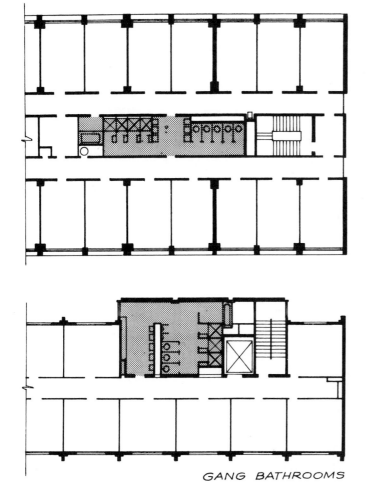

GANG BATHROOMS

0   10   20   30

Fig. 10

COLLEGE AND UNIVERSITY FACILITIES
Dormitories

job of housing to smooth the transition from green freshmen to sophisticated seniors. At Harvard University, house libraries relieve some pressure on central facilities, creating a sense of academic community as well as making books more readily available. Inexpensive paperback libraries are quite adequate for providing both stimulating and enjoyable reading materials within a residential atmosphere. Eventually these libraries will include random-access listening stations; it is therefore advisable to initially provide adequate distribution access into the structure.

Music rooms can also serve as tape and record libraries, although the centrally located equipment will be used less frequently as more students can afford their own equipment. All music involves a noise factor which must be considered.

Formal academic classes in residence halls present difficulties in mechanical services and density beyond the capability of most residence hall structures, but informal classes and seminars can be successfully held in the social spaces in the hall.

5. *Service and storage.* The university must provide facilities for (1) maintenance of buildings, (2) the mechanical and electrical equipment, and (3) overflow storage from student rooms.

Increasing affluence of students and the growth of disposable articles have increased space requirements for efficient trash collection and removal. Trash chutes, central collection facilities, and dumping trucks are required to handle present volumes of trash. Too often this involves the ugly exposure of the trash while awaiting collection, as well as the considerable fire hazard.

Efficient maintenance of electrical and mechanical systems requires easy access without the invasion of student privacy. Equipment should be so located.

Out-of-season and seldom-used student property is usually stored in inexpensive areas of a building, but these are often the least accessible. This situation could be relieved by more adequate storage provisions in the student room. Student and service storage should be in separate areas and away from heavy traffic areas such as laundry and recreation rooms. Bike shelters, surfboards, skis, and scuba gear present spatial storage problems that require careful consideration. All student storage areas must be lockable.

6. *Circulation and interrelation of spaces.* The residence hall is a social organism. The relationship of student rooms one to another and to the public and service rooms make up a total environment most conveniently studied as a hierarchy of spaces. The hierarchy is determined by the student activities and the physical characteristics of the building. Following is a hierarchy of typical unit sizes in university housing:

Student unit	Students
Room	1–2
Suite	4–12
Group	16–24
House or floor	48–72
Hall, building or college	120–800
Complex of halls	1,200–4,800
Campus	12,000–27,500

Unit size is defined by building spaces, activities related to space, and by agents of regulation and control. For example, a number of rooms served by a bathroom constitutes a suite, group, or floor. A number of rooms under the direction of a resident assistant will estab-

lish a unit. All the rooms on one floor having common access and services may also be considered as a unit.

The predominant traditional pattern is the familiar double-loaded corridor arrangement wherein the unit is one floor of a residence hall. This plan offers easy control opportunities. With a group of 48 to 72 students, it facilitates the organization of intramural and academic activities. Another source of group size derivation is the optimum number sharing bathroom facilities.

Efficient space utilization requires that the circulation area comprise the smallest possible percentage of the total area. Studies of existing student housing show the efficiency percentage varying from 7 percent to 25 percent. Although it is advantageous to reduce circulation areas, building safety codes prescribe minimum areas and arrangements. Corridors which are mean, cramped, and possibly dangerous in an emergency are not acceptable.

Economy is the obvious feature of double-loaded corridors because core plans require more circulation area. When each student has a single room, economy of circulation space is difficult since each room must have a window on the periphery of the building. This arrangement, in its simplest configuration, requires extremely long frontages. Irregular building configurations to reduce corridor space must be considered in a cost context also.

Elevators for freight and disabled students are useful in all buildings. In high-rise buildings, passenger elevators are essential, although they tend to make insular entities of each floor. This problem can be reduced by skip-stop elevators stopping at unit lounges linking two floors. The initial expense of good elevators is not offset by cheap ones requiring much maintenance. Competent servicing can be provided by including maintenance contracts in purchase agreements. The better service an elevator gives, the less likely it is to be

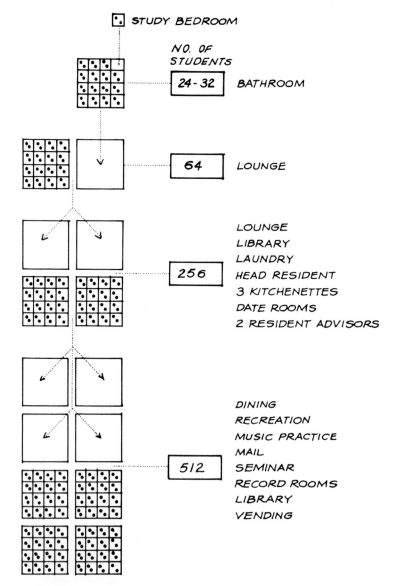

HIERARCHY DIAGRAM.
DOUBLE LOADED CORRIDOR, HIGH RISE BUILDING.

Fig. 11

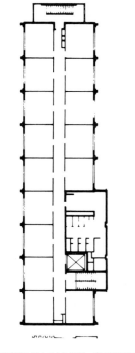

DOUBLE LOADED CORRIDOR

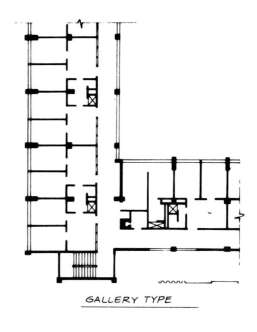

GALLERY TYPE

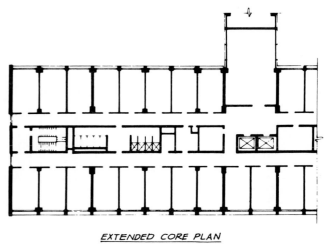

EXTENDED CORE PLAN

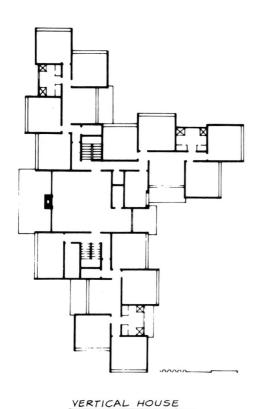

VERTICAL HOUSE

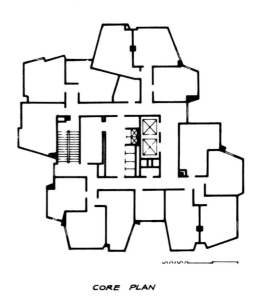

CORE PLAN

Fig. 12 Basic room-hall plan types.

COLLEGE AND UNIVERSITY FACILITIES
Dormitories

abused. Elevator switches, as common targets of student pranks, must be tamper-proof. Escalators are too expensive and have far too great a passenger capacity to be viable alternatives in residence halls.

The location and intensity of such fixed facilities as baths, stairs, and elevators are the main inhibitors of future rearrangement. The URBS approach permits choice based on requirements rather than custom and makes possible alteration to new unit sizes to satisfy rapid social change. Hence the initial placement of the fixed facilities is a critical decision.

A major determinant of environment is the access to movement from space to space. Those spaces grouped about a room or wide corridor make up a more residential environment through the use of attractive carpets, colors, and materials. Corridors can be more fully utilized; for example, conversation spaces that do not impede circulation can be provided by window seats and railed landings. Although stairs must conform to fire regulations, their configurations can be a pleasant contribution to the environment.

Structural Spans

The 40-ft span with a 20-ft bay length derived from study of many existing dormitory plans as well as proposed ideal environment spaces. On the national scale, older dormitory types were studied along with the newer ones being built. Whereas 10 years ago most structures were a simple, rectangular shell, a present-day trend seems to involve more complex configurations relating to more complex hierarchies in the social structure.

As a frame of reference, residence halls were classified in five basic plan types:

1. The Double-loaded Corridor—a series of perimeter rooms on both sides of a five-foot + corridor, usually with gang baths and stairs at either end

2. The Gallery Plan—a variation of the Double-loaded Corridor with rooms on one side only of an open or closed corridor

3. The Extended Core Plan—a series of perimeter rooms around four sides of a structure. In the center is a core of service rooms including gang toilets, janitor's closets, elevators, etc. A corridor usually surrounds the core on four sides

4. Vertical House—a series of 4, 6, 8 rooms, suites, etc. A stair serving one or two such configurations of rooms or suites is provided, creating the feeling of an individual house

5. Point Tower Plan—usually but not always high-rise with vertical circulation such as stairs and elevators in a center core along with gang baths and service rooms. The rooms, suites, and arrangements are on the perimeter. Shared baths are often used with suites of 4, 6, 8 persons

Once these five types were defined, all plans were classified accordingly, and a study of their structural requirements was begun. These plans were studied not as actually constructed but rather as they would need to be framed to permit maximum adaptability.

Based on these studies, frequency of occurrence charts showed that very few long spans over 35 ft were used and that a corresponding maximum short span of 20 ft was adequate. Coupling this study with spatial needs and assuming a fixed toilet space, it was concluded that a maximum 35- by 20-ft bay would be required. Provision by a given system of bays larger than 35 by 20 ft will, of course, be acceptable provided the required spans are taken care of.

A variety of bay sizes will be needed in addition to accommodate balconies, overhangs, stairways, and elevators. The precise conditions for these accommodations will be defined in the performance specifications for structure.

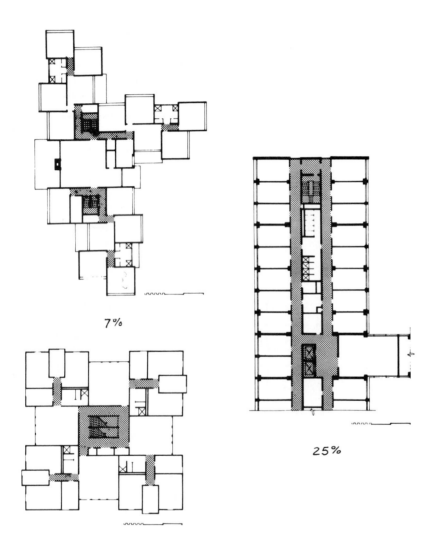

7%

14%

25%

RATIOS OF CIRCULATION TO GROSS AREA

Fig. 13

RESIDENCE HALLS

Sleeping and Study Quarters (Fig. 1)
Space There must be a minimum clear floor space in such areas of 6' [183 cm] by 6' [183 cm] enabling a 360° turn by a wheelchair.

Working Area Space clearance under counter, table, and desk tops to be used by a wheelchair student shall be a minimum of 27½" [69.8 cm] in height and 32" [81.3 cm] in width.

Beds Beds shall have minimum dimensions of 3' [92 cm] by 6' [183 cm] and between 19" [48.3 cm] and 22" [55.9 cm] in mattress height from floor level.

Mirrors Mirrors should be adjustably hung (a minimum of 2'-0" [61.0 cm] in length) so that the bottom is 30" [76.2 cm] above floor level. Where this lower height is not feasible, mirrors of greater height shall be tilted from the top to a degree to sufficiently accommodate individuals described in rational.

Electrical Outlets Electrical outlets shall be mounted no lower than 20" [50.8 cm] above floor level.

Handles and Switches Protruding desk and dresser drawer handles shall be installed. Switches for electrical fixtures and equipment shall be of a toggle or push-button type or equipped with pull-chains of a minimum length of 15" [38 cm].

Closets Where one closet is provided for each occupant, the clothes bar should provide two different heights. Three-quarters of the total length should be at 52" [132 cm] and the remaining quarter at 62" [157.5 cm]. To achieve this, the lower bar, three-quarters of the total length, can be suspended from the higher bar. Wall hooks shall be installed within a height range of 40" [101.6 cm] to 56" [142.2 cm]. Shelves of various height intervals shall be installed on the side-closed wall. The top shelf shall not exceed 45" [114.3 cm] in height. Shelves above the clothes bars shall be provided for long-term storage. (See Fig. 2.)

Windows, Heating, and Air Conditioning Windows shall close and open easily, using hardware latches, cranks, or slides which are within the accessibility range limits of 20" [50.8 cm] to 48" [121.9 cm] above floor level. Heating and air-conditioning controls and thermostats shall be mounted within the same height range.

Power Curtain Traverse Rods Power traverse rods should be installed in rooms occupied by the physically handicapped. All controls should be placed within an accessibility height range of 20" [50.8 cm] to 48" [121.9 cm].

PERFORMING ARTS

Aisles Where possible all new theater construction shall have ramped aisles (no greater

Architectural Accessibility for the Disabled of College Campuses, Stephen R. Cotler and Alfred H. Degraff, State University Construction Fund, Albany, N.Y., 1976.

than 1 in 12) with no steps (sight lines should be considered). If this is not possible, accessible and level cross aisles between seating sections shall be provided with minimum width of 7'-6" [228.6 cm]. (See Fig. 3.)

The placement of seating areas for the physically handicapped should not block egress routes used in the case of emergency.

Seating Seating space shall be set aside for those in wheelchairs who must remain in their wheelchairs and cannot transfer to the regular seating. The number of *level* floor spaces of at least 36" [92 cm] in width and 4'-4" [132 cm] in length to be provided shall be as follows:

Capacity of assembly space	Minimum number of seating spaces
0–75	2
75–300	3
over 300	3 + 1 for each add'tl. 100

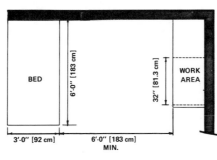

Fig. 1

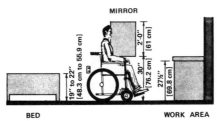

CLOSET

Fig. 2

LECTURE HALLS

Lecture Seating Lecture halls providing fixed seating and desk facilities shall provide spaces of level floor area of at least 36" [92 cm] in

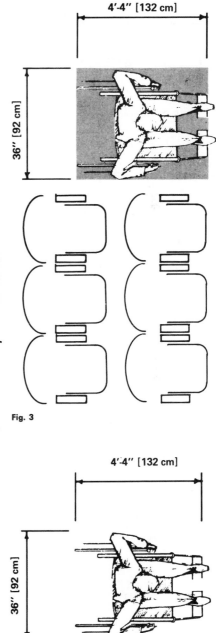

Fig. 3

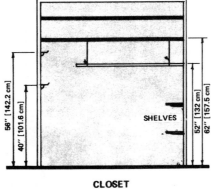

Fig. 4

COLLEGE AND UNIVERSITY FACILITIES
Handicapped Students

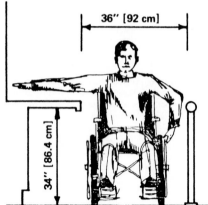

Fig. 5

width and 4'-4" [132 cm] in length. Desk space provided in this area shall have a knee clearance of at least 32" [81.3 cm] in width and a height of 27½" [69.8 cm]. (See Fig. 4.) The number of desk spaces and accompanying level floor areas shall be provided as follows:

Lecture hall capacity	Minimum number of spaces provided
0–50	2
50–100	3
101–200	4
over 200	4 + 1 for each add'tl 100

CAFETERIAS

Food Lines   Food lines of cafeterias shall employ tray slides no higher than 34" [86.4 cm] in height and, where a security wall or railing runs the length of the line, the area shall be at least 36"

[92 cm] in width for passage as measured from the outer edge of the tray slide. (See Fig. 5.)

Self-Service Areas   Salad bars, condiment areas, beverage dispensers, utensil racks, and other areas where self-service is required shall provide access within the unilateral vertical reach range of 20" [50.8 cm] to 48" [121.9 cm].

Dining Area   Tables shall be provided within the dining area which provide a knee clearance of at least 27½" [69.8 cm] in height and 32" [81.3 cm] in width.

Pedestal tables are not recommended because the center post hinders wheelchair footrests.

Aisle widths shall be at least 6'-0" [183 cm] as measured from table edge to table edge (Fig. 6, plan "A"), or 3'-0" [92 cm] from table corner to table corner (Fig. 6, plan "B"), in those areas used by persons in wheelchairs.

The width of main aisles, in areas of normal traffic pedestrian flow, shall be at least 6'-0" [183 cm] to allow two wheelchairs to pass each other (Figs. 7 and 8).

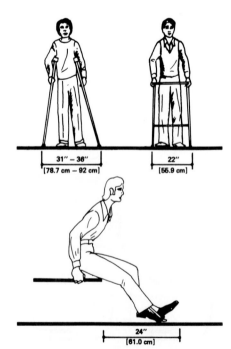

Fig. 6

Fig. 7

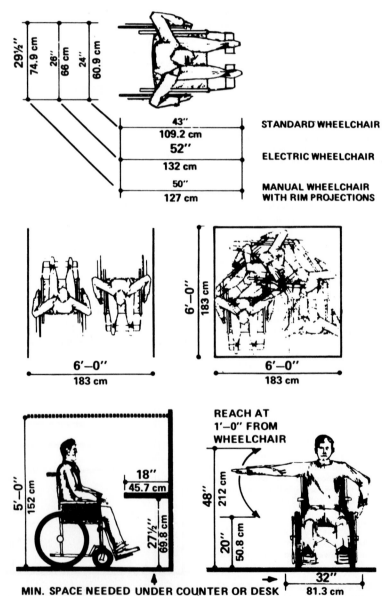

Fig. 8

RAMPS

Width A ramp shall be at least 4′ [122 cm] in width.

Length The inclined section of a ramp shall not exceed 30′ [9.14 m] in length. At both ends of each 30′ [9.14 m] (or smaller) section and at each turning point shall be a level area of at least 6′ [183 cm] in length and the width of the ramp.

Gradients *In modifying existing spaces:* If an area to be ramped has a vertical drop of 3″ [7.6 cm] or less *and* is situated either in an open area or at a door with no closing-device pressure, then a gradient of not greater than 1:4 (25%) shall be used.

In Modifying Existing Spaces If an area to be ramped has a vertical drop of 2″ [5.1 cm] or less *and* is situated at a door with a closing-device pressure, then a gradient of not greater than 1:6 (16.66%) shall be used.

In New Construction Any vertical drop over ½″ [1.27 cm] shall be ramped using a gradient not greater than 1:12 (8.33%) and preferably 1:16 (6.25%) where feasible. (See Fig. 9.)

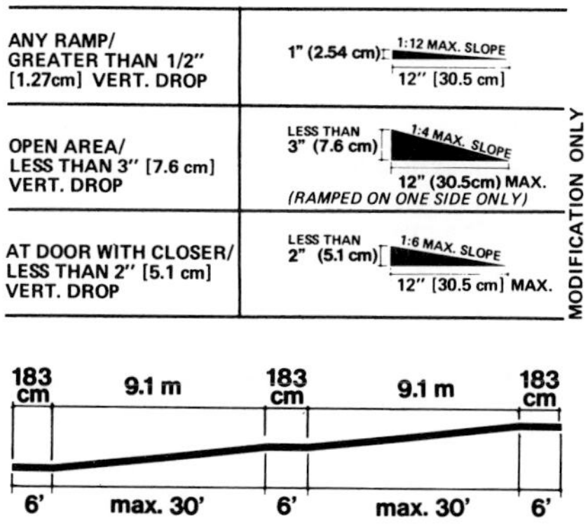

Fig. 9

By KEYES D. METCALF

LIBRARIES, ACADEMIC AND RESEARCH

Formulas and Tables

The figures given here are at best only approximations and may be altered by local conditions; they are not arrived at by exact scientific calculation.

Six groups are dealt with; those relating to:

I. Column spacing
II. Ceiling heights and floor size areas
III. Reader accommodations
IV. Book storage (excluding problems that are affected by column spacing)
V. Card catalogs
VI. Government standards

Planning Academic and Research Library Buildings, McGraw-Hill Book Company, New York, 1965.

I. Column Spacing

A. Stack Areas No one size is perfect for column sizes or column spacing.

Other things being equal, the larger the bay size, the better.

Column spacing—that is, the distance between column centers—is generally more important in concentrated stack areas than in combined stack and reading areas because in the latter suitable adjustments are easier to make.

Clear space between columns—this is not the space between column centers—in a column range should preferably be a multiple of 3 ft (plus an additional 4 in. to provide for irregularities in the column sizes and for the end uprights in the range).

Range spacing and range lengths have a greater effect on book capacity than the distance between columns in a column range. The reduction of space between range centers by 1 in. increases book capacity by approximately 2 percent. The reduction of space used for cross aisles at right angles to the ranges is also of importance. (See Fig. 10.)

If practicable, columns should be no greater than 14 in. in the direction of a range, and the dimension in the other direction should be kept down to 18 in. If over 14 in. in the direction of the range is necessary, the column might almost as well be 32 in. in that direction. It could then occupy the space of a full stack section and perhaps enclose a heating duct. If a column is wider than the range, it will jut into the stack aisle. Irregular length stack sections are inconvenient, and can often be replaced to advantage by a lectern or consultation table.

Tables 1 and 2 deal with standard layouts in commonly used module sizes.

The following comments may be useful in connection with Tables 1 and 2.

1. Spacing 3 ft 9 in. or less should be used for closed-access storage only, with ranges not more than 30 ft long and not more than 18 in. deep.

2. Spacing 3 ft 9 in. to 4 ft 1 in. can be used to advantage for large, little used, limited-ac-

TABLE 1 Square Modules with the Column Spacing a Multiple of 3 ft (Plus 1½ ft for the Column itself)*

Bay size	Sections between columns, standard 3 ft	Ranges to a bay	Range spacing on centers
19 ft 6 in. by 19 ft 6 in.	6	5	3 ft 10⁴⁄₅ in.
	6	4	4 ft 10½ in.
	6	3	6 ft 6 in.
22 ft 6 in. by 22 ft 6 in.	7	6	3 ft 9 in.
	7	5	4 ft 6 in.
	7	4	5 ft 7½ in.
25 ft 6 in. by 25 ft 6 in.	8	7	3 ft 7⁵⁄₇ in.
	8	6	4 ft 3 in.
	8	5	5 ft 1⅕ in.
	8	4	6 ft 4½ in.
28 ft 6 in. by 28 ft 6 in.	9	8	3 ft 6¾ in.
	9	7	4 ft 0⁶⁄₇ in.
	9	6	4 ft 9 in.
	9	5	5 ft 8⅖ in.

* Columns should not be wider than the depth of range. 14 by 14 in. up to 14 by 18 in. is suggested.

TABLE 2 Square Modules with Column Spacing Multiple of 3 ft*

Bay size	Sections between columns standard 3 ft	Ranges to a bay	Range spacing on centers
18 ft by 18 ft	5	5	3 ft 7⅕ in.
	5	4	4 ft 6 in.
	5	3	6 ft
21 ft by 21 ft	6	6	3 ft 6 in.
	6	5	4 ft 2⅖ in.
	6	4	5 ft 3 in.
24 ft by 24 ft	7	7	3 ft 5⅐ in.
	7	6	4 ft
	7	5	4 ft 9⅗ in.
	7	4	6 ft
27 ft by 27 ft	8	8	3 ft 4½ in.
	8	7	3 ft 10²⁄₇ in.
	8	6	4 ft 6 in.
	8	5	5 ft 4⅘ in.
	8	4	6 ft 9 in.

* Columns should not be wider than the depth of the range. 18 by 32 in. is suggested.

COLLEGE AND UNIVERSITY FACILITIES
Libraries

cess stacks with ranges up to 30 ft long. Closed-access ranges up to 60 ft long have been used successfully with ranges 18 in. or less deep, 4 ft or 4 ft 1 in. on centers.

3. Spacing 4 ft 2 in. to 4 ft 6 in. can be used for open-access stack, preferably held to 18 in. in depth with the range length based on the amount of use.

4. Spacing 4 ft 6 in. to 5 ft is generous even for heavily used open-access undergraduate stack if ranges are 15 ft long and 4 ft 6 in. on centers, and in some circumstances up to 30 ft if 5 ft on centers.

5. Spacing 5 ft to 5 ft 10 in. is unnecessarily generous for any regular stack shelving and is often adequate for periodical display cases and for heavily used reference collections.

6. Spacing 6 ft or greater is adequate for newspaper shelving and generous for periodical display cases.

Square bays are more flexible than those that form a long rectangle and are generally somewhat cheaper if the ceiling height is limited. But if the latter are used, the number of suitable sizes can be greatly increased. Table 3 shows possibilities with 22 ft 6 in. in one direction and different spacing in the other one.

Similar tables can be prepared for long rectangular bays 18 ft, 19½ ft, 21 ft, 24 ft, 25½ ft, 27 ft, and 28½ ft in one direction.

If section lengths are changed from 3 ft to some other size, such as 3 ft 1 in., 3 ft 2 in., 3 ft 3 in., 3 ft 4 in., 3 ft 5 in., or 3 ft 6 in., or in countries using the metric system to 90, 95, 100, or 105 cm. tables comparable to Tables 1, 2 and 3 above should be prepared with those lengths as a base.

B. Seating Accommodations

Column spacing is of less importance in connection with seating accommodations than with shelving. Tables 4 and 5 show the maximum number of carrels available on one side of standard-size bays and the number of studies available in such bays.

II. Ceiling Heights and Floor Areas

Minimum and maximum ceiling heights and floor areas involve basic functional and aesthetic problems. Suggestions from the functional point of view are proposed as an aid in reaching decisions.

A. Ceiling Heights
Table 6 suggests functional minimums and maximums.

B. Floor Areas
Both the number of floors in a library and the area of each floor may be important functionally and aesthetically. Decisions in regard to them may properly be influenced by the site surroundings, the slope of the ground, and the value of the property.

Table 7 makes suggestions, which at best are only approximations, as to the percentage of the gross square footage of a library building which functionally should be on the entrance or central-services level in a typical academic library.

III. Accommodations for Readers

Seating accommodations for readers and the service to readers are the largest space consumers in most libraries. The required areas depend on:

A. The number of accommodations provided

B. The types of accommodations and the percentage of each

TABLE 3 Long Rectangular Modules, 22 ft 6 in. in One Direction*

Bay size	Ranges to a bay	Range spacing on centers
22 ft 6 in. by 18 ft	4	4 ft 6 in.
22 ft 6 in. by 20 ft	5	4 ft
22 ft 6 in. by 20 ft 10 in.	5	4 ft 2 in.
22 ft 6 in. by 21 ft 8 in.	5	4 ft 4 in.
22 ft 6 in. by 24 ft	6	4 ft
22 ft 6 in. by 25 ft	6	4 ft 2 in.
22 ft 6 in. by 26 ft	6	4 ft 4 in.
22 ft 6 in. by 27 ft	6	4 ft 6 in.

* A bay of this size will give seven sections 3 ft long between 14-in. columns in the direction of the column range. The column sizes suggested in Table 2 are suitable here.

TABLE 4 Carrels*

Bay size	Open†	Double- or triple- staggered‡	Small closed§	Large closed¶
18 ft	4	4	4	3
19½ ft	4	4	4	3
21 ft	5	4	4	4
22½ ft	5	5	5	4
24 ft	6	5	5	4
25½ ft	6	5	5	5
27 ft	6	6	6	5

* A carrel, as used here, is an area in which a reader is cut off from any neighbor who is closer than 3 ft on either side or front and back and one side. The minimum desirable width of an adequate carrel working surface is 2 ft 9 in., which is as useful as 3 ft for each person at a table with two or more persons sitting side by side. Minimum depth suggested is 20 in.

† Distance apart on centers should be not less than 4 ft 3 in., unless the front table leg is set back 4 to 6 in. and armless chairs are used, in which case the distance on centers can be reduced to 4 ft. Any distance over 4 ft 6 in. is unnecessarily generous. A clear space of 27 in. or more between working surface and partition at the rear is recommended. A shelf above the table interferes with overhead lighting and makes a deeper table desirable.

‡ Distance between centers should seldom be less than 4 ft 6 in.; 5 ft is preferred; anything greater is unnecessarily generous. With triple-staggered carrels, the back of the center one should be held down to no more than 10 in. above the tabletop.

§ The distance between centers should be not less than 4 ft 6 in.; and 5 ft is preferred. Watch out for ventilation. A window is psychologically desirable. Closed carrels are not recommended for undergraduates or any student not actually engaged in writing a dissertation. Glass in the door or grills should be provided for supervision.

¶ A room less than 6 ft long at right angles to the desk will permit shelves above the desk or a bookcase behind the occupant but preferably not both. One less than 6 ft parallel to the desk will not permit a 4-ft long desk, and a second chair, and may make it necessary to open the door outward.

TABLE 5 Faculty Studies and Small Multipurpose Rooms

Bay size	Small faculty study*	Small conference room or generous faculty study†
18 ft	3	2
19½ ft	3	2
21 ft	3	2
22½ ft	3	2
24 ft	4	3
25½ ft	4	3
27 ft	4	3

* A room of this size can house a large desk, shelving, a filing case, and permit a door to open in.

† This will provide for conference rooms for four, an adequate small staff office, or a generous faculty study. It should be at least 8 ft in the clear in one direction and have a total area of over 70 sq ft.

Any small room will seem less confining if it has a window, and since window wall space is generally at a premium, a room can well have one of its short sides on the window wall.

C. Dimensions of the working surfaces for each type of accommodation

D. Average square footage required for each type of accommodation

E. Additional space required for service to readers

A. Formulas for Percentage of Students for Whom Seating Accommodations Are Required
The formula used should depend on:

1. The quality of the student body and faculty. The higher the quality, the greater the library use.

2. The library facilities provided. The more satisfactory the seating accommodations and the services provided, the greater the use.

3. The quality of the collections. Superior collections increase use.

4. The curriculum. In general, students in the humanities and social sciences use the library more than do those in the pure and applied sciences.

5. The emphasis placed on textbook instruction, which tends to reduce library use.

6. Whether the student body is resident or commuting and, if the former, whether the dormitories provide suitable study facilities. Heaviest library use in most residential institutions is in the evening; in commuting ones, during the daytime hours.

7. Whether the location is rural, suburban, or urban. Large population centers tend to decrease evening use because of other available activities and attractions.

8. Whether the institution is coeducational or for one sex only. Coeducation tends to increase library use, particularly in the evening.

9. The emphasis placed by the faculty on the library and on nontextbook reading.

10. The percentage of graduate students and the fields in which they work.

11. The institution's policy in regard to use by persons other than those connected with it.

12. The departmental library arrangements which may make available other reading facilities and reduce the use of the central library. Table 8 suggests formulas for percentage of students for whom seating is suggested.

B. Suggestions for Types of Seating Accommodations and the Percentage of Each Type

1. *For Undergraduates*

   a. Tables for four or more. Not more than 20 percent. Should be largely restricted

TABLE 6 Clear Ceiling Heights

Area	Suggested minimum*	Suggested functional maximum†
Book stacks‡	7 ft 6 in.	8 ft 6 in.
Stacks with lights at right angle to ranges§	8 ft 4 in.	8 ft 9 in.
Stacks with lights on range tops functioning by ceiling reflection	9 ft 0 in.	9 ft 6 in.
Reading areas under 100 sq ft	7 ft 6 in.	8 ft 6 in.
Individual seating in large areas	8 ft 4 in.	9 ft 6 in.
Large reading rooms over 100 ft long broken by screens or bookcases	9 ft 6 in.	10 ft 6 in.
Auditoriums up to 1,500 sq ft	9 ft 6 in.	10 ft 6 in.
Entrance or main level with over 20,000 sq ft	9 ft 6 in.	10 ft 6 in.
Floor with mezzanine¶	15 ft 6 in.	18 ft 6 in.

* Heights lower than specified have been used successfully on occasion, but ceiling lights should be recessed and good ventilation assured. Financial savings will be comparatively small.

† Greater heights may be useful aesthetically and provide added flexibility by making areas available for a wider range of purposes.

‡ 7 ft 6 in. is the lowest height which permits an adequate protective base and seven shelves 12 in. on centers (standard for academic libraries) with suitable clearance at the top. The top shelf will be 6 ft 4 in. above the floor, the greatest height that can be reached without difficulty by a person 5 ft tall. Space above 7 ft 6 in. is not useful for storage of open-access collections and will be confusing if used for other shelving.

§ This height used with fluorescent tubes, at right angles to the ranges, permits stack ranges to be shifted closer together or farther apart without rewiring, and is high enough so that heat from the tubes will not damage the books on the top shelf. If the fixtures are flush or nearly flush with the ceiling, the clear height can be reduced a few inches.

¶ Mezzanines provide inexpensive square footage if they occupy at least 60 percent of the floor area (building codes may prohibit them unless mezzanine is partitioned off and made a separate unit), and if the overall height of the two resulting levels is not much more than 6 ft greater than would be provided if there were no mezzanine.

to those in reserve-book and reference rooms.

b. Lounge chairs. Not more than 15 percent. Should in general be restricted to lounge areas, smoking rooms, current-periodical rooms, or used to break up unpleasantly long rows of other types of accommodations. In many libraries 8 to 10 percent of seating of this kind is adequate.

c. Individual accommodations. Up to 85 percent. These should provide in most cases for working surfaces cut off from immediately adjacent neighbors,

by aisles or partitions on one, two, or three sides. The partitions should be high enough—52 in. for men—so that heads do not bob up or down above them and cause visual distraction. These accommodations may include:

(1) Tables for one. These can be quite satisfactory along a wall or screen if the readers all face in the same direction.

(2) Tables for two with partitions down the center. See Fig. 5b. For limited use only.

(3) Tables for four or more with par-

TABLE 7 Suggested Formulas for Percentage of Gross Square Footage Functionally Desirable on the Central-Services Level*

Gross building area in sq ft	Size of collections in volumes	Minimum percentages of gross area on central-services level
Under 20,000	Under 100,000	40–50
20,000–45,000	100,000–250,000	33⅓–40
40,000–80,000	250,000–500,000	25–33⅓
75,000–150,000	500,000–1,000,000	20–30
135,000 +	1,000,000 +	16⅔–25

* Central services as used here include the main control point, circulation and reference services, reference and bibliographical collections, the public catalog, and acquisition and catalog departments.

These computations are approximations only, but smaller figures than those in the last column will often necessitate shifting part of the central services to other levels and incidentally may add considerably to staff payrolls.

TABLE 8 Formulas for Percentage of Students for Whom Seating Accommodations Are Suggested

Type of institution	Percentage
Superior residential coeducational liberal arts college in rural area or small town	50–60
Superior residential liberal arts college for men or women in rural area or small town	45–50
Superior residential liberal arts college in a small city	40–45
Superior residential university	35–40
Typical residential university	25–30
Typical commuting university	20–25

titions in both directions. See Fig. 3. A great improvement over a table for four without partitions.

(4) Pinwheel arrangement for four. See Fig. 8c. Satisfactory, but requires more space than (3) above.

(5) Double carrels with readers facing in different directions. See Fig. 5b. Not as satisfactory as (6) below.

(6) Double-staggered carrels. See Fig. 7a.

(7) Pairs of double-staggered carrels on both sides of a screen. See Fig. 7b.

(8) Triple-staggered carrels in place of three stack ranges or in a large reading area.

(9) Rows of single carrels at right angles to a wall in book-stack or reading area. See Fig. 1a.

(10) Single carrels in place of last stack section at the end of a blind stack aisle. See Fig. 1b.

(11) Typing carrels similar to (10) above, but with special acoustic protection.

(12) Rows of double carrels in a reading area or in place of two stack ranges. See Fig. 6.

Closed carrels are rarely recommended for undergraduates. Shelves in carrels tend to en-

TABLE 9 Suggested Working Surface Area for Each Person

Type of accommodation	Minimum size	Adequate size
Table for multiple seating	33 in. by 21 in.*	36 in. by 24 in.
Individual table or open carrel for undergraduate	33 in. by 20 in.†	36 in. by 22 in.
Open carrel for graduate student without book shelf over it	36 in. by 24 in.‡	
Carrel, open or closed, for graduate student writing dissertation, with a book shelf	36 in. by 27 in.§	48 in. by 30 in.
Faculty study	48 in. by 30 in.	60 in. by 30 in. if there is shelving over it

* Recommended only for reserve-book use or for a college for women.

† A space of 33 by 20 in. goes farther in an individual accommodation than at a large table because others do not intrude on the space.

‡ Shelves are not recommended over open carrels because they make it easier for an unauthorized student to monopolize one.

§ A shelf over a carrel table requires additional depth because it interferes with lighting. A closed carrel should preferably have a window, glass in the door, and more space around the table than an open one, or claustrophobia may result.

COLLEGE AND UNIVERSITY FACILITIES

Libraries

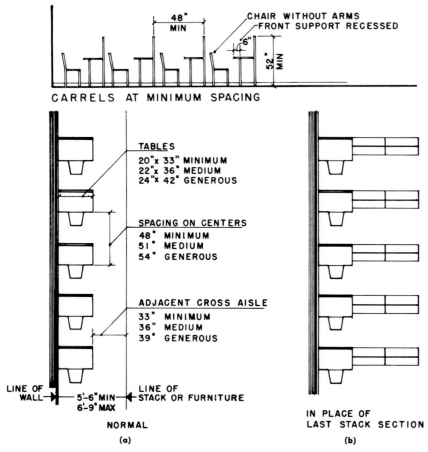

CARRELS AT MINIMUM SPACING

TABLES
20"x 33" MINIMUM
22"x 36" MEDIUM
24"x 42" GENEROUS

SPACING ON CENTERS
48" MINIMUM
51" MEDIUM
54" GENEROUS

ADJACENT CROSS AISLE
33" MINIMUM
36" MEDIUM
39" GENEROUS

LINE OF WALL — 5'-6" MIN — LINE OF STACK OR FURNITURE
6'-9" MAX

NORMAL
(a)

IN PLACE OF LAST STACK SECTION
(b)

Fig. 1 Carrels at right angles to a wall. (a) Suggests sizes and spacing and shows elevations. (b) Carrel in place of last stack section next to a wall. The working surface of the carrel should be in line with the stack range instead of the aisle in order to make it easier to get into the chair.

courage undesirable monopolization. A shelf outside the carrel with an open or locked cupboard provides for books and papers to be reserved and makes possible longer hours of carrel use.

2. *Graduate Student Accommodations*
   a. At tables for multiple seating. Not recommended.
   b. Open carrels of any of the types proposed in 1 above. Graduate carrels may have shelves over the working surface, but this will require deeper table tops because of lighting problems, unless the shelves are installed at one side. See Figs. 2a, b, and c.
   c. Closed carrels. See C and D below for working surface dimensions and square-footage requirements. Closed carrels require special care for satisfactory lighting and ventilation. Unless larger than necessary to provide adequate working surfaces, claustrophobia tends to result. A window for each carrel or an attractive grill on at least one side will help.

3. *Faculty Accommodations.* If possible, closed studies should be provided for faculty members engaged in research projects which require the use of library materials. Limited assignment periods are suggested. They should not be used as offices. See C and D below for working surface dimensions and square-footage requirements.

C. Dimensions of Working Surface for Each Type of Seating Accommodation Table 9 gives suggested minimum and adequate dimensions.

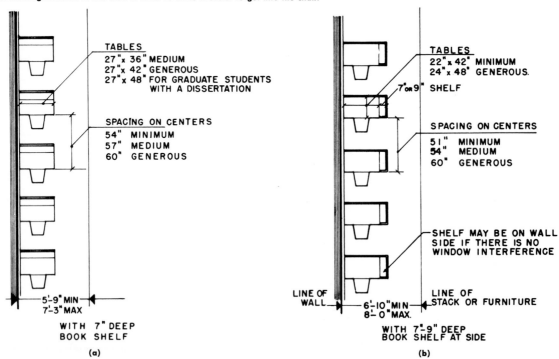

TABLES
27"x 36" MEDIUM
27"x 42" GENEROUS
27"x 48" FOR GRADUATE STUDENTS WITH A DISSERTATION

SPACING ON CENTERS
54" MINIMUM
57" MEDIUM
60" GENEROUS

5'-9" MIN
7'-3" MAX

WITH 7" DEEP BOOK SHELF
(a)

TABLES
22"x 42" MINIMUM
24"x 48" GENEROUS.

7" or 9" SHELF

SPACING ON CENTERS
51" MINIMUM
54" MEDIUM
60" GENEROUS

SHELF MAY BE ON WALL SIDE IF THERE IS NO WINDOW INTERFERENCE

LINE OF WALL — 6'-10" MIN — LINE OF STACK OR FURNITURE
8'-0" MAX.

WITH 7'-9" DEEP BOOK SHELF AT SIDE
(b)

Fig. 2 Carrels with shelves. (a) Shelf in front of reader. The table should be 5 in. deeper than one without a shelf, and adequate spacing between carrels may be difficult to arrange. (b) Shelf at one side instead of in front. (It can be at either side.) This requires more width but less depth. (c) Shelf at one side facing the aisle. This can provide more shelf capacity and greater privacy; it also demands greater total width.

D. Average Square Footage Required for Different Types of Accommodation The square-footage requirements suggested in Table 10 are at best approximations, but may be helpful in preliminary stages of planning.

E. Additional Space Required for Service to Readers Space for direct access to seating accommodations is dealt with in Table 10 and elsewhere. Additional space required includes:

Assignable Areas

The public catalog.

Space around the bibliographical and reference and current-periodical collections which is required because of heavy use.

Public areas outside service desks.

Special accommodations for microfilm reproductions, maps, manuscripts, archives, and other collections not shelved in the main stack area. These may include audiovisual areas of various types.

Staff working quarters.

Nonassignable Areas

Entrances, vestibules, and lobbies
Corridors
Areas used primarily as traffic arteries
Stairwells and elevator shafts
Toilets
Walls and columns

It is suggested that not less than 25 sq ft per reader in assignable or nonassignable areas will be required for the services in these groups, and that unless the special accommo- dations mentioned above are held to a reasonable minimum and careful planning is provided throughout, the 25 may have to be increased to 35 sq ft.

Seating Accommodations As an aid in planning layouts, suggestions are presented for arrangements for seating accommodations in reading areas and book stacks. Remember that academic and research (not public) libraries are under consideration, and the sizes and arrangements suggested are for academic and research use.

1. Single open carrels with the long axis of the tabletops at right angles to a wall. These may be in reading areas, or in book stacks with walls on one side, a subsidiary cross aisle on the other, with the end of stack ranges beyond the aisle, or they may take the place of the last stack section in a range. Single carrels should preferably be fastened to the wall or floor in some way so as not to get out of position. (See Fig. 1a and b.)

2. Single closed carrels along a book-stack wall and opening into a subsidiary stack aisle. These are quite similar to the open carrels described above, but have partitions and a door and, unless considerably larger, they may be difficult to ventilate and to light and tend to cause claustrophobia. Partitions to the ceiling are not recommended for undergraduates, but if the area, including the adjacent aisle, is at least as much as 5 ft by 6 ft 8 in., it can be used for graduate students if there is glass in the door. Light from an outside window will

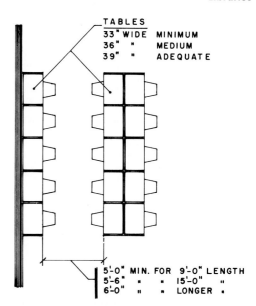

Fig. 3 Reading-room table with dividing partitions. Not very satisfactory if table seats more than four and reader is hemmed in on both sides. If he leans back, he is too close to his neighbor. If light is hung from the partition, it tends to cause an unpleasant glare. If partitions between readers sitting side by side are extended on both sides to provide more privacy, they become too confining.

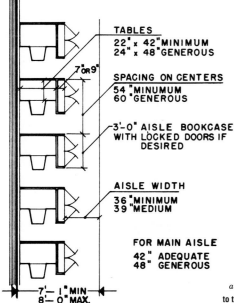

Fig. 2 (cont.) Carrels with shelves.

TABLE 10 Approximate Square-footage Requirements for Different Types of Seating Accommodations [a]

Type of accommodations	Requirements, sq ft		
	Minimum	Adequate	Generous
Small lounge chair [b]	20	25	30
Large lounge chair [c]	25	30	35
Individual table [d]	25	30	35
Tables for four [e]	22½	25	27½
Tables for more than four [f]	20	22½	25
Individual carrels [g]	20	22½	25
Double carrels [h]	22½	25	27½
Doubled-staggered carrels [i]	22½	25	27½
Triple-staggered carrels [j]	22½	25	27½
Double row of carrels with partitions between, placed in a reading room or in place of two stack ranges [k]	22½	25	27½

[a] The figures used here include: (1) area of working surface if any; (2) area occupied by chair; (3) area used for direct access to the accommodations; and (4) reasonable share of all the assignable space used for main aisles in the room under consideration.
[b] These chairs if in pairs should be separated by a small table to prevent congestion and to hold books not in use.
[c] Large lounge chairs are expensive, space-consuming, and an aid to slumber. Rarely recommended.
[d] Individual tables are space-consuming, are generally disorderly in appearance because they are easily moved, and result in a restless atmosphere from traffic on all sides. Not recommended except along a wall or screen.
[e] Tables for four are the largest ones recommended, unless pressure for additional capacity is great.
[f] Tables for more than four are space savers, but few readers like to sit with someone on each side. They will avoid using them as far as possible.
[g] Individual carrels are economical in use of space if placed at right angles to a wall, adjacent to an aisle that must be provided under any circumstances. They reduce visual distraction if partitions 52 in. or more in height are provided on at least two of the four sides. See Fig. 5a and d.
[h] Double carrels are useful, but the staggered ones described below are preferred.
[i] Double-staggered carrels are as economical of space as tables for four and reduce visual distractions. See Fig. 7a.
[j] Triple-staggered carrels are as economical of space as tables for six or more and reduce visual distraction.
[k] Double rows of carrels are economical in space use and reduce visual distraction. See Fig. 6.

COLLEGE AND UNIVERSITY FACILITIES

Libraries

help. Fig. 4b shows a closed carrel with a door.

3. Single carrels in place of a stack section at the end of a book range. (See Fig. 1b.) As far as space use is concerned, this is the most economical way to provide a seating accommodation, and it gives a great deal of seclusion, which many readers want. It presents four problems, however, as follows:

a. The space from front to back is limited to the distance between range centers, which in some cases is minimal.

b. Unless the table top is specially designed to occupy the full depth of the double-faced range, as shown in Fig. 3, it may be difficult to get into the chair because the table top will jut out into the aisle.

c. Some readers, particularly if there is no adjacent outside window, will feel too shut in for comfort.

d. Since the seat is at the end of a blind aisle, the length of the range should not be more than half that of a range with cross aisles at both ends.

4. Single seats facing a reading room or stack wall or a high partition down the center of a regular reading room table, sometimes with a high partition at the sides projecting 6 in. beyond the table top into the aisle, to cut one off from his neighbors. There is no place to look out, except directly at the neighbor to the right or left when leaning back in the chair. They are not recommended, except in an open area in groups of four where the reader can look out in at least one direction, because few students enjoy facing a blank wall, unless they can look out at least a few feet on one side without seeing a neighbor close at hand. (See Fig. 3.) Single carrels in a sawtooth, or what is known as a dog-leg arrangement, shown in Fig. 4c, are preferable to those directly facing a wall, as the reader can look out on one side and still is protected from his neighbors. They require no additional space.

5. Double carrels in rows in a reading room

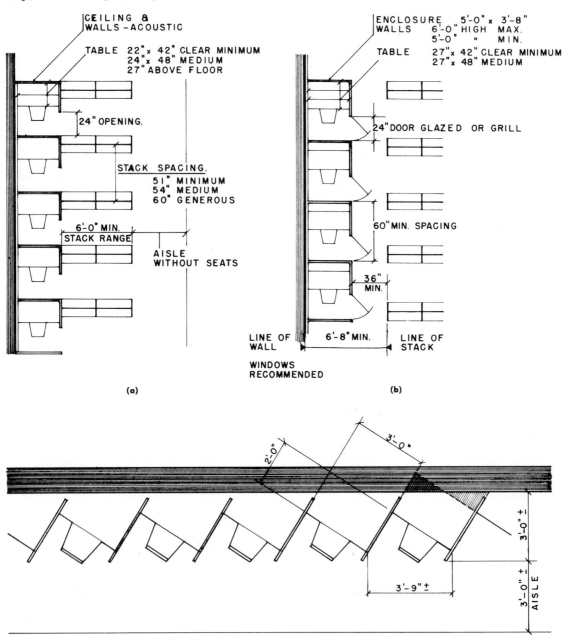

Fig. 4 Other types of single carrels. (a) Partly open typing carrel in place of last stack section with acoustically protected walls and ceiling aided by adjacent books. Absence of other seating close at hand makes doors unnecessary. (b) Closed carrel with door and shelf. If there is no window, wider spacing is desirable to prevent claustrophobia. Ventilation and lighting will present problems. (c) A dog-leg carrel is a compromise for one facing a wall, which is disliked by many, if partitions are extended enough to provide seclusion. The carrel is open on one side.

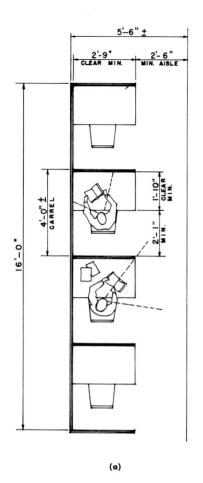

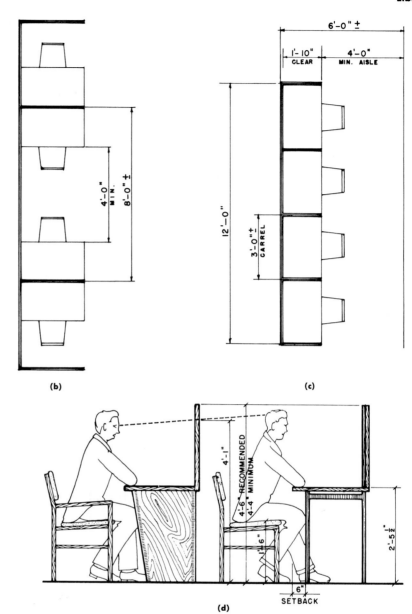

Fig. 5 Open carrels along a wall or a partition at least 52 in. high. (a) Carrels along a wall all facing the same way. (Recommended.) (b) Carrels along a wall in pairs. (Possible, but they back up to each other unpleasantly.) (c) Carrels facing a wall. (Not recommended. If there are side partitions, reader has "blinders." If he leans back, his neighbor is close at hand.) (d) Carrel elevation to show desirable height of partitions to prevent visual distraction. The left-hand carrel shows a rounded type of construction and the right-hand one a square type.

separated by partitions which are at least 52 in. in height in the front and on one side of the working area. Partitions in front can be held down to no more than 3 to 10 in. above the table top because a full view of one's neighbor all the time is less distracting than a head bobbing up and down occasionally; but 52 in. above the floor is preferable. (Fig. 5d.)

6. Double carrels in rows in place of two stack ranges. A size of 33 by 22 in. can be used in place of two stack ranges when ranges are 4 ft 3 in. on centers. A size of 36 by 22 in. can be used comfortably with ranges 4 ft 6 in. on centers. By placing one or both end pairs at right angles to the others, the carrel range and the stack range length can be made to match with table tops and distances between centers of standard size. (See Fig. 6.)

7. Double-staggered carrels with the adja-cent table tops overlapping by one-half their depth, placed along walls, with 4½ ft minimum on centers and 5 ft preferred.

8. "Pinwheel" groups of four carrels, pref-erably in a reading alcove. If the alcove is 12 by 12 ft in the clear, table tops 22 by 36 in. are recommended, with partitions at least 52 in. in height, which extend 6 in. beyond the end of each table. Shelves are ordinarily not rec-ommended for these cases, particularly if the table top is less than 27 in. deep.

This arrangement fits perfectly in a 27-ft column spacing with two alcoves to a bay. If the module size is 25 ft 6 in., the space in each alcove will be reduced a total of 9 in., and one of the shelf sections will be only 27 in. It can be used for shorter shelves or set up as wall space for a bulletin board or for a picture or other decoration.

If ventilation is adequate, alcoves can be partially closed in on the fourth side by a single or double-faced book section, which may help to use space to advantage and make possible the best utilization of the available bay size. The main aisle between double rows of alcoves can be as narrow as 4½ ft. (See Fig. 8b and c.)

Pinwheel groups have been successful in large reading areas, but they tend to give an impres-sion of disorderliness when not in an alcove.

9. Carrels in alcoves with tables for four installed with 52-in.-high partitions in each direction. These alcoves may be as little as 9 ft deep and 11 ft 3 in. to 12 ft wide in the clear. With a 25 ft 6 in. bay and 4 ft 6 in. main aisle, an unusually large capacity is possible. (See Fig. 8b and c.) With a 27-ft bay, the space utilization is still good, and the main aisle can be widened to 6 ft.

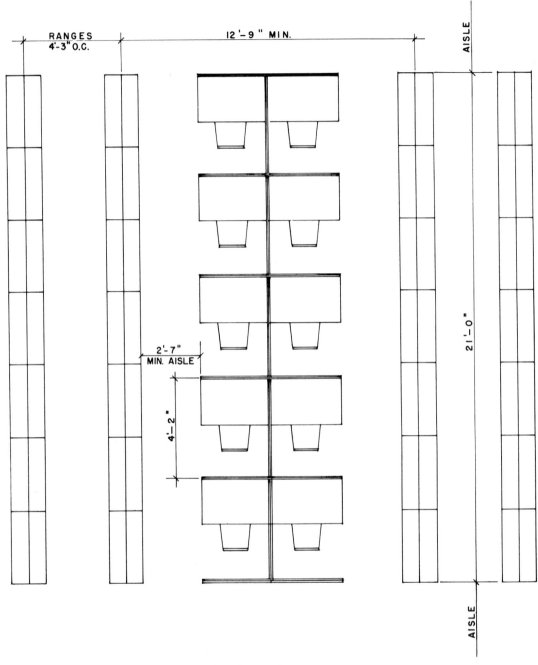

Fig. 6 Double rows of carrels in bookstack or reading area in place of two stack ranges.

IV. Book-Stack Capacity

Book-stack capacity is based on:

A. The number of volumes shelved in a standard stack section

B. The square-footage requirements for a standard stack section.

A. The Number of Volumes Shelved in a Standard Stack Section The number of volumes that can be shelved in a standard stack section depends on: (1) Book heights and the number of shelves per section; (2) book thickness; (3) the decision in regard to what is considered a full section.

1. *Book Heights and Shelves per Section.* Stack sections in academic libraries are considered standard if they are 7 ft 6 in. high and 3 ft wide. Sections of this height make possible seven shelves 12 in. on centers over a 4-in. base. This spacing is adequate for books which are 11 in. tall or less, which, as shown in Table 11, include 90 percent of the books in a typical collection.

It is suggested that most of the remaining 10 percent will be concentrated in a comparatively few subjects, that 70 percent of this 10 percent will be between 11 and 13 in. tall, and that six shelves 14 in. on centers will provide for them.

2. *Book Thickness and the Number of Volumes That Can Be Shelved Satisfactorily on Each Linear Foot of Shelving.* No two libraries

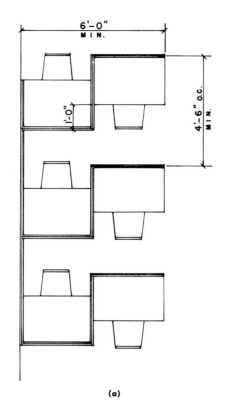

(a)

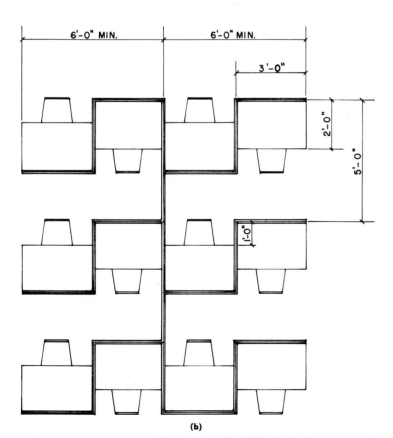

(b)

Fig. 7 Double-staggered carrels. (a) Double-staggered carrel adjacent to a wall. The carrel by the wall will be helped by a window. Partitions should be 52 in. high or higher. Recommended. (b) Double-staggered carrels on each side of a screen or partition. A space saver, but recommended only when necessary to provide required seating capacity. The backs of the inside carrels should be no more than 40 in. high.

are alike in this connection. The average thickness will depend on (a) The definition of a

TABLE 11 Book Heights*

8 in. or less	25%
9 in. or less	54
10 in. or less	79
11 in. or less	90
12 in. or less	94
13 in. or less	97
Over 13 in.	3

* Adapted from Rider's Compact Storage, p. 45, which was based to a considerable extent on research done by Van Hoesen and Kilpatrick on the height of books in academic libraries.

volume; (b) binding policy, particularly for pamphlets and serials and periodicals; (c) the collection under consideration.

A commonly used formula for thickness of books is shown in Table 12.

TABLE 12 Volumes per Linear Foot of Shelf for Books in Different Subjects*

Subject	Volumes per foot of shelf	Volumes per single-faced section
Circulating (nonfiction)	8	168
Fiction	8	168
Economics	8	168
General literature	7	147
History	7	147
Art (not including large folios)	7	147
Technical and scientific	6	126
Medical	5	105
Public documents	5	105
Bound periodicals	5	105
Law	4	84

* This table is in common use by stack manufacturers.

3. *The Decision on When a Section Is Full.* In Table 10 a suggested number of volumes per single-faced section is proposed. It is evident that if books are shelved by subject, it is unwise to fill the shelves completely, and any estimate must be an approximation. For many libraries 125 volumes per stack section is considered safe.

B. Square-footage Requirements for a Standard Stack Section. The square-footage requirements for a standard stack section depend primarily on: (1) range spacing; (2) range lengths; (3) the number of cross aisles and their widths; (4) cross aisle area charged against adjacent reader accommodations; (5) nonassignable space.

1. *Range Spacing.* Range spacing should be based on column spacing, on shelf depths, which are discussed in *a* below; and on stack-aisle widths, dealt with in 2 below.

a. Shelf depths. Depths as used here are based on double-faced bracket shelving with 2 in. between the back of the shelf on one side of the range and the back of the shelf on the other side. Shelf depths specified by stack manufacturers are 1 in. greater than the actual depth, that is, a 7-in. "actual" shelf is called an 8-in. "nominal" shelf, because 8 in. is available if half the 2 in. noted above is assigned

COLLEGE AND UNIVERSITY FACILITIES
Libraries

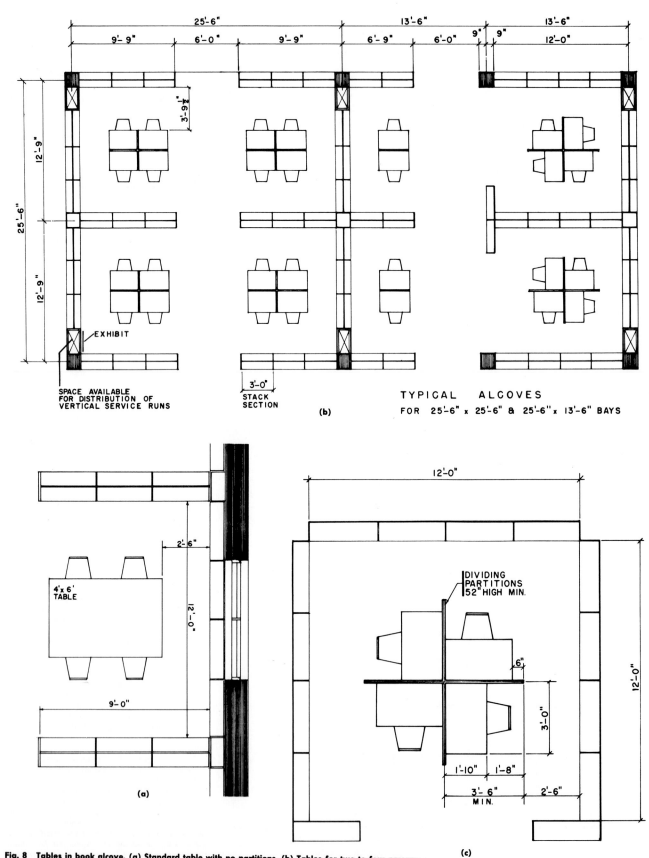

TYPICAL ALCOVES
FOR 25'-6" x 25'-6" & 25'-6" x 13'-6" BAYS

Fig. 8 Tables in book alcove. (a) Standard table with no partitions. (b) Tables for two to four persons, with partitions fitted in different column spacing and with exhibit space replacing a short section. (c) Nest of tables in pinwheel form to give additional privacy.

to the shelves on each side of a double-faced shelf section.

Table 13 shows depths of books. If these figures are correct (the author believes they

TABLE 13 Percentage of Books in an Academic Collection Below Different Depths Measured from the Back of the Spine to the Fore Edge of the Covers*

5 in. or less	25%
6 in. or less	54
7 in. or less	79
8 in. or less	90
9 in. or less	94
10 in. or less	97†
Over 10 in.	3

* Adapted from Rider's Compact Book Storage, p. 45.
† An 8-in. actual, i.e., a 9-in. nominal depth shelf, will house a 10-in.-deep book without difficulty, unless there is another deep book immediately behind it. Most books over 10 in. deep will be more than 11 in. tall and should be segregated on special shelving which is more than 9 in. in nominal depth.

represent the average in research and academic libraries), a shelf with 8 in. actual depth, together with the space available between shelves on the two sides of a double-faced section, will provide for practically any book that does not have to be segregated because of its height, and 8-in. actual depth shelves (they are designated by the manufacturers as 9-in. shelves) are recommended in place of the 7- or 9-in. actual-depth shelves which are commonly used. In many libraries a 7-in. actual-depth shelf is suitable for a large part of the collections.

2. Stack-aisle Widths and Stack-range Lengths. Stack-aisle widths should be based on the amount of use by individuals and by trucks and the length of the ranges before a cross aisle is reached. Other things being equal, the longer the range, the wider the aisle should be. Table 14 suggests desirable stack-aisle widths in conjunction with stack-range lengths under different types and amounts of use.

Do not forget that stack-aisle widths must be based, indirectly at least, on the column spacing, and are affected as well by the shelf depths discussed in 1a above, if columns are not to obstruct the aisles. The distance between column centers should be an exact multiple of the distance between the center of parallel stack ranges within the stack bay, which in turn is determined by the sum of the depth of a double-faced range and the width of a stack aisle.

3. Widths for Main and Subsidiary Cross-stack Aisles. Cross-aisle widths should be based on amount of use and are inevitably affected by the column spacing. Column spacing often makes it difficult to provide any cross-aisle widths except 3 ft or a multiple of 3 ft. Table 15 suggests desirable cross-aisle widths under different types and amounts of use.

4. Cross-aisle Area Charged against Adjacent Reader Accommodations. The effect on square-footage requirements per stack section and volume capacity per net square foot of stack area, resulting from the provision of reader accommodations in the form of stack carrels, is shown in Figs. 10 and 11. These indicate that the assignment of one-half of the adjacent cross-aisle areas to reader space when carrels are on one side of the cross aisles

TABLE 14 Suggested Stack-Aisle Widths and Stack-Range Lengths*

Typical use of stack	Aisle width, in. †		Range lengths ‡	
	Min.	Max.	Min.	Max.
Closed-access storage stack	24	30	30	60
Limited-access, little-used stack for over 1,000,000 volumes	26	31	30	42
Heavily used open-access stack for over 1,000,000 volumes	31	36	24	36
Very heavily used open-access stack with less than 1,000,000 volumes	33	40	15	30
Newspaper stack with 18 in. deep shelves	36	45	15	30
Reference and current-periodical room stacks . . .	36	60	12	21
Current-periodical display stacks	42	60	12	21

* These are suggestions only and not to be considered definite recommendations. Circumstances alter cases.
† Stack-aisle widths of 24 in. should be considered an absolute minimum and are rarely justifiable. Anything under 26 in. is difficult with a book truck, even when the use is light. The minimum range lengths suggested.
‡ Stack-range lengths are often determined by available space, rather than by their suitability. The maximum lengths shown in the table should generally be used only with the maximum aisle widths suggested.

TABLE 15 Suggested Cross-Aisle Widths*†

Typical use of stack	Main aisle		Subsidiary cross aisle ‡	
	Min.	Max.	Min.	Max.
Closed-access storage . . .	3 ft	4 ft 6 in.	2 ft 6 in.	3 ft 6 in.
Limited-access stack	3 ft	4 ft 6 in.	3 ft	3 ft 6 in.
Heavily used open-access stack.	4 ft	5 ft	3 ft	4 ft
Heavily used open-access stack for large collection and ranges 30 ft or more long	4 ft 6 in.	6 ft	3 ft 3 in.	4 ft 6 in.

* These are suggestions only and not to be considered definite recommendations. Circumstances alter cases.
† In determining minimum or maximum widths, keep in mind the length and width of the book trucks used, as well as the amount of use. Minimum width stack aisles should not be accompanied by minimum cross aisles. From the widths shown in the table, up to 4 in. may have to be subtracted to provide for adjacent stack uprights and irregularities in column sizes.
‡ If open carrels adjoin a subsidiary aisle, they will make it seem wider, but traffic will tend to be disturbing to the carrel occupants.
If closed carrels open from a subsidiary aisle, they will make it seem narrower.

TABLE 16 Square Footage Required for One Single-faced Standard Section

Range spacing	Square feet with minimum cross aisles *	Square feet with generous cross aisles †	Square feet with adequate cross aisles combined with carrels ‡
5 ft 0 in.	8.25	9.00	8.4375
4 ft 6 in.	7.425	8.10	7.60
4 ft 3 in.	7.0125	7.65	7.225
4 ft 0 in.	6.60	7.20	6.75

* Based on Fig. 10, with a 15-ft blind-aisle range on each side of a 3-ft center aisle.
† Based on two 3-ft side aisles and a 6-ft center aisle separated by 30-ft stack ranges.
‡ Based on 3-ft side aisles between carrels and 30-ft stack ranges, the latter separated by a 4 ft 6 in. center aisle. One-half of the side aisles are charged against the carrels, but even on 5-ft centers the carrels occupy only 22½ sq ft, and square footage for a section is low.

and book-stack ranges are on the other, may increase rather than decrease book capacity per square foot of net stack area, and in addition provide desirable and economical seating accommodations adjacent to the books. See Table 16.

It is evident that a large number of variables are involved in book-stack capacity. Table 16 is based on the square footage required for a single-faced standard section in stack layouts, with different range spacing, range lengths, and cross-aisle widths, as well as stack carrels.

Table 17 shows stack capacity per square foot of area if 100, 125, 150, or 160 volumes per standard stack section is used in connection with 7, $8\frac{1}{3}$, 9, or 10 sq ft occupied by each section.

5. *Nonassignable Space.* Nonassignable space includes, as far as its effect on book capacity is concerned, the floor space occupied by columns, mechanical services, and vertical transportation of all kinds. We mention it here simply to call attention to it. In a carefully designed stack for 25,000 volumes or more on one level, nonassignable space should not amount to more than 10 percent of the gross stack area, and with a larger installation considerably less than that.

V. Card Catalog Capacity

In planning a card-catalog room, estimates quite similar to those used for book-stack capacity must be made. They should include:

A. The capacity for each card catalog unit used

B. The square footage of floor space required to file 1,000 cards comfortably

A. The Capacity of Each Card Catalog Unit The capacity of each card catalog unit depends on:

1. The number of trays it contains
2. The depth of each tray and the number of inches of cards that can be filed in it without undesirable and uneconomical congestion
3. The thickness of the card stock, that is, the number of cards that will occupy 1 in. of filing space

1. *The Number of Trays in a Card Cabinet.* This depends on the number of trays in each direction, that is, vertically and horizontally. Cabinets are made in a great many different sizes, but for large installations 6 trays wide and 10 to 12 high are considered standard, giving 60 or 72 to a unit.

A cabinet with trays 14 or even 16 high is possible, with fairly low bases so that the top one will be within reach. This will give 84 or 96 trays to a unit.

Cabinets 5 trays wide of different heights are also available, but may be more expensive per tray unless purchased in large quantities. They have the advantage of fitting into standard 3-ft-wide stack units.

2. *The Depth of the Trays.* Trays can be purchased in almost any depth, but just over 15, 17, and 19 in. might be considered standard. A tray under 15 in. is uneconomical in floor space used if the catalog is large. Those over 19 in. are so heavy when full as to make their use a doubtful blessing.

3. *The Thickness of Cards and the Number That Will Occupy 1 in. of Filing Space.* Experience indicates that 100 average cards to 1 in. of filing space is a safe figure to use today. Cards tend to thicken somewhat as they get older.

Table 18 shows the capacity for cabinets 6 trays wide with different heights and different tray depths, based on 100 cards to 1 in., with the net available filing space filled to a comfortable working capacity. The term "tray

TABLE 17 Volume Capacity per 1,000 sq ft of Stack Area with Different Number of Square Feet and Different Number of Volumes per Section

Sq ft per section a	No. of sections in 1,000 sq ft	Volumes per 1,000 sq ft with different no. of vols. per section b,c			
		100 h	125 i	150 j	160 k
10 d	100	10,000	12,500	15,000	16,000
9 e	111	11,100	13,875	16,650	17,760
$8\frac{1}{3}$ f	120	12,000	15,000	18,000	19,200
7 g	143	14,300	17,875	21,450	22,880

a Examination of Table 16 and Figs. 9 to 11 should help in determining area to allow for a single-faced section. This matter has been covered in IVB.

b Volumes per section has been covered in detail in IVA.

c If a period is used instead of a comma in the volume count in the last four columns shown above, it will give the number of volumes per square foot available under different conditions.

d 10 sq ft per section is the cubook formula proposed by R. W. Henderson.

e See Table 16 for an example.

f The author suggests that this is a satisfactory and safe figure to use for a large collection accessible to graduate students and a limited number of undergraduates.

g Adequate for a very large collection with limited access.

h 100 volumes per section is the cubook formula.

i The author suggests that this is a safe figure for comfortable working capacity in an average library. See IVA.

j The number of 150 volumes per section is too often proposed by architects and librarians. While it is a possible figure, it should be realized that it approaches full capacity and should be used only in cases where additional space is immediately available when capacity is reached. The time to consider what comes next will have passed.

k The number of 160 volumes per section should not be considered for most academic libraries, unless the collection has an unusually high percentage of abnormally thin volumes and individually bound pamphlets.

depth" refers to the overall depth of the cabinet in which the trays are housed. From it 3 in. should be subtracted to obtain the gross filing space available, and comfortable working capacity can be estimated at between 70 and 75 percent of the gross filing space, with a somewhat larger percentage usable with the longer trays.

The capacities noted above can be increased by at least 10 percent before they become completely unmanageable, but it is strongly recommended that the lower figure be used in estimating comfortable working capacity.

B. Square Footage of Floor Space Required to File 1,000 Cards Comfortably The space requirements depend on:

1. The depth of the trays is a somewhat variable factor, as already noted.
2. The height of the cabinets.

TABLE 18 Card Capacity for Standard Card Cabinets Six Trays Wide*

Trays high	Tray length		
	15 in. †	17 in. ‡	19 in. §
10	51,000	60,000	69,000
12	61,200	72,000	82,800
14	71,400	84,000	96,600
16	81,600	96,000	110,400

* Cabinets six trays wide occupy approximately 40 in. in width. Five-tray-wide cabinets occupy approximately $33\frac{1}{3}$ in. in width and can be placed in a standard 3-ft-wide stack section. They will probably cost more per tray, but they may fit into the available space to advantage, sometimes combined with the wider units.

† A 15-in. tray is estimated to provide 12 in. of net filing space, which, if filled to 7.1 percent capacity, will house comfortably approximately 850 cards which average 1/100 in. in thickness.

‡ A 17-in. tray is estimated to provide 14 in. of net filing space, which, if filled to 72 percent of capacity, will house comfortably approximately 1,000 cards which average 1/100 in. in thickness.

§ A 19-in. tray is estimated to provide 16 in. of net filing space, which, if filled to 73 percent of capacity, will house comfortably approximately 1,150 cards which average 1/100 in. in thickness. These trays may be uncomfortably heavy when filled to capacity.

3. The space between cabinets set aside for consultation tables and for those who use the catalog. This should depend on the intensity of use at the time of peak loads. A small catalog with heavy use requires much more square footage for 1,000 cards than does a large one with light use.

4. The space assigned to main and secondary aisles used to approach the cards.

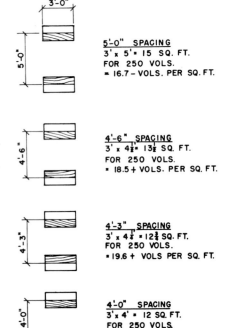

Fig. 9 Stack capacity with different range spacing. No allowance is included here for cross aisles. See Figs. 10 and 11 for their effect. Stack capacities used here are on the basis of 125 volumes to each single-faced section.

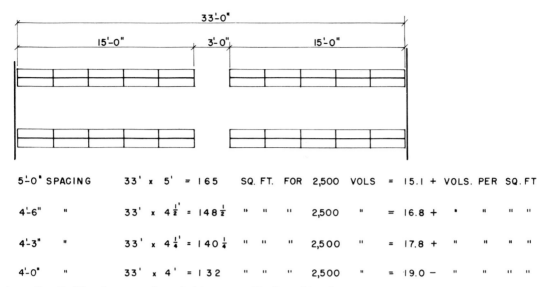

5'-0" SPACING   33' x 5' = 165   SQ. FT. FOR 2,500 VOLS = 15.1 + VOLS. PER SQ. FT

4'-6"   "   33' x 4$\frac{1}{2}$' = 148$\frac{1}{2}$ "   "   "   2,500   "   = 16.8 +   "   "   "   "

4'-3"   "   33' x 4$\frac{1}{4}$' = 140$\frac{1}{4}$ "   "   "   2,500   "   = 17.8 +   "   "   "   "

4'-0"   "   33' x 4' = 132   "   "   "   2,500   "   = 19.0 −   "   "   "   "

Fig. 10   Stack capacity with different range spacing and minimum cross aisle. Cross aisle = $\frac{1}{11}$ area.

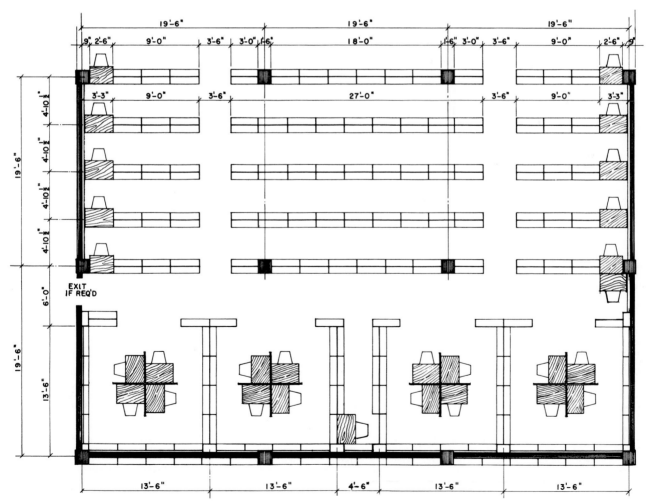

Fig. 11   Stack combined with stack alcoves. Nonstandard bay sizes can sometimes be used to advantage without seriously affecting capacity per square foot.

COLLEGE AND UNIVERSITY FACILITIES
Libraries

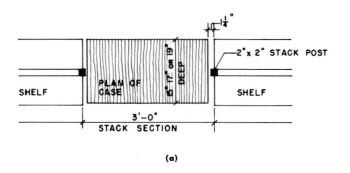

(a)

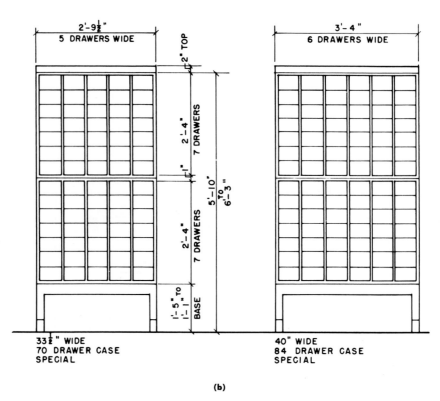

(b)

Fig. 12 Width of catalog cases. (a) Cases which are five trays wide can be fitted into a standard 3-ft wide book section, an arrangement which is sometimes useful. (b) The right-hand case is a standard six-tray width; both cases are in two parts, each seven trays high for additional capacity. Additional horizontal support provided by thicker cross pieces (not shown) will be required in each part.

Figs. 17 and 18 show different arrangements based primarily on the intensity of use and secondarily on the size of the catalog which result in all the way from 1,000 to 4,000 cards per sq ft of floor space for the whole area.

Every library building program should indicate the number of cards that should be housed and any available information about the amount of use at the time of peak loads.

Card catalogs are generally placed in double-faced rows parallel to each other, at suitable distances apart, so spaced that it is possible to go around either end of each row to reach the next one. As catalogs become larger, it may be desirable and perhaps necessary to fill in one

of the ends, making an alcove closed on three sides. This may add to the capacity of the area by as much as 50 percent, but it must be remembered that, if corners are tiight together, there is danger of bruised knuckles when a tray from the row next to the corner is pulled out. A 4- to 6-in. break, preferably covered with a filler, is desirable on each side of the corner. A double row of alcoves with a corridor in between, perhaps 6 ft wide, may give the largest possible capacity in a given area.

Suggested layouts for three libraries, each representing a different situation as far as size and use are concerned, are shown in Figs. 16, 17, and 18.

VI. Government Standards

It is possible and in some cases necessary to base space-assignment figures on standards promulgated by governmental authorities supervising the institutions concerned. These standards can be helpful but, like all formulas and tables, they should be used with caution because, as has been emphasized throughout this section, situations differ and circumstances alter cases. With this word of warning, standards for three different groups are noted:

A. California State Colleges Library Standards Based upon library volumes to be housed, the fol-

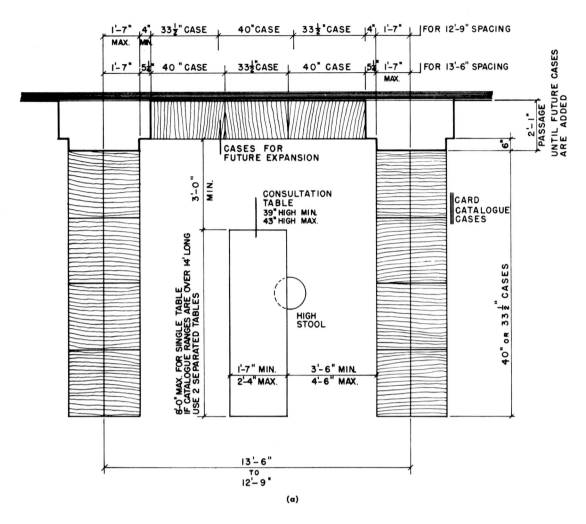

(a)

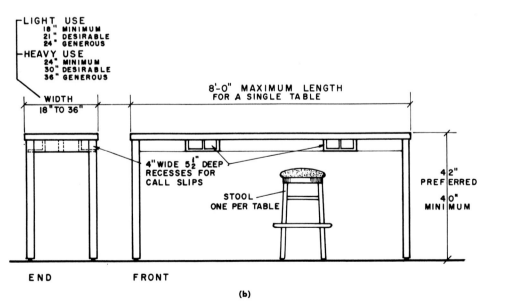

(b)

Fig. 13 Consultation table adjacent to catalog cases. (a) If the table is placed between parallel rows of cases with aisles of suitable width, it will prevent obstruction and not require the trays to be carried uncomfortably long distances. (b) This shows an end and front elevation of a consultation table indicating possible widths, heights, and accessories.

COLLEGE AND UNIVERSITY FACILITIES

Libraries

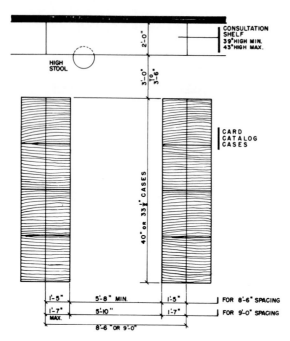

Fig. 14 Consultation table along a wall at right angles to catalog cases. With this arrangement, cases can be placed closer together but trays must be carried considerably farther, and there will be a tendency to try to consult cards without removing trays. Congestion and damage to cards may result.

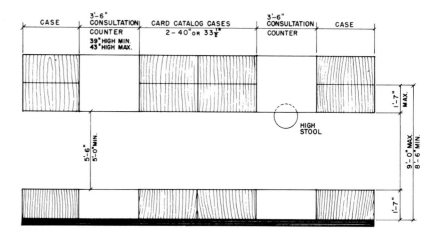

Fig. 15 Consultation tables in line with and between catalog cases. Consultation tables arranged in this way save steps but partially obstruct use of adjacent trays.

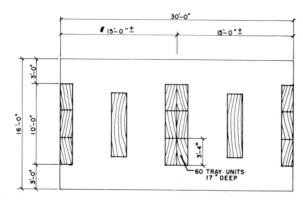

Fig. 16 Catalog for a small library. With 3-ft-wide aisles at end of each row of standard cases six trays wide and ten high, 720,000 cards can be housed in 480 sq ft, giving 1,500 to a square foot. This is adequate spacing for a library with 300 seats.

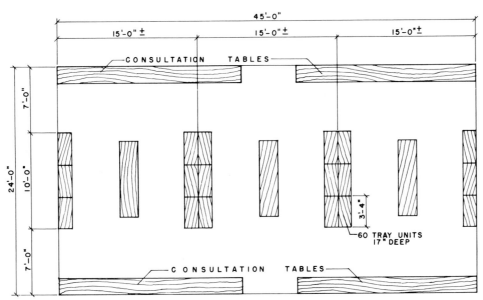

Fig. 17 Catalog room for a small university library with 1,000 seats. A larger proportion of the area is required for consultation tables and only 1,000 cards per square foot of floor space is provided.

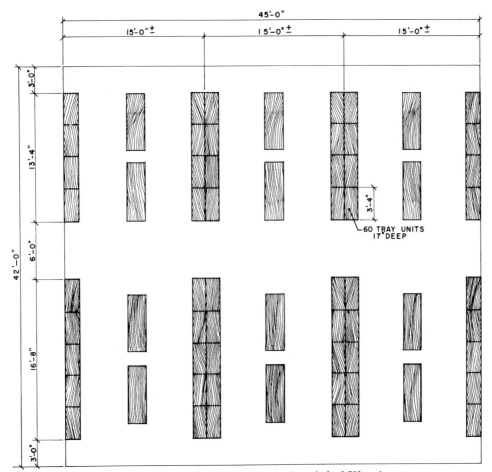

Fig. 18 Catalog room for typical large university library. Provision is made for 1,500 cards per square foot of area with adequate space at tables for readers consulting them.

COLLEGE AND UNIVERSITY FACILITIES
Libraries; Individual Study Carrels

lowing space standards are to serve as guidelines for the design of new buildings or additions to existing buildings:

1. Book-stack areas at the rate of 0.10 sq ft per volume.

2. Readers' stations at the rate of 25 sq ft per station, with stations to be provided for 25 percent of predicted FTE (full-time equivalent students).

3. Special materials. An additional area equal to 25 percent of the bound-volume area should be the budget standard for special materials: unbound periodicals, maps, courses of study, and sample textbooks.

4. Special functions.

(These data relate to each person employed in any of these categories)

	Square feet
Administration	150
Administrative conference room	150
Secretary-reception	160
Technical services	
Division head	150
Department head	110
Asst. catalog librarian	110
Asst. order librarian	110
Serials librarian	110
Documents librarian	110
Clerical—per position	80

INDIVIDUAL STUDY CARRELS
From an Educational Facilities Laboratories Report*

	Square feet
Public services	
Division head	150
Department head	150
Reference librarian	110
Special services	110
Circulation librarian	110
Clerical—per position	80
Public services points	
Per librarian's station	125
Per clerical station	80

B. The California State Department of Education in 1955 included this statement in *A Restudy of the Needs of California in Higher Education.*

Libraries.—Total library space requirements, including study halls and all library-staff work areas, were computed on the basis of the following estimates:

1. Reading rooms and study halls, including circulation desks and staff offices: 30 net square feet per station and one station for every four full-time students, or 7.5 net square feet per full-time student.

2. Collections housing the volumes listed below, including work areas, assuming progressively greater use of closed stacks as collections increase in size, and the use of central storage facilities for the larger collections:

First 150,000 volumes	0.10 net sq ft per volume
Second 150,000 volumes	0.09
Next 300,000 volumes	0.08
Next 400,000 volumes	0.07
Second 1,000,000 volumes	0.05

(Note: The total floor area allowed by 1 and 2 above will, it is estimated, provide for the necessary carrels, microfilm and audio-visual facilities, etc.)

3. Size of collection:

State college: 30 volumes per full-time student for the first 5,000 students, plus 20 volumes per full-time student beyond 5,000 students.

University: 100 volumes per full-time student for the first 10,000 students, plus 75 volumes per student for the second 10,000 students, plus 50 volumes per student beyond 20,000 students.

C. The United States Veterans Administration has prepared tables to indicate library space assignments which are based on the number of beds in different types of hospitals. They are hoping by the use of these tables to determine through a computer the square footage to be assigned in a library for each group of space users, library staff, hospital staff, patients, shelving equipment, and so forth.

Fig. 1 A variety of possible shapes and arrangements for small-group rooms.

* "The School Library, Facilities for Independent Study in the Secondary School," by Ralph E. Ellsworth, Ph.D., and Hobart D. Wagener, A.I.A., edited by Ruth Weinstock, Educational Facilities Laboratories, New York, 1963.

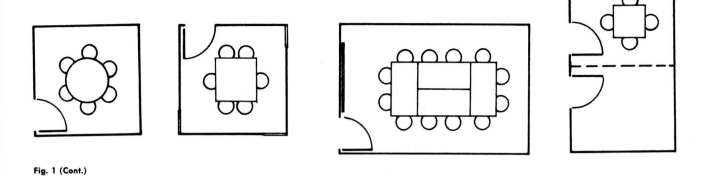

Fig. 1 (Cont.)

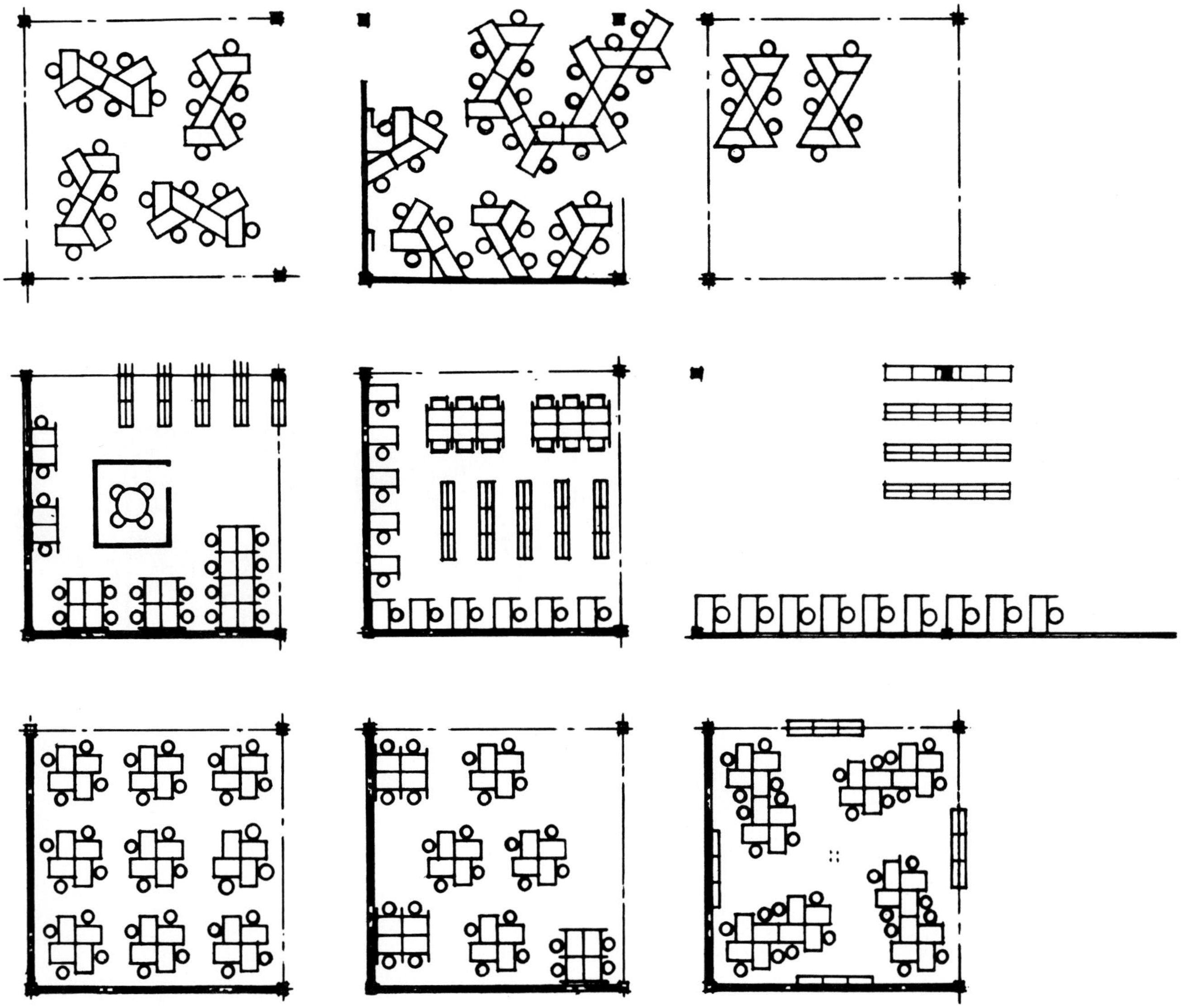

Fig. 2 A variety of possible carrel arrangements.

COLLEGE AND UNIVERSITY FACILITIES
Individual Study Carrels

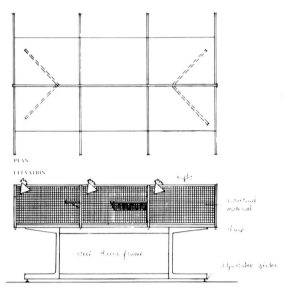

Fig. 3 Carrels with panel dividers.

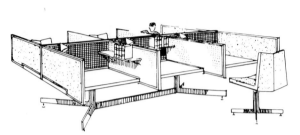

Fig. 4 Conventional library table subdivided by panels.

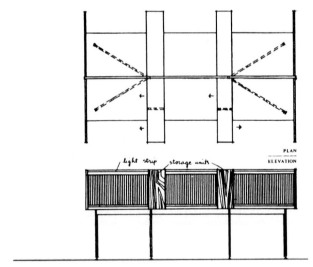

Fig. 5 Carrels with storage dividers.

Fig. 6 Library table with storage units as dividers.

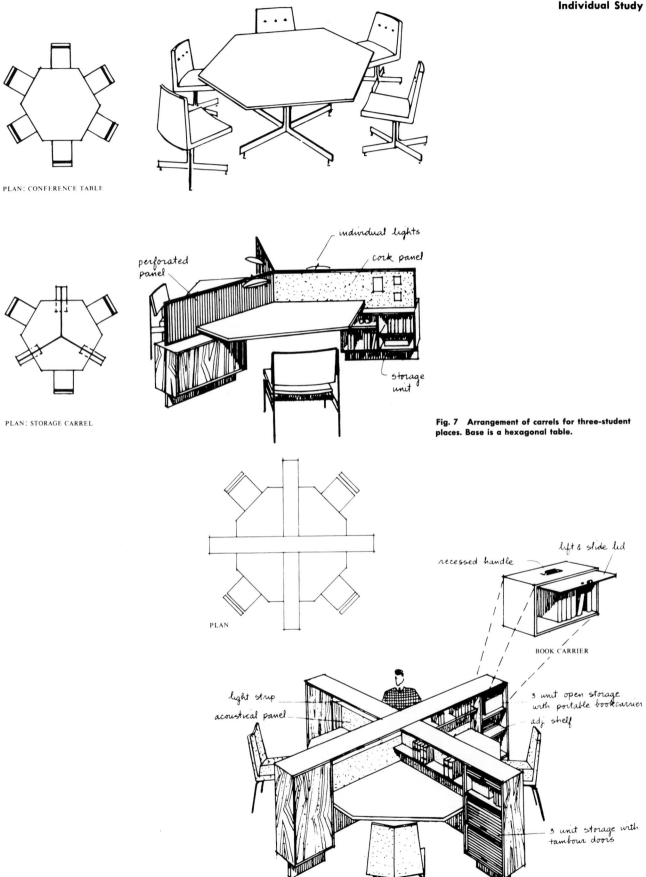

PLAN: CONFERENCE TABLE

PLAN: STORAGE CARREL

perforated panel

individual lights

cork panel

storage unit

Fig. 7 Arrangement of carrels for three-student places. Base is a hexagonal table.

PLAN

recessed handle

lift & slide lid

BOOK CARRIER

light strip

acoustical panel

3 unit open storage with portable bookcarrier

adj shelf

3 unit storage with tambour doors

Fig. 8 Carrels for four student places using octagonal table.

317

COLLEGE AND UNIVERSITY FACILITIES
Individual Study Carrels

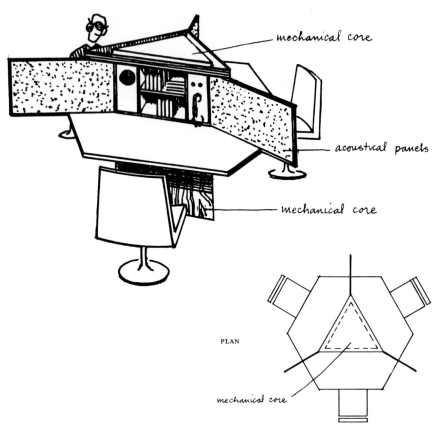

Fig. 9 Hexagon-based carrel with mechanical core.

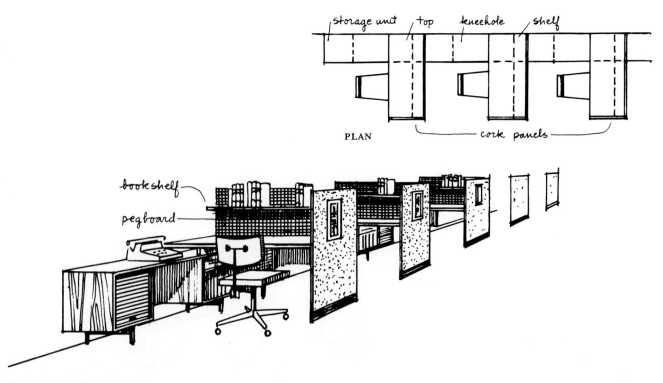

Fig. 10 Carrels with typing unit.

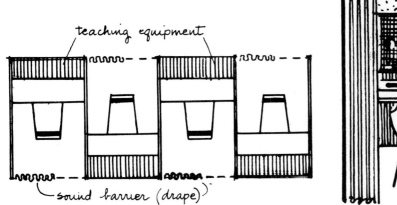

Fig. 11 Closed carrels for sound and visual equipment.

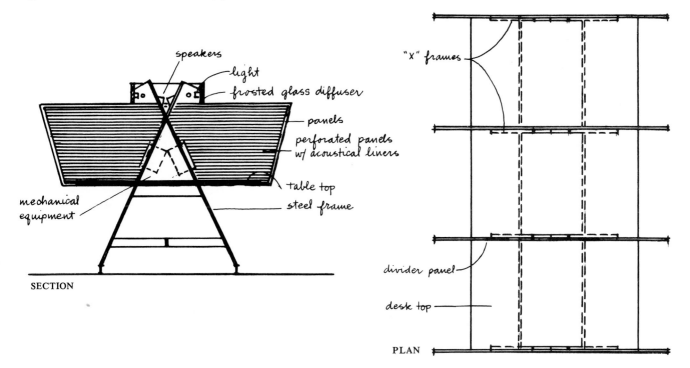

SECTION

PLAN

Fig. 12 Carrels with mechanical equipment built in, based on a steel or aluminum "X" frame. Frame folds up like a card table, can be used for other purposes as well.

COLLEGE AND UNIVERSITY FACILITIES
Individual Study Carrels

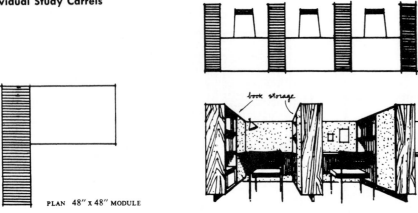

PLAN 48" x 48" MODULE

book storage

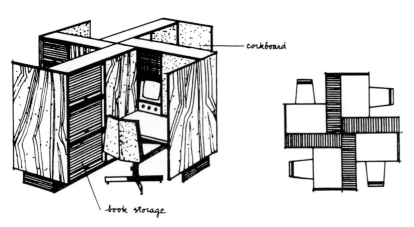

corkboard

book storage

Fig. 13   Carrel arrangements using standard bookcases and tables.

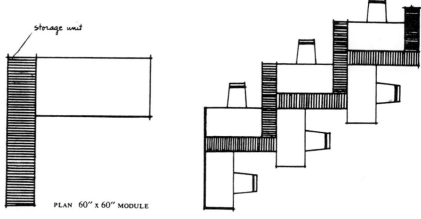

storage unit

PLAN 60" x 60" MODULE

luminous panel

book storage

cork or acoustical panel

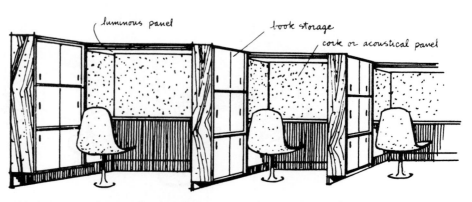

Fig. 14   Carrels with storage lockers for books.

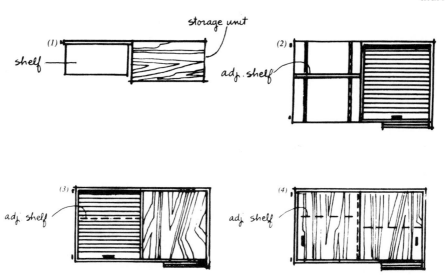

Fig. 15 Various storage units: (1) plan, (2) elevation, (3) tambour door, and (4) sliding doors opening to opposite sides.

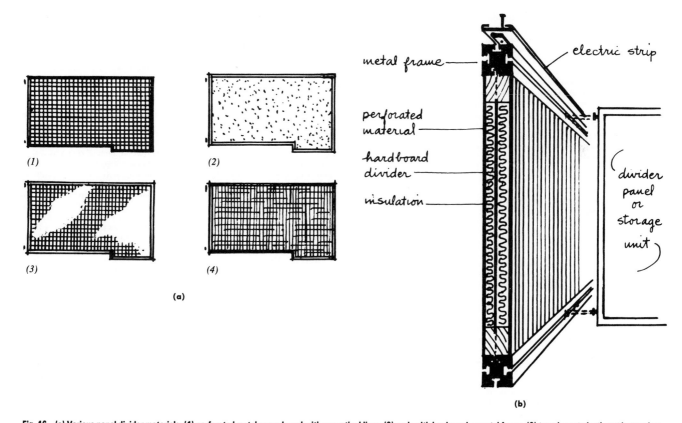

Fig. 16 (a) Various panel divider materials: (1) perforated metal or pegboard with acoustical liner, (2) cork with hardwood or metal frame, (3) translucent plastic set in wood or metal frame, and (4) fabric covered fiberboard set in metal frame. (b) Divider panel and center divider: side panels or storage units can be slid along tracks of center divider to change carrel size.

Educational

COLLEGE AND UNIVERSITY FACILITIES
Student Unions

By CHESTER ARTHUR BERRY, Ed.D.

STUDENT UNIONS

Organization

Since by definition the term college union has two meanings—organization and building—it is necessary to investigate the nature of each. The organization of students, faculty, and alumni which composes the union usually operates with a governing board at its head. This board, which may or may not include representatives of the three groups, is responsible for the operation of the union, although much of the detail is handled by trained staff members and much of the guiding philosophy is originally that of the professional staff. The board itself is concerned largely with questions of policy and implements its policies through the work of various volunteer committees and the paid staff of the union.

The committees consist almost entirely of students and may or may not include members of the governing board. At Michigan State University the following standing committees operate: education, library, merit, outings, publications, publicity, social, and tournament. At the University of Nebraska standing committees for 1950–51 included: general entertainment; special activities; convocations and hospitality; music activities; house and office; public relations; recreation; dance; and budgets, orientation, and evaluation. Regardless of the titles and varying functions, most of the committees serve as the links which connect the boards with the general campus population. The committees plan and execute programs, attending to such details as scheduling, publicizing, decorating, and budgeting. They may choose records for the music library, prints for the art collection. They may help in the orientation of freshmen or study a proposed change in furniture arrangement. They may run the billiards tournament or a book review hour. The committees, sensitive to campus needs and interests, keep the union dynamic, flexible, and busy.

Building

The nature of a college union building varies with each structure, whether approached from either the functional or the physical standpoint. Functionally it is a community center of the first order. It may be a library, art gallery, art workshop, theater, billiard and bowling room, dance center, scene of concerts and forums, informal outing and sports headquarters, office building, hotel, public relations agency, ticket bureau, general campus information bureau, convention headquarters, and post office. The uniqueness of college unions demands custom planning, with the result that, physically, union buildings differ as local situations differ. While the overall purposes of unions remain relatively alike, their functional and structural natures vary.

The functions housed by the union building ideally are those needed to make it the focus

Planning a College Union Building, Teachers College Press, New York, 1960.

of the recreational, cultural, social, and civic life on the campus. Needless to say, many existing campus facilities such as the library, art museum, gymnasium, or theater cannot and should not be duplicated in a new union building, but the inclusion of as many such facilities as are feasible is desirable to assure that the widest possible range of educational experiences are made available by the union.

Structurally, of course, the union building must house efficiently the facilities required by the union functions while suggesting its purposes by its appearance and design. Its atmosphere should meet the local requirements. If the union is considered "the living room of the campus," it is logical that it reflect the friendliness and warmth of a living room. If it exists largely to serve as a convention center and hotel, it might well offer a more formal environment but, it should be pointed out, such an approach may result in a building and an operation which do not meet the terms of definition of a college union. Whatever the local requirements may be, it seems well to remember that much of the activity of a union is informal in nature and that most of the participation in its activities is carried on by informal college students. The nature of a college union building, then, might well be largely informal to reflect the character of the activities which it houses.

The well-planned union building separates its areas by functions to permit efficient communication, supervision, and operation. It does not place bowling areas next to conference rooms or information desks on upper levels. By separating yet coordinating its components, it continually offers the opportunity for new experiences, so that the walk from the coffee shop to the games area, for example, may lead students past a music room or by an art exhibit. It literally surrounds those who use it with opportunities, and this pervasiveness is a part of the nature of a union.

Facilities and Activities

The diversity of facilities and activities of a union building makes their classification into a few major categories difficult. Nevertheless, there are some aspects of similarity of use, such as noise, service, or supervision, which appear to recommend it. The eight classifications include:

1. Administrative, service, and maintenance
2. Food
3. Quiet
4. Theater
5. Hobby
6. Games
7. Outdoor
8. Miscellaneous

Insistence on rigid separation of activities into areas is, of course, fruitless. Thus, listening to records or working on the college newspaper are hobbies which might well take place in the quiet area, and a bridge tournament held in the main lounge would defy cataloging, involving as it does a quiet hobby which is a game.

Far from definitive, the table merely indicates the type of program which can fit into each area. Much of the duplication of function

which occurs among areas is caused because all facilities are not likely to be found in any union building, with the result, for example, that the ballroom or meeting rooms of a theaterless building may assume many of the functions which are best performed in the theater. Conflicting events also demand alternate expedients, such as showing motion pictures in a large meeting room on dress-rehearsal night or holding a club meeting in a rehearsal room on an evening when meeting rooms are at a premium. The table does not exhaust the flexibility of use by any means. Obviously the small building without cardroom, chess room and ballroom can use its lounges for many of the events listed for those areas. The success and attendance (not necessarily synonymous) of various programs also determine their locations, so that an exceptional music recital might well be held in the theater while a bridge tournament might never require the use of the ballroom.

Not all of the facilities mentioned are discussed here. Some, such as cooperative groceries or ice skating rinks, occur so seldom in connection with unions that they can scarcely be considered as union facilities. Others—bookstore, faculty space, hotel unit, swimming pool, university administrative offices, beauty and barber shops, or chapel—are facilities about which there is widely varying opinion and are usually justified only by local circumstances.

Administrative, Service and Maintenance Areas

A glance at the Classified Facilities Table reveals that union program activities as such are infrequently held in most of these facilities. The program potential of the barber shop and check rooms, for example, is not very high. Closer examination of the table shows that nearly all of the activities are in the nature of services and most of them, in all probability, are performed by paid staff members. If the union board has its offices located away from the administrative offices, the function of staff members is even more pronounced, since many of the services rendered, such as interviewing and training union committee applicants or operating a talent agency or a date bureau, are carried on in the student offices.

Food Areas

Examination of the Classified Facilities Table shows that the variety of food services offered by union buildings equals that of large, modern hotels. They include soda fountains and grill, cafeterias, private dining rooms, service dining rooms, coffee shops, faculty dining rooms, commuters' lunchrooms, women's dining rooms, and banquet rooms.

Since the dining service is the main source of union revenue and caters regularly to a large segment of the campus, it is extremely important that it be planned, constructed, and operated properly.

Functionality As in other union building facilities, the functions of the food service areas vary with the institutions. The existence of other eating facilities on and off the campus, the policies of such facilities (a la carte, five- or seven-day board bills, semester contracts), the location of existing places as well as that of the union building, the prevalence and size of conferences and conventions, and the institution's future plans are some of the items which should be considered.

Food Area Components An all-inclusive union food operation, embracing soda fountain and grills; cafeteria; private, women's, faculty, banquet, and service dining rooms; coffee shops; and commuters' lunchroom includes many components in common with other food operations elsewhere, since the flow process is basically the same. Such components include receiving, storage, meat cutting, vegetable preparation, cooking, bakery, ice cream, salad, service (cafeteria counter or waitress pantry), dining, pot-washing, dishwashing, garbage and trash storage, maintenance, employees' facilities, rest rooms, coat rooms, and offices. All unions neither need nor are able to afford such a comprehensive plant, and only the largest can use all components. Certainly few small unions can afford to hire a butcher for a meat-cutting room, and many provide only refreshment services through a soda fountain or grillroom.

Receiving The receiving facilities of the food area need not be separate from those for the rest of the union building. If combined to serve all the other areas, they may permit the employment of a receiving clerk. A central storeroom for nonperishable items is quite feasible as well, and such arrangement may make it possible for even the smaller unions to use a receiving clerk-storekeeper. Obviously, both vertical and horizontal transportation is needed in such an operation and, since the frequency and perishability of food deliveries are high, the receiving room should be near the food service department.

Storage Storage in the food area includes dry stores or nonperishables, day stores, refrigerated stores, frozen stores, garbage and trash storage. Some may include several subdivisions such as freezers for meat, fruit, vegetables, and ice cream or dairy and meat, fruit, and vegetable refrigerators.

Service Areas The service areas are directly between the various preparation areas and the dining areas in the flow chart. They are usually the places where the food is placed on the individual plates and distributed and may take the form of a cafeteria counter, a serving kitchen or pantry, a waitress station, a serving counter in the kitchen, or a station in a short-order kitchen. In this area food must be kept hot or cold and dishes stored. Dispensing of food occurs here for consumption in the dining area. Refinements and variations of this basic operation differ according to the type of food service being offered.

The prepared food in larger union buildings may go in several directions from the central kitchen. Cafeterias, counters, banquet service kitchens, soda fountains, coffee shops, employees' cafeteria counters, private and public dining room kitchens, and commuter lunchrooms may all be served from this single area, with auxiliary food preparation completed at the serving scene.

Supplying food to these service areas calls for various kinds of transportation. Cafeterias demand a rather steady stream of food for two or more hours at a time, while banquets and private dinners demand that all persons be

Classified Facilities Table

Administrative, Service, and Maintenance:

Offices	Duplicating area
Check and coat rooms	Rest rooms
Information center	Janitorial spaces
Bookstore	Bulletin boards
Non-union offices	Bank
Ticket office	Delivery area
Barber shop	Trash rooms
Beauty shop	Elevator
Post office	Mechanical rooms
Maintenance shop	Storage
Lobby	Employees' lockers and rest rooms
Western Union office	Pay telephones
Shops	Corridors
Lost and found	P-A system

Food:

Soda fountain and grill	Banquet room
Cafeteria	Offices
Private dining rooms	Kitchen
Service dining rooms	Dishwashing room
Coffee shop	Garbage room
Faculty dining room	Refrigeration room
Commuters' lunchroom	Trash room
Women's dining room	

Quiet:

Meeting rooms	Commuters' lockers
Lounges	Box lunch lockers
Music listening room	Commuters' sleeping rooms
Library	International center
Guest rooms	Student activities area
Dormitory	Student organization offices
Chapel	Art room
Other faculty space	

Games:

Table tennis room	Bowling alleys
Cardroom	Chess room
Billiard room	

Hobby:

Photographic studio	Outing club headquarters
Art shop	Amateur radio transmitter
Craft shop	Lending art library

Theater:

Auditorium	Stage house
Stage	Costume shop
Dressing rooms	Costume storage
Shops	Rehearsal room
Lobbies	Ticket office
Projection booth	Offices

Outdoor:

Cement slab	Games
Sun decks	Parking
Picnic areas	

Miscellaneous:

Ballroom	Swimming pool
Music recital room	Ice skating rink
Music practice room	Cooperative grocery
Television room	Ski slide
Convention hall	

Non-Union:

Campus newspaper	Student amateur radio club
College yearbook	Religious advising
Student government	Outing club
Student radio station	Others

served nearly simultaneously. Public dining rooms, coffee shops, and soda fountains require more individual service.

Many unions do a brisk take-out business with coffee, sandwiches, and similar refreshment being purchased for consumption outside the building. Much of this business occurs late in the evening when food is taken back to living units for consumption during study hours. The soda-fountain–short-order facilities with their long operating hours and particular menu are best equipped to handle this operation.

Dining Rooms Basically, the function of the dining room is the housing of eaters. If this were its only function, the most economical and efficient way to fulfill it would be achieved by using long tables with stools stored under them and with one large room used for all eating. Since some of the union's education and service programs are carried out in the dining areas, they must do much more than just house eaters. In addition to eating, such activities as card and chess playing, dances, carnivals, entertainment, concerts or recitals, radio forums, or speeches may occur in them. They may house displays or serve as polling places. Meetings and private parties may take place in some of them, classes in etiquette or homemaking in others. In some, conferences or conventions for hundreds may be occurring simultaneously with intimate tête-a-têtes in others. Therefore, more than mere feeding stations, the dining rooms are really gathering places for people. They are important in bringing students, faculty, alumni, staff, and the public together, and they further the unifying concepts of the term union.

The variety of dining facilities found in the larger union buildings attests to the variety of dining functions demanding service. There are the soda fountains or snack bars where a quick bite or cup of coffee may be obtained or where acquaintanceships are made and friendships cemented. This, more than any other single spot on campus, is apt to be *the* gathering place. Smoke, juke box music, laughter, conversation and crowds typify it, and informality is its keynote. The coffee shops offer informal dining, with or without table service, for a relaxed meal or casual entertaining; the cafeteria provides the low-priced three meals a day; and the dining room, with its linen, service, crystal, and other fine appointments, is the place for a full-course meal, special date, or folks from home. The banquet hall provides for the numerous student, faculty, and other organizational dinners that occur throughout the year but which abound each spring, and the private dining rooms cater to luncheon or dinner meetings for groups, classes, guests, or others.

Quiet Areas

All the quiet areas of the union building need not be connected, but they should be isolated from the noisier sections such as kitchens, workshops, or game areas. Actually, quiet areas subdivide quite easily by function to permit separation. Thus, the living quarters such as guest rooms, guest dormitories, or commuters' sleeping rooms should be separated from the busier lounges and meeting rooms, and their combination permits more efficient operation, supervision, and housekeeping. Student activity areas (rooms with desks and files not permanently assigned) and student offices (permanently assigned spaces) should be together for ease of communication and supervision. The facilities for day students, if they are distinguished from those normally used by all students, should adjoin each other, including their lunchroom and lounge. The location of meeting rooms near each other permits flexibility of use, easy transfer of furniture and equipment, proper supervision and maintenance resulting from concentration of people, and economy of time between meetings. Lounges may be spread throughout the building to serve various sections and may vary in kind with the sections they serve.

Some of the quiet areas may well be served by separate entrances, included among which could be the chapel, guest quarters, faculty lounge, international center, and student activities and office spaces. Problems of control arise when this situation occurs and it may have some divisive effect on the union, but late operating hours in the newspaper office or guest wing may dictate separation of such areas from the whole building, as may the partial operation of the building during vacation periods.

Music listening (properly soundproofed), library or browsing, and art display rooms can be located together in a sort of cultural center. If this is done, the issuing of records, books, and periodicals and prints from a central location and supervision of that area proves economical. These areas are likely to offer less attraction than the game areas, for example, while supplying experiences of value in broadening the horizons of undergraduates. Their location, however, in a fairly prominent spot may encourage more patronage, but since heavy traffic and accompanying noisiness may result, a choice may be necessary between prominence and peacefulness of position.

Meeting Rooms *Expansibility.* A glance at the Classified Facilities Table shows a wide variety of uses to which meeting rooms and lounges may be put and the degree of interchangeability which exists between the functions of the two areas. If lounges are not to be used for formal programs but solely for spontaneous, informal use, the number of meeting rooms required is larger than that demanded when the use of lounges permits more flexibility. It seems quite certain, at any rate, that the meeting room facility will require expansion early.

The need for many small meeting rooms does not eliminate the demand for larger ones. Enough of each is expensive and the compromise of dividing large rooms into smaller ones by means of folding or sliding walls is a widely accepted one, even though it is a compromise with faults centering largely around the acoustic problem.

Some small meeting rooms, equipped with tables and seating, may double as conference rooms, and the tables themselves may serve as rostrums for meetings as well as conference tables.

The addition of a small 16 mm projection booth at the end of a meeting room simplifies the showing of motion pictures to small groups and eliminates much of the need for transporting and setting up equipment in a room where its noise, light and extension cords detract from the film showing. Such a booth, separated from the meeting room by a wall and glass port, can serve many groups and relieve much of the load normally placed on a theatre, particularly if this booth looks into a larger room which may be subdivided.

Lounges A variety of lounges—men's, women's, faculty, commuters', mixed—may be included in a union building. To a certain extent, the kind of institution involved determines the kinds of lounges which are desirable. A residential college does not need a commuters' lounge; a women's college probably finds a men's lounge superfluous, although it may wish to have a room available which can be converted to serve such a purpose on special occasions. The existence and location of a faculty club may determine the desirability of a faculty lounge, and the facilities and entertaining regulations in living units bear on the size and number of mixed lounges. The presence and availability of other lounges on campus should be considered in planning the union building lounges.

Reading Rooms While all colleges have libraries, they seem to be considered primarily places for work, so that much can be done by a union browsing or reading room to stimulate good recreational reading habits on the campus. Avoidance of the "library stigma" may be achieved by using comfortable surroundings with air conditioning, fireplaces, decorative plants, proper lighting, by not numbering the binding of books and by meeting the reading needs through a selection committee. Certainly atmosphere is important if the browsing room is to be the sort of place where students and others go for intellectual stimulation or satisfaction, or to while away some time.

The normal functions most likely to be carried out in the browsing room are book, periodical and newspaper storage, reading and book selection. Books are usually shelved around the periphery of the room, and this area should be separated from furnishings and equipment by an aisle wide enough to permit persons to select their books easily. Periodicals and newspapers require less browsing room and may be incorporated in a lounge arrangement of furniture by use of standard racks, or by storage on coffee or other tables.

Music Rooms Marked changes have occurred in the field of music listening. Record changers, the long playing record, tape recorders, and high fidelity have increased tremendously the interest in reproduced music and have offered unions, among others, a real opportunity for improving the level of musical understanding and interest of their students. At the same time, problems of control and usage have been raised since record and tape playing equipment is costly and complex, records easily damaged and the noise potential great enough to transform the so-called quiet areas of the union building into pandemonium. The whole music listening program must be thought out well in advance because this aspect of the union building is dependent to a very great extent upon the manner in which the program functions. Individuals listening to music may do so in booths, small rooms or lounges of varying sizes. They may be using earphones which can disturb no one, commercial combination phonograph-radios, or custom-built high fidelity sets. They may be playing the records themselves or may have requested selections which an attendant is playing from the control point. Records and tapes may be kept with the player and used by anyone, they may be issued by an attendant or they may be private property. Persons using record players may be required to pass a test in the operation of the equipment. Planned group listening such as record coffee hours may be held in a multipurpose lounge equipped with a player or a speaker from a master system, or they may take place in a music lounge specifically designed for music listening, recorded and live. Economy may demand that listening booths be connected with the reading room where group concerts are held. Obviously, many of these items must be considered before the building is planned, because such items as conduits, storage racks, acoustics, equipment, furniture, electrical outlets, glazed doors for supervision, and cataloging methods determine much of the utility of the music room.

Commuters' Areas Nonresident students at colleges near or in metropolitan centers afford many problems to unions, a number of which center around their nonparticipation in most of the union's programs. Their demands on the college naturally differ from those of the residents. They need parking space on the campus, a place to eat a bag or light lunch, storage place for books, lunches, and similar equipment, a spot for resting or, perhaps, an occasional overnight stay. While the union is not necessarily the only location on the campus where such services may be rendered, it seems to be the logical place for many of them. Furthermore, many of the day students are quite likely to eat in the union and to use it as their headquarters, and so it seems logical to plan to meet as many of their demands as possible in advance. If the union building is to be a unifying factor on the campus, it must be prepared to serve the offtimes large [nonresident] segment of the student body.

Guest Rooms Many union buildings contain overnight guest facilities, the extent of which ranges from a single room or suite through large, barracks-like halls to elaborate hotels with full commercial service. The facilities may be intended primarily for university guests, such as convocation speakers, for visiting groups such as athletic teams, for parents or returning alumni, for the guests of students or for conventions. They add to the service aspects of the union building and offer little to its educational program aside from the training the larger units afford to student employees and to students who are majoring in hotel administration. The inclusion of guest rooms in the union building depends upon many diverse elements, such as present and future needs, facilities existing elsewhere, nearby hotels, curricular development, operating hours, operating costs and other union facilities, and careful study is indicated. The fact that the Association of College Unions lists hotel units among the doubtful facilities to be included in union buildings should serve to reinforce the need for careful study.

Student Activities Area A student activities area is a space housing a number of desks and filing cabinets which can be used by varying student organizations for a portion of the academic year. Thus groups which do not need an office or room of their own can be accommodated with a minimum of space allocation. The number of groups and activities on each campus that might use such an area determine its size, and it appears wise to consider that the existence of such an area might well increase requests for its use, thus making a somewhat oversized original plan advisable.

Theater

Need Like so many other parts of the union building, the theater must be custom-built to suit its campus. It is quite likely that a union building located near a modern, well-equipped theater can utilize these facilities for its program and not need a theater of its own. On the other hand, the demands on such a theater by dramatic and other groups may render the theater unavailable for the variety of activities

which the Classified Facilities Table indicates may be held therein, thus making desirable the inclusion of a theater in the union building. With a well-housed drama program already in operation, the theater requirements may be pared down so that nothing more than an auditorium and platform suits the union's needs. Such a solution appears most questionable, however, since it provides little more than a forum for speakers, a location for motion pictures and stage for formal music concerts. Such activities as variety or vaudeville shows, fashion shows, orchestral and choral concerts, sing contests and dance recitals become difficult to present without proper stage, scenery, dressing, shops, wing and lighting facilities. The use of road shows—ballet, drama, opera, and the like—by the union is obviated. It may be that such activities can be housed elsewhere, but the demands on theaters of dramatic groups for practice and for rehearsal and staging time, of music groups for practice and concert time, of assemblies, meetings and conferences for auditorium time, of departments and organizations for space for motion pictures, lectures and demonstrations, indicate that a close study of all present demands upon theater facilities be studied and that future possibilities, particularly as suggested by other campuses with adequate union theaters, be considered before plans are drawn up. The place of other existing theaters and assembly halls in the campus scheme of things, including policies governing their use, should be given grave consideration.

A union theater would seem to suit most of its purposes if it houses the requirements of a fairly orthodox collegiate drama program and adds such items as an elevating forestage-orchestra pit; audience access to stage for variety shows, sing contests and the like; fluctuating seating capacity by means of sliding panels or draperies; reception or lobby lounge; broadcasting facilities; possible combination craft-scenery shops, and still and motion-picture equipment to achieve the flexibility which is an earmark of the union building.

To function completely, the union theater would be composed of:

Auditorium	Projection booth
Stage	Sound system
Forestage	Screen
Orchestra pit	Stage house
Proscenium arch	Lobby
Dressing rooms	Ticket office
Scene shop	Scenery storeroom
Costume shop	Control board
Light booth	Rest rooms
Makeup room	Coat room
Rehearsal room	Lounge or green room

Some of these facilities, such as lounge, coat room, rest room or rehearsal room, may be a part of the union building and serve a double purpose, so that a nearby lounge may be used for receptions or a properly shaped meeting room double for use during live rehearsals.

Arts and Crafts Shops

The variety of offerings which the union's shops can provide is large. Some of these offerings, such as photography, demand specialized facilities and equipment; others, such as leatherwork or jewelry making, require little and can be accommodated in a general shop area. The tools of some crafts may be used in common by participants in other union activities, so that the scene, maintenance, and woodworking shops may use the same power tools

and central materials sources and the camera club and campus publications the same studios. The size of the union and the university, the organizational scheme and expected use of the various shops would determine the possibility of such a combination. Among the arts and crafts activities which a union might embrace are:

Painting	General woodworking
Sketching	Picture framing
Block printing	Cabinet making
Poster making	Metal and jewelry work
Silk screening	Ceramics
Clay modeling	Drafting
Weaving	Photography
Rug making	Leatherwork
Drawing	Graphic arts
Fly tying	Sewing
Plastic work	Knitting

While adherents of nearly each art or craft could develop a list of reasons why their favorite activity should be allocated separate space and equipment, much of it with special requirements such as north light for sketching or humidity control for clay modeling, enough compromises and combinations can be effected to provide a variety of activities within a reasonable area.

Outdoor Games

The extent to which the games area should be developed is dependent in large degree on what is available elsewhere on the campus. The number of games within the union's province which can be played outside might include badminton, bowling on the green, boccie, croquet, curling, clock golf, horseshoes, shuffleboard, table tennis, giant checkers, deck tennis, roque, quoits, and a variety of table games such as chess, checkers, or cards.

Integration of Areas

Some union facilities must be located on the street level; others operate most efficiently on other levels. There are strong reasons for placing food services, information center, bookstore, ticket offices, ballroom, and administrative offices on the ground floor, while other areas such as publication offices or student activity offices may be in less accessible locations. Guest rooms, which receive relatively little traffic and function better in quiet, fit nicely into higher floors and more remote wings. The task of putting the various elements of a union building together so that each fulfills its own function while complementing that of the others is nearly certain to demand compromises. Realism may dictate that such revenue-producing facilities as a bookstore or soda fountain take precedence in location over a music room or browsing library, even though it may be educationally desirable to expose, at least by propinquity, those entering the building to the latter rather than the former. Traffic to the most popular areas of the union building should not be so directed that it causes great crowds of people to throng its passages and stairways to the disturbance of other sections and to the detriment of building maintenance. Some seldom-used facilities, such as a ballroom or hobby shop, may finally be placed on the top floor because there is no room elsewhere for them.

Segregation by Function Whenever practical, areas should be separated by function, as previously described in the section on game rooms, where supervision, instruction, and equipment control for all were made possible. Such areas

Educational

COLLEGE AND UNIVERSITY FACILITIES
Student Unions

may assist others in their functions when properly located and so, while complete in themselves, they can nevertheless help and be helped by others. Thus, a self-contained game area receives players from a nearby coffee shop, and the presence of such a shop induces gamesters to stop for refreshments when leaving. It is to be hoped that persons walking by a corridor case containing a craft display might be interested in utilizing the out-of-the-way hobby shop.

Some principles in combining the elements of the union building into an entity are elementary. The games area is noisy and should not be next to sleeping rooms or private dining or meeting rooms. Kitchens demand considerable delivery, removal, and storage, hence they should be near driveways, storerooms, and receiving spaces. The information center should be near the main entrance. The theater should have its own exits and entrance and is probably best situated in its own wing. Similar or related activities may suggest combinations such as the ballroom-banquet room or theatre-radio station. The browsing, music, and art

rooms can be worked into a unit which is serviced and supervised by one central control or which, at least during rest periods or emergencies, can be satisfactorily administered by one person.

The kitchen should connect with the ballroom and with certain of the lounges and meeting rooms, even if only by conveyors or elevators, to provide adequate service for receptions, coffee hours, intermission refreshments, and, possibly, banquets. Thus, those areas served by the kitchen but not on the same level must be vertically aligned with it if they are to be serviced by a dumbwaiter.

Public Spaces So far, then, the food areas are best located largely on the ground level with the games rooms not too remote from the refreshment area and with some meeting rooms and lounges directly above the kitchen. The theater crowds at intermission may use the refreshment service if it is not too far distant, hence this wing, which offers some meeting space while sometimes needing additional reception and rehearsal room, might well ad-

join the foot–meeting-room section. A review of this portion of the building so far reveals it to be a busy place with many persons using it for eating, meeting, and theater work. Service facilities such as coat rooms, toilets, and public telephones are needed, and multipurpose lounges prove valuable. If the costume and stage shops are to have any connections with the hobby shops, the latter must be included in this section of the building. By the same token, if the darkroom facilities are to be used by the campus publications, these offices might well be located here.

Reception Center The main entrance, lobby, and information desk go together. In some union buildings the information center includes ticket, cigarette, and other sales, a lost and found service, and, possibly, some office functions.

Figures 1–21 are reprinted from *Planning College Union Facilities for Multiple-use,* Association of College Unions—International, Madison, Wisconsin, 1966.

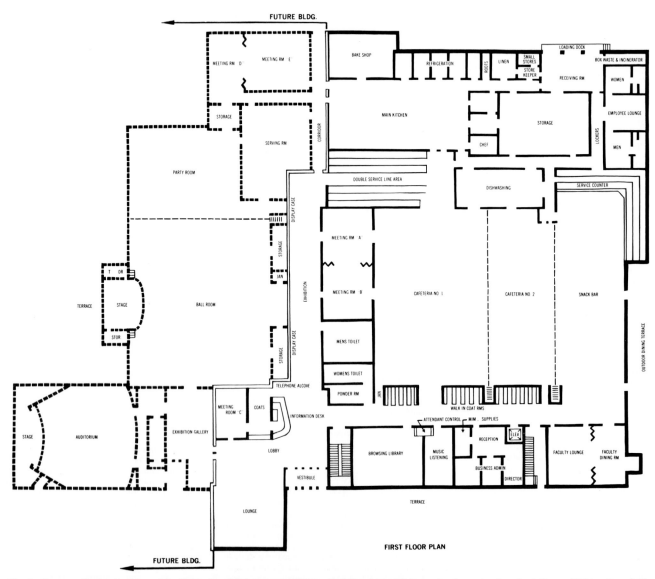

Fig. 1 The core of union facilities at the University of Delaware—solid lines. And the planned future extensions, showing circulation and integration of all units (including how food would be delivered to the future ballroom and private dining rooms)—dashed lines.

326

Smaller unions combine this center with an administrative office and even make it the issuing and supervising center for the music and browsing rooms. Many unions may wish to place a large lounge for receptions next to the main entrance. Coat rooms should adjoin this area, and toilets should be near by.

Administrative Spaces If the advantages of adjoining offices outweigh those of decentralized offices, an administrative suite can be planned wherein equipment and personnel can be used with flexibility. Some office space is needed in the various departments but can be reduced if centralization is adopted. Should decentralized offices be used, the social director might well be housed in the student activities section where the various student government organizations, union committees, and publications hold forth. In this way communication among the various groups and with the social director is improved and a relatively quiet group of activities kept together. If decentralization of offices is adopted, other offices besides the social director's can serve double duty. The business office near the food or bookstore area can offer closer supervision and emergency as-

sistance. A maintenance superintendent's office near the maintenance shop or a reservation office near the information center can provide bonuses in the form of added service.

Quiet Areas The quiet areas, logically enough, occur away from the noisier, highly trafficked ones. Offices; conference and meeting rooms; art, music, and browsing rooms; and lounges go well together, but they cannot entirely be separated from the noisier sections. Meeting rooms with their periodic traffic introduce some noise to an otherwise quiet facility, particularly when larger rooms are in use, and it may be that larger meeting rooms and lounges fit into the noisier section, which includes the food services, while smaller meeting rooms and lounges and conference rooms are combined in a quiet section which embraces of-

fices and other less noisy facilities. While outside noise can interfere with the music room, the considerable amount of sound which originates therein makes the music room a most unlikely component of a quiet area unless it is well soundproofed.

By and large, the quiet areas of the building present most of the demands for late or vacation-time operation. Guest rooms and administrative and publications offices are quite likely to function late at night or during the Christmas or summer vacations, and locating these together with separate access permits their use after the union's normal operating hours. With this in mind it may seem advisable to place the campus radio station alongside the various student offices. Separate use of other areas of the building should also be considered in laying out the floor plans.

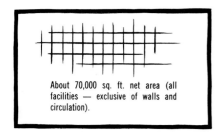

About 70,000 sq. ft. net area (all facilities — exclusive of walls and circulation).

Fig. 2 A union embracing typical facilities usually required at a university for about 6,000 students:
- Food Service
- Social Facilities
- Recreation Rooms
- Small Auditorium
- Meeting & Conference Rooms
- Offices
- Service Auxiliaries

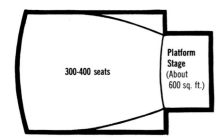

300-400 seats | Platform Stage (About 600 sq. ft.)

Fig. 3 Union auditorium—Needed for union cultural program, movies, conferences.

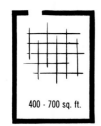

400 - 700 sq. ft.

Fig. 4 Separate TV lounge—At minimum size needed for special event broadcasts.

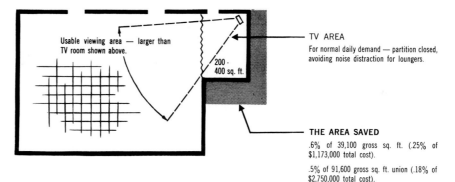

Usable viewing area — larger than TV room shown above.

200 - 400 sq. ft.

TV AREA
For normal daily demand — partition closed, avoiding noise distraction for loungers.

THE AREA SAVED
.6% of 39,100 gross sq. ft. (.25% of $1,173,000 total cost).

.5% of 91,600 gross sq. ft. union (.18% of $2,750,000 total cost).

Fig. 5 Main lounge—Used to expand TV viewing area during special event broadcasts, with folding partition open.

St. | Office mail boxes

Fig. 6 Information desk—Requires full-time attendant.

MEETING ROOM A (700 sq. ft.)

A typical need afternoons and evenings.

MEETING ROOM B (500 sq. ft.)

Fig. 7 Private dining or meeting rooms.

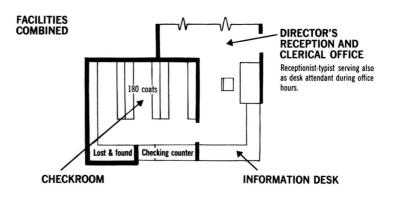

FACILITIES COMBINED

180 coats

Lost & found | Checking counter

CHECKROOM

DIRECTOR'S RECEPTION AND CLERICAL OFFICE
Receptionist-typist serving also as desk attendant during office hours.

INFORMATION DESK

Fig. 8 Combined facilities.

COLLEGE AND UNIVERSITY FACILITIES

Student Unions

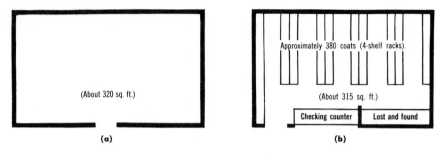

(About 320 sq. ft.)

(a)

Approximately 380 coats (4-shelf racks).

(About 315 sq. ft.)

| Checking counter | Lost and found |

(b)

Fig. 9   Normal main-floor facilities: (a) conference room; (b) coat checkroom.

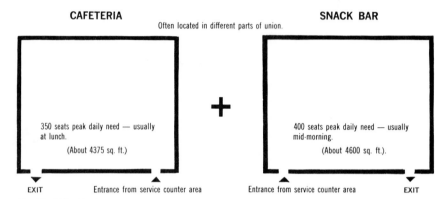

CAFETERIA

Often located in different parts of union.

SNACK BAR

350 seats peak daily need — usually at lunch.

(About 4375 sq. ft.)

+

400 seats peak daily need — usually mid-morning.

(About 4600 sq. ft.).

EXIT   Entrance from service counter area

Entrance from service counter area   EXIT

Fig. 10   Union food services.

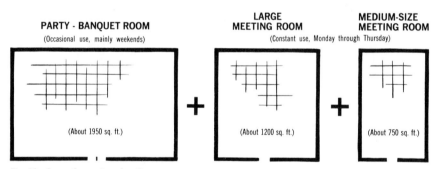

PARTY - BANQUET ROOM

(Occasional use, mainly weekends)

(About 1950 sq. ft.)

+

LARGE MEETING ROOM

(Constant use, Monday through Thursday)

(About 1200 sq. ft.)

+

MEDIUM-SIZE MEETING ROOM

(About 750 sq. ft.)

Fig. 11   Space for various functions.

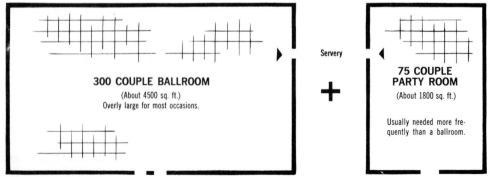

300 COUPLE BALLROOM
(About 4500 sq. ft.)
Overly large for most occasions.

Servery

+

75 COUPLE PARTY ROOM
(About 1800 sq. ft.)

Usually needed more frequently than a ballroom.

Total area: 6300 sq. ft.

Fig. 12   Facilities for social functions.

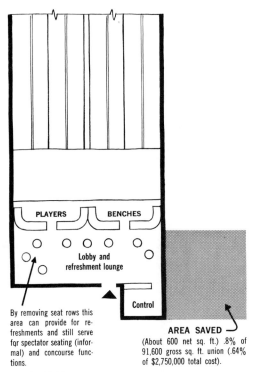

PLAYERS BENCHES

Lobby and refreshment lounge

Control

By removing seat rows this area can provide for refreshments and still serve for spectator seating (informal) and concourse functions.

AREA SAVED
(About 600 net sq. ft.) .8% of 91,600 gross sq. ft. union (.64% of $2,750,000 total cost).

Fig. 13 Multi-use spectator area.

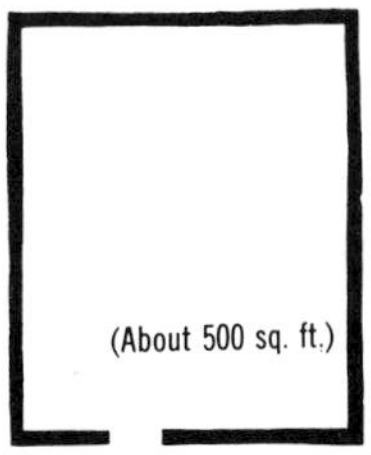

(About 500 sq. ft.)

Fig. 14 Meeting room (plus storage).

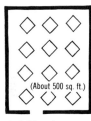

(About 500 sq. ft.)

Fig. 15 Separate bridge-chess room (game-playing only).

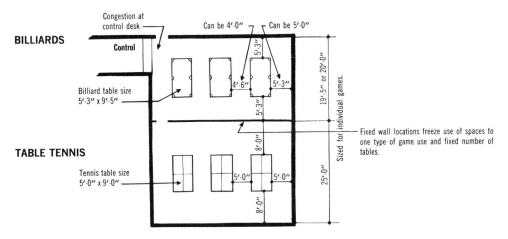

BILLIARDS

Congestion at control desk.

Control

Can be 4'-0"   Can be 5'-0"

5'-3"

4'-6"   5'-3"

Billiard table size 5'-3" x 9'-5"

5'-3"

19'-5" or 20'-0"

Sized for individual games.

Fixed wall locations freeze use of spaces to one type of game use and fixed number of tables.

8'-0"

TABLE TENNIS

Tennis table size 5'-0" x 9'-0"

5'-0"   5'-0"

8'-0"

25'-0"

Fig. 16 Game facilities.

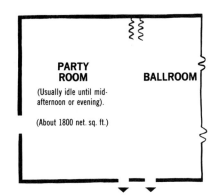

PARTY ROOM   **BALLROOM**

(Usually idle until mid-afternoon or evening).

(About 1800 net. sq. ft.)

Fig. 17

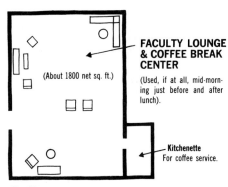

FACULTY LOUNGE & COFFEE BREAK CENTER

(Used, if at all, mid-morning just before and after lunch).

(About 1800 net sq. ft.)

Kitchenette For coffee service.

Fig. 18

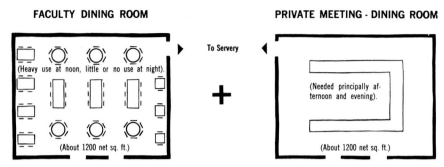

FACULTY DINING ROOM — (Heavy use at noon, little or no use at night). (About 1200 net sq. ft.)

To Servery

PRIVATE MEETING - DINING ROOM — (Needed principally afternoon and evening). (About 1200 net sq. ft.)

Fig. 19   Special dining facilities.

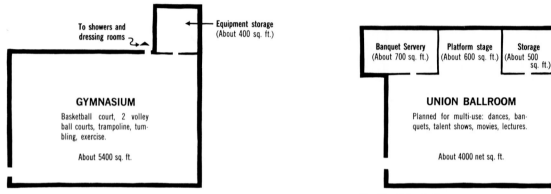

GYMNASIUM — Basketball court, 2 volley ball courts, trampoline, tumbling, exercise. About 5400 sq. ft. — To showers and dressing rooms — Equipment storage (About 400 sq. ft.)

Fig. 20   Gymnasium.

UNION BALLROOM — Planned for multi-use: dances, banquets, talent shows, movies, lectures. About 4000 net sq. ft. — Banquet Servery (About 700 sq. ft.) — Platform stage (About 600 sq. ft.) — Storage (About 500 sq. ft.)

Fig. 21   Union ballroom.

COMPUTATION CENTERS

Most experts in the field agree that a computation center for a college or university should be an all-campus facility, administratively under the control either of the Graduate School or of an all-campus committee, rather than an adjunct of an academic department such as mathematics, statistics, or electrical engineering. A currently emerging pattern is the formation of a separate department of computer science with some teaching duties; it usually has some affiliation with the department of mathematics and is possibly not fully responsible for the service activities of the computation center.

Location of a Computation Center, Public Access, and Parking

In choosing a central or peripheral location for a computer, the rapid development of computer use by medical schools, business schools, and behaviorial science groups, as well as by physical scientists and engineers, should be considered. Proximity to users must be weighed against the almost certain needs for expansion in the near future. New means are being developed whereby a fast central computer can service simultaneously a number of different input-output stations that may be placed strategically at several points on a campus.

A computation center is visited daily by large numbers of people who come either as clients to have problems done on the com-

Buildings and Facilities for the Mathematical Sciences, Conference Board of the Mathematical Sciences, Washington, D.C., 1963.

puter or as visitors to see the facilities. Hence it is important that adequate parking be provided near the computation center to accommodate both its own staff and these visitors.

Access to the computer facilities must also be provided for the computing machinery and for the supplies that will be needed in its operation.

The functions of a computation center may be different at different institutions, and must be considered in planning its location and space requirements.

A small center with more limited objectives may require a relatively small amount of space at first. However, experience has often indicated that after a small computer has introduced research workers in many areas on the campus to the potentialities of computer use, a larger center is not only desired but justified. Wise planning must take this into account.

Furthermore, experience both on university campuses and in industrial organizations suggests that a single computer of great capability is preferable to a collection of several much slower machines, since both the machine cost and programing cost per unit of computing are cheaper on the single large machine than on several minor machines. It is assumed that the large machine is satisfactory to all parties concerned, is capable of handling the combined workload, and is not idle much of the time. The tenfold increase in cost required for a fast machine may possibly provide a hundredfold increase in capability, thereby reducing the *cost per unit of computing* by a factor of ten. This is a real saving if the fast machine is used to capacity, but not if it is used only 10 percent of the time.

Perhaps even more serious than the direct dollar cost is the fragmentation of knowledge that takes place when each small computer has its own staff, communicating poorly, if at all, with similar groups on the same campus. Despite this, groups frustrated by inconvenient or inadequate access press strongly and sometimes successfully for their own installation. A separate problem here is the need for analogue or digital equipment tied directly (i.e. "on line") to a real time experiment, such as a reactor, jet engine test stand, or a human being under some form of medical observation or treatment. Techniques for interrupting large-scale problems for brief uses of the computer are under very active development, but it is difficult at this time to predict whether additional machines of about the present size will be installed or whether even larger machines will be shared by many users, perhaps with the aid of off-site input and output devices.

Public Viewing and Briefing

The main computer room itself is an important showplace. Good public relations require that it be located where visitors can easily see it from a corridor or viewing room through a glass wall. Otherwise, there will be crowding that interferes with the work. A classroom, briefing room, or auditorium, equipped with adequate chalkboard in front, should be placed near the viewing area. This room can be used both for briefing groups who may come to see the computer and for regular instruction in computer science, either in short courses, institutes, or regular university courses.

Computer Space

The main computer room is the heart of a computing center. It must be accessible to the computer staff who operate the machines and to the maintenance engineers who repair the machines and keep them in running order, as well as being strategically located for public viewing (Figs. 1 and 2). It must also be accessible to appropriate storage spaces and to the power supply. Efficient operation requires that the individual machine units in the main computing room be so placed that they are easily accessible for quick repair in emergency, as well as being conveniently located for the operators and the public. If the distance from the back of the computer units to the walls were made 18 in. greater than the distance needed to open the cabinet doors and carry out repairs, this wall space could be used for storage that would be accessible except during maintenance. (However, fire regulations demand that only the absolute minimum of records required for efficient operation shall be kept in the computer room itself.) An upper limit to the distances between computer units may be set in some installations by the available lengths of information cable.

The machines in the main computer room need proper support, cable connections, and air conditioning. In the main machine rooms for most of the larger computers, the underlying fixed floor is built about 18 in. lower than the floors in adjacent preparation rooms or corridors, and it is covered by a strong elevated floor beneath which cable connections can be installed without obstructing the passageways (Fig. 3). The panels may be covered with carpeting or other types of flooring materials, but it is important that the floor be kept free from dust, lint, and static electricity.

In buildings without a recessed subfloor, such as those remodeled for computer use, ramps should be used to connect the elevated floor with floor areas at a different level in order to permit carts with tape or punch cards, or other equipment, to be rolled in.

Auxiliary card-punch machines, tape preparation units, and printers may be included within the vapor seal enclosing the main computer units, but they should probably be separated from the main room by glass panels to reduce the noise level and dirt. Acoustic treatment of the ceilings is important for noise reduction. Adequate and well-diffused lighting should also be installed in the ceilings of the computer areas.

Some information storage media, such as punched Hollerith cards, punched tape, or magnetic tape, are needed for current use and should be readily accessible; a fireproof storage closet for such items should be adjacent to the computer room. Magnetic tapes are commonly stored in flat, cylindrical cans, placed on racks so that their circular bases are in a vertical plane. Metal file cabinets with drawers designed for standard punched cards are also commercially available.

Maintenance and Mechanical Areas, Power, and Air Conditioning

Adequate space should be provided near the main equipment room for the use of maintenance engineers, whether they be local personnel or representatives of the equipment manufacturer on contract to repair the machines. Undue economy in the space available to maintenance engineers may be no economy at all in the long run, since time wasted in repairing a fast computer may be worth several dollars a minute.

Spaces for auxiliary mechanical equipment for the computer, including the power supply and air conditioning, must be provided close to the main computer room. There are some advantages in having this area adjacent to the working areas for maintenance personnel.

Preparation Areas

For programming there should be a preparation room, or "ready room," near the auxiliary machine room, where programmers may put their programs on tape or cards that the computer can read, and where they may check their programs for errors. A ready room should be equipped with work tables and desk calculators in addition to the auxiliary punch units that may be needed for preparing programs to be read by the computer.

For efficient operation, many people who do not have permanent offices in the computer area need temporary work space there.

A reception desk or counter may be provided in or near the ready room to accept and check in programs to be run on the machine, record completed work, and return it to an appropriate cubbyhole in a large rack, where it may be picked up by the person who submitted it.

Offices, Conference Rooms, Library, and Lounge

Spaces required by the computer personnel, in addition to the preparation areas just described, include offices, conference rooms, library, and lounge or refreshment corner. Conference rooms are needed in which several persons, including the proposer of the problem, may get together to discuss possible methods of attack for its solution. Private offices are needed where people working on problems can concentrate without interruption on the complicated series of steps necessary to program a problem.

A reference library should be readily available to computer personnel. This library should include not only a collection or "library" of subroutines and other programs that may be stored on tape or punched cards but also at least a minimal collection of technical books and journals relating to computing and numerical

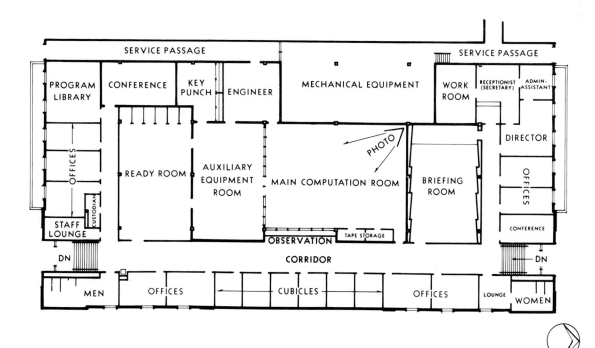

Fig. 1 Plan of computation center, University of Texas.

COLLEGE AND UNIVERSITY FACILITIES

Computation Centers

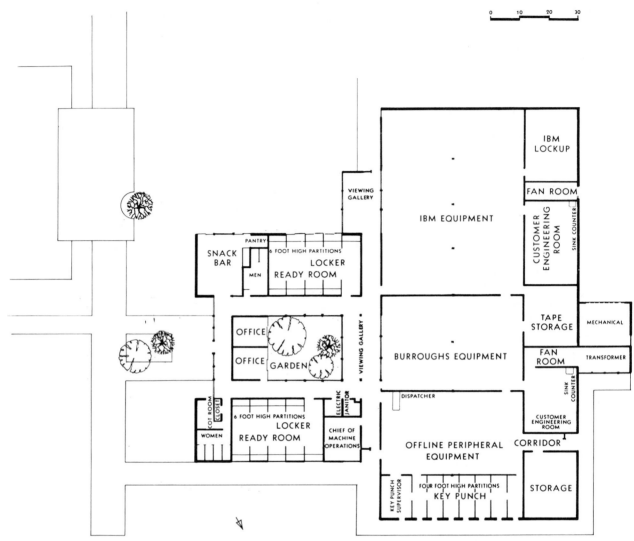

Fig. 2 Plan of computation center, Stanford University.

analysis. A larger departmental collection in a separate room, including duplicates of some pertinent mathematics books, may be justified if the computing center cannot share a library with mathematics or statistics and is not near the main library.

Offices for computer personnel should include the same essentials as for mathematics professors, namely, a desk, chairs, bookshelving, telephone, and adequate chalkboard on at least one wall. However, the computer specialist may have more need than the pure mathematician for electrical equipment such as desk calculator or a tape punch. These require electrical outlets and either a table or writing shelf on which to work.

Regular staff members of a computer center should not only have individual offices where they can work without distraction but also a staff lounge where they can get together to exchange ideas and charge their mental batteries. At the University of Texas Computation Center (Fig. 1), ten offices of 180 square ft each and six cubicles of 100 sq ft each are provided for the use of staff and graduate students, and there is a small lounge in which

coffee can be served. Since a computer may be in operation 24 hours a day and programming activities require long periods of meticulous work, a kitchenette or at least a hot plate may be needed to restore the energy and efficiency of the staff.

Reception, Administration, Duplicating, and Storage

The administrative space for the computing center may closely resemble the administrative space for a mathematics department. Not to be forgotten are offices for the director and his assistant, office space for reception and for secretaries and typists, and a workroom equipped with duplicating machines and plenty of shelving space for all the reports and notes that must be reproduced. Of course, adequate space with controlled temperature and humidity must be provided for the storage of punched cards. Clearly, such general facilities as toilets must not be overlooked.

A computer installation uses large quantities of materials, such as punch cards, paper tapes,

ditto paper, and paper for a high-speed printer. Suitable provision must be made for receiving and storing these supplies. Printing by machine at slower speeds directly on multilith masters permits the reproduction of computer-produced information without the errors arising from human intervention. Supplies for such work will require storage.

Fire Protection and Emergencies

To prevent damage to the computer by fire or water hazards arising outside the computer room itself, the equipment should be housed in a fire-resistive building and should be protected by fire doors from the rest of the building; the flooring should be of noncombustible construction, and the roof or floor above the computer room should be a watertight slab to which the walls are sealed. Waterproofed walls and proper drainage may be needed to prevent water damage in a basement installation. Local fire protection for certain key computer units may be provided by approved automatic carbon dioxide fire extinguishers rather than by water sprinklers.

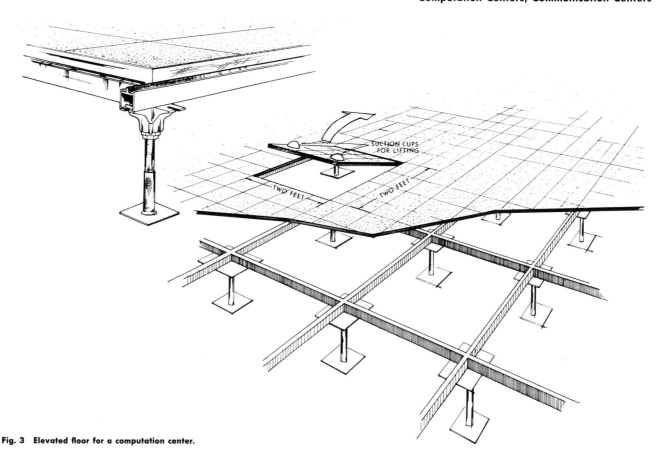

Fig. 3 Elevated floor for a computation center.

Cards, disks, and drums should be kept in waterproof, noncombustible metal cabinets with controlled temperature and humidity if required. Those not in current use should be stored in a separate room close to the computer room. Magnetic tape itself is highly flammable. Duplicate copies of programs and records might be stored in a remote place as insurance against their total loss by a fire in the computer center. Adequate controls should prevent the ducts of the computer air-conditioning system from circulating smoke and fire in case of emergency; it is best to have the computer air ducts independent of the other air ducts in the building. All office furniture in the computer room should be metal.

Hazards other than fire and water that may need to be considered in planning and maintaining a computer installation are those from radiation, magnetic fields, static electricity, dust, insects, or rodents. To protect stored rolls of magnetic tape from loss of information due to local magnetic disturbances, it is best to place their containers on edge in a magnetically protected storage place. To minimize the effects of dust and static electricity, carpets and drapes should be made of materials free from lint and static; the use of dustcloths or dry mops for cleaning should be avoided.

If the incoming power supply for the computer is subject to occasional interruptions, a secondary source of power may be needed to provide continuity of operations. Failure of the air-conditioning system may also cause the computer to shut down within a short time, so there should be a warning alarm that will immediately call attention to such a failure.

COMMUNICATIONS CENTERS

A new building type resulting from new thinking and practice is the communications center. The emphasis of this type of facility is on large-group instruction and on the media to support it. For this reason, it is becoming a college building, centrally located on the campus to accommodate many hundreds of students in large groups throughout the day. It may also be part of an educational park with its facilities available to all school groups in the area. (See Fig. 1.)

The philosophy behind the communications center is a simple one. If the institution feels that large-group instruction fits its needs for economical but effective instruction (as many colleges do believe), it makes sense to put these expensive "supporting" functions together. The communications center can economically provide:

• Shared projection areas, allowing expensive equipment to be kept together in one room. This not only ensures better care of the equipment, but through consolidation, utilization rates can go up.

• Special and expensive lighting and mechanical systems. It is cheaper and less cumbersome, for instance, to air-condition one whole building rather than little pieces of many buildings.

Educational Facilities with New Media, Department of Audiovisual Instruction, National Education Association in collaboration with the Center for Architectural Research, Rensselaer Polytechnic Institute.

• Special and expensive electrical installations.

• Accommodation for weird room shapes; placing one pie-shaped lecture room in many separate buildings creates waste space and odd configurations. Putting many such rooms together in one building allows the good designer to cut down if not eliminate these wasted spaces. (See Fig. 2.)

• Centralization of production facilities. Since many of the items produced will be used in the large-group lectures, it makes sense to consolidate all production and "support" activities in the building (Fig. 2).

• A central "focal" point for faculty training in effectively using presentation and other instructional media.

The communications center does not become the property of any one discipline or department on campus; its use will be encouraged for all departments needing it. It will occupy a focal point on the campus, probably at the crossroads of major circulation paths.

The types of facilities the communications center may include cover those in many areas. (See Fig. 3.)

• Lobby and Circulation
   Include display, exhibition, reception, kitchen areas
   Generous to accommodate many large groups in the building
• Instructional Spaces
   Lecture halls (capacity determined by local programming)
   Storage and preparation areas
   Seminar and small-group rooms

333

Educational

COLLEGE AND UNIVERSITY FACILITIES

Communication Centers

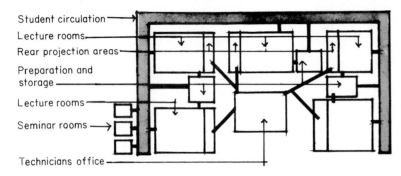

Student circulation
Lecture rooms
Rear projection areas
Preparation and storage
Lecture rooms
Seminar rooms
Technicians office

SPACE RELATIONSHIPS

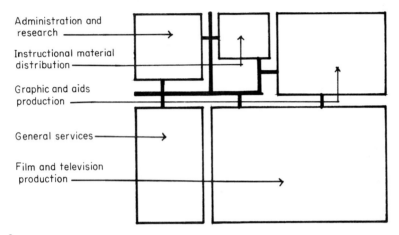

Administration and research
Instructional material distribution
Graphic and aids production
General services
Film and television production

Fig. 1

- Film and TV Production
  TV and film studios
  Central engineering and control
  Dressing and ante areas
  Equipment storage and work rooms
  Prop storage and work rooms
  Staff and faculty offices
  Film processing and editing
  Preview and conference rooms
- Graphics and Aids Production
  Art and finishing studios
  Photo and finishing studios
  Staff and preview areas
- Instructional Materials Distribution
  Storage of materials and equipment
  Check-out area
  Office, records, and work area
- Administration and Research
  Office and conference
  Library
  Records storage
- General Services
  Workshop areas
  Shipping and receiving
  Building maintenance

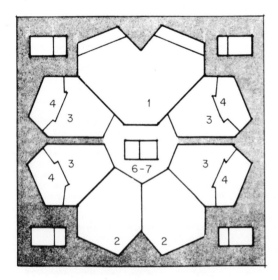

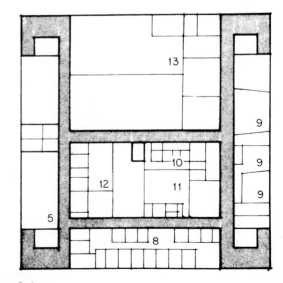

1 Lecture (480)
2 Lecture (240)
3 Lecture (120)
4 Lecture (60)
5 Assembly area
6 Rear projection
7 Preparation and storage
8 Office and conference
9 TV studios
10 Graphic arts
11 Photo area
12 Production storage
13 Mechanical and storage

Fig. 2   Communications lecture hall center, State University of New York, Oswego, N.Y. Skidmore Owings & Merrill, Architects.

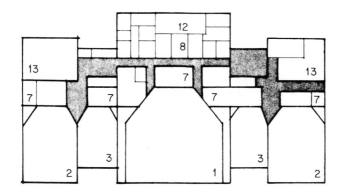

1 Lecture (480)
2 Lecture (240)
3 Lecture (120)
4 Lecture (60)
5 Assembly area
6 Rear projection
7 Preparation and storage
8 Office and conference
9 TV studios
10 Graphic arts
11 Photo area
12 Production storage
13 Mechanical and storage

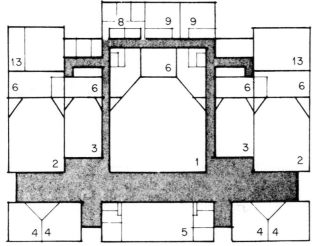

Fig. 3 Communications lecture hall center, State University of New York, Oneonta, N.Y. Toole & Angerame, Architects.

Necessary work areas
Shipping and receiving
• Production Services
Regional office and conference
Research, testing, and evaluation
Equipment mock-up and repair
Radio origination studios and support
TV origination and support
Film origination and support
Photographic and film processing
Graphics center
Writing and editing publications areas
Publications mock-up areas
Central reproduction facility
Shipping and receiving
• Curriculum Services
Regional office and conference
Curriculum development and project center
Resource rooms for the various disciplines
Spaces for adjunct and consulting staffs
Student testing area
Pupil personnel services staff area
In-service training areas
Demonstration classrooms
Exhibit areas
• Administrative Services
Legal advisory office
Financial planning, audit, and control office
Transportation, maintenance, etc. offices
Central personnel interviewing and records center
• Supporting Services
Lobby and central exhibition spaces
Large-group area
Conference and assembly areas
Cafeteria and kitchen
Central receiving and storage
Central workshop
Maintenance, toilet, services, etc.

Many of these facility types have already been discussed elsewhere. The design of the regional center will necessarily become a process of "putting them together" with the necessary offices, conference areas, circulation, and other "support" areas.

Figures 1 and 2 show the kinds of space relationships that might exist in a regional center undertaking a broad range of programs and services.

Regional Education Laboratories

While the regional supplementary center can perform services and conduct localized research for its members, there is still a need for educational research on the larger scale. This larger-scale research has been growing steadily in this post-Sputnik era, but much remains to be done. Moreover, overall coordination of projects and widespread reporting of findings are needed if the research is to become an effective part of contemporary education.

These concerns stand behind the creation of the regional education laboratory. The laboratory steps in to undertake the research and fill the gaps always present between projects and dissemination of results.

So far, attempts at these regional research and development centers have been sporadic; some highly successful ones have been set up in large universities to attack specific educational problems, but the educational laboratory concept has yet to be adopted on any scale. Title IV of the Elementary and Secondary Education Act of 1965 calls for aid to support and maintain these kinds of centers, though, and growth in this direction is bound to result.

While these laboratories will take on different tasks, they will have some similar goals in mind, such as the following:

REGIONAL EDUCATION CENTER (SUPPLEMENTARY)

This concept is not new. There are already many attempts to provide regional programs, resources, and services; some are little more than country film libraries while others (like Toronto's Education Centre) provide a whole variety of services, classes, materials, and publications. Title III money will begin to fill in the gaps in our fragmented efforts so far, and the future points toward more "comprehensive" supplementary centers.

Despite the constant use of the term "center," these regional activities may not be accomplished in a central facility at all. The best possibilities for coordination and cross-fertilization exist in the central facility, but economics may preclude this. Many of the programs and

Educational Facilities with New Media, Department of Audiovisual Instruction, National Education Association in collaboration with the Center for Architectural Research, Rensselaer Polytechnic Institute.

services can be accomplished in outlying or adjacent buildings; most "centers" will probably be a combination of a central building with many of these scattered adjunct buildings housing various parts of the effort.

The types of spaces that might be included in the supplementary center are many, including

• Regional Administration
Administrative office and conference areas
Clerical staff areas
Regional research and conference areas
Central records and storage areas
Data processing center
• Program Coordination
Administrative and staff areas
Facilities for the programs themselves
• Resource Services
Regional office and conference
Professional resource library
Search and bibliographic work area
Central examination area for books, resources, and equipment
Central ordering and processing
Central collection of materials for area borrowing

COLLEGE AND UNIVERSITY FACILITIES
Regional Education Center (Supplementary)

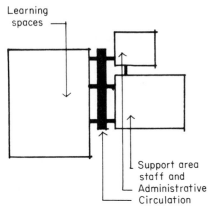

PROGRAM-ORIENTED

Fig. 1

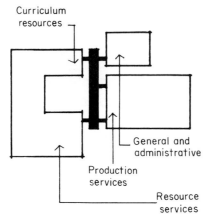

SERVICE-ORIENTED

Small project offices closely tied to central media and information complexes
- Central Information Complex
  Warehouse of resources, reports, data files, etc.
  May include information retrieval and storage
  Entire complex readily accessible to all in the center and wired to adjunct units of the laboratory
- Central Media Complex
  Production and origination facilities as required
  Work areas for testing and mocking-up media units
  Accessible to all functions in the laboratory
  Can be used for media research and support for other research
- Evaluation and Processing
  Office and conference area for the evaluation team

• To carry on a concentrated and coordinated program of educational research activities. These activities will most likely be accomplished by eminently qualified persons and will have widespread rather than limited application and use.

• To develop new curriculum units, with special attention to ways of supporting them. This will make media research, testing, and evaluation an important part of the laboratory's program.

• To test, evaluate, and disseminate innovations on a broad scale.

• To provide direction and to encourage innovation in other quarters.

• To supplement and coordinate research throughout the region.

• To provide a training ground for educational research personnel.

In order to achieve these goals, the various regional education laboratories will have a number of common characteristics,

• Projects may be undertaken "in-house" or in collaboration with other educational and community groups.

• Staffing will include at least a corps of administrators to coordinate activities, a professional evaluation staff, and a professional dissemination unit. Actual project research may be carried on by other staff members, interim staff, consultants, or a combination of these.

• The laboratory will remain flexible. It will adapt to the situation as necessary, changing its own character as it undertakes different kinds of projects in different fields.

The regions covered by these laboratories will be necessarily large; some now envision perhaps a dozen large centers around the country. Smaller, more specialized units in colleges and universities may supplement the laboratories or extend their work into specific areas.

Implications for facilities, then, are not concrete. Most laboratories will require a variety of spaces, some of which may be "eked out" of local college buildings or those of other cooperating groups. While many of the laboratory's activities may be scattered around the region it serves, it is reasonable to believe that there will be at least a central administrative facility and staff. Kinds of facilities may include
- Administrative and Project
  Central administrative offices
  Conference areas

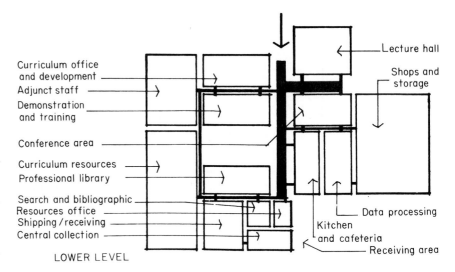

LOWER LEVEL

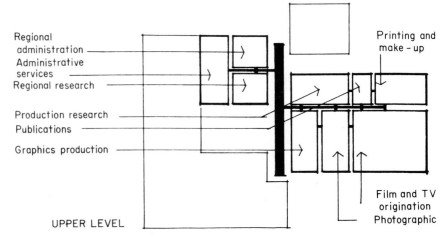

UPPER LEVEL

Fig. 2

Data processing center serving all units of the laboratory
- Demonstration and Mock-up
  Area for mocking-up different facility types
  Large open space that can be arranged in many ways
  Central location for access by staff, students, visitors
  Provision for visitors and viewing
- Dissemination Area
  Office area for professional dissemination staff
  Publications editing and mock-up areas
  Printing and finishing areas
  Shipping and receiving
- Service and Workshop
  Large workshop to serve for all "carpentry" activities in the laboratory
  Conventional building service spaces

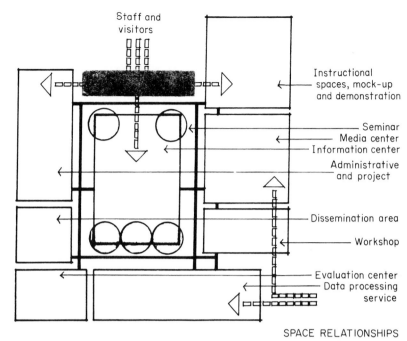

SPACE RELATIONSHIPS

Fig. 1

RESOURCE FACILITIES (LIBRARY)

No other educational facility is receiving more attention today than the library and its descendant, the resources center. There are many concepts and philosophies for the new form of the library, and as is appropriate in a time of change and innovation, the form of the library is certainly not set. One fact is certain; the library (it will be called the resources center from here on) is more than a repository for books and printed materials available for checkout or for use by students at long, drab tables with stiff chairs. The functional characteristics of the library are still present—the acquiring, cataloging, indexing, storing, retrieving, use, and restoring of information, but the information has taken on many new forms. It is in the form of books, periodicals, and standard references, but also films and slides, audio tapes and programs, videotapes and kinescopes, film strips and miniaturized equipment. The problem is how to handle these various types of resources logistically and still have them readily available for student use as required by the educational philosophy of the institution. (See Figs. 1 and 2.)

It is certainly the educational philosophy and the way it is translated by faculty and staff that dictate how a resources center is used. It may be simply a more complex library—a place where students come and check out materials as required to complete assignments. It may also be the whole focus of the educational program for the institution—a place where a student comes and learns independently, and a place from which information is delivered to students throughout the entire school plant working in a number of different learning situations. More and more, the resources center is becoming the focal point, philosophically and physically, for many new school plants. Whatever the philosophy, it must be spelled out in terms of educational objectives before any architectural planning can begin.

A resources center may function as part of the system of education within a school plant in a number of different ways. Figure 3 indicates a "little school" or "school-within-a-school" concept in which each subdivision contains a

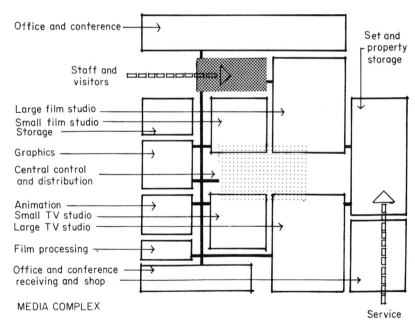

MEDIA COMPLEX

Fig. 2

resources center, either discipline-oriented or general in content. In such an institution, the resources center will contain independent study facilities and seminar and project rooms, as well as the resources themselves. These resources centers may be interconnected for call-up of material from any one of them, and in turn, all the resources centers may be connected with a large, regional electronic storage and retrieval facility.

Figure 4a indicates a single resources center as the focus of the school and serving the entire school. Not only would students come to

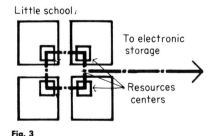

Fig. 3

Educational Facilities with New Media, Department of Audiovisual Instruction, National Education Association in collaboration with the Center for Architectural Research, Rensselaer Polytechnic Institute.

Educational

COLLEGE AND UNIVERSITY FACILITIES
Resource Facilities (Library)

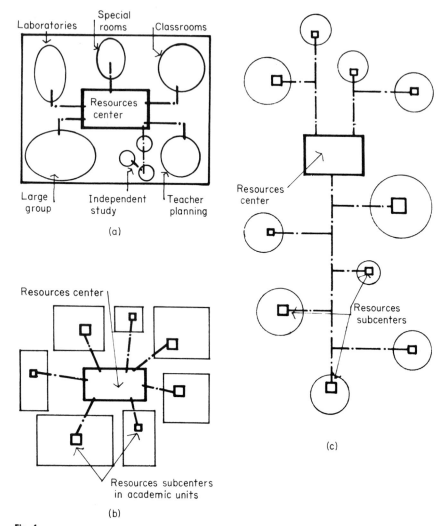

Fig. 4

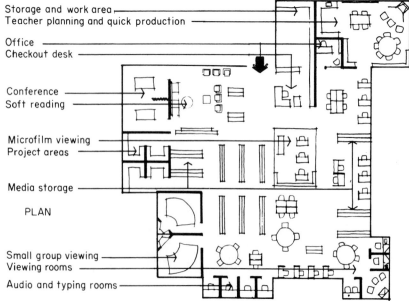

Fig. 5 Resources center.

the resources center to use the resources, but audio and video materials would be distributed from the center to carrels and independent study facilities, classrooms, seminar rooms, and other kinds of spaces throughout the school plant. In this case, a student does not have to come physically to the resources center to partake of its resources.

Figure 4b might illustrate a large educational complex—a college or university, an educational park, or a large, centralized school plant. A large central resources center serves the entire complex and, in turn, a number of subcenters located within specialized academic units. Here resources will be distributed in a number of ways and the student will have the choice of either using his local subcenter or going to the larger centralized facility. In turn, the central unit could draw from large regional or national information centers.

In Fig. 4c a central, electronically based storage and retrieval facility serves a number of schools within a district, and each school contains a small resource subcenter. It should be noted that in this type of system all materials must be distributed electronically or physically from the central facility to the schools for student use.

In programming and planning resource facilities, the following points may prove of assistance:

1. The resources center in school buildings should be considered as a learning facility as well as a place to store and use materials. This means that the spaces must be readily accessible, inviting in character and environment, well equipped, humanely administered, and an integral part of the school plant.

2. Independent study and learning facilities within or associated with resources centers are more than "electronic carrels." A comfortable lounge chair, some carpeted flooring, a seat at a table, tables with low dividers, small separate rooms, and writing cubicles are all independent study facilities and should be represented along with the electronic carrel. There should not be a choice of only "wet" or "dry" carrels, but a mixture of these and other accommodations for individual students learning with resources.

3. A concern with space utilization has led to some solutions for independent study facilities in resources centers that consist of monotonous row upon monotonous row of carrels. Such planning seems to completely deny a basic philosophy of the resources center—individualization.

4. In bringing a resources center to physical reality, it may follow a variety of solutions—centralized in a single large space, decentralized in small units which are dispersed about, or a combination of both. Whatever the planning scheme, the resources center will include a number of common components. These would include administrative and work areas, media storage, book and periodical storage, soft reading area, independent study area, simple production and reproduction facilities, and conference, project, and seminar facilities.

5. In planning a resources center, consideration should be given to the rapid advances that have been made in computer-based library operations—processing acquisitions, printing out bibliographies and special lists, handling checkouts and due and reserve notices, and requisitioning materials. Certainly this type of system should be studied with the idea of initially incorporating compatible components allowing expansion of the basic system serving several centers and subcenters.

6. Electronically based information storage and retrieval systems will certainly be a

338

planning factor in designing resources centers. Some carrels will be "wired into" such systems for instant access to information, and in some cases, the resources centers may be part of the "input" into a retrieval system. The hardware and economies of such systems have not been clearly defined, and they are not universally available. However, planning must anticipate their eventual role.

Resource Facility Study – 1

This resources center combines many different types of facilities into a single center. As such, it would form the resources focus for a high school, middle school, and, with modifications, an elementary school. In addition, it has many of the characteristics appropriate for a re-source subcenter found at many points in a large educational complex.

The central area consists of storage facilities for books, media, independent audiovisual equipment, and a variety of facilities for inde-pendent study and learning—soft reading ar-eas, electronic carrels, reading and writing carrels, reading tables and chairs, etc. Sur-rounding this center are a number of significant supplementary facilities. Small viewing rooms provide for independent and team work using projected media. Typing or audio rooms pro-vide soundproof cubicles for individual use. Seminar rooms, project areas, and conference facilities all provide for the use of various kinds of resources by small groups working together. Naturally, storage, workrooms, and office facilities must be provided, as well as reference files, indexes and a control center. Finally, the teachers' planning, preview, and simple pro-duction facility is provided as part of this par-ticular resources center. (See Fig. 5.)

This center would be located at the heart of a school plant with other educational facilities surrounding it, all easily accessible.

Resource Facility Study – 2

This resources center would be appropriate as a subcenter in "schools-within-schools." It can be either a general resources subcenter or discipline-oriented, and provides for long-term, independent student utilization. Carrels for audio and video use, and reading and writing, are provided, as are a soft reading area, tables and chairs, and enclosed and semi-enclosed rooms used for typing and recording. The adjunct facilities include small group viewing rooms, project rooms, conference rooms, a small teacher production facility, and office work and storage space for the administrators of the center. (See Fig. 6.)

As a resources subcenter, this facility would be surrounded by other types of learning spaces, and the line of demarcation between the resources and other educational facilities would be indistinguishable. In fact, if properly dsigned, students would move between these spaces freely without feeling that they were moving from one educational world to another.

Resource Facility Study – 3

This resources center introduces the basic philosophic concept that teachers themselves are significant resources and coordinators in the use of resources. Therefore, they should be part of the resources center, and this study includes a teacher planning and conference suite composed of teachers' work cubicles

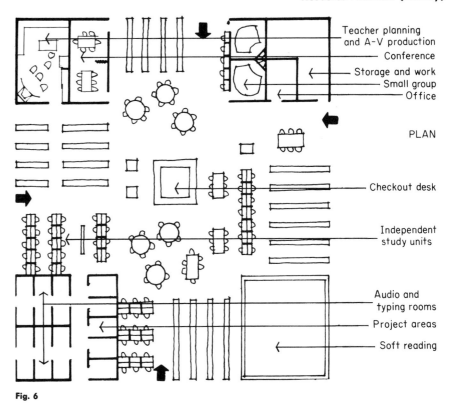

Teacher planning and A-V production
Conference
Storage and work
Small group
Office

PLAN

Checkout desk

Independent study units

Audio and typing rooms
Project areas
Soft reading

Fig. 6

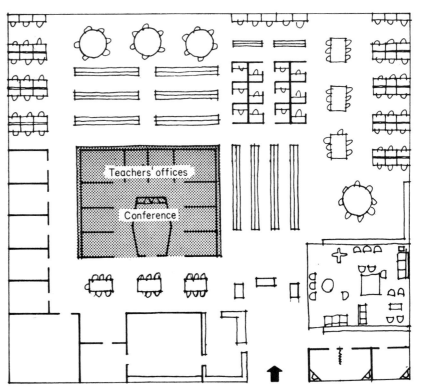

Teachers' offices

Conference

Fig. 7

339

surrounding a common conference and work area. Here students may come on appointment, or on a "drop-in" basis, and consult with their instructors as readily as they could consult with the other resources contained in the center. This type of facility would be most appropriate for a non-graded or continuous-progress type of educational philosophy. It might serve either as a resource subcenter in a "school-within-a-school" concept or as the basic resources center in a school which is moving toward continuous progress, but which is initially designed for a significant program in team planning and teaching. (See Fig. 7.)

The remainder of the resources center includes accessibility to a variety of resources which may be used individually and in small groups.

LARGE-GROUP FACILITIES

It seems that the effectiveness of media in education has been tested most extensively in large-group learning situations. Certainly in the last ten years many public schools and a large number of colleges and universities have adopted large-group instruction using media for an increasingly large proportion of the instructional load. In fact, it is through the utilization of learning media that large-group instruction may become truly effective—by bringing to this type of learning system means for magnifying and displaying information, presenting information from a remote location, introducing information that otherwise would be impossible to present, and introducing information in a more demonstratively effective way.

There is a current reexamination of large-group instruction following on the heels of a general concern for more independent and individualized learning experiences. Even though there are proponents of each to the exclusion of the other, the logical solution for most institutions will be the incorporation of both types of learning experience—and indeed a variety of learning experiences in between—and in turn the necessary facilities for their effective use. This "mix" of learning experiences is the basis for many organizational patterns, and is at the heart of the systems approach to designing learning.

For these reasons an examination of the planning of large-group facilities with media is essential, particularly because the design criteria and planning considerations in large-group facilities with media are probably the most critical of any type of space that might be provided. The following points summarize these design and planning criteria:

1. An optimum viewing area, as defined by the various display surfaces which are considered critical for student viewing, will determine the most effective room shape. This optimum area is not a fixed function of the combination of screens and/or monitors but will vary with the type of material presented, the duration of the presentation, the quality of the equipment, the type of screen, and other factors of environment. (See details of projection systems and viewing areas.)

2. Stepped or sloped floors will always be required in order to provide optimum viewing conditions. Both horizontal and vertical sight lines in these rooms are major design factors. Also, raised seating introduces more intimacy in these rooms and may allow the interaction desired for case presentations and discussions.

3. Once the viewing area has been established, the actual capacity of the large-group space becomes a function of the seating type and arrangement. Seating types run the gamut from loose seats to fixed seats and built-in counters. Whenever possible, aisles and circulation spaces should be kept out of the viewing area to assure the maximum number of seats located within optimum viewing conditions.

4. As long as the display of information and the use of media are a significant function in the large-group room, windows and natural light are a liability rather than an asset. Although means may be found for controlling natural light, the size of required images in the room mitigates against natural light with its inherent problems of control and "washed out images" caused by ambient light.

5. Complete climatic conditioning is necessary for this type of space by virtue of the number of students involved, the lack of natural windows and ventilation, and the concentration required by this type of learning experience. Such conditioning will include cooling, air change, filtration, and humidity control.

6. Proper acoustical design, from the outset, is necessary for the successful functioning of this type of room. Not only should sound originating within the room be easily heard by all students but the space should be thoroughly acoustically isolated from interfering sounds from the outside.

7. Likewise, the planning of lighting is an important consideration. Generally, three levels of illumination will be necessary for the display methods used in these spaces; control of ambient light on projection screens is likewise essential.

8. Because lighting, acoustics, and climatic conditioning are such critical design features in the large-group room, their integration and design must be considered from the outset. Too often this kind of space suffers badly because these design features are neglected until too late in the planning process.

9. Educationally, the key to the proper functioning of this type of space is the integration of the systems for displaying information and other media uses. The studies which follow illustrate the fact that the display surfaces are an integral part of the room, and that equipment should be located for proper functioning and not to interfere in any way with the process of learning. This consideration includes the location and planning of the teacher's lectern or control center and suggests that lighting and equipment be tied in and controlled from this lectern.

10. Finally, the success of these rooms will depend on the inclusion and relationship of adjunct storage, projection, and preparation areas. This is particularly true when rooms are to be used for science courses requiring equipment and demonstrations. In addition,

these adjunct spaces may include project areas, conference rooms, and other smaller-group activities used to complement large-group presentation.

Large-group instruction can include learning functions other than the simple presentation of information. Manipulative and laboratory types of experiences have been employed for many years, and this study suggests a combination of laboratory and lecture-demonstration functions within the same facility. The resulting "lecture laboratory" permits the experimental and information presentation functions to be carried on simultaneously and without changing rooms. The advantages of being able to demonstrate and present information to a group of students seated at laboratory stations is one that may help overcome the problems of amalgamating media and instruction in science areas.

The lecture laboratory is a suite of facilities including a large area containing over a hundred student laboratory-desk stations, two smaller demonstration and special equipment areas, a rear projection area, a special projects room, and storage and preparation space serving all parts of the facility. The student area is arranged on three platforms with a ramp at one side for wheeling in special equipment, reagents, and other materials for student use. Each laboratory station consists of a stand-up, sit-down work area with complete utilities serving every two students. The smaller demonstration areas in the front of the room permit small groups of students to work more intimately as a team or with an instructor, and also provides space for special equipment used by students during the laboratory exercises; these can be shielded from the larger area by movable partitions. (See Fig. 1.)

The projection area allows two 10-ft images to be projected simultaneously, and further information display can be provided through two overhead projectors. The front of the room also provides area for demonstrations which are prepared and supplied from the adjacent work and storage room. These types of demonstrations will probably be magnified by closed-circuit TV and projected on the rear projection screen.

Production-Support Facilities

To reiterate a basic point, the effective and efficient utilization of learning media in education requires three broad types of space—learning spaces, resource facilities, and production-instructional support facilities. In addition to classrooms, lecture rooms, laboratories, and seminar rooms designed and equipped with appropriate media, it is necessary that film, slide, and tape materials and other media resources be made accessible to students and staff for individual use. Also, facilities must be provided in which learning media may be produced and which house the staff and functions that support the teaching faculty in their work.

The following points are offered as guidance in the design and planning of productional-instructional support facilities:

1. Production and support functions and in turn their facilities vary in complexity and size with their location and level within the educational system. Within an academic department or "little school," simple facilities should be available for teachers and students to produce transparencies, photocopies, slides, multiple copies, graphs, and charts. Usually, this local, simple production area will be located within

New Spaces for Learning: Designing college facilities to utilize instructional aids and media. Report of Research Project DASFEE: (Design of Auditorium-Studio Facilities for Engineering Education) supported by grant from Educational Facilities Laboratories, Inc., revised ed., June 1966.

Stand-up/sit-down
laboratory work stations

Demonstration table
with overhead projection

Special project area

Rear projection area

Preparation, storage and control

Small-group demonstration areas

PLAN

Scale: $1/16'' = 1'-0''$

Egress

Rear projection area

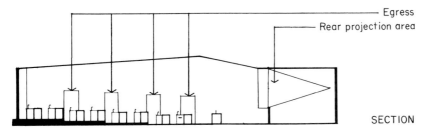

SECTION

Fig. 1

the resources center or instructional materials center.

At the other end of the spectrum may be a very large and complex production facility as part of a large regional service and production center. Such facilities may form a part of the regional service center or educational laboratory. In between these two extremes are production centers which will serve a university, a college, a large high school, several schools within a district, an entire school district, or all the institutions located in an educational park.

The important objective is to provide several echelons of production and support ranging from the very large and complex covering a region to the very simple and local serving a few teachers. Also, to adequately support the uses of media, all of these echelons of production and support should eventually be represented so that the instructional staff has many levels to draw upon, depending on the complexity and needs of the particular learning situation.

2. Production support centers may be composed of a variety of components, each of which is related according to the echelon of production and the types of services to be offered. Some of these components are:

Graphic arts production
Photographic production
Motion picture production
Audio recording
Animation
Television origination
Television control, distribution, and recording
Film editing and processing
Graphic materials production and assembly
Scene, set, and model production
Equipment storage and repair
General storage
Administration and offices for production staff and visiting faculty and teachers
Conference and preview facilities
Film and tape materials and equipment storage and distribution.

In programming an instructional support center, it is the manner in which these components are arranged and placed together that creates the appropriate center for a particular institution.

3. The instructional support center can perform several major services in addition to producing films, slides, tapes, and other instructional materials:

• It can design and produce materials that are not commercially available but which are needed for specific instructional purposes.

• It can provide technical assistance to teachers and professors in using instructional technology effectively. It is this type of assistance which helps teachers overcome a fear of mechanical devices about which they have little knowledge and great anxiety.

• It can be the catalyst which causes teachers to begin planning instruction and learning together. Producing televised instruction may bring cooperation among teachers who otherwise would always function as independent entities.

• An instructional support center can provide pedagogical assistance to teachers in designing learning. The learning systems designers—the pedagogical consultants—would logically be housed within this center.

• These facilities can provide the professional focus for teachers and faculty members by making available professional references, material, journals, and consultants.

4. Instructional support facilities may be an integral part of an educational plant or a separate, free-standing building or unit. In either case, consideration should be given to designing the area to permit changes in areas and relocation of walls, services, and cables. Flexibility of this type is very important, as the functions, staff, and faculty develop. A "loft space," free of interior partitions and permitting economical changes, may be the best type of space.

5. One of the changes anticipated above involves the planning of TV studios. Often when studios are initially planned, the faculty will wish to provide for a class of students to be present in the studio during production. However, as the faculty becomes more comfortable with television, the need for students in the studio is less significant. The building should be designed to permit this evolutionary change.

6. Obviously there is not single instructional

COLLEGE AND UNIVERSITY FACILITIES

Large-Group Facilities

support facility which solves all needs at all levels. There are many, many different systems of production and support which can be diagrammed. Figure 2a indicates a regional center which supports a number of subcenters within schools throughout the system. From the subcenter, further production and support activities are provided to individual classrooms, resources center, independent study facilities, and special rooms. It should be noted that within the resources center there is the small, simplified production area for teacher use. The same diagram might illustrate the activities within a college or university campus where, from a central location, major production and support feeds out into schools and departments and then into individual facilities and areas.

Figure 2b illustrates a center within a large central school which not only supports that school but feeds into other, smaller schools throughout a school district. This might be the appropriate diagram to illustrate production-support facilities within an "educational park."

Production-Support—1 This production-support center might serve a high school, a couple of middle schools, several elementary schools, or a combination of all. Figure 3 shows the basic facilities to support uses of television, graphic arts, and projected media while providing the administrative and instructional support activities necessary for such a situation. The multi-use studio can be used for live and recorded television production, film production, still photography, and, possibly, audio recording. Control of all of these production activities would come from the central control and distribution room.

The graphics room includes drafting space, copying machines, film editing and copying equipment, assembly and work tables, and other equipment associated with these types of production. The preparation and storage area adjacent to the studio is used for building and storing sets and models; next to it is maintenance and repair area for AV equipment used both within this production facility and throughout the schools it serves. The administrative facilities include waiting and exhibit areas, preview and conference rooms, and offices.

Production-Support—2 Figure 4 illustrates a center producing basic institutional aids and media, with an emphasis on film production. The production process is initiated by a conference between faculty and production staff, at which time the nature and instructional requirements of the materials are defined and a production schedule is set up. After production, the finished materials are distributed to the faculty concerned. Eventually the material may be deposited in the library of resources center where it is available to the student for review; it may also be distributed to cooperating institutions.

Production-Support—3 Figure 5 illustrates a center designed for originating televised instruction for distribution to a number of receiving points on the campus or to cooperating institutions. This center may fulfill a number of related functions such as reception and distribution of "off the air" programs, recording of televised instruction (videotape or kinescope), distribution of film materials, and coordinating of remote origination from labs, research centers, and other potential "studios." These related functions affect space considerations only as far as requirements of engineering

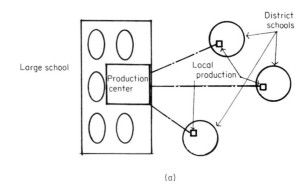

(a)

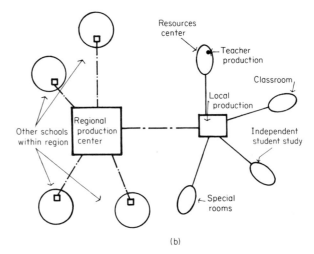

(b)

Fig. 2

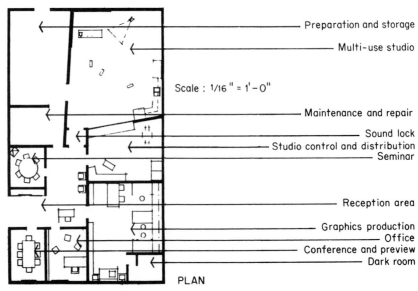

Scale : 1/16 " = 1'-0"

PLAN

Fig. 3

342

and control, and storage of materials and equipment. Distribution of the television image may be by open or closed circuit or both; the method of transmission does not basically affect the design of the facility.

Such a unit would probably serve an entire campus, or, possibly, in the case of the large university, one or more colleges on the campus.

Production-Support — 4 An institution venturing into a broad program utilizing the aids and media may well consider providing a single facility that combines all the production functions. In the long run such an approach can probably be justified from the standpoint of economy of space, equipment, and personnel, as often a single activity will support several production processes. A graphic arts studio,

for example, can produce not only visuals and graphic materials for direct classroom use but also the materials used in film production and television production. This total, more complex center is represented in Fig. 6.

Projection Systems

Too frequently the hardware used in audiovisual presentations is regarded as a collection of individual items—a projector, a screen, and a speaker—each performing its function more or less independently. A much broader concept is essential if media are to be used with maximum effectiveness. Not only these hardware items but also the seating area and the environment itself must be considered as integrated components of a system, each influenced by and depending on all of the others in producing the

total effect. None of these components, even the hardware, can be selected on its merits alone.

Regardless of the projected material or method, the effectiveness of the presentation depends upon the ease with which the viewers receive the message. With any normal audience, the quality of viewing conditions is chiefly determined by four factors:

1. The appropriateness and efficiency of the projection equipment and screens
2. The quality of the projected material
3. The location of the viewer in relation to the screen
4. The visual and auditory environment

Front and Rear Projection Before considering any of the above matters, it is important to recognize that two different methods may be used

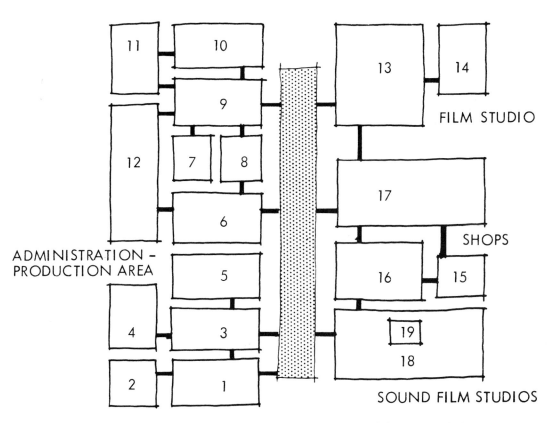

1. clerical and shipping - location of receptionist, secretaries and personnel involved in distribution of materials.

2. film vault - storage of completed film materials.

3. conference-rehearsal - rooms for faculty-production staff conferences, rehearsals prior to recording or filming, and periodic staff conferences.

4. production staff offices.

5. recording and radio studios - making of audio-tapes, dubbing of sound on films and possibly radio broadcasting.

6. graphic-art studio - production of graphs, charts, "visuals" and some slide materials for both direct classroom and film production use.

7. still photography.

8. animation - filming of art work.

9. processing - darkrooms for limited developing and printing of film materials.

10. editing-assembly - editing of motion pictures and assembly of all instructional materials.

11. previewing - small projection rooms for viewing incomplete as well as finished film materials.

12. offices, storage, and toilets - located as needed adjacent to the various production areas.

13. film studio - a large, open studio for the filming of silent motion pictures on which the sound may later be added. The studio can be flexibly divided into filming areas by using demountable flats. This will permit simultaneous filming of one or more productions.

14. external slab - concrete slab (possibly covered) adjacent and accessible to the studio for exter-

nal filming. It may also be used as a receiving platform for materials taken directly into the studio.

15. model and set shop - production of models and demonstration apparatus for direct instructional or production uses, and the making of sets and flats for use in the studios.

16. storage - a large area for storage of materials used in the studios or awaiting distribution for classroom use.

17. equipment receiving, storage and maintenance.

18. sound studios - several studios in which both the sound and image are recorded simultaneously. This permits only one production at a time per studio.

19. control-engineering - glass-fronted booths accessible to each studio for control-engineering personnel and equipment.

Fig. 4

Educational

COLLEGE AND UNIVERSITY FACILITIES
Large-Group Facilities

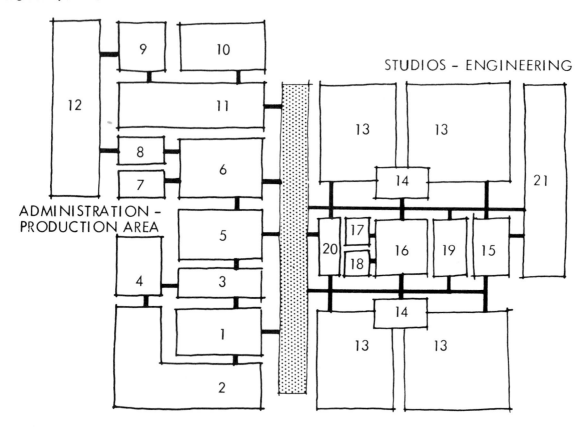

1. reception and secretarial – space for secretarial staff and reception area for visitors.

2. TV faculty offices – offices for faculty members instructing by television and provided to permit coordination between "on-camera" faculty and production staff. (The faculty may also have academic office elsewhere on the campus).

3. production staff offices.

4. conference rooms – spaces for planning

5. film and graphic materials storage – storage of materials used by the faculty in preparation and presentation of televised instruction and includes space for previewing projected materials.

6. graphic arts studio – production of art work

7. still photography.

8. processing – darkrooms for limited processing of film materials.

9. workshop – making or assembling of models, sets, flats and apparatus for studio use.

10. equipment shop – receiving, maintenance and storage of camera, sound, control, lighting and other production equipment.

11. storage – large area for flats, sets, apparatus, and other production materials.

12. offices, storage, toilets and mechanical equipment areas – located as needed throughout the unit.

13. television studios – origination of televised production. The size, location and functioning of the studios will vary depending on the philosophy and scope of televised instruction.

14. studio control – glass-fronted booths which serve one or more studios and house the producer-director and control equipment. (Booths do not require direct visual contact with studios; control may be handled by monitors.)

15. storage – adjacent to the studios to avoid loss of production areas within the studios given over to storage.

16. central control, engineering and distribution – electronic "nerve center" for receiving "off-the-air", coordinating remote and studio signals, and maintaining control of all origination and distribution.

17. projection – location of camera chains for distribution of film, slide, and opaque materials.

18. recording – location of kinescope or video tape recorders.

19. equipment storage – storage of camera equipment available for studio use.

20. dressing and make-up areas.

21. external slab – televising of equipment and apparatus too large or cumbersome to be moved into a studio.

Fig. 5

for projecting images onto a screen, and that the choice of method will influence the design of a projection system. These two methods are:
• Front projection, in which both the projector and the viewers are on the same side of an opaque screen which reflects the image, and,
• Rear projection, in which the projector and the viewers are on opposite sides of a translucent screen upon which the image is displayed.

Either one may be used for any type of projector, including the TV projector, but customarily the overhead and opaque projectors are used in front projection. (See Fig. 7.)

Both front and rear projection have their inherent advantages and disadvantages, which become clear by comparing them in respect to the most important areas of difference. These are:
• The effect of ambient light
• Space requirements, and
• Interference with the projected image

The ambient light level in the room is much more critical with front projection than with rear projection. This means that with present equipment a much higher level of room lighting can be tolerated in the viewing area when rear projection is employed. This is considered to be the chief advantage of rear projection,

particularly in larger rooms. In rooms where small image sizes are appropriate, ambient light effects may not be critical providing proper equipment is used. Current developments in the improvement of equipment indicate that the size of acceptable images possible with front projection under useful levels of ambient light will be increased.

An undeniable disadvantage of rear projection is that additional space behind the screen must be provided to accommodate the projectors and their throw distances. To conserve space, projectors with short focal length lenses are desirable and mirrors may be used to "bend" the projection rays. Also self-

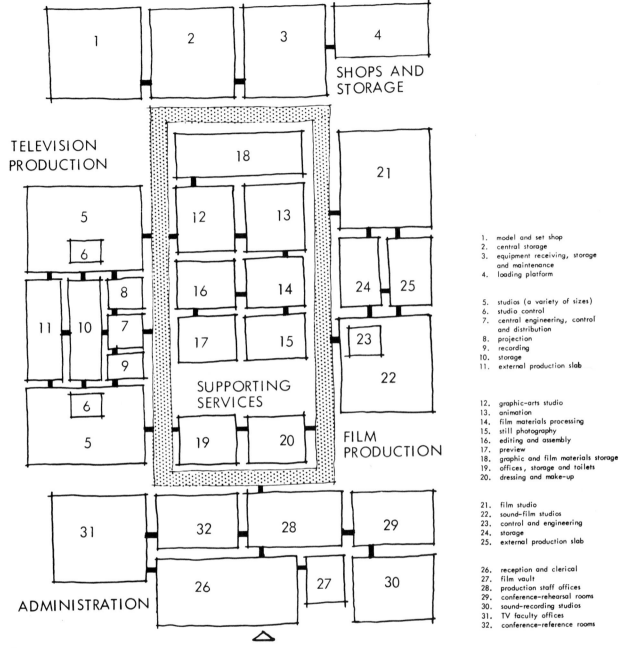

1. model and set shop
2. central storage
3. equipment receiving, storage and maintenance
4. loading platform

5. studios (a variety of sizes)
6. studio control
7. central engineering, control and distribution
8. projection
9. recording
10. storage
11. external production slab

12. graphic-arts studio
13. animation
14. film materials processing
15. still photography
16. editing and assembly
17. preview
18. graphic and film materials storage
19. offices, storage and toilets
20. dressing and make-up

21. film studio
22. sound-film studios
23. control and engineering
24. storage
25. external production slab

26. reception and clerical
27. film vault
28. production staff offices
29. conference-rehearsal rooms
30. sound-recording studios
31. TV faculty offices
32. conference-reference rooms

Fig. 6

contained screen-projector units or media modules may be used. It must be recognized, however, that shortening the focal length of the projector decreases the width of optimum viewing areas, and the use of mirrors generally diminishes the effective brightness of the projected image.

One of the important advantages of rear projection is that the projection rays are protected from interference by either the instructor or the viewers. The instructor can stand in front of the image to point out details without casting shadows. With front projection this is impossible; distracting shadows are cast by any object or person in the path of the projection

beam, and the freedom of the instructor is limited accordingly.

It has been assumed that in both methods the projectors are located in reasonably sound-proof enclosures and that remote control is provided for the instructor who remains at the front of the class. Such assumptions are frequently not valid for front projection, however. With relatively small groups of viewers, portable front projection equipment is often used, and the instructor himself may operate the projector. Used in this way, front projection has several additional disadvantages which should be recognized. Unless precautions are taken to minimize it, the noise of the projector

is distractive to viewers, and if the instructor must double as an operator, his effectiveness as a teacher is necessarily diminished.

Screens The design of any projection system must necessarily recognize "the human factor" —the needs and limitations of the observer. The impact and effectiveness of the image displayed largely depend on such matters as its brightness, its legibility and its contrast values.

The human eye can tolerate and adjust to a remarkably wide range of conditions, but if eyestrain is to be avoided, these critical variables must be controlled within established

Educational

COLLEGE AND UNIVERSITY FACILITIES

Large-Group Facilities

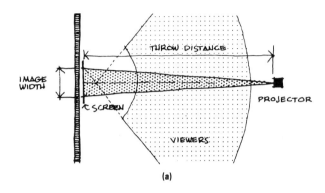

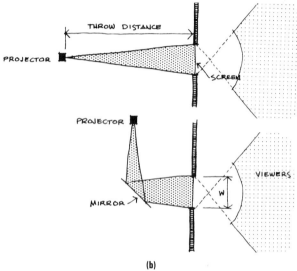

Fig. 7 (a) Front projection; (b) rear projection.

limits of acceptability. The projection screen is a major component in determining visual comfort.

A variety of screen types are available for both front and rear projection. They differ significantly in their characteristics, affecting both the appropriate size of viewing area and the tolerable level of ambient lighting.

Projectors The reader is cautioned that any discussion of projection devices can only report on the existing ranges and characteristics of commercially available equipment. Technological developments can render much of today's equipment obsolete; at the time equipment is selected, the newest models should be investigated for improvements in optical systems, lumen output, remote capability, ease of operation, and cost.

Overhead Projector. The overhead projector currently is one of the most popular projection devices in classrooms. Ease and speed of transparency-making, high lumen output, elimination of the need for room darkening, and ease of operation are among its good characteristics. The only special requirement for this projector is a tilted screen in order to prevent keystoning of the image. Projectors range from fanless desktop models to those which include the projection of slides and filmstrip through the projector's optical system.

35 mm Slide Projector. The classroom use of 35 mm color slides has substantially increased with the production of inexpensive,

foolproof 35 mm cameras and remotely controlled projectors. With the low cost of slide production and the space savings in storage, the 35mm slide is being used more and more extensively than the 3¼- by 4-in. slide. For efficient use in classrooms, the projectors should be capable of remote on-off, forward-reverse, and focus. Ideally, the fan should have a thermal device to allow cooling of the projector after the lamp is turned off. Highly desirable characteristics for a projector will be ease of loading, low cost of slide trays that accept all sorts of mountings, and freedom from jamming. Lenses are available that will allow projection from as short a distance as 1 W (1 width of the screen) for rear projection to 6 W for front projection in larger auditoriums. With improvements in lumen output, mirrors can be used to reduce the space required for rear screen projection. Projectors are available with xenon light sources, random access, digital readout, and audio projector programming.

3¼- by 4-in. Slide Projector. Most 3¼-by 4-in. slide projectors manufactured today are of the manually operated type. For the purpose of this report and where remote control of the projection device is necessary, the few remotely operated projectors currently available are discussed. Some of the most desirable characteristics of these projectors are high lumen output, the capability with an adapter of projecting 35 mm slides, the ability to handle polaroid slides, and short-throw lenses for rear screen projection.

Motion Picture Projectors. Currently the 16 mm projector has a monopoly on motion picture projection in the classroom. However, with the introduction of the new, large-frame 8 mm film and sound cameras, there may be a marked changeover to 8 mm for small-group use, and it will be introduced for independent study. Film projection using 35 mm film has never found extensive educational application.

Film Strip Projectors and Previewers. The low cost and availability of film strips on almost every subject make this form of visual aid attractive to many teachers. Projectors with remote control are required for rear-screen projection. Simple film strip previewers may adequately serve the student studying independently. In between are projectors appropriate for front projection with small groups.

Television Projectors. Television projection has its greatest implications for large-group instruction. Its use as a method of displaying and magnifying gross images is excellent. Its promise as a first-rate teaching tool is dependent not only on its ability to have good contrast, brightness, and definition but also simple maintenance. Projectors are available for closed circuit or broadcast in either black and white or color and black and white. In general, the more expensive the projector, the more acceptable the image and the higher the lumen output. Projected television requires slightly more than a 2 W throw distance. Prices vary tremendously from $2,800 to $50,000 or so.

More Information. For more comprehensive information on projection equipment the reader is directed to the *Audio-visual Equipment Directory,* National Audio-Visual Association, Inc., 1201 Spring Street, Fairfax, Virginia.

Space for Rear Projection. In designing for rear projection, one of the problems the architect faces is the allowance of the correct amount of space for the location of the projection equipment. Figure 8*a* shows a projector located at a 1 W throw distance and indicates the maximum bend angle for seat A as over 75. This is unsatisfactory for this seat; the allowable bend angle is established by the screen characteristics, and at present, the maximum bend angle is 60. Figure 8*b* shows a 2 W throw distance and a maximum bend angle at seat A of about 60, which is satisfactory. Figure 8*c* shows a total depth of rear projection area as 1 W, but by using a mirror, it still permits a 2 W throw distance and a 60° bend angle.

Mirrors Reduce Light. The use of mirrors, however, has its drawback in that about a 10 percent loss of image brightness occurs. One must also be careful of reflections of ambient light of other projectors or classroom light passing through other screens and affecting either the mirror or the screen. This can be combatted by locating black drapes to mask the projectors from this stray light.

Some General Rules. A few general rules are helpful in locating projectors and establishing space for rear projection equipment:

• The larger the screen, the longer the throw distance.

• Conversely, the smaller the screen, the shorter the throw distance.

• Mirrors may be used to fold the projection beam for space saving with smaller screens or with projectors with high lumen output on larger screens.

• For initial schematic design a 2 W depth behind all the screens should be allocated for the rear projection area.

• The use of extra closeup lenses decreases the viewing area, and may result in some distortion around the edge of projected images.

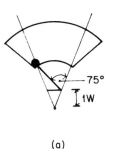 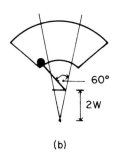 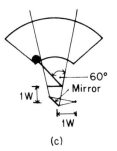

(a)   (b)   (c)

Fig. 8

The Viewing Area *Viewing Area Not Critical in Most Classrooms.* Before projected materials were introduced, the objects to be viewed in the usual schoolroom were the instructor, the chalkboards, and sometimes maps and charts. The instructor was free to move about the room, and the other objects of visual attention were usually distributed over several wall areas. All of them received their illumination by the general lighting of the room itself. With no fixed area of attention, sightlines and viewing were not critical as long as the general lighting was adequate.

Projected Images Restrict Viewing Area. For the effective use of visual aids, however, the requirements for good viewing are much more demanding. The projected image necessarily occupies a fixed position, and, except on the TV receiver, is in a flat plane. Whereas a three-dimensional object may well be viewed from the side, a flat picture can be seen intelligibly only within the limits of a "cone of view." To see the image properly, the viewer must be within the limits of this cone, and neither too near the image nor too far from it. The area defined by these limits is referred to as the viewing area. Its importance in the planning of spaces for image viewing is fundamental, whether the space be a small informal conference area or a large formal lecture hall.

Shape of the Viewing Area. The shape of the viewing area, then, is approximately as shown. Its size is always based on the size of the image to be viewed. The human eye comprehends detail only within a limited cone angle (about $2\frac{1}{2}$ min of arc), and the length of chord subtending this arc, e.g. the image width, varies with its distance from the observer. Thus an object 20 ft away and 6 ft long appears the same as a similar object 10 ft away and 3 ft long. The size of the viewing area is determined by three dimensions, as shown in Fig. 9.

• The minimum distance (1), which is the distance from the nearest part of the image to the eye of the closest viewer

• The maximum distance (2), which is the

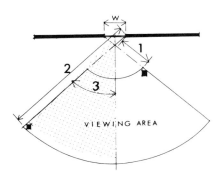

Fig. 9

distance from the furthermost part of the image to the most distant viewer

• The maximum viewing angle (3), which is the angle between the projection axis and the line of sight of a person located as far from this axis as he can be and still see all image detail in proper brilliance

Two Ways of Establishing the Viewing Angle. Whether the apex of the maximum viewing angle should be located at the screen or at some other point on the projection axis is a moot point. There is some disagreement among authorities, too, as to how it should govern the side limits of the viewing area. Some prefer the use of the "edge angle," while others use the angle at the center of the screen. By either approach, the limits defined are essentially similar. In this study, an edge angle of 40° has been used in laying out viewing areas for rear projection, since it is felt this best represents average screen characteristics. With front projection, the use of the "center angle" is probably more common practice, and its values range from 20° to possibly as high as 50°. The maximum value of the angle used in determining the viewing area for receiver TV is 45°.

Minimum and Maximum TV Viewing Distances

Size of TV tube	Min viewing distance, 4 W	Max viewing distance, 12 W
17 in.	4 ft-11 in.	14 ft-9 in.
19 in.	5 ft-1 in.	15 ft-2 in.
21 in.	6 ft-4 in.	19 ft-0 in.
23 in.	6 ft-6 in.	19 ft-4 in.
24 in.	7 ft-5 in.	21 ft-5 in.
27 in.	9 ft-8 in.	24 ft-5 in.

Defining Minimum and Maximum Viewing Distances. Practical minimum and maximum distances are both expressed as multiples of the image width (W). They vary both with the medium being used and with the type and quality of material being projected, and may be affected also, in some degree, by personal preferences. They have not yet been precisely determined by scientific methods, and it is doubtful that such data would have much practical value anyway. The generally accepted values, resulting from numerous studies, are these: (See Fig. 10.)

	Film, slides and projected TV	TV receivers
Minimum distance . .	2 W	4 W
Maximum distance . .	6 to 10 W	12 W

Relation of Screen Size and Viewing Area. Since the size of the viewing area is a function of the image width, it follows that the proper

screen size for any given space will be determined by the number of viewers intended. Conversely, a given type and size of screen automatically establishes the size of the viewing area, and consequently the size of audience that can be properly accommodated. The viewing area is the pattern which determines the seating arrangement in any learning space where projected images are to be used, and in the larger spaces, at least, it also influences the shape of the room. (Fig. 11.)

Planning the Projection System *Steps in Design.* Whether front or rear projection is to be used, the design of the projection system itself involves determining:

1. The size of viewing area required
2. The appropriate screen size
3. The proper type of screen
4. The appropriate projector(s)—the required lumen output, focal length and location
5. The maximum permissible level of ambient lighting on the screen.

Trial and Error at First. The desired audience size is usually predetermined. In some cases, the size of the viewing area, too, may be established by existing conditions. Otherwise, its size and shape should be tentatively

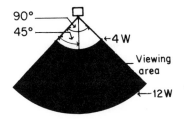

Fig. 10

approximated in accord with the principles already discussed. Because of the relationship between its dimensions and the width of screen to be used, the inexperienced designer necessarily proceeds by trial and error until he arrives at a satisfactory arrangement accommodating the specified audience in proper relationship with the screen. Sometimes, the problem may be reversed, requiring a determination of the optimum audience and seating arrangement for projection equipment already at hand.

Standards Professional standards accepted by the Society of Motion Picture and Television Engineers have been developed for viewing front and rear projected images. These standards provide excellent images. However, for the purpose of economy in classroom use of projected media, it is felt that some standards based on the poorest seat in the room can be lowered, particularly for gross images. The following resumé of standards indicates by asterisk (*) those that are less than the professional standards.

Screen Brightness
Motion pictures:

    5 ft L—Minimum* (gross images)
    10 ft L—Satisfactory
    15 ft L—Excellent
    20 ft L—Maximum (flicker threshold for some
        observers)

Slides:

    2.5 ft L—Minimum* (gross images)
    5 ft L—Minimum for slides with detail
    10 ft L—Satisfactory
    20 ft L—Excellent

COLLEGE AND UNIVERSITY FACILITIES
Large-Group Facilities

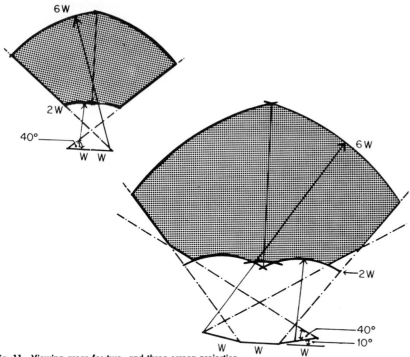

Fig. 11 Viewing areas for two- and three-screen projection.

Projected TV:

2 ft L — Minimum* (gross images)
20 ft L — Maximum (flicker threshold for some observers)

TV monitors:

100 lumens per square foot

Brightness Ratio

2:1 — Excellent
3:1 — Very good
10:1 — Acceptable* under some conditions

Contrast Ratio

100:1 — Pictorial scenes
25:1 — Good legibility of printed characters
5:1 — White letters on black background
30:1 — Minimum* contrast ratio for poorest seat dictated by higher levels of classroom light and many types of projected materials

Contrast ratio is determined in part by non-image brightness which, in turn, is related to screen reflectance and room ambient light. Therefore, controlling the amount of ambient light reaching the screen is important. For large screen installations, if the amount of ambient light occurring at the screen is held to 1–2 ft C, the contrast ratio will normally be adequate.

Writing Surface Lighting Levels Ideally, an average ratio of 1:1 between writing surface brightness and screen brightness should be maintained, while not spilling excessive ambient light on the screens. Since screen brightness varies for each seat in the viewing area, the average condition of brightness for each broad class of projected material should be approximately satisfied. For a medium to large size room, three lighting levels would be in the range of:

5–10 ft C — Projected TV and films
10–20 ft C — Slides
30 + ft C — Other class activities

Media Module This study led to the design and development of a self-contained media cabinet which might be used in many types of small and medium group situations. These "media modules" can be of several types:

• A fixed cabinet with self-contained equipment, rear projection screen, and several additional "swing-out" display surfaces.

• Same as above, only the entire media module would be mobile.

• A basic fixed cabinet with rear projection screen and "swing-out" display surfaces. Projection equipment would be mounted on mobile carts which would roll into the cabinet and which would permit the interchanging of projectors.

• Same as above with both the basic cabinet and the equipment carts mobile.

• Any of the above, but with a cabinet and rear projection screen sized to accommodate two rear projected images side-by-side.

Media modules have several attractive features. They can be fabricated in a shop and installed in existing classrooms with little disruption of normal class meetings; in this way, media modules can quickly and inexpensively convert existing facilities for uses of media. Both in building new facilities and remodelling old, the media module is a rela-

tively inexpensive answer initially, which also readily adapts to new and improved equipment. Mobile units can be designed for flexible spaces where the regrouping of students frequently is an important functional requirement; fixed installations of media might not be feasible in such circumstances. As illustrated in this study, media modules can be used to increase the utilization of facilities such as dining rooms and gymnasiums by also allowing them to be used for instruction.

The accompanying figure (Fig. 12) shows one type of media module which was designed and built. The basic cabinet with screen and display surfaces could be either fixed or mobile. Various types of projectors can be mounted in the cart, which is rolled into position for projection on the rear projection screen. Remote controls operate the equipment and the rear screen is of the flexible type. This media module has a screen surface 32 in. square and the entire unit stands 6 ft–8 in. high. Naturally, these dimensions will vary from module to module.

Furniture *Planning Furniture an Integral Part of the Design Process.* For effective uses of media in education, the manner in which classrooms, seminar rooms, independent study facilities, and other learning spaces are furnished is an important design decision. Unfortunately, too often the selection and purchase of furniture are left until too late in the planning process when energies, funds, and professional services have been expended. Furniture, as part of the learning environment, should be considered an integral part of any space in which media are to be employed; its selection should be based on careful study and professional advice early in planning. Most importantly, functional, aesthetic, and economic criteria should be established during the programming stages when the functional requirements of the spaces are spelled out.

Fixed Seating — Continuous Counters with Fixed Seats. Many types of seating for learning spaces are available, but their individual appropriateness varies from space to space. Of the three basic types of seating (fixed, movable, and combined) fixed has had the advantage of guaranteeing that, once properly positioned, every student will always be in the proper relationship to screens and other display surfaces. Of the various types of fixed seating, the continuous counter with individual fixed chairs provides a desirable surface for writing and for holding references. This is particularly important in secondary and higher education where the learning process may require extensive use of various types of materials and resources during a class. Also,

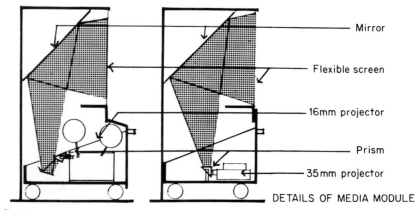

Mirror
Flexible screen
16mm projector
Prism
35mm projector

DETAILS OF MEDIA MODULE

Fig. 12

a continuous counter works well when portable, audiovisual equipment, small demonstrations, or various forms of teaching machines are to be used by students at their seats, or when student response systems, requiring the use of a response panel at each station, are to be installed initially or planned for later installation. This type of seating does require more floor area per unit than most other types of fixed seating, but this may be compensated for by the provision of cross aisles between each row of seating, allowing students to move freely to and from their seats.

Fixed Seating — Theater Types. There are many so-called "theater-type" of fixed seating employing a seat with a folding or lifting individual writing surface. Unfortunately, many of the tablet arms provided with this type of seating have the disadvantage of being too small to accommodate writing and reference materials. Lately, some improvements in seating have resulted in folding tablet arms that are adequate in size. Generally, fixed seating of this kind requires less floor area than the continuous counters, but student access to his individual seat is more limited. Also, the necessary moving parts to raise and lower the tablet arms can create maintenance and upkeep problems. Installation of response devices and outlets for equipment can be handled in seating with movable tablet arms, but this again introduces maintenance problems.

Movable Seating. Movable seating also introduces a variety of alternatives, and again the provision of an adequate writing surface is extremely important. In rooms where regrouping of students is important, separate table units or seat-table units that are modular to allow conference and discussion groupings are desirable. Movable seating mitigates against the use of any individual student instructional device requiring wiring, such as response systems, portable recorders or projectors, and power-operated teaching machines. Particularly with movable seating, seating should be scaled and designed with the age and character of the students in mind.

Combined Seating. Combined seating is basically of one type — continuous counter with loose seats. This type has the advantages of flexibility, accommodation to many body postures, and reduced cost over the continuous counter with fixed seats. However, the interpretation of building codes may prohibit continental seating in large rooms. The accompanying diagram (Fig. 13) shows several of the fixed and combined types of seating that are available, together with the average size of writing surfaces and the floor area required.

A Mix of Seating Is Often the Answer. In many instances, several types of seating in one space may best meet functional needs. For instance, loose tables and chairs on a flat floor area at the front of a large teaching room can be used for case studies, moot courts, and other instructional methods, while the remainder of the seating is fixed on a sloped or stepped floor. Also, in rooms requiring raised seating, rows of seating may alternate between riser-mounted and floor-mounted types. Particularly in medium group spaces, various types of loose seating may meet the varying requirements dictated by multi-age, multi-class, and nongraded approaches to learning.

Importance of Good Sight Lines from All Seats. Certainly in rooms where projected media are to be used extensively, good sight lines from all seats to all screens are important. Where 40 or more students are involved, this will generally require stepped or sloped floors. However, steep slopes such as seen for years in college lecture halls or amphitheaters are not always necessary. These slopes have usually been dictated by a functional requirement that every student be able to see the top of a demonstration table at the front of the room. Rather than thus increasing the volume of the room, and the cost of the room, electronic means of magnification should be employed which shifts the functional requirement from viewing a demonstration table to the more easily accommodated viewing of screens. By offsetting the rows of seating, and by using platforms containing two rows of seating each, the volume of the room can be reduced without impairing the viewing of screens and information display surfaces.

Investigate the Advantages of Continental Seating. In laying out seating in the larger rooms, continental seating, which allows cross aisles between the rows of seats, should be explored. This arrangement can move aisles outside the viewing area, can allow longer rows of seats, and can permit students to move to and from their seats without disturbing other students. The square footage per seating unit based on the total room area may not be much greater than that for more conventional arrangements. Each such solution must be judged in accordance with the applicable building code.

Educational

COLLEGE AND UNIVERSITY FACILITIES
Large-Group Facilities

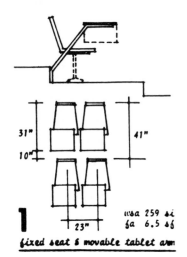

1 fixed seat & movable tablet arm

wsa 259 si
fa 6.5 sf

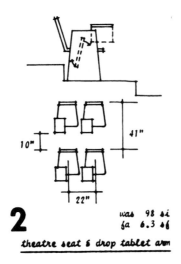

2 theatre seat & drop tablet arm

wsa 98 si
fa 6.3 sf

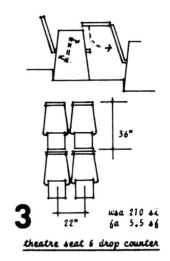

3 theatre seat & drop counter

wsa 210 si
fa 5.5 sf

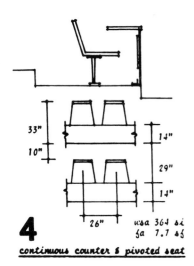

4 continuous counter & pivoted seat

wsa 364 si
fa 7.7 sf

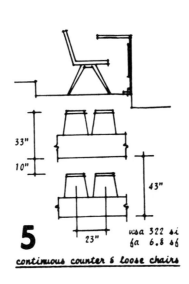

5 continuous counter & loose chairs

wsa 322 si
fa 6.8 sf

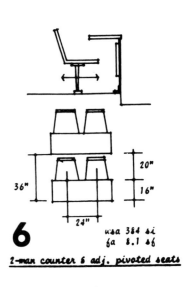

6 2-man counter & adj. pivoted seats

wsa 384 si
fa 8.1 sf

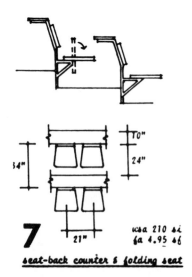

7 seat-back counter & folding seat

wsa 210 si
fa 4.95 sf

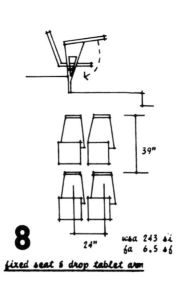

8 fixed seat & drop tablet arm

wsa 243 si
fa 6.5 sf

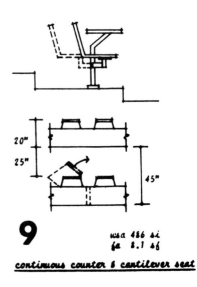

9 continuous counter & cantilever seat

wsa 486 si
fa 8.1 sf

wsa – writing surface area
fa – floor area

Fig. 13 Seating types.

350

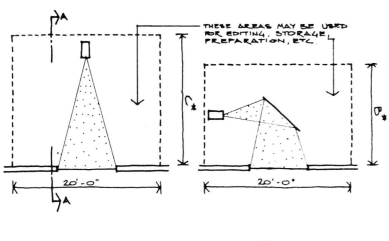

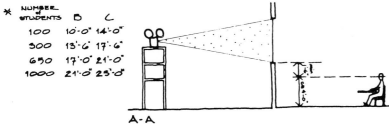

Fig. 1 Rear-screen projection area.

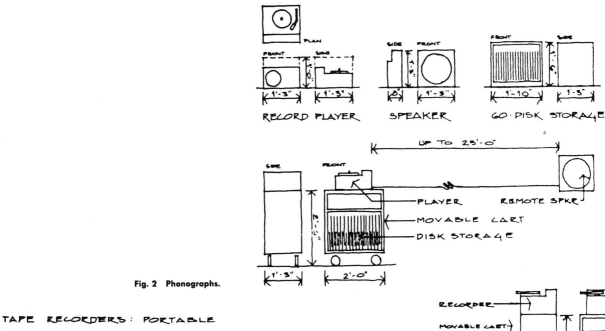

Fig. 2 Phonographs.

TAPE RECORDERS: PORTABLE

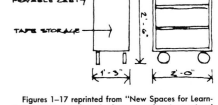

Fig. 3 Tape recorders.

Figures 1–17 reprinted from "New Spaces for Learning: Designing college facilities to utilize instructional aids and media." Report of Research Project DASFEE: (Design of Auditorium-Studio Facilities for Engineering Education) supported by grant from Educational Facilities Laboratories, Inc., revised ed., June 1966.

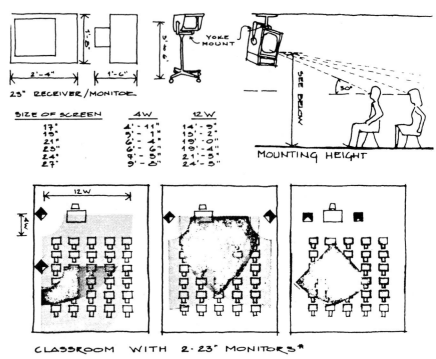

23" RECEIVER/MONITOR

SIZE OF SCREEN	4W	12W
17"	4'-11"	14'-5"
19"	5'-1"	15'-2"
21"	6'-4"	19'-0"
23"	6'-6"	19'-4"
24"	7'-5"	21'-5"
27"	9'-0"	24'-5"

MOUNTING HEIGHT

CLASSROOM WITH 2·23" MONITORS*

Fig. 4 Classroom monitors.

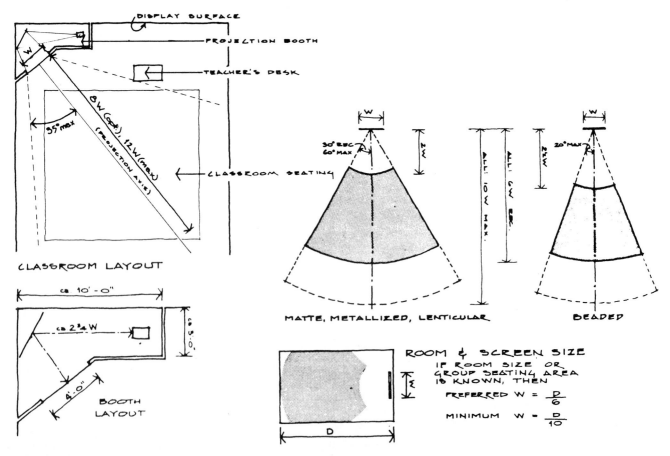

CLASSROOM LAYOUT

BOOTH LAYOUT

MATTE, METALLIZED, LENTICULAR

BEADED

ROOM & SCREEN SIZE
IF ROOM SIZE OR GROUP SEATING AREA IS KNOWN, THEN

PREFERRED W = $\frac{D}{6}$

MINIMUM W = $\frac{D}{10}$

Fig. 5 Rear-screen projection cabinet.

Fig. 6 Front projection screens.

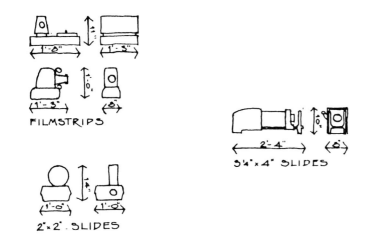

FILMSTRIPS

2"x2" SLIDES

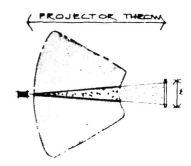

3¼"x4" SLIDES

Fig. 7 Slides and filmstrips; projectors.

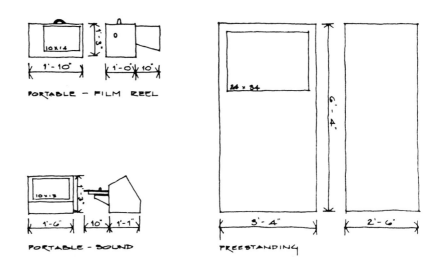

PORTABLE – FILM REEL

PORTABLE – SOUND

FREESTANDING

Fig. 8 Repetitive film projectors.

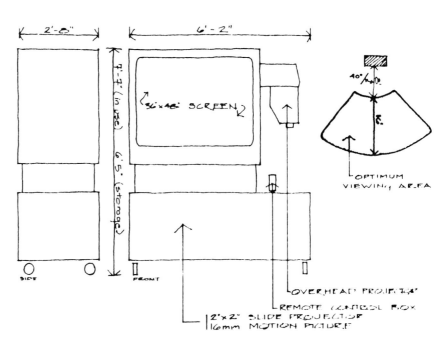

OPTIMUM VIEWING AREA

OVERHEAD PROJECTOR

REMOTE CONTROL BOX

2"x2" SLIDE PROJECTOR
16mm MOTION PICTURE

Fig. 9 Multiprojector console.

COLLEGE AND UNIVERSITY FACILITIES
Audiovisual

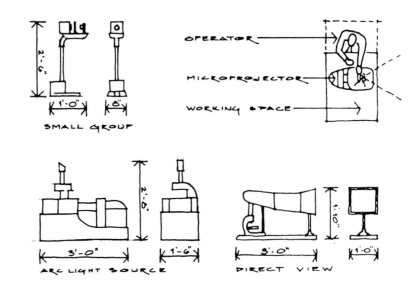

Fig. 10   Microprojectors.

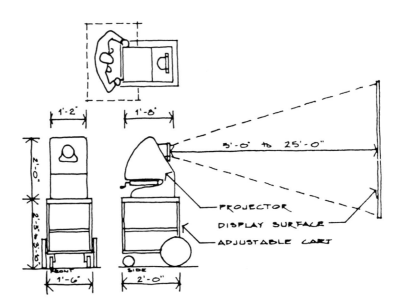

Fig. 11   Opaque projector.

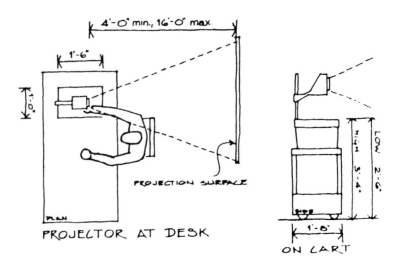

Fig. 12   Overhead projector.

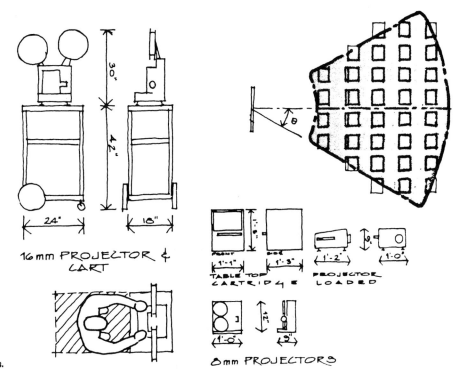

Fig. 13   8-mm and 16-mm motion-picture projectors.

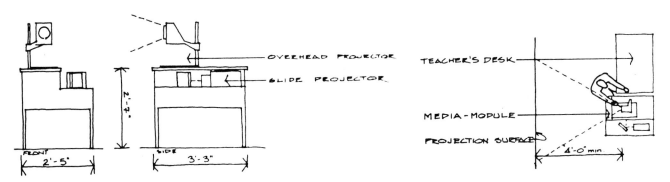

Fig. 14   Multiprojector module.

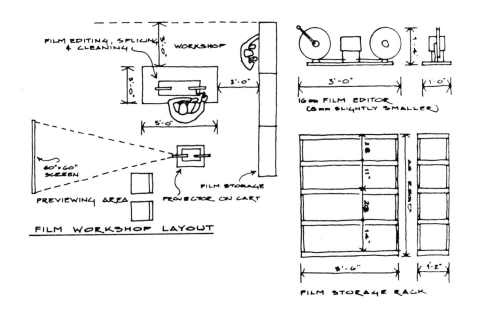

Fig. 15   Film workshop.

COLLEGE AND UNIVERSITY FACILITIES
Audiovisual

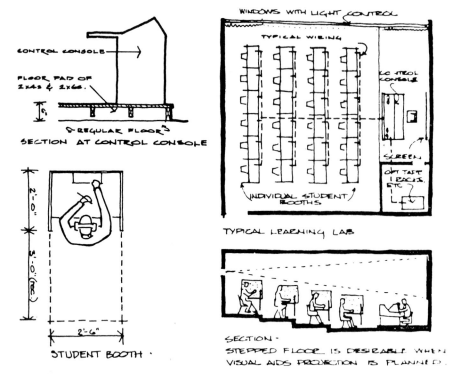

SECTION AT CONTROL CONSOLE

TYPICAL LEARNING LAB

STUDENT BOOTH

SECTION -
STEPPED FLOOR IS DESIRABLE WHEN
VISUAL AIDS PROJECTION IS PLANNED.

Fig. 16

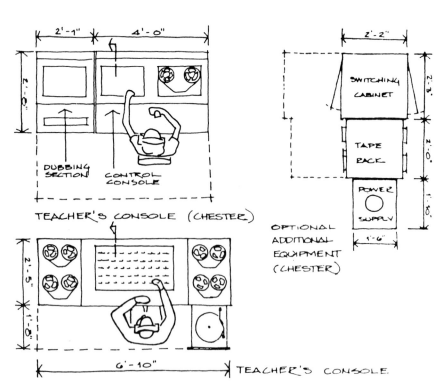

TEACHER'S CONSOLE (CHESTER)

OPTIONAL ADDITIONAL EQUIPMENT (CHESTER)

TEACHER'S CONSOLE.

Fig. 17   Language laboratory

THEATER-ARTS-LABORATORY TEACHING STATION

There are many types of space facility which may be employed in the Theater-Arts program. The Theater-Arts-Laboratory Teaching Station is primarily a classroom which is designed for, and specifically allocated to, the teaching of theater-arts subjects. It is presumed that this room will probably be assigned to a single teacher, or to a small group of teachers, employed in a team-teaching concept. With only slight expansion, however, it might serve in some instances as a very comfortable and pleasant place for public performances. It is not designed primarily as a replacement for a conventional school auditorium. Its existence, however, will emphasize the fact that the well-appointed auditorium is not essential for the successful pursuance of a theater-arts program. Under ideal circumstances, such a facility is employed on a day-to-day basis by the teacher in the normal progress of instruction, and therefore may be considered a supplement to the auditorium employed for the larger public performances. In addition to the normal daily class functions, it is entirely appropriate to employ the teaching station, on occasion, for public presentation of material adapted to this space, if the seating will accommodate a small invited, or even paying audience.

Although some dimensional data are provided, it should be remembered that they represent only a suggested treatment and that, in specific instances, a room might change its shape perceptibly and be increased or decreased in size. The basic concept of this room implies that its primary function is that of a classroom, and a continual enlargement of this facility approaching a small auditorium would be undesirable. The term "teaching station" is employed rather than "little" or "studio theater" in an attempt to emphasize its classroom function.

Separate Service Facilities

If the school has separate auditorium facilities, it is recommended that the teaching station be nearby in order that some of the service areas might be employed by both of these theater units. As an example—it would be possible for the teaching station and the auditorium to use the

Architecture for the Educational Theatre, H. W. Robinson, 1970. Reprinted by permission. Copyright © 1970 by University of Oregon.

Fig. 1 Functional and space relationships of auditorium to teaching station. It is highly desirable, as the text indicates, to have both a stage–auditorium and a teaching station in an efficient academic theater plant. If both are provided, it is not necessary to duplicate all of the support functions; avoiding unnecessary duplication will save space and construction costs. This diagram illustrates the desirable functional and positional relationships between the two complementary theater forms.

same dressing rooms, the same lobby space, the same ticket offices, the same rest rooms, the same shop area, and some of the same storage area (see Fig. 1). Although it is true that on occasion both of these producing units might be in performance simultaneously, it is not probable that this would occur frequently enough to warrant complete duplication of all these service areas. However, such support space is absolutely essential, and, if it is not provided in connection with some other function of the building, it will be necessary to plan it in connection with the teaching station. In the description which follows, it will be apparent that there are a number of advantages to having the teaching station accessible from four sides. The dimensional data suggest the possibility, but do not demand that the teaching station

occupy space equivalent in size and shape to two standard classrooms. The recommended plan includes space for normal classroom function, space for arena-type presentation, space for proscenium and thrust stage presentations, and allows all of this space to be converted to other multiple-theater purposes.

The area designated as the teaching station divides roughly into three parts (see Fig. 2). Part one: some fixed seating on an inclined floor accommodating about 30 students, with chairs equipped with movable tablet arms. Within some individual teaching practices the area might be preferred with a flat floor with movable chairs. Part two: an elevated stage, presumably at the opposite end from the fixed seating just described, and with the usual physical and electrical

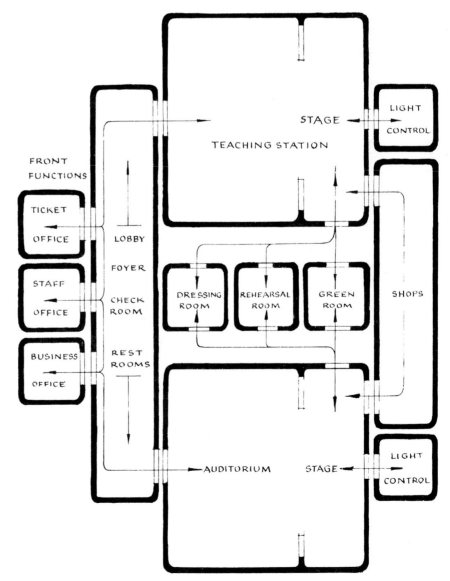

equipment. When employed as a proscenium stage, there would be space for seating approximately 80 in the fixed seating described combined with the temporary seating in the space next described. Part three: a flat floor area between part one and part two for rehearsal, demonstration and arena staging, a playing area of at least 14 by 18 ft, and with the usual lighting and mechanical equipment. When this area is employed for arena staging, and all other areas adapted to seating, it can accommodate approximately 140. The minimum width of this room is 24 ft; widths up to 36 ft would prove additionally desirable. The total length of the room, if the areas described are laid end-to-end, is about 70 ft.

If the fixed seating plan is employed for some 30 to 50 seats, and if they are on a raked (inclined) or terraced floor, it is recommended that there be at least a 5-in differential in the height of the rows. Back-to-back spacing of 36 in is recommended for rows, and 20–22 in for individual seat widths. Other seating to be provided should be of padded metal folding chairs with arm rests. Linkable chairs have some advantages in terms of ease of movement, for regrouping, and for cleaning.

The center area of the room is recommended for general demonstration, classroom space, and as an arena playing area for productions to be viewed from four sides. It is suggested that the recessed space might be twenty-one to twenty-four inches below that of the surrounding areas, including the service halls. This provides a depressed area for the arena stage with some seating at that level, with other raised seating on all sides, and it also allows for the elevated proscenium and thrust stage to be above the central floor area. Although the raised stage at the end of the room may be employed as a proscenium stage, it should not be thought of as that exclusively. Its design lends itself to other, flexible treatment. There is no fixed proscenium—the bounding edges of the opening are established by movable sections of wall or by a simple curtain framing. This stage space should be the full width of the room at that end, and should be at least 14 ft deep. Although more-than-usual classroom height is desirable over the stage area, it is not necessary to provide the usual stage house or fly space. It is suggested that two levels (each 3 ft deep) running the full width of the stage be provided in front of the fixed platform area with one-third stage height differential for each, namely 7 or 8 in. These levels can be created by separate, collapsible, or nesting boxes and reemployed as terraced seating spaces for the arena concept, or as variable forestage space as suggested by the accompanying diagrams (see Fig. 4).

A projection room may be provided at the end of the room opposite that of the fixed stage,

to serve as a sound room and a listening room, as well as to accommodate projection equipment.

The ceiling of this room should be approximately 14 ft above the stage level, and should provide, in addition to standard room lighting, other arrangements for the hanging of special stage lighting instruments and other hanging units. These supporting members can be exposed or concealed above a false ceiling. Lighting control may be located either in the offstage area on the fixed stage floor or in the projection room described above.

A walkway at least 42 in wide should be provided on the two long sides of the room which connect the stage level at one end with the entrance level at the opposite end. For classroom use, these levels will be employed as display and work areas at low table height. When the room is employed for arena staging, they serve as elevated rows of seating on the two sides. For end staging, they serve as additional side stages or for walkways approaching the stage for entrance, tableau, or processional purposes. If slightly enlarged, the space beneath these walkways may be employed for storage for seating or other theatrical equipment.

No attempt will be made here to specify a minimum of equipment for this teaching station, but it is obvious that it must have the usual complement of front traveler, cyclorama, switchboard, and lighting equipment.

Although it is not planned that all three of these areas will be used simultaneously in a classroom teaching station, it is possible to have on stage the fixed stage scenic, lighting, and property elements to be used for a public presentation or for the use of another class while the teacher lectures or conducts a demonstration in the central area without having to clear this material. In the same way a set-up can remain in the arena section and the teacher will still have a lecture area and a drill or rehearsal area unencumbered.

The essential features of this classroom teaching station are designed specifically to serve the purposes of theater instruction, but if, in scheduling, it appears that the room will not be in contin-

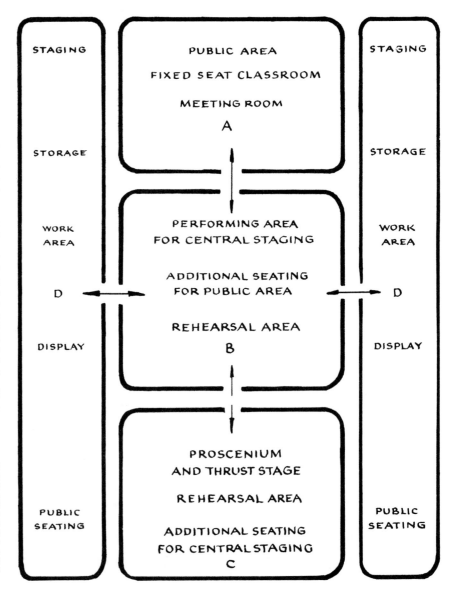

Fig. 2 The teaching station. The teaching station provides space for all theater functions such as work areas, rehearsal areas, classroom, and public seating for all three basic theater forms: thrust, arena, and proscenium. It is multifunctional in terms of space, but can seldom accommodate more than one function at one time. The basic concept calls for three major tandem spaces, A, B, C, and two flanking spaces, D; all are multifunctional. The dimensions of these spaces are optional (see text). This diagram shows the interrelationship of the spaces and their function, and introduces the plan presented in Fig. 3.

ual use, it may be employed quite effectively in the true multiple-function sense. Although specifically designed for theater purposes, it has not lost its usefulness as a general classroom regardless of subject matter. It has a raised stage for any type of classroom performance, a large flat floor space for activities such as dance, and may even be used as a small lecture hall.

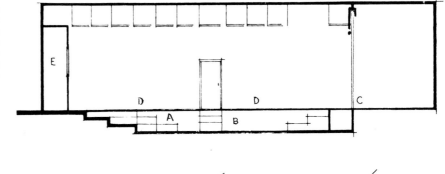

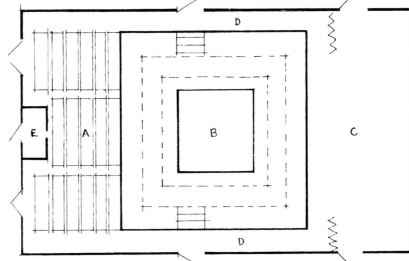

Fig. 3 Teaching station: section and plan. A. Fixed seating; B. potential arena staging; C. elevated stage, no fixed proscenium; D. elevated walkways on each side of the room serve as work tables and arena seating and provide chair and platform storage underneath; E. projection room.

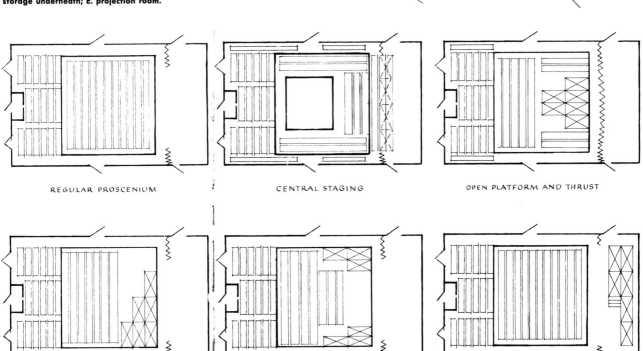

REGULAR PROSCENIUM

CENTRAL STAGING

OPEN PLATFORM AND THRUST

VARIABLE SHAPE AND LEVEL

SIDE STAGES

VARIABLE ONSTAGE PLATFORMS

Fig. 4 Teaching station: platform and seating alternatives. The standard teaching station is readily convertible to many staging forms. A few of the alternates are suggested in this diagram. Portable platforms of standard modular dimension such as 3 by 6 ft may be used as a base for audience seating on varying levels, or stacked to change the height of playing levels. These units are stored, when not in use, under the forestage and under the elevated walkways at each side of the room. Stair units of compatible height increase the flexibility of the system. Infinite variety is available with the exercise of imagination (note that the fixed seating remains the same for each alternate).

Educational

COLLEGE AND UNIVERSITY FACILITIES
Programs and Programming

By JAMES A. PADDOCK, Dober, Paddock, Upton and Associates, Inc.

PROGRAMS AND PROGRAMMING

Until recent years large building projects were launched by nothing more than a conversation between an individual client and the architect of his personal choice with, perhaps, some reference to a historical precedent with which both were familiar. The resulting inconvenient planning and lack of facilities and equipment in buildings of all types appeared to be of little consequence. Labor was cheap and plentiful; space was at a discount; client and architect could afford to waste space.

Recently several changes in society have affected the way in which new building is brought into being: the autocratic statesman, industrialist, and educator has been supplanted by the building committee; the personal fortune has been replaced by the finance committee and program budgeting; and building requirements have become vastly more exacting in response to the technological revolution in government, industry, and education. At the same time, the private conversation and occasional letter between client and architect has given way to a wordy document by which a many-headed client instructs an architectural organization and many specialists in building design and construction. This document is sometimes called "user requirements" or "building specifications"; more frequently it is known as the "program." Generally, programs are of two types, serving different purposes.

Master Plan Program

The program for the master plan is concerned with large-scale development to be accomplished in several phases over many years. It deals in building space to the nearest thousand square foot and required site area in acres. The master plan program may be used to determine the area of land to be acquired for the new development, to assess the adequacy of an existing site and utilities to accommodate future requirements, to estimate development costs, and to raise funds.

Building Program

The building program is concerned with detailed space descriptions for immediate new construction and deals in building space to the nearest hundred square foot. The detailed building program may be used as the basis for the architect's design. It also may be used to conduct an architectural competition for the selection of an architect, to estimate construction costs, to estimate furniture and equipment requirements, and to raise funds.

A program may be concerned with the expansion of existing physical facilities to accommodate a growing organization, or with the development of new facilities on a site not yet selected for an organization in process of formation. In either case, the program is a set of instructions and criteria derived from consideration of many factors, including at least the following:

1. *Policy.* The organization's goals and objectives for future growth and change. In an educational institution this would be known as the academic plan.

2. *Projection.* Anticipation of numbers and characteristics of people to be accommodated at some point in the future or at some selected level of activity, population, or enrollment.

3. *Criteria.* Space planning standards for people and equipment and other factual requirements which must be met.

4. *Spatial relationship.* The desired relationship among individuals, groups, and the equipment they use; their relationship to visitors,

TABLE 1   Sample of Typical Program Sheet

	Audio visual and TV
Existing operations	Function:
	The Audio Visual and Television Centers, although headquartered together, are independent operations. The Audio Visual Center is financed by the College; the Television Center is financed by the Education Department.
	The Audio Visual Center conducts courses required of all Education majors and prepares and distributes all films and other audio visual aids, distributes all television tapes prepared by the Television Center, and provides projection and other technical personnel to all departments.
	The Television Center prepares television tapes for teaching purposes.
	Facilities:
	Existing space is cramped and inappropriate to the function housed. (The television repair center is in a mechanical equipment room containing steam-operated hot-water boiler and reaches 100° during the summer.)
Anticipated changes	Function:
	The trend toward interdisciplinary operations will bring the two centers closer together.
	Facilities:
	Although the Audio Visual and Television Centers will each require their own office and studio facilities, technical and support spaces may be shared.
Location criteria	Located adjacent to a space easily vacated to accommodate unforeseen future expansion.
Planning assumptions	Separate graphic arts and photography facilities will be provided for the Audio Visual Center and College Relations and Publications.

TABLE 2   Space Program

	Number of existing	Stations projected	Net sq ft per station	Total net sq ft
Audio visual center:				
Coordinator	1	1	140	140
Faculty office	1	1	100	100
Supervisor	1	1	100	100
Secretary	3	3	60	180
Projectionist's study room	. . .	. . .	. . .	100
Reception	. . .	. . .	. . .	80
Student viewing cubicles	. . .	15	30	450
Student/faculty laboratory	. . .	6	40	240
Previewing studios:				
Group (15)	. . .	1	225	225
Individual	. . .	4	40	160
Audio visual class/laboratory	. . .	20	60	1200
Repair shop	. . .	1	400	400
Subtotal				3,375
Television:				
Coordinator of educational activities of TV	1	1	140	140
Faculty office	1	1	100	100
Technical coordinator	1	1	100	100
Higher education officers	2	2	80	160
Secretary	1	1	60	60
Student work stations	. . .	3	60	180
Control room	. . .	1	400	400
Shop	. . .	1	400	400
Subtotal				1,540

TABLE 3   Sample of Detailed Building Program Space Description

Area Number:	MM-11
Name of Space:	Biology/chemistry preparation room
Number:	One
Floor Area:	180 sq ft
User:	Faculty, lab technician
Purpose:	Preparation and setting up of movable demonstration bench, storage of chemicals and apparatus, storage of bench
Ceiling Height:	No special requirements
Lighting Requirements:	No special requirements
Heating, Ventilating, Air Conditioning, Exhaust:	Fume hood
Suggested Materials for Floors Walls: Ceiling:	Acid resistant floor and base
Doors:	If direct access is provided to hall, then door to hall to be solid core or equivalent, gasketted; window with sliding panel, door width to allow passage of movable bench
Equipment and Furniture:	1. Chemical bench 12 ft long with sink, hot and cold water, gas, vacuum, and air, chemical resistant stop, cupboards and drawer under; reagent shelf, acid drain
	2. Storage cabinets and shelving
	3. Fume hood
	4. Electric wall clock
	5. Steel chalkboard, 4×3 ft
	6. Pegboard, 4×3 ft for drying glassware
	7. Stool
Special Utility Requirements:	Plugmold on wall above bench
Spatial Relationships:	Adjacent to hall at stage level and to service access

the public, and others outside the immediate organization; and the flow of information, supplies, and material.

5. *Constraints.* Limitations of budget, time, area of site, zoning restrictions and availability of special equipment.

Programming

The process by which the program is produced is called programming. This may be done by the client (the people who are going to use the building), the architect, or a consultant. In any case, the process is essentially the same and consists of the following steps.

1. *Existing data.* Assembly and review of all existing documents concerning policy decisions, enrollment projections, corporate plans, and other papers that describe the present and future structure of the organization.

2. *Planning committee.* Appointment of a planning committee to review the programming

work as it proceeds, to resolve possible conflicts over such matters as the allocation of space or other resources among competing divisions, and to approve the completed program document. The committee should include a representative of each functional area within the organization. Most of these functional areas can be identified prior to the beginning of the programming process by reference to organization charts and telephone directories and through consultation with administrators. The size and, consequently, the number of functional areas specified depend largely on the level of detail to which the programming is expected to go. For example, all administrative functions might be subsumed under an Office of the Vice President for Administration. If more detail is required, subdivisions might be made to establish separate offices for fiscal planning, personnel, buildings and grounds, etc.

3. *Interviews.* Interviewing individuals and groups representing each functional area within the organization. The purpose of these interviews is to ask the individual, Who are you, what do you do, how do you do it, with whom, and in what kind of space? Ideally, these discussions should almost never touch on the question of how much space is needed. The programmer should know from the space inventory how much space exists, if any; and he will be able to observe overcrowding or gross under-utilization. The person using the space is the expert regarding *how* it is used. The programmer is an expert in translating need into square feet. The success of the discussions depends upon each party's ability to stay within his own area of expertise.

4. *Draft program.* Following the interviews, the programmer writes a detailed sheet for each functional area (see Tables 1 to 3). The draft program sheet will include the programmer's analysis of the spaces required and their sizes. The sheet is then sent to the person interviewed. Review and further discussion take place as required until he is satisfied that the program sheet represents his explicit understanding of need.

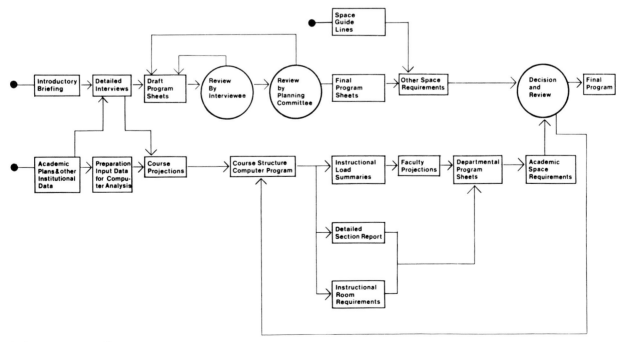

Fig. 1   Program process outline.

5. *Committee review.* The planning committee meets to review the draft program sheets. The committee must judge individual space requests in the context of the whole organization. It must ensure that requests are not redundant but complementary and that no interests have been ignored.

6. *Estimate of building size and cost.* The program consultant totals the net square foot space, requests, and estimates the building area needed in gross square feet. This is done by applying a "net-to-gross" multiplier to allow for circulation space, washrooms, mechanical equipment areas, and wall thicknesses. Typical multipliers are 1.66 for offices, 1.35 for undergraduate libraries, and 1.25 for auditoria. The total gross square footage is now used to make an approximate estimate of construction cost. Other costs such as furniture, equipment, site works and professional fees may be estimated in order to arrive at a total development cost.

7. *Final decision and review.* The committee now has a list of carefully considered statements concerning the amount and type of space required by each functional area based on specified assumptions concerning its responsibilities, and an approximate estimate of the cost of developing a building or buildings to accommodate the programmed spaces. It is highly likely that the total demands exceed the organization's resources. The task now is to decide how much space should be allotted for each purpose. The planning committee may resolve the conflict, or the president of the organization and some representative group of advisers may make the final decisions concerning allocations of space or development funds.

The process outlined above reduces a vast amount of data to a reasonable set of statements concerning any one of which there should be little or no argument, and so the decision-making process should be comparatively easy. When the decisions have been made, the organization will have clarified its goals and established a reasonably firm basis for physical planning and architectural design. Figure 1 illustrates the programming process as it might apply to an educational institution.

3

Cultural

MUSEUMS	365	THEATERS	392
SMALL MUSEUMS	372	Sight Lines	402
EXHIBITION SPACES	377	Stage Space	405
Visual Arts Facility	378	MUSIC AND DRAMA CENTERS	411
LIBRARIES	380	House	411
Diagrams of Essential Library Elements	380	Basic Seating Data	419
Branch Libraries	382	Stage	423
Space Requirements	383	SPACE FOR DANCE	429
Service and Space Relationships	386	COMMUNITY THEATERS	433
Library Location	387	AMPHITHEATERS	439
Accessible to Handicapped	389	MUSIC FACILITIES	442
Branch Buildings	390	ARTS AND CRAFTS CENTERS	451
Bookmobiles	390	PERFORMING ARTS CENTER	463
Bookstack Data	391		

By BRUNO MOLAJOLI

GENERAL OBSERVATIONS

Whenever it is proposed to build a museum—whether large or small—there is usually one preliminary matter to be settled: the choice of a site. Where several possibilities are available, the drawbacks and advantages of each must be carefully weighed.

Should the site be central, or on the outskirts of the town? This appears to be the most usual dilemma. Until 20 or 30 years ago there was a preference for the center of a town, with its better transport facilities. But as the use and speed of public and private transport have gradually increased and it has become easier to get from one point to another, it has been realized that the convenience of a central situation for a museum is outweighed by the many and substantial advantages of a less central position. These include a greater choice and easier acquisition of land (at lower cost), less fatigue from the noise of traffic—a growing and already very real problem—and an atmosphere less laden with dust and with gases which when not poisonous are, to say the least, unpleasant.

A museum should always be readily accessible from all parts of the town by public transport and, if possible, be within walking distance as well, and must be within easy reach of schools, colleges, university, and libraries. As a matter of fact, all these institutions have similar problems and stand equally in need of topographical coordination; it would be advisable to take this into account at the town-planning stage, rather than deal with each case separately, as it arises, a method which may involve the sacrifice or neglect of many desiderata.

Museums tend nowadays to be regarded more and more as "cultural centers." It must therefore be remembered that as such they are visited not only by students but by people with different backgrounds who, if a museum is near enough and easy to reach, may come to it, even with little time to spare, in search of instructive recreation.

Though there is still a prejudice against the building of museums in parks or gardens—on the plea that this makes them more difficult to reach and disturbs the tranquillity of such places—these are becoming very popular as the sites of new museums. They offer considerable advantages—a wider choice of detached positions, thus reducing the risk of fire; a relative degree of protection from dust, noise, vibrations, exhaust gases from motor engines or factories, smoke from the chimneys of houses and from municipal heating plants, the sulphur content of which is always harmful to works of art.

A belt of trees surrounding the museum building serves as an effective natural filter for dust and for the chemical discharges that pollute the air of a modern industrial town; it also helps to stabilize the humidity of the atmosphere, to which paintings and period furniture are often sensitive. It is said that large trees, if unduly close to the building, cut off or deflect the light and thus diminish or alter its effect

Museums, The Organization of Museums, UNESCO, Place de Fontenoy, Paris, 1967.

on color; but this disadvantage would appear to be unimportant, or in any case easy to overcome.

The surrounding land may offer space for an annex, built at a suitable distance from the museum itself, to house various types of equipment and services (heating and electricity, repair shop, garage, etc.), or the stores required for them (wood, textile materials, fuel oils, etc.), which it would be unsafe or, for some reason, inconvenient to stock in the main building.

Moreover, space will always be available—at least in theory—for future expansion, either by enlargement of the original building or by the construction of connected annexes; this is particularly important if the first project has to be restricted in scale for reasons which, though unavoidable, are likely to be transitory.

The beauty of a museum is considerably enhanced if it is surrounded by a garden which, if the local climate is propitious, can be used to advantage for the display of certain types of exhibit, such as ancient or modern sculpture, archaeological or architectural fragments, etc.

Part of the surrounding grounds may also provide space for a car park.

The planning of a museum is an outstanding example of the need not only for preliminary and specific agreements but for close and uninterrupted collaboration between the architect and his employer.

There is no such thing as a museum planned in the abstract, suitable for all cases and circumstances. On the contrary, every case has its own conditions, requirements, characteristics, purposes, and problems, the assessment of which is primarily the task of the museum director. It is for him to provide the architect with an exact description of the result to be aimed at and of the preliminary steps to be taken, and he must be prepared to share in every successive phase of the work—failing which the finished building may fall short in some respects of the many and complex technical and functional demands which a modern museum must satisfy.

Another point to be considered is whether the new building is to house an entirely new museum (whose contents have yet to be assembled) or to afford a permanent home for an existing collection. In the first case we have the advantage of a free approach to the problem and can decide on an ideal form for the museum; but with the attendant drawback of beginning our work in the abstract, on the basis of entirely vague and theoretical assumptions which future developments will probably not confirm. In the second case we must take care not to go to the opposite extreme by designing a building too precisely adapted to the quality and quantity of the works or collections which form the nucleus of the museum; future needs and possibilities of development should always be foreseen and provision made for them.

All this is part of the director's responsibility.

Due regard should also be given to the special character of the new museum—the quality it already possesses and by which it is in future to be distinguished—in relation to its collections. This may, of course, be of several kinds (artistic, archaeological, technical, scientific,

etc.) and respond to various needs (cultural, general or local permanence or interchangeability, uniformity of the exhibits or group display, etc.).

Naturally, every type of collection, every kind of material, every situation has its own general and individual requirements which will considerably influence the structure of the building and the form and size of the exhibition rooms and related services. It is no use attempting to present a series of archaeological or ethnographical exhibits, whose interest is chiefly documentary, in the space and surroundings that would be appropriate to a collection of works of art, paintings, or sculpture of great aesthetic importance, or to apply the same standards to a museum arranged chronologically and one whose exhibits are classified in artistic or scientific categories; nor is it possible to display a collection of small works of art, such as jewelry, small bronzes, medallions, miniatures, etc., in rooms of the size needed for large objects of less meticulous workmanship, which require to be seen as a whole and from a certain distance.

Even a picture gallery cannot be designed in such a way as to serve equally well for the exhibition of old pictures and modern ones: for, apart from the fact that aesthetic considerations recommend different settings for the two groups, it is obvious that a gallery of old paintings is comparatively "stabilized," whereas the appearance of a modern gallery is to some extent "transitory," owing to the greater ease and frequency with which additions, changes, and rearrangements can be made, In the latter case, therefore, not only the architectural features of the building but also its actual construction must be planned with a view to facilitating the rapid displacement and changeover of exhibits. The transport of heavy statues, the adaptation of space and the use of the sources of light in the way and on the scale most appropriate for particular works of art, should be taken into account as well as the possibility either of grouping or of displaying them singly, according to the importance and emphasis to be attributed to them.

A museum must be planned not only in relation to its purpose and to the quality and type of its exhibits, but also with regard to certain economic and social considerations. For instance, if it is to be the only institution in the town which is suitable for a number of cultural purposes (theatrical performances, lectures, concerts, exhibitions, meetings, courses of instruction, etc.) it may be desirable to take account in the initial calculations of the financial resources on which it will be able to rely, the nature of the local population, the trend of development of that population as revealed by statistics, and the proportion of the population which is interested in each of the museum's activities.

In fact, the word "museum" covers a wide range of possibilities, and the architect commissioned to design one must make clear—to himself first of all—not only the specific character of the museum he is to build but the potential subsidiary developments and related purposes which can be sensed and foreseen in addition to the dominant theme.

The future may see substantial changes in

our present conception of museums. If the architect who designs one allows in his plan for easy adaptation to new fashions, new developments, new practical and aesthetic possibilities, his work will be all the sounder and more enduring. A museum is not like an exhibition, to be broken up after a short time and brought together later in an entirely different form. There should be nothing "ephemeral" in its character or appearance, even where the possibility of changes or temporary arrangements is to be contemplated.

These considerations should be borne in mind when the architectural plans for the building are drawn up.

According to a prejudice which, though gradually dying, is still fairly common, a museum building should be imposing in appearance, solemn, and monumental. The worst of it is that this effect is often sought through the adoption of an archaic style of architecture. We are all acquainted with deplorable instances of new buildings constructed in imitation of the antique; they produce a markedly antihistorical impression, just because they were inspired by a false view of history. Another outmoded prejudice is that which demands a "classical" setting for ancient works of art, as though their venerable dignity would suffer and their aesthetic value be diminished if they were placed in modern surroundings.

But though the style of the building should be frankly contemporary and governed by the creative imagination of its designer, architectural interest must not be an end in itself but should be subordinated to the purpose in view. In other words we must not devote our entire effort to designing rooms which will be architecturally pleasing; it is at least equally important that attention be concentrated on the works exhibited, that their *mise en valeur* be ensured and their predominance established. A museum in which the works of art were relegated to the background and used to "complete" a pretentious architectural scheme, could not be regarded as successful; but neither could a museum which went to the other extreme, where the construction was subordinated to cold, mechanically functional considerations so that no spatial relationship could be created between the works of art and other exhibits—a museum with a completely impersonal atmosphere.

The ideal would seem to lie somewhere between these two extremes—the aim being to allow for that sense of proportion which should always be in evidence when a museum is planned, to ensure that the visitor will find there the friendly, welcoming atmosphere, the attractive and convenient features that he enjoys in his own house.

It is the difficult but essential task of the architect, no less than of the director of a museum, to bring the place into conformity with the mentality and customs of every citizen of whatever rank and standard of education. Much will depend on the level of taste of both men, on their human qualities of sympathy and sensibility, which must go hand in hand with their professional abilities and which cannot be prompted or taught.

PLANS FOR SMALL MUSEUMS

The foregoing remarks apply to every new museum, whatever its size. We shall now consider more particularly the principles and characteristics on which the planning and construction of small museums should be based.

By "small museum" we understand any institution whose program and finances are restricted so that, at least at its inception, the premises built for it will be of limited size, in most cases only one story high.

It is not so easy to determine precisely within what limits the idea of the "little museum" is to be confined; for while it may, at its smallest, consist of one room, it may on the other hand be of an appreciable extent, though still too small to be properly described as a medium-sized or large museum.

For the present purpose it may be assumed that the "small museum" will not consist of more than 10 to 12 medium-sized exhibition rooms (16 $\times$ 24 sq ft) in addition to its other services.

A new museum, even on this small scale, cannot function efficiently unless it respects the general principles of museography and the special possibilities for applying them which are provided by the particular circumstances governing its construction.

There are certain museographical considerations which must have a decisive influence on the structure of the building, for instance, on the arrangement of the rooms or the type of roof chosen, and which are therefore of technical importance in the construction.

Consequently, the successful planning of a museum entails the well-considered choice and unerring application of these deciding principles, whose chief theoretical and practical aspects I shall now briefly describe.

Natural Lighting This is one of the subjects most keenly discussed by museum authorities, and is, indeed, of outstanding importance. It was believed at one time that electric light, being easy to switch on, adaptable and unvarying in its effects and able to give full value to architectural features, might provide not merely an alternative to the use of daylight in museums, but a substitute for it. But experience has forced us to recognize that—especially where running expenses have to be considered—daylight is still the best means of lighting a museum, despite the variations and difficulties which characterize it at different seasons and in different places. The building should therefore be so planned as to make the best use of this source of light, even if certain other structural features have to be sacrificed as a result.

Daylight may come from above or from the side. In the former case suitable skylights will be provided in the ceilings of the exhibition rooms. In the latter case, one or more walls will be pierced by windows, the height and width of which must be decided according to individual requirements (see Fig. 1a-j.).

Lighting from Above This type of lighting, sometimes called overhead lighting (I dislike this term, which seems too restrictive, ignoring the possibility of directing the light from above at any desirable angle), has long been favored by the designers of museums, for it presents certain obvious advantages.

1. A freer and steadier supply of light, less liable to be affected by the different aspects of the various rooms in the building and by any lateral obstacles (other buildings, trees, etc.) which might tend, by causing refraction or by casting shadows, to alter the quantity or quality of the light itself.

2. The possibility of regulating the amount of light cast on the pictures or other exhibits and of securing full and uniform lighting, giving good visibility with a minimum of reflection or distortion.

3. The saving of wallspace, which thus remains available for exhibits.

4. The maximum latitude in planning space inside the building, which can be divided without requiring courtyards or light shafts.

5. The facilitation of security measures, owing to fewer openings in the outside walls.

Compared with these advantages, the drawbacks seem trifling and can in any case be reduced or overcome by suitable technical and structural measures. They are:

1. The excess of radiating light, or of diffused light interspersed with irregular rays.

2. The disadvantages inseparable from any system of skylights (increased weight of the roof or ceiling supports; liability to become coated with dirt; risk of panes being broken; danger of rainwater infiltration; condensation of moisture; admission of sun rays; irradiation and dispersion of heat, etc.).

3. The monotony of the lighting, and oppressive claustrophobic effect produced on visitors called upon to walk through a long succession of rooms lit from above.

4. The greater complexity of the architectural and technical problems to be solved in providing a roof which, while adapted to this form of lighting, will effectively serve its various purposes (problems relating to weatherproof qualities, heating, maintenance, cleaning, security, etc.).

Lateral Lighting This is provided either by ordinary windows of various shapes and sizes, placed at suitable intervals in the walls, or by continuous openings; both windows and openings may be placed either at a level at which people can see out of them or in the upper part of the wall.

The solution adopted will be determined by the type of museum and the nature of its exhibits, as the advantages and disadvantages vary from one to another.

Windows at the usual level, whether separate or continuous, have one serious drawback, in that the wall in which they are placed is rendered useless and the opposite wall practically useless, because showcases, paintings, and any other object with a smooth reflecting surface, if placed against the wall facing the source of light, will inevitably cause an interplay of reflections which impedes visibility. These windows will, however, shed full and agreeable light on exhibits placed against the other walls and in the center of the room at a correct angle to the source of light.

Advocates of lateral lighting point out that this is particularly successful in bringing out the plastic and luminous qualities of paintings and sculpture created in past centuries, when artists usually worked by such light.

All this must be considered in conjunction with the proper use of the floor space, the shape, arrangement, and sequence of the different rooms, their size and depth in relation to the outer walls—the aim being to make the most of the sources of light and to obtain the greatest possible uniformity of lighting throughout each room.

A definite practical advantage is, however, that of rendering possible the utmost simplicity and economy in the style of building, permitting the adoption of the ordinary, nontransparent roofing (flat or sloped) customary in the district, and providing, thanks to the side windows, a convenient and simple method of regulating ventilation and temperature in museums which cannot afford expensive air-conditioning apparatus.

Another advantage of windows placed at the ordinary level is that some of them can be fitted with transparent glass, allowing pleasant views of the countryside, gardens, or architecturally interesting courtyards. This provides a

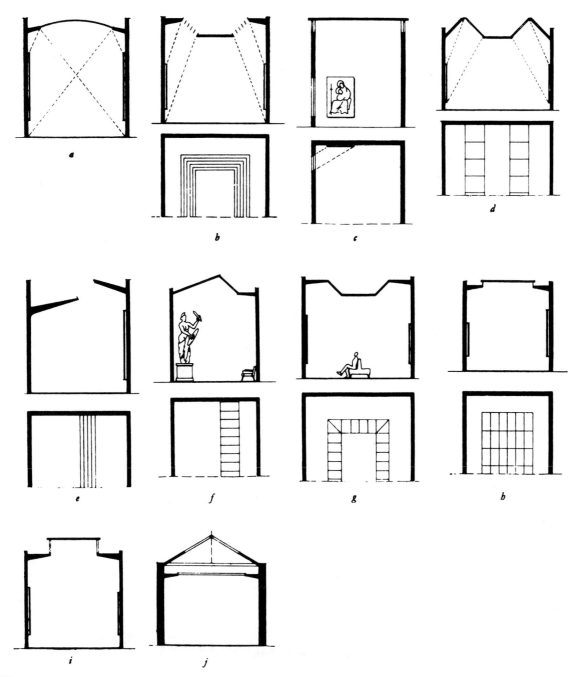

Fig. 1 Different methods of admitting natural light from above. (a) Cross section. (b) to (h) Cross section and view from above. (i) and (j) Cross section.

diversion, resting the visitor's eyes and refreshing his mind.

For this purpose it may be wise, even where overhead lighting is adopted, to arrange a few lateral openings for the passing visitor.

High-placed windows, especially if they occupy more than one wall, provide more light, more closely resembling that supplied by skylights, and leave all four walls free for exhibits: but as they must be placed at a considerable height, if visitors are not to be dazzled, the rooms must be comparatively large and the ceilings lofty. This means that considerable stretches of wall will be left blank, and building expenses will increase owing to the larger size of the rooms.

The tendency nowadays is to abandon uni-form lighting in favor of light concentrated on the walls and on individual exhibits or groups of exhibits, which are thus rendered more conspicuous and more likely to attract the visitor's attention. Consequently, instead of lighting the whole room, it is found preferable to light the showcases from within, either by artificial lighting or by backing them with frosted glass which admits daylight from outside.

This is a possibility which the architect of a small museum can bear in mind, making use of it in special cases and for objects (glass, ceramics, enamels, etc.) whose effect can be heightened by such lighting. But it entails special structural features which may complicate the general budget.

Moreover, if the lighting system is too rigid, too definitely planned to suit a particular setting and to establish certain relationships between that setting and the exhibits, it will form an impediment by imposing a certain stability, tending to reduce the museum to the static condition from which modern institutions are striving to emerge—the present-day being that a museum should make a lively, dynamic impression.

It therefore seems preferable, especially in small museums, to choose an intermediate system which can be adapted to varying needs and necessary changes, even if it thus becomes more difficult to achieve ideal results.

Utilization and Division of Space In designing a museum the architect will also be decisively in-

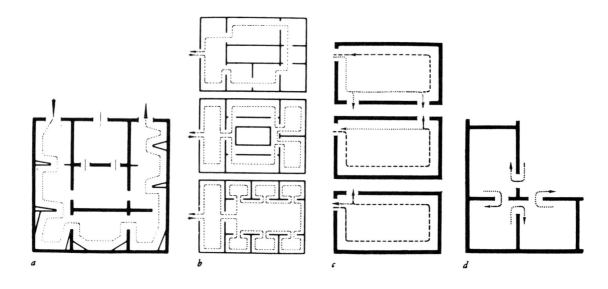

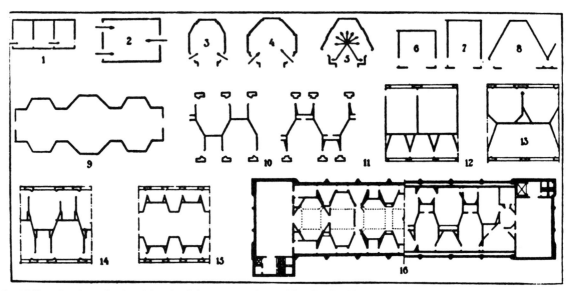

Fig. 2 (a) to (d) Floor plans for the location of doors in relation to the use of space. (e) 1 — Traditional location of doors. 2 to 8 — Secondary doors. 9 to 15 — Polygonal enclosures.

fluenced by the way in which it is intended to utilize and divide the space to be devoted to the displays. This, too, is of course closely connected with the question of lighting, which we have already discussed.

The modern tendency is to create large unbroken spaces, which can then be divided up by movable partitions or lightweight structures, to be grouped or displaced as required.

The traditional system is the contrary one of dividing the space, by means of permanent walls, into rooms of various sizes, which may be either communicating or independent (connected, in the latter case, by passages or side galleries) (see Fig. 2a–e).

A small museum may do well to adopt an intermediate system with a succession of average-sized rooms (for the display of permanent collections whose contents will not change, such as those received through bequests, donations, etc.) and one or more large rooms which can be variously divided up when required by movable partitions or light structures.

The structure of the building and, with it, the interior and exterior technical features,

will vary according to the purpose for which it is intended. Requirements and costs will be different in each separate case, for it is evident that the larger the surface to be roofed in one span without intermediate supports, the greater the technical problem and the cost of the roof. Furthermore, the architect's calculations for the various features of a coordinated project (plan, circulation, lighting, etc.) will not be the same if the project relates to rigid construction subdivided by permanent walls, or to flexible construction, adjusted to the changes periodically effected in the museum.

Museum Services Before considering the planning of the museum it is essential to determine the size and location of the various services. In other words, we must decide how much space can and should be allocated for subsidiary activities, or for those necessary to the functioning of the museum in its relationship with the public (offices, rooms for meetings and lectures, library, documentation service) on the same floor as the exhibition rooms, and which services and technical plant (heating and electrical apparatus, storerooms, work-

shops, garage, etc.) can be housed in the basement or, if possible, in special outlying buildings to be built as annexes, at a convenient distance from the main building.

It should be remembered that the usual custom is to set aside for these purposes an area which may be as much as 50 percent of the total space available. In small museums this proportion may be reduced. But the fact remains that two conflicting needs have to be reconciled: on the one hand there must be easy communication between the public rooms and the museum services, since this makes for smooth relations between visitors and staff; on the other hand it must be possible to separate these two sections, so that they can function independently at any time. This is necessary chiefly to safeguard the collections at times when the building is closed to the public while the curators or office staff are still at work and the library and lecture hall in use.

Planning

It is hardly necessary to explain, before embarking upon a discussion of the different questions that may arise when a small museum is being planned and built, that my aim is merely to put forward certain suggestions to serve as practical pointers, based on experience of the subject, with no intention of trespassing upon the domains of the various technical authorities who must inevitably be consulted.

The Exterior A museum which is to be built in an isolated spot or reserved space (park, garden, etc.) needs to be surrounded by an enclosure, especially if the site forms part of an extensive area. For the visitor, this enclosure will provide a foretaste of the museum's architecture, and thus must not constitute a "psychological barrier," though the fundamental aim of security, which it has to serve, must not be sacrificed.

If, on the contrary, the museum is to overlook a public street, it will always be advisable: (a) to separate it from the stream of traffic by a belt of trees or even by flowerbeds; (b) to set back the entrance in a quiet corner: (c) to allow space for a public car park.

The architect should think of the building he has been asked to design as an organism capable of growing, and therefore provide from the outset for suitable possibilities of expansion, so that when the time comes for this it will not require far-reaching and costly alterations. He should regard the portion to be built as the nucleus of a cell, capable of multiplying itself or at least of joining up, according to plan, with future enlargements.

Where space permits, it is best to allow for horizontal expansion, as this, though more expensive, has the twofold advantage of enabling all the display rooms to be kept on one level and of leaving the roof free for overhead lighting.

Renouncing all pretensions to a monumental style, the outward appearance of the building—especially if overhead lighting is adopted, so that there are no windows to break the surface—should be distinguished by a simple balance of line and proportion and by its functional character.

Arrangement Any general plan of construction which entails an apportionment of premises is closely bound up with the purpose of the museum and the nature, quality, and principal components of its collections. Each type of museum has different requirements, which may be met by various architectural methods.

It is difficult to give any exact classification of the different types of collections, but we can offer a very brief one, if only to indicate the wide range of demands the designer of a museum may be called upon to meet:

1. *Museums of art and archaeology.* The size of the rooms and height of the ceilings will be determined by the nature and dimensions of the works to be exhibited. It is not difficult to calculate a practical minimum capable either of accommodating old paintings, which are usually large, or medium-sized modern canvases; a suitable room might measure about 16 by 23 ft, with wall accommodation to a height of about 14 ft. In the case of furniture, or of examples of decorative art (metal, glass, ceramics, textiles, etc.) to be displayed in showcases, the ceiling need not be as high. If pictures and sculpture are to be shown separately, their settings must be different from the point of view of space and lighting. For silver, jewelry, or precious objects, it may be better to use showcases set in the walls—which can thus be equipped with locking devices and antiburglar safeguards—lit from within, the rooms being left in semi-darkness. Rooms lit by artificial means rather

than by sunlight are best for drawings, engravings, watercolors, and textiles. Such rooms may be long and narrow rather than square—rather like corridors or galleries—as the visitor has no need to stand back in order to look at the exhibits, which will be arranged in showcases against the longest walls.

2. *Historical or archival museums.* These need less space for the showcases in which their exhibits are placed, and comparatively large and numerous storerooms for the documents kept in reserve. Relics and papers are best shown in rooms equipped with suitable protective devices and artificially lighted, though some use may also be made of indirect natural light.

3. *Ethnographic and folk museums.* The exhibits are usually displayed in showcases. They are often large and cumbersome, requiring a good deal of space. Considerable space is also needed for reproducing typical surroundings, if this is done with genuine pieces and properties or full-sized replicas. Strong artificial lighting is generally used as being more effective than daylight.

4. *Museums of physical and natural sciences, technological or educational museums.* Owing to the great variety of collections involved, their division into sections and the necessary scientific cataloging, these museums differ in size and in architectural and functional characteristics. Where the exhibits are arranged in series (minerals, insects, fossils, dried plants, etc.), medium-sized rooms may suffice, whereas reconstructions and built-up displays of animals or plants demand considerable space and special technical features (for instance, means of keeping the special materials and preparations in good condition, unaffected by the atmosphere, or equipment for maintaining aquaria, permanent film displays, etc.). This type of museum needs laboratories for the preparation and upkeep of certain exhibits (stuffing, drying, disinfecting, etc.).

It thus rests with the architect to decide, for each of these types of museum, what arrangement will best satisfy the particular conditions, purposes, and requirements involved.

There can never be any objection to adopting the modern principle of a building so constructed that its interior can be adapted, divided, and altered to meet the varying demands of successive exhibitions. If this is done, the most important thing is that the construction shall be "flexible," that is, capable of adaptation to the different features it must simultaneously or successively contain, while preserving unchanged its general framework—entrances and exits, lighting system, general services and technical installation. This principle is particularly valuable in small museums and in any others which must allow for enlargements not always foreseeable at the outset.

The internal arrangement of the available space, the distribution and style of the galleries can then be either temporary or comparatively permanent. In the former case, use will be made of movable partitions, panels of lightweight material (plywood or thin metal frames covered with cloth, etc.) fitted into special supports or into holes or grooves suitably placed in the floor; these can either be separate or arranged in groups held together by bolts or hinges.

This system is very practical for small museums which intend to follow a definite cultural program including successive loan exhibitions of works of art, and are therefore obliged to make frequent changes, dictated by circumstances, in the size and appearance of their galleries. It has, however, the draw-

backs that all the interior structure is independent of the outer walls of the building and made of comparatively fragile materials which are expensive to keep in repair; moreover the place never looks settled, but rather mechanical and disjointed—an effect which is displeasing to the eye unless the architect designs the component parts with great taste.

Other objections to this method include the difficulty of preparing new catalogs and guides to keep pace with the changes, and of overcoming the conservatism of a great proportion of the public; and, above all, the consequent impossibility of arranging circulation within the building, and other matters affecting the division of space on a permanent basis. These things have to be left to the organizers of each successive exhibition, and therefore cannot be included in the architect's original plan.

If, on the other hand, the interior space is to be divided up in a more or less permanent manner, the question of "flexibility" being set aside until the comparatively distant time when the original plan of the museum comes to be radically altered, than the dividing walls can be really "built" to last, even if lightweight materials are employed. For their role will be reduced to providing a background for works of art, for showcases, or for any exhibits hung on them, and to supporting their share of whatever type of roof or ceiling is chosen.

In this case the interior arrangement will be very similar to, if not identical with, that of a museum of the traditional type, planned as a complete building with all its sections permanently fixed and the size and shape of its rooms settled once and for all.

In this kind of structure it is more than ever necessary to plan with a view to enabling the public to circulate and to arranging the collections and services in the most rational and functional manner possible.

The question of circulation must be studied attentively, so that the arrangement and the itinerary will be clear not only to anyone looking at the ground plan of the museum but also to anyone walking through the rooms. It should be planned to fit the logical order of the exhibition, whether that order is governed by chronology, by the nature of the material displayed, or as in a scientific museum, aims at providing a connected sequence of practical information.

Though a compulsory, one-way route may not be entirely desirable in a large museum, it is satisfactory and one might say logical in a small one, as it saves space and facilitates supervision. Visitors should not have to turn back and return through rooms they have already seen, in order to reach the exit. They should, however, be able to turn off on their way round if they wish to cut short their visit or confine it to certain things that particularly interest them.

So, even if a museum is to show a series of selected works of the first quality, we should consider the possibility of arranging them in proximity to one another in such a way that they can be seen without the necessity of traversing the entire building. For example, in a succession of rooms surrounding an inner courtyard (see Fig. 3).

Care should always be taken, however, to avoid the confusion of too many adjacent doors, or of rooms running parallel to one another; visitors must not be made to feel that they are in a maze where they can easily lose their way.

If the designer's preference or the demands of space result in a series of rooms all set along the same axis, it may be desirable to connect them by a corridor. But this should not be the only means of access to the rooms, for if the visitor is forced to return to it each

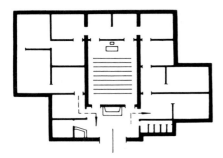

Fig. 3 Suggested floor plan for a small museum.

time, fatigue and bewilderment will be much increased.

Entrance However many outside doors may be found necessary for the various museum services (but these should be as few as possible, to facilitate supervision and security measures), there must be only one public entrance, placed quite separately from the others. This should lead into a vestibule where certain essential services will be located—sale of tickets, information service, and sale of catalogs and postcards. In a small museum one person will of course be responsible for

all this, and the necessary installation must be carefully planned to ensure the most practical form and arrangement. The official in charge should not be confined to a booth behind a window, but should be able to move about freely and leave his [her] position when circumstances require.

In a little museum it would be particularly unsuitable to design the entrance hall on a massive or pompous scale, as was customary in the past, making it unnecessarily lofty, and to decorate it in would-be monumental style, like the atrium of a classical temple, with arches and pillars. Modern architects tend increasingly to reduce overhead space and give the greatest possible width and depth, producing a balanced effect of greater intimacy and attraction. It is important for the entrance hall to seem attractive even to the casual passerby—who is always a potential visitor to the museum. It should provide an easy introduction to the building, a point from which the individual visitor can find his way without difficulty and where large parties can be greeted and assembled. It must therefore be fairly spacious, and provided with the strict minimum of sturdily built furniture (one or two tables for the sale of tickets, catalogs, etc., a cloakroom, a few benches or chairs, a notice board, a general plan of the museum to guide visitors, a clock, and perhaps a public tele-

phone booth and a letterbox). It is not advisable to have only one door from here into the exhibition rooms; there should be two, an entrance and an exit, far enough apart to prevent delay should there be a crowd but placed in such a way that both can be easily watched at the same time.

In museums where arriving and departing visitors are to be mechanically counted, an automatic turnstile should be installed, serving both doors but placed at a sufficient distance from the main entrance and the ticket office. Another possible method is that of the photoelectric cell, but the objection to this is that when visitors are crowding through the turnstile the record may not be accurate. In museums where admission is free, attendance can be computed for statistical purposes more simply by the custodian with a manual counter—which will avoid adding an unnecessary complication to the fittings of the entrance hall.

Exhibition Rooms—Shape and Requirements A museum in which all the rooms are the same size becomes very monotonous. By varying their dimensions and the relation between height and width—and also by using different colors for the walls and different kinds of flooring—we provide a spontaneous and unconscious stimulus to attention (see Fig. 4a–f).

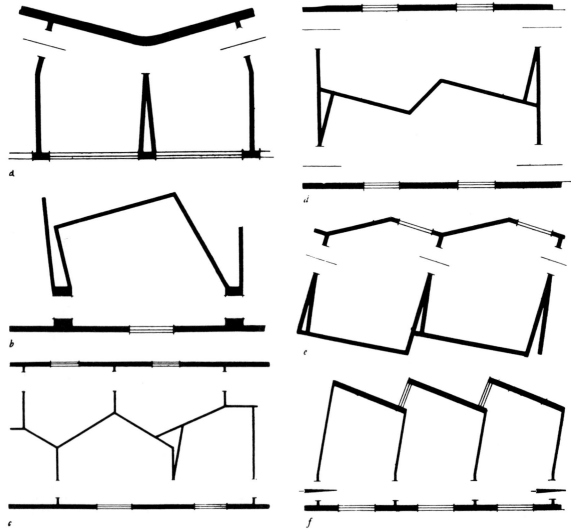

Fig. 4 Different ways of dividing up exhibition space.

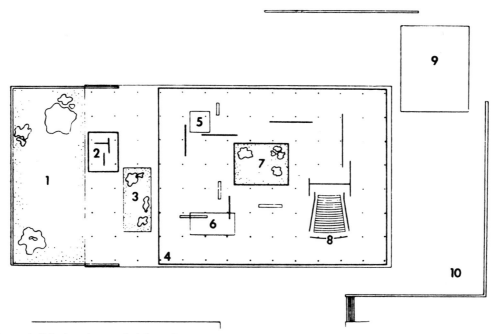

Fig. 5 In 1942, Mies van der Rohe devoted a great deal of attention to the theoretical design of a museum for a small city to provide a setting for Picasso's painting Guernica. The building is designed to be as flexible as possible, consisting simply of a floor slab, columns, roof plate, free-standing partitions and exterior walls of glass.

The relative "absence of architecture" intensifies the individuality of each work of art and at the same time incorporates it into the entire design.

One of the museum's original features is the auditorium which consists of free-standing partitions and an acoustical dropped ceiling.

"Two openings in the roof plate (3 and 7) admit light into an inner court (7) and into an open passage (3). Outer walls (4) and those of the inner court are of glass. On the exterior, free-standing walls of stone would define outer courts (1) and terraces (10). Offices (2) and wardrobes would be free-standing. A shallow recessed area (5) is provided, around the edge of which small groups could sit for informal discussions. The auditorium (8) is defined by free-standing walls providing facilities for lectures, concerts and intimate formal discussions. The form of these walls and the shell hung above the stage would be dictated by the acoustics. The floor of the auditorium is recessed in steps of seat height, using each step as a continuous bench. Number (6) is the print department and a space for special exhibits. Number (9) is a pool." (From P. C. Johnson, "Mies van der Rohe," Museum of Modern Art, New York, 1947.)

Monotony also results when a number of rooms follow one another in a straight line. Even where this cannot be entirely avoided, the rooms should be so constructed that the doors are not opposite one another, providing a "telescopic" view through the building. An uninterrupted prospect of the long route ahead is usually found to have a depressing effect on visitors.

There are, however, undoubted advantages in being able to see into several rooms at the same time; it is a help, for instance, in directing visitors, and for security purposes.

On the other hand, by varying the positions of the doors we are also able to place the visitor, from the moment of his entrance, at the point chosen by the organizer of the display as the best for conveying an immediate and striking impression of its general contents, or for giving a view of the most important piece in that particular room. In principle, the door should be placed in such a way that a visitor coming through it will see the full length of the opposite wall. It is therefore not advisable for it to face a window, since the visitor will then be dazzled just as he comes in.

With regard to the shape and size of the rooms, I have already pointed out that dimensions should be varied so as to stimulate the attention of the public and should also be adapted to the size of the exhibits.

I ought perhaps to repeat here, for the sake of clarity, that the form and size of the rooms will also depend to some extent on the lighting system chosen. Overhead lighting allows greater diversity of shape (rectangular, polygonal, circular, etc.) because the lighting can always be arranged on a scale to suit the room. Oblong rooms, divided by partitions to a certain height, but with one ceiling and skylight, should however be avoided; this system has proved unsatisfactory both from the aesthetic and from the functional points of view.

The practice of rounding off the corners of rectangular rooms is also going out of fashion, as it has been found that the advantage of unbroken walls and the impression of better use of light in a more compact space are offset by the resultant monotony, and that the general effect is not pleasing to the eye.

Lateral lighting requires shallow rooms, their walls set at an oblique angle to the source of light. But the larger the windows, the more difficult it becomes to prevent light from being reflected in the works placed against the opposite wall. It is undeniably difficult to give a pleasing appearance to these asymmetrical rooms; the taste of a fine architect is needed to give them character and harmony, either by careful attention to spatial proportion or by the use of different colors for the walls and ceiling.

Theoretically, the door between two laterally lit rooms should be placed near the wall next to the windows, because otherwise the two walls meet in a dark corner where nothing can be exhibited. But if the daylight is admitted not through a vertical or comparatively narrow window, but through a "ribbon" of glass running the whole length of the wall, the problem is not the same. In this case the two end walls, meeting the outside wall from the normal direction, or at a slight angle, will be well lit throughout their length; the doorways can therefore be placed at the furthest extremities, thus adding to the effective depth of the room.

One important fact should be remembered when the shape of the rooms is being decided. A square room, when it exceeds a certain size (about 23 sq ft), has no advantage over an oblong one, either from the point of view of cost (roof span) or from that of the use of space in the satisfactory display of the exhibits, expecially if they are paintings.

It is sometimes found advisable to place a work of art of outstanding interest and exceptional value in a room by itself, to attract and concentrate the greatest possible attention. Such a room need be only large enough to accommodate a single work; but there must always be enough space for the public to circulate freely. Galleries intended for permanent exhibitions may, on the contrary, be of considerable size, though it is never advisable for them to be more than about 22 ft wide, 12 to 18 ft high, and 65 to 80 ft long.

SMALL MUSEUMS

PLANNING THE SMALL MUSEUM

The objective of the proposed museum should be clearly defined, as well as the geographic region, the subject (history, natural history, or art) and extent of display and other services.

The following is an example of a suitable basic statement for a small museum:

The basic objective of the Museum is to collect, preserve, study and exhibit significant objects of the community, and provide related educational services in order to increase public knowledge and stimulate creative activity.

This statement should have further definition by incorporating a reference to the type of collections, whether human history, natural history or art.

A good museum includes these basic functions: (1) curatorial, (2) display, (3) display preparation, (4) education. In order to realize both objectives and functions, certain facilities and spaces are essential.

There must be sufficient diversification of spaces to allow each function to be undertaken separately while at the same time combining certain activities in a single area as required for economy in a small museum. Because of the many and varied kinds of tasks which a museum has to perform, it is absolutely impossible to maintain good housekeeping and curatorial procedures without separation of functions into separate rooms. This relation between functions and physical facilities is summarized in the following.

Functions	Space required
1. Curatorial Functions	
a. Collection, preservation, identification, documentation, study, restoration.	a. Office-workroom, Workshop
b. Storage of collections.	b. Reserve Collection Room
2. Display Function	
Thematic and changing displays of selected objects and documents from the collections arranged to tell a story.	Display Gallery
3. Display Preparation Function	
The preparation of exhibits.	Workshop, Office-workroom
4. Educational and Public Functions	
This term has been expanded to include all public functions.	
a. Lectures, school tours, society meetings, films, and social functions.	a. Lecture room, Chair storage closet, Kitchenette
b. Reception, information, sales, supervision of display gallery.	b. Lobby, Sales and Information Counter
c. Public requirements.	c. Cloak room, Washrooms
5. Other Services	
a. Mechanical.	a. Heating-ventilation plant
b. Janitorial.	b. Janitor's closet

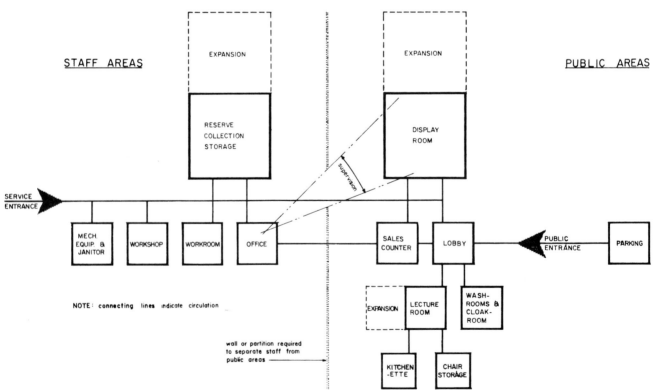

Fig. 1 Space organization diagram.

The Technical Requirements of Small Museums, Raymond O. Harrison, M.R.A.I.C. Technical Paper No. 1, Canadian Museums Association, Ottawa, Ontario, 1966.

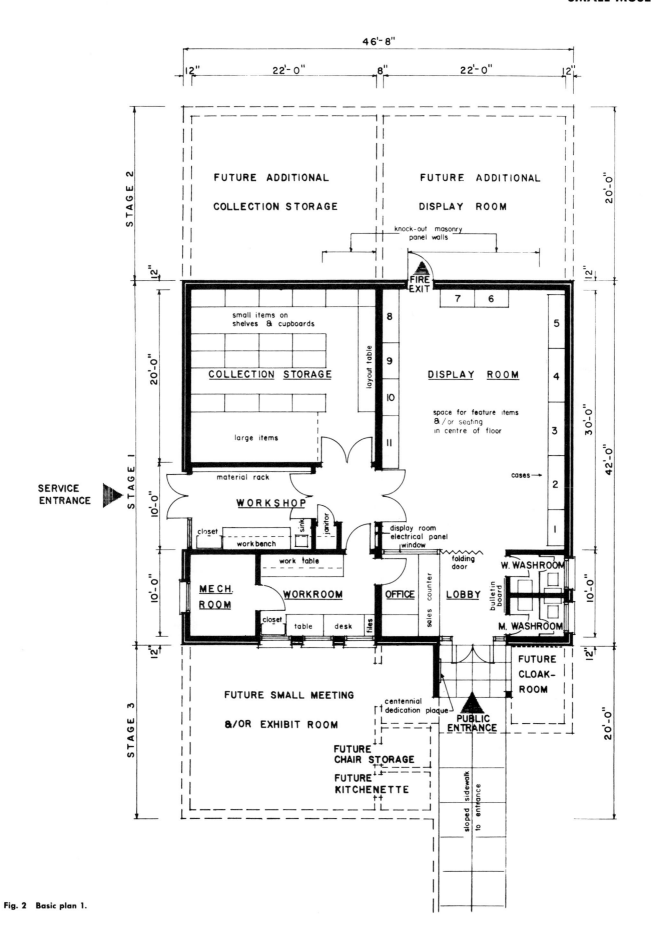

Fig. 2 Basic plan 1.

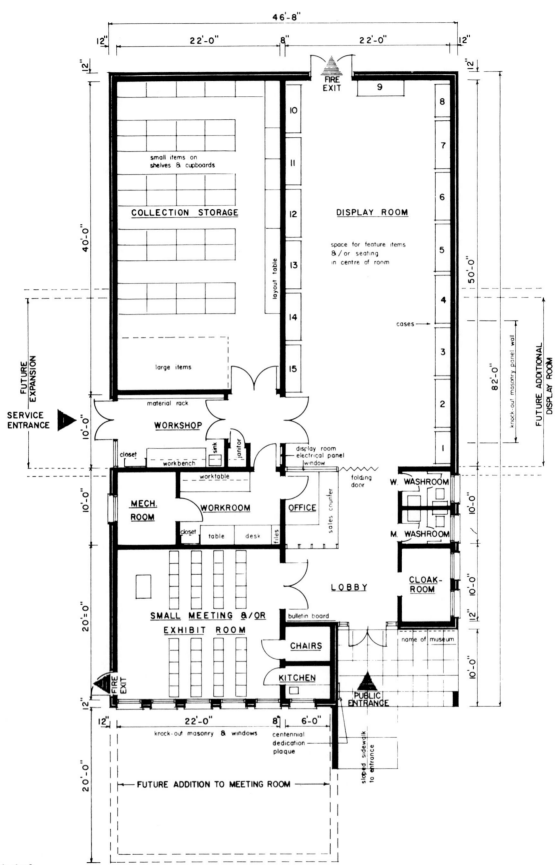

Fig. 3 Basic plan 2.

ORGANIZATION OF SPACE

The next step in the planning of a museum is the working relationship between these various functions. The planning of a good museum must reflect the most efficient manner in which the various tasks are carried out individually and in relationship to each other, without one adversely affecting the other. A major consideration in this planning is the matter of future expansion and construction in several stages.

The diagram (Fig. 1) illustrates the most efficient working arrangement,

To illustrate the manner in which a good small museum may be planned on the basis of the organizational diagram, three basic plans are presented as examples, ranging from the smallest possible at 1960 sq ft, up to 3823 sq ft, and therefore representing three different capital expenditures and operating costs. All plans incorporate provisions for future expansion and construction in several stages as a basic principle.

It should be further noted that the museum plans shown are based upon collections comprising smaller types of specimens and artifacts. Large equipment, vehicles, and farm machinery would require considerably more space although the basic functions outlined earlier would still apply. The following is a summary of some main features.

Basic Plan 1

This plan (Fig. 2) shows the absolutely minimum sizes of spaces required for an effective minimum museum. It will be noted that the display area is only about 40 percent of the area of the building.

Future expansion of the existing collection storage room can take place as the collections grow, while the existing display room also can be increased in size as required. Future addition of a lecture room off the lobby can also be achieved so that the educational functions of the museum can be expanded. Note that these additions can be made without complication to the roof structure of the original plan. The number of perimeter display cases shown would be ample to maintain and ensure changing displays.

Basic Plan 2

This (Fig. 3) is an expansion of Plan 1, with allowance for further expansion of the display, collection, and educational functions in the future. The number of perimeter cases shown would be ample for the story theme and changing exhibits while the center of the room may have larger items, photographic panels or special feature displays. The display room is 33 percent of gross.

GALLERY DESIGN*

The average American museum visitor (Fig. 4), if a man, is about 5 ft 9¼ in tall, and his eye level is 5 ft 4¾ in; the average woman is about 5 ft 3¼ in tall, and her eye level is 4 ft 11¾ in. Thus, the mean adult eye-level height is about 5 ft 2¼ in. With little eye movement, people usually see and recognize with ease things that are within an approximately elliptical cone of vision, with the apex of the cone at the eye-level height. Studies have shown that, in general, the

* Reprinted with permission from Technical Leaflet # 52, *Gallery and Case Exhibit Design,* by Arminta Neal, Copyright 1969 by the American Association for State and Local History, 1400 8th Avenue South, Nashville, TN 37203.

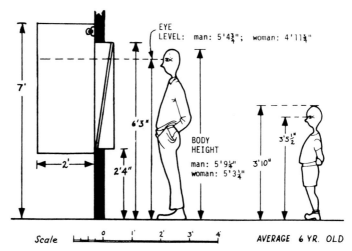

Fig. 4 Measurements of adult and six-year-old visitors in relation to cases.

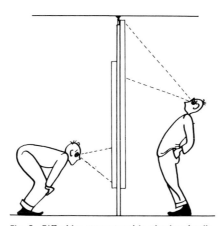

Fig. 5 Difficulties encountered in viewing details more than 3 ft below or 1 ft above one's eye level.

adult museum visitor observes an area only a little over 1 ft above his own eye level to 3 ft below it at an average viewing distance of 24–48 in (Fig. 5). Arranging objects and labels above and below these limits places a strain on seldom-used muscles and produces aching backs, tired feet, burning eyes, and stiff necks. Some quite large objects, such as totem poles or dinosaurs, will inevitably soar above these viewing limits, and, in this event, the visitor must be permitted space to back far enough away from the object to comprehend it without becoming a case for an orthopedic specialist (Fig. 6).

The flow of visitors is like the flow of water in a stream. If the cases are arranged with gently curving lines to take advantage of this pattern of movement (Fig. 7b), visitors will find the room more attractive and can progress easily with the line of the case. Often the arrangements can be staggered (Fig. 7c) which produces a certain mystery and a desire on the part of the visitor to peek around corners to see what is next. It is not always necessary to have a wide opening into a hall. Cases that are arranged to narrow the entrance a bit (Fig. 7d), so that the hall inside then opens out, provide a certain amount of interest.

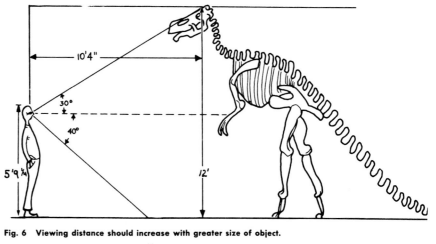

Fig. 6 Viewing distance should increase with greater size of object.

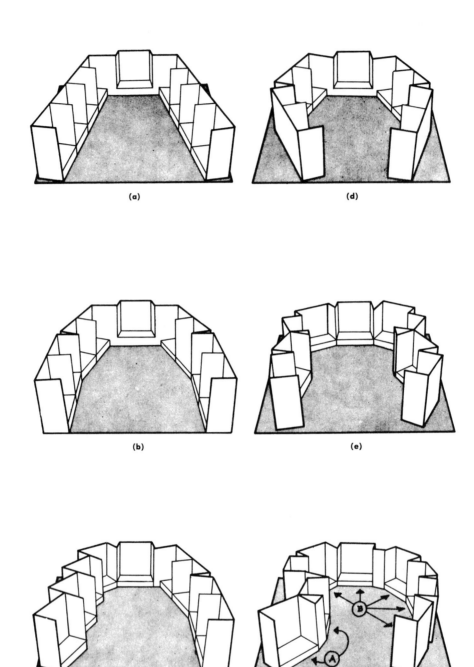

(a)

(b)

(c)

(d)

(e)

(f)

Fig. 7 Possible gallery arrangements.

EXHIBITION SPACES

The first step in designing exhibition spaces is to have a clear idea of what you will be showing. How many exhibits are planned per year, and how often will they change? What kinds of traveling exhibitions do you hope to schedule? If you have a permanent collection, how many pieces will remain on view? Will you be showing some very large-scale art? Mostly small pieces? Three-dimensional objects to be displayed in cases or on pedestals? Fragile prints and drawings?

With firm program plans in hand, you can determine the degree of flexibility you need, the layout of your galleries, and the size and environmental qualities of the spaces. There are few fixed rules, so the guidelines in this section are necessarily general.

The guidelines here reflect the belief that exhibitions of paintings, prints, drawings, photography, and sculpture will continue to be the "bread and butter" of any visual arts facility's annual programming. Providing for such newer developments as video and performance art is not that difficult, even for the small or medium-sized museum or art center. The key is flexibility: Can you turn gallery space into a performance art site for an evening with a minimum of fuss? Do you have sufficient, conveniently located outlets to accommodate video monitors? If you plan to emphasize nontraditional art forms, be sure to talk with artists who work in these media about their specific needs.

Orient the Visitor

Unlike the performing arts, in which the audience stays in one place to watch the action on stage, the visual arts require movement and choice on the part of the spectator. Your galleries and other public spaces must be designed to help the viewer organize the experience of looking at and considering a sequence of objects.

The entry and lobby areas should direct visitors to the galleries, where they should be able to survey what there is to see, select a starting point, and move to it as directly as possible. From that point, you want the arrangement of spaces to yield a continuously unfolding experience, allowing the visitor's attention to be drawn easily from object to object, gallery to gallery.

Some factors to keep in mind when designing your exhibition spaces:

- Viewers should be able to move through the exhibit without being forced to walk past objects they have already seen.
- There must be adequate space for visitors to move at different speeds. Some will move continuously, while others will stop to examine particular objects in greater detail.
- A viewer tends to turn to the right upon entering a gallery. Circulation patterns should be designed with this in mind.
- The ability to survey the gallery area in one sweep will help viewers understand what is on display and decide what they want to see.

Provide a Pleasant, Varied Environment

A crowded, warm, or noisy environment can make the most ardent art lover irritable. Be sure the facility has sufficiently roomy corridors and aisles as well as other "transitional" areas such as courtyards or skylit spaces. Viewers need places to sit down and rest, reflect on the art, take a break from the visual richness of the galleries, or simply get their bearings. Frequently, these spaces are illuminated by daylight, in contrast to the gallery areas, which are lit primarily with electric light. Seats at appropriate distances from large, important works of art give visitors a chance to pause and examine the art without standing for long periods of time.

These amenities also vary the "pace" of the visit—an important element in the design of a visual arts facility. When viewers become tired, satiated with the sheer quantity of the art, or discomfited by noise, their gallery experience ceases to be rewarding. Visual diversity helps keep the viewer interested. A low level of ambient lighting in the gallery area can be contrasted with dramatic highlighting. Variations in ceiling heights and different wall colors throughout a sequence of galleries help ward off visitor fatigue. Of course, none of these features should ever upstage the art.

It is essential to control noise and vibration in the exhibit space; air conditioning and other equipment should be selected and located accordingly. The mechanical engineers on your project should be aware of the need to mask distracting sounds.

Critical Dimensions for a Visual Arts Facility

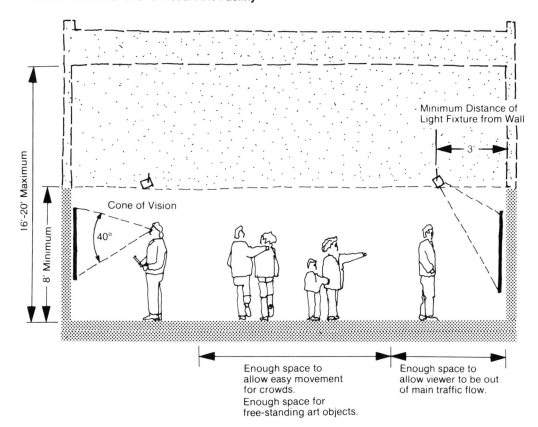

EXHIBITION SPACES
Visual Arts Facility

Functional Diagram of a Small Visual Arts Facility

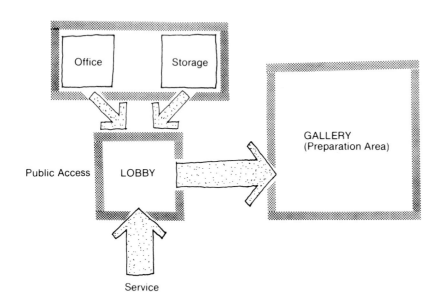

Functional Diagram of a Large Visual Arts Facility

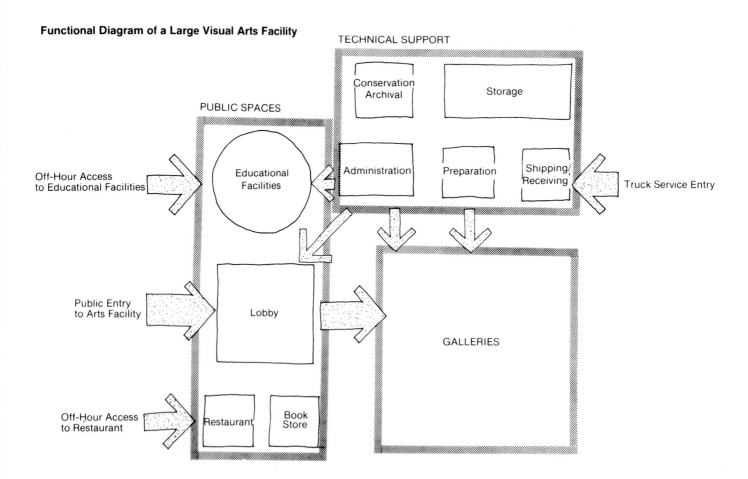

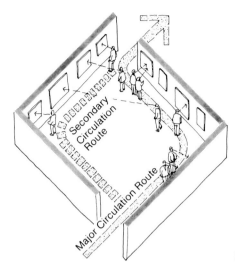

Right Hand Preference Circulation Patterns

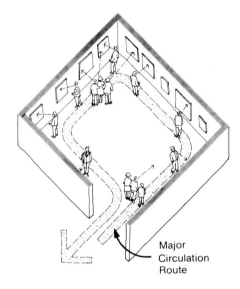

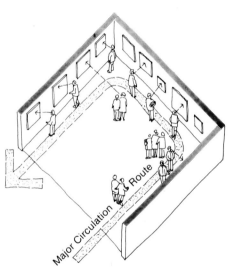

LIBRARIES
Diagrams of Essential Library Elements

DIAGRAMS OF ESSENTIAL LIBRARY ELEMENTS

Three diagrams have been prepared as an aid to visualizing the functional relationships of the principal areas in typical small libraries. These diagrams are for libraries for towns of 5,000, 10,000 and 25,000 persons respectively.

They are meant to clarify relationships and circulation patterns. They definitely are *not* building plans, nor do they constitute the only possible relationships between the program elements. It is intended that they assist in understanding the interrelationships between the major program elements.

They are intended to suggest a starting point for the planning of the library and represent *minimum standards.* They are derived from "Interim Standards for Small Public Libraries: Guidelines Toward Achieving the Goals of Public Library Service." ALA—Public Library Association, Chicago, 1962. (See Table 2 on p. 345.)

I. The Library for the Town of 5,000 Population

The basic principles when planning for the library (Fig. 1) are:
1. Location to insure maximum accessibility
2. Simplicity of design concept
3. Ease of supervision by library staff
4. Provision for future expansion

The basic statistics of the library are:

Staff: One and one-half persons, including a professional librarian and a part-time assistant.

Book Collection:	15,000 volumes
Space for book collection:	1,000 sq ft
Space for readers:	700 sq ft
Staff work space:	500 sq ft
Estimated additional span for utilities, circulation, and miscellaneous:	800 sq ft
Total estimated floor space:	3,500 sq ft

These are approximates only and will, of course, vary with each community.

II. The Library for the Town of 10,000 Population

This library (Fig. 2) in many respects is an expanded version of the first one. The basic principles and relationships are the same. The staff and space requirements are approximately twice those of the first.

The larger size permits the development of special areas that add to the usefulness of the library and enable it to provide better services. Some of these may be: a special area in the children's section for storytelling and related activities, expanded reference, and separate periodical areas. A small meeting room may be a useful addition to the program.

The basic requirements for this library are:

Staff: Three persons: a professional librarian, an assistant, and part-time clerical and page help equivalent to one full-time person.

Size of book collection:	20,000 volumes
Space for the book collection:	2,000 sq ft
Space for readers (40 seats min.):	1,200 sq ft
Staff work space:	1,000 sq ft
Estimated additional space for utilities, circulation, and miscellaneous:	2,800 sq ft
Total estimated floor space	7,000 sq ft

III. The Library for the Town of 25,000 Population

This library (Fig. 3) in function is more complex than the previous libraries. To the three basic functional areas of the library, which are expanded and elaborated on, there usually is added a fourth, a community function, often in the form of a meeting room or small auditorium. There may also be (Fig. 4):

Special exhibition space
Special exhibition rooms
Study area with carrels near the stacks
Small meeting rooms
Audiovisual rooms or booths

The circulation pattern is more complex. A separate entrance for children is highly desirable. Access to the community facility by the public after normal library hours is required. A library of this size may be a two-level structure. On the diagram (Fig. 3) we have indicated these circulation requirements. Note the separate staff and public circulation between levels. The basic requirements for the library for the town of 25,000 persons are:

Staff: Ten—this might be broken down to include two professional librarians, a college graduate, three assistants, and four other persons, divided between clerical and pages.

Space for book collection:	5,000 sq ft
Reader space (minimum of 75 seats):	2,250 sq ft
Staff work space:	1,500 sq ft
Estimated additional space required for special uses, utilities, and miscellaneous:	6,250 sq ft
Total estimated floor space:	15,000 sq ft

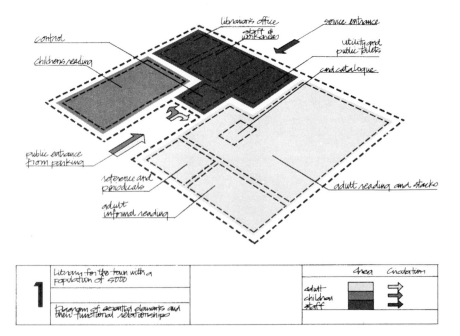

Fig. 1

A. Anthony Tappé, ALA., *Guide to Planning a Library Building,* Huggens and Tappé, Inc., Boston, 1968.

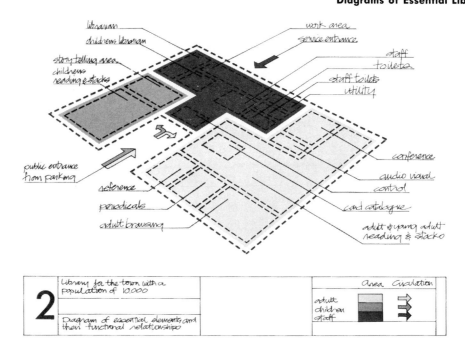

Fig. 2

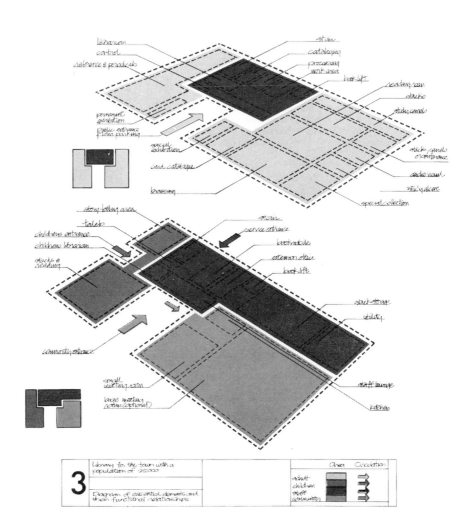

Fig. 3

Cultural

LIBRARIES
Branch Libraries

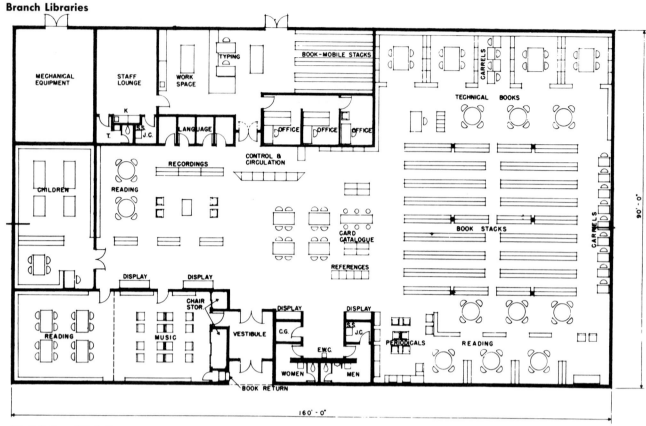

FLOOR PLAN AREA SHOWN: 14,364 SQ. FT

Fig. 4 Floor plan of a library. *Source:* U.S. Naval Facilities Engineering Command, Department of the Navy, Washington, D.C.

BRANCH LIBRARIES

A branch library can play an important role as a cultural center. In addition to providing books, it can provide record and tape lending, music-listening facilities, visual-aid facilities, and lecture series as well as act as a general information center. With such an expanded role, the library or cultural center will be an important element in the neighborhood. Figs. 1 and 2 are possible floor plans.

Regardless of the size of the community, its library should provide access to enough books to cover the interests of the whole population.

Manual of Housing/Planning and Design Criteria, De Chiara and Koppelman, Prentice-Hall, Inc., Englewood Cliffs, N.J., 1975.

1. Libraries serving populations from 5,000 to 50,000 require a minimum of 2 books per capita.

2. Communities up to 5,000 persons need access to a minimum of 10,000 volumes, or 3 books per capita, whichever is greater.

The library building should provide space for the full range of library services. All libraries should have designated areas for children's, young adult, and adult materials.

Multipurpose rooms should be provided for meeting, viewing, and listening by cultural, educational, and civic groups unless such facilities are readily available elsewhere in the community. They should be located for easy supervision so that they may be used for quiet reading and study when not needed by groups.

No single type of building is satisfactory for all public libraries. Each building is likely to be different, and its differences should be directly related to its service program.

The library building should be located in or near the community shopping center and at street level if possible. Adequate parking should be available nearby.

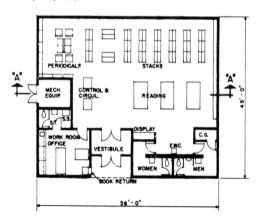

Fig. 1

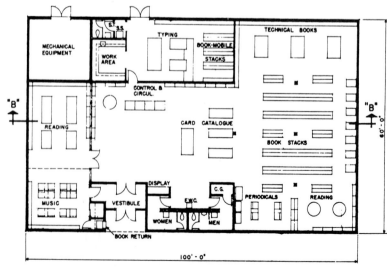

Fig. 2

382

SPACE REQUIREMENTS

The program statement, which includes objectives, activities, and requirements, will spell out total needs in terms of square feet of floor space. Generally speaking, the total need may be divided into five categories: space for (1) books, (2) readers, (3) staff, (4) group meetings, and (5) mechanical operations and all other (stairways, elevators, toilets, etc.). Actual space allocations will tend to vary in accordance with the library service program in relationship to community needs.[1] Table 1 provides general guidelines for programming the total building, and Table 2 provides guidelines for interior space in relation to population and size of the book collection.

Space for Books

To a large extent the amount of book shelving required will depend on the size of the library service area and whether the library is a member of a library system. Most library planners, when estimating the size of the book collection, apply a standard which ranges from three books per capita (smallest communities) to one and one-half books per capita (largest cities). In any event enough book shelving should be provided to plan for 20 years' anticipated growth.

The program statement should also include a detailed analysis of the amount of shelving needed. It should be presented in terms of category, location, and linear feet. Categories found in nearly all public libraries include adult fiction and nonfiction; children's books; books for young adults; reference books; bound, unbound, and microfilmed newspapers; bound, unbound, and microfilmed periodicals; local history books; less used books for the bookstacks; and special subject collections. Allowances should be made also for nonbook materials (i.e., phonograph records) which are often accommodated on library shelving.

Despite the fact that there is considerable variation in the size of books, there are several reliable formulas which may be used to estimate the amount of space required for books. These are: open reading rooms, 7 volumes per lineal foot, or 50 books per foot of standard height wall shelving, or 100 books per foot of double-faced shelving; bookstack areas, 15 books per square foot (includes aisles), or 2

books per cubic foot. Approximately 50 long-play phonograph records may be shelved in one lineal foot of wall shelving. It is important to note that these formulas are given for full capacity. Under normal conditions, one-third of each shelf should be left for future expansion. (See Figs. 1 to 3.)

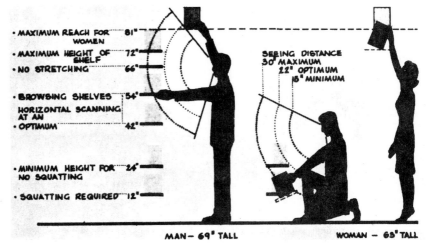

Fig. 1 Optimum shelving conditions for adults.

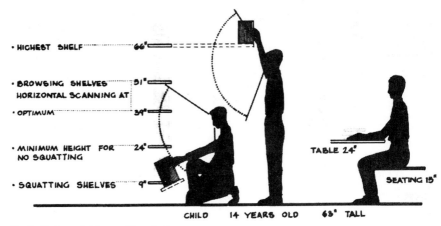

Fig. 2 Optimum shelving conditions for teen-agers.

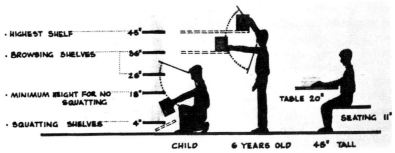

Fig. 3 Optimum shelving conditions for children.

Space for Readers

Reader seating requirements should be determined for at least 20 years ahead. Two principal sources of information which library building planners will find equally useful for this purpose are first, a careful analysis of

Local Public Library Administration, International City Managers Association, Chicago, Ill., 1964. With illustrations from Harold L. Roth, Ed., *Planning Library Buildings for Service,* American Library Association, Chicago, 1964.

[1] Much of the discussion on space standards is based on Joseph L. Wheeler, *The Effective Location of Public Library Buildings* (Urbana: University of Illinois Library School, Occasional Papers, No. 52, 1958), 50pp.; Joseph L. Wheeler and Herbert Goldhor, *Practical Administration of Public Libraries* (New York: Harper and Row, 1962), pp. 553-60; American Library Association, Subcommittee on Standards In Small Libraries, Public Library Association; *Interim Standards for Small Public Libraries: Guidelines Toward Achieving the Goals of Public Library Service* (Chicago: The Association, 1962), 16pp.; and Russell J. Schunk, *Pointers for Public Library Building Planners* (Chicago: American Library Association, 1945), 67pp.

Figures 1 to 9 by Francis Joseph McCarthy, FAIA.

Cultural

LIBRARIES

Space Requirements

purely local needs, and second, existing, time-proven formulas applied as a basic guide.

The most important factor in determining reader space needs is of course the reading potential of the people who will use the library. A conveniently located, attractive library will stimulate dramatically increased library use. Serious errors can result when estimates are based on use of the old, existing library.

As noted earlier an additional problem that must be carefully evaluated is providing an adequate number of seats for use by readers during peak periods. This problem has been intensified in recent years due to the increase in school attendance and the newer methods of instruction which involve extensive use of reference and supplementary materials by students of all ages. Since these periods of peak use occur irregularly, it is not economical to provide reading rooms which will be large enough to accommodate abnormally large crowds. Therefore, some libraries have attempted to solve this problem by locating multipurpose rooms adjacent to adult reference

TABLE 1 Experience Formulas for Library Size and Costs

Population size	Book stock — volumes per capita	No. of seats per 1,000 population	Circulation — volumes per capita	Total sq ft per capita	Desirable, first floor, sq ft per capita
Under 10,000	3½-5	10	10	0.7-0.8	0.5-0.7
10,000-35,000	2¾-3	5	9.5	0.6-0.65	0.4-0.45
35,000-100,000	2½-2¾	3	9	0.5-0.6	0.25-0.3
100,000-200,000	1¾-2	2	8	0.4-0.5	0.15-0.2
200,000-500,000	1¼-1½	1¼	7	0.35-0.4	0.1-0.125
500,000 and up	1-1¼	1	6.5	0.3	0.06-0.08

SOURCE: Joseph L. Wheeler and Herbert Goldhor, Practical Administration of Public Libraries (New York: Harper and Row, 1962) p. 554.

TABLE 2 Guidelines for Determining Minimum Space Requirements

Population served	Shelving Space*			Reader space, sq ft	Staff work space, sq ft	Estimated additional space needed, sq ft‡	Total floor space, sq ft
	Size of book collection, volumes	Linear feet of shelving†	Amount of floor space, sq ft				
Under 2,499	10,000	1,300	1,000	Min. 400 for 13 seats, at 30 sq ft per reader space	300	300	2,000
2,500-4,999	10,000, plus 3 per capita for pop. over 3,500	1,300. Add 1 ft of shelving for every 8 vols. over 10,000	1,000. Add 1 sq ft for every 10 vols. over 10,000	Min. 500 for 16 seats. Add 5 seats per 1,000 over 3,500 pop. served, at 30 sq ft per reader space	300	700	2,500, or 0.7 sq ft per capita, whichever is greater
5,000-9,999	15,000, plus 2 per capita for pop. over 5,000	1,875. Add 1 ft of shelving for every 8 vols. over 15,000	1,500. Add 1 sq ft for every 10 vols. over 15,000	Min. 700 for 23 seats. Add 4 seats per 1,000 over 5,000 pop. served, at 30 sq ft per reader space	500. Add 150 sq ft for each full-time staff member over 3	1,000	3,500, or 0.7 sq ft per capita, whichever is greater
10,000-24,999	20,000, plus 2 per capita for pop. over 10,000	2,500. Add 1 ft of shelving for every 8 vols. over 20,000	2,000. Add 1 sq ft for every 10 vols. over 20,000	Min. 1,200 for 40 seats. Add 4 seats per 1,000 over 10,000 pop. served, at 30 sq ft per reader space	1,000. Add 150 sq ft for each full-time staff member over 7	1,800	7,000, or 0.7 sq ft per capita, whichever is greater
25,000-49,999	50,000 plus 2. per capita for pop. over 25,000	6,300 Add 1 ft of shelving for every 8 vols. over 50,000	5,000. Add 1 sq ft for every 10 vols. over 50,000	Min. 2,250 for 75 seats. Add 3 seats per 1,000 over 25,000 pop. served, at 30 sq ft per reader space	1,500. Add 150 sq ft for each full-time staff member over 13	5,250	15,000, or 0.6 sq ft per capita, whichever is greater

SOURCE: American Library Association, Subcommittee on Standards for Small Libraries, Public Library Association, Interim Standards for Small Public Libraries: Guidelines Toward Achieving the Goals of Public Library Service (Chicago: The Association, 1962), p. 15. This brief 16-page report is based on standards set forth in ALA's, Public Library Service; A Guide to Evaluation with Minimum Standards. It is intended to provide interim standards for libraries serving populations of less than 50,000 until these libraries can meet the standards of ALA's Public Library Service.

*Libraries in systems need only to provide shelving for basic collection plus number of books on loan from resource center at any one time.

†A standard library shelf equals 3 lin ft.

‡Space for circulation desk, heating and cooling equipment, multipurpose room, stairways, supplies, toilets, etc., as required by community needs and the program of library services.

and study areas. Arrangements of this type have proved to be most effective in smaller libraries and in branch library buildings.

The following formulas, developed by Joseph L. Wheeler, are based on building analyses made over a period of more than 30 years. If the estimated future population is less than 10,000, allow 10 seats per thousand; if more than 10,000 but less than 35,000, allow 5 seats per thousand; between 35,000 and 100,000, 3 seats per thousand; between 100,000 and 200,000, 2 seats per thousand; between 200,000 and 500,000, allow $1\frac{1}{4}$ seats per thousand; and 500,000 and up, 1 seat per thousand.[2]

As an established rule of thumb, minimum allowances are made of 30 sq ft per adult reader and 20 sq ft per child. These allocations for reader seating are in terms of net space for readers, chairs, tables, aisles, and service desk. Seating requirements should be listed according to the several areas of the building. In addition, the program statement should estimate the proportion of table seating to informal seating (See Figs. 4 to 6.)

Space for Staff

Space requirements for the staff must also be stated in the program. These estimates will be conditioned by (1) anticipated growth for a 20-year period and (2) the nature and extent of the library's service program. The American Library Association recommends that space for staff be calculated on the basis of "one staff member (full-time or equivalent) . . . for each 2,500 people in the service area."[3] It is a minimum standard that includes pages but not maintenance personnel. Although suitable for application to most situations, it must not be regarded as inflexible. As an example, a library that is not affiliated with a system will probably require a somewhat larger staff than libraries that have joined together in cooperative arrangements, such as centralized technical processing centers. Moreover, something as fundamental as the number of hours per week the library is open will affect the size of the staff and, consequently, space requirements. There are striking differences in staff requirements between libraries open 20, 38, or 72 hours per week.

Staff space requirements should be calculated on the basis of 100 sq ft per staff member. It is important that this standard be met for there is ample evidence that space for staff has been outgrown more rapidly than any other type of space in most library buildings. Only too often is it easy to forget that an expanding service program will require the support of an enlarged staff. The unit of measurement of 100 sq ft per staff member includes space for desk, chair, books, and equipment.

A checklist of staff work areas should include (1) administrative offices, (2) work rooms, and (3) staff lunch and lounge rooms.

Administrative offices should include a combination librarian's office-trustee room; spaces for the assistant librarian and a secretary-receptionist; business office; and other related offices. Work room areas should be provided for technical processing; reference, circulation, extension, and other departments; subject specialists; and supply storage. Comfort facilities for the staff should include cooking and lunchroom areas as well as appropriate locker, lounge, and toilet facilities for both men and women. Comfortable working conditions contribute to effective personnel administration as well as to efficient library service.

[2] Wheeler, *op. cit.*, p. 18; Wheeler and Goldhor, *op. cit.*
[3] *Public Library Service, op. cit.*, p. 43.

Meeting Rooms

With the exception of the very smallest libraries, most public libraries should provide some group meeting space, at least one multipurpose meeting room. At the other extreme, a small auditorium and a series of conference rooms may be required. The services proposed by the library together with community needs for facilities of this type will be the final determinants.

Multipurpose rooms meet two general classes of need. First, they can be utilized for children's story hours, discussion groups, staff meetings, and other library-sponsored activities. Second, various community, educational, cultural, and local government groups will make frequent and varied use of a multipurpose room. To be of maximum value, however, the room should be arranged for easy and effective use of audiovisual equipment. In addition, there should be adjacent closet space for storage of blackboards, folding tables, chairs, and related equipment.

Many libraries provide a small "pullman" type kitchen in an area adjoining group meeting rooms. Serious consideration should be given to including this facility since there are many occasions when it is highly appropriate to serve simple refreshments. A kitchen featuring a compact combination stove-sink-refrigerator unit will not cause administrative or maintenance problems provided regulations governing its use are stated clearly. Separate

provisions should be made for staff kitchen and lounge facilities.

Small auditoriums may feature sloping floors along with elaborate lighting, stage, and projection equipment, or they may be austere with major emphasis placed on flexibility. It is recommended that no auditorium ever be included in a library building program statement without first consulting community leaders. Such facilities are expensive to maintain and, as a result, can place an invisible but dangerous strain on the library's budget unless fully justified. Whenever group meeting spaces are provided, it is important that they be located where there can be access for community use without opening the rest of the building. It is customary to allow from 7 to 10 sq ft per seat for meeting room and auditorium seating.

Space for Mechanical Operations

Included within this category are halls, stairways, toilets, elevators and lifts, air ducts, heating and air conditioning equipment, closets, and shops.

Because it is exceedingly easy to underestimate the amount of space required for mechanical operations, it is recommended that the best available technical advice be secured to assure inclusion of an accurate estimate within the program statement. Fortunately, with the development of new construction materials and techniques combined with new concepts in planning, much less space is needed for these

Fig. 4   Minimum clearances for various body positions in library stack areas.

385

LIBRARIES
Service and Space Relationships

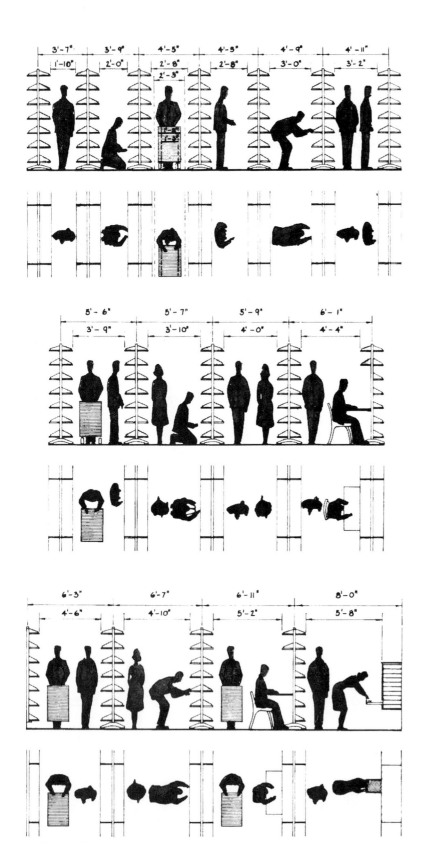

Fig. 4 (cont.)   Minimum clearances for various body positions in library stack areas.

purposes than was formerly the case. It is suggested that an allowance of 20 percent be made for mechanical operations. In comparison, some planners allowed twice as much space not too many years ago. It is of utmost importance that this space requirement not be overlooked. After the amount of space needed has been estimated, it should be added to the total required for the other activities to be provided in the building.

SERVICE AND SPACE RELATIONSHIPS

As a logical extension of the program statement, it is important that the members of the planning team, especially the architect, acquire an understanding of the interrelationships between areas within the library. It is not enough to simply know how much space is needed; it is equally important to determine which element is to be placed where—and why. Toward this end, service and space relationships can be most readily clarified by analyzing all of the activities that take place in the library. This analysis of both public and staff use can be facilitated through preparation of work flow studies.

The central objective for the library planner is to arrange the several elements in a manner which will assure maximum flexibility. Reduced expenses for supervision, personnel, and construction are among the benefits derived from an "open," flexible building.

More specifically, flexibility implies successful, long-time use of the building. The same area may be used for one or more purposes at different times. The amount of space allocated for a certain use may be shrunk or expanded without structural changes. Furniture and equipment are not fixed and may be relocated.

Ideally, all public services should be located on the main floor of a library in the interests of user convenience, economy, and simplification of operation. Where this is impossible, as in the case of libraries in large cities, every effort should be made to visualize the vertical movement of persons and materials. Under any circumstances, a careful study of the flow of traffic and material is basic to the development of successful service and space relationships. Members of the planning team will find it useful to visualize the traffic flow of library users according to age and purpose of their visit to the library from the point of entrance into the building to the time of departure. Another test that will help to clarify space relationships is to trace a book from the placement of its order to the time it is placed on the public shelves and the cards are filed in the card catalog. (See Figs. 7 to 9.)

In addition to locating a maximum number of public services on the main floor, the following points should be kept in mind:

1. Only one complete card catalog should be maintained. It should be located conveniently as near as possible to the reading and reference areas, circulation desk, and the processing department. Department catalogs, a children's catalog, and shelflist and other processing records should be placed in their respective areas as needed.

2. Except for large libraries, there should not be more than one circulation desk. It should be near the main entrance where there will be direct visual control of the movement of both children and adults.

3. There should be a single public entrance within short distance of the circulation desk. Auditoriums and meeting rooms need not be directly accessible from the main entrance.

4. Public toilets, telephones, and display cases should be located where they can be supervised by circulation desk personnel.

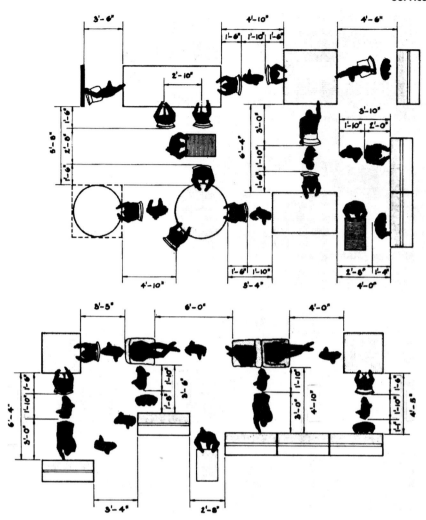

Fig. 5 Minimum clearances for people and equipment in reading rooms.

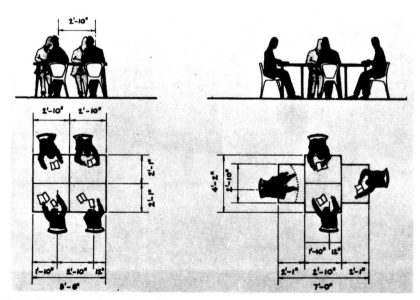

Fig. 6 Table space requirements for readers.

5. Every public service area should be supported by book storage, office, and work areas. Reading rooms should be grouped so that they may be served by common book storage, office, and work area.

6. A librarian or attendant should not be responsible for areas more than 55 ft beyond his desk.

7. Load bearing walls should be kept to a minimum and maximum use of shelving and furniture made to separate different service areas.

Other factors, such as exterior light and noise, also may influence the location of various areas within the building.

Finally it may be said that the success or failure of a building is measured by the degree to which planners succeed in applying the foregoing principles of desirable interrelationships. Whether it is a simple village library or a complex large-city library, every effort should be made to facilitate supervisory control, flexibility, and convenience of readers. Careful attention to supervisory control together with a flexible layout of public services will pay off in savings in staff time and ability to handle peak loads with a minimum staff. By the same token, failure to achieve effective service and space relationships can be a financial burden for many years and the source of continuing inconvenience for countless readers.

LIBRARY LOCATION

Central Location

A library is a service organization intended to serve people. Therefore, it should be centrally located where it will be accessible to the largest number of potential readers and information seekers.

This principle is neither new nor revolutionary. It has been advocated by a vast majority of experienced public library administrators for well over a half century. The concept of a centrally located library is just as valid now when there are more than 70 million registered motor vehicles as it was when the first successful American automobile was introduced in 1892.

A central location is usually associated with a heavy concentration of retail stores, office buildings, banks, public transportation points, and parking facilities. "This means that it [the public library] should be near the center of general community activity, i.e., the shopping and business district. Just as dime store operators study the flow of pedestrian traffic before locating one of their units, so should library planners consider carefully the best location to reach John Q. Public. A building located just around the corner from the most advantageous spot can lose a great deal of its potential patronage."[4]

The importance of a central location was reaffirmed in this statement: "A prominent, easily accessible location is required to attract a large number of persons. Therefore the library should be placed where people naturally converge—in the heart of the shopping and business district, rather than in a remote location such as a park, civic center or quiet side street."[5] The American Library Association's standards for public library service also emphasize the need of "maximum accessibility."

Unquestionably, a location which affords maximum accessibility to the greatest number of people is fundamental to the success of

[4] Russell J. Schunk, *Pointers for Public Library Building Planners* (Chicago: American Library Association, 1945), p. 6.
[5] Charles M. Mohrhardt and Ralph A. Ulveling, "Public Libraries," *Architectural Record,* December, 1952, p. 152.

LIBRARIES

Library Location

every new public library, be it the central library or a branch. It is equally true that a site which is located in the heart of a shopping and business district will usually cost far more than a site which is located in a remote or secondary area. Once confronted with the reality of the high cost usually associated with the acquisition of a prime location, there is a tendency toward "instant" compromise. Fortunately, ever increasing numbers of municipal officials, architects, and citizens recognize that the public library cannot fulfill its functions in a second-rate location and that operating costs are proportionately higher for an off-center library than for one which is centrally located. Maximum use is synonymous with lower service-unit costs, and strategically located sites are synonymous with maximum use.

The Site

In addition to central location, several other important criteria should be considered in library site selection:

1. The site should be prominent. A corner site at a busy intersection where the library can easily be seen is preferred. Maximum use should be made of display windows and views of the interior.

2. The site should permit street level entrance. Although a site that slopes to the rear has certain advantages, a level site should be acquired if possible.

3. The site should be large enough for expansion, accessibility for service vehicles and bookmobiles, and a modest amount of landscaping.

4. The site should permit orientation of the front of the building to the north in order to minimize glare from the sun. When this is not possible, orientation to the east is the second choice. However, an otherwise excellent, centrally located site should not be eliminated for lack of appropriate orientation. Modern year around temperature control devices and artificial light can be used effectively to minimize sun exposure problems.

5. Rectangular service areas within a building lend themselves to easy supervision. As a result, a site which is rectangular in shape and permits construction of a rectangular building should be obtained if possible.

6. Ideally, a site should have uniform foundation conditions, either rock or soil. Test borings should be made, preferably before a site is purchased.

Certain other conditions should be met if the community is to be adequately served. First, the library should be located reasonably near adequate automobile parking. Second, parking provisions should be made for bookmobiles, other official library vehicles, and library staff members. Third, automobile access to drive-in service windows should be provided where this feature has been incorporated into the library building design.

Although emphasis has been placed on acquiring a site which would be large enough to permit easy horizontal expansion, it is important to note that under certain conditions purchase of a strategically located smaller site can be justified provided there is enough space to locate primary adult public service areas at street level. Both Norfolk and Dallas acted accordingly when they acquired their choice downtown sites. In both instances, multistory buildings were erected with provision made for vertical expansion.

Where Not to Locate a Library

Despite the overwhelming evidence that can be offered in support of central locations for cen-

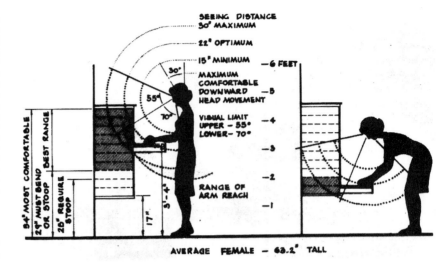

Fig. 7   Desirable heights for catalog tray consultation.

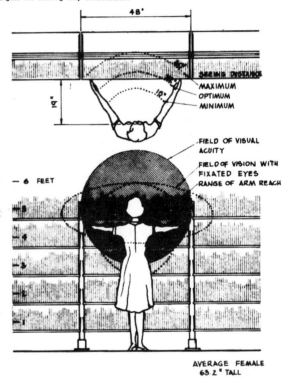

Fig. 8   Study for feasibility of scanning the 48-in. shelf.

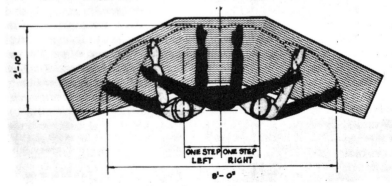

Fig. 9   Study for charge desk —maximum usable space from one position or station.

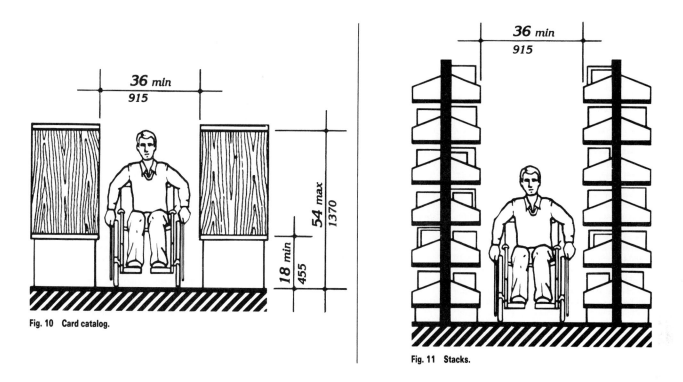

Fig. 10 Card catalog.

Fig. 11 Stacks.

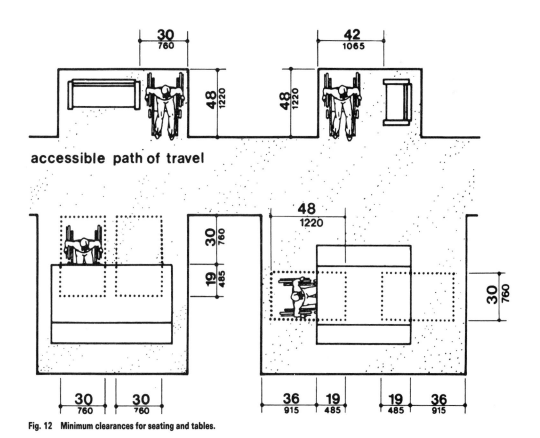

accessible path of travel

Fig. 12 Minimum clearances for seating and tables.

LIBRARIES
Library Location; Branch Buildings; Bookmobiles

tral libraries and branches in cities both large and small, library planners continue to encounter seemingly plausible arguments from those who believe that libraries should be located in civic or cultural centers, parks, or on sites where avoidance of noise or provision for parking is the major consideration. Usually these misconceptions are held by those who are not qualified to choose a library site.[6] They do not understand the significance of the library in the daily life of its constituents. Quite to the contrary, they associate the library with a setting of monumental buildings, large landscaped grounds, and quiet, aloof surroundings. Libraries are not mausoleums, they are dynamic educational centers whose services and resources must be easily accessible to the greatest number of potential readers.

Specifically, then, remote locations should be avoided. By definition, "remote" means (either literally or psychologically) to be situated at a distance, out of the way, secluded, separate, not primary. Hence the aloof and inaccessible civic and cultural center fits this definition because it is separated from the daily life of the community and is used principally for attendance at special events. How much more satisfactory it is to be where there are bright lights at night rather than in a civic center where governmental offices close at 5 P.M. and there is little activity at night or on weekends.

The San Francisco Public Library is in a civic center and is a classic example of a poorly located library. Removed from the mainstream of community life, it is flanked by municipal buildings, the civic auditorium, and large landscaped areas. The Carnegie Library of Pittsburgh, which is located in a cultural and educational center, has attempted to overcome its problem of remoteness by establishing lending and business reference branches in the downtown area. Such operations are expensive, unsatisfactory, and would not be necessary if the central library were located downtown.

By the same token, it is almost always a serious mistake to place a library in the geographic or population center of a community. Except in those rare instances where there is coincidence between trade center and geographic or population center, such centers are remote and unrelated to the everyday activities within the life of the community.

Another argument that may be encountered is that the library should be located away from noise. Again, if this point is heeded, it will mean placing the building in a remote location. Fortunately, modern technology has provided acoustical materials, air conditioning, and lighting methods which have completely invalidated this argument.

The argument encountered most often, however, is the one that the library should be placed where there is ample parking space for the library's public. Again, the implication is clear, for if the library is to assume full responsibility for providing enough parking, it will be necessary to locate the building in a secondary location where land is cheap.

Although there are some individuals for whom parking is the main consideration in using the library, numerous surveys have reaffirmed the point of view that a downtown, pedestrian-oriented location in the thick of things is the most important consideration affecting use of the public library. To illustrate, the Knoxville Branch, Carnegie Library of Pittsburgh, is located on the main street of a busy commercial district near banks, post office, liquor and variety stores, and public transportation. Its sister West End Branch, two blocks removed from the neighborhood shopping center, enjoys ample parking facilities in a parklike setting.

The centrally located Knoxville Branch, of course, lends more books for considerably less money than does the West End Branch.

As another comparison, a well-stocked bookmobile will lend many more books at a busy suburban shopping center than will secluded nearby community libraries that offer the very same books *plus* parking, peacefulness, and higher service unit costs!

The parking problem cannot be overlooked. On the other hand, it is a communitywide problem that must be solved by the community rather than by the library alone. In fact, choked highways and overtaxed parking facilities are matters of increasing concern to all governments. Perhaps new concepts in mass transit will help to alleviate parking problems throughout the nation. In the meantime, many libraries have attempted to ease the parking problem through provision of curbside book return boxes. Others are experimenting with drive-in return and "will call" windows, similar to those used by banks for drive-in service.

BRANCH BUILDINGS

Branch libraries usually are established as a result of population growth and community expansion. Generally, it is their purpose to provide books and services which will meet the everyday reading needs of children and adult general readers who live within the local neighborhood. The person who requires more advanced information and special materials will use the collection at the headquarters library.

Although there is a definite trend toward the establishment of larger and fewer branch libraries, there are hundreds of branch libraries which vary widely in both size and responsibility. They range from the small subbranch, open but a few hours each week, to large regional centers which provide a full range of library service.

Branch libraries may be found in busy urban shopping centers and quiet rural communities. Many are housed in their own buildings while others occupy rented quarters. In smaller communities, branch libraries sometimes share space in public buildings planned for joint municipal use.

Whether small or large, rural or urban, owned or rented, branch library buildings should be planned with great care. The object of this planning is a building strategically located for the area which it is to serve. It should be attractive, functional, flexible, and economical to operate. Toward this end, it is essential that a written program statement be prepared for the guidance of the architect. This statement should include objectives, services and their interrelationships, physical requirements, and operational procedures. Physical requirements specify the spaces which will be needed for books, readers, staff, meeting and community service rooms, and other auxiliary spaces.

Of equal or even greater importance is the need for adhering to accepted location and site selection standards. The most functional attractive building can never realize its full potential unless it is located where it will be easily accessible to the largest number of people. The following criteria are suggested as a basis for evaluating sites for a new branch building:

1. A branch library usually should serve a minimum of 25,000 to 30,000 people within a 1- to 1½-mi radius of the branch, subject to topographic conditions.

2. A branch library should be located within reasonable proximity of a residential area so that a sizable number of children and adults will be within walking distance.

3. A branch library should be near an important street or highway intersection, especially wherever public transportation is available.

4. A branch library should be either within or on the fringe of a major neighborhood or regional shopping center.

5. A branch library should be located where it can be clearly seen.

6. A branch library should provide parking space equal to its interior area if general parking facilities are not available.

Other factors to be considered by the planning team are parking space for bicycles and space for delivery trucks. In certain communities where bicycles are used heavily, it will be necessary to make appropriate provisions. Where the terrain is rugged, the use of bicycles may be limited. Planners must also make allowances for library system delivery and repair vehicles. The latter may be station-wagon types, full-size trucks, or both.

In addition to a highly accessible location, a branch library building should incorporate the same basic building details found in a headquarters or central library building.

1. A branch library should be at street level entrance with as little setback as possible.

2. When space permits, it should be a one-floor plan with all public service at ground level.

3. It should have a minimum number of fixed partitions.

4. A branch library should be planned to permit easy expansion.

5. It should have enough windows on its street frontage so that the books and people within can serve as a living advertisement and constant invitation to use the library.

6. It should not have more than one single control desk, thereby reducing operating costs.

7. It should be air conditioned and adequately illuminated.

8. It should have one multipurpose meeting room available for both library and community purposes if such use is anticipated.

Branch library buildings, as well as central libraries, should be located in the heart of retail shopping districts in order to serve the greatest numbers at the lowest cost, for the more who are served the less each service performed will cost. In other words, there are certain fixed operating costs which pertain wherever the library may be located. With the maximum exposure gained from a good location, unit costs are reduced accordingly.

It can be safely assumed that the most successful branch library will be the one that is based on a carefully stated written program and is located in the thick of things. It is of great importance that the accepted principles of planning and site selection not be overlooked merely because a "small branch" is being planned. To bypass any of these steps in planning is to invite mistakes which might prove to be costly. This holds true for new branches, rented storerooms, leased branch buildings built according to library specifications, and branch facilities incorporated into other public service buildings.

BOOKMOBILES

Because of obvious space restrictions, a bookmobile is a book distribution service which cannot serve as a substitute for a branch library, since there are neither reference nor study facilities. Known to many as "one-room libraries on wheels," bookmobiles have become a widely and enthusiastically accepted form of library service.

Although they are used principally to serve sparsely populated fringe and pocket areas where a full-scale library cannot be justified, they are used often to serve densely populated areas until branch libraries can be planned, financed, and built. As a natural by-product and

[6] Wheeler, *op. cit.*, pp. 3–5.

added benefit deriving from their mobility, bookmobiles pretest the validity of potential branch library locations.

Wherever the bookmobile goes, it is met and used by crowds of book-hungry men, women, and children, who are entitled to the use of a facility which provides maximum safety and comfort. As a result, it is important that bookmobiles be chosen with great care. Following a thorough study of local service requirements, the bookmobile planner should visit and inspect bookmobiles being used by other libraries which have comparable requirements. Major attention should be given to equipment. Shelving, desks, electric power, heat, light, ventilation, air conditioning, chassis, and convenience accessories are items which relate directly to function as well as reader and staff comfort.

Bookmobile size will be determined in part by population to be served, terrain, roads, climate, number of books to be carried, and the amount of work space required by the staff. To illustrate, while a tractor-trailer rig may be most appropriate to serve the densely populated Youngstown area, it would not be feasible for use on the mountain roads of sparsely populated rural New Hampshire.

Another item to be explored is bookmobile storage and service facilities at the headquarters library. When a new library is being planned, adequate provisions should be made for the support of bookmobile service.

Library and other officials responsible for the selection of a bookmobile should be guided by the standards for structural design and equipment as established by the American Library Association.

BOOKSTACK DATA

Unit Stack Weights

Books
25 to 30 lb per cu ft of ranges.
Stack Construction
Quoted as 5, 8, and 8 to 10 lb per cu ft, depending upon the manufacturer.
Deck Framing
2 to 4 lb per sq ft of gross deck area.
Deck Flooring
3-in. reinforced concrete slab, 38 lb per sq ft; $3\frac{1}{2}$-in. reinforced concrete slab, 38 lb per sq ft; gross area, with $\frac{1}{8}$-in. tile or linoleum covering, 45 lb; flanged steel plate floor, 12 lb per sq ft of gross area; $1\frac{1}{4}$-in. marble or slate, 18 lb per sq ft, aisle area.
Live Loads
Building codes vary, but in general, for column loads, assume 40 lb per sq ft of aisle area for live load and reduce this figure 5 percent for each deck below the top deck.

Bookstack Capacities

Among formulas suggested for use in computing the size of stacks necessary to house a given number of books is the "cubook" method, devised by R. W. Henderson of the New York Public Library.[7] The cubook is a measurement of stack capacity, defined as the "volume of space required to shelve the average book in the typical library." According to this formula, a single-faced section of stack 3 ft long and 7 ft 6 in. high has the following capacities:

100 cubooks (85 percent octavos, 13 percent quartos, and 2 percent folios)[8]

[7] *Library Journal,* Nov. 15, 1934, and Jan. 15, 1936.
[8] According to American Library Association, an octavo is about 8 to 10 in. high; a quarto, 10 to 12 in.; and a folio, over 12 in.

117 volumes (87 percent octavos and 13 percent quartos)
132 volumes (octavos only)
67 volumes (quartos only)
12 volumes (folios only)

The cubook method makes provision for 10 percent of each shelf to remain unoccupied, since it often is impractical to load shelves to their full visible capacity.

To determine the number of sections required when the number of volumes to be shelved is known, the following formulas are used:

Let N = number of single-faced sections required (1 section = 100 cubooks)

1. For a typical library, when the cubook is considered directly applicable: N = Vols. ÷ 100
2. For a library made up of octavos and quartos only: N = Vols. ÷ 117
3. For a library made up of octavos only: N = Vols. ÷ 132.3
4. For a library made up of quartos only: N = Vols. ÷ 67.5
5. For a library made up of folios only: N = Vols. ÷ 11.7
6. For a library made up of various size groups when the ratios are known:

$$N = [\text{Octavos} + (\text{quartos} \times 1.96) + (\text{folios} \times 11.3)] \div 132.3$$

Shelf Size The foregoing formulas indicate the number of sections required but do not cover the number of shelves or the proportion of shelves of each width (8 in., 10 in., or 12 in.). In general, the following shelf data applies:

For folios—thirteen 12-in. shelves per section

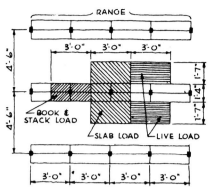

TYPICAL STACK LOADING DIAGRAM

For octavos and quartos—usually 7 shelves per section, divided as follows:
85 percent 8-in. shelves
10 percent 10-in. shelves
5 percent 12-in. shelves

Area and Volume Requirements The cubook can be reduced to approximate terms of area and volume requirements for bookstacks, as follows:
11.08 cubooks require 1 sq ft of stack floor area
1.48 cubooks require 1 cu ft of space in a stack
These values can be used as follows:
Required stack floor area = No. cubooks × 0.090
Required space (cu ft) = No. cubooks × 0.676

Stack Loads: General Variation of Stack Loads for from One to Twelve Tiers

	8-in. shelving											
Tiers	1	2	3	4	5	6	7	8	9	10	11	12
A	495	2,320	4,120	5,890	7,630	9,340	11,029	12,670	14,290	15,880	17,440	18,970
B	990	3,000	4,990	6,960	8,910	10,840	12,750	14,640	16,510	18,360	20,190	22,000
C	495	1,500	2,600	3,590	4,570	5,540	6,500	7,450	8,390	9,320	10,240	11,150
	10-in. shelving											
A	620	2,570	4,490	6,380	8,240	10,070	11,870	13,640	15,380	17,090	18,770	20,420
B	1,240	4,000	6,240	8,460	10,660	12,849	15,000	17,140	19,260	21,360	23,440	25,500
C	620	1,750	2,870	3,980	5,080	6,170	7,250	8,320	9,480	10,530	11,570	12,600

Including stacks, books, live load, and $3\frac{1}{2}$-in. concrete deck floor. (A = typical aisle and support; B = typical intermediate support; C = typical wall end support).

Shelving Data for Special Collections*

Type of book	Vols. per foot of shelf	Vols. per foot of single-faced range	Vols. per shelf	Maximum vols. per single-faced section	Shelf depth, in.	Shelves per section
Circulating (nonfiction)	8	56	24	168	8	7
Fiction	8	56	24	168	8	7
Economics	8	56	24	168	8	7
General literature	7	49	21	147	8	7
Reference	7	49	21	147	8 & 10	6-7
History	7	49	21	147	8	7
Technical and scientific	6	42	18	126	10 & 12	7
Medical	5	35	15	105	8 & 10	6-7
Law	4	28	12	84	8	7
Public documents	5	35	15	105	8	7
Bound periodicals	5	35	15	105	10 & 12	5-7
U.S. patent specifications	2	14	6	42	8	7
Art	7	42	21	126	10 & 12	5-6
Braille	4	24	12	72	15	5-6

* To be consistent with cubook method, figures shown should be reduced by 10 percent to avoid overcrowding shelves.

By JO MIELZINER

The twentieth century brought an entirely new attitude toward shaping our theaters. Whereas in the past, a consistent, developing production technique gave rise to a single, if gradually developing theater shape for each period, in the last 60 years several theater shapes have been available for our use. Due partly, no doubt, to nineteenth-century historicism and scholarship, a revival of earlier stage forms sprang up to accompany the mainstream tradition of the proscenium stage. There began to be a multiple choice of theater shapes for plays in the twentieth century—a situation that was unknown in previous times. This movement clearly underscored the tremendous activity in theater arts —the thinking and lack of it—being done by all people involved.

Proscenium Theaters

From the turn of the twentieth century to the present day, the proscenium theater—a direct-line survival of the horseshoe opera house that originated in the Renaissance—has continued as the most generally accepted and widely built theater shape in this country. By definition, a proscenium theater is a shape in which the audience faces the performing area on one side only and sees the performing area through an architectural opening that often has an elaborated architectural frame—although that is not an essential element. The performing area is not always limited by that opening; it can project out a nominal distance into the auditorium in the form of what is called a fore-stage or apron. In essence, this is not an intimate theater shape, since the audience and the actors are each in separate, but connected, interior rooms (see Fig. 1).

At the turn of the century, many American proscenium theaters were outmoded and run down, despite the fact that the theater itself was prosperous. Unlike European theaters of the time, in the United States experiments were hampered by the lack of space, prohibitive

The Shape of Our Theatre, Clarkson N. Potter, Publisher, New York.

Fig. 2   The typical early-twentieth-century American theater had meager and often inadequate stage and supporting facilities.

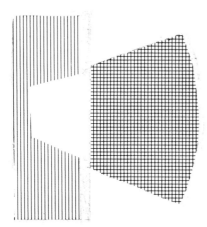

Fig. 1   The proscenium shape.

labor costs, and the overriding profit motive of the commerical American theater. Very few of these theaters were built with adequate machinery—stage elevators or turntables. Tenants were expected to bring everything with them, including turntables and all lighting equipment. Consequently, early-twentieth-century producing groups dedicated to the new stagecraft and contemporary American playwrights found their theaters woefully inadequate in shape and meager in equipment.

The absentee landlord's profits were not put back into the buildings or into new equipment, particularly stage lighting equipment. Actually, landlords were not absent physically. What was missing was any real love of the arts of the theater; instead they substituted a love of profits. If they were away from their theaters for any length of time, their general managers were on hand to keep a watchful eye on financial operations.

One New York City landlord-builder ordered a theater constructed with as little space as possible for the stage, the lobby, and between-legroom rows. In one instance the box office was omitted entirely. In spite of the owner's concern over his new theater's capacity to operate on a profitable level, the absence of any professional theater people on the owner's or the architect's staff was responsible for the amazing omission. Only in a last-minute inspection by the owner did this situation reveal itself, and a hastily designed and very cramped box office was quickly put in.

One theater builder in Philadelphia forgot to include dressing rooms and later had them constructed in a separate building across an alley, back of the theater. This little convenience meant that the artist, to get from his dressing room to the stage, had to go down to the basement, literally duck under sewage and steam pipes, and then go up into the other building. All this showed little understanding for the art of the theater—and no respect for its artists (see Fig. 2).

Because of this general situation, it was the

producer, not the theater owner, who was forced to keep up with the times and pay for proper facilities and equipment to install portable dressing rooms backstage. I note these almost unbelievable instances not in the spirit of gossip, but to stress the need for the constant presence of a professional theater expert —not on the outskirts of a projected theater design, but in a position of responsibility.

However, some producer-managers who were clients for their own theater buildings had a real love of theater itself, and an understanding of the latest European stagecraft developments. Among them were the Frohmans, David Belasco, and Florenz Ziegfeld; the latter retained architect-scene designer Joseph Urban to design his own theater. Winthrop Ames, a wealthy amateur of the arts, and a thoroughly professional producer, put up the Century Theater on New York's Central Park West. This 2,000-seat theater was notably ahead of its time, but was soon demolished because no contemporary repertory company could fill it.

If the absentee theater owners had been more knowing, if they had even more materialistic imagination, they would have made the kind of improvement that Billy Rose later made to his Ziegfeld Theatre (since demolished). There he equipped the backstage as well as the auditorium with the latest, most efficient lighting equipment and lighting control systems. Even if motivated solely by financial self-interest, this produced lucrative rentals from his tenants, and also provided presentational potential for the users.

Because the picture frame theaters were badly designed and therefore nearly unusable, they have recently been much downgraded. They were not bad simply because they were old or because they had proscenium forms, but because of their initial poor design. What most of us have forgotten is that the proscenium stage has been for centuries and will remain one of our most useful theater shapes.

A Revival of Ancient Shapes

As early as 1914, a group at Teachers College in New York used the simplest bleachers and seats on four sides of a medium-sized room to create an arena stage. An ancient theater shape, the arena stage was used in the great coliseums and arenas of Greece and Rome— but never specifically for drama. This new usage was the beginning of a revival.

The arena is a theater-in-the-round. The stage is surrounded on all sides by the audience. This arrangement puts the greatest number of the audience in intimate proximity with the performer. Both the audience and actor are in the same room. Others were gradually won

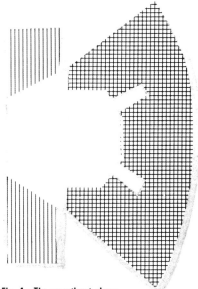

Fig. 4 The open-thrust shape.

to this cost-saving stage form which automatically minimizes the expensive, elaborate scenery usually associated with the proscenium tradition. (See Fig. 3.)

The period following World War I was exciting both in Europe and America. Inspired by a fresh approach to writing and the new European expressionistic stage designers and producers—Adolphe Appia in Switzerland, Max

Reinhardt and Leopold Jessner in Germany— our best young playwrights, Eugene O'Neill, Elmer Rice, and John Howard Lawson, helped launch and stimulate a new attitude toward stagecraft in the United States.

Expressionistic scene development in Germany and Russia was also reflected in America. Lee Simonson, Norman Bel Geddes, and Robert Edmond Jones produced designs of dramatic imagination for scenery and stage. However, since they were not in the mainstream of commercial thinking, few of these new stages were actually built.

Conventional Broadway was not the only vital place; community and college playhouses sprang up all over the country. But the time and cost of producing scenery led directors to by-pass that traditional problem and to investigate other techniques of stagecraft.

Early in this century, the ancient open-thrust stage, which had been used before the development of the proscenium theatre, was revived by several directors and producers. High costs of proscenium productions, which required elaborate and sometimes complicated scenery as well as high operating costs, led to this revival. Coupled with this was a desire to bring greater intimacy to the theater again. (See Fig. 4.)

The open-thrust stage had experienced an earlier revival in Europe. Davioud and Bourdais' unexecuted 1875 opera house design proposed a stage of extreme thrust, extending 50 ft into the auditorium with seating on three sides. And in the twenties, the Parisian actor-director Jacques Copeau conceived a truly open theater chamber of intimate proportions in his Theatre Vieux Colombier. His open stage had multiple

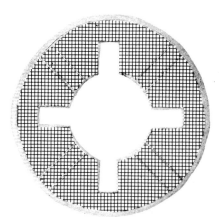

Fig. 3 The arena shape.

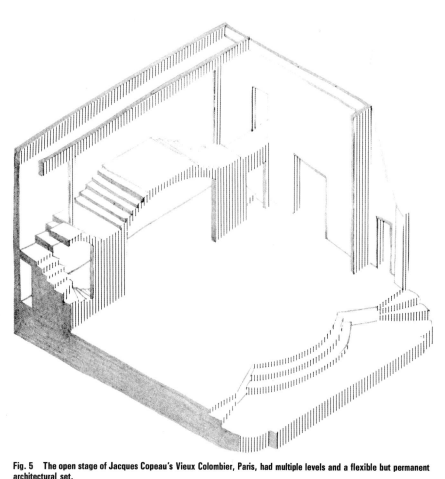

Fig. 5 The open stage of Jacques Copeau's Vieux Colombier, Paris, had multiple levels and a flexible but permanent architectural set.

levels, a number of entrances and exits, and a flexible architectural set, which was permanent and therefore cost-cutting. Neither of these European theater designs directly influenced American stage designs, however, until the educational theater did so much to spur the revival of the open-thrust stage. (See Fig. 5.)

American educators felt that the proper method of teaching Shakespeare was to permit students to act and to observe performances of his plays on the type of stage for which they were written. Educators often attempted makeshift open-thrust stages in whatever theaters were available to them. Scenery of the proscenium tradition was virtually eliminated in open-thrust stagecraft. And ultimately permanent open-thrust stage theaters were constructed by the producers of Shakespeare festivals for such regional and community groups as those at San Diego, California; Portland, Oregon; and later the Folger Shakespeare Library in Washington, D.C.

A thrust stage must not be confused with extended forestages in proscenium theatres, which utilize techniques of acting, direction, and designing that do not differ from standard proscenium stagecraft. A true thrust stage is a platform extending into an open auditorium in which the audience truly surrounds the stage on three sides. There may be exits in the back of the stage, as well as under the audience through vomitory tunnels. A thrust stage is an area deep and wide enough on which to play a full scene. When an apron or forestage is only an adjunct to a proscenium stage, it should not be considered a thrust stage (see Fig. 6).

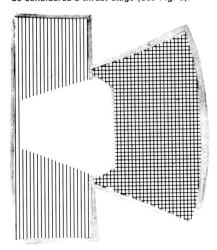

Fig. 6 The apron shape.

Thus, by the end of the twenties, theater professionals had a choice of not only the traditional proscenium stage but also the revived open-thrust and the arena stage forms.

Hiatus in Theater Building

The Depression of 1929 brought a virtual end to theater building in the United States until the end of World War II. No commercial theaters were built in major American cities between 1929 and 1950. The sole exception was Rockefeller Center's Center Theatre, built in 1936 and demolished in 1950. In the thirties, only a few colleges and universities had the funds to build modern theaters with stages designed for modern stagecraft and modern repertory requirements.

After World War II, America was ripe for a "cultural explosion." Mid-twentieth-century Americans were more affluent, better traveled,

and more cultivated. There was a new boom in theater construction. The quarter-century hiatus in building, however, had left its mark. A whole generation of architects and designers had been passed by, and the new generation was unschooled in the development of stage design. This ignorance led to rampant confusion in theater design.

Multiple Choice at Midcentury

When theatre building activity was resumed, the proscenium was the only widely known theater shape; therefore it continued to be popular. To make the proscenium more effective for mid-twentieth-century use, new developments were introduced by architects and designers. Electrically operated flying scenery, electronic control systems like those that preset positions for stage elevators, and predetermined lighting plans made the designing of theaters as complicated as it made the physical operation simpler. More and more sophisticated attention to good sight lines and seating furthered the continuation of the proscenium tradition.

Clients, on the other hand, sometimes continued a status-seeking reverence for seventeenth- and eighteenth-century European models that could not, in all ways, take advantage of these new techniques. A significant example of this reactionary view was the attitude of the Metropolitan Opera Board of Directors toward commissioning a new opera house in Lincoln Center. I am not criticizing the architects' designs or even their execution. The design was chosen with the conviction that the "Golden Horseshoe" of their old (1882) house was sacrosanct. A sentimental attachment to the past, as well as a lack of sympathy with contemporary design, may well have influenced the Board's decision. But I would suspect that the fear of alienating the few, but financially critical constituents was the dominant factor in their decision.

I am well aware that backstage the mechanical facilities of the new Metropolitan Opera House are up to date and undoubtedly do much to keep down the backbreaking operational overhead.

That they did not attempt to peer into the not-too-distant twenty-first century is understandable. The life-span of contemporary structures—particularly those associated with the performing arts, is shortening so quickly that new theater shapes may serve satisfactorily for only a generation or two. But in delib-

erately choosing a multitiered eighteenth-century horseshoe seating plan, the directors were guilty of a graver error than just inflicting substandard sight lines. That error was the failure to recognize that our twentieth-century visual art forms are not just passing fads, but are deeply dyed in our daily lives, in our means of communication and our social behavior. It seems strange that the impresarios of an art form as abstract as music should allow themselves to close their eyes to even the most universally acceptable visual arts of our midcentury.

Today, only after careful consideration, proper planning and design will the proscenium theater regain its usefulness. A modern proscenium theater need not be rigid in its dimensions—either in width or height. Side panels adjacent to the proscenium can have facilities for openings and side stages. Offstage rooms—right and left, up and down, traps and fly loft—all have to be provided. All these elements lend great flexibility to the Proscenium stage, but also make it more complex and more expensive to build. Basically, the proscenium is one of the most flexible theater shapes because any and all styles of production can be effectively realized. For the director, the problems of sight lines and other questions inherent in proscenium productions are fluid. In stagecraft, particularly lighting and settings, everything from the most stylistic and simple designs to the most elaborate and imaginative settings can take full advantage of this shape. Even a play such as *Hair*, which was first performed on an open stage, was successfully produced on Broadway in a proscenium theater. (See Fig. 7.)

The limitation of this theater shape is that it tends to be less intimate than either the Theater-in-the-round or the open-thrust stage. Yet it also must be remembered that many playwrights want the kind of separation between actor and audience that the proscenium shape gives. On the whole, if I were limited to a single stage form, I would choose a flexible proscenium with an ample forestage.

During the 1950s, labor and material costs again led clients as well as producers and designers to seek new methods of stagecraft. So it was that arena stages or theaters-in-the-round gained wider acceptance as a suitable setting for spoken drama. They were less expensive to build and required virtually no conventional scenery. A strong influence during the theater explosion, the arena stage in Washington, D.C., clearly demonstrates how sophisticated theater-in-the-round can be. De-

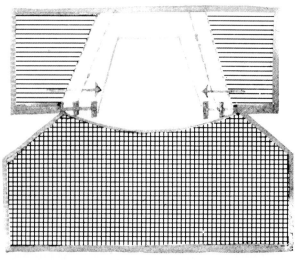

Fig. 7 In today's proscenium theater, the width of the proscenium opening can often be varied by adjustable panels.

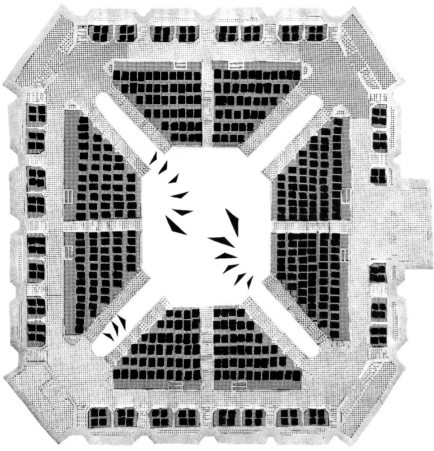

Fig. 8 The arena stage in Washington, D.C., designed by architect Harry Weese in 1961, is an exemplary modern arena-shaped theater.

signed for Zelda Fichandler in 1961 by Chicago architects Harry Weese & Associates, it is a far cry from the frequently seen, makeshift theaters-in-the-round. Well planned and successful, it is actually a theater-in-the-rectangle, but the principle of an audience surrounding the stage is identical. Here both the architect and the owner worked carefully to meet the needs of the company and to solve the technical problems and limitations of such a theater shape (see Fig. 8).

One built-in limitation of arena stages is applicable to all stages surrounded, or partly surrounded, by the audience: the director must constantly change his axis to prevent one group of viewers from being presented with poorer images than other sections of the audience. Actors, as well as the director, must use entirely different attacks on performance and movement. Lighting is also more difficult in arena staging because of the mandatory economy; however, when handled by an artist, this flexible medium can stress the nonillusionistic approach to a design.

In addition, the ability to vary settings is a limitation, both because architectural forms are impractical, and because elevations on the stage have to be limited in scale. In choosing a repertory for an arena stage company, certain plays—such as the classical plays of Sophocles, Euripides, Shakespeare, Molière, and Sheridan—succeed while, on the other hand, some plays written for the proscenium stage must be omitted.

One of the primary advantages of an arena theater is intimacy. Even with 1,000 seats, the most distant member of the audience need not

be much more than 32 ft from the nearest part of the stage. Although in more sophisticated theaters-in-the-round, it is possible to use traps and to fly elements overhead from a modified grid above the center of the stage, scenic investiture is ordinarily reduced to only the most expressive and economical forms of lighting and projection, costumes, props, and simple portable scenic elements that do not mask the actor from any part of the surrounding audience. On the whole, I think the advantages far outweigh the disadvantages of arena theaters. The fact that presentation style stresses imagination and simplicity is surely a strong argument.

Throughout the fifties and sixties a major innovative force in theater architecture has been Irish theater director Sir Tyrone Guthrie. In the fifties, after much acclaimed experimentation in England and Scotland, Guthrie was invited by the bright, ambitious young community leaders of Stratford, Ontario, to establish a theater. Intended primarily for the classics, the theater was first set up inside a tent, and later rebuilt under a permanent architectural structure (see Fig. 9).

Tyrone Guthrie's concept for Stratford, which was worked out with theater designer Tanya Moisewitsch, was appropriately a classical one. The auditorium is based on a steeply banked, semicircular, Greco-Roman, three-sided seating arrangement; it surrounds an open-thrust stage that has many basic elements of the Elizabethan stage. Besides entrances from the rear wall, Guthrie also used vomitories, which are entrances and exits to the stage from below the audience seating areas.

Little if any background scenery is used. Stress is on costumes, props, and lighting, which the director/designer team use in the most imaginative and simplest way to create scenic atmosphere. Light is used almost entirely as illumination, with very little sophistication in movement, color, or image projection. On the other hand, their sophisticated use of costumes and properties has been extremely important in creating a sense of mood and character. The impact of the theater was international. It was intimate and vital, and extremely suitable for the classics.

A few years later, after the Ontario theater had been built, Guthrie himself initiated, with Oliver Rea, a similar venture in Minneapolis, Minnesota. There, he planned with architect Ralph Rapson a variation on the Stratford, Ontario, theater. Corrections were made, for example, in the sight lines at extreme left and right. He included facilities for hanging scenery behind the thrust. It is a token proscenium behind the thrust stage. This combination of the two theater forms was a major innovation. And thoughtful architects and designers throughout the country and abroad studied it with great interest.

An open-thrust stage can be extremely simple, like Tyrone Guthrie's Stratford, Ontario, theater. It can then be elaborated by planning an adaptable grid for lights, props, and scenic elements to be hung directly over the thrust. Yet all this fits into the basically simple staging that is germane to the shape.

The advantages of thrust are clear and strong, but so are its disadvantages. Of the advantages, the greatest is perhaps the heightened sense of involvement gained by both the audience and the actor. Intimacy naturally is enhanced; the movement and pace of the play are swift; and the technique is fluid and cinematographic. The open-thrust stage does, however, diminish the significance of the "illusionistic" style of stage design. (Depending on one's point of view, admittedly, this may be counted either as one of its advantages or as one of its limitations. For me, illusion is one of the lesser achievements of the contemporary theater.) The open stage requires a totally different approach. The cast cannot be directed to act only toward the front, because the audience is on the sides as well. And, in a sense, they must act dimensionally within a scenic scheme, rather than in front of it. Costumes also become more important as do the few but choice properties with which the actors work. And finally, because background pictures are not being created, lighting must become a living element through which players move.

Generally, the open-thrust stage is more flexible than the arena. With the open-thrust stage, the director does not have to worry so much about the actor's back being to the audience. But because the open-thrust is more complicated to design, it may turn out to be more expensive to build than the arena or proscenium theatre.

Perhaps the most outstanding disadvantage is that the more realistic a play is, the less effective it may be for the open-thrust stage. Shakespearean plays and other earlier classics are easily adaptable since in their writing and production they were presented on open Elizabethan stages with a minimum of scenic effects. Much of nineteenth-century drama is considered ill-suited for the open-thrust stage; but this also presents an opportunity for an imaginative director to approach these plays with a radically fresh style.

Of the multiple choices in theater shapes at midcentury, then, three were prominent—proscenium, arena, and open-thrust; but more involved, complex choices of theater shapes were

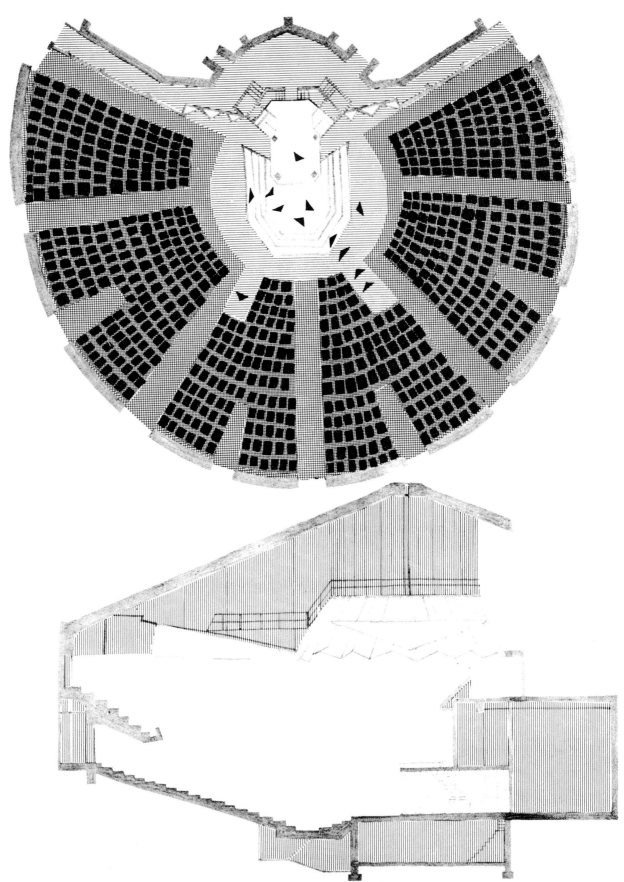

Fig. 9   The Stratford, Ontario, Shakespeare Festival Theatre has been an influential interpretation of the open-thrust stage. It combines an Elizabethan stage with a Greco-Roman audience seating plan.

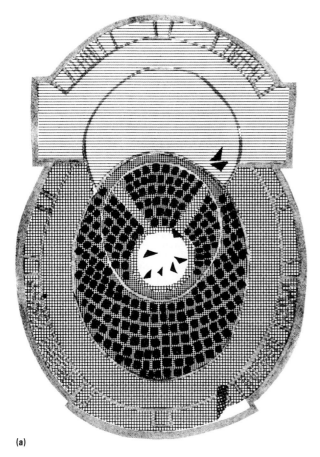

(a)

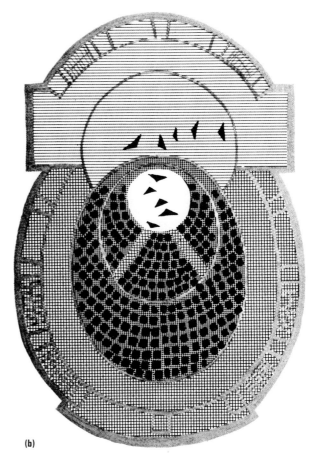

(b)

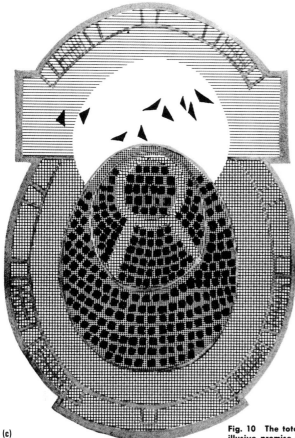

(c)

yet to confuse the decision-making and design processes of architects and clients.

MULTICHOICE IN A SINGLE THEATER

Besides the choice among three traditional, historical theater shapes, which are available to theater planners and designers today, a new combination of multiples has appeared. Now, we can attempt to have several, or all three of these stage forms in a single building —even in the same auditorium. This unique possibility has led to the extreme complication of present-day theater design and to the utter confusion of present-day theater designers.

The educator's desire to perform Shakespearean plays in the original setting has been extended to a desire also to perform eighteenth- and nineteenth-century plays in the theaters for which they were originally produced. Not content with an open-thrust stage theater for plays written for that basic shape, from the days of classical Greece to the Middle Ages, producers also want a proscenium theater, in which to present Renaissance and later plays. This desire has now spread from the educators to the producers of community and regional theater as well.

Where sufficient funds are available, the building of two theaters—one proscenium and one open—splendidly accommodates this desire. (It must be remembered that in no age but our own were plays written expressly for arena theaters.) However, sufficient funds do not always seem available for such a splendid solution. As a compromise, and it must immediately be recognized as that, architects,

Fig. 10 The total theater scheme, designed by Walter Gropius in 1929, is a chimera holding forth the illusive promise of a multiform stage. It could be changed from (a) the proscenium shape to (b) the open-thrust shape, and (c) the arena shape.

stage engineers, and designers have attempted to build, within a single theater, multiform stages, which can be changed from one shape to another (Fig. 10).

The Multiform Stage

Inspired by the total theater scheme of the late architect Walter Gropius, which was designed in 1929, but never executed, engineers have attempted tour-de-force theaters that could be altered from proscenium stage arrangements to open-thrust stage arrangements—and even to the arena shape. Engineering and mechanical ingenuity, coupled with accurate electric controls, have made these chimeras appear attainable. It is my feeling, however, that this concept has never been successfully realized.

Multiform stages were developed for clients who felt they could afford to build only one theater, but were unable to commit themselves to a single stage form. The mechanical multiform stage was also intended to make flexible space operational for theaters of large size, and to save manpower and time in rearranging stage form and audience seating plans.

In Fig. 11 I have illustrated one theater interior that can be used for two types of stage productions by rearranging some of the seating and changing the proscenium proportions. The first is a true proscenium technique. Then, by using an elevator to bring up a thrust stage and readjust the seating elements, this same theater can be used for a second technique—the open-thrust stage.

At the Loeb Drama Center at Harvard University, mechanical means have been provided to create three entirely different relations between acting area and audience seating. De-

signed by architect Hugh Stubbins and theater engineer George Izenour, the Loeb Theatre interior itself does not essentially change—only the mobile units within its walls and under its ceilings. The avowed purpose of this highly selective and mechanical complex was to satisfy the needs of student directors, actors, and authors to create any and all stage shapes at will (see Fig. 12).

For all multiform stages, there is a price paid —not only in dollars, but also in sacrifice of function. No multiform stage can be either a perfect thrust or a perfect proscenium stage. Yes, they work. But the additional expense, both in design and construction and ultimately in operational costs, is not worth the loss of unified purpose that characterizes a theater with a single stage shape. Such experiments fail basically for the very reason that in none of their two or three or five alternate adjustments has one a feeling of a well-designed, simple, clean, direct, single-form theater. In order to make a collective multiform that works at all, each single arrangement must be a compromise.

It has been my experience that impressive and technically practical as some of the experiments may be, in none of their various chameleon-like changes are they as effective in either arrangements or elements as the stages designed for a specific purpose.

Even a theater that can be changed to create only two of the basic stage shapes is a compromise. But such dual-form or "hybrid" theaters appeal to clients who desire some of the advantages of the thrust stage and, with a minimum of changeover, the use of the same auditorium as a proscenium stage. And it must be admitted that a stage that can be changed from

arena shape to open-thrust shape may not be so serious a compromise. The real difficulty is in designing a theater that will accommodate both the axial vision demanded by the proscenium stage and the radial vision that is basic to the open-thrust stage.

I have been involved (although after instinctive personal protest) in designing a number of dual-form theaters. An honest architect or designer must hold a Monday-morning quarterback session with himself, if not in public, upon the completion of an important job. I feel that a public session here will provide a valuable share of my experience.

It was tragic that one of the great architects with a true and sensitive understanding of theater, the late Eero Saarinen, should have lived to complete only the Beaumont Theater of Lincoln Center. It was a privilege to be codesigner with him on the stage and auditorium. When Eero and I were given the responsibility for designing the two theaters for the Lincoln Center Repertory Company, we met privately for long, honest studies. I found, to my pleasure, that our basic concepts were in agreement. First, neither of us believed in anything but single-form stages; we both were completely opposed to a multiform stage. If our original proposition had been accepted, we would have had the upstairs theater slightly smaller and the downstairs theaters slightly larger. One of them would have been pure thrust stage and the other pure proscenium. The question of which form would be which size would have been left to the building committee. That is, if the committee voted that the larger theater should have a proscenium stage, we wanted that theater to be a pure proscenium theater, in the best sense, and the other to be a pure open-thrust stage—and vice versa. (See Fig. 13.)

We were overruled. In fact, some members of the committee even talked about a basic multiuse scheme for the Beaumont. We turned that down completely, but we realized that we would have to accept the compromise of a dualform design. Our original proposition would have been the wiser decision, and ultimately far cheaper in both initial costs and in subsequent operating costs.

However, Lincoln Center gave us months of exploratory time and supported the costs of experimental designs and models which were shown to the building committee of the Repertory Company and to a group of theater critics. A small, but very volatile minority of them supported the idea that the open-thrust stage should be the dominant form. But at the end of the investigation, the consensus was that we should design the larger theater so that it could be used as a proscenium theater and as an open-thrust stage; and that we, as designers, should find some practical means of making the changeover relatively simple.

We pointed out that to meet the production schedule of a repertory company for a two-hour changeover between matinee and evening, it would be imperative to install expensive automatic mechanical equipment. For example, if a production using open-thrust was completed at 5 or 5:30 and the evening schedule called for proscenium staging, an enormous amount of work would be required not only in changing the scenery and lighting, but in changing the seating plan and the open-thrust stage itself. What we designed at the Beaumont Theater for this changeover can be effected in 2 hours.

It is achieved by locating the front group of seats on a large lift that descends to the subbasement where a turntable rotates them, substituting an open-thrust stage, which is then raised into position. Proscenium panels at the Beaumont can be opened to make a maximum

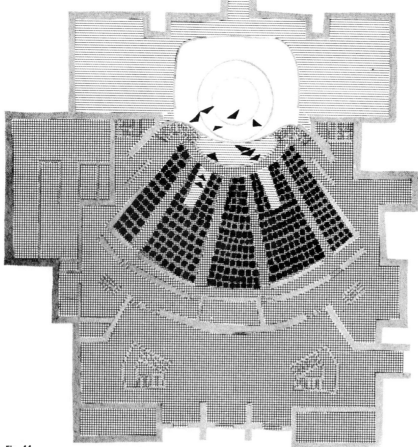

Fig. 11

(a)

(b)

proscenium opening that is 50 ft across. When the thrust is in use, the panels are completely closed; then actors can enter from right and left downstage of the proscenium panels and from two vomitory entrances under the front orchestra seats.

It must be stated categorically that multiform stages are designed for dramatic productions of plays only. In the case of the Beaumont, the acoustical characteristics are specifically for the spoken word. The theater cannot be used successfully for opera or musical recitals.

Multiuse Auditoriums

An approach to theater shapes born of the mid-twentieth-century electronic era, and perhaps twentieth-century indecision, is the multi-use auditorium. It is an attempt to satisfy the client who wants an auditorium so adaptable in relationships that any and all the performing arts can be accommodated. Not only do performing groups want a theater to house plays, but they also hope to use their new auditoriums for opera and musical productions, concerts, and recitals. But music reverberation time demands a greater spatial volume than that for the spoken word. What results is an attempt to build one hall that can be suited to both music and drama by altering the very volume of the auditorium. This implies large-scale physical changes being made to ceiling elements and even to the side walls of the auditorium. In some instances, an entire balcony can be shut off for the purpose of changing acoustical characteristics and audience capacity.

Colleges and universities have led the race in building such facilities. High schools have built structures that attempt to accommodate the basketball court, as well as the performance of Ibsen and the choral society recital. Combinations such as the gymnatorium and the cafetorium have been tried as a means of saving

(c)

Fig. 12 The Loeb Drama Center at Harvard University, designed by architect Hugh Stubbins and theater engineer George Izenour in 1960, is a small-scale realization of the multiform stage. Electrically operated mobile seating units and stage sections can be rearranged to create (a) a basic proscenium shape, (b) a basic open-thrust shape, and (c) a modified arena or center stage shape.

space and construction funds. Such schemes appealed equally to builders, architects, and engineers, as well as clients. The multi-use theater thus spread to fantastic degrees. And it has become a byword of confusion in the 1960s. Not only the idea but the definition of the words "multi-use" or "multipurpose" have become confused, even by theater experts.

It is understandable that members of boards of trustees or college regents cried out for a single design to meet all the needs of all the performing arts. Even in affluent times, it is not easy for a large university or regional theater group to raise enough money to build more than one good theater. And there will inevitably be an avid army of architects, engineers, and acoustical specialists willing to take on that challenging desire of clients to accommodate all the performing arts in a single auditorium. Even when the architects or consultants are men of integrity and theater experience, they may find difficulty in persuading building committees that however well an auditorium may suit the combined needs of the choral society and the music school opera, it cannot possibly be used for intimate drama as well.

This is when the dangerous plea is made to bring in the engineering magic that we see in so many regional and college theaters today, and in such community auditoriums as the Jesse Jones Hall in Houston.

During the 1960s, engineering firms devised astounding mechanical systems that changed the very shape of an auditorium, pitched the floor, tipping the ceiling and cutting off the balconies, pivoted the walls, and rolled banks of seating across the floor and stage. In too many of these cases, these electronic tails wagged the theatrical dogs.

Not all engineering developments were futile, however. Certainly in terms of stagecraft, electronic controls for rigging and lighting systems, which were often developed for such auditoriums, have been astonishing in their programs of complicated presentational problems, but these are mechanical contributions to the backstage area and are not to be confused with the mechanical manipulation of the architectural front-of-the-house arrangements.

It is certainly human on the part of an owner or manager to feel that a single auditorium with adjustable elements serves in place of what might otherwise be a complex of two or three separate theaters. But every medium in the dramatic and musical arts cries for a specific scale for the performing area and the audience. With the spoken word in drama, the sense of intimacy is essential both visually and aurally. Add music and singing from a musical comedy, and the scale of the auditorium can increase appreciably.

An auditorium that is good for the actor's voice is technically ineffectual for the singing voice and for musical instruments. The reverse is equally true. On an everyday level, we know that when we want to say something intimate to a friend, we do not shout it across a courtyard. We approach closely, eye to eye, and speak quietly in close contact, as in intimate drama. If we want to sing an aria to that same friend, we would back away or choose a room of sufficient size. The same principle holds in choosing a theater shape.

Specifically, the distance between the last viewer and the performer can increase because when acting is augmented by broader techniques, the audience can be much farther away from the performer and still enjoy an acceptable contact. From operetta to grand opera, an even greater change in scale is acceptable. In fact, the patron who enjoys second-row-center seats at a drama would find grand opera completely unacceptable at

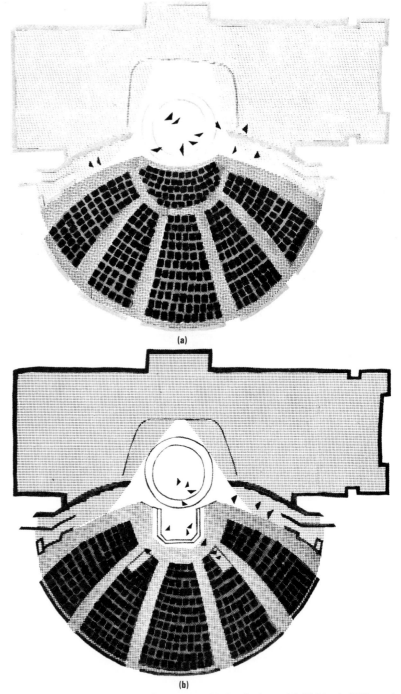

(a)

(b)

Fig. 13 The Beaumont Theater at Lincoln Center, designed by Eero Saarinen and Jo Mielziner in 1960, can change its shape from (a) an open-thrust stage to (b) a proscenium stage with a modified apron.

this close range. To many followers of opera, of course, the aural appreciation is almost complete without the visual.

The scale that I have been referring to is not only the distance between the audience and the forestage but also the width of the playing stage or proscenium opening. As an example, a good width for a legitimate play is not much more than 35 ft; whereas opera stages will open 60 to 80 ft in width.

It is self-evident that the solution to housing all these art forms in one building must be a magic one, if technically successful. Furthermore, this technical magic must be a dominant part of the basic design. The multi-use auditorium is one of the most serious mistakes in the history of theater design. The notion that

any single design can be used for all purposes is nonsense.

Uncommitted Theater Spaces

Still another theater design approach that developed during this period of "theater explosion" is one for which there is no historical precedent in the tradition of our indoor theaters. It is based on the idea that neither of the basic elements that make up a theater—audience or stage—should be predetermined so far as their location or configuration within the theater are concerned.

In effect, this concept says that within the space provided by the architect, an undetermined stage area and seating area may be set

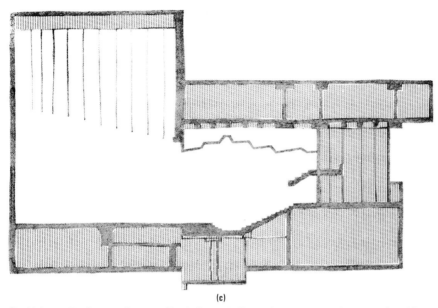

(c)

Fig. 13 (cont.) The Beaumont Theater at Lincoln Center. (c) The section shows a very deep stage planned for a repertory schedule. The deep stage, combined with large stage wagons, and a "saturation lighting" system as well as the multiform stage mechanism make it possible to change stage shapes and scenery from production to production in a matter of hours with minimum labor.

at will in a wide variety of relationships, arrangements, and relocations. This final theater concept goes one step further than the mechanized theaters. It rejects any and all means for creating a specific playing area or an audience area. Its proponents say, "Give me a cocoon that shuts out the outer world, and in it we will create our concepts without the aid of predetermined form." They feel that it frees future theater users from any "set interior arrangement." They also proffer what they feel is the advantage of a simultaneous and multiple approach to dramatic problems. Theirs is the "uncommitted theater space."

Back in the 1890s, the great scenic artist Adolphe Appia said, "Let us abandon theaters to their dying past, and let us erect simple buildings instead, merely to cover the space where we work—no stage, no amphitheatre, only a bare and empty room." This bold pronunciamento, like many manifestos, bears some analysis. Any serious student of the theater who admires Adolphe Appia's magnificently conceived stage settings knows, however, that to achieve the subtlety of his mood lighting and the perfectly proportioned grandeur of his plastic forms, the most complex and technically sophisticated equipment must be available. Much of this equipment must be located not only backstage but in the auditorium itself and subtly related to the stage area. In other words, Appia's "bare empty room," once equipped to meet the high standards of his production concepts, would lose all semblance of nudity and emptiness and might become a well-conceived and carefully predetermined theater.

The limitations of mechanized multiform schemes are even greater in these uncommitted theater spaces. On the economic side, the budget for such an indeterminate theater must be greatly increased for purely mechanical equipment, if for no other. In order to justify the alleged freedom, a maximum amount of mechanical support must be available in every corner of the uncommitted area. Naturally egresses and exits, ventilating and heating equipment, supporting technical elements and power outlets for lighting must be predetermined and fixed. And the operating costs for moving this equipment are major restrictions on the alleged freedom.

Any rational study of the intricate problems relating to sight lines, acoustics, or lighting must also lead one to the conclusion that to keep these relationships in an undetermined plan can mean only that the ultimate quality of any single interior relationship is bound to be below par.

The only logical justification for this nonmechanical, multiform approach is for a university that offers a course in theater architecture. As a really effective working laboratory for the study of acting, direction, and stage design, it is one to be researched and explored.

Uncommitted Spaces for Involvement?

Another current trend in stagecraft is the desire for even further involvement of the actor and audience. I refer to a greater psychological and physical contact between audience and actor, and to a greater use of sensory as well as visual involvement throughout the theater. It has been suggested that the uncommitted theater space fosters this involvement.

Ever since the 1900s, nonobjective and totally abstract experiments in the arts have been expressed beyond the painter's and sculptor's studio. Changes in all communication arts—written and visual—have influenced dramatists in a revolutionary way. Poetry, prose, and journalism have all been affected by the tempo of the radio, recorded music, and their extension into cinematography and television. Poets have rejected rhyme, meter, and syntax. Prose writers have made equally insurrectionary demands on their medium. In the first 50 years of this century the theater reflected very little of this movement. In recent years, avant-garde writers and directors have plunged into radical experiments in what they felt was a new theater-oriented field that furthers audience involvement.

When I refer to total involvement, I do not mean what is currently referred to as a "Happening." The talk about Happenings is based on a valuable instinct—the genuine desire for greater contact, for greater participation of both audience and actor, but it is practiced and preached in an undisciplined and, I think, uncreative way. It is undisciplined because it makes a point of the fact that there is ostensibly no premeditated play, no rehearsal, no restrictive texts.

Although the charade, the conversation, the story, and the extemporaneous narrative have

value, they are not basically theater. Any theater form—like all serious art forms—is born of deliberation, self-discipline, and creativity. To rely on improvisation, no matter how talented the actor, or how receptive the audience, is to misunderstand freedom.

Freedom in art is not license. The artist can be free only if he masters and accepts the limitation of his medium. I have always believed that authors and directors must be given the greatest freedom in staging. In the auditorium and on the stage, the greatest range of lighting, scenic equipment, and spatial freedom must be available. If a new play needs one hundred different visual indications of mood and background, it must be provided.

I have worked with directors and authors who desperately wanted to be free of any set format. But gradually, to have effects, lights, and scenic elements meet the needs of an actor at a precise moment, we started to reintroduce a theatrical limitation—dramatic form.

Similarly, we must accept and work with the physical limitations of our stages. If I have a stage that is only 10 ft deep, and I want to give the impression of unlimited space, I accept that 10 ft and do something with it. Suggestions and implications, whether they are visual, oral, or aural, are means of working with one's limitations. It might be the use of the magic of poetry or of music's abstract sounds. The power of the creative artist is infinite, but only when he masters the technique in which he creates. Yet all these production aids, these minute details, must be made practical and must be carefully timed and rehearsed. All the environmental background, born in excitement and high imagination, must be transposed into controlled and disciplined technique.

I feel I must state that I am not, on principle, anti-Happening. It must be said on behalf of Happenings that they do accentuate some of the better trends fostered by all contemporary dramatists and stage directors. They have one outstanding characteristic in common with other modern theater movements—the desire to accentuate actor-spectator relationships.

The advocates of Happenings question the accepted concepts of actor-audience spatial relationships. Michael Kirby states in the *Tulane Drama Review* (Vol. 10, No. 2, p. 40, Winter, 1965):

> Performance and audience are both necessary to have theatre. But it might be thought that it is this very separation of spectator and work which is responsible for an "artificiality" of the form, and many Happenings and related pieces have attempted to "break down" the barrier between presentation and spectator and to make the passive viewer a more active participator. At any rate, works have recently been conceived which, since they are to be performed without an audience—a totally original and unprecedented development in the art—might be called "activities."

It would be pointless at this early stage of the avant-garde experiments in Happenings even to suggest what formalized theater shape they might take, or if they will have any influence at all on theater shapes. Their most vocal leaders seem to disagree about the best environment in which this new and exotic hybrid will flourish.

At this writing, this theater of protest does find what seems to be adequate housing in a large variety of structures—both in and out of the theater. So varied are they, that this particular form of dramatic expression does not easily fit into this discussion of theater shapes. If and when it matures into a new art form, then it may develop a stage and auditorium especially designed for its own needs. I doubt that it will be a totally uncommitted theater space.

By HAROLD BURRIS-MEYER and F. G. COLE

SIGHT LINES

If the patron is to see satisfactorily, plan and section must conform to a number of limitations which are set forth in the following list. To design an auditorium is to determine a seating area within these limitations and to establish position (not shape) of walls and shape of floors therefrom.

1. The horizontal angle of polychromatic vision (no eye movement) is approximately $40°$.

2. The horizontal angle to the center line at which objects onstage, upstage of the curtain line, cease to bear the intended relationship to other objects onstage and to the background is approximately $60°$.

3. The horizontal angle to a flat projection sheet at which distortion on the screen becomes substantially intolerable is $60°$ measured to the far side of the projected image. Curvature introduced into the screen may render the distortion less from the extreme seats on the opposite side of the center line of the house but will increase distortion from the seats on the same side of the center line (see Fig. 14).

4. Judged by the audience's ability to recognize shapes, and confirmed by free audience choice of seats, the following is the order of desirability of locations:
   a. front center (except when the screen is close to the front row)
   b. middle center
   c. middle side
   d. front side
   e. rear center
   f. rear side

5. Audiences will not choose locations beyond a line approximately $100°$ to the curtain at the side of the proscenium.

6. The vertical angle beyond which ability to recognize standard shapes falls off very rapidly is approximately $30°$ (see Figs. 15 and 16).

7. The recommended maximum angle of motion picture projection to the horizontal is $12°$.

PLAN

If the foregoing limitations are applied in the horizontal plane for any given proscenium opening, they will limit an area of maximum value as seating space which is approximately elliptical. It is interesting to note that this shape for an auditorium plan was pioneered by the late Joseph Urban who had little of the present data to work with and may safely be assumed to have chosen the shape largely on esthetic grounds. A fan shape provides additional seating space at minimum sacrifice of sight lines, but nobody wants the seats in the extreme rear corners.

Seating

Occupants of all seats are visually related to the performance when the seats are oriented toward the stage. This necessitates curving the rows of seats. The center of curvature is lo-

Theatres and Auditoriums, 2d ed., copyright © 1964 by Litton Educational Publishing, Inc., by permission of Van Nostrand Reinhold Company.

cated on the center line of the auditorium approximately the depth of the house behind the proscenium. Budgetary limitations may dictate that seats be in straight rows to simplify construction; these rows can at least be related to the center of attention on stage by being placed on chords of the optimum row curvature.

Stagger

To provide best visibility from any seat, no patron should sit exactly in front of any other

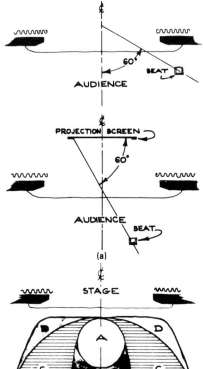

(a)

patron unless more than one row distant. This requirement makes it necessary to stagger seats. Staggering is accomplished by the non-uniform placement of seats of varying widths in succeeding rows. Unless the walls of the theatre are parallel (which is acoustically hazardous), it is extremely unlikely that more than a very few rows can be made up of seats of uniform width. The lack of uniformity thereby introduced provides the means by which staggering can be accomplished. Seats are made with uniform standards and interchangeable backs and seats so that a wide variation of seat width is possible; a variation from seat to seat of an inch or two, cumulative enough to accomplish satisfactory stagger and make rows even, is not noticed by the patron.

Various seating companies have their own schemes and formulas for seat stagger, some of them patented. The client may ask a seating company for a seating plan and should examine it critically for (1) insufficient stagger in occasional areas of the house and (2) the introduction of seats narrower than the acceptable minimum.

Aisles

Aisles are of questionable desirability except in the largest houses. They must, however, be employed in many localities because of building laws which make no provision for continuous-row or so-called continental seating in which all rows are widely spaced and serve as transverse aisles. Many a bad sight line has resulted from putting the maximum legal number of seats, usually 14, into each row in every section. Obviously, for purposes of seeing, radial aisles are best, with curved aisles only slightly less efficient. Aisles perpendicular to the curtain line often have the accidental result of making side section seats undesirable because people using the aisles interrupt the view toward the stage. The box office would

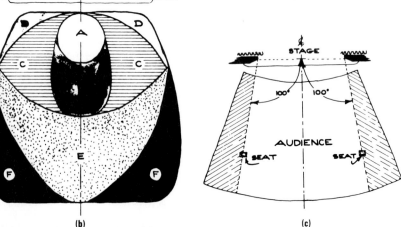

(b)   (c)

Fig. 14   (a) The horizontal angle to the center line at which objects onstage, upstage of the curtain line, cease to bear the intended relationship to other objects onstage and to the background is approximately $60°$. The horizontal angle to the projection screen at which distortion on the screen becomes substantially intolerable is $60°$. (b) Based on the ability to recognize shapes and confirmed by sequential seat selection of unreserved seats, the order of desirability of locations is: A, front center, except when the picture screen is close to the front row; B, middle center; C, middle side; D, front side; E, rear center; F, rear side. (c) Audiences will not choose locations beyond a line approximately $100°$ to the curtain at the proscenium. The shaded areas contain undesirable seats.

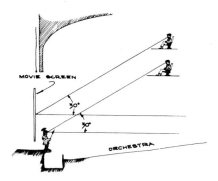

Fig. 15 The vertical angle above which ability to recognize familiar shapes falls off very rapidly is 30°.

like a theatre with all seats in the center section. A center aisle wastes the most desirable seating area in the theater and inevitably causes the objectionable condition of seats near the aisle being directly in front of each other. (See Fig. 17.)

Depth of House

There are many formulas used to determine the depth of the house, or more accurately, to determine the relationship between depth of house, width of house, and width of screen or proscenium. They vary considerably and are all empirically derived on the basis of existing theaters, with too little reference to whether such theaters are good or not. Typical are the following: Optimum depth equals 4 times screen width. Maximum depth equals 6 times screen width. Depth equals 1.25 to 2.35 times

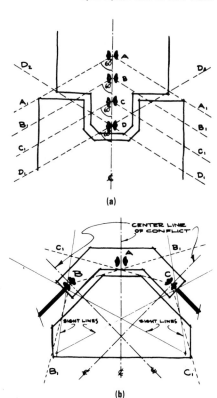

Fig. 16 (a) A scene of direct conflict loses its visual significance to spectators outside the angles D_1-D-D_1, etc. One performer covers the other for spectators inside the angles D_1-D-D_2. (b) Scenes of direct conflict staged anywhere between B and C on an extended stage retain visual significance for all spectators between lines BB_1 and CC_1.

house width when house width is 2.5 to 3.5 times screen width. Practically, there are only two significant considerations in planning the depth of the house:

1. Visual acuity. Normal human vision can perceive a minimum dimension or separation equal to 1 minute of visual arc. Translated into space measurement this means that at 10 ft a normal eye can perceive a dimension of 0.035 in., at 50 ft, 0.175 in., and at 100 ft, 0.35 in. Details of actors' make-up and facial expression are not plainly recognizable at distances of more than 50 ft from the stage.

2. Capacity. The larger the house, the lower can be the price per seat or the greater the gross. If the box office is not to be considered, capacity may be limited by optimum seeing requirements, and the last rows kept within 50 ft of the stage. As various requirements

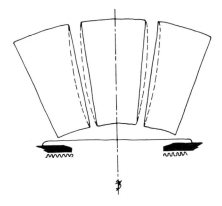

Fig. 17 Straight radial aisles are better than aisles which curve or bend.

operate to increase capacity, the distance of the rear seats from the stage must be increased and seeing conditions impaired in proportion. The theater operator may compensate the occupants of these seats by charging less for them. For shows involving live human actors, 75 ft is generally accepted on grounds of visibility as maximum house depth. (See Fig. 18.)

In theatrical entertainment which has as its chief visual component human actors (live shows), the degree to which these performers must be seen to satisfy the audience and put the show across varies.

A. Details of facial expression and small gesture are important in legitimate drama, vaudeville and burlesque, intimate revue and cabaret.

B. Broad gesture by single individuals is important in grand opera presentation, musical comedy, and the dance.

C. Gesture by individuals is unimportant and movement of individuals from place to place is the smallest significant movement in pageant.

It follows then that theaters planned for the types of entertainment listed under A must be limited in depth of auditorium so that visibility from the remotest seat still allows the occupant to perceive facial expressions (not over 75 ft).

Theaters planned for the types listed under B may have greater distance from the stage to the remotest seat, but this distance is set at a maximum beyond which the individual actor is diminished to insignificance (approximately 125 ft).

Spectators in the last rows at the Radio City Music Hall in New York, looking through a distance ranging from 160 to over 200 ft, depending on the location of the performers onstage, see a ballet reduced to the size of midgets, and an individual performer, even with the dramatic enhancement of a follow spot, is a very insignificant figure indeed.

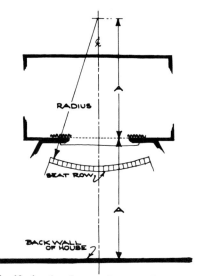

Fig. 18 Location of center of curvature for rows of seats.

Summary

Given the proscenium opening and capacity, laying out the orchestra and balcony or balconies in plan becomes a simple and straightforward process. Sight lines determine proscenium splay and house width. Visibility limits and capacity determine depth. Minimum distance from stage or screen to first row is determined in the section.

As can be realized from the foregoing requirements for seeing, any scheme which attempts to provide flexible audience-performance relationships sacrifices something, usually in every form attempted. The multiform theater cannot be justified except as a laboratory, where certain limitations are an acceptable price for flexibility and the box office does not need to support the enterprise.

SECTION

The vertical angle of 30° at the spectator's position establishes the distance from the closest seat to the screen or to the highest significant object on the stage. The lowest seat in the orchestra must be located where the patron can just see the stage floor (except in the case of theaters built for motion pictures only). The highest seat in the balcony must be on a line which is not more than 30° to the horizontal at the front curtain at the stage floor if it is not to be above the limit of reasonable distortion. The standing patron at the back of the orchestra must be able to see the top of the screen, which is usually as high as any significant portion of a stage setting. Each spectator must see the whole stage or screen over the heads of those in front of him. Within these limits the floor slope of orchestra and balcony can be laid out: the first step in determining auditorium section. (See Fig. 19.)

Several methods have been offered heretofore for developing the floor slope. Doubtless others will be offered in the future. The authors present the following method as one which assures unobstructed vision from all seats. It may be noted that this system produces a floor slope considerably steeper than that in many existing theaters. It also produces better seeing conditions.

To determine floor slope, establish eye position of spectator in first row on center line by approximately 30° vertical angle above. For live shows, stage floor will be approximately 2

THEATERS
Sight Lines

in. below this level. For theaters designed solely for motion pictures, the location of the stage floor is not critical; the position of the bottom of the screen is. (See Fig. 20.)

A point 3 ft 8 in. below, and 18 in. in front of the eye position will be the floor level for the front row. (1) Draw a sight line from the eye position to downstage edge of stage, and extend it back of the eye position for the front row, step off horizontal seat spacing (back to back), and draw vertical lines at the points thus established. (2) Establish a point 5 in. above the intersection of the extended sight line and the next vertical line. (3) This is the eye position for the second row and the floor level at the front edge of the second row seat is 3 ft 8 in. below and 18 in. in front of the eye position. Repeat steps (1), (2), and (3) to the back of the house and draw in the floor slope. Where the slope exceeds 1½ in. per foot, platforms are required under the seats, and steps in the aisles. A cross aisle which divides the orchestra into front and back sections entails the elevation of the first row of seats behind it to make up for horizontal width of the aisle.

The standing spectator's eye level behind the rear row of seats is assumed to be 5 ft 6 in. above the floor level of the last row. The sight line from this position to the top of the screen or highest probable curtain trim establishes the minimum height for ceiling under balcony. (See Fig. 21.)

Raising the stage will make it possible to reduce the floor slope but at the penalty of producing upward sight lines in the first two or three rows which are uncomfortable and unnatural for viewing stage setting and action. If the stage floor is above the elevation of the first row eye position, the upstage floor out of sight by perhaps as much as 6 in. from the first row is generally preferable to having an excessive floor slope, especially if more than one balcony is used.

When planning for motion pictures only, the lower sight line from the first row will come to the bottom of the projected picture, approximately 24 in. above the stage floor, or still higher if a reverse floor slope is planned.

In laying out the balcony, sight lines are laid out from rear to front because it is unsafe to change balcony slope. The focal point onstage is the point farthest downstage at which visibility is requisite, or, in the case of motion pictures only, the bottom of the screen. The maximum forward extensity of the balcony is then determined when the location of the spectator's eye position has been moved forward to a point beyond which the floor and supporting structure would intersect the upper sight line of the spectator standing at the rear of the orchestra.

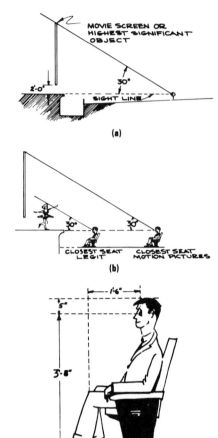

(a)

(b)

(c)

Fig. 20 (a) Maximum tolerable upward sight line angle for motion pictures. (b) Maximum angle determines location of closest seats. (c) Basic dimensions for plotting floor slope.

The pitch of balcony floors should not change since that would entail a change of riser height for aisle stairs and introduce attendant hazards. If vision from the rear row in the balcony is adequate, the rest of the balcony is satisfactory.

In theaters designed only to show motion pictures, the first row need not be located so that the patron can see the stage floor. It is satisfactory if he sees without obstruction the bottom of the screen which is seldom placed less

than 2 ft above the stage floor. Raising the screen makes it possible to flatten the contour of the orchestra floor. The reversed floor slope developed by Ben Schlanger makes use of this relationship to get the maximum number of seats into the zone of least visual distortion, and to hold the height of motion picture theaters to a minimum. A result of the reversed floor slope is to place balcony seats in the zone of optimum seeing.

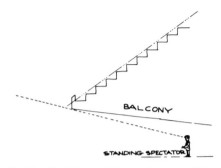

Fig. 21 The sight line of the standing patron limits the balcony overhang.

It is apparent that a theater designed for maximum efficiency for motion pictures (reverse floor slope) is almost completely useless for any other sort of production except large-screen television. The principle survives in the angle of the car stands in the drive-in motion picture theaters.

Floor Dish

The planning of the floor slope is not completed when pitch of orchestra and balcony has been laid out on the center line. It depends also on the curve of the rows of seats. The whole row must be at the same elevation if the seats are to be level. The floor therefore is not a sloped plane, but a dished surface in which horizontal contours follow the seat row curve. The floor section at the center line, rotated horizontally about the center of curvature of the rows of seats, will determine the orchestra floor shape. The balcony is planned the same way save that the floor is terraced to take the seats. (See Fig. 22.)

Comment

It has been established that conditions of seeing limit the depth of the house. Since capacity is a function of depth and width, increasing the width increases the capacity. However, since sight lines from the side seats limit the angular spread of the side walls, the width can be increased only by increasing the proscenium opening. The width of the proscenium opening is a function of the kind of production contemplated for the theater. The dimensions given in Table 1 are derived from the requirements of the types of produc-

TABLE 1 Proscenium Widths, in Feet, for Kinds of Theatrical Production

	Minimum	Usual	Reasonable maximum
Drama	26	30 to 35	40
Vaudeville, revue . . .	30	35	45
Musical comedy, operetta	30	40	50
Presentation, opera	40	60	80

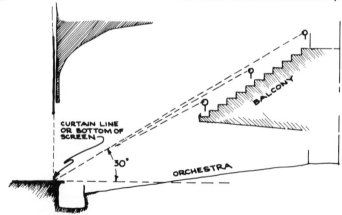

Fig. 19 Maximum tolerable downward sight line angle from balcony.

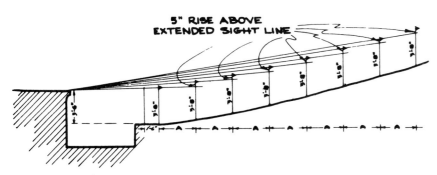

Fig. 22 Developed floor slope for unobstructed vision.

tion noted when the performances are so staged as to assure maximum effectiveness.

Where budget permits building to have better than minimum visibility standards, wall angles may be narrowed, floor angles increased, and balcony omitted, and visibility from the worst seats thereby improved to a point considerably better than what is just salable. A very real problem, however, is to prevent precedent or personal prejudice from so influencing auditorium design as to cause the inclusion of large numbers of unsalable seats. One manager insisted, after floor slope and stage height had been determined and the auditorium floor laid, that the stage floor be lowered some 10 in. below the height called for in the plan, in the interests of, as he put it, "intimacy." From the middle of the orchestra in that theater it is hard to see below the level of the actor's navel. (See Fig. 23.)

Greek theaters were semicircular (horizontal sight-line angle 90° to center line). This was all right in Greece where there was no proscenium. It is obviously not all right where a proscenium is used. Yet, a misguided reverence for ancient practice still gives us some theaters with impossible sight lines.

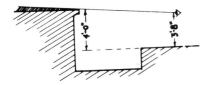

Fig. 23 Zone of invisibility. Causes: stage too high, front seats too low.

Opera houses of the Renaissance had side boxes for the very good reason that the people in the boxes competed (often successfully) with the stage show for audience attention. This condition persists, but it is worth noting that the best example of such a theater in America has not made a nickel for a generation. Nevertheless, theaters with at least vestigial side boxes are still built.

It is perhaps unnecessary to add that theaters planned in conformity with the principles here set forth may adhere in spirit to almost any architectural style by the discreet planning of service and decorative elements which do not affect the basic shape of the theater. In theaters which are being rebuilt, it is often possible to retain the desirable features and still provide a good theater.

Open Stage and Extended Stage

The open stage form in which sight lines must be directed to the edge of the acting area necessitates steep balconies. The balcony of a theater which is convertible from proscenium to open stage form must follow the requirements for open stage. Any theater in which performance extends beyond the proscenium onto either forestage, open stage, or extended stage requires very careful planning to provide good seeing from all balcony seats to all parts of the acting area.

Arena Stage

Few, if any, arena-form theaters have balconies, nor are they likely to have since the all-around seating of the arena form seems to satisfy seating capacity demands without balconies. Moreover, to satisfy the requirements of good seeing in arena, it is necessary to elevate successive rows of seats more than in proscenium form as a partial solution of the insoluble problem of actors covering other actors from some spectator's direction. (See Fig. 24.)

If seat rows are successively and sufficiently elevated, the audience may see over the heads

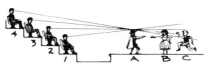

Fig. 24 The sight line problem inherent in the arena form: A hides B and C from first two rows.

of near actors to the heads, and partially the bodies, of actors farther away.

The stage is easily defined: it is that part of the theater where the performance takes place.

Its size, shape, arrangement, and equipment, therefore, must logically develop from the nature of the performance. Inasmuch as architectural acoustics and the electronic control of sound can provide for optimum audience perception of the auditory components, regardless of the form of the stage, development of the requirements for the stage may proceed from a consideration of the visual components and the routine of performance.

STAGE SPACE

For all production types, the visual components divide into two categories: performers and scenic investiture. These indicate the functional divisions of the stage: (1) the space in which the performers work, which, though actually three-dimensional, is usually referred to as the acting *area*, and (2) the space wherein the scenic investiture is arranged, which will be called hereafter the scenery *space*. A corollary of the presence of scenic investiture is the need for its operation and storage. This indicates a third functional division of the stage: working and storage space.

There is a functional relationship between acting area, scenery space, and working and storage space. The size, shape, and arrangement of the acting area must be determined before the other spaces can be logically developed. (See Figs. 25 and 26 and Table 2.)

Performance-Audience Relationship

The theater situation is fundamentally one of the relationship between the performers and the audience. The audience wants to hear and see the show without distraction and in comfort and safety, as stated, but its ultimate objective in attending the show is to receive the utmost sensory stimulation toward the maximum emotional and intellectual experience. Maximum appreciation and enjoyment of, and in a very real sense participation in, the theater experience by each individual member of the audience depend upon the maximum enjoyment of it by the entire audience. Group reaction to a single performance stimulus is something less than total unless that stimulus be perceived *at the same time, in the same measure, and with the same significance by the entire group.*

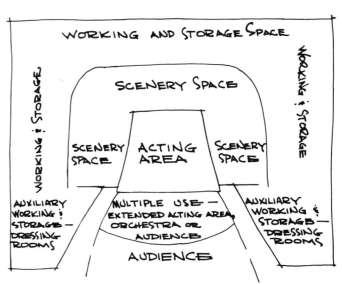

Fig. 25 Position of backstage areas relative to each other. This diagram must not be interpreted in terms of size or shape.

TABLE 2 Spatial Requirements for Various Types of Theatrical Productions

	General characteristics	Acting area size	Shape
Pageant and symphonic drama	Dramatic episodes, processions, marches, dances, and crowd scenes. Masses of performers engaged in simple but expansive movements before very large audiences.	From 2,000 to 5,000 sq ft, depending on the scale of the pageant.	Rectangular with aspect ratio between 1 to 3 and 2 to 3.
Grand opera.	Large numbers of performers on the acting area at one time; often more than one hundred in big scenes and finales. Movement is martial processions and group dances and the costumes are elaborate. Soloists perform downstage center, close to the footlights but within the bounds of the conventional proscenium, principals play twosome and group scenes in the area near the audience, and choruses and supernumeraries require space upstage. The ballet and the chorus of soldiers, pilgrims, peasants, or what not, sometimes fill the entire acting area. The performance is viewed objectively by the audience and does not benefit by intimate contact between performance and audience.	Minimum: 1,000 sq ft Usual: About 2,500 sq ft Reasonable maximum: 4,000 sq ft	Quadrilateral with an aspect ratio between 1 to 2 and 2 to 3. Sides converge toward the back of the stage, following the sight lines from the extreme lateral positions.
Vaudeville, revue.	Vaudeville and revue emphasize the human scale. Although the vaudevillian keys his performance for the last row in the gallery, the form is characterized by intimate direct relationship between performer and audience: monologues straight to the front, confidential asides to the front row, and audience participation in illusions. Other acts (acrobatics, etc.) are played across the line of audience vision for maximum effect.	Minimum: 350 sq ft Usual: About 450 sq ft Reasonable maximum: 700 sq ft	Rhomboid with aspect ratio about 1 to 3. Sides converge toward back of stage following the sight lines from the extreme lateral seats.
Dance	Graceful and expressive movements of human figures in designed patterns, chiefly in two dimensions but with the third dimension introduced by leaps and carries. Occasional elevation of parts of the stage floor. Singles, duets, trios, quartets, groups. The movement demands maximal clear stage space.	Anything under 700 sq ft is constricting. Reasonable maximum: 1,200 sq ft	Rhomboid with aspect ratio about 3 to 4. May project into and be surrounded by audience (open stage or arena) since frontal aspect of performers has minimal and space-filling quality has maximal significance.
Musical: folk opera, operetta, musical comedy, musical drama	These forms embody on a smaller scale the production elements of grand opera, plus a certain freedom and a quest for novelty which encourage the development of new performance devices. Close audience contact of soloists and specialists is borrowed from vaudeville and revue. Big scenes involve many dancers, singers, and showgirls, often with space-filling costume and movement. Fifty people on stage at one time is not unusual.	Minimum: 600 sq ft Usual: About 1,200 sq ft Reasonable maximum: 1,800 sq ft	Proscenium: Rhomboid with aspect ratio between 1 to 2 and 2 to 3. Sides converge toward the back of the stage following the sight lines from the extreme lateral seats. Arena: Circle, square, or rectangle (3 by 4 aspect ratio) or ellipse (3 by 4 aspect ratio).

Arrangement	Proscenium	Orchestra	Comment
Long dimension of acting area perpendicular to general sight line. Audience entirely on one side, elevated to perceive two-dimensional movement. Large openings at ends and in side opposite audience for processions, group entrances, and exits. Some elevation of portion of acting area opposite audience, purely for compositional reasons.	Either no proscenium with performers entering the "pageant field" from beyond the lateral sight lines, or structural or natural barriers to delineate the side limits of the acting area and conceal backstage apparatus and activity. "Curtains" of sliding panels, lights or fountains for concealing the acting area; often the concealment is by blackout only.	Space for 100 musicians between audience and acting area. Conductor must see performance.	Primarily an outdoor form, it is often staged in makeshift or adapted theatres, utilizing athletic fields and stands or natural amphitheatres. A few permanent pageant theatres have been built.
Long dimension perpendicular to the general sight line. Audience elevated to perceive two-dimensional movement.	Width equal to the long dimension of the acting area.	Pit for 60 to 80 musicians. Conductor must have good view of action.	Movement in two dimensions in acting area is a significant visual component, predicating elevation of the seating area to make this movement visible.
Long axis of the acting area perpendicular to the optimum sight line. Audience grouped as close as possible to the optimum sight line. The forestage is an essential part of the acting area; steps, ramps, and runways into the house are useful.	Width equal to the long dimension of the acting area. Flexibility is to some advantage in revue but of little value in vaudeville.	Music and music cues closely integrated with both vaudeville and revue performances. Pit space for from 15 to 30 musicians. Conductor and percussionist must have good view of the action.	Most of the visual components of vaudeville and revue are such that they are perceived best in the conventional audience-performance relationship. The comic monologist who must confront his audience is defeated by the open stage and arena arrangements.
Nearly square acting area so that dance patterns may be arranged in depth and movement may be in many directions including along the diagonals. Many dance figures require circular movement. Many entrances desirable, especially from the sides of the acting area.	Proscenium not really necessary; though useful as concealment for lighting instruments and dancers awaiting entrances, other devices such as pylons, movable panels, and curtains may be substituted.	Music almost always accompanies dancers. For dance as part of opera or musical show, orchestra is in pit. For dance as specific performance, as in ballet, orchestra may be in remote location and music piped in. Maximum orchestra for dance: 60 musicians in pit for classical ballet. Minimum: one drummer.	Dance in its various manifestations is the performance form best suited to the open stage or arena since it possesses the least amount of facial-expression significance and the greatest amount of movement and pattern in two or three dimensions. Elevation of the audience to perceive best the patterns of dance is desirable.
Proscenium: Long axis of acting area perpendicular to the optimum sight line. Mechanized mobility of structural parts to produce changes in acting area arrangement are desirable. Forestages, sidestages, acting area elevators. Arena: Numerous wide entrances for actors and stage hands via the aisles or through tunnels under the seating banks. Ramps preferable to stairs or steps. Experimentation possible in rendering stage flexible by lifts, and in development of flying systems over the acting area.	Usually as wide as the acting area, but should be adaptable to changes in the arrangement of the acting area described in the preceding column. Arena: None	Music an integral auditory component, sometimes integral visually. Elevating orchestra pit to accommodate from 20 to 40 musicians. Arena: Orchestra pit beside the acting area parallel to long axis and opposite principal entrance. This unavoidably imparts a performer orientation toward the orchestra and favors the seats in that general direction.	The assumption by ballet of a greater share in the performance of musical comedy indicates the need for a high general sight line from the audience. A phenomenon of the last 20 summers has been the growth of the musical theatre arena under canvas by which huge audiences have been enabled to see revivals of standard and Broadway musicals at popular prices though with general reduction of scenic investiture to that which is possible in the arena form. The movement has been economically feasible and generally profitable.

TABLE 2 Spatial Requirements for Various Types of Theatrical Productions (Continued)

	General characteristics	Acting area size	Shape
Legitimate drama.............	Of all production types, legitimate drama places the greatest emphasis upon the scale of the human actor. The importance of the individual actor requires that stage space and scenery do not dwarf him. Dominance of plot, locale, and characterization requires verisimilitude in the size and relationship of scenic objects. Too small an acting area crowds actors and furniture, hampers stage action, and detracts from the dramatic effect which is the sole aim of the performance. Too large an acting area diminishes the actor in scale and renders his performance ineffective by weakening the effect of his gestures and movement.	Minimum: 240 sq ft (12 by 20 ft) Usual: About 525 sq ft (15 by 35 ft) Reasonable maximum: 1,000 sq ft (25 by 40 ft)	Proscenium: Quadrilateral with an aspect ratio about 1 to 2. Sides converge toward the back of the stage following the sight line from the extreme lateral seats. Open stage: Semicircle, quadrilateral, or polygon projecting from a proscenium or from an architectural facade. Arena: Circle, square, rectangle, polygon, or ellipse with about 3 by 4 aspect ratio. Entrances from diagonal corners and in middle of one or both long sides.

Total Uniform Effect

If the theater does not permit total uniform stimulus and reaction, the performance can never reach its peak of effectiveness. The best efforts of theater artists stand the best chance of appreciative reception by audiences if the audience-performance relationship fosters total uniform stimulus and reaction, hereinafter called *total uniform effect*.

The producer and the theater artists have requirements consistent with these: they want the physical facilities which will allow their show to stimulate the audience to the maximum of intellectual and emotional appreciation. The skilled theater artist applies knowledge of audience reaction to the preparation of every part of the performance. If, because of inadequacies of the theater building, the audience cannot perceive the performance as the artist has planned it, the artist fails through no fault of his own, and the audience is disappointed.

Not only is it the height of theatrical artistry for the showman to achieve this condition of total uniform effect, but it is good business. The spectator who does not see or does not hear or does not comprehend a speech or action because of inadequate physical orientation toward the performance feels to some degree cheated of his admission fee and less inclined to return to the theater than does the spectator who perceives all the components of the performance fully and who feels that the performance is projected toward him and those close to him.

Expert showmen and artists use their productional knowledge and skills to the fullest within the limits of the physical plants at their disposal. It is the duty of the theater planner to provide them with facilities which neither limit nor hinder their efforts.

The performance and the audience can be related to each other in a limited number of combinations with some degree of variation possible in each arrangement.

Performance-Audience Arrangements

Audience Looking in One Direction toward the Performance: Proscenium This has been the conventional arrangement of the twentieth-century theater in the United States. It has the following attributes:

It affords the maximum confrontation of performers and audience and is best for lecturers, concert singers, recitation and dramatic presentation. It establishes a limited orientation of performers to audience. The audience

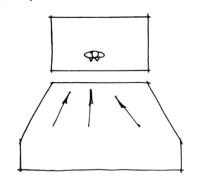

Fig. 27

being in one compact group within a narrow horizontal angle, the performers can relate their actions to the whole audience simultaneously. (See Fig. 27.)

It creates a limited, unified, fixed frame for the pictorial composition of the performance. Scenery can approach the quality of fine art in the refinement of its design elements.

It permits the director and designer to relate performers to scenery, secure in the knowledge that the whole audience will perceive the relationships in the same way.

It is the best arrangement for presenting to an audience a dramatic action of conflict or opposition of forces because the line of action of the opposition or conflict is across the line of vision of the audience and hence is maximally perceptible.

It is the form most conducive to the production of total uniform effect.

Being the established conventional form, it stands vulnerable to attack by avant-gardists who often seek change for the sake of change.

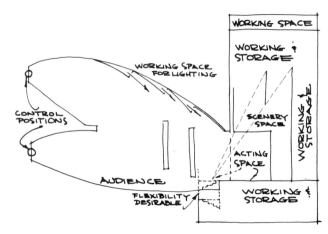

Fig. 26 Position of backstage spaces.

Arrangement	Proscenium	Orchestra	Comment
The realistic style of dramatic production confines the performance to an acting area entirely inside the proscenium. The apron is not used. Most historic styles and much modern dramatic theory demand more freedom of audience-performance relationship than the realistic style and call for the projection of the performance toward, into, and around the audience. For this projecting aprons, forestages, sidestages, runways, steps and ramps into the aisles are all to some degree useful. To meet the demands of different styles and stylists, the acting area for drama must be capable of assuming many shapes. To confine it within the proscenium opening is adequate for the realistic style but inadequate for the others; to project it toward, into, or around the audience in any rigidly unalterable form is likewise adequate for one style but inadequate for others.	Width equal to long dimension of the acting area. Moving panels to vary width, openings in proscenium splay to form side-stages, movable pylons or columns by which opening may be subdivided are all desirable. Flexibility and mobility are increasingly desirable. The application of motive power under remote control to the movement of structural parts to produce different arrangements appears desirable but is costly. Manually alterable parts, particularly forestage proscenium panels and sections of the stage floor, if not unwieldy, are reasonable substitutes.	Orchestral music is sometimes an integral visual part of the performance, but most generally it is a purely auditory component. It is not generally necessary for the orchestra to be seen by the audience, but because cueing of music is so exacting, the conductor must see the action. It is reasonable to provide a pit for from 15 to 30 musicians, but the flexibility cited at the left must be provided, either by portable pit covers, steps, and platforms or by mechanized orchestra lifts. There is opportunity for originality of arrangement.	The various forms of theatre used by legitimate drama are discussed fully earlier in this chapter.

It is limited in seating capacity because the principal direction of expansion is away from the performance; the limit of good seeing becomes the limit of expansion. Expansion laterally tends to destroy total uniform effect by making occupants of the side seats view the performance from widely divergent angles and thus see the actors, action and scenery in nonsignificant relationship.

Theatrical production refuses to be contained within a strictly limited space behind a rectangular opening. The existing proscenium form has been called the picture frame stage, and the peep show stage, and even during its incidence and rise to prevalence there were objections to its restrictive character. The theory of theater admits, and numerous modern plays contain, instances where the contact between performance and audience must be more intimate than the formal frame permits. History of theater shows 24 centuries in which the picture frame was either nonexistent or modified by the use of acting areas in front of it, against the last century and a quarter during which the proscenium developed in prominence. Modern theatrical practice contains frequent instances of the performance's attempting to come through the frame, into, about, and around the audience.

Audience Partially Surrounding the Performance: Open Stage In several variations this arrangement has gained in popularity during the midcentury. Essentially an old arrangement descended from Greek, Roman, Renaissance, and Elizabethan theaters, it has been readopted for several reasons:

It places the performers in the same space envelope as the audience. This is said to produce a unity of experience between performers and audience, though the authors believe that the essential dichotomy of function between performers and audience persists regardless of spatial relationship and that attempts to resolve this dichotomy are futile, fallacious, and irrelevant. (See Fig. 28.)

It places more spectators closer to the performance than does the proscenium arrangement and in this way contributes to good

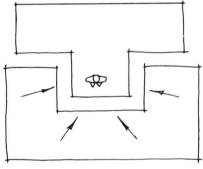

Fig. 28

seeing, but it places a burden of diffused orientation upon directors and performers and makes impossible the achievement of total uniform effect.

It contains inherent difficulties in the entrance and exit of actors which are usually solved by providing entrances beneath the seating area.

Difficulties pertaining to the scenic investiture which are common to both this arrangement and the arena arrangement will be considered together.

Audience Surrounding Performance: Arena or Central Staging Variously called *bandbox, arena, theater-in-the-round, circle theater* and deriving certainly from circus, ancient amphitheatre (*double theater*), and primitive ritual sites, the arrangement of the acting area in the center of a surrounding ring of audience has gained in popularity in the twentieth century for a number of reasons:

Expediency. At a time when formal theaters have been decreasingly available and increasingly expensive to build, while simultaneously the number of play production groups has been increasing rapidly, the arena arrangement, achievable in any large room, makes a rudimentary theater possible.

Economy. As well as seating maximum audience in the minimum enclosure, this arrange-

ment seats the largest audience within the shortest distance from the acting area. It is therefore attractive to the showman and also to the spectator who attaches value to proximity to the stage. (See Figs. 29 and 31.)

The claims of intimacy which are voiced for the open stage arrangement are repeated for the central stage and the same demurrers apply with the additional statement of positions *pro* and *contra* the feature of seeing the audience across the acting area. The argument *pro* is that seeing other members of the audience enjoying the show stimulates one's own enjoyment. The argument *contra* claims that the opposite audience seen beyond the actors is no part of the performance and is therefore a negative factor to the degree that it is distracting. It is surely a negative factor in that it is not a part of the design and plan of the performance; it is not scenic investiture.

Economy is also affected by the effective limitation of scenery: There can be no scenery or properties that the audience cannot see over, under, or through. This restricts scenic investiture to paint or other coverings on the stage floor, very low platforms, devices suspended above the acting area, outline representations of such objects as must be set on the

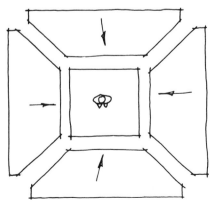

Fig. 29

stage for use by the actors (doors, windows, and similar architectural details), and low pieces of furniture.

Disadvantages. Because the audience is seated all around the acting area, it is unavoidable that viewpoints will be maximally different and it becomes impossible for director and actors to compose the performance so as to produce a total uniform effect. Furthermore because the conditions of *covering* (one actor blocking audience vision of another actor) are also maximized, it is necessary to prevent covering by increasing the pitch of the seating area.

An unavoidable disadvantage of this form lies in the anterior-posterior aspect of every actor and the fact that the most dramatically expressive side is oriented in only one direction. The summary comment on this aspect was made by the late David Itkin: "I have seen one-half of the show; now I will buy a ticket on the other side of the house and see the other half of the show." Unfortunately, because the performance must (at times) be oriented toward the sides where he has not yet sat with his two tickets, he would have had to buy two more tickets, four in all.

Performance Extending around Audience: Extended Stage Variously called *side stages, multi-proscenium, theater-all-around,* and even *theatrama,* this arrangement has gained some acceptance in the midcentury decades. (See Fig. 30.)

This form begins as an extension of the conventional acting area to left and right, usually as *parodoi* entrances on the audience side of the proscenium, or as doors in the side wall splays which may be used when desired as frontal entrances onto the stage. Its fullest development is in the four-stage form which requires that the audience sit in swivel chairs.

Its uses in production are various:

1. Small scenes played on side stages while scenery is being changed on the main stage.

2. Processions entering from the side stages and moving into the main stage.

3. Expansion of acting area for simultaneous showing of several settings or locales.

4. Elimination of changes of scenery by having all scenery set up on the various stages and moving the action and even rotating the audience. (This form relates directly to the television studio method of having several settings set up and moving actors and cameras from one set to another.)

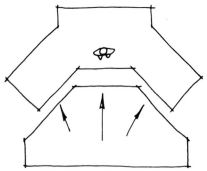

Fig. 30

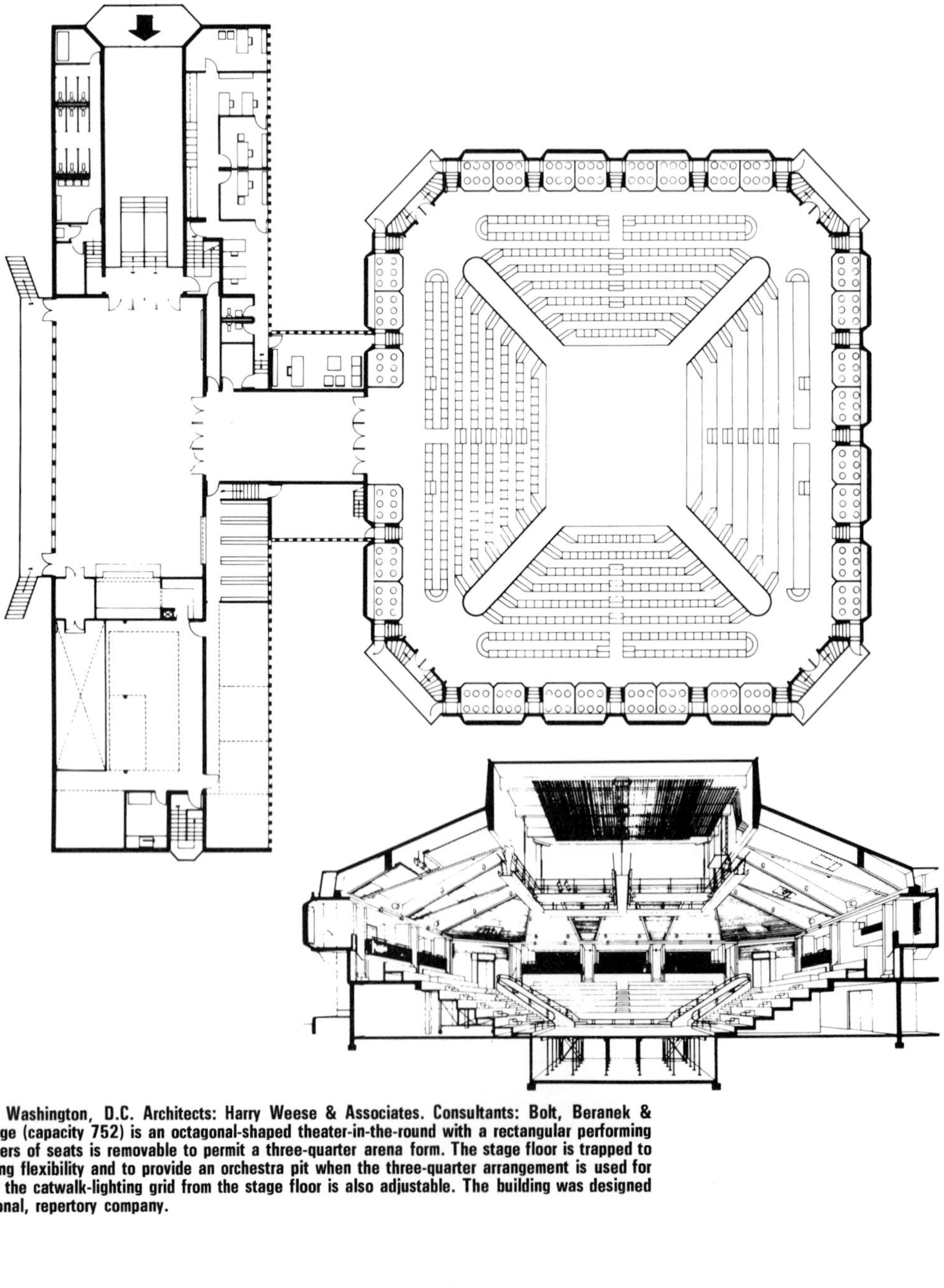

Fig. 31 Arena stage, Washington, D.C. Architects: Harry Weese & Associates. Consultants: Bolt, Beranek & Newman. The arena stage (capacity 752) is an octagonal-shaped theater-in-the-round with a rectangular performing area. One of the four tiers of seats is removable to permit a three-quarter arena form. The stage floor is trapped to provide additional staging flexibility and to provide an orchestra pit when the three-quarter arrangement is used for musicals. The height of the catwalk-lighting grid from the stage floor is also adjustable. The building was designed for a resident, professional, repertory company.

HOUSE

The House is one half of the Room. Investigation reveals two general concepts about it. Vision criteria, the major organizing principles of Drama uses, define the distribution of people in the House while hearing criteria, the major organizing principles of Music uses, define the distribution of boundary surfaces. Second, varying the size of a Drama audience mainly influences the linear and planar geometry of the House, while varying the Music audience mainly influences volumetric geometry.

In this section, Drama (vision) and Music (hearing) considerations will be applied to the audience portion of a Room, in terms of the primary attributes of size, shape and arrangement. A Frontal arrangement is assumed, either legitimate drama or orchestra on stage.

Drama Houses

1. Seating Area Dimensions The number and arrangement of seats defines the net floor area of the House (an aspect of size). Reckoning of area includes allowance for aisles and varies from 6 to 10 square feet per seat. Generally, a figure of 8 s.f. is good for first estimates although a higher number is usually needed for smaller capacities. This variation is caused less by differing seat dimensions than by conditions of arrangement. Sharp radius curves and ragged aisles introduce triangular residual areas. If seating is moveable, additional allowance must be made for imprecision and maneuvering clearances (13–15 s.f. is commonly used).

To assure a speedy exit in emergencies, conventional seating usually limits row length to seven seats accessible from one aisle or fourteen from two, with rows spaced not less than 33". Row spacing must be greater for continental seating, which is practically unlimited in row length. Continental requires wider end aisles with closely spaced exit doors. Continental gives more legroom seated, but more interference from latecomers. It also heightens the sense of vastness in a large Room. On balance, floor area per seat is the same for both methods.

7 to 12 SF/Person

Continental Row Spacing

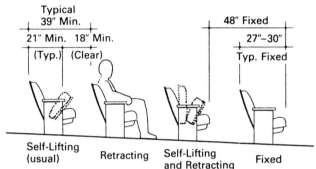

Conventional Row Spacing

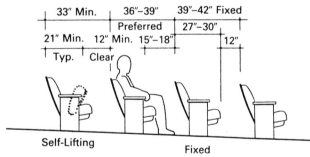

Fig. 1 Seating area units.

Area Comparison
(incl. 20% aisles)

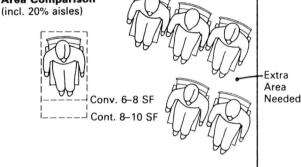

Conv. 6–8 SF

Cont. 8–10 SF

Extra Area Needed

Typical Seating Dimensions

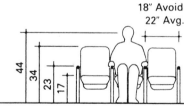

Widths
18" Avoid
22" Avg.

MUSIC AND DRAMA CENTERS
House

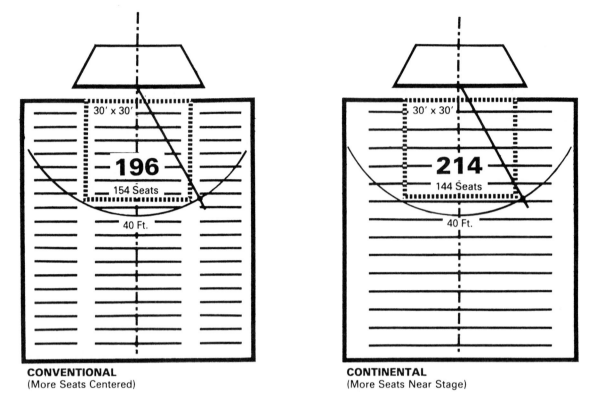

CONVENTIONAL
(More Seats Centered)

CONTINENTAL
(More Seats Near Stage)

Fig. 2 Conventional vs. continental seating.

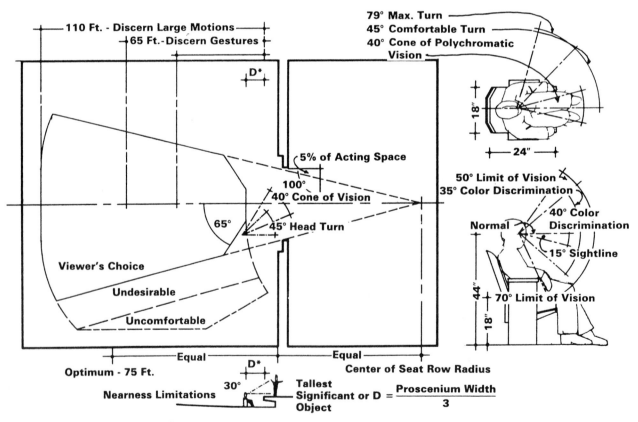

Fig. 3 Plan definition of frontal seating.

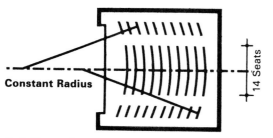

Constant Radius — 14 Seats

Fixed Radius — 14 Seats

Fig. 4 Plan curvature.

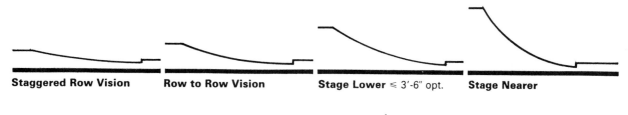

Staggered Row Vision | **Row to Row Vision** | **Stage Lower** $\leq$ 3'-6" opt. | **Stage Nearer**

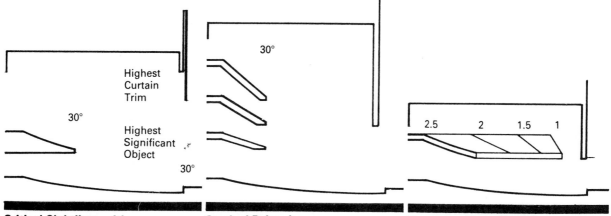

30°

Highest Curtain Trim

Highest Significant Object

30°

30°

2.5 2 1.5 1

Critical Sightlines with Inclusion of Balcony Maximum Acceptable Vertical Aspect @ 30°

Stacked Balconies Necessary Slope Increases with Elevation

Necessary Floor Slope Increases as Balcony Nears Stage

Fig. 5 Floor slope-sightline relationship.

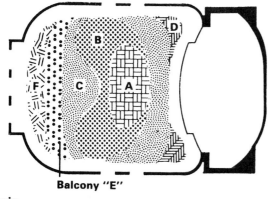

Balcony "E"

Music
Based on Auditory Quality

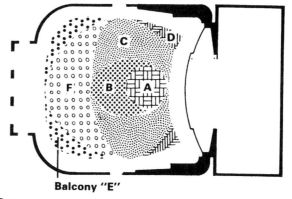

Balcony "E"

Drama
Based on Visual Quality

Fig. 6 Audience seating preferences.

MUSIC AND DRAMA CENTERS
House

2. Plan Arrangement with Respect to Stage Vision criteria define the horizontal proportions (plan shape) of the Room with reference to the stage configuration and proscenium width. The dominant side-to-side movement on a Frontal stage places value on proximity to the Room centerline, while the desirability of short viewing distance works in the other direction. The objective logically should be to maximize the number of seats in the center front region.

Actors' expressions are difficult to see beyond 40 feet, gestures past 65 feet, and only large body movements can be seen between 65 and 110 feet. Location of drama audiences should be within 65 feet, if possible. Viewing at an oblique angle foreshortens the image and may require neck craning. The normal cone of optimum vision covers 30 degrees vertically and 40 degrees horizontally. Viewing angle works against front corner seats, which have the most oblique view from which portions of the acting area may be obscured. For that matter, any "front row" seat requires a lot of head movement to take in the entire acting area. A 45 degree pivot is considered maximum tolerable exercise.

The intimacy of Drama is enriched by focused

orientation. Curved rows reinforce the impression of uniformity by centering attention. If the center point of curvature is on stage, the nearest rows are sharply arched. But the longer the radius, the less appreciable its effect. If conventional seating is employed (with longest rows of 14 seats) the radiating aisles eliminate a number of near-center seats. An alternate conventional plan places a cross aisle nearer the stage, which eliminates seats within the optimum vision distance. Continental seating avoids these radial geometry issues entirely.

Curved rows of gentle arc can have identical radius with the focus somewhat reduced, but allowing uniform, maximum row length and flush aisles with conventional seating. This "rectangular" arrangement requires varied seat unit size in order to provide staggered seats from row to row. Staggered seats permit one viewer to see between heads in the next row.

3. Vertical Arrangement with Respect to Stage Sight line criteria in the vertical dimension help define floor slope (an aspect of sectional shape). Flat-floor Rooms are limited in capacity by the problem of seeing past a few rows of people. A straight rake

(ramped) floor improves conditions for a short distance only. With each successive row, the steepness of slope must increase in order to accomplish the same geometric sightline clearance from row to row—optimum 5 or 6 inches—every two rows if seats are staggered. The relative stage level is a factor here—a lower stage favors a steeper floor. Since concern for comfort and safety limits the maximum ramp slope and discourages single risers in aisles, a limit is implied for the number of rows before a cross aisle or other device breaks the pattern. Where steps are necessary, they should be between 4½" and 8" high and clearly marked or illuminated. Aisle slopes should not exceed one foot in eight.

Rising curvature is a difficult construction condition. When compounded with horizontal radii a "dish" or "teacup" is formed. Converging aisles become a necessity, which for safety should run in the direction of slope.

Dished floors present slight disadvantages in terms of adaptability to other arrangements. If level terraces are desired on a temporary basis (dinner theater or experimental forms) no section of infill platform is alike. A constant radius or rectangular plan is more easily adaptable at some expense to intimacy of focus.

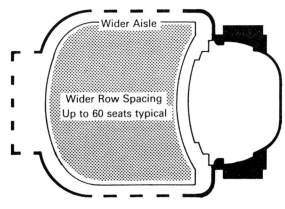

Continental

+ **Economic Use of Space**
+ **More Leg Room**
− **Less Comfortable Seat Access**
− **Numerous Exit Doors**

Fig. 7   Large house problems.

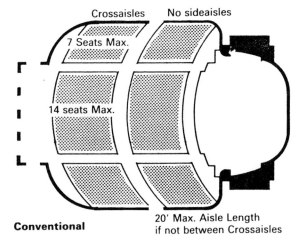

Conventional

+ **Easy Seat Access**
+ **Fewer Exits**
− **Less Leg Room**
− **Aisles take up space**

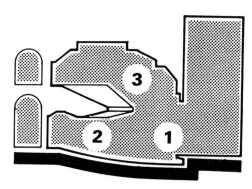

Balcony: 3 places

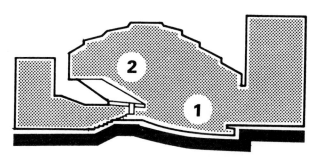

Ledge: 2 places

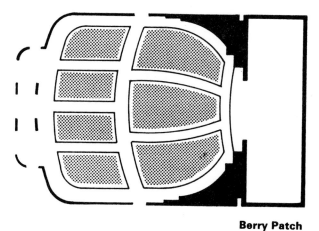

Berry Patch

Fig. 8 Larger house subdivisions.

4. The Large Room Special problems are associated with size increase, including the impression of scale conveyed by a sea of people. It makes the performance seem more remote, the individual less important, the experience less intense (aspects of arrangement).

Continental "wall-to-wall" seating can heighten this impression, although it is more efficient at large capacities because cross aisles are not needed. Nevertheless, aisles do help define smaller units of seating, which may make the Room seem smaller.

As distances increase, the effects of floor slope are amplified. Entry and exit doors occur at greater elevational differences, not necessarily in equal increments, which affects design of surrounding spaces and access patterns. Further, as aisle length increases with conventional seating good practice requires cross aisles to ensure reasonable travel distance to exits. The cross aisle is a means of collecting exiting audience from more than one aisle, and is consequently quite wide. It eliminates two or more rows of seats.

Increased seating area can also have a psychological effect on performers confronted with fractional attendance that seems even smaller relative to empty seats. There are several alternatives to choose from in countering the results of larger size.

Berry-patching, or horizontally offsetting sections of the audience area, answers the questions of aisle length and to some degree identifies smaller reference units for viewers, but introduces cross aisles.

A *ledge* may be incorporated, with or without a cross aisle, vertically offsetting the house floor and defining two places in the Room. Also, assigning seating priority to the lower section reduces apparent emptiness.

Finally, a *balcony* solution brings about three places of different flavor. Each place provides a strong visual frame of reference more intimate than the total.

The ability to shut down or darken the balcony effectively removes it from the actors' estimate of the house. The problem of aisle slopes exceeding maximum is removed; essentially, the steep area at the rear is lifted to form the balcony, acquiring an even steeper slope navigable by steps. Entry/exit is distinctly "two-story". Finally, lifting and tilting (the balcony) may enable it to be moved forward slightly, bringing more front row audience within range of the actor, and partially obscuring the rear of the house where the empty seats are.

Sitting under a very deep balcony can sometimes be like sitting in another room. The rearmost row should at least be able to see the top of the proscenium. Balconies also tend to blanket an area acoustically, preventing reflected sound from reaching back rows. The acoustically acceptable overhang can be greater for Drama than for Music since the reverberant contribution is smaller. Moreover, since speech intelligibility favors a proportionally high direct/reverberant ratio it improves with steeper floor rake and short throw.

If amplified or pre-recorded sound is employed, correct positioning of loudspeakers may influence Room shape. Normally, a central loudspeaker cluster is located over the stage so that actor and loudspeaker are equidistant from listener. The acoustic shadow cast by a low balcony can be a problem best dealt with by raising the balcony.

Cultural

MUSIC AND DRAMA CENTERS

House

VISUAL PRINCIPLES THAT INFLUENCE THE DESIGN OF THE HOUSE

An optimum view of the stage throughout the house depends on three factors:

- Slope of the house floor
- Staggering of seats
- Elevation of the stage

The Slope (Rake) of the House Floor

If the floor is flat, patrons have a hard time seeing over the people in front of them. For this reason, most theater floors slope gently upward toward the back of the house. The floor may be ramped (a continuous slope) or stepped. For safety reasons, a ramped floor is limited to a maximum slope of 10 percent; steeper slopes must be stepped. Be sure to provide for wheelchair-bound patrons and standing room positions when figuring the slope of the house.

Staggered Seats

The positioning of seats in the rows depends on the degree of the rake. *One-row vision,* in which seats in each row line up directly with those in front, requires a very steep rake to allow for proper viewing angles. *Two-row vision* involves staggered seating and permits an unobstructed view between the two seats in front of the patron. Because this arrangement does not involve a steep rake, it is highly recommended.

Elevation of the Stage

The stage should always be below eye level of patrons sitting in the first row. Ideal height is between two feet, six inches and three feet, six inches from the floor at the first row of seats. The viewing angle of the audience varies with art form. In dance, for example, patrons must be able to see the dancers' feet. Make sure the stage floor is level with all support spaces backstage to expedite movement of scenery and equipment.

Flat Floor Stage

416

5"
Eye Level

Edge of Stage

3'8"

Rake of floor is steep enough
for row A to see over
heads of row B

One-Row Vision

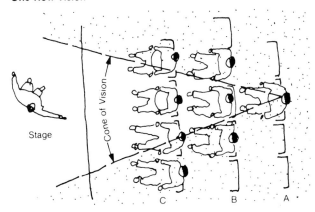

Stage

Cone of Vision

C   B   A

Plan of One-Row Vision

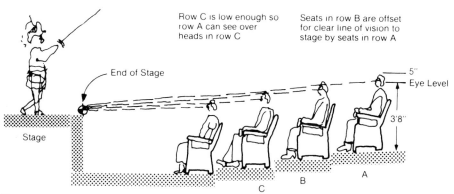

Row C is low enough so
row A can see over
heads in row C

Seats in row B are offset
for clear line of vision to
stage by seats in row A

End of Stage

5"
Eye Level

3'8"

Stage

C   B   A

Two-Row Vision

Requires the Lowest Angle Rake

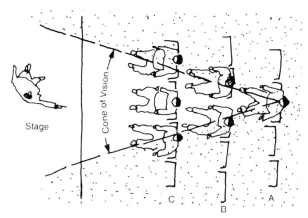

Stage

Cone of Vision

C   B   A

Plan of Two-Row Vision

MUSIC AND DRAMA CENTERS

House

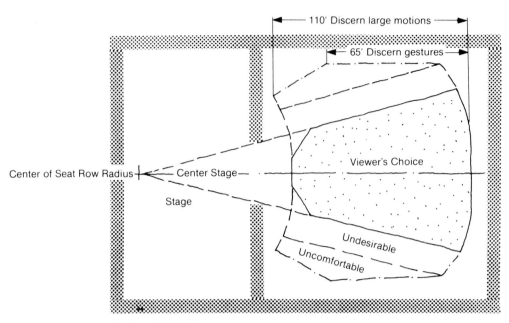

110' Discern large motions

65' Discern gestures

Center of Seat Row Radius

Center Stage

Stage

Viewer's Choice

Undesirable

Uncomfortable

Horizontal Sightlines

BASIC SEATING DATA

Seating standards for use in theaters, auditoriums and similar buildings are developed on this and the following pages, which give tabular data and methods for laying out seating plans. Material is the result of research by Frederic Arden Pawley. Sources include seating manufacturers and architectural offices specializing in theaters.

Types of Seats

Construction and Finish Upholstery variations include *spring-edge* seats (most luxurious, more expensive); *box-spring* (nearly as comfortable);

spring-back; and *padded-back*. Veneer-back seating is suitable only for conditions subject to hard usage, as in schools. Acoustical control is more satisfactory with upholstered types.

Sizes Seats are designated by width, the depth front-to-back varying only slightly. Common sizes and recommended uses are shown below. In pew seating without individual arms, as in churches or arenas, a "sitting" is usually 18 in. wide.

Pitch of Back This will vary according to the vertical angle of vision to the center of interest. In general, greater pitches are used for front

portions of orchestra floors and more nearly vertical backs for elevated banks such as balconies.

Clearances In addition to those noted diagrammatically below, the following points should be considered: *Coves* at intersection of floor and walls (or risers) should be kept small (1½-in. radius) to permit close fitting and leveling of seat standards. *Balcony risers* cause cramped knee-room when 12 in. high unless back-to-back seat spacing is increased. End clearances in balconies should be increased to 2½-in. *Pitch of back* greater than average (see Fig. 1) also requires increased back-to-back spacing.

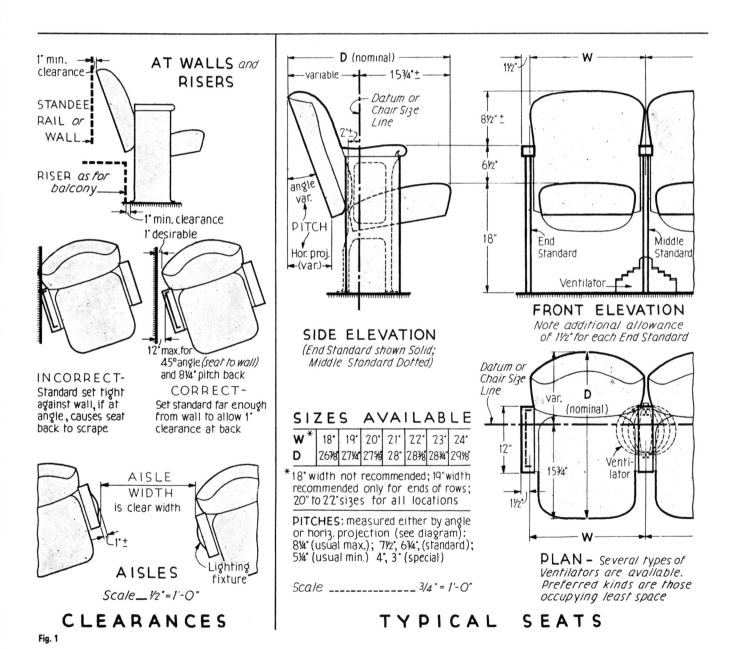

Fig. 1

MUSIC AND DRAMA CENTERS
Basic Seating Data

Types of Layouts

Rows These may be straight across entire theater, side banks may be canted, or entire rows may be curved. Advantages of each type are shown in Fig. 2. Min. radius for curved rows, due to seat construction, is 20 ft. Center for radii of rows and center of screen or stage need not coincide, although this is the ideal case. When rows are curved, a sloping auditorium floor should be a compound curve or amphitheater type to prevent tilted side seats.

Aisles These may be straight or curved, parallel or radial. Aisles should run at right angles to rows to eliminate "pockets."

Combinations of row and aisle types commonly used are shown in Fig. 2.

Continental Seating, most commonly used abroad, involves use of rows with unlimited number of seats. Local codes in this country often either prohibit its use or impose many restrictions. However, existing examples have proved safe and comfortable due to increased back-to-back seat spacing (up to 42 in.) which is essential to scheme. Larger than usual side aisles or foyers and many side exits are required.

Code Requirements These govern (1) maximum number of seats in a bank, (2) aisle width, (3) crossovers (not uniform). Usual requirements are: (1) no seat more than seven seats from an aisle; (2) min. aisle width of 3 ft, increasing by varying factors in relation to length of aisles. (3) Requirements for crossovers, not uniformly subject to codes, vary. Consult local authorities.

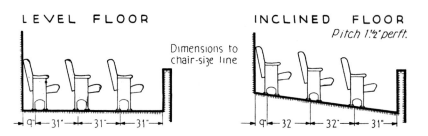
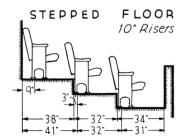

MINIMUM SPACINGS FOR VARYING FLOOR CONDITIONS
Based on stock sizes with 5¼" pitch back

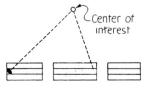

STRAIGHT ROWS
Uncomfortable for spectators at side, unequal stress on seats and backs

STRAIGHT, CANTED SIDE-BANKS
Same defects as straight rows though to less degree. Note that rows do not line up. Steps if required in aisles will be unsafe

CURVED ROWS
Recommended for comfort, ease of vision and safety

TYPES OF ROWS

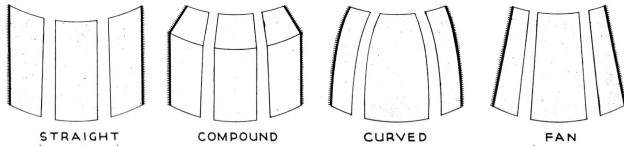

STRAIGHT
(poorest type)

COMPOUND

CURVED

FAN
(ideally best)

COMMON THREE-BANK LAYOUTS
see also "Continental Seating" in text

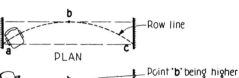
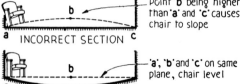

SIDE RAKE *(Curved Rows)*

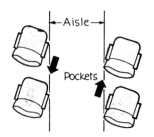
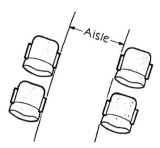

Aisles cutting diagonally across rows produce dangerous "pockets" and waste space

Curved or straight radial aisles reduce number and size of "pockets"

DIRECTION OF AISLES

Fig. 2

420

AUDITORIUM DIMENSIONS

Preliminary estimates may be based upon the "Rule of Thumb" which is sufficiently accurate for rough sketches.

Tables. For such purposes as financing, working drawings, etc., follow method outlined in Examples A, B, C and D. Variations between the two methods are to be expected.

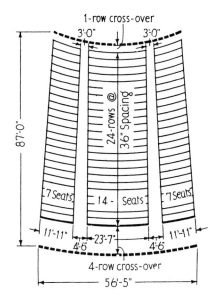

EXAMPLE A: Given auditorium area = 87'-0" x 56'-5" or 4900 + sq. ft., how many 20" seats, 36" back-to-back?

1. Rows: In Table I, 36" col., at 87'-0" depth, No. rows = 29
   less cross-overs (1 row at front, 4 at rear) = — 5
   Rows available for seats = 24
2. Aisles: Table II, increase in aisle width per row = 0.75"; 0.75 x 24 =
   Total increase = 1'-6"
   Min. aisle = 3'-0"
   Max. aisle = 4'-6"
3. Seating Scheme: Select tentative scheme; 2 aisles, 2 dead-end seat banks, 1 center bank. From typical code, dead-end rows may be 7 seats long, center rows 14 seats. In Table IV 14—20" seats = 23'-7"
   7—20" seats = 11'-11"
   7—20" seats = 11'-11"
   From (2) above, 2 aisles = 9'-0"
   Total width = 56'-5"
   Seats per row = 28
4. Total No. of Seats: (Table III)
   or 28 x 24 = { 672 seats }

EXAMPLE B: Given capacity of 672 seats, what are auditorium dimensions?
This problem is the converse of "A".

EXAMPLE C: What is radius of any row?
To radius of back of first-row seats add desired value from Table I.

EXAMPLE D: How many and what sizes of seats can be used in rows shortened by curved or radial aisles? See Table IV.

RULE of THUMB for SEATING AREA:
Allow 7½ sq. ft per Seat, including Aisles and Cross-overs.
This is sufficiently accurate for preliminary planning.

Table I - Depth Dimensions (Ft.-In.) for Various Spacings

No. Rows	Overall Depth for Seat Spacing (Back-to-back) of:										
	32"	33"	34"	35"	36"	37"	38"	39"	40"	41"	42"
1	2-8	2-9	2-10	2-11	3-0	3-1	3-2	3-3	3-4	3-5	3-6
2	5-4	5-6	5-8	5-10	6-0	6-2	6-4	6-6	6-8	6-10	7-0
3	8-0	8-3	8-6	8-9	9-0	9-3	9-6	9-9	10-0	10-3	10-6
4	10-8	11-0	11-4	11-8	12-0	12-4	12-8	13-0	13-4	13-8	14-0
5	13-4	13-9	14-2	14-7	15-0	15-5	15-10	16-3	16-8	17-1	17-6
6	16-0	16-6	17-0	17-6	18-0	18-6	19-0	19-6	20-0	20-6	21-0
7	18-8	19-3	19-10	20-5	21-0	21-7	22-2	22-9	23-4	23-11	24-6
8	21-4	22-0	22-8	23-4	24-0	24-8	25-4	26-0	26-8	27-4	28-0
9	24-0	24-9	25-6	26-3	27-0	27-9	28-6	29-3	30-0	30-9	31-6
10	26-8	27-6	28-4	29-2	30-0	30-10	31-8	32-6	33-4	34-2	35-0
11	29-4	30-3	31-2	32-1	33-0	33-11	34-10	35-9	36-8	37-7	38-6
12	32-0	33-0	34-0	35-0	36-0	37-0	38-0	39-0	40-0	41-0	42-0
13	34-8	35-9	36-10	37-11	39-0	40-1	41-2	42-3	43-4	44-5	45-6
14	37-4	38-6	39-8	40-10	42-0	43-2	44-4	45-6	46-8	47-10	49-0
15	40-0	41-3	42-6	43-9	45-0	46-3	47-6	48-9	50-0	51-3	52-6
16	42-8	44-0	45-4	46-8	48-0	49-4	50-8	52-0	53-4	54-8	56-0
17	45-4	46-9	48-2	49-7	51-0	52-5	53-10	55-3	56-8	58-1	59-6
18	48-0	49-6	51-0	52-6	54-0	55-6	57-0	58-6	60-0	61-6	63-0
19	50-8	52-3	53-10	55-5	57-0	58-7	60-2	61-9	63-4	64-11	66-6
20	53-4	55-0	56-8	58-4	60-0	61-8	63-4	65-0	66-8	68-4	70-0
21	56-0	57-9	59-6	61-3	63-0	64-9	66-6	68-3	70-0	71-9	73-6
22	58-8	60-6	62-4	64-2	66-0	67-10	69-8	71-6	73-4	75-2	77-0
23	61-4	63-3	65-2	67-1	69-0	70-11	72-10	74-9	76-8	78-7	80-6
24	64-0	66-0	68-0	70-0	72-0	74-0	76-0	78-0	80-0	82-0	84-0
25	66-8	68-9	70-10	72-11	75-0	77-1	79-2	81-3	83-4	85-5	87-6
26	69-4	71-6	73-8	75-10	78-0	80-2	82-4	84-6	86-8	88-10	91-0
27	72-0	74-3	76-6	78-9	81-0	83-3	85-6	87-9	90-0	92-3	94-6
28	74-8	77-0	79-4	81-8	84-0	86-4	88-8	91-0	93-4	95-8	98-0
29	77-4	79-9	82-2	84-7	87-0	89-5	91-10	94-3	96-8	99-1	101-6
30	80-0	82-6	85-0	87-6	90-0	92-6	95-0	97-6	100-0	102-6	105-0
31	82-8	85-3	87-10	90-5	93-0	95-7	98-2	100-9	103-4	105-11	108-6
32	85-4	88-0	90-8	93-4	96-0	98-8	101-4	104-0	106-8	109-4	112-0

Table II - Aisle Width Increase (in inches) Per Row of Length

Seat Spacing Back-to-Back	Fire Underwriters Code: 3'-0" plus ¼" per 1'-0"	N.Y. City Code: 3'-0" plus 1½" per 5'-0"
32"	0.67	0.80
33"	0.69	0.83
34"	0.71	0.86
35"	0.73	0.88
36"	0.75	0.90
37"	0.77	0.93
38"	0.79	0.95
39"	0.81	0.98
40"	0.83	1.00
41"	0.85	1.03
42"	0.88	1.05
Proper factor x no. of rows = total increase in inches, Add to 3'-0" minimum aisle width		

Table III - Seating Capacities, 1-32 Rows

No. of Rows	7 Seats	14 Seats	28 Seats	No. of Rows	7 Seats	14 Seats	28 Seats
1	7	14	28	17	119	238	476
2	14	28	56	18	126	252	504
3	21	42	84	19	133	266	532
4	28	56	112	20	140	280	560
5	35	70	140	21	147	294	588
6	42	84	168	22	154	308	616
7	49	98	196	23	161	322	644
8	56	112	224	24	168	336	672
9	63	126	252	25	175	350	700
10	70	140	280	26	182	364	728
11	77	154	308	27	189	378	756
12	84	168	336	28	196	392	784
13	91	182	364	29	203	406	812
14	98	196	392	30	210	420	840
15	105	210	420	31	217	434	868
16	112	224	448	32	224	448	896

MUSIC AND DRAMA CENTERS
Basic Seating Data

Table IV - Numbers of Seats (Stock Sizes) for Any Row Length

Group 1

Row Length Ft.-In.	In.	19"	20"	21"	22"
5- 0	60	3			
5- 1	61	2	1		
5- 2	62	1	2		
5- 3	63		3		
5- 4	64		2	1	
5- 5	65		1	2	
5- 6	66			3	
5- 7	67			2	1
5- 8	68			1	2
5- 9	69				3
6- 7	79	4			
6- 8	80	3	1		
6- 9	81	2	2		
6-10	82	1	3		
6-11	83		4		
7- 0	84		3	1	
7- 1	85		2	2	
7- 2	86		1	3	
7- 3	87			4	
7- 4	88			3	1
7- 5	89			2	2
7- 6	90			1	3
7- 8	91				4
8- 2	98	5			
8- 3	99	4	1		
8- 4	100	3	2		
8- 5	101	2	3		
8- 6	102	1	4		
8- 7	103		5		
8- 8	104		4	1	
8- 9	105		3	2	
8-10	106		2	3	
8-11	107		1	4	
9- 0	108			5	
9- 1	109			4	1
9- 2	110			3	2
9- 3	111			2	3
9- 4	112			1	4
9- 5	113				5
9- 9	117	6			
9-10	118	5	1		
9-11	119	4	2		
10- 0	120	3	3		
10- 1	121	2	4		
10- 2	122	1	5		
10- 3	123		6		
10- 4	124		5	1	
10- 5	125		4	2	
10- 6	126		3	3	
10- 7	127		2	4	
10- 8	128		1	5	
10- 9	129			6	
10-10	130			5	1
10-11	131			4	2
11- 0	132			3	3
11- 1	133			2	4
11- 2	134			1	5
11- 3	135				6
11- 4	136	7			

Group 2

Row Length Ft.-In.	In.	19"	20"	21"	22"
11- 5	137	6	1		
11- 6	138	5	2		
11- 7	139	4	3		
11- 8	140	3	4		
11- 9	141	2	5		
11-10	142	1	6		
11-11	143		7		
12- 0	144		6	1	
12- 1	145		5	2	
12- 2	146		4	3	
12- 3	147		3	4	
12- 4	148		2	5	
12- 5	149		1	6	
12- 6	150			7	
12- 7	151			6	1
12- 8	152			5	2
12- 9	153			4	3
12-10	154			3	4
12-11	155	8		2	5
13- 0	156	7	1	1	6
13- 1	157	6	2		7
13- 2	158	5	3		
13- 3	159	4	4		
13- 4	160	3	5		
13- 5	161	2	6		
13- 6	162	1	7		
13- 7	163		8		
13- 8	164		7	1	
13- 9	165		6	2	
13-10	166		5	3	
13-11	167		4	4	
14- 0	168		3	5	
14- 1	169		2	6	
14- 2	170		1	7	
14- 3	171			8	
14- 4	172			7	1
14- 5	173			6	2
14- 6	174	9		5	3
14- 7	175	8	1	4	4
14- 8	176	7	2	3	5
14- 9	177	6	3	2	6
14-10	178	5	4	1	7
14-11	179	4	5		8
15- 0	180	3	6		
15- 1	181	2	7		
15- 2	182	1	8		
15- 3	183		9		
15- 4	184		8	1	
15- 5	185		7	2	
15- 6	186		6	3	
15- 7	187		5	4	
15- 8	188		4	5	
15- 9	189		3	6	
15-10	190		2	7	
15-11	191		1	8	
16- 0	192			9	
16- 1	193	10		8	1
16- 2	194	9	1	7	2
16- 3	195	8	2	6	3

Group 3

Row Length Ft.-In.	In.	19"	20"	21"	22"
16- 4	196	7	3	5	4
16- 5	197	6	4	4	5
16- 6	198	5	5	3	6
16- 7	199	4	6	2	7
16- 8	200	3	7	1	8
16- 9	201	2	8		9
16-10	202	1	9		
16-11	203		10		
17- 0	204		9	1	
17- 1	205		8	2	
17- 2	206		7	3	
17- 3	207		6	4	
17- 4	208		5	5	
17- 5	209		4	6	
17- 6	210		3	7	
17- 7	211		2	8	
17- 8	212	11	1		9
17- 9	213	10	1	10	
17-10	214	9	2	9	1
17-11	215	8	3	8	2
18- 0	216	7	4	7	3
18- 1	217	6	5	6	4
18- 2	218	5	6	5	5
18- 3	219	4	7	4	6
18- 4	220	3	8	3	7
18- 5	221	2	9	2	8
18- 6	222	1	10	1	9
18- 7	223		11		10
18- 8	224		10	1	
18- 9	225		9	2	
18-10	226		8	3	
18-11	227		7	4	
19- 0	228		6	5	
19- 1	229		5	6	
19- 2	230		4	7	
19- 3	231	12	3	8	
19- 4	232	11	1 2	9	
19- 5	233	10	2 1	10	
19- 6	234	9	3	11	
19- 7	235	8	4	10	1
19- 8	236	7	5	9	2
19- 9	237	6	6	8	3
19-10	238	5	7	7	4
19-11	239	4	8	6	5
20- 0	240	3	9	5	6
20- 1	241	2	10	4	7
20- 2	242	1	11	3	8
20- 3	243		12	2	9
20- 4	244		11	1 1	10
20- 5	245		10	2	11
20- 6	246		9	3	
20- 7	247		8	4	
20- 8	248		7	5	
20- 9	249		6	6	
20-10	250	13	5	7	
20-11	251	12	1 4	8	
21- 0	252	11	2 3	9	
21- 1	253	10	3 2	10	
21- 2	254	9	4 1	11	

Group 4

Row Length Ft.-In.	In.	19"	20"	21"	22"
21- 3	255	8	5	12	
21- 4	256	7	6	11	1
21- 5	257	6	7	10	2
21- 6	258	5	8	9	3
21- 7	259	4	9	8	4
21- 8	260	3	10	7	5
21- 9	261	2	11	6	6
21-10	262	1	12	5	7
21-11	263		13	4	8
22- 0	264		12	1 3	9
22- 1	265		11	2 2	10
22- 2	266		10	3 1	11
22- 3	267		9	4	12
22- 4	268		8	5	
22- 5	269	14	7	6	
22- 6	270	13	1 6	7	
22- 7	271	12	2 5	8	
22- 8	272	11	3 4	9	
22- 9	273	10	4 3	10	
22-10	274	9	5 2	11	
22-11	275	8	6 1	12	
23- 0	276	7	7	13	
23- 1	277	6	8	12	1
23- 2	278	5	9	11	2
23- 3	279	4	10	10	3
23- 4	280	3	11	9	4
23- 5	281	2	12	8	5
23- 6	282	1	13	7	6
23- 7	283		14	6	7
23- 8	284		13	1 5	8
23- 9	285		12	2 4	9
23-10	286		11	3 3	10
23-11	287		10	4 2	11
24- 0	288		9	5 1	12
24- 1	289		8	6	13
24- 2	290		7	7	
24- 3	291		6	8	
24- 4	292		5	9	
24- 5	293		4	10	
24- 6	294		3	11	
24- 7	295		2	12	
24- 8	296		1	13	
24- 9	297			14	
24-10	298			13	1
24-11	299			12	2
25- 0	300			11	3
25- 1	301			10	4
25- 2	302			9	5
25- 3	303			8	6
25- 4	304			7	7
25- 5	305			6	8
25- 6	306			5	9
25- 7	307			4	10
25- 8	308			3	11
25- 9	309			2	12
25-10	310			1	13
25-11	311				14

End Allowances: Normal 3" allowance to accommodate 2 end standards per row is included above. For balconies with steps in aisles allow 2" additional.

Seat Sizes: Common sizes shown. Seats are also available 18", 23" & 24" wide. 18" size not recommended. Limit use of 19" seats to ends of rows for comfort.

Choice of Seats: Note that for longer rows two choices of seat sizes are available. Example: Row length = 14'- 9"; six 19" seats and three 20" may be used; or, two 21" and six 22". Dotted lines separate choices. Dimensions not fitted by stock sizes are omitted.

STAGE

Stage dimensions and volumetric relationships have a fundamental effect in establishing the geometries of the House. This section will build on discussion of the House to help determine what makes one Stage configuration different from another.

The physical characteristics of the Stage are functions of its intended use. Seven performance types pertinent to Frontal Stage criteria will be looked at briefly to see where they differ.

A. General Considerations

Variations among Stage forms have two levels of impact on Room design—Vision parameters (location of audience) and Hearing parameters (location of boundary surfaces).

1. Vision Parameters These are related to the dimensions of performing (acting) area:

- Width/depth/shape of acting area.
- Height of proscenium (if any).
- Elevation and/or rake of stage.
- Location of acting area relative to proscenium.

2. Hearing Parameters These are related to boundaries of the Stage enclosure:

- Size/shape of enclosing shell (if any).
- Nature of coupled volumes (if any).
- Absorptive properties of enclosure.
- Location of sound source relative to enclosure.

The corresponding functional elements depend on the use for which the Stage is designed. A few categorical terms will be of help in comparative treatments of stage types. Performing (acting) area is the portion of stage space meant to be seen. The stage enclosure defines a volume contiguous with the stage space, communicating with the house. Together, these constitute the bare minimum Open Stage. The stage floor may be stepped or sloped ("raked"). If a wall divides the stage space from the house the opening in it is the proscenium and the volume behind it is stagehouse.

For Music, an enclosure within the stagehouse is a shell, its overhead extension into the house a forestage canopy. If a portion of the remaining stagehouse volume communicates with the house, it is said to be coupled.

For Drama, scene space surrounds the acting space, and is surrounded by working space within the stagehouse—around, above or below. An open stage can have scene and working space, but scenic material may not be withdrawn vertically unless there is a proscenium wall and flyloft—i.e., a stagehouse—separable from the audience house by a fire curtain closure. Below stage working space (trap room) must also be separated from the house except through the proscenium. An orchestra pit communicates with the house in front of the proscenium and fire curtain.

B. Functional Requirements

The following are desirable Stage characteristics for various performance types. Discussion here stresses key functions and design rationale.

1. Legitimate Drama The medium includes speech, action and scenic context. The human figure is extremely important; scenic illusion refers to this for dimensional scale. Dominant movement across the acting area, entering left and right, makes other entries special events. Drama usually works through sustained continuity over a series of unfolding, developing events and situations; the ability to control changes in context, pace, center of attention and atmospheric tone is essential.

Performance Space Acting area is approximately 35' w × 20' d (40' × 25' usual maximum). This defines the downstage zone of most action; however, the full stage depth is utilized. It has a level floor that can be built upon, normally 30–36" above front row of house. Traps are recommended in key acting area.

Enclosure A stagehouse is recommended, with a proscenium portal 35' w × 26' (can be larger). Stagehouse configuration is related to scene handling methods; flyloft is recommended strongly.

Scene/Working Space Wrap-around scene space is required for flats, drops, wagons. Allow ample horizontal working space for the largest set piece plus actors' waiting areas, technicians' workspace, counterweights and pinrail, curtain space and switchgear. Use inside clearances and keep the plan shape compact and rectangular. Overhead working space must accept the longest flown piece plus borders plus gridiron and line space plus manhigh passage above grid. Understage working space should be at least eight feet clear height. If any portion of working space is omitted by design, stage level allocation should be increased 50%.

2. Dance The medium consists of action with music and some scenic context. Large movements of dancers in two directions (to-fro, side-side) physically occupy a region 15 feet above the floor. Dancers' entry from scene space on all sides is important. Scenery is often minimal, but not stage lighting. Although recorded music can be used, a dance facility should provide for a live orchestra. A dance concert usually consists of a series of separate pieces or events with rest periods between during which the stage is reset and the audience must be otherwise occupied. The technical qualities that help sustain continuity during performance should be versatile and sophisticated, especially lighting controls. Also, music is to be heard on stage distinctly.

Performance Space Acting area is typically 50'w × 40'd, although 40' width will accommodate modern dance and small troupes. Higher sightlines (lower stage in steeper house) improve perception of deep movements. Construction of a resilient dance floor is essential, e.g. on built-up criss-crossed sleepers with neoprene cushions between. Sponge mats are not springy enough, and injuries can result. Often, a removable linoleum, vinyl or hardboard surface is put down, with seams taped.

Enclosure A high proscenium is needed in large Rooms for clear view of the dancers' space, or no proscenium at all in intimate Rooms. Stagehouse requirements relate to scenery components.

Scene/Working Space Scene space at each side is usually devoted to entry legs and tabs for the depth of the stage. A cyclorama or backdrop is frequently used. Unimpeded crossover passage is very important, preferably wide enough for costumed dancers to pass each other without disturbing drapery, etc. Wing space must accommodate assembled dancers. An orchestra pit is very desirable, for 20–50 musicians.

3. Music-Drama Speech, music, action and scenic components are all incorporated in this form of presentation, sometimes called light opera or musical comedy. It is similar to straight drama in its storyline continuity, which demands directorial skill in successfully alternating speech, song and dance, and also relies heavily on stagecraft and technical support. The musical component is a key feature of transitions, requiring expert control. A relatively large cast and crew are typical with up to 50 people on stage at once and quantities of scenery to manage. Coordinating all this activity is a major problem requiring, besides extensive preparations, an excellent communications system during performance.

Performance Space Although principal attention is generally focused downstage, background "chorus" activity and the ability to have "cross talk" at the same time makes a wide, deep acting area desirable, about 60' × 45' deep. For a given production, this can be masked down. The floor should be danceable, although it needn't be very sophisticated in construction; the ability to build on and anchor to it is as important. Traps and pit-type cyclorama are desirable.

Enclosure A 30'–35' high proscenium arch is recommended, along with flyloft stagehouse. Stagehouse proportions recognize that wing-space is as important as loft space.

Scene/Working Space Wrap-around scene space must accept a large variety of rather elaborate scenery. The dimension of this zone must allow for structural support of stand-up sets with recesses and overhangs, often in combination with flown portions. Wagon sets are very useful as well, but require substantial working space in addition to that for cast assembly, other properties and technicians. Symmetrical working space is advised, to simplify maneuvering during scene changes. Since live music is essential, provide an orchestra pit for 15–30 musicians.

4. Orchestral Music First identify the kind of orchestra for which the facility is primarily intended. Both its size and instrumental composition have a part in determining its characteristic sound, intensity, the literature emphasized, and requirements of physical arrangement. This suggests a Room designed for its "most likely" users nevertheless involves tolerances for variations. Music concerts consist of a series of uninterrupted performance periods of varying length. In the intervals instrumental components may be changed, reorganized and returned while the audience, immobilized during performance, refreshes itself. The sometimes subtle alterations must be carefully prearranged in a rehearsal situation as similar to concert conditions as possible.

Performance Space Orchestra set-ups are usually as compact as practicable, in order to hear each other, see each other, and share sheet music. Stage area averages 16–20 square feet per musician and proscenium widths range from 55–80 feet. For various groups, this amounts to:

- Ensemble or band, 30–50 musicians, 800–900 s.f.
- Medium orchestra, 50–80 musicians, 1200–1500 s.f.
- Medium orchestra and chorus, 50–100 voices, 1800–2300 s.f.
- Symphony orchestra, 80–125 musicians, 2000–2400 s.f.
- Symphony and large chorus of 100–200 voices, 2800–3500 s.f.

MUSIC AND DRAMA CENTERS

Stage

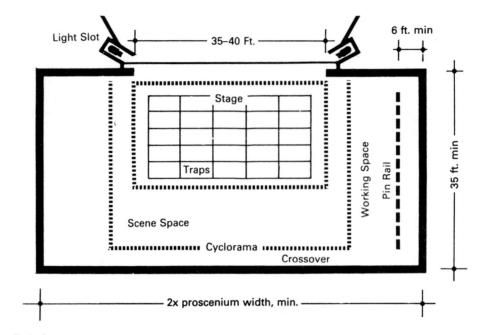

Fig. 1   Drama stage.

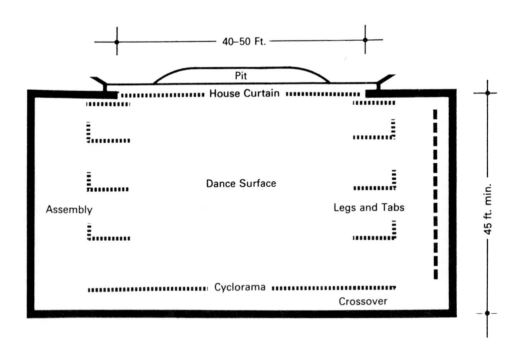

Fig. 2   Dance stage.

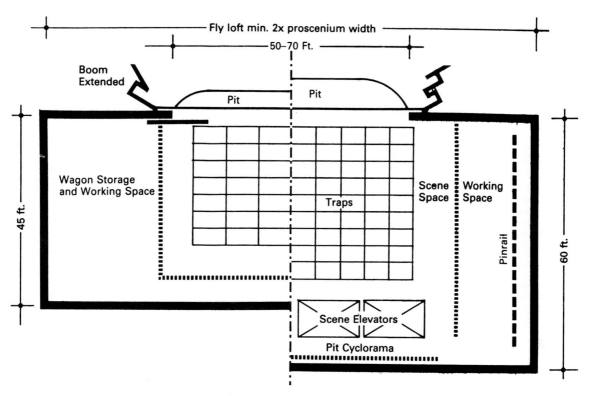

Fig. 3   Music-drama 50 ft. proscenium stage; grand opera 70 ft. proscenium stage.

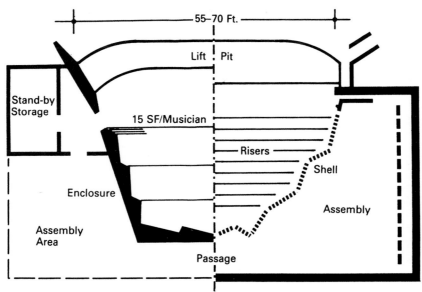

Fig. 4   Orchestral-choral stage.

MUSIC AND DRAMA CENTERS
Stage

Flexibility will help achieve sectional balance. A flat floor with portable riser platforms is advised, although some orchestras will not use risers. Performances with musicians and chorus often require extension forward and split-level arrangement with chorus behind orchestra. This can be accomplished on a large symphony stage with reduced orchestra, or by extension of an apron over the pit. Moving the orchestra forward alters the relationship to the enclosure. Smaller music ensembles and bands can be accommodated on a theoretically large stage with suitable adjustment of enclosure and musician arrangement. Therefore, the suggested approach is to size the stage for the largest likely group.

Enclosure Disregarding open stage forms applicable to small Rooms, two kinds of "sending end" enclosures are possible; the "hole in the wall" associated with traditional drama prosceniums and the "horn" that gradually becomes the Room. The latter is permanent construction especially designed for Music use, with structural qualities similar to the House. The first type (proscenium) is normally employed in multi-use Rooms or theater conversions, consisting of a demountable shell erected in the stagehouse. Both types have a degree of geometric adjustability.

Scene/Working Space Stagehouse functions, if any, are minimal for Music; most support activity takes place backstage or from control areas in the House. However, space adjoining the performance area should be allotted for performers' assembly and temporary instrument standby (pianos, extra chairs and stands). There may also be separate rooms for broadcast, recording equipment and lighting switchgear. If there is a story below stage, thoughtful planning of freight lifts is needed to make stage loading efficient. Installing a lift platform in the orchestra pit is recommended only if the acoustic enclosure design makes provision for the platform's use as performance area—i.e., if a proper forestage canopy is installed.

5. Recital Instrumental and vocal recital rooms are the most intimate music spaces. The presentation format is similar to orchestral concerts, but musicians are fewer in number and share a much more personal relationship with the listener. Recital acoustics provide greater definition among instruments.

Performance Space The platform area depends somewhat on anticipated music group sizes, 400–600 square feet typically. A low elevation, 24"–30", is usual and portable risers may be employed for the larger groups or for choral performances.

Enclosure The surfaces near the platform may be treated with adjustable panels that are reflective, absorptive or both. These are normally intended to adjust hearing on stage rather than project sound to the house, and a high degree of diffusion is desirable. The ceiling over the stage, or suspended reflectors, should be within 20 feet and no walls parallel. Occasionally, a false or openwork proscenium is used to support and screen lighting and audio equipment.

Scene/Working Space No scenery is involved, unless the Room has secondary uses. Piano, risers and chairs are stored adjoining the stage. There should be a lounge to which musicians may retire, and dimmers for house and stage lights.

6. Choral Basically a musical medium, group singing can have some of the characteristics of dramatic speech depending on the literature presented. Intelligibility is more important for secular works in terms of lyric continuity than for liturgical and choral-symphonic combinations. Choral requirements fall somewhere between those of a large recital hall and medium-sized orchestral facility, depending also on the number of voices.

Performance Space A rather close packing of singers is desirable in most cases to facilitate their mutual hearing and visual contact. Instruments and music stands are not involved. Singers may be seated for long or intermittent performance, or may stand throughout. Between 5 and 9 square feet of stage area is needed per singer. Additional area should be allowed for piano or instrumental accompaniment. Portable adjustable risers in 8 inch increments are a definite advantage over fixed risers. The floor area is normally twice as wide as deep.

Enclosure Recital or orchestral considerations are similar, although a shaped enclosure or shell is more likely to prove successful in larger Rooms. The human voice is relatively directional but not as powerful as many instruments until carefully trained, and rarely for sustained periods. The enclosures' function to blend, balance and contain sound energy is important.

Scene/Working Space Similar considerations pertain to recital, although offstage assembly space must be larger and is best with entries provided from both sides of the performance area. For orchestral accompaniment a pit is desirable, and actually necessary for large scale events. The alternative is a very large open stage arrangement.

7. Opera Musical drama is the middle ground between operatic recital and grand opera, since it makes more or less equal use of song, speech, music, dance and scenic elements. Operatic recital emphasizes music and song over action and scenery, and grand opera may be considered song, music and spectacle. The storyline is often well-known and diminishes in importance compared to musical execution. Traditionally lavish costumery and settings are involved along with a large cast of singers and musicians supporting lead soloists. Opera recital may involve two or more small groups on a stage similar to that for musical drama or smaller, with minimal scenic devices and dance activity. Grand opera involves a great deal of background movement, multiple entry points, stagecraft, special effects, and scene changes.

Performance Space Wider and deeper than others, it is typically 75' × 55'd. Traps, multilevel constructions, stage elevators and lifts are used extensively. The great depth and width of stage is

not merely a tradition, nor the requirement of elephants, camels and chariots. Dramatic part-singing demands a great deal of movement on stage, reassembling of voices, and accommodation of a large chorus. Since it is difficult to sing while moving, the cast moves to new relationships with the soloists.

Enclosure The opera proscenium is typically 65–80' wide and 40–50' high. This promotes acoustic coupling of the deep stage to the house and recognizes the probable height of a multitiered audience requiring good sightlines. The enormity of stage and stagehouse places premium value on trained, powerful voices and dramatic presence.

Scene/Working Space Opera stages are often the most technically sophisticated, the scenery vast and expensive because of its importance to performance. A person on an empty opera stage is dwarfed. He must move from prop to carefully selected prop, in order to maintain continuity of

scale. Grand opera requires substantial scene space and offstage working space on all sides. A large, fully equipped flyloft, or a combination with scene elevators from below stage, is also needed. The flyloft must furnish generous flexible lighting points behind the proscenium and above stage, often including sidelighting towers in the wings.

An orchestra pit is essential to grand opera. The pit locates musicians properly relative to the action, but out of direct line of sight. It enables eye contact between the conductor and musicians and singers. It also enables singers and musicians to hear themselves best. Grand opera requires an especially large pit (80 musicians) and careful acoustic design. This design often reflects the nature of opera music; the pit has a mainly reverberant contribution at low intensity so as not to overpower voice intelligibility. The deep Bayreuth pit was developed expressly for Wagnerian opera, giving an eerie non-directional sound.

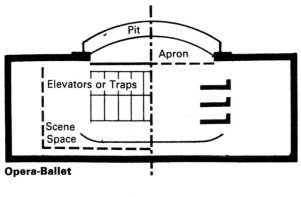

Opera-Ballet

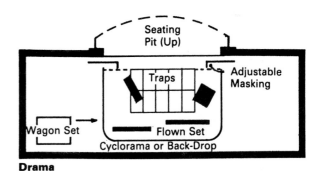

Drama

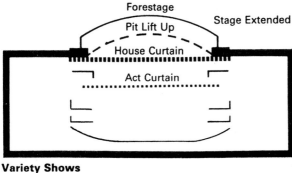

Variety Shows

Fig. 5 The multi-use stage.

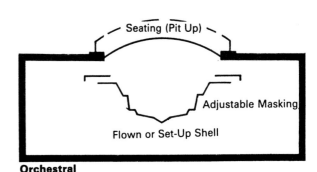

Orchestral

MUSIC AND DRAMA CENTERS

Stage

C. Functional Relationship of Stage to Room

No single stage form can best satisfy the functional requirements of all performance types. But a given stage form can often accommodate more than one performance type.

While single-purpose Rooms are typically best suited to their uses, the likelihood is that some degree of multi-use will exist. Unfortunately the prevalent tendency to begin with multi-use as a major design objective too often leads to disappointing, costly failures. Attempts to "install" flexibility take the form of mechanical devices; apron lifts and moving walls are the usual culprits.

Performance types can be grouped according to similarity of stage requirements as a first step, but it is important to bear in mind that both Stage and House are interdependent parts of the total Room. Any alteration of selection criteria for one has impact on the other particularly with regard to vision and hearing parameters. The audience arrangement in the House is based on the task of seeing action on the Stage, and this basis changes with the stage form and type of performance. The enclosure construction for both House and Stage corresponds to hearing tasks, and if the tasks or any part of the enclosure varies, adjustment may be required to obtain the best conditions.

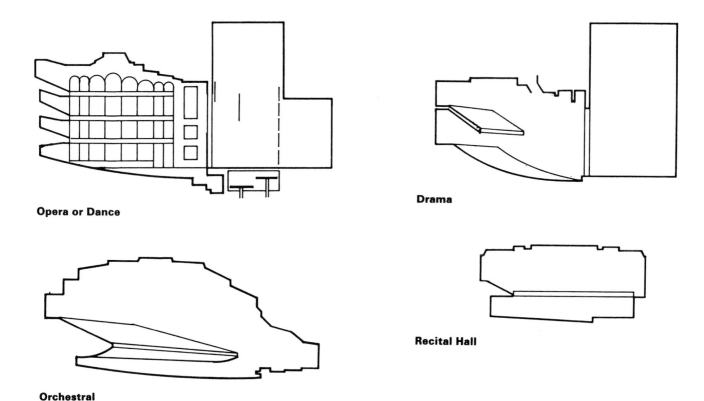

Opera or Dance

Drama

Orchestral

Recital Hall

Fig. 6   Four kinds of single-purpose rooms.

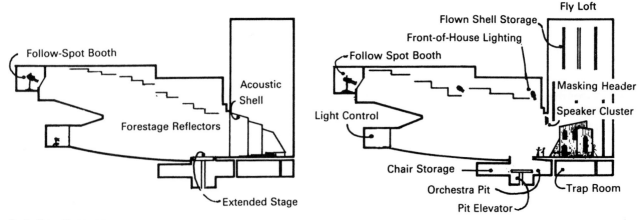

Fig. 7   The multi-use room.

While each company stages its own version, most consider a performing area 45 feet wide by 40 feet deep the minimum necessary. Many prefer a space 60 feet wide.

But the dance stage must be wider than the actual performance space. A proper stage includes a minimum of 10 to 15 feet of wing space on each side. These are transition zones between the performing area and offstage. Performers preparing for an entrance need wing space in which to warm up, to catch their breath, or to concentrate on a difficult passage. An entrance can be ruined if the dancer, crowded into a tiny area, is bumped by another performer or a stagehand.

Exits, when a dancer runs or leaps into the wings, or departs the stage holding another dancer aloft, also require ample space. At one New York theatre, where wing space is almost nil, dancers are said to lean mattresses against the walls, and to station themselves in the wings to catch colleagues making fast exits. Dance is demanding, but leaping offstage into a mattress seems one demand too many.

The wing space is occupied by more than dancers entering and exiting. Lighting equipment mounted on vertical steel booms (known as torms, trees, or ladders) is positioned in the wings for side-lighting effects. Dancers expect to cope with booms; but where there is ample wing space, booms can be positioned to be less obstructive.

The height of the stagehouse is dictated by the height of the stage picture demanded by the companies that will use the theatre.

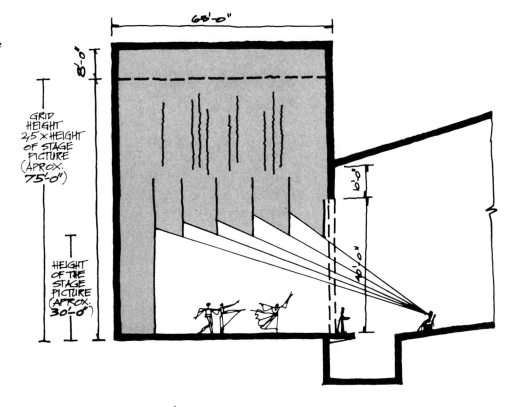

The orchestra pit must permit the conductor to see every member of the orchestra as well as the performers on stage without interrupting the audience's sightlines.

429

SPACE FOR DANCE

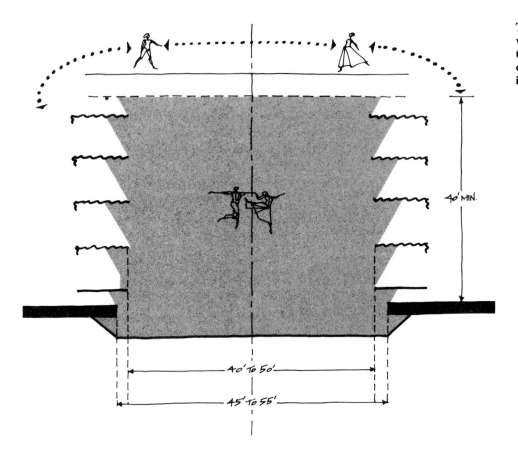

The floor plan of the performing area within a proscenium stagehouse shows the critical dimensions and principal components of stage drapery and masking used for dance.

40' MIN.

40' TO 50'

45' TO 55'

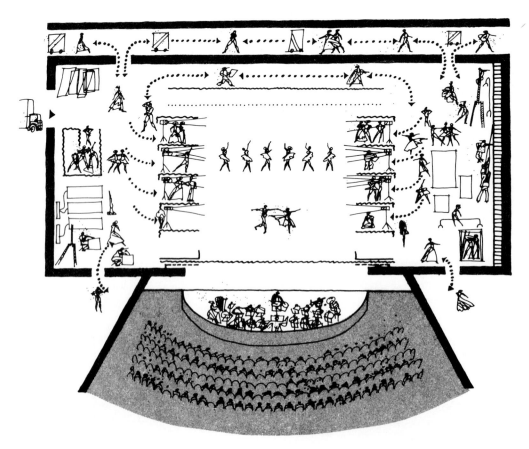

The proscenium stage—in full operation.

The "best seat in the house," located on the centerline of the auditorium, provides a clear view of the entire performing area and masks the wings.

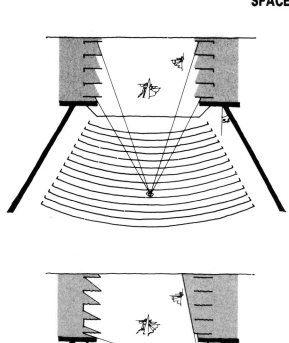

If the angle of the seating fan is limited to 60 degrees, people seated at the extreme ends of rows will have an adequate view of the stage and will not see too far into the wings.

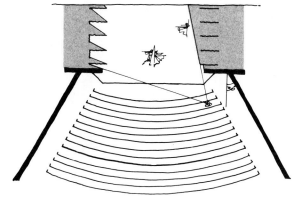

If the angle of the fan is widened in an effort to increase the seating capacity of the house, persons seated at the ends of rows cannot see a significant portion of the stage, and wing space cannot be masked. This illustration shows the angle at 80 degrees.

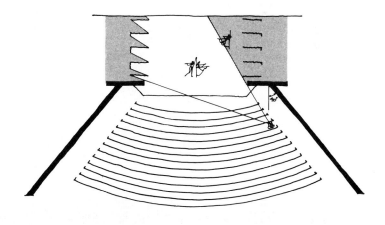

Keeping the 60-degree fan but increasing the width of the proscenium in order to increase the seating capacity is no solution because dance companies cannot increase the width of their performing area, as defined by their masking, because this would change the choreography.

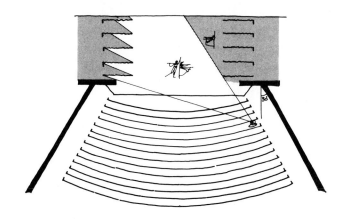

SPACE FOR DANCE

The rehearsal studio must be larger than the performing area on stage in order to allow space for entrances and exits, for dancers waiting their turn to rehearse, for rehearsal instruments or sound equipment, and for the choreographer and rehearsal director to have an adequate view of the work in progress.

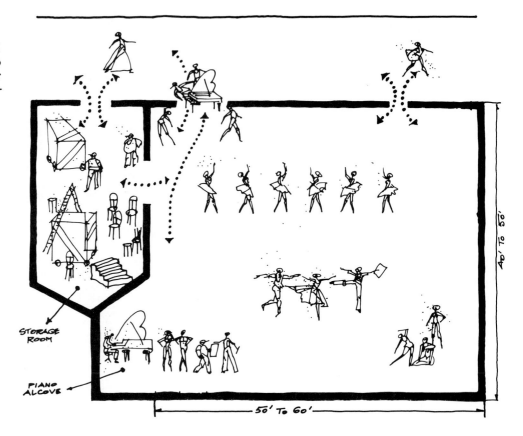

A well-equipped rehearsal studio needs barres, full-length mirrors (and curtains to cover them), a piano alcove, windows for fresh air and natural light, and ceiling fans for circulation.

Typical dimensions for rehearsal studio barres, mirrors, and draperies.

The community theater usually contains 500 to 1,000 seats and serves amateurs, semiprofessionals, and visiting professional groups. Most of the scenery and costumes are designed and made at the theater and require a special type of workshop. Because of its varied use, and the rather indeterminate responsibility of its management, its planning should be as simple and as foolproof as possible. This study will not include experimental theaters, since these present special problems.

A properly selected site offers (1) Accessibility by normal means of transportation. (A central location is essential for walking only. Automobiles should not have to traverse congested traffic zones when this can be avoided.) (2) Sufficient separation from bus and streetcar lines, principal highways, and other sources of noise. (3) Parking space. (4) Convenience to complementary community activities, educational or recreational, in order to reduce interbuilding traffic and minimize supervision and maintenance.

ARRANGEMENT

"Front" or public areas, and "backstage" or work groups, constitute the two major elements. Spectators should find everything necessary for their needs accessible from the foyer once they have presented tickets. Included are toilets, coatrooms, drinking fountains, lounges, and smoking areas. The lobby should provide waiting space and circulation to areas other than the theater, which may be contained in the building. The manager's office is convenient if adjacent to the box office and accessible from the lobby. In the work group, control of the stage entrance will avoid interference from unauthorized persons and facili-

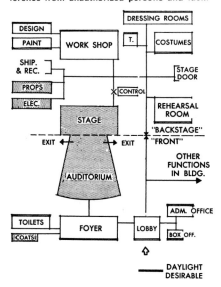

Fig. 1 Organization chart.

Time-Saver Standards, 1st ed., McGraw-Hill, Inc., New York, N.Y., 1946.

tate accounting of players, properties, and scenery. Rehearsal rooms are part of the work area and should be near other work elements. Movement of heavy furniture and other properties demands close relation between work spaces and stage proper. Dressing rooms may be more remote but within supervisory distance. (See Fig. 1.)

GENERAL REQUIREMENTS

Requirements for community theaters, although derived from the same sources and from the same historical background as those of the commercial, or "professional," theater, exhibit fundamental differences. Emphasis upon creative effort leads to demands for a different type of accommodation than does the necessity for financial profit. Two general types of creative community activity, directly related to the theater, require special provisions.

Audience Activity This is great before and after a performance and between acts, due to the social nature of the occasion. Spaces for lounging, talking, smoking, are all necessary. Easy access to such spaces is of prime importance. At times, audience and actors may intermingle; for this a combination of lounge and rehearsal room is needed. Since refreshments may be served, a small kitchen or serving pantry is essential.

Production Activities These consist of preparation for and presentation of the performance. In a community theater, scenery, costumes, and properties are mostly prepared within the theater plant. Separate workshops are ordinarily provided, one for costumes, and one for scenery and properties. Used materials are salvaged insofar as possible, stored within the plant, and reused. Ample storage space is needed.

Presentation problems may be solved differently in the community theater than in its commercial prototype. Both types demand ample stage space; but, whereas in the "professional" theater, urban real-estate values have forced a vertical development with lofty stage houses for lifting scenery vertically ("flying"), tiered dressing rooms, and often inadequate wing space, the community theater, built on less expensive land, may be expanded horizontally. Scenery can be shifted horizontally, perhaps on wagon stages. Proscenium size and shape may be variable. Such flexibility and multiplicity of uses are not only financially desirable, but some theater authorities call them essential for the theater's progress. Types of stages which are considered impractical in the average commercial theater, become available.

Limitations Because the theater has such highly specialized requirements, this study is limited in scope to those items within the creative center which are strictly community theater needs. Emphasis in the community theater being on amateur participation in all phases of the theater, there is to be expected less efficiency of personnel, and a necessity for greater

flexibility of facilities, than in commercial theaters.

Capacity of the auditorium for the type of theater here discussed averages approximately 800 persons, often less. If, for financial reasons, provisions for road shows must be included, minimum seating capacity has to be increased to 1,200, preferably 1,500 persons. This increase brings many disadvantages, among which are lack of intimacy and lack of flexibility in auditorium shape and stage type.

Public Circulation A prime requisite for public areas in the community theater is ease of movement. Access between the various parts needs to be as free as possible, to permit their full use by the audience before the show, between acts, and after the final curtain. Code requirements as to doors and exits are minima for safety; the community theater needs even greater circulation facilities. Depending upon site, nature of surrounding developments, disposition of plan elements, and requirements for acoustics, lighting, etc., the number of openings to vestibule, lobby, auditorium, and lounge may be increased far beyond the minimum.

Access to Auditorium If possible the principal entrances from the lobby to the auditorium should be arranged without doors. In order to achieve this it is necessary to make a careful acoustical analysis; in all probability sound-deadening material will be required on the walls of approaching corridors or lobbies, to prevent parallelism.

Types of Space It is always desirable to have both vestibule and lobby. In most cases, it would be well to provide a separate lounge which on occasion may be used for social meetings, lectures, discussion groups, etc. The lounge may also serve as rehearsal space.

Vestibule The lighting in the vestibule adjoining the street may be quite brilliant. Telephone booths should be provided, accessible from the vestibule. In general the addition of other features, such as small bookstores, etc., which will attract the public to the theater as a part of their daily lives, is desirable.

Ticket Office This should, if possible, both command the entrance to the inner lobby and at the same time permit the lines to form without obstructing it. There are preferably two ticket windows, one for reserved seats and one for current seats. Necessary also is sufficient free wall space for a small ticket rack which can be made locally.

Lobby While the theater in the large city has no particular need for oversize lobbies, in the community theater the performance must be considered as a social occasion as well as dramatic entertainment. Therefore, the lobby should be arranged to show off groups of people and their clothes to advantage.

A combination of exhibition space and lobby is easy to achieve, and is generally desirable in the community theater. It is hoped that the community will take an interest in the produc-

Cultural

COMMUNITY THEATERS

Community Theaters

Typical space requirements			Typical Space Requirements		
Spaces	Areas* (sq ft)	Remarks	Spaces	Areas* (sq ft)	Remarks
Vestibule and gallery	1,200	Less area would hamper use of space as gallery and meeting place. Area may be increased in proportion as auditorium capacity exceeds 800. Good lighting is necessary.	Stage	3,500	Ample; 2,800 sq ft minimum; 3,500 usual avg. except for encircling stage. Air conditioning in conjunction with auditorium desirable; no outside light; top of stage house louvered (consult codes); if conventional stage, minimum height, floor to grid, is 70 ft.
Checkroom	240	Minimum unless checkroom does not serve auditorium or unless patrons do not check overcoats.			
Lobby	1,000	See Vestibule; mechanical ventilation needed here.	Stage workshop	1,500	Sometimes reduced to 1,200 sq ft. Outside light, if clear glass, preferably from north; if obscure, orientation unimportant.
Ticket office	50	Minimum; for larger houses additional administration office (50–80 sq ft) is required. Ticket windows (2) and wall space (approx. 4 by 8 ft) are necessary.	Scene storage	1,000	Minimum; larger if possible.
			Costume workshop	420	May reduce to 300 sq ft; north light desirable.
Lounge-rehearsal room	750	Minimum size, equal to acting area of stage; mech. vent. needed.	Costume storage	210	Minimum; no outside light; preferably ventilated; must be dry.
Administrative	350	Minimum; area varies. Outside light and air needed.	Costume dyeing	80	Minimum; no outside light required; unless outside air provided, must be mechanically ventilated.
Men's toilets	250	Consult codes; areas ample for 800 capacity; either mech. vent. or outside light and air needed.	Six dressing rooms†	680	Each room requires access to two lavatories; size not changed with size of building; stars' dressing rooms each need private toilet and shower; all preferably air-conditioned.
Women's toilets	250				
Auditorium	5,600	Minimum for conventional seating; may increase to 7,000–8,000 sq ft for aisleless seating. Area includes forestage (removable seats). Outside light undesirable.	Makeup room†	130	Minimum; used also for dressing, requires two lavatories; preferably air-conditioned.
Radio studio	300	Can be reduced to 200 sq ft; no outside light; mech. vent. needed.	Two chorus rooms†	440	Reasonable minimum; three lavatories needed in each; preferably air-conditioned.
Control room	70	Minimum; mech. vent. needed.	Two bathrooms	300	Reasonable minimum.
Director's room	20	Minimum, but adequate.	Stage manager	150	Minimum.
Quiet room	30	Acts as sound insulation between circulation and radio unit.	Discussion room	750	Can be used for rehearsal; area determined by acting area.
Projection room	200	Ample, includes toilet and lavatory; consult code requirements.			
Spotlight booth	400	Area may be divided into three booths: one on center with stage, one at each side of auditorium.			

* Based on auditorium capacity of 800.
† Dressing, chorus, make-up rooms require mirrors, preferably 3-sided type, movable; and overhead lighting, mirror-lighting equipment.

tion of a play as well as in its presentation, and, therefore, exhibition space is desirable to show the various developments: costume designs, sketches for stage settings, etc., even though the space is not used as an actual art gallery.

Checkroom This should be either adequate or omitted entirely. If included it should open from the main lobby and provision should be made to have a sufficient number of attendants and a sufficiently large opening to the lobby so that standing in long lines after the performance is not necessary. In community theaters the expense of the proper number of attendants may become a problem. The checkroom serves not only the theater, but also other facilities in the building, and therefore should have an entrance to the main vestibule.

Auxiliary Spaces These include areas not always essential to the theater, but usually desirable. Projection rooms are fairly well standardized. If provisions for radio broadcasting are desired, for either instruction and study of new dramatic techniques, or actual broadcasting, the minima outlined in the table above may be provided. Discussion or viewing rooms are

similar to radio studios, and, like them, usually need loudspeakers. Here an instructor and class, or the theater director and assistants, may discuss a production freely while it is in progress.

AUDITORIUM AND STAGE

Maximum Seating Distance Even in theaters of 1,200 to 1,500 capacity, the last seat is preferably not over 75 to 100 ft from the stage, and much less in smaller houses. When balconies are used, the front of the balcony is preferably within 50 ft of the stage.

Sight Lines The apron of a forestage may be excluded from view to prevent sight lines angled sharply downward from rear seats. In auditoria of 800 or less capacity, when balconies are not used, a complete view of the forestage should be possible. Side proscenia of encircling stages do not require perfect sight lines; balconies may help improve them. Sight lines for the side seats in the auditorium should permit a minimum of two-thirds of the main acting space to

be seen through the conventional proscenium; conversely, care should be taken that areas beyond the acting space are masked.

Seating Facilities Seat spacing preferably always exceeds the minimum of the New York Code of 32 in., back-to-back; and, if possible, seats are not less than 20 in. on centers. Use of "Continental" seating, in which each seat row becomes an aisle, should be limited to small auditoria, where it does not force the rear row to be located too far from the stage. Aisle widths and number of aisles are generally determined by building codes.

Auditorium Capacity and Type Need to vary the capacity of an 800-seat auditorium is not urgent. However, when necessary, this may be accomplished with curtains, placed in such a way, perhaps under the lip of a balcony or at a natural break in the auditorium, that they do not appear to change the essential proportions of the auditorium. Empty seats visible to actors are a detriment to good performances. Experts should be consulted as to the acoustical effect on the auditorium. A solid partition will very probably cause havoc in the acoustics.

434

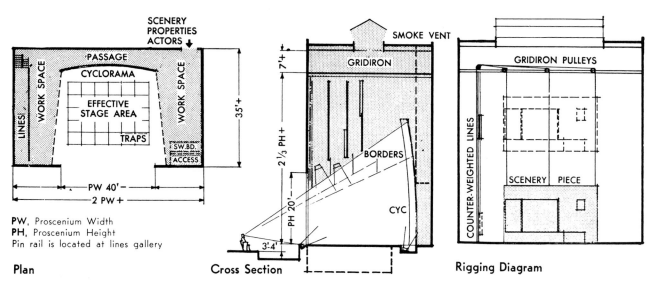

PW, Proscenium Width
PH, Proscenium Height
Pin rail is located at lines gallery

Plan   **Cross Section**   **Rigging Diagram**

STAGE DIAGRAMS

Advantages or disadvantages of stadium houses versus balconies are subject to much discussion. The best opinion seems to agree that a stadium house for a capacity of over 800 or 1,000 will have a rear row of seats too far from the stage for "comedies of errors," although satisfactory for spectacle pieces.

Auditorium Lighting The object of lighting in the auditorium is to concentrate attention upon the stage, even before the curtain goes up. In most cases, lights with reflectors, in coves hidden from view, will prove most satisfactory. Fluorescent lighting, though efficient, is difficult to use because it cannot be dimmed. The color of the light should be neutral though warm. Chandeliers are usually considered objectionable.

Stage Area Space is the most vital consideration. It is necessary that the stage be so arranged that up to five sets can be set up and stacked in succession, without being seen during the performance; and that this be done without acrobatics on the part of amateur stage hands. Furthermore, open-air (plein-air) scenes require the appearance of great height. Again, a high stage loft and an expanse of unimpeded wall space are desirable for storing current sets. This means confining openings to one wall if possible, or, at the most, two. It is also necessary that the stage provide a "crossover," i.e., a passage for actors across the stage, either behind the stage through a corridor, possibly through the stage shop, or behind the cyclorama.

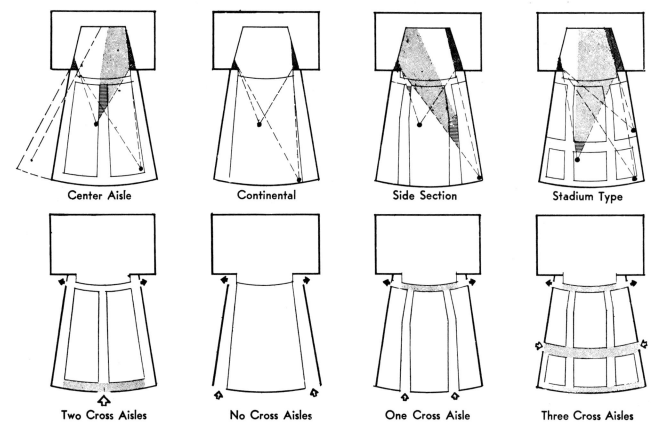

SEATING AND AISLE ARRANGEMENTS: Heavily shaded areas represent stage and seating area losses from comparative visual position in various systems.

COMMUNITY THEATERS

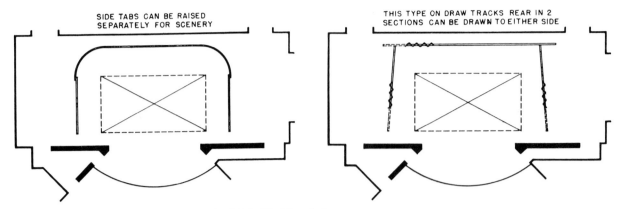

SIDE TABS CAN BE RAISED SEPARATELY FOR SCENERY

THIS TYPE ON DRAW TRACKS REAR IN 2 SECTIONS CAN BE DRAWN TO EITHER SIDE

Fig. 2 Two of the many types of cycloramas; one on the right is difficult to adjust.

Acting Facilities The *acting area* extends slightly more than the width of the proscenium, and is, at the least, 20 ft deep. It should be trapped throughout its extent, with unimpeded space below.

All types of stages are preferably provided with an ample forestage. Even though this is not carried to an extreme, it is desirable for performances which are to be seen in the "round" rather than through a picture frame, and for soloists or lecturers. It can include provisions for removable seats, thus varying the auditorium's capacity.

The stage manager requires at least a desk, with direct access to stage, and to dressing rooms. The prompter needs a small space from which he can hear and follow action without being seen.

Scenic Provisions *Cycloramas,* or background surfaces, are illustrated by diagram and are susceptible to great variation, both as to material, number of units, and shape. In planning for the type of cyclorama to be used, provision must be made for moving scenery horizontally. Permanent solid cycloramas, made of plaster, are particularly desirable for use only as a back wall of an encircling stage. Curves must be acute, and as a rule it will be found desirable to tilt the cyclorama back slightly to reduce objectionable sound reflection. (See Fig. 2.)

The *gridiron* consists of a number of structural steel shapes suspended from 70 to 90 ft above the stage floor. Its exact location and composition are best determined by a stage equipment specialist. The *pinrail* is located along one wall of the stage, and serves as a means of securing grid lines. It is commonly 14 to 15 ft above the stage floor.

Two doors, each at least 8 by 12 ft, are usually required for loading scenery. One should open to the scene shop, the other to a street or alley. The latter door may be omitted when no provisions are made for road shows.

Revolving or elevator stages may also be desirable, but are often too costly.

Nonconventional Stages If great flexibility is required in the stage, as would seem desirable for the community theater, a greater amount of stage area and cubage may be added to the wings. With certain exceptions, it is obvious that a given amount of cubage up in the air does not have the multiplicity of use that it will have at stage level. The result may be a long, circular, low stage surrounding the better part of the audience, closed off from the auditorium by a series of panels which may be shifted at will. Gridiron is usually eliminated unless funds are available for both grid and "encircling" stage.

With this "encircling" type of stage, additional storage space should be provided adjacent to the shop; and scenes may be shifted on

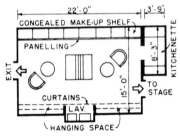

Combined Green Room and dressing room for women's chorus (20 people). The Green Room is an actor's recreation and discussion space, to which a few visitors may be admitted. Lights and mirrors are similar to those in other dressing rooms.

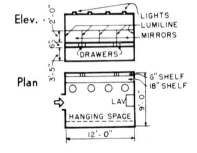

Typical dressing room for four people. Overhead lights are necessary for adjusting wigs and costumes, and for final inspection of make-up. Lights at mirrors are preferably designed to illuminate the actors' faces evenly, rather than to light the mirrors.

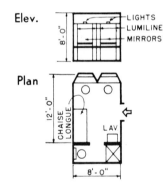

Typical "Stars'" dressing room for two people. Triple mirrors are desirable. Chaise longue is desirable but not essential. Adjoining toilet should contain a shower and water closet.

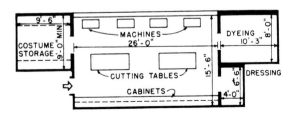

At left, plan of typical costume shop. Good light, preferably natural, is essential for sewing machines. In many respects the costume shop is similar to the sewing department of a modern high school.

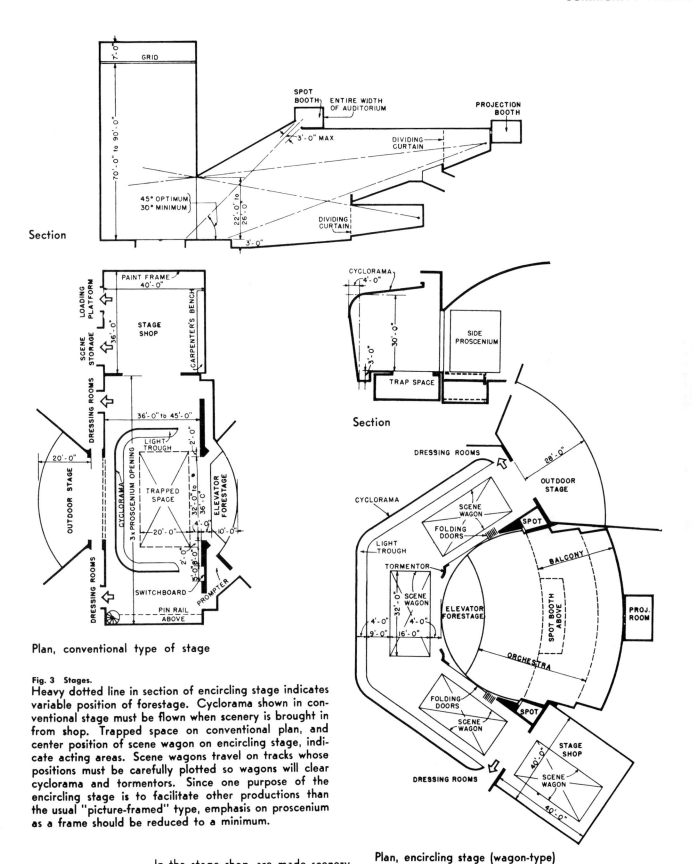

Section

Plan, conventional type of stage

Section

Fig. 3 Stages.
Heavy dotted line in section of encircling stage indicates variable position of forestage. Cyclorama shown in conventional stage must be flown when scenery is brought in from shop. Trapped space on conventional plan, and center position of scene wagon on encircling stage, indicate acting areas. Scene wagons travel on tracks whose positions must be carefully plotted so wagons will clear cyclorama and tormentors. Since one purpose of the encircling stage is to facilitate other productions than the usual "picture-framed" type, emphasis on proscenium as a frame should be reduced to a minimum.

In the stage shop are made scenery and properties. Facilities for woodworking, metalworking, and painting, and storage space for lumber, nails, tools, canvas, and painting materials, are all needed.

Plan, encircling stage (wagon-type)

wagons. When the encircling stage is used with all panels open, wagons are dispensed with and scenery is formalized. If structurally possible, the entire proscenium should be unimpeded by fixed columns. However, two columns placed at either side of an imaginary proscenium may be very useful for concealing vertical banks of lights. These light housings (in this case the columns) are called "tormentors," and are preferably movable. (See Fig. 3.)

Diagram of the encircling stage shows three spaces for two wagons (excluding the shop). If there is unlimited space, more wagons may be made available; but the ensuing complications are considerable and the gains small. The encircling stage becomes less practical as the size of the auditorium increases. Even with auditoria for 800, good sight lines are difficult to obtain unless stage area is substantially increased. It should be noticed, however, that productions which need side stages do not require perfect sight lines.

One may conclude that encircling stages are both economically and functionally desirable for the smallest auditoria, while for those of 800 seats and up, their cost may become prohibitive.

Outdoor Stage Size of outdoor auditoria varies considerably. The stage, of necessity, is some-

what formalized. If possible it should have immediate access to the inside stage, preferably through the wall, unless this arrangement is prevented by a built-in cyclorama.

Stage Shop Adequate area is a prime consideration. Equally important is the height to be allowed for the paint frame. When the conventional type of stage, with gridiron, is used, the height for a paint frame is at least 30 ft. Even with the comparatively low "encircling" stage, a 30-ft paint frame is necessary, since the effective height of scenery remains the same. It is possible to rig the paint frame on the rear wall of the auditorium, or on a stage wall. However, when this is done, no scenery can be painted on the frame during productions or during rehearsals. The shop is the center of most of the dramatic activities and includes subdivisions for carpentry, electrical, metal, and painting work. It should be provided with good outside light, preferably diffused. It should immediately adjoin the stage storage space, the desirable clear ceiling height of which is 15 ft. Less height can be used in storage spaces, but this necessitates laying flats on their sides, which is considered unsatisfactory.

Costume Shop This, too, is a vital element in the community theater, because, of necessity,

most of the costumes are made on the premises. The costume-storage space should adjoin the costume shop.

WORKSHOPS, DRESSING ROOMS, STORAGE

Dressing Rooms Requirements for individual dressing rooms vary, depending upon the likelihood of producing professional shows and the funds available. Most satisfactory would be provisions for 18 to 20 actors in a number of dressing rooms, each providing for 3 to 4 actors, and two chorus rooms, one for men and one for women, each providing for about 20 actors. One chorus room may be used as a Green Room or lounge for actors.

Rehearsal Rooms The number of rehearsal rooms is determined entirely by how much use is made of the building and how often the stage is available for rehearsal. Rehearsal rooms should be in the same proportion and somewhat larger than the acting area of the stage; and, acoustically, should reproduce stage conditions as closely as possible. The public lounge, adjacent to the auditorium lobby, may also serve for rehearsals.

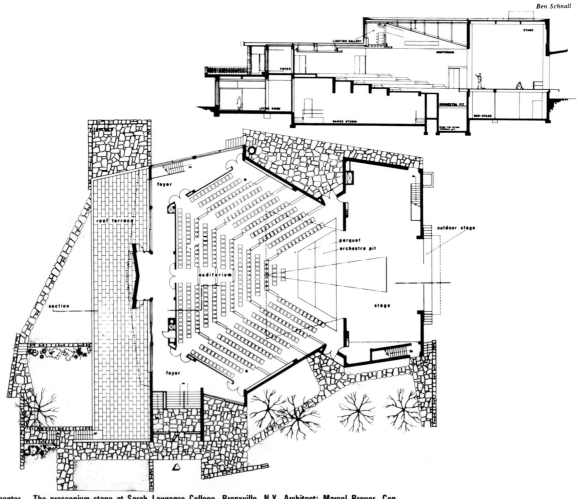

Ben Schnall

Arts center. The proscenium stage at Sarah Lawrence College, Bronxville, N.Y. Architect: Marcel Breuer. Consultants: Stanley C. McCandless, E. C. Cole, Sidney K. Wolfe. This multipurpose auditorium (capacity 500) is steeply raked and the stage floor is low to allow better audience perspective, especially for dance performances. Alternate rows of seats are removable to permit installation of tables or desks. The lighting gallery is close to the stage so that the control board operator's sight lines are similar to those of the spectators. The backstage wall opens onto tennis courts so the stage may be used for outdoor performances, commencement exercises, and special events.

By SAMUEL SELDEN

NOTE: No fixed specifications have yet been drawn which are applicable to outdoor theaters everywhere. The following suggestions should be regarded as tentative, to be modified to suit particular local needs and available facilities.

THE SIZE OF THE THEATER

An outdoor theater can be planned to seat as many as 3,000 spectators without the use of amplification for the actors' voices. What is recommended, however, as an upper limit for the seating, is about 2,500. The suggestions in this outline are scaled for a structure of between 1,500–2,000 seats, which is nearer the ideal.

OUTSIDE THE THEATER

1. *Parking Lot (or Lots) should be—*
   Large enough to handle one car for every three spectators.
   Designed to permit convenient and speedy exit following the performance, with good access from traffic routes.
   Surfaced with gravel or asphalt and provided with good drainage under all conditions.
   Well lighted for ease and security in parking and walking.
   So arranged as to permit the quick departure of any car in case of an emergency during the performance.
   Convenient to the box office and the entrance to the theater.
   Located where the noises and lights of late-arriving cars will not disturb the performance.
   Well marked with signs.

2. *A Business Office*
   If the theater is on or very near a main traffic route, the office of the manager may be placed at the theater.
   Usual practice, however, is to have this office in the center of the nearest town where it is readily accessible to patrons stopping in hotels and motels.
   In any case, the business office should have an information center and display space in addition to work space for the manager and promotion director and their assistants.
   It should include a place for the display of folders, a desk for handling rooming accommodations, and the like.

3. *A Box Office*
   Convenient to both the parking lot and the entrance to the theater.
   With shelter for patrons buying tickets in bad weather.

An Amphitheatre for Epic Drama, Institute of Outdoor Drama, University of North Carolina, Chapel Hill, N.C., 1966.

Provided with windows for advanced sales, reserve seats, and general-admission (if any), clearly marked with prices.
With telephone connections to the business office (if not in the same building) and to the stage.
Near toilet facilities and a water fountain.

4. *Other Facilities (Desirable Though Not Completely Necessary)*
   A first aid station.
   A nursery for patron's children.
   A pay telephone.
   A concession stand or house.

5. *The Entrance to the Theater*
   Well marked, simple, and attractive.
   Near enough to the parking lot to keep older people from tiring themselves while getting to the theater.
   Far enough away from the lot to let patrons lose the sound of traffic and fall under the quiet spell of the general setting before stepping into the theater.
   Sometimes provision can be made for bringing very old or crippled patrons by car along a separate path right to the theater entrance.

6. *A Separate Entrance and Parking for Cast and Crew*

THE AUDITORIUM

Of primary importance are good hearing and good sightlines to every part of the performance areas. This means that an effective compromise must be made between width and depth. A very wide auditorium may have good acoustics but poor sight lines, while a very narrow auditorium will tend toward the reverse.

Effective acoustical planning depends on the correct placement of reflective surfaces for all sounds involved in the performance. Care must be taken, for instance, not to place opposing walls backing the side stages exactly parallel to each other (as they may cause a disturbing reverberation in the lower part of the amphitheater). Remember that the sound waves tend to bounce off mirror surfaces at the same angles that light does.

One of the first aids to good sightlines is an effective slope. Seats may be set on a rising parabolic curve, or on two different inclines, a fairly mild slope for the lower half of auditorium (the half near the main stage) and a steeper slope for the upper (rear) half. The slope recommended for the lower portion is $12°$ (that is, a rise of about 1 minute in 7), and for the upper $24°$ (about 1 minute in $3\frac{1}{2}$) or steeper.

There should be at least five aisles, two down the center, two down the outside, and one cross aisle at the break between the two slopes. If the central seating area in the back section of the auditorium is very wide, it can be broken by an additional longitudinal aisle extending from the top down to the cross aisle.

All stepped sections should be illuminated by small hooded aisle lights.

The seating may be provided by sturdy wooden benches with plank backs, by benches surmounted by clamped-on plastic sport seats, or by individual metal seats with or without arms. If single seats are used, they may be so mounted or racked together that patrons will not shift them around.

The most satisfactory seats seem to be either sturdy metal and canvas folding chairs or chairs with tough, preformed plastic seats. These can be lifted for cleaning, tilted to avoid water puddles during a rain, and can be stored indoors when not in use at the close of the season. All seats should be clearly numbered. The width of each seat should not be less than 18 in. and need not be more than 23 in. A comfortable width is about 21 in. The distance between rows of seats should be 3 ft. Other details about the auditorium which need to be kept in mind are:

1. Toilet facilities, placed and housed where they are convenient to both sides of the auditorium but are not noisy, and of sufficient number to accommodate the peak requirements which occur just before performance and during an intermission.

2. Rain shelters on both sides of the seating area or at the back, for use in case of sudden showers.

3. Concession booths on each side (walled in to reduce the noise of refrigerators and the handling of bottles).

4. Good paving (not loose gravel which is very noisy) and good drainage everywhere.

5. Sufficient auditorium lighting to let patrons read their programs easily, and high enough to be out of their eyes.

6. Signs placed where they will indicate clearly to the patrons where the various sections of seats are, as well as the toilets and the refreshment centers.

7. A public address system for announcements to the audience on rainy nights.

THE STAGES

The usual arrangement of acting areas in an outdoor theater is a large main stage and two smaller side stages in front of the proscenium wall and to the right and left of the main stage. This plan allows for flexible and continuous action since, by taking a scene off to one of the side stages, it permits the technical crew to change a setting on the main stage. Thus the play does not have to be broken at any point, except for the intermission.

These features are recommended for the main (central) stage:

1. A level 3 ft above the base of the lowest row of seats in the auditorium.

2. A proscenium opening of about 70 ft.

3. A depth of about 40 ft from the line of the proscenium walls. (The apron in front of this line should be as narrow as possible.)

4. Plenty of wing space—at least 50 ft—at each side of the acting areas.

5. A height for the proscenium wall on each side of the opening of 16 to 18 ft and of a

length sufficient to mask from the audience all activity back stage.

6. An appearance for the proscenium wall which is simple, fairly neutral, and thoroughly in keeping with both the natural setting of the theater and the style of the play being performed (log, board, stone, or brick).

7. Level ground, well drained and preferably surfaced with either cement or asphalt (where scene changing does not require a smooth clear floor, the dancers can be helped by giving them several inches of sand as a dance cover).

8. Some amphitheaters have been built with a second, slightly higher, level with one or two longitudinal steps leading up to it, about 20 ft upstage, in an effort to increase the variety of acting spaces available. Careful consideration should be given to its effect on scene shifting, dancing, or other theater uses before this is incorporated as part of the permanent design.

9. In some cases it will be necessary to include anchoring devices for jacks, flanges, and stage braces supporting heavy movable scenery set directly and permanently into the hard surface of the stage floor.

10. Electrical outlets for stage lighting and for the convenient attachment of cable to special effects such as campfires.

11. Circuits for an intercommunication system between departments.

12. Unless a steep embankment or a clump of tall trees can serve as an acoustical background, a high wooden or masonry wall should be erected behind the stage to provide a sounding board at the rear of the acting areas. There should be masking wings for side entrances on the main stage and for mounting of lighting equipment and for convenient scene shifting space. A back wall for a 70-ft proscenium opening would be about 110 ft.

These features are suggested for each of the two side stages (right and left of the proscenium opening):

1. A level 2 ft above that of the main stage (5 ft above the base of the lowest row of seats), with easy access from both backstage and the main stage.

2. The area covering a quarter of a circle with a radial center on the proscenium wall of the main stage, starting about 30 ft back from the opening (giving a cut-of-pie-shaped acting space on the side stage of about 30 by 30 ft with the curve toward the audience).

3. No proscenium frame of any kind is needed for this side stage (the proscenium wall of the main stage forms the rear wall for these side stages).

4. Three steps or a ramp at the front corner to connect the side stage with the apron of the main stage.

5. Level ground, drained and surfaced like the main stage.

6. A door or concealed passageway connecting this stage to the wing of the main stage for the use of actors.

7. Considerable working space, right or left, beyond this acting area for the manipulation, and possibly the storage, of scenery and properties to be used on this stage. (If these are to be stored backstage in a wing of the main stage and brought out front when needed, an adequately concealed passage should be provided for them.)

Careful thought must be given to the far background of the three stages. The view of the stage and beyond it to the trees or distant mountains should be attractive and mood-creating from the moment the spectator first comes into the theater area.

THE BACKSTAGE AREA

In the wings:

1. There should be plenty of free space for the assembling of actors, the organizing of groups, and the massing of crowd voices for offstage effects.

2. Property tables should be placed in locations convenient to both sides of the main stage and the entrances to the side stages.

3. There should be adequate spaces for the storing and sheltering of the portable scenery units and properties.

4. There should be proper drainage in every part.

5. All the permanent wiring should be run under ground where it cannot trip the actors or interfere with the movement of scenery and properties.

6. Some controlled illumination should be provided for backstage operations, well shielded so no direct or reflected lighting will be seen by the spectators.

7. There should be sufficient space for the drying of scenery, costumes, and properties the morning after a rain.

8. A bulletin board for nightly directions to actors and technicians should be set up in a free and convenient spot, a little away from any of the main traffic lanes onto the stage.

9. There should be an efficient intercommunication system over which messages can be sent from one side of the stage to the other, from the stage manager to the electrician, the organist, and the house manager.

The area behind the main stage should not be used for any large operation. There should be no lighting here except what may be planned for stage effects, and all trees should be left standing to maintain a good background screening for the stage pictures.

A spacious passageway should be provided for the actors and technicians who have to cross behind stage from one wing to the other.

THE DRESSING ROOMS

The placement and size of the dressing rooms will depend to a great extent on local topography and on the number of actors in the show.

The dressing rooms should be put as near the wings as possible without interfering in any way with the backstage movement of scenery and actors.

At the same time, the dressing rooms should be completely out of view of the audience. Care should be taken to see that no light shining through a door or window finds its way directly or indirectly to the eyes of the spectator, and that noises in the dressing rooms are not heard out front.

The dressing rooms may be laid out as a group of small units to take care of small groups of actors, or as larger rooms capable of taking care of big groups of men or women.

The best arrangement has smaller dressing rooms for selected groups of male and female actors; one for the leading men, one for female leaders, and other rooms for groups of secondary players.

If there are any in the show who have to use unusual makeup, like Indian body wash and war paint, these should be given an area partitioned off so that their body makeup will not rub against other actors' costumes. They should have also their own shower facilities.

A shelf-type makeup table of 18 in. width and 30 in. height should be built around the walls of the dressing rooms with a 2 ft 6 in. or 3-ft space for each actor. In front of each actor will be a makeup mirror with a 75-watt light on each side. Benches or chairs 18 in. high, sufficient for all of the makeup positions, should be provided.

Ample space and equipment should be furnished each member of the cast for dressing and for the hanging of costumes, especially if they are of period design. Some permanent costume racks are recommended.

It is desirable to have at least one full-length mirror in each dressing room.

Showers, lavatories and toilet facilities must be supplied for each large dressing room or dressing room area. There should be at least:

• One toilet for each six persons
• One shower to each six persons
• One wash basin for each four persons
• Several urinals for men
• More toilets for women

If the production has only a few actors who use body makeup, the need will be for fewer showers and more wash basins.

Hot and cold running water must be furnished. It will be needed by the actors in the evening and by the costumer during the day. The hot water heater must be large enough to furnish hot water to a large number of actors in a short space of time. There might be one 400-gal heater or two 200-gal heaters, one for each side. Oil, coal, or gas heaters are better than electric since the electric require a longer warming-up period than can usually be tolerated.

The dressing rooms must be properly ventilated. Louvers and large circulating fans are suggested. Windows, if used, should be placed away from the stage and the audience area to minimize light leaks.

Light baffles for doors can be used to avoid these leaks. The doors should be placed in such a way as to be of convenience to the actors wanting to reach the backstage areas, while keeping to a minimum the danger of light spills.

SHOPS AND OFFICES

The Costume Shop

The shop should be conveniently close to the dressing room area. The size of it and the equipment of it will depend on whether it is to be used simply for the maintenance or also for the preparation of costumes. If it is to serve as the main construction center it should contain space for a large cutting table (about 3 by 6 ft) and at least four sewing machines, sewing tables, and chairs. The shop must be large enough to house one or more washing machines. It should also have space for the storing of materials and accessories. The shop should be at least 30 by 30 ft. It would be wise for the architect to consult the costumer before the final plans for this room are drawn.

The costume shop should be weatherproofed and well ventilated to prevent mildewing of the costumes in damp weather. If the shop is to be used as the winter costume storage room, it will require a more carefully constructed building than one used only in the summer months.

Very important is an indoor drying room for the rapid drying of laundered costumes on rainy days, and the drying of suits and dresses caught in summer showers during a performance.

The costume room should be well lighted by fluorescent lamps.

The Scene Shop

The scene shop should be located in the backstage area, and it should not be in view of the audience. Unless it is to be used also for the nightly storage of scenery it does not necessarily have to be immediately adjacent to the stage areas. However, it should be built for the convenient removal of built and painted scenery and properties from the shop to the stage. It is very important that the building be weatherproofed, and that it be large enough and of proper height for the construction and painting of all shapes of scenery. It is well to consider the width and the height of the doors, since the completed scenery unit may be rather high and wide and will therefore require an opening large enough to permit its being carried out easily.

The size of the scene shop should be at least 30 ft long by 30 ft wide by 20 ft high. It must be long and wide enough for the construction of a big two- or three-fold flat. The scene shop must be high enough to allow a 16-ft flat to be moved around easily in an erect position. There should be large doors at the end of the building most convenient to the stage. The doors should be at least 12 ft wide by 9 ft high.

The shop should be well ventilated to speed the drying of the freshly painted scenery and make the technical crew comfortable while working in hot weather.

The shop should be well lighted, preferably by fluorescent lamps.

It should be equipped with hot and cold running water. A shower would be desirable.

Desirable is an outdoor space for the building and painting of scenery and properties during periods of good weather.

There should be a weathertight storage room for the preservation of the scenery and properties during the winter months. Precaution should be taken to prevent damage by rats. (Sacks of "Warfarin" or other rodent repellents may be placed around both the scenery and costume storerooms.)

Offices

It is desirable to have backstage office space for the director, technical director, lighting director, choir director, and stage manager. The stage manager should have at least desk space. The costumer and technical director can use a section of their costume and scene shops respectively as offices.

LIGHTING TOWERS AND OTHER LIGHTING STATIONS

A special problem which will come into the architect's planning is that concerned with the design of the lighting for the three stages. This should be worked out carefully in consultation with a lighting expert.

The first part of the problem involves the shape, size and placement of the two lighting towers (for front illumination of the acting areas) on each side of the auditorium. They should be close enough to the main stage to provide it with maximum spotlighting, far enough in—toward the center of the auditorium—to make the angling of the light lines to the corners of this stage effective. At the same time the towers should be far enough up the hill away from the side stages to permit getting good illumination down onto them. (Some of the spotlighting for each stage will come from the near tower, some from across the auditorium from the tower on the other side.) Each tower should be high enough to let the light fall on the near side stage at an angle of about 45°, illuminating clearly figures on that stage without spilling light onto the main stage beyond. If the side stage extends 30 ft out from the proscenium wall and the tower is placed about 15 or 20 ft up the hill from this—that is, 45 or 50 ft from the proscenium wall—the tower may have to rise 30 or 35 ft above the level of the main stage.

At least two banks of large spotlights will be hung in the top of each tower. In the bottom of one tower might be placed the control board for all stage lighting, and in the bottom of the other the console of the electric organ, together with the control of any sound equipment (such as that for a narrator) that may be employed in the play. Some theaters use space below the lighting towers for rest rooms for the audience, after providing separate access for the lighting crew.

While the towers are being placed for effective illumination, they must be arranged in such a way as not to interfere with the sight lines from the rear side corners of the auditorium to the acting areas on the side stages. In order to keep the sight lines clear, the architect will have to put the towers closely contiguous to the side aisles, and he may have to modify the width of the auditorium at the back.

Some of the smaller and newer theaters, concentrating on use of the Quartz-Iodine lamped long-throw spotlights, have minimized the use of lighting towers by mounting a battery of spotlights on top of the rain shelter at the rear of the audience. A few years ago the spotlight cost would have been too great, but new lens systems developed for quartz lights now allow this type of mounting as an increasingly popular solution for lighting both main and side stages. At present most theaters still use lighting towers as well as the newer rain-shelter mounting.

Other stations for stage lighting will be on pipe framing just behind the edge of the proscenium walls on both sides, and in narrow footlight troughs at the front edges of the main and side stages. The play will doubtless require additional incidental stations, but since these will probably be on or behind scenery units they will not involve the architect.

All permanent wiring which is to be run in conduits under the ground from the towers to the stages, between the towers and between the stages, and to controls, should be laid before any paving is done.

LIGHTING CONTROL EQUIPMENT

The lighting control booth should allow the operator full vision of all acting areas which are to be lighted. The best location in the 1,500–2,000 seat theater is above the rain shelter high over the rear of the audience.

Some theaters use a booth built in the center of the auditorium, but this causes a loss of valuable revenue seats. Others use space in the ticket office building, or space at the base of one of the lighting towers.

Location of lighting control consoles backstage is considered old fashioned and inefficient.

Many good lighting control systems are on the market and a number of them should be investigated to determine the best possible choice for your production situation. A minimum of 85,000 to 100,000 watts will be required in any standard situation.

ROOM AND AREA REQUIREMENTS

Music facilities can be divided into two general classifications depending upon their function: those used for instructional activities and those serving in an auxiliary capacity such as storage areas, workrooms, and offices. A typical large music facility for an institution of higher education will require a wide variety of rooms and work areas. The needs of elementary and secondary schools will probably be somewhat less but will incorporate many of these functional areas. (See Fig. 1.)

1. *Instructional areas*
    Rehearsal halls
    Practice rooms
    Class piano rooms
    Regular classrooms
    Listening facilities
    Studios
    Recital hall
    Combinations
2. *Auxiliary areas*
    Storage areas
    Music library
    Work rooms
    Broadcast control booth
    Additional facilities

Instructional Areas

Rehearsal Halls — Instrumental Rooms An instrumental rehearsal room obviously should be large enough to accommodate the largest band, orchestra, or combined group expected to use the facility. The needs may vary from one section of the country to another, but 80 to 120 pupils may be taken as the normal range. In some areas which emphasize large bands it is not unusual, however, to find groups containing up to 180 pupils. The use of the school for community music activities should also be considered. Combined school and community groups may make it desirable to construct somewhat larger rehearsal facilities and provide additional storage space.

Room Size. In estimating the approximate number of square feet of floor space that should be provided for instrumental groups, one should allow 20 to 24 sq ft per student (i.e., 1,600 to 1,920 sq ft of floor space for an 80-piece band or a 60-piece orchestra). This will provide the necessary space for aisles, music stands, and other equipment. No student should sit against a wall or stand within $7\frac{1}{2}$ ft of the ceiling. This is especially true of the basses and percussion instruments, which are frequently placed on the highest riser in the back of the ensemble.

Room Height. The height of an instrumental rehearsal hall depends on the number of students involved as well as the shape of the room. One of the common faults of music facilities is the lack of sufficient ceiling height. Ceiling height must be planned for acoustic purposes even if a split-level effect is created

Music Buildings, Rooms and Equipment, Music Educators National Conference, 1902 Association Dr., Reston, Va., 1966.

on the floor above the music suite. Not all such rooms will be designed with a ceiling that is parallel to the floor, so that an average ceiling height figure may be more meaningful than a simple number. This average will be in the neighborhood of 14 to 18 ft. Anything less than a 14-ft ceiling in an instrumental rehearsal room should be questioned. Another check to ensure adequate space for proper acoustics in a rehearsal room is to allow approximately 400 cu ft per performer.

Risers. Differences of opinion will be found concerning the desirability of providing risers in instrumental rooms. Pupils sitting in the back of the room and the far sides may have some difficulty in seeing the conductor unless they are seated on an elevation of some sort. No decided preference for flat floors or for risers has been demonstrated. Architects are currently designing music rooms of both types according to the preference of those planning the facilities. Whichever is used, flat floors or risers, it will be necessary to make the appropriate adjustments to provide for diffusion of sound. With the use of risers, additional room height will be needed. Some schools feel that semipermanent or portable risers solve the problem and provide room flexibility. The provision of sets of risers—one to be kept in the auditorium and another for the rehearsal hall—avoids some of the logistical problems, but many directors who have risers in the rehearsal room find the flat floor of the stage satisfactory. Many symphony orchestras have abandoned the use of risers, their conductors having discovered that when the brass and percussion sections are elevated, they often overbalance the strings. This may be even more true with school orchestras. The problem presented by the lack of stage enclosures (shells) far outweighs the problem of whether or not to use risers on the stage. Risers that telescope into the wall are another possibility, but the expense involved may prohibit their use in many situations.

If risers are used, a width of 60 in. for most terraces will prove adequate. A 60-in. step will be wide enough for a single row of instrumentalists or two rows of singers. The top riser should be wider (up to 120 in.) since the back of the room ordinarily accommodates the larger percussion and bass instruments. Ordinarily, an elevation of 6 to 8 in. is adequate (sight line is a good indication of ear line). A white strip of paint or a rubberized nonskid tread on the edge of all risers provides an element of safety. The number of terraces will range from one to five, depending on the size of the room and the needs of the organizations using the rehearsal facilities.

Other Considerations. The instrumental rehearsal room will probably be used for instrumental classes and possibly even for theory or other music classes. Mounted chalkboards are therefore desirable. Since rehearsing is the room's principal function, however, no decision should be made that will detract from its ability to fulfill that role. The straight chairs required for performing groups should not be sacrificed for tablet armchairs. Provisions for closed-circuit television and a projection screen should be considered. Many rehearsal rooms being currently planned and

built incorporate microphone outlets with adequate wiring leading to the control room.

If the room is to be used for orchestra rehearsals or cello classes, some thought should be given to the effect of cello end pins on tile or wood flooring. One solution is to provide for $\frac{1}{4}$-in. plywood floor panels large enough to serve the player and his instrument.

Finally, it should be noted that there is some doubt as to the advisability of bands and orchestras using the same rooms. Recent research has indicated that, for teaching purposes, the band requires a much less reverberant room than does the orchestra.

Rehearsal Halls — Choral Rooms The specialized requirements of choral rehearsal rooms are somewhat different from those of facilities used exclusively for instrumental groups. Space requirements are simplified since it is not necessary to provide floor area for music stands and instruments. If the vocal groups are to stand for rehearsals, 6 sq ft per pupil will suffice. The use of fixed chairs on risers will require more space; at least 10 sq ft is necessary for each pupil if the risers are the minimum width of 30 in. Extra space should be planned if wider (36- or 40-in.) risers are preferred, 15 to 18 sq ft per person being not unusual. Choral room ceilings do not need to be as high as those in instrumental rehearsal halls, but should be higher than those in an ordinary classroom.

Risers. Few if any large choral groups rehearse or perform without the use of risers. They are used to avoid having the tone of singers in the back rows obstructed by the bodies of the singers in front. They are also essential for easy observation of the conductor. An elevation of 6 to 10 in. and a width of 40 in. are adequate for permanent or semipermanent choral risers.

Few choral directors desire an aisle in the center of the room. This may be avoided if the width of the riser and the distance between seat rows are sufficient to allow convenient passage. Safety regulations differ, but risers 40 in. wide are adequate to meet the requirements in most areas.

Since the choral room is most likely to be used as a general classroom in nonchoral hours, folding tablet armchairs will be useful for both classroom and rehearsal functions. Fixed opera (theater) chairs are sometimes employed in choral rooms, especially when the room is designed to serve as a recital hall. In all probability choral directors will want to make recommendations concerning the chairs to ensure proper support for the lower back of the singers. Not less than 125 cu ft of space per seat should be provided in recital hall-choral rooms.

Some choir directors prefer to have their groups stand for rehearsals as well as for concerts. In such cases the risers should have a width of approximately 15 in. and a height of 8 or 10 in. per step. A permanent or portable stage is an advantage for a choral room. Three or four steps from the floor of the room to the stage can be designed to serve as permanent standing risers.

Other Considerations. The use of the choral room for other than rehearsal functions suggests the advisability of providing chalkboards, a projection screen, and closed circuit television. Microphone outlets for recording and broadcasting should be considered. Schools being built now should be planned to make possible the use of performing groups for broadening the cultural life of the whole school.

Rehearsal Halls – Combined Vocal-Instrumental Facilities Let it be said at the outset that acoustically, one room cannot serve for both vocal and instrumental rehearsals with completely satisfactory results. Some communities, however, find it economically unsound to provide space for both instrumental and vocal groups while employing only one teacher. It is therefore expedient to consider space for the combined vocal-instrumental situations. Provisions for changing the reverberation characteristics of such a room with drapes or other materials are a possibility.

In many one-teacher situations, one room is the nucleus of all music activities. In the small-

50 music majors	$\times$	16 hr per week $=$	800 hr per week
40 on secondary instruments	$\times$	6 hr per week $=$	240 hr per week
80 theory students	$\times$	2 hr per week $=$	160 hr per week
150 elementary education students	$\times$	2 hr per week $=$	300 hr per week
			1,500 hr per week

$$\frac{\text{Practice hours per week}}{\text{Hours available for use per week}} = \frac{1,500}{60} = 25 \text{ practice rooms needed}$$

est of music departments, a single all-purpose room can be planned *in terms of space* to accommodate the vocal and instrumental group rehearsals, small ensembles and individual rehearsals, library, instrument and equipment storage, instrument repair facilities, office, and teaching studio as well as various other music classes insofar as the scheduled school day permits. Although space can be provided for this multipurpose situation, few of these activities can be adequately housed in one room without creating undesirable acoustical

conditions for the other activities. It may be dangerous to ask elementary school children and the majority of junior high school pupils to sing in such compromise situations. While variable acoustical control may be employed, the installation of such materials may be more expensive than providing additional facilities. When possible, separate special rooms for instrumental and choral activities should be provided, since vocal groups require a much "warmer" room than do bands and orchestras.

Space in such a combination room will have to be figured on the basis of the suggestions made for instrumental rehearsal halls. The room might be thought of as the future instrumental room, expansion to separate facilities being the ultimate goal.

Practice Rooms Practice rooms are a facility peculiar to the teaching of music, with some special problems not encountered by administrators or architects in planning other elements of the school. Among the factors which must be considered are isolation of sound, size, ventilation, amount of use, and supervision.

Number. The number of practice rooms needed by a music department should be related to the number of students involved and the administrative policies concerned with their use rather than by the amount of space created by the architect in splaying the back wall of the rehearsal hall. Some authorities recommend that students practice as much as possible in school, so that assistance and supervision are possible. Many feel that it is particularly important that practice room facilities are available for those students who play the larger instruments because of the difficulty in carrying the instruments home. These practice rooms should be convenient to the large rehearsal room, so that the moving of heavy, large instruments is minimized. In determining the number of practice rooms needed by a collegiate school or department of music, a calculation similar to that shown at the top of the page might be used.

Size. Practice rooms vary in size according to their various functions. Individual practice rooms are quite satisfactory in the 55 to 65 sq ft range. This provides sufficient space for an upright piano, a chair, and a music stand—but little more. Public schools, once planned with several rooms of this size in the music suite, are now being built with slightly larger rooms for ensemble practice, reflecting the increased emphasis on small groups, both vocal and instrumental. Colleges which plan large blocks of small practice rooms will also want to provide a number of larger rooms for ensemble practice, or to accommodate grand pianos (2) or organs.

Other Considerations. More and more school buildings in the North as well as the South are being air-conditioned, and this is a distinct advantage where practice rooms are concerned. In fact, there is no other way to provide proper sound isolation. If the building is air-conditioned, the practice rooms can be arranged in blocks, spaced compactly, and planned without outside windows. Sound filters should be provided for the air ducts to

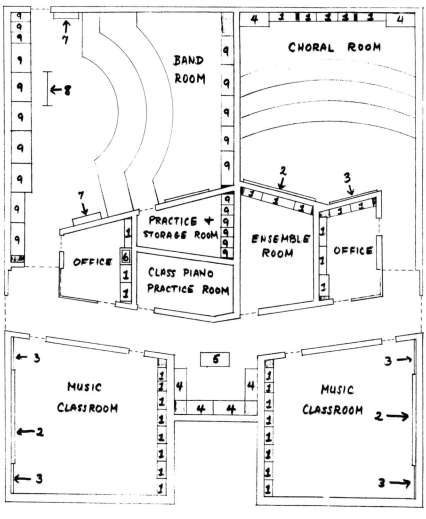

1 Shelving and/or cabinets for storage of books, records, etc.
2 Chalkboard
3 Tackboard
4 Gown and/or uniform storage
5 General storage cabinet
6 Sink
7 Sorting rack
8 Portable chalkboard
9 Instrument storage

Scale: 1/8" = 1'0"

Fig. 1   Governor Thomas Johnson High School, Frederick, Md. Henry Powell Hopkins and Associates, Architects.

MUSIC FACILITIES

prevent transmission of sound from one room to another, and the return air ducts should be placed in the ceilings or walls, not in the doors. Construction to ensure adequate transmission loss will make practice rooms more expensive than ordinary classrooms, but economies may be effected here with more justification than in some other parts of the music suite.

Nonparallel walls have been widely used to avoid reflection of sound in these small rooms. Double glass windows in the doors, or opening on the rehearsal hall or teacher's office in schools, permit supervision without interruption. Electronic monitoring devices are sometimes incorporated.

Class Piano Rooms Many school systems are now providing class instruction in piano as well as in the band and orchestra instruments. Some schools have constructed specially designed rooms for this type of instruction. These rooms should be as near as possible to the other music rooms in order to realize complete utilization in a coordinated music program. There should be acoustical treatment of the walls and ceilings, and insulation against sound transmission to and from other classrooms as prescribed by the acoustical consultant. Careful consideration should be given to sound conditioning of rooms for class piano if several pianos are used, due to the percussive action of tone production of several performers. The front wall should be equipped with blackboard (plain and with music staves), bulletin board space, music cabinet, and electrical outlets. Space should be provided for television, phonograph, and recording facilities.

If electronic pianos are used in such a room, it is useful to provide an adequate number of electric outlets in the floor to avoid the need for extension cords and the hazard they present. Organ class instruction is now finding increasing favor in several of our larger cities, and properly wired rooms should be planned if this activity is to be part of a school's program.

Regular Classrooms Regular academic classrooms are used by many schools for classes in music history, appreciation, theory, composition, arranging, and other music education classes. Though the acoustical treatment may not need to be as extensive or expensive as in some other parts of the music suite, if the learning to take place in the room is to involve listening to music, more than ordinary care must be taken to block out extraneous sounds. A classroom that will be used primarily for general music classes needs ample storage space for books, records, rhythm instruments, autoharps, piano keyboards, pictures, and similar equipment. Provision should be made for a projector screen mounted at ceiling height or in a ceiling recess.

In some situations it may be possible to provide a projection room adjoining the classroom, or even between two classrooms so that the projector can be prepared without losing class time. If a classroom is to be used primarily for theory classes, it will be desirable to have staff lines painted on the chalkboard. Conversely, if music literature classes are to be the principal occupants, painted staff lines are less desirable. If a college classroom is to be used largely for music education classes, it will need adequate locked shelf space or will need to be planned adjacent to a storage room (with shelves) for the large amount of material used in such classes. In a campus school situation, classrooms may need to be provided with rows of coat hooks and shelf space.

Listening Facilities Several types of listening facilities are in common use in collegiate music schools today, and each presents specific planning problems. As independent study becomes more common in secondary schools, some similar facilities will become desirable in the music department or in the school library. The principal systems include the following:

1. A number of soundproofed listening rooms or cubicles are each provided with a record player. The student receives phono recordings from a central location (often the departmental office) and is his own operator.

2. A bank of record players or turntables is placed in a central control room. Worktables in an adjoining room are supplied with a number of receiving channels and sets of earphones. The student requests a particular recording, which is played by the monitor in charge of the control room, and the student listens through earphones.

3. Tapes are made available to the student, who listens either in a cubicle as in (1) above, or in a central room (in which earphones are necessary).

4. Tapes are administered through a control room, as in (2) above, and the student listens through earphones.

The planning of a listening facility is dictated first of all by the kind of equipment the department uses, or the kind to which it wishes to change. The number of listening rooms or cubicles, the size of the control room and the number of channels available, the number of places at the worktables can be calculated by a method similar to that employed in the case of practice rooms. The design of the system, if methods (2) or (4) are used, must of course precede the planning of the area. Other than providing for adequate space and convenient location in relationship to other music areas, no general observations will be needed in this section.

In many cases a college will set aside certain classrooms as theory laboratories. It may be desirable to provide cubicles in which students may work with individual tape recorders, phono records, or similar equipment. Certain storage and control requirements must also be planned in such situations.

Studios Traditionally much of the teaching of music has been done on a one-to-one basis. Though this country has accomplished much through group instruction, it is still true that advanced instruction is almost always given to a single student. In colleges and conservatories this is carried on in studios which also serve as the faculty members' offices. It is desirable also for schools to provide an office for each full-time music instructor. Most frequently it is located adjacent to the teacher's rehearsal hall and is provided with windows that enable him to keep an eye on ensemble rehearsals being conducted by students in the hall or in practice rooms.

In a college it is not difficult to determine the proper number of office-studios, since the figure corresponds directly with the number of applied music teachers. More difficult is the matter of assuring the responsible authorities that space devoted to the studios will be fully used. A college instructor teaching applied music is likely to have a teaching schedule of 18 to 24 hours per week, and he will wish to do his own practicing and professional work in his studio. Occupancy of somewhere between 30 and 40 hours per week may thus be expected. Administrators may expect a 50 to 60 hour-per-week occupancy as they do in the case of classrooms and practice rooms. They may need help to see that an applied-music teacher cannot work effectively if he has to share a studio.

Size. The music teacher's office needs to be larger than a small practice room since he will, in all probability, have his desk and files there. There should be enough additional space for group lessons if he has the need. Music files, instrument storage, and work areas frequented by students should not be in the office-studio.

College studios will vary in size with the instructor's specialty. Studios of the senior piano staff will ideally be large enough to accommodate two grand pianos and the usual office furniture of desk, file cabinets, and bookshelves. Studios of instructors of voice and other instruments, traditionally requiring only one piano, can be a bit smaller if acoustic conditions are otherwise met. Nonparallel walls are recommended, but the studio should not be designed in such a way that piano placement and disposition of furniture are made difficult.

The size of the studio may also be determined by other duties of the faculty member. As an academic adviser, he may need additional space for file cabinets; if he uses the room for seminars he may require space for a table and chairs. In virtually all cases a small mounted chalkboard in each studio will be a valuable asset.

Recital Hall A room intended for recitals or for performances by chamber music groups or small ensembles may be termed a recital hall. Anything larger falls into the category of theater or auditorium. Thus, planning the recital hall may well begin with a decision about the hall's intended use and its seating capacity. This will in turn influence the size of its stage and bring about certain limitations of use. A hall seating 250 people, say, can scarcely have a stage large enough to seat an orchestra and chorus, or even a large band. Schools may combine the idea of a recital hall or little theater with the need for areas for large-group instruction.

As in the case of other large special-use rooms, one may think of a recital hall as including several subareas also. Chief among these are performers' dressing room or rooms, pipe-organ chambers (if the hall is to have an organ), recording or broadcasting control room, and box office. In each case, the location of these subareas should be considered in relation to ease of concert operation. For example, a control room should have a view of the entire stage, and performers' rooms should be located on the same floor as the stage rather than a floor above or below; otherwise both lose much of their convenience.

The seating capacity of the recital hall having been determined, its shape, proportions, etc., become matters for the architect. But a number of practical considerations, often overlooked even by experienced architects, may be listed here. For example, the lighting panel or dimmer panel should be located on the same side of the stage as the dressing room, for that is the side at which the stage manager will normally stand in order to communicate with the performers. A bell or phone system should connect the backstage area with the box office, for efficiency in concert operation. Doors leading from the wings onto the stage must be wide enough to provide for the passage of a grand piano—a small detail, yet one that has often been missed. If delivery of pianos or other large equipment is anticipated, the stage should have access to a loading dock. And even if the music building caters primarily to campus audiences, provision for parking areas should be considered.

Even at the college level, the recital hall, as in the case of the large rehearsal rooms, will probably double as a classroom or large lecture hall at certain times. It may be necessary, therefore, to provide theater-type seats with folding tablet arms so that the needs of both concert audience and note-taking students may be met. A large ceiling-mounted projection screen may be found desirable, as well as connections to the recording studio. Some thought should be given to the location of a projector, since a special projection booth is unlikely in a small recital hall.

Fine Arts Combinations Many schools are adopting the administrative policy of establishing fine arts departments and housing art, drama, and music in units separate from the classroom area. Buildings of this nature usually consist of a music complex, a drama complex, and a visual arts complex. Dance may sometimes be included (see Fig. 2).

The music complex has been described earlier. The drama complex consists of a small theater with a capacity of 300 to 500, workroom, dressing areas, one or more classrooms, storage rooms, radio-television control and listening areas, costume storage and work area, and library.

Auxiliary Areas

Storage Areas Adequate storage areas, planned with traffic patterns in mind, are important to the proper functioning of a music facility. Storage, with proper heat and humidity control, is necessary for musical instruments, robes and uniforms, music, records, and various types of equipment. With careful planning, the

storage areas can be conveniently placed and at the same time serve as a buffer between two sound-producing areas such as the instrumental and choral rehearsal halls (see Fig. 3).

Instrument Storage. Instrument storage facilities should be located so as to minimize the moving of instruments. Sufficient free floor space should be provided to permit smooth flow of traffic. Storage cabinets located within the rehearsal areas are inaccessible during rehearsal periods and frequently cause congestion during period changes.

Uniform and Robe Storage. Storage facilities should be planned for the school-owned band and orchestra uniforms, choir robes, or vestments. This closet space should be cedarlined. A well-constructed, close-fitting door will help protect against moths and dust. The closet space should be high enough so that the uniforms and robes will not touch the floor when hanging on the racks. Some provision should be made to space the uniforms and robes at equal intervals and to facilitate identification. A separate (pigeonhole) compartment for the caps, belts, and other miscellaneous equipment should also be provided.

Music Library Music libraries will range from a single set of filing cabinets in the music room to the school of music library complete with stacks, reading rooms, charging desk, listening facilities, and work areas. In most colleges there will also be smaller libraries (band,

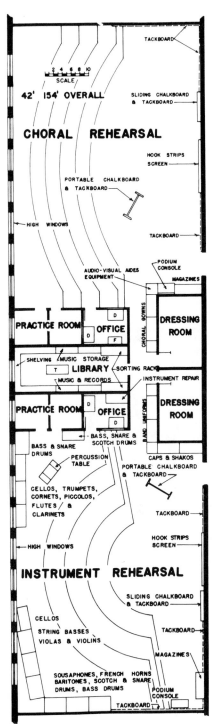

Fig. 3 Plan for a two-teacher music department.

orchestra, choral) which are more like the school situations described here.

Workrooms *Instrument Repair.* Some sort of facility should be provided for emergency instrument repairs. A special room is recommended, although many schools will use a section of the music library room or director's office for this purpose. Larger school systems will employ specially trained men to take care of all instrument and equipment repairs. The minimum provision should be a workbench, stool, and a supply of tools for repairs. Cabinet

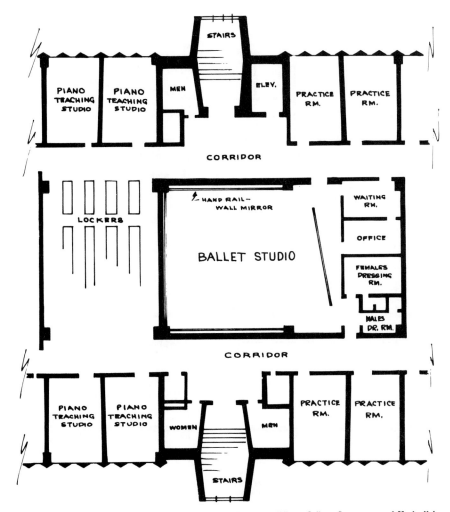

Fig. 2 Provisions for instruction in dance may be included in some buildings. College Conservatory of Music, University of Cincinnati. Edward J. Schulte and Associates, Architects.

space with small drawers should be provided to hold pads, pad cement, springs, cork, and other miscellaneous equipment. If a great deal of repair work is done in the school, the workbench should have a gas connection, electrical outlets, wood and steel vises, and other specialized equipment. Running water and a large sink for cleaning brass instruments should be included.

Duplicating Room. School music departments will have the facilities of the general office at their disposal in most cases and may not need duplicating equipment in the music suite itself. Most collegiate departments or schools of music and some school departments housed separately in a campus-type school will find a duplicating room invaluable. There are many times when the music department needs items copied—rehearsal schedules, instrumental parts of a student composition, football show routines, trip itineraries, vocalizes for the choir, songs in the public domain—that equipment should be readily available. The room should include enough counter space for several types of machines, space for collating, and a sink.

Offices. A music program that functions smoothly should provide a well-located director's office. The size of the office and the types of equipment included in it will depend on the size and organization of the school. The room need not be especially large unless it is also to serve as a studio in which small-group

instruction may be carried on. It should, however, be able to accommodate a desk, two or three chairs, filing cabinets for correspondence, cabinets for miscellaneous storage, and any special equipment such as electronic tuners, piano, phonograph, radio, and tape recorder.

Music teachers who teach in several locations in a school (e.g., harmony in a classroom, choir in the recital hall, general music in a specially equipped center) need an office to organize the many materials and instruments and pieces of equipment with which they work. Offices are also essential for the department head or the director of performing groups because of the frequent contact they have with members of the community.

Broadcast Control Booth The recent improvements in recording equipment and television education have resulted in many schools being constructed with facilities to make possible the use of these new techniques. Educational programs of all types are made available to the school and community; therefore, school space should be allowed for both receiving and broadcasting of music. The control booth should be well insulated for sound and should have slanted double glass windows for viewing the performing groups. Such a control booth is sometimes located adjacent to the stage of the auditorium or recital hall and sometimes between the rehearsal halls. (See Fig. 4.)

Additional Facilities *Washroom and Toilet Facilities.* Because the music suite is frequently used at night when the remainder of the building is locked, washroom, toilet facilities, and custodial work areas must be provided within the music unit. In many instances they may be necessary for the changing of uniforms and must be convenient to the rest of the department. These facilities require about 15 percent of the total floor space if adequate room is to be provided. If recitals to which the public is invited are given within the music unit, additional rest room space may be needed.

Lounge. Collegiate music departments may need to consider the desirability of a lounge in which students can relax. If other study areas on the campus are some distance from the music facilities, one portion of the lounge might provide desk or table space. An area might also be provided for vending machines.

Elevator. Because of the heavy instruments and equipment which it is frequently necessary to move in a music department, an elevator is a most desirable feature in a building of two or more floors. Also recommended is a loading dock adjacent to the parking area.

THE AUDITORIUM

An auditorium should be designed so that the activities can be maintained and operated with a minimum of time and labor consumed in the

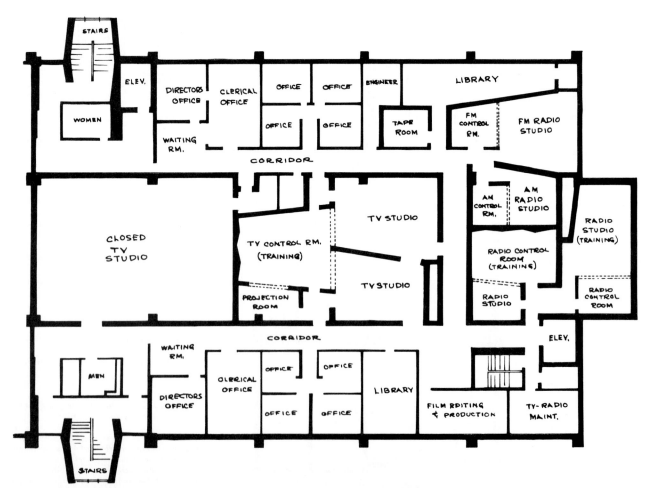

Fig. 4   The recent improvements in recording equipment and television education have resulted in facilities to make use of these new techniques. College Conservatory of Music, University of Cincinnati, Edward J. Schulte and Associates, Architects.

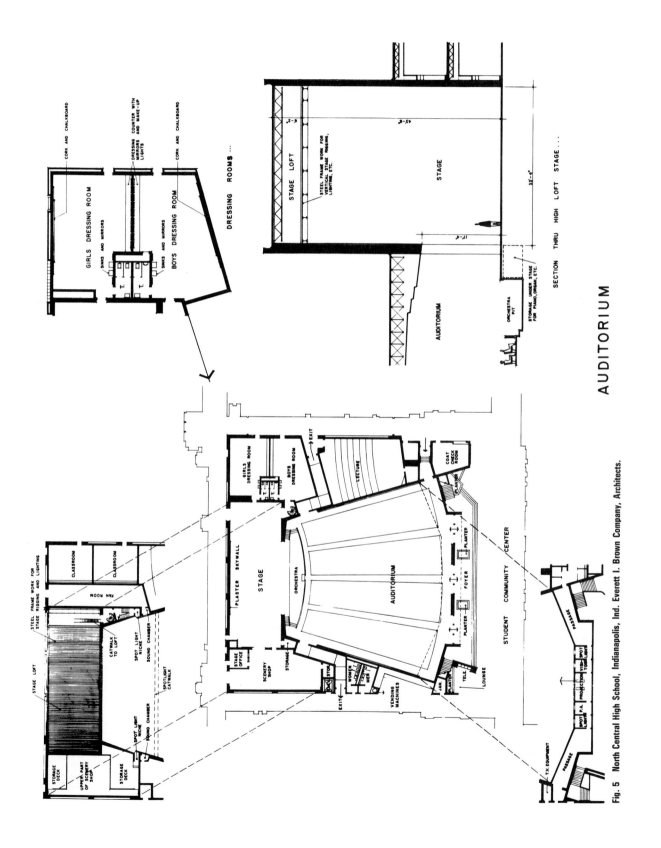

DRESSING ROOMS . . .

SECTION THRU HIGH LOFT STAGE . . . .

AUDITORIUM

Fig. 5 North Central High School, Indianapolis, Ind. Everett I. Brown Company, Architects.

preparation of an event. In schools, this area is being designed for education, not commercial purposes.

Stage

The stage is considered first because it is the part of the auditorium most frequently abused by the designers.

The proscenium arch size is dependent upon several factors—the size of the auditorium, the playing area of the stage, the height of the stage loft or grid (Fig. 5), the size of the community using the auditorium, and the seating capacity of the auditorium. For general purposes, the proscenium arch should not exceed 65 or 70 ft in width and the height of the auditorium should be in practical or artistic proportion to the width. This height is an important factor that will determine the location of the grid. The grid will be the subject of a separate discussion. All of these items are interrelated, and the architect must consider all of them and their interrelationships.

The playing size of the stage will be determined by the sizes of the musical organizations, the stage requirements of musical or dramatic productions, and the scope of other activities proposed for this stage. Clarence J. Best recommended in his survey that an orchestra player be allotted 18 sq ft of floor space for himself, his instrument, and his music stand. This is a generally accepted figure for the minimum seating area and is much less than recommended for the rehearsal hall, because the space needed at the front of such a room need not be figured here. A 100-piece orchestra would require about 1,800 sq ft of floor space, or an area about 50 ft wide and 36 ft deep. For practical purposes the requirements for band are about the same. The stage will have to be proportionately larger if the instructor is planning to rehearse and use combined choral and orchestral groups. This is the type of information the music educator must supply to the architect.

The stage area of 1,800 sq ft mentioned above merely refers to that part of the stage visible to the audience and usable inside the shell or legs. The offstage area is often overlooked, yet it is a very important functional part of the stage. In presenting concerts, operettas, and plays, some offstage area is necessary to handle personnel, scenery, and equipment. These areas are often too small. The left and right offstage areas should each be approximately one-half the size of the stage plus 10 percent. In addition, there must also be sufficient offstage area for the pin rail, switchboard, and similar permanent features. A large proscenium opening can always be made smaller through the use of curtains, flats, teasers, etc. If the major architectural construction is too small, increasing the size of the proscenium is very difficult.

A good proportion to follow in determining the depth of the stage is that the depth should be 75 percent of the width of the proscenium arch, and this depth area should continue on both sides of the stage. To use simple figures, if the proscenium arch is 48 ft, the depth of the stage should be 36 ft. The offstage areas would be approximately 27 ft wide and plus that additional space necessary for permanent equipment on the right-hand side. Both offstage areas would be 36 ft deep. This offstage area could handle stage wagons that would cover the entire playing stage. It would be of sufficient size to store a number of stage sets for musical and dramatic performances. A trap in

the stage floor is handy for moving equipment from work areas below and makes possible special effects in dramatic productions.

The offstage areas should be readily accessible to adequate dressing room space. There should be adequate space close to the stage to take care of lighting machines, lighting cables, repair and supply parts, and storage for curtains and other stage equipment. In all educational situations it is practical to have the rehearsal rooms for chorus, orchestra, and band in close proximity to the stage in order to facilitate the preparation for rehearsals, concerts, and recitals.

The instrumental storage rooms, library rooms, scenic shops (including painting racks), and construction areas should be close enough so that properties can be shifted onto the stage with a minimum of effort and damage.

Apron

The floor area in front of the proscenium arch is called the stage apron. This apron should be at least 8 ft wide, so that pianos and other equipment may be used in front of the main curtain. The apron may extend out over the orchestra pit. The front of the apron should be finished with a hard oak or maple flooring, and that part in back of the proscenium should have close-grained pine in order that the floor will not splinter and yet will be soft enough to take stage screws. Much money has been wasted on hardwood floors for school stages, to the extreme exasperation of stage directors and their crews. The oak or maple floor should be finished with a high gloss but not waxed, and the pine floor should be finished with many coats of oil and the oil allowed to penetrate the wood thoroughly so that it will be fairly seasoned. On both sides of the stage leading from the auditorium to the stage apron there should be appropriate steps. These steps should be wide enough to enable personnel to carry musical instruments and other small properties to and from the auditorium to the stage, or so that the students may approach the stage at least two abreast.

Grid

One of the paramount faults of school auditoriums is that the grid over the stage is often not high enough to allow the scenery to be pulled out of sight. The grid should be at least the height of the proscenium arch times two plus a minimum of 8 ft. Then there should be from 4 to 7 ft above the grid to the top of the building structure, so that the people who find it necessary to work on the grid, changing pulleys, etc., will have sufficient room. The overall height must be sufficient to make it feasible to hang scenery and pull it out of sight in changing sets.

Often when there is no space overhead and scenery must be pulled into the wings of the stage there is also not enough space to stack this scenery offstage. Thus the only solution is to make the stage smaller, masking out with drapes or flats and reducing the proscenium arch so that the stage is much narrower. Then the stage crews will have to work behind the drapes as a backstage area. *If dramatic productions are anticipated, space should be provided for a grid.*

One not too familiar with stage operations or requirements often finds the grid an ideal place to run ventilating pipes, conduits, steam lines, and water pipes. Just because this large grid area presents a wide open space, it is a

tempting area for various trades; however, this area must be kept entirely free for the necessary stage equipment. Nothing is more distressing than to have guide ropes fouled among ventilating ducts, or to have steam pipes leak in the center of a stage set during a performance or concert.

Battens

A proper stage will have a number of battens suspended from the grid. These battens are long pieces of pipe extending the full width of the stage and continuing backstage, so the curtains and legs may be hung backstage in order to mask off this area from the view of the audience. Battens are part of the permanent fixtures of a stage. The common way to counterbalance the battens is through installation of a pin rail. The standard counterbalancing equipment as supplied by the major manufacturers of stage equipment is usually satisfactory. Makeshift installations should be avoided. Battens should be placed 6 in. apart. There never seem to be enough pipe battens to take care of the stage needs. All the lights, border lights, teasers, a border in front of each strip light, three or four legs on each side, the front curtain, oleo curtain, back drops, and sky drops are all standard pieces of equipment that are hung from battens. By the time a light batten or light bridge is added at the fore part of the stage and sufficient battens are provided for scenery changes, it is not at all unusual to use about 25 or 30 battens.

Cyclorama

Most stages require a cyclorama and a set of cyclorama lights. This cyclorama should not be taken as a substitute for a stage shell. A cyclorama is usually a continuous curtain starting close to the proscenium arch on one side of the stage. It extends to the rear of the stage, across the back of the stage, and comes forward, ending close to the other side of the proscenium arch.

Shell

Every stage must be equipped with an adequate shell. For lectures, concerts, and recitals on theater stages, the purpose of a shell is to project the sound into the auditorium. This shell should not attempt to use border lights for lighting but should have lights installed in each section of the ceiling so that the stage will be flooded with about 60 to 70 footcandles of lighting. The lights should be arranged so that the back row will have sufficient light, and so that the lights will not throw a glare back into the audience. The shell should be made the full width of the proscenium. The ceiling can hang from the battens. The size of the shell can be varied by adding or subtracting flats and adding or subtracting ceiling sections.

Doors

All doors entering on a stage must be of sufficient height and width to provide ready access to the stage. This is especially true of the scenery doors. They must be high enough to accommodate wide stage wagons, large instruments, and permit (if necessary) entrance of motor vehicles. The door for scenery should be at least 8 ft wide and 14 ft tall, and all other doors leading to and from the stage should be unusually wide double doors. Doors leading into the auditorium should be solid, with no

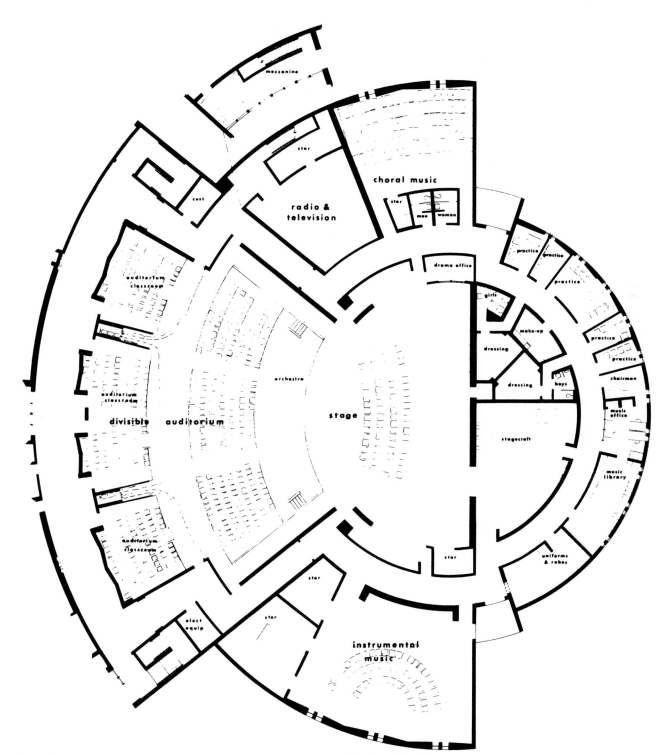

Fig. 6 Divisible auditoriums provide a means of increasing the use of large areas. Huron High School, Ann Arbor, Mich. Lane, Riebe, Weiland, Architects.

windows, in order to avoid light leaks. All doors should operate silently. Panic bars on exit doors are generally required by law but are sometimes rendered useless by padlocks and chains, an extremely dangerous practice.

Lights

There are many new concepts in stage lighting, whether the facility to be lighted is the proscenium theater, the open stage, or the modified proscenium stage. The border and footlight installations once popular in school auditoriums are no longer considered adequate. In addition to sufficient downlights for concerts and other nontheatrical presentations, school auditoriums need stage lighting for a number of specific dramatic purposes. The amount of lighting and the types required will of course depend on the design of the auditorium and the nature of the productions which are projected for it.

Front lighting from slots in the auditorium ceiling serviced by catwalks is highly desirable. Ellipsoidal spotlights are used to light the acting area. Additional spots may be desired in wall slots, and a follow spot operated from a booth in the rear of the auditorium is common. Spotlights (generally softer Fresnel types) are needed on battens or on stands or tormentor pipes to provide further illumination of the acting area. Borderlights and sometimes footlights are employed for toning and blending. Beamlights are used for backlighting. Floodlights are used for background effects and special footlights are needed for a cyclorama. Sidelighting is sometimes provided by spotlights from a mobile tower in the wings. An elaborate college or community theater installation may wish to provide a light bridge.

Open stages and modified proscenium stages frequently provide for projected backgrounds. The lamp house for scenic projection may be located above the stage area or in a ceiling slot above the front curtain.

The stage switchboard may be located at the rear of the auditorium in a lighting booth; it may be located offstage on the stage floor, but out of the way of other operating equipment; or it may be located in an elevated position off the stage floor. They should be able to take care of an adequate number of floor pockets, three or four locations on both sides of the stage. These will vary in accordance with the size of the auditorium, stage, and its lighting equipment. A

dimmer system should be part of most school lighting installations.

Risers

Portable risers should be provided as part of the regular stage equipment. These risers, if adjustable to suit choral groups, orchestra, or band, make it possible to stage all kinds of musical activities even if the instrumental groups alone prefer to perform on the flat. Dramatic productions require a different type of riser and in addition to the standard construction, occasionally adjustable hydraulically controlled risers are used. Storage space for risers should be planned.

Orchestra Pits

Most school auditoriums need an adequate orchestra pit. The pit should be in direct proportion to the size of the stage and the size of the auditorium and above all, should be sufficient to house the potential orchestra of the school. That is, the potential school orchestra that would be required for performances of a musical play, operetta, or opera. The stage with a 45-ft proscenium would probably have an orchestra pit of sufficient size to seat 60 players, allowing 18 to 20 sq ft per player. Likewise, a stage with a 60-ft proscenium should have a pit large enough to accommodate a 100-piece orchestra. With a larger or small stage, the pit should be in direct proportion.

The pit should be deep enough so that the orchestra is completely out of sight of the audience. The director's podium should be high enough for him to be able to see the back area of the stage yet remain in full view of the orchestra.

The railing around the entire orchestra pit must be high enough to hide the orchestra yet low enough not to interfere with the sight lines of the audience. The head and the shoulders of the director may be visible over this orchestra pit railing. It is preferable, however, that the director be hidden from view of the audience so that there will be no distraction of any kind while the director is giving cues to the orchestra, cast, or performers.

A movable pit floor, usually known as a hydraulic pit, is a highly desirable though not inexpensive feature. The hydraulic pit floor should come up to stage level and then be lowered to the floor below. In this event the ac-

cess will be a simple matter through double doors and the problem of determining adequate pit levels for performance is immediately solved. The hydraulic pit floor will act as a good sound reflector when not being used as an orchestra pit. At that time the pit will probably be located slightly below the stage level.

Seating Area

A factor that is often overlooked in the design of an auditorium is the seating capacity. In a commercial theater and in certain other specific situations a hall is designed with the idea that it is necessary to have the entire potential attendance at one performance. The larger the attendance, the less expense involved, the more money made.

In an educational situation, however, the auditorium or theater is for an educational purpose, no matter at what level—elementary, secondary, or college—it is used. A fine program is prepared and, so far as the performance is concerned, there is value in having repeat performances. From this viewpoint it might be logical to reduce the seating capacity of the auditorium or theater and spend some of the limited funds in seeing that the auditorium has better equipment so that the performances can be presented adequately. This should be considered by school administrators and teachers when building the theater or auditorium.

There are other reasons for considering smaller seating capacity. Although audiovisual aids can be presented to large mass groups, it is difficult to hold the personal student-to-teacher relationship that can be attained in smaller groups. In addition to a projection booth at the rear, consideration should be given to a projector platform closer to the stage for use with short-range equipment. All booths and platforms should be located to clear the heads of people seated or standing.

The divisible auditorium is a concept finding increasing favor with those who need to justify the number of hours per day school facilities are used. Such auditoriums are designed to be divided by sound-retarding partitions into three or more areas for large-group instruction. Partitions may run from front to rear as well as across the auditorium. Provision for projecting films and other audiovisual materials should be planned for all areas. (See Fig. 6.)

A typical Arts and Crafts Center may be divided into four basic functional areas: a shop for woodworking; an area for photography; a multi-purpose studio for arts and crafts; and utility and service areas. Variations may be made in the allocation of space for specific arts and crafts activities.

Arts and crafts activities are classified under basic categories. Each primary category includes a number of other activities. A minimum of the seven basic arts and crafts constitutes the essential program. Additional activities may be added to the program as demand and resources permit.

The activities, participants, equipment, physical and technological requirements, space allocations and relationships for the following primary arts and crafts will be discussed here:

Handcrafted Pottery and Ceramics Glasswork, mosaics

Glassblowing

Drawing and Painting Printmaking, serigraphy, lay out and advertising design

Jewelry and Art Metal Enameling, lapidary, casting

Weaving, Textiles, and General Handcrafts Leather, clothing and accessories

Sculpture and Three-Dimensional Design Plastics, display models, interior decoration

Photography Film making, experimental processes

Woodwork and Repair Upholstery, refinishing

There are also support activities which generate space requirements such as lobby, lounge, exhibit areas, library, studio/classroom, office, sales area, tool issue area, storage, rest rooms, and service areas.

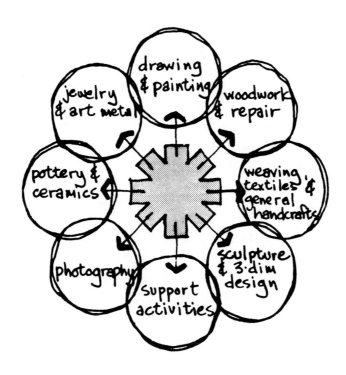

Functional Areas

Cultural

ARTS AND CRAFTS CENTERS

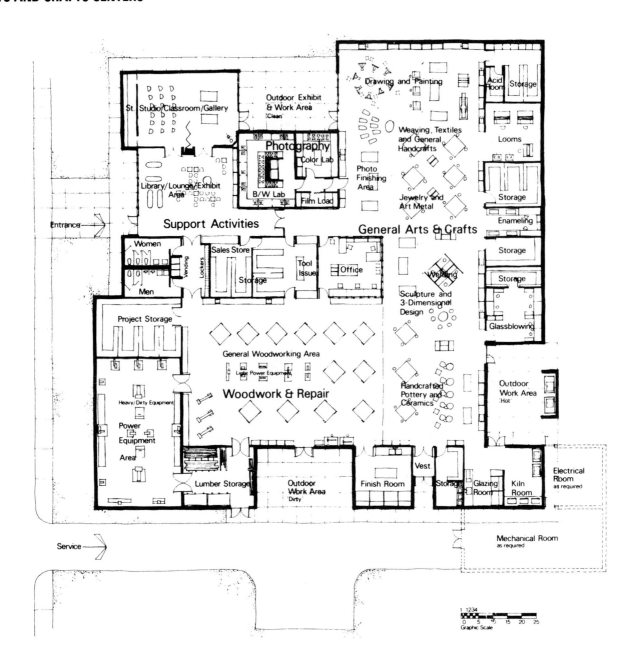

The area within the Arts and Crafts Centers basically conforms to the following space distribution:

Activity	Percent of Total Areas
General Arts and Crafts	40%
Photography	10%
Woodwork and Repair	35%
Support Activities	15%

It should be recognized that the percentage of total area allocation listed for the activities above may vary as the gross building area changes. For instance, in the larger Arts and Crafts Centers more space might be devoted to new or expanded programs in general arts and crafts than to a proportional increase in the size of the woodwork shop. Nevertheless, the percentages given are a solid base for providing adequate facilities for a diversified program.

452

HANDCRAFTED POTTERY AND CERAMICS

Activities

(1) The process whereby earth clays and minerals are transformed into utilitarian and decorative objects is one of civilization's earliest forms of expression. Clay is worked by several methods including hand modeling, throwing on a potter's wheel, and casting. After pieces have dried, they are fired to form a bisque, glazed, and fired again. A comprehensive program includes clay preparation, forming techniques, decorating, firing procedures, and glaze formulation. The process by which a novice is familiarized with the techniques includes demonstrations, lectures, graphic presentations, and practice.

(2) Mold making is an activity related to pottery reproduction. The actual making of molds of one's own design is a creative experience. Casting of clay in ceramic molds is a repetitive process which relates more to commercial manufacturing. Such ceramic mold activities are not normally a function of the Arts and Crafts Center and if provided should be housed in a separate facility.

(3) Additional activities in the clay and mineral category involve working with glass. Mosaics, stained glass and etching, designing, forming and slumping of glass can be performed in the general arts and crafts studio as they are compatible with most other craft processes. However, glassblowing does have a considerable influence on facility design and is treated separately in this chapter.

Physical Requirements

(1) Ceramic/pottery activities may be conducted within the common area of the general arts and crafts space. This includes work areas for designing, forming and glazing. However, kilns, which generate a great amount of heat, should be separated from the general work area. Working with clay can be dusty and, where possible, should be separated from other craft works. Materials often come in large containers, so storage rooms should be convenient to service entrances. Room surfaces should be nonporous and easily cleaned. Sloped floors with drains are desirable. Storage for drying of pottery is required in an area separate from the general work space.

(2) Studio layout should reflect the step by step progression of the process. Correct operation of the kilns is crucial and should be under the visual control of a supervisor. Electric kilns generate a low amount of heat and may be used for bisque and low fire glazing; they are the most commonly used type at Arts and Crafts Centers. Gas kilns are high-heat units used for high fire and are in demand where more sophisticated programs are offered.

(3) Outside covered work space is desirable in moderate climates. This is especially true for high-heat generating kilns which can be built outdoors.

Related Areas

The office and tool issue room should be nearby. Clay storage should be near a service entrance. Kilns and glass-glowing furnaces are compatible and can be isolated together, preferably on exterior walls or outdoors where climate permits.

Furnishings—Equipment

Major items of equipment include: wedging boards, kiln carts, electric ceramic kilns, gas ceramic kiln, enamel kilns, portable clay storage cabinets, dampproof cabinets, drying cabinets, potter's wheels, work tables with metal tops, sinks, and spray booths.

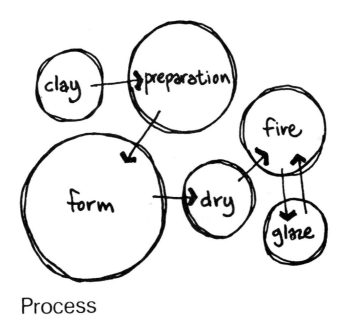

Process

GLASSBLOWING

Activities

The popularity of glassblowing has grown rapidly, and there is an increasing demand for facilities and programs for free blowing in Arts and Crafts Centers. Although it is actually a part of Handcrafted Pottery and Ceramics, glassblowing is treated separately since it is so specialized and has its own specific physical and technological requirements. The basic process starts with the production of molten glass within a refractory container in a furnace. Molten glass can be made either by melting glass or by fusing together the raw materials that form glass. The molten glass is then gathered on the tip of a hollow-iron blowpipe and is inflated, spun, tooled, sheared and manipulated to the desired shape. The glass on the end of

the tube is maintained in a molten state by a small furnace called a "Glory Hole". The glass is finally tempered in an annealing oven.

Physical Requirements

Glassblowing produces a great amount of heat, requires a generous amount of space per participant, and therefore is an incompatible activity to include in the general arts and crafts area. More suitably it belongs in a covered outdoor space or in a well ventilated foundry-type room. If indoors, furnaces should be near an exterior wall and have mechanical exhaust systems. Concrete floors, masonry walls and exposed ceiling construction are all appropriate. Storage is required for materials and tools.

Related Areas

Outdoor work areas for gas kilns. Storage Areas.

Furnishings—Equipment

The prime equipment items are the melting or pot furnace, "Glory Hole" furnaces, and annealing oven. Craftsmen work at special benches with arms for rolling the blowpipes. A marver where glass is chilled and molded is essential. A portable yoke is provided at the entrance to the "Glory Hole" furnace. Water buckets placed on the floor are required to clean blowpipes. Small drop-off boxes catch pieces knocked from blowpipes. A heavy-duty work counter with asbestos top should be provided. Storage shelves or cabinets for annealed products, materials and tools are required.

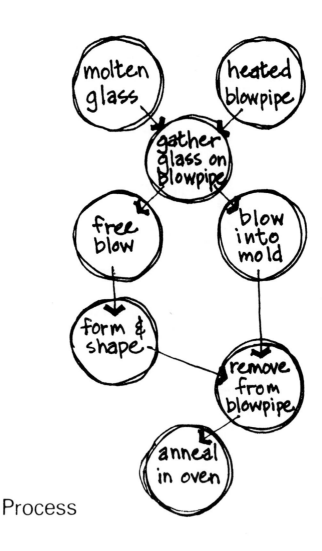

Process

DRAWING AND PAINTING

Activities

In addition to painting and drawing in a variety of media, the graphic arts program includes design projects, drafting, wood and linoleum block printing, etching, lithography, and silkscreen painting.

Physical Requirements

The general area used for graphics can be typical studio space. Painted block or panel walls and acoustic ceilings are adequate. Surfaces should be washable. Acid-resistant, impervious floors such as treated concrete or quarry tile are very desirable in graphic arts areas. However, since the area serves several arts and crafts, it may be necessary to compromise on floor covering and use high quality resilient flooring throughout. Natural north light is desirable for painting and drawing areas, as is convenient access to an outdoor painting court. Toxic chemicals are used in etching and silkscreen processes and for safety they should be used away from other activities. An outdoor area for cleaning silkscreens or an acid room is desirable. Storage may be required in a general storage area with secure provisions for acid storage.

Furnishings—Equipment

Major items of equipment include printing presses, block printing presses, drawing tables, paper cutters, easels, paper storage cabinets, chairs and stools, display cases, work tables with surfaces for cutting, drying racks for prints, slatted storage for canvases, a slide projector with screen, portable easels, and work sinks.

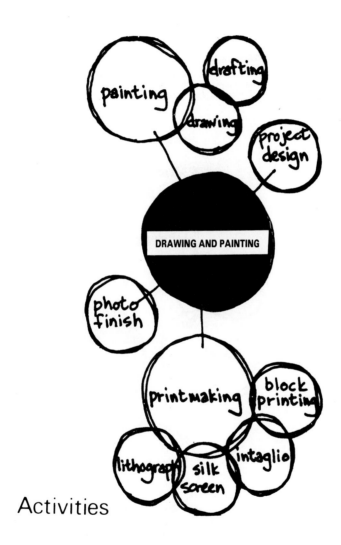

Activities

JEWELRY AND ART METAL

Activities

A knowledge of the properties of metals is basic to activities in the program. Processes include designing and construction with sheets, wires and tubes and soldering, welding and casting. Projects include various forms of jewelry, ornaments, hollow ware, welded metal sculpture and utensils executed in copper, bronze, silver, pewter, tin, lead and gold. Hand and power tools are used in the various processes. Design and construction of jewelry may require the addition of stone settings and coloring. Additional activities in this category include procedures for lapidary (cutting or polishing stones) and metal enameling (fusing color to metal in a kiln).

Physical Requirements

This program takes place within the general arts and crafts area. While the characteristics of the multi-purpose space are suitable for many activities in jewelry and art metal, there are some cautions that should be exercised in planning, depending on the extent of the program. For instance, welding and hot-metal casting should be set aside in an alcove with a hardened concrete floor. Acetylene torches should have a shielded work space with good mechanical ventilation. Special gas jets may be installed over work tables for fine soldering. Enameling involves the use of acids, kilns and blowtorches; therefore, the area where enamel is applied and dried should be apart from other areas to prevent spreading metal dust or jarring enamels that are drying. The dust from clay in the ceramics area is incompatible with the enameling process, and these two functions should be separated.

Furnishings—Equipment

Much of the jewelry work can be done at standard work counters with accessory V-blocks, anvils, gas fixtures and vises attached. Alternatively, two to four jeweler's workbenches can be provided in the general work space. At least one asbestos-covered work top is needed. Hot metal casting requires furnaces which should be vented. Slab saws and flat laps are floor mounted items. Combination lapidary units can perform several operations but limit the number of active participants. Therefore in a large shop, separate lapidary units for cutting, grinding, polishing and buffing are preferable. Water connections are required for some grinders. Buffing machines, drill presses, trim saws, centrifugal and vacuum casting machines, faceting machine, grinding arbors, burn out kilns, sanders and gem tumblers can all be bench mounted. Lapidary equipment should be so placed as to facilitate the progression of operations from slabbing, trimming and grinding through polishing and faceting.

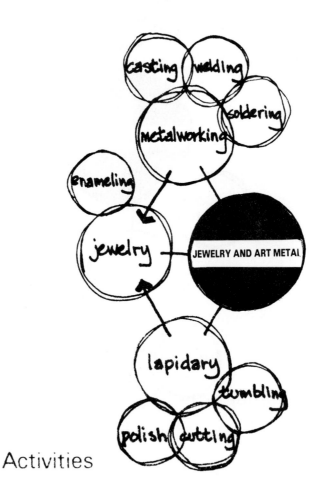

Activities

WEAVING, TEXTILES, AND GENERAL HANDCRAFTS

Activities

This program covers a wide variety of activities. Loom weaving, tapestry work, batik, tie-dye, macrame, soft sculpture, banners, fabric collages, needlepoint, stitchery, and sewing are all part of this general category. In addition, leather craft, with its braiding, lacing, sewing and tooling, and other general crafts such as bookbinding, basketry, candle making and puppetry fall within the general handcrafts nomenclature.

Physical Requirements

The general work area should be flexible to allow for frequently changing needs. Some activities will require a permanent setup, such as floor looms and sewing machines, and these may be installed in alcoves. The predominant arrangement, however, will be one of movable work tables and counters which can be adapted for a variety of crafts. Storage should be provided within a common room.

Furnishings—Equipment

The basic furnishings consist of workbenches, tables, and stools. Much of the specialized equipment is portable. Foot powered looms occupy considerable floor space when in operation but may be moved together and stored when not in use. Table looms, rug looms, and tapestry frames can be utilized on table tops and stored when not in use. Heavy-duty sewing machines are essential in a textile program. Enamel pans, hot plates and drying racks are necessary for dyeing.

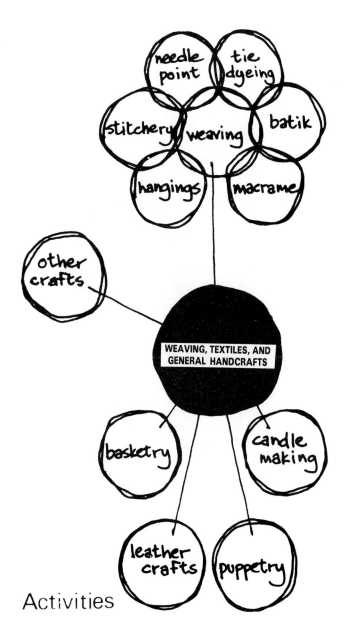

Activities

SCULPTURE AND THREE-DIMENSIONAL DESIGN

Activities

This branch of the program covers the use of materials and techniques to produce three-dimensional objects, figures, or construction in the round or half round. Processes in sculpture involve clay modeling, wood carving, stone cutting, plastic work, metal casting and welding. Model building, paper mache work, displays and exhibition properties and interior decoration are additional activities within this category.

Physical Requirements

Many activities will take place in the general arts and crafts area without special modifications. Projects such as clay sculpture, welding, or wood-carving can utilize the same areas provided for pottery, art metal, woodwork, and outdoor projects. Large exhibition work requires unobstructed space.

Furnishings—Equipment

Major items include floor and table sculpture stands, several sets of hand chisels, portable electric chisels, grinding and buffer arbor, welding equipment and a heavy anvil. Workbenches and stools already provided in the general arts and crafts area are adequate for most projects. Woodworking power tools, kilns and furnaces used in other activities can be shared.

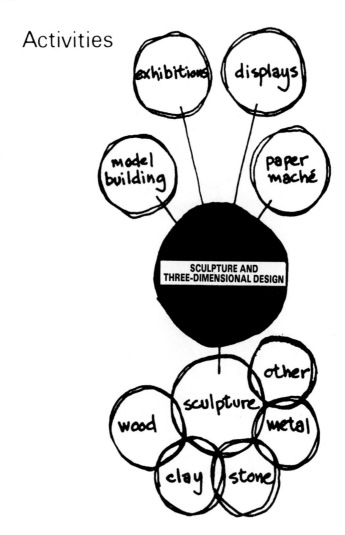

Activities

458

PHOTOGRAPHY

Activities

(1) Basic processes of photography remain the same although there are wide differences in sophistication of equipment, techniques of still and motion pictures, and variations between monochromatic and color film. Film processing consists of loading, developing, enlarging, print washing, drying, trimming, and mounting. Other elements of the center's photography program include studio work, film and slide projection, demonstrations, classroom instruction, and exhibits.

(2) There are three basic functional areas in a photography department: the studio/classroom/gallery which may be shared with the other craft activities; the photographic laboratory where film processing takes place; and the finishing work area where prints are dried, trimmed and mounted. The photographic laboratory should be divided into two separate areas when both monochromatic and color film are processed.

Physical Requirements

(1) The studio/classroom/gallery is a multi-use area that should be designed with flexibility in mind. For use as a portrait studio, it should have effective light control at windows to bar extraneous light. An adjacent closet for storing chairs, props and equipment is desirable, as is a pull-down screen for projection. When used as a gallery, continuous wall tracks and wall systems for hanging displays reduce special exhibit requirements and simplify hanging backdrops for portrait use. A chalkboard should be included for instruction. A folding partition adds to the flexible use of this space. Ceilings should be designed to allow for spotlights to be attached for illuminating exhibits.

(2) The photo lab encompasses all activities of film processing. It starts with film loading which takes place in totally dark cubicles. The monochromatic film processing darkroom is used with safe lights, but conventional color film processing requires a separate darkroom with total darkness. However, recent advances in color films will undoubtedly reduce light safeguard requirements. A red glass partition (red plastic over glass) has been successful in some photo lab work areas. Dark rooms require light-trap entrances. Room surfaces in the processing area should be nonporous, easily cleaned and chemical resistant.

(3) The finishing work area need not be a particularly specialized space. There are no special lighting or isolation requirements. In fact, except for the storage of some special equipment, there is no real impediment to using shared space for this activity. In particular, it relates closely to the graphic arts.

(4) In larger photo facilities, thought should be given to providing separate space for a staff office and a central storage room.

(5) Physical arrangements can be varied from the large general dark rooms to smaller activity centers with work areas for two to four people.

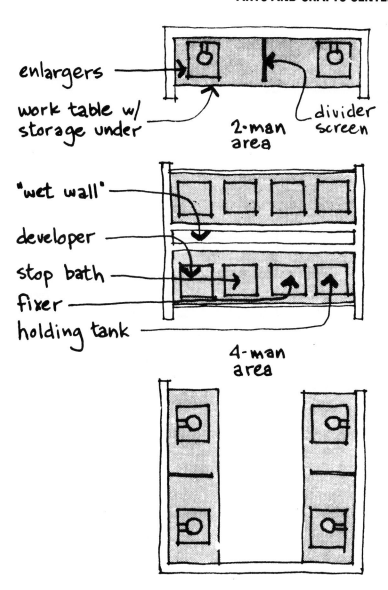

enlargers

work table w/ storage under

2-man area

divider screen

"wet wall"

developer

stop bath

fixer

holding tank

4-man area

Optional 2-4 Man Work Areas

Cultural

ARTS AND CRAFTS CENTERS

Related Spaces

(1) The studio/classroom/gallery should be near the main entrance, library/lounge/exhibit area, and office.

(2) The finishing area should be convenient to the graphic arts area. Possibly it can be a shared area.

Furnishings—Equipment

(1) Equipment requirements may vary depending upon the emphasis of particular programs. The following list is general in nature:

(2) Studio/Classroom/Gallery—Backdrops, mobile rear screen projector, stacking chairs, film and slide projectors.

(3) Photo Finish Area—drymounting presses, papercutter, sink, print drying cabinets, print dryers, copy camera, work tables and counters.

(4) Photo Laboratories—enlargers, refrigerator, contact printers, developing sinks, film drying cabinets, papercutter, paper cabinets, metal-lined cabinets, print washers, safe light, timers.

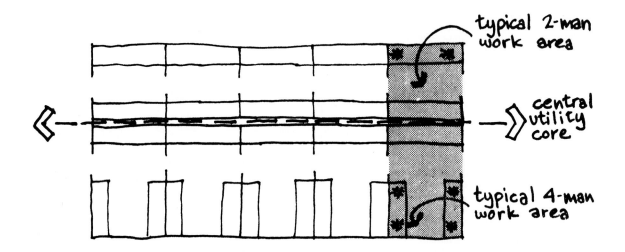

WOODWORK AND REPAIR

Activities

(1) The woodworking program requires space and equipment for a variety of general carpentry and cabinetry activities. These include furniture design, construction, repair and refinishing, upholstery, turning, pattern work, picture framing and rough carpentry projects.

(2) Although the woodworking portion of the arts and crafts program includes repair of small appliances, radios, television sets and other electronic equipment, it should not be done in the woodworking area. Repairs of this nature should be done in the more dust-free areas, such as the general arts and crafts area.

Physical Requirements

(1) Within the woodworking area, space must be provided for the following activities: receiving and storing lumber, using fixed-power equipment, building projects both large and small, using hand tools, finishing, hand sanding, storing projects, issuing tools, demonstrations, and controlling the operations of the shop.

(2) Shop layout will depend on the overall approach to sharing space with other activities in the center. In any case, noisy, dusty machines should be separated from the general work area. Finishing and drying requires a separate dust-free space. Where possible these activities should be in separate rooms. Consideration might be given to the use of a self-contained auto-type spray booth as a finishing room with access arranged through a vestibule serving both the shop and an outdoor work area. A small space with drawing board is desirable for project planning. The lumber storage area should be near the major fixed equipment.

(3) The plan should be based on safe functional operation of activities and flow of materials and personnel. Operational clearances required for various types of power equipment are shown in Fig. 1.

(4) Hardened concrete floors are most common in woodworking shops. Wood floors offer a softer walking surface and better acoustics, but they have higher initial cost and greater maintenance. Floors should be nonslip. Low windows are not desirable but windows may be provided above door head height. All glazing should be wire glass or plastic.

Related Spaces

The woodworking shop should be located in an area of the building which isolates noise. A supervisor's station should be near or part of office and tool issue room. The service and material receiving entrance should be under staff supervision. Convenient access is needed to the technical reference library. Wash-up areas and lockers for work clothes should be provided near the shop entrance.

Furnishings—Equipment

(1) The National Safety Council urges that special precautions be taken in all woodworking areas to prevent accidents to participants. All fixed power tools should be surrounded by "safety islands" marked with tape and should be separated from general circulation and arranged so that ample space is provided for the operator and task. Aisles should be generous enough to permit free two-way passage. Workbenches should be grouped and spaced according to sizes of anticipated projects. Tools and equipment should be of industrial quality. Each machine must have a guard attached and locked on and a safety cut-off switch in addition to the master switch for the area. Power tools should be grounded. Floors should have a non-slip finish. Color coding machinery will contribute to safe operations. It is recommended that the center's director and the supervisors of the woodworking activities become familiar with the safety requirements for woodworking power tools as set forth in the Occupational Safety and Health Act of 1970.

(2) The following list notes the major items of equipment which are typical for a woodworking facility of approximately 7,225 square feet: Radial arm saws, wood lathes, four-station work benches, band saws, drill presses, jig saws, circular saws, disc sanders, belt/disc sanders, jointers, shapers, panel saws, surface planers, hand tools, vises, lockers, and storage cabinets.

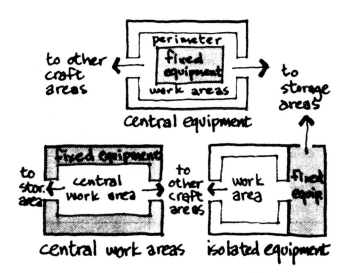

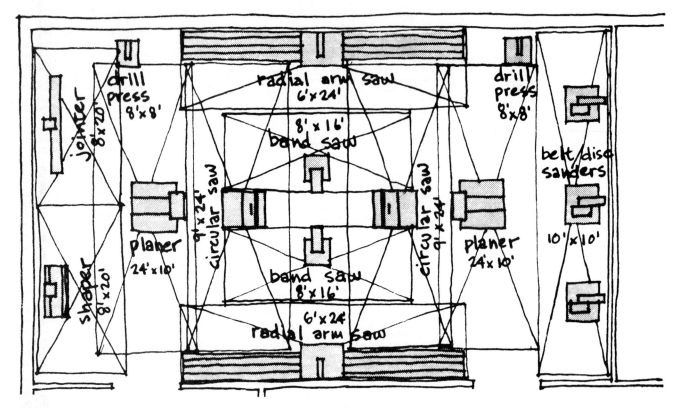

Fig. 1 Operational clearances. [Note: For safe working conditions an allowance of 75 to 125 square feet per person is required (including machinery) in woodworking according to type of activity in progress.] Width/length ratio of work area: minimum 1/1, maximum 1/2. Minimum width of general work area: 30 feet. Minimum ceiling height: 12 feet.

Process

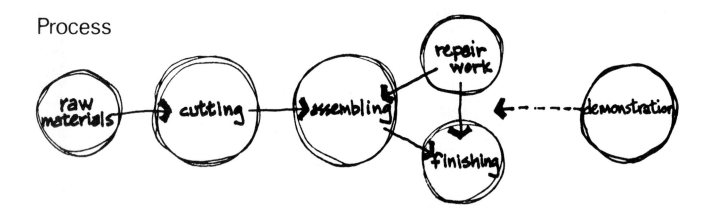

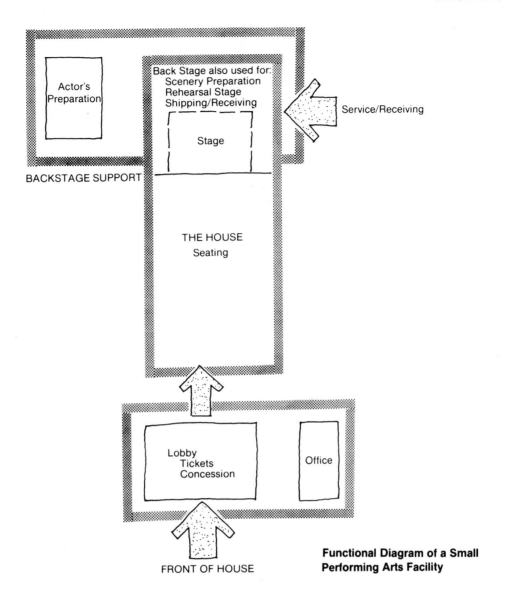

BACKSTAGE SUPPORT

Functional Diagram of a Small Performing Arts Facility

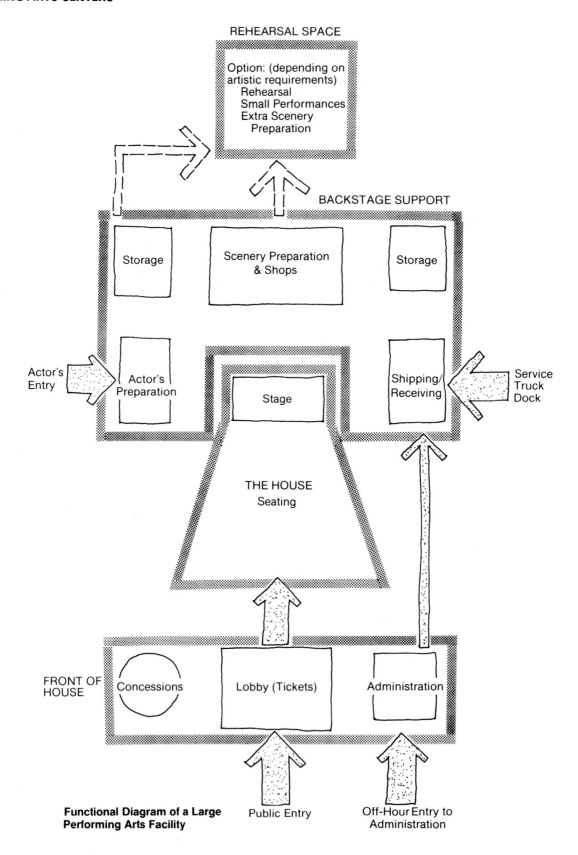

REHEARSAL SPACE

Option: (depending on
artistic requirements)
Rehearsal
Small Performances
Extra Scenery
Preparation

BACKSTAGE SUPPORT

Storage

Scenery Preparation
& Shops

Storage

Actor's
Entry

Actor's
Preparation

Stage

Shipping/
Receiving

Service
Truck
Dock

THE HOUSE
Seating

FRONT OF
HOUSE

Concessions

Lobby (Tickets)

Administration

**Functional Diagram of a Large
Performing Arts Facility**

Public Entry

Off-Hour Entry to
Administration

Health

HOSPITALS	**467**
Introduction and Flow Charts	467
Bedrooms	467
Nursing Units	474
Surgical Suite	475
Nursery	477
Pediatric Nursing Units	480
Diagnostic X-Ray Suite	484
Pharmacy	490
Teletherapy Units	492
Electroencephalographic Suite	496
Physical Therapy Department	497
Occupational Therapy Department	500
Community Mental Health Center	503
Laboratory	503
Labor-Delivery Suite	509
Radioisotope Facility	511
Outpatient Activity	513
Emergency Activity	528
EDP Unit	530
REHABILITATION CENTERS	**533**
MENTAL HEALTH CENTERS	**548**
NURSING HOMES	**554**
CHILD HEALTH STATION	**561**
MEDICAL SCHOOLS	**562**
DENTAL SCHOOLS	**583**
NURSING SCHOOLS	**600**
YOUTH TREATMENT CENTERS	**616**
MULTIPHASIC HEALTH SCREENING CENTERS	**622**

By AUGUST HOENACK, Chief, Architectural and Engineering Branch, Division of Hospital and Medical Facilities, Public Health Service, U.S. Department of Health, Education and Welfare

INTRODUCTION AND FLOW CHARTS

The hospital as a building type is composed of complex components, each of which could well tax the talents of architects, mechanical engineers, and the other professions and skills involved in their design and construction. Material relating to *all* these components would fill a book. Therefore, the following have been selected for discussion in this section:

Bedrooms
Nursing units
Surgical suite
Nursery
Pediatric nursing units
Diagnostic x-ray suite
Teletherapy units
Electroencephalographic suite
Physical therapy department
Occupational therapy departments
Community mental health center
Laboratory
Labor-delivery suite
Radioisotope facility
Outpatient activity
Emergency activity
EDP unit

The material presented here has been selected, not necessarily as a guide from a functional standpoint or to indicate what the hospital may need, but rather as examples of critical space organization involving specialized equipment and facilities which are peculiar to a hospital. The extent of services, kind of equipment, space requirements, etc., will vary with each hospital and must be related to the services the hospital is to perform. Consequently, the information presented here must, of course, be adapted in each case.

Much has been written on the subject of the design and construction of hospitals. An adequate bibliography of this material is beyond the scope of this section. The architect who is not acquainted with hospital design should obtain additional information and bibliographies from such sources as the Bacon Library of the American Hospital Association in Chicago and the U.S. Public Health Service in Washington, D.C.

Figure 1 shows generalized flow charts for the hospital as a whole and for various departments which are not discussed in the following pages.

BEDROOMS*

It was not the committee's purpose to include an analysis of the number of beds per nursing unit, or the proportions of single, double and four-bed rooms within given units. This study is limited to the individual room *per se,* to a review of numerous small but often vital details that make either a good room or an unsatisfactory one. These details are fine points that an administrator or architect should be familiar with before departing to something more original, if that should be his wish.

In general, the many room plans reviewed

*Report by the AIA Committee on Hospitals & Health

have basic similarities but many variations in detail. Accompanying plans have been specially drawn to illustrate the majority of features that will be discussed. It must not be construed that these represent ideal or minimum standards. (See Figs. 2 to 6.)

Size

First point of interest is the considerable variation in room sizes. Ranges of net clear floor area from corridor door to window stool, not including built-in wardrobes, are:

Single rooms: 117 to 172 sq ft (deluxe are larger)
Double rooms: 157 to 210 sq ft
Four-bed rooms: 308 to 401 sq ft

Major differences are found in depth of rooms from inside of exterior wall to room side of corridor partition, all the way from 14 ft–6 in. for single rooms or 15 ft–0 in. for double and four-bed rooms to 21 ft–8 in. for all types. These differences are caused principally by varied space requirements of one or two beds in combination with various plumbing facilities—they reflect the endless search for a common denominator which will have flexibility to accommodate several combinations of room and toilet requirements within a uniform building dimension and fenestration without waste of expensive space.

In the two and four-bed rooms a clear distance of 14 ft–0 in. for two beds and two bedside tables is "snug," but it should be noted that the majority of rooms studied measure nearer to 15 ft–0 in. clear, which is the USPHS standard. Lavatory, toilet door, or wardrobe door do not encroach into these clear dimensions in the better rooms.

In the other dimension, comments of administrators evoke no complaints about single rooms as narrow as 10 ft–0 in. to centers of partitions—rooms up to 12 ft–0 in. on centers draw comments from "excellent" to "more than ample." Majority of double bedrooms are 12 ft–0 in. on centers and are well regarded—smaller ones are criticized for being too tight. Four-bed rooms range from acceptable minimum of 20 ft–0 in. on centers to more than 24 ft–0 in.

Closets

In almost every case individual hanging space is provided for each patient, often in the form of built-in metal wardrobes—sometimes these are in combination with dressers, with mirrors over. One caution was offered that mirrors should not be so placed as to reflect light into patient's eyes.

Furniture

There is uniformity in every plan reviewed in the way beds are set parallel to exterior wall, so that patients can look out window without facing directly into the bright sky. Motor-operated high-low beds are also uniformly popular—it should be noted that they may be a full 7 ft–3 in. in overall length.

There is no uniformity in position of bedside table. It may be placed on near side of bed as

one enters room, or on far side, or sometimes on patient's right or left, whichever way the bed faces. No preponderant preference can be detected. The typical bedside table measures about 16 in. x 20 in.

Plans reviewed did not concern themselves with other furniture. In single rooms, especially, the presence of a bureau, side chair, arm chair, ottoman, or television set is partly dependent on economic status of patient being served. These items take space and deserve attention in the planning stage—they may well affect overall room size.

Plumbing Fixtures

Next to room size the most important architectural problem is disposition of plumbing facilities. Although minimum budget hospitals are still being built without a toilet connecting to every bedroom, a private toilet is now regarded as a basic feature with each bedroom. It is perhaps axiomatic that in almost every case a bedpan cleansing device is incorporated. 2 ft–10 in. to 3 ft–2 in. by 3 ft–10 in. to 4 ft–10 in. are the dimensions noted for individual toilet rooms, usually with grab-bars on one or both side walls. Locating water closet slightly off-center in the room allows a little more space on wider side for manipulating cleanser—the latter needs only cold water and is usually on the right as you face back wall. Some plans indicate bedpan rack or cabinet within toilet room—otherwise bedpan is stored in bedside table.

Several plans were reviewed which showed shared toilets between two single or double rooms. While this arrangement may save some space and expense, it presents its own problems such as added disturbance to patients, special door hardware, and lack of flexibility in room assignment to patients of opposite sex. It is interesting that the administrators with this type of accommodation offered no comment on these points. The committee infers that the shared toilet is valid only in large hospitals, in which separation of sexes is a lesser problem.

Location of lavatory reveals about an even choice between placing it in bedroom proper, where it invites more frequent use by attending nurses and physicians, or in toilet rooms, where it is less institutional-looking to patient and visitors. It is known that some thoughtful hospitals purposely set lavatories at 3 ft–0 in. above floor—in other plans studied, the lower, conventional residential height is observed.

Not many toilet rooms have tubs, which make them complete bathrooms off bedrooms. This choice is undoubtedly a matter of economics of the particular hospital. The fact that almost no shower stalls appear leads the committee to conjecture that most hospitals are content to have shower heads in tubs, relying on suction-cup rubber mats and strong grab bars to avoid injury to patients from slipping.

Doors and Windows

Standard bedroom door width is 3 ft–10 in. or 4 ft–0 in. This can be reduced by 2 in. with offset hinges. A slight majority of doors to single

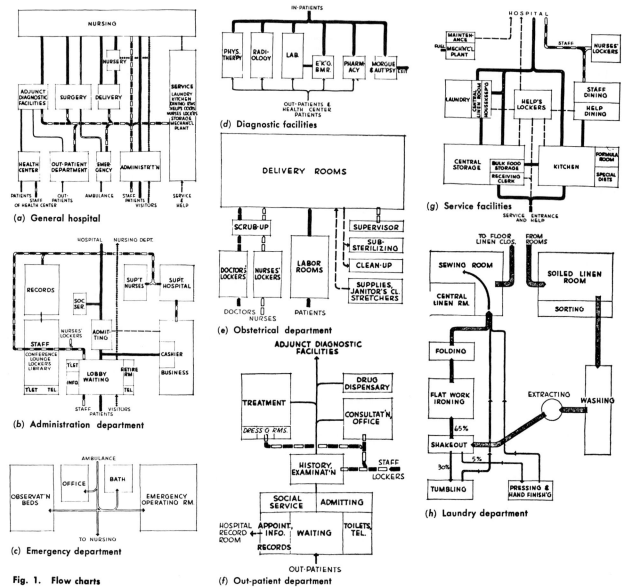

(a) General hospital

(b) Administration department

(c) Emergency department

(d) Diagnostic facilities

(e) Obstetrical department

(f) Out-patient department

(g) Service facilities

(h) Laundry department

Fig. 1. Flow charts

From Design and Construction of General Hospitals by Public Health Service, U.S. Department of Health, Education and Welfare (1953).

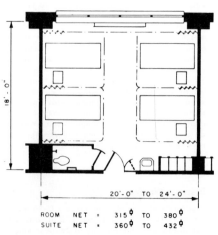

ROOM NET = 315 ☐ TO 380 ☐
SUITE NET = 360 ☐ TO 432 ☐

Fig. 2 Four-bed room

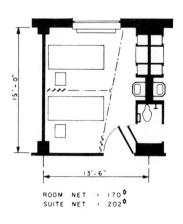

ROOM NET = 170 ☐
SUITE NET = 202 ☐

Fig. 3. Double bedroom, small, shared toilet

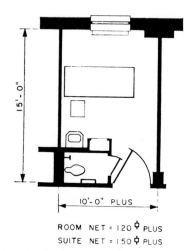

ROOM NET = 120 ☐ PLUS
SUITE NET = 150 ☐ PLUS

Fig. 4. Single room, small

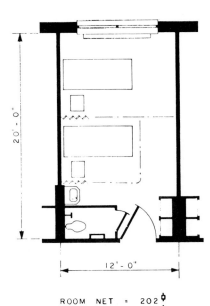

ROOM NET = 202 ⏀
SUITE NET = 240 ⏀

Fig. 5. Double room, medium size

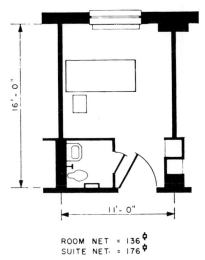

ROOM NET = 136 ⏀
SUITE NET = 176 ⏀

Fig. 6. Single room, medium size

and double rooms are hinged on side toward beds, so that door ajar serves as screen to patient. Toilet room door widths are 2 ft-0 in. to 2 ft-4 in. swinging out into bedroom, except where surface-bolted or pivoted hinges are used, so that doors can be removed in the event a patient in toilet room faints and falls against door.

The wide variety of window treatment suggests that climate, orientation, esthetics, economics and other considerations do more to govern this architectural feature than any predetermined optimum standard. It is interesting that administrators' comments in this general area say little about psychological or therapeutic values of wide vs narrow or high vs low windows, but do offer practical complaints about windows that are drafty or difficult to clean and wood stools that spot too easily. Preferences are expressed for marble and laminated plastic stools. A definite division of opinion is found between those who prefer nothing but drapes and those who favor only Venetian blinds at windows. The committee notes that low window stools offer patient an opportunity to see out when his motorized bed is in its low position.

Room Finishes

There is no strong preference for one type of flooring material over another. Inquiries made about oversize sloping bases to keep furniture away from walls reveal that those few who have them seem satisfied, whereas only one administrator without them expressed a wish that he might have had them. Wall behind bed is the only location within a bedroom where a sloping base appears to have merit. Plaster walls are most common. Acoustical ceilings are not considered essential, even in multi-bed rooms—use of a suspended acoustical system is more valuable for access to mechanical work than for its acoustical properties.

Built-in Equipment

Built-in wardrobe-dresser-recessed-mirror combinations have been discussed above. Some emphasis is also found for separate 9 in. wide flower shelves bracketed on wall beside or opposite bed, about 4 ft-6 in. above floor. There are a variety of cubicle curtain arrangements in multi-bed rooms, from the simplest cross-room tracks to complete enclosures around each bed.

Lighting

A study of the rooms shows that no single, a few double, and most four-bed rooms have ceiling fixtures for general illumination. In almost all rooms there is a wall fixture over head of bed, mounted from 5 ft-2 in. to 6 ft-6 in. above floor. There are numerous fixtures on the market today for this purpose, providing varying combinations of direct and indirect light. The one prevailing comment of a number of administrators is that no wall light gives adequate illumination for examining the patient. Another caution is to control light in multi-bed rooms so that it will not shine in another patient's eyes—this frequently happens across the room in four-bed rooms. Almost all rooms have night-lights, either set in wall at a low elevation or incorporated in over-bed light. The one prevailing comment here recommends switching the night-light out in corridor or near room door, rather than at bedside. (See Fig. 7.)

A special wrinkle for single rooms, where private duty nurses may be in attendance, is a ceiling down-light over a chair near door into the room, at which location the nurse can guard patient from unwanted visitors and at same time read comfortably day or night without bothering patient.

Other Electrical Work

The audio-visual nurse's call is almost universally used and gets a popular rating among administrators who commented—except for use in pediatrics. In some cases the speaker is located in ceiling over bed. In one instance a request is made for the pilot light also in ceiling, as being more easily seen by patient. On walls with two beds the use of one call for two beds or provision of separate calls is about an even choice.

In a small percentage of hospitals several radio channels are piped in at head of bed. In fewer instances the same is true of TV; most TV sets are portable and provided through a rental agency.

Oxygen and Suction

Oxygen is piped in from a central source in most rooms studied. Outlets are 4 ft-0 in. to 5 ft-6 in. above floors—5 ft-0 in. minimum is the *NPFA Bulletin 565* standard if outlet is not recessed. There is an even division of opinion concerning location of oxygen outlets,

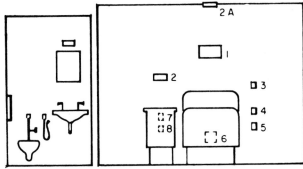

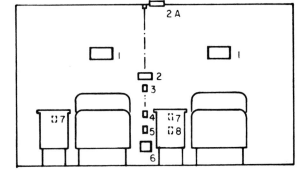

Fig. 7. Wall elevation of single room (left) and double room (right)

Legend

1. Overbed light
2. Nurses' call
2A. Micro speaker in ceiling

3. Oxygen outlet
4. Suction outlet
5. Suction bottle bracket

6. Night light—switch outside room door
7. Double duplex outlet
8. Telephone, radio, TV jacks

ADMITTING DEPARTMENT FUNCTIONAL FLOW CHART

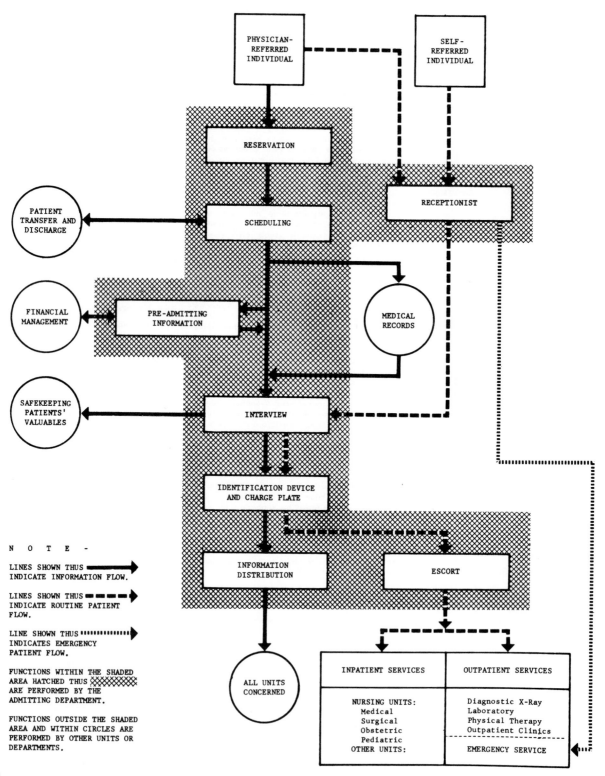

Fig. 8

Figures 8–12 from *Administrative Services and Facilities for Hospitals,* Health Services and Mental Health Adm., Dept. of Health, Education, and Welfare, Washington.

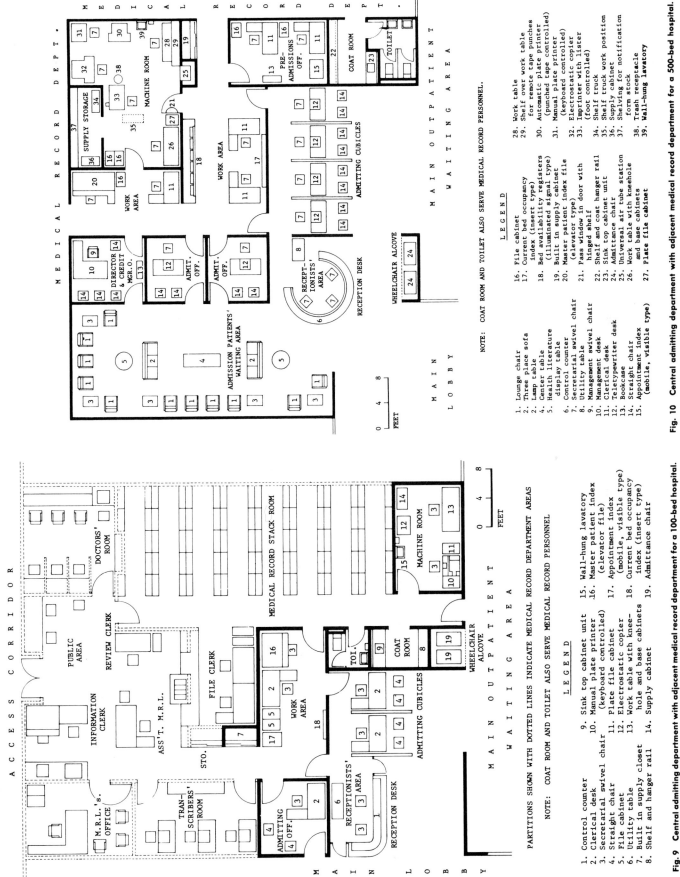

Fig. 9 Central admitting department with adjacent medical record department for a 100-bed hospital.

Fig. 10 Central admitting department with adjacent medical record department for a 500-bed hospital.

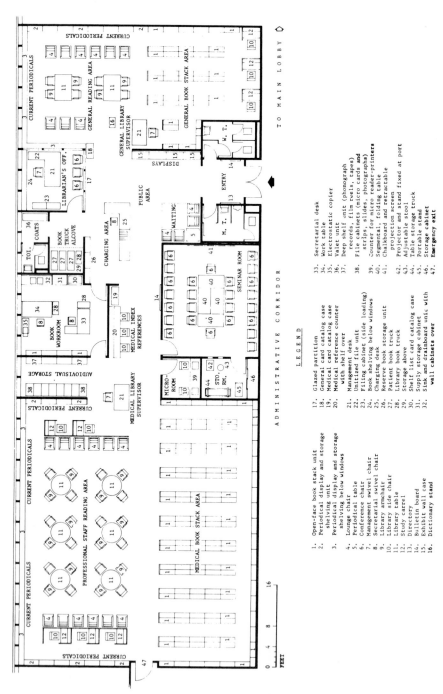

LEGEND

1. Open-face book stack unit
2. Periodical display and storage shelving unit
3. Periodical display and storage shelving below windows
4. Lounge chair
5. Periodical table
6. Conference chair
7. Management swivel chair
8. Secretarial swivel chair
9. Library armchair
10. Library side chair
11. Library table
12. Study carrel
13. Directory
14. Bulletin board
15. Exhibit wall case
16. Dictionary stand

17. Glazed partition
18. General card catalog case
19. Medical card catalog case
20. Medical reference counter with shelf over
21. Management desk
22. Unitized file unit
23. Filing cabinet (side loading)
24. Book shelving below windows
25. Charging desk
26. Reserve book storage unit
27. Patient book truck
28. Library book truck
29. Storage above
30. Shelf list card catalog case
31. Supply storage cabinet
32. Sink and drainboard unit with wall cabinets over

33. Secretarial desk
34. Work table
35. Electrostatic copier
36. Valet unit
37. Deep shelf unit (phonograph records, film reels, tapes)
38. File cabinets (micro cards and strips, slides, photographs)
39. Counter for micro reader-printers
40. Segmental, folding table
41. Chalkboard and retractable projection screen
42. Projector and stand fixed at port
43. Adjustable stool
44. Table storage truck
45. Portable stand
46. Storage cabinet
47. Emergency exit

Fig. 11 Medical library unit with patient and general library facilities adjacent for a 500-bed hospital. This is generally similar to a unit for a 300-bed hospital.

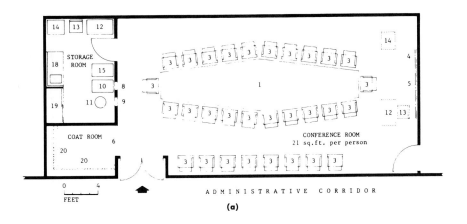

(a)

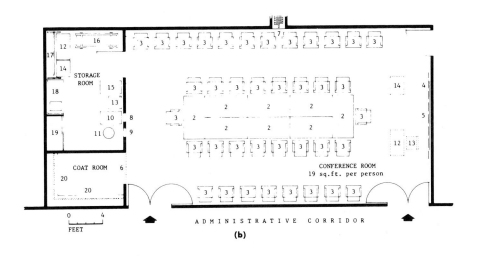

(b)

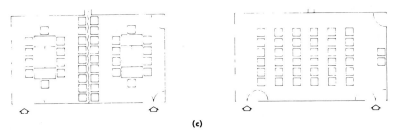

(c)

L E G E N D

1. Conference table	8. Projection port	15. Utility truck
2. Segmental folding table	9. Operator's view port	16. Folding table truck
3. Conference chair	10. Projector stand at port	17. Portable chalkboard
4. Chalkboard	11. Adjustable stool	18. Coffee bar unit
5. Retractable projection screen	12. Recording secretary's table	19. Storage closet
6. Drop ceiling	13. Secretarial swivel chair	20. Hat shelf with
7. Folding partition	14. Portable speaker's podium	clothes rod below

Fig. 12 Conference and board-meeting unit: (a) for a 500-bed hospital (Unit for a 300-bed hospital would be generally similar.); (b) for a 100-bed hospital; (c) alternate seating for a 100-bed hospital.

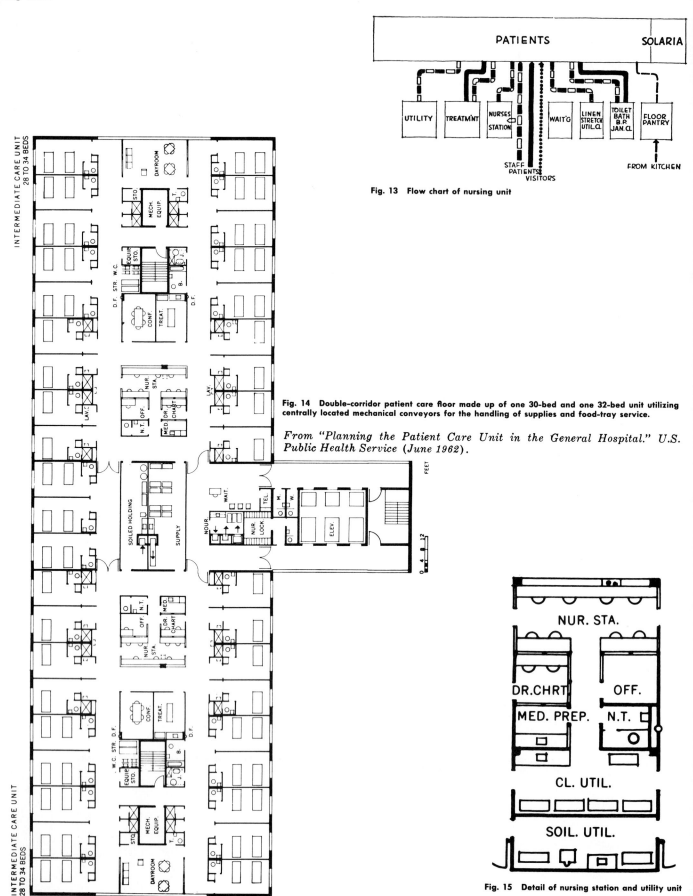

Fig. 13   Flow chart of nursing unit

Fig. 14   Double-corridor patient care floor made up of one 30-bed and one 32-bed unit utilizing centrally located mechanical conveyors for the handling of supplies and food-tray service.

From "Planning the Patient Care Unit in the General Hospital." U.S. Public Health Service (June 1962).

Fig. 15   Detail of nursing station and utility unit

either on near side of bed, as one enters room, or on far side. Suction is provided in all rooms in approximately one-third of the hospitals, in some rooms in one-third, and in no rooms in one-third. Outlets are either grouped in same plate with oxygen or they are separate, beside or below oxygen. Piped compressed air in bedrooms is noted only occasionally.

Air Conditioning

The incidence of airconditioning is still something that depends on climate and economics. Individual room units present no problems of cross-contamination of air from one room to another. Central systems do create problems if recirculation is desired. A check across the country indicates that opinion is divided on extent to which central recirculation should be permitted.

Organization of Wall Outlets

An overall glance at the numerous room layouts studied by the committee emphasizes the clutter of wall outlets and paraphernalia of many kinds at head of each bed. In general they detract from appearance of room. A checklist for a well-equipped bed in a single room will include some 24 different facilities! In order to minimize the scatter effect at normal eye level, the committee suggests that half of these facilities could be consolidated in a low-wall outlet through a single flexible cable to bedside table, where many items would be within reach of patient. Only two items might then occur on wall at eye-level — oxygen outlet (code requirement) and over-bed light (if used). Following check-list gives an indication of the thinking of some of the committee on this point:

Portable Bedside Panel (Patient's Control)

- Nurses' call switch, pilot light, monitor light
- General room illumination switch, dimmer control
- Reading light switch
- Room thermostat remote control
- Electric blanket control
- Electric clock
- Duplex convenience receptacle
- Radio station selector (central radio system)
- Jack for pillow speaker (ceiling speaker in private rooms)
- Provision for TV remote control to be clipped onto panel
- Provision for telephone instrument (bracket type)

NURSING UNITS

Integral with bed
- Bed control (within patient's reach, but with nurse-controlled cut-off feature)
Ceiling
- Nurses' call micro-speaker
- Radio speaker (private rooms only)
High on Wall (60 in. or higher)
- Over-bed light fixture (direct and indirect)
- Oxygen outlet
Low on Wall (approximately 24 in.)
- Receptacle for portable bedside panel
- Night light (switched from corridor)
- Telephone jack
- Double duplex receptacle (bed, oxygen tent, portable x-ray, heating pad, etc)
- Remote recording instrument receptacles (temp, pulse, respiratory)
- Suction outlet
- Bracket for suction bottle

Double Corridor Nursing Floor

Figure 14 shows a typical double-corridor nursing unit which is often utilized in hospital planning. It has the following advantages:

1. It permits a closer relationship between the patient bedrooms and the nursing station and other service areas.

2. It permits greater flexibility in segregation of patients for various medical reasons.

3. Much of the staff activity and particularly conversation can be carried on within the service unit complex, thus cutting down noise in the patient corridor.

Figure 15 indicates more clearly the nursing station and utility room arrangement. The clean utility is designed to accommodate carts for storing linens, utensils, and other supplies, which would be brought from a central supply and sterilizing unit. Elevators are located outside the nursing unit to cut down on the amount of noise. This would also permit a future nursing unit to be located on the other side of the elevators.

The success of this plan depends, to a great extent, on well-designed air conditioning and lighting, particularly for the center unit. While this nursing floor consists of two 25-bed nursing units, many authorities believe that greater efficiencies are obtained in having a larger ratio of beds per nursing station. This particular nursing floor might easily be extended one or two bays, increasing the capacity to 62 or 70 beds.

This plan also demonstrates how an intensive nursing service can be integrated into the same module or bay which accommodates the typical patient room. One 6-bed intensive ward is shown, and the adjacent typical double rooms can accommodate intensive-care patients when the need arises.

By AARON N. KIFF and MARY WORTHEN
Kiff, Colean, Sounder & Voss (Office of York and Sawyer)

SURGICAL SUITE

The surgical suite of the general hospital is a very complex workshop. It is one of the most important departments of any hospital, and its planning is complicated by the diversities of opinion and experience of the many persons involved in policy decisions essential to development of a good program of requirements.

We say a "program of requirements" rather than "plan." Before any intelligent planning can be done by the architect, there must be a meeting of minds on the size of department; i.e., the number and type of operating rooms and the work methods to be followed in the supportive areas. Administrators, surgeons, anesthetists, surgical nurses, all must participate in the preplanning analysis of needs and functional methods. The architect must have a wide understanding of various management procedures to be sure that all are discussed in reaching any conclusions with the particular group involved.

The number and type of operating rooms is the first major decision. In the general hospital, the tendency is to have all major operating rooms as nearly identical as possible to facilitate scheduling of various surgical procedures. Free floor space should be 18 ft by 20 ft, or approximately 350 sq ft. Many surgeons and surgical supervisors recommend 20 ft by 20 ft free floor space.

The planning and equipping of each operat-

ing room are based on a series of questions, such as: (a) size, (b) usage, (c) environmental control*, (d) lighting—surgical and general illumination*, (e) intercommunications and signal systems*, (f) electronic equipment and monitoring system*, (g) service lines, such as suction, oxygen, nitrous oxide, compressed air, (h) provision for x-ray, not only x-ray tube stand but control, transformer, and necessary lead protection, (i) provision for TV camera, movie cameras, other recording equipment, (j) safety precaution in hazardous areas, (k) cabinet work, supply cabinets and storage for operating table appliances, (l) need for clocks, film illuminators.

The rapid development of cardiac and neurosurgery is creating a demand for one or more extra-large operating rooms. This type of surgery calls for a larger team of surgeons, nurses and technicians, plus a great deal of extra equipment, such as heart-lung machines, hypothermia equipment, etc.; also electronic devices for measuring bodily functions, i.e., electrocardiograph, electroencephalograph, blood pressure, respiration, body temperature, etc. Today many architects are providing an "instrumentation" room adjacent to or between two extra-large operating rooms to accommodate such equipment, which is frequently not explosion-proof. The floor of any such room is usually elevated approximately 3 ft above the operating room floor. Plate glass panels permit vision into operating rooms, and through-wall conduits accommodate wires and other leads of various appliances in the instrumentation room to the surgical field. Such an area can also house the TV control and monitor (if used), x-ray controls, etc.

In the hospital as a whole, the actual patient area is only a very small per cent of the total. The same is true within the surgical suite. The operating rooms themselves will account for only about one-fourth of the total area required for the suite with its supportive functions such as—

Offices and administration areas, scrub areas, work and supply rooms, laboratory, dark room, post-anesthesia recovery, holding or induction areas, lounge, locker and toilet rooms for various personnel groups, conference or teaching rooms, and circulation within the department.

The analysis of various suites illustrating this article show a spread from 1115 sq ft to 1585 sq ft total gross area per operating or cystoscopic room (if included)—and every suite could use more gross floor area for storage, according to comments. Thus, a suite of eight operating rooms averaging 350 sq ft each $= 2800$ sq ft $\times 4 = 11,200$ sq ft estimated total area required—or 1400 sq ft per operating room.

Within the surgical suite we have three basic zones predicated on three types of activity and circulation involved, and the degree of sterility to be maintained. The preplanning analysis of these areas is just as important as the determination of the number and type of operating rooms.

Outer zone: Administrative elements and basic control where personnel enter the department, patients are received and held or sent to proper holding areas of inner zone; conference, classroom areas, locker spaces, any outpatient reception, etc.

Intermediate zone: Predominantly work and storage areas; outside personnel will deliver to this area but should not penetrate the inner zone. The recovery suite, if completely inte-

---

*These subjects have so many ramifications they are only mentioned here.

grated with the surgical suite, is an intermediate or outer zone activity.

Inner zone: The actual operating rooms, the scrub areas, the patient holding or induction areas. All alien traffic should be eliminated. Here we want to maintain the highest level of cleanliness and aseptic conditions.

Outer zone administrative areas have increased in importance. Offices are needed for the surgical supervisor, the clerks who manage scheduling and paper work, the clinical instructor (particularly if there is a school of nursing), possibly the chief of staff. There must be provision for surgeons to dictate medical records.

And don't forget the patient. After all, he is the primary concern. Who is responsible for his transportation to the surgical suite, and on whose bed or stretcher? How is he checked in and where does he wait if the room for which he is scheduled is not ready? Who has not seen surgical corridors lined with occupied stretchers for want of adequate holding, preparation or induction areas? Another factor is added if any ambulant outpatient work is to be done. There must be provision for receiving, controlled waiting, dressing rooms and toilets.

A variety of persons must be provided with lounge, locker and toilet space—surgeons (male and female), nurses, technicians, aides, orderlies. Coffee and cola seem to lubricate the entire department; some systematic provision for their supply is warranted.

A conference or classroom for departmental meetings and in-service training programs is easily justified.

The access to all these areas should be removed from strictly surgical areas, as people are entering and leaving in street clothes and should not penetrate into other zones until after changing shoes and clothing.

The planning and equipping of the intermediate zone are based on the method of processing and storing of the thousands of items involved. It is fairly common practice for the central sterile supply department, elsewhere in the hospital, to be responsible for the prep-

aration and autoclaving of all surgical linen packs, gloves, syringes, needles, and external fluids. The storage of these items to be used in surgery becomes the responsibility of the surgical department and adequate space must be provided for a predetermined level of inventory. (See Fig. 1.)

The method of processing surgical instruments has been the subject of various research projects, notably at the University of Pittsburgh (see *The Modern Hospital,* November 1955). The new ultrasonic cleaning equipment is eliminating a time-consuming, laborious process. The cost of the equipment discourages duplication and encourages the consolidation of work areas where lay personnel can be trained under close supervision to carry out approved processing techniques.

The method of packing and sterilizing instruments and utensils will determine the size, type, and location of autoclaves needed. Consideration must be given to inclusion of an ethylene oxide sterilizer for cystoscopes, bronchoscopes and delicate surgical instruments which cannot be sterilized by steam or high temperatures. How and where instruments will be stored is another decision to be made.

Suitable storage space must be provided for: (a) clean surgical supplies such as extra linen, tape, bandage materials, etc.; (b) parenteral solutions, external fluids or sterile water; (c) essential drugs and narcotics; (d) blood supplies, bone bank, tissue bank, eye bank, etc.; (e) radium and isotopes used in surgery.

It seems impossible to provide adequate centralized garage-type spaces for bulky equipment not in constant use. Dr. Carl Walter has estimated that an average of 80 sq ft per operating room is needed.

The intermediate zone also houses the facilities for handling waste, soiled linen, etc., and janitorial equipment for routine housekeeping.

The anesthesia service cannot be shortchanged. It may spread over all zones of the surgical suite. Office space is required, work and storage space for equipment. And most im-

portant is the decision on where induction of the patient is to take place: centrally to all rooms, locally in induction areas (sometimes referred to as preparation or holding rooms) or in the operating room proper. There are acknowledged hazards in moving anesthetized patients and equipment. Induction areas should permit quicker turnover in operating room usage, but they also require more anesthetists and nurses to administer.*

The post-anesthesia recovery room has become an integral part of the surgical suite in most cases. The size will vary from one-and-a-half to two beds per operating room. There is a close relationship between the anesthesia department and the recovery room.

Any frozen section laboratory should be located near the entrance of the surgical suite so that laboratory personnel need not penetrate the inner zone.

Any dark room facilities should be located to serve those rooms generating greatest load of film, normally the cystoscopic, urological and orthopedic services. It should be accessible from a corridor to prevent alien traffic through any operating room.

Inner zone planning includes the operating rooms and their essential supportive elements. Decisions must be made on the type of scrub-up sinks or troughs and their location providing minimum travel to the operating room to eliminate chance of contamination after scrub procedure.

The need for local "substerilizing" rooms is being questioned by many authorities. The trend toward centralization of work areas and sterilizing equipment, and the changing techniques of instrument packaging are reducing the importance of the substerilizing area. Circulation travel distance and work patterns are factors determining the need for decentralized work areas. When such areas are provided there should be staff access for servicing and stocking them without going through an operating room.

The program of need dictates the gross area required for the surgical suite. Recent developments indicate that more efficient departments with minimum travel distances can be planned in bulky squarish areas. This tendency has affected the location of the surgical suite in relationship to the hospital as a whole. The suite has come downstairs to a lower floor where it is more possible to spread out and achieve the desired shape, divorced from the usually narrow structural pattern of a nursing unit. Planning within the squarish areas has been made possible with the parallel development of air conditioning and artificial lighting. Dependence upon windows for ventilation and light is a thing of the past. The optimum conditions of temperature, humidity, and light level can be controlled by mechanical means far better than by nature. (See Fig. 2.)

The surgical suite location must mesh with the total circulation pattern so that patients can be moved to and from surgery with a minimum of travel through other hospital services. Its location is also affected by its close relationship to three other major hospital services—the x-ray department, the clinical laboratories, and the central sterile supply.

One other important factor in the location of the surgical suite is future expansion. Anticipate ways and means to permit growth in an orderly fashion without upsetting the basic relationship of internal organization—or without extending lines of travel to unacceptable or uneconomical lengths.

Fig. 1 Flow chart

From Design and Construction of General Hospitals by U.S. Public Health Service, U.S. Department of Health, Education and Welfare (1953).

*Experience with various suites indicates that what was planned for induction frequently is converted to other causes.

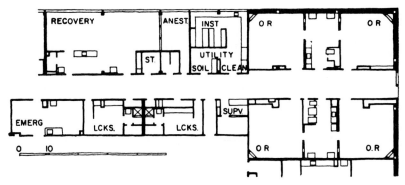

(a) *Sherlock, Smith and Adams, Architects.*

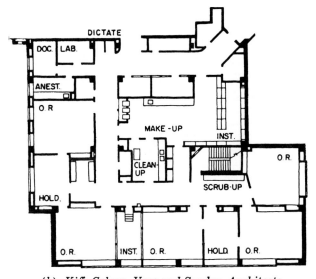

(b) *Kiff, Colean, Voss and Souder, Architects.*

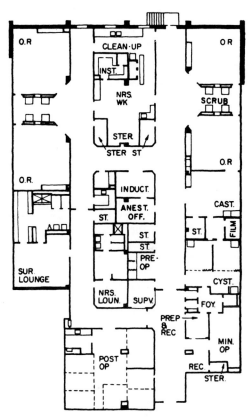

(c) *Louis Allen Abramson, Architect.*

Fig. 2 Typical plans of operating suites

NURSERY*

As one of the areas in the hospital where patients are most vulnerable to infection, the nursery should be planned to provide the best means for the care, safety, and welfare of the infants. Although the plans and diagrams, shown here, have been developed for hospitals of specified sizes, the principles set forth apply to all hospitals, large or small, new or old.

Basic recommendations for planning nurseries that have been developed, based on clinical experience and study, include: limiting the number of infants in each nursery; wide spacing of bassinets within each nursery; separation of bassinets by cubicle partitions; promoting the use of aseptic techniques and individual care by providing, among other things, ample space and handwashing facilities; limiting the number of bassinets served by one nurses' station; separating facilities for premature infants and for observing infants suspected of having infectious conditions;

*The study from which this article was condensed was prepared for the Division of Hospital and Medical Facilities, Public Health Service, and the Children's Bureau, Social Security Administration, by O. Bernard Ives, architect. Copies of the study may be obtained from Superintendent of Documents, U.S. Government Printing Office, Washington

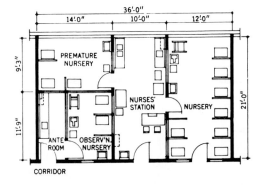

NURSERY FOR 440 LIVE BIRTHS PER YEAR IN HOSPITAL OF APPROXIMATELY 50 BEDS.
The number of bassinets and maternity beds required is based on number of live births expected in hospital per year, rather than a rule-of-thumb relationship to the over-all bed complement. Six to 8 per cent (up to 12 per cent in poor economic areas) of the total live births will be premature (low birth weight of 5 pounds 8 ounces)

Fig. 1 Plans for nursery in 50-bed hospital.

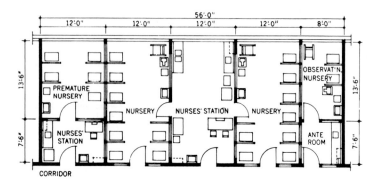

NURSERY FOR 880 LIVE BIRTHS PER YEAR IN HOSPITAL OF APPROXIMATELY 100 BEDS. The estimated number of premature births divided by 18 (number of 20-day average stay periods in a year) will equal the average number of premature bassinets or incubators required. This figure must be adjusted for 100 per cent occupancy (often assumed at 70 per cent). A premature center nearby would eliminate need for such facilities in the hospital

COHORT SYSTEM NURSERY FOR 880 LIVE BIRTHS PER YEAR IN HOSPITAL OF APPROXIMATELY 100 BEDS. In hospitals using the cohort system, babies born within 48 hours of each other are kept in the same nursery, arriving and leaving together, in theory reducing cross-infection through the elimination of over-lapping of babies with infections. Cohort nurseries are thoroughly cleaned and disinfected between discharge of one cohort and admission of the next

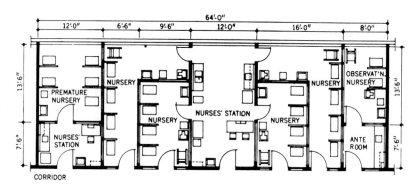

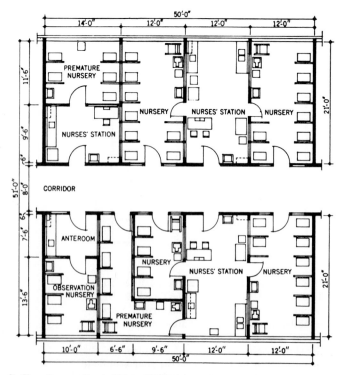

NURSERY FOR 1,500 LIVE BIRTHS PER YEAR IN HOSPITAL OF APPROXIMATELY 200 BEDS. Size of full-term portion of this nursery, as well as the others shown, is based on estimated number of live births per year less the premature births. This figure is then divided by 73 (the number of five-day average stay periods in a year) and adjusted from this 70 per cent occupancy total to a 100 per cent occupancy figure. Observation bassinets are provided at rate of 10 per cent of full-term bassinets, in nurseries with capacity of 20 or more. In smaller nurseries a minimum of two observation bassinets are provided

Fig. 2 Plans for nurseries in 100- or 200-bed hospitals.

DETAIL PLAN, TWO EIGHT-BASSINET FULL-TERM NURSERIES AND NURSES' STATION. Typical arrangement of a pair of full-term nurseries with nurses' station between allowing two nurses to tend 16 bassinets (or a maximum of 20) from one position. Recommended items of furnishings and equipment are shown located in what is considered their proper relationship to each other and to the complete nursery-nurses' station layout

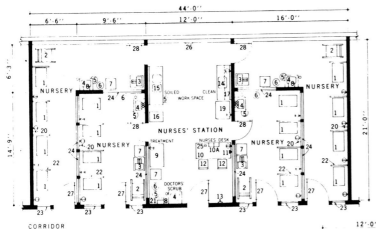

DETAIL PLAN, TWO PAIRS FOUR-BASSINET COHORT SYSTEM NURSERIES AND NURSES' STATION. A cohort system arrangement similar to the layout above, and of the same size. As in the conventional plan *(above)*, the four cohort nurseries may be tended by two nurses working together from a single centrally-located nurses' station. Workspace required will be approximately the same in both types

LEFT: **DETAIL PLAN, FIVE-INCUBATOR NURSERY WITH NURSES' STATION.** *MIDDLE AND RIGHT:* **MAXIMUM (THREE-BASSINET) AND MINIMUM (TWO-BASSINET) OBSERVATION NURSERIES.** The minimum and maximum size observation nurseries have anterooms between nurseries and corridors, provided with approximately the same facilities as work and treatment areas of full-term nurseries

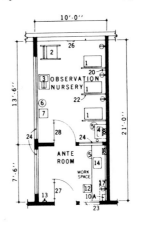

LEGEND

1. Bassinet with cabinet, pull-out shelf below, on 3-inch ball-bearing casters, with wheel lock
2. Rocking chair with armrests, washable finish
3. Utility table, 16 by 20 inches, with top drawer to hold infant scales
4. Lavatory, 18 by 22 inches, with gooseneck spout, knee or foot controls, shelf over
5. Waste receptacle, foot-controlled cover, removable waxed liner
6. Soiled diaper receptacle, foot-controlled cover, removable waxed liner
7. Soiled linen hamper on 3-inch ball-bearing casters, removable waxed liner, foot-controlled cover

8. Paper towel dispenser, enclosed type
9. Treatment table, 24 by 36 by 36 inches high, on 3-inch ball-bearing casters, with wheel lock
10. Nurse's desk, 30 inches high
10A. Chart rack
11. Telephone outlet
12. Office chair, swivel, without arms
13. Hookstrip
14. Sink with gooseneck spout, knee or foot controls, in counter 36 inches high, open below
15. Double compartment sink with gooseneck spout, knee or foot controls, in counter 36 inches high
16. Bottle warmer on portable carriage
17. Wall cabinet
18. Incubator, on 3-inch ball-bearing casters, with wheel lock

19. Refrigerator, with built-in thermometer
20. Double oxygen outlet, one for each four full-term—or each two premature—bassinets
21. Shelves (three), starting 42 inches above floor, for clean gowns, supplies
22. Cubicle partition, starting 30 inches above floor, with 2-foot-high clear glass or lucite panel, wall- and ceiling-hung metal frame
23. Clear wire-glass view panel in steel frame, 1,296 square inches maximum, bottom 42 inches above floor
24. Clear plate-glass or lucite view panel, bottom 42 inches above floor
25. Hand-wind clock, desk type
26. Electric clock
27. Door with upper panel of wire glass
28. Door with upper panel of clear glass

Fig. 3   Detail plans for three types of nurseries.

and providing optimum conditions of temperature, relative humidity and ventilation. Figures 1 to 13 show a variety of nursery plans.

Full-term nurseries should be located in the maternity nursing unit as close to the mothers as possible and away from the line of traffic of other than maternity services. An area of 30 feet per infant is recommended, exclusive of the nurses' station.

The extent of the spread of infection in a nursery can be reduced as the number of infants in each nursery room is reduced. The optimum number of full-term infants that can be cared for by a member of the nursing staff is in the range of 8 to 10.

Bassinets should be at least 2 feet apart and, if partitions are used, cubicles should be large enough to permit bedside care. Partitions should be glazed or transparent so that the infants can be easily observed by the nurse. To facilitate cleaning, partitions should not extend to the floor. Cubicle partitions might extend only from the bottom of the bassinet to 24 inches above. The supporting frames of the partitions may be attached to the ceiling and wall. Where a wall is not available, as in an island arrangement, some supports must extend to the floor.

In nurseries without cubicle partitions bassinets are often crowded together side by side. Although cubicle partitions may be objectionable from the standpoint of cleaning (and are often unsightly), they help to ensure that bassinets are properly spaced.

Fixed-view windows between the nursery and the corridor permit visitors to view the infants from the corridor. There windows must be wire glass set in steel frames and must conform to National Fire Code requirements. Fixed view windows in partitions between nurseries and the nurses' station or between two nurseries facilitate observation of all infants in the area. These windows may be of clear plate glass or lucite and should be as large as practicable.

A door direct from each nursery to the corridor is recommended to permit faster evacuation in case of fire and easier movement of bassinets from the nursery to the mothers at feeding time and to avoid traffic through the nurses' station. This door, hung in a steel frame, should have a wire glass panel and must conform to National Fire Code requirements.

Furnishings and equipment for each full-term nursery should include, in addition to the items shown in the plans, a suction bulb or a mechanical device with a soft rubber tip and individual catheters for individual infants for each full-term (and premature) nursery. Controls of the suction device should include a regulator to limit the suction to avoid injury to the infant. Suction should be provided from a central system.

A four-bassinet nursery lends itself well to the "cohort" system, in which babies born during the same interval (no more than 48 hours) are kept in the same nursery. Babies arrive and leave together. After the departure of each cohort, the nursery is thoroughly cleaned and disinfected before admission of the next cohort, thereby—in theory—breaking the chain of possible cross-infection by eliminating the overlapping of babies with infections.

The use of four-bassinet nurseries does not imply increased staff. Two four-bassinet nurseries may be under the care of one nursing

person if she wears a scrub gown and scrubs properly between visits to each nursery. Two such nurseries may be considered the equivalent of one eight-bassinet nursery in assigning nurses' station and work space. Furnishings and equipment will be the same as those for full-term nurseries.

Since premature infants require more specialized care than full-term infants, a reasonable ratio of staff to premature infants is set at one to five. Thus, a premature nursery room should accommodate no more than five infants and should have a minimum area of 30 square feet per infant. A separate nursery is usually not indicated if less than five infants are to be cared for at one time. In such cases, space for them can often be provided in the full-term nursery. One nurses' station may serve two premature nurseries, or a premature nursery and a full-term nursery if the nurseries are paired.

In a premature nursery where suitable environmental temperature and humidity are maintained, only 50 to 75 per cent of the premature infants may require incubators. Furnishings for premature nurseries will be similar to those in full-term nurseries, aside from the incubators.

An observation nursery should be provided for infants suspected of infection. When positive diagnosis is made, the infant is transferred elsewhere in the hospital and placed on isolation precautions. However, if diagnosis is not positive the infant may be returned to the regular nursery provided he has not been exposed to an infected infant in the observation nursery.

The observation nursery should be a completely separate unit, but it should be located adjacent to a full-term nursery with a glazed partition between to permit observation by the nursery staff. A minimum of 40 square feet per bassinet is recommended to provide adequate space for bedside care and treatment of the infant.

Observation bassinets should be provided at the rate of 10 per cent of the full-term bassinets. A minimum of two—and a maximum of three—bassinets are recommended for each observation nursery. These nurseries may be repeated as many times as necessary to provide the required complement of observation bassinets. Furnishings and equipment will be similar to those in full-term nurseries.

An anteroom should be provided between the nursery and the corridor. This area should contain the same facilities as the work and treatment areas for full-term nurseries.

The nurses' station serves as a control point and also provides workspace for the nurse and an area for treating infants. The nurse's desk should be placed so that the entrances from the corridor and from the station to the nurseries can be supervised. The nurseries should be visible through observation windows in the partitions.

A station between two nurseries will require a double desk for two nurses. No more than two full-term nurseries, each housing 8 to 10 bassinets, should be served by one nurses' station. In the cohort system, four nurseries, of four bassinets each, may be so served.

The nurse's workspace should occupy a separate area at one end of the nurses' station. This arrangement affords the nurse full view of the infants while attending to most activities. The treatment area should be located near the entrance to the nurses' station so the physician need not walk through the workspace. Routine

examinations and treatments should be carried out at the bassinets in the nursery. A physicians' scrub area should be located at the entrance of the nurses' station. The description of the full-term nurses' station also applies to premature nurseries, except that the treatment table is omitted. Other necessary areas, not shown in the plans, include formula rooms, nurses' locker rooms, demonstration rooms and storage.

Air conditioning will be required for nurseries to ensure the constant temperature and humidity conditions so beneficial to care of the newborn. In addition, the air-conditioning system, through the ventilating features, will remove odor and will materially reduce the bacterial contamination of the environment.

PEDIATRIC NURSING UNITS*

The floor plans of pediatric nursing units shown in Figs. 1 and 2 illustrate suggested arrangements of the patient rooms and the supporting facilities described in the text. These plans are designed also to conform with other nursing units of the hospital.

The total bed count in each plan exceeds the recommended maximum of 20 beds per nursing unit because provision has been made for parents to sleep in. The number of sleep-in beds will vary with hospital policy and with the number of parents who are able or who wish to sleep in. All bedrooms are sized and equipped to accommodate full-size hospital beds as well as smaller youth beds and cribs.

Another feature is the extensive use of glass in partitions between rooms and in corridor partitions. This provides the visual control most necessary in pediatric nursing.

Rooms for sick infants and isolation rooms are located for direct observation from the nurses' station. The nurses' station is centered in each unit, thus reducing travel distances and allowing general observation of activity and traffic.

Workrooms are centrally located in the single pediatric nursing unit (Fig. 1) and conveniently accessible to both nursing units as shown in Fig. 2.

An important therapeutic area is the dayroom-playroom which may be used for dining and schoolwork as well. At least 50 percent of the children may use this room. It is located for ready observation and control from the nurses' station and at the same time designed to avoid disturbing patients in their rooms. Furnishings and equipment are selected for multiuse in these various activities.

The dietary facility for the unit is located adjoining the dayroom-playroom to provide convenient and sanitary service of snacks and meals.

The library-classroom is located at the quiet end of the nursing unit, convenient to the adolescent patients.

Waiting and interview rooms are located at the entrance to the unit. This provides an office for the physician and a place where the child's medical history may be reviewed with the parent.

* U.S. Department of Health, Education, and Welfare, Public Health Service, Health Service and Mental Health Administration, Division of Hospital and Medical Facilities, Architectural and Engineering Branch.

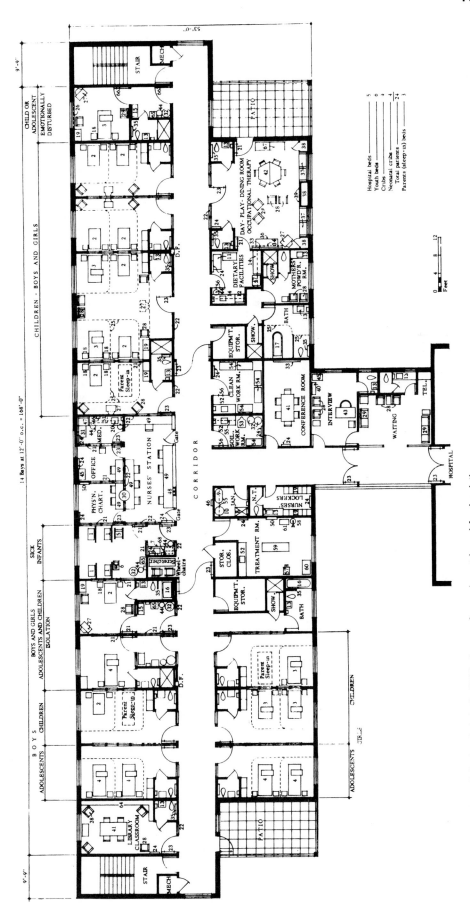

Fig. 1 Pediatric nursing unit for hospitals in the 200-bed range. See equipment legend for description of items numbered. Items of equipment are identified in only one typical room. These are to be repeated in other similar rooms unless otherwise numbered. The components of this plan are designed to conform with those of other nursing floors of the hospital.

HOSPITALS
Pediatric Nursing Units

Equipment Legend for Figures 1 and 2*

1. Sick infant's crib.
2. Crib.
3. Adjustable youth bed with overbed table.
4. Adjustable hospital bed with overbed table.
5. Rocking chair with arm rests, washable finish.
6. Infant scale.
7. Sink with spout at least 5 in above rim of sink and foot- or knee-action valves, in counter 36 in high, open below, wall cabinet above, soap dispenser and enclosed-type paper towel dispenser.
8. Depressed floor sink with mop-handle rack.
9. Mop buckets on roller carriage.
10. Wet-dry vacuum machine.
11. Small enclosed cart, 4 to 6 trays capacity.
12. Ice-making machine, self dispensing.
13. Lavatory, with spout at least 5 in above the flood rim of the fixture, wrist-action valves, soap dispenser and enclosed-type paper towel dispenser, mirror, shelf, and waste receptacle with foot-controlled cover and removable waxed liner.
14. Sink with spout at least 5 in above the flood rim of the sink and wrist-action valves, in counter 36 in high, cabinets below and above, soap dispenser and enclosed-type paper towel dispenser.
15. Utility supply cart.
16. Bathtub, normal height with controls on wall.
17. Bathtub, pedestal type, with controls on wall.
18. Bedside cabinet.
19. Lockers.
20. Sink with spout at least 5 in above the flood rim of the sink and knee- or wrist-action valves, in counter 36 in high, open below, with only one drawer directly under the counter, soap dispenser and enclosed-type paper towel dispenser. Wall cabinet above with double-locked narcotics compartment and inside light.
21. Clear glass, bottom 40 in above floor.
22. Clear wire glass in metal frame (1,296 sq in max.), bottom 40 in above floor.
23. Door, upper panel clear wire glass.
24. Bulletin board, 26 x 24 in.
25. Cubicle curtain.
26. Detention screen.
27. Portable TV on stand or on wall shelf.
28. Easy chair.
29. Sofa.
30. Circular type chart.
31. Medication cart.
32. Soiled linen hamper on 3-in ball-bearing casters, foot-controlled cover, removable waxed liner.
33. Chalkboard.
34. Projection screen, roll-up type.
35. Grab bar.
36. Desk with drawers.
37. Window seat, hinged at back, storage space under for toys.
38. Storage cabinet.
39. Sliding doors.
40. Bookcase.
41. Conference table.
42. Multipurpose type table.
43. Executive type desk and chair.
44. Waste receptacle, foot-controlled cover, removable waxed liner.
45. Filing cabinet.
46. Electric clock.
47. Refrigerator.
48. Pneumatic tube station.
49. Counter, open below, with only one drawer directly under the counter and form rack on top at the back.
50. Recessed double x-ray illuminator.
51. Graduated shelving with cubicles for individual medications and slots for identification cards.
52. Sink with spout at least 5 in above the flood rim of the sink and foot-, knee-, or wrist-action valves, in counter 36 in high, open below, soap dispenser and enclosed-type paper towel dispenser.
53. Clinical sink with wrist-action valves and a bedpan-flushing attachment with foot-action valves.
54. Adjustable metal shelving on casters.
55. Shelf above.
56. Vision panel clear wire glass.
57. Mayo table.
58. Examining light.
59. Examining table.
60. Instrument table, 24 x 36 in.
61. Automatic ascending trayveyor.
62. Automatic descending trayveyor.
63. Dumbwaiter.
64. Built-in bookcases.
65. Lavatory, with spout at least 5 in above the flood rim of the fixture and knee- or wrist-action valves, shelf over, soap dispenser and enclosed type paper towel dispenser.
66. View panel with safety glass, approx. 6 x 12 inches and 4 feet 6 inches from floor.
67. Vending machines.
68. Undercounter refrigerator.

* Figures 1 and 2 from "Manual for the Care of Children in Hospitals," U.S. Dept. of Health, Education, and Welfare, Division of Hospital and Medical Facilities, Architectural and Engineering Branch, 1968.

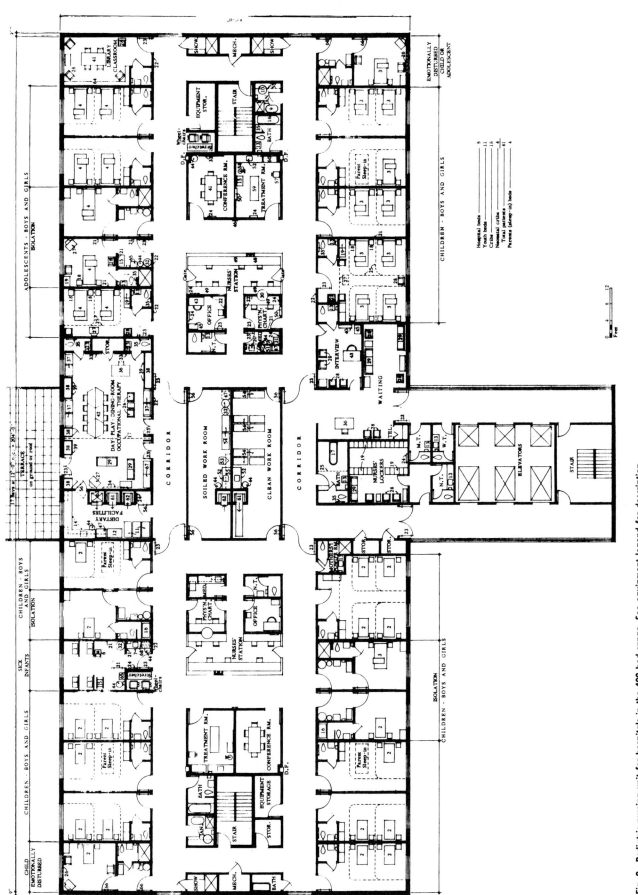

Fig. 2 Pediatric nursing unit for hospitals in the 400-bed range. See equipment legend for description of items numbered. Items of equipment are identified in only one typical room. These are to be repeated in other similar rooms unless otherwise numbered. The components of this plan are designed to conform with those of other nursing floors of the hospital.

Health

HOSPITALS
Diagnostic X-Ray Suite

By WILBUR R. TAYLOR,
CLIFFORD E. NELSON, M.D., and
WILLIAM W. McMASTER

DIAGNOSTIC X-RAY SUITE

In a recent study it was found that many hospitals allotted inadequate space to the x-ray department, and expansion was often impractical. Adequate space for waiting, toilets, and dressing rooms helps insure continuous routines in handling patients. The lack of adequate space results in needless waste of effort and time in efficiently scheduling examinations. An unsatisfactory layout is a handicap to both the hospital and the radiologist since the hospital loses potential revenue, and the radiologist's time, as well as that of the staff, is needlessly wasted. This is particularly important to a small hospital which has a visiting radiologist for it is to the advantage of the hospital and radiologist to schedule as many examinations are possible during his visit.

Location

The diagnostic x-ray department should be located on the first floor, conveniently accessible both to outpatients and inpatients. It is also desirable to locate the department close to the elevators and adjoining the outpatient department and near other diagnostic and treatment facilities.

The functional requirements of the department are usually best satisfied by locating the x-ray rooms at the end of a wing. In this

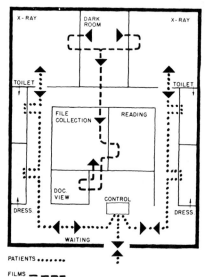

PATIENTS ......

FILMS ━ ━ ━ ━

Fig. 1

The authors are all engaged in work for Public Health Service, Mr. Taylor and Mr. McMaster as architects in the Architectural and Engineering Branch, Division of Hospital and Medical Facilities, Bureau of Medical Services; Dr. Nelson as a radiologist, Division of Radiological Health, Bureau of State Services.

location, the activity within the department will not be disturbed by through traffic to other parts of the hospital, and less shielding will be required because of the exterior walls. (See Fig. 1.)

Plan A

Plan A illustrates an x-ray suite that will provide an efficiently operating service for about 8400 patient examinations yearly, or an average of about 35 examinations daily. This average workload is typical in a hospital of approximately 100 beds (or somewhat more) with an out-patient x-ray service. Unforeseen scheduling problems, of course, will occasionally cause the average of 35 examinations per day to be exceeded. (See Fig. 2.)

The staff needed for this volume of work usually includes: 1 radiologist, 2 or 3 technicians, 1 secretary-receptionist, 1 secretary-file clerk, 1 orderly (as needed).

This plan will permit the workload to be augmented at least 50 percent by increasing the staff, if no more than 20 percent of the x-ray work is fluoroscopic.

Among the desirable characteristics that this plan attempts to provide for is the need for correlating the functions of the working group to obtain maximum efficiency. The arrangement of patient areas and examination rooms around the perimeter, with the administrative staff in the center, makes it possible for these units to operate more efficiently. The technicians' corridor in the rear of the department provides for easy access to the x-ray rooms, film processing rooms, and distribution areas without interference from patients' cross traffic.

Administration Spaces

Every radiologist has specific ideas on the most suitable ways for arranging and operating the administrative functions of the x-ray department. Some of the variables involved are assignment of personnel and functions, reception of patients, sequence of patient examinations, film distribution, and staff viewing facilities. This plan provides for flexibility of space arrangements by allowing for variation of several of the operations within the administrative unit.

Waiting Room General waiting space for about ten patients is located at the entrance to the department. From here the patient is directed to an assigned dressing room. A separate area, to the left of the entrance and in sight of the secretary-receptionist, is provided for wheelchair and stretcher patients. This section is partitioned off by a curtain which may be partially drawn to provide privacy, yet afford the necessary surveillance of unattended patients from the secretary-receptionist's desk. Additional chairs in this area can be used to accommodate the attendants of these patients or for an overflow of waiting patients when needed.

Secretary-Receptionist The administrative functions and business records of the department, scheduling of appointments, receiving of patients, typing of the necessary identification forms and requisitions for examinations, and assigning of patients to dressing rooms are handled by the secretary-receptionist. If time permits, the secretary-receptionist assists in typing the radiologist's reports. The desk is centrally located, directly in front of the entrance between the waiting room and administrative area, so that the secretary-receptionist may supervise waiting patients and have access to correspondence and report files.

Secretary-File Clerk The secretary-file clerk assembles, sorts, and files all films and reports, assists the secretary-receptionist when needed, and transcribes and types the radiologist's reports. These functions are not rigidly fixed and can be interchanged, if desired. For example, a technician may be assigned to assist the file clerk with film assembling and sorting, or the file clerk may be given other functions as needed. The desk is located near a counter-partition in the film collection and distribution area. The low counter and the gate (No. 79) are designed so the entrance to the department can be observed and patients directed when required.

Doctors' Viewing Room The doctors' viewing room is located near the office of the radiologist so that he may be immediately available for consultation. The room is near the film files, convenient to the secretary and file clerk, and situated so as not to intrude upon the functional flow of the work. Its location within the administrative unit provides privacy so that diagnostic comments and discussions will not be overheard by patients.

Radiologist's Office This office is conveniently situated near the x-ray rooms, the secretary-receptionist's desk and the filing distribution area, and is not too easily accessible to the public; it is also provided with a door which opens directly to the technicians' corridor. The fire exit which is located off the technicians' corridor provides a second exit from the department for the radiologist.

Film Files The film files are located in the collection and distribution area and convenient to the radiologist's office. Since it is desirable to keep active films for at least five years, approximately 125 linear feet of filing space is provided. After that time, additional storage space elsewhere will be needed for the less active files. Closed front metal x-ray files are recommended (see Fire Safety). Teaching files may not be needed in a hospital of this size, but if desired, a section of the active files may be allotted for this use.

General Facilities

Dressing Rooms Three dressing rooms for each x-ray machine should be provided so that the

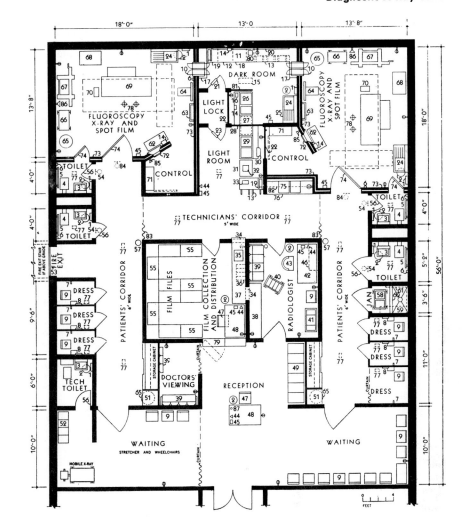

LEGEND

1. Paper towel dispenser
2. Waste paper receptacle
3. Lavatory
4. Wall-hung water closet
5. Continuous grab bar
6. Emergency calling station (push button)
7. Hook strip
8. Mirror and shelf below
9. Straight chair
10. Cassette pass box
11. Film loading counter
12. Film storage bin
13. Film hanger racks under counter
14. Safelight
15. Ceiling light, white and red
16. Timer
17. Counter with storage cabinets below
18. Cassette storage bins
19. Trash deposit cabinet
20. Cassette cover retainer and wall guard
21. Door with light-proof louver in upper panel
22. Access panel
23. Door with light-proof louver in lower panel
24. Utility sink with drainboard
25. Refrigerating unit under drainboard
26. Developing tank with thermostatic mixing valve
27. Through-the-wall fixing tank
28. Light-proof panel
29. Washing tank
30. X-ray film illuminator (wet viewing)
31. Film dryer
32. Film dryer exhaust to outside
33. Film corner cutter
34. Film pass slot
35. Flush-mounted counter illuminator
36. Film sorting bins above counter
37. Film sorting counter
38. Counter with cabinets below
39. On-wall or mobile film illuminators
40. Temporary film file cart
41. Stereoscope
42. Executive type desk
43. Executive type chair
44. Telephone outlet
45. Intercommunication system outlet
46. Bookshelves, 42 in. by 14 in.
47. Typist chair
48. Typist desk
49. Filing cabinet, letter size
50. Gown storage, open shelves, storage cabinet above
51. Gown storage, open shelving with laundry hamper below
52. Technicians' lockers
53. Fire door
54. Dome light, buzzer and annunciator at receptionist's desk
55. Closed metal film files, 5 shelves high
56. Hook on toilet side of door

57. Fire extinguisher
58. Mop truck
59. Shelf
60. Curb and receptor on janitor's sink
61. Mop hanging strip
62. Storage cabinet and writing counter
63. Fluoroscopic apron and glove holder
64. Fluoroscopic chair
65. Laundry hamper
66. Clean linen cart
67. Cassette changer
68. Transformer
69. Radiographic fluoroscopic unit with spot film device
70. Foot stool
71. Control unit
72. Leaded glass view window
73. Lead lining (or other shielding material) as required
74. Lead-lined door, light proofed
75. Barium sink
76. Barium storage (below counter)
77. Red light for dark adaptation
78. Fluoroscopic ceiling light
79. Counter with gate
80. Film identifier, cabinet below
81. Anti-splash panel
82. Wall cabinet over sink
83. Curtain, floor to ceiling
84. Warning light
85. Microphone
86. Loudspeaker
87. Annunciator (for emergency calling station)

Fig. 2 Diagnostic radiographic suite, Plan A.

HOSPITALS
Diagnostic X-Ray Suite

equipment and staff can function without delay. Each dressing room should be equipped with a straight-back chair, clothes hook, mirror, and a shelf below the mirror. For the protection of patients' valuables, the doors may be equipped with locks, or centrally located lockers may be provided. Where doors are installed, they should swing outward to avoid the possibility of being blocked by a patient and should be at least 12 inches from the floor.

For the convenience of patients in wheelchairs, an outsized dressing room is provided. Instead of a door, it is equipped with a curtain so that the patient can maneuver easily.

Patients' Toilet Rooms Toilets should be immediately available for patients undergoing fluoroscopy, and similar facilities should be conveniently available for waiting patients. A minimum of two toilets should be provided for each x-ray room. All toilets should be located near the x-ray rooms.

At least one toilet room should be directly accessible to each x-ray room and have an opening into the corridor. To prevent the patients from accidentally opening the door between the toilet and x-ray room, this door should be equipped with hardware which is operable only from the x-ray room. The doors of the toilet rooms which open into the patients' corridor should be equipped with bathroom locks, which are operated by knob latch bolts and dead bolts from both sides.

One of the patients' toilet rooms is designed to accommodate a patient in a wheelchair. The room is larger than the others, for easy maneuvering, and has a 3 ft door. The lavatory is set on wall brackets 6 in. out from the wall and 2 ft 10 in. from the floor.

One toilet should be provided with a bedpan flushing attachment. Water closets should be suspended from the wall to simplify cleaning. Each toilet room should be equipped with a grab bar for use by elderly or weak patients. A dome light and buzzer system with an emergency call station in each toilet room and an annunciator at the secretary-receptionist's desk are recommended.

Technicians' Toilets and Lockers During busy periods it is essential that the staff be available at all times. Separate toilet and locker facilities are provided for technicians. This reduces the time technicians must be absent from the area and contributes to the efficiency of the department.

Storage Facilities

General Storage For bulk supplies, a storage cabinet equipped with sliding doors and adjustable shelves is located inside each patients' corridor near the entrance. Materials such as films, opaque solutions, developing solutions, and office supplies are stored here.

Daily Linen Supplies (X-Ray Rooms) Clean linen, requisitioned from the hospital central supply, is stored on a cart (No. 66) in each x-ray room; soiled linen is placed in a hamper (No. 65).

Gown Storage Open adjustable shelves for gown storage are placed next to each general bulk supply cabinet, just inside the corridor entrance. The shelving for clean gowns starts about 4 ft from the floor, leaving space beneath for a linen hamper (No. 65) for soiled gowns.

Janitor's Closet The janitor's closet must be readily available for emergency cleaning and it should be convenient to the x-ray rooms and toilets. The closet should contain a floor receptor with a curb or a janitor's service sink, a mop-hanging strip and a shelf, and provide space for parking the mop truck.

Diagnostic X-Ray Rooms

X-Ray Equipment Both rooms are equipped with combination x-ray and fluoroscopic machines with spot film devices. An overhead type tube support is indicated in the plan, as this facilitates x-raying a patient in bed or on a stretcher. For reasons of economy, however, it may be desirable to equip one room with a floor-ceiling track. If an overhead mounted track is used, it may be supported from the floor by columns or may be bracketed from the wall, although a ceiling suspension makes a neater installation.

The optimum size of the x-ray room is about 14 by 18 ft. Ceiling height requirements vary for different x-ray machines, but a minimum of 9 ft 6 in. is recommended. The machine and transformer should be placed so as to allow adequate space for admittance of a bed or stretcher in the room. Mounting the transformer on the wall is recommended to save floor space. However, sufficient clearances (at least 2 ft above the transformer) for servicing the transformer should be provided.

The sink and drainboard, for handwashing and rinsing utensils and barium equipment, is equipped with a gooseneck spout. It is located near the foot of the x-ray table. The drainboard can also be used as a barium counter.

It is recommended that the control panel be wired to a signal outside each x-ray room to indicate when the machine is on, to prevent other personnel from inadvertently entering the room. A red light bulb will be satisfactory as a signal for most installations.

Control Booth It is essential that the control booth be located to the right of the machine so that the patient may be observed when the table is inclined, since machines with end-pivoted tables tilt to the right. In the plan, no door is shown on the control booth as the radiation will have scattered at least twice before it reaches the control booth area. This is in accordance with Handbook 60, as amended, issued by the National Bureau of Standards. The arrangement of the control booth to the right and the cassette changer to the extreme left, as shown in the plan, fully meets this requirement. In addition, since the beam is directed toward the outside wall, radiation exposure to other personnel is lessened, and the amount of shielding required is decreased.

If the cassette changers are placed to the right of the machine (on the wall opposite to that indicated on the plan), a door on the control booth or a baffle placed in the room is required to protect the technician in the booth. Furthermore, additional shielding is required to protect films and personnel in the department because the primary beam would not be directed toward the outside wall. In the present scheme, the shielding necessary in the interior walls is principally to safeguard against the scatter radiation.

Storage Cabinet and Writing Counter A storage cabinet (No. 62), with a safety light above, serves also as a writing counter for the radiologist and technicians. Shelves in the cabinet provide space for storage of accessory items such as sandbags, measuring devices used with x-ray machine, and disposable items needed for patients' examinations.

Film Processing and Distribution Area

Darkroom This room is located between the two x-ray rooms to facilitate handling of films. Cassettes are loaded and unloaded on the counter (No. 11). Space is provided for loading and stacking cassettes at both ends of the counter.

A utility sink with a drainboard (No. 24), located opposite the processing tank, is provided for mixing chemical solutions and handwashing. A refrigerating unit (No. 25) for the tank is located in the space beneath the drainboard.

X-ray films are processed in an area separated from the loading counter by a partition (No. 81) at the end of the developing tank which helps to avoid accidental splashing and damage to the screens and films on the loading counter. A through-wall processing unit tank permits the radiologist or staff doctors to read the wet films in the lightroom area without interrupting darkroom procedures.

A lightlock between the darkroom and the lightroom, equipped with interlocking doors, is necessary to allow entrance into the darkroom of other personnel during film processing. Although a maze has some advantages over the lightlock, the additional space needed is not justifiable in a facility of this size. Access panels (No. 22), located in the lightlock and in the control space, are provided to simplify installation and servicing of the processing tanks.

Film Processing Area To reduce unnecessary traffic, the film processing rooms are located near the collection and distribution area. This layout allows the technician to work without interruption during the processing routine. Processing of films begins at the developing tank (No. 26) in the darkroom, and continues to the final rinsing tank (No. 29) in the lightroom where the films may be wet-viewed at an illuminator, if desired, and then dried. After the films are dried, they are brought to the counter (33) in the technicians' corridor for final trimming, and passed through to the film collection and distribution area.

Collection and Distribution Area Film sorting bins (No. 36) are provided above the counter in the collection and distribution area for temporary filing. After all films have been assembled, they are passed through the film pass slot (No. 34) to the radiologist for interpretation. He returns the films in a file cart or through a slot which leads into a box under the distribution counter. The films may then be temporarily filed for viewing by staff doctors or placed in the active files.

Barium Mixing Facilities

A two-compartment sink (No. 75) in a counter, located in the technicians' corridor and accessible to both x-ray rooms, is provided for mixing barium. A duplex outlet for plugging in an electric mixer or a heating element is located above the counter unit. Barium supplies for daily use are stored in cabinets under the counter; the bulk supplies can be stocked in one of the general storage cabinets located in the patients' corridors.

Dark Adaptation

Patients must be allowed to become accustomed to the low lighting level in the x-ray

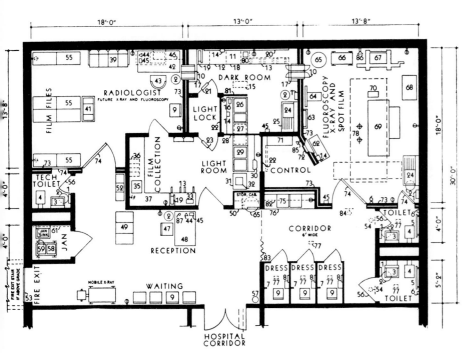

Fig. 3 Diagnostic radiographic suite, Plan B.

rooms and the staff must retain their dark adaptation despite the opening of the doors of the fluoroscopic rooms between patients' examinations.

To facilitate dark adaptation, curtains are shown at the intersections of the technicians' and the patients' corridors. In addition to the illumination normally provided in the corridors, patients' toilet rooms, and dressing rooms, it is recommended that these areas be equipped with an independently controlled dim lighting system of red bulbs for dark adaptation.

Miscellaneous Services

It is assumed that the central sterile supply department of the hospital will provide all such services for the x-ray department.

The mobile x-ray unit should be stored in the radiology department where it will be under the supervision and control of the department and available when needed.

Optional Facilities

Intercommunication System Provision of a system within the department increases the efficiency of the staff and speeds up service. Outlets are shown at the desk of the secretary-receptionist, in the x-ray rooms and the darkroom, and in the technicians' corridor. It is recommended that a one-way intercommunication system, with a microphone in the control booth and a loudspeaker at the cassette changer, be installed so that the technician need not leave the control booth to give instructions to the patient at the far end of the x-ray room.

Refrigerator Some items used in the x-ray department, such as barium suspensions for fluoroscopic examinations of the upper gastrointestinal tract, cream for a gall bladder series, and carbonated beverages for carbon

dioxide distention of the stomach, require refrigeration. The space under one end of the barium counter at the sink (No. 75) in the technicians' corridor may be used for an under-counter type refrigerator.

High-Speed Film Dryer The plan provides sufficient space for an anhydrator, if desired, in lieu of the dryer shown (No. 31).

Finish Materials

Materials used in this department are generally similar to those usually provided in hospitals. However, special attention should be given to some of the areas in the x-ray suite.

Darkroom The cassette loading counter surface should be of a material which is static-free; wood or linoleum is often preferred. Vinyl or vinyl-asbestos tile, $\frac{1}{8}$ in. thick, appears to be a satisfactory material for floors in this size department. Experience indicates, however, that asphalt tile and linoleum floors do not stand up well under the effects of spilled solutions. A pattern of alternating dark and light tiles improves visibility when working under a safe light.

X-Ray Rooms No special finishes are required for the x-ray rooms. Asphalt tile floors are satisfactory and a pattern of alternating dark and light tiles is also desirable here. Plaster walls and ceilings are acceptable, but accoustical tile ceilings are preferred since they aid in reducing reverberation.

Toilets Tile floors and wainscot are highly desirable for easy cleaning.

Doctors' Viewing Room Acoustical treatment is recommended to lessen the possibility of doctors' conversations being overheard by nearby waiting patients.

Electrical Installations

Voltage supplied to the x-ray unit should be constant so that fluoroscopic images and radiographs will be uniform. An independent feeder with sufficient capacity to prevent a voltage drop greater than 3 percent is recommended. To minimize voltage fluctuations, a separate transformer for the x-ray feeder is required for most installations.

Illumination

Illumination intensities in the various areas of the suite should comply with recommendations given in the Lighting Handbook, 3rd Edition (1959), published by the Illuminating Engineering Society. Briefly, the general illumination should be not less than 10 footcandles in corridors and in rooms where reading is not required. The waiting room should have 15 footcandles, with supplemental lighting for reading. Offices and areas where clerical work is performed should have at least 50 footcandles, preferably 70.

Indirect or cove lighting fixtures are recommended for the x-ray rooms so that patients need not be inconvenienced by glare when lying face upward during examinations.

Primary barriers should be provided on all surfaces of the x-ray rooms which are exposed, or which may be exposed, to the useful beam between the x-ray tube and occupied areas. Secondary barriers should be provided on all other room surfaces where protection is needed. In determining secondary barriers, consideration should be given to direct or leakage radiation which passes through the tube housing, and also to the secondary or scattered radiation emitted from objects being irradiated by either the useful beam, leakage radiation, or other scattered radiation.

Air Conditioning

Air conditioning with positive ventilation and a well-defined pattern of air movement within the department is necessary to provide an acceptable environment. In order to prevent the spread of odors from the radiographic and fluoroscopic rooms, darkroom, toilets, and janitor's closets, the ventilation system should be designed so that a negative air pressure relative to the adjoining corridors will be maintained in these rooms. This can be done by exhausting more air from these rooms than is supplied to them, and by reversing this procedure in the corridors. Doors to the toilets and the janitor's closet should be undercut or louvered so that air from the corridors may flow into these areas and be exhausted without recirculation.

Because of the odor problem, the air from the fluoroscopic and x-ray rooms should not be recirculated during the time these rooms are in use, unless adequate odor removal equipment is incorporated in the ventilation system. For economical operation, where odor control equipment is not used, the exhaust system should be provided with motor-operated dampers, switched from within the room, which will direct the air to the outdoors when the rooms are being used, or recirculate the air during idle periods.

As the darkroom will be used for longer periods than the x-ray rooms, an independent system to exhaust the air to the outdoors should be provided. The exhaust from the darkroom should be controlled from a switch in the room and the system should be dam-

HOSPITALS
Diagnostic X-Ray Suite

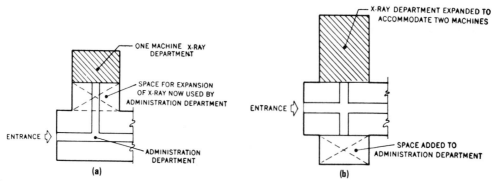

Fig. 4   X-ray department. (a) Before expansion. (b) After expansion.

pered to regulate the amount of air handled. The exhaust from the film dryer in the lightroom should be connected into the darkroom exhaust system.

The following conditions are recommended for the comfort of patients and personnel:

Administration and Waiting Areas A temperature of 72°F with a relative humidity of 50 per cent and a ventilation rate of 1–1½ air changes per hour.

Patients' and Technicians' Corridors A temperature of 75°F to 80°F with relative humidity of 50 per cent and a ventilation rate of 2 air changes per hour.

Fluoroscopic and X-Ray Rooms A temperature of 75°F to 80°F with relative humidity of 50 per cent and a ventilation rate of 6 air changes per hour.

Darkroom A temperature of 72°F with rela-

tive humidity of 50 per cent and a ventilation rate of 10 air changes per hour.

Fire Safety

To provide an adequate measure of fire safety for the patients and the staff in this department, consideration must be given to factors of design and construction relating to fire prevention and fire protection. The basic structure should be built with fire resistive materials and incombustible finishes and provided with approved equipment.

Closed metal files are recommended for storage of x-ray films. If open shelves are used instead, an automatic sprinkler system should be installed over this storage area to neutralize the hazard of the large volume of combustible materials which would be exposed to possible fire.

Fire extinguishers (carbon dioxide type preferred) should be provided, as located on the plans, to assist in controlling fire.

In accordance with good fire safety practice, two means of egress are provided in the plan: one at the entrance to the department and an emergency exit located off the patient's corridor (door No. 53). The emergency fire exit should lead directly to the ground level outside the building, through an appropriate exit stairway.

Plan B—Design for Expansion

This one-machine department, designed to handle a daily average of about 20 patient examinations, could satisfactorily serve a hospital of 50 to 100 beds, depending upon the extent of outpatient services provided. As in Plan A, its volume of examinations can be increased, depending on the staffing pattern and other factors, discussed previously. (See Fig. 3.)

The staff usually required for this work-

1. Overhead tube conveyor (O.T.C.)
2. O.T.C. ceiling tracks
3. Image intensifier carriage
4. Negator with TV and 90-mm
5. Table
6. Table
7. Pedestal table
8. Stretcher
9. Control
10. Transformer
11. High-voltage adapter kit
12. Planigraph mounted on ceiling track
13. Franklin headstand
14. Mobile TV monitor
15. Wall-mounted cassette holder
16. High-capacity autoprocessor
17. Cassette transfer cabinet
18. Multibank film viewer
19. Replenisher tanks
20. Wall-mounted cable catch
21. Intensifier power supply mounted on shelf above control
22. TV control mounted on shelf above control
23. Planigraph control
24. High-speed starter mounted on wall
25. Single-plane film changer
26. Program selector
27. Single-plane parked

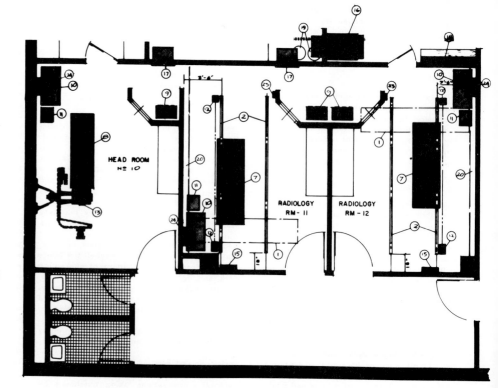

Fig. 5   Typical radiographic room.

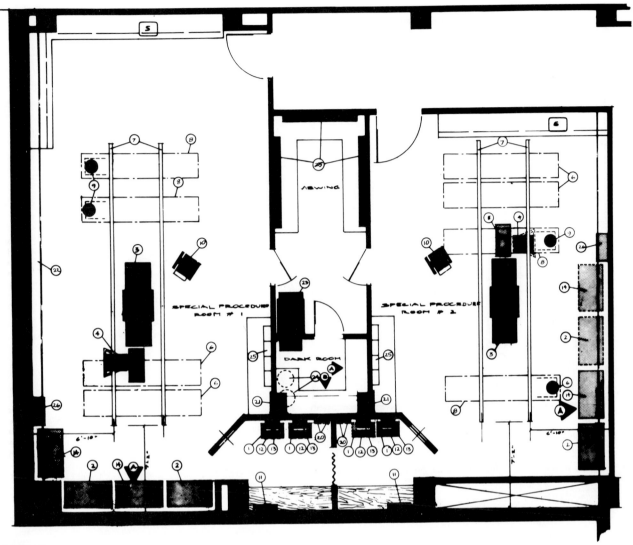

Equipment list

1. Control
2. Power units cabinets
3. Spectrum special procedure table
4. Plane film changer
5. Single-plane film changer
6. Overhead tube conveyor (O.T.C.)
7. O.T.C. ceiling track
8. Intensifier carriage
9. Negator mounted with TV and 35-mm cine

10. TV monitor mounted on cart
11. Program selector
12. Intensifier power supply mounted on shelf above control
13. TV control unit mounted on shelf
14. Additional power unit cabinet to house cine equipment
15. High-voltage adapter kit
16. Cine bias tank
17. Cine smoother tank
18. Cine powerstat

19. Cine control cabinet
20. Operator's control
21. Cassette transfer cabinet
22. Wall-mounted cable catch
23. High-capacity processor
24. Replenisher tanks
25. Multibank film viewer
26. Airflex biplane control

Fig. 6   Typical vascular layout. Equipment shown dotted is for future installation.

load includes: 1 part-time radiologist, 1 technician, 1 secretary-receptionist-technician, 1 orderly (as needed).

This plan will result in a functional unit. It has another important advantage in that it may be expanded to include all the features of Plan A. Such expansion is usually indicated when the hospital is served by a full-time radiologist, when the average daily load approaches 30 examinations per day, and when the proportion of time-consuming examinations becomes high.

Expansion problems frequently occur in a hospital of 100 beds or less, where there is only one x-ray machine and a part-time radiologist. As the volume of work increases, the radiologist spends more time at the hospital, and a second machine is installed. Unfortunately, in most of these cases, the lack of

planning for a future expansion program and expansion area results in an inefficient layout. This limits the usefulness of the equipment and the efficiency of the staff. Examples of such limitations are: poor location of the darkroom in relation to the new x-ray room, inadequate size of the darkroom, insufficient number of toilet facilities and dressing rooms, lack of office and waiting areas, and limited film filing space.

Remodeling an x-ray department is more expensive than remodeling other areas of a hospital because of the shielding, wiring, and plumbing. Expansion of the x-ray department should be incorporated in the original plan. Roughing in the plumbing and building in the shielding and electrical conduits in the expansion space will result in future savings and an efficient x-ray suite.

Minimum alterations to Plan B necessary to duplicate the facilities of Plan A would be the remodeling of the film collection area to accommodate a new control booth, the elimination of the partition between the lightroom and reception space, the elimination of the dressing rooms and of the partition behind them.

Until the need for remodeling becomes apparent, part of the administration offices of the hospital may temporarily be situated in the expansion space. When enlarging the x-ray department, other space may then be added to the administration department. The dotted lines on Fig. 4 illustrate how this expansion may be designed.

A typical radiographic room is shown in Fig. 5; a typical vascular layout is shown in Fig. 6.

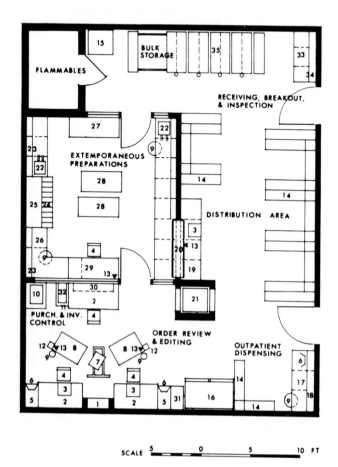

Legend
1. Pneumatic tube station
2. Desk
3. Typewriter, electric, nonmovable carriage
4. Chair
5. Files, intermediate height
6. Files, swinging panel, strip insert type
7. File, revolving on two levels
8. Table, movable, 2 feet by 3 feet
9. Waste receptacle
10. Photocopier
11. File, 2-drawer
12. Utility pole
13. Telephone
14. Shelving, adjustable, 12 inches
15. Safe
16. Refrigerator, with freezer
17. Counter, with file drawer, bins
18. Shelving, adjustable, 7 inches
19. Counter, dispensing
20. Two-shelf unit above counter
21. Dumbwaiter, open both sides
22. Cabinet, with sink, drain board
23. Cabinet, wall-mounted
24. Bins, on top of hood
25. Hood, laminar airflow, vertical or horizontal
26. Counter, with open adjustable shelving beneath
27. Cart, storage
28. Carts, utility
29. Desk, small
30. Bookcase, wall-mounted
31. File cabinet, 5-drawer
32. File, visible index type
33. Counter, with adjustable shelves beneath
34. Shelving, wall-mounted, 9 inches
35. Shelving, adjustable, rail-mounted

Fig. 1 Pharmacy department in a 100-bed hospital. (From *Planning for Hospital Pharmacies,* DHEW Pub. No. (HRA)77-4003, U.S. Department of Health, Education, and Welfare, Washington, D.C., 1977.)

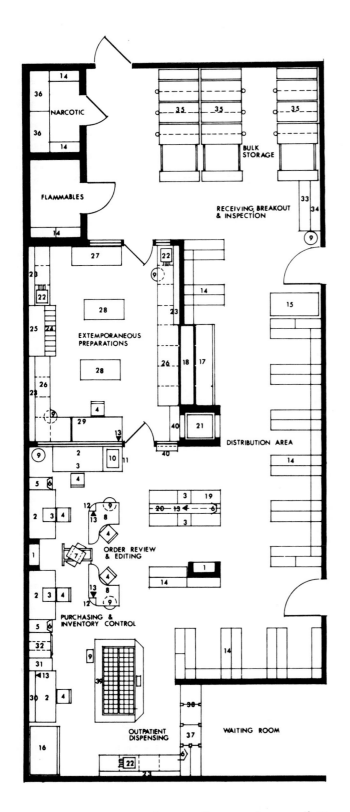

Legend
1. Pneumatic tube station
2. Desk
3. Typewriter, electric, nonmovable carriage
4. Chair
5. Files, intermediate height
6. Files, swinging panel, strip insert type
7. File, revolving on two levels
8. Desk, special design
9. Waste receptacle
10. Photocopier
11. Photocopier, cabinet
12. Utility pole
13. Telephone
14. Shelving, adjustable, 12 inches
15. Delivery truck
16. Refrigerator, with freezer
17. Refrigerator, open front type
18. Refrigerator, pass-through, counter height
19. Counter, dispensing
20. Two-shelf unit above counter
21. Dumbwaiter, open both sides
22. Cabinet, with sink, drainboard
23. Cabinet, wall-mounted
24. Bins, on top of hood
25. Hood, laminar airflow, vertical or horizontal
26. Counter, with open adjustable shelving beneath
27. Cart, storage
28. Carts, utility
29. Desk, small
30. Bookcase, wall-mounted
31. File cabinet, 5-drawer
32. File, visible index type
33. Counter, with adjustable shelves beneath
34. Shelving, wall-mounted, 9 inches
35. Shelving, adjustable, rail-mounted
36. Shelving, adjustable, 24 inches
37. Counter, with adjustable shelves beneath
38. Panels, acoustical
39. File, rotary mechanical
40. Ledge

Fig. 2 Pharmacy department in a 300-bed hospital. (From *Planning for Hospital Pharmacies,* DHEW Pub. No. (HRA)77-4003, U.S. Department of Health, Education, and Welfare, Washington, D.C., 1977.)

By WILBUR R. TAYLOR,
WILLIAM A. MILLS, and
JAMES G. TERRILL, JR.

TELETHERAPY UNITS

Radiation and Architectural Considerations for Cobalt-60 Unit

By the term teletherapy, we are restricting ourselves to the use of radiation at a distance; that is, the subject and source are separated by a distance of 50 centimeters or more. In particular, we are concerned with the use of the radioactive isotopes cobalt-60 and cesium-137 as sources of radiation in teletherapy units.

We have restricted our discussion to ^{60}Co and ^{137}Cs, primarily because they are the more familiar of the isotopes suggested for use in teletherapy units. We are not including the use of radium and high energy x-rays, since some of the problems associated with these are quite different in their solution and nature.

The primary purposes of this article are to furnish architects who are anticipating a teletherapy unit with information on basic radiation protection ideas and techniques, and to serve as a guide in the solutions of certain architectural problems. We are by no means attempting to evaluate the advantages and disadvantages of ^{60}Co and ^{137}Cs units against other types of units.

For a discussion of the fundamentals of radiation shielding and a glossary of radiation terminology, see *Architectural Record*, November, 1957, pages 218–220.

In planning a cobalt installation, it should be understood that each type of machine and its location within the building will present a different problem which will require an individual solution. Consequently, no one type plan can be designed which will take care of the various shielding requirements presented by the different machines and installations. The architect is dependent upon other professionals for specific technical information he needs before he can intelligently design a building containing a cobalt teletherapy unit. The problems incurred may materially affect the orientation, location, and structural and functional design of the building. Therefore, during preliminary design stages, close cooperation between architect, radiologist, and radiation physicist is necessary to develop an efficient and economical layout.

It should be noted that the Atomic Energy Commission places responsibility upon the applicant for conditions of installation and use of the facility. Since the use of a facility is largely dependent upon the conditions of installation, it is to the applicant's advantage to secure the services of a radiation physicist at the inception of a project. His function is to advise the applicant and architect on radiation

Wilbur R. Taylor is a Hospital Architect in the Division of Hospital and Medical Facilities, Bureau of Medical Service, Public Health Service, Department of Health, Education, and Welfare; and William A. Mills and James G. Terrill, Jr. are respectively Radiation Physicist and Chief of Radiological Health Program, Division of Sanitary Engineering Services, Bureau of State Services, Public Health Service.

requirements, assume responsibility for the final design as to shielding provided and furnish the supporting information required in Application Form AEC-313 relative to exposure rates in areas surrounding the teletherapy room and occupancy factors assigned.

Fundamental decisions as to: (1) the type of machine, (2) strength of the source, (3) desired location, and (4) the shielding required for floor, walls, and ceiling must be made before the building's structural system can be designed. During the early design, it may be determined that the structural system cannot support the weight of the shielding, or perhaps soil conditions will not permit sufficient excavation for a subgrade installation. It may then be necessary to change or alter one or more of the following: the machine or its operation, the source strength or the location of the room.

To those not familiar with such shielding problems, the included plans have been developed to illustrate the shielding necessary for three types of machines in specific locations. However, before considering the detailed plans, it may be desirable to discuss some of the general requirements of such facilities.

Location

The cobalt suite should adjoin the x-ray therapy department. This location permits the joint use of waiting, dressing, toilet, examination, work and consultation rooms. In addition, it offers the important advantage of having the staff concentrated in one area, thereby eliminating the considerable loss of time involved in traveling to a remote location. This is an important consideration and justifies the cost of any additional shielding that may be necessary to achieve it.

A location below grade, unoccupied above and below, will require less shielding. However, if such a location separates the cobalt and the x-ray therapy departments, it may be more costly in both loss of staff time and efficiency than the cost of concrete shielding amortized over several years. If, for example, twenty-five minutes per day are lost in traveling to a remote location, one additional patient could be treated in this time each day—or 240 patients per year. Assuming a staff salary of $20,000 per year, this loss of twenty-five minutes per day results in an indirect salary loss of $1032 per year, which would soon equal the cost of shielding in a new facility.

A corner location for the cobalt room is usually desirable since through traffic is eliminated, only two interior walls require shielding, distance to the property line utilizes the inverse square law to reduce shielding and the structural requirements are more easily solved.

Teletherapy Room Details

Size The room size may vary to suit different manufacturers' equipment. A room approximately 15 ft by 18 ft by 9 ft-6 in. plus the necessary entrance maze, will accommodate most of the machines commercially available with the exception of the largest rotating models. For reasons of cost, the room should be as compact as possible after allowing space to install the equipment and to position the treatment table.

Shielding The shielding necessary for a room must not only be considered in terms of floor, ceiling and wall shielding, but also such things as doors, windows, ventilation and heating ducts, and safety locks. Radiation that might

escape through such possibilities could result in overexposure to personnel, if proper precautions are not taken.

Entrance The primary purpose of specific entrance construction is to protect personnel. It should also provide sufficient space to admit a stretcher and the largest crated piece of equipment. In some cases, a considerable savings in cost of assembling equipment may be had by making the door and maze large enough to admit the crated assembled machine. For this purpose, some manufacturers specify a door opening of 4 by 7 ft and a minimum distance of 6 ft at the end of the maze.

Rather than add large amounts of lead to doors, the shielding problem may be solved to some degree by having the door to the teletherapy room open into a maze. This maze should be built so that no primary radiation could fall directly on the door. In designing doors for such a room, a good practice is to have a door of wood with a layer of lead. This lead can either be on the inside surface, or between layers of wood. Commercially available x-ray doors serve well for this purpose. The space between the door and floor can usually be shielded by using a lead strip under the door or by making a slight rise in the floor containing lead, on the outer side of the door. Lead shielding at the jamb and head between the frame and buck may be eliminated by the use of a combination frame and buck set in concrete.

For safety precautions, the door lock should be such that the door can be readily opened from inside the cobalt room.

Control View Window It is standard practice to locate this window at a height which will permit the operator to be seated during the treatment period, 4 ft-0 in. from the floor to the center of the window being an optimum distance. In plan, the window should be located in the area of minimum radiation and for convenient observation of the patient. This position, for a rotational machine, would be along the axis of rotation, and for a fixed beam unit, 90° to the plane of tilt.

From the control view window the entire room should be in full view, using mirrors when necessary. The glass should contain lead or other materials in amounts which would provide shielding equivalent to the surrounding concrete. The frame is usually packed with lead wool and should be designed to offset the shielding loss of the reduced concrete thickness at beveled areas. The cost of such special glass and frame increases rapidly with size and an 8 by 8 in. window is considered an optimum size.

Heating and Air Conditioning The only problem in relation to heating and air conditioning not encountered in other buildings is that of providing shielding where walls are pierced with supply and return ducts. The usual solution is to locate ducts and openings in walls which are least subject to radiation and offset the path of ducts through the wall, lead or other high density material being added, where necessary, to maintain the shielding value of the wall displaced by ducts.

Electrical Electrical service required for the machine will vary with each manufacturer's equipment. Voltage will vary from 110-single phase to 220-three phase for large machines.

Room lighting should assure good over-all illumination, preferably from cove lighting or an indirect type of fixture. It is essential

ROOM FOR COBALT-60 FACILITIES

By U.S. Public Health Service

Fig. 1 Fixed beam unit.*

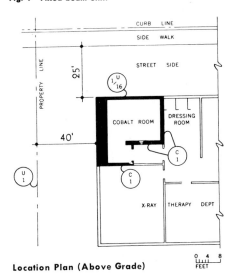

Location Plan (Above Grade)

SYMBOLS

- (C/1) Full Occupancy Controlled
- (U/1) Full Occupancy Uncontrolled
- (U/¼) Partial Occupancy Uncontrolled
- (U/16) Occasional Occupancy Uncontrolled

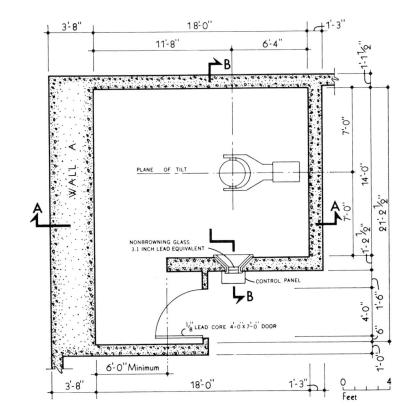

For Design Requirements see next page.

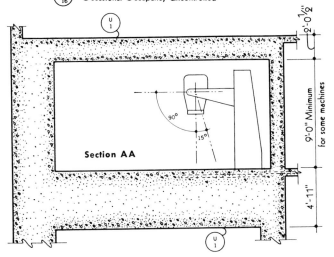

Section AA

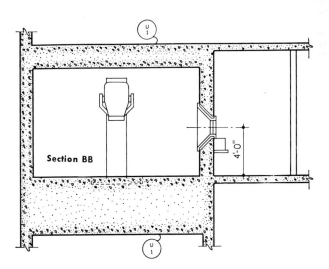

Section BB

The shielding indicated on the accompanying plans was computed on a basis of a 5,000 curie source. Because of its high cost, it is not now commonly used. Reduction of the source, however, does not decrease the shielding requirements significantly. For example, in the plan, use of a 2,000 curie source would result in a reduction of the thickness of wall A by 3 in.; for a 500 curie source, a reduction of 5 in. more. Since greatest cost is in forming, such savings are relatively small.

In new construction, the cost of concrete shielding will, in most cases, be a small part of the total cost of the installation.

To illustrate the maximum required shielding for floor and ceiling, the thicknesses shown have been computed for locations with full-time uncontrolled occupancy above and below. With controlled occupancy less shielding would be necessary and with no occupancy, these slabs could be reduced to the minimum structural requirements. An underground location is the only way, short of limiting the machine, of reducing the thickness of exterior walls.

*With Primary Beam Restricted to Floor and One Wall

Health

HOSPITALS
Teletherapy Units

Fig. 2 Rotational unit with primary beam absorber.

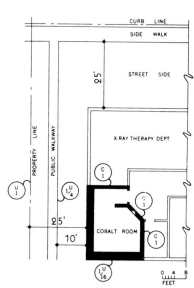

Location Plan (Above Grade)

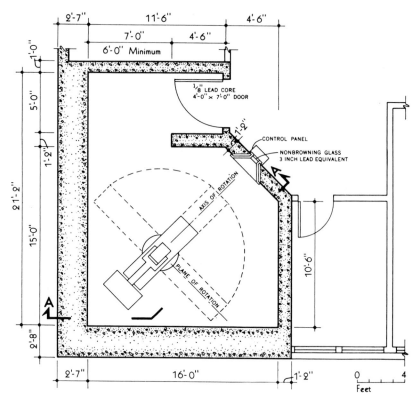

Plan of Cobalt-60 Room

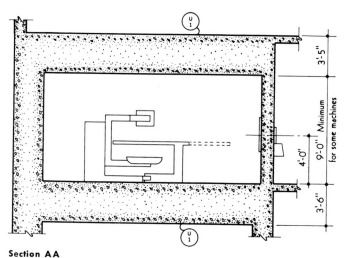

Section AA

SYMBOLS

(C 1) Full Occupancy Controlled

(U 1) Full Occupancy Uncontrolled

(U ¼) Partial Occupancy Uncontrolled

(U 1/16) Occasional Occupancy Uncontrolled

DESIGN REQUIREMENTS

Controlled Area $MPD = 5.0 \frac{Rem}{Yr} = 5.0 \frac{Rem}{60 Wk} = 100 \frac{MRem}{Wk}$

Uncontrolled Area $MPD = 0.5 \frac{Rem}{Yr} = 0.5 \frac{Rem}{52 Wk} = 9.6 \frac{MRem}{Wk}$

Full Occupancy $T = 1$

> Control space, residences, play areas, wards, office work rooms, darkrooms, corridors and waiting space large enough to hold desks and rest rooms used by radiologic staff and others routinely exposed to radiation.

Partial Occupancy $T = \frac{1}{4}$

> Corridors in X-ray departments too narrow for future desk space, rest rooms not used by radiologic personnel, parking lots, utility rooms.

Occasional Occupancy $T = \frac{1}{16}$

> Stairways, automatic elevators, streets, closets too small for future workrooms, toilets not used by radiologic personnel.

Source 5000 Curies

Fig. 3   Rotational unit without primary beam absorber.

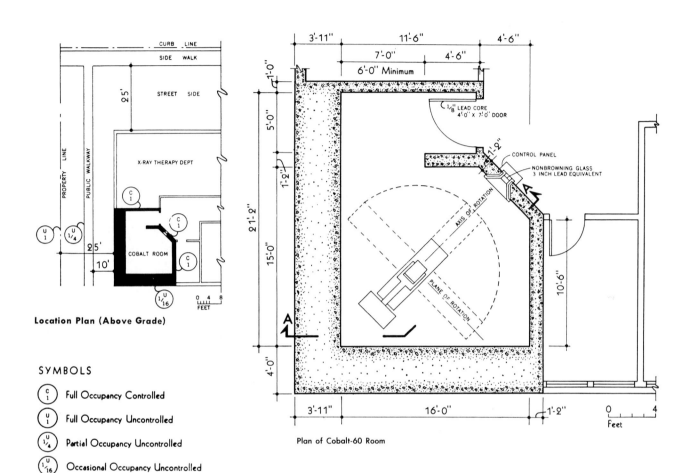

Location Plan (Above Grade)

SYMBOLS

- $\begin{smallmatrix}C\\1\end{smallmatrix}$ Full Occupancy Controlled
- $\begin{smallmatrix}U\\1\end{smallmatrix}$ Full Occupancy Uncontrolled
- $\begin{smallmatrix}U\\1/4\end{smallmatrix}$ Partial Occupancy Uncontrolled
- $\begin{smallmatrix}U\\1/16\end{smallmatrix}$ Occasional Occupancy Uncontrolled

Plan of Cobalt-60 Room

For Design Requirements see previous page.

A primary beam absorber on a machine reduces the shielding requirements considerably. However, some radiologists prefer to use a machine without the absorber, because of its greater flexibility, and for this reason some machines are designed to be used with or without the absorber. Under these conditions the room shielding should be designed for use either way. The plan and section shown here illustrate the necessary shielding.

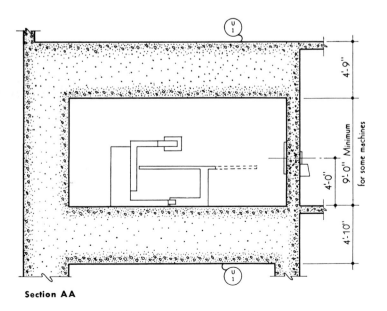

Section AA

that the operator be able to observe any movement of the patient during treatment and shadows produced by a rotating machine interfere with observation.

In providing a safety lock for the door, it has been found of great value to interlock the machine control with the door, so that opening the door automatically shuts off the machine.

Conduits should be provided for power and control wiring.

Environment The general effect to be created in this department should be one of cheerfulness and restfulness. Color and even murals have been used effectively on the walls of the cobalt room.

The usual hospital finishes such as acoustical ceiling tile and resilient flooring are desirable in this area.

Remodeling Unless previously designed for super voltage x-ray, remodeling an existing building can be expensive. It is often impossible to build in sufficient shielding which makes it necessary to control nearby occupancy and restrict direction of the beam, thereby handicapping the usefulness of the machine. Other problems such as relocating plumbing, heating, electrical services and disturbing the normal operation of the building during remodeling must be considered.

In new construction, concrete shielding is relatively cheap, but in remodeling the cost is high. For this reason the use of masonry units may be preferable since no form work is necessary and the work can be performed intermittently. Good workmanship, of course, is necessary to prevent voids in mortar joints.

In some cases it might be better to add to the building, rather than to remodel an existing portion. Normal hospital operation would not be interfered with, costs may be lower and a more efficient layout would probably result.

By NOYCE L. GRIFFIN, Electrical Engineer, Architectural and Engineering Branch, Division of Hospital and Medical Facilities, Public Health Service, U.S. Department of Health, Education and Welfare.

ELECTROENCEPHALOGRAPHIC SUITE

Introduction

An electroencephalographic (EEG) examination consists of the measurement of electrical potentials of the brain as measurable at the scalp. It requires an extremely sensitive instrument located so as to be as free as possible from outside electrical disturbances. The examination requires careful preparation of the patient and involves securing several pairs of electrodes to the patient's scalp, connecting the conductors from the electrodes to the EEG unit, operating the EEG unit to obtain recordings under definite physical conditions of the patient, removing the electrodes and any adhesive, if used in attaching the electrodes.

Suitable space must be provided for the neurologist and his staff to examine patients, read the recordings, prepare reports, and keep records. The suite should be arranged to provide office facilities for the neurologist and typist or secretary, a workroom for technician,

space for preparation and examination of patients, and storage space for supplies and voluminous EEG recordings. The preparation and examining space should, as a minimum, comprise two rooms: one with a hospital-type bed and equipment for the preparation of the patient; the other containing the EEG instruments, a desk or table, and other facilities needed by the technician (Fig. 1). A more efficient layout may be had by dividing the preparation and examining space into separate rooms. This would increase the patient-handling capacity of the unit, as one patient could be prepared while another is examined (Fig. 2). Toilet facilities should be conveniently available for patients' use.

Although shielding of the patient's room against electrical disturbances is not always required, it is usually desirable. Where such disturbances are excessive for the quality of work required, a completely shielded room may be necessary. The most common electrical disturbances are caused by high-frequency equipment such as diathermy and radio, static electricity, high-voltage transmission lines, large transformer banks, large motors, nearby powerful FM broadcast stations, and conductors carrying heavy currents. To minimize disturbances from power systems, all power conductors in the vicinity of the EEG machine should be metal armored or installed in metal raceway. Large or main electrical conductors should be routed as far away from the EEG examining locations as practicable, both horizontally and vertically, and use of fluorescent lighting in the vicinity of the EEG unit should be avoided.

A reasonable amount of soundproofing of the examining room is desirable.

EEG recordings and case records are bulky and require considerable space for filing. Open shelving of the large pigeonhole type is reasonably satisfactory for filing the large folders of active case records. This filing space should be located in the office or preferably in an adjacent room convenient to the neurologist.

Workroom

The workroom facilities and equipment normally consist of the EEG unit, preferably the console type, photo-stimulator panel, a supply cabinet for recording paper, preparation materials, an electric clock with sweep second hand, a workbench with wood top and cabinet below for EEG maintenance and general use, and a general office-type desk or table. Switches for control of lights in workroom and examining room should be located in the workroom. Shelving for EEG recordings and case records may be located in this room unless other suitable space is provided, and should be approximately 12 in. deep.

Examining Room

Doors through which patients must pass to enter the examining room should be 3 ft 10 in. wide to permit easy passage of stretcher or wheelchair. The size of the examining room should be sufficient to accommodate a hospital bed and allow enough additional space to permit the technician to work efficiently. For sleep inducement, exterior windows should be equipped with shades to partially darken the room. As it is desirable that the patient be in full view of the operator, the examining room should have sufficient width to permit the bed to be placed parallel to the wall nearest the workroom. This wall should have two 3-in.

openings, 20 in. above the floor, one for passing the EEG electrode cable with plug attached, the other for passing the photostimulator conductors.

The partition between the workroom and the patient's room should be provided with a glass window not less than 24 in. high and 36 in. wide, mounted with the lower edge 43 in. from the floor. This window should be located to provide good vision of the patient. In the preparation area, floor and sink are subjected to staining and eroding effects of chemicals such as acetone and collodion used for setting and removing electrodes to and from patient's scalp. The sink should be vitreous china set in a countertop resistant to acid and alkali, with cabinets below.

A masonry-type floor such as tile or terrazzo is recommended in the preparation area. Solvents such as acetone used for removal of electrode adhesive, when spilled or dropped on the floor, are injurious to the resilient type of flooring materials such as vinyl, asphalt, rubber, or linoleum.

When air-drying paste is used in setting electrodes, means should be provided for quick drying. Hand-held hair dryers are sometimes used, but a low-pressure compressed-air outlet is preferred. Some technicians use a self-supporting conducting paste for electrode attachment that requires no drying; others use pin-type electrodes, which do not require paste or adhesive, for insertion into the scalp.

Shielding

Shielding may be required, depending upon the equipment used and its location with respect to sources of disturbances and the quality of recordings required. It is recommended that in new construction shielding be provided in all examining rooms, and that omission of shielding be considered only when converting existing rooms.

Properly installed shielding of the examining rooms will eliminate or minimize outside disturbances caused by static electrical discharges and high-frequency equipment. It has little effect on magnetic disturbances such as those produced by power transformers, high-voltage equipment, and current-carrying conductors. For minimizing disturbances due to magnetic forces, the most effective means is distance.

Where shielding is required, panels and equipment for completely shielding the room may be obtained from several manufacturers, or as an alternate, satisfactory shielding may be constructed with copper insect screening. The strips of shielding material should be bonded and soldered at intervals of about 2 ft or less and should entirely cover all walls, floors, ceiling, doors, and windows. The screening should pass on the room side of any lighting fixture or electrical device without making contact with it. Wall and ceiling finish materials and the floor covering may be applied over the shielding if desired. In this case, the shielding material should be copper sheeting to preclude the possibility of interferences developing in the shielding due to the installation of plaster or mastic materials.

The shield should be grounded at one point only. The ground connection should be brought out to a terminal arrangement convenient for connection to the EEG unit and for disconnection for testing. Double screening produces a more effective shield than single screening. Shielding efficiency is further increased by insulating one layer of screen from the other

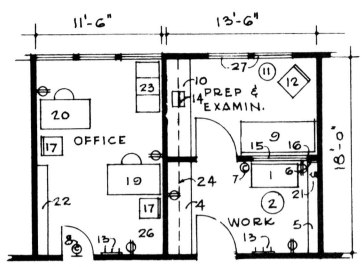

Fig. 1 Minimum EEG suite.

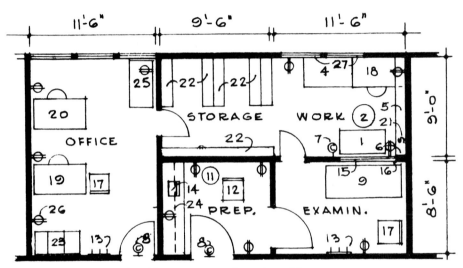

Fig. 2 Recommended suite with separate preparation and examining rooms.

Equipment list

1. Electroencephalograph, console type
2. Stool
3. Steel cabinet with shelving and door
4. Work bench, cabinet below
5. Shelf
6. Photostimulator panel (if used)
7. Clock with sweep second hand above glass panel
8. Clock outlet
9. Adjustable hospital bed
10. Sink in counter, cabinets below
11. Sanitary waste receptacle
12. Chair for patient preparation
13. Hook strip
14. Mirror above sink
15. Glass window
16. Two holes through wall, 3 in., 20 in. from floor
17. Armchair
18. General office-type desk and chair
19. Typist's desk and chair
20. Executive-type desk and chair
21. Two-pole switch for light in patient's room
22. Filing compartments for EEG recordings
23. File cabinets, legal size
24. Cabinet above for electrodes, etc.
25. Work table
26. Duplex outlets
27. Venetian blind

except at the one ground point. If a screened room is provided, all electric conductors entering the screened area should be equipped with filters to prevent disturbances by these conductors.

PHYSICAL THERAPY DEPARTMENT*

Of the many environmental factors which condition the effectiveness of physical therapy service to patients, the most important are

*This material is condensed from the chapter "Suitable Environment" in the manual Physical Therapy Essentials of a Hospital Department prepared by the Joint Committee of the American Hospital Association and the American Physical Therapy Association.
Planning is by Thomas P. Galbraith and Peter N. Jensen, Hospital Architects of the Architectural and Engineering Branch, Division of Hospital and Medical Facilities, Public Health Service.

space, location and work areas. Ventilation, lighting, interior finish and related considerations also contribute toward providing a suitable environment. The keynote is function.

Location

Location is closely related to function. The area selected for physical therapy should be centrally located to minimize problems of transporting patients and to facilitate giving bedside treatment when necessary. At least half of the patients treated in a general hospital physical therapy department are likely to be out-patients. With this in mind, special attention should be given to accessibility, and to having as few steps as possible to climb, as few long corridors and heavy doors to negotiate. A ground floor location, convenient for both in- and out-patients and for access to an outdoor exercise area, is recommended.

Availability of daylight and fresh air should also be considered in selecting a location.

In new hospitals, physical therapy is frequently placed in an area which includes other out-patient services, social service, occupa-

tional therapy, recreation. It is particularly important that physical and occupational therapy be in close proximity.

Amount of Space

The amount of space needed depends on the number of patients treated, the kinds of disabilities and the treatments required. Also to be considered is the fact that some space-consuming equipment—such as a whirlpool bath, treatment tables, parallel bars, etc.—are minimum essentials for even a one-therapist department. These pieces of equipment will not be multiplied in direct proportion to increases in staff and patient load.

Efforts to correlate bed capacity and physical therapy space requirements are not satisfactory. Hospitals with 50-100 beds may serve large numbers of out-patients. The amount of space given over to physical therapy in a small hospital is, justifiably, out of proportion to the bed capacity.

No absolute standard can be recommended as the amount of space needed for physical therapy in a general hospital. The most that

HOSPITALS

Physical Therapy Department

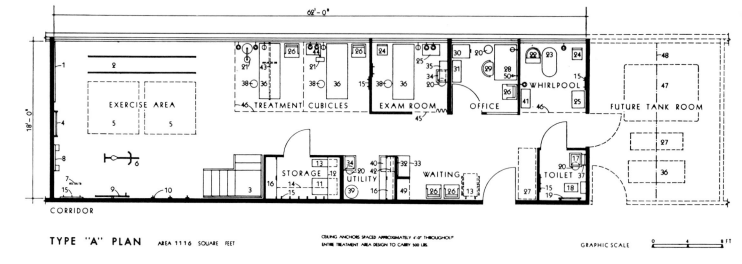

TYPE "A" PLAN   AREA 1116 SQUARE FEET

CEILING ANCHORS SPACED APPROXIMATELY 4'-0" THROUGHOUT
ENTIRE TREATMENT AREA DESIGN TO CARRY 500 LBS.

GRAPHIC SCALE   0   4   8 FT

NOTE: MAJOR PIECES OF EQUIPMENT RECOMMENDED FOR ONE
PHYSICAL THERAPIST AND AID INDICATED ON TYPE PLANS

Equipment list

1. Posture Mirror
2. Parallel Bars
3. Steps
4. Stall Bars
5. Gym Mat
6. Stationary Bicycle
7. Sayer Head Sling Attached to Ceiling
8. Pulley Weights
9. Shoulder Wheel
10. Gym Mat Hooks
11. Cart with Open Shelves
12. Open Shelves
13. Wheel Chair
14. Shelf
15. Wall Hooks
16. Wall Cabinet
17. Lavatory, Gooseneck Spout
18. Water Closet
19. Hand Rail
20. Waste Paper Receptacle
21. Portable Equipment
22. Adjustable Chair
23. Whirlpool
24. Chair
25. Table
26. Chair, preferable with arms
27. Wheel Stretcher
28. Desk
29. Swivel Chair
30. File Cabinet
31. Bookcase
32. Bulletin Board
33. Wall Desk (counter, shelf below)
34. Lavatory, Gooseneck Spout and Foot Control
35. Wall Cabinet with Lock
36. Treatment Table, Storage below
37. Mirror and Glass Shelf over Lavatory
38. Adjustable Stool
39. Laundry Hamper
40. Sink with Drainboard
41. Paraffin Bath
42. Glass Shelf over Sink
43. Overbed Trapeze
44. Three Single Outlets on separate branch circuits. 1 outlet 2-pole, 2 outlets 3-pole
45. Folding Door
46. Cubicle Curtain
47. Under Water Exercise Equipment
48. Overhead Lift
49. Coat Rack
50. Telephone Outlet

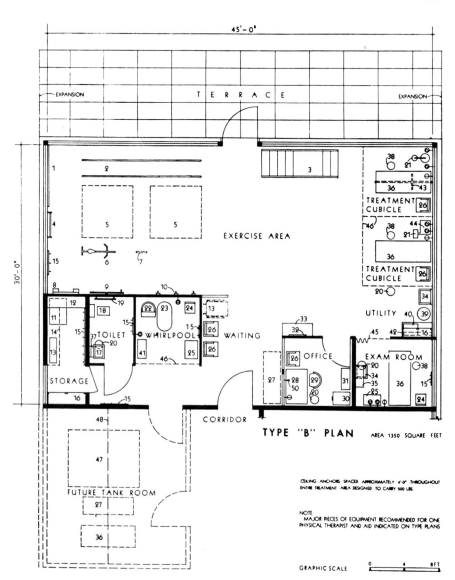

TYPE "B" PLAN   AREA 1350 SQUARE FEET

CEILING ANCHORS SPACED APPROXIMATELY 4'-0" THROUGHOUT
ENTIRE TREATMENT AREA DESIGNED TO CARRY 500 LBS.

NOTE
MAJOR PIECES OF EQUIPMENT RECOMMENDED FOR ONE
PHYSICAL THERAPIST AND AID INDICATED ON TYPE PLANS

GRAPHIC SCALE   0   4   8 FT

Fig. 1

can be said is that, if possible, it is desirable to plan for at least a thousand square feet of floor space, free of structural obstructions. About half of that should be exercise area. (See Fig. 1.)

This does not mean that a hospital cannot begin an effective physical therapy service in smaller quarters. Many have done so successfully, using to full advantage whatever space resources they had. But crowded quarters do subject the staff to strain and call for more than ordinary ingenuity and good humor in order to make it possible for patients to obtain maximum benefit from treatment.

Work Space Components

Whatever the eventual size of a physical therapy department, from the very beginning plans must be made to provide certain kinds of work space. These essential components can be expanded, multiplied or refined as the physical therapy department grows but the fundamental requirements are the same for a small or large department. They include: (1) reception area, (2) staff space, (3) examining room, (4) treatment areas, (5) toilet facilities, (6) storage.

Experienced physical therapists have many suggestions for increasing the efficiency of physical therapy departments by giving attention to details of planning and arranging these component work areas. For example:

Reception area: Accommodations for in-patients and out-patients, if possible. Adequate space for stretcher and wheelchair patients.

Staff space—private: Office space suitable for interviewing patients, attending to administrative and clerical duties, housing files, etc. Writing facilities for the staff adequate for dictation, record keeping. There should be space

for staff lockers and dressing rooms separate from the patient area, either within the department or near to it.

Examining room: Floor to ceiling partitions for privacy. Arranged so that necessary examining equipment can remain in the room permanently. Possible to use this space for special tests and measurements or for treatment when privacy is desirable.

Treatment area: There are three types of treatment areas: cubicle (dry), underwater exercise (wet) and exercise (open). Each is designed to meet the particular requirements of the special equipment used for different kinds of treatment.

Cubicle: Each unit large enough for the physical therapist to work on either side of the table without having to move equipment belonging in the cubicle. Preferably cubicles divided by curtains for easier access for wheelchair and stretcher cases, for expansion of usable floor area for gait analysis, group activity or teaching purposes.

Curtain tracks should be flush with the ceiling and curtains should have open panels at the top for ventilation when drawn. Both curtains and tracks should be sturdy. In or near the cubicles, out-patients need a place or locker for their outer clothing.

Underwater exercise area: All equipment requiring special plumbing and water supply concentrated in one section of the department but accessible and adjacent to other treatment areas. Should include a treatment table, especially in the room with a tank or exercise pool. Fixed overhead lifts are absolutely essential for the efficient use of tanks and failure to provide lifts severely limits the usefulness of this valuable equipment. Plumbing and other installation requirements, humidity and noise

from motors call for special care and attention. Electrical and metal equipment in other treatment areas may suffer damage unless the underwater exercise area is carefully planned.

Exercise area: Very flexible open space planned to accommodate patients engaged in diverse individual or group exercise activities. Used extensively by people in wheelchairs, on crutches or canes, or with other disabilities which limit their motion and agility. At least one wall should be reinforced for the installation of stall bars and similar equipment (see Fig. 2).

Toilet facilities: Separate toilet facilities for patients and staff, if possible. Patient facilities should be designed to accommodate wheelchair patients. If the department serves small children, seat adaptors with foot rests should be provided.

Storage: Designed to meet special needs in and near work areas. Should also be storage space on the wards for equipment and supplies usually needed for bedside treatments. For wheelchairs, stretchers, etc., it is best to plan "carport" space, not closets. All storage space should be accessible, simple, well lighted.

Special Considerations

Ventilation Adequate, controlled ventilation is of extreme importance in a physical therapy department. Many of the treatment procedures require the use of dry or moist heat, or active exercise, which raise body temperatures. A continuous, reliable flow of fresh air is essential to the comfort of patients and staff. This includes protection from drafts.

Air conditioning, desirable for the entire department, will be a necessity for certain areas of the physical therapy department, in most

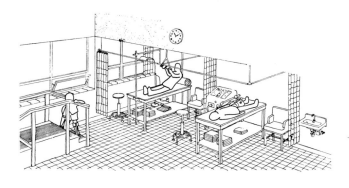

Perspective sketches by William McMaster

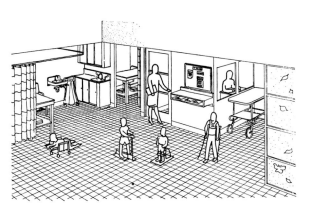

Fig. 2

HOSPITALS

Physical Therapy Department; Occupational Therapy Department

sections of the country. The reduction of humidity for comfort, protection of equipment and reduction of the hazard of slippery floors makes air conditioning vital in the underwater exercise area. It has been demonstrated as desirable in the exercise area and in treatment cubicles, especially where heat producing equipment is used. Air conditioning engineers should be consulted before ventilation equipment is installed.

Sinks Hospitals hand washing lavatories with hot and cold water mixing outlets, preferably foot operated, should be located at the proper height in convenient places. At least one sink should be of sufficient width and depth to accommodate the care of wet packs and other special washing needs.

Interior Finishes The activity of patients in wheelchairs, on stretchers and crutches subjects floors and walls to heavy wear. Materials which will stand up under such rough usage, remain attractive and require a minimum of maintenance should be specified despite higher costs.

All interior wall surfaces of the department should have a durable and attractive wainscot to protect them against damage by wheelchairs, stretchers and carts. Ceramic wall tile or glazed structural units will serve the purpose but they emphasize the institutional character of the hospital. In patient areas this should be minimized as much as possible. In the last several years vinyl wall covering has gained in popularity as a wainscoting material, and to some extent for the entire wall. Two weights of the material are available; the heavier weight for areas subjected to severe abuse, the lighter weight for other parts of the wall.

The use of decorative colors for interior finishes and equipment is, of course, highly desirable in this department as it is in other parts of the hospital. Research in "color therapy" for hospitals adds to decorators' ideas the therapeutic value of combinations of pastel colors. "Cool" pastels—green, blue, violet and their many derivatives—are considered mildly restful. Some light colors in general are stimulating and may be of advantage in the exercise area.

Doors For accommodation of stretcher and wheelchair traffic, doors within the department should be at least 40 inches wide. Raised thresholds should be eliminated.

Ceiling Moorings These moorings, strategically located in the ceiling in treatment areas, have been found useful for attaching overhead equipment such as hoists, pulleys, bars, counterbalancing equipment, etc. They should be constructed and attached to joists in such a manner that each supports at least 500 pounds.

Layout

It is impossible to anticipate all of the practical problems of layout in a particular building or to say in advance that one plan or another is the right one. A few guidelines, however, may be useful in making decisions about layout.

Expect to expand and plan for it from the beginning. It is impossible to overestimate the value of the exercise area. Give it as many square feet of appropriate space as possible.

Note the need to have the underwater exercise equipment grouped in one area, separate but adjacent and accessible to the other treatment areas.

When deciding which units to place next to each other or group together, consider how they are used by patients, especially the flow of traffic from one unit to another. Try to avoid needless traffic. Try to conserve the energies of staff.

Visit other physical therapy departments and find out what the physical therapists like or would like to change in the layouts of their own departments.

By ALONZO W. CLARK, AIA with the collaboration of the American Occupational Therapy Association

OCCUPATIONAL THERAPY DEPARTMENT

The increasing recognition of occupational therapy as an integral part of the medical rehabilitation program has resulted in its becoming an increasingly important element of hospital planning.

These pages present a summary of the recommendations of the American Occupational Therapy Association on the planning of typical occupational therapy departments. These basic plans and discussions were developed to serve only as guides for designing similar units, and will not be universally applicable without some modification. This material was presented at length in the October, 1950, issue of *HOSPITALS, Journal of the American Hospital Association*. For reprints of this article, which contains extensive equipment and supply lists for planning storage, write American Occupational Therapy Association, 6000 Executive Blvd., Suite 200, Rockville, MD 20852.

Basic solutions for occupational therapy departments are largely dependent on the following factors:

1. *Number of patients to be treated.* On the basis of hospital surveys and committee recommendations, it was agreed that 30 per cent of hospital patients should normally be referred for occupational therapy. About 40 per cent of these would be treated in the clinic, and 60 per cent treated in their beds or on the wards. One occupational therapist in the clinic can generally accommodate about 15 patients in each of two daily sessions, one in the morning, one in the afternoon. This number will vary according to the type of patient—more psychiatric patients, fewer physically disabled patients.

2. *Floor space required by patients.* Approximately 54 to 61 sq ft per patient is recommended for the entire department, including clinic, office and storage. For the clinic alone, 42 to 47 sq ft per patient is suggested to allow for easy circulation and use of equipment. These figures are based on a study of the needs of a typical department.

3. *Types of treatment media to be used.* Some 70-odd activities are used in occupational therapy departments throughout the country. Basic requirements for small units are as follows; these should be expanded for larger units:

a. Bench work—carpentry, plastics, metal work including painting and finishing of completed projects.

b. Table work—leather, blockprinting, flytying, sewing and art work.

c. Loom work—weaving, braiding.

d. "Functional equipment" (not an active classification)—bicycle, jig saws and other adapted equipment for treatment of physical disabilities.

Storage facilities should provide for at least 3 months' supply, as many institutions order on a quarterly basis. All the above items must, of course, be adapted to suit a particular type and size of hospital.

4. *Location of the department in a hospital.* Daylighted space as close to patient areas as possible and readily accessible to toilet facilities is recommended. Proximity to the physical therapy department is advisable. Necessary facilities include running water, gas, and electric outlets; dust collectors for power woodworking tools are recommended.

The Smaller Unit

For hospitals up to a 250-bed capacity, a basic plan was evolved (see next page). At the rate of referral cited, up to 30 patients should be accommodated. These could be cared for by one therapist, with a possible second therapist for ward service. On the basis of 15 patients per session at 54 sq ft per patient, the entire unit was allotted 813.75 sq ft (17½ by 46½ ft). The clinic area, planned at 42 sq ft per patient, totals 638.75 sq ft (17½ by 36½ ft). The minimum basic activities were provided for with 20 work stations for flexibility in selection. Activities requiring bulky equipment such as printing and advanced ceramics were omitted. It was assumed that preparation and finishing could be done in the clinic or on a counter top in the storeroom. The following considerations were made for the three specific areas within the department:

1. *Clinic area.* The first obvious requirement is space for free circulation around the required equipment (see general list following). Space for parking at least 3 wheel chairs is also necessary. Double doors at shop entrance simplify moving equipment and supplies. Sliding doors for upper cabinets avoid interference with patients working at counter tops. No display case for finished articles was included as it was felt that this emphasized the product rather than therapeutic objectives.

2. *Storage area.* Space was provided for a mobile cart for servicing ward patients. A cabinet with work top was included for preparation and finishing work. It was assumed that only 8-ft lengths of lumber and plywood would be stored in this basic unit, and that other closets, rooms, etc. in various parts of the hospital could be used for "dead storage."

3. *Office area.* Space was provided for the usual office furnishings. A large glass panel in front of the desk facilitates control and supervision of the unit.

Variations for Hospital Types The basic plan is directly applicable to *psychiatric* and *general medical and surgical* hospitals. In the latter case, a bicycle jig saw is recommended in place of a drill press stand (a table model drill press could be used).

Tuberculosis hospitals require two minor changes: replacement of one floor loom and the braid-weaving frame with two industrial sewing machines.

Pediatric hospitals need the following changes: a plan adaptable to division into two parts—one for small children, one for adolescents. For equipment changes, see plan. Tables should adjust in height.

Physical disability hospitals can use the basic plan with a few variations in equipment. Although fewer patients can be treated per therapist, fewer will be able to come to the clinic for treatment; a second therapist will be needed for treatment in the wards.

The Larger Unit

A basic plan for a typical occupational therapy unit for large hospitals of approximately 500

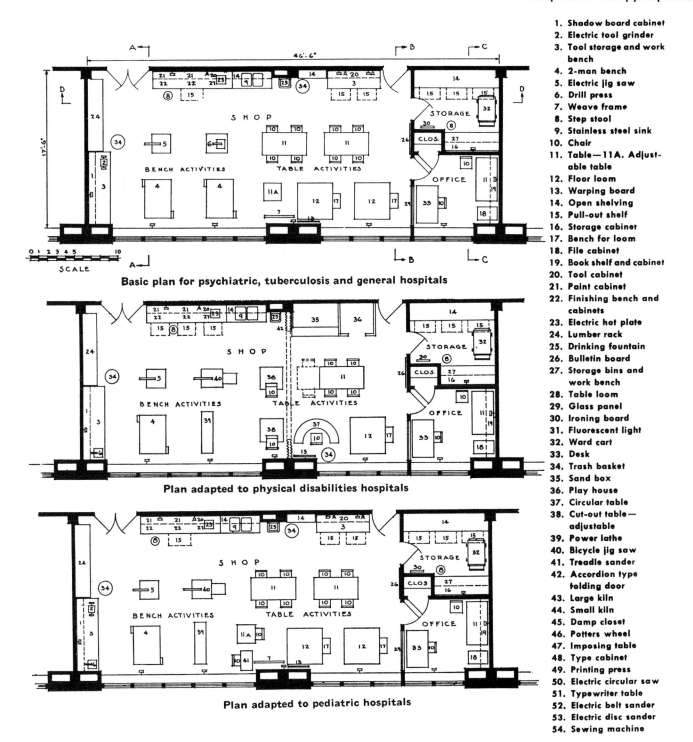

1. Shadow board cabinet
2. Electric tool grinder
3. Tool storage and work bench
4. 2-man bench
5. Electric jig saw
6. Drill press
7. Weave frame
8. Step stool
9. Stainless steel sink
10. Chair
11. Table—11A. Adjustable table
12. Floor loom
13. Warping board
14. Open shelving
15. Pull-out shelf
16. Storage cabinet
17. Bench for loom
18. File cabinet
19. Book shelf and cabinet
20. Tool cabinet
21. Paint cabinet
22. Finishing bench and cabinets
23. Electric hot plate
24. Lumber rack
25. Drinking fountain
26. Bulletin board
27. Storage bins and work bench
28. Table loom
29. Glass panel
30. Ironing board
31. Fluorescent light
32. Ward cart
33. Desk
34. Trash basket
35. Sand box
36. Play house
37. Circular table
38. Cut-out table—adjustable
39. Power lathe
40. Bicycle jig saw
41. Treadle sander
42. Accordion type folding door
43. Large kiln
44. Small kiln
45. Damp closet
46. Potters wheel
47. Imposing table
48. Type cabinet
49. Printing press
50. Electric circular saw
51. Typewriter table
52. Electric belt sander
53. Electric disc sander
54. Sewing machine

Basic plan for psychiatric, tuberculosis and general hospitals

Plan adapted to physical disabilities hospitals

Plan adapted to pediatric hospitals

Fig. 1   Floor plans for typical occupational therapy department in hospitals up to 250-bed capacity.

Health

HOSPITALS
Occupational Therapy Department

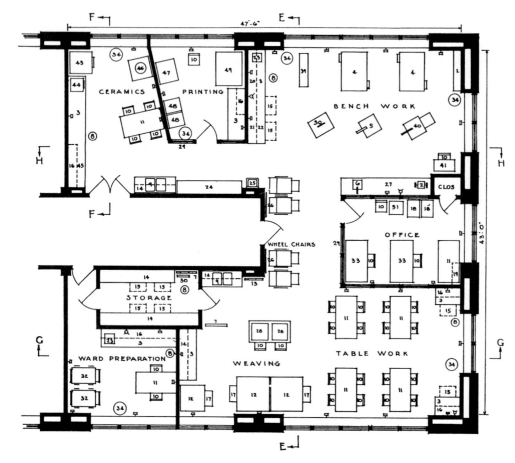

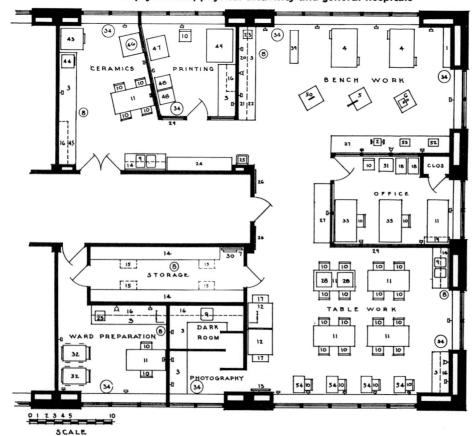

Plan for psychiatric, physical disability and general hospitals

SCALE

Fig. 2 Floor plans for typical occupational therapy department in hospitals up to 500-bed capacity.

1. Shadow board cabinet
2. Electric tool grinder
3. Tool storage and work bench
4. 2-man bench
5. Electric jig saw
6. Drill press
7. Weave frame
8. Step stool
9. Stainless steel sink
10. Chair
11. Table—11A. Adjustable table
12. Floor loom
13. Warping board
14. Open shelving
15. Pull-out shelf
16. Storage cabinet
17. Bench for loom
18. File cabinet
19. Book shelf and cabinet
20. Tool cabinet
21. Paint cabinet
22. Finishing bench and cabinets
23. Electric hot plate
24. Lumber rack
25. Drinking fountain
26. Bulletin board
27. Storage bins and work bench
28. Table loom
29. Glass panel
30. Ironing board
31. Fluorescent light
32. Ward cart
33. Desk
34. Trash basket
35. Sand box
36. Play house
37. Circular table
38. Cut-out table—adjustable
39. Power lathe
40. Bicycle jig saw
41. Treadle sander
42. Accordion type folding door
43. Large kiln
44. Small kiln
45. Damp closet
46. Potters wheel
47. Imposing table
48. Type cabinet
49. Printing press
50. Electric circular saw
51. Typewriter table
52. Electric belt sander
53. Electric disc sander
54. Sewing machine

beds was shown previously. Again using the same basis for rate of patient referrals to the department (30 per cent of rated bed capacity), the large unit should accommodate 150 patients a day. The actual clinic load would be 60 patients (40 per cent of 150), or about 30 in each of two sessions.

The unit as presented was planned on the basis of 31 patients. Using 61 sq ft per person, the gross area allotted the entire unit is approximately 1,880 sq ft. Net area of the clinic is about 1,450 sq ft, or 47 sq ft per person.

This increased space per person over that allowed in the smaller unit is the result of adding two activities requiring bulky equipment and separate rooms. These are ceramics and printing. It was also deemed essential to have a separate ward preparation room to serve the increased number of ward patients. To allow for a necessary dispersion factor, 10 extra work stations are provided in the clinic. The larger unit therefore contains the following sections:

1. *Clinic*, including weaving and table activities area, bench activities, printing unit, ceramics unit.
2. *Office*.
3. *Storage*.
4. *Ward preparation area*.

Three therapists plus three assistants could run clinic and wards.

Space requirements for the various activities were determined from the following estimate:

Activity	% of patients	No. of patients
Wood, plastics, metal	22	7
General crafts (table activities)	64	19
Ceramics	9	3
Printing	5	2
	100	31

Variations for Hospital Types The larger plan is suitable for *general medical and surgical hospitals, psychiatric hospitals* and, with minor changes in equipment, for hospitals treating *physical disabilities*. Several units might be used for very large psychiatric hospitals. *Pediatric hospitals* are seldom as large as 500 beds; if so more personnel are needed.

Compiled by the Architectural and Engineering Branch, Division of Hospital and Medical Facilities, U.S. Public Health Service; August Hoenack, Branch Chief

CHECKLIST OF SPACES FOR A COMMUNITY MENTAL HEALTH CENTER

Facilities listed are those that may be required in the overall programs of mental health centers. They can be in one or several buildings on one or several sites, even under one or several cooperating ownerships. The list is for review by architects and administrators whenever new facilities are planned.

ADMINISTRATION

Office space for:
1. Director
2. Assistant director
3. Nursing director
4. Secretaries and typists
5. Business office

Ancillary spaces:
1. Record room
2. Staff lounge
3. Library
4. Conference room
5. Lobby and waiting
6. Toilets: public, personnel

DIAGNOSTIC & TREATMENT

Laboratory:
1. Office
2. Clinical
3. Pathology
4. Bacteriology
5. Washing and sterilizing

Suites:
1. Basal metabolism and electrocardiology
2. Morgue and autopsy
3. Dental
4. Eye, ear, nose and throat
5. Electroencephalography
6. Radiology

Physical therapy:
1. Electrotherapy
2. Hydrotherapy with exercise
3. Small gymnasium

Pharmacy department

Occupational therapy:
1. Space for small woodworking tools and benches for carpentry, metal work, leather work, printing, weaving, rug making, etc.
2. Office
3. Storage room

OUTPATIENT EXAMINATION AND TREATMENT

Office space for:
1. Psychiatrists
2. Psychologists
3. Social workers
4. Nurses
5. Health educators
6. Occupational therapists
7. Rehabilitation counselors
8. Recreation therapists
9. Clerical operators
10. Aides
11. Research analyst
12. Group therapy and conference

(Lobby, waiting space, and toilets may be combined with those in the administrative area.)

INPATIENT FACILITIES

Facilities may be required for the following types of patients grouped in accordance with the local program. (Separate spaces for male and female. Treatment and diagnosis spaces for each category.)

Patients' categories:
1. New admissions
2. Quiet ambulant
3. Disturbed
4. Alcoholic
5. Criminalistic
6. Day care
7. Night care
8. Children
   a. Emotionally disturbed
   b. Retarded

Each patient care unit:
1. Waiting space for visitors
2. Doctors' offices and examination rooms
3. Offices for psychologists, social workers, therapist or others as required
4. Nurses' station and toilet
5. Conference room
6. Therapy space
7. Day room(s)
8. Utility room
9. Pantry or nourishment preparation
10. Dining room
11. Washroom and toilets
12. Patients' lockers
13. Showers and bathrooms
14. Storage (for recreational and occupational therapy equipment)
15. Supply and linen storage
16. Janitors' closet
17. Stretcher alcove

Minimum room areas:
1. 80 sq ft per bed in alcoves and four-bed rooms
2. 100 sq ft in single rooms
3. 40 to 50 sq ft per patient in day rooms, preferably divided into one large and one small room

STERILIZING AND SUPPLY FACILITIES

(Sufficient to serve both outpatients and inpatients.)

SERVICE DEPARTMENT

Dietary facilities:
1. Main kitchen and bakery
2. Dietitians' office
3. Dishwashing room
4. Refrigerators
5. Garbage collecting and disposal facilities
6. Can washing room
7. Day storage room
8. Staff dining room

Housekeeping facilities:
1. Laundry
2. Separate sorting room
3. Separate clean linen and sewing room
4. Housekeeper's office and storage (near linen storage)

Mechanical facilities:
1. Boiler room and pump room
2. Engineer's office
3. Shower and locker room

Maintenance shops:
Carpentry, painting, mechanical, repair rooms

Employees' facilities:
Locker, rest, toilet and shower rooms for various categories

Storage:
1. Medical records
2. General storage (a minimum 20 sq ft per bed to be concentrated in one area)

LABORATORY

Preliminary Planning

Locate the department as favorably as possible for the laboratory staff and the ambulant inpatients and outpatients. A space on the first floor near an elevator is preferable. Also, another determinant in locating the laboratory is the consideration for future expansion.

In determining the overall size of the laboratory, the first concern is the individual technical units. It is only after the size of these units has been established and an architectural layout has been developed to fit the program that the sum of the areas can accurately reflect the size of the laboratory department.

The square-foot-per-bed ratio is no longer considered a desirable guide in determining the size of a hospital department because of the wide variation of such factors as type and size of hospital, pattern of usage, growth of the community, and medical practice. Plans for the

Planning the Laboratory for the General Hospital, Public Health Service, Dept. of Health, Education, and Welfare, 1963.

laboratory area should be based on work volumes within specific ranges, such as 40,000–75,000 tests, or 75,000–120,000 tests. The key to this method is to estimate the work volume and its breakdown into work units for hospitals of different sizes.

The following is an outline of the procedure which may be used in estimating needed laboratory space, based on the number of tests performed, personnel, and equipment.

1. Break down the total volume of work into units, such as hematology, urinalysis, chemistry, as previously noted.

2. Determine the number of technologists required in each department. The data shown in Table 1 may be used as a basis for this determination.

3. Determine the necessary equipment and space for the number of technologists required.

For the purpose of developing guide material, the Architectural and Engineering Branch of the Division of Hospital and Medical Facilities collected data from 360 hospitals in addition to the data compiled by the Committee on Laboratory Planning of the College of American Pathologists. Tables 2, 3, 4, and 5 present these data.

Many laboratories show annual workload increases of about 10 percent, thus doubling the work volume in approximately nine years.

This annual increase should be considered during the planning stage of the laboratory. However, improved techniques and automation suggest that it may be possible for a greater volume of work to be done in the same work area size.

Laboratory Guide Plan

Plan A is a suggested plan for a hospital laboratory service with an estimated workload of 70,000 to 120,000 laboratory tests annually. For planning purposes, this laboratory is designed to serve a general hospital of 150 to 200 beds. The nontechnical staff would include one or more laboratory helpers in the glasswashing and sterilizing unit and a clerk-typist and secretary in the administrative unit. (See Fig. 1a.)

The laboratory services of a general hospital having this work volume would require work areas for six main technical units: hematology, blood bank, urinalysis, biochemistry, histology, and serology-bacteriology.

The block plan has been utilized here, as it provides a good functional relationship for all units. The pathologist's office in the center provides for easy supervision of the work stations; the hematology unit is near the waiting room; the bacteriology unit is at the end of the

laboratory, yet near the washing and sterilizing areas; and the histology unit is near the pathologist's office.

Other schemes similar to that shown in Plan D or a typical wing arrangement with a corridor down the center would also be satisfactory.

In the technical area of Plan A, the open plan arrangement (except for the histology and serology-bacteriology units) has several advantages over the "separate room for each unit" scheme for hospitals of this size. These advantages include: easier supervision; common use of such equipment as desks, refrigerators, and centrifuges; flexible use of personnel; and more available space since many doors and partitions are eliminated. If desired, partitions could be erected between each unit, as indicated on the plan for the histology and serology-bacteriology units.

Laboratory Module for Techical Area Maximum flexibility is desirable in the technical work areas of the laboratory department. In the plans, this has been achieved by using a module of approximately 10 by 20 ft, with a similar arrangement for each module. Each one consists of two standard laboratory workbenches 12 ft long, 30 in. deep, with a working surface or counter of about 23 in., and a reagent shelf. Knee spaces are indicated where needed for

---

TABLE 1 Tests Performed Annually per Medical Technologist*

Laboratory Unit	Tests
Hematology	13,400
Urinalysis	30,720
Serology	11,520
Biochemistry	9,600
Bacteriology	7,680
Histology	3,840
Parasitology	9,600

* These figures were derived from data developed by Seward E. Owen and Edmund P. Finch, presented in two articles published in *Modern Hospital*, June and October, 1957. Titles of the articles are: "How to Calculate the Laboratory Work Load" and "How to Measure Laboratory Productivity"

TABLE 2 Tests Performed Annually in General Hospitals

Hospital Bed Size	Number of Tests		
	Low	High	Median
50- 99	12,000	25,000	19,000
100-149	24,000	75,000	39,000
150-200	55,000	163,000	69,000

TABLE 3 Utilization Index of Laboratory Services in General Hospitals

Hospital Bed Size	Tests per Patient Day		
	Low	High	Median
100-149	1.05	2.02	1.29
150-200	1.08	2.67	1.32

TABLE 4 Tests Performed Annually in Each Laboratory Unit

General Hospitals—150-200 Beds

Unit	Low	High	Median	Technologists Required	
				Median	High
Urinalysis	6,200	20,100	11,300	0.4	.7
Hematology	29,800	81,200	35,800	2.5	5.6
Serology	3,600	13,500	6,800	0.6	1.1
Biochemistry	2,300	19,600	6,600	0.7	2.0
Parasitology*	—	—	—	—	—
Bacteriology	400	4,700	1,800	0.2	0.6
Histology	700	5,100	1,800	0.5	1.3
Basal Metabolism	30	700	400		
Electrocardiograms	800	4,200	1,300		
Blood Bank Tests	130	23,200	4,500	1.0	2.0
Transfusions	800	2,000	1,000		
Other	500	9,600	1,700		
			TOTALS	5.9	13.3

* Included with urinalysis

TABLE 5 Tests Performed Annually in Each Laboratory Unit

General Hospitals—100-149 Beds

Unit	Low	High	Median	Technologists Required	
				Median	High
Urinalysis	3,000	9,000	4,800	0.2	0.3
Hematology	9,000	37,000	20,200	1.4	2.5
Serology	220	5,600	3,500	0.3	0.4
Biochemistry	1,300	5,300	2,800	0.3	0.6
Bacteriology	85	3,800	700	0.09	0.5
Histology	700	3,100	1,500	0.4	0.8
Parasitology	200	250	200	0.02	0.02
Basal Metabolism	20	300	60	—	—
Electrocardiograms	500	3,300	650	0.5	1.0
Blood Bank Tests	20	9,200	2,800		
Transfusions	400	1,300	700		
Other	80	7,300	400		
			TOTALS	3.21	6.12

personnel who perform tests from a sitting position. Drawers, cabinets, and shelves are provided below the work counter for daily equipment and supplies. This arrangement provides a 5-ft aisle between workbenches, which is considered optimum for movement within the working area. Equipment such as centrifuges, refrigerators, and desks, which may be used jointly by the personnel, is located opposite the units along the interior of the technical work area.

Technical Areas *Hematology-Blood Bank Unit.* A standard module is assigned to the hematology-blood bank unit. One half of this module is provided with a workbench for procedures such as hemoglobin tests, sedimentation rates, staining, and washing of pipettes (in Plan A, counter No. 7 on left side of unit). Knee space and storage cabinets are provided below the counter. In the other half of the module, a workbench 30 in. high, with three knee spaces, is provided for technologists who are seated during tests, such as those involving microscopic procedures.

The micro-hematocrit centrifuge, because of its noise and vibration when in use, is placed in the general technical area along the interior wall directly opposite the hematology unit. The other equipment needed by this work unit, such as a refrigerator, centrifuge, and recording desk, is located conveniently opposite the unit, where it is shared with the urinalysis and the chemistry units.

It is assumed that the laboratory will obtain blood for transfusions from other sources, and, therefore, needs only facilities for blood storage. A blood bank refrigerator is provided for this purpose in the examination and test room. Compatibility tests on the blood are done in the hematology unit. A hospital which operates a selfcontained blood bank, that is, collects and does complete processing of all blood, should provide a separate bleeding room, processing laboratory, donors' recovery room, and an office available for preliminary physical examinations.

Urinalysis Unit. The urinalysis unit is assigned one half of a standard module, consisting of a workbench, 12 linear ft long and 30 in. high, and serves as the work area for the microscopic and chemical examinations. Five linear ft of the workbench and a knee space are provided for personnel performing the microscopic examinations; the remainder of the workbench is used for the chemical examinations. A sink located at one end of the workbench provides a continuous working surface for the technologists.

Biochemistry Unit. The biochemistry unit requires an area that occupies one and a half standard laboratory modules. The half module is shared with the urinalysis unit and is used for the necessary preliminary procedures that are done prior to the actual chemical analyses. A knee space is provided in this workbench for personnel who perform titrations and other procedures while seated. The adjoining module provides workbench area where a variety of chemical procedures may be performed and includes a fume hood for removal of vapors and gases.

The workbenches for the chemical procedures are about 36 in. high, with drawers and cabinets below. The reagent shelves are used to hold the chemicals needed during the procedures. Two utility sinks are provided, one in each chemistry work area. Apparatus used in this unit is cleaned by the personnel in the unit; test tubes, pipettes, and flasks are sent to the central glass-washing area nearby.

An instrument table 36 in. high is located along the interior wall opposite this unit where chemical apparatus, such as colorimeter, flame photometer, spectrophotometer, and carbon dioxide gas apparatus are placed. Adjacent to the instrument table is an analytical balance on a vibration-free table or other type of support. By placing this apparatus away from the busy preparation and test procedure work areas, personnel can use the apparatus without interference from other procedures. It also lessens the possibility of damage to the equipment by the accidental spillage or splattering of chemical reagents.

A centrifuge, refrigerator, and desk are provided along the interior wall opposite the unit for the use of the personnel in this unit. The desk and refrigerator are shared with the urinalysis and the hematology units.

Histology Unit. The histology unit is assigned a standard module, separated from the other units by a partition to prevent odors from spreading to other areas. It is located near the pathologist's office since the medical technologist here works under his direction and supervision.

Along one half of the module, an area is utilized by the pathologist to examine surgical and autopsy specimens and to select the tissues for slide sections to be prepared by the technologist. An exhaust hood is provided over this section, as shown in the plan (No. 53), to draw off disagreeable odors from specimens and solutions. The remainder of the module is used for the processing and staining of tissues. Knee spaces are provided, one at each of the specialized work areas. The workbench is 30 in. high with a 22- or 23-in.-deep working area, cabinets and drawers below the counter, and a reagent shelf. Wall-hung cabinets are provided for additional storage. A utility sink is provided at the end of the workbench.

Serology-Bacteriology Unit. The serology and bacteriology work is combined in one standard laboratory module, where a half module is assigned to each unit. Culture media for use in bacteriology are prepared in the bacteriology work area and sent to the sterilizing unit for sterilization.

The workbenches are 30 in. high with a 22- or 23-in.-deep working area, and are provided with reagent shelves. A knee space is provided in each workbench since most of the procedures are done in a sitting position. A utility sink is provided for the personnel in both units, but the bacteriology unit also requires a sink for the staining of slides. A fume hood is provided to prevent the spread of possible infection to personnel when preparing specimens from suspect cases of tuberculosis, fungus, or virus diseases.

A centrifuge, refrigerator, and incubator are provided along the interior wall within the unit. A desk is also conveniently located for the use of the personnel.

This module is partitioned and separated from the other units by a door to reduce contamination of air and the hazard of infection to personnel in the other lab areas.

Administrative Area The administrative area is separated from the technical work areas so that the nonlaboratory personnel need not enter the technical areas. This is the central control and collection point for receiving specimens and is the reception area for the patients and the hospital staff who come to the laboratory.

Waiting Room. A waiting area, with conventional waiting room furnishings, is provided for the ambulant patients. In this area, a desk is provided for a clerk-typist. An intercommunication system between the technical areas of

the laboratory and the clerk-typist is recommended. This enables her to quickly notify the technical personnel when a patient arrives and also to transfer phone calls for information concerning a laboratory report.

The pathologist's secretary is also located in this area, near the pathologist's office. She takes dictation and handles all the pathologist's correspondence, surgical pathological reports, and autopsy protocols.

Venipuncture Cubicle. A venipuncture cubicle is provided where blood specimens are taken from the ambulant patients sent to the laboratory.

Specimen Toilet. A specimen toilet is provided in this area for the collection of urine and stool specimens; a pass window opens directly into the technical area near the urinalysis unit.

Basal Metabolism-Electrocardiography Room. A room is also located here for basal metabolism tests and electrocardiograms, and when necessary, to obtain blood from donors. A desk is provided in this room to permit handling of paper work. A lavatory is also provided.

Pathologist's Office. The pathologist's office is located so that he may have easy access to the technical areas of the laboratory, particularly the histology unit. This office is separated by a glass partition which permits the pathologist to observe the technical work areas. A draw curtain may be used when he desires privacy. Those who wish to consult the pathologist have access to his office through an entrance from the administrative area.

Auxiliary Service Areas The auxiliary service units are located adjacent to the administrative area and are easily accessible to the technical areas.

Glass Washing and Sterilizing Unit. The glass washing and sterilizing unit is close to the serology-bacteriology and the biochemistry units which will utilize such services more often than the other units. A separate door leads directly into the serology-bacteriology unit so that contaminated glassware need not be transported through other work areas.

Within this unit are located a water still, pressure sterilizer, sterilizing oven, and pipette washer. Storage cabinets are also provided for stock items of glassware, chemicals, and reagents. A hood over the sterilizers and water still is used to exhaust the heat generated by the equipment. Utility carts used to transport dirty glassware from the various laboratory units to this area are parked in this unit.

Locker and Toilet Facilities. Separate locker and toilet facilities are provided within the laboratory department for the medical technologists. This convenience reduces the time personnel must be away from the work areas. Since most medical technologists are females, lockers have been provided for them in the department. However, where male technologists are employed, lockers should also be provided for them, either in the laboratory or in another location.

Optional Services. Clinical photography, medical illustration, and research facilities are not included in the plan because of their specialized requirements. If these services are to be part of the laboratory department, revision and expansion of the plan will be necessary.

Guide Plans for Smaller Hospital Laboratories

Plan B is a suggested guide for a general hospital laboratory service having an anticipated

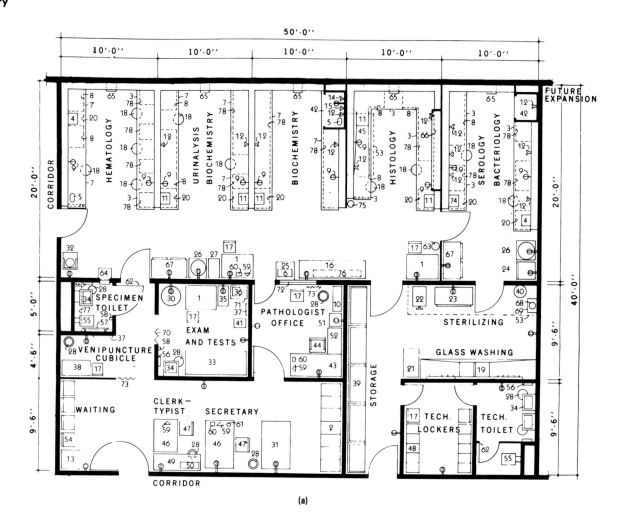

(a)

LEGEND

1. Desk, 30 by 40 in., single pedestal
2. Filing cabinet, letter size
3. Counter, 30-in. high
4. Staining sink
5. Cup sink
6. Analytical balance
7. Counter, 36-in. high
8. Cabinets with adjustable shelves, below counter
9. Electric strip outlets, continuous
10. Bookcase
11. Utility sink
12. Gas outlet
13. Table for magazines
14. Suction outlet
15. Compressed air outlet
16. Table for instruments
17. Straight chair
18. Stool
19. Two-compartment sink 8-in. deep; drainboards-noncorrosive metal; peg boards above drainboards
20. Cabinet with trash receptacle on inside of door
21. Utility cart
22. Laboratory pressure sterilizer
23. Hot air oven
24. Incubator
25. Shelf or table for analytical balance
26. Centrifuge

27. Table for Harvard trip balance
28. Waste paper receptacle
29. Refrigerator, 8 cu. ft.
30. Refrigerator, blood bank
31. Worktable
32. Micro-hematocrit centrifuge
33. Examination table
34. Lavatory
35. Basal metabolism apparatus
36. Electrocardiograph
37. Hook strip
38. Table, 24 by 36 in.
39. Storage cabinets
40. Water still, 2-5 gals. per hr.
41. Adult scale
42. Fume hood
43. Double-pedestal office desk
44. Office chair, swivel, with arms
45. Noncorrosive metal work surface; pitch to sink
46. Typewriter desk
47. Posture chair
48. Technicians' lockers
49. Specimen receiving table
50. Request file with pigeon holes
51. Slide file cabinet
52. Microscope table
53. Exhaust hood

54. Easy chair
55. Wall-hung water closet
56. Paper towel dispenser
57. Grab bar, continuous
58. Emergency call station (push button) connected to buzzer at secretary's desk
59. Telephone outlet
60. Intercommunication system outlet
61. Buzzer at receptionist's desk from emergency calling stations
62. Hook on toilet-side of door
63. Fire extinguisher
64. Pass-through between toilet and laboratory
65. Exhaust air grills near floor
66. Wall cabinet
67. Refrigerator, 11 cu. ft.
68. Pipette washer
69. Shelf, for pipette washer, 10 in. above floor
70. Folding door
71. Table for electrocardiograph
72. Window
73. Curtain
74. Sink with electric waste disposal
75. Carbon dioxide cylinder
76. Gas cylinders under table
77. Shelf for urine bottles
78. Drawers with adjustable shelves, below counter

Fig. 1 (a) Plan A (70,000 to 120,000 tests annually) for average size of 150 to 200 beds. (b) Plan B (40,000 to 75,000 tests annually) for average size of 100 to 150 beds. (c) Plan C (20,000 to 30,000 tests annually) for less than 100 beds.

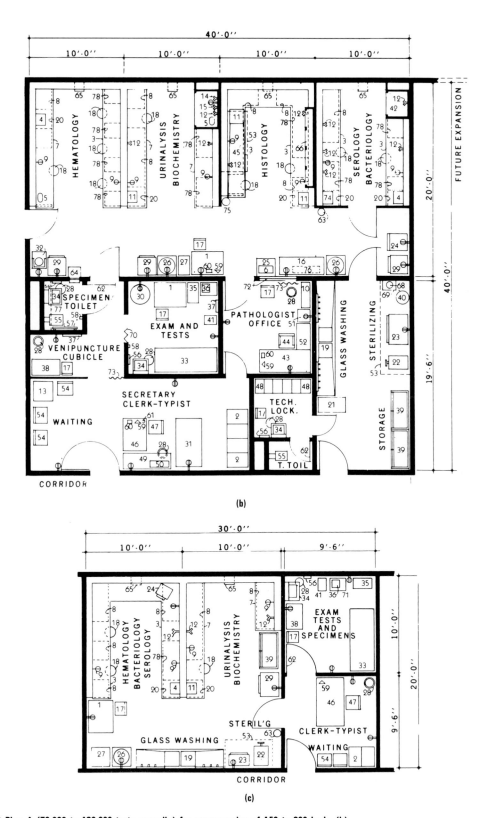

(b)

(c)

Fig. 1 (cont.) (a) Plan A (70,000 to 120,000 tests annually) for average size of 150 to 200 beds. (b) Plan B (40,000 to 75,000 tests annually) for average size of 100 to 150 beds. (c) Plan C (20,000 to 30,000 tests annually) for less than 100 beds.

annual workload of 40,000 to 75,000 tests. The estimated technical staff required to handle this workload is 4 to 7 medical technologists, based on the annual workload per technologist (Tables 1 and 5). The nontechnical staff would include one or more laboratory helpers in the glass washing and sterilizing unit and a secretary to handle the administrative work. This plan provides for a laboratory department having a full-time pathologist. It is assumed that a histology unit will be needed.

A laboratory service performing a yearly volume of 40,000 to 75,000 tests requires the same types of technical units as one that handles 70,000 to 120,000 laboratory tests. The space requirements for the technical work areas of the units are reduced, however, because the workload is less and fewer technologists are needed. (See Fig. 1b.)

Technical, Administrative, Auxiliary Areas. The plan provides four laboratory modules where the technical procedures performed include hematology, urinalysis, biochemistry, histology, and serology-bacteriology. Only the biochemistry unit is reduced in area because of less work and simpler procedures. The decreased work volume in the other units does not warrant further reduction of their work areas.

The principle of having equipment such as centrifuges, refrigerators, and recording desks close to the working unit which is to use them was followed as in Plan A.

Because of the decreased workload, the working area and the space for clerical personnel also are reduced.

The glass washing, sterilizing, storage space, and technicians' locker facilities also are reduced.

Plan D presents a design which might be used for a laboratory service in a small hospital. It allots the same areas for the technical, administrative, and auxiliary service units that Plan B provides, but the total square footage is less. However, more difficulty is encountered in providing as efficient a relationship between the administrative and auxiliary services and the technical laboratory units as in the plans for larger departments. (See Fig. 2.)

Plan C is a suggested plan for a general hospital laboratory service handling an annual workload of from 20,000 to 30,000 tests. The estimated technical staff required to handle this workload is 2 to 3 medical technologists, based on the workload per technologist and the annual volume of tests (Tables 1 and 2). The nontechnical staff would include one laboratory helper and a clerk-typist. (See Fig. 1c.)

The utilization of the standard laboratory module previously described permits even the small laboratory to be divided into technical, administrative, and auxiliary service work areas where the technologists may work in an area designed for the specific task.

Because of the decreased workload in a laboratory of this size, it is feasible to combine the hematology, bacteriology, and serology units by providing half a module for hematology and the other half for bacteriology and serology. A second module is provided for urinalysis and biochemistry, storage space, and refrigerator. Only the more common and simple laboratory procedures would be done in these units.

A glass washing and sterilizing area is provided directly opposite but apart from the technical work areas.

The administrative area provides a small waiting room where a clerk-typist receives patients and laboratory requests and specimens. In this area, a room is also provided for performing basal metabolism tests and

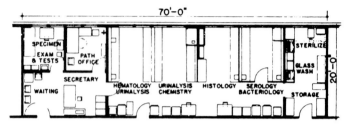

Fig. 2 Plan D alternate plan (40,000 to 75,000 tests annually).

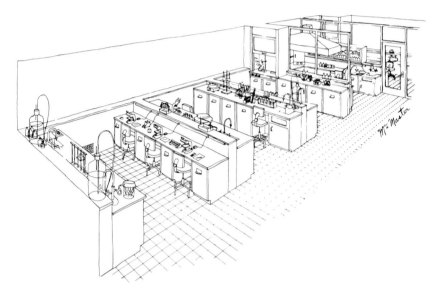

Fig. 3 Perspective view of laboratory for general hospital of 150 to 200 beds.

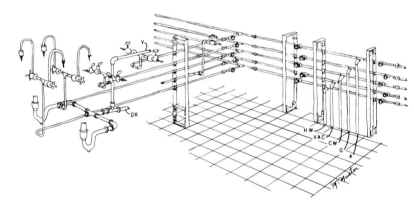

Fig. 4 Diagram of piping behind laboratory workbenches.

electrocardiograms. This room also can be used for obtaining blood specimens from ambulant patients.

Utility Services

The utility service systems required in the operation of the laboratory include water, waste, gas, vacuum and compressed air. Because of the importance of these systems, the need for continuity of service, and the probability of future expansion, careful study is necessary in designing them for safety and efficiency.

Piping systems should not be exposed because they create housekeeping problems as dirt collectors and may be hazardous; many are noisy and unsightly. They should be located where they will be easily accessible for service

and repairs with a minimum of disruption of normal laboratory services. A sufficient number of valves, traps, and cleanout openings should be installed and should be located so as to permit maximum use of the facilities during repairs.

Laboratory benches are usually placed at right angles to and adjoining outside walls to effectively utilize space. This location of the benches simplifies, to some extent, the arrangement of the piping systems by installing vertical lines in the outside wall and mounting the horizontal piping on this wall. This arrangement is particularly advantageous for the waste vent stacks which must be carried vertically to the roof. Removable panels between the bench islands on the outside wall provide easy access to the main piping systems and sectionalizing valves. Branch lines may be carried from the horizontal wall piping through the center of the island to serve the benches on both sides. (See Figs. 3 and 4.)

For safety purposes and to facilitate repairs, each individual piping system should be plainly identified by color, coding, or labeling. All waste piping should be of a noncorrosive material and should be discharged to a dilution pit or should be carried to a point in the piping system where the discharge will be diluted by waste from other areas.

Laboratory sinks should be made of noncorrosive material and should be designed for laboratory service. A waste grinder under the sink in the serology unit is highly desirable for disposal of clotted blood which may otherwise clog the drain.

LABOR-DELIVERY SUITE

Locating the Delivery Suite

Since the labor-delivery unit is basically self-sufficient, it may be located adjacent to the newborn nursery and maternity unit or elsewhere in the hospital; wherever possible, it should be located on the same floor. Transportation of mother and infant is reduced and maximum utilization of staff is obtained when all three units are together.

However, in large hospitals requiring more than one maternity nursing unit, another location may be required.

Planning the Labor-Delivery Unit in the General Hospital, Public Health Service, Department of Health, Education, and Welfare, 1964.

Functional Arrangement of the Delivery Suite

The delivery suite includes three areas of activity: labor, delivery, and recovery. Proper sequential arrangement of labor, delivery, and recovery areas within the labor-delivery unit facilitates patient care and aids the staff in carrying out proper medical techniques and practices. (See Fig. 1.)

Labor, delivery, and recovery rooms should be located and related for easy movement of patients from one area to another and for good patient observation. In large suites, locating service facilities on subsidiary corridors may help to reduce and control traffic.

From the standpoint of asepsis, location of delivery rooms and service facilities is critical. A location as remote as practicable from the entrance to the suite will reduce traffic, cause less air turbulence, and provide greater privacy for the patient.

Scrub-up areas should be adjacent to delivery rooms so that attending physicians can observe delivery room procedures and the condition of the patient.

A medical preparation facility serving labor and delivery areas should be convenient to both, accessible only to authorized personnel. This is usually located at the nurses' station or control area.

Storage for flammable anesthetics may not connect directly with anesthetizing areas.

A soiled holding room should be convenient for preparing the delivery room for a subsequent patient and for retaining soiled articles for disposal, processing, or return to central service.

Since the exact time of birth can seldom be determined, labor rooms should be close to delivery rooms but not so close that the two areas are intermixed or that patients in labor can overhear or view delivery room procedures.

A subsidiary corridor, if placed with a separate access to labor rooms, will permit the husband to visit in the labor room without passing through the main corridor and may also serve as a lounge area for ambulant patients and authorized visitors.

A recovery room should be located within the unit in an area: (1) adjacent to delivery rooms, or (2) near the main entrance to the unit. The determining factor may be the policy on permitting visitors to the recovery room. If no visitors are permitted, the first location has the advantage of immediate accessibility to delivery rooms and close proximity to the attending staff. The second location enables the husband to visit the patient without entering more restricted areas of the unit.

The location of the nurses' station will be determined to some extent by the size of the delivery suite and the nursing staff. A nurses' station for a unit of more than two delivery rooms should be placed near the entrance to serve as a control center for admitting and directing patients and performing other administration procedures without permitting these activities to interfere with other areas of the unit. If continuous attendance is difficult because of a small staff, the nurses' station may be located between labor and delivery areas so that nurses' travel to observe patients, keep charts, and participate in delivery room procedures is reduced.

Locker and toilet facilities for the obstetrical nursing staff and attending physicians should be included within the unit and arranged so that they will not enter clean areas in street clothes and will avoid exposure to contaminated areas after changing to obstetric garments. Where possible, entrances to these facilities from outside the unit are desirable.

The doctors' lounge and sleeping accommodations should be located within the unit

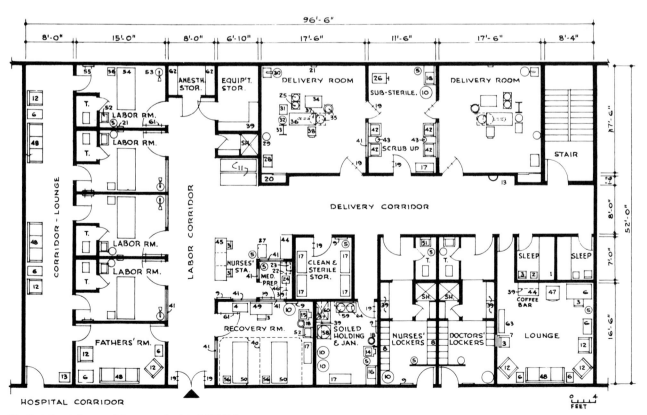

Fig. 1 Labor-delivery unit for approximately 1,500 births per year.

Health

HOSPITALS
Labor-Delivery Suite

adjacent to their locker facilities so that the physicians may be immediately available for patients' needs. Even in the smallest hospitals, sleeping accommodations near the labor-delivery unit should be available to attending physicians.

Dictation facilities should be located in or near the doctors' lounge.

Admitting and Preparation Various methods are used to admit maternity patients:

1. Through the main hospital admitting desk and then either to a maternity nursing unit or to a labor room in the delivery unit.

2. Directly to labor rooms in the delivery suite.

3. In an admitting and preparation unit. An admitting and preparation unit is desirable in hospitals where a large daily patient load makes it necessary, after observation, to group patients: those to be returned home, those to be sent to the nursing unit, and those to be admitted to the labor-delivery unit.

If such a unit is provided, two locations are feasible: (1) adjoining the hospital admitting area, and (2) adjacent to but not a part of the delivery suite. The first location facilitates the admitting process and permits immediate patient examination, provided the obstetrical staff is available, and it also prevents patients not in labor or those destined for isolation from entering maternity nursing areas. The second location concentrates obstetrical staff activities in a single area of the hospital and allows immediate availability of the delivery suite in emergency cases.

Labor Rooms Labor rooms should provide maximum comfort and relaxation for the patient and should have facilities for examination, preparation, and observation. Unless an admitting and preparation unit outside the labor-delivery unit is available, the patient may be admitted directly to the labor room.

Although traditional practice has permitted two or more beds in labor rooms, single occupancy rooms are recommended. They eliminate the necessity for a patient preparation room, separate infectious patients, provide greater privacy, and if in accordance with hospital policy, permit the husband to visit the patient during labor. These rooms should have a minimum floor area of 100 sq ft. Multiple occupancy rooms should have not less than 80 sq ft per bed. If only one delivery room is required, one labor room should be arranged as an emergency delivery room and should have a minimum floor area of 180 sq ft.

A toilet and lavatory for each labor room provides privacy for the ambulant patient, and reduces bedpan services; however, patient's use of the toilet should be controlled. If individual toilet rooms are not provided, a single toilet room convenient to all labor rooms will suffice.

One shower and dressing cubicle is sufficient for the labor room area. If admittance, preparation, and shower facilities are located outside the unit, the labor area shower may be omitted. Each labor room should have a lavatory with gooseneck-type spout and foot- or wrist-operated controls, soap dispenser, and paper towel dispenser for handwashing by the patient, the nurse, and the physician.

The minimum width for labor room doors is 3 ft 8 in. However, to provide for the passage of beds or stretchers, 4 ft is recommended. Each labor bed should be furnished with oxygen and suction outlets and nurses' calling stations. Controls to provide adjustment of the level of general room lighting and the bed light are desirable. Air conditioning is recom-

mended. Music, piped into each labor room and controlled at the nurses' station, may be considered for the comfort of the patient. A cut-off in each room is required.

Delivery Room In designing and equipping the delivery room, every facility for the welfare and safety of the mother and the newborn child should be incorporated. Basic considerations include the immediate availability of equipment and supplies, built-in protection against anesthetic explosion, auxiliary electrical systems in case of power failure, an adequate air-conditioning system, and finishes that promote aseptic conditions.

Space allowance for equipment and for the staff to circulate freely is a primary factor in determining the size of a delivery room. A clear floor area approximately 17 ft 6 in. square is generally large enough.

The position of the anesthesiologist in the delivery room is determined by the arrangement of the backup table in the delivery room. This table is located in the cleanest area of the delivery room, away from all traffic and opposite the entrance to the sterilizer and scrubup areas. The feet of the patient are usually located nearest the backup table with the obstetrician at that end and the anesthesiologist at the opposite end. Since most anesthesiologists are right-handed, their equipment is located on the right, and it is desirable to place the door so that the anesthesiologist's equipment can be located where it need not be moved when the patient is brought in.

The view box should be located behind the anesthesiologist so that the circulating nurse may insert or remove films and the obstetrician may observe it without turning.

It is assumed that cesarean sections will be performed in the surgical suite.

A minimum ceiling height of 9 ft is required for an obstetrical light. Additional height is advantageous and may be required for some types of lighting fixtures.

Oxygen and vacuum wall outlets should be installed near the bassinet location for use in resuscitation.

Built-in cabinets in the delivery room should be kept to a minimum and used for storage of such supplies as sutures and special instruments.

The minimum width for the delivery room door is 3 ft 8 in.; however, 4 ft is recommended since patients will often be moved to the delivery room on a labor bed.

An emergency call system, foot- or elbow-operated, must have stations in each delivery room with a dome light and buzzer in the corridor over each delivery room door and in locker rooms, lounge, nurses' station, and other such areas. A nurses' intercom system must be provided between these same areas.

Recovery Room The recovery period, after delivery, is critical and may last from 1 to 3 hours. During this period the mother requires close observation and special care by the labor-delivery nursing staff. Some hospitals insist on continuous bedside attendance during this time. Various locations may be used for patients during the recovery period: a delivery room, a labor room, a bed in the maternity nursing unit, or a recovery room used exclusively for this purpose.

The recovery room has generally been accepted as a necessary facility in the delivery suite and should be considered for any hospital requiring three or more labor beds. A recovery room provides a location for recovering patients, frees the delivery or labor room for cleanup prior to occupancy by another patient,

concentrates patients in similar condition, and facilitates the special nursing care required.

In designing the recovery room, provision should be made for easy movement of stretchers or beds. If a number of patients will be cared for, a separate entrance and an exit may be advisable. Space should be provided for a nurse's desk, an instrument cart or table, a clean supply cart, a soiled linen hamper, and a waste receptacle. The nurse's desk should be large enough for a telephone, charts, a nurses' calling station, and forms and writing material. Cubicle curtains at each stretcher location should allow clearance for attending the patient from either side. Oxygen and suction outlets and a nurses' calling station should be installed at each stretcher position. Glass view panels between the room and the corridor facilitate observation.

Nurses' Station The nurses' station is the administrative and control center of the labor-delivery unit. Its size, complexity, and location will be determined by the extent of responsibilities charged to the obstetrical supervisor as well as by the size and staffing of the suite.

If patients are admitted directly to the labor-delivery unit, the nurses' station may be responsible for admitting procedures. Inventory and requisitioning of supplies may be handled at the nurses' station, although central service would assume this responsibility under a complement system.

If office records are extensive, file cabinets may be necessary. In large units, an office for the obstetrical supervisor may be required. A bulletin board should be provided for work schedules and hospital bulletins. A desk-height counter for the master station of the nurses' calling system, medical records, and a telephone may be adequate if the daily workload is small.

Doctors' Lockers and Lounge This area should contain a locker room, a toilet and shower room, a lounge, and sleeping accommodations. If the staff is not large enough to warrant separate facilities, a toilet-shower room and combined locker-lounge-sleeping room may serve staff needs.

In hospitals with only one delivery room, a minimum of 6 lockers is recommended; in those with more than one delivery room, a minimum of 5 lockers per delivery room is recommended. The minimum size recommended for a locker is 12 by 18 by 60 in.

Space should be provided in the locker room for a cart for clean scrub suits and a hamper for soiled linen.

The lounge should accommodate a couch, chairs, bookcase, magazine table, and a television set. A recessed film illuminator should also be provided. If dictation booths are not provided, a suitable desk and chair for this purpose should be included in the lounge.

Sleeping accommodations for the attending staff should be provided. For flexibility of use by either male or female doctors, it is preferable to provide single occupancy rooms for this purpose. In addition to the bed, furnishings should include chair and night table. If only a combined locker-lounge-sleeping room is required, the couch should open to make a bed.

Scrub-up and Substerilizing Areas Hand scrubbing by the obstetrician and nurse is an essential part of delivery technique. Facilities should be next to the delivery room so that the physician can see into the delivery room through a glass view-panel while scrubbing. On the plan shown in this publication the scrub-up and substerilizing areas are combined in one room. A door between this room and the delivery room is recommended. The area used for scrubbing should be deep enough so that persons scrubbing will not interfere with traffic and so that splashed water will not constitute a hazard.

If one scrub-up area is to be used for two delivery rooms, at least three scrub sinks should be provided.

The substerilizing area should contain a high-speed washer-sterilizer for emergency sterilization or for processing instruments.

Supply and Equipment Storage *Supplies.* The main factor in determining the space allocation for supply storage in the labor-delivery unit is the method and frequency of issuing supplies from central supply areas. Supplies include all items processed by the laundry and central sterile supply and those issued from central service. Excluded are pharmacy, anesthetic, or equipment items. All supplies should be kept in hospital central service and issued to the labor-delivery unit only after the required processing.

A more recent storage method uses the same carts on which supplies are delivered from storage of clean and sterile items. Supplies used only in the delivery room are packed on one cart and those for other use on other carts. Clean supply carts may also be assigned to doctors' and nurses' locker rooms for scrub clothes and towels. This method requires a clean supply room near the delivery rooms for carts containing clean or sterile items.

Equipment Storage. Equipment that is infrequently used, such as delivery table parts and duplicate equipment not in use, should be stored in an equipment storage room in the unit. This room should have shelves for small items and floor space for larger equipment.

Medications A medication preparation room or unit should be located near labor and delivery rooms for storage and preparation of drugs, including narcotics.

Medication preparation requires uninterrupted concentration by the nurse, and an enclosure or room with glass viewing panels is suggested for this function. A work counter with storage for syringes and accessories and a sink with gooseneck-type spout and foot or wrist controls for handwashing are recommended. If stepped shelves, sized for the smaller medicine bottles, are provided, the nurse can read labels quickly and arrange medicines in the order desired. A wall cabinet is suggested for bottles of solutions, and an eye-level locked cabinet for narcotics should be furnished. Since some medicines must be maintained below room temperature, a refrigerator is also required.

Anesthesia Facilities The anesthesiologist should be consulted early in the planning stage to determine design requirements for anesthesia facilities including what gases are to be piped; the number, size, and location of gas cylinders to be stored; and space required for cleaning and checking the anesthesia equipment.

Piping oxygen and vacuum to delivery rooms and other areas of the hospital is standard practice. In some hospitals, nitrous oxide is piped to the delivery room.

A room should be provided in the unit for storing gas cylinders. Flammable gases should be stored separately from oxygen and nitrous oxide, which may be stored in any location since there are no hazards involved. Small cylinders sized to fit the anesthesia apparatus may be stored in racks. Cans of volatile liquids

may be stored on shelves in the same storage area. Shelves should be provided for equipment such as pressure gauges. Large cylinders should be stored upright in racks. Space for a gas cylinder truck or carrier may be necessary. The primary purpose of storage for these gases and volatile liquids within the unit is to assure availability over weekends and at night when main hospital supply rooms may be closed. Storage space for a 48-hour supply of gas is considered maximum, and additional storage space on the unit is not desirable.

Instrument Processing The processing of instruments includes washing, preferably in a washer-sterilizer or by hand, disassembling where necessary, arranging for future use, and sterilizing.

One of several methods may be followed for instrument processing.

1. Soiled instruments are washed in the washer-sterilizer and sent to central sterile supply for processing. The plan shown is based on this assumption.

2. Soiled instruments are sent directly to central supply for processing. The washer-sterilizer is required for emergency sterilization.

3. Processing may take place in the unit under the direction of the obstetrical supervisor. In this case a workroom is required.

Soiled Holding Room All cleanup techniques including housekeeping are originated in this area, and soiled materials are placed here for disposal or return to central sterile supply for processing. This room will require a sink with drainboards for gross cleaning, a flushing rim sink for disposal of liquid wastes, a cart for storage of cleaning materials, carts and hampers to receive soiled articles, and a waste receptacle. Germicidal solutions and utensils used in cleaning should be stored here. If placentas are saved, a domestic-type deep freeze will be required.

RADIOISOTOPE FACILITY

Suggested Plans

Plans 1 and 2 in Fig. 1 show the relationship between the workload and facilities required.

Plan 1 Plan 1 is intended for a hospital anticipating limited isotope use in which the bulk of the workload will consist of relatively simple diagnostic tests such as thyroid uptake studies and occasional therapy using iodine-131 or phosphorus-32. Intracavitary therapy with colloidal suspensions of radioisotopes is not anticipated, nor are diagnostic procedures involving organ scanning. The one-room arrangement shown on Plan 1 may be sufficient in this case. (See Fig. 1a.)

A work counter (4) with built-in sink (5) and splashback is provided. Cabinets (3) and (1) located above and below the counter, respectively, provide storage space. Isotopes are stored on the work counter at area marked (A) behind lead bricks. Note that the area of the counter reserved for the isotopes is at maximum distance from the radiation detection instruments in the room, to minimize the possi-

Radioisotope Facilities in the General Hospital, Public Health Service, Department of Health, Education, and Welfare, 1966.

bility of the radiation from the stored containers interfering with the use of these instruments. Also, the isotope area is on an outside wall and as far as possible from the corridor.

Two instruments are utilized in this plan, both of which, for the sake of economy, can be operated from the same scaler (10), mounted on a cart. However, in terms of flexibility, a separate scaler for each of the instruments might be preferable. The scintillation well counter (6) is located on the work counter, at the opposite end from the isotope storage area. The detector for thyroid uptake work (8) is used in conjunction with a patient examining table (7); both can be enclosed by a curtain (17) for patient privacy. A hook strip (18) is provided in this area for patient clothing.

The desk (12), chair (14), and filing cabinet (13) are for the use of the isotopes technician. It may be desirable to file records for patients, radiation monitoring, and isotope shipments in this area.

Because certain radioactive drugs require refrigeration, a small under-counter refrigerator might be added to this room. On the other hand, because the quantity of this heat-labile material commonly on hand in a limited isotope operation is small, the use of refrigerator space in another department, such as the clinical laboratory, might be feasible. If refrigerator space in another department is used, the radioactive material should be adequately labeled as to its radiation hazard and properly shielded before it leaves the isotope department. A third possibility would be the acquisition of one of the new miniature refrigerators, which are inexpensive, can be used on a counter top, and provide approximately 1 cu ft of interior space.

Plan 2 Plan 2 shows a two-room arrangement in which facilities are included for diagnostic scanning procedures and for occasional intracavitary therapy with radioactive phosphorus or gold, in addition to the general types of diagnostic procedures that would be done in the facilities shown in Plan 1. A larger overall isotope workload with more frequent therapy cases is also assumed. (See Fig. 1b.)

In the main room, two separate sinks are utilized. The clean sink (5) is used only for handling nonradioactive items, whereas the disposal sink (5a) is used to wash glassware contaminated with radioisotopes and to dispose of radioactive waste. To minimize contamination, the disposal sink should have an elbow or knee control.

Isotopes are stored, as in Plan 1, behind lead bricks on the work counter (4) at space marked (A). A refrigerator (15) is provided below the counter top conveniently nearby for the storage of heat-labile items, and space is also planned for a floor-type centrifuge (16) in this area.

The detector for thyroid uptake work (8) and the scintillation well counter (6) are operated in this plan from two separate scalers (10). Because of the larger volume of work, more work counter area is provided in this room than in Plan 1. The open floor space in the center of the room is larger than might be anticipated for a standard laboratory, to allow for the positioning of a patient stretcher, so that occasional intracavitary isotope therapy can be carried out here. The use of this room instead of the patient's room for intracavitary instillations has two advantages: the isotope area is more easily and safely decontaminated should spillage occur during the procedure; and movement of radioactive material through the hospital is minimized. Curtains hung from a ceiling track are used for privacy during these procedures.

The smaller room accommodates the scan-

HOSPITALS
Radioisotope Facility

LEGEND

1. Cabinets below counter.
2. Cabinets and drawer units below counter.
3. Wall cabinets.
4. Work counter.
5. Sink with foot, knee or elbow control with splashback, spout outlet mounted 5 inches above flood rim, hot and cold water.
5a. Disposal sink with foot, knee, or elbow control with splashback spout outlet mounted 5 inches above flood rim, hot and cold water.
6. Scintillation well counter.
7. Patient examination table.
8. Detector and stand.
9. Scanner.
10. Scaler mounted on cart.
11. Stretcher.
12. Desk.
13. Filing cabinet below.
14. Chair.
15. Refrigerator below counter.
16. Space for floor type centrifuge.
17. Curtain track at ceiling.
18. Hookstrip.
19. Kneespace under counter.
20. Telephone outlet.
21. Drainboard.
22. Bookshelf over desk.

"A" Space for storage of isotopes on top of the counter.

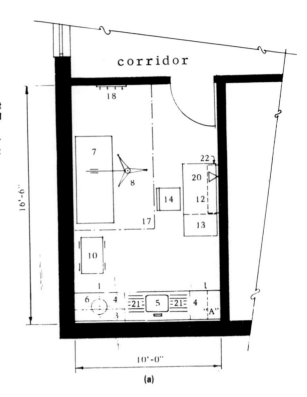

(a)

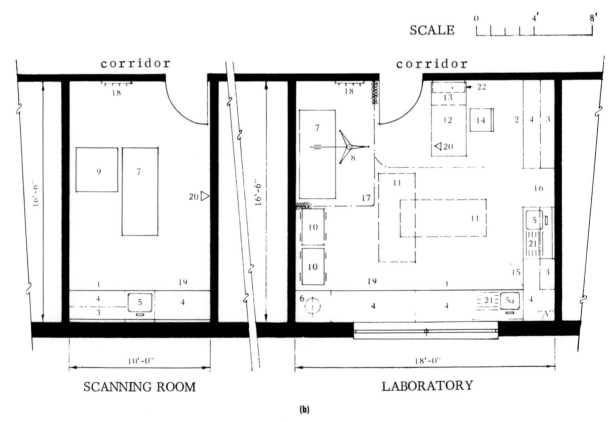

(b)

Fig. 1 (a) Plan 1: minimum radioisotope facility. (b) Plan 2: radioisotope facility with separate scanning room and laboratory.

ner (9), and the examining table (7) with which it is used. A hook strip (18) is affixed to one wall for patient clothing, and cabinets (1 and 3) are provided for storage of equipment and supplies. The sink (5) is for staff use prior to patient examination.

In the initial planning of the installation, consideration should be given to possible expansion of scanning facilities. Scanning procedures are time-consuming; as an overall guide, no more than four scans per day can be expected from each instrument. This will vary, of course, depending upon the diagnostic procedure performed. As the workload grows, a second scanning room may be required.

Hazards

There are two ways in which radioactive materials may be hazardous: First, some of their radiations present an *external* hazard to persons in their vicinity, as in the case of X-ray machines; second, when used in unsealed solution or powdered form, radioisotopes may be accidentally ingested or inhaled as a result of spillage or inexpert handling, thus becoming an *internal* hazard to personnel. Therefore, careful attention must be given to safe techniques and facilities to eliminate unintentional and potentially harmful radiation exposure to both personnel and patients when radioactive medicines are handled and administered.

Radiation Protection

In designing and constructing radioisotope facilities, the possibility of both external and internal hazards must be considered. To protect personnel against the radiation from *externally* located radioactive materials, *shielding,* usually made of lead, should be provided where necessary. In most instances, simple lead bricks arranged around radioisotope containers provide sufficient shielding. The most important factor in protection against the *internal* hazards of radioactive materials is the prevention of their ingestion or inhalation through safe operating techniques. The use of these techniques can be encouraged by providing facilities in the design of the radioisotope installation which lend themselves to safe working procedures. For example, smooth, nonporous counter tops and sinks should be provided to facilitate the cleanup of accidental spills.

Location

From the standpoint of safety and control, it is usually preferable that the hospital designate one department for radioisotope handling rather than allow all departments to administer radioisotopes to patients. In many hospitals, the radiology department is in charge of radioisotopes. If the radioisotope unit is located near its parent department, operations are facilitated because this allows for the efficient overlapping of staff duties and permits the sharing of examination and waiting rooms. Thus the location of the radioisotope unit will be dependent to some degree upon the location of the department that assumes responsibility for it.

Other factors will also influence location. For example, because many patients receiving diagnostic doses of radioisotopes will be handled on an outpatient basis, the radioisotope facility should provide convenient access from the street or elevators. Furthermore, locating the radioisotope facility at an exterior corner or corridor end permits the control of traffic.

OUTPATIENT ACTIVITY

Because physical medicine in the Outpatient Activity is used by both inpatients and outpatients, it is situated for the convenience and accessibility of both types of patients. Patients arriving at the Emergency Activity are evaluated (triage), and appropriate disposition is made of each case. The surgical suite is located close to the Emergency Activity to ensure the most rapid conveyance of a patient in a life-threatening situation. Cardiac arrest patients will receive immediate treatment by the code blue alert team within the Emergency Activity. After the crisis, the patient will be transferred to an adjoining intensive coronary care unit.

Since patients entering the Emergency Activity are frequently assigned elsewhere, close working relationships should exist with other areas of the hospital such as the surgical suite, intensive care units, and the main X-ray department.

Some additional working relationships between the Outpatient Activity and other hospital services are indicated in Fig. 1. Since these do not require immediate adjacency, they assume less importance on the relative scale of values established by either the overall planners or the designer.

Intradepartmental Relationships

Although the program of functions may delineate certain specific constraints and preferences as to disposition of the elements of an Outpatient Activity, the final outcome often is a compromise that represents the best acceptable solution to all parties concerned. (See Figs. 2 and 3.)

In one example, elements of the Outpatient Activity are arranged along the main circulation route. Since considerable traffic is expected, this corridor is 10 ft wide and forms the spine of the scheme. Branch corridors, each 8 ft wide, which separate other elements from each other, originate from the spine and provide access for people and goods to respective elements.

Since new patients do not know locations of the various clinics, some method must be devised to assist them. The architect can help by incorporating into the physical design a simple, easily understood system of signs. They might be either wall-mounted or incorporated into the floor surface, adding what can be an exciting physical design element to relieve the monotony of a long hospital corridor.

Becoming oriented within a modern hospital can be difficult even for a well person and especially confusing to a patient who is debilitated. Ability to control the internal environment has resulted in many windowless spaces in a hospital which are interconnected by a maze of corridors, especially in the diagnostic and treatment areas. To help resolve the orientation problem, specialty clinics (except pediatric) are grouped in one area. The pediatric clinic is in close proximity to the entrance to reduce travel distance for the mother carrying an infant.

The control and administration or business office should be the primary contact between the patient and the institution. This is the point of origin of the service where disposition is made as to what is appropriate for the patient.

The two categories of outpatients are: (a) new

Guidelines to Functional Programing, Equipping, and Designing Hospital Outpatient & Emergency Activities, DHEW Publication No. (HRA) 77-4002, U.S. Department of Health, Education, and Welfare, Washington, D.C., 1977.

patients for whom admission records and other documentation must be prepared and (b) repeat patients whose documentation is on file.

Administration

All patients enter the facility through a vestibule which provides protection from inclement weather. They are greeted by a control officer in the business office who has an overview of all incoming people and orients patients to processing. (See Fig. 12.)

Admitting On the first visit, the patient is directed to one of the admitting interview cubicles which form an integral part of the business office. On completion of the admitting procedure, a clerk summons a messenger whose station, which should be large enough to store wheelchairs, is adjacent and connected to the business office. He [she] escorts the patient directly to the intake screening center or, if it is fully occupied, to the public waiting area.

The repeat patient who has an appointment to a specific clinic stops at the check-in station where he [she] receives instruction. He [she] may go directly to the clinic or wait in the public waiting space until notified by the control officer. (The business office is responsible for checking patients in and out and for collecting fees, if applicable.)

Despite rigorous efforts and best intentions in establishing schedules and appointments, delays due to unforeseen circumstances will occur. Hence, patients and family members must be afforded an appropriate waiting place also needed by patients awaiting prescriptions issued from the pharmacy dispensary. This suggests that the dispensary be directly accessible from the public waiting area and that visual signals be installed near the issue windows indicating when the prescription is ready.

All patients, upon completing their visit, report to the check-out station where they are issued instructions for a repeat visit, if necessary. The architectural design accommodates these requirements.

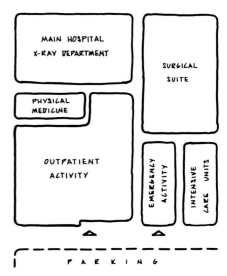

INTERDEPARTMENTAL RELATIONSHIP SCHEME

Fig. 1 This diagram illustrates graphically one design solution

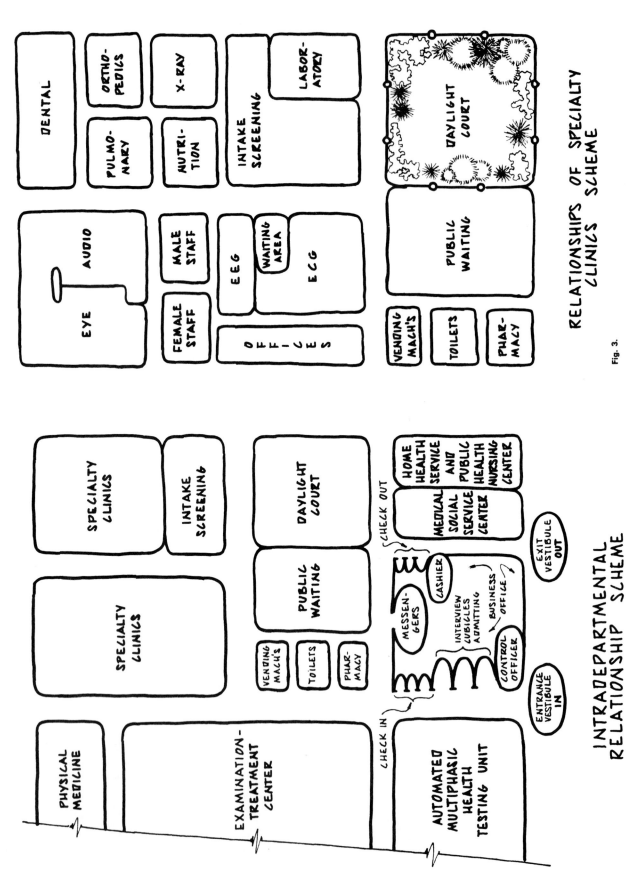

RELATIONSHIPS OF SPECIALTY CLINICS SCHEME

Fig. 3.

INTRADEPARTMENTAL RELATIONSHIP SCHEME

Fig. 2.

Medical Record Unit The medical record room is strategically placed near the business office and adjacent to the examination-treatment center for easy access. It is served by a pneumatic tube station and messenger service.

Medical Social Service Center An important outpatient service is health education and follow-up care that may extend into the patient's home. The center provides a base of operations for medical social service for evaluation and future follow-up, if indicated. The follow-up extends patient care into home and community.

A large multipurpose room is provided for large-group health education. Conveniently placed near the entrance, it can be used when the rest of the Outpatient Activity is closed.

Home Health and Public Health Nursing Center Adjacent and interconnected to medical social service is the home health and public health nursing center. Both have reception and patient sub-waiting areas.

Specialty Clinics

Adjacent to both the Administration and the Examination and Treatment Center are the clinics designed and equipped for special procedures. (See Figs. 2 and 3; see also Fig. 11.)

All new patients pass through the intake screening center where medical evaluation and disposition are made regarding subsequent medical treatment. Medical history and documentation are initiated and routine laboratory testing performed. Therefore, provision must be made for separate specimen collection spaces for men and women, a routine testing laboratory, and a sub-waiting area with a registered nurse in attendance. Appropriate spaces and fixtures are provided for handicapped persons.

The laboratory and x-ray unit will serve the Outpatient and Emergency Activities. The laboratory, with pass-through windows for specimens, will use pneumatic tubes for forwarding specimens to the main hospital's laboratory. An x-ray unit

for diagnostic purposes should be large enough to accommodate stretcher patients.

Patients requiring extensive diagnostic tests can be referred to the main hospital's radiology department and pathological and pulmonary function laboratories.

While the EEG and ECG clinics are located within the Outpatient Activity, they serve the entire hospital.

Examination-Treatment Center

A large portion of outpatient workload will be handled in the examination-treatment center rather than in the specialty clinics. Hence, a waiting room with public conveniences is provided. The layout of the center, Fig. 4, was called for by the program of functions which designates three work components herein called clusters. Each cluster consisting of ten examination-treatment rooms surrounds its own central utility work space designated as a personnel corridor. (See Fig. 5.) Other configurations may be equally appropriate.

In the first phase, 30 examination-treatment rooms are provided. Future expansion to add 30 rooms must, of necessity, be linear along the utility work space. This corridor must be limited in length to approximately 100 ft because experience shows greater distance to be undesirable. All the examination-treatment rooms are accessible from a system of patients' corridors stemming from the waiting room. In addition, personnel corridors are accessible from the outside corridor.

With the exception of general and special surgery, proctology, and urology, all examination rooms are similar in size and design.

No special provision is made for patient disrobing since either a ceiling track curtain or a folding screen may be used. It is assumed that the physician examines one patient while another undresses in an adjacent examination room. In most cases, allocation of two or more examination rooms per physician allows economic use of his [her] time.

The following scheme will apply throughout:

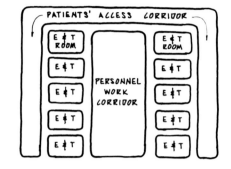

EXAMINATION-TREATMENT CENTER INDIVIDUAL CLUSTER SCHEME

Fig. 5.

- Each examination room will have not less than 80 net sq ft of usable floor area. Rooms also used for treatment shall not have less than 120 net sq ft of usable floor space.
- Examination or treatment tables are to be accessible on three sides allowing for working space of not less than 30 in clear on each side.
- Handwashing facilities for attending staff must be provided.

The clinics of the center are grouped by similarities of medical specialties. All are identically equipped except those listed below which have individual needs:

General and special surgery	Metabolic
Proctology	Neurology
Urology	Allergy-
Diabetic	Dermatology
	Cardiovascular

See also Fig. 9, for specific equipment recommendations.

Physical Medicine and Rehabilitation

This unit which incorporates physical and occupational therapy, although an integral part of outpatient service, is a separate entity. Serving both outpatients and inpatients, the unit's location may cause somewhat of a dilemma. In the scheme illustrated in the example (Fig. 6), it is clearly identifiable and its functions are administered by unit personnel.

The services provided reflect the functional programing requirements rather than what this department should or should not be. Other programs could include a prosthesis workshop, fitting rooms, and multidiscipline conference rooms, among others. That every individual situation or program requires an individual planning solution to meet specific local needs cannot be overemphasized.

Although an element of outpatient service, Physical Medicine and Rehabilitation (PM&R) also serves the inpatient hospital population. Accessibility from outside as well as from inside the hospital without impeding outpatient services requires the designer's special consideration.

PM&R consists of two principal elements: physical therapy and occupational therapy. While these activities are subject to interpretation, the elements and equipment provided are expected to constitute a comprehensive approach to the normally recognized concept of an Occupational Therapy Department. The two departments are

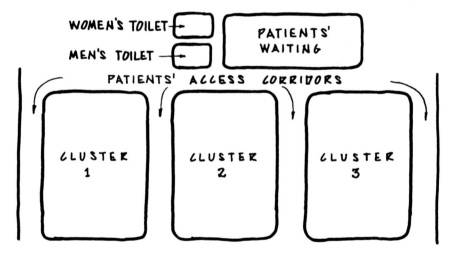

EXAMINATION-TREATMENT CENTER RELATIONSHIP SCHEME

Fig. 4.

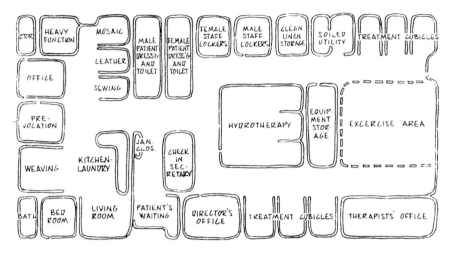

PHYSICAL MEDICINE AND REHABILITATION
RELATIONSHIP SCHEME

Fig. 6

adjacent but separate with their own staffs; administration and control may be shared. Figure 6 illustrates the relationships between individual spaces within the departments and reasons for them as understood by an architect.

PM&R is under the physiatrist-director whose office is accessible from the outside corridor, the secretary's office, and from within the department, thus facilitating overall supervisory duties.

Special attention is given to the fact that many patients are physically incapacitated and use prosthetic appliances or wheelchairs. Some inpatients may be brought in on stretchers. Therefore, corridors are a minimum of 6 ft wide. Wheelchair patients are provided special plumbing fixtures, drinking fountains, and large cubicles for dressing and undressing.

Corridor wall handrails are controversial. Those against maintain that patients should learn to be independent and not have handrails. Those for believe that the weak, uncertain patient needs assistance which he [she] can ignore later. Because patients in PM&R should be under continuous supervision or attended by staff, the decision must be made by the institution. To be a useful aid for handicapped persons, the handrail must be designed to meet the users' anthropometric requirements. It must be substantial, offset from the wall, and well secured to prevent anchorage failure and possible injury.

Opinions differ regarding provision of a tank in hydrotherapy for total immersion of the patient's body. Some authorities recommend elimination of the tank. Others advocate provision of a swimming pool. Obviously, the latter cost implications are so great that the issue can only be resolved by each individual program.

Hydrotherapy produces a large volume of soiled wet linen which is often overlooked or given insufficient recognition. Adequate provision should be made either for collecting, temporarily holding, and transporting this linen to the hospital laundry or for processing in the physical medicine department.

The spaces indicated in Fig. 6 accommodate the equipment recommended (see Fig. 10). The physical therapy entity is based on the racetrack corridor principle, facilitating movement of people and equipment from one part of the facility to another. Wet activities such as hydrotherapy are purposefully placed in an enclosed room. The exercise area is placed apart from other activities to help preserve patients' dignity and alleviate their apprehension and self-consciousness as they try to regain their previous mobility or agility.

The Occupational Therapy Department shares some facilities with the physical therapy entity. These are control-administration and patients' dressing and toilet facilities. Unless the function of a particular space dictated that it be enclosed, the PM&R facility should be as open as possible which facilitates needed visual supervision. For example, windows are provided in room 27 [Fig. 10]—the heavy function activities area—to enclose noise and airborne particles, yet allow visual observation.

Automated Multiphasic Health Testing Unit

Multiphasic health testing or multiphasic screening is a system which involves collecting, organizing, storing, and presenting medical data for the purpose of detecting body malfunctions before symptoms become obvious. Thus, the physician is enabled to initiate early treatment.

This type of service involving multiple tests is in a developing stage. The example presented in this publication, therefore, should be evaluated carefully against local clinical and diagnostic requirements.

The tests are similar to but more extensive than those usually given by an internist or a general practitioner during a complete physical examination. Multiphasic testing differs in that it is systematized and automated with maximum reliance on electronic recording instruments; the tests, in most cases, can be administered by a technician rather than by a medical practitioner. An electronic technician must be available to ensure that the electronic and mechanical instruments are functioning properly and recording the results. Operating personnel must understand how the instrumentation works. Only with the use of automated methods are testing programs designed for large population groups economically feasible.

Automated instrument packages are of three types: (1) instruments that either come in contact physically with the patient or scan and record a function, such as vision; (2) laboratory test instruments used on samples taken from the patient; and (3) interpretive instruments or computer hardware.

Tests should be grouped so that they will be carried out expeditiously. Careful grouping minimizes the feeling by patients that they are on an assembly line. However, the more tests given at one component, the greater the operator skill required. Furthermore, if it takes twice as long to go through a component, the number of parallel stations must be doubled to maintain the patient flow rate. Thus, test equipment must be duplicated.

Generating the individual medical report is the primary function of multiphasic screening. The report will convey to the physician all information gathered during the examinations. This is the rationale for using electronic data processing for large volume operations in the storage, analysis, and retrieval of test information. The ultimate goal is to have all results automatically fed into a computer so that immediately after the testing is completed all subsequent diagnostic procedures may be scheduled. Many instruments used do not have this capability and many tests require manual processing or visual observation reporting.

Data processing should, therefore, be incorporated only after careful analysis and justification. Use of semiautomated procedures frequently must be considered. Card forms may be designed that can accept pencil entry of all clinical data. A mark-sense document reader may serve as one type of data entry terminal to the computer. Of course, data entry keyboards may be used for manual input of data as well as automated instrument input of test results.

The Automated Multiphasic Health Testing Unit described in the pro forma example (Fig. 8) is located near the entrance so it may be used and operated separately from the other clinics and on a different time schedule, if desired, or even omitted. It is incorporated in the Outpatient Activity to illustrate one aspect of preventive medicine.

A self-contained entity having its own supportive staff and resources capable of acting independently, the unit is related organizationally to the overall outpatient service. Patient flow through the facility should be expeditious with no backtracking. The clinic is oversized in anticipation of future increases in the number of patients.

The health evaluation procedures and tests are carried out at test stations or rooms; they follow a definite established sequence as shown in the pro forma example. The sequence and timing have special importance for medical reasons. An example is the time interval that must elapse between administration of drops for pupil dilation and the eye examination.

Opinions vary as to the time interval required for certain tests. Therefore, the tests which take place between critical events must be fitted in according to individual situations encountered. No universal rule can be established regarding the number of testing stations or their sequence.

Figure 7 illustrates the sequence of events. Patients arrive at the reception registration area, A-1 (in Fig. 8), which is large enough to accommodate several people. Following admitting procedures, they take glucose in space A-2 and proceed to A-3 to execute their medical history. Afterwards they go to their respective locker rooms (A-5 for women and A-13 for men) and change into a hospital gown, depositing street clothing in lockable lockers. The next station is A-8 where tests are performed for audio and visual acuity.

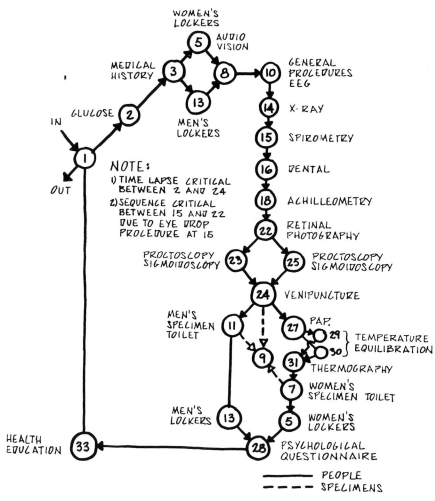

Fig. 7. Automated multiphasic health-testing sequence.

The next stop is A-10, general procedures room, which also accommodates two ECG testing stations. The next stations are A-14 for chest x-ray and A-15 for spirometry. Eye drops are also administered at A-15. A subwaiting area, A-17, is an alcove where patients may wait when delays occur between tests without obstructing corridor traffic. The next stations are dental examination, A-16; achilleometry, A-18; retinal photography, A-22, where eye examinations, including tonometry, are performed. Sufficient time has elapsed between administration of the eye drops at A-15 for the fundus photo to be performed.

The next station (either A-23 or A-25) is where proctoscopy and sigmoidoscopy (i.e., endoscopic) examinations are performed. Both rooms have toilet facilities. A-24 accommodates venipuncture where blood samples are drawn. (The elapse of a prescribed time period is essential from the time of glucose ingestion in A-2 to venipuncture in A-24. This pro forma example requires 2 hours for this procedure, with a ±15-minute deviation.)

After A-24, the flow of patients divides. Men, after providing specimens, go to locker room A-13 to don street clothing. A specimen toilet is provided for each sex. Each toilet is provided with a pass-through window to room A-9 which is a laboratory pick-up station. Specimens are collected from patients and transferred by messenger to the main hospital laboratory for processing. Women, after leaving A-24, proceed to the Papanicolaou smear examination room, A-27, through temperature equilization rooms, A-29 or A-30, for the thermography examination in A-31. After completion of these procedures, they give their specimens at A-7, and go to the locker room, A-5, to dress. All patients are required to fill out the psychological questionnaire in A-28. Round-table discussions on health education are conducted by staff in A-33. The screening process ends in A-1 where the receptionist/registrar checks out the patient.

The facility has a storeroom, A-12, for general and medical supplies. A lounge room, A-19, and record storage room, A-32, are provided for the automated multiphasic health testing unit staff; staff toilets for both sexes, A-20 and A-21, are also provided. There is a director's office, A-4, and chief nurse's office, A-6, and a janitor's closet, A-26. All designated spaces or rooms are provided with the necessary furniture and equipment to carry out medical and administrative tasks.

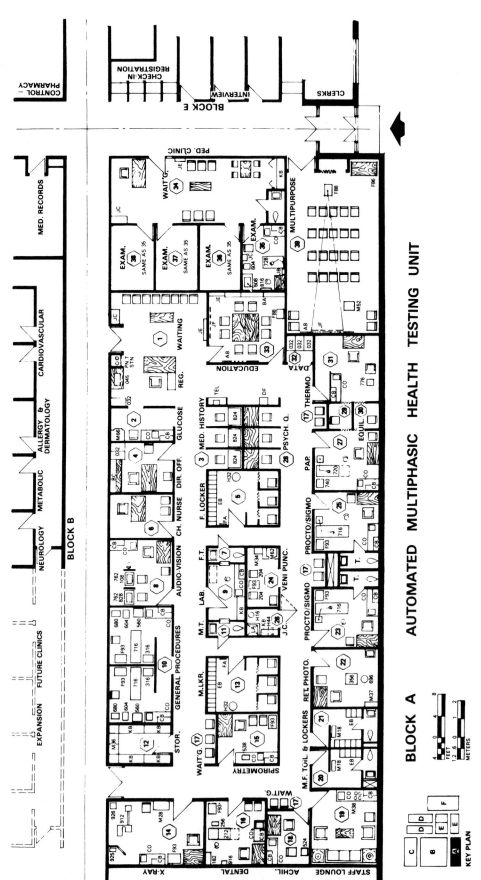

Fig. 8.

BLOCK A   AUTOMATED MULTIPHASIC HEALTH TESTING UNIT

Equipment Legend for Fig. 8

Nonmedical Equipment—Fixed

AB	Board, chalk
BC	Bookcase
CB	Cabinet, storage
CO	Counters
DF	Drinking Fountain
EB	Lockers, clothes
FA	Mirror
JB	Chart rack
JC	Clothes rack
JE	Rack, magazine
JF	Screen projection
KB	Shelving, supply
LA	Receptor, floor

Nonmedical Equipment—Movable

F-86	Table, folding
F-88	Table, projection
F-93	Table, utility
H-16	Bucket, mopping
H-32	Hamper, linen
H-44	Vacuum cleaner
M-18	Bench
M-28	Cabinet, film filing
M-34	Cabinet
M-36	Cabinet, storage
M-37	Cabinet, storage
M-52	Podium
M-62	Refrigerator
M-66	Refrigerator
O-32	Cabinet, filing
O-45	Computer terminal

Medical Equipment

108	Audiometer
182	Cabinet, dental
204	Chair, blood-drawing
212	Dental chair
256	Dental unit, complete with light
316	Electrocardiograph
356	Fundus Camera, complete with table
524	Photomograph [sic]
538	Pulmonary function screener
560	Pulse Monitor
604	Scale
608	Scale, infant
680	Stool, foot
696	Stool, adjustable
716	Table, examining and treatment
720	Table, examining and treatment
728	Table, examining
740	Table, instrument
762	Table, vision testing and audiometer
776	Thermography unit
816	Viewer, X-ray
824	Visual display console
828	Vision tester
912	X-ray, chest unit
916	Dental X-ray
925	X-ray, generator, control
926	X-ray, generator, transformer

HOSPITALS

Outpatient Activity

Fig. 9

Equipment Legend for Fig. 9

Nonmedical Equipment—Fixed

AA	Board, bulletin
BC	Bookcase
BD	Cabinet
CA	Cabinet
CO	Counter
CP	Counters with sink
DF	Drinking Fountain
EA	Lavatory
JC	Rack, clothes
JE	Rack, magazine
KB	Shelf, storage
LA	Receptor, floor

Nonmedical Equipment—Movable

F-12	Bed, single
F-21	Chair, two-seat base unit
F-24	Chair, three-seat base unit
F-27	Chair, four-seat base unit
F-33	Chair, plastic shell
F-42	Chair, straight
F-45	Chair, swivel
F-66	Sofa
O-28	Cabinet, filing
O-36	Cabinet, filing
H-16	Bucket, mopping
H-20	Cart, housekeeping
H-36	Machine, floor maintenance
H-44	Vacuum cleaner
M-30	Cabinet
M-36	Cabinet, storage
M-66	Refrigerator

Medical Equipment

132	Basal metabolism, apparatus
140	Bed, hospital
168	Sphygmomanometer
192	Cart, surgical
228	Chair, specialist
280	Diagnostic Set
316	Electrocardiograph
320	Electroencephalograph
384	Kickbucket
404	Lamp, table
416	Light, operating
604	Scale
660	Stand, Mayo
680	Stool, foot
688	Stool, operator
720	Table, examining and treatment
744	Table, operating, minor
756	Table, proctologic
760	Table, urological
816	Viewer, X-ray

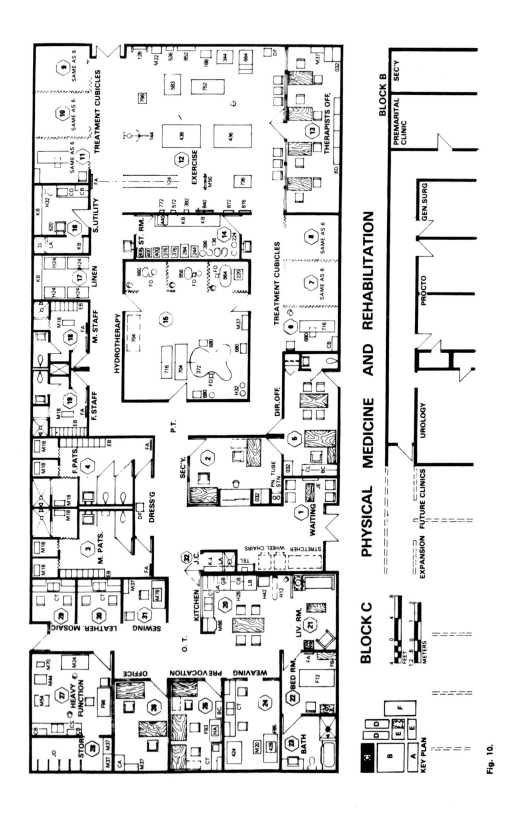

Fig. 10.

Equipment Legend for Fig. 10

Nonmedical Equipment—Fixed

BC	Bookcase
BD	Bookcase
CA	Cabinet, filing
CB	Cabinet, storage
CL	Counter
CO	Counters
CS	Counters with sink
CT	Counters
DF	Drinking Fountain
EB	Lockers, clothes
FA	Mirror
GA	Oven, (range) floor, electric
GB	Oven, wall, electric
HA	Printing press
JC	Clothes rack
JD	Rack, wall for lumber, storage
JE	Rack, magazine
KB	Shelving, supply
LA	Receptor, floor
LB	Washer

Nonmedical Equipment—Movable

F-12	Bed	M-18	Bench, locker
F-15	Chair, easy	M-20	Bench, loom
F-64	Dresser	M-22	Bench, stall bar
F-66	Sofa, 3-seater	M-24	Bench, work with vises
F-85	Table, loom	M-37	Cabinet, storage
F-93	Table, utility	M-44	Kiln, electric
F-96	Table, work	M-50	Mirror, movable
H-12	Board, ironing	M-54	Potter's wheel
H-24	Cart, linen	M-66	Refrigerator-freezer
H-28	Dryer, front loader	M-70	Sander, electric
H-32	Hamper, linen	M-78	Sewing machine
H-42	Tray, laundry	O-32	Cabinet, filing

Medical Equipment

124	Bars, parallel	572	Rack, dumbbell
128	Bars, stall	583	Restorator
136	Bath, paraffin	620	Sink, clinical
144	Bicycle	664	Stairs, exercise
188	Cart, weight plates	680	Stool, foot
220	Chair, therapy	704	Stretcher, adjustable
224	Chair, arm and hand whirlpool	716	Table, examining and treat-
244	Cold therapy unit		ment
284	Diathermy	736	Table, hand, wrist, and forearm
344	Exercise unit	752	Table, standing, tilt
372	Hubbard and wading tank	772	Tensiometer
376	Hydrocollator	796	Traction machine
392	Ladder, shoulder	808	Ultrasonic treatment unit
396	Lamp, infrared	840	Wheel, shoulder
400	Lamp, ultraviolet	852	Weight, chest pulley
424	Loom, floor, rug	856	Whirlpool, arm (fixed tank)
428	Loom, table	860	Whirlpool, arm (movable tank)
436	Mat, exercise	864	Whirlpool, arm, leg, hip
440	Medcolator	872	Wrist, machine
536	Pulley, weight	876	Wrist, roll

HOSPITALS
Outpatient Activity

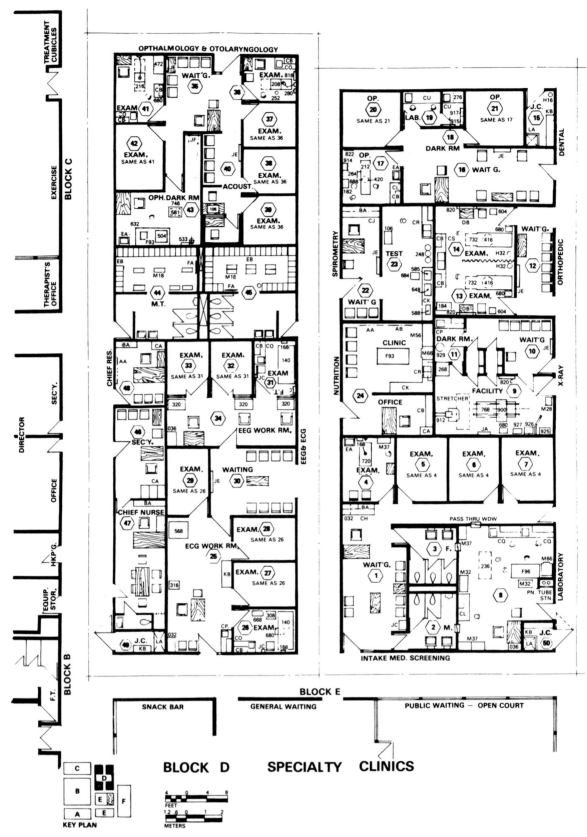

BLOCK D   SPECIALTY CLINICS

KEY PLAN

Fig. 11.

Equipment Legend for Fig. 11

Nonmedical Equipment—Fixed

AA	Board, bulletin	CT	Counter
AB	Board, chalk	CU	Counter
BA	Bookcase, built-in, open shelving	DB	Desk
CA	Cabinet, filing	EA	Lavatory
CB	Cabinet, storage	EB	Locker
CH	Counter	FA	Mirror
CK	Counter	JA	Rack, apron and glove
CL	Counter	JC	Rack, clothes
CO	Counter with inset sink	JE	Rack, magazine
CP	Counter with inset sink	JF	Screen, projection
CQ	Counter	KB	Shelving, supply
CR	Counter	LA	Receptor, floor
CS	Counter		

Nonmedical Equipment—Movable

F-93	Table, utility	M-32	Cabinet, cart
F-96	Table, work	M-37	Cabinet, storage
H-16	Bucket, mopping	M-56	Range, oven
H-32	Hamper, linen	M-66	Refrigerator
M-12	Basket, waste	O-32	Cabinet, filing
M-18	Bench	O-36	Cabinet, filing
M-28	Cabinet, film filing		

Medical Equipment

106	Analyzer, blood, gas and pH	581	Refractor, acuity
108	Audiometer	585	Recorder, pulmonary function
140	Bed, hospital	588	Respirometer
168	Blood pressure device	604	Scale
182	Cabinet, dental	632	Lamp, slit
184	Cart, orthopedic supply	648	Spirometer
208	Chair, examining	660	Stand, Mayo
212	Chair, dental	668	Step assembly
216	Chair, ophthalmic	680	Stool, foot
236	Clinical analyzer, automatic	684	Stool, high support unit
248	Compressed gas cylinder carrier	688	Stool, operator
252	Cuspidor unit	720	Table, examining
264	Dental unit	732	Table, fracture
268	Developer, film, automatic	746	Table, instrument, adjustable, ocular
276	Processing tank	768	Table, X-ray
280	Diagnostic set	816	Viewer, X-ray
308	Electrocardiograph	820	Viewer, X-ray
316	Electrocardiograph	900	Tube, X-ray
320	Electroencephalograph, complete with cabinet	912	Chest unit, X-ray, automatic
		914	X-ray, dental
340	Emergency drug cabinet	915	Film, hanger, dental X-ray
416	Light, examining	917	Rack, film dryer
420	Light, dental	925	Generator, control, X-ray
472	Ophthalmic instrument stand	926	Transformer, X-ray
504	Perimeter	927	Power module, X-ray
533	Projector, acuity complete with slides	929	Tank, replenisher
568	Recorder, physiological		

HOSPITALS
Outpatient Activity

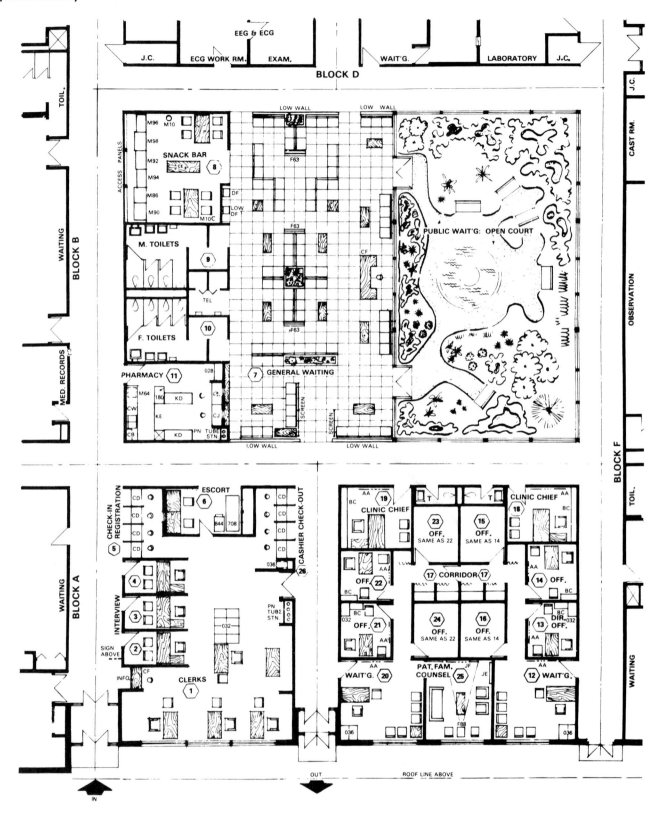

KEY PLAN

BLOCK E   ADMINISTRATION

FEET

METERS

Fig. 12.

526

Equipment Legend for Fig. 12

Nonmedical Equipment—Fixed

AA	Board, bulletin
BC	Bookcase
CB	Cabinet, storage
CD	Counter, check-in stations
CE	Counter, stand-up
CF	Counter
CJ	Counter, issue
CW	Counter, work
DF	Drinking fountain
JE	Rack, magazine
JF	Screen, projection
KD	Shelf, supply
KE	Shelf, supply

Medical Equipment

180	Cabinet, filing, patient medication
708	Stretcher
844	Wheelchair

Nonmedical Equipment—Movable

F-63	Rack, magazine
F-88	Table, projection
M-10	Basket, waste
M-32	Cabinet, cart
M-64	Refrigerator, undercounter
M-86	Vending machines, cold beverages
M-90	Vending machines, hot beverages
M-92	Vending machines, candy, assorted
M-94	Vending machines, desserts, assorted pastry
M-96	Vending machines, food items, hot canned foods
M-98	Vending machines, food items, sandwiches, pies, milk, refrigerated
O-28	Cabinet, filing
O-32	Cabinet, filing
O-36	Cabinet, filing

Health

HOSPITALS
Emergency Activity

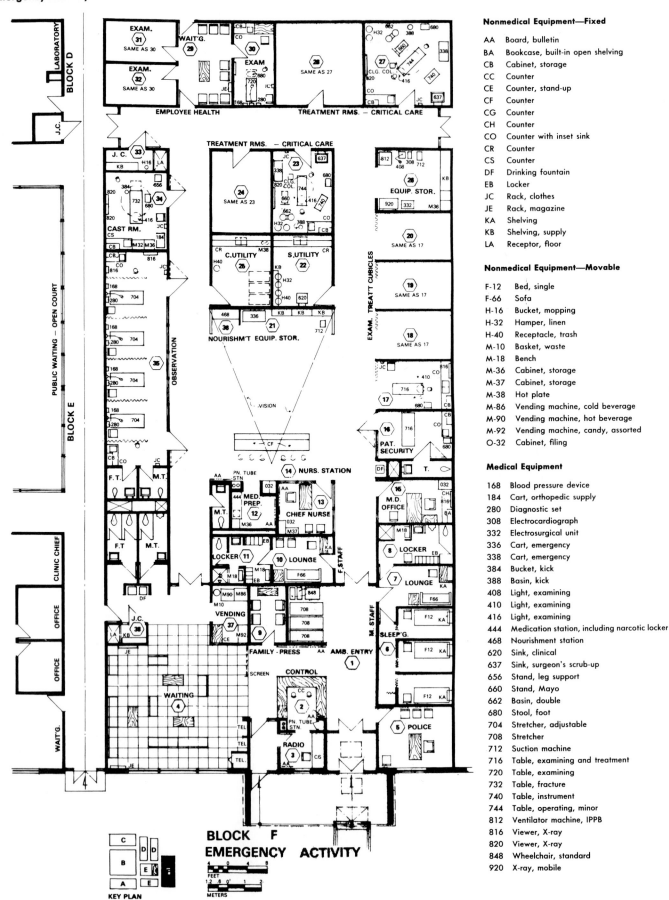

Fig. 1.

Nonmedical Equipment—Fixed

AA	Board, bulletin
BA	Bookcase, built-in open shelving
CB	Cabinet, storage
CC	Counter
CE	Counter, stand-up
CF	Counter
CG	Counter
CH	Counter
CO	Counter with inset sink
CR	Counter
CS	Counter
DF	Drinking fountain
EB	Locker
JC	Rack, clothes
JE	Rack, magazine
KA	Shelving
KB	Shelving, supply
LA	Receptor, floor

Nonmedical Equipment—Movable

F-12	Bed, single
F-66	Sofa
H-16	Bucket, mopping
H-32	Hamper, linen
H-40	Receptacle, trash
M-10	Basket, waste
M-18	Bench
M-36	Cabinet, storage
M-37	Cabinet, storage
M-38	Hot plate
M-86	Vending machine, cold beverage
M-90	Vending machine, hot beverage
M-92	Vending machine, candy, assorted
O-32	Cabinet, filing

Medical Equipment

168	Blood pressure device
184	Cart, orthopedic supply
280	Diagnostic set
308	Electrocardiograph
332	Electrosurgical unit
336	Cart, emergency
338	Cart, emergency
384	Bucket, kick
388	Basin, kick
408	Light, examining
410	Light, examining
416	Light, examining
444	Medication station, including narcotic locker
468	Nourishment station
620	Sink, clinical
637	Sink, surgeon's scrub-up
656	Stand, leg support
660	Stand, Mayo
662	Basin, double
680	Stool, foot
704	Stretcher, adjustable
708	Stretcher
712	Suction machine
716	Table, examining and treatment
720	Table, examining
732	Table, fracture
740	Table, instrument
744	Table, operating, minor
812	Ventilator machine, IPPB
816	Viewer, X-ray
820	Viewer, X-ray
848	Wheelchair, standard
920	X-ray, mobile

EMERGENCY ACTIVITY

In planning the Emergency Activity, particular attention must be paid to movements of people (patients and staff) and material (equipment and supplies). The first priority, of course, must be the movement of those patients who require immediate or urgent medical attention and the responding members of the medical staff. The time factor in terms of minutes can make the difference between life and death. All necessary equipment and lifesaving apparatus must be located in designated spaces so as not to impede the movement of staff yet be readily accessible when needed.

According to the pro forma example (Fig. 1), the Emergency Activity is intended to be a casualty center offering services 24 hours per day. Medical, surgical, and nursing services as well as first aid are provided. A main premise is that dignity of patients and their families will be respected and protected at all times. During the early years, about 35,000 visits annually are expected which will rise to 50,000 in about ten years. Supportive services such as laboratory, diagnostic x-ray, electrocardiographic and pulmonary function facilities will be located at the boundary between the Emergency and Outpatient Activities, assuring easy access to both.

The Emergency Activity should be located on the ground floor to ensure easy access for patients arriving by ambulance or auto. A separate entry for walk-in patients is required. These entrances, which are separate from the Outpatient Activity, must be easily identifiable, protected from inclement weather, and accessible to handicapped patients. The emergency facility also must be easily accessible from the hospital to patients and to the house staff performing their routine duties or being summoned for consultation or emergency action.

Intradepartmental Relationships

Since they share some supportive facilities, the emergency and outpatient facilities are adjacent to each other. Good planning practice requires that the Emergency Activity be easily accessible to the hospital's surgical suite, coronary intensive care unit, and the primary radiological facilities. (See Fig. 1.)

The relationships within any Emergency Activity may be arranged according to individual preference and needs. The following should be considered for any complete emergency activity:

Public Sector Areas
- Entrance for patients arriving by ambulance, other modes of transportation, or conveyances
- Entrance for walk-in patients
- Control station
- Public waiting space with appropriate public amenities

Treatment Facilities
- Patients' observation room
- Treatment cubicles
- Examination rooms
- Cast room
- Critical care rooms

An Emergency Activity may also include a patient's security room and areas providing supportive services and staff accommodations.

Guidelines to Functional Programing, Equipping, and Designing Hospital Outpatient & Emergency Activities, DHEW Publication No. (HRA) 77-4002, U.S. Department of Health, Education, and Welfare, Washington, D.C., 1977.

Figure 2 is a graphic interpretation showing space relationships. As stated earlier, the first priority is the movement of patients requiring immediate medical attention. The patient brought by ambulance is conveyed on the ambulance stretcher directly to either a treatment cubicle or to a critical care room. An alcove holds stretchers and wheelchairs for patients arriving by vehicles. If the situation requires use of an operating room, the patient is admitted administratively to the Emergency Activity and conveyed through the door by the critical care room to the surgical suite.

Public Sector Area The admitting procedure is accomplished at the control center either by a family member or another individual accompanying the patient. The walk-in patient enters through the vestibule left of the control center and registers for admission at the center. Afterwards he may be asked to wait until called in public waiting space with his escort or family member. Admitting personnel exercise their medical judgments in each case as to the degree of medical urgency

and, if necessary, request a physician to make a disposition. In some cases, the patient may be referred to the adjacent Outpatient Activity.

The control center is placed strategically to provide visual control of all incoming traffic and observation of the public waiting area so personnel may be aware of any medical emergency that may arise there. Near the entrance, the control center has an external window so an approaching ambulance may be observed. Vestibules to eliminate drafts at the entrances provide a certain amount of comfort for control center personnel. The center could be enclosed with a glazed partition but, although transparent, it is perceived by patients as a physical barrier. The counter at the control center also serves as a barrier against cold drafts. It must be emphasized that the response the patient receives at admission leaves lasting impressions. Thus, special attention should be given to provide an atmosphere of professional competency.

The radio room, incorporated with the control center, serves as a communication link with ambulance crews or rescue units in the community. The

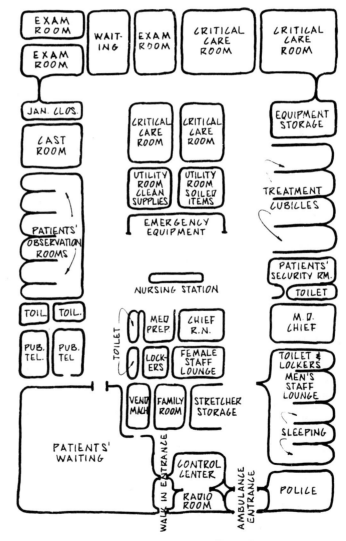

EMERGENCY ACTIVITY
INTRADEPARTMENTAL RELATIONSHIP SCHEME

Fig. 2.

529

police room may also be used by reporters and attorneys. Immediate members of the family may retire to the family room pending the outcome of medical intervention involving a life-threatening situation of a patient; here, doctors and clergymen may converse with the family.

Waiting in an Emergency Activity is a particularly difficult time for every patient since each perceives his medical urgency as unique. A state of anxiety predominates. The environment, obviously, should not only cater to physical needs and comfort but should also instill a feeling of confidence and relieve anxiety or fear.

Toilets for both sexes adequately screened from the public view, telephones ensuring privacy, vending machines with beverages or snacks, comfortable seating arrangements (not benches) all contribute to physical comfort. The general design of the waiting space (including color, texture, decor, acoustical control) all contribute to the welfare of waiting patients. The public waiting area should be screened visually from incoming ambulances discharging patients. A daylight window to the outside is often desirable but care should be taken to avoid location that will focus attention of the patients on ambulance arrivals.

Treatment Facilities Patients are treated in spaces surrounding the nursing station, the hub of all activities. This station is backed up by the medical preparation room and the office of the chief nurse who supervises all operations. Therefore, a glazed partition is provided which ensures acoustical privacy and affords visual control.

Staff amenities include toilets, lounge, and locker room for female staff. Lounge and sleeping accommodations are provided for three full-time physicians and resident medical staff who often work long hours and, although not continuously, are on call.

The chief physician's office is located in close proximity to that of the chief nurse since they often communicate face to face. Emergency equipment, to be readily accessible in case of urgent need, is deliberately placed in an alcove in front of the nursing station.

The patient's security room, with an unbreakable view window for observation, is placed close to the nursing station. Curtains may be installed outside the room, if necessary, to eliminate a view from the room itself. The door to the room and to its toilet must open outward to prevent the patient from locking himself [herself] in. To prevent self-injury, the room should be devoid of any sharp-edged appurtenances, and the light fixture, preferably tamperproof, should be flush with mounting surface. Surfaces should be smooth without any crevices with coved wall bases to facilitate easy cleaning in case of gross soiling by a disturbed patient.

It is important to emphasize that this is not a prison cell or a dry-up tank for an alcoholic. The patient confined in this security room is there for medical treatment although he may be under police control or may be mentally unstable. Physical design that provides a pleasant atmosphere is of paramount significance.

Treatment cubicles have curtains for privacy, if necessary, and are equipped to handle examinations and minor treatments. More severe injuries are treated in critical care rooms which are of two sizes. For a coronary patient, the emergency team may consist of a number of specialists using numerous kinds of portable equipment; therefore, larger space is required to accommodate both. Conductive flooring must be provided if explosive anesthetic gases are used and all

safety regulations must be observed. Each critical care room is provided with a scrub sink. Special attention should be given to the scrub sink area because of the hazards of infection and a slippery floor.

The cast room, used for closed reduction of fractures, is equipped similarly to a treatment cubicle with the addition of a plaster sink and trap. All supplies, splints, and fracture frames are kept in the room. The door must allow passage of a patient on a stretcher who, after treatment, may be immobilized by means of orthopedic accessories and attachments to the stretcher.

The patient's observation room must be in full view of the nursing station. Privacy between patients may be achieved by a cubicle curtain. Toilets for both sexes are provided. Nurses' work counters are at each end of the room.

The entire Emergency Activity is easily accessible from the hospital and the x-ray and laboratory facilities which, located between the two activities, are shared with the Outpatient Activity.

Fig. 1 Shared terminal service electronic data processing unit.

EDP UNIT

Data Entry and Transmission Room (Shared Terminal Service System)
Function This area accommodates equipment and personnel necessary for encoding source data onto computer compatible magnetic tape, transmitting the encoded data to outside computer facilities for processing, and receiving the processed data in conventional printed copy form.

Occupancy Two tape entry operators, one tape transmission operator, and occasionally the programer-analyst.

E.D.P. Secretarial Office
Function This area provides facilities for reception and secretarial service to the E.D.P. director and systems analyst(s).

Occupancy Secretary and waiting for three visitors.

Adjacent Areas E.D.P. director's office, systems analyst's office(s), and administrative corridor.

Systems Analyst's Office(s)
Function Each subject office area or work station (one is assumed for the shared terminal service E.D.P. unit and two for the medium system E.D.P. unit) provides for a systems analyst who is responsible for planning, scheduling, and coordinating activities required to develop systems for processing data and obtaining solutions to complex problems. He [she] is concerned with developing

Administrative Services and Facilities for Hospitals: A Planning Guide HEW Pub. No. (HSM) 72–4035. U.S. Department of Health, Education, and Welfare, Washington, D.C., 1972.

methods for computer usage in the various areas of hospital operation, such as financial management, material management, admitting, medical records, clinical pathology, outpatient service, and others. He [she] works with the management engineering unit personnel to improve operating methods and systems which provide for more efficient interdepartmental operation.

After determining the exact nature of the data processing problem, he [she] defines, analyzes, and structures it in a logical manner so that a system to solve the problem and obtain the desired results can be developed. He [she] obtains all the data needed and defines exactly the way it is to be processed. He [she] prepares charts, tables, and diagrams and describes the processing system and the steps necessary to make it operate. He [she] may recommend the type of equipment to be used, prepare instructions for programers, and interpret final results and translate them into terms understandable to management.

When working with systems already in use, the systems analyst is also concerned with improving and adapting the system to handle additional or different types of data.

In 500-bed hospitals, one of the senior systems analysts is designated "Chief."

Occupancy Systems analyst and seating for three visitors in each office.

Adjacent Areas Shared terminal service system: E.D.P. secretarial office, E.D.P. director's office, and data entry and transmission room.

Medium system: E.D.P. secretarial office, E.D.P. director's office, and E.D.P. programing area. Convenient communication with the E.D.P. supervisor's office and E.D.P. machine room essential.

E.D.P. Programer's Office(s)
Function This area provides for the E.D.P. programers who prepare step-by-step instructions that tell the computer exactly what to do. Three programers, each with a separate work office or cubicle within this area, are assumed for the medium system E.D.P. unit.

Every problem processed in a computer must be carefully analyzed so that exact and logical steps for its solution can be worked out. This preliminary work is generally the responsibility of the systems analyst. When it has been completed, the program or detailed instructions for processing the data can be prepared by the programer. Exactly how he [she] does this depends not only on the type of computer hardware available but on the nature of the problem. These determine what programing techniques will be used. Still other techniques are required in writing aids which reduce the amount of detail associated with programing.

The programer usually starts an assignment by determining exactly what information must be used to prepare assigned documents and their exact final format. He [she] then makes a flow chart or diagram that shows the order in which the computer must perform each operation and for each operation prepares detailed instructions. These when relayed to the computer's control unit, instruct the machine exactly what to do with each piece of information to produce the documents anticipated. The programer also prepares an instruction sheet for the console operator to follow when the program is run on the computer.

The final step in programing is debugging or checking on whether the instructions have been correctly written and will produce the desired re-

ELECTRONIC DATA PROCESSING UNIT (Medium System.)

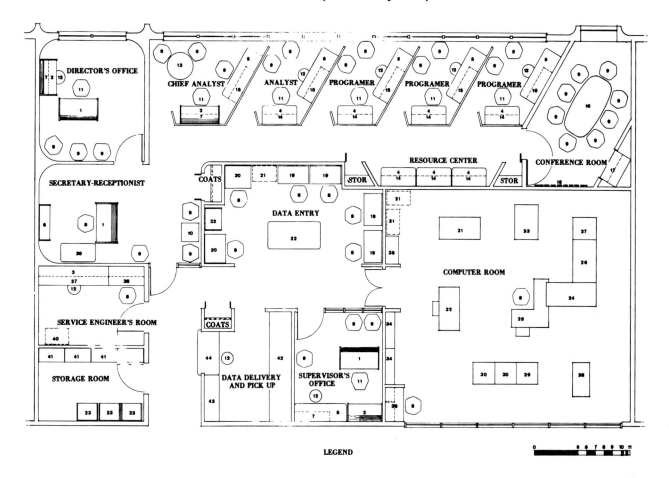

LEGEND

1. Work surface, roll top
2. Work surface, roll top, wall hanging
3. Work surface, typewriter
4. Work surface, wall hanging
5. Work surface, sloped top
6. Bin, file
7. Shelf
8. Clerical swivel chair
9. Arm chair, shell type
10. Table, end
11. Management chair
12. Stool
13. Table
14. Shelves
15. File bin under 72" work surface
16. Table, conference
17. Kitchen, efficiency
18. Projector screen
19. Data entry units
20. Key punch desks
21. Utility shelf truck
22. Table

23. Locker with drawers and shelves on truck
24. Processing unit
25. Console work-shelf and printer
26. 3 drive disc storage
27. 2 drive disc storage
28. Power unit
29. Tape control unit
30. Magnetic tape facility
31. Card read punch
32. Printer
33. Control unit
34. Tape storage units
35. Disc pack storage
36. Built in desk and book case with 3 lockable drawers
37. Work counter complete with base units
38. Desk unit
39. Wall cab storage unit
40. Tool and test equipment cart
41. Shelf units
42. Burster complete with table
43. 1 decollator (mobile) 6-ply
44. Counter top

Fig. 2.

sults. A program is debugged in two steps. First the programer takes a sample of the data to be processed and reviews step-by-step exactly what will happen as the computer follows the series of instructions which make up the program. Then, after revising the instructions to take care of any difficulties that have appeared, the programer completes the test by making a trial run in the computer. The console operator sometimes helps with the latter part of the debugging process.

A simple program can be made for a computer within a few days; a complex problem may re-

quire many months. To improve efficiency, existing programs must be updated to keep pace with administrative changes. Introduction of larger or newer model computers often requires that many programs be rewritten.

Information to be processed by a computer is encoded first onto some type of medium which is compatible with the computer such as magnetic tape, paper tape, or punchcards. Most computers are designed to accept data in punchcard form.

Occupancy One E.D.P. programer and seating for one visitor per office or work station. A total

of three offices or work stations is assumed for the medium system E.D.P. programing area.

Adjacent Areas E.D.P. secretarial office, systems analysts' offices, E.D.P. machine room, and E.D.P. supervisor's office. Convenient communication with the E.D.P. director's office, conference room, E.D.P. supply storage room, and data entry room is essential.

Conference Room
Function This area provides for private discussions, inservice education, and meetings.

HOSPITALS
EDP Unit

Occupancy Eight persons.

Adjacent Areas E.D.P. director's office, analysts' offices, programers' offices, and resource center.

Resource Center
Function This area provides for a library of programs, computer literature, related files, and software required to facilitate an efficient operation. A resource center should provide work surfaces for analysts and programers in order to minimize the amount of material stored in individual work stations.

Occupancy None.

Adjacent Areas E.D.P. director's office, analysts' offices, programers' offices, and conference room.

E.D.P. Director's Office
Function This area provides for the E.D.P. director who with the concurrence of the hospital administrator is responsible for the total activity of the E.D.P. service system, including formulation, development, and implementation of overall policies, programs, plans, and procedures for control of the system in general and the E.D.P. unit in particular.

The director reviews and analyzes the various inter and intra workflow activities and methods of all hospital operating programs in relation to the total E.D.P. function. On the basis of these analyses, he [she] formulates and institutes management controls designed to improve the efficiency of the programs through the application of E.D.P. techniques with due consideration for quality requirements, optimum use of personnel and/or other resources, and time and cost limitations.

He [she] establishes training programs to orient hospital personnel in the potentials of the E.D.P. services and to teach them the methods and techniques which will enable them to fully utilize these services in their areas. He also institutes research activities to improve E.D.P. uses in the hospital and maintains a technical library of materials relative to all elements of data processing.

He [she] maintains statistical records as a basis for evaluating the effectiveness of the service and the improvement of the hospital's operation through the use of E.D.P.

He [she] provides advice and exchange of information, resolves problems, and participates in meetings and conferences with key staff members and department heads to discuss present and expected work and to develop broad plans.

Occupancy E.D.P. director and three visitors.

Adjacent Areas
Shared terminal service system: E.D.P. secretarial office, systems analyst's office, and data entry and transmission room.

Medium system: E.D.P. secretarial office and systems analysts' offices. Convenient communication with the programing area and E.D.P. supervisor's office essential.

Data Entry Room (Medium System)
Function This area accommodates equipment and personnel necessary for encoding information onto computer compatible media for electronic data processing application. It also accommodates limited facilities for occasional card punching relative to programing.

Occupancy Three data entry operators and occasionally one programer for a short period of time.

Computer Room
Function This area accommodates most basic electronic equipment or hardware required for the electronic data processing activities program. Limited expansion and access space are essential.

Occupancy One operator for each shift.

Adjacent Areas E.D.P. supervisor's office. E.D.P. service engineers' workroom, programing area, data entry room, and data delivery and pickup area. Convenient communication with the E.D.P. director's office, the systems analysts' offices, and the E.D.P. supply storage room.

Comment The raised floor of this area allows future layout changes with minimum alteration cost, protects interconnecting cables and power receptacles, provides personnel safety, and permits the space between the two floors to be used for air supply ducts or as a plenum where necessary.

The environment for this room area should be maintained at 75°F. and 50 percent relative humidity. The air should be supplied through a filter of at least 90 percent efficiency based on the National Bureau of Standards discoloration test using atmospheric dust. Use of the space beneath the raised floor as a plenum will depend upon the recommendations of the electronic equipment manufacturer and the design engineer. Pressurization to minimize dust infiltration from adjacent areas is an important consideration.

To function properly, magnetic tapes require the same temperature and relative humidity levels as the electronic hardware. Because of this, and also for their easy retrieval, those tapes in frequent use are generally stored in cabinets and shelf tables within the computer room. Sometimes a separate storage room remotely located is provided for extra protection of vital records. These include master tapes which would be irreplaceable or those which would be needed immediately after a fire or could not be quickly reproduced. If an approved data safe is provided for storage of vital records, it can be located within the computer room.

In laying out a computer room, the manufacturer's specifications regarding maximum lengths for the control cables which interconnect the various machines and the minimum service clearances for the machines should not be exceeded. Another important layout consideration is adequate working area for operating personnel and space for auxiliary equipment such as worktables, cabinets, and utility trucks.

E.D.P. Supervisor's Office
Function This area accommodates the supervisor responsible for the physical production aspects of the E.D.P. operation, for quality controls, and some cooperative functions relative to programing.

Occupancy E.D.P. supervisor and two visitors.

Adjacent Areas E.D.P. machine room, data entry room, and data delivery and pickup area. Convenient communication with the E.D.P. director's office, E.D.P. programing area, and E.D.P. supply storage room is essential.

Data Delivery and Pickup Area
Function This area serves as a receiving station for unprocessed data and also as a pickup point for processed data. Decollating, bursting, collating, and binding of data forms and documents prior to pickup are done in this area.

Occupancy One person.

Adjacent Areas Data entry room, E.D.P. machine room, and administrative corridor. This area should be visible and easily accessible from the E.D.P. supervisor's office.

E.D.P. Service Engineer's Room
Function This area facilitates the maintenance and service engineering activities essential to the continuing operation of the E.D.P. equipment.

Adjacent Areas E.D.P. machine room.

Occupancy One person.

E.D.P. Supply Storage Room
Function This area provides readily available holding space for short-term inventories of standard and special machine-mated paper forms. It also provides holding for a small reserve of new magnetic tapes, and in the case of the medium system E.D.P. unit, a small reserve also of blank cards. A one-week supply of forms is generally preferred holding.

Occupancy No permanent personnel.

Adjacent Areas Data delivery and pickup area to be easily accessible to the data entry room, the E.D.P. machine or transmission room, and the administrative corridor.

By F. CUTHBERT SALMON, AIA, and CHRISTINE F. SALMON, AIA

Planning means thinking in terms of spatial and human interrelationships.

The interrelationships between the several areas of activities are varied and complex; add to these the problems of site selection, considerations of finance, and provision for future expansion, and it becomes apparent that sound planning requires rigor and thoroughness. (See Fig. 1.)

One of the most basic planning principles is organization: the best organization for the purpose intended. When that purpose is rehabilitation, one must take into account the limited mobility and acute sensitivity to physical environment of those for whom the building is intended.

With limited mobility, the wheelchair becomes a basic unit or module of design. The range of the dimensions of a standard wheelchair must be borne in mind. Design is governed not only by these basic dimensions, but also by the dimensions of the paths of action of the chair. Variations in disability permit variable limits of maneuverability, and the relationship of the wheelchair to basic equip-

ment must also be recognized in the development of the planning data.

MEDICAL

The medical area of a rehabilitation center provides the following services: medical evaluation, performed by the physician and his staff; physical therapy, including hydrotherapy; occupational therapy; speech and hearing therapy. It also furnishes the services of a prosthetic and/or orthetic appliance shop. The detailed character of the medical area will vary with the program of the center itself.

The emphases in the medical program will be determined by the needs of the patients and by already existent community medical facilities.

The medical area provides the basis for the patients' total program at the center. It must be accessible to all other areas and be well integrated with the administration and admissions services. (See Fig. 2.)

This section will contain much specialized examination, treatment, and therapy equip-

ment. Some of this will be heavy, requiring a floor designed to accommodate such concentrated loads; the electrical service to these machines is important.

Patients will be wearing lightweight examination or treatment gowns here, and the heating system will have to compensate for this. The records for all sections of this area are extensive; therefore, adequate storage for them is mandatory. Conferences with patients and staff make further demands on the available space. Many different kinds of activities will be housed here and the space needs to be adjustable accordingly. Accessibility to all other areas is also essential for the medical area of activity.

Physician

Medical diagnosis is the basis for development of the patient's successful rehabilitation program.

On admission, a medical examination is essential, whether the patient is prescribed a program in one or several of the center's areas of activity: physical medicine, social adjustment, or vocational rehabilitation. A nurse is usually present during the examination.

Complete evaluation of the patient may require the services of consulting medical specialists, staff specialists in the several medical therapies, psychologists, social workers, and vocational counselors. A total integrated program is developed for the patient, with medical considerations as the initial frame of reference.

Location Within Building As all patients receive medical evaluation, the physician's unit should be near the center's main entrance.

For purposes of admission, and for the keeping of records, location of the unit near the administrative department is desirable.

If an in-patient nursing unit is included, the physician should have, if possible, convenient access to the nursing unit.

In smaller centers, the main waiting room for the building may serve as the waiting area for the physician's unit.

Place the unit in a quiet zone.

Staff-Patient Ratios The physician-patient ratio will depend entirely on the nature of the program. Centers accommodating in-patients will necessarily need a greater amount of physician service per patient than the out-patient type of center.

Physician-patient ratios can be established only on an individual basis.

Organization of Space The physician's unit should form a self-contained area, with access to the consultation room and the medical examination room by means of a subcorridor, if possible.

To make full use of the physician's time, there should be two examination rooms for each consultation room.

Recommended for the area is a toilet designed for wheelchair occupancy, accessible from the examination room.

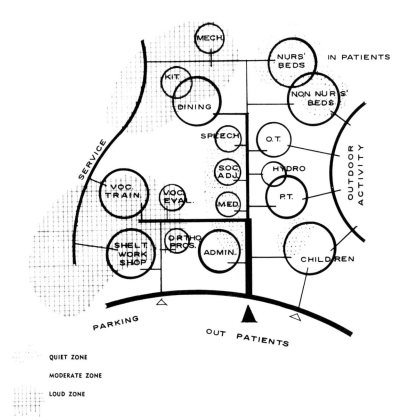

Fig. 1 Interrelations of main elements of space of a rehabilitation center. Activities may be grouped according to relative noise levels.

REHABILITATION CENTERS

Although a clinical scale is essential equipment for the examination room, a wheelchair patient's scale constructed from a modified platform scale is very desirable. These scales should be conveniently accessible from the other parts of the building and may be placed in the physician's unit, or near the physical therapy exercise room or gymnasium.

Waiting Room Arrange the furniture to allow space for wheelchair patients. Also, include coat hanging facilities.

Secretary Include in the furnishings a secretary's desk, writing table, and letter size file cabinets.

As certain records must be available to department heads in other areas of the center, placement of such files in the central records room of the administrative area is the usual practice. However, some centers prefer to keep medical records in the physician's unit. A physician's records are traditionally privileged communications, and, if kept in the central records room, should be made available only to the responsible professional personnel.

Consultation Room Include in the furnishings for the physician's office and consultation room an executive desk and chair, bookshelves, and film illuminator. Allow space for two visitors' chairs and a wheelchair. Provide a convenient coat closet. (See Fig. 3.)

Examination Room Include in the furnishings for this room an examination table with clearance on all sides, an examination light, a lavatory and mirror, clinical scales, a film illuminator, an instrument and supply closet, a small electric pressure sterilizer (if no lab-utility room is provided), and a chair. Standing bars are optional equipment.

Lab-Utility Room If a lab-utility room is provided, equip it with a pressure sterilizer, sink, plaster cart, work counter, and storage cabinets.

Radiology Radiology is usually provided for rehabilitation centers by x-ray departments of hospitals, clinics, and other institutions. If radiology is to form a part of the center's services, standard practice in the design and construction of the department should be followed. (See Fig. 4.)

Physical Therapy

Physical therapy is administered under medical supervision and performed by graduates of a school or course approved by the Council on Medical Education and Hospitals of the American Medical Association.

The objectives of physical therapy are to correct or alleviate bone and joint or neuromuscular disabilities. This entails a concern with all types of physical disabilities, such as neurological diseases, arthritis, amputation, paralysis, spasticity, structural and postural malalignments, crippling accidents, postsurgical conditions, etc. Measures are used to retain or reestablish circulation, muscle tone, coordination, joint motion leading to mobility, ambulation, and activities of daily living.

In carrying out his aim, the therapist will make use of heat, cold, water, light, and electricity as well as the training effects of active, passive, resistive, and reeducation exercises.

Organization of Space There should be two major treatment areas, dry and wet. The dry area includes the exercise room or gym and treatment cubicles; whereas the wet area includes all hydrotherapy treatment, tanks, pools, and related facilities.

Hydrotherapy equipment should be grouped in one area, separate from, but adjacent and accessible to other treatment areas.

Space considerations for a physical therapy department must take into account circulation areas for patients and staff. Situate the equipment for efficient and safe use, and provide storage space for equipment and supplies.

Flexibility and expansion of facilities should be considered in basic planning to meet changes in requirements.

It is advisable to consult with the chief physical therapist, the center's director, and the center's physician to determine equipment needs and the program of activity for this department.

Location Within Building The place for physical and occupational therapy, as well as for activities of daily living, should be in close proximity, as many patients will receive treatment and training in all three areas.

Arrange the areas so that scheduled patients may proceed directly to physical therapy without interfering with circulation to other departments.

As physical therapy may take advantage of certain outdoor activity, place the exercise room or gym near the outdoors.

As physical therapy involves some noisy activity, this area should be removed from quiet zones, such as the place where speech and hearing therapy is administered, or the nursing unit. (See Fig. 5.)

The area should be convenient to the center's physician and the nursing unit (if provided).

Staff-Patient Ratios One physical therapist can treat an average of 10 to 15 patients per day.

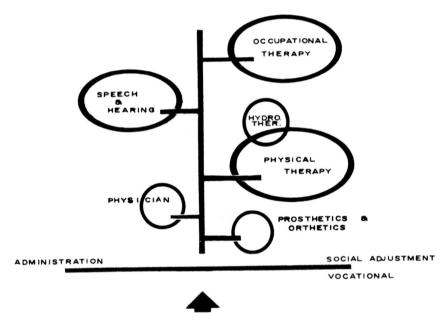

Fig. 2

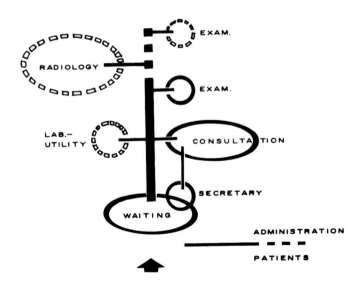

Fig. 3

534

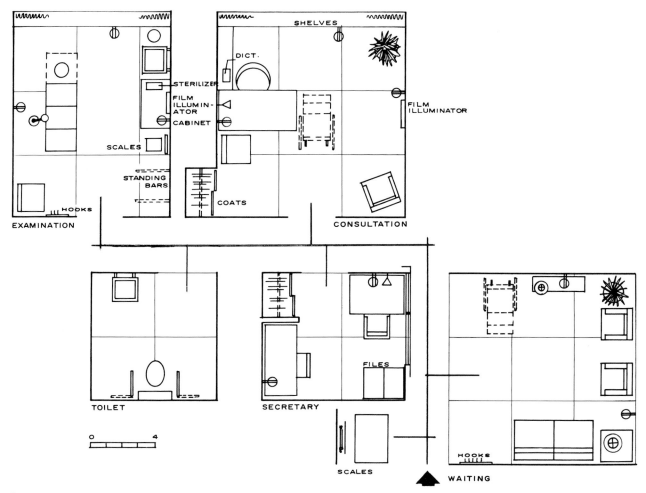

Fig. 4

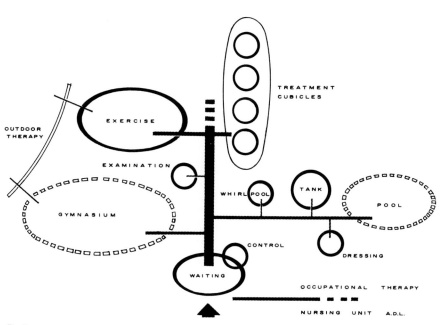

Fig. 5

Group services may increase this to 20 a day.

If the physical therapist is assisted by non-professionals and if the work space and scheduling are well planned, a maximum staff-patient ratio may be achieved. Nonprofessional assistants, paid or volunteer, can be trained to prepare patients for treatments, attend to equipment, and transport patients, if necessary.

There are many variables involved in staff-patient ratios.

Treatment Cubicles Divide the cubicles with curtain tracks for easy access by wheelchair and stretcher patients and for flexibility in use of space, as for instructional activity or gait training. Curtains should not extend to the ceiling or floor, so that when drawn, they may not interfere with ventilation. (See Fig. 6.)

Equip cubicles with a treatment table with adequate work space on each side and at the head. Treatment tables with drawers or shelving provide convenient storage space for sheets and other requirements.

Provide in the cubicles a place for the patient's outer clothing, such as hooks or lockers.

Provide a lavatory convenient for the therapist's use.

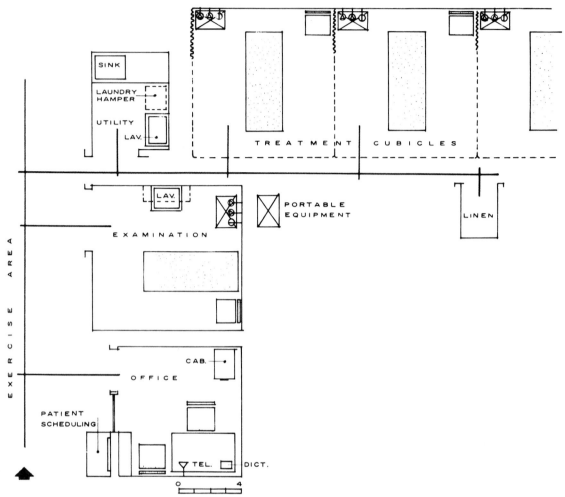

Fig. 6 Treatment cubicles and examination room.

Equipment for this department may include infrared and ultraviolet lamps, diathermy, hot pack and electrical stimulation apparatus, ultrasonic equipment, suspension apparatus (Guthrie-Smith), electrical diagnostic apparatus, moist heat equipment, sand bags, powder boards, powder, oil or lotion, alcohol, and linen.

In many cases patients will be lying on their backs during treatments. Ceiling lighting should be indirect or semi-direct to avoid glare. Therapists making tests or examinations require shaded or nonglare spotlights.

Waiting Area Provide space for wheelchair and ambulant patients; and if there is a nursing unit, space also for a stretcher.

Place the therapist's office near the waiting area for control.

From the waiting area, the patient should be able to go to the exercise room, hydrotherapy, or treatment cubicles with a minimum interference of activities.

Therapist's Office There should be staff office space for interviewing patients and attending to administrative duties, as well as space for

files, and a desk with a dictating machine.

Partition the office so that interviews may have acoustical privacy.

Situate it near the patients' entrance to the physical therapy department and design it to provide maximum supervision of activities.

A patient scheduling board and writing surface are recommended. Locate them conveniently for all physical therapists.

Staff lockers and dressing rooms (separate from patients) should be near this department.

Examining Room The room should be convenient to the entrance of the physical therapy department.

Equip it with an examination table, lavatory, and space for examination equipment.

Provide floor-to-ceiling partitions for privacy.

The room may be used for special tests and measurements, or for treatment when privacy is desirable.

Scales for weighing patients (including patients in wheelchairs) are sometimes provided in this room.

Exercise Area This area should be a flexible, clear space for individual and group exercise activities. (See Fig. 7.)

The most frequently used items of equipment are: exercise mats (sometimes raised 24 in. off the floor for the convenience of therapists and wheelchair or crutch patients—if area is of sufficient size, mats may remain in place), shoulder wheel, shoulder overhead and wall weights, shoulder ladder, steps, curbs, ramps, stall bars, parallel bars, posture mirror, stationary bicycle, counterbalanced and individual weights, sand bags, and paraffin bath. Some of this equipment may be made by a skilled carpenter rather than purchased. Purchased equipment should be accompanied by satisfactory repair and maintenance service.

Certain equipment relationships should be maintained. Place the posture mirror 4 ft from the end of the parallel bars. When mats and other movable equipment are removed, there should be sufficient space for gait training, also related to a posture mirror.

Doors to the exercise area should be wide enough to accommodate not only patients but also equipment. Double doors, each 3 ft wide, are recommended.

The layout shown suggests a minimum exercise area for a physical therapy department with one therapist and an aid. For an expansion

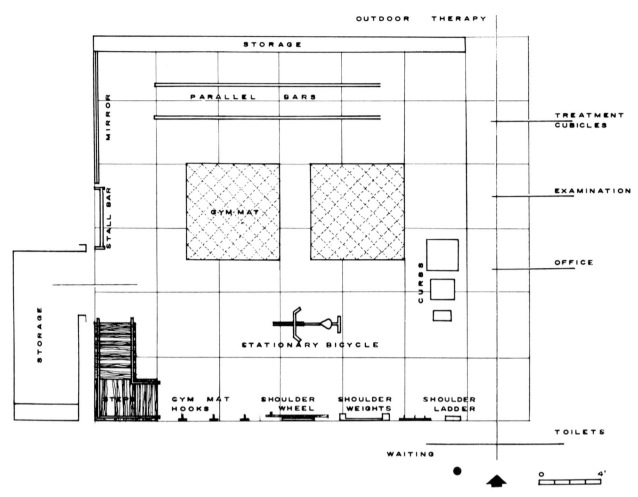

Fig. 7

of the exercise area see "Gymnasium" in this section.

The exercise area may be divided by open partitions which allow for the attachment of equipment and subdividing of activities, yet which permit circulation of air and easy supervision of the total area.

An observation cubicle with one-way vision glass may sometimes be used to advantage in order that visitors will not interfere with patients' activities.

Reinforce the walls for installation of exercise equipment, such as stall bars.

Provide storage for equipment not in use.

Toilets should be accessible to the patients and designed for those who are confined to wheelchairs.

A wall clock in the room for timing exercises is recommended.

Vinyl wall covering to a minimum height of 5 ft will protect walls and ease maintenance.

There should be adequate ventilation. Fresh air without drafts in the exercise and treatment cubicles is very important. Air conditioning of this area is highly desirable.

Windows or room exposure should be designed to provide privacy within the exercise room.

Gymnasium In larger centers or centers with inpatients, a gymnasium is recommended. It serves a variety of uses, such as individual and group exercises, recreational programs, and meetings.

The gymnasium will augment the program of the physical therapy exercise room, permitting the therapist to conduct group wheelchair and mat classes. The room should be furnished with parallel bars, wall bars, stairs, curbs, gradients, wall mirrors, etc., for individual instruction.

The room will also be used for recreational activity such as group volleyball, basketball, moving pictures, and wheelchair square dancing. A minimum clear ceiling height of 14 ft is recommended. If the gymnasium meets standard space requirements, rental of its use to community athletic organizations will be facilitated. Providing a recreational program is particularly important where inpatients are involved.

The gymnasium will also be used by the social group worker in the social adjustment program of some patients.

As the gymnasium is a multipurpose room, equipment and furniture within the area should be movable. Provision for its storage is essential.

As a meeting room to be used by selected groups within the community, this facility provides an excellent opportunity to acquaint the public with the problems of rehabilitation and to arouse interest in the center's program. For this purpose, the gymnasium should be easily accessible to the public.

To make maximum use of this multipurpose room, it is important that activities be controlled to avoid conflicting schedules.

Hydrotherapy The space for hydrotherapy is frequently the most expensive area of the center; consequently, it should be planned with considerable selectivity.

Whirlpool tanks for arm, foot, hip, and leg immersion are considered inadequate by many centers serving multiple disabilities unless augmented with facilities for complete body immersion. (See Fig. 8.)

Almost all exercises and treatments can be conducted with a Hubbard tank and a wading pool and tank. Combinations of Hubbard tanks with wading facilities are available where space is limited.

Therapeutic pools are expensive to construct; consequently, they are usually considered only for larger centers.

All hydrotherapy activities require linen and towel storage. Also provide a wringer and dryer for bathing suits and a storage space for wet and dry bathing suits of both staff and patients.

Tank and pool areas require storage space for wheelchairs and stretchers, adequate

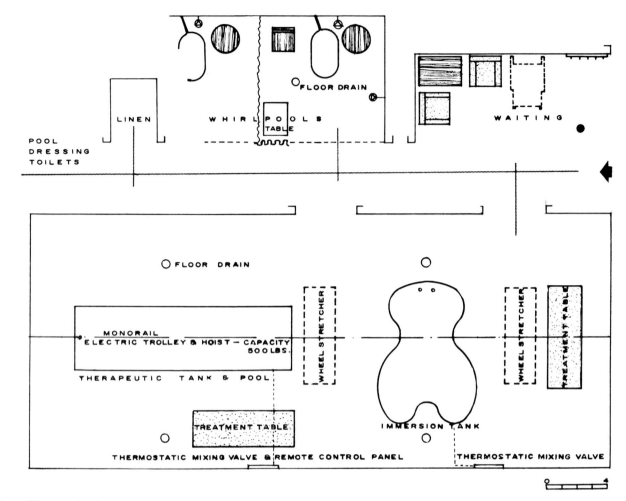

LINEN

FLOOR DRAIN

WHIRLPOOLS
TABLE

WAITING

POOL
DRESSING
TOILETS

FLOOR DRAIN

MONORAIL
ELECTRIC TROLLEY & HOIST — CAPACITY
500 LBS.

WHEEL STRETCHER

WHEEL STRETCHER

TREATMENT TABLE

THERAPEUTIC TANK & POOL

TREATMENT TABLE

IMMERSION TANK

THERMOSTATIC MIXING VALVE & REMOTE CONTROL PANEL

THERMOSTATIC MIXING VALVE

Fig. 8 Whirlpools and tank room.

dressing cubicles, or dressing rooms to permit maximum use of pool, showers, and toilet facilities.

As hydrotherapy is a moderately noisy activity, it should be removed from areas requiring sound control.

Floors should be of unglazed ceramic tile with drains for spilled water and tank overflow.

As equipment is heavy when filled with water, a structure must be designed for these additional loads.

Overhead monorails with lift mechanism are essential for efficient use of Hubbard tanks and waders. Ceilings should be a minimum of 9 ft 6 in. The location of the monorail with proper relationship to equipment is essential.

All pipes for hydrotherapy should be accessible but concealed. Waste lines should be adequate for rapid changes of water.

All hydrotherapy equipment should have thermostatically controlled mixing valves. Adequate pressure and an ample source of 160° F. water are essential.

Humidity reduction is a major concern in planning the hydrotherapy department. Adequate air conditioning is essential for the comfort of patients and staff.

Whirlpools This includes equipment for the treatment of arms, hips, and legs. Some models are available as movable units, in which case a sink or lavatory is required in the cubicle for drainage of the unit.

Provide space for chair, table, and a stool of adjustable height.

In small centers where hydrotherapy equipment consists only of whirlpool tanks, place them near treatment cubicles and near the exercise room for easy supervision by the therapist.

Tank Room A treatment table with storage space is an essential requirement.

Allow space for wheel stretchers and provide 44-in.-wide doors. (A 56-in.-wide opening is necessary to install combination treatment and wading tank.)

Allow space for stretcher and wheelchair storage.

Showers and Dressing Rooms Directly related to the efficient use of a hydrotherapy pool is the provision of adequate dressing room facilities.

Dressing facilities do not necessarily have a size relationship to the pool indicated. For example, some programs will require several dressing tables in order to accommodate the patients.

Hydrotherapy Pool Many variations in size are possible.

The depth of the pool should be graduated. Variations of depth in 5-in. increments are recommended. For children the shallow end should be 2 ft deep, for adults, 3 ft. The deep end of the pool should be 5 ft.

There should be a continuous gutter around the pool for the use of the patients and for the purpose of attaching plinths.

A portion of the floor surrounding the pool may be depressed to form an observation area for the therapist.

Occupational Therapy

Occupational therapy is administered under medical supervision and performed by graduates of schools of occupational therapy approved by the Council on Medical Education and Hospitals of the American Medical Association.

The objectives of occupational therapists are to assist in the mental and physical restoration of the disabled person, enabling him to adjust to his disability, increase his work capacity, and to want to become a productive member of his community.

In addition, the occupational therapist is concerned with the training of patients in the activities of daily living.

To achieve these goals, occupational therapy utilizes, on an individual basis, remedial activities which are found in creative skills and manual arts. (See Fig. 9.)

Location Within Building Occupational therapy should be adjacent to the physical therapy department, since many patients will use both areas.

Locate the area so that scheduled patients may proceed directly to occupational therapy without interfering with the circulation of other departments.

As some phases of occupational therapy involve noisy activity, this area should be removed from quiet zones in the building, or provision should be made for acoustic control.

Certain occupational therapy activities, such as those characteristic of daily living, may be conducted out of doors in favorable weather. It is recommended that, if possible, access to an outdoor area be provided.

The area should be accessible to the center's physician, the social adjustment area, and the vocational counseling area. As occupational therapy involves coordination with the nursing unit (for dressing and toileting particularly), the occupational therapy department should be conveniently related to it.

Staff-Patient Ratios One occupational therapist can treat eight to fifteen patients per day. The number of patients depends upon types of disabilities and the severity of the cases.

Where highly individual treatments are required, the daily load will decrease. Also, if the therapist is relieved of administrative responsibilities and assisted by nonprofessional persons, the daily load will increase.

For orthopedic patients, special equipment must frequently be devised under close supervision of the occupational therapist.

There are many variables applicable to staff-patient ratios.

Organization of Space The activity area may be so planned that each activity has a separate unit, or it may be planned to separate quiet from noisy and dusty from clean activity. The unit system facilitates assignment of special instructors to special activities and is also a more orderly arrangement of the space. However, this method increases the number of staff, makes supervision more difficult, and can be considered only in larger departments.

The activities of daily living (ADL) area, which is used to teach the patient how to live self-sufficiently in his home environment, should be closely related to the main occupational therapy treatment room.

As the occupational therapist works closely with the social adjustment staff and the vocational counselors, his office should be near their areas.

Activities of Daily Living The activities which are indicated include most situations found in the home (see Fig. 10).

Some training, particularly bathroom and

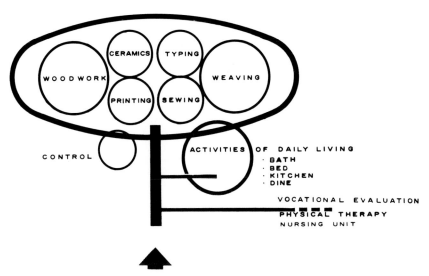

Fig. 9

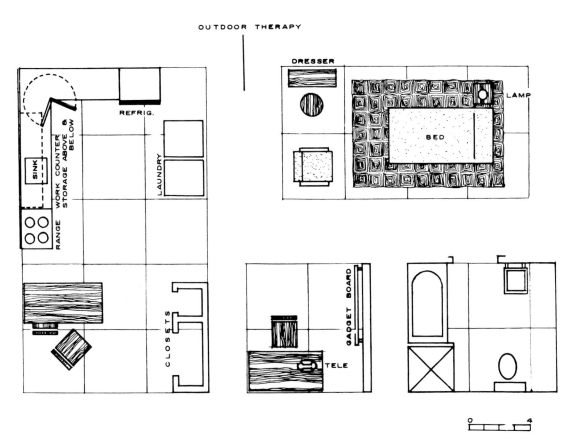

Fig. 10   Activities of daily living.

bedroom activities, will require cooperation with physical therapists. Consequently, the ADL area should be easily accessible from the physical therapy department.

A gadget board containing numerous items of hardware, light switches, faucets, and other items frequently used should be included. The board should be adjustable in height.

The bathroom should be arranged to accommodate wheelchair patients (see "Inpatients").

The kitchen plan may include, in addition to the type illustrated for wheelchair use, standard counter and cabinet arrangements to test the patient's ability to cope with "normal" situations. Counters of adjustable height may be used to advantage in training patients.

A front loading washer and dryer, as illustrated, is desirable for wheelchair patients. Controls at the front of the range are recommended. However, the purpose of this training is to show the patient how he may use, if possible, appliances that are standard in his community.

A standard clothes closet is recommended as a part of the training in dressing.

A broom closet, vacuum cleaner, and adjustable ironing board should also be included.

Table space should be provided for training in eating and for use as a writing surface.

A rug can also be used to test the patient's ability to cope with that type of floor covering.

Speech and Hearing

The speech and hearing unit serves those with disabilities of deafness, stuttering, or delayed speech and voice disorders which may result from various basic abnormalities, diseases, or injuries.

A wide variety of programs is possible. Some provide for treatment of postoperative disorders resulting from tonsillectomies and ear operations, cerebral palsy, meningitis, cleft palate, hemiplegia, vocal cord anomalies.

Services may range from testing and treating of all conditions to emphasis on disorders associated with certain specific disabilities.

The center may include speech therapy only or audiological testing as well.

The program may serve adults or children, or both.

The center may include a teaching and research program in speech and hearing.

Staff-Patient Ratios Although ratios vary widely with different patients, an approximation of staff-patient ratios is as follows:

1. For audiometric screening: one audiometric technician may screen one patient every five to eight minutes.

2. For audiometric testing: the audiologist may test four to eight patients per day during the initial screening process. For a complete test for hearing aid evaluation, three hours is needed per patient, and the test is usually conducted in two visits.

3. For individual therapy: one therapist for six to ten patients per day (one half-hour to one-hour periods). The audiologist may also act as therapist.

4. For group therapy: five to eight persons per therapist; one therapist for twenty-four patients per day.

Organization of Space Patients' toilet facilities and coat racks should be accessible from the waiting room. It is recommended that the sound control room, test room, and audiometric testing rooms be located on a subcorridor off the waiting room in order to reduce noise. In a children's program, a play and ex-

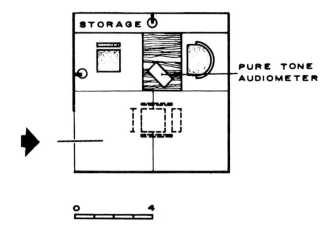

PURE TONE AUDIOMETER

Fig. 11

amination room near the test room is recommended.

Audiometric Testing The audiometric testing room (or, in some cases, booths) is a facility for pure-tone threshold testing and short form hearing screening tests (see Fig. 11).

Space should be provided for the audiologist's desk with an audiometer and one patient's chair or wheel chair. Furniture should be arranged so that the audiologist may face the patient and operate the audiometer. Provide storage and shelving.

The room should be treated acoustically for an overall residual noise level of not more than 40 decibels as measured on the "C" scale. This involves the treatment of walls, ceilings, and floors. (See Fig. 12.)

Control Room and Test Room This facility is essential for an audiology program.

It is preferable to place these rooms off the subcorridor or hall, and to control the activity in surrounding rooms in order that extraneous noises be eliminated.

For a children's program it is highly desirable that, outside the test room, a play and examination room be provided to accustom the child to his environment and to make the transition to the test room as easy as possible. This room should be equipped with children's furniture and toys.

Equipment for the control room will include a work surface for the audiometer, earphones and microphone, tape recorder, and tape and record storage, and may include other equipment such as a Bekesy audiometer.

If hearing aid evaluation is part of the program, provide storage space for hearing aids either in the test room or the control room.

The control room should be treated acoustically to achieve an overall residual noise level of not more than 40 decibels on the "C" scale.

An observation window approximately 18 by 20 in. is required. For adequate control of sound transmission, three pieces of glass of different thicknesses and nonparallel in construction are recommended. One-way vision glass in the control room is optional.

Equipment for the test room includes a speaker, microphone, and headphone. Microphone and headphone jacks should be located near the patient's chair. Additional auxiliary wall- or ceiling-mounted speakers are sometimes provided, particularly for the testing of children. These speakers should be separately switched. All this equipment is wired to the audiometer. Additional spare jacks in both the control and the test room are recommended

for other items of equipment. Conduits between the jacks should be installed in a manner that avoids sound transmission.

For complete diagnostic service, a galvanic skin response audiometer may be used in the test room. For diagnostic testing, delayed auditory feedback equipment may be used. For a children's program, children's furniture and toys should be part of the test room.

The test rooms should be acoustically treated to achieve an overall residual noise level of not more than 30 decibels on the "C" scale. This requires carefully supervised construction of a "floating room." In new construction the subfloor may be depressed to eliminate the high step or ramp at the entrance to the test room. If built on grade, the floating slab for the room may be placed on a sand bed.

To achieve this degree of acoustic control, it is essential that the floating room have adequate "mass" and that all necessary precautions are taken to avoid the conduction of sound.

Proper air circulation is a frequent problem.

Orthetic and/or Prosthetic Appliance Shop

Orthetic appliances are medically prescribed for the support of weakened parts of the body and to increase or control their function. Prosthetic appliances are medically prescribed artificial substitutes for a missing body part. Such devices are constructed by orthetists and prosthetists in cooperation with the physician, the physical therapist, and the occupational therapist. (See Fig. 13.)

The type of facility for orthetic and prosthetic services will vary widely with rehabilitation centers and is dictated at times by the availability of commercial services.

Frequently, arrangements are made for a representative of a commercial firm to visit the center. For this purpose a fitting room is recommended as a minimum facility, although an office or treatment cubicle is sometimes used and minor adjustments and repairs to appliances are made in the occupational therapy department.

However, a small shop (as illustrated) within the center provides close liaison between the patient, the medical team, and the orthetist or prosthetist. In such a shop, small devices such as feeders and page turners may be fabricated and adjustments and repairs made to wheelchairs, braces, limbs, and crutches.

If a minimum facility is established, consideration should be given to its future expansion, not only in terms of space, but with respect to electrical services, ventilation, gas supply, etc.

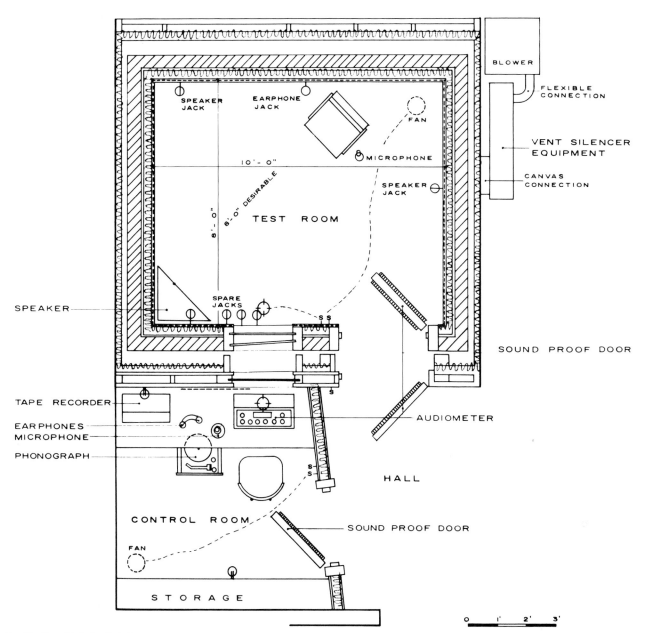

Fig. 12 Plan of typical audio-testing area.

The fabrication of major appliances requires much heavy and noisy equipment. Isolation of such a shop is essential to the control of noise and reduction of the fire hazard.

Location Within Building As the orthetic and/or prosthetic appliance shop will serve outpatients requiring minor adjustments or repairs to their devices, the unit should be easily accessible to entrances.

The unit should be located in a noisy zone, and, if possible, near the gymnasium, so that the patient may try out his prostheses or braces. The fitting room, however, may be made sufficiently large for this purpose.

SOCIAL ADJUSTMENT

Social adjustment requires psychiatric and social services for the treatment of social and emotional problems.

Psychiatric Service: Frequently the psychiatrist is employed on a part-time basis and is primarily called upon to provide the following services:

1. Psychiatric screening to diagnose emotional problems
2. Staff consultations on how these problems should be managed in relation to the patient's total rehabilitation program
3. In-service staff training for the purpose of developing greater understanding of the psychological factors in disability

Psychological Services include:

1. Psychological evaluation, accomplished by means of various psychological testing procedures and interviews which evaluate the patient's intelligence and personality
2. Interpretation of clinical findings to members of the staff
3. Counseling (therapy) on either an individual or a group basis, usually carried out with the psychiatrist and social service staff

4. In-service training of psychologists and participation in psychological research.

The minimum recommended psychological facilities would include a psychologist's counseling room and test room.

Social Services include the following:

1. Social study and evaluation, including the collection of relevant information from the patient, his family, and other agencies, and the appraisal of such information with respect to the patient's rehabilitation potential
2. Social casework, where the social worker (medical social worker or psychiatric social worker) works with the patient to improve attitudes toward self-support and motivation toward treatment and work
3. Social group work, including the correction of abnormal living patterns by using planned group activities, recreational in nature but therapeutic in value. It may include hobby activities, group discussions, and activities of an adult education nature.

REHABILITATION CENTERS

Location Within Building The services should be administered in a quiet area of the building.

As most incoming patients will receive some services in this area, it should be readily accessible from the main entrance of the building.

If the program involves large numbers of children, the psychological therapy room for children should be in the children's treatment-training unit.

(See Fig. 14.)

Organization of Space The flow pattern for patients within this area will vary considerably. A typical pattern for the evaluation of a new patient would have the sequence of receptionist, waiting room, social worker (for case history of patient), medical evaluation (for all incoming patients), psychological testing, and psychiatric screening. The two latter services are not needed by all patients.

Vocational counseling, and appraisal of the patient's employment potential in the vocational evaluation unit may also be included in the initial evaluation. Also for this purpose, audiometric screening and speech evaluation are often helpful.

Staff-Patient Ratios As psychiatric screening and psychological therapy will vary widely with individual patients, no approximation of staff-patient ratios is possible.

For psychological testing a recommended average is two patients a day per psychologist for brief psychological evaluations. This includes the time required for interpretation and writing reports. Extensive psychological evaluation requires one work day per patient, including time for preparation of the report. Other activities such as training, research, and therapy will detract from these averages. This does not provide for evaluation of vocational skills, aptitudes, and interests, which is a function of vocational services.

For social caseworkers, the number of cases per worker will vary with the number of intake studies and the number receiving continuing service. Where there is a balance between these two types of service, an individual caseworker may handle a caseload of from 25 to 35 patients.

Waiting Room If the program is of sufficient scope, provide a separate waiting area with a receptionist for the psychological-social unit. In smaller centers, this facility may be incorporated in the main waiting room for the center.

The receptionist schedules patient interviews with the psychological-social staff.

Access to interview and test rooms by means of a subcorridor will provide privacy and reduce extraneous noise from the rest of the building.

Psychological Training and Research Programs For a training program, provide observation facilities in the children's play therapy and activity group rooms, such as observation cubicles with one-way vision glass or, preferably, television cameras with screens in a central viewing room. (See Fig. 15.)

Provide a separate office for each psychological trainee.

Research programs are of a wide variety. Some involve much equipment; others, no equipment. Provide a separate area for this facility.

VOCATIONAL

The vocational area of a rehabilitation center provides the following services: counseling,

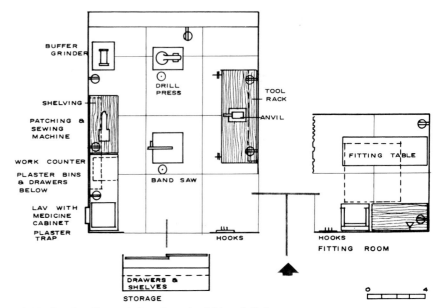

Fig. 13   Orthetic and/or prosthetic appliance shop (minimum facility).

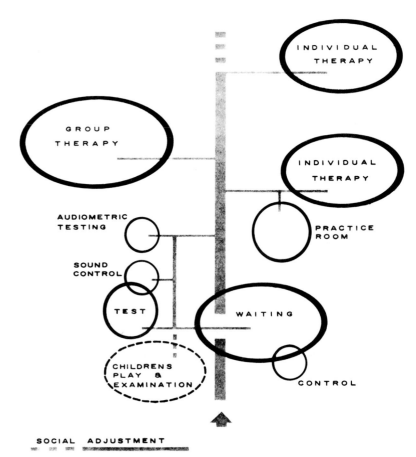

SOCIAL   ADJUSTMENT

Fig. 14

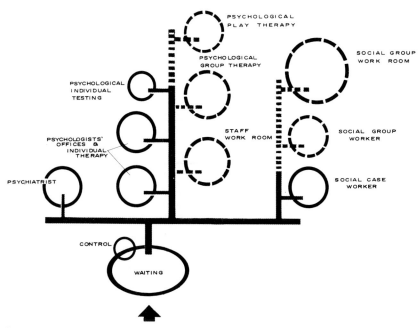

Fig. 15

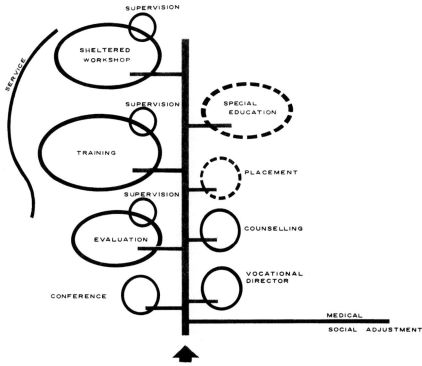

Fig. 16

evaluation, training, and placement; the sheltered workshop (or rehabilitation workshop) is part of this area, and in some cases, certain aspects of special education will be included. The vocational program is determined by the needs of the patients and the needs and opportunities of business and industry in the community served by the center. This program is a most important part of the patient's total rehabilitation process. (See Fig.16.)

This area has the responsibility of acquainting the patient with situations in industry or in business and of preparing him for job competition. Realistically designed workshops and offices will be required to create a job situation atmosphere for the patient.

This area should present to the patient a very wide range of job possibilities. Few centers will contain an extensive number of job situations; some may have none if this need has been satisfied through the cooperation of a trade school or some other agency. Patients should not be trained for jobs which they cannot obtain later.

Changing types and techniques in industry make it essential that this area have maximum flexibility, especially in heating, ventilating, plumbing, lighting, electrical installations, and equipment placement. The vocational area must offer training in small segments of a job operation and present advanced types of vocational opportunities.

Vocational counseling provides an opportunity for the patient to obtain an understanding of his vocational abilities and potential, and to learn the scope of their possible application. The center may choose to work with cooperating counselors already established in the community, if it does not provide this service within the center. Sometimes counselors are loaned to centers by the State Vocational Rehabilitation Agency and conduct their work at the center.

Vocational evaluation is the process of collecting and appraising data on the patient's interests, aptitudes, and ability in work situations. This section needs to be quite broad in scope in order to find the vocation best suited and most satisfying to the disabled person. This section of the center's program is frequently referred to as a prevocational unit.

Vocational training provides the discipline necessary for the patient to attain his job potential established in vocational evaluation. Vocational training requires carefully supervised instruction in vocations best serving the patient's needs with full regard to employment possibilities.

Sheltered workshop provides employment for disabled persons within the center. This is productive work for which wages are paid; the work is usually obtained on contract or subcontract basis. In this area, further vocational evaluation and training are possible.

Special education will be found in this area when enough patients have difficulties with certain areas of academic or vocational achievement. If children need this service, it may be located in their area. Frequently, this is provided through cooperation with the public schools.

Placement service is to be offered when the number of job placements and contacts warrants it; otherwise this service is performed by other agencies. In smaller centers placements may be handled by the vocational counselor. Placement may mean the patient's return to his former job, full employment by selective placement or partial or special employment either at home or in the sheltered workshop.

543

Supervisors will be in charge of the separate units of this area and will be responsible for integrating their unit with the total vocational effort.

The *director* will be in charge of the total vocational area and responsible for integrating this area with the rest of the rehabilitation center program.

Vocational Training

Vocational training is prescribed after evaluation of the patient's abilities, interests, and job training has begun.

The vocational training unit provides opportunity for growth in ability and assurance in actual job situations or experiences as close to reality as possible. During this period of training, the patient may continue to receive services from the medical unit, the social adjustment unit, or any other part of the rehabilitation center. (See Fig. 17.)

Differences in disabilities and the nature of the community will dictate differences in the kind of training program to be employed. In addition to working with local industry, the local training resources will supplement the center's training programs whenever practicable and suitable. Trade schools may accept only the more capable candidates who do not have emotional or medical problems, and in some cases, they may not be able to give the personal attention needed. The rehabilitation center deals with complex problems and disabilities; therefore, its vocational training unit will need to give greater emphasis to limited training objectives which are often more suitable to the restricted educational and cultural backgrounds of many of its patients.

Training in a range of vocations should be offered to accommodate several levels of abilities, skills, and interests. In addition, the changing personnel needs of industry make a representative range important.

There follows a sampling of some of the vocational training fields that the architect may be called upon to plan for:
1. Commercial
2. Tailoring
3. Drafting
4. Watch repair
5. Shoe repair
6. Furniture repair and upholstering
7. Machine shop operation
8. Radio, television, and appliance repair
(See Fig. 18.)

Sheltered Workshop

The sheltered workshop provides additional opportunities for further evaluation, training, and eventual employment of the handicapped individual. The sheltered workshop was once thought of as a place for terminal employment of those who could not benefit from further training. Today this concept has changed, and it is established as one of the steps in the rehabilitation process. There will, perhaps, always be some patients who, because of extensive or complicated disabilities, require the environment of the sheltered workshop as the only means of permanent employment.

The sheltered workshop is never an isolated unit in terms of program, but is part of the total vocational area which in turn is an integral part of the center. For selected patients, it is the best means of developing work tolerance, work habits, confidence, and skill. It also provides a means for the development of industrial quantity standards. The added incentive of pay for work done is often the motivation needed to help the disabled person carry through his rehabilitation program. This work is most frequently secured from industry or other sources on subcontract basis.

This work must be done within the most businesslike atmosphere and framework, yet without undue pressures of time; however, it must meet the standards of quality and guarantee delivery of the required quantities on time schedules. It must provide payment for services rendered and rewards in terms of individual growth and development.

Location Within Building   The sheltered workshop should be conveniently related to the other areas of vocational services. It may be a detached or semidetached unit with a separate patient entrance, as patients engaged in the shop usually work an eight-hour-day program and no longer require the intensive services of the medical department.

Depending upon its closeness to the medical department of the center, the shop may require a first-aid room. In the larger workshop a full-time nurse may be required.

As work within the shop may be noisy, separation from quiet areas in the center is recommended.

For delivery and shipment of goods, it is essential that the unit be adjacent to a loading area.

Organization of Space   This area will closely resemble industrial space and will house industrial operations. The heating, ventilating, and dust collection systems will need to be planned accordingly, with floors designed for adequate loads and an electrical system to meet many different kinds of demands.

The type of work carried out in the shop will be subject to frequent change. Flexibility in organizing the space is, therefore, essential: the area should have a high ceiling and be free of columns. Floors should be designed to take heavy loads of equipment and stacked materials. Much of the work under contract in the shop will be of an assembly line nature. However, the products may merely require work surfaces for their assembly or they may require special equipment (frequently supplied to the center by the contracting firm if it is for a particular job). In laying out equipment in the shop, it is advisable to obtain expert industrial advice in order to assure efficient flow patterns and simplified handling and storage of materials and products.

Some work surfaces should be adjustable in height and all should be designed for the use of wheelchair patients.

Electrical power outlets should be frequently spotted along bench walls and/or the ceiling grid. Floor outlets for power tool use in the central area of the shop are recommended. Wiring should be sized to take a varying power demand.

Adequate general illumination should be provided with increased intensity at work stations as dictated by the task.

A time clock for the patients' use is sometimes provided in the workshop to encourage punctuality and to determine the patients' production rate.

All necessary safety precautions should be taken to protect the patient from power tool hazards, fire hazards, falls, and other mishaps. A potential hazard exists when there is insufficient space for the storage of materials and products. Ample storage space should be provided for the orderly, safe arrangement of bulky items. A sprinkler system installed in the shop will reduce fire risk.

Storage is a major problem and is related to the volume of items handled. The space for storage will vary from 15 percent to 50 percent of the work area.

Receiving, shipping, and handling of bulk items require additional space. This space

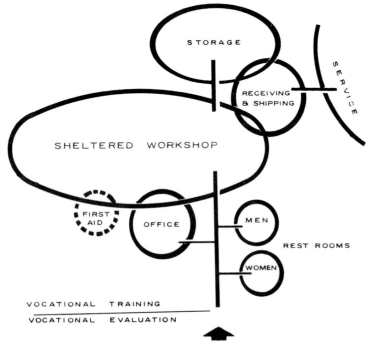

Fig. 17

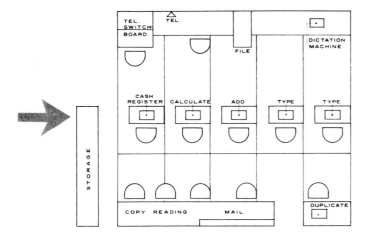

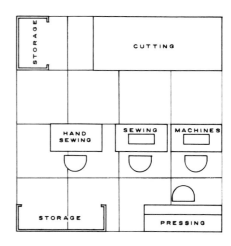

I. Commercial
- i) typists;
- ii) secretaries;
- iii) bookkeepers;
- iv) telephone operators;
- v) cashiers;
- vi) business machine operator;
- vii) copy readers;
- viii) bank tellers;
- ix) ticket agents;
- x) receptionists;
- xi) shipping and receiving clerks;
- xii) file clerks;
- xiii) sales clerks.

II. Skilled and Semiskilled
  A. Sewing and Tailoring
- i) spreaders;
- ii) markers;
- iii) cutter;
- iv) trimmers;
- v) pattern makers;
- vi) pattern graders;
- vii) tailors;
- viii) pressers;
- ix) hand sewers;
- x) sewing machine operators;
- xi) weave-bac specialists;
- xii) chair cover makers.

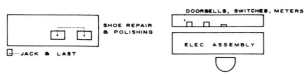

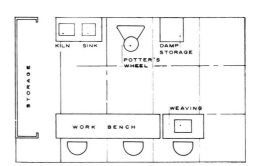

Skilled and Semiskilled
  B. Drafting:
- i) electrical draftsmen;
- ii) automotive draftsmen;
- iii) architectural draftsmen;
- iv) mechanical draftsmen.

  C. Commercial Art:
- i) layout men;
- ii) illustrators;
- iii) letterers;
- iv) window display artists;
- v) show card layout.

Skilled and Semiskilled
  D. Arts and Crafts:
- i) ceramics;
- ii) leather;
- iii) metal work;
- iv) weaving;
- v) jewelry;
- vi) electroplating.

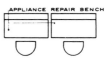

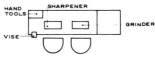

Skilled and Semiskilled
  E. Repairmen:
- i) business machines;
- ii) watch repairing;
- iii) assemblers;
- iv) tool sharpening;
- v) camera repairing;
- vi) shoe repairing.

  F. Electric Light, Power, and Electronics:
- i) meter readers;
- ii) meter men;
- iii) assemblers;
- iv) inspectors and testers;
- v) radio, television, electronic machine repairmen.

Skilled and Semiskilled
  G. Building Trades:
- i) carpenters;
- ii) painters;
- iii) plumbers;
- iv) masons;
- v) electricians.

  H. Woodwork Trades:
- i) patternmakers;
- ii) cabinet makers;
- iii) furniture repairmen.

  I. Plastics Production:
- i) bench grinders;
- ii) hand filers;
- iii) drill press operators;
- iv) assemblers.

Fig. 18

III. Machine Shop Operations:
   i) tool and die makers;
   ii) machine tool operators.

IV. Unskilled
   A. Restaurant Occupations:
      i) waiters and waitresses.

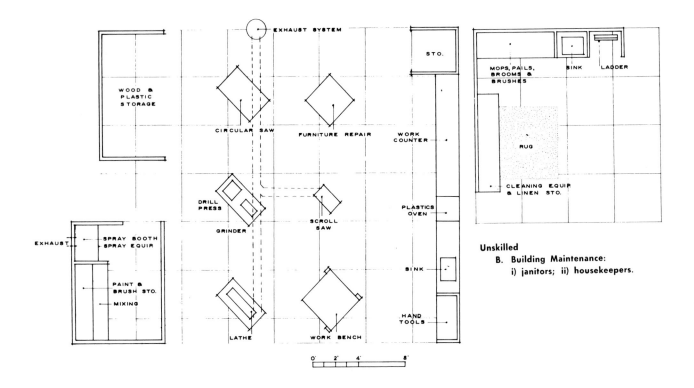

Unskilled
   B. Building Maintenance:
      i) janitors; ii) housekeepers.

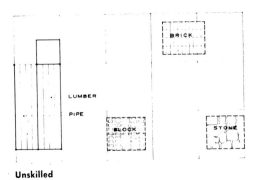

Unskilled
   C. Building Material Handling

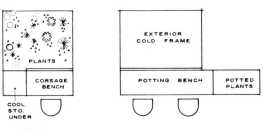

Unskilled
   D. Greenhouse and Floriculture:
      i) greenhouse worker;
      ii) flower preparation (corsages, etc.).

Fig. 18 (continued)

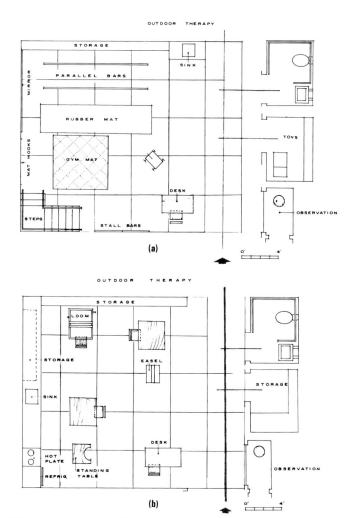

Fig. 19   (a) Children's physical therapy. (b) Children's occupational therapy.

program, facilities for snacks—refrigerator, hot plate, and sink—are indicated. Or locate this facility within the children's treatment and training area to serve the nursery as well as the occupational therapy room.

Exterior circulation involves both vehicular and pedestrian traffic. Buses, taxis, automobiles, and service trucks must be considered. *Parking spaces* should be located so that neither patients nor visitors need cross driveways to enter the building. Separate areas of the parking space should be designated for patient, staff, and visitor use. Appropriate directional signs should be considered for the efficient control of traffic. In some centers where many outpatients drive their own cars, a carport designed for wheelchair patients is a considerable convenience. (See Fig. 20.)

All centers will require a *service area* for the delivery of equipment, supplies, and fuel. However, centers with kitchen facilities, vocational training programs, and a sheltered workshop will have a greatly increased service problem; and the service area and its relation to other traffic must be studied accordingly.

Adequate *maintenance shop* facilities are essential. The shop not only will serve general maintenance purposes, but frequently will be used for the repair, modification, or fabrication of furniture and equipment used in the center.

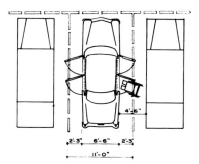

should be related to a loading dock and truck service area. The service area should be planned so that it does not interfere with other vehicular or pedestrian circulation.

As patients working in the shop will usually work an eight-hour day, facilities for their comfort should not be overlooked. If the center has no dining facilities, a lunchroom convenient to the shop is recommended, as some patients will bring their lunches with them. Provision of a cafeteria is also considered a desirable facility where the number of patients warrants it.

Most states have specific requirements for rest areas for men and women. These requirements should be checked carefully before planning lounges, toilet facilities, and lockers for the patients in the workshop.

A small office for the workshop supervisor should be provided, and so designed that there is maximum supervision of the shop activity from the office. Additional office space will be required for records, cost accounting, and estimating. The size of this area will be determined essentially by the volume of work and number of contracts handled by the workshop.

Physical Therapy Exercise Room   The requirements here are similar to those needed in the exercise room for adults, except that the equipment is selected for the child's size and interests. (See Fig. 19.)

The space indicates a minimum exercise area staffed by one therapist.

Treatment cubicle requirements are the same for children as adults; equip them with treatment tables and ceiling-mounted mirrors above.

Relate the area to outdoor therapy for outdoor exercises.

Provide a sink for the therapist's and children's use.

Toilet facilities for children should be immediately convenient to the exercise room and outdoor therapy.

Special equipment may have to be designed for individual cases. Figure 19 illustrates a movable stall bar and parallel bars adjustable in height and width for children of varying ages.

Occupational Therapy   Equipment should be selected for the child's physical and mental age level. The plan indicates an area staffed by one therapist.

Place toilet facilities convenient to the therapy room.

Relate the room to the outdoors so that some activities may be conducted outside.

Although special equipment may be required for individual cases, equipment indicated includes standing tables, typing tables, work tables (all with adjustable heights), loom, easel, and workbench.

Provide a sink within the room for the children's and therapist's use.

As training in eating may form a part of the

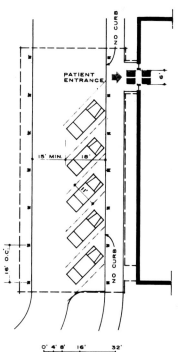

Fig. 20   Parking space for cars operated by disabled persons.

547

The Physical Plant

The physical plant shall provide a safe and sanitary environment with adequate diagnostic and therapeutic resources.

The design and construction of the physical plant should be appropriate to the type of services it houses, to the staffing and organizational pattern of the facility, and to local geography and style. It will, therefore, be unique for each facility, but it must be safe and must make a positive contribution to the efficient attainment of the facility's goals. It must satisfy the physiological as well as the psychological needs of patients and staff.

Sleeping units for patients are designed to promote comfort and dignity and to ensure privacy consistent with the patients' welfare. In the absence of other state or local requirements, there is a minimum of 80 sq ft of floor space in single rooms and 70 sq ft of floor space per person in multiple patient rooms. It is desirable that multiple patient rooms be designed to accommodate no more than six patients, but preferably four. There may be a need for appropriate security measures incorporated into the physical design of some wards.

There is a minimum of one lavatory for each six patients, one toilet for each eight patients, one tub or shower for each fifteen patients, and one drinking fountain on each ward. A lavatory is installed in each toilet area. Appropriate provisions are made to ensure privacy in toilet and bathing areas.

Since psychiatric patients are generally ambulatory and need to associate with other patients and with staff, there is provision for day rooms and recreational areas. At least 40 sq ft of floor space per patient is required for dayrooms. There are also usually solaria, a dining room or cafeteria where many patients take their meals, a vistors' room, a gymnasium, an exercise area in the building or perhaps on the grounds, and rooms for special treatment, interviewing of patients, group and individual therapy, etc. Other facilities for patients might include a locker room or individual lockers in the sleeping units, a small laundry room, a snack kitchen on each ward, and a coffee shop, clothing shop, and cosmetic shop for patients as well as employees.

Offices are provided for physicians, psychologists, social workers, nursing administrators, dietitian, and other staff members, and these are conveniently located to encourage effective communication with patients and other staff. Nurses' stations should be centrally located to permit full view of recreation areas and immediate access to patients and to treatment areas. Appropriate conference rooms are also provided, and there are suitable arrangements for clerical staff for each department or unit.

Standards for Psychiatric Facilities, The American Psychiatric Association, Washington, D.C., 1969.

SIX TYPES OF PSYCHIATRIC FACILITIES

Community Mental Health Centers

The community mental health center represents the formal reflection of the professional objectives of providing comprehensive services and continuity of care for the prevention, early detection, treatment, and follow-up care of mental disorder within a designated population. The comprehensive center is essentially a program rather than a building complex; it is a program that seeks to plan and coordinate the range of mental health services required to meet the mental health needs of a population. It is a combination of services either under a single administration in a discrete physical entity, under a single administration in multiple physical facilities, or under various administrations which, by contracts and/or agreements, are organized to provide the continuity of services noted above.

A center may be under governmental, philanthropic, or private auspices, or it may be supported by a combination of resources. If it is to be an effective agency, however, the community served by the center should participate in establishing the major needs, goals, and priorities of the mental health center. The community and the staff of the mental health center must define the goals and establish a priority system for the attainment of these goals. The community is ultimately responsible for identifying resources and needs, obtaining sufficient financial support to assure adequate numbers of competent personnel, adequately paid and given an adequate physical plant to implement the programs to achieve the stated goals.

As a minimum, the center must provide outpatient, inpatient, partial hospitalization (including day care) services, community consultation and professional education for other than the staff of the center, and clinical diagnosis and treatment on an emergency basis. It is also desirable that it participate in public education to promote or conserve mental health research to increase the body of knowledge about mental illness and the effectiveness of services utilized, home care and follow-up, nursing home care, vocational rehabilitation, guidance for the families of emotionally disturbed persons, and otherwise contribute to maintaining the optimal functioning of individuals with residual sequelae or complications of mental disorders. Services of the center should be easily accessible and widely publicized to the community served.

To provide comprehensive services and continuity of care, the community mental health center should have easy relationships with other "people-serving" agencies, and particularly with the public psychiatric hospital serving the area. Patient care must be coordinated between the center and other agencies, and patients must move from one element of service to another within the center with ease, as treatment needs indicate. For example, in mental health centers that are part of or closely related to general hospitals, the necessary inpatient, dietetic, laboratory, pharmacy, medical, and surgical services might be provided by the general hospital. Arrangements need only be made to ensure availability and ready accessibility for patients in the mental health center.

To be truly comprehensive, the mental health center must be responsible for the adequacy of services provided to persons with special problem mental disorders or to populations facing unusually chronic and severe emotional stress and who are alienated from their community or the broader community's supportive social systems. It may not be feasible for the center to provide all of the clinical services necessary in managing the difficult biological and social problems presented by drug dependency, alcoholism, aging, delinquency, mental retardation, or the many other special problems included among the mental disorders or in which mental disorder is suspected of playing a significant part. The center should, however, identify the population at risk for each of the special problems and plan a program to provide preventive, diagnostic, therapeutic, rehabilitative, or supportive services for each of these populations. It should identify the community's most likely agents for early intervention to assist or support individuals in each of these populations or identify agents who are providing therapeutic and rehabilitative care. The program should indicate the ways in which the center would be most useful to these community agents.

The responsibility for the mental health needs of a population implies that the mental health center should help various social systems of the community function in ways that develop and sustain effectiveness of individuals participating in these systems. The center should aid these systems in their support of persons with mental disorder. The implications for prevention, diagnosis, treatment, and rehabilitation are obvious; the recipient of mental health services includes the patient but the services extend to his family and to a variety of social systems. Consultation and education in the community are important functions of any center. In these ways the center responds to the community's need for interlocking, strengthening, and expansion of all its resources that have a bearing on mental health. Community consultation and education offer possibilities for influencing mental health beyond the confines of hospitals and offices and thus contribute to the prevention of mental disorder.

To deliver this broad range of services, a flexible organization with a multidisciplinary staff is required. In addition to the usual professional staff of psychiatrists, psychologists, social workers, nurses, and activity therapists, there may be a variety of nonprofessional personnel, volunteers, and social scientists to add new perspectives to the center. Staff may be organized by services (prevention, diagnosis, intensive treatment, extended treatment, rehabilitation, etc.), by programs for specific population groups (children, adolescents, the aged, alcoholics, mentally retarded, etc.), or by geographic areas of the community served. Regardless of the organization, there must be adequate qualified leadership, administrative and clinical, to assure thoughtful supervision, planning, evaluation, and coordination required to blend the array of available talents and resources into an effective center of services.

Responsibility and commensurate authority should be delegated to ensure optimal utilization of each person's skills, respecting principles of ultimate legal and clinical responsibility. As stated elsewhere by the APA, "The need for cooperatively defining the area of activity and responsibility for professionals who participate in the care of patients requires that physicians or their designees be recognized as having the ultimate responsibility for patient care. They, and they alone, are trained to assume this responsibility. In the public interest, other professionals or nonprofessionals, when contributing to patient care, must recognize and respect this ultimate responsibility.[1]

Psychiatric Outpatient Clinics

In a psychiatric outpatient clinic, a psychiatrist assumes responsibility for providing diagnostic, consulting, and therapeutic services for outpatients with the help of a professional staff that includes at least the disciplines of psychiatry, psychology, and social work. This staff nucleus may be supplemented as needed by representatives of related disciplines, such as pediatrics, internal medicine, neurology, mental health nursing, speech therapy, remedial techniques, physical and occupational therapy, and rehabilitation.

Members of the various disciplines not only work on the staff but also function on the team in daily practice, coordinating their skills to meet the needs of patients. The psychiatrist who serves as director sees that this coordination is effective. He assumes responsibility for all clinical functions and is on duty sufficient time, on a regularly scheduled basis, to adequately discharge his responsibility. He assures adequate evaluation of all new patients, supervision of the staff, and sustained direction of the total program of services. The psychiatrist-in-charge retains overall authority, but may delegate administrative, as distinct from clinical, responsibility to a nonmedical executive or administrator.

In addition to diagnosing and treating patients, the clinic provides training for professional psychiatric personnel and those of other disciplines as well as education for the public; it participates in various community endeavors related to the mentally ill and carries out research. The methods of implementation and the proportionate emphasis given to the various functions differ according to local circumstances, community needs, and clinic policy.

The clinic may serve patients for whom appropriate psychiatric assistance in a convenient outpatient clinic may prevent more prolonged illness, those recovering from a stage of illness that required hospitalization and who may need further outpatient care as they resume a regular way of life, those who are referred for prehospitalization evaluation, and those who can benefit from temporary therapeutic intervention to overcome a life crisis.

[1] *Principles Underlying Interdisciplinary Relations Between the Professions of Psychiatry and Psychology* — A Position Statement by the Council of the American Psychiatric Association, February 1964.

Admission policies for outpatient clinics vary. Many clinics have an "open door," or "walk-in," policy, indicating that they accept both self-referrals and referrals from community agents. Others accept only those cases that have been referred by another professional source. Some clinics specialize in the diagnosis and treatment of children, adults, or special populations, such as people with alcohol problems. Each clinic has a written plan indicating the scope of its admission policy and referral plan, and the plan is well known to all referring sources.

The services of a clinic may be offered on either a full- or part-time basis, according to local circumstances. Whatever its arrangement, the clinic should be accessible to the members of the community it serves. For example, a clinic serving an area where many working people are paid by the day or hour with little or no provision for sick leave should be open some evenings or weekends so as not to discourage or penalize those who would have to take a loss in pay to begin or continue treatment.

The clinic's participation in community service plans is an important responsibility. Some individuals may have a problem that can best be removed or alleviated by another agency, and the clinic cooperates with other community resources wherever possible. Some patients need help from several sources, and the professionals involved must clarify the needs and outline areas in which each can be most effective. Working relationships with surrounding inpatient facilities are maintained to achieve easy flow of patients in and out of inpatient services and to avoid administrative delays and failure of communication about patients.

The clinic may be affiliated with a medical school, hospital, welfare or public health department, or other appropriate professional organizations for the exchange of services, scientific advancement, and professional and administrative support. If not, it achieves these aims through the use of qualified consultants or by establishing a professional advisory board of appropriately qualified persons.

The psychiatric outpatient clinic is often asked to furnish an evaluative report regarding a patient. The content of a report is determined by the purposes of the agency for which it is prepared and it is in keeping with ethical practice.

Psychiatric Services in General Hospitals

All general hospitals should have a well-known plan for receiving, management, and disposition of psychiatric patients. If the general hospital has a psychiatric service or department, there must be a qualified psychiatrist in charge, with appropriate allied personnel, particularly nursing personnel who have had training in the management of psychiatric patients.

Every general hospital must think through its responsibilities for the person presenting himself with psychiatric symptoms, in order either to admit the patient or to assist in quickly referring him to the nearest treatment resource capable of providing prompt diagnosis and treatment for the particular case. The feasibility of establishing a psychiatric service in a general hospital as a part of the network of the total community health program will depend upon many factors, including local needs, the availability of other facilities, the availability of staff, and the orientation of the medical professional in the hospital and community.

Whether a separate psychiatric service can or cannot be provided, it is frequently possible to use some general medical, minimal care, or other beds for psychiatric patients and to secure the services of a consultant psychiatrist. All good general hospitals have a plan for handling psychiatric emergencies, such as acute toxic reactions, suicide attempts, and acute behavioral disturbances. Small hospitals may have two or more rooms for such patients, pending their transfer to a hospital where special psychiatric facilities are available. It is advisable that no patient with suicidal tendencies be released without psychiatric consultation if a psychiatrist is available.

When the general hospital has a psychiatric service, the service provides for the care and treatment of patients admitted for psychiatric disorders and also for those patients who, in the course of hospitalization for another reason, experience a psychiatric illness. Most patients are admitted voluntarily, although occasionally the hospital seeks legal authority for detaining one who is very disturbed. Any limitations on admissions, such as those imposed by the physical construction of the unit or by the training and experience of its staff, are clearly stated in the plan of the hospital.

Because of the small size of the psychiatric unit in most general hospitals, the unit usually focuses on intensive short-term therapy and diagnostic services. Some general hospitals have, however, found it possible to develop suitable facilities and staffing to admit and treat psychiatric patients who are expected to remain over 30 days. Some hospitals also have provision for partial hospitalization, in addition to round-the-clock services, and for outpatient services to former patients and others who do not need full-time hospitalization.

Experience has indicated that, expressed as a percentage of the bed capacity of the hospital, the number of psychiatric beds required will vary from 3 to 15 percent, the most usual figure being about 10 percent of the total beds. A capacity of 20 to 26 beds in one nursing unit seems to be most efficient. When a hospital is capable of supporting more than this number of beds, they are usually provided in two or more nursing units. Experience has shown that men and women may be treated in one unit if adequate facilities are available.

Since the psychiatric service operates as an integral part of the hospital, many of its functional services are provided by the hospital administration. These might include most of the general professional services: i.e., medical, surgical, and dental; dietetic, laboratory, x-ray, pharmacy, library, chaplaincy, and medical records; and administrative and maintenance services.

Private Psychiatric Hospitals

Private psychiatric hospitals are nongovernmental specialty hospitals. Like general hospitals, they may be operated on either a nonprofit or for-profit basis. They have the responsibility of providing treatment programs with definitive goals for the welfare of the patient, with the realization that the period of hospitalization may be only a segment of the total treatment plan.

The medical staff should make use of the opportunity provided by a high ratio of medical staff to patients to regulate the therapeutic program and to observe the processes of illness and the response to therapy. The most advanced approaches to treatment, and individualization of program to meet each patient's

MENTAL HEALTH CENTERS

needs, should be employed. The hospital should take advantage of around-the-clock observations by many trained observers, and multidisciplinary views in conference, in the evaluation of therapy and the integration of theory and practice. There should be a periodic evaluation of the effectiveness of the hospital therapeutic program. Although the primary function of the hospital is to maintain excellence in psychiatric treatment, the professional and administrative staff should be encouraged to utilize the unique opportunities for education and research.

Most private psychiatric hospitals serve their geographic communities—local, state, and regional—although a number of them, because of their special or unique treatment programs for specific categories of patients, receive referrals from wherever in the world these patients come.

Private psychiatric hospitals, therefore, vary greatly. Each follows the program determined by its medical staff, its approach to treatment and its goals. Each private psychiatric hospital must have established written procedures by which it will either admit a patient or quickly refer him to the nearest, most appropriate, treatment facility. A qualified psychiatrist must be responsible for the treatment of the patient, and there must be other mental health professionals, including nursing personnel with training in psychiatric nursing.

The length of stay in a private psychiatric hospital should be commensurate with the goals of therapy and the patient's illness. In keeping with the current concepts that early and effective intervention may result in the return of the patient to his community after a very short period of hospitalization, the average length of stay is less than 60 days in three-fourths of the private psychiatric hospitals. To meet the ultimate needs of the patient, many hospitals maintain medium- or long-term intensive treatment programs as well. The primary goal of hospital treatment is not the shortest possible stay but the most effective therapy. Within the limits of therapeutic goals, the hospital should provide the type and amount of treatment that will result in the patient's resumption of healthy functioning.

Public Psychiatric Hospitals

A public psychiatric hospital is defined as an institution provided by the community—whether city, county, state, provincial, or federal government—for the diagnosis, treatment, and care of patients with psychiatric and neurological disorders. Most hospitals in this group are state or provincial hospitals. They provide both short-term and long-term treatment and admit patients both voluntarily and by legal commitment.

While it is recognized that variations in the usual type of state hospital organization are suitable in certain localities, the essential professional, diagnostic, treatment, and administrative and maintenance services described in the preceding section on general standards can be applied to all public hospitals by individual interpretation. Each public hospital has an important function to perform in providing necessary psychiatric services to its community and in promoting psychiatric education and research. Recognizing the advantages of affiliation with medical schools and other medical centers in their areas, many public hospitals have established formal programs of participation in cooperative educational and research efforts.

Whether the total treatment program of the

hospital is separated into discrete units depends upon its size, its type of organization, and the medical administrative philosophy. However, patients have individual and differing needs, and the treatment program, however administratively organized, seeks to serve these various needs.

The hospital should be large enough to meet the community's needs for psychiatric services, but not so large as to compromise its ability to meet the needs of each patient for individual treatment. Optimal size might be described as the most efficient and effective balance between the facility's ability to meet the unique needs of the community and its ability to meet the unique needs of each patient. One method that has been devised to achieve this balance is the unit system.

Larger hospitals may operate under this system, with several semiautonomous patient care units making up the complex. The treatment programs are organized into separate units of similar size, staffing, and types of patients. Regardless of how long he stays, each patient is admitted, treated, and discharged within the same unit. His treatment is the responsibility of the same group of staff members from admission to discharge and aftercare. In some instances, the units represent specific geographical areas; this enables the professional staff to work closely and continuously with professional and lay community agencies from that region. Other facilities do not find this geographic admission plan practical and prefer to admit patients to each unit in rotation. Regardless of how admissions are handled, the goal of each unit is appropriate treatment for each patient at the most appropriate site.

The treatment program may include separate wards for certain types of patients with special treatment, educational, and rehabilitation needs, such as children, adolescents, alcoholics, patients with tuberculosis, and others who require intensive medical treatment in addition to psychiatric care.

Increasingly, public hospitals are following the mental health center concepts of comprehensiveness of service and continuity of care. They are, therefore, developing a range of services, including programs of varying degrees of partial hospitalization, outpatient services, rehabilitation, vocational guidance, and aftercare in addition to the intensive inpatient treatment programs. A proper balance of these other programs allows for the more efficient use of the inpatient services.

The concept of the "open door" has been applied to the majority of wards in most psychiatric hospitals. The open hospital encourages early treatment by emphasizing the voluntary nature of hospitalization and the expressed confidence of the staff that the patient can accept responsibility for his own management. Freedom of movement enables patients to do many things for themselves that might have to be done by staff members under other conditions, and thus allows more staff time available for the promotion of active treatment. It is necessary for some facilities to maintain a closed ward or wards, however, for those patients who may be likely to endanger the safety and welfare of themselves and/or others. Confidence in the facility can best be maintained if appropriate precautions are taken to protect the community from the exceptional patient who has in the past caused it concern.

The hospital encourages and participates in community planning for the development of appropriate alternative resources and facilities to deal with social problems that have in the

past often been assigned to the public psychiatric hospital due to the lack of available alternatives. The most appropriate and efficient use of scarce psychiatric resources requires that all possibilities for securing the best treatment and care for each individual patient be explored by the patient's family, the family physician, and community social agencies, and that a broad range of resources be available in the community to meet the multiplicity of needs.

The hospital encourages community provision for diagnostic, treatment, rehabilitation, and educational and preventive mental hygiene services for former patients, and for those for whom hospitalization may be averted, to ensure a comprehensive network of mental health care services. Within this network some services may be provided by the hospital's mental health clinic, which functions on a regular, scheduled basis, either in a fixed location or on a traveling basis. The clinic assists in the rehabilitation of former hospital patients, advises those about to enter the hospital, offers treatment to those who do not need hospitalization, and diagnoses and/or treats children with behavioral or educational problems. The staff of the clinic includes as a minimum a psychiatrist, a social worker, and a psychologist, and, if the hospital has adopted the unit system, the same team follows the patient from preadmission interview to discharge and follow-up care. The services of the clinic also include follow-up counseling, evaluation of adjustment after discharge, and medical supervision of drug dosage.

Services for the Mentally Retarded

The past ten years or more have brought about a dramatic change of basic concepts regarding the care and treatment of persons with the mental retardation syndrome. Consequently, requirements of care and treatment have shifted to an extent that the newly developed or developing facilities can no longer be considered as one compatible group of "hospitals and schools for mental defectives" as was the case in earlier years.

First of all, the care, treatment, education and training of mentally retarded persons in the low borderline and educable range have shifted significantly from residential facilities to day schools. Trained or qualified educators along with other specialists (medicine, audiology, speech, and physical therapy) provide meaningful and adequate services within the public school system or in schools operated by affiliates of the National Association for Retarded Children.

Secondly, the care, treatment, and training for more severely retarded children (trainables) are being provided in many communities in a manner similar to that in which these services are rendered for the youngsters who are educable.

As a third observation, it must be acknowledged that, for some years now, there has been an observable trend for those persons who suffer from the rather severe to severest degrees of retardation (decerebration syndrome) to outnumber either the educable or the trainable retardates in state institutions. Their demand upon the availability of total lifelong care has become a dominant factor.

Thus, it is no longer possible to establish meaningful standards based upon traditional concepts. A new approach is indicated that takes into consideration factual changes and continued transition.

The complexities of needed services can best

be dealt with by projecting various life-span requirements as known to us. However, we shall not attempt to make specific recommendations for those services that are non-medical in nature.

The Infant and Small Child Most mentally retarded children are retarded at birth (prenatal and paranatal retardation), although it may not be evident at the time. They require diagnostic, prognostic, and treatment services.

The pre-school-age medical clinic may operate as an independent agency, a part of a general hospital, or a part of the state hospital-training school system. In any event, utilization of existing services and efforts at integration in regional areas will be made and standards must be established and maintained to meet existing needs.

It is desirable that the director of the clinic be a well-qualified pediatrician. He will have medical consultants on his staff (neurologist, child psychiatrist, ophthalmologist, dentist, physiatrist, nutritionists, public health nurses, and others as needed). Essential are full-time or part-time qualified social workers, clinical or developmental psychologists, audiologists, speech, occupational, and physical therapists and medical secretaries. The number of staff employed must correspond to the needs of the patients referred to the clinic.

The clinic must have adequate space to function. It must have available all diagnostic tools and procedures that are necessary to establish an inclusive and comprehensive diagnosis, such as roentgenology, clinical and anatomic pathology, biochemistry, genetics, and electroencephalography.

All personnel must meet licensing and/or certification requirements of their respective professions. The clinic, if it is eligible, must meet the standards of the Joint Commission on Accreditation of Hospitals.

The Younger School-Age Child Mentally retarded children, once properly diagnosed, will re-quire a broad range of varying services:

Children who are ambulatory and without significant adjustment problems are, generally, entered into nursery schools with subsequent promotion into subprimary and appropriate grades of the public school system. State licensing procedures establish necessary standards for personnel and facilities.

Children who are not ambulatory or who have major adjustment problems that cannot be dealt with in the public school system or the private home may require in-residence facilities that provide special orthopedic or psychiatric services or services to the blind, deaf, or others. All children in this category will be given the required additional diagnostic, treatment, rehabilitative, and educational services that are needed to assist them to develop their optimal potential. Such programs must be multidisciplinary, under qualified medical direction. Thus, they must meet the requirements of the Joint Commission on Accreditation of Hospitals.

As the process of treatment and rehabilitation progresses, a differentiation of each child's long-range needs will become evident. It may lead to discharge into the community and referral to a child guidance clinic and to the public special school system. It may require prolonged hospitalization because of specific medical requirements. Or, it may result in providing lifelong protective care in an accredited institution for the chronically ill (extended care unit), a licensed nursing home, or a licensed boarding home. In any event, local, state, and/or federal licensing requirements must be met and the facility should be accredited by the Joint Commission on Accreditation of Hospitals if it is eligible.

The Progressing Preadolescents and Adolescents Most of the mentally retarded youngsters in the educational and training programs will reach the limit of their academic potential before the age of sixteen. Therefore, it is necessary that meaningful and adequate prevoca-tional programs be available at the appropriate time. Whether such a program is part of a public school system or an integral part of a private or public residential care facility, it must meet the licensing and certification requirements of the state and/or federal government. Under the current legal definition, a mentally retarded youngster capable of rehabilitation, as interpreted by the Division of Vocational Rehabilitation, qualifies at age sixteen to participate in this program.

Adequate day care programs and/or domiciliary facilities must meet the program needs of the clients. Also, they must meet licensing or certification requirements of each licensing body (department of health, department of labor, department of education, the fire marshal, department of insurance, etc.).

The Young Adult and the Adult By the time a retarded person is eighteen years of age, his future role in our society can be assessed fairly accurately, in most instances. The need may range from living more or less independently in the community or in a supervised group-living program (hostel, sheltered workshop) to residence in a licensed boarding home, a licensed nursing home, or in an institution for chronically disabled or ill persons. Correspondingly, he may be economically independent, partially self-supporting, or receive public support through Medicare, Medicaid, Social Security, or aid to the permanently and totally disabled.

In any event, adequate legal and social provisions must be made to protect the person with the mental retardation syndrome against physical, emotional, social, or economic exploitation and abuse. Also, regardless of where the retarded adult lives, he must have adequate access to all community resources that he may need at any given time in his life span. This will require programmed supervisory services that can be included in an adequate protective mechanism (Guardianship Act).

MENTAL HEALTH CENTERS

SPATIAL NEEDS OF PROGRAM ELEMENTS

NOTE: Design of all spaces should be noninstitutional. The following are suggestions for consideration in all program element needs indicated below:

Openers in space-planning
Live plants
Design for groupings of 4 to 8 persons
Comfortable light level (natural light, desk lamps, incandescents instead of neon, etc.)
Freedom for hanging pictures
Warm surface finishes in natural materials
Views outside
Contact with outdoors
Visual access to mainstream of activity.

The following does not assume that all services must be located under one roof (see Location of Services).

1. Inpatient Unit

This is a short-term residential facility for living under a supervised therapeutic program, requiring a domestic or college-dormitory rather than a hospital atmosphere. Architectural Section, NIMH, recommends this area be classified residential occupancy (NFPA No. 101) where permitted by local authorities.

Patient Needs

Privacy for sleeping, dressing, and bathing.
Provision for personal grooming needs.
As few regulations for use of facility as possible.
Patients should be able to rearrange furniture, hang pictures on wall, etc.
Patient belongings should not be out of reach—lockable storage space should be provided in each patient's bedroom unless specifically prohibited by program.

Domestic Needs to Be Provided   Laundry and snack kitchen for use by each living group (16–24 patients).

Socialization Areas   A variety of settings is necessary:
Space for small conversational groupings or quiet individual use (2–4 persons). Example: small living space in a suite of two or four bedrooms.
Activity spaces for games, dancing, music, group living (16–24 persons). Two living areas are desirable to allow noisy and quiet activities to occur simultaneously. Quiet activity space could also be used for group therapy. Example: a large living room as the focus of living group activities with a smaller, comfortably furnished lounge adjacent.

Visiting Area   Space should be provided for private visiting with family and friends. Example: an out-of-the-way alcove for 6 persons, located near the entrance to the unit and the nurse's station, allowing visual and conversation level acoustical privacy.

NOTE: each group of 16–24 patients requires the above spaces. Design should allow natural groupings of 4–8 persons.

Physical Planning Guidelines for Community Mental Health Centers, Clyde H. Dorsett, AIA, Architectural Consultant, National Institute of Mental Health, Bethesda, Md., 1978.

Recreation—*physical exercise*   Space in the form of an exercise room, gymnasium, or outdoor space (especially in warm climates) should be provided. Example: small exercise room for group setting-up exercise program with agreement to use high school gym and playing fields located within easy walking distance.

Staff needs

Lounge area
Storage for personal property
Staff toilet
Area for charting/private discussion with therapists
Security for drugs
Multiuse patient interview space, family discussion, etc.
Minimal barriers to interaction with patients. Example: desks are preferable to glazed nursing stations.

Housekeeping Needs

Domestic housekeeping:
Linens—in patients' bedrooms or locate for central distribution
Each bedroom unit to have own linen supply
Bathroom and personal items
Central janitor's closet
Dietary services:
Snacks, patients' activities in kitchen
Feeding—hospital cafeteria and kitchen service on units; storage for dishes, linens, etc.
Icemakers
Complete domestic kitchen—exhaust system must be adequate

Intensive care

Acoustical privacy
Social space for contact with staff and freedom to leave confined room
Close supervision by staff
Controlled access to toilet, wardrobe, light switches outside patient's room
Security
Tamperproof equipment and fixtures within patient's room and toilet (but not obviously tamperproof to patient)
Tempered plate glass or removable-type detention screens
Treatment room—first aid, emergency physical examination items for special programs such as drugs, alcohol, etc.
Laboratory with storage
Direct access from nurse's station and from emergency rooms in general hospitals
Audio communications between nurse's station and patient's room
Patient rooms may be used for medical care when needed.
Necessary equipment not removable from the room must be lockable and concealable.
We recommend occupancy for this area be institutional.

2. Emergencies

Emergency can occur in any element of service at any time. Most common:
1. walk-in
2. escorted emergency
Walk-in: arriving at any element of service for the first time to get help. This person may come in alone or with others. He [or she] is ambulant and functioning.
Escorted emergency: ambulant but not functioning.

Physical Space for Walk-in:

Inviting entrance
Must have immediate relationship to outside while patient is in waiting-reception area
Privacy with receptionist in stating his [her] needs
NOTE: all spaces for walk-in interview and initial treatment, admitting of walk-in emergency can be those used by outpatients.

Escorted emergency

Will utilize all staff and space in emergency suite of general hospital.
Additional spaces may be needed in general hospital emergency.
Space:
Interview space that promotes communication between patient and physician.
Holding space—waiting bed space—for patient to wait while disposition for treatment is considered (i.e., sedated patient).
Entrance available directly to intensive care area for escorted emergencies.
NOTE: design and location should motivate interaction and communication between all agencies and elements of service utilizing the facility.

3. Outpatient

Admitting Offices   Should be convenient to receptionist

Ancillary Services

Waiting areas
Secretarial space
Public and staff toilets, lounge (coffee, sink, refrigerator), and library-workroom

Waiting Areas

Limited to 8–12 patients
Distributed throughout office areas
Receptionist by front door—open, friendly, encourage contact between receptionist and patient

Office space	Conference and interview	Meetings (with consultation and educational service)
Play therapy	Group therapy*	Larger groups
Individual	Staff conferences	Community groups
Family	Interagency professional groups	General meetings

* Group therapy rooms to be utilized through total programs

Children's Treatment Adjacent to entrance and child therapist's office
Provide for observation
Provide for work sink (as part of "messy area"), and locked storage
Provide for separate toilet available to children; separate waiting area, with possibility of observation by parent; outdoor play space; scaled for children; cleanable surfaces

Office Space Should motivate communication between patient and therapist, should contain doctor (staff) and at least four or more patients and be flexible in arrangement of furniture.

Conference Spaces
Sufficient to accommodate 16 people
Suitable for audiovisual presentations, staff meetings, staff work area
Accessible to main entrance and/or office spaces and rest rooms
Suitable for group therapy
Provides storage closet

Staff Lounge Should be comfortable for 8 people adjacent to staff toilets, storage, and small kitchenette (coffee-making, lunch, refrigerator); also adjacent to staff library and workroom.

Need for large meeting room depends on availability of space in the community. Such a room needs audiovisual facilities, storage space, and sufficient toilet areas; it should be located between central facilities and community.

4. Partial Hospitalization
Day Care This requires a primary social area (living-room-type space)
1. Staff needs
   Office space for day program director
   Work area for staff
   Medications
   Nurses' lockers and toilet
   (All located in position for information and control for particular hospital program)
2. Patient's needs
   Storage for wraps and for personal articles
   Telephone, drinking fountain
   Toilets
   Kitchen suitable for social groups and therapy

Occupational Therapy This consists of quiet and noisy activities and depends on the program. The most flexible design requires at least two rooms of classroom size with two kinds of storage: for patients' projects and materials and for equipment. The office for the program director is mostly program space for patient occupational therapy activities with the occupational therapist as part of the therapy team. It may be without staff offices and consist of large rooms divided by movable storage cabinets.

Recreational Therapy Social recreational therapy has the following requirements:
Large social space
Outdoor terrace for gardening, outdoor games, and an inactive outdoor area for quiet
T.V.—music
Quiet indoor space
Movies
Kitchen, canteen-type
Library (quiet)
Quiet social area
Not minimal but desirable are a swimming pool with its own dressing rooms and toilets; and table games.

Structured recreational therapy programs require a small gym, for 8–12 patients at one time, with its own showers, dressing rooms, and lockers. One should inventory the community facilities that can be used: YMCA, schools, shopping centers, public parks, public pools, and other mental-health related programs in the community. An active outdoor area must be available with a playing field, large space for active games, etc.

The R.T. office can be same as for O.T. Weekend and night-evening program can be held within the same space as the inpatient program.

5. Children's Day Care

General needs include a staff office, a central reception room—gathering place, and classrooms. The program could utilize the adult gym. Toilets and a small snack kitchen should be available. (They could be used for other parts of the center's program.)

Classrooms need an area for messy (wet area) work (sink, etc.), an outdoor area, a teacher's work area with a desk (no desk in classroom), and also, for problem kids, quiet study; this class is separated from main classroom area by a curtain. Children's outdoor play space must be separated from adult outdoor areas.

6. Administration

Reception-waiting area
Director's office—meeting room nearby
Offices for program directors
Volunteers and part-time office and lounge—with lockers and toilets
Conference room
Library-workroom—staff lounge
Business—secretarial pool
Central records for all service elements

7. Consultation and Education

Meeting rooms and office spaces are located adjacent to or within central office groupings. Center can multiuse spaces for other elements of program for this purpose. (Basis of operations for C&S is out in the community and will use facility only to conduct business and for meetings.)

CIRCULATION

1. Use for Socialization

Circulation space can be used for more than transportation from one area to another. Informal contacts, pausing along the way to look at views, stopping for a cup of coffee at a coffee bar are activities that also encourage *social contact*.

Entry–Waiting Area Entrance through the front door to all program elements located in the facility should be possible. Arriving persons should be greeted by a staff person out in the open. Example: volunteer behind a desk located in sight of front door. Waiting areas should be small—groups of 4 to 6—in sight of receptionist. Waiting area allows view of mainstream of activity, but is located in well-defined area out of main traffic pattern.

Drinking fountain, toilets, and pay telephone are adjacent to entry-waiting area. A coffee pot is preferable to vending machines.

Contact with Staff Staff persons (volunteers, secretaries) should be located to be visible to persons moving in circulation pattern of building. Example: secretary for outpatient offices located in alcove with chairs for waiting adjacent to circulation space.

Provide informal social areas as part of circulation space leading to meeting rooms, partial hospitalization, etc. places where numbers of people congregate, and also at "nodes" in circulation system—places where people are likely to pause. Example: gathering space with area for coats, bathrooms outside community meeting room.

Waiting for outpatient appointments should be adjacent to outpatient staff offices. Director of Center should be located adjacent to other staff offices to encourage interstaff contact.

2. Orientation

Use of views outdoors and natural light—clear inside/outside circulation.
Clear relation of program spaces to front door: go here for outpatient, go there for day program, go around corner for inpatient.
Privacy or separation provided by single turn in corridor or by screens—minimum of closed doors.
Staff person to greet arrival to program area—secretary for outpatient area, nurse or volunteer located by entrance to inpatient unit, etc.
Use staff and design of circulation space rather than barriers (locked doors) for control.

3. Time use

Locate community meeting areas near front door for night-time use—lock off rest of facility.
Partial hospitalization/inpatient section could have its own entrance for day/night use.

4. Variety

Circulation spaces should contrast light, dark, outside, inside, narrow, wide, free, controlled, stimulating (warm colors), subdued (cool colors) to provide clues to kind of activities associated with nearby program spaces and to maintain orientation. Example: corridor outside day program area widens to allow informal socialization and use of lockers located against one wall and is lit by skylight.

5. Zoning

Program elements should be related to:

Public accessibility
Acoustical separation
Heavy circulation/noisy activities
Quiet/private activities
Scheduled use/nonscheduled use
Frequency of use
Day/night use
Unique or common use
Sole staff use
Sole patient use
Joint use by staff and patients
Relation to other program spaces
Relation to front door
Need for outdoor space and natural light
Need for privacy/controlled access

NOTE: The prevalent dichotomy between circulation/service spaces and program spaces should be minimized where possible.

Health
NURSING HOMES

By WILLIAM BREGER, AIA

INTRODUCTION

Current thinking in health planning emphasizes the concept of providing a spectrum of care which serves the health needs of the entire community. This spectrum includes general medical and surgical facilities, mental, rehabilitation, and tuberculosis hospitals, and long-term care facilities, hereafter referred to as LTC, which provide care beyond acute, short-term medical and nursing care and may be in either chronic hospitals or nursing homes.

While the functions of a chronic hospital are relatively clear, what is understood by a nursing home can be somewhat ambiguous. For our purposes, an LTC may be defined as a facility which is operated either independently or in connection with a hospital and provides nursing care and medical services under the general direction of persons licensed to practice medicine or surgery. Furthermore, unlike the chronic hospital, the LTC generally does not have resident physicians and limits its medical services to minor treatment, diagnostic x-ray, and minor laboratory analysis. Although good medical practice should be available wherever and whenever a patient needs it, the fact is that major medical and surgical treatments are almost always performed in other facilities.

Eight categories of LTC facilities are readily identifiable: general hospitals with long-term-care beds, voluntary chronic hospitals, local government chronic hospitals, public home infirmaries, convalescent homes, voluntary nursing homes, proprietary nursing homes, and infirmaries or homes for the aged. Other nomenclature for the categories listed above are *extended care facilities, intermediate care facilities, shelter homes for the aged, geriatric homes for the aged,* and *long-term-care facilities,* homes for adults, foster homes, boarding homes, etc.

Each type has its own criteria for admission based for the most part on the type of care required; but reimbursement, whether through private payment, private medical insurance, Medicare or Medicaid, etc., may as well be a determining factor in patient placement. Whatever problems are involved, the fact is that patients often require a wide range of services beyond initial acute medical care, and these services may cross several "institutional lines," from intensive nursing and rehabilitative care through lesser degrees of nursing care to perhaps simply convalescent attention.

SOCIAL PLANNING CRITERIA

The basic criterion used in determining the needs for all health care facilities is the ratio of beds to the population served. Generally, we find that there are approximately 13.2 beds

Hospital statistics from Health and Hospital Planning Council of Southern New York, 1970 and Long-Term Care, (LTC) Projection, 1973. Illustrations from Michael B. Miller and William N. Breger, "How to Plan for Extended Care Service." *Modern Hospital,* October 1966

per thousand population. A characteristic distribution of these beds is shown in Fig. 1.

Thus, the characteristic distribution of LTC in all categories is 4.8 beds per thousand, and, equally important, is the understanding that the most significant single characteristic of this patient population is that they are elderly. Their age characteristics are indicated in Fig. 2.

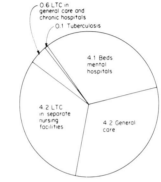

Fig. 1 Ratio of beds to population served.

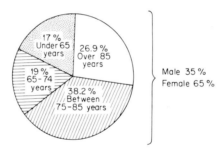

Fig. 2 Age characteristics of patient population.

As Dr. Michael Miller says,[1] studies of this aging population in terms of their characteristics from a medical viewpoint have indicated that terminal cancer is seen in only 3 to 5 percent of the patient population. Varying degrees of organic brain syndrome, as manifested by memory, intellectual, and judgmental deficits associated with confusion and disorientation, with or without locomotion disability, constitute at least 70 to 75 percent of the patient population. Recent studies indicate that 20 to 30 percent of a nursing home population may be expected to have experienced a significant psychiatric decompensation in the pre-aged period. Of the whole, 40 to 50 percent will demonstrate significant cardio-renal-vascular disease in varying degrees of decompensation. Arthropathies are virtually a universal occurrence, although only 20 to 30 percent may

[1]"Synthesis of a Therapeutic Community for the Aged III," published in *Geriatrics,* vol. 21, pp. 151–163, August 1966.

require specific management techniques. Fifteen to twenty percent of the patient population will present significant visual deficits, and there will be approximately the same number with auditory deficits. Other organ system involvement in the same patient is the rule rather than exception, such as gastrointestinal, pulmonary, neurological, and metabolic disorders. Multiorgan pathology in the chronically aged is a distinguishing characteristic of disability in contrast to other age groups.

The utilization rate differs as well. Extended care facilities, both independent and attached to general hospitals, have an average turnover of 7 to 8 patients per year per bed, or approximately 40 to 50 day stays, and there are less rapid turnovers for other LTC facilities (proprietary nursing homes, 1.17; voluntary nursing homes, 1.69; voluntary chronic hospitals, 1.30; public home infirmaries, 0.91; average of all LTC facilities, 1.43 per year).

One can conclude as well both from the demographic changes in a society that is proportionately growing elderly and the societal changes of placing the elderly members of society in medically oriented facilities that the LTC facility would have a greater percentage of beds allotted to it proportionately in the future and that this area of health concern would experience real as well as proportional growth.

Another aspect of social planning is the translation of social data into the architectural program. We have found that the ideal method of determining the physical facilities of the building is in terms of the proposed patient population rated by their capacities to perform activities, including daily living, both in terms of their physical capabilities and their behavioral capacities. Tables 1 to 4 describe the clinical nature of the patient population under study and give some index of the percentage of patient population in each group. At the conclusion, we will indicate the physical configuration of the nursing units that each group generates.

Group I—Physically Disabled (15–25 percent)[2]

Patients having significant physical disabilities but with emotional and intellectual intactness and the ability to socialize in an open, unsupervised environment. (See Fig. 3.)

Group II—Mentally and Physically Disabled (25–30 percent)

Patients with severe physical disabilities with superimposed substantial handicaps of organic brain disease, thus requiring total nursing care for physical disabilities and major supervision for social activities. (See Fig. 4.)

Group III—Custodial (15–25 percent)

Patients presenting moderate or no physical handicaps with either no or minimal emotional or social disabilities, thus able to function in an uncontrolled social milieu. However they

[2]Based on 1,050 patient survey by W. Breger at Columbia School of Public Health and Hospital Administration, 1970.

function best in a professionally supervised environment. (See Fig. 5.)

Group IV — Mentally Disabled (30–50 percent)

Patients having minimal to mild physical disabilities with major emotional and social disabilities, who therefore require minimal nursing care on a purely physical level but because of the advanced degree of organic brain disease (senility) these patients are essentially totally and permanently disabled. (See Fig. 6.)

DESIGN CRITERIA

The design problems unique in this facility mainly involve the nursing units and supportive facilities that are required in terms of the projected patient population. The problems in-

herent in dietary, mechanical maintenance, and general and building storage facilities are fairly uniform regardless of the type of projected patient population and have a basic similarity to medical facilities of the same size, such as general hospitals, tuberculosis hospitals, etc. It should be noted that supply storage facilities, linens, equipment, etc., would depend to some extent on the projected patient population.

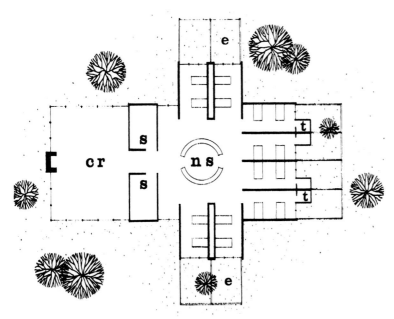

Fig. 3 Group 1, physically disabled. Symbols represent the following facilities: CR, community room; NS, nursing station; T, toilet; S, services (i.e., utility rooms, treatment, bathing, pantry, nonpatient storage); P, pantry, E, outdoor environment. (This list applies to Figs. 3–6.)

TABLE 1 Group I Facilities*

Area	Design requirements
Community room	Unsupervised
Physical therapy	Combined with community living
Exterior environment	Unsupervised
Bedrooms	Sufficient area for wheelchairs, walkers, crutches; half of rooms with bedside flush toilets
Toilets	20-22 in. from floor
Bathing	Near nurses' station, must be supervised
Utility room	Near nurses' station
Pantry	Supervised, near nurses' station
Storage area, personal	Limited vertical storage; increase in horizontal storage
Nonpersonal storage	Limited vertical storage; increase in horizontal storage
Treatment room	Near nurses' station
Family counseling	Near nurses' station
Nurses' station	Located for convenience of nurses

* Group I patients suffer severe physical handicaps but are emotionally and physically intact.

TABLE 2 Group II Facilities*

Area	Design requirements
Community room	Supervised
Physical therapy	Combined with community living
Exterior environment	Supervised
Bedrooms	Sufficient area for wheelchairs, walkers, crutches; half of rooms with bedside flush toilets
Toilets	20-22 in. from floor
Bathing	Near nurses' station, must be supervised
Utility room	Near nurses' station
Pantry	Supervised, near nurses' station
Storage area, personal	Limited vertical storage; increase in horizontal storage
Nonpersonal storage	Limited vertical storage; increase in horizontal storage
Treatment room	Near nurses' station
Family counseling	Near nurses' station
Nurses' station	Located for convenience of nurses

* Group II patients suffer severe physical and behavioral disability. Therefore they require total nursing care as well as major supervision of social activities.

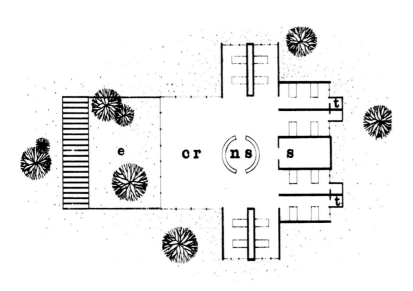

Fig. 4 Group II, mentally and physically disabled.

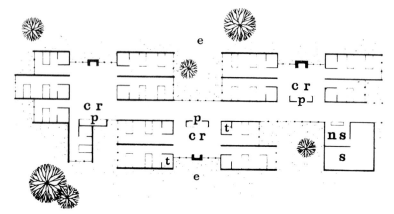

Fig. 5 Group III, custodial.

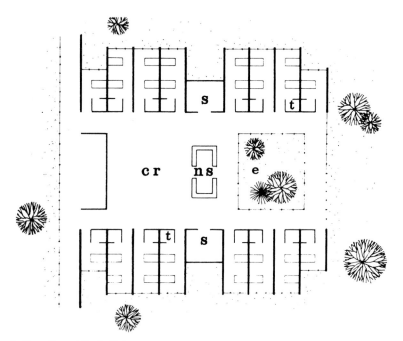

Fig. 6 Group IV, mentally disabled.

TABLE 3 Group III Facilities*

Area	Design requirements
Community room	Unsupervised
Physical therapy	Not indicated
Exterior environment	Unsupervised
Bedrooms	Conventional
Toilets	Conventional
Bathing	May be located conveniently; nonsupervision permissible
Utility room	Not indicated
Pantry	Unsupervised, near community room
Storage area, personal	Increase in vertical storage; conventional horizontal storage space
Nonpersonal storage	Increase in vertical storage; conventional horizontal storage space
Treatment room	Not indicated
Family counseling	Near nurses' station
Nurses' station	Located for convenience of nurses

*Group III patients require little supervision because they present no, or very moderate, physical and emotional and social disability.

TABLE 4 Group IV Facilities*

Area	Design requirements
Community room	Supervised
Physical therapy	Not indicated
Exterior environment	Supervised
Bedrooms	Conventional
Toilets	Conventional
Bathing	Supervised, but located conveniently for patient
Utility room	Not indicated
Pantry	Supervised, near nurses' station
Storage area, personal	Increase in vertical storage; incease in horizontal storage space
Nonpersonal storage	Increase in vertical storage; increase in horizontal storage space
Treatment room	Not indicated
Family counseling	Near nurses' station
Nurses' station	Located to permit control of patient areas

* On the purely physical level, patients in Group IV need little nursing care but require maximum supervision because of emotional disability.

Because, generally speaking, nursing home administrators cannot determine patient population beforehand—or they choose because of administrative and economic patterns to have a wide mix of patients, the common interpretation of the structure is to have the nursing and activity functions not flexible. This type of building is in a great degree determined by the relevant codes and the most economical means of construction. It has been our experience, however, that the criterion of initial low construction cost results in high administrative, maintenance, and operational costs, and as building costs are a very small percentage of what the patient pays, a debt service of $2.50 to $5.00 a day, it appears a false economy. Another factor that should be explored is that operational care could be improved even in the uniform nursing unit if the design were determined to a greater extent by an awareness of the proposed patient population.

Regardless of what overview decisions are made, the design of the typical LTC is basically concerned with (1) the relationship of area size to the daily census in the facility, (2) the analysis of these areas in terms of the different functions, and (3) the criteria used in discerning the nursing unit layout and supportive facilities.

1. In most instances the program delineates the size of the LTC facilities. It is determined by such factors as available money for construction; the need within a community as determined by demographic factors or methods of health care, code requirements, site limitations; and, finally, the kind of operation as foreseen by the administrator or nursing home operator. The nursing unit is a prime factor in operational cost, and thus the size of the facility is usually a multiple of the number of nursing units. Because of the cost of operation of feeding, therapy, and administration, the larger the facility, usually the more economically efficient it will be, although too large a unit might not allow for adequate patient service functions. The average size in 1970 was 80 beds, and the present recommended criterion is that it should not be less than 120 beds. In high-operational-cost areas, economically viable nursing homes require a minimum of 200 beds. Once the number of beds has been determined,

the areas of the building can be calculated, bearing in mind such factors as the care given, the stipulation of single-bedded or multi-bedded rooms, and the community facilities provided. Again, in the typical facility at present, where community functions are non-existent or minimal and where the number of single- and multi-bedded rooms are determined by code or FHA regulations, etc., the size varies between a total building area of 250 and 400 sq ft per bed.

2. Although, as previously noted, it is desirable that the inter- and intraconfiguration be determined by the medical and social patterns of patient care, there are common facilities that are required for operation by codes and public agencies. Thus, in an overall sense, the design of all independent long-term care buildings will contain the following component parts:

1. Administrative facilities
2. Staff facilities
3. Public facilities
4. Medical, treatment, and morgue facilities
5. Dietary service
6. Storage areas
7. Work area and maintenance areas
8. Mechanical facilities such as boiler, air conditioner, pump
9. Patient, staff and visitor circulation patterns.
10. Nursing units including ancillary facilities—i.e., nurses' station, nursing unit dayroom
11. Supportive and rehabilitative facilities for patients, such as recreation, dining, therapy areas

The component parts listed above, except for items 10 and 11—the nursing unit and supportive facilities—are similar to those of general hospitals, and thus criteria developed for general medical facilities, as indicated in the section on "Hospitals," may be applied to the LTC facilities. Some indication of the ways in which the areas of the LTC differ from those of the general hospital are listed below.

1. Administrative Facilities Although there has been a great increase in staffing patterns in recent years nursing home administration facilities still require significantly less area and have fewer employees than do general medical facilities. The reasons for this are that nursing homes provide fewer medical, surgical, and laboratory services; administrative problems are reduced by the lower turnover of patients (less record keeping and billing); and, usually, there are fewer visitors per patient per day, although there may be more family counseling. The administrative employees in a nursing home would number between 5 and 10 per 200 patients, and the area required would be about 150 sq ft per employee. However, with the administrative and bookkeeping problems involved in government aid programs and other funding, there has been a remarkable increase in the required area for administrative purposes in recent years, and it is expected that this trend will continue. Generally speaking, there are the following areas: a business office; a lobby and information center; an administrator's office; an admitting and medical records area; an administrative staff toilet room, supervising nurses' areas; social service office; and staff conference room.

2. Staff Facilities As stated above, the reduced medical services provided, as well as the usual absence of staff physicians, results in a concomitant reduction of staff in an LTC facility as compared with a general hospital. Often the staffing is determined by patient population and is indicated in administrative codes, such as at least two registered nurses per facility,

one licensed practical nurse per 20 patients, and one aide per patients.[3] These are usually female, whereas other employees, such as porters and kitchen workers, are mixed. Generally speaking, LTC facilities have $\frac{1}{2}$ to 1 employee per patient, and 80 percent of them are female.

The facilities needed are locker rooms, toilet and shower facilities, and dining room. There is some question as to the location of these facilities—whether they should be grouped in a separate area or distributed on each nursing floor with a smaller central grouping. There should be a central lounge, and it should be accessible to the employees' dining room.

3. Public Facilities The type and size of the public facilities depend to some extent on the type of sponsorship of the LTC facility; but one factor is constant: the number of visitors in the LTC facility is much smaller per patient than in an acute general hospital. This is often reflected in parking criteria and internal visiting areas. Where the general hospital may require one visitor parking space per bed, the LTC facility requires one visitor parking space for between 3 and 20 beds. Architectural features that are desirable are a visitors' lavatory on each nursing floor and, when the building is large enough, a small lobby with perhaps a snack and gift shop. When an LTC facility is community sponsored, a variety of public functions may be provided for it, but these would be similar to what is provided in a community supported general hospital.

4. Medical, Treatment, and Morgue Facilities As we have mentioned, both legislative requirements and medical practice require that major treatment of the acutely ill patient in the LTC be available within general medical and surgical hospitals. This gives the community an economical use of both staffing and facilities. Sometimes chronic hospitals in nonurban areas provide as part of their facilities intensive medical and surgical units; but with the notion of regional health care, this is not considered by most health planning agencies to be desirable today. The facilities in the LTC which are provided, where the law permits, are a diagnostic x-ray unit, a laboratory for hematology, biochemistry, etc., and, usually as part of the nursing unit, treatment rooms. It is desirable that spaces for dentistry, podiatry, and, on occasion, optometry, be provided if the patient population can support them. However, all these operations can usually be carried out in comparatively small areas.

The requirements for a morgue facility have varied with different localities and different regulations. It is ultimately a problem of operation whether they should be provided or not, but if required because of geographic or administrative reasons, the morgue is at best a small area used for storage of bodies for a few hours or a day or two at most. The autopsy procedure is a hospital function.

5. Dietary Facilities In the LTC as in the general hospital, the dietary requirements and the space and equipment required to support them are extensive and the basis for involved research and analysis.

Feeding is required for nourishment and as a patient activity, and, quite understandably, the social functions of dining are important

[3] Another way of interpreting staff requirements is by using the New York State Code which requires of staffing time one hour of nursing care for ambulatory patients, two hours of nursing care for the semiambulatory, and four hours per day for the bedridden or wheelchair-confined patient.

therapeutically. Feeding is accomplished in five different methods in medical facilities: (1) Intravenous infusions, naso-gastric tube feeding, gastrostomy feeding; (2) with trays in bed; (3) at tables in patient rooms; (4) with trays in a controlled recreation room on the patient floor; and (5) family style in a controlled dayroom, in the nursing unit, or on a separate floor. It is understandable that methods 4 and 5 will be favored and used more frequently in the LTC. Here the social dynamics of group situations can be developed, and it is also a more efficient way of providing patient dining. Many have held that feeding intravenously or with trays in bed are undesirable in terms of an LTC facility, but they are occasionally used, depending on patient conditions. Feeding at tables in patient rooms is used more often because it is possible to control behavioral problems in this dining context. The size of the facility, however, is smaller, as the number of employees is much lower than in a general hospital.

6. Storage Facilities In the recent past considerable thought has been given to ways of resolving the storage problems of LTC facilities. Formerly large patient storage areas, as much as 25 sq ft per patient, were required, and there were minimal requirements for household supplies, linen, and furniture. However, the idea of the patient bringing possessions to the LTC to be stored is considered anachronistic, and the criterion used in designing storage areas today is about 5 sq ft per patient for personal storage and 5 sq ft for general hospital supplies and goods. The latter is less than what is allotted in a general hospital, because, as previously mentioned, the type of care required in a nursing home does not demand as many linens, pharmaceuticals, and supplies. However, the elements of hospital storage should be provided, and the importance of ensuring the flexibility of the compartments for this cannot be overemphasized.

7. Work Area and Maintenance Areas In general these are quite similar to those of the community hospitals, except that there is a minimum of medical equipment to maintain and that, although the number of patients may be similar to the general hospital, the total amount of equipment in the LTC requiring maintenance or repair is considerably less. We have found a single large room to be more than adequate in these areas for most LTC facilities.

8. Structural and Mechanical Factors During the last few years, the LTC facility has been designed to meet the structural and mechanical standards of the general hospital. As in most other medical facilities, problems, particularly of fire safety, have required fireproof buildings, often with sprinkler protection, smoke detectors, zoned floor areas, and rigid standards of fire resistance in terms of flooring, surfaces, and materials used. It is, of course, a fact that fire safety in a building housing many patients with behavioral problems (often involving carelessness and disorientation) is one of the major, if not the major factor in construction. While this appears evident, there are also other aspects of mechanical equipment criteria that are somewhat different than those for the short-term general hospital:

a. Lighting It has been our experience that the level of illumination required for the LTC, bearing in mind the elderly patient population and their reduced sensory awareness and perception, is somewhat higher than that required in the patient areas of the general hospital. Furthermore, the problems of safety require that all electric lamps and fixtures be firmly connected to a surface to avoid tipping.

b. *Heating and Cooling* An imperative decision that has concerned the LTC administrator has been the method of heating and/or cooling. It is generally found that the elderly are far more likely to complain of being too cold than of being too warm. Therefore, in terms of the patient population, the provision of adequate heat without provisions for cooling has been considered satisfactory. Another factor is that the confused patient cannot be expected to reliably perceive or control his environment. Presently, the thinking is that the use of air-conditioning facilities is desirable, ideally with individual controls. However, even here there are problems for the patients in multi-bedded rooms.

c. *Ventilation* A characteristic of many LTC facilities, because of the behaviorally difficult patient, is the problem of ventilation and the control of odors. It is a much more serious problem, at least for the staff and public, in this facility than in the general hospital and must be resolved by proper ventilation methods, the use of surface materials that do not retain odors, and the use of plumbing and furniture that allow for easy mopping and cleaning. The professional literature on this subject is extensive, and this aspect of mechanical equipment should be thoroughly researched before the LTC facility is designed.

9. Circulation Patterns The movement of people, goods and equipment in the LTC is for the most part similar in nature, if not in intensity, to that in general hospitals. The one special problem is the need of adequate control for the circulation of the behaviorally difficult patient, for often the need to control the movement of this type of patient comes into conflict with the need to provide free movement in terms of fire department regulations. The use of mechanical devices such as buzzers attached to fire doors, the shortening of corridors, the visual control of elevator doors, and controlled exits from the building are some of the factors that can help control the traffic problems involved with this patient population.

10. Nursing Units and Supportive Facilities An almost seminal practice in the design of LTC facilities is the placement of patients in autonomous nursing units, as it is believed that the control and management of patients can best be achieved in this manner. This nursing unit can be defined as a self-contained grouping of rooms, supportive facilities with unified control, all on one level. A basic decision is the size of the nursing unit, and while ideally the size of the unit will have a direct relationship to the degree and type of patient care provided in the unit, nursing home codes and governmental regulations generally set the number of patients cared for in a nursing unit between 30 and 60. In principle, the range could be even greater, as the spectrum of patients in LTC facilities is so varied. Thus as Table 3 shows, patients in Group III (custodial patients) could be in units of up to 100 beds, while patients in Group II (mentally and physically disabled patients) might be in units of 20 beds.

Concomitant with the decision as to the number of beds per nursing unit is the determination of the number of beds per room. Here the guidelines are medical operational criteria, hospital and administrative codes, and financial mechanisms. But also a very important consideration is the aesthetic and social values that the patient may have, and, even more important, those of the people placing him in the home. Thus, often patients with minimal cognitive awareness, requiring as much group support as possible, may be erroneously housed in single rooms because of social pressures.

Most thinking today is that the two-bedded room with adjoining or private bath should be the basic room pattern regardless of nursing unit size or type of care required, and that there should be a certain number of single rooms as well within the unit for medical and behavioral problems.

Codes require at least one single room per patient unit as an isolation suite with its own toilet, but often the requirements are that single rooms be available for 10–33 percent of the patients. However, the problem of the single or the multi-bedded room, as well as the other functions of the nursing unit, should (once the minimum code requirements are resolved) be determined by the criterion of what patient population would be served in the program given to the architect, and, as pointed out above, the criteria can range from minimum requirements to aesthetic and social values.

Supporting the idea of the autonomy of the nursing unit are the types of ancillary facilities that are part of it. The functions that must be provided are the control of the unit from the nurses' station, the preparation of medicines, the cleaning and providing of the entire range of supplies necessary for the patients, the supplying of supplementary food, and whatever bathing, recreation, dining, and training facilities are required. The question of whether patient treatment (e.g., surgical dressings, etc.) should be done in the room or in a separate treatment room depends on the choices that the nurses make. All of these functions are usually translated into representative areas as determined by the relevant codes. Listed in Tables 1 through 4 is an analysis of the types of areas, the required equipment, the minimum size, the function, and the relationships that seem to be generic in terms of regulations. The fact, of course, is that, depending on the projected patient population, the types and sizes of these facilities would vary. Thus, in Group III, medical preparation and treatment might be eliminated and the pantry might be made much larger than for other patient populations. However, most codes do allow, if not flexibility in the type of function required, a fairly wide range in terms of the size required.

The essential thrust in the design of the LTC is ultimately in the configuration of the nursing unit, and, as mentioned, the genesis of the choices available for this is in the operational program initially presented to the architect, or, even more salutary, when developed with the architect. In the overwhelming percentage of buildings, as has been stated, most of the plans are made for a variable patient population, ideally with a central nursing station adjacent to ancillary nursing functions that the nurse directly uses, with visual control of the patient corridors, recreation area, and means of entrance and egress. The size of the units, both for economy of structure and operation, is as large as the relevant code would allow. However, as has been pointed out, there is really little difference between this nursing unit

and a general hospital nursing unit, despite the fact that one is meant for an average 5-day stay and the other for an average 400-day stay. On a theoretical basis, Figs. 3 to 6 illustrate the correlation of possible unit configurations based on the patient population. While these designs would obviously be modified by code, medical practice, economy, and a difficult problem of determining the projected patient population, we believe they are valuable as abstractions indicating the correlation of care and planning.

11. Rehabilitative Facilities Rehabilitation and physical medicine is the primary medical discipline involved in LTC facilities. Present thinking is that, in terms of the aged patient population, rehabilitation should properly be both a physical and behavioral therapeutic process. For the most part, this therapy is not centered on making the patient operational in society but rather on providing adjustments for the patients to live with their disabilities. Just as difficult an aspect of this adjustment as the physically based problems are those problems generated by behavioral disabilities. While, broadly speaking, spaces for therapy have meant facilities for physiotherapy, hydrotherapy, and heat therapy, the fact is that facilities for social therapy or facilities for developing social groupings should be part of the overall planning.

The areas for physically based rehabilitation are required by code, but the type of medical care given in these spaces is usually determined by the medical staff and administration. Often, physiotherapy, both in exercise and manipulation, has been considered sufficient for the patient population, and the location of this space has been both in separate rooms and as part of the dayroom, as this would induce a greater incentive for the individual patient to perform in terms of a peer group. Whether this area is separate or part of other areas, the fact remains that the use of such apparatus as parallel bars, exercise wheels, etc., under proper supervision, is a vital part of the patients' care. The need for hydro and heat therapies in the LTC facility has often been questioned. Ultimately, the decision to use these latter therapies is either an administrative or governing regulation.

Recreational spaces are needed for the behaviorally based therapies or what is sometimes called occupational therapy, which can be considered both physical and behavioral therapy. Whereas a central area is desired, often the actual therapy takes place within the nursing unit dayroom.

Often considered the best behaviorally based therapy is participation in a social community, whereby, as it has been demonstrated, many of the anxieties and much of the loneliness that is a concomitant of the aging process can be reduced. These group situations may take the forms of religious services, lectures, group games, group teas; even a bar has been used. However, the most important aspect that generates one of the most difficult planning decisions is the development of a community within the LTC, whereby patients will be providing support for others. In terms of architectural configurations, spaces for this activity have been arranged so that sleeping rooms open directly onto living rooms, or they have been provided by eliminating halls and having spaces open into large community areas. It is through the exploration of this problem that architectural planning may be considered an aid of therapy as well. The size of these

TABLE 5 Typical Regulatory Requirements for LTC Facilities

		Nursing unit		
Type and size of room	Activity	Equipment and sizes	Relationship	Comments
Single (125 sq ft) Multi-bedded (100 sq ft per bed), cubicle curtains required	Depends on patient population. Will serve for both sleeping and general activity, and may also include dining, recreation, and therapy	Beds (usually gatch type) with side rails, 36 by 86 in.; overbed tables (usually not required); bedside cabinet, 18 by 20 in.; chairs, straight back and arms (at least one chair per bed) Storage Space: Vertical storage—robes, outdoor clothing in closets or wardrobes, 1 ft 8 in. wide by 1 ft 10 in. deep, should contain shoe rack and shelf Horizontal storage—cabinets or built-in drawers, 1 ft 6 in. deep (Note: Ideally, vertical storage areas should be increased for ambulatory patients and horizontal storage increased for nonambulatory patients.) Optional Equipment: Small table, ideally round with a heavy pedestal base; platform rocking chairs, where patient conditions permit; lavatory; cabinet for storing patient toiletries (Note: Where private toilet is used, lavatory may be placed in toilet.)	Not more than 120 ft from nurses' station	See plans; desirable distribution should be based on administrative practices
Toilet (3 by 6 ft) Toilet and lavatory (3 by 8 ft and/or 6 by 5 ft)		Required: Grab bars, toiletry cabinet and/or space for toiletries, mirror (Note: lavatory should be accessible to wheelchair patients.) Optional: Divert-a-valve, bedpan washer		
Nurses' station (minimum 6 lin ft of counter with access space on both sides)	Control of nursing unit charting communications, storage of supplies and nurses' personal effects	Patient charts (9 by 12 in.—May be movable or set into the desk), chart rack for 40 charts (4 ft wide by 16 in. deep), writing desk, legal files, cabinet storage area, outlets for nurses' call system, telephones		
Nurses' toilet room (5 ft by 4 ft 6 in.)		Toilet, lavatory, toiletry cabinet, mirror	Convenient to nurses' station	Although not desirable, often used as visitors' toilet as well
Clean workroom (minimum 8 by 6 ft)	Storage and assembly of clean supplies such as instruments, etc.	12-ft-minimum work counter with back splash, instrument sterilizer, 2 sinks, drawer and cabinet storage	No more than 120 ft from patients' rooms	
Medicine room, 1 ft 6 in. by 5 ft cabinet (mediprep unit)	Storage and preparation of medicine	Sink, refrigerator, locked storage (Note: Facilities for preparation of medication can in mediprep unit.)	Adjacent to nurses' station	May be a designated area within clean workroom if self-contained cabinet is provided
Soiled workroom (minimum 8 by 6 ft)	Cleaning of supplies and equipment	Clinical sink-bedpan flusher, work counter, waste and soiled linen receptacles	No more than 120 ft from patients' rooms	
Enclosed storage space (4 by 4 ft)	Clean linen storage			May be a designated area within the clean workroom
Nourishment station 5 lin ft of counter and work space in front	Supplemental food for patients during nondining hours	Storage area, stove, sink, refrigerator Optional: Icemaker, coffeemaker		May serve more than one nursing unit
Equipment storage room (4 by 6 ft)	Storage of intravenous stands, air mattresses, walkers, similar bulky equipment			
Patient baths (showers not less than 4 sq ft)		One shower stall or bathtub for each 15 beds not individually served, grab bars at bathing fixtures, recessed soapdishes		At least one bathtub in each nursing unit

TABLE 5 Typical Regulatory Requirements for LTC Facilities (Continued)

		Nursing unit (cont'd)		
Type and size of room	Activity	Equipment and sizes	Relationship	Comments
Stretcher and wheelchair parking area (8 by 5 ft)		Open space	Easily accessible from hall, near exit and entrance of nursing unit	
Janitor's closet	Storage and cleaning of house equipment	Housekeeping supplies and equipment, floor receptor or service sink		Larger cleaning area desirable with garbage and linen chutes in vertical-type buildings
		Nursing unit and patient activity areas		
Dayroom; total area for patient activities, 30 sq ft per patient. Minimum size, 300 sq ft	Controlled and multigroup activities, religious services, lectures, group games, group teas, dining (most frequently this is combined with the dayroom, but it can be separate). Recreational therapy often combined with this area	Upholstered sofas and armchairs, preferably with straight backs and designed for ability of patients to sit and get up; straight chairs similar to those in patient rooms; rocking chairs similar to those in patient rooms; tables with firm supports and round or rounded edges, accessible to and of a height for wheelchair patients (preferably with pedestal supports and round tops); television sets on low tables or ceiling-mounted lectern	Required floor day room ideally to be controlled by nurses' station; different medical programs generate different relationships	Generally nursing unit dayroom is 15 sq ft per patient; common day and dining room is 15 sq ft per patient
Physiotherapy minimum 300 sq ft, approximately 3 sq ft per patient)			Central to LTC circulation from nursing units	
a. Exercise space	Exercising, treatment and training in ambulation, stair-climbing, and activities of daily living	Parallel bars, exercise wheel, ambulation track shoulder ladder, convertible exercise steps		Structural reinforcement necessary for ceiling mounted ambulation track and wall-mounted exercise wheels
b. Examination and massage space	Manipulations and massaging	Treatment tables with pads (3 by 6 ft)		
Hydro and heat therapy area may be combined with physiotherapy. Size included in area above	Use of water movement and heat as massage	Mobile stands, hydrocollater (2 by 3 ft high), infra-red lamp, whirlpools (partial- and full-immersion tanks), paraffin bath, patient lift, ultrasonic generator, microwave diathermy unit		Not usually required by code
Occupational or recreational therapy	Social and physical support in terms of creative actions	Hand looms, potter's wheel, painting equipment, easels, leatherworking tools, woodworking tools, sewing machines		Size of room varies depending on where activity is done. Often area is used primarily as a storage facility and for fixed equipment (i.e., kiln, etc.).

areas for social rooms is often delineated by relevant codes and average about 30 sq ft per patient, but usually the codes allow the distribution in either a nursing unit dayroom, floor lounges, or a common LTC dayroom to be done in terms of the administrative program. Again, the only rule we can recommend would be to arrive at this through the analysis of the particular patient population of the proposed facility. Listed in Table 5, in terms of the usual codes and regulations, are the typical patient activity areas, their size, the equipment they usually contain, and their relationships.

CONCLUSION

Mentioned above have been only the rough planning data of the design of LTC facilities. Microscopic analyses based on the kind of hardware patients with reduced manipulative ability can use, the types of furniture (such as seating that would allow easy access without strain, beds that would be sufficiently protective, and tables that would be sufficiently sturdy), the kind of plumbing fixtures that the elderly patient needs, and the kinds of interior surfaces are part of the literature of professional magazines and should be examined in detail. The essential basis, though, for understanding these aspects of the LTC is the understanding of the patient.

Nor is it our intention to discuss the major problem of aesthetic values in terms of this patient population. The range of what aesthetic an LTC facility should generate, whether the criterion should be what society wants, what the employees want, what the children of the patient want, or what the patients want is a question that individual decisions must resolve, and these can, it is hoped, be based on some empirical data. It is believed as well that the extended care LTC program should generate a building that emphasizes the quality of space required for a longer patient stay and that this quality should be different from that of the community hospital in both plan and form, visually and functionally. Finally, we should arrive at an architectural expression for this space that would be a rejection of institutional forms, such as long hallways, sterile color schemes, mechanistic furniture, purely utilitarian finishes, and an acceptance of the fact that sunlight, casualness, and comfort not only are desirable patterns but also are part of the therapy and well-being of the LTC patient.

The task of resolving this fundamental social problem of providing support for the ill aged is a social action that we have just begun to explore and to which architects can make a most meaningful contribution.

CHILD HEALTH STATION

The diagram (Fig. 1) shows the desirable space organization for a child health station.

Preferred location for the carriage shelter is within the building if space permits. If the shelter must be outside, it should be placed in the lee of the building.

The various rooms shall have space for the following equipment:

N.Y.C.H.A. Memo to Architects.

Waiting Room

Desk and chair at control point between waiting room and entrance to weighing and undressing room, etc.; movable chairs, with ample space between and around them; demonstration table; play pen, within the waiting room, minimum area 60 sq ft; small chairs and table; bookshelves, 36 in high.

Public Toilet

Located off waiting room. Provide one normal-sized toilet, and one child's toilet, one lavatory, set 28 in from floor.

Weighing, Undressing, and Dressing Room

Table; Bench-type clothes hamper; 25 cubicles; slop sink.

Anteroom to Doctors' Offices

Chairs.

Doctors' Offices

In each office: desk; two chairs; large table; smaller table; lavatory (standard apartment type).

Utility Room

Table; refrigerator; four-burner gas range; combination sink and laundry tray (standard apartment type).

Nurse's Office

Located adjacent to the waiting room, it can be used also for isolation space. It will need a desk and a chair.

Staff Room

Table and chairs.

Staff Toilet

Lavatory and toilet.

Consultation Room

Desk, two chairs, table, and three file cabinets.

Slop Sink Closet

Must have space for cleaning equipment.

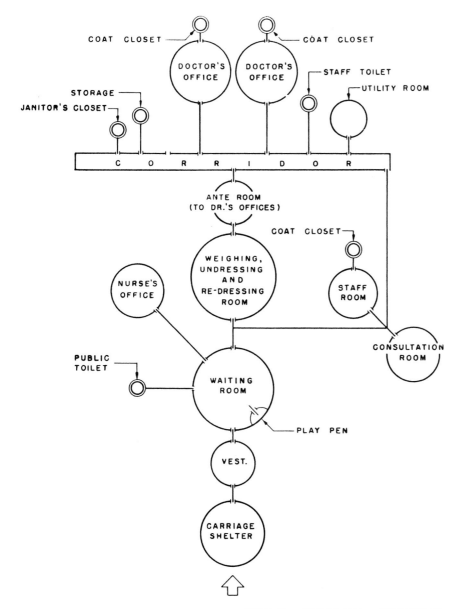

CHILD HEALTH STATION
SPACE ORGANIZATION

Fig. 1 From New York City Housing Authority, *N.Y.C.H.A. Memo to Architects.*

SITE AND PLANNING CONSIDERATIONS

Site

The modern medical center is so large and so complex that it should be located on the edge of the university campus rather than within it. This location will emphasize the fact that the medical center is a satellite in the university orbit, but has a degree of autonomy. It is important that students and staff in the medical center have easy access to the main university campus, and that the medical center be accessible to all areas of the university.

The site should be large enough to accommodate growth of the school programs and concurrent parking for at least 20 years. The minimum size recommended for a medical center including a teaching hospital is 50 acres, and 50 to 150 acres is preferable. Buildings should be placed on the site so that additions can be made as programs develop and as enrollment increases.

The service functions of the medical school involve patient care in hospitals and outpatient clinics. Growth of research and service responsibilities frequently leads to the development of specialized hospitals, such as children's, veterans', psychiatric, chronic disease, rehabilitation, or others. The site should permit location of these facilities in relation to the major teaching hospital so that staff and students can be within a five- to ten-minute walk. The teaching hospital and clinical science facilities should be placed on the site so that the educational functions relate to and connect with the basic science facilities. Outdoor facilities for rehabilitation of patients related to the clinic and recreation facilities for students related to housing should be provided. The extent of these facilities varies widely among schools. Adequate space for housing should be provided nearby. Apartment-type housing with play areas for children, within five minutes' walking distance of the hospital, is preferable.

Adequate parking facilities should be provided for students, staff, patients, and public convenient to each element of the medical center including housing. This may take the form of divided shopping-center-type parking, preferably with trees, various types of paved surface parking, or multilevel parking garages.

If possible, the site should be sloping so that more than one level of entrance to the buildings can be obtained and horizontal movement of supplies can take place at one level without conflicting with horizontal movement of people at another level.

The direction of prevailing wind should be studied so that buildings can be placed in relation to each other and to the campus and community to avoid windblown odors from cooking and incineration of animal waste and trash, bacteria from infected patients, chemical fumes, and low levels of radioactive isotopes.

The site for the animal farm is not usually contiguous to the medical center. However, a minimum site of about 25 acres should be

Medical School Facilities, Public Health Service, U.S. Department of Health, Education, and Welfare, Washington, D.C., 1964.

provided; recent studies indicate that 120 acres may be required. It should be located for convenient transportation to and from the animal quarters.

Functional Relationships

Of prime importance in planning medical schools is the relationship of its three major components: the basic science facilities, the clinical science facilities, and the teaching hospital. For the most efficient movement of students, faculty, patients, and supplies, the three should be interconnected, but for maximum flexibility in expansion each should be an independent element. Fig. 1 illustrates this relationship.

The basic science and the clinical teaching and research facilities, in turn, should be attached to the hospital to permit easy access to patient units and other hospital facilities. The diagram also shows the possibility of expansion inherent in this relationship.

In the basic science facilities, the departments can be stacked above each other with teaching laboratories, faculty, research and office space, and lecture rooms for each department located on the same floor. The cadaver preparation and storage department is usually located on a floor accessible to grade for convenience in handling cadavers. Central animal quarters serve teaching and research areas for both basic science and clinical departments. A location with direct connection to the circulation center and at grade level for access to a delivery entrance for animals is important.

Other common-use areas should be located where they are accessible to both the basic science and clinical departments. Thus, a basement location for such facilities as the radioisotope laboratory and technical shops is acceptable. Administrative facilities, school post office, snack bar, student lounge, and bookstore should be accessible from a circulation center and are generally placed on the first floor. Study cubicles for basic science students

should be convenient to both the medical library and teaching laboratories. The medical illustration area should be located for north light if possible.

Locating the clinical science facilities in connection with the circulation center provides access to the common-use facilities mentioned above. These clinical science facilities, similar to those provided in the basic science departments, consist of faculty research and office space, since third- and fourth-year students are taught in the hospital. Individual departments should be on the same floors as the patient-care units which they serve in the adjoining hospital. Study cubicles for third- and fourth-year students and house officers can be provided in the teaching hospital. Lecture rooms should be placed near the circulation center for greater flexibility of use.

The arrangements and relationships of the elements of the departments in both the basic and clinical sciences are generally similar. Facilities for an individual department should be on the same floor insofar as possible. Teaching laboratories and their auxiliary spaces in basic science departments should be separate from but near faculty offices and research laboratories.

Elements such as floor animal rooms and cold rooms, which are found in each department, should be stacked for economy. These facilities, together with lecture rooms, should be sized initially and located to take care of later expansion.

Toilet facilities should be designed to accommodate expansion. If located on a circulation center they will be accessible to adjacent departments. Separate elevators for passengers and supplies are recommended.

Program Assumptions

Because of the variations which exist among present schools and programs, it is apparent that space requirements for a new school cannot be stated dogmatically. There is great need,

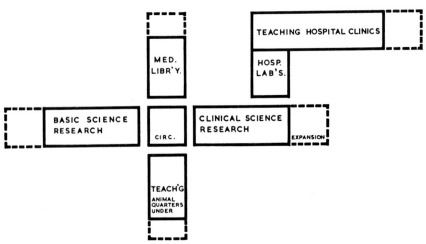

Fig. 1 Functional relationship of medical school elements.

however, for some benchmark for planning a new school.

In this section, it is assumed that the basic science facilities, clinical science facilities, and teaching hospital are contiguous.

The space considerations and requirements presented in this section are for two hypothetical schools including basic science facilities, clinical science facilities, and a teaching hospital. The first is School A, with an entering class of 64 students and a hospital of 500 beds; the second is School B, with an entering class of 96 students and a hospital of 700 beds.

School A

1. Is a four-year university-based school.

2. Provides space to house an entering class of 64 medical students, with a planned expansion to an entering class of 96 students. Enrollment in third- and fourth-year classes will be 60, with future expansion to 90.

3. Provides office and laboratory space for a full-time faculty of 35 in the basic science departments and 60 in the clinical departments.

4. Provides space for 40 graduate students and postdoctoral fellows in the basic science departments and 30 in the clinical departments.

5. Provides either conventional or multi-discipline teaching laboratories for the basic sciences.

6. Has its own library, with ultimate capacity of 100,000 volumes.

7. Has its own teaching hospital of 500 beds.

9. Has its own technical and maintenance shops, but heat is supplied from a central source.

10. Does not provide space for teaching students in other health professions such as dentistry or nursing.

School B

1. Is a four-year university-based school.

2. Provides space to house an entering class of 96 medical students with third- and fourth-year enrollment of 90 per class.

3. Provides office and laboratory space for a full-time faculty of 50 in the basic science departments and 85 in the clinical departments.

4. Provides space for 55 graduate students and postdoctoral fellows in the basic science departments and 40 in the clinical departments.

5. Provides either conventional or multi-discipline teaching laboratories for the basic sciences.

6. Has its own library with ultimate capacity of 100,000 volumes.

7. Has its own teaching hospital of 700 beds.

9. Has its own technical and maintenance shops, but heat is supplied from a central source.

10. Does not provide space for teaching students in other health professions such as dentistry or nursing.

GENERAL ADMINISTRATION AND SUPPORTING FACILITIES

General Administration

The dean of the medical school is responsible for the formulation and execution of policies of the teaching programs and for the general administration of the basic sciences, the clinical sciences, and the teaching hospital. Because of the magnitude and complexities of these programs, the dean will require assistance from competent persons in these fields. Table 1 gives the net area for administration.

TABLE 1 Net Area for General Administration

Type of facility	School A (entering class of 64 students)		School B (entering class of 96 students)
	Square feet		
Total	3,900		4,700
Dean's office	400		400
Assistant dean's office	200	(2)	400
Secretaries' offices	450		600
Conference room	500		500
Business offices	400		500
Registrar and alumni	250		300
Postgraduate office	250		300
Scholarship and grants	250		400
Records	200		300
Public information and publications	200		200
Public toilets	200		200
Waiting room	500		500
Storage	100		100

Medical School Library

The medical school library includes the offices, work areas, stacks, carrels, vaults, reading rooms, alcoves, conference rooms, audiovisual rooms, and other related spaces required by the maintenance and service responsibilities connected with the care and use of recorded medical information.

In programing and designing the medical school library, consideration should be given to the probable impact of future regional branches of the National Library of Medicine and the computer-based bibliographic retrieval and publication system called MEDLARS— Medical Literature Analysis and Retrieval System.

The medical school library should be located so that its resources are quickly available to students, research workers, faculty members, hospital staff, and practicing physicians. Unless there are large medical research collections nearby, the library should be equipped to accommodate 100,000 volumes and 1,600 scientific periodicals.

Table 2 gives the net area for a medical school library of 100,000 volumes and 1,600 periodicals. Since medical library collections tend to increase rapidly, the library should be planned for future expansion.

In designing the library, maximum flexibility should be a prime consideration with necessary divisions in the form of partitions which can be moved.

Shelving, whether in stacks or in reading areas, should be standard library equipment, with standard interchangeable parts. Standard sections, usually 3 ft long, should be used throughout, with only such exceptions as floor layout may demand. Those for medical books have a shelf depth of 10 in. One 3-ft-long single-faced section will accommodate approximately 100 volumes.

Service aisles between stacks should not be less than 3 ft wide. Main aisles should be at least 3 ft 6 in. wide. If bookstacks are on more than one level, or are not on the level where books are received, vertical transportation must be provided.

Students and faculty members should have free access to stack areas, which should be provided with carrels for work and study.

These are usually alcoves, preferably adjacent to windows, each equipped with a desk, reading light, and chair. They should be provided at the rate of one for each ten students. However, fewer may be required if individual study cubicles for students are provided elsewhere.

Other rooms often associated with the stack area are a microfilm storage and viewing room and a room for the storage of motion-picture films and slides. A relatively soundproof room for photoduplication facilities is necessary. An area for general reading and open-shelf reference work may be supplemented by a number of smaller reading areas, rooms, or alcoves. The main reading area should be near the main catalog and circulation desk. If individual student study cubicles are not provided in the school, student reading areas in the library should accommodate from 25 to 50 percent of the total enrollment of the medical school and students from other programs who require access to the collection. Students seated at tables require a minimum of 25 sq ft of space each. Additional seating allowance should be made for faculty and research staff and other users.

A separate alcove with shelves, or a section of shelving in the main reading area, should be

TABLE 2 Net area (in Square Feet) of Facilities Required for a Medical School Library of 100,000 Volumes and 1,600 Periodicals

Type of facility	Schools A and B (entering classes of 64 and 96 students)
	Square feet
Total net area _ _ _ _ _ _ _ _ _ _ _ _ _ _ _	29,560
Public services:	
Total _ _ _ _ _ _ _ _ _ _ _ _ _ _ _ _ _	24,950
Vestibule _ _ _ _ _ _ _ _ _ _ _ _ _ _ _	100
Reception area and display _ _ _ _ _ _ _ _	400
Charging and reserve areas _ _ _ _ _ _ _ _	450
Card catalog area _ _ _ _ _ _ _ _ _ _ _ _	150
Information and reference areas _ _ _ _ _ _	400
Browsing collection _ _ _ _ _ _ _ _ _ _ _	150
Main reading area _ _ _ _ _ _ _ _ _ _ _ _	6,070
Microreading area _ _ _ _ _ _ _ _ _ _ _ _	200
Paging-reading area _ _ _ _ _ _ _ _ _ _ _	400
Periodicals area including indexes _ _ _ _ _	1,200
Seminar-study areas _ _ _ _ _ _ _ _ _ _ _	1,350
Historical collection room _ _ _ _ _ _ _ _ _	630
Sound demonstration room _ _ _ _ _ _ _ _	450
Slides and movie room _ _ _ _ _ _ _ _ _ _	450
Bookstack areas _ _ _ _ _ _ _ _ _ _ _ _ _	10,000
Unenclosed carrels _ _ _ _ _ _ _ _ _ _ _ _	1,200
Closed carrels _ _ _ _ _ _ _ _ _ _ _ _ _ _	200
Audiovisual storage _ _ _ _ _ _ _ _ _ _ _	400
Microfilm storage _ _ _ _ _ _ _ _ _ _ _ _	200
Food vending machine area _ _ _ _ _ _ _ _	300
Public toilets _ _ _ _ _ _ _ _ _ _ _ _ _ _	250
Work area:	
Total _ _ _ _ _ _ _ _ _ _ _ _ _ _ _ _ _	4,610
Receiving and mailing room _ _ _ _ _ _ _ _	500
Acquisitions department _ _ _ _ _ _ _ _ _	600
Cataloging department _ _ _ _ _ _ _ _ _ _	520
Preparation room _ _ _ _ _ _ _ _ _ _ _ _	150
Photoduplication _ _ _ _ _ _ _ _ _ _ _ _	800
Binding and mending _ _ _ _ _ _ _ _ _ _ _	240
Serials work area _ _ _ _ _ _ _ _ _ _ _ _	200
Chief librarian's office _ _ _ _ _ _ _ _ _ _	200
Reception-secretary's office _ _ _ _ _ _ _ _	200
Assistant librarians' offices _ _ _ _ _ _ _ _	120
Historical librarian's office _ _ _ _ _ _ _ _	120
Office storage _ _ _ _ _ _ _ _ _ _ _ _ _ _	80
Staff room _ _ _ _ _ _ _ _ _ _ _ _ _ _ _	400
Staff toilets and lockers _ _ _ _ _ _ _ _ _	240
Housekeeping _ _ _ _ _ _ _ _ _ _ _ _ _ _	240

provided for unbound journals. If sloping display shelves are used for current issues of journals, open shelving underneath for housing unbound earlier issues are more convenient than closed compartments.

A room with paging facilities may be provided for the use of those on call. Small study rooms for group conferences of four to six persons each should also be included. An area should be provided in the lobby or near the reference desk containing nontechnical books for browsing. A film- and slide-projection room and a sound-tape room, each to accommodate 16 students and an instructor, may be required depending on the program. Both rooms should be soundproofed and designed so as not to distract readers in other areas. A microfilm reading room is necessary. A medical history room may be required and may be a combined medical history and rare medical book room, in which case protected windows, doors with locks, a fireproof vault, and special air conditioning will be required. Well-lighted exhibit cases should be provided adjacent to the entrance to the library and its main lanes of traffic. Public toilets, rest rooms, coat rooms, and janitor services should be convenient to the reading areas.

The book charging desk, located near the entrance, should control the exits from reading areas, workrooms, and stacks to minimize book loss. The card catalog should be close to the main entrance and near the circulation desk and the acquisition and cataloging rooms. In the staff workroom a sink should be provided. Provisions should be made so that noise generated by activities at these areas does not distract readers.

One workroom subdivided into alcoves by double-faced bookshelves may be provided, instead of separate workrooms, for acquisition and cataloging. These rooms should be near the public catalog and should have direct access to the stackroom; 100 sq ft should be allowed for each staff member.

The reception-secretary's office should be adjacent to the head librarian's office. A departmental conference room may be required. The head librarian's office should be accessible both to the staff workrooms and library clientele.

The receiving room is best located on the ground floor with access to an unloading platform. A work table, shelving, and shipping equipment should be provided. Lift service, preferably an elevator which will hold loaded book carts, between the receiving room and the acquisitions department should be provided where these areas are on different floors. Vending machines for food and drink should be located outside the library proper and be provided with space for tables.

Animal Quarters

The need for controlled care of animals to meet teaching and research requirements is reflected in the provision of a central animal service in an increasing number of medical schools.

The location of animal quarters on the ground floor, where direct-connected outdoor animal runs and truck unloading facilities can be provided with complete separation from any other function, has many advantages. A separate entrance to serve the animal quarters is essential. Provision should be made for expansion in the initial planning.

However, a vivarium in an adjacent wing with its own vertical transportation for animals, animal supplies, and personnel may serve the needs of research better than an animal facility at grade level. The floors of the vivarium should communicate with those of the adjoining structure so that animal rooms are horizontally contiguous to the research and teaching laboratories using them and so that animals can be transferred to the laboratories without traversing corridors of other areas. If a vivarium is provided, animal-holding rooms are not usually required within research areas.

Animal quarters are composed of a number of different kinds of areas. Each has its own requirements in terms of space and location. In animal areas, provision must be made for the reception, quarantine, and isolation of incoming animals near the animal entrance; for housing different species; for exercising animals; and for specific research projects. Isolation rooms for infected animals, each with a vestibule containing facilities for gowning and scrubbing, are required.

Table 3 gives the net area for animal quarters.

Animal rooms should be isolated from each other with no connecting openings and arranged to separate clean and contaminated functions. A service corridor may be provided in addition to the main access corridor to allow the removal of soiled bedding and other material at the rear of a range of cages rather than through the main corridor. Borrowed light in corridor partitions and between rooms should be avoided since light bothers some animals. Windows, if used, should be placed at least 6 ft above the floor so that animal cages can fit below them. Each room should have a sink

TABLE 3 Net Area for Animal Quarters

Type of facility	School A (entering class of 64 students)	School B (entering class of 96 students)
	Square feet	
Total net area	11,980	14,860
Animal rooms:		
Total	9,730	11,830
Coldblooded animals and aquarium	140	200
Guinea pigs, rabbits, hamsters, rats, and mice	1,800	2,700
Primate	280	400
Cats	250	370
Dogs	2,100	3,000
Animal reception-quarantine	(3) 300	(3) 300
Cage washing and sterilization	350	350
Cage storage	280	280
Bedding storage	300	300
Food storage and preparation	750	750
X-ray and fluoroscopy	400	400
Sterile isolation	(3) 600	(3) 600
Routine laboratory	200	200
Veterinarian's research laboratory	630	630
Veterinarian's office	250	250
Isolation	230	230
Autopsy	300	300
Animal morgue	70	70
Incinerator	220	220
Keeper's locker	280	280
Animal surgery rooms:		
Total	2,250	3,030
Operating	(3) 900	(5) 1,500
Scrubup	180	360
Recovery	200	200
Cleanup	300	300
Instrument	270	270
Central sterilizing	400	400

and soap dispenser. A vestibule at the entrance to a block of rooms where the attendant can change clothes and shoes is recommended to help reduce infection.

The construction of animal quarters should be fire resistant, vermin- and insect-proof, and above all easy to clean. Recesses, cracks, and pockets should be avoided. Bases should be coved. Special attention should be given to such openings between rooms as pipes, conduit, and telephone wiring. Doorsills will prevent water from leaking into the corridor when floors are washed down, but are not as convenient for moving cage racks in and out of rooms.

Wall surfaces should be smooth, hard, and easily cleaned. Ceramic tile is often used but is easily damaged by cage racks. For protection of wall surfaces from such damage, a 6-in. curb may be provided. Cinder- or concrete-block walls must be laid up with tight joints and covered with a moisture-resistant material.

Doors should be 3 ft 6 in. wide to permit easy passage of cage racks, and all hardware should be recessed.

Floors should be able to resist the disintegrative action of the organic salts and acids in animal urine. Quarry tile with acid-resistant joints is satisfactory but should not be used in the corridor because of the noise created by cage carts as they bump along the joints. Concrete floors, well compacted and troweled, are also satisfactory. Asphalt, rubber, and vinyl tile floors are not recommended.

Floor drains are suggested for monkey and dog rooms. These should be 6 in. in diameter of the flushing type with special hair traps to avoid clogging. Use of floor drains in smaller animal rooms will depend on whether the rooms are hosed down regularly or swept and wet-mopped.

Departmental Offices

Each basic science and clinical science department faculty member requires office space for his departmental activities and laboratories for research. The head of each department requires an office with a desk, reference table, and space for a conference of several persons located near his research laboratory and adjacent to a secretary's office (see Fig. 2).

The conference room, which will be used for meetings of groups of students, should accommodate about 20 persons. Shelving for departmental books and periodicals and storage space for slide projectors, models, and other visual-aid equipment, chalk boards, and roll-up projection screens should be provided. In the clinical departments, x-ray view boxes are required.

The secretary's office may handle the secretarial work for the entire department and should be sized for the ultimate expansion of the department.

For space estimating, a unit of sixteen modules may be used as the primary unit for each department. The balance of the staff can be housed in additional eight-module units each accommodating five or six people and providing laboratory, office space, and supporting facilities. An additional two-module space is required for each additional faculty member.

Research Facilities

Research laboratories should be provided for faculty members, postdoctoral fellows, and graduate students in each department.

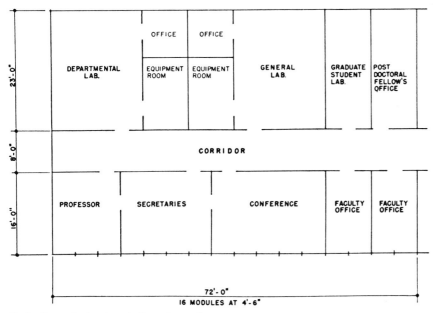

Fig. 2 Diagram for departmental office and research area.

The use of modules in planning laboratory facilities permits flexibility in utilization of space where changes in space requirements are common. Utilities and duct connections should be so provided that when space is changed utilities are available without undue pipe runs or perforations of walls or ceilings.

The equipment of research laboratories will vary with the kind of activity performed in them. It should be possible to rearrange work counters, microscope benches, and sinks, and to vary the size of the room as required without undue labor, inconvenience, or expense. This is most easily accomplished if all utilities and ducts are properly sized and located so as to make them available to all parts of the laboratory wing. This includes space not designed originally for laboratory use.

Some possible arrangements of research laboratories are shown on Fig. 3. The fume hood is shown on the corridor wall for convenient relation to the duct space.

Counter heights will vary—31 in. for sit-down work and 37 in. for stand-up work are most commonly used. The choice of a peninsula or island counter in larger laboratories may vary with the research project. Island counters can be used on all sides but are more expensive to install and alter; peninsula counters are more flexible with respect to air, vacuum, water, gas, drainage, and electrical services required.

An additional two-module space adjacent to the large laboratory can be divided to provide an office for an instructor and a special instrument or storage room. A two-module space may be used for four study cubicles for post-doctoral fellows.

Cold rooms are required in the laboratory wing of each department. They are refrigerated rooms for several workers who do procedures at low temperatures. A counter with sink, undercounter cabinets, and shelving are usual equipment. Electrical, air, and vacuum connections are required. All safety features such as safety door latches and warning lights should be installed.

The term "animal-holding room" is used to designate areas within a basic science or clinical department where small animals are held for a short time. These holding rooms, located close to an elevator which also serves the central animal quarters, eliminate the hauling of animal cages through public corridors. The animals are assigned to a staff member conducting studies requiring close, periodic observation or experimentation over a short time for a limited number of animals. These rooms may also be available to medical students performing animal experiments. Space is required for racks of cages, often placed back to back in the center of the room, with a single line of racks placed against the walls.

Animal operating and recovery rooms should be located in central animal quarters. Where vivaria are provided on each floor adjacent to departments, they should substitute for animal-holding rooms.

If properly located and provided with the necessary utilities, storage rooms can be used for expanded research activities. Those shown on the accompanying space diagrams are located and sized to allow for expansion. A four-module central equipment room should be provided in each department.

Auditorium and Lecture Rooms

The auditorium and lecture rooms are important teaching facilities for all the medical

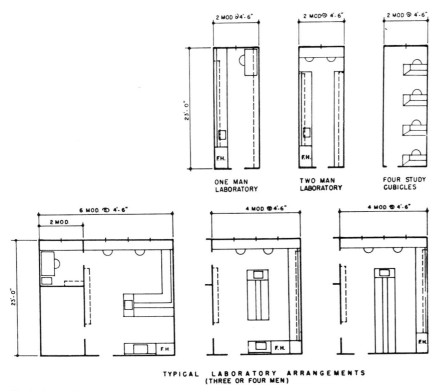

Fig. 3 Layouts for research laboratories.

school departments and the teaching hospital. They should be located for convenient use by faculty and students from the clinical departments, the teaching hospital, the basic science facilities, and by outside groups.

Auditorium The hospital auditorium is necessary to any medical education program. It is used for demonstrating patients to students and should be attached to the teaching hospital so as to provide maximum convenience and the least movement of patients. Ramps should be provided for bringing in wheelchair and stretcher patients.

The minimum seating capacity required for teaching in a university hospital auditorium is equal to the total number of students in the third- and fourth-year classes plus 50 percent additional seats.

A second auditorium or additional lecture rooms may be required since prolonged use of the lecture facilities may conflict with regular undergraduate teaching schedules.

For auditoriums, most authorities prefer fixed seats with dropleaf tablet arms, arranged in theater fashion with a sloping floor. The auditorium should have a low stage to facilitate the demonstration of patients and should be equipped for the installation of closed-circuit television. Projection facilities for sound films and slides, lighting controls, chalkboards, public-address systems, and closed-circuit television for doctors' paging should be provided.

Lecture Rooms A significant portion of the instruction in a medical school involves the use of lecture rooms.

A minimum of three lecture rooms should be provided in the *basic science facilities* as follows: two sloping or stepped-floor lecture rooms of 120–150 seats each for use primarily in basic science courses, and one sloping or stepped-floor lecture room of 80 seats for graduate-student instruction, continuation education, and other programs. Table 15 gives the area for lecture rooms for a hypothetical basic science facility.

Two 150-seat lecture rooms of sloping or step-floor type should be provided as part of *the clinical department facilities and the teaching hospital.*

Lecture rooms included in the tables are sized to accommodate a class of 96 students, with 25 percent additional seats. Although a class size of less than 96 students may be contemplated in the initial planning of a new medical school, it will be advantageous to construct lecture rooms on the basis of the maximum class size.

The main entrances to lecture rooms should be located at the rear, although corridor access to the demonstration areas of lecture rooms is essential for bringing in tables and other large equipment.

A minimum distance of 10 to 12 ft should be provided between the first row of seats and the back wall of the demonstration space.

Fixed seats with dropleaf tablet arms are generally preferred for lecture rooms. Such seats are usually 26 in. in width and require a minimum back-to-back spacing of 36 in. For a rough estimate of lecture-room seating-area size, including aisles and crossovers, 10 sq ft per person may be used.

Demonstration areas in all lecture rooms should be equipped with chalkboard, x-ray film illuminators, and roll-up projection screens. A lavatory may be necessary for the demonstration areas.

A projection area with platform, projector table, and convenient electrical outlets should be provided in each lecture room. Sound amplification equipment with conduits for loudspeakers for sound movies should be installed. Projectors are noisy and some sound-absorbent baffling may be required if a separate booth is not provided.

Auxiliary spaces which may be required for the use of the lecture rooms, such as storage rooms for visual aids and portable equipment, coat-rooms, toilet rooms, and telephone booths, will be determined by the individual school. Public toilets should be convenient to lecture rooms.

Study Cubicles Consideration should be given to the use of study cubicles within the basic science and clinical departments for postdoctoral fellows, and in the teaching hospital for the house staff.

Cubicles for medical students in the first two years should be located in the basic science area. For third- and fourth-year students, cubicles should be in the teaching hospital. Table 15 gives the net area for cubicles for hypothetical schools.

Each cubicle contains a desk with drawers on one side; a cabinet above the desk for books with a built-in fluorescent study light underneath; and a locker which, in addition to hanging clothes, may be used for microscope storage. A duplex outlet is necessary to attach the microscope. The locker not only provides privacy by forming a barrier, but also eliminates the necessity for separate locker rooms.

An allowance of 50 sq ft per cubicle is adequate. This includes desk, locker, chair space, and adjacent aisle. If aisles are double loaded (cubicles on either side), privacy for the student may be obtained by staggering the cubicles so that desks are not directly opposite each other.

It is desirable to have a lounge area nearby where discussions among small groups can be held without disturbing students in the study cubicle. Chalkboards and tackboard should be provided in this area and vending machines should be available.

If the study cubicle-clothes locker combination is not used, separate *student locker rooms* for male and female students should be provided. To conserve students' time and to ease elevator traffic, locker rooms should be located close to the line of travel to teaching areas. The proximity of the hospital should determine the necessity for separate locker rooms for third- and fourth-year students.

A *toilet room* should be connected to each locker room or study cubicle area and showers should be provided in the basic science area. If study cubicles with lockers are installed, a dressing room is required adjacent to toilet and shower room in the basic science facilities. A rest room for women should be included.

Student Activity Facilities

Lounge Space may be provided for such activities as pingpong, billiards, and card playing. A recessed or screened area with vending machines is desirable. A kitchenette for preparing coffee and snacks is provided in some schools. Shelving for books and current magazines, an aerial for TV, and a storage closet adequate for card tables, phonograph records, and other equipment should be provided. Public and house telephones should be available.

Table 4 gives net area for various student activity facilities. Facilities should also be provided for outdoor recreation.

Activities Office A student activities office near the student lounge may serve as headquarters for such activities as student organizations, honor medical societies, student publications, and student council, and may be the center of inquiry regarding athletic, recreational, and social events. There should be space for typewriter desks, file cabinets, and shelving. If the activities office is to serve as an information center, a service counter and bulletin board would be desirable. If the office is to be used for student publications, space for duplicating machines will be required.

Laundry Collection The medical student often wears more than one coat per day in the basic science courses. To maintain a supply of clean linen, a laundry collection station convenient to the student lounge or locker room should be provided with a pickup and delivery counter.

Bookstore The bookstore, although primarily for students, should be available to all persons using the building. Its location on a main floor of the medical school is preferable.

Health Office A student health office will serve the entire four-year student body, half of which will be studying in the basic science areas, the other half in the hospital. Locating the health office adjacent to medical school administrative offices may be desirable if they are near the hospital. Otherwise, a hospital location is suggested.

The health office should have a waiting area, an office area, and an examining room and should provide space for a medical cabinet, a small domestic refrigerator for storing pharmaceuticals, an examining table, a portable examining light, weighing scales, storage cabinet for incidentals, a clothes rack, and a lavatory.

Medical Illustration Service

The demand in medical schools for visual material to implement teaching, research, and patient-care programs is so great that a centralized medical illustration service for the production of such material is required.

Space required will depend on the extent of activities and number of personnel. The activities of a medical illustration service are divided into graphic arts, plastic arts, and photography. Closed-circuit television as a teaching aid is usually a separate service but may be a part of the medical illustration service. The medical illustration service usually is responsible for

TABLE 4   Net Area for Student Activities

Type of facility	School A (entering class of 64 students)	School B (entering class of 96 students)
	Square feet	
Total	1,850	2,400
Lounge and toilets	1,000	1,200
Student activities office . . .	200	200
Laundry collection.	200	400
Bookstore	450	600
Health office and examination area*		

* May be in hospital or part of general university health service.

maintaining the slide and movie projectors used throughout the school and facilities for repair and storage of such equipment should be provided. (See Table 5.)

Activities to be considered in planning the *graphic art section* include drawing, painting, and airbrush work, drafting for charts and technical diagrams, mechanical lettering, and general art work required in preparing displays or scientific exhibits. A large, well-lighted room, subdivided into work areas, is usually satisfactory. If possible, the area should be provided with natural north light.

The activities of the *plastic art section* include the skilled operations required to produce three-dimensional models of the organs of the body. These activities require a room for working with the patient in addition to the main work studio. Since the activities involve close color matching, both the studio and patient room should have north light.

TABLE 5   Net Area for Medical Illustration

Type of facility	School A (entering class of 64 students)	School B (entering class of 96 students)
	Square feet	
Total net area	2,020	3,170
Administration:		
Total	370	370
Chief's office	140	140
Secretary and files	140	140
Equipment and supply room	90	90
Medical illustration: Artists' work area.	600	950
Photography:		
Total	1,050	1,050
Photo studio and dressing	420	420
Photomicrography room	90	90
Light lock	50	50
Darkrooms . . . . (2)	140 (2)	140
Loading room	30	30
Mixing room	60	60
Laboratory	190	190
Finishing room	70	70
Audiovisual: TV studio (including control area)		800

Activities to be considered in planning the *photographic section* of the department are photographing patients, both still and cine, photomicrography, copying, film processing and printing, film and print drying, film loading, chemical mixing, print and slide finishing.

Photographing human and animal specimens is a regular activity of a photographic section, but, because of the hazards involved in handling fresh specimens, this work should be done in or near the autopsy rooms.

A studio for photographing patients is required; two are preferable—a main studio for full-length studies and a "closeup" studio for phtographing the head, extremities, eyes, and mouth. The wall of the main studio serving as a background should have a plain, smooth surface for at least 12 ft of its width. The adjacent floor space or patient area should be the

same tone as the wall with a 3-in.-radius cove at the base of the wall to prevent a strong line of demarcation between the floor and wall in full-length studies. A height scale on the wall at one side of the background area is desirable. Electric outlets should be provided at either side of the patient area for floodlamps and other portable lighting equipment. An adjacent patients' dressing cubicle and a lavatory with wrist-action valves are necessary. The door for admitting patients to the studio should be at least 44 in. wide.

For making 16-mm. motion pictures, about 35 ft between background and camera is required to prevent distortion. However, it is possible to back the camera into an adjacent work area to attain this distance. Sometimes a draw curtain is provided between the main studio and the "closeup" studio to facilitate this arrangement.

A separate room for photomicrography permits the photographer to work in the dark, which is frequently necessary; permits him to leave the equipment set up; and minimizes dust. The room should be near a darkroom.

Copying charts and drawings is frequently done in the main studio. Copying radiographs, however, requires a small room that can be darkened. Both types of copy work can be done in this room.

The smallest photographic section will require two darkrooms, one for films and one for contact prints, enlargements, and lantern slides. If color films are to be processed, a special darkroom for this purpose should be provided. The volume of color printing will indicate whether a special darkroom for this purpose is warranted. Darkrooms should have a sink along one wall and a bench along the other, with 3 ft of work space between them for one occupant or 4 ft for 2. Film and print driers may be located in any open work area near the darkrooms.

A room for loading film holders reduces traffic. A small, well-ventilated room, with a sink for chemical mixing, is necessary to protect equipment and materials against chemical fumes.

It is desirable to provide a small room for motion-picture film editing and titling, and for binding slides. Other finishing operations such as spotting, trimming, and mounting may also be done in this room. If projection equipment is included, motion pictures and slides may be checked.

A storage room for supplies should be provided. At least one refrigerator should be included for storing color material.

A storage room should also be provided in the general storage area of the building for the service. Some of the material handled may be a fire hazard and protective provisions should be made.

Technical Shops

Central technical shops are required as a supportive facility to all departments of a medical school. However, specialized shops may be required in some departments. The use of shops elsewhere on the university campus is not usually satisfactory from the standpoint of time or accuracy.

Technical shops usually include separate areas for metalwork, woodwork, glassblowing, and electronics. A metalworking shop usually requires a metal lathe, a drill press, two milling machines (one horizontal and one vertical), a metal-cutting band saw, a bench grinder, and a universal tool and cutter grinder. Storage

racks for bar and plate stock, tool cabinets and racks, and a machinist's bench will also be required. The woodworking shop needs space for a table saw, a thickness planer, a jointer, a wood lathe, and a drill press. A heavy wood bench, lumber racks, and tool cabinets should also be included. The glassblowing and electronics shops may be similar to those described for the department of biochemistry but on a larger scale.

Each technical shop should have space for a desk and files to record stock purchases and maintain requisitions from individual departments. The area for technical shops is given in Table 15.

Service Facilities

Table 6 gives the area for service facilities.

Telephone Facilities The teaching hospital will need switchboards. If the medical school is close by, a central telephone system may be advantageous. Combining the switchboard and information center is not recommended for a medical school complex. The switchboard is therefore best located in an area inaccessible to the public. A doctors' call system will be required in the hospital.

Postal Facilities A postal facility in the medical school may assume the normal duties of a post office and handle the distribution of interoffice correspondence. If the teaching hospital is adjacent, a central facility of this type will reduce duplication of mail handling and delivery.

TABLE 6   Net Area for Service Facilities

Type of facility	School A (entering class of 64 students)	School B (entering class of 96 students)
	Square feet	
Total net area_____	13,700	16,050
Total_____	6,000	8,350
Telephone equipment room__	800	1,100
Post office_____	550	1,000
Personnel and purchasing [1]__	400	400
Employees' lockers and toilet facilities_____	2,000	3,000
Maintenance shops_____	900	1,100
Plant engineer_____	150	150
Housekeeping_____	600	600
Duplicating_____	200	400
Snark bar_____	400	600
Central storage: [2]		
Total_____	7,700	7,700
Basic science departments:		
Anatomy_____	1,000	1,000
Biochemistry_____	500	500
Physiology_____	500	500
Microbiology_____	500	500
Pathology_____	1,500	1,500
Pharmacology_____	500	500
Clinical departments:		
Medicine_____	500	500
Surgery_____	500	500
Pediatrics_____	500	500
Obstetrics-gynecology_____	500	500
Psychiatry_____	300	300
Radiology_____	600	600
Preventive medicine_	300	300

[1] 2 offices and secretaries.

[2] Central storage spaces for each department are listed on the department tables. However, areas for this storage are grouped here.

Central Storage Storage spaces within the department are discussed under other headings, but, in addition, separate storage space should be provided for each department elsewhere in the building. The amount of space for departments should be determined by their needs and designed for expansion.

A general storage room near maintenance shops should be provided for fixtures and equipment required for building maintenance and operation.

Each department should have a partitioned space for bulk storage. Because of variable loads of stored items, it is preferable to locate storage areas on a basement floor to avoid special floor live loads.

Central areas for storage and dispensing of bulk supplies of gases such as acetylene, argon, and hydrogen, and flammable liquids such as alcohol, acetone, and xylene, require specially designed space readily accessible to loading platforms and receiving areas. These areas must comply with applicable codes.

Locker and Toilet Facilities Locker and toilet facilities should be provided for male and female service personnel convenient to the employee entrance.

Snack Bar Vending machines for food and drink serve as a convenient type of snack bar.

Another type includes facilities for short-order foods, a service counter with stools, a table seating area, and a preparation-storage room. Allocation of space for a cashier counter and vending machines may be desirable. The snack bar should be convenient to the center of activity.

Maintenance Shops Maintenance shops required by the medical school and hospital usually include a mechanical and plumbing shop, an electrical shop, a carpentry shop, and a paint shop. Where the medical school and hospital are under one roof or in close proximity, a single set of maintenance shops may serve both.

The plant engineer usually has the responsibility for coordinating maintenance and repair activities. He requires an office with space for a desk and correspondence files, a secretary's office suitable for one secretary, files, and waiting space, and usually needs a separate drafting room with tables and plan-filing facilities.

Duplicating Room A central duplicating facility may be required if each department does not have duplicating facilities within the department. Some schools have set up a print shop in addition.

BASIC SCIENCE FACILITIES

Ideally, basic science, clinical science, and teaching hospital facilities are contiguous because of the close interrelationship of their functions in the teaching of clinical medicine.

Conventional and Multidiscipline Laboratories

Basic science departments have certain common elements, the most outstanding of which are the teaching laboratories. Two types of laboratories are in use in medical schools today: conventional laboratories, where each department has its own laboratories or shares laboratories with another department requiring similar facilities and students move from one laboratory to another; and multidiscipline laboratories where students are assigned

work spaces and all disciplines except gross anatomy are taught in this laboratory.

With the exception of gross anatomy, the basic sciences may be taught in either conventional or multidiscipline laboratories.

Conventional Laboratories If conventional laboratories are used, the following considerations must be taken into account:
- Laboratories are usually sized to accommodate an entire entering class. They are sometimes arranged for division, by means of folding partitions, into groups usually of 16 students (Figs. 4 and 5). One laboratory is usually assigned to each of the disciplines in the basic sciences, although in some instances several departments—for example, physiology and pharmacology, and pathology and microbiology—may use the same laboratory.
- Laboratories are generally referred to as sit-down or stand-up laboratories. Sit-down laboratories are provided for microbiology, microanatomy and neuroanatomy, and pathology. In physiology, pharmacology, and biochemistry, most of the work is done standing up. In sit-down laboratories, however, some stand-up work is done, and it is customary to provide stand-up counters for special instruments and reagents which may be shared by groups of students.
- Auxiliary rooms are required. These include preparation and issuing rooms, glassware processing rooms, storage rooms, and media-preparation rooms. Some schools place large and noisy pieces of equipment shared by groups of students in a separate instrument room.
- Graduate students usually use the same laboratories as medical students for classroom laboratory work. If separate facilities are provided, they are located close to the

auxiliary rooms. The design is similar but size will vary with the teaching program.

Multidiscipline Laboratories The multidiscipline laboratory is sized to take the number of students assigned to one teacher, usually 16 students, although some schools assign 24.

Except for dissection, the student will do all his laboratory work in this room; therefore, both sit-down counters, 31 in. high, and stand-up counters, 37 in. high, are required. In addition, movable tables 37 in. high are required for animal work for physiology (Figs. 6 and 7).

Table 7 gives the area for multidiscipline laboratories.

Each student is assigned a space containing about 4 ft of stand-up counter and the same length of sit-down counter opposite.

Utilities, storage, sinks, and general design and finishes of both stand-up and sit-down space will be similar to that for conventional laboratories. Chalkboards should be visible from each student space. Bulletin boards should be located near the entrance.

An equipment room is provided adjacent to or between each pair of multidiscipline laboratories in some designs. Equipped with a fume hood, counter space with utilities and cabinet space, it houses equipment required for the work in adjoining laboratories. Equipment such as centrifuge, freezers, and refrigerators are available to more than one laboratory.

The laboratory manager's office, secretary's office, and office space for one or two assistants should be provided. In addition, a ready storage room, a student issuing and supply room, a chemical storage room, cold room, and glass-washing room are required. If media preparation or slide preparation are to be done here, space for these should be provided.

TABLE 7 Net Area for Hypothetical Multidiscipline Laboratories

Type of facility	School A (entering class of 64 students)		School B (entering class of 96 students)	
	Square feet			
Total		22,500		29,960
Gross dissecting rooms (4 students/table):				
Medical students		2,560		3,840
Graduate students		720		720
Utility room		160		160
Storage room		250		250
Neuroanatomy		280		280
Multidiscipline laboratories:				
1st year medical students	(4 @ 940)	3,760	(6 @ 940)	5,640
"Interlab" equipment rooms	(2 @ 400)	800	(3 @ 400)	1,200
2d year medical students	(4 @ 940)	3,760	(6 @ 940)	5,640
"Interlab" equipment rooms	(2 @ 400)	800	(3 @ 400)	1,200
Ancillary teaching facilities:				
Cold rooms	(2 @ 200)	400	(2 @ 200)	400
Regulated temperature rooms	(2 @ 410)	820	(2 @ 410)	820
Human experiments laboratory		780		780
Glass washing, sterilizing, and storage		630		630
Media preparation room		280		280
Clinical pathology tissue room		570		570
Balance rooms	(2 @ 100)	200	(3 @ 100)	300
Calculating and drafting rooms	(2 @ 280)	560	(2 @ 280)	560
Animal rooms	(4 @ 410)	1,640	(6 @ 410)	2,460
Conference rooms	(4 @ 350)	1,400	(6 @ 350)	2,100
Stockrooms	(2 @ 410)	820	(2 @ 410)	820
Laboratory management:				
Laboratory manager's office		210		210
Secretary's office		210		210
Assistant managers' offices	(2 @ 140)	280	(2 @ 140)	280
Laboratory		410		410
Cold room		100		100
Animal room		100		100

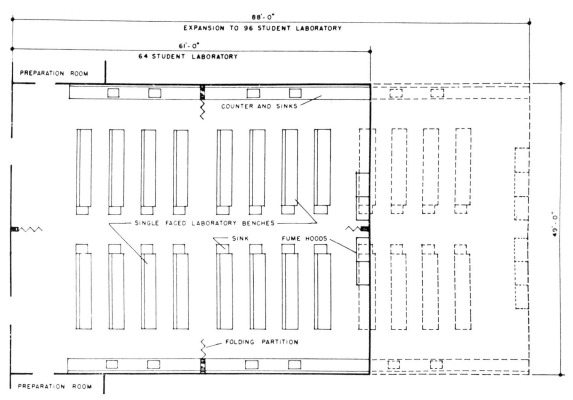

Fig. 4   Layout for a conventional teaching laboratory with single-faced benches.

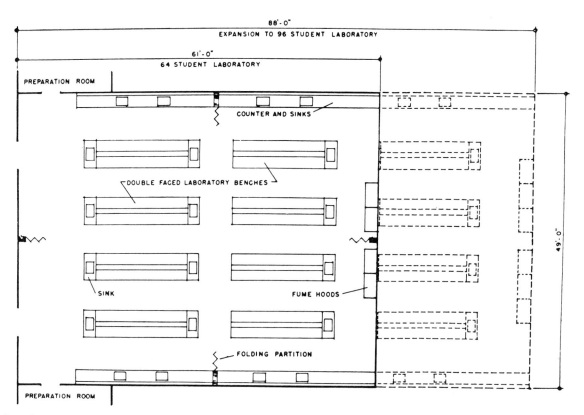

Fig. 5   Layout for a conventional teaching laboratory with double-faced benches.

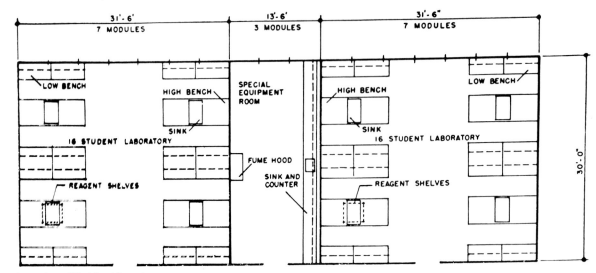

Fig. 6 Layout for multidiscipline laboratories.

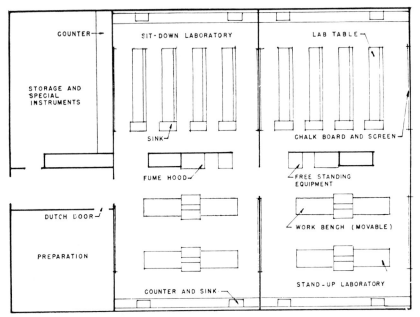

Fig. 7 Floor plan for multidiscipline laboratories.

Additional unassigned conference rooms sized to accommodate 20 persons may be provided in the basic science facilities for use by unscheduled groups.

Basic Science Departments

Anatomy Figure 8 shows a space diagram for a minimum department of anatomy. Table 8 provides a list of net areas for an anatomy department.

Dissecting Room. The teaching area for gross anatomy is usually one large room with stand-up height dissecting tables to accommodate all the students in the course. Convenience for faculty and students and proximity of elevator service to be used for transporting cadavers are important considerations in the location. Provisions should be made to prevent viewing of dissection procedures by unauthorized persons. One dissecting table for each four students is usually required.

Tables should be arranged to allow ample work space on all sides. Additional space to accommodate one or two portable tables for use in demonstrations or by special students may be required. If dissecting tables are movable, a folding partition may be installed to provide a screen behind which the tables may be stacked during off-semesters, freeing the room for other uses.

Handwashing facilities for students should be provided in the dissecting room. Surgical scrub-up sinks, three for each sixteen students, with wrist- or foot-action valves or industrial-type fixtures are recommended. Counter units should have reagent ledges, knee spaces, and under-counter drawers and cabinets for storage of student's dissecting equipment and demonstration microscopes. Electrical service outlets for microscope illuminators should be provided. Counter tops should have resilient surfaces.

Wall-mounted x-ray illuminators, one for each sixteen students, a bank of four to eight, should be located for easy viewing by a group. Chalkboards located for easy viewing by each sixteen-student group should also be provided.

Storage for fixed specimens and models used in demonstrations and for x-ray film should be provided. Cabinets in a connecting area, such as a utility room, may suffice.

The *utility room,* which may serve as a diener's work room, should have a flushing-rim service sink accessible to the dissecting area. The sink should have flush valve and wrist-operated valves.

Graduate-student dissecting room. It should be adjacent to auxiliary rooms of the medical students' dissecting room. Fixed equipment and mechanical facilities should be similar to those furnished the medical student.

Microneuroanatomy Teaching Laboratory A conventional student teaching laboratory for microanatomy and neuroanatomy instruction usually requires a demonstration area with a table, chalkboard, projection screen, and sit-down laboratory benches to accommodate all the students of either course. Benches should seat four students on the same side to face in the same direction for an unobstructed view of the demonstration area.

Each bench position should have knee space, drawers, and a cabinet for storing slides and microscope case. Water, air, gas, electrical outlets, and vacuum should be provided at each position. Liquid waste receptors in bench tops may be either lead cup sinks or continuous drain troughs with stone end sinks. Bench top material should be resilient and alcohol- and stain-resistant.

In addition to sit-down benches, some stand-up bench space should be provided for each sixteen students. Bulletin boards and tack boards should be provided.

Graduate-student teaching laboratory. It should be adjacent to auxiliary rooms of the medical students' microneuroanatomy teaching laboratory. Fixed equipment and mechanical facilities should be similar to those furnished the medical student.

Gross Neuroanatomy Room. This room is a supplementary teaching area. Usually the area serves also as a departmental storage center for specimens, in which case adjustable shelv-

TABLE 8   Net Area for a Department of Anatomy

Type of facility	School A (entering class of 64 students)		School B (entering class of 96 students)	
	With conventional departmental laboratories	With multidiscipline laboratories	With conventional departmental laboratories	With multidiscipline laboratories
Assumed size of faculty	7	7	10	10
Number of graduate students and postdoctoral fellows	7	7	10	10
	Square feet			
Total net area	19, 330	(¹)	22, 950	(¹)
Faculty offices, research laboratories, and related facilities:				
Total	11, 640	11, 510	12, 660	12, 530
Professor's office	210	210	210	210
Secretary's office	280	280	280	280
Conference room	350	350	350	350
Faculty offices	(4) 560	(4) 560	(4) 560	(4) 560
Postdoctoral fellows' office	200	200	200	200
Data room	280	280	280	280
Special-projects room	280	280	280	280
Research laboratories:				
Departmental	610	610	610	610
General	(3) 1, 830	(3) 1, 830	(4) 2, 440	(4) 2, 440
Graduate students	(2) 400	(2) 400	(3) 600	(3) 600
Special	(2) 400	(2) 400	(1) 200	(1) 200
Electron microscopy rooms	610	610	610	610
Storage room	280	280	280	280
Tissue staining and embedding and technician's office	1, 140	1, 140	1, 140	1, 140
Microneuro preparation and technician's office	570	570	570	570
Special instrument storage	200	200	200	200
Coldroom	200	200	200	200
Animal room	(1) 410	(1) 410	(2) 820	(2) 820
Gross neuroanatomy and neurological storage room	410	280	410	280
Cadaver storage rooms (60 bodies) and compressor room	(2) 720	(2) 720	(2) 720	(2) 720
Embalming room	560	560	560	560
Embalming room storage	160	160	160	160
Crematory	200	200	200	200
Morgue (pathology)	210	210	210	210
Mortician's office	140	140	140	140
Urn storage room	430	430	430	430
Departmental central storage ²				
Conventional teaching:				
Total	7, 690	(¹)	10, 290	(¹)
Gross dissecting rooms (4 students/table):				
Undergraduate students	2, 560		3, 840	
Graduate students	720		720	
Utility room	160		160	
Storage room	250		250	
Microneuroanatomy teaching laboratories:				
Undergraduate students	3, 000		4, 320	
Graduate students	720		720	
Conference room	280		280	

¹ For total net area for multidiscipline laboratories, see Table 7.
² For central storage areas, see Table 6.

ing for supporting a number of jars of formalin is required.

The demonstration table, located at the center of the room to accommodate four students on each side, is usually provided with a stainless-steel top with raised edge and an integral sink at one end. Lighting should be designed for close observation at tabletop level. Hand-washing facilities, an x-ray film illuminator, and a chalkboard should be provided. Storage for formalin should be considered.

Tissue Staining and Embedding. This unit may be subdivided into a head technician's office, an embedding area, a sectioning and tissue-staining area, and a slide storage-and-issue area with access to the teaching laboratory, preferably by way of a dutch door for issuing slides and materials.

In the embedding room small tissue specimens are prepared, processed through a number of solutions by hand or in an automatic tissue-processing machine, then embedded in small cubes of paraffin or celloidin. Preparing the specimens requires the use of a refriger-

ator for gross tissue storage and a sit-down counter with sink.

For processing specimens and mixing solutions, a stand-up counter with sink, under-counter cabinets for equipment, and wall cabinets for chemicals and reagents are usually sufficient. For embedding procedures, an island bench of stand-up height with paraffin oven at or near one end should be provided. Cabinets with drawers for paraffin molds and mounting blocks and for filing embedments in frequent use should be provided. A storage room for embedments and for fixed gross tissue specimens not frequently used should be provided in the general storage area of the building. Glazed partitions may be installed to separate sectioning and mounting activities from the staining procedures.

Sectioning and mounting activities require sit-down counters with knee space and drawers for storing slides and equipment. Counters for tissue staining and stain mixing should be of sit-down height. Each work position should have a sink, knee space, cabinets for equipment, and chemical storage. For

attaching cover glasses and labels, a sit-down counter with knee space and drawers is satisfactory. Hand-washing facilities should be provided. Counter-top surfaces should be resilient and stain and alcohol resistant.

The slide storage-and-issue area requires standard microscope slide file cabinets, and cabinets for storage of boxed sets of slides.

Microneuro Preparation. To prepare microscope slides used in the neuroanatomy course, a microneuro preparation unit is required similar in design and equipment to the tissue staining and embedding unit for microanatomy. The head *technician's office* should have access to the unit and to the corridor.

Electron Microscopy. In the preparation-room, stand-up and sit-down counters and a fume hood are required. Air, gas, vacuum, and electrical outlets should be available. A refrigerator is necessary for chemical storage. The electron microscope should be located away from electric motors, elevators, fans, and other equipment that may generate vibration and stray magnetic fields. The room should be shielded to minimize dust, and the room should be windowless.

Electron microscopy requires a darkroom next to the microscope room. Table 9 gives the area for an electron microscope suite.

TABLE 9   Net Area for Electron Microscope Suite*

Type of supporting area	School A (entering class of 64 students), square feet
Total	610
Electron microscope rooms	(2) 230
Darkroom	70
Preparation area	280
Entry	30

*See departments of anatomy, microbiology, and pathology.

Cadaver Preparation and Storage. The unit should be so located and designed that no unauthorized persons may enter. Its location relative to the dissecting and autopsy rooms should not require transportation through any public areas. It should be located at grade with a receiving entrance accessible to a low loading platform. Where design permits, the platform may also serve the animal-receiving entrance.

The mortician's work area or *embalming room* should permit working on all sides of the embalming table and handling by stretcher cart, portable lift, or other means. An embalming table with built-in sink at one end is generally preferred. A combination instrument and scrub sink with knee- or foot-operated valve, service sink, and a floor drain should be provided. Floor and wall materials should be washable.

A connected *storage room* for supplies and equipment is necessary. Shower and dressing facilities for use of the mortician should be provided. A *mortician's office* should be adjacent to the area.

Cadaver storage should be adjacent to the embalming room. There are several methods of storing cadavers, some more demanding of space than others. An efficient method is storage on individual tray shelves on both sides of a service aisle. Thirty-five tray positions are usually adequate for a school with a 64-

Health

MEDICAL SCHOOLS

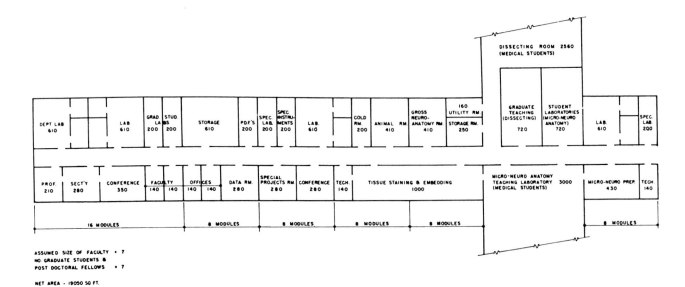

ASSUMED SIZE OF FACULTY = 7
NO. GRADUATE STUDENTS &
POST DOCTORAL FELLOWS = 7

NET AREA - 19050 SQ FT.

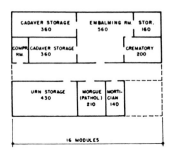

Fig. 8 Diagram for a department of anatomy.

student entering class; provision should be made in the original planning for approximately 60 tray positions to accommodate enrollment increases up to 96 students.

A crematory, if provided, should be located in the cadaver preparation and storage unit.

The department will require storage space for tissue embedments and gross organs. The same type storage as that described for pathology should be provided.

Biochemistry Figure 9 shows a space diagram for a minimum department of biochemistry. Table 10 gives the area for the department for the 64- and 96-student class hypothetical schools.

Teaching Laboratory. The conventional teaching laboratory is similar to those of other basic sciences. Island-type laboratory benches approximately 16 feet long will accommodate eight students, four on either side. The bench should have a stone sink at one or preferably both ends and a continuous drain trough or cup sinks (one for each two students), a continuous reagent shelf, and individual service outlets for each student. Services required are gas, air, vacuum, cold water, and electricity. Bench tops should be stone or acid-resistant composition surfaces.

A large chalkboard, smaller chalkboards for each 16 students, a retractable projection screen, and a bulletin board should be provided. An instructor's table of desk height with knee space, cabinets, cup sink, electrical outlets, cold water, and gas should be provided for demonstration to the class.

The teaching laboratory should be adjacent to auxiliary rooms of the medical student teach-

ing laboratory. Fixed equipment and mechanical facilities should be similar to those furnished the medical student.

Preparation Room. A preparation room adjacent to the teaching laboratory is used for mixing reagents and for storing chemicals and glassware. It may be divided by partitions into alcoves for separating issue, storage, and preparation. These alcoves should have laboratory benches, sinks, and cabinets for use as a research area. The storage of glassware, chemicals, and other stocked items requires adjustable shelving. The issuing area requires cabinets with small drawers and an issue window or door opening into the teaching laboratory.

Glassware Washing and Storage. Commercial glass washing and drying machines are often employed. In addition, a large sink with drainboards is required, with space for glassware carts, a worktable for glassware sorting, and shelves for storage.

Physiology Figure 10 shows a space diagram for a minimum department of physiology. Table 11 gives the net area for a physiology department.

Teaching Laboratory. A conventional teaching laboratory may be used by more than one department. The laboratory described here is a conventional laboratory designed for specific use by the department of physiology. With only minimal additional equipment this laboratory is suitable for pharmacology teaching.

Many animals are used in physiology teaching and stand-up tables 37 in. high with casters to accommodate four students, two on each side, are suggested. A shelf under the top

should be provided as storage space for animal boards. A service island may be provided with gas, electrical, air, and vacuum outlets. Distilled water should be piped into *one place* in each laboratory or preparation area and carboys should be used at work stations. A floor drain should be installed between each pair of service islands.

A 4-ft fume hood should suffice for eight students. Space for incubators should be considered unless they can be placed on counters.

Chalkboards, a bulletin board, and a retractable projection screen should be furnished similar in size and number to those in other teaching laboratories. Space for an instructor's table at the front of the laboratory is required.

Graduate Student Teaching Laboratory. It should be located adjacent to auxiliary rooms of the teaching laboratory. Fixed equipment and mechanical facilities should be similar to those furnished the medical student.

Student Research Laboratory. Furniture and mechanical facilities may be similar to those of a typical research laboratory.

Equipment Storage. An equipment storage area, adjacent to the teaching laboratory, is needed, as is desk space for a stock clerk and technician. A 31-in.-high counter with gas, air, vacuum, and electrical outlets and cabinets should be installed for testing and preparing equipment. An issue window or door opening into the teaching laboratory is desirable. Space for assembly of equipment to be issued and for glassblowing and soldering should be provided.

Shielded Room. If required by the program, a shielded room distant from obvious electrostatic interference must be provided.

572

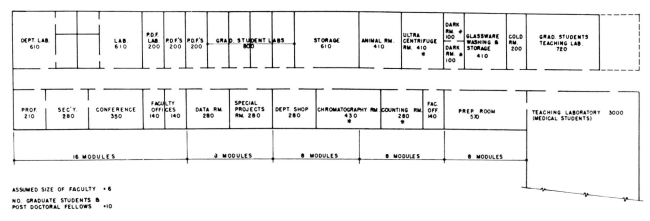

ASSUMED SIZE OF FACULTY = 6

NO. GRADUATE STUDENTS &
POST DOCTORAL FELLOWS = 10

* SPECIAL ROOMS WILL VARY WITH
TYPE OF RESEARCH PROGRAM.

NET AREA - 11960 SQ FT

Fig. 9 Diagram for a department of biochemistry.

TABLE 10   Net Area for a Department of Biochemistry

Type of facility	School A (entering class of 64 students)		School B (entering class of 96 students)	
	With conventional departmental laboratories	With multidiscipline laboratories	With conventional departmental laboratories	With multidiscipline laboratories
Assumed size of faculty	6	6	9	9
Number of graduate students and postdoctoral fellows	10	10	14	14
	Square feet			
Total net area	12,240	(1)	14,980	(1)
Faculty offices, research laboratories, and related facilities:				
Total	8,670	8,670	10,090	10,090
Professor's office	210	210	210	210
Secretary's office	280	280	280	280
Conference room	350	350	350	350
Faculty offices	(3) 420	(3) 420	(3) 420	(3) 420
Postdoctoral fellows' offices	(2) 400	(2) 400	(2) 400	(2) 400
Data room	280	280	280	280
Special-projects room	280	280	280	280
Research laboratories:				
Departmental	610	610	610	610
General	610	610	(3) 1,830	(3) 1,830
Postdoctoral fellows	200	200	200	200
Graduate students	(4) 800	(4) 800	(5) 1,000	(5) 1,000
Storage room (future laboratory)	610	610	610	610
Storage room	280	280	280	280
Glassware washing and storage	410	410	410	410
Cold room	200	200	200	200
Special-equipment room 2	430	430	430	430
Centrifuge room 2	410	410	410	410
Darkrooms 2	(2) 200	(2) 200	(2) 200	(2) 200
Counting room 2	280	280	280	280
Departmental shop	280	280	280	280
Animal room	410	410	410	410
Graduate students' teaching laboratory	720	720	720	720
Departmental storage 3				
Conventional teaching:				
Total	3,570	(1)	4,890	(1)
Teaching laboratory	3,000		4,320	
Preparation room	570		570	

1 For total net area for multidiscipline laboratories, see Table 7.
2 Special rooms will vary with type of research.
3 For central storage areas, see Table 6.

Audio Room. If an audio room is provided, it should consist of a test room and a control room with a triple-glazed clear-glass observation window between and with acoustical treatment, including reduction of floor vibration.

The test room should have a microphone and a speaker cabinet. The control room should have a sit-down counter with cabinets located on the observation window side.

Physio-optics Room. If the student curriculum includes exercises in physio-optics, a special room will be needed with 20-ft separation between the subject and the vision chart. A sink for hand washing and a sit-down counter for recording are necessary.

Treadmill and Gas Analysis. A room close to the laboratory is preferable. The room should also contain a cot and table for recording.

Supply Room. This room should be near the teaching laboratory. Shelving and racks for volatile solvent storage should be within a fire-resistive closet off the mixing and issue areas. Counter tops, 37 in. high, with gas, air, vacuum, and electrical outlets, cabinets with varying sized drawers, and a sink are required for mixing solutions and preparations for student use. Glassware washing and storage require a large sink, drainboards, provision for distilled water, and base cabinets for glassware. An issue window is suggested. Space should be allocated for solution carts and assembly of materials to be issued. A head technician's office may be required depending on the quantity of material handled.

Department Shop. A minimum machine shop should contain a drill press, a metal lathe, a milling machine, and wood and metal bandsaws. A workbench, stock racks, and tool bin are required.

In the electronics area, a sit-down work counter with electrical outlets of appropriate voltages, drawers, and locked storage cabinets for electronic equipment and space to bring in floor-mounted equipment for testing will be required. Noise and vibration associated with technical shops should be considered in their relation to other areas.

Constant Temperature Rooms. Constant-temperature rooms should have access to the corridor and to a work area. Doors from the corridor should accommodate beds or animal

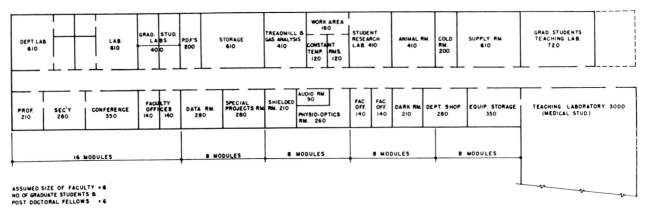

ASSUMED SIZE OF FACULTY = 6
NO OF GRADUATE STUDENTS 8
POST DOCTORAL FELLOWS = 6

NET AREA - 11950 SQ. FT.

Fig. 10 Diagram for a department of physiology.

racks. Floor and wall surfaces should be similar to those suggested for animal quarters.

The work area associated with these rooms should have 31-in.-high work counters, a sink, and gas, air, vacuum, and electrical outlets.

Microbiology Figure 11 shows a space diagram for a minimum department of microbiology. The net area for a microbiology department is given in Table 12.

Teaching Laboratory. The conventional teaching laboratory is usually designed to accommodate the second-year class. Satisfactory results can be obtained with the use of an island-type laboratory bench to position four students all on the same side facing demonstrations.

Laboratory benches may be 31 in. high for sitdown work with microscopes. Each student should have knee space, drawers for supplies, and a cabinet for microscope storage. Bench service outlets should be water, gas, air, vacuum, and electrical for each position. A cup sink at each position, or continuous drain trough, and a shelf for storing bottles above are required. Bench tops should be resilient and stainproof.

In addition to island benches, it is desirable to have counters 37 in. high, with reagent shelves equipped with gas, air, vacuum, electrical outlets, and sinks with wrist-action valves for hand washing.

A chalkboard, a bulletin board, a retractable projection screen, and space for the instructor's desk at the front of the laboratory are required. Space in the teaching laboratory may be required for incubators and refrigerators. One domestic refrigerator per sixteen students and one stationary incubator per eight students should be provided. A stationary centrifuge, one per sixteen students, may be provided depending on the curriculum.

Facilities should be available to maintain and observe such small animals as rabbits, guinea pigs, and mice close to the teaching laboratories.

Graduate Student Teaching Laboratory. It should be adjacent to auxiliary rooms of the teaching laboratory. Fixed equipment and mechanical facilities should be similar to those furnished the medical student.

Research Laboratories The microbiology

TABLE 11 Net Area for a Department of Physiology

Type of facility	School A (entering class of 64 students)		School B (entering class of 96 students)	
	With conventional departmental laboratories	With multidiscipline laboratories	With conventional departmental laboratories	With multidiscipline laboratories
Assumed size of faculty	6	6	8	8
Number of graduate students and postdoctoral fellows	6	6	8	8
	Square feet			
Total net area	12,230	(¹)	14,160	(¹)
Faculty offices, research laboratories, and related facilities:				
Total	6,940	6,940	7,550	7,550
Professor's office	210	210	210	210
Secretary's office	280	280	280	280
Conference room	350	350	350	350
Faculty offices	(4) 560	(4) 560	(4) 560	(4) 560
Postdoctoral fellows' office	200	200	200	200
Data room	280	280	280	280
Special-projects room	280	280	280	280
Research laboratories:				
Departmental	610	610	610	610
General	610	610	(2) 1,220	(2) 1,220
Graduate students	(2) 400	(2) 400	(2) 400	(2) 400
Storage room (future laboratory)	610	610	610	610
Storage room	280	280	280	280
Constant-temperature rooms	(2) 240	(2) 240	(2) 240	(2) 240
Shielded room	210	210	210	210
Dark room	210	210	210	210
Departmental shop	280	280	280	280
Animal room	410	410	410	410
Cold room	200	200	200	200
Graduate students teaching laboratory	720	720	720	720
Departmental central storage ²				
Conventional teaching:				
Total	5,290	(¹)	6,610	(¹)
Teaching laboratory	3,000		4,320	
Equipment storage room	350		350	
Supply room	610		610	
Student research laboratory and work area	570		570	
Audio room	90		90	
Physio-optics room	260		260	
Treadmill and gas analysis room	410		410	

¹ For total net area for multidiscipline laboratories see Table 7.
² For central storage area, see Table 6.

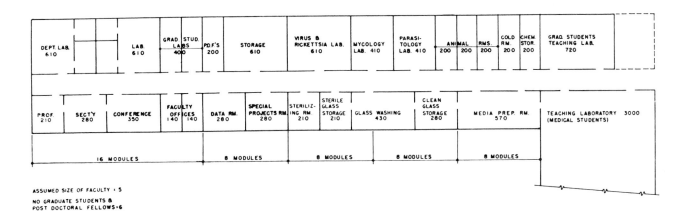

ASSUMED SIZE OF FACULTY = 5

NO GRADUATE STUDENTS &
POST DOCTORAL FELLOWS=6

NET AREA = 11960 SQ FT

Fig. 11 Diagram for a department of microbiology.

TABLE 12 Net Area for a Department of Microbiology

Type of facility	School A (entering class of 64 students)		School B (entering class of 96 students)	
	With conventional departmental laboratories	With multidiscipline laboratories	With conventional departmental laboratories	With multidiscipline laboratories
Assumed size of faculty	5	5	7	7
Number of graduate students and postdoctoral fellows	6	6	8	8
	Square feet			
Total net area	12,240	(1)	14,170	(1)
Faculty offices, research laboratories, and associated facilities:				
Total	9,240	8,970	9,850	9,580
Professor's office	210	210	210	210
Secretary's office	280	280	280	280
Conference room	350	350	350	350
Faculty offices	(2) 280	(2) 280	(2) 280	(2) 280
Postdoctoral fellows' office	200	200	200	200
Data room	280	280	280	280
Special-projects room	280	280	280	280
Research laboratories:				
Departmental	610	610	610	610
General	610	610	(2) 1,220	(2) 1,220
Graduate students	(2) 400	(2) 400	(2) 400	(2) 400
Storage room (future laboratory)	610	610	610	610
Storage room	280	280	280	280
Media preparation room	570	430	570	430
Sterilizing room	210	210	210	210
Sterile glass storage	210	210	210	210
Glass washing	430	430	430	430
Clean glass storage	280	210	280	210
Chemical storage	200	140	200	140
Virus and rickettsia laboratory	610	610	610	610
Mycology laboratory	410	410	410	410
Parasitology laboratory	410	410	410	410
Animal rooms	(3) 600	(3) 600	(3) 600	(3) 600
Cold room	200	200	200	200
Graduate students teaching laboratory	720	720	720	720
Departmental central storage 2				
Conventional teaching:				
Total	3,000	(1)	4,320	(1)
Teaching laboratory	3,000		4,320	

1 For total net area for multidiscipline laboratories see Table 7.
2 For central storage areas, see Table 6.

research laboratories will, in many instances, be similar in equipment and design to laboratories in other basic sciences. However, laboratories used for bacteriological and virus research have additional requirements. Glassware of an unusually large size is often used. One sink in each laboratory should be sized to wash this glassware.

Separate animal rooms are provided in the microbiology department to prevent cross-contamination. If highly contagious material is to be handled, a vestibule may be needed at the entrance to microbiology animal rooms to permit the attendant to change clothes and shoes to reduce infection and cross-contamination.

Electron Microscopy. Facilities for this purpose would be similar to those described for the department of anatomy.

Media Preparation. Media preparation areas should be adjacent to teaching areas and designed to eliminate through traffic to prevent drafts and the introduction of contaminating organisms. A media kitchen requires a range, or portable hot plates on a counter 37 in. high, for cooking the material. Counter-top sinks and cabinets with drawers ranging in width from 6 in. to 2 ft 6 in. and wall cabinets with shelves for storage are desirable. Counters should have air, gas, vacuum, and electrical outlets. Distilled water should be piped to one location over a sink and distributed in carboys.

After the unsterile liquid culture media has been prepared in bulk quantities, it is dispensed into test tubes or plates. This requires counter space similar to the media kitchen, including wall and base cabinets and service outlets.

An autoclave is required for sterilizing prepared culture media after it is poured into previously sterilized petri dishes. A flushing-rim sink near the autoclave is desirable for disposal of spoiled media.

The issue room will contain glassware and equipment storage, shelving and cabinets for glassware and equipment, and an issue window opening into the laboratory.

Glassware Washing and Storage. If this is to be done as a central unit for the department, it should be divided into sterilizing, sterile storage, glassware washing, and clean glass storage.

An autoclave to sterilize glassware prior to washing, a sink and drainboard area, and space for chemical jars and for soaking extra dirty glassware are required. Commercial glass

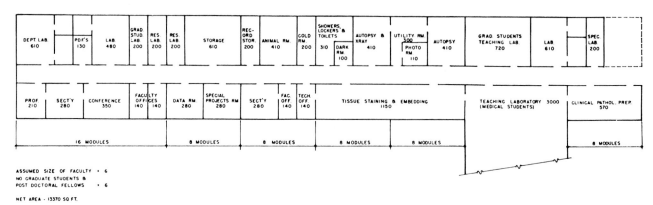

ASSUMED SIZE OF FACULTY · 6
NO GRADUATE STUDENTS &
POST DOCTORAL FELLOWS · 6

NET AREA - 13370 SQ FT.

Fig. 12 Diagram for a department of pathology.

washers and dryers may be employed and space for these should be provided beside the sink. Space should be available at sink and washer area for glassware and petri dish carts and cart storage.

Storage areas should be furnished with adjustable shelving, as some glassware may be exceptionally long or high. An issue window or door from sterile storage to corridor should be provided.

Chemical Storage. Bulk storage of chemicals should be provided for in basement areas.

Pathology Figure 12 shows a space diagram for a minimum department of pathology. Table 13 gives the net area for a pathology department.

Teaching Laboratory. A conventional teaching laboratory similar to that described for micro- and neuroanatomy is usually adequate for teaching the second-year pathology course.

Graduate Student Teaching Laboratories. These should be adjacent to auxiliary rooms of the medical students' pathology teaching laboratory.

Tissue Staining and Embedding, Technician's Office. A unit similar in design and equipment to the tissue staining and embedding unit described for microanatomy should be provided.

Clinical Pathology Preparation Unit. This unit usually has a head technician's office and a preparation room with direct access to the teaching laboratory, preferably by a dutch door. For preparing some types of specimens as well as stains and reagents for direct issue, a stand-up counter 37 in. high is desirable. For other types of specimens, particularly those such as blood and bone marrow, a sit-down counter 31 in. high is more convenient. Both counters should have reagent shelves, counter-top sinks, air, gas, vacuum, and electrical service outlets, knee spaces, cabinets for storing equipment and chemicals and reagents. Work surfaces should be alcohol- and stain-resistant and resilient to minimize glass breakage. A refrigerator for storage of clinical material and a lavatory with wrist-action valves for handwashing are necessary. Space for parking a specimen cart should be provided.

Autopsy Room. This should be located convenient both to the teaching hospital and to the pathology department and arranged so as to prevent unnecessary contact of unauthorized persons with autopsy procedures. If the basic science building is separated from the teaching hospital, autopsy facilities should

TABLE 13 Net Area for a Department of Pathology

Type of facility	School A (entering class of 64 students)		School B (entering class of 96 students)	
	With conventional departmental laboratories	With multidiscipline laboratories	With conventional departmental laboratories	With multidiscipline laboratories
Assumed size of faculty [1]	6	6	9	9
Number of graduate students, postdoctoral fellows and residents	6	6	8	8
	Square feet			
Total net area	14,100	[2]	17,390	[2]
Faculty offices, research laboratories, and associated facilities:				
Total	11,100	11,100	13,070	13,070
Professor's office	210	210	210	210
Secretary's offices	(2) 560	(2) 560	(2) 560	(2) 560
Conference room	350	350	350	350
Faculty offices	(3) 420	(3) 420	(3) 420	(3) 420
Postdoctoral fellows' office	130	130	200	200
Data room	280	280	280	280
Special-projects room	280	280	280	280
Research laboratories:				
Departmental	610	610	610	160
General	(2) 1,099	(2) 1,090	(3) 1,830	(3) 1,830
Graduate students	200	200	200	200
Special	200	200	200	200
Residents' laboratories	(2) 400	(2) 400	(3) 530	(3) 530
Electron microscope	610	610	610	610
Storage room	280	280	280	280
Tissue staining and embedding and technician's office	1,290	1,290	1,290	1,290
Clinical pathology preparation	570	570	570	570
Record storage	200	200	410	410
Autopsy rooms	410	410	(2) 820	(2) 820
Darkroom	100	100	100	100
Utility room	300	300	300	300
Photo room	110	110	110	110
Autopsy and X-ray	410	410	410	410
Gross pathology conference room	310	310	310	310
Dictation room	140	140	140	140
Showers, lockers and toilets	310	310	310	310
Morgue (see department of anatomy)				
Animal rooms	410	410	(2) 820	(2) 820
Cold rooms	200	200	200	200
Graduate students teaching laboratory	720	720	720	720
Departmental central storage [3]				
Conventional teaching:				
Total	3,000	[2]	4,320	[2]
Teaching laboratory	3,000		4,320	

[1] For teaching responsibility only.
[2] For total net area for multidiscipline laboratories see Table 7.
[3] For central storage areas, see Table 6.

Note. — These areas do not provide for the permanent professional or resident staffs performing services for clinical pathology in the teaching hospital.

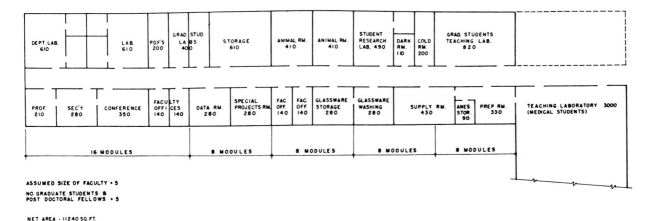

ASSUMED SIZE OF FACULTY = 5

NO. GRADUATE STUDENTS &
POST DOCTORAL FELLOWS = 5

NET AREA - 11240 SQ.FT.

Fig. 13 Diagram for a department of pharmacology.

TABLE 14 Net Area for a Department of Pharmacology

Type of facility	School A (entering class of 64 students)		School B (entering class of 96 students)	
	With conventional departmental laboratories	With multidiscipline laboratories	With conventional departmental laboratories	With multidiscipline laboratories
Assumed size of faculty	5	5	7	7
Number of graduate students and postdoctoral fellows	5	5	7	7
	Square feet			
Total net area	11,520	(1)	13,450	(1)
Faculty offices, research laboratories, and associated facilities:				
Total	7,700	7,700	8,310	8,310
Professor's office	210	210	210	210
Secretary's office	280	280	280	280
Conference room	350	350	350	350
Faculty offices	(4) 560	(4) 560	(4) 560	(4) 560
Postdoctoral fellows' office	200	200	200	200
Data room	280	280	280	280
Special-projects room	280	280	280	280
Research laboratories:				
Departmental	610	610	610	610
General	610	610	(2) 1,220	(2) 1,220
Graduate students	(2) 400	(2) 400	(2) 400	(2) 400
Storage room (future laboratory)	610	610	610	610
Storage room	280	280	280	280
Supply room	430	430	430	430
Glassware washing and storage	560	560	560	560
Anesthesia storage	90	90	90	90
Darkroom	110	110	110	110
Animal rooms	(2) 820	(2) 820	(2) 820	(2) 820
Cold room	200	200	200	200
Graduate students teaching laboratory	820	820	820	820
Departmental central storage 2				
Conventional teaching:				
Total	3,820	(1)	5,140	(1)
Teaching laboratory	3,000	--------	4,320	--------
Preparation room	330	--------	330	--------
Students research laboratory	490	--------	490	--------

1 For total net area for multidiscipline laboratories, see Table 7.
2 For central storage areas, see Table 6.

be located in the hospital to avoid transporting bodies from one building to another.

Each autopsy room should be equipped with a scrub-up sink with knee- or foot-action valve; a sink with drainboards, cold-water manifold, and gas and electrical service outlets; an adjacent work counter with drawers and cabinets for storage of supplies; a flushing-rim clinical sink; wall cabinets with adjustable shelves and glazed doors for storing instruments; a wall-mounted four-bank x-ray film illuminator; and a chalkboard. An instrument sterilizer and a storage cabinet for fixed specimens should also be provided if they are not available in an adjoining utility or clean-up room.

Water and ac electrical service outlets with waterproof caps are required. A table with downdraft top for removal of contamination and odors directly at their source, with an integral sink at one end of the top, and service outlets, is generally preferred. Provision should be made for foot-operated dictation equipment. A ceiling-mounted 35-mm. still camera should be located over the table for *in situ* photographs during the autopsy. The same mount may provide for TV to remote monitors.

Space to accommodate a portable observation stand opposite the table for convenient viewing of autopsy procedures by students and house staff should be provided.

Floor and walls should be of water-resistant material, and a floor drain should be installed.

Autopsy and X-Ray Room. A mobile x-ray machine should be provided. X-ray protection should be in accordance with the recommendations of the applicable handbooks of the National Bureau of Standards.

Utility and Clean-up Room. This room should be located between two autopsy rooms with direct access to each and to the corridor. Equipment for this area includes a sink with drainboard; a flushing-rim service sink; provisions for storage of glass jars, formalin, and alcohol; wall cabinets for fixed specimen storage; and an instrument washer-sterilizer unless provided in each autopsy room.

Photo Room. The photo room should adjoin the autopsy room.

Fixed equipment in a photo room usually includes a stand-up counter with sink and electrical outlets, a cabinet for instruments and supplies, and shelves for photographic accessories.

For photographing gross specimens, a 3-ft-square light box is used. Electric outlets for table and floodlamps should be 30 amperes.

Darkroom. Wet and dry areas of the darkroom should be separated. A refrigerator for storing color film should be provided, and water supply at all processing sinks is required.

Bench tops should be chemically inert, watertight, and wear resistant. Floor surfaces should be waterproof, resistant to chemicals, resilient for foot comfort, and not slippery when wet.

Cold Room. A cold room separate from the research cold room but adjacent to the autopsy areas for holding tissue and organs for later study is required. A deep-freeze unit and adjustable metal shelving may be provided for preservation of fresh gross material for class use. Stand-up counters with sinks and air, vacuum, and electrical service outlets are required. Floor surface should be smooth, waterproof, and wear resistant.

A separate room for storing gross pathological specimens should be provided.

Gross Pathology Conference Rooms. A stand-up table with sink at one end and down-draft top similar to that described for the gross neuroanatomy room is appropriate. Other equipment includes adjustable shelving, x-ray film illuminators, bulletin board, and scrub sink with knee or foot controls. Where possible, this area should have direct access to the cold room.

Dictating Room. This is a small room equipped with desk and equipment for writing or dictating autopsy records.

Record Storage. Open-faced shelving with shelf dividers designed for vertical stacking of the records with a reference table and chairs should be provided. A storage room for records of less frequent reference should be provided in basement storage.

The pathology department requires areas for storage of embedments, fixed tissue, gross organs, microscope slides, and protocol records not in frequent use. Tissue in solution is kept in glass jars, paraffin sealed, and stored on wood shelving designed for jar height.

Microscope slides are usually contained in metal slide files, and this area should be separated from areas where formalin vapors are present. Protocol records are often bound and placed on shelving or in legal-size file cabinets.

Pharmacology Figure 13 shows a space diagram for a minimum department of pharmacology. Net area for a pharmacology department is given in Table 14.

Teaching Laboratory. The conventional pharmacology teaching laboratory may be similar to the physiology teaching laboratory.

Graduate Student Teaching Laboratory. This should be adjacent to auxiliary rooms of the medical student teaching laboratory. Fixed equipment and mechanical facilities should be similar to those furnished the medical student.

Student Research Laboratory. A student research laboratory, if provided, should contain facilities similar to those in typical pharmacology research laboratories. Where possible, it should be located within the teaching area but adjacent to research areas.

Glassware Washing and Storage. Glassware washing and storage facilities similar to those indicated for the biochemistry department are adequate in the pharmacology department; they should be located near the teaching laboratory.

Preparation Room. This should be adjacent to the pharmacology teaching laboratory.

Anesthesia Storage. An anesthesia storage room should be provided with cylinder storage racks to lock cylinders in an upright position and shelving for pressure gauges and other anesthetic equipment. Space at ground level should be provided for bulk storage of cylinders.

Supply Room. A supply room in pharmacology may be divided into two areas: one for instruments and general supplies and the other for chemicals used in research.

Some instruments require floor space while others should be placed on shelving. A desk-high counter with drawers and file cabinet is needed. Since some instruments may be used here, electrical outlets should be provided.

If narcotics are to be stored, a built-in safe should be provided.

Space must be provided for the care of animals used in experimental work in pharmacology.

A summary of space estimates for all basic science facilities is given in Table 15.

Clinical Science Facilities

The departments generally include internal medicine, surgery, pediatrics, obstetrics and gynecology, psychiatry, preventive medicine, and radiology. Pathology, although usually considered a basic science department, nevertheless has many of the characteristics of a clinical department and, therefore, functionally and structurally, usually bridges both.

Space diagrams for the departments of medicine, surgery, pediatrics, obstetrics-gynecology, psychiatry, and preventive medicine are shown in Figs. 14 through 19 for a hypothetical school with an entering class of 64 students (60 in the third and fourth year). Tables 16 through 21 give the net area for a minimum facility for each clinical department for hypothetical schools with entering classes of 64 and 96 students. Table 22 gives a summary of space estimates for all clinical science departments.

For convenience of operation, clinical department facilities should be located between, and connecting with, the basic science building and the teaching hospital. This allows for joint use of teaching, research, and supporting facilities provided in the basic science building and makes it convenient for the medical staff to take care of their hospital responsibilities. Departments should be located on the same floor or floors as the patient-care units they serve.

Research facilities in the form of laboratories should be provided for each department member.

Teaching activities of all departments will be carried out, for the most part, in common lecture rooms, on the wards of the hospital, and in the outpatient department.

Medicine The department of medicine consists of physicians specializing in internal medicine and includes the subspecialties of allergy, cardiology, dermatology, gastroenterology, hematology, infectious diseases and immunology, metabolism, neurology, and pulmonary diseases. The members of the department will have responsibility for the care of hospitalized patients, for ambulatory patients in the medical clinics of the outpatient department, and for medical consultations on patients under the care of other clinical services. They will have major teaching duties for second-, third-, and fourth-year medical students, interns, residents, and clinical fellows.

Surgery The department of surgery consists of physicians specializing in general surgery or in one of the surgical specialties, which include anesthesiology, ophthalmology, otolaryngology, orthopedics, neurosurgery, plastic surgery, thoracic surgery, and urology. The members of this department will have responsibility for the care of patients who are hospitalized on the surgical service; who visit the surgical clinics of the outpatient department; and who require surgical consultation while on some other service. Often the emergency service of a hospital is under the direction of the department of surgery, as may be the professional aspects of disaster planning. The department of surgery will have teaching responsibilities for second-, third-, and fourth-year medical students, interns, residents, and surgical fellows. Each full-time member of the department may be expected to engage in research.

Pediatrics The department of pediatrics consists of physicians specializing in the developmental aspects of physiological processes and expressions of disease. They are as concerned about the long-term health effects of early disease and with their prevention, as with the immediate care of infants and children. In most

TABLE 15 Summary of Space Estimates for Basic Science Facilities for Hypothetical 4-Year Medical Schools with Entering Classes of 64 and 96 Students [1]

Type of facility	School A (entering class of 64 students)		School B (entering class of 96 students)	
	With conventional departmental laboratories	With multidiscipline laboratories	With conventional departmental laboratories	With multidiscipline laboratories
	Square feet			
Total gross square feet (rounded) [2]	152,000	135,000	183,000	158,000
Total net square feet (rounded)	99,000	88,000	119,000	103,000
Departmental facilities:				
Anatomy	19,330	11,510	22,950	12,530
Biochemistry	12,240	8,670	14,980	10,090
Physiology	12,230	6,940	14,160	7,550
Microbiology	12,240	8,970	14,170	9,580
Pathology [3]	14,100	11,100	17,390	13,070
Pharmacology	11,520	7,700	13,450	8,310
Multidiscipline laboratories and adjunctive areas		22,500		29,960
Lecture rooms	3,780	3,780	3,780	3,780
Unassigned conference rooms	(2 @ 350) 700		(3 @ 350) 1,050	
Study cubicles [4]	6,110	([5])	9,400	([5])
Technical shops	1,500	1,500	2,000	2,000
Departmental central storage	4,500	4,500	4,500	4,500
Toilets	1,200	1,200	1,200	1,200

[1] This table does not include the supporting facilities which are a necessary part of both the basic science and clinical science facilities.

[2] To compute gross area, it is estimated that 65 percent of the total gross area is available as usable space, and the remaining 35 percent will provide space for exterior walls, partitions, corridors, stairs, elevators, and duct ways and chases for mechanical and electrical requirements.

[3] Space for service functions in the teaching hospital is not included.

[4] Study cubicles for 3d- and 4th-year students and for house officers in teaching hospital.

[5] Optional.

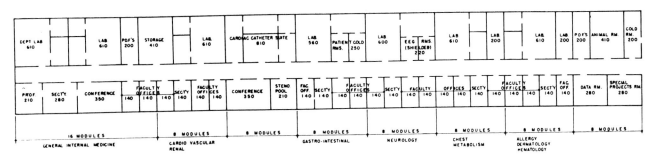

ASSUMED SIZE OF FACULTY : 18
POST DOCTORAL FELLOWS : 8

NET AREA - 12350 SQ FT

Fig. 14   Diagram for a department of medicine.

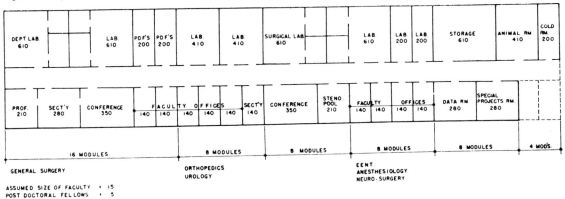

Fig. 15   Diagram for a department of surgery.

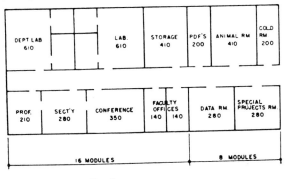

ASSUMED SIZE OF FACULTY = 5
POST DOCTORAL FELLOWS = 3

NET AREA - 4120 SQ. FT.

Fig. 16   Diagram for a department of pediatrics.

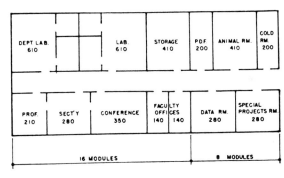

ASSUMED SIZE OF FACULTY = 3
POST DOCTORAL FELLOWS = 1

NET AREA - 4120 SQ. FT.

Fig. 17   Diagram for a department of obstetrics-gynecology.

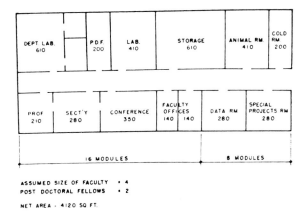

ASSUMED SIZE OF FACULTY = 4
POST DOCTORAL FELLOWS = 2

NET AREA - 4120 SQ FT.

Fig. 18   Diagram for a department of preventive medicine.

579

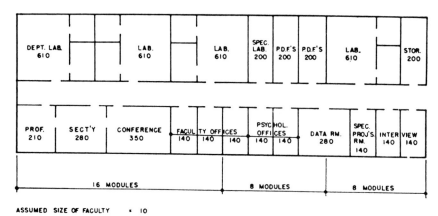

ASSUMED SIZE OF FACULTY = 10
POST DOCTORAL FELLOWS = 8

NET AREA - 5480 SQ FT

Fig. 19 Diagram for a department of psychiatry.

TABLE 16   Net Area for a Department of Medicine for Hypothetical Schools with Entering Classes of 64 and 96 Students

Subspecialty and type of facility	School A (entering class of 64 students)	School B (entering class of 96 students)	Subspecialty and type of facility	School A (entering class of 64 students)	School B (entering class of 96 students)
Assumed size of faculty [1]	18	25		Square feet	
Postdoctoral fellows	8	11	Faculty facilities—Continued		
			Metabolism:		
	Square feet		Total	480	690
Faculty facilities:			Faculty offices	(2) 280	(2) 280
Total net area	13,440	15,490	Laboratory	200	410
General internal medicine:			Allergy:		
Total	2,400	3,150	Total	890	890
Professor's office [2]	210	210	Faculty offices	(2) 280	(2) 280
Secretaries' office	280	280	Laboratory	610	610
Conference room	350	350	Dermatology:		
Faculty offices	140	(2) 280	Total	420	1,030
Postdoctoral fellows' office	200	200	Professor's office	140	140
Departmental laboratory	610	610	Secretary's office	140	140
Additional laboratories	610	(2) 1,220	Faculty office	140	140
Cardiovascular-renal:			Laboratory	(?)	610
Total	1,030	1,170	Hematology:		
Professor's office	140	140	Total	340	340
Secretary's office	140	140	Faculty office	140	140
Faculty offices	140	(2) 280	Laboratory	200	200
Laboratory	610	610	Common-use facilities:		
Gastrointestinal:			Total	4,510	4,710
Total	1,170	1,170	Special laboratory	610	610
Professor's office	140	140	Postdoctoral fellows' offices	200	(2) 400
Secretary's office	140	140	Conference room	350	350
Faculty offices	(2) 280	(2) 280	Steno pool	210	210
Laboratory	610	610	Data room	280	280
Neurology:			Special-projects room	280	280
Total	1,170	1,310	Storage room (future laboratory)	410	410
Professor's office	140	140	Storage room	280	280
Secretary's office	140	140	Cardiac catheter suite	810	810
Faculty offices	140	(2) 280	Patients' cold room	(2) 250	(2) 250
Office	140	140	EEG rooms	(2) 220	(2) 220
Laboratory	610	610	Cold room	200	200
Chest:			Animal room	410	410
Total	1,030	1,030			
Professor's office	140	140			
Secretary's office	140	140			
Faculty offices	140	140			
Laboratory	610	610			

[1] For teaching responsibility only.
[2] Chairman of department.

TABLE 17   Net Area for a Department of Surgery

Subspecialty and type of facility	School A (entering class of 64 students)	School B (entering class of 96 students)	Subspecialty and type of facility	School A (entering class of 64 students)	School B (entering class of 96 students)
Assumed size of faculty [1]	15	21		Square feet	
Postdoctoral fellows	5	7	Eye, ear, nose, and throat (EENT):		
	Square feet		Total	1,090	1,230
Faculty facilities:			Professor's office	140	140
Total net area	8,840	11,120	Faculty offices	140	(2) 280
General surgery:			Laboratory	610	610
Total	2,740	4,300	Laboratory	200	200
Professor's office [2]	210	210	Anesthesiology:		
Secretary's office	280	280	Total	340	690
Conference room	350	350	Faculty offices	140	(2) 280
Faculty offices	(2) 280	(3) 420	Laboratory	200	410
Postdoctoral fellows' offices	(2) 400	(3) 600	Neurosurgery:		
Departmental laboratory	610	610	Total	340	690
Additional laboratories	610	(3)1,830	Faculty offices	140	(2) 280
Orthopedics:			Laboratory	200	410
Total	550	690	Common-use facilities:		
Faculty offices	140	(2) 280	Total	2,950	2,690
Laboratory	410	410	Conference rooms	350	(2) 700
Urology:			Steno pool	210	210
Total	830	830	Data room	280	280
Professor's office	140	140	Special-projects room	280	-------
Secretary's office	140	140	Storage room (future laboratory)	610	-------
Faculty office	140	140	Storage room	-------	280
Laboratory	410	410	Surgical laboratory	610	610
			Cold room	200	200
			Animal room	410	410

[1] For teaching responsibility only.
[2] Chairman of department.

TABLE 18   Net Area for a Department of Pediatrics

Type of facility	School A (entering class of 64 students)	School B (entering class of 96 students)
Assumed size of faculty [1]	5	8
Postdoctoral fellows	3	4
	Square feet	
Total net area	4,260	5,010
Faculty facilities:		
Total	2,680	3,430
Professor's office	210	210
Professor's office	140	140
Secretary's office	280	280
Conference room	350	350
Faculty offices	(2) 280	(3) 420
Postdoctoral fellows' office	200	200
Departmental laboratory	610	610
Additional laboratories	610	(2) 1,220
Common-use facilities:		
Total	1,580	1,580
Data room	140	140
Special projects room	280	280
Storage room (future laboratory)	410	410
Storage room	140	140
Cold room	200	200
Animal room	410	410

[1] For teaching responsibility only.

TABLE 19   Net Area for a Department of Obstetrics-Gynecology

Type of facility	School A (entering class of 64 students)	School B (entering class of 96 students)
Assumed size of faculty [1]	3	4
Postdoctoral fellows	1	1
	Square feet	
Total net area	4,390	4,390
Faculty facilities:		
Total	2,540	2,540
Professor's office	210	210
Secretary's office	280	280
Conference room	350	350
Faculty offices	(2) 280	(2) 280
Postdoctoral fellows' office	200	200
Departmental laboratory	610	610
Additional laboratory	610	610
Common-use facilities:		
Total	1,850	1,850
Data room	140	140
Special-projects room	280	280
Storage room (future laboratory)	410	410
Storage room	410	410
Cold room	200	200
Animal room	410	410

[1] For teaching responsibility only.

TABLE 20   Net Area for a Department of Preventive Medicine

Type of facility	School A (entering class of 64 students)	School B (entering class of 96 students)
Assumed size of faculty [1]	4	6
Postdoctoral fellows	2	3
	Square feet	
Total net area	4,260	4,870
Faculty facilities:		
Total	2,340	2,950
Professor's office	210	210
Secretary's office	280	280
Conference room	350	350
Faculty offices	(2) 280	(2) 280
Postdoctoral fellows' office	200	200
Departmental laboratory	610	610
Additional laboratories	410	(2) 1,020
Common-use facilities:		
Total	1,920	1,920
Data room	140	140
Special-projects room	280	280
Storage room (future laboratory)	610	610
Storage room	280	280
Cold room	200	200
Animal room	410	410

[1] For teaching responsibility only.

university hospitals, the age range extends to the fourteenth or sixteenth year. Pediatrics is a nonsurgical specialty. Consequently, surgery on patients in the pediatrics age is generally handled by the department of surgery. As in internal medicine, a number of subspecialties generally based on organ systems such as cardiology, neurology, and endocrinology are usually represented in the department of pediatrics.

The general requirements for departmental offices, teaching spaces, and laboratories are the same in pediatrics as in other clinical departments. Teaching is generally concentrated within one or both of the last two clinical years. In addition, there are teaching responsibilities for interns, residents, and postdoctoral fellows in pediatric training.

Obstetrics and Gynecology Obstetrics concerns itself with the processes of conception, gestation, and delivery in women, whereas gynecology deals with the specific diseases of the female reproductive tract.

Requirements of the department of obstetrics and gynecology for administrative office, teaching and research space are not essentially different from those of any other clinical department. Usually this department confines its teaching activities to students in one or both of the third and fourth years. Teaching activities may expand to include such courses as reproductive biology. In addition, there are teaching responsibilities for residents and fellows. Interns are generally not assigned to this service except as part of a rotating program. Student groups may be smaller than in some services and, therefore, teaching space should be sized accordingly.

Psychiatry The department of psychiatry consists of specialists concerned with the functions and disfunctions of the mind and emotions.

Offices for members of the department of psychiatry may be used for somewhat different purposes than staff offices of other clinical departments. For example, not only do psychiatrists use their offices for desk work, study, and conferences with students and others, but they may also use them as interview rooms for psychiatric patients. Clearly, this will have an effect upon the design of the psychiatric departmental office suite in that it may be necessary to incorporate waiting rooms for patients and space for the administrative control of patients in addition to the usual departmental administrative space, teaching space, conference rooms, and reference libraries.

Consultation rooms connected by a one-way viewing screen or TV with an adjoining observation area are frequently required.

In general, studies involving psychiatric patients are best carried out in research facilities associated with the psychiatric bed area, and laboratory studies not involving patients are best carried out in departmental research laboratories.

Preventive Medicine In general, however, the discipline of preventive medicine comprises physicians who are concerned with the natural history of disease and the factors in the environment which have an effect upon morbidity and mortality. They are interested in reducing the incidence of avoidable disease and premature death through control of those factors which may contribute to disability and incapacity.

There is usually a close relationship between the staffs of pediatrics, medicine, obstetrics-gynecology, psychiatry, and preventive medicine, and this should be borne in mind in the location and assignment of office space.

TABLE 21   Net Area for a Department of Psychiatry

Type of facility	School A (entering class of 64 students)	School B (entering class of 96 students)
Assumed size of faculty [1]	10	14
Postdoctoral fellows	8	10
	Square feet	
Total net area	5,480	6,660
Faculty facilities:		
Total	5,000	6,100
Professor's office	210	210
Professor's office	140	140
Secretary's office	280	280
Conference room	350	350
Faculty offices	(3) 420	(5) 700
Postdoctoral fellows' offices	(2) 400	(2) 400
Interview offices	(2) 280	(2) 280
Psychologists' offices	(2) 280	(2) 280
Departmental laboratory	610	610
Additional laboratories	(3) 1,830	(4) 2,440
Special laboratory	200	410
Common-use facilities:		
Total	480	560
Data room	140	140
Special-projects room	140	140
Storage room	200	280

[1] For teaching responsibility only.

TABLE 22   Summary of Space Estimates for Clinical Science Facilities for a Hypothetical Four-Year Medical School*

Type of facility	School A (entering class of 64 students)	School B (entering class of 96 students)
	Square feet	
Total gross area† (rounded)	69,000	80,000
Total net area (rounded)	45,000	52,000
Departmental facilities:		
Medicine	13,440	15,490
Surgery	8,840	11,120
Pediatrics	4,260	5,010
Obstetrics and gynecology	4,390	4,390
Psychiatry	5,480	6,660
Preventive medicine	4,260	4,870
Auditorium‡		
Lecture rooms‡		
Central storage	3,200	3,200
Toilet rooms	1,200	1,200
Radiology‡		
Anesthesiology‡		
Pathology§		

* This table does not include the supporting facilities which are a necessary part of both the basic science and clinical science facilities.

† To compute the gross area, it is estimated that 65 percent of the total gross area is available as usable space, while the remaining 35 percent will provide space for exterior walls, partitions, corridors, stairs, elevators, and duct ways and chases for mechanical and electrical requirements.

‡ In the teaching hospital.

§ Preclinical pathology is taught in the basic science facilities. Space for clinical pathology may be provided in the teaching hospital.

SELECTING THE SITE

Preferred Locations

Dental educators generally prefer certain locations for a dental school. The obvious choice, a university campus, has impressive advantages. It offers students and faculty a richer cultural life and often a more pleasant environment. Adequate housing and student facilities may be more readily available than in other locations. If the university also has a medical school on campus, students and faculty can enjoy a close association with other health professions.

Location in a health center is also advantageous, since it offers access to a complex of health facilities and provides day-to-day opportunity for close cooperation between the health professions. A metropolitan location generally assures the school an ample supply of patients for teaching clinics.

The Site Itself

Topography and Dimensions. High ground with natural drainage is desirable, but the elevation should not be so high that approach on foot is difficult. A patient entrance at ground level and a service drive to the basement area should be feasible. A gently sloping lot has advantages, since it offers entrances on two levels; traffic in and out of the building is automatically divided between them, and the movement of people and supplies can more easily be diverted over separate routes within the building. The site selected should be of sufficient size to permit later expansion.

Where land costs are favorable and where parking facilities are planned, a building site covering a minimum of 10 to 12 acres is advisable.

Utilities. Sewerage, water, electricity, telephone, and gas must be available on the site or be extendible to it at reasonable cost. Utilities must also have adequate capacity.

Transportation and Parking. Convenient public transportation is a necessity. Runs should be frequent, with adequate peak-hour service. Good public transportation materially reduces the parking problem. It also makes it easier for the school to secure and retain service and clerical employees. Even with good public transportation, first-class roads should connect the school directly with local traffic arteries.

The site should permit adequate parking areas for students, faculty, and patients. Generally, one parking place for each full-time faculty member and one for every two part-time members is advisable. A site in a suburban area should also allow two parking places per entering class student (ECS) for students, if possible, and another two places per ECS for clinic patients.

In determining how much land will be needed for parking, allow 130 cars per acre (for 45°

parking) as a guide if parking lots are to be used. Parking lots, however, are likely to become desirable building sites, and multilevel garages or underground parking may prove a more permanent solution to the parking problem.

SPACE RELATIONSHIPS

The Effect of Traffic Patterns

The arrangement of the many elements of a school is determined largely by the movement of students, faculty, patients, and materials.
Clinics. The most common and effective way of reducing traffic within the school is by physical separation of the clinical facilities from the remainder of the school. Staffed by a separate faculty and visited daily by large numbers of patients whose presence elsewhere in the school could be disruptive, the clinical facilities are logically a physical entity. For this reason, physical separation will continue to be advisable even though efforts to break down the rigid separation which exists between the clinical and basic science teaching programs are successful.

However, if they are successful, there probably will be a need to locate certain clinical areas so that students can move between the clinics and the basic science areas without disturbing the clinical routine. Planning committees should therefore consider the possible

implications of this change for traffic patterns within the school.
Basic Science and Preclinical Laboratories. The activities of freshmen and sophomores are largely confined to these areas; by locating them in reasonable proximity, with other facilities used by these students nearby, traffic within the school could be materially reduced. However, since laboratory sessions are normally scheduled for a full half day, with students shifting between laboratories only once a day, locating these areas on separate floors or in separate wings may well resolve a particular school's problems of space arrangement.

A Design which Controls Traffic Flow

Figure 1 is a space diagram showing the relationships between and within the clinical and preclinical dental science areas of a school which will locate its basic science facilities in another wing or on another floor.

All student facilities are located close to their major areas of activity. Note the proximity of student lounges and locker rooms to the teaching facilities used by the students. Freshmen and sophomore locker rooms are adjacent to the preclinical laboratories, while locker rooms for junior and seniors are close to the clinic. Locker rooms for both groups adjoin the student lounge and bookstore and are located near the student entrance. Lecture rooms, used by both preclinical and clinical students, are readily accessible from all student areas.

Public Health Service, U.S. Department of Health, Education, and Welfare, 1962.

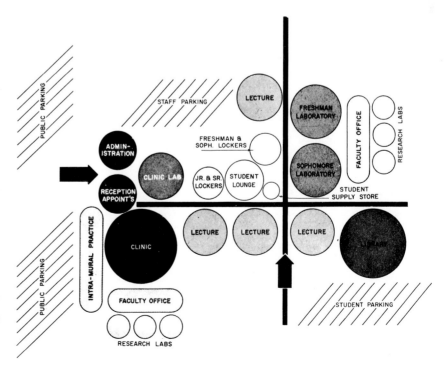

Fig. 1 Space relationships: preclinical and clinical dental science areas.

DENTAL SCHOOLS

The need for a location as free of vibration as possible makes the basement the preferred site for the electron microscope suite, for example, though this location is seldom convenient for users of the laboratory. Facilities which will be used after normal school hours—auditorium, libraries, and study areas—provide another example. Ideally, they should be located so that they can be left open after the remainder of the school is locked.

THE PHYSICAL PLANT: DESIGN AND STRUCTURE

Modular Planning for Flexibility and Efficient Use of Space

Modular planning is particularly adaptable to the design of schools, hospitals, and other buildings in which repetitive elements lend themselves to the systematic and uniform spacing of certain structural features. The module should be a multiple of the basic 4-in. module recommended by the American Standards Association Project A62.

Many building components are prefabricated on this basis, and the floor plans in this section are based on modular design, using a module of 4 ft 8 in.

In Laboratory and Office Planning In the dental school, modular design is particularly applicable to the planning of research laboratories and offices. Figure 2 shows a section of a typical basic science laboratory based on the 4-ft 8-in. module. It is a two-module laboratory, approximately 9 ft in width. When allowances are made for the equipment and laboratory benches extending into the room from the wall, the two-module unit is the smallest size practical but yet adequate for its function.

Examples of Modular Planning When modular planning of areas is combined with modular planning of utilities, various combinations of offices, laboratories, and storage space are practical. (See Fig. 3.)

Figure 3b is a sectional drawing of a research floor of a school. Figure 3c is a partial plan of the corridor wall. Columns are located at every fifth module. Vertical utility shafts, which supply the laboratories with water, drainage, gas, and other utilities, are located at every fourth module.

Figure 3a shows the arrangements of laboratories, office, and equipment storage areas possible with this design. For example, if a series of laboratories of four-module width is desired, either index A or B can be followed. Index A has the laboratory bench at the side walls, while index B shows a center island or peninsula type of laboratory. If an office and equipment room is desired with each laboratory, these can be substituted for alternate laboratories.

Indexes C and D illustrate smaller laboratories suitable for one or two researchers. Index C is a series of laboratories only, and index D is a combination of two-module laboratories, offices, and equipment storage rooms. One or more four-module laboratories can easily be provided in combination with two-module laboratories.

Advantages and Limitations Modular design can be applied to structures in which utilities are located at or in the exterior walls. It can also be used, and with perhaps greater flexibility, in research laboratories in which a central utility core is utilized. (Fig. 4.)

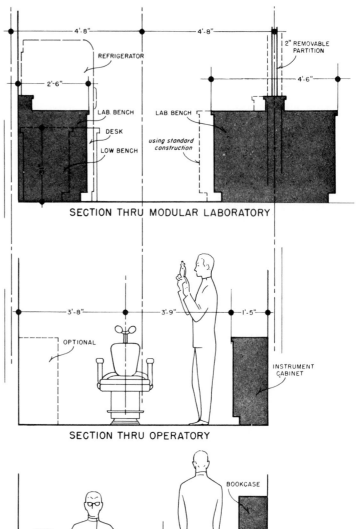

SECTION THRU MODULAR LABORATORY

SECTION THRU OPERATORY

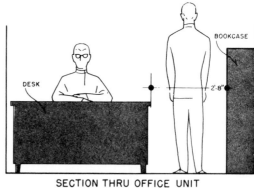

SECTION THRU OFFICE UNIT

Fig. 2 Building module.

Modular design provides a basis for determining the width of laboratories and offices. In estimating depth, at least 24 or 25 ft should be allowed. In Figure 18 the bay depth is 28 ft—the equivalent of six modules; a sufficient allowance when utility shafts are located along the corridor wall.

Caution should be used in following modular planning for other elements of the dental school. Where location of columns is important, strict adherence to the selected planning module may result in obstacles in aisles and other areas. This is a particular problem in the clinics, where chair layout may be adversely affected by a lack of coordination with the structural and mechanical features of the building. In the clinic area, modular design is of lesser importance in those plans in which op-

eratories, laboratories, offices, and other small rooms are not located along the exterior walls.

BASIC SCIENCE FACILITIES—IN GENERAL

Few decisions made in the initial stages of programming will have a greater influence on the space and structural requirements of the dental school than those reached in defining the school's teaching and research objectives in the basic sciences.

Departmental Facilities

The head of every department needs a private office with space enough to accommodate small staff or student conferences. An adjoin-

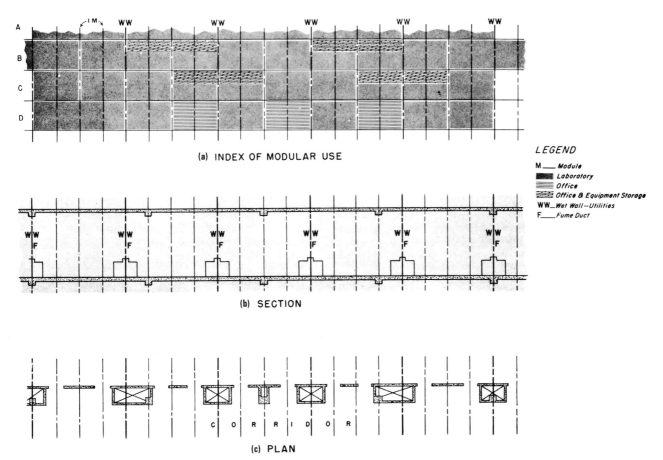

(a) INDEX OF MODULAR USE

LEGEND

M ___ Module
▓▓▓ Laboratory
≡ Office
▨ Office & Equipment Storage
WW ___ Wet Wall—Utilities
F ___ Fume Duct

(b) SECTION

(c) PLAN

Fig. 3 Modular planning of research areas.

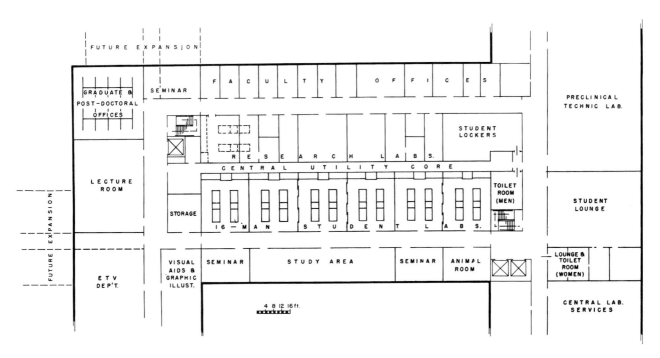

Fig. 4 Plan for a basic science area utilizing a central utility core.

ing office should be provided for the department secretary. A conference room and a seminar room accommodating a 16-student group should also be provided. In addition to chalkboards and bookshelves, each room should be equipped with or adaptable to the use of slide and film projectors and ETV. Both can be used for staff or student conferences, or for formal but unscheduled classes or seminars. A data processing room for use both by faculty and graduate students is also an advantage. Special equipment need not be elaborate, and may include an adding machine, a calculator, and a typewriter.

A storage room easily accessible to staff offices and research facilities is a major convenience. Properly planned, it can always be converted into office space—a much-needed insurance against eventual overcrowding.

Every full-time faculty member and graduate student will need office and research laboratory space. In addition, an unassigned research laboratory should be considered for each department.

Laboratories

The traditional arrangement for basic science teaching provides a laboratory of class size for every department. This calls for a separate laboratory for anatomy, biochemistry, physiology, microbiology, pathology, and pharmacology.

Considerably less space will be needed for undergraduate teaching if multidiscipline laboratories are used, and dental schools have generally found that more than one discipline can easily be scheduled for a single laboratory. Schools which use integrated systems of instruction or which need to assure a marked degree of flexibility will necessarily plan multidiscipline laboratories.

If they are equipped with movable partitions and four- or eight-man position benches, both departmental and multi-discipline laboratories of class size are easily divided into smaller units to accommodate research projects or small-group teaching. Many educators, however, look with increasing favor on the laboratory designed specifically for the smaller number of students. Figure 5 is a floor plan showing how items of equipment are placed. Sophomore laboratories have no anatomy table but are otherwise similar.

Unit laboratories accommodating a larger number of students and designed for teaching only the basic science disciplines are more widely favored. Figure 6 is a floor plan of a 16-student laboratory in which physiology, biochemistry, and pharmacology are taught. More detailed information on the arrangement and equipment of teaching laboratories, and the special facilities associated with them will be found in a following section. Suggested space allowances are shown in Table 1.

BASIC SCIENCE LABORATORY FACILITIES

Three teaching laboratories—two multidiscipline and one single discipline—are described in this section. Together, the three can accommodate all of the basic laboratory sciences taught in a dental school.

Each of the multidiscipline laboratories described may be laid out as a series of self-contained units accommodating small groups of students, or retained as a class-size laboratory and equipped with folding partitions to permit division of the room into smaller units.

The ancillary and special facilities required by the different disciplines using these labora-

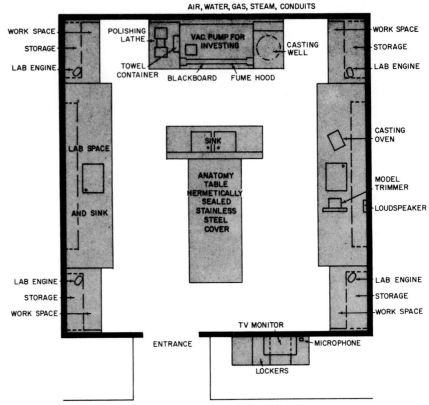

Fig. 5 Layout and equipment of unit laboratory for both basic and preclinical sciences.

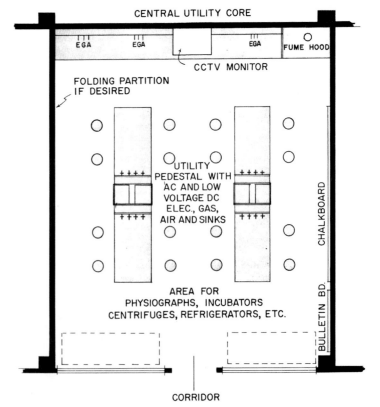

Fig. 6 Sixteen-man teaching laboratory.

TABLE 1 Summary Space Allocations — Ten Hypothetical Schools

Type of Area	Size of entering class									
	In schools with facilities for all basic sciences					In schools with facilities for clinically oriented basic sciences only				
	112	96	80	64	48	112	96	80	64	48
Net square feet — all areas	215,545	186,875	165,205	141,135	122,175	156,220	134,400	120,230	104,700	89,510
Basic science facilities	60,600	53,750	47,200	39,350	35,500	11,250	9,900	8,750	7,650	6,650
Teaching laboratory and ancillary facilities	22,600	19,950	17,300	14,550	12,200	5,900	5,100	4,400	3,700	3,000
Special laboratory facilities	1,900	1,900	1,900	1,900	1,900	700	700	700	700	700
Faculty offices and research laboratories	17,100	14,400	12,300	9,000	8,100	2,100	1,800	1,500	1,200	900
Graduate study and research areas	6,100	5,400	4,600	3,400	2,800	750	600	450	450	450
Other departmental facilities	12,900	12,300	11,100	10,500	10,500	1,800	1,700	1,700	1,600	1,600
Clinical (and preclinical) facilities	88,375	73,585	67,425	59,665	51,205	88,375	73,585	67,425	59,665	51,205
Operatories and ancillary facilities	53,475	44,385	40,325	36,865	32,305	53,475	44,385	41,325	36,865	32,305
Laboratories and ancillary facilities	18,800	16,400	14,000	11,400	8,800	18,800	16,400	14,000	11,400	8,800
Faculty offices and research areas	13,200	10,600	10,600	9,400	8,200	13,200	10,600	10,000	9,400	8,200
Graduate study and research areas	2,900	2,200	2,100	2,000	1,900	2,900	2,200	2,100	2,000	1,900
Common facilities	31,570	28,440	23,780	19,820	16,670	24,395	22,615	19,455	16,985	14,555
Lecture rooms	7,100	6,200	4,900	4,000	3,100	5,300	4,600	3,700	3,000	2,300
Library	10,780	9,950	9,120	8,290	7,560	10,780	9,950	9,120	8,290	7,560
ETV and visual aids	4,790	4,590	3,660	2,830	2,510	4,190	4,090	3,260	2,520	2,320
ETV	2,650	2,550	2,200	1,650	1,500	2,550	2,550	2,200	1,650	1,500
Visual aids	2,140	2,040	1,460	1,180	1,010	1,640	1,540	1,060	870	820
Special supporting facilities for laboratories and clinics	8,900	7,700	6,100	4,700	3,500	4,125	3,975	3,375	3,175	2,375
Animal quarters	6,900	5,700	4,700	3,500	2,500	2,525	2,375	2,275	2,175	1,575
Technical shops	2,000	2,000	1,400	1,200	1,000	1,600	1,600	1,100	1,000	800
General supporting facilities	35,000	30,900	26,800	22,300	18,800	32,200	28,300	24,600	20,400	17,100
Administration	5,700	5,300	4,900	4,300	3,800	5,500	5,100	4,700	4,100	3,600
Special facilities for students and faculty	13,600	12,100	10,300	8,700	7,300	12,000	10,700	9,100	7,700	6,500
General maintenance and building services	15,700	13,500	11,600	9,300	7,700	14,700	12,500	10,800	8,600	7,000

tories are generally described, and they are substantially the same whether small-group or class-size laboratories are utilized.

Low-Bench Disciplines

Teaching Laboratory The disciplines which share the low-bench teaching laboratory are those employing microscopy as their principal technique — histology (the microscopic study of normal tissue), pathology (the microscopic study of diseased tissue), and microbiology (the study of microorganisms).

Laboratory Benches and Arrangement. Laboratory benches are usually 30 to 32 in. high to permit students to sit comfortably for long sessions at the microscope. Stools have back rests and adjustable seats. Either single or double-width benches may be used. However, because all students sit along one side of single-width benches, these can be more easily arranged to permit all students to face the demonstration area. A four-position bench is particularly desirable in the class-size laboratory, since it permits the division of the class into groups of 16 or less without splitting the group at any bench. If double benches are used, the eight-position bench is preferred.

Clearances of 3 ft between single-width benches and 4 ft 6 in. between double-width benches are required. Side aisles, center aisle, and main cross aisle should be 6 ft wide.

Work Station at the Bench. Each position at the bench should be at least 42 in. wide to allow both adequate knee space and room for a base cabinet containing drawers for storing slides and supplies and a cupboard for storing a microscope. Water, gas, and electricity should be available at each position. The need for an air outlet is limited, and a vacuum is seldom used. A lead cup sink at each position

(or a bench-long drain trough with a sink at one end) is necessary.

Bench Tops. Bench-top surfacing should be resilient, to minimize slide breakage, as well as stain and alcohol resistant. Bench tops should be as free of joints as possible.

Stand-up Work Areas. Wall counters (37 in. high) are located along the sides of the laboratory area. These provide bench space of stand-up height, where students may set up portable equipment, conduct experiments with animals, or take part in other assigned projects. Counter-top handwashing sinks with knee- or foot-operated valves should be installed and supplied with hot and cold running water. Gas, air, and electricity outlets will also be needed. One set of outlets for every four work stations at the counter is adequate.

Demonstration. The demonstration area should have a table, retractable projection screen, and a chalkboard at least 4 ft high and as long as the supporting wall permits. Additional small chalkboards — 3 by 4 ft — should be available throughout the laboratory. At least one for every 16 students should be provided, and all chalkboards should have adequate illumination. A bulletin board is also advisable. Because small-group laboratories easily accommodate demonstrations, no separate areas are needed for this purpose in schools employing the unit arrangement. Each of the small-group laboratories will require its own projection screens, chalkboards, and a bulletin board.

Stationary Equipment. One noncorrosive fume hood should be provided for every 16 students. Stationary centrifuges in the same ratio are desirable for microbiology. Space will be needed for incubators — one for every eight students — and for refrigerators — one for every 16 students.

Ancillary Facilities Each discipline sharing the low-bench teaching laboratory must have certain ancillary facilities available.

Space for the preparation of microscope slides is necessary for any laboratory in which histology and pathology are taught. Preferably, this area consists of two interconnecting rooms. In one, the embedding room, tissue is processed and embedded in paraffin. This room should have two counters, 31 in. in height, one to be used as a workbench for preparing and processing specimens and the other for mixing solutions. Placing a plain worktable at one end of the paraffin oven provides an efficient arrangement for the embedding procedures. For easy access from either side, the worktable should be located near the center of the room. Wall cabinets for storing solutions and other supplies should be provided.

The second room is used for sectioning, staining, and storing the completed slides. Counters 31 in. high and 2 ft wide should be provided in this room. Each work station at the counter should have knee space of sufficient width and a base unit with drawers for storing blank slides. All of the countertops in these slide preparation rooms should be resilient and stain-resistant.

For microbiology, a media preparation room should be provided adjacent to the teaching laboratory. Usually the work of a trained technician, media preparation requires space for several items of equipment, including a range or hot plates for cooking the material, an autoclave for sterilizing test tubes and media, a refrigerator for storage of culture media, and often an incubator for testing the sterility of media prior to use. This area should be dust-free. Wall counters 37 in. high, equipped with base cabinets and air, gas, distilled water and electrical outlets, are needed both in the kitchen area and in the area where media are transferred to test tubes. In the latter, burette stands are normally placed on the counter top.

A fairly large area for glassware washing and sterilization should adjoin the teaching laboratory. Commercial glass-washing and drying machines, an autoclave, and often a hot air sterilizer must be accommodated, as well as sink and drainboards, space for storing the carts which carry glassware and Petri dishes to and from the area, and a worktable for glassware storage.

Storage rooms for chemicals, glassware, equipment, and other materials are necessary. Among the items of portable equipment which may be used and will require space for storage are water baths, incubators, and spectrophotometers.

An animal holding room where small animals may be held for observation or experimentation completes the list of the larger ancillary areas required in conjunction with this laboratory.

Special Facilities Additional facilities which are of special value for research and teaching in the low-bench disciplines include a cold room and electron microscope setup.

The cold room is essentially a refrigerator room. It contains counter space and sink for work that must be done at low temperatures. Safety door latches and warning lights are mandatory features.

An electron microscope unit requires at least three rooms: one to house the microscope itself, another for slide preparation, and a third —a darkroom—for developing, enlarging, and printing electron micrographs.

High-Bench Disciplines

Teaching Laboratory The disciplines which share the high-bench teaching laboratory are those for which laboratory work requires that the student stand and move about to perform experiments. These include physiology (the study of the process of living organisms), pharmacology (the science of drugs), and biochemistry (the study of the chemical compounds and processes occurring in organisms).

Laboratory Benches and Arrangement. Laboratory benches are usually 37 in. high. Stools of adjustable height are provided. Except for their height, benches may be similar in design and arrangement to those in the low-bench laboratory. The four-position bench has particular merit because much of the work, especially in physiology, consists of special projects undertaken by a team of four students.

Work Station at the Bench. The student's work station is also similar to that in the low-bench lab. Each station should have a base cabinet with both drawer and cupboard space. Adequate knee room should be provided, even though students stand a good share of the time.

Hot, cold, and distilled water should be available at each bench position. Gas and electricity are also required. In addition, low-voltage direct current and control circuits should be available from a central panel.

Bench Tops. Bench tops should be of stone or of acid-resistant composition stone because of the reagents used in biochemistry.

Sit-down Work Area. Low counters, with resilient counter tops, and under-counter cabinets are placed along one or more of the laboratory walls. Gas, hot and cold water, air, and electric outlets will be needed, and counter-top sinks should be equipped with knee- or foot-operated valves for hand-washing. Stools with adjustable seats should be provided.

Demonstration Area. The demonstration space and equipment are like that of the low-bench lab. In addition, physiology teaching makes extensive use of electric polygraphs and the Van Slyke machines, often to the extent of one to each four students. If the unit laboratory is used, no demonstration area is necessary since each unit can easily accommodate demonstrations.

Stationary Equipment. Fume hoods—one to every 16 students—should be provided. Because flammable and explosive chemicals are used, the hoods should be installed a safe distance from fire exits. Burette stands, approximately 5 ft in length, are used by both biochemistry and pharmacology students. One to every 16 students is an accepted ratio.

Movable Equipment. A great variety of movable equipment may be used. A few movable tables of stand-up height may be required for some of the experiments in pharmacology and physiology involving animals. Table tops are of laminated wood with a stain resistant finish, and a shelf is provided for storing animal boards. In addition, a deep-freeze unit, centrifuges, refrigerators, incubators, and much of the electronic apparatus used in physiology are part of the movable equipment used in the laboratory for which space is required. First aid kits and blankets are necessary, although these generally occupy no floor space but are mounted on the wall.

Ancillary Facilities Both biochemistry and pharmacology require a preparation room adjacent to the teaching laboratory for mixing reagents and storing chemicals and glassware. Storage and washing facilities are included in this room. Wall counters similar to those in the teaching laboratory and wall cabinets permit this room to be used as a research area during off periods.

Each discipline requires storage and supply areas, some of them special in nature. Special provisions must be made, for example, for storing anesthetics. Although only a limited supply of cylinders holding oxygen or anesthetics should be kept here (additional storage should be allotted at ground level), the storage area should be located along an exterior wall, with floor and ceiling louvers installed to provide gravity ventilation. The room should be locked. For chemical storage areas, fire hazards must be minimized. Narcotics require locked storage. Generally, rooms used to store instruments and equipment should be amply supplied with electrical outlets so that equipment can be used without being removed from the room.

Animal rooms and cold rooms are among the other facilities used regularly in conjunction with the teaching program of the high-bench laboratory.

Special Facilities Many of the special facilities used for research and teaching in the high-bench disciplines require unusual construction or safety features.

The *chromatography* room is a biochemistry research laboratory where various processes are employed to separate organic substances. In laboratories where paper or column chromatography is performed, fume hoods capable of exhausting toxic or inflammable vapors are required, and the laboratory must be maintained under negative air pressure to prevent the spread of vapors. Where gas chromatography is used, it must also be possible to seal off the laboratory in the event of fire. Some instruments used in this laboratory depend upon radioactivity as an ionization source; if these

are installed, safeguards must be provided, even though the radioactivity level is low.

In the *ultracentrifuge* room, another small laboratory often used in biochemistry research, the selection of equipment will largely determine the requirements. Depending upon its anticipated use, the ultracentrifuge may be either electrically powered or air driven. At least part of the housing for this equipment is of heavy armor plate. Additional cooling may be needed in the room to offset heat produced by operation of the equipment.

Constant-temperature rooms, or controlled-temperature rooms, as they are sometimes called, are used to house small animals under constant temperature and humidity conditions. The work area in this room usually consists of 31-in.-high counters, with a sink and outlet for gas, air, and electricity. Space may be needed for counter-top food storage. At least one floor drain will be required so that the room may be completely washed down.

The space allotted for the *radioisotope laboratory* should be divided into two rooms, the radioisotope laboratory proper (radiochemistry laboratory) and the uptake-measuring room (counting room).

The radiochemistry laboratory is the room where shipments of radioisotopes are received and stored. Here, too, specimens are made ready for examination, and dosages are prepared and administered. Items contaminated with radioisotopes are either cleaned, held for decay of radioactivity, or stored prior to disposition.

In the counting room, the uptake of the radioactive substance is prepared and the radioactive content of specimens is accurately determined. If the counting room is separated from the radiochemistry laboratory by a corridor, the possibility that stored isotopes will interfere with counting can be substantially reduced.

The location of the radioisotope laboratory some distance away from x-ray equipment prevents interference with measurements of radioactivity. The basement is usually the best location, since it simplifies provisions for waste disposal and shielding. In most schools, a basement laboratory will also be convenient to the central animal quarters, and this is highly desirable. If the main radioisotope laboratory is some distance away from these animal quarters, schools may want a separate and specially designed radioisotope laboratory within the animal quarters.

Safety features and special devices are essential to guard against radiation contamination.

Wall shielding is a necessary safeguard against radioactive penetration, and the average building partition will not usually suffice for this purpose. Plastic, wood, or other light material is adequate shielding against beta radiation. Solid concrete or solid brick walls will be necessary for protection against gamma rays.

Interior wall surfaces should always be of a smooth, nonporous material. High-gloss enamel paint is best suited for this purpose. To facilitate decontamination, strippable vinyl plastic or replaceable wall panels are installed near sinks and other critical areas.

The floor in a radioisotope laboratory is usually a concrete slab. The slab must have a protective covering or coating to prevent radioactive contamination from spillage. The floor should always have a heavy wax coating, which will fill cracks and serve as waterproofing. Counter tops should be stainless steel, with splash-back trims. Sinks should be made of

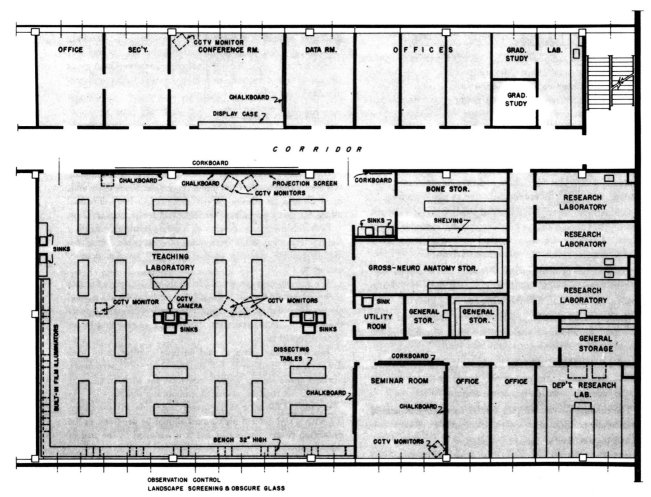

Fig. 7 Layout of anatomy laboratory of class size.

stainless steel and equipped with foot or knee controls. Each sink should have two drainboards.

Holding tanks must be provided for the collection of large amounts of radioactive materials or small amounts of the more dangerous isotopes.

Special radio-chemical fume hoods are necessary. Because of the dangers of air movement, hoods should never be placed near windows, doors, or ventilators.

A deluge shower will also be needed.

Anatomy

The Dissection Room Dissection tables are the basic laboratory equipment. They are approximately 24 by 78 in. Aisles at the table sides should be 5 ft wide and those at the ends 3 ft 6 in.

Dissection rooms are, as a rule, planned to accommodate full classes. Though class size largely determines room size, space should be allowed to accommodate a few additional tables for use by graduate students and for demonstrations. (See Fig. 7.)

Good table lighting is essential. Often, adjustable lighting fixtures are attached to both sides of each table. If tables are on casters, cleaning of the room will be considerably easier.

The dissection room should be equipped with an adequate number of hand basins.

Round, industrial sinks are a good choice, since they accommodate more students simultaneously than those of standard design. One sink for every four tables is an accepted ratio.

The dissection room should include counter units with drawers and cupboards for storing students' instruments. Storage space should also be provided for such supplies as wood blocks, mallets, arm rests, embalming fluids.

Because of the odor of the preserving fluids, air conditioning with a 100 percent air exhaust should be provided in the dissection room.

As the anatomy dissection room is frequently washed down, durable, waterproof flooring is required. Providing storage space for the dissection tables will make it possible to use the dissection room for other purposes.

Ancillary Facilities

Several additional rooms either near or adjacent to the dissection room are required. Storage space for cadavers must be provided and bone storage space will also be needed. If neuroanatomy is taught in the dissection room, storage for gross specimens must be available, too.

Generally, schools will need sufficient storage capacity for 1.5 cadavers for every four ECS. If the school policy is to hold cadavers for one year prior to use, storage requirements will double. Cadavers are commonly stored in large walk-in refrigerators. Because the

method of preservation and storage affects ancillary space requirements, the system to be used should be determined early in the programming stage, and specifics should be worked out with the aid of qualified consultants.

A room equipped for embalming is often provided, though dental schools with access to medical school facilities will probably need only a minimum of space for this purpose. As for final disposal, cadavers are usually cremated. The dental school can either provide its own crematory for this purpose, share facilities with a medical school, or arrange periodic transfer of cadavers to public facilities for cremation.

Because it should never be necessary to move cadavers through public areas, facilities for cadaver storage and embalming should be as near as possible to the dissection room, and all three should be located at ground level. Wherever practical, loading platforms should open directly into the cadaver storage area to facilitate delivery and removal.

PRECLINICAL FACILITIES

The Preclinical Laboratory The preclinical laboratory is designed to accommodate the entire class of freshman or sophomore students in a single session. (See Fig. 8.)

Though it is not often so-called, the pre-

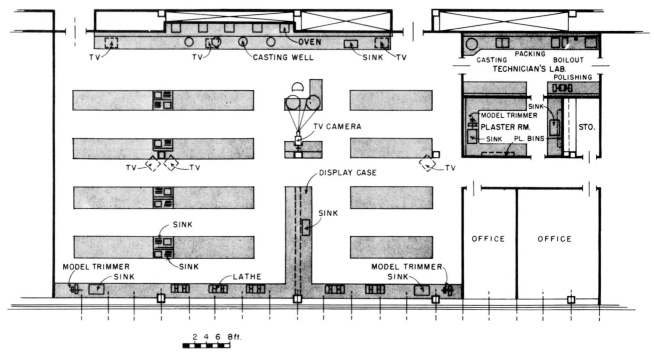

Fig. 8 Preclinical laboratory of 96 student positions utilizing closed-circuit television for demonstrations.

clinical laboratory is actually a multidiscipline laboratory, for all the preclinical dental science courses are taught here: the instructors of the several subjects take over the laboratory in turn while the students remain in their assigned places.

Seating. In the arrangement most common to preclinical laboratories, students sit on each side of a bench, their backs to those of students at the next row of benches. The aisles separating the rows are at least 4 ft 6 in. wide, so that the instructor may move easily between the benches as he inspects the students' work.

In some of the newer laboratories, benches are arranged so that all students face in one direction—usually toward the instructor's podium. The aisles between benches—a 3 ft minimum is satisfactory—are not as wide as those required for back-to-back seating. On the other hand, back-to-back seating is economical. It conserves floor space and reduces the cost of bench work and utilities.

In either of the two seating plans, high or low benches can be used, but the low bench—32 in. in height—will perhaps be the more satisfactory. With low benches, a standard adjustable typing chair on casters can be used and is less costly than the laboratory stool. All benches should be equipped with gas, air, and duplex electrical receptacles. Each student station at the bench should be at least 3 ft wide, and 3 ft 6 in. is actually more satisfactory. If the latter figure is used, an over-all allowance of 38 sq ft per student position will provide adequately for the teaching facilities.

Every preclinical technic laboratory should provide the instructor with a table or desk, equipped with gas, air, and electricity for demonstration purposes. In large classes which require more than one instructor, each should be allotted desk space.

Ancillary Facilities. To reduce the tracking of plaster from the laboratory into the public corridors, the processing room, which is used for pouring wax forms, molds, impressions, and flasks for denture processing, can be located adjacent to the preclinical technic laboratory. Also nearby should be a small storeroom.

ETV in the Preclinical Laboratory Figure 8 shows a preclinical dental technic laboratory of 96 student positions together with an adjoining processing room. Demonstrations within the laboratory are given with closed-circuit television. There are 16 students per monitor. The monitors are also coupled to the television studio of the school.

This layout is also adaptable to the monitoring of students' work by closed-circuit television. In such a system, the picture is relayed to the console at the demonstration position.

While the principal medium of demonstration is ETV, facilities for chalk talks and for projection of motion pictures or slides are provided. Display cases, some of which permit viewing from both sides, should be provided for models and examples of student work. The laboratory shown has the equipment used in common by students, such as lathes, model trimmers, sinks, ovens and casting machines, located at the perimeter walls.

THE CLINICS: FUNCTION AND OPERATION

In the clinics, dental students gain experience in the correction and control of dental diseases and disorders. Here, too, the community finds an additional source of dental services, some of which are frequently unobtainable outside the dental school.

Patient Movement in the Clinics Figure 9 illustrates patient movement through the clinics. The new patient first reports to the information desk located in the lobby or main waiting room of the clinic area. He then proceeds to the regis-

tration desk, where a case record is opened for him. At the appointment desk, his next stop, he is scheduled for an oral examination.

The patient then undergoes, either on the initial visit or a subsequent one, a screening examination. This procedure enables the school to select patients with varied dental problems.

Following the screening examination, the patient goes to the radiology clinic for full-mouth roentgenograms and then to the diagnostic clinic for a thorough oral examination, performed by a dental student working under the direction of an instructor. When the examination is completed, the patient returns to the appointment desk where he is referred for subsequent visits either to the general dental clinic or to one of the special clinics. On later visits, the patient reports directly to the waiting room of the clinic where he will receive treatment.

Reception and Screening Area The reception area in the main waiting room is the control center of the clinics, coordinating the flow of patients and records to clinics in the treatment area. In addition, the work of the appointment desk is closely coordinated with that of the clinic business office.

Frequently the information, registration, and appointment desks are combined, but they may be separate in large schools, or information and registration may be handled at one desk while appointments are made at a second. Similarly, one or more of these desks may be located either in the main waiting room or in adjacent rooms.

The reception area will require a records office. The convenience with which records can be dispatched to the clinics is an important consideration in the location of the area. However, storage space for inactive records need not be provided here, as these are frequently microfilmed or moved after two years to storage rooms in other areas of the school.

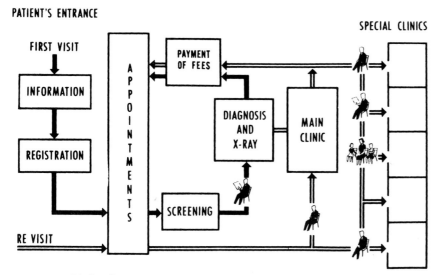

Fig. 9   Dental clinic flow diagram.

Screening. For the screening of new patients, an examination room separate from the diagnostic clinic is desirable. This room should be equipped with dental chairs. Dental units are not necessary unless the room will also be used for emergency treatment.

Emergency treatment rooms function as a part of the reception and screening area. Either a series of single-chair rooms or a large room with two or three dental chairs is practical. Although emergency treatment rooms are sometimes included in each of the clinics in the treatment area, the provision of central facilities is more likely to assure that the rooms are not preempted for some other purpose.

Examination, Diagnosis, and Treatment Planning Area

It is in the diagnostic and radiology clinics that the incoming patient's need for dental care is determined and a plan of treatment formulated.

The Diagnostic Clinic Essential facilities in the diagnostic clinic include operatories or examination rooms, a clinical diagnostic laboratory, and a treatment planning and consultation room. Faculty offices and faculty research areas should be provided nearby.

Although multiple-chair rooms are sometimes used for examinations, a series of single-chair rooms assures privacy for the recording of patients' case histories. Each position should be equipped with an x-ray viewer. Estimating that 16 patients can be accommodated daily in each chair, an eight-chair facility could handle over 120 patients each day. In addition to dental chairs, the examination rooms should be furnished with desks for the convenience of those students who are recording case histories.

The clinical diagnostic laboratory is used for hematological and other diagnostic procedures. It is equipped with laboratory benches similar to those used for the low-bench basic science disciplines, but since students are assigned here in blocs, eight positions are usually sufficient. Air, gas, and electricity should be available at each position, and both hot and cold water are desirable. A hand washing sink should also be provided. One stand-up laboratory bench should be located at the outer wall. Because patients seen in this laboratory are referred directly from the diagnostic clinic, no waiting room is needed.

The treatment planning and consultation room, where students and instructors meet to discuss cases, should be equipped with a chalkboard, demonstration table, projection screen, and x-ray viewer, in addition to a dental chair and unit. The room can also be used for small-group demonstrations.

Radiology Clinic Because roentgenograms are made for every incoming patient, the radiology

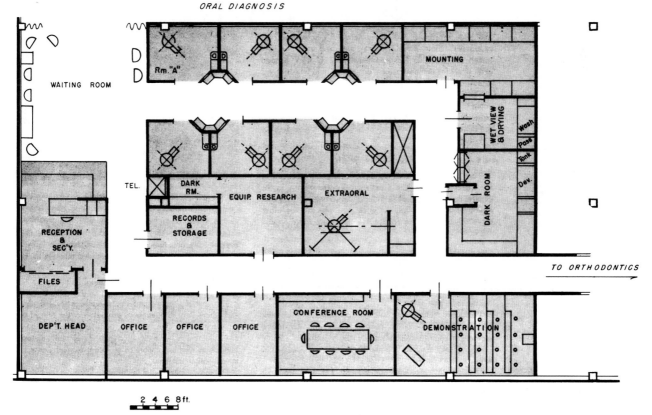

Fig. 10   Radiology clinic.

clinic is included in the examination and diagnostic area. However, the radiology clinic also serves all the other clinics, and patients undergoing treatment are directed here for additional roentgenograms.

Shielding Against Radiation. Rooms containing x-ray machines must be shielded through the use of lead-lined walls and partitions or appropriate building materials of an adequate thickness. In addition, controls for x-ray machines should be located behind shielded partitions.

In general, shielding should be sufficient to limit the exposure of personnel to a minimum amount of radiation, certainly no more than 0.1 roentgen per week. In rooms equipped with 90 kvp x-ray machines, for example, the walls should be shielded with 1.2-mm sheet lead (3 lb per square foot) to a height of 7 ft. Stone concrete at least 3 in. thick should be used for ceiling and floor.

The Layout of the Clinic. Figure 10 shows the components and equipment of the radiology clinic. This plan includes eight rooms where the roentgenograms utilized in routine oral examinations are taken, and one extraoral radiology room.

In the radiology rooms, the machine is located behind the dental chair and up to 20 degrees to either side, the recommended position. Observation of the patient is made through a lead glass viewing window which has a speaking slot. Each of the rooms is equipped with a small chalkboard, illuminator, lavatory, and shelf. Room A, slightly larger than the others, has a 4-ft-wide opening to facilitate handling of wheelchair and stretcher patients.

The extraoral radiology room is of slightly greater depth than the intraoral, because a long-focus film distance is required for the facial-profile roentgenogram.

Each of these rooms is lead-shielded, and the x-ray machine controls are located behind lead-protected partitions.

Film Processing. A suite of rooms for film processing includes a darkroom, oversized to permit group instruction, a wet viewing and drying room, and a mounting room. A framed opening in the wall between the drying and mounting rooms is used for passage of film. The mounting room accommodates eight students. Each student position has a 14- by 17-in. view box built into the surface of the bench.

Air conditioning in the darkroom and wet viewing room is desirable not only for the comfort of personnel but for the protection of exposed film. Maintaining air at positive pressure will prevent dust from entering around windows and doors.

Ancillary Facilities. The special demonstration room, which accommodates 16 students, has provisions for movie and slide projection and closed-circuit television monitors. An exodontist's chair, a mobile x-ray unit, and a mobile lead screen are available for demonstrations. If ETV is used extensively for demonstrations, this room could be converted to a film library.

The departmental research area includes a small darkroom. A conference room, suitable for seminars and equipped with chalkboard, projection equipment, and an illuminated viewer, and a group of faculty offices complete the radiology clinic.

Treatment Area

The General Clinic
Because the general clinic is typically the largest and busiest of all the clinics, the main waiting room and control

desks and many of the other elements already described are considered a part of it.

Treatment components include operatories, treatment planning and consultation rooms, supply and dispensing services, and sterilization and sterile supply facilities. Study and laboratory areas for the use of graduate students should adjoin.

The operatories, or work stations, into which all the clinics are divided, consist of dental chairs and units, instrument cabinets, sterilization units, and other necessary equipment. Each station should be large enough to accommodate the patient, the student who is treating him, the supervising instructor, and frequently a dental assistant. Several fully partitioned work stations should be provided to accommodate patients whose emotional reaction to dental care makes privacy mandatory.

The Special Clinics
The special clinics—periodontic-endodontic, orthodontic, and others—are differentiated primarily by the type of treatment rendered. One, however, is distinguished by the type of patient treated—the chronically ill, the mentally disturbed, and others who are unable to receive treatment under regular clinical conditions.

The same departmental facilities and most of the treatment facilities required in the general clinic are needed for each of the special clinics. Every special clinic should have at least one fully partitioned work station. Generally, each will have a small waiting room with control desks separate from the main waiting room. However, related specialties such as pedodontics and orthodontics often share a waiting room.

Specific Requirements. Except for some variations in the design of the instrument cabinet, the basic equipment of the special clinics is the same as that of the general clinic. Most of the special clinics are equipped with standard dental chairs and units. The pedodontic clinic, however, requires a smaller chair and the oral surgery clinic special chairs or operating tables. And a few of the special clinics require additional components and highly specialized equipment. Clinics where general anesthetics are administered must have recovery rooms and toilets. A ceramics laboratory is sometimes maintained in the crown and bridge clinic.

The orthodontic clinic requires a number of special facilities. Among these are a measure room, a record room, a tracing room with a light table for routine tracing, and an office for technical personnel. This clinic usually contains two or more rooms with specialized equipment. At least one dental chair which can be used when general anesthetics are administered is required.

Frequently facilities for periodontic and endodontic treatment and for oral medicines are combined in one clinic. If x-ray machines are provided, the clinic must be shielded in the same manner as the radiology clinic or a lead-lined partition provided around the x-ray machines.

Oral Surgery Clinic: A Special Case. Perhaps the greatest variation in the components and equipment is found in the oral surgery clinic.

Figure 11 illustrates an oral surgery department planned to accommodate blocs of eight students. Eight of its nine operatories are equipped for surgery requiring local anesthe-

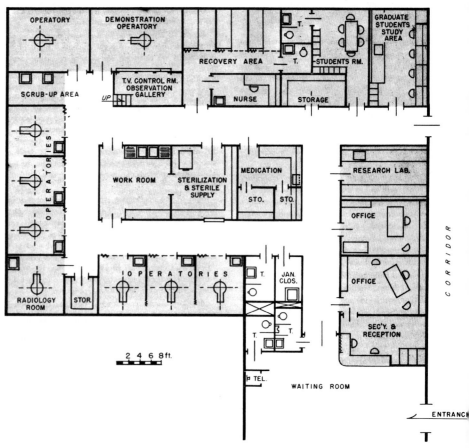

Fig. 11 Oral surgery department.

sics. Six of these, grouped in threes, are semi-enclosed. Folding partitions make full enclosure possible.

Of the three remaining operatories, the largest is equipped with an x-ray machine. Centrally located to the other operatories, this room is lead-lined. The demonstration operatory is equipped for cases requiring general anesthesia as well as local. So is the adjacent operatory (upper right). In addition, the demonstration operatory is designed for closed-circuit television. A glass-enclosed gallery can be used for observation of treatment procedures, or as a control booth for television.

Both of the operatories equipped for general anesthesia are located adjacent to their supporting facilities. A scrub-up area is provided at the entrances. Nearby is the recovery area containing bunks and toilet facilities. A glass-partitioned nurse's station permits observation of patients. Also conveniently located are the sterilizing and sterile supply rooms, which serve only this clinic. Of the two rooms provided for storage of medication, one is used for narcotics and other medicines which must be kept locked.

Ancillary Facilities. Student facilities include a locker room with toilet, located near the secondary exit from the main operational area. The combination graduate student study area and laboratory accommodates four students. It contains desks, lockers, and a laboratory bench with a sink and electrical outlets. Locating the two administrative offices at the entrance to the clinic permits greater control and accessibility. A departmental research laboratory is provided, as in other clinical departments.

A patient waiting room seating 16 people would be adequate in a clinic of this type. Toilet rooms should be provided nearby. Although patients would normally enter and leave the clinic through the main waiting room, a secondary exit is provided for those requiring assistance after surgery.

Supporting Facilities

Central Supply and Dispensing Services Although each clinic in the treatment area will have its own small supply facilities, centralized service is necessary for the receiving and distribution of bulk supplies. Locating the central service near the clinics will permit greater efficiency. In a multistory building, stacking the smaller units on different floors will simplify the placement of service elevators and dumbwaiters.

Clinical Laboratories Most schools today believe the provision of two large general laboratories of full-class size—one for the juniors, one for the seniors—to be the most effective. Small separate laboratories in each of the special clinics are also a possibility. Schools should make every effort to see to it that each junior and senior student is provided with assigned, individually locked cupboards and supply drawers.

If the full-class laboratory for each of the upper classes can be provided, the design and layout will be approximately the same as that of the freshman-sophomore preclinical laboratories. Though no special demonstration position need be set aside, facilities for ETV should be included.

The processing laboratory, which contains special equipment such as heavy duty ovens, boilout tanks, and packing and curing units, must be large enough to accommodate not only students but the dental laboratory technicians employed by the school.

CLINICS: SPACE ALLOCATIONS AND RELATIONSHIPS

Dental educators today favor the adoption of the cubicle clinic. The privacy of the cubicle, a factor appreciated by patients as well as students, and the overall atmosphere of the cubicle clinic engender self-confidence and efficiency on the part of the student. (See Figs. 12 and 13.)

Planning the Cubicle Clinic

Influence of Dental Assistants Cubicles accommodating the student-assistant team must be narrower and deeper than those in which a student works alone. The size (7 ft 6 in. by 7 ft 6 in.) and the arrangement of the cubicle in Fig. 15a, with the instrument panel at the right of the operator, is satisfactory for the dental student working alone.

The cubicles in Fig. 15b and c are planned for utilization of assistants. The cubicle in Fig. 15b, which is 6 ft 9 in. by 9 ft 2 in., is slightly narrower and deeper than the one in Fig. 15a. The added depth of the cubicle in Fig. 15b permits the location of the instrument cabinet and sink at the rear of the cubicle, convenient to the operator and the assistant. Figure 15c is another variation, adaptable to the 4 ft 8 in. planning module.

A cubicle clinic designed for utilization of

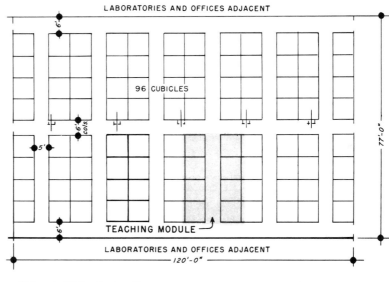

9240 sq.ft. *(96.3 sq.ft./CHAIR)* CLEAR SPAN – NO COLUMNS
9360 sq.ft. *(97.5 sq.ft./CHAIR)* CENTER ROW OF COLUMNS

Fig. 12 Cubicle clinic.

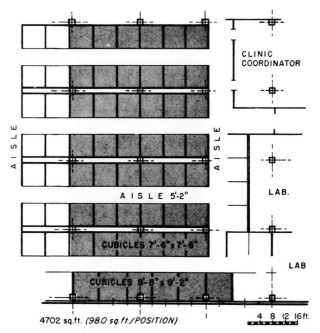

4702 sq.ft. *(98.0 sq.ft./POSITION)*

Fig. 13 Variation of cubicle clinic.

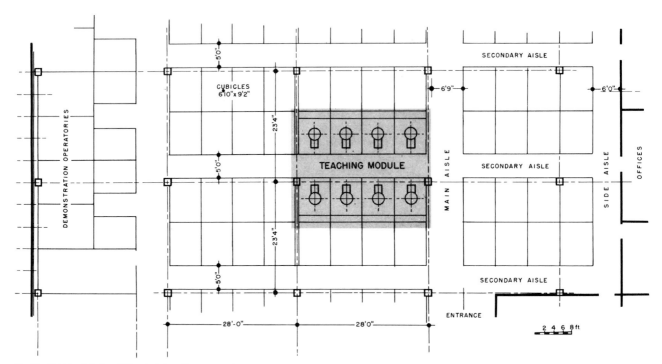

Fig. 14 Cubicle clinic for utilizing dental auxiliary personnel.

auxiliary personnel is illustrated by Fig. 14. The location of the main and secondary aisles permits the instructor to move from one work station to another without retracing his steps.

Cubicle Dimensions Cubicles in existing dental schools range in size from 6 ft 4 in. by 7 ft to 7 ft 8 in. by 9 ft 6 in. Where dental assistants will be used, a cubicle of 6 ft 9 in. by 9 ft 6 in. is desirable. For students working alone, a cubicle of 7 ft 6 in. by 7 ft 6 in. is adequate.

Cubicles may be either partially or fully enclosed. A partition height of approximately 5 ft is recommended for most cubicles. This provides privacy, yet allows for expansion and gives an impression of spaciousness. A 4-ft partition topped by a 1-ft-high translucent plastic panel may be used. Allowing an open space between partition and floor facilitates cleaning. However, one or two fully enclosed cubicles are desirable in every clinic.

Determining the Number of Clinic Positions

For the clinics as a whole, at least two operating positions should be provided for every entering class student—one in the general clinic and one in the group of special clinics.

Every school should also plan additional clinic positions for its graduate and postgraduate students. The equivalent of one student module is desirable in the general clinic for even a modest program of advanced study. Additional positions will also be needed in the special clinics, with the number dependent upon the goals of the school and the particular dental specialities emphasized in its graduate curriculum.

Estimating Space Requirements

Space allowances for each operating position will also vary in the different clinics. The diagnostic clinic will require 85 sq ft per position, an allotment also sufficient for oral surgery.

In the radiology clinic, 115 sq ft per position should be allowed, and in the clinic for the chronically ill and handicapped, 125 sq ft. For other clinics, an allowance of 100 sq ft per student position should be adequate.

Space allowance for some of the supporting facilities of the clinical departments will be fairly standard. For demonstration operatories, for example, a uniform allowance of 200 sq ft each may be used.

INSTRUCTION ROOMS, STUDY AREAS, AND LIBRARY FACILITIES

Seminars

The seminar is a room especially planned to accommodate small-group instruction for 16 students or less, usually at an advanced level of training.

In most schools, one or more seminar rooms will be needed for the use of each basic science department—at least one for instruction and perhaps one for departmental conferences.

In the clinical facilities of most schools, each of the special clinics will need one seminar room for treatment planning and consultation, and the general clinic will need more than one. In programming, a reasonable standard for the general clinic would allow four rooms for a class size of 96, increasing or decreasing the number by one for each 16-student module added or subtracted.

Allow a minimum of 300 sq ft for each seminar room, with increments of 75 sq ft for every four students beyond the 16 accommodated in the standard room.

Seating arrangements in seminar rooms are a matter of choice. Usually the instructor and his students sit around a central table, but some seminar rooms are furnished with standard tablet-arm chairs. Unitized folding tables and folding chairs permit maximum flexibility in seating arrangements, however, and their

use is increasing, especially in the seminar room used for showing slides, 16mm films, and other visual aids. If it is so used, a small adjoining room for storage of visual aid materials is also helpful. A seminar, like any other instruction room, should be equipped with a chalkboard.

Lecture Rooms

Although they accommodate a minimum of 50 people, all lecture rooms need not have the same capacity. The smallest should, however, seat at least a full class, plus an overrun of 20 percent. If the school expects a later expansion in class size, lecture rooms should be planned from the beginning to accommodate it, and the 20 percent overrun allowance should also be based on the larger figure.

A good rule of thumb is to provide seating capacity for one additional 16-student module beyond class size in schools with 96 ECS. An allowance of 12 sq ft per seat (roughly 200 sq ft for a student module of 16) is sufficient to permit an adequate aisle on either side of the seating area and, in a large lecture room, a center aisle as well.

A minimum of three lecture rooms should be provided, one for use of the basic science departments and located near them, one for clinical and preclinical instruction and accessible to the clinics, and one for special courses or for multiple use. In the school which will have no auditorium, the multiple-use lecture room might be designed to provide $2\frac{1}{2}$ positions per ECS. All lecture rooms should be located so as to minimize noise and traffic congestion in the corridors.

Layout. It may be difficult to decide whether the lecture room should be long and relatively narrow, like the usual hall, or wider and shallower, like an amphitheater. Because of its wide viewing angle, the amphitheater is not particularly suitable for the showing of slides and films. On the other hand, instructors favor-

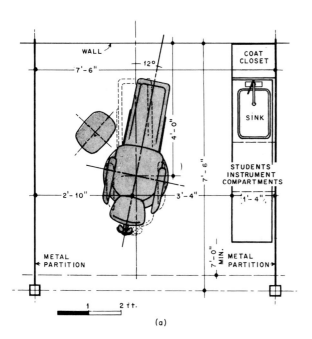

(a)

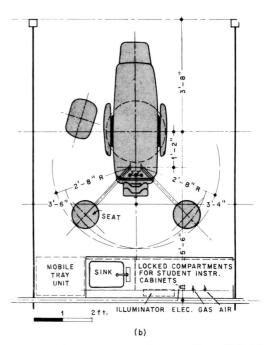

(b)

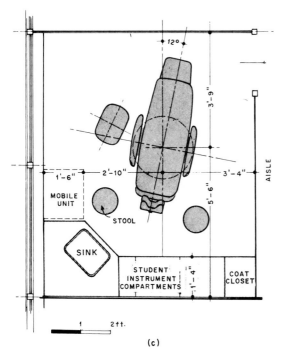

(c)

Fig. 15 (a) Cubicle for student working alone. (b) Cubicle for student and assistant. (c) Variation for student-assistant team.

ing the chalk talk technique often dislike a long room. Television monitors can be used in either type.

Every lecture room should be equipped with a large chalkboard; a minimum of 12 lin ft is recommended. If, because of the size of the room, a raised platform is provided, it should be long enough to extend 2 ft beyond each end of the chalkboard. Projection screens which can be automatically lowered and raised may also be a part of the permanent equipment.

The floors of lecture rooms should be sloped or terraced slightly to provide a good view of the chalkboards and projection screen.

Some larger lecture rooms are split level or have a balcony. Whenever possible, students should enter from the rear.

Furnishings. Fixed or movable tablet-arm chairs, or auditorium seats equipped with tablet arms, are commonly found in lecture rooms. If the latter are used, the aisle seat at the left of each row can be fitted with an outside tablet arm for the use of left-handed students. Writing counters with individual seats are also frequently used.

Auditoriums. For schools that have ready access to them, auditoriums sometimes serve as lecture or examination rooms. As a rule,

however, programming committees will find it difficult to justify a large auditorium solely for the use of a dental school, since it is generally more economical to rent a hall for occasions such as graduations which require large seating capacity.

If an auditorium is planned, it should be located on a ground floor. Direct entry from the outside is necessary, because the auditorium will often be used by the public when the remainder of the school is closed. Seating capacity should be sufficient to accommodate students enrolled in every program of the school as well as the total faculty.

Auditoriums must have public toilets and cloakrooms; a small lounge off the foyer is advisable. Areas for the preparation and storage of demonstration materials should be provided backstage, as should a toilet room.

Areas for Study, Reference, and Research

Study Areas Places for first- and second-year students should probably be located near the basic science laboratories, and those for third- and fourth-year students near the clinics. If possible, they should be so situated that students will have access to them at all times, even when the rest of the school is closed. *Space.* About 19 sq ft per ECS should be allowed in planning standard study places for a school providing one study place for every two students. This type of study place can be in a common room, and is usually unassigned. However, some schools may prefer the partially partitioned cubicle. Requiring approximately 48 sq ft per student position, the cubicles are furnished with a desk and chair, a coat locker, and storage space for books, microscopes, and school supplies. Because a cubicle is permanently assigned to each student, space requirements are based on the total enrollment.

Library Facilities The following guidelines, though general, may be helpful.
Reading and Study Rooms. The main reading room should accommodate from 25 to 50 percent of the total number of students. Reading room exits should be controlled by book

595

charge-out or loan desks, and the card catalog and circulation desk should be nearby.

Carrels. Unenclosed desk areas of about 12 sq ft are useful for individual study and should be available in the ratio of one for every 10 students. Small study rooms reserved for graduate and postdoctoral students are also an advantage. Either they should be soundproofed or located far enough away from the main reading room to permit students to use typewriters without disturbing others.

Microfilm. Auxiliary facilities such as a microfilm reading room, a sound tape room, and a rare book room are also desirable.

Stacks. Stacks should be arranged to facilitate both storage and use of books. The stacks should be located as close to reading rooms as possible, preferably at or below the level of the main reading room.

Stack area varies in proportion to volumes. Generous allowances should always be made for future expansion. Stack sections are usually 3 ft in length and 7 ft 6 in. in height, with a shelf depth of at least 10 in. One single-faced section 3 ft long will accommodate approximately 100 volumes. Service aisles between stacks should be at least 3 ft wide, and the main aisles at least 3 ft 8 in. wide. A microfilm room for processing and storage may be associated with the stack area.

Other Facilities. Acquisition and catalog rooms should be near the public card catalog and have direct access to the stacks.

Offices should be provided for the head librarian and an assistant, with the head librarian's office accessible both to staff rooms and to readers. Storage space for office supplies should be available.

A library stocked with 25,000 volumes and amply supplied with space for reading rooms and auxiliary facilities would require approximately 10,000 sq ft for a school with 96 ECS.

EDUCATIONAL TELEVISION AND OTHER VISUAL AIDS

The location of the ETV department should be carefully chosen to hold distribution distances to a minimum. A top floor or penthouse would be a logical location. Preferably, the visual aids department should be nearby. The studio should not be less than 1,300 sq ft, completely visible from the control room. The ceiling height of the studio (13 to 14 ft) is another factor that must be considered in planning. One area of the studio should contain a dental operatory setup, with chair, unit, and instrument cabinet. A movable (on casters) laboratory demonstration bench will be required for demonstrations of experiments in the basic sciences. The televising of anatomical dissection will require a large overhead mirror. A smaller bench for dental technic demonstration, chalkboards, flip stand, and tack boards are additional requirements. Ample maneuvering area for the television cameras and operators must also be provided. Figure 16 shows an ETV department of approximately 2,500 sq ft.

The control room should be elevated and built as close to the ceiling as possible for maximum visibility. Entry into the control room should be possible without going through the studio.

Provision should be made for a film chain installation requiring a room approximately 12 by 15 ft. Kinescope recorders and videotape recorders should be planned for in areas adjoining the control room.

The amount of prop storage space required will vary with the emphasis placed on television and on the availability of other storage areas.

The director and assistant director will require office areas.

Visual Aids Department

The increasing use of ETV has not eliminated the need for a complete visual aids department, but has increased it. Figure 16 shows a visual aids department. In larger schools, 18 to 20 sq ft per ECS would provide centralized visual aids facilities for both the basic sciences and the dental science divisions.

Graphic Arts. Drafting tables, plan file cabinets, and a sink or lavatory should be provided.

Another room is needed for production of the three-dimensional models. A workbench with sink and utilities is required.

Photography. The room provided for the photographic section should be large enough to permit the photographing of patients, photomicrography, copying, film processing and printing, and print and slide finishing. It might also include equipment for preparing and projecting printed pages and similar opaque materials. The studio should be not less than 12 ft wide and approximately 35 ft long for making 16 mm motion pictures and for their projection.

Distribution and Storage of Visual Aids. Administrative offices are required for the maintenance of files and cataloging of material, control of distribution and the requisitioning of visual aids materials, and adequate space should be provided for storage of slides and films and for the storage, maintenance, and operation of all projectors.

SUPPORTING SERVICES FOR LABORATORIES AND CLINICS

The Feasibility of Centralized Laboratory Supply Services

Figure 17 is an example of a reasonable plan for a fully centralized laboratory service. Since the operation of four-student laboratories for all

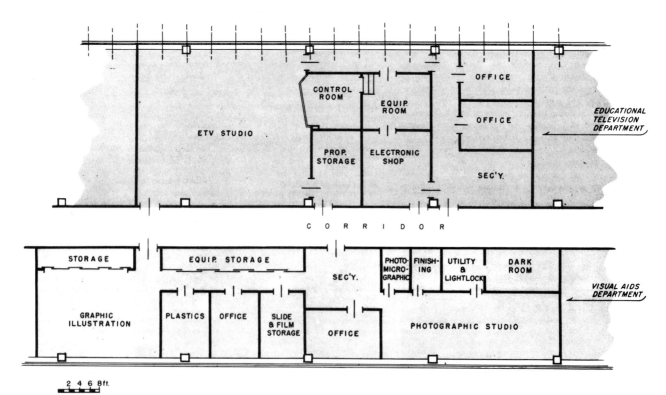

Fig. 16 ETV and visual aids departments.

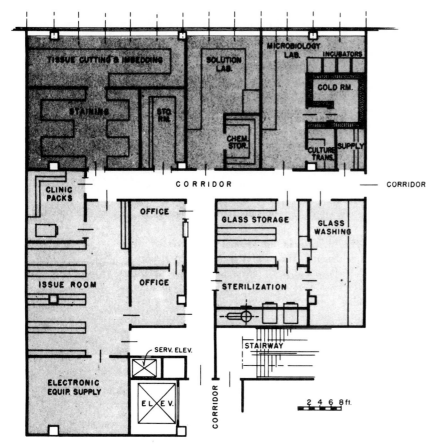

Fig. 17 Central laboratory services department.

ceiving of animals is simplified and the possibility of their escape minimized. The preferred location is on the ground level or in a properly air-conditioned basement area.

Technical Shops The technical shops are responsible for the upkeep and repair of the more complex equipment and devices employed by the various school departments. They also design and fabricate unique apparatus required for research and experimentation.

Though smaller shops of this type are attached to one of the basic science departments, the services of the central technical shops, with their larger staffs and more extensive equipment, should be available to all departments, including the basic sciences, of the dental school.

Even schools which do not require these specialized technical activities will need to provide the modest facilities required for the routine maintenance and repair of standard dental equipment, such as engines, lathes, and dental chairs. Because major repairs of this type are ordinarily made under contract, only limited equipment is necessary.

FACULTY FACILITIES

Office Facilities

A uniform allowance of 200 sq ft for each full-time faculty member will provide enough space to assure an individual office for each teacher with the rank of instructor or above as well as sufficient additional space for department heads and others with administrative responsibility.

Research Facilities

Space requirements for faculty research are particularly difficult to anticipate. An allowance of 100 sq ft for each full-time faculty member represents the equivalent of one small laboratory for each two teachers.

Function and Location

Faculty facilities are usually included in the area of major dental school activities, a location with obvious functional advantages (Fig. 18). If they are housed separately from undergraduate areas, however, future expansion of offices and research space is simplified. Also, if faculty facilities are grouped together in a separate area and their assignments controlled by the office of the dean, rather than by the department, the problem of transferring assigned facilities from one activity or faculty to another will be simplified. The relative merit of separate or departmentally integrated facilities should be carefully weighed before final decisions on exact locations are made.

GRADUATE AND POSTGRADUATE FACILITIES

In the basic science departments, an allowance of 150 sq ft per student will permit a two-module office and a four-module laboratory for each four graduate students. In the clinical departments, an allowance of 100 sq ft per student will permit one small combination study and research area for each four students. Additional operatories will also be needed.

Graduate programs should also be adequately provided with study cubicles and reserved library study rooms for the specific use of their students.

---

basic science departments requires that equipment and supplies be in the individual laboratories prior to the beginning of a scheduled experiment, the central service facilities make delivery by placing each laboratory's equipment and supplies on trays. The trays are then placed on carts which circulate between the laboratories on regular delivery rounds.

Services Requiring Both Departmental and Central Facilities

Animal Quarters Although holding rooms for small animals adjoin research and teaching areas, a dental school must still provide one large and centrally located animal area.

To avoid the possible spread of disease, different species of animals should never be housed in the same room. Ideally, then, the central animal area should consist not of one large room but of a number of smaller ones. No room should be larger than 600 sq ft—a size which will amply accommodate 32 large dog cages.

Space requirements for smaller animals vary, and the following table provides examples of the net footage needed:

Mice . . . . 7 per sq ft
Guinea pigs . . . . 2 per sq ft
Rats. . . . . 5 per sq ft
Rabbits. . . . . 1 per 2 sq ft

In addition to this net space, allowance must be made for corridors and vestibules within the quarters, as well as for storage.

Storage places no major demand upon available space. Adequate facilities permit the storage of bedding, housekeeping supplies, and enough food for one day near the central holding rooms. Bulk storage is not necessary.

Ancillary facilities of the central quarters will, however, occupy substantial amounts of space. These should include a receiving or isolation room where animals can be held for observation during laboratory tests, and at least one adjoining small laboratory and perhaps more, depending upon the size of the school's research program.

There should be a small room for preparing food for the animals, and a much larger area for washing and sterilizing cages. The washers and sterilizers used here must be big enough to accommodate the largest cage. (Fixed cages, which must be washed within the holding rooms, are so arranged that refuse can be washed into a gutter and then into a flushing drain.)

Other facilities found in the larger animal quarters include animal surgery rooms, equipped with their own ancillary facilities for instrument sterilization and storage, recovery rooms, an autopsy room, an incinerator room, and a refrigerated storage area. Offices for a veterinarian and for an animal keeper are also provided.

The planning of the central animal area should not be undertaken without thorough consideration of such factors as insect and pest control, the reduction of noise and odors, and the sanitary disposal of refuse. Animal quarters should not be visible to the public, and they should be arranged so that the re-

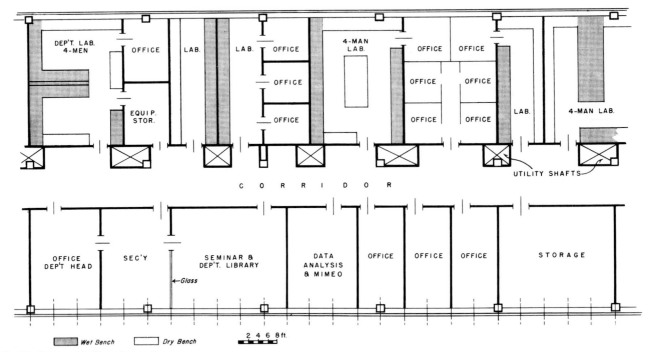

Fig. 18 Departmental office and research area.

AUXILIARY PERSONNEL

Training Facilities for Dental Hygienists

Dental hygiene students may share classroom space, facilities of the x-ray department, and the library, for example, with dental students. If ample laboratory space is available in the dental school, this, too, may be shared, although a separate laboratory for hygiene students facilitates class scheduling for courses like dental anatomy and prophylaxis technics, which have heavy clock-hour laboratory requirements. The laboratory should be equipped with low benches having electricity, gas, and air outlets. Sufficient laboratory positions to accommodate an entire class are needed. A space allotment of 600 sq ft per 16-student module should be adequate.

The clinic space for the dental hygiene program may be either in a section of the main clinic or in a separate clinic.

If any increase in enrollments is planned for a later date, enough space should be allocated originally and utilities installed to provide for the added students, even though all space is not immediately equipped.

Hygienists will require lounge, locker, and toilet facilities. In some schools, they will share these facilities with other women.

The careful location of a hygiene clinic is one way of providing flexibility in school planning. If, at some later date, it should become necessary to expand the school's clinical facilities, the dental hygiene clinic can be relocated and its former facilities incorporated into other clinics.

ADMINISTRATIVE FACILITIES

One of the focal points of dental school activity is the administrative area. Though it should be readily accessible to visitors, it need not be in a predominant location. In some schools, it is located on an upper floor, convenient to an elevator or stairway.

In general most dental schools will to some extent undertake duties which fall into three broad categories—academic policy, student affairs, and business and personnel management.

Academic Offices

In planning the office of the dean, space must be allotted for the dean's private study and for his secretary—with due regard paid to the need for bookshelves, filing space, and office supply storage. A conference room may also be necessary. In addition, offices will be required for an assistant or associate dean and his secretary. Whether or not the dean's offices should be grouped so that the secretarial staff may share a large single office is a decision for the individual school. In programming, approximately 1,500 sq ft should be adequate for these rooms. In larger schools, an office for another assistant dean may be needed.

Where the programs warrant it, graduate and postgraduate divisions will have their own officers and offices, and extensive research activity will require a research coordinator, who will also need an office. Schools training dental hygienists or dental assistants will need office accommodations for the director of these programs. Some schools also include an office for part-time faculty members in the administrative area. In programming, allow 200 sq ft for each office and 300 sq ft for each conference room required in connection with these programs.

Student Affairs

Schools which do not depend upon the university for such services will require a registrar's office to process applications for admission, to supervise registrations, and to maintain student records.

Many schools also offer active programs of student assistance, including counseling and advisory services, and office space is required for the professional personnel who conduct them. In some schools, offices are provided for the chaplains appointed to serve their students. All schools will probably need space to house expanding scholarship and loan activities, and, in some, additional space will be needed to handle student housing services. In small schools or in schools with very limited responsibilities for directing student affairs, these activities will probably be combined with those of a business or personnel office.

Business and Personnel Management

Some schools have little more than a cashier's office and a minimum of clerical help. Others maintain a complex accounting and fiscal operation, headed by the office of the bursar.

A public relations department, personnel offices, and stenographic-dictaphone pools may also be needed in larger institutions. Adequate space for stock rooms and administrative records is always essential. The advisability of employing an administrative director of clinics should be considered, and some schools today strengthen this service by adding a social worker.

In some activities—printing and publications is one—the type of equipment largely determines space needs. Offset printing presses will be desirable in some schools; others need little more than mimeograph machines, and their space requirements will vary accordingly.

Mail rooms which consistently handle bulk mailing require a special space allotment.

The actual allocation of space for the various business functions and for the administration of student affairs will vary widely. For the average school, however, total space needs for these two groups of functions will probably be adequately met by an allowance of 25 sq ft per ECS.

STUDENT FACILITIES

Bookstores

For most schools, an allowance of from 8 to 10 sq ft per ECS—with a minimum of 500 sq ft— is a good preliminary estimate of bookstore space. This will provide room enough both for open displays and for some storage. If possible, the store should be located near the student lounge or the cafeteria.

Student Lounges

The student lounge is important—perhaps indispensable—to a dental school, and the availability of similar facilities elsewhere on the campus does not, in this case, reduce the need for a lounge in the dental school itself. The lounge is the students' social center.

Although the number of women enrolled in undergraduate dental schools is small, schools should provide separate lounges for their convenience. In some schools, women dental students will be able to share the lounges provided for student dental hygienists and dental assistants.

In programming, the committee should estimate lounge space at 23 sq ft per ECS for a class size of 96. For classes of different sizes, 200 sq ft should be added or subtracted for each group of 16 students. These amounts permit simultaneous occupancy by approximately 25 percent of the total enrollment.

Locker Rooms

Adjoining the lounge areas should be adequate toilet facilities and—if feasible—the student locker rooms. Locker rooms should at least be convenient to the part of the school where the student spends most of his academic day— near the basic science and preclinical technic laboratories for freshmen and sophomores, near the clinics and associated clinical laboratories for juniors and seniors.

The locker room area required for male students can be estimated at 1,800 sq ft for an entering class of 48 (or three 16-student modules); this amount should be increased by 500 sq ft for each additional group of 16 students.

As to the lockers themselves, the types chosen should depend on the use to which they are put. If dental students are expected to keep their instrument cases in clothing lockers, the size of the case should be established and a prototype made so that the suitability of the lockers can be tested before they are purchased. The lockers chosen should also be large enough to accommodate other dental equipment.

Health

NURSING SCHOOLS

INTRODUCTION

This section deals with design for the following nursing programs, respectively: the diploma, associate degree, baccalaureate and graduate degrees, and practical nursing. In each section, a description is presented of special aspects of each program. A hypothetical school has been described and space requirements determined. No attempt was made to compare the space requirements of one program with another, since each has its special needs, precluding a common basis for comparative purposes. For example, each program differs in purpose, curriculum, and graduation requirements.

The second half of this chapter sets forth planning considerations which will affect the architectural design of a facility. No attempt is made to outline finished plans since this should be the decision of the individual school, after a careful evaluation of various alternatives. Moreover, before the architect begins to develop his plans, the school must first establish its educational program.

DIPLOMA NURSING PROGRAMS

The diploma nursing program is conducted by a single-purpose school and may be either hospital-sponsored or independently incorporated. This program serves the interests and needs of qualified high school graduates who want (1) an education centered in a hospital, and (2) an early and continuing opportunity to be with patients and with personnel who provide health services. (See Fig. 1 and Table 1.)

Program Characteristics

Diploma programs emphasize the basic scientific principles of nursing care and of recognizing indications of diseases, disabilities, and patient needs. The curriculum is planned to equip graduates with the skills necessary to organize and implement a nursing plan that will meet the immediate needs of one or more patients, to be responsible for the direction of other members of the nursing team, and, to the degree possible, to promote the restoration of the patient's health.

Some graduates of diploma programs may wish to fulfill requirements for a baccalaureate degree in nursing. Admission is granted in accordance with the admission policies of the particular college or university they wish to attend.

THE ASSOCIATE DEGREE NURSING PROGRAM

The associate degree nursing program is generally established as a division or department of a community junior college, although some are in four-year colleges or universities. This program is designed to fulfill the educational

Nursing Education Facilities, Public Health Service, Department of Health, Education, and Welfare, Washington, D.C., 1964.

needs of qualified high school graduates who want (1) to prepare to practice nursing as registered nurses, and (2) to study in a college where they may share responsibilities and privileges as well as intellectual and social experiences with students in other educational programs. (See Fig. 2 and Table 2.)

Program Characteristics

The following characteristics identify associate degree nursing programs:

1. The college controls, finances, and administers the program.

2. The program conforms with the overall standards and policies of the college and operates within the framework of its organization, administration, interdisciplinary curriculum committees, and the student personnel program.

3. The policies and procedures promulgated for faculty in other college departments also apply to the nursing faculty.

4. Members of the nursing faculty plan, organize, implement, and teach the nursing courses. They select, guide, and evaluate all learning experiences including those in the patient care areas.

5. The college, by means of written agreements with hospitals and other agencies in the community, provides clinical facilities essential to nursing education.

6. Students meet the requirements of the college and its nursing department for admission, continuation of study, and graduation.

7. The nursing program is organized within the framework of the community junior college curriculum pattern leading to an associate degree.

Graduates of the associate degree nursing program are prepared to give patient-centered nursing care in beginning general-duty nurse positions. They are prepared to draw upon a background from the physical, biological, and social sciences in administering nursing care to patients. They relate well with people and are self-directive in learning from experience as practicing nurses. They are prepared to cooperate and share responsibility for the patients' welfare with other general-duty nurses, head nurses, supervisors, attending physicians, and others. As all other beginning practitioners, these graduates need to be oriented to new work situations and given time and opportunity to become increasingly effective in the practice of nursing.

The program is complete for its purpose. Some graduates from associate degree programs may later wish to fulfill requirements for a baccalaureate degree in nursing.

BACCALAUREATE AND GRADUATE NURSING PROGRAMS

Program Characteristics

Undergraduate Programs A nursing program leading to a baccalaureate degree is conducted by an educational unit in nursing (department, division, school, or college) that is an integral part of a college or university and is organized

and controlled in the same way as other units in the institution. (See Table 3.)

The baccalaureate degree program is designed to serve the needs and purposes of persons who want (1) to learn and practice the humanistic and scientific bases for care of patients, (2) to prepare for nursing at the baccalaureate level, (3) to share with students preparing for other occupations all the general advantages of a college or university preparation, and (4) to acquire a baccalaureate education as a prerequisite for graduate study to prepare to practice in such specialties as teaching, administration, or research.

Graduates of baccalaureate programs are prepared for nursing positions in community health services and may advance without further formal education to positions, such as head nurse and team leader, which require administrative skills. Graduates also have a foundation for continuing personal and professional development and for graduate study in nursing.

Some graduates of associate degree and diploma programs in nursing may wish to fulfill requirements for a baccalaureate degree in nursing. Admission requirements vary with different colleges and universities.

Graduate Programs A graduate nursing program is organized similar to other graduate programs within the university. With only few exceptions, these are offered in conjunction with a baccalaureate nursing program. (See Table 4.)

The graduate program is designed to prepare nurses for leadership positions in teaching and administration in all types of educational programs. Such a program also provides an opportunity to study for supervisory and administrative positions in nursing service. Consultants, clinical specialists, and research workers also require graduate study.

(See Fig. 3.)

PRACTICAL NURSING PROGRAMS

Seventy-five percent of the state-approved nursing programs leading to a practical nurse certificate are controlled by educational institutions or agencies. The majority are under state and local boards of education. The remainder are mostly under the control of hospitals, with the exception of about six which are under other community agencies. (See Tables 5 and 6 and Figs. 4 and 5.)

Program Characteristics

The practical nursing program which leads to a certificate or diploma is usually one year in length, self-contained, complete, and satisfactory for its own purpose, providing preparation exclusively for practical nursing. (California and Texas call these programs "Vocational Nurse Programs" and license the graduates as Licensed Vocational Nurses.) This program's objective is to prepare a needed worker in nursing service who will share in giving direct care to patients. Graduates of practical nursing programs perform two major functions:

600

TABLE 1   Space Requirements for a 3-Year Diploma Program with a Total Entering Class of 64 and a Total Enrollment of 148

Spaces	Nursing education area			Remarks
	Number of rooms	Group size, each room	Total net area (sq. ft.)	
Teaching	–	–	9,330	
Lecture-demonstration room	1	75	1,940	
Classrooms	2	38	1,370	
Conference rooms	3	16	900	Additional required in hospital.
Multipurpose room with storage and utility room	1	–	2,000	8 beds.
Science laboratories	–	–	–	Optional.
Storage—teaching aids	1	–	120	
Library	1	–	3,000	3,000 books; 1,000 bound periodical volumes.
Faculty	–	–	2,277	
Offices	15	1	1,500	
Conference room	1	20	377	
Lounge	1	–	300	Shared with administrative staff.
Washrooms, toilets	1	–	100	1 watercloset and 2 lavatories.
Lockers	–	–	–	
Administration	–	–	1,660	
Lobby—reception area	1	–	100	
General office	1	5	400	
Secretary-receptionist.				
Clerk-typists.				
Storage area	1	–	120	
Duplicating area	1	–	100	
Director's office	1	–	340	With coat closet and toilet.
Director's secretary office	1	1	100	
Assistant director's office	1	1	120	
Registrar's office and admissions office	1	–	140	Combined function.
Students' counselor's office	1	1	160	
Students' health service	–	–	–	Shared with hospital employees' health service.
Staff lounge				Shared with faculty.
Visitors' toilets:				
Men	1	–	40	1 watercloset, 1 lavatory.
Women	1	–	40	1 watercloset, 1 lavatory.
Supporting	–	–	1,580	
Students' toilets:				
Men	1	–	120	1 watercloset, 1 lavatory, including 10 full-size lockers.
Women	1	–	280	7 waterclosets, 7 lavatories.
Students' lounge	1	–	300	
Lockers	–	–	240	30 full-size lockers.
Janitors' closets	1	–	40	Or as required.
Coat alcoves	–	–	–	As required.
Vending machines	–	–	–	As required.
Telephone booths	–	–	–	As required.
Drinking fountains	–	–	–	Minimum of 4—recessed or as required.
General storage	1	–	600	
			14,847	Net area.
			9,898	For walls, partitions, corridors, stairs, and mechanical space.
			24,745	Total gross area.
			167.2	Area per enrolled student.

If the sciences are taught in the home school, add the following:

Teaching	–	–	4,368	
Classrooms	1	38	648	These should be added if the sciences are taught in the home school.
Science laboratories	2	–	3,600	
Storage and preparation room	1	–	120	
Faculty	–	–	500	
Offices	5	1	500	
			19,215	Total net area.
			12,810	For walls, partitions, corridors, stairs, and mechanical space.
			32,025	Total gross area.
			216.4	Area per enrolled student.
Assembly room	1	200	3,000	Flat floor.
			22,215	Total net area.
			14,810	For walls, partitions, corridors, stairs, and mechanical space.
			37,025	Total gross area.
			250.2	Area per enrolled student.

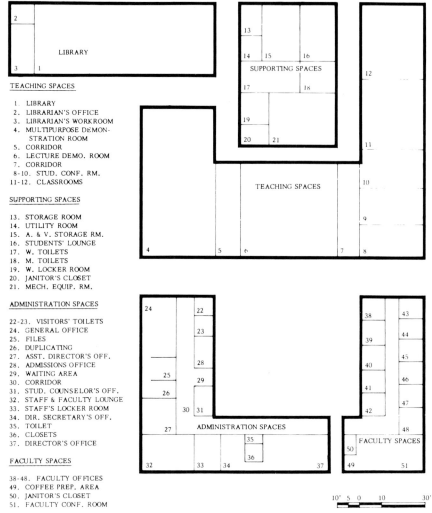

TEACHING SPACES

1. LIBRARY
2. LIBRARIAN'S OFFICE
3. LIBRARIAN'S WORKROOM
4. MULTIPURPOSE DEMON-
   STRATION ROOM
5. CORRIDOR
6. LECTURE DEMO. ROOM
7. CORRIDOR
8-10. STUD. CONF. RM.
11-12. CLASSROOMS

SUPPORTING SPACES

13. STORAGE ROOM
14. UTILITY ROOM
15. A. & V. STORAGE RM.
16. STUDENTS' LOUNGE
17. W. TOILETS
18. M. TOILETS
19. W. LOCKER ROOM
20. JANITOR'S CLOSET
21. MECH. EQUIP. RM.

ADMINISTRATION SPACES

22-23. VISITORS' TOILETS
24. GENERAL OFFICE
25. FILES
26. DUPLICATING
27. ASST. DIRECTOR'S OFF.
28. ADMISSIONS OFFICE
29. WAITING AREA
30. CORRIDOR
31. STUD. COUNSELOR'S OFF.
32. STAFF & FACULTY LOUNGE
33. STAFF'S LOCKER ROOM
34. DIR. SECRETARY'S OFF.
35. TOILET
36. CLOSETS
37. DIRECTOR'S OFFICE

FACULTY SPACES

38-48. FACULTY OFFICES
49. COFFEE PREP. AREA
50. JANITOR'S CLOSET
51. FACULTY CONF. ROOM

Fig. 1 Space relationships in the diploma program.

1. Under the direction of a registered nurse or physician, they administer nursing care in situations relatively free of scientific complexity.

2. In a close working relationship, they assist registered nurses in providing nursing care in more complex situations.

ARCHITECTURAL CONSIDERATIONS

The physical essentials of the various spaces required for any type of program of nursing education are briefly described in this section. All the spaces noted, however, are not necessarily required for all programs. Moreover, many of the spaces may be used in conjunction with other departments of a community college, a university, or institution to which the nursing education program is related. Where possible, variations are noted.

The diagrams of teaching spaces are only suggestive of one method of arranging these spaces. The final scheme used by a nursing education program will depend on its particular needs expressed in the written program. The

degree to which the architect can effectively design a facility depends largely on how thoroughly the functional program of the proposed facility was prepared.

Although each nursing education facility will find it necessary to determine its own space requirements in light of its own needs, the spaces required by most schools might be grouped under seven categories. These categories include teaching spaces, research facilities, faculty offices, administrative unit, students' facilities, supporting areas, and continuing education.

Teaching Spaces

Lecture-Demonstration Rooms The lecture-demonstration room (Fig. 6) is used for the purpose implied in its name. Factors to be considered in determining physical dimensions are requirements for the following: (1) teaching station, (2) demonstration area, (3) seating area, (4) projection space or room, and (5) storage closets. A brief description of each follows:

Teaching Station. The teaching station should be equipped with chalkboards, tack

boards, projection screens, and map rails above to support diagrams and charts.

Demonstration Area. The demonstration area in front of the teaching station should be large enough to permit the use of equipment such as an adult-size bed or movable sectional counter units which have locking wheels. These units, which have storage space underneath, provide greater flexibility than fixed counters, since they can be assembled into any arrangement or length and can be stored elsewhere when not in use.

A lavatory will be needed in the lecture-demonstration area for use whenever a patient care demonstration is presented. The doors into this room should be a minimum of 3 ft 8 in. wide to provide an adequate passageway for a bed and other equipment used during a demonstration.

Seating Area. Since good visibility of the instruction and demonstration area should be assured from all seats, a stepped floor should be considered. Steps should be so designed that each sight line misses the row ahead by 4 in. Fixed seats equipped with hinged or removable tablet supports for writing are recom-

TABLE 2   Space Requirements for a 2-Year Associate Degree Program in a Community College with an Entering Class of 64 and a Total Enrollment of 104

Spaces	Nursing education area			Remarks
	Number of rooms	Group size, each room	Total net area (sq. ft.)	
Teaching	–	–	6,120	
Lecture-demonstration room	1	104	2,300	
Classrooms	1	44	800	
Conference rooms	3	16	900	Additional required in hospital.
Multipurpose room with storage and utility rooms	1	–	2,000	8 beds.
Storage—teaching aids	1	–	120	
Science laboratories	–	–	–	In the college.
Library	–	–	–	In the college.
Faculty	–	–	1,580	
Offices	10	1	1,000	
Conference room	1	20	400	
Lounge	–	–	–	In the college.
Washroom and toilets	–	–	180	
Administration	–	–	840	
Lobby-reception	1	–	100	
General office	1	–	320	
Secretary-receptionist	–	1	–	
Clerk-typists	–	3	–	
Storage area	1	–	80	
Duplicating area	–	–	–	In the college.
Director's office	1	1	340	With coat closet and toilet.
Registrar's office	–	–	–	In the college.
Admissions office	–	–	–	In the college.
Student counselor's office	–	–	–	In the college.
Students' health service	–	–	–	In the college.
Staff lounge—washroom and toilet	–	–	–	In the college.
Visitors' toilets:				
Men	–	–	–	In the college.
Women	–	–	–	In the college.
Supporting	–	–	1,300	
Students' toilets	–	–	420	
Men's toilet	–	–	–	1 watercloset, 1 lavatory, 1 urinal.
Women's toilets	–	–	–	5 waterclosets, 5 lavatories.
Students' lounge	–	–	–	Located in college.
Lockers	–	–	240	104 full-size lockers. (Additional may be needed in the hospital.)
Janitors' closets	1	–	40	Or as required.
Coat alcoves	–	–	–	As required.
Vending machines	–	–	–	As required.
Telephone booths	–	–	–	As required.
Drinking fountains	–	–	–	Minimum of 3—recessed or as required.
General storage	1	–	600	
			9,840	Net area.
			6,560	For walls, partitions, corridors, stairs, and mechanical space.
			16,400	Total gross area.
			157.7	Area per enrolled student.

mended. Ten percent of the seats should be for left-handed students.

Projection Room. A projection room separated from the classroom is desirable because it eliminates such disturbing factors as noise and light. However, certain disadvantages of a separate projection room such as the need for an operator and for communication facilities between the operator and the instructor should be considered.

In lieu of a projection room, a console for projection equipment is a good compromise. This console will contain all lighting and projection controls and will have locked storage space for equipment when not in use.

If such a room is provided, it may also be used for editing and storing material to be projected. Provision, therefore, should be made for counters with storage space underneath. One of the counters should have a sink. Open shelves or wall cabinets with glazed doors may be provided above the counters.

The projection wall should have two small windows so that two projectors can show two images on the screens simultaneously. The width of the screen should be approximately equal to one-sixth of the distance to the last row of seats. Projection screens can be the roll-up type, either manually or mechanically operated, or the fixed type. Mechanical operation, although noisy, prevents accidental demage to the screen.

Storage Closets. Storage closets with standard-height doors may be provided. Among other things, skeletons and full-scale models of the human body may be stored here if there is no centralized storage.

Classrooms. The classroom (see Fig. 7) should provide an optimum setting for communication between the instructor and the students.

The room's shape and size should permit easy visibility of written material on the chalkboard as well as the projected image on the screen. The need to maintain as close a verbal distance as possible between students and the instructor should also be considered.

Acoustical treatment to support verbal communication and sound insulation to prevent the penetration of outside noises must be considered in selecting structural and finish materials.

In addition to the floor area required for seating, space should be allocated for teaching and demonstration and for mounting a projector.

If central storage of such teaching aids as skeletons and full-scale models of the human body is not provided, storage closets will be required in classrooms.

A lavatory should be provided in the room near the teaching station so that it will be easily accessible for use whenever patient care is being demonstrated.

The classroom door should be a minimum of 3 ft 8 in. wide to permit easy transportation of an adult-size bed which may be required for demonstration.

Equipment which will be needed for classrooms includes chalkboards, tack boards, and projection screens. x-ray film illuminators, either portable or wall mounted, may also be used.

Multipurpose Room The multipurpose room (see Fig. 8) may be used for student practice of patient care as well as for classroom functions. Thus, the room should accommodate:

1. Adult-size beds which may be separated by curtains suspended from ceiling curtain tracks.

2. A medicine preparation area including movable sectional counter units and fixed counters located at the wall, with sink and storage cabinets underneath and wall cabinets with glazed doors above.

3. A handwashing demonstration unit and a minimum of three lavatory basins, with foot, wrist, or knee control.

4. Dressing cubicles. One method for providing privacy is through the use of curtains suspended from ceiling curtain tracks.

5. Storage closets for small equipment, linen, charts, and diagrams. These closets should have a full-size door and should be large enough to store skeletons and full-size models of the human body, if necessary.

6. Chalkboards, tack boards, projection screens.

7. Seating around tables for seminar-type lectures for 16 students.

8. Space for projector mounting.

X-ray film illuminators may be used in all teaching areas. They can be either wall mounted or portable. If portable, storage space should be allocated for them when not in use.

Utility Room. The utility room can either be a part of the multipurpose demonstration room or may be separated by a solid partition.

Although each facility must determine its own specific equipment needs, the following built-in features are recommended:

1. A counter with sink and storage underneath with wall cabinets above

2. Roughed-in plumbing to accommodate future fixtures

Students' Conference Rooms (Teaching) Student conference rooms will be required in all programs. (See Fig. 7.) The number of such rooms will depend on the anticipated enrollment. Major planning considerations include:

• Seating arrangement at tables for group discussions or lectures

• Placement of chalkboards and tackboards

• Adequate sound isolation from one room space to another

Science Laboratories Students enrolled in associate and baccalaureate degree programs in nursing attend science courses with other undergraduates. The trend in diploma programs is to purchase instruction in the sciences from a local junior college, a college, or a university. To avoid the unnecessary duplication of expensive facilities, diploma programs should plan science laboratories only if such facilities are not available from other institutions. (See Fig. 9.)

Library Library facilities are required in all nursing education programs. Wherever feasible, a library may be shared with other types of programs; however, the diploma school will usually have its own library. An example of library facilities for a diploma program is shown in Fig. 10.

The information presented is considered minimum for the needs of a nursing education facility whether it is part of a larger library or an independent library. In any event, future expansion should be a major planning consideration.

Principal elements to be considered in designing a library include (1) the library room; (2) the librarian's office; (3) the librarian's workroom; and (4) the storage area for audiovisual equipment and models.

Library Room

Reference and Study Area. Study space should accommodate a minimum of one-third of the total student body. Reference tables may be provided for one-half of these students and carrels for the other half. Teaching machines may be used in carrels.

The reference and study area should occupy 55 to 60 percent of the total floor space of the library room.

Service Area. Card catalog and circulation activities should be located near the library entrance and reading area.

Storage Area. All nursing programs should have an adequate amount of space for stacks to accommodate necessary titles and bound volumes of periodicals. Appropriate filing arrangements should be provided for reports, pamphlets, bulletins, microfilms, microcards, and programmed material for teaching machines. For the diploma program, stacks should be provided for a minimum of 3,000 titles and 1,000 bound periodical volumes.

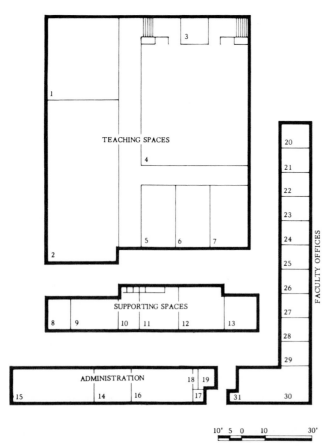

TEACHING SPACES

1. CLASSROOM
2. MULTIPURPOSE DEMONSTRATION ROOM
3. PROJECTION ROOM
4. LECTURE DEMO. ROOM
5-7. STUDENTS' CONF.

SUPPORTING SPACES

8. UTILITY ROOM
9. STORAGE ROOM
10. MEN'S ROOM
11. WOMEN'S TOILETS
12. MECH. EQUIP. ROOM
13. A. & V. STORAGE ROOM

ADMINISTRATION SPACES

14. LOBBY
15. GENERAL OFFICE
16. DIRECTOR'S OFFICE
17. TOILET
18. CLOSET
19. JANITOR'S CLOSET

FACULTY SPACES

20-29. FACULTY OFFICES
30. FACULTY CONF. ROOM
31. COFFEE PREP. AREA

Fig. 2 Space relationships in an associate degree nursing program.

TABLE 3 Space Requirements for a 4-Year Basic Baccalaureate Nursing Program with an Entering
Class of 96 and a Total Enrollment of 240

Spaces	Nursing education area			Remarks
	Number of rooms	Group size, each room	Total net area (sq. ft.)	
Teaching	–	–	14,064	
Lecture-demonstration rooms	2	120	4,608	
Classrooms	2	60	2,200	
Conference rooms	6	25	3,696	Additional required in the hospital.
Multipurpose room with storage, utility, and observation rooms	1	–	3,000	8 beds.
Science laboratories	1	–	–	In the college.
Storage-teaching aids	1	–	160	
Reference reading room	1	16	400	
Library	–	–	–	In the college.
Faculty	–	–	3,980	
Offices	27	1	2,700	
Research space added	–	–	–	Depending on the program.
Graduate assistants' office	1	4	240	
Conference room	1	40	720	
Lounge	1	–	320	Shared with administrative staff—with 5 lockers.
Administration	–	–	1,500	
Lobby-reception	1	–	100	
General office	1	9	720	
Secretary-receptionist. Clerk-typists.				
Storage area	1	–	80	
Duplicating area	1	–	80	
Dean's office	1	–	340	With coat closet and toilet.
Dean's secretary's office	1	1	100	
Registrar's office	–	–	–	In the college.
Admissions office	–	–	–	In the college.
Student counselor's office	–	–	–	In the college.
Students' health center	–	–	–	In the college.
Visitors' toilets:				
Men	–	–	40	1 watercloset, 1 lavatory.
Women	–	–	40	1 watercloset, 1 lavatory.
Supporting	–	–	1,940	
Students' toilets	–	–	660	1 lavatory.
Men	1	–	–	1 watercloset; 1 urinal.
Women	2	–	–	13 waterclosets; 13 lavatories.
Students' lounge	–	–	–	In the college.
Lockers	–	–	600	250 full-size lockers or as required.
Janitors' closets	2	–	80	As required.
Coat alcoves	–	–	–	As required.
Vending machines	–	–	–	As required.
Telephone booths	–	–	–	As required.
Drinking fountains	–	–	–	Minimum of 7—recessed or as required.
General storage	1	–	600	
Continuing education	–	–	2,560	
Assembly room	1	100	1,600	Folding partitions to divide the room into 4 spaces (optional).
Conference room	–	–	–	Optional.
Lounge and reception area	–	–	700	
Toilets:				
Men	1	–	130	1 watercloset; 1 urinal; 1 lavatory.
Women	1	–	130	1 watercloset; 2 lavatories.
Drinking fountains	–	–	–	
			24,044	Total net area.
			16,029	For walls, partitions, corridors, stairs, and mechanical space.
			40,073	Total gross area.
			166.97	Area per enrolled student, approximately 167 sq. ft.

Librarian's Office
The librarian's office should be separated from the library room by a glazed wall partition or a view window to enable the librarian to oversee activity in the library. The office should be sufficiently large to accommodate several people for an informal conference and should be equipped with necessary furniture including bookshelves, desk, and typewriter stand.

Librarian's Workroom
The workroom should be adjacent to the library room and to the librarian's office. Direct access should be provided into the corridor to permit easy deliveries by either a 3-ft 8-in. clear opening or double doors.

The room should include:
• Counter worktop with sink and storage cabinets underneath; part of the counter should have knee space underneath
• Storage shelves or wall cabinets above
• Adequate number of electrical outlets
• Space allocation for desk, worktables, movable book carts

Reference Reading Room
Nursing education programs which use adjacent library facilities may need only a small reference-reading room in the nursing education facility. Standard references and professional periodicals should be kept in this room, where study space should also be provided.

Equipment such as shelves, storage cabi-

nets, reference tables, and seats around tables for 16 people should be provided.

Storage Area
Some nursing education programs may wish to centralize all teaching aids under the librarian's supervision. Such a center is sometimes referred to as the Instructional Materials Center (IMC). If provisions for storing skeletons and full-scale models of the human body are not made elsewhere (i.e., lecture-demonstration room, classrooms, or multipurpose demonstration room), a central storage facility should be provided. This room should be placed close to the library and should be equipped with sturdy open shelving to hold heavy equipment. In planning the space to be

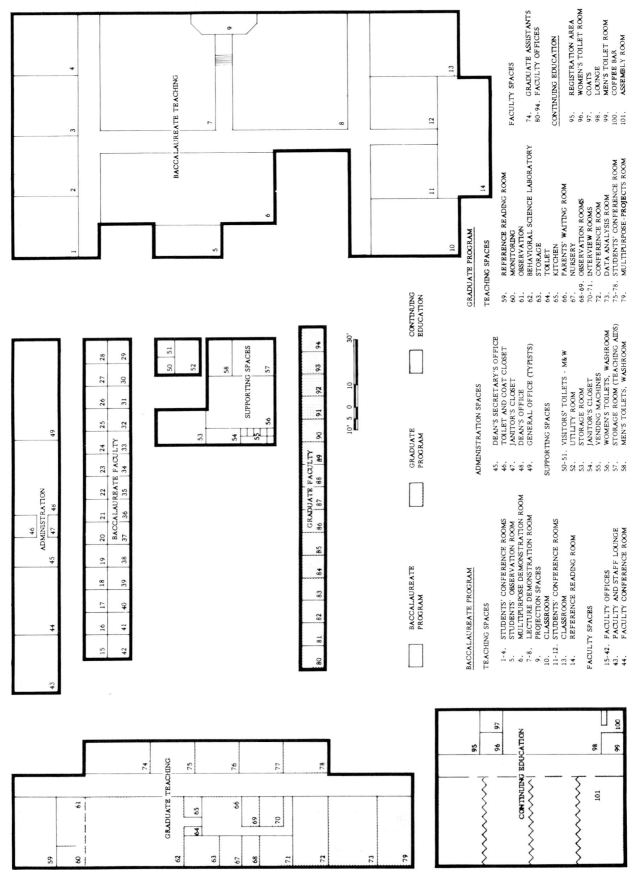

BACCALAUREATE PROGRAM

TEACHING SPACES

1-4. STUDENTS' CONFERENCE ROOMS
5. STUDENTS' OBSERVATION ROOM
6. MULTIPURPOSE DEMONSTRATION ROOM
7-8. LECTURE DEMONSTRATION ROOM
9. PROJECTION SPACES
10. CLASSROOM
11-12. STUDENTS' CONFERENCE ROOMS
13. CLASSROOM
14. REFERENCE READING ROOM

FACULTY SPACES

15-42. FACULTY OFFICES
43. FACULTY AND STAFF LOUNGE
44. FACULTY CONFERENCE ROOM

ADMINISTRATION SPACES

45. DEAN'S SECRETARY'S OFFICE
46. TOILET AND COAT CLOSET
47. JANITOR'S CLOSET
48. DEAN'S OFFICE
49. GENERAL OFFICE (TYPISTS)

SUPPORTING SPACES

50-51. VISITORS' TOILETS - M&W
52. UTILITY ROOM
53. STORAGE ROOM
54. JANITOR'S CLOSET
55. VENDING MACHINES
56. WOMEN'S TOILETS, WASHROOM
57. STORAGE ROOM (TEACHING AIDS)
58. MEN'S TOILETS, WASHROOM

GRADUATE PROGRAM

TEACHING SPACES

59. REFERENCE READING ROOM
60. MONITORING
61. OBSERVATION
62. BEHAVIORAL SCIENCE LABORATORY
63. STORAGE
64. TOILET
65. KITCHEN
66. PARENTS' WAITING ROOM
67. NURSERY
68-69. OBSERVATION ROOMS
70-71. INTERVIEW ROOMS
72. CONFERENCE ROOM
73. DATA ANALYSIS ROOM
75-78. STUDENTS' CONFERENCE ROOM
79. MULTIPURPOSE-PROJECTS ROOM

FACULTY SPACES

74. GRADUATE ASSISTANTS
80-94. FACULTY OFFICES

CONTINUING EDUCATION

95. REGISTRATION AREA
96. WOMEN'S TOILET ROOM
97. COATS
98. LOUNGE
99. MEN'S TOILET ROOM
100. COFFEE BAR
101. ASSEMBLY ROOM

Fig. 3 Space relationships in baccalaureate, graduate, and continuing education programs.

TABLE 4 Space Requirements for a 2-Year Graduate Nursing Program in Conjunction with a Basic Baccalaureate Program with a Total Entering Class of 30 and a Total Enrollment of 60

Spaces	Nursing education area			Remarks
	Number of rooms	Group size, each room	Total net area (sq. ft.)	
Teaching	–	–	1,280	
Lecture-demonstration room	–	80	–	Shared with undergraduate program.
Classrooms	–	40	–	Shared with undergraduate program.
Seminar rooms	4	12	880	
Reference-reading room	1	16	400	
Library	–	–	–	Shared with college.
Research laboratories	–	–	7,735	
Behavioral science	–	–	–	
Waiting area	–	–	–	
Nursery	–	–	–	
Observation rooms	–	–	–	
Interview rooms	–	–	–	
Conference room	–	–	–	
Data analysis room	–	–	–	
Multipurpose projects room	–	–	–	
Faculty	–	–	2,726	
Offices	15	1	1,500	
Research space added	–	–	–	Depending on program.
Graduate assistant's office	1	8	576	
Secretaries' office	1	5	400	
Toilets:				
Men	1	–	100	1 water closet, 1 urinal, 1 lavatory.
Women	1	–	150	3 waterclosets, 3 lavatories.
Supporting	–	–	–	Shared with undergraduate program.
			11,741	Total net area.
			7,827	For walls, partitions, corridors, stairs, and mechanical space.
			19,568	Total gross area.
			326.1	Area per enrolled student.

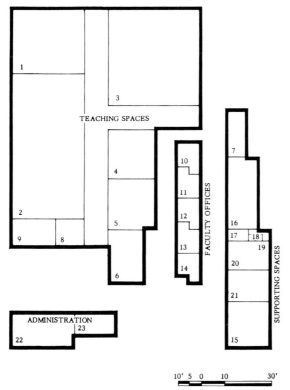

TEACHING SPACES

1. CLASSROOM
2. MULTIPURPOSE ROOM
3. LECTURE DEMONSTRATION ROOM
4-5. STUDENTS' CONFERENCE ROOM
6. REFERENCE READING ROOM
7. STORE ROOM - TEACHING AIDS
8. UTILITY ROOM
9. STORE ROOM

FACULTY SPACES

10-14. FACULTY OFFICES

SUPPORTING SPACES

15. STUDENTS' LOCKER ROOM
16. STUDENTS' LOUNGE
17. JANITOR'S CLOSET
18. VENDING MACHINES
19. TELEPHONE BOOTHS
20. M. TOILETS & WASHROOM
21. W. TOILETS & WASHROOM

ADMINISTRATION SPACES

22. DIRECTOR'S OFFICE
23. LOBBY-RECEPTION AREA

Fig. 4 Space relationships of a practical nursing program in a vocational school.

TABLE 5 Space Requirements for a 1-Year Practical Nursing Program in a Vocational School with an Entering Class and Enrollment of 64

Spaces	Nursing education area			Remarks
	Number of rooms	Group size, each room	Total net area (sq. ft.)	
Teaching	–	–	5,368	
Lecture-demonstration room	1	64	1,600	
Classrooms	1	36	648	
Conference rooms	2	16	600	Additional required in hospital.
Multipurpose room with storage and utility rooms	1	–	2,000	8 beds.
Storage-teaching aids	1	–	120	
Reference-reading room	1	16	400	
Library	–	–	–	Shared.
Faculty	–	–	500	
Offices	5	1	500	
Lounge	–	–	–	School faculty lounge.
Toilets and lockers	–	–	–	Shared.
Administration	–	–	580	
Reception and general office	1	2	160	
Storage area	1	–	80	
Duplicating area	–	–	–	Shared.
Director's office	1	1	340	With coat closet and toilet.
Registrar's office	–	–	–	Shared.
Admissions office	–	–	–	Shared.
Student counselor's office	–	–	–	Shared.
Students' health service	–	–	–	Shared.
Staff lounge	–	–	–	Shared.
Washroom, toilets, and lockers	–	–	–	Shared.
Visitors toilets:				
Men	–	–	–	Shared.
Women	–	–	–	Shared.
Supporting	–	–	1,825	
Students' toilets:				
Men	1	–	180	2 waterclosets, 2 urinals, 2 lavatories.
Women	1	–	180	4 waterclosets, 4 lavatories.
Students' lounge	1	–	400	
Lockers	–	–	400	1 full-size locker for each new student and each staff member.
Janitors' closets	1	–	40	Or as required.
Coat alcoves	–	–	25	Or as required.
Vending machines	–	–	–	As required.
Telephone booths	–	–	–	As required.
Drinking fountains	–	–	–	Minimum of 2 recessed or as required.
General storage	1	–	600	
			8,273	Total net area.
			5,515	For walls, partitions, corridors, stairs, and mechanical space.
			13,788	Total gross area.
			215.4	Area per enrolled student.

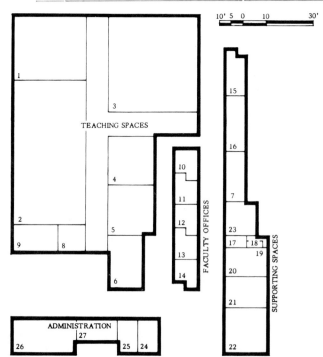

10' 5 0   10   30'

TEACHING SPACES

1. CLASSROOM
2. MULTIPURPOSE ROOM
3. LECTURE DEMONSTRATION ROOM
4-5. STUDENTS' CONFERENCE ROOM
6. REFERENCE READING ROOM
7. STORE ROOM - TEACHING AIDS
8. UTILITY ROOM
9. STORE ROOM

FACULTY SPACES

10-14. FACULTY OFFICES

SUPPORTING SPACES

15. STUDENTS' LOCKER ROOM
16. STUDENTS' LOUNGE
17. JANITOR'S CLOSET
18. VENDING MACHINES
19. TELEPHONE BOOTH
20. M. TOILETS & WASHROOM
21. W. TOILETS & WASHROOM
22. MECHANICAL EQUIPMENT ROOM

ADMINISTRATION SPACES

23. STAFF LOUNGE
24. ADMISSION & REGISTRAR'S OFF.
25. FILES & STATIONERY STORE ROOM
26. DIRECTOR'S OFFICE
27. LOBBY-RECEPTION AREA

Fig. 5 Space relationships of a practical nursing program in a hospital.

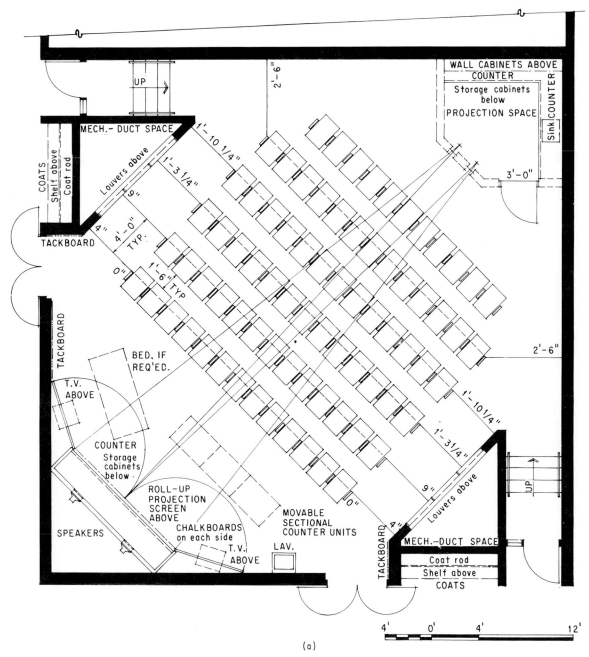

Fig. 6 Lecture-demonstration rooms.

provided for storing charts and diagrams, consideration should be given the need for easy identification and accessibility.

Full-scale skeletons and models of the human body, preferably mounted on a small cart for easy transportation, should be stored in full-size closets. Small models of parts of the human body may be stored in wall cabinets with glazed doors for easy identification. It may be preferable to store certain audiovisual items within the room in which they are used. In addition, a general storage area or room is required, and provision for storing teaching machines should be made.

A building with more than one story will need at least one service elevator for transporting heavy equipment.

Research Facilities

Research facilities will be required only by the baccalaureate and graduate nursing education programs. Typical laboratory arrangements are shown in Fig. 11.

In some instances, nursing education programs will need to develop research facilities either for graduate students or faculty members. The amount of laboratory space required depends upon the type of research program offered. Therefore, before architectural plans are developed, the needs should be carefully evaluated and defined by the faculty members and others who will use the laboratory facilities.

The building program for research facilities

will vary among schools since it must be based on each school's individual requirements. Research facilities may include:
- Biological science laboratories
- Behavioral science laboratories
- The data analysis room including offices and conference room
- Multipurpose project room(s)

Biological Science Laboratories Biological science laboratories will need the following spaces:
- Separate offices for each researcher
- Storage or supply preparation room to serve several laboratories, for equipment, glassware, and supplies
- Deluge shower and eye bath for emergencies

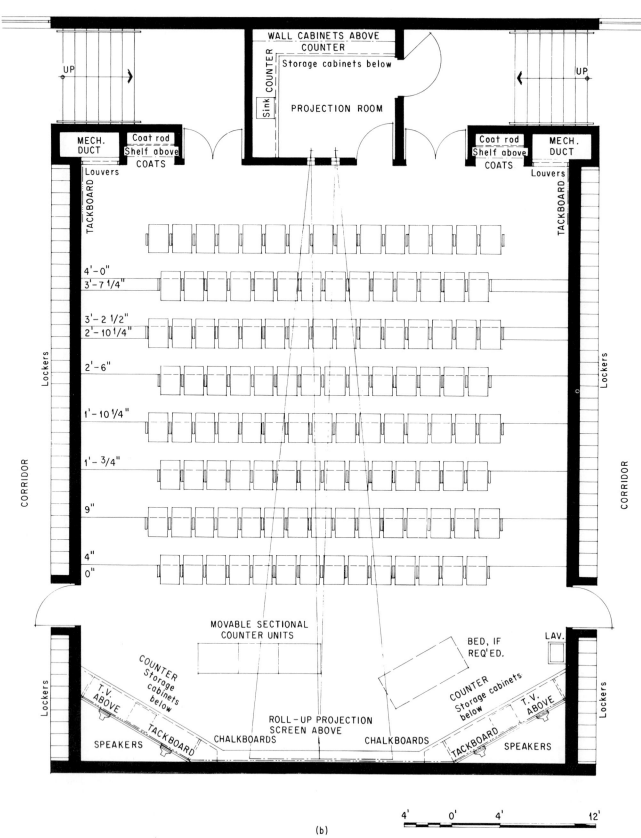

(b)

Fig. 6 (cont.)   Lecture-demonstration rooms.

TABLE 6 Space Requirements for a 1-Year Practical Nursing Program in a Hospital with an Entering Class and Total Enrollment of 64

Spaces	Number of rooms	Group size, each room	Total net area (sq. ft.)	Remarks
Teaching	–	–	5,368	
Lecture-demonstration room	1	64	1,600	
Classrooms	1	36	648	
Conference rooms	2	16	600	Additional required in hospital.
Multipurpose room with storage and utility rooms	1	–	2,000	8 beds.
Storage-teaching aids	1	–	120	
Reference-reading room	1	16	400	
Library	–	–	–	Shared with a hospital.
Faculty	–	–	500	
Offices	–	–	500	
Administration	–	–	780	
Lobby-reception area	1	2	160	
Storage area	1	–	80	
Duplicating area	–	–	–	Shared with hospital.
Director's office	1	1	340	With coat closet and toilet.
Staff lounge and washroom	1	–	200	
Toilets and lockers	–	–	–	
Supporting	–	–	1,265	
Students' toilets:				
Men	1	–	180	2 waterclosets, 2 urinals, 2 lavatories.
Women	1	–	180	4 waterclosets, 4 lavatories.
Students' lounge	1	–	140	
Lockers	–	–	100	
Janitors' closets	1	–	40	Or as required.
Coat alcoves	–	–	25	Or as required.
Vending machines	–	–	–	As required.
Telephone booths	–	–	–	As required.
Drinking fountains	–	–	–	Minimum of 2 recessed or as required.
General storage	1	–	600	
			7,913	Total net area.
			5,275	For walls, corridors, partitions, stairs, and mechanical space.
			13,188	Total gross area.
			206.06	Area per enrolled student.

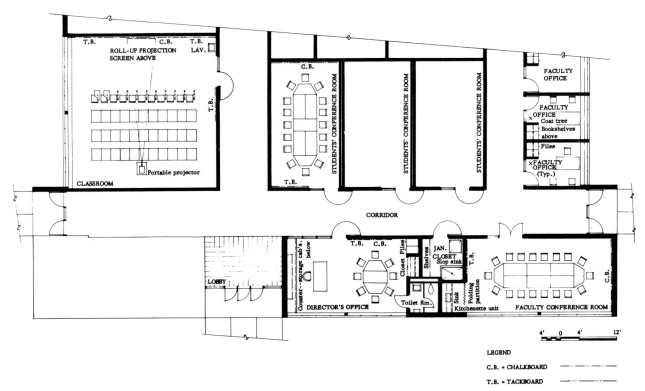

Fig. 7   Student-faculty areas.

Design factors to be considered for these laboratories are:

• Counters of different heights with knee space underneath and reagent shelf. These may be located along the walls or, if the space permits, an island-type counter similar to others should be provided.

• Chemical-resistant sinks with hot and cold water.

• Gas, air, and electrical outlets.

• Fume hoods with adequate exhaust system and sprinkler heads.

• A refrigerator or freezer may be needed for these laboratories.

It is assumed that the animals needed for research will be supplied from a central location, since it would not be economically feasible to construct special animal housing facilities within the nursing education unit.

Behavioral Science Laboratory The primary requirement in the behavioral science laboratory is that the human subject be observed unobtrusively by the students. (See Fig. 12.) Thus, the following design factors should be considered:

1. The laboratory should be large enough to accommodate a bed and various patient care activities. Space is also needed for research personnel and equipment.

2. An adjacent observation room with a one-way viewing glass partition will provide an overall view of the laboratory. The one-way viewing glass partition should be double glazed with sealed airspace between the glass to ensure sound isolation between the two rooms. The viewing screen should be unobtrusive floor-to-ceiling panels rather than a view window which in itself may suggest its purpose. Not all panels need be two-way glass—only those necessary for viewing.

3. The observation room should accommodate 16 students. A stepped seating platform, either permanent or temporary, might be considered to assure all the participants a good overall view of activities within the laboratory. Since the subject should not be disturbed while being observed, observation rooms should be carpeted and should have sound-absorbing materials on walls and ceilings.

4. Provision should be made for communication facilities between the two rooms as well as for concealed recording and audio and physiological factor monitoring equipment.

5. Both the behavioral science laboratory room and the observation room should be equipped with a dimmer switch to control the illumination level. Temperature and humidity controls are also important.

6. Facilities which should be directly accessible from the behavioral science laboratory include:

• Toilet room with lavatory for hand-washing

• Kitchenette or alcove with kitchen accommodations

• Storage room for storing equipment such as children's toys

In conjunction with behavioral science lab-

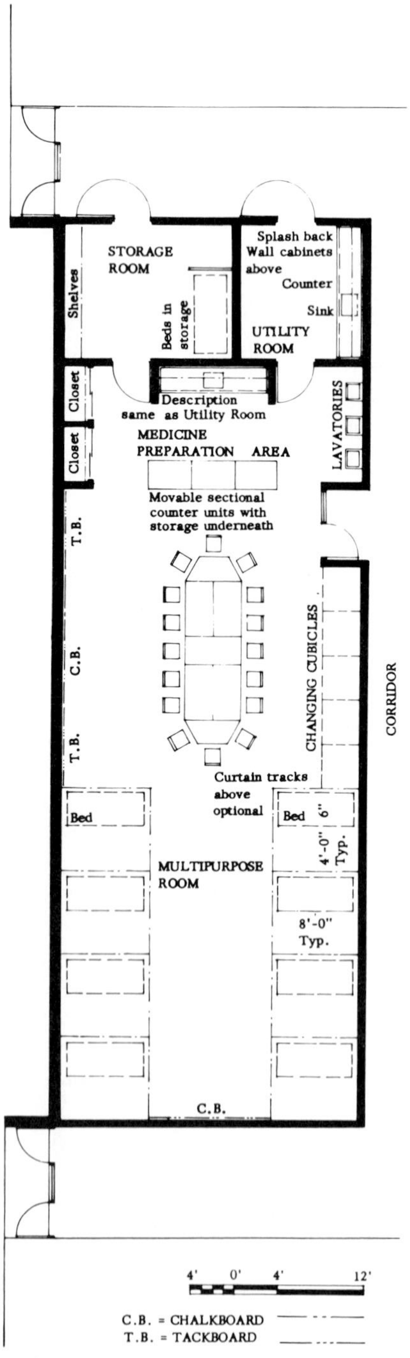

Fig. 8 Multipurpose room.

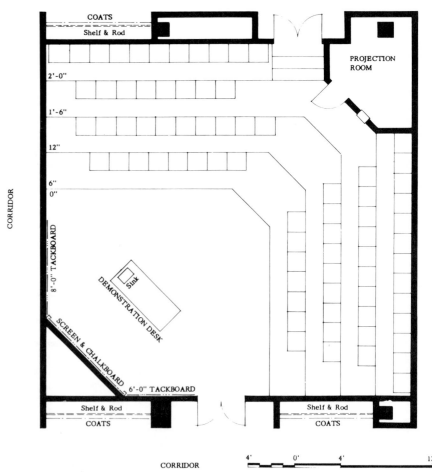

Fig. 9 Lecture-demonstration room at Texas Woman's University College of Nursing, Houston, Texas. (Freeman and Van Ness, Architects.)

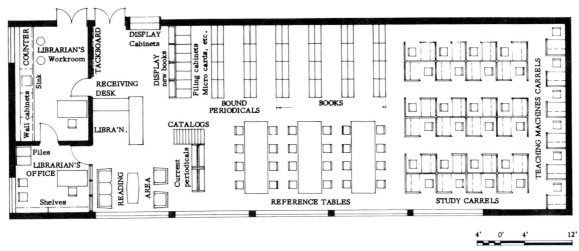

Fig. 10 Library facilities for a diploma nursing program.

oratories, the following should be considered:

1. Waiting room or area, suitably furnished for adults or adults with children.

2. Play nursery for children with provision to oversee the activities from the waiting room. Special attention should be paid to acoustical treatment of this room and its decor.

3. Interviewing rooms, with adjacent observation room, separated by one-way glass viewing partition. (Items 2–5 cited above also apply here.)

Faculty Offices

Faculty offices may be grouped together to form the faculty offices suite. In programs having a small faculty, administrative and business offices may be grouped together with faculty offices forming a unit that is separate in character from the teaching spaces. (See Fig. 7.) In addition to offices for each faculty member, one or more offices might be provided for guest lecturers or visiting faculty.

The faculty offices suite should include:

• Individual offices for each faculty member. Each office should have ample space for furniture, bookcases or shelves, and files.

• Conference room or rooms. The size of the conference room depends on the number of people to be accommodated. Chalkboards and tack boards are necessary in these rooms.

• Faculty lounge. An alcove or small room off the lounge may be provided to accommodate a kitchenette unit and a counter with sink and storage cabinets underneath.

• Toilet facilities including a washroom and locker room or lockers, located in proximity to the lounge or adjoining it. An alcove off the washroom or small room accommodating a sofa, cot, or other suitable furniture might be considered.

• Graduate assistants' office. This room should be furnished with desks for use of teaching assistants or graduate assistants. In addition to the teaching machines located elsewhere in the school for students' use, some teaching machines may be needed in the faculty office suite for use by members of the faculty who may be engaged in developing programed materials.

Data Analysis Room The data analysis room will require space for calculating machines, tables, and office-type furniture. Area allocation should be made for storing data. Other requirements include individual offices and a conference room that can be used by research personnel.

Offices and Ancillary Supporting Areas Requirements for office space and for supporting areas and services will vary from school to school. Each program, therefore, should determine its particular needs. Some of the spaces to be considered include:

1. A lobby and reception area with an information desk as a point of control. The information desk or counter may be incorporated in the general office. In small schools the lobby or reception area may also be the secretary's office and the secretary may also be the receptionist. Toilet facilities for visitors should be conveniently located.

2. General office including space for secretarial staff. The amount of space needed will be based on the ratio of secretaries to faculty members established by the school's policy.

3. Space for filing cabinets for the students' active records. This may be either a part of the general office or a small room directly accessible from the general office. A storage area should be provided for inactive files. Programs organized under hospital control must provide space for permanent storage of student and school records.

4. Space for duplicating equipment including a counter with sink and storage cabinets underneath. This space may be either an alcove in the general office or a small room directly accessible from the general office.

5. Storage room for stationery directly accessible from the general office.

6. Small room for receiving, dispatching, and distributing mail and packages. This room also may serve as a message center for faculty members.

7. An intercommunication control system (switchboard) within the general office. Intercommunication between the rooms within the facility for nursing education is highly desirable. Outside calls should be handled by one

person who would transfer them to the party concerned or, when necessary, take messages.

8. Wall space should be allocated for official bulletin boards either in the lobby waiting area or outside the general office.

9. Storage room for miscellaneous office equipment or furniture.

10. An office for the dean or director. The office should be large enough to accommodate several people for small conferences. A private toilet room with handwashing facilities and a coat closet adjacent to this office is highly desirable. (See Fig. 7.)

11. An office for a secretary adjoining or accessible to the office of the dean or director.

12. Office or offices for assistants or associates of the dean or director. These offices should either be adjacent or in proximity to the office of the dean or director.

13. Office for registrar with ample space for filing cabinets.

14. Office for admissions officer with ample space for filing cabinets.

15. Students' health service and observation area.

16. Office for students' counselor, incorporating waiting area.

17. Office for graduate assistants and fellows, each of whom should have a desk.

18. Janitors' closets and storage space of housekeeping supplies.

Students' Facilities

Provision of student facilities should be governed by such factors as enrollment and the school's physical setting. Whether the facility is a self-contained unit or is a part of a larger education complex is an important consideration. The needs should be evaluated and established individually for each program.

Spaces for the following should be considered:

• Toilet room and washroom for women students with adjoining room or alcove to accommodate a sofa or cot.

• Toilet room and washroom for male students, if any.

• Locker rooms or lockers in corridors.

• A student lounge may be found desirable,

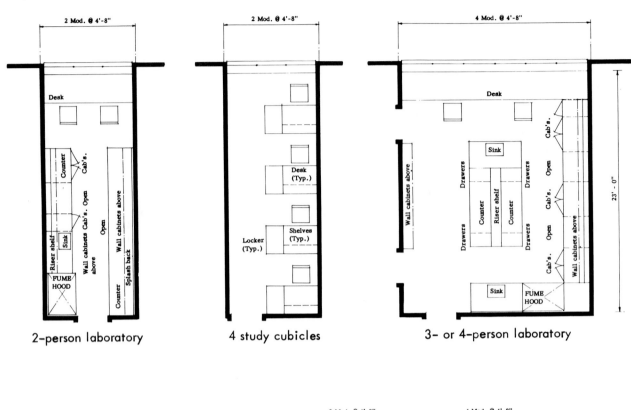

2-person laboratory

4 study cubicles

3- or 4-person laboratory

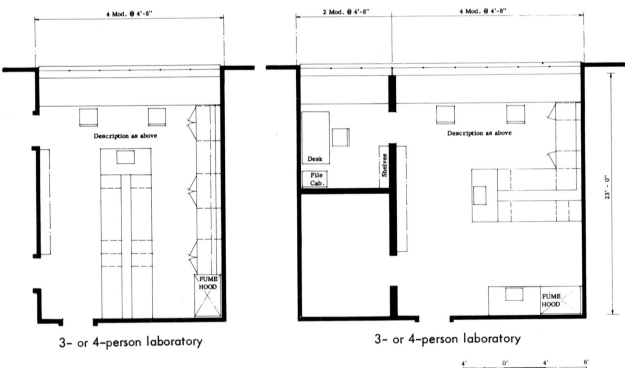

3- or 4-person laboratory

3- or 4-person laboratory

Fig. 11 Typical research laboratory arrangements.

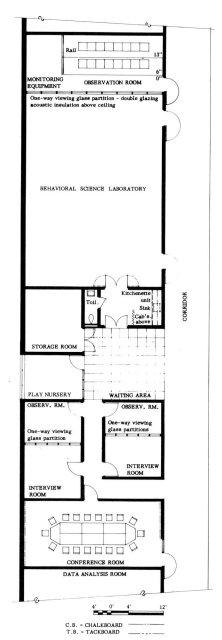

C.B. = CHALKBOARD
T.B. = TACKBOARD

Fig. 12 Behavioral science laboratory for a nursing graduate program.

particularly if no other lounges in the facility are available to nursing students. A lounge may be provided in the students' residence, which may be physically connected with the nursing education facility. In some facilities, students' lounge or lounges are provided, either in the student union building or elsewhere on the college or university campus.

Supporting Areas

Listed below are planning considerations for supporting areas:
- The provision of coat alcoves in corridors may be desirable.
- The need for general storage rooms should be determined by each program.

- Housekeeping and maintenance rooms, including janitors' closets and storage areas for housekeeping supplies and equipment, will be needed.
- Space should be allocated for vending machines either in alcoves of corridor or centralized in one room assigned for this purpose.
- An adequate number of public pay telephone booths should be located in strategic locations in alcoves off corridors so that traffic will not be obstructed.
- An adequate number of drinking fountains or water coolers should be placed in alcoves off corridors or recessed in the wall so that traffic flow will not be obstructed.

Continuing Education

Continuing education is usually a part of the overall school facility. However, for the purposes of nursing education, it would have the following elements:
- Assembly room to seat a large group
- Conference rooms
- Lounge room and space for coffee service
- Reception and registration area
- Men's and women's toilets
- If warranted, offices for the continuing education director and staff

Assembly Room The number of people to be accommodated in the assembly room will depend upon the individual facility. In general, provision should be made for 100 or more persons, seated along rows of tables or groups of sectional tables. A movable platform to elevate the speaker should be considered.

If found desirable, this room may be subdivided into from two to four conference spaces by means of folding partitions which should preferably stack up in a wall alcove designed for this purpose. They should be selected for maximum sound-retardant properties to limit the passage of sound from one space to the other. Sound reduction of at least 25 to 30 decibels is considered minimum. These conference spaces should have chalkboards and tack boards.

Conference Rooms In some institutions it may be desirable not to subdivide the assembly room, in which case four or five small conference-type rooms should be provided, each to accommodate from 20 to 25 persons. These rooms should have separate entrances, should be equipped with chalkboards and tack boards, and should be arranged with seats around tables for face-to-face conferences.

Reception and Registration Area Definite allocation for the reception and registration area should be made. Coat room or alcove for depositing the outer garments should be incorporated.

Lounge Room. A lounge room should be provided large enough to accommodate the anticipated number of participants in the Continuing Education Program. An alcove accommodating a kitchenette unit, counter for coffee service, and vending machines may be considered desirable.

An adequate number of toilets should be convenient to this area.

Health

YOUTH TREATMENT CENTERS

By Kenneth Ricci, Architect

BACKGROUND

The residential treatment concept has its foundation in the *halfway house* program originally developed for men returning from prison to the outside world. Residence in the halfway house, as its name implies, was an intermediate stage between prison and freedom, during which the ex-convict could readjust to normal responsibilities, look for a job, and resume an independent life, all within the security of the house. It was a temporary situation providing bed, board, advice, and company. From the halfway house the newly freed man was expected to begin an independent, constructive life.

The basic attribute of the halfway house was that it provided independence within a framework of emotional and financial security. The house was used for adults as well as juvenile ex-offenders. Perhaps the most famous house for adolescents is the Highfields House, established in New Jersey in 1948. Highfields was the model for virtually all the initial juvenile halfway houses. The concept has spread widely because of its humane approach and its recorded successes, until presently the residential treatment concept is being used for narcotics treatment, youth offenders, probation cases, and social service shelters.

Unlike the original halfway house, which was a way station between prison and the outside, the residential treatment centers presently are operated for ex-offenders as well as for those with no criminal conviction who are referred to the program. The efficacy of this approach is considered to lie in the residential, as opposed to the institutional, character of the facility—maximum size is usually between 25 and 30—and in the *treatment* of residents rather than their punishment or neglect.

TARGET POPULATION

Community-based residential treatment centers are now being operated for a variety of programs. Correction, narcotics, and probation agencies now include residential, neighborhood-based programs as part of their treatment spectrum. Youth agencies, on both municipal and state levels, operate programs for adjudicated youths as well as youths referred from family court as a condition of probation or referred from public or private agencies with parental consent.

Private agencies also operate residential facilities for young people referred from their family counseling bureaus with attitudinal or behavioral problems. Among private drug treatment programs, the "house" concept is widely used, with many variations ranging from in-city programs to monastic retreats.

Whatever the program, the target population includes those young people who express a desire to improve their life; those who can relate to people—adults, peers—either negatively or positively, but who are willing to deal with others; those who can recall their past and are willing to discuss it; those first offenders who

would be brutalized by a large institution or even those who are not convicted of crime but need a release from pressures in the home environment.

GOALS

The basic goal of this type of program is *treatment*, rather than punishment, for antisocial behavior. Other goals usually are *control* of activity within the facility and in the immediate neighborhood, *services* for the residents (i.e., medical, educational, employment, recreation), and proper *administration* of the total program.

The purpose of this report is not to delve into the conceptual foundations too deeply, especially since these vary from agency to agency, but to set forth some general goals and examine how these can be translated into an architectural approach (see "Architectural Considerations," below).

Treatment in these centers is currently focused on peer group interaction. Through the use of pressure from peers in group therapy sessions, individuals are forced to deal with their behavior, its motives, and its consequences. These therapy groups, with no more than 10 to 12 members, are led by staff members. Ideally, members of the group should share living and sleeping areas in the program. This becomes an important design concern. Individual *counseling* is also done by various staff members, from ex-residents through psychiatrists. An important aspect of treatment comes through coping with the simple routine of daily living with peers, neighbors, employers, teachers, and staff. Exposure to nonprofessional staff, like the woman cook or custodian, provides important links to parental or big-brother figures. Often the cook is the only woman accessible to the young resident in the facility.

Control in the residential center is not applied as it is in the prison, with walls and barriers, but instead it is implied through behavior standards set by the staff and peer group. In this way, self-control will hopefully become internalized and remain active while the resident is out of the facility and especially

Illustrative Area Requirements

(Typical Program for 21-bed unit — intended only as a guide)

Space	Area, sq ft	Remarks
Administration:		
Director's office	175	
Secretary, reception, files . . .	200	Preferably near entry for control.
Assistant director	150	
Interview offices, 2, at 100 sq ft each	200	For private interviews between resident and caseworker.
Kitchen	350	
Food storage, garbage room, and receiving room	250	Depends on purchasing patterns and delivery schedule of supplies.
Dining room (capacity: 30).	600	Family-style service. No serving counter. Staff and residents share dining room.
Lounge	600	Quiet activities.
Recreation	600	Active activities.
Public toilet	As required	Men's and women's lavatories accessible to above spaces.
Bedrooms, 21 at 100 sq ft each	2,100	
Residents baths.	As required	5 W.C., 5 lavatories, 5 tubs or showers.
Counselor's bedrooms, 2, at 150 sq ft each	300	
Laundry room	As required	
Linen storage	As required	
Director's apartment	1,500	Should have private entrance.
Net total	7,025	
Gross total*	10,725	

*Gross = 1.5 net; includes mechanical equipment space, corridors and stairs, toilets and baths, janitor's closet, custodian's room, construction thickness.

616

after he has left the program. Of course, audio and visual control are necessary for general security. Ease of supervision should be built into the building so that staff can generally see and hear what is happening without deliberate snooping.

Access is usually through only one door, and this will have to be controlled in order to keep track of who comes and goes. Electrical security devices include remote sensors for doors, closed-circuit television, smoke detectors, etc. These devices are used only with utmost discretion, especially the television eye, since they could seriously compromise the treatment approach.

Services such as medical care, education, employment, and recreation may be supplied by the facility but should ideally be accessible in the community. Since most programs stress learning to adjust to "real life," education, recreation, and employment in the neighborhood are encouraged. Larger facilities may have to provide these services; the more community services are available, of course, the more economical and effective the smaller program will be, insofar as it simulates home environment.

Administration varies according to the facility. Basic staff usually includes a director, assistant director, secretary, live-in counselors, visiting counselors, and cook. According to the type of program, teachers, social workers, and work supervisors may be included as optional. Since therapy groups include all or half of the residents, they are usually run by the director or his assistant with the aid of the counselors. This minimizes staff numbers and maximizes interaction.

Quarters are often provided within the facility for the director and/or assistant director (sometimes including family) as well as the live-in counselors. The director's quarters ought to be distinctly separate but adjacent; live-in counselors reside within the facility, adjacent to their respective groups. Live-in directors are a departure from institutional precedents but are quite frequent in this type of program. When staff and residents live together, confidence and stability are encouraged. The architect should keep in mind the privacy requirements of the family in residence. Since programs are located in a community, isolation of the live-in family is less a problem than it would be on the grounds of an institution.

With regard to the tabulated area requirements, it should be noted that

• Twenty-one beds is an arbitrary size, used here for illustration only. Any program with a few less residents will not efficiently utilize the facilities listed; any program with a larger number of residents might lose the residential quality. Numbers will vary from agency to agency, but rule of thumb puts optimum size between 21 and 30. The total population should ideally be a multiple of a therapy group.

• Making efficient use of administrative staff while maximizing residential milieu is the rationale for the seven-bed-unit approach. Three physically separate seven-bed units are each run by a pair of houseparents, all under the supervision of one administrator. Neighborhoods apparently accept seven more readily than twenty or thirty new young residents, especially since seven youths plus two houseparents can move right into an existing two-family home. Renting the home keeps it on the tax rolls. One seven-bed unit was set up in an apartment in a New York City housing project. The seven-bed unit operates like a private household and has just about the same type of residential requirements that a family of nine has.

• Certain spaces, like lounge or recreation spaces, can be made accessible to community groups for their use. These spaces should have access directly from entry and should adjoin public toilets. Directors like to make their facilities available to neighbors in order to build good relations.

• The irreducible design element in this type of program is the therapy group. The residents who share the same group therapy sessions are usually grouped together in sleeping areas, so that throughout the design the group's size and integrity ought to be reflected in the layout of the various spaces.

SITE SELECTION

The entire concept of community-based residential treatment hinges on the location of the facility in a neighborhood setting similar to that to which the resident will return.

Each locale will have different criteria for site selection. Each will have specific problems. The most common problems are zoning restriction, building code restrictions, and the opposition of local residents. Local resistance can be quite intense initially; one architectural reaction to this problem is to purchase and renovate an existing building in order to keep low visibility. For such purposes programs should be kept to smallest size feasible (see table, above, showing area requirements), like the seven-bed unit. Leasing a building keeps it on the tax rolls. Renovation can be a trap if the building is not sound; examine foundations and floors, and especially plumbing, electrical wiring, and heating. Client's patience can be worn very thin and extras can mount on a bad choice. (See "Special Considerations" below.)

Programs should be near transportation to schools, jobs, recreation. The more outside services are accessible to the residents, the less services the program itself needs to provide. Likewise, proximity to transportation will make it easier to attract staff personnel and for visitors, family, university consultants, etc., to reach the program. On-site parking spaces may be compulsory in some suburban neighborhoods.

Where conditions permit, an outside recreation area is desirable. In the urban facility, the rooftop of a new building can be made to fill this function provided that it meets local codes. Too much land around a program can, however, isolate it from the community and reinforce an institutional attitude on the part of residents and staff. The spatial distance between community and facility can often be overcome by mechanical means; the social distance between the two must be overcome by staff and residents in order to allow the program to bear fruit. Making spaces available to local groups, for example, decreases the social distance between home and neighborhood. Proper site selection can accomplish much in reducing social distances.

ARCHITECTURAL CONSIDERATIONS

This discussion of some typical areas of the building designed is intended to be illustrative, not definitive. It gives an indication of the various interwoven considerations—economic, behavioral, administrative—that play upon the design process.

Territory and Status

For the architect, two key conceptual tools in arranging spaces in a facility like this are *territory* and *status*. The provision of clearly defined territorial boundaries—private, semi-public, public—in institutional situations is an aid to residents in guiding themselves and their actions. Certainly territory—one's room, one's den—is at issue even within a family, and still more so in a program, regardless how intimate

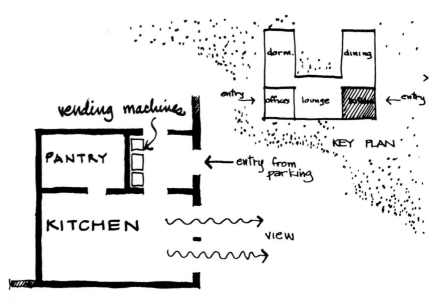

Fig. 1 Kitchen planning concepts in a suburban residence.
In this enlarged plan of a kitchen it can be seen that location near the entry yields several benefits: the cook has full-time view of entry and parking lot; ease of deliveries; interaction of woman cook with boys—boys do chores in return for snacks and recognition. Visual control: view of parking and entry. Aural control: vending machine noise, door hinges tell of activity at door. Interpersonal control: most boys use entry at kitchen side while staff and secretaries use entry at office side. Kitchen has more action, more status, more snacks.

YOUTH TREATMENT CENTERS

or small-scale. As intimacy and trust increase, the pressure to defend territory seems to decrease. That is the point when some programs remove locks from personal belongings—to test out the group's attitudes.

Likewise by sharing territory, one shares an extension of oneself. When the cook asks residents to help, to do favors, run errands, she returns the favor by sharing her territory—her status—with the youngsters. By the same token, some spaces have no status. The notoriously empty "lounges" in some facilities bear witness to this, while young people crowd into the room of a favorite counselor. The spaces in these cases have a certain value because of the status of their inhabitants, while other spaces have little or no status. In so intensely social a situation as the residential center, the design of spaces must be modulated by acute behavioral considerations such as territory and status. Each person ought to be able to easily identify his territory—room and belongings, office or kitchen—while at the same time he should be able to share all or part of it with another. This goes for both staff and residents. Often staff use their authority to control or lock off certain spaces, and in the process they convey the sense of dominance so often associated with institutions. The architect cannot control the inhabitants, but he can make himself aware of the issues and learn to modulate the design of space to account for their relation to behavior. These concepts—territory and status—are only two among many. Further reference vectors are found in "Information Resources," below.

Kitchen

In the smallest facilities (seven-bed), the kitchen is simply residential in design. Since program sizes vary, it is not constructive to enumerate kitchen equipment or kitchen area. General performance criteria for kitchens are as follows:

• Residents almost universally help in the kitchen. This is part of the responsibility of all residents to lend support to the house. All equipment, furnishings, and detail should therefore be of extra heavy-duty construction since it will be exposed to hard and inexperienced personnel. A safe and easily maintained design could have tiled surfaces, floor drains, and metal pan ceilings for fire retardance, washability, and sound dampening.

• Relation to dining room can be informal, since family-style service is often used.

• The cook, often the one accessible woman in the facility, should not be isolated by the kitchen design. The kitchen should be, if not central, at least conveniently located in regard to the common and entry areas.

• In smaller programs the kitchen can be designed as a control point near the main entry in order to capitalize on the full-time presence of the cook during the day. This is economically wise from the staffing viewpoint. Young people will gravitate toward the kitchen for available snacks. Figure 1 illustrates a kitchen serving several goals in a 20-bed program: food preparation, entry supervision, and interaction of boys and cook.

Bedrooms

• Single room occupancy is usually preferred in these programs. For many residents this will be the first time that they have had a private room, private territory, of their own. For economy, bedroom sizes are usually minimal. While the value of privacy is considered

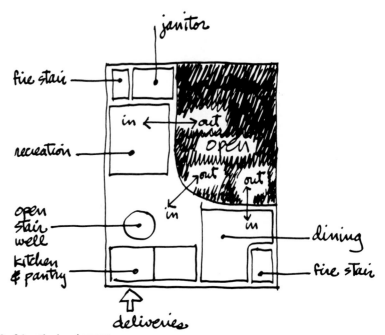

Fig. 2 Schematic plan—basement.
The basement lets out onto the open yard. Dining, recreation, and circulation connect with the outdoors. Kitchen connects to the street side. Open stairwell communicates sights and sounds to the first floor.

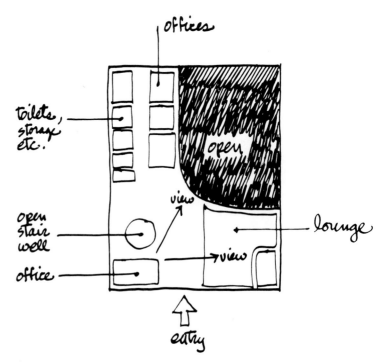

Fig. 3 Schematic plan—first floor.
The first floor is the hub. Use of the lounge by local folks can reduce social distance between program and community, so it is placed near entry and toilets. Office near entry has a view of inside and outside, of upstairs and downstairs. The eye and the ear replace the foot for control.

great, it is important to arrange the individual rooms so that the resident cannot deliberately isolate himself from the activities of the program.

• Dormitories and four-man rooms are often used, while two-man rooms are often discouraged because of aggression, turnover rates, and homosexuality. In the dormitory situation, the strains of daily communal living are multiplied. The supply of private "territory" is at a minimum and constantly subject to aggression, theft, damage, etc. In dormitory design, therefore, it is important to give thought to provision of easily identified and defensible territory in the form of furniture, storage, shelving, bed, textured or colored floor surface or change in floor levels, ceiling heights, etc. (see Furnishings, below). For most residents, their sleeping area and belongings constitute their entire worldly possessions; therefore the maintenance of these becomes very important. The diagram (Fig. 5) indicates an approach to creating an immediate private zone around the bed, providing easily defined space and lockability and meeting personal storage needs.

Control

Residential, community-based programs usually require no overt physical constraints on residents. No walls. No locked doors. Instead of physical control, these programs aim initially at developing a sensitivity to social control in youths and ultimately at a sense of self-control. The mechanisms for creating these internal controls are group therapy sessions, individual counseling, exposure to community living from a stable, supportive residential base, and a frankness and intimacy among staff and residents. In short, the aim is to simulate a domestic environment with responsibilities shared by youths and staff. For this reason, residents must help in the kitchen, residents and staff eat together, and staff lives on the premises (with family or without).

Physical controls in the traditional sense are usually not used. Nevertheless, a certain measure of supervision by the staff must be pos-

sible, just as a well-designed house enables a mother to keep track of her children, either indoors or out. The architect has at his disposal three unobtrusive supervision methods: aural, visual, and movement supervision. The relation of corridors, windows, and key rooms like kitchen and offices, will enable staff persons to hear if not see the activity of the house. Open stairwells (building codes permitting) and courtyards carry sounds. Sounds carry messages. By locating vending machines properly, the cook in the illustrated kitchen (Fig. 1) can keep track of activity near the door. Visual supervision is the most difficult to achieve without resorting to long corridors, view panels on bedroom doors, etc. By using hard materials in key areas, sounds can be reinforced and transmitted. The control of movement through architectural design can enhance supervision. Judicious placement of entry, kitchen, and lounges—the natural gravitation points of hungry teen-agers — can ensure a view of moving people by staff. A window overlooking a parking lot or an office by a stairway are effective means of supervision in a small center. See accompanying diagrams (Figs. 2, 3, and 4).

SPECIAL CONSIDERATIONS

Renovations

Renovations are attractive to many agencies because of the public pressure for action and the budget restrictions on capital construction. When operating with a tight schedule or a tight-fisted comptroller, the lure of renovation is strong. Under such conditions, renovation should not be extensive. Mechanical, electrical, and plumbing facilities should be in good enough condition to remain, otherwise cutting and patching for a new system will drive up the cost. Extensive renovation is exceedingly time-consuming and contractors competent in such work are scarce and expensive. The only reason to consider renovation on a large scale would be if the building has special historic or esthetic value to the community or the program.

While the cost per square foot of major renovation can be 20 to 30 percent less than new construction, a well-planned new facility often needs less square feet than an existing building. Ultimately the total costs of renovation and new construction will not be far apart. As a rule of thumb, say that if renovation cost is 75 percent or more of comparable new construction, new construction is preferable since it can be completed faster, will have less contingency costs, and can be designed much more efficiently.

Mechanical Equipment (H.V.A.C., electrical, plumbing, elevators) Saving existing equipment may be false economy for two reasons. First, it may inhibit efficient, effective planning. Second, the original equipment may be faulty. Check existing maintenance and expense record if available; this will give an inkling as to past performance. Installing new mechanical equipment in an existing structure is costlier than installation in a new structure; add 15 percent of equipment cost for cutting and patching.

Code Checklist When considering the renovation potential of an existing building, some basic factors ought to be considered.

a. Multiple dwelling codes and/or social service regulations may place restrictions on the number of occupants per room, regardless of room size. Check applicable codes to determine the building's capacity for sleep-in occupants.

b. The required fire protection devices (alarms, smoke or thermal detectors, sprinkler systems) are based on the construction classification of the building; its area and height; and the number, age, and physical condition of its residents. When considering renovation, check the area, height, and construction class of your building against the fire protection requirements of the building code as well as municipal or state social service regulations. Fire protection regulations for public agencies are strict even when there are as few as seven or nine residents in a standard residential dwelling; certainly they are far stricter than requirements for one-family dwellings.

A new water service and sprinkler systems can be expensive in urban areas. Additional expenditures for a pump to provide adequate water pressure may be needed. In some areas, a water meter must be attached to the sprinkler system by law.

c. Egress requirements are usually stringent. The entire building (especially if multi-storied) should have two means of egress via fire-rated corridors and openings. Assembly areas (dining, auditorium, lecture) should also have direct, unobstructed egress. One egress may be acceptable if protected by sprinklers, smoke or heat detector, and alarm system.

d. Local fire departments may also have rules calling for special equipment for group occupancy structures: smoke detectors, alarm systems, fire extinguishers, and perhaps persons trained in emergency techniques.

e. Rooftop areas, especially in urban sites, often have the potential for excellent recreation areas when proper protection, egress, and area requirements are met. Rooftops may require separate certificate of occupancy.

f. Floors should be capable of carrying the large live loads required for assembly areas (dining, auditorium, recreation, corridor). It is often difficult to prove live load capacity to a building department if the original plans of an old building are lacking. Replacing existing floors with capable floors is tricky and expensive.

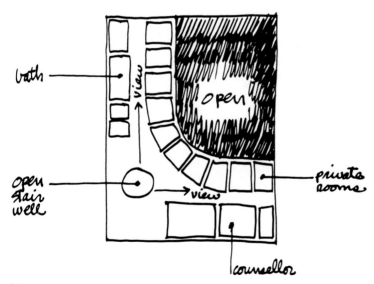

Fig. 4 Schematic plan—bedroom floor.
The concept illustrates a group of private areas or rooms around a common territory, the open yard. Open stairwell gives a view down each corridor. A counsellor lives on each floor. The plan is open, yet each territory is defined.

YOUTH TREATMENT CENTERS

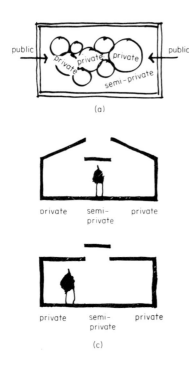

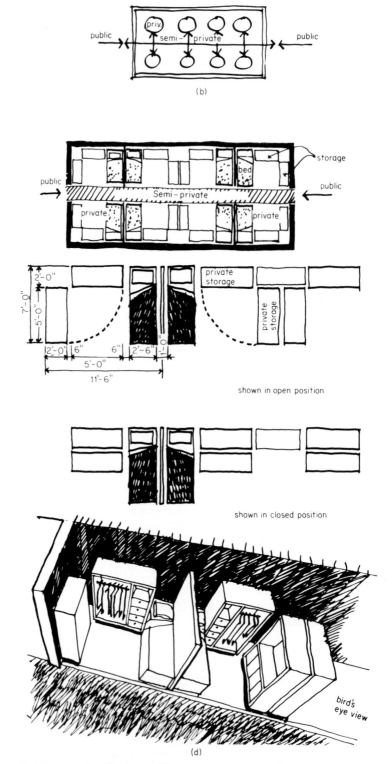

Building Codes These can be flexible. If a particular building is well suited to your needs and yet cannot be made to comply with local codes in certain categories, a reconsideration may be requested based on need and on a willingness to provide extra safeguards or concessions in other categories of the code.

Leasing

The leasing of small, sound residences ready for immediate occupancy has been done for seven-bed units. This is the quickest and least obtrusive means of filling the architectural needs of a program, since the houseparents and residents move right in without disturbing the physiognomy of the neighborhood. The decision to lease or buy will be made according to the agency's financial policy. Leasing keeps the property on the local tax rolls; this can be a benefit when developing rapport with the community. The relatively modest investment in such a situation gives the agency great freedom to cope with a changing neighborhood, changing treatment concepts, or budget fluctuations by returning the lease or allowing it to lapse when the facility is no longer viable.

CONSTRUCTION, FURNISHINGS, AND SPECIAL EQUIPMENT

Construction

• *Generally*, surfaces should be finished to provide ease of cleaning or painting, resistance to heavy wear and defacement, fire retardance, and noise dampening. The general starkness of such surfaces in bedrooms, corridors, stair halls, etc., can be relieved with use of chromatic colors and, in the lounge areas (for example), by use of carpet on floors and walls. Youngsters usually respond to unusual textures and strong colors. Administrators usually

Fig. 5 Graphic concepts of territory in group living.
(a) Undefined territories. Definition of territory varies from occupant to occupant, depending on his status within the peer group. (b) Defined territories. Definition of public, semi-private, and private areas is accomplished by using architectural elements. Therefore, size and shape of private territory are not dependent on individual's status. Private areas can be defined as zones within a dormitory or as individual rooms along a corridor. See accompanying diagrams. (c) Dormitory with defined territories. Bed and lockable storage units (see enlarged sketch) form private territory zones along semi-private walkway. Walkway can be defined by using space texture, color. (d) Private territory.

do not. Sound dampening increases the intimacy of a room and lessens the institutional feeling.

• *Glass areas* should be kept small; large areas ought to be tempered or wireglass. Window dimensions—opening size, height above finished floor—should reflect the more intimate scale required for children in a domestic setting.

• *Hardware.* The open nature of residential treatment usually calls for nothing more than a sturdy grade of domestic hardware. This will depend on the program director. All individual bedrooms and offices should have key locks; provide a master key for staff personnel. Bathroom privacy is kept intact normally, with doors on all toilet stalls.

Furnishings

Domestic furniture, sturdy, ample, and colorful, fills the bill for most areas, including dining, lounge, and group rooms. Bedrooms are discussed below. In many programs residents build their own furniture as an economy measure. Some administrators believe that residents take better care of such furniture and equipment than of ordinary institutional furniture. Administrative areas require file cabinets, typing desks, etc., all of which should fit into the domestic scale.

Individual Bedrooms These should have a writing and reading surface, clothing storage (hanging and folded), suitcase storage, seating for two or three, and a single bed. Storage areas should have key locks, as should the room doors. Seating and storage might be built in and/or incorporated in the architecture (a window seat, for example). Ample tack board and shelves should be provided for pinups, posters, etc. For many residents, especially young people, this will probably be the first time they have had a private room; the room is considered an individual's "territory" and as such should be susceptible to some rearrangement according to his/her idiosyncrasies—often the arrangement of a room will give the staff an indication of the occupant's character.

Group Bedrooms or Dormitories These should provide the same basic "territorial" needs as the private rooms: sleeping, sitting, writing/reading, locked storage, display surfaces (tack board, shelves). The necessity for easily identified and defensible territory is acute in institutional programs, especially in communal living arrangements, since there is less privacy in these circumstances. Conflict between residents is lessened when personal belongings can be securely stored. Some programs remove locks when they feel that intragroup trust has been built up. The architectural solution to this territorial question has an important impact on group living. In a dormitory situation, compact, foldaway territory provides one type of solution. See Fig. 5.

Special Equipment (Optional)

• Intercom between staff areas
• Emergency lighting and power system
• Central smoke detection system and/or fire alarm system

• Closed circuit television and videotape facility for group therapy sessions
• Master antenna system
• Elevator
• Garbage disposal or condenser

INFORMATION RESOURCES

Agencies

The following agencies either operate community-based, residential treatment centers themselves or advise on and regulate the operation of such centers. Contact agencies of a similar nature in your area for material, permission to visit, and interviews with staff and administration. Most programs are quite enthusiastic about visitors. Those listed are intended only as examples of such agencies. The persons named are those with whom the author has been in communication.

New York

New York State Division for Youth
2 University Place
Albany, N.Y. 12205

Operates rural and urban programs ranging from 7-bed units to 60-bed camps.

New York State Department of Social Services
1450 Western Avenue
Albany, N.Y. 12203

Responsible for designing and operating public programs and for regulating and licensing private programs of various sizes.

California

State of California
Department of Corrections
California Rehabilitation Center
P.O. Box 841
Corona, Calif. 91720

Operates many treatment modalities within a large compound and has experimented with concepts in innovative institutional living.

Florida

State of Florida Division of Youth Services
311 South Calhoun
Tallahassee, Fla. 32304

Operates youth programs on a residential scale at several urban and suburban locations and is expanding these facilities rapidly.

Ohio

International Halfway House Association
2316 Auberncrest
Cincinnatti, Ohio 45219

Organization representing halfway houses of many modalities, run for many types of individuals by both public and private agencies. A good central source for locating programs in practically all the states of the Union.

Federal

National Clearinghouse for Criminal Justice and Planning
Department of Architecture
University of Illinois
1102 W. Main St.
Urbana, Ill. 61801

National Institute sponsors inventories of current correctional programs, research into correctional modes, and demonstration projects. Contact the Institute for list of projects and publications.

Publications

Most agencies produce many unpublished but informative papers, monographs, memorandums, etc., dealing with their particular approach. These are valuable and should be ferreted out. A representative sampling of published material follows:

Design for Change

Model Treatment Program
Bradley, Smith, Salstrom
National Council on Crime and Delinquency
Crocker/Citizens Savings Bank Building
Sacramento, Calif.

A project, sponsored by the Ford Foundation, which studies the restructuring of the entire treatment milieu—staff, clients, administration, architecture.

The Non-Prison

A New Approach to Treating Youthful Offenders
Bruce Publishing Company
Milwaukee, Wis. 1970
Introduction by Richard McGee,

Book version of Model Treatment Program.

Survey of Halfway Houses in the United States

Oliver J. Keller
Center for Studies in Criminal Justice, Chicago, Ill., 1968.

Youthful Offenders at Highfields: An Evaluation of the Effects of Short-Term Treatment of Delinquent Boys.

H. Ashley Weeks
Ann Arbor, University of Michigan Press, Ann Arbor, Mich., 1958.

The Hidden Dimension

Edward T. Hall
Anchor Books, Doubleday & Company, Inc., Garden City, N.Y., 1969.

Study of proxemics, the distance regulations in the animal world and in man's culture. A good, basic book on spaces and their messages.

On Social Control and Collective Behavior

Robert Ezra Park
Selected papers, edited and with introduction by Ralph H. Turner,
University of Chicago Press, Chicago, Ill., ca. 1967.

A good sampling of this sociologist's work and views, including concepts of social distance and human ecology, both basic and vital to architectural design.

Others Basic readings in "social ecology" and behavior can be found in the works of Erving Goffman, Humphrey Osmond, Robert Sommer, et al., both in book form and in periodicals.

Health

MULTIPHASIC HEALTH SCREENING CENTERS

GENERAL HISTORY OF MULTIPHASIC SCREENING

Present multiphasic screening programs could be considered an extension of the mass chest x-ray program begun in the 1940s. As the incidence of tuberculosis declined, the usefulness of these particular screening units diminished. However, in the 1950s with the control of most acute diseases, there was a renewed interest in chronic disorders and mass-screening for them.

Today, not only the medical profession but also business and industry are beginning to realize the importance of preventive medicine. Some examples are: the Kaiser Foundation, an industry-founded trust in California, offers computerized screening to its 1.5 million members; the Metropolitan Life Insurance Company plans to provide automated tests for over 50,000 employees; and the Cannery Workers' Union in California, which can screen 20,000 workers during the three-month canning season, makes multiphasic screening available to its members in three 60-ft long trailers.

This use of comprehensive screening both in specialized clinics and in mobile units is the beginning of providing preventive medical care and health education for all people.

FUNCTIONAL ANALYSIS

The following is a resumé of tests that could be performed in a multiphasic screening unit. Some procedures are more sophisticated than others and, therefore, might be more difficult to adapt to this situation. The more common tests are enumerated: however, this order does not necessarily reflect proper test sequence. Equipment necessary for the various stations has been included with the appropriate test description.

The screenee presents his appointment card to the volunteer or receptionist. This may be in the same area as registration or it may be in a separate location.

History

A semienclosed cubicle or private room is desirable for registration in order to obtain an accurate medical history. The screenee may be reluctant to answer personal questions in an area where others may overhear him. One solution to this problem is to have the screenee fill out a history questionnaire at home before his appointment; however, those who do not read or speak English fluently and those who are illiterate may need help in answering these questions. During return appointments, screenees should fill out an interval medical history.

Relocatable Multiphasic Health Screening, Research and Graduate Center, School of Architecture, Texas A & M University, College Station, Texas Health Services Research, Federal Health Programs Services.

Dressing Area

Dressing areas may be provided for use before or after cardiopulmonary tests, chest x-ray, mammography, thermography, pap-smear, and proctoscopy/sigmoidoscopy. The screenee removes all clothing to the waist and dons a radiolucent disposable gown.

Anthropometry

At this station, the screenee's height, weight, and temperature will be measured and recorded. Various other body measurements may be taken at this time for anthropometrical research projects. A skinfold thickness test (subscapular and triceps) is performed to determine the degree of obesity. (See Fig. 1.)

Vision

The screenee may be examined for visual acuity with a Snellen chart or various types of stereoscopic screening devices may be used to test for fusion, acuity level, color and binocular vision, thus eliminating the need for a Snellen chart. (See Fig. 2.)

After receiving proparacain HCl eye drops or a similar medication as a topical anesthetic, he is tested for glaucoma, increased intraocular pressure, by means of a tonometer. If the electronic tonometer is used, no drops are needed.

He is prepared for retinal photography with phenylephrine HCl or similar drops in one eye 20 minutes before the test to dilate the pupil.

If photography is not used, he may be examined with an ophthalmoscope; however, this requires trained personnel.

Retinal Photo

A fundus camera is used to take a 35 mm photograph of the retina 20 minutes after mydriatic eye drops are instilled to detect any pathology (e.g., disc changes, retinal arteriosclerosis, hypertensive angiopathy, diabetic retinopathy, etc.). Depending on the type and strength of mydriatic drops used, the 20-minute limit may be exceeded. (See Fig. 3.)

Hearing

Hearing perception is tested through measurement of tone thresholds. Various frequencies are tested using increasing and decreasing tone volumes. Audiometric testing may be primarily self-administered by means of a special audiometer. Quality of the earphones is more important than the degree of soundproofing. (See Fig. 4.)

Glucose Ingestion

The screenee is given a 75 gm glucose medium to ingest. This may be dispensed in bottles or in a refrigerated carbonated beverage unit. The time of administration is recorded on the appropriate card. At the end of one hour (determined by the screening unit), a blood sample will be drawn and tested for glucose. Testing exactly on the predetermined hour is vital to this test's accuracy.

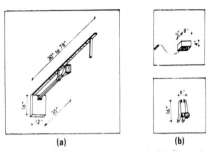

Fig. 1 (a) Scale with measuring rod. (b) Electronic thermometer skinfold calipers.

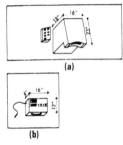

Fig. 2 (a) Vision tester. (b) Electronic tonometer.

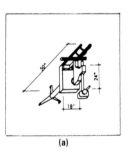

Fig. 3 (a) Fundus camera. (b) Portable fundus camera.

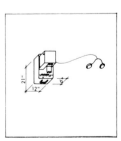

Fig. 4 Audiometer.

Besides diabetes, numerous latent conditions may result in abnormal glucose levels.

Dental

This station consists of a dental and soft tissue examination. Disposable instruments may be used. Teeth are not cleaned or filled in the unit. (See Fig. 5.)

Cardiopulmonary

Vital Signs The screenee lies down on an examining table where his pulse, respiratory rate, and blood pressure are checked and recorded. With the monitor shown, temperature may also be taken. Modular monitoring equipment is available which measures and digitally displays vital signs, including the respiratory rate.

Electrocardiogram An electrocardiogram is taken to detect abnormal cardiac rhythm, conduction disturbances, myocardial damage, coronary insufficiency, and other conditions which alter the normal electrical activity of the heart. The most common method of electrocardiography in this country today employs twelve leads (I, II, III, aVR, aVL, aVF, V1, V2, V3, V4, V5, V6), taken sequentially. An EKG may also be recorded using a single oblique chest electrode. Cady has described a method by which he determined that the "ordered importance of standard electrocardiographic leads were leads V6, V2, and III." An EKG chair has been developed, but it is not yet in production. It consists of an electrocardiograph and an ordinary artificial leather reclining chair with lithium chloride impregnated electrodes. (See Fig. 6.)

Graded Exercise Tolerance EKG A preliminary EKG is recorded. If this is normal and there is no prior history of significant myocardial damage or ischemia, an exercise EKG may be performed to help detect coronary insufficiency. This should not be done without a physician present because of complications that could arise in performing such a test on older patients and members of other high-risk groups.

Phonocardiogram This test is done to record and detect heart murmur and abnormal heart sounds. (See Fig. 7.)

Spirometry The screenee is shown how to use the spirometer (or vitalometer) to determine lung capacity. He exhales into the disposable mouthpiece of a vitalometer tube or into the large double-lumen catheter of a spirometer. The amount of exhaled air and the flow rate indicate the degree of respiratory impairment. A more basic test consists of measuring the screenee's chest circumference before and after inhalation. If inhalation does not increase the dimension properly for age and sex, there is some degree of respiratory impairment. (See Fig. 8.)

X-Ray

Chest A 70-mm posterior-anterior chest x-ray is performed to determine pulmonary, cardiac, or neoplastic conditions. High speed processors currently on the market can be used to develop films in approximately 90 seconds. If 70-mm x-ray is used, a radiologist familiar with such films must be used for their interpretation. (See Fig. 9.)

Flat Plate of Abdomen A flat plate x-ray may be taken to visualize any abdominal pathology. (See Fig. 10.)

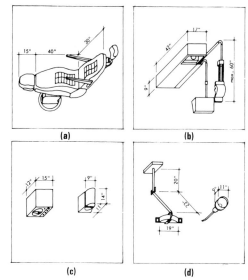

Fig. 5 (a) Dental chair. (b) Light, instrument table, cuspidor. (c) Sterilizers. (d) Light and cuspidor.

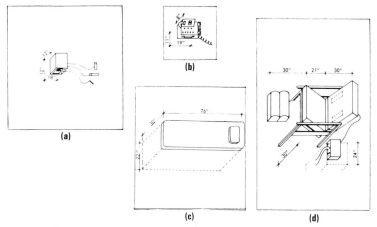

Fig. 6 (a) Monitor (B/P, pulse, temperature). (b) Electrocardiograph (connectable to computer via phone). (c) EKG table. (d) EKG chair.

Fig. 7 Phonocardiograph.

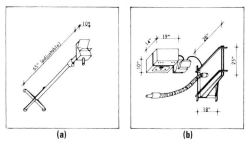

Fig. 8 (a) Spirometer (portable). (b) Spirometer (connectable to computer).

MULTIPHASIC HEALTH SCREENING CENTERS

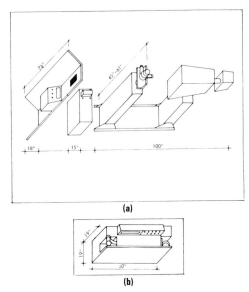

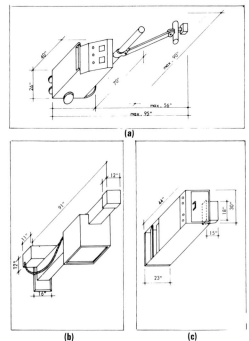

Fig. 9 (a) X-ray unit (70 mm). (b) Developer (70 mm).

Fig. 10 (a) X-ray unit (14 by 17 in.). (b) X-ray cassette holder (14 by 17 in.). (c) Developer (rapid process).

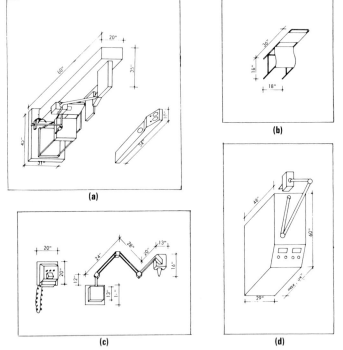

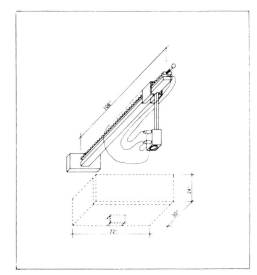

Fig. 11 (a) Panoramic dental x-ray unit with controls. (b) Dental x-ray chair. (c) Controls and wall-mounted dental x-ray unit. (d) Dental x-ray unit (portable).

Fig. 12 Mammography unit.

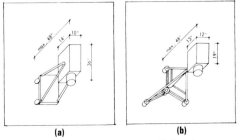

Fig. 13 (a) Thermographic display unit. (b) Scanning camera.

Dental Both panoramic and apical films of the anterior incisors may be taken at this station. (See. Fig. 11.)

Mammography Various x-ray views are taken of each breast to visualize neoplastic conditions in menopausal women. (See Fig. 12.)

Thermography

This test is performed on menopausal women to determine the presence of breast tumors, which are shown by an increase in thermal level at the tumor site. It is more time consuming than a mammogram, since a "cooling down" period of approximately 10 minutes is required (in order to obtain accurate thermal patterns of body heat emitted from the skin's surface). The screenee then sits on a stool 10 ft from the infra-red scanning camera, in which the natural thermal radiation from the breast is recorded and converted to thermal patterns on the cathode ray tube. These patterns may be photographed. Three thermograms (one AP and two oblique) and approximately five isotherms (superimposed pictures which map thermal levels) may be taken. (See Fig. 13.)

Laboratory Tests

Blood Blood chemistry tests can be performed by means of automated multichannel analyzers using a minimum of sample. Techniques such as automatic reagent addition to sample, synchronous flow techniques, reagent-sample mixing by centrifugal force, time-controlled incubations in self-enclosed plastic packages containing chemical reagents, and automatic presentation of sample plus reagents to a colorimeter or spectrophotometer are all available at the current state of the art. Automatic sample blanks and removal of protein or other interfering substances by dialysis can also be accomplished. There are a large number and variety of clinical tests available in different combinations and these comprise almost all of the commonly requested chemical parameters. All multichannel devices currently available possess the capability of interfacing to computers either directly or indirectly (paper or magnetic tape, data cards, etc.) and independently produce bar chart or printed output.

CBC (complete blood count) and STS (serological test for syphilis) should be done on all specimens. Automated equipment is available for both of these tests. The blood sample may also be checked for the presence of the rheumatoid factor (indicative of rheumatoid arthritis) by means of latex fixation test. (See Fig. 14.)

Urinalysis The urine specimen is obtained in the unit. Toilet facilities may be provided near the lab. It should be tested for color, specific gravity, pH, sugar, albumin, acetone, and bacteria.

Parasite Detection Depending on the needs of the screening group and the geographical location, tests to detect parasites may be necessary. Gross examinations of the feces may reveal the presence of worms; however, a microscopic examination may be necessary to detect parasite eggs and small worms. (See Fig. 15.)

Immunization

Space may be provided for administering immunizations against communicable diseases

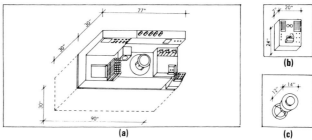

Fig. 14 (a) Compact multiple channel analyzer. (b) Blood count unit. (c) Centrifuge.

Fig. 15 Microscope.　　　　**Fig. 16** Jet injector.

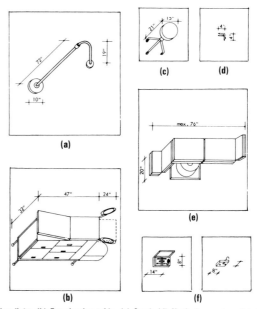

Fig. 17 (a) Examination light. (b) Examination table. (c) Stool. (d) Vaginal speculum. (e) Examination table. (f) Proctoscopes, sigmoidoscopes, battery box for light.

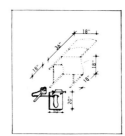

Fig. 18 Achilles reflex meter.　　　　**Fig. 19** Pressure tolerance set.

MULTIPHASIC HEALTH SCREENING CENTERS

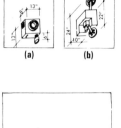

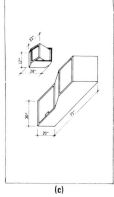

Fig. 20 (a) Slide projector. (b) Movie projector, 16 mm. (c) Table model and freestanding rear-screen projectors.

Fig. 21 (a) An enlarged data collection sequence for multiple health evaluation, usable in either a dual automobile or a small transportable unit (12 phase). (b) A comprehensive data collection sequence for multiple health evaluation, usable in a complex transportable unit (17 phase).

such as diphtheria, measles, polio, smallpox, tetanus, typhoid, and whooping cough (pertussis). Those which are given depend on individual, area needs and age groups. (See Fig. 16.)

Tuberculin Skin Testing

This method of testing for tuberculosis is better than a chest x-ray for preliminary case finding in low risk groups. If the screenee develops a positive reaction after 48 hours, he may then be given an x-ray to confirm or rule out active pulmonary TB.

Pap Smear

Pap smears to detect cervical cancer may be done on all married women, single women over 21, those who have been pregnant, and those under 21 who have proper consent. The exceptions are those in the last trimester of pregnancy. Disposable vaginal specula are available. (See Fig. 17d.)

Proctoscopy, Sigmoidoscopy

Examination of the rectum and the sigmoid (lower portion of the descending colon) by means of a lighted instrument (scope) may be done to detect polyps or cancerous lesions. Disposable sigmoidoscopes are now available which eliminate the need for autoclaving or sterilization (See Fig. 17f.)

Achilleometry

Achilles Reflex This is a test to detect hypothyroidism. The screenee places one knee on a chair or stool with his foot and ankle extending over the edge. His Achilles tendon is struck with a percussion hammer. The reflex action (plantar reflex and extension) is similar to that of the knee jerk. It is exaggerated in upper motor neuron disease and absent in lower motor neuron disease. A photomotograph may

be used to record the test results. (See Fig. 18.)

Pressure Tolerance This test is performed on the Achilles tendon to determine the pain threshold of each screenee in order to test for neurological damage. (See Fig. 19.)

Psychological Questionnaire

The screenee either fills out a psychological questionnaire or uses prepunched cards, placing them in yes or no, true or false slots where the results may be tabulated by computer. This test may be performed to evaluate the screenee's mental processes (association, intelligence, imagination, emotion) as well as his responses to various stimuli. Various tests can be used.

Health Education

All screenees should receive specific health counseling at each screening station during or after each test. In addition, provision could be made for a special health education station at the end of all testing procedures for (1) any further questions that may have arisen, (2) guidance regarding the follow-up process, and (3) general health information. This instruction could be done by persons such as physicians, registered nurses, health educators, or trained volunteers.

Visual Aids At this same station, provision should be made for showing health related slides and films and using a rear-screen projector. (See Fig. 20.)

Library A small library area should be provided in which printed health brochures are made available for the screenees to take home. Health related magazines as well as basic books on health and hygiene should be made available for reading in the unit.

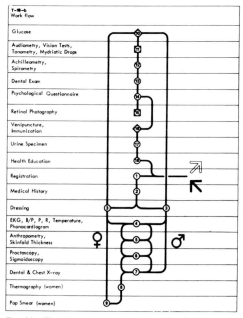

Fig. 22 Work flow of unit with 18 stations. Square and diamond symbols indicate critical interdependence between tests.

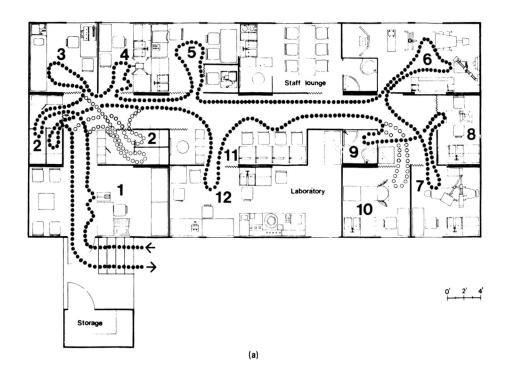

(a)

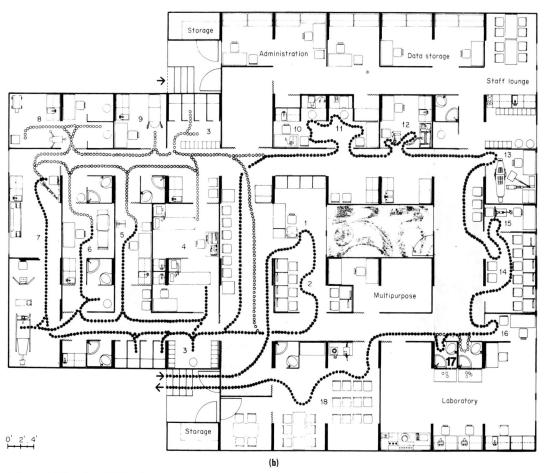

(b)

Fig. 23   Circulation plan (a) 12 stations, (b) 18 stations.

MULTIPHASIC HEALTH SCREENING CENTERS

First Aid

Space for this station should be provided for the physician or RN to handle any emergencies that might arise during the screening process.

Basic Test Sequences

Basic patient flow charts are represented in Fig. 21a and b. The individual health evaluation tests are grouped according to the ease and convenience of administering each one, and according to equipment size and/or similarity. Functional body systems were given only secondary consideration where grouping of tests was concerned. Each testing group is referred to as a phase, with different numbers of phases comprising a complete data collection sequence. Testing sequence was determined by convenience of arrangement and by required time intervals between phases, e.g., 20 minutes between instilling mydriatic drops and taking the retinal photograph. Phases which are heavily outlined are those whose position in the data collection sequence may not be altered because of critical interdependence with another phase. All other phases may be rearranged as long as the number of phases between those marked as invariable remains constant. (See Fig. 22.)

Test Durations

Individual test durations have been estimated. After consulting the USPHS, staff members of operational multiphasic screening units, nursing personnel, and medical literature, the following list of assumed times was compiled. Actual times will vary depending on factors such as the type of screenee, staffing pattern, and type of equipment used.

Entrance and exit for the screenees are combined, but the unit provides a separate personnel entrance. The health evaluation process consists of 18 phases. Characteristics of this unit are the separate corridors for men and women and many separate screening stations to use during those tests which require their wearing disposable gowns. After these tests they will undergo the remainder of the test sequence together. The unit also contains a consultation room. (See Fig. 23.)

Test	Assumed Time, minutes
Achilleometry	4
Audiometry	5
Dental exam	8
Dressing	4
EKG, B/P, P, R	6–8
Glucose	2
Health education	24
Height, weight	3–4
Immunization	4
Medical history	24
Mydriatic drops (instillation)	2
Pap smear	4–5
Phonocardiogram	4
Proctoscopy, sigmoidoscopy	12
Psychological questionnaire	24
Registration	4–5
Retinal photography	4–5
Skinfold	1–2
Spirometry	4
Temperature	1–4
Thermography	12
Tonometry	2
Urine specimen	2–4
Venipuncture	4
Vision	7
X-ray (chest)	3–4
X-ray (dental)	1–2

5

Religious

CHURCHES, GENERAL	631	TEMPLES AND SYNAGOGUES	655
CHURCHES, LUTHERAN	638	CHAPELS	662
CHURCHES, UNITED METHODIST	643	CHURCH SCHOOLS	665

By MARIA A. BENTEL, AIA, and FREDERICK R. BENTEL, AIA,
Bentel & Bentel, Architects, Locust Valley, L.I.

CHURCHES—BUILDINGS FOR WORSHIP

Church design, which for many years followed long-established rules governing the organization of the space, has been affected by the liturgical renewal all denominations are currently undergoing. In fact, each particular building committee is confronted by some quite disturbing questions and doubts. There are those who ask "Why build?" as well as being concerned with "fixing the form of worship," so that future change is, at best, difficult.

Assuming that these questions are satisfactorily resolved, the building committee and architect can commence developing a program. The church is essentially a gathering place for worship and other congregational activities. There is a functional need not only to provide a comfortable environment but also a special quality that makes worship possible as well as meaningful. It is precisely this search for quality which makes church design so challenging to most architects.

The Site

The "house of worship" is by its very nature an important public building. It speaks to the entire community about the beliefs and aspirations of the congregation. Unfortunately, some congregations worship in churches considerably more "triumphant" than their creed, and it is advisable to strive for simplicity and subtlety.

The church's position on the site will be somewhat determined by this "public image," but some functional considerations also exist. On a limited urban site the church may occupy so much of the land that only building entry and egress are possible. However, if there is room on the site for parking spaces, these will be useful even if the majority of the worshipers walk. The possibility of pulling wedding and funeral cars out of the stream of street traffic as well as dropping off worshipers during inclement weather is worth investigation. The suburban or country church site is usually larger and, with a dispersed congregation, the car parking capability is no longer optional, it is indeed essential. Ample parking areas reached by convenient driveways are functional necessities. There is a stronger entrance relationship to the parking areas and driveways than there may be to the street. Many otherwise successfully designed churches are flawed by the fact that most of the congregation is always coming in the back door. The more generous site permits the consideration of outdoor worship as well as other outdoor activities. The building program must consider these possibilities very thoroughly.

The Plan

The basic determinant of the plan is the programmed relationship between the congregation and the altar area. The emphasis of all faiths is on the involvement of the congregation in the action of the worship service. Plans which suggest an auditorium, with the altar platform viewed through a proscenium arch, have an unfortunate "performance" aspect. Likewise, plan forms which destroy the oneness of the congregation are less favored.

Since all faiths place emphasis on the spoken word, it is important to consider the ability of the preacher to maintain eye contact with the congregation. "Theater in the round" is not a recommended approach for this reason. Great care must be exercised if the structure requires columns or piers within the worship space for obvious reasons having to do with the sight lines. Although there is no liturgical requirement for seating, the length of most services requires the utilization of a seating device. It is in this particular aspect that the concept of flexible use collides with reality. The church pew has in its favor its relatively modest cost and its orderly appearance. The much more flexible individual chair generally requires more space per person and, even when ganged, requires straightening by custodial help. The desire of the congregation for nonworship uses of the church will determine the type of seating. It is worth noting that some church plans, with the assistance of movable altar platforms and chairs, permit more than one arrangement of the congregation. This is an attractive possibility for church groups interested in innovation.

Plan types are discussed below. All other elements of the church building are related to the worship area. Listed below are the required supporting facilities.

Entry The minimum function of the entry area is as a vestibule from the out-of-doors. However, this space must be sized in relation to the number of occupants, as it will oftentimes act as a lobby. Coat storage may be located here, as well as any required toilet facilities or usher's room and janitor's closet. Pamphlet racks, bulletin boards, and memorial plaques or books are wisely located here rather than in the worship room.

Vesting Room or Sacristy Although each denomination favors a particular nomenclature, the function remains the same. The celebrant requires a room for robing and the storage of vestments and the ceremonial utensils. It is prudent to consider a toilet connected to this room. Often this room will accommodate a guest speaker or another clergyman. Vestments should be stored flat or hung no tighter than three per foot.

It is important that this room be located thoughtfully in relation to both the entry and the worship space. While it is convenient to consider a position close to the altar platform, it will work at a disadvantage if the worship ceremony involves procession through the congregation or if the minister is to greet or bid farewell to the congregation at the entry. Acolytes or altar boys also require a vesting space, which should be near the vesting room for supervision.

Work Sacristy This room may also have many different names, but its function is to provide space for flower arranging, the storage of altar cloths (sometimes also their washing and pressing), ceremonial utensil storage and cleaning, and candle and candlestick storage. A sink is required, as well as storage cupboards or closets. This room is best located near the altar platform if at all possible.

Optional Support Facilities

Choir Robing Room Depending on the size of the choir, this room may have to be very spacious. Closet space for robes is essential, and it will serve the coats of the choir also. Choir robes should not be stored more densely than four per foot of hanging. Provide a lockable closet for women's handbags.

The choir room can also serve as a rehearsal room if acoustic isolation from the balance of the building is provided. A piano or small electric organ would be necessary.

Church Meeting Room Depending on the congregation, the requirements for a meeting or conference room will vary. A small kitchenette is also desirable.

Expansion Space The sometimes great fluctuations of attendance at worship can be overcome by programming for expansion space. The relationship to the worship area should be planned to ensure good sight lines when in use. If the two spaces are utilized for separate functions at the same time, an acoustic separation is essential.

Plan Types

Rectangular The most commonly utilized plan form is the rectangular, with the altar platform at one end and the seating oriented in rows looking toward the single focal point. A central aisle is usual. This plan is simple, and as long as the altar platform is within the congregational volume, there is no excessive "performance" quality. The primary difficulty arises when the seating capacity exceeds 500, because the viewing distance becomes overly long and worshipers in the rear seats experience a diminished sense of participation.

The illustrated plan (Fig. 1a) shows an entry stair within the seating from an on-grade vestibule. The rear pews are on elevated steps for good sight lines. The choir in this case is part of the altar area. The vesting room is on the vestibule floor level adjacent to the main doors. While the plan is very simple, the movement is almost into the middle of the worship space. This arrangement has some aesthetic impact as well as counteracting the tendency for worshipers to concentrate at the usually more convenient rear seats.

Cruciform Plan forms which have symbolic significance are not unusual. The altar area is often in the head of the cross or at the crossing (see Fig. 1b). Depending on the seating arrangement within the arms of the cruciform plan, there may be a loss of a sense of congregational unity.

The church shown in Fig. 1b is constructed with glass walls looking into walled gardens. The altar platform is at the transept. Note that

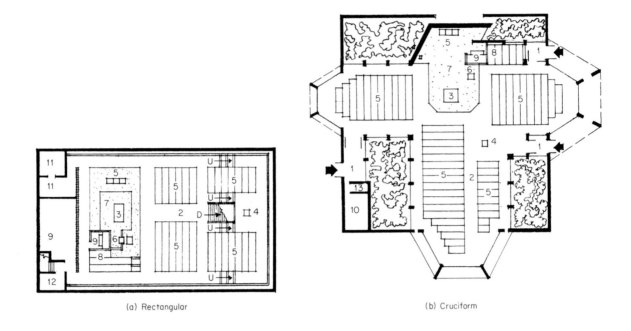

(a) Rectangular

(b) Cruciform

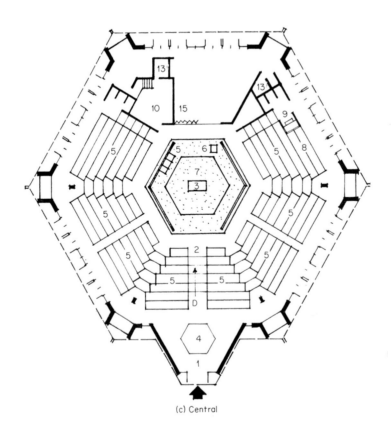

(c) Central

Fig. 1 (a) Rectangular. Church of the Redeemer, Merrick, N.Y. (b) Cruciform. St. Anthony, Nanuet, N.Y. (c) Central. St. Jude's Church, Napanoch, N.Y.

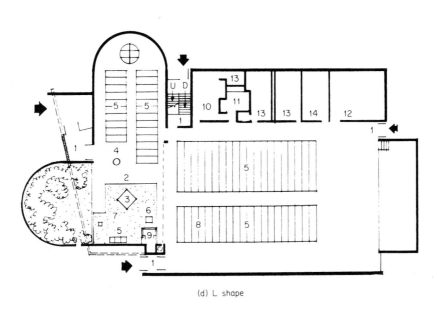

(d) L shape

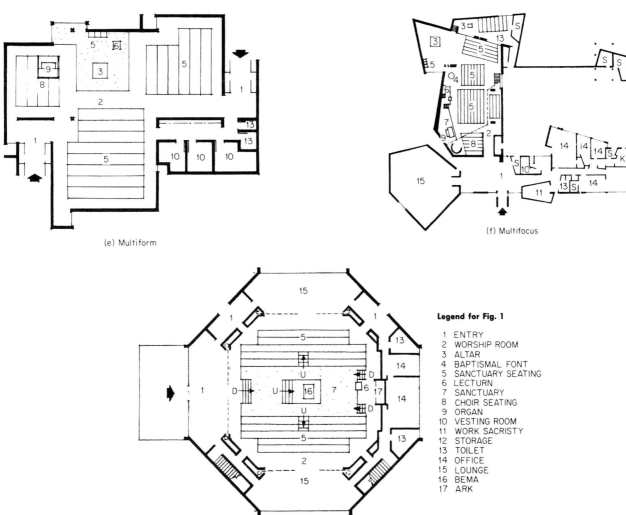

(e) Multiform

(f) Multifocus

(g) Parallel seating

Legend for Fig. 1

1 ENTRY
2 WORSHIP ROOM
3 ALTAR
4 BAPTISMAL FONT
5 SANCTUARY SEATING
6 LECTURN
7 SANCTUARY
8 CHOIR SEATING
9 ORGAN
10 VESTING ROOM
11 WORK SACRISTY
12 STORAGE
13 TOILET
14 OFFICE
15 LOUNGE
16 BEMA
17 ARK

Fig. 1 (cont.) (d) L-shape — expandable. St. John-Vianney, Flushing, N.Y. (e) Multiform. Mount Snow Chapel, Wilmington, Vt. (f) Multifocus. Thomas Kerk Reformed Church, Amsterdam, The Netherlands. Karel Sijmons, Architect. (g) Parallel seating. Orthodox Synagogue, Lakewood, N.J. Davis, Brody, & Wisniewski, Architects.

there are numerous entrances, which are related to parking areas.

A fairly large congregation (600) is accommodated without a "gymnasium" effect or very large structural spans. Many times the cruciform plan is chosen less for the inherent symbolism than for the smaller scale imparted to the building exterior.

Central Plans based on the concept of an encircling congregation are to be found in quite ancient churches. Liturgical reevaluation has generated renewed interest in this concept. In addition to the previously discussed problem concerning loss of eye contact by the preacher, certain nonreligious activities taking place in the church may also suffer. Not all the seats will have good viewing angles for motion pictures or slides. Likewise, a lecturer may also find an audience distributed for a span of 270° around the lectern an unusual condition.

Nevertheless, the sense of intimacy and oneness is very great and may overcome all objections. While the accompanying example (Fig. 1c) is hexagonal, many geometric forms are possible. The portion of the space not utilized for seating in this example is used for support facilities. There is the immediate problem that the external form is not internally complete, and this can be a grave fault. The architect should be equally concerned about the deleterious effect on a clearly expressed worship space form when a multitude of small support facility spaces are "tacked on."

"L" or "T" Expandable As stated previously, the varying requirements for worship space seating have caused a variety of plans that are expandable to be developed. The most compelling argument for this type of plan is that the space can be tailored to the number of participants. Unfortunately, this argument has resulted in the building of many churches that are flexible, but in which those who worship in the overflow area feel like outsiders. The ceiling height, floor and wall finish, and lighting of the expansion space should be in harmony with those of the smaller worship area to which it is joined. Worshipers in the expansion space should not get the feeling that they are looking through a doorway. Undoubtedly the best approach is to design the total worship area and then to introduce dividing partitions.

Figure 1d illustrates a church for over 600, of which only 120 are accommodated in the permanent chapel. The expansion space is

sized for basketball, with a small stage platform at one end. The orientation of the seats is deliberately reversed from performance to worship. The enclosed garden visible from the chapel is related more to the expansion space than to the chapel. The altar is rotated depending on the size of the congregation.

Multiform Current interest is focused on a rather random deployment of the congregation around the altar platform. The plan then reflects this arrangement by articulating each group of pews. This nonrigid plan is informal and invites innovation if a movable altar platform and seating are used.

Figure 1e is the plan of a small interfaith chapel with parking on two sides and vesting space for the three chaplains. Fairly conventional wood framing is supported on columns so located as to avoid interference with viewing angles.

Multifocus A relatively new liturgical innovation has been included in the illustrations since it may develop into a significant plan form. Here the thought is to move the focus of interest with the liturgical actions around the space. Fixed seating is not compatible with this approach, nor is it likely to be used for large congregations because of the possibility of confusion.

The Dutch church plan (Fig. 1f) shows the seating used for preaching and singing, with a large standing space about the communion table for that part of the service.

Parallel Seating While not entirely unique in the history of church design, parallel seating is not a common arrangement. As illustrated in the synagogue plan (Fig. 1g), this approach is worthy of thoughtful examination. The problem of expansion is also neatly solved.

Organ and Choir Location

For many years, the choir has been located in the church either in monastic fashion before the altar or in the "voice of angels" position in the choir loft. Due in no small part to the relocation of the altar so that the celebrant can face the congregation, the choir location is being rethought.

Possibly just as worship service is losing its performance quality, so too the choir is being asked to lead the congregation's singing rather than to perform before it. Hence locations of

the choir within the congregation are being considered.

Illustrated are five alternatives:

1. Behind altar (Fig. 2a), the choir is less visible but still easily heard. Unfortunately the members of the choir are not part of the congregation and have poor opportunity to worship properly or to feel that the sermon is also directed to them.
2. Before the altar (Fig. 2b). Here, the choir is segregated but part of the congregation.
3. Rear of the church (Fig. 2c). The choir is part of the congregation, but this situation is not much different from that in the choir loft.
4. Choir alcove (Fig. 2d). This arrangement has many variants, and it can be very effective.
5. Within the pews (Fig. 2e). A simpler version of the "before the altar" arrangement. The significance of the choir is very much reduced.

It should be emphasized that in all cases the organ will be best located where the organist can see the action at the altar as well as cue the singers by virtue of being seen when giving signals. The organist is a potential distraction to the rest of the congregation, and it is therefore prudent to construct low walls about the instrument.

Pipe organs are too expensive and take too much room to be treated as an afterthought. A church which expects to install a pipe organ must plan for that instrument, since introducing an instrument later without proper provisions is almost always unsuccessful. While other musical instruments have been successfully used in churches, the advent of sophisticated electronic organs permits even very small congregations to consider their use without sacrificing quality.

Other Planning Considerations

Acoustics Small churches seldom have acoustic problems if the space is "live" (i.e., somewhat reverberant). More errors are committed by excessive use of sound absorbing materials than by restraint in their use.

Echoes and "dead spots" will have to be anticipated in churches sized for more than 600, but even then reasonable precautions will suffice.

Public address systems are recommended

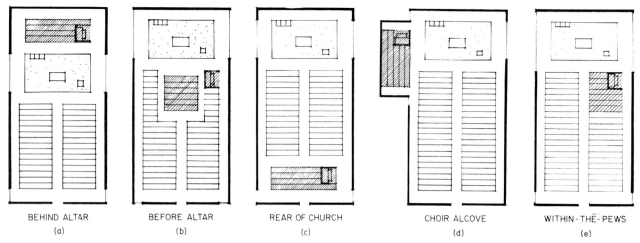

BEHIND ALTAR	BEFORE ALTAR	REAR OF CHURCH	CHOIR ALCOVE	WITHIN-THE-PEWS
(a)	(b)	(c)	(d)	(e)

Fig. 2 Possible locations for the choir.

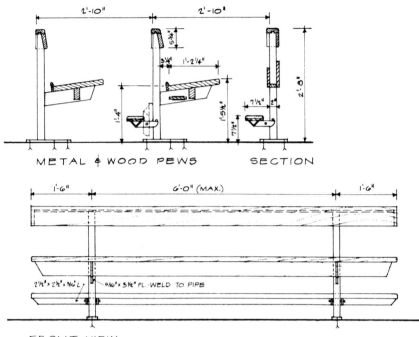

METAL & WOOD PEWS — SECTION

FRONT VIEW

Fig. 3

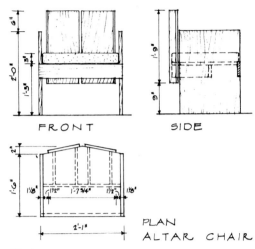

FRONT — SIDE

PLAN ALTAR CHAIR

Fig. 4

for all but the smallest churches. A trained speaker can usually be very well heard, but amplification is a help to the many untrained and unaccustomed speakers using the lectern.

If an ambitious music program (chamber groups or recitals) is programmed, then a competent consultant is recommended.

Air Conditioning In an age when every public space is usually air-conditioned, it is imprudent to overlook this aspect of providing a comfortable environment for worship. The use of the church during the summer months, the hour and length of the worship service, and the anticipated size of the congregation will determine the best type of system. However, it is imperative that the architect and his consultant give due consideration to equipment and air noise. A church with a high background noise generated by poor equipment and register selection has failed to provide a proper environment for worship.

Lighting *Natural* The introduction of natural light into a worship area can animate the space and create that sense of the unique which should be part of the architect's goal. The programmatic and liturgical emphasis will dictate how natural light will be admitted and what it is to do.

One word of caution: avoid the common pitfall of forcing the congregation to look into the sun. If the celebrant is silhouetted against backlighted glass (even diffused or stained), it will create considerable discomfort. Although most worship services are in the morning hours, there will be weddings, etc., which can make low-lying westerly sun a great problem.

Artificial High light levels are not required in worship spaces. Thirty to fifty footcandles are quite adequate for most visual tasks in a church. Hanging fixtures in churches are not mandatory and are potentially distracting if there are too many or if they are too ornate. It is prudent to consider how the fixtures will be relamped, since the life of an incandescent lamp is relatively short and the pews make ladder erection difficult. Locate lighting controls so that proper control is possible for non-worship uses. Outdoor lighting is also important, since the church will be utilized at night and the access paths to the building must be defined.

Churches have been the targets for some of the increasing vandalism all buildings have experienced. Therefore outdoor security lighting, controlled by a timer, is recommended.

Sizes

Gross Area For purposes of establishing pre-

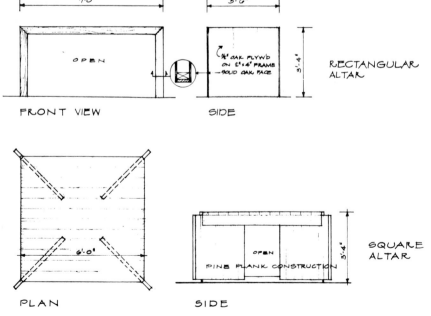

FRONT VIEW — SIDE

RECTANGULAR ALTAR

PLAN — SIDE

SQUARE ALTAR

Fig. 5

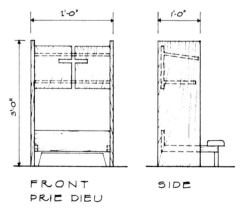

FRONT PRIE DIEU — SIDE

Fig. 6

635

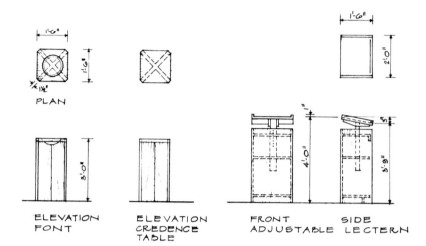

PLAN

ELEVATION FONT

ELEVATION CREDENCE TABLE

FRONT ADJUSTABLE

SIDE LECTERN

Fig. 7

liminary space requirements, allow 10 to 12 sq ft per seat. This would include moderate space for altar platform, work sacristy, vesting room, and vestibule. If only the seating area is considered (including aisles), allow 8 sq ft per person.

Seating If pews are utilized, some building codes will gauge capacity on the basis of 18 in. of pew length per person. Actually, this density will only rarely be achieved, and the usual space per person will be 22 to 24 in. Back-to-back dimension will average 36 in., with a minimum of 33 in. (especially if a kneeler is contemplated) and a maximum of 42 in. The widest

spacing will actually be uncomfortable for kneeler use. It is wise to provide storage space for prayer books or hymnals on a shelf below the seat ahead or mounted on the seat back. The foregoing dimensions will hold true for folding or stacking chairs. Allow space in the aisle for funeral catafalques and candles. (See Fig. 3.)

Altar Size varies from 5 ft-6 in. to 8 ft long by 28 to 48 in. wide by 40 in. high. The altar need not be rectangular, but in any event its historical beginning was as a table and it is reasonable to retain some of that image. (See Figs. 4 and 5.)

Altar Platform Four to six inches in height is generally sufficient. It is imperative to plan the platform for the furniture and the movements of all those on it.

Weddings are often performed on the platform and space between the altar and the platform edge will have to accommodate the clergyman and the nuptial couple (sometimes kneeling at a prie dieu or kneeling device). (See Fig. 6.)

Confessional In those churches requiring them, the custom is to provide a space for the seated priest with the penitent kneeling within a small cubicle and speaking through a heavily veiled opening at the priest's ear. It is also possible to use a more natural conference room setting, but the arrangement must be such that the confessor (priest) cannot see the penitent, in order to preserve the required anonymity.

Candlesticks Candles varying in size from 1 to $2\frac{1}{2}$ in. and in length from $9\frac{1}{2}$ to $33\frac{1}{2}$ in. The holder can be on the altar or on the floor beside the altar. Overly tall candlestick and holder combinations may obstruct the view of the clergyman. It should be mentioned that an airstream directed toward the altar will cause annoying flickering of the candle flame and uneven wax burning.

Lectern or Pulpit Provide a sloped (adjustable height) surface with lip to retain a book placed on the surface. The pulpit width varies from 24 to 36 in. Depth measured horizontally is a minimum of 16 in. (See Fig. 7.)

Communion Rail If a rail is required, the height should not exceed 36 in. The communion rail is considered to be a symbolic extension of the altar table, and as such it is desirable that it have a broad top (6 to 8 in.).

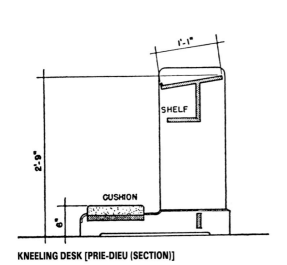

KNEELING DESK [PRIE-DIEU (SECTION)]

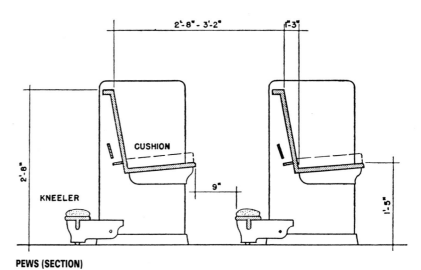

PEWS (SECTION)

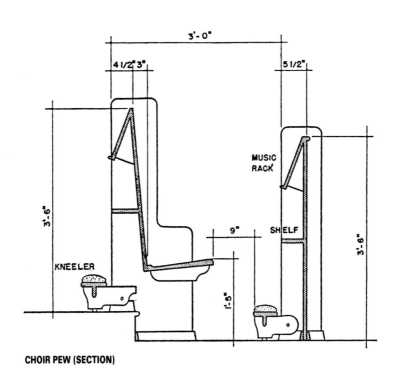

CHOIR PEW (SECTION)

Religious
CHURCHES, LUTHERAN

By MAURICE R. SALO, AIA, Consulting Architect to the Lutheran Church in America

THE SELECTION OF THE SITE

The selection of the site is the most important decision to be made by the building committee, since it sets limitations for the potential area and volume of the proposed church structure and profoundly shapes its character and determines its future growth, development, and importance to the community and parish. The following factors are major considerations:

1. The character and stability of the environs of the site
2. Accessibility to the site for the membership
   a. Relationship to highways and secondary roads
   b. Coordination into the regional plan and traffic pattern of area affected
   c. Provision of ample parking area
   d. General contours of the property
   e. Soil characteristics
   f. Presence of rock and ledge outcroppings
   g. Presence of water problems
   h. Availability of utilities

The practical elements and component spaces required by the church are as follows:

1. The church room (liturgical center) areas for intimately related activities
   a. Narthex (entrance vestibule)
   b. Chancel (including altar, pulpit, and lectern)
   c. Choir and organ facilities
   d. Baptismal font and facilities
   e. Sacristy
   f. Minister's study
   g. Church tower
2. Administration
   a. Secretary's office
   b. General office
   c. Mailing, printing, and reproduction rooms
   d. Minister's office
   e. Assistant minister's office
3. Church school
   a. Kindergarden
   b. Intermediate classes
   c. Junior classes
   d. Senior classes
   e. College group facilities
   f. Adult facilities
   g. Family counseling facilities
   h. Visual education facilities
   i. Boy Scout rooms
   j. Brownie rooms
   k. Library facilities
4. Social hall
   a. Auditorium with stage or dais
   b. Kitchen facilities
   c. Coat rooms
   d. Toilet facilities
   e. Storage rooms (generous for materials, seats, and equipment)
   f. Lobby or foyer
5. Church parlor with fireplace
6. Kitchenette
7. Parking
8. Landscape—gardens and similar features

Note: The above facilities are desirable for complete church activities. However, each parish has its own special requirements, which

are specified in the building committee's brief. There some elements can be omitted and some areas may be assigned to multiple use. All these elements are critical in determining the design and establishing the cost of the building program.

After the selection of the site, the following practical elements and spaces required for a church structure must be considered by the committee and incorporated into their program or brief. (See Fig. 1.) Administration is centrally located for control. Other elements are related but adapted to dictates of site, to the architect's interpretation of the problem, and to suggestions of building committee.

THE NARTHEX

The narthex is the vestibule or entry into the church room. Its shape is, of course, suggested by the basic plan of the church complex. It is recommended that it be at least 10 ft wide to permit facile movement of the congregation and the usual personal greetings to the parishioners by the minister. It is well to locate toilet facilities, coat rooms, and similar conveniences discreetly off the narthex or in other accessible areas, since there is no rigid rule except convenience to determine their disposition.

THE CHURCH ROOM

The church room on the main body of the church today may assume many forms due to the demands of site and the architect's interpretation of the building committee's brief.

Essentially the space must have dignity and strength to carry out the spirit of worship and logically contain the twelve elements outlined subsequently in this article.

A center or direct aisle from the seating area is essential to permit weddings and similar activities to function properly. The center aisle should not be less than 5 ft wide. Side aisles should not be less than 3 ft wide.

Sculpture, painting, and stained glass may be used, but with good taste and properly placed to enhance the room and to express its special character. Art has always been a basic vehicle of man to express the beauty and logic of the universe and for a moment's escape from the sometime prosaic reality, and therefore, it is a fitting agent to bring about the awareness of divine truth.

The church room (liturgical center) and appurtenant areas for intimately related activities are as follows:

UNICAMERAL SPACE (CHANCEL)

The chancel is the climactic point of the churchroom and the main center of liturgical activities. Therefore special attention should be given to all its elements and appointments. The chancel or unicameral area in today's church is an integral part of the church room. A distinct separation of these elements should

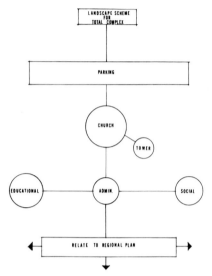

Fig. 1 Diagrammatic relation of elements of the Lutheran church.

be avoided and the clear separation of celebrants and worshipers should not be stressed. It follows that the chancel space should extend as far as practical limits permit into the church room, so that all can equally participate in corporate worship.

It is the present feeling that all liturgical centers are equally holy. The historic liturgical center with its concentration of worship at the altar and reredoes as an essential element in the church room, is changing, although some Lutherans still preserve an attachment to this traditional treatment.

There are great possibilities in the placement of the chancel and its elements. It may be located centrally or asymetrically as long as its activities are within a comfortable vision range.

The chancel should be raised three steps, each of which is not more than 6 in. high, with treads a minimum of 16 in. wide. A clear aisle with a minimum width of 5 ft should be provided for convenient circulation around the perimeter of the chancel. We are not illustrating characteristic arrangements since the range of possibilities is too great. However, in the discussion of the choir arrangements, some suggestions will be made.

ALTAR

The altar is the most sacred element in the chancel, traditionally as well as in terms of today's worship. It usually reflects the concept of the Last Supper and should bear the character of a table. Its design treatment should reflect dignity and should have meticulously thought out details. The special treatment of this element must be the responsibility of the architect. He must properly relate its material and character to the total church room design. Figure 2 is a sketch of an altar, with dimensions to be used solely as a guide.

THE PULPIT

The pulpit is the most actively used element in the chancel. It is dynamic, as opposed to the more static holy appointments. It is a setting from which the preacher brings the Gospel and the word of God to the worshipers. It should be prominently placed in the chancel without obscuring the view of the altar and other elements of the chancel. The centrally placed pulpit in a circular room, in the author's opinion, is not sound, since it does not permit the preacher to be seen by all. It should be comfortably located, seen by all, so that the preacher's visage, movement, and use of hands can be viewed, enabling him to deliver his message forcefully and to have complete communication with every worshiper. We suggest that the pulpit be raised two or three steps to raise the preacher's stature—to give him greater dignity—for at these moments he is the apostle of God and more than an ordinary man.

The pulpit must be provided with the following elements:

1. Bible rest
2. Shelf under Bible rest for notes and papers
3. A light over the Bible rest for reading purposes
4. Microphone—with all its conduits and devices shrouded in the construction of the pulpit

The design character should be left to the architect, as a standard form is not possible due to the variability of the church room design. Materials are optional, but they are related to the church design and should have inherent dignity and strength. Figure 3 is a sketch of a pulpit with critical dimensions to be used solely as a guide.

THE LECTERN

The lectern is a smaller reading desk and is an element in liturgical activities. It is used in conjunction with the pulpit during services.

It may be omitted at the discretion of the building committee. This is particularly true in the design for smaller churches. The following elements are essential to the lectern:

1. Bible rest
2. Reading light over the Bible rest
3. Microphone (electrical elements to be concealed)

Figure 4 shows the lectern's critical dimensions, but this sketch is not to be taken as a criterion for its design.

THE COMMUNION RAIL

In many Lutheran churches the communion rail is omitted and the communion elements are served directly from the altar table while the communicants are standing.

In such instances where a communion rail is desired, it should not be more than 2½ ft high and located around the elements of the chancel to permit maximum participation at one time with easy movement flow to the rail and to the pews. The step before the rail should not be less than 2 ft wide. As in the case of the other elements of the chancel, the design should reflect and be in character with the design idiom of the church room. Figure 5 shows critical dimensions, which may be used as a guide.

CHOIR AND ORGAN FACILITIES

The particular location of a choir is usually determined by the minister, choirmaster, and

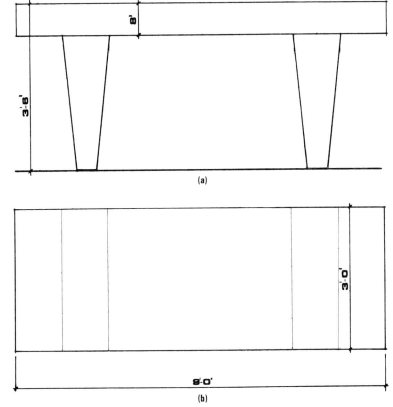

Fig. 2 (a) Schematic altar elevation. (b) Schematic altar plan.

organist for its suitability to the required services. The decision on its placement must be made by the committee early in its deliberations and the architect must be advised as soon as possible, since the choir is a major element affecting the shape of the church room.

There are five possible arrangements for the choir and many interpretations for each type. These five basic choir locations are as follows:

1. Split choir in the chancel
2. Choir centrally located behind the altar
3. Asymmetrically located choir placed on one or the other side of the chancel
4. Choir placed in the seating area of the church room
5. Choir in the rear balcony

An analysis of the five basic locations of the choir and their relative merits follows.

The Split Choir in the Chancel

This type of choir setting (see Fig. 6a) is traditional, but most churches today have found it the least suitable for present-day needs. It has the following advantages:

1. The members of the choir are a visible part of the congregation and participate in the total worship.
2. The altar, placed between the ranks of the choir pews, has a dominant focal position.
3. The service is enriched by the color of the choristers' vestments, by their trained behavior, and by their organized singing.
4. Musically, this arrangement creates some problems, since the singers cannot be centrally directed. The organist needs the aid of mirror devices to see the singers perform in unison.
5. It creates further a sense of separation between the singers, the professional clerical celebrants, and the laic worshippers, reflecting

the complete separation of these functions which was characteristic of the medieval church.

6. This scheme frequently forces the location of organ pipes to be opposed on the side wall, since it implies a central reredos. Musically, the organ should speak directly to the worship room. Although this side arrangement can be reasonably handled, it would be a compromise. As stated earlier, this scheme is not sympathetic to today's church concept. There are other approaches to the problem which should be studied for their suitability to the congregation before type of choir plan is decided upon.

Choir Centrally Located

The choir may be located centrally, behind the altar. Theoretically this is sound. This arrangement permits a central position for the organ console. It enables the choirmaster to face the choir directly and to conduct the music properly. (See Fig. 6b.)

However, it places the choir personnel behind the altar and the pulpit, which can distract from the serenity of the service. A number of devices can be used to offset this difficulty. For instance, the choir stalls may be lowered, so that singers are not too visible when performing. Another possibility would be to use perforated screens to make the choir's movements less conspicuous.

The organ screen, of course, is best located behind the singers, so that it voices directly to the church room. This arrangement has many advantages, but it makes the organ conflict and compete with the altar and pulpit. With a disciplined choir, however, this plan has interesting possibilities.

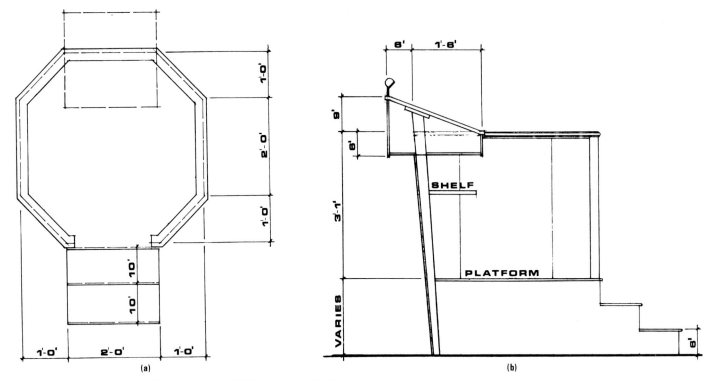

Fig. 3   (a) Schematic plan of pulpit. Minimum dimensions. (b) Schematic section of pulpit.

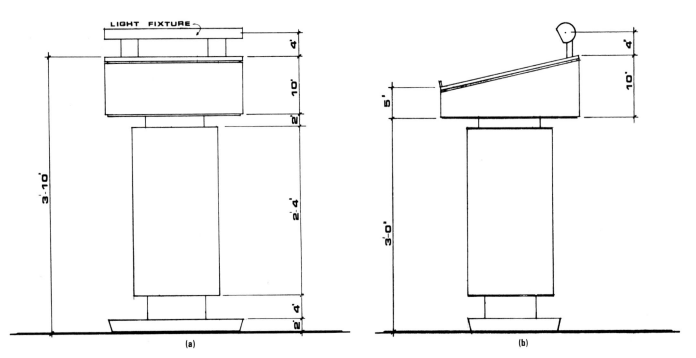

Fig. 4   Schematic lectern elevation. (a) Front. (b) Side.

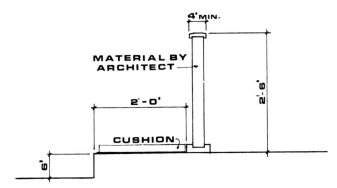

Fig. 5 Schematic section through communion rail.

THE BAPTISMAL FONT

This unit is an important part of liturgical activities and must be placed in a prominent area of the church room—that is, in the chancel or in a space conveniently close to it. It must be in the visual range of the congregation so that all can participate in the baptismal rites.

The baptismal font may be a fixed element or it can be a movable unit which can be placed conveniently when required. If it is a fixed unit, a proper setting must be provided.

Figure 7 gives some basic dimensions to be used as a guide for its design. The concept can be simple or elaborate, but it must be related in character to the overall design of the church room.

Choir Located Asymmetrically

This arrangement (see Fig 6c) places the choir facilities at the front of the church next to the chancel area. It causes the design of the church itself to be asymmetrical in plan and volume, and it poses a difficult problem for the architect who seeks to develop a design of proper repose with ecclesiastical dignity. This plan has the advantage of avoiding direct competition between the choir and the chancel and placing all liturgical activities within comfortable vision range of the congregation. It permits good musical direction and provides a control position for the console and organist.

Choir Placed in the Seating Area of the Church Room

This (see Fig. 6d) is a novel departure from tradition. It has the advantage that the choir and parishioners worship in concert. Perhaps it also deemphasizes the choir and its colorful role in the worship ritual. The decision for this arrangement must be based on the minister's attitude toward the service and on the feelings of the building committee. The console of the organ can be membered into the pens of choir area and so arranged that the organist faces the choir and has complete control of the singing. The organ space and its elements must be closely related to the choir's location.

Choir in the Rear Balcony

This (see Fig. 6e) arrangement is ideal from the musician's point of view since the direction of the music is good and the organist can be so placed as to be in perfect control of the singing. The organ can be effectively located behind the choir. From the point of view of the worship, the choir is remote from the main church room and not visible.

This arrangement will provide an effective musical background for church services, and many successful examples of this scheme exist. It does, however, conflict with the present-day concept of corporate worship. The committee must decide to what extent its ideas on worship conflict with this musically excellent arrangement.

THE ORGAN

The organ is a major element in the design of a church space, and adequate volume for its housing, air supply, and electrical elements must be provided.

Often today, pipes are exposed in the interior walls of the church room and become an interesting part of the church decor. We noted earlier that an organ builder must be consulted in the earliest stage of church planning as the organ cannot be installed as an afterthought. The form of the church must be designed to ensure maximum purity of tone and to provide the proper acoustics. The excessive use of sound-absorbing acoustical material will strip the overtones of the various pipes—particularly double reed sounds, bases, and tones in the treble clef.

THE SACRISTY

The sacristy is a room located adjacent to the chancel. It is a practical space for flow arrangement, for the preparation of communion elements, and for the storage of items required for the activities in the chancel. It generally contains a double sink with hot and cold water, a refrigerator, and base and wall-hung cabinets. Its design may be simple and materials may be chosen as economically as desired as long as they are in good taste.

No illustrative drawing is required for this space since it varies in so many instances, but it must function smoothly. At least two people must be able to work here at the same time. It must have direct access to the chancel and a secondary exit to a hall or corridor outside the church area.

MINISTER'S STUDY

A minister's study or room is adjacent to the chancel, with direct access to the chancel and egress to a hall or corridor. This room should provide space for a desk and a number of chairs, files, coat closet, toilet, and a shower bath. It is convenient for last-minute reviews of his sermon, guest speakers, conferences, and similar purposes.

This room should be a dignified space and should have a reverend atmosphere. Since this area varies a great deal in its form—because it is related to the particular church form of which it is a related element—no sketches will be provided.

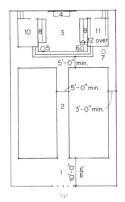
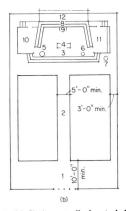
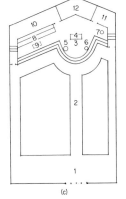
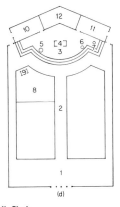
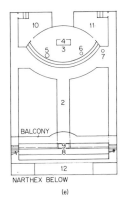

Fig. 6 (a) Split choir in chancel. (b) Choir centrally located. (c) Choir located asymmetrically. (d) Choir located in seating area. (e) Choir located in balcony.
(1) Narthex, (2) church room, (3) chancel or unicameral space, (4) altar, (5) pulpit, (6) lectern, (7) baptistry, (8) choir space, (9) organ console, (10) ministers' room, (11) sacristy, (12) organ loft.

CHURCHES, LUTHERAN

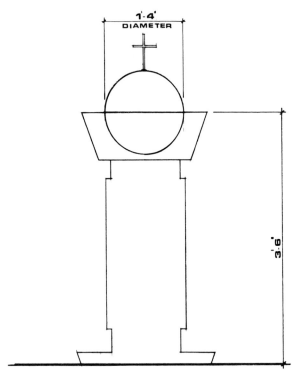

Fig. 7 Schematic section through baptistry.

CHURCH TOWER

The church tower, though not an integral part of the church room itself, will be discussed herein since it is a symbol of the church and expresses the religious character of the total church complex.

Today it is often felt that the church tower involves an unnecessary expense and that a properly designed church is sufficient to express the spirit of Christian worship. However, a church tower or campanile has long been associated with ecclesiastical structures and to many it has a symbolic value beyond its cost or its logic. Perhaps it does conflict with the criteria of present-day attitudes. But it is an understandable symbol of worship and an abstract witness to the Christian spirit; therefore it may justifiably be used.

It does provide an opportunity for abstract sculptural expression and keynotes the total spirit of the church building complex. This is a matter for the building committee to decide. We believe that it is a valuable device to proclaim positively that this is a church. No sketches are provided, for there are infinite possibilities in its design. It has another positive value in that it can house a carillon.

ADMINISTRATION

Administration consists of elements outlined earlier in this article. These rooms are sized to meet the specific requirements of the committee's brief.

Special attention should be given to the minister's offices, to give them ecclesiastical char-

acter. The minister's office should not be less than 12 by 20 ft clear and should contain closets, bookshelves, and toilet facilities.

CHURCH SCHOOL

Classrooms should not be less than 24 by 32 ft. Small rooms are too restrictive and are not adaptable to program changes. It is best that adequate natural light be provided, and light areas should not be sacrificed for design effects.

The kindergarten should provide 30 sq ft per pupil because of the nature of kindergarten activities.

The architectural treatment should reflect the rhythm and character of the church building.

SOCIAL HALL

This should provide seating equal to that of the nave. It should be a pleasant area and well correlated to the exterior landscape features if possible. The ceiling should not be less than 14 ft clear if possible.

CHURCH PARLOR

This is a very desirable space and serves many functions. It should not be less than 24 by 14 ft in plan dimensions and should have a ceiling at least 12 ft high. The room should have a clublike character with suggestions of its basic religious relationship. It should be comfortable and pleasantly furnished and decorated.

PARKING

Parking should provide one parking space for every five persons in the church room seating. Its arrangement necessarily is a function of the total landscape pattern.

LANDSCAPING

The landscape is an integral part of the total architectural concept and should properly relate to building plans and mass. It is recommended that a professional landscape architect be consulted to achieve the best results.

ORGANIZATION

The main entrance to the building should be easily accessible from the parking area, and should be designed with a drive up and canopy entrance. This permits covered access to the building during inclement weather.

The building should be organized so that people can easily orient themselves once inside the front doors. A key feature in this kind of arrangement is a large, centrally located narthex that serves as the circulation hub of the building. A person should be able to proceed directly from the narthex to the sanctuary, fellowship hall or classrooms. For convenience, the church offices and restrooms could also be located off this area. Not only does this make them more accessible, but it also enables the secretary to monitor the main entrance from the church office. Fig. 2 illustrates this kind of arrangement.

SANCTUARY

Basic Premises on Which the Recommendations Are Based

I. The purpose of erecting a building is to provide a place where people may assemble for worship, fellowship, education and prepare for service.

II. People and what they do are the major concern of the church. The building forms a background for the action and is secondary to the gathered congregation and the liturgy.

III. The essential elements for worship consist of a place for the preaching of the word and the right enactment of the sacraments.

IV. The aim of worship is "to focus attention and to suggest and direct appropriate human responses to the divine-human encounter."*

V. Theology does not directly influence architecture. Theology (or beliefs) does influence liturgy (what we do). Architecture is a result of efforts to provide a setting for the liturgy.

VI. Our church buildings should celebrate the conviction that God is present in our lives in this age.

WORSHIP ROOM

The worship room is to be designed to assist the liturgy. The liturgy consists basically of provisions for the preaching of the word and the sacraments of baptism and holy communion. Since the ministry of the word and the sacraments are of equal importance, the architectural plan should give emphasis and stress to the pulpit, table and font.

The worship room may also be used for other functions such as: confirmation and reception of members, weddings, funerals, choir programs, drama, education, and fellowship. Because of this, the pulpit, table, and font should be portable.

* Professor Albert C. Outler, "A Methodist Comment About Methodism," *Worship and Christian Unity,* April 19, 1966, p. 2.

Materials taken in part from publications of the Office of Architecture, National Division, Board of Global Ministries, the United Methodist Church. For further information write Douglas Hoffman, Office of Architecture, United Methodist Church, 475 Riverside Drive, Room 307, New York, New York 10027.

The design and arrangement of the worship room should reflect the fact that the minister and congregation come together in a corporate act of worship. The platform on which the pulpit, table, and font are located is a distinct area because of the functions involved, but it should not be separated from the congregational seating space.

Since the major emphasis is upon preaching, baptism, and communion, architectural features such as windows, reredos, or dossal should not distract from the liturgy. The seats for the minister should also be located so that they do not compete visually with the more liturgical centers unless used as such.

Sermon

The pulpit is a place designed specifically for the preaching and reading of the word of God. This does not exclude the possibility that in some instances this function may take place elsewhere in the room.

The location of the pulpit affects the relation-

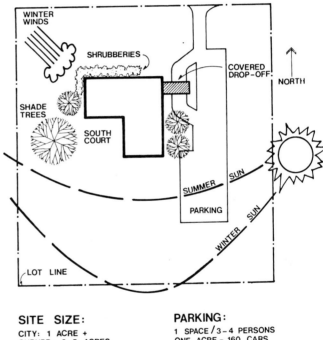

SITE SIZE:
CITY: 1 ACRE +
SUBURB: 3–5 ACRES
RURAL: 3 ACRES +

PARKING:
1 SPACE / 3–4 PERSONS
ONE ACRE = 160 CARS

Fig. 1   Site location.

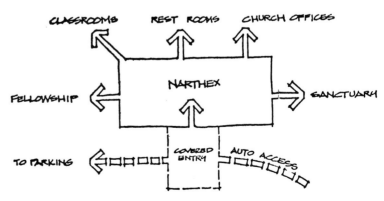

Fig. 2.

643

CHURCHES, UNITED METHODIST

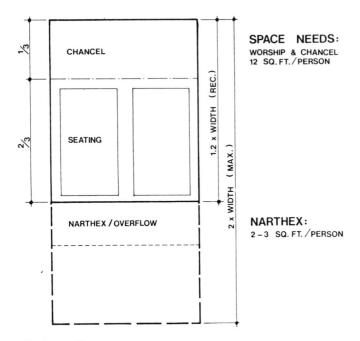

SPACE NEEDS:
WORSHIP & CHANCEL
12 SQ. FT./PERSON

NARTHEX:
2-3 SQ. FT./PERSON

Fig. 3 Worship.

ship between the sermon and the congregation. The minister must be able to see the congregation and the congregation must be able to hear and see the minister.

Listening to a sermon is a corporate activity. The minister must be aware of the response of the congregation to the sermon even though the response is unspoken. Conversely, the congregation needs to see the minister. They need to see his facial expressions and his gestures. This can be achieved by elevating the pulpit, so that even those seated in back of the room can see the minister.

The rapport between the minister and congregation can be destroyed, however, if the pulpit is raised too high or if it is located at too great a distance from the congregation. If raised too high, the viewing angle becomes oppressive for those seated nearby. If placed too far from the congregation, the contact between the minister and the people is lessened.

Choir

The function of the choir is to lead congregational singing (hymns), to sing to the congregation (anthem), and to sing on behalf of the congregation (choral responses). In addition, many choirs offer sacred concerts on special occasions. The choir should be located so as to best fulfill these functions.

The choir should not be placed behind the pulpit or table facing the congregation or in divided choir stalls in a deep chancel where they may be a visual distraction during the service. Their task is to lead worship, not to be performers of musical acts.

The organ console should be located so that the organist can direct the choir. The organ chambers should be located so that the organist may balance the music of the organ and choir. The director should be easily seen by the choir without being conspicuous to the congregation.

Space should be allowed in the design of the worship room for the use of instruments or unusually large choir groups on special occasions. If

chairs instead of pews are used in the choir loft, this space may then be used for the placement of musical instruments.

Congregational Space

The worshiping assembly should be situated so as to suggest their active role as participants in worship. Worship is a corporate activity. It involves the minister, the choir, and the congregation. It does not represent a performer-spectator

relationship. The size, shape, and arrangement of the room should emphasize the understanding that worship involves the entire congregation in the service. This can be achieved by bringing the congregation closer to the liturgical centers and by planning for a level floor. Conversely, long narrow rooms which place a large number of the congregation at a great distance from the minister and rooms which have sloping floors and balconies which emphasize the spectator-performer relationship should be avoided.

In order to provide as much flexibility as possible in adjusting the seating for different occasions, services, numbers of worshipers and future trends, chairs are recommended instead of pews. The chairs should be comfortable, attractive, durable, and reasonable in cost. They should be firmly linked together when in use and designed to be stacked when not in use.

Chairs are recommended for the following reasons:

1. For some services, such as those which emphasize preaching, there may be advantages in eliminating the center aisle so that the congregation sits together as one group, further emphasizing the corporate aspects of worship.

2. For those occasions when the attendance is lower, the number of seats may be reduced, the aisles may be made wider, and the spacing of the seats and rows increased.

3. For some communion services the church may desire to place the communion table in the congregational seating space with the people grouped around the table.

4. The church may desire to use the sanctuary for youth or adult church school classes. Chairs would allow several groups to meet and arrange their seats in a circle or small group.

5. Different functions require aisles of varying widths. For a choir or offertory processional, a 5-ft aisle is usually sufficient. A wedding processional could use a 6-ft aisle, and a funeral processional needs a 7-ft aisle. (See Fig. 4.)

Fig. 4 Aisle widths in the sanctuary: the minimum recommended sanctuary aisle widths needed for the various liturgies.

Order of Worship

The normal service for most churches places emphasis on the spoken word—invocation, prayers, reading of the scriptures, responsive reading, affirmations, sermon, and benediction. The worship room should be designed to provide the best possible acoustical environment for these functions. It is imperative that the minister be able to communicate directly with the congregation without having to resort to artificial aids such as a public address system. The size and shape of the room and the materials employed should contribute to the effectiveness of the spoken word.

The Order for the Administration of the Sacrament of Baptism

The baptismal font should be located so that it is convenient for all to see. The ceremony should be visible to the entire congregation. The candidates should be able to approach the font if baptism by pouring is desired, and there should be sufficient space for the minister, parents and sponsors. The basin should be sufficiently large to make pouring possible (no less than 15 inches in diameter), and the use of water should be visible and audible. The font should be of sufficient size and prominence to remind people of their baptism and to suggest the importance of this sacrament.

The Order for Confirmation and Reception into the Church

The service should take place in view of the entire congregation. It might be helpful if the candidates step up into the raised chancel area so that they may be easily seen when they stand or kneel. There should be sufficient space for a considerable number of candidates to kneel, only one row deep, and space for the minister to conveniently lay his hands upon their heads while they kneel.

The Order for the Administration of the Sacrament of the Lord's Supper or Holy Communion

Traditionally, Methodists have served the elements to those who kneel at the communion rail. Because of the time this method may consume if individual table dismissals are considered necessary, many large churches serve the elements to those seated in the nave.

Both methods will probably be continued, and in addition it may also be possible to consider serving communion to those who stand around the table. Apparently this was one of the methods used by the early church.

If communion is to be served to those who stand around the table, a rail is no longer needed. In this case the table should be easily accessible to the congregation, and there must be sufficient space around the table for the minister and his assistants as well as a large number of communicants. The entire congregation should be accommodated in at least ten tables and five would be a better goal, either standing or at a rail.

The communion rail was originally designed to protect the table from profane and irreverent treatment. It now serves as a rail for support while people are kneeling and to hold the empty cups. It should no longer be designed as a barrier to prevent one from entering a "holy of holies."

The architectural solution should not determine whether the elements will be offered in the chancel or in the nave seats. The church should decide how the service is to be conducted and the architectural plan should be a result of efforts to provide a meaningful setting for the liturgy.

Ideally, the room should be designed to accommodate both methods of serving communion. This will allow communion to be served in the pews now, if this be the wish of the church, and yet it will permit others to conduct the service in the chancel if this be their desire.

The Commission on Worship of The Methodist Church does not recommend self-service communion. With this method, the elements are placed at the rail before the start of the service and each person serves himself.

The communion table provides a surface for the placement of the communion elements. It is essentially a table. The size of the table should be scaled to the person or persons involved and the liturgical action about it.

The table should be free-standing so that the minister may stand behind the table and face the congregation for parts of the service. The table may also be used to receive the offering and provide a place for a small, portable book rest.

It is often desirable to provide a small table or credence shelf to hold flowers, empty offering plates, the communion cloth, lids, or other items while not being used.

The Order for the Service of Marriage

The aisle leading to the chancel should be of ample width (6 to 7 feet) for the procession of the wedding party. There should be a way to signal the organist when the bride is ready to make her entrance.

There should be sufficient space at the front cross aisle for the wedding party. If the ceremony takes place on the raised chancel area, the wedding party will not block the congregation's view of the couple. There should be provision for the couple to kneel after the ring ceremony.

The Order for the Burial of the Dead

There should be sufficient space for carrying the casket from the front door of the church with a minimum number of stairs and slopes. The doors should be sufficiently wide. The aisle leading to the chancel should be at least 6 feet, 6 inches wide and 7 feet is better if pallbearers are to walk alongside of the casket.

SUPPLEMENTAL DATA

Balcony

Balconies are not generally recommended, especially in churches of moderate size, because those seated in a balcony tend to become isolated from the rest of the worshiping congregation. Balconies emphasize the spectator role of the worshiper rather than his participation in the service.

In larger churches a balcony is often a useful device for seating a greater number of persons within an effective radius for seeing and hearing.

If those seated in the balcony are to see the chancel it will be necessary to step succeeding rows up from the front. These steps should not exceed 6½ inches each in height, and the risers should extend across the full width of the balcony, including the aisles. The balcony should not extend out over more than two rows of the nave pews. There should be two separate sets of stairs to the balcony.

Candles

If the communion table is to be free-standing, the candles could be placed on a credence shelf on the rear wall of the chancel, behind the table;

but large candles standing free on the floor might be more in scale with the chancel. Candle splicers or joiners may be used, so that only the top part of the candle is burned and replaced when necessary.

Chancel Rail

There is a trend today to modify or eliminate the chancel rail in order to reduce or eliminate the effect of separation between nave and chancel. Its height is usually the same as the choir screen, approximately 36 inches.

Chancel Window

A chancel window facing the congregation, while it may be an aesthetically satisfactory solution, creates a problem of diverting attention from the cross and table to the window, or what is beyond the window. If it is a well-designed window it draws attention to itself. If it is clear glass, it could draw the attention of the congregation to a point outside the sanctuary.

Clear or lightly colored glass may create a problem of excessive glare which impairs the visual contact between the worshipers and the minister. Even the *darkest* chancel windows under certain conditions may be a problem.

If the intention of the church is to focus the attention of the congregation upon the liturgy and the physical symbols of worship, such as the cross, table, pulpit, etc., we question the desirability of a chancel window.

Credence Shelf

To provide a definite place for the candles, flowers, and/or empty offering plates, etc., we suggest an adaptation of the ancient credence shelf in the chancel. This shelf could be placed on the wall behind the communion table, and it should be large enough to accommodate the above pieces and high enough so that they can be seen by the congregation. The credence shelf does not replace the communion table but is an addition to it.

Cross

As late as 1920 the cross was unheard of in nearly all Protestant churches in America, but in a generation it has come back into almost general use. The problem today is not *whether* there should be a cross, but rather how many and what size. No church should have more than two crosses—one on the exterior and one in the chancel. The tendency to treat the cross as a decorative symbol to be used with abandon throughout the building is regrettable.

Flags

We do not recommend placing flags in the chancel for the following reasons:

1. We live in a day of growing stress on ecumenical Christianity. At the same time, our missionaries are hindered in preaching the gospel because Christianity has become so closely identified with western culture, "Yankee imperialism," etc. To correct an error of the past, it might be a wise and discerning policy not to permit flags (or any other secular symbol) to share the honor which attaches to the symbols of the Divine Presence.

2. Flags in the chancel create separate and static centers of interest in competition with the action of the liturgy and such essential physical centers as the cross, table, and pulpit.

3. Aesthetically, the colors of the flag often

clash with the liturgical colors of the paraments and the chancel itself.

Hymn Boards

Hymn boards have been used to indicate to the congregation the numbers of hymns to be sung and the responsive reading for the day. Since nearly all churches now use a printed bulletin to give this information, we feel that hymn boards are no longer necessary. They cost money, and like the flags, create unnecessary centers of interest.

Lectern

The pulpit, table, and font are all that is needed for worship in most of our churches. There are times, however, when it may be advantageous to have a small portable lectern. Some ministers prefer to reserve the pulpit for preaching only, and use the lectern for the reading of the Scriptures, etc. This leaves the pulpit bookstand free of a large pulpit Bible, more easily usable for sermon notes or manuscript. Announcements and addresses or talks other than sermons are delivered from the lectern. Also if more than one minister is involved in the service, an additional place from which to speak or conduct the service may be helpful.

Offering Plates

Apparently there are two basic ways of receiving the offering. In most cases the offering plates are in the chancel and the minister hands them to the ushers who come forward to receive them. In other churches the empty offering plates are kept at the rear of the room and are brought forward by the ushers, only after the offering is taken. In any case, empty offering plates should never be placed on the table. After the offering has been received, the minister or ushers places the plates upon the table. If the empty plates are kept in the chancel we suggest that they be placed on the credence shelf, or on a small table provided for that purpose.

Organ Grille

If the organ pipes are located prominently on the chancel wall (so that they would become the visual center of interest if left exposed), we recommend that the pipes be screened from view by an organ grille. The screening material should be acoustically transparent. If an electronic organ is used, the grille will conceal the speakers and other electronic equipment. Exposed pipes are acceptable on side walls or at the rear.

Pews

If pews are used, provide for a center aisle and two sections of pews. Local building codes may specify the width of aisles and the seating space per person. We recommend side aisles in all but the smallest churches so as to provide direct access to both ends of the pews. On special occasions when additional seating space is needed, a row of chairs can be placed in the side or cross aisles, providing the local fire regulations are not violated.

Unless local ordinances require otherwise, allow a maximum of 14 persons per pew when both ends open out onto an aisle, and a maximum of 7 persons per pew when there is access to only one aisle. For pews to seat up to 8 persons the minimum pew spacing is 32 inches back-of-pew to back-of-pew. For pews to seat 9, 10 or 11 persons allow 33 inches and for 12, 13 or

14 persons per pew allow a minimum spacing of 34 inches.

Width of seat per person:	18" minimum
	20" good
	22" excellent
Spacing of rows of pews:	32" minimum
	34" good
	36" excellent
Spacing of screen in front of first pew:	36" minimum
	38" good
	40" excellent
Height of seat above floor:	17"

Aisles

Center aisle minimum requirements:	4' small church
	5' medium church
	6' large church
Side aisle minimum requirements:	2'-6" small church
	3'-6" medium church
	4'-6" large church
Front cross aisle minimum requirements:	5' small church
	6' medium church
	7' large church
Rear cross aisle minimum requirements:	4' small church
	5' medium church
	6' large church

Prayer Desk

A prayer desk (prie-dieu) provides a place for the minister to kneel. Since it is portable, it may be placed in front of the clergy seat or out in the chancel in front of the table. Here it is sometimes used for the wedding service. It should not compete with the more important liturgical centers.

Predella

The predella is a raised floor area or platform beneath the communion table. It is usually 6 inches or so higher than the rest of the chancel floor. Its function is to elevate the table so that it can be seen by the entire worshiping congregation. Many planners forget that virtually everything below head height (approximately 48 inches) will be masked from view by the heads and shoulders of people seated in the first few pews in the nave.

There should be a minimum of 36 inches and preferably 42 inches between the edge of the table and the edge of the predella. In larger churches 48 inches is desirable. This allows ample space for the officiating minister to present the offering or administer holy communion.

The steps leading up to the predella and/or chancel should be broad, 14 to 18 inches in width, with 6-inch risers.

Reredos and Dossal

The reredos is a vertical screen of wood or carved stone in back of the altar, usually ornate in design and intended to enhance the appearance and focal importance of the altar. The reredos developed in the Middle Ages as a successor to the ciborium when the altar was moved to the rear wall of the chancel.

Since we recommend a free-standing commu-

nion table, not an altar, the reredos becomes a distraction and an unnecessary item of expense.

The dossal is a fabric hanging on the wall in back of the altar or table. Like the reredos, its purpose is to give visual prominence to the worship center and its appointments. In fact, it is in fabric what the reredos is in carving.

The main disadvantage of a dossal (beside the danger of drawing attention to itself) is that it creates a large sound-absorbing surface in an area where you would normally want a hard surface to reflect sound out into the nave. We do not recommend its use.

FELLOWSHIP HALL UNITS OF VARIOUS SIZES

A Fellowship Hall and Lounge Seating Approximately 100 (70 + 28)

The floor plan below (Fig. 5) illustrates how a small fellowship hall may be used as a first unit for a congregation expected to eventually number 300–350 persons.

Space for dining in this building:

70	at tables in the fellowship hall
28	at tables in the lounge
98	total seating capacity

Assembly seating for worship:

81	in the temporary sanctuary
10	in the choir
32	overflow seating in the lounge
123	total seating capacity

Church schoolroom assignment and capacity:

Kitchen:	5	Younger children at 30 sq ft per person
Lounge:	17	Elementary children at 25 sq ft per person
Fellowship hall rear	20	Youths at 20 sq ft per person
front	28	Adults at 15 sq ft per person
up to	70	Total average attendance

A Fellowship Hall-Lounge Unit Seating Approximately 200 (144 + 48)

The floor plan in Fig. 6 shows a somewhat larger fellowship hall for a congregation eventually expected to number 700–750 persons.

Assembly seating for worship:

66	in the temporary sanctuary
16	in the choir
110	overflow seating in the rear of the fellowship hall
66	additional seats in the lounge
258	total seating capacity

Space for dining:

144	at tables in the hall
48	at tables in the lounge
192	total seating capacity

Church schoolroom assignment and capacity:

Kitchen:	15	Younger children at 30 sq ft per person
Lounge:	26	Elementary children at 25 sq ft per person
Fellowship hall rear	36	Youths at 20 sq ft per person
front	55	Adults at 15 sq ft per person
up to	132	Total average attendance

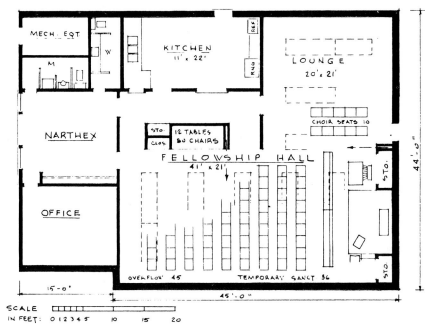

Fig. 5.

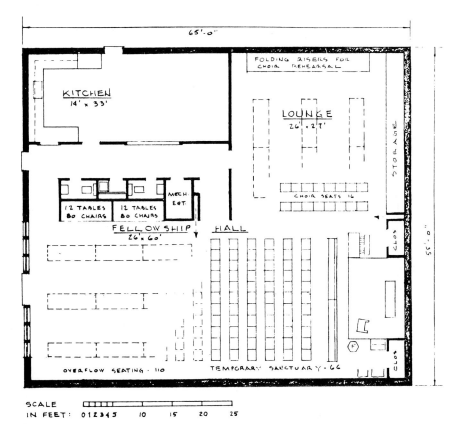

Fig. 6.

UTILITY, SIMPLICITY, FLEXIBILITY AND INTIMACY

In planning buildings designed to meet the needs of present and future generations, it is questionable whether we should continue to treat worship as something apart from the rest of life requiring a special place for this sole purpose. This approach presumes that all other activities are secular in nature and must take place elsewhere. In practice this has led to the building of one room for worship and other rooms for education, fellowship, or community services.

The early Christian church apparently made no such distinction. Homes were used for formal rites as well as a full range of domestic activities. A church building is essentially a house to permit the Lord's people to gather for worship and witness. The building itself is neither sacred nor holy. It is only the relationship between people that can be considered in these terms.

In addition to the more important question of what activities may take place within the church, the demand for adequate facilities for both new and old congregations in the inner city as well as in suburban and rural areas, places a heavy burden on funds available for building. In many instances it would be better to invest financial resources in program and additional trained personnel rather than continue to build single purpose structures.

At a recent meeting of the Commission on Worship it was suggested that churches be planned around the following axioms:

Utility A church should be designed for the several types of worship which will be used.

Simplicity Concentrate on the essentials and eliminate the superfluous.

Flexibility A church should be adaptable for many different services and occasions.

Intimacy Our buildings should foster a sense of oneness in the doing of our work.*

The sketches in Fig. 8 illustrate ways of accomplishing these means. Apparently maximum use can be made of a rectangular room with a level floor. Not shown in the sketches are such facilities as narthex, sacristy, organ space, choir room, kitchen, or storage areas which would normally be needed. The size and location of these spaces would vary with each architectural solution. To change the character or atmosphere of the room, movable wall panels, light cloth hangings or other devices might be used. The following abbreviations are used:

T = Communion table
P = Pulpit
L = Lectern
F = Baptismal font

* Professor James F. White in paper prepared for the Commission on Worship, Dallas, Texas, April 11, 1967.

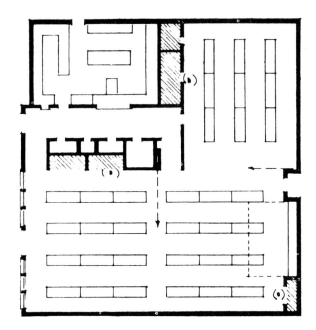

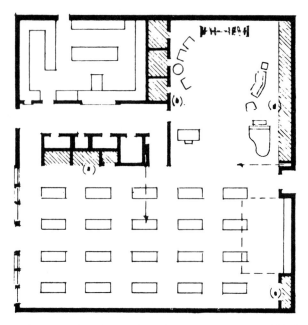

A. This arrangement for maximum seating at table in the Fellowship Hall shows 192 places with 72 additional in the lounge—or 264 total. If tables are placed perpendicular to the platform, the diners will have maximum visibility of an after-meal speaker or program. Tables for 8 are shown. Per person, this is the least expensive size and the one most commonly used. Storage: At (a), tables and chairs for hall; at (b) are tables and informal furniture for the lounge, scouts' storage; at (c) recreational equipment, speaker's stand, drama props, etc., for platform use, and materials for the adult classrooms (see arrangement K following).

B. Tables for 6 are better—they place everyone in conversational range. They are also lighter to handle, more flexible in usage; but they are slightly more expensive (about 8 percent). We recommend the smaller size, if possible. In this arrangement, the hall holds 120, comfortably seated. The lounge is shown arranged as an assembly and waiting space for diners, with desk for tickets, coatrack brought in from other area, and chairs. The piano could furnish dinner music or be used later in leading singing. Storage: At (a) 24 tables for 6 with 120 chairs over; at (d) is space for choir robes, recreation equipment, schulwerk [sic] or rhythm-band instruments.

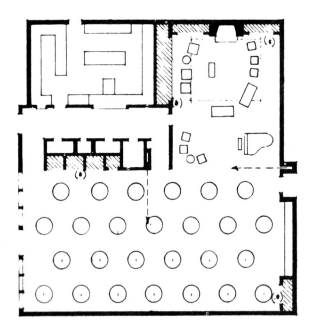

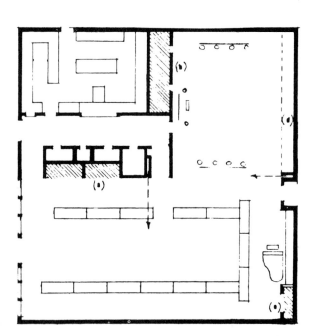

C. Round tables (48-in diameter) seat 6 comfortably or will accommodate 8. They are best for placing diners in face-to-face contact, and they cost slightly less than the 8-ft rectangular tables. At 6 per table, the arrangement shown seats 156; at 8 per table, 208. In the lounge, informal furniture about a fireplace provides the living-room atmosphere which many churches desire. Storage: at (a) there is space for 36 round tables or carts, 120 chairs over, and church-school or recreational materials in the extra closet; at (b), additional tables, lounge furniture, etc.; at (c) and (e), materials for classroom and platform use.

D. Here the tables in the Fellowship Hall are arranged in a conventional U shape, for a banquet of 100-plus diners. The lounge area is cleared of all furniture, etc., for a scout meeting, with flags and backdrop on one side and stations for a relay race at the ends. Storage: At (b) a 5-ft-square [area] is enough for most scout troops. There is also space for furniture, etc. If needed later, the right-hand wall could become a storage area (for choir robes, instruments, special equipment, etc.). Note that by drawing the accordion-fold partitions separate groups could (at least theoretically) dine simultaneously in each of the three areas.

Fig. 7 Seating arrangements for optimum use of a Fellowship Hall.

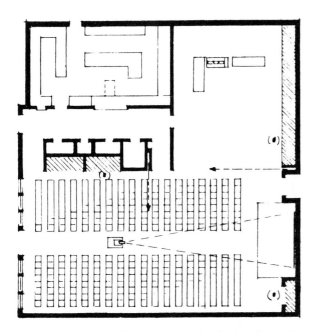

E. In this sketch, the hall is arranged for the showing of a motion picture. The screen is a pull-down installation on the wall behind the platform. There are 288 seats for the viewers. The lounge is set up for buffet refreshments (coffee, a light meal, or more) after the program in the hall. The portable serving unit from the kitchen has been wheeled out into the lounge for direct service of hot food. Such a buffet setup could be used with or after dancing, games, or any meeting in the hall, or for a "covered dish" meal to be enjoyed at the tables in the Fellowship Hall.

F. In this sketch, the combined hall and lounge is [sic] set up as an MYF or Youth Club center or canteen. In the well-lit hall, markings for large-scale recreation (volley ball, four-square, and shuffleboard, etc.) are shown in the flooring. Table games like skittles, table golf, or ping-pong could be included. Recreation equipment is stored on the high shelf at (a) or in closet (e). The dimly lit and more intimate lounge is suitable for small-group sharing. Pull-out partitions at (b) make several intimate boothlike groups possible. A demountable, prefab fireplace at (d) makes a larger conversation center. This and other equipment can be stored at (d) or (b).

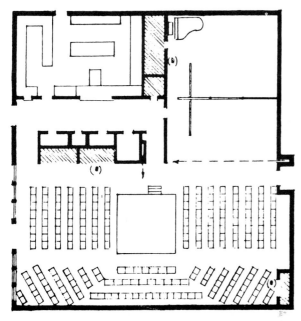

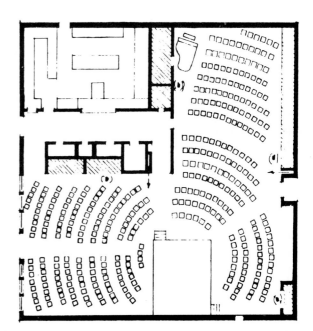

G. Here, the platform has been set out into the hall for a theater-in-the-round or other event suitable for such a setup (string group, chamber music, dance, etc.); 210 people can be seated, none further than 25 ft from the stage. The lounge has been temporarily converted into "dressing rooms" with portable partitions rolled in from the church school. Special storage for the drama workshop (floodlights on stands, paint, tools, props, etc.) is shown at (b), opening into the corridor.

H. In this scheme, the platform has been set against an outside wall to permit maximum seating in the combined area (350 people plus). Two "entrances" for the performers are shown. The kitchen or some area of the church outside the Fellowship Hall wing could be used for "dressing." Storage for drama equipment is again shown at (b).

Fig. 7   (Cont.)

CHURCHES, UNITED METHODIST

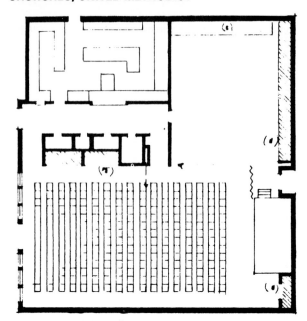

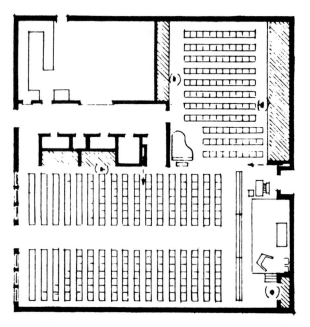

I. Here, the Fellowship Hall is arranged for assembly seating with no center aisle. Better viewing is possible using this system, since the choice center section is filled, but local regulations covering this arrangement must be carefully noted; 238 seats are possible. Incidentally, we do not recommend the use of pews at any time in this area of the church—all the indications are for chairs. The lounge is shown cleared of all furniture, etc., to serve as a waiting area, preparation space, or dressing room for the platform. A setup of this kind is suitable for a fashion show, for church-school "exercises," for a recital or musical program, for speaker(s), or drama. Center-section seating can also be provided for services of public worship, using the same chancel-platform setting as in J. We recommend a chair spacing of 18–20 in, and a row spacing of 36 in, back to back. Folding risers for choir at (c).

J. This arrangement shows the Fellowship Hall set up for public worship, as it would when the Hall is a first unit. The normal seating of 238 in the hall can be supplemented by overflow seating for 88 additional worshippers in the lounge. In churches which must also use the Fellowship Hall for church-school classes, the platform end of the hall could be prepared for worship beforehand, the rear of the hall closed off after class and set up for church while the front rows are filling. Divided seating as shown is suitable if the rows are too long for single-group seating. A 5-ft-wide storage area is shown at (d) for general use in the first unit. Later, this area, fitted with pull-out and turn-around racks like those used in department stores, could be used for choir robes.

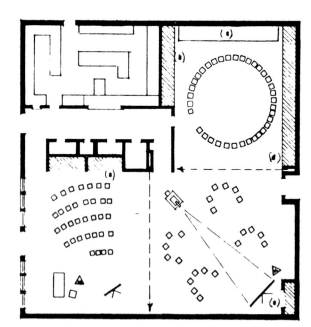

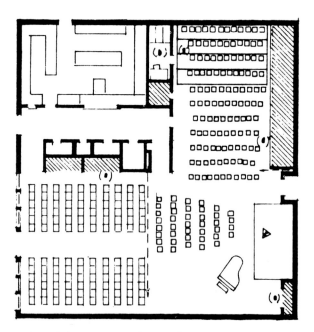

K. This Fellowship Hall arrangement shows three church-school classes in progress behind the drawn accordion-fold partitions. In one, a circle of chairs brings the whole group into face-to-face discussion. In the next class, an audiovisual is being watched by small groups who will later form buzz-groups for discussion. The teacher stands beside the screen to aid in presentation. In the third room, a class seated in informal rows faces the teacher, his or her desk-table, and a map-stand or other teaching aid. For most churches, we recommend that these Fellowship Hall areas be assigned to adult classes, even though they be oversize rooms. In first-unit halls, it will be necessary to house the whole school in this area. And in first-unit churches, the kitchen will be only partly furnished (as in J), so that it could be used as a classroom too. Classroom storage for the separate groups will be at (a), (d), and (e).

L. In this sketch, the Fellowship Hall–lounge is shown in combined use as a music room. The rear of the Fellowship Hall is shown being used as overflow seating for the sanctuary across the narthex; 120 overflow worshippers may use this space, plus those who may sit in the narthex itself. If it is needed, the rest of the hall may be overflow seating space as well. A very large choir rehearsal is shown in progress in the lounge, which has been thrown open to the hall. Folding risers, usually seating all the choir or instrumental group in view of the director, now hold only part of the combined groups. The lounge is especially good for music use. Not only can it be made larger, but it is near rest rooms and can be separately heated or cooled. At (b), a small office for the Music Director is possible, with file cabinets and desk. At (c) are double choir-robe racks, rhythm-band or schulwerk [sic] instruments, etc.

Fig. 7 (Cont.)

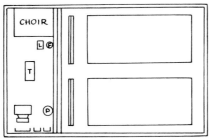

A. FORMAL WORSHIP
All furnishings are portable with the possible exception of the organ console. The emphasis is upon the pulpit, table and font. The nave seats 240 and the choir from 21 to 24.

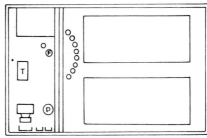

B. BAPTISM
The pastor and the one being baptized would stand on the level of the chancel platform so the ceremony could be seen by the congregation. The parents and sponsors would stand before the font on the nave floor.

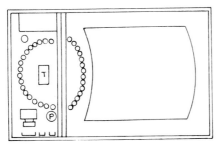

C. COMMUNION
Communion is served by the pastor to the congregation as they stand around the table. The center aisle has been eliminated and the rows of chairs placed 42" apart allowing 20" per person.

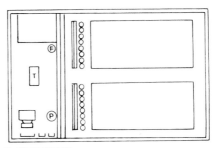

D. COMMUNION
The communicants are served by the pastor at a portable communion rail and kneeling step. The rows of chairs in the nave are spaced 32" apart allowing 18" per person.

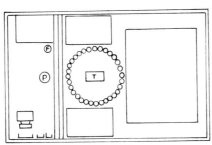

E. COMMUNION
The communion table has been moved down into the nave with the congregation grouped around it. The pulpit has been moved to the center of the chancel platform. Communion could be served standing or the portable rail and kneeling step could be used for kneeling.

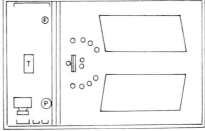

F. WEDDING
The width of the center aisle has been increased from 5' to 7' and the width of the front cross aisle increased to allow adequate space for the bridal party and pastor. A prayer desk or prie-dieu is used for kneeling. This plan seats 98 although the capacity could be increased.

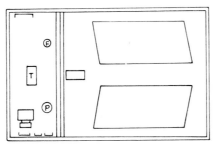

G. FUNERAL
The width of the center aisle has been increased to 7' to allow the pallbearers to bring in the casket. The actual seating capacity would depend upon the need. The normal practice is to place the casket as indicated, perpendicular to the table.

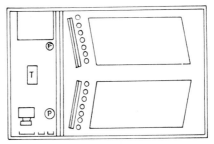

H. RECEPTION OF MEMBERS
Those being received in membership are shown at the communion rail. The same arrangement would serve a confirmation service where kneeling is required.

Fig. 8.

651

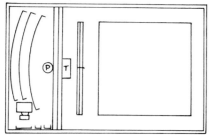

I. EVANGELISTIC MEETING
The congregation has been grouped together in front of the pulpit, which has been placed in the center of the chancel. The choir is grouped in back of the pulpit. The communion table and rail are forward of the pulpit.

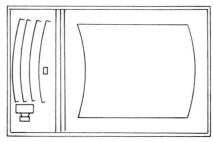

J. CHOIR PROGRAM
The choir is grouped together on the platform facing the choir leader and congregation. Special choir programs (cantatas, oratorios, etc.) are popular in many parts of the country. There is considerable freedom in these plans in providing space for instrumentalists near the choir.

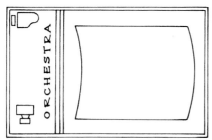

K. CONCERT
Ample space is available in this arrangement for large musical instruments and a piano on the platform.

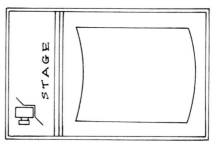

L. DRAMA
The chancel platform serves as a stage for drama, interpretative dancing, church school pageants, etc. In this illustration, the organ console is screened from view.

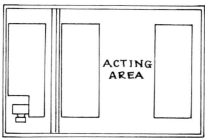

M. DRAMA
The acting area is in the center of the nave and the chancel is used for seating. This is similar to theatre-in-the-round productions.

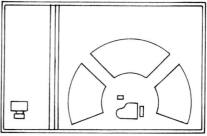

N. GROUP SINGING
For community or groups singing the congregation is grouped around the piano and the song leader.

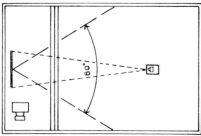

O. AUDIO-VISUAL
The screen is located on the platform so that the majority of the audience would be within the recommended 60° viewing angle. Beyond this angle the picture becomes distorted.

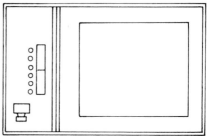

P. MEETINGS
In this illustration two tables have been placed in the center of the platform with the leaders seated behind the tables. This could be used for debates, lectures or church or community meetings.

Fig. 8 (Cont.)

652

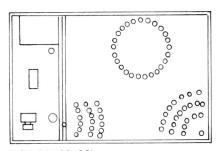

Q. CHURCH SCHOOL

Three classes for youth or adults are shown in different parts of the room. We are assuming that separate classes would be provided for children.

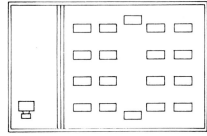

R. STUDY HALL

The 40' x 65' room could also be used after school hours as a study hall. Separate tables are shown for each two to four students, as well as tables for those in charge.

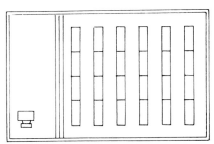

S. DINING

Using standard size tables (30" x 96") the room would accommodate 192 persons allowing 8 persons per table. The 15' x 40' platform could serve for the speaker's table, additional tables or for a program.

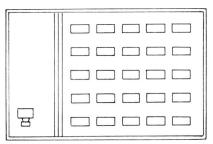

T. DINING

If smaller tables (30" x 72") were arranged with space between each table, the room would accommodate 150 persons allowing 6 persons per table. If the tables were moved together to provide space for 5 additional tables, the room would seat 180 persons.

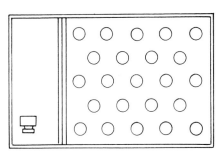

U. DINING

Round tables encourage a greater sense of fellowship since all persons are within conversation range of each other. This arrangement around 48" diameter tables seats 138 at 6 persons per table, or 184 at 8 persons per table.

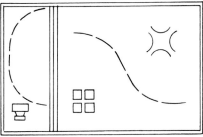

V. DISPLAYS

The room is arranged for such displays as paintings, sculpture, book exhibits, schools of mission displays, church school exhibits or any other type of exhibition which requires space for large numbers of people and ample viewing areas. The arrangement is planned to encourage the flow of traffic through the exhibitions.

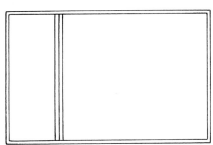

W. GROUP ACTIVITIES

If all the furniture in the rooms were movable, the entire area could be cleared for group activities. This would require ample nearby storage space for all furniture.

Fig. 8 (Cont.)

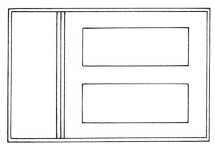

X. MINIMUM SEATING

The use of chairs allows the church to set up seats for the anticipated attendance. For each of these arrangements the room would appear to be full. (12 rows of chairs, 24" per person, 36" per row, seats 144).

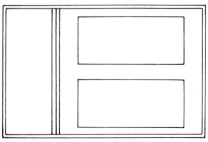

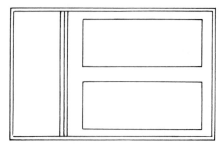

Y. AVERAGE SEATING
By reducing the spacing between chairs and between rows and by reducing the width of aisles, the room would seat 234 persons. (13 rows of chairs, 20″ per person, 33″ per row, seats 234).

Z. MAXIMUM SEATING
For those occasions requiring maximum seating the chairs are placed closer together. This will still allow ample seating space for most individuals. (15 rows of chairs, 18″ per person, 32″ per row, seats 300).

Fig. 8 (Cont.)

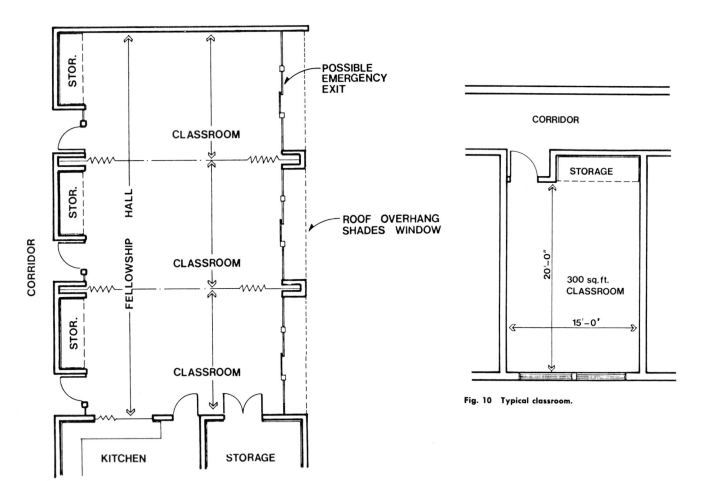

Fig. 9 Fellowship/classrooms.

Fig. 10 Typical classroom.

By KEITH I. HIBNER, AIA
Consultant: MYRON E. SCHOEN, FTA, Director, Commission on Synagogue
Administration, Union of American Hebrew Congregations, and Central Conference
of American Rabbis

GENERAL

Organized Judaism and the synagogue are found in nearly all of the civilized areas of the world except eastern Asia. Jewish culture, through the ages, has not developed an indigenous architectural style or expression primarily because Jews have been frequently denied social, economic, and educational opportunities, i.e., the owning of property and the establishing of permanent roots. Temple and synagogue designers have, for the most part, emulated regional architecture. Current congregations tend to welcome the best in contemporary architectural design and art work. The architect undertaking a temple or synagogue commission should become familiar with Jewish customs, traditions, art forms, and the magnificent literary expression of the religion.

Religious Judaism in the United States today consists of the Orthodox, Conservative, and Reform movements. Each group has readily distinguished ceremonial practices and a divergent approach to programming. Furthermore, within each of the three main divisions there exist considerable variations of viewpoints and practices. Hence, the architect will find it mandatory to collaborate closely with the individual synagogue building, religion, and education committees.

In the United States, the terms *temple* and *synagogue* are used interchangeably. This text will use the generic terminology *the synagogue.*

Site

If possible, the architect should advise on the selection of a site. Most community zoning and building jurisdiction will permit religious structures within any of their zoned areas. A site location on a secondary street at the approximate center of the congregation neighborhood is desirable. An optimum off-street parking ratio of one car per congregation family is desirable but seldom achieved. It should be noted that Orthodox congregations prohibit the use of autos or public transportation on the Sabbath and hence must be placed in close proximity to membership.

Materials

Since funds are usually limited, the majority of synagogues are designed for conservative initial cost. Construction materials and mechanical equipment should be specified for considerations of permanence, durability, and low cost of maintenance. The selection of better materials and equipment may increase initial cost but can result in considerable long-term maintenance economies.

Master Plan

Both budget limitations and anticipated congregation growth normally require a staged program and multiple use of facilities. An "ultimate growth" master plan should be designed so that the initial and later stages of construction can be readily expanded and integrated into the master plan (final) concept.

SPACE CRITERIA

Elements shown in Figs. 1 and 2 are those most commonly programmed in temple and synagogue buildings.

Worship Areas

Sanctuary. The sanctuary will traditionally, if site use permits, orient with the bimah platform to the east. The bimah platform height will vary from 24 to 36 in. Center steps (6-in. rise, 12-in. tread) are normally used. The focal point of the sanctuary is the ark, which is located on the rear wall area of the bimah. The ark cabinet houses the congregation's Torah — or Scrolls — the written doctrine of the divine rule for Jewish religious life. The ark platform is one or two steps above the bimah floor level. Suspended in front of and above the ark is the eternal light, which traditionally remains constantly lighted. Located on the bimah platform are reading lecterns for the rabbi and cantor, occasionally standing art work, and chairs for the synagogue officers and trustees. Note that all Orthodox congregations and some Conservative congregations separate the bimah area and the cantor's station from the pulpit area and ark. The specific requirements and physical facilities of the religious areas must be thoroughly programmed in the early design stage. The architect should seek advice from the rabbi and the congregation's religious committee.

Seating Data Reform and Conservative synagogues commonly use the conventional fan or auditorium seating pattern with the bimah platform placed at the front end (preferably east). The Orthodox and Sephardic synagogues traditionally place the bimah platform in the center of the U-shaped rectangular seating pattern in the sanctuary. Men and women are seated in separate sections (usually divided by an aisle), and a more Orthodox group will require visual separation also between the men's and women's sections.

The number of permanent seats (pews) provided in the sanctuary is commonly 40 to 50 per cent of the anticipated ultimate adult congregation size. A synagogue with 400 to 500 members will provide 200 to 225 permanent seats (10 sq ft per person) for the average attendance at weekly services. However, the yearly observance of High Holy Days (Rosh Hashanah, the Jewish New Year; and Yom Kippur, the Day of Atonement) will require maximum seating (of several times more than regular attendance) with direct view to the bimah. Hence it is practically mandatory planning that the sanctuary seating area expand into multipurpose areas and social hall areas. Sliding or folding soundproof doors are commonly placed between the religious and social areas. Folding or stacking chairs (6 to 7 sq ft per person) are used for the temporary seating requirements.

Choir Seating for the choir is usually in an area

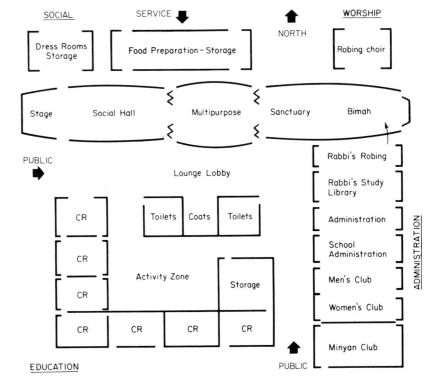

Fig. 1 Flow diagram.

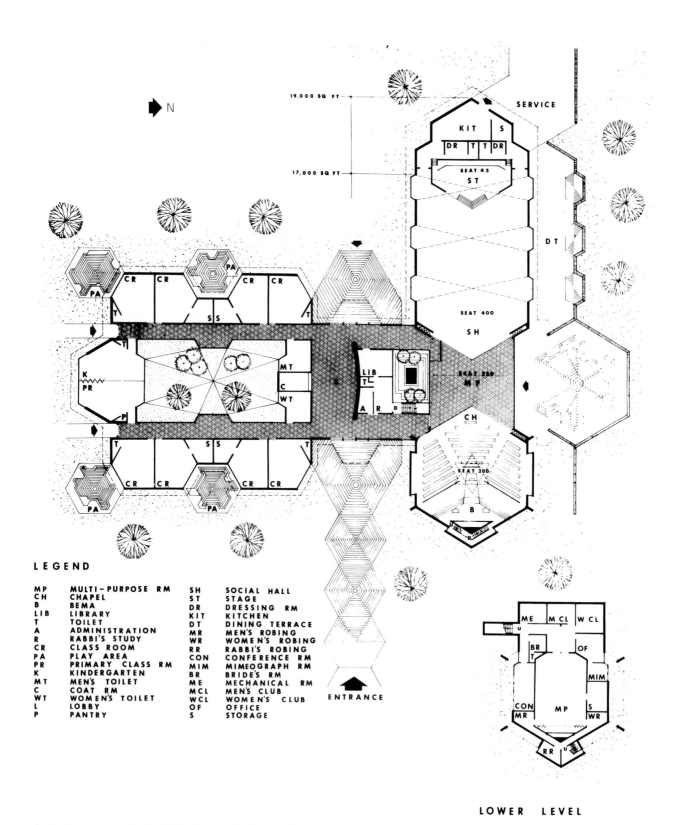

LEGEND

MP	MULTI-PURPOSE RM	SH	SOCIAL HALL
CH	CHAPEL	ST	STAGE
B	BEMA	DR	DRESSING RM
LIB	LIBRARY	KIT	KITCHEN
T	TOILET	DT	DINING TERRACE
AR	ADMINISTRATION	MR	MEN'S ROBING
R	RABBI'S STUDY	WR	WOMEN'S ROBING
CR	CLASS ROOM	RR	RABBI'S ROBING
PA	PLAY AREA	CON	CONFERENCE RM
PR	PRIMARY CLASS RM	MIM	MIMEOGRAPH RM
K	KINDERGARTEN	BR	BRIDE'S RM
MT	MEN'S TOILET	ME	MECHANICAL RM
C	COAT RM	MCL	MEN'S CLUB
WT	WOMEN'S TOILET	WCL	WOMEN'S CLUB
L	LOBBY	OF	OFFICE
P	PANTRY	S	STORAGE

LOWER LEVEL

Fig. 2   **Plan for a reform temple.** (Keith I. Hibner, Architect.)

656

concealed from direct congregation view. Movable screen partitions are utilized occasionally, so that the choir is visible for various functions such as weddings. The choir members and the organist must have a direct and easy view of the cantor and rabbi. Men's and women's robing rooms should have direct hidden access to the choir seating area or loft.

Minyan Chapel Such chapels are used for small groups—10 to 25 male congregants—for daily religious observance. Frequently a multipurpose area will suffice for minyan services where budget does not permit separate facilities.

Education

The Hebrew school normally functions in the late afternoon, after the public school sessions. Classes are ideally limited to from 15 to a maximum of 20 students. Normal public school desk and seating data apply to classroom size. Ample storage and display areas are required. Classrooms can also double as meeting rooms for adult game/craft clubs and education in the evenings. A teen-age or secondary social area is desirable and should include a small kitchenette facility. Outdoor supervised seminar and play areas are desirable.

Social Areas

Multipurpose Area Such a room is desirable when budget and space permit. The area is located between the sanctuary and a social hall and will open by means of movable doors to one or both adjoining rooms. The multipurpose room serves for overflow sanctuary seating or for larger social functions. Also, of course, the area is frequently used as a smaller social meeting room. The multipurpose area acts as an effective sound barrier between the chapel and social hall. A small kitchen unit for serving coffee and snacks is often incorporated.

Social Hall This area is used for larger social functions, i.e., dining, dancing, Bar Mitzvahs and wedding parties, little theater productions, and temporary seating for High Holy Day religious services. Storage space for folding chairs and dining tables is normally provided under a stage.

The stage should have a minimum area and facilities for amateur theatrical productions. A minimum depth of stage is 18 ft. A proscenium width of 24 ft is satisfactory. Minimum wing space is 10 to 12 ft. Overhead facilities for stage drop and lights should be provided. Small dressing rooms and toilets for men and women should be located backstage. The stage area platform is used also for High Holy Day seating.

Kitchen Requirements for the kitchen facilities vary greatly in individual synagogues. Smaller congregations will program minimum cooking-serving areas for use with off-premises catering establishments. Larger congregations will require a large self-contained food preparation center. The Orthodox and Conservative synagogues mandate kosher kitchen facilities with absolute separation between meat and dairy food functions.

It should be noted that many large synagogues will rent their kitchen and social hall facilities to an outside professional caterer, who will, in turn, operate the premises and supply food for social affairs sponsored by the synagogue as well as outside groups. This arrangement provides an income to the temple

and assures professional, readily available service.

Administration Areas

Administration Office An administration office (150 to 170 sq ft) should have visual control over the main public entry. Desk and file space is required for one or two secretaries. The rabbi's study is normally contiguous.

General Office A further general office (175 to 200 sq ft) is desirable. It includes the school administrative area, desks and counter for mailing and general filing, and storage facilities. A separate but adjacent soundproof room is desirable for mimeographing, mailing, etc. The school administrative portion of this general office should be so located as to have visual control of the classroom facilities area.

Rabbi's Study A room should be provided (175 to 200 sq ft) for lounge and seating space for small informal meetings, rabbi's desk or work table, and adequate shelf and storage facilities. The rabbi's study should have nonpublic access to a robing room and private toilet. It is most desirable that the rabbi be able to robe and enter directly to the rear or side of the bimah platform in the sanctuary without walking through the sanctuary's public seating aisles.

Library A room (220 to 250 sq ft) for the housing of religious books is required in many programs. The library is frequently used for synagogue executive board meetings. Furnishings normally include a table seating 12 to 16 and informal lounge facilities. The library should have access from the rabbi's study and the public lobby.

Men's Club and Women's (Sisterhood) Club Offices When required, provide (120 to 150 sq ft) room with desk and file space and seating for club officer meetings.

Miscellaneous Areas

Bride's Room This area (120 to 150 sq ft) is used for seclusion and final dressing of a bride prior to a wedding. A private toilet should be provided. It is desirable to locate the bride's room adjacent to a multipurpose room where the bride may receive well-wishers.

Public Toilets In a modest budget program, one set of toilet facilities can reasonably service the school as well as the sanctuary and social areas and hence should be easily accessible to both. This is possible because educational, religious, and social functions do not normally occur simultaneously. If budget permits, two separate toilet facilities should be programmed.

Coat Room Spaces for coat hanging and shelving should be provided (100 to 150 sq ft of floor area is adequate).

Public Spaces Lobbies, corridors, and circulation should be designed for direct, easy movement. Large lounge and congregating areas are required for social functions as well as religious recesses. Where possible, outdoor courtyards, terraces, and atriums are most desirable.

Storage Areas Ample storage space should be provided within the area of the separate synagogue functions (education, social, religious, kitchen, etc.). Provide storage area for the out-

door functions (deck chairs, lawnmowers, landscaping tools, etc.).

Mechanical Equipment Areas The location and size of rooms having utility services, heating, and air-conditioning equipment will be determined from criteria supplied by the mechanical engineering consultant. Exterior as well as interior access to these areas is desirable.

ADDITIONAL DESIGN CONSIDERATIONS

Landscaping

A landscape architect should be retained as a member of the planning team. Hardy, easily maintained shrubs and plantings should be specified. Service areas should be screened. Care should be taken to incorporate landscaped areas for congregation use in the outdoor celebration of the festival holidays, i.e., feasts of Shabuoth and Sukkoth.

Aesthetics—Art Work

Nineteenth-century American synagogues were predominantly routine copies of churches. The meaningless six-pointed star (Mogen David) was the distinctive (typical) form of art decoration. Today, however, architects and artists are making significant contributions to Jewish culture by incorporating Jewish religious symbolism in structure and ornament. Ideally, the religious artist will work under the direction of, and collaborate closely with, the architect. The artist should be retained in the preliminary planning stages. The art program will include such items as decorative ark doors, the design of the eternal light, stained glass windows, exterior and interior lettering and sculpture, woodcarvings, weavings, lecterns, choir screens, paintings, mosaics, etc. While Jewish tradition still leans strongly to the omission of the human face or form in the sanctuary and strictly prohibits the depiction of the Deity in any form whatsoever, there has been a decided return to the human and animal form in art work in contemporary buildings.

Mechanical Design

The master plan criteria of staged construction will necessitate careful consideration by the mechanical engineering consultants, i.e., electrical service or heating and air-conditioning plants may be oversized to accommodate future requirements. Economical heating, ventilating, and air-conditioning design will utilize multizone operation consistent with time-staggered synagogue facility use. A checklist prepared by the architect will include detailed design criteria for multiple mechanical building facilities. These will include exterior, interior, and stage lighting requirements; acoustic considerations; fire alarm systems; intercom and public address sound systems; kitchen design; pipe organ installation; fire hydrants; in-ground sprinkling system; design of toilet facilities and exterior ramps for the handicapped; site and building drainage, etc.

Information Sources

The most knowledgeable and comprehensive source for synagogue design information in the United States today is the Commission on Synagogue Administration of the Union of American Hebrew Congregations, 838 Fifth Avenue, New York, N.Y. 10021. A list of their books and publications is available on written request.

Religious

TEMPLES AND SYNAGOGUES

By RICHARD M. BENNETT, FAIA

THE SOCIAL CENTER

The three principal functions of the synagogue are to provide a place for worship, a place for education, and a place for the Jewish community to carry on some of its social activities. The latter function—the community function— is what makes the synagogue such an unusual religious building.

It is fair to say that the extent to which a modern synagogue fulfills that community function will determine whether the congregation thinks of its building as a symbol of a *living* religion or whether the building and the activities within it will seem divorced from the realities of everyday life.

The community or social functions of a synagogue have always constituted one of its main purposes. Certainly, the outer courtyards of Solomon's Temple served a visiting and meeting-in-fellowship need. There, too, one found chambers for the preparation of food, and special rooms for those with special interests. History also shows us that subsequent synagogues were true community centers in that they were built around a congregation and its needs rather than centered upon a royal priesthood. Even beyond areas for the immediate use of its members, the synagogue had rooms for the reception of travelers who paid for such hospitality many times over with their tales of foreign places and news of the outer world.

So the importance of the synagogue as a community center is not a recent development. Only its ways of serving the community are modified—the purposes remain unchanged. The basic need is for a place for friendly, social intercourse; a place to discuss common day-to-day problems in the outer world; a place for healthy common activities, for the young folks to meet and to prepare to assume their places in the community; a place to enjoy the company of those with the same interests; and, finally, a place in which, from time to time, one might be stimulated by considerations beyond the immediate horizon.

Today, these fundamental needs are reflected in the increasing complexity of synagogue plans. Spacious corridors, foyers, and lobbies have taken the place of the ancient open courtyards. There are club rooms for men, women, and children. There are kitchens for the preparation of food and large spaces for dinners and suppers. There are areas for dances, plays, lectures, concerts, and exhibitions. There are classrooms for adult education as well as craft and hobby rooms. And there are offices where the organization and direction of these activities can be guided and publicized to ensure their success.

Naturally, there is a tremendous range in the size and extent of the facilities provided depending upon the size and means of each congregation. Few synagogues have a separate space for every function, and the multi-use of space is the rule rather than the exception.

Corridors and Vestibules

The most elementary social function is the meeting, greeting, and visiting with fellow congregants before and after religious services. This requires generously sized corridors, aisles, lobbies, foyer, and vestibules. If these elements are generous in size, they permit friends to pause and talk without obstructing the flow of traffic. For the same reason there should be wide walks outside the building, and a large paved area or courtyard that invites "stopping to chat" without blocking sidewalks. A few feet added to a corridor makes it useful also as an exhibition space and does much to enhance the dignity and serenity of a structure.

The Social Hall

The social hall is probably the most important community facility. With a kitchen it becomes a banquet hall; adding a stage makes it a theater or lecture hall; removing chairs and tables makes it a dance hall or game room; by means of folding doors it can become overflow space to be merged with an adjoining sanctuary for High Holy Day services.

In determining its size one can estimate its capacity by allowing about 7 sq ft per person for seating on folding chairs in rows and about 12 sq ft per person for seating people at long tables. Main aisles from the kitchen to dining tables should be at least 5 ft wide and other spaces between tables can be 3 ft wide. Such approximate standards are useful only for preliminary planning, since each room becomes an individual problem which must take into account the position of entrance doors, the kitchen access, stage platform, exits, and so on. Careful attention to seating arrangements is most important in achieving quick, smooth, and efficient service of meals.

The height of the social hall is an architectural consideration. If the room is to be used for games, such as basketball, that may determine its height; if it is to open into the main sanctuary through folding doors, the merger of these two spaces may be a deciding factor.

Sometimes there will be a projection room for movies; but the wide availability of 16 mm film, which is fireproof and does not require a professional operator, makes such an elaborate installation less necessary. If, however, a projection booth is desired, it should be large enough to make possible the use of color and spot lighting of the stage. Phone and buzzer connection to the stage manager is then essential. Even if it is planned for the use of 16 mm projectors or slides alone, a signal system and conduit connections for sound should be provided.

Plays and movies make light control of windows a serious problem. Windows might be eliminated entirely to escape this problem, but a frequent objection to that is that the same space is used for many different purposes and should therefore be capable of reflecting a number of different moods. The answer is that this can be accomplished effectively by several *artificial* lighting schemes. For example, one could have a down-light only from the ceiling for dances and lectures; light "washed" by wall brackets over ceiling and walls (and no other lights) for dining; and all the light fixtures turned on for games. Many congregations do not allow their social hall to be used for games

that are liable to give the room too much wear and tear. If the room is used for games at all, any windows will have to be specially guarded against breakage; and if large windows are used, care must be taken to have them screened on the outside by planting (or have them look out on an enclosed area) to ensure privacy from anyone passing by. So that, by and large, a good case can be made for a windowless social hall.

Here are some specific details that must be watched in planning the social hall:

• As in all public buildings, durability is a prime consideration in the choice of building materials. By using natural materials on which any scratches will uncover the same color (and more or less the same texture) as the original surface, one can make sure that a room will last longer and look better for a longer period of time than if one had used synthetic surface materials and unprotected plaster and paint.

• In a room that is to serve so many functions a rather neutral color scheme will make decoration for specific occasions a good deal easier and more effective than a strong initial decorating scheme.

• There should most certainly be some acoustic treatment to quiet the room, and the designer should investigate the acoustic properties of the room for its use as an auditorium.

• If the room has a large seating capacity, artificial ventilation is needed during some of the events that may take place in it.

• Generally speaking, a hardwood floor is recommended for a social hall.

• Among the drawbacks of multipurpose rooms—which must have level floors—are less comfortable sight lines for stage, lecture, and movie purposes.

The Stage

The stage itself can vary in elaborateness from a temporary platform at one end of a room to a complete professional setup. But in all stage designs there are certain basic principles that must be followed: The first is to augment the playing area (the part visible from the audience) with space at both sides for the exits and entrances of the players, for temporary placing of props and of scenery necessary for other acts, as well as for positions for stage crew and actors awaiting their part. Experience suggests that the horizontal handling of scenery is preferred for amateur theatricals. "Flying," the hoisting of backdrops and unused scenery, is expensive and relatively dangerous to untrained people. The stage floor should be of soft wood to allow for stage screws to brace the scenery.

A most vital element of the stage design is good, flexible lighting. Folding footlights, border lights above, and a method of lighting the entire proscenium from the front, coupled with heavy-duty outlets for spot and floodlights backstage, should all be included.

Dressing rooms are necessary—but sometimes Sunday school rooms must double for that purpose. Most needed is storage space. Old scenery, props, makeup material, stage braces, extra lights, should all have a space where they can be kept safely. It must be remembered that several different groups will probably make use of the stage—groups of different ages and degrees of responsibility. In such cases some groups should have space to keep their own accessories under lock and key.

No matter how elementary the stage setup, there will, of necessity, be some making of scenery with its attendant painting and mess. In other words, the stage should not be a "finished" space, but a workshop within which one can simulate a variety of environments.

If the auditorium is to be used for many different purposes, chair storage may be found under the stage. Most often the chairs are stacked on carts which can be pushed into position under the stage. This method requires the stage to be about $3\frac{1}{2}$ ft above the floor. Occasionally, one or two sections of the stage floor can be made removable, but such a provision is not mandatory. Access from outside to the stage area must be considered in relation to the size of the scenery and props that will be used. This access should be convenient to a service drive.

The Kitchen

The layout should not be that of a commercial kitchen. A greater number of people will have to be accommodated; its use will be rather sporadic; and the kitchen help will not be so well trained to work together—which means that they will need more space than would be provided in a commercial kitchen.

The basic scheme for kitchens usually develops from the route waitresses follow in returning from the dining room. The planning sequence is for them immediately to pass a *soiled dish station,* behind which is the dishwashing equipment, and (if space permits) the dish storage. Next, the waitresses pass the cook's table which is backed up by ranges, ovens, space for meat and vegetable preparation, and storage, including refrigerators. They then pass a cold table where salads are prepared. At this station, ice cream is picked up —if that is the dessert. Next comes the pastry table where milk as a beverage is usually found as well. Finally the waitress passes by the coffee station.

The synagogue kitchen differs here from the usual commercial kitchen: first, all plates are served with the same menu; second, returned plates all come at the same time, but they do not need immediate washing for immediate reuse. This means there may have to be greater stacking area, but the dishwashing equipment may not have to be so elaborate or work so fast. Finally, attention to special requests is at a minimum, and each waitress need merely pick up plates and portions already prepared and waiting. Checking stations and cashiering can be dispensed with under this arrangement.

If at all possible, kitchens should be planned so that the entering traffic moves from the right to the left. The kitchen should be entered and left through vestibules which deaden the noise so that after-dinner activities in the social hall are not disturbed by the sounds of finishing up in the kitchen. Attention must also be paid to ventilating the kitchen, both to prevent odors from permeating the rest of the building and to ensure comfort for the volunteer workers. In smaller kitchen installations, pass-through openings may be used as pickup stations for the waitresses rather than having them file through the kitchen. A similar slot can be located for the return of used dishes.

Here are some additional points to consider in kitchen planning:

• For congregations adhering to the dietary laws, separate dish storage is demanded, as well as separate sinks for washing the double set of plates.

• Since the kitchen will be used by different groups of women, glass cupboard doors are often specified so that those unfamiliar with the kitchen can more readily find stored articles.

• Cupboards should be planned for utensils, silver, paper cups and napkins, and linen storage.

• Storage space should also be provided for canned goods, soft drinks and other supplies for special events, as well as lockers or clothes closets and toilet facilities for kitchen help.

• Stainless steel equipment, quarry tile or greaseproof mastic floors, tile walls, and acoustic ceilings are recommended.

• The kitchen should be close to a service entrance, which should give access to a screened, walled-in service court large enough to take care of the necessary refuse.

• A telephone in the kitchen is a necessary convenience and should connect with the administration office.

• In addition to the main kitchen, it is not uncommon to find kitchenettes for use at small teas and for the staff to use for their lunches. If a separate kitchenette is not used, a smaller stove for small occasions should augment the main range.

Parlors and Lounges

A parlor or lounge can serve many purposes. Teas, coffee and cake refreshments and visiting after evening affairs, club and committee meetings, as well as weddings and receptions need that kind of space. The relation of such a room to the rest of the temple is important.

Open and flexible planning does not conceive of a synagogue plan as a series of cells strung along corridors but as a series of large spaces that flow into each other. They can still be closed off one from the other whenever a desire for privacy or use by smaller groups makes this necessary.

The parlor or lounge should be near the main kitchen or near a kitchenette.

Changeable lighting effects for different purposes make the room more useful; furniture that can be shifted without too much difficulty is similarly desirable. If this room can be designed to open onto a patio, court, or garden, its charm and usefulness will be tremendously enhanced.

Club Rooms

Economy usually suggests that the same club room should be shared by a number of organizations. If that is so, individual closets, or even storage rooms, which can be locked up to enable each organization to store its own possessions, will give each the sense that its needs were considered in planning the building.

Craft Rooms

Art studios, photographic dark rooms, woodworking and sewing rooms, and the like are often used by both adults and children, day and night. This raises several problems: there must be storage space for materials and for projects under way; the rooms must be located in such a way that they can be used independently of the rest of the building; furniture suitable for both children and adults must be provided; there should be plenty of steady, clear light; they should have durable wall and floor finishes; they should be sound-conditioned to

keep their noise away from other rooms; and, in some instances, they should have special safety devices to prevent the use of dangerous equipment without adequate supervision.

Games and Sports

In the small synagogue, the social hall may, on occasion, be used as a game room. As noted above, such necessarily rough usage demands materials and details which are often not desirable when the room is used for more formal occasions. Ping pong and less strenuous (and destructive) games are then indicated.

In some cases basement space can be created quite economically and playrooms can then be located at half grade or below.

If a gymnasium is to be included it should be big enough to house a regulation-size basketball court. In addition to the playing floor, there must be a locker space, shower and drying rooms for both boys and girls, and storage space for equipment. While it is possible to build one gym for boys and another for girls (or to build one large gym that can be divided into two), a single gym used alternately seems more reasonable.

How to Publicize Community Activities

The office space of the synagogue must include space for those who organize, schedule, and publicize the community activities. Desk and work-table space, filing space, space for duplicating devices and for envelope stuffing and kindred tasks must all be provided. Often publicity is taken for granted in a small congregation, since it is informally accomplished by word of mouth. With expansion, this situation often changes and organized publicity is needed to get full advantage of the opportunities offered by a new building. In addition to this office space, bulletin boards in key spots, with adequate space for posters and notices and good illumination, are important. Display space for objects created in art, sewing, and craft classes also provide a stimulus for those taking part in such programs as well as encouragement for others to enroll.

Storage Facilities

Large closets in each room are often of greater value than large storage rooms somewhere else. Desk drawers, table pedestals, chests, and cabinets often turn out to be more flexible and cheaper than built-in equipment.

One of the vexing problems created by large community facilities is the disposition of hats and coats. Lockers that can line the corridors are probably best, though they are expensive. In more modest plans, hook strips and a shelf have proved to be perfectly satisfactory. A checkroom (supplemented by the use of classrooms for peak loads) offers another sensible solution. In classrooms, wardrobes whose doors open in unison have turned out to be usable. Sometimes the doors can have blackboards on their outer faces.

How the Community Function Affects the Overall Plan

The section of the synagogue devoted to community affairs should be located—and its various entrances should be arranged—so that it can be used independently of the rest of the building when necessary. This means, incidentally, that the heating and ventilating system can be zone-controlled to reduce operating cost. Any intelligent plan will group together areas of similar use.

As a principle this is obvious. But in practice there are a number of factors that must be remembered. Though the building may be divisible into zones according to function, each zone must have access to toilets. The office area probably should function in relation to each zone; and certain classrooms must be considered both as part of the religious school and as part of the community center. This is especially true of classrooms that may double as dressing rooms for the stage; of the arts and crafts rooms and the camera studio; and of classrooms that may on occasion double as coat rooms.

There is a natural temptation for a congregation to try to arrive at a fixed and final plan solution. Only rarely will we accept the fact that future generations may discover new needs—and may wish to abandon some activities we now hold dear. The wisest planning will allow for additions and make future changes easy. This is accomplished best by the elimination of interior bearing walls, by extending corridors to the full length of any wings, and above all, by starting with a site that will allow for healthy growth. For the community functions of the synagogue have grown and changed radically over the past centuries, and there is no reason to believe that this growth and change will not continue.

By MAX B. SCHREIBER and T. P. DEIS

THE EDUCATIONAL CENTER

In planning the educational facilities of a synagogue, several general considerations must be kept in mind from the very start.

Future expansion is one. This can be accomplished in several ways. One is by *horizontal extension*, i.e., either by increasing the size of the wing of the building or by constructing an additional wing. In this connection it is important to secure sufficient land at the outset so that there will be adequate space for the extension; or else, there should be an agreement whereby adjoining land may be secured when required. Future expansion may also be provided by *vertical extension* in the form of adding one or more stories.

While horizontal extension is usually more desirable than the vertical (since it reduces walking up and down stairs), it is frequently impossible to acquire the necessary land. In that case future stories can be planned by slight increase in the foundations and other supporting members. The additional cost is negligible compared to the resulting benefits.

The one-story educational unit is undoubtedly the best arrangement. It permits direct access to the exterior for outdoor play, with quick and easy dismissal in case of an emergency. If conditions require more than one story, then stairways must be introduced and there should be a sufficient number of stairs to permit quick exit. Usually, local building codes are very specific about the number and width of stairs required as well as their location, construction, and arrangement.

Children should not be required to walk more than two flights of stairs; therefore, the modern school must be limited to a three-story building. Only in extreme cases (where horizontal planning is impossible because of high land cost or for other reasons) is it permissible to build more than three stories—and that only if an elevator is provided. This of course is only a last resort since the elevator is expensive to install and costly to operate and maintain.

Great care should be given to the exposure of the classrooms. For the academic classroom an east or west orientation is desirable. Special rooms like nature study, science, should face south. The ideal exposures for the kindergarten or nursery are south and east.

Here are several specific questions that arise in the design of a synagogue school wing:

How Many Classrooms and What Size?

The size of the school, and therefore the number of classrooms, depends on the number of pupils expected to attend and also on the type of school. Classrooms for an all-day school will vary slightly in requirements from those for a part-time school. Since finances are of utmost concern to most institutions, the classrooms are frequently planned to accommodate a large number of pupils in order to reduce the number of teachers. But conditions vary from year to year, so that a large room may be wasted if only a small number of pupils will use it. Good education practice, on the other hand, dictates smaller classes for greater efficiency; between these two extremes a happy medium must be selected. A class of 25 pupils has proved satisfactory in most instances. Since most schools have shown considerable variation in the size of classes for different grades, it is often possible to construct classrooms of varying sizes to accommodate from 20 to 35 pupils.

The number of children to be provided for will depend largely on the community. A careful survey must be made to determine how many pupils may be expected to attend the school. From that figure the number of classrooms can be arrived at, using the average-size class as a basis. For an all-day school, provision must be made for at least one classroom for each grade in order to permit a full school curriculum.

The actual size of the classroom is based on a minimum of 15 sq ft for each child. This figure provides only for the area devoted to seats and aisles; if the educational program calls for activity space, then the room must be based on a larger amount of between 20 and 25 sq ft per child.

The advantages of the larger room can readily be understood. With it an air of informality and spaciousness can easily be achieved. From nearly every point of view it permits greater flexibility in use. It provides increased flexibility in the arrangement of furniture and class groups; in the accommodation of changing class sizes; in the education program which can be carried out in the classroom; and in the accommodation of adult activities.

On the other hand, the special suitability of the smaller room for the work of small groups and committees should not be overlooked.

Movable Partitions in Classrooms: Pros and Cons

Various types of movable partitions may be used to separate one room or area from another. One type becoming increasingly popular is the folding partition which extends or closes with ease and operates in a fixed track. A second type is the wood accordion door—which is hinged so that it may be extended to form a wall or folded back out of the way against opposite walls. A third type is a curtain of cloth, reed, or bamboo, operating in or on a fixed track. A fourth type is the movable area separator, which is really a portable screen generally extending to a height of 6 or 7 ft. Finally, a partition might be made in modular units in such a way that these can be disassembled and moved to a new location. This last type probably is not a movable partition in the narrower sense.

Multiple Use of Schoolroom

Most of the factors mentioned in the two preceding sections, such as the size and flexibility of classrooms, have a direct bearing on the extent to which classrooms can be used for multiple purposes. If there is no large assembly hall or auditorium available, a row of classrooms separated by folding or accordion type doors can quickly and easily be converted into a large assembly, meeting, or banquet hall. A smaller classroom, however, accommodates the smaller group or committee admirably. In this way, both large and small classrooms can serve subsidiary uses such as for meeting, working, and social gathering places.

In the dual use of a room, the selection of the type of furniture is of utmost importance. If a classroom is also to be used as a meeting room for adults the *fixed* type of children's desks and seats will be impractical for the adults. It will be necessary to select the upper-grade classroom to be used for adult meetings since there the furniture will be of a larger size and more suitable.

For the afternoon type school, a large space must be set aside for the pupils to gather in inclement weather before time for classes; this is required since the classrooms may be occupied by a previous session and the pupils will not be able to go directly to their classes until the previous period is ended. In the all-day schools the problem does not generally exist, since the pupils can go directly to their classrooms.

The Kindergarten as a Nursery

A kindergarten and nursery can be a powerful force in attracting younger families to the synagogue who otherwise would be unwilling to leave their small children at home or who could not otherwise all attend at the same time. The kindergarten and nursery may well be combined; in fact, there is a worthwhile advantage in this. In the case of families with two or three children in the nursery and kindergarten age group, keeping them all together helps them adjust much more quickly to the new surroundings, cuts down the fears and insecurities which children naturally feel under the circumstances, and makes the work of the adult attendant much easier.

This kindergarten area should be well soundproofed. Consequently, a movable partition separating this room from another might be inadvisable.

The room should have adequate tackboard area for mounting large, colorful posters and displays. For the smallest children, and for those who become sleepy, the necessary number of cots should be provided.

It is important that the kindergarten and nursery be large and roomy. Children of the age to be accommodated here often play on the floor and delight in active games. These demand generous space. Adequate room is needed for the storage of toys, materials, and other play equipment. From a health point of view, congestion in this space particularly ought to be avoided because it encourages the

Peter Blake (ed.), *An American Synagogue for Today and Tomorrow*, The Union of American Hebrew Congregations, New York, 1954.

spread of disease. In general, it can be said that an air of attractiveness and commodiousness in the nursery and kindergarten area will return worthwhile dividends in increased family attendance and participation in all the activities of the synagogue.

In order to provide as much sunlight as possible, the kindergarten room should face south and east. The ideal location is on the first floor to avoid steps and also to provide easy access to an outdoor playground, which is of utmost importance to this kind of a class. *The area of this room should be based on 30 sq ft per child and the class should be limited to a maximum of 20 children.*

Window areas should be generous—the more light the better. If the windowsills are more than a few feet above the exterior ground, some type of window guard must be provided to protect the youngsters from falling out. Windowshades are necessary, since the kindergarten pupils frequently rest during the day and require a darkened room. Also the heat of the sun and strong glare can be minimized by lowering the shades.

Since the kindergarten pupils must be kept under constant observation, it is mandatory to provide the toilet room directly off the main playroom. In this way the teacher can control the children and help those who require assistance without leaving the room itself. At least two water closets and two washbasins should be provided in each kindergarten toilet room, and these fixtures should be of the small, low type to suit the age of the children. Soap dispensers and paper towels are provided for purposes of cleanliness and to teach the children good health practices. A wash sink in the playroom itself is standard equipment, since children love to play with water. Drinking facilities must be provided either in the form of a drinking fountain or by means of paper cups adjacent to the sink.

Clothing facilities should be located in the playroom itself or as close to it as possible. The cubicles containing five or six spaces have proved quite satisfactory since they are easy to move from place to place. The top portion of each section is devoted to a blanket or hat, the center portion is for the coat, and the lower part for rubbers or boots.

There should be a sufficient number of movable toy storage cabinets. These cabinets are used not only for the storage of toys and equipment but also to form alcoves of varying sizes and shapes to section off various play activities. Since the children play on the floor a good part of the time, a sanitary material must be provided which is easy to clean, warm to the touch, and colorful.

While many of the rooms in the education center may be used for other purposes, the kindergarten should never be used for any other purpose. Frequently, the children work on a project of building which may take several days or a week, and this must not be disturbed.

In connection with the kindergarten room, an outdoor playground is necessary since the children spend considerable time outdoors in good weather. Sand pit, swings, slides, seesaws, are the commonly used items of equipment. The playground should be so arranged that the sun will strike it and not be cut off by adjoining buildings.

Design and Furnishing of a Classroom

Research of late years has established that the planning of physical environmental factors of the classroom—such as seating, lighting, decoration, temperature, and sound—contributes greatly to the learning progress and well-being of the children. Coordinating the environment in this way is particularly important where the children spend several hours in sustained visual activity.

The proportions of an academic classroom should be such that the width is about three-fourths of the length. The long, narrow room provides better control for the teacher than a classroom which is wide and shallow. In the latter room the light from the windows will not penetrate to the far side and thus the last rows of seats will be poorly lighted. The windows should be arranged on the long side so that when the pupils face the front of the room the natural light will come from the left side.

Windows may be as large as possible, starting at approximately 3 ft above the floor and rising to the ceiling or as high as structural members permit; the higher the heads of the windows the farther the light will penetrate toward the opposite side of the room. The areas of the windows should never be less than 10 percent of the floor area of the room. Shades or other sun-control devices should be provided to cut the glare and strong sun and for use if motion pictures are shown.

The following description of a typical classroom should not be taken as a rigid formula, for many variations in design are possible. This is merely one good way of designing such a room: the front of the classroom should be provided with a chalkboard across the entire wall, with a cork tack board above. On the corridor wall toward the front of the room is the door. This door should swing into the room if the local law permits, in order to keep the corridor clear. If the law requires that the door swing outward towards the corridor, then it should be set back into the room in the form of a recess. The door itself should be provided with a glass vision panel, and a glass transom should be provided over the door to admit light into the corridor. On the room side of the corridor wall, beginning at the entrance door, there should be a series of cabinets in this order: teachers' locker, storage cabinet, pupils' wardrobe, material cabinet, exhibit cabinet with a cupboard under, magazine rack. The wardrobe is composed of a series of doors which contain tack board or chalkboard sections. The Austral type wardrobe doors are the most acceptable since they pivot out of the line of travel; they are, however, the most expensive, and if finances are limited, then the sliding or hinged type of wardrobe doors may be used. Within the wardrobe are hooks and a shelf for hats. The wardrobe compartment must be ventilated, either by mechanical means if the building is equipped with an air-conditioning or ventilating system or by means of a grille in several of the doors.

Two types of flooring are generally used in classrooms: the wood floor and the asphalt tile floor. With fixed furniture, the wood floor must be used to provide a surface for fastening the desks and seats. The tendency in modern education, however, has been toward movable

furniture, and in that connection asphalt tile has proved most satisfactory.

Classroom furniture of the best design and quality is available at moderate cost. Since the equipment will be moved frequently, it is important that it possess the needed strength and durability. The soundest equipment for individual student use is a desk with swivel seat and a top adjustable to $20°$ slope. Depending on the extent to which the room is to be used for different purposes, individual tables with sloped tops and separate chairs provide greater flexibility. These individual tables can easily be grouped to form larger working surfaces. Probably the greatest all-round flexibility can be achieved by the use of larger multi-place tables with adjustable-height steel standards and folding chairs. For kindergarten and primary grades, however, folding chairs are not satisfactory.

Painting the classroom does more than any other single item to make the room attractive and cheerful. The painting scheme should produce high reflectivity without glare and yet maintain the practical quality of easy maintenance.

Adequate artificial overhead light should be provided to supplement daylight and for evening activities. At least one electric outlet must be provided for showing moving pictures and for similar purposes.

The Library, Visual Aids, etc.

Depending again upon the scope of the services the synagogue means to offer, it can provide files of periodicals, newspapers, motion picture films, and recorded music, which might not otherwise be conveniently available to members.

The library might also be made available for small meetings, teas, and receptions.

Beauty and attractiveness are just as important as health and usefulness in planning the library. Informality without loss of discipline can be obtained by the proper selection of furniture, equipment, and decoration. The shelves must be suited to the age groups for which they are intended. Best possible natural daylight should be obtained and bilateral fenestration is desirable. Artificial illumination must be carefully worked out. If the library is to be used by outsiders after school hours, then the room should be located in such a position that it is easily accessible from the exterior; yet it should be removed from the noisy side of the building.

Modern education is making more and more extensive use of visual aids in an unending variety of motion picture films, slides, maps, charts, photographs, and other non-book aids. These items are usually controlled by the school library and are made available for use in such a manner as has been traditionally employed for books. Special provision must be made for storing and handling the items mentioned and cabinets and shelving or special racks are required. The circulation and storage of records and portable record players and radios also come under the jurisdiction of the library.

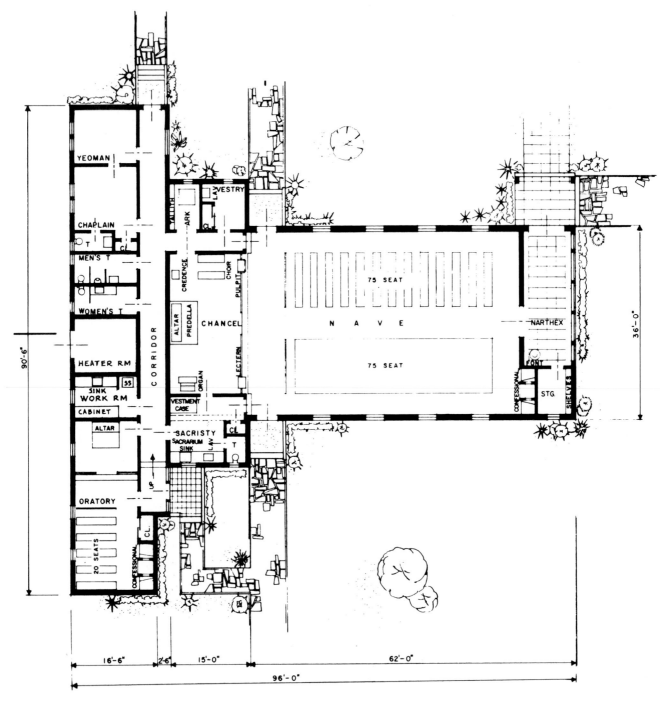

Fig. 1 150-Seat chapel

Department of the Navy, Bureau of Yards & Docks, Washington, D.C., Williams, Coile & Blanchard and Associates Architects, Engineers, Washington, D.C.

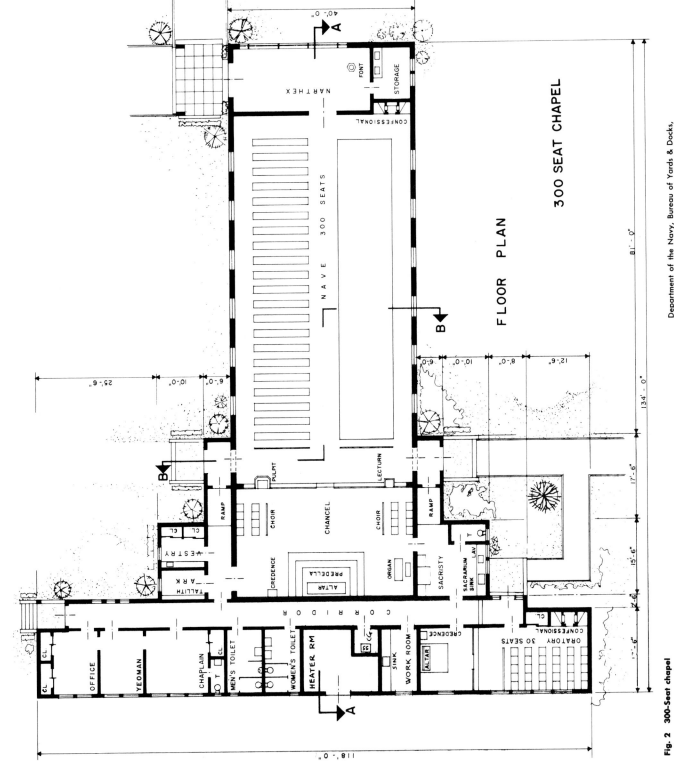

300 SEAT CHAPEL

FLOOR PLAN

Department of the Navy, Bureau of Yards & Docks, Washington, D.C.; Williams, Coile & Blanchard and Associates Architects, Engineers, Washington, D.C.

Fig. 2 300-Seat chapel

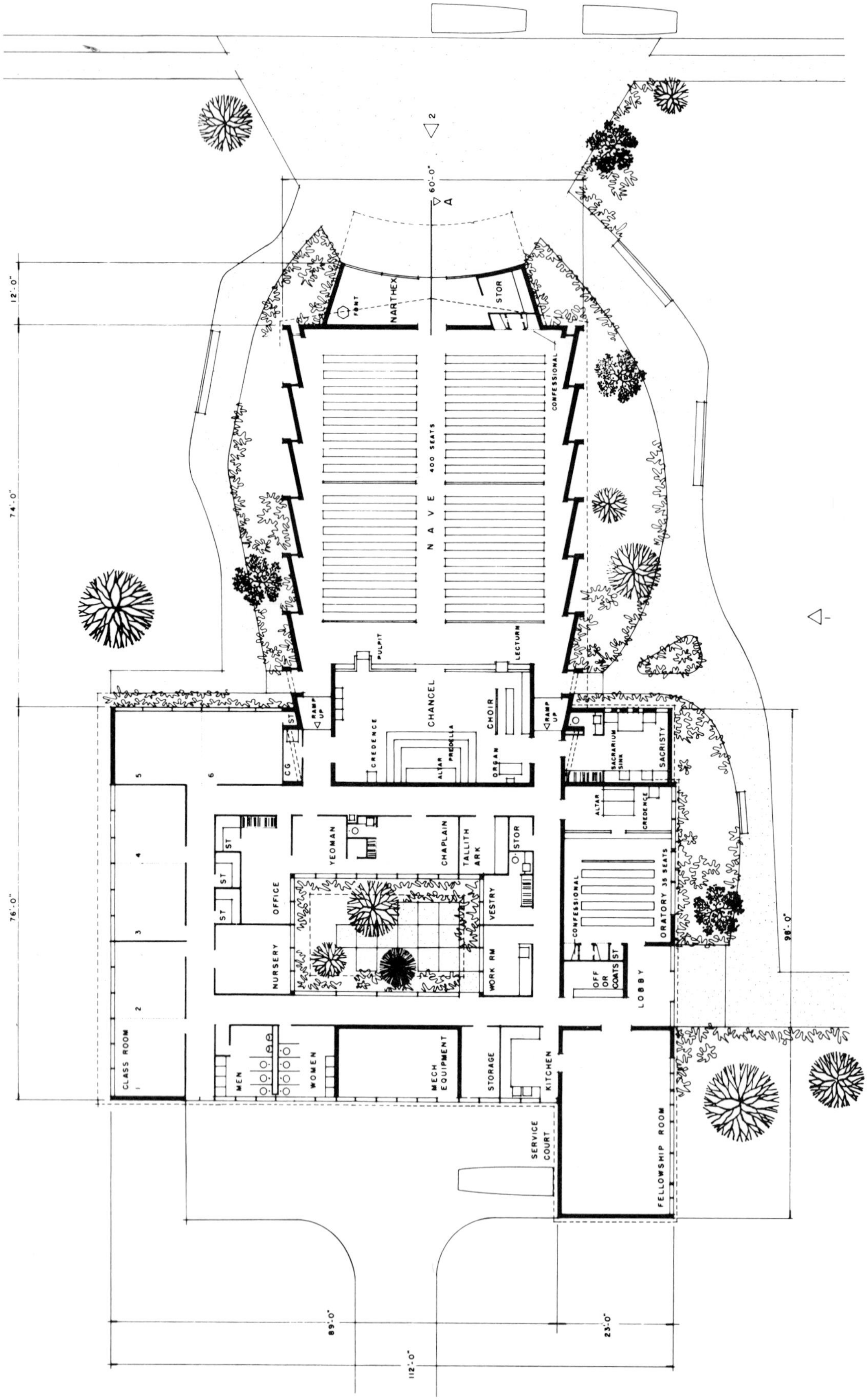

Department of the Navy, Bureau of Yards & Docks, Washington, D.C., Williams, Coile & Blanchard and Associates Architects, Engineers, Washington, D.C.

Fig. 3 Chapel and education center.

By MILDRED C. WIDBER and SCOTT TURNER RITENOUR

TABLE 1   Rooms Needed in Relation to Program and Size of Church School — Through Sixth Grade

	Very small church school, 1-99 pupils		Small church school, 100–199 pupils	
	Enrollment	Housing facilities	Enrollment	Housing facilities
Nursery, infants and toddlers under 18 months		None unless separate space is available.		None unless separate space is available.
Toddlers, ages 1½ and 2		Same as above.		Same as above.
Nursery class, age 3	12	May be necessary to house several 3-year-olds in same room as kindergarten. Try to keep in a separate area of the room with one helper.	18	One room that may be kept just for the 3-year-old group. If church sponsors weekday nursery school, this room and kindergarten room may be used. Rooms should be near each other.
Kindergarten, ages 4 and 5	12	Separate room. Do not encourage attendance of 3-year-olds at expense of 4- and 5-year olds.	20	One room that may be used both during church school hour and church hour. Limit use by others.
Primary, grades 1 and 2	12	One room where age group can meet, but if necessary, along with the entire church school session. May meet separately in a large, divided space.	16–20	Separate room for each 16–20 pupils. Beyond those numbers, two sessions or additional space needed. Grades one and two may meet together or separately.
Lower junior: Grades 3 and 4	10	Same as for primary.	16–25	Separate room, 16–25 in group. Beyond 25, additional space or two sessions needed.
Grades 5 and 6	8	One room or part of room in which juniors may be alone for at least 45 minutes a Sunday. Note: In all cases boys and girls should be grouped together.	16–25	Same as above for lower juniors.

Seventh grade

Grades 7 and 8	6	If necessary, church school class may meet in church pew or in nearby home. For other types of activity, see below.	10–20	One room. (See notes below.)
Grades 9 and 10	6	Same as for grades 7 and 8.	8–15	One room.
Grades 11 and 12	10	Meet in church pews for church school classes. Junior highs and seniors may meet together for activities other than study and discussion. Ordinarily the church sanctuary, a home nearby, or the fellowship room is available for such use.	8–15	Same as above Program activities room may be coordinated for use by all junior and senior high groups. (See notes below.)
Older youth		If older youth are working, they may wish to form a group of their own or they may join with college students. If they are attending college away from home, let the college pastor know. If they are attending college at home, provide for a college-age fellowship. Facilities needed are both those listed in this section and those on chart for adults. In all cases boys and girls should be grouped together.		

Focus: Building for Christian Education, United Church Press, Philadelphia, 1969.

Religious

CHURCH SCHOOLS

Medium church school, 200-299 pupils		Large church school, 300-599 pupils		Very large church school 600 or more pupils
Enrollment	Housing facilities	Enrollment	Housing facilities	
6-10	Provide separate room with cribs and play-pens for those under 18 months.	10	Separate crib and playpen room.	Similar to large church school, but these usually operate in two or three sessions and so have more adequate space for each age group.
6-10	Separate room needed for toddlers — or one room for above, with separate spaces for infants and toddlers.	12	Separate room for toddlers.	
30-36	Two rooms or two sessions. No more than 18 children in any one nursery class group. 15 a better figure.	30-36	Two rooms to be used by 3-year-olds only, or one room used for two or three sessions. No more than 15-18 in any one group.	
40	Two rooms, one for 4-year-olds, one for 5-year-olds. 20 limit in any one group. Or, two 4-5-year-old groups, 20 in each.	50-80	Four rooms — two for 4-year-olds and two for 5-year-olds or two rooms (one for each age) if there are two or three sessions. 20 limit.	
32-60	Two or three rooms, one for each 16-20 pupils. Grades may meet together or separately. May come together occasionally for common interests. These rooms may be used during the week by parents or other groups. Should be multipurpose.	64-80	Four rooms — or two if there is a second session. 16-20 pupils in one group. Grades 1 and 2 may meet together or separately.	
16-75	Same as for primary. May have up to 25 in one group.	64-100	Same as for primary. May have up to 25 in one group.	
16-25	Grades 5 and 6 may meet together or separately, boys and girls together. 16-25 the limit for each group.	32-75	Two or three rooms depending upon enrollment. See medium church school for further details.	
through youth				
20-30	One room large enough for entire group. Smaller spaces for conversation and discussion. Class groups, 8-10. Flexible arrangement possible.	30-60	Flexible arrangement. One room needed where entire group may gather for sings, recreation, dramatics. Small rooms for conversation and discussion groups of 8-10 each.	Enrollment, 60 — similar to large school. Multiple sessions provide more adequate space for each group.
15-25	Same as above for middle high, and senior high.	25-50	Same as above for middle high and senior high.	

The important arrangements for all three youth groups are:
1. A large space for the entire group for varied activities, such as recreation, sings, dramatics.
2. Small, intimate class groupings of 8-10 members each, in which there may be vigorous discussion, research, and study. This means use of the large space for two or three such groups (possibly), with use of other smaller rooms when enrollment necessitates. It is better not to have many small groups meeting in a single space. Intimacy and privacy of class groupings are essential at this age.
3. Formal worship provided by attendance at regular church service.

For any church to consider: When possible, the room used in the church school should be used for the Sunday evening or through-the-week program. Therefore, it should be suited to a variety of activities and provided with ample storage space for supplies and equipment.

Classrooms should be attractive, efficiently designed, and large enough for ample movement.

Recreation, crafts, hobbies, art activities, and drama are part of the ongoing program, and facilities should be provided for them. A kitchenette is desirable.

For a weekday schedule of activities, rooms should be near a building entrance for easy access.

TABLE 2 Summary — School Equipment

Age group	Maximum children per room*	Floor space per child	Toilets, sinks, drinking fountains	Wraps	Cabinets
Nursery I, babies and toddlers birth to age 2	8-10 (Cribs at 3 ft intervals)	35 sq ft — good; 30 sq ft — fair; under 25 sq ft — poor. Separate room for babies and toddlers.	Toilets and wash basins within pre-school room area preferred. Otherwise, observe strictest sanitation facilities for storing and warming food.	Rod hangers in the room (preferably in storage cabinet with shelf above and below), 30 in. above floor. Full length for teachers. Hooks are hazardous. Not recommended.	Movable, ample for supplies.
Nursery II, age 2	8 — good 10 — fair 12 — poor	35 sq ft — good; 30 sq ft — fair; under 25 sq ft — poor. (Warm clean floors for children to sit on. All preschoolers.)	Adjoining room with junior fixtures or wooden step if adult fixtures used. Toilets 10 in., basins 24 in. above floor.	Rod hangers in the room (preferably in storage cabinet with shelf above and below), 30 in. above floor. Full length for teachers. Hooks are hazardous. Not recommended.	Movable, ample for supplies needed. Low open shelves for toys.
Nursery III, age 3	Up to 15 — good 15-18 — fair Over 18 — poor	35 sq ft — good; 30 sq ft — fair; under 25 sq ft — poor.	Adjoining room with junior fixtures or wooden step if adult fixtures used. Toilets 10 in., basins 24 in. above floor.	Rod hangers in the room (preferably in storage cabinet with shelf above and below), 36 in. above floor. Full length for teachers. Hooks are hazardous. Not recommended.	Movable, ample for supplies needed. Low open shelves for toys. Space for filing pictures and materials used in room. Open shelves for toys.
Kindergarten I, II, ages 4 and 5	Up to 20 — good 20-25 — fair Over 25 — poor	35 sq ft — good; 30 sq ft — fair; under 25 sq ft poor.		Rod hangers in the room (preferably in storage cabinet with shelf above and below), 42 in. above floor. Full length for teachers. Hooks are hazardous. Not recommended.	Movable, ample for supplies needed. Low open shelves for toys. Space for filing pictures and for materials used in room. Open shelves for toys.

* Rooms on first floor and above grade level.

TABLE 3 Rooms Needed in Relation to Program and to Size of Church School — Preschool Children

Age group	Church school, 1-99 pupils	Church school, 100-299 pupils	Church school, 300-499 pupils	Church school, 500-899 pupils	Church school, 900 or more pupils
Nursery I, infants and toddlers, under 18 months Nursery II, ages 1½ and 2	Omit — unless suitable separate space is available.	Omit — unless suitable separate space is available.	Possible here to provide one room for toddlers. If there is a need, consider separate room with cribs and playpens, etc., for those under 18 months.	Separate crib and playpen room. Separate room for toddlers.	Similar to larger church schools.
Nursery III, age 3	May be necessary to house several 3-year-olds in same room as kindergarten. Try to separate parts of the room, using one helper.	Enrollment 8-18. One room that may be kept for just the 3-year-old group. If the church sponsors a weekday nursery school, this room and kindergarten room may be used. Have rooms near each other.	Enrollment 20-30. Two rooms. These may be used during the week by parent groups, etc., particularly if a folding partition separates them.	Enrollment 32-54. Three rooms to be used by 3-year-olds only, or one room used for each of two or three sessions.	These usually operate in two sessions.
Kindergarten I, II, ages 4 and 5	Enrollment up to 12. Separate room. Do not encourage attendance of 3-year-olds at expense of the 4- and 5-year-olds.	Enrollment 16-25. One room to be used both during the church school hour and church hour; limited use by others.	Enrollment 40-50. Two rooms, one for 4-year-olds and one for 5-year-olds. It is helpful to have rooms adjoining for possible use by adults.	Enrollment 64-100. Four rooms, two for 4-year-olds and two for 5-year-olds; or two rooms (one for each age) used for two or three sessions.	Three sessions would provide more adequate space for each age group.

Display space	Furniture	Other materials
Grooved picture rail 14 in. above floor. Tack board extending from 14 to 38 in. above the floor.	Cribs — preferably bassinets on metal frames with rubber tires. Playpens, bed linen, plastic mats for playpens.	
Grooved picture rail 17 in. above the floor. Tack board extending 17 to 43 in. above the floor.	Chairs 6 in. from floor. Not needed for every child. Tables — height 16 in. — small. Tops 18 by 24 in. A book table — not essential if space limited.	Large blocks (2 x 4 x 8 in. and 2 x 4 x 12 in.); floor toys (peg wagon, wooden, train, cars); books, pictures; a Bible; cuddly toys (stuffed animals, rag dolls); housekeeping toys (doll, doll bed, tea table and dishes); ball; picture rail; offering container; wastebasket; growing plants or other nature materials; a songbook, or collection of songs, recommended in the literature for use by the leaders. Add later (where space permits) walking board; more housekeeping equipment (pans, telephone, small rocking chair); push and pull toys; small wagon, resting mats; washable rug or rugs for floor.
Grooved picture rail 20 in. above the floor. Tack board extending from 20 to 48 in. above floor.	Chairs 8 in. from floor. A few 6 in. Tables, height, 18 in. Tops, 24 by 36 in. or 28 by 42 in. Teacher's table, 18 by 24 in. Piano — not essential but desirable.	Large blocks (2 x 4 x 8 in. and 2 x 4 x 12 in.); floor toys (cars, trucks, train, boat); ball, books; a Bible; pictures; housekeeping toys; a songbook, or collection of songs, recommended in the literature for use by the leaders; offering container; wastebasket; growing plants or other nature materials. Add later (where space permits) easels for painting; paint; set of steps; large hollow blocks; more housekeeping toys (broom, ironing board, iron, clothesline, doll carriage — large enough to come to waist of child); large puzzles, sets of wooden animals and people for block play; low bench or stools near place for wraps.
Grooved picture rail 24 in. above floor. Tack board extending from 24 to 54 in. above floor.	Chairs 10 in. from floor. Tables, height 20 in. Tops 24 by 42 in. or 28 by 48 in. Piano desirable.	Large blocks (2 x 4 x 8 in. and 2 x 4 x 12 in.); floor toys for dramatic play; books; a Bible; pictures; housekeeping toys; paper scissors; large crayons; a songbook or collection of songs, recommended in the literature for use by the teachers; offering container; wastebasket; growing plants or other nature materials; display or tack strip space. Add later (where space permits) easels for painting; paint; large hollow blocks; large puzzles; sets of wooden animals and people for block play; small aprons, nurses' caps, pocketbooks, ties, for dramatic play in housekeeping center.

TABLE 4 Rooms Needed by Elementary Children as Related to School Size

	Church school, 1-99 pupils	Church school, 100-299 pupils	Church school, 300-499 pupils	Church school, 500-899 pupils	Church school, 900 or more pupils
Primary, grades 1, 2, and 3	Enrollment up to 18. One room where age group can meet, but if necessary along with the entire church school session. May be part of large space divided.	Enrollment 24-54. One room; or one large room and one medium size room for approximately 25. Two grades can use large room for all purposes. One grade can use smaller room for all purposes or unite with the other two grades.	Enrollment 60-90. Three rooms — one for each school grade to be treated as three separate groups; or may come together occasionally for worship or other purposes.	Enrollment 96-162. Six rooms — or three if there is a second session. Handle as separate groups.	Have more adequate space for each age group.
Junior, grades 4, 5, and 6	Enrollment up to 15. One room or part of room in which juniors may be alone for at least 45 minutes a Sunday. May have to worship some of the time with older groups in the church school.	Enrollment 20-45. Same as requirements for primary children.	Enrollment 50-75. Three rooms, one for each grade; or one large room and one medium size for approximately 30.	Enrollment 80-135. Same as for primary.	

TABLE 5 Summary of Space and Equipment for Elementary School Children

Age group	Maximum children per room*	Floor space per child	Toilets, basins, drinking facilities	Wraps
Primary, grades 1, 2, and 3; ages 6, 7, and 8	Up to 25 — good 25-30 — fair 30-35 — poor (See comment below for assembly)	30 sq ft — good 25 sq ft — fair 20 sq ft — poor	Separate toilets for boys, girls. Readily accessible on same floor. Washbasins 28 in. from floor. Toilets 14 in. from floor. Sink with running water and double drain board in room preferred.	Some prefer in room. Use rod hangers 42 to 48 in. above floor, shelf above.
Juniors, grades 4, 5, and 6; ages 9, 10 and 11	Up to 25 — good 25-30 — fair 30-35 — poor Up to 45 pupils, 3 rooms; 1 larger for assembly at times.	20-30 sq ft — good 25 sq ft — fair 20 sq ft — poor	As above except basins 30 in; toilets 16 in. from floor.	Some prefer in room, otherwise in recessed corridor storage space. Use rod hangers 48-54 in. above floor, shelf above.

* Preferably on first floor, above grade level.

TABLE 6 Rooms Needed in Relation to Program and to Size of Church School — Youth Division

	Church school, 1-99 pupils	Church school, 100-299 pupils	Church school, 300-499 pupils	Church school, 500-899 pupils	Church school, 900 or more pupils
Junior high	Enrollment up to 12. Church school class may meet in church pew or in nearby home. For other types of activity, see below.	Enrollment 12-35. Church school classes may be held in sanctuary if necessary but a meeting space is needed for other program activities.	Enrollment 35-60. Department Assembly Room, plus two classrooms large enough for classes of 15-20. Assembly room may be used for through-the-week activities.	Enrollment 60-100. Department Assembly Room with classrooms for groups of 15-20. Assembly room should be available for activities of junior highs throughout the week.	Enrollment 100 or more. Three departments should be provided, one for each grade. Provide each section with an Assembly Room and classrooms.
Senior high	Enrollment up to 10. Meet in church pews for Church school classes. Junior highs and seniors may meet together for activities other than study and discussion. Ordinarily the church sanctuary, a home nearby, or the fellowship room is available for such use.	Enrollment 10-30. Same as above. Separate room should be available for program activities.	Enrollment 24-40. Assembly Room with two classrooms. A third class may meet in the assembly room itself. Such a room also becomes a headquarters for the Youth Fellowship.	Enrollment 50-90. Department Assembly Room with classrooms for groups of about 20.	Enrollment 90. Department Assembly and Room with classrooms over for groups of not more than 25.
Older youth	If older youth are working, they may wish to have a group of their own, or they may join with college students. If they are attending college away from home, let the college pastor know. If they are attending college at home, provide for a college-age fellowship. Facilities needed are both those listed in this section and those under "Adult."	For any church to consider: Where possible the same room should be used for assembly and worship in the church school and also for Sunday evening or through-the-week program. Therefore, it should be suited to a variety of activities and provided with ample storage space for supplies and equipment. Classrooms should be attractive, efficiently designed, and large enough to allow for ample movement. Recreation, crafts, hobbies, and drama are part of the ongoing program and facilities should be provided for them. A kitchenette is desirable. For a weekday schedule of activities, room should be easy of access, near building entrance.			

Cabinets	Display space	Furniture	Other materials
Ample space carefully planned for pupils' and teachers' supplies, handiwork, picture storage. Open shelves for books.	Grooved picture rail 30 in. above the floor. Tack board 30 to 62 in. above the floor. Portable blackboards or turnover charts made for handling and tack boards on one or two sides of room.	Chairs 14 in. from floor, some 12 in. Table tops 30 by 48 or 54 in., 24 in. high. Small tables for beauty or worship centers. Piano. Record player.	Recommended literature, one or more Bibles, paper, pencils, crayons, paste, scissors. Songbook for pianist and teacher's use (one recommended in the literature). Pictures, books chosen according to unit being studied; simple reference books. Song charts. Growing plants or other nature materials, wastebasket, picture rail, movable blackboard or large sheets of newsprint on an easel may be desired.
Same as above but provide storage for maps, large objects.	Grooved picture rail 36 in. above the floor. Tack board 36 to 72 in. above floor.	Chairs 16 in. from floor. Table tops 30 by 48 or 54 in., 26 in. high. Piano. Small tables for beauty and worship center. Record player.	Recommended literature, a Bible for the department, a Bible for each child. Songbooks for children's use (one recommended in the literature), pictures. Books chosen according to unit being studied, paper, pencils, crayons, paste, scissors; offering container. Wastebasket, growing plants or other nature materials, picture rail, movable blackboard or large sheets of newsprint on an easel may be useful. Add later Bible dictionary; Bible atlas, maps, a globe, reference books, copies of different translations of the Bible, a dictionary.

TABLE 7   Summary of Space and Equipment for Youth*

Age group	Maximum pupils per room	Floor space per pupil	Furniture and equipment
Junior high I, II, III, and grades 7, 8, and 9; ages 12, 13, and 14	20 pupils — good 10–15 pupils — preferred	15–18 sq ft — good 12–15 sq ft — fair 10–12 sq ft — poor	Lightweight tables without drawers. Space to store extra tables and chairs. Comfortable, sturdy chairs, blackboard or turn-over chart frames with large sheets of paper. Display board, wall maps, youth library, pianos, record player and record storage, recreational equipment and place to store it. Bibles, textbooks, etc.
Senior high and older youth; grades 10, 11, and 12; ages 15, 16, and 17	25 pupils maximum	Same as above	Equipped for audiovisuals. Nearby accessible cloak storage space, toilet facilities. Storage cabinets for pictures, hymnals, materials and supplies. Colorful, attractive furnishings in keeping with decor of building.
Older youth, 18–23 years			

* Provision should be made for recreation, worship, handicraft and hobbies, dramatics, youth choirs, and refreshments.

TABLE 8   Rooms Needed in Relation to Program and to Size of Church School — Adult Division*

	Church school, 1-99 pupils	Church school, 100-299 pupils	Church school, 300-499 pupils	Church school, 500-899 pupils	Church school, 900 or more pupils
Young adult	Enrollment up to 10. Church school class may meet in sanctuary or in nearby home. Social, recreation, and service activities of class, and of young adult fellowship, may use church dining room or homes of members.	Enrollment up to 30. One classroom advisable especially for parents' class, or a mixed group. Class may use sanctuary. For other class and young adult fellowship activities use may be made of church fellowship hall, or similar room and homes of members.	Enrollment up to 50. Two classrooms advisable; one for parents' group, one for a mixed group. Sanctuary pews may be used. Young adult fellowship Sunday night and week night activities in fellowship hall or other rooms, or in homes. Provision needed for dramatics, recreation, and audiovisuals.	Enrollment up to 50. Same needs in general as medium church school, except provision for more class groupings according to interest needs. A church hobby room would enlist many young adults. Provision needed also for dramatics, recreation, and audiovisuals.	Enrollment 100 or more. Same needs in general as large church school. More activities on Sunday night and week nights will need church space because homes cannot usually accommodate larger attendance.
Middle adult	Enrollment up to 10. Church school class may meet in sanctuary or nearby home.	Enrollment up to 30. One or two class meeting places in sanctuary or available rooms in other parts of the church.	Enrollment up to 50. Same general space and equipment needs as medium church school, with allowance for larger attendance and provision for informal interest groups.	Enrollment up to 90. Same general space and equipment needs as medium church school, with allowance for more classes, especially short-term interest groups.	Enrollment 100 or more. Smaller classes of 20 to 30 preferable to one or two large classes.
	Middle adults will also be active in men's fellowships, women's associations, and other organized groups and will need space and equipment for such activities. However, these meeting places will probably be used by other age groups at other times, thus making it unnecessary to build and equip these rooms for adults only. Storage space must thus be provided for equipment that will serve the different age groups.				
Older adult	Enrollment up to 7. No special facilities needed. Older adults will probably participate in middle adult study and activities.	Enrollment up to 21. May participate with middle adults. If separate class is needed, a section of the pews in the sanctuary will probably be available	Enrollment up to 35	Enrollment 65 or more	Enrollment up to 65

* The enrollment figures used in this chart are based on a sampling of a variety of church schools. It was found that there were approximately 27 adults to every 100 pupils enrolled in the church school. The figure 27 was broken down into 10 young adults, 10 middle adults, and 7 older adults. However, church school situations are so varied in proportionate age groupings that many exceptions must be made.

Space should also be considered for meeting of entire adult department of the church school. An office for administration of the adult department, and for records, is desirable. A fellowship hall with stage, kitchenette, provision for audiovisuals, hobbies, recreation, and service activities will provide for a multiplicity of uses for almost every kind of adult need.

TABLE 9   Summary of Space and Equipment for Adults*

Age group	Maximum persons per room	Floor space per person	Furniture and equipment
Young adults, ages 24-35	20-25 preferred 50 persons maximum	Lecture type, 8-10 sq ft per person	Facilities for study groups and discussions, tables for discussion groups and study, comfortable chairs, blackboards or turnover charts, lecterns, pictures, Bibles, books, pianos, cabinets for supplies, provision for dramatics and audiovisuals.
Adults, ages 36-64		10-12 sq ft for activity-type teaching	Facilities for teas, light refreshments, suppers, hobby and recreation, and informal fellowship weekday clubs, recreation, etc.
Older adults, age 65 up			Small meditation room apart from the nave or chapel.

* For adults and older adults, rooms should be on first floor, if possible.

Religious

CHURCH SCHOOLS

TABLE 10   Rooms Needed in Relation to Program and to Size of Church School Administrative Functions

Persons and functions	Church school, 1-99 pupils	Church school, 100-299 pupils	Church school, 300-499 pupils	Church school, 500-899 pupils	Church school 900 or more pupils
Pastor	Study and work room. Built-in table and shelves with curtain or doors to conceal mimeograph equipment when not in use.	Study and separate work room. Closet for supplies.	Study and office for secretary with equipment for records. Work room with cabinets for supplies.	Study with office for secretary. Office for church secretary. Offices for other staff members and their secretaries. Work room and supply closets.	Same as for 500–899 church school with addition of conference or board room adequate for largest group, should have table, exhibit space, blackboard, A-V equipment.
Director of Christian Education	None.	None.	Office large enough for desk, table, bookcases, and chairs. Space for counseling and small committee work.	Office large enough for desk, table, bookcases, chairs, with space for counseling and committee work. A separate office for secretary.	Same as for 500–899 church school plus offices for age group assistants and their secretaries.
Church School Supt., Secretary, and Treasurer	Desk space with shelves or chest of drawers for literature, supplies, and records.	Room with desks and cabinets for records, literature and supplies.	Room with desks, cabinets for records, literature, and supplies.	Room with desks, work table, filing cabinet for records. Storeroom for literature and supplies.	Same as for 500–899 church school but with increased space.
Choir Director	Desk or table space. Cabinet for filing church music. Closet or cabinet for choir robes.	Room with desk or table. Cabinets for music and choir robes. Shelves for hymnals used by choir.	Office with desk, cabinet, and piano. Room with table, and cabinets for music, choir robes, hymnals.	Office and studio with piano. Room for robing of choir with cabinets for music, robes, and hymns.	Same as for 500–899 church school but with more ample robe closets and robing space.
Library	Built-in bookcases with locks, or space for movable units. Filing cabinets for records.	Room with bookcases (built-in or movable), table, chairs, filing cabinet for records. Cabinet for picture files.	Room with bookcases, table, chairs, cabinets for records, filing pictures and maps. Exhibit cabinets.	Large room with tables, chairs, with space for reading and study. Picture and files. Cabinet for records. World friendship museum.	Same as for 500–899 church school but with increased space and equipment.

Governmental and Public

CITY AND TOWN HALLS	675	YWCA BUILDINGS	742
COURTHOUSES	680	BOYS' CLUBS	755
FIRE STATIONS	700	RECREATION CENTERS	761
FIREHOUSES	703	NEIGHBORHOOD SERVICE CENTERS	767
POLICE STATIONS	708	EMBASSIES	769
POLICE FACILITY	718	POST OFFICES	773
JAILS AND PRISONS	725	ACCESS RAMPS FOR THE HANDICAPPED	774
YMCA BUILDINGS	741	PUBLIC TOILET ROOMS FOR THE HANDICAPPED	775

Steps to be taken in planning and constructing a city hall are (1) determining need, (2) determining space requirements, (3) selecting an architect, (4) acquiring a site, (5) approving layout, design, and architectural features, and (6) developing a financial plan. These steps are not a one-two-three process; frequently they must be done simultaneously. It is important to have an idea of what is wanted before selecting an architect, but the architect can be helpful in delineating wants. It is important to remember that the city hall must last 60 years or more. The following "dos and don'ts" provide a guide to officials engaged in planning a new city hall.

Do:

1. Locate the city hall where it will be most convenient and if possible where land values are reasonable.

2. Be prepared to provide the architect with information on departments to be housed, the number of employees, types of furnishings and equipment, and special requirements such as vault and storage space.

3. Provide ample off-street parking space for both employees and the public.

4. Put most or all city department headquarters in the city hall.

5. Provide for structural expansion and flexibility in office layout.

6. Plan the city hall from the inside out with emphasis on work flow, convenience to the public, and convenience for employees.

7. Provide for the comfort and efficiency of employees with controlled ventilation and adequate lighting.

8. Provide for employee lounges and rest rooms.

9. Use materials, construction, and furnishings which make the city hall easy to maintain.

10. Provide open, unobstructed counters for transactions with the public.

Don't:

1. Don't locate in an area of declining property values except when part of a comprehensive urban renewal program.

2. Don't try to remodel an old post office, school building, convention hall, or other building designed for some other special use.

3. Don't forget that the city hall is an office building, not a monument or an ornament.

4. Don't underestimate space needs; the average commercial office building lasts 67 years.

5. Don't tie up valuable space with indoor pistol ranges, drive-through garages, private exits, wide corridors, and other gadgets.

6. Don't cut up the city hall into cubbyholes for minor officials.

Planning the New City Hall, Report #212, Management Information Service, International City Managers' Association, Washington, D.C., September 1961.

7. Don't build the city hall over two stories in height if at all possible.

8. Don't let the public come in contact with police or criminal activities.

9. Don't provide in the main lobby any facilities, such as a cigar and soft drink stand, which encourage loitering.

DETERMINING NEED

The need for a new city hall may seem obvious to those who spend their working hours at the city hall. Ceilings are high; heating costs are twice what they should be; space originally meant for storage has been converted to offices; electrical wiring violates code provisions; and the present facility is just old anyway. All of this—and more besides—may be true, but what is not known is how extensive the need is. This must be determined by careful study. In determining the need for a city hall alternate courses of action should be studied.

Factors Influencing Need Determining the extent of need involves two areas: (1) condition of building, and (2) space needs.

The condition of the building is the easiest to evaluate. Things to be considered are type of construction, structural condition, electrical wiring, heating and ventilating, and facilities such as rest rooms. Nothing may be seriously wrong and a new facility still needed, but it is important to know these points. Careful and professional review may bring factors to light heretofore not considered.

At an early stage it is important to have some idea of space needs. This can be determined in general terms by having each department submit their space needs for review and study. If departments are already crowded, additional space needed now is not hard to estimate. The real problem in determining space needs is what will be needed in the future. The building may be adequate now, but will it be in 5, 10, 20 years? Few cities decide to build a new city hall and do so almost immediately. Experience seems to indicate that a new city hall is the outgrowth of a number of years of careful planning and, once built, lasts a long time.

In estimating future needs not only must traditional services such as police and building inspection be considered but also what future services the city may be required to provide. One of the "dos" is to provide for structural expansion. However, provision for such expansion must be in reason, and should be based on projections of future needs. Knowledge of the community and its people is essential to space planning. City officials should know the population projections for the next 20 or 25 years, the economic level of the community, and present and probable social and economic characteristics.

SELECTING THE LOCATION OF THE CITY HALL

Civic Centers In selecting the location for a city hall, the first consideration is whether it should be placed on a site by itself or whether it should

be combined with a group of related buildings in a civic center. The civic center has had great appeal to the city planner because it offers certain advantages and at the same time provides for latitude in design. The buildings that are included in civic centers range from a grouping of strictly administrative offices and service buildings to a complex of office buildings, auditoriums, libraries, and so on.

The great advantage of a civic center is that the grouping of public buildings may prove to be convenient to the public in transacting business that requires visits to more than one public agency. It also may result in one or more governmental units being able to use the facilities of the other. Finally, it often is convenient to have certain facilities grouped together in order to expedite interagency and governmental relations.

Obviously if a city hall is to be part of a civic center, it must be planned in relation to the other facilities. For instance, the San Jose, California, city hall is part of a civic center consisting of a health building, communications building, police garage, county office building, sheriff's department and jail, criminal-legal building, and a juvenile center. Some of the facilities, such as the administrative offices in the health building, did not have to be repeated in the city hall.

Site selection for a civic center must consider the factors listed below for locating a city hall. In addition, several other points are important. The site for a civic center must permit flexibility in building arrangement. Since more land is necessary, street patterns may have to be altered, and additional land will be needed for parking. Once the site has been selected, means must be found to preserve it for gradual development of all the units. Also, the site must be located so as not to interfere with the normal development of the business district.

On the surface the civic center idea has great appeal. There are those who feel that center concept has limitations. An article by Richard A. Miller entitled "Are Civic Centers Obsolete?," *Architectural Forum,* January, 1959, highlights these objections. Miller points out that cities range in size "from mammoth concentrations" to small cities. "As a rule, the concentration of community buildings can be increased in inverse ratio to the size of the city." One of the strong points made in the article relates to the discussion above on decentralization of city offices:

> Government buildings—the city hall, fire station, and police stations—which were long the nucleus of most civic centers, tend themselves to be dispersed today. The reason is obvious. Fire and police buildings, for example, are best located at a central point in the street network, and with the building of expressways, this point rarely intersects with the best location for the mayor's office or the council chamber. Service agencies (such as the water and park departments) increasingly favor headquarters locations adjacent to their operating facilities. In Philadelphia, where two new government office-type buildings will be erected, the city also plans to remodel and expand the old city hall in Penn Center to

CITY AND TOWN HALLS

house the mayor and the council—thus retaining a symbolic center of government in the heart of the city.

City-County Building The county-seat city should investigate the possibility of constructing one building to serve the needs of both the city and the county. At least 40 cities and counties occupy the same building.

The city-county building has two major advantages. First, local governmental facilities are together, which is frequently a convenience to the public and to city and county agencies that have contact with each other. The second advantage is cost savings. Depending on conditions, a joint building can be constructed for less money than two separate facilities when all costs are considered: land, engineering and architectural fees, financing charges, and so on. Joint occupancy can result in operating savings.

The majority of cities that occupy office space with the county feel that the arrangement is very satisfactory. The most often stated disadvantage is lack of room for expansion. A joint city-county building must be carefully planned so that both governmental units have area to expand in. A city and a county have different as well as similar needs. When the differences are too great, a city-county building can cause problems. The other drawback is that expenses and responsibilities for operating the building are not always distributed equitably. It is thus extremely important that an agreement for building operation and maintenance be worked out in advance of construction.

Location The selection of a site for a city hall will be influenced by a number of circumstances. Some of these conditions are limiting in nature, such as the availability of land. There are, however, certain guiding principles that should be considered. When Tacoma and Pierce County decided to build a city-county building the planned commissions of each governmental unit jointly developed a set of location factors. The six applicable principles for a city hall location are as follows:

1. "Government must serve and be accessible to the people. . ." Efficiency of service is related to how convenient governmental facilities are for the majority of those citizens using the facility.

2. "Since public services must serve every citizen as well as, and as conveniently as possible, those activities must be located near the center of transportation and the center of business activity. In the large city public transportation comes to a head in the central business district. Major arterial streets are planned to bring people in and out of the city center. In most cases the city hall should be located near public transportation, if any, and certainly near major arterial streets.

The city hall should be near the center of business activity because this is where the principal users of the facility are most frequently located. As an example, attorneys frequently must use records that are housed in city hall. A city should determine what groups most often come to city hall and place the facility as close to those groups as possible.

3. "Government offices must have integration with, not isolation from, other offices in order to serve the public efficiently and effectively." City government agencies use the services of professional men and other businesses. Locating the city hall near the center of business activity helps expedite the work of the agencies located in city hall.

4. "Maximum use of transit systems will result in the least public parking areas and

cause the least congestion on city streets." Obviously this applies only to the city having some form of public transit. People travel either by walking or by using cars, taxis, or public transit. If the city hall is readily accessible to automobiles only, parking requirements would increase in direct ratio to the increased use of the car. For the city that does not have transit systems, location in the center area of the city may help to reduce parking requirements. People come to the city center to do a variety of things; frequently they park and walk between different places of business.

5. "The central business district is the real civic center of the 20th century." A lot has been said about the deteriorating central business district. The impression has been given that the central city is drying up; that everything is moving out. Thus why not the city hall. In the first place there is good reason to believe that the moving out has largely been the retail store and to a lesser extent the office building. Secondly, in the large city, the concentration of people makes it possible for certain types of business, including retail, to operate more efficiently; in the small city the general business area is staying intact for the same reason. A city cannot afford to allow the central business district to dry up because of the investment it represents. The proper placement of the city hall in the central business district can contribute to the life of this area.

6. "More than the initial land cost must be included under the economic considerations of the site. . ." The site should allow for expansion. Site development cost must be considered. These expenditures include demolition of existing structures, if any, grading utilities, and flood protection.

LAYOUT, DESIGN, AND CONSTRUCTION FEATURES

General Building Layout Building arrangement is the next step in planning a city hall. It is helpful as a starting point to use the following checklist of departments, offices, special-purpose rooms, and service areas in analyzing interior building requirements:

1. Departments requiring constant contact with the general public and the collection or payment of money—for example, the finance department and tax collector

2. Departments requiring contact with special classes of the public—for example, city-owned utilities, building permits, personnel, city planning, and city clerk

3. Other departments including public works, recreation, police, fire, etc.

4. City council chamber and office space for use by the mayor and councilmen

5. Offices for the chief administrator

6. Courtrooms

7. Storage vaults and record rooms

8. Locker rooms, rest rooms, janitor closets, public telephones, and space for heating, ventilating, plumbing, and electrical equipment

9. "Circulating areas" for lobbies, corridors, elevators, and stairways

The relationship of one room or functional area to another is important. No room exists by itself, and many of the problems of living in a building arise from the neglect of this fact. Departments related in function should be located near one another and consecutive operations planned in production-line style. Excessive lobbies and hall space add to the cost of construction without adding usable space.

The height of the building will depend upon the amount of ground available and the amount of office space needed. Land generally is cheaper than additional height. Taller buildings

are more difficult to maintain and require more planning of the interior to get related functions on adjacent floors. Also any city building of more than two floors should have an elevator, especially if the public has any great use of the top floor.

Provision for a full basement housing general offices is not often made in new city office buildings. Most professional organizations advise against locating general offices in the basement. The basement can be used for storage and service activities such as duplicating, receiving and shipping rooms, heating and air-conditioning equipment, and central switchboard.

Departmental Layout Departmental layout will depend on the activities carried on by the department and the tools or special equipment used. For example, a finance department layout may require an open area for accounting clerks and collectors with one or two private offices, a machine room, and a vault. The public works department, on the other hand, may require private offices for the director, the engineer, and individual inspectors, a drafting room, a vault, a plan or map room, and conference rooms.

The first step in departmental layout is to survey the work done by the department. Work flow should be especially studied. A complete list should be made of all employees and equipment to occupy the space. The possibility of future expansion should be anticipated and provision made for additional personnel. Provision also should be made for peak rather than average work loads. Flow of work should, as nearly as practicable, be in a straight line. Normally, work should come to the employees rather than their going to the work. Minor activities can be grouped around areas of major activity.

Private Offices A major factor in the determination of space needs is the question of who should get private offices and under what circumstances. More space is required for private offices; space utilization is restricted through segregation of areas for private offices; and considerable expense is involved in rearranging and reerecting partitions. Ventilation, lighting, and heating problems are complicated by a number of small offices; supervision and coordination of work, flow of work, and communications are made more difficult. An open, well-arranged office has a more orderly and businesslike appearance than a series of small offices.

Certain conditions justify private offices. First, transactions of a confidential nature require private facilities. General conference rooms, however, where confidential meetings may be held as occasion demands, may reduce the need for private offices. Second, privacy is often desirable not so much because of the confidential nature of the work, but because of the number of persons interviewed or because the work is of an independent nature which requires more quiet and privacy than the open office will allow. There is little agreement as to who should have private offices except for the chief administrative officer and department heads.

Chief Administrator's Office The location of the chief administrator's office is important to good public relations. It should be located so as to give the impression of being easily reached and open to any caller, but it should not be too prominent. The second floor ordinarily is a good location since some effort must be expended to visit it, and the casual or merely curious individual is less likely to intrude.

A first-floor location, however, can be just as good if callers are properly screened by a secretary or receptionist. It has the additional advantage of being close to the offices most frequented by the public. Of interest to council-manager cities is the fact that the mayor has an office in the majority of cases located very close to the city manager's office. See the

second-floor plan of the Alhambra, California, city hall (Fig. 1) for a typical executive layout.

The administrator's office should be large enough for meetings of department heads unless a conference room adjoins his office. A conference table that will accommodate up to 12 people is desirable. Space should be provided adjacent to the administrator's office

for a secretary and one or more assistants, depending upon the size of the city. The secretary's office would also serve as a reception room for people who call on the administrator.

Council Members The council meeting room should be carefully planned if full use is to be made of it. Location of the council chamber is

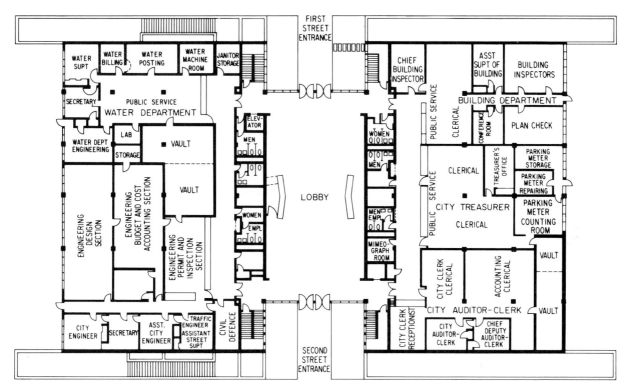

FIRST FLOOR PLAN

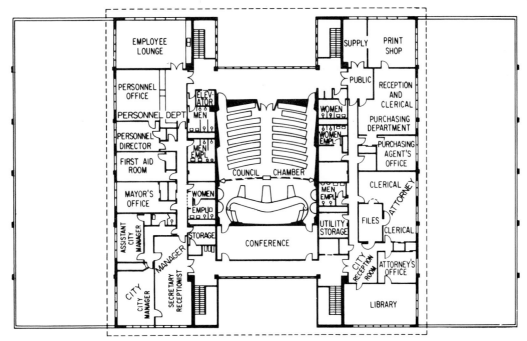

SECOND FLOOR PLAN

Fig. 1 Alhambra, California, City Hall.

important because of the public nature of the business transacted there. Most of the cities with multistoried buildings have located the council room on the first or second floor.

The offices located near or around the council chamber are usually those of the city clerk, city attorney, and city manager. Small meeting rooms and an office for the mayor and councilmen may be located nearby.

In most cities surveyed, councilmen sit at separate desks or at a semicircular table, the open end of which faces the citizens. In only a few cities do the councilmen have their backs to the public. The mayor usually sits in the center flanked by the manager, clerk, and attorney. The council table often is put on a dais 18 in. or 2 ft above the main floor (see Fig. 2).

It is well to plan the council chamber so that it also can be used for other purposes. In many cities it is used as a general courtroom for public hearings held by city agencies, as a meeting room for the city planning or zoning commission, for general conferences, and as a public meeting room.

Finance Activities The collection activities of the finance department have more contact with the public than any other municipal activity with the possible exception of the police and building departments. A prominent location near the front entrance is therefore desirable. Avoidance of cubbyholes for separate functions and provision for a large work area enhance the appearance of the building and give the impression of a well-planned and efficient layout. Collection functions should be located near the public counter with billing, assessing, accounting, budgeting, and purchasing at a greater distance. These activities should be so grouped and arranged that the supervisor can observe the work of all his employees. A drive-in collection window should be provided where possible.

A separate, soundproofed machine room should be provided where machines are used in accounting or billing. Acoustical ceilings and walls, thermopane glass partitions, and carpeted floors will absorb much of the machine noise and make for more efficient working conditions in the general office. A vault for safekeeping of records should be provided unless one is provided near by in the city clerk's office.

Police Department The police department is singled out for discussion because of the special facilities it needs other than regular office space. As noted, the police department is frequently not included in the city hall. When it is, however, it should be basically separate from other city hall activities, and public and criminal activities should be separated.

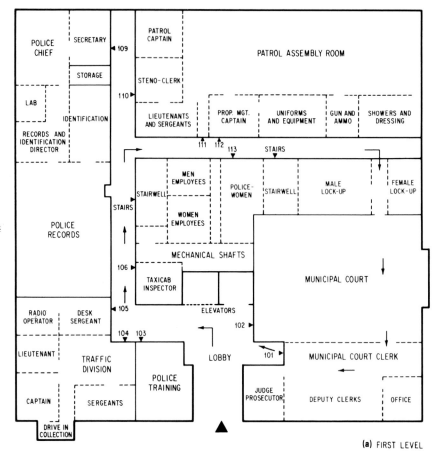

(a) FIRST LEVEL

Fig. 3   Raleigh, North Carolina, City Hall.

The extent of facilities will depend largely on the size of the community and the size of the department. In planning police station facilities, several basic needs should be considered by all cities. Jail cells should be away from public areas. Prisoner retention for any period requires toilets, kitchen facilities, and separation of men and women prisoners. Because of the expense of cellblocks, the possibility of using county jail facilities should be investigated. Many communities contract with the county for prisoner care. This may be impractical for very large cities, but cities up to 100,000 certainly can effectively use this method of reducing police station cost. If county facilities are used, it is then necessary only to pro-

vide a retention room or rooms with toilet facilities. Such rooms do not need to be regular cells.

The communications center should be isolated from the general public and other work areas. However, in smaller communities where it is necessary for communications personnel to act as receptionists, this is not possible. In such a case the communications section might be located in a glass enclosure with a sliding panel.

Fingerprinting, photographic, identification, and booking areas should be located together, although not necessarily in the same room. Where possible, a separate prisoner entrance leading directly into the area for booking should be provided. The essential element is to provide a continuous process of booking, fingerprinting, photographing, and identifying of prisoners in the same area of the building. Where possible, it is desirable to have the area near the jail or retention area.

Provide plenty of space for storage. Firearms and other equipment should be stored in locked cabinets. Room for confiscated, lost, and abandoned articles is necessary if such items are to be kept properly.

When patrolmen change shifts on beats it is not necessary to have a large assembly room, but it is desirable to provide space for officers to fill out reports. In large departments, the detective force will need a separate room with lineup facilities.

In the very large departments separate rooms for interrogating prisoners are neces-

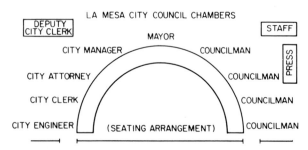

Fig. 2   City Council seating arrangement, La Mesa, California.

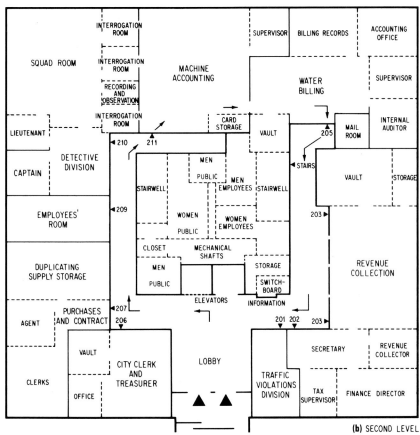

(b) SECOND LEVEL

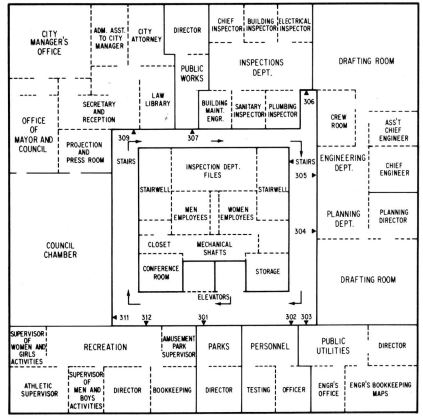

sary. In the medium-sized department, the detective squad room can be used for interrogation. A separate room for the use of prisoners and their attorneys or visitors is important when the station has facilities for housing prisoners. Finally the large city should have a courtroom near the jail or detention facilities of the police department.

The police department facilities of the Raleigh city hall are well planned (Figs. 3a-c). Separation is achieved by having the police department on ground level except for the detective bureau. The detective bureau is reached by a stairwell located so that the general public would not have use for it. Notice that the traffic violations division is on the second level right across from the city clerk and treasurer's office. This places money collecting in one area and very convenient to the public. The municipal court is off the lobby on the ground level and next to the male and female lockups.

Design of the City Hall The city hall is essentially an office building, not a monument or an ornament. The building should be so designed as to be economical in construction and maintenance. True long-range economy is achieved by a judicious balance between original cost and maintenance cost. A building with cheap materials and equipment for the sake of low first cost may be quite expensive in maintenance and replacement.

Even though the city hall should be basically functional and not a monument, originality in design is not precluded.

Fig. 3 (cont.)   Raleigh, North Carolina, City Hall.

(c) THIRD LEVEL

Governmental and Public

COURTHOUSES

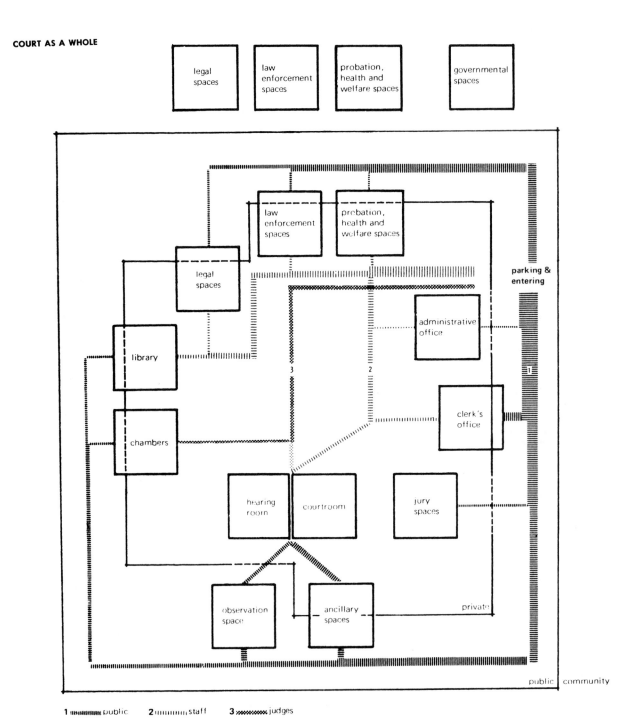

COURT AS A WHOLE

1 ▥▥▥ public   2 ▥▥▥ staff   3 ✕✕✕✕ judges

Fig. 1 Movement and access to internal spaces in the general trial court.

The American Courthouse: Planning and Design for the Judicial Process, The American Bar Association and The American Institute of Architects Joint Committee on the Design of Courtrooms and Court Facilities, The Institute of Continuing Legal Education, Ann Arbor, Michigan, 1973.

680

GENERAL TRIAL COURT

Trial Operations

Jury trials, whether civil or criminal, involve five general operations: opening preliminaries (including impaneling of the jury), opening statements, presentation of evidence by each side, closing statements, and deliberation and decision.

1. The opening preliminaries start with the bailiff's announcement that the court is in session and the naming of the presiding judge, who enters and calls the first case. The attorneys first have the opportunity to make motions in the case, then they signify that they are ready for trial. After the jury has been impaneled and sworn, an attorney may ask that all witnesses other than the parties be excluded from the courtroom. If the judge so rules, he informs the witnesses where they should wait. The court may recess a number of times, and it may adjourn to reconvene the following day or at some later time.

2. The prosecutor or the attorney for the plaintiff generally presents the first opening statement, followed by the defendant's opening statement. Each attorney tries to present the strong points of his case in his statement, defining the issues and describing the evidence he intends to present in support of his contentions. Motions may be made during or at the end of the opening statements.

3. The attorneys for each side then present their evidence. The prosecution in a criminal case, or the plaintiff in a civil action, goes first. Evidence consists of all exhibits and testimony by witnesses, including parties. Absent [sic] a priori stipulation on its admissibility, the opposing attorney may challenge the admissibility of any exhibit. The jury may be dismissed while the attorneys present their arguments to the judge on the matter, or the arguments may occur at the judge's bench or outside the courtroom. Each exhibit received in evidence is given an identifying number by the reporter or clerk.

When the attorneys request the isolation of witnesses, private and secure waiting facilities outside the courtroom are necessary. After each witness is called and sworn by the clerk, the attorney who called the witness proceeds with direct examination. The opposing attorney then cross-examines the witness and the first attorney may then examine on redirect.

4. Each attorney makes a closing statement to present the merits of his [her] case forcefully and persuasively. Although practices vary, the judge usually has had an earlier conference with the attorneys about the length of these statements and the content of instructions to be given to the jury. Generally, each attorney prepares the instructions which he [she] wishes the judge to give to the jury. The judge may use any of these or, in most jurisdictions, may frame his [her] own instructions. Opposing counsel may object to specific instructions given by the judge. A growing number of states are adopting "pattern" jury instructions, which are standardized expositions of points of law to be used in every case where they are applicable. Such instructions should reduce the number of inconsistent and conflicting decisions in the trial courts of the state and eventually reduce the number of appeals.

5. Jury deliberation and decision continues until agreement is reached or the jury informs the bailiff that it cannot agree upon a verdict. Deliberations can continue for days, and unless facilities are planned so that the trial courtroom can be utilized for other proceedings during this period, the space is not being used efficiently.

TABLE 1. Unit Space Requirements of the Courtroom

Participants	Furniture area per person, sq ft	Movement area per person, sq ft	Total area per person, sq ft
Judge	20–25*	25–30	45–55
Clerk	15–18	15–17	30–35
Reporter	8–9	3–6	11–15
Bailiff	8–9	3–6	11–15
Attorney	15–18†	17–22	32–40
Party	11–13	5–7	16–20
Witness	7–9*	8–11	15–20
Juror	4–5*	4–5	8–10
Press	6–7	4–8	10–15
Public	3–4	3–4	6–8

* Add a nonencroachment distance of 5–6 ft.

† Add 4–5 sq ft for a movable podium.

After the jury returns a verdict, the losing attorney may ask that the jury be polled; the judge then asks each juror if the verdict properly states his decision. Judgment may be entered on the verdict forthwith, or judgment may be reserved until the judge has ruled on post-trial motions filed by counsel.

Space Requirements

Table 1 shows the areas for movement and furniture (including working and seating surfaces) which each person in the courtroom requires. The nonencroachment distance of 5–6 feet for the judge insures a degree of privacy commensurate with his role. A nonencroachment distance surrounding jurors and witnesses helps prevent violation of the jurors' impartial role by attorneys and lessens the impact of attempts to intimidate witnesses.

Numerous cases involve several parties and more than one attorney for each side. Space should be provided for four attorneys and four parties, an area of 192–240 square feet. In addition, a space of 112–140 square feet must be provided for twelve jurors and two alternates.

Thirty jurors are usually called for examination (voir dire); if thirty spectators are assumed, the total public and observation seating area required would be 180–240 square feet, with perhaps an additional 50–75 square feet for the press. A total space of 534–695 square feet is required to accommodate all active (304–380 square feet) and passive (230–315 square feet) participants. This does not include general circulation space.

Communication and Spatial Patterns

The four types of communications in every courtroom are visible, audio, movement of people, and document transfer. By studying the frequency and importance of communications, a communication pattern is developed for each person in relation to every other person in the courtroom. The communication pattern is then utilized to show how each person should be spatially related to every other person. The patterns for the four types of communications, together with the unit space requirements, provide the analytical basis for a courtroom plan.

A Total Communication System By combining the separate analyses of visual and audio communications, movement of people and document transfer, a total pattern of communications is achieved (Fig. 2). The attorneys and judge are the main nodes of communication, followed in importance by the witness and the jury.

Figures 3 and 4 are the final composite spatial disposition diagrams resulting from a superimposition of separate diagrams. These diagrams reveal that if the visual requirements of the active participants are met, most of the other requirements are fulfilled.

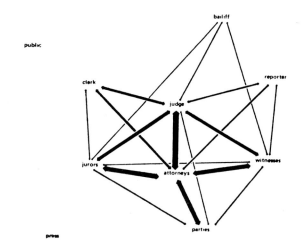

Fig. 2 A total communication system for jury trials.

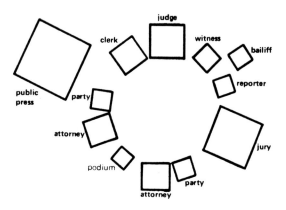

Fig. 3   Spatial disposition for jury trials, based on a total communication system (alternate A).

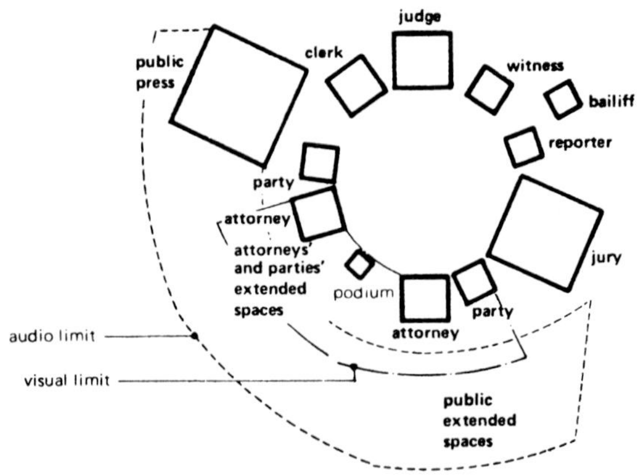

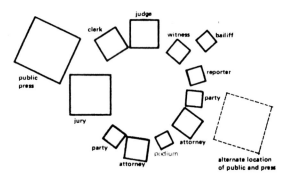

Fig. 4   Spatial disposition for jury trials, based on a total communication system (alternate B).

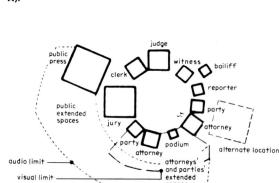

Fig. 5   Enlarged public and press areas for jury trials (alternate A).

Fig. 6   Enlarged public and press areas for jury trials (alternate B).

In Fig. 3 (alternate A) the bailiff can move unobtrusively to judge, witness, and jury; easily supervise and escort witnesses and jurors; run errands for the judge; and keep the public and press under constant surveillance. In Fig. 4 (alternate B), he has to cross the room to reach the jurors.

In both diagrams the witness is located within the private conversation zone of the judge. To keep him [her] out of this zone and still meet the visual requirements, the space around which the active participants are grouped must be expanded. Failing this, the judge's bench should be designed so that the end farthest from the witness box can be used for private talks between judge and counsel with the reporter present.

Only visual and audio requirements need be considered in the location of the public and press. No satisfactory visual location of the observation area permits it to fall wholly within the desirable audio zone, although alternate A is better in this respect than any other disposition.

Observation Space Problems   The space allocated to public and press in Figs. 3 and 4 may not be sufficient for cases that attract a large attendance. Figures 5 and 6 show its possible expansion.

The ability to satisfy visual and audio requirements decreases as the observation space expands beyond its optimum position. With an extension sideways, the public and press move behind the primary participants and are less able

to see faces clearly. If the public and press space is extended around the rear of the jury box, observers would still be able to view all the other participants. If the observation space is extended around the rear of the attorneys' and parties' stations, the public and press would see the attorney only from behind when he addresses the court. Such extension would also conflict with any expansion of the area for attorneys and parties in cases involving several of each. Alternate B (Fig. 6) therefore appears more satisfactory for courtrooms requiring large observation seating capacities.

Providing a large public observation space in every courtroom to accommodate an occasional well-publicized case is unrealistic and expensive. Most courtrooms require only sufficient space to accommodate relatives and friends of the defendant or people directly related to the case.

In jurisdictions where the impaneling of jurors, including the voir dire questioning, is performed in the courtroom, there should be adequate space for the seating of prospective jurors. The observation area is the natural place for this purpose. If thirty persons are required from which to impanel a jury, the observation area should provide seating for this number plus some observers, perhaps a total of forty. If the jurors are impaneled outside the courtroom, twenty seats would be quite adequate for observers.

In each jurisdiction, average and maximum public attendance for each type of case should be recorded and analyzed to assist in the formula-

tion of space requirements for future facilities. Occasional cases for which a large public attendance is anticipated can be assigned to courtrooms equipped with larger public observation spaces. One judge writes: "With respect to courtrooms for jury trials, I believe they must be basically of one size. The need for larger space for the public during an important trial would have its drawbacks. Basically, we are interested in the litigants, their witnesses and relatives and friends—not to provide an amphitheatre for those interested in watching a particular procedure."

A recent survey indicates that most news reporters want a court location where they can clearly see and hear the primary participants; leave the courtroom with minimum disturbance; have adequate writing surfaces, an unobstructed frontal view of all participants and a clear close-up view of all exhibit boards; and be close enough to the witness to hear every word.

Because they fear it would set a precedent for excluding the press from the courtroom, most news reporters see little merit in seating the press in another room behind a one-way window with a view of the proceedings. However, there is some interest in an enclosed press area behind a one-way window which would permit the use of phones and possibly courtroom photography. A one-way window would give news reporters maximum freedom to converse and move about and enable them to have instant communication with their offices in order to meet deadlines. Some news reporters, on the other hand, think that a courtroom should be designed primarily for the trial proceedings and that no special provisions should be made for the press.

In most general trial courtrooms today, the space ratio between the action area and the public observation space is approximately two to one, with the latter being a physical part of the courtroom. The public is usually placed behind the attorneys and parties as a visually integrated part of the courtroom.

If the observation space were separated from the courtroom by a glass wall and a sound system were installed, there would still be a possibility of visual distraction from the audience. This would not be the case, however, if one-way glass were used as the separating wall. Depending on the number of people to be accommodated, the observation area could be placed in two or more locations. Whatever its size and location, this area requires different spatial and other environmental considerations than does the courtroom action area.

Should closed-circuit television be accepted in a public trial, the spatial relationship between the public observation space and the courtroom would be revolutionized. Then the public observation space would no longer have to adjoin the courtroom, which could lead to several drastic design and planning changes.

- There would be a significant reduction in the size of the courtroom. Few jury courtrooms would need to exceed 1,500 square feet, and the area of nonjury courtrooms could be considerably smaller.
- In a multilevel courthouse, more courtrooms could be grouped together on each floor. Public traffic could be more readily separated from the traffic of courtroom participants; thus, more courtrooms on each floor would not necessarily mean greater traffic congestion.
- Public observation spaces could be centralized on the lower floors of a multilevel building, concentrating the public traffic to avoid overload of the vertical transportation system and minimizing unnecessary movement throughout the building.

Courtroom Accessibility

Participants entering the courtroom should be able to get to their respective locations as directly as possible, a goal best achieved by placing access points close to their locations (Figs. 7 and 8). The diagrams are not meant to pinpoint the exact location of each entrance, but simply to indicate its general position; nor is it implied that each type of participant should have a separate entrance.

Movement of participants from spaces outside the courtroom to their points of access should also be as direct as possible. The judge and the court staff, coming from their chambers and staff offices, should not have to go through the public areas of the courthouse to get into the courtroom. This is not merely a matter of convenience. Personal contact between jurors and the public should be avoided under all circumstances to minimize the risk of mistrial. Separate public, private, and security zones must be established in the courthouse, with similar zones of access to the courtroom.

The alternate plans show the judge, court staff, and jurors coming from their outside private zone and going directly to their stations within the courtroom. The public and the press should be able to enter their observation area directly from the public zone. Attorneys, parties, and witnesses

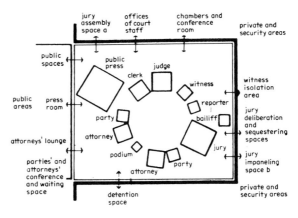

Fig. 7 Optimum access to the jury trial courtroom (alternate A). *a.* If jury impaneled in courtroom. *b.* If jury impaneled outside courtroom.

should be able to enter their waiting areas from the public zone and from there go directly to their stations in the courtroom. Prisoners should come directly through a separate security zone to a detention space near the bailiff's station.

NONJURY TRIALS, HEARINGS, AND ANCILLARY FUNCTIONS

The current trend in the court system is toward achievement of a speedier and more effective administration of justice. In the nonjury trial, participants are few and the operations are simple; in formal and informal hearings, the participants are even fewer and the operations simpler. Thus, the physical requirements of these proceedings are modified accordingly from those of the jury trial.

Courtrooms equipped for full jury trials can, of course, be used for nonjury trials and hearings. A flexible arrangement of furniture, with front rows which can double as an attorneys' table is desirable.

Objectives

Nonjury Trials In comparison with jury trials, nonjury trials reduce the emotional and monetary costs; they also require less time for disposition. The nonjury trial encourages a substantial reduction in the real or apparent hostility of attorneys and allows the judge to dispose of many more

disputes. The time for impaneling a jury is eliminated, and opening and closing statements can be much briefer since the judge is presumed to be an expert. Arguments can be heard immediately because repeated recesses for discussion out of hearing of the jury are not required. There is no need for the preparation of instructions to the jury, and the time for jury deliberation and decision is eliminated.

The needs of news reporters and the general public are essentially the same as in jury trials. However, there is generally much less public interest in nonjury trials; the physical facilities for news reporters and public observers can be reduced without impairing any privileges.

Hearings Whether a hearing is formal or informal, its primary characteristic is variety. There is a broad spectrum of legal proceedings ranging from adoption to bankruptcy to arraignment to general motion practice. There is an equivalent range in the extent to which hearings can dispose of cases. A hearing may result in final disposition, temporary resolution, resolution of one part of a larger proceeding or a temporary postponement. The degree to which a hearing is an adversary proceeding can also range widely within the same type of hearing, whether formal or informal. The same is true of the number and types of persons involved, as well as the degree of simplicity or complexity of their activities. Despite this

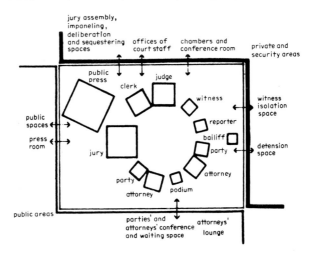

Fig. 8 Optimum access to the jury trial courtroom (alternate B).

diversity, certain general observations can be made about the objectives of both formal and informal hearings.

Formal hearings require flexibility seasoned with appropriate solemnity and restraint. Flexibility is needed because of the variety of matters which may come before the presiding officers, who may or may not be judges. Appropriate solemnity and restraint are needed because of the hostility which may be present.

Informal hearings require flexibility seasoned with kindly or businesslike responses from the presiding officer. The hearing should aim at maximum interchange within a quasiprivate environment. Informality can be achieved without loss of dignity and with minimum restraint on all participants, including the presiding officers. Flexibility is required because of the great variety of legal proceedings heard informally. When personal problems are involved, an atmosphere of calm and friendly concern is needed. For fiscal matters like bankruptcy or small claims, an atmosphere of efficiency and businesslike involvement is desirable.

Operations

Nonjury Trials The general operations of the nonjury trial include the opening preliminaries, opening statements, presentation of evidence, closing statements, and deliberation and decision by the judge.

With the elimination of a jury, activities are simplified. Opening preliminaries involve only convening of the court and determining that all parties or their representatives are ready for trial. Opening and closing statements tend to be briefer. Presentation of evidence may evoke objections, but these can be argued and ruled upon immediately by the judge. Closing statements are usually confined to questions of law raised by the case. The judge either gives his decision immediately or takes the case under advisement. In the latter instance, he often asks for briefs from each side. After the decision, post-trial motions are filed and later considered by the judge, and a judgment, final unless appealed, is given.

Hearings Certain hearings are almost indistinguishable from trials without a jury and, further, the dividing line between formal and informal hearings is as nebulous as the line of demarcation between informal hearings and conferences.

Hearings, both formal and informal, may be related to a trial or may be used as a substitute for a trial to dispose of cases in certain specialized legal proceedings involving, for example, minors, incompetents, injunctions or probate matters.

Most hearings related to trials involve motions, which are typically requests that the court decide a single issue such as jurisdiction or a change of venue, discovery requests, a motion for a new trial or postponement of sentencing. Motions can be made verbally at the hearing or presented in writing, and arguments can be verbal or in the form of briefs. Decisions can be expressed as an opinion or a verbal assent or dissent.

The operations in the formal hearing include the opening preliminaries; presentation and argument, in which the presiding officer may play an active role; and decision by the presiding officer. They are not too different from nonjury trials—somewhat less elaborate but still retaining the formal qualities of a trial. The presiding officer may be a judge or a court officer such as a referee in bankruptcy cases. Typically, a clerk and a court reporter make an official transcript of the proceeding.

Opening preliminaries include convening the hearing and determining that all necessary parties or their representatives are ready to proceed. Depending on the type of hearing, the presiding officer may actively participate in examination of a party or witness or may sit as a disinterested overseer of the proceeding. In the latter instance, the hearing operates in much the same fashion as a nonjury trial. Decision by the presiding officer may be made immediately, or he may take the matter under advisement and hand down a decision at a later date.

Informal hearings are similar, but less stylized and often private. Attorneys are frequently not present and usually a small number of persons attend. Very often court reporters are not necessary and in some instances the presiding officer does not use a clerk or bailiff. Official orders are either prepared and signed during the hearing by the presiding officer or prepared, signed, and transmitted at a later date.

Exploration of the problem and its possible solutions may involve ordered presentations by the parties or their attorneys, or it may only be a conversation between the presiding officer and someone who has a problem. The problem can be extremely complicated, or it may only require a necessary signing of a document. Usually, the decision of the presiding officer is made immediately.

Requirements of Nonjury Trials and Formal Hearings

Each nonjury trial and formal hearing exhibits different characteristics, but even in the largest metropolitan areas it is impractical to design a formal hearing room to serve each type of case. Instead, it is more practical to have one room which can be adapted to fewer participants and differing degrees of formality. Furniture should be movable and adjustable in height, so that its arrangement can conform to the degree of formality. Adjustable partitions and ceilings allow for change in the size and character of the room as needed.

Except for the elimination of jury activities and the space required for the jury box, the activity, space, and communication (visual, audio, movement, and document transfer) relationships in nonjury trials and formal hearings are the same as in jury trials. There is only a slight variation in the degree of importance of the bailiff.

Composite Spatial Disposition As might be expected, the composite spatial disposition for communications (Fig. 9) is much the same as that for the jury trial (Figs. 3 and 4). The absence of a jury enables the participants to be closer to each other, and the attorneys and parties can be moved toward the judge. The diameter of

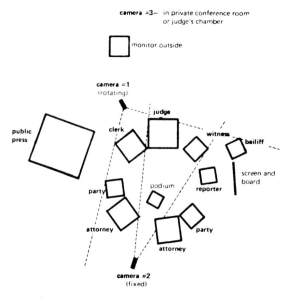

Fig. 9 Spatial disposition based on a total communication system (nonjury trials, formal hearings)

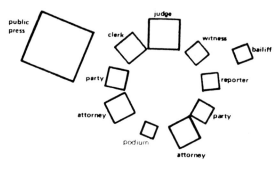

Fig. 10 Location of visual equipment and display board (nonjury trials, formal hearings)

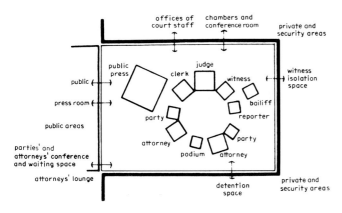

Fig. 11 Access to the courtroom from related spaces (nonjury trials, formal hearings)

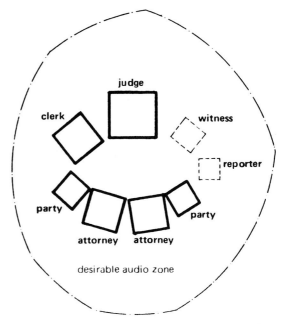

Fig. 13 Spatial disposition for informal hearings, based on audio requirements

the trial area is also reduced by approximately 5 feet.

The use of movable furniture in the trial area below the judge's bench will allow rearrangements to conform to proceedings of differing complexity and formality. With fewer participants, the distance between them can be reduced or they can be brought into a less formal relation to each other.

Figure 10 shows the location of television cameras related to a video tape system. The camera behind the clerk is capable of panning 180 degrees while the second camera is fixed on the judge and the witnesses. The only variation from the jury trial is that the exhibits display board is now within the range of the first camera. Figure 11, showing courtroom access, uses the same criteria as Figs. 7 and 8.

Requirements of Informal Hearings

Compared with trials and formal hearings, everything is simplified and condensed in the informal hearing. Frequently, the only participants are the judge or hearing officer, the clerk, and the party or parties, although attorneys or other representatives of the parties, a court reporter, and witnesses also attend at times. Even if open to the public and press, the degree of public interest

is so low that observers can readily be accommodated with a few extra chairs.

The communication patterns among participants in such hearings are similar to those in trials, but simplified by the absence of the bailiff, jury, public, press, and others.

The smaller number of people and the informality require a more intimate arrangement of participants. A spatial disposition for visual communication based on the maximum visual angle of 150 degrees reduces the distance between the judge and the attorneys to less than 15 feet and between the court reporter and the farthest party to less than 25 feet (Fig. 12).

Beyond the maximum audio angle of 140 degrees, speech intelligibility reduces rapidly. In Fig. 13, optimum audio conditions exist within the

area enclosed by the broken dotted line, the result of drawing 32-foot arcs from the major participants.

Movement during informal hearings is minimal, although sometimes the judge and the attorneys may discuss matters privately at the bench outside the hearing range of the parties and witnesses, with the reporter also moving to the bench. Occasionally attorneys and their respective clients may have private conferences. For the most part, however, all remain seated throughout the proceedings (Fig. 14).

Spatial disposition based on the transfer of documents between participants is shown in Fig. 15. Again the attorneys are the most active participants, transferring documents and exhibits to the judge, clerk and witnesses. Figure 16 shows the composite spatial disposition of participants. The attorneys and parties are placed in front of the judge who is flanked on one side by the clerk and by the witness, if any, on the other. The court reporter is adjacent to the witness and is approximately equidistant from the judge and the attorneys. This results in a generally elliptical

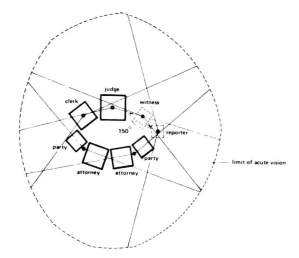

Fig. 12 Spatial disposition for informal hearings, based on visual requirements

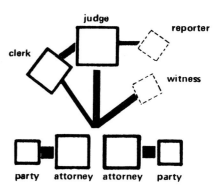

Fig. 14 Spatial disposition for informal hearings, based on movement

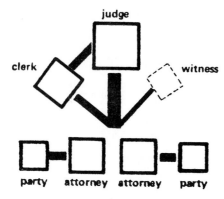

Fig. 15   Spatial disposition for informal hearings, based on document transfer

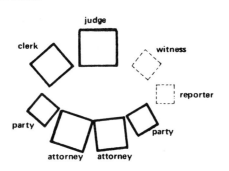

Fig. 16   Spatial disposition for informal hearings, based on a total communication system

shape, but where witnesses and a reporter do not attend, a flexible furniture arrangement permits parties and their representatives to be moved closer to the judge.

To emphasize his role, the judge's bench should be raised, but not so high as to prevent informality in the proceeding. Since all participants remain seated when speaking, it is sufficient for the judge to be one step above the eye level of the other participants. The nonencroachment distance between attorneys and the judge and between the witness and attorney during examination should be maintained at a minimum of 5–6 feet.

Ideally, there should be three separate points of access into the informal hearing room, as shown in Fig. 17. The judge and the court staff,

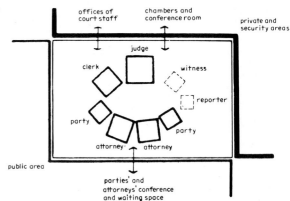

Fig. 17   Access to the informal hearing room from related spaces

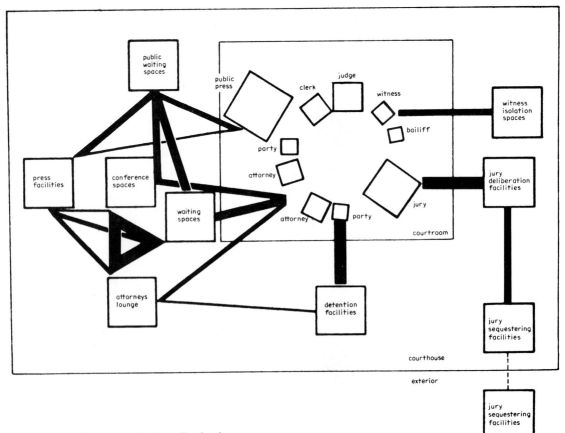

Fig. 18   Interspatial movement pattern for ancillary functions

including the clerk and the court reporter, should have separate private entrances into the room. The attorneys and the parties can enter either from their waiting spaces or from the public waiting space. Witnesses involved in informal hearings do not normally require isolation, so seating space could be provided for them within the room.

Ancillary Functions

Several ancillary functions primarily identified with trials and hearings may also have some relation to other court functions. Conferences between attorneys and parties call for conference rooms. Attorneys should be able to relax and work in the privacy of an attorneys' lounge, while the public and news media should have separate facilities. When witnesses are isolated, they are the responsibility of the bailiff and must remain in witness isolation spaces until called to testify. Temporary detention of the accused or defendant in detention facilities is the responsibility of the law enforcement officers, but the security and safety of jurors during jury deliberation and sequestering are the responsibility of the bailiff.

Analysis of movement among these activities shows their relative importance to be in the following descending order: trial and hearing, waiting, working and relaxing, public waiting, conference, news reporting, jury deliberation, detention, witness isolation, and jury sequestering.

Figure 18 shows the interspatial movement pattern for ancillary functions. Witness isolation and jury deliberation and sequestering spaces should be located in close proximity to the witness stand and to the jury box, respectively. The other ancillary activities are related to each other and should be grouped together near the courtroom. The attorneys' lounge should preferably have a separate access into the courtroom and be readily accessible to the detention space. In addition, the detention space should be close to the defendant's station in the courtroom, with direct access. Press facilities should be located near the courtroom and reasonably near the conference and waiting spaces. The public waiting space should provide access to the conference and waiting spaces, press facilities and the attorneys' lounge, as well as to the public observation space in the court-

room. If audiovisual devices are used, however, the public observation space does not have to be located in the courtroom. Table 2 shows unit space requirements for each ancillary activity both on a per person basis and as modules for minimum requirements.

TABLE 2 Unit Space Requirements of Ancillary Functions

Space	Area per person, sq ft	Area of combined spaces, sq ft
Conference space	20–27	80–108 (4 persons)
Waiting space	13–20	260–400 (20 persons)
Witness isolation	44–63	
Attorney's lounge		
Lounge space	13–20	130–200 (10 persons)
Work space	44–63	
Press room		
Interview space	20–25	200–250 (10 persons)
Offices	69–75	

THE DISTRICT COURT

Court spaces most frequently required in federal buildings are for the district court which holds sessions in the principal cities of its judicial district and generally has its headquarters in the largest or most centrally located city in the district.

Part 1. Description

Jurisdiction The district court is the federal court of original jurisdiction where cases are given their initial trial. Each state comprises at least one judicial district and, depending upon the volume of business and its geographical distribution, a state may be divided into two or more judicial districts.

Spaces Required With a few exceptions, a United States district court sits at more than one place within each judicial district. The following spaces are always required:

Courtroom
Judge's suite
Court officers quarters
Petit jury rooms
Grand jury suite
Witnesses' room

In some instances, a district court library, jurors' assembly room, press room, pretrial hearing room, and attorneys' conference room will also be required.

Court Officers Requiring Quarters At each place of holding court, space will be required for the following officers:

United States district judge (one or more, depending upon the volume of business within the district)
Clerk of the court
United States attorney
United States marshal
Probation and parole office
(one or more)
Court reporter (one or more)

Additional Offices at Major Installations Wherever a major installation of the district court is required, facilities will be needed in it for the following additional officers, if specified:

Referee in bankruptcy (one or more)
United States commissioner
Jury commissioner

Space Arrangements in District Court Suite Certain parts of the court must be closely connected. Courtrooms and their related rooms should ordinarily be above the first floor. In multistory buildings, all of the court activities should be located on consecutive floors. It is not desirable to place agencies unrelated to the court on the same floor with it. The need for simple, direct circulation for the public and for the court officers will influence the location and arrangement of the units of the court.

GSA Handbook, Public Buildings Service, General Services Administration, Washington, D.C.

Part 2. The District Courtroom

Location The court's activities revolve around the courtroom, so it should be centrally located. Spaces for the officers of the court should be placed with regard to their functions in the courtroom and their responsibilities to the judge. (Figs. 1 to 3).

Illumination Natural lighting may be restricted to auxiliary offices, the courtroom itself having no outside exposure.

Dimensions The minimum size of a district courtroom is $38\frac{1}{2}$ ft in width by $58\frac{1}{2}$ ft in length. The ceiling height of a courtroom should be proportionate to its size and to the requirements of proper illumination, ventilation or air conditioning, and acoustics. In a large installation with many courtrooms, most of them should be of minimum size. One or more courtrooms with additional space for the audience may be necessary to accommodate trials that attract the public and are attended by many representatives of the press.

Courtroom Entrances

Public Entrance. This is located at the end of the courtroom opposite the judge's bench and fitted with double doors swinging out into a courtroom lobby.

Jury Entrance. This entrance should permit the jury to pass directly from the courtroom to the jury rooms, preferably without crossing the courtroom or passing through any public corridor or space. If the prisoners cannot use the jurors' entrance door, provide a special entrance through which they may be taken to the detention cells.

Side Entrance. Provide an entrance, for attorneys and press reporters, to the courtroom area in front of the railing and benches for the public.

Coat Closets For the use of attorneys, provide one or more coat closets off the judicial end of the courtroom to accommodate not less than 20 coats. For the jurors selected, provide a coat closet or alcove either immediately off the courtroom or off a secondary lobby which is not accessible to the public.

Furniture

Built-in Furniture. The jury box shall accommodate 14 jurors and should be located at the judge's left. The following items must be provided:

1 Judges' bench and witness stand
1 clerk of court desk and court reporter
1 jury box
12 benches with gate and railings

Fixed Chairs. The jury type courtroom must accommodate the following fixed chairs:

1 armchair for witness stand—rotary, fixed-pedestal
14 armchairs for jurors, rotary—fixed-pedestal

Movable Furniture. Limited to the following:

3 judges' chairs
1 clerk of court armchair—rotary
1 court reporter armchair—rotary
1 lectern, Fig. 1
10 attorneys' armchairs—rotary
10 armchairs for general use
2 attorneys' tables—120 by 48 in.
1 press reporters' table—120 by 48 in.
1 flagstaff—shaft top $9\frac{1}{2}$ ft above floor

Part 3. Judge's Suite

Components Judge's entire suite includes the following rooms:

Judge's office
Judge's library
Judge's reception room
Judge's toilet
Judge's coat closet
Secretary and reception room
Crier's vestibule
Law clerk's office
Coat closet
Supply closet

Location The judge's suite must be located adjoining the courtroom. A corner office for the judge is generally preferred, but it may be necessary to place it elsewhere to get maximum freedom from street noises. See Fig. 4. Locate the judge's office to provide access to the bench either directly from his office or through a private passage, so that the judge will not have to go through any public space. The judge's office must connect with a corridor, so that he may enter or leave without passing through any other office.

Entrances The entrances required for circulation within the judge's chambers are shown on Figs. 1 and 4. Where several courtrooms are grouped on a floor, judges may pass to the courtrooms through a common private corridor. In multistory buildings, it is desirable to have the judges' suites adjacent to the courtrooms so that the judges do not have to go through public spaces or use public elevators when going to or from court. Public entrance must be provided for the secretary's office.

Judge's Office

Area and Furniture. As informal pretrial hearings are often held in the judge's office, the minimum area shall be 750 sq ft.

Height. Ceiling height shall be not less than 9 ft.

Shelving. Usable wall space of the judge's suite shall be lined with flush, adjustable wood bookshelves 10 in. wide and extending from the floor to the top of the doors. The walls above shall be furred out to the face of the shelves.

Clock. Install a wall electric clock on a wall visible from the judge's desk and not hidden by a lighting fixture.

Toilet. It is desirable to locate the judge's toilet so that the entrance is not directly from his office. The toilet shall be equipped with a noiseless type water closet, a lavatory, a medicine case with mirror, paper holder, towel bar, and robe hook. The fixtures shall not be mounted on the courtroom wall. Refer to Fig. 4.

Coat Closet. It is desirable but not mandatory to locate the judge's coat closet off a passage outside his office. The closet shall be not less than 3 ft wide and 2 ft deep; it shall be equipped with two 12-in. shelves, hanging rod, and coat hooks.

Secretary and Reception Room–Crier's Vestibule

Location. Locate the secretary and reception room between the judge's private office and the law clerk's office. Refer to Figs. 2 and 4. The first point of entrance to the suite by the public is through the vestibule occupied by the crier.

Area and Furniture. The room shall have a minimum area of 350 sq ft and the secretary's space shall be divided by a railing and gate from the reception space, which shall be not less than 7 ft wide.

Entrances. Figure 4 shows the preferred arrangement of entrances between the rooms. It is not desirable to put closets or toilets between the secretary's office and the judge's office.

Law Clerk's Office
The law clerk's office usually should adjoin the secretary's office so that the secretary can receive the clerk's visitors as well

as those for the judge. There need not be an independent public entrance unless the plan naturally permits one. Usable wall space shall be lined with flush, adjustable, built-in wood bookshelves from the floor to the top of the doors. The office shall have a minimum area of 400 sq ft (500 to 600 sq ft in metropolitan areas) including shelving.

Judge's Library
When a judge's library is provided, no separate space for the law clerk will be supplied, since he will have his office in the library. It is best located adjoining the secretary's office and shall be large enough to store the number of law books required. Provide adjustable, built-in wood bookshelves.

Part 4. Petit Jury

Description The petit jury usually consists of 12 jurors, but there may be one or more alternates. It is assumed that in actual practice the number of jurors and alternates in the jury box during a trial will not exceed 14. At the end of the trial, the alternates, if any, withdraw, and the jury retires to the jury room to consider its verdict. The jury later returns to the courtroom to report to the court the jury's verdict or disagreement. The jury panel from which the petit jury is selected consists of persons chosen by the jury commissioner and the clerk of the court according to law. The names of those constituting the panel from which the petit jury is selected have been drawn by the commissioner and the clerk from

the jury wheel and summoned by the court to report as jurors. The panel of jurors ordinarily assembles in the courtroom. At a trial the names of the qualified jurors in attendance and not excused by the court are placed in a jury wheel. The clerk draws from the wheel one name at a time. The jurors who are finally accepted for the trial of the case sit in the jury box, and those who are not accepted withdraw and their names are replaced in the jury wheel by the clerk. If the court has a jurors' assembly room, the prospective jurors assemble there and do not go into the courtroom until a case is called for a trial in which a jury is required.

Location of Jury Rooms Locate jury rooms so that jurors may go to them from the courtroom without going through a public corridor or going across the courtroom. It is desirable to have jury rooms on the courtroom floor level, as indicated on Fig. 2, for convenience of aged or crippled jurors. Frequently two jury rooms are required where there is but one courtroom in the building. When there are two or more courtrooms, $1\frac{1}{2}$ jury rooms are usually provided for each courtroom.

Area and Furniture Jury rooms shall have a minimum area of 350 sq ft and must be proportioned to accommodate a table, 120 by 48 in., and 14 armchairs.

Coat Closet and Toilet Rooms Each jury room must have a coat closet or alcove, a toilet room for men, and also one for women.

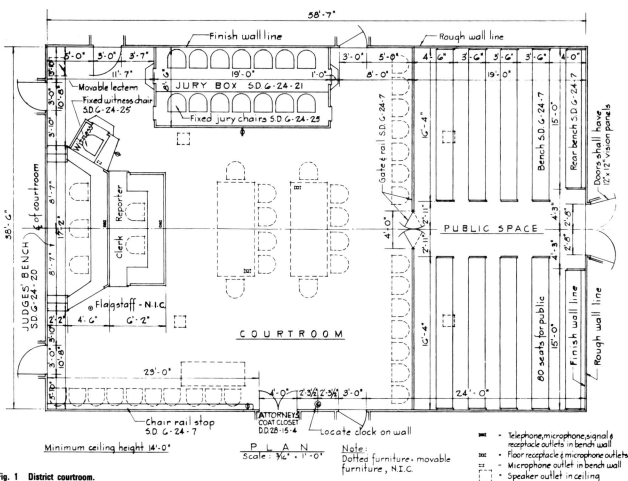

Fig. 1 District courtroom.

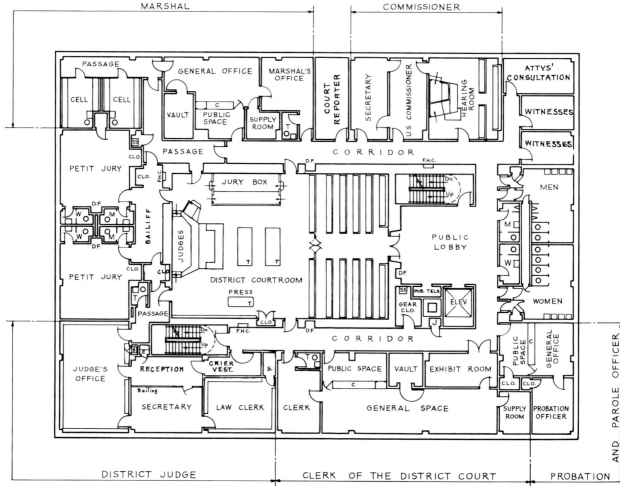

Fig. 2   District court plan, first floor.

Entrances If there are two or more jury rooms, they may open into a common lobby under the control of a bailiff.

Signaling Equipment In each petit jury room, install equipment to operate a flashing signal in the bailiff's lobby and in the courtroom.

Panic Exits If entrance to a jury room is directly from a common lobby, such jury room or common lobby must have a second exit door of panic type, equipped with suitable panic hardware, local alarm signal, and explanatory sign on the jury side of the door.

Soundproofing The walls of the jury room must be soundproofed, as the jurors' discussions would otherwise be audible in adjoining rooms. The jury room should have an acoustic ceiling.

Auxiliary Occupancy When court is not in session, the jury room often serves as a waiting room, a roll-call room, or a conference room.

Part 5. Witness Room

Locations This is for the use of witnesses waiting to testify before the court and should be located as near the courtroom as possible, preferably on the same side as the marshal's office. A deputy marshal or bailiff calls the witnesses into the courtroom. Refer to Fig. 2.

Area The witness room shall have a minimum area of 200 sq ft.

Auxiliary Uses When the court is not in session the witness room may be used as a conference or committee room.

Part 6. Jurors' Assembly Lounge

Three Courtroom Requirements This lounge may be required if there are two or more courtrooms. The size of the lounge will be determined by allowing 15 sq ft per occupant. The lounge shall have a private toilet for men and also one for women. Provide an entrance from the public corridor and a drinking fountain. When a jury commissioner's suite is required, the jurors' assembly lounge forms part of that suite, but it need not be adjoining or adjacent. Telephone recesses and cloak room should have direct access from this lounge.

Furniture The number of selected jurors will determine the number of varied style chairs, tables, magazine racks, etc., to be installed in this jurors' lounge.

Part 7. Grand Jury Suite

Description, Location, and Components The grand jury is impaneled by the court and consists of not less than 16 nor more than 23 jurors. The grand jury hears evidence presented to it and conducts investigations to determine if charges or violation of federal criminal statutes shall be prosecuted. It is presided over by a foreman, named by the court, and usually the cases considered by it are presented by the United States attorney. Outsiders must not be able to overhear or observe grand jury proceedings. The plan of the grand jury suite shown, Fig. 5, indicates the relationship of the rooms and the entrances required. The grand jury suite includes the following rooms:

Grand jury room
Witnesses' room
Bailiff's vestibule
Coat closet and toilet for men and women

Grand Jury Room The grand jurors' chairs are in either three or four rows, depending upon the width of the room. This room shall have a minimum area of 600 sq ft to accommodate

23 jurors' armchairs — rotary and fixed
1 table — 96 by 42 in.
1 table — 54 by 42 in.
6 armchairs
1 drinking fountain

Witnesses' Room This is for the use of witnesses until called by the bailiff to testify in the grand jury rooms. The witnesses' room shall have a minimum area of 300 sq ft.

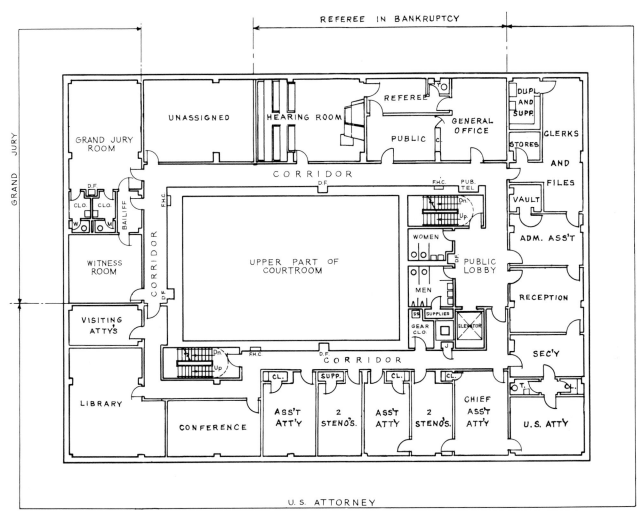

Fig. 3   District court plan, second floor.

Bailiff's Vestibule   This shall have a minimum of 40 sq ft and must accommodate a desk and one armchair.

Coat Closets – Toilets for Men and Women   Figure 5 shows a desirable combination of coat closets and toilet rooms, but a common coat closet or alcove and separate toilet rooms are acceptable.

Part 8. United States Attorney

Duties and Location   The United States attorney represents the government in all cases, both civil and criminal, to which the government is a party or in which it has an interest. Since much of the time of the United States attorney and the assistant attorneys is spent in the courtroom, their offices should be located convenient to it, but not necessarily on the same floor.

Components   The United States attorney has a headquarters at some designated city in the judicial district, not necessarily the same city where the judge's headquarters are located. His suite in a courts building varies in size in accordance with the amount of work he must handle. A typical suite, Fig. 3, will include the following.

United States attorney's office
Coat closet and toilet
Reception room
Secretary's office
Chief assistant, United States attorney's office
Assistant, United States attorney's office
Stenographer's office (two stenos each)
Conference room
Visiting attorneys' room
Library
Administrative assistant's office
Vault
Clerks and files room
Supply room—general—duplicating
Storage room

United States Attorney's Office   The office of the United States attorney shall have a minimum area of 300 sq ft.

Reception Room   In large installations a public reception room, readily accessible to callers, shall be provided. It adjoins the secretary's office and should be located between the office of the United States attorney and that of the administrative assistant. Refer to Fig. 3. The minimum area of the reception room shall be 300 sq ft. It shall be planned to seat visitors and to permit control of intercommunicating doors by the receptionist.

Secretary's Office   In metropolitan areas where there is a great deal of work, the United States attorney may require the services of a private secretary, whose office usually is located between the office of the United States attorney and the reception room.

Chief Assistant United States Attorney's Office   The office of the chief assistant United States attorney shall have a minimum area of 250 sq ft. Locate it adjoining the office of the United States attorney.

Conference Room   The conference room shall have a minimum area of 250 sq ft. A large installation may require several conference rooms, located for the convenient use of the attorneys. This room should be sound treated.

Assistant United States Attorneys' offices.   Offices of the assistant United States attorneys should be adjacent to each other and convenient to the chief assistant United States attorney. Each office shall have a minimum area of 180 sq ft.

Library   The library is used by all of the attorneys in the suite and therefore should open on a corridor.

Administrative Assistant's Office   The office of the administrative assistant should be located adjoining the reception room on the side opposite the United States attorney's office and shall have a minimum area of 230 sq ft.

Vault A vault for the administrative assistant, opening into his office, shall have a minimum size of 6 by 9 ft.

Work and Supply Room A general work and supply room convenient to the administrative assistant's staff shall have a minimum area of 50 sq ft. It may be necessary to provide a separate room with electrical outlets for a mimeograph machine, photostat machine, or other duplicating equipment.

Stenographers' Office Provide administrative assistant/stenographers' office between the offices of assistant United States attorneys, allowing a minimum area of 100 sq ft per desk. Generally there will be a ratio of two stenographers for three attorneys.

Clerks and Files Room The room for the clerks and files shall adjoin and connect with the administrative assistant's office.

Smaller Installations United States attorney's suites differ in size and requirements in accordance with the work in the district. They may be as small as three rooms in cities where

court is held for a very short period or where no assistant United States attorney is regularly stationed. Where no United States attorney is regularly stationed at a place of holding court, his offices will not have a private toilet or coat closet and the rooms may be used for conference or committee rooms when court is not in session. Room sizes will average about 200 sq ft each and furniture will correspond with that of similar rooms in a major installation.

Part 9. United States Marshal

Duties The United States marshal is charged with the custody of prisoners and their production in court, the maintenance of order in the courtroom, the service of processes, the appearance of witnesses, the collection and disbursement of certain monies and fees, the custody of certain property in the possession of the court, and other special duties assigned by the court.

Location The marshal's suite should be so located with relation to the courtroom that prisoners can pass directly to it from the detention cells without exposure to public contact or view. If the suite is located one floor above or below the courtroom, a private stair

which offers no opportunity for escape must be provided for prisoners. In multistory buildings with courtrooms on different floors, a private elevator to transport prisoners from a lower floor or basement entrance to the marshal's detention cells and to and from the courtrooms is usually required. A freight elevator may often serve in lieu of a private elevator for this purpose. On large installations, the detention cells may be put in the basement. In that case, no additional detention cells are provided on other floors.

Components The United States marshal has a headquarters at some designated city in the judicial district, not necessarily the same city where the judge's headquarters are located. The marshal's suite varies in size according to the amount of work in the district. A typical suite for large installations includes:

Marshal's office
Toilet
General office
Vault
Bookkeepers' office
Deputy marshals' office
Interviewing room
Fingerprinting room
Detention cells for men and for women
Holding cells
Storage room
Evidence storage room (may be in basement)

Marshal's Office This shall have a minimum area of 300 sq ft. Provide a private toilet of not less than 30 sq ft.

General Office Provide a general office with a minimum area of 500 sq ft. The public space is separated from the rest of the general office by a counter and gate. The public space should have a minimum width of 8 ft.

Vault Opening into the general office, provide a vault with a minimum area of 100 sq ft. and accommodating a money safe. Locate the vault so that the interior is not visible from the public space.

Bookkeepers' Office Provide a bookkeepers' office adjoining the general office with a minimum of 300 sq ft. One desk is provided for each occupant.

Deputies Adjacent to and connected with the bookkeepers' office (by passage if necessary), provide an office with a minimum area of 300 sq ft for the marshal's deputies. One desk is provided for each occupant.

Fingerprinting Room Provide a fingerprinting room with a minimum of 120 sq ft adjoining and connecting with the deputies' office. In the smaller offices, the fingerprinting cabinet and lavatory may be placed in the deputies' office and the fingerprinting room omitted.

Interviewing Room Provide an interviewing room with a minimum area of 150 sq ft, located so that prisoners can be brought from the detention cells as directly as possible. The room shall accommodate one table and four side chairs.

Detention Cells for Men and for Women

Cells for Men. Usually, provide two detention cells with observation passage. The cells shall be not less than 10 ft wide and be large enough to accommodate the maximum number of prisoners detained at one time. The size of a cell shall be determined by allowing for each prisoner a minimum of 25 sq ft.

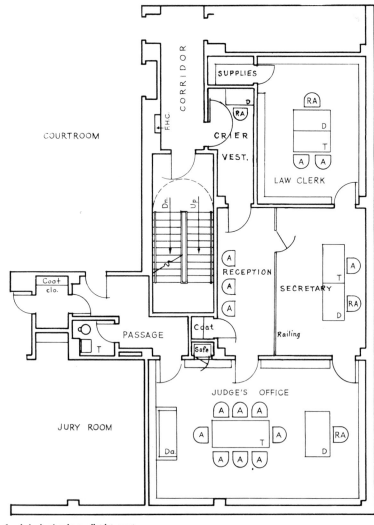

Fig. 4 Judge's chambers, district court.

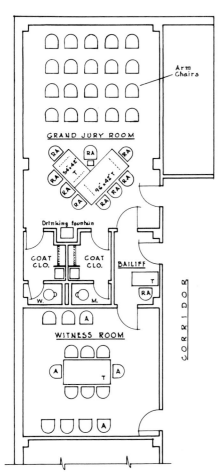

Fig. 5   Grand jury rooms.

Cells for Women Prisoners. Similar to detention cells for men.

Observation Passage. An observation passage at least 4 ft wide shall be located along the exterior wall of the building and be separated from the cells by a prison-type grille partition. The entire cell must be visible from the observation passage.

Holding Cells   If required, provide holding cells for projects with three or more courtrooms. They should be located in back of the courtrooms near the prisoners' entrance.

Supply and Storage Room   Provide a supply and storage room of required size convenient to the deputies' office.

Evidence Storage   At times marshals have custody of bulky evidence, requiring a large storage area. A storage room (preferably in the basement) of 300 sq ft minimum should be provided.

Smaller Installation   This suite will require fewer and perhaps smaller rooms than the headquarters suite in the same district, but the arrangement and relationship of its rooms will be similar to that of the corresponding rooms in a major installation.

Part 10. Clerk of the District Court

Duties   The clerk is the administrative officer of the court. He receives cases for filing in the court, maintains the records of its proceedings and actions, organizes its calendar, receives and disburses its money, and gives information to attorneys and interested parties regarding the disposition of cases as recorded in his office.

Location   It is desirable to locate the clerk near the courtroom and convenient to the judge. In multiple courts the clerk should be easily accessible to the public.

Components   The offices of the clerk of the court vary in size and number in accordance with the volume of business. The rooms include:

Clerk's office and toilet
Chief deputy clerk's office
General office, with public space and files
Examination room
Supply room
Work room
Vault
Exhibit room
File rooms as required
Naturalization clerk's office, with public space

Clerk's Office   This shall have a minimum area of 500 sq ft and be connected with a private toilet with a minimum area of 30 sq ft.

Deputy Clerk's Office   This shall have a minimum area of 300 sq ft and be located between the clerk's office and the general office.

General Office with Public Space   The size of the general office ordinarily will be determined by the number of desks, tables, and file cases used. But if it requires so many cases for active files that they would cause the general office to be disproportionately large, provide additional file rooms. Preferably they should be connected to the general office: but if located on adjacent floors, provide direct stairways and dumbwaiters. The public space is separated from the rest of the general office by a counter with one or more gates. The public space shall have a minimum width of 8 ft. In a very large general office, the counter will be U-shaped or L-shaped to accommodate the required length. Provide a cashier's grille with returns on the counter. Refer to Fig. 6.

Examination Room   This is provided for attorneys and others who are permitted to inspect the

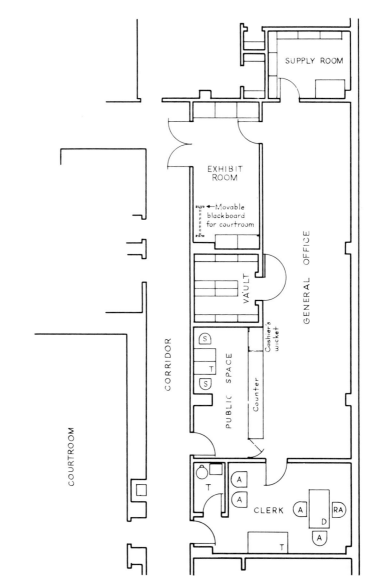

Fig. 6   Clerk of the district court's suite (small installation).

records. It shall have a minimum area of 150 sq ft and be connected to the general office.

Supply Room This should be close to the general office and have a minimum area of 100 sq ft.

Work Room This should be near the supply room. It shall have a minimum area of 300 sq ft. The clerk of the court may install a photostat machine with developing equipment and other duplicating machines that will require water, waste, and electrical connections.

Vault The vault, which holds a money safe, shall open into the general office and be planned to prevent public view of the interior. It shall have a minimum area of 80 sq ft, lined with steel shelving in sections 3 ft long and 12 in. wide.

Exhibit Room This shall have a minimum area of 250 sq ft. Entrance shall be from a corridor through double doors. The portable blackboard for courtroom use is usually stored in this room.

Smaller Installation This suite will require fewer and smaller rooms, but the rooms will be similar in character and relationship to corresponding rooms in a major installation. Refer to Fig. 6.

Naturalization Clerk's Office, with Public Space If an office for the naturalization clerk is required, it should be adjacent to the general office of the clerk of the court. The office shall have a minimum area of 400 sq ft, with a public space.

Part 11. Jury Commissioner

Duties and Components of Suite The jury commissioner, together with the clerk of the court, selects the persons who are eligible to serve on the grand and petit juries. Quarters for this officer are ordinarily not required except in major installations. A typical plan, Fig. 7, for a jury commissioner's suite in a major installation, will contain:

> Jury commissioner's office
> Examination room
> Jurors' assembly room
> Men's and women's toilets
> File room

Jury Commissioner's Office This shall have a minimum area of 250 sq ft, a width of 15 ft. and a direct entrance from the public corridor.

Examination Room This shall have a minimum area of 200 sq ft and connect to the jury commissioner's office.

Jurors' Assembly Room When quarters for the jury commissioner are required the jurors' assembly room should be part of his suite; but the room is frequently required as a separate unit, when no provision is made for a jury commissioner. It shall have toilets for men and women and a centrally located drinking fountain.

File Room This shall have a minimum area of 150 sq ft and be located adjacent to the jury commissioner's office.

Part 12. United States Commissioner

Duties The commissioner is a magistrate who exercises certain judicial functions and before whom persons are arraigned immediately after arrest. He holds preliminary hearings of prisoners to determine whether they shall be held for the grand jury, discharged, or released on bail. He issues warrants and writs, fixes bail, and sometimes handles juvenile cases.

Location and Components The preferred location of the commissioner's suite is near the freight elevator or the prisoners' elevator. The suite, Fig. 8, need not be on the same floor as the courtroom. Usually it will include:

Hearing room
Commissioner's office
Secretary's office (required only in larger jurisdictions)

Hearing Room This shall have a minimum area of 400 sq ft and accommodate:

> 1 Built-in combination bench, witness stand and attorney's table, built-in benches to seat a minimum of 16 persons
> 1 rotary armchair, fixed-pedestal—for witness
> 1 judge's chair—for the commissioner
> 5 armchairs
> 10 side chairs

Commissioner's Office This shall have a minimum area of 200 sq ft and adjoin and connect with the hearing room and the secretary's office.

One-Room Type In certain jurisdictions, the work of the commissioner may be insufficient to justify a separate hearing room and then only a single office of not less than 250 sq ft will be required.

Part 13. Probation and Parole Officer

Duties The probation and parole officer supervises the probationers referred to him by the court and the persons released on parole from

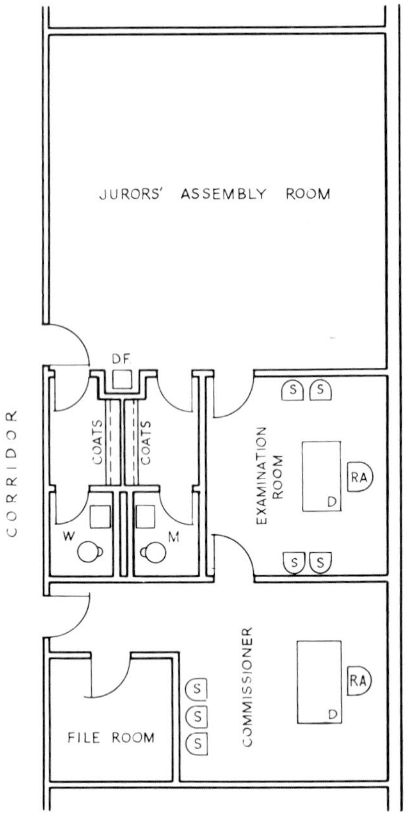

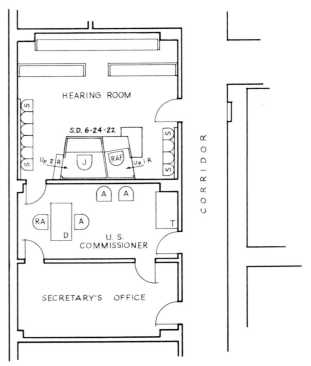

Fig. 7 Jury commissioner's suite.

Fig. 8 United States commissioner's suite.

penal institutions by the Department of Justice. For a stated period the probationer or parolee is required to report to the officer at specified intervals. He confers with the officer, who helps him solve his problems and adjust himself to society. To aid the judge in determining a sentence, the officer, when requested by the judge, makes presentence investigations of persons convicted of violations of the law.

Location and Components The suite should be located where it is accessible to the public by elevator or stairs, and preferably near the marshal's office, but not necessarily on the courtroom floor. The number of rooms in a suite varies with the amount of work handled by the officer. See Figs. 9 and 10. A suite may consist of the following:

Office for the probation and parole officer
Offices for one or more assistant officers
General office, with public space
File room
Supply closet or supply room

General Office with Public Space This shall have a minimum area of 275 sq ft when there are no assistant officers and 350 sq ft when there are one or more assistant officers.

Office of Probation and Parole Officer This shall have a minimum area of 200 sq ft. In an office staffed by two or more officers, the area for the chief may be increased. The office should connect

to the general office. In the case of a one-man office, it is desirable but not mandatory for the probation and parole officer to be able to pass directly from his office to the public corridor. Where there are two or more assistant officers, it is mandatory that each officer be able to pass directly from his office to the public corridor.

Offices for Assistant Probation and Parole Officers Each of these shall have a minimum area of 200 sq ft.

File Room This will be required only when there are two or more assistant probation and parole officers. It shall have a minimum area of 14 sq ft of file space for each assistant.

Part 14. Referee in Bankruptcy

Duties The referee conducts hearings, holds conferences, makes findings, and reports to the judge the findings and disposition of bankruptcy cases. Refer to Figs. 11 and 12.

Full-Time Referee, Chief Clark and Two or Three Assistant Clerks

Components. The referee's work varies in the different districts, and the rooms and personnel in each office will vary accordingly. The referee's suite, Fig. 11, generally will include the following rooms:

Hearing room
Referee's office (with toilet)
General office with public space
Chief clerk's office
File room
Trustees' room

Hearing Room. This shall have a minimum area of 600 sq ft, be conveniently accessible to the public, and accommodate:

1 built-in combination bench and witness stand
1 judge's chair
1 armchair for witness, rotary, fixed-pedestal
2 attorneys' tables
7 armchairs
Built-in benches to seat a minimum of 25 persons

Referee's Office. This shall have a minimum area of 250 sq ft and adjoin and connect with the hearing room.

General Office with Public Space. This shall have a minimum area of 350 sq ft and connect with the referee's office and the chief clerk's office.

Chief Clerk's Office. This shall have a minimum area of 200 sq ft and adjoin and connect with the general office.

File Room. This shall have a minimum area of 250 sq ft and connect with the general office.

Trustees' Room. One or more rooms, approximately 250 sq ft, shall be provided for trustees in the larger courts.

Referee and One or Two Clerks This small suite shall contain the same rooms and equipment provided for referee, chief clerk, and two or three assistant clerks, except that the file room and chief clerk's office shall be omitted. Refer to Fig. 12.

Part-Time Referee and One Clerk In a district where there are very few bankruptcy cases to be heard, only one room may be required. When this one-room office is provided, the referee may hold hearings in a vacant hearing room elsewhere in the building or use his own office if only a few persons are to be accommodated. It shall have a minimum area of 300 sq ft.

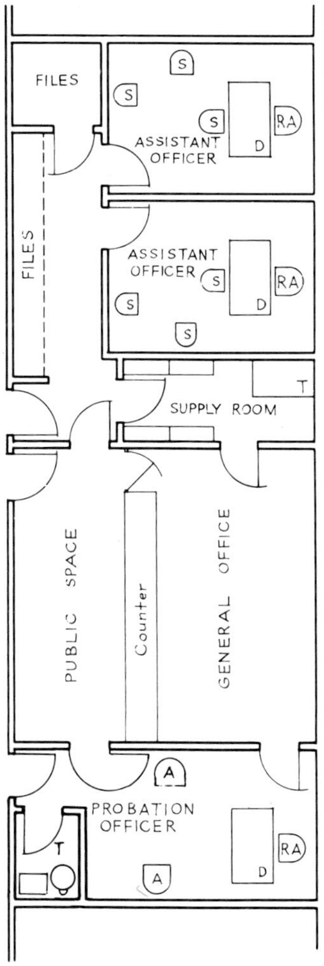

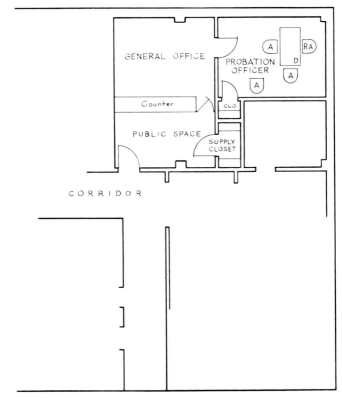

Fig. 9   Probation officer with two assistants.

Fig. 10   Probation officer's suite (small installation).

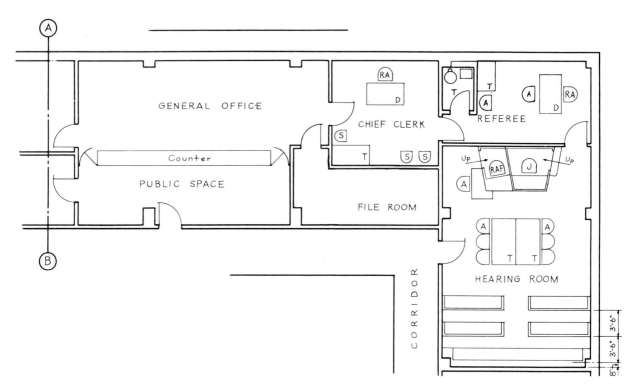

Fig. 11   Referee in bankruptcy.

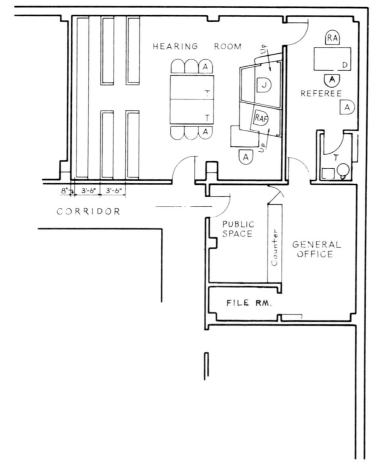

Fig. 12   Referee in bankruptcy's suite (small installation).

Part 15. Miscellaneous Assignments

Quarters for Visiting Judges   When these are required, the spaces shall be generally similar to those provided for the resident judge.

Court Reporter

Duties and Location.   The court reporter makes the official verbatim record of the court proceedings and furnishes transcripts when required. His office may be located anywhere in the building. Refer to Fig. 13.

Components and Furniture.   The reporter's quarters will include a general office, with file space, having a minimum area of 200 sq ft if the building has one courtroom. For each additional courtroom, add 50 sq ft to the general office.

District Court Library

General.   When there are two or more courtrooms, a general law library may be required, convenient to the judges' chambers.

Arrangement.   Reading tables should be located in front of windows. When window spacing will permit, put tables in small alcoves formed by bookstacks as separating partitions. Provide a main aisle at least 4 ft in width extending the full length of the room and separating the reading section from the general stack section.

Areas and Furniture.   The size of the library will accommodate readers to be seated.

Bookstacks.   Legal volumes average 2 to $2\frac{1}{2}$ in. in thickness, 6 to 10 in. in width, and 8 to 11 in. in height. Thus a stack section 3 ft long and 7 ft 3 in. high with shelves 12 in. on centers will store about 98 legal volumes. Stack sections are made up on single-faced wall sections and double-faced freestanding sections, which must be arranged in rows with the range isles, 2 ft 6 in. wide, and accessible from the main aisle.

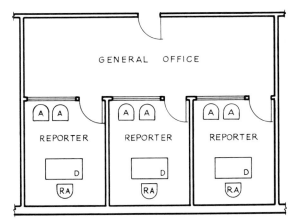

Fig. 13 Court reporters' offices.

Reading Tables. Each of these seats four people.

Press Room The location may be at any place in the building. Telephone booths with coin telephones will be installed. This room for news reporters may be required in buildings with two or more courtrooms. The minimum area of the room shall be 200 sq ft.

CIRCUIT COURT OF APPEALS

Part 1. Description

Jurisdiction The circuit court of appeals and the Court of Appeals for the District of Columbia are the intermediate federal appellate courts, each having the power to review the decisions of the district courts within its judicial circuit and the orders and decisions of

certain federal boards, commissions, and other regulatory agencies. There are ten judicial circuits, each composed of several states. The District of Columbia is a separate jurisdiction. There may be several places of holding court within each judicial circuit, but each circuit court of appeals has a headquarters court within its circuit.

Spaces Required A courtroom with its auxiliary facilities, and spaces for each of the following will be required at each court:

Circuit judges (three or more)
Clerk of the court
Library
Marshal (only if court is in the District of Columbia)

Location The location of the circuit court within the building, and the relationship of its rooms, is determined by the same conditions that govern in the case of the district court. Refer to Figs. 14 and 15.

Part 2. Courtroom

Dimensions. The minimum size of the courtroom shall be $38\frac{1}{2}$ ft in width by 50 ft in length; the ceiling height should be in proportion to the size of the room and be designed to meet the requirements of good illumination, ventilation or air conditioning, and acoustics.

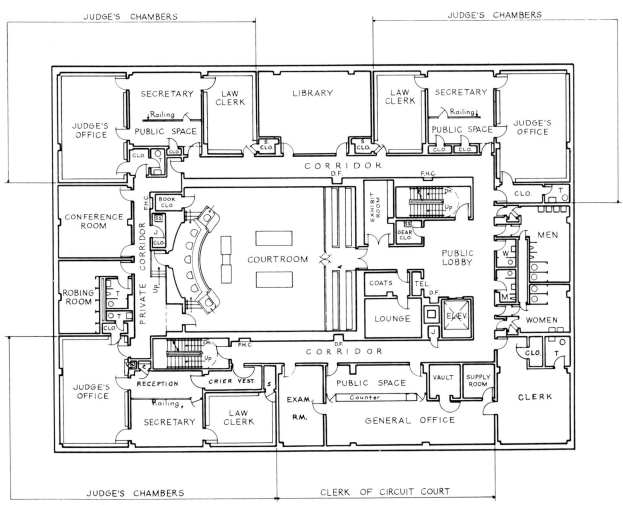

Fig. 14 Circuit court of appeals.

Entrances The public entrance, the judge's entrance, and corridor entrances are indicated on Fig. 14.

Built-in Furniture It shall include:

Combination judge's bench, clerk's desk, and bailiff's desk
Railing and gates
Benches in public space to seat 32 persons at 2 ft o.c.

Movable Furniture This shall include:

     5 judges' chairs
    12 lounge chairs
     1 pedestal armchair for clerk
     1 pedestal armchair for bailiff
     2 attorneys' tables, 60 by 34 in.
     1 lectern
    20 rotary armchairs for attorneys
     2 attorneys' tables, 120 by 48 in.

Part 3. Judges' Suite

Location There will be three or more judges' suites for the circuit court of appeals. Each judge's suite shall be similar in size, arrangement, and equipment to the district judge's chambers except that more space for books may be required. The judges' suites need not adjoin the courtroom but shall be adjacent to it and preferably on the same floor.

Judges' Conference Room This shall have a minimum area of 400 sq ft, should be connected to the judges' robing room and toilet, and must accommodate:

     1 table, 120 by 48 in.
    10 armchairs

Judges' Robing Room and Toilet Provide a robing room with a minimum floor area of 200 sq ft, so located that judges may enter the courtroom without passing through any public space. When the plan permits, the robing room may open directly into the courtroom. Provide a robe closet for each judge.

Part 4. Assignments

Clerk of Circuit Court — Large Installation This large suite shall be the same in location, size, arrangement, and equipment as that described for the clerk of the court except that there will be no naturalization clerk's office.

Library This shall be similar in location and size as shown on Fig. 14.

CUSTOMS COURT

Part 1. Description

Jurisdiction The United States Customs Court has exclusive jurisdiction over all civil actions arising under the regular tariff laws, the internal revenue laws relating to imported merchandise, and the provisions set forth in the various reciprocal trade agreements. Cases coming before the court for trial are handled under the legal procedure established by the Customs Administrative Act of June 10, 1890, and the several acts supplemental thereto. The court's function is to interpret the law and the facts respecting the classification of merchandise and the rates of duty imposed thereon. In addition to the court's exclusive authority to determine the dutiable value of imported merchandise, it also has sole jurisdiction in proceedings wherein relief is sought from so-called penalty or increased duties imposed by law because the final appraised value exceeded the value declared on entry.

Location

Headquarters. The United States Customs Court is in New York City. In addition to the regular trials during the year at New York, various circuits are held by the customs court in approximately 49 customs districts covering the entire United States and its possessions, embracing more than 298 ports or subports of entry. All its cases are tried without juries. In some forms of its litigation, the court consists of three judges, and in other cases the court is composed of only one judge. When cases are heard on circuit, the court usually consists of one judge or three judges. The judges on circuit are accompanied by a court reporter who also acts as calendar clerk. When the records have been transcribed by the court reporter, they are forwarded to New York and assigned to a judge or division for consideration and decision.

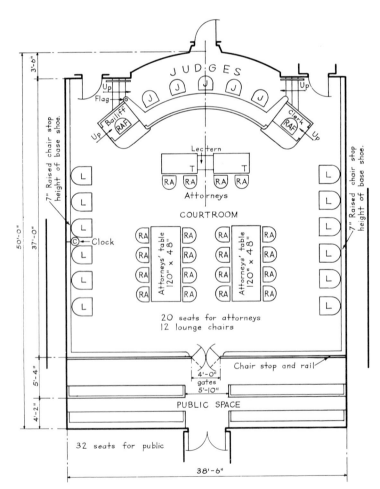

Fig. 15 Courtroom for circuit court of appeals.

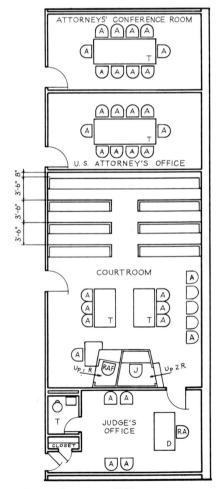

Fig. 16 Customs court (field).

Field Quarters. The customs court field quarters, Fig. 16, are sometimes located in appraisers' stores buildings so that they are convenient to the customs examiners; but it is considered more desirable to have the courtrooms located in the federal courthouse, when practicable.

Ports of Entry. Facilities for customs courts should be provided at all ports of entry.

Space Required The field quarters suite is indicated in Fig. 16. It will include:

Courtroom
Judge's office (with toilet)
United States customs attorney's office
Attorneys' conference office

Part 2. Courtroom

Size The courtroom should have a minimum area of 820 sq ft. The entrance door should be at a point to the rear of the attorneys' tables to assure minimum disturbance by people entering or leaving during trials.

Built-in Furniture The standard built-in bench for three judges with witness stand and built-in benches to seat 40 persons are required.

Movable Furniture The movable furniture will be furnished and installed by the government. It includes

  3 judges' chairs
  1 witness' armchair, rotary and fixed-pedestal
  2 attorneys' tables, 72 by 40 in.
12 armchairs

Part 3. Assignments

Judge's Office This shall have a minimum area of 500 sq ft.

United States Attorney's Office Provide a room with minimum area of 250 sq ft.

Attorneys' Conference Room Provide a room with minimum area of 250 sq ft.

Governmental and Public
FIRE STATIONS

By GEORGE H. TRYON and GORDON P. McKINNON

FIRE DEPARTMENT STATIONS AND BUILDINGS

Fire department buildings include administrative offices; "stations," "houses," or "halls" housing the apparatus and equipment; fire alarm and communications centers; fire training facilities; and maintenance and supply facilities, including shops and storerooms. In some relatively small fire departments, all or several of these functions, insofar as provided, may be housed in one facility.

A. Administrative Offices

The administrative offices may be housed in a municipal office building or city hall, or at a headquarters or central fire station. Headquarters may include offices and facilities for the chief of department, the fire prevention division, the planning and research staff, the budget or fiscal bureau, the personnel department, the fire investigation bureau, and the medical officer. The exact facilities needed will vary with the organization of the individual department. It is desirable to arrange the headquarters offices so that the general public will not have to pass through the apparatus room or fire fighters' quarters to reach the offices.

B. Fire Stations

General There are two types of fire houses: one is operated by a paid fire department, the other by volunteers. Equipment for both is essentially the same. Differences occur in facilities provided for personnel.

Modern practice is to group companies and apparatus needed to protect a given neighborhood in order to provide better teamwork and administrative control. Most fire stations house at least one pumper company, with its assigned first line and reserve apparatus, and other companies, including aerial ladder, aerial platform, squad, rescue, salvage, and various auxiliary types of apparatus. Ample space is needed for reserve apparatus, both to provide a replacement when needed and as equipment for use by off-duty personnel recalled in an emergency.

Far too many fire stations have outgrown their usefulness because inadequate consideration was given to the future needs of the district. The cost of providing adequate apparatus storage space is relatively modest when compared with the total cost of a fire station facility. A desirable policy is to provide an apparatus room large enough to house at least six major fire department vehicles. Even where it is intended initially to house a single first line piece of apparatus, a prudent minimum would be a two-track station capable of housing two first line and two reserve or special-duty pieces. Space should also be provided for additional men, who will be needed when further apparatus is obtained.

Elements of fire house design are shown

Fire Protection Handbook, National Fire Protection Association-International, Boston, Mass., 1969.

in Fig. 1. All facilities indicated are desirable but not mandatory. In paid departments, one company generally consists of 14 men; in a volunteer department, quarters are provided for paid drivers only.

Apparatus Rooms It is preferable that the apparatus floor be unobstructed by columns. Future use of the space should not be circumscribed by having major rooms protrude into the apparatus storage area. For multitrack stations, a minimum width of 20 ft per track is recommended. This should be increased to at least 24-ft width for a single-track station. A suggested desirable unobstructed depth is 80 ft, with ceiling height of 13 ft (minimum).

Ample space is needed to permit work around the apparatus, changing of hose, putting on fire clothing when responding, and to permit free movement of personnel when answering alarms. Space is needed along walls for clothing racks, slop sinks, battery chargers, water tank fill connections, etc. Space should be provided for hose storage racks without obstructing access to apparatus. Table 1 gives sizes of apparatus.

Floor should be of concrete, designed to carry a load of 125 lb per sq ft.

Wall surfaces should be of an easily cleaned material, and floor should have sufficient drains to permit flushing with hose. Hot and cold water connections are needed at center of side walls.

If apparatus room is to be used for repairs, provide a repair pit. Also, carbon monoxide gases have to be exhausted to outside, usually by means of under-floor piping to which

motor exhaust may be connected with flexible tubing. (Recreation room on first floor should be raised at least 6 in. for protection against gas.)

Fire stations should have adequate office space and facilities for all officers on duty. This includes not only the various company officers but offices and quarters for district and deputy chiefs. Among the other facilities needed in fire stations are a watch room, a dormitory, a locker and washroom, storerooms, study rooms, a kitchen, recreation room, and hose drying facilities.

The watch room should be so located that the man on patrol can see the apparatus floor, observe all persons entering the building, and preferably see the street in front of the property. It should be the center of the station's fire alarm facilities and have facilities for turning on house lights and alerting and dispatching fire fighters. If a watch desk is to be used, it should be on platform raised 6 in. above apparatus room floor to allow man on duty to remain during cleaning. Floors of closets, toilets, oil room, stair landings, etc., should also be raised for same reason.

Volunteer fire departments frequently require other facilities at their stations including social halls or meeting rooms, recreation facilities, and ladies' club rooms or lounges, particularly where the volunteer fire company's quarters serve as a community center.

Apparatus Room Doors Doors for fire apparatus should be large enough to permit quick passage without accident. An opening at least 14 ft by 14 ft is recommended.

Table 1. Fire apparatus sizes

Note: Turning radius varies from 26 to 48 ft, according to type and make. "Cab-over-engine" type of apparatus is slightly shorter over all.

Village-Size Pumping Engine, 500 g.p.m.	
Length over all	24'-0''
Width over all	7'-6''
Height over all	6'-5''
Triple Combination Pumping Engine, 750 g.p.m. (most used)	
Length over all	28'-0''
Width over all	8'-0''
Height over all	6'-11''
Hook-and-Ladder Truck (removable hand-raised ladders)	
Length over all	41'-3''
Width over all	8'-0''
Height over all	7'-3''
Hook-and-Ladder Aerial Truck (4-wheel type)	
Length over all	58'-9''
Width over all	8'-0''
Height over all	8'-7''
Hook-and-Ladder Aerial Truck (tractor-drawn type, 6-wheel)	
Length over all	63'-6''
Width over all	8'-0''
Height over all	8'-7''
Clearance required	12'-0''

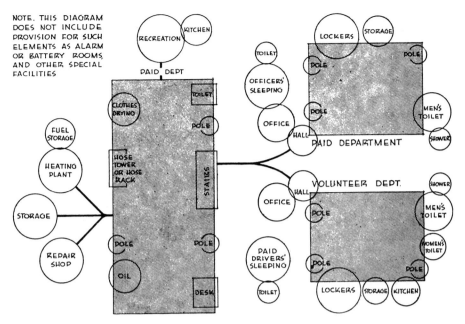

NOTE. THIS DIAGRAM DOES NOT INCLUDE PROVISION FOR SUCH ELEMENTS AS ALARM OR BATTERY ROOMS, AND OTHER SPECIAL FACILITIES

Fig. 1 Elements of a firehouse.

Designs for Stations Figure 2 shows suggested minimum space requirements for a district fire station intended for urban or suburban service where the station is to be mainly manned by full-paid personnel. The shape of the lot may vary with local circumstances, but it is considered very poor practice to start with a lot of inadequate size. A larger lot tends to have considerably more reuse or resale value at such time as it may be desired to add to the fire department facilities or to relocate the station.

The plan for an urban station shown in Fig. 4 provides space for two pumper companies (or a pumper company and a squad company) plus an aerial ladder or aerial platform company. Space is provided for reserve apparatus to be manned by off-shift personnel when needed. If desired, two-piece engine or truck companies can be operated out of such a station. Separate quarters with a garage are provided for the district fire chief so that he can come and go without opening up or lighting the main station and so that major apparatus can be taken out without moving the chief's car.

Unless required by the terrain or grade, a basement is not recommended under the main apparatus room as this tends to add materially to the cost. However, where the terrain makes a basement necessary, the main apparatus room may be reduced in size and a garage for reserve apparatus provided on the lower level. A basement may be desirable under the living quarters to provide room for heating equipment, storage, and other facilities.

The apparatus area should be of modern garage-type construction. It is good practice to provide automatic sprinklers for a fire department station. This has training value as well as providing fire protection for a type of garage occupancy which has a rather poor fire record. The heat for the garage area (where required) may be controlled by a separate thermostat from the company quarters. Where a hose drying tower is provided (see NFPA No. 198) it may also be equipped as a drill tower.

For a rural fire station manned chiefly by call or volunteer firemen (Fig. 5), space should be provided initially for not less than four pieces of major apparatus including a pumper, water tanker, booster squad or forest fire truck, and a reserve pumper or second tanker. Often a rescue truck or ambulance also must be housed. Far too many rural fire departments have quickly outgrown their stations and have been forced to leave part of their apparatus outside or in a private garage where it is not readily available for use or under close fire department supervision.

Adequate meeting room space is needed, with proper exit facilities. The station should be located on a plot large enough to permit doubling the apparatus room when the department grows and to provide future office space

and quarters for paid apparatus drivers who may be subsequently employed.

It is bad practice to crowd three pieces of apparatus abreast in space designed for two trucks; this slows response and makes it difficult to properly service apparatus.

In Figs. 4 and 5 apparatus doors are shown at the front and rear of the stations. These are desirable so that the apparatus in the second line can leave the building in event of mechanical failure of a first-line piece. In some cases, where the lot has a long road frontage, it may be desirable to provide more apparatus doors facing the road and to reduce the depth of the building to about 50 ft. However, care should be taken to allow ample depth for major apparatus which may be purchased, such as large "nurse tankers" or apparatus with long ladders or an aerial platform. Normally, fire stations are expected to give 50 to 60 years of service, and what starts as a purely rural district fire station often has major properties to protect as business and industry move into the area. This may require facilities to house additional major apparatus and manpower.

Parking Facilities Parking areas for firemen's cars should not be overlooked. The station should have a parking area large enough to provide off-street parking for each fireman on duty or scheduled to respond to fires. Where call or volunteer firemen are to respond to the station to man apparatus, ample parking space should be provided adjacent to the front of the station. With paid departments, parking should be at the sides or rear. Additional yard space should be provided for company drill work. Figures 2 and 3 show plot plans for urban and rural stations respectively.

The apron or ramp in front of the station should be large enough to permit washing of apparatus and safe entry of vehicles into traffic.

C. Fire Alarm and Communications Buildings

The communications building or fire alarm office should be of fire-resistive construction and isolated from all hazards that might interfere with the prompt transmission of alarms. Where the fire alarm office is part of a fire station or administration building, it should be

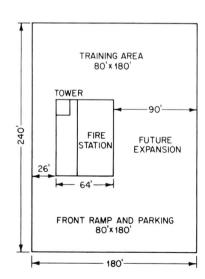

Fig. 2 Plot plan for a typical district fire station for urban and suburban services. Minimum recommended plot size is 43,200 sq ft.

Fig. 3 Plot plan for a typical rural fire station. Minimum recommended plot size is 43,200 sq ft.

isolated from the rest of the structure and protected against all hazards both internal and external. Ample emergency power should be provided so that the station and communications equipment can continue to operate should outside power fail.

The communications office includes the operating room where all alarms are received and transmitted to the department. It also should have the telephone switchboard for the department, the radio control console, voice amplification controls, fire alarm circuit panels, and test equipment. Frequently, a central console is provided containing all communications controls and information needed by the dispatchers. There should be an office for the fire alarm superintendent, drafting room for plans, battery room, storerooms for fire alarm supplies, garage for fire alarm vehicles, and facilities for fire alarm personnel.

D. Fire Training Facilities

Facilities needed for the fire department training program include study rooms and library facilities in each fire station. A fire training center should include adequate classrooms and training aids. The better training centers have an apparatus room where major apparatus can be brought indoors for instruction purposes, and the operation of various items of fire protection equipment (hydrants, fire alarm, and automatic sprinklers) can be demonstrated. Other desirable features include an auditorium where various fire protection conferences and training meetings can be held, facilities for preparation and reproduction of training manuals and bulletins, and a fire protection library.

Outdoor training facilities should include large grounds with various structures for demonstrations and practice fires, a drill tower for hose and ladder evolutions, tanks for practice on flammable liquids fires, electrical and gas utility installations for fire training purposes, hydrants and pumper suction facilities, and other equipment duplicating situations that may be encountered at fires. When an individual fire department is too small to provide all the necessary training facilities, the practice is to supplement the local training program by use of regional or state fire schools which do provide more adequate facilities and curricula. The NFPA book, *Firemen's Training Centers,* gives additional suggestions for planning such facilities and contains illustrations of some typical centers.

E. Maintenance Facilities and Shops

Facilities for maintenance and repair work on fire apparatus should be provided. A repair shop includes an area where major apparatus, including ladder trucks, can be serviced and repaired.

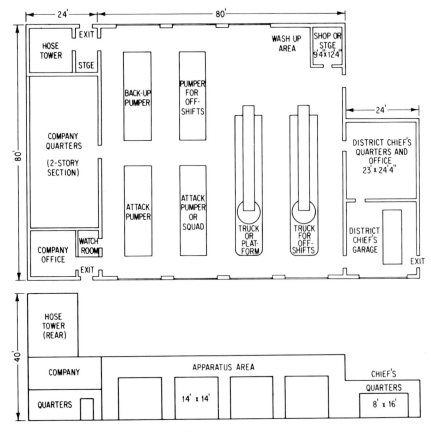

Fig. 4   Elevation and plan view of a typical urban fire station.

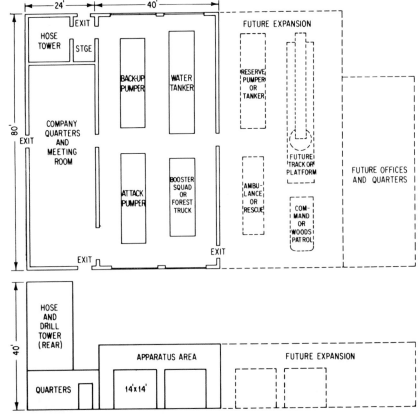

Fig. 5   Elevation and plan view of a typical rural fire station.

By EMMANUEL MESAGNA, R.A.

FIREHOUSE PLANNING

Over the past decade, Firehouse Planning and Design has become increasingly sophisticated and complex. Years of study and experience have made it apparent that by planning a firehouse properly, a safer and quicker turnout can be made. This is accomplished primarily by arranging traffic flow patterns within the firehouse to be as direct as possible. The integration of the "primary adjacency" concept for planning the firehouse will deduct considerably from the turnout time by "grouping" the firefighting personnel in the "highest activity" areas of the firehouse. Turnout time along with dispatching time and travel time are three of the key elements in the successful containment of fire which is one of the primary goals of a firefighting unit.

The improvements in firehouse planning have created a total upgrading of human comforts with great emphasis on physical fitness. These include well-planned kitchens, air conditioning, better lighting, well-planned toilet-shower facilities and dormitory spaces, acoustical improvements, safety features in building planning and the integration of a small gymnasium-like area, for physical fitness purposes in firefighting needs, into the firehouse plan.

Concept Planning for the Firehouse and Plan Types

Turnout time is the key element in firehouse planning. When planning the firehouse the most important feature is to group various functional spaces in a primary adjacency pattern so that movements to exit from the firehouse are minimized. Dispatching, travel, and turnout time are the key elements in the successful containment of the fire.

The one-story firehouse has a series of plan types which can be categorized in the following manner (see Fig. 1):

(A) One-Way Straddle of the Apparatus Area
All of the support functions for this plan type are located to the left or right of the apparatus area. This plan type is the least desirable in that the plan has the longest travel distances to reach the apparatus area and therefore adds to the turnout time of the fire company. This plan type by its nature creates a circulation pattern which can be eliminated in other plan types. Other plan types have supporting areas responding directly onto the apparatus area.

(B) Two-Way, U Wraparound of Apparatus Area
This plan type is the most desirable for purposes of minimizing the turnout time in firehouse planning. Using the same gross area for the standard two-company unit, it places all areas at the shortest possible distance from the responding apparatus. Another key element in this type of planning concept is that it separates the noisy areas of the firehouse from the quiet areas by the natural separation of the apparatus area.

Chief Architect, Fire Department, City of New York, Director of Facilities Planning and Design, 1978.

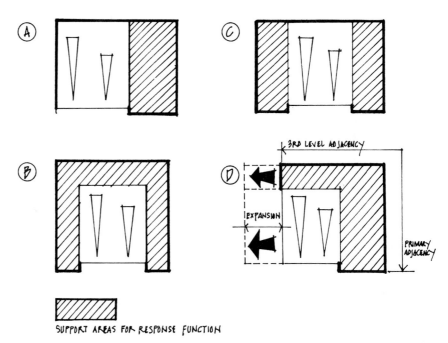

Fig. 1.

(C) Two-Way Straddle of the Apparatus Area
This plan type is the second most desirable for purposes of minimizing the turnout time in firehouse planning. The plan clearly separates the noisy areas of the firehouse from the quiet areas and may create circulation patterns in the support areas by not taking advantage of the back of the firehouse for support area use. This plan type is the same for the two-story firehouse with the quiet volume stacked over the apparatus area (see Figs. 2 and 3).

(D) L Wraparound of the Apparatus Area This plan type is unique in that the location of the L arrangement allows for the natural progression in locating the primary adjacency areas through the third-level adjacency areas as the L wraps around the apparatus area from the leg of the L to the toe. The key turnout spaces are placed in normal sequence by virtue of its form. One of the advantages of this plan type is the flexibility for expansion along the apparatus area and the toe of the L. This plan type is the third most desirable with the advantage of potential for expansion.

Adjacency Relationships for Space Planning of a Firehouse

The key concept in planning a firehouse for the shortest turnout time possible is the development of an adjacency planning concept. The main purpose of this concept is an in-depth study of spaces in a firehouse which require an "adjacency rating" for purposes of functional planning of the firehouse to verify where the greatest amounts of activity occur. These "activity locations" will then be joined in such a manner that a minimum amount of grouping time is required for the firefighting personnel to respond to the fire. This grouping time is extremely valuable to the response action. At this time the company officers develop a response strategy for the shortest route to the fire location and the problems of the fire condition.

Primary Adjacency Spaces in this category must be directly connected in a physical manner to each other or directly to the apparatus area which is the key turnout location in the response action.

Secondary Adjacency Spaces in this category must be placed at a midway location in the firehouse plan because of the dependency of function during day-to-day operations that are not of primary importance.

Third-Level Adjacency Spaces in this category are the least used in a firehouse and have no direct day-to-day operational relationship to the primary and secondary adjacency spaces.

Primary Adjacency Spaces
Dispatcher-housewatch area, lobby area
Administrative—company offices
Kitchen/recreation area/gym area/training area
Lounge area
Classroom facility with accommodations for television, videotape teaching
Basic toilet area (close to high-use areas)
Dormitory areas

FIREHOUSES

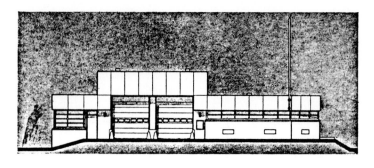

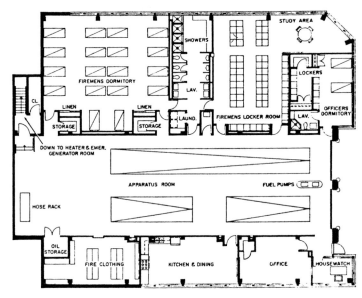

Fig. 2 Typical plan and elevation of a one-story firehouse. Front elevation and floor plan of one-story firehouse which features "active" and "quiet" sections of the firehouse divided by the apparatus floor, a good example of the two-way straddle of the apparatus area.

Turnout gear storage (can be third-level adjacency according to response action strategy)

Secondary Adjacency Spaces
General shop, storage, repair area
Cleanup areas
Hose storage/drying area

Third-Level Adjacency Spaces
Apparatus parts storage
Boiler plant, utilities, and emergency generator area
Locker room area
Miscellaneous storage areas
Major toilet-shower area, clothes washing and drying area
Administrative area—not related to the response action
Conference/public areas
Any other function not directly related to the response action

Note: Adjacency levels must be ascertained through in-depth interviews with fire department administrators and may change accordingly.

Space-Planning Analysis to obtain the Gross Area Requirements for the Firehouse

Prior to site selection it is essential that an architect/space-planning analyst be retained for purposes of ascertaining the gross area requirements for the firehouse. A space-planning analyst is a new breed of expert whose main responsibility is to arrive at the most efficient total gross space required for the building. High building costs have necessitated the use of a space-planning analyst to obtain the *least* gross area for the building function with maximum efficiency.

The space-planning analyst will make in-depth studies of equipment, personnel, utility needs, and circulation and arrive at the optimum gross area requirements for the building. Prior to planning a firehouse, it is essential that all equipment and personnel needs are clearly delineated in numbers and size so that proper circulation allowances can be made for the proper functioning of the firehouse; these in turn will give the gross area requirements. As part of the study by the space-planning analyst many options will be offered which will examine the level of *maximizing* or *minimizing* the space needs and the ultimate advantage and disadvantage of each as they relate to the function of the building.

Building and Site relationship

Three of the major considerations related to the building and site relationship are the building setback, training area requirements, and the onsite parking requirement for firefighting personnel. The minimum setback is 30 ft and should ideally be standard at 65 ft to accommodate the largest piece of apparatus in the fire service. This will give optimum visibility for apparatus exiting from the firehouse. The apron area shall have the smallest possible slope to drain water and may include a hot-water underground piping system or electrical cable de-icing system to clear the apron for response purposes. All building sites require an open area to one side of the firehouse for purposes of training with the largest piece of apparatus available to the firefighting unit. A parking area to accommodate all personnel on duty at any one time is absolutely necessary, plus a minimum of 50 percent more as extra space for administrative personnel. Beyond this point the parking requirement is a subjective judgment which may include parking spaces for public and social functions. The parking area is to be located adjacent to the dispatcher-housewatch area with visual control of the activity in the parking area.

The main arterial street shall be wide enough to accommodate the apparatus with the largest turning radius. It is also essential that traffic controls be installed on extreme ends of the front property line to stop traffic during a response action.

As a secondary consideration, any responding of apparatus directly into the low sun orientations shall be eliminated to do away with the vision problem of the quick transition from basic darkness to brightness and the ensuing accident potential, by orienting the building properly.

Wherever possible additional land should be allocated to the site footage for purposes of integrating the drive-through apparatus area arrangement in the floor plan. This method of returning from the response action creates less disruption in the street and potential for accident during the backing up of apparatus.

DISCUSSION OF THE VARIOUS SPACE COMPONENTS IN FIREHOUSE PLANNING

Dispatcher-Housewatch Area

This key communication area is being formed as an independent operating space, completely sound-controlled for optimum hearing ability. It must be completely air-conditioned and have maximum visual control of the quarters and street conditions. Glass areas in the front of the housewatch are arranged in such a manner, that 180° of visibility in front of the firehouse is possible. The alarm lights button at the fire communications console is not limited to activating the alarm lights as in the past. The alarm button also activates the apparatus fume-exhaust system and a series of floodlights mounted on the front face of the building. These lights illuminate the apron area and street for a safer response. An adjustable timer turns off the floodlights and the fume-exhaust system after the overhead doors have been electrically secured shut. They can be activated manually through an override switch by the housewatchman in other than response situations.

Control Functions of the Dispatcher-Housewatch Area This key communication area is also the center of all electronic switching devices which control the security and functioning of the firehouse and include:

1. Gasoline and diesel pump operation
2. Manual operation of floodlights mounted on the front of the building
3. Security lights surrounding the problem areas of the building
4. Manual control of fume-exhaust system
5. Alarm lights for various parts of the building during response action

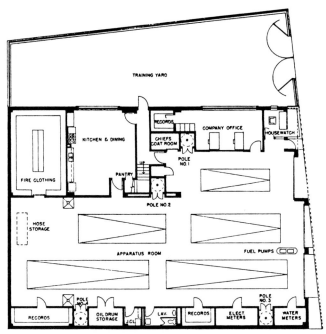

First-floor plan of the two-story firehouse.

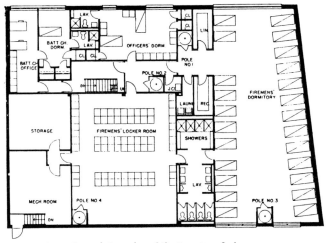

Second-story plan of the two-story firehouse.

Front elevation of the firehouse.

Fig. 3 Typical plans and elevation of a two-story firehouse, a good example of a two-way straddle of the apparatus area with the "quiet" section stacked over the apparatus area.

6. Daily-use light control

7. Control of overhead doors with up and stop buttons only for safety purposes; down button located at overhead door location only

8. A complete intercom system for immediate verbal communication to all areas of the firehouse plan

Management Adjacency The planned adjacency of the housewatch and the company offices affords excellent audible communication between the dispatcher-housewatch area and the company offices—the management arm of the firehouse. Both areas also face the apparatus storage area and have glass walls, allowing for visual control of the apparatus floor. This adjacency of space is ideal for all aspects of communication and decision making during initial turnout action.

The Apparatus Storage Area

This is the heart of every firehouse; its location, shape, flexibility, size, layout, and column-free approach will provide for easy, quick access from all areas in the four major concepts in planning a firehouse. These factors will provide the fire-fighting units with a good functional design for response purposes. The integration of the large areas such as the apparatus area and hose storage area into one large, open apparatus area and the elimination of the turnout gear storage from the apparatus area have allowed for "clear space" mobility. The single open space now offers greater flexibility in the apparatus storage area and may also function as an area for training and for storage of spare or down apparatus.

Apparatus storage areas are now being equipped with a sophisticated fume-exhaust sys-

tem. The fume-exhaust system is activated from the alarm lights button located on the fire communications console unit. The fume-exhaust system is capable of a massive exhaust pull of 5000 cfm which is the equivalent of six changes of air per hour. A timer will automatically shut the system down after a set time lapse. Provisions have been made for the manual control of the fume-exhaust system when companies are not in a response action. A study of fume-exhaust pipe locations on the apparatus has allowed us to place intake grilles at optimum locations for greatest intake pull. Our goal is for the maximum elimination of fume-exhaust gases on the apparatus floor. Upon the return of the apparatus to quarters, a manual switch operation can be utilized and the fumes can be exhausted as long as required for the comfort of the personnel.

It is recommended that all apparatus areas

utilize single apparatus doors approximately 12 ft wide by 14 ft high. Wide, single-opening apparatus doors are not recommended because of the possibility of having the door frozen closed due to a breakdown in the mechanized door operation. This situation will put the responding apparatus out of service and increase the response time of first-due apparatus. A pair of doors is more functional in that a breakdown in one door will allow the responding apparatus to maneuver through the other door. This will eliminate the turnout problem in case of an emergency breakdown of one of the mechanized overhead doors. It is essential to include a totalizer on all apparatus doors so that tension springs may be replaced on a preventive maintenance schedule based on predictive breakdown of the equipment. This standardization of door-opening size will simplify the storage of spare parts for repair purposes. All door operators, springs, track, turning shafts, and other accessory equipment of a single size will simplify the storage of parts while minimizing the inventory burden. It is recommended that all overhead doors be opened with electrical operators for purposes of decreasing the turnout time. Electrical operators shall have the capability of manual operation in case of breakdown of the motorized equipment. It is essential that the overhead-door-operating equipment be put on the emergency generator in case of electrical failure in the community.

Generally throughout the fire service, the hose tower is being eliminated as a functional need in the operation of a firehouse. With the use of sophisticated hose drying equipment and the use of polyester hose which does not require drying, the hose tower is being phased out in both new and existing firehouses.

Turnout Gear Storage

A well-planned firehouse shall have facilities for storing helmets, coats, and boots with accommodation for washing and drying out, as well as a floor drain system. The turnout gear storage area shall be secured with a pull-down see-through mesh gate arrangement and locking device to secure the area while the company is out of quarters. Included as part of the equipment for this area shall be an electric heater for drying and an exhaust fan to clear out the humidity in the area. The wall and ceiling finishes in this area are critical for maintenance and shall include maintenance-free finishes such as permanently glazed surfaces.

Slide Pole and Enclosures

There is a movement in the fire service to generally eliminate the slide pole as a means of circulation from the second floor of a firehouse. Serious injuries have occurred in the use of slide poles. Their use is generally discouraged in favor of a stairway or the trend toward the one-story firehouse, wherever the land value permits, in all areas of the country. In some areas of the country, particularly in the urban areas, the air rights over firehouses have been sold to developers to offset the high land cost.

Classroom—TV Amphitheater for Training Purposes

The future of all training programs will be in the firehouse through the medium of closed-circuit television and videotape. For this purpose a sophisticated space is required in order to create a positive environment for learning. The space will

require complete acoustical treatment, theater-type viewing chairs, a sloped floor arrangement for viewing purposes, and a desk top writing surface. In terms of adjacency level, this space is classified as a primary adjacency and shall have direct access to the firefighting apparatus area.

Kitchen—Dining Room—Recreation Area

The kitchen—dining room area is completely planned for reduction of maintenance and efficiency of operation. Each component shall be planned for the level of commercial use completely in stain-

TYPICAL SPACE REQUIREMENTS SURVEY FORM FOR OBTAINING THE GROSS AREA REQUIREMENT FOR A NEW FIREHOUSE

• SPACE REQUIREMENTS SURVEY • • GROSS AREA REQUIREMENTS FOR A NEW FIREHOUSE BUILDING. • UNIT • PRESENT LOCATION • UNIT HEAD, NAME & TITLE • PERSON INTERVIEWED			• FIRE DEPARTMENT • KEY CONTACT PERSON • TELE. NUMBER • DATE	
• SPACE OR EQUIPMENT TYPE	SQ FEET PER UNIT	MULTIPLY	TOTAL NUMBER OF ITEMS REQUIRED	AREA REQUIRED INCLUDES INTRA-CIRCULATION FACTOR.
• LADDER - TILLER OPERATED 53'	1040	X		
• LADDER - TOWER 33'	800	X		
• LADDER - REAR MOUNT 36'	752	X		
• PUMPER - STANDARD 26'	592	X		
• PUMPER - SQUIRT 33'	800	X		
• RESCUE TRUCK 29'	640	X		
• AIRPORT CRASH TRUCK 30'	656	X		
• AMBULANCE 20'	496	X		
• BRUSH FIRE UNIT 20'	496	X		
• LIGHT TRUCK 26'	592	X		
• COMMUNICATION VEHICLE 25'	576	X		
• SPECIALTY VAN 25'	576	X		
• CHIEFS CAR 25'	576	X		
• HOSE STORAGE RACK	100	X		
• HOSE DRYER UNIT - ELECTRIC	60	X		
• HOSE WASHER UNIT	100	X		
• TURNOUT GEAR STORAGE	8 SQ. FEET PER PERSON	X		
• COMMUNICATIONS CONSOLE UNIT STANDARD 3' x 8' -	120	—		
• STANDARD DESK AREA	90	X		
• LEGAL FILE	9	X		
• TABLE, 36" x 60"	60	X		
• SHELVING UNIT, 36"W x 12"D	12	X		
• SIDE CHAIR	8	X		
• TELEPRINTER, COMPUTERIZED RESPONSE	9	X		
• KITCHEN AREA, FOOD PREPARATION 14' COUNTER SERVICE LENGTH, SINK, DISHWASHER, RANGE AND WORK COUNTER FOR NUMBER OF PERSONS	120	—		
6	120	—		
8	160	—		
10	200	—		
12	240	—		
14	280	—		
16	320	—		
18	360			
• CONFERENCE ROOMS SEATING FOR: 6	100	—		
12	200	—		
15	300	—		
20	375	—		
SIZE OF CONFERENCE ROOMS TO VARY IN ACCORDANCE				

Fig. 4   Check-list form for firehouse planning.

WITH SEATING CONFIGURATIONS AND SPACE NEEDS.

• GASOLINE AND DIESEL REFUELING AREA.	24 PER PUMP UNIT.	X
• TOILET FACILITIES (PER UNIT)		
WATER CLOSET	27	X
URINAL	8	X
LAVATORY	16	X
SHOWER AREA W/ BENCH	27	X
CLOTHES WASHER	24	X
CLOTHES DRYER	24	X
SLOP SINK- STORAGE AREA	40	X
• VEHICLE MAINTENANCE AREA	100	X
• LOCKER ROOM AREA 2'x 2' LOCKER UNIT	15	X
• DORMITORY AREA 5'x 7' BUNK SIZE	100	X
• LINEN STORAGE ROOM	80	—
• GENERATOR ROOM	200	—
• GENERAL STORAGE - ALL FLOORS	400	—
• BOILER ROOM	360	—
• ELECTRICAL ROOM	50	—
• WATER METER ROOM	50	—

SUB-TOTAL ___ SQ. FT.

• BUILDING CORE PRIMARY CIRCULATION, ENCLOSING WALLS, INTERIOR WALLS, STAIRS, FLUES, VENTS, STACKS, PIPE SHAFTS, VERTICAL DUCTS AND OTHER SPACE CONSUMING ITEMS. — 10 to 13% OF NET AREAS ABOVE (SUB-TOTAL)

LOWER LIMIT-1 STORY F.H.   UPPER LIMIT-2 STORY F.H.

BUILDING CORE ___ SQ. FT.

GROSS AREA REQUIREMENT   SQ. FT.

Fig. 4 (Cont.).

less steel. Included also are a large refrigerator and a six-burner range (commercial type) with a grill unit and oven. This is a heavy-duty commercial range with a proven successful performance. Included is a stainless steel range hood with removable and washable stainless steel filters. The ceilings are of washable acoustical tile and the floor and wall are finished in a ceramic or quarry tile, which has eliminated maintenance except for simple cleaning.

Dormitory–Locker Room

New planning concepts have the dormitory and locker-room spaces straddling the toilet-shower and clothes-washing core areas. This provides sound isolation between the noisy locker room and quiet dormitory area. In cases where the dormitory area faces onto a traffic street it is best not to provide any windows on the dormitory walls facing the street. This type of planning will give maximum sound isolation and privacy for this quiet area of the firehouse.

Chief's Quarters

A refinement of the planning of the chief's quarters has produced a unique privacy aspect and efficiency of response. The chief's car and his turnout gear storage closet are located at the base of the egress stair or circulation corridor at the apparatus floor level, with his office and dormitory having direct access to his response vehicle. In the typical two-story firehouse illustrated (Fig. 3), the chief's quarters are located at the head of the stair at the second floor and he goes directly into his suite of rooms from the egress stair. This eliminates many unnecessary steps by giving the responding chief direct access to his response vehicle. This will eliminate circulation patterns which in the past carried the responding chief through the company locker room and dormitory. There is a continuity of function between the chief's car area, the chief's turnout gear storage, the egress stair, and the responding chief's office and dormitory; the adjacency of these spaces indicates a minimum circulation pattern.

DISCUSSION OF THE ADVANTAGES OF THE ONE-STORY FIREHOUSE OVER THE TWO-STORY FIREHOUSE

There is a national movement generally to eliminate the two-story firehouse as a planning concept in firehouse design.

The arguments in favor of the one-story firehouse are mainly based on positive facts and response action strategy:

1. Injuries to members of the responding fire companies resulting from the use of stairs and slide poles will be eliminated.

2. Elimination of the physical exertion required in the constant up and down activity of a high-activity firefighting unit.

3. It is apparent that the most economical solution to firehouse design is the one-story firehouse. It is approximately 10 percent lower in cost than the two-story firehouse and becomes a trade-off when evaluating low land cost and the difference in construction cost between the one-story firehouse and the two-story firehouse. Although the one-time land costs have been made an obstacle to the one-story firehouse, the determining factors in the decision for a one-story or two-story firehouse shall be the efficiency of response and the reduction of maintenance and operational burdens which are life/cycle determinants. This maintenance and operation burden will far exceed the original cost of the land.

4. As a secondary option for high land cost, the value of the land can always be recouped by selling the air rights over the property for future development or for additional floor area to adjacent parcels as allowed by the zoning regulations in the particular municipality.

HOUSING

Perhaps no item of police equipment or property has the potential for providing or denying optimal utilization of command and supportive services personnel in any greater degree than the police headquarters building itself. Earlier this century the automobile reduced the need for large numbers of officers to provide on-street police service or for emergency standby purposes, but no such dramatic invention has reduced the nonline personnel requirements of a police agency. Indeed, the complexities of staff and auxiliary services and the utilization of sophisticated automated data processing equipment and systems, the growth of planning and research activities, the increase in training requirements—all emphasize the need for sound planning of police facilities if both space and personnel are to be used effectively and economically.

When an old building is recognized as inadequate several alternative responses to the problem may be identified: (1) doing nothing about the building or its floor plan and employing additional personnel in numbers sufficient to overcome the operational handicaps of the existing facility, (2) reducing service to the public and to the line or field elements of the department whenever the physical and functional relationships of people and their work are such that they require more time and/or personnel than is presently available, (3) researching the departmental and public needs and redesigning and modifying those portions of the structure which present operational or administrative problems, or (4) designing and constructing a new facility.[1]

In some situations, the handicap of a poorly arranged building may be overcome by minimal reconstruction or relocation of offices and work areas, though this approach may not always be used to great advantage in cases where unusual problems exist. It is generally unwise, however, to attempt to redesign the police station in an existing structure. Experience throughout the nation has shown that such moves may eventually cost more than new construction, and the results are seldom satisfactory. The most economical approach, if viewed from a 20- to 40-year vantage point, probably will be in the design and construction of a new facility. This is true because the expenses of reconstruction are essentially a one-time cost, but the personnel costs of employees whose work performance is limited or wasted through poor building design continue year after year. Moreover, delaying new buildings when the need is apparent can be costly because of rising construction costs.

If only one unnecessary 24-hour per day posi-

[1] Whenever a new building or a major restructuring of an old one is under consideration, the key decision to be made does not concern building design at all—it is analysis and appraisal of departmental program and organization. All too often a building is designed to fit an antiquated, unrealistic agency structure. Thus a review of department organization should be made, accompanied by necessary changes, before a new building design or modification of an old one is attempted.

Municipal Police Administration, 1971, International City Management Association, Washington, D.C.

tion is saved or eliminated by such a move, the annual salary savings amounts to approximately five times the cost of one person's salary and fringe benefits. Unnecessary recurring personnel expenditures are a major consideration in building design. The luxury of poor working quarters is beyond the reach of most police departments in the United States. Given an already undermanned field force, the additional cost burden for personal services occasioned by poor building design is a major consideration. Fortunately, there is a developing awareness of the impact of poor design on police efficiency and costs for personal services.[2]

DESIGN OF A POLICE BUILDING

In designing modifications of an existing structure, or when plans are drawn for a new police facility, many factors should be considered. These involve functional relationships, economy of space, public convenience, security, etc.

Functional Relationships Offices and work areas of elements performing essentially the same tasks should be grouped so as to achieve maximum use of physical facilities, thereby avoiding duplication of equipment or furnishings. For example, the work of records and communication units are so interrelated and mutually supportive that space arrangements should assure direct access from one to the other. Further, temporary reassignments of personnel could easily be made between the integrated elements as work loads vary between the two. Administrative line officers should be grouped closely. Booking, identification, and detention operations must be so related that time and travel distance are shortened to conserve personnel resources and to avoid security problems.

Public Considerations Public access should not conflict with prisoner passageways or areas; this will avoid exposure of prisoners to the public and will eliminate the possiblity of harm to either. The public, of course, must be restricted in its movement within designated areas of the building. Avoidance of prisoners' public contact eliminates the possibility of embarrassment, particularly to women and children, and criticism of the agency and its procedures. Also eliminated is the possibility of passing weapons to prisoners and escape efforts.

Public counters or business windows should be within reasonable distance of the building entrance to avoid public confusion and to limit the public's need to move about the police buildings. The public information and complaint desk should be adjacent to the communications or dispatch area. This is particularly important in the smaller departments. Equally important is provision of a single complaint counter or center; this avoids

[2] Under modern conditions of employment—the 40-hour week, generous vacation and holiday leave, and in-service training, for example—about five persons, give or take small percentage differences, are required to man one fulltime post 24 hours per day throughout the year.

duplication of services or permits better administrative control and convenience. Public telephones for the use of attorneys, bondsmen, visitors, and the public should be located away from the main counter to avoid confusion and disruption of on-going police services.

General Design Considerations Building design should make possible the use of only one floor, or a section of one floor, during those hours when the administrative offices are closed. This concept has full applicability to both small and large agencies. Such design tends to keep operating costs low and improve general security. Whenever possible, walls for offices, rooms, and assembly areas should be of modular construction which permits expansion and flexibility of operation. Metal and glass partitions, and even file cabinet dividers should be used for functional allocation of space whenever privacy is not a major consideration; open space should predominate. Lighting, decor, and acoustical treatment should be planned carefully to increase comfort and efficiency of personnel.

Adequate parking facilities should be provided, including space for vehicles belonging to all agencies using the building, on-duty personnel, and clients and visitors, plus reasonable space for emergency needs. A distinction should be made between official and public needs. Location of parking space should provide for close access to the building by kinds of use.

Communications, Records, and Evidence The communications operation, including radio consoles, monitoring units, teletype machines, alarm systems, and telephones, should be housed in an air-conditioned, acoustically treated room. Teletype machines may require separate and acoustically treated cubicles to minimize the effect of their noise. The room should be designed to assure privacy and security; only police personnel on duty in communications and records and certain other authorized personnel should have access to it. In addition, the communications center should be on a raised, paneled floor to allow for adequate conduits and wiring and to provide flexibility when rearrangement is necessary.

Design of the records facility should provide for utilization of under-the-counter files in appropriate locations. In addition, vertical shelf files should be used whenever practicable to reduce storage space; closed shelf files provide all the features of standard file cabinets but require less room. As suggested earlier, file cabinets of five or more drawers can be used effectively as space dividers which provide for a measure of privacy. Acoustical treatment, false floors, and air conditioning are essential in the design of space for electronic data processing equipment. Duplicating and printing machines which create noise problems should be housed in acoustically treated cabinets within the services area.

Automatic multitape typewriters should also be located in a separate, acoustically treated room rather than in the general office area. Provision for the safekeeping of evidence and recovered property should be made within the services of-

708

fices and should be separate from those facilities used for prisoners' property.

Detention and Related Facilities All prisoner facilities should be located near the services element to enable personnel to perform booking and turnkey duties whenever possible, thus minimizing the need for jailkeeping staff. Provisions should be established whereby prisoners may be held in separate security areas prior to being booked. This will prevent prisoners not yet booked from disposing of possible evidence in their possession or from passing dangerous weapons through cells to prisoners already in custody.

The outside entrance to the jail and detention facilities should open to a drive-in garage. Police vehicles should be able to drive into the interior of the police building, with the outer garage door opened and closed remotely from within the area, and still remain outside the main detention and booking area. A second door which separates the unloading area from passage to the jail, also electrically controlled from within, should be provided. Means of providing security for the transportation of prisoners or material witnesses to court from the detention areas should be planned carefully, and conflicts with routes of nonpolice traffic within the building avoided.

Visitors' and attorneys' rooms must maintain all but audible and visual separation between prisoner and visitor.

A separate, secure storage area for prisoners' personal property should be provided within the booking area, preferably under a counter. It should contain enough cubicles to allow each to be numbered to correspond to the cells and bunks within each cell. For example, the first compartment logically would be 1-A, meaning Cell Number 1, Bunk A. It would contain property only if a prisoner were occupying that cell and bunk. This procedure would permit booking or detention personnel to immediately return property to a prisoner as he is released, avoiding unfortunate loss or destruction of property which has been mislaid or forgotten at the time of his release.

Closed-circuit television may be installed at various vantage points within the security areas for protection of police and detention personnel and for observation of prisoners, if direct observation of prisoners cannot be accomplished because of jail location or design without additional station personnel. A special portable extension telephone should be provided for prisoner use and located in a secure and private area within the detention facility. A gun reception and storage area should also be provided near the jail entrance where police officers may turn in their weapons to the officer in charge before entering the detention areas.

Provisions for Multiple Use Often classrooms, assembly, and other rooms may be designed to form a complex of interrelated multipurpose areas, giving sufficient flexibility to allow use for roll call, training classes, police community relations meetings, public hearings, scout troop meetings, and other purposes. A little foresight in the design of this section of the building can save a considerable amount of wasted space which is used only sporadically. Coupled with careful planning of class or meeting schedules, the same space can often be used for almost the entire day.

Service Facilities

It is important to the progressive police administrator that staffing requirements of the depart-

ment's administrative and service elements be kept at the lowest level, consistent with continued high-quality service to other elements within the department and to the public. This is possible only when the design and physical layout of the police facility are responsive to this need.

Important in the design of any building is the location of the records and identification files and the communications center. These are intimately related in function and purpose. If possible, the communications center and the records office should be located back-to-back, with facilities provided to allow for the direct exchange of information during those hours when clerks are on duty in the records office. In those departments where records clerks normally are not on duty around the clock, direct access to current records must be provided for the communications personnel; otherwise the lack of immediate availability of previously gathered information will handicap field forces.

The property room should also be located in or near the records center and close to the public information counter or desk. The communications center should be a room of sufficient size to provide an adequate number of dispatchers' positions, status boards, a supervisor's monitoring and backup position (perhaps only a desk initially, later to be replaced by a complete radio console), and teletype transceiver units. The records staff should be trained so that its personnel can provide additional manpower in the communications center during periods of maximum dispatching need. Unless appropriate physical facilities are provided to allow mutual assistance, additional personnel must be assigned to the communications section to allow it to handle overloads as well.

The auxiliary services work area should be air conditioned to provide optimum comfort for personnel and citizens conducting business there. Provisions for rest rooms, filing cabinets, and space for additional personnel during peak work periods should be provided near the communications center. It is axiomatic that the greater the distance to these areas, the greater the manpower cost to the department.

Administrative and Investigative Offices

The location of offices for the chief of police, division command offices, and the working offices and areas for criminal investigators, vice officers, youth officers, and administrative and staff support personnel, while not perhaps as critical as that of the records and communications center, has far-reaching operational and public relations implications.

Depending upon the size of the department, the chief of police and top-level command officers should have some freedom of movement and privacy. Some chiefs find it nearly impossible to function effectively while in their offices because of constant interruption by visitors who should normally be assisted by desk officers or other personnel. Frequently a visitor will demand to see the chief, rather than the proper officer or employee, simply because of inadequate provision for privacy. Too few persons see this as a design or office layout problem, insisting that "with proper control the interruptions will be kept at a minimum." The chief of a small or medium-sized department will soon find that the sight of him at his desk, with no one else in the room, indicates to many citizens that he should be available to talk to anyone. Therefore, certain offices should not be located immediately adjacent to the main public entrance unless some screening

or physical separation is provided which allows privacy and freedom of movement to and from the offices.

For the same reasons, offices of the youth unit, the vice unit, and the intelligence unit should be located away from the normal public traffic flow areas. However, they should be relatively close to the police officers' entrance to the records area. Often the desired degree of isolation can be provided by rear entrances or alternate routes of exit. Informants, victims of potentially embarrassing crimes, parents of youths apprehended for offenses, and cooperating officers from other agencies generally do not wish to expose themselves to persons in the building for fear of recognition, injury, or other reasons. The feeling that the department is concerned with their privacy or their personal safety frequently assists investigators in persuading citizens to cooperate in investigations in which they would normally maintain silence. Further, the damage caused by the unexpected exposure of a witness, informant, criminal partner, or an otherwise unknown officer to a suspect who happened to be in the station for some other reason is often irreparable.

The layout of investigators' work areas should be kept simple and free of the honeycomb or cubbyhole design found in many stations. Private offices should be provided only for the commander of the unit in small and medium-sized departments and only for the top-level subordinate commanders in the larger agencies. Investigators should have individual lockers for clothing and equipment required for normal work, with nominal filing cabinet space for paperwork associated with current cases.

A good investigator can seldom justify a private desk and file cabinets, for most of his work will be in the field, in the preparation of reports, and in attendance at court, inquests, and hearings. Many agencies utilize a series of tables or salesmen's desks for the investigators' use while reading records, taking notes, or dictating reports, thus minimizing the need for furniture and space. In such situations, a number of semiprivate interview areas are sometimes provided for questioning witnesses, informants, and other persons. However, responsibility for providing interview facilities for prisoners remains with the auxiliary services element so that prisoners need not be removed from within the security area. The same precautions apply for line-up or show-up rooms, and they should not be placed in the investigative office areas.

The offices of division commanders need not be removed from the general area of their subordinates' work areas, but patrol and traffic personnel assembly and roll-call rooms may be multipurpose facilities some distance from the division offices. Whenever possible, the highest ranking commanders' offices should be close to the chief's office and the conference room.

Other administrative offices such as those used by training personnel, planning, and internal affairs personnel also should be located in the same area so that the command staff will be close to these support units. These working areas also should be predominantly open space with a minimum of private offices or rooms. Modular wall dividers and desk or filing cabinet separators are sufficient to divide space among several major elements performing similar or related work.

One major consideration involves the location, design, and use of the police garage. Generally speaking, no attempt should be made to combine the auto maintenance or storage garage with a prisoner unloading area except in smaller depart-

POLICE STATIONS

ments. The garage and prisoner entrance may use the same door, but there should be a secure "tunnel" or section set aside which would allow the vehicle carrying prisoners to be completely isolated inside the security area after the door is closed. Sufficient space must be allowed so that several prisoners may be taken from the prisoner van without endangering the officers involved. Preferably, this area should not be visible from within the remainder of the garage.

Vehicle storage facilities located inside the garage should provide enough space to house most vehicles not in use, especially in areas where the weather is severe. The garage entrance should not open directly onto a public street or a heavily used alley unless sufficient space is provided so that police vehicles need not be backed out into oncoming traffic. If also used for maintenance and repair of departmental vehicles, the garage should be provided with additional space for a small office, parts and storage, and the actual repair and maintenance area. If possible, the garage should not occupy prime first-floor space, especially in larger communities where the police building is situated in the congested downtown area.

A final matter of building design involves the departments' marksmanship program. A department often will need an indoor as well as an outdoor target range, but careful planning minimizes the space required. If properly designed and constructed, the range may sometimes be combined with other training facilities, especially in smaller agencies where the shooting program does not require fulltime use of the area.

By JOSHUA H. VOGEL, AIA

Police stations represent one of the necessary governmental functions requiring careful planning. One of the most serious administrative problems confronting most police forces is lack of adequate or proper space and facilities for a police headquarters and jail.

There are two main objectives to be considered in the construction of the police department building: first, the handling and processing of the prisoners; second, the service to the public. The arrangement should be such that prisoners may be handled within the police department itself, without allowing those prisoners to be in contact with the public generally.

Plans Developed for this Section

The plans shown represent the results of the field survey and study by the police chiefs' advisory committee and subcommittees. Particular attention was given to room sizes and the arrangement in the plan of these various spaces in relation to one another, so as to ensure safe flow of traffic within the building by the public and security control of the prisoners by the police force without unnecessary duplication of staff.

The ideas reflected are based on past experiences with similar police stations now in use, and the explanation which follows each plan directs attention to some of the important elements suggested for inclusion in new structures.

SITE REQUIREMENTS

A. General

Police stations should be planned as if they are to be in a separate location from other structures. If analysis of site locations for a police station permits other structures housing other city functions (such as city hall or fire station) to be erected on the same site without interfering with the proper discharge of functions, then one central site can be chosen.

The jail section of a building should be above the ground and set back far enough from the property line to prevent contact between prisoners and persons outside of the building. Jail quarters should be accessible to a loading space at, or within, the building for the transportation of prisoners. It should be located where the vehicular traffic is not too heavy.

Off-street parking, space for expansion, light and air on all sides, and separate entrances must be provided whenever possible.

Small Cities and Towns

It has been found in small, compactly built cities and towns that one location will serve all city departments under one roof. When the city or town area extends only a few blocks in any direction, access to arterial streets

Police Stations, Planning and Specifications, Bureau of Governmental Research and Services, University of Washington, Seattle, Wash., 1954.

is readily possible. Such a central site, however, should be so laid out that it gives an opportunity for the public to enter the administration rooms from one street, the fire department from another side street, and the police department from a third side or from the rear.

In all these cases, the location in relationship to the various land uses, the street pattern, and size of the site itself makes it possible that this central site can have all the governmental units in one location and still meet all the site requirements of the individual functions separately.

GENERAL DESIGN INFORMATION

A. Horizontal Plan

A building with the least number of floors is more economical to supervise because less personnel is required to supervise it. While a building of several floors may cost less in construction and be a saving in site costs, the extra outlay for administrative personnel, year after year, will never cease; in time it may be far greater than the additional cost of the desirable horizontal plan.

B. Construction Building Code

The building should be fire resistant, properly lighted, heated, and ventilated. The plans should be arranged to prevent smoke and hot gases, from cooking or heating units, from passing through the building at any time.

Fire safety devices such as standpipes, fire hose, extinguishers, and alarms should be amply provided.

If the building is of two stories or more, two or more enclosed stairways should be provided according to building regulations for fire hazards.

C. Facilities

1. **Windows** Windows adjacent to jail quarters should have steel bars or steel detention sash with screening devices and be inaccessible to prisoners. All parts of detention quarters should be separated from exterior walls by a mesh partition, parallel to outside walls and 3 ft inside them, to prevent passing of contraband, exhibitionism, and to give passage for supervising personnel.

2. **Storage** A safe storage place should be provided for cash and valuable articles.

3. **Firearms** Firearms, weapons, and medicines should be stored in strong, securely locked cabinets inaccessible to prisoners; i.e. they should be kept in locations removed from jail quarters and corridors.

4. **Firefighting Apparatus** All fire hazards should be guarded against. Avoid exposed electrical installations, wood partitions, straw ticks, paper, rags, and other combustible materials. Fire hose in locked cabinets should be easily

accessible for inspection, for jail personnel to have for drilling, and for use in event of fire or emergency.

5. **Telephone, Radio** The telephone and radio service should include equipment for fire calls and auxiliary fire alarm as well as provision for right-of-way calls, conference calls, watch calls from stations of duty, and supervisory calls.

6. **Detective Division** The location of a detective division will depend upon the workload involved and the number of detectives employed. There should be a main detective office large enough to permit all detectives to get together for briefing and instructions. In addition, there should be small rooms located adjacent to the main detective office, which can be used for interrogation purposes. These need not be elaborate and require only a desk and two or three chairs.

7. **Show-up Room** In case a show-up room is desired, it should be located in such a manner as to permit the shuttling back and forth of prisoners from the confinement quarters to the show-up room without coming into contact with the public.

8. **Visitors' Room** A visiting room should be provided so as to promote informal interviews under adequate supervision. This visitors' room can serve for visitors for the prisoners or as a conference room between an attorney and a prisoner. It should be so located that the prisoners' entrance is on the jail side and the visitors' and attorneys' entrance is from the public side. A separation between prisoners and visitors inside the room should be provided by at least a fine meshed double screening or heavy plate glass windows. Another type of separation is the use of a table at least 3 ft wide with a partition extending to the floor and the partition above the table running to the ceiling so that it is impossible to pass even the smallest item of contraband.

9. **Interview Room** A separate interviewing room should be provided for the use of attorneys, probation officers, and social welfare workers.

10. **Examining Room** This same room, if properly located, can also serve as an examination room for the medical officer. For medical facilities, a locked steel cabinet for the medical equipment can be placed on the wall in one of the examination rooms.

11. **Kitchen** When the jail averages more than 15 prisoners a day, a properly equipped kitchen has been found advisable. There should be a refrigerator room and locked storage closet. The kitchen should be equipped with a stove for top and oven cooking. If it is a two-story building, one kitchen only on the first floor is recommended and dumbwaiters may be used, with a pantry on the second floor. In cases where the food is brought from the outside and not cooked on the premises, the kitchen or

POLICE STATIONS

pantry should at least have modern sterilizing dishwashing equipment.

12. Laundry A laundry should be included in the jail, with modern-type equipment and a sterilizer for clothing and bedding.

13. Janitor's Slop Sink A janitor's slop sink should be placed in an open space large enough so that mops and cleaning gear can be hung on racks exposed to sun and air. This janitor's room should be well ventilated and inaccessible to prisoners.

14. Segregation Male and female prisoners must be kept entirely separate. Other segregations are necessary, such as separations of juveniles, sentenced from unsentenced prisoners, those with crime records and disciplinary cases separated from drunkards, vagrants, traffic violators, and witnesses. Prisoners of unsound mind, contagious disease carriers, and known sex perverts must be isolated. Plans should provide close and readily maintained supervision of the jail sections housing drunks, the insane, or the mentally disturbed.

15. Cells The cells should be arranged so that maximum security is provided for prisoners serving time, and these cells must be separated from those housing material witnesses. The maximum number of individual cells makes possible segregation of prisoners. Individual cells are advised for small jails where accommodations are limited. Cells for women prisoners, where women prisoners are rarely housed, can be used for juveniles. One cell should be capable of heavy padding for violent prisoners and should be unfurnished.

16. Cell Furniture Cells should be equipped with toilet, washbowl, a locker or cabinet (preferably an under-bed type), a table, and a chair or stool. The cell beds should be metal, equipped with a clean mattress, clean sheets, mattress cover, blankets, pillow, and pillowcase. The bed should have a rigid bedspring frame bracketed to the wall. The washbowl and toilet should be prison type.

17. Dormitories Dormitories should have at least 75 sq ft of floor space per prisoner, have 10 ft ceiling height, and there should be at least one toilet and one washbowl for each eight inmates or fraction thereof.

18. Tanks Tanks can be equipped with a fastened bench and open toilet and urinal for prisoners. Tanks should be limited to accommodate not more than 15 men each.

19. Floor Drains All the various portions of the building should contain floor drains to make it possible to flush out the floors to avoid odors.

20. Lighting It is desirable, where possible, that the prisoners' living quarters be accessible to the entrance of sunlight, and the walls should be painted in light colors. Where light is dependent upon electrical fixtures, the fixtures should be the built-in, tamperproof type with tempered plate glass front for protection of the lamp.

21. Plumbing Adequate water and sewage systems should be provided. Provision for prisoners to obtain drinking water should be provided by the installation of recessed sanitary drinking fountains installed throughout the jail. Bathing facilities (showers) should be available for daily use. In the larger police stations, some tub baths for women are recommended. Thermostatically controlled, concealed mixing valves should be provided for all showers and hot water supply to lavatories. For flushing devices, the control should be vandalproof, pushbutton-operated, and flushing type valve adjustable for flushing time. Toilets and urinals should have a similar type of pushbutton valve. Lavatories should be equipped with self-closing, pushbutton-operated valves and integral supply spout and nozzle and an integral slow-draining strainer. Hand-operated valves, which are easily damaged, should not be used. Waste and vent stacks, as well as supply and exhaust ducts, must be properly constructed so that the prisoners cannot use them for communication. Plumbing fixtures should be wall-mounted in the tanks and individual cells. For padded cells, a flushing-rim floor drain is the only toilet fixture which can be used, and its flushing valve should be located in the pipe space to be operated only by supervisory personnel outside the cell.

Showers shall have vandalproof head with concealed pushbutton-operated flushing-type valve with adjustable flushing time, and, as mentioned above, all hot water should be thermostatically controlled to prevent scalding.

22. Receiving Garage A receiving garage should be built immediately adjacent to the building or made a part of it, so that cars could drive in off the street or alley directly into the garage. This garage should not be used for parking purposes but merely for the discharge of prisoners when they are brought to the police station. The jail elevator should be in such a position as to be easily available directly from this garage.

POLICE STATION—CITIES OF 3,500 AND 7,000 POPULATION

A. General Needs

Although a city with 3,500 or 7,000 population requires less jail space, nevertheless, space for traffic reports and courtroom is needed, and it is most important to have a one-story plan well arranged, as personnel is very limited.

The same requirements for circulation, isolation, and public and private entrances, as described for the larger cities, are equally important.

The prisoner booking room, jail, and general office should be arranged so that one officer can book and supervise prisoners, handle communications, and serve the public without leaving the main office. The entrance to the jail and routing of prisoner traffic must be separate from the public area traffic. There should be an enclosed, escapeproof hallway or area for conducting prisoners from the jail to the courtroom.

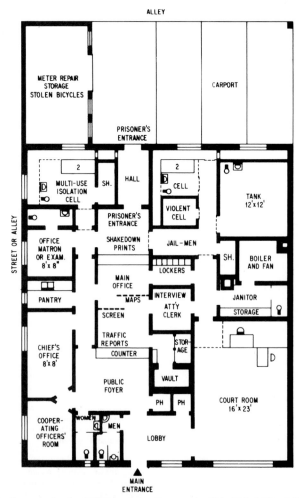

Fig. 1 Plan of police station for city of 3,500 population. One story, lot 48 by 74 ft, building 2,784 sq ft.

B. Police Station—City of 3,500 Population

The floor plan for 3,500 or less population on a small lot on a corner street has all the needed central control but has few offices and a small jail (see Fig. 1).

1. Courtroom The courtroom is located so as to be accessible to men prisoners, while women prisoners can be brought through the office to court.

As the courtroom is sometimes used for special meetings, it is planned to have a separate entrance lobby so the public need not pass through the police station foyer and disturb the office at night.

2. Men's Cells One padded cell, one two-bed cell, and a large tank are provided. The tank can serve as a dayroom in this plan. Beds could be placed in the tank.

3. Multiuse Cells The multi-use isolation cell with two beds can be for isolation, for two inmates, for juveniles, or, in rare cases, it can be used as a women's cell, in which latter case a matron must be called in and the examination room is for her use. The multipurpose cell could be arranged for two two-beds so that altogether six inmates could be accommodated. If beds are placed in the tank, up to ten inmates could be housed.

4. Pantry The pantry is for service and dishwashing in case meals are so arranged. It can be used as a small laboratory if not used as a pantry.

5. Possible Expansion If the particular city has a greater maximum number of prisoners, it should be noted that the men's jail could be expanded into the carport space by placing the carport space farther back on the lot and building more cells on the cell side of the corridor. A dayroom in back of the tank side of the corridor could be provided.

Summary of Requirements
Population: Less than 3,500. See Fig. 1 for plan
Number of Persons in Police Department: Male officers, 4
Parking: Space for police officials' cars and public's vehicles, 4 (min.)
Estimate of Space and Facilities, Requirements for
I. *General Police Administration Operations:*
   A. *Executive's Requirements* (Room or space sizes in feet):
      1. Chief's office: 8 by 14
      2. Private entrance
      3. Conference room: Combined with courtroom
      4. Cooperating officer's room: 8 by 10
   B. *Records and Clerical:*
      1. Central records maintenance: Combined with main office, traffic records, and personnel records.
      2. Map space: In main office
   C. *Communications:*
      1. Telephone and radio: In main office
   D. *Training:*
      1. Classroom: Combined with courtroom
      2. Library: Combined with chief's office
      3. Supplies storage: Combined with main office
   E. *Identification:*
      1. Prints: Combined with shakedown room

II. *Prisoners and Jail Facilities:*
   A. *Receiving, Processing, and Confinement:*
      1. Drive-in garage: 12 by 25
      2. Booking, searching room: 10 by 10
      3. Medical examination room: 8 by 8
      4. Isolation cell: One, 7 by 8
      5. Violent cell: One, 7 by 7
      6. Tank: 12 by 12
      7. Dayroom: Combined with tank
      8. Toilet: In cells
      9. Shower: 3 by 7
      10. Attorneys' interview room: 9 by 9
      11. Storage: Combined with janitor's room
      12. Storage prisoners' property: Vault 4 by 6
      13. Prisoners' waiting space to courtroom: 4 by 8
      14. Pantry: 6 by 8
   B. *Separate Rooms, Facilities for Women Prisoners:*
      1. One multi-use isolation cell: 12 by 12
      2. Shower, toilet: 3 by 8
      3. Matron's room: Combined with examination room: 8 by 8
      4. Matron's toilet: 3 by 8
   C. *Separate Rooms for Juvenile Prisoners:*
      1. Use multi-use isolation cell
III. *Receiving and Assisting Public:*
      1. Separate entrance foyer: 10 by 14
      2. Public toilets: Men's and women's, each 5 by 10
      3. Public telephone: In foyer
      4. Complaint counter: Combined with main office, traffic violations and reporting accidents
IV. *Police Personnel Requirements:*
      1. Male locker room: 6 by 8
      2. Toilet: Combined with janitor's room
V. *Police Property Requirements:*
      1. Storage of recovered, stolen bicycles: Combined with meter repair, 12 by 24
      2. Storage of recovered stolen property
      3. Storage of Police Department supplies: 8 by 8, near vault
VI. *Police Building Maintenance Requirements:*
      1. Janitor's room: 6 by 10
      2. Boiler and fans: 10 by 10
      3. Heating, ventilating: Combined with boiler room
      4. Repairs: Combined with meter repair room
VII. *Courts:*
      1. Police courtroom: 16 by 23
      2. Clerk's office: Combined with attorney's room, 9 by 9
      3. Attorney's room: Combined with interview room
VIII. *Public Safety Education:*
      1. Safety: Combined with main office

C. Police Station—City of 7,000 Population

The plan shown in Fig. 2 for 7,000 population is for a narrow site on a street corner.

1. Offices and Courtroom Offices for officers and the central record office and courtroom are provided. A 4-ft wall space is needed for the intercommunication system in the office. The attorney-clerk's room must serve also as

visitors' room in conjunction with prisoners' waiting hall back of the courtroom.

The matron's office must serve for visitors' room for women; and the attorney-clerk's office, in conjunction with the corridor for men prisoners, must serve for visitors' room for men.

2. Women's Jail The women's cell for four inmates and adjacent cell for two inmates could be used for juvenile or isolation cells.

3. Pantry The kitchenette is a pantry for serving food brought in from outside and placed in trays, and for dishwashing.

4. Men's Jail For men there are two isolation cells, one padded cell, and four four-bed cells, thus housing 18 men besides those in the tank. Dayroom for the privileged is provided.

Summary of Requirements
Population: Less than 7,000, See Fig. 2 for plan.
Number of Persons in Police Department: Male officers, 8 to 10
Parking: Off-street parking area for police vehicles adjacent to the police building; 2 cars. Area required for parking cars of persons who visit police headquarters; 2 cars. Total, 4 cars (min.).
Location of Police Headquarters Facilities: In the business district or manufacturing district. The building should be by itself if possible. If not, with the city hall. If it is combined, the lights, heating, and ventilation for the police department are to be operated separately. The police station should have separate entrances, one for the public and one for prisoners.
Estimate of Space and Facilities, Requirements for
I. *General Police Administrative Operations:*
   A. *Executive's Requirements* (Room or space sizes in feet):
      1. Chief's office: 11 by 14
      2. Private entrance: Yes
      3. Conference Room and Classroom: Combined with courtroom
      4. Chief's office toilet: 3 by 8
      5. Chief's office clothes closet: 2 by 4
   B. *Records and Clerical:*
      1. Central records maintenance: Combined with main office, traffic records, and personnel records
      2. Map space: In main office
      3. Mimeographing: In main office
   C. *Communications:*
      1. Telephone and radio in main office
      2. Public telephone in foyer
   D. *Training:*
      1. Classroom: Combined with courtroom
      2. Library: In chief's office
      3. Firearms range: At city sportsmen's range
      4. Supplies storage: Combined with main office
   E. *Identification:*
      1. Photographing and Fingerprinting room
      2. Darkroom: 6 by 10
      3. Lineup or show-up: Combined with courtroom.
II. *Prisoners and Jail Facilities:*
   A. *Receiving, Processing and Confinement:*
      1. Drive-in garage: 12 by 24
      2. Booking and searching room: 10 by 10

3. Medical examination room: Combined with booking room
4. Isolation cells: Two, 7 by 8 each
5. Violent cells: One, 7 by 7
6. Group cells: Four, four bunks each
7. Tank: 10 by 12
8. Dayroom: 12 by 19
9. Toilet and shower room: One in dayroom

10. Attorneys' interrogation room: 8 by 8
11. Prisoners' visiting: Space in corner courtroom
12. Matron's room: 7 by 10
13. Storage, bedding: 7 by 14
14. Storage, prisoners' property: Vault 5 by 5
15. Enclosed vestibule to prisoners' waiting space: 3 by 12

16. Prisoners' waiting space adjacent to courtroom: 3 by 10
17. Kitchenette-pantry: 7 by 12
18. Food storage: 4 by 7
   B. *Separate Rooms for Women Prisoners:*
      1. One group cell: 12 by 12, four bunks
      2. One isolation cell: 8 by 10
      3. Shower, toilet
      4. Matron's room: Combined with examination room, 7 by 10
III. *Receiving and Assisting the Public:*
      1. Separate entrance foyer: 8 by 15
      2. Public toilets: Men's and women's: Each 6 by 6
      3. Public telephone: In anteroom
      4. Complaint counter: Combined with traffic violations' bureau and traffic accident reporting counter
IV. *Police Personnel Requirements:*
      1. Male locker room: 8 by 10
      2. Coffee bar: Combined with kitchenette
V. *Police Property Requirements:*
      1. Storage of recovered stolen bicycles: 14 by 14
      2. Storage of recovered stolen property
VI. *Police Building Maintenance Requirements:*
      1. Janitor's room: 4 by 7
      2. Boiler and fans: 8 by 14
      3. Heating and ventilating system
      4. Electrical controls
      5. Water controls
VII. *Courts:*
      1. Police courtroom: 17 by 30
      2. Court clerk's office and city attorney's office: 8 by 8
VIII. *Public Safety Education:*
      1. Safety education office: Combined with main office

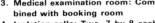

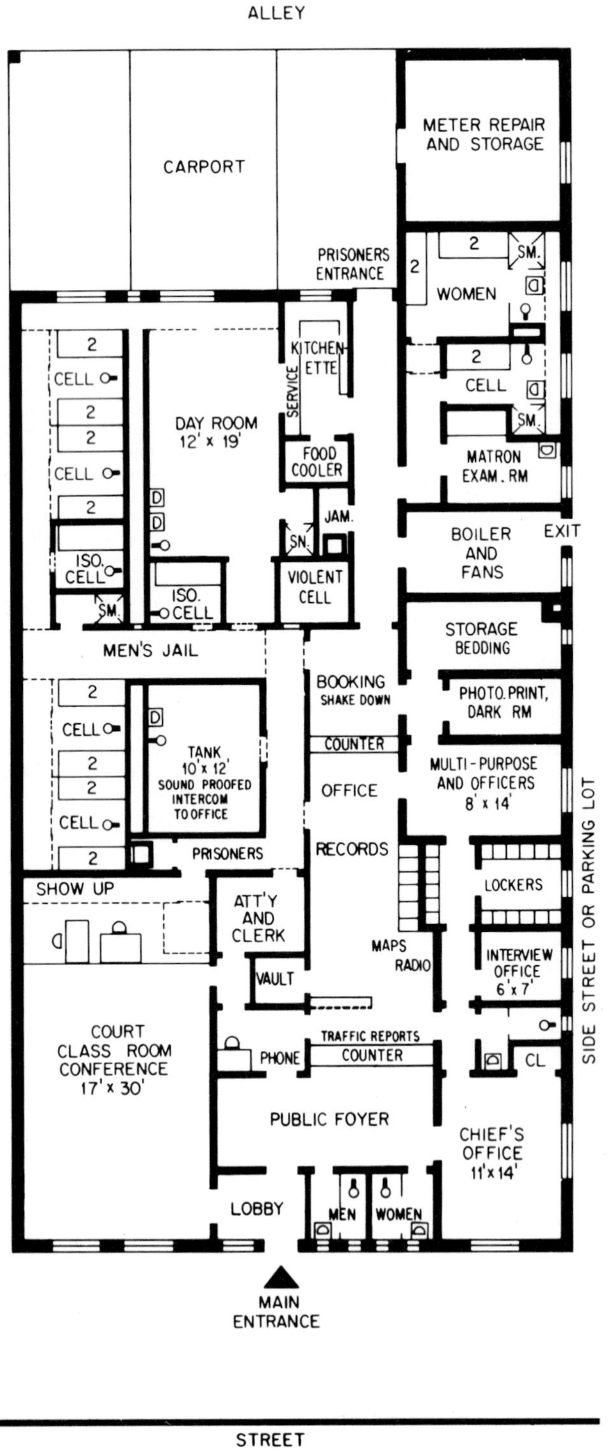

Fig. 2   Plan of police station for city of 7,000 population. One story, lot 50 by 100 ft; building 4,300 sq ft.

POLICE STATION—CITY OF 15,000 POPULATION

A. Plan

The sketch plan illustrates how arrangements provide for central control with public and private entrances and separated, isolated quarters for juveniles, men, and women without any necessity for different classes of prisoners to cross each others' quarters or intermingle.

For 15,000 population or less, a plan of a one-story building is shown in Fig. 3.

B. Room Spaces

1. Central Offices   All the necessary offices for administrative functions are provided. Offices for chief and assistant officers are accessible to the jail or to the public. The public, however, is separated from prisoner areas. The main office oversees the whole first floor with a minimum of personnel on duty at any one time.

2. Courtroom, Prisoners' Waiting Room   The courtroom has the public entrance at one end, and at the other end the prisoners' waiting room adjoins. In this case the prisoners' waiting room is also arranged to be used in conjunction with the visitors' room.

3. Booking Room   The booking room or shakedown is central to the men's jail and the juveniles' or women's quarters. The interrogation room can also be used as a matron's office as needed.

4. Juveniles' Women's Cells There are cells for four juveniles. For the women's jail, there is a cell for four inmates and a small tank, which can also serve as an isolation cell.

5. Men's Jail For the men's jail there is one eight-bed group cell which can be used for trusties, two isolation cells, one padded cell, and one sixteen-bed and one eight-bed group cell with dayrooms. A maximum number of 34 men can be housed, besides those in the tank.

6. Second Floor Alternate It should be noted that if the men's jail is on the second floor, the jail quarters are not over the juveniles' or women's jail quarters. Intercommunication thus is impossible and there are no special construction problems. The second floor, however, requires one more officer on duty than would be required in the case of the one-story plan.

7. Stairs The enclosed passage and/or stairs to the courtroom for men prisoners is provided for whether a one-story or a two-story plan is adopted.

Summary of Requirements

Population: Less than 15,000. See Figs. 3 and 4 for plans.
Parking: Off-street parking area for police vehicles adjacent to the police building: 6 cars. Area required for parking cars of persons

who visit police headquarters; 3 to 6 cars. Total, 9 to 12 cars (min.).
Estimate of Space and Facilities, Requirements for

I. *General Police Administration Operations:*
  A. *Executive's Requirements* (Room or space sizes in feet):
   1. Chief's office: 12 by 12 to 12 by 15
   2. Private entrance: 3 by 6
   3. Conference room: 10 by 10
   4. Chief's office toilet: 6 by 8
   5. Chief's office clothes closet: 2 by 4
   6. Assistant chief's office: 9 by 10
   7. Chief's secretary's office: Combined with main record room, 10 by 17
   8. Other: waiting room or public lobby: 15 by 20
  B. *Records and Clerical:*
   1. Central records maintenance, in main office, 12 by 18
   2. Map room and library (accidents and crime data): Combined with officers' briefing room, 9 by 15
   3. Old records storage: 4 by 6
   4. Men staff toilets and lockers: 8 by 10
   5. Women staff toilets and lockers: 8 by 10
   6. Meter repair room: 10 by 12

  C. *Communications:* Combined with general office
  D. *Training:*
   1. Classroom: Combined with courtroom, 17 by 24
   2. Library: Optional, 10 by 12
   3. Firearms range: 15 by 70
   4. Supplies storage: 6 by 6
  E. *Identification:*
   1. Photographing and fingerprinting rooms: Combined with record room, 9 by 12
   2. Photographic dark room: 6 by 8
   3. Identification records: Combined with main office
   4. Storage: 6 by 6 or combined with hall lockers
   5. Lineup or show-up: Combined with courtroom
  F. *Office for Use of Other Enforcement Agencies' Representatives (Military Police, Federal Agents, Parole Officers):* 10 by 10, optional
II. *Prisoners and Jail Facilities:*
  A. *Receiving, Processing, and Confinement:*
   1. Drive-in, escapeproof garage: 15 by 25
   2. Booking and searching rooms: 10 by 12
   3. Physician's office and medical examination and treatment

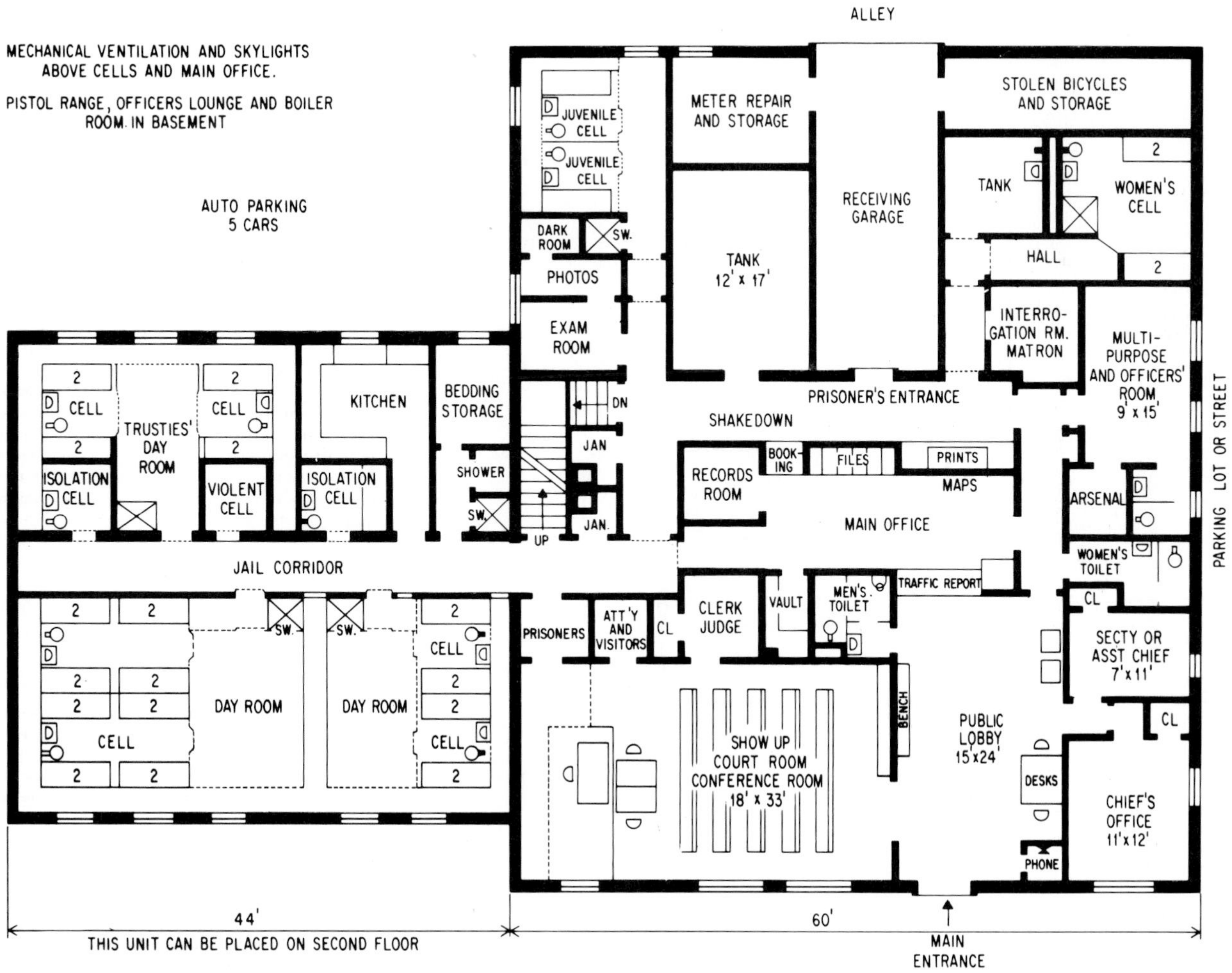

Fig. 3 Plan of police station for city of 15,000 population. Building 6,000 sq ft. (a) First floor plan. (b) Second floor plan.

rooms: Combined with interrogation room

4. Isolation cells: Two, 7 by 8 each
5. Violent cells: One, 6 by 7
6. Group cells: Two, 8 by 13
7. Cellblock: One 10 by 24; One 15 by 24
8. Tank: 12 by 17
9. Dayroom: Two, 9 by 20 and 12 by 20
10. Toilet in cells and shower room: Two, 4 by 6
11. Attorneys' interrogation room: 9 by 10
12. Prisoners' visiting room: 8 by 8
13. Delousing room: 6 by 6
14. Laundry: 8 by 8
15. Storage, cleaning utensils: 9 by 13, combined with storage
16. Storage, bedding: 6 by 8
17. Storage, prisoners' property: 4 by 6, or lockers
18. Prisoners' waiting room adjacent to courtroom: 7 by 8
19. Kitchen: 8 by 10
20. Refrigerator: 4 by 6, optional
21. Food storage: 4 by 6

B. *Separate Rooms for Women Prisoners:*
1. One isolation cell: 8 by 12
2. One violent cell: 7 by 7, optional
3. One tank: 9 by 10
4. One shower in tank, one in cell, toilet in each cell
5. Matron's room: 10 by 14, plus 4 by 6 toilet optional

C. *Separate Rooms for Juvenile Offenders:*
1. Two cells: 7 by 8
2. One shower, One toilet in cell

III. *Receiving and Assisting Public:*
1. Separate entrance
2. Public waiting room: 10 by 14 to 15 by 24
3. Public toilets: Men's and women's, 8 by 8 each
4. Public telephone: One pay phone, 3 by 3
5. Information center: Desk sergeant
6. Complaint counter: Combined with general office, 12 by 18
7. Traffic violations bureau: Combined with complaint counter
8. Traffic accident reporting counter: One 3 by 5 desk

IV. *Police Personnel Requirements:*
1. Male employees' lounge: 10 by 12, optional in basement
2. Male locker room: Ten lockers in 9 by 12 room
3. Women's locker room: One locker in women's office toilet
4. Male shower and toilet room: Two toilets, one shower combined with lounge
5. Gymnasium: 27 by 23, in basement
6. Lunchroom and coffee bar: 9 by 10, in squad room in basement

V. *Police Property Requirements:*
1. Storage of uniforms: Lockers in basement

2. Storage of guns and ammunition: 5 by 6
3. Storage of police vehicles: Two cars, 20 by 24
4. Storage of recovered stolen bicycles: 10 by 12
5. Storage of recovered stolen property: Combined with storage
6. Storage of police department supplies: Two cupboards in officers' room

VI. *Police Building Maintenance Requirements:*
1. Janitor's room and lockers: Closets on each floor
2. Boiler and fuel: 14 by 16
3. Heating and ventilating system
4. Electrical controls: Emergency 8 kva electric generator unit for radio and lights
5. Repair and construction: 12 by 15

VII. *Courts.*
1. Police courtroom: 18 by 33, Combined with courtroom
2. Judge's chambers: 9 by 9
3. Court clerk's office: Combined with item 2

VIII. *Police Divisional Operations:*
A. *Detective Division:*
1. Office of officer-in-charge: 8 by 10, Combined with interrogation or assistant chief
2. Interrogation rooms: 8 by 8, Combined with examining room
B. *Women's (Morals) Bureau:*
1. Office of officer-in-charge: 9 by 15, Combined with interrogation room
C. *Juvenile Division:*
1. Office of officer-in-charge: 8 by 10, Combined with interrogation room
D. *Public Safety Education:*
1. Bicycle licensing room: 8 by 10

DESCRIPTION OF PLAN FOR A SMALL TOWN HALL WITH POLICE STATION

A. Site Location

The site location can be anyplace centrally located in town. Distances across a small town are too short to present special problems. Usually the fire department is a rural fire district with the fire station located on separate property, although it could be on the same lot. In some cases the library can be planned on the same site if the entrance is on the opposite side from the prisoners' entrance.

B. Plans

A plan of a small town hall is shown in Fig. 4.

C. Room Spaces

1. Court and Council Room For a small town in a rural fire district, with few utilities to operate, a combined city hall and police station is desirable, as the council room can serve as a courtroom, and only one heating unit is needed.

2. City Hall Offices To provide for best use of personnel, since the clerk-treasurer may serve only part time, the marshal's office is located to oversee the town hall's public lobby as well as the prisoners' entrance and jail. The requirement of reporting traffic accidents warrants the office being kept open daily.

3. Offices This small plan has an office for the mayor or conference room, one clerk-treasurer

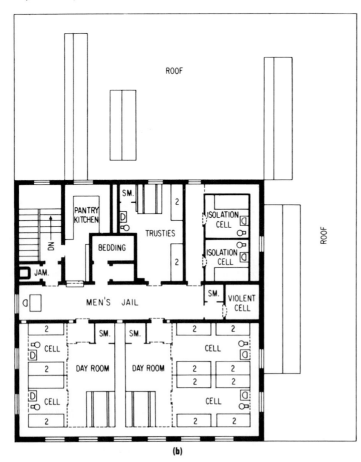

Fig. 3 (cont.) Plan of police station for city of 15,000 population. Building 6,000 sq ft. (a) First floor plan. (b) Second floor plan.

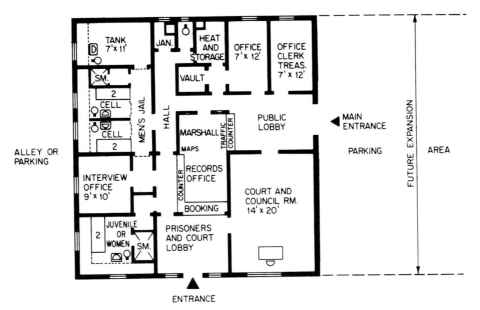

Fig. 4 Small town hall with police station.

office, a vault used by the marshal and city clerk, and a court-council room. The records room and the marshal's office are in one unit.

4. Juveniles' and Women's Cells One two-bed isolated cell can serve for juvenile or women prisoners, or as an isolation cell. Seldom is it needed for all such uses at the same time.

5. Men's Cells The men's jail includes the tank and two two-bed cells. Altogether six inmates, besides those in the tank, can be housed. Toilets and heating plant are included.

Governmental and Public

POLICE FACILITY

SITE SELECTION

Accessibility

From a total program standpoint, several possible sites should be inspected for a proposed law enforcement building. Several factors should be taken into consideration when selecting the site including location, available land area, configuration, and relationship of the site to major arteries and main highways that extend throughout the area. Additionally, the relationship of the proposed building to existing governmental structures should be considered, with particular emphasis placed on the relative proximity to the existing courts, jails, and prisons.

Primary consideration should be given to the selection of a site that will provide maximum accessibility to the community being served. The facility should be as close to the centers of business, industries, schools, welfare agencies, and the courts as circumstances permit and in an area which can be served by public transportation. Not only will this facilitate the use of such resources, but problems in staffing are simplified when there are not tiring and complicated daily trips to and from the facility. For prisoners who are selected to participate in programs of work release, study release, clinical services, or other community activities, transportation problems can contribute heavily to the success of such programs.

The facility should be easily accessible to the public and not hidden on a side street or on a site with very limited street frontages. The building should be related to one or two of the main streets connecting both north and south and east and west portions of the city. The building should not face an extremely busy highway or through-city thoroughfare, which might make access into the traffic lanes difficult.

The site should be accessible to two streets, rather than one. Several entrances and exits should be provided for police vehicles to ensure immediate access and egress to and from the site in the event one of the entrances might be temporarily blocked.

Residents can best be served by the central location of all criminal justice components and activities in a centralized design concept.

Parking

The site should be adequate, not only for the building itself, but to accommodate a police motor-court activity, staff parking area, and public off-street parking requirements. The parking space allocated for employee vehicles and for police vehicles is important when making shift changes and removing prisoners to and from jail. In the case of a combined police/jail facility, a private jail booking entrance (sally port) and prisoner processing area, easily accessible to automobiles, should be included in the plans.

In some instances, a basement-level parking

Police Facility Design, Bureau of Operations and Research, International Association of Chiefs of Police, Gaithersburg, Maryland, 1978.

garage for police vehicles may be desirable. A ramp leading from the basement level would provide adequate street access. Placing the garage and official parking facilities in the basement will reduce noise levels at shift change times and during the conduct of daily activities, thereby avoiding inconvenience to adjacent land owners.

The parking lot or roof of the structure should also be considered as a possible site for a helicopter landing pad.

THE BUILDING

A police building should be regarded as a viable and flexible structure. It should be capable of growing with the community and the department it serves. The architect should be fully aware of the growth potential of the department and should design a facility that will meet not only the present needs of the agency, but also its future needs.

Police Function Only

Ideally, the building should house only the police component of the criminal justice system. Except in very small communities, the building should be exclusively oriented to the police function. Consideration should be given to separating the police from the incarceration function and the associated stringent design features necessary when the jail is made a part of the police building.

Similarly, the judicial functions would best serve the needs of the people if they were not located in the same building as the police. The framers of our Constitution made it perfectly clear that there must be separation of power between the executive, legislative, and judicial branches of government; therefore, we urge physical separation of the police facility, the courts, and the jail.

Exterior Design Philosophy

All public buildings should reflect an atmosphere of restrained dignity, permanence, security, beauty, and strength. It is imperative that a police facility impart the sense of strength and permanence to a greater degree than other governmental structures. To the public, the police building should represent a friendly, businesslike, professional building complex. Security provisions must, of course, be incorporated into the design because of the volatility of our times; however, it is possible to artfully disguise them so that the fortress image is not the predominant feature of the structure.

The police facility should be constructed of noncombustible materials. The design of the building, including the exterior surfaces, landscaping, and other elements, should be planned to reduce the number of areas where explosives may be hidden. Reinforced masonry on the exterior walls and either concrete or a lightweight concrete layer on the roof, will improve the building's resistance to manmade [sic] or natural disasters. Many refinements to increase building safety and security can be provided at little additional cost. All or most of the glass areas, both interior and exterior,

should be of bullet-resistant material. An interior garden court could be one of the methods used to create a quiet, beautiful, and serene atmosphere that could psychologically benefit the entire staff and eliminate the feeling of being enclosed in a windowless fortress. Whenever possible, the exterior of the building should not include windows.

The so-called "windowless" building may contain considerable glass, but the glass is positioned in such a manner that none of the interior activities can be viewed from the exterior areas. Psychologically, glass used in this manner can completely eliminate the feeling by the staff that they are working in a windowless facility.

The police building should be designed to provide services to the public as well as to fulfill the everyday working needs of the police. The structure should be readily accessible with ample public and private parking space. Properly designed landscaping, flagpoles, and identifying illuminated signs can and should be attractive and functional components of the building.

Horizontal Plan

A building with the least number of floors is more economical because less personnel are required to supervise it. While a multistory building may cost less in construction and be a saving in land costs, the extra outlay for administrative personnel, year after year, will never cease. In time, it will probably be far greater than the additional cost of the more desirable horizontal plan.

The horizontal design philosophy lessens the need for stairs and elevators which, when utilized, add hazard potential when moving prisoners, for bomb placement, for fire, and so on.

Human Needs

A law enforcement agency deals with many people. Basically, however, they can be divided into three categories:

- Department personnel
- General public
- Prisoners

Each group has specific needs in a police building and the needs of each should be considered as they relate to the entire facility.

Department Personnel The term "department personnel" includes all employees of an agency—executives, managers, supervisors, officers (both uniformed and plainclothed), clerical, and special employees.

Uniformed personnel who constitute the bulk of employees usually report to a central location which should include lockers, showers, and physical exercise area. A briefing room with the capacity to accommodate approximately two-thirds of the patrol force should be located near the locker rooms. A separate entrance into the building should be provided for use by police employees only. Unnecessary mingling of police officers, the public, and prisoners should be avoided in the police facility.

718

General public The majority of persons visiting the police headquarters will have business only at the central information center. Therefore, the public information lobby should be a part of the information center operation and should be easily accessible from the *main entrance.* Employees in the information center can then handle inquiries and refer callers to the proper official or office. As a general rule, the building should be planned and equipped to avoid confusing the public. Offices should be plainly designated by functional titles on the doors. A conveniently placed building directory in the lobby is also an important feature that should not be overlooked.

Prisoners When the jail facility is located within the police building and/or when prisoner booking is done at police headquarters, special design features must be incorporated to accommodate this function. Prisoners should enter the building through a separate secure entrance. A sally port with automatic doors and drive-in provision should be part of the security entrance. A model prisoner-processing arrangement is shown in Fig. 1.

The reader should refer to Fig. 2 to better understand the relationship of the three separate entrances, public parking, employee parking, and police vehicle parking. Note in Fig. 2 the security feature of the gate separating the police vehicles from public access. Whenever the police facility is located in a residential area, high shrubbery and, more preferably, a masonry wall surrounding the police parking area should protect the adjacent residents from the glare of vehicle lights at night.

Interior Design Features

One of the basic requirements of a functional floor plan in a modern police facility is the control of internal circulation. Efficiency and safety dictate that the public enter the building through a single entrance into a controlled lobby. The public should not penetrate beyond the lobby

and should be allowed further access only after the need has been demonstrated. Figure 2 shows the functional relationships of the three entrances.

Space Allocation The functional policy facility should be as flexible as possible for efficiency and economy. A flexible building is one in which

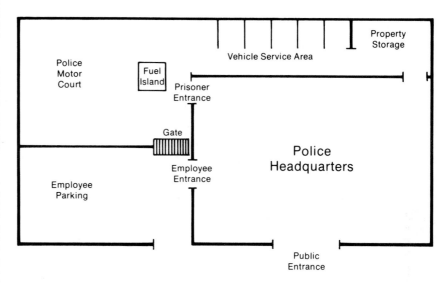

Fig. 2 Exterior design relationship.

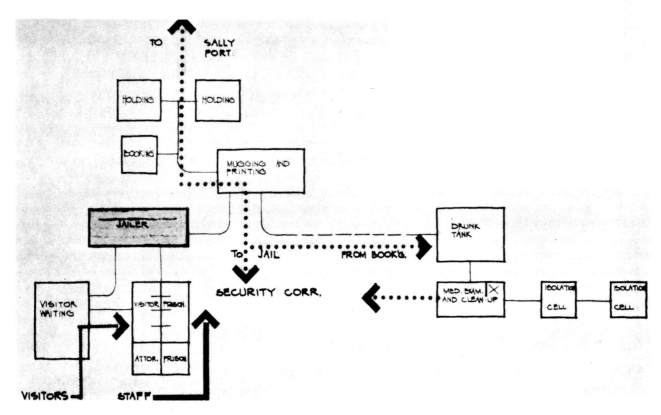

Fig. 1 Model prisoner-processing arrangement.

POLICE FACILITY

the interior space is adaptable to a broad variety of occupancies and the exterior walls are expandable to meet future growth needs.

In some cases, interior flexibility may be attained by the installation of movable partitions which can provide necessary privacy and also may be shifted to meet future functional space needs. Partitions approximately 6 feet in height afford sufficient privacy without affecting light or air conditioning. Private offices and small rooms should be kept to a minimum.

Private offices make supervision more difficult; occupants are tempted to turn their attention to outside matters and to engage in activity not strictly police-related. The potential for this situation is lessened when the partitions forming the offices are glass and, in some instances, the partitions may be less than ceiling height.

Glass partitions facilitate supervision and tend to assist in maintaining a businesslike appearance on the part of personnel by providing an unobstructed view for supervisors. Each area that must be kept secure, such as places where prisoners are confined or moved, the communications center, and areas for property and evidence storage, require special design features. Permanent partitions should be used in these areas and wherever the need is justified.

The building should contain large open floor areas in which a broad variety of furniture and equipment may be arranged. These areas may be subdivided with a minimum of structural or mechanical operation and expense through the use of standardized, movable, and interchangeable nonstructural elements.

Space can also be separated effectively by counters. The counters can also serve as receptacles for file cabinets.

ADMINISTRATIVE AREA

One portion of the police facility should be reserved exclusively for the administrative command staff. This staff includes the chief of police, planning and inspectional services commanders, and the commanders of the primary organizational entities with departmentwide jurisdiction, such as the uniformed division, criminal investigation division, administrative services division, and technical services division.

Chief of Police

Immediate public access to the chief of police is not always necessary or desirable. Many citizens with minor problems, who at first demand to see the chief, can have their problems adequately resolved by talking to subordinate personnel. Constant interruptions of this sort would distract the chief from his primary obligations to the department. Thus, we recommend an office area that is away from the mainstream of public and staff, preferably near the rear of a one-story building or on the second floor of a two-story building. It is customary and worthwhile for the chief to have a private entrance, private toilet facility, closet, and a conference room immediately adjacent to his office. The normal space allowance for the chief's private office should be approximately 300 square feet. The separate conference room should be large enough to seat all officers above the rank of lieutenant, i.e., the executive staff. Access to the conference room should be from both the chief's office and from a common hallway for staff use.

The chief should be provided with a private secretary and, in larger agencies, an administrative officer. These two staff assistants should, of course, be provided sufficient office space immediately adjacent to the chief's offices.

Figure 3 shows model layouts for the office of the chief of police in cities of varying size. Figure 4 shows model layouts for conference rooms.

Executive Command Staff The chief's executive staff should occupy offices which surround his own. Each staff office should be approximately 200 square feet in size. These staff offices could conceivably share secretarial services, e.g., one secretary for every two staff commanders.

CENTRAL RECORDS AREA

Records

The public entrance into a police facility should be primarily through a single main entranceway into a common lobby. This single public entrance should be controlled and supervised from the central records center.

This central records center should be placed in full view of the main facility entrance. The location should be such that records personnel can individually screen all citizens entering the building. Provision should be made in the lobby

area for public seating, public telephones, showcases for display of exhibits, and public restrooms. The public restrooms should be constructed of materials that would limit damage to the building in the event of a concealed, incendiary explosion.

The records area should be separated by glass from the public areas and staff access counter to ensure complete security of the entire records area.

The majority of persons visiting the police station will have business at the records center. Therefore, a public counter should be part of the records center. The employees in the records center can then handle inquiries or refer callers to the proper official or office. As a general rule, the building should be planned to reduce the necessity of having the public wander about the building seeking assistance. Public circulation within the building should be controlled and limited by separating the public lobby area from other corridors and doors that should be controlled electrically.

The interior of a police facility should be decorated in a professional manner. Bright, warm, but soft colors combined with careful use of complementary accents should greet the public. Rotary records systems should enhance the appearance of the records center as well as provide for a

12 X 16 = 192
+38
230 S/F

CITIES TO 15,000 POPULATION

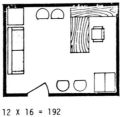

14 X 15 = 210
+42
252 S/F

CITIES 15,000 TO 30,000

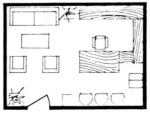

14 X 20 = 280
+56
336 S/F

CITIES 30,000 TO 75,000

Fig. 3 Office for police chief.

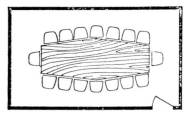

18 PERSONS
14 X 29 = 324
+66
390 S/F

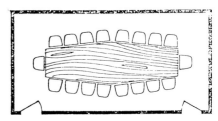

16 PERSONS
14 X 25 = 270
+54
324 S/F

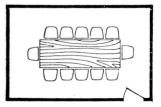

12 PERSONS
12 X 21 = 252
+50
302 S/F

Fig. 4 Conference rooms.

functional records storage and retrieval operation.

The records room, in addition to serving the public, should also be the center for collection and dissemination of information to police officers. Therefore, a private counter should be provided for police officers so that they may more effectively utilize records without using the public area and without permitting them complete freedom of access to the records room itself. Only personnel assigned to the records function should be permitted in the room. This recommendation is made to preserve the integrity of the records and accountability for their proper maintenance.

The size of a records area should, of course, reflect the needs and space requirements of personnel assigned to the records function. A useful guide, when in doubt as to size, is to allocate approximately 100 square feet of space for each 15 police officers in the department.

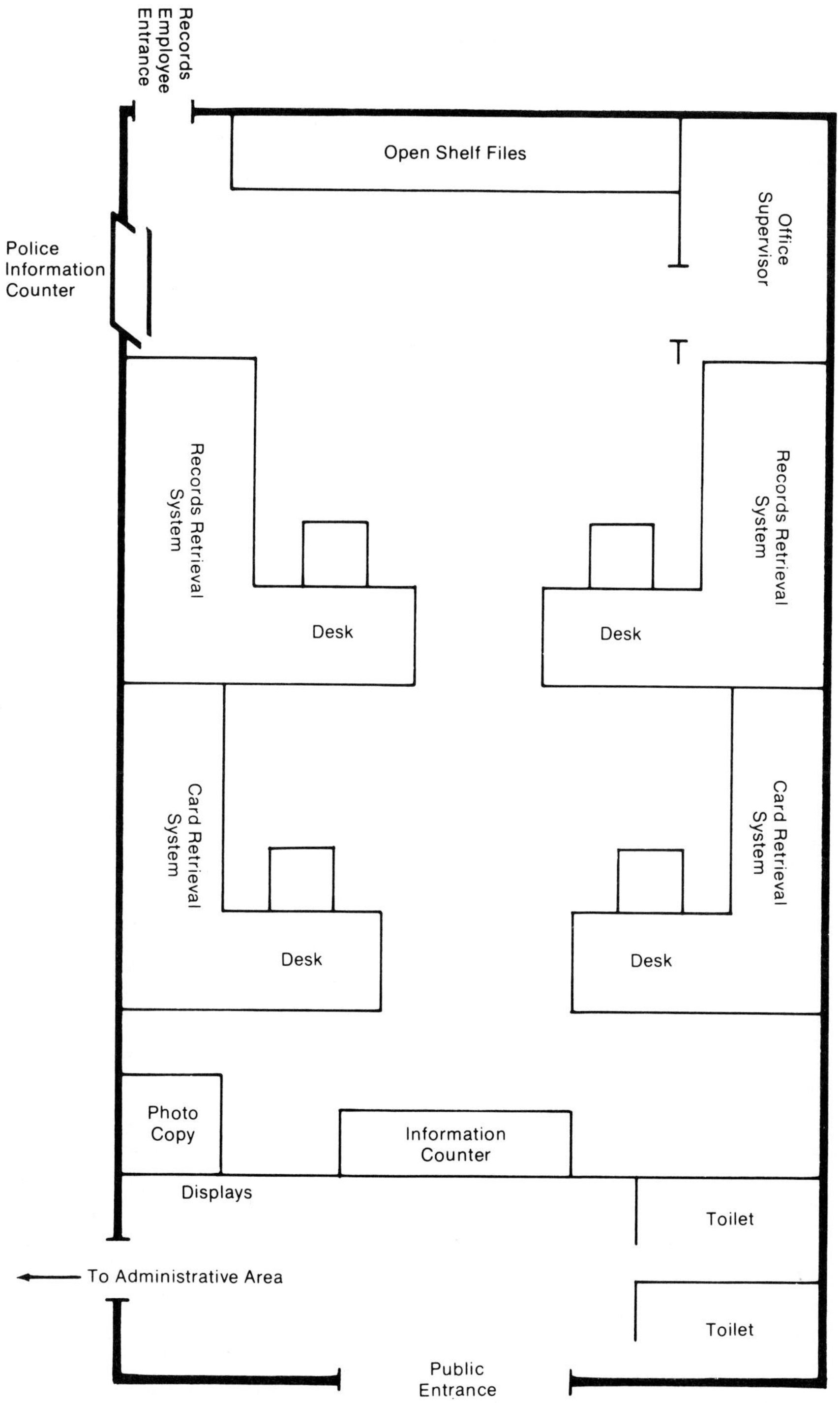

Because of the heavy floor weight that will be required in the records area of the building as a result of files and other equipment, structural design requires that the floor be reinforced.

A model police information center is shown in Fig. 5.

COMMUNICATIONS

Dispatching Facilities

The police communications command center and its related equipment should be isolated from public contact in one of the more secure areas of the building. Other electrical and mechanical systems should also be protected to reduce the possibility of sabotage or vandalism.

Most police practitioners would agree that locating the dispatching and records units in close proximity offers advantages of expediting the flow of information and makes more efficient use of personnel. This philosophy is most practical in small agencies where a minimum number of persons on a late tour of duty could conceivably handle both communications and records responsibilities. When this arrangement is necessitated by department size, we recommend that the entire records and communications area be bullet-resistant.

Radio Console In addition to radio, the dispatch console should contain all electronic systems such as television surveillance of the jail and outside of the building, smoke and fire detection and warning devices, detention area audio surveillance, remote control for doors, and vehicle status boards, recorders, intercom, and TV monitors.

Status Board Status boards are devices used to indicate the availability of field units. Such a device is justified as a dispatching aid in the smaller as well as the larger departments. Switch control pilot lights may be used, with indicators at each dispatching position, on a large map visible to all positions. The switches must be wired so that actuation in any position causes the same indication at all other positions. Placing of pilot lights on a large map showing beat boundaries is particularly valuable to dispatchers responsible for deployment of large numbers of field units. Each unit's status cannot be accurately recalled from memory, nor can time usually be taken to query a number of units to determine which is the closest to the assignment at hand.

Recording Device The elimination of the log-keeping requirement by the FCC, which for many years required a transmission by transmission entry in a written form, has eased the dispatching burden considerably. However, the value of such a record for internal administrative purposes remains. The use of a multichannel tape recorder to fulfill this need is recommended. Space should be allocated for such a device when designing the communications center.

Complaint Operator/Dispatcher

Two types of complaint/dispatch operations are generally acceptable, depending upon the size of a particular agency. In the smaller departments, a single person usually can handle both the complaint-reception function as well as the dispatch operation. Whereas, in the larger agencies, complaint processing may require extensive specialization, perhaps with operators subdivided for geographical areas of responsibility. An alternate approach to the latter is to combine the complaint operators' and dispatchers' duties in

Fig. 5 Model functional space design, police information center.

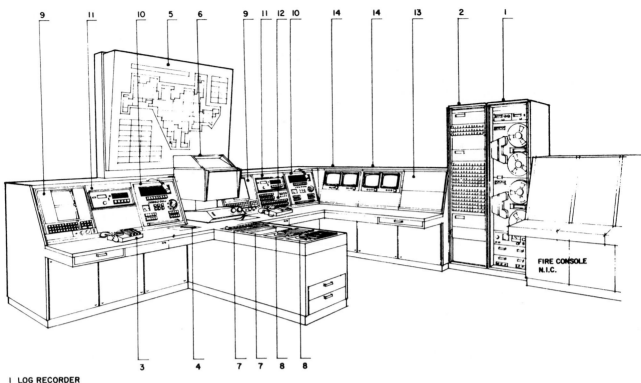

I LOG RECORDER
2 CONTRACT ALARM SYSTEMS
3 CALL DIRECTOR TELEPHONE
4 DATE-TIME STAMP
5 STATUS MAP
6 3M READER PRINTER
7 CARD SLOT STATUS SW. PANEL - W/ FUTURE
8 INTERCOM MASTER
9 FLIP CARD
10 RADIO MONITOR - RADIO CONTROL
11 INSTANT RECALL RECORDER
12 SECURITY CONTROLS - BLDG. ALARMS
13 SPARE PANEL
14 CCT V MONITORS

COMMUNICATIONS CONSOLE
DOVER TOWNSHIP   N. J.

Fig. 6.

one position and add personnel as message volume demands. Difficulties arise in this method, however, when the message volume would justify either a separate complaint operator and a dispatcher or two combined operators/dispatchers (or any multiple thereof). The architect and the agency consultant will have to make the decision as to individual agency needs regarding communications according to the volume of complaint traffic, prior to the design of the command center.

Command Center Supervision

The function of supervising a police communications center should not pose any unusual problems arising out of the nature of the task. The sensitive nature of the process demands at least constant availability of supervision. In larger installations, provision should be made for the supervisor to monitor both landline and radio communications as they are carried on; performance of complaint operators and dispatchers may thus be evaluated to determine training needs and to correct improper procedures. A monitoring position is also useful for instruction of newly assigned personnel, and for intercepting and/or assisting in high priority calls.

Environmental Considerations

The communications command center should be made adequate in terms of sound conditioning, lighting, air conditioning, room configuration, ability to expand facilities, and total security from potential sabotage. This area should be a complete self-contained unit with toilet, lunch room, locker space, and supervisor's area. See Fig. 6.

Emergency Power Supplies

Radio and landline communications are vulnerable to several influencing factors, the most important of which is electrical power. In the event of failure of normal power sources, the communications center should have some method of obtaining standby electrical service to the base station to insure its continued operations; therefore, the base station should be equipped with an emergency power source. This equipment should be capable of supporting not only all communications equipment, but also lighting requirements for the command center and primary operational portions of the building.

Figure 7 is intended to provide the reader with a visual display of a conceptual design model for a communications command center where telephone reception and dispatching are performed by the same person.

CRIMINAL INVESTIGATION AREA

Several design features should be considered when allocating floor space for criminal investiga-tors. Investigators make extensive and constant use of records; therefore, it is practical to place investigators as near as possible to the records center. A great number of people coming to the police facility do so in order to confer with investigators; public access is an important feature that must be considered when physically locating detectives.

The area allocated to detectives should provide for individual work space and a degree of privacy for each officer. Collectively, however, detectives should be in constant contact with one another. Therefore, a single spacious room is recommended to house all detectives. The room could then be divided into individual office areas by movable partitions.

Interrogation rooms are another important feature that should be located near the detectives.

Again, in the same general vicinity, the architect should provide for office space for both the unit commander and supervisors.

Figure 8 shows a practical solution for all of the individual requirements needed in order for detectives to conduct their daily operation.

Figure 9 shows model interview rooms.

UNIFORMED OPERATIONS AREA

Although uniformed operations requires the largest number of officers, the physical space needs in a police facility for uniformed personnel are

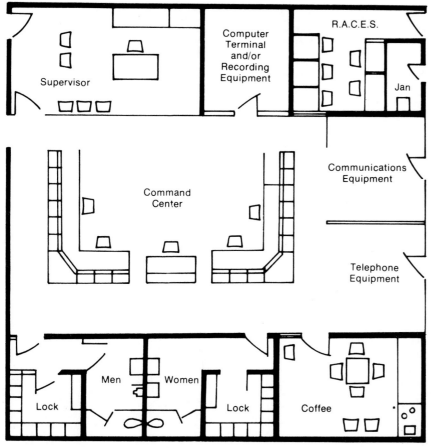

Fig. 7 Model communications command center.

substantially less than those of other departmental units. Uniformed officers, of necessity, must remain to a great extent in the field. They require the use of a locker room, toilets, squad room, physical exercise area, briefing room, and writing area.

Commander/Supervisor

The patrol commander and/or shift supervisor should have an office accessible to the public, uniformed personnel, and the communications center. The close proximity to the communications center is important so that the commander can assist dispatchers, or take over the operation when necessary, under emergency conditions.

Special Operations

Office space should also be provided for traffic and tactical supervisors. These offices should be of sufficient size to accommodate crime and traffic accident location maps, charts, and other crime, accident, and special event analysis materials.

Roll-Call Room

Uniformed personnel, who constitute the bulk of employees, will report for roll call (briefing) prior to going on their assignments. Special features of a roll-call room should be planned by the architect. It is wise policy to have this room as private as possible. The public, upon seeing numerous members about an office (especially uniformed members), inevitably concludes that they are nonproductive. Roll call, with its attendant inspection, training, reading of orders, and special instructions, should be conducted in a place out of public view. It is equally important to provide space, which cannot be seen by the public, where officers may prepare reports that are not completed in the field because of time or importance.

Special Features

It is wise to plan for a recreation area and lunch area with commissary provisions. The recreation area should be large enough to accommodate

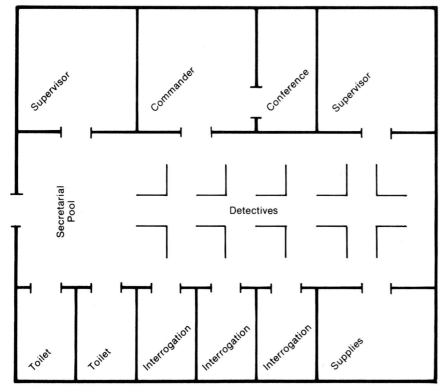

Fig. 8 Model detective area.

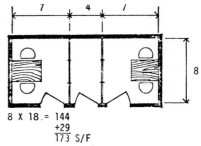

8 X 18.= 144
+29
173 S/F
TWO INTERVIEW ROOMS WITH MONITOR

8 X 8 = 64
+13
77 S/F
INTERVIEW ROOM FOR TWO OR THREE PERSONS

Fig. 9 Interview rooms.

a universal gym and other physical exercise equipment that would encourage officers to maintain excellent physical condition, as well as provide space for defensive tactics and other training.

Squad or roll-call rooms should be designed so that desired privacy can be maintained during roll call and training sessions. Lockers should not be placed in these rooms thereby making it necessary for officers to change clothes or use lockers while the roll call for the next shift is in session. The squad room should not serve as a traffic path to other portions of the building.

Movable seating should be provided where roll-call training is conducted. The room should be acoustically treated and equipped with wall-mounted bulletin boards, chalk boards, individual mail slots for distribution of printed material, and wall-mounted clothes and hat racks. An ideal work flow pattern would show the locker room adjacent to the roll-call room.

Locker Facilities

An individual clothes locker should be provided for each uniformed officer in the department. The locker facility should be coupled with shower-room accommodations.

Training

Where possible, a training room should be separate from the roll-call room. This would allow uninterrupted training sessions. In the event that space is at a premium, the roll-call room could be designed as a multipurpose room large enough to conduct training sessions.

Library

A police library is a reflection of the philosophy of a police administrator and his agency to achieve the best possible law enforcement through constant staff study and improvement.

Savings of police budget dollars can be used to justify a professional library. It can save money on duplicate subscription costs, long-distance telephone calls, and duplication of files, space, effort, and materials. Ordering subscriptions to journals for each supervisor and administrator can be an unnecessary and excessive expense.

A library should be provided with a sufficient number of bookshelves and seating capacity to accommodate approximately five percent of the work force. Tables in the library should be at least 5 to 6 feet from each other if the chairs are to be placed back to back. Between the tables and the walls, there should be an aisle approximately 5 feet wide. The length of the shelving should not be more than 3 feet per section.

PROPERTY ROOMS

Department Property

Department-owned property such as report forms, stationery, blank books, pencils, and other office equipment should be stored in a single room. Likewise, the department armament and munitions should be stored in a dustproof, moistureproof, secure room. It is recognized that armament must be immediately available to operational personnel; however, the supervisor in charge of property management must, of necessity, have the armament under his [her] immediate control and provide for routine inspections and inventory of such equipment. Both of these factors must be considered when planning for the location of the armory.

Evidence Room

An evidence storage room should be included in any planning for a police facility. The room should be secured against unauthorized intrusion and should allow for four different types of storage modes:

- Open bins
- File cabinets
- Safe
- Possible refrigerator

Open bins should constitute the majority of the room area. The bins should be approximately 3 feet wide and should be designed to allow for expansion upward. The balance of the evidence room can best be utilized by installing standard, letter-sized file cabinets. Small items that are more subject to loss are better stored in cabinets.

A good-sized safe should constitute the third storage mode for inclusion in an evidence room. This receptacle should be used to safeguard monies, jewelry, and other such valuables.

A refrigerator should be used to store narcotics, blood samples, and other perishables.

Since the evidence room would not normally be open 24 hours a day, it is necessary to establish temporary holding lockers into which evidence can be placed until it can be secured by the department evidence custodian. These lockers should be either self-locking or equipped with open padlocks. Officers coming into possession of evidence should properly mark it and deposit it in a locker. The door can then be snapped shut or padlocked. It should thereafter be opened only by the duly designated evidence custodian.

All evidence should be kept in the evidence storage room when not otherwise being examined or presented at trial.

LABORATORY FACILITIES

The location of the laboratory in a police building is relatively unimportant, and some advantages are gained in having it in a remote area. Space requirements and utility connections are the principal considerations; space needs are strongly influenced by the size of the laboratory staff and the equipment used. A police laboratory should be designed to meet future requirements.

Every agency should have at least a rudimentary laboratory. Depending upon the department's expertise and size, a laboratory could range in size from a single photography darkroom to a complex facility with separate rooms to accommodate: a darkroom; copy and other photographic work; chemical examinations; other laboratory instruments; evidence storage; a repository of standards for comparison; a director's office; a reception room; and a polygraph room.

Needless to say, those agencies that are physically located near a county, regional, state, or federal laboratory facility would require less laboratory space.

FIREARMS RANGE

An indoor firearms range should be considered as a very necessary component of every police facility. Such a range would most likely be situated in the basement or, in the case of only one floor, adjacent to the main facility. A minimum area for a range should be approximately 100 feet in length with a minimum of 4 feet in width for each shooting position desired.

By JOHN J. GROSFELD, AIA

GENERAL

Man is responsive to his physical environment. Traditionally, architects have relied on intuitive design processes to achieve desired responses, but recently a collaboration between architecture and the social sciences has enabled us to apply vast information resources to the problems of practical design. However, an architect seeking information finds a scarcity of scientific data about men in confinement. Until there are more studies and until collaboration becomes more general and more systematized, the correctional architect must continue to rely largely on experience and intuition.

One begins, however, with some general knowledge. Life in correctional institutions has been destructive of the human spirit; in a large proportion of cases the goal of rehabilitation has been utterly frustrated! The removal of a man from society and the attendant loss of his freedom, privacy, and independence as well as the deadeningly strict daily routine result in a totally depersonalized, totalitarian environment. Long-standing conventions in the design of correctional institutions and outmoded concepts of efficiency and functionalism have led to the repetitious and symmetrical arrangements of space and forms characteristic of the corrections field. Long corridors, highly polished floors, and hard finishes that reflect light and sound are hypnotic and result in impersonal surroundings.

The developing science of human behavior has led to an increased emphasis on the rehabilitation of offenders through treatment and academic and vocational training. Basic to these programs is a concern for the inmate as an individual. This knowledge should be applied in the design of new correctional facilities to create an environment that will foster positive responses. (See Fig. 1.)

TYPES OF FACILITIES

Increased emphasis on restructuring correctional systems to effect maximum change in offenders has resulted in the growth of various interrelated facility types, each serving different functions, often under separate jurisdictions.

Lockups

Lockups, or holding cells, are security facilities for the temporary detention of persons held for investigation or preliminary hearings following arrest. These facilities are usually operated by the police department and detention in them generally does not exceed 48 hours. Persons who must be held longer are transferred to the city or county jail.

Jails

Jails, or detention facilities, house accused persons awaiting trial and convicted offenders serving short sentences, usually a maximum of 1 year. As a rule jails are under local jurisdiction, such as the sheriff's office. Since the

Fig. 1 This correctional institution for younger offenders functions as a therapeutic community. The basic programs of the facility, namely diagnosis and treatment, are expressed by individualized building units of limited size in a nonregimented setting. (St. Albans Correctional Center, Vermont, Litchfield Grosfeld Weidner, Architects.)

inmates have not been extensively classified and the likelihood of attempted violence or escape has not been determined, security provisions in jails are at their maximum. It is entirely possible that a person brought to a jail to await trial for a misdemeanor (minor crime) might be wanted in another state for murder. This information may not be known to the jail staff until fingerprints are cleared through the FBI and other interrelated identification systems, sometimes a matter of several weeks. Traditionally, jails have not provided any rehabilitation programs because of the limited local financing and the erroneous belief that inmates spend too short a time there to benefit from a sustained treatment program. Recently, however, trends in correctional thinking and practice envision the possibility of new and more constructive uses of local jails. Through massive grants for planning and implementation, the federal government is encouraging development of extensive special rehabilitation programs directly geared to short-term incarceration. They recognize that jail represents an offender's first contact with the criminal justice system and thus it presents an optimum opportunity for intervention in a criminal career.

Jails are usually located in urban centers due to the need to be close to the courts. When site availability does not allow an adjacent court-jail relationship, a transportation system must be established to provide inmates quick and secure access to the courts.

Correctional Institutions

Correctional institutions, or prisons, are facilities for convicted persons serving sentences.

Since rehabilitation is a fundamental aim of these institutions, current correctional philosophy calls for individualized treatment to the greatest extent practical, even in maximum security institutions. Essential elements of a well-rounded individualized correctional program include scientific classification and program planning based on complete case histories and examinations, medical and dental services providing corrective as well as curative treatment, individual and group therapy and counseling, academic and vocational training, indoor and outdoor recreation, casework services for prisoners and their families, and preparation for parole or release.

The variety of treatment programs which correspond to the different needs of offenders require a system of specialized correctional institutions so classified, coordinated, and organized in staff and program as to meet the specific needs of offenders.

Some correctional institutions are under local control, such as a city or county penitentiary or workhouse, but the majority are under the jurisdiction of a state department of correction. Traditionally, such institutions have been located outside the urban centers isolated on large tracts of state-owned land. These self-sustaining communities have a complete complement of personnel and services, including medical, educational, recreational, religious, food and maintenance services. The trend toward isolating the correctional institution from the community is slowly being reversed because of an increased awareness of the need to involve the community in the correctional process and because of the rising costs of providing services in an institution which already exist in the community.

Governmental and Public

JAILS AND PRISONS

Community Correctional Centers

Community correctional centers are the result of the new emphasis in correctional theory to build or rebuild solid ties between the offender and the community, to integrate or reintegrate the offender into community life. This type of facility is located within the community and can serve to contain both pretrial and sentenced offenders.

The basic premise of such a facility is maximum utilization of community resources in the correctional process by providing existing services to the facility on a contract basis. For example, the educational and commercial-industrial resources of the community can be utilized for the training and rehabilitation of offenders. Thus the community correctional center can function as an outpatient clinic, providing a treatment center for an expanded probation and parole system, and ultimately relieving the overcrowded conditions in the existing penal institutions.

THE PLANNING TEAM

Planning for detention facilities involves many individuals at governmental and local community levels. Since no single planner or organization can adequately consider all the needs of the community in planning a detention facility, the architect's role during this early stage must be as a member of a specialized team.

In large metropolitan jurisdictions, a professional planning agency initially projects the detention facilities, integrating the scheme with broad-scale plans for community develop-ment. Close collaboration with the administrations of the principal agencies involved, such as law enforcement, judicial, corrections, probation and parole, is mandatory. Also, a citizens' advisory committee may be formed, consisting of competent and concerned community members, whose support can be crucial in community acceptance of the new detention facility.

Since smaller communities have more limited technical or professional resources, the planning responsibility may be assigned to a group of local administrators, a local crime commission, or a citizens' council. In such instances, an architect knowledgeable in correctional facilities design can play a major role in the planning stage, coordinating all the available resources.

DEVELOPING PLANNING INFORMATION

Of utmost importance in planning a detention facility is a clear idea of the ends to be served and the means of achieving these ends.

The steps involved in initial planning for a new detention facility consist of a process of outlining a series of priorities of needed improvements based on a number of assessments which are supported by as much firm data as may be available. These basic steps are discussed below.

Assessment of Needs

Basic to the planning of a new facility is an analysis of the numbers and types of persons to be served. This task is made more difficult by the need to consider the various areas that peripherally affect the field of law enforcement and determine increases or decreases in inmate population. For example, the initiation of an effective bail reform program will significantly reduce the number of persons held in pretrial detention. Acting in reverse, any substantial increase in the number of accused persons accepting their right to legal counsel and choosing their right to a jury trial will increase court operation costs and extend jail time from arrest to final disposition. A marked increase in law enforcement effectiveness can result in more arrests and an increase in jail population. A judicial reform program that initiates measures as a substitute for pretrial detention, such as issuing of summons or release on recognizance with promise to appeal in court, will substantially reduce jail populations. The planners need to consider all these programs and anticipate their effect on the projected inmate population.

Inmate population projections consist primarily of estimates of the numbers and kinds of people coming into the correctional system. Information must be broken down by age, sex, offense, and tendency toward rehabilitation. This task may be most difficult if the statistical data available to the planners are not broken down in specific categories. The following is a partial list of the type of information needed for planning:

1. Number and dates of arrests by major categories
   a. *Felony crimes.* Breakdown by crimes against property, against persons, against public order; narcotics and drug sale and use, and sex

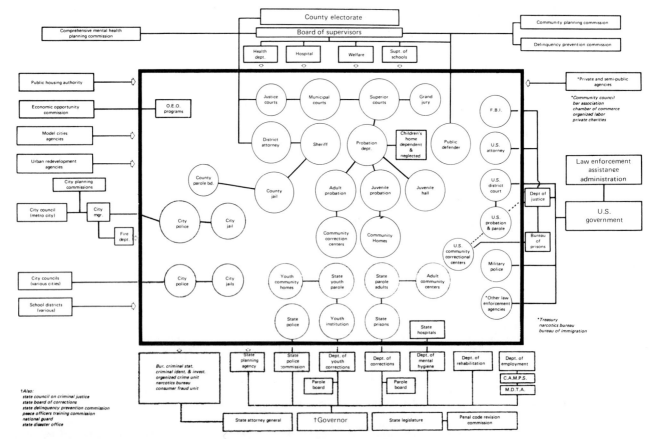

Fig. 2 Jurisdictional structure of a criminal justice operation at the community level within a typical county government boundary. (U.S. Bureau of Prisons.)

726

    b. Misdemeanor crimes. Same breakdown as for felonies. Separate alcohol-involved arrests and minor traffic arrests
2. Number and dates of judicial actions
    a. Adjudication actions. Number dismissed, transfers to other jurisdictions, pleas as charged, pleas to reduce charges, to trial, convictions
    b. Sentencing actions. Numbers of
      • Fines, restitution orders and suspended sentences
      • Jail sentences
      • Probations granted
      • Prison and reformatory sentences
      • Commitments to community correctional centers
3. Number and movements of sentenced offenders by
    a. Time served in jail before discharge
    b. Time served in state institutions before parole or discharge
    c. Time served on probation before discharge
    d. Time served on parole before discharge

Analysis of Existing Systems

To plan a new facility, a clear understanding of the function of the existing criminal justice system is essential. Basic analyses should be made of the flow of offenders through the system, specific functions of the system, and costs incurred.

Figure 2, a schematic diagram, represents all the criminal justice activities which may be found at the county level, as well as the various organizations and agencies that provide programs and services for these activities. This configuration will not be applicable to all localities. By formulating such a chart for a particular local governmental jurisdiction, planners will see where duplicate and overlapping functions occur within the existing system, enabling them to restructure these areas.

Figure 3 is a schematic flow chart showing the various stages and directions an offender moves through from arrest to release. The complete comprehension of the offender flow for a particular jurisdiction is critical in order to make the flow more efficient, especially at points where decisions are made. Vital statistics, such as the number of offenders involved in each step of the process and the average time for completion of each step, must be included in the chart.

The analysis of cost-effectiveness of correctional programs and facilities will involve looking at the entire correctional process of a particular system. Capital required for a new facility, cost of construction, and operating cost per inmate can be estimated with some degree of accuracy. The effect on the overall corrections system should also be weighed to fully justify the new facility, using data on the costs of community-based services, probation and parole. Projected costs can then be compiled to show the anticipated effect of the system and its new facility on the crime rate of the community. These projections of cost effectiveness of criminal career intervention should be compared with the costs likely to be borne by the community if the offender were to continue his criminal career.

Identification of Resources

Before planners can consider what new programs or facilities should be introduced or expanded, they must clearly identify the types and amounts of support that presently may be available from all sources. Some of these sources may be outside the jurisdiction of the correctional system, such as certain governmental agencies or private agencies and organizations. Services may exist within the community such as paraprofessional volunteer help. Identification of these existing resources involves exploration of legislative groups, governmental agencies in the field of education, health, mental health, social welfare, employment services, and vocational rehabilitation as well as industry, labor, and civic groups.

The resulting inventory or resources then can be evaluated in the light of the professed goals of the correctional system to determine the new resources needed to attain these goals and the steps needed to tap new resources.

The resulting tabulation of existing and new resources will then provide the operative framework for the proposed new facility.

Analysis of Funding

After the correctional programs, services, and new facilities have been defined, the task of estimating basic costs of implementation and the identification of funding sources remains. Included in this analysis must be investigation of other agencies that contribute services or personnel. The sequence, timing, and amount of funds needed and the basic components of an operating model require delineation. A plan for the establishment of a new correctional facility will not start immediately as a full-scale operation but will be implemented gradually, involving construction of the physical plant, setting up of new correctional programs, hiring and training of staff, and finally, occupancy and program implementation.

Basic sources for funding are local government capital budgets and state or federal subsidy programs. Most funding programs combine several sources, devising intricate formulas for matching funds and allocating subsidies to specified programs. Guidelines for governmental subsidies vary from year to year and therefore need to be continually evaluated for applicability. Applications for subsidies should be filed as early as possible during the initial planning stage, since the bureaucratic process delays the date of ultimate approval.

Planners who inform themselves about the specific programs of existing subsidies can structure their new programs and facilities to take optimum advantage of available assistance programs. For example, if the federal government desires to promote the development of community-based correctional facilities that utilize maximum existing community resources, then perhaps a proposal from a local government to establish such a facility as a model project will receive maximum federal funding assistance under the "Discretionary Grants" section of the federal subsidy program. Funding assistance is available for every phase of criminal justice development, including planning, construction, staffing, and operation of new facilities.

Systems for Implementation

Another early planning function is determination of the systems and administrative machinery required to implement the new program. There may be an ongoing system which will absorb the new program with a minimum of expansion or change. More likely, however, it will be necessary to establish an administrative body carefully allied to supportive agencies (parole, employment, etc.) to ensure the most effective delivery of programs and services. This procedure can involve decisions on shared responsibilities, which may require new enabling legislation. By categorically identifying the range of proposed programs

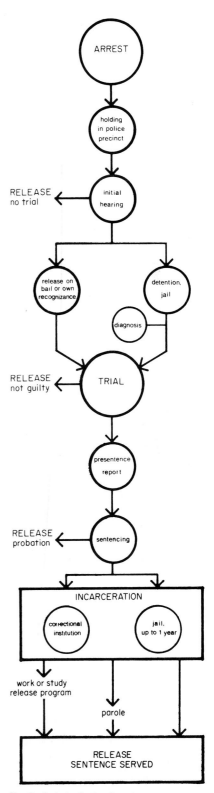

Fig. 3 Typical offender flow through the criminal justice system.

and services, planners are in a position to effectively mold the administrative system's needs into a comprehensive whole.

Planning for the Future

Comprehensive criminal justice planning is concerned with present and future effectiveness of the overall system. Budget allowances often limit the progressive development of programs and facilities, but the establishment of master plan timetables can accomplish the required improvements within the limitations and within a realistic schedule. Planning for future capacities will enable architects to allow for orderly expansion of facilities with a minimum interruption of the ongoing facility. As new methods of treatment are developed, the programs change and therefore maximum flexibility is required. By establishing a clear program of development, necessary preparatory steps may be taken well in advance to facilitate transition into future stages.

SITE SELECTION

Numerous factors must be considered in the selection of a site. Initially, the geographical area for the new facility is determined by the source of the majority of inmates to be served, although many other factors are important. Within a geographical area the factors to be considered in site selection are as follows. (See Fig. 4.)

Availability of Resources

In relation to maximum program effectiveness, the facility should be as close to the centers of business, industry, schools, medical facilities, welfare service agencies, and the courts as possible, and accessible to public transportation. Close proximity to a major college or university is highly desirable, in order to encourage development of a curriculum in law enforcement, using the facility as a teaching laboratory. Consideration should be given to community areas that could supply staff personnel, although an innovative and rehabilitation-oriented facility will attract high-caliber staff anyway. Accessibility to major industries and business facilities is essential for a successful work-release program.

Land Costs

Unless a facility is to be very small, the site cost will represent a very small percentage of the total cost of the completed facility. A mediocre or poor site should not be selected just because the saving might be 50 percent greater than that of a good site. This type of economy might be very expensive in the long run. For example, the initial capital outlay for an inner-city facility undoubtedly would be substantially greater than in an outlying area because building sites are scarce, expensive, and affected by zoning ordinances. Construction costs for an inner-city facility would be more expensive, requiring vertical high-rise development to achieve the required separation of functions. Against these factors must be weighed the increased operating costs of an outlying site: longer transportation time and additional man-days for inmate escort duty.

Topography and Utilities

The site should be reasonably level with sufficient slope to provide good drainage. Ample acreage is required for the physical plant and its roads, parking, and recreation areas. A "buffer zone" of vacant land is desirable to avoid encroachment of private construction to a point where it would influence the free flow of inmates within the facility. Studies should be conducted by professionals to determine subsoil conditions, water supply, and availability of all major utilities.

Access to Community

Family visiting can play a major role in reorienting an inmate's antisocial attitude and alleviating bitterness and dispair over his imprisonment. Therefore, the facility ought to be within easy reach of the communities served. Also, utilizing a new and relatively untapped resource —the community volunteer—requires ready access to community areas.

Acceptance by Community

This consideration is of major importance to the ultimate success of a new facility. The community must be receptive to the establishment of a new correctional institution in its midst. This is a most sensitive area for many citizens, and a well-planned and early campaign of public relations and information dissemination will pay high dividends in community acceptance. Meetings should be scheduled during the initial planning, with local community leaders invited to speak and to explain the function of the proposed facility to the townspeople. Alienation toward prisoners can be overcome by developing interests in an active volunteer program that cultivates advocates for the facility within the community.

DESIGN PRINCIPLES

Basic to the development of design principles related to correctional architecture is the criminal justice system as it has existed in the past, as it exists today, and as it will exist in the future. Present and future in particular must be considered by correctional planners as the framework for the design of innovative models for correctional management.

Historical Background

The development of corrections theory in the United States can be traced from the early nineteenth century, where punishment and restraint were the major components of the criminal justice system. Gradually penologists became aware of the need to rehabilitate prisoners, but early attempts to do so called for encouraging offenders to contemplate their sins in solitude and silence. This method only replaced physical maiming of prisoners with a psychological maiming which is potentially more destructive.

By 1870 some concerned penologists recognized that the methods employed to rehabilitate offenders were not working. They drew up a Declaration of Principles adopted at the first meeting of the American Correctional Association in Cincinnati. It included the following objectives:

- Reformation, not vindictive suffering, should be the purpose of penal treatment.
- The prisoner should be made to realize that his destiny was in his own hands.
- Prison discipline should be such as to gain the will of the prisoner and conserve his self-respect.
- The aim of the prison should be to make industrious free men rather than orderly and obedient prisoners.
- Prisons should be small, and separate institutions should be constructed for different types of offenders.
- There should be established a system for the collection of uniform penal statistics.
- Society at large should be made to realize its responsibility for crime conditions.

(The reader who is unfamiliar with the history of corrections will be interested to know that in 1970 The American Correctional Association met in Cincinnati and found the same faults existing today and reiterated the same recommendations.)

With the coming of the reformatory era, corrections evolved its own identity as a profession by emphasizing vocational training and education, followed by individual casework. Crime came to be seen as a symptom of sickness. Group therapy and counseling, the therapeutic community approach, and community-based treatment are the current dominant correctional concepts, but punishment and revenge have remained a basic part of the correctional structure.

Security Grading

The stated goals of today's correctional system include the protection of society, deterrence

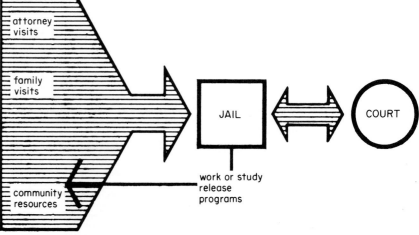

Fig. 4 Major elements in site selection for a detention facility.

of crime, and rehabilitation of prisoners. Most penologists acknowledge that the majority of offenders in our correctional system do not represent a repeated threat to society. Due to the lack of a reliable means of determining risk potential, a majority of offenders are imprisoned without necessity.

Although the emphasis placed on rehabilitation of offenders seems to meet with society's approval, correctional administrators are generally inhibited in innovative measures because of a lack of valid information about public attitudes. An escape or a crime committed by a probationer is met with outrage and indignation by the public, providing correctional administrators only with the most negative public opinions upon which to base decisions. Only too often the response to innovation is "the public isn't ready for that," when the administrator has no positive means of assessing public readiness.

Ideally, a correctional system should include several types of institutions offering varying degrees of custody and types of treatment programs. The following describes the three basic types of specialized institutions.

Minimum Security Sometimes referred to as the open institution, this facility operates without armed guard posts. If it has a fence at all, it is only for the purpose of keeping the unauthorized public out.

The inmate housing facilities of a minimum-security institution may be comprised to a large extent of open dormitories, which are by far the most economical type of housing facility. Individual rooms, however, are preferable to dormitories for a sense of privacy not readily available in a regimented institutionalized setting. The ideal housing situation would be single rooms that allow inmates to lock their own rooms but which are accessible to the staff by master key. Dormitories are particularly unsatisfactory as housing in women's institutions, based on our society's traditional standard of modesty and privacy for women. Regardless of whether dormitories or individual rooms are selected, planning must provide easy supervision of the inmates' quarters.

The open institution is certain to play an increasingly important role in future correctional systems. The term originated with an emphasis on young offenders or prisoners nearing release date, but it currently covers a broad range of facilities having in common only the absence of barred windows and armed guards. These would include open camps or farms adjacent to security prisons that operate as satellite facilities, or separate independent camps for reforestation, land reclamation, or farming. An idea as yet unexplored is the open camp related to urban industrial activity.

Medium Security Custody in a medium-security institution is generally achieved by a perimeter control system that allows considerable free movement within the facility. Perimeter control consists of two lines of fencing 12 to 15 ft high separated by a space of at least 20 ft. Varying degrees of surveillance techniques, ranging from staff patrol to electronic detection systems or both, keep the perimeter fence under scrutiny. Perimeter control can be extended to include the exterior skins of housing units. In this manner, control is effected by the exterior walls, windows, doors, openings, and roof construction, while still allowing relatively free inmate movement inside.

Inmate housing in a medium-security institution should consist of individual outside cells, rooms, or dormitories. Dormitory housing always remains a compromise between

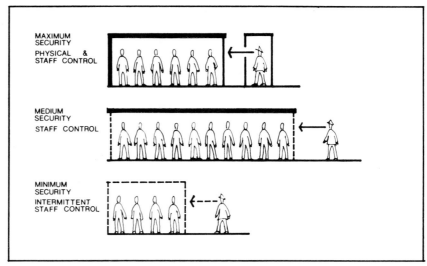

PRETRIAL DETENTION

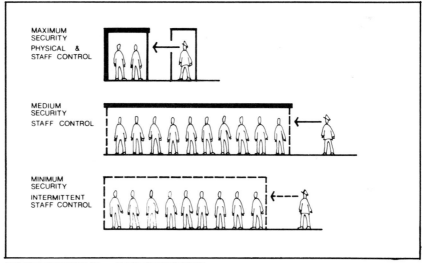

CORRECTIONAL INSTITUTIONS

Fig. 5 This diagram shows approximate proportions of security grading of inmate populations in multicustody detention and sentenced facilities.

construction costs and the more ideal arrangement of individual rooms or cells, since rooms or cells with exterior windows provide inmates with a sense of individuality and territory.

Maximum Security Emphasis in this type of facility is on control and supervision via a perimeter fence or wall system in housing units and in all building areas accessible to inmates. Perimeter control is often effected by strategically located towers containing armed guards or by circulating patrol cars in constant contact with the control center which monitors an electronic intrusion-sensing system along the perimeter enclosure.

Housing facilities in maximum-security institutions are characterized by individual cells with their own plumbing and sanitary facilities. A small percentage of the housing may be composed of interior cellblocks consisting of groups of cells not directly accessible to outside walls or windows. Planning must consider maximum staff surveillance of all inmate areas

and activities, with cells readily observable by staff.

This degree of custody is required for less than 15 percent of the total inmate population in a correctional system.

Multisecurity While ideally it is desirable to provide separate institutions for each type of security system, such compartmentalization is available only to correctional systems with a high inmate population. For the smaller systems, such as those of counties, cities, or low-density states, it is unlikely that funds will be available for separate facilities. In these instances, a single institution will house the total inmate population of the system. Maximum separation is needed between custody groups to avoid inhibiting the full participation in the correctional program of minimum-security inmates due to restrictions imposed on inmates under maximum custody.

It is impossible to prescribe a formula for determining proportions of maximum-, medium-, or minimum-security offenders that apply to all correctional projects. This proportion must be determined at the initial planning stage and should consider the effectiveness of services and programs that provide diversion from incarceration, such as bail practices, release on recognizance, probation, parole, and extra-agency referrals. It is certain that a system that does not incarcerate low-security risk persons awaiting trial will require a higher proportion of maximum- and medium-security facilities in its jail. Likewise, a system that does not have a strong probation and parole system will require a higher proportion of minimum-security facilities.

Figure 5 lists suggested proportions of basic security types to be provided in a multisecurity facility. These proportions are a general guide only and are given here to provide a basis for the planning described above.

Physical Image

A structure communicates its identity and goals to its users and to the community through its physical appearance. The attitudes of community residents toward the corrections system will be influenced by what they perceive as the physical image. In the past, the character of correctional buildings was expressed by a monolithic, fortresslike, and generally forbidding appearance.

The basic design of correctional architecture should clearly identify the function and purpose of the facility. The need for a variety of external controls, such as fences, locks, and detention windows, still remains. But these external controls need not be the dominant theme of the perceived environment, since the avowed purpose and goal of modern corrections are to build up the offenders' internal control over their own behavior. Because social controls replace external controls to a large extent, external controls where required should be subtly and unobtrusively integrated into the building form. The type of external controls recommended are the minimum consistent with the goals and methods of the correctional program.

Building Massing

After determining the correctional program, planners need to consider what basic form a new correctional facility will take. Certainly the character of the site plays a dominant role: an urban site limited in area will undoubtedly require vertical stacking of functions. This arrangement will apply particularly to urban jails that need to be easily accessible to the

courts. The resulting jail requires an efficient vertical transportation system for both inmates and staff. Major problems confronting the planner involve communication between inmates and pedestrians, vehicular traffic to and from the facility, and the provision and furnishing of outdoor recreation areas. (See Figs. 6 and 7.)

Where larger tracts of land are available, horizontal arrangement of functions will allow a more flexible expression of the program. A connected plan lends itself well to high-custody facilities where maximum control of inmate movement is required, while the multiunit plan permits a greater freedom of movement between units, with basic control provided by the perimeter enclosure.

Size of Facility

The size of a new facility should be determined from estimates of the rate of commitment of inmates and their length of stay. The absence of uniform data makes this assessment a most difficult and uncertain task.

The maximum inmate population for a correctional facility should not exceed 500. Any institution operating as a single unit becomes increasingly inefficient and unsafe when its population exceeds that number. An ideal population should not exceed 200. There are institutions with capacities of 5,000 or more because the practicalities of state government make it easier to obtain funds to add to an existing institution in a piecemeal fashion than to acquire a new site and build a completely new facility. An analysis of operating costs often indicates that a high capacity means lower per capita costs. Such figures are easily computed and readily understood by legislators and the lay public, but the negative effects of large overcrowded institutions are clear only to the prison administrator.

All authorities involved in corrections and in the science of human behavior agree that a maximum homogeneous population of 200 offers the best milieu for treatment. The larger the institution population, the more its inmates and staff lose their identity and individuality. Conversely, the per capita cost of operating a fully programmed institution that is too small would be prohibitive. It is obvious that a compromise must be reached between the ideal treatment population and the funding capacity of the system.

A viable compromise is the satellite concept of planning. This approach involves the breaking up of a large institution into several smaller units, but still operating as a single administrative unit. Such a facility potentially has the

economy and program range of the large institution, yet retains the personalized treatment and safety valves inherent to the smaller facility.

Flexibility

Not only are the types of prisoners and purposes of their confinement undergoing constant change, but also the methods used to deal with them. New techniques, programs, and services present new requirements, necessitating the capability of self-modification through feedback and evaluation. Modification must also be aided by the physical design of the facility for this evaluation to be effective. Design for a number of indeterminate future conditions rather than a single set of fixed functions implies a "loose fit" between form and function at any point in time. It is far more desirable to have a facility with some "float" space than a building that fits today's needs so tightly that it becomes obsolete immediately when programs begin to develop and change.

In addition to responding to their own internal expansion needs, correctional facilities serve as a catalyst for the location of other nearby public and private community services. For example, a single unit could grow into a community resources mall, in effect an administrative subcenter of county-state-city social services, justice, and other governmental functions (see Fig. 8).

The degree of flexibility in spatial arrangement and convertibility of space that can be realized is determined by:
- The location of fixed circulation elements, such as stairs, elevators, and entrances
- The location of fixed service elements and utilities
- The structural module, including spans and location of fixed elements such as columns
- The design of mechanical, distribution, and lighting systems
- The design of flexible systems of partitions and interior finishes

The creation of flexible spaces requires early decisions in the design process about the extent and degree of flexibility required. All component building systems, especially the structural and environmental control systems, need to be organized into a pattern to allow maximum flexibility. Considerations of economy and performance ought to be made in conjunction with the degree of flexibility desired, for example, comparing a totally flexible, movable wall system with a semiflexible system of nonbearing partitions constructed of permanent materials. The movable system would initially be the more expensive, but frequent plan revisions in the semiflexible system would more than use up any savings initially gained by its selection. Noneconomic factors, such as use appropriateness (sound control, security, resistance to use and abuse) must also be taken into account.

Circulation and Security Control

The movement of inmates and staff within a correctional facility is a problem of major dimensions. Due to the complex functions, circulation from living quarters to dining halls, to work assignments, to school, to recreation, to infirmary, to canteen, to the administration building, and to numerous other parts of the institution needs to be planned not only to provide easy flow, but also to allow required supervision and custody control. The problem of supervision and circulation is just as important to the movement of supplies and materials throughout the institution.

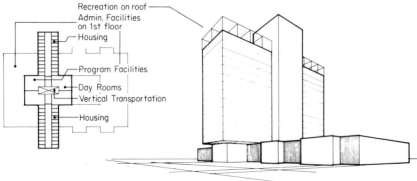
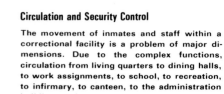

Recreation on roof
Admin. Facilities on 1st floor
Housing
Program Facilities
Day Rooms
Vertical Transportation
Housing

Fig. 6 Vertical massing is a response to limitations imposed by an urban site.

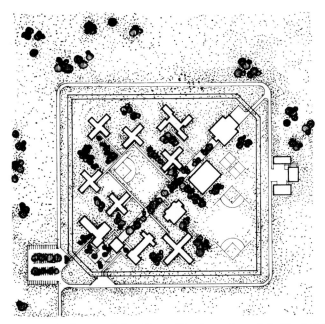

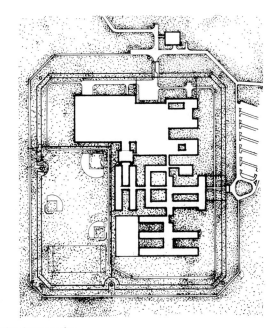

Fig. 7 Horizontal development as indicated by two different concepts unrestrained by site limitations but expressing distinct levels of custody through massing.

Security in a correctional setting can be obtained in numerous ways: by technological advances in electronics, such as audio- and visual-monitoring systems; by more effective interpersonal relationships between staff and inmates; by more effective inmate diagnosis and classification; and by providing achievement-oriented correctional programs.

Basic security control can be attained in either of two ways. Primary reliance can be placed on a strong perimeter security system, with armed towers and sophisticated fence alarm systems. This method permits the inner compound area to be fairly open and allows greater freedom of movement within. Relatively little security is provided by internal structures. Conversely, reliance can be placed on the internal structural security of the facility's units themselves. This approach promotes minimal controlled movement between units and, therefore, there is less of a need for a strong perimeter security, but inmate participation in the correctional program is generally limited to that which can occur within the respective units.

Neither of these extremes is wholly appropriate for most institutions. The process of zone control more closely approximates in structure and operation the varied security needs of diverse programs and services. There are facilities that operate around the clock

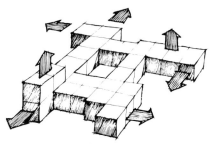

Fig. 8 Flexibility must allow for growth in response to program changes in the future.

and, therefore, require the greatest security and supervision, such as housing units, infirmary, control center, and main entrance. However, some facilities, such as the dining hall, may operate from 12 to 16 hours a day, others will operate 8 hours a day for 5 days during the week, while still other activities will occur for only 3 or 4 hours during the evening. By grouping the facilities in accordance with the schedule of use and by carefully planning access to these areas, portions of the institution not in use during certain periods may be closed off entirely to the inmate population, thus reducing the need for custodial control.

BASIC ELEMENTS OF A CORRECTIONAL FACILITY

Housing

The choice of inmate housing type is directly related to several factors: the type of facility planned, what programs, staff, and funding, both for construction and for operation, will be available. There are few guidelines regarding the ratio of cells to dormitory space. The guidelines that do exist often conflict, depending on the balance of priorities between maintaining security, providing an effective rehabilitative environment, or having an adequate professional staff. Planners will find that it is impossible to satisfy fully all these criteria.

Individual cells are advisable for institutions handling maximum-security inmates who require constant supervision. Inmates who are not maximum-security risks and are allowed more freedom of unrestricted movement in the housing units can be housed in individual rooms or in dormitories. Since jails and detention centers confine inmates whose requirements for supervision and control are virtually unknown upon arrival, a fairly high proportion of single cells or rooms is advisable, while open institutions and minimum-security camps can have a higher proportion of dormitory space (see Figs. 9 to 15).

One of the factors that influences the ratio of cells to dormitory space is the extent to which the institution has the staff and facilities to gather information essential for inmate classification. Since the total inmate treatment and training program is conditioned largely by custody requirements, its success is almost wholly dependent on flexibility of custody classification and handling of prisoners. When such basic data about offenders is available, management of the inmate population is made easier, and housing assignments can reflect the actual security problems which individual offenders present.

Interior Cells These are usually placed back-to-back in the center of the cellblock with a continuous utility space separating the two rows of cells. The utility space provides a means of running plumbing, ventilation, and electrical utilities in an area accessible for easy maintenance. Plumbing fixtures are fitted into the rear cell wall that defines the utility space. The piping extends directly into the chase, with tamper-proof pushbutton valves the only item exposed within the cell. Wall-mounted water closets are preferable to facilitate cleaning of the floor, but where fixtures may be damaged through abusive use, floor-mounted units should be installed. Mild-steel grilles along the front of the cell admit light and air, while allowing for maximum supervision of the occupant. Continuous fresh air should be provided by mechanical ventilation through the front of the cell and exhausted through registers in the back wall of the cell. It is expedient to firmly anchor steel beds and desks to floors and walls. Cell walls may be constructed of mild steel plate $\frac{1}{4}$ in. thick, with vertical splice joints every 3 ft, or of concrete or masonry blocks. Steel plate is often more economical, requiring less space than concrete or masonry and reducing the cell-block length. Masonry is preferable for noise control since its semi-absorbent surface is able to reduce the high level of background noise, a characteristic of multiple steel cells.

731

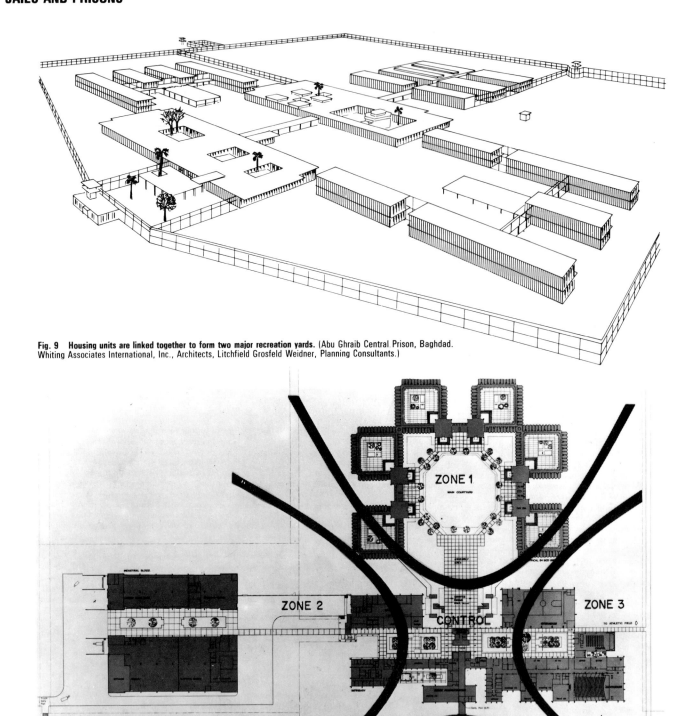

Fig. 9   Housing units are linked together to form two major recreation yards. (Abu Ghraib Central Prison, Baghdad. Whiting Associates International, Inc., Architects, Litchfield Grosfeld Weidner, Planning Consultants.)

Fig. 10   Zone control is established by the plan of this correctional institution, simplifying supervisory activity throughout day and night. Zone 1, inmate housing units, dining hall; zone 2, prison services and work areas; zone 3, rehabilitation facilities; zone 4, administration, guard facilities. (Medium Security Prison, Leesburg, N.J., Gruzen & Partners, Architects.)

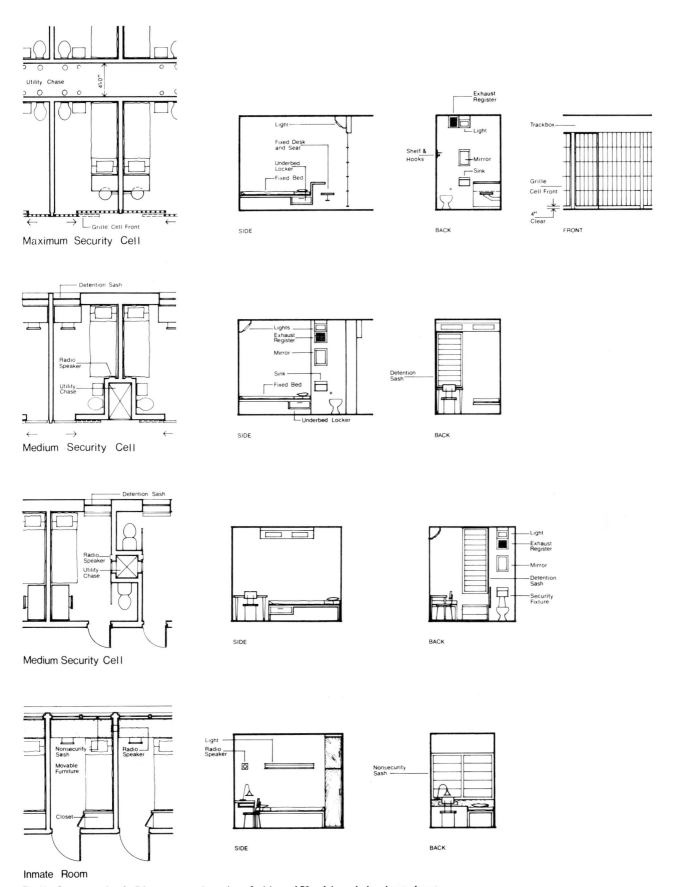

Maximum Security Cell

Medium Security Cell

Medium Security Cell

Inmate Room

Fig. 11 Some suggestions for living spaces are shown above. A minimum of 70 sq ft is required per inmate. Layouts and materials should reflect a concern for the privacy and dignity of the occupant.

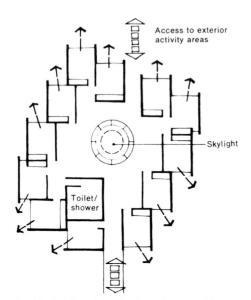

Fig. 12 Low internal security. Personal spaces with potential for individual inside locking. Central group space for informal or structured activity. (Guidelines for the Planning and Design of Regional and Community Correctional Centers for Adults, University of Illinois.)

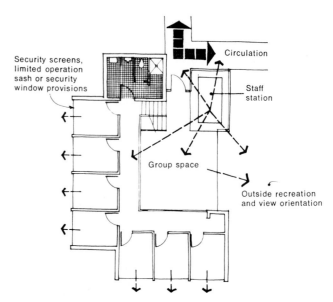

Fig. 13 Medium internal security. Seven rooms at upper level, seven at lower; group space and entry at middle level, providing separation of private space from group space with staff supervision of movements. (Guidelines for the Planning and Design of Regional and Community Correctional Centers for Adults, University of Illinois.)

Exterior Cells These are located on the outside wall of a housing unit, each with a window. A traditional arrangement consists of two rows of cells with a central corridor, but new imaginative planning concepts are breaking out of this mold by grouping cells around common activity spaces or arranging them along single-loaded corridors. Sliding or swinging doors open into the cell and are fitted with vision ports for nighttime bed checks. Toilet fixtures are attached to individual pipe chases, back-to-back for two cells, with access for maintenance. Furniture may be built-in or movable, depending on the degree of security required. Ventilating air, introduced into the center corridor, is drawn into the cells through door undercuts and exhausted through a register in the pipe chase. Walls are of concrete or masonry units; floors are concrete with a steel-troweled finish. Cells may be provided with radio speakers broadcasting programs from a central station with a limited selection of stations.

Inmate Rooms These are individual living spaces that resemble college students' rooms. Furniture is movable; toilet fixtures are centrally located for common use by the members of the housing group. Swinging doors can be wood or hollow metal, and the room occupants may have a key that controls the door lock, although there is provision for an overriding custodial deadlock. Rooms have outside windows with sashes of varying degrees of security. Radio hookups should be provided as well as an electrical outlet for use of an electric shaver. Wall and floor surfaces ought to be selected for durability and ease of maintenance, but with a concern for livability.

Dormitories or Squad Rooms These should be planned for ease of visual supervision, avoiding, for example, double-deck beds because of blind spots created by the high units. Each inmate usually has a locker for his belongings, which can be an integral part of his bed or located in a bank of lockers. Beds are best

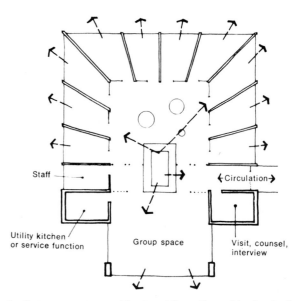

Fig. 14 High security. Cluster component arranged for close staff surveillance of functions by direct observation. (Guidelines for the Planning and Design of Regional and Community Correctional Centers for Adults, University of Illinois.)

arranged in informal groupings that permit circulation and avoid a rigid grid pattern. A floor area of 55 sq ft for each bed and its circulation space is recommended. Maximum densities of dormitories should not exceed 30 persons in a single group, and 20 persons is even better. In order to provide a more livable environment for each inmate and offer him some privacy, lightweight panels can be erected to form cubicles around bed areas. Although this arrangement makes supervision less easy, this problem can be solved easily by orienting the open ends of cubicles towards the control area. Chairs and tables ought to be provided in dormitory areas particularly if there is not an adjacent dayroom.

Housing Support Functions

In addition to the raw housing space required for inmates' sleeping accommodations, certain housing support functions are needed for the operation of the unit. Each housing group should have a casual recreation area, generally called a dayroom, adjacent to the living quarters. Dayrooms should allot a minimum of 15 sq ft of space per inmate and should contain a large closet for equipment storage. Activities that might take place in the dayroom are casual games (cards, dominoes), ping-pong, television watching, reading, and dining (as opposed to central dining). Separation of areas by noisy and quiet activities is highly desirable.

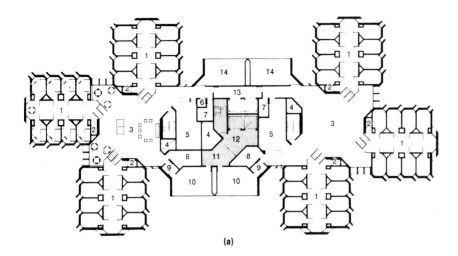

(a)

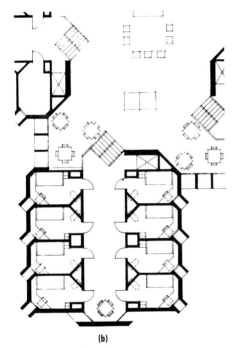

(b)

1 8-man suite
2 Shower
3 Multipurpose dining
4 Mechanical
5 Food service, pantry, dish wash
6 Barber, storage
7 Linen
8 Janitor, storage
9 Strip check
10 Visiting
11 Sally port
12 Nonsecure lobby
13 Secure lobby
14 Activity

Fig. 15   Small group living expressed by this design for a metropolitan correctional center. Each floor provides a full range of program activities. (a) Typical living unit floor plan. (b) Typical 8-man suite. (Federal Correctional Center, New York City, Gruzen & Partners, Architects.)

Utility functions to support a housing unit include group toilets (except for cells which have individual fixtures), showers, and a janitor's sink. In addition to these basic functions, housing units may require closet space for storage of clean and soiled linen and clothing, depending on the institution's method of distributing such articles.

It is recommended to provide small laundry facilities near housing units utilizing commercial machines so that inmates can do their own personal clothing, particularly in a detention center where an institutional clothing system may not exist.

ADMINISTRATION

An essential first step in the planning of administrative functions for a correctional facility is to determine the organizational pattern of authority. The agency having jurisdiction over the facility establishes the pattern, generally without the participation of the planners, although it will form the basis for space planning.

Administrative functions can be grouped to include those facilities that are located *outside* of security controls of the institution, and those *within* the basic security system. Functions to be located outside of security are those in which the staff needs to be accessible to the public and requires ease of ingress to and egress from the institution. Such functions include those of the office of the head of the institution, the business manager, certain deputy wardens whose duties relate to the public, and their various administrative, clerical, and secretarial staffs.

Those administrative officers whose work relates directly to the inmate population should have their offices within the basic security system of the institution, preferably near the most vital area of his function. The deputy warden in charge of custody would, for example, have his office adjacent to the central control room and the key control points of the institution. The deputy warden in charge of the inmate program ought to be located in the heart of the institution so that he is not isolated from the inmate population that he serves. Similarly, administrative officers such as directors of education, recreation, and vocational training should have their offices located within the operating areas of their programs.

An idea gaining acceptance is the inclusion of arraignment court facilities within a detention facility. With a courtroom directly within the portion of the institution under security, the elaborate precautions involved in guarding prisoners and transporting them to the courts is unnecessary. The judge and attorneys come to the jail instead. There are problems created by admitting judges and attorneys within the controlled zones of the institution, but these are minor compared to the difficulties involved in transporting prisoners to the courts.

CORRECTIONAL PROGRAM

Program functions include all areas of activity which involve the professional treatment of inmates to influence change in attitudes and behavior. Some basic program functions in a correctional institution are:

Counseling
Casework
Clinical services
Education
Vocational training
Work-release or study-release

Counseling

Counseling is the establishment of a direct relationship, either at a personal or group level, in an attempt to solve specific personal problems or develop over a period of time increased self-understanding and maturity. Counseling may be the natural outgrowth of personal relationships between staff and inmates developing through day-to-day contact or the deliberate structuring of groups for mutual discussion of inmate and staff problems. Arranging living accommodations in small groups provides a natural setting for the development of counseling relationships between custodial staff and inmates. Optimum size of the counseling group seems to be from 8 to 12 persons, and a multiuse space within the housing unit where such activity can take place on a scheduled basis is highly desirable. Each housing unit should also include office space which can be utilized for individual interviews and private discussions.

Casework

Casework comprises services by professionally trained personnel (study, diagnosis, and treatment of psychosocial problems) administered individually or on a group basis. Casework activity involves obtaining the inmate's social history, solving immediate problems with family or other persons, exploring problems of social adjustment, and providing supportive guidance and information for release. In addition to the general institution program, other situations aided by casework services are presentence investigations of

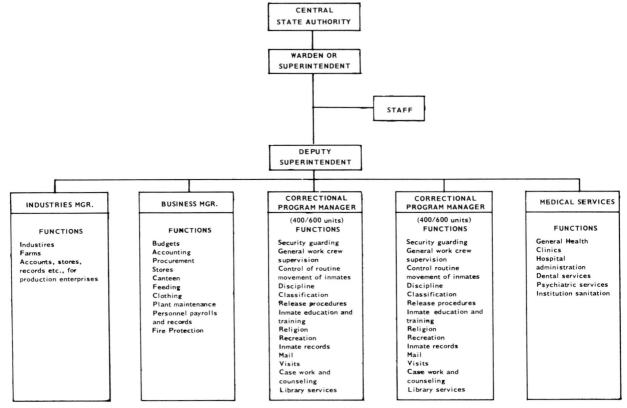

Fig. 16 A suggested organizational framework for a correctional institution with a diverse rehabilitation program.

detainees (for probation), the reception process, and postinstitutional supervision (parole). Casework activities are most effectively carried out in a centralized area that has ready access to typing services and records, although it is possible that a caseworker might go to see his client in an interview room in a housing unit.

Clinical Services

Clinical services rely on a professional staff such as psychiatrists, clinical psychologists, psychiatric nurses, occupational therapists, and other specifically trained technicians. These services provide intensive diagnostic and treatment techniques to discover causes and cures for individual maladjustments. The clinical staff also provides guidance and support to other staff members to aid them in their custodial responsibilities, including conducting sessions on personality theory and psychodynamics for line personnel. Allowances should be made in the maximum-security unit of the institution for individual and group treatment by the clinical services personnel. The general inmate population could go to a centrally located clinic.

Education

Education in prison is basic to any comprehensive correctional program. From 10 to 30 percent of all prison inmates are functional illiterates with an inability to surpass minimum test scores for the fourth grade. Only 1 to 3 percent have completed high school. Statistically, retardation in educational achievement is highly correlated with the extent of criminal behavior. While the median school level

attained by the United States population as a whole exceeds the tenth grade, prison inmates have a median of eighth grade. This is a clear indication that inmates would be better prepared for today's job market and for the other responsibilities of a noncriminal life if they had more education (see Figs. 16 to 18).

Design standards for educational facilities in prisons are the same as for other schools, with perhaps more emphasis on flexibility, such as interior partitions that can be moved as the curriculum changes. A basic correctional education program should provide for the following subjects:

Academic
General education
Institution orientation
Prerelease instruction
Commercial training
Music
Health education
Arts and crafts
Dramatics
Audio-visual room

The educational unit should be located on a major circulation corridor for maximum accessibility to inmates. Many classes will be taught in the evening by the extension service of a state university or by a teacher from a nearby college. It must be possible to use the educational unit during these hours without undue traffic through areas that are normally open during the daytime only. A close connection should exist between the educational unit and the library. It is wise to make the audio-visual room adaptable for a range of uses, with ample ancillary storage space for additional chairs and musical instruments. The music room, of course, must be situated for minimum inter-

ference with classroom areas. Adequate space ought to be set aside for the education director and staff. Toilets for inmates and staff need to be provided within the unit to minimize unnecessary movement through the main entrance to the unit.

Vocational Training

Vocational training programs in prisons have to extend beyond those operations which are necessary solely for the maintenance of the institution and prison industries. In addition, the inmates' level of educational achievement needs to be considered in assigning them to training programs involving high technical skills. Vocational program planning calls for a careful analysis of current market conditions to determine what jobs are actually available to inmates upon release. This analysis includes investigations of union and governmental job restrictions because of certain criminal histories.

Shop and maintenance areas should be supplemented with adjacent classrooms and special training facilities for instruction on new techniques and procedures.

The regulation and inspection of tools are critical functions in a prison. Since all tools must be accounted for each day, they should be stored on shadow boards which automatically indicate when any tool is out of place.

Work Release or Study Release

These programs are usually administered through correctional units detached from the basic prison. These units house those inmates who have qualified for a program of partial release into the community in order to work

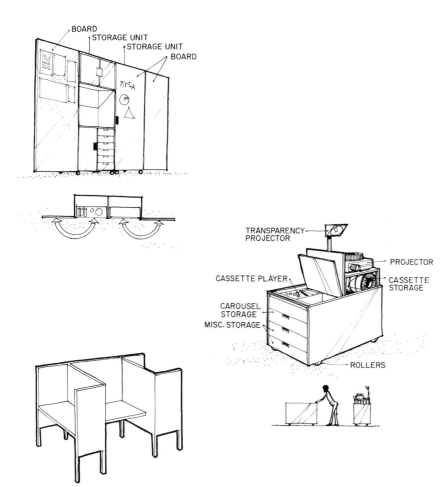

Fig. 17 Educational component providing range of spaces in five sizes to offer choice of space appropriate to particular staff-inmate or inmate activity. Folding partition offers opportunity for larger group presentations or dialogues. (Guidelines for the Planning and Design of Regional and Community Correctional Centers for Adults, University of Illinois.)

Fig. 18 Teaching components include a multiuse instructional support unit, a mobile audio-visual unit, and a modular carrel unit for individual study. (Guidelines for the Planning and Design of Regional and Community Correctional Centers for Adults, University of Illinois.)

or study. This program is often administered as a prerelease phase where inmates generally are transferred to the unit a short time before their release. Work-release inmates must not be mixed with regular prison inmates, since they are often coerced by insiders to bring in contraband from the outside.

Since the occupants of the work-release units are free to work in the community, no physical constraints are necessary in their housing facility. The structure becomes comparable to a college dormitory, and often a private residence is acquired for this purpose, as long as it conforms to normal occupancy, health, and fire standards.

Consideration should be given to locations close to public transportation and within communities where the neighborhood atmosphere permits racially integrated housing. Space needs to be provided for offices, recreation, dayrooms, kitchen, dining room, laundry, and storage, in addition to sleeping areas.

INMATE SERVICES

Library

Library services function as the information and library materials center supporting the total institutional program. The library will provide a significant type of recreation for certain inmates, especially those not interested in or not able to participate in sports. The heaviest use comes during the evening hours, therefore, the library should be located so that adjoining areas with limited operating hours may be closed off without impairing access to the library. The library is best located far from such noisy areas as music rooms or workshops, but easily accessible to housing and close to the educational unit.

The quantity of reading matter in a very small facility, such as a small county jail or prison camp, would be a small reference collection supplemented by a program of book interchange from a general library. Larger facilities need libraries with no fewer than 6,000 volumes, or at least 10 books per inmate. Institutions with high populations of long-term prisoners should provide a minimum of 15

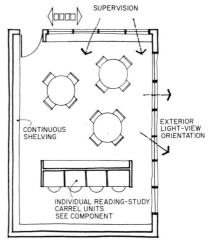

Fig. 19 Library component utilizing individualized reading-study area located remote from distraction of entry circulation-active usage area near entry for ease of access. (Guidelines for the Planning and Design of Regional and Community Correctional Centers for Adults, University of Illinois.)

to 20 volumes per inmate. The institution library ought to have access to a general library with a collection of at least 100,000 volumes for reference or interlibrary loan service. Seating space should be allotted for not less than 5 percent of the institution's population, with an allowance of 30 to 35 sq ft per reader for bookshelves, tables, chairs, and circulation. (See Fig. 19.)

Supporting facilities can include a librarian's office and workroom, a magazine storage room, and a listening room with record player. Provisions should be made for transporting books to the segregated maximum-security and infirmary areas to serve inmates who cannot travel to the library. In warmer climates an outdoor area is highly desirable to serve as a reading garden.

Commissary

This is where inmates purchase personal items, such as cigarettes, combs, candy, juice, and as many minor items as the administration wants to stock. A commissary operation may be centralized, so that inmates come in shifts to make their purchases, or it may be the traveling type, with a cart moving to and from the housing units. As a variation of the centralized commissary operation, inmates fill out request slips in their housing area, the slips are then taken to the central commissary where orders are placed in containers and marked for the ordering inmates. The containers are then distributed to them in the housing units.

A central commissary needs sufficient space and display counters for inmates to see the items available, so that they can order without delay. If ice cream or cold drinks are sold, refrigerated storage units must be provided. Ample space must be allotted for storage of stock and for the commissary officer's bookkeeping operation. (See Fig. 20.)

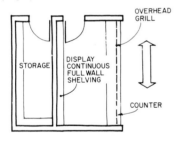

Fig. 20 A commissary component with adjacent storage room for stock, corridor located for easy access. (Guidelines for the Planning and Design of Regional and Community Correctional Centers for Adults, University of Illinois.)

Barber

Barber facilities may be located centrally or in individual housing units. If they are decentralized, the chair(s) should be movable for storage while not in use. Generally inmates shave themselves, and barber services only apply to haircuts.

RECEPTION AND DISCHARGE

The reception and discharge unit is the point of institutional entry or departure for all prisoners. The entry process can be important in determining the inmate's later attitudes and behavior since it is his initial institutional impression. The reception process involves booking, examination, clothing issue, classification interview, fingerprinting, photographing, and assignment to a housing section. Sufficient holding areas must be provided where incoming inmates can congregate until the staff is prepared to administer the reception procedure. The holding areas require benches for sitting and toilet facilities in each area. Showers and drying areas should be provided at the reception area, and an examination room and doctor's office ought to be included for medical examinations. Prisoners beginning the process should not have access to those who have completed the process and are awaiting assignment to a housing unit. Most institutions assign new inmates to a special reception housing unit where they undergo orientation, classification, diagnosis, and withdrawal from drugs, as required. Due to the high percentage of drug addicts received by detention facilities, a major segment of newly received prisoners will undergo withdrawal, which is no longer a problem if methadone is administered. The withdrawal period takes from 3 to 5 days, and medical observation must be maintained during this time. (See Fig. 21.)

MEDICAL SERVICES

The correctional institution has an explicit responsibility to protect and maintain the health of inmates and to prevent the spread of disease among the prisoner population. Preventive medical services in a prison begin with the physical examination of each newly received inmate, encompassing any laboratory or x-ray evaluations that may be necessary. Those inmates who are found to be ill upon admission should be placed in the infirmary for treatment. The initial examination demands the identification of chronic illness in new inmates, such as a cardiac condition, tuberculosis, or diabetes, as well as drug addiction.

The centralized medical facilities of a prison consist of an inpatient and outpatient department. The outpatient function consists of the regular daily procedure under which inmates who are ill or require medical attention can report to the physician for examination and treatment. In small facilities the physician may tour the institution personally, but this is not as desirable as having the inmates go to a central facility for sick call. At least 10 percent of an institution's inmate population may be expected to report to sick call daily. An ample waiting area that includes toilet facilities is thus required for inmates waiting for medical attention. Consultation and treatment rooms should be located in close proximity to the clinical laboratory, x-ray, and pharmacy areas.

Inpatient facilities ought to have a full range of accommodations for inmates requiring formal medical attention. Sufficient beds need

to be supplied to accommodate 3 to 5 percent of the total population that will be housed in single rooms and wards. Areas need to be allotted for the isolation of patients with contagious disease, and special facilities for psychiatric patients who require special security and safety devices to prevent self-injury. The range of treatment facilities will vary, depending on general medical facilities available in neighboring communities. Normally, major surgery is performed at a nearby general hospital, although larger institutions may offer partial or full operating suites for emergency use. Basic treatment areas include general examination and treatment, hydrotherapy, physiotherapy, and eye, ear, nose, and throat services. These areas should be closely related to each other and under the direct supervision of the office of the medical director. Support facilities for these treatment areas comprise an x-ray suite, an EKG-BMR room, a clinical laboratory, and a pharmacy. The pharmacy must allow for a secure storage for drugs.

In addition to general medical treatment, a program of dental care requires a dental suite consisting of one or more treatment rooms and a laboratory. The dental suite should be adjacent to the medical waiting room. The dentist will function more efficiently if he has at least two chairs, thus permitting a trained inmate helper to prepare the next patient for treatment.

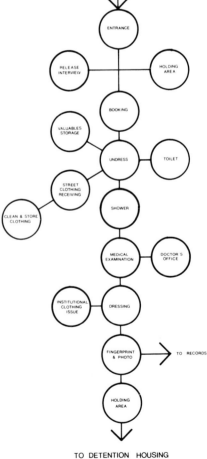

Fig. 21 A diagram showing inmate flow through the reception component of a detention facility.

FOOD SERVICE

One of the most important and difficult operations in any correctional facility is the preparation and serving of three meals a day to the inmate population and to the staff. Most of the kitchen work will be done by inmates with varying levels of experience or interest, under the direction of a steward and a limited staff. Food service can be improved by providing vocational culinary training as part of the correctional program.

With few exceptions, the food preparation is accomplished in a central kitchen facility having major areas for receiving, storage and preparation of food, cooking, dishwashing, and garbage disposal. The amount of space required for storage of foodstuff depends upon the frequency and characteristics of the food-purchasing and delivery program in the institution.

The point of entry for receiving food items requiring a substantial amount of storage should be supervised by a storekeeper who checks incoming deliveries against orders and designates storage areas in the institutional warehouse. The steward replenishes his daily stock from the warehouse or, in smaller installations with more frequent deliveries, food items are stored near the kitchen for continuous use.

The steward supervises the main kitchen, and his office should be strategically located to promote this control, with maximum glazed vision lights. Facilities for the inmate kitchen detail generally include a lounge, classroom (for special culinary instruction), and toilet. Generally, these inmates will put on their kitchen clothing in their housing unit, but some institutions provide clothing in the kitchen itself which necessitates inclusion of a locker room.

There are several basic methods of inmate feeding, each method having its advantages and disadvantages. An appropriate choice of methods depends upon consideration of the correctional goals of the facility, types of inmates served, available custodial manpower, and relationship to the overall program. The basic feeding patterns are

Central dining room(s) adjacent to kitchen
Local dining rooms in housing units
Feeding in inmates' cells
A combination of the above

Central Dining

Central dining adjacent to the kitchen facilitates delivery of prepared food and return of soiled dishes to the dishwashing area, generally located in the kitchen. Dining may take place in a single room or be sectioned off to reduce an excessively large group of inmates congregating in a single space. The process is usually carried out in shifts or on a continuous basis where inmates leave after they have finished with their meals and other inmates take their seats. Careful planning allows a sufficient area for inmates on line waiting to be seated so that they will not interfere with inmates already eating. The institutional sound system should be extended into the dining area to enable broadcasting of announcements and music programs.

Localized Dining

Localized dining in housing units eliminates the problem of large numbers of inmates congregating together and is more ideally suited to the type of facility that promotes a correctional program based on a group interaction. The local dining room can be used for other program purposes between meals. The distribution of food from the kitchen is achieved by heated food carts, which function as serving steamtables in the dining area. It is generally preferable to return dirty dishes to a central dishwashing facility in the kitchen, since cleaning in accordance with health code requirements necessitates special equipment too difficult and expensive to supply in dispersed locations.

Cell Dining

Cell dining is the least desirable method and should be restricted only to that small minority of inmates who pose disciplinary problems. Even for this group, cell feeding should be avoided by providing a special high-security housing unit with its own dining room. Thus cell feeding will be restricted to the most uncontrollable inmates who generally are a very small percentage of the total population.

Staff Dining

Staff dining is generally treated as a separate function from inmate dining, except in small correctional units that promote a close rapport between staff and inmates. The staff dining hall often is divided into areas for custodial staff and areas for superior officers. These dining facilities should be near a main traffic artery, so that in case of an emergency there can be quick access to the main control points of the institution.

RECREATION

Recreation has been recognized as an integral part of a good correctional treatment program. It alleviates the dull monotony of prison life, acts as a safety valve for the release of pent-up energies that otherwise might lead to disturbances, and can be directed toward helping inmates confront some of their personal problems. A well-rounded recreation program should embrace active, competitive sports and strenuous activities for all inmates who are physically fit and interested. For those inmates who cannot take part in active sports, corrective physical fitness programs and other forms of recreation ought to be made available.

Indoor facilities naturally are essential for a full year-round recreation program. It is expedient to plan the gymnasium area for multiple program uses, so that movies and other auditorium functions can take place there. Without question, the most popular sport among inmates is basketball, particularly when the majority of inmates come from urban centers. The main floor of the gymnasium needs to be available for basketball, volleyball, and other floor games, so a separate area should be allotted for boxing, wrestling, and weightlifting, another popular prison activity. Spectator seating ought to be portable to increase the maximum activities space when seating is not required, yet easily brought in for movies or shows. Lockers and showers need to be supplied for inmates and visiting teams.

To meet requirements for basketball and volleyball activities, a gymnasium floor has to be at least 60 ft wide and 100 ft long, with a clear height of 20 ft. For competitive play, a gymnasium floor length of 100 ft is desirable. In addition to a main basketball court, allowances ought to be made for side practice courts to accommodate a maximum number of users at a time. Floor inserts will enable the quick installation of a volleyball net as an alternate activity.

Besides the indoor facilities, outdoor recreation space is necessary for a complete recreational program. On urban sites where outdoor space is not available, it is wise to use roof surfaces to their maximum. These areas generally require fencing enclosures at the sides and top. Where the site is not restrictive, yard and field areas should be provided to supplement the indoor programs. It is expedient to locate outdoor recreation fields adjacent to the gymnasium if possible, to permit common use of lockers and controlled distribution of athletic equipment. The athletic field needs to be adequate for football, baseball, soccer, softball, basketball, and handball, with smaller activity areas for shuffleboard, horseshoes, and bocci ball supplementing it.

VISITING

There are two basic types of visiting done in a correctional facility, visits with family and visits with attorneys and caseworkers.

Visits with family are encouraged to sustain family ties until the inmate's release. Each institution establishes controls for the frequency and length of visits, depending primarily upon the staff available for supervision. Different types of institutions and different kinds of prisoners impose varying custodial restraints, requiring diverse visiting accommodations. Some prisoners and visitors require separation by physical barrier to maintain safe custody and prevent passage of contraband. Others can meet without incident in an informal furnished living room where they may embrace and sit alongside one another under observant supervision.

Closed Visiting

Closed or secure visiting room consists of a booth with a complete physical barrier separating the inmate and visitor. A large expanse of tempered or laminated glass permits visual contact while aural contact can be effected by telephone or microphone-speaker arrangement.

Open Visiting

Open visiting allows contact and normal conversation between inmates and visitors. Since constraints are more relaxed, it is desirable to provide an outdoor area adjacent to the visiting room for use in warm weather. Visitors should leave packages and handbags outside of the visiting room, however, and for this purpose an alcove containing small lockers is attached to the visitors' waiting room. In some instances, prisoners change clothing for visiting and are thoroughly searched before and after an open visit, a security measure intended to guard against the introduction of contraband.

Conjugal Visiting

Conjugal visiting deserves serious consideration for any sentence institution that hopes to encourage normal sexual adjustment among inmates. While the problems associated with conjugal visiting are numerous and its practice under present prison regulations might not completely fill the sexual needs of an inmate, conjugal visiting does allow a man to retain his masculine self-esteem and reduce the need to establish it through homosexual conquests. These facilities should be totally removed from the prisoner population and offer complete privacy to the couples, with quarters that do not reflect the institutional character of the prison.

Attorney and Caseworker Visiting

Attorney and caseworker visitation ought to occur in a central location close to the institution's main entrance to avoid excessive outside traffic into the heart of the prison. The privacy and confidentiality of visits between a prisoner and his attorney must be completely respected, and visiting rooms should be fully enclosed with liberal glassed-in areas for visual observation by custodial officers.

RELIGION

The actual services that take place in a chapel are only a small part of a complete religious program, which includes religious education, counseling, and contact with inmates' families and visitors. The institutional clergymen require individual offices, preferably near the chapel, to carry out their administrative responsibilities. In many institutions, the chapel is used for other nonreligious functions and may act as an auditorium or gymnasium. Within a limited physical plant, this may be an efficient multiuse of a space, but it is obvious that if conditions permit, it is far more desirable to designate a chapel area exclusively for religious activities. Separate chapels for each faith group are preferable, but an interfaith chapel can be equipped with a revolving altar to serve the three major faiths.

SECURITY CONTROL

Security control in a correctional institution is effected by every component of the institution, including layout and design of building elements, details of operation and construction, and the skilled and intelligent supervision of prisoners by a competent staff.

Central Control

Central control is monitored by a control room that functions as the nerve center of the institution. This area is constantly in complete operation, acting as the custodial center for key control, communications, alarm, and traffic control.

The control room operates a series of electrically interlocked doors to fully supervise entrance and exit from the custody zone of the

institution. Ideally, the control room should have visual access along the major traffic corridors. If a system of closed-circuit television is used to view key points in the institution, the monitor screens also must be located in the central control room. All institutional keys should be stored in the key cabinet of the control room and furnished to officers at the beginning of their tour of duty and returned upon tour completion. The communications network of the institution, including security telephones, public address systems, and paging systems, ought to be controlled from this area, as well as all alarm systems, including general emergency alarms, and indicators for opening key doors or operating elevators. It is wise to locate a system of traffic control in or adjacent to the central control room to indicate at any given time the housing location of each inmate.

Firearms

Firearms should be stored in a secure depository at the main entrance of the institution. Many official visitors to a detention or sentence institution will be in possession of firearms, but these must never be permitted inside the custody portion of the facility.

Vehicular Access

Vehicular access to an institution with a perimeter security enclosure should be through an entrance vestibule with doors and gates at each end, both of which ought never to be unlocked at the same time. Frequently, large vehicle gates are motor-operated, controlled from a nearby tower or other control point.

Locks and Locking Devices

Locks and locking devices in correctional institutions ought to be fabricated and installed by manufacturers who specialize in these devices and have a proven record of satisfactory installation. Prison locks should be of the deadbolt type, requiring the officer to turn the key in the lock for positive proof of security. Locking devices for rows of cells are generally controlled from cabinets at the front corridor of a cellblock. Basic sliding cell door locking devices fall into four categories.

Manual Gang Locking All doors can be deadlocked or unlocked as a group by moving levers in a control cabinet. Individual doors are locked or unlocked by a key at the door. Doors are moved manually by the inmates.

Electromechanical Selective All doors are locked or unlocked and operated individually or in groups from switches in a control cabinet.

Any door can be manually unlocked or locked by a key at the door without interfering with the electrical operation.

Manual Keyless Selective All doors are locked or unlocked and operated individually or in groups by moving levers in a control cabinet.

Keyless Electric Selective All doors are locked or unlocked and operated individually or in groups from switches in a control cabinet. There are means of unlocking and locking doors individually or in groups in the event of an electrical power failure.

SUMMARY

In the past, when an architect was assigned to a correctional project, he was relegated to the status of technician or draftsman by the corrections agency or local sheriff. He was handed an outline of basic area requirements and given instructions about their predetermined functional relationships. He rarely interviewed correctional staff representing the various program disciplines and did not explore extensively any alternative solutions to program requirements.

The result? In 1970 a survey of the nation's 4,037 jails found that 86 percent had no facilities for recreation or even exercise, 89 percent lacked educational facilities, 49 percent lacked medical facilities, 26 percent were without visiting facilities and 1.4 percent even lacked toilets.

Attempts have been made to liberalize and develop programs hampered by archaic physical plants, where environment is measured not by its effect on men, but by the strength of steel. There the difference between maximum- and medium-security construction is defined by the time it takes to cut through a steel bar or by the height of a wall.

Change is apparent. Today's architect should question the very need for a correctional institution to begin with. He should challenge the program's constraints, including requirements concerning security, indestructibility, location, and he should analyze the program's capability to ensure that past mistakes are not repeated. The era of the stereotype prison is over. Each community must plan and design in accordance with its own needs. New facilities need to be drawn into populated areas where professional staff, services, educational institutions, and human contact can integrate the offender into community life. The new corrections theory is not based on brick, mortar, and steel, but rather on the interaction between skilled professionals and the offenders within a therapeutic setting.

Fig. 1 **Typical plan for YMCA building.** (National Council of the Young Men's Christian Association of U.S.A.)

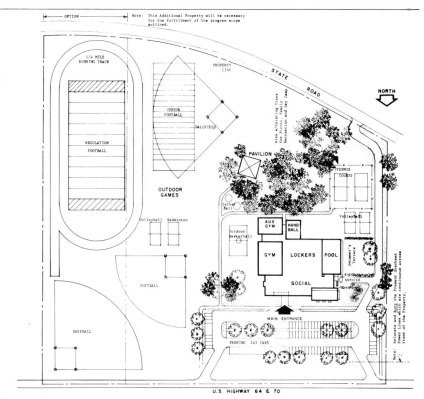

Fig. 2 **Site plan.** (National Council of the Young Men's Christian Association of U.S.A.)

Government and Public
YWCA BUILDINGS

By IRIS ALEX, AIA., Building Consultant, and GLADYS L. BROWN, Health, Physical Education, and Recreation Consultant

BUILDING SITE

The decision to build a new building or to undertake major renovations is the end result of a long process of study, analysis, planning, and fund-raising on the part of the local YWCA. The geographical location of a new facility is determined by community needs for the services to be offered.

The architect, it is hoped, will be involved in the selection of the site. The YWCA may have options on one or more parcels of empty land or land with existing structures on it. The following factors should be taken into account in choosing the site:

• *Proximity to public transportation and availability of parking facilities.* Depending on the locality, participants will arrive by bus or other available means of public transport or by private car. Since the building should attract all kinds of people, easy access to it is of prime importance. If the lot is not large enough to accommodate parking, there should be parking lots in the vicinity.

• *Size of site.* The site should be large enough to accommodate the proposed building, any possible future additions, on-site parking if required and desired, and outdoor activity space if this is included in the program.

• *Visibility.* The site should be easily seen and easy to find. There should be adequate road frontage for the building and for driveway entrances. Identifying signs should be visible from a distance.

When the building site is the property where the present YWCA building is located plus an adjacent lot, and the present building is to be demolished and replaced, careful consideration should be given to building the new structure in phases. Since the YWCA is a membership organization, a long interruption of services is detrimental. It is desirable to be able to carry on programs as long as possible and with as little disruption as possible in the old facilities while the new building is in the construction process. If the size of the site does not allow for phased construction, then the YWCA will have to move to temporary quarters.

GENERAL DESIGN PRINCIPLES

Thoughtful consideration should be given to the things the YWCA wishes to express through a building as well as to its adaptability and usefulness for the activities it is to house. The building should be a friendly place, attractive to different kinds of people. As a community investment, it should be designed for maximum use at minimum operating cost.

It should be designed so that people coming to it or just going by are aware that it is a busy place. Offices at the front of the building present a dark and lifeless appearance after office hours even though the rest of the building is teeming with activity. If it is evident from the outside that something is going on within, potential users will be more apt to investigate, and the contributor to the building or to the community fund will feel that he is helping to provide something that is really being used.

Maximum effectiveness in use of staff time

is essential. The element of control of the building should be given major consideration, so that staff on duty at a front desk can be alert to all people coming into or leaving the building. Additional exits for safety should be under the control of the person supervising the area during the periods when such exits are open. When space is provided for drop-in use, it should be located within the range of vision of either the front desk or a staff office during the time it is open. Program staff offices should be related to the activity areas to be supervised by the staff member. This gives opportunity for the supervision of the groups and for informal contacts with individuals before and after the activities.

Ease of maintenance is important, especially in small buildings not requiring the full-time services of an engineer or janitor. Heating should be as automatic as possible; mechanical equipment should permit operation with minimum attention and upkeep. In the long run it will save both money and man-hours if portable equipment is stored in a location related to its use, even though that may be more expensive to provide than a single storage room.

Since the building will be used by individuals of all ages—from toddlers to the infirm—details of construction should be designed so as to avoid offering temptation to the young. Everything from light switches to swimming pools should be viewed as having potential "attractive nuisance" qualities, and all possible safeguards should be provided. Rooms to be used for public meetings should be on the main floor, if possible, or otherwise readily accessible and located so as to reduce unnecessary traffic.

Interior construction and decoration should provide a colorful appearance and at the same time be durable and easy to maintain. Many materials now in use can make an attractive looking building and still meet the requirements of ease of maintenance. Furnishings can be both sturdy and attractive. The feminine touch can be achieved without wallpaper and ruffles or fragile furniture. Ingenuity in planning is required; it pays off both in long-term satisfaction and in economy of operation, so that the maximum possible amount of the yearly budget can go into staffing and otherwise supporting the program. (See Table 1.)

Another essential point is flexibility in use, with the amount of space for single-purpose use kept to the minimum. Additional storage for equipment for several groups, features that can be shut off from a room, or flooring and other elements in construction may increase the original cost of a single room but may greatly enhance its use. The standby cost of single-purpose rooms with limited use is even higher in the long run and is an extravagance during the life of the building. Wherever possible, the plan must permit flexibility so that later adaptations or modifications can be made without undue expense or waste.

MAIN ENTRANCE AND LOBBY

The front entrance should be inviting and accessible, avoiding steep steps and providing

sufficient platform space on the outside so that there is adequate clearance for doors that open out. Access for the handicapped must be provided. Doors should be sturdy but not too heavy. They should give some vision into the immediate lobby into which people enter.

Space inside the doors and on traffic lanes to other parts of the building should be sufficient and routed to cause a minimum of congestion at periods of peak use. Since the trend is away from huge lobbies and lounges, space actually needed for traffic should be achieved, insofar as possible, by planning for maximum use rather than for large areas. To avoid a "sitters' lounge," which tends to attract people who do not participate, only a limited lounge space should be planned, with the furnishings so arranged as to avoid interference with the traffic lanes. Wall space for displays and bulletin boards should be provided in the lobby.

The main entrance should be located carefully so that it is accessible to the street and to any parking area nearby, either one on the building site or a public lot in the neighborhood. If most participants arrive by car, it is important that they reach a main entrance by the shortest route from their cars. Very often, people find a side or rear door more conveniently located and enter the building by that means, thus complicating the control of traffic in the buildings. Have the lobby so arranged that the entrances from the street and from the parking area can easily be supervised from the reception desk. (See Fig. 1.)

RECEPTION DESK

The main front desk is both a key public relations contact and a control point for the entire building. It should be located so that people entering the building can find it quickly and so that the lobby and lounge are within the line of vision of the front desk staff.

The size of the main desk area will depend upon the volume of use and the number and kinds of services to be performed there. In a large building, especially when the front desk serves both an activities and a residence building and/or handles registration for activities involving large numbers of people, the counter should be large enough to permit two or more people to give service at the same time. It should be located so that traffic flows in one direction and people will not crowd in front of it, impede movement, slow down the service, or cut off the view.

Equipment should be planned and conveniently located for service at slack periods when a minimum staff is on duty and must be alert to what is going on in the lobby. If there are times when the person covering the counter must also operate the switchboard, it must be placed where she can save steps yet watch the lounge. Mailboxes, storage space, and file boxes or drawers for registration cards should be readily accessible. If, during their slack periods, the front office employees do any of the processes for large mailings, counter space should be provided away from the congestion of the regular working equipment. Provision should be made for the easy and safe handling

742

of cash and the issuing of receipts. An adjacent office is needed for the office supervisor and for jobs requiring concentration, such as record keeping or the counting of money. It is better to have the safe located in this office instead of in the main desk area. Sufficient storage space should be provided for supplies and equipment.

SPACE FOR BUSINESS AND ADMINISTRATION

Whether a business and purchasing office should be in the same area as the main desk and its related office space will depend on the size of the association and the number of people employed. In a small building, offices can be planned so that people doing several kinds of jobs can work nearby. Such a plan may include space for mimeographing and assembling, record keeping, bookkeeping, and other business or administrative tasks. In a large association with a sizable volume of business and a number of staff employed in the different kinds of operations, it will be better to locate the business and administrative offices elsewhere and in relation to each other so that as much of the main floor as possible can be kept free for activities. (See Fig. 2.)

Lavatory and coat storage space should be provided for the use of the staff in each total unit of offices.

Administrative offices should be provided for all administrative staff. The offices of the executive and any associates or assistants and the related clerical staff should be located so that they are accessible to the people who need to come to them but away from major activity areas. When possible, it is also advisable to have a separate office for the president, with a desk of her own and a telephone so that she can have privacy when she needs it. Sometimes this office can be used by other volunteers or staff. If the volume of work of the treasurer is large, she needs an office or a desk in the business office.

Storage space is essential in administrative offices, and small offices uncluttered by needed materials or equipment can provide a better work setting than large floor spaces with makeshift storage arrangements. Offices of professional staff should not be arranged so that they give a sense of remoteness or inaccessibility. The offices for clerical staff should be adjacent to those of the professional staff with whom they work, so that they can work efficiently and screen unnecessary interruptions. If counseling or other individual services are offered, the office for that staff will need to be readily accessible to the hesitant or timid person and ensure a degree of privacy and freedom from interruptions. It is essential for a counselor to have an attractive private office for individual consultations. (See Fig. 3.)

The offices for the administration and management of the business and property of the association have been described at this point because of their relationship in a small building. Their exact location in larger buildings will vary according to other features. In any event, they will occupy a relatively small space as compared to that used for activities. The amount of space for administration and management may be increased where offices for metropolitan staff are housed in the central building. The total ratio of office to activities space should be studied in order to achieve maximum use of the building for program but also enough office space to serve the requirements of good administration.

SPACE FOR ACTIVITIES OR GROUP USE

The number and types of rooms to be included for program use will be determined by the space budget previously prepared by the YWCA building committee and the degree to which multiple-purpose use can be made of each area.

Few buildings, even large ones, should have big rooms for single-purpose use. An auditorium with slanted floor and permanent seating is a luxury unless there is such heavy demand for it that it will actually be in use a large amount of the time.

The largest room for which an organization should make provision should be one that can house several kinds of activities and will be used to maximum capacity frequently enough to justify its inclusion in the plan. It is not advisable to consider providing for the largest group the association will want to assemble at any one time or even several times during a year. It is less costly to rent that kind of space elsewhere in the community for a limited number of events than to construct and maintain space that will in all or in part be standby space during most of the year.

The same principle applies to construction of health education facilities for competitive sports that are limited in the agency program and for which other community facilities are or should be made available.

On the other hand, a room for mass activities of several kinds can be justified, especially if it can be converted into two or more smaller rooms for other types of groups to use in between times.

A large multiple-purpose room in a building without a complete health and recreation department may have to be used for gym classes and also for mass activities. In order to make it useful for other things, there will be some limitations on the kinds of gymnasium programs and equipment that may be used. However, unless the primary use is for health education programs, it is probably too expensive to provide the special features required for competitive sports or other activities involving high-cost facilities that will not give maximum return on the investment.

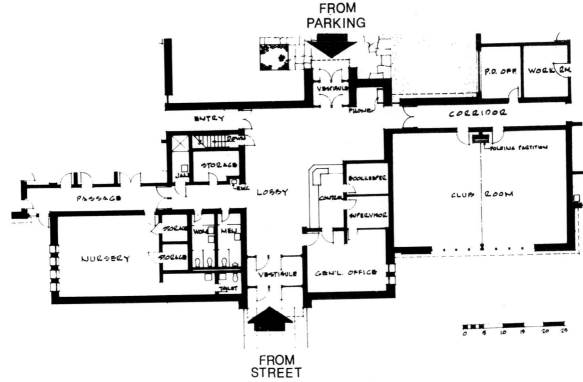

Fig. 1   Summit, New Jersey, YWCA. Entrance area, offices, child care, activity room. Small city association. (Ludlow and Jefferson, Architects.)

Government and Public

YWCA BUILDINGS

TABLE 1 Recommended Finish Schedule for General Areas*†

Rooms	Floors								Walls									Ceilings				
	Resilient tile or sheet	Carpet (replaceable)	Carpet	Hard maple	Terrazzo (cement or epoxy)	Quarry tile	Ceramic tile	Dustproof concrete	Epoxy or cold-glazed cement coating on concrete block	Painted concrete block	Glazed tile or brick	Brick or other exterior wall	Wood paneling	Tackboard paneling (partial)	Vinyl wall covering	Steel and glass partition	Unfinished	Lay-in exposed-grid acoustic panels	Acoustic tile	Acoustic plaster	Plaster	Unfinished
Entrance vestibule	1								1			1									1	
Lobby, Lounge	2	1	1	1					1			1	1	1	1			2	1	1		
Corridors	1	1		1	2				1		1				1			2	1			
Offices	1	1											1	1	1	1		2	1			
Activity, class, club rooms	1	1							1	2			1	1				1	2			
Child care room	1	1							1	2			1	1	1			1	2			
Multipurpose room	2		1						1				1		1			1	2			
Crafts rooms	1					1		1	1	2	1				1			1	2		2	2
Storage	1							1		1												1
Service areas								1		1						1						1
Toilets							1			1					2						1	

*1, 2 = Order of preference.
†Painted surfaces to be kept to minimum.

Adequate public toilet facilities for women and men should be provided in a location convenient for participants in activity areas. These should not be located too close to the front entrance and/or out of sight of the reception desk or some other control point.

Multipurpose Room

A room that can be used for dances, for informal mass activities, or as an auditorium and a banquet room can be designed to serve all those purposes satisfactorily if proper atten-

tion is given to the particular requirements of each.

For use as an auditorium, the size and type of stage and dressing rooms will depend upon whether the room will have frequent use for dramatic productions. For frequent use, a permanent stage with accessible dressing rooms is recommended. Dressing rooms can be designed for other uses provided there is adequate closet and storage space for each use.

Adjacent storage space must be provided for stage properties and surplus chairs in order to clear the room for dances and similar activi-

ties. A stage high enough to be seen from the back of a flat-floor auditorium will usually have room for some storage under it. Dollies which can easily be rolled in and out of such space save labor in setting up and clearing the room. If a portable stage is used, storage space must be provided.

If games or other activities may take place in the room, there should be adequate storage for that equipment. This may sound like a lot of storage, but it must be provided somewhere and more storage can result in more use of the available floor space for program. Proximity of storage to location of use can save time and effort for the maintenance staff and speed up the conversion of the space for different uses.

Checkrooms should be considered in relation to the large room and to other parts of the building. It is more economical to provide small checking areas located near activities space than to have one large checkroom requiring an attendant even at times of minimum use. Portable racks within sight of the groups or supervisor may be practical and can be moved into temporary checking areas when there is unusual demand. A checkroom should not be located in a heavy traffic area and should have a marked one-way traffic lane when a large group is to be served. A kitchen should be located for ease of service to the large room, directly connected with it or adjacent to it. Food should not be carried a great distance or across a hall or other space where people may be congregated or passing. Such functions will not necessitate a continuous or even frequent use for the kitchen and do not require elaborate refrigeration to carry over perishable foods. There should be a service entrance so that deliveries can be made and waste removed independently of the main lobby or heavy traffic lanes. It should be controlled when deliveries are being made. A buzzer connection should be installed to the main office facilities

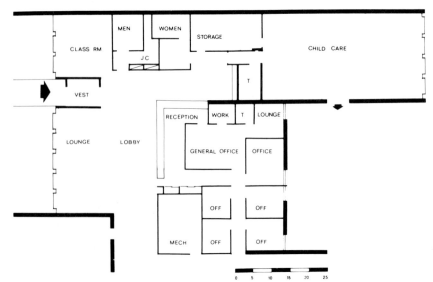

Fig. 2 Oakland Branch, YWCA of Metropolitan Detroit, Michigan. Entrance area, offices, child care. Branch building. (O'Dell, Hewlett & Luckenbach, Architects.)

744

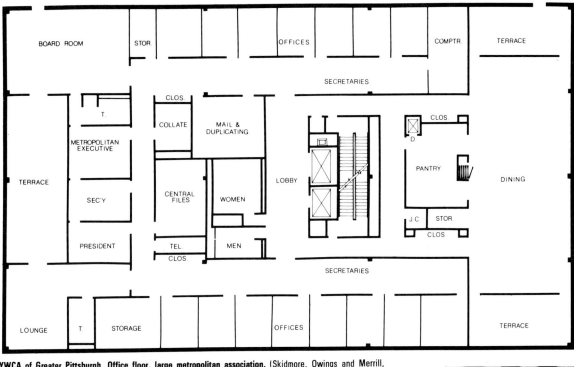

Fig. 3   YWCA of Greater Pittsburgh. Office floor, large metropolitan association. (Skidmore, Owings and Merrill, Architects.)

to call a janitor to take deliveries so that he will not have to waste his time waiting for them.

Storage for dishes can be provided by cupboards that open in the dining area or are adjacent to an opening for transfer to the dining area. The size and arrangement of other kitchen equipment will depend somewhat on the kind of service planned. If it is to be catering service, the total preparation of a meal may not be done on the premises. Sufficient heavy-duty equipment should be provided for normal use, but again it is not advisable to install all that would be needed for the unusual events.

Smaller Activity Rooms

Other rooms will be needed for small-group use and should be so arranged that they can be combined for different sized groups. A room that can be used for meetings of 150 to 200 people can be divided to form several small units. Good-quality acoustic folding partitions for dividing rooms can make the smaller units satisfactory for simultaneous use.

Entrance into each section of the room must be from a hallway, so that no group will be disturbed by people passing through and so that one or more sections need not serve as a passageway.

If several types of groups are to use the rooms, each group should have the equipment it requires, and the equipment adapted to several uses should be available as needed. A craft room has frequently been considered a single-purpose room, especially if, in addition to sinks, benches, and other usual equipment, the organization has a kiln or machinery for crafts. It is possible, however, to group these pieces of equipment at one or both ends of the room and shut off those areas with movable partitions that can be locked in place, thus converting the remaining area into a room for classes or other small meetings. Drying racks for craft products should be out of reach of the curious but accessible to the craftsmen. A well-organized display arrangement can offer

stimulation and new ideas to others. A similar plan can be used to convert activities space for use as a chapel or quiet room. An altar or other arrangement for worship that can be opened for use when the room becomes a chapel might be at one end.

The rooms used by several groups and the special-purpose areas should be grouped to facilitate supervision of the activities and provide a variety of programs close together. Meeting rooms, classrooms, craft and similar space should in general be located on one floor or on consecutive floors to permit ease of movement from one area to another and to limit the amount of elevator use (where there is one) and/or stair climbing.

Food service is needed in relation to program activities, and building plans should provide facilities for it. A kitchen that can be used for meals for large groups should be related to the area that will be used for such affairs. Kitchenettes should be provided to serve small groups, and if a residence is to be included in the plan, cooking facilities must be furnished for permanent residents. A snack bar adjacent to a drop-in lounge or recreation space may be provided.

Vending machines are often included in the program, and electrical and plumbing connections should be provided in locations where machines may be installed.

CHILD CARE FACILITIES

If a program is to be carried out for mothers of young children, a nursery with special lavatory facilities will be required. The proper standards are essential, both in the building arrangement and the supervision, and should meet local ordinances and health department requirements. If the space is to be used for other purposes, the special equipment will require storage space where it can be out of the way and properly protected. (See Figs. 1 and 2.)

Local ordinances dictate the space allotted per child, the maximum number of children per

room, and special facilities to be provided. An outdoor, enclosed play space adjacent to the indoor facilities is desirable.

HEALTH, PHYSICAL EDUCATION, AND RECREATION FACILITIES

If a YWCA is planning to include HPER facilities, particularly a swimming pool in new building plans, or to add these facilities to an already existing building, meticulous research and care must go into choosing construction methods, mechanical, electrical, and filtration systems, finishing materials, and into designing the area for the best traffic flow and use of space. (See Figs. 4 to 6.)

The operating costs of HPER facilities are rarely subsidized by the local community chest agency, and the YWCA must pay all operating and maintenance costs for these facilities out of the income from classes and rentals. Since construction costs are so high for these facilities, the design must provide for the maximum utilization of teaching-staff time and ease of maintenance and operation by the custodial staff.

There should be an easy flow of traffic from the main lobby. Having the swimming pool visible from the lobby will attract participants. Spectator space in the natatorium is desirable if the budget allows for it.

It is preferable to have the entire HPER unit on the ground floor. If this is not possible, the locker rooms and swimming pool must be on one level, and the gymnasium or multipurpose room, dance and exercise studios can be located on a different floor but with a means of access directly from the HPER lobby area. It is important to avoid cross traffic of participants in gym attire with other traffic in the main lobby.

The HPER facilities should be so situated in the building that they can be open for rental by outside groups when other parts of the building are closed.

745

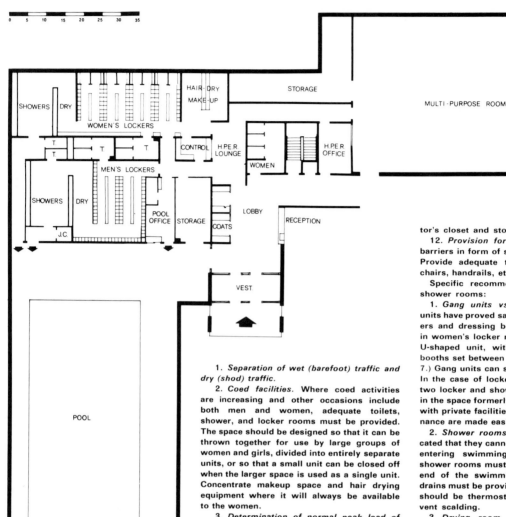

Fig. 4 Bangor, Maine, YWCA, HPER addition.
(Higgins, Webster and Partners, Architects.)

Elements in a Total HPER Unit

Lobby Lounge

A separate lounge adjacent to the locker rooms should be provided for HPER participants. A control office with a counter from which an attendant may dispense locker keys and towels, keep records, etc., should open into this room. Doors to locker rooms should be within sight of the attendant. Lounge furniture, bulletin boards, and vending machines should be provided. Access to gymnasium or other small exercise rooms should be through this space. Participants in gym attire can wait here for classes in order to relieve the occupant load in the locker rooms.

Ideally, the locker room entrances can be closed off and the space used as a social lounge during recreational and social programs.

Locker and Shower Rooms Important considerations in locker-room design include the following:

1. *Separation of wet (barefoot) traffic and dry (shod) traffic.*

2. *Coed facilities.* Where coed activities are increasing and other occasions include both men and women, adequate toilets, shower, and locker rooms must be provided. The space should be designed so that it can be thrown together for use by large groups of women and girls, divided into entirely separate units, or so that a small unit can be closed off when the larger space is used as a single unit. Concentrate makeup space and hair drying equipment where it will always be available to the women.

3. *Determination of normal peak load of users.* Estimate can be based on the number of people expected for swimming and other classes scheduled within a two-hour interval during popular program hours. This figure should determine the approximate number of lockers needed. The extent of private vs. gang facilities to be offered (depending on local community's custom), the kind of lockers (long or short), methods of checking and control, and the number of showers and toilets required by state health codes and good practice also figure in determining the size of the locker facilities. Adequate dressing and circulation space are important. Ten to fifteen sq ft per person should be allowed.

4. *Safety of program participants.*

5. *Provision for storage of coats and bulky belongings.* This is a factor in locker size. Lockers should be large enough to accommodate a dress hanger. If necessary, coats can be stored on racks under the supervision of the attendant.

6. *Protection of participants' belongings.*

7. *Supervision of locker rooms.* This is especially important if there is a heavy emphasis on children's program.

8. *Method of control and dispensing keys, towels, etc., and checking valuables.* Possible need for washing machine and dryer.

9. *Attractiveness of area.* Layout, materials, colors, lighting.

10. *Comfort of participants.* Temperature, humidity, acoustics, good traffic patterns, adequate space.

11. *Ease of maintenance.* Well-located janitor's closet and storage, choice of materials.

12. *Provision for handicapped people.* No barriers in form of steps or narrow doorways. Provide adequate turning space for wheelchairs, handrails, etc.

Specific recommendations for locker and shower rooms:

1. *Gang units vs. private facilities.* Gang units have proved satisfactory, but a few showers and dressing booths should be included in women's locker rooms. Recommended is a U-shaped unit, with two or three dressing booths set between rows of lockers. (See Fig. 7.) Gang units can save a great deal of space. In the case of locker room remodeling, often two locker and shower units can be installed in the space formerly occupied by a single unit with private facilities. Supervision and maintenance are made easier, and costs are reduced.

2. *Shower rooms.* These should be so located that they cannot be bypassed by persons entering swimming pool. Doors from the shower rooms must be located at the shallow end of the swimming pool. Adequate floor drains must be provided. Temperature of water should be thermostatically controlled to prevent scalding.

3. *Drying room.* This should be placed between showers and locker room to keep dressing area dry. Participants remove suits here and dry off before returning to lockers.

4. *Lockers.* Ideally, most lockers should be the long type. Some short lockers can be used if space is limited. These can be used by children. Lockers should have sloping tops to facilitate maintenance and should be set on raised, coved bases. Lockers finished in bright colors are an excellent means of providing a cheerful atmosphere. Benches can either be floor-supported between rows of lockers or cantilevered from the base below the lockers.

5. *Toilet facilities.* Two sets of toilet facilities are needed, one "wet" and one "dry." The wet unit can consist of a single toilet without washbasin located off the shower room. The user reshowers before going back to the swimming pool. The dry unit is located near the locker room entrance and makeup area and contains washbasins in addition to toilets. Toilets should be wall-hung and partitions ceiling-hung to facilitate maintenance.

6. *Makeup area.* This is an essential area and should be located out of the main traffic flow. Adequate space should be provided to accommodate large groups. Provide deep shelves at standing height and adequate mirror area. This should be located in the women's locker room but should also be available to the second locker room when both are used by women and girls.

7. *Hair dryers.* These should be located adjacent to the makeup area. Automatic, wall-hung dryers are recommended and should be set at

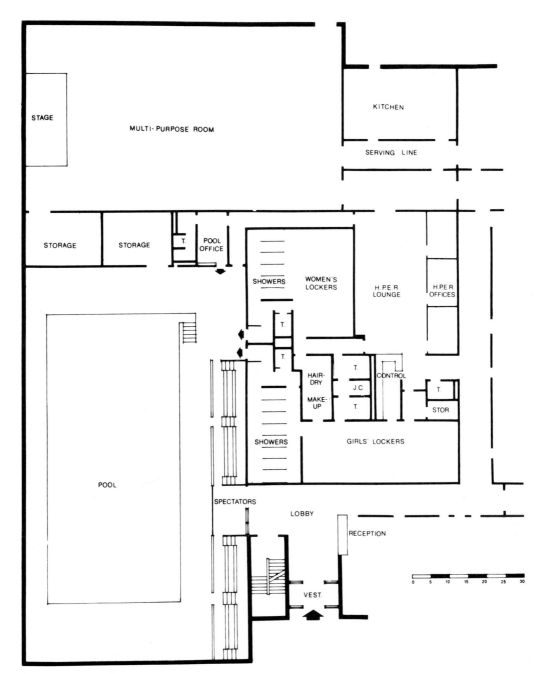

Fig. 5   Orange, New Jersey, YWCA, HPER facilities. (Emil Schmidlin, Architect.)

suitable heights for girls and women. Some hair dryers should be placed in the men's locker room. Do *not* locate hair dryers near the shower rooms. Hair clogs the floor drains, and participants should dress before using hair dryers.

8. *Materials used in locker-room construction.* The ideal floor material is nonslip ceramic mosaic tile. Unfinished concrete usually encourages fungus growth and attracts dirt. If the budget is too restricted for ceramic tile throughout the locker area, it should be used in the shower and drying rooms, and a good concrete sealer should be used for the dry dressing areas.

All floors must pitch to adequate drains, and hose bibbs should be provided. See sched-

ule for recommended floor, wall, and ceiling finishes. (See Table 2.)

9. *Lighting, Heating, Ventilating.* Lighting should be in the form of recessed, vaporproof fixtures. Illumination should be evenly distributed over the entire area, with fixtures located over dressing spaces between rows of lockers. The recommended footcandle level is 30. Provide concentrated and flattering lighting at the makeup area.

In designing the heating, ventilating, and air conditioning system, the locker room and shower areas humidity control is a prime factor. This area should be zoned separately. Too high a velocity of air is chilling to the wet skin. The shower and locker room temperature should be about 80°.

Offices The number of offices required reflects the size and scope of the program. At minimum, the following are required:

1. *Director's office.* This office should be located either off the HPER lounge-lobby or off an adjacent corridor. This office should be easily accessible to the public and closely related to the HPER unit. When a swimming pool is not included in the HPER unit, a staff dressing room and shower should be connected to this office.

2. *Pool office.* A second office is needed when a pool is included. This office opens off the HPER lounge or locker-room complex and has a door opening directly onto the pool deck. This office, which should have a large sliding glass window for supervision of the

Government and Public
YWCA BUILDINGS

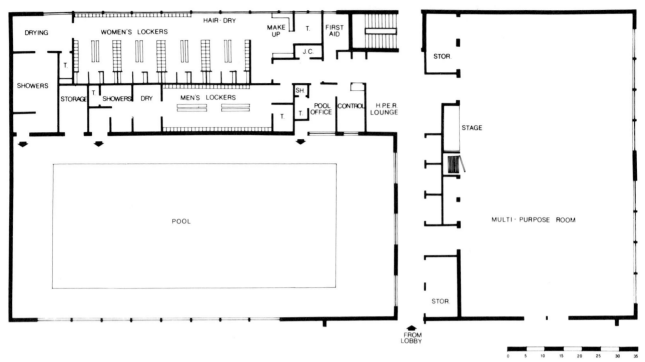

Fig. 6 **Greenville, South Carolina, YWCA, HPER facilities.** (Charles Potter, Jr. — Alison Lee, Architects.)

pool, contains controls for the natatorium and underwater lights and sound system, first-aid equipment, a telephone, teaching aids, and audio equipment. There should be a staff dressing and shower room opening off this room. The pool office should be large enough to accommodate a first-aid cot.

3. *Control office for locker-room attendant,* previously described.

Gymnasium or Multipurpose Room Previously determined budget and program factors dictate whether there will be a regulation gymnasium or a multipurpose room. Very few YWCAs can

afford the luxury of two large rooms, so that a multipurpose room usually serves for physical activities as well as large meeting, social, and food service events. The floor must be suitable for all uses and preferably should be wood. Court markings and floor sockets should be provided as required.

TABLE 2 Recommended Finish Schedule for HPER Facilities *†

Rooms	Floors								Walls							Ceilings						
	Cushion-edge nonslip ceramic tile	Abrasive Terrazzo	Trowel-on epoxy coating	Resilient tile or sheet	Hard maple	Synthetic gym flooring	Carpeting	Dustproof concrete	Ceramic tile	Glazed block or brick	Epoxy or cold-glazed cement coating on concrete block	Wood paneling	Painted concrete block	Vinyl wall covering	Unfinished	Perforated metal panels	Perforated asbestos-cement panels	Kiln-fired, waterproof mineral-fiber tile	Lay-in exposed-grid acoustic panels	Glass-fiber acoustic units	Plaster	Unfinished
Natatorium	1	2							1	1	2					1	1	1		1		
Shower rooms	1	2							1	1						1		1				1
Locker rooms	1	2	3					3	1	1	1		2					1	1			
Toilets	1								1	1	2			3					2		1	
Offices, lounge				1			1				1	1	2	1					1			
Gymnasium				1	2				1			1	2						1			
Multipurpose room			2	1						1	1		1						1			
Dance, exercise rooms . .				1						1	1	2							1			
Fitness studio			2			1				1	2	1							1		2	
Storage								1						1								1

*1, 2, 3 = Order of preference.
†Painted surfaces to be kept to minimum.

748

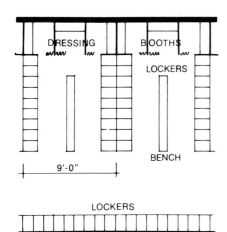

Fig. 7 Recommended U-shaped unit of lockers and dressing booths.

Collapsible bleachers, a viewing balcony, and a portable or permanent stage may be included in the program and budget.

Consult *Planning Areas and Facilities for Health, Physical Education, and Recreation,* published by the American Association for Health, Physical Education, and Recreation, 1201 Sixteenth Street, N.W., Washington, D.C. 20036, and available on order from the YWCA National Board, 600 Lexington Avenue, New York, N.Y. 10022. This volume gives regulation floor areas, court markings, ceiling heights, and other pertinent design data.

Provide as much flat, clear wall space as possible. Avoid column and other projections inside the room. Lighting fixtures should be shatterproof, and an exposed grid, lay-in acoustic board ceiling is the most practical, since panels can be easily replaced in case of damage. Separate storage rooms adequate for gym equipment and for chairs and tables should be provided. If the program calls for the large room to be divided, provide an acoustically rated folding partition. Adequate power outlets should be provided. Other possible program requirements are sound systems, bulletin boards, projection screens, etc.

Smaller Activity Rooms Some physical education activities call for smaller rooms: corrective exercise and dance classes, for example. These rooms should have wood floors and mirrors. Ballet bars and other required apparatus should be included. If there is a fitness studio in the program, provide adequate space for all contemplated equipment. A carpeted floor may be desirable.

Natatorium The natatorium is a large, clear-span room, with adequate heating, ventilating, and humidity controls, which houses an indoor swimming pool. Sufficient width must be provided for adequate deck space around the pool.

The interior walls of the natatorium should be flush. Avoid column projections and recessed areas, including entrances from locker rooms and offices. The lifeguard on duty must be able to see the entire space. The exterior walls and roof should be well insulated to prevent condensation.

The YWCA swimming program is primarily intended for teaching, with recreation secondary. Both functions must be income-producing, and maintenance and operating costs must be kept low.

It is often tempting to envision an indoor-outdoor pool situation, but the necessary provisions for this kind of design feature are costly

to construct and keep in repair, whether they are sliding glazed walls, movable roofs, pressurized enclosures, or a battery of hinged, glazed doors. The outdoor setting is not used sufficiently in YWCA programs in most parts of the country to justify the cost. Sunbathing space is not income-producing, and added staff supervision is required.

The inclusion of any windows is not recommended, since sunlight reflects on the water surface, making it difficult for the lifeguards to see the swimmers. It also causes algae growth and consumes large quantities of chlorine.

Important considerations in natatorium design:

1. *Ceiling height.* A minimum height of 15 ft must be maintained over a 1-meter diving board.

2. *Materials.* All materials used in the natatorium must be moisture- and chemical-resistant. A schedule of recommended materials is shown. Any metal doors, trim, railings, etc. should be stainless steel. Any other metal will require too much maintenance.

3. *Ventilation.* Controlling the humidity in the natatorium is essential. Introducing dry, heated air and removing moist air should produce a comfortable environment. Temperature must be kept constant and at a minimum of 80° for swimmers' comfort. When spectators are present for a competitive event, the temperature can be lowered. Air velocity should be kept low to avoid chilling wet skin. A flat ceiling surface is desirable to allow air to move freely.

4. *Adequate acoustic control.* This is essential for a teaching program. An acoustic ceiling of moisture-resistant material can be supplemented by wall-mounted acoustic units.

5. *Good lighting.* Light fixtures should be located over the pool deck only for easy relamping and should provide a minimum uniform lighting level of 60 footcandles. The light source should be diffused to avoid glare on the water surface. An emergency lighting system must be provided.

6. *Spectator space.* Desirable for teaching and for special events. Spectator space must be separated from the pool deck by a low wall. The spectator entrance should be controlled from the reception desk. It is preferable to have the spectator space at or slightly above the deck level rather than at balcony height.

7. *Miscellaneous provisions.* An adequate storage room is required for instruction and other pool equipment such as lane markers, starter blocks, a canoe if called for in the program, etc. Maintenance equipment should be stored separately.

Hot and cold recessed hose bibbs, a drinking fountain, a clock, and an adequate number of power outlets should be provided. Include hooks or inserts on the upper walls for displays and decorations. Provide means of hanging rescue equipment (pole and ring buoys) so that it can be reached when needed.

Swimming Pool Important considerations in swimming pool design:

1. Conformance to state or local regulatory agency regulations. Submission of plans and specifications for approval.

2. Careful study of soil mechanics, results of test borings to determine best pool shell and foundation construction, drainage, need for hydrostatic relief valves, etc.

3. Thorough inquiry and research into YWCA's proposed program use of swimming pool. Requirements for instructional, recreational, and competitive uses of a pool are sometimes in conflict, and program emphasis will be a decisive factor in choice of size, water

depth, and overflow system. The pool must be easily accessible to handicapped persons.

4. Initial construction costs and ongoing maintenance costs. Construction savings that will require extensive future maintenance and repairs must be avoided. There is no comparable substitute for a properly engineered reinforced-concrete pool shell. Some savings can be made in finishes by restricting ceramic tile to a minimum area at the water line and plastering the rest of the tank. By incorporating adequate surge tank area, either in a separate tank or in an integral trench, savings in the heating and filtering of water can be made. Architects should avoid inexpensive pool "packages" which seem to afford savings. Often much of the equipment included is inferior.

Count on your combined architectural and engineering experience or engage the services of a qualified pool engineer to design a suitable installation. The National Swimming Pool Institute in Washington, D.C. may be contacted for suggested names of qualified engineers throughout the country.

If the YWCA does not have the funds to build a well-designed pool of the size desired it is advisable to cut down the size of the pool rather than sacrifice construction quality.

5. Thorough investigation of source of potable water supply (for sufficient volume and for chemical composition), waste and sewer connections, power supply and fuel supply in the vicinity.

6. Read and follow applicable suggestions in the following reference materials:

a. *Suggested Minimum Standards for Residential and Public Swimming Pools,* National Swimming Pool Institute, 2000 K Street, Washington, D.C. 20006.

b. State or local health codes covering public swimming pools.

c. *Swimming Pools, A Guide to their Planning, Design and Operation.* Council for National Cooperation in Aquatics. Hoffman Publications, Inc., Sunrise Professional Building, Fort Lauderdale, Florida 33304, 1969.

d. *Planning Areas and Facilities for Health, Physical Education and Recreation,* previously cited.

Specific Recommendations for Pool Design

1. *Size and shape.* A rectangular pool with vertical side walls is recommended, with deep water at one end and shallow water at the other.

Pool size will be determined by program needs. If schools and other agencies will be using the facility, cooperative planning is necessary.

Standard pool sizes (in feet):

60	by	25
60	by	30
75	by	25
75	by	30
75	by	35
75	by	42*
82.5	by	42*

Competitive requirements:

For recognized competition, a 75-ft pool is essential. (Actual length is 75 ft 1 in.) Swimming lanes should be 7 ft wide. A minimum of four lanes is needed, with 1 ft extra on outside lanes. If the YWCA will be building the only pool in the community, it may be necessary to meet competitive requirements. If a heavy

*Not generally recommended for YWCAs.

749

instruction program is anticipated, especially using the station teaching method with several teachers at the same time and large classes, the 75-ft pool with a large shallow water area is desirable.

2. *Depth.* Minimum depth of water allowed is 3 ft. Recommended shallow depth is 3 ft 6 in. This is required for a competitive pool. Approximately 60 to 65 percent of the pool area should contain water less than 5 ft deep. The slope of the shallow water area must be gradual. In depths under 5 ft, it should not slope more than 1 ft in 15.

Minimum deep water depth is 9 ft for a 1-meter diving board, although some state codes require a 10-ft minimum. Recommended pool bottom contours are shown in the National Swimming Pool Institute Standards. The deepest point in the pool should be under the plummet line from the end of the diving board. For good water circulation, the pool bottom should rise gradually from this point to the deep end of the pool.

3. *Pool construction.* Any choice of material for construction or finishing that requires frequent repair, refinishing, or painting is not economical. Certified boring logs should be obtained and expertly interpreted so that the appropriate shell construction can be determined. Poured reinforced concrete is preferred. Adequately reinforced pneumatically applied concrete has been used, but the curved bottom contour interferes with full use of the pool for teaching. Metal shell construction requires constant repainting, which causes disruption to teaching schedules and subsequent loss of income.

4. *Pool tank finishes.* Ceramic tile remains the classical permanent swimming pool finish. Tile should be vitreous square-edged tile to permit smooth tile grout. White tile should be used within the tank, with required lane and target markings in black. Properly filtered water is blue and looks best in a white tank. If the use of tile must be restricted, it can be installed in a 1-ft-deep band along the long sides and extend 3 ft 6 in. down at the ends. The rest of the tank can be plastered. A white cement plaster with a "marble dust" finish should last from four to eight years. Pool markings can be delineated by having lines cut or by setting tile strips before plastering.

Pool markings must be carefully indicated on the detail drawings. Required markings for competitive swimming can be found in *Swimming Pools, A Guide to their Planning, Design and Operation,* previously cited. Recessed cup-type anchors and inserts for lifelines and lane dividers must be provided for.

5. *Pool ladders and entrance steps.* Ladders should be recessed in side walls only, adjacent to deep and shallow ends. If deck space and budget permit, a short flight of steps leading into the shallow end should be incorporated into the design.

6. *Overflow systems.* There is a wide choice of overflow systems: fully recessed or semi-recessed gutters; roll-out, rim-flow, or deck-level systems; surface skimmers; and pre-fabricated steel semirecessed gutters.

Cost factors influence the choice. For example, a fully recessed tile gutter is the most expensive to install, while a deck-level installation with large coping stones will have a minimum cost both in construction and associated piping.

Proposed program use influences the choice. Deck-level, rim-flow, or roll-out systems offer ideal conditions for teaching and recreation but are not ideal for competition, where the ends of the pool must be defined. This problem can be solved by setting up temporary turning boards for competitive events.

An important element in the general hydraulic performance of the system is adequate surge tank capacity. The function of a surge tank is to provide storage area for large volumes of overflow or gutter water that are likely to accumulate at rates faster than the circulating pump can accommodate. This capacity is required to maintain a continuous skimming of the overflow perimeter edge for proper sanitary conditions in the pool. The tank can be a separate chamber of concrete or steel, or it can be integrally accommodated (as in the trench of the deck-level and rim-flow systems). The National Swimming Pool Institute recommends a minimum of $\frac{1}{2}$ gal of water for every square foot of pool surface.

Whatever overflow system is used, the coping or edge must be installed dead level and must provide a comfortable handhold for swimmers. The number of drains and the size of the piping from the overflow system must be adequate to prevent flooding of the gutters, which would interfere with the skimming of the surface water.

A comparison and evaluation of overflow systems follow:

a. *Fully recessed gutter.* No drawing is shown. This is an old-fashioned system with many drawbacks and is not recommended for YWCA pools. It is the most expensive to build, difficult to clean, and contrary to good pool operation.

b. *Semirecessed gutter.* (See Fig. 8.) Similar to fully recessed, but water level is closer to deck and gutter is easier to clean. System must be piped to surge tank.

Advantages	Disadvantages
Provides visible pool edge for competition	Water level 5 or 6 in. below deck. Difficult to climb out of pool
Cuts down surface roughness when gutters are flooded	Some cleaning difficulty
Water surface closer to deck than in fully recessed	Requires pipe tunnel for access
	Narrow edge of gutter lip provides precarious footing for diving off edge

Recommendations: Acceptable for YWCA pools.

c. *Roll out.* (Fig. 9) Basically a deck-level installation. Drains are located either in horizontal portion of shallow trench or in corner.

Advantages	Disadvantages
Comfortable pool use and egress	Decks may flood if adequate number of drains are not provided
Ideal for teaching and recreation	Pool edge not visible for competition. Temporary turning boards can be used
Gives beginner swimmers feeling of security by allowing wide visibility	Requires pipe tunnel for access
Easy cleaning	
Low construction costs	

Recommendation: Excellent for YWCA pools.

d. *Deck-level or rimflow system.* (Fig. 10.) These two systems have many similarities but they differ in their hydraulic characteristics. The *deck-level* installation has side inlets and a bottom main drain. The integral trench serves as surge capacity for surface skimming, and supply piping can be run in the trench. The *rimflow* installation has bottom inlets and the integral trench serves as the main drain. All the pool water is drawn over the edges. Both systems incorporate a precast coping and precast concrete slotted trench cover.

Advantages	Disadvantages
Trench serves as integral surge tank	Deck can flood if not properly pitched
Minimum construction costs	Pool edge not visible for competition. Temporary turning boards can be used
No pipe tunnel needed	Care must be taken in choosing cleaning materials for deck since some deck water enters pool recirculation system
Comfortable pool use and egress	
Ideal for teaching and recreation	
Gives beginner swimmers feeling of security	Bottom inlets in rimflow system are inaccessible for servicing
Easy cleaning	

Recommendation: Excellent for YWCA pools.

e. *Surface skimmers.* No drawing is shown. This system consists of container devices set in the top of the pool wall. The skimmers operate by suction of the pool pump. There is no surge tank required, and the water is constantly skimmed by movable weirs. Skimmers are not approved by all state boards of health. The disadvantages are the continuing expense and nuisance of maintaining the movable weirs and the fact that skimmers do not eliminate surface turbulence in large pools. Surface skimmers are suitable for very small pools only. They are not recommended for large YWCA pools.

f. *Prefabricated stainless steel recessed gutter.* No drawing is shown. This system is usually part of a commercial "package." The disadvantages are numerous: skimmer weirs needing manual adjustments several times a day, water-line inlets that disturb swimmers in end lanes, and exposed rings for lane and life lines among them. The main advantages are that a pipe tunnel is not required, and the manufacturer substitutes a large diameter return pipe for a surge tank. This system is not recommended for YWCA pools.

7. *Underwater lights.* Lights can be either wet-niche or dry-niche type. Dry-niche lights require a pipe tunnel or manhole for servicing. Wet-niche lights are reached from inside the pool and the fixture brought up to the deck for relamping. Follow requirements of Article 680 in the National Electrical Code.

Underwater lights are desirable for safety and for synchronized swimming programs,

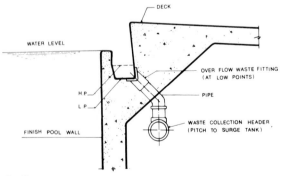

Fig. 8 Semirecessed gutter.

pool shows, and pageants. An acceptable lighting level is 1 watt per square foot of pool area.

Lights should be located in side walls only, and not directly opposite each other. Depth below water line should be at least 3 ft in the shallow area, and about 6 ft 8 in. in the diving well.

If the budget does not allow for complete installation of lights, provide conduit, junction boxes, wall niches, and other provision for future installation. Controls for underwater lights must be located in the pool office.

8. *Underwater speakers* are useful for coaching and for synchronized swimming.

9. *Decks.* Decks must completely surround the pool. For side decks, the minimum width is 5 ft, but the side used for instruction should be wider. Decks at both ends should be 13 to 15 ft wide. Decks should have nonslip surfaces, preferably of cushion edge mosaic ceramic tile 1 by 1 in. or 2 by 2 in. in size. Depth and distance markings should be in a contrasting color. Deck surface must be properly pitched to an adequate number of drains. It is important to pitch decks so that water splashed on the decks does not return to the pool. Provide corrosion proof anchors and inserts for deck equipment.

10. *Deck equipment.* Deck equipment may include diving boards (no higher than 1 meter recommended), lifeguard chair, starter blocks, and a hydraulic lift for the handicapped. Lifeguard chairs are essential for large pools as specified in state codes. Some form of vacuum cleaner must be provided. Recommended are automated pool-bottom cleaners that require only a power outlet. This kind of cleaner cuts down considerably on maintenance time.

An adequate number of recessed hot and cold hose bibbs should be provided to allow any part of the pool and natatorium to be reached with a 75-ft hose.

11. *Water circulation and filtration systems.* There are three interrelated and interacting systems required to clarify and disinfect water in the swimming pools:
- Recirculation and distribution of water
- Removal of particles by filtration
- Feeding chemicals for disinfection and control of pH

Pool water should be pumped, filtered, chemically treated, heated, and circulated continuously at a minimum turnover rate of eight hours —six hours if the pool is heavily used. Water is introduced into the pool through inlets (normally located on the sides, although the rimflow system has bottom inlets), dispersed uniformly, and removed through main bottom drains located at the deepest point of the pool. (In the rimflow system, all water is drained

over the pool edges.) Supplementary drainage is by means of the overflow system which continuously skims the surface water. The highest degree of contamination is found at or just below the water surface.

A note of caution about main bottom drains —the grating must be heavy enough so that swimmers can't remove it, and the openings must be so small that divers' fingers can't be caught in them.

Brief description of interrelated systems: Return water is piped from *main drain line* and *surge tank* through *hair and lint catcher,* pumped through a *flowmeter* to the *filters.* (Note: If vacuum-type diatomaceous earth filter is used, this kind of filter precedes the hair and lint catcher on the suction side of the pump. Granular media (sand and gravel) filters and pressure diatomaceous earth filters are on the pressure side of the pump.) Chemicals are introduced into the water through *mechanical feeders.* Then the water is heated and returned to the pool through the inlets. All equipment and piping must be sized for the recommended turnover rate.

Some recommendations:

Pumps. Pumps are preferably located below the water line, or self-priming pumps must be specified. Dual pumps should be provided, in case of breakdown.

Filters. The most commonly used filters are either pressure granular media filters (sand and gravel or anthrafilt) or pressure or vacuum diatomaceous earth filters. A comparison follows:

- Pressure granular media filters:
  High initial costs, low operating costs.
  Require little maintenance and no replacement of filter medium.
  Backwashing is simple but requires a large volume of water.
  Require large floor area. Filters are usually installed in batteries of three or four which enables one to be backwashed while the others operate. (Smaller highrate sand filters are on the market. These have been installed in a few YWCA pools recently and have proved satisfactory.)
  Traditional granular media filters are recommended for YWCAs because of their low maintenance costs and simple operation.
- Diatomaceous earth filters, pressure or vacuum:
  Low initial costs, high operating costs.
  Require extensive care. Filter medium must be replaced each time filter is backwashed.

Possibility of medium entering pool and clouding water if not skillfully handled.
Requires less water to backwash.
Diatomaceous earth does not remove some water discoloration, specifically if the water supply contains iron.
Recommended for YWCAs only if a skilled pool maintenance man is available.

Water treatment. Chlorine is the most widely accepted agent for water purification. While bromine and iodine are being used in some areas, they are much more costly and have not been given broad approval by public health authorities.

Chlorine is available in gas form, delivered in sealed tanks; as calcium hypochlorite in powder form; or as sodium hypochlorite in liquid form. Whichever form is used, application through a mechanical feeder is required. The feeder must be capable of supplying 1 lb of chlorine per eight hours for each 10,000 gal of pool water.

Chlorine gas is dangerous to handle, although less costly than other types.

Calcium hypochlorite is safer and easier to handle but is still combustible. This type is recommended for YWCA pools.

Sodium hypochlorite delivered in jars is bulky and hard to handle. The chemical breaks down under warm conditions.

All the above chemicals lower the pH factor in the water, so that an acid neutralizing agent like soda ash must be added.

Delivery, storage, and handling of pool chemicals must be taken into account when designing and locating the filter room. When the filter room is below grade, a sidewalk elevator can be provided or some means of lowering deliveries of supplies. Adequately sized doors and areaways facilitate delivery and replacement of bulky equipment. The pool filter room should have good ventilation and a water supply.

SERVICE FACILITIES

Provide space for maintenance equipment and storage, janitor's closets in strategic locations, maintenance workers' dressing rooms, office space for the chief maintenance man, and unloading and receiving facilities.

Provide public telephones and drinking fountains in convenient locations.

MECHANICAL EQUIPMENT

The proposed mechanical systems for the building must be presented and explained to the building committee and board of directors. The anticipated capability of the maintenance staff is a factor to consider in the choice of systems. Automatic controls should be considered in order to cut down on maintenance time.

If there are not sufficient funds available to complete air-conditioning systems, for example, install roughing provisions for future completion which will cause the least disruption and renovation when funds can be raised to complete the installation. Air conditioning is recommended for most YWCA buildings so that facilities can be used to their maximum effectiveness all year long.

SPECIAL FACILITIES

Two special features may or may not be included in the building plans. One is food service in the form of a cafeteria or coffee shop, and the other is residence (Figs. 11-13).

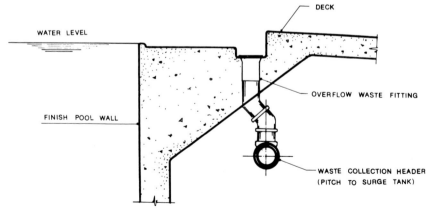

Fig. 9 Roll out.

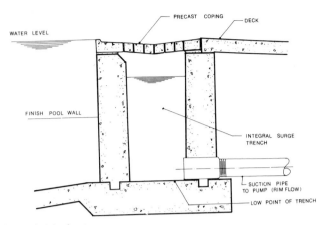

Fig. 10 Rimflow or deck level system.

The situation has changed over the years in most communities where reasonably priced meals are available in restaurants and other eating places, to the point where the YWCA may no longer provide a unique service. Often the food service operation in the YWCA now is unable to compete and again must be subsidized or closed. Private operators rightly question the use of contributors' money to subsidize a competitor and, in addition, feel that the YWCA has an unfair advantage because of its tax-free status. In some instances the association has rendered itself liable to property tax because of its food service.

The inclusion of an extensive food service operation in a new or remodeled building should be the result of an established program need for residents or for members, staff, and volunteers engaged in varied YWCA programs. Among the factors to consider in reaching the decision to include such facilities are the location of the building in relation to nearby eating places, the size of the building, the kinds of programs offered, and the numbers of people present in the building during meal hours.

The food service facilities noted earlier—a kitchen to serve group meals, kitchenette units, vending machines, and cooking facilities for residents—may suffice for food needs in a small building. In a large building, it may prove economically feasible to install more extensive facilities if the need is present.

Food Service

Cafeterias serving individual meals at cost are features associated with the YWCA for many years. Originally, food service was for the benefit of women and girls at a time when public food service was not readily available. The cafeteria idea was developed by the YWCA in many communities in order to provide whole-some food at prices employed women and girls could afford, and in a suitable atmosphere. Subsidy of such a feature was accepted as long as it was recognized as a necessary service for the girls and women for whom the organization assumed responsibility. The success of the idea and the quality and price of the food attracted other clientele, whose patronage tended to decrease the subsidy.

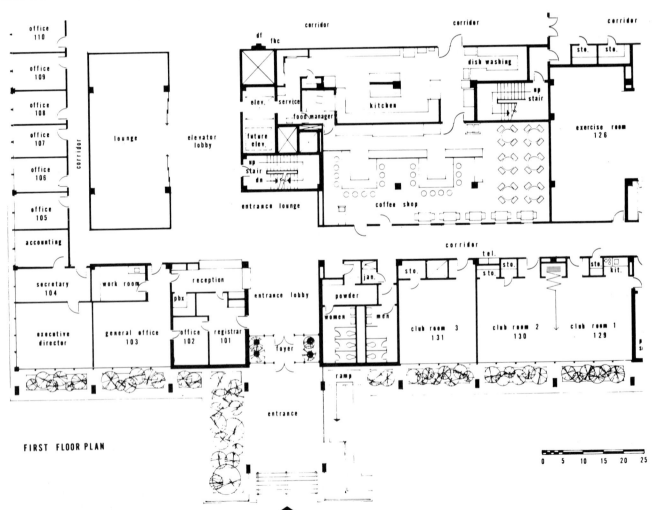

Fig. 11 Charlotte, North Carolina, YWCA, coffee shop. (J. N. Pease Associates, Architects.)

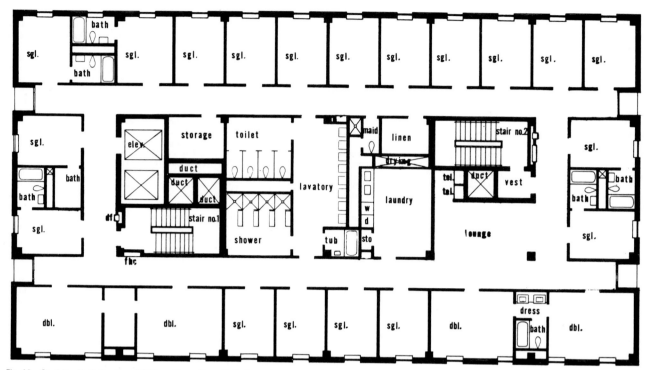

Fig. 12   Charlotte, North Carolina, YWCA, residence floor. (J. N. Pease Associates, Architects.)

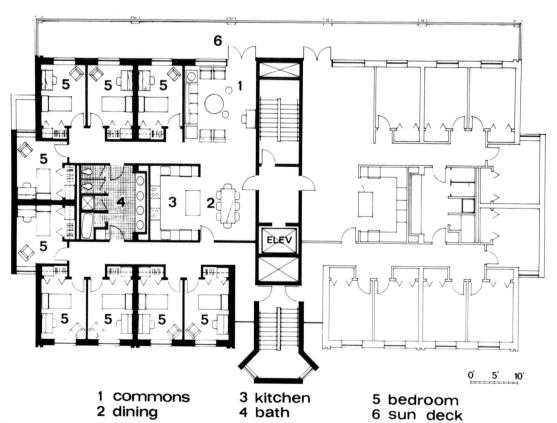

1 commons   3 kitchen   5 bedroom
2 dining   4 bath   6 sun deck

Fig. 13   YWCA of White Plains and Central Westchester, New York, residence cluster. (James D. Lothrop, Architect.)

Residences

One of the earliest services the YWCA undertook for the benefit of women and girls was that of providing housing within the budget of employed girls and offering a protected living situation. For many years that service was considered essential and sufficiently in the interest of the community and the individuals to warrant a sizable subsidy. Increasingly, as the need for the protective aspect has decreased and as other housing for employed women has become available, subsidy of YWCA residences has been withdrawn.

Because the YWCA has an obligation to maintain high standards of residence operation, a residence should not be continued nor included in a new building unless the long-term demand will be sufficient to provide enough residence income to carry the full cost of operating the unit according to these standards.

A decision to include a residence in a new YWCA building should be based on a careful study of the need for it in the years ahead as well as on current demand for that type of housing. The changes in the demand for YWCA residence facilities and the requirement that the operation pay its own way, with all legitimate costs charged to it, make the decision a serious one.

If a residence is contemplated in a new facility, it can be considered either in relation to and as a part of an activities building or as a separate unit. If it is part of an activities building, there will be certain economies in operation that will decrease operating cost. On the other hand, if demand for those facilities does not hold up, it is not easy to adapt the space to other uses; and, if that were possible, there is no assurance of a need for that much additional activities space. A separate unit may be more costly to construct and will be more expensive to operate. Services like those of the front desk must be duplicated and additional lounge and other space must be provided. The advantage of a separate unit located so that sale of it will not unduly affect the use of the activities building is that it gives a certain amount of flexibil-

ity. It must be remembered, however, that a building designed for a specific use is less salable than one that can be converted to other uses.

In an entirely separate housing unit, a large bed capacity will be required to support such things as lounge, front-desk utilities, and night service to admit late arrivals. Office space need not be provided for the business and administrative aspects if these are carried at the branch or metropolitan level. However, there should be an office for individual interviews of applicants for rooms and for counseling. Lounge space should be provided on the first floor for residents to entertain their guests and should permit supervision from the main desk. In addition, there might be a small lounge on each floor or so for the exclusive use of the residents.

If food service is provided, it should be located on the main floor so that residents can entertain guests without taking them into the living area. It takes a large residence to support food service unless it is also open to participants in the program in the activities building and/or to the public. It might be feasible to have kitchenettes with refrigerator, locker space for limited storage of food, and dining space for the permanent residents.

Most of the rooms for residents should be single. A limited number may have twin beds, but the trend is definitely toward singles for both permanent and transient use. There should be a lavatory in each of the rooms if there is no private bath. Preferably, bathrooms should provide a shower or tub and a toilet for every five to six occupants. Transient space should be separated from that for permanent residents so far as possible.

The floor space needed in permanent rooms will depend somewhat on the amount of storage space and the amount and location of built-in units. A small room can be more comfortable to live in and more easily cleaned if there is sufficient closet space. A storage room for large suitcases and boxes should be readily available so that it is possible to require that they not be kept in sleeping rooms.

In addition to a limited amount of drying

space in each room, laundry facilities should be provided for the use of permanent residents.

Built-in furniture may represent a real economy, but some furniture should be movable so that room arrangements can be changed. Electric outlets should be placed so that regrouping of furniture, including lamps, will not present the hazard of long extension cords on the floor. Provision of a bulletin-type board or some other device for hanging pictures or ornaments will save walls. Furnishings should be such that curtains and floor coverings can be changed for different color combinations.

The residence director needs a suite with bedroom, bath, living room, and a small kitchenette located where she can be aware of activity yet have privacy when off duty. Unless the residence is large enough to have a night matron on duty, the director's rooms and also one other room for a relief person should have a buzzer connected to the front door so that guests arriving after closing hours can be admitted.

There is a recent experimental trend toward providing apartments within the YWCA residence. In communities where there are industries employing large numbers of young, single women and where there is a shortage of apartments for rent, the YWCA can provide an answer to the need for private living accommodations if this can be made economically feasible.

Another experimental type of residence facility, along the lines of the Evangeline Residences in England, consists of clusters of rooms grouped around a common kitchen, dining, and living room. These clusters vary from seven to nine rooms generally and provide a small group setting.

In addition to and in conjunction with the traditional purpose of the YWCA residence, many associations provide transitional housing for girls and women with special problems. The YWCAs have used their facilities in working relationships with the Job Corps, mental hospitals, probation agencies, schools, and other agencies for housing women who need supportive, counseling, and educational facilities.

By HOWARD M. WILLIAMS, Director, National Building Consultation and Supply Services, Boys' Clubs of America

A boys' club building is what the name implies—a building designed primarily for use by boys. For that reason alone, it is unique. It should contain adequate facilities for a well-balanced program of recreational, physical, social, and educational activities. The size of the facilities should be in proportion to the number of boys to be served, and facilities should be provided to serve approximately one-fourth of the active membership of a boys' club at any time. Where permitted, single-story buildings are highly desirable because they are easier to supervise than multistory structures. Avoid construction of buildings with more than two stories because of increasing cost of fireproof or fire-resistant building materials. Roof playgrounds also are not recommended because they are expensive to construct and difficult to keep free from leaks.

Types of Space

A boys' club building contains two general types of space—program and service. The program space is divided into recreational, social, educational, and physical areas. (1) Recreational space includes a games room for "midgets," juniors, and intermediates and a lounge for older boys. (2) Social program space consists of clubrooms and lounges. (3) Educational program space contains rooms for shops, classes, and library. (4) Physical program space consists of a gymnasium, natatorium, special exercise room, and dressing and shower rooms. (5) Service space includes offices, toilet rooms, stairs, corridors, storage rooms, and boiler rooms. Usually the percentage of boy capacity of a building is distributed as follows:

Physical education facilities . . . . 40 percent
Recreational facilities . . . . 25 percent
Educational facilities. . . . . 25 percent
Social facilities . . . . 10 percent

A kitchen is also essential. In many clubs, kitchens are used for social events and cooking classes, and by boards of directors, women's auxiliaries, mothers' clubs, parents' clubs, and service organizations.

It is desirable to provide some space for health services, such as physical and dental examinations, but a room designed expressly for this purpose is not essential. If a club has a visitors' or girls' dressing room, it can be easily adapted. (See Figs. 1 to 3.)

With the exception of the games room and the dressing rooms, boys should not be required to pass through one activity space to reach another. If all facilities cannot be placed on one floor, it is desirable to locate activity spaces accommodating large numbers of boys, such as games rooms, gymnasiums, swimming pool, and locker rooms, on the first floor within easy access of the lobby.

Locate offices and control desks or counters at strategic points along lanes of travel where one staff member can overlook or give visual supervision to two or more areas. Offices and toilet rooms should be adjacent to the lobby,

Manual on Boys' Clubs Building, Planning, and Construction.

games room, or corridors, thereby accessible without passing through an activity area.

Provide as much storage space as possible within the limitations of the structure. It is a well-known fact that most boys' clubs do not have adequate space for storage of equipment and operating supplies. A roomy closet on each floor for maintenance supplies is also essential. This closet should contain a slop sink and shelves and should be large enough for mops, brooms, a polishing machine, vacuum cleaner, and other cleaning supplies. This room should be well ventilated.

There is no basis for determining the minimum amount of storage space which should be provided, but again, few boys' clubs ever have enough. Some authorities estimate that at least 4 percent of the total floor area should be allocated to storage. Too often, when limited funds require a plan to be reduced in size, the storerooms are first in the process of elimination. When sufficient storage space has not been provided, it generally becomes necessary to use some activity space for this purpose, thus reducing the amount of service which can be rendered to boys.

Minimum office space in a building includes room for the following: general office or control desk, executive office, and an office for the physical director. An office for other staff members is desirable but not essential.

Other Facilities Which May Be Added:

Regulation gymnasium (60 by 80 ft)
Swimming pool
Additional rooms, which might include a room for older boys
Health examination room
Larger kitchen

Additional offices for staff members
Enlarged or additional crafts rooms
More storage space
Group club rooms and an auditorium, depending upon requirements of the community

When planning a small boys' club building, it is important to bear in mind the possibility of future expansion. It is especially desirable to

consider the addition of a swimming pool, no matter how remote the idea may appear at the time. A minimum boys' club building should contain facilities for 100 boys (in simultaneous occupancy). Minimum facilities should include the items indicated in Table 1.

TABLE 1   Minimum Facilities for Building

Room	Approx. minimum dimensions, ft	Boy capacity
Games room.	28 by 42	42
Gymnasium (not necessarily regulation size)	30 by 60 with 20-ft ceiling	30
Dressing room	15 by 24	(30)
Library-group meetings	17 by 17	14
Crafts room	17 by 18	14
Toilet rooms		
Storage rooms		
Offices		
Kitchen		
Total boy capacity. .		100

RECREATIONAL ACTIVITY SPACE

Games Room

The games room is one place in a boys' club where any boy may participate. The high cost of construction and supervision has made it necessary to reduce the number of games rooms to one or two. It is desirable to have separate rooms for the younger and older boys. Most clubs prefer a midget-junior room and a senior lounge.

Twenty-five to thirty percent of the boy capacity of a building should be devoted to recreational or games room activities. The basis for determining the size of a games room is as follows:

Cadets or "midgets" . . . . 20 sq ft per boy
Juniors . . . . 25 sq ft per boy
Intermediates. . . . . 25 sq ft per boy
Seniors . . . . 30 sq ft per boy

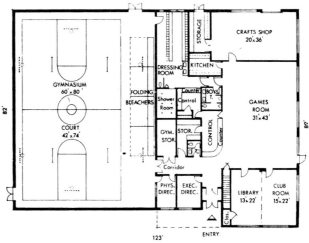

Fig. 1   Boys' Club (building 136).

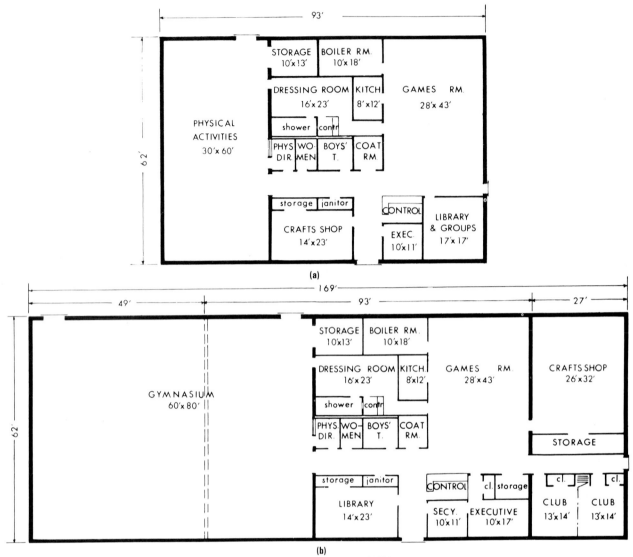

Fig. 2 Boys' Club building 100-200. (a) Unit one, regular program capacity: 100 boys simultaneously. (b) Unit two, regular program capacity: 200 boys simultaneously.

Where it is necessary to provide for more than one age group in a games room, the largest square foot factor should be used.

Locate the general games room near the club entrance. It is desirable to locate the senior lounge where it can receive some supervision from the general games room attendant.

Provide a variety of games for individual and group participation in the general games room. The room and equipment should be flexible enough to permit games tables to be rearranged or changed to meet the needs of the membership. Games tables should be sturdy and *not* fastened to the floor. Most tables are 30 in. high; some should be lower for use by younger members.

Where space and funds for building are limited, it is often necessary to combine programs in one room. It has been established that certain craft activities can be carried on in a games room. These should be of a quiet nature, such as soap carving, plastic pins, gimp work, leathercraft, shell craft and bead or cork work. (Activities such as woodworking are obviously not practical.) These programs may be operated simultaneously rather than

closing down the games activities, but combined activities should be considered only as a last resort.

There should be a counter for storage and display of game equipment that can be checked.

The older boys' or senior room should be a combination lounge and games room. Equipment should include games tables, easy chairs and sofas, a piano, hi-fi or television, and a writing desk. However, where space for building is limited, the basic facilities of a boys' club must be included first.

Games room ceilings should be at least 12 ft high to minimize damage from pool cues. Acoustical treatment is highly recommended.

SOCIAL ACTIVITY SPACE

Club Rooms

Every boys' club should have at least one room for group meetings, and larger clubs usually need about three group club rooms. For maxi-

mum use of these rooms, they should be located adjacent to each other and separated by sound-resistant, flush-folding partitions. These folding partitions permit flexible combinations of small rooms, one small and one large room, or just one very large room to accommodate any type of meeting, luncheon, or dinner.

A kitchen should be located adjacent to the club room or within proximity for snacks, meals, and luncheon or dinner meetings. Ample storage rooms are essential to accommodate equipment.

Fifteen square feet per boy is the basis for determining the size of a club room, minimum capacity for this room being not less than 10 boys.

Kitchen

A kitchen is one of the minimum essentials for a boys' club building. This room should be large enough to accommodate cooking classes. The kitchen may also be used in combination with a canteen. (See Fig. 4.)

Kitchens should have ranges, refrigerators,

sinks, and cabinets of sizes and capacities proportionate to the room area and to the extent to which they will be used. The average club kitchen seldom prepares and serves food to groups exceeding 100. Service for larger gatherings (banquets, etc.) is generally delegated to local caterers who are better equipped.

EDUCATIONAL ACTIVITY SPACE

Crafts Shops

Larger boys' club buildings usually have several rooms devoted to arts and crafts. These may include space for fine arts, ceramics, woodworking, photography, and small crafts.

The importance or popularity of arts and crafts in a boys' club depends on the leadership available and the geographical location of the community. Usually every club has one room set up for woodworking because it is popular with boys all year long. If this room has a variety of tools and enough electrical 110- and 220-volt outlets, it is possible to vary the arts and crafts classes to conform with members' desires.

A crafts room to accommodate at least 20 boys is desirable. Leadership available for various crafts will determine the size of classes, but the minimum should be space for 20 boys. In a small club, a room for 14 boys is acceptable.

Forty-five square feet per boy is the basis for determining the size of a woodworking shop. This includes space for workbenches, some storage cabinets, power tools, and aisles. Forty square feet per boy is acceptable for a woodworking shop without machine tools. The size of a room for small arts and crafts is determined on the basis of 35 sq ft per boy.

Since many crafts use the same tools, it is possible and desirable to carry on more than one craft at the same time in the same room, provided there is ample storage space and leadership. There is a definite trend toward having one large room to accommodate all arts and crafts. Such rooms are equipped for lapidary or ceramics, woodworking, and electronics. Larger clubs usually have a separate room for art work. Some may have two or more shops.

Every arts and crafts room should have ample storage space for tools, materials, and unfinished projects. A separate finishing room for painting handicrafts is desirable. This room should be well ventilated with access to the outside so that fumes from painting and paint staining will not remain.

Provide a sink with both hot and cold water in every arts and crafts room.

Library

The library is usually located along a route which large numbers of boys use to travel through the building. The room should be attractively furnished so boys will want to go in to read or do homework. The library should be able to accommodate about 10 percent of the daily boy attendance. The acceptable basis for determining the size of a library is to allow for not less than 20 nor more than 25 sq ft per boy. This is sufficient to include space for furniture, bookshelves, and a desk for the librarian.

If space is available, two or three study cubicles are very desirable.

Adjustable bookshelves, not exceeding 5 ft in height, should be located along one wall. Additional shelves may be added as required. Informal furniture is suggested and should include round tables, straight-back chairs, low stools, easy chairs, librarian's desk, and a magazine rack. All furniture should be sturdy enough to withstand the rigors of use by youth. Some small chairs and tables for the seven- and eight-year-olds are recommended, since this group cannot sit comfortably in regular chairs at regular table height.

A small reading room should have a variety of furniture suitable for space limitations. Provide at least one table.

PHYSICAL ACTIVITY SPACE

Gymnasium

A boys' club building, especially if it is to be used by older boys, should have a gymnasium large enough to provide at least a regulation junior high school basketball court. The gymnasium, however, should be more than just a basketball court. Floors and overhead construction should be strong enough to support various types of gymnastic equipment. The most desirable size for a gymnasium is 60 by 80 ft overall inside dimensions. Such a room will accommodate a 42- by 74-ft regulation junior high school basketball court with minimum 3-ft sidelines around three sides, and five rows of folding bleachers along the fourth side. Two 40- by 60-ft cross or practice courts can also be included in this area. These are desirable not only for basketball but also for volleyball, etc. Senior high school and college size courts are acceptable when funds for construction and space are available.

As noted, small buildings with inadequate gymnasiums are undesirable when older boys are to be served. However, in minimum-sized buildings or when extension or branch clubs are planned, smaller gymnasiums are acceptable.

Space for spectators is needed in any gymna-

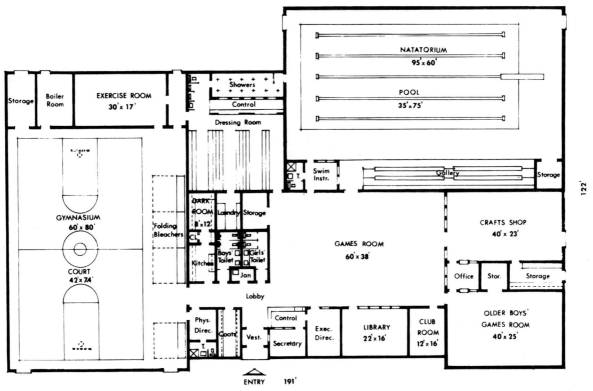

Fig. 3 Boys' Club building. (a) 215–320. (b) 288–393.

sium regardless of size. This space should be on the gymnasium floor where it can be easily supervised. Second-story balconies for spectators are costly to construct, difficult to supervise, and usually do not permit full vision of all parts of the gymnasium floor. Folding bleachers are best for use in spectator space, but movable bleachers are acceptable. There should be no permanent bleachers or chairs on the gymnasium floor because they present a hazard to participants in the physical program and reduce the width of the room for cross-court purposes. Generally, the maximum number of spectator seats is 150. In some communities, much more spectator space might be wanted.

Clear height from floor to bottom of trusses must be 20 ft for a 60- by 80-ft gymnasium. Amateur Athletic Union rules and some building codes require more than 20 ft of clear height.

Many boys' club gymnasiums are used at times as auditoriums. Very often a stage is provided at one end. However, because some building codes place so many conditions and restrictions on built-in stages, it is not always economical to provide one. In such cases, portable stages or platforms may be used.

A good-sized storage room for gym equipment is essential. Doors to these rooms should be 6 ft wide and 7 ft high to accommodate flat mat trucks and a trampoline.

An office for the physical director is necessary. This should be located on the same level with the gym floor and preferably in a spot where people will not have to cross the gym floor to reach it.

Simultaneous use by 40 boys is considered maximum capacity for a gymnasium, as it is difficult for one instructor to handle any more at one time.

Swimming Pool

An indoor swimming pool is a tremendous attraction to the boys' club. Swimming is one of the most beneficial activities in maintaining physical fitness and health. A swimming pool encourages cleanliness and personal hygiene, since each boy must take a shower with warm water and soap just before entering a pool. Swimming is a group activity that helps build self-confidence and gives each boy a chance to play with his friends and develop socially. In surveys of popular boys' activities, swimming is at the top of the list.

The 30- by 75- and 35- by 75-ft pools have been recommended as desirable sizes for boys' clubs by the Boys' Clubs of America National Committee on Aquatics. The Amateur Athletic Union's requirement for the length of a pool is 75 ft 1 in. in order to take care of any irregularities in construction. A boys' club swimming pool should never be less than 60 ft in length. Since there is very little difference in cost between a 60- or 75-ft pool, the shorter pool should be considered only when site limitations prohibit a 75-ft pool. The minimum size is 25 by 60 ft. Other sizes are 30 by 60 ft, 25 by 75 ft, 30 by 75 ft, 35 by 75 ft, 42 by 75 ft, and T-shaped pools with a tank of either 30 by 75 ft or 35 by 75 ft.

Seventy-five-foot pools are acceptable for competitive swimming. The recommended width of swimming lanes is 6 ft for pools up to 30 ft in width, and 7 ft for pools 35 ft and over in width.

Space for spectators should be provided in the swimming pool room. Most state public health regulations require spectator space to be separated from the pool deck to prevent people in street shoes from walking on the deck. It is desirable to have the spectators' gallery near the pool deck level, not at second-

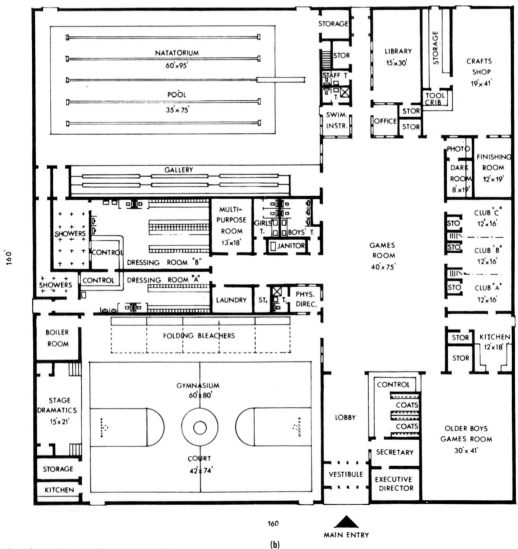

Fig. 3 (cont.)   Boys' Club building. (a) 215-320. (b) 288-393.

758

story height. The gallery is needed for parents and visitors and also for class instruction.

Overall minimum ceiling heights in natatoriums are sometimes determined by local ordinances. In any case, the minimum clear height in the diving area should be not less than 15 ft above the diving board. This clear height should be maintained for a minimum distance of 10 ft in front and 5 ft to the rear of the front or tip, and at least 10 ft on each side of the diving board.

Boys' club swimming pools should have 1-meter diving boards only. Three-meter boards and diving towers are not recommended because they are very difficult to supervise.

Depth of the swimming pool at the deep end should be not less than 8 ft 6 in. in front of a 1-meter diving board. Depth at the shallow end should start at 3 ft and slope to 3 ft 6 in. in a distance of 22½ ft for a pool 60 ft long and 35 ft for a 75-ft pool. Although local regulations may dictate otherwise, the foregoing is recommended for boys' club pools because more shallow-water area is desired for teaching purposes. If local or state codes require the pool floor to be pitched more, a variance should be obtained.

Minimum recommended width for decks around any pool is 5 ft. A 10-ft-wide deck on one side (preferably the side with the spectators' gallery) is useful for instruction purposes. The recommended width of the deck at the diving end of the pool is 13 ft 6 in.

Windows in the natatorium should be carefully planned. If they face south and/or west, the windows should be close to the ceiling. Large windows, especially those facing south and west, permit too much sunlight to enter the room. Excessive natural light places too much glare on the pool surface, thus making it difficult for the swimming instructor or lifeguard to see the bathers. Too much sunlight also encourages the growth of algae, which will make the water cloudy. Many colleges, universities and boys' clubs are now building natatoriums with no exterior windows of any kind. Since artificial illumination is used whenever the pool is in operation, windows are not needed. (See Fig. 5.)

Underwater lights are desirable not only for their esthetic value but also for safety, as they make it possible for the instructor to see all boys in the pool. These lights should be cast into the concrete walls and staggered along the sides of a pool for even distribution of light. They should never be located directly opposite each other. Do not place underwater lights in the ends of a pool.

Most state public health regulations require public and semipublic swimming pools to use the "recirculation" water purification system. This means water is continually drawn from the pool and replaced by freshly processed water. The drawn-off water is screened, filtered, chemically treated, and heated until restored to its original purity.

Recirculation pools can be divided into two categories: The conventional scum gutter and the water level or flush deck. The physical difference between the two is that the former has a scum gutter set into the walls of the pool, while the water level deck has moved the gutter from the side walls to the deck. Water level in the scum gutter pools varies from several inches to as much as 2 ft below the decks; water in the flush deck pool is always within ½ in. of deck level.

The primary operational difference is that many state public health ordinances require water entering scum gutter drains to flow directly to the sewer. Any water drawn off through the scum gutter is thus irretrievably

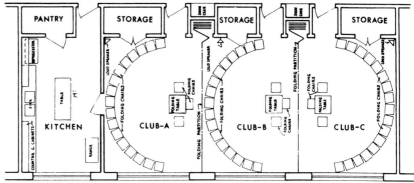

Fig. 4 Three-club-kitchen combination. Serving 20 boys per hour in each club room.

lost, as is the heat it contains. Water overflowing into the drains of the water level deck pool is carried to a balancing tank or reservoir where it is held until it is chemically treated and the pump can recirculate it through the filters back to the pool. No large quantities of water or heat are lost in this process.

The idea of water level deck swimming pools originated in Boys' Clubs of America in the late 1930s. Since that time most new boys' club pools have used the design, as have recreation departments, schools, the U.S. Navy, the Royal Canadian Air Force, and various youth organizations. Water level deck pools are ideal for teaching swimming. The instructor does not have to stand at the very edge of the pool to see everyone in the water, and nonswimmers feel safer because they can see the whole room and the instructor. This is not true of some of the old scum gutter pools where the bather can see only the ceiling and the sides of the pool. Nonswimmers and beginners also feel safer in a flush deck pool because they can get out of it at any point around the pool's perimeter merely by placing hands on the deck and kicking the feet. Ladders are not necessary, although some local ordinances require their installation. Actually, ladders are more of a liability than an asset in water level deck pools, but if they are required by law, make sure that they are the removable type.

Water level deck pools must be carefully designed so that all water washed over the decks will drain quickly into the overflow trenches. Overflow water must never be permitted to wash back into the pool. Also, to be efficient, the reservoir or balancing tank *must* have sufficient capacity to store the overflow water until it is recirculated through the filter system and pumped back into the pool.

Chlorine is the most widely acceptable agent for purifying pool water. Bromide, iodine, and other chemicals are also used, but these have not been approved by all public health authorities. There are two types of chlorine—liquid and gas. Gas chlorine is less expensive than liquid, but it is extremely poisonous and is dangerous if handled incorrectly or if a leak should develop in the tank in which it is stored. Several times during any given year, articles appear in newspapers about the many people who are critically or fatally injured because of a chlorine leak or because a tank of chlorine gas fell off a truck and exploded. Some cities now prohibit use of gas chlorine in swimming pools. Liquid chlorine is a bit more expensive but much less dangerous. It will bleach dyes and eat holes in woolen material, and it is poisonous if taken internally in its concentrated form. But liquid chlorine will not contaminate the atmosphere. Chlorine can be purchased as a liquid or in powder or tablet form to be dissolved in water. It should be fed into the water

recirculation system by means of a mechanical chemical feeder to ensure proper dosage and mixing.

Filters most commonly used for boys' club swimming pools are the pressure sand and gravel filters and the vacuum diatomaceous earth filter. In recent years, high flow pressure sand filters have been developed. These are smaller and less costly than the sand and gravel filters. No matter which type is chosen, filters and the pumps used with them should be of sufficient capacity to recirculate the pool water at least every eight, or more preferably, every six hours.

Dressing Rooms

Dressing rooms should be located adjacent to and on the same level with the gymnasium and/or swimming pool.

Before the size of a dressing room is determined, consideration should be given to the climate of the area in which the boys' club is to be located, the age groups and number of boys to be served, and the activities requiring dressing room use. As a general rule, for the younger or midget group, small lockers approximately 12- by 12- by 12-in. are recommended. In most cases, the small lockers are also suitable for the junior group. The 12- by 12- by 30-in. double-tier locker is recommended for intermediates and seniors. Regardless of the size of lockers, there should be enough to accommodate the maximum capacity of the gymnasium and/or swimming pool plus an equal number to provide for change in groups —this means a gymnasium with 40-boy capacity should have 80 lockers (see Fig. 6).

Minimum distance between rows of lockers should be 8 ft 6 in., measured from back to back of lockers. This allows a minimum of 12 in. on each side for lockers, 16 in. for a bench attached to the base of each row of lockers, and 3 ft 10 in. for aisle space. Benches are essential in dressing rooms, regardless of the type of lockers used.

Basket and bag systems are acceptable under certain conditions. They are less expensive than lockers and occupy less space. The principal objection to these systems is the difficulty in managing them. An attendant has to handle each basket or bag four times to service one boy.

It is essential to provide toilet facilities close to the shower room entrance. If such facilities are not immediately available, the shower room floor will be used as a substitute. When a dressing room is used to service a swimming pool, toilet facilities are usually required by law. Small dressing rooms should have at least one water closet, urinal, and lavatory; large dressing rooms should have two of each. The use of dressing room toilet facilities for the

PLAN

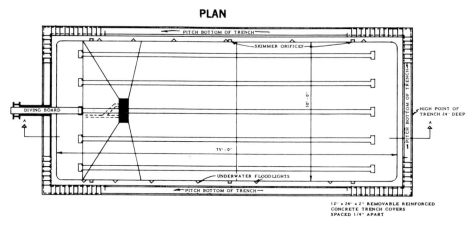

SECTION A-A

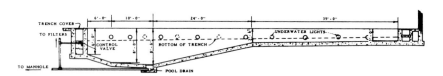

Fig. 5 Natatorium.

entire boys' club is not recommended, since such combined use increases problems in supervision and results in water being tracked into the club.

Plan locker rooms so the attendant in the control cage can see the entire room and also the shower room.

Shower Room

The number of shower heads recommended for a dressing room serving a gymnasium is five. The number of shower heads recommended for a swimming pool dressing room is twelve.

Shower heads should be suspended from the ceiling with the bottom of the head not less than 8 ft nor more than 9 ft above the floor. Ceiling shower heads, rigid and without ball joints, are recommended because four boys can shower under one head. Wall shower heads can accommodate a maximum of two boys.

Any wall projections in shower rooms are a source of injury to boys.

SERVICE SPACE

Executive's and Secretary's Offices

Locate the secretary's office directly adjacent to the club entrance so the person working there can see who enters or leaves during the morning and afternoon when the building is not completely staffed.

The executive's office should be next to the secretary's office and also close to the club entrance, where it is easily accessible to boys, parents, and visitors.

In communities where the boys' club has one or more branches or where the club must have a more complex office arrangement, the unit director's office should be adjacent to the entrance. The secretary's and executive's offices and a workroom may be located in a different section of the building.

Windows are recommended for interior walls so the executive can see what is going on outside. Provide venetian blinds or draw curtains

over these windows to ensure complete privacy during consultations and interviews.

Control Counters

As previously stated, control counters should be located where the attendant can see the area to be served as well as other areas.

Height of control counters should be no more than 40 in. A low section of 33 in. for young boys to fill out membership applications is recommended.

Games control counters should have cabinets below them for storage of supplies.

Toilet Rooms

Locate boys' toilet rooms adjacent to the lobby or corridor where they are easily accessible. It is desirable to have toilet entrances near a con-

trol desk from which an attendant can see those who enter or leave the room.

Local codes in many cities and states govern the minimum number of water closets, urinals and lavatories which must be installed in public buildings. These are usually determined by the maximum capacity of a building. In communities having no codes or ordinances requiring adequate toilet facilities, the following formula is recommended:

1 water closet (toilet) for each 50 boys
1 urinal for each 50 boys
1 lavatory for each 100 boys

Wall-hung water closets, lavatories, and urinals are preferred. Some wall-hung urinals should be set lower than standard heights to accommodate small boys. Stall urinals are acceptable. With fixtures on the walls, floors are easier to clean.

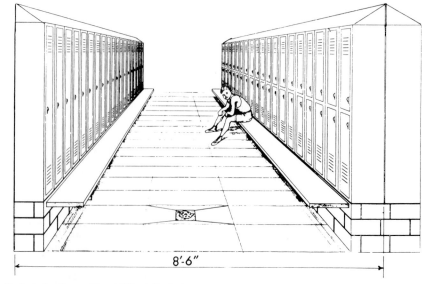

Fig. 6 Locker diagram. 60- and 30-in. double-tier lockers.

760

Recreation buildings should be functionally designed to make possible a varied program of activities for all ages and both sexes. These buildings should be designed and dedicated to meet the needs of all people in their respective neighborhoods and communities.

Recreation buildings should provide a safe, healthful, and attractive atmosphere in which every person in the community or neighborhood has the opportunity to enjoy his leisure by participation in activities of a social, creative, cultural, or physical nature.

Planning Areas and Facilities for Health, Physical Education, and Recreation, rev. 1966, The Athletic Institute, Merchandise Mart, Chicago, Ill., American Association for Health, Physical Education, and Recreation, Washington, D.C.

Due to advances in medical science, people live longer. Thus, the percentage of the aging in our population is increasing. In addition, it is approximated that one out of seven people in our nation has a permanent disability. Therefore, there is a greater challenge than ever before to prevent the construction of architectural barriers which make it difficult for the aging and the disabled to participate in the recreation program.

Almost without exception, recreation areas require some type of structure which will fulfill program needs and yet blend aesthetically into its surroundings. In terms of function, building types may range from the simple picnic shelter to the complex community recreation building with its variety of special service facilities. Such buildings may vary in design from the rustic, depicting the style of early colonial

days, to the contemporary, representing the most modern architectural concepts.

In many neighborhoods and communities, school facilities are adequately equipped to provide recreation programs for youth, but other existing age groups are not always served. In such instances, the community must depend upon public recreation facilities which are planned and operated independently to accommodate a recreation program for the total community. Since the school is an integral part of the community, it should have a part in the planning of public recreation facilities. Conversely, when school buildings are being designed, cooperative planning with community recreation authorities is essential in order to assure that the new structures will include facilities needed for joint school and community use.

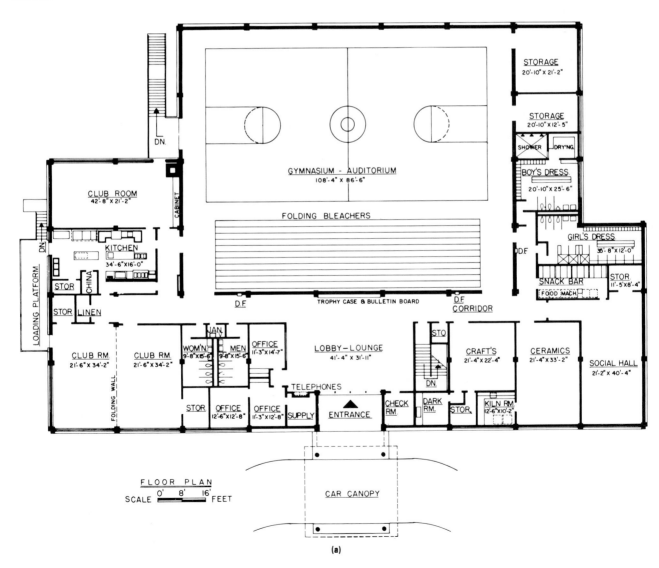

(a)

Fig. 1 Collett Street Recreation Center, Morganton, N.C.

Government and Public
RECREATION CENTERS

PLANNING OBJECTIVES

The planning and designing of a recreation building demand a precise and logical approach. Since a recreation building reflects the unique needs of a neighborhood or community, the specific plans and design will vary, but the preliminary considerations and planning objectives will be the same.

The successful incorporation of accepted planning objectives will ensure maximum utilization of the building. The preliminary plans and the continuous reevaluation of the functional design of the building prior to its construction should be considered in terms of the following questions:

• Has the most effective use of the entire area been determined, and does it utilize all of the natural resources?

• Does the preliminary plan include all of the essential areas and facilities necessary to fulfill the program objectives?

• Does the design provide for flexibility in use and for future expansion?

• Does the floor plan permit convenient access to, and facilitate circulation within, the building?

• Does the floor plan provide for ease in supervision and administration of the building?

• Have individual rooms been located and designed so as to encourage multiple use within safety limits?

• Has the building been designed so as to ensure opportunity for its use by all members of the community, including the aging and disabled?

• Does the design encompass accepted aesthetic qualities that relate harmoniously with the surroundings?

• Is the building designed and constructed so as to ensure joint use with other public or private agencies?

• Is the building so designed that it will permit economy in construction and maintenance?

CLASSIFICATION OF RECREATION BUILDINGS

Growth in the scope and complexity of the recreation program has created a need for buildings which will provide facilities adapted for a wide variety of recreation activities. Unlike many of the early structures, present-day buildings provide for adaptability and multiple use. This change from the simple to the complex has stimulated the development of a variety of recreation buildings. These are classified by function and then categorized by size.

The standards used for determining the size requirements of recreation buildings are usually based upon a square-footage-to-population ratio. This may be determined by allowing 1 to 2 sq ft per person to be served. For example, if the building is to serve 8,000 persons, it should be approximately 12,000 sq ft in size. This footage ratio may vary where cities build one center to accommodate the entire population.

Type I Recreation Buildings

The plans in Fig. 1. illustrate a Type I recreation building. This type of building is usually constructed in larger subdivisions or suburban areas of a metropolis. However, recent trends reveal that many smaller cities (30,000 or less) have constructed such facilities to serve the total community.

This type of building encloses 20,000 sq ft or more and usually includes the following facilities:

Multipurpose	Game room
Gymnasium	Photography room
Shower and locker rooms	Office (administration)
	Office (staff)
Club rooms	Rest rooms
Arts and crafts room	Kitchen
Lounge and lobby	Large storage areas

Type II Recreation Buildings

The Type II recreation building is illustrated in Fig. 2. This is the most common type and can be used in any city or community. It is believed by many recreation experts that the most efficiently operated building is the one designed to accommodate a neighborhood or area of approximately 8,000 persons.

This building encloses 10,000 to 20,000 sq ft and includes basically the same facilities as the Type I structure. Room sizes may vary and emphasis may be placed on those facilities that will best serve the program objectives.

Type III Recreation Buildings

These buildings are used in many communities to satisfy the needs of less populated areas and usually include most of the following facilities (Fig. 3):

Social hall or gymnasium
Shower-dressing room
Club room
Lobby-lounge
Office
Rest rooms
Kitchenette
Adequate storage areas

Social Hall–Gymnasium

In order to obtain maximum benefit from the social hall-gymnasium, this facility is ordinarily used for a variety of social activities, such as folk, square, and social dancing, banquets, and roller skating, in addition to basketball and other forms of athletics.

The size of a community recreation building's social hall-gymnasium should be at least 90 by 100 ft, with a minimum height of 22 ft. This will permit a basketball court of 50 by 84 ft.

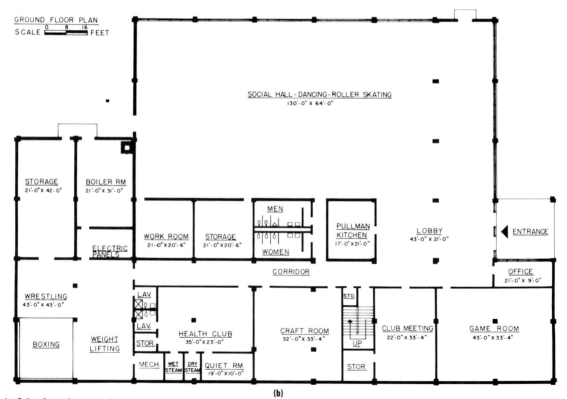

Fig. 1 (cont.) Collett Street Recreation Center, Morganton, N.C.

762

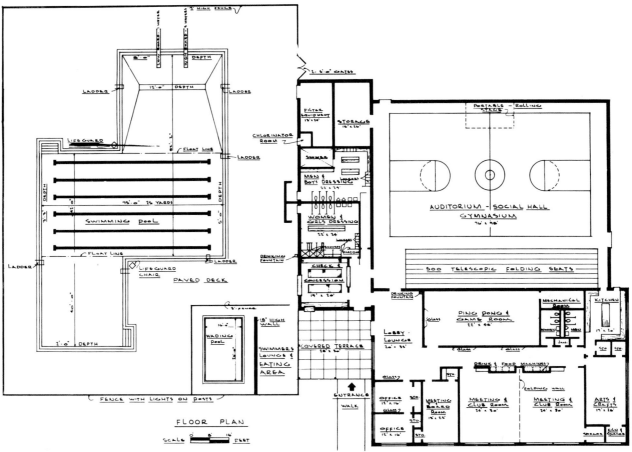

FLOOR PLAN

Fig. 2 Thomaston-Upson County Recreation Center, Thomaston, Ga.

These dimensions will permit seven tiers of telescopic bleachers on one side of the social hall-gymnasium, seating approximately 325 spectators.

Provision should be made for a mechanical ventilating system (forced air). The wainscoting should provide clear, unobstructed wall space from the floor to a height of 12 ft. If the room contains windows, they should be placed above the wainscoting on the sides and should be provided with protective guards. There should be no windows at either end of the social hall-gymnasium.

It is preferable to have no windows in a social hall-gymnasium as they have little functional value. If it is necessary to use windows, they should be placed on the north side, or if used on two sides, then on the north and south, never on the east or west. Where sky domes are installed, they should be waterproof, and the room should be equipped with vent domes and exhaust fans for ventilation.

Maple flooring is commonly used. The cork spring clip or other type expansion joint should be installed on all four sides. If suspended apparatus is used in the social hall-gymnasium and wall attachments for control ropes and chains are affixed to the wall, these attachments should be at least 7 ft above the floor level and should be recessed.

This room should be equipped with stainless steel or aluminum portable and removable handrails attached to all wall surfaces, and also along the face of folding bleachers to provide a handhold for roller skaters.

Whenever possible, noncontact (nonmarring) furniture should be used. Design characteris-tics of such furniture also facilitate safer use by the aging and disabled.

In a masonry building, particularly in one with concrete reinforced frame, stainless-steel eyebolts should be installed in each corner and at each column for the hanging of decorations for special parties. These bolts should be located within 12 ft of the ceiling in the smaller rooms, and at least 15 ft high in the social hall-gymnasium. The use of eyebolts will eliminate the necessity of driving nails or screws into the walls.

THE COMMUNITY RECREATION BUILDING

The community recreation building functions beyond the primary purpose of serving a single neighborhood. It is designed to offer a more diversified program in order to meet the complete recreational needs of all people in the community. The community building is normally larger than a neighborhood building and is usually located in a major recreation area such as a community park or playing field.

As stated previously, community recreation buildings vary in function and design, but, generally, they contain most of the facilities described on the following pages.

Multipurpose Room

The multipurpose room should be designed to accommodate such activities as general meetings, social recreation, active table games, dancing, dramatics, orchestra practice, concerts, and banquets.

The area of this room should be approximately 2,000 to 3,000 sq ft. It should be rectangular in shape with a minimum width of 40 ft. The minimum ceiling height should be at least 16 ft.

The floor should have a nonskid surface to prevent many common accidents. The floor should also be level in order to permit multiple use for meetings, dancing, dramatic presentations, etc.

Stage

A stage and related facilities are frequently included in a community center. They may be built in conjunction with the multipurpose room or, preferably, as a separate unit.

The stage proper should be about 20 ft in depth, and the proscenium opening should be at least two-thirds the width of the room. It is desirable that the approach to the stage from the floor of the main room be by inclined ramp with a nonskid surface to facilitate the physically disabled and aging and to accommodate the movement of equipment.

Consideration might be given to the construction of an outdoor stage contiguous to the multipurpose room. Some buildings have been successfully constructed with a revolving stage for outdoor and indoor programs. Portable or recessed stages might also be considered.

It is desirable that the room be equipped with a modern public-address system, permanently installed with matched speakers and with outlets for additional microphones and phonographic equipment. Consideration should be

763

given to a master control from the office of the building. All stage lighting should be modern and should be controlled from a dimmer-control cabinet equipped with a rheostat. Provisions should also be made for television installation.

Recessed drinking fountains and cuspidors should be provided and should be located in areas where they will cause a minimum amount of interference. Water fountains should be hand or hand-and-foot operated, with up-front spouts and controls. Protective floor covering or drainage at the base of the fountain should be considered to avoid floor damage.

Dressing-Locker Room

A room for the purpose of changing clothes is necessary and should be in close proximity to the social hall-gymnasium. There are two accepted plans for checking personal apparel: (1) The use of locker rooms with metal lockers; and (2) The use of dressing rooms with a checkroom for checking clothing in wire baskets or nylon bags.

Locker Room If the lockers are to be used in connection with outdoor sports, they should be located so the players will have access to them without going through the entire building. The suggested requirements for the locker room in a community recreation building are as follows: for men and boys, 200 lockers; for women and girls, 150 lockers. The placement of lockers should take into account the space requirements of the disabled.

The floor of the locker room should pitch to a central drain or drains to facilitate cleaning and washing. The junction of the wall and floor should be coved. In the women's locker room,

dressing booths should be supplied in the ratio of 10 percent of the total number of lockers. Hair driers and nonbreakable liquid-soap dispensers are also recommended.

Dressing Room with Checkroom The use of galvanized-wire baskets or nylon or plastic bags is growing in popularity. This system will accommodate the same number of users in about one-fourth of the space required for metal lockers. However, there is no saving of space required for dressing.

If there is a possibility of a swimming pool being constructed on this site at some future time, dressing rooms should be located and arranged so as to serve both the gymnasium and the pool.

Shower Rooms

The size of shower rooms is dependent upon the extent of the facilities and the number of persons to be served at one time. Adequate ventilation should be a primary consideration.

For men and boys, it is suggested that approximately 12 shower heads be provided, spaced a minimum of 4 ft apart and 6 ft above the floor level. For women and girls, it is recommended that a minimum of 6 group shower heads and 3 individual shower-and-dressing booths be provided. Shower heads should be 4 1/2 ft above the floor level. Nonbreakable liquid-soap dispensers are recommended, and hair driers are suggested for the ladies' locker room.

To accommodate the disabled, two folding "L" seats should be placed in opposite corners of each group shower to facilitate both right-hand and left-hand approaches.

In the construction of the shower-room

floor, drainage gutters 4 in. deep and 8 to 10 in. wide placed around the perimeter of the shower room will provide a sanitary means of drainage. The central portion of the shower floor, raised above the depressed area, should drain toward the shower drains. A carborundum-impregnated ceramic tile, or its equal, will provide a nonslip surface.

The temperature of water feeding into the shower heads should be 120°F, controlled by means of a mixing chamber rather than by individual control. Vandalproof shower heads should be used.

Club Rooms

Experience indicates the desirability of providing a minimum of 500 sq ft of floor space per club room. For community recreation buildings, at least three to five club rooms should be provided for multiple use. At least one large club room should be located adjoining the kitchen.

When windows in club rooms and lounges are placed high in a wall, they are not broken as often as low windows and they also provide more space for furniture, bulletin boards, pegboards, chalkboards, and exhibits. Since broken window glass is a major problem, a nonbreakable type of windowpane is preferable. Windows may be omitted and sky domes and vent domes used. By omitting windows, the need for drapes, venetian blinds, and curtains—all items subject to vandalism—is also eliminated.

A chair rail or wainscoting to prevent the marring of walls should be installed to a height of 3 ft above the floor. Whenever possible, noncontact (nonmarring) furniture should be used.

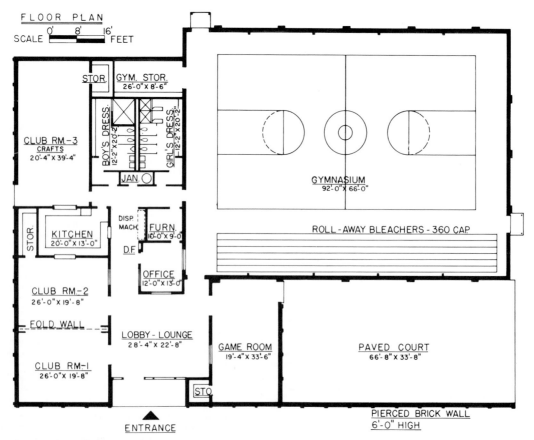

Fig. 3 Glenwood Community Center, Greensboro, N.C.

Arts and Crafts Room

A separate arts and crafts room is desirable. However, if this is not possible, then at least one club room should be equipped for crafts, with provision for gas, compressed air, and a modern sink with hot and cold water. The sink should have a clay trap.

Ample storage cabinets, closets, or lockers should be included for the safe storage of craft materials, unfinished projects, and exhibit materials. Base and wall plugs should be provided in all club rooms for the operation of electric irons, sewing machines, power tools, movie projectors, etc. If a kiln is used, it should be placed in an adjoining room for reasons of safety and should be equipped with a heavy-duty 220-volt electrical outlet. Bulletin boards and exhibit cases may be used to display completed projects.

Lounge and Lobby

The lobby of the community recreation building is the space just inside the entrance. The lounge should open off the lobby, and, if possible, should be close to the central office and to the multipurpose room and/or social hall-gymnasium. The lounge and lobby are often combined into one room. When they are combined, it is suggested that the size of the lobby-lounge be about 600 to 800 sq ft.

This facility should be attractively lighted and should contain a wall-mounted, recessed drinking fountain and a built-in electrically lighted trophy case and bulletin board. Appropriate space should be allowed for public telephones, and at least one telephone should be installed so as to accommodate a person in a wheelchair. Provision should also be made for aquariums and for growing plants and flowers. Adequate space, preferably recessed, and electrical and water connections for automatic vending machines should be included.

The office, club rooms, game room, and rest rooms are usually adjacent to the lobby-lounge.

The entrance doors of the lobby present a problem from the standpoints of aesthetics, safety, security, and vandalism. Solid glass panels—from ceiling to floor—and solid glass doors are quite popular and attractive, but their use must be carefully studied. Since glass doors and panels can be easily broken, good aluminum doors with a minimum of glass are preferable.

One of the main causes of damage to floors is the habit of many individuals of dropping a cigarette on the floor and stepping on it. This habit causes definite damage to asphalt or vinyl-asbestos tile, disfiguring and discoloring light colors and, to some extent, even marring darker colors. Therefore, terrazzo, quarry tile, and patio tile are preferable.

Game Room

The game room, approximately 30 by 64 ft in size, is designed for a variety of games, including billiards and table tennis. In planning this room, sufficient storage space should be provided for various items of game equipment and supplies to be used.

This room should be in close proximity to office supervision. It should also be acoustically treated, due to the noise factor.

The choice of floor material should be carefully considered because of the heavy traffic usually prevalent in this room. Windows should be placed high in the walls to reduce glass breakage. A chair rail or wainscoting to prevent the marring of walls should be installed to a height of 3 ft above the floor. Whenever possible, noncontact (nonmarring) furniture should be used.

Photography Room

A special room can be provided and equipped as a darkroom. Ventilation should be provided through the use of lightproof ventilators. Hot and cold running water, special light plugs—both wall and base—and photographic sinks for developing and washing prints should also be provided.

A mixer is desirable to accurately control the water temperature. A filter should also be provided if the water quality is not good. Doors should be lightproof.

Director's Office

An office of approximately 120 sq ft in size is suggested, with sufficient window space to provide maximum supervision of the lobby, lounge, club rooms, and social hall-gymnasium. At least three walls should have windows. If there is a window connected to the social hall-gymnasium, a nonbreakable-type glass is preferable.

It is often recommended that there be an adjoining shower-dressing unit with a floor-surface area of not less than 100 sq ft. This unit should contain a shower, toilet and lavatory, clothes closet, and first-aid supply cabinet.

Opening off the director's office should be a storage closet with a burglarproof door for storing valuable supplies and equipment, such as the motion-picture projector and public-address system.

Rest Rooms

Rest-room facilities should be designed to serve both indoor and outdoor areas. Provision should be made for direct access from the exterior of the building at a point adjacent to such activity areas.

Rest rooms should include multipurpose units, combining automatic towel and soap dispensers, mirror and shelf, and a combination paper-towel dispenser and waste receptacle. These units should be recessed in the wall.

Mirrors should have metal frames and be recessed into the wall so they cannot be torn off. The preferred soap dispenser is built into the lavatory since this type is less subject to vandalism than the wall-installed type.

Dressing-room benches should be of a permanent type and should be securely anchored to the floor so they cannot be turned over, stacked against the wall, broken, or removed from the building. Toilet fixtures should be hung from the wall for ease in cleaning. In rest rooms where several fixtures are used, one fixture of proper height for young children and the disabled should be included. Lavatories should be of enamel-coated iron or other unbreakable material rather than vitreous china.

A flush-valve water closet with the valve 24 in. above the top of the fixture—or 3 ft above the floor—is preferred over a tank-type toilet fixture. Automatic valves for water taps in showers and lavatories are recommended to reduce water loss caused by taps being left open. Hose bibbs should be installed in each rest room and/or shower room, at a proper height so buckets can be placed under them.

Toilet facilities should be made accessible to the disabled.

Kitchen

The Pullman or kitchenette-type kitchen is usually desirable for most community and neighborhood recreation buildings. If large dinners or banquets are to be served, provision should be made for a full-size modern kitchen that con-

forms to local health regulations and has a free floor space at least 54 in. wide.

The kitchen should be located near the club rooms and the social hall-gymnasium. This will make the kitchen available to small gatherings in the club rooms and to large banquet gatherings in the social hall-gymnasium. The kitchen is often placed between two club rooms and made available to both rooms by the use of aluminum roll-up doors.

Adequate storage space, cabinet space, and electrical outlets for such appliances as the refrigerator, the range, the dishwasher, and can openers should be provided. Exhaust fans should also be installed.

Storage Areas

One of the most common errors found in many recreation buildings is the lack of sufficient storage space for equipment, maintenance, and custodial purposes.

Equipment Storage Room Provision should be made for storing apparatus and equipment. There should be an opening 6 ft wide with louvered flush doors between the social hall-gymnasium and the storage room. This will permit passage of the most bulky equipment. There should be no raised threshold.

The minimum size of the storage room should be approximately 250 sq ft. Provision should be made for storage of inflated balls, bats, softballs, and other supplies, either in separate cabinets or a special closet. Appropriate bins, shelves, and racks are suggested. In addition, a recessed alcove for the storage of a piano is desirable.

Maintenance Storage Room The maintenance storage room varies in size, depending upon the adjacent outdoor space and the size of the building. The room is ordinarily located on the ground level, adjacent to the outdoor areas. An outside entrance should be provided by means of a burglarproof door sufficiently large to permit the passage of motorized and other maintenance equipment.

This facility is used as a headquarters for all outdoor maintenance. It may have to house rakes, shovels, hose, marking equipment and supplies, hand tools, power tools, and other equipment. A repair shop and its facilities are usually incorporated in this area. The room should have sufficient base and wall outlets to serve both the workbench and power-equipment needs.

Recessed wall shelving and cabinet storage should be provided for tools, supplies, and equipment. This space should also contain hot and cold water, a slop sink, a lavatory, a water closet, and a clothes closet.

The floor should be concrete and should be pitched to a central drain. The junction of the floor and wall should be coved.

Custodial Storage Rooms A supply closet equipped with a slop sink and space for mops, pails, brooms, and cleaning supplies should be centrally located on each floor level.

NEIGHBORHOOD RECREATION BUILDINGS

The neighborhood recreation building will include many of the features of the community recreation building, as previously described. The neighborhood building, however, is usually intended to serve a smaller number of people. The size of the facility will ordinarily fall into the Type III (under 10,000 sq ft) or Type II (10,000 to 20,000 sq ft) classification. In all cases, the building should be so designed that rooms can be easily added.

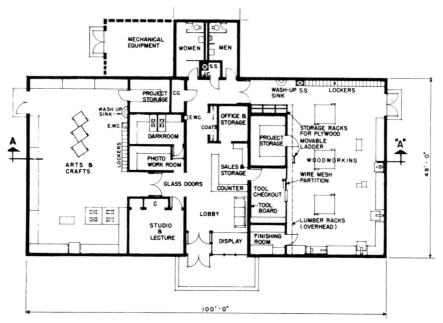

Fig. 4.

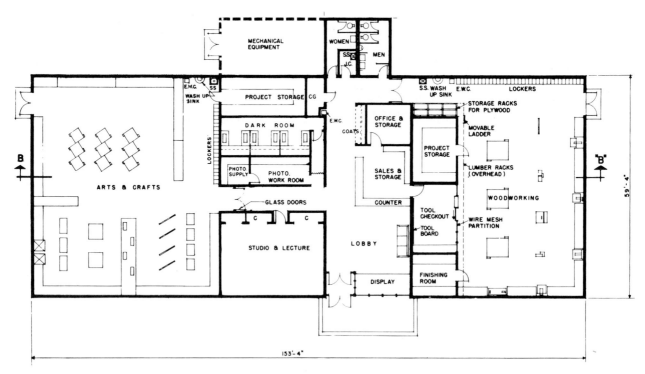

Fig. 5.

U.S. Naval Facilities Engineering Command, Department of the Navy, Washington, D.C.

NEIGHBORHOOD SERVICE CENTERS

By ROBERT PERLMAN and DAVID JONES

A neighborhood service center may be defined as a conveniently located facility, staffed by professional workers and community residents with no training, designed to provide specific and speedy services to people with a wide variety of simple and complex problems. On the philosophical level, the centers comprise one important element of a broad attack on crime and poverty. On the action level, they are one way of dealing with problems of inhabitants of the inner city, a "place to go" for help.

Services dispensed by centers may range from on-the-spot advice on problems requiring immediate attention to long-term assistance with legal, employment, and personal problems. In addition to furnishing these services, a growing number of neighborhood centers are planning for, and implementing, programs designed to mobilize neighborhood groups to participate in decision-making processes that directly affect their lives, to become a vital force for social change. These centers feel that they must not only help to resolve specific problems but must also work to correct those faults in the society that create these problems.

Those who have developed and worked in such centers are generally very enthusiastic about this "new" way to deliver services. National organizations, as well as local, governmental, and voluntary agencies, are becoming increasingly interested in utilizing this particular organizational device.

The goals of the center are to promote and facilitate effective involvement of neighborhood residents in the solution of neighborhood problems and to improve the quality of programs which are designed to aid the elimination of poverty. As such, the neighborhood center is the focal point of the local community action program in a neighborhood.

A center can gather and share information about new and existing programs. It can deliver the resources of many public and private service agencies to those who need them. It can coordinate the programs and services of these agencies to answer the needs of the individual and the total community. At the same time, it can work to modify and enrich existing programs and services so that they respond more effectively to the unique poverty problems of the neighborhood.

In order for the center to have effect on the elimination of poverty, it must belong to the neighborhood it serves. It must be what the people want it to be. It should be a place where people will want to go, not simply because they can get free medical treatment or legal advice but because it is a comfortable, familiar, friendly, and exciting place to be.

The neighborhood center's most important function is to provide the people of a neighborhood with a structure and a program design to enable them to act. The center should help people gather and use their own resources as well as those in the community at large; it should help them develop the competence to

Neighborhood Service Centers, Office of Juvenile Delinquency and Youth Development, U.S. Department of Health, Education and Welfare, Washington, D.C., 1967.

work in their own behalf toward the resolution of the social and economic problems of poverty in their neighborhood.

The first step in planning a neighborhood center is the determination of the neighborhood to be served. The best way to decide if a given geographical area is a neighborhood is to discover if the people in the area think of themselves as being neighborhood residents. In Appalachia, a neighborhood may be a "holler" or a "creek." In the South, a rural town and the surrounding farms may be a neighborhood. In cities, a neighborhood could be one or more public housing projects. In many cases, the definition of the neighborhood may be so obvious a consideration that it demands very little thought. It may simply be the section of town where poor people live.

It is important that neighborhood centers be placed in more or less distinct neighborhoods. Some consideration should be given, however, to the size of the population served. Harlem is a neighborhood, but it clearly cannot be served by just one neighborhood center. As a general rule, a center that serves more than 35,000 people will probably be too large for effective neighborhood communication. On the other hand, some neighborhoods will be too small for a full-scale facility. In such cases, particularly in sparsely populated rural areas, nearby neighborhood centers may consider placing outposts to perform outreach and referral functions and to provide communication with the center and other service groups.

Another important consideration in the determination of the neighborhood is the transportation system, public and private, in the area to be served. The neighborhood center should be located within easy reach of area residents or should develop its own transportation system to bring itself as close as possible to the people it serves.

Determining the Neighborhood Needs

The second step in planning a neighborhood center is the determination of the area's particular needs. Local conditions and the expressed desires of neighborhood residents should be the most important considerations. Asking simple questions of a number of residents is one way to get the necessary information.

The processes of neighborhood involvement and participation can develop in the people served by a neighborhood center an active concern about services by making the programs, both existing and locally initiated, respond directly to needs that they themselves have indicated.

Responding to Neighborhood Needs

Once the neighborhood's unique mix of needs are pinpointed, arrangements should be made to decentralize into the center existing programs which can meet these needs. Written agreements between the service agency and the center can govern the terms of each decentralization. These agreements should clearly define the organizational chain of command within the neighborhood center: what kind of

program will be offered, and what procedural and other changes are agreed to by both parties in operating the program through the facilities of the center.

Programs must not be imposed on neighborhoods but should grow out of expressed neighborhood needs and the capacity of neighborhood people to use them. Where no existing program can adequately respond to definite neighborhood needs, the center may want to develop and operate new programs.

Decisions about what programs and groups will operate through the center will help determine the physical requirements of the facility. At the present time, centers vary in size and function from single-deck referral units to highly complex, specially designed facilities incorporating a wide range of services. There is no single model.

In an urban environment, the neighborhood center may operate out of a single storefront, from many offices scattered throughout the area, or from a cluster of buildings. In a rural environment, where transportation is more difficult and neighbors are more widely dispersed than in cities, certain variations may be more feasible.

Rural Variations

In rural areas, the neighborhood center may be a system of facilities on wheels, a fleet of service buses that continually travel from place to place within the area served by the center. Operating from a small administrative center, one kind of mobile unit can travel throughout a county, spending a day or two every week or every other week parked near a neighborhood of poor people. Such units may serve only for recruitment, intake, diagnosis, and referral to nonmobile, nondecentralized services. They may also take the form of single-purpose units. Mobile public health units are an example of a traveling single-purpose service that has proved successful in many areas. The eventual goal should be truly multipurpose units which go where the poor are and serve as many of their needs as possible. Mobile units do not have to operate from a single administrative center. Another variation involves carrying programs, on a rotating schedule, to a number of neighborhood centers scattered throughout the service area. These centers may be located in abandoned schoolhouses, old homes, grange halls, church halls, or other available space which has been turned into an appropriate facility. Each of these in-the-field centers would have a skeleton staff of resident workers who would do outreach work on a full-time basis.

The individual community will have to decide which of these models is most appropriate to local conditions. For many communities, a combination of the two may be the most workable solution.

Some typical service programs could consist of the following:

The Housing and Rent Clinic would advise and assist tenants on their problems, conduct housing inspections and verify complaints, and work with city agencies on the prompt handling of housing problems.

Government and Public

NEIGHBORHOOD SERVICE CENTERS

Tenant and Block Organization and Education would help existing tenant groups identify and act on problems, conduct conferences and training sessions on tenants' rights, emergency action, self-help techniques to improve apartments and evaluation of urban renewal needs, and would organize new groups.

Coordinated Processing of Housing Service and Community Facilities, Complaints, and Requests. The central offices of the neighborhood boards would coordinate complaints on housing and requests for public facilities and take them up with city agencies, maintain records, and conduct studies of the effectiveness of city services.

Housing Repair and Maintenance Service. A nonprofit corporation would repair and rehabilitate housing, employing (and training) youth and unemployed adults as the labor force.

Consumer education clinics would help people get the most for their money by providing information through lectures and the distribution of written material. *Parents workshops* would assist parents to understand the school system and encourage them through group discussions to take a more active part in working with the schools for the education of their children.

Employment services would primarily offer information and referral to appropriate sources of jobs and training.

A Health Conservation and Education Unit would assess the health needs of residents, develop programs to meet them, and facilitate the delivery of the city's health services.

Ancillary services would consist of social services and legal services. *Social services* would provide counseling to individuals and families on a short-term basis—for example,

a dispute with an employer or getting a child reinstated in school—and long-range help with such problems as material and child-rearing difficulties. Teams of indigenous workers would operate under a supervisor. In addition, there would be homemakers and home technicians to help with management of family budgets, to provide temporary child care so that mothers can keep appointments at other agencies, and an escort service for the aged. There would be special educational programs for unwed parents, with a particular effort to involve fathers; a service for the aged and isolated; and the use of mental health resources on a contractual basis.

Throughout, referrals would be made to these programs by the neighborhood staff and there would be a referral program to facilitate coordination within the centers and with other community agencies.

DESIGN CONSIDERATIONS FOR OFFICE BUILDINGS

The building character should express:
- Its representational and office building nature
- The nature of the building in terms understood by and compatible to the host country
- Quality without ostentation or luxury
- A deference to local architectural tradition and materials

General planning should include:
- Easy and direct pedestrian access and egress, including provisions for the physically handicapped.
- Easy vehicular access and egress with provision for adequate visitors, and staff parking along with the necessary service access to building. Shelter should be provided at main entrance for protection during inclement weather.
- Arrangement of public spaces for convenient service to the public.
- Arrangement of sensitive areas remote from public.
- Efficient circulation employing maximum use of double loaded corridors.
- Provision for building expansion either vertically, horizontally or both.
- Physical security of building by perimeter walls and/or fences, setbacks from property lines, exterior lighting, easy control of entrances and visual control of stairways and elevators.

Climatic and local considerations include:

Humidity
Dust control
Extreme temperatures
Insect control
Sun and inclement weather control
Earthquakes
Flooding

The Basic Space Module

The basic space module of 75 sq ft represents the normal space allocation for individual desk personnel engaged in clerical activities. Increments of this module will provide offices of proper size for individuals or groups having other functional space requirements. Thus, an office of 150 sq ft will accommodate a single reporting officer or two clerk-typists; an office of 225 sq ft will provide for an officer of supervisory rank, two secretaries, or three clerk-typists. The 75-sq-ft module thus establishes a means by which the building can be systematically designed for flexibility of partitioning to suit space needs.

The typical single office of 150 sq ft represents a preferred room shape of 8 ft 8 in. wide by 17 ft 6 in. deep. These proportions have been proved to accommodate required furniture for one or two persons depending on rank and function. Similarly for offices of larger size, furniture and space needs will be satisfied if the 17-ft 6-in. depth is retained uniformly and the widths are varied in accordance with net area requirements.

Dimensional Limitations

The following represent minimum clear ceiling heights. Adjustments may be required in some instances to accommodate specific requirements.

Classified conference room . . . . 10 ft
Classified mail and
  communications space . . . . 10 ft
Mechanical space . . . . Varies — to be
  ascertained in
  each case
Typical office space . . . . 9 ft
General storage areas . . . . 10 ft

Planning Flexibility

The following space standards are established for purposes of planning consistency and cost control and for these reasons should be adhered to. This does not preclude variations where such are necessary to provide for special requirements at a particular post. In addition to specific space variations, the site and locale may dictate that the service functions may preferably be located in a structure separate from the office building.

SPACE STANDARDS FOR EMBASSY OFFICE BUILDINGS

The following net areas are recommended for the various typical embassy staff requirements and functions. Space variations between the class I, II, III, and IV posts are indicated under

the post classifications. An asterisk (*) indicates those functions or spaces requiring additional evaluation specifically to accommodate the special need at each post.

Office of the Ambassador

This section is a sensitive area and should be located on an upper floor and separated from the general public areas. Access to the ambassador's and deputy chief of mission's offices should be through and controlled by the secretaries' office. The reception area should be separate but convenient to the secretaries' office. (See Table 1.)

Political Section

This is a sensitive section which reports directly to the ambassador and should be located accordingly. (See Table 2.)

Economic Section

This section should be conveniently located for easy public access although not necessarily on the main ground floor except in the case of the commercial library. This latter function and any directly associated office should be immediately available to the public. (See Table 3.)

Consular Section

The size of this section will vary greatly according to the volume of the consular activity. At

TABLE 1   Embassy Space for Ambassadorial Section

	Class post, net sq ft			
	I	II	III	IV
Ambassador's office	600	525	450	450
Private lavatory	75	75	50	50
Coat closet				
Deputy chief of mission	450	375	300	300
Secretaries (two)	300	225	225	225
File alcove and kitchenette	75	75	75	75
Reception area	300	225	225	150
Conference room	600	525	450	375

TABLE 2   Embassy Space for Political Section

	Class post, net sq ft			
	I	II	III	IV
Chief political section	375	300	225	225
Secretary	225	225	150	150
Political reporting officer	225	150	150	150
Reception area	225	150	150	150
Political officers (each)	150	150	150	150
Clerk-typists (150 sq ft				
first, plus 75 sq ft each additional)				

TABLE 3   Embassy Space for Economic Section†

	Class post, net sq ft			
	I	II	III	IV
Chief of economic section	375	300	225	225
Secretary-receptionist (including waiting area)	300	225	225	225
Economic reporting officer	225	150	150	150
Labor officer	225	225	150	150
Commercial officer	225	225	150	150
Others	150	150	150	150
Agricultural officer	225	150	150	150
Assistants (each)	150	150	150	150
Commercial library*	425	375	375	300
Clerk-typists (each)	75	75	75	75
Translators (each)	75	75	75	75

†Note: At some posts one of the above, such as agricultural, may be large enough to warrant a separate section.

some posts this work would be handled by one officer requiring one room; at others, the complete operation would require one or more floors and several waiting rooms. Its varied function is to process visas, citizenship, veterans' affairs, notarials, shipping, and social security. This section will require its own file room, its own waiting areas (for larger posts preferably two, one for immigrants and one for nonimmigrants), toilet facilities, fingerprinting facilities, confidential interviewing room, and mail storage boxes for American citizens. By its public nature it should be on the ground floor near the main entrance or possibly have an entrance of its own.

Only minimum areas are recommended here because of the wide variation between consular activities in and between classification of posts. Specific space allocations will be determined by need on an individual case basis. (See Table 4.)

TABLE 4   Embassy Space for Consular Section

	Basic minimum* net sq ft
Consular officer	225
Junior officer	150
Clerks (each)	75
Stenographers (each)	75
Waiting rooms	225
Two toilets for above	75
File rooms for immigrant or visa files	150
Vault (visa, notarial fees, etc.)	75
Veterans' affairs	150
Citizenship officer	150
Notarials	150
Shipping and storage	150

Administration Section

The operation of this section will not be confined to one area of the building but will be distributed throughout. The responsibilities consist of general housekeeping of the post, supervision of building personnel, post expenditures, message center or communications complex, maintenance personnel, Marine Guards, etc. The administration officer and

his immediate staff, especially those coming in contact with local businessmen and tradespeople, should be on the ground floor near the main entrance. The communications complex should be separate and in a more remote area, preferably near the ambassador, as it will contain the mail and file rooms, communications room, vault, and incinerator for classified material. This area will be contained in a concrete vault accessible through one controlled entrance.

Communications Complex* This facility is subject to changing requirements and to sharp variations between posts. Therefore, it is impractical to establish general space requirements. Instead, required areas will be determined by the department on a case basis for each building planned.

This function is to be designed and constructed in accord with "Minimum Physical Security Standards of Foreign Service Office Buildings" and should be located on the top floor remote from all public areas and access.

TABLE 5   Embassy Space for Administrative Section

	Class post, net sq ft			
	I	II	III	IV
Administration				
Administrative officer	375	300	225	225
Administrative assistant	225	225	150	150
Secretary-waiting	300	300	225	225
Stenos and clerks (150 sq ft first, plus 75 sq ft each additional)				
General services†				
General services officer	300	225	150	150
Assistant general services officer(s), each	150	150	150	150
Secretaries, stenos, clerks (150 sq ft first, plus 75 sq ft each additional)				
Budget and fiscal				
Budget and fiscal officer	225	225	150	150
Disbursing officer	150	150	150	150
Vault (if required)	25	25	25	25
Accounting clerks (each)	75	75	75	75
Waiting space* (provide counter)	225	150	150	150
Time and payroll*	300	225	150	150

†Note: Additional non-desk personnel such as chauffeurs, maintenance and char force will occupy space designated under Maintenance and Service Space.

TABLE 6   Embassy Space for Liaison Attaché

	Class post, net sq ft			
	I	II	III	IV
Chief of liaison	225	225	150	150
Liaison officers (each)	150	150	150	150
Secretaries (150 sq ft first, plus 75 sq ft each additional)				
Reception	225	225	150	150
Photo and dark room	225	225	150	150
Vault and incinerator*	150	150	75	75

TABLE 7   Embassy Space for Military Attaché

	Class post, net sq ft			
	I	II	III	IV
Military attaché.	300	225	225	150
Military assistant.	150	150	150	150
Enlisted men (150 sq ft first, plus 75 sq ft each additional)				
Civilian assistant	150	150	150	150
Clerk stenographers (150 sq ft first, plus 75 sq ft each additional)				
Reception room and receptionist*.	300	225	225	150
(This reception room can be shared by the three services)				
File-communications* (varies)	375	300	225	150
Vault and incinerator*.	150	150	75	75
Photo and dark room	225	225	150	150
Storage area* (basement)	300	225	225	150

The communication complex will normally consist of the following:

> Ante and reading room
> Classified mail and file room
> Vault
> Incinerator
> Communication room(s)
> Office(s)
> Lavatory

Liaison Attaché

This section should be located on or near the top floor of the building, usually adjacent to the communications area. (See Table 6.)

Military Attachés (Army, Navy, Air)

This space will vary according to post. The post may have one or all three services represented. For the most part, this operation will be of a classified nature and should be remote from the public. In some posts the military attachés will have their own communication complex and vault. A photo laboratory may be required for each service. (See Table 7.)

United States Information Service

This section may not always be located at a post. It is also possible that this activity may be located away from the office building proper and in a more advantageous location in the midtown section. The library is the largest unit in the Information Service. Many posts include a projection room or theaterette for motion pictures. This activity should be on the ground floor or basement.

Since USIS activities often take place after hours, when the mission is closed, the service should have a separate entrance so that the rest of the building can be separated and locked for security reasons. (See Table 8.)

USIS Library   The supervisors' offices should be 150 sq ft net and library assistants' offices should be based upon 75 sq ft per desk personnel required. Because of the extreme variation of the size of libraries between posts, it is impractical to stipulate standard spaces for the various library functions. Instead, the USIS space recommendations should emanate from the post and should be based upon an accurate survey of the need in each case. This need should be established by the number of volumes in the collection and the average peak number of people patronizing the library. USIS Library spaces include the following:

TABLE 8   Embassy Space for United States Information Service

	Class post, net sq ft			
	I	II	III	IV
Public affairs				
Public affairs officer.	375	300	225	225
Junior officers (each)	150	150	150	150
Secretary-steno (150 sq ft first, plus 75 sq ft each additional)				
Reception room.	225	225	150	150
Cultural affairs				
Cultural affairs officer.	225	225	150	150
Secretary-steno	150	150	150	150
Assistants or translators (150 sq ft first, plus 75 sq ft each additional)				
Press section				
Press officers (each).	150	150	150	150
Translators (150 sq ft first, plus 75 sq ft each additional)				
Clerk-stenographers (150 sq ft first, plus 75 sq ft each additional)				
Publications officers (150 sq ft first, plus 75 sq ft each additional)				
Press morgue*	300	300	225	150
Storage*.	300	300	225	150
Duplication unit* (or photo lab.).	375	300	225	150
Motion picture section				
Motion picture officer	225	225	150	150
Assistants (150 sq ft first, plus 75 sq ft each additional)				
Projectionists (150 sq ft first, plus 75 sq ft each additional)				
Clerk-stenographer (150 sq ft first, plus 75 sq ft each additional)				
Film library and editing*	225	225	150	150
Film and projector* repair and storage.	300	300	225	225
Projection and viewing room* (min. 300 sq ft)				
Dark room.	150	150	150	75
Radio section				
Radio officers.	150	150	150	150
Assistants (150 sq ft first, plus 75 sq ft each additional)				
Clerk-stenographer (150 sq ft first, plus 75 sq ft each additional)				
Audiovisual studio*				
Studio.	375	375		
Control room.	300	300		
Storage room*	150	150	75	75
Exhibits section				
Exhibits officer	150	150	150	150
Assistants (150 sq ft first, plus 75 sq ft each additional)				
Studio workroom*	375	300	300	225
Exhibits area* (in lobby)	375	300	225	150
Storage room (basement)	600	450	300	225
Miscellaneous USIS areas				
Separate lobby	600	450	375	300
Mail room (near service entrance).	375	300	225	225
Conference room.	450	375	300	225
Distribution and mailing unit	450	375	300	225

Reading room and stacks
Reference section
Workroom (book repair)
Periodicals section
Private reading room (research)
Music room
Children's library
Cataloging
Supervisor's office
Library assistants
Book storage

Roof Penthouse

On the roof may be located the elevator machine room and the building's air-conditioning equipment. Space for these should be allocated as required by equipment and need. (See Table 9.)

Garage or Parking Area

To the areas noted above there may be added garage facilities or outside parking, or a combination of both, depending on site. The following items are to be considered as necessary:

Parking area (x number of cars)
Wash and grease rack
Dispatcher's office
Chauffeur's dayroom and toilet
Bicycle racks
Underground gasoline storage tank
(including pump)
Vehicle repair shop and tool storage

TABLE 9 Embassy Space for Miscellaneous Functional and Service Areas

	Class post, net sq ft			
	I	II	III	IV
Conference room (unclassified)	600	525	450	375
Women's rest room (adjacent to a toilet)	225	225	150	150
Lobby and reception area	750	600	525	450
Marine guard room (off or near lobby)	225	225	150	150
Extra offices	150	150	150	150
V.I.P. offices (150 sq ft each)	450	300	150	150
Medical*	525	450	375	300
Service entrance (loading dock and receiving)	300	225	150	75
Unclassified mail room (near service entrance)	300	225	150	150
General supply room*	450	375	225	150
General storage room*	900	750	600	450
Snack bar* (kitchenette and food storage)	750	600	450	300
Telephone equipment room*	525	225	150	75
Mechanical equipment* (heating and air conditioning)	1,050	900	750	600
Repair shop(s)	600	450	450	300
Char force (lockers and toilets)	450	450	300	225
Trash and incinerator room	200	225	150	150
Electrical transformer and switchboard	450	375	300	150
Standby generator room (if required)	525	375	225	150
Messengers' locker room	150	150	75	75
Water storage tanks* (basement or separate from building)	—	—	—	—

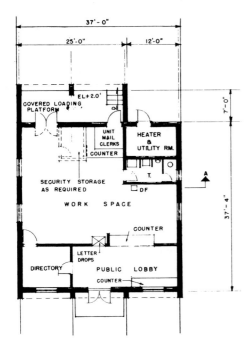

Fig. 1 Gross area, 1,500 sq ft.

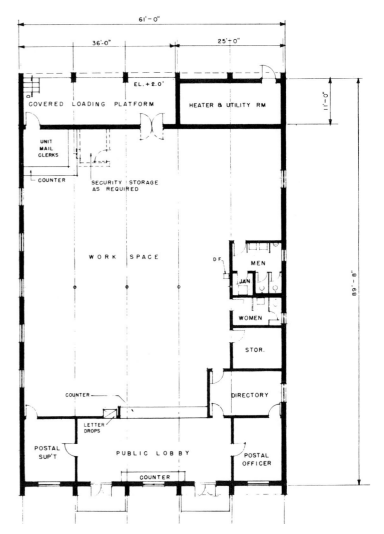

Fig. 3 Gross area, 5,300 sq ft.

U.S. Naval Facilities Engineering Command, Department of the Navy, Washington, D.C.

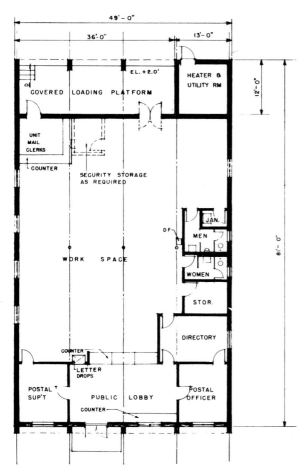

Fig. 2 Gross area, 3,750 sq ft.

ACCESS RAMPS FOR THE HANDICAPPED

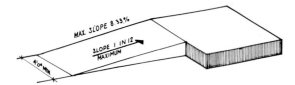

Fig. 1.

A ramp is defined as a sloping walkway which is attached to a building as a means of moving from one floor elevation to another without encountering any obstruction.

A ramp must be at least 4 ft wide. Ramp slopes must not be greater than 8.33 percent (1 inch in 12). (See Fig. 1.) If a ramp slopes 5 percent (1 inch in 20) or less, and there is no dropoff, then no handrail will be required. If ramp slope is greater than 5 percent, and there is no dropoff, then one handrail will be required. See handrail requirements in Fig. 5.

Ramps shall have at least a 5'-0" straight level surface at the bottom to allow stopping distance for wheelchairs. (See Fig. 2)

Ramps shall have a 3'-0" long intermediate-level platform at 30'-0" intervals for rest and safety. (See Figs. 3 and 4.)

Ramps shall have level platforms wherever they turn to allow turning and stopping space for wheelchairs.

An Illustrated Handbook of the Handicapped, Section of the North Carolina State Building Code. Ronald Mace, AIA, and Betsy Laslett, Raleigh, N.C., 1977.

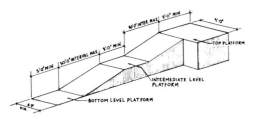

Fig. 2   Straight-run ramp.

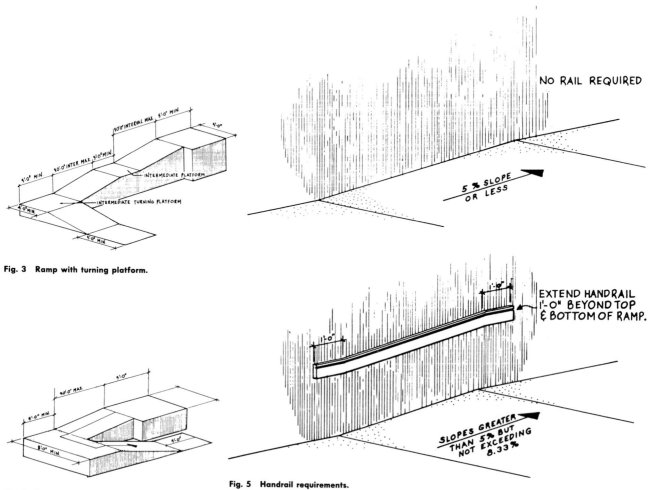

Fig. 3   Ramp with turning platform.

Fig. 4   Ramp with intermediate switchback platform.

Fig. 5   Handrail requirements.

NO RAIL REQUIRED

5 % SLOPE OR LESS

EXTEND HANDRAIL 1'-0" BEYOND TOP & BOTTOM OF RAMP.

SLOPES GREATER THAN 5% BUT NOT EXCEEDING 8.33%

PUBLIC TOILET ROOMS FOR THE HANDICAPPED

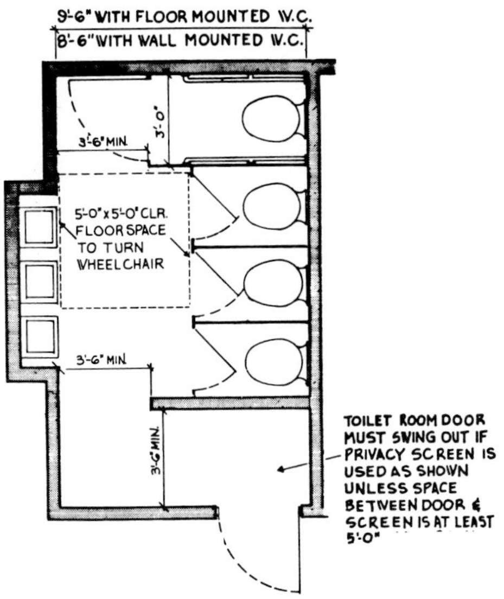

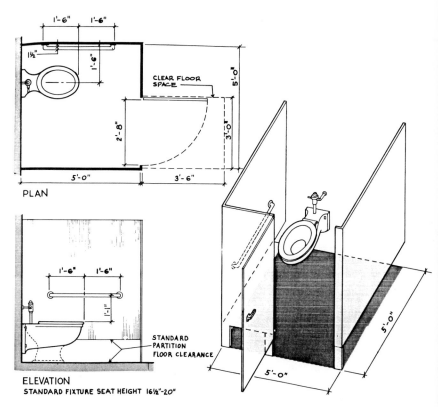

TOILET STALL

A 5' x 5' stall is usable by most people and has the following requirements.
1. Stall must be 5 x 5 ft
2. W.C. center line is 1 ft 6 in from side wall
3. 32 in door diagonally opposite W.C.
4. Handrail extends 1 ft 6 in in front of W.C. 1½ in O.D., 1½ in from wall, 13 in above seat
5. Standard partition toe clearance

Fig. 1 Due to additional length of handicapped toilet stalls it is suggested they be located at end of toilet rooms as shown here.

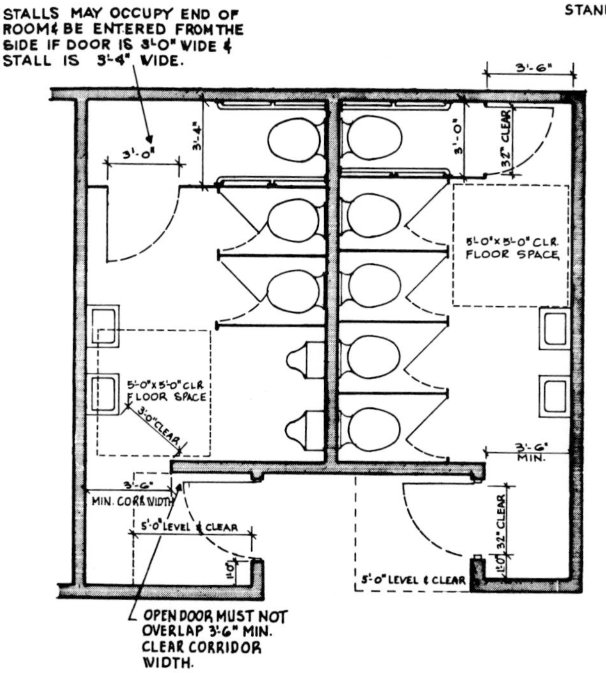

PLAN

ELEVATION
STANDARD FIXTURE SEAT HEIGHT 16½"-20"

Fig. 3 Toilet stall elevation and plan.

An Illustrated Handbook of the Handicapped, Section of the North Carolina State Building Code, Ronald Mace, AIA, and Betsy Laslett, Raleigh, N.C., 1977.

Fig. 2 Suggested entry and privacy screen arrangement to prevent door swinging out into the corridor. Doors may swing in or out.

7

Commercial

REGIONAL SHOPPING CENTERS	779
RETAIL SHOPS	796
General	796
Principles of Retail Shop Design	796
Interiors	796
Layouts and Dimensions	798
Show Windows	807
Women's Wear	808
Men's Wear	811
Bookshops	812
Gift Shops	812
Jewelry Shops	813
Barber Shop	815
Tailor and Cleaner	815
Beauty Shop	816
Shoe-Repair Shop	816
Florist Shops	816
Drugstores	817
Liquor Stores	818
Shoe Stores	820
SUPERMARKETS	823
BANKS	825
RESTAURANTS, EATING PLACES, AND FOODSERVICE FACILITIES	827
KITCHENS	843
OFFICES, GENERAL	855
Furniture	857
Work Stations	859
Private and Semiprivate	871
Conference Rooms	873
Layout	874
Space	875
Planning	876
Clearances	887
WASHROOM FACILITIES	889
MEDICAL OFFICES	891
Radiology	896
General Practice	898
Pediatrics	899
Internal Medicine	899
Ophthalmology	900
Plastic Surgery	900
General Surgery	901
Orthopedic Surgery	901
DENTAL OFFICES	902
General Dentistry	905
Orthodontics	908
LAW OFFICES	909
OPHTHALMOLOGICAL OFFICES	913
PARKING	916
Automobile Dimensions	916
PARKING GARAGES	922
PARKING LOTS	934
AUTOMOBILE SERVICE STATIONS	938
Automotive Shop	942
Gas-Filling and Service Stations	943
AUTOMOBILE BODY SHOP	944
AUTOMOBILE DEALER CENTERS	947
TRUCK DEALER AND SERVICE FACILITIES	956
RADIO STATIONS	960
TV STATIONS	967
HOTELS	972
Space Allotments	991
Guestroom Floor	993
Guestroom Design	998
MOTELS	1004
COMPUTER (EDP) FACILITIES	1017
PHOTOGRAPHIC LABORATORIES	1020
FUNERAL HOMES	1021

REGIONAL SHOPPING CENTERS

By LATHROP DOUGLASS, FAIA

BASIC HISTORY AND TRENDS

A shopping center is a complex of retail stores and related facilities planned as a unified group to give maximum shopping convenience to the customer and maximum exposure to the merchandise. The concept is not new. The agora of the typical city of ancient Greece was essentially a shopping center in the heart of the business district. The Emperor Trajan's architect, the Greek slave Apollodorus, built a shopping center adjacent to the Roman Forum in A.D. 110. It had a two-level enclosed and ventilated mall lined with open-fronted shops startlingly similar to today's most up-to-date concept. The typical Arabian *souk,* or market, of the Middle Ages also had narrow, weather-protected malls lined with open-fronted shops.

The past two decades, however, have seen such a tremendous development in planned shopping facilities in the United States that today's center has, in fact, become a new building type.

First, population growth led to outward expansion of the cities and the building up of the vast residential suburbs. Downtown congestion, due to increased car ownership and inadequate streets, weakened the downtown merchants and prompted them to set up branches in the suburban periphery in order to be more convenient to their customers. As a result of these activities on a large scale, a whole new industry was born. Each suburban district soon had its own major shopping center and several minor ones. Such districts each had clearly defined trade areas.

Another major change then set in: Vastly improved, high-speed circumferential highways soon tended to put all these suburban centers in competition with each other. At the same time, the decline of retail business and decay of buildings in the central business districts began forcing, in self-defense, a revitalization of downtown.

As a result of these two new factors, the shopping center industry is today pointing in two new, significant directions. First, the suburban centers are becoming megacenters, complete with several department stores, office buildings, motels, amusements, and, of course, parking facilities. Second, the central business districts are making a determined stand to counteract the ever-growing suburban competition by embarking on programs for construction of new high-speed connector routes to downtown and construction of major downtown renewal projects, also complete with stores, offices, hotels, amusements, and parking facilities, usually in decked garages due to the high downtown land cost.

TYPES OF CENTERS

Neighborhood Center (Suburban)

This is a row of stores customarily (but not always) in a strip, or line, paralleling the highway and with parking between the line of storefronts and the highway. Service is by alley in the rear. Ranging from 20,000 to 100,000 sq ft of space, these projects usually contain a supermarket and a drugstore, often a variety store, and a half-dozen or more service-type stores. They cater to a very limited trade area and are not normally competitive with the major centers. A few of the newer of these centers have their retail units clustered around an enclosed "mini-mall."

Intermediate or Community-Size Center

This also is usually a strip of stores but substantially larger than the neighborhood center and usually containing a so-called "junior" department store as the major unit. This type is vulnerable to competition from the larger centers and hence has declined in desirability. The parking pattern is normally similar to that of the neighborhood center.

Regional Center (Suburban)

This contains one to four department stores plus 50 to 100 or more satellite shops and facilities, all fronting on an internal pedestrian mall, or shopping walkway. Parking completely surrounds the building group so that all stores face inward to the mall with their "backs" to the parking (Fig. 1).

With today's rising land costs and diminishing supply of suitable large tracts, there has been a growing trend toward double-decked parking to save land area. It is simply a matter of the relation between the land cost and the cost of the parking deck (Fig. 2).

There is also a strong trend toward double decking of the stores themselves so that the central pedestrian mall has two interconnecting levels, each lined with shops. The double-level mall is also due, in part, to the need to keep horizontal walking (shopping) distances within reason. As land costs continue to rise and projects to grow larger, three- and four-level malls will, no doubt, become common.

Renewal Projects (Downtown)

Because of their complexity in matters legal and political—as well as physical—downtown centers are still, to some extent, in the experimental stage. The trend is toward a close integration, on two or more shopping levels, of department stores, shops of all sorts, restaurants, etc. The multilevel malls may connect directly or by bridges to other shopping facilities, hotels, office buildings, theaters, and parking garages. Because of high land costs, all parking is normally multidecked and can be above, below, or, better, laterally contiguous to the shopping facilities. The downtown trend is toward a multilevel pattern interconnecting the essential parts of the central business district.

DEVELOPMENT AND FINANCING

Shopping centers are customarily promoted and owned by developers whose primary motive is a return on their investment and, to a lesser extent, by department stores or

2 DEPARTMENT STORE PLAN ON 1 OR 2 LEVELS WITH FUTURE 3RD DEPARTMENT STORE

FUTURE DEPARTMENT STORE

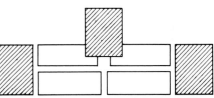

ONE OF VARIOUS 3 DEPARTMENT STORE PLANS; ONE OR TWO LEVELS

CLASSIC 2 DEPARTMENT STORE PLAN; 1 OR 2 LEVELS. PLANS WITH ONE DEPARTMENT STORE ARE RARELY UNDERTAKEN

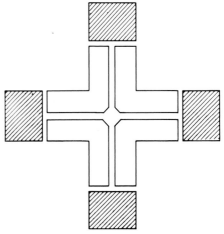

ONE OF VARIOUS 4 DEPARTMENT STORE PLANS; 1 OR 2 LEVELS

▨ DEPARTMENT STORE
☐ SHOPS

Fig. 1

779

Commercial
REGIONAL SHOPPING CENTERS

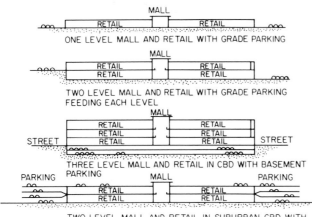

ONE LEVEL MALL AND RETAIL WITH GRADE PARKING

TWO LEVEL MALL AND RETAIL WITH GRADE PARKING FEEDING EACH LEVEL

THREE LEVEL MALL AND RETAIL IN CBD WITH BASEMENT PARKING

TWO LEVEL MALL AND RETAIL IN SUBURBAN CBD WITH MULTI-DECK CONTIGUOUS PARKING FEEDING EACH LEVEL

ONE LEVEL MALL AND RETAIL WITH LEASABLE BASEMENTS AND TRUCK SERVICE TUNNEL; GROUND LEVEL FOR SALES ONLY; BASEMENTS FOR SERVICES

Fig. 2

other merchants who are looking for new outlets to increase their sales volume. With the advent of rapid inflation, there is also a strong trend toward participation in ownership by the institutions, such as insurance companies, who in the past confined their activity merely to lending money to the developer or merchant.

Customarily the developer, regardless of what individual or group he represents, can, with good judgment and skill, set up the project on the basis of, let us say, a 10 percent investment of his own money and the remaining 90 percent as a long-term loan from an insurance company or other institution. As the long-term loan usually does not become available until completion of the project, the developer borrows needed interim money, or short-term financing, usually from a bank. The dollar value of the long-term loan is primarily calculated as a multiple of the anticipated rent roll; that is to say, it is based on a certain number of times the total projected annual rent collectible from all the committed tenants who have acceptable credit ratings. As the loan is based primarily on the rents and, therefore, is not affected by overruns in the construction cost of the job, it is obvious that the construction budget becomes of utmost importance. With only, say, 10 percent of the total job cost as his investment and 90 percent borrowed, an overrun of 10 percent will, in actuality, *double* the amount of money that the developer must invest. Otherwise, he will have to sell out, go bankrupt, or cut every possible cost he can, even if it damages the popularity of the project. The vital importance, as a result of this pattern, of a realistic and inviolable budget should be clear.

THE TEAM

At the earliest possible stage in the concept of the project, preferably even before acquisition of the land, a developer, i.e., owner, should assemble his *professional team*. For a small neighborhood center, such a team might consist solely of the owner and the architect, especially if the owner is experienced in this type of leasing.

For today's regional centers and downtown renewal programs, however, the essential team involves, in addition to the developer (who may be an individual or a large development corporation), the architect; the market analyst; the leasing agent; the mortgage broker; the engineers (usually retained by the architect and including mechanical, structural, and site); the attorney; the public relations advisor; and other occasionally needed specialists. The larger and more complex the proposed project, the more necessary it is that each of these members of the team be experienced not only in his own profession but also in the specific field of shopping center development. It is desirable, in fact, that they participate, as part of the team, in major decision making.

THE ECONOMIC SURVEY OR MARKET ANALYSIS

Prior to any planning activity and often prior to acquisition of the land, the market analyst makes a complete survey of the anticipated trade area surrounding the proposed site for the center. The boundaries of the trade area customarily depend on acceptable automobile driving time to the center. Frequently the trade area is broken into a primary area, where a high percentage of the inhabitants would shop at the center, and one or more secondary areas where, due to competition or to driving times or other reasons, a smaller percentage would be anticipated. The analyst assembles data on existing population, future population trends, income levels, car ownership, existing shopping facilities and their probable future competitive effect, and also projected facilities already announced or likely to be announced by other developers. He estimates the probable mortality rate of these proposed projects—i.e., how many will never be built—and the competitive effect of any survivors. The analyst, from his available statistical records, and based on the income level, population, ethnic origins, and other characteristics of the trade area, then makes estimates of the amount of family income likely to be allocated to such categories as food, drugs, furniture, women's and men's

clothes, shoes, department store purchases, etc., etc.; and, from these estimates, he prepares charts indicating the recommended total amount of floor area to be built and how much of this floor area should be devoted to the various kinds of merchandise and services. These data then form the basis for the architectural planning. No major project should be undertaken without an adequate market analysis.

It is axiomatic that success goes to the developer who "gets there the fustest with the mostest," as the old saying goes. If the project is too slow in coming to fruition, a competitive center, securing a firm hold on the available business, may be built.

If a project is too large for the trade area, it cannot be sufficiently rented, and the unrented space may cause it to fail. If it is too small for the trade area, it will invite the construction of competitive centers and may lose out due to this competition. In the past this determination of size, i.e., total store area, was perhaps the most vital decision to be made and one that could be readily pinpointed from a thorough market survey by a firm of sound judgment. Today, however, with the vast increase in circumferential highways, it has been conclusively established that trade area boundaries no longer can be pinpointed. A surprising number of shoppers now take advantage of centers on the opposite side of a city because of the new high-speed peripheral highways. Today every aspect of a center's concept, planning, and design must be of the best for survival in the face of competition.

A school can be unfunctional, but the children still have to go to school. A home may have many bad features, but the family will still live there. Even a factory building can have its faults. A shopping center, however, depends on the whims of its customers, mostly female, for its success. If, because of inconvenience or unsuitable merchandise or for any other reason, it does not have the proper appeal, the customers simply will not go there to shop, and the project may become a failure.

SITE SELECTION

The following criteria normally apply:

• A site available for development and located within the trade area recommended in the market analysis.

• Location easily accessible to at least one existing or shortly to be constructed major highway, preferably to two or more major highways. A location literally bordering on one or more major highways is desirable for its advertising impact on passing cars, but this is not necessary if suitable access roads exist between the highway and the site.

• Adequate present and future capacity of adjacent highways for through traffic *plus* that to be generated by the center.

• Land cost in proper relation to total capital cost and to obtainable rents.

• Adequate size and suitable shape to permit proper planning of the merchandising area and a proper number of parking spaces. Where acreage is limited and high land costs are justified, parking can be on decks and the whole project can be multilevel.

• Zoning suitable for proposed use or at least a reasonable chance that such zoning may be obtained. Zoning changes are often difficult, expensive, and time-consuming to make.

• Utilities available or installable at acceptable cost.

• Subsurface ground conditions that can

780

be overcome at acceptable cost, such as rock, swamp, trunk sewers, streams, etc.

• No easements or other legal restrictions that will interfere with proper planning.

• Topography that will permit as near to an ideal plan as possible without incurring excessive grading or drainage costs. It is noted, however, that it is usually better in principle to move a million yards of earth than to compromise a plan that will give maximum customer convenience and proper store relationships.

Other criteria that are desirable but not essential include:

• Adequate site area for future expansion and inclusion of supporting facilities, such as office buildings, motels, etc. There is little risk in the acquisition of such additional land, as land values always go up with the construction of a major center.

• Proximity to public transportation (in the case of larger cities).

• Possibility of integrating the land with other mutually beneficial uses such as town centers, recreation, housing, etc.

• Protection of the project from undesirable neighboring developments through achievement of suitable zoning of adjacent land.

SCHEMATIC PLANNING

Following acquisition of the site and completion of the economic survey, it is customary for the developer to retain a suitably experienced architect who proceeds to work out, from the market survey and physical information pertaining to the property, a simple schematic solution. This shows building sizes and arrangement, gross leasable areas, malls and public space, parking layout, access roads, method of servicing, and other basic aspects of the concept, including all pertinent statistics. This material, in conjunction with the economic survey, is then used by the developer in approaching the department store prospects. The architect's work normally is suspended at this point until the department stores are committed. Many projects never go beyond this stage and, in any case, there is usually a substantial lapse of time before the project goes ahead.

The major principles of schematic planning, in addition to conforming to the leasable area recommendations of the economic survey, are (1) convenience and comfort for the customer, and (2) maximum merchandising potential for the tenant stores. Customer convenience demands ease of vehicular access to and from the site; ease and adequacy of parking; reasonable walking distances; simple, direct pedestrian shopping routes with minimum obstructions and inconveniences. It is axiomatic that a shopper rarely goes where there is inconvenience of any sort.

Maximum merchandising potential means the giving to each tenant in the project of a reasonably equal opportunity to capture a portion of the customer's trade. The means of achieving this is normally based on the concept of "anchors," or "pulls," that is to say, those merchandising units that have maximum appeal to the customer. The typical shopper is usually attracted to a center primarily by the type and range of merchandise offered by the major department stores. This appeal is supplemented by the opportunity for convenient comparison shopping in the many smaller or satellite stores. Because of the customer activity generated by the appeal of the department stores, these major units are spaced at strategic spots, such as at each end of a one- or two-level pedestrian mall

whose length is lined on each side with the smaller satellite stores. The flow of customers from these major units to each other then draws people past the smaller stores, where they stop en route for impulse and comparative shopping.

The key to this planning is the avoidance of any dead ends or out-of-the-way locations for the smaller stores and the concentration of all shopping on clearly defined routes connecting with major "anchors," or "pulls," i.e., the department stores.

Data on store sizes, mall design, parking layout, etc. are included in other sections of this article.

INTEGRATION WITH THE COMMUNITY

For many years the typical shopping center has been a low, flat building mass resembling an island surrounded by a vast, barren ocean of asphalt. Landscaping has been inadequate, and integration of any sort with the community has been completely lacking. With the competitive need, however, for increasing the size of centers and including within their general scope office buildings, hotels, housing, etc., the resulting more complex planning requirements have given rise to a better opportunity, as well as to greater urgency, for the true integration of the stores and parking within a larger major complex, such complex in turn properly integrated with the existing neighborhood. The importance of this integration has been emphasized in the concepts of the "new towns" arising in Europe and elsewhere. Plan integration with the neighborhood has, in fact, become a must for large centers and a factor not to be ignored even for the smallest ones. Such integration involves the space interrelationship between the neighborhood and project's buildings, roadways, parking, landscaping, and pedestrian walks. It can be a powerful means of assuring long-range future real estate values, both for the shopping project and for the entire surrounding community, whether commercial or residential.

Where land costs permit, it is obviously desirable to obtain control of the land surrounding the center, not only to protect the center but to take advantage of the inevitable increase in value and development potential of such land.

PLANNING FOR EXPANSION AND STAGED CONSTRUCTION

It has always been considered good practice to build retail space as nearly as possible commensurate with market survey recommendations. Today, however, two problems often confront the developer:

a. With the increasing extent of peripheral highways and the spectacular growth of the suburbs in many cities, it has become increasingly difficult to estimate the *future* potential of a particular center and hence the amount of *future* space needed to maintain its competitive position.

b. With the increasing number of centers with two to four department stores, the situation arises in which one or more such stores, however necessary they may be to the project and however eager they may be to be included, may for good reasons of their own wish an opening date a year or more later than the official opening date set for the center.

Therefore, it has become more and more customary to do either or both of the following:

a. Plan for a more or less indeterminate expansion at some unspecified future date.

b. Plan for one or more specific stages of construction, each to be undertaken as a successive part of a more or less continuous construction operation.

In the latter case, i.e., two or more specifically scheduled construction stages, the problem becomes more one of leasing than of planning. The project is planned for the final stage, and it becomes the leasing broker's problem as to how much space he can lease at top rents in the first stage and how much it becomes necessary to leave for the later stage or stages due to the initial absence of one or more department stores. There also arises the problem of the construction contract. If stage one is completed before stage two is sent out for bidding, then the bidding can be truly competitive. But when the second stage begins before completion of the first stage, it may be difficult to secure bids or to negotiate a reasonable price with the contractor already on the job. A method occasionally used on large centers, and one which applies in this situation, is for the general contractor or the owner's building organization to clearly establish that more than one subcontractor in each major trade will be utilized and thereby to ensure a continuing competitive atmosphere. This procedure also has the advantage of allowing smaller subcontractors to bid on parts of large jobs.

In the case, however, of providing for expansion at some *undetermined* future date, the situation is different and much more difficult to resolve. Merely to provide excess land area for future use is usually an unacceptable solution. This is because proper integration of the future unknown facilities with the existing center may turn out to be difficult if not impossible. This, in turn, weakens the trade potential of the overall enlarged project. The proper procedure usually is to master-plan the entire available site so that a thoroughly acceptable final project can result. It is noted, however, that any master plan for the enlargement of a center at some indeterminate time, say three years or more in the future, must in every case take into consideration the following:

The most critical time for any center whatsoever is the year it opens and usually also the succeeding two years of its life. It either becomes a success within those years, or it becomes, for the time being at least, a failure. Few developers with their small equity investment and high mortgage payments can afford to retain ownership of a losing operation for a sufficient length of time to take advantage of any ultimate success.

Therefore, the master plan for the site must provide for as nearly perfect an *initial* stage as is possible. If, then, in five or ten years the center becomes so popular that the developer decides to enlarge it, the center's popularity and sales potential are already clearly established and the perfection of the final plan is of much less importance.

Expansion of individual stores is a different problem. Special provision for such expansion may be made by (1) adding future floor(s), (2) lateral contiguous construction, (3) use of areas held in reserve for this purpose in basements and mezzanines, or (4) eliminating adjacent tenancies and taking over their space.

In all cases involving an increase in the project's gross leasable area (G.L.A.), added parking must be provided to compensate and maintain proper ratio of G.L.A. to car stalls.

Regardless of the program of phased construction or of future expansion, there are two additional items that must at all times be taken into consideration in any schedule:

1. A shopping center does by far its greatest

amount of business in the two months before Christmas. Its next busiest season is before Easter, and the next busiest, after that, is prior to "back to school." Therefore, shopping centers in general and department stores in particular customarily set opening dates that are inviolable. Any serious postponement can jeopardize the heavy investment in merchandise for that particular season. It is customary, therefore, in all shopping center operations to schedule the work *backward* from the mandatory and inflexible opening date and allow adequate time for fixturing and stocking the stores.

2. For public impact and general public acceptance in a shopping center's early years, it is generally desirable to schedule the leasing, planning, and construction so that *all stores can open at once.* This avoids the public inconvenience and bad public relations of a mall with many barricades, etc., due to unfinished stores, as well as the unfavorable customer reaction from limited merchandise.

GENERAL DESIGN AND PLANNING CRITERIA

Column Spacing

Significant dimension is along the mall as this involves the widths, i.e., frontages, of stores. Often used spaces are 20, 25 and 30 ft, with the last the most flexible. Dimension from mall to rear of store can be set by the most economical structural system. It is essential to arrive at the most economical structural system, as the roof is a major cost factor.

Store Depths

For one-story stores in America, buildings are usually 120 to 140 ft deep, sometimes more to accommodate larger stores. If there are basements or mezzanines, the depth dimension usually can be reduced 20 to 25 percent. In European centers and others with many very small stores, there is a problem in how to achieve shallow depth without incurring higher costs from greater mall lengths in relation to floor area. One often used and desirable device is to "dog leg," or "ell," a larger store around a smaller store.

Clear Heights

These vary from 10 to 14 ft or more, with 12 ft a good average. Above this clear height, there must be adequate space for air-conditioning ducts, recessed lights, structural system, etc.

Ducts and Shafts

The shells of the buildings must be flexible enough to accommodate any reasonable tenant requirements. It is essential that the mechanical engineer set up a schedule of the location and sizes of the principal duct runs and shafts to avoid serious future space problems. This requirement includes special exhaust ventilation through the roof and all other mechanical items that can be anticipated.

Central Plant vs. Individual HVAC System

Regardless of which method is used, the space to be occupied by all equipment must be determined, both in size and location, in the earliest planning stages. Central plant equipment can be in a separate building, on the project roof, or elsewhere so long as it is

economical as to design and length of runs. Individual plants in each store require roof space, cooling towers, etc.

Roof Equipment Concealment

The inexcusable eyesores so often seen can be avoided by proper coordination of work between the leasing agent, the architect, and the mechanical engineer and the resulting provision of properly located and designed roof screens and enclosures.

Exterior Walls

As these may have, depending on each store's requirements, service doors, public entrance doors, trash rooms, show windows, etc., a modular design that can suitably accommodate for visual effect any of these features is very desirable. Show windows and public entrances are rare on parking lot facades, as it has been found that the great majority of customers enter stores from the mall rather than directly from the parking lot. Public entrances from the parking lot usually occur only for department stores, for stores open on Sundays, and for such tenants as restaurants, drugstores, and the like.

Anarchy vs. Regimentation

In the original shopping centers, there often was no design control at all, with a resulting anarchy of signs, materials, and design. This situation gradually changed to one where so much rigid control was exercised that the projects became far too monotonous. Proper design calls for a homogeneous whole with the widest possible latitude for individual design of each store. Generally the greatest possible latitude (in good taste) should be given to the *mall* facades, with fairly severe restrictions placed on the *exterior* facades. This gives interest in the interior, where it is desirable, and unity of design for the exterior.

Traffic

The car capacity of all contiguous roadways used for ingress and egress must be sufficient to accommodate present and future through traffic *plus* the traffic generated by the shopping center. Proper signal controls, reservoir

lanes, divider strips, and other traffic control features must be provided. It should always be kept in mind that a center with, say, 5,000-car parking and an average turnover on Fridays of, say, four cars per parking space, accommodates a total number of cars per day that would stretch, if traveling in a line on the highway, all the way from New York to Boston. Because of the complexity of the traffic problem, the developer or his architect frequently hires a traffic engineer to assure himself that the highways have adequate capacity and that the center can accommodate smoothly the ingress and egress of customers' cars. The traffic engineer is, however, interested in speed and smooth flow of traffic, while the architect for the project should be more concerned with convenience, simplicity, and customer's freedom of choice in selecting her route and parking procedure (Fig. 3).

LEASING

Customarily the satellite stores and all other facilities, retail or otherwise with the exception of the department store, are leased by the developer. The developer may lease one or all the department stores and build them to the tenant's requirements, or he may sell or lease the land to one or more, in which case the department store designs and constructs its own facilities within the established limits and requirements of the overall project.

The satellite leases usually provide for a minimum annual rent (on which the mortgage calculation is based) plus or against an *overage* rent consisting of a percentage of the store's gross annual sales. It is the latter provision which makes the success of each individual store so important to the developer and which compensates him for future inflation. It puts the developer and tenant into a sort of partnership.

It is obvious that the individual rent terms must reflect not only the cost of the land and overall project costs but also the amount of special work done by the developer for the individual tenant. In the past, the developer installed much of the tenant's special requirements and received a proportionally higher rent. The trend today, however, is for the developer to supply the shell of the premises only, with each tenant installing at his own

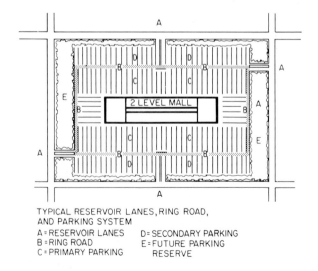

TYPICAL RESERVOIR LANES, RING ROAD, AND PARKING SYSTEM
A = RESERVOIR LANES   D = SECONDARY PARKING
B = RING ROAD   E = FUTURE PARKING
C = PRIMARY PARKING   RESERVE

Fig. 3

expense the ceiling and floor finishes, decor, mall storefront, and some of the air-conditioning equipment items. Trade fixtures, except in unusual circumstances, are always installed by the tenant.

As the leasing program takes time to consummate, it is absolutely essential that the leasing proceed *simultaneously* with the architectural design and drawings and that the leasing agent and the architect and his engineers keep in continuous communication. Otherwise, long delays and expensive changes ensue.

In view of the importance of the department stores in generating customer traffic for the project, their lease terms usually provide only a minimum (if any) profit for the developer. The profit on the development as a whole must then come from proportionately higher rents from the satellites. For this reason, when the owner of a center is a developer and not a department store, it is essential that at least half the total retail area be occupied by high-rent satellites.

TENANT MIX

Tenant "mix" is the name for the *plan* relationship to each other of the various types of stores and facilities. Proper tenant mix exposes the customer to a varying sequence of differing types of merchandise. If each store type is properly located in relation to every other store type, it has been demonstrated that each store will receive its maximum sales volume. In such cases, the center will be successful and all tenants, plus the developer, will profit. If the relationships are not correct, many of the stores may not receive their fair share of the customer's dollar, and both the individual store and the developer will suffer. The developer may not, in such cases, receive any rent based on percentage of sales volume, and the strength of the center as a whole will be weakened. There are many theories on proper tenant mix. It has been fairly well established, however, that with few exceptions and regardless of length of malls or number of mall levels, a generally *mixed* pattern of high and low prices, soft goods and hard goods, retail and services produces the best individual sales volumes and overall success.

THE MALL

The pedestrian mall has become the feature of today's shopping center, whether the project is in the suburbs or in the central business district. The pedestrian mall has the following characteristics:

a. The mall usually consists of the principal mall, the major pedestrian shopping street of the project, and one or more subsidiary approach malls or access routes connecting the main mall with the parking areas or adjacent streets.

b. With few exceptions, all stores have their principal entrance on the main mall or, less desirably, on approach malls, whether or not these stores have additional entrances to parking lots or adjacent streets.

c. The mall can be on one level or on two or more superimposed levels. Each mall level should, however, avoid slopes or steps within its own walkways to avoid hindrance to shopping and a source of accidents.

d. The mall can be (1) open, with weather protection consisting solely of continuous

canopies along the store fronts, (2) completely covered but open to the air, or (3) completely enclosed, necessitating heating in winter and air-conditioning in summer.

The trend has been almost exclusively toward the enclosed climatized mall except where weather conditions are ideal or some other factor makes the open mall preferable.

Enclosed malls have been in the form of huge courts; they have been wide, narrow, straight, circuitous, empty, or filled with amenities; they have had one level or two or more levels; and they have been lighted by skylights or solely by artificial means (Fig. 4).

The trend has been steadily away from wide malls and court-type malls. Currently widths of 30 to 40 ft are outnumbering widths of 50 ft or more. The wider malls require more land-

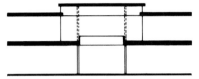

TYPICAL SECTION OF 2 STORY MALL SHOWING NARROWER LOWER LEVEL SOMETIMES USED TO GIVE BETTER VISIBILITY BETWEEN LEVELS AND INCREASE LEASABLE AREA.

Fig. 4

scaping and features to avoid a barren atmosphere. They also require more cubage and hence are less economical despite the possibility of high rents from kiosks and similar features spotted along their lengths. Furthermore, and most important, narrow malls facilitate back and forth comparison shopping from one side to the other and hence significantly aid the customer's exposure to the merchandise. A logical trend is toward stretches of narrow mall, generally devoid of amenities, punctuated by moderate-sized courts in front of department stores or elsewhere which become customer magnets. The courts have greater lighting intensity, greater height, and spectacular features such as fountains, lush landscaping, and monumental sculpture.

The length of malls generally should not be more than 800 ft (preferably less) between department stores or other major features; but, in the case of more than two department stores, total length can be substantially more.

Because of the high downtown land costs and increasing land costs in the suburbs, plus the shortage of sites of adequate area, the two-level mall is becoming a standard solution; in due course, malls of three levels or more will doubtless increase in number. Such multilevels make the shopping area much more compact and walking distances shorter.

In connection with any two-level (or more) mall, it is virtually mandatory that *each level be as important as every other level;* otherwise, one level will become *the* level, all the stores will want to be on that level, and the other level will be second choice, will command lower rents, and hence, in all probability, will not economically justify its construction.

To achieve this equality of desirability, of customer appeal, and of rent balance, it is essential that both (or all) levels have:

a. Equally convenient accessibility from parking areas by means of two or more levels of immediately adjacent parking, whether on grade or on decks or by means of other devices to equalize the parking convenience.

b. No mall dead end on any level without a department store as its terminus.

c. Adequate vertical transportation between levels, usually one or more sets of escalators and several sets of convenient stairs.

d. Visual interconnection of levels through the maximum use of open wells permitting maximum visibility of one level's shops and customers from the other.

MALL AMENITIES

With the advent of the pedestrian mall came the need to give it interest and glamour as an enhancement to the overall customer appeal of the center. This interest or glamour is normally non-income producing; but, in the case of small retail kiosks for such items as keys, stockings, photo supplies, and soft drink facilities, very high rents can be obtained because of the conspicuous and high-exposure locations.

Mall amenities generally include, in addition to landscaping, which will be elaborated on in another section, most of the following items:

• Trash and ash receptacles, a mandatory aid in preventing litter.

• Directories of one sort or another to facilitate finding specific stores.

• Public telephone installations.

• Seating groups and individual benches for resting, although many planners believe it is better to have frequent coffee stands both for better control and to produce income. Many also believe that, in downtown areas, it is often better to avoid benches so as to discourage loitering by undesirable elements.

• Fountains, properly designed for public protection from water hazards. (Water seems to have a universal appeal.)

• Kiosks of various sizes and shapes, generally less than 250 sq ft, though there is a trend to larger ones.

• Lockers (occasionally) for storing purchases while continuing to shop.

• Sculpture or other art forms as major design features.

• Miscellaneous items occasionally used to catch the public interest, such as birdcages, kiddy mazes, fashion mirrors, closed-circuit TV, clocks, continuous music, fashion platforms, exhibit areas, etc. It is noted that in the case of exhibit areas, it is necessary to provide adequate mall-access doors for bringing in large items to be exhibited.

Mall lighting should be low-keyed and incandescent, should lend interest to dark or monotonous areas, and should, except in major courts, allow the storefronts to be the main attraction. Natural light is often used in moderation to give variety of effect and sometimes to save power cost, but generally natural light must be limited in order to avoid dilution of the impact of the storefronts along the mall. As malls are customarily open late afternoons and evenings, adequate artificial illumination must be provided regardless of the extent of the natural light.

Mall materials are of great importance. Generally speaking, they should reflect the quality level of the project, be sturdy enough to resist vandalism, and require minimum maintenance. As an example, floor materials on projects vary from hardened cement to terrazzo, tile, or marble, and now, occasionally, to carpeting. It is noted that the floor of a mall is very conspicuous and the character, quality, and ease of maintenance of its surface materials should be primary considerations.

REGIONAL SHOPPING CENTERS

STOREFRONTS AND SIGNS ON THE MALL

Open malls require glazed storefronts, and hence their requirements are similar to those of the typical city street. Enclosed, climatized malls can have open storefronts, i.e., the major part of the store's frontage can be without show windows and completely open, so that the shopper can enter the store virtually without being aware she has done so. At night the store is protected by sliding glass panels or roll-up grilles.

Generally speaking, except for certain limitations on use of materials and, more particularly, on store signs, the tenant is encouraged to use as much imagination and variety in his store frontage as possible to give glamour, interest, and appeal not only to his own store but to the mall as a whole. Customarily the storefront as well as the store interior is designed by a firm retained by the individual store rather than by the developer.

Except for whatever devices are used to achieve overall unity and harmony, the mall frontage can be treated completely at the will of each tenant, subject only to such restrictions as are recorded in the lease terms. It is essential, however, that such terms give the developer and his architect the right of final approval at their sole discretion. Signs are primarily either for store identification or for general advertising of the store. The former has a legitimate place in the shopping center concept. The latter generally does not. The larger the store, the greater the justification for a sign, as the larger stores are the magnets that attract the public. Endless exterior signs for the smaller stores are confusing, unsightly, and useless to store, owner, and customer. The passerby cannot read the confusion of smaller signs, and the shopper who has already parked gets no identification value from small-store exterior signs as there is literally no way for her to relate any such sign to its own store once she has parked her car and entered the mall system.

Signs, on the other hand, are a necessity within the mall to identify the individual stores. Signs should be simple, easily grasped, in good taste, and so arranged as to be visible at close range as well as at a distance. Too often store identification to the passing potential customer is omitted in favor of huge signs legible only at a distance that may not exist. Properly designed and lighted signs can greatly enhance the interest and appeal. Sign regulations should accompany each lease, and all signs must be subject to final approval from the owner and his architect to ensure proper harmony.

Signs or pylons on the exterior to identify the shopping center itself are a common practice but of dubious value. A regional project with its half-mile of construction is so conspicuous that anything more than simple identification is usually unnecessary.

EXTERIOR FACADES

Some of the major satellite stores desire storefronts on the exterior of the complex, i.e., parking lot facades. The trend, however, whether by store preference for simpler control or by developer preference for economy, is to reduce to a minimum the number of show windows and public entrances on the exterior facade. Experience has shown that the public does not like to enter a mall through anything but the regular mall entrances or else through major stores such as department stores. Furthermore, the whole theory of the present-day shopping center is to get the customers as quickly as possible into the mall, from which the shopping process originates. Department stores insist on having direct entrances on the parking lot as well as the mall, but here again, exterior show windows are usually cut to the minimum.

Even in the central-business-district projects, where some of the stores front on both city streets and the mall, experience has shown that the majority of the shoppers enter the stores from the malls rather than from the city streets, and many street entrances have been closed off.

In the matter of materials, the trend is toward permanence through good but not elaborate quality and the use of masonry and related types of material.

A major problem of recent origin that requires careful solution is that resulting from the fact that there may be several department stores, in addition to the satellite stores, each designed by a different architect. Achievement of harmony of design can, therefore, become difficult.

The problem of visible mechanical equipment is always a serious one. Mechanical design and drawings should always be carefully checked for visual aspects, and when such equipment is visible, consideration has to be given to suitable methods of concealment, whether by masonry screens or whatever.

SERVICING

Servicing involves the delivery of goods to the various stores and also the removal of trash and garbage. In the simple strip center, the servicing is customarily by an alley in the rear of the strip of stores. It is desirable to conceal the alley from adjacent neighborhood areas by a wall or landscaping.

In the one-level regional suburban center, servicing is customarily by one of the following:

a. Underground service tunnel, usually under the mall, connecting directly to tenant-leased basements which connect, in turn, to the stores above. This system avoids all unsightly trash, keeps parked trucks out of the way, and avoids allocation of prime parking space to servicing. It also relegates non-selling activities to the basement, reserving the main floor for sales. The tunnel adds, however, 3 percent or more to the total cost of the construction and more or less necessitates the inclusion of basements. This, in turn, calls for realistic leasing and financing of these basement areas if they are to be self-supporting financially.

b. Service courts on the periphery of the building complex. These are usually partially shielded from public view by masonry walls 6 to 10 ft high or higher. Their cost is minimum, but they occupy space that is expensive if land costs are high and that could otherwise be utilized for prime parking. The interiors of the courts are objectionable in appearance and can rarely be adequately screened. Furthermore these courts can usually be made directly accessible to only a portion of the stores present. This type of project normally has no basement space.

c. Over-the-curb and sidewalk directly from the street. This is the cheapest and uses the least land, but it requires rigid enforcement of cleanliness by the project management, delivery of merchandise and removal of trash generally before or after business hours, and the mandatory inclusion of trash rooms in each store.

Generally speaking, markets, department stores, restaurants, and drug and variety stores have the greatest demand for adequate service facilities.

Service trucking routes on the site are often separated from customer routes, but this arrangement is generally not necessary as the relatively few number of trucks per day in a typical shopping center presents no traffic problem. In the case of sidewalk delivery, the parked trucks pose problems, and policing may be required to prevent the accumulation of trash.

In multilevel projects, the use of strategically placed freight elevators is necessary. These usually connect to fireproof passages at the rear of the stores (whether on an upper level or below grade) and often serve also as fire exits. With this type of project, necessitating service corridors, service courts can usually be fewer and more concentrated.

Mezzanines are occasionally used to provide storage and non-selling space. Such facilities have value in that they reduce the depth of space required and hence the land occupied, but they rarely produce savings in construction cost because of the need for greater height of store-building roofs for adequate clearances.

CLIMATE CONTROL

Today virtually all commercial space such as stores, offices, hotels, and pedestrian malls are maintained the year round within certain limits as to temperature and relative humidity. In most climates this means heating and humidification in the winter, cooling and dehumidification in the summer, and at least ventilation in the intermediate seasons.

The problem of cooling is proportionately more important than heating, even in relatively cold climates, because of the necessity to compensate for the body heat and moisture emitted by crowds of people and the heat from electric lighting, especially the incandescent type. It is not uncommon, even in the north, for the cooling system of a department store to operate almost into the winter season.

When this climatization of commercial space began to be adopted in the earlier shopping centers, it was frequently a matter of tenant choice and expense. The developer would supply the minimum heating required by the code, and each tenant would then decide whether or not to install his own air-conditioning system. This method is still used in neighborhood strip centers. As air-conditioning became more universal, however, it became logical for the developer to take advantage of his stronger buying position and have the air-conditioning installed on his own account as individual systems in each of the stores of his project, charging each tenant enough more rent to compensate for the cost and having each tenant responsible for operation and maintenance. Compressors and fans, as well as "cooling towers" required in the case of larger stores, were installed in basements, on mezzanines, and on roofs. Roof installations, necessary both for lower cost and engineering requirements, became large and unsightly. This led to efforts to concentrate the equipment as much as possible and to surround it with lightweight or, preferably, masonry screen walls creating penthouses on the roofs. With this system of air-conditioning, each tenant always paid the retail electric rate applicable to the service required by him.

In the late 1960s, a new trend set in for the larger regional centers. The developer and his mechanical engineer found they could profitably work out a system involving a central cooling and heating plant for the entire project, metering and selling chilled water and hot water to each of the tenants and, of course, providing complete air-conditioning and heating for the mall and other public space. In this type of operation the developer installs the central plant, all the equipment for the mall, and the distribution lines for the heated and chilled water to the individual tenant spaces. Usually each tenant and/or store owner then installs the heat exchanger, fans, and distribution ducts within his own premises. The developer buys electric power at low rates because of the large amount purchased, and the individual tenant pays the developer for the water used at a lower rate than that which he would have had to pay in the case of his own individual plant. However, the tenant still pays enough to allow the developer to make a profit on the overall central plant operation. Because of this demonstrable and sometimes very substantial annual profit from the sale of heated and chilled water, the developer can finance the central plant so that it does not increase his equity investment. This had not been true before the 1960s.

In some states the developer can go even further and set up a so-called *total energy plant*, producing the electricity itself by means of gas or other fuels. Such systems are, in effect, private utility companies and subject to state law.

Should the developer wish to stay out of the problems of negotiation with tenants and operation of the central plant, there are companies that will undertake, for suitable remuneration, the construction, operation, and ownership of the system on behalf of the developer. In this case, it is obvious that financial and engineering responsibility of the operating company must be clearly established.

It is always *essential* that design provision be made in the earliest stages of the planning for all items of mechanical equipment, with allowance for floor space, for weight, for ceiling clearances, and for suitable visual effects of supply and exhaust grilles, especially in malls.

PARKING AND TRAFFIC

The need for parking was one of the primary factors leading to the development of the shopping center concept. Provision of adequate and convenient parking is, in fact, a basic requirement of any shopping center, regardless of its size or location. In suburban areas where almost all the trade comes by automobile, a ratio of between 5 and 6 car spaces per 1,000 sq ft of leasable store area is mandatory. In the central business district, where mass transportation and walk-in trade can be counted on for a substantial part of the clientele, the ratio can go down to as low as 2.5 to 3 cars per 1,000 sq ft.

In strip centers, customer parking is generally between the roadway and the line of storefronts.

In regional suburban centers, the parking normally is on grade and completely surrounding the shopping complex. Where land costs approach the cost of parking decks, it is be-

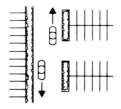

IDEAL LOCATION FOR HEDGES (3 FT. MIN. HEIGHT) TO CONCEAL "OCEAN OF ASPHALT."

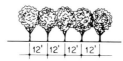

SPACING FOR CONTINUOUS TREE HEDGE

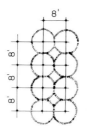

SPACING FOR BOSQUE OR FORMAL MASS OF SMALL TREES.

COMPACTED MASS OF TREES FOR SCALE EFFECT

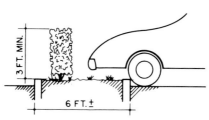

SIMPLE CONTINUOUS HEDGE FOR CONCEALING "OCEAN OF ASPHALT."

Fig. 5

coming more frequent to deck at least a portion of the site area, often where topography aids the situation.

In central-business-district projects, because of very high land cost, the parking usually has to be multidecked and is preferably contiguous, connecting directly with different levels of the center. It can also, for further economy of land use, be above the retail floors on decks as roof parking; or, more customarily, it can be below the retail levels in basement or partial basement locations. Though basement parking is the least desirable from the viewpoint of the shopper's normal psychology and is also least desirable from the construction cost point of view, it is a relatively common arrangement due to inadequate land area and to the legal aspects of the federal urban renewal programs. In such programs, in order to conserve land area and cost, the developer frequently can build the complex on air rights over multidecked garage facilities built by one or another government agency.

It has been stated by authorities on the subject, however, that for customer acceptance it is better to have parking above grade, even up to six or eight levels, than to have it more than one or two levels below grade.

In the matter of parking layout, car stalls can be set at angles (say, $70°$) to the lanes, which then requires *one-way* traffic; or stalls can be at $90°$ to the lanes, permitting *two-way* traffic. The former is easier for the actual positioning of the car in the stall but more complicated and inflexible for the customer, due to the one-way pattern. Although both are commonly used, the $90°$ arrangement is somewhat more frequent for grade parking whereas the angled system is more customary for garages and decks.

Parking lanes, including the stalls on each side, range from 60 to 64 ft in width for $90°$ parking and from 56 to 58 ft for angled parking. In any decked parking layout, it is important that deck widths be multiples of these standard dimensions. Otherwise, wasted deck area substantially increases the cost per car of the parking without any offsetting advantages. In the case of multi-use central-business-district structures, the proper column spacing, requirements of parking, merchandising, offices, and hotel use vary considerably, and the planning becomes very involved. Practical decisions must be made as to which facility governs, and in no case must the "tail be allowed to wag the dog."

In the typical shopping center, parking is provided by the developer. In the case of central-business-district renewal projects, however, parking may be provided by a parking authority, renewal agency, or others. It may or may not be leased to the developer, or it may be built by the developer and leased to a parking authority or others.

In the case of double-level malls in the suburbs, topography can be an aid rather than a hindrance through provision of on-grade parking at two different levels—one parking area at the level of the upper mall, the other at the lower, thus equalizing the parking access and convenience for each level of the mall.

There are a number of ramp systems for decked parking and various patterns of parking lanes or bays for both ramped and grade parking. In the case of grade parking, lanes or bays should generally be at right angles to the building facades to enable shoppers to walk directly to the building complex without threading through parked cars, as with lanes parallel to the facades.

LANDSCAPING

This visually important element of shopping center design rarely receives the attention and budget its importance deserves. Most suburban customers have gardens and are landscape-conscious. Nevertheless, there are literally hundreds of shopping centers that are surrounded by barren oceans of monotonous asphalt. The primary reason for this situation is that the landscaping is installed last, is not related directly to the building construction operation, and consequently is vulnerable to "corner cutting" by the developer, especially if the project cost is running over the budget.

The landscaping in the regional, that is to say, suburban center usually has two components: interior, i.e., the landscaping in the mall, and exterior, i.e., that outside the buildings and in the parking areas. Because of the climate control in the typical enclosed mall, tropical planting can be maintained provided that adequate light, water, and drainage are supplied and there is proper maintenance. Although mall landscaping should not be luxurious to the point of blocking views of stores and interfering too much with cross-mall shopper traffic, mall landscaping can become a very powerful attraction to shoppers and provide a great deal of advertising and public relations value. When conditions are not suitable for living plants, good results can sometimes be obtained with properly fabricated artificial material.

For the exterior landscaping of the project, the principal problems are (1) the budget; (2) proper scale and effect in relation to the buildings; (3) suitable maintenance, including the problems involved in snow removal; (4) the necessity for obtaining maximum visual impact the first year of the center's operation.

As to this last item, the developer is not so concerned with how the planting will look in 10 years because the first 3 years of the center's operation are the most critical. It is during those years that everything must be at its best, and success is or is not established.

As to scale and effect, it is obviously difficult to obtain satisfactory results when a building mass may be as much as 2,000 ft long and only 20 ft high, and where vast acres of parking must be laid out with maximum convenience for those parking their cars (Fig. 5).

The following basic criteria, if used with imagination and a reasonable budget, can produce maximum effects for minimum costs:

a. Mass effects through close spacing of several trees or bushes in clumps or rows. Better to group five trees a few feet apart than to spot them *singly*, such as at ends of parking lanes, where they will be lost visually.

b. Concentration of the planting near the buildings where it will have the most effect, and not on the periphery.

c. Use of long lines of hedges (*not less* than 3 ft high, and of inexpensive plant material if necessary) wherever the parking pattern will permit. The hedges cut the line of sight from the normal eye level at 5 ft and, especially inside a car, at 4 ft. If the hedges are properly located, they can effectively conceal from view large areas of the parking pavement. This can go a long way toward preventing the "sea of asphalt" effect.

d. Installation of the maximum-sized plant material the budget will permit. Better to omit parts of the planting and use cheaper varieties of material than to have to wait 10 years for the plants to produce the proper effect.

As the regional centers must grow larger, more complex, and more glamorous to maintain their competitive positions, the quality and extent of the landscaping on future projects should steadily improve.

LIST OF STORES BY LOCATIONS

For reference purposes, the alphabetically arranged lists below represent a check list of stores that the Council[1] considers are suitable for the several categories of real estate location in shopping areas.

No. 1 Locations (100 Percent or "Hot Spot")

1. Bakery
2. Boys' clothing
3. Candy store
4. Children's wear
5. Cosmetics and perfume
6. Costume jewelry
7. Department store
8. Drugstore
9. Five and ten
10. Florist
11. Gift shop
12. Girls' apparel
13. Grocery (cash and carry)
14. Handkerchiefs and handbags
15. Hosiery shop
16. Infants' wear
17. Jewelry
18. Leather goods and luggage — (depends on ability to pay high rent)
19. Lingerie
20. Men's clothing
21. Men's furnishings
22. Millinery
23. Novelties
24. Optical shop
25. Paperback book store
26. Photographic supplies and cameras
27. Popcorn and nuts
28. Prescriptions (may not be possible because of drugstore)
29. Restaurant
30. Shoes, children's
31. Shoes, men's
32. Shoes, women's
33. Sportswear, women's
34. Tobacconist
35. Toilet goods
36. Variety store
37. Women's wear

The following shops may go equally well in either No. 1 or No. 2 locations:

1. Cafeteria
2. Dry goods
3. Newsstand
4. Service grocery

No. 1 locations should be held largely for shops that keep open on certain common nights.

No. 2 Locations (Near the 100 Percent Area)

1. Art store and artists' supplies
2. Athletic goods
3. Auto supplies
4. Bank

A bank should not be in a no. 1 location, as it has limited open hours and when closed has a deadening effect on adjacent shops.

5. Bar (liquor)
6. Barber shop (basement in the no. 1 location)

When deciding on width of a barber shop, consider carefully the number of lines of barber chairs in order that space will not be wasted.

7. Beauty shop

J. Ross McKeever (ed.), *The Community Builders Handbook*, Urban Land Institute, Washington, D.C., 1968.

[1] Community Builders Council of the Urban Land Institute.

8. Bookstore
9. China and silver
10. Cleaners and dyers (pick-up)
11. Cocktail lounge
12. Corset shop
13. Delicatessen (also in no. 1 location in some cases)
14. Electrical appliances
15. Fruit and vegetable market (should be considered in relation to regular grocer)
16. Glass and china
17. Laundry agency
18. Linen shop
19. Liquor store
20. Maternity clothes
21. Pen shop
22. Radio and television
23. Sewing machines and supplies
24. Sporting goods
25. Stationery and greeting cards
26. Telegraph office
27. Theater (or no. 3 location)
28. Woolens and yarns

The following shops may go equally well in either no. 2 or no. 3 locations:

1. Gas, power, and light company offices
2. Ticket offices
3. Toy shop

No. 3 Locations

1. Army goods store (or in no. 4 location)
2. Art needlework shop
3. Baby furniture
4. Building and loan office
5. Chinese restaurant
6. Christian Science Reading Room (or second floor in no. 2)
7. Dance studio (or no. 4 location)
8. Doctors and dentists

Doctors and dentists are not favored in central locations. Janitorial expense for doctors' offices is at least twice as high as for ordinary office space. Also, they are hard tenants to please as to maintenance.

9. Drapery and curtain shop
10. Electrical equipment and repair
11. Express office (a popular service that helps build up a retail area)
12. Furniture (pays low rent per square foot)
13. Hardware
14. Health foods store
15. Hobby shop
16. Interior decoration
17. Ladies' and men's tailor (or second floor in no. 1 or no. 2 locations)
18. Mortgage loan office (or second floor in no. 2 location)
19. Office supplies and office furniture (pays low rent per square foot)
20. Optometrist and optician (or no. 1 or 2)
21. Paint store
22. Photographers (or second floor in no. 1 or no. 2 locations)
23. Piano store (low rent)
24. Pictures and framing (low rent)
25. Post office
26. Power and light offices
27. Real estate offices (or no. 4)
28. Shoe repair
29. Tavern
30. Ticket offices
31. Travel bureau (or no. 2 location)

No. 4 Locations

1. Automatic family laundry service
2. Bowling alleys
3. Carpets and rugs, oriental
4. Diaper service
5. Dog or cat hospital (without outside runs)
6. Drive-in eating places
7. Radio and television broadcasting station

By VICTOR GRUEN, *AIA**

The shopping center is one of the few new building types created in our time. Because shopping centers represent groupings of structures and because of the underlying cooperative spirit involved, the need for environmental planning for this building type is obvious. Where this need has been fully understood, shopping centers have taken on the characteristics of urban organisms serving a multitude of human needs and activities.

SELECTING THE SITE

Location

For the purposes of this discussion, the term "location" indicates the general area in which to select a shopping center site. The merits of location, whether the land has already been acquired or is being sought, must always be subjected to careful economic analysis. If the site has already been acquired, the economist directs his study toward the economic characteristics of the location in an effort to decide whether the particular property should be developed as a shopping center project, and if so, what its size and character should be. If the site has not yet been acquired, the economist must make a study of the general area within which the most suitable location can be pinpointed. This over-all study may involve as large an area as the metropolitan area of a large city.

First, an analysis is made of the total available economic potential of the general area. The search is gradually narrowed down through analysis of various segments of the larger area; a specific area within the chosen segment that seems to offer the most advantageous potential is then examined, and finally, a defined location within this specific area is chosen. If properly undertaken, this procedure will usually establish the most suitable location for a shopping center.

Inherent in any economic analysis is a study of the following factors:

Population
Income
Purchasing power

* The illustrations and certain other material in this section have been reprinted, with permission, from Shopping Towns USA by Victor Gruen and Larry Smith, published by Reinhold Publishing Corp., New York (1960).

Competitive facilities
Accessibility
Other related considerations.

Attention must be paid not only to the existing population but also to prospects for future growth, which may be forecast by reference to past growth rates, the trend of population shifts, and the availability of remaining suitable land for residential development.

Population

In forecasting the population trend for ten or fifteen years, consideration must be given to such factors as existing population density, zoning restrictions, physical or man-made barriers to the development of new residential areas (mountains, waterways, industrial areas, public parks, cemeteries, airports), and other land uses that would forestall residential development.

The composition of the population in the trade area, as far as racial or economic characteristics are concerned, is important in various regions of the country.

In areas where strong traditions or prejudices exist, it may be unreasonable to expect that various ethnic groups will shop together. Also, it is unreasonable to expect that persons of low- or middle-income groups will patronize a high-quality type of shopping center or, conversely, that persons in the highest income groups will shop generally in centers that feature medium- or low-priced merchandise.

Trade area

The term "trade area" is normally defined as "that area from which is obtained the major portion of the continuing patronage necessary for the steady support of the shopping center."

The defining factors used in delineating a trade area vary from center to center. They include, but are not limited to, the size and influence of the proposed retail facilities, planning and design characteristics, travel time to and from the location, the existence of natural or man-made barriers—such as railroads and rivers—that

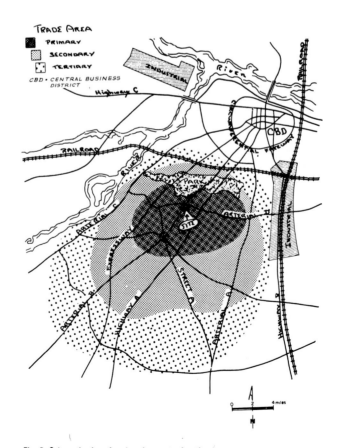

Fig. 6. Schematic plan of a shopping center location

Shown in the plan are trade areas, means of access, and various barriers to accessibility.

would limit accessibility either in fact or psychologically, and the existence of competitive facilities. Thus the trade areas for various locations will not necessarily assume similar sizes or shapes (Fig. 6).

Site qualifications

It is important that the land to be used possess, to the greatest degree possible, the following qualifications:

1. The site must be located in the most desirable general area as established by the economic survey.

2. The site must be owned or controlled by the developer, or offer the possibility of acquisition.

3. Land cost must be in keeping with over-all economic considerations.

4. Existing zoning must permit shopping center development, or a reasonable likelihood of rezoning must exist.

5. The site must contain sufficient land to permit construction of facilities to meet the sales potential.

6. The land must be in one piece, free of intervening roadways, rights-of-way, easements, major waterways, or other ob-

stacles that would force development in separated portions.

7. The topography and shape of the site must permit advantageous planning and reasonably economical construction.

8. The surrounding road pattern and accessibility must allow full utilization of the business potential.

9. The structure must be visible from major thoroughfares.

14. Surrounding land uses should be free of competitive developments, and, if possible, should be of a nature that enhances the operation of the shopping center.

Rarely will a site completely fulfill all the above requirements, and advantages will have to be weighed and balanced against shortcomings. If the site already exists, it is sometimes difficult to separate the affection an owner may have for it (because of family sentiment or other reasons) from the hard facts of suitability, but it is well to remember that most poorly operating centers in the United States are located on just such "accidental" sites. It is, of course, possible that an existing site

may also fulfill the standard requirements, but determination should be made only after the same thorough scrutiny and analysis that would be given to a site to be purchased.

The following list indicates the relative importance of various considerations in site selection:

Location (value of 50)	*Value*
Population within 1 mile—quantity	5
Population within 1 mile—quality	3
Population within 5 miles—quantity	7
Population within 5 miles—quality	4
Population from rural area—quantity	2
Population from rural area—quality	1
Pedestrian traffic shopping at adjacent stores	4
Pedestrian traffic nearby for other purposes	3
Public transportation	5
Automobile traffic—quantity	4
Automobile traffic—availability	4
Direction of population growth	7
Area (value of 15)	
Size of plot	15

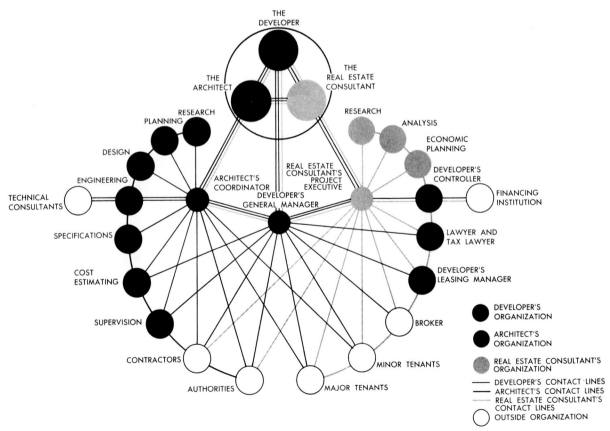

Fig. 7. The planning team

Physical characteristics (value of 25)

Shape of plot for design	4
Plot not divided by traffic lanes	8
Location on arterials for ease of traffic control	4
Cost of clearing and grading	2
Cost of utilities and drainage	2
Visibility	3
Surrounding areas	2

Availability (value of 10)

Ease of acquisition and time	6
Cost	4
	100%

ZONING

Contrary to nineteenth-century precepts of strict separation of industrial and residential land, brought about by rapid industrialization, most progressive planners and zoning boards today recognize that not all types of nonresidential activities are necessarily undesirable in predominantly residential areas.

The modern shopping center that integrates commercial, business, entertainment, and cultural facilities within a carefully planned framework, separates various modes of traffic from one another, and provides for the protection of surrounding residential areas from any objectionable uses, has made a significant contribution in this direction.

The developer may encounter any of the following zoning conditions:

1. The site is commercially zoned, or zoned for a "lower" use, in which case there is no problem.

2. The community has not yet adopted a zoning master plan, and the local planning board is willing to grant suitable zoning.

3. The entire site area is zoned residentially, or only a small portion, usually a narrow strip along the highways, is zoned for commercial use. The owner will then have to apply for rezoning of all or part of the site.

THE PLANNING TEAM

Depending on the size and complexity of the project, the planning team might, in neighborhood and intermediate centers, consist of the developer, the architect, and in some instances, a leasing consultant or lease broker. In projects of greater complexity and size, such as regional shopping centers, it may be well to add to the team an experienced consultant in real estate matters, well versed in shopping center economics (Fig. 7).

THE PLANNING SCHEDULE

Shopping center planning is a lengthy process in which each step must logically follow from the previous one. Impatient or snap decisions may result in catastrophe. First, a tentative planning and construction schedule is outlined which may be divided into five phases:

Exploratory phase
Preliminary phase
Final planning phase
Construction phase
Opening phase.

For regional centers, each of these phases is likely to be clearly defined and even subdivided into various stages; for smaller centers the activity may be consolidated into fewer stages.

1. *Exploratory phase:* All pertinent circumstances and conditions are thoroughly probed, and the conceptual image of the shopping center is established.

2. *Preliminary phase:* Negotiations with major tenants and financing institutions are undertaken, and necessary adjustments are made. Preliminary drawings indicating all architectural and engineering aspects are completed. Preliminary specifications are written, and a reliable preliminary cost estimate is arrived at.

3. *Final planning phase:* Working drawings and specifications are completed, establishing a reliable basis for competitive bidding and for construction. Building permits are obtained. Invitations to bid are written.

4. *Construction phase:* Contracts are awarded. The architect is engaged in general supervision, supported by clerks-of-the-works who are usually retained by the developer. The architect chooses materials, selects colors, and integrates landscaping and art work. The developer and the economist are active in completing leasing, getting the center on an operational basis, and preparing for the opening.

5. *Opening phase:* The opening is an important event that calls for imagination as well as careful planning. In recent years, shopping centers of varying size throughout the country have been opened with ceremonies ranging from the quiet, unobtrusive opening of a few stores at a time, to mass opening ceremonies lasting for several days and featuring various kinds of attention-getting promotions.

Timing

It is difficult to estimate the time periods necessary for each phase of the planning

schedule, because of fluctuations in size and complexity of the project, availability of major tenants and of financing, climatic conditions, and the like. The following tabulation gives time ranges for regional projects proceeding under normal conditions:

	Time span, weeks
Exploratory phase (26 to 56 weeks)	
Feasibility study	8 to 12
Conceptual planning stage	4 to 6
Presentation stage	4 to 8
Development stage	10 to 30
Preliminary phase (10 to 22 weeks)	
Adjustment stage	4 to 10
Consolidation stage	6 to 12
Final planning phase	20 to 30
Construction phase (62 to 114 weeks)	
Bidding	4 to 6
General building construction	52 to 100
Tenants' building—interior construction	6 to 8
Total for planning and construction	118 to 222
	(27 to 51 months)

For intermediate centers (100,000 to 300,000 sq ft), a reasonable time span is 18 to 40 months; for neighborhood centers the span, depending largely on tenant availability, is likely to range from 12 to 24 months.

SPACE ALLOTMENTS

The architect's work starts with the planning of the site. For this task he must have at his disposal the findings of the economic analysis establishing the total rental area that can be supported by the shopping potential, broken down into main merchandising categories. He must have some idea of other uses to which the land should be devoted, and an idea of other probable zoning problems. On the basis of feasibility studies, he now has a general idea of traffic and accessibility, as well as full information about physical conditions of the site (including a topographic survey) and, as a result of test borings, about soil conditions. Sometimes he also knows the basic requirements of the potential major tenant or tenants.

With this information, he begins planning by carefully allocating portions of the land to specific uses. These uses fall into seven basic categories:

REGIONAL SHOPPING CENTERS

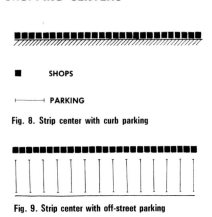

■   SHOPS

⊢——⊣ PARKING

Fig. 8. Strip center with curb parking

Fig. 9. Strip center with off-street parking

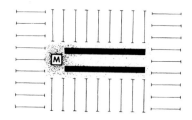

Fig. 11. Mall center with only one magnet

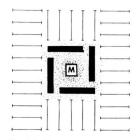

Fig. 13. Cluster-type center

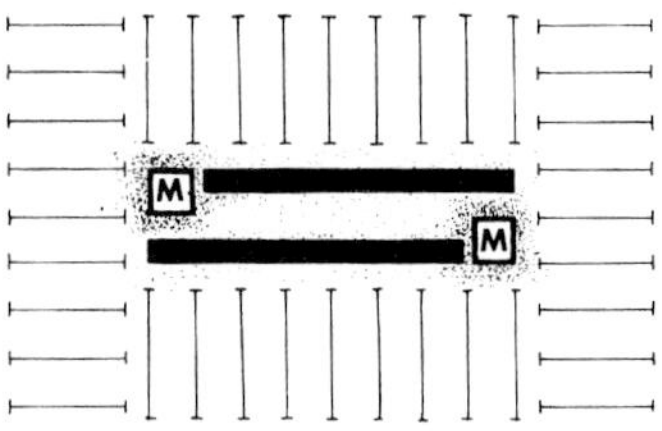

Fig. 10. Double-strip center with off-street parking

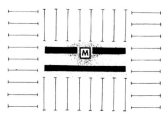

Fig. 12. Mall center with magnet centrally placed

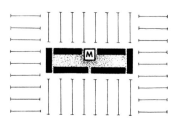

Fig. 14. "Introverted" center

1. *Structures*
   a. For retail purposes (retail areas)
   b. For service purposes (heating and air-conditioning plants, electric substations, maintenance shops, truck roads, loading docks, and equipment storage)
   c. For other commercial uses (offices and recreational facilities)
   d. For public use such as civic and social facilities (community center, auditorium, exhibition space, and children's play areas)
2. *Car storage areas*
   a. Surface parking lots
   b. Double-deck or multiple-deck garages
3. *Pedestrian areas*
   a. Malls, courts, lanes, and plazas
   b. Covered pedestrian areas, such as public corridors and covered malls or courts
4. *Automobile movement areas*
   Distribution road system on site
5. *Public transportation areas*
   Bus roads, bus terminals, and taxi stands
6. *Buffer areas*
   Landscaped areas separating car storage areas or service areas from the public road system, or areas separating parking areas from one another or parking areas from service areas
7. *Reserve areas*
   Portions of site to be held in reserve

for the planned growth of the shopping center.

SITE PLANNING PRINCIPLES

The allocation of space for these and possibly other uses should be guided by certain planning principles in order to attain the highest feasible productivity of the land over an extended period of time: (1) Safeguard surrounding areas against blight; (2) Expose retail facilities to maximum foot traffic; (3) Separate various mechanized traffic types from one another and from foot traffic; (4) Create a maximum of comfort and convenience for shoppers and merchants; and (5) Achieve orderliness, unity, and beauty.

Foot traffic

Exposure of all individual stores in a shopping center to the maximum amount of foot traffic is the best assurance of high sales volume. Suburban business real estate often has been evaluated on the basis of passing automobile traffic—an evaluation which overlooks the fact that automobiles do not buy merchandise. It is only after the driver of even the most expensive car leaves it and becomes a pedestrian that he can become a buyer. Therefore, if shopping centers are to prosper, dense foot traffic must be created. "Shopping traffic," the act of walking from store to store, creates the lifeblood of a

shopping center; and proper circulation of this shopping traffic ensures business success.

Bearing in mind the relative importance in each instance of the size of the center, the shape of the site, the character of the tenancy, and other related circumstances, it is possible to weigh the advantages and drawbacks of various types of site planning to achieve the desired foot traffic. The manner in which site planning can influence the quantity of shopping traffic is illustrated in the schematic plans (Figs. 8 through 14) discussed **below.**

The degree of completeness of the separation between transportation and pedestrian areas depends on the size of the shopping center. In a single commercial building, this separation becomes effective only after the customer has entered the store. If there are two buildings, it might be possible to arrange a separated pedestrian area between them. The chances to create separated pedestrian areas are slightly higher in an intermediate center. In a regional center, complete separation is almost always possible and should be effected. Even in the smallest grouping of stores, such as a neighborhood center, it is possible to achieve a certain amount of separation by means of broad sidewalks with landscaping, low garden walls, and the like.

Strip center with curb parking (Fig. 8): In this plan, the shopping center is comprised of a row of stores extending 2,000 ft along the highway. The shopper parks at the curb in front of the store, transacts his business, and then is likely to enter his car and drive off. Shopping or foot traffic is limited.

Strip center with off-street parking (Fig. 9): This shopping center consists of a 2,000-ft-long row of stores set back from the highway sufficiently to permit parking in front. The sidewalk, or covered walkway, encourages foot traffic along the store fronts. This plan generates a certain amount of shopping traffic and thus is clearly superior to the type shown in Fig. 8. Shopping traffic is nevertheless limited, chiefly because of the 2,000-ft distance between the extreme ends of the strip. The shopper may return to his car after each transaction and drive to the next store on his list, ignoring intervening merchants.

Double-strip center with off-street parking (Fig. 10): Here, the strip is divided into two rows of stores, facing each other along a pedestrian mall, with parking on four sides. A "magnet" (department store, junior department store, or other major tenant store) is placed at each end. The 2,000-ft strip of stores is now divided into two 1,000-ft-long strips. With the distance between the two magnets now only half as great, foot traffic will be greater and the intervening stores will profit accordingly. Also, the creation of a highly desirable pedestrian area shielded from the noise, smells, confusion, and hazards of automobile traffic will contribute to greater shopping traffic.

Mall center with only one magnet (Fig. 11): In this plan, the existence of only one magnet, located at the extreme end of the pedestrian mall, reduces shopping traffic because of lack of interchange. The stores farthest from the magnet will participate very little in the traffic it generates.

Mall center with magnet centrally placed (Fig. 12): The arrangement of the pedestrian mall is the same as that shown in Fig. 11, except that the magnet is moved to a center position on one side of the mall. This modification represents a considerable improvement over the previous example.

Cluster-type center (Fig. 13): The major tenant is placed in the center of a cluster arrangement. Nearly all stores thus become neighbors of the most powerful shopping-traffic puller.

"Introverted" center (Fig. 14): This type exemplifies what might be called the "introverted" center, in which all store fronts are turned toward the inside of the building cluster. Entry into individual stores directly from the parking lot is diminished

or completely excluded. Shopping traffic is funneled through a limited number of entrance arcades into pedestrian areas—a plan that markedly increases the density of shopping traffic and controls its direction.

Separation of traffic types

1. *Pedestrian from transportation:* The separation of pedestrian areas from transportation areas is one of the cornerstones of good planning. The constant movement of vehicles within transportation areas inevitably creates a certain amount of danger, noise, fumes, and confusion, which distract the shopper and diminish shopping enjoyment.

2. *Service from customer traffic:* Service traffic in shopping centers represents a considerable portion of mechanized traffic. Even in the smallest shopping center, service vehicles for deliveries, pick-ups, garbage and trash collection, repair crews, construction and fixture contractors, and utility companies create a significant portion of the over-all traffic. Separation of service traffic from customer traffic is essential and may be accomplished on one or two levels.

Service areas on the merchandising or ground level in the form of truck roads, service courts, and other types of loading facilities, are practical in the neighborhood and intermediate centers. Good planning principles demand that such areas be properly shielded by screen walls or landscaping and that service vehicles be able to enter or leave without interference from automobiles or pedestrians.

Service areas on nonmerchandising levels permit the most productive space to be totally freed from service functions. Only the large center can achieve this separation, for which there are a number of possible arrangements. The truck tunnel under the shopping center mall is an expensive solution that is more talked about than used. Service roads located at the basement level provide a less expensive solution and are widely used. Where subsurface or topographical conditions make the construction of basements impractical, service and storage areas may be placed above the merchandising level and connected to it by ramps.

3. *Public transportation from customer traffic:* Separation of public transportation from customer traffic is essential. The designer must also consider the space needs for public transportation. Generous arrangements for public carriers with well-located and well-protected waiting areas will encourage transportation companies to

use them. Space requirements for existing and future public transportation facilities should be discussed at the outset of site planning work, and if possible, provisions should exceed the required minimum. Storage space for buses should be provided on or near the site so the transportation company can make extra facilities available for peak periods, especially at closing hours.

Orderliness, unity, and beauty

The concept of orderliness, unity, and beauty is a major planning principle; it must be applied to every major and minor aspect of the project, and must permeate all architectural expressions. Landscaping, signs, the architecture of structures, architectural treatment of spaces between structures, composition of structures in relation to one another, colors, and materials—all must adhere to this vital principle.

PLANNING THE SURROUNDING AREA

The term "surrounding area" can be understood either in its narrowest sense, that is, strips of land on the opposite side of the public roads adjoining the shopping center, or in its widest sense: the entire community within which a shopping center is located.

A reciprocal relationship exists between a shopping center and its surrounding area. A well-planned center can exert a highly invigorating influence on the area surrounding it, while a well-planned surrounding area can add in large measure to the prosperity of the center. Conversely, a poorly planned or unplanned commercial grouping of stores can have a deteriorating effect on its surrounding area, while the success of even the best-planned center can be endangered by a poorly planned or blighted surrounding area. The degree to which effective planning can be applied depends on the general location of the center, the size of the center, the investment policy of the developer, and existing zoning and economic conditions.

In general, if the site for a shopping center is the one remaining piece of land within a completely built-up area, there will obviously be meager possibilities for influencing the character of the surrounding area. Shopping centers in such areas usually operate under the handicap of having to be fitted into existing area and traffic conditions. On the other hand, one should consider the undoubted advantage of being provided with a fully developed buying potential.

Commercial
REGIONAL SHOPPING CENTERS

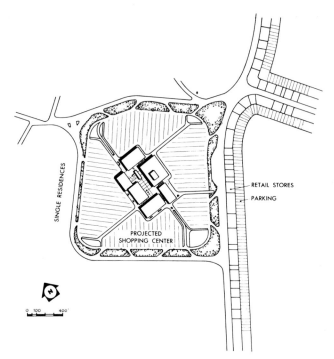

Fig. 15. Original zoning plan

The plan shows zoning conditions as they existed when the original shopping center was projected.

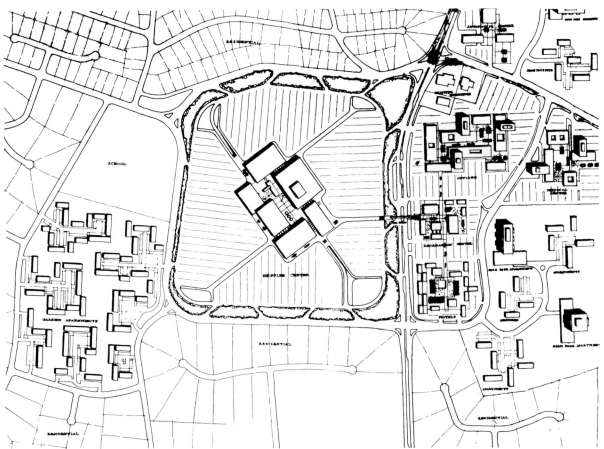

Fig. 16. Revised zoning plan

The plan represents the architect's suggestions for the surrounding land use for the same shopping center shown in Fig. 15. The revisions ensure control of the surrounding land by the developer.

792

Most shopping centers do not fall into this category since it would be rare to find a sufficiently large site for such construction within a fully built-up area. Large tracts of land can usually be found only on the fringe of suburban developments or in comparatively empty areas between suburban growth. This fact applies especially to the large regional shopping center and, to a lesser degree, to the intermediate one. With some planning, however, both types can create sufficient pulling power to reduce the disadvantage of being at some distance from densely populated areas.

The greatest opportunity for effective planning of surrounding areas in relation to the shopping center is afforded when new communities are projected. Then it is often possible to set aside, in the master plan, sites of ideal size.

Whether the shopping center developer acquires surrounding land with the intention of developing it himself, or intends to negotiate with the owners of such land in order to persuade them to develop along the lines of best common interest, it is important to make a comprehensive plan for the land use of the surrounding area (Figs. 15 and 16).

PLANNING FOR EXPANSION

Planning for expansion should be considered if the shopping center is located in a steadily growing area. In such a situation the department store and other major stores will often express the desire to enlarge when their sales volume reaches a stated figure.

In order to make planning for expansion feasible, certain prerequisites must exist. The carrying potential of surrounding public roads must be sufficient to absorb additional traffic loads. The site must be large enough to permit the developer to hold space in reserve for additional building, parking, and traffic areas; alternatively, additionally created income must be such as to justify capital investment for double-deck or multiple-deck parking structures at the time of enlargement. Most important, the developer must be reasonably certain that the growing buying potential of the area will not be more efficiently served by existing or future competition. For example, if suitable shopping center sites exist within the trade area, the likelihood of such future competition is great. These and other related factors must be carefully considered before making a decision to plan for expansion.

If it is decided to plan with a view to expansion, certain measures must be taken. Since the desire of department stores and other major tenant stores for growth is

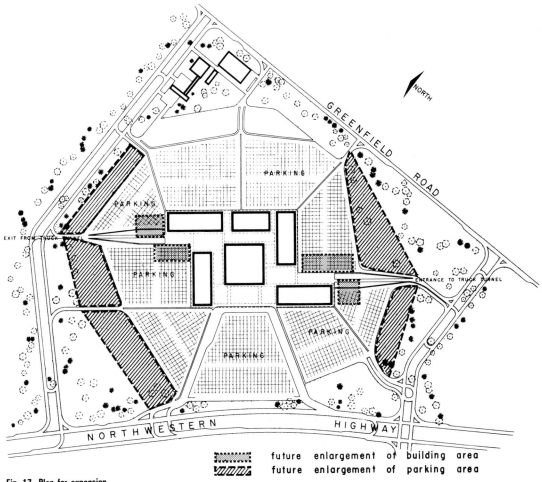

■■■■■■ future enlargement of building area
▨▨▨▨ future enlargement of parking area

Fig. 17. Plan for expansion

Northland Center, Detroit; Victor Gruen Associates, Architects.

usually best met by provisions for vertical additions, the construction of larger foundations and heavier columns as well as roof slabs strong enough to carry future floor loads are required. Horizontal growth is difficult to accomplish without destroying the relationship between shopping center buildings and other elements. Land must be held in reserve for the enlarged parking needs that will be created by expanded shopping facilities. When the original construction is completed, these reserve areas will have to be properly landscaped in order not to mar the over-all appearance of the center. Central air-conditioning and heating-plant structures must be dimensioned to provide space for additional equipment, and all underground utility lines should be of sufficient size to meet ultimate needs. The general plan shown in Fig. 17 indicates existing structures and provisions for expansion.

PLANNING FOR DEVELOPMENT IN STAGES

Planning for development in stages should be considered if the shopping center site is located in an area that has not reached its ultimate population potential and if a quick acceleration of population growth may be expected. Another motivation for development in stages may be the desire of a land owner to make some immediate use of his land even though full utilization will be practical only in future years.

Planning for development in stages can be successfully accomplished only if a total master site-use plan is completed before construction or even detailed planning of the first stage is undertaken.

TRAFFIC

Traffic planning, an integral part of planning the site and the surrounding area, plays an important role in the proper functioning and success of the shopping center. It should be borne in mind, however, that the shopping center is not to be planned to serve traffic; rather, traffic is to be planned to serve the shopping center. Basic traffic planning concerns the planning team as a whole and the architect in particular.

Before the site is finally decided upon, serious consideration must be given to its accessibility. It is essential to gather all information about existing roads and the traffic-carrying capacities of the surrounding road system, as well as to establish the expected additional traffic load generated by the new shopping center.

Although the architect will avail himself of the assistance of a traffic engineer, the specialist should not be expected to furnish basic concepts but should assist the architect in finding solutions within the framework of general and specified planning aims. Traffic planning is the responsibility of the architect since it is part of the general planning of the center.

Aims of traffic planning

1. *Easy traffic flow on surrounding road system.* The existence of enterprises that would result in a constant entering and exiting of cars along the roads opposite the shopping center would disrupt the flow of traffic and is therefore highly undesirable. (This is one reason why proper planning of the surrounding area is so important.) The existence of many side roads opposite the shopping center would also interfere with good traffic flow. The planner's main task is to see to it that automobiles can enter the site without slowdowns.

2. *Effective transfer of road traffic onto the site.* If automobiles were driven directly from an adjoining highway onto parking-lot lanes, chaos would result. The circulatory road that functions as a turn-off lane from the highway, making possible a gradual change of speed from fast-moving traffic to slower parking-lot traffic, plays an extremely important role.

3. *Even and effective distribution of traffic on the site.* The customer should be free to drive to any of the parking areas that surround the center so that he may come as close as possible to the store where he will make his first purchase. Secondary traffic movements within the parking area must be facilitated. In larger centers, arrangements must be made to guarantee the easy flow of circulatory traffic, avoiding any interference with pedestrians walking to and from the center's structures.

4. *Convenient and efficient arrangement of car storage facilities.* The aim of the parking-lot layout should not be to achieve the greatest possible number of parking stalls, but rather to ensure the greatest possible turnover of cars during a given period. Parking capacity is a valid measuring stick only if it denotes the number of conveniently arranged and dimensioned parking stalls.

Walkways for pedestrians will result in greater safety for shoppers and will eliminate the slowing down of vehicles, but will reduce the number of parking spaces in any area. Surfacing of good quality will speed parking and reduce maintenance costs. Lanes should be clearly numbered with signs visible to the motorists when entering the lot as well as when returning from shopping. Proper illumination is essential for safety and speed of parking operations.

No formula for proportioning parking area to sales area is recommended. Existing successful shopping centers provide from 3 to 9 car spaces per 1,000 sq ft of rentable area; however, each project must be decided on its own merits. An allowance of 400 sq ft per stall, including drives, walks, and landscaping, is recommended. Wide stalls arranged at a 45-deg angle permit the fastest and most comfortable parking. The maximum size recommended for a single parking lot is 800 cars.

5. *Separation of service vehicles from customer car traffic.* For service vehicles (trucks, trailers, and garbage- and trash-collecting vehicles), separate roads, branching off from the general road system at points removed as far as possible from the shopping area, should be provided. Ideally—and this can be accomplished in large regional shopping centers—separate entrances and exits to the public road system should be planned. If this arrangement is not feasible, the service roads should branch off from the perimeter circulatory road or, in smaller centers, from general entrance and exit roads before such roads take on the characteristics of parking lanes. Under no circumstances should service vehicles cross roads that directly serve parking operations. Public transportation vehicles should be similarly separated from customer car traffic.

CHARACTER OF THE BUILDINGS

The shopping center establishes a new environment resulting from the banding together of individual businesses in cooperative fashion with the aim of creating greater commercial effectiveness through unified endeavor. It is important that the individual characteristics of the participants not be suppressed, but encouraged. It is equally important, however, that a strong common denominator be created to tie the individual enterprises into a homogeneous unit. These dual aims can be achieved by skillful planning and design. Buildings for single tenancy, for example, are planned not only in accordance with the specific requirements of the specific tenant, but also in harmony with the character of the overall shopping center architecture. Such buildings thus offer a variation of the main theme rather than the introduction of a new one (Fig. 18).

Regimentation is as much to be shunned as anarchy. Complete control of store-front design results in monotony and dullness, and diminishes the enjoyment of window shopping, which thrives on excitement created by ever-changing designs and colors.

Small depth is needed if service facilities are in basements and pedestrian traffic moves only on one side of structure

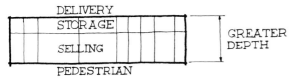

Greater depth is needed if delivery is at back of store on ground level and storage facilities have to be provided on ground level for each tenant

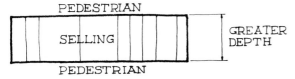

Greater depth is needed if shopping traffic moves on both sides of individual stores

Fig. 18. Depth requirements for tenant stores

The cooperative spirit is best expressed if individual design of tenant stores is encouraged within established limits; around these individual design areas there must be a framework of architecturally controlled areas large enough and treated with sufficient forcefulness to hold the varying expressions firmly together (Fig. 19).

PEDESTRIAN AREAS

Open spaces must be more than narrow lanes between long rows of stores. They must be busy and colorful, exciting and stimulating, must make walking enjoyable,

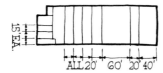

Stores of varying depth and width can be arranged between multiple-tenant structures by skillful division and orientation of stores

and provide places for rest and relaxation. All the senses should be rewarded. Trees, flowers, fountains, sculpture, and murals, as well as the architecture of freestanding structures, are vital parts of the over-all scheme. Public events such as fashion shows, holiday celebrations, and exhibitions are all parts of the life in these open spaces, as are snack bars, outdoor cafes, and restaurants.

Shopping must thus be understood as more than a utilitarian activity. The environment should be so attractive that customers will enjoy these trips, will stay longer, and return more often. This will result in cash registers ringing more often and recording higher sales.

Anarchy in store-front design

Regimentation in store-front design

Individuality in store-front design within a strong architectural framework

Fig. 19. Store-front design

Commercial

RETAIL SHOPS
General; Principles of Retail Shop Design; Interiors

By MURRAY S. COHEN, AIA, Architect

GENERAL

People love to look, window-shop, and buy. Shopping as an experience should provide fun, which in turn provides profits. A successful store or shop is one that is designed to merchandise in addition to looking good. A store can be divided into two principal parts: the *exterior,* which gives identification, encompasses the storefront, show windows, and displays, and the *interior,* where the promise of the storefront display is delivered. Briefly stated, the storefront initiates the sale, and the interior consummates it.

The storefront and the design of the facade must be attractive in order to catch the shoppers' attention and to draw the customers in from the street or from the mall in shopping centers. Graphic identification, with bold color, lighting, lettering, and logos, and attractive display of merchandise are the initial steps.

In enclosed malls, the glass-enclosed show windows are often eliminated or minimized. The "show window" displays are set up in a large vestibule, perhaps elevated or on portable platforms, and become part of the interior. Hence the demarcation between the exterior and the interior is not physical, rather the two are integrated, and it is difficult to define where one ends and the other begins. This is particularly true in enclosed shopping malls. The open or no front generally promotes more impulse buying; department stores will often make their entrances an extension of the mall so that the shopper will be easily enticed into the store. When doors are used, either on the street or on the mall, they should be well marked and easy to find. Entrance to the interior should be easy, related to interior traffic flow and layout, and should be accessible to vertical transportation, if any.

PRINCIPLES OF RETAIL SHOP DESIGN

In order to design satisfactory shops, the first requirement is an understanding of those portions of current merchandising theories which affect the design problem. Briefly, "merchandising psychology" consists of, first, arousing interest; second, satisfying it.

With staple goods the first phase is almost automatic. When nonstaples, accessories, or specialties other than "demand" goods are to be sold, methods of arousing interest may become more complex.

The second phase—the actual sale—involves factors of convenience which are desirable in order to make buying easy, to satisfy customers completely, and to achieve economy of space and time for the store management.

Both phases affect the design of retail shops, and are closely interrelated. In some cases the planning problems involved cannot be segregated. A more detailed listing of steps in the merchandising process, as they affect shop design, follows:

Attracting Customers

This can be accomplished by means of advertising, prices, show-window displays, or new or remodeled quarters, which occupies much of a merchant's efforts. Of these, storefronts and display windows are important to the store designer.

Inducing Entrance

Show windows, in addition to attracting passersby, should induce them to enter the store. Show windows may be opened up to display the shop's interior; or closed in, to give privacy to customers within. Door locations require study in relation to pedestrian traffic flow, grades of sidewalks and store floors, and interior layout of the shop. In colder climates drafts and outdoor temperature changes can be controlled at the door.

Organizing Store Spaces

Organizing store spaces, and consequently the merchandise to be sold, into departments, enables customers to find objects easily, and permits storekeepers to keep close check on profits or losses from various types of goods. Store lighting and "dressing" are simplified. Even small shops benefit from a measure of departmentalization; in large shops, the practice becomes essential as methods of training salespeople, of handling, controlling, and wrapping stock become more complex.

Interior Displays

Interior displays require particular attention in specialty shops. Types range from displays of staple goods which assist customers in selection, to displays of accessories which the sale of staples may suggest to the customer. Problems of arrangement with regard to merchandise, departments, and routes of customers' approach are involved.

Relief from the repeated impact of merchandise sales efforts and displays is necessary in most shops. Experienced salespeople can tell at a glance the customer who is satiated with shopping and too bewildered to buy. After he has been refreshed by a brief rest, the customer's interest can be recaptured quickly. Such relaxation may be mental or physical, or both.

Conveniences

Conveniences intended primarily for the customers' benefit, while not strictly allied to the problems of attracting trade or selling goods, are necessary to some types of shops. A florist, for instance, provides a card-writing desk or counter in his shop. In other shop types, particularly those whose prices are above the average, such extra provisions are often highly desirable. Conveniences of this kind include: telephone booths, drinking fountains, lavatories or powder rooms, desks for writing cards or checks, stools or chairs at counters or in special sales rooms, and vanity tables or triplicate mirrors for certain types of apparel fitting rooms.

In regard to finishes and equipment, the idea may be extended to include: floor surfacing for comfort; acoustic treatment of ceilings and possibly walls; illumination of pleasant, sometimes special, quality; and air conditioning. All these have been found profitable investments in various cases. Their necessity or desirability depends to an extent on the type of shop, its location, or the climate of the locality.

INTERIORS

The successful retail shop is an efficient selling machine or sales factory. In addition to servicing the customers, the employees have to be considered so they can give better service to the customer.

Merchandise and space must be organized to help the customer in making a selection and to help the sales person in selling. Easy circulation and exposing the customer to the maximum amount of merchandise are part of good design. Avoid monotony in circulation and dis-

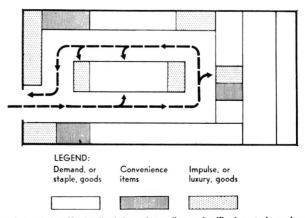

LEGEND:
Demand, or staple, goods   Convenience items   Impulse, or luxury, goods

Fig. 1 **Principles of shop design. Merchandise is located according to classification: staple goods are unobtrusively yet accessibly placed; luxury items are spotted where the prospective customer cannot help but be attracted to them. White counter areas are allocated to services: cashier, wrapper, information, etc.**

796

play of merchandise. Where possible, do not hesitate to be bold or even shocking. This stimulates the customer and his urge to buy.

The location and design of the cashier and wrapping unit are important and provide for several persons to be serviced. Often this acts as a control center.

Flexibility so that fixtures and departments can be moved or modified is part of present-day merchandising. Fixtures should be minimized and merchandise emphasized. Design and use fixtures so that full attention is thrown on the merchandise. Surveys must be made for each particular type of store, its merchandise, operation, and personnel to determine actual sizes and requirements. Do not design fixtures so that a salesperson has to reach merchandise on too high a shelf or stoop too low.

Determine what customer accessories are required: seating in general, counters, tables, mirrors, telephones, drinking fountains, rest rooms, special lighting, and floor coverings. Accessories will vary, depending on the store's location and the type of customer, as well as the nature of the merchandise.

Location of stock rooms, or of reserves, must be carefully considered so that the salesperson does not have to leave a customer for too long a period.

Fitting and dressing rooms should be located conveniently near the item being sold.

Selling Areas

Departmentalization Benefits to be derived from segregation of merchandise by types have been touched upon previously. All these are factors in decreasing the average time per sale, an important figure in large-store accounting and in small stores with rush periods (Fig. 1).

Within each department, and as a guide when relating departments to each other and to the path of the typical customer through the store, merchandise and services can be analyzed by classification. Most objects can be placed in one of the following classes, relating them to the needs of customers:

Impulse, or luxury, goods are high-profit articles, usually (but not necessarily) high in price.

Convenience items are stocked for the passerby who happens in, but who may return for other purchases if properly impressed. Often these are not in themselves strictly profitable merchandise.

Demand goods are also staples, like conveniences, but are articles which the customer starts out with a definite idea of purchasing. These attract him to the store and he buys them—other goods must be sold to him.

These classifications necessarily overlap; but, in a shop whose type of customer can be forecast, divisions along some such lines are possible. Signs are not always necessary; each department may be designated by display of typical articles as a kind of poster.

Customer Flow The accompanying diagrams based upon analyses of traffic indicate the possibility of organizing departments in relation to the flow of customers through the store.

Interest in articles on display was found to be inversely proportional to the number displayed after a low limit had been reached. A central location in a group seemed to lead to increased interest in a picture. One important conclusion is that what a customer sees is more influenced by the arrangement of the space and the walking habits of customers, than by the intrinsic quality of the objects exhibited. Tendencies to turn to the right, to be attracted by doorways, to choose the wider of

two aisles, and to be fatigued by too much material on display are all of utmost importance to the store planner.

Store services must also be analyzed in relation to customer flow.

Self-Service Operators of large stores have found that self-service speeds up selling. For that reason their stock is easily accessible to the shopper. Often, too, customers insist upon handling merchandise, and are more easily sold when they can get these first-hand impressions. As a result, many stores have abandoned the selling-over-the-counter plan, which decreases free sales space, and rely upon open wall fixtures, wall displays, and display tables whenever possible.

In direct contrast to this type is the exclusive shop which keeps its stock in closed fixtures or in the stockroom, permitting selection of merchandise only by sample displays. Some specialty shops work entirely on this basis.

Shop Sizes These are far from standardized. However, as determined by real estate values, and merchandising, structural, fixture, and aisle space requirements, shops with one customer's aisle only are usually 12 to 15 ft wide by 50 to 60 ft long in large cities; and 15 to 18 ft. wide by 60 to 80 ft long in smaller cities. These dimensions apply particularly to shops in 100 percent retail districts.

Heights are more easily determined. Basements 8 to 9 ft high, in the clear, permit economical stock storage. Ground floors are preferably approximately 12 ft high if no mezzanine is included; mezzanines at least 7 ft 6 in. above floor level will accommodate most fixture heights. Height from mezzanine floor to ceiling may be as low as 6 ft 6 in. if used for service space only; 7 ft is the preferred minimum for public use.

Typical Counter and Case Layouts

Center Island Type illustrated, $L = 13$ ft avg. min.; $W = 9$ ft 6 in. to 13 ft. Islands composed of showcases only, $L = 10$ ft min.; $W = 5$ ft 10 in. to 6 ft 3 in. For floor tables, $L = 4$ to 7 ft; $W = 2$ ft 6 in. to 3 ft.

Aisle Widths For clerks, min. = 1 ft 8 in.; desirable, 2 ft to 2 ft 3 in. For main public aisles, min. = 4 ft 6 in.; avg., 5 ft 6 in. to 7 ft; usual max., 11 ft. Secondary public aisles, 3 ft to 3 ft 6 in.

See Figs. 2 and 3.

Displays

The segregation of displays in areas specifically designed for the purpose, and in locations selected with respect to entrances and customer traffic flow, is easily accomplished in departmentalized store planning (Fig. 4).

Display Surfaces Locating display surfaces perpendicular to the line of entrance may result in angular plans, or in the use of screens or freestanding display cases, as indicated in the diagram. Locations for display niches, alcoves, etc., may depend on space requirements of the various shop departments and upon the relationship to customer flow lines.

In a shop, "architecture" is preferably secondary in importance to the merchandise displayed. This does not mean that every inch of space must be crowded with goods "on display," because such practice causes loss of customer interest.

Scale An important factor in display is the relation between the possible viewing distance and the scale of the merchandise. Thus a stair-

way side wall or narrow passage is suited for small scale display only. Vistas, on the other hand, and displays opposite doorways, have more carrying power and consequently can be bolder. Vistas, or a sense of perspective, can also be created by lighting emphasis. When a lighted display is placed at the rear wall under a mezzanine space which is slightly darker than the store proper, a spatial relationship is set up which depends more upon the relative intensities of light than upon actual distance. It is possible to dramatize objects on display, to make them stand apart from their neighbors and in this way suggest that they are more desirable. On the other hand, it is not always best to separate costly and inexpensive objects. Low-priced merchandise may often be sold by contrast with high-priced objects, and vice versa. Choice of method depends to an extent on the problem under consideration.

Accessible zones, rather than low or high displays, are particularly valuable in self-service portions of the shop. Just as show-window bulkheads are rising and glass heights decreasing, so the fixtures inside the store are bringing merchandise within reach and concentrating it for emphasis.

Show Windows These are designed primarily with the effect upon potential customers in mind; ease in changing displays is also important. Windows must be "dressed" quickly; if they are hard to work with, they will not be changed as often as merchandising policies indicate to be necessary. Variety and timeliness of displays are considered essential.

The diagrams in Fig. 5 illustrate one set of principles whose use increases the value of displays. The same principles may be applied to horizontal planning; the "shadow-box" type of window, with limited display space, is considered most effective by display designers. In conjunction with these, it should be noted that bulkhead heights tend to increase as the size of objects displayed decreases, to permit more minute examination of merchandise.

Glazing of types which do not interfere with vision will materially increase the show window's value. Patented systems, which eliminate reflections, are available; so are types of glass suited to special conditions, such as heat-resisting glass.

Window backs may be closed or open, depending on the type of shop and the degree of customer privacy desired. When backs are open, confusion of display and shop interior may be avoided by using temporary or permanent screens or panels as backgrounds.

Window dressing may be done in full public view in certain types of shops, as jewelry or gift shops. In other cases, venetian blinds or other types of glass curtains may be required. Apparent size of glass area may be changed to accommodate varying displays by using variable valances and side-pieces.

Storage space is required for display accessories, forms, blocks, platforms, panel backgrounds, and seasonal changes of floor pads or carpets.

Ease of window dressing may be aided in several ways. Access panels should be large enough for easy passage for men and materials. Access passages, segregated from the shop's interior, may be provided. Dummy windows may be provided, sometimes on rolling platforms.

Show-Window Lighting In many stores other than specialty shops, light intensities have been increased far above requirements for ordinary vision, in an effort to overcome reflections. This has also been considered a means of competing with adjacent store windows.

Commercial

RETAIL SHOPS
Layouts and Dimensions

There are two basic planning guidelines for laying out a retail sales floor. Six basic plans can help the designer to carry them out. These are certainly not the only plans that can be developed, but they form the foundation on which others can be created.

The guidelines

- Use 100 percent of the space allocated.
- Do not sacrifice function for esthetics. Successful plans combine both to the fullest.

Six basic plans

- Straight
- Pathway
- Diagonal
- Curved
- Varied
- Geometric

Straight Plan

The *straight plan* is a conventional form of layout that utilizes walls and projections to create smaller spaces. It is an economical plan to execute and can be adapted to any type of store, from gift shops to apparel outlets, from drug and grocery stores to department stores.

Variety in the straight plan can be introduced by creating niches with the merchandise. To define transition from one section of the store to the other, displays can be placed to help lead customers. Elevate floor levels for a change of pace.

This plan lends itself well to pulling customers

to the back of the store. In a bookstore, for example, special sale merchandise can be placed at the rear, with signage informing shoppers of the items and directing them in the right direction.

Pathway Plan

Applicable to virtually any type of store, the pathway plan is particularly suited to larger stores over 5000 square feet and on one level. The *pathway plan,* a good architectural organizer, gets shoppers smoothly from the front to the rear of the store.

This plan is recommended for apparel stores because of its ability to minimize the cluttered feeling which tends to discourage or disturb shoppers who do not care to fight their way to the racks in the back. This plan also focuses the shoppers' attention to other merchandise on the path. The designer can create designs off the path using the floor or ceiling as directional elements.

Diagonal Plan

For self-service stores, a *diagonal plan* is optimal. The cashier is in a central location, with sight lines to all areas of the space. Soft goods or hard goods stores, including drug and food stores, can take advantage of the diagonal plan.

Visually, the plan has an exciting and dynamic quality. Because it is not based on a straight line, it invites movement and circulation.

Curved Plan

For boutiques, salons, or other high-quality stores, the *curved plan* creates an inviting, special envi-

ronment for the customer. It also costs more to construct than angular or square plans.

The curved theme can be emphasized with walls, ceiling, and corners. To complete the look, specify circular floor fixtures.

Varied Plan

For products that require back-up merchandise to be immediately adjacent (shoes and men's shirts, for example), the *varied plan* is highly functional. It is a variation of the straight-line plan with sufficient square footage allowed for box or carton storage off the main sales floor with perimeter wall stocking.

As shown in the illustration on page 799, the varied plan has a "bellows" effect, a tapering back or space delineation that focuses on a special-purpose area in the back. Service departments in stereo, jewelry, or hardware stores can be located in this narrow end. For a tobacco shop, it is a fine place for the humidor.

Geometric Plan

The designer creates forms with shapes derived from showcases, racks, or gondolas in a *geometric plan*. This plan is the most exotic of the six basic plans, and the designer can use wall angles to restate the shapes dominating the sales floor.

The geometric plan comfortably allows for fitting rooms without wasting square footage; this benefit makes the plan especially suitable for apparel stores. Also, it can nicely accommodate adjacent stock, making it an alternative to the varied plan for shoe stores and gift shops.

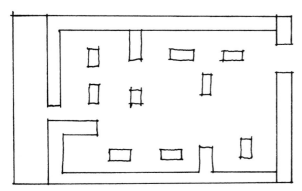

This straight plan uses walls and projections to create smaller spaces and is economical.

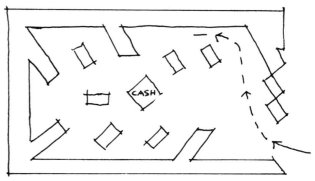

This diagonal pattern permits angular traffic flow and creates perimeter design interest and excitement in movement. The central placement of the cash-wrap permits security and vision.

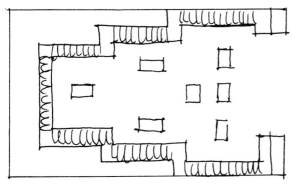

This varied plan illustrates added variety of forms which can work to a designer's advantage.

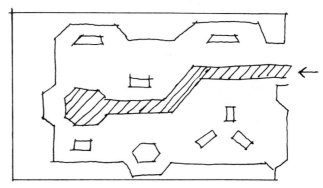

This pathway plan pulls patrons through the store to the rear without interruption by floor fixtures. The merits of such a layout are that the path can take any shape and that it creates a design pattern.

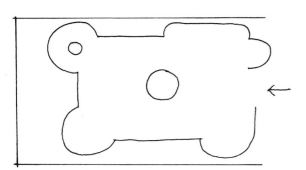

People respond to circular and curved shapes such as those shown here, which soften the angular and square plan.

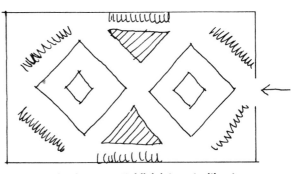

A geometric plan can establish interest without excessive cost, if the store's product can accept it. Ceiling and floors can be lowered or raised to create zones and departments.

Alternate plan arrangements

Commercial

RETAIL SHOPS
Layouts and Dimensions

The drawing at the top of the page shows the clearances required for a medium height display counter. The suggested seat height of 21 to 22 in, or 53.3 to 55.8 cm, requires a footrest for the seated customer. The counter height shown will allow the display to be viewed by both the seated customer and the standing sales clerk. The customer activity zone allows adequate space for the chair. Knee height, buttock-knee length, popliteal height, and eye height sitting are all significant human dimensions to consider in the design of counters to be used by a seated customer.

The drawing at the bottom of the page is of a low 30-in, or 76.2-cm, display counter also for use by a seated customer. The anthropometric considerations are the same. Although the counter height is responsive to the anthropometric requirements of the seated customer, it is less than ideal for the standing clerk. For the standing user's optimum comfort, the counter height should be about 2 or 3 in, or 5 to 7.6 cm, below elbow height. This will allow a person to handle objects comfortably on the counter surface or use the counter as support for his or her arms. The 30-in height is too low to permit such use.

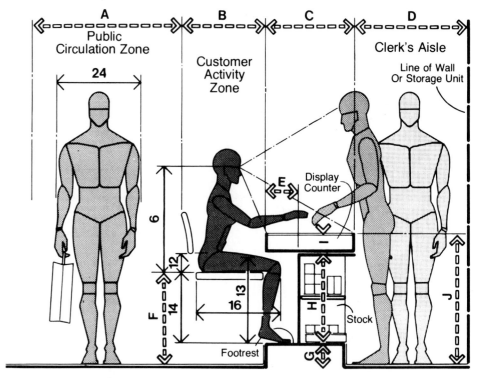

SEATED CUSTOMER / DESIRABLE COUNTER HEIGHT

	in	cm
A	36	91.4
B	26–30	66.0–76.2
C	18–24	45.7–61.0
D	30 min.	76.2 min.
E	10	25.4
F	21–22	53.3–55.9
G	5	12.7
H	23–25	58.4–63.5
I	4–6	10.2–15.2
J	34–36	86.4–91.4
K	30	76.2
L	16–17	40.6–43.2

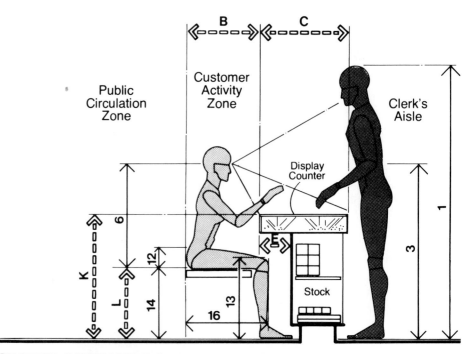

SEATED CUSTOMER / LOW COUNTER HEIGHT

800

The top drawing shows the clearances involved for a 42-in, or 106.7-cm, high counter to service a seated user. By filling the recess with an additional display, however, the counter can also be used exclusively as a typical sales counter. It should be noted, however, that although sometimes used for special display situations, such a counter height is not recommended. Both the customer and the sales clerk of smaller body size would find coping with such a height uncomfortable anthropometrically, particularly when one considers that the counter would be higher than the elbow height of slightly over 5 percent of the population. From a merchandising viewpoint, where customer convenience is of paramount importance, it would be unwise to exceed 39 to 40 in, or 99 to 101.6 cm, as a counter height. In addition, the smaller sales clerk forced to tend such a counter for extended periods of time could be subjected to severe backaches and pains. Getting on and off a high stool for elderly and disabled people or those of smaller body size can be not only difficult, but hazardous. The bottom drawing illustrates the clearances for a typical sales counter.

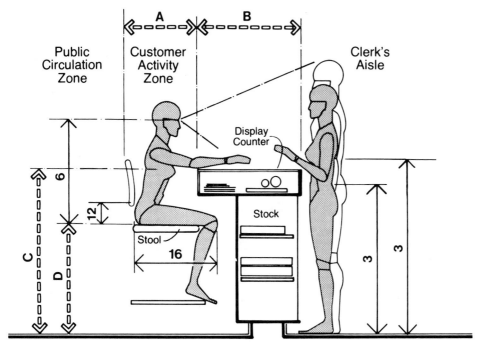

SEATED CUSTOMER / HIGH COUNTER HEIGHT

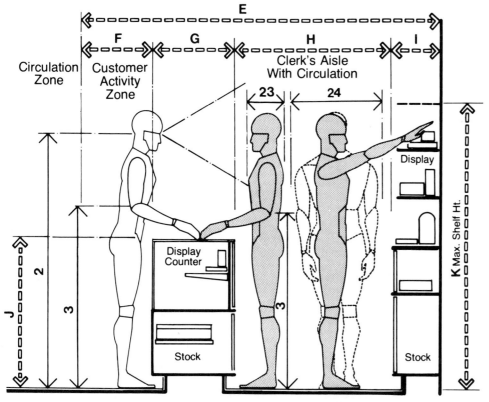

TYPICAL SALES AREA / STANDING CUSTOMER

	in	cm
A	26–30	66.0–76.2
B	18–24	45.7–61.0
C	42	106.7
D	28	71.1
E	84–112	213.4–284.5
F	18	45.7
G	18–24	45.7–61.0
H	30–48	76.2–121.9
I	18–22	45.7–55.9
J	35–38	88.9–96.5
K	72	182.9

Commercial

RETAIL SHOPS
Layouts and Dimensions

Shelving is probably used more than any other single interior component for the storage and/or display of merchandise. Not only must the merchandise be within reach anthropometrically, but it must be fairly visible as well. The heights established must therefore be responsive to vertical grip reach dimensions as well as to eye height. In establishing height limits, the body size data of the smaller person should be used. Since in retail spaces, departments may cater exclusively to members of one sex or the other, two sets of data are presented. One is based on the body size of the smaller female and the other on the body size of the smaller male. The suggested heights reflect a compromise between reach requirements and visibility requirements.

The drawing at the bottom of the page illustrates the clearances involved in hanging-type merchandise cases. Rod heights should be related not only to human reach limitations, but in certain cases to the sizes of the merchandise displayed. There is usually no conflict in respect to garments.

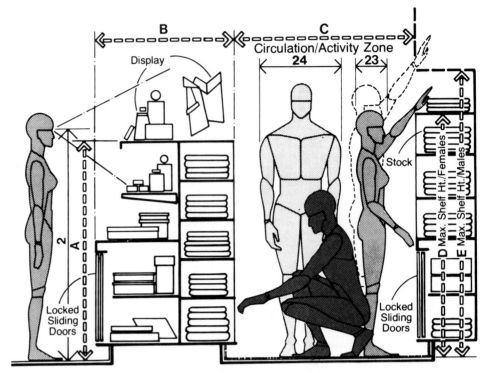

TYPICAL MERCHANDISE CASES

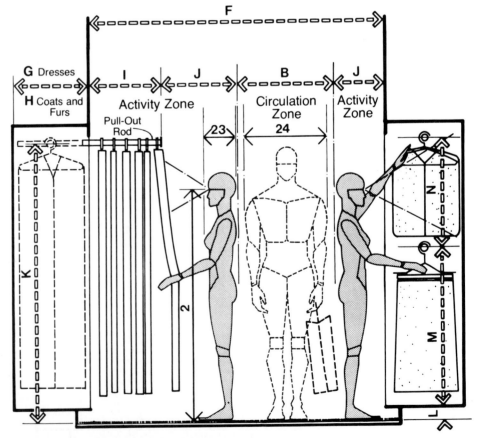

	in	cm
A	48 max.	121.9 max.
B	30–36	76.2–91.4
C	51 min.	129.5 min.
D	66	167.6
E	72	182.9
F	84–96	213.4–243.8
G	20–26	50.8–66.0
H	28–30	71.1–76.2
I	18–24	45.7–61.0
J	18 min.	45.7 min.
K	72 max.	182.9 max.
L	4	10.2
M	42	106.7
N	26 min.	66.0 min.

HANGING MERCHANDISE CASES

802

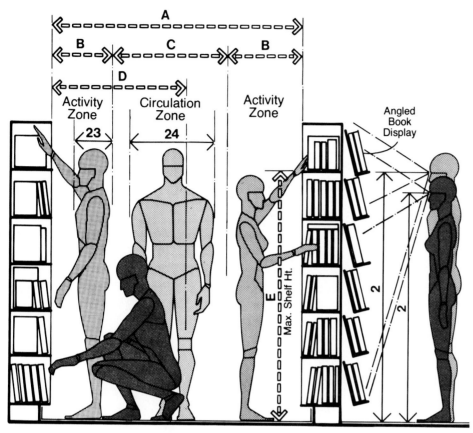

BOOK STORE / DISPLAY AREA

The drawing at the top of the page concerns book and magazine displays and suggests the anthropometric considerations involved. The rationale is essentially the same as that indicated for the general merchandise shelving on the preceding page. In regard to books, however, the question of visibility is even more critical. To perceive the basic form, shape, and color of general merchandise may be sufficient, but for books and magazines the legibility of printed matter must be taken into account. The distance between the customer and the display lighting, and angle of sight should all be considered.

The drawing at the bottom of the page deals with human dimension and the fitting area of a shoe store. The fitting zone clearance should accommodate the body size of the seated customer and that of the sales clerk. The 60 to 66 in, or 152.4 to 167.6 cm, clearance should be viewed as a minimum. The buttock-heel length of the larger person was considered in anthropometrically establishing the clearance dimension. In regard to the workzone, vertical grip reach measurements of the smaller male and female should be used in establishing shelf heights, while maximum body breadth and maximum body depth of the larger person should be considered in establishing clearances.

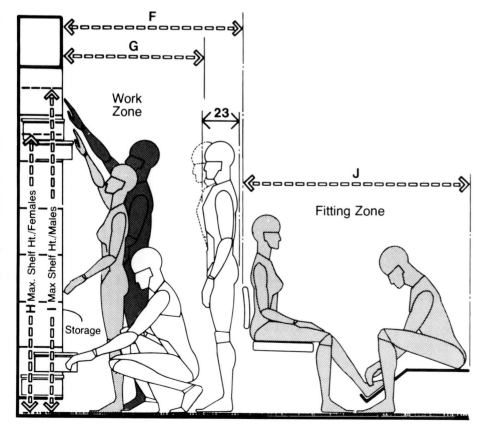

SHOE STORE / FITTING AREA

	in	cm
A	66 min.	167.6 min.
B	18 min.	45.7 min.
C	30 min.	76.2 min.
D	36	91.4
E	68	172.7
F	48	121.9
G	36 min.	91.4 min.
H	66	167.6
I	72	182.9
J	60–66	152.4–167.6

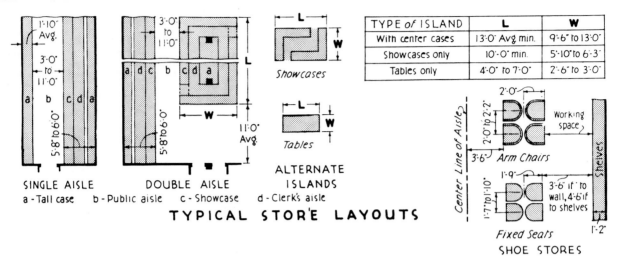

TYPE of ISLAND	L	W
With center cases	13'-0" Avg min.	9'-6" to 13'-0"
Showcases only	10'-0" min.	5'-10" to 6'-3"
Tables only	4'-0" to 7'-0"	2'-6" to 3'-0"

Showcases

Tables

SINGLE AISLE

DOUBLE AISLE

ALTERNATE ISLANDS

a - Tall case   b - Public aisle   c - Showcase   d - Clerk's aisle

TYPICAL STORE LAYOUTS

Arm Chairs

Fixed Seats

SHOE STORES

SECTIONS thru TYPICAL FIXTURES and AISLES

CLERK'S AISLES: *Minimum width 1'-8"; recommended 2'-0" to 2'-3" wide (as for grocery) 3'-0"*

PUBLIC AISLES: *Main, min width 4'-6"; avg. 5'-6" to 7'-0"; maximum 11'-0"*

Secondary, min. 3'-0"; recom. 3'-6"

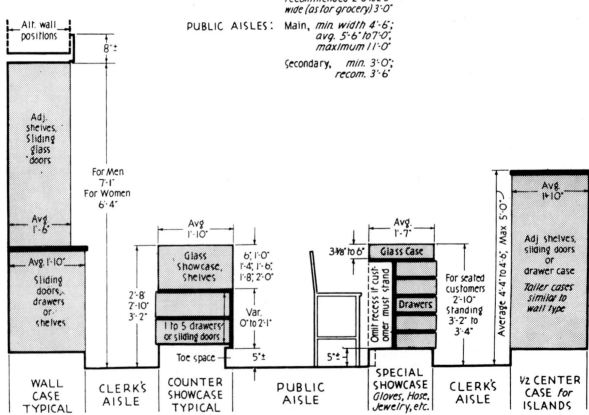

WALL CASE TYPICAL

CLERK'S AISLE

COUNTER SHOWCASE TYPICAL

PUBLIC AISLE

SPECIAL SHOWCASE *Gloves, Hose, Jewelry, etc.*

CLERK'S AISLE

½ CENTER CASE for ISLANDS

Fig. 2

804

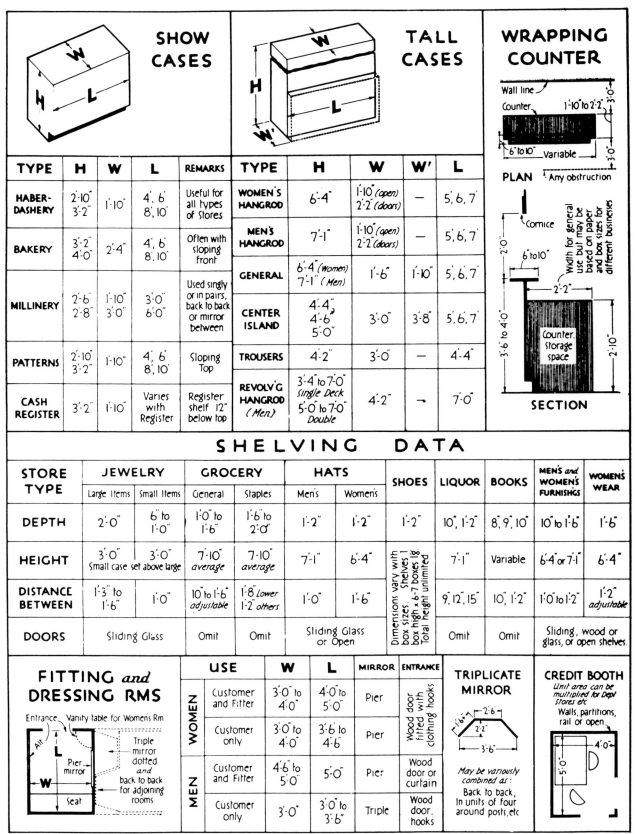

SHOW CASES

TYPE	H	W	L	REMARKS
HABER-DASHERY	2'-10", 3'-2"	1'-10"	4', 6', 8', 10'	Useful for all types of Stores
BAKERY	3'-2", 4'-0"	2'-4"	4', 6', 8', 10'	Often with sloping front
MILLINERY	2'-6", 2'-8"	1'-10", 3'-0"	3'-0", 6'-0"	Used singly or in pairs, back to back or mirror between
PATTERNS	2'-10", 3'-2"	1'-10"	4', 6', 8', 10'	Sloping Top
CASH REGISTER	3'-2"	1'-10"	Varies with Register	Register shelf 12" below top

TALL CASES

TYPE	H	W	W'	L
WOMEN'S HANGROD	6'-4"	1'-10" (open), 2'-2" (doors)	—	5, 6, 7
MEN'S HANGROD	7'-1"	1'-10" (open), 2'-2" (doors)	—	5, 6, 7
GENERAL	6'-4" (Women), 7'-1" (Men)	1'-6"	1'-10"	5, 6, 7
CENTER ISLAND	4'-4", 4'-6", 5'-0"	3'-0"	3'-8"	5, 6, 7
TROUSERS	4'-2"	3'-0"	—	4'-4"
REVOLV'G HANGROD (Men)	3'-4" to 7'-0" single Deck, 5'-0" to 7'-0" Double	4'-2"	—	7'-0"

WRAPPING COUNTER

Wall line
Counter 1'-10" to 2'-2" 3'-0"
6" to 10" Variable 3'-0"

PLAN Any obstruction

Cornice
Width for general use but may be based on paper and box sizes for different businesses
2'-0" 6" to 10"
2'-2"
3'-6" to 4'-0"
Counter. Storage space 2'-10"

SECTION

SHELVING DATA

STORE TYPE	JEWELRY		GROCERY		HATS		SHOES	LIQUOR	BOOKS	MEN'S and WOMEN'S FURNISH'GS	WOMEN'S WEAR
	Large Items	Small Items	General	Staples	Men's	Women's					
DEPTH	2'-0"	6" to 1'-0"	1'-0" to 1'-6"	1'-6" to 2'-0"	1'-2"	1'-2"	1'-2"	10", 1'-2"	8", 9", 10"	10" to 1'-6"	1'-6"
HEIGHT	3'-0" Small case set above large	3'-0"	7'-10" average	7'-10" average	7'-1"	6'-4"	Dimensions vary with box sizes. Shelves 1 box high x 6-7 boxes lg. Total height unlimited	7'-1"	Variable	6'-4" or 7'-1"	6'-4"
DISTANCE BETWEEN	1'-3" to 1'-6"	1'-0"	10" to 1'-6" adjustable	1'-8" Lower, 1'-2" others	1'-0"	1'-6"		9", 12", 15"	10", 1'-2"	1'-0" to 1'-2"	1'-2" adjustable
DOORS	Sliding Glass		Omit	Omit	Sliding Glass or Open			Omit	Omit	Sliding, wood or glass, or open shelves.	

FITTING and DRESSING RMS

Entrance. Vanity table for Women's Rm
Triple mirror dotted and back to back for adjoining rooms
Pier mirror
Seat
Alt.
L
W

	USE	W	L	MIRROR	ENTRANCE
WOMEN	Customer and Fitter	3'-0" to 4'-0"	4'-0" to 5'-0"	Pier	Wood door fitted with clothing hooks
	Customer only	3'-0" to 4'-0"	3'-6" to 4'-6"	Pier	
MEN	Customer and Fitter	4'-6" to 5'-0"	5'-0"	Pier	Wood door or curtain
	Customer only	3'-0"	3'-0" to 3'-6"	Triple	Wood door, hooks

TRIPLICATE MIRROR

2'-6"
1'-6"
2'-2"
3'-6"

May be variously combined as:
Back to back, In units of four around posts, etc.

CREDIT BOOTH

Unit area can be multiplied for Dept Stores etc
Walls, partitions, rail or open
5'-0"
4'-0"

Fig. 3

DISPLAYS
OPPOSITE
DOORWAYS

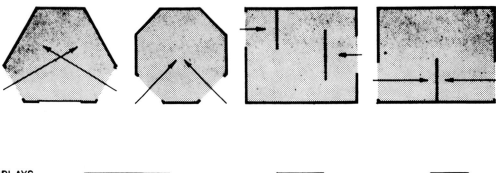

ISOLATION OF DISPLAYS
BY ANGULAR PLANNING

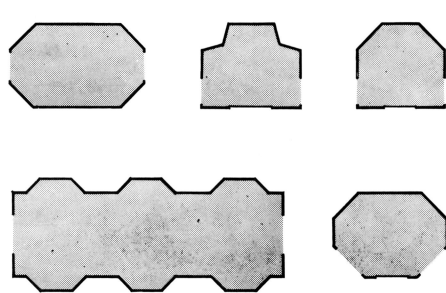

NO SCALE

Fig. 4

Shop Entrances Show windows cannot stop at merely attracting and stopping passersby. Patrons must be induced to enter the shop.

Steps are considered inadvisable. When a change in grade is necessary, and it is too great for a ramp, the steps may be in the store, well lighted.

It is necessary to provide some form of protection from drafts at entrances, particularly in cold climates. In air-conditioned stores, in order to maintain the conditioning system's efficiency at a maximum, a seal between indoor and outdoor air may be needed.

Vestibules offer such protection, and may be made removable in summer months. Revolving doors are often essential where wind pressures are high, when volume of traffic is great, or when air conditioning is used.

Work Areas

Wrapping and Cash Register Counter Locations for these require study. The type of shop will determine whether these services should be out in the open or concealed, near or remote from the door; positioned to permit a sales-clerk to make change while facing the doorway, or, as some managers prefer, to do nothing else when ringing up sales. In other shops, a cashier is considered to provide better control and efficiency. Some shops have a separate room or curtained alcove for wrapping and cashier space, or a basement or mezzanine

served by dumbwaiter and pneumatic tube (Fig. 6).

A cash register and wrapping counter in an alcove near the door, which permits the clerk to face the shop and doorway, is desirable in small shops where business is hurried, or where for long periods one clerk must sell, order, wrap, ring up sales, make change, and watch the shop. A store with a narrow entrance might better have these services remote to avoid crowding at the doorway. The separate wrapping room, basement, or other space is used in stores with a more leisurely trade, or when, as in many gift shops, goods are fragile and rarely carried out by the customer. It is less confusing and less "commercial" in appearance for the shop as a whole to have this service outside of the selling space. However, such planning increases customers' waiting time.

Proper location of the cash register for safety may also be dependent upon a wide variety of factors such as number of salespeople, type of show-window back (open or closed ones which conceal the shop from the sidewalk), and type of neighborhood (busy or quiet).

There is in the more exclusive small shops a tendency away from the use of cash registers. Some merchants consider them too commercial in appearance and provide a simple cash drawer, sometimes without a bell alarm. This naturally is a case of individual preference and reliability of personnel.

Waste Basket Space for waste baskets should be provided in each department. This can be

arranged under a counter or in a back fixture near the wrapper by omitting the base. When in a counter with recessed toe-space at the front, such waste basket space will have a small ledge—the top of the toe space—which should be continuously braced.

Offices Mezzanine space overlooking the store is the most popular location for management offices. Venetian blinds are often used as a screen; semi-obscure glass may be used; transparent mirrors can also be used, but the space they conceal must be darker than the store side. A practical way of doing this on a mezzanine used for working offices is to run the corridor along the front of the mezzanine, separating the mirror-screen from the offices.

WOMEN'S WEAR

This type of store is usually one of two types:

1. A chain-store operation, usually selling at lower prices with greater quantities, which requires mass display and mass selling, sometimes a multiple-floor operation. There is usually more self-service and less contact and selling required by the salesperson. All merchandise is up forward in selling areas.

2. A medium- and higher-price operation, usually a small store, most often owner-operated. There is more personal selling and closer contact between salesperson and customer. The smaller stylish store does not necessarily

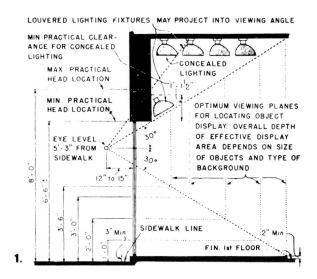

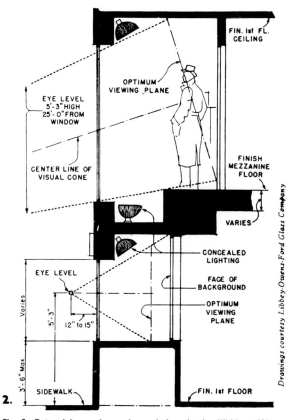

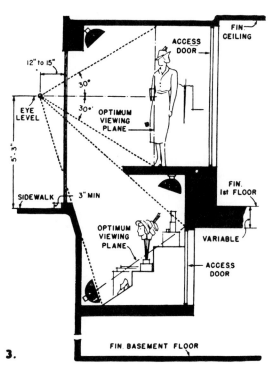

Fig. 5 Determining optimum show-window depths. Within a 60° cone, the average human eye sees comfortably, without appreciable physical effort. Optimum viewing planes are those in which objects on display can be seen in their entirety without causing the eye to encompass arcs greater than 60°. Diagram 1 illustrates a graphic method of determining optimum viewing planes for given bulkhead heights. Diagram 2 shows the application of these principles to second-floor windows; sight lines are limited by practicable window dimensions. Diagram 3 extends basic principles to include both basement and first-floor levels, seen through one window.

RETAIL SHOPS
Women's Wear

have all demand merchandise on display. The merchandise is brought out from stock rooms. (See Figs. 7 to 9.)

The exterior of the lower-price store, like the interior, will have large displays, hence large show windows with low bulkheads. The vestibule, or distance from the building line to the entrance doors, is usually greater than for the average store. The smaller stylish store will have a smaller show window, or perhaps no show window, only a display platform which is really part of the store.

The interior for both types of stores is departmentalized, and the store is divided into related departments. The front part of the store will have the impulse items such as bags, gloves, hosiery, lingerie, sweaters, and costume jewelry, with the cashier and wrapping counter. The rear will have the demand merchandise such as dresses, coats, suits, robes, and sportswear. The cases for this merchandise are often set away from the walls to provide space behind for the fitting rooms, stock, alterations, and work room.

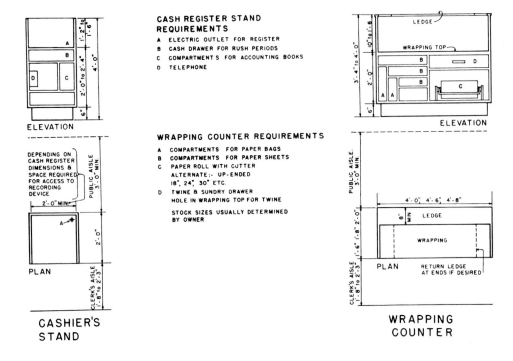

Fig. 6

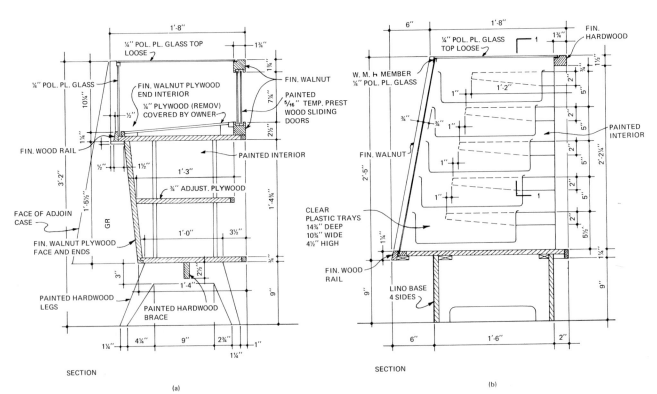

Fig. 7 (a) Jewelry and lingerie. (b) Neckwear and panties.

808

Good general lighting for main areas, lighting pattern in areas architecturally separated, can vary from the general light pattern. Adjustable spotlights for changing displays and special lighting should be provided at fitting mirrors or over counters. Carpet should be used throughout except in stock or work rooms.

In shops for women's clothing and haberdashery, the turnover of stock must be rapid, as styles quickly become obsolete. Most articles, other than accessories which are easily damaged or lost, are currently at least partly sold on a self-service basis.

Nonselling Areas

A workroom for marking merchandise, making small repairs, and preparing articles for display is needed. A hanging pole, some shelving, and space for ironing board use are required. The minimum area can be 4 by 6 ft. Larger shops may have a complete alteration department (Fig. 10).

Sales and Display Areas

Departmentalizing is necessary, due to the varied kinds of merchandise sold. Novelty jewelry, stockings, gloves, and sweaters are all placed near the store entrance; coats, dresses, and hats are farther back in the shop. Sweaters and knitted suits are kept on shelving, usually glass, because hanging stretches them out of shape. The hat department requires some separation from the rest of the shop.

It has been found important in all apparel shops to have several display niches, really interior show windows with or without glass, which should be lighted, for the display of ensembles and related accessories. This is almost essential to suggest associated articles.

Triple mirrors are needed where clothing is to be tried on. Double mirrors, angled to one another, may prove as satisfactory as triple mirrors. Hand and table, wall or counter mirrors are needed in millinery departments (Figs. 11 and 12).

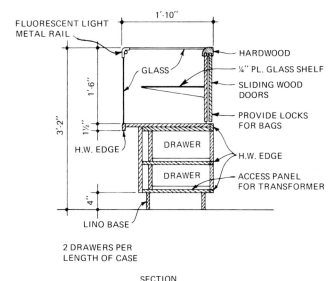

Fig. 8 Blouse and lingerie or bag and scarf counters.

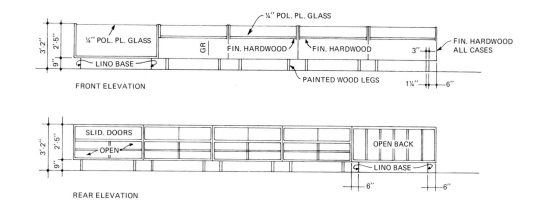

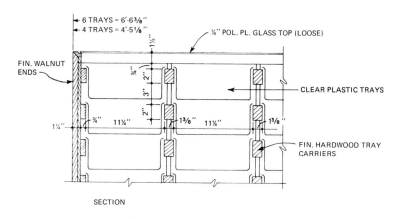

Fig. 9 Display and storage units.

RETAIL SHOPS
Women's Wear

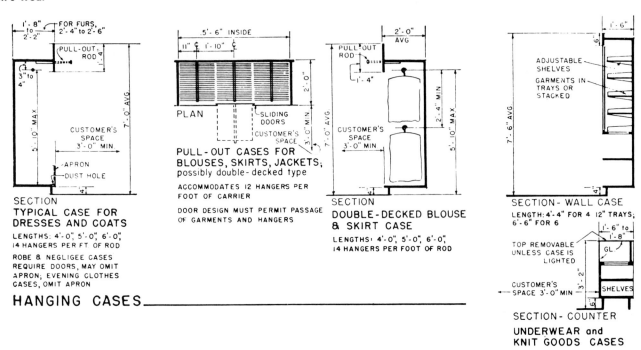

HANGING CASES

ACCESSORY CASES

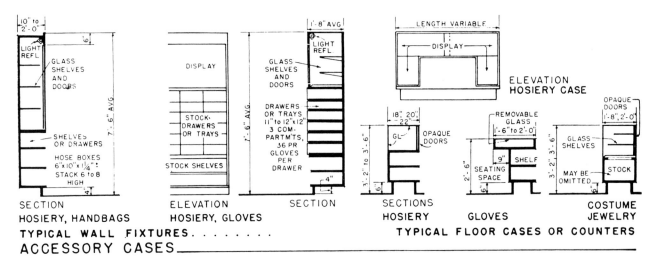

MILLINERY FIXTURES

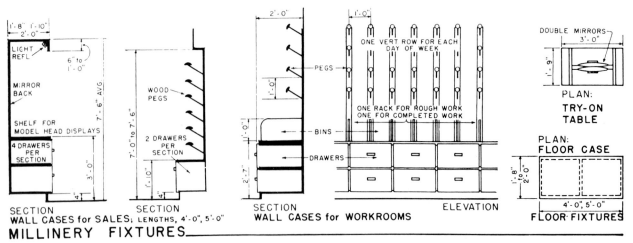

Fig. 10 Women's wear cases.

Mechanical Systems Lighting of triple and other mirrors and fitting rooms is extremely important. Strong direct overhead lights are to be avoided because they cast unflattering shadows. Well-diffused indirect light with direct side light has been found fairly satisfactory. Special "daylight" fixtures and lamps are helpful in color matching.

MEN'S WEAR

Counters and clerks' aisles are seldom, if ever, included in clothing sales space, but are ordinarily required in combination with wall cases for haberdashery and accessories. One or more fitting rooms are necessary in clothing departments; a small fitting platform, one step high and approximately 4 ft by 4 ft, is sometimes needed. Chairs and smoking stands are standard equipment. "Daylight" lighting fixtures aid in matching or determining colors.

Nonselling Areas

Stock rooms, with space for about 20 percent of the store's total stock, are usually sufficient for peak-load seasons. If alterations to clothing are made on the premises, a tailor shop, with water and electrical connections for pressing and sewing machines, is required. Wrapping counters for clothing departments are often located in workrooms; for haberdashery, wrapping counters are usually combined with cashier's space, which is located conveniently to both departments (Figs. 13 to 15).

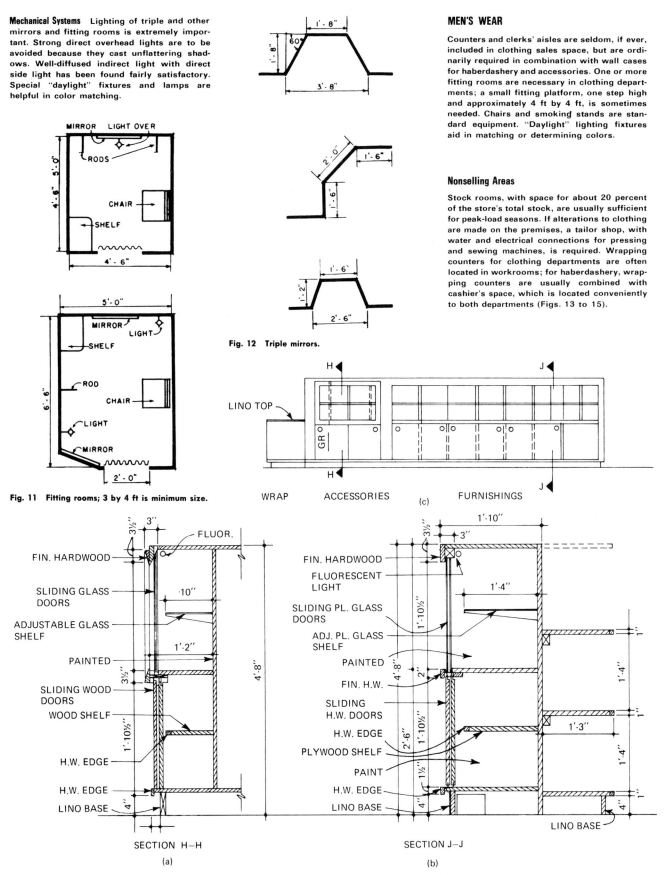

Fig. 11 Fitting rooms; 3 by 4 ft is minimum size.

Fig. 12 Triple mirrors.

Fig. 13 Island display cases. (a) Boy's furnishings accessories. (b) Men's furnishings stock shelving. (c) Front view.

RETAIL SHOPS
Men's Wear; Book; Gift

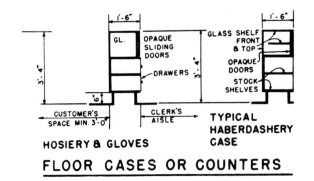

HOSIERY & GLOVES

TYPICAL HABERDASHERY CASE

FLOOR CASES OR COUNTERS

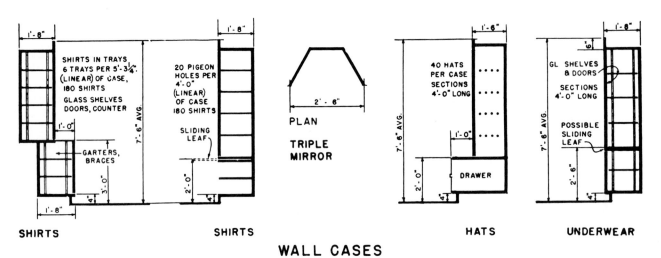

SHIRTS   SHIRTS   PLAN TRIPLE MIRROR   HATS   UNDERWEAR

WALL CASES

Fig. 14 Men's wear cases.

BOOKSHOPS

Each customer in a bookshop requires privacy, direct access to the books displayed, and sufficient light for comfortable vision while reading. Bookbuying customers like to browse, and nothing is less attractive to them than crowded circulation.

Sales and Display Spaces

The first requirement is a plan which by means of low book shelving provides alcoves or selling recesses into which customers can be drawn out of the main circulation. Such an arrangement increases lineal feet of shelving.

The second important step is to assure fairly high intensities of lighting, not only on shelves and displays, but everywhere to permit book reading without discomfort at any place in the shop.

The third step is the design of store fixtures which sell books.

Design of Store Fixtures

This requires considerable study. The front cover of a book is three or four times as wide as the backstrip. Consequently, display which features this maximum dimension secures the maximum display value of jacket design and title lettering. For this reason there is a trend,

particularly noticeable in chain bookshops, to use the most accessible area of the fixture, at about hand height, for front-cover display. There are some disadvantages to this practice, including loss of stock space and untidiness resulting from piling books too high on counters. This latter practice also makes access to lower display shelves difficult. Some otherwise waste space behind vertical "front-cover" displays may be used for stock. Use of sloping counters, with rims high enough to retain only one layer of books, will prevent the second practice.

All shelving should be within normal reaching distance; the maximum height to which the average adult can reach is from 6 ft 3 in. to 6 ft 6 in. Display and stock tables may be introduced in wider alcoves. Aisles not less than 3 ft wide are preferred; main circulation aisles are not usually greater in width than 6 ft or 6 ft 6 in., for large shops.

Nonselling Areas

These consist of wrapping and cash register space, small office and employees' lavatory, and necessary room for mechanical system equipment. Location of all of these varies with each job. In small, "one-man" shops, wrapping, cash register, and office space may be combined and located near the entrance for easy supervision. In no case should these areas obtrude upon customer space.

Lighting and Air Conditioning

Lighting is preferably high in intensity and without glare.

Direct lighting concentrated on the fixtures' selling zone—the area of the counter and of the two or three shelves immediately above counter height—has been found satisfactory. Light sources are best concealed. Complete air conditioning will aid in preserving stock, and is often necessary to increase the comfort of customers in the rather confined alcove spaces.

GIFT SHOPS

The problem in designing gift shops is complicated by the variety and number of objects which must be displayed. Merchandise is seldom bought without seeing and handling either the actual object or a sample. Cleaning and arranging such a varied, fragile stock is a serious maintenance problem.

Selling and Interior Display Areas

Departmentalizing the stock is valuable but difficult to achieve, and is ordinarily accomplished differently for each job, depending on the general type of merchandise. Objects may be arranged according to material, texture, and color; or according to function; or in mixed groupings coordinated according to probable use. Both classified and mixed groupings are considered essential. Times and seasons for various types of merchandise must be considered and display space provided to accommodate these changes in positions and importance relative to the regular stock.

Shelving is required for all small objects, such as glassware, pottery, silver, etc. Sizes range from 8 to 12 and even 20 in. in width; below counter height, shelf or stock space is often enclosed to protect objects which might be damaged by dust. Sales counters are usually eliminated; although, again, for small, perishable articles, glass show cases may be advisable. Closed displays with concealed soffit lighting have been found valuable for such objects of special value or fragility, articles which deteriorate if left in the open (leather, silver, plaster, unglazed terra cotta). Sale of gift merchandise implies the writing of cards and notes for enclosure, and of checks. One or more desks should be provided for customers for these purposes. It has been suggested that space should be provided for telephone books for addresses.

Show Windows

Most gift shop window backs are open, or partially so, in order to give views through into the shop. Lighted interior displays visible through open backs often attract customers. Flexibility is sometimes demanded; that is, a window with a back which may be open or

closed at will. Lighted recessed shelving in the window side or backs, or on adjustable brackets, exploits varied display levels.

Nonselling Areas

Stock rooms require a range of sizes of shelving, from 8 to 12 or 20 in. wide, as well as closed cupboards for objects which might be damaged by dust.

The receiving and packing room will have to handle large quantities of inflammable packing material.

A wrapping table, 3 ft 6 in. by 5 ft, with two paper rolls, 18, 24 to 30 in. long is usually sufficient. Weighing scales are required.

JEWELRY SHOPS

Jewelry stores range from the small shop which sells fine, expensive, and exclusive items to the commercial credit store which displays and sells in volume, and then to the costume jewelry shop. Jewelry, at all prices, is an impulse item and so needs good visual appeal.

The better jewelry store is a small store with a small front and may be the open or see-through type. Displays are on an individual basis, uncluttered, very well illuminated, and up high for easy, close examination. This store is never self-service; it requires individual leisurely attention to the customer. Displays and counters are individual units. Small tables, sometimes combined with a small display or

showcase (Fig. 16), are for the customer and sales person to sit down during the transaction.

Very exclusive shops will have private salesrooms for special customers. Sometimes these are glass enclosed and have drapes that are drawn when the room is used and complete privacy required.

Wall displays are shallow, individual, glass-enclosed, and intensely illuminated. The repair department should be located at the rear of the store and completely visible to the customer through glass.

A larger store may have several departments such as silverware, gifts, crystal, glass, and china which may be displayed on and sold from open shelves against the walls, with no counters, or from island counter units.

All jewelry items are removed from the show windows, displays, and cases and put into the vault when the store is closed. Display cases have small removable trays that are transferred with the jewelry into a special section of the vault made to receive these trays. Protection is important and must be considered in the early part of the design with the agency that will provide the service. Lighting is critical, primarily incandescent, with blue fluorescent to offset the yellow in the incandescent.

Provide sufficient counter mirrors and occasional full-length mirrors.

In the better store cash is generally handled from a cash drawer at the wrapping counter located in the rear or in the office. The entire store must be inconspicuously visible from the

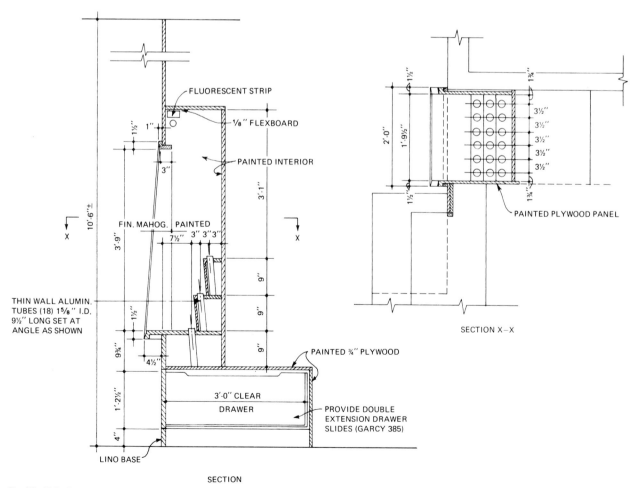

SECTION

Fig. 15 Umbrella display.

RETAIL SHOPS
Jewelry

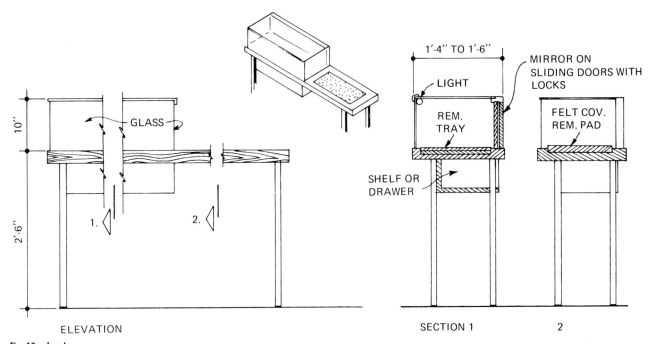

ELEVATION

SECTION 1   2

Fig. 16 Jewelry.

stock room or office. This may be done with the use of one-way mirrors.

The credit jewelry store, or the popular price store, caters to volume in both customers and merchandise. Counters are of the stand-up type; not individual (Fig. 17). Two, three, or more are combined into a single long unit. Displays on the interior and the show windows will have a mass display of items. The cashier and wrapping desk are located at the front of the store for better control.

Jewelry is sold by persons trained to give individual attention to each customer. Patrons are given little opportunity to handle merchandise except in the presence of a salesperson. Valuable stock is ordinarily locked in a vault each night, and the entire store must be "dressed" each morning.

Sales and Display Areas

These are divided into a general salesroom for ordinary customers, and one or more private rooms for customers who wish to buy expensive items, usually precious stones.

No counters, in the ordinary sense, are provided; it has been found preferable to have nothing between customer and salesman. Both sit at tables, 2 ft by 3 ft in size, which are spaced at 9 to 10 ft intervals for privacy. A few display cases are used, and stock drawers to hold jewelry trays. Display tables for stationery and watches are sometimes fitted with display drawers, the full size of the table, and visible through a glass top. Wall cases are often recessed in salesroom walls.

Private sales cubicles may be from 6 to 7 ft by 8 to 10 ft. Furniture should include 3 or 4 chairs and a sales table.

Show Windows

They usually have high bulkheads, are small in size, and have opaque backs. Displays are usually limited, and small in scale. Glazing should interfere with vision as little as possible.

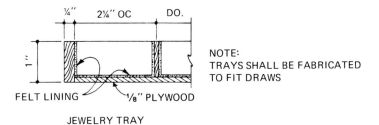

NOTE:
TRAYS SHALL BE FABRICATED TO FIT DRAWS

JEWELRY TRAY

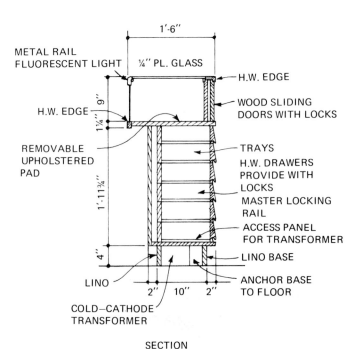

SECTION

Fig. 17 Costume jewelry.

Nonselling Areas

Protection of stock is important, although there are few deleterious influences against which jewelry must be protected. Pearls and ivory will not stand heat. Silver will tarnish; watches and clocks must be oiled and regulated. A jewelry polishing shop may be needed in a room adjacent to the general offices. This is about 8 by 8 ft with benches, shelves, sink, and electrical tools.

Protection against theft is provided ordinarily by keeping stock in a vault at night, and by installing alarm systems at all windows and doors. Where available, various private, police, or similar protective agency systems are usually interconnected.

Conveniences installed for customers' comfort include private telephone booths, drinking fountains, and a lavatory, as well as vanity tables.

Offices may include spaces for manager, clerical department, telephone switchboard, and registry (accurate records of purchases are usually required by law). Offices are often in mezzanines. Shipping departments may be in basements or first floors.

CHAIR UNIT

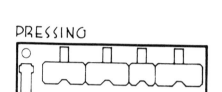

BARBER SHOP

The typical five-chair barber shop can be accommodated in a store 14 by 42 ft. in size. A shop for a small community ordinarily has a single shampoo basin; if individual basins are required at all barber chairs, space requirements have to be slightly increased (Fig. 18).

SHOP CLEARANCES

a. 10'-9"   **e.** 0'-10"
b. 4'-6"   **f.** 12'-0" to 14'-0"
c. 7'-6"   **g.** 2'-6"
d. 4'-0"   **Manicure table:** 1'-4" x 2'-6"

CHAIR UNIT

a. 3'-0"   **d.** 4'-6"   **g.** 6'-0"
b. 1'-6"   **e.** 1'-0"   **h.** 0'6"
c. 1'-6"   **f.** 1'-0"   **i.** 0'-3"

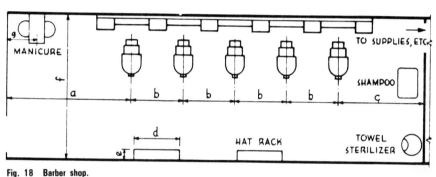

Fig. 18   Barber shop.

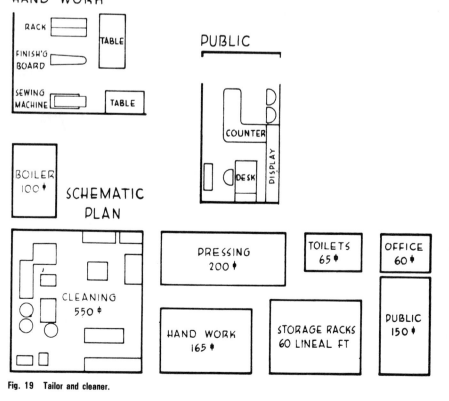

Fig. 19   Tailor and cleaner.

TAILOR AND CLEANER

The schematic plan here presented shows areas required for the various functions in a complete small tailoring and cleaning establishment. If a tailor's shop is the only requirement (for pressing and repairs) and cleaning work is sent out, cleaning and boiler-room areas may be omitted (Fig. 19).

PRESSING UNIT

Vacuum steam unit: 2'-6" x 5'-9"
Pressing machine: 5'-9" x 3'-0", 5'-0", or 6'-0"
Tables and racks: 2'-0" wide, 15 lin. ft.

HANDWORK AREA

Tables: 3'-0" x 6'-0", 2'-6" x 5'-6"
Sewing: 3'-6" x 6'-0"
Finishing board: 4'0" x 6'0"
Hanging rack: 2'-0" wide, 4½ lin. ft.

RETAIL SHOPS

Beauty; Shoe-Repair; Florist

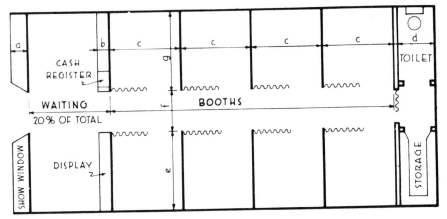

Fig. 20   Beauty shop.

BEAUTY SHOP

The typical small beauty shop has to contain at least six to eight booths in order to do enough business to be successful. If manicuring is to be done in booths, 20% of the shop's total area is devoted to waiting room. If manicure tables (15 by 30 in., with 5 ft. between tables) have to be placed in waiting space, the 20% proportion may have to be enlarged (Fig. 20).

DIMENSIONS

a. 1'-0" to 1'-6"   **d.** 3'-0"
b. 1'-0"   **e.** 6'-6" to 7'-0"
c. 5'-0", 6'-0", 7'-0"   **f.** 3'-6" to 7'-0"
   (for standard   **g.** 6'-6" to 7'-0"
   wall cabinets)

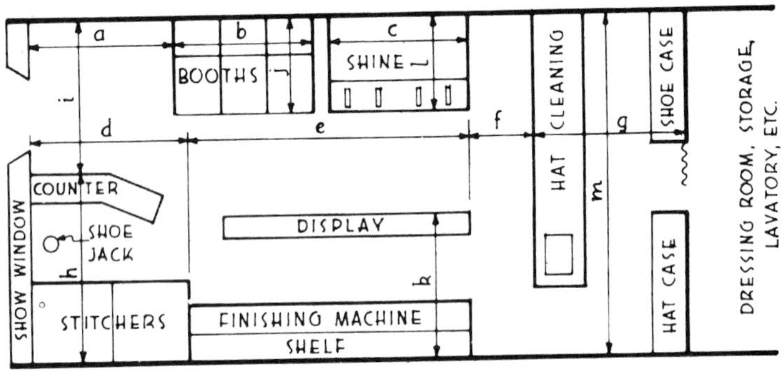

Fig. 21   Shoe repair shop.

SHOE-REPAIR SHOP

Data are based on requirements for a one-man shop, possibly with helper. Door is always at one side of show window; small window is sometimes omitted. Large window contains 10- to 12-inch-wide workbench. Booths for "while-you-wait" are standardized at 1 ft. 8 in. wide, with 2-in. arm rests between; depth is variable. Shoeshine benches are never placed opposite waiting booths (Fig. 21).

DIMENSIONS

a. 5'-6"   **d.** 6'-0"   **i.** 6'-0"
b. 5'-8"   **e.** 11'-0"   **j.** 3'-6"
c. 5'-0" std. for **f.** 2'-6"   **k.** 5'-6"
   2 chairs; 6'-   **g.** 6'-0"   **l.** 3'-6"
   0" size also   **h.** 7'-0"   **m.** 13'-0"
   available

FLORIST SHOPS

In flower shops, selling and display areas are combined, and temperatures must be kept low to prevent loss of stock. Show windows are almost always completely open, to display the entire shop's interior.

Selling and Interior Display

Refrigerated cases inside the store are usually raised off the floor on a bulkhead for ease in reaching in and in cleaning. Maximum depth for reach-in cases is four feet. Sliding glass doors are usually standard.

Shelving and racks are required for vases and pottery. Shelf dimensions depend on the stock to be carried. Desk space for several persons, for writing gift cards, is another requirement. Desks may be of the stand-up type, possibly attached to columns.

Finishes   Floors both in public spaces and in refrigerated cases, must be impervious to water; linoleum, tile, glass brick, and similar materials have proved satisfactory. Walls are often mirrored, since repeated reflections are found to be helpful to the sale of stock.

Mechanical systems   Store temperatures are held down to approximately 50°F for best conditions. Refrigerated cases are kept at 42 to 50°F for roses and some other species of flowers.

Cooling coils are usually placed in the tops of cases, with compressors in basement spaces.

Nonselling Areas

Workrooms are required for preparing special displays, floral pieces, and for storing watering cans, ribbon, twine, paper, boxes, and additional pottery. Workroom sizes are not standardized. A sink with a high cold water tap, or hose, is required for filling watering cans.

Ribbon is stocked in rolls from $\frac{1}{4}$ to 10 in. wide. Boxes are stacked on tables or shelves for each day's trade; 150 boxes is an average for moderately large shops. Table may be 4 by 8 ft; box shelves may be 1 to 3 ft deep.

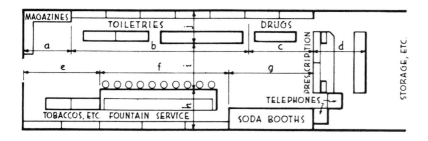

DRUGSTORE

PLAN DIMENSIONS
a. 8'-6''
b. 32'-6'' (wall cases, counter, stepped counter)
c. 10'-6''
d. 9'-0''
e. 13'-0''
f. 21'-6''
g. 14'-6''
h. 6'-9'' to 7'-0''
i. 5'-9'' to 8'-0''
j. 4'-6'' to 5'-8'' (varies with counter depth)

SODA BOOTHS
a. 1'-4''
b. 2'-0''
c. 4'-8'' min.
d. 3'-6'' min.

SODA BOOTHS

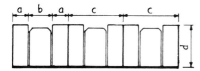

Fig. 22 Drugstore.

DRUGSTORES

Today's drugstore is no longer the small neighborhood pharmacy or "wet" store that included a soda fountain with tables. It is now either a small "dry" store, primarily handling prescriptions, sundries, and cosmetics, or the large variety type of store, very often part of a chain operation with certain departments leased out. In addition to the departments already mentioned for the small store, it may have a complete luncheonette and departments for tobacco, film, greeting cards, books, and certain household items typical of the variety store. The larger store very often is part of a shopping center complex.

Storefronts are simple, generally the open or see-through type, with shallow display windows with high platforms.

Interior must be well organized and grouped or departmentalized. The prescription department usually is in the rear of the store, with a small seating or waiting area. This is similar to typical department store selling, which forces the prescription customer through the entire store and past the impulse items. Very often the tobacco section will also be located in the rear, for the same reason, though some operations prefer to handle tobacco at the cashier along with film. The luncheonette normally is at the front, as is the cosmetics department, with drugs and sundries centered, and the book department and telephones again favored in the rear.

Large operations will have several controlled check-out counters at the front, with separate cash registers at the pharmacy and luncheonette.

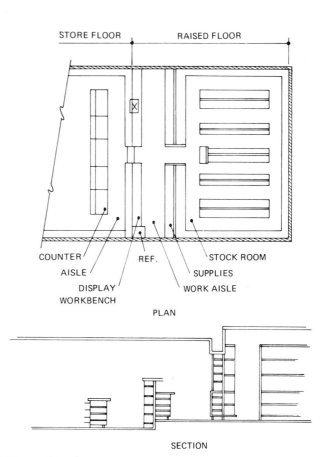

Fig. 23 Pharmacy area of drugstore.

RETAIL SHOPS
Drug; Liquor

The only departments requiring or using counter service are prescriptions, cosmetics, tobacco, film, and radios. All other selling is from open displays, gondolas, and wall shelving, usually continuous for flexibility identical to that used for supermarkets and with a curtain wall and continuous light cornice at the top of the shelving.

If the prescription and pharmacy work area is elevated one or two steps above the main floor, it provides a better view and control of the entire store. The layout and operation of the prescription department varies with the individual pharmacist. The work area is divided into a wet and dry area with a worktable, stainless-steel sink with hot and cold water, and a refrigerator. In addition to bottle and container storage, generally under the workbench, space is required for prescription files, current and past. Keeping good records is mandatory by law (Fig. 23).

By A. PETER FLORIO Designer-Consultant

LIQUOR STORES

The liquor store will consist of many ideas such as:
1. Zoned and cold wall refrigeration
2. Perpetual inventory systems
3. Refrigerated gondolas
4. Electronicair filter system to remove dust and dirt from sales area
5. Automatic check-out systems
6. End of pilferage
7. New approaches to exterior store design
New product ideas such as:
1. Frozen and refrigerated cordials, liqueurs
2. Complete lines of powdered cocktails, mixed drinks

The rapidly growing "spendable income" of the American public is the single largest factor, for the perpetual stream of new products and new packaging that enters the retail liquor industry constantly is slowly bringing about new ideas in product development and product presentation which, in turn, create new demands and new requirements for equipment manufacturers and store designers.

All these new items create new problems of merchandising techniques. In conjunction with these new products, the percentage of women customers is ever increasing. Within the next 10 years, women will outnumber men customers, as liquor in one form or another is becoming more and more of a staple item in the average American home.

Women shoppers are more demanding, more critical, and more susceptible to a properly designed merchandising layout in an attractive well-lighted store, and they are bigger impulse item buyers than men. (And they also control most of the family money.)

The selling area will either be covered with carpeting, which will be specially designed with a foam backing that will eliminate a large percentage of bottle breakage in the sales area, or floor tile that will never need polishing.

The merchandising layout will be completely different than we know today, with the use of

Liquor Store Management Manual, reprinted from *Liquor Store Magazine*, March 1968. © 1968 by Jobson Publishing Corp., New York, N.Y.

zoned and cold wall refrigeration. Appearancewise, the shelving will basically look as it does presently, but each shelf will have temperature control as required to hold each category of merchandise at a correct holding temperature. Walk-in coolers will be eliminated as a means of refrigeration.

One example of the usage of the cold-wall method is as follows: 99 percent of every liquor store in the United States today has a partition wall separating the back room from the sales area, and in almost every case the cooler is either in front of this partition or the partition is built flush with the front of the cooler, with the cold-wall idea, when the partition is built. Cold panels will be built right into the wall with uprights placed every four feet for adjustable shelving. All the can beer and beverages can be merchandised this way, for combination case beer, can beer, and beverage merchandising.

The zoned refrigeration idea will be used so that case beer can be stacked 2 or 3 cases deep and with adjustable shelves for loose merchandise. This method can be applied to any length and width of floor space required, This same idea will be used to encompass the wine wall shelving. The shelf merchandise will maintain a temperature range of $37°$ to $61°$ which can be adjusted to hold at a preselected temperature, and percentage of humidity to properly contain the product.

The same method of zoned refrigeration will be used on all gondolas that will be used to merchandise estate and chateau bottling of wine; cordials and liqueurs (that can be held in a frozen or refrigerated state, thereby offering more true flavor and taste than is now possible); gourmet foods and can beer.

It will have an electronic pilferage detection system such as the sensormatic detection system which uses a sensitized dot in the price tag or sticker. It is almost impossible to find the dot without special equipment.

If the package or article is properly checked out through a cashier, the dot is desensitized by equipment under the counter. If the shoplifter conceals the package or article and gets by the cashier, the dot continues to give off electronic signals that are picked up by a sensitive detector at the exit, notifying security officers that a theft is taking place.

Location Analysis

Downtown City Location
• Advantages   Pedestrian traffic is principal advantage. Also availability of business market.
• Disadvantages   High rentals, competition, lack of parking facilities.

Suburban
• Advantages   Upper income customers. Considerable home entertainment. Good gift market.
• Disadvantages   Lack of street traffic. High delivery costs.

Industrial
• Advantages   Excellent customer pool. Both business and labor.
• Disadvantages   Peak selling periods. Pay days, after working hours. Need for lots of small sizes.

Residential
•Advantages   Regular customers. Opportunity for promotion.
•Disadvantages   Customers in mixed income groups. Therefore, need to maintain variety of services.

Shopping Center
• Advantages   Heavy traffic locations. Good parking facilities.
• Disadvantages   Mostly female traffic. Distraction of other types of stores.

Highway Location
• Advantages   Customer convenience.Heavy automobile traffic.
• Disadvantages   Not easy to "stop" customers. Need for extensive parking facilities.

As mentioned above, there are opportunities to do business regardless of the location.

Considerations in Liquor Store Design

Among the positive marketing trends that are affecting liquor store design today are the following:
1. The change in buying trends of the consumer public
2. The new drinking sophistication of consumers
3. The emergence of women as liquor store customers
4. The home entertainment boom
5. The constant flow of new brands, new products, new sizes entering the market to meet the new demands of consumers

There are also some negative trends, and stores must be designed to cope with them. They are:
1. The shortage of experienced personnel
2. The high cost of overhead and daily operation
3. Extreme price competition in many sections of the country
4. Pilferage problems in some city areas
5. Regulations, regulations, regulations

In order to properly lay out and design a liquor operation, the following points must be covered in order to achieve the utmost efficiency, flexibility, economy of operation, and profit:
1. Location analysis
2. Structural arrangement
3. Liquor merchandising "problem" areas
4. Product placement
5. Check-out system
6. Traffic control
7. Financing
8. Interior designing
9. Signs and display techniques
10. Refrigeration requirements
11. Electrical requirements
12. Plumbing requirements
13. Air conditioning requirements
14. Heating requirements
See Fig. 24 for some possible layouts.

Interior Design

The basic plan and operation of a liquor store is that of self-service, i.e., open shelving, but with a sufficient number of clerks available to help customers. Women are doing more shopping in liquor stores, particularly the neighborhood store, and are impulse buyers—they need and expect assistance in making selections.

Storefronts are usually the completely open, see-through type without any window backs since many states require the entire interior of the store to be visible from the street. Before starting any plans or sketches, check carefully with local and state liquor authorities about any specific requirements or restrictions because they vary in each area. Merchandise in show windows may be protected by grilles or similar devices. Often only one entrance may be permitted, except when the store is within a shopping center. A separate delivery entrance is desirable, but must be well controlled from the office and, if possible, from the cashier. Exterior hardware should be omitted on this door.

Show-window platforms should not be too deep, from 4 ft 0 in. to 5 ft 0 in. and should be on the low side, from 6 to 24 in. maximum above the floor. On the exterior, provision must be made for protection when the store is closed by use of an overhead rolling grille or a folding gate. This protection should be over all show windows and the entrance door. The entire premises including all wall and roof openings, such as air intakes and exhausts, must be protected by a well-designed alarm system.

The interior will be departmentalized to the extent that hard liquors, wines, and beer are all grouped and displayed differently. Hard liquors are displayed and sold from shelving not unlike that of a supermarket or super-drugstore, including the typical price or label holder on the shelf edge, and are well illuminated from a light cone at the top of the shelving.

Domestic, inexpensive wines may be displayed and sold from shelving similar to that for hard liquor. Generally wines are stored lying down as in a wine rack except that several bottles would be grouped in one opening and directly under or over the opening would be an upright bottle carefully displayed to give good visibility for reading the label. Being able to read the label on a wine bottle is a must for the customer. Another method is to have sloping shelves with the angle changing to give a better view of the label. Again, all shelving is to be well illuminated. An illuminated wine chiller, with displays, is a must since many wines must be served chilled and a good, steady customer can be developed if he or she knows that a chilled wine can be picked up for immediate use. Pull-out shelves, which hold several bottles, are also handy so a customer may accumulate a selection or await a decision on final selection.

Beer and mixers should be located at the rear and to the side and, if possible, stored and displayed in reach-in refrigeration. Where possible, build these accommodations into the wall. Loading or refilling from the rear is highly desirable for this bulky merchandise.

A gift, or specialty, section and impulse items should be adjacent to or part of the cashier or service counter. Other impulse items, such as gourmet foods, bar accessories, and giftware should be located so that they are easily visible from the exterior.

The cashier, or service counter, is generally located toward the rear of the store, except for very large operations where check-out counters and service carts, as in supermarkets, are sometimes used. When in the rear, the counter should be large enough to accommodate at least two customers at the same time. Discuss with the operator of the store the special requirements for the working side of the counter: the various sizes of bags, wrapping materials, receiving compartments for inventory tags, handling of cash, and cash register security. An office working area is required. If possible, locate it so that from it deliveries can be controlled and a view of the cashier and of the entire store is possible. The entrance door must be equipped to announce the entering or leaving of any person. Liquor stores are prime targets for hold-ups and pilferage.

The center of the floor is generally kept free of fixed fixtures; use portable gondolas or islands. Displays often are made up of merchandise and containers and with material furnished by the suppliers. By keeping the center of the floor flexible, direction and location of displays can be changed.

In addition to the general lighting and lighting over shelving, provide adjustable spotlights throughout the ceiling area to highlight displays and accent downlights over the cashier.

For floor covering, carpet is preferred in the selling areas, or perhaps wood, and hard floor covering for the storage areas.

If storage is on a level above or below the selling floor, a belt conveyor should be installed. To expedite the handling of the heavy merchandise, portable roller conveyors should be used where there are long stock aisles.

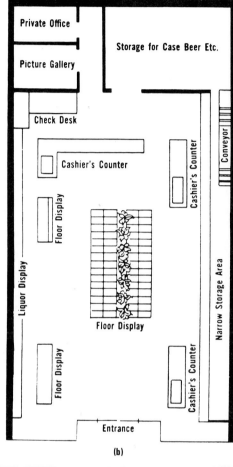

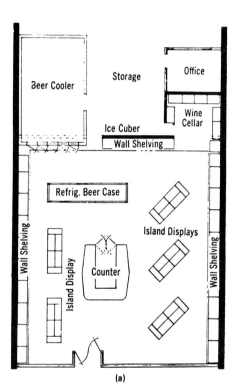

(a)

(b)

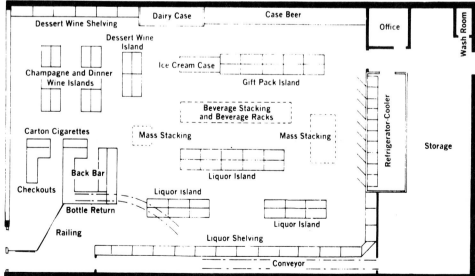

(c)

Fig. 24   Typical liquor store layouts. (a) Small, self-service. (b) Semi-self-service. (c) Large self-service.

By MURRAY S. COHEN, AIA, Architect

SHOE STORES

Different requirements and customer demands have generally required separate stores for men, women, and children. A shoe store is a volume trade operation and is highly competitive.

The storefront is the see-through type, with a large enclosed show window for display of the maximum number of shoes. Average depth of the show window is from 4 ft 6 in. to 5 ft 0 in. with platforms 2 ft 0 in. above the floor. Dust on shoes shows up very quickly, downgrading the merchandise, thus show windows should be enclosed and have tight sliding or hinged access doors. A ceiling display grid facilitates the handling of suspended items. In show windows, lighting must be predominantly incandescent; fluorescent lighting is used only to provide general illumination. Provide an exhaust to reduce the heat buildup from the lights. Floors will sometimes have removable plywood panels to which changeable materials are fastened by the window trimmer.

The interior of this type of store must be arranged to accommodate the maximum number of seats allowing efficient circulation for the salemen's traffic route from stock to customer and not crowding the fitting spaces in front of customer's chairs. Chairs must be comfortable and have arms to provide separation between customers. Provide plenty of fixed or portable shoe-level fitting mirrors as well as occasional full-length mirrors so that customers can get a full view of their entire figure. The shoe shelving generally has some exposed space in the sales area and some concealed in rear or side stock rooms or areas. Exposed shelving in sales areas should not be higher than can be reached without a step stool; concealed or stock-room shelving can extend up to 10 ft 0 in. Where the height is available, two levels, like library stacks, can be used. A cellar storeroom is required for reserves. (See Figs. 25 to 27.)

Cashier counter should be centrally located for good control and accessibility. The hose bar, accessories, and impulse items are generally located near or adjacent to the cashier.

If possible, arrange for rear delivery of merchandise. An employee toilet, a combination workbench for minor repairs, and a desk should be provided in the stock room, with quick access to sales room. In certain men's stores selling a better or higher-priced shoe there will be a shoeshine stand serviced by the porter or handyman.

Floors in the selling area must be carpeted. In enclosed shopping malls the carpet is often extended out into the vestibule. Stock rooms can have hard floor covering.

Women's stores usually are more plush, have more of a salon setting, and have less exposed stock in the sales area. Seating is more informal, with love seats and groupings in addition to the individual well-upholstered seat.

Adjacent to or part of the cashier counter there is an extensive hosiery, glove, handbag, and other matching accessories area. A slipper bar is usually a separate section.

In the area or store for children it is highly desirable to have a raised platform, accessible by steps, so that the salesman can better observe the fitting and walking without having to bend or lie down on the floor.

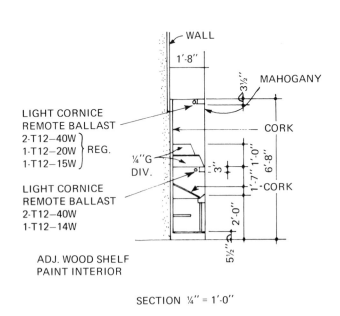

(a)

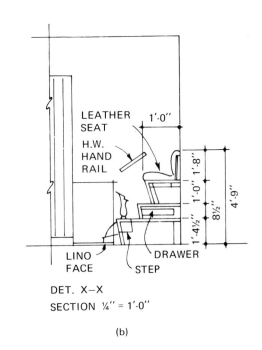

(b)

Fig. 25   (a) Sock bar. (b) Shoeshine stand.

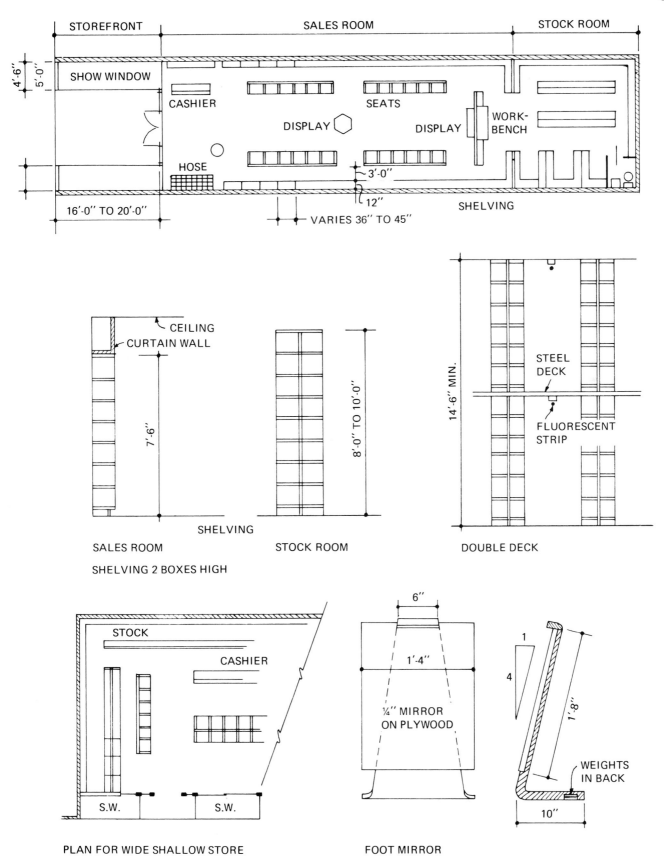

SHELVING 2 BOXES HIGH

SALES ROOM · STOCK ROOM · DOUBLE DECK

PLAN FOR WIDE SHALLOW STORE

FOOT MIRROR

Fig. 26   Men's shoe store.

RETAIL SHOPS
Shoe

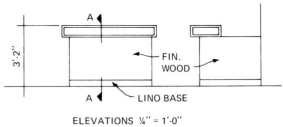

ELEVATIONS ¼" = 1'-0"

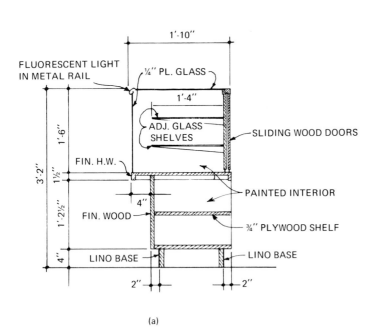

(a)

SECTION A–A

(b)

Fig. 27 (a) Showcases: open stock shelves (b) Hose counter.

By **HERBERT ROSS**

Architecturally, the supermarket is a large-scale emporium of merchandise that doesn't have to shout to be noticed.

Properly situated on its site, the supermarket and any "satellite shops," attached or not (shops which can be entered from the market or from a separate outside entrance) offer a parking ratio of 3.6 sq ft to 1 sq ft of total store area. To obtain the necessary parking area in areas with high land costs, rooftop and basement parking should be considered. The satellite shops such as convenience grocery stores, liquor and drugstores, and a carry-out food shop remain open after the supermarket has closed for the day.

New, free-standing supermarkets average 22,700 sq ft to 31,000 sq ft with 75 to 80 percent of the total store devoted to selling space and the remaining 20 to 25 percent of floor space devoted to service areas such as storage coolers, prepackaging areas, grocery storage, etc. Weekly sales per square foot of selling space vary from $3.10/sq ft to $3.75/sq ft (Fig. 1).

About 50 percent of the supermarkets total equipment and fixture investment is in refrigeration equipment—meat, dairy, produce, frozen food, delicatessen, and the storage coolers necessary for each department. The remaining 50 percent is devoted to grocery items—half of which can be nonfood items, such as housewares, soft goods, glassware, health, and beauty aids. The most important square footage is that required by the check-out stands—one for each $10,000.00 of projected weekly volume plus an additional check-stand for future expansion (this is only a rule of thumb figure and varies with the region of the country and the type of service the market provides the customer). The accompanying plan, adapted to the individual operation requirements, provides a practical guide in the layout of a supermarket.

Assuming proper location of the store on the site, one which makes it most accessible to traffic and parking, the next step would be to decide on the configuration of the store.

Generally, free-standing markets tend to be rectangular in shape, with the narrower portion forming the front-to-rear dimension. Since most often the deliveries are at the rear, the various back room areas (preparation and storage) are located at the rear of the building, leaving the selling space more or less square.

At this point, the method of construction must be considered, particularly the location of any columns. Ideally, these should be kept out of the shopping aisles. Assuming a 7 ft 0 in. aisle between 4 ft 0 in. wide shelving islands, columns spaced in a multiple of 11 ft 0 in. will keep the columns out of the aisles. (Shelving can be cut to fit around columns, and this is preferred to columns in the shopping aisles.)

Although refrigerated fixtures have been and can be located almost anywhere on the sales floor, most often they are located at the walls. They tend to be too large and bulky to be placed in any central location, where they

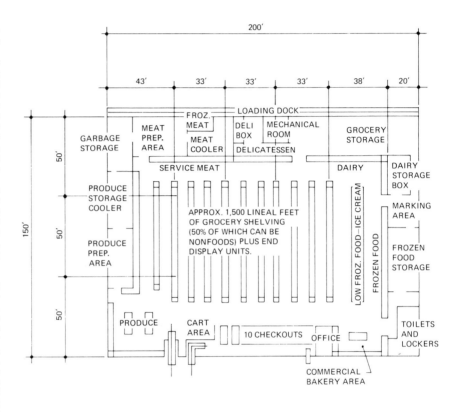

Fig. 1 Typical free-standing supermarket.

would obstruct the overall view of the store. The refrigerated cases should be placed as near as practicable to their associated work rooms and storage coolers. This also applies to the service departments such as the delicatessen, in-store bakery, and snack bar.

Since all merchandise purchases must be funneled through the check-out counters, they are all located in one location (usually at the front of the store near the exit door).

The size of today's supermarket makes the use of self-contained refrigerated cases (with a few exceptions) impractical. Therefore, some sort of centralized refrigeration system is employed. (All major refrigeration equipment manufacturers offer a form of centralized refrigeration system and all are basically alike.) Such a system utilizes a bank of compressors and condensers (air- or water-cooled) located in one room with liquid refrigerant running to the individual cases and the heated gas being returned to the condensers.

823

Commercial
SUPERMARKETS

By EGMONT ARENS, Industrial Designer

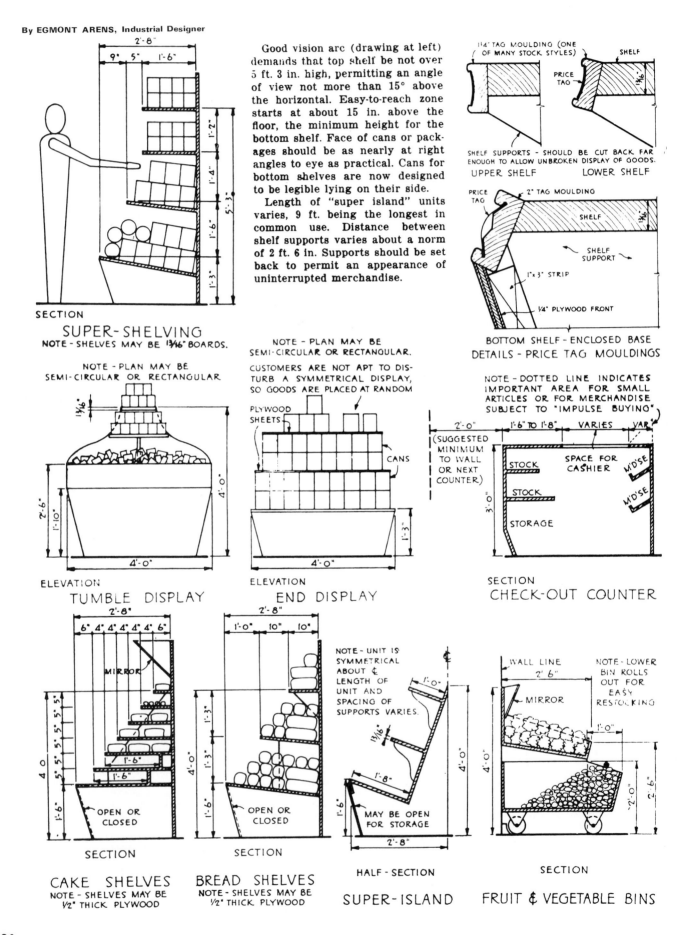

Good vision arc (drawing at left) demands that top shelf be not over 5 ft. 3 in. high, permitting an angle of view not more than 15° above the horizontal. Easy-to-reach zone starts at about 15 in. above the floor, the minimum height for the bottom shelf. Face of cans or packages should be as nearly at right angles to eye as practical. Cans for bottom shelves are now designed to be legible lying on their side.

Length of "super island" units varies, 9 ft. being the longest in common use. Distance between shelf supports varies about a norm of 2 ft. 6 in. Supports should be set back to permit an appearance of uninterrupted merchandise.

SECTION
SUPER-SHELVING
NOTE - SHELVES MAY BE 13/16" BOARDS.

NOTE - PLAN MAY BE SEMI-CIRCULAR OR RECTANGULAR

ELEVATION
TUMBLE DISPLAY

NOTE - PLAN MAY BE SEMI-CIRCULAR OR RECTANGULAR.

CUSTOMERS ARE NOT APT TO DISTURB A SYMMETRICAL DISPLAY, SO GOODS ARE PLACED AT RANDOM

ELEVATION
END DISPLAY

SHELF SUPPORTS - SHOULD BE CUT BACK FAR ENOUGH TO ALLOW UNBROKEN DISPLAY OF GOODS.
UPPER SHELF   LOWER SHELF

BOTTOM SHELF - ENCLOSED BASE
DETAILS - PRICE TAG MOULDINGS

NOTE - DOTTED LINE INDICATES IMPORTANT AREA FOR SMALL ARTICLES OR FOR MERCHANDISE SUBJECT TO "IMPULSE BUYING"

SECTION
CHECK-OUT COUNTER

SECTION
CAKE SHELVES
NOTE - SHELVES MAY BE 1/2" THICK PLYWOOD

SECTION
BREAD SHELVES
NOTE - SHELVES MAY BE 1/2" THICK PLYWOOD

NOTE - UNIT IS SYMMETRICAL ABOUT ℄ LENGTH OF UNIT AND SPACING OF SUPPORTS VARIES.

HALF-SECTION
SUPER-ISLAND

NOTE - LOWER BIN ROLLS OUT FOR EASY RESTOCKING

SECTION
FRUIT & VEGETABLE BINS

824

New bank merchandising systems have been followed by a new bank architecture which no longer needs to follow the old idiom that a bank must retain its aloof dignity. Stability and strength are still to be preserved in the image of the bank, but not to extremes.

Bankers of today have recognized the increased mobility of the nation and the financial needs of the average homeowner, and in combining the two have arrived at a new expression and image for the bank. In projection of future trends, these bankers indicate that the bank of the next decade will blend excitement and attraction with dignity and a modern feeling of solidity. "The banks will be made more inviting through the further use of glass, color, and art; and by offering their services more conveniently; and through increased point of contact at the street and through drive-in facilities."[1]

The innovation of the drive-in and walk-up window recognizes today's informal, mobile living and extends the bank's services to make them more attractive and more convenient to the public. Elements that remain open after regular banking hours, such as a meeting room, savings department, and safety deposit vault, serve the needs not only of the customer of the bank but of the general public as well. Flexibility, then, becomes a key word in bank design. The bank of today cannot subsist under the old idea that a bank is for money only, especially when its image is concerned with public activities along with regular banking activities.

The place in which the bank's transactions take place should be attractive, friendly, and unimposing; a minimum obstruction between the customer and the bank's representatives is a must.

However, before any design requirements can be made, the building requirements (both personnel and departmental) must be firmly established and the basic philosophy of banking operations and building design agreed upon.

DESCRIPTION OF SPACES

1. Public spaces
   a. Lobby. This must be easily accessible to the public. It contains reception/information, loan officers, tellers, and check-writing desks.
      (1) If located on the lower level or

[1] *Banking*, vol. 56, pp. 57–58, February, 1964.

second floor of a building, escalators are recommended for public conveyance to the lobby.
      (2) Tellers should be located so that they are easily accessible and so that the spaces surrounding them allow easy circulation of the public.
      (3) Loan officers and others who have direct contact with the customer should be readily available.
      (4) Check-writing desks should be placed so as not to block circulation, especially of the lineup space in front of the tellers.
   b. Tellers are usually located at one side of the bank to allow for expansion. This is usually considered to be the most flexible of all schemes.
   c. Officers' platform. This should provide open space for contact officers, cubicles for collection officers, and offices for the installment loan and commercial loan officers. A conference room should be provided in this area unless the need warrants more than one.
   d. Access to the safety deposit vault should be provided for customers. Access to the money vault for tellers should be provided.

2. Operations. This is the department that makes sure the bank is run on a steady, professional basis. It takes care of all the clerical work required to run the bank and keep its records in order.
   a. Bookkeeping department. This should be in close proximity to tellers, since this is where the tellers receive and give all the information they need.
   b. Proof department. This is not accessible to the public. It can be separated from the other areas, but should be fairly close to the data processing area.
   c. Data processing area. Special air conditioning is required here. False floors are recommended to house the electric cables.
   d. Clerical, mail, and other various minor services as required by the individual situation. The mail room is usually located in close proximity to the proof department.
   e. Fireproof records vault, to service proof, trust, and bookkeeping departments. This does not have to be adjacent to all three, but access must be provided for all three.

   f. Safety deposit vault, fireproof. This provides boxes for the storage and safekeeping of customers' valuables. Coupon booths of minimal size and a conference room large enough to hold 10 to 20 people should be provided.
   g. General services. This includes toilets, employees' lounge, snack bar, mechanical equipment, maintenance, and PBX.
   h. Drive-in and walk-up tellers. These teller windows are an essential part of a bank. Their design should be carefully considered with regard to flow of traffic and security.
   i. Trust department. This is one of the bank's major services to the public. It is here that trusts, probates, accounts, etc., are put in effect and carried out. This area also needs a lawyers' department.
   j. Auditorium/meeting room able to seat 200 to 300. This room is mostly used by the public and is often loaned rent free. Rest room facilities, a stage, storage space, and coffee bar should be included. This room should be thought of as an all-purpose room. In addition to serving as a meeting room, it will facilitate the training of bank personnel.

3. Executive suite. Usually includes offices for the senior vice-presidents, board members, and president plus all the personnel they need to continue their business. A conference room and board of directors' meeting room are required.

4. Buildings. It is the duty of this department to maintain the physical building, keep records, and collect rental fees for all spaces in the building owned by the bank.

5. Legal department. This department keeps the bank's legal business in order. A library/conference room is usually included in this area.

6. Data processing. This department helps to facilitate and process the bank's checking, payroll, operations, and other procedures.

7. Mail room. The mail room usually contains the addressograph, microfilm equipment, duplicating machines, and other equipment necessary to run this operation. This area should be located near a service yard or elevator and in conjunction with the printing/purchasing department.

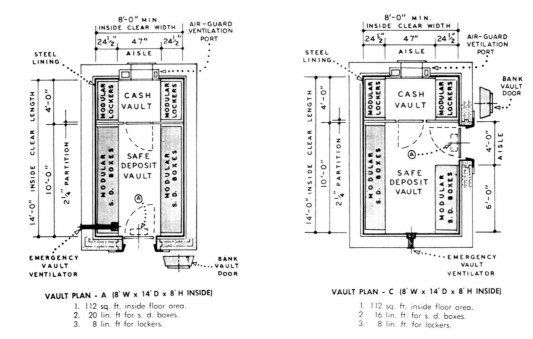

VAULT PLAN - A (8' W x 14' D x 8' H INSIDE)

1. 112 sq. ft. inside floor area.
2. 20 lin. ft for s. d. boxes.
3. 8 lin. ft for lockers.

VAULT PLAN - C (8' W x 14' D x 8' H INSIDE)

1. 112 sq. ft. inside floor area.
2. 16 lin. ft. for s. d. boxes.
3. 8 lin. ft. for lockers.

Fig. 1 The above plans are recommended for single-aisle vaults up to 14' inside clear widths. Interior vault dimensions should be established in accordance with individual requirements and the emergency vault ventilator should be located through a convenient wall area that is exposed inside the building. Location of the vault alarm control cabinet is designed [sic] by "A" and should be recessed in the vault wall when it interferes with the removal of the bond boxes. When the vault width is 14' or more, refer to double- or multiple-aisle vault plans. (Mosler Safe Co.)

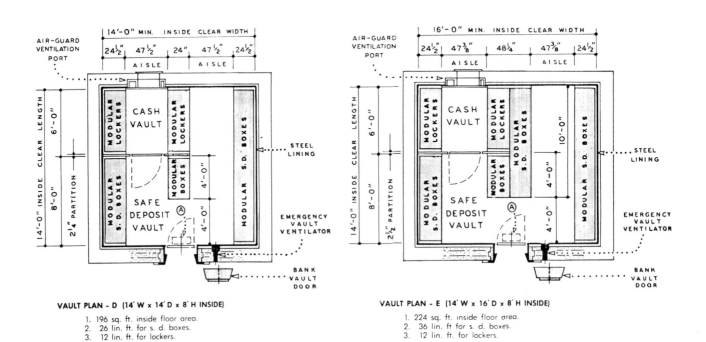

VAULT PLAN - D (14' W x 14' D x 8' H INSIDE)

1. 196 sq. ft. inside floor area.
2. 26 lin. ft. for s. d. boxes.
3. 12 lin. ft. for lockers.

VAULT PLAN - E (14' W x 16' D x 8' H INSIDE)

1. 224 sq. ft. inside floor area.
2. 36 lin. ft for s. d. boxes.
3. 12 lin. ft. for lockers.

Fig. 2 The above plans are recommended for double-aisle vaults from 14' to 16' inside clear widths. Interior vault dimensions should be established in accordance with individual requirements and the emergency vault ventilator and emergency door should be located through a convenient wall area that is exposed inside the building. Location of the vault alarm control cabinet is designed [sic] by "A." When planning vaults with three or more aisles, refer to the multiple-aisle bank vault plans. (Mosler Safe Co.)

By LENDAL H. KOTSCHEVAR and MARGARET E. TERRELL

SPACE REQUIREMENTS

Adequacy of space will influence building and operating costs and efficiency. When space is too small, labor time and effort are likely to increase and the volume and quality of output decrease. When it is too large, building and maintenance costs are excessive.

Decisions pertaining to space allowance may be strongly affected by the limitations of investment funds and available space. Ample space is sometimes provided by means of low-cost materials and equipment of such inferior quality that they have short and unsatisfactory service life. In other instances, space is restricted to a point where it prohibits profitable volume or the best utilization of labor. Space allowances in relation to investment should be balanced in terms of (1) proposed permanence of the facility, (2) acuteness of need for the specific operation, (3) essentials for operating efficiency, (4) desirable standards in terms of appearance, sanitation, and good quality of production and service, and (5) immediate and future costs, depreciation, upkeep, and maintenance.

Facts peculiar to the particular establishment should be used as the basis for determining space needs. Requirements will vary for facilities of a given type and volume. Location; type of operation; clientele; frequency of deliveries of supplies; kind of food used, such as fresh, frozen, or canned; and the completeness of processing to be done will cause variation in production and storage requirements. The policies of those in charge will have an influence. Certain general information, such as numbers to be served, turnover, arrival rate, and type of service, will be helpful in deciding dining area needs.

Study is required to clarify immediate and future needs in food production. Choices should be made between meat cutting or portion-ready meats, a baking section or use of commercially baked products, and the use of unprocessed versus processed foods. If enlargement is probable, studies made before the building is planned as to how space may be added and how the initial plan should be designed to minimize ultimate cost, will be helpful.

It is well to block out space allowances according to functions that the facility is to perform. Calculate area requirements in terms of: (1) volume and type of service, (2) amount and size of equipment to be used, (3) number of workers required, (4) space for needed supplies, and (5) suitable traffic area. The dining area location and space allowance are usually determined first, the production areas next in terms of specific relationship to the dining area, and the other sections as required to these. Planners should be careful in accepting general space recommendations. There are many variations.

Food Service Planning, John Wiley & Sons, New York, 1967.

Dining Area

Space for dining areas is usually based on the number of square feet per person seated times the number of persons seated at one time.

Space Requirements The patron's size and the type and quality of service should be considered. Small children may require only 8 sq ft for a type of service in which an adult would need 12 sq ft for comfort. A banquet seating allowance might be as little as 10 sq ft per seat and that for a deluxe restaurant as much as 20 sq ft. The amount of serving equipment in the dining area and lineup space will influence needs. Lost space must be considered.

The diner's comfort should govern allowance. Crowding is distasteful to many people. It is likely to be tolerated more readily by youngsters than by adults. It is more acceptable in low-cost, quick-service units than in those featuring leisurely dining. Both young and old enjoy having sufficient elbow room and enough space so that dishes of food and beverage are not crowded. Place settings for adults usually allow 24 in. and for children 18 to 20 in. (Table 1).

TABLE 1   Square Feet per Seat Used for Various Types of Food Operations

Type of operation	Square feet per seat
Cafeteria, commercial	16–18
Cafeteria, college and industrial	12–15
Cafeteria, school lunchroom. . . .	9–12
College residence, table service	12–15
Counter service	18–20
Table service, hotel, club restaurant	15–18
Table service, minimum eating	11–14
Banquet, minimum	10–11

All of the areas in a dining room used for purposes other than seating are a part of the square footage allowed for seating. This does not include waiting areas, guest facilities, cloakrooms, and other similar areas. Excessive loss or use of space for other than seating in the dining area will, however, increase needs. Structural features of the room should be considered. Width and length of the room, table and chair sizes, and seating arrangements affect capacity.

Service stations may be estimated in the proportion of one small one for every 20 seats or a large central one for every 50 to 60 places. The advisability of having a central serving station will be influenced by the distance of the dining area from the serving area. It is of special value when production and dining are on different floors. Plumbing and wiring and whether supplies are delivered mechanically will influence location of the stations. Small substations for silver, dishes, napery, bever-

ages, ice, butter, and condiments may measure 20 to 24 in. square and 36 to 38 in. high. The size of central stations varies from that for a small enclosed room to that of a screened section measuring approximately 8 to 10 ft long by 27 to 30 in. wide by 6 to 7 ft high.

Table size will influence patron comfort and efficient utilization of space. In a cafeteria, for example, where patrons may dine on their trays, it is important that the table be of adequate size to accommodate the number of trays likely to be there. Four trays 14 by 18 in. fit better on a table 48 in. square than on a table 36 or 42 in. square. Small tables, such as 24 or 30 in. square, are economical for seating but are uncomfortable for large people. They are only suitable in crowded areas for fast turnover and light meals. Tables having common width and height allowing them to be fitted together will give flexibility in seating arrangements. These are particularly good for banquette or cocktail-type bench seating along a wall. Tables for booths are difficult for waitresses to serve if they are longer than 4 ft. The width of booths including seats and table is commonly 5½ ft. A lunch counter will have a minimum width of 16 in. and a maximum width of 24 to 30 in. The linear feet are calculated on the basis of 20 to 24 in. per seat. The maximum area best served by one waitress is generally 16 ft of counter. This will give eight to ten seats. U-shaped counters make maximum use of space and reduce travel. Space in depth of 8½ to 11 ft will be required for every linear foot of counter. This will provide 3 to 4 ft of public aisle, 2½ ft for aisle space for employees. A width of 4½ ft is desirable where employees must pass.

Calculate aisle space between tables and chairs to include passage area and that occupied by the person seated at the table. A minimum passage area is 18 in. between chairs and, including chair area, tables should be spaced 4 to 5 ft apart. Aisles on which bus carts or other mobile equipment is to be moved should be sized according to the width of such equipment.

The best utilization of space can often be arrived at through the use of templates or scaled models. Diagonal arrangement of square tables utilizes space better than square arrangement and yields a more trouble-free traffic lane. Lanes that pass between backs of chairs are likely to be blocked when guests arise or are being seated.

Table heights in schools should be chosen for the comfort of children. In units patronized by many grades a compromise height will be needed between the 30 in. normally used for adults and the 24 in. suitable for children, or two sizes may be used in different sections of the room. A table length to seat four, six, or eight is preferable to longer ones.

Number of Persons Allowance The number of persons to be seated at one time is the second point of information needed for calculation of the dining room size. The total number of seats required at one time, multiplied by the space required for each seat, will give the total number of square feet needed in the

RESTAURANTS, EATING PLACES, AND FOODSERVICE FACILITIES

dining area. The number of times a seat is occupied during a given period is commonly referred to as "turnover." The turnover per hour, times the number of seats available, gives the total number of patrons who can be served in an hour. If peak loads, or number to be served at one time, are known, the number of seats required can be estimated.

Turnover rates tend to vary, for they are influenced by such factors as the amount of food eaten, the elaborateness of the service, and the diner's time allowance. A breakfast meal of few foods may be eaten more quickly than dinner, and a simple fare faster than a many-course meal. Turnover is quickest in dining rooms where food has been prepared in advance for fast service and where patrons serve themselves and bus their soiled dishes. The turnover time is speeded up 10 percent by patrons removing their soiled dishes so that tables are quickly available for other guests. Deluxe service for leisure dining, involving removal and placement of several courses, takes the longest time. Although specific turnover may vary from 10 minutes to 2 hours, actual eating time is normally 10 to 15 minutes for breakfast, 15 to 20 minutes for lunch, and 30 to 40 minutes for dinner.

The calculation of occupancy of seats in a dining room must take into consideration a certain percentage of vacancy, except where a given number are seated at one time according to assignment. In table-service dining rooms this has been estimated as 20 percent of total capacity, in cafeterias from 12 to 18 percent, and for counter operations 10 to 12 percent. Many factors influence this percentage, such as patrons arriving at different times, irregular rate of turnover, and reluctance to share a table with strangers.

The table sizes used in the dining room will affect occupancy. It is often desirable to provide for groups varying from two to eight, with a predominance in most dining rooms of those for two people. The "deuces" may be of a size and shape that can be put together to form tables for larger groups. In metropolitan areas where many tend to dine alone, wall bench-type seating and tables for two with a center ridge or line denoting space for one have been used successfully. Chairs with a "tablet-arm" that will hold a tray have been used for fast turnover in crowded areas.

The utilization of seating capacity tends to be greater for cafeterias than for table service. The patron may spend 25 to 50 percent of the time while seated at the table waiting for service. The cafeteria diner may begin eating as soon as he is seated. One cafeteria line can serve four to eight patrons per minute depending on (1) the speed of the servers, (2) the elaborateness of food selection, (3) convenience of the layout, and (4) the type of patrons. At these rates, 240 to 480 patrons will need to be seated within an hour. If the turnover rate is two per hour, then from 120 to 240 seats will be used. However, if 15 percent of the total capacity at the peak period remains unfilled, then between 140 and 280 seats will be required. An additional 14 to 28 seats or 10 percent would be needed if the patrons do not bus their soiled dishes.

Patronage estimates for facilities of different types may be guided by the number of persons in residence, enrollments in a school, an industry's payroll, the membership of a club, or the amount of traffic in an office or shopping area. In each case a certain percentage may normally be expected to dine in the facility provided. The percentage will be influenced by such factors as its location in relation to other facilities, the patron's buying power,

the price plan (on the basis of subsidy or profit), patron's mealtime allowance, and convenience of the location.

The patronage estimate for a college cafeteria should take into consideration the number of students who live at home, are members of a live-in group, such as an organized house, and the number of other dining facilities available on or near the campus. A college residence providing table service may have to allow a seating capacity that is 110 percent of occupancy if a policy exists for having "special guest" occasions and seating all at one time.

An industrial lunchroom may serve as few as 25 percent and as many as 90 percent of the payroll. Clues to probable patronage may be drawn from such factors as nearness to other eating facilities, wage rates, type of work, prices to be charged, convenience, quality, and attractiveness. The attitude of management toward the lunchroom may affect patronage also. Pride in providing a good service for the industrial family as opposed to a take-it-or-leave-it attitude tends to win favorable response.

The size of a dining room in a hospital should be determined as to whether it is to be used for employees, patients, or guests, or any combination of these. The type of hospital and the number of ambulatory patients should also be considered. The type of hospital will also influence the number of personnel employed. The ratio of personnel to patients will vary from 1 to 3, depending on how much special care is required or how much teaching and research are done. Good food and reasonable prices will attract a high percentage of those eligible to eat in the facility.

School lunch participation varies 25 to 75 percent and a good percentage for planning is 60 to 75 percent of enrollment. Where prices are low, the food good, meal selections appealing, and the food service carefully integrated with the educational program, the percentage will be high.

Banquet seating requires planning because maximum seating potential means maximum profits. Folding tables 30 in. wide are popular. These are obtained in varying lengths, but 72 and 96 in. are commonly used. The spacing for the legs should be such as to allow for comfortable seating when the tables are joined end to end and place settings are laid on 24-in. centers.

Restaurant operators should consider space in relation to patronage volume essential for a profitable business. Labor, food, and operating costs must be met and a profit realized that covers risk-bearing effort expended and return on investment. Essential income is weighed in the light of probable patronage and probable average check. The number of seats provided in planning must cover this need.

Flexibility in seating capacity is often desirable. People do not like to be crowded nor do they enjoy the lonely experience of being seated in a huge area occupied by only a few. Sparse patronage creates an impression of poor popularity. Separate rooms, folding doors, screens, or other attractive devices can be used to reduce size of an area during slack periods. Sections left open should be those easiest to serve. Balconies, back rooms, or other less desirable space can often be used for overflow numbers that occasionally require service.

A common experience in many dining room operations is the need for more seating at one meal than at others. This may be due either to increased numbers or different turnover rates. A residence cafeteria serving

600 men has an overflow room seating 100, which it uses only at dinner. The night meal is not only larger but the men dine in a more leisurely fashion. The room is available for serving other groups at breakfast and lunch.

Commercial restaurants located in shopping or office areas often have a heavier demand at noon than at the dinner hour. Rooms used for general patronage at noon may be closed at night or provide space for private dinner parties. Entrances to these rooms should not require passage through the main dining room. Convenience for special service is important.

Production Areas

A frequently used rule for allotting space for the kitchen is that it should be one-third to one-half the area of the dining room. It has been found unsatisfactory, however, to go by a set space allowance for this area. Detailed study of space allocations leads to the conclusion that percentages in relation to the dining area are "completely unrealistic and unreliable." An analysis of specific needs is required. Many factors influence space requirements, such as:

1. Type of preparation and service
2. Amount of the total production done in the unit
3. Volume in terms of the number of meals served
4. Variety of foods offered in the menu
5. Elaborateness of preparation and service
6. Amount of individual service given, as in a hospital tray service
7. Seating and service plan, whether on one floor or many

The cost of providing space, equipment, and labor is sufficient to merit careful calculation of the best type of operation before planning. New products on the market, new cooking methods, and new equipment available should be evaluated. The use of preprocessed products in many metropolitan areas has made a pronounced change in the amount of space allotted for bake shop, meat cutting, and vegetable preparation areas. Where portion-cut meats are readily available, it is questionable whether even a large establishment can afford to equip and provide skilled labor for a butcher shop. The use of large quantities of frozen foods affects storage needs. The cost and quality of market products, their availability, and the frequency of deliveries are all to be considered.

Variety in menu selection and elaboration of foods tend to increase space needs in work areas and storage. Small amounts of numerous items do not permit stacking and bulk packaging. Elaboration of food often involves individual portion treatment, with individual casseroles, for example, as compared to bulk steam table pans. A hospital food service requiring many special diets serves as a common example of menu variety and individual portion treatment imposing special space requirements.

The equipment provided will affect the space needs. Garbage and refuse, for example, may require a sizable area for storage awaiting pickup. Disposal units for food garbage, incinerator for burnable refuse, and a crusher for tin cans will greatly reduce the amount to be held. Frequency of garbage collection will minimize the space needs.

Structural features of the building may influence the utilization of space. The shape of the kitchen, location of ventilation and elevator shafts, support columns and partitions should be considered in relation to an efficient layout for work. The location of entrances and exits for a good flow of traffic, window placement, suitable space, and relationship of sections need consideration. Eliminate partitions whenever possible; this will reduce space needs and also permit easier supervision of production areas.

Kitchens serving a smaller number require a larger square footage per meal than those serving a larger number. The following data used for industrial cafeterias show the rate at which space needs per meal tend to decrease as the number served increases (Table 2).

TABLE 2 Variation in Space Needs in Relation to Numbers Served

Meal load	Square feet per meal	Variation in square feet
100-200	5.00	500-1,000
200-400	4.00	800-1,600
400-800	3.50	1,400-2,800
800-1,300	3.00	2,400-3,900
1,300-2,000	2.50	3,250-5,000
2,000-3,000	2.00	4,000-6,000
3,000-5,000	1.85	5,500-9,250

Planners are often asked to make estimates of space needs before having an opportunity to make policies or detailed plans for operations. Figures that will be found useful in making such estimates are given in Table 3. These figures pertain to average kitchen areas found in different types of food facilities. Their use is to be regarded as *tentative and to be measured carefully in terms of specific needs.* The square footage given is to be multiplied by the maximum number of meals estimated per hour of service, in order to find the total space requirement.

After production policies have been established, work areas may be blocked out in terms of the equipment needs and the number of workers required to do the work in a section. Linear space, depths, and heights for work centers should be controlled in terms of average human measurements. This will include the reach to and grasp of material or equipment used in working. The length and width of the work table is adjusted in terms of the amount and size of equipment that will rest on it during the progress of work. The linear measurement will vary in terms of the number of workers using it at one time.

The width of the table may be 24 to 30 in. unless dishes or food containers are to rest at the back of the table. Tables 36 in. wide are preferable when the back of the area is used for such storage. Where two workers work opposite each other, a table 42 in. wide may be used. A work area of 4 to 6 lin ft will be within convenient reach of the average person. Tables 8 to 10 ft long are used if two people are working

side by side. A height of 34 in., commonly used as a working height, should be evaluated in terms of specific work done and equipment used.

Aisle space should permit free, easy movement of essential traffic. The minimum width for a lane between equipment where one person works alone is 36 and 42 in. where more than one is employed and where workers must pass each other in the progress of work. Where mobile equipment is used, 48 to 54 in. are recommended. At least 60 in. are needed for main traffic lanes where workers regularly pass each other with mobile equipment. If workers or equipment must stand in the lane while working, appropriate space should be allowed for this. Thought should be given to space for doors opening into an aisle and for handling large pieces of equipment, such as roasting pans, baking sheets, and stock pots.

Main thoroughfares should not pass through work centers. Compactness is essential for step-saving. It is well for the work centers to be in close proximity to main traffic lanes, with easy access to them. It is important both to avoid distraction from outsiders passing through work centers and to conserve space. Work centers at right angles to traffic lanes are efficient (Fig. 1).

The percentage of floor area covered by equipment varies according to production needs and the type of equipment used. A satisfactory layout may claim less than 30 percent of total space for equipment while work areas, traffic lanes, and space around equipment for easy operation and cleaning may require 70 percent or more.

For hospital production and service areas, 20 to 30 sq ft per bed is suggested. The need is reduced as the number of beds increases— approximately 30 sq ft per bed for a 50-bed, and 20 sq ft per bed for a 200-bed hospital. This allowance does not include major storage areas, dining rooms, employee facilities, or floor serving pantries.

Serving Areas

Space allowance of serving areas should be adapted to the needs of the specific facility. The menu, organization of work, and number served will influence size. The type of service will also be influential in dictating space needed.

In cafeterias the counter length should be regulated by the variety and volume. Excess space partially filled is unattractive, but crowding is also undesirable. An estimate that may be used for allotting width is 14 ft. This allows for 4 ft as patron lane space, 1 ft tray slide, 2 ft counter width, 4½ ft for workers, and 2½ ft for back bar. The size of the tray should dictate the width of the tray slide. The average length of counters in college residence halls and hospitals is found to be 30 to 32 ft, while those

in school lunchrooms average around 15 to 20 ft. Some commercial cafeteria counters may be 70 to 80 ft long, but counters over 50 ft long are frequently considered inefficient. Twenty feet is usually thought of as a minimum but, under special conditions and where a limited menu is served, 6 to 8 ft may be sufficient. The trend is toward shorter counters with mobile serving units or dish holders set at right angles to the counter. Smoother service and greater speed are achieved. Counter height may be set at comfortable levels for workers and patrons. Schools may have lower counters so that children may see the food and push their trays along a slide as they are served. For little folk, 28 to 30 in. is desirable, with counters narrow so that servers may reach over to assist a child. A solid tray slide tends to result in fewer accidents than those made of bars or tubing. Plastic trays measuring 9 by 12 in., compartmented, and of pastel colors are popular. Slides for these may be on the servers' side of the counter for ease of service and to eliminate spillage or accidents. The child picks up the completed service at the end of the line.

Some planners use, as a rough guide, one counter or line for every 250 to 300 patrons served, but arrival rate, speed of service, and turnover are more reliable factors to consider in establishing the number of lines required.

Hospital service space will depend upon whether central or floor service is used, trays are set up in serving pantries, and modified diets are set up in line or in a diet kitchen. Space must be allowed for bulk food trucks, tray trucks, small tray carts, or special dispensing units used.

Short-order units where food moves directly from production to the consumer require the least service space. The need for an intermediate station is eliminated. Step-saving compactness saves space. The units requiring the most space are those furnishing elaborate or highly individualized service.

Receiving and Storage Areas

Space allocation for receiving and storage must be based on specific needs. The volume and type of items received and stored should be considered. Although the average operation may find a dock 8 ft deep and 12 ft long sufficient for receiving items, this would not be sufficient for a large one. The space requirement in square feet for food storage for 30 days has been calculated by some as approximately one half the total served or, if 1,000 are served, 500 sq ft may be used as a tentative figure for total food storage needs. Cases of 6/10's stacked 6 cases high on flat trucks will have a bearing weight of approximately 250 to 300 lb per sq ft. Skid sizes should be 3 by 2½ ft by 8 to 12 in. high. Where heavy items, such as 10-gal cans of milk, are stored, bearing weights may be increased. One case of 6/10's, 24/2½'s, or 24/2's weighs approximately 50 lb and occupies 1 cu ft.

Common Storage The volume of canned food needed to serve 100 persons three meals daily for one month is estimated at approximately 45 cases of 6/10's or equivalent. The maximum stack height will be 8 or 9 cases or approximately 72 in. Accessibility of items that differ, as well as volume, will govern the number of stacks needed. A total of 3 cu ft per stack is estimated to include floor space covered by a case of canned food, plus a share of aisle space. One thousand cases piled eight high in 125 stacks will require 375 sq ft or a storage area approximately 20 by 20 ft. Storeroom aisles may be as narrow as 36 in., but 42 or 48

TABLE 3 Square Feet of Kitchen Space per Meal for Food Facilities of Different Type and Size

Type of facility	Estimated maximum meals per hour				
	200 or less	200-400	400-800	800-1,300	1,300-7,500
Cafeterias	7.5-5.0	5.0-4.0	4.0-3.5	3.5-3.0	3.0-1.8
Hospitals	18.0-4.5	12.0-4.5	11.0-4.5	10.0-4.0	8.0-4.0
Hotels	18.0-4.0	7.5-3.0	6.0-3.0	4.0-3.0	4.0-3.0
Industrial lunchrooms	7.5-5.0	4.0-3.2	3.5-2.0	3.0-2.0	2.5-1.7
Lunch counters	7.5-2.0	2.0-1.5			
Railroad dining car	1.6				
Restaurants (service)	7.0-4.0	5.0-3.6	5.0-3.6	5.0-3.0	5.0-3.0
School lunchrooms	4.0-3.3	3.3-2.2	3.0-2.0	2.5-1.6	2.0-1.6

Commercial

RESTAURANTS, EATING PLACES, AND FOODSERVICE FACILITIES

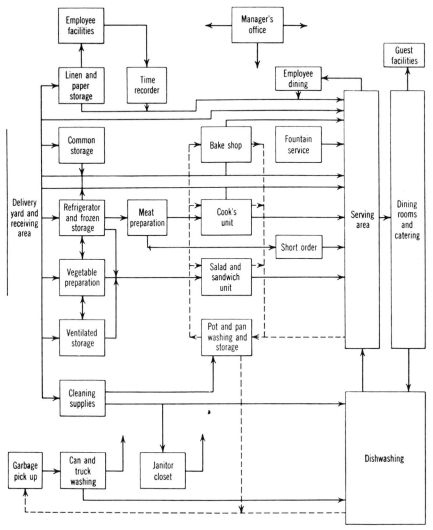

Fig. 1 Flow diagram showing functional relationships.

in. are preferred. Wider aisles may be required if trucks are used. A 3-ft skid on a hydraulic jack needs maneuvering room. If rolling bins or garbage cans on dollies are used for storage, plan location for these. If cans or bins are under shelves, adjust height of bottom shelf to clear and allow for work space for removing food from these containers. Fixed shelving will be best when planned to suit the sizes of items stored. Consider both interspace and depth suitable. Condiment bottles, cereal packages, and canned goods differ in package sizes and in stacking quality. The depth of a shelf should accommodate either the width or length of the case, and the interspace should be adequate for the number to be stacked one on top of another. Allow $1\frac{1}{2}$ to 2 in. as free space for ease of positioning. Add thickness of shelving to interspace when stating measurements between centers.

Position heavy items to reduce lifting and facilitate dispensing. Drums of oil and vinegar should have spigots and be equipped with pumps or located on cradles. Table surface and scales should be located for convenient issuing of dry stores. Plan to have all products at least 6 in. above the floor or movable to facilitate cleaning of storage area. Limit height of top shelf for easy reach without aid of stool or stepladder. The average vertical reach of

men is $84\frac{1}{2}$ in. and of women 81 in. Use of the top shelf for light, bulky packages, such as cereal, is recommended.

Refrigerated and Low-Temperature Storage There are many factors affecting space needs for refrigerated and low-temperature foods. Across-the-board figures generally should be used only in preliminary estimates. The quantity stored at one time will dictate the storage needs. Variation in the type of storage also will be indicated by the types of items to be stored. Allocation in preliminary planning may be as follows: 20 to 35 percent for meat (portion-ready meats require $\frac{1}{2}$ to $\frac{1}{3}$ less space than carcass or wholesale cuts); 30 to 35 percent for fruits and vegetables; 20 to 25 percent for dairy products, including those in serving areas; 10 to 25 percent for frozen foods; and 5 to 10 percent for carry-over foods, salads, sandwich material, and bakery products. A requirement of 15 to 20 cu ft of refrigeration per 100 complete meals has also been used by some planners. Others state 1 to $1\frac{1}{2}$ cu ft of usable refrigerator space should be provided for every three meals served. Analysis of a number of award-winning installations indicated that approximately 0.25 to 0.50 cu ft of refrigerated walk-in space was provided per meal served, and frozen walk-in space approxi-

mated 0.1 to 0.3 cu ft per meal served. Additional low-temperature or refrigerated space in terms of reach-ins was not calculated. In some climates, refrigerated space must be provided for dried fruits, nuts, cereals, and other foods to prevent weevil and insect infestation.

A walk-in becomes feasible for an operation serving 300 to 400 meals per day, and refrigerated pass-throughs can be added when from 400 to 500 meals are served per day. A walk-in 5 to 6 ft wide does not permit storage on both sides with adequate aisle space. Storage space of $1\frac{1}{2}$ to 2 ft should be allowed on either side of the aisle. If crates or cases are stored, this may have to be increased. Aisles of 30 in. are usually too narrow; 42 in. are desirable. If mobile equipment is moved in and out, aisles may have to be wider. Walk-ins that are 8 to 9 ft wide and about 10 ft long are minimum size. This allows for two storage areas 30 in. wide with a 3 to 4 ft aisle. If added width is desired for storage space in the center, allowance for storage areas of about 3 ft wide and 42 in. minimum aisles should be provided. Large walk-ins may be designed for lift truck operation, with doors opening from the receiving dock on one side and into the kitchen opposite. If this is done and lift trucks are used, space must be provided in storage aisles for their working and turning around. Doors should be a minimum of 42 in. wide to admit large crates and containers or be sized to suit mobile equipment. Doors to low-temperature areas are most often planned to open into a refrigerated area. If this is not done a heating device may have to be installed on a door opening into a warm area to prevent its freezing tight from condensation. About 12 to 15 sq ft must be kept free for every door opening. About 45 lb of frozen food, if stacked in cases, can be stored per cubic foot. About 30 to 35 lb of refrigerated food can be stored per cubic foot.

Sanitation Areas

Dishwashing Area The space required for the dishwashing operation depends on the methods and equipment used. In all instances there must be adequate room to receive the volume of soiled dishes likely to arrive at any one time, plus space for scraping, stacking, and placing in baskets on a conveyor of a machine or into a prerinsing operation. The dimensions may be only 30 to 36 in. for a single tank machine, 60 to 72 in. for sinks, or 7 to over 30 ft for a conveyor-type machine. The requirements in the clean dish area will vary. It is important that there be enough space for dishes to be exposed to air for sufficient time to air-dry before stacking. For a basket-type machine, it is well to allow space equal to that required for three baskets, a stack of trays, and three or four stacks of dishes. For basket machines, it is usually recommended that the clean dish area occupy 66 percent of the total table space and the soiled dish area, 40 percent.

Methods used for transporting and storing dishes will influence space needs. Where mobile storage equipment is used, more space is needed for the several units than where one cart is used for transporting and is repeatedly loaded and unloaded. A table surface is desirable for sorting, treating, or inspecting silver and other tableware. The installation of a domestic washer and drier in the dishroom may require space.

Pot and Pan Section Provide a soiled utensil collection area adequate for the largest volume that normally arrives in the section at one time. The busiest periods are likely to occur when preparation containers are emptied for service

830

RESTAURANTS, EATING PLACES, AND FOODSERVICE FACILITIES

Introduction

Accurate determination of the space requirements for a foodservice facility is a very difficult problem, involving considerable research and computation. The space required for each functional area of the facility is dependent upon many factors which are not constant for all types of operations. The factors involved include the number of meals to be prepared; the functions and tasks to be performed; the equipment requirements; the number of employees and corresponding workplaces required; storage for materials; and suitable space for traffic and movement. The importance of accurately evaluating these factors cannot be overemphasized. Overestimating or underestimating any of them can lead to an excess or a shortage of space for the facility.

Space Estimates

The general guides and "rules of thumb" that will be given are to be used for preliminary space estimates only. They are to be regarded as strictly tentative and subject to easy change. The "rules of thumb" are used to get a general idea of the overall size of a facility in order to make preliminary cost estimates for feasibility studies, or to determine approximate land requirements for the building. One problem with using guides and "rules of thumb" is that the figures given are usually based on existing operations and do not reflect newer methods of foodservice operation. Another difficulty is that these figures are not given for all types of foodservice operations and consequently they would be of little use for certain types of projects. Most of the figures available are for general facilities that have no unusual space requirements.

Total Facility Size

Depending upon the type of foodservice to be planned, a general estimate of the total building size can be obtained by relating it to the number of seats to be provided. The estimated square footage of total space per seat is given in Table 4. These figures can be related to the number of meals to be prepared by considering the turnover rate for a particular meal period. A range of space estimates is given to allow for variations in the methods of operation. The smaller figures are used for limited menu and limited-space operations; the larger figures are suitable for operations with extensive menus and allow more spacious areas.

Figures for estimating the total facility size of other types of foodservice, such as tray service, car service, or take-out service, are not available because of the great variations that exist in these types of operations. The only guides available would be to evaluate similar existing operations and make adjustments as needed.

Dining Areas

Estimating the space required for dining areas is based on the number of persons to be seated at one time and the square feet of space allowed per seat. The number of persons to be seated at one time is determined by considering the total number of customers to be served for a given time period, and the turnover. Turnover refers to seat usage and is expressed by the number of times a seat will be occupied over a given time period. Turnover is usually expressed on a per-hour basis, although it can be determined on a per-meal basis.

TABLE 4 Estimated Total Facility Space for Foodservice Facilities

Type of operation	Area per seat	
	ft^2	m^2
Table service	24–32	2.23–2.97
Counter service	18–24	1.67–2.23
Booth service	20–28	1.86–2.60
Cafeteria service	22–30	2.04–2.79

The turnover is determined by estimating the average time a seat is occupied for the time period desired. For example, if the turnover is to be expressed on a per-hour basis and the average estimated time the seat is occupied is 20 minutes, the turnover is 3. If the average seat occupancy time is 30 min, then the turnover rate is 2 per hour. Determining the turnover rate per meal period is useful for determining the total seating capacity based on estimated sales volume.

Turnover rates are affected by the method of serving and serving time as well as by the type of customer, menu offerings and the dining atmosphere. Typical turnover rates for some types of foodservice operations are shown in Table 5.

Turnover rates can be increased to some extent by many design and operational factors. This is not to suggest that all facilities should be designed for high turnover rates. However, if high turnover is one of the basic objectives, then the planner and subsequent manager can use the following to accomplish this:

Use menu items that require short processing times, or use predominately preprocessed items.

Provide ample production space and equipment to handle the peak periods.

Use well-lighted and light-colored painted areas for serving and dining.

Arrange dining tables in close proximity to each other.

Develop a somewhat uncomfortable dining seat design.

Provide sufficient service personnel so guests are served promptly after they are seated.

Provide for prompt clearing of the tables when a customer is finished with a course or the entire meal.

Make sure guest checks are presented to customers as soon as they are finished eating.

TABLE 5 Turnover Rates for Foodservice Facilities

Type of operation	Turnover rate (per hr)
Commercial cafeteria	1½–2½
Industrial or school cafeterias	2–3
Counter service	2–3½
Combination counter and table service	2–3
Leisurely table service	½–1
Regular table service	1–2½

Note that a number of factors identified above are characteristic of the management policy after the facility has been built. This again emphasizes the close working relationship that has to exist between the owner or manager and the planner during the planning process. A foodservice facility designed for high turnover must also be managed for high turnover if the anticipated volume of sales is to be generated.

The square feet of space allowed in the dining areas is governed by the amount of comfort desired. Crowding in dining areas is not desirable except in some quick-service fast-food operations. Most individuals would like to have sufficient elbow room and table space to enjoy their meal.

TABLE 6 Estimated Dining Area Space for Foodservice Facilities

Type of facility	Dining space per seat	
	ft^2	m^2
Table service	12–18	1.11–1.67
Counter service	16–20	1.49–1.86
Booth service	12–16	1.11–1.49
Cafeteria service	12–16	1.11–1.49
Banquet	10–12	0.93–1.11

Suggested space requirements for dining areas are given in Table 6. The figures on the high end of the range are used where ample space or leisurely dining are to be provided. The figures on the low end of the range will result in minimum space requirements.

The estimates for dining areas include space for tables, chairs, aisles, and service stations. They do not allow for waiting areas, rest rooms, or other similar areas. Space requirements for these areas have to be determined separately. The size and arrangement of tables, chairs, booths, and counters selected for the dining area are important to the efficient use of the space allowed.

Production Areas

The space estimates for production areas include room for all the functional areas, such as receiving, storage, preparation, cooking, and warewashing, that are required to produce the menu items. Estimates for production areas for typical foodservice facilities are given in Table 7.

Facilities that will be processing primarily fresh items should use the higher space estimates. This allows for the additional equipment and worker space needed. The smaller figures are used for operations using preprocessed foods and require minimal production space.

TABLE 7 Estimated Production Space for Food Facilities

Type of facility	Space per seat	
	ft^2	m^2
Table service	8–12	0.74–1.11
Counter service	4–6	0.37–0.56
Booth service	6–10	0.56–0.93
Cafeteria service	8–12	0.74–1.11

RESTAURANTS, EATING PLACES, AND FOODSERVICE FACILITIES

TABLE 8 Estimated Percentage of Production Space Allowed for Functional Areas

Functional areas	Space allowed (%)
Receiving	5
Food storage	20
Preparation	14
Cooking	8
Baking	10
Warewashing	5
Traffic aisles	16
Trash storage	5
Employee facilities	15
Miscellaneous	2

A suggested percentage breakdown of the production space for general table service operations is shown in Table 8.

These percentage figures assume a typical operation using fresh products. Baking of rolls, pastries and cakes are also assumed to be done in the facility.

Space Calculations

Another approach to the problem of determining space requirements is to calculate the space needed for each of the functional areas separately. This is done by identifying and determining the pertinent variables involved for the different functional areas. It is assumed at this point that the individual workplaces and pieces of equipment for the facility have been determined and will now be grouped together. The space required for the flow of materials and workers between the workplaces and pieces of equipment is added as needed to develop the space to allow for each function.

A brief discussion of some of the functional areas and the variables affecting their space requirements will be given to illustrate this procedure. Computational operations are presented as applicable. Consideration of the traffic aisles is one of the common variables for all areas and is therefore included.

Traffic Aisles Traffic aisles are used for the movement of materials and workers, and should not be confused with work aisles that provide floor space for the worker to perform the task. The primary purpose of traffic aisles is to allow easy movement between workplaces, equipment, and functional areas. Since traffic aisles are not productive space, they should be kept at a minimum both in numbers and size. Traffic aisles should be just wide enough to provide easy movement of the materials and workers required for efficient operation of the facility.

In general, work aisles and traffic aisles should be separated as much as possible. This can usually be accomplished by locating traffic aisles perpendicular to the work aisles. In some instances, combined work and traffic aisles may be used if the traffic is light and if they offer a better solution to the design problem. Traffic aisles that serve two or more functional areas will minimize the amount of space required. Placement of traffic aisles along walls and other perimeter locations is not desirable for the same reason.

The width of traffic aisles is dependent upon the type of traffic to be accommodated. If it consists of only people who are not carrying anything, a minimum aisle width of 30 in. (762 mm) will allow persons to pass without difficulty. For workers who will be carrying containers and materials or pushing mobile carts and trucks an aisle width of 24 in. (610 mm) plus the width of the container or material carried or the mobile cart width will allow enough space. For example, if one worker has to pass another worker pushing a 20-in. (508 mm) wide cart, an aisle width of 44 in. (1118 mm) (24 plus 20) would be needed. The traffic aisle widths required for special types of movement such as carrying large trays have to be sized accordingly.

In those instances where a combined work and traffic aisle is needed, a minimum of 42 in. (1067 mm) is required to allow one person to pass another person at the workplace. Aisles where there are persons working in a back-to-back arrangement have to be a minimum of 48 in. (1219 mm) wide to allow passage of people between them. An important point to remember is that the less movement required to operate the facility, the less aisle space is needed.

Receiving Area

The main variables affecting the amount of space needed for the receiving function are the number, type and size of deliveries that are to be handled at one time. Many operations can have deliveries scheduled so they will have to handle only one delivery at a time. The types of materials to be received are considered because of the variety of containers and packaging methods available. Ease of opening, checking, moving, and stackability all have a bearing on the space required.

The size of deliveries to be handled may depend on the storage space available in the facility, and is determined in conjunction with storage space requirements. Storage space in turn can be modified by the frequency of deliveries. A greater frequency of deliveries can reduce the size requirements of the receiving area as well. Therefore, storage space and receiving space requirements should be determined together after these factors have been evaluated.

Needless to say, all equipment and work areas for the receiving function must be provided for.

Storage Areas

The amount of dry, refrigerator and freezer space required for the facility is determined by the number of days of storage to be provided for. A general recommendation for dry storage of foods is to provide space for 2–4 weeks supply, depending on the availability of the food items. The total volume of goods to be stored can be estimated as follows. First determine the number of meals for which storage is to be provided. An operation planning on serving 600 meals per day and desiring a two weeks supply will need storage for 8400 (600 meals per day $\times$ 14 days) meals. Next, estimate the weight per meal of items that will be stored in the dry storage area. This calls for an evaluation of all menu items. A general estimate between ¼ and ½ lb (0.113 and 0.227 kg) per meal may be used; it is based on a total weight estimate per average meal of 1–1½ lb (0.454–0.680 kg). These figures are for full meals and adjustments for partial meals have to be made. If an estimate of ½ lb (0.227 kg) per meal is used, then the total weight to provide storage for is 4200 lb (1905 kg) (8400 meals $\times$ 0.5 lb per meal). Then the total weight computed is divided by an average density of 45 lb per ft^3 (721 kg per m^3), which will give the total volume of goods to be stored. In this example, the total volume in cubic feet is 4200 lb $\div$ 45 lb/ft^3 = 93.3. This indicates that space for 93.3 cubic ft (2.64 m^3) of goods, exclusive of aisle space, will be needed.

If the goods are to be stored on shelves, the total square footage of shelving can be computed by considering the height to which the materials can be stored on the shelf. If the materials can be stored to a height of 1 ft, then 93.3 (93.3 ft^3 $\div$ 1 foot) ft^2 (8.67 m^2) of shelving will be needed. If a height of 1½ ft (0.457 m) can be used, then 62.2 (93.3 $\div$ 1.5) ft^2 (5.78 m^2) of shelving is required.

The length of shelving is computed by dividing the square feet by the width of shelving to be used.

This same method of computation can be used for the refrigerator and freezer storage areas. The weight per meal of items that will be stored in the refrigerators and freezers will vary between 0.75 and 1 lb (0.340 and 0.454 kg). The average density of refrigerator items can be assumed to be 30 lb/ft^3 (481 kg/m^3). Items that will be stored in freezers can be assumed to have a density of 40 lb/ft^3 (641 kg/m^3).

The number of days of storage for refrigerator items may vary from one day to a week or more, depending on the method of operation used for the facility. Freezer items can be stored for longer periods of time and are determined by the frequency of deliveries available. An economic lot size analysis may be made to determine the optimum size of storage to provide. The analysis compares ordering, purchasing and receiving costs to the cost of the storage.

Serving Areas

Serving areas for most table service facilities are planned as a part of the main cooking area and separate space determinations are not usually needed. The pick-up area is included in the space requirements for the main cooking area. Additional serving stations for table service can be considered in computations for the dining area.

Cafeteria operations require separate space for the serving function to allow room for the serving counter, room for guests and room for servers. Variables affecting the size of the serving area are the number of people to be served and the serving time allowed. Serving line rates vary from 2 to 10 persons per minute for straight-line cafeteria counters. The serving line rate is dependent on the number of choices and the number of servers. Shopping-center counter arrangements can handle up to 20 or more persons per minute.

The length of cafeteria counters is determined by the variety and volume of food items to be displayed. Adequate space for merchandising food items should be allowed.

The space required for straight-line counters may be roughly estimated at 10–15 ft^2 (0.929–1.39 m^2) of floor space for each linear foot (0.305 m) of counter. This provides room for the counters, customer aisles, room for servers, and back-bar equipment. Shopping-center arrangements generally require 18–20 ft^2 (1.67–1.86 m^2) of floor area for each linear foot (0.305 m) of counter.

The sizing of serving facilities for cafeterias is directly related to the capacity of the dining area. Ideal design results when the flow of people from the serving facility is balanced with the seating available in the dining room. At equilibrium conditions, the flow rate of people leaving the serving areas and entering the dining area should equal the flow rate of people leaving the dining area. In other words, the number of seats provided in the dining area has a direct relationship to the rate of people leaving the serving line for a given average eating time. This relationship can be expressed by the equation:

$$R = N/T$$

where R = rate of people leaving serving area, N = number of seats in dining area, and T = average eating time.

For example, a 200-seat dining room where the average eating time is 20 minutes should have serving facilities capable of handling 10 (R = 200/20) persons per minute. If the eating time is 30 minutes, a serving facility must be able to handle 6.7 (R = 200/30) persons per minute.

Dining Areas

Calculating the space requirements for dining areas can be difficult because of the many choices available. For example, the final space required for a dining room is dependent upon the following variables:

1. Types of seating to be provided:
   a. Tables and chairs
   b. Booths
   c. Counters
   d. Banquettes
   e. Combinations
2. Table sizes desired
3. Table shapes desired
4. Pattern of table arrangements
5. Aisle space desired
6. Number of service stations needed

A suggested approach that allows a planner to evaluate these variables and their effect on the dining space per seat is the modular concept. For this situation the module contains space for the table, the seats, and the appropriate share of the service and access aisles. The modular concept enables designers first to evaluate the space requirements for different choices that may be made before reaching their final decisions.

The following example will illustrate this concept for a dining room that will use tables and chairs only. The first step in the modular concept is to select the size and shape of table to be considered. This is done in relation to the customer, the menu, the type of service, and the type of atmosphere desired in the dining room. Some typical sizes and shapes of dining tables are given in Table 9.

The second step is to select the aisle spaces to be used. Aisle space in dining areas may be divided into service aisles and access aisles. Service aisles usually range from 2.5 ft (0.762 m) minimum for a limited menu operation to as wide as 4.5 ft (1.37 m) for a dining room featuring cart service or table side food preparation. Access aisles are provided to allow people to get into and out of the chairs easily. Thus the type of customer, size of chairs and the desired atmosphere (crowded versus spacious) are the critical factors in selecting the access aisles. Access aisles are generally 1.5 ft (0.457 m) to 2 ft (0.610 m) wide as a minimum. Combined service and access aisles or aisles for cafeterias where people carry their own trays are usually sized from 3 ft (0.914 m) to 4.5 ft. (1.37 m).

Having selected the table size and shape and the desired aisle space, the next step is to consider possible table arrangement patterns. Square or round tables may be arranged into a rectangular or diagonal pattern, as shown in Fig. 2. The diagonal pattern is more efficient in the use of space than the rectangular pattern.

TABLE 9 Typical Sizes and Shapes of Dining Tables

Type	Shape	Minimum size (in.)	Spacious (in.)
Tables for 1's or 2's	Square	24 × 24	30 × 30
	Rectangle	24 × 30	30 × 36
	Round	30	36
Tables for 3's or 4's	Square	30 × 30	42 × 42
	Rectangle	30 × 42	36 × 48
	Round	36	48
Tables for 5's or 6's	Rectangle	30 × 60	42 × 72
	Round	48	60
Drop leaf tables	30 × 30 in. opening to 42 in. round		
	36 × 36 in. opening to 52 in. round		

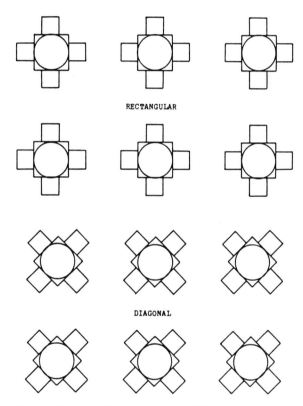

RECTANGULAR

DIAGONAL

Fig. 2 Rectangular and diagonal arrangement of tables.

RESTAURANTS, EATING PLACES, AND FOODSERVICE FACILITIES

The module used for evaluating the factors mentioned is drawn as illustrated in Fig. 3. The module contains one-half of the aisle space selected. The following choices were used for the module:

1. Square table, 36 × 36 in. (914 × 914 mm), for four diners
2. 18 in. (457 mm) seating space (occupied position)
3. Combined service and access aisle of 3 ft (0.914 m)
4. Rectangular pattern of table arrangement

The module size for this example is 9 ft (2.74 m) by 9 ft (2.74 m), which results in a total area of 81 ft² (7.52 m²). Considering that the module is for four persons, the space per seat for this module is 20.25 ft² (1.88 m²)/seat. If this module were to be used for a dining room with 100 seats, the total area required would be 2025 ft² (188 m²).

The module for a diagonal pattern of table arrangement using the same choices for the table size, seat space and aisle space is shown in Fig. 4. The size of the module for the diagonal pattern is 8 ft 4 in. (2.54 m) by 8 ft 4 in. (2.54 m), which gives a total area of 69.44 ft² (6.45 m²). The space per seat is 17.36 ft² (1.61 m²)/seat, which is 2.89 ft² (0.27 m²) less than for the rectangular pattern. For the 100 seat dining room, the diagonal pattern would require 1736 ft² (161 m²), which is 289 ft² (26.8 m²) less than the rectangular pattern.

Similar modules for other sizes or types of seating arrangements can be developed. Care must be taken when using different size tables so that the modules developed for each size table are compatible at least on one side. For example, when tables for twos and tables for fours are to be used, the modules can be adjusted by selecting table shapes or sizes that give the same module dimension along one axis. This would allow a mixing of the tables without affecting the pattern of aisle ways in the dining area.

The possible seating configurations for dining areas are endless, and careful planning is required to make the most efficient use of space.

These procedures illustrate the preferred method of arriving at space requirements for a foodservice facility. Each type of food facility to be planned will have differences that will result in different space requirements.

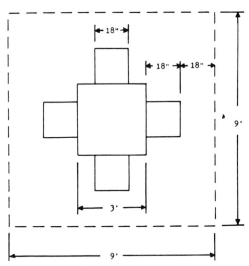

Fig. 3   Module for a square table to be arranged in a rectangular pattern.

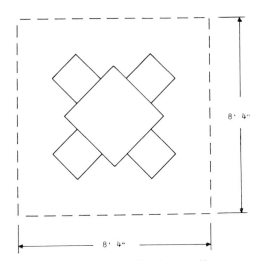

Fig. 4   Module for the square table to be arranged in a diagonal pattern.

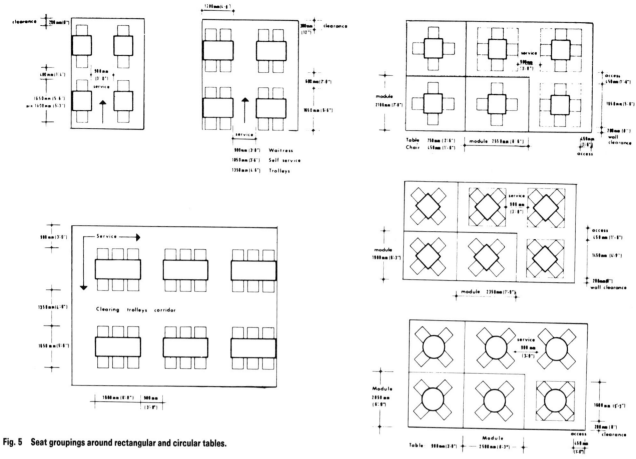

Fig. 5 Seat groupings around rectangular and circular tables.

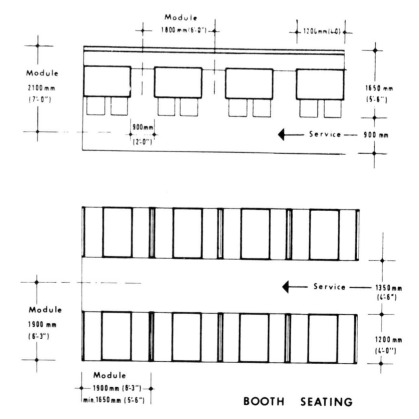

Fig. 6 Banquette seating arrangements and limiting dimensions including space for access and service.

Fred Lawson, *Restaurant Planning and Design,* The Architectural Press, Ltd., London, 1973.

BOOTH SEATING

RESTAURANTS, EATING PLACES, AND FOODSERVICE FACILITIES

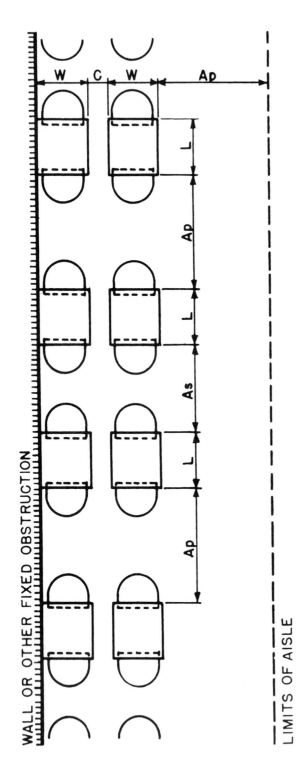

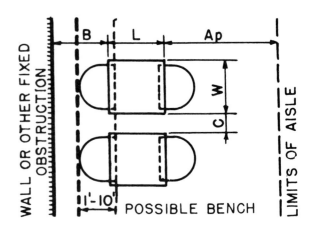

		Abs. Min.	Des. Min.	Comfort-able
Ap	Public circ'n	3–0 to 4–6	3–6 to 5–0	3–9 to 5–0
As	Service aisle	3–6 to 4–6	4–0 to 5–0	4–0 to 5–6
B	To wall	1–8 to 2–0	2–0 to 2–6	2–0 to 3–0
C	Between units	0 to 8	6 to 1–0	1–0
	Length	1–8 to 2–0	2–3 to 2–4	2–4 to 2–6
	Width	1–8 to 2–0	2–2 to 2–3	2–4 to 2–6

all dimensions in feet and inches

		Abs. Min.	Des. Min.	Comfort-able
Ap	Public circ'n	*1–10 to 4–6	2–3 to 5–0	3–0 to 5–0
As	Service aisle	3–0 to 3–6	3–6 to 4–0	3–9 to 4–0
C	Between units	0 to 3	4 to 6	6
	Length	1–8 to 2–0	2–3 to 2–4	2–4 to 2–6
	Width	1–8 to 2–0	2–2 to 2–3	2–4 to 2–6

*Lower range only if chairs, etc., do not project into aisle

Fig. 7   Table and chair units.

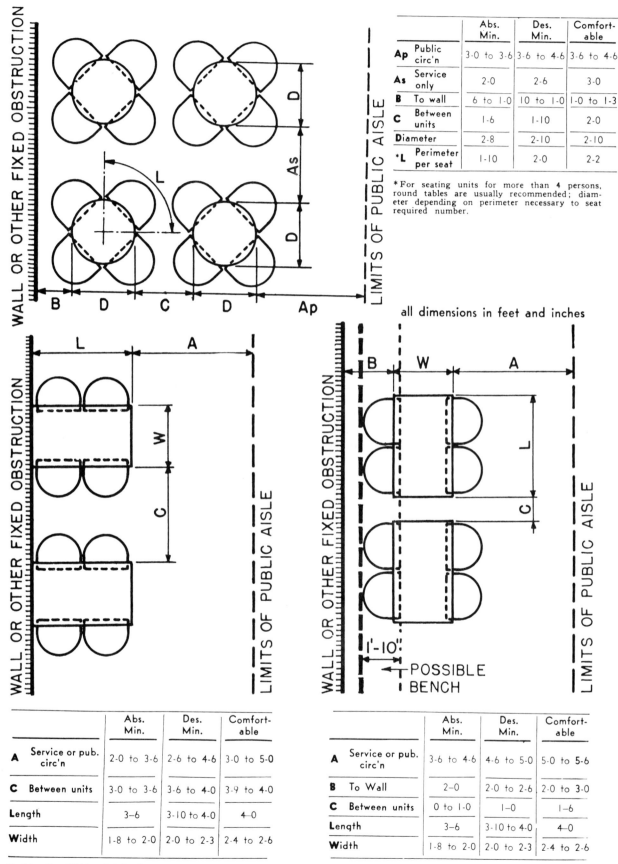

		Abs. Min.	Des. Min.	Comfort- able
Ap	Public circ'n	3-0 to 3-6	3-6 to 4-6	3-6 to 4-6
As	Service only	2-0	2-6	3-0
B	To wall	6 to 1-0	10 to 1-0	1-0 to 1-3
C	Between units	1-6	1-10	2-0
Diameter		2-8	2-10	2-10
***L**	Perimeter per seat	1-10	2-0	2-2

* For seating units for more than 4 persons, round tables are usually recommended; diameter depending on perimeter necessary to seat required number.

all dimensions in feet and inches

		Abs. Min.	Des. Min.	Comfort- able
A	Service or pub. circ'n	2-0 to 3-6	2-6 to 4-6	3-0 to 5-0
C	Between units	3-0 to 3-6	3-6 to 4-0	3-9 to 4-0
Length		3-6	3-10 to 4-0	4-0
Width		1-8 to 2-0	2-0 to 2-3	2-4 to 2-6

		Abs. Min.	Des. Min.	Comfort- able
A	Service or pub. circ'n	3-6 to 4-6	4-6 to 5-0	5-0 to 5-6
B	To Wall	2-0	2-0 to 2-6	2-0 to 3-0
C	Between units	0 to 1-0	1-0	1-6
Length		3-6	3-10 to 4-0	4-0
Width		1-8 to 2-0	2-0 to 2-3	2-4 to 2-6

Fig. 7 (continued) Table and chair units.

RESTAURANTS, EATING PLACES, AND FOODSERVICE FACILITIES

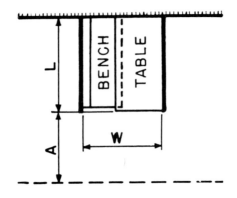

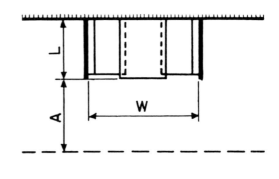

2 PERSONS SIDE BY SIDE

	Abs. Min.	Des. Min.	Comfort-able
Service A and pub. circ'n	2–6	3–0	3–6
Length	3–6	3–9	4–0
Width	3–0	3–3	3–6

Note: This type not ordinarily recommended.

2 PERSONS FACE TO FACE

	Abs. Min.	Des. Min.	Comfort-able
Service A and pub. circ'n	2–6 to 3–0	3–0 to 4–0	3–6 to 5–0
Length	2–0	2–2 to 2–6	2–6
Width	4–10 to 5–6	5–2 to 5–6	5–8 to 5–10

dimensions in feet and inches

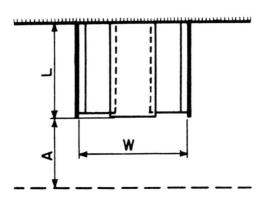

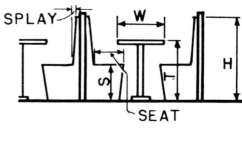

4 PERSONS

	Abs. Min.	Des. Min.	Comfort-able
Service A and pub. circ'n	2–6 to 3–0	3–0 to 4–0	3–6 to 5–0
Length	3–6	3–9 to 4–0	4–0 to 4–2
Width	4–10 to 5–6	5–2 to 5–6	5–8 to 5–10

BOOTH FURNITURE HEIGHTS

	Abs. Min.	Des. Min.	Comfort-able
H	3–0 to 3–6	3–6	4–0
S	1–5 to 1–6	1–5 to 1–6	1–6
T	2–5	2–5 to 2–6	2–6
W	1–8 to 2–0	2–0 to 2–2	2–4 to 2–6
Seat	1–4 to 1–5	1–5 to 1–6	1–6 to 1–8
Splay	0 to 0–3	0–2 to 0–3	0–3½ to 0–4

Fig. 8 Booths.

RESTAURANTS, EATING PLACES, AND FOODSERVICE FACILITIES

The top drawing shows some of the basic clearances required for a typical counter: 36 in, or 91.4 cm, for workspace behind the counter; 18- to 24-in, or 45.7 to 61 cm, for the counter top; and 60 to 66 in, or 152.4 to 167.6 cm, between the front face of the counter and the nearest obstruction. The bottom drawing shows a section through the counter and back counter. Most counters are about 42 in, or 106.7 cm, in height. The clearance from the top of the seat to the underside of the counter top and the depth of the counter top overhang are extremely important. Buttock-knee length and thigh clearance are the key anthropometric measurements to consider for proper body fit. Footrest heights should take into consideration popliteal height. In most cases this is ignored, and 42-in counters are provided with 7-in, or 17.8-cm, footrests that are 23 in, or 58.4 cm, below the seat surface, which cannot work. The popliteal height of the larger user, based on 99th percentile data, is only about 20 in, or 50.8 cm. Therefore, the feet dangle unsupported several inches above the footrest and the body is deprived of any stability. The footrest shown on the drawing, although higher, only serves a portion of the seated users and is intended primarily for standing patrons. The most logical solution is a separate footrest, integral with the stool.

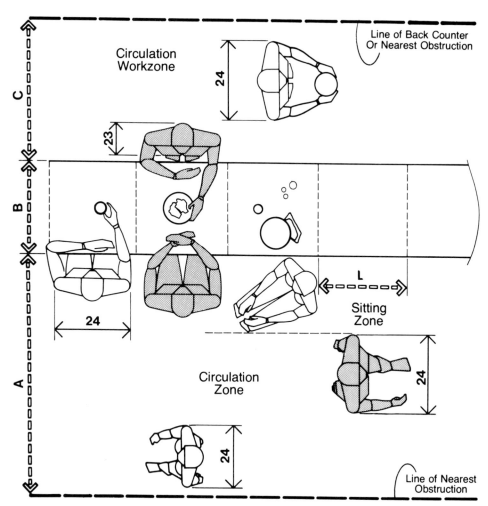

LUNCH COUNTER

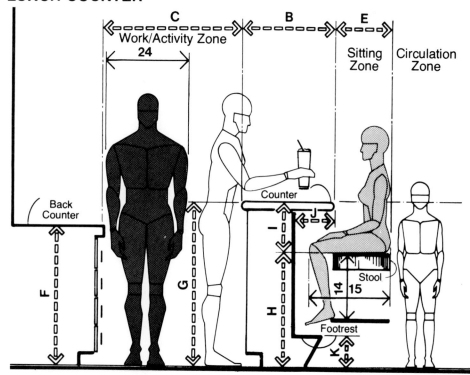

LUNCH COUNTER

	in	cm
A	60–66	152.4–167.6
B	18–24	45.7–61.0
C	36	91.4
D	24	61.0
E	12–18	30.5–45.7
F	35–36	88.9–91.4
G	42	106.7
H	30–31	76.2–78.7
I	11–12	27.9–30.5
J	10	25.4
K	12–13	30.5–33.0

Commercial

RESTAURANTS, EATING PLACES, AND FOODSERVICE FACILITIES

The distance between bar and back-bar should allow adequate workspace. A minimum of 36 in, or 90 cm, should provide space for one bartender to serve and another to circulate behind him. Maximum body depth and maximum body breadth are the primary anthropometric considerations in establishing clearance. A one-bartender operation would require a 30-in, or 75-cm, clearance.

In regard to bar stools, clearance between the stool seats is more critical than center line spacing, and it should allow patrons of larger body size a comfortable side approach and departure from the stool without body contact with the next person. A 12-in, or 30-cm, wide stool on 24-in, or 61-cm, centers, which is quite common, will allow only less than 5 percent of male users access to the stool without disturbing the next patron, while a 30-in, or 75-cm, spacing will accommodate 95 percent of the users. The tradeoff, however, would be the loss of two seats for every 120 in, or 300 cm, of bar length. A spacing of 12-in stools on 28-in, or 70 cm, centers is suggested as a compromise. The ultimate decision is an individual one and must reconcile human factors with economic viability.

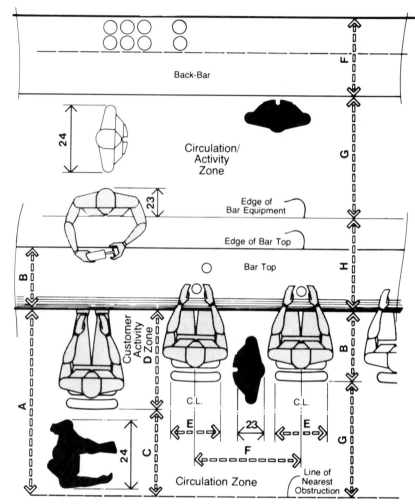

BAR AND BACK-BAR

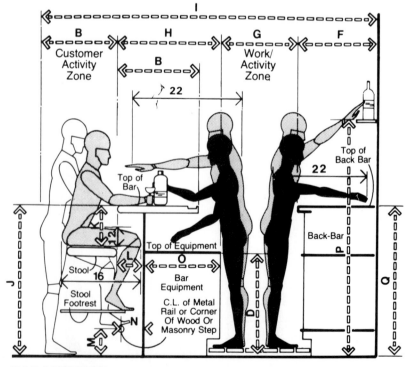

BAR / SECTION

	in	cm
A	54	137.2
B	18–24	45.7–61.0
C	24	61.0
D	30	76.2
E	16–18	40.6–45.7
F	24–30	61.0–76.2
G	30–36	76.2–91.4
H	28–38	71.1–96.5
I	100–128	254.0–325.1
J	42–45	106.7–114.3
K	11–12	27.9–30.5
L	6–7	15.2–17.8
M	7–9	17.8–22.9
N	6–9	15.2–22.9
O	22–26	55.9–66.0
P	60–69	152.4–175.3
Q	36–42	91.4–106.7

840

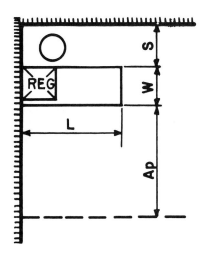

CASHIER'S DESK and COUNTER

		Usual Minimum
S	Cashier's Aisle	2-0 to 2-6
Ap	Public Aisle	3-6 to 5-0
	Length	4-0 to 8-0
	Width	2-0 to 2-4

Fig. 9 Nondining spaces.

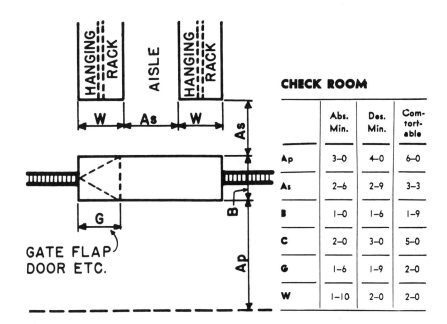

CHECK ROOM

	Abs. Min.	Des. Min.	Comfortable
Ap	3-0	4-0	6-0
As	2-6	2-9	3-3
B	1-0	1-6	1-9
C	2-0	3-0	5-0
G	1-6	1-9	2-0
W	1-10	2-0	2-0

dimensions in feet and inches

and immediately following service when service equipment is brought from the serving areas. A disposal or a removable strainer above a drain is desirable for waste removal.

When allowing space for the pot and pan section, 40 sq ft is generally regarded as a minimum for the smallest unit. The free work aisle between the sinks and other equipment should be 4 ft wide. The space allowance above the minimum will vary widely depending upon the type equipment used and the volume of pots and pans handled. Less space in relation to the maximum load may be required where a mechanical washer is used and fewer labor hours will be spent in handling a large volume per unit handled.

Miscellaneous Sanitation Areas For washing mobile equipment, space is needed where splashing can be confined and that has satisfactory drainage. This area may be adjacent to the dishwashing section or to the place where can washing is done. The size and type of equipment to be handled will govern the space needs.

A storage area for emergency cleanup equipment is needed in convenient relationship to dining rooms and work sections. Spillage and breakage create unsightliness and are accident hazards. Immediate care usually does not require heavy or large equipment but may be handled by a small broom, dustpan, small mop, and bucket not used for major cleaning. A mobile unit may be designed to carry these things, or a small closet may be provided.

Major cleaning equipment required will depend on the floors, finishes, and furniture to be cleaned. Determine whether a power sweeper, scrubber, and waxer are to be used. Space may be required for storage of janitor supply carts and for miscellaneous replacement items, such as light bulbs. Provision will be needed

for storing, emptying, cleaning, and filling mop trucks and for cleaning and air-drying wet mops.

Employee Facilities

Facilities for employees may include locker and lounge area, toilets, showers, time-recording equipment, hand basins near work areas, and dining rooms. An employee entrance should be so located that the employees may go directly to the dressing rooms without passing through the dining room or production area.

Locker and Lounge Area Employee possessions should be protected in a suitably safe and sanitary condition while the employees are at work. Whether individual lockers or common cupboard, sufficient space should be allowed for personal clothing to hang without crowding or wrinkling. If cupboards are used for clothing, a separate space should be afforded for street clothing and for uniforms, and individual parcel lockers should be provided for storage of purses and other valuables. The height of the space for clothing should permit the longest garment to hang straight without wrinkling. The depth from front to back should be a minimum of 20 in.

Suitable size for an employee lounge depends largely on scheduling of workers and the policies of individual establishments. Many operators discourage lounging in the dressing room and recommend the employees' dining area for this. Others having broken shifts on their schedules favor an extra room for lounging. In all cases benches or chairs are to be provided upon which workers may sit while changing clothes and shoes. A cot or daybed, 36 in. by 6 ft, should be provided in the women's room.

Toilets and Showers The location of toilet facilities near work areas is preferred over a remote location in promoting good health habits, lessening loss of labor time, and permitting closer employee supervision. Separate facilities should be provided for men and women. They should be separated from food areas by a hallway or double entrance. Supply one wash bowl for every 8 to 10 workers, one toilet stool for every 12 to 15 women, and one urinal and one toilet stool for every 15 men. Toilet compartments measure approximately 3 by $4\frac{1}{2}$ to 5 ft.

The type of employees, the climate, kind of work, and conditions of work will influence the need for shower facilities. Showers will be appreciated and used by employees working in hot, humid kitchens. Experience has demonstrated that they are little used in localities where the weather is cool most of the year, the work areas well ventilated, and workers drawn from an income group who have good facilities at home.

Time-recording Equipment Provide space for a recorder near and within view of the office. Wall-hung card racks of sufficient capacity are recommended for the number of workers, both full and part time, who are likely to be employed during an accounting period. Estimated space for a clock recorder is approximately 18 in. wide by $12\frac{1}{2}$ in. deep and 18 in. high, and a rack of 50 cards approximately $1\frac{1}{2}$ by $2\frac{1}{2}$ by $34\frac{1}{2}$ in.

General Considerations The size of employee facilities has been found to vary widely. Small operations may not supply lockers and may have only a toilet and lavatory for workers. Some do not provide separate dining areas. Expediency in allowing ample space may be tempered by cost of space, available room, and the acuteness of need. Total space used

Commercial

RESTAURANTS, EATING PLACES, AND FOODSERVICE FACILITIES

may be increased where main toilet and locker areas are remotely located and additional facilities are provided near work areas. It may be decreased where the food facility is a part of a larger organization providing facilities for other workers as in a hospital or in a hotel.

Guest Facilities

Comfort and cordiality should characterize the entrance and waiting area for guests. The size of the area should be based on probable need for waiting, type of service, and number of persons likely to congregate at one time. If there is a lounge or hallway adjacent to the dining room, this may provide some waiting space.

Locate the public telephone, coat rack, and toilet facilities in convenient relationship to the waiting area. In college dining rooms provide ample space for books as well as coats. In residences, a hallway approaching the dining room will lessen the wear on the lounge. Attractive benches or seats are recommended.

TABLE AND CHAIR UNITS

Data on space allocations and clearance contained in Figs. 2 to 8 is presented as an aid in determining capacities, desirable seating layouts, and necessary clearances. Information was furnished by the John Van Range Co. and Albert Pick Co., restaurant equipment specialists; Louis A. Brown, architect; and the Brunswick-Balke-Collender Co.

Tabulations are divided into three groups. The most luxurious establishments ordinarily use as minima the largest figures given, and vice-versa.

BOOTHS

There are, in some localities, code and other restrictions on booth furniture dimensions. Authorities having local jurisdiction should be consulted. One designer consulted regarded the 2-person booth (side-by side) as a waste of space; others recognize that conditions may arise when no other type of furniture will suffice. Booths for more than four persons are not commonly encountered.

NONDINING SPACES

Diagrams, tables and other data given in Fig. 9 and below illustrate only a few of the many types of nondining spaces and clearances required. Data included here may, however, suggest methods of solving most problems.

Cashier

Preferred location for the cashier's desk or counter, according to the Albert Pick Co., is on the right hand side of the door when leaving, in order to avoid cross-traffic and resulting congestion. Dimensions vary from those given in the table according to what merchandise is sold by the cashier and can best be determined in

conjunction with each job. If quantities of tobacco, etc., are sold, a back wall case may be necessary.

Coat Checking

Figure 9 illustrates only one type of check room layout; selection of type and size depends on the job under consideration. It is generally considered uneconomical, except in the most luxurious restaurants, to provide check rooms capable of accommodating garments for the peak load of patrons, for the following reasons: (1) Women usually do not check coats; (2) not all male patrons check coats; (3) space required can usually be used otherwise to greater advantage. The Albert Pick Co. estimates that approximately 5 garments can be hung per linear foot on each side of the type of racks diagrammed.

Use of coat trees in dining areas is termed "necessary but never desirable." These occupy approximately 20 by 20 in., are 72 in. high, and can accommodate 8 garments per costumer. Overshoe racks are considered undesirable; umbrella racks, desirable in check rooms.

Telephone Facilities

Booths are usually preferred to telephone jacks, probably because of costs of installation and of relocating wiring when redecorating or replanning. Booths should be out of direct vision yet convenient to dining and lounge areas. One booth per 50 seats is the usual ratio or one phone jack per dining booth.

The greatest areas for efficiency in manufacturing have been in the areas of reduced work flow. Industrial engineers learned a long time ago that the movement of a product from one spot to another does not of itself improve the product. The process of moving takes time, costs money, is dehumanizing and may, in fact, cause product damage. Industry has evolved all types of imaginative methods for reducing travel and, where it was essential, cause it to happen with the least amount of human assistance and at the lowest possible cost.

The food service industry, until recently, has generally felt that these techniques were not appropriate, primarily because of the past availability of low-cost help and the acceptance of what were considered traditional work methods. With sharply rising labor costs and with the need for gaining the full productivity of technically trained people, the industry is rapidly adopting improved material handling concepts.

The evolution of a food service scheme which requires the smallest number of steps or distances to be traveled is developed using 80 percent common sense and 20 percent technical know-how. In planning a new or modernized facility, the designer must continually ask two questions: "Why?" and "How?" And the classic answer, "It's always been done this way," is no longer acceptable.

Since the architectural relationship, both horizontally and vertically, of the various elements in the project is the first consideration, the "why" question must be asked first at every step in the process. Many designers establish a work-flow plan before endeavoring to effect the interrelationship of the various areas. Each operation has its own unique features and only by continually asking at each step the question, "why," will the most effective plan evolve.

Usually foodstuffs are received and immediately stored. Generally there are refrigerated, frozen, and dry storage areas and these logically should be adjacent to receiving areas and should also be readily accessible to the preparation facilities. It is often appropriate to have not only major storage areas but also interim, smaller storage facilities. As the cost of labor increases, many designers are rethinking the old concept of having a single walk-in refrigerator, for example, and locating smaller process refrigerators strategically throughout the layout.

Certain of the preparation processes may be located in separate floors. A bakery, for example, may be tucked out of the way, but thought must be given to the flow of materials to and away from this area. Generally the plan is a continuous process, always moving forward from one step to the next, with backtracking or cross-overs limited as far as possible.

In most feeding operations, all of the production ultimately ends in the serving area, and care must be taken to establish the flow of the finished food to the customer, whether

Kitchen Planning Magazine, vol. 7, no. 4, fourth quarter, 1970. *Harbrace Encyclopedia of Professional Kitchen Planning.*

it be in a sit-down dining room on the same floor or to patients in a multi-story hospital. This, in essence, comprises the heart of the primary work flow and if any steps can be eliminated in the process, this will be of benefit to those who will operate the facility.

In addition to this basic flow, we find peripheral flow patterns which may be cyclical in nature; for example, the preparation utensils have to be scraped, washed, stored, and then returned to the work areas; dining room serviceware undergoes a similar but more complex process. And during all the processes there is a generation of waste, sometimes from the receiving area; certainly from the preparation and serving areas, as well as from the washing facilities. All this waste material must travel to some point of disposal which in many cases is adjacent to the receiving area. The work flow in each of these supplementary processes likewise must be considered and minimized (Fig. 1).

There are other architectural features that must be considered in addition to the interrelation of the spaces: the proper height of loading trucks, the elimination of door saddles, walk-in refrigerators and freezers at floor level, the design of elevators and dumbwaiters which are the proper size and which stop floor flush and for loading.

The means or equipment necessary for the transport of food in process is the next consideration, and the question "how" must be answered. All things considered, the wheel is the basic "how." Wherever possible, dollies, trucks, carts, wagons and rolling racks should be employed.

The source of supply and method of delivery are the first considerations. There are many suppliers who offer their products palletized for quick, easy transfer to the receiving area. Others strap quantities of boxes together. The designer must concern himself not only with what is currently in practice but what might be done, and adapt his equipment to meet the nature of incoming products. Once in the building, various methods are used. Some facilities have been designed around a single tier rack which is used for everything from the initial receiving to final service. Other designs involve the use of a variety of special purpose vehicles: often the heavy duty platform truck, rolling shelves or movable pallets for the receiving and storing process; then going to special purpose pan racks for moving food in process to the serving area, with still other special purpose carts for soiled and clean dish handling. There are as many variations of these combinations as there are food service operations and there are trucks and carts for every conceivable use. It behooves the designer to make the selection of the proper carts in evolving the food service scheme.

Dumbwaiters, elevators, dish tables, serving counters, work tables, doorways and refrigerators all must be designed keeping in mind the specific vehicles to be used. In major installations, there are some exciting new concepts using carts which are transported by overhead monorails. Another new technique utilizes buried cables in the floor along which carts

move from place to place without assistance, following electric impulses in the cable.

There are special considerations to which the designer must address himself, such as security, supervision, safety and employee morale. Next to the banking business, the food service industry involves itself in a product which has great universal appeal. Security, therefore, must be an overriding consideration. On paper, the walk-in refrigerator that opens directly onto the loading area may seem great, but unfortunately, human nature being what it is, employees working where they would be out of view are often tempted to conspire to accept short deliveries or slip merchandise out for their own use. Receiving areas, therefore, should be open and visible to management.

Supervisors should be located in strategic areas where they have a commanding view of the important operations. Some schemes include elevated offices where supervisors can scan a major portion of the entire operation, seeing not only the preparation areas but also serving areas.

Safety considerations include providing adequate width of aisles, limiting weights on carts, protecting passageways adjacent to dangerous machinery, etc.

Employee morale is increasingly important. Minimizing the isolation of employees in dull storerooms by themselves can improve productivity.

It would be impossible for the designer to create all the work areas in such a fashion that transport was eliminated. It would also be impossible to make use of every special purpose cart available. It is the designer's job to weigh all of the factors involved and to consider frequency, quantities to be moved, the weights involved and then compromise these various relationships to come up with a workable scheme.

After the size of each area has been determined, many designers create a scheme of space relationships to the proper scale irrespective of the architectural configuration to which they must conform. And only after they have evolved the best theoretical scheme do they try to fit it into the space available. Unfortunately, in the past the work areas of the food service facility frequently have been left to the end and fitted in as best they could. With the tremendous cost of building, equipment and the mechanical services required plus the increasing cost of labor, this is one of the major planning considerations that should be given priority not only in the allocation of space but its relationships to food service and other building functions.

AISLE SPACE

Many of the problems which exist in kitchens are due to inadequate thought of the flow sequences of food through the kitchen. The matter of aisle spaces is of great importance in the food facility. There are some general rules, comments and recommendations which can be made for typical establishments.

1. Separate work and traffic aisles as much

Commercial
KITCHENS

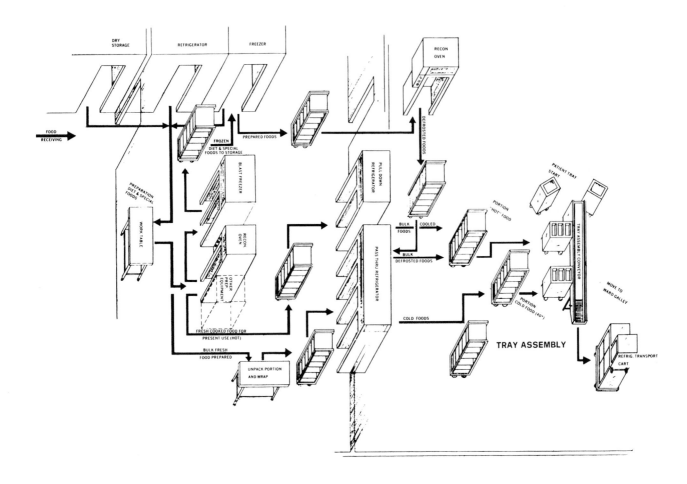

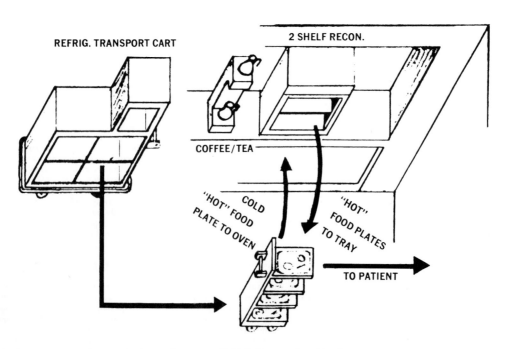

Fig. 1   Ward galley. Work-flow rendering for a hospital food service program. (Cold distribution and ward heating method.)

as possible. This may be done by locating traffic aisles parallel or perpendicular to the working aisles.

2. Traffic aisles should be made to serve two departments where possible. Traffic aisles against walls can serve only the one department adjacent to the aisle.

3. Aisles around the perimeter of kitchen have several disadvantages:

a. They serve only one department.

b. They utilize a large area when compared to the remaining area. For example: a 5-ft-wide aisle running around the entire perimeter of a 40-sq-ft area uses almost 25 percent of the total area available.

c. Paths along the perimeter of a room are the longest paths available between departments, requiring increased moving time. Remember, movement per se adds nothing to a product except cost.

4. Traffic aisles and especially work aisles that are too wide require many extra steps, often while personnel are carrying relatively heavy loads. Aisles should be sized according to the guides above.

It is definitely not recommended to move traffic through aisles where workers must constantly cross between two stations on either side of the aisle. The width of the aisle becomes excessive and this could become dangerous (Fig. 2).

Work aisle guide	Width, in.
For 1 person working	24 to 36 (Keep to minimum)
For 2 persons working back to back	42
For personnel who must pass equipment which projects into the aisle	30 + the distance of projection into the aisle
Traffic aisle guide	
For 2 persons to pass	30
For 1 truck to pass one person — one-way traffic	24 + maximum truck width
For 2 trucks to pass — one-way traffic	20 + maximum truck width
For 2 trucks to pass — two-way traffic	30 + the sum of truck widths
Multi-usage aisle guide (these are not recommended but must sometimes be employed)	
For personnel passing 1 worker at his station	42
For personnel passing 2 workers, back-to-back at their stations . . .	48
For trucks passing 2 workers, back-to-back at their stations . . .	60 + truck width

LOCATING FOOD WASTE DISPOSERS

Food waste disposers can be supplied with a number of different type assemblies making them suitable for practically any position where food waste occurs.

When trying to decide upon the disposer and assembly most suitable for use at the soiled dish table, a number of questions should first be answered:

1. Is there sufficient room on the soiled dish table for a cone bowl or sink — or must space be conserved?

2. Will the disposer be used to handle preparation waste in addition to the waste returned to the dish table?

3. Will there be a quantity of milk containers and other paper waste to dispose of?

4. Will more than one operator be using the same machine?

5. Does the dishwashing machine have built-in prewash, or will the prerinsing operation be done over the disposer, or made a part of a machine incorporating both features?

6. Will compartment-type trays be used?

In installations where the unloading area for soiled dishes is very limited and the designer cannot afford the space that a cone bowl or sink requires, there is a disposer assembly that takes no more space than that allowed for a scrap-block. This would be strictly a disposer operation.

When the food waste disposer is to be used for disposing of both preparation waste and table scraps, the assembly should have built-in flexibility. A cone bowl with removable stainless steel sleeve offers this. With the stainless steel perforated sleeve removed, the cone bowl becomes a large receiving hopper — one that accepts leafy waste with ease. With the stainless steel perforated sleeve and scrap-block in position, the assembly is then suitable for scraping of waste and control of silverware that might accidentally be pulled or dropped into the cone bowl.

Overhead prerinse can be installed above the disposer if desired. However, it is difficult to prevent the stream from traveling over the table. Recessing the cone bowl in a shallow sink will assist in confining the rinse water.

When one disposer is to be used by two or more operators, placement of the machine and the design of the table takes on added importance. Where two operators are to use one machine, an island type of installation satisfies the requirement. If more than two operators are to be served by one disposer, a trough is most suitable.

Knowing that the scraping of waste is but the first step toward preparing tableware for the washing operation and that size and type of dishwashing machine governs the amount of preparatory work needed, you may be interested in two machines that incorporate disposers which have been specifically designed for work ahead of the dishwasher machine.

When working ahead of a dishwashing machine that does not incorporate prewash, the preparatory operation must be performed as a separate operation in the prewash sink or as a scraping, preflushing, and disposing and this makes for an excellent preparatory operation. Basically this machine consists of a wash tank, a recirculation pump, a separator conveyor, silver-salvage basin and a food waste disposer.

The machine should occupy a position between the point where the soiled dishes land and where they are to be sorted while waiting to be racked.

Since water may be used to transport waste from the food waste disposer, this machine first uses the water for scraping, then reuses it as a transporting medium. For most efficient operation, the machine should be used while sorting, as a combined, rather than a separate operation.

Sorted tableware that is waiting to be racked carries sufficient water to actually soak small pieces of food waste that may still be clinging to the tableware.

On the dish table installations where there will be two or more operators preparing tableware at the soiled dish table and where the dishwashing machine incorporates built-in prewash, a trough type scraping and disposing operation offers speed and flexibility. The operators then can move to the work load rather than moving the load to some one position. An installation of this type can be one

that uses fresh water flowing within the trough or one where there is a large volume of recirculated water mixed with a small amount of fresh water conveying the waste to the food waste disposer.

In planning for the most suitable installation, thought must be given to the width and length of the trough and whether it will be straight, L shape, or some other design.

If the trough is short and straight, a fresh water trough installation works well. The disposer is usually attached to the lower end of the trough section and the fresh water brought in at the opposite end and at intermediate positions along the trough. Since water is the carrying agent for the ground food waste leaving the disposer, a trough installation offers double usage for the water as it is first used to move the scraped waste along the trough to the disposer. The same water is then used to transport the ground waste to the sewage system.

In installations where a recirculating water conveyor and food waste disposer is to be used in conjunction with a trough application, the designer or consultant is permitted to use imagination in his planning. L-shape or U-shape troughs serving an entire area can become reality where there is 65 to 70 gallons per minute of recirculated water with which to work.

With quantities of water moving in a trough, waste moves freely without operator assistance. On some installations tableware is actually presoaked in certain sections of the prefabricated trough without interfering with the forward flow of food waste to the disposer.

Vegetable Preparation

When choosing a food waste disposer for installation for a vegetable preparation area, the designer should keep in mind that he will be wanting to dispose of large, leafy waste, and the opening into the disposer should be able to handle this waste. He should choose an assembly along with the disposer that offers this convenience.

Where there is to be a fairly heavy work load in the vegetable preparation area, some consultants have found a two-compartment sink desirable. The first compartment measures 24 by 36 by 6 in. It is here the trimming and disposing of food waste takes place. The vegetables are then rinsed in the second compartment that measures 18 by 24 by 12 in.

Should a designer choose to install the disposer in the work table adjoining a sink, there are a number of assemblies that are designed for this application. Generally, the assembly consists of a cone bowl fitted with a rubber scrap block. Water can either be directed into the cone bowl through a water inlet elbow or an elevated gooseneck. With the latter type of inlet, the water serves a double purpose in that the vegetables can be washed under the stream. The water entering the disposer then carries the ground waste through the waste line.

Pot Sink

The pot and pan area is another location where consideration should be given to the installation of a food waste disposer because there is considerable amount of waste returned on the utensils.

The disposer can be fitted with a sink drain fitting and installed at the base of the sink or included with a suitable assembly and made a part of the work table adjoining the sinks.

Commercial
KITCHENS

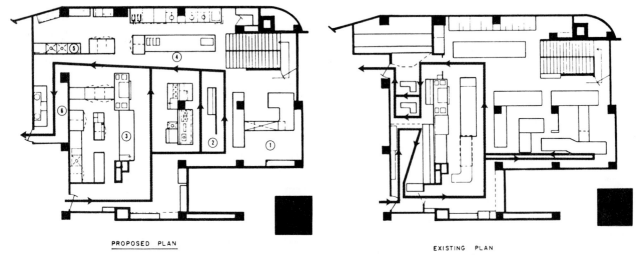

PROPOSED PLAN

EXISTING PLAN

Area Designations
1. Warewashing
2. Waiters' Pantry
3. Cold Food Preparation
4. Hot Food Pick-up
5. Hot Food Preparation
6. Checking Area

Fig. 2   Movement through traffic aisle at the cafe/bar kitchen facilities, Hotel Commodore.

Although there is no hard and fast rule when choosing the proper size disposer, there is a relationship between horsepower, size of opening to the disposer and the size of the grinding chamber.

THE MAIN COOKING AREA

The main cooking department is the heart of the kitchen and deserves special care in designing. Both meat and vegetables are usually cooked in this area. Serving in table service restaurants may take place from or near this area. In other installations, the cooked food is transported a considerable distance to the serving area. In general, it has been found advisable to cook such items as vegetables in small batches as close as possible to the serving time. This consideration requires that at least the vegetable cooking should be done as near to the serving area as possible. In fact, some installations utilizing cafeteria counters have provided small, high speed vegetable steamers directly on the cafeteria counter.

Meats may be prepared in large batches but the trend is towards staggering of the start and completion of meat cooking even though no equipment may be saved because of the long processing time as compared to the serving period.

The trend in the design of the main cooking area has been towards the provision of roast ovens separate from the ranges. This reduces friction between those using range top and the oven.

The flow chart below indicates the relation of the main cooking area to the other kitchen departments. (Fig. 3.)

Fig. 3

The layout of the main cooking department varies greatly from installation to installation. In general, the table service restaurant will serve from this area, and this requires consideration. In many cases where food is cooked to order, insufficient refrigerated or frozen food storage space has been provided in the main cooking area.

Several considerations are necessary before typical departmental layouts are presented.

1. The broiler should be at the end of the line—away from the traffic in front of the cooking equipment. Adequate refrigeration and work space should be provided for the broiler operator.

Traditional French kitchen arrangements assign the broiling, carving and roasting duties to the broiler operator. It is not always necessary to follow this practice in today's kitchens.

2. Fryers may be located near the broiler if the same person will operate them or they may be located at the far end of the range battery. Sufficient work table space and an area to drain fried foods must be provided in addition to refrigeration and in some cases freezer storage space.

3. The steam table or serving area, if it is to be from the same area as cooking, should be near the broilers and fryers.

4. The space between cook's table and cooking equipment should be at a minimum but should provide for opening of range ovens, steamers, etc. If traffic or trucks are anticipated, greater space than normal is required.

5. All heat-producing equipment should be vented to an effective exhaust hood. Local laws should also be checked on this point.

6. Equipment which is placed against a wall should have sufficient space for cleaning behind the equipment. One to two feet are recommended.

7. It is preferable to provide breaks in extended cook's or serving tables for access by cooks. Extended parallel, back-to-back arrangements may require breaks in the equipment for similar reasons.

8. Plate warming facilities have traditionally been placed in front of the cook's table in waiter service restaurants. The trend, however, has been toward provision of plate warming facilities which are directly accessible to the servers.

PREPARATION AREAS

Meat Preparation

The meat preparation departments take meats as delivered and convert them into products suitable for further processing in the main cooking area. The specific duties of this department have changed significantly in recent years. There was a time when cooks did most of the preparation at the main cooking area. This gave way to a meat preparation department where butchers prepared the meats for the cooks. The meat was then issued to the cooking department in such a ready-to-cook quantity that portion control was readily obtainable. The trend now, in all but the very large installation, has been towards the increasing purchase of meat in a ready-to-cook state. The theory, which often is valid, is that the various packing houses with their skilled mass-production workers can perform this operation more economically. A further benefit is that meat storage space is decreased—often up to 40 percent—by the purchase of ready-to-cook meats.

The flow chart for a typical meat preparation area with its relationships to the other kitchen departments is shown in Fig. 4.

Holding in a refrigerated area may precede cooking. In some instances, meats are prepared a day or more prior to cooking.

Fig. 4

846

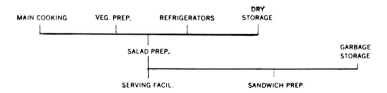

Fig. 5

Salad Preparation

The salad preparation section utilizes ingredients prepared in the vegetable preparation section and/or items from the fruit and vegetable refrigerator. Some minor amount of meat and dairy products may also be used in various salads. In table service restaurants, the salad departments may be included with the pantry or *garde manger*. Such typical departments are shown with the serving departments. Some installations, however, combine the salad and vegetable preparation departments. In those installations using cafeteria counters, the salads pass directly from the salad preparation area to the counter. Pass through refrigerators are quite useful in minimizing the steps required to service the cafeteria counter especially if salads will be prepared during the serving period.

The flow chart (Fig. 5) for a typical preparation area shows the relationship of this department to the other kitchen departments. The number of trips, method of transportation and amounts which are to be transported between the departments should determine the relative location of the salad preparation area. For example, if salads are to be made with a constant flow of materials from the vegetable preparation department and a storing of completed salads in mobile refrigerated trucks until ready for moving to the service area, then the location of this department should be as close to the vegetable preparation department and refrigerator as possible. With such a production system, it is not necessary to locate this department near the service facilities. On the other hand, supplies may be batch delivered and a constant flow of salads to the serving areas will be maintained. For such an operation the location of the salad preparation area should favor the serving facilities.

The work methods to be followed in the preparation of salads determine the precise layout of this department. As with the other kitchen departments, food should flow as much as possible in a continuous direction from the start of the department through processing and on to the next department. Some installations, especially those processing large numbers of the same or similar salads, are able to apply the principles of mass production and mass assembly to the design of the salad preparation department.

Vegetable Preparation

The vegetable preparation department prepares fresh vegetables for cooking and salads. In some installations, as previously noted, vegetables used in salads are prepared in the salad preparation department. Prior to the layout of this department, the precise functions and operations which will be performed should be determined.

The flow chart for the vegetable preparation area (Fig. 6) shows its relationship to the other departments in the kitchen.

In many instances vegetables are prepared the day before their usage by the salad and main cooking units. In such cases the prepared vegetables must be stored in holding refrigerators. The vegetable refrigerator is usually used for this purpose, but very large installations and those installations which do not have the walk-in refrigerators on the same floor as preparation and cooking will provide holding refrigerators.

The layout of the vegetable preparation should follow as closely as possible the processing steps. Typical layouts vary depending on the state of the raw materials and the operations to be performed.

Sandwich Stations

Efficient food production requires planned arrangement of equipment. The size of the operations to be handled will determine dimensions. It must provide ample space for ingredients, tools and a logical work flow. The height must permit the worker to maintain good posture, use the least amount of energy, and stand in a relaxed position. Where short handled tools are used, the average recommended height is 36 in. Allow adequate toe space at the bottom edge of counter. The width of the work counter must provide comfortable reaching areas, without the necessity of the worker stretching. Sixteen inches from each elbow in all working directions is the average comfortable reaching areas, without the necessity of the worker stretching.

A counter top of hard maple or synthetic rubber-plastic composition is preferred. If the installation has a metal or other top, a large cutting block with a hard surface can be placed on it. Have counter top project at least $1\frac{1}{2}$ inches beyond the front of unit to prevent crumbs from collecting on shelf or door gasket below.

Provide a food-waste container recessed in the right hand side of the counter for "as you go" cleaning of the working surface. It should be easily accessible for removal, emptying and cleaning.

Both the placement angle of the filling containers and their sequence arrangement for left to right working of the sandwich maker will streamline operations. The fillings are more accessible if the containers tilt slightly forward toward the worker. Spreading of sandwiches is an automatic reach-and-touch procedure if each filling container is put in its customary place.

The "in-use" bread supply should be kept at the left of the sandwich board. Many food-service establishments use a container which holds 3 to 4 varieties of bread or a self-leveling bread dispenser which moves each slice into position.

For the efficient handling of serving plates, there is a self-leveling dish dispenser, which allows the dishes to "pop" into position. This equipment can be recessed at the right hand corner of the counter top for the final step in sandwich preparation. These dispensers are available with hot or cold controls.

Select toasters and grills for performance, capacity, thermostatic controls, and easy cleaning. Production volume is the determining factor in their size and arrangement, but accessibility to the worker is of prime importance.

Adjacent to the sandwich center should be a double compartment sink. In installations where the salad and sandwich centers are adjacent, this sink can, of course, serve both units.

Provide an accessible storage area for small working tools, such as knives, spatulas, scoops, spoons, cutters, and other related equipment.

The layout of a sandwich center must often fit different shaped spaces. The equipment listed above can be arranged in a straight line, a U-shape, a circle, a corner, or as an aisle. In each available space, the equipment should be arranged as efficiently as possible.

WORK FLOW IN OTHER AREAS

Serving Facilities

The type and arrangement of serving facilities varies greatly from installation to installation. Restaurants use pantries and range batteries. Employee feeding facilities use cafeterias, snack bars, etc. Hospitals use tray makeup conveyors, cafeterias for employees and staff, and sometimes decentralized tray makeup facilities as floor pantries.

The major service departments in a table service restaurant are the range battery and pantry. The departmental layouts for the main cooking department illustrate typical arrangements of this area with provisions for service. The pantry and cold service are often united in one area of the kitchen. In other installations, salads and cold meats are prepared in one area and desserts, beverages, and some other items in the pantry.

The trend seems toward the combination of these two areas and toward the movement of many of the pantry items as rolls, butter and beverages to waitress stations located at strategic points in the dining room. Self-service of salad, cold meat and pantry items by the waiters and waitresses is ever increasing in

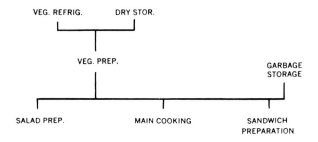

Fig. 6

table service restaurants, especially if speed of service and minimization of kitchen workers is of importance.

Bake Shop

Of all the preparation departments which might be located away from the main kitchen, the bake shop is usually least affected by such a location. The major differences of a remote bake shop are the requirements of additional pot washing and refrigeration facilities. Ovens should then be located in the bake shop, and this usually prevents their dual usage by the main cooking department.

Though some food service installations still prepare their own yeast breads, it is generally advisable to have this service rendered by a commercial bakery. Some bakeries will prepare yeast breads to special order if demand is sufficient. The completely self-contained installations and some of those featuring specialties do—and will continue to—prepare their own yeast breads.

Many installations do prepare pastries on the premises.

Successful freezing of prepared items for baking has enabled the typical shop to become much more efficient in recent years. Studies have shown that freezing of some items may even be helpful with respect to the quality of the finished product. This has made it possible to prepare relatively large quantities of an item using mass production techniques of preparation and baking them as needed. For such an operation, a freezer capable of freezing as well as storing prepared items is necessary. Such a freezer is called a sharp freezer.

In general, the bake shop should be near the storage area, both dry and refrigerated, and near the pot washing area. Location near serving facilities is of relatively minor importance if mobile racks are used to transfer sufficient quantities of baked goods to minimize the number of trips required. The flow chart (Fig. 7)

Fig. 7

shows the relationship of the typical bake shop to the other kitchen departments.

The layout within the bake shop should follow the typical processing steps as much as possible. The oven should be near the landing table with sufficient space in front of the oven to remove baked goods with a peel which reaches to the innermost corners of the oven. In general, as much clear space should be provided in front of a bake oven as the bake oven is deep, front to back. The proof box should be near the oven as should the baker's table. The mixer, pastry stove or hot plate and steam-jacketed kettle, if used, should be near the baker's table.

Fig. 8

Refrigerated Storage

The production processes in a kitchen are characterized by relatively few receipts of refrigerated supplies compared to movements between the refrigerated storage area and the preparation departments. For this reason, it is suggested that location of the refrigerated storage be close to the preparation departments (see Fig. 8).

In some instances the flow chart will be modified by preparation procedures which are to be followed. For example, some installations will partially prepare vegetables prior to storage.

Too often when the refrigerated storage areas and preparation departments are located on different floors, the time required to wait for elevators is excessive.

Another arrangement is to have the refrigerated storage and preparation departments near receiving, then move to the final preparation and production departments. This arrangement is better than that above but is still limited by vertical transportation. An advantage of such a location is that the part of the meat and vegetables which is scrap is closer to the garbage storage area.

In general it is recommended that the freezer storage open into a refrigerator rather than directly into the warmer kitchen. With such an arrangement, the refrigerator might be made for dual purpose usage, as a refrigerator or freezer. This will probably be quite useful in the future with the trend toward increasing usage of frozen foods. An alternate location of the storage freezer is near the main cooking area. This minimizes the distance traveled on the part of the cooks in obtaining food which is purchased in a ready to cook state.

Dishwashing

In the past, extreme emphasis was placed on locating this department either adjacent to a cafeteria service dining room or as the first "port-of-call" in a kitchen serving a table service dining room. With the increasing usage of vertical and horizontal conveyors, this becomes of lesser importance, and increasing attention can be placed on locating the dishwashing area near the location of dish usage— the serving and/or preparation areas as the mode of operation dictates. It is not unusual, nor impractical, to locate the dishwashing on a floor other than the dining room floor.

A separate dishwashing room which is well ventilated, lighted and has noise-absorbing surfaces will be found a great aid in lowering the high—often objectionably high—noise level commonly found in kitchens.

The large operation utilizing horizontal conveyors can apply industrial engineering principles to the breakdown of patron or patient trays.

Glass washing, long a major problem in food service, is now being better handled largely through the control of washing, rinsing and water additions. In most instances, it is not at all impractical to wash glasses in the same machine as dishes, if they are washed shortly after the water has been changed. Other installations utilize a glass washer with a separate soiled glass table or use the same tables as for soiled dishes.

Some installations, especially larger hotels, find it necessary to provide a separate silver room where hollowware may be correctly cleaned, burnished and maintained. Such an area usually can provide a better means for control of expensive silver.

The flow chart (Fig. 9) shows the typical relationship of this department to others within the food service installation.

Fig. 9

Pot Washing

Many smaller installations try to utilize the same sinks for pot washing and vegetable or salad preparation. This practice is not recommended. A minimum of two compartments— preferably three compartments with a grease or skimmer compartment between the first two compartments—is recommended. The main cooking, baking and serving departments are the major source of pots, pans and other utensils. In many installations, a relatively large storage area for soiled pots is required as they are not washed at the same time as received in the pot washing department. This is especially true if the same personnel operate the dishwashing machines and the pot washing department.

Fig. 10

The flow chart for a typical pot washing department is shown in Fig. 10. Note that pot, pan and utensil storage, while not shown on the flow chart, must be considered. This is apt to occur in each department from which pots arrive and in two places in the pot washing area: prior to cleaning and subsequent to cleaning.

By Max Fengler

KITCHEN PERSONNEL AND THEIR FUNCTIONS

- Chef de cuisine (kitchen chef) is responsible for purchase of goods, cost control, setting up the menu, and supervision of personnel and hygiene in the kitchen area.
- Sous-chef (kitchen chef's assistant) represents the kitchen chef in his absence; in a large organization, he takes over some of the chef's duties.
- Saucier (sauce cook) prepares all sauces and the meals that go with them, as well as all fish dishes (although in large organizations there is a poissonier); he is responsible for the work at the kitchen range, and in medium-sized establishments he assumes the functions of the chef's assisant.
- Rotisseur (roast, fry, and grill cook)
In large restaurants, there is, in addition, a grilladin.
- Entrémetier (soup, vegetable, and side-dish cook)
In large restaurants a potagier prepares soups and broths.
- Garde-manger supplies the ready-to-cut meat and fish preparation, the cold appetizers, hors d'oeuvres, and salads. In large restaurants, this work is divided between the hors d'oeuvrier (appetizer cook) and the boucher (butcher).
- Pâtissier makes cookies, cakes, ice cream, and other desserts; in large restaurants, the work is divided among the glacier (ice cream maker), confiseur (fine pastry cook), and boulanger (baker of bread, rolls, and other baked goods).
- Commis (junior cook) is available to chefs of sections.
- Salad man or girl produces and serves various kinds of salads and in some restaurants is responsible for the smorgasbord (hors d'oeuvres) and is subordinate to the gardemanger.
- Casserolier cleans, cares for, and services all pans, cooking equipment, and kitchen machines.
- Kitchen boy cleans the kitchen, helps with the preparation of dishes, and has other duties.
- Contrôleur is in charge of supplies, controls their placement and storage, and does the inventory bookkeeping.
- Gouvernante accepts goods, exercises control, supervises the economat, dry storage, linen, and cleaning materials, and hands out staples.
- In European restaurants, the bar lady is responsible for all beverages and often is the representative for the management, and, in smaller restaurants, oversees the waiters.
  - Argentier is responsible for the care of silver.
  - Office boy
  - Dish washer

Restaurant Architecture and Design, Universe Books, New York, 1971.

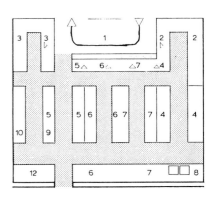

Fig. 1 Hotel or restaurant kitchen or French restaurant of high standard. Capacity for main meals: Hotel—100–200 persons/menu, 100 persons/à la carte. Restaurant—200–300 persons/mealtime from 11:30 to 1:30. Waiters' passageway: tangential. Kitchen: Linear arrangement with large installations in the rear. See Legend for explanation of numbers.

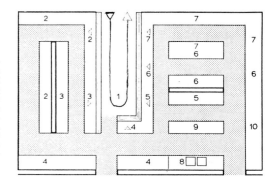

Fig. 2 Hotel or restaurant kitchen. Capacity: With this layout, a 200-seat restaurant will be able to handle three full sittings. This layout can also take care of a hotel with 100 guests and can also accommodate a restaurant open to the general public, an outdoor restaurant, and a private dining area for parties and conferences (altogether, 400 guests). Waiters' passageway: in the center. Kitchen: Linear arrangement with large installations in the rear. See Legend for explanation of numbers.

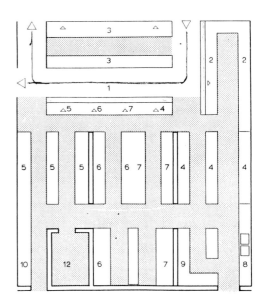

Fig. 3 Large restaurant kitchen for restaurants with many private party and conference facilities or with commissary and catering capacity for other businesses. Suitable also for large hotel with large restaurant for the general public. Capacity: 800–1,000 persons (e.g., 200 seats and fourfold reoccupancy). Waiters' passageway: tangential, with food buffet situated in front. The waiter has access to beverages and other items from the waiters' passageway in the kitchen and from the dining room side as well. The buffet looks over the dining rooms. Kitchen: Linear arrangement with fitted berths for large apparatus. See Legend for explanation of numbers.

Commercial
KITCHENS

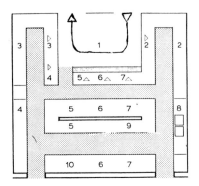

Fig. 4 Restaurant kitchen especially suited for city or excursion restaurants. Capacity: as in Fig. 1. Waiters' passageway: tangential. Kitchen: The cooking, roasting, grill, and frying apparatus are planned as wall structures. See Legend for explanation of numbers.

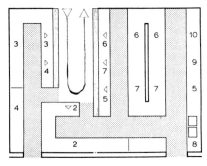

Fig. 5 Restaurant kitchen. Capacity: This arrangement is conceived for a very busy city restaurant of good quality (approximately 600 persons—e.g., 150 seats with fourfold reoccupancy). Waiters' passageway: in the center. Kitchen: The cooking, roasting, grill, and frying apparatus are planned as wall structures. See Legend for explanation of numbers.

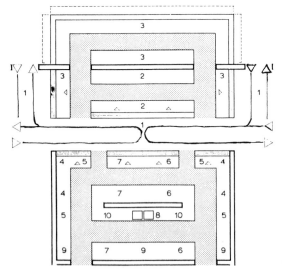

Fig. 6 Large restaurant kitchen for restaurants with many auxiliary rooms, bowling alleys, garden, and a snack bar projecting into the main dining room. Suitable for a highly frequented city restaurant or for an excursion spot with various conference rooms, etc. Capacity: 1,000–1,200 persons. Waiters' passageway: tangential. Buffet and washing-up zone (dish return) placed in front. The waiter can pick up drinks and other items at two places in the kitchen, the drinks coming partly from the bar. Kitchen: Warm kitchen as wall structure with central serving area; cold kitchen and pastry area divided with two serving areas each, symmetrically arranged. See Legend for explanation of numbers.

Legend for Restaurant and Hotel
Kitchen Layouts (Figs. 1 to 6)

(Layouts: Scale 1:300)
 1. Waiters' passageway—meal and beverage counter—dish return
 2. Dishwashing area (dishes, glasses, silver)
 3. Beverages—preparation and serving
 4. Pastry (cookies, cakes, ice cream, dessert)—preparation and serving
 5. Cold kitchen (cold appetizers, salad, fish)—preparation and serving
 6. Warm kitchen—saucier/rôtisseur area (sauces, roasts, grill, fish)—preparation including large apparatus area and serving
 7. Warm kitchen—entremétier area (soups, vegetables, entrées)—preparation including large apparatus area and serving
 8. Pot and pan washing—casserolier area
 9. Vegetable preparation
10. Meat preparation
11. Vegetable cold storage
12. Meat cold storage
13. Economat (dry storage)
14. Beverage cold storage
15. Linen, dish, cleaning supplies storage
16. Staple goods storage
17. Goods acceptance and control
18. Empty goods and garbage collecting rooms

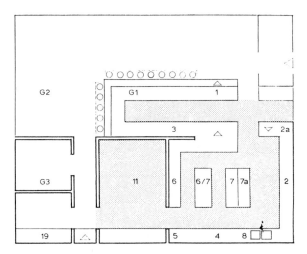

Fig. 7 Snack bar (Pub, tavern, bistro, café, or restaurant). Capacity: 55–60 seats (five- or six-fold reoccupancy over lunchtime, twofold in the evening; at other times, a well-run café, cake, and snack business). The kitchen deals primarily with ready-to-serve articles. In a city business with daily delivery, the storage space does not have to be especially large.

Legend:
 1. Meal and beverage serving counter
 2. Dishwasher
2a. Dish return
 3. Beverage buffet with mixer, toaster, ice-cream container, etc.
 4. Oven and small pastry station
 5. Garde-manger
 6. Saucier/rôtisseur
6/7. Range
 7. Entremétier
7a. Cooking vat and high-performance steam cooker
6/7b. Warming cupboard and warm serving counter with warming lamps
 8. Pot and pan washing
11. Storage, empty goods, office; instead of cold storage rooms—cold storage and freezer cupboards
19. Employees' toilets
G1. Bar counter—also for meals
G2. Dining room with table seating
G3. Guests' toilets/make-up room/telephone booths

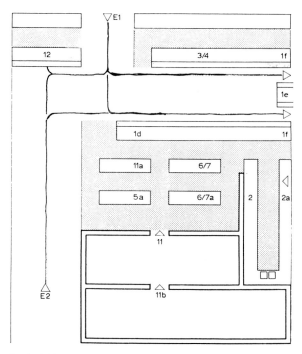

Legend:

1d. Self-service buffet with grill and fry unit
1e. Salad dressings, spices, cutlery reserves
1f. Cashier
2. Dishwasher
2a. Dish return
3/4. Sandwich unit, cakes, ice cream, coffee, beverages; service available at an outdoor café
5a. Cold preparation table
6/7. Defrosting, warming-up apparatus front, serviceable on two sides (convection ovens, heating appliances for the Nacka system or Régéthermic ovens)
11. Cold storage and storage (varies in size according to system of servicing and rhythm of delivery)
11a. Refrigerator front, serviceable on two sides
11b. Delivery, empty goods, intermediary storage, personnel cloakroom
12. Kiosk—sales on the inside and to customers on the street
E1. Entrance from street
E2. Entrance from building (department store, office building, etc.)

Fig. 8   Self-service restaurant suitable for department stores or office buildings. Kitchen: no independent production; outside delivery and preparation via deep-freeze, boiling-in-the-bag (Nacka), or Régéthermic methods.

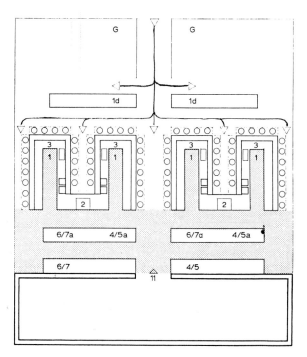

Legend:

1. Service passage for U-shaped or finger-shaped counter
1d. Automats for self-service
2. Connection of two fingers with dishwasher having two covers serviceable on both sides; adjoining are two sinks each
3. Coffee machine, refrigerators, soup vat storage
4/5. Salad and ice cream preparation
4/5a. Cold counter—salad, ice cream, dessert
6/7. Frying pan, soup cooker, and other cooking equipment
6/7a. Warm counter—bain-marie, fryer, grill plates
11. Economat, cold storage, and freezer space, staples room (delivery, empty goods room, office, personnel cloakrooms and washrooms not included)
G Guest rooms with standing room and seats (automat service with disposable dishes)

Fig. 9   Restaurant with finger-shaped bar and automats for quick lunch service in restaurants for passersby, cafeterias, department stores, highway restaurants. Capacity: 500 persons per hour. Kitchen: preparation of precooked meals, salads, and ice cream.

Commercial
KITCHENS

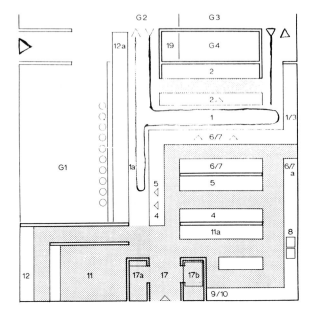

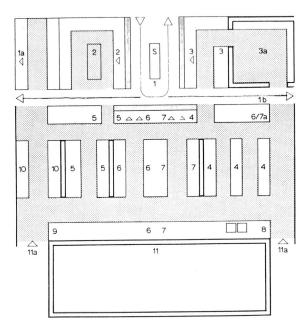

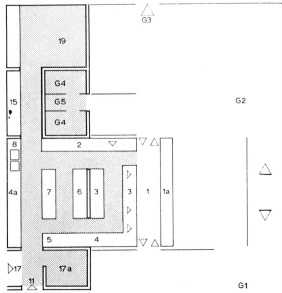

Fig. 10 Restaurant for travelers (Highway restaurant, or café-restaurant at a busy intersection in the city). Capacity:
- Snack—45–50 seats (200 persons every hour)
- Restaurant—80 seats—(two- or threefold reoccupancy during meals; at other times, coffee, ice cream, pastry, and sandwich service)
- Grill—40 seats (one- or twofold reoccupancy, high standard service) Kitchen: Linear-wall arrangement, approximately equal balance between freshly prepared meals and ready-to-serve meals. Storage, empty goods, and personnel cloakrooms in the cellar.

Legend:
1. Waiters' passageway
1a. Service corridor for snacks, and cold meal and pastry-serving counter for restaurant
1/3. Waiters—Beverage self-service
2. Dishwasher
4. Pastry
5. Cold kitchen
6/7. Warm kitchen (roast, grill, fry), bain-marie in the serving counter
6/7a. Cooking and frying apparatus (2 vats, 1 pan)
8. Pot and pan washing
9/10. Meat and vegetable preparation
11. Storage for the day
11a. Cupboard group, cooled and not cooled
12. Kiosk facing the street
12a. Cigarette machine
17. Goods delivery
17a. Office
17b. Elevator to cellar
19. Employee toilets
G1. Snack area with about 40 seats and seats at the bar
G2. Restaurant
G3. Grill restaurant, possibly with small bar for espresso coffee, aperitifs, whisky, and other spirits
G4. Guests' toilets

Fig. 11 Large hotel-restaurant kitchen also for large restaurants with some auxiliary rooms and with outside deliveries or production for other organizations (variant of Figs. 3 and 6). Capacity: 800–1000 persons. Waiters' passageway: in the center, with a special serving link to the garden (or, for instance, to a bowling alley) and directly connecting to the auxiliary rooms. Kitchen: Linear arrangement with rear side of large apparatus.

Legend:
1. Waiters' passageway
1a. Meal and beverage serving to garden
1b. Access to auxiliary rooms
2. Dishwashing area
3. Beverage serving area
3a. Beverage cold storage (day cellar)
4. Pastry
5. Cold kitchen
6. Warm kitchen—saucier/rôtisseur area
7. Warm kitchen—entremétier area
8. Pot and pan washing
9. Vegetable preparation
10. Meat preparation
11. Cold storage and storage rooms
11a. Accesses to delivery, empty goods room, and intermediary storage, office, personnel cloakrooms and toilets
S Service accessories (cash register)

Fig. 12 Café-restaurant with tearoom, or a city restaurant in a busy district.
- Café: alcohol-free beverages, except for bottled beer; pastry and small meals—cold and warm
- Tearoom: alcohol-free beverages, pastry, sandwiches. Capacity: About 150 seats (continuous service from early morning to midnight or later). Kitchen: extensive use of precooked meals; little storage.

Legend:
1. Waiters' passageway
1a. Serving stations and cash register
2. Dishwasher
3. Beverage buffet with mixer, toaster, ice cream container, etc.
4. Pastry
4a. Pastry oven
5. Sandwich unit
6. Defrosting and heating equipment, soup vats
7. Oven, grill, frying apparatus
8. Pot and pan washing
11. Day stores, empty goods (staple goods in cellar)
15. Linen storage
17. Delivery
17a. Office
19. Employees' washrooms, cloakroom for waiters (cloakroom and washrooms for kitchen employees in cellar)
G1. Tearoom
G2. Café-restaurant
G3. Terrace or garden
G4. Washrooms
G5. Telephone booths

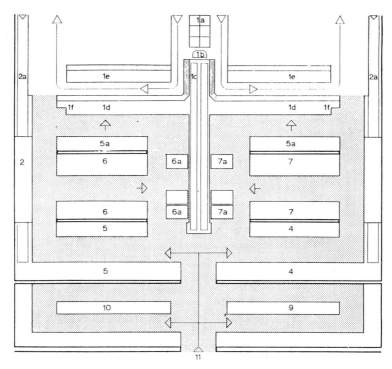

Fig. 13 Student dining hall or cafeteria with two-sided self-service buffet and conveyor belt. Capacity: 12 persons per minute $\times$ 2 = 24 persons. Without cash payment: hourly capacity, 1,400 persons. With cash circulation: hourly capacity, 1,100 persons. Seating: at least 340 seats. Kitchen: fully equipped linear arrangement, planned for automatic equipment.

Legend:

1a. Platter and cutlery trolley
1b. Distribution help, regulation of conveyor-belt speed, dietary food storage
1c. Conveyor belt for standard menu
1d. Self-service buffet—Menu:

1 soup of the day	various salads
1 stew	various desserts
1 standard menu	dairy products
1 dietary food	5 cold beverages (beer, wine, carbon-
2 cold meals	ated beverages, juice)

1e. Salad dressings, condiments, cutlery
1f. Cash register
2. Dishwasher

2a. Soiled-dish conveyor belt
4. Pastry
5. Garde-manger
5a. Portioning table for cold meals, salads, and desserts
6. Roast kitchen, possibly with roasting automats
6a. Warm-storage trolleys—portioning of meat, sauces, dietary foods
7. Cooking kitchen, possibly with automatic steam cookers
7a. Warm-storage trolleys for portioning of vegetables, entrées
9. Vegetable preparation
10. Meat preparation
11. Access to the storage rooms, delivery, and auxiliary rooms

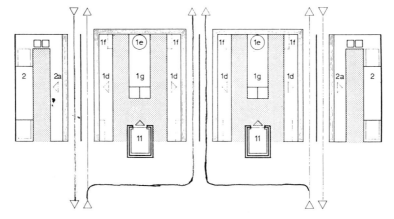

Fig. 14 Student dining hall or cafeteria with four self-service buffets. Capacity: at least 1,500 persons per hour. Seating: at least 400 seats. Kitchen: outside delivery of meals with standard or conveyor-type elevator.

Legend:

1d. Self-service buffet—menu as in Fig. 13
1e. Circular device for salad dressings, condiments, extra cutlery, etc.
1f. Cash register
1g. Preparation table with trolley stand
2. Dishwasher
2a. Soiled-dish return
11. Standard or conveyor-type elevator connection to meal-preparation kitchen

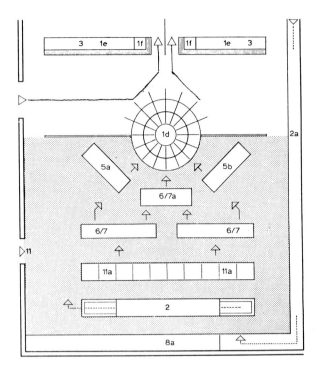

Fig. 15 Student dining hall or cafeteria with self-service carrousel. Capacity: after the initial phase, 1,400 persons per hour. Seating: at least 400 seats. Meal delivery from a central kitchen—deep-freeze, boil-in-the-bag (Nacka), and Régéthermic system.

Legend:

17. Linear-arrangement kitchen with automats. For large output, there are appropriate appliances for steaming and baking.

18. Linear-arrangement kitchen with transport-equipment system. In the foreground: dish washing; soup, vegetable, and entrée vats; stove for general purposes and dietary foods; sauces and meats.

19. Three-tier carrousel (Maison Tricault, Paris) of 2-meter diameter, with a tray slide.

1d. Self-service three-tiered carrousel
    Below: 2 cold dishes, various salads, desserts (partly on ice)
    Center: warm meals, 3 warm dishes, 2 grilled or fried dishes (with warming lamps above)
    Above: sandwiches, pastry, etc.

1e. Salad dressings, condiments, extra cutlery, etc.

1f. Cash register

2. Dishwaster (stacking area, 3 tanks, drying zone)

2a. Soiled-dish conveyor belt

3. Beverage self-service area

5a. Portioning table for cold dishes and salads

5b. Portioning table for desserts, sandwiches, etc.

6/7. Warming and defrosting appliances

6/7a. Portioning table for warm meats

8a. Trolley storage

11. Meal delivery from the central kitchen, access to the supply and auxiliary rooms

11a. Storage cupboards for cold goods and other goods delivered from the central kitchen

By FRANK MEMOLI

CORE LOCATION

Central (Interior)

This location has a number of advantages. It allows all window space to be utilized as rentable office space and depending upon the configuration of the building plan will permit offices of varying depths to receive natural light. The central location is also extremely convenient in terms of access and in some cases may be equidistant for all sides. This simplifies area division and provides good flexibility of tenant distribution in the same way. Horizontal utility runs may also be relatively equidistant from the core. Combined with a square building plan, bearing exterior, and core walls this location permits a floor plan free of columns and thus totally flexible for office layout.

While this core location has definite advantages, it also has some drawbacks. One disadvantage is that the central interior location limits the depth of offices in the midzone of each floor, thus affecting the element of flexibility in office layout. Another floor-area-consuming characteristic of this core is that it requires an access corridor around its perimeter.

Off-Center (Interior)

Like the central-interior core, the off-center interior core permits all window or building perimeter space to be used for offices. However, it presents somewhat more flexibility in maximum depth and arrangement of spaces. This can be particularly desirable where large open spaces such as secretarial or clerical pools are required. It also affords the opportunity of developing small secluded spaces in the relatively narrow portion of the floor plan where the core is closest to the exterior walls.

This core location may present some problems of access. Because it is off-center, it is somewhat remote and thus less convenient to the far sides and corners of the building. If there is multiple-tenant occupancy on any given floor, a long access corridor will be required as will be a perimeter corridor around the core itself. The off-center location may also lessen flexibility of tenant distribution.

Split (Interior)

The principal advantage of a split core is that it virtually eliminates the need for a peripheral corridor on the core. Access to this core is from the area between its split elements and not from the area around its edges. This permits more flexibility of floor-area division, leaving even the area immediately adjacent to the core available for office space. Depending on the width of the access space in the center of the core, this space may be put to different uses on different floors. At the ground, or entry, level this area can become a lobby, while on floors where elevators do not stop this space can be used for additional office space.

Exterior

Unlike the three interior core locations discussed, the primary advantage of an exterior core arrangement is that it leaves the entire floor area of the building available for tenant use. In addition, the core does not complicate the floor plan either functionally or structurally. With this type of arrangement, maximum flexibility is achieved with respect to tenant distribution, office depth, and layout. Since the core creates a "dead wall" or portion thereof, it may be used as a buffer between the building and an adjoining property which may have objectionable characteristics. Location on the outside of the building also permits the core to act as a point of transition between one building and another of possibly different scale.

Some problems are also created by placing the core on the outside of a building. The primary drawback is that, in the case of multitenant occupancy, the core requires a long access corridor lessening flexibility of tenant distribution. In addition, the core occupies desirable window space so that the offices immediately adjacent to the core may not receive any natural light.

GENERAL PRINCIPLES

Work Flow

The relationship of individuals, as determined by operating procedures, must be the governing factor in any layout. The development of a layout which conforms to and complements the predominant work flow requirements of an office is perhaps the most important phase of space planning. By the systematic study of the operations, processes, and procedures involved in individual (or group) tasks, the planner can assist management by providing work station patterns which ensure a smooth, straight-line flow of work. It should be understood that space planning does not conflict with or overlap the field of methods and systems analysis. The role of the space planner is to gain a knowledge of the functions, as developed, and to translate them into the best space layout possible within the limitations imposed by building characteristics, fiscal allotments, etc.

Straight-Line Principle In a well-planned office, paper goes from one desk to another with the least amount of handling, traveling, and delay. Work should progress in a series of straight lines with a general forward movement, avoiding criss-cross motion and backward flow. When the layout is being developed, the flow pattern can be traced from desk to desk. Caution must be exercised, however, since the straight-line work principle cannot be adapted to all activities, particularly those headquarter or departmental offices whose staff activities do not lend themselves to assembly-line processing.

Guide for Space Planning & Layout, General Services Administration, Public Buildings Service, Washington, D.C.

Work Stations

All work stations, whether in a private office or in open space, are reduced to units of furniture and equipment. See Fig. 1 for the work stations most frequently used. The basic unit of work stations are desks and therefore require the most consideration. The following general rules are applicable in positioning desks:

1. Desks should face the same direction unless there is a compelling functional reason to do otherwise. The use of this technique provides for straight work flow patterns, facilitates communications, and creates a neat and attractive appearance.

2. In open area, consideration should be given to placing desks in rows of two. This method will permit the use of bank-type partitions as a divider for those activities which require visual privacy while still obtaining maximum utilization.

3. Desks should be spaced at a distance of 6 ft from the front of a desk to the desk behind it. This distance should be increased to 7 ft when desks are in rows of two, ingress and egress is confined to one side of the aisle, or in instances where more than two desks side by side cannot be avoided.

4. In private offices the desk should be positioned to afford the occupant a view of the door.

5. In open work areas the supervisor should be located adjacent to the receptionist or secretary. Access to supervisory work stations should not be through the work area.

6. Desks of employees having considerable visitor contact should be located near the office entrance. Conversely, desks of employees doing classified work should be away from entrances.

"Executive Core" Concept

Most new building designs produce a block-type structure which is well lighted and air conditioned, and which is divided by a few access corridors radiating from a central service core. This type of construction permits development of space plans based on the "Executive Core" concept. This concept, or technique, places all or a majority of the private offices in the core area and allocates space along the building perimeter for others. It has proved very satisfactory in many cases where it has been used and has potential in most new buildings in which large, or relatively large, groups of "lower echelon" employees will be housed.

This concept arises from the premise that employees performing routine tasks which keep them at their desks almost the entire work day require the psychological advantages of window space. On the other hand, supervisors and executives are frequently called upon to leave their offices for meetings, supervisory tours, etc., and interior offices, if properly designed and decorated, are completely acceptable for them. Also, the occupants of private offices generally receive the greatest number of visitors; in fact, the need to receive many visitors is perhaps the justification most frequently given for private offices. The location of private offices in the core facilitates the handling of visitors and keeps them from the general work areas.

Other Planning Considerations

The application of the following considerations will assist the space planner to attain functional effectiveness in the final layout:

1. Employees performing close work should be in the best-lighted areas. Glaring surfaces which affect vision should be identified and corrected.

2. Clothes lockers in an office layout are out of date and wasteful. Large rooms or open areas should be provided with hanging space for coats and shelves for hats, packages, and other material. Space not suitable for work stations should be used whenever possible.

3. Heavy equipment generally should be placed against walls or columns in order to avoid floor overloading.

4. Be safety conscious. Do not obstruct exits, corridors, or stairways. Comply with fire safety codes governing aisles, exits, etc.

5. Where frequent interviews with the general public are required, as in personnel offices, the use of interview cubicles should be considered. Such cubicles need only be large enough for the interviewer, the applicant, and a small desk or table.

6. In operations which require employees to work away from their office, with only infrequent visits there to file reports, etc., consideration should be given to assigning two or more employees to each desk. Other considerations include the provision of 45-in. desks and the use of common work tables, with the assignment of file cabinet drawers to each employee in which to keep papers, etc.

Private Offices

The private office is the most controversial problem facing the space planner. The assignment of private offices and the type of partitioning to be used are issues to be settled by top management acting on the advice and recommendations of the space planner. Private offices should be assigned primarily for functional reasons, i.e., nature of work, visitor traffic, or for security reasons. When private offices are provided, they should be only large enough for the occupant to conduct his normal business with a reasonable degree of dignity (Fig. 2). The following are some of the factors requiring consideration prior to making the assignment:

Classification Grade The necessity for a private office cannot be directly related to the classification grade of the employee.

Supervisors in Open Space Supervisors who are working with their employees, rather than planning for them, should generally be in the same room or open space with them. The supervisor may be separated from the balance of his section by a distance of several feet which permits a degree of privacy.

Prestige A frequent justification for a private office is to impress visiting representatives of industry, and the general public, with the importance or dignity of the official being contacted. Recent studies of office planning in private industry tend to refute such a position. They show many highly paid employees housed in attractive open space. Moderately sized private offices are provided only for upper-echelon officials. The offices of many top executives of large, nationally known companies are less than 250 sq ft each. The provision of a private office, or too large a private office, for a Gov-

ernment official may give the taxpayers an adverse impression.

Security Requirements The space planner hears many reasons why people in Government need places where confidential discussions can be held and a variety of suggestions as to how this should be accomplished. The private office is the most popular, if not always the most practical, solution. The Federal establishment undoubtedly has a greater problem in this respect than many branches of business.

In addition to the security requirements, the Government is faced with privacy situations involving investigative agencies and other activities which have occasion to inquire into the most confidential aspects of individuals' personal lives and the operations of business concerns. There is no question as to these persons' entitlement to reasonable privacy regardless of whether they are summoned to the office, appear voluntarily to render assistance, or avail themselves of services offered by the agency. There are alternatives, however, in determining the methods to be used to satisfy the various requirements.

Sizes of Private Offices It is desirable that private offices be a minimum of 100 sq ft and a maximum of 300 sq ft each in size, depending upon the requirements of the occupant. See sketches of most widely used private offices. Only in cases where it is necessary for the occupant to meet with delegations of 10 or more people at least once a day should the size approach 300 sq ft. For the average Government function, the private office should not exceed 200 sq ft.

Semiprivate Offices

The semiprivate office is a room, ranging in size from 150 to 400 sq ft, occupied by two or more individuals. These offices can be enclosed by ceiling-high, three-quarter-high, or bank-type partitions. Examples of semiprivate offices are shown. Because of the loss of flexibility introduced by the use of the partitions required to enclose these offices, the same rigid review given private offices should be employed. Generally, the need to house members of a work team or other groups of employees assigned to a common task is an acceptable justification for semiprivate accommodations.

General or Open Space

The following paragraphs describe some of the factors affecting good office layout in general or open space:

General "General office space" refers to an open area occupied by a number of employees, supervisors, furnishings, equipment, and circulation area. Large open areas permit flexibility and effective utilization, aid office communications, provide better light and ventilation, reduce space requirements, make possible better flow of work, simplify supervision, and eliminate partition costs. In many cases, however, open-space housing for more than 50 persons should be subdivided either by use of file cabinets, shelving, railing, or low bank-type partitions.

Open-Area Work Stations The space allocated to these work stations is based on the furniture and equipment necessary to perform the work assigned as well as on circulation area. The space assigned to any specific work station may be increased due to special furniture and equipment requirements associated with the particular position.

Circulation

This is the area required to conveniently permit ingress and egress to work stations. The size of an aisle should be governed by the amount of traffic it bears. The following standards with regard to internal circulation will be applied in space planning surveys:

1. Aisles leading to main exits from areas which carry substantial traffic (main aisles) should be 60 in. wide.

2. Aisles which carry a moderate amount of traffic (intermediate aisles) should be 48 in. wide.

3. Aisles between rows of desks (secondary aisles) should be approximately 36 in. wide.

Conference Requirements

Conferences, meetings, and assemblies are an important part of Government operations. Since there is no established standard suggesting the number of conference rooms based on the number of people, the needs will vary widely among agencies or agency components, depending largely on the nature of their work. Whenever possible, the establishment of conference rooms should be based on need established from past records and experience, rather than on anticipated needs. Unnecessary conference space is often allowed because planning is not based on such records of demonstrated need. The space planner should always evaluate the utilization of existing conference rooms before recommending others (Fig. 3).

Conference Space in Private Offices vs. the Conference Room Conferences are best conducted in space designed for that purpose. Conference space should not be provided in private offices. In lieu of large offices, it is desirable to provide a conference room adjoining the office of a top official who holds a large number of conferences and nearby conference rooms for officials with more limited requirements. Separate conference rooms permit maximum utilization through scheduling at an appropriate level of management. Where feasible, training and conference requirements should be pooled and conference space used as auxiliary office area for visitors.

Location of Conference Rooms The conference room should be centrally located to the users. Interior space, which is not the most desirable for office purposes, is well suited for conference use. This location eliminates outside distraction and the need for window coverings during visual presentations. Access to conference rooms should be through corridors or through reception areas.

Sizes of Conference Rooms Conference rooms should be designed to accommodate average but not maximum attendance. Extra chairs can be used to achieve additional seating. See illustrations of preferred layout of conference rooms of various sizes.

Reception Areas and Visitor Control

Visitors receive their first impression of an organization from the decor and layout of the reception area. It should be attractive, neat, businesslike, and above all, adequate to accommodate normal visitor traffic. An allowance of 10 sq ft for each visitor to be served may be used for space allocation. For example, if space is required for a total of five visitors at any given time, a total of 50 sq ft should be used in planning the space. Size, decor, and equipment will depend largely on the type and volume of visitor traffic; thus special

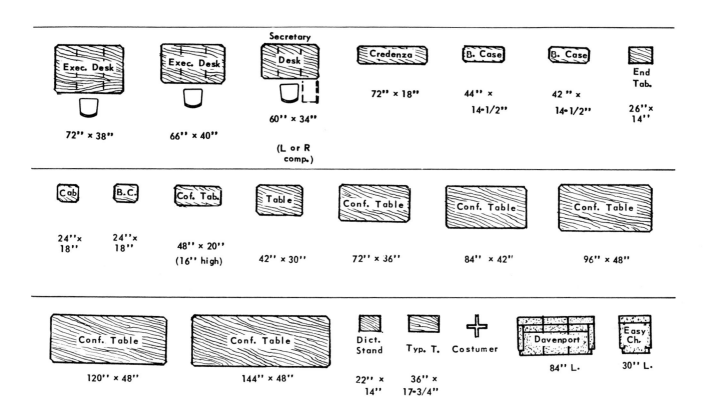

Exec. Desk — 72'' x 38''

Exec. Desk — 66'' x 40''

Secretary Desk — 60'' x 34'' (L or R comp.)

Credenza — 72'' x 18''

B. Case — 44'' x 14-1/2''

B. Case — 42'' x 14-1/2''

End Tab. — 26''x 14''

Cab — 24''x 18''

B.C. — 24''x 18''

Cof. Tab. — 48'' x 20'' (16'' high)

Table — 42'' x 30''

Conf. Table — 72'' x 36''

Conf. Table — 84'' x 42''

Conf. Table — 96'' x 48''

Conf. Table — 120'' x 48''

Conf. Table — 144'' x 48''

Dict. Stand — 22'' x 14''

Typ. T. — 36'' x 17-3/4''

Costumer

Davenport — 84'' L.

Easy Ch. — 30'' L.

EXECUTIVE WOOD-METAL (CONTEMPORARY DESIGN)

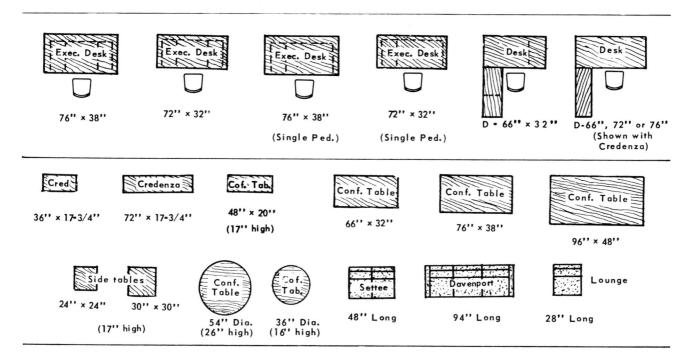

Exec. Desk — 76'' x 38''

Exec. Desk — 72'' x 32''

Exec. Desk — 76'' x 38'' (Single Ped.)

Exec. Desk — 72'' x 32'' (Single Ped.)

Desk — D - 66'' x 32''

Desk — D-66'', 72'' or 76'' (Shown with Credenza)

Cred — 36'' x 17-3/4''

Credenza — 72'' x 17-3/4''

Cof. Tab. — 48'' x 20'' (17'' high)

Conf. Table — 66'' x 32''

Conf. Table — 76'' x 38''

Conf. Table — 96'' x 48''

Side tables — 24'' x 24''   30'' x 30'' (17'' high)

Conf. Table — 54'' Dia. (26'' high)

Cof. Tab. — 36'' Dia. (16'' high)

Settee — 48'' Long

Davenport — 94'' Long

Lounge — 28'' Long

857

Commercial

OFFICES, GENERAL
Furniture

METAL

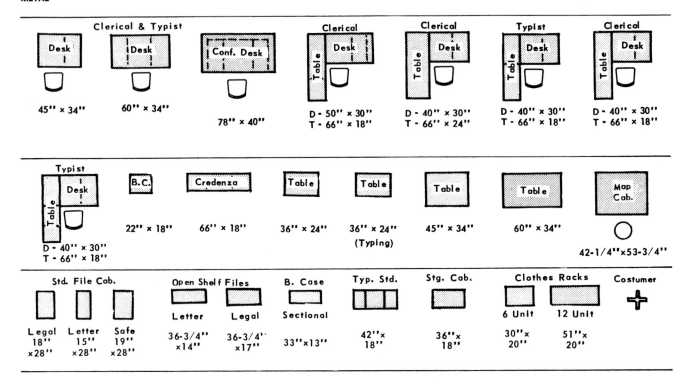

WOOD

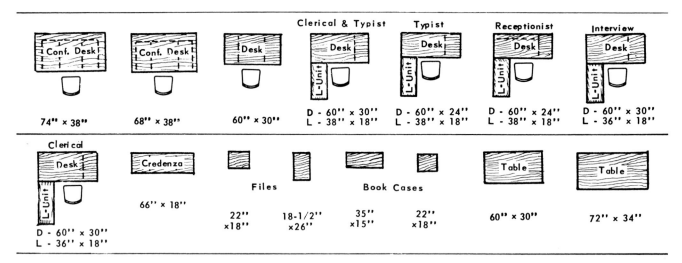

858

FURNISHINGS

Workstation furnishings depend more on the options available than on conventions that are more honored in their breach than observance by office designers generally. Office layout is typically structured by independent workstations or clustered groupings (i.e., workcenters) organized in a variety of configurations. Within these configurations, electronic equipment as well as other necessary furnishings are typically shared or allocated to an individual workstation. Configuration patterns tend to support adjacency requirements of people to people and define zones or departmental boundaries within the work area.

Further, in connection with the selection of workstation furnishings, Fig. 1 illustrates how a small number of standard or custom-made units can be combined with ordinary desks and tables to introduce substantial economies in space usage and flexibility at modest cost.

The key to successful workstation furnishing is that it support a sustained and time-efficient interface between people and machines. Complaints of eye strain, fatigue, and musculoskeletal problems and negative attitudes toward and anxieties about the quality of working life have been shown repeatedly to stem mainly from association with VDTs. Prevention of these problems depends upon workstation specifications that comply with two principal furnishing design criteria: (1) All components are designed to accommodate the specific task and equipment requirements. This involves a fully evaluated task, examining the configuration alternatives and integrating the workstation design with building systems re-

quirements. (2) All components are engineered to support the physical and psychological needs of the user. This factor involves the design quality of the product, that is, detailing and construction that permit flexibility in size, shape, height, configuration, ease of use, and adaptability.

Storage and filing components such as lateral file banks, shelving cabinets, and media closets come in a variety of sizes and shapes and as such become planning elements within either open or a closed floor space. File banks and cabinets provide physical separation between work areas, visual privacy, spatial definition, and partial acoustic control when sheathed with sound-retardant panels. They can also be used to introduce color, planting, and signage into the office interior.

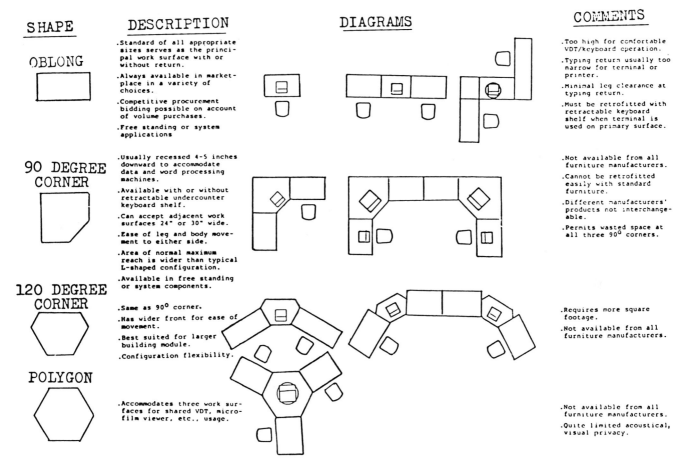

Fig. 1 Work surface expansion methods.

Commercial

OFFICES, GENERAL
Work Stations

Electronic and micrographic media, as well as hardcopy computer printouts that are infrequently referenced but that must be centrally located for general reference purposes or that do not require individual workstation storage, are generally allocated to separate storage components somewhere within the work area.

Reception and conference areas are essential for informal group gatherings and require access to a degree consonant with security, privacy, and/or environmental control. For example, sensitive operations, confidential information, or the need for controlled air quality/temperature may require special protection against unauthorized manipulation or access. Attention to foot traffic, circulation throughout the work area layout, and/or specific hardware and surveillance controls ensures proper design of access/reception areas. Proper layout planning and design considerations may include separation of access from general office areas by full-height partitions or locating equipment and work-centers away from public foot traffic patterns. Providing separate entrances for workers and visitors can also improve security.

Ancillary areas such as specialized computer rooms, media libraries, video tape centers, and a microfilm processing facility are typical examples of the need for planning and designing of a unique type. Ancillary space will also be needed for computer-related supplies and for such personal services locations as a lounge, a first aid center, food service, vending machines, a mail room, and duplication/copy, etc., facilities.

AUTOMATED AND CONVENTIONAL WORKSTATION PLANNING

It will be observed in Table 1 that the layout differences in automated and conventional workstations are subtle, but their physical requirements are markedly different. The equipment and task requirements, workstation size, number of components, adjustment alternatives, lighting, filing facilities, storage places, and equipment accessories are some of the most prominent functional differences. Table 1 does not evaluate the differences, but rather identifies the important design considerations applicable to each.

Workstation Furnishings

Office furniture manufacturers consistently expand both the types and the styles of their products. Generally, their product lines include filing cabinets, desks, chairs, tables, storage units, modules, screens, and related items suitable for use in conventional as well as automated and OOL applications. The common types of automated office furnishings are discussed below and illustrated in Fig. 2.

Desks are the universal symbol of office work. A cardinal rule is that anywhere a desk is found, paperwork is a principal, if not *the* principal, workstation activity. A desk is a suitable work surface with drawers for stationery, office supplies and tools, and personal effects. As such, the desk is the central feature of the workstation.

Cost is important in considering the size of office desks because, in most cases, even when a company owns its office building, estimates are made of space rental that should be charged against each activity.

TABLE 1 Conventional and Automated Workstation Design Factors

Conventional workstation	Automated workstation
Minimal standard equipment	Larger work area required
Standard tasks accommodated, such as writing, referencing, conferencing, telephoning, filing, typing, and transcribing	More work surface needed
Reduced acoustical privacy	More equipment and accessories such as retractable keyboard shelves and disk drive hangers
Minimal adjustment requirements	More filing facilities
Task lighting optional	Acoustical and visual privacy
Stationary work surfaces	Task lighting may require adjustable light at equipment location
Transcriber optional depending on dictation system used	Adjustable work surfaces
Document holder by typewriter optional depending on word processing system and/or personal preference	Adequate primary work surface
	Ease of leg movement
	Footrest often required

860

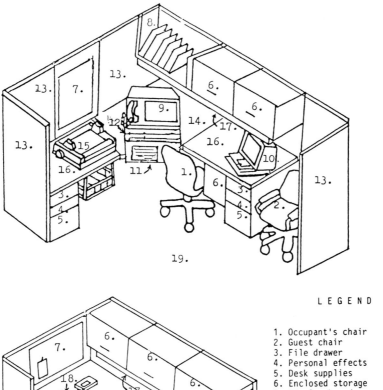

LEGEND

1. Occupant's chair
2. Guest chair
3. File drawer
4. Personal effects
5. Desk supplies
6. Enclosed storage
7. Display board
8. Shelving with organizer for CPO filing.
10. Microfilm viewer
11. Adjustable keyboard
12. Disk drive
13. Acoustical panel
14. Recessed VDT stand
15. Computer printer with paper manager below
16. Textured work surfaced (for lower eflection)

17. Task lighting from under cabinets.
18. Electronic typewriter with playback device
19. Workstation may be enclosed by the addition of wall panels.

Fig. 2   Automated workstations.

Double-pedestal desk

Generally available in various models
with desk tops from 24" to 38" deep,
60" to 78" wide, and with many combinations of file, box, personal drawers,
and a controlling lock.

Single-pedestal desk

Made in 24" and 30" depths, single-
pedestal desks can have from two to
nine drawers, at left or right side.

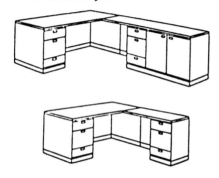

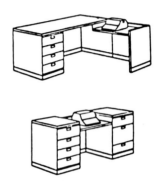

L-shaped desk

Various executive and clerical models
that feature L-returns at desk height.
Tops range from 24" to 36" deep, 60"
to 75" wide; side tops are 19" deep
and 30" to 75" wide. Available with
numerous drawer and cupboard combinations.

Typewriter desk

Many L-shaped models have typing returns 30" and 40" wide, with 60" work
surface tops 24" to 30" deep. Single-
and double-pedestal space-saver desks
have recessed machine platforms that
are 24" deep, 45" and 60" wide. Most
models have built-in organizers for
typing supplies.

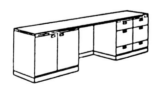

Credenza

Credenzas that match single- and
double-pedestal desks come with
various combinations of drawer and
cupboard pedestals with or without
kneespace in 19" and 24" depths,
and in several widths from 15" to
90".

Fig. 3 Desk components.

862

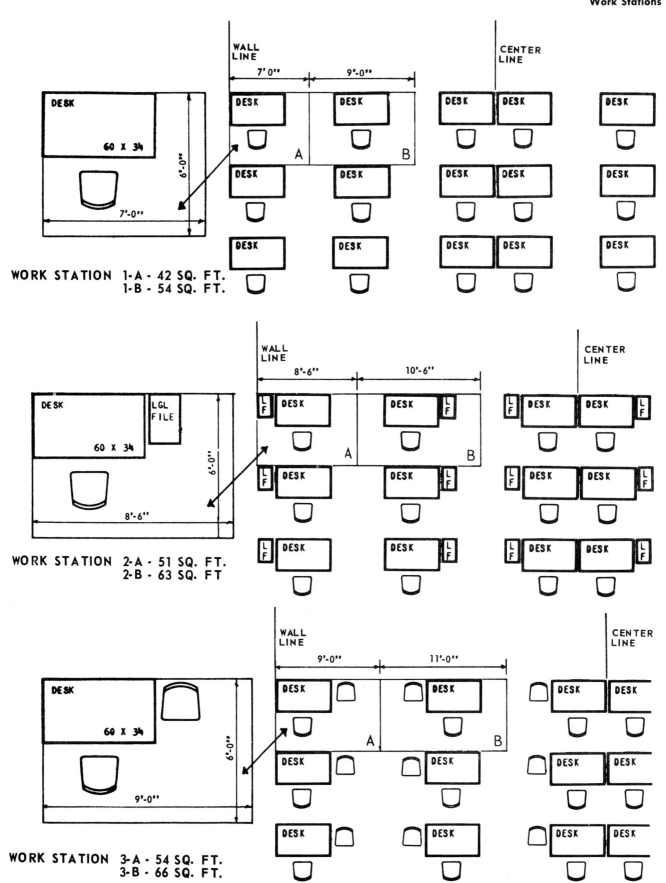

WORK STATION 1-A - 42 SQ. FT.
1-B - 54 SQ. FT.

WORK STATION 2-A - 51 SQ. FT.
2-B - 63 SQ. FT

WORK STATION 3-A - 54 SQ. FT.
3-B - 66 SQ. FT.

Fig. 1 Recommended work stations.

OFFICES, GENERAL
Work Stations

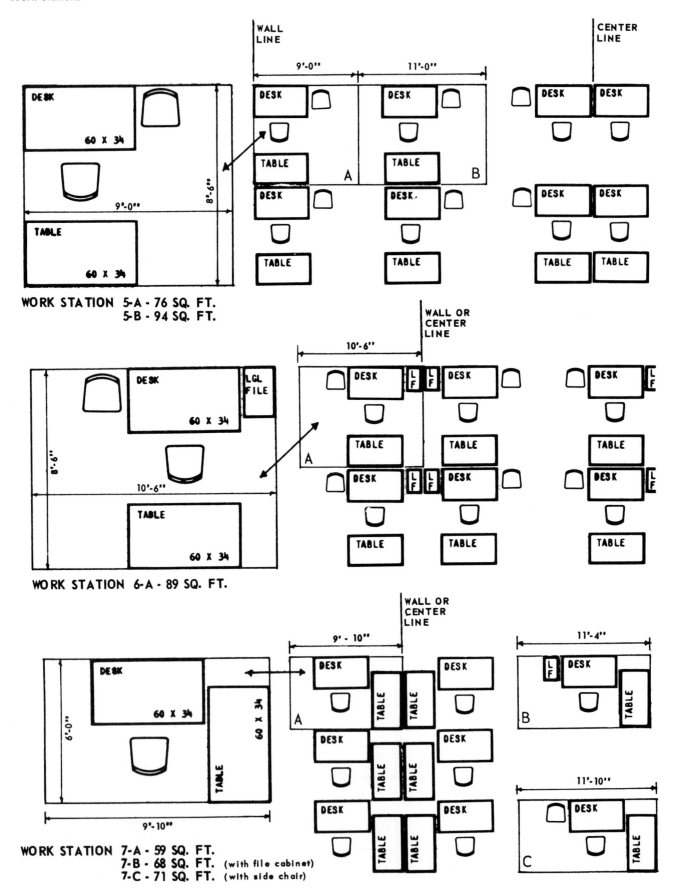

WORK STATION 5-A - 76 SQ. FT.
5-B - 94 SQ. FT.

WORK STATION 6-A - 89 SQ. FT.

WORK STATION 7-A - 59 SQ. FT.
7-B - 68 SQ. FT. (with file cabinet)
7-C - 71 SQ. FT. (with side chair)

Fig. 1 (cont.) Recommended work stations.

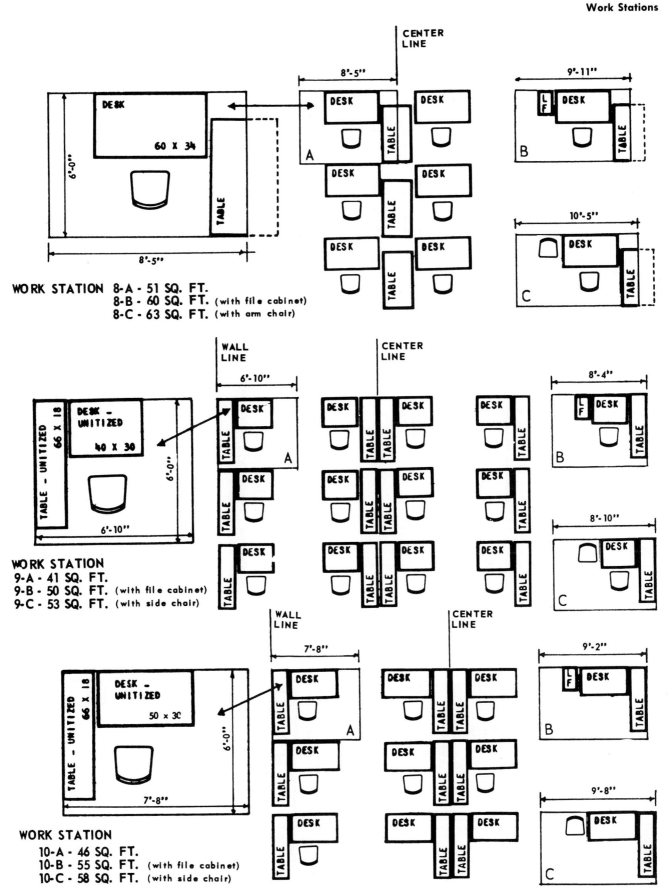

WORK STATION 8-A - 51 SQ. FT.
8-B - 60 SQ. FT. (with file cabinet)
8-C - 63 SQ. FT. (with arm chair)

WORK STATION
9-A - 41 SQ. FT.
9-B - 50 SQ. FT. (with file cabinet)
9-C - 53 SQ. FT. (with side chair)

WORK STATION
10-A - 46 SQ. FT.
10-B - 55 SQ. FT. (with file cabinet)
10-C - 58 SQ. FT. (with side chair)

Fig. 1 (cont.) Recommended work stations.

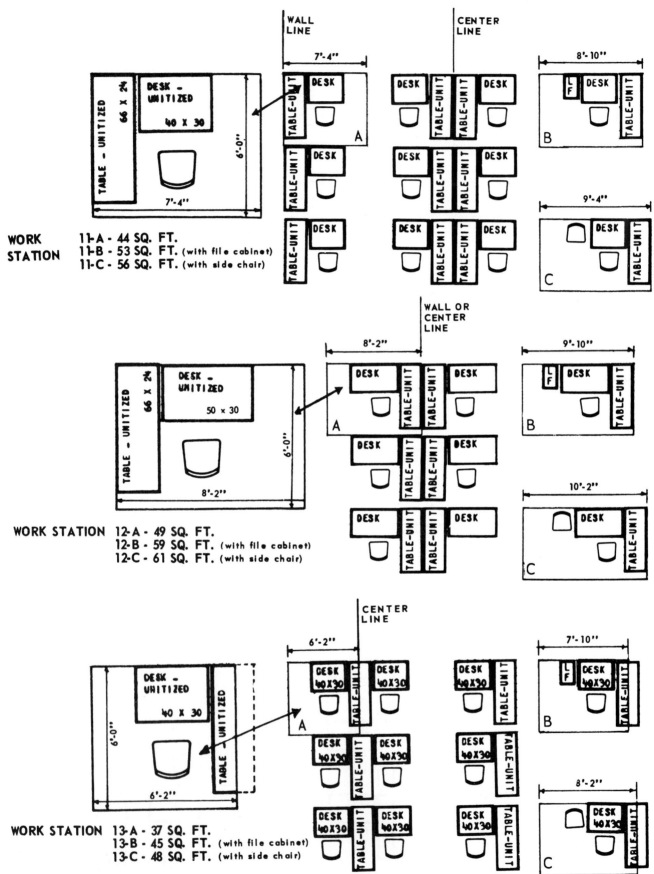

WORK
STATION
11-A - 44 SQ. FT.
11-B - 53 SQ. FT. (with file cabinet)
11-C - 56 SQ. FT. (with side chair)

WORK STATION
12-A - 49 SQ. FT.
12-B - 59 SQ. FT. (with file cabinet)
12-C - 61 SQ. FT. (with side chair)

WORK STATION
13-A - 37 SQ. FT.
13-B - 45 SQ. FT. (with file cabinet)
13-C - 48 SQ. FT. (with side chair)

Fig. 1 (cont.) Recommended work stations.

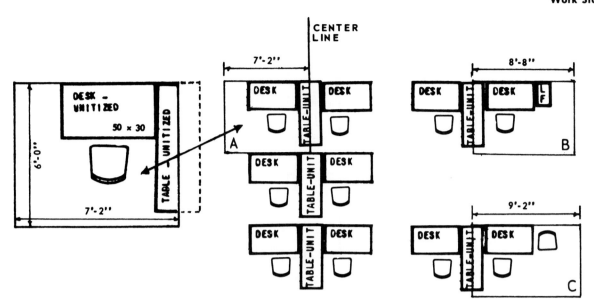

WORK STATION 14-A - 43 SQ. FT.
14-B - 52 SQ. FT. (with file cabinet)
14-C - 55 SQ. FT. (with arm chair)

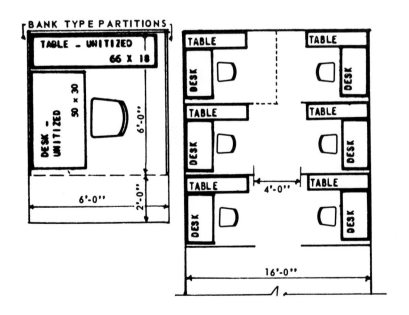

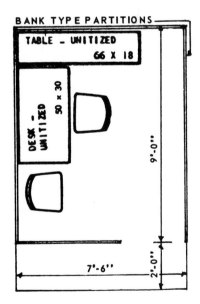

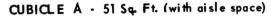

CUBICLE A - 51 Sq. Ft. (with aisle space)

CUBICLE B -

Fig. 1 (cont.) Recommended work stations.

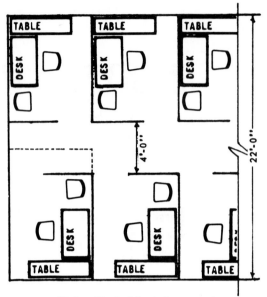

83 Sq. Ft. (with aisle space)

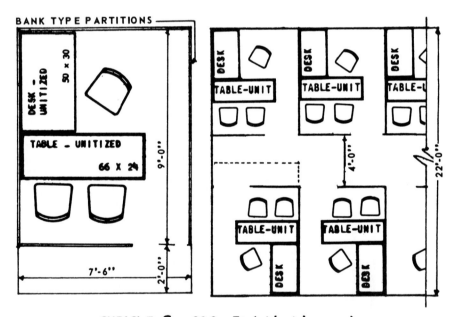

CUBICLE C - 83 Sq. Ft. (with aisle space)

Fig. 1 (cont.)   Recommended work stations.

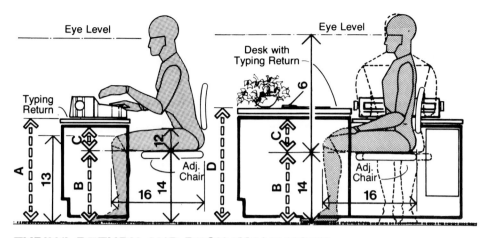

TYPING RETURN AND DESK / MALE USER

The two elevations at the top illustrate the major anthropometric considerations for the seated male and female user at both workstation and typing return. What should be noted is the seat height of the chair (a function of popliteal height) and its relationship to the specific task. When the worksurface is lowered to accommodate a specialized function, as in the case of the typing return, special attention must be given to the requirements for thigh clearance. Most standard office typing returns have been geared to the anthropometric requirements of the female user. The popliteal height and thigh clearance requirements of the larger male user may not be readily met.

The plan at the bottom shows the typical workstation expanded into the basic U-shaped configuration. The work/activity zone dimension range is shown as 46 to 58 in, or 116.8 to 147.3 cm; additional space is needed to allow for drawer extension of the lateral file. Not only does it provide more storage, the lateral file unit is generally the same height as that of the worksurface and is often utilized as a supplementary worksurface. The distance between this unit and that of the primary worksurface must be sufficient to allow for movement and rotation of the chair.

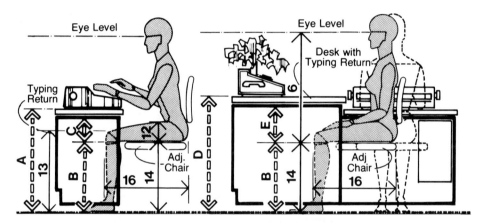

TYPING RETURN AND DESK / FEMALE USER

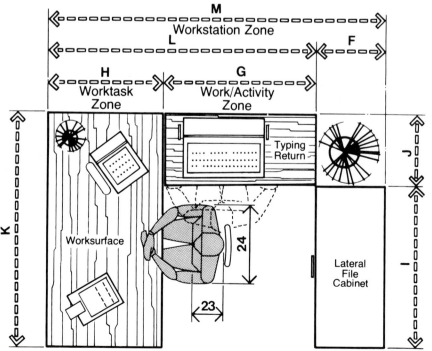

BASIC U-SHAPED WORKSTATION

	in	cm
A	26–27	66.0–68.6
B	14–20	35.6–50.8
C	7.5 min.	19.1 min
D	29–30	73.7–76.2
E	7 min.	17.8 min.
F	18–24	45.7–61.0
G	46–58	116.8–147.3
H	30–36	76.2–91.4
I	42–50	106.7–127.0
J	18–22	45.7–55.9
K	60–72	152.4–182.9
L	76–94	193.0–238.8
M	94–118	238.8–299.7

The basic workstation, as illustrated in both plan and section on this page, is the fundamental building block in understanding the anthropometric considerations for the planning and design of the general office. The worktask zone must be large enough to accommodate the paperwork, equipment, and other accessories that support the user's function. The work/activity zone dimension, shown on the top drawing, is established by the space requirements needed for use of the typical return. In no case should this distance be less than the 30 in, or 76.2 cm, needed to provide adequate space for the chair clearance zone. The visitor seating zone, ranging in depth from 30 to 42 in, or 76.2 to 106.7 cm, requires the designer to accommodate both the buttock-knee and buttock-toe length body dimensions of the larger user. If an overhang is provided or the desk's modesty panel is recessed, the visitor seating zone can be reduced due to the additional knee and toe clearances provided. The specific type and size of the seating (i.e., if it swivels or if it has casters) also influence these dimensions.

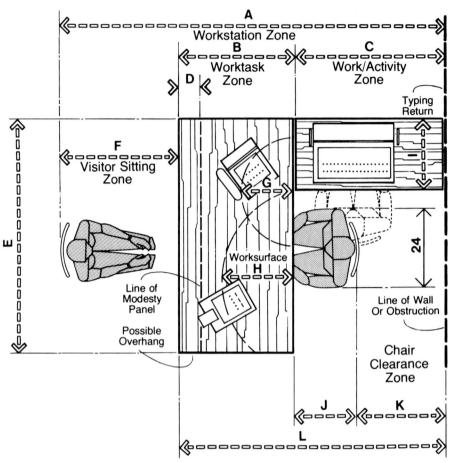

BASIC WORKSTATION WITH VISITOR SEATING

	in	cm
A	90–126	228.6–320.0
B	30–36	76.2–91.4
C	30–48	76.2–121.9
D	6–12	15.2–30.5
E	60–72	152.4–182.9
F	30–42	76.2–106.7
G	14–18	35.6–45.7
H	16–20	40.6–50.8
I	18–22	45.7–55.9
J	18–24	45.7–61.0
K	6–24	15.2–61.0
L	60–84	152.4–213.4
M	24–30	61.0–76.2
N	29–30	73.7–76.2
O	15–18	38.1–45.7

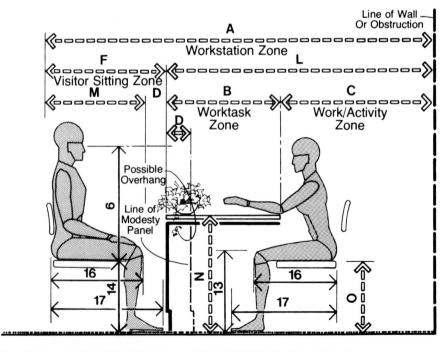

BASIC WORKSTATION WITH VISITOR SEATING

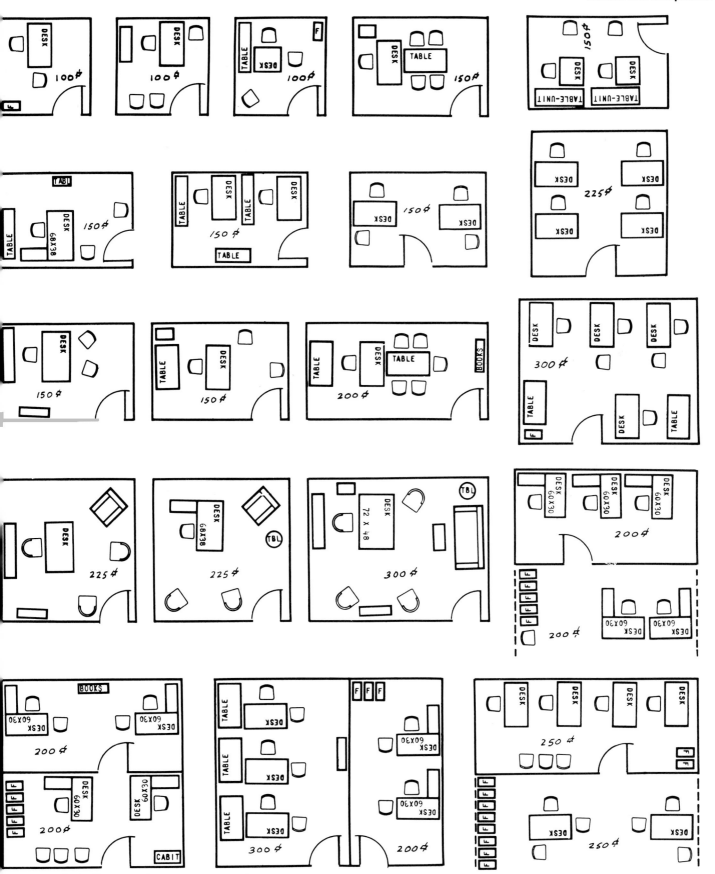

Fig. 2   Recommended layouts for private and semiprivate offices.

Commercial

OFFICES, GENERAL
Private and Semiprivate

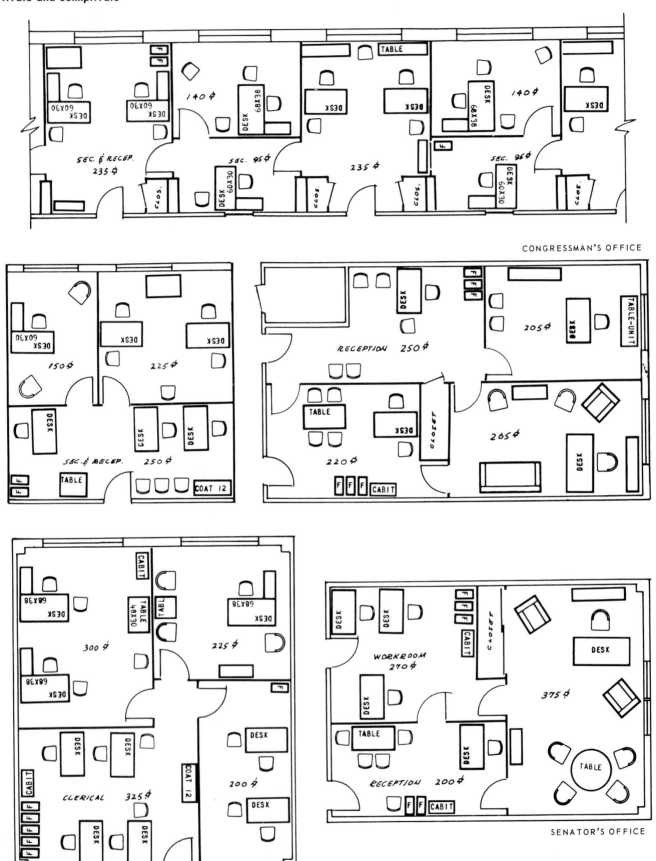

CONGRESSMAN'S OFFICE

SENATOR'S OFFICE

Fig. 2 (cont.)   Recommended layouts for private and semiprivate offices.

872

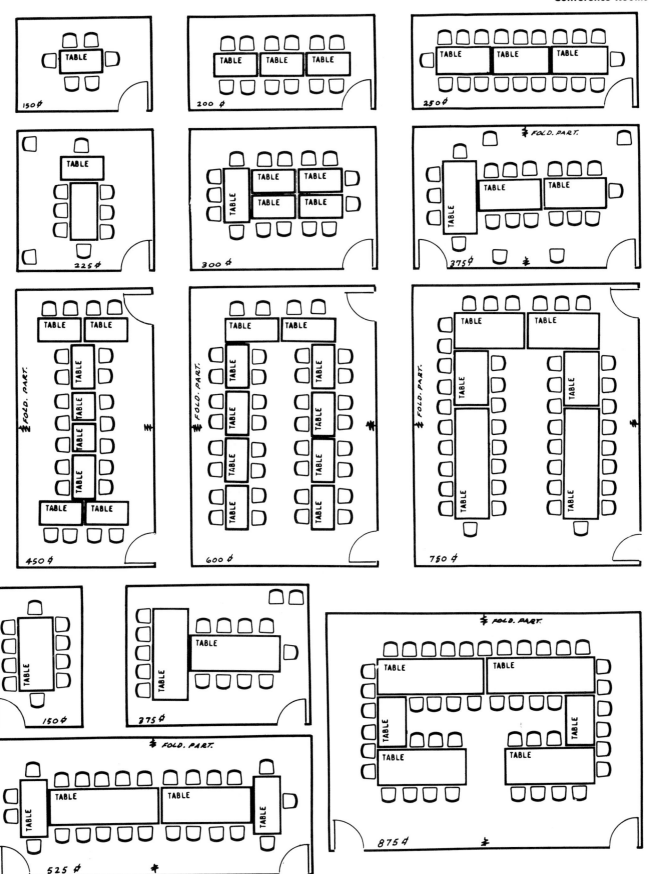

Fig. 3 Recommended layouts for conference rooms.

Commercial

OFFICES, GENERAL

Layout

planning will be required to meet specific needs. The receptionist should be placed so as to command a clear view of those entering and be easily accessible to visitors.

Storage Space

Office space should not be used for bulk storage. Only working inventories of office supplies and other materials should be maintained in offices, preferably in standard supply cabinets. Secondary space, such as basement areas, should be used to locate supply operations.

Special Requirements

"Special requirements" refers to space other than that required for furniture and equipment usually found in office operations and which is essential to the work of the agencies. The space planner must identify these special requirements in the early stages of the space planning.

Interim Space Allowances Table 1 gives allowances to be used by The General Services Administration in space planning for agencies, or elements thereof, which do not have Occupancy Guides, including agency headquarters activities. These allowances are canceled immediately upon publication of the appropriate Occupancy Guide.

TABLE 1 Interim Space Allowances

Grade	Type assignment	Allowance, sq ft per person
GS 1–16		60
GS 7–11	Supervisory	100
GS 7–11	Nonsupervisory	75
GS 12–13	Supervisory	150
GS 12–13	Nonsupervisory	100
GS 14–15	Supervisory	225
GS 14–15	Nonsupervisory	150
GS 16–17–18 . . .		300

OFFICE LAYOUT BY FUNCTION

The office operation is like a large machine which needs to have all of its parts synchronized and moving smoothly. Each office function must mesh smoothly with the others with a minimum of friction.

The office machine's source of power is information, and it is the purpose of good office layout design to permit this information to flow smoothly, avoiding unnecessary turns and traps. There is certainly no one office layout that will fit all companies, any more than there is an all-purpose machine, but there are some reasonably good principles of layout by function that could be applied to any office situation.

Six Basic Office Functions

If you were to make a list of the typical office functions, you would find it quite a long one. Every office needs management, communications, filing, billing, payments, payroll, purchasing, and accounting. Other functions are added according to the purpose of the busi-

How to Plan Your Office Space, National Office Products Association, Washington, D.C., 1968.

ness, such as production, production engineering, quality control, shipping and receiving, cost accounting, industrial engineering, data processing, inventory, etc.

However, all office functions can be cataloged into one of these six groups:

1. Management
2. Finance
3. Sales
4. General services
5. Technical services
6. Production

Here are some pointers for placing these groups in the best office layout position to permit smooth operation.

The Management Group The top management group is usually arranged together, often in a sort of chain of command. They will be reasonably isolated from general office traffic and casual interruptions. They are frequently around the edge of the office, but they may also be in the center. The top official is perhaps the chairman of the board or the president, and he naturally will have the largest and best appointed office. The top executives need more space not only for prestige but because they have more than the usual amount of visitors and meetings. If a conference room is used, the size of the individual offices can be reduced somewhat. There is a trend away from the overabundant office for the top executives, undoubtedly encouraged by the high cost of office space rental. The newer designed, space-saving furniture, however, makes the reduced space practical from an efficiency standpoint. It is not unusual in the newer offices to find the top management men in offices about 12 by 15 ft in size.

The Financial Group Although the financial executives have responsibilities that extend into the general office and involve a considerable percentage of the clerical force, the executives need not be on the spot. Supervisors can run the show with little more connection to the boss than through intercoms or interoffice mail.

It is probably more important to put the accounting function near where it picks up the orders from the sales department. The accounting functions usually line up according to the system procedure, going in a straight line through such activities as credit checks, order processing, inventory control billing, and finally accounts receivable.

The purchasing department has a lot of contact with vendors, so it should be near the entrance or reception room to avoid excessive traffic. Part of purchasing has to be tied to the accounting function through the handling of requisitions, shipping notices, and vendors' invoices.

The personnel department is usually close to the reception area so that they can interview job applicants and other callers without general disruption of the office area.

The data processing activity usually comes at the end of the line, but it should be out of the traffic swirl and in a spot where the noise can be confined.

The Sales Group Every firm has some sort of a sales function which starts the activity of the company. For this reason there is a considerable amount of communication between it and all the other functions of the office. The sales group frequently has visitors and needs a lot of space for catalogs and specification files, so that each person there probably has a little more than the average amount of floor space. Pricing, estimating, and correspondence are large functions in the sales group. Many

sales groups need a conference room or an all-purpose room that can be used for training, meetings, demonstrations, and conferences with the engineering and product development group.

The General Office Group This is the group that provides general services for all of the other functions, such as central files, stenographic service, library, mail handling, duplicating, and general communications.

The reference functions like central files, the library, and the stenographic pool are normally in the center of all the other functions in the office. The mail handling is at either end of the office work flow. Duplicating services are normally isolated because of the noise and fumes, and may be near the function that calls most frequently for this service, such as shipping and receiving rooms.

The telephone switchboard is part of the job of the receptionist, and is naturally in the reception area. In a more complicated communications setup it might be in a center by itself, convenient to the other office activities.

Technical Service Group Technical services such as the engineering, drafting, and design people are normally located near the activities they assist, such as manufacturing, sales, and production. When they deal with production and systems work they are frequently out in the plant.

The Production Group The production group is usually in a second office, set up out in the production plant. It is just as important to the business as the general offices and should have the same amount of considerations, dignities, and facilities. This is not always the case, unfortunately, but where it has been the policy to put this office group on a par with the general offices, an improvement in work and general morale has been accomplished.

In any large-scale planning, other factors besides available space will naturally influence the decision for the final placing of any particular department. The shipping and receiving departments, for example, could hardly be placed on the top floor even though their space requirements would fit perfectly into a given area on the top floor.

Study the Organization Chart

The arrangement of the office functions will actually be a projection of the organization chart of the firm, located with respect for the flow of work and the physical requirements of each department.

The organization chart will show the departments and sections which make up the firm, like the executive, offices, sales, accounting, engineering, production, research, and purchasing. The chart will also give a clue to the interrelationship of the departments.

Relatively minor activities are better placed around the major office activities rather than integrated with them. When more space is needed, the major activities can be expanded with less disruption simply by moving a minor activity over a desk or two.

Each department and division has a good reason for being in one location rather than another. Here are ten guides for determining what that location should be. When the department is properly assigned to a major area, minor changes can be made later without an upheaval in the basic pattern. Some departments will naturally qualify in several of these guides, and then it will be a matter of choosing the locations which seem to offer the best compromise.

874

1. Convenience to the Public Those departments having the greatest number of visitors should be located so that the visitors have a short, direct, and convenient route from the main entrance to the department sought. The sales, purchasing, and employment or personnel departments usually have the most visitors. Convenient access is not only enjoyed by the visitors but it offers the least disturbance to the work of employees.

2. Flow of Work Departments having the closest working connections should be placed closest together. When this is done, the work flows with a minimum waste of time between operations. Sales and advertising departments normally work together; so do the sales and credit departments, cost and payroll departments. When they are too far apart, unnecessary walking time is increased or the telephone switchboard or intercoms are overworked.

3. Equipment Used Some departmental operations require the use of special equipment requiring extensive wiring, plumbing, or ventilation equipment. Moving departments of this type requires expensive alterations. Obviously, two such departments should not be located together because of the difficulty of later expansion.

Some sections of a department may use noisy equipment. They may use teletypes, tabulating equipment, reproduction equipment, and similar specialized equipment. Typing and stenographic sections, because of their concentration, will produce a higher noise level than a similar number of machines scattered throughout the area. To minimize disturbance to the rest of the employees, these sections are commonly segregated into sound-treated rooms.

4. Centralized Functions Sections and facilities that serve the entire office should be centrally located and easily accessible to all who use them. Correspondence and stenographic pools, central files, cost accounting, and tabulating are examples. Of course, rest rooms, water fountains, and supply cabinets should be provided in sufficient numbers and conveniently located.

5. Confidential Areas Certain functions of a business may be of a confidential nature that requires them to be isolated from others in the office and from the general public. Central files, the paymaster, the controller, and legal offices are examples.

6. Conference Rooms Conference and training rooms should be reasonably near those departments that use them the most. If the office is air conditioned, the room can be in the interior of the space to eliminate the distraction of windows and to provide more wall display area.

7. Freight Elevators Departments receiving and delivering large quantities of materials should be located near the freight area for ease of handling, less time and labor, and less distraction of other workers. Mail, stockroom, and machine departments are in this category.

8. Shipping Dock Shipping and receiving activities and mail rooms should obviously be near the point of entrance and exit of material.

9. Service Facilities Eating, medical, and lounge facilities are generally on the lower floors to reduce elevator traffic. The number and type of employees in a particular department might be considered in locating it near these facilities.

10. Passenger Elevators When an office occupies more than one floor, elevator service will be more effective when the departments with large clerical forces are on the lower floors.

The fundamental unit (module) for office space planning is the *individual worker*, seated at his or her desk or work station. The space allowance assigned to each worker can be either liberal or economical depending upon space limitations or the kind of atmosphere desired in the office.

In larger offices where there are many routine jobs, space standards tend to be economical. Where the work is specialized, where there are many visitors, or where high morale is promoted, space assignment is apt to be more generous. Larger firms tend to be more economical than smaller ones, for the extra space means extra rental costs or more buildings. Smaller firms have fewer routing operations and tend to have more generous space allowances.

In the general office area, allotment of 100 sq ft per clerical worker is generally considered a liberal standard; 65 sq ft is an economical standard. Eighty square feet would be a reasonable average.

FIVE GUIDES FOR SPACE ALLOWANCES

Good space utilization does not necessarily mean allocating the least possible working space per person. On the contrary, too little working space may reduce the worker's efficiency and waste many times the savings made by any reduction in the square-foot rental costs. Good space utilization, in its broad meaning, allots more space to those positions whose activity justifies it, and reduces the space where there is a surplus.

There is no accurate scale of space allowances which will make layout planning automatic. We can give you here, however, some guidelines which have been established from a large number of surveys made of offices, both commercial and governmental. These suggestions will help you make a broad estimate of your space requirements or will serve as a check against your own utilization of space.

We can break down the types of space required in the typical office into five categories as follows:

1. Office space
2. File space
3. Special equipment
4. Storage space
5. Special rooms

Let's discuss these five space categories separately.

Office Space Allowance

The following typical allowances include space for departmental aisles, space to move about, space for occasional visitors and consultation, rest rooms, fountains, special files, general office equipment, bookcases, and coat racks. It does not include main aisles, corridors, or the space covered by the other four space categories.

	Square feet
Top executive	400–600
Junior executives	100–200
Supervisors	80–100
Operator at 60 in. desk	55
Operator at 55 in. desk	50
Operator at 50 in. desk	45

Operators are assumed to be at desks side by side, two in a row. Add space for file and side chair if needed.

The use of L-shaped furniture for work stations will give more *surface* room than the standard desks, but the *floor space* will be roughly equivalent when the width is the same as desks above.

File Space Allowance

The actual space taken up by a file cabinet and its open drawer is easily measured. It is difficult to estimate how much should be added to these measurements for working area until decisions are made on arrangement of the filing area.

In general, each open file cabinet will require the following space allowance without consideration of any working area in front of the open drawer:

	Square feet
Standard letter file	6
Standard legal file	7
Side-opening letter file	6½
Side-opening legal file	7½

Special Equipment Allowance

Certain special types of office machines require more space than normally allowed in an estimate based on the average clerk or typist position. Any space taken up by the following equipment and their operators should be added to that considered for the regular office space.

1. Tabulating equipment
2. Duplicating equipment
3. Telephone switchboard
4. Teletype equipment
5. Time clock space
6. Other special equipment

Storage Space Allowance

Storage requirements depend on the nature of the firm's work, its age, and the inclination of the administration to retain records. Here are some storage space requirements which should be considered:

1. Vaults
2. Stockrooms
3. Transfer files
4. Shelving
5. Janitor supplies and equipment
6. Stock rooms
7. Coat rooms

Special Rooms Allowance

Depending on the type of business, offices will require rooms of a size matched to their use. These will include:

1. Reception room
2. Waiting room
3. Interviewing room
4. Examination room
5. Conference room
6. Exhibit room
7. Medical room
8. Lunchroom
9. Employee lounge
10. Rest room
11. Mail room

The more common rooms will have the following typical space allotments, based on their use by 15 people.

	Square feet
Reception room	400
Waiting or interviewing room	200
Conference room	500

Add approximately 10 sq ft for each additional person to be provided for.

Commercial

OFFICES, GENERAL
Planning

By JOSEPH KLEIMAN, Architect, Freidin, Kleiman, Kelleher, New York, N.Y.

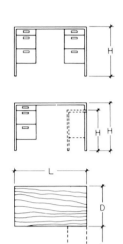

DESK DIMENSIONS

		DESKS			RETURNS	
		DOUBLE PEDESTAL		SINGLE PEDESTAL		FOR EXECUTIVE DESK RETURNS ARE AVAILABLE AT SAME HEIGHT AS DESK
	STANDARD	RANGE	STANDARD	RANGE	STANDARD	RANGE
D	2'-6"	2'-0"–3'-3"	2'-6"	2'-0"–3'-3"	1'-6"	1'-3"–1'-8"
H	2'-5"	2'-4"–2'-6"	2'-5"	2'-4"–2'-6"	2'-2"	2'-1"–2'-3"
L	5'-0"	4'-6"–7'-0"	5'-0'	3'-9"–7'-0"	3'-0"	2'-0"–5'-0"

DESKS-SINGLE OR DOUBLE PEDESTAL

WORK TABLES ARE OF SIMILAR DIMENSIONS.

FOR EXECUTIVE DESKS WITH RETURNS, RETURNS ARE AVAILABLE AT THE SAME HEIGHT AS THE DESK SURFACE.

A MINIMUM CLEAR WIDTH OF 22" SHOULD BE PROVIDED FOR KNEE ROOM, 24" IS NORMAL.

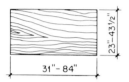

15"-18"

1 BOX 1 FILE | 3 BOX | 2 TRAY 2 BOX | 6 TRAY

VARIOUS DRAWER ARRANGEMENTS FOR PEDESTALS

23"–43½" | 31"–84"

ARTIST AND DRAFTING DESKS OR TABLES

PEDESTALS FOR SECRETARIAL RETURNS WILL BE REDUCED IN HEIGHT THE EQUIVALENT OF ONE PENCIL DRAWER.

STANDARD SIZE ENGINEERING OR ARCHITECTURAL DRAFTING TABLES ARE 37½"x 43½"D x 60"-72"-84"W x 37"H.

Fig. 4 Office planning: desks — sizes.

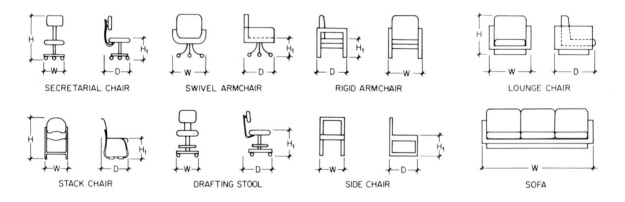

SECRETARIAL CHAIR   SWIVEL ARMCHAIR   RIGID ARMCHAIR   LOUNGE CHAIR

STACK CHAIR   DRAFTING STOOL   SIDE CHAIR   SOFA

CHAIR DIMENSIONS

	SECRETARIAL		SWIVEL ARMCHAIR		RIGID ARMCHAIR		STACK CHAIR		RIGID AND ADJUSTABLE DRAFTING STOOL		SIDE CHAIR	
	STD.	RANGE	STD.	RANGE	STD.	RANGE	STD.	RANGE	STD	RANGE	STD.	RANGE
W	1'-5"	1'-4"–1'-8"	2'-4"	1'-8"–2'-6"	1'-10"	1'-6"–2'-3"	1'-9"	1'-6"–1'-11"	1'-6"	1'-5"–2'-0"	1'-8"	1'-4"–2'-0"
D	1'-7½"	1'-6–2'-0"	2'-3"	1'-8"–2'-6"	1'-10"	1'-7"–2'-8"	1'-9"	1'-7"–1'-10"	1'-8"	1'-6"–2'-0"	1'-10"	1'-6–2'-8"
H	2'-6"	2'-5"–2'-10"	2'-9"	2'-6"–3'-0"	2'-6"	2'-4"–2'-10"	2'-6"	2'-4–2'-9"	3'-0"	2'-11"–3'-6"	2'-6"	2'-4–2'-10"
H₁	1'-5"	1'-4"–1'-8"	1'-5"	1'-4"–1'-10"	1'-6"	1'-4"–1'-7"	1'-5"	1'-5"–1'-6"	2'-4"	1'-5"–2'-10"	1'-6"	1'-5"–1'-7"

LOUNGE CHAIR AND SOFA DIMENSIONS

	LOUNGE CHAIR		SOFA
	STD.	RANGE	
W	2'-6"	2'-6"–3'-4"	D, H AND H₁ SIMILAR
D	2'-7"	2'-2"–3'-4"	2 SEATS-5'-0"–6'-7"
H	2'-6"	2'-1"–3'-4"	3 SEATS-6'-0"–7'-6" 4 SEATS-7'-8"–9'-0"
H₁	1'-3"	1'-0"–1'-6"	

Fig. 5 Office planning: seating — sizes.

876

TYPICAL VERTICAL FILE AND OVERFILE STORAGE DIMENSIONS

			OVERFILE STORAGE	
			OVER 2 LETTER	OVER 3 LETTER
DEPTH		2'-4½"	2'-4½"	2'-4½"
WIDTH	LETTER	1'-2⅞"	2'-5¾"	2'-11¾"
	LEGAL	1'-5⅞"	3'-8¾"	4'-5¾"
HEIGHT	2 DR.	2'-6"	2'-2" and 3'-1"	2'-2" and 3'-1"
	3 DR.	3'-5"		
	4 DR.	4'-3"		
	5 DR.	4'-11"		

DIMENSIONS OF VARIOUS MANUFAC-
TURERS WILL VARY SLIGHTLY

VERTICAL FILES

TYPICAL LATERAL FILE AND OVERFILE STORAGE DIMENSIONS

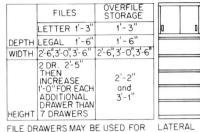

		FILES	OVERFILE STORAGE
DEPTH	LETTER	1'-3"	1'-3"
	LEGAL	1'-6"	1'-6"
WIDTH		2'-6", 3'-0", 3'-6"	2'-6", 3'-0", 3'-6"
HEIGHT		2 DR. 2'-5" THEN INCREASE 1'-0" FOR EACH ADDITIONAL DRAWER THAN 7 DRAWERS	2'-2" and 3'-1"

FILE DRAWERS MAY BE USED FOR
STORAGE IN LIEU OF OVERFILE
UNITS

LATERAL FILES

FILES AND OVERFILE STORAGE

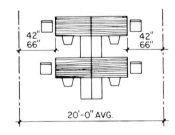

4 LEGAL FILES = 6'-0"
4 LETTER FILES = 5'-0"

PLAN-VERTICAL FILES

	CABINET DIMENSIONS
DEPTH	1'-6", 1'-10", 2'-0"
WIDTH	1'-6", 2'-0", 3'-0"
HEIGHT	2'-6", 3'-6", 5'-6", 6'-6"

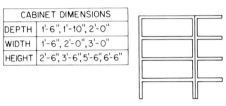

	SHELVING DIMENSIONS
DEPTH	6", 9", 1'-0", 1'-3", 1'-6" 1'-9", 2'-0", 2'-6", 3'-6"
WIDTH	2'-0", 2'-6", 3'-0", 3'-6", 4'-0"
HEIGHTS	AS DESIRED

3'-36" UNITS = 9'-0"

NOTE: SIMILAR AISLE CLEARANCES SHOULD BE
APPLIED TO STORAGE OR BOOK SHELVING

STORAGE AND WARDROBE CABINETS   STORAGE AND LIBRARY SHELVING

Fig. 6   Office planning: files and storage — sizes.

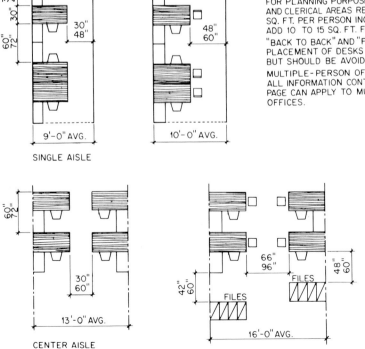

SINGLE AISLE

9'-0" AVG.   10'-0" AVG.

NOTES:

DIMENSIONS SHOWN ARE BASED ON
2'-6" x 5'-0" DESKS

FOR PLANNING PURPOSES SECRETARIAL
AND CLERICAL AREAS REQUIRE 45 TO 60
SQ. FT. PER PERSON INCLUDING AISLES,
ADD 10 TO 15 SQ. FT. FOR SIDE CHAIRS

"BACK TO BACK" AND "FACE TO FACE"
PLACEMENT OF DESKS CAN SAVE SPACE
BUT SHOULD BE AVOIDED IF POSSIBLE.

MULTIPLE-PERSON OFFICES
ALL INFORMATION CONTAINED ON THIS
PAGE CAN APPLY TO MULTIPLE PERSON
OFFICES.

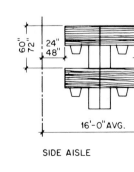

20'-0" AVG.

CENTER AISLE   13'-0" AVG.   16'-0" AVG.   FILES

SIDE AISLE   16'-0" AVG.

Fig. 7   Office planning: clearances for secretarial areas and general clerical offices.

Commercial

OFFICES, GENERAL
Planning

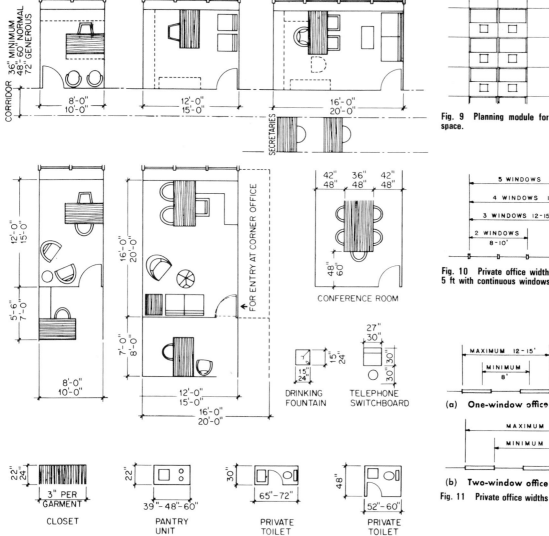

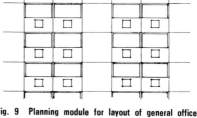

Fig. 9 Planning module for layout of general office space.

Fig. 10 Private office widths using a module of 4 to 5 ft with continuous windows.

(a) One-window office

(b) Two-window office

Fig. 11 Private office widths using a module of 4 to 5

Fig. 8 Office planning: layouts for private offices.

Office layout is often based upon a module derived from standard furniture and equipment and the necessary clearances. For large general offices, the planning unit or module is based upon one desk and chair and is thus about 5 by 6 ft. Since this dimension is also satisfactory for aisles between rows of desks the module can be used to form a regular grid for the planning of large office areas (Fig. 9).

In the layout of private offices the controlling factors are the minimum practical office layout with the wall and window design. A planning module of 4 to 5 ft works reasonably well for this purpose. With this module the smallest office (2 modules) would be 8 to 10 ft wide, and a convenient range of office sizes is provided in increments of one module (Fig. 10). If the exterior wall consists of continuous windows, one module in width, then the office widths are limited to even modules. If windows alternate with solid walls, then office widths do not have to be in even modules but may vary widely (Fig. 11). This type of wall

design permits greater flexibility in office layout at the expense of less natural light in the offices.

The planning module and the exterior wall module must be reconciled with the structural module or column bay. If all these modules coincide, then the wall or window units adjacent to the column must be smaller than the intermediate units (Fig. 12a). If the wall units are kept uniform in size, then the planning module is interrupted by the column width (Fig. 12b). If the columns are set inside the walls, they do not interfere with the wall module but they create a serious limitation on the layout of private offices (Fig. 12c). If the columns are set outside the walls, then the planning module and the wall module are not affected by them (Fig. 12d).

Column spacing most frequently used in multistory steel-framed office buildings is around 25 ft, center to center. Recent trend is toward larger spacing; 30 to 35 ft is not uncommon. Flexibility of interior space is so important in office building design that the extra cost of clear span framing with the elimination of all interior columns is sometimes considered worthwhile; clear spans of 60 to 70 ft have been used.

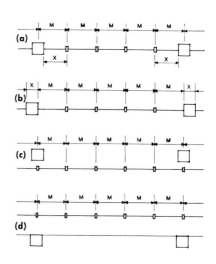

Note: all plans drawn with outside at bottom

Fig. 12 Relation of planning module and wall module to column spacing and location.

878

Efficiency of an office building design is measured by the ratio of rentable space to total space. Average efficiency is about 70 percent; maximum possible is about 85 percent. The non-rentable space consists of the elevators, stairs, and toilets and their associated lobbies, corridors, pipe and duct shafts, and janitor's closets. These facilities are usually planned in a compact unit called the service core. For preliminary assumptions, the number of elevators required may be estimated on the basis of one elevator per 25,000 sq ft of rentable area. Elevator lobbies should be 6 to 9 ft wide if elevators are on one side only; 10 to 12 ft if elevators are on both sides. Corridors are usually 5 to 6 ft wide (Fig. 13), wider if very long, narrower if very short.

Since the floor space within 25 to 30 ft from the exterior wall brings premium rentals, office buildings (site or zoning consideration aside) tend to assume a slablike shape, 60 to 70 ft wide by 150 ft or more long, with the service core in the center (Fig. 14). For greater flexibility in the rental space, the service core may be moved completely outside the office space. When this scheme is combined with clear span framing, the ultimate in flexibility is achieved (Fig. 15).

Floor-to-floor heights are usually about 12 ft, ranging from 11 to 14 ft. Finished ceiling heights are generally about 8 to 8½ ft. The space above the ceiling is required for ducts and recessed lighting. In order to avoid excessive depths in this utility space, girders are sometimes designed with openings in the web to permit the passage of ducts.

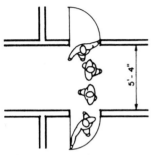

Fig. 13 Corridor width based on requirements of human figures.

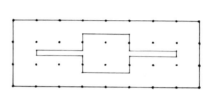

Fig. 14 Typical slab plan with service core at center.

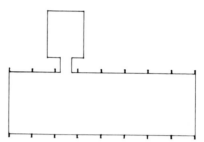

Fig. 15 Maximum flexibility of rental area achieved by use of clear-span framing and separate service tower.

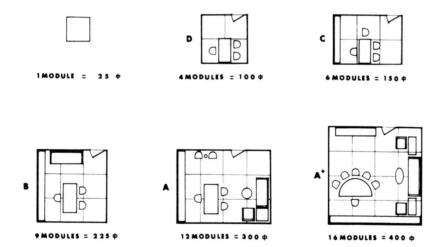

Fig. 16 Typical modular office plans.

1 MODULE = 25 φ

4 MODULES = 100 φ

6 MODULES = 150 φ

9 MODULES = 225 φ

12 MODULES = 300 φ

16 MODULES = 400 φ

Commercial

OFFICES, GENERAL

Planning

The Office Planning Concept

The office planning concept has a strong effect on design. The concept is properly dealt with in programming, since it influences building size and form. Two main concepts may be considered: The *conventional plan* in which most of the building perimeter is taken up by fully enclosed private offices and the *open plan,* which assigns all or most occupants to spaces enclosed by low screens or modular furniture. Of course, the concept is closely related to the decisions made when creating space standards and, accordingly, the issue may need to be discussed during data collection.

There are several pros and cons for each of the two main concepts. As implied by its name, the *conventional plan* for many years has been the customary way of arranging office space, and it may be ingrained in the attitudes of at least the older generation of management. In a corporate headquarters, where the ratio of managers to clerical and technical people may be quite high, application of the conventional plan may result in the use of almost the entire perimeter for enclosed offices.

The *advantages* of the conventional plan are:

1. Visual and aural privacy can be provided for the offices of executives and managers.
2. The plan is well suited for a company that wishes sharp lines drawn between ranks of its staff and that considers a private office a measure of promotion.
3. The need for conference space is minimized.

The *disadvantages* include:

1. Partitions must be demounted or demolished when space changes are necessary
2. Natural light and a view of the exterior is denied to those working in the interior
3. The energy savings made possible by directing natural light to the interior are minimal.

The *open plan* has its ultimate application in the *office landscape* concept, whereby even senior executives are situated in open areas screened by low partitions or plantings. Office landscaping originated in Europe and was introduced in the USA in the 1960s, where the concept was employed in such major corporate headquarters as Uniroyal and Weyerhauser. In recent years, open planning has gained acceptance, but few headquarters today are designed without enclosed offices for senior executives and high-level managers. In the resulting compromise plan, managers below a certain level may be assigned to comfortably sized work stations. Inherent in the open planning concept is the need for an acoustical environment that affords aural privacy.

The *advantages* of the open plan are:

1. Most employees enjoy natural light and a view of the exterior
2. The plan is highly flexible. Space can be rearranged or offices moved with relative ease
3. By using modular work stations, variations in the user's needs can easily be accomplished
4. The plan is compatible with energy conserving design.

Disadvantages include:

1. There is, inevitably, some loss of aural and visual privacy.
2. The plan is not feasible in buildings with narrow wings or many obstructions.
3. Orientation for visitors may be more difficult than in the conventional plan.
4. More conference space may be necessary than for the conventional plan.

As noted above, recent office plans represent a compromise between the two basic concepts. This usually requires that part of the management staff be assigned to open locations. However, such offices can be placed on the perimeter to preserve the intent of the conventional plan. Another compromise involves the executive core concept, which places fully enclosed offices (with glazed wall sections) at the interior, thus keeping the perimeter open to the interior.

The Office Planning Module

The space allocations in the facilities program are usually based on a consistent space module. The module is derived from analysis of needs, compatibility with manufacturers' standards, and an existing module if a headquarters building is being expanded. The modular approach is most applicable to offices, so the office module will control the planning of the building.

The greatest advantage of modular planning is the flexibility that can be attained. The basic module is extended to the structural grid and to ceiling and underfloor systems, thus making for ready change or interchange of space. There is a minor penalty in overall space in modular planning versus exact sizing of individual spaces. However, considering a headquarters' vulnerabil-

ity to change, the benefits outweigh the disadvantages.

The $5' \times 5'$ office-planning module is commonly used, and it is the basis for sizing most partitions, work stations, ceiling and underfloor systems. The schedule below shows applications of the $5' \times 5'$ module to typical office sizes and comparisons to the offices based on $4' \times 4'$ and $6' \times 6'$ modules.

It may be seen that a $5' \times 5'$ grid, using a consistent depth of $15'$ for the larger offices, affords a good range of sizes and requires minimum perimeter for average-size spaces. Considerations in selecting and applying a module include the following measures:

It is usually necessary to depart from the module at corridors and core spaces in which case a "half module" should be used.

The Type D offices are the smallest that should be considered for rooms with full-height partitions. Placing them on the perimeter necessitates breaks in aisles, or wasted space, unless the offices occupy a full end or side of a floor.

The types of offices on the perimeter should be kept to a minimum number; avoid, if possible, creating a variety of sizes using half-modules.

Different grades of offices can be created by varying the furniture and furnishings within spaces of similar size.

Staying on the module is most important for spaces with full-height partitions. Working positions in regular office areas should be planned in general conformance with the grid, but some latitude is possible in a flexible underfloor system.

Type	5 × 5			4 × 4			6 × 6		
	D × W	Square feet	Perimeter	D × W	Square feet	Perimeter	D × W	Square feet	Perimeter
A	15 × 25	375	25	16 × 24	384	24	18 × 18	324	18
B	15 × 15	225	15	16 × 16	256	16	18 × 12	216	12
C	15 × 10	150	10	16 × 12	192	12	12 × 12	144	12
D	10 × 10	100	10	12 × 8	96	8	—	—	—

Typical Office and Work Station Arrangements

The programmed allocations for all occupants of office space result from analysis of the users' needs. A number of factors, including modularity, dictate a degree of uniformity in the types and arrangements of working spaces for all but the senior executives in a headquarters.

Usually, the items of furniture in each office are assumed and the typical spaces are tested by making layouts showing alternate arrangements. (Figure 17 shows such a study.)

The availability of a wide variety of modular work stations affords almost limitless opportunities for adapting individual spaces to the users' needs. However, space management and inventorying are greatly simplified if all or most of the occupants' needs can be satisfied by a few typical work stations. In making this determination, it is well to establish a basic type that serves the largest number of users. Variations can then be made for the atypical needs of certain groups. Usually, a careful study discloses commonality in the requirements of many office occupants. Three or

less typical work stations can often fulfill the needs of such users as analysts, accountants, auditors, computer programmers, and supervisors, with only minor variations in equipment and storage units. Figure 18 shows two such typical work stations for a headquarters. The basic types shown are suitable for assistant managers and all professionals below that rank. Figure 18 also shows two work stations designed for secretaries and clerical workers. Considerations in establishing typical work stations include:

A program is usually written before a work station manufacturer is decided upon. The typical stations should therefore be based on units that can be supplied by several vendors.

A basic determination involves whether a work station employs freestanding desks, credenzas, and other furniture; or whether a "hang-on" system is contemplated that attaches all furniture and equipment to the space-dividing screens. The former method allows existing furniture to be used, while the second offers the great versatility

and high degree of standardization made possible through integrated furniture/partition systems.

Modular systems can be extended to work stations for secretaries, clerks, equipment operators, and other workers in a general office.

Groups of work stations can be arranged in clusters, pinwheels, or linear fashion. Screens or storage units can be employed to define the groups, or to give a degree of privacy.

Space Allocations for General Office Areas

The term *general office* applies to space used primarily by secretaries, typists, clerks, machine operators, and the like. In an open plan that uses work stations, there may be a blurring of the distinction between private and general office areas, except that the private offices will be larger and provided with a different grade of furniture. However, the general office areas require space allocations for items other than desks and chairs, and it is important that the program reflect allowance for these items.

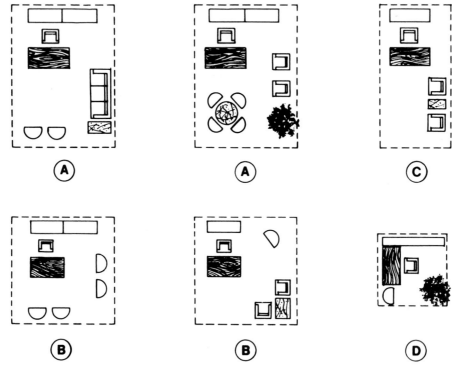

Fig. 17 Alternate furniture arrangements in typical offices.

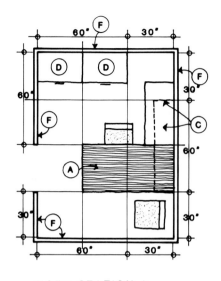

WORK STATION 2

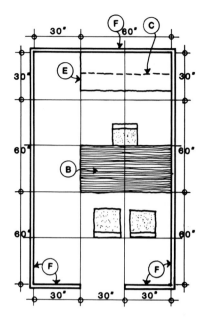

WORK STATION 1

● **LEGEND**

A- 30" x 60" L DESK W/42" ± EXECUTIVE HEIGHT RETURN

B- 30" x 60" DOUBLE PEDESTAL DESK

C- FLIPPER DOOR PANEL HUNG CABINET W/TASK LIGHT UNDER

D- 30" WIDE 2 DRAWER LATERAL FILE (FREE STANDING)

E- 60" WIDE CREDENZA W/STORAGE CABINET AT CENTER BOX
   & FILE DRAWER EACH SIDE

F- 66" H.± ACOUSTIC STRUCTURAL PANELS, WIDTH AS NOTED ON PLAN

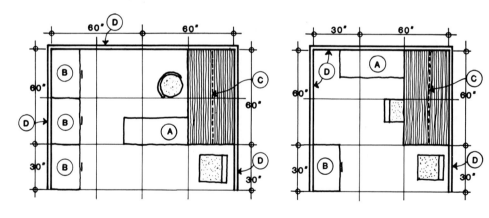

SECRETARIAL STATION   **CLERICAL STATION**

● **LEGEND**

A- 30" x 60" DESK W/42" TYPING RETURN

B- 30" WIDE 2 DRAWER LATERAL FILE (FREE STANDING)

C- 60" WIDE PANEL HUNG FLIPPER DOOR CABINET W/TASK LIGHT UNDER

D- 66" H.± ACCOUSTIC STRUCTURAL PANELS , WIDTH AS NOTED ON PLAN

Fig. 18 Typical work stations: managers and analysts; secretaries and clerks.

Open-Office Landscaping

Figuratively as well as literally, office walls and partitions are tumbling down as architects and interior designers imaginatively implement concepts in new and recycled buildings to achieve more attractive office accommodations, reduced construction costs, and increased space utilization.

The term "open-office landscaping" (OOL) refers to a relatively recent development in the layout and structural arrangement of office space. Its principal feature is space that is free, or almost free, of conventional walls, corridors, private offices, and straight-line passageways between rows of desks and office equipment. Instead, the available space is divided into "clusters" or workcenters, and individual workstations are delineated by high, medium, and low screens and cabinets, plants, bookshelves, modular furniture, and fixtures designed to suppress noise and promote working efficiency. Instead of in rows, desks are arranged at various angles to each other as dictated by the natural lines of work flow and communications.

In the typical landscaped office, eye appeal is also a main objective, but such other environmental considerations as lighting, acoustics, air conditioning, noise abatement, functionally designed furniture, and the use of color and decorations such as plants, statues, and other artwork are incorporated in OOL designs. Apart from environmental considerations, the absence of fixed partitions between workcenters and, in most cases, private offices permits a maximum degree of flexibility in the initial OOL design, as well as making it possible to accommodate new activities, or extend those already in existence, at minimum cost and inconvenience.

OOL Elements

1. A principal feature of OOL is entirely open office space, free of conventional walls and corridors.

2. Workstations comprise movable elements such as desks, chairs, free-standing screens, shelving, files, and foliage usually without relocation of fixed installations such as light fixtures, heating and air conditioning outlets, partitions, or floor covering. Recently, this characteristic of non-changeability of fixed installations has been extensively modified, especially in new offices, but the use of self-contained workcenter modules having built-in ambient and task lighting and access to electric and communication lines located either above the ceiling or below the flooring continue to be interior design trends.

3. Each individual grouping of workstations are arranged without regard for windows or other conventional constraints, in non-uniform fashion, usually dictated by natural lines of information flow and one-to-one personal communication.

4. As originally conceived, the OOL office plan provided for no private offices because privacy could be achieved by the use of foliage and movable sound absorbing screens wired for electricity and sometimes for optionally located telephone and/or computer connections. The original OOL plan has been somewhat modified (referred to as the American Plan) so that higher-echelon executives may have walled-in offices to provide a greater degree of privacy for confidential conferences and concentration and as recognition of their higher organizational status.

5. The status of workers in OOL, as compared with executives, is determined more by their work assignments than by their locations. Upper-echelon personnel, however, may have a greater amount of floor space, a distinctive color of desk top, and possibly a differently shaped desk. Beyond these, there are few visible signs of organizational rank.

6. Perhaps the most significant characteristic of the OOL plan is that it provides flexibility for layouts that shift as work assignments shift. Only simple tools are required to rearrange the panels and component parts that make up each workstation. Furthermore, the cost of relocating the parts of the OOL plan to create new designs is substantially less than the cost of rearranging offices with fixed partitions.

7. Approximately 20 percent fewer light fixtures are needed to light a particular workcenter, since the reduction of walls between offices allows a more efficient placement of the fixtures. Further, it is estimated that a lighting system that is part of an OOL plan reduces energy consumption by about 40 percent.

8. Construction costs are approximately 50 percent lower when using the OOL plan. When the cost of furnishings and equipment is added, the cost differential narrows, since OOL-plan furniture and component parts are somewhat more expensive than traditional office furniture and equipment. It should be noted, however, that the cost is partially offset by the OOL's greater flexibility and the lower cost of later rearrangement.

9. The amount of usable space, expressed as a percentage of the gross available space, is greater than the conventional grid layout with its usual rows of desks, files, etc. In the landscaped office, the usable space may run as high as 80 to 90 percent. This means that square footage under the OOL plan can be reduced by as much as 20 to 30 percent. In turn, the rental cost per square foot of usable space is much less than in a traditional fixed-wall office. To illustrate, through the use of workstations that utilize vertical space for storage, the OOL plan reduces the amount of floor space required for each workstation while at the same time providing for a more efficient work area for the individual.

10. The psychological effect on employees of removing physical barriers is pronounced. Their positive feelings about OOL are manifested in productivity—one measure of the success of the plan. It is contended that when walls are torn down, the communication barriers between managers and employees tend to diminish. Employees in clusters or groupings seem to feel freer to ask questions and come into a supervisor's workstation to discuss problems. Managers and supervisors, too, have more opportunity to observe interactions among employees, since they are less isolated in private offices and more in touch with their workers. See Fig. 19.

Cost Both the initial cost of an OOL-plan application as well as continuing maintenance are lower than those of conventional arrangements, while employee morale has usually improved, except in a few cases where executives have felt that being deprived of a private office has lowered their status in the eyes of their subordinates and peers.

TABLE 2 Open-Office Landscape Design Guidelines

A. Recognize (and act accordingly) that the open plan requires total planning before, during, and after implementation.

B. Consider both present and expected personnel and equipment needs when determining space requirements and layout.

C. Consult with the workers who will be affected by the conversion to the open-plan concept.

D. Educate office personnel about the advantages of the open-plan over the conventional layout office.

E. Face the issue of privacy and noise in relation to the psychological and physiological needs of the workers and those of the organization as a whole.

F. Exercise control over unauthorized rearrangements whereby office workers abuse the open plan by encroaching on their neighbors' space and unnecessarily disturbing others.

G. Locate noisy equipment such as TELEX, word processing printers, and duplicators in well-insulated, enclosed rooms to avoid disturbing others in open-plan modules or enclosures.

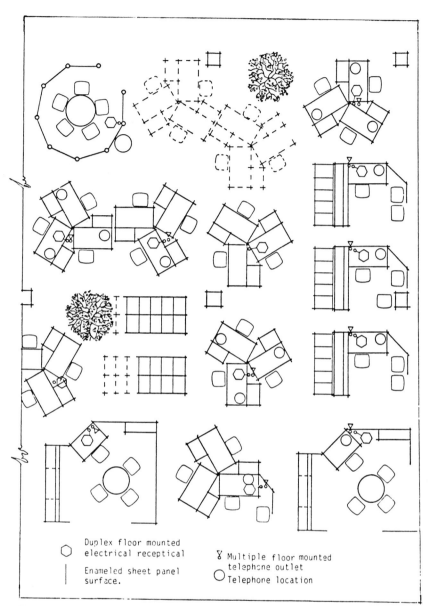

Duplex floor mounted electrical receptical

Enameled sheet panel surface.

Multiple floor mounted telephone outlet

Telephone location

Fig. 19   Example of open-office landscape concept.

OFFICES, GENERAL

Planning

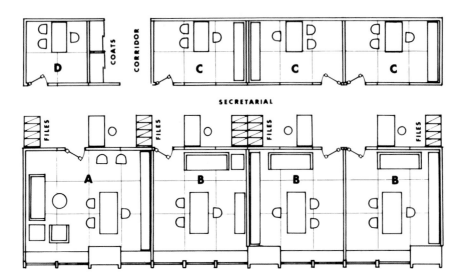

Fig. 20 Typical modular private office plan with secretarial area.

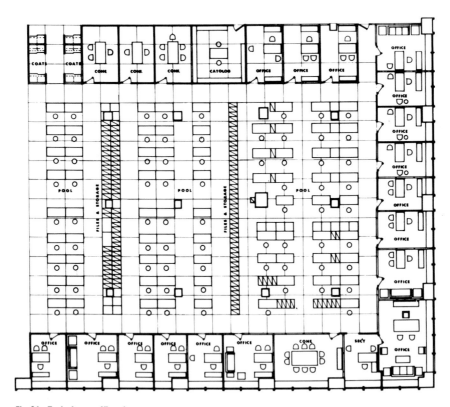

Fig. 21 Typical open office plan.

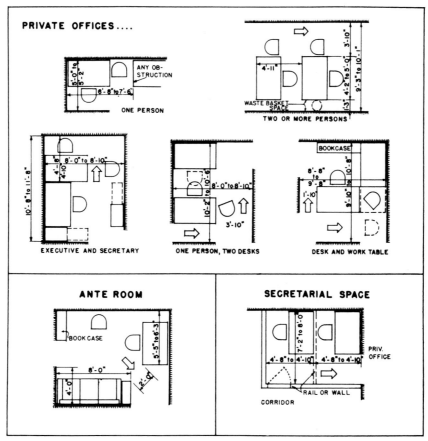

Fig. 1   Clearances in various types of offices.

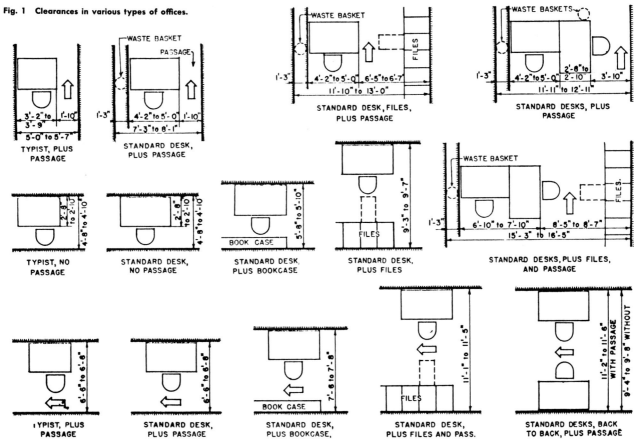

Fig. 2   Desk clearances.

Commercial

OFFICES, GENERAL

Clearances

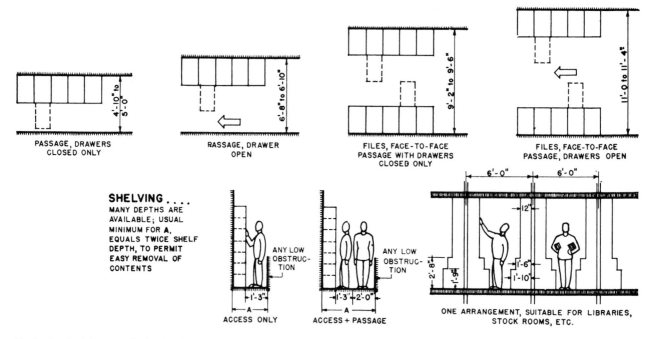

PASSAGE, DRAWERS CLOSED ONLY — 4'-10" to 5'-0"

RASSAGE, DRAWER OPEN — 6'-8" to 6'-10"

FILES, FACE-TO-FACE PASSAGE WITH DRAWERS CLOSED ONLY — 9'-2" to 9'-6"

FILES, FACE-TO-FACE PASSAGE, DRAWERS OPEN — 11'-0 to 11'-4"

SHELVING.... MANY DEPTHS ARE AVAILABLE; USUAL MINIMUM FOR A, EQUALS TWICE SHELF DEPTH, TO PERMIT EASY REMOVAL OF CONTENTS

ANY LOW OBSTRUCTION — 1'-3" — A — ACCESS ONLY

ANY LOW OBSTRUCTION — 1'-3" + 2'-0" — A — ACCESS + PASSAGE

6'-0" — 6'-0" — 12" — 2'-8" — 1'-9" — 1'-6" — 1'-10" — ONE ARRANGEMENT, SUITABLE FOR LIBRARIES, STOCK ROOMS, ETC.

Fig. 3 Standard clearances for legal and letter-sized files.

888

LARGE PUBLIC WASHROOMS

In multiple stall restrooms, be sure: (1) The entry is properly laid out. (2) All passageways are 3'-8" (1118 mm) wide minimum. (3) There is a 5'-0" × 5'-0" (1524 mm × 1524 mm) wheelchair turn around space. Space under the lavatory may be used as part of this space, but only that portion which is clear to a height of 27" (686 mm). (4) The working parts of at least one of each type of dispenser, receptacle and vendor (coin slots, push-buttons, dispenser openings, etc.) are no more than 40" (1016 mm) above the floor. (5) Waste receptacles are recessed into the wall, out of everyone's way. Free-standing, moveable receptacles may block the corridor and become a barrier for the handicapped.

Usually the end toilet compartment is designed to accommodate the handicapped. The door is outswinging and hinged on the wall side to avoid interference with other compartments.

Toilet compartments for the handicapped should be at least 38" (965 mm) wide for front entry and 42" (1067 mm) wide for side entry compartments and have 4'-0" (1219 mm) of clear space in front of the toilet to allow the wheelchair to enter and the door to close.

Toilet compartments with side entry require a wider door than those having front entry to provide additional turning space for wheelchairs. Side entry compartments may occupy the entire end of the room when room width does not permit sufficient depth for a front entry toilet compartment for the handicapped.

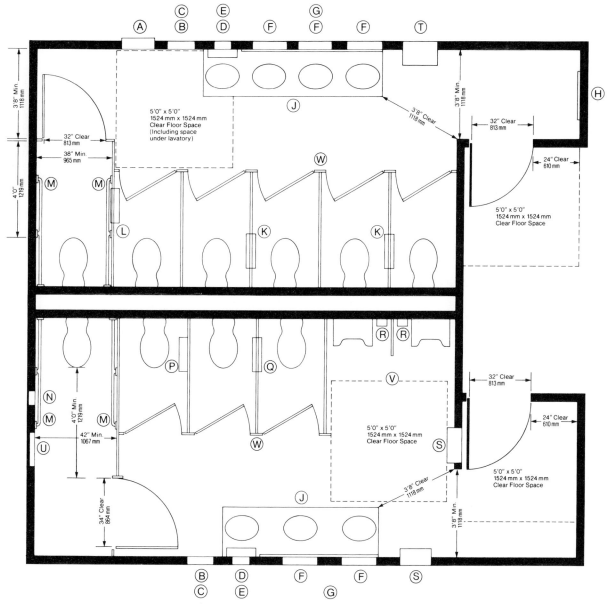

Legend

A Recessed Feminine Napkin-Tampon Vendor
B Recessed Waste Receptacle
C Recessed Paper Towel Dispenser
D Recessed Soap Dispenser
E Fixed Tilt Mirror 16" × 30" (406 mm × 762 mm)
F Multi-Purpose Unit with Paper Towel Dispenser and Soap Dispenser
G Mirror
H Full Length Mirror 24" × 60" (610 mm × 1524 mm)
J Laminated Plastic Countertop. Mounting height 34" (864 mm) from countertop to floor; 30" (762 mm) clear from bottom of 4" (102 mm) apron to floor
K Partition Mounted Toilet Seat Cover Dispenser, Feminine Napkin Disposal, Toilet Tissue Dispenser
L Partition Mounted Toilet Seat Cover Dispenser, Feminine Napkin Disposal, Toilet Tissue Dispenser
M Wheelchair Toilet Compartment Grab Bar, 1½" (38 mm) diameter, 1½" (38 mm) clearance from wall
N Recessed Multi-Roll Toilet Tissue Dispenser (below bar)

P Surface Mounted Toilet Seat Cover Dispenser, Roll Toilet Tissue Dispenser
Q Partition Mounted Toilet Seat Cover Dispenser, Roll Toilet Tissue Dispenser
R Stainless Steel Wall Mounted Ash Tray
S Recessed Waste Receptacle
T Recessed Waste Receptacle
U Recessed Toilet Seat Cover Dispenser
V Laminated Plastic Wall Hung Urinal Screen
W Ceiling Hung Laminated Plastic Toilet Compartments

Commercial
WASHROOM FACILITIES

SMALL OR PRIVATE WASHROOMS

All three of these washrooms are usable by those in wheelchairs.

Each has a 5'-0" × 5'-0" (1524 mm × 1524 mm) clear turn around space. Area under the lavatory may be used as part of this space, but only that portion which is clear to a height of 27" (686 mm).

Do not obstruct approach to a toilet by using a wall to floor grab bar. When side walls are not within arm's reach, use a horizontal grab bar on the wall behind the toilet. The design on the lower left is particularly well suited for hospital use.

As a safety measure, it is recommended that horizontal grab bars be installed in place of towel bars. Every horizontal grab bar can serve as a towel bar, but a towel bar and its wall attachment are *not* designed to function as a grab bar.

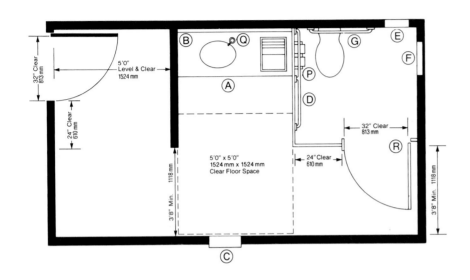

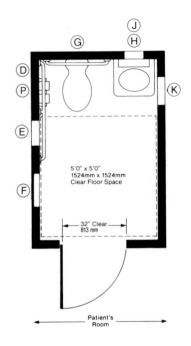

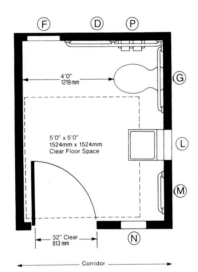

Note: These illustrations represent layouts using the minimum space to meet code requirements when outswinging doors are used. The door should swing into another room such as a patient's room in a hospital, a hotel room, an office, or an entry way and not into a corridor.

If a small washroom is located off a corridor, it is recommended that the door swing into the washroom and that the size of the room be increased to provide the required 5'-0" x 5'-0" (1524 mm x 1524 mm) clear space inside the washroom. A door that swings into a corridor or passageway is a hazard to everyone.

Scale: ¼" = 1'-0"

Legend
A Laminated Plastic Vanity Center. Includes Paper Towel Dispenser and Waste Receptacle. Mounting height 34" (864 mm) from countertop to floor
B Mirror 60" × 36" (1524 mm × 914 mm)
C Recessed Feminine Napkin-Tampon Vendor
D Horizontal Grab Bar, 48" (1219 mm) long, 1½" (38 mm) diameter, 1½" (38 mm) clearance from wall
E Recessed Feminine Napkin Disposal (below bar)

F Recessed Toilet Seat Cover Dispenser
G Horizontal Grab Bar, 30" (762 mm) long, 1½" (38 mm) diameter, 1½" (38 mm) clearance from wall
H Recessed Soap Dispenser
J Fixed Tilt Mirror 16" × 30" (406 mm × 762 mm)
K Recessed Paper Towel Dispenser and Waste Receptacle
L Recessed Hospital Console Unit
M Horizontal Towel Bar/Grab Bar, 18" (457

mm) long, 1¼" (32 mm) diameter, 1½" (38 mm) clearance from wall
N Recessed Waste Receptacle
P Surface Mounted Roll Toilet Tissue Dispenser, without controlled delivery (below bar)
Q Lavatory Mounted Soap Dispenser
R Ceiling Hung Laminated Plastic Toilet Compartment

The eight basic elements of a medical office are:

1. Receptionist—control station—business office
2. Waiting room
3. Consultation room
4. Examination and treatment room
5. Laboratory including EKG and BMR
6. X-ray
7. Utility and service areas
8. Toilet

A medical practice facility can have no fixed, ideal plan. First, no two individuals or groups of individuals think alike or work alike. Second, the physical and geographical limitations which characterize a medical practice facility, whether for a new building, a remodeled building, or rental space, do not permit the adoption of any single plan. Each facility must be custom-made to express the individuality and to satisfy the working habits of those who will use it.

The eight basic elements found in nearly all medical offices can be thought of as the "building blocks." While these eight elements may change in size and shape depending on methods of operation, they are always integrated in the medical practice facility, or their counterpart is conveniently available (Fig. 1).

In the following pages will be found draw-

A Planning Guide for Physicians' Medical Facilities, edited by the American Medical Association and published through a grant made by the Sears-Roebuck Foundation.

ings and explanations of each of the eight elements, and further examples of how they can be combined and expanded.

1. RECEPTION AND BUSINESS OFFICE

The receptionist, who, in the small medical practice facility is also the doctor's assistant, the bookkeeper, and the bill collector, is the hub around which the office revolves. She should be so placed that she can keep an eye on all the workings of the office. She should see and acknowledge the arrival of the patient and must follow the progress of the doctor so that the patient flow has proper direction. If she discusses bills and appointments, the space should be large enough for others besides herself, and private enough that her conversations are not generally overheard.

For the larger office the functions mentioned above may be split among two, three or even more persons. The receptionist still should be able to see the entrance and the waiting room. If she is too far removed to watch the progress of the doctor she has to be informed by the nurse assistant of this progress so she can keep the flow of patients coming.

If there is a separate business manager-bookkeeper, a private space should be provided for working on records, and discussing bills with patients. It is advisable this office be located so that it is accessible to outgoing patients. The exit from this office should permit patients to leave without backtracking, or

going through the waiting room. Proper relationship to the entrance will also assist in the control of deliveries to the office (Fig. 2).

2. RECEPTION—WAITING ROOM

The patients receive their first impression from the waiting room. Its appearance may indicate the type of care they can expect to receive. A wait in a crowded, out-of-date room can depress and disgruntle even the best and steadiest of patients.

The chairs, tables, and lamps should be adequate in number and well spaced so as to make reading possible and to give the patients a feeling of freedom. The patient load provides the only criterion for the number of chairs you must provide. If the schedule is always well maintained, the waiting area need only be a minimum. If the doctor is burdened with emergency calls and extended house or hospital calls, then the waiting room should be more ample.

Needless to say, some educated thought should be given to decoration: the walls, upholstery, pictures, and drapes. Tasteful, harmonizing colors which are cheery rather than drab are desirable. The overall effect should be homelike and restful.

The waiting room preferably should permit a view of the outside and, if possible, the view should be a pleasing one. Flowers, trees, or distance are the best, but when this is impossible an interesting view of people and activity is the second choice (Fig. 3).

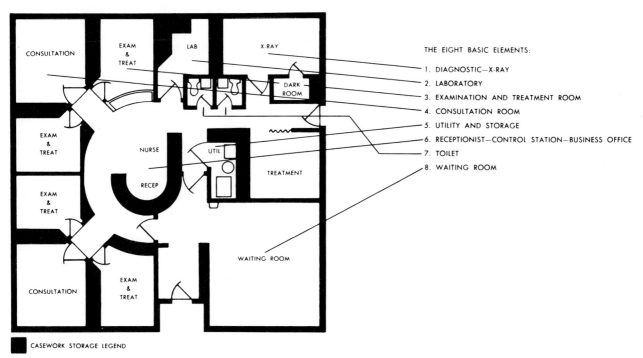

THE EIGHT BASIC ELEMENTS:

1. DIAGNOSTIC—X-RAY
2. LABORATORY
3. EXAMINATION AND TREATMENT ROOM
4. CONSULTATION ROOM
5. UTILITY AND STORAGE
6. RECEPTIONIST—CONTROL STATION—BUSINESS OFFICE
7. TOILET
8. WAITING ROOM

CASEWORK STORAGE LEGEND

Fig. 1

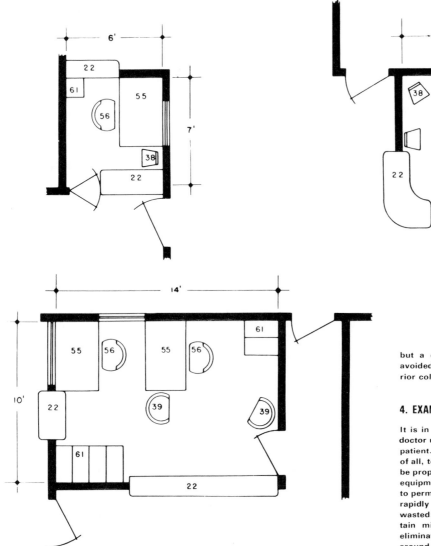

Fig. 2 Reception and business office.

The waiting room should be removed from the actual office activity. It should not be a thoroughfare for traffic, nor should it be an office for the discussion of bills and appointments between the receptionist or office manager and patients. If one enters the office directly from out-of-doors, it is well to have a lobby to prevent drafts. If the business office opens on the lobby, it may well serve to receive the incomer and to determine his business. This, in turn, allows some to be directed to the waiting room and others to be taken directly to the doctor without incurring hurt feelings and arguments from patients in the waiting room.

3. CONSULTATION ROOM

This space is generally the stopping point, at some time, for all patients passing through the office. The patient is usually directed there first for a discussion of symptoms and progress and for simple examinations. He is then sent to an examination or treatment room, from which he may return to the consultation room for further discussion and prescription. However, there seems to be a trend to simplify and speed up this procedure, in a majority of instances, by concentrating the entire patient visit to the examination room.

This enables the physician to utilize another room for patient examination and treatment.

The theory that all space be used for examination and treatment or for purely professional use has merit. However, the average examining room is sparsely equipped and very impersonal. Patient discussions and diagnostic reviews are better handled in more comfortable and professional surroundings. A properly furnished consultation room can have a beneficial effect on both the patient and the physician. In addition physicians are called on by many professional detail men and other individuals in the medical field. Such contacts are better handled in a nicely furnished—but not elaborate—consultation room.

The consultation room need not be spacious, but a cramped, closed-in feeling should be avoided. Tasteful furniture, pictures and interior colors are desirable (Fig. 4).

4. EXAMINING AND TREATMENT ROOM

It is in this room, with its variations, that the doctor usually has his closest contact with the patient. This is his workroom. It needs, first of all, to be efficient. In other words, it should be properly and adequately lighted, with all the equipment necessary placed in such a way as to permit the doctor and his assistants to work rapidly and easily. Here space cannot be wasted; neither can it be reduced beyond a certain minimum. Unnecessary steps must be eliminated; yet there should be room to move around easily and without interference.

This is one room in which the design must be determined by the needs and the working habits of the doctor. These must be investigated carefully and thoroughly in order that he may have what best meets his needs and desires. While he has been trained to do many things well, despite adverse conditions and scanty equipment, there is no need to handicap him on his home grounds.

Seldom is one examination or treatment room enough. Two rooms can often more than double the doctor's capacity, and some doctors have as many as eight. Where there are several rooms, patients can be prepared ahead of time by the assistants. Furthermore, a number of procedures can be handled by the assistants, on direction of the doctor, while he is putting his time to better use with other patients. When this practice is followed intelligently and it does not slip into an impersonal production line technique, it results in increased efficiency.

Where the examination-treatment room is used for most of the doctor-patient contacts, it is necessary to provide a few things not formerly found there. It is also necessary to provide for the patients' comfort and convenience. For the doctor, a desk or writing space, and perhaps a satisfactory chair for use during discussions with the patient, may be ample additions.

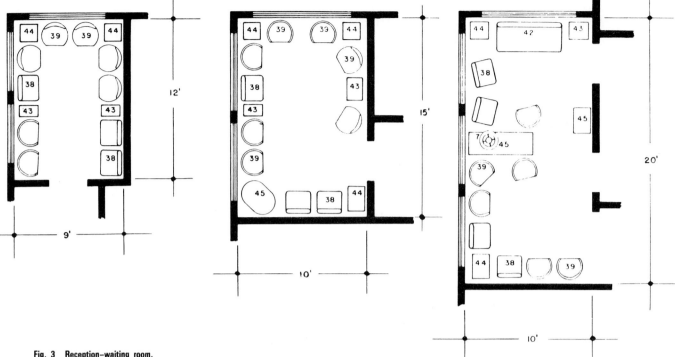

Fig. 3 Reception–waiting room.

For the patient, dressing facilities, cubicle, mirror, clothes hooks, slippers, chairs or low bench in or immediately adjacent to the examination-treatment room are a great convenience. A comfortable chair, magazines, and an ash tray are also advisable to ease the patients' waiting time when the doctor is delayed with some other patient (Fig. 5).

5. LABORATORY

This room varies from a few shelves, sink, sterilizer, etc., in the corner of the examination room to a complete laboratory in a separate room.

In the smaller office it is best combined with other uses for the saving of space and of steps. The nurses' workroom, the store room, the recovery room, and a spare examination room are all possible elements which can, under certain conditions, be combined with the lab-

oratory. The ideal, of course, is a room designed for specific laboratory procedures with adequate equipment and supplies. However, the extent to which each doctor desires to carry on his own procedures determines the extent to which this ideal is approached.

In planning laboratory space, it is best to keep two factors in mind. A common mistake is to provide too little counter space, so be generous with it. Secondly, regardless of size, laboratory space should be contiguous with toilet facilities and a pass-through should be provided between the two areas (Fig. 6).

6. X-RAY

If the doctor is planning to use an x-ray machine, provisions for housing it must be made in the planning stage. It is best to decide early exactly what kind of x-ray, darkroom, and

developing equipment the doctor will buy. The planning representatives of the manufacturers can be a part of the planning team then, working closely with the architect or consultant in the preliminary stages of planning.

Nearly all state and city codes now require lead or concrete protection in all interior walls and doors of rooms housing x-ray equipment. If spaces above or below are inhabited, protection is also required in floors and ceilings. Exterior walls need not be protected.

Likewise, there are rather stringent code requirements for the wiring of x-ray rooms and equipment—including separate entrance service in many cases. This should be checked carefully. In most cases, the manufacturer's representative will be familiar with wiring requirements, but if he is not a local resident, he may not be familiar with all the local rules. For this reason, it is best to have this reviewed independently. If a pass-through system is to

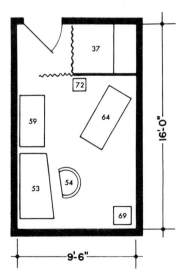

Fig. 4 Consultation room.

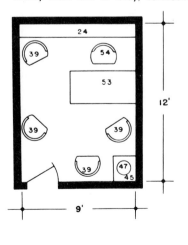

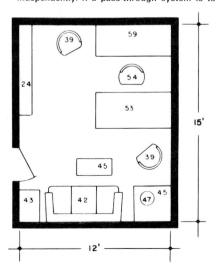

MEDICAL OFFICES

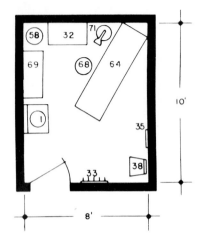

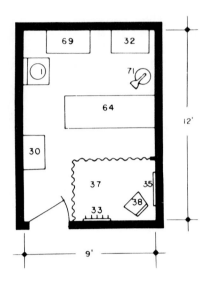

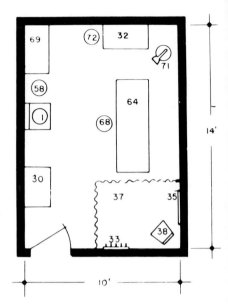

Fig. 5 Examining and treatment room.

be installed, or the through-wall immediate developing system used, the viewing room must be located adjacent to that wall of the darkroom (Fig. 7).

7. UTILITY AND SERVICE AREAS

The location of utility and service areas should be planned carefully in every medical building. These areas include:

Utility Room In a one-story building this room should contain heating and air-conditioning equipment, hot water heater, janitor's sink and space for janitor's supplies. Some states will require separation of the janitor's space from the heating space. This room should not be more than 15 to 20 ft from an outside wall unless the compressor is to be on the roof. Size of the room will depend on the equipment size, and this should be carefully checked in prelimi-

nary planning. A pegboard wall will be handy in the janitor's area. Some states will require one or two fire wall partitions and a fire door in this room.

Storage Spaces Storage and utility space must be provided for patient wraps, staff wraps, utility paper goods and towels, office supplies, old files, and treatment and medicinal needs for at least one full day in each workroom. Casework walls in treatment rooms, laboratory, EKG and BMR room, cast room, and other workrooms, with self-contained sink and counter top, will largely solve the latter problem. The other closets and storage spaces will have to be located convenient to the place of principal use.

Lavatory Rooms The number is dependent upon convenience desired and the expense the doctor wishes to undertake. Facilities adjacent to the waiting room for patients, in the work

area for staff, and at least one adjoining the laboratory are all desirable. The doctor must decide how many he wants in relation to the cost. Wall hung stools and lavatories are recommended.

EQUIPMENT LIST

The numbers appearing in the drawings refer to the equipment list below. This list should be used in conjunction with the diagrams.

1. Lavatory with mirror and towel bar
2. Sink with gooseneck spout
3. Water closet
4. Shower stall
5. Gas line
6. Air line
7. Vacuum line

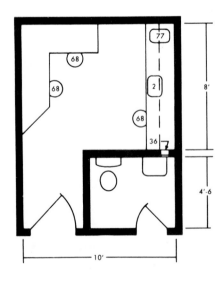

Fig. 6 Laboratory.

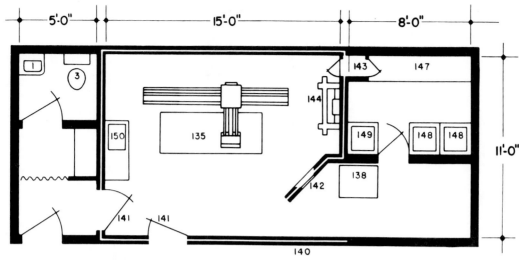

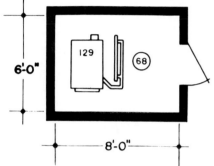

Fig. 7 X-ray.

8. Piped oxygen
9. Sink disposal unit
10. Sterilizers—stills, etc.
11. Ceiling light
12. Convenience outlets, 110
13. Convenience outlets, 220
14. Wall light
15. Intercom systems and buzzer calls
16. Telephone system
17. Heating controls
18. Air-conditioning controls
19. Radiological devices
20. Special operating lights
21. Room dividers
22. Receptionist's desk and counter
23. Special desk
24. Bookcases
25. Counter open where stool is shown
26. Backsplash
27. Reagent shelf
28. Wall hung shelf
29. Wall cabinet
30. Wall hung charting desk
31. Instrument case
32. Equipment table or stand
33. Hook strip
34. Dressing table with mirror
35. Mirror
36. Specimen passbox
37. Dressing cubicle
38. Straight chair
39. Occasional chair
40. Easy chair
41. Love seat
42. Sectional seat
43. End table
44. Magazine table
45. Occasional table

46. Floor lamp
47. Table lamp
48. Costumer
49. Umbrella rack
50. Toy cabinet
51. Play desk
52. Children's chair
53. Executive's desk
54. Executive's desk chair
55. Secretary's desk
56. Secretary's chair
57. Bookcase
58. Waste receptacle
59. Work table
60. Desk lamp
61. Filing cabinet
62. Supply cabinet
63. Step stool
64. Treatment table
65. Treatment chair-table
66. Physiotherapy table
67. Couch
68. Adjustable stool
69. Instrument and supply cabinet
70. Instrument sterilizers
71. Examining light
72. Waste receptacle with foot lever
73. Clinical scale
74. Industrial treatment chair
75. Refrigerator (biological)
76. Pegboard with drip pan
77. Pressure sterilizer
78. Incubator
79. Serological water bath
80. Paraffin oven
81. Laboratory table
82. Centrifuge
83. Bunsen burner
84. Hot plate
85. Basal metabolism apparatus
86. Electrocardiograph
87. Portable operating light
88. Operating table
89. Mayo table
90. Specialist's chair
91. Cabinet with suction pump and compressed air
92. Ultraviolet lamp
93. Infra-red lamp
94. Diathermy short wave unit
95. Electrosurgical unit
96. Audiometer
97. Accessory table
98. Woods light
99. Baby scale
100. Examining table
101. Urological x-ray table

102. Irrigator unit
103. Proctoscopic examining table
104. Irrigator unit
105. Instrument and supply cabinet with suction apparatus
106. Galvanic unit
107. Plaster cart
108. Wheelchair
109. Whirlpool bath
110. Paraffin bath
111. Stall bars
112. Shoulder wheel
113. Pulley weights
114. Timing device
115. Couch
116. Reading light
117. Eye operating light
118. Greens' refractor
119. Binocular ophthalmoscope
120. Lens case on cabinet
121. Vertometer
122. Vision chart
123. Tangent screen
124. Chin rest
125. Slit lamp
126. Kertometer
127. Troposcope or synoptophore
128. Perimeter
129. Fluoroscope
130. Film illuminator
131. Stereoscope
132. Movable lead-lined screen
133. Film filing cabinets
134. Film storage bin
135. Radiographic and fluoroscopic combination unit
136. Superficial x-ray therapy unit
137. Deep therapy unit
138. Control unit (current control)
139. Movable lead-lined screen
140. Lead protection
141. Lead-lined door (lightproof)
142. Leaded glass view window
143. Cassette pass box
144. Cassette changer
145. Film dryer
146. Storage cabinet (4½ ft high)
147. Loading counter with film storage bin and cabinets below, safe light and film rack above
148. Developing tank with (size)—(timer) and (safe light) above
149. Film washing tank, with illuminator above; without illuminator above
150. Barium sink in counter, cabinet below, recessed cabinet above
151. Folding screen

Commercial

MEDICAL OFFICES
Radiology

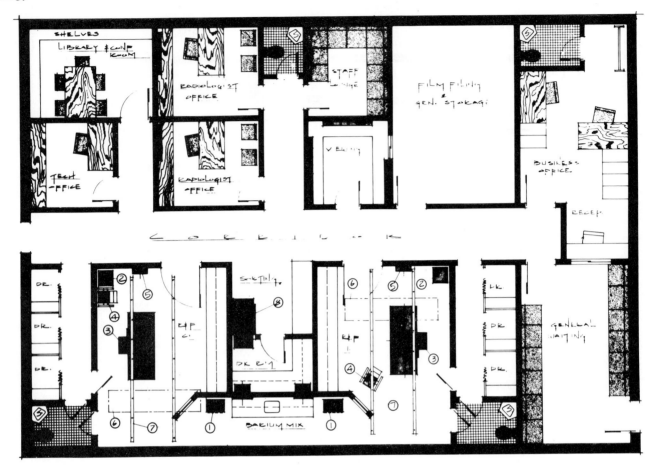

Equipment list
1. Control
2. X-ray transformer
3. Table
4. TV monitor on mobile cart
5. Cassette holder
6. Overhead tube conveyor
7. Ceiling-mounted rails
8. Autoprocessor

Fig. 1   Typical radiologist's office.

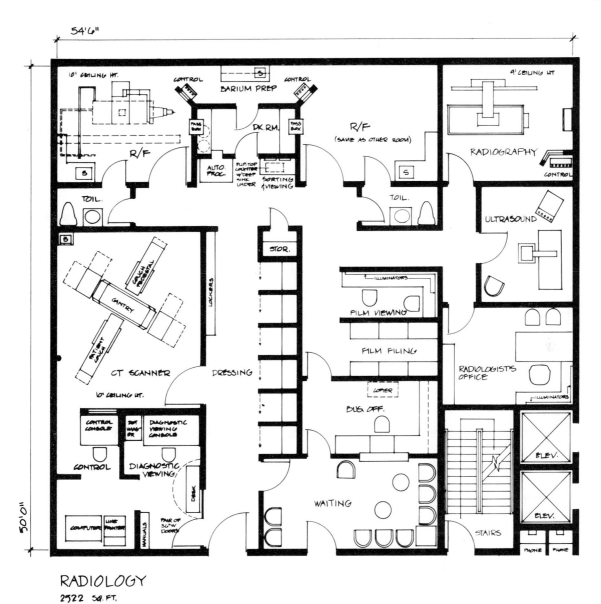

RADIOLOGY
2522 SQ. FT.

Fig. 2   Suite plan for radiology, 2522 square feet.

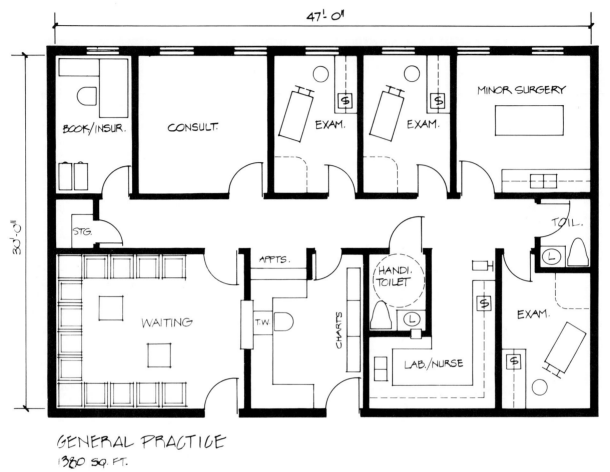

GENERAL PRACTICE
1380 SQ. FT.

Fig. 3 Suite plan for general practice, 1380 square feet.

TABLE 1 Analysis of Program: General Practice

No. of Physicians:	1	2	3
Consultation	12 × 12 = 144	2 @ 12 × 12 = 288	3 @ 12 × 12 = 432
Exam Rooms	3 @ 8 × 12 = 288	6 @ 8 × 12 = 576	9 @ 8 × 12 = 864
Waiting Room	12 × 14 = 168	14 × 18 = 252	20 × 24 = 480
Business Office	12 × 14 = 168	14 × 16 = 224	18 × 30 = 540[a]
Nurse Station	8 × 10 = 80	10 × 12 = 120	12 × 12 = 144
Toilets	2 @ 5 × 6 = 60	2 @ 5 × 6 = 60	3 @ 5 × 6 = 90
Storage	4 × 6 = 24	6 × 8 = 48	8 × 10 = 80
Cast Room	Use Minor Surgery	Use Minor Surgery	12 × 12 = 144
EKG	Use Minor Surgery	Use Minor Surgery	8 × 12 = 96
Staff Lounge	—	8 × 12 = 96	10 × 12 = 120
Minor Surgery	12 × 12 = 144	12 × 12 = 144	12 × 12 = 144
X-ray Area[b]	—	12 × 20 = 240	12 × 20 = 240
Laboratory	—	8 × 10 = 80	16 × 16 = 256[c]
Subtotal	1076 ft²	2128 ft²	3630 ft²
15% Circulation	161	319	545
Total	1237 ft²	2447 ft²	4175 ft²

[a]Includes insurance clerk, bookkeeper, and office manager.
[b]Includes darkroom, control, film filing, and dressing area.
[c]Includes lab, waiting, and blood draw.

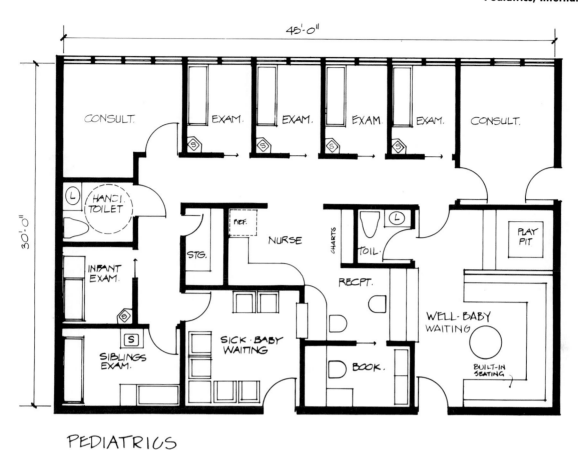

PEDIATRICS

1350 SQ. FT.

Fig. 4   Suite plan for pediatrics, 1350 square feet.

INTERNAL MEDICINE   2238 SQ. FT.

Fig. 5   Suite plan for internal medicine, 2238 square feet.

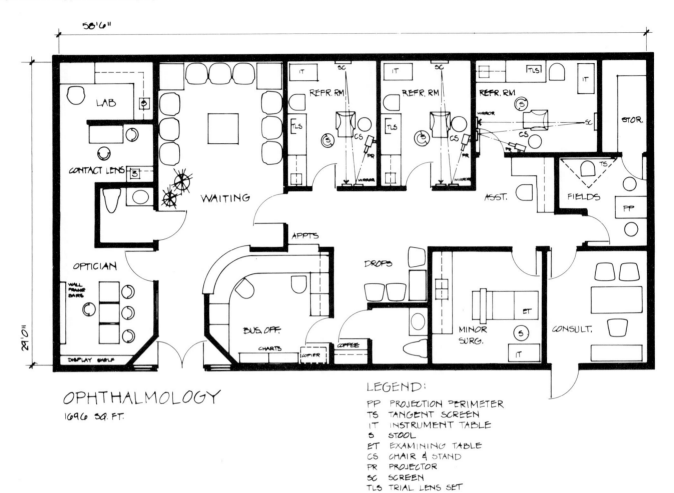

OPHTHALMOLOGY
1696 SQ. FT.

LEGEND:
PP PROJECTION PERIMETER
TS TANGENT SCREEN
IT INSTRUMENT TABLE
S   STOOL
ET EXAMINING TABLE
CS CHAIR & STAND
PR PROJECTOR
SC SCREEN
TLS TRIAL LENS SET

Fig. 6 Suite plan for ophthalmology, 1696 square feet.

PLASTIC SURGERY
2750 SQ. FT.

Fig. 7 Suite plan for plastic surgery, 2750 square feet.

GENERAL SURGERY
2747 SQ FT.

Fig. 8 Suite plan for general surgery, 2747 square feet.

ORTHOPEDIC SURGERY
2257 SQ. FT.

Fig. 9 Suite plan for orthopedic surgery, 2257 square feet.

Commercial
DENTAL OFFICES

By MARVIN CUTLER, AID

ELEMENTS OF A DENTAL OFFICE

Reception (waiting area)
Business office
Auxiliary business area
Consultation or study areas
Audiovisual, patient education
Hygienist (variable)
Treatment rooms (variable)
Laboratory (variable)
Darkroom
X-ray (variable)
Sterilizing area (variable)
Staff lounge
Preventive area (patient education)

Environment and the Professional Image

The dentist, as opposed to a physician (unless a specialist), is *locked* into his environment. In order for a dentist to treat his patient, he must use extensive tools and dental equipment which require fixed or semifixed plumbing and other built-in operating instruments and services. The plumbing services that are necessary to facilitate the operation are water (filtered), air (dry, filtered), suction (wet or dry), waste (vented), and electricity. These are basic and essential input and output elements.

The proper location of services to be performed is essential. The relationship, volume, and use of each area will vary according to individual concepts and needs. Whether the dentist is a general practitioner or a specialist, training and developed concepts or working habits vary, often greatly (Fig. 1).

With the advent of semifixed or flexible equipment, the dentist can change or modify his operative procedures. Recent years have seen radical changes in dental concepts. Government participation through health, educa-

tion, and welfare programs has made dental services readily available to large numbers of the population. This has caused the dentist to expand his facilities and increase the number of auxiliary and paradental personnel. As a result of both the increase in patients and the constantly changing dental concepts, the need for flexibility in the office is essential.

Reception

The ideal area for a single practitioner should be approximately 150 sq ft minimum, with three walls unbroken by doorways. This allows perimeter of space for maximum seating of five

to seven people. Lighting should be incandescent and diffuse. Both recessed and below-ceiling light sources should be used.

Business Office or Secretarial Area

This is the key or control point in the management of the office. The drawing (Fig. 2) reflects the position the receptionist assumes in relation to waiting area. Full visual control is maintained through closed sliding glass window. Appointment and financial arrangements are consummated at this point. All traffic and flow control is regulated by the nurse/secretary.

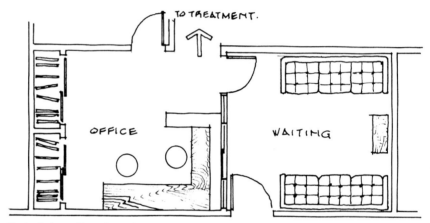

Fig. 2   Business office and reception room.

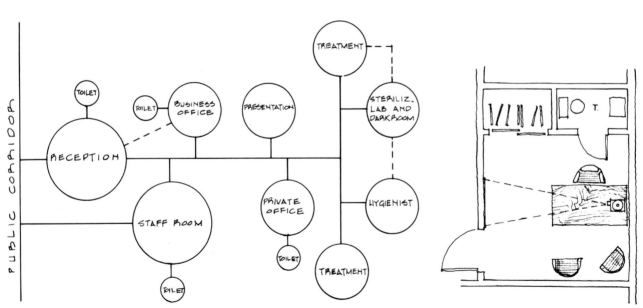

Fig. 1   Dental office flow diagram.

Fig. 3   Private office.

Private Office

In many offices the private consultation room serves multiple functions, particularly in the last few years, when the cost of space has become so prohibitive and the doctor is interested in increasing the number of treatment rooms within a small overall space. Consultation room desks may take on several shapes, depending on the practice concept of the doctor. He may wish to maintain a formal relationship whereby he faces the patient, who sits opposite the desk. He may prefer an informal arrangement where he and the patient sit around a "table" rather than a formal desk. Active study models and diagnostic models should be located in shallow desk drawers in the desk or in the nearby storage system (Fig. 3).

Treatment Room

The heart of any dental practice is the treatment room. Storage, instrumentation, and comfortable arrangement of equipment and instru-

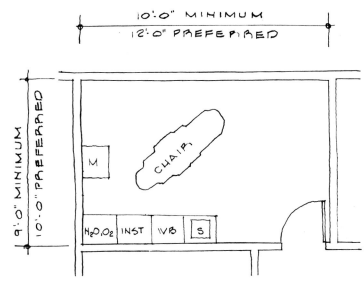

Fig. 4   Treatment room.

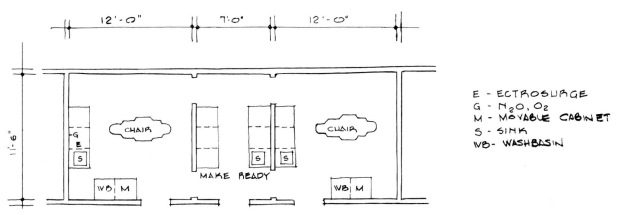

Fig. 5   Treatment rooms.

E - ECTROSURGE
G - H_2O, O_2
M - MOVABLE CABINET
S - SINK
WB- WASHBASIN

ments vary with each doctor and doctor's concept as well as with field conditions. The main consideration is to permit the doctor to work in a stressless or comfortable working position and environment. The use and placement of one or two sinks depend upon doctor's concept. Figures 4 and 5 show us a fair amount of storage for supplies and instruments. Adequate work space and counter permits doctor to do bench work without interfering with his chair-side assistant. During the past few years, doctors have experienced a constant change in concepts. Therefore, a degree of flexibility must be reflected in the planning. A mobile instrument cabinet can be tucked under the counter. This is necessary to allow doctor a greater degree of change in his position while treating his patient. The emphasis in the treatment room should be on efficiency, ease of maintenance, and a pleasant atmosphere for the patient, doctor, and staff.

Hygienist's Room

Although the size and function of the hygienist's room may differ from those of the regular treatment room, it is not uncommon to equip this room in the same way as the regular treat-

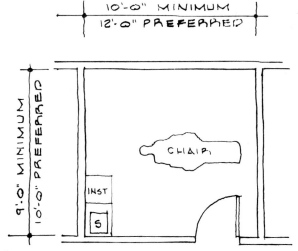

Fig. 6   Hygienist's room.

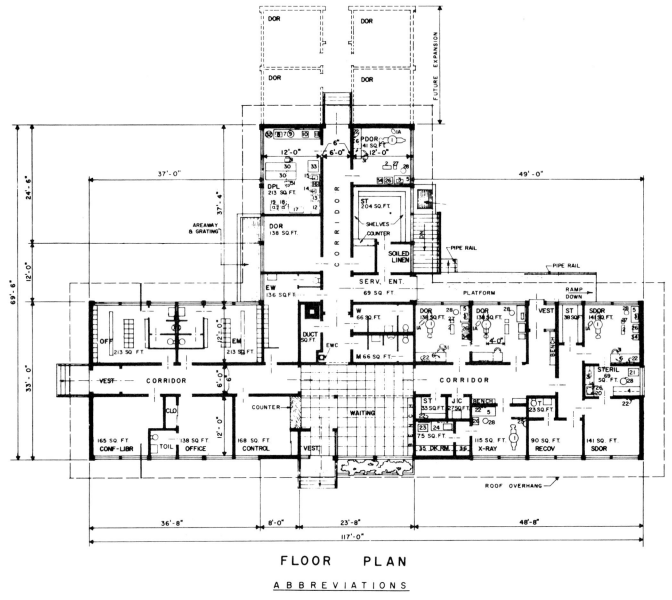

FLOOR PLAN

ABBREVIATIONS

ADMIN	— ADMINISTRATION	OFF	— OFFICERS	
CONF - LIBR	— CONFERENCE - LIBRARY	PDOR	— PROSTHETICS DENTAL OPERATING ROOM	
DK RM	— DARK ROOM	RECOV	— RECOVERY	
DOR	— DENTAL OPERATING ROOM	SDOR	— SURGICAL DENTAL OPERATING ROOM	
DPL	— DENTAL PROSTHETICS	ST	— STORAGE	
EM	— ENLISTED MEN	STERIL	— STERILIZATION ROOM	
E W	— ENLISTED WOMEN	T	— TOILET	
J C	— JANITOR'S CLOSET	VEST	— VESTIBULE	
M	— MEN	W	— WOMEN	

Fig. 7 Dental clinic plan.

ment rooms. This will allow the dentist to use this room, when needed, as an additional treatment room (Fig. 6).

Sterilizing Area

The location of the sterilizing area is determined by various factors: dental procedural concepts, the available space in the office, and the psychological image the doctor wishes to obtain. The materials used here should be about the same as those in the laboratory. There should be adequate storage space for

trays and supplies, including the pre-prepared trays as well as those which will be cleaned up at various intervals during the normal working day. The autoclave should be placed out of the reach of children, and the ultrasonic cleaners can be used more efficiently if recessed into the work-counter tops.

The size and location of support areas such as sterilizing, laboratory, dark room, x-ray area, etc., will depend in part on doctor's *concept* as well as the logistics of the space. A small laboratory unit is merely used for model pouring, trimming, and storage. The size of many

labs is often larger to accommodate expanded technical skills and services. Some doctors split lab duties into two areas.

In conclusion, the dental office is a professional home. Like it or not, the dentist spends the most productive years of his life in it—more than half his waking moments. The office does, therefore, reflect his personality as well as his professional image. It can either assist the doctor to aspire to greater success and satisfaction, or it can sentence him to a professional life of mediocrity and apathy.

Figure 7 shows a plan for a dental clinic.

GENERAL DENTISTRY

Office Circulation Patterns

The traffic flow within a dental office is from waiting room to X-ray (either a special room for this purpose or located in a standard operatory) to operatory. The patient should be able to enter the operatory and sit down on the right side of the chair (for a right-handed dentist) without walking around the chair or through the assistant's work area (Fig. 8). At the end of the procedure the patient walks to the reception area, repairs makeup or combs hair at the vanity or in the toilet room, books a future appointment if required, and pays for services.

The dentist's circulation is from private office to operatory and between operatories. He or she should be able to enter the operatory without having to walk around the chair or through the assistant's work area, wash hands, and be seated on the patient's right (if he or she is right-handed), as in Fig. 8. The assistant's path is from the sterilizing area to the operatories, darkroom, and lab. The assistant (also called the auxiliary), in most cases, will have to walk the greater distance in order to reach her work area since it is more important to maximize production that the dentists have the shortest route (Fig. 9, Plans A, C, D, and Fig. 10, Plan F). The office should be laid out to save as many steps as possible. Since the dentist and assistant are working in such confined areas, it is critical that these spaces be well planned and efficient. As with a medical office, a dental office should have a private entrance/exit for the staff and dentists so that they do not have to pass through the waiting room.

The Dental Assistant

The dental assistant or auxiliary performs many duties. Among them are cleanup of operatories, seating of patients in dental chair, preparing tray setups, taking X-rays, sterilizing instruments, loading anesthetic syringes, pouring impressions, mixing amalgams, charting and numbering teeth, handling suction, air, and water syringe, and assisting the dentist in dozens of restorative and surgical procedures.

Design Operatories for Flexibility

A right-handed dentist will work to the patient's right and a left-handed dentist to the patient's left. Traditionally, operatories were designed either for a right-handed dentist *or* a left-handed one. Today, flexibility is the key. New equipment is designed to accommodate change. In a practice composed of right-handed and left-handed dentists, an *ambidextrous* operatory can be designed (Fig. 11) in which the utilities are brought up under the toe of the chair and are mounted near the chair on a swing-away bracket that is designed to swing to either the left or the right of the chair. The X-ray head should be mounted over the fixed cabinet behind the patient, and the mobile cabinet used by the assistant may be used on either side of the chair. The mobile cabinet would slide into an opening in the fixed cabinet when not in use, and the hoses for water, compressed air, and suction would come from the wall behind the fixed cabinet or from a swing-away bracket

on the chair, negating the need for a mobile cabinet.

Size of Operatories

Operatories may be as small as 8×10 feet or as large as 10×12 feet, 100 square feet is the average size. Figure 12 shows the minimum distances between the dental chair, cabinetry, and perimeter of the room. Dentists used to prefer small operatories when they worked alone so that while seated (or standing) they could reach everything they needed without walking. Now that most dentists use an assistant and the trend is toward longer appointments (it is more efficient to do a lot of work at one sitting), many dentists feel more comfortable working in a large operatory. If the dentist uses large mobile cabinets, a more spacious operatory is desirable so that the cabinets can easily be moved to any position in the room.

Number of Operatories

There is no rule governing the number of operatories per dentist since the dentist's temperament and practice methods have a lot to do with it. A dentist who works slowly or who does a lot of restorative work with long appointments can be comfortable with two operatories. A dentist with many short appointments will need four operatories in order not to lose time during the change of patients and the preparation or cleanup of operatories. A rule of thumb is three operatories per dentist in a general practice.

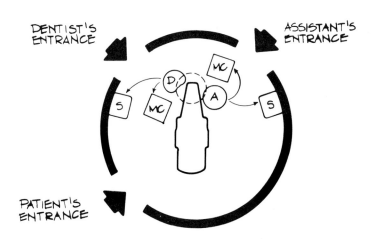

LEGEND

D = DENTIST
A = ASSISTANT
MC = MOBILE CABINET
S = SINK
FC = FIXED CABINET

OPTIMUM TRAFFIC FLOW PATTERN FOR OPERATORY. DOTTED LINE INDICATES INSTRUMENT TRANSFER ZONE.

Fig. 8   Optimum traffic flow pattern.

Commercial

DENTAL OFFICES
General Dentistry

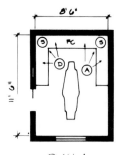
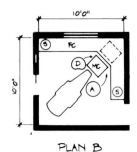

PLAN A
"U" DESIGN OPERATORY. DENTIST AND ASSISTANT WORK OFF OF FIXED CABINETS.

PLAN B
DIAGONAL CHAIR PLACEMENT WITH SINGLE MOBILE CABINET BEHIND PATIENT'S HEAD. DENTIST AND ASSISTANT WORK OFF OF MOBILE CABINET.

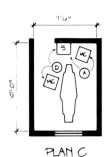
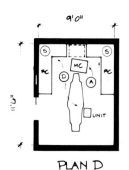

PLAN C
ASSISTANT AND DENTIST WORK OFF OF SPLIT MOBILE CABINETS. NO FIXED CABINETRY IN ROOM.

PLAN D
MODIFIED "U" ARRANGEMENT WITH OPENING IN FIXED CABINETS FOR STORAGE OF MOBILE CABINET. ASSISTANT WORKS OFF OF MOBILE CABINET BEHIND PATIENT AND DENTIST WORKS OFF OF A DENTAL UNIT WITH INSTRUMENTATION DELIVERED OVER THE PATIENT'S CHEST.

Fig. 9 Plans A, B, C, D.

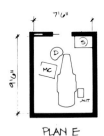

PLAN E
AN OPERATORY FOR A DENTIST WHO WORKS WITHOUT AN ASSISTANT.

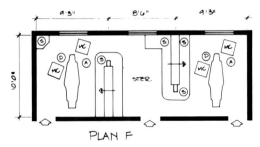

PLAN F
DENTIST AND ASSISTANT WORK OFF MOBILE CABINETS. BOTH OPERATORIES HAVE PASS-THROUGH FEATURE WITH STERILIZATION AREA WHICH PERMITS CLEAN TRAY SET-UPS TO BE PLACED IN OPERATORY (AND DIRTY ONES REMOVED) WITHOUT ENTERING THE ROOM.

Fig. 10 Plans E, F.

Design of the Dental Operatory

This is the most important room in a dental office. Although analogous to the physician's examination room, it is far more critical to a dentist's practice than the medical exam room is to a physician's practice since the physician has ancillary rooms for diagnosis, testing, and treatment, but the dentist has only the operatory. In terms of economics, the physician has the opportunity to enhance his or her income from laboratory tests, X-ray films, and the use of medical aides to give injections, administer EKGs and EEGs, or to do physical therapy. But the dentist has only the operatory plus the laboratory and X-ray work from which to derive income. For this reason many time and motion studies focusing on operatory efficiency have been published in dental journals. And, in recent years, certain major changes have evolved as a result of these studies. Patients now recline in a contour chair with the dentist working from a seated position at the side of the patient. If right-handed, the dentist will be seated to the right of the patient and will work in an area that could be designated at from 9:00 to 12:00, imagining the face of a clock surrounding the patient. Most dentists use an assistant, which is called *four handed dentistry*. Some dentists use two assistants. Figure 8 illustrates the optimum traffic flow pattern for an operatory. However, the exigencies of the fixed structure of the space, the location of windows and other "given" features, have an impact on the layout of the space, and compromises sometimes must be made.

Instrumentation There are four categories of instrumentation.

Handpiece Delivery System This is composed of rotary tools with drill bits that are used to cut and shape teeth.

Evacuation System Blood, debris, and water are removed from the mouth usually by suction (a vacuum system). This is normally performed by the dental assistant.

Hand-held Instruments These tools include probes, scalers, forceps, etc.

Three-way Syringe Often used by both the dentist and the assistant for spraying water, compressed air, or a combination thereof. In a well-equipped operatory, the assistant will have her own three-way syringe for drying or moistening preparations as well as for washing debris from the patient's mouth.

Methods of Delivery The instrumentation can be delivered to the oral cavity of the patient by three methods.

Mobile Delivery System The utilities (water, air, suction, electricity) can be delivered via mobile carts in *split* fashion (the dentist's cart has the handpieces and syringe, while the assistant's cart has a syringe and suction), or via a *single* cart from which the dentist's as well as the assistant's instruments are delivered. The single cart is usually located to the rear of the patient (Fig. 9, Plan B), while the split cart (for a right-handed dentist) would be located just below the patient's right shoulder and the split cart for the assistant would be located to the left of the patient's head (Fig. 8 and Fig. 9, Plan C).

906

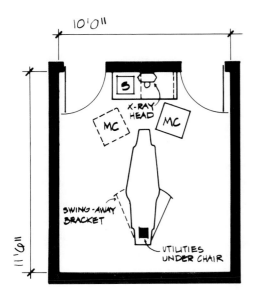

Rear Delivery System Both the dentist's and the assistant's instrumentation are delivered from behind the patient's head from a fixed cabinet (Fig. 9, Plan A) with the systems built in. Delivery of instrumentation from a mobile cabinet behind the patient is discussed above.

Over-the-Patient Delivery System Instruments and utilities are delivered from an area near the patient's left or right elbow or over the patient's chest. These kinds of delivery systems are usually attached to the chair so that even as the chair is adjusted up or down, the relationship of instrument location with respect to the oral cavity is constant (Fig. 9, Plan D and Fig. 10, Plan E).

There are combinations of the above delivery systems as well as other variables that must be considered. Two such items are the use of the cuspidor versus the more efficient central suction, and the number and placement of sinks in the operatory. Cuspidors (spittoons) can be purchased with central suction operation or with gravity drain. However, most modern dental offices use central suction with no cuspidor. The suction hoses at each operatory work off of a vacuum pump located in an equipment room near the operatories.

AMBIDEXTROUS OPERATORY

THIS ARRANGEMENT SERVES A PRACTICE COMPOSED OF RIGHT-AND-LEFT-HANDED DENTISTS. THE X-RAY HEAD IS MOUNTED BEHIND THE PATIENT. UTILITIES ARE UNDER THE TOE OF THE CHAIR AND THE ASSISTANT'S MOBILE CART CAN MOVE TO EITHER SIDE.

Fig. 11   Ambidextrous operatory.

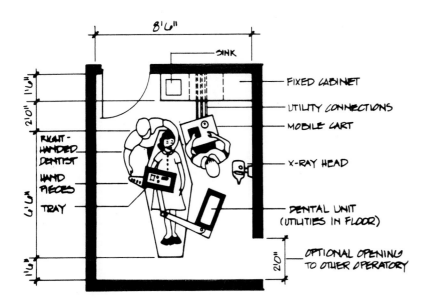

OPTIMAL SIZE OF OPERATORY

Fig. 12   Optimal size of operatory.

DENTAL OFFICES
General Dentistry; Orthodontics

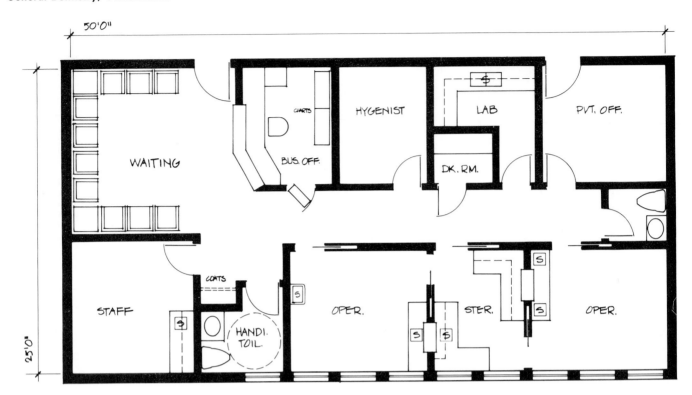

GENERAL DENTISTRY
1250 SQ.FT.

Fig. 13 Suite plan, 1250 square feet.

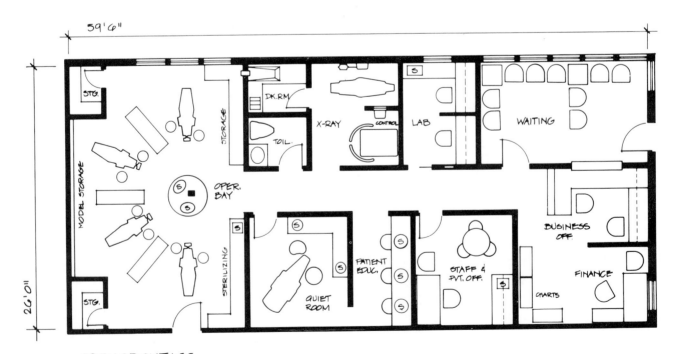

ORTHODONTICS
1547 SQ.FT.

Fig. 14 Suite plan for orthodontics, 1547 square feet.

The rental area per lawyer varies from 230 to 1,212 sq ft. The median is 455 sq ft, and the average is 484 sq ft.

A minimum-size office is illustrated by Fig. 1, which is two modules wide by three modules deep. If a 48-in. module is adopted, the clear dimensions without allowance for partitions will be 8 by 12 ft. The clear dimensions (with partitions 4 in. thick) are given in feet and inches, the maximum desk size is given in inches, and the net area is given in square feet. Larger offices are illustrated by Figs. 2 to 8, and suites are illustrated by Figs. 9 to 19. With each illustration of a suite of rooms comprising a law office, the dimensions and the following square-foot areas (using a 48-in. module) are given:

• Rental area as customarily measured
• Architectural area as measured for preliminary cost estimates
• Area (rental) per lawyer

The following abbreviations and symbols are used with these diagrams:

P—private office
R—reception room or area
S—secretary or stenographers
F—file room or space
L—library or library and conference room
C—conference room
V—vault
U—utility, storage, or work room
T—toilet room
N—north exposure
>—north exposure
←—exit

THE SMALL OFFICE

Figure 9 shows possible arrangements for a firm composed of only one lawyer. If a single lawyer's office must serve as a library and conference room, and perhaps also accommodate the files, it should be large enough for a conference-type desk and four or five chairs. It is almost essential to have a second room for use as a reception room and secretary's office. It is better to have a separation between the secretary's space and the reception space. The files may be of sufficient volume to require a separate file room.

Figure 10 illustrates arrangements for two lawyers (either partners or cooperators). In Fig. 10c, with a combination library and conference room, the private offices could be somewhat smaller. Figure 11 shows offices for three lawyers. Files should be separated from the reception room and convenient to the clerical employees as in Fig. 11a, or in a separate room as in Fig. 11b. If one office is large enough for conferences and the book collection not too large, the library and conference room may be eliminated. On the other hand, some firms with only two principals have a large enough collection of books to warrant inclu-

Law Office Layout and Design, Committee on Economics of Law Practice of the American Bar Association.

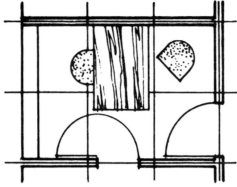

Fig. 1

Module	Office	Desk	Area sf
3'-8"	7'-0" x 10'-10"	52 x 32	76
4'-0"	7'-8" x 11'-10"	60 x 40	91
4'-4"	8'-4" x 12'-10"	66 x 40	107

Module	Office	Desk	Area sf
3'-8"	10'-8" x 10'-10"	66 x 34	116
4'-0"	11'-8" x 11'-10"	66 x 40	138
4'-4"	12'-8" x 12'-10"	66 x 40	163

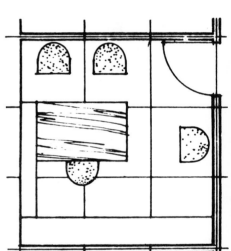

Fig. 2

Module	Office	Desk	Area sf
3'-8"	14'-4" x 10'-10"	60 x 40	155
4'-0"	15'-8" x 11'-10"	60 x 40	185
4'-4"	17'-0" x 12'-10"	60 x 40	218

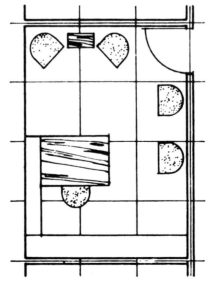

Fig. 3

909

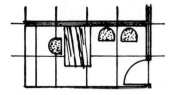

Module	Office	Desk	Area sf
3'-8''	7'-0'' x 14'-6''	52 x 32	102
4'-0''	7'-8'' x 15'-10''	60 x 40	123
4'-4''	8'-4'' x 17'-2''	66 x 40	142

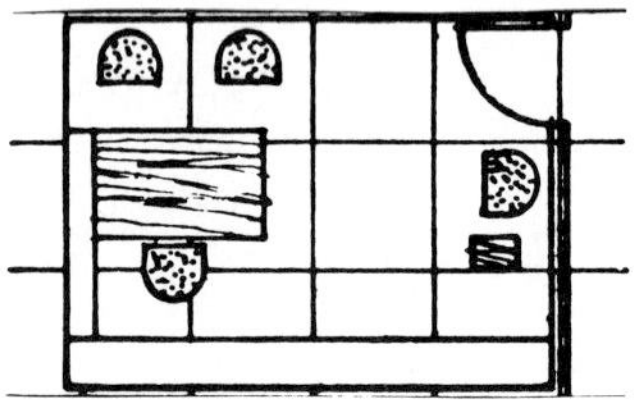

Fig. 4

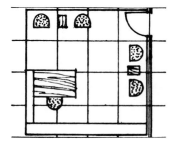

Module	Office	Desk	Area sf
3'-8''	10'-8'' x 14'-6''	60 x 34	155
4'-0''	11'-8'' x 15'-10''	66 x 40	186
4'-4''	12'-8'' x 17'-2''	66 x 40	217

Fig. 5

Module	Office	Desk	Area sf
3'-8''	14'-4'' x 14'-6''	66 x 40	208
4'-0''	15'-8'' x 15'-10''	66 x 40	248
4'-4''	17'-0'' x 17'-2''	66 x 40	290

Fig. 6

Module	Office	Desk	Area sf
3'-8''	18'-0'' x 14'-6''	66 x 40	256
4'-0''	19'-8'' x 15'-10''	66 x 40	312
4'-4''	21'-4'' x 17'-2''	66 x 40	357

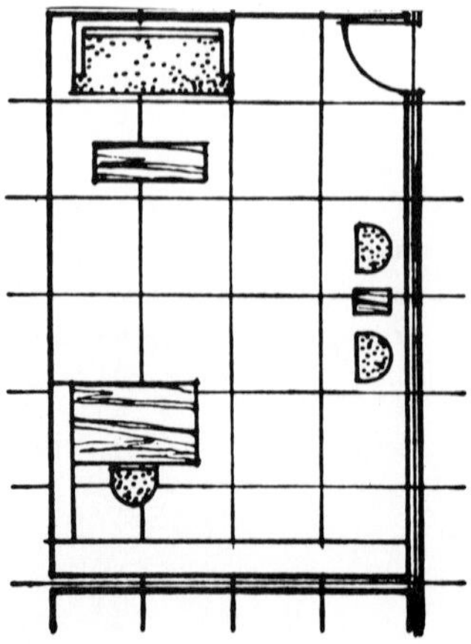

Fig. 7

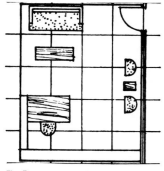

Module	Office	Desk	Area sf
3'-8''	21'-8'' x 14'-6''	66 x 40	314
4'-0''	23'-8'' x 15'-10''	66 x 40	378
4'-4''	25'-8'' x 17'-2''	66 x 40	438

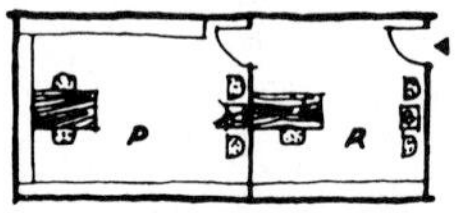

Fig. 8

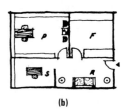

(a)

(b)

Fig. 9 Offices for one lawyer. (a) Rental area: 366 sq ft, 12 by 28 ft. (b) Rental area: 560 sq ft, 20 by 28 ft.

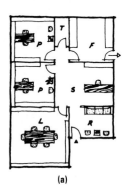

(a)

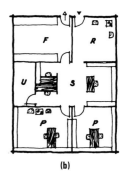

(b)

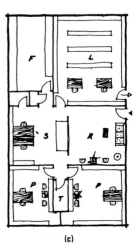

(c)

Fig. 10 Offices for two lawyers. (a) Rental area: 1,008 sq ft, 36 by 28 ft. Architectural area: 1,140 sq ft, 504 sq ft per lawyer. (b) Rental area: 1,008 sq ft, 36 by 28 ft. Architectural area: 1,140 sq ft, 504 sq ft per lawyer. (c) Rental area: 1,536 sq ft, 48 by 32 ft. Architectural area: 1,600 sq ft, 768 sq ft per lawyer.

sion of a sizable room for use solely as a library as in Fig. 10c. Figure 10a is suitable for a separate building and Figs. 10b and c are for rental space in an office building.

THE MEDIUM-SIZE OFFICE

While firms composed of more than ten lawyers generally carry on a diversified practice and hence choose central locations, some firms of five to ten lawyers may locate near their principal clients. The selection of space in the first story of a commercial building or the erection of a building may be considered. If the clientele is concentrated in a suburban center or small satellite city, or a city of 50,000 or smaller, the scale of land values may be such that first-story space near the commercial center could be considered. Because of the high cost of land in the center of large cities, buildings, to be feasible, must be larger than needed by a single law office; hence selection of space in an elevatored office building is often the only answer.

The same area which is planned for three lawyers, as is indicated in Fig. 11a, may be rearranged to accommodate five lawyers, as indicated by Fig. 12a. As rearranged, the area of most of the private offices is too small for conferences with more than one or two visitors, and secretarial space may be insufficient; but where rental rates are high this degree of crowding may be justified. Offices for firms with from five to twelve lawyers are indicated by Figs. 13 to 17. The arrangement shown in Fig. 17 may be expanded or contracted to provide for as few as four lawyers or as many as twenty.

Secretaries' desks should be close to the lawyers' offices. Some firms prefer each lawyer's secretary to be just outside his office door or in an adjacent private office, as in Fig. 17. In general, however, more use can be made of secretarial, stenographic, and clerical employees if some are in a pool to be drawn upon as needs arise.

THE LARGE OFFICE

The planning of space for a large law office may be influenced by the size and shape of the space available. The possibility of securing adequate, well-planned space is enhanced when the firm actively participates in the promotion of an office building.

Figure 18 indicates possibilities of planning large spaces. The same scheme with larger offices could provide for 11 to 18 lawyers, or could be enlarged to accommodate up to 40 or more lawyers. The plan should be based upon a study of the special needs of each lawyer and the relations between members of the firm.

SPACE FOR A COOPERATIVE GROUP

In buildings planned for occupancy by a number of law firms, facilities may be pooled, such as library, vault, utility space, and reception room. Files should be kept in the separate offices and secretaries' spaces. (Fig. 19.)

PLAN ELEMENTS

The most desirable orientation for offices and workrooms varies in different locations, but north is generally preferred. In Figs. 9 to 17, the most desirable orientation is indicated by the location of the letter N. Outside exposure

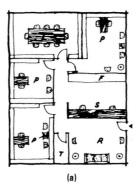

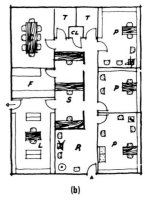

(a)   **(b)**

Fig. 11 Offices for three lawyers. (a) Rental area: 1,152 sq ft, 36 by 32 ft. Architectural area: 1,292 sq ft, 384 sq ft per lawyer. (b) Rental area: 1,584 sq ft, 44 by 36 ft. Architectural area: 1,748 sq ft, 523 sq ft per lawyer.

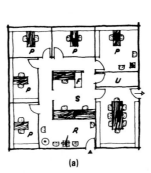

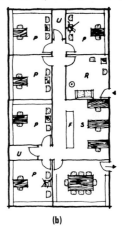

(a)   **(b)**

Fig. 12 Offices for five lawyers. (a) Rental area: 1,152 sq ft, 32 by 36 ft. Architectural area: 1,292 sq ft, 230 sq ft per lawyer. (b) Rental area: 1,456 sq ft, 52 by 28 ft. Architectural area: 1,620 sq ft, 291 sq ft per lawyer.

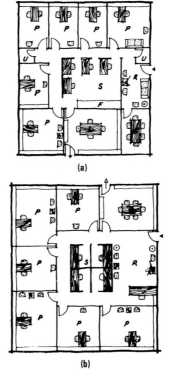

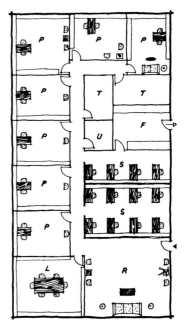

(a)

(b)

Fig. 13 Offices for six lawyers. (a) Rental area: 1,440 sq ft, 40 by 36 ft. Architectural area: 1,596 sq ft, 240 sq ft per lawyer. (b) Rental area: 1,760 sq ft, 44 by 40 ft. Architectural area: 1,886 sq ft, 293 sq ft per lawyer.

Fig. 14 Offices for seven lawyers. Rental area: 3,250 sq ft, 80 by 44 ft. Architectural area: 3,772 sq ft, 503 sq ft per lawyer.

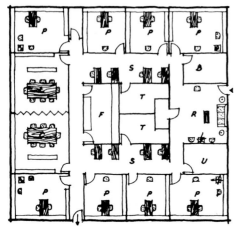

Fig. 15 Offices for eight lawyers. Rental area: 3,120 sq ft, 52 by 60 ft. Architectural area: 3,348 sq ft, 390 sq ft per lawyer.

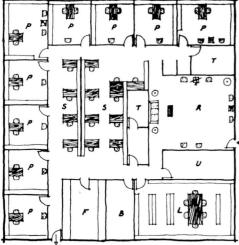

Fig. 16 Offices for nine lawyers. Rental area: 4,096 sq ft, 64 by 64 ft. Architectural area: 4,356 sq ft, 455 sq ft per lawyer.

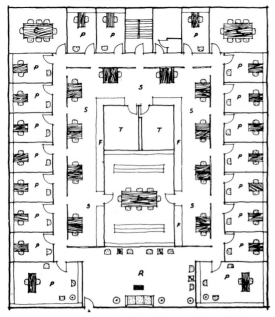

Fig. 18 Arrangement for large firms: 19 lawyers. Rental area: 23,040 sq ft, 144 by 160 ft. Architectural area: 23,652 sq ft, 1,212 sq ft per lawyer.

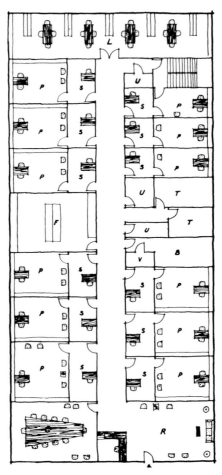

Fig. 17 Offices for 12 lawyers. Rental area: 6,720 sq ft, 56 by 120 ft. Architectural area: 7,076 sq ft, 560 sq ft per lawyer.

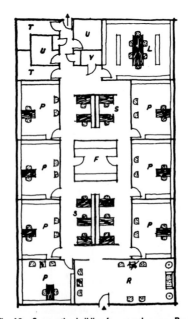

Fig. 19 Cooperative building for seven lawyers. Rental area: 3,340 sq ft, 44 by 76 ft. Architectural area: 3,588 sq ft, 477 sq ft per lawyer.

is desirable for offices and advantageous for large work areas, conference rooms, library, and rest rooms. Central locations are preferred for library, file room, and conference rooms.

The size of rooms is determined in part by the purpose and effect desired, and the furniture chosen. The desirability of commodiousness may be weighed against the rent or its equivalent. If space is air conditioned, smaller spaces may be tolerated. Lack of commodiousness may be offset by the use of rich materials and effective decoration.

FURNITURE

The reception room should have adequate seating in addition to the receptionist's desk, and perhaps side tables for ash trays and magazines. The minimum equipment for a private office is an executive's desk and chair, one or two chairs for visitors, and desk-height bookcases. If desk drawers are not adequate, one or more letter files may be required. For large offices, a sofa, side tables, coffee table, and even a conference table may be included. The furniture of conference rooms may be limited to a table and chairs, but some ornamental furniture may be included. If the room may be divided by a folding partition, two tables may be needed. Lawyers' libraries are for reference, and unless they are to be used also as conference rooms, only one or two small tables are needed. Each secretary's space must have its desk and chair, and files should be placed nearby. For security, file rooms may be included in the plan, and a vault may be needed for valuable papers. Storage spaces may be equipped with shelves, coat hooks, etc., combined with work space for duplicating equipment. Utility rooms are usually required only in separate buildings (rather than rental space) for heating and air conditioning equipment, transformer vault, main switch and meters, etc. A small kitchen or coffee bar may have a hot plate and sink, or more complete conventional kitchen equipment. Toilet facilities are usually required only for large law offices or when the offices occupy complete separate buildings. A couch should be provided in the women's toilet room or in a separate rest room.

INTERIOR DESIGN

Lawyers' offices require little interior decoration, but there is a discernible tendency to make offices homelike. Accessories used should be carefully selected. The most common wall decorations found in lawyers' offices are the certificates of admission to the bar and diplomas. These serve the purpose of assuring clients of the lawyer's qualifications.

By BERNARD SPERO and ERNEST J. HASCH

Efficient office layout calls for the use of certain basic principles which must be modified to meet the requirements of available space, personal habits, and individual preferences. What might be considered efficient by one practitioner is not necessarily so deemed by the next. It is axiomatic that the ones who seem most pleased with their office layouts are the ones who have worked in one or more offices before designing their final suites. Their layout better serves their own habit patterns. Therefore, it is wise to consider each factor as an individual problem and solve it according to the individual requirements as well as to limitations of space.

Waiting Room

The size of the waiting room depends on the practitioner's style of operation. Some adhere closely to their appointment schedule; others do not. Some must accommodate a great many children or expect a family group with many patients. Some use a production-line modus operandi in which assistants process the patients through drop areas or other checkup stations; others prefer to do all patient workup themselves. So perhaps a "kiddie area" or a "drop area" or both are required. In general, the busy practitioner should be able to accommodate from 10 to 12 people and provide emergency space for 3 or 4 more. About 2 ft of wall space is needed for each person. The idea that waiting room space is nonproductive and therefore wasteful is a fallacy. Few practitioners decrease their waiting room space in subsequent offices; most of them increase it.

If the waiting room is inadequate to contain the patient load, it is helpful to use a system of traffic control in which patients are transferred from the waiting room, in proper order, to operational rooms to await the doctor. This means that extra refraction rooms or combination refraction-treatment rooms are required—or even a field room, a muscle room, or a photography room, if these functions are to be performed independently.

Closets

Space must be provided for patients' wraps. If the space available does not lend itself to installation of a clothes closet, then racks or decorative wall-mounted clothes hangers can be used. Although less efficient, cloakroom facilities can be placed in the receptionist's quarters or in the passageways into the doctor's working areas.

Storage

Storage is an important, and often forgotten, item in office planning. A multitude of supplies are essential to sustain a busy practice, and they should be readily available when needed. Professional accessories and adjuncts are usu-

"International Ophthalmology Clinics" Uveitis, *Efficient Office Management*, vol. 3, no. 2, June 1963, Little, Brown and Company, Boston, Mass.

ally kept in small cabinets in the examination rooms, but general office supplies should be under the commission of the nurse or secretary. Storage cabinets can be built along corridors or above files. Advantage should be taken of any natural structural indentations due to columns or other structural irregularities; these are most useful for construction of cabinets, as they are normally waste space otherwise.

Files

The type of record charts to be used must first be determined and then the appropriate files selected. Room for future files should be apportioned, especially if the office is to be occupied for several years. Files should be accessible to the receptionist and the nurse, and are generally located in the receptionist's office. At times it is advantageous to recess file cabinets into a partition so that only the fronts show, while their bodies jut into a less-needed area of a contiguous room. This can have both aesthetic and functional value. If other space is not available, the file-cabinet area is also a good place for a small refrigerator.

Receptionist

The receptionist should be able to observe the entire waiting room and also control the flow of traffic of patients. After registering the patient, the receptionist usually pulls the record chart or starts a new one if necessary. The chart is placed at the doctor's disposal by means of the particular system used. Different systems are used. The chart can be placed in a rack outside the examination room to be used next, or on a desk in the examination room; some prefer just to select the chart from a rack or a counter top in the reception area or passageway.

Depending on the locality of the practice, the habits of the community, and the duties given the receptionist, one of several reception arrangements can be used. If the practice is located in a community where an informal relationship between public and profession is the rule, the receptionist can be placed behind a desk right out in the waiting room or behind a counter top. Office fees, if uniform, can be quoted and collected over a desk or a counter top. But if histories are to be taken, it is normally advisable to install the receptionist at a desk behind a partition, or to compromise with a half partition.

If the practice is large, or expected to be, it is advisable to provide space for two girls in the receptionist area. This is particularly true if the location is considered a permanent one. If not, a small business office should be planned for any future exigency.

Consultation Room

This is an arbitrary thing dependent on availability of space and on personal preferences. Many physicians prefer to interview patients initially in a private office. Others do so in the examination rooms, thus saving the time involved in transferring the patient from con-

sultation room to examination room. Those who work straight through and then must dash off to other commitments have little need of a private office, per se; but those who wish to stop and rest during the day need the privacy of some office to which they can retire. If excessive space must be taken in order to acquire a particular suite, one room can be adapted for use as a relaxation room, with a cot and beverages and other comforts; or it can be used as a dressing room for the assistants. A room of this type can always be converted to an examination room later, if the need should arise.

Examination Rooms

Examination rooms can be refraction rooms, treatment rooms, minor-surgery rooms, field rooms, photography rooms, muscle and orthoptic rooms, or any combination thereof. There was a time when refractions were done in one room, treatment in another, fields in another, and perhaps slit-lamp microscopy in yet another. Now, there is a trend toward more consolidation, so that practically all phases of a complete eye examination can be done in a single room, thus obviating the transfer of patient from room to room. This arrangement is a time-saver, especially if all parts of the examination are done by the eye doctor; but if assistants do part of the work-up, such as fields or muscle testing or even preliminary visions, there must be separate rooms for the different functions.

Refraction Room

Although only one refracting lane can be used at a time, it is generally conceded that more than one is needed by the busy ophthalmologist. Much time can be lost each day waiting for hats to be donned or doffed, waiting for makeup to be applied, listening to well-meant but time-consuming farewells, and finally waiting for another patient to be brought in and properly settled into position. With a second room available, it is a simple matter to give final instructions, bid a courteous farewell and step into the next room, where a patient has already been seated, with records laid out in a convenient place and instruments properly positioned for immediate use. Someone else can assist the departure of the patient just finished. This is not a very important item when the practice has just started, but as it flourishes, time becomes extremely important.

If it is not possible to have two identical refraction lanes, it is helpful to set up a second lane in a smaller room, perhaps a treatment room, which can be used when the patient load gets unduly heavy. Mirrors or special visual charts can be used, and still the room can be devoted primarily to some other function.

The size of a refraction room depends not only on the space available, but also on the predilections of the practitioner. Some insist on at least a 20-ft lane; others feel that this is relatively unimportant. Most feel that a visual lane of from 15 to 20 ft is satisfactory. Disregarding other factors, the characters on vision charts can be sized appropriately for any dis-

Commercial

OPHTHALMOLOGICAL OFFICES

tance used. The size of projected characters can be altered by optical means; charts with reverse characters can be used in conjunction with a mirror; charts with direct characters for a 10-ft distance are available; and sometimes it is feasible to use a two-mirror setup, in which one of the mirrors becomes a secondary projector to gain length of projection.

If the longer visual lane is considered necessary, and space is limited, it is sometimes feasible to use tunnels to attain the desired distance and yet conserve space. Tunnels can extend from floor to ceiling, or can even be constructed above files which open out into a different room. In any case, if there is no objection to the so-called "tunnel effect" in the mind of the eye doctor, many space-saving arrangements are possible with this method.

As mentioned before, many doctors now prefer to do a complete eye examination, including treatment, in a single room. Then there must be room for the visual lane with the routine examining equipment (chair, stools, trial lenses, refracting accessories, slit lamp) as well as some field equipment (perimeter, tangent screen) and, no doubt, a consultation desk. There should also be room for medicines, treatment cabinet, and perhaps a treatment table. This would require a minimum of 150 sq ft.

The type of equipment selected will determine, to some extent, the size of the space needed or, conversely, the space available determines, to some extent, the type of equipment which should be used. If the larger "deluxe-type" patients' chair is used, it should be positioned about 4 ft from a wall in order to utilize its adjustable and reclining features; and then a treatment table might not be considered necessary. On the other hand, the smaller, less adjustable chair can be placed close to the wall; but a treatment table is needed for tonometry, treatment, and minor surgery unless these functions are to be done in another room.

Sometimes the positioning of the projector (for vision lanes) presents a problem, perhaps because of corners or extraneous paraphernalia around the patients' chair. A recent innovation is the use of remote-control projectors. These projectors, now available, can be mounted in an out-of-the-way position and be completely controlled by fingertip switches on or around the lens cabinet. With this arrangement, there is no need to reach in front of a patient, or turn awkwardly, to change the characters projected.

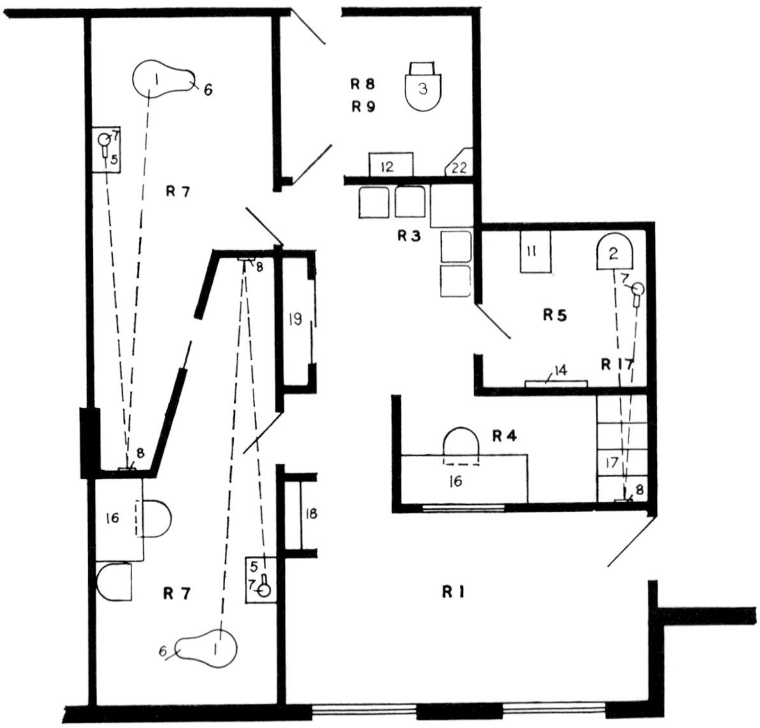

Furnishings
1. Deluxe refracting unit
2. Small adjustable chair
3. Reclining treatment chair
4. Casual chair
5. Lens cabinet
6. Slit lamp
7. Projector
8. Screen
9. Vision chart
10. Mirror
11. Perimeter
12. Treatment cabinet
13. Treatment table
14. Tangent screen
15. Clothes rack
16. Desk
17. Files
18. Clothes closet
19. Storage cabinet
20. Storage cabinet 40 in. high
21. Storage cabinet over files
22. Sink
23. Wall mount
25. Refrigerator
26. Shelf
27. Clothes hooks

Areas
R1 Waiting room
R2 Waiting room—children
R3 Drop area
R4 Receptionist—business office
R5 Nurse's office
R6 Personnel lounge
R7 Refraction room
R8 Treatment room
R9 Minor surgery
R10 Private office
R11 Field room
R12 Orthoptic-muscle room
R13 Photography
R14 Storage room
R15 Files
R16 Washroom
R17 Tunnel

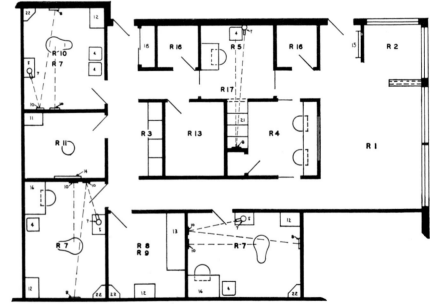

Area: 752 sq ft, 32 by 26 ft
Office personnel: One doctor, one nurse, one receptionist
Units available:
  One waiting room 17 ft 3 in. by 8 ft 9 in — 11 people
  One drop area 6 ft 2 in. by 5 ft 6 in. — 4 people
  One reception office 11 ft 9 in. by 5 ft

Two refraction rooms — one 18-ft lane — 21 ft by 8 ft 8 in.; one 18-ft lane — 20 ft 9 in.; by 8 ft 8 in.
One treatment and minor-surgery room 9 ft by 7 ft 6 in.
One nurse's office-field room 7 ft 9 in. by 7 ft 4 in. — with 12-ft projection lane above files

Fig. 1 Plan for one-doctor opthalmological office.

Area: 1,150 sq ft, 44 by 29 ft
Office personnel: Two doctors, one nurse, one secretary, one receptionist
Units available:
  One waiting room 13 ft by 11 ft 2 in. — 10 people
  One children's room 6 ft 3 in. by 5 ft 10 in.
  One drop area 8 ft by 2 ft 6 in. — 4 people
  One reception-business office 10 by 8 ft

Three refraction rooms — two 20-ft lanes — by using "double mirror" setup — 12 ft 6 in. by 9 in.; by using "double mirror" setup — 11 ft by 9 in.
One treatment and minor-surgery room 9 ft by 8 ft 6 in.
One field room 9 by 7 ft
One photography room 8 ft by 6 ft 6 in.
One nurse's office — 13-ft lane — 8 ft by 7 ft 10 in.
Two washrooms 4 ft 6 in. by 4 ft. 6 in.

Fig. 2 Plan for two-doctor opthalmological office.

914

If two refraction rooms are to be used, it is better to have them adjacent or adjoining, or separated by no more than a smaller treatment or minor-surgery room.

Miscellaneous Rooms

Since the various services required of the ophthalmologist are so interrelated, refraction rooms now usually contain some treatment facilities. But it is still helpful to have a room available, possibly smaller, which can be used for treatment, minor surgery, and fields. One such room for every two refraction rooms should be adequate, even in the larger multimanned practices. It is advisable to have a vision lane in the miscellaneous rooms whenever possible. Almost any distance can be used to create a satisfactory vision lane.

Minor surgery can be done in any chair with a headrest and a reclining back, but a chair-table or a stationary treatment table is considerably more comfortable to the patient. The examining chair which can be converted into a flat treatment table can serve several purposes. It can serve as a general treatment chair for tonometry or minor surgery; it can be a refraction chair; and it can be positioned at the prescribed distance from a tangent screen so that central fields can be taken from the same chair, thus making efficient use of a smaller room.

Orthoptic rooms, as such, are seldom used unless the volume of the practice affords the use of an orthoptist. The diagnostic work performed by most eye doctors is done in one of the other operational rooms; but if orthoptic treatments are to be given, a separate orthoptic room is indicated.

Treatment, minor surgery, and fields can usually be done in a room of about 100 to 130 sq ft, with smaller rooms serving well for any single one of the functions.

Figure 1 is a plan designed to give the nurse and the receptionist complete control of the traffic flow. The receptionist controls the patients in the drop area and refers them to the nurse, who does primary work-ups. Then the patients are directed to one of the doctor's refraction rooms. The refraction rooms are identical, and should be equipped identically. There is a room for treatment and minor surgery, and the nurse could also use it in addition to her field room. Storage is centrally located in the corridor.

Figure 2 shows three refraction rooms, one nurse's office, and three miscellaneous rooms to facilitate processing a large practice through this suite. The nurse and any other assistants have access to all parts of the suite, and the nurse has a 13-ft vision lane over the files. All assistants to the doctors can cooperate efficiently to route patients properly according to the system used, and still oversee the overall operation from various vantage points. The doctors, under a proper system, will have several rooms in which they can perform the various functions required. For instance, the photography room, which is seldom used as such, can be used for tonography, gonioscopy, and orthoptics, or even as a personnel lounge. The children's waiting room can be kept under constant surveillance.

Turning Diameter Dimension

Wall to Wall Turning Diameter is the diameter of the smallest circle which will enclose the outermost points of projection of the vehicle while executing its sharpest practicable turn. This is equal to the minimum turning circle plus twice the radial overhang beyond the turning radius.

Curb to Curb Turning Diameter is the diameter of the smallest circle within which the vehicle will clear a curb 6 in. high, while the vehicle is executing its sharpest practicable turn. This is equal to the turning circle plus twice the horizontal distance from the center of tire contact with the road to the arc subtended by a chord drawn between the points of intersection of the outermost projection of the tire shoulder on a horizontal plane 6 in. above the surface on which the tire rests.

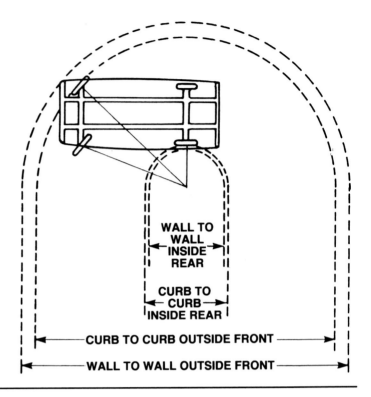

Exterior Length Dimensions

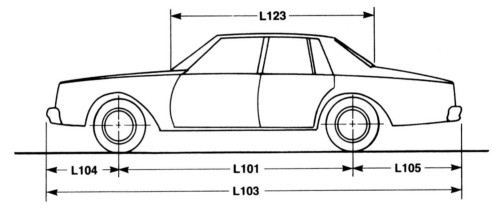

L101 – Wheelbase (WB). The dimension measured longitudinally between front and rear wheel centerlines. In case of dual rear axles, the dimensions shall be to the midpoint of the centerlines of the rear wheels.

L103 – Vehicle length. The maximum dimension measured longitudinally between the foremost point and the rearmost point on the vehicle, including bumper, bumper guards, tow hooks and/or rub strips, if standard equipment.

L104 – Overhang – front. The dimension measured longitudinally from the centerline of the front wheels to the foremost point

on the vehicle, including bumper, bumper guards, tow hooks and/or rub strips, if standard equipment.

L105 – Overhang – rear. The dimension measured longitudinally from the centerline of the rear wheels; or in the case of dual axles, the dimension shall be midpoint of the centerlines of the rear wheels, to the rearmost point on the vehicle, including rear bumpers, bumper guards, tow hooks and rub strips, if standard equipment.

L123 – Upper structure length. The dimension measured longitudinally from the cowl point to the deck point.

Fig. 1 Parking dimensions for 1988 passenger cars. (See pages 918-921.)

Exterior Width Dimensions

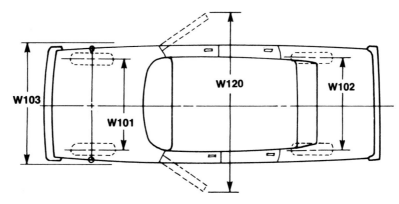

W101 – Tread – front. The dimension measured between the tire centerlines at the ground.

W102 – Tread – rear. The dimension measured between the tire centerlines at the ground. In case of dual wheels, the dimension will be measured to the centerline of tire and wheel assemblies.

W103 – Vehicle width. The maximum dimension measured between the widest point on the vehicle, excluding exterior mirrors, flexible mud flaps, marker lamps, but including bumpers, moldings, sheet metal protrusions or dual wheels, if standard equipment.

W120 – Vehicle width – front doors open. The dimension measured between the widest point on the front doors in maximum hold-open position.

Exterior Height Dimensions

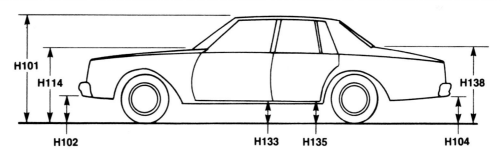

H101 – Vehicle height. The dimension measured vertically from the highest point on the vehicle body to ground.

H102 – Front bumper to ground. The minimum dimension measured vertically from the lowest point on the front bumper to ground, including bumper guards, if standard equipment.

H104 – Rear bumper to ground. The minimum dimension measured vertically from the lowest point on the rear bumper to ground, including bumper guards, if standard equipment.

H114 – Cowl point to ground. Measured at zero "Y" plane.

H133 – Bottom of door closed – front to ground. The dimension measured vertically from the bottom outside corner of the door on the lock pillar side, in maximum closed position, to ground.

H135 – Bottom of door closed – rear to ground. The dimension measured vertically from the bottom outside corner of the door on the lock pillar side, in maximum closed position, to ground.

H138 – Deck point to ground. Measured at zero "Y" plane.

Ground Clearance Dimensions

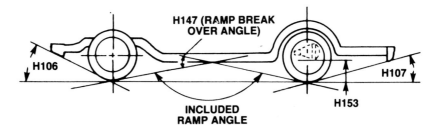

H106 – Angle of approach. The angle measured between a line tangent to the front tire static loaded radius arc and the initial point of structural interference forward of the front tire to ground. The limiting structural component shall be designated.

H107 – Angle of departure. The angle measured between a line tangent to the rear tire static loaded radius arc and the initial point of structural interference rearward of the rear tire to ground. The limiting component shall be designated.

H147 – Ramp breakover angle. The angle measured between two lines tangent to the front and rear tire static loaded radius and intersecting at a point on the underside of the vehicle which defines the largest ramp over which the vehicle can roll.

H153 – Rear axle differential to ground. The minimum dimension measured from the rear axle differential to ground.

H156 – Minimum running ground clearance. The minimum dimension measured from the sprung vehicle to ground. Specify location.

Fig. 1 (cont.)

Commercial

PARKING
Automobile Dimensions

TABLE 1 Overall Dimensions—1988 (figures in inches) [as shown in Fig. 1]

Models	Wheelbase, L101	Overall length, L103	Overall width, W103	Overall width— doors open, W120	Overall height, H101	Minimum running ground clearance, H156
Chrysler Motors						
Chrysler 5th Avenue, Dodge Diplomat, Plymouth Gran Fury	112.6	204.6–206.7	72.4	143.9	55.1	6.0
Chrysler New Yorker/Landau, Dodge Dynasty	104.3	193.6	68.5	137.9	53.5	5.0
Chrysler LeBaron (K-Body)	100.3–100.4	179.0–179.2	68.0	135.1	52.9–53.2	4.6–4.7
Plymouth Reliant, Dodge Aries	100.3–100.4	178.5–178.6	68.0	135.1–158.2	52.5–53.2	4.6
Chrysler New Yorker Turbo, Plymouth Caravelle, Dodge 600	103.3	185.2–187.2	68.0	135.1	53.1	4.7–5.0
Chrysler LeBaron GTS, Dodge Lancer	103.1	180.4	68.3	138.2	52.4–53.0	4.2–4.8
Dodge Omni, Plymouth Horizon	99.1	163.2	66.8	130.7	53.0	4.6
Dodge Daytona, Pacifica and Shelby Z	97.0	178.4–179.2	69.3	151.5	50.1–50.6	4.3–4.7
Plymouth Sundance, Dodge Shadow	97.0	171.7	67.3	135.1–160.4	52.7	4.6
Chrysler LeBaron (J-Body)	100.3–100.4	184.9	68.5	156.1	50.9–52.1	4.6–4.7
Plymouth Voyager, Dodge Caravan	112.0–119.1	175.9–190.5	72.0	142.3	64.4–64.7	2.7–3.4
Chrysler Conquest	95.8	173.2	68.3	141.5	50.2	4.6
Plymouth/Dodge Colt	93.7	157.2–169.3	63.8–64.4	129.9–149.0	50.8–53.7	3.5–5.1
Plymouth/Dodge Colt Vista	103.3–103.5	176.6	64.8	130	57.3–59.4	4.3–5.1
Medallion	102.4	183.2	67.5	141.7	52.8	5.5
Premier	106.0	192.8	70.0	143.1	53.3	5.0
Eagle	109.3	180.9	72.3	140.4	55.4	7.35
Ford Motor Company						
Ford, Mercury	114.3	211.0–219.0	77.5–79.3	142.9	55.5–56.5	5.2
Thunderbird, Cougar	104.2	200.8–202.1	71.1	159.0	53.4–53.8	5.0
Tempo, Topaz	99.9	176.5	68.3	131.0–150.8	52.7	5.1
Mustang	100.5	179.6	69.1	153.5	51.9–52.1	4.5
Lincoln	117.3	219.2	78.1	144.4	55.9	5.6
Escort, Lynx, EXP	94.2	166.9–168.4	65.9	125.4–144.2	53.3–53.7	4.8–5.7
Tracer	94.7	162.0	65.2	148.6	53.0	5.1
Festiva	90.2	140.5	63.2	147.2	55.3	—
Continental	109.0	205.1	72.7	—	55.6	5.6
Mark VII	108.5	202.8	70.9	169.5	54.2	6.4
Merkur XR4Ti	102.7	178.4	68.0	151.6	53.8	—
Taurus, Sable	106.0	188.4–191.9	70.8	140.6	54.3–55.1	5.1–5.8
Scorpio	108.7	186.4	69.5	142.8	54.6	5.2
General Motors Corporation						
Cadillac DeVille, Fleetwood Limousine, Buick Electra; Oldsmobile Ninety Eight	134.4–110.8	218.6–196.4	72.5–72.4	164.9–138.5	55.1–54.3	6.2–5.6
Cadillac Fleetwood Brougham "RWD"	121.5	221.0	76.5	129.8	56.7	5.5
Chevrolet Caprice, Pontiac Safari	115.9	220.5–212.8	79.8–75.4	157.6–129.6	59.3–56.4	8.0–6.2
Oldsmobile Delta 88, Buick LeSabre, Pontiac Bonneville	110.8	198.7–196.1	72.4	164.9–139.6	55.5–54.7	6.6
Buick Riviera, Oldsmobile Toronado, Cadillac Eldorado, Seville	108.0	191.2–187.5	71.7–70.9	154.3–134.3	53.7–53.0	6.0
Chevrolet Monte Carlo	108.1	202.4	71.8	157.0	54.9	5.4
Pontiac Grand Prix, Oldsmobile Cutlass Supreme, Buick Regal	107.5	193.9–192.1	72.5–71.0	162.8–157.8	53.5–52.8	5.3
Chevrolet Celebrity, Pontiac 6000; Oldsmobile Cutlass Ciera, Buick Century	104.9	194.4–188.3	72.0–69.3	149.6–130.3	54.5–53.3	6.4–5.6
Pontiac Grand Am, Oldsmobile Calais, Buick Skylark	103.4	180.1–177.5	66.7	146.9–146.6	52.6–52.4	5.8–5.7
Chevrolet Cavalier, Pontiac Sunbird, Oldsmobile Firenza, Buick Skyhawk, Cadillac Cimarron	101.2	181.7–167.1	66.3–65.0	145.0–126.7	54.5–52.0	5.9–5.6
Chevrolet Camaro, Pontiac Firebird	101.0	192.0–188.1	72.8–72.4	155.1	50.4–49.7	5.0–4.5
Cadillac Allante	99.4	178.6	73.5	154.7	52.2	—
Pontiac LeMans	99.2	172.4–163.7	65.7–65.5	146.4–129.9	53.7–53.5	5.4–5.3
Chevrolet Corvette	96.2	176.5	71.0	145.9	46.4	4.7
Pontiac Fiero	93.4	165.1–160.7	69.0	150.0	46.9	5.4–5.3
Chevrolet Sprint	92.3–88.4	148.4–144.5	60.2	138.2–123.9	53.1	6.9
Chevrolet Spectrum	94.5	160.2–157.4	63.6	136.6–125.4	52.0	5.4
Chevrolet Nova	95.7	166.3	64.4	128.9	52.8	5.3
Volkswagen						
VW Fox	92.8	163.4	63.0	—	53.7	5.5
Golf, GTI, Jetta	97.3	158.0–171.7	65.6–66.1	—	55.7	4.6
Scirocco, Cabriolet	94.5	151.5–165.5	64.8	—	51.4–55.6	4.3–4.9
Quantum, Syncro	100.4	179.5–180.7	66.7–67.2	—	54.8–58.0	5.0
Audi 80–90, Quattro	99.9–100.2	176.3	66.7	—	54.8–55.0	5.0
Audi 5000, 100, 200, Turbo, Turbo Quattro	105.8	192.7	71.4	—	55.9	5.4
Vanagon, Camper	96.9	179.9	72.6	—	75.9–80.9	6.3
Volvo						
244	104.3	190.0	67.7	129.9	56.6	—
245	104.3	190.7	67.7	129.9	57.0	—
740	109.1	188.4	69.3	138.6	55.5–56.5	5.9
760	109.1	188.4	69.3	138.6	55.5–56.7	5.9

TABLE 2 Front of Car Dimensions—1988 (figures in inches) [as shown in Fig. 1]

Models	Bottom of front bumper to ground, H102	Height, bottom of front door to ground, H133	Cowl at rear to ground, H114	Length		Width tread, W101
				Upper structure, L123	Overhang, front, L104	
Chrysler Motors						
Chrysler 5th Avenue, Dodge Diplomat, Plymouth Gran Fury	13.8	11.2	37.1	93.9–95.3	40.0	60.5
Chrysler New Yorker/Landau, Dodge Dynasty	11.7	10.2	37.2	95.9	43.5	57.6
Chrysler LeBaron (K-Body)	11.7–11.9	10.4	36.0–36.1	88.1–115.6	39.4	57.6
Plymouth Reliant, Dodge Aries	11.8	9.9–10.1	35.9	88.1–115.6	38.8	57.6
Chrysler New Yorker Turbo, Plymouth Caravelle, Dodge 600	11.9–12.5	11.2	36.0	97.5–97.6	39.4–39.6	57.6
Chrysler LeBaron GTS, Dodge Lancer	10.0–10.6	9.3–9.8	36.2–36.8	106.9	40.5	57.6
Dodge Omni, Plymouth Horizon	14.4	10.6	35.1	101.5	31.5	56.1
Dodge Daytona, Pacificia and Shelby Z	8.6–11.4	10.0–10.5	36.6–37.0	104.9	42.7–43.8	57.6
Plymouth Sundance, Dodge Shadow	9.7	9.3–9.5	35.9	95	38.3	57.6
Chrysler LeBaron (J-Body)	10.0	9.6–9.9	36.9–37.0	91.7–97.8	43.2	57.6
Plymouth Voyager, Dodge Caravan	13.5–13.6	12.5–12.6	44.8–44.9	—	33.1–33.8	59.9
Chrysler Conquest	13.8	10.2	36.0	102.4	38.2	57.7
Plymouth/Dodge Colt	8.7–9.3	8.9–10.4	34.6–35.2	94.9–115.4	33.5–33.7	55.5
Plymouth/Dodge Colt Vista	13.6–16.5	9.8–12.2	38.8–41.3	122.8	34.6–34.8	55.3–55.5
Medallion	9.1	10.8	35.0	107.9	41.9	57.2
Premier	14.6	11.1	35.7	112.2	42.0	58.2
Eagle	16.4	13.8	40.2	96.3	33.5	59.6
Ford Motor Company						
Ford, Mercury	13.4–13.6	11.5–12.2	37.6	106.3–142.3	42.4–45.5	62.2
Thunderbird, Cougar	14.8	10.4	38.8–38.9	96.4–103.6	45.4–46.7	58.1
Tempo, Topaz	9.8	10.0	36.6–36.7	100.0–100.1	34.4	54.9
Mustang	15.4	10.1	37.7	92.6–95.8	40.0	56.6
Lincoln	12.9	11.7	37.8	106.5	46.0	62.2
Escort, Lynx, EXP	14.9–15.4	11.2–11.3	36.3	105.6–110.6	35.4–36.4	54.7–54.9
Tracer	9.4	10.2	35.6	104.6	33.8	54.9
Festiva	8.6	10.4	36.8	97.9	26.9	55.1
Continental	9.3	—	37.6	113.7	45.0	62.3
Mark VII	14.7	11.4	39.1	107.8	43.7	58.4
Merkur XR4Ti	7.0	11.8	37.4	113.2	34.7	57.2
Taurus, Sable	13.5–15.7	11.3–11.4	36.8–37.2	108.8–133.6	39.2	61.6
Scorpio	9.5	11.9	38.0	120.4	34.3	58.1
General Motors Corporation						
Cadillac DeVille, Fleetwood Limousine, Buick Electra; Oldsmobile Ninety Eight	15.0–10.4	11.5–10.9	33.9–37.0	105.3–97.3	43.0–41.7	60.3
Cadillac Fleetwood Brougham "RWD"	10.0	11.1	39.9	97.7	42.7	61.7
Chevrolet Caprice, Pontiac Safari	13.0–12.0	12.1–11.2	40.1–39.4	138.0–93.1	44.3–40.6	62.2–61.7
Oldsmobile Delta 88, Buick LeSabre, Pontiac Bonneville	20.1	12.2	38.5–38.1	107.8–98.9	43.3–41.3	60.3
Buick Riviera, Oldsmobile Toronado, Cadillac Eldorado, Seville	14.1–12.5	11.2–10.6	43.7–36.2	96.6–93.7	44.1–43.4	59.9
Chevrolet Monte Carlo	12.5	11.1	39.0	90.7	44.4	58.5
Pontiac Grand Prix, Oldsmobile Cutlass Supreme, Buick Regal	13.9	12.0	33.5	111.2–104.6	44.1–42.4	59.5
Chevrolet Celebrity, Pontiac 6000; Oldsmobile Cutlass Ciera, Buick Century	14.3–9.6	19.2–10.9	37.0–36.6	128.6–94.5	43.2–40.7	58.7
Pontiac Grand Am, Oldsmobile Calais, Buick Skylark	11.0–8.4	11.4–11.1	36.8–36.6	89.9	39.7–38.5	55.6
Chevrolet Cavalier, Pontiac Sunbird, Oldsmobile Firenza, Buick Skyhawk, Cadillac Cimarron	14.8–8.0	11.9–11.1	37.3–36.3	115.1–91.9	42.6–30.0	55.6
Chevrolet Camaro, Pontiac Firebird	13.7–10.7	14.3–9.8	35.6–34.9	105.1	46.5–42.8	60.7–60.0
Cadillac Allante	—	12.7	37.6	84.3	40.2	60.4
Pontiac LeMans	8.9–8.7	10.9–10.7	36.6	105.1–99.2	33.1	55.1
Chevrolet Corvette	4.9	9.8	33.3	90.9	40.6	59.6
Pontiac Fiero	13.1–12.4	9.6	32.8	59.8	40.5–36.4	58.3–57.8
Chevrolet Sprint	8.7	12.8	36.2	98.5–94.6	28.9	52.6
Chevrolet Spectrum	9.1	9.6–9.5	36.0	104.6–94.3	32.1	54.7
Chevrolet Nova	15.0	10.8	35.2	110.0–97.4	33.3	56.1
Volkswagen						
VW Fox	—	—	—	—	—	53.7
Golf, GTI, Jetta	19.7–20.1	—	—	—	—	55.7–56.3
Scirocco, Cabriolet	19.8	—	—	—	—	54.7
Quantum, Syncro	20.4–20.7	—	—	—	—	55.6–55.7
Audi 80–90, Quattro	15.9	—	—	—	37.2	55.6
Audi 5000, 100, 200, Turbo, Turbo Quattro	15.4–15.6	—	—	—	41.9	57.8
Vanagon, Camper	12.0–17.3	—	—	—	—	62.4
Volvo						
244	14.6	12.8	38.7	98.2	37.8	56.3
245	14.6	12.8	38.7	—	37.8	56.3
740	14.3	12.5	38.0	99.4	36.2	57.9
760	14.3	12.5	38.0	99.4	36.2	57.5

Commercial

PARKING

Automobile Dimensions

TABLE 3 Rear of Car Dimensions—1988 (figures in inches) [as shown in Fig. 1]

Models	Bottom of rear bumper to ground, H104	Axle differential to ground, H153	Deck at rear window to ground, H138	Bottom of rear door to ground, H135	Overhang, rear, L105	Width tread, W102
Chrysler Motors						
Chrysler 5th Avenue, Dodge Diplomat, Plymouth Gran Fury	10.6–10.7	6.9	36.5	11.0	52.0–54.1	60.0
Chrysler New Yorker/Landau, Dodge Dynasty	9.7	—	37.4	9.5	44.9–45.8	57.6
Chrysler LeBaron (K-Body)	11.4	—	33.8–35.0	7.2	39.3–39.5	57.2
Plymouth Reliant, Dodge Aries	10.8–11.6	—	33.8–34.9	9.7	39.3–39.5	57.2
Chrysler New Yorker Turbo, Plymouth Caravelle, Dodge 600	10.9–11.4	—	37.2–37.4	9.9	42.5–44.3	57.2
Chrysler LeBaron GTS, Dodge Lancer	10.9–11.5	—	35.9–36.5	8.0–8.6	36.8	57.2
Dodge Omni, Plymouth Horizon	11.9	—	33.1	10.5	32.6	55.7
Dodge Daytona, Pacificia and Shelby Z	11.1–11.8	—	33.2–33.8	9.5–10.0	38.4–38.7	57.6
Plymouth Sundance, Dodge Shadow	10.3	—	36.3	9.1	36.4	57.2
Chrysler LeBaron (J-Body)	10.6–11.4	—	36.1–37.3	8.9–9.2	41.3–41.4	57.6
Plymouth Voyager, Dodge Caravan	12.6–13.0	—	—	12.5–12.7	30.7–39.0	62.1
Chrysler Conquest	11.8	—	35.2	—	39.2	57.3
Plymouth/Dodge Colt	9.3–11.2	—	32.3–35.2	8.7–10.4	30.1–41.9	52.8
Plymouth/Dodge Colt Vista	11.8–13.6	5.1–4×4	37.6–39.4	9.8–12.0	38.4	54.1–54.5
Medallion	10.4	—	37.8	10.8	39.0	55.4
Premier	11.6	—	36.0	10.9	44.7	57.1
Eagle	14.0	7.5	39.8	13.5	38.2	57.6
Ford Motor Company						
Ford, Mercury	11.1	6.1	36.5–38.0	11.4–12.1	54.3–59.3	62.0
Thunderbird, Cougar	13.7	5.7	38.5–39.6	—	51.3	58.5
Tempo, Topaz	14.0	—	37.0–38.1	9.7–9.8	42.4–42.7	57.6
Mustang	13.2	6.1	35.1–35.7	—	39.1	57.0
Lincoln	9.5	6.4	38.9	11.6	56.0	62.0
Escort, Lynx, EXP	12.3–13.2	—	33.1–37.1	10.5–10.9	37.3–38.4	56.0
Tracer	10.7	—	35.1	10.2	33.5	56.0
Festiva	10.0	—	36.4	—	23.4	62.2
Continental	12.6	5.9	39.7	—	51.1	61.1
Mark VII	15.0	6.4	40.1	—	50.6	59.0
Merkur XR4Ti	7.6	—	36.5	—	41.0	57.8
Taurus, Sable	10.5–14.3	5.7–6.2	35.4–39.1	10.9–11.0	43.2–46.7	59.9–60.5
Scorpio	9.1	7.1	38.7	11.8	43.4	58.1
General Motors Corporation						
Cadillac DeVille, Fleetwood Limousine, Buick Electra; Oldsmobile Ninety Eight	13.1–12.6	8.8–6.4	38.5–38.1	11.9–10.1	44.0–42.4	59.8
Cadillac Fleetwood Brougham "RWD"	10.2	6.5	41.0	11.8	56.9	60.7
Chevrolet Caprice, Pontiac Safari	14.3–11.9	14.1–7.5	42.7–40.3	12.3–11.7	60.3–55.9	64.1–60.7
Oldsmobile Delta 88, Buick LeSabre, Pontiac Bonneville	21.8	6.1–6.0	40.1–39.7	12.4	42.7–42.4	59.8
Buick Riviera, Oldsmobile Toronado, Cadillac Eldorado, Seville	13.1–12.7	11.6	43.3–38.5	11.2	36.6–36.5	59.9
Chevrolet Monte Carlo	14.2	6.8	39.8	11.1	49.9	57.8
Pontiac Grand Prix, Oldsmobile Cutlass Supreme, Buick Regal	10.3	5.4	36.4	—	42.3–41.7	58.2–58.0
Chevrolet Celebrity, Pontiac 6000; Oldsmobile Cutlass Ciera, Buick Century	15.5–12.2	6.2–5.1	38.9–37.8	19.3–11.1	47.0–42.2	57.0–56.8
Pontiac Grand Am, Oldsmobile Calais, Buick Skylark	12.7–12.1	6.6–6.5	38.2–37.7	11.5–11.1	37.0–35.6	55.2
Chevrolet Cavalier, Pontiac Sunbird, Oldsmobile Firenza, Buick Skyhawk, Cadillac Cimarron	13.7–8.8	7.0–6.4	52.7–37.4	12.0–11.1	38.9–28.8	55.2
Chevrolet Camaro, Pontiac Firebird	14.1–12.5	12.0–6.8	36.1–35.9	—	44.6–44.2	61.6–60.9
Cadillac Allante	—	—	40.3	—	39.1	60.4
Pontiac LeMans	12.8–12.1	6.8	39.4–37.9	10.8	40.1–31.4	55.4
Chevrolet Corvette	13.0	6.8	—	—	39.7	60.4
Pontiac Fiero	13.5–13.1	10.6–6.1	34.4	—	31.2–30.9	59.3–58.7
Chevrolet Sprint	9.3	6.5	—	12.9	27.2	51.2
Chevrolet Spectrum	7.7–7.5	—	35.6–34.3	9.3	33.6–30.8	54.3
Chevrolet Nova	13.8	—	37.8	10.8	37.4	55.3
Volkswagen						
VW Fox	—	—	—	—	—	53.9
Golf, GTI, Jetta	21.4–22.2	—	—	—	—	56.3
Scirocco, Cabriolet	19.3	—	—	—	—	53.5
Quantum, Syncro	19.5–21.8	—	—	—	—	56.0–56.5
Audi 80-90, Quattro	19.6	—	—	—	38.8	56.3
Audi 5000, 100, 200, Turbo, Turbo Quattro	15.1–15.4	—	—	—	45.1	55.8
Vanagon, Camper	14.6–16.9	—	—	—	—	61.8
Volvo						
244	14.4	6.5	39.4	12.8	48.3	53.5
245	14.4	6.5	—	12.8	49.1	53.5
740	14.3	6.4	38.0	12.5	43.1	57.5
760	14.3	6.4	38.0	12.5	43.1	57.5–59.8

TABLE 4 Angles of Approach and Departure, Ramp Breakover Angle, and Turning Diameter—1988 (as shown in Fig. 1)

Models	Angle of approach (degrees), H106	Angle of departure (degrees), H107	Ramp breakover angle (degrees), H147	Turning diameter (feet)			
				Outside front		Inside rear	
				Wall/ wall	Curb/ curb	Wall/ wall	Curb/ curb
Chrysler Motors							
Chrysler 5th Avenue, Dodge Diplomat, Plymouth Gran Fury	19	12	12	43.6	40.7	24.3	24.7
Chrysler New Yorker/Landau, Dodge Dynasty	17	12.7	13.5	—	40.5	—	—
Chrysler LeBaron (K-Body)	19	17	12	39.1	36.2	20.7	20.9
Plymouth Reliant, Dodge Aries	18	16–17	11–12	38.1	35.2	19.8	20.1
Chrysler New Yorker Turbo, Plymouth Caravelle, Dodge 600 ...	19	15–16	11	39.1	36.2	20.7	20.9
Chrysler LeBaron GTS, Dodge Lancer	16.6–17	17–17.9	10.8–11	38.7–44.9	36.2–42.9	20.6–28.1	20.9–28.4
Dodge Omni, Plymouth Horizon	20	21	15	39.1–40.8	37.2–39.1	22.4–24.5	22.8–24.8
Dodge Daytona, Pacificia and Shelby Z	12–15	16–18	11–12	37.0–42.9	34.3–40.7	19.0–26.1	19.3–26.3
Plymouth Sundance, Dodge Shadow	16	16	12	36.2	33.9	18.75	19.0
Chrysler LeBaron (J-Body)	15	16–17	11–12	38.1	35.2–39.3	19.8	20.1
Plymouth Voyager, Dodge Caravan	24	20–24	13–14	—	41.0–43.0	—	—
Chrysler Conquest	16	19	12	35.1	31.5	—	—
Plymouth/Dodge Colt	18–20	13–27	13	32.8–35.1	30.2–32.5	—	—
Plymouth/Dodge Colt Vista	17–22	15–18	8–14	37.4	34.8	20.3	19.7
Medallion	16.0	15.0	13.3	—	34.4	—	—
Premier	15.7	15.0	11.2	38.9	35.9	20.1	20.4
Eagle	29.7	28.6	16.8	39.5	37.2	20.6	21.1
Ford Motor Company							
Ford, Mercury	17.8–19.3	9.6–11.8	12.9–14.4	43.1	39.1	22.0	22.6
Thunderbird, Cougar	18.9	14.7	11.8	—	41.2	—	—
Tempo, Topaz	19.0	16.2	13.1	—	37.3–40.7	—	—
Mustang	16.8	12.7	12.7	—	37.4–41.2	—	—
Lincoln	17.4	11.0	13.2	44.1	40.0	22.7	23.4
Escort, Lynx, EXP	15.8–25.8	14.8–21.8	13.8–15.2	—	35.7–37.2	—	—
Tracer	18	16	12.5	33.1	30.8	—	—
Festiva	22	32	—	15.7	14.1	—	—
Continental	15.6	15.8	—	—	38.0	—	—
Mark VII	16.3	16.0	13.5	42.2	40.1	24.7	25.2
Merkur XR4Ti	19.5	14.5	—	37.1	35.4	—	—
Taurus, Sable	16.7–17.9	14.3–16.7	17.7–18.4	—	38.1	—	—
Scorpio	20.4	13.9	16.8	36.1	34.1	17.5	—
General Motors Corporation							
Cadillac DeVille, Fleetwood Limousine, Buick Electra; Oldsmobile Ninety Eight	18.3–14.2	19.0–17.0	23.1–10.8	48.6–42.0	45.8–39.1	24.3	23.0
Cadillac Fleetwood Brougham "RWD"	14.8	15.3	11.3	44.1	40.5	22.5	23.2
Chevrolet Caprice, Pontiac Safari	18.5–17.0	14.0–9.8	17.5–12.3	45.3–42.5	39.7–38.5	23.3–21.9	23.1–22.3
Oldsmobile Delta 88, Buick LeSabre, Pontiac Bonneville	20.3	23.3	10.5–10.0	48.6–41.7	40.8–38.5	24.3	23.0
Buick Riviera, Oldsmobile Toronado, Cadillac Eldorado, Seville ..	15.5–11.5	21.5–20.5	12.9	42.7–41.2	40.3–35.8	24.7–22.8	24.9–23.0
Chevrolet Monte Carlo	19.3	15.9	15.7	42.6	37.1	22.9	23.4
Pontiac Grand Prix, Oldsmobile Cutlass Supreme, Buick Regal ..	18.0	11.5	10.5	40.1–38.0	39.0–37.5	—	32.7
Chevrolet Celebrity, Pontiac 6000; Oldsmobile Cutlass Ciera, Buick Century	20.3–14.0	18.8–8.9	22.5–13.9	42.5–40.0	38.5–37.0	23.3–22.6	23.1–23.0
Pontiac Grand Am, Oldsmobile Calais, Buick Skylark	15–14	18–17	15–14	40.5–37.8	37.8–35.4	22.9–19.6	23.0–19.9
Chevrolet Cavalier, Pontiac Sunbird, Oldsmobile Firenza, Buick Skyhawk, Cadillac Cimarron	20–16	20–17	16–15	37.2	34.3	19.2	19.4
Chevrolet Camaro, Pontiac Firebird	16.5–12.2	18.8–15.6	13.4–10.7	42.6–39.4	40.0–36.9	—	—
Cadillac Allante	—	—	—	35.8–37.3	36.1	35.4	35.4
Pontiac LeMans	18.0	17.0	10.0	34.9	32.8	17.7	17.9
Chevrolet Corvette	10.6	20.2	12.3	41.4	40.4	25.0	25.0
Pontiac Fiero	17.9–13.7	26.5–23.9	13.6	37.7	37.1	23.6	22.9
Chevrolet Sprint	20.5	26.2	20.0–19.0	—	—	—	—
Chevrolet Spectrum	20.8	16.6	13.0	34.8	32.8	—	—
Chevrolet Nova	19.0	17.0	14.5	40.2	37.0	19.7	20.9
Volkswagen							
VW Fox	—	—	—	—	31.5	—	—
Golf, GTI, Jetta	—	—	—	—	34.4	—	—
Scirocco, Cabriolet	—	—	—	—	31.2	—	—
Quantum, Syncro	—	—	—	—	31.5	—	—
Audi 80–90, Quattro	—	—	—	—	33.8	—	—
Audi 5000, 100, 200, Turbo, Turbo Quattro	—	—	—	—	34.2	—	—
Vanagon, Camper	—	—	—	—	35.8	—	—
Volvo							
244	18.7	12.5	12.6	35.4	32.2	16.1	16.4
245	18.7	12.5	12.6	35.4	32.2	16.1	16.4
740	15.8	14.5	12.6	35.7	32.5	15.7	16.1
760	15.8	14.5–14.8	12.6	35.7	32.5	—	—

Ramp Breakover Angle

The ramp breakover angle is the measure of ability of the car to break over a steep ramp, either climbing or descending, without scraping (see Fig. 2). The Society of Automotive Engineers calls for a minimum of 10 degrees as a design standard. A number of models have not met this standard in recent years. The average for all groups has remained relatively constant during the period 1958–1971 despite appreciable vehicle height reductions.

The ramp breakover angle influence can be altered thru use of design techniques. Transitional blends top and bottom of ramps composed of two or more break points can multiply the ramp steepness, with workable break angles, beyond the normal capacities of car or driver. In existing structures these problems are overcome by building a pad of asphalt or concrete each side of the break point. In this manner cars having a low breakover angle

can negotiate potential critical points without scraping.

Long wheelbase cars combined with low center clearance are most susceptible to inadequate breakover angles. Buick Riviera, Pontiac Tempest, Oldsmobile Toronado, and Lincoln had lower ramp breakover angles in 1970 than Society of Automotive Engineers design standards recommendation.

Angle of Departure

A reasonable minimum value is necessary to reduce the incidence of tailpipe and rear bumper dragging. The standard calls for a minimum of 10 degrees, violated only in the 1957–1959 period. Only one 1970 car, Mercury, met the minimum standard. Most cars are substantially above 10 degrees. The most critical condition is at driveways where the apron is steep, or a combination of excessive crown to gutter and apron slope.

Angle of Approach

The trend of approach angle of domestic cars from 1948 to 1962 indicates a drop in the 1957–1959 period below 15 degrees. The standard developed in 1960 by the Society of Automotive Engineers calls for a minimum value of 15 degrees. The standard has been maintained up to 1970 when reduced by Chrysler and Dodge to 14.0 and 14.6 degrees respectively. (See Fig. 3.)

Ramp Slopes

The maximum ramp slope should be 20 percent. For slopes over 10 percent, a transition at least 8 ft long should be provided at each end of the ramp at one half the slope of the ramp itself. (See Fig. 4.)

Driveway Exits

A ramped driveway exit rising up to a public sidewalk must have a transition section that is

Fig. 2 Ramp breakover angle.

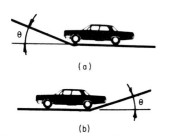

Fig. 3 (a) Angle of approach. (b) Angle of departure.

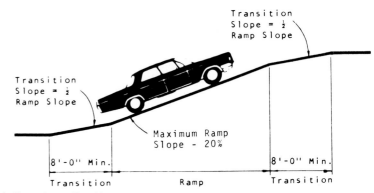

Fig. 4 Ramp slopes. (Transitions are required only if ramp slope exceeds 10 percent.)

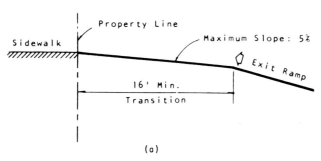

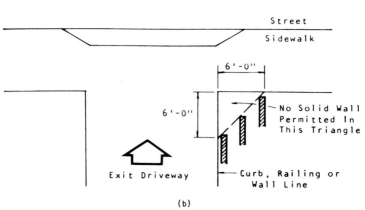

Fig. 5 Driveway exits.

almost level (maximum slope: 5 percent) before intersecting the sidewalk to prevent the hood of the car from obscuring the driver's view of pedestrians on the walk. This transition should be 16 ft long. (See Fig. 5a.)

Property line walls should also be regulated so as not to interfere with the driver's view of pedestrians on a public sidewalk. Wherever an exit driveway is parallel and adjacent to a property line wall which extends all the way to a sidewalk, the edge of the driveway should be physically established, by curb or railing, at least 6 ft from that wall. For each foot that the wall is held back from the sidewalk, the required distance between driveway and wall may be reduced by one foot. (See Fig. 5b.)

RAMP SYSTEMS*

A number of different interfloor ramp systems can be used to enable vehicles to traverse the approximate 10-ft (3-m) elevation between parking levels. Some of these systems provide separate and exclusive ramps, while others make use of continuous sloping floors that accommodate both parked vehicles and interfloor travel.

Ramps may be straight, curved, or a combination. No single ramp system is best for all applications. The choice should be based on site shape and dimensions and parking demand characteristics. Ramps may be designed for one-way or two-way traffic movement. However, one-lane-wide ramps should not be operated on a reversible two-way basis.

In some instances, site topography will allow direct access to several parking levels from the street system. This is a desirable arrangement, since it leaves more space for parking and provides more flexibility for traffic distribution between the street system and parking facility.

Time and convenience are important to ramp travel and should be considered in any comparison of ramp types. Actual travel time on ramps varies little among different ramp system types; however, some ramp systems have more potential for delay caused by conflicting traffic movements that limit ramp capacity. Other factors influencing ramp design include accident hazards, construction cost, and ability to accommodate vehicles and drivers conveniently.

Analysis of Ramp Movements

A ramp system includes any portion of storage floors used by vehicles moving between levels. Nearly every successful ramp system requires vehicles to follow an approximately circular path when traveling between parking levels. The number of 360-degree rotations required to circulate through the garage and parking structure height are major concerns, particularly in self-park designs.

It is generally desirable to limit the maximum number of complete rotations to five or six. Depending on ramp system type, this will control the maximum desirable number of parking levels and limit the number of parking spaces a driver must pass during garage travel.

Drivers are sometimes distracted or disturbed by the awareness of height when traveling on upper parking levels—a condition that can be accentuated if parking levels extend higher than adjacent buildings. To reduce driver distraction,

parapet walls along driving ramps should be designed to limit the driver's view of surroundings outside the parking structure.

Clearway and Adjacent Ramp Types Ramp systems may be divided into two types, based on the amount of interference between ramp traffic and parking-unparking operations. Ramp systems designed on the "clearway" principle provide interfloor travel paths completely separated from potentially conflicting parking-unparking movements. Ramp systems in which part or all of the ramp travel is performed on access aisles may be called the "adjacent parking" type. The number of parking stalls adjacent to the ramp may vary from a small number to the total capacity of the facility. (See Fig. 1.)

Clearway ramp systems provide the safest movement with least delay and, except for sloping floor designs, are preferred for self-park designs. However, the clearway ramp system is seldom feasible for small garage sites.

An adjacent-parking layout requires less area per parking stall because of the twofold use of travel paths, and consequently can be used to advantage on smaller land parcels. However, adjacent-parking ramp designs are more susceptible to traffic movement delays and potential accident-causing situations.

The actual travel speeds for free-moving vehicles on the two types of ramps do not vary greatly. Delays on the adjacent-parking type ramp system caused by parking-unparking maneuvers are difficult to measure but must be recognized as a sizeable quantity. Delays will be greater on parking levels nearest the street level, since these levels always have larger numbers of vehicles in the circulation system.

Concentric Versus Tandem Ramp Design Ramp systems also can be classified as concentric or tandem, depending on whether the travel paths of vehicles moving up and down between parking levels revolve about the same or separate centers. Helically-curved (spiral) ramps are usually built concentrically to save space and to provide flatter grades. Straight ramp systems are designed in either concentric or tandem configurations.

Vehicles traveling on a ramp system may move either clockwise or counterclockwise. Counterclockwise rotation is generally preferred in the United States and other countries where drivers customarily sit on the left side in vehicles since it places drivers on the inside of turns, enabling better vehicle handling.

Parallel Versus Opposed Ramp Design For vehicles to rotate in the same direction on a ramp system, up and down ramps must slope in opposite directions, requiring ramp surfaces to be op-

posed. If up and down ramps slope in the same direction, ramp surfaces are parallel and vehicles must rotate in opposite directions.

While no significant difference has been observed in operational ease, it is obvious that opposed ramp types are safer, since all vehicles must travel in the same direction. Parallel ramp systems are considerably cheaper to construct, however.

Geometric Ramp Types

For safety, convenience, and traffic operating efficiency, the path followed by the ramp through traffic on any floor of a parking garage should be short, with minimum turns and traffic crossings. Ramp arrangements within a garage should be consistent, in order to be as simple and comprehensible as possible.

Ramp design and arrangement are influenced by (1) orientation of ramp traffic flow to main-floor street entrance and exit points and to other ramp systems that might exist in larger garages, (2) conformance of ramps with access aisles throughout each floor area, and (3) site dimensions.

Straight-Ramp Systems Ramps within a straight-ramp system usually should be "stacked" one over another for construction economy and traffic circulation uniformity. The stacking of ramps creates a "ramp-well." From a plan view, the sum of the system's ramp-well areas and the floor area containing aisles used by ramp portal-to-portal traffic is the ramp system's area, or envelope. This extends vertically through the parking structure (with the possible exception of roof and/or basement levels).

For straight-ramp garages, the ramp system is usually rectangularly shaped (ignoring curved ramp ends), with the ramp well(s) along the structure's longer-side dimension. This is because more horizontal distance is required to satisfy ramp grade criteria than to accommodate vehicular movement between ramp ends.

Figure 2 illustrates a basic straight-ramp system having a ramp-well on one side only. In this system, vehicles follow an elliptical path, most of which is on flat surfaces. Figure 3 is a parallel straight-ramp system, with ramp-wells on two sides of the structure. Turning movements for the up and down ramps are performed in different areas, while the floor travel is performed in a two-way movement along the same aisle. Depending on structure width, the floor travel could be directionally separated. The systems represented in Figs. 2 and 3 are both very adaptable to entrance and exit points on the same street.

Figure 4 is an adjacent-parking type opposed straight-ramp system. Travel paths for through up and down movements fall in the same aisle,

* *Parking Garage Planning and Operation,* Eno Foundation for Transportation, Inc., Westport, Conn., 1978.

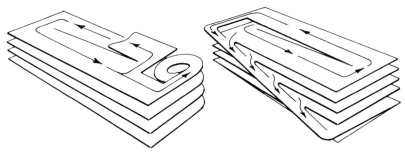

Fig. 1 Parking garage examples that incorporate adjacent-parking ramp systems for traffic entering and clearway ramp systems for traffic exiting the facilities.

eliminating traffic crossing points. Figure 5 illustrates a clearway type opposed straight-ramp system. Ends of opposed ramps on the main floor are pointed in opposite directions, making this type suited to structures with entrance and exit points on separate streets. This design can be adapted to entrance and exit points on the same street, but requires a 180-degree turn on the main floor—necessitating additional space.

Straight-ramp systems are advantageous in relatively narrow buildings. They require less floor

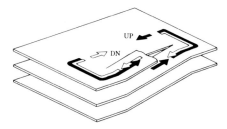

Fig. 2 Parallel straight-ramp system with ramp-wells on two structure sides.

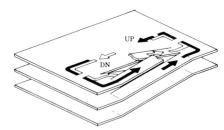

Fig. 3 Straight-ramp system with one ramp-well.

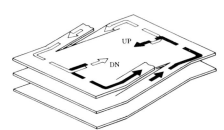

Fig. 4 Adjacent-parking type opposed straight-ramp system.

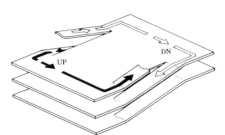

Fig. 5 Clearway-type opposed straight-ramp system.

area than helically-curved ramps and are simple to construct, particularly in existing structures being converted to parking garages. However, sharp turns, necessary to get on and off straight ramps, are disadvantages.

Split-Level or Staggered-Floor Systems. The staggered-floor parking garage, invented by Fernand E. d'Humy, is now generally referred to as a split-level garage. It is constructed in two sections, with floor levels in one section staggered vertically by one-half story from those in adjacent sections. Short straight ramps, sloped in alternate directions and separated by the distance required to easily make a 180-degree turn between ramps, connect the half-stories.

Any combination of straight ramps can be applied to the split-level floor systems. Traffic rotation direction may be the same, in which case the aisles are one-way, thereby reducing conflicts. Turning paths may overlap, requiring less space for the ramp system. Rotation can be provided also in opposite directions, which simplifies ramp construction by having up and down ramps on the same plane.

The division between split-level structure halves

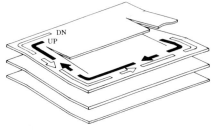

Fig. 6 Two-way staggered-floor ramp system.

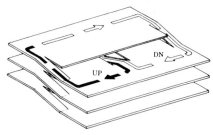

Fig. 7 Tandem staggered-floor ramp system.

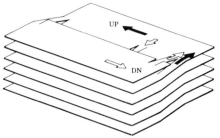

Fig. 8 This staggered-floor system provides parking on level floors and desirable one-way traffic flow.

may be perpendicular to the street or parallel. In the latter case, either the front or back half may be elevated. Split-level floors can overlap as much as 5 to 6 ft (1.5 to 1.8 m) to increase space efficiency and make narrow sites workable.

Figures 6 through 9 illustrate various types of split-level configurations. Figure 8 is the most common type.

Split-level designs are particularly applicable to small, high-cost sites where maximum use of space must be achieved. Construction is relatively simple, and the design fits well on rectangular sites. This system is efficient in terms of floor space per vehicle parking stall but, like all ramp systems employing adjacent parking, frequent conflicts may arise between circulating traffic and parking-unparking vehicles.

One variation in the split-level system uses three separate sections, with the two end sections at equal elevations and staggered one-half story with respect to the center section (see Fig. 9). Fifty percent fewer turns are required, thereby reducing travel time. However, vehicles parked on the end sections must be driven an extra half-floor when entering or leaving. "Wrong way" ramp travel is also a greater possibility with this type of design.

Sloping-Floor Systems The sloping-floor parking garage, in its simplest form, contains two adjacent parking modules tilted in opposite directions, with cross-aisles at each end so that vehicles traveling the length of both aisles make a 360-degree turn to move up or down one complete parking level (Fig. 10). Thus, there is no area set aside for ramps in the ordinary sense. The cross-aisles may be sloped or level.

Parking industry experience indicates that the sloping-floor design is well-suited to self-park operations. The relatively flat floor slope (customarily ranging between 3 and 5 percent) permits comfortable parking and pedestrian walking. Because parking is adjacent to the interfloor circulation system, each entering customer has an oppor-

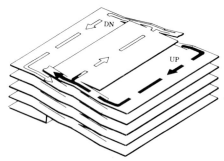

Fig. 9 Three-level staggered-floor ramp system.

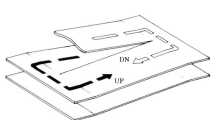

Fig. 10 Basic sloping-floor concept.

tunity to park in the first available space. However, the operational problems in adjacent parking can cause congestion during peak outbound movements if clearway-type express ramps are not used.

Floor-to-floor travel distance is greater in sloping-floor garages than in other types of ramp garages. However, this is offset somewhat by the opportunity for greater travel speeds due to flat slopes and longer tangents.

For large structures it is desirable to have only part of the floor area sloped, with level floor sections at ends to form cross-aisles. Ramp connections at midpoints of opposite sloping floors permit one-way traffic circulation (Fig. 11). It is possible to achieve one-way traffic circulation in sloping-floor layouts, with parking along aisles on every level, by using two sloping-floor garage units placed end-to-end. In the level center section where the two units meet, traffic flow can change from up to down and vice versa. This permits flexibility for angled parking, limited only by available site width (Fig. 12).

Helically Curved Ramp Systems The helix (spiral) ramp can be a single surface that permits vehicles to travel on a continuous helical path between parking levels. When two-way traffic is handled on a single helix, the outer lane is used for up movements, since it has a larger radius of curvature and lower grade. Up movements are usually counterclockwise and down movements clockwise.

Helical-ramp entrance and exit points can be located on the same side or opposite sides of the ramp coil. In either case, ramp access points are located directly above each other on each succeeding floor. Helically curved ramps should be of the clearway type. Examples are illustrated in Figs. 13 and 14.

The double helix system (Fig. 14) uses two helical-path surfaces that are sloped in opposite directions. One surface can be used for up movements, the other for down movements. The two sloping helical surfaces may be separated or they may be interwoven. Vehicle movements for both up and down travel directions are made in the same direction of rotation. In the United States and other countries using left-side drive vehicles, counterclockwise rotation is preferred.

Interwoven double helix systems are popular in tall structures (10 to 12 parking levels) because the number of 360-degree turns can be reduced by using two separated helical surfaces to serve alternate parking levels.

Traditionally, curving ramps are said to be continuous where they provide 360 degrees of rotation between two parking levels. The noncontinuous helically curved ramps that provide rotation through 180 degrees are commonly referred to as semicircular—although this definition is not quite correct, since the curved section is helical in shape.

Helically curved ramps are most often located in corners of rectangular structures to minimize floor-space loss, or they are located outside the structure when additional site area is available. Helically curved ramps require more space than straight ramps, but they can offer better traffic operation by providing gradual turning as compared to sharp turning movements usually required at ends of straight ramps. In addition,

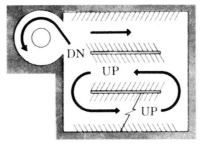

Fig. 13 Helical ramps such as this one can be used effectively for express exiting.

superelevation at ends of straight ramps may require undesirable warping of floor areas.

Express Exit Ramps Large parking structures with frequent high-turnover conditions may be served best with an express ramp for one direction of travel—usually for exiting traffic. Express exits can be curved or straight, and are designed always on the clearway principle, providing one-way traffic movement (Fig. 15). They are generally desirable to serve high-turnover transient patronage. They improve operating efficiency by reducing travel time and conflicts—but may add significantly to structure costs, since they increase the area prorated to each parking space in determinations of space-use efficiency.

Ramp Standards

Ramp design parameters governing the acceptability of such ramp features as maximum gradient and minimum radius of curvature have evolved from garage operating experience. The following discussion presents standards generally used by the parking industry.

Ramp Grades Ramp grade (slope) is computed by multiplying floor-to-floor height by 100 and dividing by the ramp length. The difference between ramp length measured along the slope or horizontally is negligible. Grades on curving ramps are measured along the outer ramp pavement edge.

Maximum practical ramp grades are principally limited by safety considerations and the psychological effect on drivers, with hill-climbing and braking abilities of automobiles being a secondary factor. Steep ramps slow traffic movement and can be particularly hazardous when wet, requiring drivers to be excessively cautious.

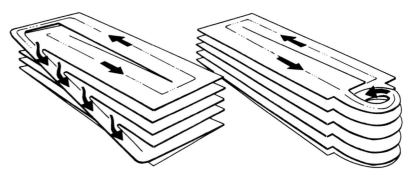

Fig. 14 Helical ramp systems can often be advantageous for structures situated on odd-shaped sites.

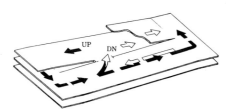

Fig. 11 Sloping-floor system with crossover ramp of mid-point.

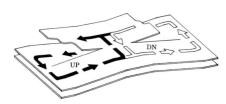

Fig. 12 Double sloping-floor system with mid-point crossover.

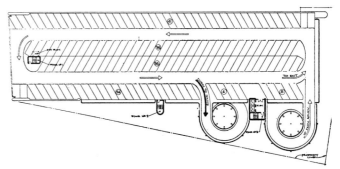

Fig. 15 Examples of straight and helical express exit ramps.

925

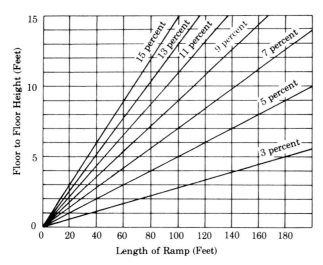

Fig. 16 Relationship between floor-to-floor height, ramp grade, and length. (SOURCE: Edmund R. Ricker, *Traffic Design of Parking Garages,* The Eno Foundation for Highway Traffic Control, 1957, p. 115.)

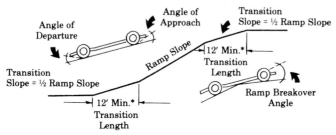

*Ramp slopes (grades) less than 10 percent can be blended satisfactorily with an 8-foot transition length.

Fig. 17 Method of blending ramp and floor grades. Vertical scale is exaggerated to show detail. (SOURCE: Adapted from Edmund R. Ricker, *Traffic Design of Parking Garages,* The Eno Foundation for Highway Traffic Control, 1957, p. 117.)

Fig. 18 Curved ramp system with tangent sections.

Minimum radius is 32 feet to outer pavement edge for helical ramp or other turning path. A 35- to 37-foot radius is most desirable.

Fig. 19 Helical ramp dimension standards.
(SOURCE: *Parking Principles,* Special Report 125 Highway Research Board, 1971.)

For self-park designs, maximum ramp grades should not exceed 15 percent; however, 20 percent maximum ramp grades for attendant-parking garages are acceptable. In parking structures where pedestrians are expected to walk on vehicle ramps, grades preferably should be no more than 10 percent.

Figure 16 graphically relates ramp grade and length with floor-to-floor heights. For instance, this graph shows that for a slope of 13 percent and a rise of 9 ft or 2.7 m (floor-to-floor height), a ramp length of 70 ft (21.3 m) long is required. Similarly, a floor-to-floor height of 11 ft (3.4 m) and a ramp length of 90 ft (27 m) results in a slope (ramp grade) of 12 percent.

The maximum preferable grade for sloping-floor self-park garages is 4 percent, and in attendant-park garages, 10 percent. Angle parking in sloping-floor garages should be 60 degrees or greater, to minimize gravity roll-back of vehicles.

Ramp Grade Transition Design Critical vehicle clearances, driver comfort, and safety considerations influence the design of ramp ends where they meet flatter floor surfaces. Ramp breakover angle, and the angles of approach (affecting front overhang of vehicles) and departure (affecting rear overhang) are critical vehicle clearance points. These angles are established for stationary vehicles with normal equipment and load, including passengers and fuel.

Ramp breakover angle is limited by wheelbase and vehicle ground clearance, and is a measure of an automobile's ability to be driven over the crest formed by two converging surfaces without scraping its underside. Ramp breakover angle varies inversely to wheelbase.

Angles of approach and departure are limited by vehicle front and rear overhang and ground clearance. These vehicle clearance angles determine an automobile's ability to roll over the sag point (lower end of ramp) formed by different grades without scraping or touching the pavement surface. The angle of departure is more critical because the rear overhang of vehicles is generally longer than the front overhang.

Standards established by the Society of Automotive Engineers limit the ramp breakover angle to no less than 10 degrees; angle of departure, no less than 10 degrees; and angle of approach, no less than 15 degrees. Vehicles designed to these minimum standards theoretically are able to traverse sag and crest sections at the bottom and top of a 17.6 percent ramp grade, and to move to flat floor grades without need for a grade transitioning (blending) area.

However, centrifugal force, causing vehicle suspension to compress when crossing a sag point, even at low speed, can result in vehicles scraping pavement surfaces. Without grade transitioning at the ramp crest, driver sight-distance can be limited momentarily, and crossing abrupt grade changes can be uncomfortable for drivers and passengers. Therefore, ramp grades should be blended gradually or transitioned to flatter floor surfaces.

A practical method of blending ramp grades to relatively flat floor levels involves using a minimum 12-ft-long (3.7-m) transition slope equal to one-half of the ramp grade. Figure 17 illustrates this ramp grade transitioning method. Ramp grades of less than 10 percent can be blended satisfactorily with a transitioning slope shorter than 12 ft (3.7 m).

Ramp Width and Radii For one-way straight ramps, minimum acceptable width is 12 ft (3.66 m); and for two-way straight ramps, where opposing traffic flows are not separated, 22 ft (6.71 m) is the recommended minimum width. Where a barrier is used between lanes to separate traffic flows, each lane should be at least 12 ft (3.66 m) wide for tangent lengths. Circular ramp lanes generally should be 14–18 ft (4.3–5.5 m) wide.

The repeated turning movements of vehicles traveling between parking levels is a primary design consideration. The spiraling path radius must be kept minimal to conserve space and reduce travel distance. However, very sharp and unrelieved turning will produce a dizzying effect on drivers. To minimize this effect, ramp systems can be laid out with sharp curves separated by short tangents or less sharply curved sections (Fig. 18).

Lateral clearance for a vehicle traveling a curved path is determined by a vehicle's outermost corner point radius (usually the front bumper) when it is turning on a minimum radius. The inside edge of travel lane radius must be less than the minimum inside rear-wheel radius—but not much smaller, or drivers will attempt to enter the ramp at too sharp an angle. The relationship between these radii depends on relative vehicle position, which is determined by maximum steering angle and driver steering input, extreme corner dimensions, and speed. Clearance is usually provided for the vehicle with the largest outermost corner point radius.

Minimum outside radius for a single-lane helical

ramp is 32 ft (9.75 m); however, an outer radius of 35–37 ft (10.67–11.28 m) is desirable. With helically curved two-lane ramp surfaces, the outer lane need not be as wide as the lane used on the inside path. The outer lane radius is less restrictive, allowing drivers to turn at a flatter angle that requires less effective width for a travel path (Fig. 19).

Ramp Turn Superelevation Vehicles traveling on curved paths are acted on by centrifugal force proportional to the square of the velocity and inversely proportional to the radius of curvature. This centrifugal force must be balanced by other forces that are developed by side-friction of the tires on pavement, and superelevation (banking) of the ramp surface. Although speeds in parking garages are low, turning radii are much smaller than those required for street or highways, thus resulting in rather large centrifugal forces. Ramp curves should not be superelevated too steeply, because very slow drivers may have difficulty in keeping away from the inside edge of the ramp pavement and fast drivers may be encouraged to drive at speeds greater than conditions of grade and sight-distance safely permit.

Garage ramp superelevation should be approximately ½-in/ft (approximately 4 cm/m) of ramp width at the point of sharpest turning, with lesser amounts adjacent to straight sections or storage floors.

Ramp Appearance Some motorists are reluctant to use ramp garages because travel paths in parking garages may combine narrow lanes, steep grades, and sharp turns. Even drivers accustomed to garage parking depend on appearance and "feel" in maneuvering their vehicles.

Consequently it is desirable to use architectural and optical effects that will give drivers confidence and reduce possible adverse psychological effects of driving in restricted spaces. An obvious means is to make sight distances as great as possible and to provide abundant illumination.

The optical trick of obscuring horizontal and vertical lines of reference may be used to reduce the apparent steepness of ramp grades. Ramp walls can be painted with stripes contrasting to wall color, parallel to ramp surface or at steeper angles. The normal angles between vertical columns and the travelway can be obscured by paint markings, or adjacent structural features may be built with architectural lines parallel or perpendicular to ramp surfaces.

Ramp structures should be as open as practicable, to provide sight distances and to reduce closed-in impressions. In locations where icing conditions are common, ramp systems should be placed in building interiors or otherwise protected from weather.

Ramp illumination should be given special attention. Wall openings should not be allowed where outside light sources could blind drivers. Artificial lighting should take the form of diffused illumination, and reflectors should be pointed away from the direction of travel.

PARKING GARAGES

Typical Designs

In the following pages the functional plans and design features of five self-parking facilities are presented. They are typical of the modern

Parking Garage Operation, The Eno Foundation for Highway Traffic Control, Saugatuck, Conn., 1961.

garage planning that has evolved during the past several years.

In Fig. 1, the plan for a twin-spiral garage is shown. The ramps, situated in opposite corners, are angled to facilitate the movement from the floors to the ramps. Entrances and exits have been provided on two streets on separate levels to take advantage of the different elevations.

The waiting area—two elevators, rest rooms, cashier's booths, and vending machines—is in the center of the garage. A retail area extends along the entire frontage of one of the streets and has a depth of about 85 ft. The fourth level of the garage, or roof deck, extends over the retail area. Ninety-degree parking is employed throughout the facility.

A staggered-floor or split-level garage is shown in Fig. 2. The ramp systems feature separated one-way operation, and access is on only one street. The overall dimensions of the 352-space facility are 120 by 240 ft. Ninety-degree parking is utilized throughout the four floors. The cashier's booth is at the entrance,

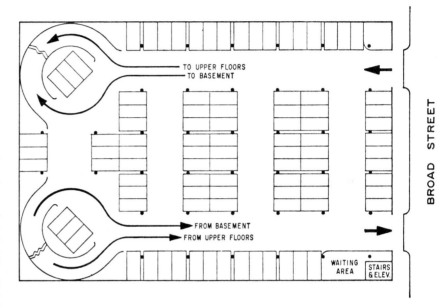

MAIN FLOOR

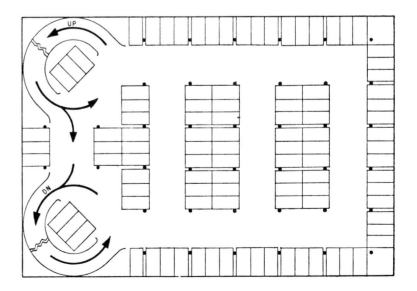

TYPICAL FLOOR

Fig. 1 Functional plan for twin-spiral garage.

PARKING GARAGES

and the stairs and elevators are strategically located in the center of the facility to take advantage of the split-level and to afford minimum walking distances.

In Fig. 3 a functional plan is presented for a facility with straight ramps. The garage has one-way aisles and angle parking. Actually, a portion of the aisles is used in the floor-to-floor circulation. There are three pedestrian elevators and four stairways to serve the eight floors. Though the entrance and exit were on the same street, they are widely separated to reduce conflicts. The overall dimensions of the facility are 183 by 165 ft.

In a sloping-floor or continuous-ramp garage, the aisles serve two purposes: access to the parking stalls, and floor-to-floor circulation. In Fig. 4, a typical garage is shown which provides 90° parking. One pedestrian elevator and three stairways have been provided for the five-level facility. The entrance and exit are on one street. The direction of travel on the ramps has been reversed to reduce the conflict at the contact with the one-way street. Overall dimensions are 122 by 157 ft.

The preparation of a design for an irregular-shape site presents many problems, especially when self-parking is to be provided. An example of a good design is presented in Fig. 5 where a spiral ramp is in the center of the garage. The aisles are one-way and two-way, and 90° parking is used throughout the facility.

For the three-floor garage, there is one

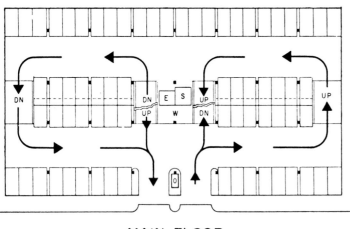

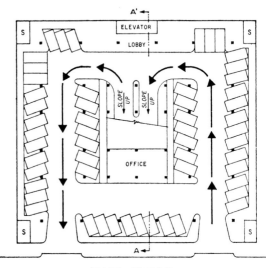

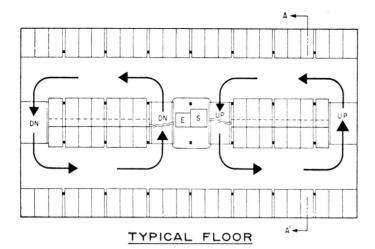

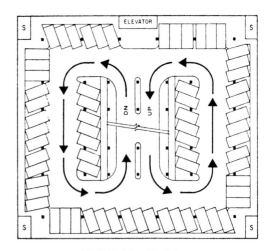

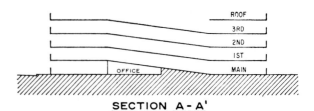

Fig. 2   Functional plan for staggered-floor garage.

Fig. 3   Functional plan for straight-ramp garage.

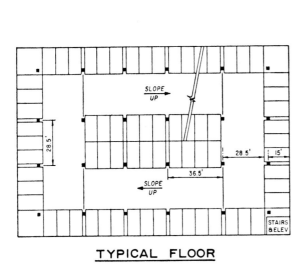

TYPICAL FLOOR

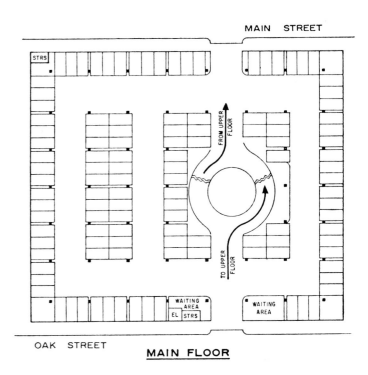

MAIN FLOOR

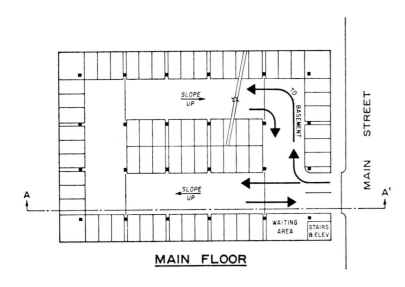

MAIN FLOOR

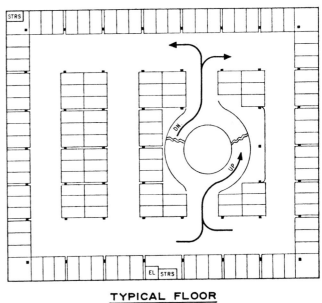

TYPICAL FLOOR

Fig. 5 Functional plan for concentric-spiral garage.

SECTION A - A'

Fig. 4 Functional plan for sloping-floor garage.

Commercial

PARKING GARAGES

pedestrian elevator available at present. Plans and areas are provided for an additional elevator when warranted. There are four stairways. In the operation of the facility, an entrance has been provided on one street and two streets are used for exiting.

Many variations may be used in garage design. The previous examples are typical designs. Design criteria and standards were assembled in a recent study.[1] The designs must be tailored to the available land.

By GEOFFREY BAKER and BRUNO FUNARO

RAMP GARAGES

Ramp garages do not simply multiply the parking capacity of a lot by the number of parking levels added. Considerable space on each level will be taken by ramps and circulation ways which must be kept free of parked cars. Only on the uppermost level (or the lowermost in the case of an underground garage) can cars be temporarily stored in the aisles as they normally are in an attendant-operated parking lot.

On a sloping lot, developed with only two or three parking levels, space normally required for ramps may be reduced. By connecting adjacent streets to the different parking levels, the street system is, in effect, incorporated into the garage ramp system.

As most garages henceforth will be designed, we believe, for customer self-parking, we have taken 12 percent (i.e., a rise of 12 ft in every 100, or a 7° angle of slope) as the maximum convenient ramp grade.

Actually public use and acceptance of a ramp slope depends less upon the mechanical power and body dimensions of the car than upon the apparent hazards to the timid driver of steep, narrow slopes, and sharp, blind turns. For some also the terror of coming down a ramp is likely to be greater than that of going up, especially now that so many cars have automatic shifts which prevent them from stalling or running backward on hills.

To make a ramp seem less confined and hazardous, it should be one-way, well-lighted but without distracting glare, and separated from opposing traffic with a wide divider strip. Camouflage painting devices may be used to make the slope appear less steep. Horizontal lines of reference can be obscured with wall stripes parallel to, or at a steeper angle than, the roadway. A long sight line, particularly at the upper end of a ramp, will guard against drivers hesitating. This in turn will increase speeds (without decreasing safety), and so increase the ramp's traffic capacity.

The shallower and longer the ramp, the more space it requires on each parking level. The only exception to this is where the whole garage becomes in effect a shallow-angled ramp, a wide roadway with a line of 90° parking on each side. This spirals up and around in a con-

tinuous line of warped rectangles fitted into the rectangular shell of the building.

The second factor governing ramp length is floor-to-floor height. The smaller this dimension, the shorter can be the ramps. However, the floor-to-ceiling clear height should not be less than $7\frac{1}{2}$ ft, and even this will require many radio aerials to be retracted or tied down at the garage entrance. Thin-floor structural slabs are particularly worthwhile in garage construction.

Each end of the ramp, where it joins the parking level, must be blended into the floor grade over a minimum distance of 12 ft. The sections of a modern car most likely to scrape ground at top or bottom of a slope are the long overhangs in front and rear beyond the wheelbase.

The area required for a ramp system will be most important in determining whether a given piece of land can be profitably developed with a multistory garage structure. A floor-to-floor height of $8\frac{1}{2}$ ft requires a 12 percent ramp 71 ft long (see Table 1). Another 45 ft beyond this will be needed for a reasonably convenient turning radius in circulation lanes on each parking floor.

So the minimum length needed for the simplest form of parking deck, with a straight ramp and on more than two levels, is 90 ft in

in attendant-operated garages will be set by the time required to walk between the furthest parked car and the central interfloor man lift which connects with the entrance check-in point where cars are collected and delivered.

This interfloor communication point should be as near as possible to the centroid of the parking floor. For attendants' average walking speed is found to be 5 ft per second; their driving speed averages 13 ft per second.

The layout of parking stalls should be designed to minimize travel time. One 100 ft of extra travel distance to and from a parking stall will add $7\frac{1}{2}$ seconds to driving time, 20 seconds to walking time, thus reducing each attendant's parking rate by one car per hour. In a large operation with high turnover, this will be revealed by either an increase of labor costs, or by long delays in the delivery of cars to outgoing customers, or by need for a larger reservoir to prevent delay in reception of incoming cars.

For customer-parking garages the same standards of walking distance should apply as in parking lots: a maximum walk of 300 ft from parked car to garage entrance. Most important here is allowance for peak periods of interfloor travel by customers entering or leaving.

TABLE 1 Ramp Length for Straight Ramps (to the nearest foot)

Angle, degrees	Ramp grade, percent	Floor-to-floor height					Split-level floors	
		8 ft	9 ft	10 ft	11 ft	12 ft	4 ft	5 ft
3	5	160	180	200	220	240	80	100
$3\frac{1}{2}$	6	133	150	167	183	200	67	88
4	7	114	128	143	157	172	57	77
$4\frac{1}{2}$	8	100	112	125	138	150	50	63
5	9	89	100	111	122	134	45	55
6	10	80	90	100	110	120	40	50
$6\frac{1}{2}$	11	73	82	91	100	109	37	46
7	12	67	75	83	92	100	34	42
$7\frac{1}{2}$	13	61	69	77	85	92	31	39
8	14	57	64	72	79	86	29	36
$8\frac{1}{2}$	15	53	60	66	73	80	27	33

addition to the ramp length, which will vary according to steepness (see plan, Fig. 3).

Minimum economical width totals 108 ft. And still, with these minimum dimensions, there is a quite uneconomical ratio of circulation space to storage space on each parking floor. Only by enlarging the floor areas, which usually means enlarging the available lot size, can more storage space be served by the same amount of circulation space.

Ramp length, of course, can only be reduced by steepening the ramp angle or reducing the floor-to-floor height between parking floors. The shape of a ramp can be changed and condensed by coiling it into a helix.

Location and shape of the ramp system is particularly important on the entrance floor of attendant-operated garages. The further away the ramp from the street entrances, the larger the reservoir space, and the better the cushion against delay and congestion at periods of peak arrival.

In general, as we have seen above, the larger each parking floor, the more advantageous the ratio between storage space and circulation ways. The upper limit on floor area

In a large garage, customer-operated elevators may be insufficient for these peak periods. Escalators will give much better service under these conditions; but they will probably be justified only in a very large garage.

In a parking garage of three floors or less, stairs are still accepted by the public. It will, however, generally be wiser to fill the top floor with long-term parkers, who (perhaps tempted by lower monthly rates) will be more willing to make the climb.

Types of Ramp Garages

Types of ramp garages vary widely. No one plan is best for all sites or all types of garage. The shape of the lot, anticipated parking demand, whether the garage is to be designed for parking by customers or by attendants, limitations of cost and of structure (particularly if the garage is part of another building such as an office block or an auditorium)—all are important factors when deciding what is the most efficient type of ramp design for the job.

Parking, Reinhold Publishing Corp., New York, 2d ptg., 1963, by permission of Van Nostrand Reinhold Company.
[1] Ricker, *Traffic Design of Parking Garages*, Eno Foundation, 1957.

To improve the ratio between ramp area and parking area, the ramp can be steepened, a one-way ramp can be used for two-way traffic, the ramp can be designed to double as a parking aisle with stalls on each side, cars may be parked in the aisles, and more rows may be double-parked. Every one of these will lower operating efficiency. None of them, except possibly the ramp which doubles as a parking aisle, are even to be considered in a modern customer-parking garage.

All ramp systems except the helical need circulation lanes kept clear on each parking floor for a continuous path upward and downward through the building.

Actually all ramp systems must circle in order to gain sufficient length within the building to go upward at a reasonable slope. In helical ramps this circling is confined to the ramp. In all other types the turning movement (through 360 or 180 according to ramp type and floor layout) is made not on the ramp but on the parking floors. This turning movement can be made more easily on a banked helical ramp than on the flat parking floors.

Minimum site width required for a ramp garage is 100 to 110 ft, as shown below; and even then there is a quite uneconomical ratio between parking area and ramp space. A helical ramp would fit a narrower site but waste even more space. For a narrow site, particularly a corner lot, the elevator garage may be most economical. Minimum width of the structure alone may be as little as 60 ft. But there must be access on both sides of this, for entrance and exit. There should also be off-street reservoir space. So minimum site width, with a street on the front and one side, is 80 ft. (see Fig. 6). If there is no side street, another 20 ft must be added to the frontage for exit lanes.

Of helical ramp types the least costly to construct is usually that shown in Fig. 7. One-way up and down lanes are on a single-banked surface. The outer lane is used for up traffic, usually counterclockwise, so that cars keep to the right in normal fashion.

The diameter of the ramp is controlled by the required turning radius: a minimum of 45 ft to the face of the outside curb of the outer lane. There is crossing of traffic at each parking floor connection, but drivers have a clear view each way.

In the circular ramp shown in Fig. 7 there is no crossing of up and down traffic, even at the parking floor connections. Each traffic stream is confined to its own ramp all the way from top to bottom of the building.

As entrance and exit points are at opposite sides of the ramp cylinder, the best position for this type of ramp will be near the center of the parking floor.

The surface of these ramps can be fully banked between floors, but they must be flattened at the point of connection with each park-

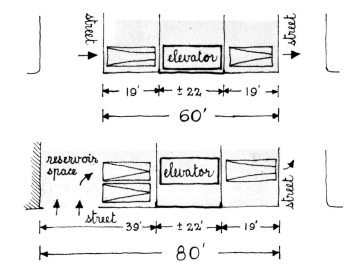

TRAFFIC CIRCULATION ON PARKING FLOORS *(BELOW)* IS IMPOSED BY THE RAMP LAYOUT CHOSEN

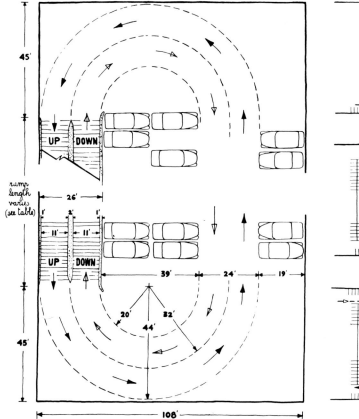

Fig. 6

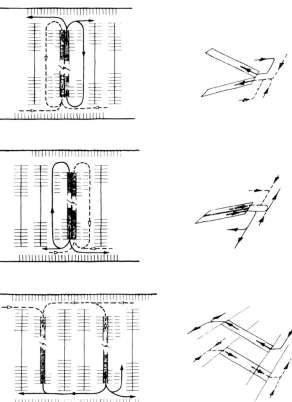

TABLE 2   Helical Ramps—Minimum Dimensions for Two Lanes Side by Side, feet

Radius to inside face of outer curb of outer lane	45
Radius of inside lane to inside face of outer curb	32
Width of inside lane between curbs	12
Width of outside lane between curbs	11
Width of border curbs (curb height: 6 in.)	1
Width of median curb (curb height: 6 in.)	2
Maximum super-elevation on ramp turns	0.1 ft per ft of width

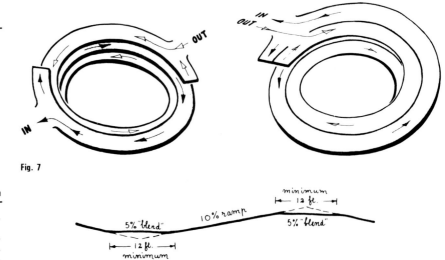

Fig. 7

ing floor, so that cars can turn off and on without too sharp a break in grade.

To avoid scraping the floor with front or rear overhangs or some part of the underbody of the car, change of grade between floor and ramp must not be too sudden. The blending

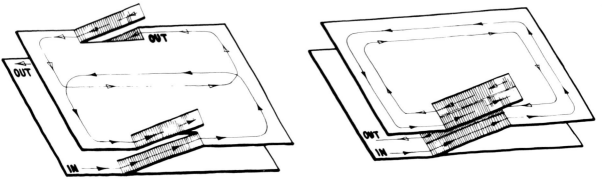

Fig. 8

Fig. 9

distance must be at least as long as most wheelbase lengths—about 10 ft. As precise construction in concrete is not to be expected, it is wiser to set 12 ft as minimum. A simple rule of thumb is to make this transition grade half the ramp grade. (See Fig. 8.)

Halfway between the circular and the straight ramp is what may be called the rectangular circle. This is so large and so shallow that it normally fills the whole building, and so wide that there is a line of right-angle parking along each side. The floors of the garage become tilted planes. A basic disadvantage of this plan is that a two-way circulation road must also serve as a parking aisle—and a very long one too. The inevitable result is congestion and delay, particularly at the lower levels during outgoing rush hours.

Probably the simplest types of ramp in structure, planning, and operation are the two-way divided ramps set one above the other at one edge or in the center of the parking floor. (See Fig. 9.)

This is quite economical of space, particularly on a lot that is rather long and narrow. Two-way circulation lanes on the parking floor may be hazardous.

Here the up and down traffic streams have been separated. This plan still has the advantages of rectangular shape and small ramp area. But the up and down circulation lanes intersect on the parking floor unless the floor area is so large that each circulation can be kept within its own half on one-way lanes.

Fig. 10

On some sites it may be an advantage to have in and out traffic widely separated at street level, as it is here.

If the up and down ramps crisscross at each floor (like an X in elevation), the two traffic streams flow in the same direction on each parking floor, and conflicting traffic movements are immediately reduced.

By placing up and down ramps at alternate edges of each floor, the up and down circulation in the ramp type shown in Fig. 10 is completely separated. Moreover, the turning movements have been cut in half. The car has to turn through only 180° (instead of 360° as in the preceding ramp plans) to go up or down through one parking level to the next. The travel distance on each floor is also reduced, so this type of ramp layout usually shows excellently fast driving time between floors.

At ground level the in and out ramps point in opposite directions, so this plan is particularly well fitted to any piece of land which runs through a block so that it has frontage on two streets.

The Split-Level Garage

The split-level garage is the parking equivalent of the split-level house. One section of a garage is offset vertically by half a story from the remainder of the building. (See Fig. 11.)

The length of each floor-to-floor straight ramp can then be divided into two halves separated from one another in plan sufficiently to allow a 180° turn on the parking floor. This means a minimum distance of 45 ft center-to-center of the ramps.

Climbing upward, or on the return trip down,

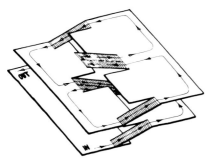

Fig. 11

the motorist negotiates these short ramps easily, so that parking in a ramp garage seems no more complex or frightening than any other sort of driving.

At the junction point between the two sections of the building, where the floors are offset vertically, they also overlap horizontally. In these few feet along the edge of each floor there is only half the normal floor-to-ceiling height found in the rest of the building; but this is sufficient height for the end few feet of a car, front or rear. So here the parked cars actually overlap one above the other, to give a saving of perhaps four to five feet in the overall width of the structure. On a narrow lot these may be the few extra feet necessary to accommodate minimum parking lot dimensions to the dimension of the lot.

Any of the ramp and circulation systems discussed earlier can be applied to the split-level garage structure.

Mechanical Elevator Garages

Mechanical elevator garages are most suitable on expensive sites which are too small for economical development with a ramp garage. They are the only practical means of developing garage space on deep lots with narrow frontage.

Mechanical elevator garages can be structurally very light and open if local building codes allow.

The two principal makes—Bowser and Pigeon Hole—both impose similar circulation patterns. Cars enter the central elevator hoistway on one side and exit on the other. So this type of garage is particularly well suited to corner sites, or any interior lot where the long side abuts on an alley which can be used for exit. In such cases the main street frontage required will be only 80 ft.

If entrance and exit must be on the same frontage, the minimum width required will be approximately 100 ft. On a structure above 10 stories in height, however, if sufficient reservoir space is provided at ground level to cushion peak arrival periods (without cars having to line up on the street outside), the lot size may have to be greater than this minimum.

Up to a point this will depend also upon the number of elevators used (the more elevators, the higher the speed of storage and delivery),

which in turn will affect the capital cost of such a garage structure.

In mechanical elevator garages a minimum of one quarter of each parking level area is occupied by circulation. When there is no double-row parking (which may entail moving front-row cars to reach those in the back), circulation space, i.e. the elevator hoistway, occupies one third of the area on each parking level. On the other hand, on a site 100 by 100 ft a circular ramp (the most condensed type) would occupy almost two-thirds of the area on each level.

The Pigeon Hole hydraulic elevator equipment moves on rails set on the ground; the Bowser electric elevators are hung from an overhead crane track. In both systems the elevator car moves simultaneously in a horizontal and a vertical direction. This is the all-important difference between these elevator systems and those which proved unsuccessful in the thirties.

Pigeon Hole uses a dolly, controlled by the elevator operator, for moving the car in and out of the elevator. Bowser elevator operators drive the car on and off. The elevator control panel is within easy reach of the operator as he sits in the car. An intercom and signal light system connects the elevators with the cashier's control booth.

The Bowser elevators are counterweighted so that, if the electric power fails, the garage can still be unloaded. These elevators will rise without power when empty. Loaded with a car, they descend at a controlled rate.

Commercial
PARKING LOTS

By FRANK HARRISON RANDOLPH, P.E., Professor of Hotel Engineering, Cornell University

Parking stalls should be built to accommodate the larger cars frequently used, although not necessarily the very largest. Planning in hopes of just medium and small size cars invites difficulties. The larger cars have an over-all length of 19 ft, over-all width 6 ft 8 in., with a wide open door projecting 3 ft 4 in. beyond the over-all width. The ramp angle must not exceed 7 deg. The limit of the front approach angle is 14 deg, while the corresponding angle at the rear is limited to 9 deg. When parked at right angles to a curb or buffer, the front overhang[1] generally does not exceed 2 ft 10 in., and the rear overhang[1] seldom exceeds 4 ft 6 in. These dimensions need consideration when planning widths of sidewalks affected by the overhang. A 5-ft sidewalk would have its usable width reduced almost to zero by the rear overhang. The front overhang may be taken at 1 ft 6 in. when figuring closely the minimum feasible spacing between buffers for a minimum width parking lot. When a central driveway is used with 90 deg parking on both sides, the space required is 62 ft wide, but the space between buffers need be only 59 ft because of the overhang.

A single stripe, 4 to 6 in. wide, may be used to mark the parking stalls. Better results in centering the car are obtained by using two 5-in. stripes, separated by 1 ft 6 in., to mark the stalls. The stripes, about 18 ft long, are joined by a semi-

[1] Overhang beyond curb or buffer is about 6 in. less than overhang dimensions (see section on "Dimensions") which are measured from the center of the wheel.

circular arc at the incoming end to form an elongated U (Fig. 3). Experience has shown this method to be very satisfactory and fully worth the extra painting.

Parking stalls should be at least 9 ft wide, 10 ft wide if space is not too restricted. Parking stalls 8 ft 6 in. wide are unsatisfactory because with the car 6 ft 8 in. wide, there is only 1 ft 10 in. between cars. If an adjacent car is only 6 in. off center and the car door is 4 in. thick, only 1 ft remains through which to squeeze, if possible.

Motel parking lots planned for maximum guest convenience, mark off parking stalls 11 ft wide and 23 ft long, allowing

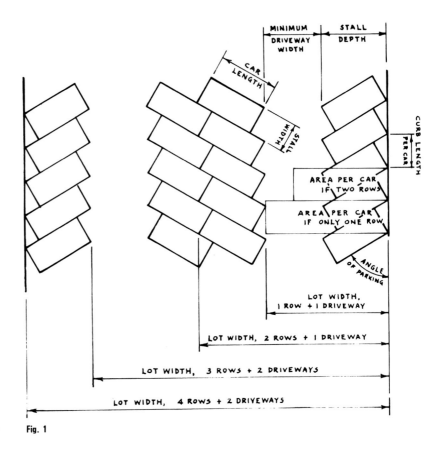

Fig. 1

Table 1. Parking lot dimensions

Angle of Parking	Stall width	Curb length per car	Stall depth	Minimum driveway width	Lot width 1 row + 1 driveway	Sq ft per car	Lot width 2 rows + 1 driveway	Sq ft per car	Lot width 3 rows + 2 driveways	Sq ft per car	Lot width 4 rows + 2 driveways	Sq ft per car
Along curb = 0°	9'	23'	9'	12'	21'	483	30'	345	51'	391	60'	345
	10'	23'	10'	12'	22'	506	32'	368	54'	414	64'	368
30°	9'	18'	17'4"	11'	28'4"	510	45'8"	411	66'2"	397	83'6"	376
	10'	20'	18'3"	11'	29'3"	585	47'6"	475	68'0"	453	86'2"	431
45°	9'	12'9"	19'10"	13'	32'10"	420	52'8"	336	79'0"	376	98'10"	315
	10'	14'2"	20'6"	13'	33'6"	490	54'0"	383	80'4"	379	100'10"	358
60°	9'	10'5"	21'0"	18'	39'0"	407	60'	313	95'0"	330	116'0"	305
	10'	11'6"	21'6"	18'	39'6"	455	61'	351	95'6"	366	116'6"	335
90°	9'	9'	19'	24'	43'	387	62'	279	105'	315	124'	279
	10'	10'	19'	24'	43'	430	62'	310	105'	350	124'	310

Refer to Fig. 1.

934

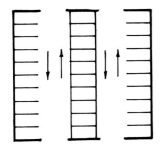 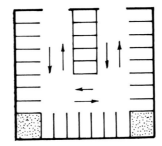 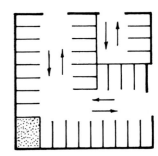

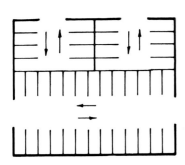 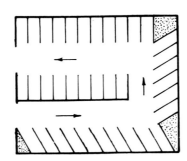 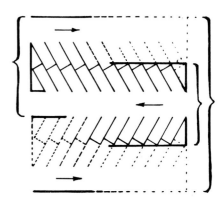

Fig. 2

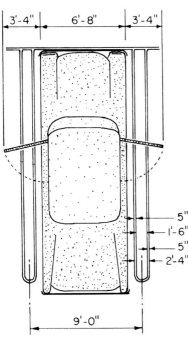

Fig. 3

4 ft behind the 19-ft car for unloading space which is advisably clear of the driveway.

Parking lots, exclusive of drives for entering them, require 350 sq ft per car as a very rough, preliminary figure. The width of the available space and the desired angle of parking are determining factors in economy. The area per car varies from 279 to 585 sq ft under conditions covered in the tabulation of parking lot dimensions. A central driveway with two rows of cars and 90 deg parking gives the best economy. Diagonal parking is easier for the driver, reduces the necessary driveway width, but requires more total space (Fig. 1).

In designing parking spaces, end stalls should be about 1 ft wider than usual, especially if bounded by a building or other obstruction or a driveway. Parking spaces under buildings should be 11 ft wide, watching out for columns, and should have 7 ft height in the clear.

The parking pattern that will be most satisfactory fully warrants careful thought. It depends upon many factors including the possible locations of access drives. These should be 20 ft wide for two-way traffic or 12 ft wide for one-way traffic (Fig. 2). If a restricted site frontage requires a right-angle turnoff, the driveway should be 25 ft wide and the curb should have a 30 ft radius. A curb radius of less than 18 ft is inadvisable.

A slope of 6 per cent is the usual maximum for state highways. A slope of 12 per cent is customary for ramps, but may be as much as 15 per cent. The parking lot should be nearly level. The central driveway may be crowned, with a 1 per cent slope draining to the edges so that persons on foot will find the driveway relatively free from water after rain or from ice in winter weather.

Commercial
PARKING LOTS

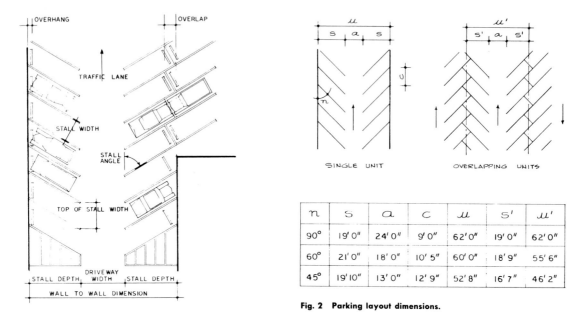

Fig. 1 Definitions.

Fig. 2 Parking layout dimensions.

n	s	a	c	u	s'	u'
90°	19' 0"	24' 0"	9' 0"	62' 0"	19' 0"	62' 0"
60°	21' 0"	18' 0"	10' 5"	60' 0"	18' 9"	55' 6"
45°	19' 10"	13' 0"	12' 9"	52' 8"	16' 7"	46' 2"

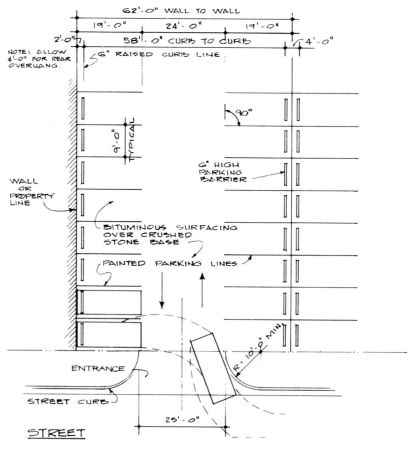

Fig. 3 Parking plan—90° parking.

SOURCE: *Design Guide for Permanent Parking Areas,*
National Crushed Stone Association, Washington, D.C.,
1970.

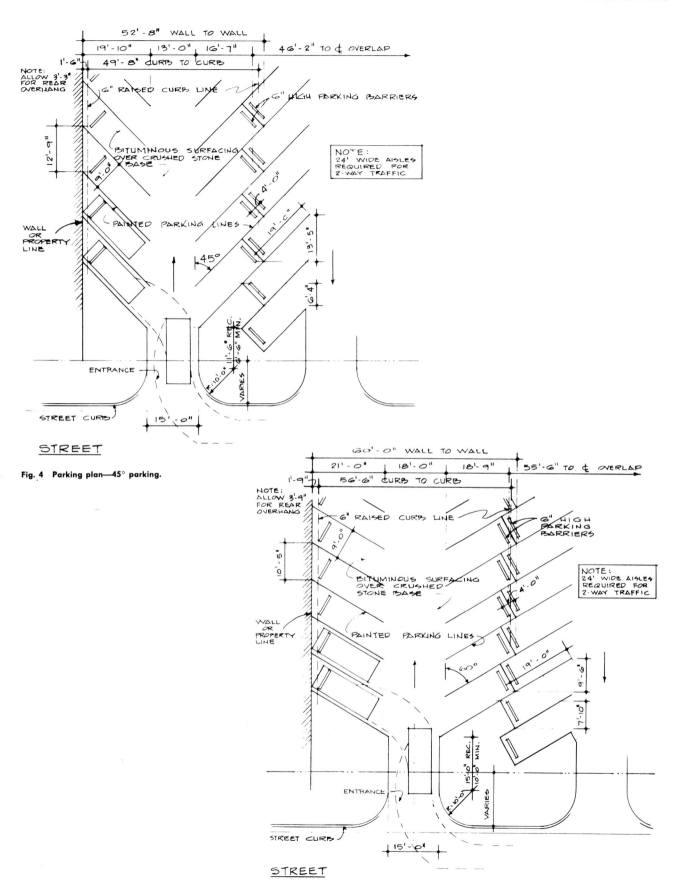

Fig. 4 Parking plan—45° parking.

Fig. 5 Parking plan—60° parking.

AUTOMOBILE SERVICE STATIONS

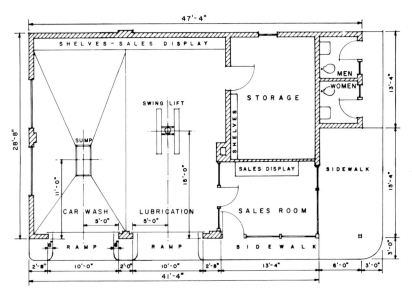

Fig. 1.　Plan of typical two-bay service station building

Drawings show the standard plan of a major oil company for a two-bay service station. Additional bays may be added for larger installations.

Minimum recommended dimensions for bay door opening is 10 by 10 ft. Overhead type doors are the most effective. Servicing pits have become obsolete, the mechanical lift being considered more practical.

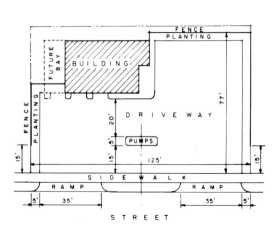

Fig. 2. Plan of service station with one pump island, midblock location

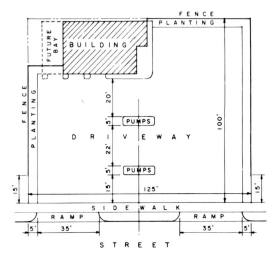

Fig. 3. Plan of service station with two pump islands, midblock location

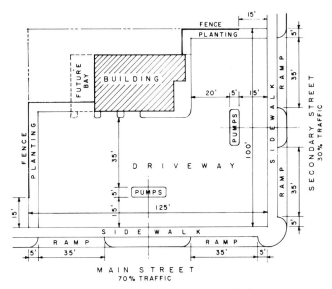

Fig. 4. Plan of service station with two pump islands, corner location

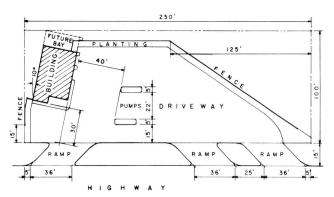

Fig. 5. Plan of service station with two pump islands, highway location

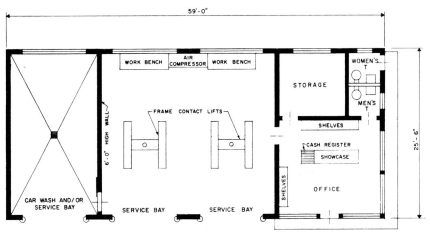

Fig. 6 Two- and three-bay stations.

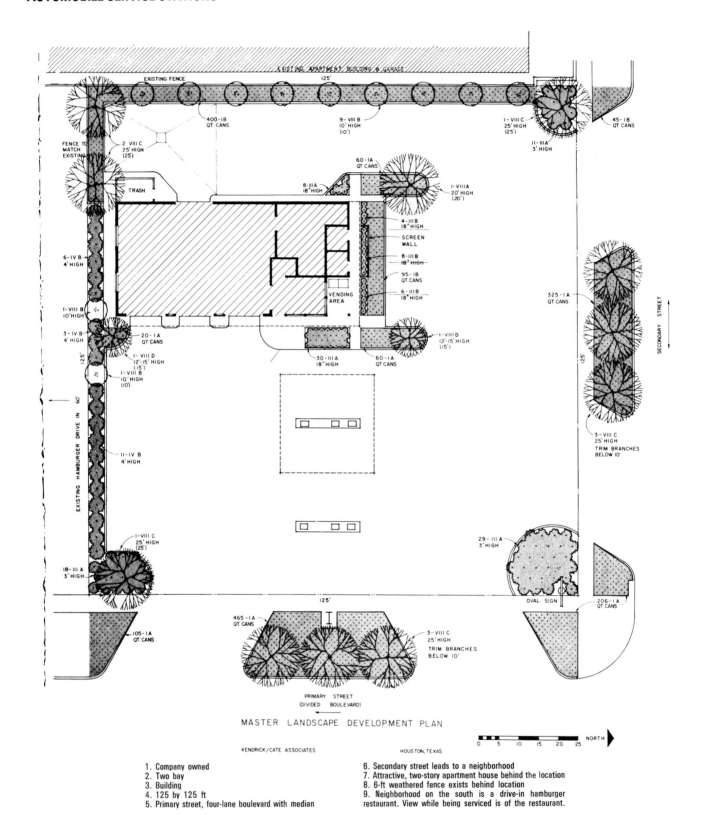

MASTER LANDSCAPE DEVELOPMENT PLAN

KENDRICK/CATE ASSOCIATES   HOUSTON, TEXAS

1. Company owned
2. Two bay
3. Building
4. 125 by 125 ft
5. Primary street, four-lane boulevard with median

6. Secondary street leads to a neighborhood
7. Attractive, two-story apartment house behind the location
8. 6-ft weathered fence exists behind location
9. Neighborhood on the south is a drive-in hamburger restaurant. View while being serviced is of the restaurant.

Fig. 7 Existing neighborhood (light commercial) location.

Compiled and edited by William J. Cronin, Jr., Marketing Department, Humble Oil & Refining Co., 1968.

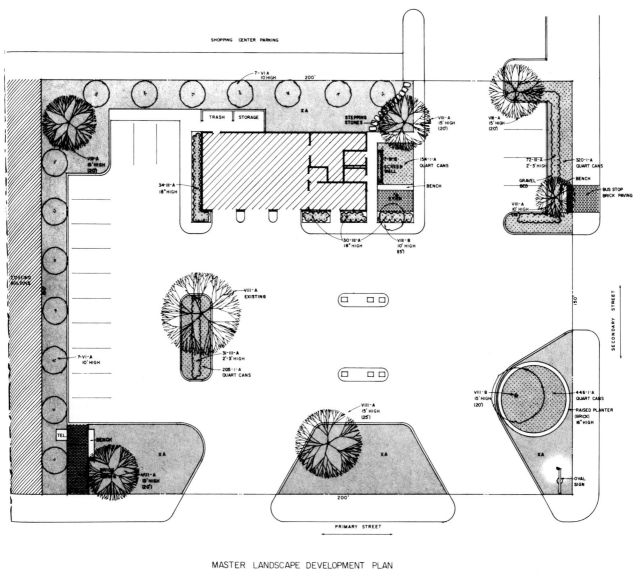

MASTER LANDSCAPE DEVELOPMENT PLAN

NEW URBAN LOCATION

KENDRICK /CATE ASSOCIATES   HOUSTON, TEXAS

1. Company owned
2. Two bay, contemporary design
3. Field stone
4. Business district 200 by 150 ft
5. Large shopping center and parking lot to the rear

6. Neighbor on the west, three-story office building extending to the sidewalk
7. Considerable foot traffic to and from shopping center
8. Purchase agreement specifies opening to parking lot

Fig. 8   Proposed new urban location.

Compiled and edited by William J. Cronin, Jr., Marketing Department, Humble Oil & Refining Co., 1968.

Commercial

AUTOMOBILE SERVICE STATIONS
Automotive Shop

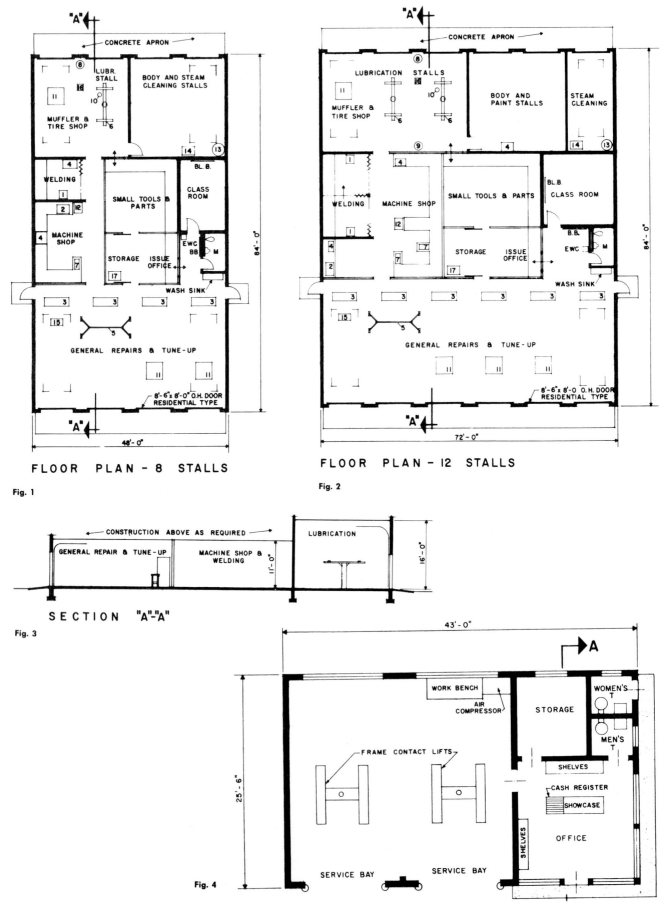

FLOOR PLAN - 8 STALLS

Fig. 1

FLOOR PLAN - 12 STALLS

Fig. 2

SECTION "A"-"A"

Fig. 3

Fig. 4

U.S. Naval Facilities Engineering Command, Department of the Navy, Washington, D.C.

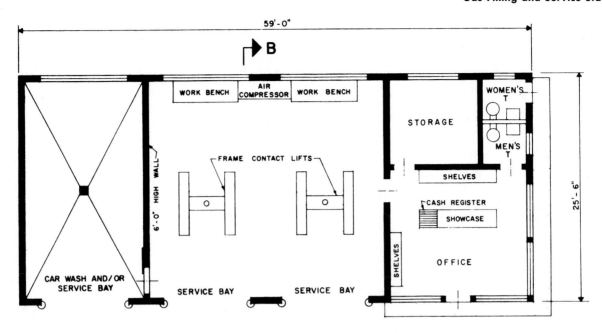

Fig. 5

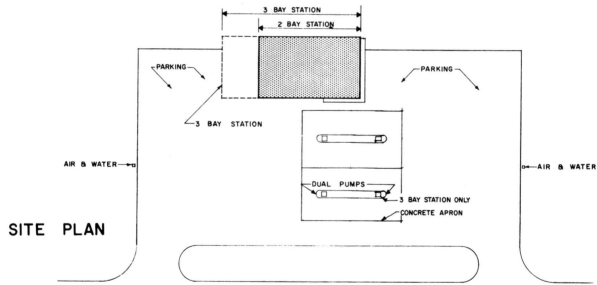

SITE PLAN

Fig. 6

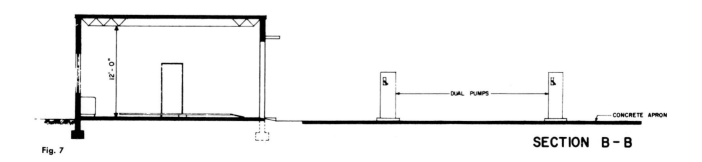

SECTION B - B

Fig. 7

U.S. Naval Facilities Engineering Command, Department of the Navy, Washington, D.C.

AUTOMOBILE BODY SHOP

STALL SIZES

Production stalls are those in which body or paint work is performed. There should be an additional outdoor parking space for each production stall to accommodate the bank of jobs to come or the jobs completed.

The general rule for stall sizes is 5 feet in front of the car for tools and work space, or 24 feet for average cars with at least 4 feet of work space between cars. This means a stall width would be the approximate width of the car plus 2 feet on either side. For stalls against the wall, add an extra foot for a 3 foot aisle between car and wall.

Stalls for passenger cars, small trucks and vans should be 12 feet wide and 24 feet deep. This size can be decreased if the shop is predominantly for compacts. Or, a ratio of compact work to the total can be determined and smaller stalls set aside for this work. Special stalls for frame straightening and other body equipment will have to be sized according to the specific piece of equipment used. Generally, 14 foot stalls are adequate for heavy metalworking. Stalls for clean-up, masking or other light duty work that does not require heavy tools may be 10 feet wide and 24 feet deep.

ESTIMATING

Since estimating may take place in many different areas, depending on the extent of the damage, it may be well to consider a separate well-lighted area for estimating.

OFFICE

A guide for planning office space allows 48 square feet for each person who will be using the office. If insurance adjusters will be using office space as well, add 48 square feet for each one.

PAINT STORAGE

A separate isolated, fireproof room for paint storage and mixing may be required by national or local codes. It will also help to control inventory and be easier to keep clean. Paint should be stored at room temperature year-round.

PARTS STORAGE

If the body shop is separate from the mechanical service shop, consider stocking body parts in the body shop and allow space accordingly. Overhead or mezzanine storage offers a good solution without taking up added floor space.

DRIVEWAY WIDTHS

Driveways for 90° parking should be a minimum of 22 feet. This width can be reduced to 18 feet with 60° parking and 14 feet with 50° parking.

Angle parking should be used only where it cannot be avoided. The awkward triangular spaces at both ends of the car and the building can seldom be used efficiently.

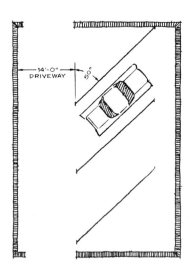

50° STALLS—14' DRIVEWAY

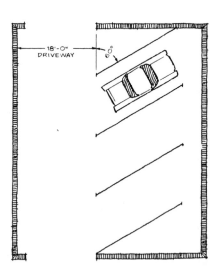

60° STALLS—18' DRIVEWAY

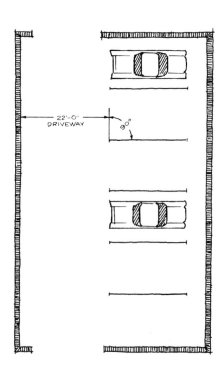

90° STALLS—22' DRIVEWAY

SPRAY BOOTH LOCATION

The spray booth should be located as far removed as possible from the area where dust and dirt is prevalent. Therefore, it should be isolated from the mechanical and metalworking portions of the shop wherever possible. This can be accomplished with partitions, walls or a separate building arrangement.

When a spray booth must be located in the same room with metalworking stalls or other locations where there is excessive dust, the intake air can be drawn from the outdoors utilizing an air replacement system. This arrangement greatly reduces the number of filter changes required in the booth doors and reduces the chances of ruined paint jobs.

STRAIGHT LINE WORK FLOW

If the volume of paint work is sufficient, a straight line work flow is recommended. Utilizing a drive-thru type spray booth, this layout is designed for maximum efficiency of manpower and equipment. Jobs are started in the metalworking stalls in the normal manner. From this point, the work flows in a production-line manner through each of the various stages all the way to final clean-up.

In this arrangement, the work is divided into its components. Each work station is manned by specialists. This enables the skilled worker (painter and metal man) to spend the greater share of his time on the tasks of his skill. A painting specialist will become more skilled and productive when relieved of unskilled chores. He may be able to handle the painting work of several metal men with paint preparation men to assist him. Another advantage is that changes in manpower requirements, due to seasonal fluctuations in the work load, can generally be made in the easiest area of replacement—the unskilled worker.

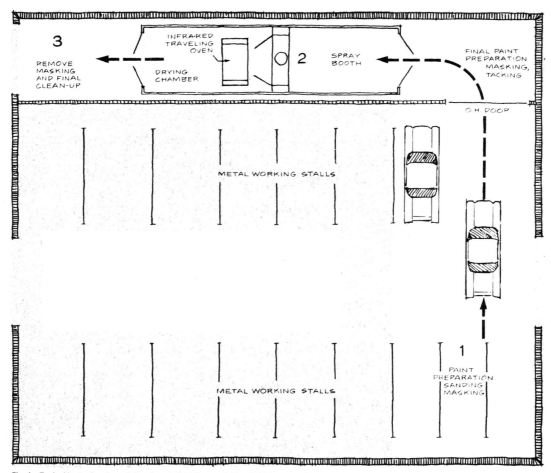

Fig. 1 Typical body shop layout showing straight-line work flow finishing operation.

AUTOMOBILE BODY SHOP

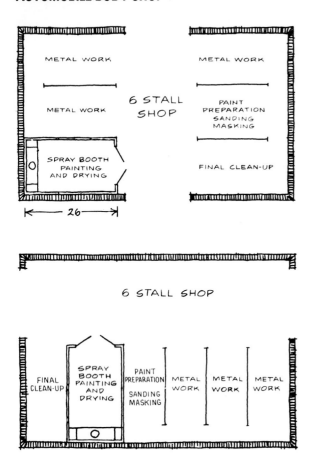

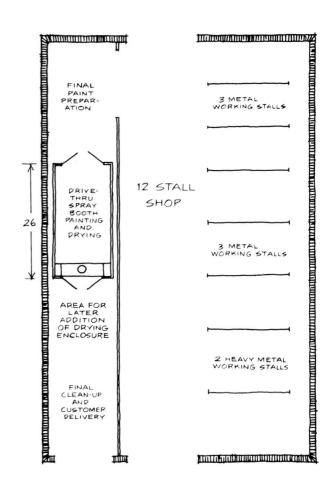

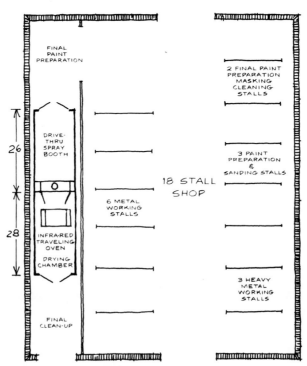

Fig. 2   Typical body shop layouts.

tion area can be considered, which is less expensive than inside roof area; and (3) customers prefer a clean, quiet atmosphere to the normal noise, dirt and congestion of the shop area.

Straight-through reception area is preferable and more conducive to service selling. Traffic control also is much more efficient, with congestion and car maneuvering kept to a minimum.

Where local climate permits, outdoor covered reception areas may be desirable as a building economy. The outdoor reception area can be designed to attractively complement the building architecture.

Customer Waiting Room

A special waiting area should be provided for customers who wait for service repair on their cars. Comfortable chairs, table, T.V., and a public telephone are desirable. Some dealers provide a waiting area in the showroom. However; a separate room, near the customer reception area and cashier, is desirable. The room size will be determined by the potential business.

Doors

The service entrance door for the customer reception area should be 16 ft wide and 12 ft high. A two-lane traffic door should have a minimum width of 24 ft. Wide doors make it easier to move cars into the stalls just inside the service entrance. Single service exit doors should be 14 ft wide and 12 ft high.

Service Control (Tower)

The service control tower should have sufficient space for efficient operation and the necessary equipment to control and schedule the service.

Write-up Area

The write-up desk adds a professional touch to the service selling function. It is desirable to have the desks located on the driver's side of the car entering the reception area.

Traffic Flow

The layout of the service department should be planned so that entrances and exits permit one-way traffic flow. Traffic flow should be a combination of dealership aisle patterns coordinated with traffic movement on public streets and alleys.

The arrangement of stalls to obtain an effi-

cient traffic pattern is one of the most critical factors in planning an efficient service department.

Stall Arrangement

Productive stall arrangement depends on size of operation, number of specialized technicians, and the dealer's preference. However, here are a few fundamentals to keep in mind—convenient location of entrances and exits, easy access to quick service stalls from customer reception area, parts counter convenient to lubrication and quick service stalls, separation of body shop, and maximum efficiency of aisle space by having one access aisle serving two rows of productive stalls (Fig. 7).

The standard 70-ft-width pattern shown in Fig. 8 provides the most efficient use of covered service space when an aisle is required. Long and narrow, it works best in small and medium-size operations. With only two main doors, heating costs are low; and when land is ample, expansion is simply a matter of adding on—without the need for major structural work.

However, if the number of stalls needed results in an excessive overall length, it makes supervision difficult and places many stalls too remote from the parts department.

Service facilities with a high percentage of "fast in—fast out" customers find the T pattern efficient. Notice that the write-up area does not conflict with the productive stall traffic flow area. Cars can be moved directly into stalls—or optionally, straight through to the service parking area, ensuring one-way traffic flow. Clear-span width is 70 ft. Like the I pattern, expansion is relatively simple (Fig. 9).

With doors on one side, it is suggested that the building should be 30 ft wide. With doors on both sides the recommended width is 60 ft. Direct drive-in stalls provide a maximum number of stalls in a minimum floor area and are very economical to construct. Although these buildings occupy less space than the 70-ft-wide buildings, they require more space on the lot for service drives and entrance to the building. The 60-ft-wide building is ideal for truck service because each double truck stall can accommodate the largest bus or tractor-trailer. Often a combination of a 70-ft-wide building with 30-ft extension on one or both sides can be used very advantageously. The larger span of the roof beams can be 70 ft because the necessary columns do not interfere. This creates a double row of stalls on each side of the central aisle. The cars in the 30-ft extension enter and leave through overhead doors in the side of the building. Here the double stalls can be used for servicing buses or tractor-trailers and, if there is a double wash rack, it

can be used for washing these large vehicles (Fig. 10).

Stall Dimensions

The width of stalls is made up of "car width" plus working space on each side of the vehicle. The total width varies from 10 ft to 14 ft according to stall function (Table 4).

Whenever a stall is next to a wall, add 2 ft to its width. Local building or fire codes supersede these recommendations if they conflict.

TABLE 4   Stall Dimensions

Stall function	Width, ft	Length, ft
Customer reception (aisle)	14	25
Lubrication (overhead equipment)	12	24
Mechanical repair	12	24
New car conditioning	12	24
Polishing and sheet metal	12	24
Paint spray booth	14	26
Wash rack	14	25
Parking	10	20

Service Stall

General-purpose service stalls should be 12 ft in width. In special situations, an 11-ft width may be acceptable, but only when structural requirements or land limitations impose the need. In buildings with direct drive-in stalls, 12-ft widths are mandatory, since lack of an aisleway means minimum walk-around and working areas. Figure 11 provides general dimensions and locations for equipment.

If the work load is light and space is at a premium, a single-stall station might be appropriate. In this suggested layout (Fig. 13) the brake testing is done on the road. Wheel alignment, front suspension hoist or jack area, and headlight testing and aiming are provided through careful arrangement in a single lane. This could be either a drive-through or drive-in-and-back-out system.

The drive-in-and-back-out safety test area could be designed around an existing front-end pit. Wheel alignment and under-vehicle inspections are made in one lane and visual inspection, brake testing and headlight testing in the other. Suggested layout could possibly be realized by the relocation of existing equipment (Fig. 14 and 15).

AUTOMOBILE DEALER CENTERS

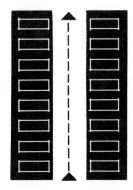

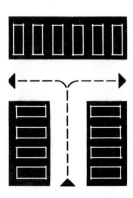

I PATTERN

As shown in the illustrations, a simple "I" pattern is the most efficient. This will work in most dealerships if the site permits such an arrangement. However, it cannot be considered a "cure-all." If the number of stalls needed results in an excessive overall length, it makes supervision difficult and places many stalls too remote from the parts department.

T PATTERN

The "T" pattern permits the same number of stalls as the "L" pattern. However, it is not suggested over the "L" pattern since it makes car movement difficult into the two end stalls near each exit. This stall and aisle pattern is useful in cases where an exit in the rear wall is impossible and the location of an alley makes two side exits more practical.

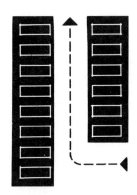

L PATTERN

The "L" Pattern is the second most efficient stall and aisle arrangement. It is normally used in those instances where straight through traffic is not possible. Note: it is necessary to sacrifice two stalls in order to accommodate one of the entrances.

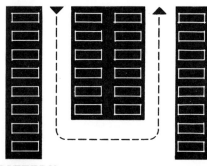

U PATTERN

The "U" pattern is used in large service operations or where no other arrangement is permissible because of existing neighboring structures or public streets. The "U" tends to centralize service traffic for more efficient control and accessibility to supporting departments.

Fig. 7   Traffic patterns.

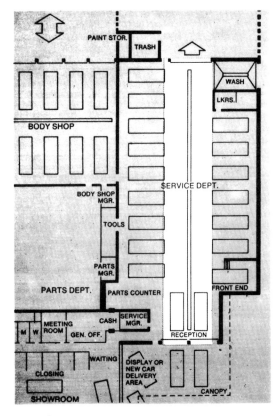

Fig. 8   Center-aisle I pattern.

952

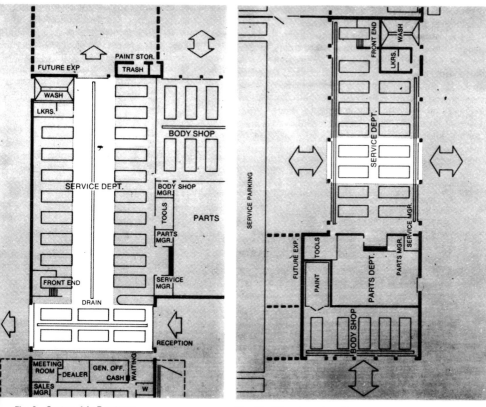

Fig. 9   Center-aisle T pattern.

Fig. 10   Drive-through pattern.

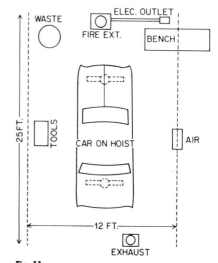

Fig. 11

30' BUILDING

60' BUILDING

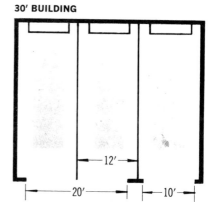

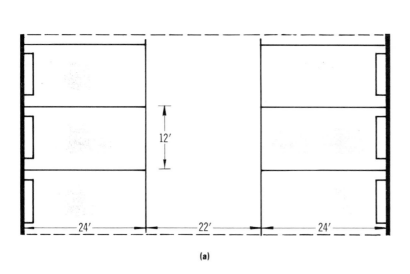

Fig. 12   (a) 90° stalls. (b) Drive-in work stalls.

AUTOMOBILE DEALER CENTERS

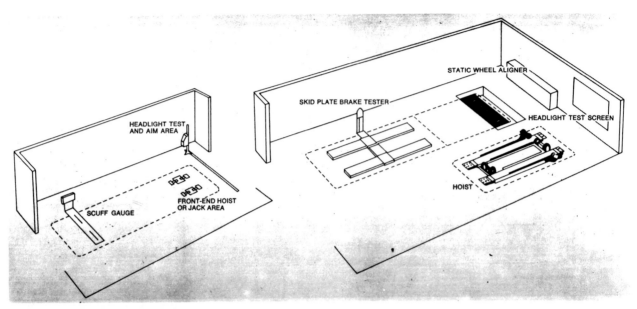

Fig. 13 Single-bay safety inspection station. **Fig. 14 Two-bay safety inspection station.**

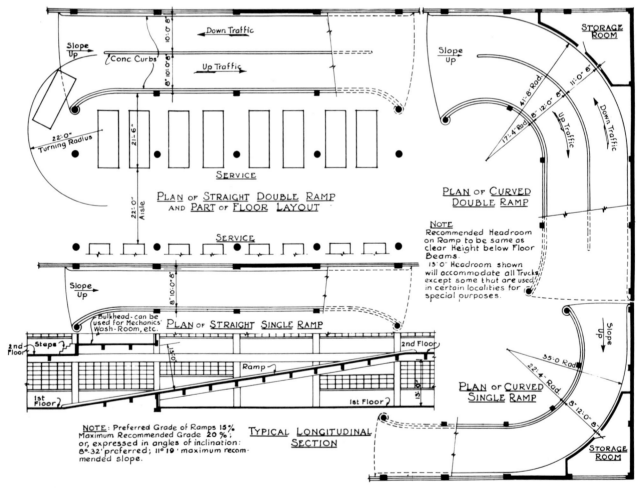

Fig. 15 Ramp design. (Chevrolet Motor Division, Building Department, Detroit, Mich.)

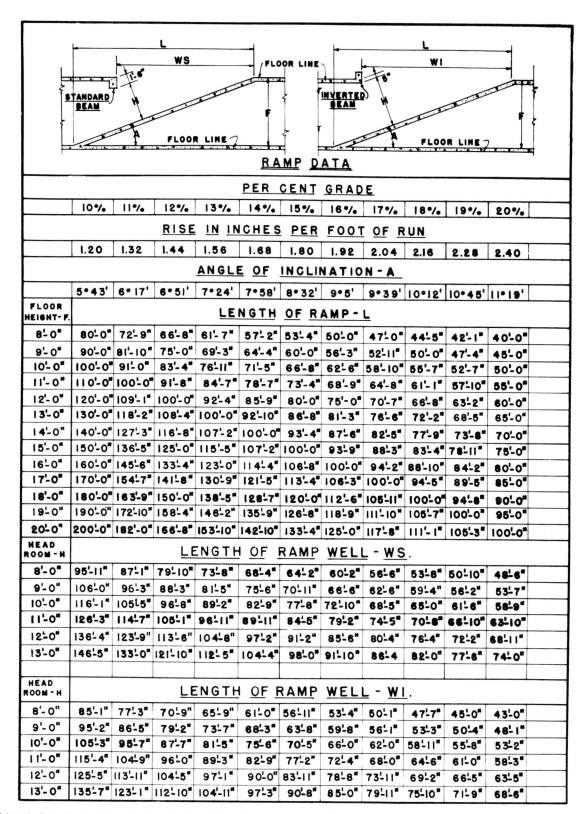

RAMP DATA

PER CENT GRADE

10%	11%	12%	13%	14%	15%	16%	17%	18%	19%	20%

RISE IN INCHES PER FOOT OF RUN

1.20	1.32	1.44	1.56	1.68	1.80	1.92	2.04	2.16	2.28	2.40

ANGLE OF INCLINATION - A

	5°43'	6°17'	6°51'	7°24'	7°58'	8°32'	9°5'	9°39'	10°12'	10°45'	11°19'

LENGTH OF RAMP - L

FLOOR HEIGHT-F.											
8'-0"	80'-0"	72'-9"	66'-8"	61'-7"	57'-2"	53'-4"	50'-0"	47'-0"	44'-5"	42'-1"	40'-0"
9'-0"	90'-0"	81'-10"	75'-0"	69'-3"	64'-4"	60'-0"	56'-3"	52'-11"	50'-0"	47'-4"	45'-0"
10'-0"	100'-0"	91'-0"	83'-4"	76'-11"	71'-5"	66'-8"	62'-6"	58'-10"	55'-7"	52'-7"	50'-0"
11'-0"	110'-0"	100'-0"	91'-8"	84'-7"	78'-7"	73'-4"	68'-9"	64'-8"	61'-1"	57'-10"	55'-0"
12'-0"	120'-0"	109'-1"	100'-0"	92'-4"	85'-9"	80'-0"	75'-0"	70'-7"	66'-8"	63'-2"	60'-0"
13'-0"	130'-0"	118'-2"	108'-4"	100'-0"	92'-10"	86'-8"	81'-3"	76'-6"	72'-2"	68'-5"	65'-0"
14'-0"	140'-0"	127'-3"	116'-8"	107'-2"	100'-0"	93'-4"	87'-6"	82'-5"	77'-9"	73'-8"	70'-0"
15'-0"	150'-0"	136'-5"	125'-0"	115'-5"	107'-2"	100'-0"	93'-9"	88'-3"	83'-4"	78'-11"	75'-0"
16'-0"	160'-0"	145'-6"	133'-4"	123'-0"	114'-4"	106'-8"	100'-0"	94'-2"	88'-10"	84'-2"	80'-0"
17'-0"	170'-0"	154'-7"	141'-8"	130'-9"	121'-5"	113'-4"	106'-3"	100'-0"	94'-5"	89'-5"	85'-0"
18'-0"	180'-0"	163'-9"	150'-0"	138'-5"	128'-7"	120'-0"	112'-6"	105'-11"	100'-0"	94'-8"	90'-0"
19'-0"	190'-0"	172'-10"	158'-4"	146'-2"	135'-9"	126'-8"	118'-9"	111'-10"	105'-7"	100'-0"	95'-0"
20'-0"	200'-0"	182'-0"	166'-8"	153'-10"	142'-10"	133'-4"	125'-0"	117'-8"	111'-1"	105'-3"	100'-0"

LENGTH OF RAMP WELL - WS.

HEAD ROOM-H											
8'-0"	95'-11"	87'-1"	79'-10"	73'-8"	68'-4"	64'-2"	60'-2"	56'-6"	53'-8"	50'-10"	48'-6"
9'-0"	106'-0"	96'-3"	88'-3"	81'-5"	75'-6"	70'-11"	66'-6"	62'-6"	59'-4"	56'-2"	53'-7"
10'-0"	116'-1"	105'-5"	96'-8"	89'-2"	82'-9"	77'-8"	72'-10"	68'-5"	65'-0"	61'-6"	58'-9"
11'-0"	126'-3"	114'-7"	105'-1"	96'-11"	89'-11"	84'-5"	79'-2"	74'-5"	70'-8"	66'-10"	63'-10"
12'-0"	136'-4"	123'-9"	113'-6"	104'-8"	97'-2"	91'-2"	85'-6"	80'-4"	76'-4"	72'-2"	68'-11"
13'-0"	146'-5"	133'-0"	121'-10"	112'-5"	104'-4"	98'-0"	91'-10"	86'-4"	82'-0"	77'-6"	74'-0"

LENGTH OF RAMP WELL - WI.

HEAD ROOM-H											
8'-0"	85'-1"	77'-3"	70'-9"	65'-9"	61'-0"	56'-11"	53'-4"	50'-1"	47'-7"	45'-0"	43'-0"
9'-0"	95'-2"	86'-5"	79'-2"	73'-7"	68'-3"	63'-8"	59'-8"	56'-1"	53'-3"	50'-4"	48'-1"
10'-0"	105'-3"	95'-7"	87'-7"	81'-5"	75'-6"	70'-5"	66'-0"	62'-0"	58'-11"	55'-8"	53'-2"
11'-0"	115'-4"	104'-9"	96'-0"	89'-3"	82'-9"	77'-2"	72'-4"	68'-0"	64'-6"	61'-0"	58'-3"
12'-0"	125'-5"	113'-11"	104'-5"	97'-1"	90'-0"	83'-11"	78'-8"	73'-11"	69'-2"	66'-5"	63'-5"
13'-0"	135'-7"	123'-1"	112'-10"	104'-11"	97'-3"	90'-8"	85'-0"	79'-11"	75'-10"	71'-9"	68'-6"

Fig. 15 (cont.) Ramp design. (Chevrolet Motor Division, Building Department, Detroit, Mich.)

Commercial

TRUCK DEALER AND SERVICE FACILITIES

AREAS

New Truck Display

Truck sales profit from good interior display, particularly light-tonnage trucks sold to families as second cars or recreation vehicles.

However, because of the wide variation in size between truck models, and because the sales of larger units are frequently made away from the dealership, indoor truck showroom displays are usually limited in size.

If you plan an interior display area, make sure that it is large enough for at least one pickup, with adequate room to walk completely around it (1,000 sq ft). The display should occupy at least 3 percent of the dealership's total area.

The display should face the majority of traffic that moves past the dealership, and be placed so that a driver does not have to turn his head to see it.

For a driver to see a display easily, it should be within $30°$ to the left or right of his straight-ahead forward vision, and close enough to catch his eye.

Display area windows should be large, but do not have to be slanted. Having strong enough lights inside the display area will usually minimize any natural glare or reflections on the outside of the glass.

Many truck dealerships rely entirely on exterior display.

This may be under a canopy or not. The advantage of the canopy is that the vehicle stays cleaner longer, doesn't spot as easily from rain or snow, and is sheltered from the sun and weather.

The disadvantage of the canopy is cost and the fact that vehicle movement can be hampered if the placing of the canopy supports is not carefully planned.

Private Offices

The dealer's or general manager's office should be the largest in the dealership.

The office should be able to accommodate four or five visitors. It should have closet and storage facilities, and if desired, its own men's room.

Consider the possibility of allowing this office to double as a meeting room for the sales staff (Table 1).

If the dealership also has a sales manager, he should have an office.

Offices for individual salesmen can double as closing rooms.

Meeting Room

A meeting room is not a luxury in a truck dealership.

When facilities have lunchrooms, these are frequently used as meeting rooms.

If it's not possible to have a separate room for meetings, consider installing a folding wall between two small private offices so that they

Profitable GMC Dealership Expansion, General Motors Corp., 1967.

can be opened up into a meeting room. Or consider using the dealer's office for a meeting room.

Wherever the meeting room is, it should be possible to darken it so that pictures can be projected.

Equipment for 16 mm motion pictures and 35 mm sound slidefilm projection should either be permanently set up or be stored in a convenient cupboard. A blackboard and/or chart stand will also be useful.

General Office

If the cashier works in the general office, then the office should be adjacent to the parts counter and the service reception area, so that the cashier's window can serve both.

The general office should be furnished with adequate desks, chairs, files, business machines, and other equipment.

It should be comfortable, reasonably quiet and well lighted.

Storage should be provided in the room for current operating records and daily supplies. Old records and infrequently used supplies can be stored somewhere else.

Vault and Storage

A vault should be provided for cash and valuable business records. If no vault is provided, essential records should be kept in special fire-resistant files or fireboxes.

Stationery, sales promotion material, model literature, and seasonal dealership decorations should be given a storage area. Obsolete records can also be stored here. This space can be in a basement, mezzanine, or on the same floor but in an out-of-the-way location.

Rest Rooms

Rest rooms for men and women employees and for customers should be provided. While local codes will dictate much of the design and equipment for these rest rooms, try to select durable and economical as well as attractive fixtures.

Floor Plan

The most functional type of layout for a truck service department is one with drive-through stalls (Figs. 1 and 2).

Trucks of varying lengths can be easily handled, including those with extremely long wheelbases. Each vehicle can be moved in or out without disturbing the others. And since no aisles are required, more floor space is useful space.

The two things that can prevent the use of this kind of stall are climate and a narrow property with limited turn-around space outside.

Where the climate is extremely cold, drive-through stalls can be too drafty and too expensive to heat.

Where there is not enough room outside for vehicles to move freely at both sides of the building, such as at some in-town locations, drive-through stalls are impractical.

However, a practical layout in this situation would be stalls where you drive in and back out through individual doors.

To preserve heat in very cold areas, it may be necessary for the department to use a common entrance door, with the trucks turning into individual stalls after entering the building. If these stalls are angled, more floor space will be required for each stall, although less will be required for the aisle.

TABLE 1   Sales Area and Building

Area	Space allowance
Interior display	
Showroom	1,000 sq ft, plus 600 sq ft for each vehicle over one
Entrance door	10 by 12 ft (pickups) 12 by 14 ft (larger trucks)
Offices (minimum):	
Dealer or general manager	180 sq ft
Sales manager.	120 sq ft
Salesmen.	90 sq ft per man
Closing office	64 sq ft
Used truck office	120 sq ft
General office	100 sq ft per person
Ceiling height	Offices — 9 ft 6 in.
Meeting room.	Allow at least 12 sq ft for each person to attend meeting, plus room for speaker and for projection equipment
Other areas:	
Rest room	30 sq ft minimum
Hall or aisle	5 ft wide
Janitor closet	32 sq ft minimum with deep sink
Customer's waiting room.	Variable

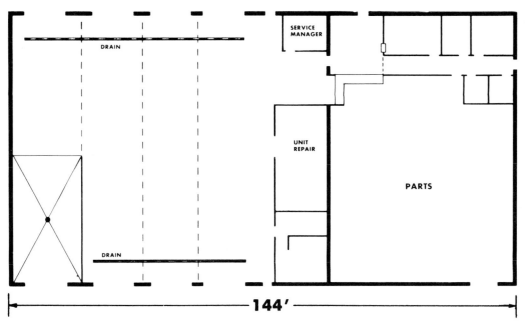

Fig. 1 Layout for small dealer.

One-way traffic through a service department door is more efficient than two-way traffic. If a common entrance must be used, try to provide a common exit at another point.

FLOW FACTORS

Four groups of things move or "flow" through the department while it is working.

How logically and easily each of these groups flows determines much of the department's ability to make money.

The four flow factors are:
1. Flow of traffic
2. Flow of people
3. Flow of parts
4. Flow of repair orders

Flow of Traffic

Start by planning where the customer traffic will wait before it gets to the service salesman or write-up man.

There must be adequate standing room outside where waiting vehicles will not get in the way of other dealership customers or street traffic.

From the service salesman, traffic must flow either to another waiting area, or to a stall where work is to be done.

If the vehicle will have to go to more than one stall (such as from diagnosis to a work stall) it should never have to backtrack.

When the work is done, the vehicle should move out to be road-checked by dynamometer and parked.

Before you approve of any service department layout, mentally move a day's traffic through it to see where the bottlenecks appear.

Flow of People

The customer should be able to get out of his vehicle, talk with the service salesman, go to the driver lounge or out of the dealership, go to the cashier and pick up his vehicle without getting in the way of sales, service, or parts employes.

The mechanic should be able to get the tools and parts he needs without going through customer areas or getting in the way of other workers.

Flow of Parts

Parts shipping and receiving should not have to be made across the flow of incoming service traffic. Parts customers should not have to wait for service customers.

Parts access for the service department should be convenient, both for the mechanic and for the parts department. To get parts, the mechanic should not have to travel far or travel through customer waiting areas. Departmentally, quick service and tune up stalls should be nearest the parts counter.

Stalls doing work that normally requires fewer parts per day (such as heavy repair) should be farther away than stalls doing general repair and maintenance.

Flow of Repair Orders

Trace the physical movement of repair order originals and copies in your current maintenance system.

Bad flow here will cause wasted mechanic time, slower billing with increased customer dissatisfaction, poorer cost accounting and maintenance control. In larger buildings a system of pneumatic tubes between offices aids in the efficient flow of paper work.

ROOMS AND AREAS

Service Manager's Office

The service manager's office should provide privacy and relative quiet, so that it can be used to handle customer complaints.

It should be closed off from the working area to keep out dirt as well as noise.

It should have windows and be located so that the service manager can easily see the main service entrance and the work areas of the department that return the highest profit.

Direct supervision from the service man-

ager's office improves work quality and reduces idleness.

Being able to see diagnosis and service stalls usually improves profit and promotes better care of the special equipment used.

In large operations, a raised office that allows the service manager to look across the entire department is effective.

General Service Area

The number and type of stalls are determined by the services (Tables 2 to 4).

Quick Service Area

Quick service is normally limited to jobs that can be done in one hour or less.

An area set aside for quick service usually produces more profit per square foot because it creates a high parts volume with relatively short labor times.

Specific quick service jobs fall into these areas:

Engine tune-up	Wheel bearings
Cooling system	Shock absorbers
Exhaust system	Universal joints
Adjustments:	Electrical
Clutches	Tires
Brakes	Lubrication
Transmissions	Body
Front end	Trim
Brake linings	
Wheel balance	

Quick service can be done in a limited way in any service operation, just by setting aside a stall for that purpose. However, the most profitable quick service results from using special methods, tools, and equipment; also in reducing the time required to get parts.

Unit Repair

A separate unit repair room can speed the rebuilding of engines and other assemblies. This room is usually most effective when separated from the general repair area. It also has all the necessary tools and equipment for

Commercial

TRUCK DEALER AND SERVICE FACILITIES

TABLE 2 Service Areas*

Area	Space allowance or dimensions
Service manager's office	Usually 120 sq ft
Paint department office (if separate)	Usually 120 sq ft
Driver's lounge	100 sq ft plus 20 sq ft for each person over 5
Lunch room	300 sq ft plus 20 sq ft for each person over 10
Showers, rest rooms, lockers	60 sq ft plus 10 sq ft for each man over 5
Unit repair	Minimum of 300 sq ft
Detroit diesel injector repair	Minimum of 48 sq ft
Toro-Flow diesel fuel pump	Minimum of 80 sq ft
Entrances:	
Individual service doors	12 ft wide, 14 ft high
One-way main service doors (or reception door on drive-through layouts)	16 ft wide, 14 ft high
Two-way main service doors	24 ft wide, 14 ft high
Ceiling height:	
General service area	15 ft minimum—floor to roof truss clearance
Over lifts	17–18 ft
Center aisles:	
With 90° stalls	22–24 ft wide for small trucks only 26–28 ft wide for large trucks
With 60° stalls	25 ft wide for large trucks
With 45° stalls	23 ft wide for large trucks

*The entire service department normally occupies 65 to 70 percent of the total area of the dealership building.

TABLE 3 Stall Dimensions

Drive-through type building		
Stalls	Dimensions	Total
Two deep (70-ft building)	15 by 35 ft	525 sq ft
Three deep (80-ft building)	15 by 26 ft	390 sq ft
Three deep (90-ft building)	15 by 29 ft	435 sq ft

Drive-in type building			
Stall angle	Dimensions	Aisle width	Total
90°	15 by 35 ft	28 ft	945 sq ft
60°	17 by 35 ft	25 ft	1,020 sq ft
45°	21 by 35 ft	23 ft	1,218 sq ft

Other areas	Dimensions
Front-end stalls	20 ft wide, 35 ft long
Wash rack	20 ft wide, 35 ft long
Lubrication stalls	20 ft wide, 35 ft long
Dynamometer stalls	20 ft wide, 35 ft long
Paint preparation, drying, and cleanup stalls	18 ft wide, 40 ft long
Sheet metal and body repair stalls	20 ft wide, 40 ft long
Paint spray booth	20 ft wide, 40 ft long
Floors	6-in. wire-mesh-reinforced concrete slab. Compressive strength of not less than 3,000 psi at 28 days. Exposed floors should be treated with floor sealer. Floor should slope $\frac{1}{8}$ in. per foot toward drain.
Compressed air lines and fittings	Designed for operating pressure of 175 lb

overhaul of units. As a result, the work done there usually produces more reliable assemblies.

By having repair stands, test equipment, and special tools in one location, close to the parts department, a specialist can do the required work in the least time.

The unit repair area should be set off from the rest of the department by wall or screen fencing. It should have a lockable door or sliding 6-ft gate.

Injector Repair

Where frequent Toro-Flow or GM Diesel work is available, a diesel injector and fuel pump repair room is profitable (Fig. 3).

Since this precision work must be done in a dirt-free area, the room must be completely enclosed, easy to keep clean, and pressurized slightly to keep outside dust from seeping in.

Smooth-surfaced walls, windows with flush sills, and benches enclosed to the floor reduce dirt traps and the time required to clean the

TABLE 4 Parts Areas and Dimensions

Area	Dimensions
Parts office	120 sq ft minimum
Parts lobby	200 sq ft minimum
Customer counter	42 in. high, at least 12 ft long
Mechanic's counter	42 in. high, at least 5 ft long
Storage and obsolete files	100 sq ft minimum

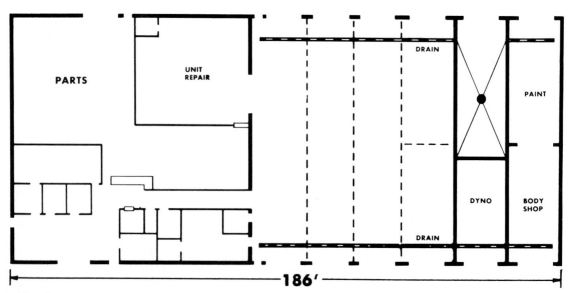

Fig. 2 Layout for medium-sized dealer.

958

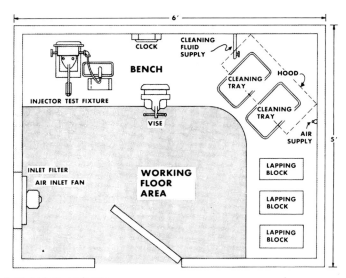

Fig. 3   Typical fuel injector repair room.

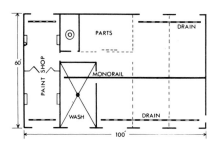

Fig. 4   Typical auxiliary paint and body shop.

room. Light-colored wall enamel also improves illumination.

To pressurize the room, use a fixed fan to draw air in through a glass fiber filter, such as those used in many air conditioners.

To let air out of the room, a hood and stovepipe with damper can be placed over the solvent pans. This will carry out solvent fumes as well. Or a roof fan can be used to exhaust air that is drawn in through filters placed at opposite ends of the room.

The room also requires an air supply to dry injector parts. The air filter and moisture trap for the air line should be placed outside the room.

Body and Paint Shop

A well-managed truck body shop will usually produce more profit per dollar invested than the dealership's general repair area.

Consult local paint and equipment companies for advice on the best possible layout for the equipment to be used and the services to be offered.

Local codes strongly govern what you can and cannot do.

If possible, plan to separate the body and paint shop from the main service building. This way you avoid the excessive noise, fumes, display of damaged vehicles, fire hazard, and increased fire insurance premiums that can come from an attached body and paint department (Fig. 4).

If the department has to be under the same roof, it must be isolated from the main service area by a firewall.

At least four stalls should be planned for complete body work: one for sheet metal repairs, one for heavy metal work and straightening frames, one for painting, and one for drying and cleanup.

Whether the body and paint shop is attached or separate, an isolated fireproof room for paint storage and mixing will lower insurance costs.

In a separate facility, you will also need to provide office space, wash-up areas, and storage for body parts.

Proper placement of the paint spray booth is a job for an expert. The booth cannot function satisfactorily if the filter doors open directly to the outside of the building. A booth exhausts 7,000 to 14,000 cu ft of air a minute. This air can't be reused because it contains volatile fumes. It must be replaced without creating a draft through the body department. Consult an expert.

EQUIPMENT

Monorail

A monorail is helpful in moving engines and other major truck components to and from the steam clean area and unit repair room.

You can't depend on a monorail alone for engine removal, since it can lift only vertically, and many truck designs require several lift positions to get the engine out.

Minimum capacity for a monorail should be 3 tons. The rail should be suspended from the ceiling structure 20 to 25 ft inside the service

doors on a drive-through layout, or near the front of a row of drive-in-back-out stalls.

One end of the rail should be in the wash rack and the other end in the unit repair area.

Hoists

Modern large truck dealerships are using hydraulic floor hoists extensively for quick service and general repair services since their use improves mechanic efficiency and morale. Hoist work also helps attract the best grade of mechanic to the business by providing better working conditions.

Where hoists are used, the best choice is one of the disappearing types. This way a creeper can be used in the stall when the hoist is not being used.

Most mechanical truck services can be provided without the use of hydraulic hoists.

Transmissions and power train components can be repaired with the truck front or rear axles up on stands. To get the unit onto the stand, a fork lift, an A-frame hoist, or a boom lift can be used. The major advantage is that all of these are portable and can move from stall to stall.

Since there is generally ample room underneath most large trucks, work may be done without any lift at all. However, hydraulic lifts can be highly advantageous.

Dynamometer

Any dynamometer needs to be isolated with sound-deadening material because of engine and tire noise.

Fork Lift

A fork lift can be a good investment for the service department and the parts department.

In the service department, it can be used to remove and install heavy truck components and to carry them to repair and cleanup areas.

In the parts department, it can be used to carry large items such as transmissions and for the shipping and receiving of stock.

The fork lift should have an 11-ft vertical beam and a capacity of at least 3 tons.

Commercial
RADIO STATIONS

By JOSEPH HOROWITZ, P.E., Manager, Planning & Design, Facilities Engineering Department, Columbia Broadcasting System, Inc.

I. PLANNING RADIO STUDIOS

A. Scope

This article deals with the planning of radio studios using the term *studios* in the broad sense of facilities for the origination of radio programs. Broadcasting facilities intended for police or other radio *communications* are not included. Application of broadcasting equipment to stadiums, arenas, concert halls, etc., is a specialized topic and will not be covered here.

Discussion will center on planning an individual station, which may be commercial or noncommercial, but principles are also applicable to centralized network facilities. Except as otherwise indicated, criteria apply to both AM and FM facilities.

B. Planning Factors

Planning of a modern radio station, while constrained by the technology of broadcasting, is determined to a large extent by the station's operating practices. It is essential to realize that, while all stations perform the same basic functions, there are wide divergences of operating practices and philosophy. Planning, therefore, starts with a careful analysis of the station's method of operation.

Following is a checklist of basic planning factors which must be known or established in order to plan the facility.

1. **Type of Programming** The most important single influence on facility requirements is the type of programming. In current practice this will usually consist of one or more of the following:

   Music
   News and public features
   Interview and panel discussion
   Production of advertising commercials

   Some stations may have special requirements for dramatic or audience participation shows, but this is no longer common. Recently, many music-oriented stations have adopted automation, which means, basically, that not only the music but announcer's commentary, time checks, station breaks, etc., are all prerecorded and all switching is handled automatically. This has significant impact on both layout and power requirement. For all stations an important planning question is the extent of "live" versus recorded programming.

2. **Hours of Operation** Stations are restricted by their FCC license provisions. Commercial stations must provide certain minimum hours of operation daily.

3. **Relationship to Talent Sources** The term *talent*, as used here, refers to the persons who participate in programs, whether as performing artists, employees, interviewees, etc.

4. **Relationship to Public** Some stations view themselves as a kind of program "factory" and limit visitors to persons having specific business with the station. Others encourage visits from schools and community groups and make elaborate provisions for them, such as viewing windows from which visitors (or passers-by) can view station operations. This decision affects circulation patterns, support facilities, and security provisions.

5. **Government Regulations** All stations are licensed by the Federal Communications Commission, whose very detailed regulations influence every aspect of operation and hence planning. Regulations, which require constant monitoring of certain devices, influence the configuration of the control room. Most stations are familiar with these requirements, but for a new station, use of an outside consultant may be desirable. As an example, an FCC regulation requiring separate AM and FM programming has generated the need for FM program facilities separate and, in some cases, apart from the AM facilities in some stations that were formerly combined.

6. **Emergency Broadcasting System (EBS)** Another area of government involvement is the Emergency Broadcasting System. Stations which agree to membership and are designated as primary EBS facilities must provide facilities capable of operation during an emergency. Government financial assistance may be available for equipment and nuclear fallout protection for the emergency studio as well as for emergency generators.

7. **Relationship of Studio and Transmitter Facilities** Studios and transmitter may be at the same or separate locations. Similarly, stations (such as an AM and FM) may share certain facilities.

8. **Operating Procedures** Most larger commercial radio stations are highly unionized. Work rules vary from one locality to the next and can have significant influence on planning of studio facilities. In some locations a disk jockey may actually operate the tape player or turntable. In other areas, this work requires a studio engineer or even a separate "platter spinner." Where regulations are less restrictive, one man may act as engineer and announcer if he meets the licensing requirements. In all cases, a careful study of operating procedures is essential.

C. Site Selection

Modern broadcasting facilities are usually quite compact and are often located within a building having other primary functions, such as an office or school. Following are some of the factors to consider in selecting a site.

1. **Location** Location is largely a function of planning factors 1, 3, and 4, that is, type of programming, relationship to talent sources, and relation to the public. If extensive interviews or panel discussions are planned, the station should be convenient to the prospective participants (show business personalities, sports or government figures). Where the station desires maximum exposure to the general public, it should be easily reached by public transportation. Sales activities of commercial radio stations likewise point to a "downtown" location.

Where these factors are less significant or good transportation is available, advantage may be taken of lower-cost suburban areas. Where studio and transmitter are combined in one building, the technical requirements of transmitters will govern the site selection. (See separate article on planning radio transmitter facilities.) This arrangement, while economical, creates a location conflict, at least for AM stations, since the ideal site for an AM transmitter is rarely convenient as a studio location.

2. **Environment** Although studio design can compensate for a hostile noise environment, reasonable freedom from excessive noise and vibration is desirable. Within a building, the area selected for studios should be free of overhead building pipes and ductwork to prevent noise and water leaks. It should also have adequate headroom, both for acoustic purposes and to accommodate air-conditioning ductwork. Surrounding tenancies should be free of objectionable noise. Otherwise, environmental factors are similar to those for an office.

3. **Utilities** A reliable power source and access to telephone and telex communications lines are essential. See Section *F* 3 for other communications.

4. **Parking** See Section *D* 5 (*c*) for possible parking requirements. Parking (or garage space) for station vehicles used for "remote" (off-premises) broadcasting is particularly important. Desire for liberal parking facilities may conflict with the need for a "downtown" location convenient to visitors, talent sources, and VIPs.

D. Description of Facilities

1. **Types of Facilities** Radio broadcasting (studio) facilities may be considered under the following groups:

   Technical (on-air) facilities
   Other broadcasting facilities
   Support facilities
   Personnel facilities
   Facilities for off-premises operations

2. **Technical (On-Air) Facilities** The on-air facilities include the studios and control rooms that form the heart of the station's operation.

   a. Studios. A studio is any room used for originating broadcast material—one in which there is a live microphone. With proper acoustical design, studios can be made just large enough to contain the desired number of persons. A two-man studio (disk jockey, newscaster) is shown in Fig. 1, and Fig. 2 shows an interview studio. In contemporary radio, music is almost always prerecorded, and broadcasts involving the public are likely to be recorded off-premises at theaters, concert halls, legislatures, etc. For these reasons large studios suitable for music or audience participation are not required in the station itself. In the exceptional case of an audience studio, the room would be designed primarily as a theater

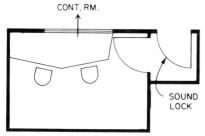

Fig. 1 One- or two-man studio (newscast, disk jockey, etc.).

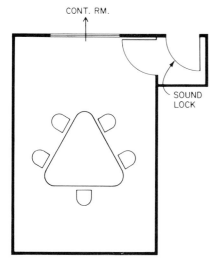

Fig. 2 Interview studio.

or auditorium with provision for taping or live broadcasting. This would be a facility apart from the radio station.

Floor areas may range from 100 sq ft for the minimum studio (news, recorded music) to 270 sq ft for a six-person studio suitable for panel discussion.

b. Control Rooms. The control room, as the name implies, contains a control console and other electronic equipment for monitoring and controlling the output from a studio. In addition, it may house tape players, turntables, and automatic switching devices as well as a small amount of disk and tape storage. Plan dimensions are dictated by the equipment to be used; occupants are one or two persons. Figure 3 shows some of the devices that may be contained in a well-equipped control room.

Many smaller stations have so-called "combo" operations, in which the engineer doubles as announcer, disk jockey, etc. In this case, the control room is also a studio and has the same sound requirements. Even when the control room does not contain a live microphone, sound characteristics are still important. The technician monitoring the program must make critical decisions based on what he hears from the loudspeakers, and any distortion caused by room acoustics will be reflected in improper adjustment of controls.

c. Equipment (Rack) Room. Electronic equipment is usually mounted in cabinets or racks, roughly the size of file cabinets. In a large station, they may be grouped for easy maintenance into a single equipment or rack room. In smaller stations, they will be located in the control rooms. In either case, access for servicing is essential. Racks are sometimes used to form the outside wall of one of the control rooms, but this is not suitable for the combo arrangement in which one room serves as both studio and control room.

d. Maintenance Shop. The maintenance shop is an electronics workshop and must be convenient to control and rack rooms. In addition to the usual workbenches and test equip-

ment, space must be available for spare parts and portable equipment for use on "remotes" (off-premises broadcasting). A 10- by 12-ft space is adequate for a small or medium-sized station. Usual occupants: one.

e. Telephone Equipment Room. In addition to the telephone equipment associated with voice communications, switchboard, etc., considerable floor space is required for telephone equipment associated with audio (sound) communications lines, including transmission to the transmitter area and receipt of incoming transmissions such as those from a radio network, etc. Local telephone company representatives should be consulted for requirements early in the planning process.

f. Automation Equipment Room. Automation equipment may be located in a control room or in a separate space. There are no special listening requirements. However, if the equipment includes card punching or tabulating equipment (used to program the automated switchers), the room can be noisy, and acoustical treatment on ceiling and walls is desirable. A glass partition will permit monitoring of the equipment while helping to contain the noise. No standards can be given for room size as this depends entirely on the equipment to be used.

3. Other Broadcasting Facilities The following facilities will not be required in all stations, but where used, they are usually closely associated with the on-air facilities.

a. Newsroom. Similar in appearance and function to the city room of a newspaper, the newsroom is the central point for gathering and editing of news stories prior to broadcast. In some cases, news may be broadcast directly from the newsroom. Special tables permit close contact between correspondents and conserve space. Newsrooms will include television monitors, an assignment board, bulletin board, and mailboxes. In some cases, particularly in large networks, separate offices are required for certain correspondents and

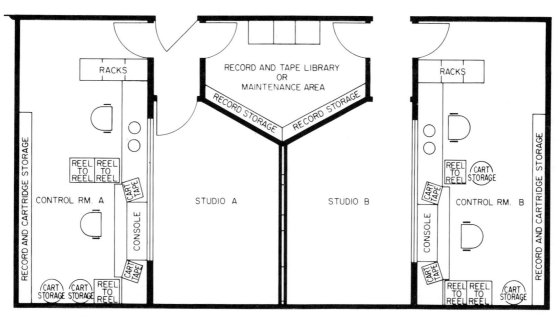

Fig. 3 Two-studio layout for a music-oriented FM station. (Designed by Fenwick S. LaBoiteaux.)

writers; these should open onto or be not far from the newsroom.

From a construction standpoint, design of the newsroom is similar to a large, very busy office. Even where news is broadcast directly from the newsroom, the background noise is usually not objectionable. (At least one all-news station plays recorded news-printer sound as background to its news broadcasts.) News facilities will vary depending on the extent of news operations at the station.

(1) The most elementary is the "rip-and-read" operation, so-called because the announcer or disk jockey leaves his post only long enough to tear off a sheet from the wire service teleprinter, which he then reads on the air. Here, the only "facility" is a printer in a closet.

(2) A typical music and news station might have a news staff of five, most of whom would be out on assignments. A room about 15 by 25 ft with three desks would suffice.

(3) An all-news station might have a staff of about 14, plus an editor. Desk space for each man is necessary. This type of newsroom is shown in Fig. 4.

b. News Printers. An important feature of the newsroom is the bank of teleprinters representing various wire services, weather, etc. These must be readily available to the newsroom, but since they are noisy, are often enclosed in a separate room acoustically treated to reduce clatter.

If operating personnel insist on locating the printers within the newsroom, consider enclosing them in a sound-proof container with hinged covers. Telex or TWX machines should also be isolated, if possible.

c. Tape and Record Library. Ideally, the tape and record library should be convenient to the studio, especially for music-oriented stations. However, since the studio area may be congested, it may be necessary to locate this elsewhere; the extent to which this can be tolerated is very much a variable and depends on local operating practices. (Fig. 3.)

For a station featuring popular contemporary music, a space 10 by 15 ft should suffice. A station with a very extensive library of classical music may require a much larger area. Normally, the library will be used by only one or two persons at a time.

Standard cabinets used for storing 12-in.-diameter long-playing records can accommodate approximately 60 records per foot of shelf, allowing enough space to permit easy insertion and removal.

Tapes, which are rapidly supplanting records, come in three forms: reels, cartridges and cassettes. Reels are stored in cardboard boxes; cassettes and cartridges do not require a separate container.

Medium	Usual dimensions	Per foot of shelf*
Reels	$7\frac{1}{2}$ by $7\frac{1}{2}$ by $\frac{3}{4}$ in.	16
Cartridges	$5\frac{1}{2}$ by 4 by 1 in.	10
Cassettes	4 by $2\frac{1}{2}$ by $\frac{1}{2}$ in.	8

* Allowing space for uprights, vertical dividers, etc.

d. Listening Rooms. As part of the library, or closely adjacent to it, should be facilities for auditing or listening to tape and records. Again, layout is a function of operating practices. If station personnel will use earphones, listening can be done in the library itself; if they insist on loudspeakers, the listening rooms should be separate and isolated acoustically from surrounding spaces, particularly studios. Provision for one or two listening positions is sufficient.

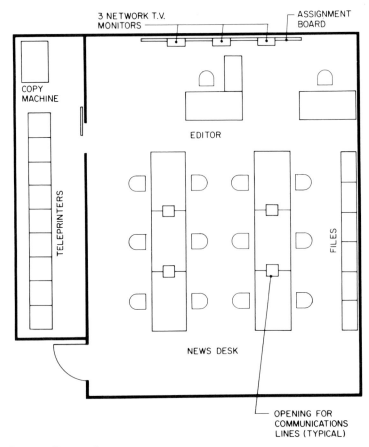

Fig. 4 Newsroom: all-news station.

e. Editing Room. Most program editing is done in the control room. However, some larger stations can effectively utilize an editing room, which is a facility akin to a control room but somewhat less sophisticated acoustically. Editing rooms are usually a part of the studio complex.

4. Support Facilities

a. Offices. Station offices will include facilities for executives, sales, programming, accounting, scheduling, operations, etc. Planning is similar to that for any other office and will not be discussed here, except to note that particular attention must be given to mailroom and telephone switchboard requirements, since activity in these areas may be high compared with a business firm of the same size.

Relation of offices to studios will depend on the size of the station and its method of operation. Some stations operate with sales, accounting, and other administrative functions remote from the studios (even in another building). Programming operations, and other functions related to broadcasting should be convenient to the studios but need not be contiguous with them.

b. Conference. For most stations, good meeting facilities are essential. They will be used for contact with sponsors and public officials as well as staff and should have provision for tape playback and other audiovisual presentations. Some stations make effective use of a conference room designed to double as a studio.

c. Reception. Planning of reception areas depends on whether visitors are limited to persons on official business or will include the general public, schoolchildren, etc. If the lat-

ter, a large lobby is desirable where groups on tour can assemble and be met by a guide. The reception area must control access effectively while still providing a welcome to bona fide visitors. Unless a receptionist or guard is on duty 24 hours a day, after-hours access presents a difficult problem. One solution is card access (similar to the system used in some parking garages) for night operating personnel, plus a night bell for other after-hours visitors. The receptionist may double as switchboard operator.

5. Personnel Facilities

a. Toilets. Plan toilets and rest rooms as for an office. Consider after-hours access. If public tours of the facility are anticipated, size toilet facilities for the visitors.

b. Cafeteria. Need for a cafeteria depends on the size of the station and the availability of other food service facilities. However, even if a complete cafeteria is not to be provided, consideration should be given to a snack bar with vending machines. This is particularly important for after-hours use when other food service facilities are not available or for operating personnel whose duties do not permit them to leave the station. The snack bar can do double duty as a lounge.

c. Parking. Parking needs are a function of local conditions, including the availability of public transportation. Planning is similar to that for offices.

Parking needs may include the following:

Station employees
Visitors
General public
Station vehicles (see following paragraph)

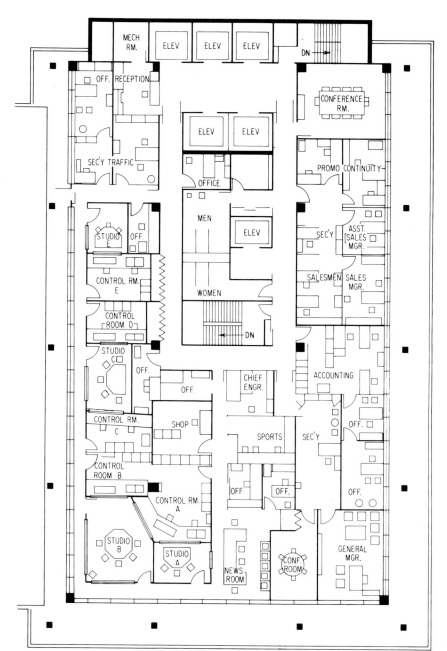

Fig. 5 Floor plan of a station serving a large metropolitan area. Files, storage, and mimeograph are on another floor (not shown).

station's needs can be determined only by careful study of its operations, including the amount of original programming planned.

b. Layout. Layout of the on-air complex requires understanding of the station's method of operation. Usually, direct visual contact is desired between studio and control room. Flexibility is provided by making it possible for each control room to handle more than one studio. Studio doors should not open directly into adjoining rooms or general corridors; where this is unavoidable, provide a sound lock at the entrance.

Although this is undesirable acoustically, operating personnel may require studio windows to the outside, either to permit the announcer to observe weather conditions or to give passersby a view of operations. A good solution in this case is use of a glassed-in corridor between studio and outer wall. Figure 5 illustrates a station where this system was employed.

c. Sound Isolation. There is an important trade-off between space requirements and complexity of construction. Isolation between adjoining rooms may be accomplished by using dividing partitions or by separating the two rooms involved. While cost is lower, the second scheme requires more floor area. Figure 6 shows a hypothetical layout for the on-air facility using corridors for sound isolation.

d. Allowance for Growth. Expansion of the on-air facility after the station is in operation is both difficult and costly. Accordingly, it is well to anticipate the need for an additional on-air facility. As an example, a room can be built to studio standards but used as a listening room, library, or office until it is required for studio purposes.

e. Three-dimensional Planning. Planning of on-air facilities requires consideration of the third dimension. In studios, maintenance of a minimum inside height of about 9 to 10 ft is important for proper acoustics. At the same time, space of 4 ft above the ceiling is desirable to accommodate ducts and other ceiling utilities.

2. Newsroom The newsroom must be accessible to the studio complex. A news-oriented station may insist on direct visual contact between newsroom and studio for signaling of "hot" news items. One solution is to place the newsroom on the opposite side of a corridor to the studio, with windows in both walls.

3. Circulation Circulation should be around, rather than through, the on-air complex. Visitors can view operations through soundproof windows. Corridors can be used to provide separation between the studio complex and adjoining spaces as well as a sound lock between the technical spaces.

F. Studio Acoustics

Acoustical design of studios, control and editing rooms requires the services of a specialist, particularly for the architect unfamiliar with such work. However, this section will touch on some of the points about which he should be consulted.

1. Objectives of Acoustical Design Basically, there are two objectives in the acoustical design of on-air facilities. The first is to attenuate or exclude unwanted sound from the room, and the second is to provide the desired acoustical characteristics *within* the room for the sounds reaching the microphone. The latter requirement has been simplified by extensive use of prerecorded music, since acoustical requirements for speech are less critical. Atten-

6. Facilities for "Remote" Operation Availability of lightweight, portable recording equipment has led to an increase in the amount of programming material originated outside the station. It is likely that this type of activity will increase and most stations will have one or more vehicles specially equipped to handle remote (off-station) operations.

Facility needs include garage space for station vehicles and storage space for portable equipment used in remote operations. Storage should be convenient to vehicle parking areas and safe from pilferage. The garage should have ac power, and space should be available for minimum maintenance or troubleshooting of mobile equipment that cannot readily be removed from the vehicle.

E. Layout Planning

1. On-Air Facilities The on-air facilities form the heart of the station and should receive primacy in planning. Since these facilities share common utilities and personnel and require sound isolation from the rest of the building, they are usually grouped together in a tight "island." This makes for operating convenience but is inflexible for changes.

a. Number of Studios. Two studios and two control rooms permit one studio to be used for editing or recording while the other is on-air. Some small stations get by with a single studio, using a second microphone position in the control room. Similarly, automation may obviate the need for the second studio. A larger

uation is still critical, particularly in stations offering contemporary rock music, where listening in adjoining rooms is done at high sound levels.

Each of these objectives will be considered in turn. In either case, the key planning factor is the nature of the broadcasting operations. It is most important that station management participate in setting acoustical design targets.

Acoustical design for control rooms is similar to that for studios. The objective is to have the sound (from loudspeakers or earphones) reaching the control operator's ear match that originated in the studio (or prerecorded) as closely as possible.

2. Room-to-Room Isolation

a. Attenuation. To exclude sounds, each studio and control room is designed as a separate "envelope," independent of the basic building structure. The first step is to establish, for each room, the permitted level of residual noise, usually expressed in noise criteria (NC) levels.[1] Typical NC levels are 20 for studios and 25 for control rooms.

The next step is to identify sources of hostile sound and to establish required room-to-room attenuation factors. Attenuation, expressed in decibels, represents the sound power loss from one space to another and determines the design of partitions, hung ceilings, windows, etc., and the need for independent "floating" floors. It should be established only after the most careful consultation with station management. As an example, if adjacent studios will be used only for news and interviews, the room-to-room attenuation may be about 40 db—using construction similar to a good private office. Where loud music is to be played, required attenuation can reach 60 db or even higher, with significant effect on cost and complexity of construction.

On the other hand, planning should also consider future program changes, since it is very difficult to upgrade a studio without total reconstruction.

b. Floor Isolation. Successful radio studios have been built using a common floor slab. Again, this is very much a function of the sound levels expected within the rooms. Where extreme sound levels are unavoidable, each studio must be placed on its own floating floor supported on springs or neoprene isolators. Note that where used, the floating floor will also support the entire studio envelope: inner walls and ceiling.

c. Doors. Doors are the Achilles' heel of every studio installation. A sound lock is an arrangement of two sound doors separated by a small vestibule. It is analogous to a light lock at the entrance to a photographic darkroom in that it prevents accidental sound leakage into a studio if the door is opened while the studio is in use. "Hostile" sounds, such as those that may become a problem when there are two separate studios, should be separated by at least two doors which should, if possible, not be opposite to each other.

Doors should be sound rated and equipped with gaskets or seals, including drop seals at the threshold. They should have hydraulic closers and handles (instead of latches) and should be provided with small viewing ports.

d. Design Details

(1) Windows must be tightly gasketed. Multiple-pane windows are common; whether

they are actually needed is a function of room-to-room attenuation. For most purposes, two panes are sufficient; but to be effective, the two panes must be in independent frames and must be of different thickness to prevent resonance.

(2) Fluorescent lighting, if used, should have ballasts remoted.

(3) Particular attention must be paid to penetrations through the envelope; entries for ductwork, conduit, cable trays, and other services must all be designed and not left to the contractor if they are not to defeat the carefully planned envelope.

(4) Corridors within the on-air complex should be carpeted to minimize foot-impact noise. Consideration should also be given to carpeting areas above the studio complex. Opinion differs on the need for carpeting within the on-air facilities themselves. While absorbing foot noise, it makes movement of equipment difficult.

(5) Studio tabletops should be of cork or felt to minimize paper-shuffling noise, and to prevent unwanted reflections of the "talent's" voice.

3. Room Acoustics

Room acoustics requires the proper balance between "hard" (sound-reflecting) and "soft" (sound-absorbing) surfaces, which is a function of the type of sound (speech, music, etc.), the room size, and the type of microphones that will be used. The tendency is towards very "dead" (absorbent) studios and control rooms. (If reverberation is desired, it can be added electronically.) Absorbent wall treatment and closely held microphones reduce the problem of reflection from parallel, hard surfaces that used to require skewing of opposite walls. Highly directional microphones may also prevent unwanted echos or "slap" from hard glass surfaces. Where a naturally "live" (reverberant) studio is required, walls should be skewed.

It is also important that sound absorption be uniform over the frequency spectrum. This is done by spacing out absorbent material such as fiber glass over a portion of the walls and ceiling.

A traditional rule of thumb for studio acoustical design is that the height, width, and length should be in the ratio of 3:4:5.

G. Utilities and Services

1. Electricity

a. Power Source. For a radio station, the most important utility is a reliable power source. Incoming service should be stable as to both voltage and frequency and free from interruptions.

b. Technical Power. Electronic equipment should be fed from a separate "technical" or "clean" power feeder. No lights or building loads should be placed on this feeder. Where voltage fluctuations are expected, provide voltage regulators for the technical power feeder.

Secondary wiring from a technical power panel within the room to the electronic equipment is usually part of the radio equipment installation, but the architect may have to provide the necessary conduits or raceways.

c. Emergency Power. Even with a reliable power source, outages and "blackouts" are still possible. The most common emergency power source is a diesel engine generator equipped with controls to start automatically when voltage drops to a predetermined level. An automatic transfer switch shifts from normal to emergency power and prevents simultaneous connection to both sources. A brief off-air period can usually be tolerated, so that the cost of no-break power is not warranted. If the station is a member of the government-sponsored Emergency Broadcasting System (EBS), it will require a *two-week* fuel supply.

2. Air Conditoning

Air conditioning is required in the studio's control and equipment rooms to

---

[1] Since the apparent loudness of a sound varies with its pitch (frequency), curves relating sound power level to frequency, known as noise criteria (NC) curves have been developed to express the levels of residual noise in a room.

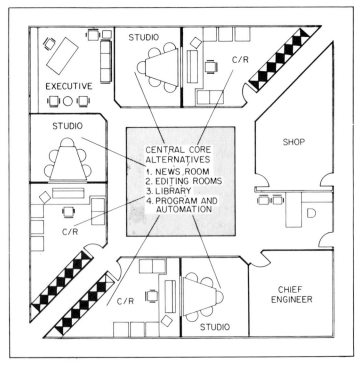

Fig. 6 Hypothetical layout for a radio studio built around a central core. (Designed by Fenwick S. LaBoiteaux.)

protect sensitive equipment, as well as for comfort, and it is usually provided in other areas in keeping with modern practices.

Special consideration must be given to acoustical requirements to prevent ductwork from carrying unwanted sounds from one room to another and to exclude fan and duct noises. Proper acoustical design of the air-conditioning system starts with equipment selection and its isolation from the building structure. It includes careful duct routing to avoid short circuiting of sound from one area to another with mains located outside the on-air complex. It also includes proper use of sound traps, turning vanes, flexible connections, and duct insulation to remove residual duct noises. Finally, careful attention to wall penetration is essential.

Air distribution inside these areas must be at low enough velocity to keep air and duct noises within the noise criteria (NC) levels selected for the space. As a rule of thumb, air velocities in branch ducts should not exceed 400 fpm at the point where the duct enters the studio. Velocity out of the diffusing element should not exceed 300 fpm, and 200 fpm is preferred. In addition to maintaining this low velocity, diffusers must also be of a type that will not in themselves generate noise.

3. Communications

a. Audio Signal Feeds. Except where studios and transmitter facilities share a single facility, broadcasting signals are transmitted from the studios to the transmitter by microwave, leased telephone lines, or a combination. Where microwave is to be used, a study must be made of terrain profile, since microwave requires a direct line of sight. Intermediate stations are used to surmount obstacles.

Central network programming may also be received by either microwave or leased telephone lines.

b. Telephone, Telex, and Wire Printers. Telephone services are important, particularly for a news-oriented station. Most stations will probably require one or more wire service teleprinters. Consideration should also be given to the need for telex and facsimile installations.

c. Point-to-Point Radio. A news-oriented station will have a significant requirement for local radio communications facilities. These are facilities for point-to-point wireless communications between the station and its reporters in field locations and are similar to police and fire radio. Usually transmission requirements can be satisfied by roof-mounted antennas. Roof antennas are also required for radio and television pickup.

4. Audio Wiring

Audio wiring is the low-voltage cabling, similar to telephone wiring, used to interconnect the electronic equipment and transmit the broadcasting signals within the studio. It is quite extensive and must be considered in design. Audio wiring may be distributed by one or more of the following:

Floor trenches with removable covers
Underfloor duct, conduit, or raceway
Hollow, elevated floors similar to those used in computer rooms
Overhead cable trays or raceways
Horizontal baseboard raceways

Floor channels and underfloor duct do not lend themselves to future changes in equipment layout. Cable trays or "ladders" are the most flexible from the maintenance standpoint, since cables are easily removed and inserted but are acceptable only if permitted by local codes. Cable system routing must be carefully checked for the interference with ducts and

lights (if in the ceiling) and to avoid compromising the acoustical "envelope" surrounding each studio and control room.

5. Other

Following is a brief checklist of some of the other systems that may be required:
a. Compressed-air and Central Vacuum Systems. Large stations and networks may require central systems serving control rooms, rack rooms, and maintenance shops. They are used for cleaning and general maintenance.
b. Loudspeaker System.
c. TV Monitor System.
d. Clock System.

II. RADIO TRANSMITTER FACILITIES

A. Description

Radio transmitters may be attended or unattended. In some smaller stations, transmitter and studios share a single building; but for AM facilities, this usually means a less than optimum location for one or the other. The following discussion assumes that studio and transmitter facilities are separate.

Besides the transmitter building, the main feature of a transmitter installation is the broadcasting antenna. For AM stations, the antenna is usually one or more radiating towers. For FM, the tower serves as a support on which a separate radiating antenna is mounted.

1. AM Transmitters

For an AM transmitter, the main structures will include the towers and their foundations, the guy anchorages (usually three, spaced radially at $120°$ about each tower base), and the transmitter building, which will be discussed subsequently. There is also a small building, of concrete or block, at the base of the tower, known as the "tuning house" or "coupling house," which houses equipment for matching the transmitter and its transmission line to the impedance of the antenna.

An important but less obvious feature of AM installations is the ground system. A copper-mesh screen, about 40 by 40 ft, is centered at the base of the tower. Buried copper cables extend outward radially from the mesh every three degrees. These are generally 6 to 12 in. below ground surface.

If the antenna is "directional," i.e., designed to broadcast in a particular, nonuniform pattern, multiple antennas (an "array") must be used instead of a single tower. Tower height is a function of the station's assigned wavelength, with most AM towers between one-quarter and five-eighths of a wavelength in height. As an example, a station with a frequency of 600 kilohertz (kHz) (1 kHz = 1,000 cycles per second) has a wavelength of 1,640 ft and could have a tower height of between 400 and 1,050 ft.

Because of the cost and land area required for an AM transmitter, some competing stations have joined forces to operate from a single tower. This arrangement calls for highly specialized design of the tower, and services of a professional radio engineer become essential.

2. FM Transmitters

FM facilities are limited to the antenna, which is usually mounted on a tower or mast, plus the transmitter itself. It is common for several FM stations to share a single mast or tower as well as for FM antennas to be mounted on a TV or AM antenna tower.

The main requirement for an FM antenna is height to clear the surrounding terrain. FCC

regulations control the relationship between height and allowable broadcasting power, which depends on the class of station. Most FM antennas are between 200 and 1,000 ft high.

B. Site Selection

1. Location

Transmitter location is determined by antenna requirements, which differ sharply for AM and FM. For AM transmitters, a rural location is usually necessary to achieve the required ground conductivity and avoid interference with reception in nearby homes, as well as to find the space needed for the ground system. FM antennas, on the other hand, require mainly height and have been successfully located in cities, on top of tall buildings.

2. Area Required

For an AM station, the site must be large enough to contain the antenna array plus the guys and ground radials. Tower guys require a radius of about two-thirds the tower height, while the ground radials should be about half the length of the station's wavelength. In the example given above of a station with a frequency of 600 kHz, the ground radials for a single tower should be about 820 ft long.

For an FM station, the site need only be large enough to contain the tower base (or the guys, in the case of a guyed tower) plus a small transmitter room. Thus, a tall building that can support the required mast makes a good FM transmitter site. A TV tower that can carry an additional antenna is also a good location.

3. Technical Considerations

Site selection for a transmitter facility is highly technical and is best entrusted to a consulting engineer specializing in this kind of work unless the station itself posesses the necessary expertise. In addition to studies of ground conductivity (for AM), careful analysis must be made of potential interference with other stations, all in accordance with detailed FCC regulations. Air traffic patterns must also be considered, as must local zoning regulations.

4. Other Considerations

In addition to the necessary technical considerations, the site should have:

All-weather access
Reliable power supply
Reliable telephone service
Parking space

It should lend itself to proper security. It should be possible to provide water and sanitary sewage either from public utilities or on-site facilities.

C. Site Planning

The ground area required by the spread of the guys and the need to accommodate the ground radial system can be quite extensive. Some of this acreage can be sold or leased out provided provision is made in the lease or deed for protection and maintenance of the ground system. Similarly, the area between the tower base and the guy anchorages, which is largely unused, can be devoted to grazing or other uses that will not disturb the ground system.

Safety should be considered in locating the transmitter building. Although structural tower failures are rare, collapses caused by accident (aircraft) or sabotage are not unknown. If possible, the transmitter building should be so placed that, in the event of such a catastrophe, the tower would be likely to fall clear of the building. An AM transmitter may be located some distances from the antenna.

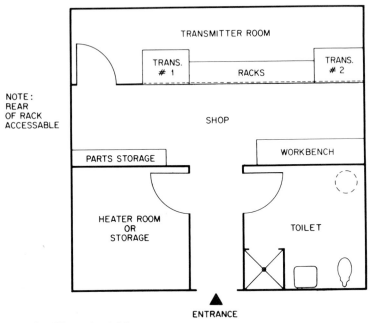

Fig. 7 Small AM or FM transmitter building.

FM transmitters must be as close to the tower as possible, to minimize line losses.

Concern over continuity of broadcasting has led some stations to provide an auxiliary antenna. This is costly both in terms of construction and land area. Perhaps a better solution is an agreement with other stations permitting some kind of dual use of their facilities in the event of an emergency.

D. Construction

1. General

a. Grounding For an AM facility, all structures within the transmitter area, including the transmitter building, must be properly grounded and tied into the ground radial system. In concrete buildings, reinforcing steel must be made electrically continuous and bonded to the ground radial system.

b. Soil Conditions AM antennas have been located in marshy or waterfront land, to take advantage of good soil conductivity. This may require pile foundations for towers and buildings. In swampy areas, consideration must be given to possible land subsidence which could affect the grounding system.

2. Towers A ground-supported tower is usually designed as a slender mast, pinned at the base and braced by one or more levels of guys. Fixed-base or cantilevered towers (without guys) are now used only for masts on the roofs of buildings. The tapered shape of a self-supporting tower is also undesirable for an AM transmitter where, as previously indicated, the tower itself is the radiating element. Electronic considerations will determine the height and general arrangement of the tower.

AM towers, which are usually of steel, are given a heavy coating of zinc galvanizing. This serves to protect the tower, but its primary purpose is to provide electrical conductivity. At radio frequencies, the "current" flows mainly along the outside periphery of the tower. Sections of the tower must be electrically bonded together for the tower to function properly.

FM towers serve only to support the separate antennas and are designed purely for structural considerations. All towers require aviation marking (alternate white and orange striping) and obstruction lighting; details are found in FCC regulations.

3. Transmitter Building In addition to space for the transmitter itself, there should be space for the associated equipment racks, maintenance, spare parts storage, and toilet facilities. Even an "unattended" facility is occupied periodically for inspection and maintenance. If the station is quite remote, minimal kitchen facilities and a shower may be desirable.

The amount of equipment which must be contained in the transmitter building depends on the station's assigned operating power. This can vary from 250 watts for very small stations to 50 kilowatts for the larger commercial stations. For the larger stations, equipment may be quite heavy, so that floor loads must be checked, particularly when locating the transmitter in an existing building.

In cold climates a carport may be desirable to protect the operator and his vehicle against ice falling from the tower. This can be a more serious hazard than it may at first seem.

When two or more stations share a single antenna system, the need for separate transmitter buildings or rooms will be determined by local operating preferences; both systems work well. Figure 7 shows the layout for an unattended transmitter in a rural location.

4. Utilities

a. Communications. Program signals may be brought to the transmitter by leased telephone lines, microwave, or a combination. Microwave requires a series of direct lines of sight.

b. Power Some transmitters have two primary power services from different substations and feeders for greater reliability; usually automatic switching between services is included.

Emergency power is required for Emergency Broadcasting System (EBS) stations and may be desirable for others, particularly where the primary power source is subject to interruptions. If provided, it should be sized to handle minimal lighting, tower obstruction lighting, and transmitter ventilation as well as the transmitter itself.

c. Heating, Ventilating, Air Conditioning. The transmitter generates considerable heat, which must be removed by mechanical ventilation. This system consists of a filtered intake with a ducted exhaust connected directly to the transmitter. Dampers are arranged so as to reduce the amount of outside air during the winter and make use of the transmitter heat. Supplemental heat is usually required to maintain comfortable working conditions in winter.

Air conditioning is not required unless the transmitter plant will be occupied for a large part of each day.

d. Lighting. Good lighting (office levels) should be provided to facilitate housekeeping and maintenance.

e. Site Development. Since an AM tower is dangerous when in operation, its base must be fenced, as should each of the guy anchor blocks, to discourage tampering with the guys. Fencing of the entire area and security lighting may also be desirable. Planting or other erosion protection for the ground around the tower should be provided.

By JOSEPH HOROWITZ, P.E., Manager, Planning & Design, Facilities Engineering Department, Columbia Broadcasting System, Inc.

TELEVISION BROADCASTING FACILITIES

A. Scope

Television broadcasting facilities range from a tiny station serving a small community to a major network facility with multiple studios and extensive supporting facilities providing programming to hundreds of city and regional markets. Because of the wide variation in requirements, this article will be limited to basic planning considerations plus a brief description of each of the facilities that *may* be required. Emphasis is on program origination facilities; transmitter installations are covered only briefly.

B. Classification

Television facilities may be classified as to purpose, type of programming, and extent of audience involvement. These factors, plus the size and budget of the station, determine the facilities to be provided and their relationships.

1. Purpose

a. Local Station. A local television station serves a defined geographical area as authorized by FCC licensing. Programming will reflect the size of the market (area served) which may range from a small town to a large metropolitan area. Many local commercial stations are affiliated with one of the major networks, which provides a large portion of their programming. Another common source of outside programming is syndicated tape and film.

b. Network. Program origination facilities for a television network differ from those of a local station in that they are usually larger, with a greater variety of supporting services. They originate program material for use by affiliated local stations.

c. Cable Television (CATV). Facilities for cable television consist of a receiving antenna and a small head end building containing the associated electronic equipment. Incoming programs are distributed over a network of cables to subscribers. Some CATV operators have austere studios suitable for local news and interviews.

d. Other. Schools and industrial concerns are making increased use of television for educational and training purposes and have set up studio facilities for this purpose. Programs may be broadcast or distributed over closed circuits. In addition, a number of cassette-type media are now available on which programs may be recorded for later playback on closed circuit.

2. Type of Programming

A basic planning factor is the extent of locally originated programming material as opposed to network-supplied or syndicated material. Locally originated programs require a studio; studio type and extent of supporting facilities will depend on nature of programming planned.

a. News studio requirements are usually quite simple. Supporting facilities will include news gathering services, plus storage and editing facilities for film and videotape. Coverage of local news events will require remote equipment.

b. Interview and panel discussions can be handled with the simplest of studios and minimal support facilities.

c. Dramatic programs (such as soap operas) call for elaborate facilities, extensive sets, props, makeup, wardrobe, and other support facilities. Studio lighting is also more elaborate.

d. Musical and variety programs are the most demanding. Studios must accommodate anything from a single performer to a large group and require great flexibility in lighting, scenery, properties, etc. Supporting facilities are similar to those for dramatic programs, but usually there is less opportunity for reuse of materials in subsequent programs.

e. "Remotes," or broadcasts originated outside the station's studios, include coverage of sports events, political conventions, news, and other public events. Facilities required for this type of operation (in addition to control room and other technical facilities required for on-premises programming) are described below.

3. Audience and Public Involvement

Studios may be further classified as audience or nonaudience. An audience studio is a cross between a theater and a studio, with the usual theater considerations of sight lines, audience acoustics, and public safety complicated by the requirements for camera operation and lighting.

The public may be involved in television facilities in ways other than as studio audiences. A station planning to encourage visitors to view the behind-the-scenes operations should make ample provision for such circulation.

Another case is the special-purpose facility which has as a major function, the training of television technicians and operating personnel. Here, control rooms and other supporting facilities must be planned to do double duty as classrooms.

C. Other Planning Factors

In addition to the classifications described, the following factors must also be considered:
1. Hours of operation.
2. Union regulations affecting technicians, stagehands, etc.
3. Management decisions on contracting out vs. work done in-house. Examples are rental of scenery props and costumes and outside film developing and storage.

D. Site Selection

Site selection has much in common with radio studios, but it will also depend on the planning factors previously enumerated. The site for an audience studio is planned much as is that for a theater, with considerations of parking, transportation, and audience egress.

All studios require truck loading facilities for delivery and removal of heavy cameras and electronic equipment and—if dramatic or variety programming is planned—scenery and properties. Insofar as possible, avoid a site subjected to vibration, such as that caused by a highway.

E. Facilities

The listing which follows includes spaces required in a larger station, a network or a college facility where exposure to all facets of television broadcasting is desired. Smaller stations will require fewer and less elaborate facilities.

1. Studios

A television studio is any room where television cameras are used. Studios range in size from that of a regular office (with the camera shooting in through a window or open door) to large studios of 100 by 100 ft used for dramatic or variety programming. Because of its importance, a brief discussion of studio planning is contained in Section G. (See Fig. 1.)

2. Control Rooms

Control rooms contain electronic equipment for monitoring and controlling the studio output. They may have separate compartments for sound (audio), picture (video), and lighting control. An announcer's booth incorporated with the control room must be acoustically isolated, since it contains a live microphone.

Control rooms must usually be accessible to the studio which they serve; direct visual contact may or may not be necessary, depending on operating practices (Fig. 2).

Acoustical considerations are similar to those for radio control rooms. Lighting should be adjustable to permit observation of television monitors.

3. Technical Facilities

Technical facilities house the extensive electronic equipment which supports broadcasting operations. Because of the space required and the fact that some of this equipment is noisy, only the smallest stations locate it in the control rooms.

To facilitate maintenance, the technical facilities are often grouped together in a Central Technical Area (CTA). CTA need not be adjacent to the studios, provided good communications are available. A dust-free temperature-controlled environment is essential. Following are the facilities that make up CTA:

a. Equipment (Rack) Rooms. The equipment room houses ancillary electronic equipment that does not require attendance or adjustment during programming, such as audio and video equipment, switching devices, transmission equipment, etc. A separate room facilitates maintenance and simplifies design of the control room. The rack room need not be adjacent to the control room(s) but should be convenient to the maintenance shop.

b. Videotape Recording (VTR). The usual medium for television recording is magnetic tape using a device called a videotape recorder (VTR), which resembles a very elaborate magnetic sound tape recorder. The VTR area for a local station may contain from two to six machines. Central network facilities will have more.

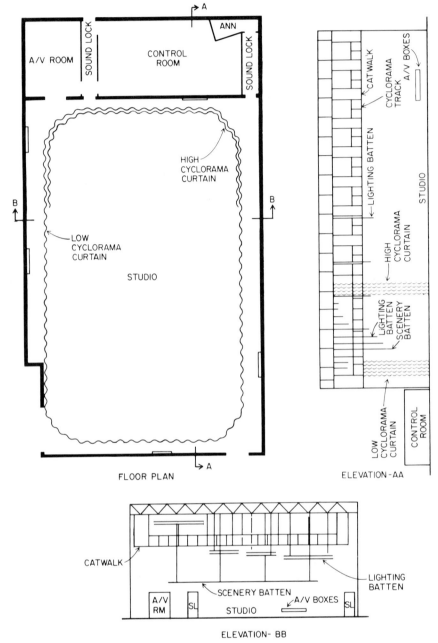

FLOOR PLAN

ELEVATION-AA

ELEVATION- BB

Fig. 1   Typical studio layout.

c. Telecine. Despite the advantages of magnetic tape, much television programming will continue to originate as motion picture film. In addition to the popularity of full-length feature film as television fare, off-station news and special events are usually easier to record with portable motion picture cameras. As the name implies (*tele*-television, *cine*-cinema), telecine contains assemblies that combine motion picture and slide projectors with a television camera. Size will depend on the number of machines to be housed.

d. Master Control. Larger stations with several studios may require a central or master control for final switching and monitoring of the on-air operation.

e. Maintenance Shop. This is an electronics workshop with considerable space for spare parts. It must be as convenient as possible to the central technical area. Ideally, it should also be convenient to the control rooms, but this is not always possible.

f. Telephone Equipment Room. For large stations and network facilities, telephone equipment associated with transmission of television programming requires a substantial floor area which is usually close to or a part of the central technical area. (This equipment is distinct from that used for normal telephone communications.)

g. Film Recording. This area contains equipment for recording, on motion picture film, material originated electronically. Before the advent of magnetic tape, this was the only method for recording television programs. Some network installations and very large stations may still require a film recording facility which can be adjacent to or part of tele-

cine. Useful adjuncts to film recording are a darkroom and viewing room.

h. Video Cartridges. New methods available for recording television programming in cartridge or cassette form include film (Electronic Video Recording), magnetic tape, plastic tape, and plastic disks. While most are not yet of broadcast quality, they may in time supplement videotape and film as program sources, much as tape cartridges now supplement phonograph records in commercial radio studios. Possible facilities' needs cannot yet be predicted.

i. Program Control. This is a room resembling a control room without a studio where television signals from various sources—such as telecine, VTR, or live remotes—are combined electronically to produce a complete program. It is useful where studios are heavily used and much off-premises work is anticipated. A program control room is required only for the largest stations or network facilities.

4. News Even the smallest station will have local news. The following facilities would be required for a large station or a central network facility:

a. Newsroom. This is similar to a newspaper "city room" with desk and telephone space for newsmen. It usually contains or is adjacent to wire service printers and is usually equipped with TV monitors.

b. Library and Archives. Just as a major newspaper will maintain a file of clippings, a large news operation will have a library of film and tape as well as reference books and other resources. This should be accessible to the newsroom.

c. Special News Studios. Since the live "action" in a news broadcast is usually limited to a man at a desk, larger stations may want a small studio opening directly off the newsroom from which news programs may originate without tying up one of the regular studios. When not in use as a studio, it serves as an office.

d. Graphic Arts. This is a facility for rapid production of charts, photos, and other visual materials. It is used extensively for news as well as other programming. It may vary from a single artist's desk in a small operation to a large room with many artists and facilities, such as a Statmaster, for photo developing and printing.

5. Studio Support Facilities The following rooms are basically similar to corresponding spaces in legitimate theaters and will not be discussed in detail. Need for them depends on the type of programming.

a. Rehearsal halls (these are best kept away from the studio to minimize sound problems).

b. Wardrobe rooms.

c. Dressing rooms (individual and group).

d. Makeup rooms.

e. "Talent"[1] lounge for performers (convenient to studios and dressing rooms). This is often called a "green room" after a similar green-painted room in a well-known concert hall.

f. Multipurpose rooms. These are rooms about the size of a chorus dressing room which can be used, as the occasion demands, for dressing rooms, rehearsal of small groups, lounge, music origination, etc.

g. Ready storage for scenery and props. This must be available as close as possible to the studios to minimize handling.

[1] "Talent" refers to the actors, announcers, and other performers who appear or are heard in programs.

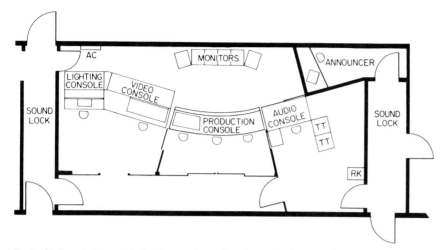

Fig. 2 Studio control room. Note that the control room shown has no visual contact with the studio; wall space is used for television monitors.

h. Crew's lounge. This should also be convenient to the studio area.

i. Storage for cameras, microphones, and lighting equipment. This should be convenient to studios, and if possible, to the maintenance shop.

6. Scenery Facilities for a large station or network will include scenic design (art studio with possibly blueprinting or photostating services), production (carpenter shop, paint shop, stage electrical shop), scenery and property (prop) storage, and facilities for disposal of unwanted scenery.

Facilities to be provided depend on business decisions as well as station size and programming, since many of these functions can be contracted out. Some networks maintain a central scenery fabricating department from which materials are trucked to and from off-premises studios. Whether made on premises or off, scenery and props constitute a significant materials handling problem. The general flow is shown graphically in Fig. 5.

7. Film Facilities for processing (developing), editing (cutting), and storage of film are identical to those in commercial film laboratories and in many cases these functions (except possibly editing) are performed for the station by a commercial film laboratory.

Film storage and handling facilities are usually strictly regulated. In the absence of local codes, refer to National Fire Protection Association pamphlets.

8. Sound Effects Central sound effects rooms—similar to small radio control rooms—are required only in the larger facilities. They need not be adjacent to the studios provided good intercommunications are available.

9. Music Origination Rooms These provide musical background to a studio program. If the instrument (piano, organ, etc.) does not appear visually, it may be located in a separate room to avoid cluttering up the studio. Usually, very close microphone techniques are used, so that acoustical requirements are not severe.

10. Viewing (Screening) Rooms A viewing room may be anything from a room with a 16 mm projector on a table for previewing films to an elaborate miniature theater for showing programs to prospective sponsors. The latter type

should be easily reached from sales and executive areas and convenient to rest rooms and offices. They are not usually related to the studio or technical facilities. Viewing rooms should have facilities for 16 mm and 35 mm motion picture film (if possible, with a separate projection booth) as well as television monitoring.

It is often possible to arrange viewing rooms so that two rooms share a single projection booth. Local code requirements will influence planning and design. The viewing room may also be designed to double as a conference room.

11. Facilities for Outside (Remote) Program Origination By contrast with radio, facilities for remote (off-premises) television broadcasting are quite elaborate. A station planning such activities will require the following:

a. Garage or parking space for the mobile vans containing remote equipment. Since these may be taller than ordinary vehicles, a careful check of overhead clearances is required.

b. A field shop for maintenance of the equipment and for storage of gear. This must be con-

venient to the garage area, since some of the equipment cannot be readily removed from the vans for servicing.

c. For a station with much off-premises work, an extra control room (without a studio) is useful. This permits putting together a remote without tying up one of the regular studios. (See 3*i*, Program Control.)

12. Echo Chambers Echo or reverberation effects are obtained in one of two ways: using "natural" echo chambers (highly reverberant rooms) or by means of artificial reverberation devices. The natural (physical) echo chambers require isolation from surrounding noise, otherwise they can be located anywhere. Need for reverberation sources depends on the type of programming contemplated.

13. Offices With the exception of those directly related to production, offices may be remote from the studios (even in another building), but they should be convenient to viewing rooms. Executive offices and conference rooms will require closed-circuit television feeds. For major network facilities, consider offices for outside "show units" (producer, director, and their assistants) as well as other employees.

14. Personnel Facilities The larger activities may require cafeteria, first aid, and other support facilities customary in an industrial building. In planning circulation and toilet facilities, consider visitors, schoolchildren, and studio audiences.

15. Building Maintenance Because of the heavy investment in facilities and equipment, television facilities are usually intensely used. Similarly, continuity of air conditioning, electric power, and other building services is essential. These factors dictate allocation of adequate space to building maintenance such as cleaning, repair shops, and spare parts storage.

Utility areas, such as transformer vaults and mechanical equipment rooms, should be liberally sized both to facilitate maintenance and to accommodate future alterations without interrupting broadcasting operations.

16. Site Development
a. Parking needs must consider:

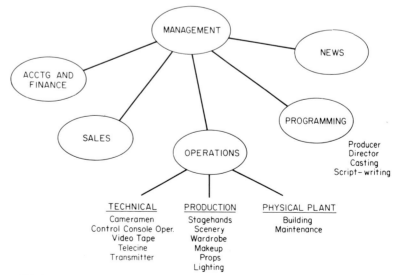

Fig. 3 Television station — schematic organization.

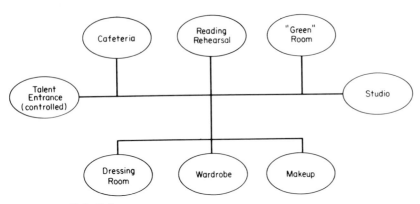

Fig. 4 Performer ("talent") flow.

> Station employees
> Visitors on business, such as customers, performers, and tradesmen
> Studio audiences
> General public (guided tours, school-children, etc.)
> Station vehicles

b. Off-street loading facilities are essential for scenery and properties as well as heavy cameras, dollies, and electronic equipment. Access is required from the loading facilities to shops, storage area, and studios.

c. Some stations make special use of their outside facilities for programs such as farm or animal shows.

F. Planning Considerations

1. Circulation Organization of a typical television station is shown schematically in Fig. 3. A television broadcasting facility includes quite divergent functions. Flows of people and materials that may be in conflict must be separated as in a manufacturing plant. Some of these flows are described below:

a. Office personnel require access to production or technical spaces only rarely. Executive and sales personnel require ready access to conference and viewing rooms.

b. Visitors should be controlled. Sponsors and other official guests should have ready access to offices and screening rooms without going through production or technical areas.

c. "Talent" (performing artists of all types) require access to studios and studio support facilities (see Fig. 4).

d. Technicians and production personnel require access to their areas and to studios.

e. Talent, technical, and production personnel should not have to pass through office areas.

f. Studio audiences, where used, should have access only to studio and toilets. Visits to production or technical spaces should be carefully controlled, as on guided tours.

g. Scenery and props involve significant materials-handling operations. Figure 5 shows the major flows which should be separated, insofar as possible, from the "people" flow.

h. "Show unit" offices (producer, director, and their staffs) are preferably located within easy access to studio facilities, although this is not always possible.

2. Expansion Studios and technical rooms are very difficult and costly to expand unless expansion is contemplated in the original construction. One approach is to build the basic shell large enough to accommodate all anticipated requirements. Interior finishes are de-

ferred and the space to be used for studios in the future is, for example, used initially for scenery storage. Where the site permits, a second approach is to locate studios next to an outside wall.

Videotape and other technical areas which do not require the ceiling heights characteristic of studios can be expanded provided the space alongside can be made available. Expansion needs should also be considered when planning fan rooms, duct routing, and other utilities spaces.

G. Studio Planning

The studio is the heart of original programmed television.

1. Audience Studio Audience studios present a particular challenge, since camera operation conflicts with the theater requirements for unobstructed sight lines. The resulting studio is usually a compromise. For a production facility with only occasional audience use, removable bleacher seating may be considered.

Television studios require a substantial camera maneuvering space between the production area and the audience seating. Camera runways project out into the seating area to permit long camera shots. Seating area is usually sloped for better audience viewing. Note that it must be possible to aim cameras at the audience as well as at the stage. Musicians are located at the same level as the rest of the production area and are usually enclosed for acoustical reasons.

Audience studios are "places of public assembly" in building code terms, with seat spacing, egress, and other aspects of audience safety and comfort to be considered.

2. Dimensions Studios can range from 20 by 25 ft for a very small station to 100 by 100 ft or more for a large facility suitable for all types of programming. Studios limited to news or similar static programming with little movement can be even smaller. A 40- by 60-ft studio is a good size for an average station.

Minimum clearance under the lighting support structure or air-conditioning ducts can range from 10 ft in the news-interview studio to 15 or 20 ft in the larger studios suitable for dramatic and variety programming. Where a walk-on grid is used for lighting, an additional 7 ft or so should be provided between bottom of grid and underside of trusses or beams forming the roof.

3. Sound and Vibration Isolation Interior acoustical requirements depend on the type of pro-

gramming. In addition to isolating the studio from outside noise, vibration that could be felt by sensitive cameras must be avoided. This may be caused by outside traffic, building equipment, or an adjoining studio. In extreme cases, the entire studio is "floated" on springs to separate it from the building structure.

4. Materials Handling Scenery, props, and other materials used in the studio may be both bulky and heavy. Entrance for large scenery flats is essential, as well as facilities for delivery of heavy items such as an automobile.

5. Floor Loading Floor loadings should accommodate the type of programming anticipated, as well as the weights of the cameras which, with their moving carriages (dollies) can be quite heavy. A live load of at least 100 psf is recommended for maximum flexibility in large studios, and some authorities recommend 125 to 150 psf. (The classic example of extreme point loading is an elephant standing on one foot.[2]) Finished floors require greater than usual freedom from irregularities and waves which would affect a rolling camera.

6. Cyclorama The production area of the studio is usually surrounded by a cyclorama, a thin, opaque curtain which provides a backdrop to scenery and conceals the walls or any storage outside the production area.

7. Lighting For smaller studios, lighting is provided by a combination of overhead and floor-mounted luminaires. Greater flexibility is obtained with an electrified raceway of the Litespan type.

For the larger studios, some type of lighting grid from which light fixtures may be hung is usually necessary. This may be serviced by ladders from the floor, but in the major studios a catwalk system is provided which permits placement and adjustment of the luminaires entirely from above. Individual light pipes or battens that can be raised and lowered are also used (see Fig. 1) permitting adjustment of lights from the studio floor.

Associated with the lighting system is a patch panel, an oversized version of a telephone switchboard, used for making lighting connections. Dimming equipment may be in the studio or centralized elsewhere and remotely controlled by a lighting console in the control room or studio.

H. Space Planning for Utilities

Color television requires very intense lighting —50 to 75 watts per square foot of production area is not uncommon. Heat generated by this lighting must be removed by air conditioning. Location of air-conditioning equipment and duct routing must be considered in original planning. Space must also be allocated to the very extensive wiring which interconnects studio, control room, and central technical area, using under-floor ducts, overhead cable trays, or other means. In one large installation, the ceiling of the central technical area was used as a kind of huge cable tray, with bundled cables laid directly on the grating that served as the ceiling. (The ceiling also served as a plenum for air conditioning.)

Power for electronic equipment ("technical" power) should be separated from that serving building equipment and may require voltage regulation. For a major station, emergency

---

[2] The weight here may range up to 5 to 7 tons.

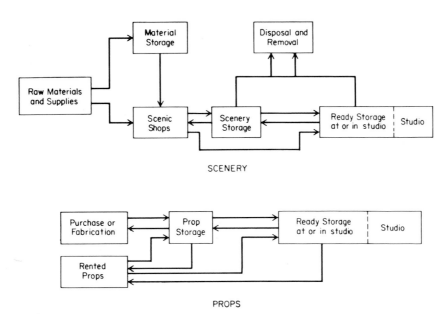

SCENERY

PROPS

Fig. 5 Materials flow, scenery and props storage.

generators should be considered to provide for continuity of minimal broadcasting, such as news, network feeds, or film. (Emergency studio operation is not usually practical because of the heavy power and air-conditioning requirements.)

I. Transmitter Facilities[3]

Transmitter facilities consist of the broadcasting antenna and the transmitter building or room. As with FM, the radiating element (antenna) is mounted on a separate tower or mast, whose function is purely structural.

[3] See discussion of radio transmitters immediately preceding this article.

There is no ground radial system as with AM radio transmitters except for lightning protection. Several antennas may be mounted on a single mast or tower.

TV transmission is primarily a line-of-sight phenomenon and is affected by buildings, mountains, etc. For this reason, antenna height is a major consideration, and many television towers are more than 1,000 ft tall.

Because of these heights, particular consideration must be given to falling ice and drifting paint spray when the tower is repainted. In general, physical site planning has much in common with radio transmitter planning.

Planning for the transmitter room also resembles that for radio transmitters, but the equipment and plant facilities are larger and

more complex. Detailed requirements depend very much on the transmitter equipment to be used, and particular attention must be paid to transmitter cooling. (UHF equipment usually requires water cooling.)

In the past, most television transmitters have been fully manned, requiring kitchen and toilet (and even sleeping facilities in some cases). While unattended transmitters are now permitted, the transmitter building will still be occupied for a part of each day, requiring some personnel support facilities. On the other hand, provision should be made for remote monitoring of building services—temperature, fire detection, electric power, etc.—for use during those periods when the station is unmanned. Where continuity of broadcasting is essential, emergency power should be provided.

Commercial
HOTELS

By **MORRIS LAPIDUS** and **ALAN LAPIDUS**, Morris Lapidus Associates

BASIC THEORIES OF HOTEL PLANNING

Before an architectural office begins planning and designing a hotel, it should know exactly how a hotel operates. Every type of building must function smoothly to achieve the end result that the client is seeking. The primary function of a hotel has not changed from the earliest recorded hostelry to the present-day hotel, whether that be a hotel of 100 rooms or 3,000 rooms, whether it be an in-city hotel or a resort hotel, whether it be a convention hotel or a family-type hotel. The earliest hostelry offered "bed and board" as well as pleasant surroundings in which to enjoy both commodities. The earliest hostelries and caravansaries worked on the same principle. The guest arrived at the front door, where he was greeted and arrangements were made for his lodging and food. A stable for horses and carriages, or a compound for camels and cargo, were provided at the rear of the establishment. A rear yard was used by the innkeeper's wife and her assistants to prepare food which was then cooked in a kitchen. We therefore had a house divided in two. The front half of the house included the reception area and the public rooms, or the covered arcades in the caravansaries, where the guests gathered to dine and to socialize. The other half of the house, or to use a term which is still applicable, the back of the house, was where food was prepared and where the guests' service amenities were taken care of, such as laundering, the shoeing of horses, or the repair of harness and traveling gear. This duality of a hotel must be thoroughly understood by an architect before pencil is put to paper to start the design. For convenience's sake and for ease in preparing a preliminary study, we will assume that all these services take place on one level. Figure 1 indicates the flow of services and hotel personnel. For the time being, we will ignore the actual rooms and concern ourselves only with the level where the "greeting" takes place and where the services are rendered. The "greeting area," for future reference, will be known as *the front of the house,* and the place where services occur will be known as *the back of the house.* It must be borne in mind that, as far as planned circulation is concerned, there must never be a mingling of the front-of-the-house services with those of the back of the house. At no time should the guest be aware of everything that is taking place at the back of the house, but, at the same time, the smooth operation of the front of the house is completely dependent upon what is taking place at the back of the house. The two functions must be kept separate and yet so interrelated that both function smoothly and efficiently.

Hotels are designed and built so that the client, owner, or operator of the hotel will get a satisfactory financial return on his investment. In order to achieve the greatest return for each dollar invested, we again face a dual problem. In the first instance, the guest must feel completely comfortable and at ease from the moment he steps through the entrance doorway, checks in, goes to his room, avails himself of the food and beverages available,

spends a comfortable night in a well-appointed, scrupulously clean room, and returns the next day to a room which is as fresh and inviting as it was the moment he first entered it after checking in. Everything for the guest's creature comforts should be carefully considered, whether it be the ease of finding the registration desk, the cashier, the bars and dining rooms, the elevators that will take him up to his room, and finally the room itself. The service at the registration desk, in the bars and dining rooms, and in the guest room itself as well as in the corridors must be such that the guest finds his every want courteously and efficiently taken care of. The physical environment becomes an important part of the guest's creature comfort. These factors include color and decor, lighting, proper air temperature, comfortable furnishings and, above all, a pleasant and relaxed atmosphere.

Everything that the guest expects and should get will be a result of what takes place at the back of the house. It is only in this area that everything that will keep a guest contented during his stay is arranged for and so ordered that everything the guest is seeking is accomplished unobtrusively and, what is most important, economically.

Economic operation of a hotel depends entirely upon the back-of-the-house services. Since these services are primarily concerned with hotel personnel, the plan must be so arranged that maximum efficiency from each hotel employee can be achieved without taxing the employee and without allowing the guest to feel the drive for efficiency that dictates every phase of hotel planning.

HOTEL ECONOMICS

The economics of a profitable hotel venture brings us to the third duality of which the architect should be extremely conscious or aware during every phase of the planning stage. This involves the economics of a new hotel, which will center upon the cost of construction and furnishing. These costs represent, together with the cost of the land, the amount of money that is to be invested. They are the base upon which the hotelier will figure his financial return. A rule of thumb devised many years ago by a prominent hotel architect still seems to be a sound rule to follow. At that time, it was stated that for every dollar of income per room, $1,000 should be spent in the construction of that room. We must bear in mind, of course, that when we speak of a room we are speaking figuratively, with the knowledge that the cost of a room would also carry its proportionate share of every other part of the structure, such as the hotel lobby, the dining rooms, the bars, the corridors, the offices, the laundry, the kitchens, and all the other facilities that will be found in a hotel. Using that rule of thumb (that is, $1 income per $1,000 invested), a room that costs $10,000 to build should bring in $10 for a night's lodging. Unfortunately, with rising costs of operation, this balance of $1 per $1,000 will not always hold, but it is still a good rule of thumb. With hotel rooms now going at from $10,000 to $40,000, we find that a $10-

per-night room is a rarity and an average of $20 and $30 is more common, while luxury hotels run as high as $40 and even $50 per night's lodging. From the above, it becomes obvious that the architect should know approximately what type of hotel his client wants, as expressed in terms of cost per room per night, in order to establish some sort of rough budget for the cost of the hotel. At this point, it should be pointed out that we are talking of cost of construction, which does not include furnishing and equipping the hotel. Another fact which does not really affect the planning of the hotel but which the architect should be keenly aware of is that preopening expenses are sizable. They are, in fact, a part of the original investment and should be charged to cost per room. More will be said of this at an appropriate place.

The second part of the financial consideration in the design of a hotel is the cost of operation. We now know what it will cost to build the hotel, and so some sort of preliminary budget becomes feasible. The architect may not know what it will cost to operate the hotel, but he should understand every facet of hotel operation and develop his plans to achieve maximum economies in the operation of the hotel. This includes the hours spent by such personnel as maids, porters, housekeepers, chefs, cooks, dishwashers, laundry workers, bellmen, receptionists, bookkeepers, reservations clerks, banquet managers, and executive staff. If we would, for a moment, think of a hotel as a plant which turns out a finished product, we would think of the finished product as the creature comforts of the guests (bed and board) and of the kitchens, laundries, and service areas as the machines. The hotel personnel would be the workers who operate the machines in order to achieve a fine product at the lowest possible cost. With these thoughts in mind, we can now take up each facet of hotel operation—front of the house and back of the house—which will be discussed in detail and illustrated with diagrams and drawings so that each part of the jigsaw puzzle which forms a hotel can be fitted into place to achieve a smoothly functioning, pleasingly desirable, and financially profitable operation.

First let us clear up the question of preopening expenses, which should be considered as a part of the total cost of the hotel. Before a hotel is put into operation—in fact, months before the first guest arrives—certain hotel personnel are employed who will eventually be charged with the operation of the hotel. Such employees would include a manager, a chief chef, a controller, an advertising and/or a public relations firm, and an engineer who will be operating the mechanical equipment of the hotel. These people will usually be found on the site of the hotel under construction anywhere from six months to one year before the hotel is completed. Their salaries are part of preopening expenses. Another factor in preopening expenses would include stationery and other supplies that various key personnel will need before the opening of the hotel as well as, ultimately, the cost of hotel stationery, typewriters, bookkeeping machinery, and office supplies. Another preopening expense will be a cost allocated for opening ceremonies, which often include cocktail parties and banquets for people from the news media and civic organizations as well as for civic authorities. All these costs are considered preopening expenses. One other item that must be considered in preopening expenses is the training of the personnel that will service the hotel. This will include maids, housekeepers, chefs and cooks, waiters and waitresses, and front-office and clerical personnel. There also will be others, such as maintenance men, bellmen, and porters. These can add at least 30 percent to the construction cost.

Another facet of costs, which the architect may or may not be involved in, involves furnishings for the hotel. In this category will be found not only the actual beds, dressers, chairs, tables, and floor coverings in the guest rooms but also the furnishings, floor coverings, special lighting fixtures, and decor items needed for all public spaces. These fall into the categories of lobbies, dining rooms, bars, cocktail lounges, coffee shops, meeting rooms, banquet rooms, and a host of other facilities which will be found in hotels.

Another large portion of the costs which normally would not be a cost of construction would be the equipment for all kitchens and bars as well as the equipment, if such a facility is to be included, of laundries and valet service. Going further, we will need lockers for employees and other amenities for the service personnel.

Finally, we come to a group of items which will include glassware, china, silver, pots and pans, linens, pillows, and uniforms for maids, bellmen, waiters, etc.

When we lump preopening expenses together with all the items enumerated above, we will find ourselves adding anywhere from 50 to 75 percent more to the actual construction costs. All these figures will not influence the budget for construction, but it would be wise for an architect designing a hotel to be conscious of these additional expenditures.

BACK OF THE HOUSE

Though rarely seen by a guest, the back of the house is the most crucial part of the plan. It must be laid out with two paramount objectives: control and efficiency. Foodstuffs, housekeeping supplies, and a great many other items must be received out of sight of the hotel guests. Such receiving is usually done at a loading dock, which should be covered so that deliveries can be made regardless of the weather. An operating hotel, even a small one, will have deliveries going on throughout the day. The receiving of shipments as well as the checking of whatever comes into the hotel and, finally, sending the various items received to their proper destination must be under tight control. This is usually the function of a receiving department that should be located directly on or adjacent to the loading dock. Tight control must be exercised in two directions. In one direction, it is not uncommon for material to be delivered and, within a short time of its having been left on the dock unchecked, for the management to find that this material has disappeared or that some parts of the shipment have gone astray. The second part of the control is to make sure that, once these shipments have arrived, they go directly to their destination without a chance of becoming lost on the way. As an example, let us say that a shipment of liquor is delivered to the hotel. It is a very simple thing to pick up a case and remove it from the loading dock before the receiving clerk has checked the shipment through his control point. It is also a very simple thing to have a case of liquor disappear on its route, once it has been checked in and before it gets to the liquor storage room. This type of pilferage will apply not only to liquor but to almost every item, including linens, foodstuffs, and even items of furnishings. A good back-of-the-house plan will be worked out in such a way that the flow of supplies is tightly controlled by the security that the architect works into his plan. Another example will suffice: It would be poor planning to have a valuable item such as liquor carted through a passageway and past an employees' locker room on its way to the liquor storage room. It would take but a moment for a case to disappear from the cart into the locker room. A tight, well-planned back of the house will have circulation patterns that will provide the utmost in control. It is this type of planning that is definitely the province of the architect. There is one further item in the control area which, at first glance, might seem highly unimportant: namely, the movement of garbage out of the hotel to a point where it will be picked up by garbage trucks. Experience has indicated that a good deal of pilferage in hotels is accomplished through

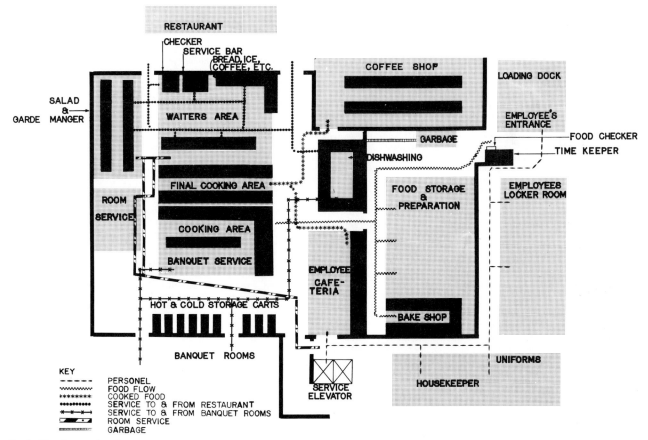

Fig. 1 Flow diagram of service areas.

the medium of garbage removal. Well-wrapped steaks and cans of food can be concealed in garbage and removed by an accomplice before the garbage haulers pick up the refuse. In the larger hotels, garbage destructors or compressors may be used, in which case tight surveillance is necessary only in the garbage receiving area. Where garbage is shipped out, it is wise to have the garbage rooms so placed (and, incidentally, refrigerated) that the receiving office has this space in full view to discourage an outside accomplice or an employee who is leaving the hotel from entering the garbage room to filch what was placed there previously by someone in the kitchen or the supply areas.

Another form of control which must be exercised and which becomes a part of the architect's planning is the flow of personnel into and out of the hotel. Hotel personnel usually come through at a point close or adjacent to the receiving area. This is not necessarily a must, but it is advisable because the same control office can observe the coming and going of the help. Usually time control is through the medium of a time clock, which is punched by the employees. It is not uncommon for thieves to attempt entry through the service area and to work their way up through service elevators to accomplish what they came for. A tight control at the point of entry and egress of all employees is highly desirable and can easily be accomplished if it is the same point as that at which food and other hotel supplies are brought in. Once again, the architect's careful planning will make it possible for employees to reach their various dressing and locker areas with a minimum of travel time lost. It must be borne in mind that there is class distinction in hotels and, as an example, that dishwashers and porters are not placed in the same locker rooms as head waiters and reception clerks. The distinction here is far from a fine line. The mix of hotel employees will be dictated by the hotel operator, and he may determine whether waiters and bellmen are to be placed together or separated. Maids and waitresses may or may not be in the same locker room, depending on the hotel operation. Locker rooms should be provided with ample toilet facilities and showers. Once the personnel have changed into their uniforms, the plan of the back of the house will make it possible for the people to get to their work stations with little time lost. Maids and porters will want to get to service elevators along the shortest possible route. Chefs, cooks, and dishwashers should get to their work areas without going through long, tortuous passages. It is usual to issue uniforms in an area as close to the locker rooms or the point of entry as possible. In this phase of planning, it should be borne in mind that uniforms are usually under the control of the housekeeper, so that the proximity of the uniform issuing room to the housekeeping department becomes a most important consideration. It should also be borne in mind that the housekeeper controls soiled and clean laundry as well as clean uniforms ready for reissue. The interplay of all of these activities will dictate a finesse in planning to bring all these activities together and to achieve as little loss in time and motion as possible. At this point, let us sum up this portion of the back of the house.

A flow diagram (Fig. 1) for a typical back of the house will indicate that the service entrance is located out of view of the main entrance to the hotel but has direct access to a street or road capable of handling truck traffic. The loading dock should be protected from weather so that food, laundry, and supplies will be off-loaded and stored and not get rain-soaked

while waiting to be checked in. All personnel will enter the hotel at this point. At least two small offices will probably be located here, one for the steward (or receiving clerk) and another for the timekeeper. Outside the steward's office there should be a floor scale to check the weight of produce as it enters. If the food storage and preparation kitchens are located on a different level, a sidewalk lift or conveyor belts should be provided. The timekeeper will check the employees in and out and help to discourage those who may be tempted to steal. Immediately past the timekeeper, the employees should be separated into two different traffic flows, one for the food service personnel, the other for everyone else. Once food service personnel enter their traffic flow, they should have no contact with either guests or other house personnel with the obvious exception of waiters. All this is simply a matter of security. If there is any deep dark secret of successful hotel service design, it is a built-in security system, which is a direct outgrowth of the architect's plans.

Uniform issue is related to the housekeeper, the housekeeper to the laundry room, and the laundry room to the soiled linen room. The soiled linen room connects by vertical linen chute to the service room on every typical floor, and every typical floor is connected by a service elevator that opens to the lower-floor service area convenient to the scrutinizing gaze of the steward and the timekeeper. For convenience, a trash chute (Fig. 2), going from every typical floor service area, should be located next to the linen chute. This will force an arrangement where the trash room is close or adjacent to the soiled linen room and both of these are near the service entrance for ease in pickup.

Laundry Facilities

A laundry is a usual adjunct of most good-sized hotels. Many hotels avail themselves of city laundry service, in which case there is no laundry room at all or only a small laundry which handles towels only. A hotel laundry that does its own uniforms and flatwork (sheets, pillowcases, linens, etc.) requires a good-sized space for washers, dryers, drum ironers, and various pressing machines—each suitable for its own type of flatwork, uniforms and guests' laundry, and men's and women's wearing apparel. If the laundry is done by a laundry service out of the hotel, then items like towels require a comparatively small space for washing and drying, since only washers and fluff dryers are necessary, together with an area for folding and stacking the clean towels. Larger hotels will maintain their own cleaning department for dry cleaning and pressing of woolens and similar garments. Such a cleaning and valet service is usually a part of or close to the laundry area, and it is definitely under the supervision of the laundry manager. It may be that, in the not-too-distant future, experiments with disposable sheets, pillowcases, and uniforms will do away with laundry services in hotels. Presently, the disposable types that have been produced are still not of sufficient strength and durability for hotel use, although the future may produce exactly that. At present some "no iron" linens are in use, thus eliminating some of the large ironers.

Housekeeping Department

The housekeeping department, having several functions, is the province of the chief housekeeper, who will usually have assistant floor housekeepers. Under the housekeeper's strict

control and supervision will be all the maids and porters. These people, after donning their uniforms, will come to the housekeeper for instructions and very often take with them supplies to take with them to the various guest-room floors. The porters will deliver to the service areas on the guest-room floors all linen and soap as well as facial tissue, toilet paper, matches, room service menus, and ashtrays. (Most hotels use inexpensive ashtrays that carry the hotel name and that the guests may take along as souvenirs.) The housekeeper's area is also a storage area, for here are kept all the supplies that become a part of housekeeping. Aside from such obvious things as a stock of linen, paper goods, soaps, etc., the housekeeper will carry in her warehouse storage area additional lamps (which are easily broken by guests) and small items of furnishings which are easily removed or destroyed. In the housekeeper's department there will usually be a place for a seamstress to mend those sheets, pillowcases, and drapes that need repair. It might be useful for the architect to know how many rooms a maid can make up during her daily tour of duty. In some areas unions control the number of rooms, and it may be as little as 12 per maid. It rarely goes beyond 15. One porter is usually assigned to each maid. In addition to the regular daytime maid, there will be, in most hotels, a night maid who will make up beds for guests ready to go to sleep. This entails the removal of the bedspreads, straightening of the room, the supplying of additional soap, toilet paper, etc., all for the guests' convenience. One night maid usually can handle twice as many rooms as a day maid handles.

Food and Beverage Service

We have now taken care of the bed portion of the "bed and board." Now let us examine the "board" part of a hotel service. The *board*, of course, refers to the old English trestle table where guests took their meals. In the earliest hostelries, the innkeeper's wife took care of the cooking, maids took care of the serving, and a large board or table sufficed for the guests. Today's food operation is a highly complicated one, and an architect should be familiar with the entire operation. Most hotel kitchens and food preparation areas are planned by experts known as kitchen engineers. It is not the architect's province to plan a kitchen, but it is certainly helpful for the architect to have a good working knowledge of what takes place in the food preparation area and in the kitchens. It will make for better communication between the architect and the kitchen engineer when they are discussing the planning of these spaces. Just one word of caution—each expert will want more space than the plan can possibly allow. They don't *really* need that much space. The kitchen engineer will conjure up visions of irate chefs stalking off the premises, but experience has indicated that the architect's knowledge of what the requirements are will temper the demands of the kitchen engineer. Let us follow the flow of the raw food from the time it is delivered to the steward until it is finally cooked and ready to be picked up by the waiters or the waitresses.

After the comestibles have been weighed in, checked, and signed for, they are sent to either dry storage or liquor storage (a room with a big lock on it) or to one of the various cold holding rooms or boxes. Canned food and other bottled or packaged food which does not need refrigeration will be sent to dry-storage rooms. In this storage space will also be kept the various condiments that the chef will need in the preparation of his food. Vegetables will be sent to an area where they will be stored ready for preparation. A refrigerator box of the proper temperature will be needed, as well as work space, sinks, and cutting boards where vegetables will be prepared for the chefs as needed. The peeling of potatoes, cleaning of carrots, trimming of lettuce, etc., are done in the vegetable preparation area and not in the kitchen area. Dairy products will go to their own cold-storage boxes. Fish, fowl, and meat will go to a separate area where boxes must be arranged with proper temperatures for their storage. Some of these items will be kept frozen, others in aging boxes, and others in simple cold storage. Fish preparation needs its own space. The hotel, in its purveying department, may buy cut and trimmed meat or portioned meat and fowl. In the latter case, only a storage area is necessary, since no preparation takes place. Where a hotel does its own butchering, it is necessary to know what size cuts the hotel intends to buy (halves, quarters, etc.), and it may be necessary to provide ceiling rails to transport them. Once again, it must be borne in mind that all these facilities are under tight control. Once the food has safely reached its destination in the rooms just described, there must be no place for it to go except into the kitchen where it will be used by cooks and chefs. Freezer, refrigerator, and cold storage boxes require heavy insulation. Slab sinkages in these areas should be provided for. If this is not done in advance, then boxes will be set on top of the slab, therefore requiring a ramp from the work area to the box. This is something that is far from desirable in a smoothly functioning kitchen. If the architect is not fed this information before construction starts, it may be necessary to depress the entire slab in this area and then, after the boxes have been placed, use fill to bring the working area up to the level of the boxes. At this point, a word or two should be said about the bakery facilities. The bakery shop should be a separate entity, having its own refrigerator boxes as well as all the pertinent equipment that a baker will use in his art—and an art it is, indeed. The baker will be called upon to bake not only the everyday bread and rolls and the run-of-the-mill cakes and pastries but also unusual designs in birthday cakes, wedding cakes, etc., and he may often be asked to carve ice figures for elaborate food displays or buffets. Here again, one should be reminded that the bakery should be close to the actual food service area so that not too many of these goodies find their way into the locker rooms or out of the hotel entirely.

We now have everything delivered, prepared, and ready for expert transformation by cooks, chefs, and *garde mangers* who will be preparing soups, ragouts, roasts, epicurean sauces, and hors d'oeuvres.

Let us take a walk through what would be an ideal kitchen, assuming that everything is happening at one level. (See Fig. 3.) The food brought in from the various prep areas consists of fish, meat, fowl, vegetables, and condiments. The food from the prep area is brought to the various points where it is to be used. One of the first areas to which a good part of the prepared food will go is the rough cooking area. Here we find the big soup kettles, the vegetable steamers, the ovens, and the hot tops where most of the bulk foods will be prepared. Since many large pots are used in this area, there is usually a pot washing area close to the rough or preliminary food cooking area. Rough cooking is usually backed up to the finished cooking area. In this finished cooking area, the chefs will be preparing sauces and gravies as well as broiling and frying and applying final flame to various types of meats, fish, and fowl.

Between the chefs' ovens, broilers, and fry-

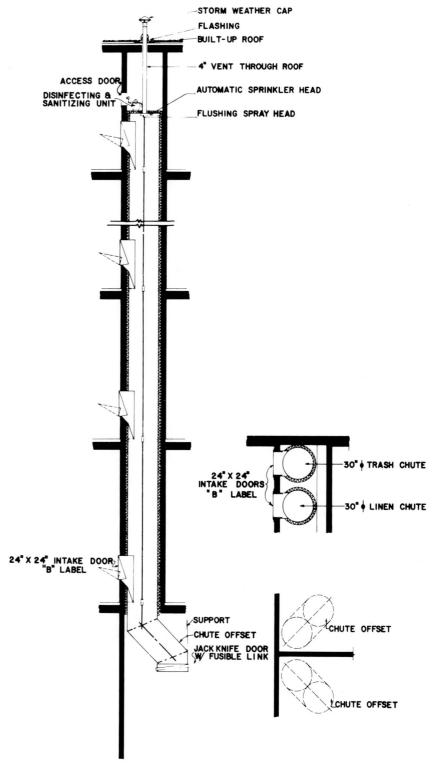

Fig. 2 Trash or linen chute.

ers, which are aligned in a straight line, there will be an aisle for the chefs. On the other side of this aisle will be the serving tables from which the waiters will pick up the finished food. At the bottom of these tables will be plate warmers which the waiter picks up and sets on the table so the chef can place the order of the specific dish that is required. Also on this table will be *bains-marie*, which are pans im-

mersed in circulating warm or hot water into which are put already prepared vegetables, gravies and soups, all kept at the proper temperature, so that the chef can ladle the required portion of food onto the dish where he has already placed his steak, broiled fish, fried food, or other entrée. Above this long serving table will be small pots and pans which the chef will take down and use to prepare the

975

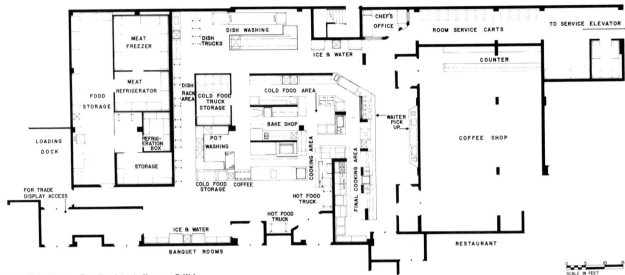

Fig. 3 Main kitchen, Paradise Island, Nassau, B.W.I.

small portions of whatever food is called for on the waiter's order. This food preparation area will have reach-in boxes for cuts of meat and fish which have been prepared and are ready for the final stage of cooking. The chef reaches in and takes out what he needs to prepare the required dish. Off to one side, somewhere in the waiter's line of traffic, will be the *garde manger* section. Here have been delivered all the prepared vegetables and fruits so that the *garde manger* can arrange salads, prepare cold desserts, and work up the various types of hors d'oeuvre as well as seafood cocktails and other cold items for the start of a meal or salads that accompany the main dish. The *garde manger*, on special occasions, will prepare special trays of cold, exotic dishes used for buffets or banquets. He will have his own reach-in boxes for all the types of fruits, vegetables, seafoods, garnishes, etc., that are used. Farther along the waiter's course will be a section, close to the exit, where such items as bread and rolls, butter, coffee, tea, ice, and other items are stored. Bread and rolls may be in a roll warmer. Here also will be found the coffee urns, toasters, and egg boilers. This entire area is for self-service by the waiters, who will pick up the items they need on their way to the guest waiting for the delivery of his food. Now let us, for a moment, leave the kitchen and go into the dining room. A bus boy has picked up the soiled dishes after a guest has completed his meal. He brings the soiled dishes into that kitchen area which is allocated for dishwashing. In some cases the waiter will pick up his own soiled dishes and deposit them in the dishwashing area. This is a very noisy operation in which sound should be carefully baffled; but because of the need to get the dishes from the dining room to the dishwasher, the dishwasher is usually placed close to the dining room area so that the dishes can be disposed of as soon as the waiter or busboy enters the kitchen. The dishwashing area is, of necessity, not only noisy but also a rather untidy operation, so it must be kept fairly isolated from the actual cooking and serving area. The reason for keeping it within the kitchen is obvious since the dishes, as soon as they have been properly cleaned, will be brought back into the kitchen area for the service of freshly prepared food. The waiter, coming into the kitchen, places his orders and follows a definite path along the cooks' and chefs' serving

tables, the *garde manger's* serving tables, and the pick-up area. Then, before entering the dining room, he will usually go by a checker's desk where he presents a check indicating the items that he is taking out of the kitchen to the diner. A checker controls all foods and beverages leaving the kitchen area to make sure that the items are correct and the prices properly indicated. One other space will usually occur in our ideal kitchen—a service bar with a bartender who will prepare the drinks that the waiter has ordered. Here again, it must be on the direct path of travel, so that after the prepared drinks have been picked up by the waiter, he will pass the checker, who will check off the drink items as to quantity and price.

Before leaving the kitchen, we must look at some other areas that we will usually find in our ideal kitchen. There will be a chef's office, which is set where the chef can observe all the activities in the kitchen. His office is usually enclosed with glass to give him aural privacy but complete visual control. Here the chef will prepare and plan menus. He will be placing orders for food and will generally be operating a rather complicated and meticulous part of the hotel service. In addition to the chef's office, there may be two other areas (once again, assuming that everything is happening on this one level). The first of these is the room-service area. Here there must be sufficient space for a fairly large number of room-service rolling tables, which are set and ready to carry the dishes that have been ordered by the guest via telephone. These tables are usually set up with their linen, glassware, and silver. In the warming compartment below the tablecloth, the room-service waiter will place the hot dishes, and on top of the rolling service table he will place the cold dishes. The room-service area is always close to the cooking and *garde manger* area. Much of the room service will consist of breakfasts or sandwiches and salads. Wherever a hot dish is called for, the room-service waiter will pick it up at the chef's cooking area. The room-service area should, of necessity, be as close to the service elevators as possible. These, of course, must come down to the kitchen from the service areas on each of the guest floors. Normally, we will find a room-service operator, who sits at a telephone taking calls from the guests. These calls are especially numerous in the morning, when many guests

are calling in for their breakfasts rather than coming down to the dining room. The cooking area, consisting mainly of griddles, will be manned by short-order chefs who are ready to prepare various hot breakfast dishes, and the *garde manger* section will be manned by a crew who are expert in the preparation of breakfast menus. For the rest of the day, sandwiches and salads coming from the *garde manger* will be most in demand. Another part of the kitchen will be devoted to the banquet area. We are assuming that this hotel is not too large and does not require a separate banquet kitchen but rather a banquet serving area. We will see again that the chefs will prepare the banquet food, managing their schedule so that it does not interfere with lunch or dinner. In the banquet area there will be mobile cabinets that take trays. These are electrified cabinets arranged to keep dishes either hot or cold. These banquet cabinets can be stocked before a banquet for certain types of menus. In other instances, where steak and roast beef are on the banquet menu, there must be areas in which the chef can broil the steaks or large ovens where a number of roasts can be prepared at the same time. A large banquet area in a hotel will require a separate banquet kitchen with its own cooking facilities as well as its own dishwashing area. Here the architect must review the food service requirements and, working with the kitchen engineer, determine the location of the banquet cooking and service area. Very often the banquet facilities are not on the same floor as the dining rooms, in which case there would have to be an elevator connecting the main kitchen with the banquet area.

Let us have one last look around. To begin with, because of what is taking place in the kitchen, the floor should be of some material which can be easily cleaned. In the past, the better kitchens used ceramic tile. There are many new types of floor preparations which can be applied directly over the concrete slab and which lend themselves to easy cleaning as well as offering a firm foothold to prevent slipping on wet spots. The walls, in most kitchens, were usually ceramic tile. Here again, the new plastic materials are by some standards even better than tile, with its cement joints and the possibility of spalling tile. By all means, every effort should be made to hold down the noise level in the kitchen, and this is best accomplished by using a perforated metal ceiling with acoustic batts above or a ceramic-treated acoustical material. Hoods over all cooking areas are a must, and the architect should check with the building code to see that the hoods conform with the standards not only of the code but also of the National Fire Underwriters to prevent the spread of fires which often occur when a dish flames up while cooking. One last observation: it is an excellent idea to have toilets and washrooms for kitchen help, so that it isn't necessary for them to return to their locker rooms, which may be at some distance. It is always advisable to keep the kitchen help within the kitchen during their stint of duty. Doors to dining rooms, and there may be several dining rooms serviced by the one kitchen, should be strategically placed and baffled so that the diners do not have a view of what goes on in the kitchen, and, what is more important, do not hear what is going on.

Most hotels have coffee shops, although the trend in many hotels today is to work out an arrangement in which a coffee shop and a restaurant are combined. This is especially true of the smaller hotels and of some of the chain hotels. For purposes of discussion, let us consider that the coffee shop is a separate entity. The ideal plan would be to place the coffee shop backed up to the kitchen, so that certain finished dishes and prepared foods can be delivered to the coffee shop work area directly from the main kitchen under complete control as it passes from prep areas to kitchen to coffee shop. In the coffee shop much of the food preparation will be done at the counters. In this area there usually will be found sandwich and salad areas as well as fryers and broilers and griddles. Also in the coffee shop will be the cold area for ice creams, desserts, etc. In the larger coffee shops, most of the cooking may be done in the kitchen and passed through to the counter for pickup by waiters and waitresses. In a coffee shop there will, of course, be counters and stools, but there will also be tables and chairs. At the counter we will usually find a pickup area where the waiters can pick up the food prepared for them without disturbing the diners who are sitting at counters. Dirty dishes will be sent back to the dishwashing area through a pass-through, or they will be carried to the dishwashing area in the main kitchen. Coffee shop diners expect quick service and, toward this end, the menus are carefully prepared for easy handling by short-order chefs and sandwich and salad men who work within the coffee shop and not in the main kitchen. Wherever specialty dishes of the day are offered, such as ragouts or soups, they are prepared in the main kitchen and placed in hot *bains-marie*, ready to be picked up for quick service.

There is another phase in the food area which may or may not be considered in a hotel, namely: food service or dining for the hotel help. Larger hotels will provide an employees' cafeteria. This space is usually planned to be close to the help's locker rooms and yet contiguous to the main kitchen. If such a plan can be worked out, the food prepared for the employees' cafeteria comes from the main kitchen, and it is served as it would be in any normal cafeteria. Employees go through a self-service line, picking up hot and cold foods as well as drinks as they go along. They are checked by the checker or cashier and carry their trays to the tables. Attention should also be paid to the fact that the dirty dishes which come out of the employees' cafeteria must be returned to the dishwashing area and here again, if at all possible, a pass-through should be arranged

whereby the dirty dishes can be passed directly to the main dishwashing area in the kitchen.

While still in the food department, let us look in on the beverage service area. This may be a bar room or a cocktail lounge. In any case, there will be a bar with stools (if local codes permit) and an area for cocktail tables and chairs. A cocktail lounge must be serviced just as the kitchen is serviced. To the bar must be brought not only liquor and bottled goods but also the usual crunchies that one finds in a bar, such as potato chips, peanuts, pretzels, etc. The bartender will also need from the commissary area oranges, lemons, limes, tomato juice, etc. Cocktail lounges will also serve cocktail canapes and, very often, sandwiches. Arrangements must be made in the plan for the delivery of all of these items to the bar without too much possibility of losing something on the way. Ideally, the delivery should be made directly to the back bar through pass-throughs from the kitchen, so that we find once again another unit backed up to the ideal kitchen. This will not always be possible.

There is a great deal more to be known about full food and beverage service in a hotel, but a general knowledge on the part of the architect will suffice. He must depend upon the kitchen engineer for advice, plans, and details, just as he must depend upon his electrical engineer, his mechanical engineer, and structural engineers to feed him the information that he will need to complete his plans for a hotel. It must be borne in mind that most hotels consider food service as a necessary evil. The percentage of profit on a food operation is always very small. Profit on beverages is much higher, and so beverage service is quite desirable as an adjunct to a food operation. A well-planned food and beverage setup, where control and efficiency are the guiding principles, will increase the rather meager profits on this hotel function. It is in this area that the architect, working with the hotel operator and his staff of experts—which includes chefs, managers, etc., as well as the kitchen engineer—can bring to bear his talents in creating an entity which will function at top efficiency.

Mechanical Spaces

Another area that should be considered in designing the back-of-the-house spaces will be the boiler or mechanical room. In this area will be found the various pieces of equipment for heating and cooling as well as all the tanks and pumps to keep all the mechanical systems in operation. Each mechanical room will be of a size and shape that will satisfy the requirements for all the creature comforts that a modern hotel has to offer. In this area will also be found all central switch gear that controls electric current for every purpose in the hotel complex. This domain belongs to the house engineer and, naturally, there should be provision for an engineer's office, with a mechanical repair shop close by. There are a number of other shops that probably will be located in this area of the hotel. These would include a carpentry shop, an upholstery shop, and definitely an area for a locksmith. Somewhere in the area, where they are easily accessible, will be storage rooms in which will be kept a multitude of spare parts to service the hotel. Some of this storage space will be used for mechanical equipment replacements, and other storage areas will contain spare parts for the furniture, carpet replacements, wallpaper replacements, cleaning materials, and cleaning equipment that will be used by the house porters.

There will be another area which, technically, belongs to the back of the house. This area will

be occupied by personnel that very often come in contact with the guests, and the strategic location of these back-of-the-house facilities will be controlled entirely by what happens in the front of the house. Included in these areas you will find accounting and bookkeeping offices (which back up the front cashiers); reservations offices (which back up to the front registration desk); and offices for management, which will include a reception area, a manager's office, and an assistant manager's office. In this part of the hotel complex one would usually find the head of the food and beverage department, who may double as the banquet manager. There will be a mail sorting room, which might well be placed behind the registration desk, since guests' mail is delivered at this point. More will be said about all these spaces when front-of-the-house operation is discussed further. Before leaving this area, we should note the fact that there will probably be a secretarial pool to handle all the spaces that have been enumerated above. We will be referring to all the above spaces as the *administrative area*.

FRONT OF THE HOUSE

We have now established the activity which controls the plan of a hotel as far as the back of the house is concerned. We will now examine what happens in the so-called "front of the house"—that area which concerns itself with the guest as distinct from that area which concerns itself with the smooth functioning of the hotel. It must be borne in mind that a hotel, like Janus, wears two faces. The guest or the paying customer sees only the front of the house, and this must be all that he desires—a wish fulfillment, an ego builder, a status symbol, and above all else a pleasant and satisfying place in which he will spend a night, a week, or a month. The back of the house, which has already been discussed, is where all that makes this happen takes place. These are the areas of burnishing, butchering, baking; of boilers, motors, compressors, and ovens. The guest never sees all this, but these unseen spaces will precisely determine his degree of contentment. These are the areas that will ultimately dictate whether the hotel will run at a profit or a loss. The front of the house comprises every area that the guest will see; lobbies, dining spaces, rest rooms, passenger elevators, corridors, hotel rooms, etc. These spaces must be handled and planned with one thought in mind: the convenience and continued approbation of the guests.

Let us now accompany our arriving guest from the time his car or taxi pulls up to the main entrance. As the guest enters the main entrance (and there should be only one main entrance), he should be overcome with a feeling of serenity, welcome, and definitely a complete absence of confusion. The registration desk and the elevators should and must be immediately apparent. The registration area consists of a front desk, behind which is a registration clerk, behind whom is the key and mail rack, and behind that the various administration spaces. At this point let us consider the registration process itself. (See Fig. 4.)

Guest Registration

A hotel registration desk must be located so that it is immediately visible as one enters the hotel lobby. The size of the desk will be determined by the size of the hotel. There is no special rule to be followed except that a hotel of let us say, 2,000 rooms might have anywhere

Fig. 4   The Churchill Hotel, London.

from four to six registration clerks, while a hotel of 100 to 200 rooms will have one or at most two spaces at which guests may register. There are certain requirements for the clerk behind the desk as far as equipment is concerned. The simplest arrangement will call for a suitable file containing advance reservation cards requesting space, so that the clerk can quickly check what room has been reserved for what particular guest. Another mandatory piece of equipment is a slip or card file which, at a glance, indicates which rooms are occupied and which rooms are open. Occupied room spaces will have a card with the name of the guest and probably the date when the guest intends to leave. As soon as the guest checks in, a card is slipped into the space for the room, indicating that the room is now occupied. This, the simplest form of registration, is applicable to the smaller hotels. Larger hotels have far more sophisticated equipment, much of it electronically controlled, which serves to indicate time of arrival of guests who have made reservations, time of departure of guests who are already checked into the hotel, and systems whereby the registration clerk can also be informed whether the room has been vacated and whether the room has already been made up by the maid on the floor and is ready to receive a new guest. The architect should acquaint himself with the requirements of the front desk and also be aware of certain companies who manufacture the filing systems and the electronic equipment which is used for reservation and guest control.

Advance Reservations

The hotel industry depends primarily on advance reservations to keep its rooms filled. The traveling public is aware of this fact, and most travelers will book their reservations in advance. Chain hotels and chain motels have developed complicated and efficient electronic systems for advance reservation bookings which are made from any point within the chain. The systems employed are very much like the systems now being used by airlines for bookings and reservations. Terminal points in the larger hotels have automatic electric equipment which types out the name, date of arrival, anticipated length of stay, and type of accom-

modations requested. Whether the system be the involved electronic system or whether it be a reservation made by telephone or wire, a reservation clerk within a reservation office in the hotel will take care of all these requests for rooms. Since questions do arise at the time when the guest is checking in, the location of the reservation office must obviously be as close to the front desk as the plan will permit. This will enable a reservation clerk to go back to the reservation department to check on a questionable reservation or to adjust any problems which may arise at the time that the new guests are checking in.

Mail and Keys

There are two other services that the front or registration desk must perform. The first and obvious one is to serve as the place where the room keys are kept. Some of the larger hotels have room-key clerks whose functions consist only of receiving keys from guests as they leave the hotel and giving the incoming guests, either upon registration or during their stay, the keys to their rooms. If the registration clerk handles the keys, then obviously the key rack is directly behind the desk, easily accessible to the registration clerk. If the hotel is large enough to require a separate area and separate personnel for handling of keys, this function will usually be alongside the actual registration desk. Since it is comparatively simple for someone to ask for a key who is not entitled to it and who may be using that key to enter and rob an absent guest, it behooves the architect to realize that some control is necessary in the handing out of keys to make sure that keys are given only to the registered guests for that particular room. Mail is also handled in most hotels at the registration desk, which dictates that keys and mail slots are designed as one unit and placed directly behind the registration desk. Where a hotel is large enough to require special key clerks, the same clerks will probably handle all incoming mail for the guests. If at all possible, mail sorting and handling should be done in an area where the guest does not see this operation take place. Ideally it would be behind the mail and key rack. A well-designed unit will be worked out so that a mail clerk can place the mail into the individual

mail slots from behind, rather than working in the front and interfering with the activity of the registration clerk.

Cashier

The average hotel usually has the cashier's counter located adjacent to the registration desk. There is no hard and fast rule concerning this close interrelationship. The larger hotels may place cashiers in the so-called "front desk" area but somewhat remote from the actual registration desk. There are times in large hotels, especially those catering to conventions, where one convention is checking out while another is checking in. This will make for traffic congestion and some confusion. Such a situation can be avoided by planning the registration and cashier facilities so that lines forming in front of the registration desk do not conflict with lines forming at the cashier's counter.

The cashier in the smaller hotels will handle most of the bookkeeping. This is done by means of today's quick and efficient electric bookkeeping machines. Very often the night cashier will handle a good deal of the bookkeeping, relieving the daytime staff of this chore. Larger hotels will have a complete bookkeeping department. This will require more than just the actual cashiers, who remain at their stations, while the bookkeeping department handles all entries and bookkeeping for the guests. It is obvious that this bookkeeping department should be close to if not backed up to the front desk cashiers, so that any questions of charges can be quickly checked and adjusted by the cashier, who will contact the bookkeeping department for clarification or corrections in the guests' bills.

Conveniences will usually be found in the cashier's area for guests who bring valuables with them, whether it be cash, jewelry, or important papers. Guests are requested by hotel management to leave such valuables in the hotel's safe deposit boxes or vault. It is desirable to have the guest transfer his valuables to a cashier out of sight of the public occupying the main lobby. Therefore, a small closed room is normally provided. The guest enters this room and gives the valuables to the cashier through a pass-through window. This pass-through window should have a view of the vault or the safe so that the guest can watch his valuables being deposited properly. Where safe deposit boxes are furnished by the hotel, the cashier will hand a key to the guest. The same procedure will be followed when the guest wishes to withdraw his valuables from the safekeeping of the hotel. This convenience is especially useful in large resort or convention hotels where women guests will be wearing jewelry on special occasions. A closed room makes it possible for the guest to deliver and receive the jewelry without being observed, a precaution that is most necessary in today's theft-prone society.

A hotel cashier must also handle the cash from restaurants and coffee shop. The cashiers in these facilities will be bringing their cash receipts to the central cashier. In a small hotel, this can be done directly without any concern about the transfer of the funds from the restaurant and coffee shop to the cashier. In large hotels, where there are a number of restaurants and other facilities which entail cash payment, special arrangements should be made for the handling of this cash and, in some instances, safety deposit boxes or vaults are provided so that the money can be stored when it is brought to the cashier space at off hours and held until

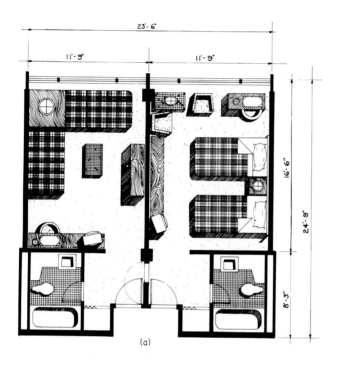

(a)

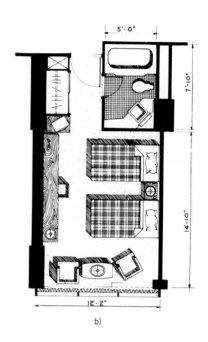

b)

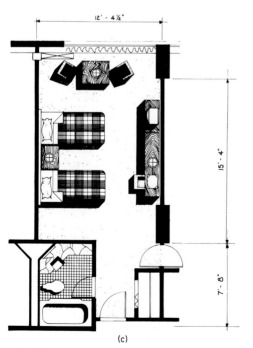

(c)

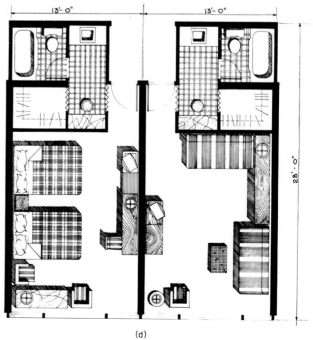

(d)

Fig. 5 (a) Uris Brothers Hotel, New York. (b) Americana Hotel, New York, typical tower room. (c) Loews N.Y. Motel, typical room. (d) Causeway Inn, Tampa, Florida.

Commercial
HOTELS

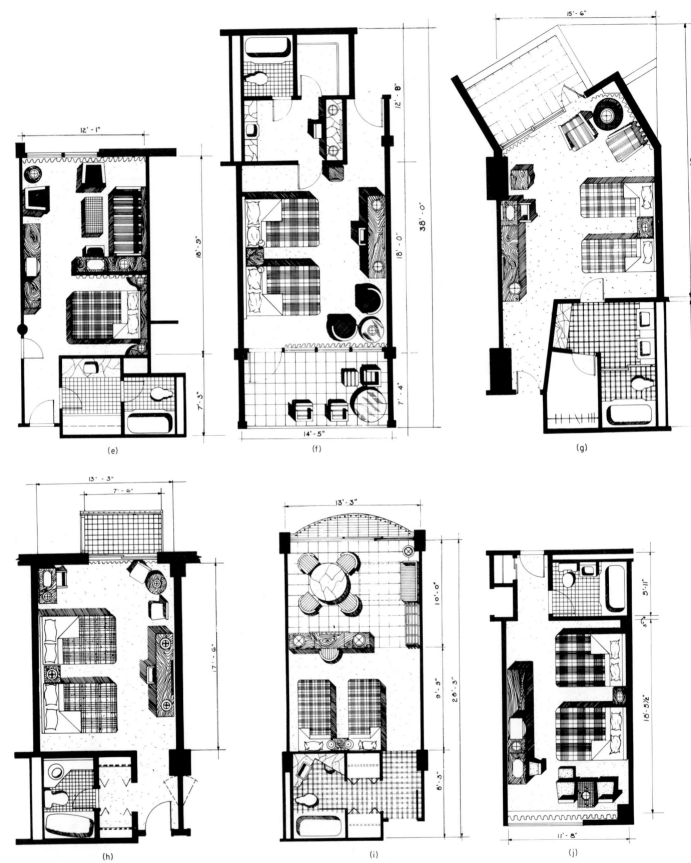

Fig. 5 (cont.) (e) Tampa International Inn, Tampa, Florida. (f) Indies House, Duck Key, Florida. (g) Americana Hotel, Bal Harbour, Florida. (h) Paradise Island Hotel, Paradise Island, Bahamas. (i) Americana of Puerto Rico, typical room layout. (j) Massena Motor Inn, Massena, N.Y.

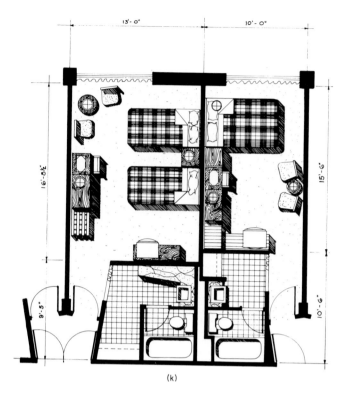

(k)

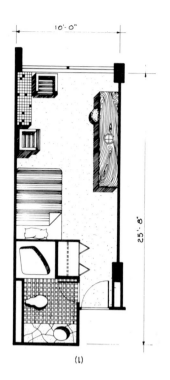

(l)

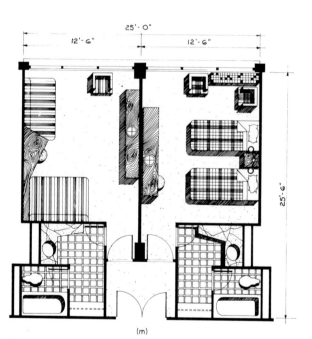

(m)

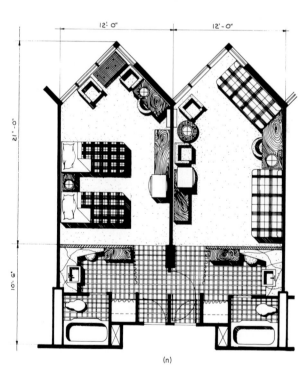

(n)

Fig. 5 (cont.) (k) Chicopee Motor Inn, Chicopee, Massachusetts. (l) and (m) Thomas Circle Motor Hotel, Washington, D.C. (n) Riverview Motor Hotel, New York.

normal cashier operations begin in the morning, at which time receipts from the night before are taken out and properly credited. This system is very much like a night depository in a bank. More and more hotels are installing pneumatic tube systems for the transfer of guests' checks directly to the cashier. These checks will be coming from various dining rooms and cocktail lounges as well as from the coffee shop and from the room-service area. These checks for food, beverages, etc., which have been signed by the guests, should be transferred as quickly as possible to the cashier. This is especially important when a guest is checking out a short time after having signed a check for food or beverages or such items as laundry and valet. Charges for telephone calls will have to be forwarded to the cashier also. Many hotels are using an electric counting device visible to the cashier which indicates the number of calls made by the guest while occupying his room. These indicators function automatically but must be supplemented whenever long-distance calls are made by guests. Such supplemental information is fed to the cashier by the telephone department.

Administrative Area

The administration of a hotel operation depends entirely upon its size. A small hotel will most likely have an office for a manager, who may have his secretary working in the same room with him. The door to his office faces the public lobby, and an additional door is provided so that he can go from his office to the front desk. This is the simplest operation and is found only in the smaller hotels. A larger, medium-sized hotel will have a manager and an assistant manager and, as a rule, there will be a reception office where one or two typist-receptionists will be acting as a buffer between the public and the manager. As a hotel project grows larger, the administrative area grows more complex. Aside from the manager and the assistant manager, there may be an office for a food and beverage manager and a banquet manager. A larger hotel, with sizable convention facilities, will also have an office for the convention manager and his assistants. Obviously, as the complexity of the office and administrative area grows, a more careful and detailed study is, perforce, made to arrange a smoothly functioning suite of administrative offices together with secretarial pools, bookkeepers, teletype machines, a mailroom for incoming mail and for voluminous outgoing mail, etc. The accompanying illustrations show how these areas have been handled in various hotels. It must be borne in mind that this front of the house works closely with the back of the house. Many of the people in the administrative area will deal with guests as well as hotel customers seeking to arrange for luncheons, banquets, and conventions. Accessibility to the public, therefore, is of the utmost importance.

Restaurant Facilities

Every hotel, whether it has 50 rooms or 2,000, must consider the feeding of guests. Small hotels may get by with a pleasant coffee shop restaurant. This type of unit is becoming more popular in the smaller hotel where feeding facilities are kept to a minimum. Such a facility would be the type where quick coffee shop service could be offered a guest, either at a counter or at a table, and where, within the same space, more leisurely dining could be provided. The difference between the two is achieved primarily through decor and atmosphere rather than any physical or struc-

tural arrangement. In such a facility, it is possible to take care of a large breakfast business using the entire facility. There are occasions when a visual separation between coffee shop and restaurant is made movable, so it can be taken away during the breakfast-hour rush. For luncheon, the division is reestablished, making it possible to serve quick meals for those in a hurry in the coffee shop area and more leisurely luncheons in the restaurant portion. In the evening, it is possible to get a more permanent type of separation between coffee shop and restaurant by pushing the coffee shop separator around the counter area, thus allowing for maximum table and seating arrangements in the so-called restaurant area when the coffee shop is doing a minimum business. Under normal situations there will be a cocktail lounge or beverage bar even in the smallest dining facility. The larger hotel will have a pleasant coffee shop for quick service and for simpler meals, whereas a restaurant, with its appropriate decor for more leisurely dining, will offer a more varied menu with probably higher cost per meal than in the coffee shop. The cocktail lounge will usually be found close to the dining room so that hotel guests can pause for a cocktail before lunch or dinner, or while waiting, before going to the dining room, to meet friends or other guests. Where convention facilities are offered within a hotel, it is wise to have a bar placed close to the convention facilities. Conventioneers seem to have a propensity for a cocktail before or after meetings. This impulse-type of beverage buying is boosted tremendously if beverage facilities are placed in the normal path of traffic. Large convention and banquet facilities usually provide a fixed or portable bar arrangement in the preassembly or foyer areas to take care of pauses between meetings and seminars and to fill those pauses with a facility that will provide a "pause that refreshes." There is no special requirement for the design of hotel restaurants, bars, cocktail lounges, and coffee shops which are in any way different from the standard requirements for any such facility. Attention is called to the fact that people staying at hotels have a tendency to seek out highly touted specialty restaurants within an area rather than eating their meals in the hotel. This is especially true for evening dining. Toward that end, hotels more and more are turning to specialty restaurants whose specialty is not only food but also decor, so that they can compete favorably with individual restaurants in the general area of the hotel. The same hotel kitchen can prepare almost any type of special food including Chinese, Polynesian, seafood, or gourmet dishes. The important thing to remember in laying out these spaces is that the decor must be developed to entice the hotel guests to eat in the hotel rather than outside in other specialty restaurants. Continuing in this vein of specialized feeding, some hotels are installing rooftop restaurants where a view of the city or the general area is available and in which fairly limited menus are offered—mostly open-hearth kitchen service which includes steaks, chops, and cuts of roast beef. Such a menu requires a very small kitchen and obviates the need for creating large, expensive facilities on a roof for specialty cooking. Wherever a rooftop restaurant is created, the architect must bear in mind that there will be increased traffic in the elevators taking diners from both in and outside the hotel to this specialized rooftop facility. And don't forget that, because of public assembly requirements, the stairs must be sized larger. Supper clubs or nightclubs will also be found in the larger hotels. When faced

with this type of dining and entertainment feature, the plans must include not only a stage of sorts, together with the attendant stage lighting, but also dressing rooms for performers and a room for the orchestra. It is highly desirable to keep such an adjunct as close to the main kitchen as possible. In the planning of large hotels that encompass all the dining facilities already mentioned, it may not be possible to operate out of one central kitchen. In this case there may be several kitchens, preferably on a horizontal core, so that there is the possibility of vertical distribution of food from the preparation areas which would probably be on the lower level.

Lobbies

Every hotel, regardless of its size, must have a public lobby. The size of the lobby is largely determined by the number of guest rooms as well as by the type of hotel that is on the architect's drawing boards. It goes without saying that the larger the hotel, the larger the lobby. The lobby will also have to be larger in a resort or convention hotel. A resort hotel will require a large lobby because guests will congregate there in the evening. A hotel catering to conventions needs a large lobby because here again there is a constant gathering of conventioneers before they go off to lectures, seminars, meetings, luncheons, and dinners. There is no rule of thumb to determine the size of a lobby. One must proceed by making a careful study of similar types of hotels and arrive at decisions after discussions with hotel operators and managers. A hotel lobby sets the mood for a hotel. This space, more than any other, will create the first and usually the most lasting impression. Furnishings, color, finishing materials, lighting, and decor must create the proper ambience regardless of whether the hotel is large or small, in a city or a resort, moderately priced or expensive. The interior designer plays a most vital part in planning and designing hotel lobbies.

Elevators

Except for one- and two-story motels, every hotel and motel will use elevators to take guests from the point at which they have checked in up to the floor where the guest's room is located. Elevators should be located so that they are immediately visible, either from the entrance of the hotel or from the check-in or registration area. Another consideration in the planning of elevators is that of their location on the guest-room floors. It is advisable to place them centrally so that the distance walked by a guest in any direction is reduced to a minimum. It would obviously be wrong to place the elevators at the end of a long corridor. It would be far better to have these elevators placed so that they are about midway between the two ends of the guest-room corridor. The number, size, and speed of the required elevators is best determined by the elevator companies themselves. It would not be wise for the architect to make a determination as to these factors. Elevator companies can give the answers when facts and figures are given to them, and it is they who will inform the architect what the number and size as well as the speed of the elevators should be. Most elevator companies are computerizing this information and can furnish it to the architect within a matter of hours. The designer should bear in mind that the elevator is part of the hotel atmosphere and, just as it is important to create the proper ambience in the lobbies, it is important to create and to carry out this pleasant feeling in the elevators, since they are the transitional points from lobby to guest-room floor.

Under no circumstances should guest elevators be used for service. Service elevators are separate and apart. Many hotel designs indicate the service elevators within the same general area as the passenger elevators, but this need not necessarily be so. Each bank of elevators should be strategically located to best service the front of the house (guests) or the back of the house.

Before leaving the subject of lobby design, attention is called to the location of the bell captain's station. The bell captain's station should be located so there is a commanding view of the hotel entrance, the registration desk, the cashier, and the elevators. If the hotel is to render the proper kind of service, it is up to the bell captain to see that the arriving or departing guest is properly taken care of. He must see to it that there is a bellman or a bellboy available for the luggage going into the hotel and the luggage going out of the hotel. Incidentally, this is also a form of safeguard to see that guests departing the hotel stop at the cashier and take care of their bills before leaving. The bell captain should have at his disposal a storage space for small parcels which may be left for absent guests and which he will eventually deliver when the guests return to the hotel. Somewhere in the lobby there should be a rather large storage space for luggage which may be left by guests after checking out but prior to departing. In very active hotels with a high occupancy, there is a mandatory check-out time. Very often the guest is not going to leave the hotel until several hours after the check-out time. Under those circumstances, the guest will leave his luggage with the bell captain after checking out, but he will remain in the hotel until it is time for him to depart via his car or to the railroad terminal or airport.

Guest-Floor Corridors

We will now accompany our guest from the elevator to the guest's room. As the elevator doors open, the guest should find himself in an area which can be designated as an elevator foyer. This may be a large open space or a space slightly wider than the corridor itself. Whatever its size, it should, by its width, denote the fact that it is the elevator foyer. It is wise to remember that no guest-room doors should be placed opposite the elevators. Guests coming or going late at night, coming out or getting into the elevators, may talk loudly or may be too noisy, in which case they would be disturbing guests whose doors open off this area. The foyer should be further demarked from the guest-room corridor by its decor and lighting. It is always a thoughtful touch to have certain appurtenances which indicate consideration for the guest in the total overall planning. One of these appurtenances would be a small bench or some type of seat for guests who may want to wait in the foyer for the elevator or who may be waiting to meet someone else on the floor. It is also a thoughtful gesture to have a full-length mirror in this area; men as well as women guests appreciate the chance to have a look at themselves before descending to the main lobby floor. There should obviously be a good-sized ash receiver for cigarettes, cigars, and other trash nuisances that the guest may want to get rid of before getting into the elevator.

The guest-floor corridors are transitional spaces between the public space, which has already been discussed, and the guest room,

which will be discussed further below. The first problem the architect faces is a question of dimension—width and length. Let us consider the advisable length of a corridor first. Good practice indicates that a corridor should, if at all possible, not be over 100 ft in length. It sometimes occurs that, because of the size of the hotel or its configuration, corridors may be longer. There are a number of hotels where corridors stretch out for over 200 ft. The architect would be well advised to introduce an interruption of some sort in his corridor planning to keep the guest from feeling as if his approach to his room were an endless path. The interruption may be by means of a change in dimension or, if the plan permits, a change in direction. The long look of a corridor may be relieved by means of appropriate lighting and decor. Where a corridor turns at right angles or at any angle, it would be well to arrange for a secondary foyer effect to give the guest a second breath, so to speak, before continuing along the corridor to his room. There is very little choice in the width of a corridor. Normally, 6 ft is considered an adequate width, although some hotels have made do with only 5 ft. This could well suffice if the corridor was a rather short one. Another expedient, which may be used either in a narrow corridor (under 6 ft) or a standard-width corridor, would be the device of recessing the bedroom or guest-room doors. Setting doors back from the corridor wall 1 ft or even as much as 2 ft gives an apparent width to the corridor and, what is more important, it gives each room entrance its own sense of privacy and individuality. It is normal to pair guest-room doors and therefore the recess or door alcove would normally be the width of two doors or a minimum of 6 ft and a depth ranging anywhere from 6 in. to 2 ft. An expedient that always helps a corridor to appear shorter is that of creating a change in the colors of the recesses, which under ideal conditions would be opposite each other on either side of the corridor. If this is possible in the plan, and it usually works out that way, a break in the carpet color or design in this area as well as a change in the color scheme for each entrance-door alcove creates a pleasant feeling of pause or interlude along a long corridor. Lighting will also play an important part in making corridors seem more interesting and less stretched out. Illuminating the alcove areas is always a pleasant device. In the first place, it makes the numbers of the doors immediately visible, and in the second place, it gives the guest a sense of comfort to know that no one could be lurking in the door alcove where deep shadows might hide him. Lighting always creates an ambiance of hospitality, and lights would be best placed in these door alcoves. This is not a hard and fast rule. In many instances, the interior designer or the architect may decide that lighting along the blank wall between the guest-room doors would serve his purpose better. All this, of course, is a matter of individual taste as well as of the wishes of the hotel operator. Another small but important factor is the design of the guest-room door itself. A flush panel door is the least expensive but also the least desirable type of door for a guest room. If only a flush door is used, strong color might be helpful, or the use of natural wood finishes would be pleasant. If at all possible, some form of decor on the door will create a sense of inviting hospitality for the arriving guest. Another thing to be borne in mind is that the guest must be able to recognize his room number, and such a room number might well be an attractive decorative adjunct in this area. Some hotels have used room numbers placed to the

side of the door rather than on the door itself. Here again, the ingenuity of the designer comes into play. It is not the intention of this dissertation to discuss color, but wall covering and wall colors in corridors are most important. It must be borne in mind that along these corridors pass endless numbers of pieces of luggage carried by the guest or the bellboy. Luggage may also be transported by means of trolleys. In any case, the lower portion of the wall will be subjected to brutal abuse by being banged with luggage or trolleys. The lower portion of the wall, therefore, might well be designed as a dado made of a bruise- and shock-resistant material or merely marked off with a contrasting color or wall covering. Thus the lower walls in the corridor can be repainted or repapered when they have been sufficiently scuffed while the upper walls may remain as they are. This can result in considerable savings to the hotel operator.

Guest Rooms

Everything that has been said about hotels thus far may be considered peripheral to the prime product that a hotel has to offer, namely, the guest rooms. This is the final product that is to be sold. In connection with this thought, it is well to remember (although this may not have any influence on the planning or the architecture of a hotel) that, unlike an item on a merchant's shelf, a guest room that is not sold one night means a complete loss. It would be as if a grocer were forced to throw out each day's unsold supply of boxed cereal and to lay in a fresh supply every morning. That is a precise analogy to the situation of the hotel man and his guest rooms. The room that is not sold and the revenue that is lost can never be recovered (Fig. 5).

Now let us have a look at the guest room itself. The first consideration is that of size. The accompanying illustrations of guest rooms in hotels designed by the authors show as wide a variety of dimensions as an architect may encounter. For the moment, let us eliminate the space taken by a bathroom and a closet and consider the actual room itself. The length and width are determined by the amount of furniture that is to go into the room and by the degree of luxury that the hotel operator wishes to achieve. Let us consider the latter first. It is an obvious truism that the luxury of space is an expensive one when considered in the light of construction costs. Space, however, does convey a feeling of luxury and, where an operator is aiming for the high-priced market, it would be well to create rooms that are sized not for the actual furniture requirements but for the sheer luxury of spaciousness.

And now to the first premise—namely, what furniture should go in and what size room should accommodate the furnishings. In order to understand furniture requirements, it is important to have a knowledge of the various types of rooms that a hotel or motel offers guests. The most common room in the hotel field today is the twin-bedded room. Then we have the possibility of a single occupancy room, and, lastly, studio rooms or suites. The twin-bedded room, the most common in hotels generally, will vary in length depending on the type of bed that the operator wishes to install. The smallest unit will have a pair of twin beds. The first question that arises in considering twin beds is whether there will be a night table between the beds or whether the two beds will be placed side by side. Rooms containing twin beds, with a night table between them, are preferred by most hotel operators because there are many double occupancies that do not necessarily involve married couples. For instance, the occupants might be two women, two men, or one adult and one child, and in these instances it is always desirable to provide separate beds. As an example, two men traveling together would much prefer to have their beds separated than to sleep side by side. Economy in space and length of room can be achieved by placing beds side by side, but although such an arrangement is often used, it is not the best one.

The next consideration is the size of the beds themselves. There are single beds which are 3 ft 6 in. wide, a full-sized bed which is 4 ft 6 in., a queen-sized bed which is 5 ft wide, and a king-sized bed which is 6 ft wide. Presently, all beds are still being made in a 6-ft 6-in. length dimension. Since the average American is growing taller and taller, it would be wise to consider 7-ft beds as a standard, since it will not be long before such beds will be introduced into most hotels. One reason for the queen-sized bed is the comfort of the guests. Many guests would appreciate the extra width of a queen-sized bed, and it is possible for families traveling together to have an adult and a child sleep in the same bed. Where king-sized beds are employed (and this will be found most often in motels), two adults may occupy one bed, so that a two-bed room may take a family of four people.

In connection with beds, it is wise to remember that the headboard, which seems like an anachronism in home furnishing, is a most important feature in hotels. Guests like to read in bed, and because of the widespread use of hair preparations, the headboard portion of the bed is subjected to heavy wear and soiling. Whether a headboard is provided or whether some other device such as a flat cushion against the wall or any other ingenious arrangement that the interior designer may come up with is used, headboards are definitely a part of hotel equipment. Beds, as a rule, come on glides or coasters in one form or another so that they can be moved when the maid comes in to make up the beds. Movement of beds is most important, so that maids and porters can clean under them. Nothing is more disturbing to a guest than to look under a bed and see an accumulation of carpet fluff and discarded cigarette butts.

Now that we have discussed beds, we know that we must have at least 7 ft 6 in. from the wall to the front edge of our newer anticipated 7-ft beds. If at all possible, there should be a 3-ft aisle and, if no furniture is placed opposite the bed (a very unlikely arrangement), then the width of the room would be a minimum of 10 ft 6 in. Where furniture will be placed on the wall opposite the bed, such furniture will most likely consist of a dresser or cupboard with drawers. Such a piece of furniture requires a minimum of 18 in. in width and most likely an optimum width of 24 in. It must be remembered that drawers have to be opened, and the guest will need room to stand in front of the dresser to open the drawer without being forced to sit down on the bed while doing so. Therefore, a 3-ft aisle again comes into play. If we consider the 7 ft 6 in. required for the bed, 3 ft for the aisle, and 2 ft for the dresser, we have an optimum room dimension of 12 ft 6 in. between walls. This is a minimum dimension, and if the plan and the budget permit, another 6 in. would be a most welcome spatial device.

Let us now consider the length of the room. This dimension will vary depending upon the types of beds used—queen, king, or standard twin—but this is only part of our consideration. It is necessary in each room to provide not only sleeping facilities but also sitting facilities.

The most common arrangement found in most hotels consists of two comfortable armchairs with a cocktail table between them. A comfortable chair will require a depth of least 30 in. and another 30 in. of leg space in front of it, which means that we need at least 5 ft from the wall before we encounter the first piece of furniture, which will probably be a bed. The furniture placement will usually call for the chairs to be placed against the window wall. The reason is obvious. A view out of the window is a pleasant experience for someone using the guest room as a sitting room. In connection with the so-called cocktail table, this may give way to a low table which may be used for dining, card playing, or writing. Many so-called "cocktail tables" are, in effect, pedestal standing lamps which combine two pieces of furniture in one: the cocktail table and the standing lamp. Such an expedient is a space saver, since the light is exactly where it is wanted and there is no need for another movable lamp. In talking of lighting, we must bear in mind that we want not only a lamp or a ceiling fixture over the sitting area but also adequate reading lights for the beds. The most often used arrangement is a twin-headed lamp sitting on the night table between the two beds. Far from enough study has been done in this type of lighting, which would make it possible to give adequate and direct light for one guest who is reading in bed while the other guest can sleep without being disturbed by the light of his roommate. Lights may be placed over the headboards, but this means that two outlets may be required and certainly two luminaires instead of one.

Another area that will need good lighting is the area which we will call the writing and makeup area. This is usually some sort of table arrangement where a guest may sit and write or where a female guest can sit down and apply her makeup It has become rather standard to combine the dresser with its drawers with another piece of furniture which is called the dressing-writing table. This type of case goods is most often used, but it is by far the least desirable for a well-appointed room. Another piece of fixed furniture that is desirable is a luggage stand. Many hotels overlook this useful piece of furniture and supply folding luggage stands. These will serve adequately but, since the guest will usually leave his piece of of luggage in the room, it is far more desirable to have a pleasant piece of furniture than a folding luggage rack. Before leaving the furnishing of the standard room, it should be noted that there should be at least one more chair in the room. This could be a straight-backed chair or a stool placed in front of the writing-makeup table. This will provide for three sitting pieces. If at all possible, a fourth chair should be considered. It is far pleasanter to have four people sitting on chairs than to have three people supplied with chairs while the fourth visitor or guest has to sit on one of the beds. Between a pair of twin beds, the ubiquitous nightstand with its small storage space below is standard. A clever interior designer can improvise and create far better furnishing arrangements than the standard nightstands—arrangements which will give the room additional storage space. The cocktail table which has been previously mentioned may well give way to a dining table, which will serve the purpose far better because it can be used for setting down a drink or a book or a package and also for serving a meal (rather than depending upon the room-service trolley). In connection with the room-service trolley, the designer should bear in mind that if a dining table is not provided, there must be sufficient space in the room to set up a room-service table. This is wheeled in

by the waiter, and it must then be possible to arrange at least two and sometimes more chairs around it for the guests who wish to dine in their rooms.

The luggage stand has already been mentioned, but at hotels where the guests may be staying for as long as a week or more (this obviously will be the case in resort hotels), the designer should bear in mind that they will come with more than one piece of luggage. Some travelers carry four and six pieces, and where to put them in the standard room becomes a serious problem.

Lighting in the room, which has been partially covered, will depend upon the interior designer. The necessary luminaires have already been discussed, but these may be supplemented with additional light to create a pleasanter ambience in the room. The control of these lights must be carefully considered. The simplest type of control will call for a switch at the door which will turn on one or two or even all the lights in the room. Most hotels and their designers give entirely too little thought to the switching arrangement for the control of lights. This leads to confusion on the part of the guest, who has to explore the room and decide which lights are controlled at their source. A great source of annoyance is the arrangement in which all the lights are controlled by one switch at the door and then each luminaire has its own ON and OFF switch. It presents an annoying and puzzling problem to the guest coming into the room or the guest who wants to turn out the lights when going to sleep. This problem has been solved in many hotels by placing one light switch at the door to turn on one of the lights and then providing a battery of light switches at the bed which control the other lighting in the room. If this is not carefully thought out, a fuming guest will often comment that one has to be a lighting engineer in order to understand how to work the intricate switching arrangement. This is especially true if two-way switches are used, one at the door and one at the bed; then you may be sure that the guests will become quite thoroughly confused. Such switching arrangements are prevalent in European hotels, but there the problem is overcome by using graphic symbols on each switch to make it possible for the traveler to figure out the intricacies of the light controls. Here we can give no advice other than to consider the problem carefully as if it were a problem in logistics.

Thus far we have been speaking only of guest rooms with normal twin- or single-bed arrangements. Another popular arrangement in hotels is that of the so-called "studio room." Dual sleep pieces have been developed which are comfortable sofas during the day and perfectly comfortable beds at night. In this context we are not speaking of the folding sofa beds. These should be used only as a last resort in hotel furnishings. They can never achieve the comfort of the standard bed. The dual sleep pieces we are talking about come in various ingenious arrangements, but they are primarily beds which have some back-up arrangement so that they become normal sofas when used for sitting. When they are moved out, rolled to a side, or adjusted in some other way to clear the backrest, they become full-width, full-length beds. The accompanying illustrations show some of the ways in which these dual sleep pieces may be used. The purpose of a studio arrangement is to enable the guest to use his room as a true sitting room. Many travelers use their rooms during the day to conduct business or to visit with friends. Obviously it is much pleasanter to sit in a room which looks like a living room than to ignore the beds, which may or may not have been made up when the guest receives company. Another reason for having these studio rooms is that they may double as sitting rooms for suites by having one room, which is a normal bedroom or guest room, adjoin another room which is furnished as a studio room. Thus the hotel can provide a two-room suite (obviously, connecting doors must be provided between these two accommodations). Before leaving the question of adjoining rooms, the architect should determine with the hotel operator how many rooms will have adjoining doors. Too often the planner decides that all rooms should have interconnecting doors. These doors are a source of annoyance because, unless the finest type of sound barriers are used on them, these doors become a nuisance in that sound will travel more easily through doors than through walls. This is true in spite of the fact that a good installation will call for one door in each room, so that actually every connecting opening has two doors. Wherever the budget permits, a high-rated door is desirable, and if at all possible, a gasketing device should be employed to cut the sound transference from one room to another. With regard to sound transference, the mechanical plans must indicate that base outlets and telephone outlets may not back up to each other. This is one of the most troublesome ways of transmitting sound from one room to the other. It is economical to back up electrical and telephone outlets, but it is a bad policy in hotels. Outlets should be staggered to avoid sound transmission. The architect should definitely consider the decibel rating of his wall construction to try and cut sound transmission from one room to another. This usually adds to the cost of the hotel, but it is highly desirable. As one guest once said, he is tired of answering his phone when it is his neighbor's that is ringing; and as another guest once complained, every time his neighbor flushes the toilet, he runs for the hills. Sound transmission is a nuisance in hotels and it should be carefully considered by the architect.

Every hotel should have arrangements for suites of a permanent nature as opposed to a combination of a studio room with a typical guest room. Suites will be furnished like fine sitting rooms. They are used not only by the affluent traveler because he can afford it but also by travelers who do a good deal of entertaining, especially business travelers who entertain clients and customers on their arrival in any given city. If a hotel offers convention facilities, it will require an inordinate number of suites. Conventions will mean that there will be a good deal of entertaining going on, and companies whose representatives are guests in the hotel will want good-sized suites for fairly large cocktail parties and other forms of entertainment. These large suites, incidentally, may double at times as seminar or conference rooms. In this context the hotel may be asked to move most of the furniture out of the suite living room and bring in seminar chairs for meetings. If such will be the case, the planner should provide for a storage room on each floor capable of holding alternate types of furniture to suit the requirements of guests using large suite-sitting rooms. These suites are also often used by two couples or by a large family, in which case the sitting room of the suite may be used for sleeping at night. In this case, dual sleep pieces will be required, but they will usually be the type that is referred to as a "davenport," or the type of sofa which opens out to become a comfortable double bed (never as comfortable as a true bed). These suites should have a good-sized dining table with a sufficient number of chairs, provision

for an adequate desk (since some business may be carried on in that room), a sufficient number of comfortable lounge chairs, and an accessory table. The decor of the room will depend upon the interior designer and the hotel operator, who usually knows what he would like in these suites. It is a good practice to arrange the sitting room of a suite so that it connects with at least two bedrooms and, if at all possible, three and sometimes even four bedrooms. This will require some intricate planning. Suites will usually be found in the corner of a building, which makes it possible for the planner to join up several bedrooms.

There are times when suites are not used, and the hotel should be able to rent each of the rooms in the suite separately. This means that each room will have its own separate key. A foyer which connects the bedrooms and the sitting area makes this separate keying of rooms possible. A single door or a pair of doors leading to the foyer of the suite will be on one key, but by opening these doors temporarily (the plans should be devised so that the doors can be swung back and out of the way), the foyer becomes part of the corridors and each room, including the sitting room, would have its own key. This makes for maximum flexibility, so that the sitting room can be rented on an individual basis. A complete bathroom should be planned for each of the sitting rooms of a suite to make it possible to rent the rooms out singly. Even if the room is not rented singly, a bathroom or lavatory facility certainly is needed in each living room or sitting room of a suite. Plumbing connections might well be arranged so that a bar can also be introduced in the sitting room. Since this room will be used for entertaining (either business or private), a bar with water connection becomes a pleasant adjunct.

There is a growing tendency in hotels and motels to create greater flexibility in meeting and seminar rooms that would be available to conventions. These rooms are so designed that they can be used as bedrooms when not required for meetings or other purposes when a convention is in the hotel. Under this concept usually two rooms are divided by a foldaway partition, so that the two rooms can be thrown into one if a larger room is required. On other occasions, the one guest room may be used for very small meetings without being opened up to the adjoining guest room. In view of the fact that these rooms are designated for meetings, whether singly or in pairs, their furnishings are different from those of the standard guest room. At the outset it must be determined that this will probably be used as a single room rather than a double room. The bed itself is placed in the wall. It is the type that swings up and is hidden in the wall. There are a number of manufacturers today who are making these hideaway beds, which are quite satisfactory for hotel use. It is possible, if so desired, to have two hideaway beds, in which case the room becomes a double room. The rest of the furniture is carefully considered so that it can be moved out of the way to open up the room for meetings or, at best, is sized so that it will not interfere with meetings in these rooms. Obviously, these rooms will be placed on the lowest floors so they can be close to the public spaces for the convenience of those who are going to use them for meetings or seminars in connection with a larger convention or meeting taking place in the hotel.

Guest Bathrooms

We are now ready to review the bathroom requirements in a hotel. The minimum bathroom will have a combination tub-shower,

a lavatory, and a water closet. Since the traveling public is very conscious of bathroom accommodations, the architect should give a good deal of thought to this feature in the hotel. The accompanying plans of the writer's projects show various arrangements of bathroom accommodations. An innovation devised by the writer's firm was the introduction of two lavatories in the bathroom facilities. These two lavatories may be right in the bathroom itself, they may be pulled out into a dressing area, or one lavatory may be placed in the bathroom and another outside the bathroom. This last arrangement is most desirable, so that if two people occupy a room, regardless of whether it is a husband and wife, two men, or two women traveling together, they have the use of the bathroom facilities without interfering with each other. It immediately becomes obvious that if, for instance, the husband is shaving, the wife can be taking a bath or shower—and other possibilities are immediately self-evident.

European hotels invariably have not only the tub, water closet, and lavatory but also a bidet. This is a particularly European custom, and we are finding that in many hotels in America the bidet is being introduced. Obviously, this additional feature is found only in the most luxurious hotels. Taking the water closet as the first of the fixtures in the bathroom, there is one word of caution. A noisy flushing toilet is a disturbing noise element not only to the occupants of the room but also to the occupants of the adjoining rooms. Flushometers are not desirable because they are noisy. There are noiseless flushometers, but they are quite expensive. The average hotel uses a silent tank-type of toilet as the most expedient type of water closet for hotels. A wall-hung unit makes cleaning of hotel bathrooms easier for the maid, but again, its economics will determine whether this fairly expensive type of installation is warranted. The tub in a guest room is normally a 5-ft tub. A good hotel installation will go for the additional expense and the additional dimension by installing 5-ft 6-in. tubs. The European hotels invariably have at least a 5-ft 6-in. tub, and there are many luxury hotels with 6-ft tubs. The normal shower head becomes standard in all hotels, although there is a growing tendency to using the so-called "telephone shower head." This is a hand-operated shower head which is more common in Europe than it is in America. Manufacturers of bathroom equipment have devised a hand-held shower head which operates as well as the normal wall shower head, and by using two movable shower-head supports, one at the normal hand level and one at the higher level where a fixed shower head normally would occur, the guest has the option of allowing the hand-type shower head to remain in a standard position or to remove it and use it as he pleases. This type of shower head, incidentally, is also convenient for women guests washing their hair.

Recently, most bathroom fixture companies have been turning their attention to some form of fiber glass or plastic tub and shower arrangements that can be delivered either in one piece or in several sections. This eliminates the necessity for the use of tile or other impervious wall material in this area. These one-piece installations are still in the early stages of development, but eventually hotels will be turning to them for economy in construction and for simplicity in installation. The standard one-piece lavatory is fast disappearing from hotels. Instead, a lavatory is becoming a shelf arrangement into which the bowl is sunk. Usually, a marble slab with a cutout to receive the lavatory bowl is used. There are many companies manufacturing synthetic marble that make the bowl and the ledge in one piece. This is highly desirable in hotels, but care should be exercised to make sure that the synthetic material can withstand cigarette burns, alcohol stains, and the general abuse that these areas get. Older hotels used to have ice-water connections in the lavatory. This is now a thing of the past because most hotels provide ice makers in corridors as a nice touch for the guests, who can fetch their own ice cubes for cold water or for cold drinks.

Another consideration in a bathroom is the so-called "medicine cabinet." Since guests really do not carry medicines any more, it is advisable to eliminate this facility entirely. If a medicine cabinet is used, very often a guest will place shaving materials, lotions, etc., in the cabinet and upon leaving the hotel forget to look in it, therefore leaving behind his or her toiletries. It is preferable to have a ledge on which toiletries may be placed, where they are conveniently reached, and where, obviously, they will not be left when the guest checks out. There are a number of appurtenances that will be placed in the washing area, such as a tumbler holder or toothbrush holder, but here again the tendency is to leave out these pieces of hardware, although a receptacle for toilet tissues is desirable and should be included. If a ledge is used, the toilet tissue holder can be placed within the recess of the ledge, as can be the tumbler holders and the toothbrush holders. Obviously, an electrical convenience outlet must be placed in this area for electric shavers, electric toothbrushes, and other electrical gadgets that today's traveler takes with him. A slot receptacle for used razor blades should not be forgotten.

Towel bars must be strategically placed so that the guest can reach for a towel regardless of whether he is stepping out of the tub or whether he is washing or shaving at the lavatory. A well-run hotel should keep an ample supply of bath towels and face towels in each guest room, and sufficient space for these should be allowed together with the necessary hardware arrangements. Hooks are often omitted, but these are necessary for a guest's pajamas or bathrobe. Of course, the ubiquitous bottle opener should not be forgotten. We still have bottles with bottle caps, although in the near future this will probably be an interesting anachronism. Another nicety which might be provided is some form of clothesline. With today's wash-and-wear apparel, many guests, especially women, like to do their washing at night and hang their garments in the bathroom. Since this has become a way of life for the traveler, an architect will be well advised to seek out one of the many tricky self-concealing wash lines on the market today.

Finally, the treatment of the walls and floors of a bathroom becomes the province of the interior designer. The use of tile, for one reason or another, is being reduced to a minimum. It will be found around the bath enclosure (where the new one-piece units are not used) and usually on the floors because they are so required by sanitary building codes. There are many new materials on the market, and such old materials as thin-slab marble may be used. Where code permits, some hotels are actually using washable synthetic carpets in bathrooms for floors. The walls are definitely no longer tiled, but some form of scrubbable wall covering material is prevalent in most hotels today. It need hardly be said but it should be noted that *good* lighting is an essential in a bathroom where men will be shaving and where women will be applying makeup. This, together with ample mirror services, is an indisputable must. A number of hotels are installing a wall-hung

mirror which is an enlarging mirror on one side and a normal mirror on the other, a very nice touch for both men and women guests. Much has been said about the bathroom, but Americans are a bathroom-conscious people. A hotel designer should realize that pleasing the guest is his prime purpose and that the bathroom can be a great guest pleaser.

Guest Room Closets

We now come to the final requirement in the guest room, namely, the closet. The size of a closet will be determined by the type of hotel. Obviously, such an accommodation in a motel is of little use. Most motels expect guests to stay only overnight, and therefore they need very little accommodation for hanging clothes. Many motels, in fact, have no closets at all but provide a neat hanging space to make sure that the motel guest who likes to check out early in the morning does not forget any clothes in the closet, which might be closed when he is leaving. Having the open hanging arrangements obviates this possibility. The longer the guest-room stay that is anticipated, then the larger the closet. The larger walk-in closet should certainly be considered where guests will be staying for any length of time. This is especially true in resort hotels, where the guest will be arriving with many pieces of luggage and the closet should be large enough to accommodate the emptied luggage during the guest's stay. It should be possible to store the luggage out of sight in the closet without diminishing the available hanging space, the shoe-rack space, or shelf space for hats and other apparel and paraphernalia. Whether the closet is a flat reach-in type or a walk-in type, the door should be such that, when the closet is opened, there are no hidden recesses where clothing may be forgotten because it cannot be readily seen by the departing guest. Another thought to be borne in mind is that closet doors can become a nuisance when opened, and their strategic location to avoid banging into open doors is definitely the province of a hotel planner. A good closet will have a hang rod with sufficient space to comfortably hold men's and women's clothes, a shelf for packages, hats, etc., and a shoe ledge or rack for placing shoes. A walk-in closet must, of course, have a good source of light. A reach-in closet should also have light outside the closet so that the guest can see what is inside.

Guest-Floor Service Space

Every guest-room floor will have a service area. A service area serves several functions. Primarily, it is a place where linen is stored and where the maids' carts are kept. We must bear in mind that each maid will handle anywhere from 12 to 15 rooms and that each maid will need a cart. The number of rooms on the floor will, therefore, determine the number of maids and, in turn, the number of carts. Aside from the space for the maids' carts, there must be a porter's closet for cleaning supplies, vacuum cleaners, pails, etc. A closed storage area should be provided for the storage of linens. In addition to the maids', porters', and linen supplies, sufficient space should be left for the storage of room-service carts. These carts will be brought to this area by the waiters after the guests have finished their meals. They may have to remain on the floor for some time waiting for the service elevator or elevators. Obviously, the service elevators will open out to this service area, so that all this activity takes place out of the sight and hearing of the hotel guests. Some hotel operators still insist on providing toilet facilities for the help in this area. Most

hotels, however, go on the assumption that the maids and porters will, in the absence of the guest, be using the toilet facilities of the guest rooms while they are working in them.

Banqueting Facilities

Most hotels and motels include meeting and banquet facilities. The smaller hotels may provide only a number of meeting rooms which may also be used for luncheons and dinners. Larger hotels will have a more diversified arrangement for meetings, luncheons, dinners, and banquets. The largest hotels are usually designed with a full banqueting and convention facility. The extent of these facilities will be determined by the hotel operator who, in turn, will convey his requirements to the architect. It is wise for the architect to have a thorough knowledge of what the feeding and space requirements for these facilities are.

The normal meeting room requirements are rather simple. The rooms will vary in size to accommodate anywhere from 10 to as many as 100 people. In most instances, wherever it is feasible, the meeting rooms will be arranged in a straight line, so that the walls separating one room from the other can be made movable. Movable, separating walls make it possible to achieve a great flexibility in the size of the rooms to accommodate meetings of various sizes. Thus, if two meeting rooms which normally might seat 25 people are thrown open to one, we would have a meeting room to take 50 people; and if another wall is opened, we would be able to seat 75 people, and so on. The numbers used are not necessarily those that will be found in hotels, they are merely used for convenience, as an example. In larger rooms, which normally qualify for conventions or large banquets, it is also possible to subdivide the space by the use of movable walls to create smaller rooms when a large room is not required. A large space which might seat 1,000 people when all folding walls have been moved back can be cut up into anywhere from four to six spaces, allowing for meeting rooms that can accommodate 150 to 250 people. In many instances both arrangements will be found in a hotel, so that there are lines of meeting rooms of a smaller nature, all subdivisible, and a really large space that is also subdivisible.

Thus far we have spoken of these spaces as meeting rooms. Most of these spaces will also be used to serve meals. These meals may consist of small luncheons or dinners for 10 or 12 people and go on up to accommodate as many as 1,000 people seated at tables for dining. Of course, in the really large convention halls, it will not be unusual to seat 3,000 or more people in one large convention banquet hall. Realizing that food must be brought to all these rooms, their juxtaposition to serving kitchens is highly important in arranging the plan. For the most part, food should be brought directly from banquet kitchens to the banquet spaces. In subdividing these spaces, the subdivision must be so planned that each space is contiguous to the kitchen and has its own doors to enable waiters to come and go between the banquet spaces and the banquet kitchen. In some instances, this is not completely possible, and it is an accepted practice, where small meeting rooms cannot be placed contiguous to the actual banquet kitchen, to arrange to serve through the same corridors that will be used by people coming and going as diners in these smaller spaces.

If the architect, working with his client, the hotel operator, has come to the conclusion that the subdivision of these spaces by means of movable walls is what will be included in

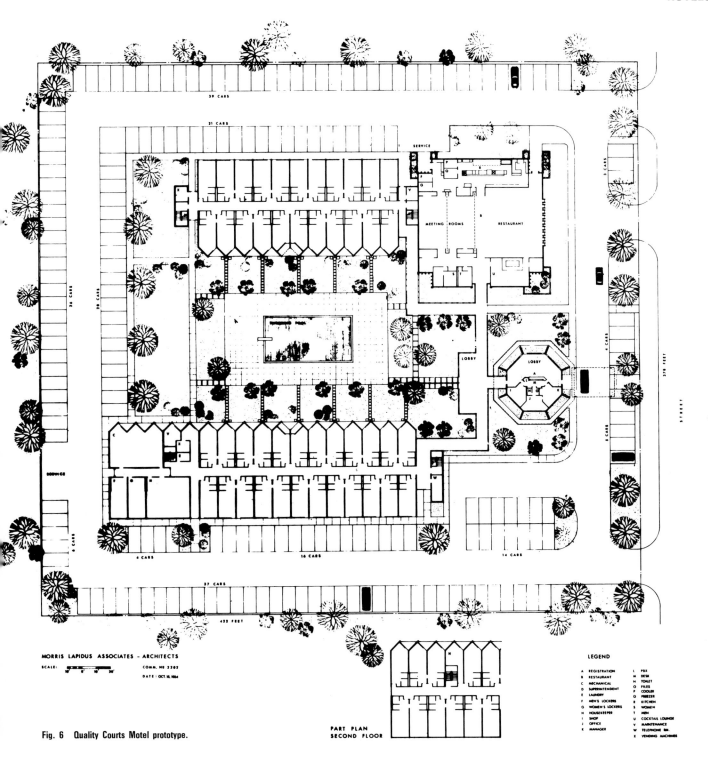

MORRIS LAPIDUS ASSOCIATES - ARCHITECTS

PART PLAN
SECOND FLOOR

LEGEND

A	REGISTRATION	L	PBX
B	RESTAURANT	M	DESK
C	MECHANICAL	N	TOILET
D	SUPERINTENDENT	O	FILES
E	LAUNDRY	P	COOLER
F	MEN'S LOCKERS	Q	FREEZER
G	WOMEN'S LOCKERS	R	KITCHEN
H	HOUSEKEEPER	S	WOMEN
I	SHOP	T	MEN
J	OFFICE	U	COCKTAIL LOUNGE
K	MANAGER	V	MAINTENANCE
		W	TELEPHONE BM
		X	VENDING MACHINES

Fig. 6 Quality Courts Motel prototype.

the plans, it behooves the architect to make a careful study of the various types of movable walls available for use in such hotel facilities. There are many manufacturers who make these walls. The architect should be careful in arranging these walls so as not to interfere with the overall concept of opening up clear spaces by moving walls.

The acoustical value of the walls must be carefully studied. Nothing is more disturbing than to have two meetings in adjacent rooms where the sound transmission is of such a high level that what happens in one space can be clearly heard in the other. Sound isolation is of the greatest importance, and this applies not only to the decibel rating of the panels themselves but also the arrangement of the joints between the sections or panels of the movable wall. The architect must also be aware of what happens above the panel as it comes up to the ceiling track and what happens to the panel as it glides along the floor. Sound isolation should be carefully studied in all these spaces, which will allow, if not properly controlled, sound to be transmitted. There are practically no walls which can guarantee absolute sound isolation when the sound reaches a high enough decibel rating. In such instances, it has been found expedient to use two sets of walls with an air space between them, which will ensure almost total sound isolation. These movable walls or panels can be operated by hand or by motor. Sweet's catalog carries all the pertinent information from every manufacturer, and an architect is well advised to carefully study not only the operation and construction of these mov-

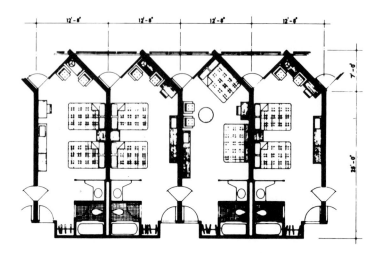

DOUBLE - WITH BALCONY

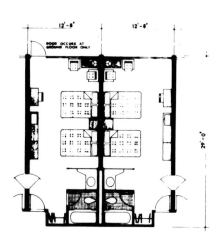

DOUBLE

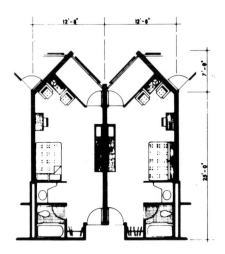

SINGLE - WITH BALCONY

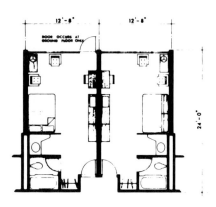

SINGLE

Fig. 7 Typical rooms, Quality Courts Motel prototype.

able wall panels but also the sound isolating devices that the manufacturer specifies.

In fairly large meeting, banquet, and convention facilities, space must be provided which is normally called "preconvention assembly space." Actually, this is a sort of foyer or gathering place for people before they go to the various meeting rooms or where they may congregate before going in to a banquet. Since most of the people who are standing are those who will eventually be seated, the proportions of the preconvention foyer space will be determined by the number of people who will be eventually seated. As a rule of thumb, a person standing in fairly close quarters will take up approximately 5 sq ft. A person seated at a table will take up anywhere from 10 to 15 sq ft. A person seated for a seminar or a meeting will require 8 or 9 sq ft. It thus becomes apparent that the ideal preconvention, prebanquet, or assembly space should be at least one-third of the area of the actual dining and meeting spaces. This one-third is arrived at empirically by comparing the amount of space required sitting or standing and by allowing for a diversity factor, knowing that not all the people who will eventually be seated will be

standing, since some of them will be latecomers and will arrive after many of the people have already gone in to be seated for their meetings or their meals. Even the one-third proportion may not be possible, and it has been found proper to use as little as 25 percent of the space for this preassembly foyer. It has been previously noted in this discussion of hotel and motel design that it is good policy to have a bar within this preconvention, premeeting space. Such bars do an excellent business. A fixed bar would be a very nice feature, but in many very large hotels it is normal practice to have movable bars set up. Very often there may be two or three bars to accommodate large groups of people.

MOTELS

Much of what has already been discussed will apply to motels. The term *motel* is rather loosely used. There are many so-called motels within cities which are, in fact, multilevel hotels providing more than the average parking found in a hotel. Where such a project occurs, it would normally be called a motor hotel.

Parking may be provided in an adjacent garage, in several levels below grade, or in several levels above grade with guests rooms starting on an upper floor above the garage levels. If property values permit, there may be an open parking area or a two- or three-story open parking garage. Whatever arrangement is eventually used, these structures should properly be called motor hotels rather than motels. Aside from the parking, everything that will be found in these motor hotels will be the same as what has been discussed under hotels.

A true motel is one which is normally found on a main highway, at an important intersection of several highways, or, finally, at a highway which enters a city and therefore is close to the city and yet not a part of it. The obvious reason is that land values within cities are too high to permit the spread that a true motel will require. Motels usually provide open parking and as a rule are only one, two, three, or at most four stories high. Usually most of the rooms will be entered from an open corridor, although this is not a hard and fast rule. There may be a combination of open corridors and closed corridors. The parking, by preference, should be placed as close as possible to the actual room that the guest will be occupying. The great advantage that motels have is the ability of guests to park close to their rooms and to carry their luggage back and forth without the assistance of a bellboy. Bellboy service is available when required, but many guests arriving by car prefer to handle their own luggage. The option should be with the guest rather than with the management of the hotel.

In the highway motel the lounge and registration area as well as administration offices may be within the buildings housing the guest rooms, or they may be completely separate as an entity which is reached from the motel rooms by means of covered or enclosed passages. Housekeeping and maintenance spaces may be placed within the management and registration area, attached to the motel wings, or housed in a separate small building to handle laundry, housekeeping supplies, locker rooms for help, and maintenance shops and storage for taking care of the grounds, the swimming pool, etc.

The restaurant which will be a part of the normal motel complex may be attached to the management and registration area or, again, may be in a separate building or in a build-

ing attached to the motel wings rather than to the building housing management and registration. In many motels the food operation is a lease arrangement and is run by chains of food and beverage companies that make a specialty of operating restaurants for individual motels or for motel chains.

Quality Court Motels are used in this context as an example. (See Figs. 6 and 7.) Our office has prepared prototypes for this company for motels ranging in size from 51 rooms, 76 rooms, 103 rooms, on up to 150 rooms. In the case of this particular organization, where the motels are usually individually owned and operated under a franchise, the food operation is a lease operation, but in every respect each of the motels contain the same basic element: namely, the registration and administrative building and a restaurant varying in size depending upon the size of the motel. A standard feature of every motel is an adequate swimming pool and pool deck (an amenity which is invariably found in all highway motels), ample parking to take care of all the guest rooms, and sufficient parking for restaurant guests who may not be staying at the motel.

Motel guest rooms differ somewhat from hotel rooms. Motels cater to two distinct clienteles. One type is the traveling businessman using a car for transportation. He usually travels alone. All he wants is a small room for his overnight stay. The other guest accommodation is for a traveling family. Here a large room is wanted. It will have two king-size beds to accommodate the parents and two children. A careful study of the location will yield the clue that will determine the mix of small and large rooms. Drawer space is not a necessity; several shelves and luggage stands are of prime importance. Closets may be and usually are omitted. Most motels are designed for single overnight stays. The use of an additional lavatory is suggested. This amenity permits a family to complete its toilet rapidly for the usual early morning start. (See Figs. 8 and 9.)

A space should be provided for vending machines that dispense hot and cold drinks, candy, snacks, and magazines. An ice maker is a must, as well as insulated ice buckets for each room. Self-service of traveler comforts and needs by means of vending machines is an extra boon for the road-weary traveler who is anxious to get his night's rest.

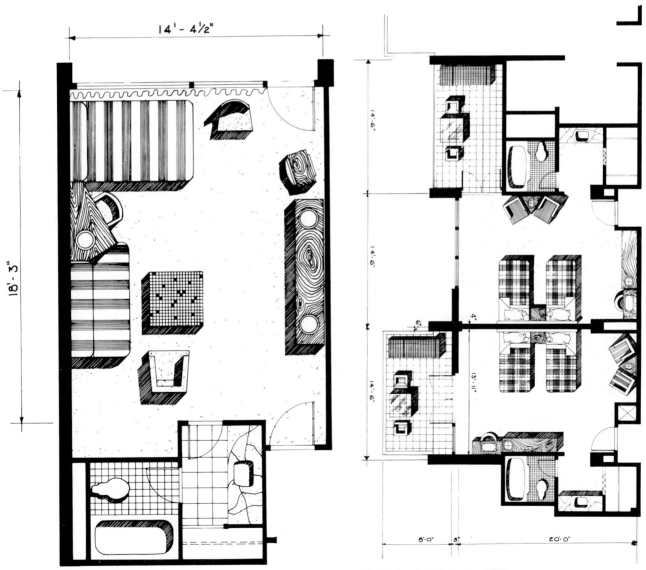

Fig. 8 Tampa International Inn, Tampa, Florida.

Fig. 9 Arawak Hotel, Jamaica, B.W.I.

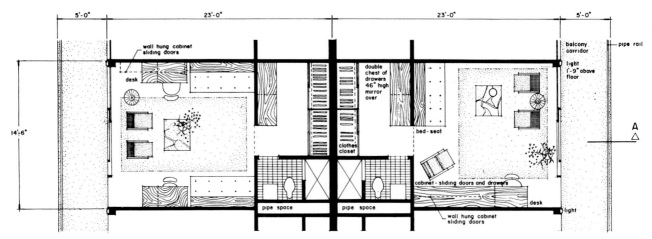

Fig. 10 Motel rooms — exterior entrance.

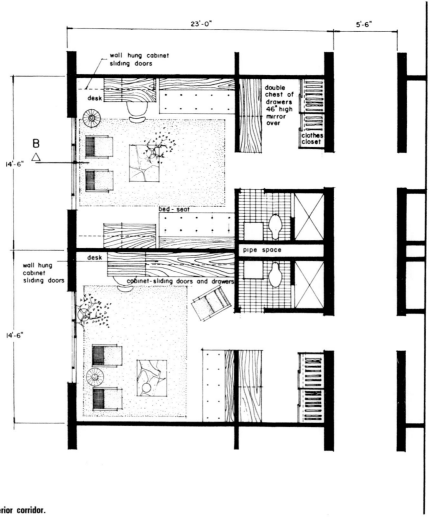

Fig. 11 Motel rooms — interior corridor.

By FRANK HARRISON RANDOLPH, P.E.
Hotel Planning Consultant and Professor of Hotel Engineering, Cornell University

PRELIMINARY SCHEDULE OF SPACE ALLOTMENTS AND FLOOR ASSIGNMENTS

The following example of applying the statistics to a proposed typical commercial hotel of 100 rooms is presented as a guide. First the general data indicate the over-all characteristics of the hotel. These data are followed by more specific space allotments.

The above schedule shows a preliminary estimate of 59 per cent productive area and 41 per cent nonproductive area, which is a more favorable ratio than is generally realized in practice.

During the preliminary planning stage, it may be decided to allocate the 1,500 sq ft area to the coffee shop, thus eliminating the main dining room and reducing the size of the main kitchen by about 250 sq ft. The banquet-ballroom, together with its three auxiliary rooms, might be omitted or, if demand for these facilities is assured, placed in the basement. The laundry would probably be omitted, although it was placed in the schedule as a possibility.

From the standpoint of efficiency, it might be convenient to have almost all areas on the ground floor. However, to make the ground-floor and basement area approximately equal, those areas designated (B) have been consigned to the basement.

Thus the area of the ground floor including 500 sq ft for stairways and elevators, but omitting the 800 sq ft coffee shop and deducting 250 sq ft from the main kitchen, amounts to 10,590 sq ft. This figure compares satisfactorily with the preliminary over-all estimate of 10,000 sq ft for the ground floor.

The area of the basement including the banquet-ballroom facilities, but omitting the laundry, and allowing 2,500 sq ft for corridors and the like, amounts to 10,440 sq ft. This figure is about the same as the ground-floor area.

The typical floor has 17 guest rooms. Two stairways, the elevator shaft, and maid's closet increase the floor area by an equivalent of 3 guest rooms, making a total area equivalent to 20 rooms per floor. Ten rooms on each side of the corridor and each room with an assumed average frontage of 12 ft gives 120 ft as the approximate length of the typical guest floor. The width is usually about 50 ft. Thus the area of the typical guest floor (120 ft by 50 ft) is 6,000 sq ft, which checks with the estimate previously made under "general data."

The summary of areas is as follows:

6 typical guest floors, each 6,000 sq ft	36,000 sq ft
Ground floor, figured at 10,590 sq ft	10,500 sq ft
Basement, figured at 10,440 sq ft	10,500 sq ft
Total approximate floor area	57,000 sq ft

The floor assignments are designated as follows: basement (B), ground floor (G), and typical guest floor (T).

SPACE ALLOTMENTS AND FLOOR ASSIGNMENTS FOR TYPICAL HOTEL OF 100 ROOMS

General data and approximations

Height of building above ground (ground floor plus 6 typical guest floors)	7 stories
Ground-floor area	10,000 sq ft
Typical guest-floor area	6,000 sq ft
Guest rooms per typical floor,	17 rooms
Stairways on the typical floor,	2 stairways
Elevators (1 guest and 1 service car)	2 elevators

The first four factors listed above are of course all interrelated and must be organized as a compatible group.

	Productive area, sq ft	Nonproductive area, sq ft
Public space		
Lobby and front office		1,100(G)
Lounge		600(G)
Corridors adjoining		200(G)
(total of above, 1,900 sq ft)		
Men's toilet for guests		150(G)
Women's toilet for guests		100(G)
Women's restroom for guests		100(G)
*Coat checkroom		120(G)
*Bellman's checkroom		40(G)

Commercial

HOTELS
Space Allotments

	Productive area, sq ft	Nonproductive area, sq ft
Concession space		
Barber shop	180(B)	
*Valet shop	100(B)	
Subrental space		
3 rented stores, (each 800 sq ft)	2,400(G)	
3 storage rooms (each 200 sq ft)	600(B)	
Food and beverage service space		
Main dining room (90 seats)	1,500(G)	
Main kitchen		1,100(G)
Bake shop		200(G)
?Coffee shop (50 seats)	800(G)	
Bar and cocktail lounge	750(G)	
Private dining rooms (250 + 500 sq ft)	750(G)	
?Banquet-ballroom	1,400(B)	
?Banquet-ballroom foyer		450(B)
?Banquet-ballroom storage		140(B)
?Banquet serving pantry		350(B)
Employees' dining room		220(B)
Steward's storeroom		400(G)
Beverage storerooms		180(B)
*China, glass, and silver storage		300(B)
Receiving room		180(G)
Garbage room		80(G)

	Productive area sq ft	Nonproductive area sq ft
Guest-room space		
102 rooms (each 250 sq ft; including bath, closet and vestibule)	25,500(T)	
Auxiliary space (add 40 per cent of above for corridors, stairs, elevators, maid's closets, walls, and partitions)		10,200(T)
General service space		
Manager's office		140(G)
*Secretary's office		100(G)
Accounting office		150(G)
?*Sales and reservations office		140(G)
*Mimeograph room		40(G)
Linen room		350(B)
?Laundry (700 sq ft; omitted)		
Men's toilet and locker room		360(B)
Women's toilet and locker room		360(B)
Maintenance shops		400(B)
Furniture storage		250(B)
*Records storeroom		250(B)
*General storeroom		200(B)
Boiler room		600(B)
*Water-heater tank space		150(B)
Fuel storage		200(B)
Transformer vault		100(B)
*Refrigeration compressor room		400(B)
*Fan rooms, ventilation equipment		400(B)
Total productive area	33,980 sq ft	
Listed nonproductive area		20,800 sq ft
Add for basement corridors, walls, stairways, and elevators		2,500 sq ft
Add for ground-floor stairways and elevators		500 sq ft
Total nonproductive area		23,800 sq ft
Grand total of areas	57,780 sq ft	

PLANNING EFFICIENCY: MAXIMUM GUESTROOM AREA

In order for the operator to realize profits, the design team must maximize the percentage of floor area devoted to guestrooms and keep to a minimum the amount of circulation and service space (service elevator lobby, linen storage, chutes, and vending). Although esthetic issues cannot be ignored, a simple comparison among alternate plans of the percentage of space allocated to revenue-producing guestrooms leads to the selection of more efficient solutions (see accompanying table on page 994).

Analyses of scores of different tower plans show that some configurations yield more efficient solutions than other types. The choice of one configuration over another can mean a saving of 20 percent in gross area of the guest room tower and of nearly 15 percent in the total building. For example, the three principal plan alternatives—the double-loaded slab, the rectangular tower, and the atrium—using the same net guestroom dimensions, will vary from 460 to 575 gross square feet (43 to 53 square meters) per room.

The study also indicates the effect of subsequent minor decisions on the efficiency of the plan—standard groupings of pairs of guestrooms, double- or single-loaded circulation, grouping of public and service elevators, and efficient access to end or corner rooms (the most difficult planning problem in certain configurations). Because guestrooms account for such a major part of the total hotel area, the designer should establish a series of quantitative benchmarks for the efficient design of the guestroom floors.

The relative efficiency of typical hotel floors can be compared most directly by calculating the percentage of the total floor area devoted to guestrooms. This varies from below 60 percent in an inefficient atrium plan to more than 75 percent in the most tightly designed double-loaded slab. Clearly, the higher this percentage the more options are available to the developer and the architect: Additional guestrooms can be built; larger rooms can be provided for the same capital investment; the quality of the furnishings or of particular building systems can be improved; other functional areas of the hotel can be enlarged; or the total construction and project cost can be substantially reduced.

The following sections contain a description, for each of the basic guestroom configurations, of the planning decisions that have the most influence on creating an economical plan. In some plans, it is the number of rooms per floor, in others it is the location of the elevator core, whereas in others the shape of the building is most critical. In general, the most efficient configurations are those where circulation space is kept to a minimum, that is, in structures with either double-loaded corridors or compact center-core towers.

Guestroom Floor Planning Objectives

Orientation/Siting

☐ Consider solar gain; generally N/S preferable to E/W exposures.
☐ Analyze wind loading.
☐ Study the potential for guestroom views.
☐ Site the structure to be visible from the road.
☐ Assess the relative visual impact and construction cost of various guestroom plan configurations.

Floor Layout

☐ Organize plan so that guestrooms occupy at least 70 percent of gross floor area.
☐ Locate elevators and stairs at interior locations rather than on exterior wall.

☐ Develop corridor plan to facilitate guest circulation.
☐ Provide elevator lobby in middle third of structure.
☐ Locate vending near public elevators.
☐ Provide service elevator, linen storage, and chutes in central location.
☐ Plan corridor width at 5′ (1.5 m) minimum, 5′6″ (1.6 m) preferred.
☐ Plan guestroom distance to exit stairs at 150 ft maximum (if fully sprinklered) or as directed by local code.
☐ Design guestrooms back to back for plumbing economies.
☐ Locate handicapped guestrooms on lower floors and near elevators.

The design of the guestroom floors, which often represents three-quarters or more of the total hotel, is critical to the efficiency of any project. Planning objectives, which help the architect assess the relative success of any particular design concept, include the points in the checklist.

SLAB PLANS

The "slab" configuration includes those plans that are primarily horizontal, including both single- and double-loaded corridor schemes (see accompanying plans). The planning variables are few; they are concerned primarily with the shape (straight or L-shaped), the layout of the core, and the location of the fire stairs. The architect must answer the following questions:

☐ Corridor loading: Given site conditions, are any single-loaded rooms appropriate?
☐ Shape: Which particular shape (straight, "offset," L, "knuckle," courtyard, or other configurations) best meets site and building constraints?
☐ Core location: Should the public and the service cores be combined or separated and where in the tower should they be positioned?
☐ Core layout: What is the best way to organize public and service elevators, linen storage, chutes, and vending?
☐ Stair location: Where should the fire stairs be located?

The high degree of efficiency of the slab plan is based primarily on the double loading of the corridors; single-loaded schemes require 4 to 6 percent more floor area for the same number of rooms. For example, only where external factors, a narrow site dimension, or spectacular views suggest single-loading should it be considered.

While slab plans as a category are the most efficient, experienced hotel architects and management company staff have found approaches to further tighten plan layouts. Configurations that bury the elevator and service cores in interior corners have several advantages. They slightly reduce the non-guestroom area, substantially reduce the amount of building perimeter, and increase the opportunities for creating architecturally interesting buildings. The "offset slab" plan, for example, is especially economical because the public and service cores are combined and, in addition, because no guestrooms are displaced from the building perimeter. The "knuckle" configuration, which bends at angles, creates interestingly shaped elevator lobbies, provides compact service areas, and breaks up the slab's long corridors. The core design is complicated by the need to connect the public elevators to the lobby and the service elevators to the housekeeping and other back-of-house areas. This often necessitates two distinct core areas at some distance from each other, although in many hotels they are located together. One common objective is to position the

elevator in the middle third of a floor so as to limit walking distances. Rather than integrate the vertical circulation into the body of the tower, the designer may, for planning reasons, add the core to the end of a compact room block or extend it out from the face of the tower facade.

The actual layout of the core is another determinant of efficiency in the typical plan. In most slab-plan hotels, the vertical cores require space equivalent to two to four structural bays. Usually, the area can be kept to a minimum; certainly fewer guestroom bays are displaced if service areas are located behind the public elevators, rather than beside them or at some distance. Clearly, the efficiency of the plan is improved when the core displaces the fewest number of guestroom units.

Surprisingly, the addition of a distinct elevator lobby is often found in the more efficient layouts. As well as creating an attractive foyer space and isolating the noise and congestion of waiting people from the guestrooms, plans with an elevator lobby tend to have many fewer awkwardly shaped and designed rooms. Thus, efficiency in the core layout comes down to the successful integration of public elevators, service elevators, linen storage, chutes, and vending into a compact vertical core.

The most frequent solutions to the placement of the fire stairs are to locate them at both ends of the corridor, as part of the elevator cores, or within the usual bathroom zone of certain rooms, thereby reducing the guestroom size. These rooms, then, require especially careful planning or are combined with others to form suites. Combining the stairs with one or both of the elevator cores often results in a more efficient overall plan than adding them to the ends of the building.

One limiting factor to the number of rooms on the guestroom floor is the typical building code requirement that there be no more than, say, 200 feet (61 meters) between stair exits. Therefore, one goal in planning the repetitive guestroom floor is to create a layout that does not require a third fire stair. Experienced hotel architects have evolved techniques for lengthening the slab, adding rooms, and manipulating the stairs and corridors to increase the building's overall efficiency.

TOWER PLANS

A second major category of guestroom floor plans are the vertically oriented towers, which are generally organized with a central core surrounded entirely by a corridor and guestrooms (see accompanying plans). The exterior architectural treatment of the tower can vary widely as the geometric shape of the plan changes from square to cross-shaped, circular to triangular. The planning considerations for towers raise similar questions for the designer:

☐ Number of rooms: How many guestrooms economically fit a particular layout?
☐ Shape: Which shape is most efficient and permits the desired mix of rooms?
☐ Corridor: How is hallway access to corner rooms arranged?
☐ Core layout: How are the elevators, linen storage, and stairs organized?

Unlike the other plan configurations, selection of the tower shape creates specific limitations on the number of rooms per floor. For the most part, towers contain between 16 and 24 rooms, depending on the guestroom dimensions, the number of floors, and the optimum core size. With 16 rooms, the core is barely large enough for two or three elevators, fire stairs, and minimum storage; on the other hand, designs with more than 24 rooms are so large at the perimeter that they contain too much central core area to be efficient.

Commercial

HOTELS
Guestroom Floor

Guestroom floor analysis

TOWER CONFIGURATION	ROOMS/FLOOR	DIMENSIONS, FT (M)	GUESTROOM (%)	CORRIDOR, SQ FT (SQ M)	PERIMETER × ROOM WIDTH	COMMENTS
Single-loaded slab	Varies 12–30+	32 × any length (10)	65	80 (7.5)	2.2–2.4	Some economy in that vertical core can be absolute minimum—not affected by room bays.
Double-loaded slab	Varies 16–40+	60 × any length (18)	70	45 (4.2)	1.6–1.8	200 ft (61 m) plus dead-end corridor for two stair scheme; can be turned into L or T.
Offset slab	Varies 24–40+	80 × any length (24)	72	50 (4.6)	1.4–1.6	Core is buried, creating lower perimeter factor; higher corridor because of elevator lobby; also other shapes.
Rectangular tower	16–24	110 × 110 (34 × 34)	65	60 (5.6)	1.5–1.7	Planning problems focus on access to corner rooms; fewer rooms/floor make it difficult to plan core.
Circular tower	16–24	90–130 diameter (27–40)	67	45–65 (4.2–6)	1.05	Smaller diameter for 16 rooms per floor; larger for 24 rooms; corridor area varies tremendously; perimeter of 16–19 ft (4.9–5.8 m)
Triangular tower	24–30	Varies	64	65–85	1.4–1.8	Central core inefficient because of triangular shape; corner rooms easier to plan than with square shape.
Atrium	24+	90+ (27)	62	95 (8.8)	1.6–1.8	Open volume creates spectacular space, open corridor balconies, opportunity for glass elevators; requires careful engineering for HVAC, especially smoke evacuation; can be shaped into irregular configurations.

Each guestroom floor configuration has certain characteristics which affect its potential planning efficiency. The table shows the basic building dimensions, the usual percentage of floor area devoted to guestrooms, the amount of area per room needed for corridors, and a "perimeter factor," a multiple of the room width required for the exterior wall. For example, the table shows that double-loaded slabs (and the "offset slab" modification) are the most efficient in terms of guestroom area percentage and that the atrium plans are the least economical in providing guestroom space.

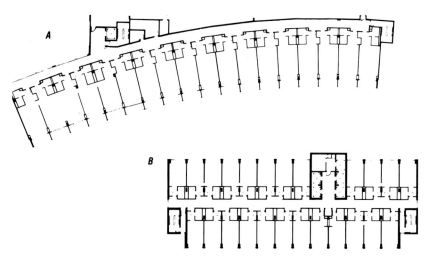

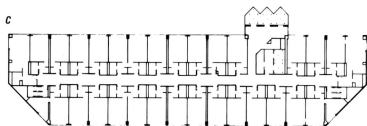

SLAB CONFIGURATIONS

A. SINGLE-LOADED PLAN (Alameda Plaza Hotel, Kansas City, MO): Plan represents typical single-loaded design with elevators and stairs unrelated to guestroom structure.

B. DOUBLE-LOADED PLAN (Sheraton Hartford, Hartford, CT): Layout illustrates economical elevator core with service area "behind" the public elevators.

C. DOUBLE-LOADED PLAN (Hyatt Regency Flint, Flint, MI): Design features elevators pulled out of the tower; stairs in bathroom zone at suite.

D. DOUBLE-LOADED OFFSET SLAB (Westin Hotel, Tulsa, OK): The core, equivalent of three guestrooms, is positioned in center of offset; stairs accommodated by extending end rooms.

E. DOUBLE-LOADED L SLAB (Boston Marriott Hotel/Copley Place, Boston, MA): Layout includes elevators buried at corner of L shape creating economies similar to offset arrangement.

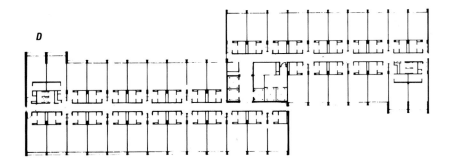

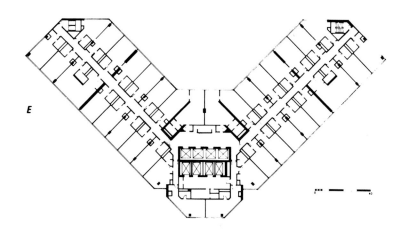

In most building configurations, efficiency is improved by adding rooms to a floor in which the core and services are only minimally enlarged, if at all, to support them. With the tower configuration, the opposite is true. The analysis of a large sample of actual hotel designs shows that, surprisingly, the *fewer* the number of rooms per floor, the more efficient the layout becomes because the core by necessity must be extremely compact and, as a result, the amount of corridor area is kept to a bare minimum. Inefficient layouts often result from *adding* rooms and by extending single-loaded corridors into each of the building corners.

The shape of the tower has a direct effect on the appearance of the structure and on its perceived scale. The efficiency of the plan, also, is a direct result of the shape because of the critical nature of the corridor access to the corner rooms in the rectangular towers and because of the design of the wedge-shaped guestroom and bathroom in the circular towers. Those plans, which minimize the amount of circulation and, in addition, create unusual corner rooms, exemplify the best in both architectural planning and interior layout.

For the circular towers, the measures of efficiency are judged by the layout of the room as well as the core design. Typically, the perimeter of the wedge-shaped guestrooms is about 16 feet (4.9 meters), whereas the corridor dimension may be less than 8 feet (2.4 meters), thus challenging the designer's skill to plan bathroom, entry vestibule, and closet.

While the design of the core in both rectangular and circular towers is less critical than the arrangement of guestrooms, certain specific issues have to be resolved. Generally, the core is centrally located, and the vertical elements are tightly grouped. The smaller hotels, those with only 16 rooms per floor, generally do not feature an elevator lobby, and the guests in rooms opposite the elevators must tolerate noise from wait-

ing guests. In a few cases, the core is split into two parts, creating roughly an H-shaped circulation zone, effectively providing an elevator lobby. The two fire stairs can be efficiently arranged in a scissors configuration to conserve space.

In the larger tower plans with 24 rooms per floor, inefficiently arranged guestrooms often create excessively large central cores. Simply, the space within the corridor may be larger than is needed for the elevators, stairs, and service areas. Some hotels have "skylobbies" to make this wasted space appear to be a positive feature, or they add conference rooms on every guest floor. Unfortunately, these solutions only show up the problems resulting from poorly conceived and designed guestroom planning. The efficient design of hotel towers requires the simultaneous study of the core layout and of the ring of guestrooms around it, with attempts to compress both as much as possible.

ATRIUM PLANS

A third major category of guestroom floor plans is the atrium design, which was reintroduced by architect John Portman for the Hyatt Regency Atlanta hotel in 1967. The atrium prototype had been used in the past century in both Denver's Brown Palace, still in operation, and San Francisco's Palace, destroyed in the 1906 earthquake and fire. The true atrium configuration has the guestrooms arranged along single-loaded corridors, much like open balconies overlooking the lobby space. The following issues must be addressed by the architect:

☐ Shape: What configuration is to be used for the guestroom structure?

☐ Public elevators: How are scenic or standard elevators to be arranged?

☐ Service core and stairs: Where are they to be located?

In addition to the open lobby volume, each atrium hotel is distinguished by the plan of the guestroom floors. While the basic prototype is the square plan with scenic passenger elevators that provide the guest with an ever-changing perspective of the lobby activity as the elevator moves to the upper floors, many of the most recent atrium designs are irregularly shaped to respond to varying site constraints. This sculpting of the building contributes to creating a unique image for the hotel, a primary goal of most developers and architects who select the atrium configuration and who accept the fact that, because of the single-loaded corridors, it is by far the least efficient of the plan types.

Practically all atrium hotels feature scenic or glass elevators, which provide views of the lobby as well as add animation to the space itself. Often these are located on an additional bridge or platform, thereby increasing the amount of circulation on each floor. In some cases, scenic elevators are placed opposite conventional ones, creating the anomaly of two very different experiences.

Service elevators, the housekeeping support functions, and the exit stairs are generally located at both ends of the wings and have relatively little effect on the efficiency of the overall plan. At a practically unfeasible 60 percent usable guestroom space, architects have sought ways to gain the prestige benefits of the atrium while increasing its efficiency. One technique that has been successful in several hotels is to combine an atrium space with double-loaded wings. This effectively and appropriately draws together the architectural excitement of the atrium space—usually on a smaller and more personal scale than in the larger atrium volumes—with the necessary economies of the double-loaded plan.

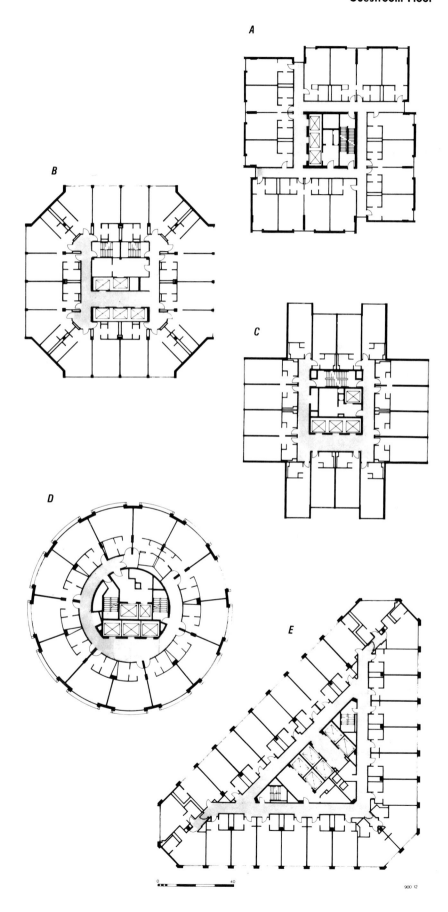

TOWER PLANS

A. PINWHEEL PLAN (Berkshire Common, Pittsfield, MA): Plan illustrates simple arrangement of 16 rooms in 4 equivalent blocks; the core is extremely efficient with scissor stair, but corridors extended to corners are excessive.

B. SQUARE PLAN, H CORRIDOR (Noble Inn, Tampa, FL): Design features extremely economical circulation and core; all bathrooms back to back; unusual yet easily furnished corner rooms.

C. CROSS-SHAPED PLAN (Holiday Inn, Ontario, Canada): Layout exemplifies economical corridor plan but increased building perimeter.

D. CIRCULAR TOWER (Westin, Seattle, WA): Arrangement shows efficient plan with very compact core and well-laid-out guest bathrooms.

E. TRIANGULAR TOWER (New Otani, Los Angeles, CA): Design illustrates well-organized and well-configured core with good access to the ends of the tower.

FURNISHINGS

The definition of the market determines not only the most appropriate bed combinations but also all the other furnishings for a particular hotel. Generally, hotels include a mixture of rooms with two beds (generally double beds), one oversized bed (either a queen or king), and suites of various types. The more common alternatives are listed in Table 2. While it is uncommon in the United States to have hotel guestrooms furnished with single, twin, or only one double bed, some hotels recently have introduced oversized twin beds in place of two double beds, primarily in convention hotels, in order to provide a more residential atmosphere and to allow more room for other furnishings.

The selection of a proper room mix is important because it influences the hotel's ability to rent 100 percent of its rooms and to generate the maximum revenue. For this reason, rooms with great flexibility, king-size bed plus a convertible sofa, for example, are increasingly popular. Typical room mix percentages for different types of hotel are provided in Table 3.

The full list of furnishings can be determined by analyzing the guestroom functions—sleeping, relaxing, working, entertaining, dressing—and their space requirements. The typical double-double room has several zones: The bathroom and areas for dressing and clothes storage are grouped next to the corridor entrance; the sleeping area is in the center of the guestroom module; and the seating and work areas are located near the window. New layouts combine the several functions in different ways or find techniques for separating them more fully. For example, suite characteristics are provided in a standard room by adding a screen to separate the sleeping and sitting portions of the space. Or a compartmentalized bathroom is created by isolating the bath and toilet area from the sink and dressing function. Such guestroom zones are shown in the illustration on p. 999.

With the continuing increase in construction and furnishing costs, it becomes more important to find new solutions to the guestroom layout, that is, designs which combine function and comfort within realistic budgets. One basic approach is to use fewer individual pieces of furniture or to scale them slightly smaller so as to give the perception of a larger or more luxurious room. The designer might include the following:

☐ Queen or 72-inch (1.8-meter) king-size bed: Beds smaller than the 78-inch (2-meter) king create more open space.
☐ Convertible sofa or wall-bed: These provide more open space and flexibility, either as the second bed with a double, queen, or king, or as the only bed in a parlor.
☐ Adequate luggage/clothes space: Sufficient drawers, luggage rack, and closet space reduce the clutter of clothes throughout the room.
☐ Armoire: Combining drawer space with a television cabinet and possibly a pullout writing ledge in a single unit eliminates the need for two or three separate pieces.
☐ Lounge/desk chairs: Lounge chairs designed to be used at the work surface eliminate the straight desk chair.
☐ Mirrors: They enlarge the space visually.
☐ Wall-mounted bedside lamps: These permit a smaller night table.
☐ Bathroom: Designs should expand the countertop, mirror, and lighting as much as possible and compartmentalize the tub and/or toilet.

TABLE 1 Hotel Guest Characteristics*

	Guest characteristics	Purpose for travel	Guestroom design factors
		Business	
Group	Single or double occupancy; 2–4 night stay; 75% men, 25% women (rising); somewhat price insensitive.	Conventions, conferences; professional associations; sales and training meetings.	King, twin, double-double; bath with dressing area; lounge seating with good work area.
Individual	Single occupancy; 1–2 night stay; 85% men, 15% women; very price insensitive.	Corporate business; sales; conventions, conferences.	King; standard bath with shower; lounge area with exceptional work area.
		Pleasure	
Family	Double-plus occupancy (includes children); 1–4 night stay, longer in resort areas; budget or midprice.	Family vacations; sightseeing; sports, family activity.	Double-double, king sofa, or adjoining rooms; lounge area and television; generous, compartmentalized bath; balcony, deck, outside access.
Couples	Double occupancy; 1–7 night stay; midprice to upscale.	Tours, clubs, associations; sightseeing; theater, sports; weekend packages; shopping, vacation.	King; dining, work surface; moderate storage; compartmentalized bath.
Singles	Single occupancy; young professionals; midprice to upscale.	Tours, clubs, associations; culture, arts, theater; shopping.	Queen; dining, work surface; standard bath.

*Guestroom design must reflect the needs of the lodger. Commercial hotels, for example, have a high rate of single occupancy and, therefore, need few rooms with two double beds. For the same reasons, they do need better designed and larger work surfaces for the businessperson and full hotel services. The table identifies the principal hotel guest markets, their characteristics, and their influence on the room design.

TABLE 2 Guestroom Bed Types†

Type	Size
Twin	2 twin beds 39×80 in. (1×2 m)
*Double-double	2 double beds 54×80 in. (1.35×2 m)
Queen	1 queen bed 60×80 in. (1.5×2 m)
*King	1 king bed 78×80 in. (2×2 m)
California king	1 king bed 72×80 in. (1.8×2 m)
Oversized twin	2 twin beds 45×80 in. (1.5×2 m)
Queen-queen	2 queen beds
Double-studio	1 double bed and convertible sofa
Queen-studio	1 queen bed and convertible sofa
*King-studio	1 king bed and convertible sofa
*Parlor	1 convertible sofa
Wall bed (Sico room)	1 wall bed

†*Guestroom bed types:* Bedrooms come in a great variety of arrangements, generally defined by the type of beds and by the number of room bays. The table provides a comprehensive listing of hotel guestroom types (the more common being identified with an *) and standard bed sizes.

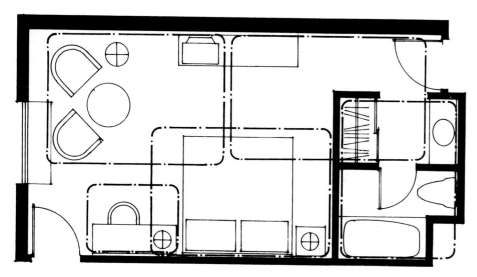

Guestroom Activity Zones. *The hotel guestroom accommodates one to four or more people, sometimes with several activities occurring at one time (for example, bathing and dressing or sleeping and watching TV). The designer needs to be alert to techniques for separating some while combining others, in both cases increasing the flexibility and adaptability of the room to different users. The plan illustrates five guestroom zones.*

TABLE 3 Guestroom Mix for Different Hotel Types*

Type of hotel	Percent of total guestrooms				Comments
	Double-double	King	King-studio	Parlor	
Budget Inn	100	0	0	0	
Motor Inn	60	28	10	2	Trend away from all double-double
Conference center	40	40	15	5	Single occupancy, except needs couples' weekend business
All-suite	10	90	0	100	All rooms connect with a parlor
Super-luxury	20	70	0	10	Double-double replaced with oversize twins
Commercial	20	60	10	10	Limited double occupancy
Resort/family	80	8	10	2	Provide room for cots
Resort/couples	20	70	5	5	
Convention	55	35	5	5	Trend toward replacing double-double with oversize twin
Mega-hotel	55	35	5	5	Double-double provides greatest flexibility for family/group business markets
Casino hotel	40	50	0	10	Depends on strength of tour markets

Guestroom mix for different hotel types: Hotel operators have established guidelines for furnishing guestrooms based on the history of the types of guests who stay at a particular type of hotel or resort. This table establishes the room mix objectives for particular types and classes of hotels.

Several details in the room arrangement and furnishing do not have any "best" solution. For example, many operators insist that the telephone should be located next to the beds, whereas others prefer that it be placed at the work area. Similarly, some prefer that the drapes be laminated and combined in a single unit to reduce the number of drapery tracks, whereas others insist on separate sheer, blackout, and overdrape to allow easy cleaning and maintenance. Throughout the room, the designer must balance the conflicting needs of function, safety, maintenance, comfort, and budget and, at the same time, must consider the varying requirements of the several different markets that a single hotel tries to attract.

DIMENSIONS

The guestroom design decision which most influences the rest of the hotel plan is the selection of the room's net width. This establishes the structural module throughout the building, including the public and service areas on the lower floors. The most common dimension is 12 feet (3.7 meters), initially used in the mid 1950s by the Holiday Inn chain as a standard for all their properties. It was designed to accommodate the furniture needed in the roadside motor inn: two double beds against one wall and a desk/luggage rack/ TV stand against the opposite wall, with adequate aisle space between. While the room has undergone some minor changes in the last quarter-century, the industry's standard room today is

essentially the same one pioneered by founder Kemmon Wilson's Holiday Inns and immediately adopted by Howard Johnson and other companies.

Until then, even the newest and best convention hotels built in the post-World War II period included a variety of room sizes, including a large percentage that were narrower than this 12-foot standard. These hotels, many of them still operating and competing with properties 30 years newer, are greatly limited by the smallness of their guestrooms. In the United States and Canada, no first class or chain-affiliated hotels (except for the budget inns) are built today with rooms less than 12 feet wide, unless, as in the case of renovations of older hotels, the size of a few rooms is limited by unavoidable architectural constraints.

In the past few years guestroom dimensions have become fairly well standardized for different quality levels within the industry (see table below). While a few hotel operators have tried to provide noticeably larger rooms than their direct competitors, guestroom size, quality, and room rate remain closely linked because of the overriding influence of construction and furnishing costs.

The guestroom layouts on pages 1001–1002 illustrate the standard room design alternatives as well as a number of more innovative solutions. The budget chains have slightly reduced the 12' $\times$ 18' (3.7 $\times$ 5.5 m) motor inn room to lower construction costs, shortening it to between 14 and 16 feet (4.3 to 4.9 meters), which is sufficient to accommodate two double beds. On the other hand, operators who are selling a more luxurious

room have experimented with larger guestroom spaces, including more sumptuous bathrooms. Increasing the width of the room module to 13 or 13.5 feet (4 to 4.1 meters) permits one major change in the room layout: two twin beds, or a queen or king-size bed can be positioned against the bathroom wall instead of the side wall, permitting many other arrangements of the furnishings. For example, several designers have placed the bed diagonally instead of against a full wall.

Generally, there is little advantage to increasing the guestroom width beyond 13.5 feet. Even this slightly larger space does not provide improved arrangements, and construction costs are increased dramatically by the increased circulation space and exterior wall area. However, at a room width of 16 feet or more a new set of design alternatives arises: the bed or beds can be positioned against one side wall and the lounge and work area against the opposite wall. Also, the greater width permits unusually luxurious bathroom arrangements, often with four or five fixtures, as well as larger entry vestibules.

The wedge-shaped rooms characteristic of circular towers present their own design problem in the layout of the guest bathroom. The smaller towers have a corridor frontage of only 6 to 8 feet (1.8 to 2.4 meters), the larger plans a more reasonable 10' feet (3 meters). Although many of these room plans show such positive features as compartmentalized bathrooms (out of necessity), minimum foyer space, a large lounge area, and expansive window wall, today's increasing competition in room size and upscale furnishings has made the smaller cylindrical towers virtually obsolete.

TABLE 4 Guestroom Dimensions

	Living area*		Bathroom		Total guestroom	
	Dimensions, feet (meters)	Area	Dimensions, feet (meters)	Area	Dimensions, feet (meters)	Area
Budget	11'6" $\times$ 15' (3.5 $\times$ 4.5)	172 (16)	5' $\times$ 5' (1.5 $\times$ 1.5)	25† (2.3)	11'6" $\times$ 20'6" (3.5 $\times$ 6.2)	236 (21.9)
Midprice	12' $\times$ 18' (3.6 $\times$ 5.5)	216 (20.1)	5' $\times$ 7'6" (1.5 $\times$ 2.3)	37 (3.4)	12' $\times$ 26' (3.6 $\times$ 6.6)	312 (29)
First class	13'6" $\times$ 19' (4.1 $\times$ 5.8)	256 (23.8)	5'6" $\times$ 8'6" (1.7 $\times$ 2.6)	47 (4.4)	13'6" $\times$ 28'6" (4.1 $\times$ 8.6)	378 (35.2)
Luxury	15' $\times$ 20' (4.5 $\times$ 6.1)	300 (27.9)	7'6" $\times$ 9' (2.3 $\times$ 2.7)	71 (6.6)	15' $\times$ 30' (4.5 $\times$ 9.1)	450 (41.8)

*Living area does not include the bathroom, closet, or entry.
†Bathroom of budget guestroom includes tub/shower and toilet; sink is part of dressing area.

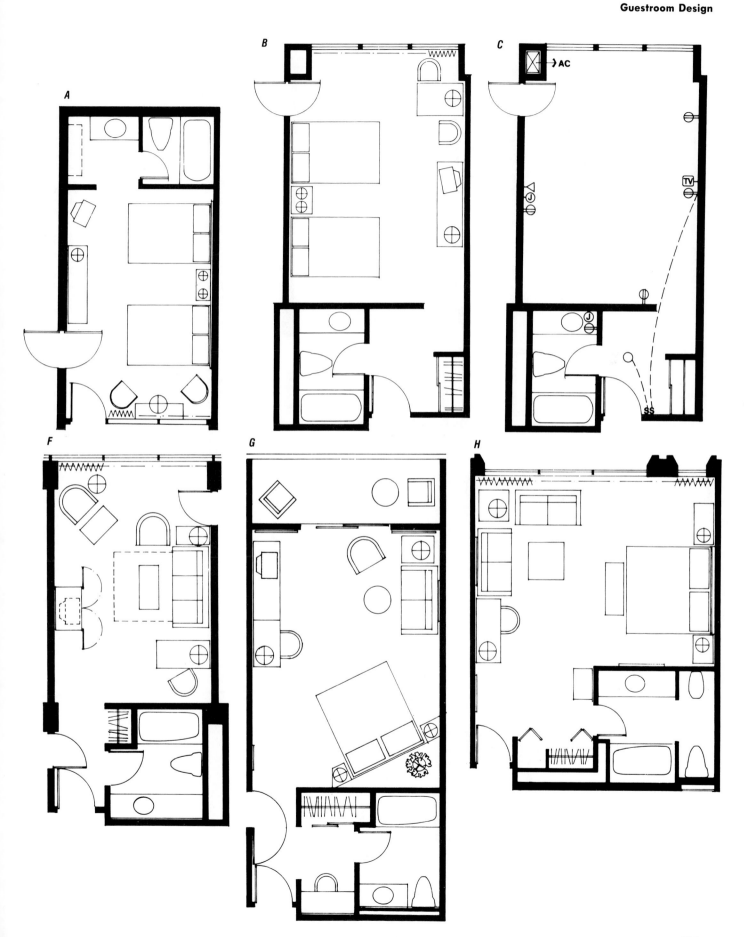

Commercial

HOTELS
Guestroom Design

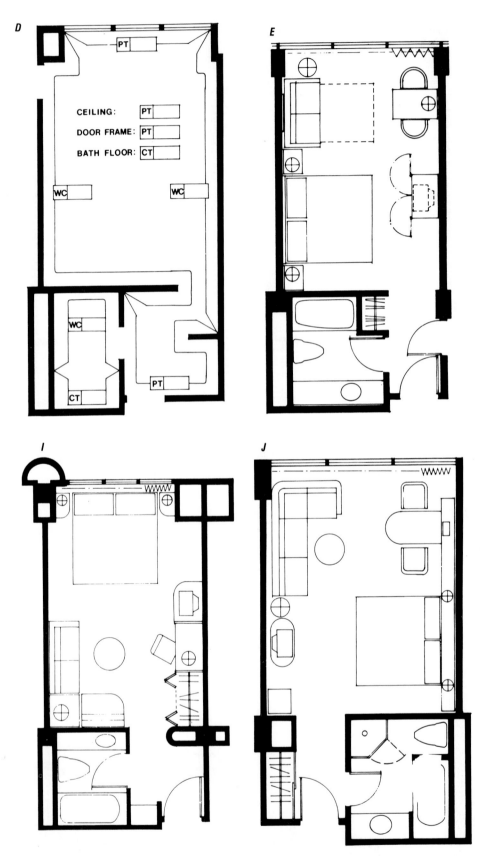

Guestroom Plans. The room layouts illustrate a variety of solutions to accommodating the family and business markets in hotels, ranging from budget to convention and luxury types. The larger rooms generally provide better lounge and work areas and oversized bathrooms.

A. Budget inn double-double (Day's Inn): Small room layout with outside rather than corridor access; limited seating (AC unit used for end table); sink and hanging clothesrod in dressing area.

B. Typical double-double: Standard motor inn and hotel room; beds take up 70 percent of living area; limited seating space.

C. Typical double-double—electrical/mechanical plan: Identify all electrical outlets, TV, phone, HVAC units; outlets and cable connections should be planned around proposed furnishings.

D. Typical double-double—finishes plan: Vinyl wallcovering (VWC), paint (P), carpet (C), ceramic tile (CT) identified and keyed to legend.

E. King-studio (Holiday Inn): Standard layout with armoire unit and large lounge area including a convertible sofa.

F. Parlor (Holiday Inn): Convertible sofa and small conference area and adjoining typical king and double-double rooms.

G. King room—diagonal bed placement (Sheraton Plaza, Palm Springs): Resort layout, larger room size, with bed splayed to reduce institutional look.

H. Luxury room (Four Seasons, Montreal, Canada): Room with wider window dimension than depth including luxurious lounge group and oversized four-fixture bath.

I. Reversed layout (Sheraton, Washington, D.C.): Unusual room with bed placed in front of window and lounge area near bathroom.

J. Luxury king room (Sheraton Grande, Los Angeles): Oversized room with shelf/ledge in place of headboard, large desk surface and lounge area; four-fixture bathroom.

SUITES

One principal way that a hotel can provide different qualities of accommodations is to include a number of guestroom suites in the room mix. A suite is defined simply as a living room connected to one or more bedrooms. Larger hotels frequently provide a hierarchy of suites, from single-bay living rooms with a sleeping alcove to multiple-bay living rooms with perhaps six adjoining rooms, including dining/conference rooms and several bedrooms. A typical suite breakdown is shown in Table 5.

Hotel suites, which make up about 10 percent of the total guestrooms, are usually positioned on the upper floors of the tower, but they may be stacked vertically where unusual conditions occur. For example, suites may be used to fill larger structural bays of the typical floor, with mini-suites tucked behind stairs or elevators and others located where the building form provides uniquely shaped rooms.

Over the last 10 years, several new amenities have been added to hotel suites. One of these is the inclusion of express checkin and concierge services on the upper floors. In some hotels, these services occur in a single room near the elevator lobby, where the staff serves light hors d'oeuvres, sells beverages, and makes newspapers available. In other hotels, this service has been expanded so that guests on the club floors or towers section bypass the busy lobby registration area and check in at the club floor. The more extensive of these tower club lounges may extend over several bays and contain space for the concierge/registration service, an office, a small seating/television lounge, a conference room, and a large lounge used for continental breakfast, afternoon tea, and cocktails.

TABLE 5 Different Types of Suites

Suite type	Living room	Bedrooms	Keys	Bays	Percent
Mini-suite	One bay	Alcove	1	1.5	2*
Conference suite	One bay	1	2	2	3
Junior suite	One bay	2	3	3	4
Executive suite	Two bays	2	3	4	1
Deluxe suite	Three bays	2	2	5	0.5

*Percentage of total rooms, that is, two mini-suites per 100 rooms.

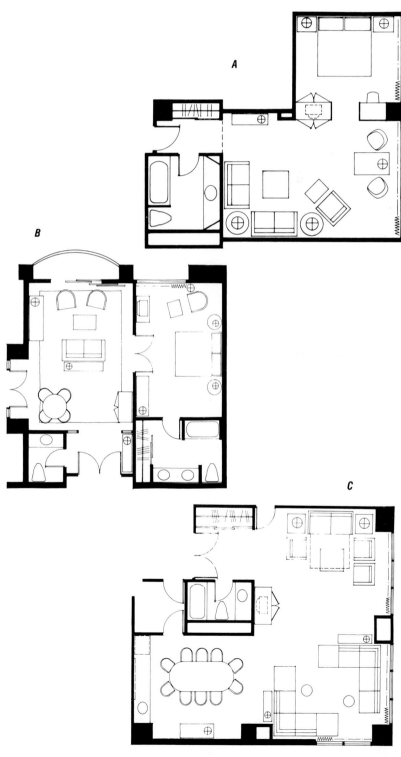

Suite Plans. *Hotel suites combine separate living and sleeping areas and are generally furnished with upgraded fabrics and casepieces. The largest suites may extend for 10 or more structural bays and combine numerous bedrooms and living areas. A range of suites includes: (A) The mini-suite, containing a single bay living room plus a king bed alcove—created by adjacent stairs or elevators. The divider between the two rooms houses the TV and a built-in dressing table.*

(B) The junior suite (Westlake Plaza, Westlake, CA) is equal to the area of two typical rooms. The living area, on an area rug over parquet floors, includes seating and dining areas, while the bedroom features a luxurious compartmentalized bathroom.

(C) Hospitality suites are intended for large groups, such as at conventions where they are the focus of corporate entertaining. The suites show two distinct lounge areas in addition to the conference/dining area with its own pantry; one or more bedrooms generally interconnect.

Commercial
MOTELS

By FRANK HARRISON RANDOLPH, *P.E.*

Hotel Planning Consultant and Professor of Hotel Engineering, Cornell University

A motel can be defined as any type of sleeping accommodation designed and operated especially for the traveler who travels by car. It may be the most primitive structure, or a virtual palace. It may be called a cabin, a court, a lodge, an inn—or simply a motel.

Growth of the motel business

Since their crude beginning in the 1920's, motels have had a phenomenal growth, paralleling that of the automobile and the highway. Long characterized by small units located on the open highway, motels are now growing larger and moving into the fringes—and even the downtown areas—of large cities. The average size, which was only 15 rooms in 1952, had by 1959 increased to 35 rooms; motels with 100 or more rooms are not uncommon since large corporations have entered the field. Motels are now considered part of the hotel business. Many of the larger motels provide the same services as hotels, and it has become increasingly difficult to draw a sharp line of demarcation between them.

Essentials for success

The success of every motel is influenced by three factors, all of immediate concern to the designer: (1) Good location, (2) Attractive appearance, and (3) Quick, pleasant, and economical service.

TYPE OF PATRONAGE

There are two main types of motel patronage: transient and terminal. The transient motorist, whether traveling on business or for pleasure, generally has certain predictable preferences. Primarily, he wants ready access to his car and quick service. The terminal guest (who may have been a transient yesterday at another motel) has different preferences because he has reached his destination. He wants pleasing surroundings and recreational facilities.

Some motels are designed primarily for transients; others cater only to the terminal guest. Still others must be planned for both types.

Commercial hotels normally derive at least 85 per cent of their room sales from persons traveling on business. The city motel, in the absence of conflicting data, should expect about the same. As a typical example, a 40-room motor court, although 2 miles from the center of a good-sized city, found that business men supplied 85 per cent of its annual business.

And it was a popular motel—its average of 80 per cent room occupancy for the year was nearly 10 per cent above the national average.

Business travel is much greater in volume than vacation or pleasure travel. The volume of business travel is, moreover, fairly constant throughout the year: only 25 per cent more business travel takes place in summer and fall than in winter and spring.

Vacation travel, however, is two to three times greater in summer than in winter. This extreme fluctuation in the volume of business makes it extremely difficult to operate profitably a motel catering solely to vacationers. Most motels of over 50 rooms need almost 50 per cent occupancy to break even. Thus some motels find it necessary to shut down during the off-season to reduce the loss. Real estate taxes and building depreciation, of course, continue nevertheless.

Vacation trips are taken by over 75 per cent of our adult population, but about 60 per cent of these people do not always go to the same place. The most popular vacation destinations in the United States are Florida, California, New York, and Michigan (in that order). Roughly two-thirds of all vacation travel takes place during the summer, and the average vacation travel period is two weeks.

There is a definite need for more acceptable motels for people in the middle- and low-income groups. A new motel should guard against pricing itself out of the market. The designer should be especially careful that construction costs do not result in prohibitively high rental rates.

FEASIBILITY

Determining the probability of financial success for a project is recommended as the first step in planning. A dependable business forecast, based on local controlling conditions, should be made by a competent concern. This forecast should determine whether there is adequate need for a new motel and should give a general indication of the number of guest rooms and the type and extent of services to be provided. The forecast should be followed by selection of the site, working out of the financial plan, and finally, determination of the functional scheme: the number, types, and sizes of guest rooms, public spaces, and food and beverage facilities, the type of building construction, and the extent of mechanical services. Only after these preliminary steps have been completed is the

project ready to be started on the drawing boards. Otherwise, much time, money, and effort may be lost in developing specific ideas that are impractical and yet difficult to discard.

Basic economic survey

Many factors will require careful study by a qualified financial advisor, such as a firm experienced in hotel and motel accounting. Ever-increasing costs of construction and operation are vital considerations. The rapidly expanding and shifting pattern of major highways should be evaluated for its effect on the site. The possibility of an overabundance of motels in the area must not be overlooked. The soundness of the title to the land may be questionable. The decision of whether to purchase the land, build on leased land, or select a sale-and-lease-back arrangement may well have a considerable effect on taxes.

It will aid greatly in planning to have in advance an idea of the type of traveler expected, the probable length of his stay, and the seasonal fluctuations expected in the volume of business. Such a survey is unquestionably a help in determining the financial feasibility of a project. Seasonal variations may require a break-even point at close to 50 per cent occupancy.

Horwath & Horwath, Hotel Accountants and Consultants, stress the importance of determining (1) the rate of economic growth of the area, (2) the probable future development of the community, and (3) the status of existing or contemplated transient housing and feeding accommodations.

LOCATION

Site location is of paramount importance. Geographically, it should be at the end of a day's run for the motorist in order to attract transient business. The average motorist is not interested in stopping for the night except at the end of his day's run, so the site should be a day's run (or a multiple of this) from one or more reservoirs of potential transient business. The typical motorist covers about 300 miles in a day, plus or minus up to 100 miles, depending upon personal preferences and highway conditions, which need individual analysis for a given area. Obviously the motorist will travel considerably farther in a day on limited-access express highways than on the usual improved routes.

Traffic surveys showing the daily volume are of value only if they indicate the number of potential customers passing the site

1004

during the critical few hours at the end of the day. The total 24-hour volume of trucks, local passenger traffic, and whatever else comes along means very little. A tally of all passenger-car license plates that passed in each direction during the end-of-the-day period, disregarding, if possible, those issued within a radius of about 200 miles, would give the most helpful indication of potential business for the day or days on which the count was taken. It would give no guarantee of volume, however, for another season or for future years.

Major highway routes are constantly changing, both in pattern and in condition. An excellent location today can become almost worthless next year because a new highway has bypassed it, taking virtually all of its long-distance passenger traffic. Or the condition of a long major route might be so greatly improved that, although the motel was formerly a normal day's drive from a potential reservoir of transient business, it would now be reached by most potential customers by midafternoon—at least two hours before their stopping time. Future highway conditions are difficult to forecast, since highway plans are often changed for unpredictable reasons with disastrous consequences for the motel, which may become virtually stranded. Careful checking with all the various planning agencies, especially the State highway department, is a precaution that must not be overlooked. Indeed, selection of the proper site requires the combined judgment of persons in many fields. The State highway department can forecast traffic characteristics. The chamber of commerce is familiar with recent civic development and building and population trends. The real estate broker knows land values. The construction engineer can report on soil conditions, excavation, and drainage, and indicate probable difficulties in building. The architect experienced in motel design will have a wealth of practical advice. The accounting firm that made the economic survey should be satisfied that the site is properly qualified. The finance company or bank that is to loan the necessary funds must be convinced of the apparent soundness of the venture. If a particular site is vetoed by any one of these qualified parties, the success of the enterprise must be considered open to serious question. There is no satisfactory substitute for an excellent location that meets these various criteria.

When the typical motorist, thinking he has travelled long enough for the day, realizes there is some difficult driving a short distance ahead, and then encounters an attractive motel, he will be nicely conditioned to decide to stop for the night. The difficulty may be the heavy traffic of a large city, a winding road over a mountain, or a tedious long stretch of road through barren country—something he would rather postpone until morning. Situating the motel suitably in advance of such an obstacle can be definitely rewarding (Fig. 1).

Some motels successfully intercept the traveler just outside a city where he had thought to find lodging (Fig. 2). If several motels are already grouped along the highway leading into a city, a new motel can be expected to be more successful if it joins the group than if it selects an isolated location. Prospective guests tend to be favorably impressed by a large group of motels, which by its very magnitude suggests abundant hospitality and a popular motel area. Once he stops, the traveler is almost certain to stay at one or another of these places (Fig. 3).

If possible, the motel should be on the right-hand side of the road, especially if traffic is at all heavy, since drivers would rather not make a left turn (Fig. 4). If the highway curves, place the motel on the right of a left-hand curve, so that it will be directly in line with the driver's vision (Fig. 5). If the site selected slopes upward from the highway, the hillside location of the motel will add to its prominence (Fig. 6).

The best motel site is the one with the greatest appeal to the largest number of potential customers. The site should of course be plainly visible from a distance. Highway intersections are often excellent places for motels. Approaching motorists will already have reduced speed and be prepared to stop, and can readily size up the situation before reaching the intersection. The order of preference of several possible site locations at an intersection may be influenced by such factors as the slope of the land and the presence of existing or future buildings (Fig. 7, 8, 9).

If travel is about equal in both directions, the motel should aim for those who are going rather than those returning, because of the opportunity for repeat business. Twenty-five per cent of the guests of some motels are repeat customers.

If a town is bypassed by the main traffic route, the motel may be placed on the right-hand side of the road leading to the town, but should be plainly visible from the main highway (Fig. 10). If two towns are not far apart on the highway, the motel should be placed to intercept the major volume of traffic before it reaches either of them. Putting the motel between the towns generally proves unsatisfactory, since most motorists would not be in the mood for stopping on such an in-between stretch (Fig. 11).

It is important to determine well in advance whether the highway department will permit the desired location. Encroachments, set-back regulations, deceleration lanes, and access drives must all be considered. The highway department may not permit direct access from deceleration or acceleration lanes. Definite approval of specific plans should be obtained from the authorities at a very early stage in the planning.

Advance signs advertising the motel and directing the motorist are essential. Often the authorities have very severe restrictions on the placement of such signs; therefore, sign locations must be assured and permissions obtained before the site may be said to be satisfactory.

TYPE OF MOTEL

Motels can be differentiated by their location and purpose. The most common types are as follows:

1. The *city motel* is built in town or on the edge of town. It is intended primarily for commercial travelers with business in the downtown area. It generally involves expensive land, a restricted site, and a structure at least three stories high. Nearly the entire site is used for buildings and parking.

2. The *motor annex*, a relatively new development, adjoins an existing hotel in the city. Whether the motel emphasizes its connection as an annex will depend on the reputation of the hotel and its advertising, location, services, utilities, supervision, and maintenance staff.

3. The *highway motor hotel* furnishes roomside parking for the traveler en route. This type of motel is usually one or two stories high, with a site of at least three acres. If space permits, not more than 15 per cent of the site area is used for buildings and parking.

4. The *resort motel* is intended primarily for guests who have reached their destination, and usually requires ample facilities for recreation. Closing during the off-season may also be necessary. The site, ideally spacious, can be small if necessary.

5. The *airport inn* is built at a major, usually intercontinental, airport. A relatively large and high-class operation, this type of motel often has 150 to 300 rooms, two-story guest-room buildings, and a site of at least 10 acres. Business is supplied by airline patrons, motorists, and guests from the metropolitan area served by the airport. The size of such a motel permits full-scale food and beverage facilities, function rooms, and often as extensive recreational facilities as are found in resort motels. The location usually borders on the outlying in-

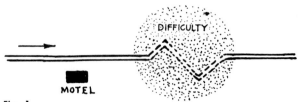
Fig. 1

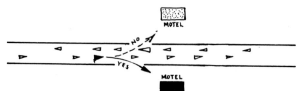
Fig. 2

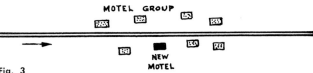
Fig. 3

Fig. 4

Fig. 5

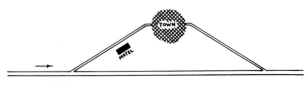
Fig. 6

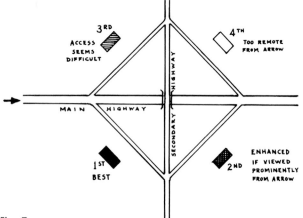
Fig. 7

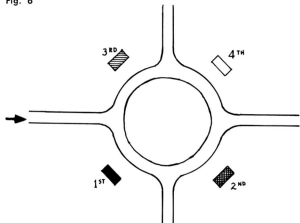
Fig. 8

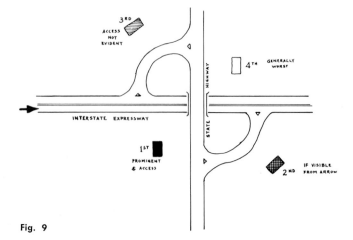
Fig. 9

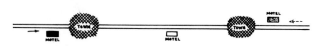
Fig. 10

Fig. 11

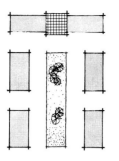

Fig. 12

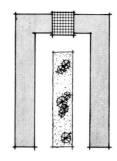

Fig. 13

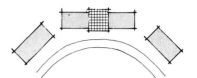

Fig. 14

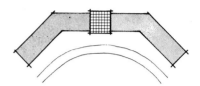

Fig. 15

Fig. 16

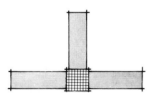

Fig. 17

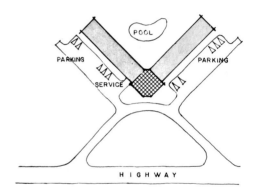

Fig. 18

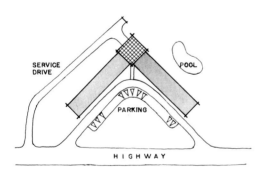

Fig. 19

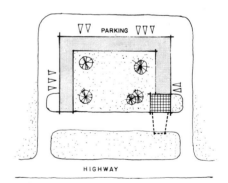

Fig. 20

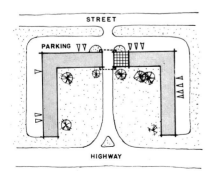

Fig. 21

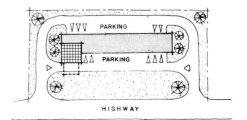

Fig. 22

dustrial area, within easy driving distance of both the suburban residential area and the city.

SITE PLAN

Pertinent factors include the size of the buildings, the area for parking, size of the site, contour of the land, and the extremely important traffic patterns for guests, employees, supplies, and refuse. The ideal arrangement should combine "pull" with privacy—two items that are difficult to attain simultaneously in any site plan. The "pull" or drawing power of an attractive appearance from the highway should be converted to privacy for the guest after arrival. Drawing power is linked with proximity to the highway; privacy is associated with quiet surroundings. Some compromise must be made on the basis of the variety of motel, the type of guest, and the site conditions. One operator may want the motel set far back from the highway; another may want the swimming pool right out in front. The designer must know the preferences of the motel owner and operator in order to produce the results desired.

If the motel is to be located on a high-speed thoroughfare, it should have a frontage of at least 500 ft. The motorist going 60 miles an hour will need about that distance to slow down comfortably in order to turn off the highway.

For a small installation, the guest units may be arranged in a U-shaped pattern, with a lawn area in the center and the guest registration building at the middle of the horizontal portion of the U (Fig. 12). The same arrangement can be modified to provide unbroken construction, with everything under one roof (Fig. 13).

A crescent-shaped arrangement is often quite appealing. The central registration building may be flanked by guest units (Fig. 14). If built as a simple structure, this arrangement usually takes the shape of a half-hexagon (Fig. 15). Or the motel might be designed as a long, straight building, with equal wings extending from the registration office (Fig. 16).

For some sites, a T-shaped structure might be most suitable. With that design, however, the service entrance can be difficult to locate (Fig. 17). The L-shaped layout is deservedly popular. Placing the registration office toward the highway extends an obvious welcome to the motorist. The sight of other cars in the parking area will also be an inducement to the prospective guest. In addition, the garden and pool area will be secluded, so that the guest can escape the noise and confusion of the highway (Fig. 18). Or the position of the L might be reversed, and the ground

areas adjoining the building attractively arranged. The swimming pool, for example, could be placed out in front as an inducement to the traveler (Fig. 19).

If the site is approximately square, and located near or in town, the registration office may best be placed at the tip of one side of a U. This familiar solution is both well-ordered and attractive (Fig. 20). If the site is longer and has access to a rear street parallel to the highway, the U may advantageously be broken by a driveway connecting the streets. The driveway could then be covered at the registration office and access to the parking areas so arranged that control could be exercised by the office over all arrivals and departures (Fig. 21).

A relatively long, narrow site on the edge of town might be developed advantageously by setting the building back from the highway and providing good visibility, roomside parking, and efficient traffic patterns (Fig. 22). If the site were somewhat deeper, the building might be designed as a half-hexagon, with a garden court and recreation area. Whether guests would prefer roomside parking or an adjacent garden court and recreation area depends on such circumstances as the purpose of their visit, length of stay, climatic conditions, and the view from windows not facing the court (Fig. 23).

A large motel in the downtown area may take the form of a hollow rectangle. The example shown in Fig. 24 provides a wide scope of services, including a restaurant, ballroom, shops, room service, year-round swimming pool, and an attractive central garden area. Street-level parking is provided under the guest rooms. A similar pattern is followed in the 68-unit motel shown in Fig. 25. The registration office, gift shop, coffee shop, cocktail lounge, and restaurant are located in the portions of the building nearest the highway. The inner court provides parking space around an island lawn with trees. This arrangement permits good control of cars entering and leaving, brings the cars near the guest rooms, and may thus seem the obvious solution to parking problems. The noise of cars arriving and departing, however, often late at night or early in the morning, will affect all guest rooms facing the court, where the noise is accentuated by reverberation. Also, the headlights of arriving cars will rake the windows facing the court. In northern climates, snow removal can be a difficult problem as well, with the hollow-rectangle arrangement.

The 150-room airport motel shown in Fig. 26 uses the inside of the enclosure for the garden, recreation, and swimming-pool area, with parking facilities around the outside. Business comes from both airline

and motor travelers. Service is comparable to that of large hotels in the city. The circular building contains a dining room and cocktail lounge on the ground floor, and a second floor meeting room.

Individuality is an asset to the motel illustrated in Fig. 27. On a site of moderate area, this motel has a convenient, covered entrance for the motorist and an adjoining circular restaurant building, backed up by an L-shaped, two-story guest section. The outside dining terrace overlooking the lawn and pool is especially inviting with its open, yet secluded atmosphere. Separate parking areas are provided for restaurant patrons and for guests.

A motel may be built on a narrow strip of valuable land between the highway and the ocean, as is frequently done in Florida. The example in Fig. 28 concentrates the three stories of guest rooms (with a double-loaded corridor) perpendicular to the shore line, providing an ocean view from every room. All guest rooms have private balconies. A garage in the semibasement accommodates self-service parking. The single-story lobby, bar, and coffee-shop portion includes a dining terrace that overlooks the circular outdoor dance floor, the pool, and the ocean. The arrangement is open, uncluttered, and inviting.

ROOM GROUPS AND PARKING

Designed for the convenience of the motorist, each room of the motel should have, if possible, at least one window with a desirable view or private outlook on a quiet area (for which landscaping may be required). Bathrooms and clothes closets should be placed along the driveway side of the rooms. The room layout should follow the usual hotel guest-room arrangement, with the central guest corridor replaced by an access driveway. Convenience, privacy, and rooms that are both quiet and cheerful are the objectives. The shape, orientation, dimensions, and topography of the individual site, of course, may necessitate some deviation from the ideal layout.

Ideally, one side of a row of guest units would take full advantage of the view, with the access drive on the opposite side of the row. Bathrooms on the entrance side would have small, high windows to increase privacy and reduce noise, whereas the guest rooms might have large picture windows to capitalize on the view. An extra doorway on the side with the view might be desirable. (See Fig. 29, 31, 32, 34, 36, 40.)

If the strip of land availabe for guest units is narrow, either because of dimensions or topography, the best solution is generally to set the units well back from

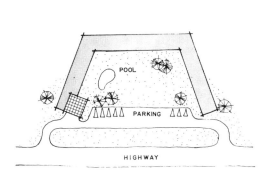

Fig. 23

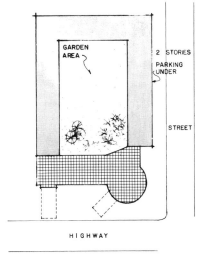

Fig. 24. Manger Motor Inn, Charlotte, N. C.;
Finn-Jenter, Architect

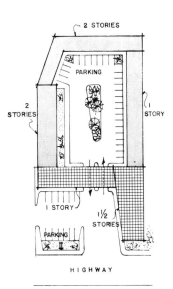

Fig. 25. Travelers Inn, Fairbanks, Alaska;
Edwin Crittenden, Architect

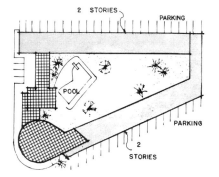

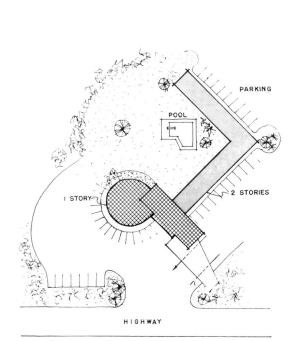

Fig. 26. Avis Motel, Midway Airport, Chicago;
Design, Inc., Architect

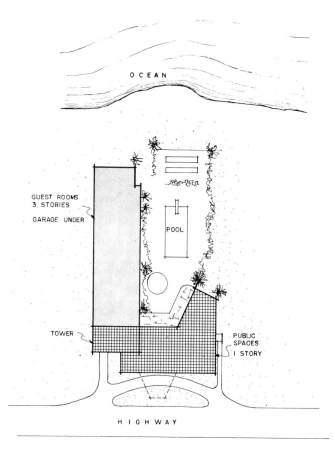

Fig. 27. O'Hare-Chicago Motor Hotel, Chicago International Airport; A. P. Swanson Associates, Architect

Fig. 28. Pan American Motel, Miami Beach, Fla.;
Carlos B. Schoeppl & Associates, Architect

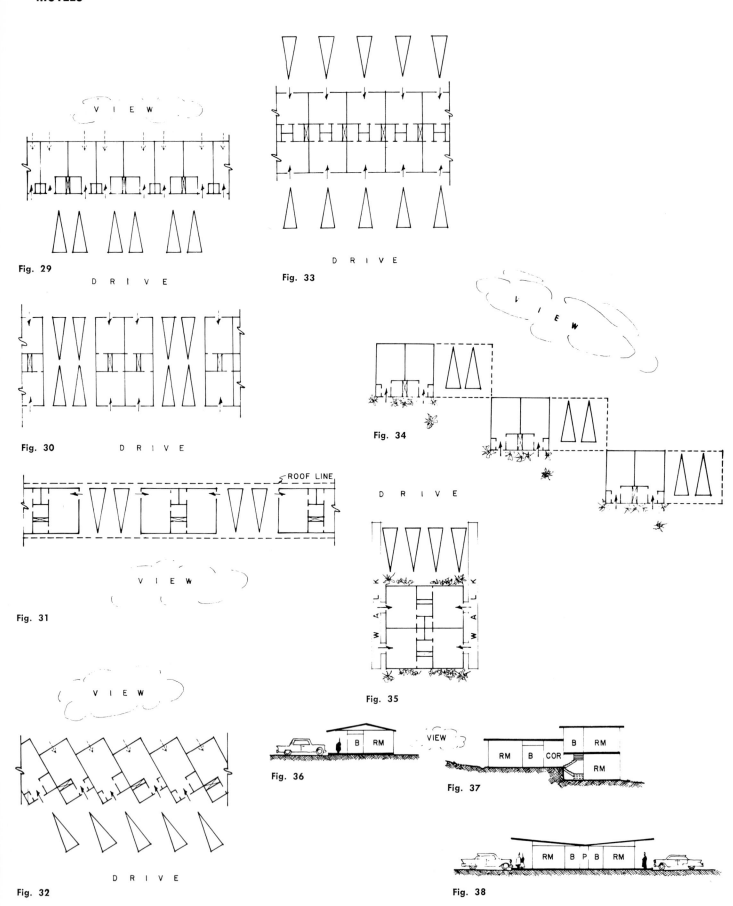

Fig. 29

Fig. 30

Fig. 31

Fig. 32

Fig. 33

Fig. 34

Fig. 35

Fig. 36

Fig. 37

Fig. 38

the road. The effect from the road will be impressive (Fig. 40). If the strip were about 25 ft wider, better results would be obtained by setting the guest units 25 ft back from the parking area, and landscaping the area between.

A level strip on a hillside, even as narrow as 43 ft, can readily accommodate both a drive and a single row of parked cars. Placing each guest room over its parked car solves the problem nicely: The cars are protected from the weather, and each guest is provided with a private balcony (Fig. 41). If the site continues downhill, it may be desirable to sink a guest room into the bank and park its car on the roof (Fig. 42). This arrangement provides privacy and a good view of the valley.

If there is no desirable view and the patronage will be mostly transient, the more economical back-to-back arrangement may be justified, despite its lack of privacy and cross-ventilation. (See Fig. 30, 33, 35, 38, 46, 48.) Two- or four-room units are often arranged with parking space between them, serving to break the monotony and add visual interest (Fig. 30, 31, 34). Another alternative is a four-room unit with all four cars parked in a row (Fig. 35).

Rooms on different levels may be advantageous, depending upon the topography and dimensions of the site, and the number of units required. Guests handling their own luggage generally do not welcome climbing a full story height, but seldom object to half that amount (Fig. 37, 45).

Corridors

An interior corridor will protect the guest in bad weather and be a great help to maid service. With protected inside corridors, a maid is customarily assigned 14 to 16 rooms; if only an outside entrance is provided, one maid would probably handle only 10 to 12 rooms. Moreover, a single interior corridor will make it easier for the management to exercise desired control; the guests, also, will probably feel more secure.

On the other hand, if the only entrance to a room is through an outside doorway, the guest can enjoy the feeling of having a private cottage. That feeling, however, will be appreciably reduced if the open corridor or public walkway is close to the building and protected by an overhanging roof, despite high windows, venetian blinds, or similar remedial devices. Privacy would be greatly improved by placing the public walkway 15 ft or more away from the building, with suitable planting between.

Compare the arrangement of two-story guest-room buildings with open corridors in Fig. 46, with the one with interior corridors in Fig. 47. Note that the construction requires floor slabs of the same width for each. An advantage of the open-corridor plan is that a quarter of the rooms have direct access to parking. The corridors, however, extend along the only windows, and thus reduce the privacy of all the guest rooms. The plan with the inside corridor offers greater privacy, better insulation from outside noise, and full protection from the weather for guests and maids. Moreover, half its guest rooms have either a private balcony or terrace.

A narrow site requiring two guest floors to secure the necessary number of rooms, may necessitate putting the building on stilts, with parking below the guest rooms. (Such an arrangement, however, increases the building height, and adds unwelcome stair climbing—or elevator problems.) With two stories, two access drives are preferable, one on each side of the building. If two drives are not feasible, however, it is possible to use a central driveway, a solution often employed in garages (Fig. 48). Both guest floors can be served by an interior double-loaded corridor, or by open corridors (one on each side) with a pipe-and-vent shaft between the guest bathrooms.

Standard motels have not yet been built. They have appeared, at times, on drawing boards, but individual circumstances—site conditions, food-service demands, and geographic location—invariably have required adjustments. Before beginning the design, the designer should thoroughly discuss with the owner and operator such matters as the choice between interior or exterior corridors, single or double loading, long guest buildings or two- and four-room units, and one- or two-story structures.

GUEST ROOMS

The motel guest wants much the same things in his room as he would want in a hotel. Reference should be made to previous pages concerning typical hotel rooms: types, sizes, design principles, and representative layouts. A motel will often increase the length and width of a similar room by a foot or two, however, to provide a greater spaciousness than would be feasible in a commercial hotel in the city. Some experienced motel operators say that 13 by 16 ft of net bedroom area is the best minimum size for a room to accommodate two persons.

Kitchenettes

Motel guests who have arrived at their destination often want cooking facilities on a modest scale. If the motel will cater primarily to overnight guests, however, the probable demand for kitchenettes should be determined by a careful study, involving a check of other motels in the neighborhood. Representative layouts including kitchenettes are shown in Fig. 49.

Complete factory-assembled kitchenettes are available in 30 to 72-in. lengths. Features included are a range top with 2, 3, or 4 burners (either gas or electric), with an oven underneath; a sink, with a utensil storage cabinet underneath; and a worktable area, with a refrigerator underneath. A storage cabinet for china and nonrefrigerated foodstuffs is usually provided on the wall above the unit.

The kitchenette unit may be placed in an alcove sized to fit it, with louvered doors or an equivalent device to screen it off or even lock it up when not desired by the guests. Or a separate room might be provided.

Wall partitions

Partitions between guest rooms should be of any construction that will reduce sound transmission by at least 45 decibels, a reduction that is usually adequate. In wood frame construction, 2 by 4's are often staggered on 8-in. centers, with a sound-insulating blanket between them. In selecting the method of construction, the designer should consider materials, labor, suitability, fire hazards, transmission loss, and cost.

Number of guest rooms

Several motel chain organizations have made careful studies to determine the minimum number of guest rooms that would be economical to operate. Their conclusions run from 64 rooms for the less elaborate forms of operation to 100 rooms for those organizations that intend all guest conveniences and services to be distinctly superior.

SPACE ALLOTMENTS

Space allotments in motels follow, in general, the pattern for allotments in hotels. Data taken from over a dozen motel plans were used to establish the space allotments listed below. Consideration was also given to the typical values for hotels, as listed on previous pages. Space allotments are directly proportional to the number of guest rooms; the figures provided below for a typical 100-room motel can be adjusted to suit any other size. (For a 60-room motel, multiply by 0.60; for 130 rooms, by 1.30.) Other modifications may be necessary to meet individual requirements. No adjustment should

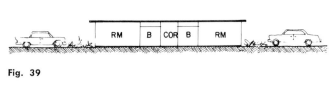

Fig. 39

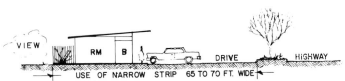

Fig. 40

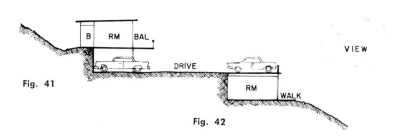

Fig. 41

Fig. 42

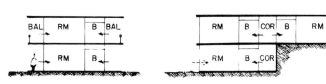

Fig. 43   Fig. 44

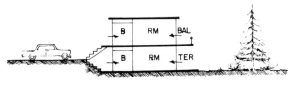

Fig. 45

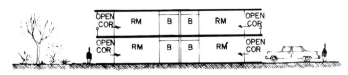

Fig. 46

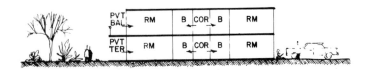

Fig. 47

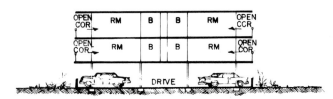

Fig. 48

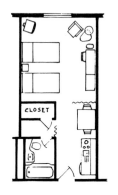

Fig. 49

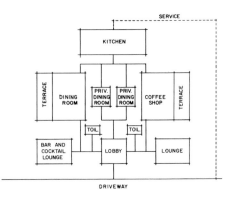

Fig. 50.   Schematic layout for motel with full dining service

be made, however, for the manager's office and the secretary's office, as each would still need about the same area.

SPACE ALLOTMENTS FOR TYPICAL 100-ROOM MOTEL

Public space	Area, sq ft
Lobby	1,100
Front office	100
Lounge	500
Corridors adjoining	300
Men's toilet for guests	140
Women's toilet for guests	120
Women's restroom	100
Coat checkroom	100

Concessions and subrentals	
Rented stores	2,000

Food and beverage service space	
Dining room (110 seats)	1,700
Coffee shop (70 seats)	1,100
Bar and cocktail lounge (50 seats)	800
Private dining rooms (75 seats)	900
Employees' dining room (20 seats)	260
Kitchen	1,300
Steward's storeroom	300
Walk-in refrigerators	150
Beverage storage	180
China, glass and silver storage	200
Receiving room	200
Garbage room	100

General service space	
Manager's office	130
Secretary's office	90
Accounting office	130
Linen room	350
Laundry	600
Men's toilet for employees	100
Men's locker room	150
Women's toilet for employees	120
Women's locker room	170
Maintenance shops	600
Furniture storage	250
General storage	600
Boiler room	750
Transformer and switchboard room	150

Extra items (if needed)

Garage for motorized lawn mowers and snow plows

Swimming pool filters, chlorinator, pump, and heater

Storage for lawn furniture and recreation equipment

Food service is not a lucrative part of the motel business; money invested in rooms would pay better dividends. The motorist, however, will want food service handy; if not actually on the premises, then only a step away. He generally dislikes to go more than a few hundred yards to find a restaurant. Therefore, unless adequate food service is already adjacent, it is advisable to provide it.

For the motel requiring strictly minimum facilities, a good solution is the factory-assembled roadside "diner" with a dozen or more seats, which can be handled by a single employee during slack hours. For the more ambitious but still rather small motel with little outside patronage, the best solution may well be a coffee shop, possibly supplemented by a bar. Such an arrangement helps to keep investment and labor costs within bounds. For the larger motel, a dining room, coffee shop, and bar with cocktail lounge may all be needed. If the motel is near a city, private dining rooms are usually added as well. Outside patronage is necessary to make extensive restaurant operations pay. The larger, more spectacular motel restaurants may derive as much as 75 per cent of their business from persons who are not overnight guests (Fig. 50).

Motel restaurant facilities average about two seats per guest room. The ratio varies, however, from one-half to three or more dining-room seats per guest room.

Care should be taken in applying the schedule of space allotments to ensure that, if any food-service area is modified, the effect on auxiliary facilities is considered.

The lobby should be designed to impress the prospective guest favorably and bid him welcome. The entrance must be easily recognizable and accessible. If feasible, the prospective guest should be sheltered from the weather, from his car to the entrance doors. Within the lobby, the registration desk should have a relatively central location, for it is the main control point of motel operation. If the guest, standing at the registration desk, can look through a large plate-glass window and see the swimming pool, attractive landscaping, or a scenic view, room sales will be greatly aided.

Parking

Parking spaces, preferably in separate areas, are generally required as follows: (1) 1 parking space for each guest room (may sometimes be reduced to 0.8 per guest room); (2) 1 parking space for every 5 restaurant seats; (3) 1 parking space for every 3 employees; (4) 2 parking spaces for delivery and service trucks (in addition to space for a truck at the service entrance).

These allotments, of course, should be modified if circumstances warrant it. A motel that is filled to capacity, with a good restaurant, bar, and banquet business from nonguests, may need 2 parking spaces per guest room. On the other hand, a downtown motel, with parking available nearby and many guests arriving by taxi, might get along with parking space equal to two-thirds the number of guest rooms.

For the design of parking areas in general, see the section of this book on "Parking." Special requirements for motel parking are discussed in the following paragraph.

Parking stalls should be adequate for the largest cars commonly used; 19 ft is the recommended minimum length. Planning for only medium and small-size cars invites trouble. Parking stalls 10 ft wide are recommended; where space is limited 9-ft stalls may be used, but this width should be considered the absolute minimum. Double stripes, $1\frac{1}{2}$ ft apart, between the stalls will result in better centering of the cars within the allotted space. Since almost all motel guests unload baggage from their cars, and reload it upon leaving, adequate and safe space should be provided for this activity. Motel parking lots planned for maximum guest convenience provide parking stalls 11 ft wide by 23 ft long, allowing 4 ft behind a 19-ft car for loading and unloading. Parking spaces under buildings should be 11 ft wide and have a clear height of 7 ft. In the design of sidewalks adjacent to parking areas, consideration must be given to the overhang of the car beyond the curb or wheel buffer; this overhang may be as much as $2\frac{1}{2}$ ft in front or $4\frac{1}{2}$ ft in the rear of the car.

Entrance drive

The turnoff from the highway to the motel should be at an angle of 30 to 45 deg; sharper turnoff angles are inadvisable. The driveway should be 20 to 25 ft wide, and the radius of the curb on the driver's right should be at least 50 ft. If a restricted site frontage should require a right-angle turnoff, then the driveway should be 25 ft wide and the curb have a 30-ft radius. A curb radius of less than 30 ft is inadvisable under any circumstances.

A slope of 6 per cent is the usual maximum for turnoffs from state highways. A slope of 12 per cent is customary for ramps, but can be as much as 15 per cent. The parking lot should be nearly level. The central driveway may be crowned, with a 1 per cent slope to the edges, so that persons on foot will find it relatively free from water after rain or from ice in winter.

Gas station

Motels sometimes include a service station where the motorist can conveniently obtain gasoline and oil, and possibly tire, battery, lubrication, and car-washing service. The decision of whether to include a gas station, however, should depend upon its being profitable in itself.

Swimming pool

About 50 per cent of the motels built in 1959 included swimming pools. The trend is to provide pools, even in motels in the downtown area of the city. Although the pool may be actually used by only a minority of the overnight guests, many more will enjoy watching the activities. Thus the pool should be surrounded by a suitable terrace at least 10 ft wide; if a diving board is provided, the terrace should be 20 ft wide in back of the board. Grass areas beyond the terrace are also recommended.

The motel pool should generally be of the recreation type. A free-form pattern, either kidney-shaped or oval, is usually suitable, but of course is subject to topography and the designer's judgment. The minimum size recommended for the pool is 20 by 40 ft, which is large enough for about 15 people in the water and 20 to 30 bathers around the edge. One motel chain prefers a 24 by 48-ft pool. Another chain, operating motels of 150 rooms and more, considers 35 by 75 ft to be the minimum.

A separate wading pool is often provided—sometimes with spray fittings or a small fountain to enhance its appearance. A fairly wide terrace should surround the pool, with benches on the terrace for parents.

Toilet facilities for men and women bathers should be accessible from the pool area. Such facilities are required by law in many states. Provision should also be made, within 40 ft of the deep end of the pool, for housing the necessary water filters, pumps, purification equipment, and heater. A water heater can extend the use of the pool over a longer season.

Other planning considerations concerning the pool and surrounding area include food and beverage service and adequate illumination for evening activities.

The inclusion of a cabana club may be considered, if there is sufficient local demand. In addition to membership fees, the cabana club may bring other profitable business to the motel. Since cabana club members are not overnight guests, however, provision must be made for dressing rooms, lockers, showers, and toilets. The

members will also expect an ample pool-side terrace area with tables and chairs, umbrellas, and reclining lawn chairs, in addition to the cabanas. The cabanas themselves, though, may serve as a windbreak, and thus help to prolong the pool season.

Recreation areas

Although the pool will probably be the most popular recreation area, a children's play yard, and areas for adult games may also be desirable. Some such games are listed below; the dimensions indicate the area for the game, including the usual surrounding border.

Game	Width x length, ft
Shuffleboard	10 x 60
Clock golf	40 x 40
Croquet	50 x 95
Horseshoes	12 x 60
Table tennis	12 x 20
Tennis	60 x 120
Handball	30 x 45

Barbecue facilities may also be desirable. An area of about 15 by 20 ft is generally ample. The play yard for small children should be enclosed by a fence. Suitable modern equipment should be selected and installed.

Indoor recreation facilities may include a television room, one or more card rooms, reading room and library, table tennis, movies, piano, and electric organ. These facilities should be discussed and decided upon in the early planning stages, because it is often impossible to fit them into a completed plan at the last minute.

Landscaping

Landscaping is important—it is one of the things the guest sees first. Well-kept, neatly defined lawns and drives will make a favorable impression; the parking arrangement should be logical and practical. Hard-surfaced walks should be so arranged that lawns may be preserved; retaining walls should be installed to prevent erosion and enhance appearance. The right varieties of trees will provide attractive shade. Undesirable views should be screened by dense plantings, trimmed hedges, stone walls, or louvered fences.

Outdoor advertising

Signs are the most effective means of attracting the attention of prospective customers. Most people stop at a motel because they like its sign.

Signs should be neat, bold, brief, and

distinctive. Their message must be grasped at a glance. The entrance sign should be plainly visible a good hundred yards from the turnoff, with letters at least 18 in. high. Copy should be reduced to a bare minimum, and only unusual services advertised.

A distinguishing emblem, trade mark, or coat of arms should be unique and easily remembered. Select one that can be used at the motel entrance, in the lobby, and on stationery, menus, and souvenir match books. Avoid using too many colors in a sign. Simplicity is effective.

Signs should be durable and suited to the climate of the location. Night illumination is essential, at least for the sign in front of the motel, but care should be taken that guests will not be annoyed by beams of light, glare, flashing off and on, or other features that might bother a person wanting to sleep. The sign at the motel customarily has a "Vacancy—No Vacancy" indication.

Heating and air conditioning

Guest rooms are best served by a central plant, with individual room temperature controls provided. A system favored by some of the more experienced organizations circulates water through convectors concealed beneath the guest-room windows. The circulating water is heated in winter and chilled in summer, the water temperature being varied in accordance with weather conditions. Each guest-room conditioning cabinet has a multispeed, manually controlled, motor-driven fan to blow air over the coils. The guest can regulate the fan speed to vary the rate of heat transfer.

Other parts of the building—such as the lobby, restaurant, kitchen, and employees' quarters—should be divided into "zones," according to their hours of use and type of air treatment needed. Each zone will have its own separately controlled equipment to supply heat or air conditioning. Air conditioning is supplied in the summer for public spaces, restaurant, and bar facilities frequented by guests. Ample exhaust ventilation will be needed for the kitchen and the employees' locker rooms and toilets. Care should be taken to avoid having to operate an entire zone of rooms with short hours of use just to accommodate one or two that will be used many hours a day.

BASIC GEOMETRY OF MOTEL SITE PLANNING

The basic element of design in motel site planning is not the rental unit alone, i.e., a living-bedroom and bathroom, but the rental unit plus a parking space, plus an access roadway, plus a pedestrian walkway, plus a certain quality which can be summed up in the term "amenity." This latter will include outlook, privacy, protection from noise, and "character." All except the last will usually imply space. In the case of outlook one may visually poach on neighboring land, but this will not in the long run be dependable without control over the development of this land.

As the basic element of design is not simple and easily defined, as might at first appear, so in its use it may be equally difficult to classify and analyze. Being composed of so many elements, it will vary greatly from one case to the next. A change in one element will change the whole balance of relative importance. We have therefore attempted to simplify and sharpen the most common requirements of this site geometry by concentrating upon a typical rental unit strip of near-minimum dimensions placed in a number of different and typical situations to demonstrate the considerations which should control the site planning of a small roadside motel. These diagrams will also provide the data for a preliminary quick check on site area and shape, as related to possible density of development and efficient utilization of the land with various types of plans.

The Rental Unit Strip Dimension   This becomes the basic planning element in these simple site plans, is made up of the rental unit, a pedestrian walkway, parking space, and access roadway. Not shown here, because too difficult to measure or reduce to a type, is amenity space, which includes outlook. The size of each of these elements will vary from one case to another, but each dimension shown here is typical.

A Shallow Site Parallel to the Highway   This will almost inevitably be best served by an elementary type of strip plan with front parking. Such a site is too narrow for the units to be turned at right angles to the highway, and if they were moved far enough forward for rear parking, the rooms would be unpleasantly close to the highway (Fig. 1).

If there is an opportunity for some outlook in the rear, even onto someone else's property, then the plan can be greatly improved by keeping access and parking on the highway side and opening up big outlook windows to the rear.

A Narrow Site at Right Angles to the Highway   This must usually be enough wider than the minimum strip dimension to allow for the side yards normally required by local building and zoning regulations. There is nothing to prevent one or both of these side yards from being incorporated into the parking space (Fig. 2).

For more intensive use of this sort of site, the strip is normally turned at the end to form an **L.** A corresponding wing might be added at the highway end but is seldom done because it would close off the motel from the view of motorists on the highway. Such wings upset the parking ratio of a typical strip; space must be found for these extra cars possibly at the rear of the wing units.

From *Motels* by Geoffrey Baker and Bruno Furno; ©1955 by Litton Educational Publishing, Inc., New York.

If the view to the rear beyond the lot line is pleasant, then it would be better to do without the rear wing. If the view is undesirable, the wing can effectively close it off, and the inside of the **L** can create an environment of its own.

For Greater Density   On a similar deep narrow site at right angles to the highway, a common plan is to pile the units two or more stories high, facing outward from a central bathroom spine. Access and parking is on each side, with access balconies along the face of the upper stories, so that pedestrian traffic is channeled immedi-

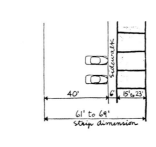
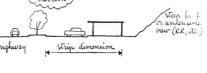
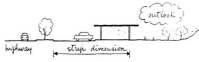

Fig. 1

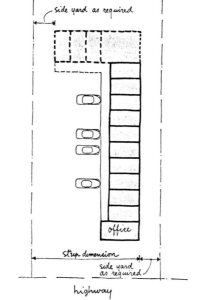

Fig. 2

ately in front of the outlook windows, killing all privacy.

The parking space must be enlarged to take care of the units above the first floor. The side yards can be usefully employed as part of the parking area. But if the second-story access balconies are reached by stairs at each end of the rental unit block, then parking space for the second-story units is most convenient if concentrated in this same area at each end of the building (Fig. 3).

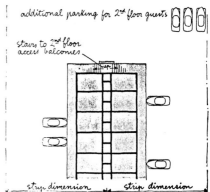

Fig. 3

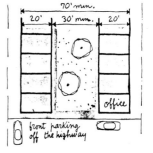

Fig. 4

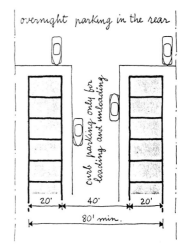

Fig. 5

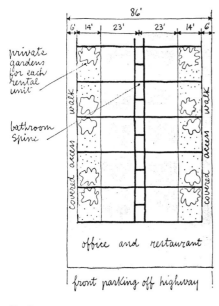

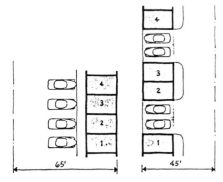

Fig. 6

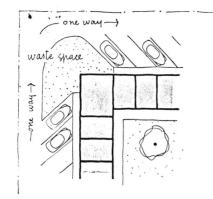

Fig. 7

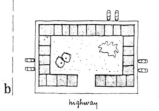

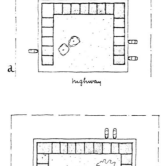

Fig. 8

The Bathroom Spine Plan May Be Improved If all parking space is concentrated at the highway end of the long narrow lot, each unit has a private fenced garden. Access is by a perimeter covered walk (Fig. 6). Plan suggested by Mayfair House, Carmel, Calif.

If Parking Need Not Be at the Unit Entrance A larger number of rental units can be fitted more successfully onto a long narrow lot by concentrating the parking area at one end. Where the central garden court becomes very narrow (Fig. 4), the only way to obtain privacy of outlook is to

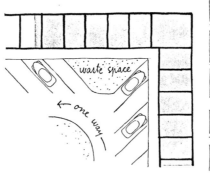

Fig. 9

Fig. 10

divide it down the center with screens or high planting.

In the plan (Fig. 5), the disadvantage of a road down the center is counterbalanced by the convenience of unloading baggage at the entrance.

Road Parking Strip and Carport Strip Compared Alternating unit pairs and double carports gives a longer but narrower strip than the conventional. For a more spacious lawn and easier drive-in, the carport strip is in practice usually made wider than shown in Fig. 7.

It's the Corners That Count When a strip plan is bent into a court, the more corners, the more waste of space; often this is of small importance. With parking on the outside front (Fig. 8) there is space for a car outside the door of each unit. With parking on the inside front (Fig. 9) there cannot be space enough for all the cars expected and corner units are left without parking stalls. The visual values of the open corner could well be combined with a road through, so that the **U** becomes two **L** courts (Fig. 10). The larger a plan, the less important are the corners.

The U Court Comes in All Patterns, All Sizes As shown in Fig. 11.

a. Opens an attractive central garden court to the highway, using this as an advertising feature.

b. Almost closed to the highway, is of less advertising value, but guests have more quiet and privacy.

c. By parking inside the **U**, the same number of units can be packed onto a smaller lot. Noisy and without privacy. Worst on a small scale.

d. For more units the **U** becomes **E**. Center line does not have parking directly outside door but can be served by interior corridor or covered walk.

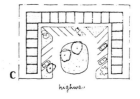

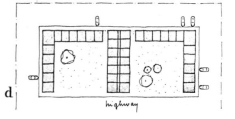

Fig. 11

Many architects and engineers who design office buildings will no doubt inevitably be engaged by a client who expects to have a computer, or more correctly electronic data processing (EDP), system installed in his building. While the needs for particular systems will ordinarily be highly individualized and complex, some general principles concerning the architectural and engineering aspects involved in planning a building for these machines can be set down. In this way, one who is faced with the design of a building which will house an EDP system may provide himself with some of the background he will need for the more detailed considerations he will be faced with later.

The use of computers for scientific or engineering calculations is well known. The use of EDP systems for the automation of ordinary business operations such as inventory controls, bank operations, clerical functions, and the like is also familiar.

EDP systems are highly demanding of the architect and his consultants. The machines refuse to function under conditions of high humidity and high or low temperature which employes might put up with. The installations are heavy and place concentrated loads on building floors. Large areas are required for the placement of many of the systems, and for the maintenance and servicing of the machines. Electric power with low variations in voltage and frequency must be furnished to the systems. Many of the systems require a raised or double floor to accommodate the large number of cables interconnecting the machines. Because of the nature of the problems involved in the design of office building spaces for EDP installations, an examination of some of their more important aspects should be of value.

The architect working on an office building which will contain an EDP system will naturally turn to the companies who produce them and to consultants who specialize in the field for detailed answers to the specific design problems. However, an examination of some of the more general and important aspects of planning should give him some background for later and more detailed study.

Electronic Data Processing System

The National Office Management Association defines a computer as "a device capable of accepting information, applying prescribed processes to the information, and supplying the results of these processes . . . from internally stored instructions, as opposed to calculators on which the sequences are impressed manually from tape, or from cards."

This is to say that computers are devices

The material in this article was developed from data supplied by the Data Processing Division, International Business Machines Corporation, White Plains, N.Y., and Air Research Associates, New York, N.Y. and was published in *Office Buildings*, McGraw-Hill Book Company, 1961.

which may receive their original instructions from tape or cards, but which also store required information within themselves. The experts in the field have tended to use the word *computer* to specifically describe devices which perform problem-solving calculations but to employ *electronic data processing system* (EDP) or more simply, *data processor,* to describe the general type of the devices.

The schematic floor plans in Fig. 1 give some indication of the units which might be used to make up three different electronic data processing systems. In practice, numerous variations of the above are possible for different purposes and problems. The plans shown are not intended to be typical, but only to serve as examples of some of the principles involved.

EDP Organization

In the simplest terms, an EDP system is composed of four major parts: input, storage (memory), processing, and output. In practice, the input will ordinarily be in the form of instructions sent to the machine by a person operating a keyboard, from punch cards, or from punched paper tape. The newer and more sophisticated high-speed systems often employ magnetic tape inputs. The storage or memory units are all magnetic devices. They include drums, disks, tape, and a system of magnetic cores. The term "solid state machines" comes from the basic characteristics of transistors. Output components are similar to the input devices. Results may be fed to keyboards, punch cards, punched paper tape, or magnetic tape. In addition, it is possible to feed the output information to high speed printers.

Schedules and Timing

It is imperative that planning for an EDP installation should begin very early. Programming of the operations the machines are to perform often takes a year or more before the actual components of the system can be selected. A year or more will usually be required between the time the system layout is approved and delivery of the equipment. Architectural and engineering considerations concerned with the building itself require a certain amount of time. The total number of months needed from the time of the decision to install an EDP system will, of course, vary with the individual problems. But, in all cases, the complete process will be spread over quite a long period. It is imperative that adequate time be allowed.

General Requirements

The first consideration in the planning of an EDP system is the provision of adequate space of the particular kind required. Proper and adequate power must be provided. Air conditioning requirements must be determined (often six times as much as for a normal office will be needed). Space must be provided for housing the air conditioning equipment. Ceilings must be high enough to allow machine

installations and, more often than not, a hung ceiling and raised floor will be necessary. The floors must be designed for the high loads to be placed upon them.

Work flow to other areas is highly important in order to obtain the utmost efficiency. Flexibility and expansion problems are acute, since EDP has a way of outmoding itself very quickly. Also, experience shows that many companies begin with systems performing limited functions but soon discover other operations that lend themselves to automation.

Space Planning

The areas required for EDP installations vary considerably. For example, one of IBM's more limited capacity systems requires about 370 sq ft, while the same company's large system may take up 3,500 sq ft. Actual space requirements for a given installation can be finally determined only by a layout of the work flow and of the machines themselves. In addition to the space for the system proper, auxiliary areas are needed for air conditioning equipment, testing, storage, and the like. Space is often required for printer form stands, card files, work tables, desks. Storage must usually be provided for permanent master document files, EDP cards (or in newer machines, magnetic tapes). These areas should be carefully located to minimize unnecessary travel time. A bulk storage room is usually required for the storage of spare filters, transformers, and other large parts.

Floor Strength and Construction

The units which compose an EDP system are heavy. Point loads on the floor may often run as high as 1,000 pounds. Even when the loads can be distributed, it is usually necessary to design the floors for 150 psf loadings, or more. As EDP installations become more common, it may be feasible to construct some buildings with all of their floors stressed for the loads of these systems. In most cases, it probably will not be economical to do so. In any case, EDP system locations will require close study and selection, followed by design for the loadings to be encountered.

Currently, the preferred method of solving the load distribution problem is by the provision of a secondary floor raised over the building floor slab. An installation of this type may have other important advantages: interconnecting power cables and receptacles may be concealed, yet remain easily accessible, the space between the floors may be utilized for housing air conditioning ducts or plenums, future changes in the layout may be effected with a minimum of lost time and expense, machines may be added easily.

While a secondary floor with raceways may be employed, a free access type, allowing complete directional freedom, is preferred. This type of floor is composed of square or rectangular panels, supported at their edges on a structural grid, and raised to the required height on pedestals of metal or other material.

Commercial

COMPUTER (EDP) FACILITIES

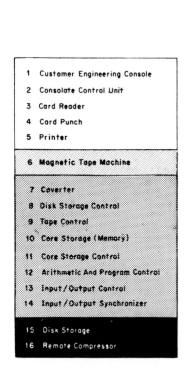

1. Customer Engineering Console
2. Consolate Control Unit
3. Card Reader
4. Card Punch
5. Printer

6. Magnetic Tape Machine

7. Coverter
8. Disk Storage Control
9. Tape Control
10. Core Storage (Memory)
11. Core Storage Control
12. Arithmetic And Program Control
13. Input/Output Control
14. Input/Output Synchronizer

15. Disk Storage
16. Remote Compressor

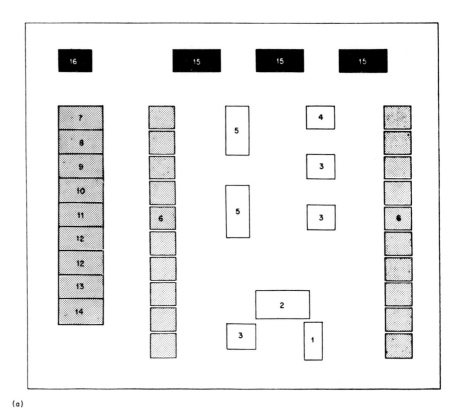

(a)

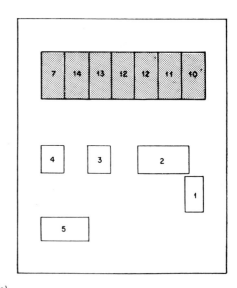

(b)

(c)

Fig. 1 (a) Schematic layout of tape/disk storage EDP. (b) Schematic layout of tape EDP system. (c) Schematic layout of card EDP system.

Air Conditioning

Electronic data processing systems require very close control of air temperature, humidity, and dust. If any of these is not held within certain prescribed limits, the machines cannot perform. Thus, the provision of adequate air conditioning is necessary. If the cooling of an office space fails, its occupants might continue to do their work, but EDP cannot. Because of this, the recommended, and usual, solution is the provision of a separate air conditioning system serving the EDP system alone. This system will be required to operate on the cooling cycle all year round.

In many cases, the preferred location for the EDP air conditioning system is in a room adjacent to the data processing machines themselves. However, if lines must be run to a cooling tower many stories away on the roof, this may prove too costly. In some cases, the tower might be located on a ledge or setback roof. Those who have had considerable experience in the design of EDP installations recommend installation of as much standby equipment as possible. Since EDP rental or purchase costs are so high, any time when the system is

1018

inoperative can be financially disastrous. It will often prove more feasible to minimize shutdowns through the use of standby equipment than to risk costly delays.

There is considerable variation in the air conditioning requirements of various EDP systems. For example, one comparatively small system dissipates heat approximately equivalent to five tons of air conditioning while with the same company's large system, heat dissipation equals about 33 tons. The IBM 7070 requires about 11 tons of air conditioning. When this machine is in operation, the temperature must be maintained in the 65 to 90°F range, and the humidity between 20 and 80 percent. When inoperative, power off, the limits are 50 to 110°F and 0 to 80 percent RH. High efficiency filters are required for use with these machines. If a mechanical filter is used, it must be rated at a minimum of 20 percent efficiency by the Bureau of Standards discoloration test using atmospheric dust. Electrostatic plate type filters must be rated at 85 to 90 percent efficiency by the same test. Special filtration will be necessary if the installation is exposed to corrosive gases, salt air, or unusually severe dust conditions.

Companies producing EDP systems recommend the installation of temperature and humidity recording instruments. Through the use of the records provided by these instruments, it will be easier to ensure that the air conditioning system is operating continuously with the required efficiency. In this way, correct functioning of the electronic data processing system itself may be more nearly assured.

Acoustical Treatment

Many of the units in an EDP system produce considerable noise. The worst offenders are such components as the card machines, printers, and blowers. For the comfort of the system operators, acoustical treatment of the area is desirable. The acoustical problems in an area containing an EDP installation are similar to those in other moderately noisy office building areas and may be solved by the usual methods. However, attention should be paid to the vibrations set up by the machines. Floor and wall construction should be capable of retarding the

transmission of the vibrations of the machines to other areas of the building.

Illumination

A minimum average general illumination of 40 footcandles measured 30 in. above the floor is recommended by systems manufacturers for all machine areas. Low levels of illumination are required for easy observation of various console and signal lights. Therefore, direct sunlight should be avoided. In larger installations, general lighting should be zoned, so that portions of the lighting may be turned on or off as required.

Vibration

An EDP installation ordinarily cannot be made in an area that is subject to large amounts of vibration. In general, the machines can withstand a sustained vibration up to 0.25G (G = gravitational acceleration). Intermittent vibrations somewhat greater than this can be withstood if their frequency is less than 25 cycles per second. In more extreme cases, steps for overcoming the problems may be recommended by the manufacturers.

Electric Power

Data processing systems place heavy loads on the electrical system of an office building. The system requirements for circuit flexibility, the need for power source dependability, and safety requirements further complicate electrical design. Exact specifications vary considerably for various installations. However, a look at the requirements for one system, the IBM 7070, might serve as an indication of the general needs. The 7070 system operates on a 208- or 230-volt, 3-phase, 60-cycle supply, and requires approximately 37 kva. The source voltage may have a total variation of ± 10 percent of the rated voltage including transient and steady state. Frequency must be within $\pm\frac{1}{2}$-cycle. Both 60-c 'e and 400-cycle power are distributed within the system, the 400-cycle being produced by a converter contained in the EDP installation. Line-to-line voltage and frequency tolerances

within the system are the same as the power source tolerances. Separate feeders from the main distribution panel of the building are most often used. However, if the building power cannot be maintained within the tolerances, a separate transformer or motor alternator may be necessary. If a transformer is used, it should be fed from the highest primary source available. The data processing system feeder should feed no loads other than those of the system. The distribution panel for the processing system should be located in the EDP area. Ordinarily, all units of the system are designed for cable entry from the floor or from under the floor beneath each machine.

Lightning Protection

Manufacturers recommend that lightning protection be installed for the secondary power sources of the systems in cases where the utility company provides lightning protectors on the primary, where primary power is supplied by an overhead power service, or where the area is subject to electrical storms or other power surges.

Tape Storage

The use of magnetic tape for feeding and receiving information from EDP systems is rapidly becoming more commonplace. Tape must be protected from dust, and from extremes of humidity and temperature. Under the usual conditions of frequent use, acetate base tapes should be stored at a temperature of 65 to 90° F, 40 to 60 percent relative humidity. If exposed to temperatures outside this range (from 40 to 120° F) for more than four hours, tape should be hermetically sealed in dustproof containers, and subsequently reconditioned in the atmosphere of use for a length of time equal to the time spent outside the use atmosphere. Other tapes (polyester base and the like) can withstand temperatures of 40 to 120°F and 0 to 80 percent RH.

When not in use tapes should be stored in dustproof containers in a vertical position. Tapes must not be placed in contact with magnetic materials or subjected to magnetic fields of greater than 50 oersteds intensity.

PHOTOGRAPHIC LABORATORIES

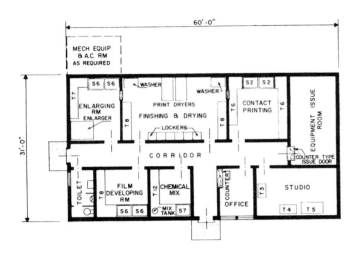

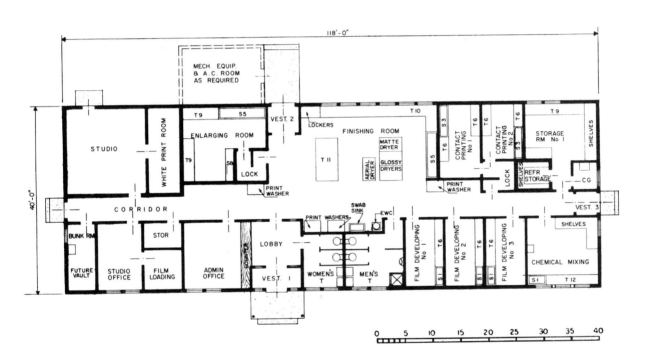

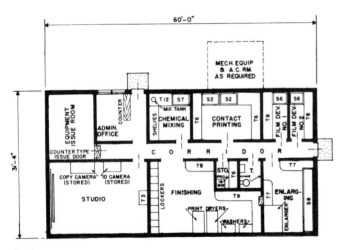

Fig. 1

By FRANK MEMOLI

The Site

The site for a funeral home should be located strategically with respect to present and future business patterns and be accessible by public as well as private transportation. A quiet location out of sight of hospitals and other organizations that might find the view of a mortuary objectionable is required, as is the availability of cemeteries and churches. Utilities should be readily obtainable.

In order to accommodate the building with parking and landscaping, and to provide for possible future expansion, a site 2 acres in area with at least 300 ft of frontage is recommended as minimum. Preferably the site should run from street to street, but where this is not possible, a corner location is acceptable.

The Building

Some specific recommendations can be applied to the building as a whole. The building should lend itself to future expansion in the event that expansion becomes necessary. On the exterior, provision should be made for exterior building lighting and a dignified sign. All service areas (loading, delivery, etc.) should be properly screened from public view. If an elevator is used, the loading dock must be at proper truck-gate height.

On the interior, all service deliveries must be accomplished without disruption of normal operations. All doorways through which caskets will pass must be at least 48 in. wide, and the corridor system must be free of sharp, narrow turns.

Parking

An ample and efficient parking facility is essential. It should provide parking space for one car for every four places of seating capacity plus one reserved space for the clergyman. A reasonable amount of reserve land for future parking facility expansion should be available.

The parking area should be freely accessible, with separate entrances and exits. Separate and clearly marked facilities should be made available to different groups such as family, cemetery, funeral service, staff, and visitors.

The area should be so planned as to facilitate cleaning, drainage, and snow removal where appropriate.

Reception Area

This area is a focal point of the funeral home and, while it affords access to all other areas, it must also protect these other areas against intrusion. It should have an air of comfort and welcome. In the event that no foyer or vestibule is practicable, this area will serve as a buffer against weather, dirt, and noise. In some instances it may double as a smoking lounge.

Adapted from *Checklist for Mortuary Planning*, by Dr. Charles H. Nichols, Director, National Foundation of Funeral Service, Evanston, Ill.

The reception area should be a unit in itself, relatively free and unencumbered, with all unnecessary doors eliminated.

Consideration should be given to the desirability of two reception areas—one for services and one for business (Fig. 1).

Selection Room

This room should be privately accessible from the arrangement office and conveniently located, especially for elderly or disabled persons. It should be relatively free from noise and other disturbances, protected from public view, and unavailable to the merely curious.

In sizing the selection room, allow 60 sq ft per casket to be displayed. The floor space should be free from unnecessary partitions and obstructions and the wall space relatively large and unbroken. Windows are not a necessity, but if provided, they should be screened from public view.

Built-in display cabinets for garments and urns may be necessary, as may be a separate vault selection room.

As with all rooms into which caskets will be placed, all doors should be at least 48 in. wide.

In case of emergency, the selection room may serve as an auxiliary chapel. It should be designed with this in mind.

Reposing (or Slumber, or State) Rooms

These rooms should be readily accessible from the preparation room, the chapel, and the reception area and should be at least 12 by 14 ft in size. They should be adjacent to one another, separated by soundproof folding doors, for use in combination. When used separately, each room should have reasonable privacy and be individually accessible to callers. The rooms may be of different sizes but must all be sufficiently flexible to double as chapels and to accommodate a variety of religious rites. The reposing rooms must all provide for attractive casket placement and floral displays.

Preparation

This room should be located well apart from public areas of the building, convenient in terms of movement of bodies, and readily accessible to the reposing rooms. If the preparation room is not on the ground floor, an elevator should be nearby. When sizing, allow an area of 14 by 16 ft for each one-table room. Each such room should contain sufficient convenient cabinet space, a sink or drain bowl at the foot of each table, arrangement for an aspirator, hot and cold water sources at the head of each table, convenient sink and sterilizer, cleanup facilities (possibly including a shower), and adequate clothing hooks and storage space. In addition to these, facilities for dressing and cosmetizing may be desired. Room walls and floors should be tiled and floor drains provided. Wherever possible, windows should be omitted. Convenient and sanitary

facilities for refuse disposal are required and provision for emergency power and lighting may be desirable.

Chapel

The chapel must be directly accessible from the main entrance or lobby and convenient to the parking area as well as in terms of post-service movement of casket, flowers, etc. A minimum clear ceiling height of 10 ft 6 in. is required. The space should be relatively free of columns and other structural elements. It should allow for a wide aisle and a clear view from all angles. The chapel must accommodate all types of religious services, and in appearance it should be sedate, dignified, and comfortable. Provision must be made for a pleasing setting for the casket, a pulpit or rostrum occupying a dominant focal point, and an unobtrusive but effective music system.

In addition to the above, the following ancillary areas will be needed: a private family room, a small study for the minister and nearby areas for overflow groups, congregation of pallbearers, and chair storage.

Family Room

The family room should be screened from public view, have a private entrance and exit, allow the family to see the casket, and enable the family to be aware of all that is going on. It should be large enough for the average family with the possibility of being adjusted in size to accommodate the occasional larger-than-average family or to serve as a reposing room. Rest rooms and first-aid facilities should be nearby. The organ should be reasonably distant from the family room.

Music Room

The music room should be located adjacent to the chapel, with the sound source at the front of the chapel but so designed as to prevent extraneous noises from drifting into that room. The musicians should be able to enter the music room without disrupting services and should have a view of the clergyman, funeral director, or signal light in order to follow cues. All music facilities will be located in this room, with ample space for organist, vocalists, standby facilities such as a piano or other self-sufficient instrument (in case of a power failure), and storage for recordings if used. Appropriate provision should be made if services are to be recorded.

Arrangement Office

This office should be private enough to be free of all disturbances during an arrangement and should afford direct private access to the selection room. It should be separate from the general business office but in reasonable proximity to it, and should be so designed as to double in use for a second purpose. It should contain a closet for wraps and have ready access to drinking water and first aid.

Commercial
FUNERAL HOMES

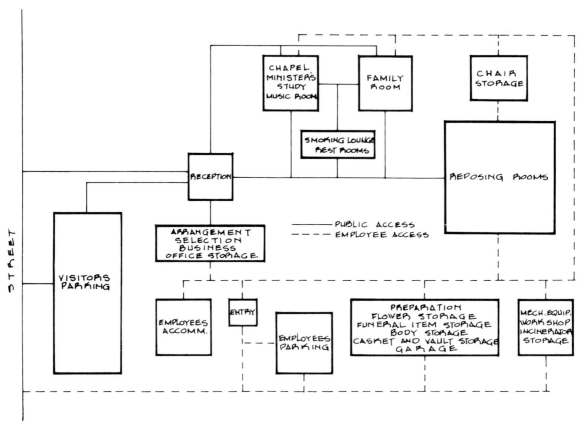

Fig. 1 Funeral home flow diagram.

Business Office

This area should be planned as a reasonably soundproof central control post for the entire operation. It should be readily but separately available for those who come on business only and should give convenient access to private offices, if any. Typical activities which occur in this office will be typing, filing, bookkeeping, mailing, accounting, etc. A safe will be required, as will sufficient storage space for business records.

Minister's Room

This quiet, secluded room must be directly accessible to the minister but to no one else. It should afford direct access for the minister to the front of the chapel. It should be a convenient place for the clergyman to review his notes and to robe and disrobe. Toilet facilities must be in close proximity.

Smoking Lounge

This room will be apart from the service areas of the mortuary but may be combined with the rest room facilities. It should be readily accessible to visitors and convey an impression of comfort and informality.

Rest Rooms

Like the smoking lounge, these rooms should be apart from the service areas of the mortuary but may be combined with the smoking lounge.

They must be conveniently located, especially with respect to the reposing rooms, and accessible to visitors.

Employee Accommodations

This area must be reasonably remote from the public areas of the mortuary and should be a place where employees can relax during off-duty periods or periods of waiting (possibly combined with the smoking lounge in smaller establishments). It should be equipped and furnished for rest, relaxation, and recreation.

If employees sleep on the premises, the sleeping rooms should be adjacent to this rest area. If a man with a family lives on the premises, a comfortable apartment must be provided.

Storage Areas

A garage apart from the mortuary and equipped for indoor car washing, general repairs, and maintenance is required.

Dry, above-ground storage for caskets and vaults must be provided and should be easily accessible. Movement from this area to the selection room should be direct.

A cool, moist room with a sink and at least 6 by 10 ft in size is required for flower storage and should be equipped for the trimming and proper care of flowers. It should have cabinets for the storage of racks, vases, utensils, etc.

Provide a room for chair storage, preferably off the chapel.

Provide a room or rooms for storage of

funeral items, preferably near the reposing rooms.

Provide ample closets for miscellaneous storage purposes, as well as adequate wardrobe facilities throughout the building.

Provide permanent fireproof storage for valuable records as well as ample storage areas, accessible to the main office, for office and printing supplies.

Provide separate storage, accessible to the cemetery service trucks, for equipment.

Provide a general storage room for miscellaneous and catch-all purposes.

If necessary, provide storage facilities for the short-term storage of bodies.

Utility Rooms

In most cases a mechanical equipment room containing heating and air conditioning equipment, set apart from the service areas, will be required.

If desired, a woodworking or carpenters shop can be provided, as well as an incinerator.

Special Facilities

In addition to required facilities listed above, the following special facilities may be needed or desirable: a crematory, a Columbarium, a lodge room, a community or civic room, kitchen facilities or coffee bar, guest apartments, guest bedrooms or a single guest room, a child's selection room, dressing and cosmetizing rooms, and an emergency power and lighting system.

8

Transportation

AIRPORTS AND TERMINALS 1025
AIRPORT CARGO FACILITIES 1075
AIR CARGO TERMINALS 1079
AIRPORT SERVICE EQUIPMENT BUILDINGS 1081
AIRCRAFT FIRE AND RESCUE STATION 1085
HELIPORTS 1087

STOL PORTS 1099
SEAPLANE TERMINALS 1103
BUS TERMINALS 1111
TRUCK TERMINALS 1117
   Truck Types and Dimensions 1123
   Docks 1125

By RICHARD M. ADLER, AIA, President, Brodsky, Hopf, & Adler, Architects & Engineers, P.C.

INTRODUCTION

An airport is like a total city devoted to dynamic movement. It comprises many varied structures that facilitate passenger and cargo movement, maintenance, and aircraft control, and other structures that provide for auxiliary support functions. The very nature of an airport's complexity makes it necessary to isolate its segments for design purposes. It is therefore the intent of this article to isolate primarily the passenger functions and to discuss how they tend to operate at an airport and what their general relationships to a community are.

Airport Operations

First, all the movements and functions of the passengers, the cargo, and the airline employees to and from an airport are regulated by a printed schedule. That is, the action that each discipline will follow is begun on the basis of this schedule, and the passenger's actions are based on the printed timetable of the airline he has chosen to fly.

The cargo movements to or from the community are based upon the normal working hours of the community. This working schedule is generally in conflict with the flying schedule of the airline. Therefore it requires special correlation by the airline.

The employees' working hours are predicated upon the functions of each discipline as it relates to the schedule. Therefore, all major elements of movement to and from the airport tend to take place upon a preestablished, programmed basis. However, the technology of the aviation industry changes so rapidly that a secondary but most important consideration arises. The technology can, overnight, change the preestablished schedules, thereby changing all relationships and movement to and from the airport. This occurs in three ways:

1. The aircraft manufacturer has demonstrated his ability to produce new aircraft with greater speeds, capable of carrying a gross load comparable to that of existing aircraft. Therefore, with the faster aircraft, time zones that had one relationship now have another. This then affects the predetermined schedule and all the related disciplines.

2. The ability to change and increase the payload of the aircraft for both passengers and cargo creates a new condition. This requires a revision of function and all disciplines in order to accept greater numbers of passengers and increased cargo movement within a short period of time. It also creates voids during other periods of the day.

3. This condition results from both increased payload and increased speed. This will totally change the predetermined schedule.

Therefore, a constant program factor in the development and design of all functions and disciplines is the fact that flexibility for future growth and expansion must be incorporated.

There is another factor to be considered within the design program, and that is the on-time record of aircraft as related to the printed schedule. The actual arrival and departure times are subject to weather conditions, me-chanical difficulties, and other special considerations that will arise from time to time.

The extent of on-time arrival or departure by aircraft and the extent of deviation from the schedule must be carefully evaluated. The airlines themselves afford the best source of information related to this problem. Although the scheduling and on-time record is good, a 10 or 15 percent deviation can raise havoc at an airport; therefore, consideration must be directed toward the capability of handling the peak condition plus an overload factor for deviation from the schedule. No two airports function in the same manner. The overload factor must be evaluated separately. However, the designer must use caution and be aware of the fact that peak capacity may be reached only at two or maybe four hours a day, depending upon the airport, and for the remainder of a 24-hour day, selected elements of the airport operate at very low efficiency. Restraint must be exercised to carefully control the amount of structure that is designed so as to provide an economically correct solution.

An airport functions as a transfer point between air vehicles and ground vehicles. There are numerous types of air vehicles designed for various functions.

The ground vehicles at an airport can take many forms. They are motor vehicles utilized as passenger cars, trucks, etc.; rapid transit systems of many descriptions; and special loading vehicles which can be utilized for supplementary transfer within the airport proper. The transfer point (passenger terminal) is generally a building structure or structures, and it is to its activities that we will primarily address ourselves. However, the understanding of the operation of this type building would be incomplete without the knowledge of a series of systems that must be correlated to its activity.

The activity is divided into public and nonpublic functions as an operating reality. The public function for both arrival and departure of passengers is described in Figs. 1 to 3. The nonpublic function is described in Figs. 4 to 6.

Relationship to Community

The operation of the airport is no different than the operation of a small city and is inherently set in motion by economic factors. It is also influenced by the fact that for the traveling passenger, air transportation makes the period of inconvenience considerably shorter than it would be with other conventional systems. However, an airport cannot be an island unto itself, and it has a great impact on a community. The very size of the airport affects the surrounding community. The careful planning of buildings and site location afford the potential for improving the environment and economics of a community.

There are many problems of noise, air pollution, and ecological balance that can be minimized or eliminated by proper site planning and building design. The community is affected by the working population of the airport, by the introduction of new industry, and by the economic impact of same.

The economic health of the airport and the architect's attempt to stay within the bounds thereby established cannot be overemphasized. The successful operation of the airport will demand total cooperation with the surrounding community. It thereby follows that every effort to establish proper working relationships among the many varied systems within the airport will be predicated upon a successful relationship with the surrounding community.

GLOSSARY

AMENITIES: That part of a terminal building housing convenience, service, and diversion facilities for the passengers, tenants, and public.

AVERAGE PEAK HOUR: The peak hour of the average peak day. The peak hour is the one-hour period of any peak day during which the highest percentage of the day's traffic is experienced. The average peak day is the average of the top 37 days (10 percent) of a year in terms of traffic volume.

BAGGAGE DIVERTER: A mechanical device for transferring baggage from a moving conveyor belt to a baggage claim counter in such manner that the baggage is evenly distributed along the baggage counter.

BOARDING CONTROL POINT: The point at which a passenger's credentials are inspected to assure that he is authorized to board a particular flight. Normally, this point is located in the vicinity of the gate from which the flight will depart.

BOARDING PASSENGER: Any originating or connecting passenger authorized to board a flight.

CONNECTING PASSENGER: A passenger who arrives on one flight only for the purpose of transferring to another flight to reach his destination. These passengers are broken down into two categories: intraline and interline passengers.

CUSTOMS: This is an area under federal jurisdiction through which passengers arriving from foreign countries are required by law to pass in order to make a declaration related to baggage which is accompanying them upon entry to the United States. This area is used for receipt of a declaration and/or examination of baggage. If duty is required, the customs agent will receive same in the customs area. Special attention must be paid to the design of this area because of changing techniques of operation.

DEPARTURE ROOM: An assembly area, including the boarding control point, located at a gate position(s) for passaengers pending availability of aircraft for boarding.

DEPLANING: Any passenger, cargo, baggage, visitor, etc., which is related to the unloading from an arriving flight.

Transportation

AIRPORTS AND TERMINALS

DOMESTIC PASSENGERS: All passengers traveling in the United States or its territories are considered as domestic. Foreign nationals within the confines and territory require no special checking and operate as domestics.

ENPLANING: Any passenger, cargo, baggage, visitor, etc., which is related to the boarding of a departing flight.

FIS: FIS is an abbreviation for Federal Inspection Services. It is utilized as an all-inclusive term for the U.S. Public Health, Immigration, and Naturalization Service, the Department of Agriculture, and U.S. Customs.

GATE: A location to which aircraft are brought for the purpose of discharging and loading passengers and their baggage.

GATE CONCOURSE: An extension from the main terminal building primarily intended to provide protected access for passengers between the main terminal building and the gates. In addition to the passenger corridor, the concourse may include airline functional areas and minimum consumer services.

GROUND TRANSPORTATION: The independently operated transportation vehicles scheduled for passengers' use between airports and the areas served thereby is called ground transportation.

IMMIGRATION: This area is devoted to the examination of passports of United States nationals and aliens seeking to enter the United States. Consideration for design and function of this area must be correlated with federal authorities.

INTERLINE CONNECTING(ION): A term used to describe passengers and baggage which arrive on the flight of one airline and depart on a flight of another.

INTOWN TERMINAL: A facility located apart from the airport, usually in the downtown area of the city, at which passengers may be processed, baggage is checked to passengers' destinations, and from which ground transportation is provided.

INTRALINE CONNECTING(ION): A term used to describe passengers and baggage which arrive on one flight and depart on another flight of the same airline.

IN-TRANSIT PASSENGER: If an internationally bound aircraft stops at an airport for refueling or discharge of passengers and a remaining number of passengers are to be detained in the aircraft for another destination, the convenience of providing a totally segregated lounge facility may be warranted for the continuing passengers. This facility is referred to as an in-transit area. No FIS inspection is required, but security of the area is important.

LONG-HAUL A term used to define flights or traffic which travel over a relatively long distance as opposed to those which travel over a shorter distance. Normally, long-haul passengers arrive at their originating airport earlier than short-haul passengers, carry more baggage than short-haul passengers, and are accompanied to or are met at the airport by more persons than short-haul passengers.

ORIGINATING PASSENGER: A passenger who is starting his trip.

OUTBOUND BAGGAGE ROOM: The area to which checked baggage of originating passengers is delivered for sorting by flights prior to its being dispatched to the aircraft for loading.

PUBLIC HEALTH SERVICE: The function of the Public Health Service is to determine whether an arriving passenger will present a health hazard to the general population. This may require inoculation, special examination, and possibly quarantine. Design requires correlation with federal authorities.

READY ROOM: An area adjacent to the normal work areas in which personnel whose duties are performed out-of-doors may assemble, be protected, and from which they may receive their work assignments. These rooms should be concealed from public view.

SELF-CLAIM BAGGAGE: A method under which passengers have direct access to terminating baggage in a controlled area. As passengers leave the area, an attendant retrieves baggage claim checks and matches them to strap checks to assure that passengers have selected only baggage to which they are entitled.

SHORT-HAUL: A term used to define flights or traffic which travel over a relatively short distance as opposed to those which travel over a long distance. Normally, short-haul passengers arrive at the airport of origin later than long-haul passengers, carry less baggage than long-haul passengers, and are accompanied to or met at the airport by fewer persons than long-haul passengers.

STANDBY PASSENGER: A passenger not holding confirmed space but who is on hand at departure time for space that might become available.

TERMINATING PASSENGER: A passenger who has arrived at his destination.

THROUGH PASSENGER: A passenger who arrives and departs on the same flight.

TRANSFER BAGGAGE ROOM: The area to which checked baggage of connecting passengers is delivered for sorting by flights prior to its being dispatched to the aircraft for loading. This may be combined with the outbound baggage room at some locations.

UNIT TERMINAL: One of several functionally complete terminal areas (which may be in the same or several buildings) each of which houses the activities of one or more airlines.

PRELIMINARY DESIGN PROGRAM AND DEVELOPMENT CONSIDERATIONS

Before planning in any form can proceed, the architect must establish a data bank and an ability to retrieve pieces of information in the most rapid manner. This includes all information from participating airlines and all programs on studies that may have been completed by the airport authority. General economic considerations must be examined and the geographical site location evaluated. The acquisition of the data, the digestion of same, and the request for supplementary information must be made at this time.

The architect must also make inquiries to the governing agency as to the requirements of the Civil Aeronautics Administration and all other government agencies. The architect must further recognize the assistance, advice, and guidance by organizations such as Air Transport Association, Airline Pilots Association, and International Air Transport Association.

The most important single element that the architect must provide for in his design is flexibility, so that all elements of the system may grow as required. In design and planning, the following must have growth capability on an individual basis without jeopardizing the total relationship of the master plan. Parking lots must be capable of growth within any specific area as demands require, and public transportation systems must be capable of individual growth. Curb frontage must grow on an independent basis. Baggage claim areas, check-in areas, gate lounge areas, aircraft positions, the number of aircraft positions—any or all of these elements and the airline operational areas must offer the capability of independent growth to meet the changing demands of the future.

The prime reason for this independence and flexibility relates to the problem of aircraft technology and the fact that the preestablished schedules may change and, as a result, congestion may become a problem at almost any point in the terminal system. These two factors make it mandatory that each element have a built in potential for expansion.

Most of the airports and the terminal structures involved have been based upon a program which is known as a *traffic forecast*. Most of the terminal buildings have been predicated on a "guesstimate" or a series of criteria and assumptions. These criteria and assumptions are further based on the guesstimate of schedule. It therefore follows that the architect would be wrong to design a structure with fixed parameters based on this information. Flexibility must be inherent in each of the elements, yet both good design and economy must be maintained. When all program information has been collected and expansion flexibility has been planned for, the architect must establish a first-stage program based upon the scheduled opening date for the airport. He must then relate this program to an ultimate date of operation. The best method for this is through the use of a computer model simulation.

The computer simulation can be established by examining the maximum number of aircraft movements that air saturation will allow and correlating this with the maximum ground area that may be available for the airport under consideration. This data can now be related back to the terminal building area for all functional disciplines that pertain. The summation of maximums and minimums will now serve as a guide for the master plan of the terminal building area. Since this analysis is extremely complex, the architect should retain specialists in this area of endeavor.

Using the computer simulation as a working tool, the architect can establish a preliminary design concept or concepts and, in addition, preliminary expansion stages for planning can be established. The architect should not take this preliminary work back to the computer at this time. Instead, he must now test and eval-

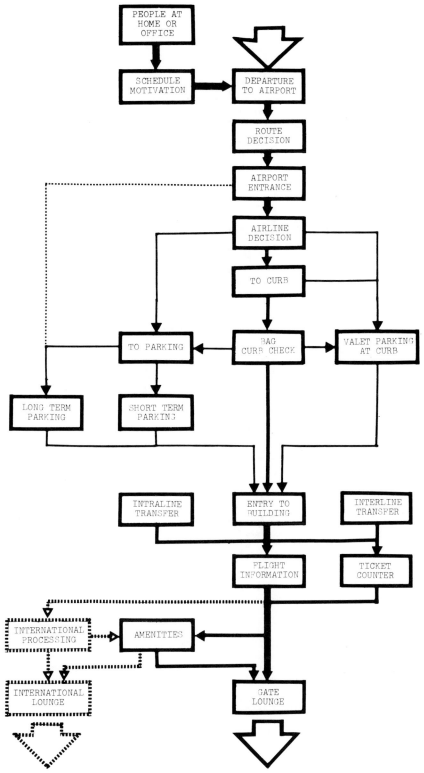

Fig. 1 Enplaning passenger flow.

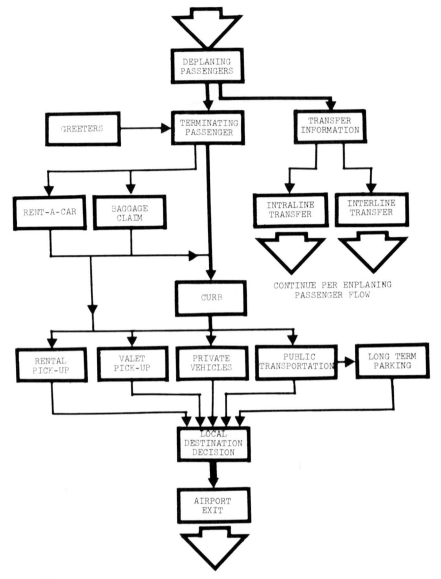

Fig. 2 Domestic deplaning passenger flow.

uate critical conditions that can occur due to changing technology, passenger growth, and expansion, and the computer will allow him to check each discipline of all the functional aspects of the terminal area. This would include all functions within the terminal building, curb-side accessibility, parking requirements (both public and employees'), road access and capabilities, public transportation, etc. Either computer simulation or analytical methods will establish time periods of congestion traditionally referred to as "average peak hours." The architect will carefully examine the average peak hour so as to ascertain simple, direct, and logical routes for all passengers, including their baggage and their vehicular transportation. He should then take these movements to the computer for analysis.

For example, assume that in the design of the terminal, average peak-hour traffic prob-

lems relate to a time span of 11 A.M. and 2 P.M. for arriving passenger flights. What will happen if, operating on the present city relationships, new aircraft traveling at considerably greater speeds become operational at this airport? It is very possible that the computer simulation will show there is no effect, or, quite the contrary, it may show that the average peaking conditions may double up.

Taking into account the time frame, the architect will be further required to work with each of the airlines to ascertain their method of operation. How do they handle passengers, baggage, cargo, amenities, food service, ramp operations, maintenance, and their own personnel? He will then attempt to provide space utilization compatible with the different users. He will also establish those space needs required by the FAA, the airport administration, etc.

Another inevitable problem directly related to the terminal building is that of providing parking space for automobiles. The architect must acquire from the operator of the parking area a system of tariffs, including those that will be applied to short-term, long-term, and valet parking. Without the tariff indication, it is impossible to determine the accrual rate of vehicular parking. The accrual rate is the factor that determines the number of parking spaces that will be required. Any change in the tariff or relationships of tariffs will change the accrual rate and therefore will change the parking space requirements.

As an additional factor, the architect must consider employee parking and the congestion that occurs during the shift changes. It therefore becomes necessary for the architect to ascertain the general character of employment practices by the airlines involved as it relates

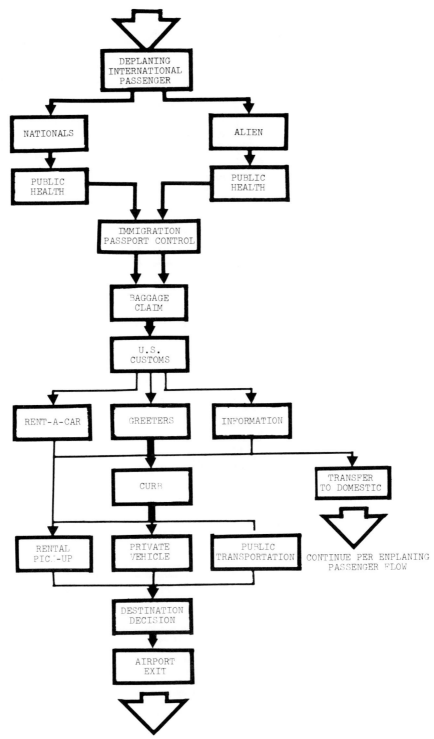

Fig. 3 International deplaning passenger flow.

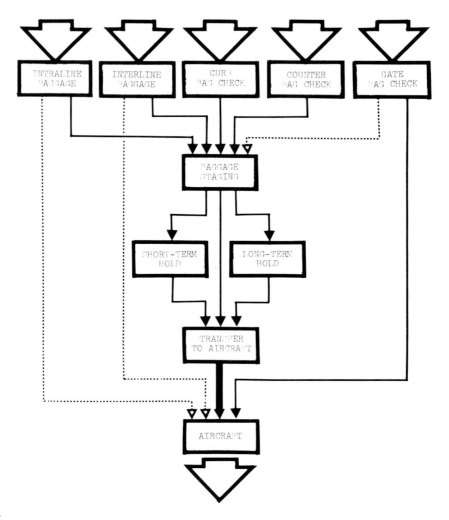

Fig. 4   Enplaning baggage.

to the schedule of time. Care must be exercised in developing access for employees to the terminal building.

In developing the passenger terminal, the architect must recognize in the early phases of planning that the new wide-body type of aircraft carries vast amounts of cargo. The economics of the new aircraft require that a sizable portion of its cargo-carrying capacity be utilized in the transportation of passengers.

Therefore the passenger terminal, if it is to serve in the best interests of the airlines and their equipment, must have the capacity to store cargo for loading into passenger aircraft. This is true for all types and sizes of passenger terminal and will tend to hold for the small terminal as well as major terminals. For with the greater use of the wide-bodied aircraft, this is becoming standard practice.

Since the passenger terminal is the transfer point between land and air, consideration must be given to the geometrics of the aircraft apron. It should afford a great degree of flexibility to include larger aircraft, aircraft mix (different types of aircraft), space required for ground equipment, the storage of cargo, and the techniques for loading people from the building to aircraft.

Any passenger terminal system will rely

heavily upon the ability of the public to secure information. It is therefore incumbent upon the architect to give consideration as early as possible to the nature and types of information systems that will be made available to the general public, so as to guide them to their desired locations.

Early planning must take into account fire safety and access to the structure as well as the probabilities of insurance premiums. The fire hazards relating to the terminal structure can be most readily identified as aircraft, fueling operations on the aircraft apron, public area hazards, baggage room areas, and cargo storage areas.

It is not unusual in smaller terminals for secondary functions of the airline to be incorporated into the terminal building. These may fall into categories such as in-flight feeding, line maintenance, and general office use.

The designer of the terminal building must at an early date include significant analyses of engineering considerations, as this will involve boiler plants, air conditioning, electrical distribution, communications systems, waste removal, and maintenance areas. Any mechanical system that is utilized must of necessity have an alternate or redundant system so that reliability of operation is guaranteed at the airport.

GENERAL DESIGN CONSIDERATIONS

Figure 7 attempts to illustrate some of the devices and systems which are available to the designer. The selection of the appropriate combination of elements will be predicated upon the carrier who will utilize same, the combination of carriers, the geographical site size and layout, and the economic considerations related to the total system development. All these techniques are constantly being improved and updated.

Design Solutions for Passenger Terminals

It is well to examine many of the historic techniques that have been utilized in the development of passenger terminals, as much can be gained therefrom.

Consolidated Passenger Terminal In this illustration, the designer can examine the technique of relating several airlines to a consolidated single structure. This structure initially provides a simple transfer stage for ground vehicles and air vehicles. The epitome of this and the most efficient in operation would be a simple airstrip with no more than a few aircraft positions and occasional aircraft scheduled.

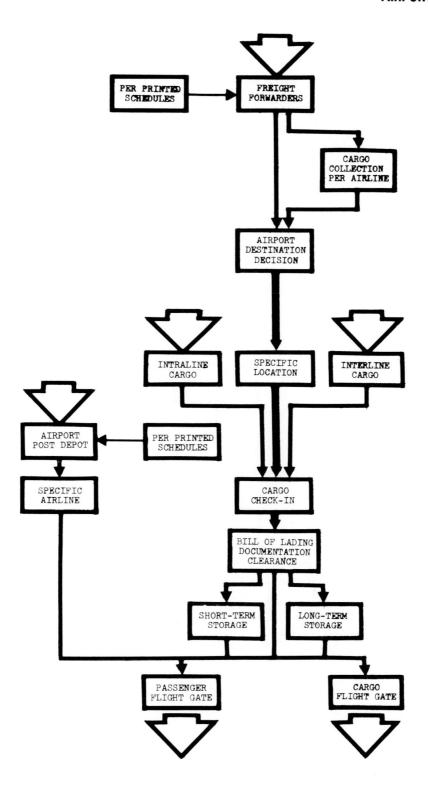

Fig. 5   Enplaning cargo.

Transportation

AIRPORTS AND TERMINALS

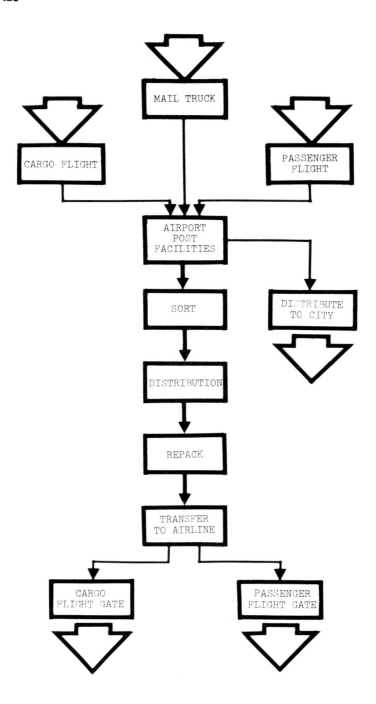

Fig. 6   Mail cargo.

The effective use of the consolidated terminal can best be measured by convenience to passengers and efficiency of operation for the airline. Major terminal complexes invariably are multiples of this small, consolidated group.

Finger Terminal (Consolidated)

Satellite Terminal (Consolidated) In these two illustrations the designer can see the evolution of a finger terminal and a satellite terminal arrangement as merely an expansion of a concept. Now the convenience to the passengers has been questioned and the increased number of aircraft positions has been related as closely as possible to the consolidated function. The evolution of these two concepts has introduced many varied problems with the single terminal. The problems are related to ground transportation needs, access to the building, prolonged walking distances, grave limitations on the aircraft apron, and the fact that all functional requirements for the airlines are totally constrained because of the physical arrangement.

Finger Terminals (Decentralized)

Satellite Terminals (Decentralized) By looking at the next two illustrations, the designer can see that decentralization offers the possibility of lessening the constraint for the individual airlines and allowing each airline to operate within its own building, but it also causes difficulties to the public in terms of rapid communications for the proper selection of a desired location. The decentralization causes further problems of interline transfers. While it also permits some advantages of more aircraft apron space, it does involve great demands upon ground vehicle transportation, problems which may possibly be solved by the use of a rapid transit system.

Drive to Gate The next illustration shows a drive-to-the-gate concept which is really the simplest form of terminal, relating back to the

1032

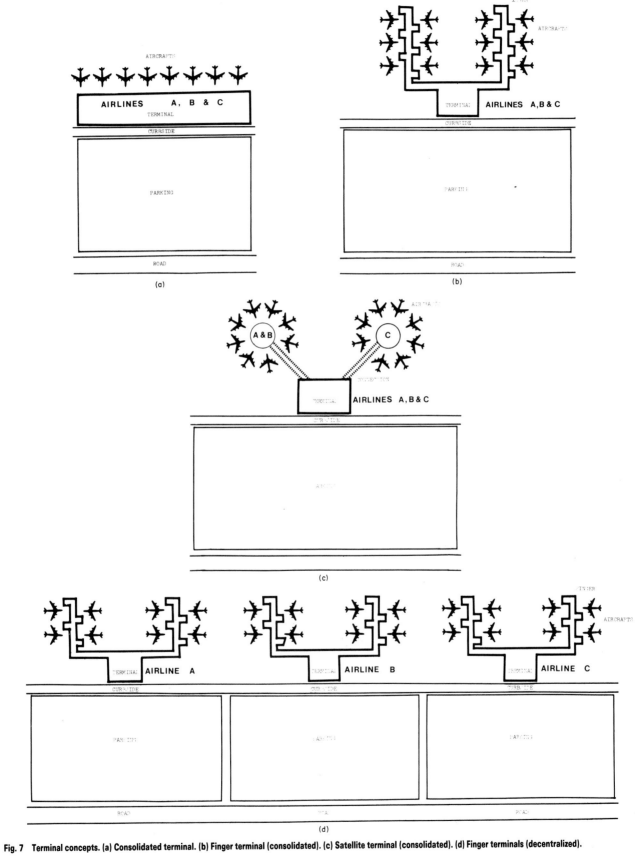

Fig. 7 Terminal concepts. (a) Consolidated terminal. (b) Finger terminal (consolidated). (c) Satellite terminal (consolidated). (d) Finger terminals (decentralized).

Transportation

AIRPORTS AND TERMINALS

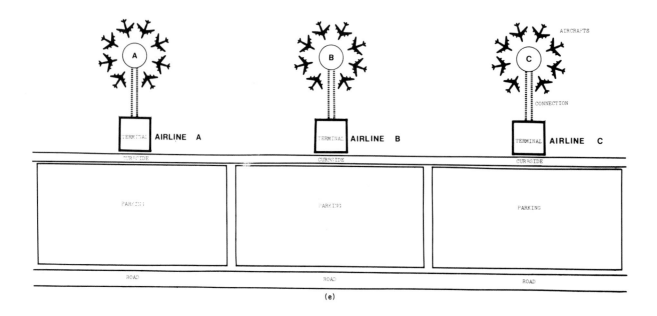

(e)

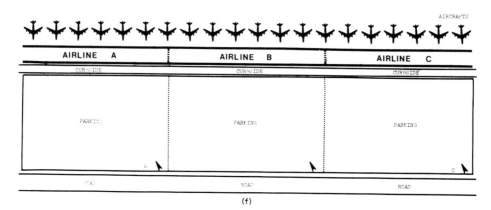

(f)

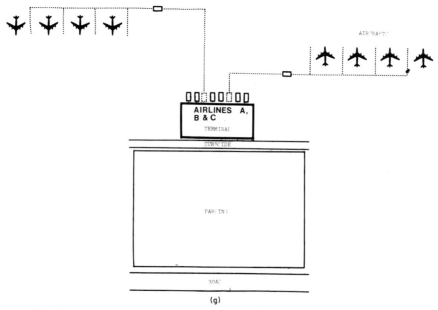

(g)

Fig. 7 (cont.) Terminal concepts. (e) Satellite terminals (decentralized). (f) Drive to gate. (g) Mobile lounge.

1034

TABLE 1   Airline Statistical Data Requirements

1. Estimated enplaning and deplaning traffic:
   Figures on enplaning and deplaning passengers should be given separately.
   a. Passengers — total number per year
      Passengers — average day, peak month
      Passengers — peak hour and time
      Passenger characteristic (business, vacation, student)
   b. Interline passengers
   c. Intraline passengers
   d. Originating passengers
   e. Air freight cargo — total tons
   f. Mail — total tons
   g. Baggage — total number per year
      Baggage — average day, peak month
2. Projected flight schedule:
   a. City pairs
   b. Originating and terminating
   c. Time frame
   d. Aircraft type
3. Aircraft:
   a. Number of gate positions
   b. Number and type of aircraft for gate size design
   c. Aircraft parking attitude
4. Terminal building spaces:
   a. Gate lounge — number and sizes
   b. Baggage claim type and size
   c. Amenities area
   d. Operational facilities — type and sizes
   e. Central ticketing facilities
5. Automobile parking requirements (airline experience):
   a. Public
   b. Valet
   c. Taxis
   d. Limousines
   e. Car rental
   f. Employees

early consolidated terminal approach with a minimum of passenger constraints. The success of this terminal approach is dependent upon a highly sophisticated information system and a ground vehicle connection between gates or related groups of gate locations.

Mobile Lounge   The mobile lounge system as a concept provides a consolidated terminal with remote parking of aircraft, and this as a system can operate efficiently and function properly as long as the gate lounges are operative (this precludes allowing drivers of the lounges the right to strike against the operator of the airport).

It poses problems in ground control on the air side of the terminal building and requires additional personnel for its total operation.

These illustrations show schematically the design concepts that are in use in present-day airports. They also point out their own efficiencies and their specific resultant problems, none of which are insurmountable. It is apparent that these basic concepts take many varied shapes and forms in present-day use and that combinations of concepts are employed. It is also apparent that substitute methods of ground transportation are in use for movement within the terminal area and for remote aircraft parking areas. However, no matter what combination of systems is designed, to reach a desired solution, it must be tested and checked for the specific requirements of any given airport for its present use and for its future growth.

AIRLINE REQUIREMENTS

The architect will carefully ascertain from the individual carriers their specific needs. This information should be correlated to the year of operations, the anticipated level of passenger and cargo, operational growth, the potential of changing route structures, and an initial and future projected flight schedule. Table 1 lists the basic data information that is required from the airlines. There are many additional technical information items which are not listed here, but the designer will determine these by inference.

Each airline demands a distinctive visual character that will make it readily identifiable to the public. All too frequently the architect tends to dismiss this requirement. The careful integration of individual airline identification in a total building design will assist the passenger. An airline will retain many professional consultants in attempting to carry a corporate image systemwide, and it will spend considerable sums of money in order to achieve this.

Undoubtedly, not all corporate identity systems are in good taste. However one should not dismiss the very special effort to achieve a simple visual image that the airlines attempt to achieve. Design judgment at this point is of paramount importance.

AIRCRAFT PARKING SYSTEMS

The placement of aircraft on the aircraft apron may be divided into two categories: push-out operations and power-out operations. The architect should determine the general technique that the airlines will utilize. The system they select will have a great effect on the aircraft apron area as well as the passenger loading system that can be utilized.

Power-out operations will involve special design considerations with regard to the wall surfaces of terminal buildings and they will require greater apron area. They will also call for blast protection in the operational areas of the terminal. This method of operation will generally mean that fewer ground personnel and less equipment are required.

The push-out operation requires the use of expensive tractors and personnel to move the aircraft out of its gate position before it powers away from the terminal area. The push-out operation does offer the advantage of requiring less apron area. It also requires less square footage at the terminal building because of a reduced linear length.

Included in the data sheets is general information related to the major types of aircraft presently in operation and some information related to future aircraft (Figs. 8 to 11).

PASSENGER LOADING METHODS

The passenger is most vocal about the technique that an airline uses for loading the aircraft. He responds rapidly to climatic conditions and will inevitably express his distress to the airport authority and the airline. Many sys-

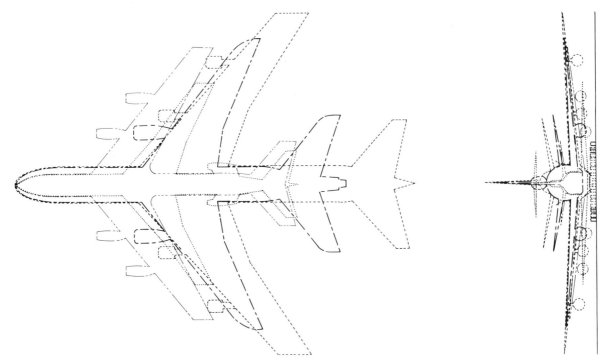

Fig. 8 Aircraft composite.

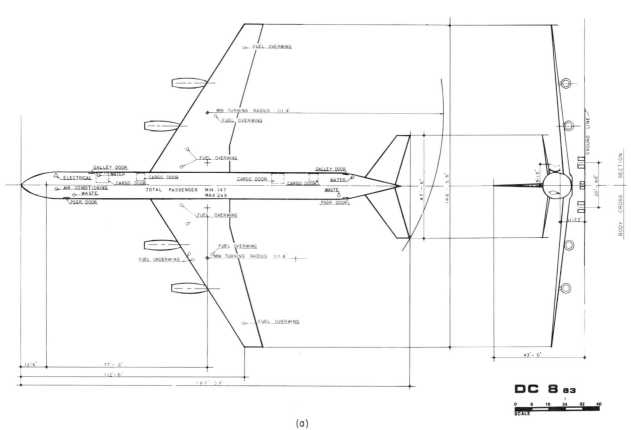

(a)

Fig. 9

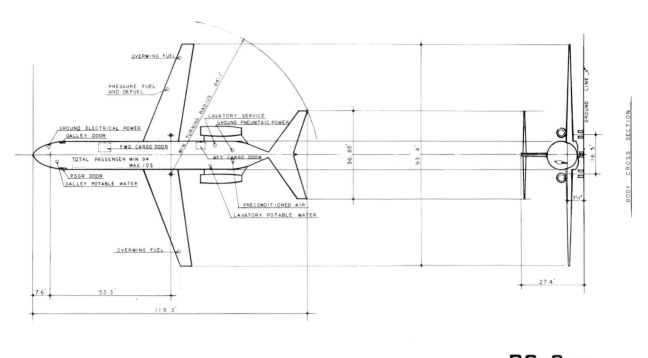

(b)

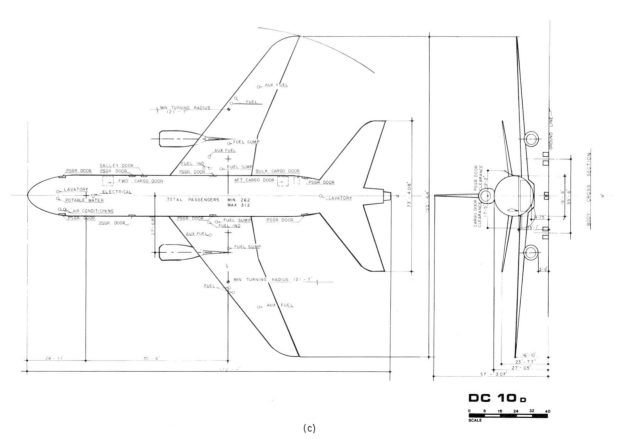

(c)

Fig. 9 (cont.)

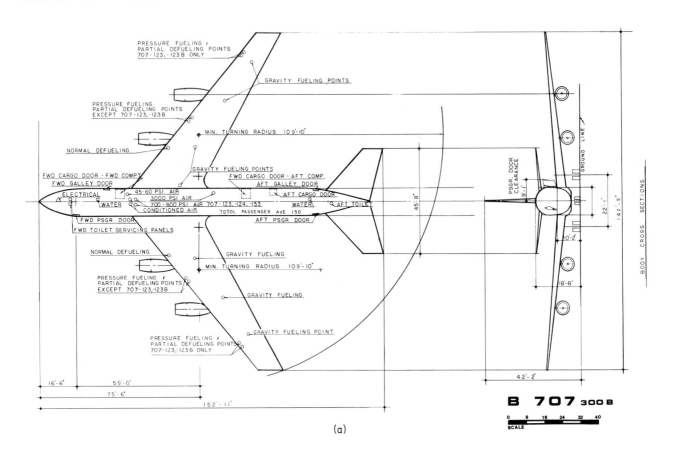

(a)

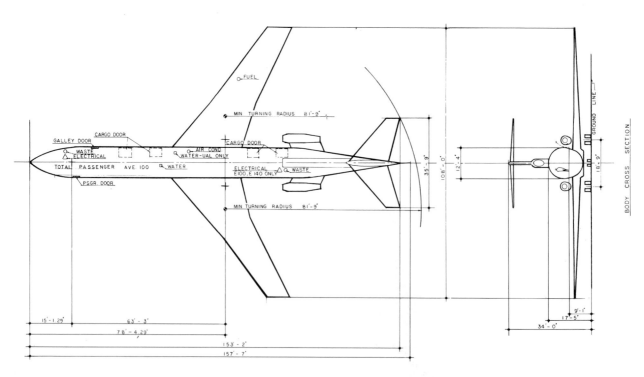

(b)

Fig. 10

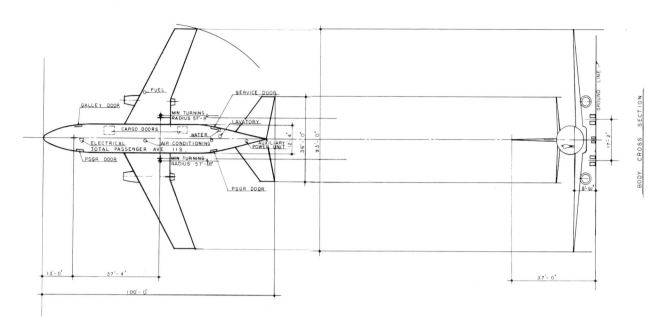

(c)

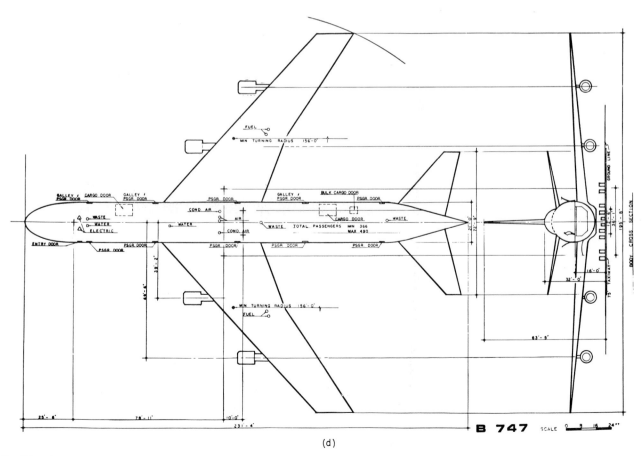

(d)

Fig. 10 (cont.)

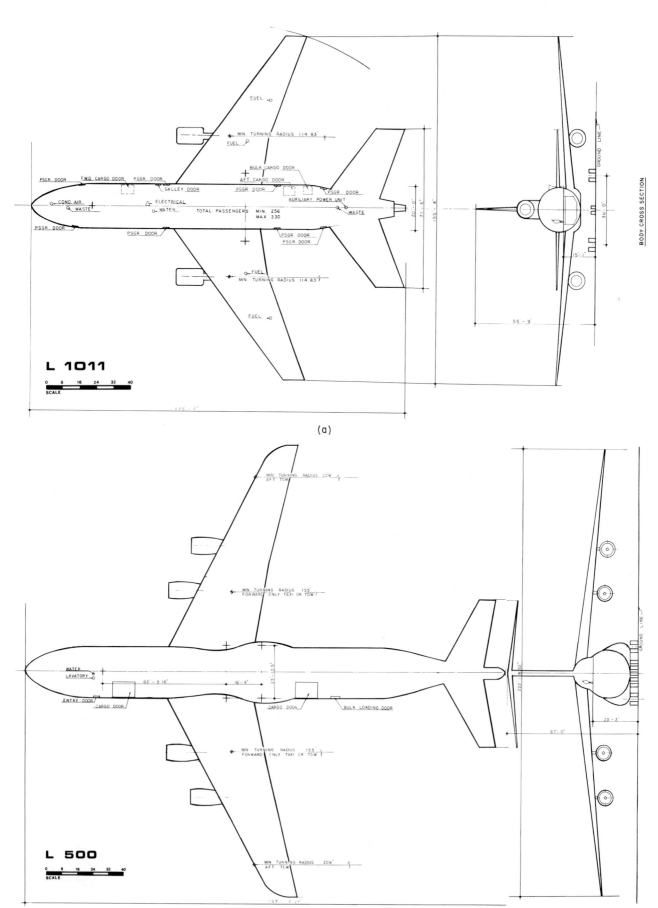

L 1011

(a)

L 500

(b)

Fig. 11

1040

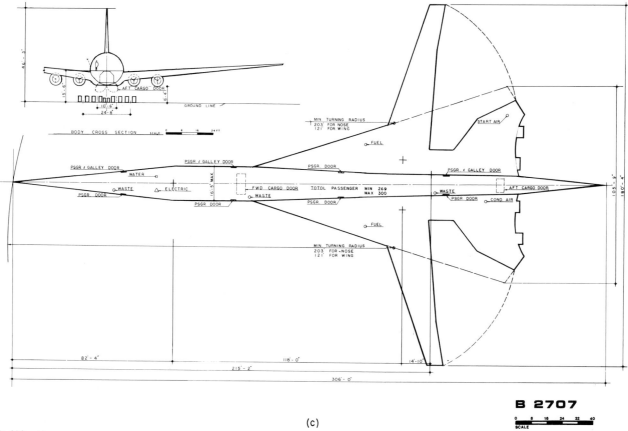

(c)

Fig. 11 (cont.)

tems have become available for passenger enplaning and deplaning depending upon the volumes of passengers, the economic considerations, and the general climatic conditions of the community. Any combination of systems is available. The following chart illustrates some of these systems (Fig. 12).

GATE LOUNGE CONCEPT

The concept and functions of the gate lounge are basically standard throughout the airline industry. The basic functional requirements are a ticket counter with all its communication equipment, a secure or semisecure seating area with sufficient seating capacity to handle the passengers, flight identification, last-minute baggage drop, and circulation pattern which separates the deplaning passenger from the enplaning passenger (Fig. 13).

However, each airline's requirements will vary in accordance with its operation procedures and level of activity.

Listed below are average sizes for gate lounges as required by each type of aircraft.

Gate lounge sizes, sq ft:

1. B-747 6,000
2. L-1011 . . . 4,000
3. DC-10 4,000
4. B2702 . . . 4,000
5. DC-8 3,500
6. B-707 3,500
7. B-737 2,000
8. B-727 2,000
9. DC-9 1,500

These sizes are approximate and should be used for preliminary planning only. Some of the airlines prefer, for the wide-bodied aircraft,

a separate ticket counter for the processing of first-class passengers, and in some cases a separate seating area is required. The type of loading bridge that an airline desires will have a direct bearing on the plan layout of the lounge. For example, Fig. 12h and i demonstrates two different loading concepts for the same type of aircraft. It is obvious that the circulation pattern within the gate lounge for these two types of loading bridges will be completely different.

BAGGAGE HANDLING SYSTEMS

The need for a baggage handling system is obvious, but the system techniques, sophistication of equipment, and the desired cost level for a system are extremely difficult to evaluate.

Examination of trends becomes important in the baggage analysis. Currently the businessman traveler will carry on one suitcase which will fit below an airline seat and a garment bag of reasonable dimension which can be hung in a wardrobe on the aircraft. Thus he bypasses the baggage system. There is also all the transfer baggage which can bypass the check-in and claim part of the system.

It is not unusual for the volume of businessmen at a given airport to reach a 30 percent level, and it can be anticipated that at least 80 percent of these businessmen will not require any baggage check-in system. Nor is it unusual for the volume of transfer passengers to vary from 10 to 45 percent of the total passenger load. Therefore, the selection of the desired system will require a complete understanding of what percentage of the passengers

utilize the terminal facilities for the particular airport.

The present-day averages of baggage that is handled by the airlines ranges from 1.6 to 1.9 bags per passenger. This will vary depending upon the airport and the airline for the type of route structure that exists. For example, the longer the stage length, the greater the probability that passengers will take several pieces of luggage—although very long international stage lengths show a reduction. Therefore, an airline which has a route structure built basically of long stage lengths will handle a much greater number of bags than an airline with a route structure based upon short stage lengths.

In providing space for a baggage handling system, the architect must have a complete understanding of each airline operation and the relationship of all the airlines combined. This understanding should encompass the percentage of baggage per passenger for originating, terminating, and transfer (both interline and intraline). It also should be related to the time schedule and the peak conditions.

A baggage check-in system can incorporate check-in points at a central ticketing counter, at the gate lounge, at the curbside, and in a parking lot. The parking lot or curbside check-in provides the greatest amount of convenience for the passenger and allows for quick acceptance of the baggage. This means that the rest of the public space in the terminal area will not be congested by baggage, taking floor space while waiting to be checked in. The curbside check-in isolates the major portion of the baggage handling with sky cap personnel and not with airline agents.

A check-in system can be serviced by a simple conveyor or a gravity chute. For large

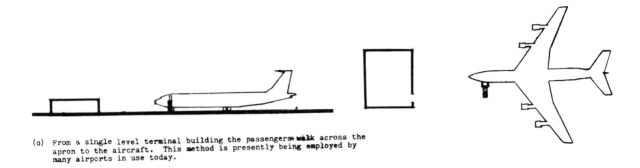

(a) From a single level terminal building the passengers walk across the apron to the aircraft. This method is presently being employed by many airports in use today.

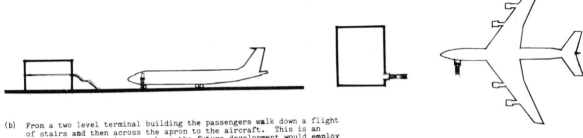

(b) From a two level terminal building the passengers walk down a flight of stairs and then across the apron to the aircraft. This is an intermediate phase in use, where the future development would employ the use of jetways.

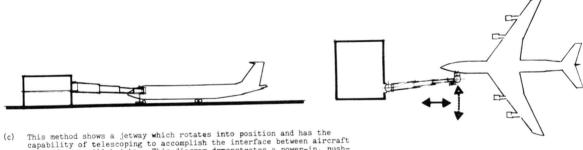

(c) This method shows a jetway which rotates into position and has the capability of telescoping to accomplish the interface between aircraft of different sill height. This diagram demonstrates a power-in, push-out gate position.

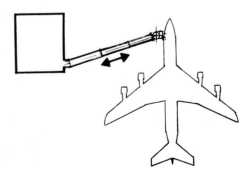

(d) This is the same as method (c) above, however, it differs only in that this diagram demonstrates a power-in, power-out gate position.

Fig. 12 Typical loading methods.

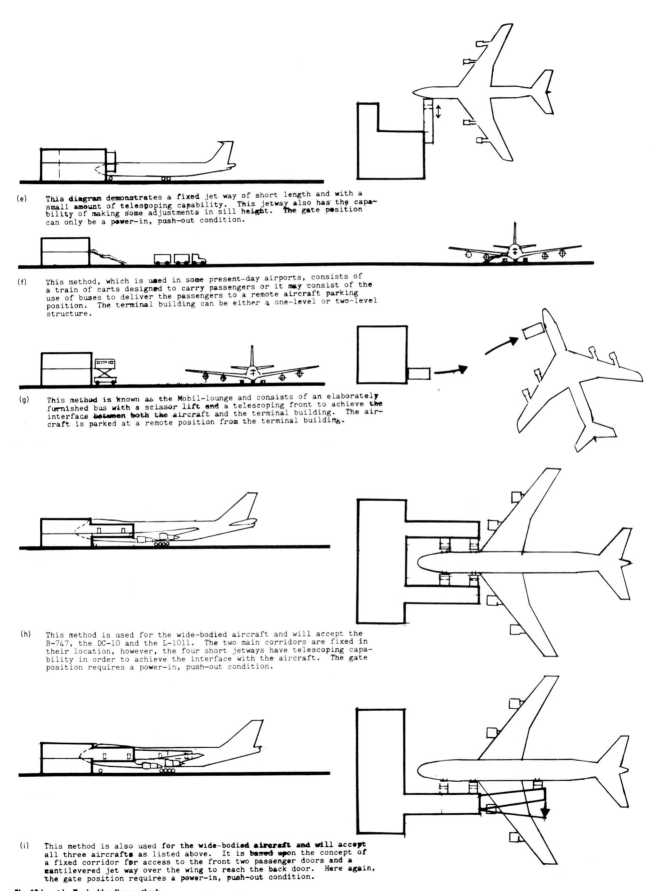

(e)   This diagram demonstrates a fixed jet way of short length and with a small amount of telescoping capability. This jetway also has the capability of making some adjustments in sill height. The gate position can only be a power-in, push-out condition.

(f)   This method, which is used in some present-day airports, consists of a train of carts designed to carry passengers or it may consist of the use of buses to deliver the passengers to a remote aircraft parking position. The terminal building can be either a one-level or two-level structure.

(g)   This method is known as the Mobil-lounge and consists of an elaborately furnished bus with a scissor lift and a telescoping front to achieve the interface between both the aircraft and the terminal building. The aircraft is parked at a remote position from the terminal building.

(h)   This method is used for the wide-bodied aircraft and will accept the B-747, the DC-10 and the L-1011. The two main corridors are fixed in their location, however, the four short jetways have telescoping capability in order to achieve the interface with the aircraft. The gate position requires a power-in, push-out condition.

(i)   This method is also used for the wide-bodied aircraft and will accept all three aircrafts as listed above. It is based upon the concept of a fixed corridor for access to the front two passenger doors and a cantilevered jet way over the wing to reach the back door. Here again, the gate position requires a power-in, push-out condition.

Fig. 12 (cont.)   Typical loading methods.

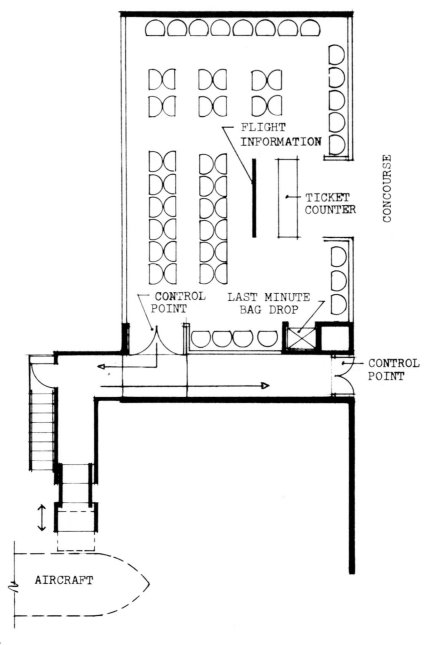

Fig. 13 Typical gate lounge.

terminal facilities where there can be many check-in points and more than one baggage makeup space, a system can comprise fully automated cars or pallets that move bags to many destinations. This type of sophisticated system is costly and, in order to justify its use, it should be considered as a total system of all baggage movement, from aircraft to passenger and from passenger to aircraft.

The acceptance of baggage from the originating passenger at the terminal is complicated by the acceptance of interline and intraline baggage for the transferring passengers. A large number of employees, for the amount of baggage handled, are utilized in interline transfers. Their route of travel by vehicle is frequently time-consuming. The transferred baggage is processed in the same backup area as the originating and terminating baggage, therefore space must be allowed in order to accom-

plish this handling. The volume of bags that is to be transferred and processed must be determined in cooperation with the airline user. The precise system used and its building space must have the capability of expansion from the initial operational level.

The selection of the correct baggage system must also be correlated to the reverse flow of baggage from aircraft to baggage claim. The baggage claim system, by its very nature, produces an acute problem of baggage handling. The terminating passenger from an arriving flight expects to claim his baggage within a short period of time. A peaking condition occurs when a combination of flights arrives within the same time frame. In contrast, the originating passengers will generally arrive at the airport over an extended period of time, therefore dispersing the handling of baggage over the same time period.

As larger aircraft, such as the 747, are utilized in greater numbers, the peaking conditions increase and decentralization of the baggage claim system becomes more desirable for the sake of passenger convenience and the elimination of congestion.

Baggage claim devices can involve many different shapes, forms, and methods of mechanical or manual handling of baggage. Figure 14 demonstrates the basic concepts that are available. The designer can see from these illustrations that the basic general technique is to produce a great display of linear feet of frontage so that passengers can readily identify their bags and claim same.

The interface between the aircraft and the claim area is still generally accomplished by towing the baggage to the terminal building, where a manual operation accomplishes the placement of baggage on the claiming device.

The ability to retrieve bags from the aircraft and transfer same to the terminal baggage handling system is a key element in rapid and efficient baggage dispersal.

The design of an automated system to transfer the baggage modules to the building system is technically feasible. This would eliminate the towing operation and provide a faster method of producing the baggage at the claim area. It would also mean that the baggage could be claimed in many different locations. However, this will depend upon the airline's required time frame, passenger convenience, and financial capabilities.

Baggage rooms must be handled with special caution to make sure that sufficient quantities of fresh air are provided if gasoline power tractors are used. Sprinkler protection must be provided and careful fire cutoff must be made between the terminal proper and baggage areas. Doors leading from the baggage room to the outside should be automated and must use rapid-acting equipment. However, it is important to provide, on all doors, safety edges which will prevent closure should an obstacle be in the way. The design concept must incorporate the capability of future expansion, and preferably this should be accomplished without disturbing the existing claiming facilities.

Area Considerations for Baggage Systems

Enplaning Baggage As indicated in the flow diagram (Fig. 4), baggage may be received from three possible sources:

1. *Curbside check-in.* This area must provide convenience of tagging and usually some mechanical conveyance back to a central bag room.

2. *Counter check-in.* This will coincide with the usual ticket counter in the main terminal area. It is customary to provide mechanization from an area directly in the back of the ticket counter to the central baggage room.

3. *Gate check-in.* In small quantities, bags are received at the gate. Bags must be checked in at this point because many passengers mistakenly believe that their suitcases will be accepted for storage in the passenger portion of the plane. A significant number of airline passengers frequently use carry-on suitcases, but unless such luggage can be stored below the seat and out of aisle space, it must be carried in the baggage compartment.

4. *Transfer baggage.* Additional bags will be received at a convenient location adjacent to the baggage room for transfer from other airlines or the same carrier. All baggage rooms which utilize mechanized equipment must be provided with sufficient room for manual handling in the event that service requirements cause a shutdown.

Deplaning Baggage For baggage claim areas, a simple square foot calculation cannot be used to determine the desired area, for there are too many variables that influence establishment of the proper layout. The basic terminal building concept will have a great influence on the baggage claim design. A terminal building which consolidates all the airlines into one claim area establishes a different set of parameters than does a terminal building concept where decentralization of airlines separates the baggage claims for each airline. In some decentralized concepts, airlines are now developing more than one claim area for each traffic level. A terminal building which processes international arrivals requires another set of parameters for the establishment of the claim area.

In order to size a baggage claim area, the architect must have the following information: the number of passengers and the amount of baggage that will be claimed within the peak condition, the type of claiming device and its physical size, its capacity, and its linear feet of frontage. Care should be taken to determine the actual working capacity of the claiming device and not the theoretical capacity as advertised by manufacturers. The architect should also determine the desired type of operation and degree of security required by either the airline or the authority. With the correlation of this material, the architect can now start to size the claim area. For an international arrivals system, the architect should allow additional space for the queuing of passengers between the claim device and the customs inspection system.

GENERAL CONSIDERATIONS

Needless to say, passengers who may be carrying baggage should be offered such conveniences of design as automated doors, sufficiently wide escalators, moving sidewalks, and similar devices. At all times the analysis of traffic flow, volume of passengers, and direction of movement should be carefully considered.

Air traffic passengers rapidly cross international boundaries, and language problems must be anticipated. The International Air Transport Association has given serious consideration to the language problem and has attempted to develop a series of glyphs which can frequently be used in lieu of bilingual messages.

Telephone communication is a necessary and important element in the passenger terminal. In some instances this will require a telephone communication center with bilingual operators.

The terminal must also provide amenities for the traveling public. These may include any of the following list and such other items as may be determined by a particular locale:

Bank	Newsstand[1]
Barber shop	Observation deck
Camera shop	Parcel lockers[1]
Candy store	Restaurant and
Car rental agencies[1]	supplementary
Cocktail lounge	eating facilities[1]
Drug store	Rest room facilities[1]
Duty free shops	Shoe shine
Employee snack bar	Showers/dressing rooms
and cafeteria[1]	Teenage lounge
Flower shop	Telegraph (desk, phones,
Gift shop	or both)[1]
Haberdashery	Telephones[1]
Hotel	Television lounge
Insurance vending[1]	Valet
Money exchange	Women's wear

In addition to the amenities, consideration should be given to traveler's aid in large installations and nursery facilities adjacent to the women's lounge in the main portion of the facility. Medical and first-aid facilities should be included in the passenger terminal if they are not provided elsewhere in the airport.

An internal telephone system may be required between the airlines, the operating authority, and/or police authorities. The size of the terminal building and the complex needs of each user should receive consideration when planning the telephone system.

[1] Considered essential by airline operators.

CURB FRONTAGE UTILIZATION

When designed correctly, curb frontage at the face of the terminal building will function properly for a very high percentage of the time. The curb frontage can be the failure point for the entire terminal operation. It can cause confusion, congestion, missed flights by enplaning passengers, and become a safety hazard to pedestrians if they must cross the road system.

The architect must devote considerable time and effort to designing the curbside frontage and the road system to it. Present design trends and concepts have separated the enplaning and deplaning road systems, but very few have eliminated pedestrian traffic across these roads. (See Fig. 15.)

In the design of the curb frontage, the architect must consider all the forms of vehicular movement, such as private passenger vehicles, valet-driven cars, rental cars, taxis, and public transportation (especially buses).

To determine the quantity of curb frontage, the following factors and assumptions must be considered:

1. All vehicles will require approximately 35 lin ft at the curb. This is a realistic interpretation of the indiscriminate manner in which vehicles tend to be parked.

2. The average time required at the curb for passenger vehicles should be surveyed for passengers by type of vehicle.

3. Duration time for valet parking will exceed the standard for passenger cars in order to provide time for an attendant to queue the vehicle prior to its being parked and so as not to impose a penalty on the need for curb frontage. The total of parking queuing time is estimated at five minutes.

4. In order to compensate for heavy congestion periods resulting from holidays, delays, etc., occurring 12 times or more per year, it is recommended that the working frontage be increased by 30 percent beyond normal calculations.

5. The system of curb frontage must be allowed for in the total master plan and thereby its expansion from the initial operation.

6. Under no circumstances should the prime arterial circulation road be used as curb frontage. Rather, a spur from the main road network should be extended to the curb frontage.

7. The curb frontage should be divided into active and passive curb. The passive curb is utilized for valet queuing or other long-term uses such as bus connections.

8. It is necessary to determine the average peak vehicular traffic for both enplaning and deplaning passengers. A graph or summation sheet should be prepared. It is helpful if this is done by 20-minute increments, and the cumulative total peaking can be determined if there is no separation of enplaning and deplaning traffic. In the event that the enplaning and deplaning functions are totally separated, the summation peak will result in isolating the time frame for the maximum parking demand as well as vehicle peak of appropriate road.

Duration Schedule in Minutes (if no survey data is available)

	Enplaning	Deplaning
Private cars	2	3
Valet cars at curb	3	3
Valet queuing	5	
Rental cars	3	3
Taxis	5	5

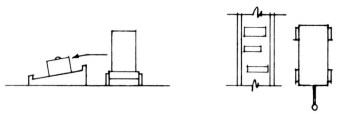

(a) The baggage is transported from the aircraft to the claiming device by a cart and is then off-loaded manually by an attendent.

(b) <u>DIVERTER</u> In this system the baggage is placed on a conveyor at one end. A diverter moves back and forth along the conveyor and disperses the baggage onto the claiming device.

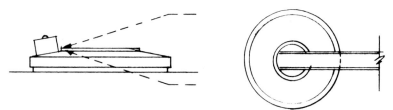

(c) <u>CAROUSEL</u> A conveyor, from underneath or from above, delivers the baggage to a rotating carousel.

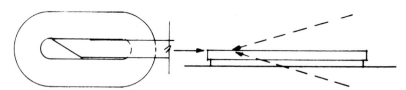

(d) <u>RACE TRACK</u> A conveyor from underneath or from above, delivers the baggage to a continuously circulating conveyor, the length of which will depend upon the terminal layout.

Fig. 14 Baggage claim systems.

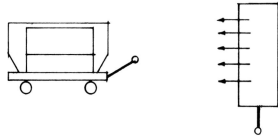

(e) <u>POD</u> The baggage pod is removed from the aircraft and delivered to the claim area. The passengers remove their baggage from the pod.

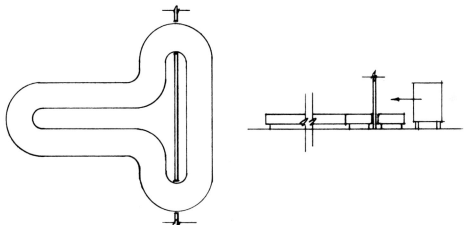

(f) <u>AMOEBA</u> This system is an extension of the race track system. The only difference being that the baggage is manually loaded directly onto the conveyor by an attendant behind a wall and out of view from the passengers.

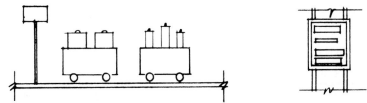

(g) <u>AUTOMATED</u> This system consists of carts that are operated by a computer system. The passenger inserts his claim ticket into a call box at a desired location, the cart then delivers the baggage at that location.

Fig. 14 (cont.) Baggage claim systems.

AIRPORTS AND TERMINALS

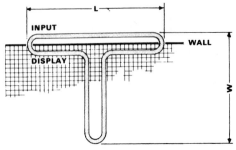

FLATBED — DIRECT FEED

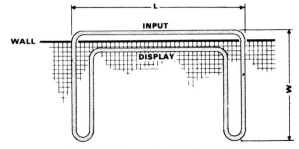

FLATBED — DIRECT FEED

SHAPE	L FT(M)	W FT(M)	CLAIM FRONTAGE FT(M)	BAG STORAGE ①
⬭	65 (20)	5 (1.5)	65 (20)	78
⊥	85 (26)	45 (13.7)	180 (55)	216
⊥	85 (26)	65 (20)	220 (67)	264
⊔	50 (15)	45 (13.7)	190 (58)	228

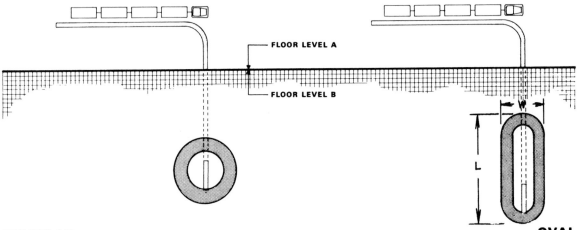

CIRCULAR
REMOTE FEED SLOPING BED

DIAMETER FT(M)	CLAIM FRONTAGE FT(M)	BAG STORAGE ①
20 (6)	63 (19)	94
25 (7.5)	78 (24)	132
30 (9)	94 (29)	169

OVAL
REMOTE FEED SLOPING BED

L FT(M)	W FT(M)	CLAIM FRONTAGE FT(M)	BAG STORAGE ①
36 (11)	20 (6)	95 (29)	170
52 (16)	20 (6)	128 (39)	247
68 (21)	18 (5.5)	156 (48)	318

① THEORETICAL BAG STORAGE — PRACTICAL BAG STORAGE CAPABILITY IS 1/3 LESS

Fig. 15 Mechanized claim devices. Source: *Planning and Design Considerations for Airport Terminal Building Development*, Advisory Circular AC 150/5360-7, DOT, FAA, 1976.

FUNCTIONAL RELATIONSHIPS AND TERMINAL CONCEPTS

Major Terminal Components

The terminal complex functions as an area of interchange between ground and air transportation modes. To accomplish this interchange, the following major components are required:

Apron The apron comprises the area and facilities used for aircraft gate parking and aircraft support and servicing operations. It includes the following sub-components:

Aircraft Gate Parking Positions Used for parking aircraft to enplane and deplane passengers. The passenger boarding device is part of the gate position.

Aircraft Service Areas On or adjacent to an aircraft parking position. They are used by airline personnel/equipment for servicing aircraft and the staging of baggage, freight, and mail for loading and unloading of aircraft.

Taxilanes Reserved to provide taxiing aircraft with access to and from parking positions.

Service/Fire Lanes Identified rights-of-way on the apron designated for aircraft ground service vehicles and fire equipment.

Connector The connector consists of the structure(s) and/or facilities normally located between the aircraft gate position and the main terminal building. At low activity airports, i.e., less than approximately 200,000 annual enplaned passengers, this component is often combined with the terminal building component. It normally contains the following elements:

Concourse A passageway for circulation between aircraft gate parking positions and the main terminal building.

Departure Lounge An area for assembling and holding passengers prior to a flight departure. In some instances, it may be a mobile lounge also used to transport passengers to a parked aircraft.

Security Inspection Station A control point for passenger and baggage inspection and controlling public access to parked aircraft.

Airline Operational Areas Areas set aside for airline personnel, equipment, and servicing activities related to aircraft arrivals and departures.

Passenger Amenities Areas normally provided in both the connector as well as the terminal components, particularly at the busier airports with relatively long connectors. These amenities include rest rooms, snack bars, beverage lounges, and other concessions and passenger services.

Building Maintenance and Utilities Areas often included in the connector component to provide terminal building maintenance and utilities.

Main Terminal Building The following elements comprise this component:

Lobbies Public areas for passenger circulation, services, and passenger/visitor waiting.

Airline Ticket Counters/Office Areas Areas required for ticket transactions, baggage check-in, flight information, and administrative backup.

Public Circulation Areas Areas for general circulation which include stairways, escalators, elevators, and corridors.

Terminal Services Facilities, both public and nonpublic, which provide services incidental to aircraft flight operations. These facilities include rest rooms, restaurants and concessions, food preparation and storage areas, truck service docks, and miscellaneous storage.

Outbound Baggage Facility A nonpublic area for sorting and processing baggage for departing flights.

Intraline and Interline Baggage Facility A nonpublic area for processing baggage transferred from one flight to another.

Inbound Baggage Facility A nonpublic area for receiving baggage from an arriving flight and public areas for baggage pickup by arriving passengers.

Federal Inspection Services A control point for processing passengers arriving on international flights.

Airport Administration and Services Areas set aside for airport management, operations, and maintenance functions.

Airport Access System This component is composed of the functional elements which enable ground ingress and egress to and from the airport terminal facility. They include the following:

Curb Platforms and curb areas (including median strips) which provide passengers and visitors with vehicle loading and unloading areas adjacent to the terminal.

Pedestrian Walkways Designated lanes and walkways for crossing airport roads, including tunnels and bridges which provide access between auto parking areas and the terminal.

Auto Parking Areas providing short-term and long-term parking for passengers, visitors, employees, and car rental.

Access Roads Vehicular roadways providing access to the terminal curb, public and employee parking, and to the community roadway/highway system.

Service Roads Public and nonpublic roadways and fire lanes providing access to various subelements of the terminal and other airport facilities, such as air freight, fuel tank stands, postal facility, and the like.

Functional Relationships of Terminal Components.

Activities within the terminal building can be categorized primarily into three functional areas: processing and servicing passengers; handling and processing of belly cargo (including passenger baggage); and, aircraft servicing. Consequently, a good terminal design necessitates a layout in which the various components are located in a sequence or pattern which coincides with the natural movement and services each requires, and those activities and operations which are functionally dependent on each other. Such a design will minimize passenger walking distances, airline servicing and processing times, and congestion caused by the intermingling of nonrelated activities.

Centralized and Unit Terminals

There are two basic concepts for the arrangement of the terminal area. In a centralized terminal, all passengers and baggage are processed in one building. Most airports utilize this arrangement. At some high activity airports, however, each airline (or several airlines combined) may be located in a separate terminal building. This is referred to as a unit terminal concept. These two design concepts are often combined in varying degrees. A single centralized terminal building has many advantages and for most situations is preferable. It represents a reasonably compact operation without the significant problem of transferring passengers and baggage between buildings. Building maintenance and operating costs for the centralized terminal will generally be significantly lower than the total costs for operating all unit terminals. A unit terminal concept can be justified only at the very high activity airports, particularly where the percentage of airline transfer passengers is relatively low. An efficient transportation system for passenger and baggage transfer between buildings is a must and should be incorporated in the design at an early stage.

Alternative Terminal Building Concepts

A terminal building design can be categorized as one of five basic concepts or a variation or combination of them. The connector is the single element that distinguishes between the various concepts, since it is different in each case. Terminal building concepts are categorized in the following manner:

Simple Terminal Concept The simple terminal consists of a single common waiting and ticketing area with exits leading to the aircraft parking apron. It is suitable at airports with low airline activity with an apron providing close-in parking for three to six commercial transport aircraft. A simple terminal normally consists of a single level structure with two to four gates with access to aircraft by walking across the aircraft parking apron. The layout of the simple terminal should take into account the possibility of pier or linear extensions for terminal expansion.

Linear Concept In the linear concept (Fig. 16), aircraft are parked along the face of the terminal building. Concourses connect the various terminal functions with the aircraft gate positions. This concept offers ease of access and relatively short walking distances if passengers are delivered to a point near gate departure by vehicular circulation systems. Expansion may be accomplished by linear extension of an existing structure or by developing two or more linear-terminal units with connectors.

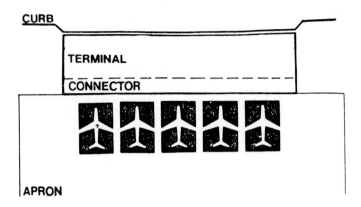

THE LINEAR CONNECTOR MAY CONSIST OF ONE OR BOTH OF THE FOLLOWING:

— A CONCOURSE, ENCLOSED AT THE FIRST OR SECOND LEVEL, CONNECTING TO THE TERMINAL ALONG A LINE OF PARKED AIRCRAFT WITH ACCESS TO THESE AIRCRAFT AT THE AIRCRAFT GATE POSITIONS

— A CONCOURSE CONNECTING TICKET POSITIONS, BAGGAGE CLAIM AREAS, ETC.

NOTE: DEPARTURE LOUNGES, CONCOURSE RELATED TO FUNCTIONAL AREAS.

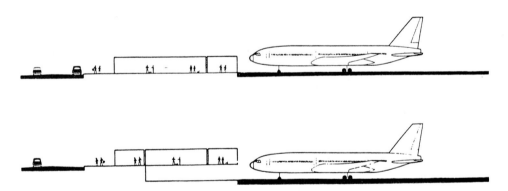

Fig. 16   The linear concept.

Pier Concept The pier concept (Fig. 17) provides interface with aircraft along piers extending from the main terminal area. In the pier concept, aircraft are usually arranged around the axis of the pier in a parallel or perpendicular parked relation- ship. Each pier has a row of aircraft gate positions on both sides, with the passenger right-of-way or concourse running along the axis of the pier and serving as the circulation space for enplaning and deplaning passengers. Access to the terminal area is at the base of the connector (pier). If two or more piers are used, spacing for aircraft maneuvering between the piers by means of an apron taxilane(s) is required.

THE PIER CONNECTOR MAY CONSIST OF:

– A COVERED CONCOURSE AT GRADE LEVEL.

– A COVERED CONCOURSE ENCLOSED AT SECOND LEVEL.

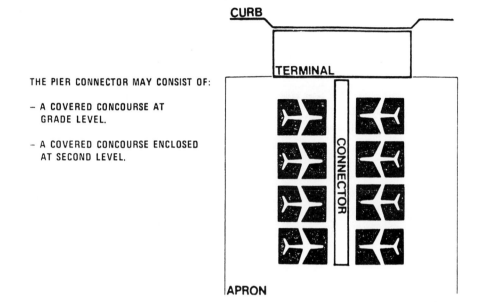

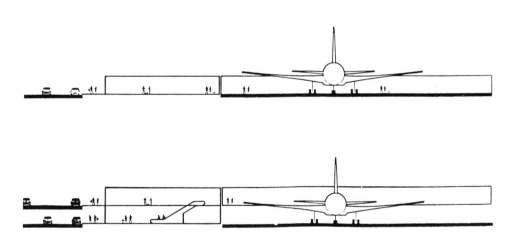

Fig. 17 The pier concept.

Transportation

AIRPORTS AND TERMINALS

Satellite Concept The satellite concept (Fig. 18) consists of a building, surrounded by aircraft, which is separated from the terminal and usually reached by a surface, underground, or above-grade connector. Aircraft are normally parked in radial or parallel positions around the satellite. The satellite can have common or separate departure lounges. Since enplaning and deplaning of aircraft are accomplished from a common area, mechanical systems may be employed to transport passengers and baggage between the terminal and satellite.

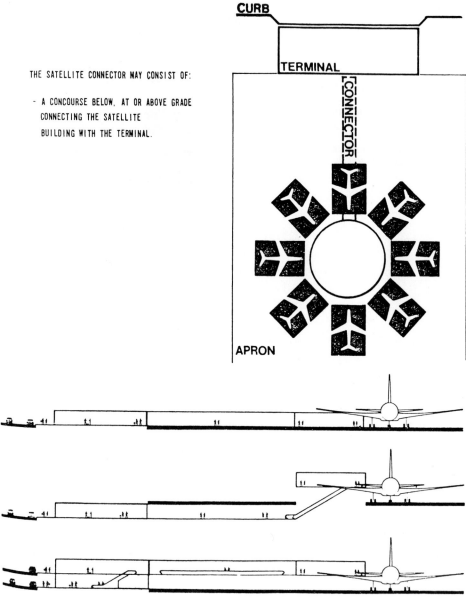

THE SATELLITE CONNECTOR MAY CONSIST OF:

- A CONCOURSE BELOW, AT OR ABOVE GRADE CONNECTING THE SATELLITE BUILDING WITH THE TERMINAL.

Fig. 18   The satellite concept.

Transporter Concept Aircraft and aircraft-servicing functions in the transporter concept (Fig. 19) are remotely located from the terminal. The connection to the terminal is provided by vehicular transport. The advantages of the transporter concept include flexibility in providing additional aircraft parking positions to accommodate increases in

schedules; ease and speed in maneuvering aircraft in and out of parking positions under their own power; separation of aircraft servicing activities from the terminal; and reduced walking distances for passengers. Transporters may also be used in establishing remote gates for charter flights. The disadvantages mainly relate to the

initial, operational, and maintenance costs associated with the transporter vehicles, although the increased transfer times required in changing airplanes can also be detrimental to airport efficiency.

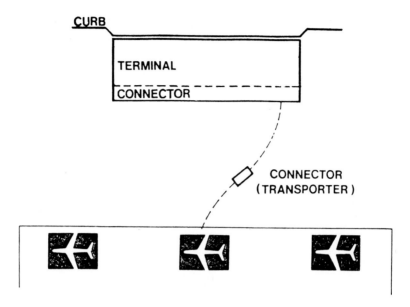

THE TRANSPORTER CONNECTOR MAY CONSIST OF:

– A NON-ELEVATING VEHICLE THAT PERMITS ENPLANING AND DEPLANING AT APRON LEVEL AT THE AIRCRAFT AND AT THE TERMINAL.

– AN ELEVATING VEHICLE THAT PERMITS DIRECT ENPLANING AND DEPLANING TO THE AIRCRAFT AND TERMINAL BY MOVING THE PASSENGER CAB VERTICALLY TO MATCH ENTRANCE LEVELS AT THE AIRCRAFT AND TERMINAL

– (DOTTED) A SECONDARY CONCOURSE CONNECTING TRANSPORTER POSITIONS.

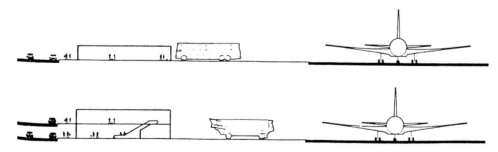

Fig. 19 The transporter concept.

Single-Level/Multilevel Terminals

The decision on whether the terminal building design should incorporate single or multilevels for processing passengers and baggage is influenced primarily by the volume of traffic. Variations of these designs are shown in the bottom elevations

depicted on Fig. 16 through 19 and are discussed as follows:

Single-level Terminal The single level terminal is the preferred design at the majority of small and non-hub airports. The processing of passengers and baggage takes place at the same level as the

apron, and the entire layout is quite simple and economical.

Multilevel Terminal At a traffic level of over 500,000 annual enplaned passengers, structures of more than one story should be investigated. In this concept, arriving and departing passengers

AIRPORTS AND TERMINALS

are vertically separated. Enplaning passengers are usually processed on the upper level and deplaning passengers on the lower level. The fingers or piers leading to the aircraft are usually two stories, whereas, the terminal enplaning and deplaning curbs may be on single or multilevels, as discussed in the following paragraph. The principal advantage of a multilevel terminal is the reduction of congestion by segregating opposing flows of passengers and baggage. The disadvantages are the higher initial investment and the continuing higher operation and maintenance costs. In evaluating the design of a multilevel terminal, the physical limitations of the site, terrain, and airline station characteristics are important considerations.

Multilevel Curbs While single level curbs may be utilized with all concepts and traffic volumes, multilevel curbs are appropriate only at multilevel terminals. Construction of multilevel curbs should be considered when passenger volumes exceed one million enplanements or when physical limitations within the terminal area or building frontage make curb separation desirable. Multilevel curbs, with their corresponding structural roads and ramps, are costly to construct and should be considered only after investigation of single-level alternatives.

Second Level Aircraft Boarding Boarding and deplaning aircraft from the second story is the usual procedure at multilevel terminals for reasons of simplicity and efficiency, unless limited by terrain features. Conversely, for the same reasons, apron-level boarding is the norm for single-level terminals. However, severe or extreme weather conditions, or other considerations, may justify second-level boarding at a single-level terminal. In such cases, two story connectors, raised pier structures, or inclined loading bridges can be utilized. Airports with over 500,000 annual enplanements are candidates for second-level boarding installations. In some situations, a combination of apron and second-level boarding gates may be a desirable alternative.

Terminal Concept Combinations and Variations

Combinations and variations of terminal concepts often result from the changing conditions experienced at an airport during its lifespan. An airport may have many types of passenger activity, varying from originating and terminating passengers using the full range of terminal services to passengers using limited services on commuter flights. The predominant type of activity usually affects the initial terminal concept selected. In

time, the amount of traffic may increase, necessitating modification or expansion of the facilities. Growth of aircraft size, a new combination of aircraft types serving the airport, or a change in the type of service may affect the suitability of the initial concept. Similarly, physical limitations of the site may cause a pure conceptual form to be modified by additions or combinations of other concepts.

Combined concepts acquire some of the advantages and disadvantages of each basic concept used. A combination of concept types can be advantageous where more costly modifications would be necessary to maintain the original concept. For example, while an airline may be suitably accommodated within an existing transporter concept terminal, a commuter operation with rapid turnovers is best served by a linear concept extension. In this case, concept combination is desirable. Thus, the appearance of concept variations and combinations in a total apron-terminal plan may reflect an evolving situation in which altering needs, growth, or physical limitations have determined the final terminal configuration. Figure 20 depicts concept combinations and variations typically utilized in airport terminal designs.

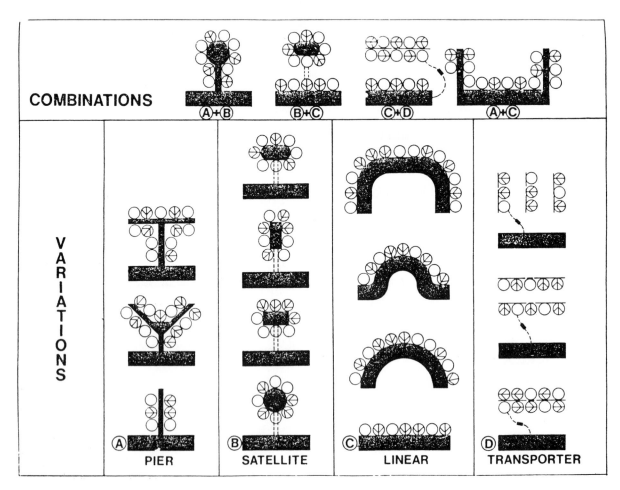

Fig. 20 Concept combinations and variations .

TERMINAL BUILDING SPACE AND FACILITY GUIDELINES

Gross Terminal Building Area Estimates

Gross Terminal Area Per Gate The relationship between annual enplaned passengers and gross terminal area per gate for a 10-year and 20-year forecast can be approximated. The profile of the curves is based on predicted growth in seats per aircraft for each forecast period; specifically, the growth in predicted aircraft mix during the peak hour of the average day of the peak month of the design year.

Rule-of-Thumb A rule-of-thumb of about 150 square feet (14 m²) of gross terminal building area per design peak-hour passenger is sometimes used for rough estimating purposes. Another rule using 0.08 to 0.12 square feet (0.007 to 0.011 m²) per annual enplanement at airports with over 250,000 annual enplanements can similarly be applied. At small airports with less than 250,000 enplanements, estimates should be based on peak hour considerations and simple sketches.

Space Allocations

The terminal building area is comprised of both usable and unusable space. Unusable space involves those areas required for building columns and exterior and interior walls, about 5 percent of the total gross area. The usable space can be classified into the two broad categories of rentable and nonrentable space. Usually, 50 to 55 percent is allocated to rentable space and 45 to 50 percent to nonrentable space. Figure 21 presents a further breakdown of these basic categories.

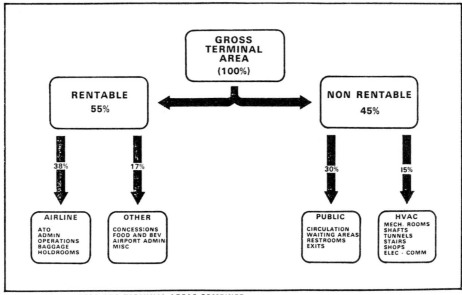

INCLUDES CONNECTOR AND TERMINAL AREAS COMBINED
STRUCTURE SPACE IS INCLUDED IN EACH AREA

Fig. 21   Gross terminal area space distribution.

Public Lobby Areas

Lobbies provide public circulation and access for carrying out the following functions: passenger ticketing; passenger and visitor waiting; housing concession areas and other passenger services; and baggage claim.

Ticketing Lobby As the initial objective of most passengers, the ticketing lobby should be arranged so that the enplaning passenger has immediate access and clear visibility to the individual airline ticket counters upon entering the building. Circulation patterns should allow the option of bypassing counters with minimum interference. Provisions for seating should be minimal to avoid congestion and encourage passengers to proceed to the gate area.

Ticket lobby sizing is a function of total length of airline counter frontage; queuing space in front of counters; and, additional space for lateral circulation to facilitate passenger movements. Queuing space requires a minimum of 12 to 15 feet (4 to 5 m). Lobby depths in front of the ticket counter range from 20 to 30 feet (12 to 15 m) for a ticket area serving 50 gates or more.

Waiting Lobby Apart from providing for passenger and visitor circulation, a centralized waiting area usually provides public seating and access to passenger amenities, including rest rooms, retail shops, food service, etc. The sizing of a central waiting lobby is influenced by the number, seating capacity, and location of individual gate waiting areas. If all gate areas have seating, the central waiting lobby may be sized to seat 15 to 25 percent of the design peak hour enplaning passengers plus visitors. However, if no gate seating areas are provided or planned, seating for 60 to 70 percent of design peak hour enplanements plus visitors should be provided.

Visitor-passenger ratios are best determined by means of local surveys. In the absence of such data, an assumption of one visitor per peak hour originating passenger is reasonable for planning purposes.

Baggage Claim Lobby This lobby provides public circulation space for access to baggage claim facilities and for egress from the claim area to the deplaning curb and ground transportation. It also furnishes space for such passenger amenities and services as car rental counters, telephones, rest rooms, limousine service, etc.

Allowance for public circulation and passenger amenities outside the claim area ranges from 15 to 20 feet (5 to 6 m) in depth at small hub airports, 20 to 30 feet (6 to 9 m) at medium hubs, and 30 to 35 feet (9 to 11 m) at those airports serving large hubs. Lobby lengths range from 50 to 75 feet (15 to 23 m) for each baggage claim device. For approximating lobby length and area, one claim device per 100 to 125 feet (30 to 38 m) of baggage claim frontage should be assumed.

Airline Ticket Counter/Offices

The Airline Ticket Counter (ATO) area is the primary location for passengers to complete ticket transactions and check-in baggage. It includes the airline counters, space and/or conveyors for handling outbound baggage, counter agent service areas, and related administrative/support offices. In almost all cases, ticket counter areas are leased by an airline for its exclusive use. Therefore, the planning, design, and sizing of these areas should be closely coordinated with individual airlines.

Ticket Counter Configurations Three ticket counter configurations are in general use. They include:

Linear Linear configuration is the most frequently used one (see Fig. 22). Multi-purpose positions indicated are those in which the agent performs several functions such as ticketing, baggage check-in, and the other services an airline may consider appropriate. During peak periods, multipurpose positions may be utilized for a single function to expedite passenger processing for those requiring only one type of service. At high volume airports, permanent special-purpose positions may be justified.

Flow-through Counters Flow-through counters, as depicted in Fig. 23, are used by some airlines, particularly at high-volume locations with a relatively high percentage of "baggage only" transactions. This configuration permits the passenger to

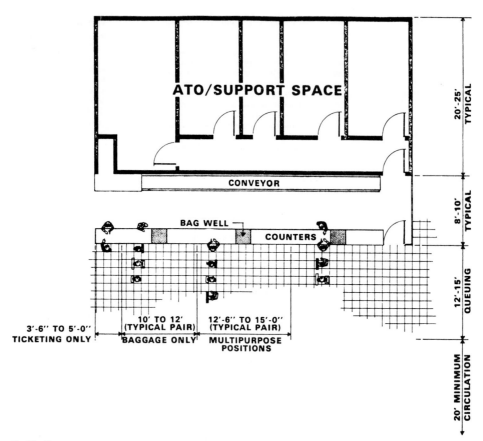

Fig. 22   Linear counter.

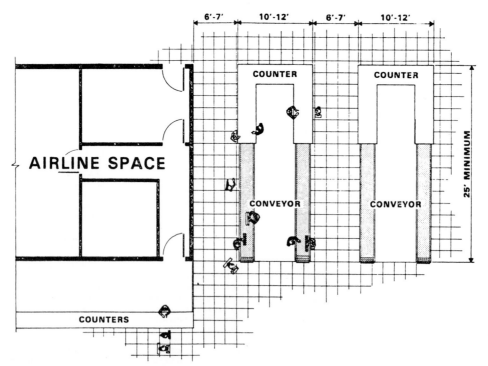

Fig. 23   Flow-through counter.

check-in baggage before completing ticketing transaction and increases outbound baggage handling capability by providing additional belt conveyors. This type of counter requires more floor space, an additional 50–70 square feet (4.7–5.1 m²), than the linear type and involves increased investment and maintenance costs. Future application will probably be limited to relatively few airports.

Island Counters The island counter shown in Fig. 24 combines some features of the flow-through and linear arrangements. The agent positions form a "U" around a single baggage conveyor belt (or pair of belts) permitting interchangeability between multipurpose or specialized positions. As with flow-through counters, this configuration has relatively limited application.

Office Support The airline ticket counter/office provides space for a number of airline support activities. These activities include: accounting and safekeeping of receipts; agent supervision; communications; information display equipment; and personnel areas for rest, personal grooming, and training. At low activity locations, the ticket counter area may provide space for all company administrative and operational functions, including outbound baggage. Figure 25 depicts two typical layouts for low activity airports with single-level terminals. At high activity locations, there is more likelihood that additional space for airline support activities will be remotely located from the ticket counters.

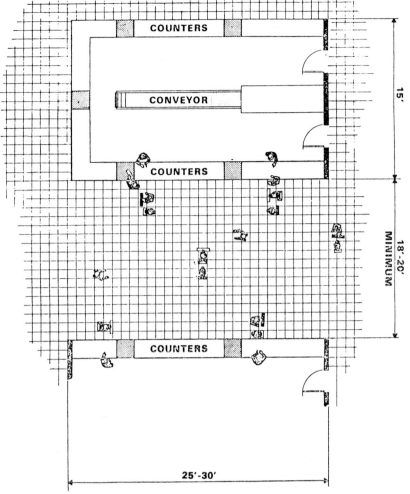

Fig. 24   Island counter.

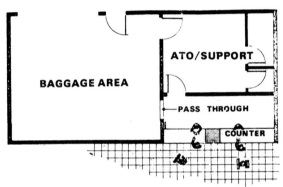

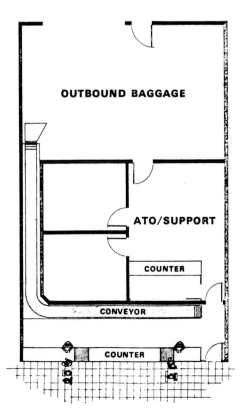

Fig. 25   Typical ATO layouts—single-level terminals.

Outbound Baggage Facilities

The outbound baggage facility is that area where baggage is received by mechanical conveyor from the ticket counters, online and offline connecting flights, and curb-side check-in. It is sorted and loaded into containers or carts for subsequent delivery to aircraft. At low-volume airports, bags may be manually moved through a wall opening.

At most airports, outbound baggage areas are located in building spaces leased by the tenant airlines for exclusive use. Each airline provides its own baggage processing equipment and conveyors. The outbound baggage area should be located in reasonably close proximity to the ticket counters to facilitate the movement of baggage between these locations. The area should also have convenient access to the aircraft parking apron by means of carts or other mobile or mechanical conveyors.

On-line and inter-line transfer baggage is best handled in the same area with other outbound baggage for optimal use of personnel, space, and equipment. An area or conveyor for receiving transfer baggage from other airlines should be considered. Often, this area is adjacent to a primary traffic aisle. Security for delivered baggage makes a conveyor or pass-through into the outbound baggage area advisable. At stations where the airlines contract with a third party for all interline deliveries, a pick-up area for baggage to be delivered to other carriers should be provided with similar provisions for baggage security and control.

Since outbound baggage area requirements are determined by individual airline policy, early input from the airlines is essential. The minimum size for an outbound baggage room is approximately 400 to 450 sq. ft. (37 to 42 m²) per airline.

At locations where an airline proposes using some type of automated sorting, additional area will be necessary. The required area should be increased by at least 150 to 200 percent for tilt-tray sorting systems and 100 percent for destination-coded vehicle systems.

Following are some common types of outbound baggage equipment:

Belt conveyors represent the most commonly used mechanized component for baggage systems, operating at speeds of 80 to 150 fpm (25 to 46 mpm) over short distances, and providing transport capacities of 26 to 50 bags per minute.

Raw belt conveyors with spill plates (Fig. 26) tend to become less efficient as the length of unloading section is increased to process simultaneous departures. In such cases, bags not removed by the baggage handler at his normal working position must be retrieved later from the end of the spill plate. That end becomes progressively more distant as the number of flights and size of aircraft increase. This condition may be alleviated somewhat by using belt conveyors with indexing features activated by photoelectric switches.

Belt conveyor capacities can be increased by adding conveyors between counter inputs and outbound baggage rooms or, marginally, by merging multiple input conveyors into a higher-speed mainline conveyor. Long segments may operate at speeds up to 30 fpm (9 mpm), with acceleration and deceleration belts at each end. This represents a practical maximum for current technology and maintenance. Accordingly, high-speed belts are primarily used to reduce transport times for long conveyor runs and seldom, if ever, increase system capacity.

Inclined belts, vertical lift devices, or chutes are used with baggage rooms located on a different floor level from the ATO counters. Chutes are the least expensive but lack means for controlling baggage movement and increase potential for damaged bags. Inclined belts should not exceed a 22-degree slope and are usually designed for 90 to 100 fpm (28 to 31 mpm) maximum. Vertical lift devices are available with capacities of 18 to 45 bags per minute.

Recirculating devices for sorting and loading baggage are normally considered when the number of departures processed concurrently exceeds the practical capabilities of a raw belt and spill plate. Equipment types include belt conveyors utilizing straight and curved segments, flat-bed devices, or sloping-bed plates devices. Each of these may be fed by more than one input conveyor and may require indexing belts and accumulators to control input flow. The recirculating feature facilitates sorting bags into carts for more flights and larger aircraft by fixing relatively stationary work positions for baggage handlers with "dynamic storage" of bags until they can be sorted into carts or containers.

Elongated oval configurations tend to be used in lieu of circular devices as the number of carts increases. Figure 27 shows carts and container dollies parked parallel to a belt-loop or flat-bed sorting device. Figure 28 shows the same carts parked at right angles to a sloping-bed device. The sloping bed may accommodate two rows of bags to increase overall storage capacity. This can offset the reduction in perimeter frontage from that afforded with parallel parking. Although right-angle parking can reduce floor space by 30 to 50 percent, some carriers also prefer parallel parking to minimize time and manpower for maneuvering and positioning of carts. In either case, the input conveyors need to be elevated to permit passage of carts and containers within the space.

Semiautomated sorting utilizes mechanical equipment to move bags onto a lateral slide or conveyor designated for concurrently processing separate departures. Figure 29 shows a linear belt sorter capable of handling about 30 bags per minute, usually where the maximum number of departures processed concurrently does not exceed 12 to 15. The operator designates the appropriate lateral after reading the tag on each passing bag. A separate sorter is needed for each input conveyor line from the ATO.

Tilt-tray sorters are considered appropriate for very high-volume stations requiring multiple inputs and greater capacities than possible with preceding types. These systems are custom designed with relatively sophisticated coding and sorting features as well as lateral conveyors accumulating baggage for each departing flight. Terminal designs should allow the flexibility for future installation of such systems.

Destination-coded vehicle systems represent highly advanced technological proposals for handling the higher volumes, longer distances, interline transfers, and elevation changes encountered in terminals serving large hubs. Although the vehicles and propulsion methods vary, all have similar design criteria. These are: speeds up to 880 ft/min (268 m/min); elevation change capability (up to 33 degrees); fixed rights-of-way; programmable control systems and vehicle encoding; and interface with load/unload stations.

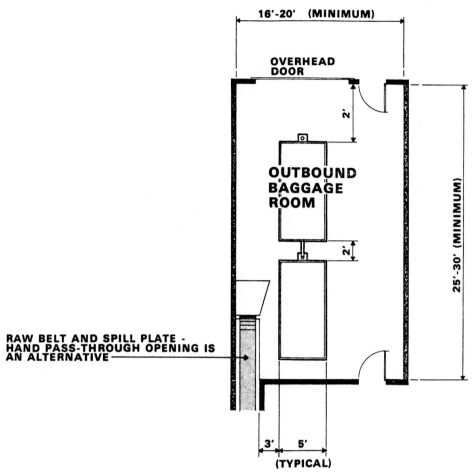

Fig. 26 Outbound baggage room typical raw belt conveyor installation.

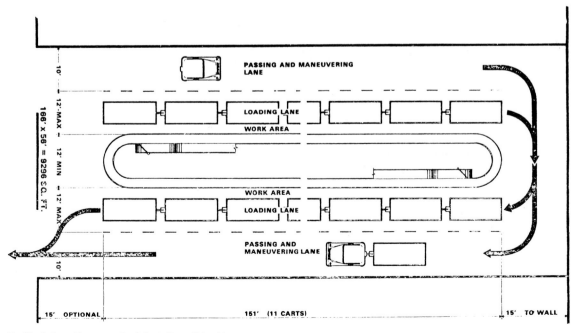

Fig. 27 Outbound baggage recirculating belt: parallel parking.

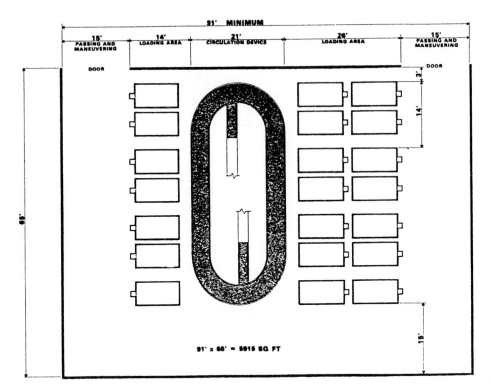

Fig. 28   Outbound baggage recirculating sloping bed: perpendicular parking.

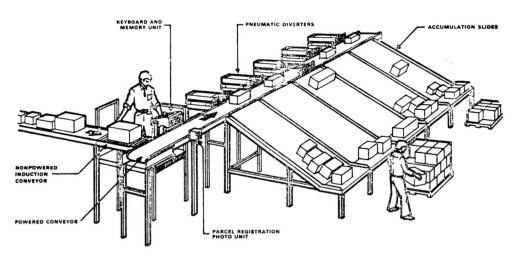

Fig. 29   Semiautomated linear belt sorter.

Security Inspection Stations

Air carriers using over 60 passenger seat aircraft in scheduled or public charter operations are required by Federal Aviation Regulations (FAR) 121.538 to screen all passengers prior to boarding in accordance with the provisions of FAR Part 108. This activity is normally handled inside the terminal building at a security screening station.

There are three types of passenger inspection stations, depending on the location of the station in relation to the aircraft boarding area. These include:

(1) Boarding Gate Station;
(2) Holding Area Station; and
(3) Sterile Concourse Station.

A Sterile Concourse Station, from both the standpoint of passenger security facilitation and economics, is the most desirable type of screening station. It is generally located in a concourse or corridor leading to one or several pier finger(s) or satellite terminal(s) and permits the screening and control of all passengers and visitors passing beyond the screening location. It thus can control a considerable number of aircraft gates with a minimum amount of inspection equipment and personnel. Pier and satellite terminal concepts are well suited for application of the Sterile Concourse Station since the single-point entrance connector element facilitates isolation of boarding areas.

Because of building geometry, especially that associated with linear and transporter terminal concepts, the Sterile Concourse Station is not always feasible. Under these circumstances, several inspection stations may be required to control a number of holding areas or departure lounges. In the worst situation, a screening station may be required at each boarding gate.

Except at low activity airports, where manual search procedures may be employed, a security inspection station will generally include a minimum of one walk-through weapons detector and one x-ray device. Such a station has a capacity of 500 to 600 persons per hour and requires an area ranging from 100 to 150 square feet (9 to 14 sq.m.). Examples of security inspection station layouts are illustrated in Fig. 30.

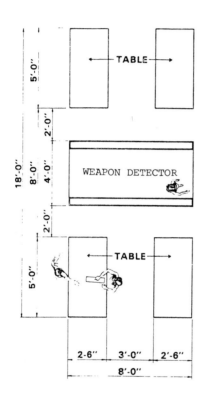

MANUAL SEARCH (144 SQ FT)

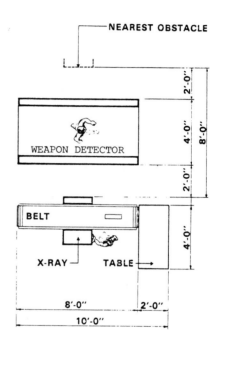

X-RAY SEARCH (120 SQ FT)

Fig. 30 Security inspection station layouts.

Space leading to the security inspection station should allow room for queuing as the flow of passengers through security is often interrupted when a passenger requires a rescreening or physical search. Queuing space should not extend into or block other circulation elements.

The boarding area beyond a security screening checkpoint, whether a holding area concourse or departure lounge, requires a design which will enable security to be maintained. In this respect, the design and location of entrances, exits, fire doors, concessions, etc., require special consideration.

Departure Lounges

The departure lounge is the waiting or holding area for passengers immediately prior to boarding an aircraft. At most airports (excepting some low activity airports), departure lounges are normally included in the space leased and controlled by individual airlines.

The departure lounge normally includes: space for one or more airline agent positions for ticket collections, aircraft seat assignment, and baggage check-in; a seating and waiting area; a queuing area for aircraft boarding; and an aisle or separate corridor for aircraft deplaning. Figures 31–33 illustrate typical departure lounge layouts.

The number of agent positions/desks is determined by the user airlines on the basis of individual airline standards for passenger waiting, processing, and boarding procedures. A queue length of at least 10 feet (3 m) in front of agent positions should be provided in departure lounges at larger airports.

The departure lounge area is a function of the number of passengers anticipated to be in the lounge 15 minutes prior to aircraft boarding. Table 2 presents information for estimating departure lounge areas on the basis of aircraft seating capacity and load factors. The average depth of lounge area generally considered to be reasonable is 25 to 30 feet (8 to 9 m).

When a lounge area serves more than one aircraft gate position, the estimated total lounge area shown in Table 2 may be reduced 5 percent for each aircraft gate position, up to a maximum of six gates.

Departure lounge seats are not generally provided to accommodate all passengers boarding an aircraft. A number of passengers will elect to remain standing in the waiting area while others will only arrive shortly before or during the boarding process. Between 15 and 20 square feet (1.4 to 1.9 m²), including aisle space, is required per seat.

The deplaning area is generally a roped aisle or separate corridor directly leading deplaning passengers from the loading bridge or apron gate to a public corridor. Separation from the rest of the departure lounge is provided to avoid interference and congestion between deplaning passengers and those waiting to board the aircraft. Six feet (2 m) is an acceptable width for this area.

TABLE 2 Departure Lounge Area Space Requirements

Aircraft seating capacity	Departure lounge area, square feet (square meters)		
	Boarding load factors		
	35–45 percent	55–65 percent	75–85 percent
Up to 80	350 (33)	515 (48)	675 (63)
81 to 110	600 (56)	850 (79)	1,110 (102)
111 to 160	850 (79)	1,175 (109)	1,500 (139)
161 to 220	1,200 (111)	1,600 (149)	2,000 (186)
221 to 280	1,500 (139)	2,000 (186)	2,500 (232)
281 to 420	2,200 (204)	3,000 (279)	3,800 (353)

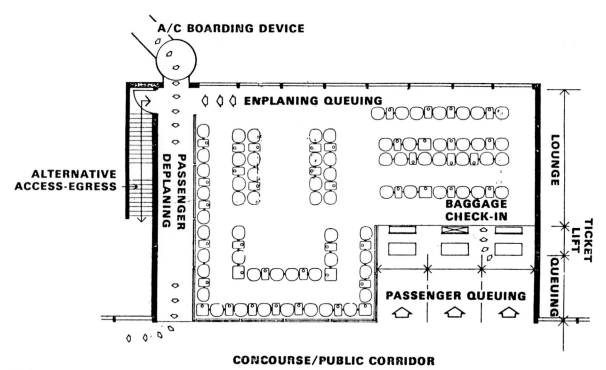

Fig. 31 Typical departure lounge layout.

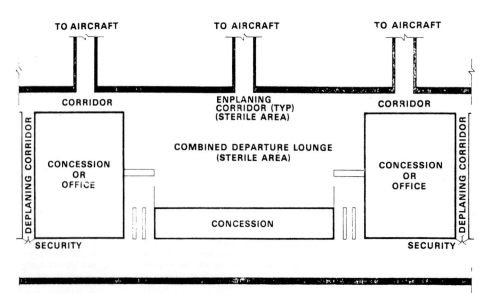

Fig. 32 Typical combined security/departure lounge layout.

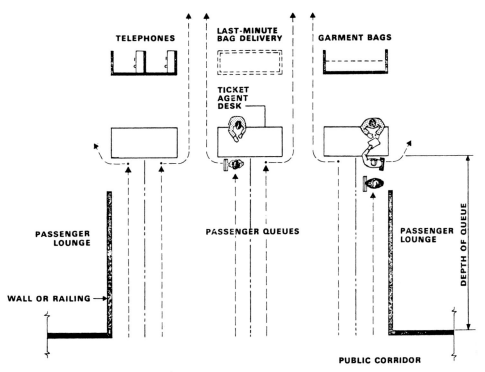

Fig. 33 Departure lounge passenger processing area

Baggage Claim Facilities

Inbound baggage handling requires both public and nonpublic building areas. The public space (claiming area) is that in which passengers and visitors have access to checked baggage displayed for identification and claiming. Nonpublic space is used to off-load bags from carts and containers onto claim devices or conveyor systems for moving into the public area.

The claiming area should be located adjacent to a deplaning curb and have convenient access to ground transportation service and auto parking facilities. Passenger access from arriving flights should be direct and avoid conflicting with enplaning passengers. The claim area should also be readily accessible from the aircraft apron by means of carts, tractors, or mechanical conveyors for quick and direct baggage delivery.

At low activity airports, a simple claim shelf is the most common baggage claim scheme. As passenger activity increases, several types of mechanical claim devices, as illustrated in Fig. 34, may be utilized to help reduce the overall required claim area length. A discussion of the more common claim schemes follows.

The simple shelf or counter is merely a shelf or counter provided in a public area on which baggage from an arriving aircraft is placed for passenger identification and retrieval. Width of the shelf is generally 30 to 36 inches (75 to 90 cm). Passengers merely move laterally along the shelf until their baggage is located and claimed.

Flat-bed plate devices are particularly applicable when direct feed loading areas are immediately adjacent and parallel to the claiming area and on the same floor level.

Sloping-bed devices are somewhat more adaptable for remote feed situations where the loading area cannot be immediately adjacent to the claiming area or must be located on a different floor level. In some cases, the width of the sloping bed is sufficient to provide storage of two rows of bags.

At low volume airports, exclusive-use facilities are not usually economically justified and claim facilities are shared or assigned preferentially to several airlines. The use of a Design Day Activity Analysis is recommended to size baggage claim facilities. In this analysis, passenger arrivals in periods of peak 20 minutes are used as the basis for sizing. However, when exclusive facilities are planned, each airline determines its baggage claim frontage and space requirements according to its own criteria for sizing space, systems, and staffing.

A public claiming area may require railings or similar separation from other public space and controlled egress to enable inspection of removed baggage for assurance of "positive claim." At some terminals, additional space may be needed adjacent to the claiming area for storage and security of unclaimed baggage and for airline baggage service facilities (lost and found).

Food and Beverage Services

These services include snack bars, coffee shops, restaurants, and bar lounges. The basic service offered at small airports is the coffee shop, although separate restaurants at some smaller city airports can be successful, depending on the community and restaurant management. Large airports usually can justify several locations for snack bars, coffee shops, bar lounges, and restaurants. Requirements for more than one of each type are highly influenced by the airport size and terminal concept involved. Unit terminals, for instance, may require coffee shops and/or snack bars at each separate terminal.

Generally speaking, a coffee shop seating less than 80 is considered an uneconomical operation at airports enplaning over one million passengers annually. At smaller airports, the seating capacity minimum may be somewhat lower, depending on such factors as local labor costs and concessionaire lease arrangements.

The following ranges appear representative for food and beverage services:

(1) Turnover rates: 10 to 19 average daily per seat. Some operators appear satisfied averaging 10 to 14 daily.
(2) Space per seat: 35 to 40 square feet (3.3 to 3.7 m²) per coffee shop/restaurant seat, including support space.
(3) Snack bars: 15 to 25 percent of coffee shop/restaurant overall space requirements.
(4) Bar lounges: 25 to 35 percent of coffee shop/restaurant overall space requirements.

The sizing of food and beverage services involves applying "use factors." Use factors are determined by dividing the average daily transactions by average daily enplanements.

For estimating and for initial planning purposes, the following average daily use factors are suggested:

(1) 40 to 60 percent at terminal airports with a high percentage of long-haul flights;
(2) 20 to 40 percent at transfer airports and through airports; and,
(3) 15 to 25 percent at terminal airports with a low percentage of long-haul flights.

Concessionaire and Building Services

The following building and concessionaire services are provided at airport terminals as appropriate for the size and activity of the airport. General area ranges for many of these services are presented for planning purposes. Larger areas may be required.

News and tobacco are physically separate at most airports where annual enplanements exceed 200,000 per year, and may be combined with other services at airports with lesser traffic. Space allowance: 150 square feet minimum, and averaging 600 to 700 square feet (56 to 66 m²) per million annual enplanements.

Gift and apparel shops operations are combined with a newsstand at smaller airports. Separate facilities normally become feasible when annual enplanements exceed one million. Space allow-

AIRPORTS AND TERMINALS

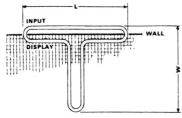

FLATBED — DIRECT FEED

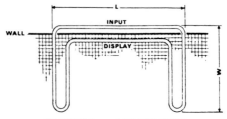

FLATBED — DIRECT FEED

SHAPE	L&W (FT)	CLAIM FRONTAGE (FT)	BAG STORAGE*
OVAL	65 x 5	65	78
⊥	85 x 45	180	216
⊥	85 x 65	220	264
⊔	50 x 45	190	228

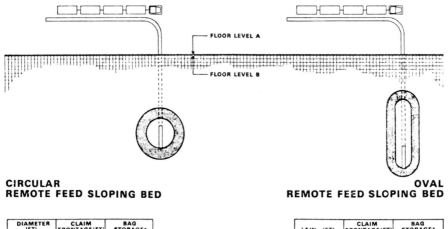

CIRCULAR REMOTE FEED SLOPING BED

OVAL REMOTE FEED SLOPING BED

DIAMETER (FT)	CLAIM FRONTAGE (FT)	BAG STORAGE*
20	63	94
25	78	132
30	94	169

L&W (FT)	CLAIM FRONTAGE (FT)	BAG STORAGE*
36 x 20	95	170
52 x 20	128	247
68 x 18	156	318

*THEORETICAL BAG STORAGE — PRACTICAL BAG STORAGE CAPABILITY IS 1/3 LESS

Fig. 34 Mechanized claim devices.

ance: 600 to 700 square feet (56 to 66 m²) per million annual enplanements.

Drug store, including sale of books, cards, and liquor, may be feasible as separate operation when annual enplanements exceed 1.5 million. Space allowance: 700 square feet (66 m²) minimum and averaging 600 to 700 square feet (56 to 66 m²) per million enplanements.

Barber and shoe shine operations at some large airports allow one chair per million annual enplanements. The most successful operations range from three to seven chairs. Space allowance: 110 to 120 square feet (10.2 to 11.2 m²) per chair with 150 square feet (14 m²) for a minimum facility.

Auto rental counters vary according to the number of companies. Space allowance: 350 to 400 square feet (33 to 37 m²) per million annual en-

planements.

Florist shop operation as a separate function may become feasible when annual enplanements exceed 2 million. The usual space allowed is 350 to 400 square feet (31.5 to 32 m²) per terminal.

Displays (including courtesy phones for hotels). Space allowance: 90 to 100 square feet (8.4 to 9.3 m²) per million annual enplanements.

Insurance (including counters and machines). Space allowance: 150 to 175 square feet (14 to 16 m²) per million annual enplanements.

Public lockers require in the range of 70 to 80 square feet (6.5 to 7.4 m²) per million annual enplanements.

Public telephones space requirement is 100 to 110 square feet (9.3 to 10.2 m²) per million annual enplanements.

Automated post offices may be found desirable

to the extent of providing one station, 125 square feet (11.6 m²) for each terminal serving at least 2.75 million annual enplanements.

Vending machine items supplement staffed facilities, especially when extended hours of operation are not justified by low volumes or multiplicity of locations. When vending machines are provided, they should be grouped and/or recessed to avoid encroaching upon circulation space for primary traffic flows. Space allowance: 50 square feet (4.7 m²) minimum or 150 square feet (14 m²) per million annual enplanements.

Public toilets are sized for building occupancy in accordance with local codes. Space allowances applied at airports vary greatly. They range from 1,500 to 1,800 square feet (140 to 167 m²) per 500 peak-hour passengers (in and out) down to 1,333 square feet (124 m²) per million annual enplanements at large hub airports.

Airport management offices' space requirements vary greatly according to the size of staff and the extent to which airport authority headquarters are located in the terminal.

Airport Police/Security Office space needs vary according to based staff and nature of arrangements with local community law enforcement agencies.

Medical aid facilities' space requirements range from that needed for first-aid service provided by airport police to that for branch operations at off-airport clinics.

USO/Travelers Aid facilities vary considerably. Space requirements are relatively minor, 80 to

100 square feet (7.4 to 9.3 m²), except at airports with annual enplanements of over one million.

Nursery facilities for travelers with small infants have been provided at airports with annual enplanements of over 1 million. The most practical solutions include a private toilet room of 50 to 60 square feet (4.7 to 5.6 m²) with facilities for changing and feeding. The number of such facilities may range from two up, depending upon terminal size and configuration.

Building maintenance and storage varies, depending upon the types of maintenance (contracted versus authority operated) and storage facilities available in other authority-owned buildings.

Building mechanical systems (HVAC) space ranges from 12 to 15 percent of the gross total space approximated for all other terminal functions. A value of 10 to 12 percent is used in relation to the connector element space. This allowance does not cover separate facilities for primary source heating and refrigeration (H&R plants).

Building structure space allowance for columns and walls is 5 percent of the total gross area approximated for all other functions.

Other space, as determined on a case-by-case basis, may be required at some airports for information services, government offices, contract service facilities and the like.

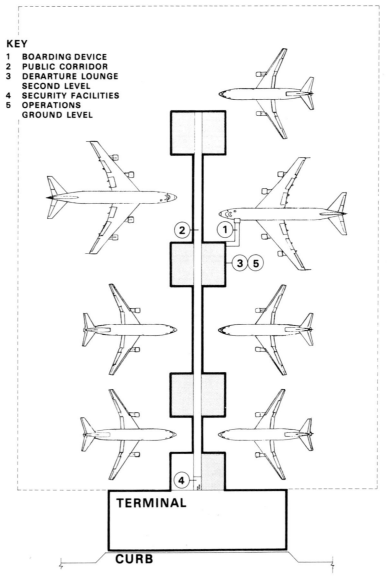

Fig. 1 Pier concept.

AIRPORTS AND TERMINALS

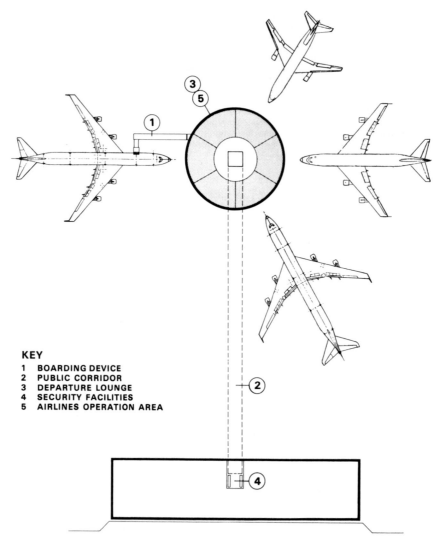

KEY
1   BOARDING DEVICE
2   PUBLIC CORRIDOR
3   DEPARTURE LOUNGE
4   SECURITY FACILITIES
5   AIRLINES OPERATION AREA

Fig. 2   Satellite concept.

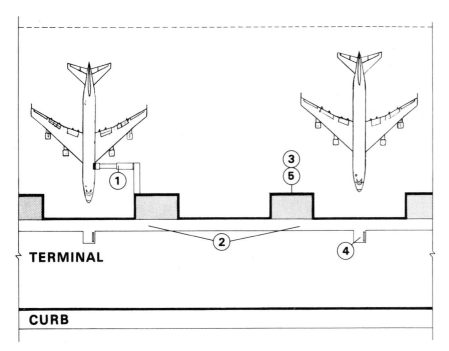

KEY
1 BOARDING DEVICE
2 PUBLIC CORRIDOR
3 DEPARTURE LOUNGE
  SECOND LEVEL
4 SECURITY FACILITIES
5 OPERATIONS
  GROUND LEVEL

TERMINAL

CURB

Fig. 3 Linear concept.

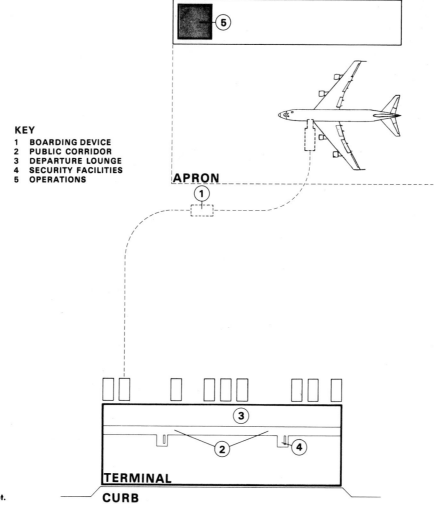

KEY
1 BOARDING DEVICE
2 PUBLIC CORRIDOR
3 DEPARTURE LOUNGE
4 SECURITY FACILITIES
5 OPERATIONS

APRON

TERMINAL

CURB

Fig. 4 Transporter concept.

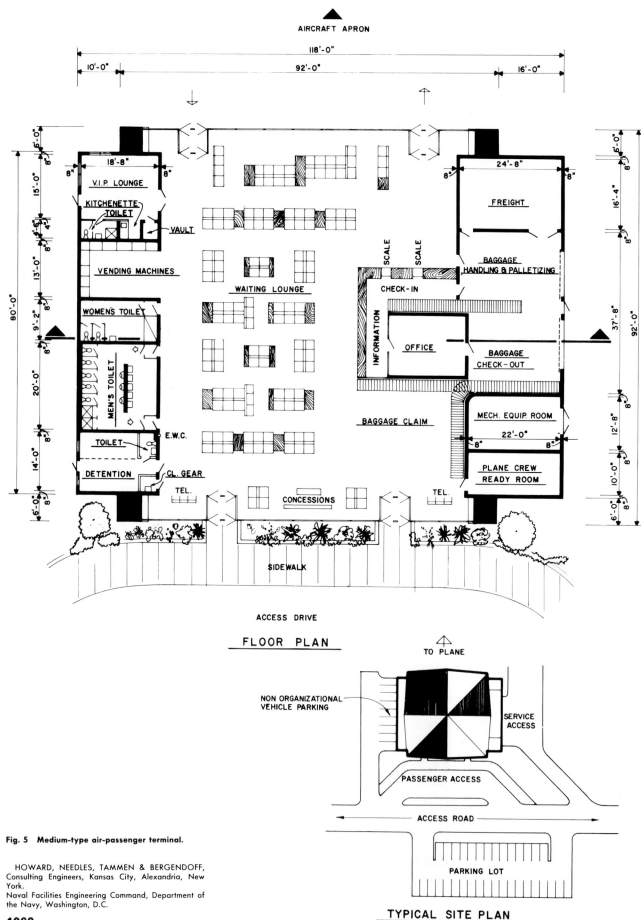

FLOOR PLAN

TYPICAL SITE PLAN

Fig. 5 Medium-type air-passenger terminal.

HOWARD, NEEDLES, TAMMEN & BERGENDOFF, Consulting Engineers, Kansas City, Alexandria, New York.
Naval Facilities Engineering Command, Department of the Navy, Washington, D.C.

AIRPORT ACCESS SYSTEMS

General

Airport access systems are comprised of a number of components which require proper spatial and sequential relationships to promote efficient traffic flows and minimize congestion. Access systems vary between airports depending on their size, complexity, physical characteristics and constraints. It is essential that the planning and design of an airport access system include a full and complete analysis which utilizes traffic flows based on current and forecasted demands.

Ground Access System Configurations

The layout and types of terminal concepts at an airport determine the integration of the components to form the ground transportation access system. The following paragraphs discuss some of the more typical ground access configurations:

Centralized Layout When the terminal complex consists of a single building or a contiguous series of buildings, the ground transportation system usually consists of sequentially and centrally located components. Except for vertical or horizontal separation, which may exist for originating and ter-

minating passenger vehicles, all passenger-related vehicles normally pass through the same series of roadways. Also, public parking and car rental facilities are centrally located. Many commercial service airports in the United States use this type of system, known as the centralized ground access concept. Some example airports are Chicago O'Hare, San Francisco International, Los Angeles International, Atlanta Hartsfield, Washington National, and Fort Lauderdale-Hollywood International. Figure 1 schematically presents this concept. This concept permits terminal unit expansion along the existing terminal area access road without loss of the original ground access system concept.

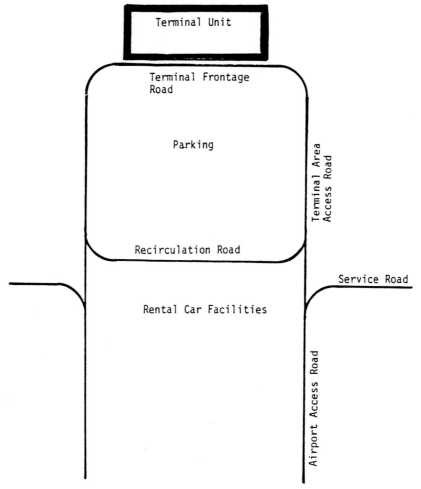

Fig. 1 Centralized ground access concept.

Transportation

AIRPORTS AND TERMINALS

Segmented Layout Division of the terminal building into originating and terminating passenger sides or grouping of airlines on either side of the building achieves flow separation on a horizontal basis. Originating passengers use one set of terminal frontage roads and terminating passengers the other; or specific airlines may group themselves on either side of the terminal unit. Orlando International, Jacksonville, and Greater Cincinnati airports use this type of ground access system layout called the segmented ground access concept. (See Figure 2.) This layout also permits expansion through terminal unit extension with retention of the same ground access system concept.

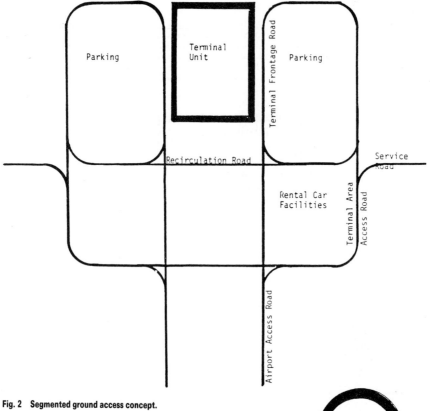

Fig. 2 Segmented ground access concept.

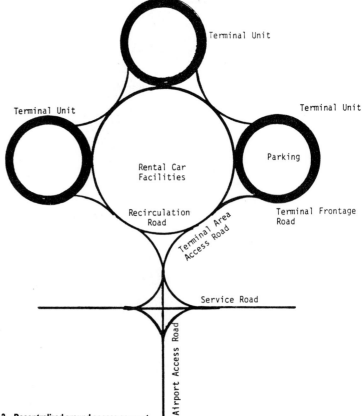

Decentralized Layout When the terminal complex consists of unit terminal buildings, vehicle flow separation on terminal access and frontage roads is possible. Airport access and terminal access roads funnel traffic to and from separate terminal facilities. Parking and car rental facilities are grouped on a terminal unit basis. Examples of this type of system use, the decentralized ground access concept, include Kennedy International and Kansas City International airports. (See Figure 3.) Expansion of the system is by addition of terminal units around the terminal access road with separate terminal frontage roads.

Fig. 3 Decentralized ground access concept.

1070

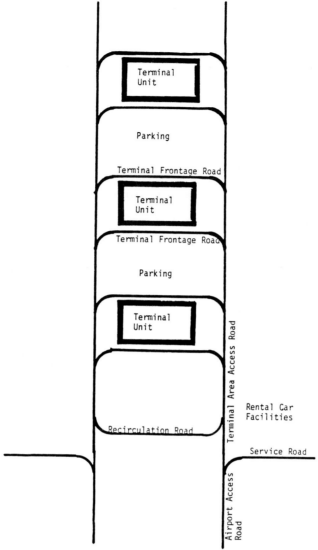

Fig. 4 Unitized ground access concept.

Unitized Layout In some cases, the terminal system may consist of a series of terminal buildings located in linear fashion. Access is from a centrally located roadway. Dallas-Fort Worth International and Houston Intercontinental airports use this type of system, the unitized ground access system concept. (See Fig. 4.) System expansion is usually accomplished by adding terminal units between terminal area access roads.

Airport Roads

The four types of airport roads are primary airport access roads, terminal area access roads, terminal frontage roads, and service roads.

Primary airport access roads provide access to the airport from the neighboring community road system. A capacity per lane of 700 to 800 vehicles per hour should be provided for at-grade interrupted flow conditions. This value approximates the flow relationship for urban arterial highways with signalized intersections; average speed range of 20 to 25 miles per hour (30 to 35 km/h); and, a demand volume to capacity ratio of approximately 0.80. For limited access highways with grade separations under uninterrupted flow con-

ditions, the recommended design is one lane for each 1,200 to 1,600 vehicles per hour. This value approximates the flow relationship for urban freeways; average speeds from 40 to 50 miles per hour (60 to 80 km/h); and a demand volume to capacity ratio approximating 0.60. A lane width of 12 feet (3.6 m), with a minimum of two lanes in each direction, is recommended.

Terminal area access roads service airport passengers, visitors, and employees and connect primary airport access roads with terminal buildings and parking facilities.

These roads should be sufficiently long to permit smooth channeling of traffic into appropriate lanes for safe access to terminal curbs, parking lots, and other public facilities. To avoid driver confusion, ample separation should be provided at locations where drivers must make directional choices. Not more than two choices should be required of a driver at any location. Traffic circulation in front of the terminal should, normally, be one-way and counter-clockwise for convenience of right-side loading and unloading of vehicles. Recirculation of vehicles to the passenger terminal should be permitted by providing road sections to link the ingress and egress lanes of the access road. When several buildings exist, it may

be advisable to provide more than one terminal road.

Traffic streams should be separated at an early stage with appropriate signing to avoid congestion and assure lower traffic volumes on each of the terminal frontage roads. Terminal area access roads should be planned to accommodate 900 to 1,000 vehicles per lane per hour. A minimum of two 12 foot (3.6 m) lanes should be provided. For recirculation roads, each lane should serve 600 vehicles per hour. If only one recirculation lane is provided, its width should be 20 feet (6 m) to accommodate stalled vehicles. For multiple recirculation lanes, the standard lane width is 12 feet (3.6 m).

Terminal frontage roads distribute vehicles directly to terminal buildings. Since considerable merging from through lanes to and from the curbfront occurs on these roadways, at least two lanes should be provided adjacent to the curb. The inside lane, sized at 8 feet (2.4 m), provides terminal curbfrontage and the 12 foot (3.6 m) outside lane serves through traffic and maneuvering to the terminal curbfrontage. While planned capacity for the outside lane should be 300 vehicles per hour, the inside lane is considered to have no throughput capacity. Additional 12 foot (3.6 m)

Transportation

AIRPORTS AND TERMINALS

through lanes should be provided at a rate of 600 vehicles per lane per hour. The terminal frontage is a critical element in the performance of the airport ground access system. Accordingly, to avoid the congestion caused by the inevitable double parking, a minimum of four lanes adjacent to the terminal curb is recommended. Four lanes are also recommended when terminal arrivals and departures are on the same level. (See Figures 5 and 6.)

Service roads are divided into two user categories—general and restricted.

General-use service roads are used for the delivery of goods, services, air cargo, flight kitchen supplies, and the like. At very large airports, to relieve congestion on airport terminal access roads, it is desirable to provide service road entrances and interchanges either before or shortly after entering the airport site. At low activity airports, the service and primary airport access roads may be coincidental.

Restricted-use service roads and traffic lanes are limited to such traffic as maintenance, fire and rescue, fuel, baggage, freight, and aircraft service vehicles. Those roads or sections of roads providing access to aircraft operating and parking areas require control points for adequate area security.

The recommended hourly lane capacity is 600 to 1,200 vehicles. Since a major portion of the road traffic is from trucks, the lower value should be used in preliminary design. The typical vehicle speed is 15 to 20 miles (25 to 33 km) per hour and frequent curb cuts are required for access to airport service facilities. Usually, these roads are two-way in nature with 12 foot (3.6 m) lane widths.

Terminal Curb Areas

Curb areas are required at terminals for loading and unloading of passengers and their baggage.

Curbfrontage The length of curb to be provided is related to the mix of vehicle types and expected curb dwell time. Table 1 shows typical curb dwell times and required vehicle slot lengths for different types of vehicles. It should be noted that, in the case of deplaning passengers, larger volumes of passengers, baggage, and ground transportation requirements peak over shorter periods of time. Strict policing is highly effective in optimizing the vehicle curb slot occupancy rate.

Sidewalk Platforms Sidewalk platforms are located immediately adjacent to curb/maneuvering lanes and terminal building entrances and exits to provide passenger walkways and safety areas for loading and unloading of vehicles.

At high activity airports, traffic curb islands are often provided to increase the curb area and, in some cases, to segregate different types of ground transportation vehicles. Airports with relatively low passenger levels may be able to accommodate both enplaning and deplaning passengers from one curb face.

Generally, the curb area is divided functionally into enplaning and deplaning curbs. It is separated physically, either horizontally at each end of the terminal building or vertically by means of structural vehicular ramps.

With a one level operation, the deplaning curb is located at the far end of the terminal with respect to approaching vehicular traffic. In the case of vertical separation, deplaning is on the lower level. Such separation minimizes the congestion which will result if opposing flows and volumes of persons, baggage, and ground vehicles are concentrated in the same curb area.

At most terminals, specific curb areas are designated for buses, limousines, courtesy cars, and taxi queues. These designated areas should be located at reasonable distances from terminal exits to reduce congestion. Overhead coverings are desirable to protect disembarking passengers from inclement weather.

Curbside Baggage Check-in Curbside baggage check-in permits baggage to be checked directly to the appropriate airline flight. The area which accommodates this service normally requires space for a baggage check-in desk (usually portable), baggage handtrucks, and a baggage conveyor or belt. Baggage may be either taken by handtruck to the ticket counter or transported directly by an adjacent conveyor belt to the outbound baggage room. The system used is economically related to passenger activity volumes, manpower, and installation cost. Terminal plans should consider design provisions to facilitate both present and future conveyor installations.

Terminal Entryways Terminal entrances should be located at enplaning curb areas and open directly into airline ticket counter lobbies. Similarly, terminal exits should be located in close proximity to baggage claim facilities and open to deplaning curbs. Automatic doors are highly recommended for: passenger baggage carrying convenience; as a weather buffer; and to increase the efficiency of passenger movement in energy conservation measures.

Pedestrian Crossings and Walkways Pedestrian crossings and walkways from terminal curbs to island platforms and parking facilities should be well marked. At high activity locations, consideration should be given to traffic-controlled crosswalks or, preferably, to grade separation by means of overpasses and tunnels.

Public Parking Facilities

Surveys at some major airports in the United States indicate that from 40 to 85 percent of the originating passengers arrive in private automobiles. Consequently, adequate public parking facilities are essential to good terminal design. Some general guidelines and recommendations for designing these facilities are discussed in succeeding paragraphs.

Locations Public parking lots should be located to provide walking distances from parked automobiles to terminals to no more than 1,000 feet (300 m). At larger airports, large volume parking needs may require provision of remote parking facilities served by shuttle bus or people mover systems.

Sizing The number of public parking spaces available per million originating passengers varies between airports, particularly at airports with over 1.5 million originations. While the range at existing airports may vary from under 1,000 to as high as 3,300 parking spaces per million originations, the suggested range is from 1,000 to 1,400. Another methodology provides parking spaces for 1.5 times the number of peak hour passengers. A better way for estimating parking needs is through a simulation based on existing parking characteristics and forecasted future needs. Simulation is expensive and time consuming, but can be justified where expansion space is severely limited or the cost of additional spaces is very high. A rule-of-thumb suggests an increase of 15 percent in the number of estimated parking spaces to minimize the amount of time required to find a parking space. In developing a parking lot plan, approximately 350 to 400 sq. ft. (31.5 to 36.0 m²), including lanes, should be allowed for each parked automobile. This is the equivalent of 109 to 124 parked cars per acre (269 to 306 per hectare) for on-grade parking.

Short-Term Versus Long-Term Parking The generally accepted definition for short-term parking is anything less than three hours. Approximately 70 to 85 percent of all parking lot users are short-term parkers, mainly greeters and well-wishers. However, this amounts to full time use of only 20 to 30 percent of the total parking requirements. Long-term parkers, the remaining 15 to 30 percent of parking lot users, are almost all travelers and occupy 70 to 80 percent of the available parking spaces. Through actual surveys and analysis of parking stubs conducted over several consecutive days, utilization charts can be developed showing vehicle volumes and length of stay. Short-term parking is usually provided nearest the terminal, since its turnover rate is often at least three times as much as for long-term lots. Short-term rates are high to discourage long-term parkers from clogging close-in lots. A rule-of-thumb suggests that separate short- and long-term parking should be provided when the total annual passenger volume exceeds 150,000 to 200,000.

Parking Lot Entrances and Exits Parking lot entrances and exits can easily become points of congestion. This congestion can be minimized by providing appropriate ticket dispensing and fee collection facilities and queuing lanes to reduce vehicle interference with access roads and parking lot circulation. Entrance and exit points should be clearly identified and sufficiently separated to avoid confusion. The total in and out airport parking lot flow can approach 25 percent of capacity in peak periods. While automatic ticket dispensers can process up to 400 vehicles per hour, a design capacity of 240 is recommended. At least two ticket dispensing machines per entrance should be provided to permit equipment maintenance without severely restricting parking operations. Attendant parking fee collection booths can process 120 to 150 vehicles hourly with variable fee parking and about 250 vehicles per hour with a flat fee. One collection position should be provided per 105 vehicles hourly in manual mode and one position per 185 vehicles per hour in a computerized operation.

TABLE 1 Typical Curbfrontage Dwell Times and Vehicle Slot Lengths

Vehicle	Curb dwell time (minutes)		Vehicle slot length (feet/meters)
	Enplane	Deplane	
Private auto	1.0 to 3.0	2.0 to 4.0	25.0/7.5
Rental car	1.0 to 3.0	2.0 to 4.0	25.0/7.5
Taxi	1.0 to 2.0	1.0 to 3.0	20.0/6.0
Limousine	2.0 to 4.0	2.0 to 5.0	35.0/10.5
Bus	2.0 to 5.0	5.0 to 10.0	50.0/15.0

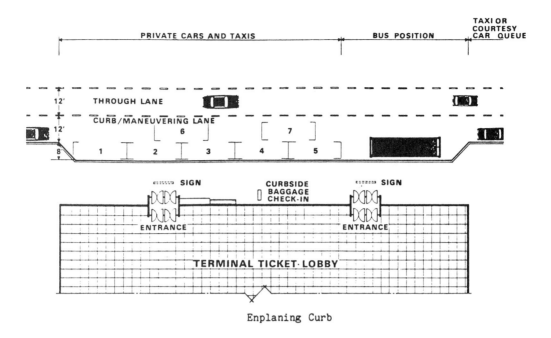

Enplaning Curb

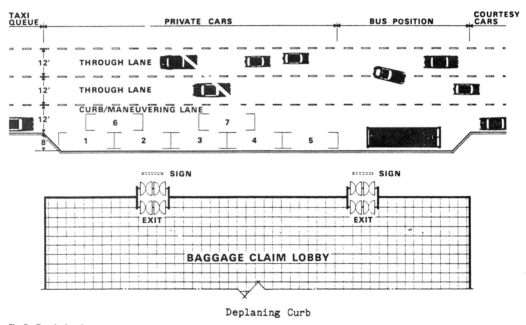

Deplaning Curb

Fig. 5 Terminal curb areas.

Circulation Counter-clockwise circulation within the parking lot is usually preferable and one-way traffic control is recommended to minimize congestion and hazards. Aisle widths should be generous and parking stalls clearly marked. The layout should be designed to minimize the number of turns and both vehicular and pedestrian travel distances. Parking lot aisles should be laid out in the direction of pedestrian-parker destination. Perpendicular parking is frequently used, since it permits parking from each side of the aisle and maximizes the number of stalls in a given area. However, parking stall layout mainly depends on the area's shape and, to a lesser extent, on local parking habits.

Parking Structures Multilevel parking structures are used at high activity airports, albeit with higher construction costs, to increase the number of parking slots in a given area and to reduce walking distances. This parking arrangement also furnishes users with protection from inclement weather.

Employee and Tenant Parking

Surveys show that approximately 90 percent of airport employees travel to work in private automobiles. Due to the variation among airports for aircraft maintenance, air cargo, and other servicing activities, a consistent relationship between numbers of employees and passengers has not been established. The number of employee/tenant parking spaces should be obtained by surveying airport management and terminal tenants. Employee and tenant parking should be provided near working areas which are not in or near terminal buildings. Otherwise, remote parking with a shuttle service to work areas is required.

Public Transportation and Rental Car Areas

Parking facilities are also required for the short-term parking of taxis, vans, limousines, buses, and for rental car ready and storage lots. Discussions should be held with the various service operators to establish parking requirements. Approximately 750 originating passengers are accommodated per rental car ready stall. The space required for taxi parking and rental car storage facilities is less than for public parking or rental car ready lots, since these vehicles are driven by professional drivers. Space for 160 vehi-

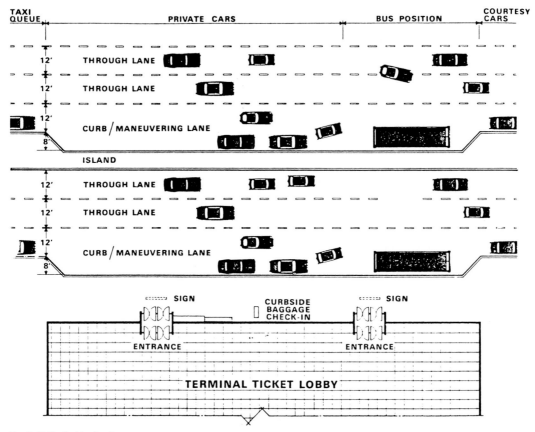

Fig. 6 Vehicular island curb.

cles per acre (395 per hectare) is recommended. Land in the immediate terminal area is at a premium. Accordingly, a trend is that on-airport rental car agencies are basing vehicles at remote locations and using vans to shuttle customers to and from these areas. Usually, short-term parking areas for buses, taxis, vans, and limousines are located away from the terminal curbfront to increase curbside operational efficiency. These vehicles can be called to the curb in a demand responsive mode and curbfront dwell time considerably reduced. Similarly, provisions can be made for exclusive lanes or dedicated auxiliary curbs for high occupancy vehicles such as vans, limousines, and buses.

AIRPORT CARGO CENTER AND ITS BUILDINGS

Interrelationships of Facilities

As the air cargo industry grows, the complex on the airport designed to handle air cargo becomes a significant element in airport planning and design. These facilities must provide for the efficient transfer of air cargo between surface transportation and aircraft. For larger airports, the complex may include a number of air carrier cargo facilities or multiple-occupancy buildings.

Design Considerations

The elements that compose the airport cargo center facilities and establish their character, size, and configuration will depend on the level of activity of the air cargo industry in the community served. The architect-engineer should work closely with the air carriers, air freight forwarders, truckers, and airport management to determine what is needed, including any special requirements peculiar to these facilities. The resulting design must satisfy present requirements and provide the flexibility necessary for future expansion. Buildings should be oriented, and land should be available to enable a logical expansion plan.

The air carrier cargo facility is the core of the cargo center, and the emphasis in this article is on that facility. It may be treated as a single building or combination of elements under one roof sufficiently integrated to permit operation as a single entity.

The design program, in the architect's vocabulary, denotes the building user's space requirements. It is one of the basic essentials for a successful solution to the design of any building. Fundamental considerations in developing a program are the elements of the building, the amount of space needed by each element, and the relationships between the spaces.

AIRPORT CARGO CENTER LOCATION

Importance of Site Planning

The complex on the airport specifically designed for the handling of air cargo is one of the major elements on the airport. The airport cargo center must be sited in a location that will contribute to the efficient transfer of cargo between surface and air transport. The selection of an appropriate site is the decision which determines to a large extent the effectiveness of the air cargo operation. The location of the elements of the complex in proper relationship to each other is of equal importance.

Location on the Airport

Four primary considerations dictate the selection of the site on an airport for the cargo complex.

1. Taxi distance from the most used runways should be as short as possible, and yet

Airport Cargo Facilities, Federal Aviation Agency, Washington, D.C., 1964.

there should not be interference with passenger operations.

2. The site should be readily accessible by surface vehicles from the passenger aircraft loading positions for efficient servicing of aircraft carrying both passengers and cargo.

3. The complex should be readily reached from all access roads to the airport to assure noninterference of vehicular traffic with aircraft movement areas.

4. Adequate space should be allowed for expansion of air cargo operations without encroaching on other airport functions, particularly without interfering with the expansion of the passenger terminal.

These four primary considerations indicate the general relationships with other functions and activities. They require extensive study to determine the degree to which they can be met on any individual airport. This study can best be made through the medium of an airport layout plan in which the advantages of possible locations and their effect on other airport facilities and operational activities can be objectively weighed.

Planning Considerations

The general location of the cargo complex having been established, a number of other factors should also be studied prior to adoption of a siting plan.

The arrangement of buildings and associated support facilities is important to satisfactory and efficient use, and it also affects future expansion of individual buildings. Important in this regard is consideration of spacing of buildings for access, vehicular circulation, and fire and safety clearances. Vehicular access and roadways, and parking areas are discussed in detail in the paragraphs that follow. Proper orientation of buildings, with respect to these factors and the prevailing winds, is essential to the functional operation of the buildings. Economical design dictates the need for balance of requirements for paved areas with other considerations discussed heretofore. Good drainage, consistent with driveway, parking, and pedestrian access requirements, is a necessary design consideration.

Noise is a consideration which must not be overlooked. Acoustical control can be achieved through proper landscape planting for sound absorption.

Cargo Center Site Plan

To illustrate the application of functional relationships discussed in this article, a diagrammatic site plan has been developed. Figure 1 indicates the relationships of facilities for a number of air carrier cargo operators, truckers, air freight forwarders, air express (REA), and airport mail facility (AMF).

The site plan orientation on the airport establishes optimum relationships of aircraft parking apron, and access and service roads discussed in the following paragraphs.

Aircraft Parking Aprons

Paved apron requirements for aircraft parking and loading positions adjoining air carrier

cargo facilities are dependent upon the type and size of aircraft used, airline schedules, and the type of materials handling system used. The need for direct access from certain facilities to the passenger loading apron, for access to both combination and all-cargo aircraft aprons for others, and for completely integrated building-apron relationships for certain materials handling systems are all important. Information on space requirements for aircraft apron parking positions can be found in the article dealing with airport design.

Access, Circulation, and Parking

Discussion of ground vehicle movement considerations is presented in general terms.

Roads Access to and egress from the airport cargo complex and circulatory roads within it should be as direct and unimpeded. There should be as little interference as possible with airport passenger vehicular traffic. In those cases, where the number and types of trucks using the access roads will cause frequent passenger traffic congestion, separate roads should be designed specifically for truck traffic leading directly to the cargo center. Visitors, passengers, and customers should be provided convenient access from the passenger terminal area.

Truck Parking Parking areas required include those designed to serve the trucker, the customer and visitor, and the employee. Planning of truck parking spaces and maneuvering areas will probably present a difficult problem because of the many variables. Maximum truck sizes vary from state to state. Trucks bringing freight to the cargo center will be of many types and sizes. Parking areas and truck-dock facilities with adequate maneuvering space must be provided for movement of vehicles without creating bottlenecks during peak loading and unloading hours.

Generally, the recommended distance for maneuvering from the loading platform to the nearest obstruction is twice the length of the largest road vehicle expected to use the facility. The Air Transport Association suggests a minimum overall depth of 100 ft for the terminal-truck apron which will allow 75 ft for maneuvering of trucks plus a 25-ft-wide access roadway. Minimum interference distances may in effect be less when tractors with smaller turning radii are used, when the spacing between trailers is increased, or when a sawtoothed loading platform design is used.

Customer and Visitor Parking Those seeking service should have the most direct access possible to the reception areas of individual air carriers, freight forwarders, and other service facilities. These parking spaces may be adjacent to the building in conjunction with the truck parking area. Permanent parking areas should not be located where expansion of buildings is being contemplated.

Employee Parking Sufficient parking should be provided for employees' cars which are generally parked for a period equal to the length of the working day. Since the employee

Transportation

AIRPORT CARGO FACILITIES

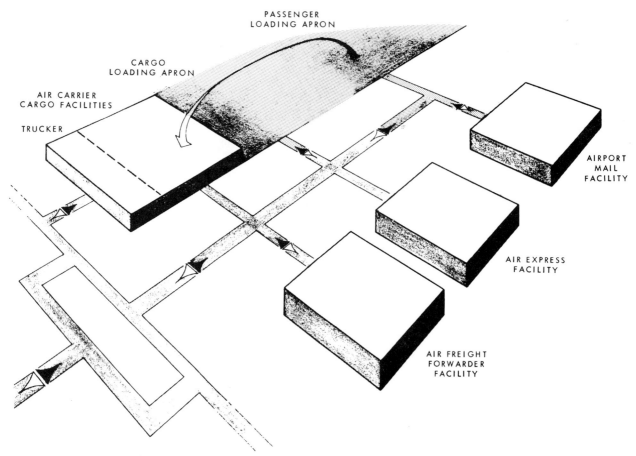

Fig. 1 Relationships of cargo facilities.

does not usually require ready access to his car during this period, it is not necessary to locate the employee parking area directly adjacent to the freight handling facilities. Where the airport is relatively small, an employee parking area common to all operational functions on the airport may be adequate for parking needs. For the larger airport, strategically located parking spaces which may be used by all employees of the airport cargo complex should be considered. There may be just one of these areas planned near the center of activity, or there may be several dependent upon the size and spread of the airport cargo complex. Administrative personnel usually require parking spaces adjacent to the office area because they may have to use their cars frequently during the working day.

AIR CARRIER CARGO BUILDINGS

Elements of the Building

An air carrier cargo building may be planned for single or multiple occupancy. The type of occupancy normally will depend on the potential for air cargo industry growth in the community being served and the volume of business generated by each of the airlines. At airports where there are a number of carriers, each generating only nominal amounts of freight daily, a multiple-occupancy building can provide adequate space to satisfy the needs of all. Single- or double-occupancy buildings with adequate aircraft apron space should be considered for those air carriers that operate all-cargo schedules and handle larger amounts of air freight.

There are four major functional elements to consider in the design of the air carrier cargo building. These are the freight-handling areas, administration area, personnel and customer accommodations, and service facilities. Figure 2 indicates diagrammatically the space relationships for functions within the air carrier cargo facilities. Airport cargo buildings should be designed for planned expansion in both length and depth, where economically feasible, and fixed support facilities so located to avoid interference with such expansion.

Truck Dock Facilities

There must be a sufficient number of truck stations to serve truckers, air freight forwarders, and others for both incoming and outgoing shipments. In addition to truck dock positions, consideration should be given to providing facilities for the airport-to-airport customers who use other than trucks to deliver or pick up small shipments.

The number of truck dock spaces will vary with the airline operation and the community. To determine the optimum number requires detailed analysis of truck arrival in a peak hour, the service time at the dock, and the acceptable waiting time for those experiencing delays.

The minimum number of dock spaces required for incoming trucks can readily be determined. Assume for example a normal "stripping" or unloading rate at each dock space of approximately 5,000 lb per hour. This rate includes time allowed for delays and spotting of vehicles. For an inbound volume from trucks of 90,000 lb of freight and a time allowed for "stripping" vehicles of three hours, the unloading would have to be accomplished

at the rate of 30,000 lb per hour. Thus, there would be a requirement for six truck spaces at the dock for this operation.

The width of each truck station should be a minimum of 12 ft to allow for parking of large vehicles. Building door openings at each station should be a minimum of 10 ft wide by 10 ft high. Extensive open platforms are not recommended because freight left in the open is subject to pilferage and damage from inclement weather. Protection from the weather for freight and personnel during stripping or loading operations should be provided by an overhang canopy of at least 5 ft. Clearance above the top of the parked freight van should be approximately 18 in.

Building floor heights may vary from 44 to 47 in. above grade. There are a number of leveling devices for accommodating truck bed heights ranging from 30 in. for a pickup truck to 50 in. for a large tractor-trailer.

Processing Area

Receiving, sorting, weighing, labeling, and building up of loads for shipment are the major activities in the processing of freight from the truck to the aircraft. There are a number of factors which have a profound effect on total space requirements.

1. *Cargo turnover* is affected by such variables as types of aircraft, frequency of service, time of day of arrivals and departures inbound, outbound, and directional preponderance of cargo.

2. *Density of cargo* accounts for considerable dimensional disparity. A ton of cut flowers occupies many times more space than a ton of machine parts.

1076

3. *Character of cargo* creates a need for specific space allocation. Refrigerated storage is required for perishable cargo, and other temperature controlled areas are needed for live cargo. Bonded storage is needed for customs, import/export control, as well as security accommodations for valuable cargo.

4. *Methods of handling and storing* cause variations in space requirements. Operations utilizing forklifts and pallets require more square footage for circulation and maneuvering.

The arrangement of space in the load build-up areas is also influenced by aircraft loading characteristics. Space should be planned for sequence loading to provide for distribution of weight in the aircraft and for easy removal of loads at destinations. Freight to be loaded on combination aircraft should be kept separate from freight to be loaded on all-cargo aircraft. Loads to be unitized on pallets, loads to be unitized in containers, and those to be loaded on aircraft manually should be controlled by providing separate but adequate space for each. The types of aircraft and the numbers of each type being served by the facility should be given careful study.

Consultation with the users as to the type of materials handling systems to be employed is essential and will be most helpful in this area of design. As materials handling systems for the air cargo industry are developed and improved, space requirements for the load build-up area and other operations may be reduced substantially. Figure 3 indicates diagrammatically suggested space requirements for receiving and processing areas.

Administrative Area, and Customer and Personnel Accommodations

Adequate administrative space is necessary for efficient management of cargo operations. A thorough analysis of the duties and responsibilities of the administrative personnel should be made prior to preparing the design program of the building. The number of employees that may ultimately be employed in the management of operations should be studied.

Reception areas should be provided to handle customers. In addition to serving as a receiving point for visitors, small packages may be claimed or bills may be paid here. There should be sufficient space for a counter, accommodations for customers, and cases for display of brochures and other sales material.

Sales offices may be required by some airlines. Space in the sales office should provide for desks, files, and facilities for telecommunications. Files should be readily accessible to all the salesmen. The sales office may serve also as a customer service center or clearinghouse for telephone inquiries. Close communication must be maintained between this office, receiving, aircraft space control, and accounting.

Management and general office space requirements are dependent upon variables such as the type of operation, the amount and type of freight processed, and the community being served. Accounting and records offices may be necessary facilities for operations of any sizable magnitude. The space required varies with the type of record keeping and accounting equipment that may be used such as automatic filing systems and data processing equipment.

Communications centers assist management in the efficient movement of freight. Each facility component must be kept informed of changes in schedule, cargo space available, and of special shipments requiring unusual attention. The communications center can serve as the central nerve system. It can provide the link between administration and operations. Space may be required for teletype machines and closed-circuit television facilities in addition to sufficient desk space for communications personnel.

Aircraft space control office requirements are dependent upon the amount of freight handling activity. This office may be placed in the receiving area or in the administration offices. Space must be provided for computing and communications equipment and for aircraft charts indicating cargo space available on the aircraft. These functions are closely related to those of receiving and processing and to those of the communications center. Provisions should be made to facilitate close liaison with these interrelated functions.

The number of personnel employed in cargo operations will vary not only with the type and volume of freight handled but also with the materials handling system used and the scheduling of aircraft loading operations. A careful study should be made of all factors including local codes and state labor laws to assure adequate provision for employee needs. Figure 3 indicates suggested space requirements. This overall area may be allocated to administration, customer accommodations, and personnel accommodations such as rest rooms, locker rooms, and lunchrooms. A first-aid room, pilot-ready room, or other specialized area may be included dependent on circumstances peculiar to proposed facilities.

Maintenance, Services, and Storage

In order to provide for an efficient operation, equipment must be kept in good working order at all times. Maintenance and storage of materials handling equipment, such as containers, should not be overlooked. The functions of maintenance and storage may be joined, or they may be completely separated. The manner in which these functions are handled depends largely on the type and amount of equipment used.

For large operations, maintenance and servicing shops may be necessary to provide repairs for such items as pallets and containers, forklift trucks, conveyors, and other materials handling equipment. Webbing used to secure freight against dislodgment in aircraft requires periodic repair. The maintenance and the servicing shops may be centrally located in the cargo complex, or they may be constructed as a part of the air carrier's individual freight handling facilities.

Garage or hangar space may be required for larger pieces of equipment, such as scissors lifts, mobile freight loaders, or other vehicles used in the freight loading operations. (In some cases, it may be economically more practical for the air carriers if this space and this type of equipment are furnished by the airport management on a rental basis.)

Space required for building utilities, such as plumbing, heating, ventilating, air conditioning, electricity, and gas depends primarily on the geographical location of the airport. Other factors, such as requirements of servicing equipment, type of fuel available in the area, and accessibility of public utilities to the airport cargo center, also must be considered. All utilities may be centrally located on the airport and furnished to users by airport management. Each building may house its own space for the provision of these utilities.

Special Handling

Some types of freight require special handling, that is, facilities and techniques not ordinarily used for normal items. Requirements depend on the policy of the air carrier in accepting shipments that require special techniques. Basically, four types of shipments which fall into the special handling category are live

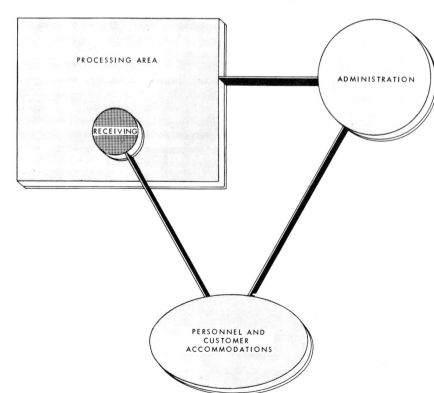

Fig. 2 Space relationships within buildings.

animals, perishables (pharmaceuticals, meats, produce, and flowers), and bonded and valuable shipments.

If the volume of live animal shipments is expected to be large, special provisions for them should be given consideration. Heating, ventilation, cleaning facilities, fresh water supply, cages and stables, and storage facilities for handling, cleaning, and feeding equipment will require study. Consultation with the local chapter of the Society for Prevention of Cruelty to Animals (SPCA) is suggested.

Perishables are being shipped in increasing quantities. Bonded and other valuable freight processed varies not only with the economic character of the community but also with the seasons.

Facilities at International Airports

Air carriers providing service for overseas shipments at international airports will require space for inspection of deplaned freight. Consultation with Bureau of Customs, Agricultural Research Service, and Public Health Service officials in addition to the airlines is essential in developing a proper design program for this area.

Building Construction

Building design consistent with functional requirements and the need for economical construction and maintenance cannot be overemphasized. Airport buildings are often constructed in areas beyond the jurisdiction of a city building code. Materials and methods of construction and design of an airport cargo building may or may not be governed by a building code of the local community or regulations established in state labor laws. When local codes are applicable, particularly in small communities, the standards designated in such codes are sometimes below those acceptable as good architectural or engineering practice for buildings on airports.

Selection of the structural system to be used for the building should be based on careful consideration of the insurance rates for various classes of building construction and occupancy. The initial cost of fire-resistant construction may be higher than other types of construction, but a lower insurance rate will often offset this higher initial cost. Fire is not the only hazard about which the designer must concern himself. Protection against pilferage, vandalism, or possible sabotage in time of emergency should be considered in choosing materials of construction. The location of the building and the types of commodities moved through the facility will also influence the type of construction.

Structural systems having the capability of economically spanning as much as 100 ft provide greater flexibility in building design and space arrangement. Clear-span structures are desirable because they allow for greater maneuverability of forklift trucks and other freight handling equipment. Large-space areas, free of columns and bearing walls, can be divided and adapted to satisfy the changing demands of functional operations. Roof construction and roof design loads vary with the area of the country.

Floor construction, according to the NBFU-recommended National Building Code, should be designed and constructed for the greatest loads that are anticipated by the user. Provision should be made for such items as floor scales, pit elevators, and recessed tracks for towveyor systems. Floors in the office areas, where extensive filing systems are maintained, should be designed to carry a minimum uni-

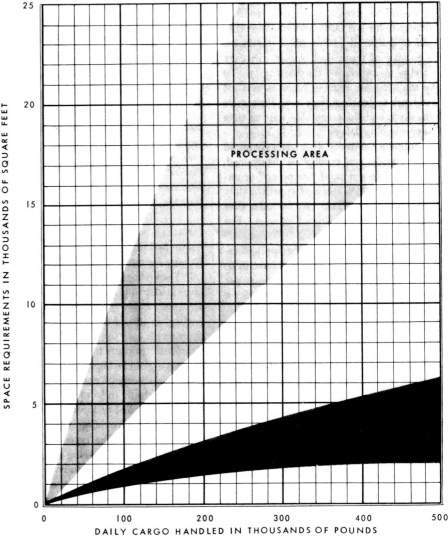

Fig. 3 Building area space requirements.

formly distributed load of 125 lb per square foot.

Selection of doors must be given careful consideration. Overhead and roll-up doors are suggested in areas where there is movement of freight. The tracks of the overhead-type door should be installed to provide as much headroom as possible within the building.

Bumpers and guards for protecting truck-dock edges are available in many designs. The nature of activity, the devices used for loading operations, and the amount of traffic are the determinants in making a selection. The use of bumpers and guards will help keep maintenance of dock areas to a minimum.

Interior finishes depend upon local factors, but they should be selected from the standpoint of minimum maintenance. The functional use of the area should be the determining factor in the selection of the finishes. In the processing and storage areas of the building, a smooth concrete finish for the floor should be adequate. A hardening additive may be used in the concrete to make a durable surface.

The toilet rooms should have floors and walls finished with a hard impervious material for ease of cleaning and maintenance. The wall finishes may be an integral part of the wall construction, such as glazed partition block or glazed brick where budgets permit. The

locker room floor should have a painted, smooth finished concrete floor if costs must be kept at a minimum. Walls may be painted masonry units or plaster. Since locker rooms are generally noisy places, an acoustic ceiling should be considered for this area.

Utilities

Heating and ventilating requirements vary with the climate and the requirements of the user. It may be possible to integrate systems with the humidity and temperature control required for handling special commodities. A system which will provide proper year-round conditioning of air particularly in administrative areas is important.

Electrical and lighting systems should be adequate for the designed functions. The requirements of the electrical service vary with the size and character of the facility. Much will depend upon the nature of the materials handling system used. Minimum required lighting levels may be governed by local codes or state labor laws; however, these may sometimes be below those acceptable as good architectural or engineering practice for buildings on airports. It is recommended that airport owners voluntarily adopt the standards from one of several recognized sources.

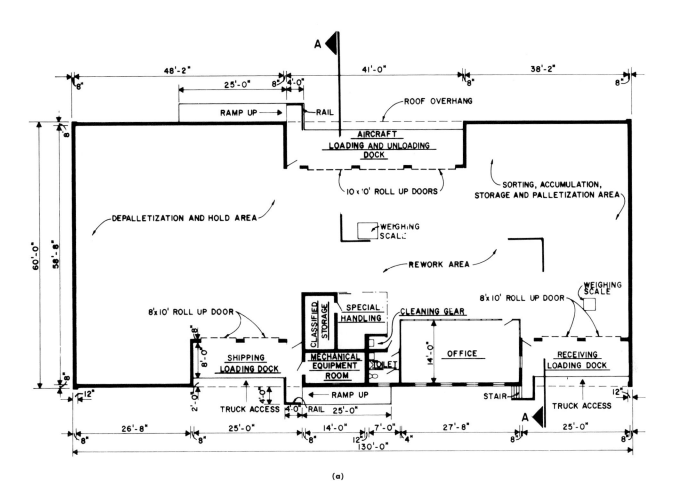

(a)

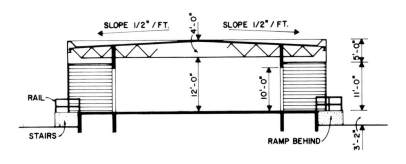

SECTION A-A

(b)

Fig. 1 SOURCE: U.S. Naval Facilities Engineering Command, Department of the Navy, Washington, D.C.

AIR CARGO TERMINALS

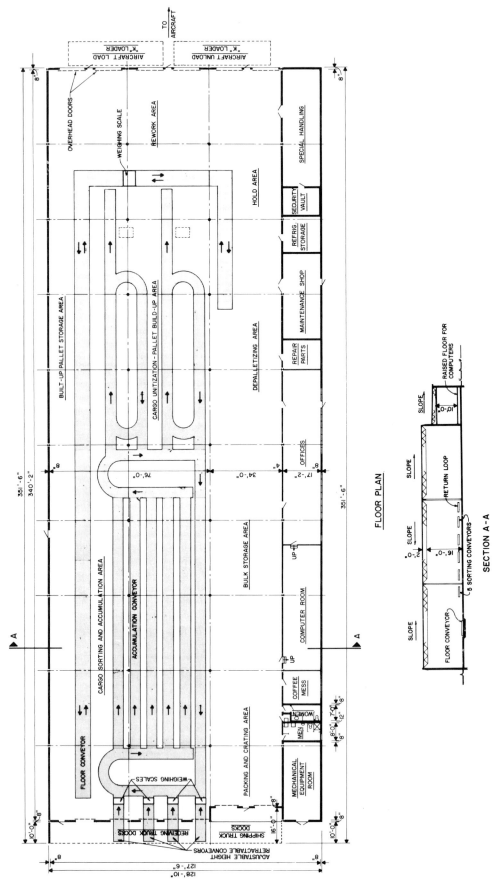

FLOOR PLAN

SECTION A-A

Fig. 2 source: U.S. Naval Facilities Engineering Command, Department of the Navy, Washington, D.C.

BUILDING SITING

Importance of Site Planning

The service equipment building must be sited in a location that will contribute to the efficient operation and performance of equipment and personnel. The analysis and study to determine the location of the building is the most important single consideration presented in this discussion.

Location on the Airport

The study to determine the location for the service equipment building should consider the proper relationships of each of the essential airport building categories identified by activities related to the terminal and to administration, to commercial aircraft facilities, to other airport oriented operations, and to aviation oriented industry which may be located on the airport. Operational activities in addition to administrative functions are generally grouped according to the relationship to the services provided by governmental agencies, air traffic control, communications, and weather; to the service provided by airport management; to the aircraft sales, storage, maintenance, and flight training; and to air cargo, express, and air mail movements. The service equipment building and fire and crash rescue building are associated with a group of operational services provided by airport management for planning purposes. It is this relationship which may lead to the combining of facilities.

There are three principal considerations that should determine the location of this functional group of operation buildings including the service equipment building. It must be close to the heart of airport operations for control of maintenance and service activities. It must be accessible to airport service roads, particularly the airport perimeter road. This will permit the equipment to reach all operational areas of the airport without having to cross active runways. It must be centrally located with respect to airport pavement areas, particularly air carrier aircraft passenger loading aprons, to other public loading and servicing aprons, and to landing area facilities. Examples of specific locations which have been selected after reasonable consideration of factors discussed are shown in Fig. 1. Site locations are indicated by order of preference.

Planning Considerations

The location of the operational activity having been established and the preliminary design concept of the building selected, a number of other factors should be studied prior to adoption of a siting plan.

The arrangement of buildings and associated support facilities is important to satisfactory and efficient use, and it also affects future

Airport Service Equipment Buildings, Federal Aviation Agency, Washington, D.C., 1964.

extensibility of the equipment building to accommodate additional garage stalls. Important in this regard is consideration of spacing of buildings for access, vehicular circulation, and fire and safety clearances. The proper orientation of the building, with respect to these factors and the prevailing winds, is essential to the functional operation of the building. In any climate, an attempt should be made to orient the building so that the large door openings will be least exposed to prevailing winds. In snow country, an effort should be made to take advantage of wind movements to reduce drifting against the building and, where possible, to remove snow from vehicular entrance doors.

Since, under most circumstances, it will not be considered practicable to site the building adjacent to aircraft operational aprons, provision should be made for adequate circulation and unobstructed access. Economical design dictates the need for balance of requirements for paved areas with other considerations discussed heretofore. Good drainage consistent with driveway, parking, and pedestrian access requirements is also important.

THE BUILDING AND ITS SURROUNDINGS

Factors Affecting Space Requirements

The need for the facility having been clearly established, the next step is the design of the building and provision for required support items in the immediate surroundings. A review of the major factors affecting the need for a facility and a review of existing or contemplated airport maintenance procedures should provide an indication of what would constitute an adequate number of garage stalls for the equipment. No two airports can be expected to need exactly the same equipment or facilities. At some airports, a number of facilities may already be furnished in another building.

Some maintenance equipment, similar to construction equipment, will not require storage in a building of the type discussed herein. Also, some types of equipment, if adequately serviced and maintained, will not require shelter at all. At some airports, all servicing of vehicles may be done off the premises.

Office space is also an essential element to be considered in the functional design of the building. Storage for hand tools and parts, although not discussed in relationship to the various types of equipment, should not be forgotten in the analysis of space requirements. In addition, consideration should be given to the space required for personnel needs such as lockers, toilet and shower facilities, multipurpose rooms, and personnel equipment storage. At airports where few personnel are employed, separate locker rooms and storage facilities may not be needed.

Space Requirements

It has been found that there exists a closer relationship between the number of vehicles used for maintenance and the amount of airport pavement than between the amount of equipment and the number of operations or passengers using the airport. Table 1 is a tabular listing of runway lengths and the number of vehicle stalls found to be satisfactory at a representative group of airports. It is based on current usage figures. The application of these figures will provide general guidance where other data are not available.

Combination Facilities

A consideration affecting space requirements and space relationships is the advantages offered by combining facilities designed to meet a number of airport operational needs. At some airports, it may be desirable to consolidate the housing for fire and rescue apparatus and maintenance and service equipment into a single building. Airport management at an airport adjacent to large bodies of water may want to consider combined facilities at a site that would permit incorporating a facility to house a rescue boat. In every case, however, there are certain overriding factors, such as siting and accessibility for example, that must be considered in evaluating the advantages and disadvantages of combining different facilities.

There is an advantage in combining fire and rescue and service equipment facilities when personnel utilized as volunteer firefighters are maintenance personnel. This is particularly true when the airport management has under-

TABLE 1 Representative Number of Stalls and Employees

| Runway length, ft | Airport mean annual snowfall | | | |
| | At least 15 in. | | Less than 15 in. | |
	Stalls	Employees	Stalls	Employees
10,000 or over	18	20	5	6
9,000 to 10,000	16	18	5	6
8,000 to 9,000	14	16	4	5
7,000 to 8,000	12	13	4	5
6,000 to 7,000	11	12	3	4
5,000 to 6,000	10	11	3	3
4,000 to 5,000	5	3	2	3
Less than 4,000	4	2	2	2

AIRPORT SERVICE EQUIPMENT BUILDINGS

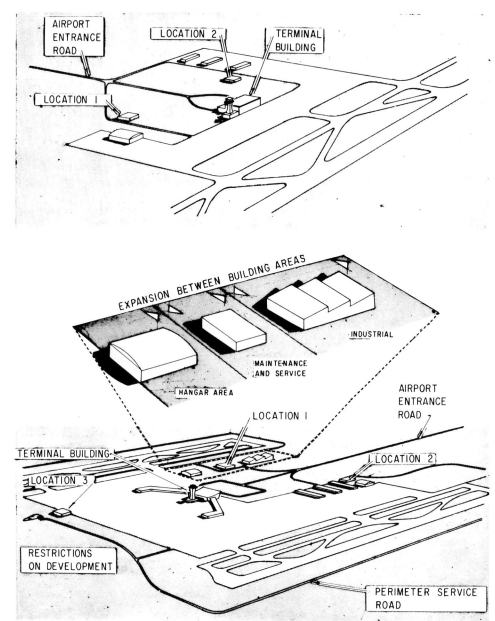

Fig. 1 Service equipment building siting.

taken the training of these men to operate fire and rescue apparatus. Even where this is not contemplated, combined facilities may be economical and satisfactory provided facilities can be made available for total needs and other requirements can be met. The requirements peculiar to the fire and rescue operation must receive just consideration.

A certain degree of isolation of facilities in combination buildings is essential for security purposes as well as for functional reasons. A full partition separating the two functional areas and isolating fire department activities and equipment is a requirement. Apparatus room requirements are such that tandem parking of vehicles is not recommended for emergency equipment. Office and storage space to satisfy the needs of the fire department should be separate from similar facilities provided for service equipment operations.

At airports where a 24-hour crew coverage requires living facilities including a dormitory

for firefighters, the disadvantages associated with combining facilities override all other considerations. All of these factors must be evaluated. They are mentioned here preparatory to the detailed discussion of space relationships and other building elements that follows. Included in Fig. 2 is a typical layout showing space relationships which may be considered for a combined equipment building.

Space Relationships

Suggested space relationships for airports having varying equipment requirements are shown in Figs. 2 and 3.

Equipment and Servicing Stalls These should normally be between 12 and 14 ft wide and 40 ft long for typical equipment in order to allow a reasonable amount of space for circulation around each vehicle. Door openings of stalls should normally be 12 ft wide and 15 ft high

for typical equipment. While most service equipment will conform to highway clearances and vehicular standards, the trend is toward larger units for special equipment developed to meet the needs of airport operation. Where stalls may be arranged to provide tandem storage of vehicles, the allowance for each vehicle space may be reduced to 35 ft with the overall interior depth of the building being 70 ft. An example of this is indicated in Fig. 3. The ceiling height should be a minimum of 17 ft.

Office Space This should be sufficient to accommodate a desk, a few chairs, and a file cabinet, which should be provided for the maintenance superintendent. A room having an area of 100 sq ft would be adequate to fulfill this need at most airports.

Storage Space Storage space for tools and equipment should be provided adjacent to the stall area in which servicing of equipment

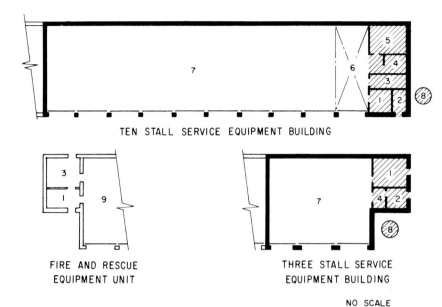

TEN STALL SERVICE EQUIPMENT BUILDING

FIRE AND RESCUE
EQUIPMENT UNIT

THREE STALL SERVICE
EQUIPMENT BUILDING

NO SCALE

LEGEND

1. OFFICE
2. HEATING ROOM
3. STORAGE
4. TOILET & SHOWER ROOM
5. LOCKERS & MULTI-PURPOSE ROOM
6. VEHICULAR SERVICE
7. EQUIPMENT GARAGE
8. SAND STORAGE
9. FIRE APPARATUS ROOM

Fig. 2 Combination equipment buildings.

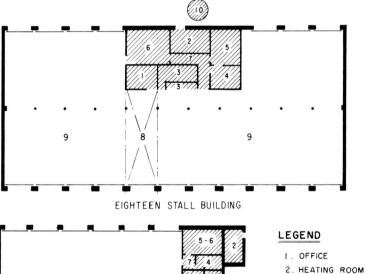

EIGHTEEN STALL BUILDING

THIRTEEN STALL BUILDING

NO SCALE

LEGEND

1. OFFICE
2. HEATING ROOM
3. STORAGE
4. TOILET & SHOWER ROOM
5. LOCKER ROOM
6. MULTI-PURPOSE ROOM
7. PASSAGE
8. VEHICULAR SERVICE
9. EQUIPMENT GARAGE
10. SAND STORAGE

Fig. 3 Service equipment buildings.

is performed. A storage area of 60 to 80 sq ft would provide reasonably adequate space for this purpose. The space may be provided along one wall of the service area in a group of secured shelves or cabinets, in a separate storage room, or both. Smaller equipment and hand tools needed in addition to those used for servicing may also be stored in the space provided.

Personnel Accommodations

1. Locker room facilities may be provided at airports where five or more persons are employed for maintenance and service work. These facilities may be combined with a multipurpose room or other personnel accommodations. When the number of maintenance personnel approaches 14, completely separate locker room facilities should be considered. One locker, 15 in. wide, 22 in. deep, and 72 in. high, should be provided for each maintenance and service employee regularly employed at the airport. At small airports, where only a few maintenance personnel are employed, facilities for clothes storage and personnel needs may be more conveniently provided elsewhere than in the equipment building.

2. Toilet, lavatory, and shower facilities allowances should be based on the total number of maintenance and service operations personnel. Toilet and shower facilities should be located adjacent to the locker room, and provision should be made for reasonable access from all working areas of the building.

3. A multipurpose room may, under some circumstances, be considered desirable for employee lunchroom space when other eating facilities are not available on the airport. An allowance of approximately 10 sq ft per employee would be adequate.

Storage Adjacent to the Building

At airports where icy conditions are experienced and sanding is used as a method of maintaining safe operating surfaces under such conditions, availability of sand is often a problem. Where airports are not located sufficiently close to a quarry from which hot, dry sand can be procured readily, an adequate amount of sand should be stored in a dry condition on the airport.

At most airports where it is necessary to store sand, it has been found that between 250 and 300 tons should be readily available on the site. Since a problem arises when sand is stored in the open, various methods of providing for sand storage should be considered. Hot, dry sand is most desirable for spreading on icy surfaces. The dryness allows the sand to be spread effectively, and the heat sets the sand in the ice to provide a reasonably good abrasive surface.

Where practicable, it is recommended that sand storage be provided adjacent to the building. One of the most effective methods of storing sand is in an elevated silo or hopper. Where this can be located adjacent to the building, access for trucks loading beneath it and problems of providing heating can be simplified. Other methods of storage at grade may be satisfactory provided mechanical loading equipment is available.

Transportation

AIRPORT SERVICE EQUIPMENT BUILDINGS

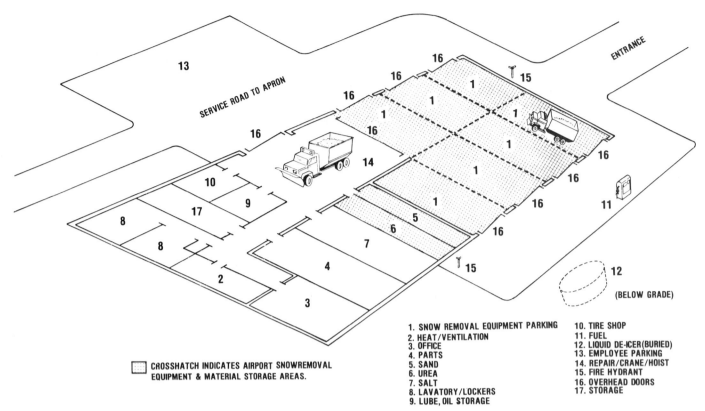

CROSSHATCH INDICATES AIRPORT SNOWREMOVAL EQUIPMENT & MATERIAL STORAGE AREAS.

1. SNOW REMOVAL EQUIPMENT PARKING
2. HEAT/VENTILATION
3. OFFICE
4. PARTS
5. SAND
6. UREA
7. SALT
8. LAVATORY/LOCKERS
9. LUBE, OIL STORAGE
10. TIRE SHOP
11. FUEL
12. LIQUID DE-ICER (BURIED)
13. EMPLOYEE PARKING
14. REPAIR/CRANE/HOIST
15. FIRE HYDRANT
16. OVERHEAD DOORS
17. STORAGE

Fig. 4   Typical building layout (drive through stall type).

Floor Area Requirement

Parking spaces are 25 feet by 40 feet (7.5×12 m) except for parking spaces for spreaders without plows, snowblowers with capacities under 2000 tons/hr, and smaller runway sweepers. Spreaders without plows and small snowblowers can normally be parked in a space 20 feet by 30 feet (6×9 m). The smaller runway sweepers can normally be parked in a space 20 feet by 40 feet (6×12 m).

Clearance Airport sweepers, snowplows, and snowblowers are normally much wider than highway type vehicles, and they often have bulky projections not visible from the operator's position. These projections can cause clearance problems as the equipment passes through most doors or other limited width openings. For this reason, it is recommended that, if possible, extra clearance be provided in door sizes. Minimum door size requirements are:

Large Equipment Large plows, blowers, and sweepers require doors 18 feet high by 25 feet wide ($5.5 \text{ m} \times 7.6 \text{ m}$).

Medium and Intermediate Equipment Medium size snow removal equipment will require doors 18 feet high by 20 feet wide ($5.5 \text{ m} \times 6.1 \text{ m}$).

Small Equipment For small equipment, doors 16 feet high by 18 feet wide ($4.9 \text{ m} \times 5.5 \text{ m}$) are adequate.

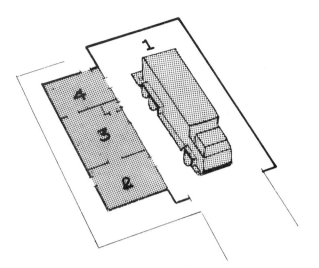

1 APPARATUS ROOM

2 ALARM ROOM

3 FIREMEN'S QUARTERS

4 STORAGE

Fig. 1   One-stall fire building space relationships.

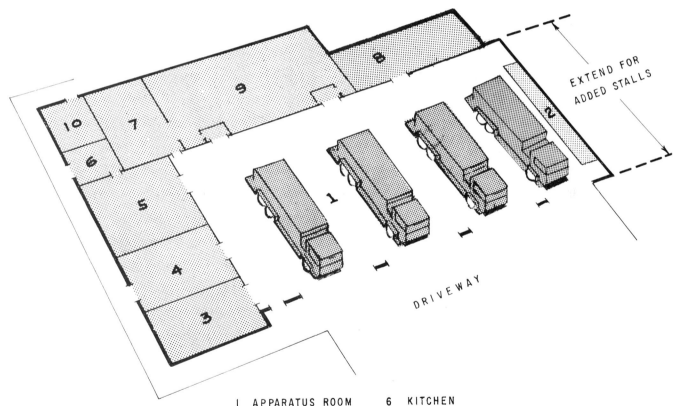

NOTE

DORMITORY IS OMITTED AT AIRPORTS
USING 8 HOUR SHIFTS AND KITCHEN
IS REDUCED IN SIZE

1 APPARATUS ROOM

2 HOSE RACKS

3 ALARM ROOM

4 CHIEF'S OFFICE

5 TRAINING ROOM

6 KITCHEN

7 LOCKER & TOILET FACILITIES

8 STORAGE ROOM

9 DORMITORY

10 UTILITY ROOM

Fig. 2   Three-stall fire building space relationships.

AIRCRAFT FIRE AND RESCUE STATION

TABLE 1 Airport Fire and Rescue Equipment Building Elements

Type station	Index number*	Number of stalls	Apparatus room			Room area (sq. ft.) provided for					
			Stall depth (width) [ft.]	Door height (width) [ft.]	Ceiling height (ft.)	Alarm	Office	Training	Kitchen	Dormitory (per person)	Storage
A	III–IV	1	35 (14)	15 (12)	17	†	100		‡	70	100
B	V	2	40 (14–16)	15 (12)	17	100	125	150	100	70	150
C	VI–VII	4	40 (14–16)	15 (12)	17	100	125	300	125	70	200
D	VIII	5	40 (14–16)	15 (12)	17	100	125	350	125	70	250

*Housing for aircraft fire and rescue equipment is not normally required at Index I and Index II airports.
†Combine with office space.
‡Alcove in office.

EXPLANATION OF TERMS

Heliport A heliport is an identifiable area on land, water, or structure, including any building or facilities thereon, used or intended to be used for the landing and takeoff of helicopters.

Helistop A helistop is an area used or intended to be used for the landing and takeoff of helicopters engaged in dropping-off or picking-up passengers or cargo.

Public Use Heliport A public use heliport is available for the takeoff or landing of helicopters without prior authorization being required to use the facility.

Private Use Heliport A private use heliport is a facility for exclusive use by the owner or other persons having prior authorization to use the facility.

Hospital Heliport A hospital heliport is a public use or private use heliport supporting helicopter air ambulance services.

Final Approach and Takeoff Area (FATO) A defined area over which the final phase of the approach maneuver to hover or landing is completed and from which the takeoff maneuver is commenced.

Takeoff and Landing Area The takeoff and landing area is a cleared area containing a FATO.

Helipad The helipad is a surface used for parking helicopters. It may be located inside or outside of the FATO or the takeoff and landing area.

Helideck The helideck is an elevated surface used for parking helicopters. It may be located inside or outside of the FATO or the takeoff and landing area.

Primary Surface The primary surface is an FAR Part 77, Subpart C, heliport imaginary surface which overlies the designated takeoff and landing area. FAR 77.29 (a) defines the primary surface as follows: "The area of the primary surface coincides in size and shape with the designated takeoff and landing area of a heliport. This surface is a horizontal plane at the elevation of the established heliport elevation." See Fig. 1.

Approach and Departure Surface The approach surface is an FAR Part 77 Subpart C heliport imaginary surface which is centered on each designated approach and departure route. The approach surface also serves as a departure surface. FAR 77.29 (b) defines the approach surface as follows: "The approach surface begins at each end of the heliport primary surface with the same width as the primary surface, and extends out-

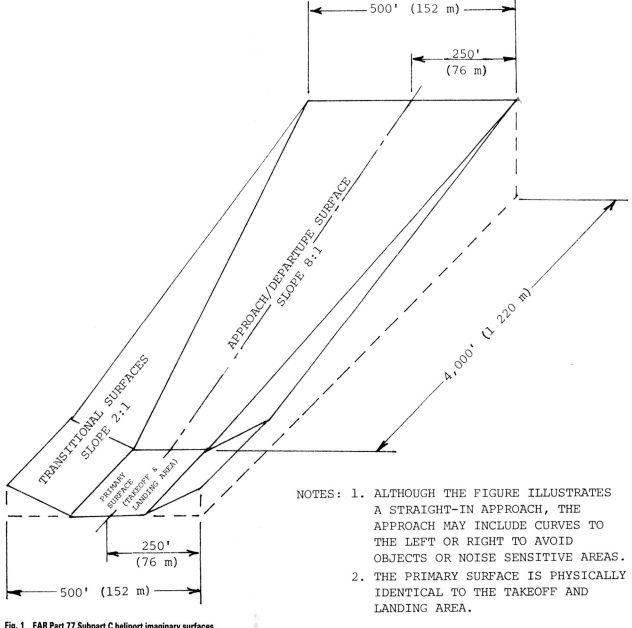

NOTES: 1. ALTHOUGH THE FIGURE ILLUSTRATES A STRAIGHT-IN APPROACH, THE APPROACH MAY INCLUDE CURVES TO THE LEFT OR RIGHT TO AVOID OBJECTS OR NOISE SENSITIVE AREAS.
2. THE PRIMARY SURFACE IS PHYSICALLY IDENTICAL TO THE TAKEOFF AND LANDING AREA.

Fig. 1 FAR Part 77 Subpart C heliport imaginary surfaces.

Transportation

HELIPORTS

ward and upward for a horizontal distance of 4,000 feet where its width is 500 feet. The slope of the approach surface is 8 to 1 for civil heliports. . . ." See Fig. 1.

Transitional Surfaces The transitional surfaces are FAR Part 77 Subpart C heliport imaginary surfaces which extend outward from the lateral boundaries of the primary and approach surfaces. FAR 77.29 (c) defines the transitional surfaces as follows: "These surfaces extend outward and upward from the lateral boundaries of the heliport primary surface and from the approach surfaces at a slope of 2 to 1 for a distance of 250 feet measured horizontally from the centerline of the primary and approach surfaces." See Fig. 1.

Obstruction to Air Navigation An obstruction to air navigation is an object which exceeds the obstruction standards of FAR 77.23.

Hazard to Air Navigation A hazard to air navigation is an object having a substantial adverse effect upon the safe and efficient use of the navigable airspace by aircraft or upon the operation of an air navigation facility. Obstructions to air navigation are presumed to be hazards to air navigation until an FAA aeronautical study has determined otherwise.

Heliport Elevation The heliport elevation is the elevation of the highest point on the takeoff and landing area expressed in feet above mean sea level.

Ground Effect An improvement in flight capability that develops whenever the helicopter flies or hovers near the ground or other surface. It results from the cushion of air built up between the ground and the helicopter by the air displaced downward by the rotor.

PRIVATE USE HELIPORTS

Takeoff and Landing Area

A private use heliport should have an unobstructed area available for the takeoff and landing of helicopters.

Location The takeoff and landing area may be located on the ground, on a water surface, a roof of a building, or an elevated platform. The location should provide at least 1/3 rotor diameter, but not less than 10 feet (3 m), horizontal clearance between the takeoff and landing area and buildings, fences, parapets, curbs, and objects which could be struck by main or tail rotors.

Size The takeoff and landing area length and width, or diameter, should be at least twice the rotor diameter of the design helicopter.

Surface Characteristics. The portion of the takeoff and landing area surface outboard of the helipad or helideck may be clear airspace. Except for essential frangible heliport visual aids which may be located in this area, the surface of the takeoff and landing area should be clear of objects, including parked helicopters, while a helicopter is landing or taking off.

Helipads and Helidecks

Size The minimum length and width, or diameter, of the helipad or helideck should be at least 1.5 times the design helicopter's undercarriage length or width, whichever is greater.

Surface Characteristics The helipad of a ground level heliport can vary from a turf to an all paved surface and normally is load bearing. Helidecks and paved helipads should have a skid-resistant surface and be designed to support 1.5 times the design helicopter's maximum takeoff weight. To assure the safety of personnel, the perimeter of a helideck raised 4 feet (1.2 m) or more above the surrounding surface should have a horizontal safety net or "shelf" installed.

Approach and Departure Route

At least one unobstructed approach and departure route is required. When surrounding conditions permit, additional approach and departure routes are desirable to allow the helicopter to take advantage of the wind direction in making a landing or takeoff.

Configuration The designated approach and departure routes may curve to avoid objects or noise sensitive areas.

Protection FAR Part 77 does not require persons contemplating the construction of objects or buildings in the vicinity of a private use heliport to give the FAA notice of their intent. Therefore, acquisition of sufficient property interests, air rights, or zoning is recommended to assure protection of at least the innermost portion of the approach and departure routes.

Parking

A parking area should be provided if more than one helicopter at a time is to be accommodated. The helicopter parking area should be of a size and location such that parked helicopters will not

obstruct the clear area used for takeoffs and landings or the approach and departure routes. Grounding rods should be provided if fueling is to be conducted at the heliport. Tie downs may be warranted.

Heliport Markings

If owners wish to identify their heliport and the boundaries of the takeoff and landing area, helipad, or helideck, these surfaces can be marked as follows:

Boundary Markings

Markers The edges of the takeoff and landing area may be marked as illustrated in Fig. 2 and 3. In-ground markers are located at the edges of the surface. Above-ground markers should be located clear of and approximately 10 feet (3 m) outboard of the takeoff and landing area. When used, above-ground markers should be as low as possible, be secured, and, if practical, be on breakaway mounts to prevent their becoming a hazard or being blown over.

Paint Lines may be painted on the boundaries of hard surfaced takeoff and landing areas, helipads, or helidecks as illustrated in Fig. 3. While white is the most commonly used color, other colors may be used. To increase conspicuity, lines may be outlined with a stripe of a contrasting color. Paint may be reflective or nonreflective.

Identification Markings Any recognizable letter, logo, initial, symbol, etc., may be used to identify the heliport and the desired touchdown location. The dimensions of the identifying marking should be as large as practical but should not be less than 10 feet (3 m) in height. The marking should be oriented to be legible from the preferred direction of approach. To assure recognition, hospital heliports and emergency evacuation facilities should be marked as illustrated in Fig. 3.

Weight Limitation A weight limit, in thousands of pounds, may be indicated by a number located to the right and below the heliport symbol as viewed from the preferred direction of approach as illustrated in Fig. 3.

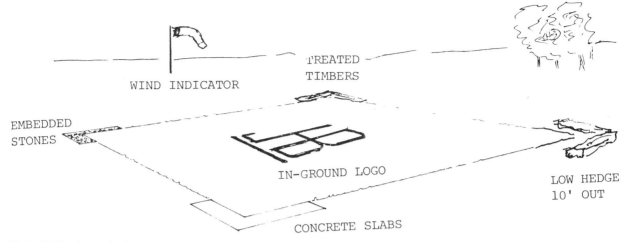

WIND INDICATOR

TREATED TIMBERS

EMBEDDED STONES

IN-GROUND LOGO

LOW HEDGE 10' OUT

CONCRETE SLABS

Fig. 2 Marking of unpaved surfaces.

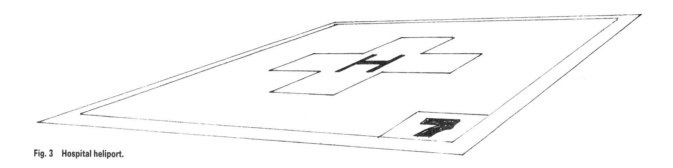

Fig. 3 Hospital heliport.

Heliport Lighting

If night operations are contemplated and ambient light is inadequate, the takeoff and landing area should be defined by perimeter lights, floodlights, or a combination thereof.

Perimeter Lights An odd number but not less then three (15 to 60 watt) lights per side is recommended for square or rectangular surfaces and 8 equally spaced lights for round surfaces. Flush in-pavement lights should be positioned no more the one foot (30 cm) in from the pavement edge. Frangible above-ground fixtures should be not more than 10 inches (25 cm) in height and located clear of and within 10 feet (3 m) of the takeoff and landing area. When necessary for snow clearance, 18 inches (45 cm) height fixtures may be located 10 feet (3 m) outboard of the takeoff and landing area. Figure 4 illustrates a perimeter lighting system. For helidecks, it may be desirable to light the perimeter of the helideck and use reflective markings to ensure the helideck can be clearly identified.

Elevated Floodlights Floodlights should illuminate the operational area and should, to the extent practicable, be mounted on buildings or poles which do not to interfere with flight operations.

Wind Direction Indicator

A means of indicating wind direction is essential. The preferred indicator is a wind cone but may be as simple as a flag on a pole. The indicator should be located so as not to interfere with flight operations and yet be able to give a true indication of the wind's direction and relative magnitude. For night operations, the wind indicator should be located in an illuminated area or be lighted.

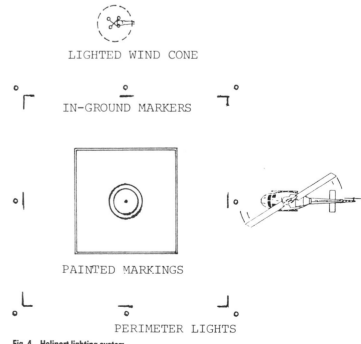

LIGHTED WIND CONE

IN-GROUND MARKERS

PAINTED MARKINGS

PERIMETER LIGHTS

Fig. 4 Heliport lighting system.

Transportation

HELIPORTS

Fences

When needed, fences should be as low as practicable, not be a hazard to flight operations, not obstruct the approach departure routes, and yet be able to prevent inadvertent or unauthorized entry. Hedges may be as effective as fences.

PUBLIC USE HELIPORTS

Takeoff and Landing Areas

Each public use heliport or helistop shall have at least one takeoff and landing area. For heliports where 10 or more operations per hour are anticipated, multiple takeoff and landing areas should be provided.

Location The takeoff and landing area may be located on the ground, on a water surface, on a roof of a building, or on an elevated platform. The location shall provide at least 1/3 rotor diameter, but not less than 10 feet (3 m), horizontal clearance between the takeoff and landing area and buildings, fences, parapets, curbs, and objects which could be struck by main or tail rotors.

Size For heliports serving single rotor helicopters exclusively, the length and width, or diameter of the takeoff and landing area shall be at least equal to twice the rotor diameter of the design helicopter. For heliports serving tandem rotor helicopters, the length and width, or diameter of the takeoff and landing area shall be at least one rotor diameter greater than the overall length of the design helicopter. When site conditions permit, a longer takeoff and landing area will increase the operational capability of the heliport.

Surface Characteristics If the FATO is marked, the portion of the takeoff and landing area outboard of the FATO may be nothing more than unobstructed airspace. If the FATO is not marked, the takeoff and landing area surface shall be capable of producing ground effect. The surface of the takeoff and landing area should be clear of objects, except for essential and frangible heliport visual aids and fire suppression equipment which is required therein.

Final Approach and Takeoff Area (FATO)

The FATO is normally centered within a takeoff and landing area. When not centered, its center is at least one rotor diameter from the edge of the takeoff and landing area.

Size The length and width, or diameter of the FATO shall be at least equal to the rotor diameter of the design single rotor helicopter. The length and width, or diameter of the FATO shall be at least equal to the overall length of the design tandem rotor helicopter.

Surface Characteristics The FATO surface shall be capable of producing ground effect.

Separation Between Adjacent FATOs When more then one FATO is provided and simultaneous same direction (side by side) diverging operations are to be conducted, a center to center separation distance of at least 200 feet (60 m) shall be provided. For sequential operations, the takeoff and landing areas containing the FATOs may overlap if the helicopters in the FATOs are clear of the approach and departure surfaces in use and are at least 1/3 rotor diameter, but not less than 10 feet (3 m), from the overlapped takeoff and landing area. Figure 5 illustrates overlapping takeoff and landing areas for sequential operations.

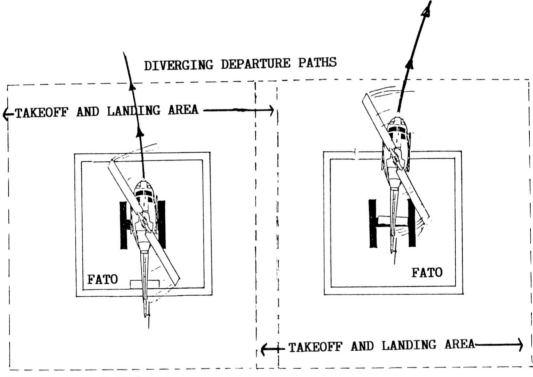

Fig. 5 Overlapping takeoff and landing areas.

1090

Approach and Departure Routes

Each takeoff and landing area shall have at least one approach and departure route. However, as many approach and departure routes as practical, separated by arcs of 90 to 180 degrees, are recommended. In configuring the routes, the heliport owner shall consider the following:

Objects and Noise Sensitive Areas The approach and departure routes should take advantage of unobstructed airspace above roadways, railroads, waterways, etc. The routes may curve to avoid objects or noise sensitive areas.

Prevailing Wind The routes should be oriented to align as near as practicable with the prevailing winds.

Heliport Imaginary Surfaces The routes locate the FAR Part 77 Subpart C heliport approach and transitional surfaces emanating from the primary surface.

Visual Glide Path Indicator Obstacle Clearance Plane If a visual glide path indicator is installed, the configuration of its approach route is fixed by the visual guide path indicator siting and clearance criteria.

Hazards to Air Navigation Objects, including parked helicopters, penetrating the imaginary surfaces are obstructions to air navigation and as such are presumed to be hazards to air navigation. The adverse effect of hazards to air navigation are mitigated by:

(1) Removing the object.
(2) Obstruction lighting and marking, if an FAA aeronautical study finds that the object would not be a hazard to air navigation if lighted and marked.
(3) Realigning the approach and departure routes.

Approach and Departure Protection Areas

Where practicable, the heliport owner should control the property underlying the innermost portion of the approach and departure surface. This area underlies the approach and departure surface from the edge of the primary surface out to a point where the approach and departure surface is 35 feet (10.5 m) above the landing surface. Figure 6 illustrates a typical configuration of a visual approach and departure protection area. While it is desirable for this area to be reasonably free of surface irregularities or objects, heliport related uses which do not create a hazardous condition are permitted. Ownership is the most effective means to protect the approach and departure routes and to provide protection to persons and property on the ground.

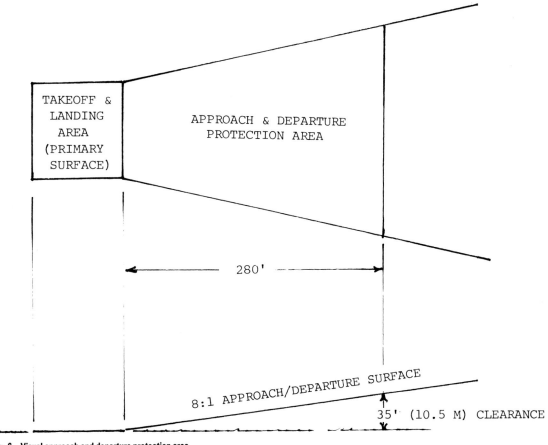

Fig. 6 Visual approach and departure protection area.

Transportation

HELIPORTS

Parking Areas

Helicopter parking shall be adequate to accommodate the number of helicopters to be served. Parking may be accomplished on a paved or unpaved apron, a helipad, or a helideck. If necessary, helipads and helidecks may be located in the FATO or the takeoff and landing area. However, a design which requires a helicopter to park in the FATO or takeoff and landing area makes that area unavailable for takeoffs or landings by other helicopters.

Location Except for helipads and helidecks located in the FATO or takeoff and landing area, the parking area shall be located such that parked helicopters are clear of the approach and departure surfaces and have at least 1/3 rotor diameter but not but not less than 10 foot (3 m) clearance from a takeoff and landing area or a fixed or movable object.

Helipads The minimum length and width, or diameter, of the helipad shall be at least 1.5 times the design helicopter's undercarriage length or width, whichever is greater. To facilitate loading or unloading of passengers or baggage or for fueling and maintenance servicing, larger pads may be desired. The helipad surface shall be designed to support 1.5 times the design helicopter's maximum takeoff weight. If hard surfaced, it should be textured or skid-resistant.

Helidecks The length and width, or diameter of the helideck shall be at least equal to the rotor diameter of the design single rotor helicopter or the overall length of the design tandem rotor helicopter. The helideck surface shall be designed to support 1.5 times the design helicopter's maximum takeoff weight and should have a textured or skid-resistant surface. To provide protection for personnel, the perimeter of a helideck raised 4 feet (1.2 m) or more above the surrounding surface shall have a 5 foot (1.5 m) wide horizontal safety net or "shelf." Figure 7 illustrates a horizontal safety net.

Tie-Downs and Static Grounding Tie-downs may be warranted. Grounding rods shall be provided at fueling locations.

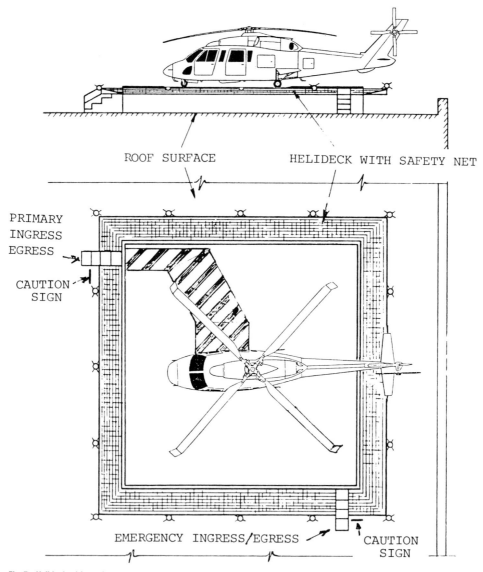

Fig. 7 Helideck with a safety net.

Taxi Routes

A cleared right-of-way for taxiing shall be provided between a takeoff and landing area and a parking area, as illustrated in Fig. 8.

Widths The taxi route width shall be at least the larger of:

(1) twice the rotor diameter of the largest helicopter which is expected to hover taxi, or

(2) one and one-half rotor diameters of the largest helicopter which is expected to ground taxi, plus 14 feet (4 m).

Parallel Taxi Route Separations The centerline-to-centerline separation distance shall be at least the larger of:

(1) one and one-half rotor diameters of the largest helicopter which is expected to hover taxi, or

(2) one and one-quarter rotor diameters of the largest helicopter which is expected to ground taxi, plus 7 feet (2 m).

Taxiways

When a hard surface taxiway is provided, it shall be centered within a taxi route and shall be at least twice the width of the undercarriage of the design helicopter.

Heliport Markings

Markings shall be painted on surfaces which are practical to paint. Paints may be reflective or nonreflective. Painted markings may be outlined with a 6-inch (15 cm) wide strip of a contrasting color to enhance their conspicuity. In-ground markers, providing color and textural differences from the natural surface, shall be used to mark turfed surfaces.

Takeoff and Landing Area Markings The edges of takeoff and landing areas not containing a marked FATO shall be painted with a 16-inch (45 cm) wide solid white line as illustrated in Fig. 9 or marked with in-ground markers as illustrated in Fig. 11. If practical, the edges of takeoff and landing areas containing a marked FATO should be painted with a 16-inch (45 cm) wide dashed white line as illustrated in Fig. 10 or marked with in-ground markers as illustrated in Fig. 11.

FATO Markings If marked, the edges of the FATO shall be painted with a 16-inch (45 cm) wide solid white line as illustrated in Fig. 10.

Heliport Identification Markings The takeoff and landing area shall be identified by a letter centered on the FATO, if marked, or otherwise centered on the takeoff and landing area. The letter shall be as large as practical, but not less than 10 feet (3 m) in height. The letter shall be oriented as viewed from the preferred direction of approach. Letter line widths shall be proportional to the letter's height. Figures 9 through 11 illustrate identification markings.

Public use heliports, except hospital heliports, shall be marked with a white capital letter H, as illustrated in Fig. 9. This represents a change from the previously recommended markings. Existing markings may remain until repainting is required.

Hospital heliports shall be marked with a red capital letter H centered in a white cross, as illustrated in Fig. 10. To increase conspicuity, the cross may be superimposed on a red background enclosed within standard edge marking.

Weight Limitations Surfaces which are limited in weight-carrying ability must be marked with a number, in thousands of pounds, indicating the weight limit. A zero indicates less than 1,000 pound load capability. Markings must be large enough to be legible from an approaching helicopter. On a FATO or takeoff and landing area, the number is located inside a box to the right and below the heliport symbol as viewed from the preferred direction of approach. A weight limit marking is illustrated in Fig. 9.

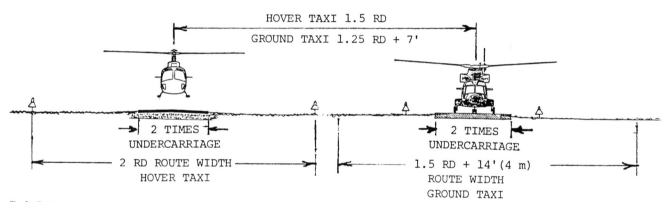

Fig. 8 Taxi route and taxiway relationship.

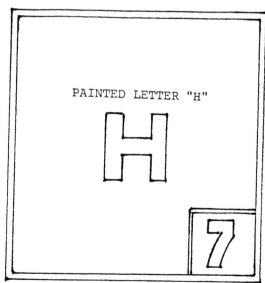

Fig. 9 Public use heliport.

Transportation
HELIPORTS

Helipad and Helideck Markings The edges of a helipad or helideck which is not analogous with a takeoff and landing area or FATO shall be painted with a 16-inch (45 cm) wide solid yellow line.

Apron Markings Parking positions for scheduled air carrier passenger service should be clearly identified and provide one rotor diameter clearance between adjacent positions.

Taxi Route Markings Routes used for hover/air taxiing should be marked with cylindrical aboveground markers having 3 equal width horizontal bands of yellow-green-yellow. Markers should be placed along each edge of the taxi route at intervals not in excess of 100 feet (30 m) on straight

sections and 50 feet (15 m) on curved sections. Markers should conform to AC 150/5345-39, FAA Specification L-853, Runway and Taxiway Retro-reflective Markers.

Taxiway Markings The centerline of a taxiway is marked with a continuous 12 inch (30 cm) wide yellow stripe and/or with green retro-reflective centerline markers meeting the requirements in AC 150/5345-39 for Type II markers. The taxiway edges may be marked with a continuous white stripe and blue reflective markers located at the taxiway entrance and exit points and along each edge at intervals not in excess of 50 feet (15 m).

Heliport Lighting

Takeoff and Landing Area Lighting If night operations are contemplated and ambient light is inadequate, the FATO or takeoff and landing area shall be defined with perimeter lights, elevated flood lights, or a combination thereof. In some cases, it may be desirable to define the perimeter of the FATO with reflective markings to ensure the FATO can be clearly identified.

Perimeter Lights Yellow omni-directional lights meeting the requirements of AC 150/5345-46, Specification for Runway and Taxiway Light Fix-

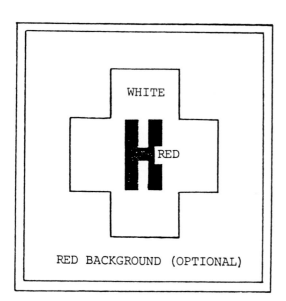

A 16' (45 cm) WIDE WHITE PAINTED LINE IS USED TO MARK THE EDGES OF A HARD SURFACED TAKEOFF AND LANDING AREA OR FATO

Fig. 10 Hospital heliport.

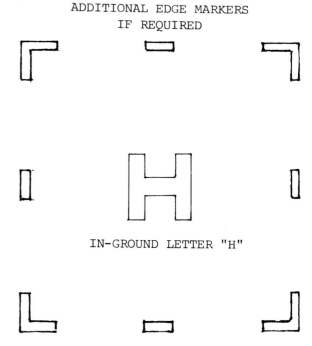

IN-GROUND MARKERS AT CORNERS OF THE TAKEOFF AND LANDING AREA

Fig. 11 In-ground markings.

1094

LIGHTED WIND CONE

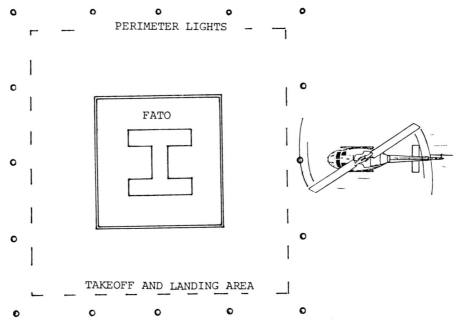

PERIMETER LIGHTS

FATO

TAKEOFF AND LANDING AREA

Fig. 12   Lighting systems for night operations.

tures, or flood lights providing at least 3 foot candle (32 lux) of illumination over the operational area, define the boundary of the FATO or the takeoff and landing area. For a square or rectangular area, an odd number of lights (3, 5, 7, etc.) shall be placed along each edge. For a circular area, at least 8 uniformly spaced lights shall be placed along its circumference. The maximum spacing between lights in either case must not exceed 30 feet (9 m).

Flush in-pavement lights shall be positioned no more the one foot (30 cm) in from the edge of a paved FATO or takeoff and landing area.

Care should be taken to ensure that perimeter lights do not create a potentially hazardous situation by being located where they may be struck by a tail rotor or skids. To minimize the potential, frangible above-ground lights shall be no more then 10 inches (25 cm) in height and located clear of but within 10 feet (3 m) of the FATO or takeoff and landing area. When necessary for snow clearance, 18 inch (45 cm) high, frangible fixtures may be located 10 feet (3 m) outboard of the takeoff and landing area. Figure 12 illustrates a perimeter lighting system for night operations.

Lights on the perimeter of a helideck may be placed on the periphery of the safety net.

Elevated Floodlights When used, elevated floodlights shall provide at least 3-foot candle (32 lux) of illumination over all operational areas and be situated and/or hooded to prevent direct or reflected light from blinding pilots. The spectral distribution of the floodlights shall be such that the colors used for surface and obstruction marking are conspicuous. Floodlights, to the extent practicable, should be mounted on buildings or poles which do not interfere with flight operations.

Taxi Route and Taxiway Lighting Guidance for designing a taxiway lighting system is found in AC 150/

5345-24, Runway and Taxiway Edge Lighting Systems. Equipment specifications are found in AC 150/5345-46, Specification for Runway and Taxiway Light Fixtures. An alternative system uses L-852 centerline lights as described in AC 150/5340-19, Taxiway Centerline Lighting Systems. Another alternative utilizes the above-ground edge or in-pavement centerline reflective markers described in AC 150/5345-39, Runway and Taxiway Centerline Retro-reflective Markers.

Taxi Route Lighting L-861T omni-directional blue lights may be used to mark the limits of a taxi route. Above-ground lights shall be spaced at a maximum interval of 100 feet (30 m) for straight sections and 50 foot (15 m) for curved sections. A minimum of three lights shall be used to define a curve.

Taxiway Edge Lights L-861T omni-directional blue lights shall be used to mark the edges of a taxiway. Above-ground lights shall be placed no more than 10 feet (3 m) out from the pavement edge.

Taxi Guidance Signs Taxi guidance signs meeting the requirements of AC 150/5345-44, Specification for Taxiway and Runway Signs, are recommended. Size 1 signs need to be installed in accordance with AC 150/5340-18, Standards for Airport Sign Systems.

Visual Aids

Wind Direction Indicator A wind cone meeting the standards of AC 150/5345-27, Specification for L-807 Eight-foot and Twelve-Foot Unlighted and Externally Lighted Wind Cone Assemblies, is recommended. The wind cone shall be located adjacent to the takeoff and landing area but not interfere with helicopter operations or be shielded by buildings or other objects that prevent it from showing a true indication of the wind's direction

and relative magnitude. The wind cone shall provide the best possible color contrast to the heliport background. Wind indicators shall be lighted for night operations.

Landing Direction Lights Landing direction lights may be used to identify the alignment of the approach route. Landing direction lights consist of a line of five L-860 or five L-861 lights with omni-directional yellow lenses spaced at 15 foot (4.5 m) intervals. Lesser spacing is permissible where physical constraints make the standard interval impractical. Landing direction lights extend out from the line of perimeter lights in the direction of the approach.

Visual Glide Path Indicator A visual glide path indicator may be used to indicate the approach path. The indicator's lowest on-course signal must provide clearance over any object in the approach path that is lying within 10 degrees of the approach course centerline. The optimum location of a visual glide path indicator is near the takeoff and landing area. Figure 13 illustrates the visual glide path indicator siting and clearance criteria.

Heliport Identification Beacon When required to aid in locating the heliport, an identification beacon flashing white-green-yellow at the rate of 30 to 53 flashes per minute should be located on or within one quarter mile (0.4 km) of the heliport. Information on heliport beacons is found in AC 150/5345-12, Specification for Airport and Heliport Beacons.

Obstruction Marking and Lighting Unless an FAA aeronautical study has determined that the absence of such marking or lighting will not impair safety, obstructions to air navigation and objects exceeding a height of 200 feet (120 m) above the level of the ground within 1 nautical mile of the heliport

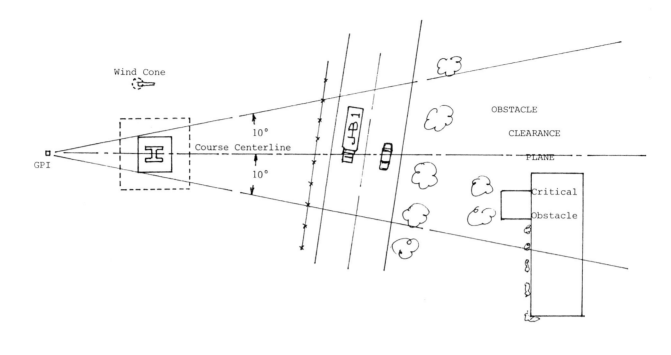

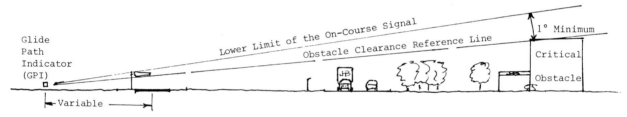

Fig. 13 Visual glide path indicator siting and clearance criteria.

shall be marked and lighted. AC 70/7460-1, Obstruction Marking and Lighting, contains guidance on how to mark and light these objects.

Heliport Facilities

The amount of property to be acquired depends upon the need to provide for helicopter fueling, maintenance, and storage, and passenger amenities such as terminal buildings, ground transportation, and automobile parking.

Fueling If provided, systems for storing and dispensing fuel must conform to federal, state, and local requirements for petroleum handling facilities.

Maintenance At larger heliports, hangars may be needed for helicopter storage and maintenance purposes.

Terminal Facilities A terminal building or sheltered waiting area should be simple, attractive, and functional to accommodate the needs of current and forecasted traffic. AC 150/5360-9, Planning and Design of Airport Terminal Facilities at Nonhub Locations, contains useful information on the design of a terminal facility.

Transportation and Parking Features such as curbside discharge and pickup areas, taxicab and rental car services may be desirable. Automobile parking areas should be large enough to accommodate employee and passenger needs. Availability of public transportation will normally reduce the requirement for vehicle parking spaces.

Safety Features

Fences When needed, fences should be as low as practical, not be a hazard to flight operations, and still be able to prevent inadvertent or unauthorized entry. When scheduled operations by certificated carries are planned, fences must meet the requirements of FAR Part 107, Airport Security.

Rescue and Firefighting Services Rescue and firefighting service requirements are as follows.

Heliports certificated under FAR Part 139, Certification and Operations: Land Airports Serving CAB Certificated Air Carriers, must provide the level of rescue and firefighting services specified in that regulation.

The National Fire Protection Association's (NFPA) Pamphlets 403, Aircraft Rescue Services, or 418, Roof-Top Heliports, provide fire protection recommendations.

To meet the NFPA recommended level of fire fighting protection, a fire hose cabinet or an extinguisher should be provided at each gate used for scheduled passenger service and near each fueling location. Cabinets and extinguishers should be located within 20 feet (6 m) of the takeoff and landing area and should not penetrate any heliport imaginary surface. Fire hose cabinets and extinguishers at helidecks should be located adjacent to but below the level of the deck.

Passenger Walkways Passenger access to operational areas must be controlled. Walkways should be marked and the primary and secondary or emergency exits should be identified with a cautionary sign. Surfaces shall slope away from passenger walkways to prevent spilled fuel from draining in these areas.

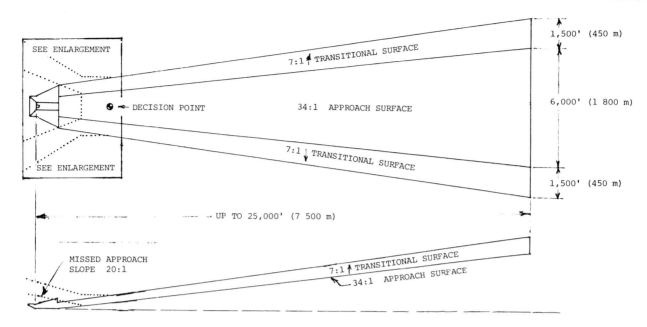

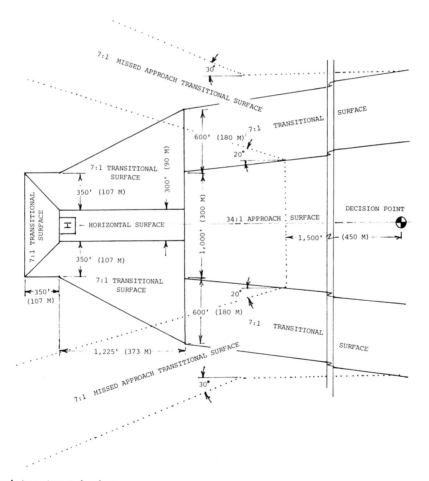

Fig. 14 Precision instrument approach surfaces.

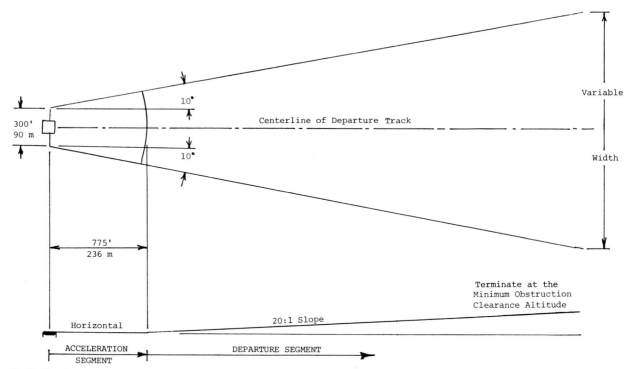

Fig. 15 Precision instrument departure surfaces.

DESIGN CRITERIA

General

During the process of developing these design criteria, certain assumptions had to be made because of the lack of commitment of large STOL aircraft to civil production. Therefore, these standards represent considered judgment of what constitutes a practical set of criteria considering available data, safety, noise, environment, and economics. It is apparent that the shorter the runway the easier it will be to locate a STOL port site, and the greater will be its compatibility with the local environment. On the other hand, the criteria cannot be so restrictive that aircraft manufacturers will be unable to produce a vehicle which can operate safely and economically from the STOL port.

Design Criteria

The following criteria have been developed based on STOL aircraft, bidirectional runway operations, and a precision instrument approach. See Figs. 1 and 2 and Table 1 for illustration of specific dimensions.

Runway Length Determination

A discussion of takeoff and landing runway lengths is needed to establish a common understanding of the terms used. This is particularly necessary for the case of the elevated STOL port, where reference to Federal Aviation Regulations (FAR) field length cannot be considered in the same context as the conventional airport.

Microwave ILS

Microwave instrument landing systems for STOL operation are currently being evaluated

Planning and Design Criteria for Metropolitan STOL Ports, Federal Aviation Administration, Department of Transportation, Washington, D.C., 1970.

by the FAA. The type of equipment has been designed specifically for steep gradient approaches. The siting of the microwave system may be relatively simple since the localizer and glide slope functions may be collocated. (See Fig. 1.) Offset instrument landing system (ILS) approaches would be advantageous under certain site conditions and are under study. Nevertheless, an offset approach should be considered only where obstructions in the approach would prevent a straight-in ILS procedure.

Obstruction Clearance

The imaginary surfaces for protection of the STOL port are shown in Fig. 3.

General The surfaces have been defined on the basis of operational tests with the microwave ILS. The 15:1 slope for the approach/departure surface is predicated on adequate obstruction clearance for steep gradient approaches and also for takeoff climb.

Curved Paths For VFR (visual flight rules) operations, a curved path for approach or departure is quite practical and may be necessary in some cases to provide a suitable route. For example, an IFR (instrument flight rules) procedure may be feasible from only one direction. Under adverse wind conditions, it would be desirable and perhaps necessary to complete the IFR approach, transition to VFR and land from the opposite direction. The radius of the curved path will vary according to the performance of individual aircraft and the angle of bank used. For planning purposes, a radius of 1,500 ft may be used.

Runway Orientation

One of the primary factors influencing runway orientation is wind. Ideally, the runway should be aligned with the prevailing winds. It is recognized that the limited number of STOL port sites will minimize the opportunity for the runway to have optimum wind coverage. On the

other hand, it is also recognized that the availability of a crosswind runway on a metropolitan STOL port will be rare. Accordingly, the designer should attempt to obtain maximum wind coverage. The minimum desirable wind coverage is 95 percent based on the total hours of available weather observations. In other words, the objective is to attain more than 95 percent usability (preferably 98 percent). The allowable crosswind component will be determined by the crosswind capabilities of the most critical aircraft expected to operate at the STOL port.

Parallel Runways – STOL Port

For simultaneous VFR operations on a STOL port, the minimum separation between the centerlines of parallel runways should be 700 ft.

Runway Capacity

The capacity of a runway is the number of aircraft operations (landings and takeoffs) that the runway can accommodate in a limited period of time. The operational capacity of a STOL runway will be lowest during IFR conditions. To obtain maximum IFR capacity, the STOL runway should be equipped with a microwave ILS and radar surveillance (including an air traffic control tower). A method for calculation of capacity values is given in Advisory Circular 150/5060–1A. This publication discusses the numerous factors which must be considered in a capacity analysis. However, as a general guideline, with current procedures, the IFR capacity of a single STOL runway will be approximately 45 operations per hour. It is expected that this capacity will be considerably expanded when adequate data have been collected and analyzed.

Potential Configurations

In many metropolitan areas, siting of a STOL port may necessitate an elevated structure. At such sites, the designer should strive to achieve vertical loading and unloading of pas-

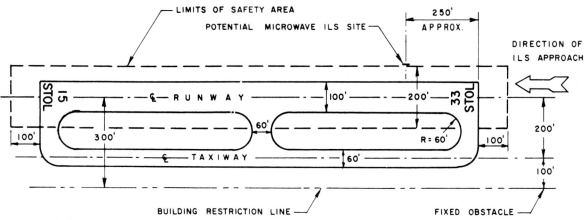

Fig. 1 Dimensional criteria.

STOL PORTS

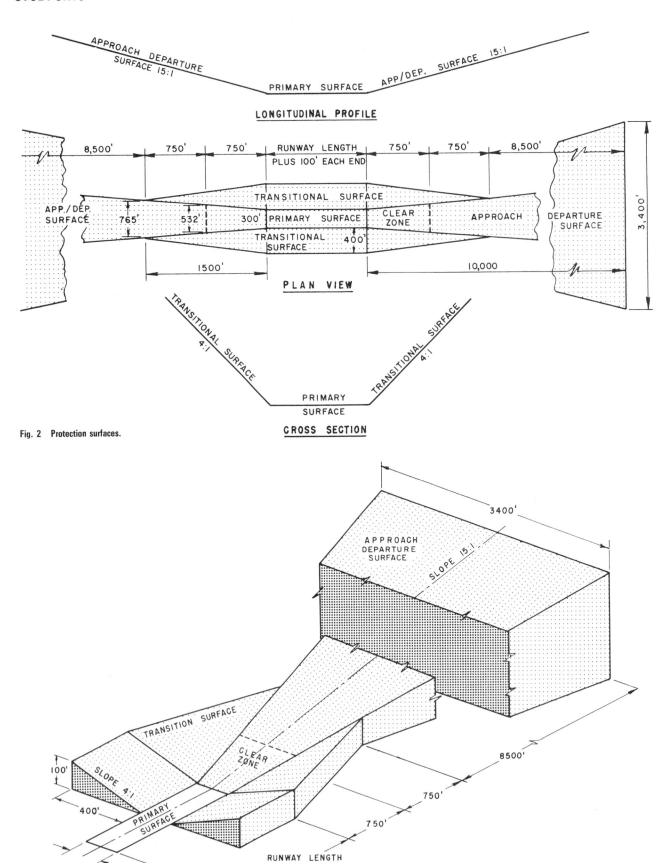

Fig. 2   Protection surfaces.

Fig. 3   Isometric of protection surfaces.

TABLE 1 Design Criteria for Metropolitan STOL Ports*

Design item	Recommended criteria	Comment
Runway length at sea level and 90°F	1,500 to 1,800 ft	Correction for elevation and temperature to be made on the basis of individual aircraft performance.
Runway width.	100 ft	Widening may be desirable if wind coverage is less than 95 per cent.
Runway safety area width.	200 ft	Widening may be desirable if wind coverage is less than 95 per cent. If elevated, a 300-ft width is recommended for the structure.
Runway safety area length	1,700 to 2,000 ft	If elevated, the structure would be within this range.
Taxiway width.	60 ft	Based on expected configuration of second generation aircraft.
Runway C_L to taxiway C_L†	200 ft	Based on expected configuration of second generation aircraft.
Runway C_L to edge of parked aircraft	250 ft	Based on expected configuration of second generation aircraft.
Runway C_L to building line	300 ft	Height controlled by transitional surface.
Taxiway C_L to fixed obstacle.	100 ft	Based on second generation aircraft.
Runway C_L to holding line	150 ft	Based on second generation aircraft.
Separation between parallel runways		See text.
Protection surfaces:		
Primary surface length	Runway length plus 100 ft on each end	
Primary surface width.	300 ft	Based on the use of microwave instrument approach equipment.
Approach/departure surface length	10,000 ft	
Approach/departure surface slope	15:1	
Approach/departure surface width at:		
Beginning	300 ft	Approach/departure surface is 765 ft wide at 1,500 ft from beginning.
10,000 feet.	3,400 ft	
Transitional surface slope	4:1	
Transitional surface maximum height	100 ft	
Clear zone:		
Length.	750 ft	
Inner width	300 ft	Begins at end of primary surface.
Outer width.	532 ft	
Pavement strength	150,000 lb gross weight on dual tandem gear	Based on second generation aircraft. Also see paragraph headed "Structural Design."

* The criteria are subject to change as further experience is gained.

†C_L = centerline

sengers and cargo; i.e., from one level to another. Such a design will allow an operational area that is virtually free of fixed obstacles. Each STOL port should be designed with due consideration of local conditions, particularly the configuration of the land available and surrounding land uses. Figure 4 shows one possible layout of the staggered runway concept. One runway is used primarily for landing and the other for takeoff. This configuration allows a considerable reduction in the total operational area by eliminating parallel taxiways. Also, the flow of traffic is optimized, since no aircraft backout or turning around is involved. Figure 5 shows the tandem runway concept. Again, one runway is used for landing and the other for takeoff, but not simultaneously. Spacing must be provided for taxiing past parked aircraft and aircraft backout for turning around. The figures are intended to illustrate the new approach which must be taken in the planning and design of STOL ports; they are not intended to require a parallel runway configuration.

ELEVATED STOL PORTS

General

The siting of a STOL port involves a series of tradeoffs. One of these is the optimum site for the origin/destination of passengers versus availability of a practical and economic site. In metropolitan areas, this causes a detailed look at elevated STOL ports. For example, in New York City, several waterfront sites on Manhattan Island have been studied. In Los Angeles and San Francisco, sites have been analyzed over railroad yards. All are intended to provide air transportation integrated with surface transportation. Such a facility appears to have a great potential for accommodating the short-haul air passenger demand. However, since it is elevated, there are some unique design problems which must be recognized.

Operational Surface

Essentially, the same standards are used for elevated STOL ports as surface facilities. Nevertheless, the question arises as to what is the recommended minimum.

Length of Structure The length of structure recommended is a range between 1,700 and 2,000 ft.

Width of Structure The recommended width of the structure is 300 ft for the runway operational area. However, this is dependent upon the emergency arresting system selected for lateral containment, the degree of wind cover-

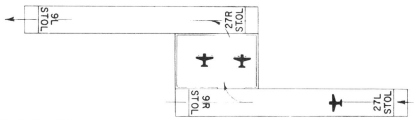

Fig. 4 Potential layout.

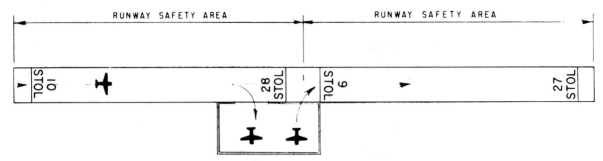

Fig. 5 Potential layout.

age, and the need for a parallel taxiway. The lateral arresting system may require a greater or lesser area width, adjacent to the runway. Also, if the runway is not aligned with prevailing winds, it may be appropriate to have a wider runway. For most STOL ports, a parallel taxiway will be needed. In this case, the structure should be at least 400 ft wide.

Structural Design

The landing area should be designed for the largest aircraft expected to use it. The maximum weight aircraft anticipated by 1985 is 150,000 lb. Other types of loads, such as snow, freight equipment, etc., should be considered in the design of the area and the structures as appropriate.

Emergency Equipment

Provision should be made for equipment on the operational area to handle emergency medical and fire situations. Consideration should also be given to some type of built-in hydrant system.

Aircraft Maintenance and Fueling

Due to the limited parking space available, it appears logical to plan only for emergency maintenance. The decision to install an aircraft fueling system will depend on several factors, among which is the requirement of the local building code.

Floating STOL Port

A STOL port located on water (floating or semi-submersed) is not truly an elevated facility.

However, many of the operational problems associated with a floating STOL port are the same as for an elevated STOL port. For example, emergency arresting systems should be provided to ensure that the aircraft does not fall into the water. On the other hand, wind flow should be considerably less of a problem. In many metropolitan areas, a floating facility, on either an interim or permanent basis, may provide the best solution to establishing STOL service.

TERMINAL AREA

General

The primary purpose of the terminal area on a STOL port is the same as the terminal area on a conventional airport—to provide for the transfer of passengers and cargo from one mode of transportation to another. However, due to the specialized function of the STOL system, attention should be given to possible innovations in the terminal area, such as gate processing and vertical movement of passengers. The STOL system, which is aimed at short-haul, high-density air transportation, must be efficient in every aspect.

Terminal Building

The terminal building should be designed to accommodate a steady flow of passengers rather than long-term holding of passengers. This means secondary features of the terminal, such as concessions and eating facilities, should be minimized. To aid in efficient passenger handling, consideration should be given to passenger processing at the gate. Since the majority of short-haul passengers are business-

oriented, time-conscious, and carry relatively little baggage, gate processing should be quite feasible. Also, mutual-use (or common use) gates appear to be a requirement.

Vertical Movement

On elevated STOL ports, it may not be feasible to locate the terminal on the same level as the operational area. This would, of course, require vertical movement of passengers and baggage. Several methods of accomplishing this have been studied. Among these are escalators, elevators, and loading bridges. The escalators would involve the least cost but would create a fixed obstacle in the aircraft maneuvering area. The elevators can be located on the side of the structure but are expensive and preclude a steady flow of passengers to the aircraft. The loading bridges completely protect the passenger from the weather but are expensive and create an obstacle. At surface STOL ports, vertical movement of passengers may be feasible between mass transit vehicles and the aircraft gate area. This should be given careful evaluation during the initial planning of the terminal.

Capacity

The size of the terminal is determined by the peak-hour volume of passengers and cargo. The forecast of the peak-hour volume must be made recognizing the maximum capacity of the runway (in VFR conditions), the aircraft passenger capacity, the aircraft load factor, and the frequency of service. Further, an analysis must be made of the maximum capacity of the surface access systems. Surface congestion has a direct effect on the efficiency of the air transportation system.

SITE SELECTION

Water Areas

In selecting an adequate site within the areas deemed feasible for water flying, it will be necessary to choose one having the proper water-area dimensions, depth, and approach or glide path ratio for the types of planes to be accommodated. Table 1 shows by comparative groups the recommended minimum standards for water landing areas. Generally, most localities will not be concerned with lengths of water areas of 5,000 ft or more. Larger installations are primarily for large commercial aircraft and military operations.

Prevailing Winds The direction and velocity of prevailing winds over the surface of the water will be the controlling factor in determining the direction of water lanes. It is not necessary to consider winds of 3 mph or less when making these determinations.

When the water landing area consists of a single lane (covering two wind directions) the greatest percentage of wind coverage should be obtained. In many cases these single-lane operating areas cannot be oriented to take maximum advantage of the prevailing winds. In this regard, a shifting of the direction of the water lane should be effected so as to utilize the greatest possible wind coverage in conjunction with water currents and approach conditions. The influence of approach zones and currents is explained under these two respective headings that follow. Where all-way landings and takeoffs can be provided, a study of the wind conditions will indicate the primary and secondary water-lane directions.

Approach Zones For seaplane operations the ideal approach zone is one which permits unobstructed approaches over water at a ratio of 40:1 or flatter, with ample clearance on either side of the approach zone center line. The width of the zone should increase from the ends of the water lanes so that at a distance of 1 mi from the end of the water lane, the zone is approximately the width of the water lane plus 1,000 ft.

Under favorable temperature conditions a water-borne aircraft will leave the water and fly level for approximately 4 seconds and a distance of about 400 ft before starting to climb. The rate of climb after this 4 second period is about 20:1. Where commercial operations are anticipated, it is recommended that the approach angle should be 40:1 or flatter.

The approach zones should be over water wherever possible, thereby permitting a reasonably safe landing in the event of power failure during initial climb or landing approach. Furthermore, for obvious safety reasons, climbs and approaches should not be made over populated areas, beaches and similar shore developments. Apart from the all-important safety factors involved, such maneuvers can create ill will and antagonism on the part of local inhabitants and boating interests. Where a suitable water area exists and the shore and surrounding development prohibits straight-away approach zones, it may be possible to establish operations in which an overwater climbing turn or let-down procedure is used.

Currents and Water-Level Variations Current and changes in water level usually will not be great enough to cause construction or operational difficulties. Only under extraordinary conditions will currents affect size requirements of the water landing area. Landing and takeoff operations can be conducted in water currents in excess of 6 knots (7 mph) but any taxiing operation between the water lanes and the shore facilities will usually require the assistance of a surface craft. Currents in excess of 3 knots (3.5 mph) usually cause some difficulty in handling seaplanes, particularly in slow taxiing while approaching floating docks, or in beaching operations. In some cases undesirable currents may be offset to some extent by advantageous prevailing winds. Locations of the following types should be avoided: (1) Where the currents exceed 6 knots (7 mph); (2) where unusual water turbulence is caused by a sharp bend in a river, the confluence of two currents, or where tide rips are prevalent.

As a general rule if the change in water levels exceeds 18 in., it will be necessary to utilize floating structures or moderately inclined beaching accommodations to facilitate handling of aircraft at the shoreline or water front. Where water-level variations are in excess of 6 ft, special or extended developments to accommodate the aircraft must be made. These developments might require a dredged channel, extended piers or special hoisting equipment depending upon the slope of the shore. It follows that the greater the water variation, the more extensive will be the facility requirements.

Water-Surface Conditions Open or unprotected water-operating areas may become so rough under certain conditions of winds and currents as to prohibit operations; hence, the varying water conditions at the proposed site must be investigated. The average light plane (3,000 lb or less), equipped with twin floats, can be operated safely in seas running to about 15 in. measured from crest to trough, while 18-in. seas will restrict normal safe operations of these aircraft. Larger float-equipped or hull-type aircraft ranging in weight from 3,000 to 15,000 lb can generally be operated safely in seas running as high as 2 ft measured from crest to trough. At the other extreme, smooth or dead calm water is undesirable because of the difficulty experienced in lifting the floats or hull from the water during takeoff. The most desirable conditions exist when the surface of the water is moderately disturbed, having ripples or waves approximately 3 to 6 in. high. Locations at which excessive ground-swell action may be encountered should be given careful consideration to determine the effect of such action on the intended operations.

Another consideration which must be taken into account, when examining the water conditions, is the presence of floating debris. Areas in which there is an objectionable amount of debris for considerable periods of time should be avoided.

TABLE 1. Recommended Minimum Standards for Water Landing Areas*

Minimum length in feet (sea level)	Minimum width in feet	Minimum depth in feet	Turning basin in feet-diameter	Remarks
2,500	200	3	None	Minimum for limited small float plane operation. Approaches should be 20:1 or flatter for a distance of at least 2 mi.
3,500	300	4	None	Minimum for limited commercial operation. Approaches should be 40:1 or flatter for a distance of at least 2 mi.
5,000	500	10	1,000	Minimum for extensive commercial operation. Approaches should be 40:1 or flatter for a distance of at least 2 mi.
10,000	700	15	2,000	Unlimited. Approaches should be 50:1 or flatter for a distance of at least 2 mi.

*The lengths indicated above are for glassy water, no wind, sea level conditions at standard temperature of 59°F. The lengths shown will be increased at the rate of 7 percent for each 1,000 ft of elevation above sea level. This corrected length shall be further increased at the rate of one-half of 1 percent for each degree that the mean temperature of the hottest month of the year, averaged over a period of years, exceeds the standard temperature. See Fig. 1.

Civil Aeronautics Administration, U.S. Department of Commerce, Washington, D.C.

Transportation

SEAPLANE TERMINALS

Sheltered Anchorage Areas A cove, small bay, or other protected area is desirable for use as a seaplane anchorage or mooring area in order to relieve floating-dock or onshore parking. A sheltered area that is protected from winds and currents is required, particularly if overnight or unattended tie-ups are to be made at locations where sudden and sometimes unexpected storms or squalls develop. Appreciable currents and winds in the anchorage area make the approach and picking up of a buoy more difficult and at times will call for the assistance of a boat. The anchorage area should be within sight and calling distance of the floating dock or ramp if possible. It also should be located so as to permit unrestricted maneuvering of the aircraft when approaching the buoys.

Bottom Conditions The type and condition of the bottom at the proposed seaplane-facility site can influence the arrangement of the various components thereof, the means of construction of the fixed structures, and the water operations to and from the shoreline.

Reservoirs and other artificial bodies of water often are flooded natural-land areas and frequently are not grubbed (stumps and logs removed) before flooding. This situation causes anchors and anchor lines to foul and, over a period of time, can create a hazard if these submerged objects rise to the surface and remain partially or totally submerged.

Obstructions which project from the bottom and constitute a hazard should be removed or, if this is impractical, must be suitably and conspicuously marked to indicate their presence to those utilizing the water area.

A hard bottom composed of shale or solid rock formations will make the construction of fixed offshore structures difficult and costly. Anchors also tend to drag over this type of bottom. Unless specially designed mooring anchors are used, precautions should be taken by selecting a more suitable anchorage area. Where boulders are found on the bottom, some construction difficulties may be encountered and anchor lines may tend to foul. Mud bottoms ordinarily present little or no difficulty.

The Onshore Facility

No site for the onshore development should be given serious consideration until it is known that adequate room is available for all of the space-taking elements required. Determination of size will require a knowledge of (1) How many planes will need hangars or tie-down space; (2) how many car parking spaces will be necessary; (3) how many patrons will use the facility; (4) whether a small office will suffice or whether an administration building with facilities for eating, refreshments, and other nonaviation activities is required; (5) how much outdoor common space, such as for lawns, walks, terrace, etc., is needed. Answers to numbers 1 and 2 can be fairly accurately measured while 3, 4, and 5 will depend upon local conditions varying from a very simple installation, in remote recreation areas, to large installations in metropolitan areas. Minimum unit requirements are as follows:

Minimum Unit Requirements for a Single Onshore Facility

Item	Facility	Area, sq ft
1 plane.	Hangar or tie-down space	3,000
1 car	Parking space	250
Office.	Small building	80
Common outdoor space	Walks, lawn, or open space	20 percent of above total

To compute the number of square feet for a given facility, multiples of the above criteria may be used. For example, a facility basing 15 aircraft in the water and 6 on land would need a maximum of 21 car-parking spaces (one for each plane) during maximum use period, plus one for each employee; i.e., approximately 25 cars or 6,250 sq ft of area. Hangar or tie-down space for 6 planes would occupy 18,000 sq ft. One small office building with food counter would require another 400 sq ft. Finally, the common outdoor use space would occupy about 4,930 sq ft (this figure representing 20 percent of the sum of the other areas). Accordingly, the total area would amount to about 29,580 sq ft or about seven-tenths of an acre.

In addition to being adequate in size, the shore facility should be located reasonably close to the water-operating area to eliminate long taxiing operations.

The availability of utilities such as electricity, water, telephone and sewage should be investigated. The basic installation may not require all utilities, but water and sanitary facilities of some sort should be provided for at all locations. In remote rural areas, established water lines and sewerage facilities will be out of the question. If such is the case, well water and chemical toilet units are feasible. State or local sanitary codes must be respected when it is planned to install water and sanitary facilities of this nature.

The most desirable sites have a moderately sloping shoreline and a water depth suitable to permit aircraft taxiing operations as close to the shoreline as possible. Excessive fluctuations in water level are not desirable since this condition requires expensive shoreline installations. Care should be taken to determine whether the water level offshore will permit aircraft operations when the water level is low.

In all cases, the area for a seaplane facility should be sufficient in extent to form a complete unit without any interior private holdings

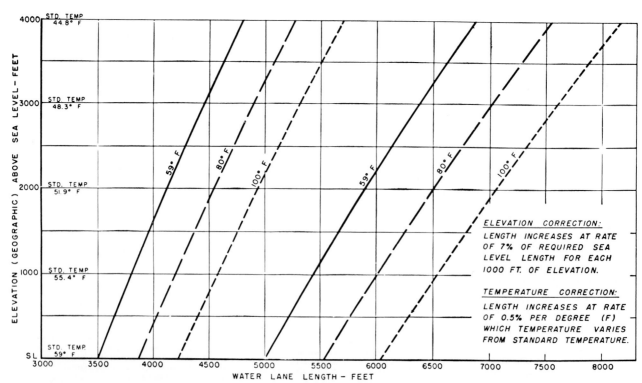

Fig. 1 Effect of elevation and temperature on water-lane lengths.

and with good boundary alignment for complete land utilization and protection. It may also be desirable in some cases to secure a liberal setback from the highway in order to protect the project and adjacent property from noise and glare and to provide room for widening any highway paralleling the property line. If sufficient land is available, a greenbelt all around the project will enhance the desirability of a seaplane facility in a neighborhood area.

General Planning Considerations

Having determined the best site available from the aeronautical point of view, other elements of community, county and state planning should be considered. These elements are accessibility and land use.

Accessibility Probably the most obvious consideration influencing the location of a seaplane facility is its proximity to the ultimate destination and source of the users. The ability of the airplane to cover long distances in a short space of time often is cited as its outstanding attribute. To retain this advantage, every effort should be made to locate the facility convenient to good streets and rapid or mass transportation facilities in urban areas, and to major highways or good roads in rural areas. Utilization of speedboats and other surface water transportation should also be carefully explored. If these associated means of access and transportation are overlooked, minimum use of the facility can be expected. In rural or recreation areas where the seaplane is used primarily for sport, location of the facility with regard to access will not be a serious problem except that the means of access or transportation for fuel, repairs, and supplies must be adequate.

Land Use Locating a facility in a residential neighborhood where let-down and takeoff procedures occur over homes may be a source of annoyance to residents in the area. Unless flight traffic procedures can be developed which will eliminate the objection of takeoffs and landings of this nature, the planner should seek a location where the existing land use will be benefited by seaplane activities. Personal seaplane flying is desired in certain neighborhoods where boating and seaplaning are of mutual interest. Here the seaplane facility will be as much an asset to the community as a yacht club. The onshore development might well include a combination office and club house for seaplane and boating interests. Normally there will be little use for a personal seaplane facility in an industrial area where local truck and auto traffic congestion make access time-consuming and undesirable.

Every effort should be made to recognize existing conditions and future proposals so that the seaplane facility can take its proper place in the community.

DESIGN CONSIDERATIONS
The Water-operating Area

Most natural water areas will provide, without modification, the required dimensions necessary for seaplane operations. Where the available water area is limited, the minimum water-operating area must consist of one water lane for landings and takeoffs and a taxi channel. A turning basin will be necessary in cases where turning must be confined to a restricted area because of water depth requirements or

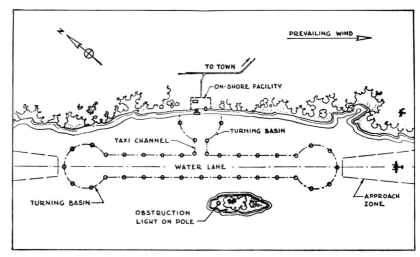

Fig. 2 General operating area.

for the segregation of other water surface-craft activities. In some cases anchorage areas may be necessary.

Water Lanes Minimum dimensions of water lanes necessary for seaplane operations are set forth in Table 1. Inasmuch as elevation and temperature affect water-lane length requirements, these factors must be considered and the lengths adjusted accordingly. Figure 1 presents a chart showing the effects of these factors on certain basic lengths. A typical layout for a single water-lane operating area is shown in Fig. 2.

Taxi Channel For small seaplanes the taxi channel should have a minimum width of 125 ft, although a width of 150 ft or more is preferred. These channels should be located to provide direct access to the onshore facility and when possible should be so oriented that approach to the ramp or floats will be into the prevailing wind. They should provide a minimum of 50 ft clearance between the side of the channel and the nearest obstruction.

Turning Basins Turning basins will be required where the use of water area is restricted. A minimum radius of 125 ft should be available for surface turns. These turning basins should be located at both ends of the water lanes and adjacent to the shoreline area. The same minimum clearance criteria, i.e., 50 ft, should be used for the separation between the side of the turning basin and the nearest obstruction.

Anchorage Areas Where anchorage areas are required, they should be located so as to provide maximum protection from high winds and rough water. The space requirements for an anchored aircraft, and the number and size of aircraft to be accommodated, will determine the size of the anchorage area. Each aircraft will swing around the mooring while anchored. To determine space needed, one must know the wingspan and length of aircraft, the length of line and bridle, and the lowest water level. The length of anchor line should be at least six times the maximum depth at mean high water at the anchor location. In cases where the aircraft swing space is limited, the length of the anchor line may be shortened to not less than three times the high-water depth, provided the normal anchor weight or holding capacity is doubled. Short anchor lines cause hard riding and should not be used where

swells or heavy wakes from boats are common. Center-to-center spacing of anchors, where small twin-float aircraft are to be moored, should not be less than twice the length of the longest anchor line plus 125 ft. For larger types of aircraft, including flying boats and amphibians this spacing should be increased by an additional 100 ft. A general layout of anchorages is shown in Fig. 3.

The Shoreline Area

Shoreline installations are partly on land and in the water. They are required to perform two general functions: (1) to provide servicing, loading and unloading, handling and tie-up facilities for seaplanes without removing them from the water, and (2) to provide haul-out facilities for removing seaplanes from the water.

The types, size, and arrangement of these installations will be determined by water conditions, the topography of the land adjacent to the water, the configuration of the bottom of the water area, the number and type of planes to be docked or removed from the water, and wind conditions. The installation will vary from a simple wood-plank platform to the more elaborate ramps with railway facilities, piers, and floats.

Ramps The simplest form of ramp consists of a wood-plank platform approximately 15 by 20 ft, laid on a sloping shore, with half its length in water. A device such as this will allow a small float plane to taxi up and out of the water. The use of such a ramp is predicated upon a relatively constant water level and the shore slope no steeper than 8 to 1.

The slope of any ramp should not be greater than 7 to 1, with gradual slopes down to 10 to 1 being preferred. Slopes less than 10 to 1 usually are too long and hence costly to construct.

Figure 4 shows the maximum draft of seaplanes of various weights and types. These data are useful in determining the depth to which the submerged end of a ramp must be lowered. A depth of ramp toe of 4 ft will provide sufficient depth for most types of water-borne aircraft in use today; a depth of 3 ft will permit handling of all but the heaviest type of amphibians. For small, light, float planes a depth of about 18 in. is adequate. In all cases, this dimension should be established for mean low water.

A ramp width of 15 ft is the minimum for small twin-float or amphibian aircraft opera-

SEAPLANE TERMINALS

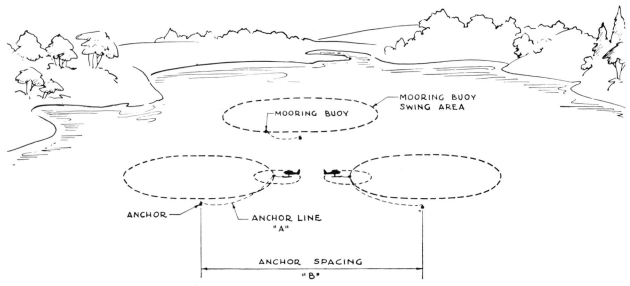

Fig. 3 General layout of anchorage areas.

tions when the water and wind conditions are relatively calm. By adding 5 ft to this minimum width, practically all water-borne aircraft of gross weights up to approximately 15,000 lb can be handled with safety, and pilots of small seaplanes can make an unattended ramp approach under adverse conditions. In figuring the ramp width, the outside-to-outside float dimensions of twin-float aircraft and the treads of amphibian aircraft are important factors and for reference are shown in Fig. 4. The maximum dimension—based on the largest aircraft to be accommodated—plus additional space on either side to allow for drift when approaching, and safe working space for personnel

when handling an aircraft on the ramp, determines the minimum practical width. Ramp-width determination does not necessitate consideration of wheel tread of present-day float plane dollies. Normally, the dolly wheels are spaced to fall between the floats, and in cases where the wheels are outside, the tread is 16 ft or less.

Piers Piers or fixed over-water structures can be utilized where the variation in water level is 18 in. or less. The pier should extend into the water to a point where the water depth is adequate for the types of aircraft to be handled. The usual design for a pier incorporates an

access walk approximately 5 ft in width with hand railings on both sides and an open-decked handling area approximately 30 by 50 ft at the walk's end. An open-decked area of this size will provide tie-up space for four small or three large seaplanes. On long piers, where the walking distance is too great for convenient handling of service equipment, a small storage shed may be located near the open-decked area. Fueling and lubrication facilities should also be located at the end of the pier.

Floats and Gangways Floats offer the greatest flexibility in providing docking facilities. This type of unit rides with wave action and is equal-

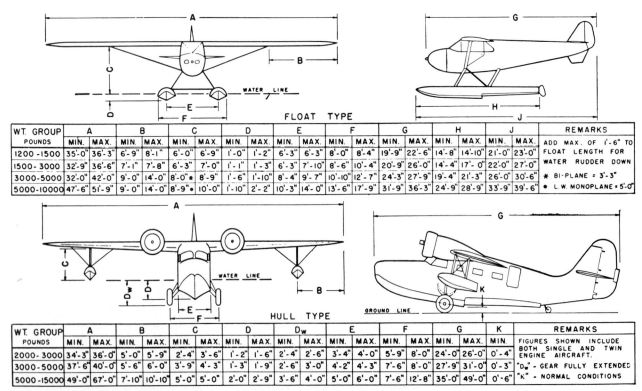

Fig. 4 Water-borne aircraft dimensional data by aircraft weight groups.

1106

ly satisfactory in areas of great or negligible water-level variations. Universal action must be provided in anchoring or attaching floats together. Figure 5 shows various types of floats for docking. A float which provides an unobstructed wing clearance of 17 ft will permit practically any twin-float seaplane or small amphibian aircraft to come along its side safely.

Floats are usually connected to the shore or pier by booms and a gangway. The maximum water-level variation dictates the length of the gangway. In no case should gangways be less than 15 ft in length and should be at least 5 ft in width. Hand rails, preferably on both sides, should be provided to assist persons using the way. A 2.75 : 1 slope ratio is the maximum

for safe and easy walking and to prevent the handrails from becoming an obstruction to wings.

In some locations it may be desirable to anchor the float offshore with anchors and anchor lines with connection to the shore by a floating walkway. A floating walkway 5 ft or less in width must have outriggers spaced longitudinally approximately every 10 ft. Outriggers 8 to 10 ft long will prevent excessive rolling of the walk.

Spacing The desired clearances between the various docking units and ramps obviously will have a decided influence on their arrangement and location. Each docking unit should

be so located that an aircraft may approach and tie up in any one of the units when adjacent units are occupied. When aircraft are operated between the various units under their own power, the recommended minimum separation between the near faces of piers, floats, ramps or marine railway is 50 ft because a waterborne aircraft can normally be taxied safely past obstructions as close as about one half of its wing span. Where aircraft are moved between units by hand, the separation between the units may be less than 50 ft to facilitate handling. A minimum of 100 ft of unobstructed water should be available directly offshore from a ramp in the direction from which approaches normally will be made.

Floating Barges The lease or purchase of land for a seaplane-facility site may be a problem at some desirable locations and yet pier or gangway rights may be easily obtained. At such locations a floating barge, anchored offshore, makes an excellent facility. An office, lounge, and service shop can be included "aboard" and by adding a floating dock alongside and ramps at the ends, a very practical and efficient facility results. The floating barge may be anchored direct to the shore or a pier by booms and a gangway, or anchored offshore in a fixed position. Some operators prefer to allow the barge to drift downwind or downwater from a single anchor. Boat transportation will be needed if the unit is mobile and moored offshore. The very uniqueness of this type of installation will, in some localities, attract many persons otherwise not directly interested in water flying. The possibility of organizing this activity on a club basis should not be overlooked. This type of installation can be made more attractive by appropriate use of paint, colorful deck chairs, awnings, marine appointments, and recreation facilities.

Some units are in operation today where an entire barge is floating but is attached to the shore. Large logs are decked over and form the base for the entire structure, which is in some cases 150 ft long by 100 ft wide, in a series of flexible units.

The Service, Tie-down, and Storage Area

This element will occupy more space than any other onshore facility. For safety and convenience, it should be separated from other incidental activities on the site, either by adequate buffer space, fencing, or both. Every effort should be made to locate floating docks and piers so that access to them by the public will not require crossing the apron or hangar area. (See Fig. 6.)

Hangars Both storage and repair hangars should be located so as to permit the off-site delivery of repair material and use by service personnel over a route as direct as possible and without interference with the movement of aircraft. The service and storage hangar area should be located in such a position in relation to the ramp or marine railway that aircraft may be moved there as directly as possible, with the least possible amount of disturbance to tied down aircraft or aircraft already in repair parking spaces.

The amount of space required for apron tiedown and hangar facilities will depend upon the number and types of aircraft that are to be accommodated. Dimensions of various aircraft are shown in Fig. 4. This information can be used to determine the space required for taxiing, turning, and storing.

Hangars should be located in an orderly and functional relation to haul-out and ramp facilities, and to eliminate as much noise and con-

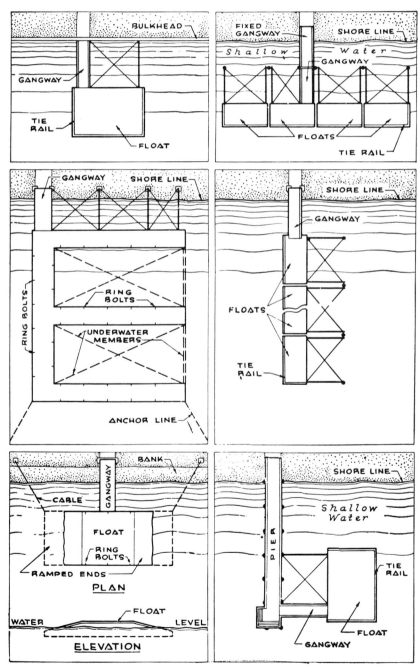

Fig. 5 Various types and arrangements of floats.

Transportation
SEAPLANE TERMINALS

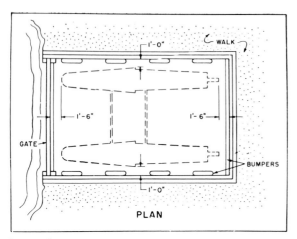

Fig. 6   Seaplane slipway.

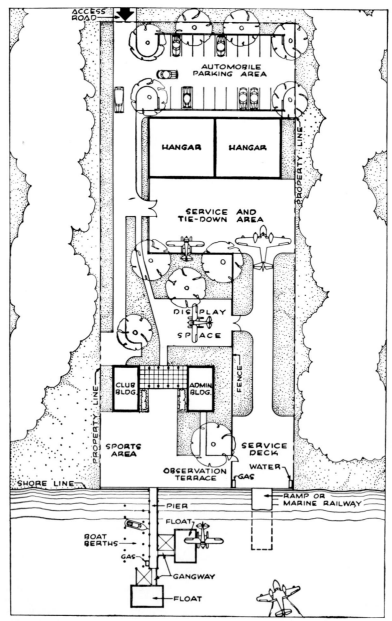

Fig. 7   Typical layout of onshore and shoreline development.

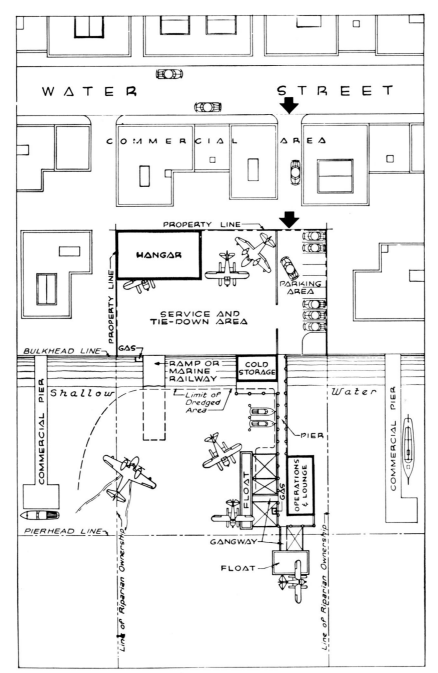

Fig. 8 Typical layout of onshore and shoreline development.

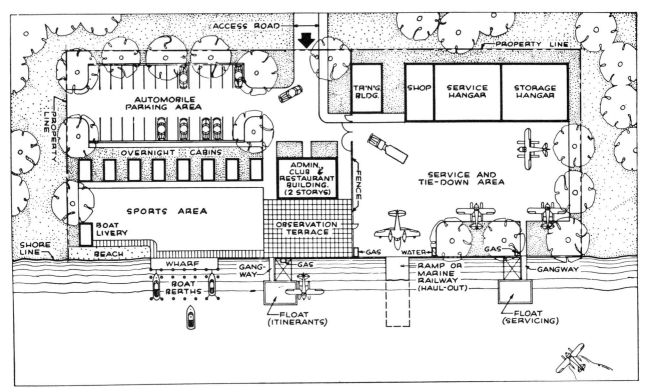

Fig. 9   Typical layout of onshore and shoreline development.

fusion as possible should be sufficiently separated from the administration building and common public-use areas.

The Administration Building and Common-Use Area

In simple installations, it may be necessary to utilize a hangar for both aircraft service and office space. In larger projects a separate administration building may be required to provide adequate space for the manager's office, passenger and pilot lounge, display space, restaurant or snack bar, and observation deck. A community room for public use, such as for lectures, meetings and classes should not be overlooked if needed. The building should not be oversized or monumental in character. Only a simple, functional design, adequate to take care of the estimated needs, is required. The location should be in a prominent position on the site, readily accessible to aircraft arrival and to customers and visitors from the onshore approach. Like airport administration buildings, visibility of the water area from the administration building is needed for the control of aircraft at locations where traffic in and out requires two-way radio communications.

Ample outdoor space reserved immediately adjacent to the administration building for public use is desirable. This space may consist of a small lawn or paved terrace on the water area side or, in more sizable installations, a larger section broken down into recreation areas, an outdoor dining terrace and lawn.

Access Access to the land area, both for customers and for service and delivery, should ordinarily be a two-way, all-weather road. However, when a long access road is required and the traffic to and from the facility is not sea-

sonal but relatively constant and without peaks, a one-way road will suffice. In such cases, turn-outs should be provided at convenient intervals. The plan should be designed for one traffic connection with the main highway or street, in order that its free-way may be preserved. A public highway should never be used as a part of the road system within a project if public use for through traffic is to continue after the project has been put into operation. Through traffic will unduly congest the land facility, could be hazardous to pedestrians, and splits the property into two separate units which is undesirable.

Roads Vehicular circulation must be provided for deliveries of gasoline, oil, fuel, and for refuse removal. These routes will influence walks and interior road system and to some extent the pattern of the master plan. In order to reduce development costs and maintenance, it is advisable to concentrate buildings for certain uses in areas with servicing facilities such as a service road, on one side. When topography and shape of tract are favorable, this type of plan effects economies.

Roads should be planned economically, but must be adequate in width to serve the anticipated traffic, to permit easy circulation and safe driving. In some instances, they may afford parking space on one or both sides, depending on the solution of a particular site problem. Some service roads may be desired for limited use. In such cases the entrance can be barred by removable posts or chains.

Parking Areas Provision of parking areas for cars must be made. As previously mentioned, one should allow one car for each based aircraft, one car for each employee, plus a ratio of visitors' cars commensurate with the judg-

ment of local interest in the use of the facility. An overall space of 250 sq ft of area will be required for each car. The type of parking space layout will, of course, depend upon the space and shape of the area available for the installation.

Parking areas should not be located so that pedestrians must cross a public road to reach the facility proper. This creates an unnecessary hazard, particularly to unescorted children who might dash across the public highway. Parking areas should be located convenient to the onshore and shoreline facilities. In no case should the pedestrians be required to walk a distance greater than 200 ft from the parking area or service road to reach buildings or shoreline.

Walks All walks should be laid out for direct access to and from the facilities to be reached. Like roads, they should not be oversized in the interest of economy of construction and maintenance. Recommended walks widths are:

Capacity	Width, ft
Public walk serving less than 100 persons	3
Normal standard walk	4
Walk serving over 400 person	5

All walks should clear obstructions (as planting, fences, etc.) by 2 ft. Avoid steps in walks; single risers should *never* be used in public walks. Avoid stepped ramps. A 10 to 15 percent gradient is preferred to steps.

Figures 7 to 9 show layouts on three distinctly different shapes of land area. These layouts indicate the inter-relationship of each use area. From arrangements such as these, studied in accordance with the previous discussion on the master plan elements and the general water-operating area shown in Fig. 2, the master plan is developed.

1110

By JULIUS PANERO, Architect and Planning Consultant

INTRODUCTION

The growth and development of bus transportation has closely followed advances in automotive technology and the improvement and expansion of the national highway network. The first bus routes were originated by individual entrepreneurs using converted passenger automobiles. These routes were short and service was generally unreliable. As the highway network expanded and more suitable bus equipment became available, these short, disconnected routes were merged into larger consolidated operations providing more reliable through services over longer distances. Our modern express highway system and the development of more comfortable and efficient high-speed buses have made bus transportation the leading means of public transport in the United States. Over the past decade bus services have evolved into several general operational categories and characteristic terminal types.

TERMINAL TYPES

Intercity Bus Terminal

The intercity terminal is usually found in the downtown core and is accessible directly by local transit, taxi, and auto. It differs from other terminal types in that it includes long-haul service in excess of several hundred miles and provides for a much greater number of bus movements. Land costs normally dictate vertical expansion capability in the denser city areas. (See Fig. 1.)

More elaborate "package express" facilities are provided in the intercity terminal and a greater amount of concession and rental space is provided to defray higher terminal construction and operating costs.

Airport-City Bus Terminal

The airport-city bus terminal provides primarily for the transportation of airline passengers from an urban center to the major airports it serves. Usually located in the urban center, the terminal is accessible by local transit systems, taxis, and autos. Oriented to departing and arriving flights, the terminal normally has provisions for arrival and departing flight information as well as preticketing and check-in facilities.

Urban-Suburban Commuter Terminal

This type of facility may be located within the downtown core, as a central passenger collection and distribution node, or on the periphery of the core, as a rapid transit feeder station. It is characterized by a diversified bus route structure and high-turnover commuter-type bus operations. Bus accessibility is an important consideration. Grade separated access by underpass or overpass connections and exclusive bus lanes on connecting highways are desirable to maintain schedule efficiency.

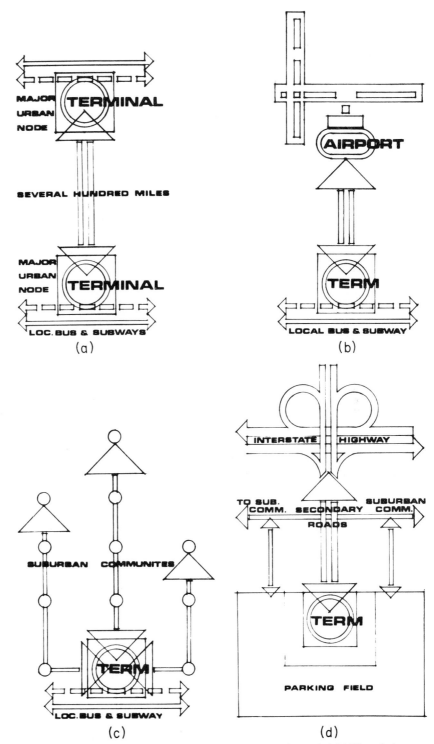

Fig. 1   Terminal types. (a) Urban located intercity terminal. (b) Airport-city bus terminal. (c) Urban-suburban commuter terminal. (d) Suburban-interstate terminal.

Transportation

BUS TERMINALS

Suburban Interstate Terminal

The suburban interstate terminal is a peripheral type designed to avoid the traffic congestion and heavy investment associated with central city and/or airport terminal facilities.

The terminal is usually located adjacent to interstate highway connections with major cities or regional airports and in many instances serves the increasing outlying "urban sprawl" areas.

In an increasing number of cases terminals of this type serve a commuter-type function where the daily journey to work in the central city may take as long as 2 hours.

Sometimes referred to as "park and ride" terminals, because access is primarily by auto, these facilities are provided with open, paved parking spaces. Investment in waiting-room and bus-berthing facilities is minimal. The terminal is usually a one-story building of simple construction.

FUNCTIONAL ELEMENTS/PLANNING CRITERIA

General functional organization of the terminal is determined by site configuration, the volume and type of bus operations, and passenger and bus traffic circulation. Although all terminal types to some extent share common planning problems, there do exist some significant differences in design rationale.

One of the most complicated terminals is the intercity type, since it is often found in a dense, developed area in the heart of the central city and its general configuration is too often inhibited by existing construction and high land costs. Moreover, the underlying design rationale should maximize provisions for short lines of flow and communication between ticketing and baggage functions and the bus interface.

An island plan with the functional elements radiating from the core allows for maximum efficiency. Such a relationship would allow the "waiting" areas to serve as the central focal point, with all bus berth positions being equidistant. As the terminal becomes more linear in plan, functional elements begin to lose their cohesiveness and often require duplication.

Although the design of all terminal types is largely dictated by bus and passenger volumes, this consideration becomes even more significant in the design of high-volume commuter bus terminals.

In such facilities the design is controlled more by bus and passenger volumes, traffic circulation, and the resultant space demands for large numbers of bus berths, while baggage handling provisions are minimal or nonexistent. These space demands may dictate a vertical, multiple-bus-level solution, with intermediate passenger circulation concourses. Traffic access, by direct exclusive highways on the bus side and by feeder transit, auto, and taxis on the passenger side are important elements of this type of terminal.

Generally, with regard to the airport-city terminal, the primary planning considerations include provisions for efficient check-in facilities, baggage handling, and flight information. Moreover, counter space requirements are usually more extensive and should include weigh-in provisions and conveyors for handling of baggage. Adequate provisions should also be made for limousine, auto, and taxi access.

The suburban interstate terminal is perhaps the simplest of the terminal types. The most

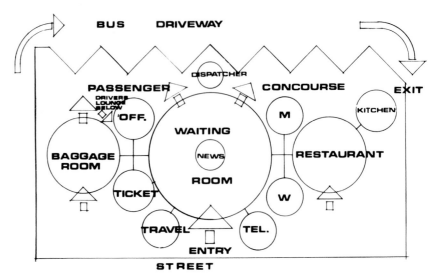

Fig. 2   Flow diagram.

significant planning requirement is adequate provision for parking. Many, if not most of the passengers drive to the facility and park their cars until their return in the evening, while others may be driven to the facility and discharged. In many instances access to the terminal may also be via local bus service and taxi.

It is essential, therefore, that the parking facilities be located so as to minimize the walking distance to the terminal and that egress and ingress be planned to avoid traffic congestion along nearby arteries. If possible, some covered walkways should be provided leading from the parking field to the terminal building.

Since there will be movement of both vehicles and passengers at the same level, provisions must be made, for obvious safety reasons, to separate the two as much as possible.

Terminal requirements should include provisions for ticket sales, vending machines and/or small snack bar, toilet facilities, office, baggage and/or storeroom. (See Fig. 2.)

Space Requirements

Public Seating Seating in any of the terminal types may be provided in the form of a separate waiting room or, in a more open plan, in the form of a simple seating area within a larger public space. This function should be directly accessible to the concourse area and should be provided with drinking fountains, trash baskets, ash urns, and clocks.

The amount of public seating varies depending on individual circumstances, terminal type, and economic priorities. As a general rule of thumb, however, an allowance of one seat for every three passengers would be adequate for an intercity terminal. The passenger quantity is calculated by multiplying the number of loading berths by an average bus capacity of between 35 and 37 people. A 10-berth loading platform therefore, would result in terminal seating of between 117 to 124.

In a high-volume commuter terminal, seating accommodations may be reduced considerably since in-terminal waiting time is much less. This would also hold true for the suburban interstate terminal.

Ticketing Facilities The trend in ticketing facilities in the modern terminal, regardless of the type, is toward open counters in contrast to the antiquated caged windows. In the larger intercity terminal, where more than one carrier may operate, separate self-contained glass-walled ticket offices may be provided, each housing their individual open ticket counters. The number of selling positions or agent stations varies with the individual operations policy of the carrier and the particular terminal type.

Perhaps the greatest number of selling positions are required in the intercity terminal. On the average, one position should be provided for each 25 to 30 waiting room seats. The lineal feet of counter space depends on individual carrier operation and the type of ticketing equipment used and may vary between 3 to 5 ft per position and/or about 50 to 60 sq ft per position. The height of the counter is usually 42 in.

In the airport-city terminal the ticketing facilities are usually in the form of continuous counters with a certain number of selling positions allocated to each airline. The length of each position is determined by the type of electronic equipment, TV equipment, and scales to be housed and usually varies between 4 to 5 ft.

Baggage Room Baggage room requirements vary significantly with terminal type and operation.

In the intercity terminal and the airport-city terminal, the baggage handling problem is more severe.

Ideally, in both cases, the sooner the departing passenger and his baggage are separated, the better. In the airport-city terminal this usually occurs at the ticket counter where the baggage is sent by conveyor directly to the loading platform or to a staging area or baggage room, where it remains before it is placed on board the bus.

In the intercity bus terminal the baggage is normally hand-carried directly onto the bus or to the baggage room, and from there it is placed on the bus. The baggage room should be accessible from both the public area and the concourse and have an area equal to about 10 percent of the total building or contain about 50 sq ft for each bus loading berth, whichever is higher. The baggage room should also be equipped with standard metal racks about four or five tiers high for baggage storage.

A portion of the baggage room may be used

for a package express service, which and should function without interfering with concourse traffic. A separate package express counter should be provided. The length of the counter depends on the scope of the operation, which varies with each location.

Public Lockers and Telephones Lockers and telephones are revenue producing, and the quantities to be provided depend to a great degree on their potential earning capacity.

Dispatch Office The dispatch office controls all bus movement and consequently should be located on the concourse so that it can observe all loading berths. The size of the dispatch office may vary anywhere from 50 to 150 sq ft.

Offices All terminals regardless of type require a certain amount of office space. The specific area to be provided depends on the terminal size and type. Although usually offices for the terminal manager, passenger agent, and switchboard are sufficient, in larger terminals more elaborate facilities are required.

Rental Space The amount of rental space to be provided for stores, shops, concessions, etc., depends primarily on the earning potential involved and the amount of space available.

By JOHN J. FRUIN, Ph.D.

PEDESTRIAN DESIGN FOR PASSENGER TERMINALS

The design of pedestrian facilities for passenger terminals is dependent on the category of terminal and its pedestrian traffic patterns. Commuter passenger terminals, with extreme but short peak traffic patterns and repetitive users, can be designed for lower standards of service than long-distance terminals, where the users are generally unfamiliar with the facility and peak traffic levels may be sustained over several hours. Detailed photographic studies of the use of pedestrian facilities indicate that maximum capacity coincides with the most crowded pedestrian concentrations, representing a poor design environment. Many of the elements of aesthetic design are lost in this type of crowded environment, as the pedestrian becomes preoccupied with the difficulties caused by the close interaction and conflicts with other persons. The challenge to the terminal designer is to balance the space requirements for a comfortable and aesthetically pleasing human environment against the space restraints caused by building configuration and cost.

The most recent approach to the design of pedestrian spaces has been the use of the level-of-service concept. On the basis of this concept, a qualitative evaluation is made of human convenience at various traffic concentrations and this is translated into appropriate design parameters. For example, it has been found through detailed photographic analysis that the maximum capacity of a corridor is ob-

From "Pedestrian Planning and Design," © (Copyright) by John J. Fruin, Ph.D.

tained when average area occupancies are about 5 sq ft per person and human locomotion is limited to a restricted, shuffling gait. Pedestrians require an average of more than 35 sq ft per person in order to select their normal walking speed and to avoid conflicts with other pedestrians. Human locomotion on stairs and the convenience and comfort of pedestrian waiting areas is similarly related to average pedestrian area occupancy.

Corridor Design

Minimum corridor widths are based on the pedestrian traffic flow volume less appropriate allowances for disruptive traffic elements such as columns, newsstands, stairways, window shoppers, etc. Where the corridor is also used as a waiting area to accommodate standing pedestrians, the maximum potential accumulation and safe human occupancy of the corridor should be determined. (See "Queuing Areas," below.) The maximum practical flow through a corridor is approximately 25 persons per foot width of corridor per minute (PFM). The flow volume that allows for the selection of normal walking speed and avoidance of traffic conflicts is equivalent to 7 PFM (or less). This standard would be used in passenger terminals that do not have severe peaking patterns or space restrictions. Where severe repetitive peaks and space restraints occur, such as in a commuter terminal, the more stringent standard of 10 to 15 PFM may be used. This standard allows the attainment of near-normal walking speed but does result in more frequent traffic conflicts with other pedestrians.

Entrances

The criteria utilized for corridor design can be roughly applied to the design of doors. The maximum capacity of a free-swinging door is approximately 60 persons per minute, but this capacity is obtained with frequent traffic disruptions and queuing at the entrance section. A standard of 40 persons per minute would be representative of a busy situation with occasional traffic disruptions. Where free-flowing traffic is desired, a standard of 20 persons per minute should be adopted.

Stairs

Human locomotion on stairs is much more stylized and restricted than walking because of the restraints imposed by the dimensional configuration of the stairs, physical exertion, and concerns for safety. As with corridors, capacity flow is obtained when there is a dense crowding of pedestrians combined with restricted, uncomfortable locomotion. The maximum practical flow on a stair is approximately 17 persons per foot width of stairway per minute (PFM) in the upward or design direction. An average of about 20 square feet per person or more is required before stair locomotion becomes normal and traffic conflicts with other pedestrians can be avoided. This is equivalent to a flow volume of about 5 PFM. This standard would be used in terminals that do not have severe peaking patterns or space restrictions. In commuter terminals, the more stringent standard of 7 to 10 PFM would be acceptable. Riser height has a significant impact on stair locomotion. Lower riser heights, 7 in. or less, increase pedestrian speed and thus improve traffic efficiency. The lower riser height is also desirable to assist the handicapped pedestrian.

Queuing Areas

A number of different pedestrian queuing situations occur in terminals which affect their functional design. Linear queues will occur where passengers line up to purchase tickets or board buses. Care must be taken that these lines do not disrupt other terminal functions. The length of a linear queue may be estimated on the basis of an average per person spacing of 20 in. The presence of baggage has little effect on this spacing because baggage is placed on the floor either between the legs or at the sides. Bulk queues may occur within a passenger terminal where passengers are waiting for bus arrivals or other services. Where no circulation through the queuing space is required, area occupancies as low as 5 sq ft per person may be tolerated for short periods. This allows standing pedestrians to avoid physical contact with each other. Where movement through the queuing space is required, such as in a passenger waiting concourse, an average area of 10 or more sq ft per person is required. Human area occupancies below 3 sq ft per person result in crowded, immobile, and potentially unsafe queues, particularly where pedestrians may be jostled off platforms.

Escalators and Moving Walks

The high costs of escalators and moving walks present difficult design quality decisions. The units are generally designed close to their practical operating capacities even though this practice causes pedestrian delays and queuing. Escalator and moving walk manufacturers will rate the theoretical capacity of their units on assumption of uniform step or space occupancies, but detailed photographic studies of pedestrian use of these units show that, even under the most crowded conditions, pedestrians will leave vacant step positions or gaps, thus reducing effective capacity. This is caused by the pedestrian's own personal space preferences and momentary hesitation when boarding these units, particularly when they operate at higher speeds. This had led to the use of a nominal or practical design capacity of 75 percent of the theoretical as shown in Table 1.

TABLE 1 Nominal Capacity — Escalators and Moving Walks

Type of unit	Capacity, persons per minute	
	Speed — 90 fpm	Speed — 120 fpm
32-in. escalator	63	84
48-in. escalator	100	133
24-in. walk		60
30-in. walk		120

Stationary stairs should be located in close proximity to escalators and inclined moving walks to allow for their alternative use in cases of mechanical failure. With a rise below 20 ft, pedestrians will also make alternative use of these stairs if escalator queues become too long. With high-rise applications above 20 ft, virtually all pedestrians will use the escalator, causing long queues and delays in the heavier traffic applications. Space for pedestrian traffic circulation and queuing should be allocated at all landing areas.

BUS TERMINALS

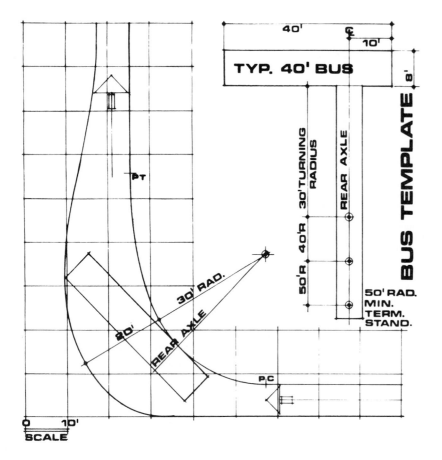

SWEEP PATH 40' BUS   90° TURN

By JULIUS PANERO,
Architect and Planning Consultant

BUS GEOMETRICS

Bus Data Bus geometrics, or the physical dimensions and maneuverability of the bus, determine the width of roadways, shapes of platforms, column spacing, ceiling heights, and other aspects of bus-level design. The apparently insignificant detail of the right-side loading of buses often restricts terminal design possibilities.

Swept Path When a bus turns normally, it always turns about a point which is somewhere on the center line of the rear axle. This is true whether motion is forward or backward.

The turns required to accomplish the movement and positioning of buses are variable and differ considerably with the equipment encountered. The turning template provides a convenient graphic method to determine minimum clearances required. (See Fig. 3.)

ROADWAY RAMPS

Bus Roadway Widths Ten-foot-wide single lanes will suffice for 8-ft-wide equipment. *Eleven-foot lanes are preferable* where ample terminal space is available and especially to accommodate equipment 8 ft wide, the use of which steadily is increasing.

Double-lane runways, enabling standing buses to be overtaken by other buses, provide a great advantage over one-lane runways because of the increased flexibility of operations that is made possible.

For the purpose of merely overtaking another

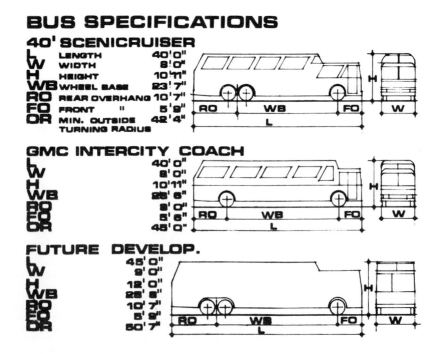

Fig. 3 Bus data.

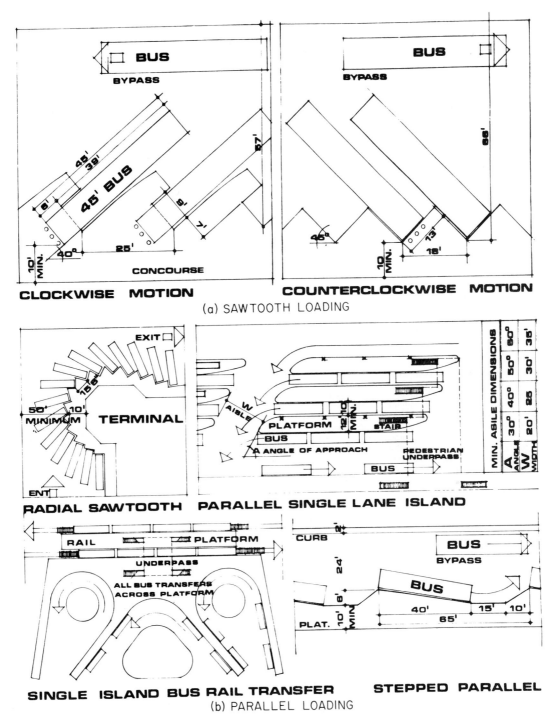

Fig. 4 Bus loading plans.

PLATFORM TYPES

Parallel Loading
- Requires *excessive* amount of space.
- Buses must usually wait until first bus exits.
- Large terminal requires pedestrian under/overpass facilities to protect passengers while crossing lanes.

Right-Angle Loading
- Disadvantages include:
  1 Outswinging bus door which forms a barrier around which passenger must pass.
  2 Bus maneuvering difficult.

Straight Sawtooth Loading
- Efficient—employed where lot is comparatively narrow and deep.
- Passenger has direct approach to loading door.
- Baggage truck can operate between buses for side loading.

Radial Sawtooth Loading
- Most efficient—buses swing into position along natural driving arc.
- Space required at front is minimum—wide space at rear making maneuvering easy.
  (See Fig. 4.)

Transportation
BUS TERMINALS

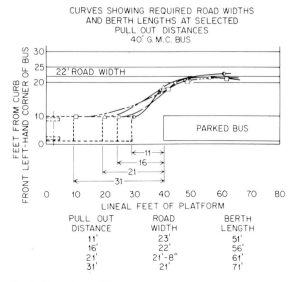

CURVES SHOWING REQUIRED ROAD WIDTHS
AND BERTH LENGTHS AT SELECTED
PULL OUT DISTANCES
40' G.M.C. BUS

PULL OUT DISTANCE	ROAD WIDTH	BERTH LENGTH
11'	23'	51'
16'	22'	56'
21'	21'-8"	61'
31'	21'	71'

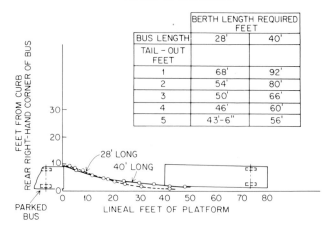

CURVES SHOWING REQUIRED BERTH LENGTHS
AS COMPARED TO BUS TAIL-OUT
28' AND 40' G.M.C. BUSES

	BERTH LENGTH REQUIRED FEET	
BUS LENGTH	28'	40'
TAIL-OUT FEET		
1	68'	92'
2	54'	80'
3	50'	66'
4	46'	60'
5	43'-6"	56'

Fig. 5 Bus roadway widths.

bus or row of buses having no appreciable tail-out, double-lane runway widths should be at least 20 ft and preferably 22 ft, especially if extra-wide equipment is to be accommodated —immediately or in the future. However, for a flexible operation under which departing buses may pull out from the platform around a standing bus, the runway width and the amount of lineal space at the platform for the pull-out maneuver are directly related. This relationship is indicated by Fig. 5, from which it is seen, for example, that a 40-ft bus having a 16-ft clearance ahead actually uses 22 ft of runway width for the pull-out. This would indicate, for practical purposes, a runway width of at least 24

ft. Also, a total minimum berth length of 40 ft plus 16 ft, or 56 ft, would be required. Obviously, the shorter the berth length allowed, the wider the runway must be, and vice versa.

Ramping Where roadway ramping down or up, at entrances or exits to runways is necessary, care should be taken to avoid sharp grade changes which will result in discomfort to passengers or rough treatment of equipment, particularly when heavily loaded. Here again, where this factor is involved, tests should be made with buses and allowance made for possible future vehicles having a longer wheelbase and overhang. Because of the longer

wheelbase of buses, critical attention should be paid to the vertical clearance where a sag curve exists, since required bus clearance will be greater. Where buses are to enter terminal buildings, doorways and other structures should allow sufficient side clearance to permit free movement of vehicles and to avoid damage and delay. Door headroom should be at least 12 ft for typical equipment, allowance being made for any use of the terminals by deck-and-a-half or double-deck buses. Actual dimensions of equipment to use the terminal should be checked before fixing critical dimensions. Minimum side clearance to all structures along the roadway should be at least 12 in.

A truck terminal is a highly specialized facility, designed for a specific function and operating plan in terms of the service standards it must meet, the area it serves, and the volumes to be handled. The objective of this article is to explain the planning required to assure that the facility will be adequate for:

1. *Dock design and yard layout.* Provide sufficient space for trucks to maneuver in and out quickly and for parking equipment. Protect freight and personnel from the weather. Design docks to provide ready access for moving material into trucks.

2. *Number of dock spots.* Provide the appropriate number of doors to enable trucks to load and unload without undue delay.

3. *Accumulation space.* Space is required immediately behind shipping and receiving spots for accumulating shipments so that vehicles can be processed quickly.

The complete design of the truck terminal, of course, depends upon first establishing the operating plan and mission. Evaluation and considerations of alternate handling systems and building designs are beyond the scope of this article.

Possible future changes must be thoroughly analyzed in establishing the design year requirements. Facilities are designed for the future, and they must be able to handle peak loads. Although the data gathering and analytical techniques required to accurately establish a design basis appear complex, they are necessary. Only with this information can the designer assure that the facility will operate as planned.

DESIGN YEAR REQUIREMENTS

The planning starts with a 5-year forecast. The planners have established the specific mission of the facility and have thoroughly estimated the needs of the future including:

1. Inbound and outbound destinations to be served
2. The nature of the workload to be handled
3. The terminal schedules required

The objective of the planning analysis is to establish a few numbers such as pounds per hour which describe what the terminal will have to do during the peak period of the design year day. The designer must know what the workload availability will be in terms of truck arrivals, dispatches, loading, and unloading times for peak operations.

1. *Determine design year peak.* Historical data are of interest only as they relate to the future. Usually, current information must be collected to describe the details of the present terminal workload, so that the data may be adjusted for the future. Determine how this current test period relates to the normal seasonal peaks and valleys encountered during the year. If the terminal is a new facility replacing an existing one, then data can usually be col-

Shipper-Motor Carrier Dock Planning Model, The Operations Council of the American Trucking Associations, Inc., Washington, D.C.

lected for one point. If the terminal is replacing two or more existing terminals or has an entirely new mission, then information may be collected for several points. The designer, of course, would like to have complete information available to make his forecast, but he must be practical and use whatever information is at hand. The type of information which can be used for evaluating seasonal peaks and valleys is:

  a. Number of shipments
  b. Pounds handled
  c. Revenue dollars
  d. Number of loads

2. *Tabulate and analyze peak period.* Establish a logical basis for a peak period. Planning the facility to handle the absolute peak day 5 years in the future is not logical. This would mean unnecessary building cost. Select a peak period somewhat lower than the average, depending upon evaluation of daily or weekly variation. For a small facility, a 40-door terminal or less, a good rule of thumb is to take an average of the 10 highest consecutive weeks during the year and use this as a base to compare other periods of the year for which you are collecting detailed information. A larger facility deserves detailed analysis. Tabulate the daily or weekly data on a bar chart. Examine it, and establish some logical cutoff for the peak period. Usually a design base which will accommodate the volume of 85 to 90 percent of the working days of the year will be suitable.

3. *Establish the design year planning base.* The new terminal should be planned for 5 years hence. Site and yard space requirements should be planned for 10 to 20 years in the future to allow for expansion of the platform facilities and other facilities beyond the design year. Design year peak should include the following:

  a. The current planning base
  b. Forecasted growth for inbound-outbound transfer and interline freight
  c. Acquisition of operating rights within present system including new distribution points and peddle routes
  d. Mergers with other carriers and possible consolidation of terminals in the same city
  e. Change in the freight pattern

The design year daily volume should be in pounds. Be careful in projecting growth based on past revenue increases, because these usually reflect rate increases, not actual growth of traffic. The final figure established should represent the planned peak design year day in terms of total pounds handled. Detailed information on current workload can therefore later be adjusted to reflect a future planning base.

4. *Tabulate data on workload availability.* Set up the test period and accumulate 4 weeks of data by maintaining daily activity logs and records. The objective of this analysis is to provide complete information on all elements of the workload, to determine the time of its availability and what must be done with it. Daily activity logs should be maintained for:

  a. Inbound arrivals by origin point
  b. Delivery loaded by route and interline carrier

  c. Inbound break-bulk by origin and destination points
  d. Interline and cartage received by carrier
  e. Pickup unloaded by route
  f. Outbound loaded by destination

The availability logs should show the workload arrivals in terms of units (or trucks), shipments, and pounds, and when it arrived. At the end of each day, summarize the information on the logs to show the workload availability by hour. At the end of the 4-week test period, summarize the vehicle and freight activity for the entire period in hourly increments. Review the daily results for a consistent pattern of vehicle and freight arrivals and for variations from the pattern.

5. *Evaluate future changes.* Before establishing the design year workload characteristics and specific terminal mission, determine those workload availability changes which might occur in the interim, either through management direction or from other sources. Key factors to consider are:

  a. Different closeout times at origin terminals
  b. Changes in routing between origin and destination terminals which may alter travel time
  c. Changes in cutoff times for interline freight
  d. Feasibility of replacing single trailer with double trailer operations, to reduce elapsed loading or eliminate combination loads
  e. Possibility that double trailer combinations may mean earlier arrival at new terminal
  f. Break-bulk traffic patterns may change by review of system operation

For new areas to be serviced by acquisition of additional rights or by merger with other carriers, estimate the workload availability based on the location of possible new terminals and estimated freight volumes to be handled. Evaluate all of these factors, and establish the design year workload availability for the new terminal.

6. *Establish service objectives.* The planner now has available a good description of the new terminal workload in terms of its content and availability. The next step is to establish two key factors:

  a. Required cutoff times for outbound loading
  b. Required time that delivery vehicles should be available on the street

The planner, therefore, will know when the workload is available and how much time the dock crew will have for processing the workload.

7. *Establish distribution of traffic by outbound destinations.* The objective is to estimate the amount of traffic to be loaded over the platform to each outbound destination to be served. Tabulate the daily average test period weight in pounds to each destination. The procedure is as follows:

  a. Tabulate daily average weight in pounds to each destination.
  b. Apply the forecasted growth factor to each destination for design year daily average weight. If forecasts are not available by destination point, use the same growth factor for all points.

c. List all new destination points acquired through operating rights or mergers with other carriers.

d. Determine design year daily average outbound weight for each new point.

A similar analysis should be prepared for inbound traffic. List all present routes, including commercial consignees and interline carriers. Evaluate these routes and determine whether future plans will call for rerouting and handling additional volume by more routes, improved delivery load averages, or more trucks on the same routes. Tabulate the expected volume of freight for each route.

At this point, the planner should have a complete description of the future workload, when it will be available, where and how it must be loaded, and what the loading and unloading—overall handling capacity required—will be for the design year day.

NUMBER OF DOORS

The number of loading and unloading doors required is based on the peak period during the design day. The peak doorway requirement may be for the inbound operation or a peak where the inbound and outbound overlap. The planner has already established the volumes to be handled, the destinations to be sorted, and the availability of freight to be unloaded. The number of doors for a given workload will therefore depend upon the number of destinations to be loaded inbound and outbound as well as the rates at which freight can be loaded and unloaded through a door. Typical truck terminal unloading and loading rates are shown in Table 1. These may be used if the planner has not already established loading and unloading rates for his own operation. The rates shown are based on the number of pounds per hour which normally can be loaded and unloaded through a doorway based on a one-man operation. The rates also include time for spotting equipment.

1. *Calculate outbound doors required.* For outbound, obviously the minimal requirement is one door per destination. Additional doors will be needed for destinations which have a greater volume of freight than can be loaded through a door in the required time period. Let us say that a carrier has four destinations and can load freight through a doorway at a rate of 6,000 lb per hour. The design year requirement for the peak period during the design day has been established. The calculation is as follows.

Example: There are four destinations, and the average loading rate is 6,000 lb per hour.

Destination	Pounds per hour to be loaded	Number of doors calculated	Number of doors allowed
A	10,000	1.7	2
B	4,000	0.7	1
C	25,000	4.2	4
D	2,000	0.3	1
Total	41,000	6.9	8

As a rule of thumb, when determining the number of doors for each destination, round all decimal values of 0.3 to the next higher whole number, and drop all decimal values less than 0.3. When calculating the number of outbound doors, be sure that all destination points are well defined. For example, Chicago might be a destination. There may be additional subdestinations required such as Chicago proper, Chicago interline, and Chicago route truck. Each of these would have to be treated as

separate destinations if the freight is sorted for them and loaded separately.

2. *Calculate number of inbound doors.* The number of doors for local delivery will depend upon the number of routes and the method used for servicing the route. Before calculating the number of doors, the operating plan must be established. The planner must know:

a. The number of dropped trailers or trucks for interline or large customers

b. Whether the plan calls for flooring freight and loading all trucks in sequence, or whether the inbound operation will be all or partially a cross-dock or direct-loading operation

c. Whether all delivery vehicles will be dispatched at once or whether there will be a second wave of local delivery

Use the planning data developed to determine the volume of freight for each route. Develop the operating plan, and provide enough truck spots for each route to be loaded at any one interval of time.

3. *Calculate number of doors required for unloading.* The calculation of the number of doors required for stripping or unloading inbound trailers or pickup and delivery vehicles is relatively simple. From the design day peak workload analysis, the planner knows the volume of traffic, its availability and how much must be stripped in a given number of hours. The only additional information needed is at what hourly rate he can expect a dockman to unload freight through a doorway.

Example

A carrier's daily peak period is during the inbound operation. The plan calls for dock crews to start in force at 2 A.M. and complete unloading inbound trailers by 7 A.M. Workload availability analysis shows that 300,000 lb of inbound is available for stripping during this period. The elapsed time for the operation is 5 hours. Stripping is planned at a continuous level rate; then the crew has 5 hours to complete the unloading. The plan will require stripping inbound vehicles at a rate of 60,000 lb per hour. Delivery can be loaded at an average rate of 4,000 lb per hour through a door; then the number of doors required for stripping is:

$$\frac{60,000}{4,000} = 15 \text{ doors required}$$

Similar calculations can be made for stripping pickup vehicles. Important factors to know are when the pickup is available, and at what continuous rate stripping should be planned in order that the unloading be completed in time to close out the outbound equipment on schedule.

TABLE 1 Loading and Unloading Rates*

Type	Shipments Average pounds	Pounds per hour†
Very small shipments‡	150	2,000– 4,000
Small shipments	300	4,000– 5,500
Average shipments.	500	5,500– 6,500
Large shipments	3,000	6,500– 8,000
Unit loads §		22,000–30,000
Containers¶		17,000–21,000
Conveyor loading		9,000–11,000

*Rates based on steady flow of freight to or from doorway. Pounds per hour will decrease if freight flow is interrupted to pick or detail inspect shipments and to travel long distances between storage and shipping or receiving area.

†Rates are based on one-man operation. With two-man operation rates will increase 50 percent to 80 percent.

‡Includes large percentage of minimum shipments and one shipment delivery or pickup. Minimum service time is 6 minutes per vehicle.

§ Includes pallet loads, skid loads, clamp loads, and slip sheet loads.

¶ Includes cages, metal, wood, and plastic containers.

SHIPMENT ACCUMULATION SPACE

Accumulation space is needed to stage shipments so that they are ready for the pickup vehicle and for placing goods received prior to disposition. Shipments should be staged in an area convenient to the truck dock.

Accumulation space may contain storage aids such as racks, bins, or shelves. Shipments may be accumulated on pallets, skids, carts, trucks, or in containers. The space might also be occupied with conveyor banks to accumulate orders or merely contain cartons stacked on the floor.

In an operation in which all freight is moved directly into vehicles spotted at the dock, accumulation space is not needed. In this case, the vehicle serves as the accumulation area, and having been filled with freight, is replaced with an empty.

1. *Determine peak accumulation.* The accumulation space should be calculated for the design year. Adequate space must be available for the total shipment accumulation volume for the peak hour of the day. The warehouse is picking orders at a certain rate and loading trucks at certain times. The accumulation space requirement, therefore, must provide storage for the cumulative total of orders picked during the day minus the cumulative total of orders loaded out. By tabulating both of these cumulative volumes by hour, the planner can determine when the peak will occur as well as what the peak volume needing to be stored will be. The peak accumulation for most facilities will generally occur sometime in the early afternoon, just prior to the peak arrival period for carriers.

2. *Calculate space required.* Convert the maximum accumulated volume for the peak into cubic feet. Convenient conversion factors can be established for converting pounds or cases into cubic feet. Finished goods, however, are not accumulated in one solid mass. Additional space must be provided for access and for separation of shipments by carrier. For most conditions, the allowance for additional space is usually about 2½ to 3 times as great as the actual cube of the product. Therefore, multiply the finished goods cubic feet by the storage space utilization factor of 2½ to 3 to obtain total storage cubic feet required.

3. *Prepare block layout.* The next step in planning the shipping accumulation space is determining the number of square feet. The procedure is as follows:

a. Determine the overall stacking height for the shipment to be stored.

b. Divide the total storage cubic feet by the stacking height.

The result will be the storage area in square feet.

Additional space must be provided for access aisles. Depending on the storage aids used, area requirements for aisles will range from 50 percent to 150 percent of the storage area, according to the size of the storage bank, type of equipment used, and whether aisles are used for more than one purpose. In most cases, the allowance for aisles is equivalent to the storage space available. Prepare a typical layout for one bay. Measure storage space and, based on aisle space needed, multiply the storage area in square feet by a factor of 1.5 to 2.5. The total square feet should provide adequate space for shipment accumulation. Draw a layout of the configuration of the area, giving the required number of square feet, and arrange the storage blocks on the layout as they actually will be. If adjustments must be made in space allowances, make them at this time.

DOCK DESIGN AND SPECIFICATIONS

The third major element in planning the shipping facility is to see that docks are the proper height for loading and unloading vehicles, that people and freight are protected from weather, and that adequate space is allowed for access and parking. Once again, plan for the design year and allow for expansion.

1. *Determine vehicle parking requirements.* Estimate the following for the design year:
Company or contract carrier vehicles

a. If company trucks or contract carrier vehicles are used for distribution, determine the maximum total number and type of vehicles on site. This maximum number will generally occur on a weekend or over a holiday.

b. Multiply the number of each type vehicle —such as 40-ft trailer, 18-ft straight truck, tractor with 40-ft trailer—by the square foot allowance for each different length of vehicle. Parking space for a vehicle should be 12 ft wide, and the length of the space should be the overall length of the vehicle plus 20 percent.

Parking space per vehicle, sq ft
$$= (\text{overall length, ft} \times 1.2) \times 12 \text{ ft}$$

c. Add total space requirement for all vehicles.

d. Subtract space for number of vehicles to be spotted at the dock.

e. Calculate truck apron area, employee parking area, and service road area. Total area for combined facilities.
Common carrier vehicles

a. Estimate the maximum number and size of vehicles which could be waiting for a door position, and provide space for these vehicles.

b. Keep apron and dock approach area clear to permit rapid removal and spotting of vehicles at the dock.

2. Provide adequate maneuvering space. The length of a vehicle's parking space or dock approach is the greatest length for the tractor-trailer combination (stall length) and the apron length necessary to maneuver the vehicle in and out of the parking spot. The apron is measured from the outermost part of the longest vehicle to be accommodated or from the outermost part of any obstruction, such as a post or part of a building structure in front of the dock. As a general rule, the dock approach should be at least twice the length of the longest tractor-trailer combination.

The width for each new parking spot or stall should be 12 ft to accommodate the longer and wider tractor-trailer combinations. This width can be used for outside parking or parking in an enclosed dock area. Use Table 2 as a guide.

TABLE 2 Minimal Parking Space or Dock Approach Length and Width (Width—12 ft)

Overall length of tractor-trailer, feet	Apron length, feet	Dock approach length, feet
40	43	83
45	49	94
50	57	107
55	62	117
60	69	129

3. *Plan for good traffic flow.* When preparing the plot plan, include:

a. *Vehicle movement on site.* Vehicles should circulate in a counterclockwise direction. Making left-hand turns with large vehicles enables the driver to see more easily the tail end of the vehicle.

b. *Service roads.* For two-direction traffic, roads should be 23 ft wide. This will allow for a 3-ft clearance between passing 8½-ft-wide vehicles with a 1½-ft side clearance. For one-way roads, the minimum straightaway width should be 12 ft.

c. *Roadway approaches and intersections.* Gates and approaches to roadways should be at least 30 ft wide for two-direction traffic and at least 20 ft wide for one-way traffic. For a right-angle roadway intersection, a minimum radius of 50 ft will be satisfactory for most vehicles. However, if the road is wider than 20 ft, the minimum radius may be decreased to 35 ft.

d. *Pedestrian lanes.* These should be located adjacent to a service road, but separated from the roadway by a physical barrier. The width of the lane can range from 4 to 6 ft, depending on the volume of pedestrian traffic.

4. *Provide proper dock height.* Truck-trailers and pickup and delivery vehicles are not built to any specific bed height; therefore, docks for vehicles at plants and distribution centers cannot be constructed to one specific height. For most trailers designed to handle dry merchandise, the vehicle bed height will vary between 48 and 52 in. For some high-cube trailers with smaller wheels, the bed height will be less than 48 in. Truck chassis with a "reefer" body will increase the bed height up to 6 in. Pickup and delivery vehicle bed heights will vary between 44 and 50 in. Vehicles with capacity loads can compress springs and change the bed height. A single-axle trailer bed height can change as much as 6 to 8 in.

To provide the best dock height for a facility, a survey should be made of the type of equipment used to determine the bed height of vehicles servicing the plant or distribution center. Different heights may be provided if all straight trucks arrive at one dock location and all trailers arrive at another. In general, selecting a dock height lower—rather than higher—will enable the driver to open or close vehicle doors while the truck is at the dock.

5. *Avoid pits and ramps.* If at all possible, grade the approach and apron area for the proper dock height and keep equipment near level. If loading pits and ramps cannot be avoided, use the following guidelines:

a. If a ramp is needed, grade the approach to the dock so that the truck or trailer is nearly level. Equipment parked at a steep angle is unsafe to load and unload. If the front end of the truck or trailer is elevated too much, the truck roof may strike the building when backing in.

b. Although most loaded trucks are designed to pull a 15 percent grade, the start-up grade for pulling away from a dock is much lower. In addition, dock facilities even if covered cannot be kept dry in wet weather. A 3 percent grade is the maximum allowable for pulling away from a dock.

6. *Specify door height and width.* Almost all shipper-consignee facilities should have truck dock doors to provide security and dock area protection from wind, rain or snow when vehicles are not at the dock. For most installations, a 9-ft door width is recommended for vehicles not perfectly spotted. Trailer widths may increase in the future to 102 inches. Door widths greater than 9 ft will cause excessive loss of heat or refrigeration; doors less than 9 ft wide will require extra maneuvering of vehicles for spotting at the dock.

To determine door heights, subtract the dock height from 14 ft. In most cases the door height will range from 9 ft 8 in. to 10 ft. This height will accommodate up to 13-ft 6-in.-high trailers. If only straight trucks deliver and pick up freight at the dock, the height of the door will range between 8 ft and 9 ft 4 in.

7. *Install permanent, self-leveling dockboards.* Installation of dock levelers enables faster turnaround of trucks and contributes to increased dock productivity. Permanently installed boards are safer to use than portable boards. The one exception to the use of dockboards would be for facilities exclusively utilizing conveyors to transport freight out of or into vehicles.

The dockboard specification will depend on the following factors:

a. Greatest height difference between the dock and bed of trucks or trailers serviced

b. Type of materials handling equipment used

c. Type of loads handled into and out of vehicles

d. Type of vehicle road equipment picking up or delivering freight

After determining the maximum height difference from dock level, the length of the dockboard can be calculated by using the allowable percentage grade for the type of handling equipment used. Allowable grades are shown in Table 3.

TABLE 3 Percent of Grade for Material Handling Equipment

Type of equipment	Allowable percent of grade*
Powered handtrucks	3
Powered platform trucks	7
Low-lift pallet or skid trucks	10
Electric fork trucks	10
Gas fork trucks	15

* Contact manufacturer and check manufacturer's specifications before operating beyond allowable percent of grade.

Most standard truck dockboard lengths range from 6 to 10 ft. For most applications, dockboards should be 6 ft wide. Use 7-ft wide dockboard for loading or unloading unit loads with fork truck.

8. *Provide area for access to trucks.* A minimum area measured inside the plant from the edge of the dock should be kept clear and unobstructed for the movement of freight and materials handling equipment. The depth of the area must allow for maneuverability of materials handling equipment in and out of vehicles and for two-way cross traffic behind the dock. If dockboards are used, provide a minimum

Transportation
TRUCK TERMINALS

depth of 12 ft behind the inside edge of the board. If dockboards are not used, allow 15 ft from the dock edge. If conveyors are used to load and unload all freight, the requirement for a clear distance behind the dock edge will not apply.

9. *Provide for weather protection.* An alternative to a fully enclosed dock is the installation of dock shelters and canopies completely enclosing the space between the building and the rear of the vehicle. Dock shelters provide a closure between the truck and dock doors. Canopies provide a roof over the dock and should be extended over the dock's entire distance. In order to reduce the effects of wind, rain and snow, the installation of canopies should also include side panel walls extending from the building at each end of the dock area.

Most shelters are designed to accommodate vehicles ranging from 10 ft to 13 ft 6 in. high. Dock shelters should be considered for plants and distribution centers which have the following characteristics:

a. Plant site is located in cold, windy or wet climate.

b. A large concentration of people work in the area and the adjacent dock area.

c. Female employees, performing stationary tasks, are located near the dock area.

d. Long loading and unloading time intervals occur at the dock.

e. There is a limited range of vehicle sizes picking up and delivering freight.

Canopies should extend a minimum of 8 ft out from the building to provide adequate protection over the rear end of parked vehicles at the dock. For level driveways, the outside edge of the canopy should be no less than 15 ft high to accommodate 13-ft 6-in. trailers. If the height of all vehicles using the dock is less than 13 ft 6 in., locate the canopy 1½ ft higher than the highest vehicle.

10. *Evaluate fully enclosed dock.* The initial cost of constructing a completely enclosed dock facility, compared with an outside dock facility, may be justified if:

a. Maximum security is needed.

b. Plant site is located in cold, windy or wet climate.

c. Vehicles are dropped for overnight loading.

d. High value merchandise is handled.

e. Merchandise handled is sensitive to temperature and water.

f. A large concentration of people work in the area and the adjacent dock area.

If a dock is completely enclosed in a building, the width of each dock position should be a minimum of 12 ft wide. The overall clear height in the vehicle docking area should be a minimum of 1½ ft higher than the highest vehicle or legal height. For most installations, this will be a 15-ft overall clear height.

The back-in type enclosure is the most common type of completely enclosed dock facility. For this enclosure, each vehicle dock position has its own doorway for direct access to the outside as shown in Fig. 1. The distance from the leading edge of the dock to the inside of the doorway where the vehicle backs in should exceed the maximum length of the vehicles using the facility or the maximum legal length of the vehicle combination by at least 5 ft. For most installations receiving tractor-trailers, an overall length of 65 ft will meet this requirement.

DOCKING FACILITIES

The primary consideration in planning modern loading and unloading facilities for motor transport equipment is to provide adequate space for efficient maneuvering into and out of loading position at properly constructed docks. No one plan will fit all requirements, but careful study of present needs and future possibilities will determine the type and size of facilities essential to efficient operation.

There is, of course, no set of standard dimensions covering the space required for maneuvering the many possible combinations of tractor-trucks and semitrailers into and out of loading position at docks or in stalls and driveways. However, the maneuvering space required is largely dependent on three factors: (1) overall length of the tractor-trailer unit; (2) the width of the position in which the vehicle must be placed; and (3) the turning radius of the tractor-truck which pulls the unit. Inasmuch as a tractor-trailer uses slightly more space to pull out than to back in, all reference to maneuvering apron space is based on the requirements for pulling out.

Length of Tractor-Trailer Unit

The length of tractor-trailer units to be accommodated will vary in accordance with state laws and differing types of operation. Analysis of the specific problem will determine the largest vehicle to be considered. For the purposes of this discussion tractor-trailer units of 35, 40 and 45 ft are considered to be the most prevalent overall lengths. If an appreciable volume of traffic is handled by "for hire" motor transport, it may be expected that the unit length to be accommodated will approximate the legal limit in the state concerned, usually between 45 and 50 ft. It is obvious that commercial haulers will use the maximum size tractor-trailer practical for efficient operation within state limitations. In general, it may be assumed that straight trucks can be accommodated in the space required for tractor-trailer units inasmuch as it has been impractical to build trucks even approaching the length and cubic capacity of modern trailers. In some states trains of more than one trailer are permitted. Such equipment is not being considered as it is assumed that each trailer in a train would be spotted separately.

Width of Position

The maximum allowable width of a truck or trailer is 8 ft and it may be assumed that virtually all units (other than those for light city delivery) are built to take full advantage of this dimension.

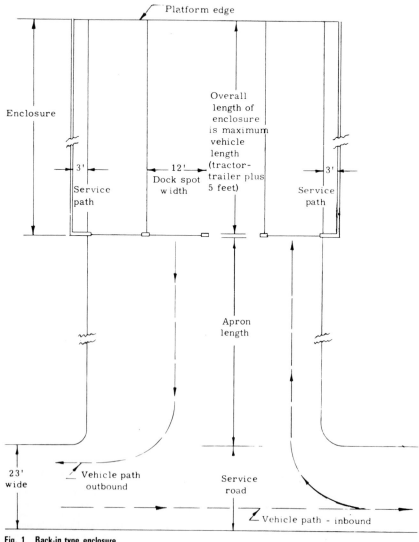

Fig. 1 Back-in type enclosure.

1120

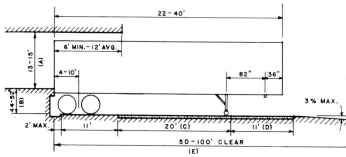

NOTES:
(A) Should be at least 6 in. over legal height for level area, more for slope.
(B) Dock height, 48 to 52 in. for road trailers, 44 in. for city trucks.
(C) Concrete apron of the dimensions shown will accommodate trailers from 22 to 40 ft long.
(D) Additional slab length recommended to support tractor wheels.
(E) General rule for distance required: total length of tractor-trailer times 2.
Trailer width—8 ft
Trailer stall width—10 ft minimum, 12 ft recommended.

Fig. 2   Recommended dimensions and clearances for truck loading docks.

The consensus among transport and traffic men interviewed is that 12 ft is a very desirable width for stalls or truck positions. Slightly narrower position widths can be utilized when necessary but should be avoided in order to reduce the possibility of damage to equipment and loss of time for jockeying into position. Also, as position width increases, the apron space required for maneuvering will decrease.

Trailer Dimensions   Average dimensions of large trailers are shown in Fig. 2, along with recommended dimensions and clearances for dock structures.

Turning Radii of Tractor-Trucks

The turning radii of tractor-trucks have a definite bearing on the apron space required for maneuvering equipment. However, because of the variation in this dimension among trucks of different types, capacities and makes, a high average turning radius has been used in arriving at recommendations regarding space requirements.

The requirements of heavy-duty units with extremely long turning radii call for special consideration. If such equipment is a factor in any operation, a special study should be made to determine the space required. Units utilizing cab-over-engine truck-tractors have somewhat shorter turning radii for the same lengths and consequently require less apron space than units with conventional tractors. Many of these tractor-trucks are in use, but few shippers can count on their exclusive use.

Apron Space Required

The apron space required to maneuver tractor-trailer units into or out of loading position in one maneuver has been worked out in practical tests with standard equipment handled by experienced drivers. Inasmuch as a high average turning radius has been arbitrarily used to provide a margin for differences in equipment, the variable factors were overall length and position width. *The apron space required is measured out from the outermost part of any vehicle or other possible obstruction in the area of the maneuver* (Fig. 4).

In the case of a single-position unobstructed dock (Fig. 4a), the distance would be measured straight out from the dock. However, if a canopy or roof, supported by posts (Fig. 4b) should be present to protect the loading area, the distance would be measured out from the posts. If it is necessary to spot a trailer alongside another vehicle (Fig. 4c), the distance would be measured from the outermost point of the vehicle obstructing the maneuver. When a stall or driveway is involved (Fig. 4d), the distance would be measured from the outermost obstruction, such as a curb, pole, or vehicle, etc.

It is highly recommended that at least the minimum apron space be allowed and that it be kept clear for the approach and maneuvering of transport units.

In locations where the proper space is not available for parking in one maneuver, trailers can be jockeyed into position. This, however, is a time-wasting, costly, and unsatisfactory process for both commercial and private transport operators.

Overhead Clearance

Standard trailers vary in height up to $12\frac{1}{2}$ ft. Consequently, it is recommended that 14-ft clearance be provided at docks or in yards, driveways, doors, stalls and interior roadways. Special transportation conditions such as delivery of large machinery may require greater clearance.

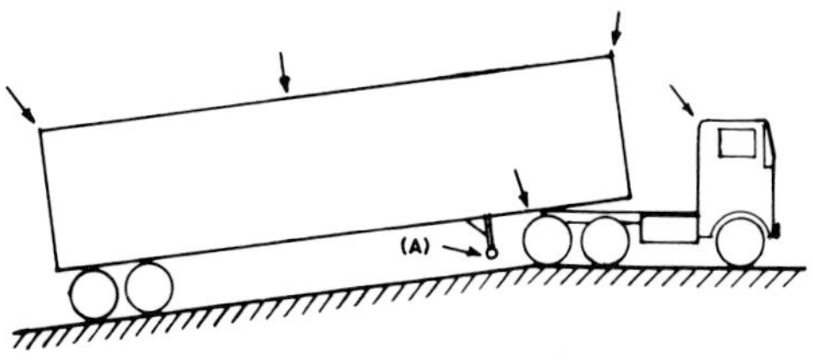

When designing for ramps, dips, or crowns in the terminal area, special care must be taken to provide clearance at the points indicated in the diagram. Actual dimensions must be obtained. Cab clearances are more critical when the combination is jackknifed. Landing gear height (A) may be as low as 10 in.

Fig. 3   Critical points for clearance.

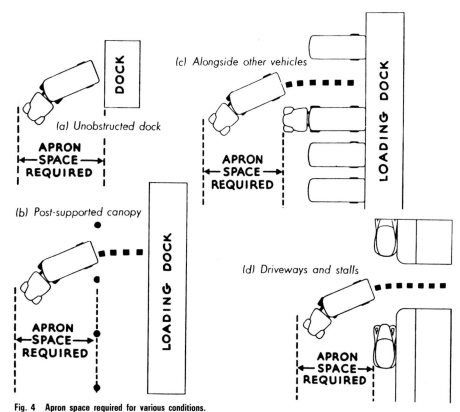

Fig. 4   Apron space required for various conditions.

Transportation
TRUCK TERMINALS

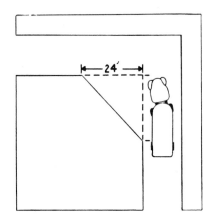

Fig. 5 Turning clearance for driveway.

Drainage

Roofs or canopies over loading docks should be constructed so as to avoid drainage into the loading area. This precaution will reduce the hazards of mud and ice and the resulting loss of traction. It is particularly important to prevent ice formation on the pavement where tractor and trailer are coupled.

Traffic Congestion

So far as possible, loading areas and approaches should be free from general traffic and obstructions. Railroad crossings, automobile traffic, parked vehicles, and material carelessly stored outside all contribute to delays in pick-up and delivery. If a right-angle turn must be negotiated in a narrow driveway, extra clear space should be provided on the inside of the turn to eliminate maneuvering.

For instance, in a driveway 12 to 14 ft wide, the triangular area, formed by the inside corner of the turn and the two points 24 ft on each side of the corner, should be left clear. This will allow proper clearance for the turning radius of the tractor-truck and the cut-in of trailer wheels.

Turning Clearance (see Fig. 5)

Site

Location: In selecting a site, consider the following factors:
1. Proximity to pickups, deliveries, and connecting carriers
2. Accessibility to main traffic arteries
3. Obstructions such as bridges, underpasses, and railroad crossings
4. Zoning
5. Urban and regional plans; future growth pattern of city
6. Transportation facilities for employees
7. Utilities

Grade: Site should be approximately level: maximum slope 3 percent; minimum slope for drainage, 1 percent. Storm drains recommended 60 to 75 ft on centers, 100 ft maximum.

Pavement: 6-in. concrete slab reinforced with 6 by 6 in. No. 8 gauge welded wire mesh; expansion joints 30 ft on centers.

Fence: 2-in. wire mesh No. 9 gauge, 7 ft high including several strands of barbed wire at the top. Protect the fence from damage by trucks by placing bumpers or 2-ft-high earth curbs 5 to 15 ft from the fence, depending upon the type of truck using the yard. In car parking areas place bumpers at least 3 ft from the fence.

Dock Building

Orientation: If possible, place the long dimension of the building parallel to the prevailing storm winds.

Column spacing: Depends upon stall width. Recommended stall width 12 ft, column spacing 24 ft.

Width of building varies from 45 to 70 ft, depending upon the type of operation: usual figure is 60 ft.

Height: Minimum clear interior height, 12 ft.

Roof overhang or canopy projection—3 ft minimum, no maximum (the longer the better); usual figure, 12 ft.

End walls: May be extended a similar distance for better weather protection.

Doors: Overhead type, 8 to 10 ft wide by 8 to 9 ft 4 in. high; the larger sizes are more usual.

Floor: Reinforced concrete designed for a live load of 150 to 250 psf; nonslip finish (float or abrasive).

Bumpers: Wood usual; steel or rubber may be used.

Steps: Iron bar rungs set in concrete dock front are less expensive than stairs; provide one set of steps per four stalls.

Light: 15 footcandles recommended; skylights optional. Floodlights arranged to shine into truck or trailer bodies are required, also floodlights for the general yard area.

Heat: Required in northern areas; suspended unit heaters or radiant heat in floor slab may be used.

Ventilation: Mechanical ventilation required if fork-lift trucks are used.

Sprinklers: Recommended for entire dock area.

(See Figs. 6 and 7.)

Offices

The office facilities may include any or all of the following:

General office
Message center
Billing office
Cashier
Telephone room
Foreman's office
Office manager
Terminal manager
Operations manager
Salesmen's room
Record room
Heater room
Central checking
Drivers' locker room
Transportation department
Dormitory
Cafeteria
Drivers' ready room

Other Facilities

Maintenance shop
Fueling area (near shop)
Weighing area
Truck and trailer parking area (two parking spaces per dock stall recommended)
Employee and visitor parking area

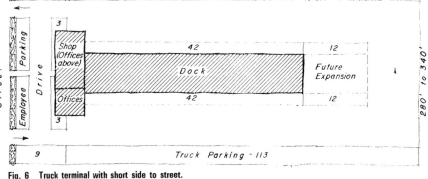

Fig. 6 Truck terminal with short side to street.

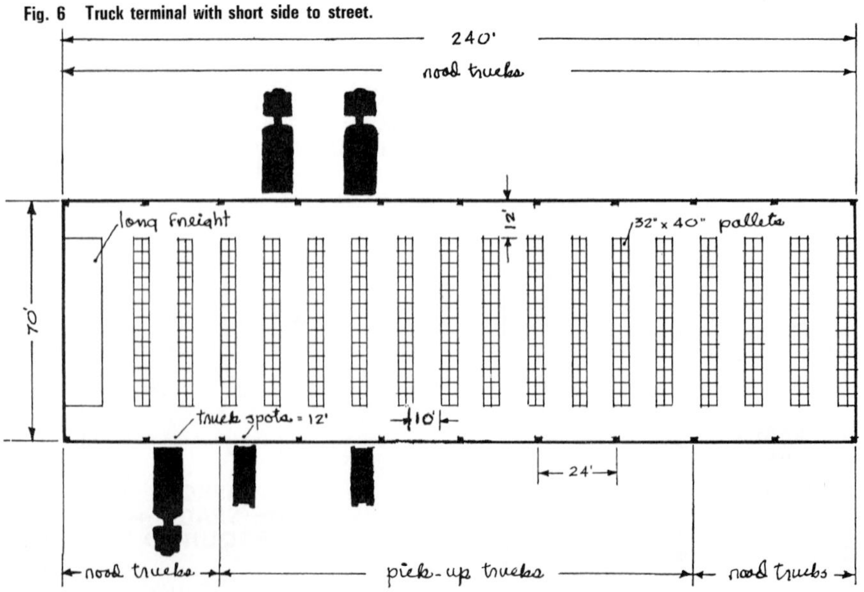

Fig. 7 Truck terminal dock plan for fork-lift truck and pallet storage.

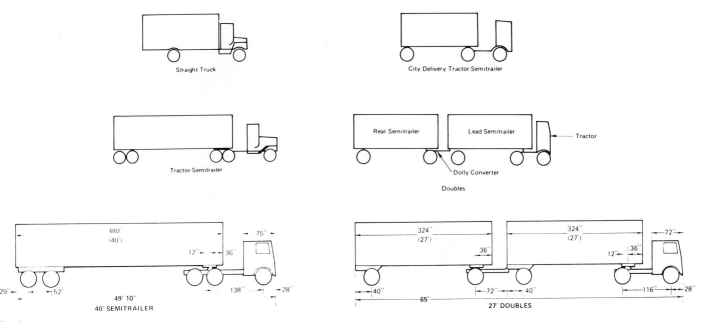

Straight Truck

City Delivery Tractor-Semitrailer

Tractor Semitrailer

Rear Semitrailer / Lead Semitrailer / Tractor / Dolly Converter

Doubles

40' SEMITRAILER

27' DOUBLES

Fig. 8

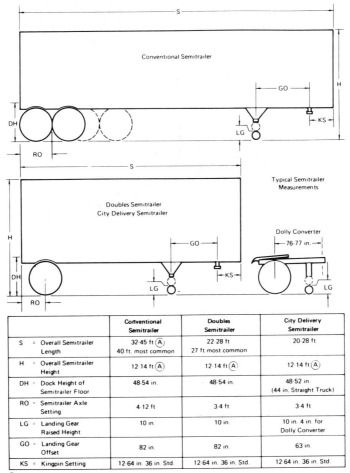

Conventional Semitrailer

Typical Semitrailer Measurements

Doubles Semitrailer
City Delivery Semitrailer

Dolly Converter 76-77 in.

		Conventional Semitrailer	Doubles Semitrailer	City Delivery Semitrailer
S =	Overall Semitrailer Length	32-45 ft (A) 40 ft. most common	22-28 ft 27 ft most common	20-28 ft
H =	Overall Semitrailer Height	12-14 ft (A)	12-14 ft (A)	12-14 ft (A)
DH =	Dock Height of Semitrailer Floor	48-54 in.	48-54 in.	48-52 in. (44 in. Straight Truck)
RO =	Semitrailer Axle Setting	4-12 ft	3-4 ft	3-4 ft
LG =	Landing Gear Raised Height	10 in.	10 in.	10 in. 4 in. for Dolly Converter
GO =	Landing Gear Offset	82 in.	82 in.	63 in.
KS =	Kingpin Setting	12-64 in. 36 in. Std.	12-64 in. 36 in. Std.	12-64 in. 36 in. Std.

(A) = Regulated by state law for various states & regions
Dimensions for empty semitrailers

Fig. 9

"How Big Is a Truck—How Sharp Does It Turn," The Operations Council of American Trucking Association, Inc., Washington, D.C., 1974.

Transportation

TRUCK TERMINALS
Truck Types and Dimensions

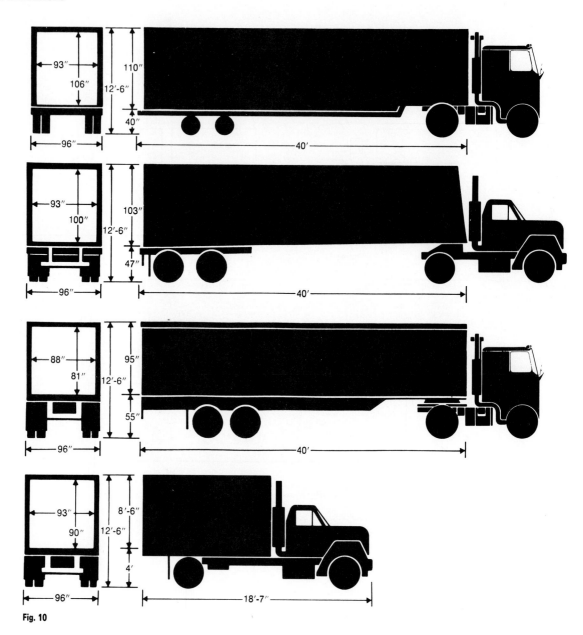

Fig. 10

1124

DESIGN

Approach Gates and Service Roads

Getting trucks to and from the dock is as important as the dock itself. Your responsibility begins when the vehicle reaches the boundary line of the property. However, before laying out the road or approach estimate the amount of car, truck, and pedestrian traffic which will be using the road or roads.

Approaches

Whatever road or gate configuration you settle upon your primary consideration is to get the trucks off the public highway quickly with a minimum of maneuvering. If at all possible, the trucks should drive into your plant, not back in. This is especially true if your plant abuts a boulevard or a one-way street. Here the driver must make a blind righthand back, which usually results in blocked traffic in both lanes. If your property abuts a narrow street you must reduce the angle of access and exit to permit up to 65' long tractor trailers (70' to 75' in Nevada and Wyoming) to turn into and off the street. This can be done with a "Y" or angle approach (Fig. 11) or a recessed approach (65' minimum, 130' optimum) to accommodate two vehicles as in Fig. 12.

If your estimates establish a high volume of truck, car, and pedestrian traffic, the best solution is to establish a "private" passenger car and pedestrian road, under the truck road where the two cross. This is a logical solution when it is realized that truck traffic may continue for a full eight hours, while pedestrian and passenger traffic is a twice-a-day, short time movement.

Recommended Standards

A. Gate and Approach Roadways. Recommended minimum width at gates are 16' for 1-way, 28' for 2-way, 32' if pedestrian traffic is involved (Fig. 13).

B. Service Roads, over which 10' wide vehicles must operate in two directions (rear view mirrors add approximately 2' to over-all vehicle width), should be no less than 24' wide to permit 2' clearance between passing vehicles with a 2' side clearance (Fig. 14).

C. One-Way Service Roads should be a minimum of 12' wide.

D. Mixed Traffic Service Roads also used by pedestrians should be a minimum of 28' wide and have 4' pedestrian lane separated from the roadway by a physical barrier.

E. Right-Angle Roadway Intersection. A 50' radius is considered a desirable minimum for most commercial vehicles. A 35' radius is satisfactory when intersecting a road 20' or more in width.

F. Traffic Circulation. Ideally, traffic should circulate counterclockwise since it is easier for drivers to make left-hand turns with large vehicles. Also, it is easier to back a trailer into the dock from a counterclockwise position.

G. Traffic Control. Speed limit regulations should be posted. Strict parking prohibitions should be maintained at points of minimum width. Proper installation of wide angle mirrors at blind corners will substantially reduce hazards.

H. Roadway Surfaces should be evenly laid and structurally sound for heavy wheel loads (40,000 lbs. on tandem axles is legal in some states). All roadways should be slightly crowned and properly equipped with drainage outlets. Scheduled, periodic maintenance is of prime importance, since ruts and pot holes can easily cause damage to merchandise as well as trucks.

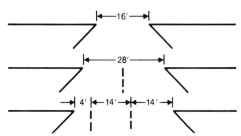

Fig. 11

Fig. 12

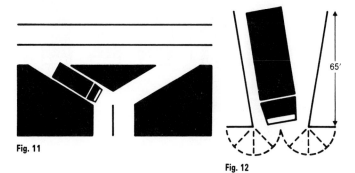

Fig. 13

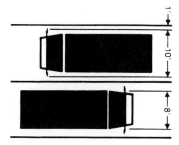

Fig. 14

TRUCK TERMINALS
Docks

Waiting Area

Unless you design your facility to accommodate peak loads, you must make provisions for a truck "waiting area." It should be adjacent to the dock approach, and large enough to accommodate as many trucks as you feel will arrive before dock positions are available. It doesn't matter how long they are to be held. Even if the wait is only five minutes, you must provide a "waiting area." The area must be designed and placed so trucks in the area will not interfere with trucks maneuvering into or pulling away from the docks.

The Maneuvering Area

In planning new or remodeling existing docks,

consideration should be given to changes in carrier size. Today all states allow over-all tractor-trailer dimensions of 55′ in length. Four years ago the average length was 50′. Some states now permit 70′ and even 75′ length combinations. Predictions are that 65′, with 70′ quite common, could be the average within the next five to ten years. If you cannot restrict the size of the trucks to be serviced, your layout should anticipate maximum size units. The length of the waiting and maneuvering area is determined by the traffic flow. If traffic flow is counterclockwise (solid arrows in Fig. 15) the maneuvering room must extend a minimum of 55′ beyond the loading area. If traffic flow is clockwise (outline arrows in Fig. 15) the maneuvering area must extend at least 115′ beyond the loading area. The figures assume a 65′

loading area and 65′ tractor-trailer combination. Longer or shorter trucks will need proportionately more or less room. Width of berths have little bearing on the maneuvering area needed.

The Loading Area

The loading area directly in front of the dock should extend a minimum of 65′ forward from the dock face and extend at least 3′ on either side of the dock itself. If the loading area is asphalted, a "landing strip" of concrete should be laid parallel to the dock to support small steel wheel landing gear. This strip should be as long as the dock and 6′ wide and cover an area from 26′ to 32′ from the face of the dock.

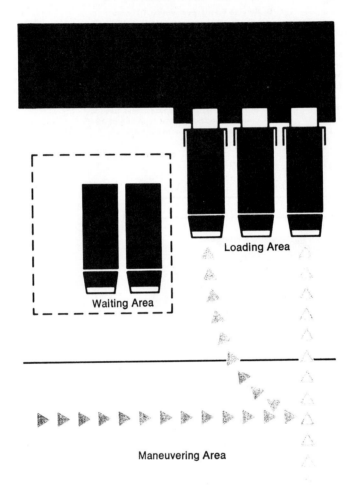

Fig. 15

PLACEMENT OF THE DOCK

It is a common practice to lump both shipping and receiving at one end or area of a plant or, in a flow-through single story plant, to put shipping at one end and receiving at the other. However, with today's sophisticated communications, truck berths might easily be placed at several points around the structure. Strategic placement would allow material to flow directly between the carrier and the proper department. Its only disadvantage is that it creates additional problems of vehicle check-in, control of berth assignment, and allocation of supervision. The savings in delivering goods directly to the proper department or area makes this design approach well worth pursuing, particularly as a means of simplifying in-plant flow of goods and processes.

Width of Berths

Regardless of other considerations, width of truck berths should not be less than 12'. If space and budget permit, 14' should be seriously considered. Often the increased width of berths permits use of space between berths for storage or staging and their convenience can quickly be offset by the additional cost of the extra width.

Scrimping on the width of the berth, even on an open dock or where there are no other considerations, will result in sprung doors, scratched equipment and lost time in maneuvering.

TYPES OF DOCKS

Flush Docks

Most modern docks fall into the flush dock category. In this construction the outside wall of the building is flush with the face of the dock. Its main advantage is that both the dock and the building wall utilize a common foundation wall. The flush design completely encloses the dock area, provides an ideal support for dock seals and canopies; virtually making the dock a part of the facility. It also prevents vandalism or pilferage of dock lights, skids, dockboards, portable plates, etc., plus permits easy heating or cooling of the entire dock (Fig. 16).

On the minus side, this design limits the length and slope of a depressed approach (see Fig. 20) and might necessitate the construction of a second interior wall and its doorways and doors. This construction also makes the installation of overhead doors, with locks, necessary for each truck berth. Most important, with this type of construction, subsequent changing or remodeling is apt to be difficult and costly.

Fig. 16

Enclosed Docks

There are two types of enclosed design: the totally enclosed and the straight-in-straight-out type. Both offer substantial advantages over any other type design.

Totally Enclosed

Although not commonly used because of high initial and maintenance cost, the totally enclosed dock and apron must be perceived as the present ultimate in design. Here (Fig. 17), two doors control all traffic, and "dispatch" trucks to the proper berth with minimum loss of time. Main advantages of this type design is total independence of outside environment, better control of pilferage, maximum dock attendant efficiency and comfort, total product and package protection, and easy installation of overhead handling capacity to load and unload open tops and flat beds. This design is also recommended for plants and warehouses where the product is subject to direct consumer pick-up in a wide variety of trucks.

The design creates two problems for the designer. He must reduce the time from the entry of the truck, until its engine is shut off to a minimum. He must also provide for adequate air-exchange.

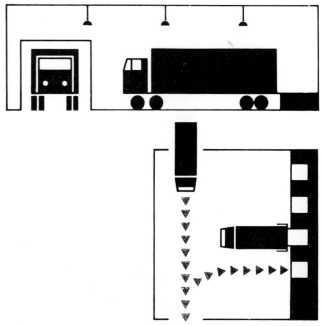

Fig. 17

TRUCK TERMINALS
Docks

Straight-In Design

Requires minimum enclosed space (Fig. 18); requires trucks to back in and drive straight out; requires more maneuvering area outside the doors than on flush docks. Generally speaking this type of design provides a double width overhead door, not less than 15' high, for each of two truck positions. Each berth should be a minimum of 12' wide with the end berths 14' for easier, safer maneuvering.

The interior floor of the enclosure must be sloped and provided with drains to catch run off or melting snow, etc. Since fumes will accumulate inside the enclosure it is good practice to equip the enclosure with some sort of exhaust system near the front end. An alternative would be an automatic fan system blowing out toward the doors.

Open Docks

Today's society with its rising crime rate, perpetuated by both professional and amateur, has virtually made open docks obsolete (Fig. 19). However in those rare instances where a combination of circumstances permits their consideration the following standards and recommendations apply.

The design should provide sufficient width to accommodate two-way cross-dock traffic. This width can easily be determined by multiplying by four the width of the material being handled. To that number add the length of the dockboard being recommended. If dockboards are being considered on both sides of the dock then add the length of both. If temporary storage space is desired and the space between truck positions or the dockboards is deemed insufficient, then space must be added to the width or length.

Considering the cost of construction, open dock widths of more than 22' are generally not practical, since in all cases they must be provided with a canopy. The canopy should extend a minimum of 3' over the edge of the dock, with 8' the ideal. Open docks cannot be heated or cooled, and provide minimum protection for goods and workers. High intensity lighting, safety surfaces, edge markings and floor drainage must also be provided.

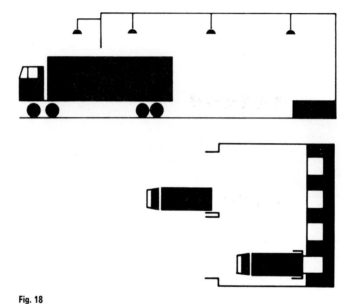

Fig. 18

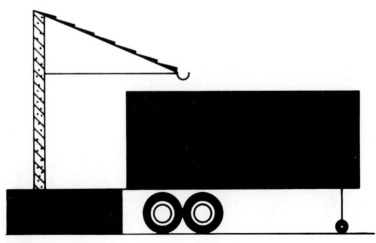

Fig. 19

1128

Depressed Driveway Approach

Modern warehouse and industrial construction often eliminates basements and dock-level buildings. Artificial dock heights can be created by depressing the driveway, without penalizing the efficiency of the dock operation. However, potential problems must be considered before construction.

Grades should never exceed 10%. Grades approaching 10% in areas where ice and snow are encountered may reduce traction to the extent loaded trucks will not be able to pull away from the dock. Provisions must be made for heating the driveways either by electrical cable or hot water pipes embedded in the concrete.

If the truck rests on a severe incline it creates three problems:

1. Loads may topple out.
2. Loading and unloading is difficult.

3. Additional burdens are placed on material handling equipment.

A depressed driveway may cause truck tops to hit the building wall. If the building wall is essentially flush with dock face, the top of the truck will strike the building before the bed of the truck contacts the bumpers (see Fig. 21).

The solution, of course, is to extend the dock face, recess the building wall or change the slope of the driveway. One of the best solutions, first proposed by one of America's leading material handling consultants, is the use of a 4' to 10' level area directly ahead of the dock, before beginning the slope (see Fig. 20).

This design approach lessens the incline angle of the truck when in position, permits easier loading and unloading and lessens the danger of goods toppling out. It, however, requires additional maneuvering area and/or a steeper incline.

So that all situations can be correctly anticipated, a detailed elevation of the dock area should be made.

Saw Tooth

Where edge of dock to street or nearest obstruction distances are less than the length of the truck to be serviced, the saw tooth design permits an effective dock operation (Fig. 22). As can be seen in the diagram, the angle cut-out reduces building and/or dock space. Angles less than 45° use twice as much per position as a 90° dock. Further, space between the positions, because of its pie-shape, is virtually useless and must also be considered as part of the penalty. All other design factors remain the same, except traffic routes must be drawn so vehicles depart with the angle of the dock and approach from the opposite side and back in with the angle of the dock.

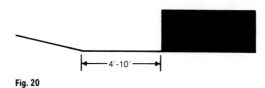

Fig. 20

Fig. 21

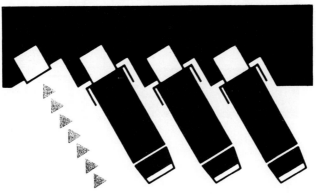

Fig. 22

TRUCK TERMINALS

Docks

Canopies

With a flush dock, a 6' to 8' wide canopy over the loading dock is recommended. However, if an open dock is contemplated, then the dock or open platforms must be protected with a canopy. A canopy can afford reasonable protection with least investment. (See Fig. 23 and Fig. 19.) The canopy should at least cover the platform. If pos-

sible extend the canopy 6' to 8' beyond the edge of the platform, particularly in areas where snow and rain are accompanied by wind.

Use of translucent material is recommended since it greatly reduces subsequent lighting problems. The canopy should be equipped with rain gutters; or sloped toward the building or center, to prevent run-off on trucks and trailers.

The leading edge of the canopy must be a mini-

mum of 15' high. However, if a movable header type dock shelter is contemplated the height of the rear of the canopy must be sufficient to accommodate the up-movement of the header.

In most situations it is best to slope the canopy away from the building and provide gutters at the leading edge. In all cases a comprehensive layout should be made to determine the lowest safe canopy height.

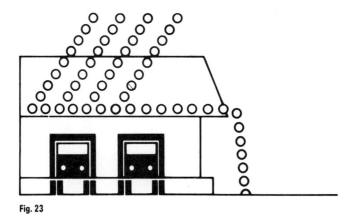

Fig. 23

Typical Flush Dock Layout

The actual dock height should be determined by the type of truck most commonly served. The other dimensions however, represent accepted practical standards.

Note the ½-inch slope from the dock face to the drain, and the wall recessed 12 inches to prevent damage from trucks backing down the incline.

Ideally a level section of drive should be provided in front of the dock, but in some cases this may result in an unacceptable increase in the approach incline.

Loading bays are spaced on 12-foot centers, and doors are 9 feet high by 9 feet wide. This height is considered a minimum. The 9-foot width offers easy fork truck maneuvering for handling

side by side pallet loads, but it also presents difficulties when dock seals are to be installed. In such cases, 8 feet is usually the maximum allowable opening.

The dockleveler positions shown are for units 6-feet wide by 8-feet long. The proper size and model will vary with operational needs.

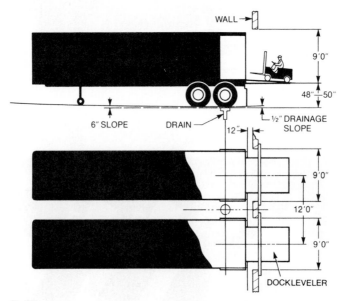

Fig. 24

1130

Most industrial truck docks are constructed 48″ high. However, many types of truck beds are considerably higher or lower than that.

For example, if your docks will serve high cube vans, plan for bed heights of 36″ to 42″. On the other hand, refrigerated trucks can range from 52″ to 56″. Drop frame trailers and furniture vans are usually 36″ high or less. The accompanying chart shows typical dimensions for a variety of truck types.

Servicing Special Trucks

Docks may occasionally serve special vehicles that vary significantly from planned dock height. For these cases, several steps can be taken:

- Portable wheel risers can elevate the rear of low bed trucks.
- Separate docks might be built for varying heights.
- An extra long dockleveler (up to 12′) with additional up-and-down travel (18″ versus 12″) minimizes the grade, allowing flexibility for varying truck heights.
- Truck levelers, installed in the driveway approach, can raise and lower the bed height to the desired level.
- Consider installing one low dock and using a hydraulic dock lift.

TABLE 4 Truck Bed Height

Type of truck	Total range	
	Min.	Max.
Container	56″	62″
Reefer	50″	60″
Dbl. axle semi	46″	56″
Straight semi	48″	52″
City delivery	44″	48″
High cube van	36″	42″
Furniture van	24″	36″
Step van	20″	30″
Panel truck	20″	24″
Stake truck	42″	48″
Flatbeds	48″	60″
Low boys	20″	24″

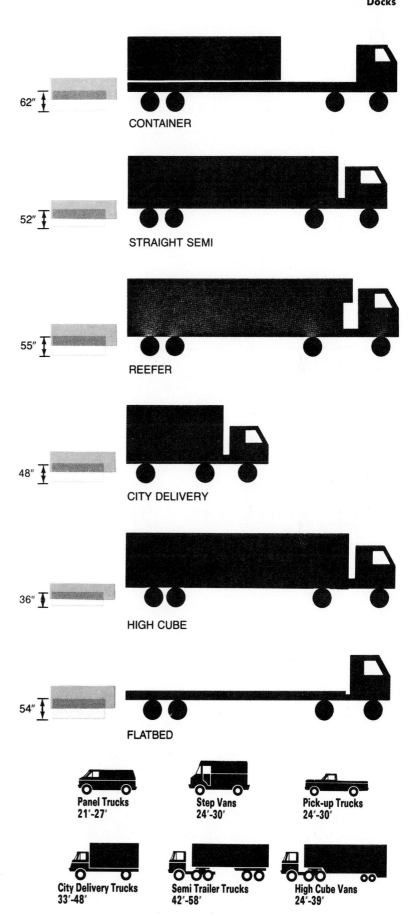

62″ — CONTAINER

52″ — STRAIGHT SEMI

55″ — REEFER

48″ — CITY DELIVERY

36″ — HIGH CUBE

54″ — FLATBED

Panel Trucks 21′-27′

Step Vans 24′-30′

Pick-up Trucks 24′-30′

City Delivery Trucks 33′-48′

Semi Trailer Trucks 42′-58′

High Cube Vans 24′-39′

9

Industrial

INDUSTRIAL PARKS	1135	RESEARCH LABORATORIES	1155
INDUSTRIAL BUILDINGS, GENERAL	1141	WAREHOUSES	1167
INDUSTRIAL PLANTS	1148	WATERFRONT WAREHOUSES	1170
INDUSTRIAL RAILROAD DOCKS	1154	AIRPORT INDUSTRIAL PARK	1174
		INDUSTRIAL PLANTS, PARKING	1178

DESIGN CONSIDERATIONS

Site Planning—Some Physical Design Guidelines

Planning specific building sites in industrial developments requires a number of considerations. These considerations include setback requirements, truck loading and maneuvering depths, vehicular parking needs, building coverage, and rail service requirements.

Building setbacks from the fronting street will vary between setting the building on the property line and therefore having a zero front yard, to a setback of 50 ft or more. If vehicular parking is placed in front of the buildings, and allowed on one side only, 40 to 45 ft should be provided for the driveway and parking stalls. If parking is allowed on both sides of the driveway, 60 to 65 ft should be provided. Side and rear building setbacks usually will be less than front setbacks. They typically range from no setback required to 15 ft. Truck and rail loading needs may control building setbacks along side and rear lot lines.

Truck loading and maneuvering depths from edge of dock to edge of maneuvering area are variable depending upon anticipated traffic. Successful warehousing operation can occur with as little as 85 ft of truck docking and maneuvering depths, whereas the recommended depth for trucking terminals for larger trucks (45-ft trailer length) is as much as 129 ft. (See Fig. 1.)

Vehicular parking needs will depend on building use. Warehousing generally will have fewer occupants which enables auto parking to be accommodated near the front end of the truck loading area. Higher densities will require devoting as much as one side of the building to vehicular parking. Seventy-five feet should be allowed for parking and landscaping if one aisle, and parking stalls on either side, are considered sufficient. The ratio of parking spaces required to building will relate to employee densities and to employee commuting habits. Keeping the area of pavement to the minimum required to accommodate parking needs will have significant effect on storm drainage design. The developer, users, and public agencies will be well advised to design parking standards with this objective in mind and to provide minimum parking with initial site development with provision for additional expansion as empirical studies indicate.[1]

SOURCE: Industrial Development Handbook, ULI—The Urban Land Institute, Washington, D.C., 1975.

[1] *Special Traffic Generator Study—Industrial Generations*, Report no. 2 (Dover, Delaware: State of Delaware, Department of Highways and Transportation, 1973). This report prepared detailed analyses of 22 industrial users, the parking ratios ranged from 0.21 spaces per 1,000 square feet of floor area to 20 spaces per 1,000 square feet of floor area. The firm with the lower ratio manufactured chemical products; the firm with a higher ratio was a clothing manufacturer. Of the 22 industrial firms studied, 11 had ratios of less than one space per 1,000 square feet of floor area; six had ratios of less than two spaces per 1,000 square feet of floor area; and only five had over two spaces per 1,000 square feet of floor space and with the exception of the one with 20 spaces per 1,000 square feet of floor area, all of these were below a four-to-one ratio.

To provide maximum return on investment, building coverage which gives the highest percentage site coverage is generally desired by the developer. However, building coverage may be limited by zoning or by parking needs of the occupants. Building coverage above 50 percent often can be achieved for warehouses whereas offices and light manufacturing, with their sizable parking needs, may be in the 30 percent range of building coverage.

Rail service requires about 15 ft from the centerline of the spur track to the rear property line when the drill or lead track is centered on the property line. If, however, the rail drill track is in its own right of way, then inside building rail service is most economical of land and improvement costs if the building can be constructed to the property line. An allowance of 150 feet should be made for bringing the rail from the lead track to a point parallel with the building. This is important in planning the distance from the building to the side property line because rail spur geometrics will require an easement on the property next door if the building must be set near the side property line.

Building dimensions are variable; however, most structures fall within the square to two-to-one ratios of length to width.

Platting Techniques

A primary objective in preparing a preliminary plan for industrial development is to provide maximum flexibility. Because the needs of prospective users cannot be known in advance, the layout of streets and rail leads must be done to create a plan which provides lots of various depths. Lots 200 to 300 ft in depth are popular. Large lots

may range from 500 to 700 ft in depth. Establishing lots for such depths will permit later introduction of a short cul-de-sac street to break these deeper lots into two medium-depth parcels.

Cul-de-sac streets should end in a paved turnaround 100 ft in diameter. This diameter will accommodate larger trucks, including 45-ft trailers, and will allow a 180-degree turn without backing.

A further objective of lot layout should be to minimize the number of at-grade rail crossings of major roads within the development. In areas with high density uses, such vehicular traffic interruptions are particularly annoying; and automatic crossing protection is often required at the developer's expense.

Submittal of a preliminary plan to the community reviewing agency will establish a pattern for the orderly submittal of record plats. While practices vary, it is desirable to make a minimum initial commitment when filing a record plat of roads and parcels. This minimum commitment will retain flexibility and will provide control over the amount of funds paid in filing fees, when these fees are based on area recorded. (See Fig. 2.)

Rail Service

When rail service to industrial developments is contemplated, the developer should contact the railroad company's industrial development department as early as possible to determine which provisions are necessary for service. As ULI Industrial Council member O. G. Linde points out, such things as reciprocal switching limits, frequency of switching service, car supply, and general rate considerations, can be very important. He suggests, "A project might experience slow development simply because the development is located

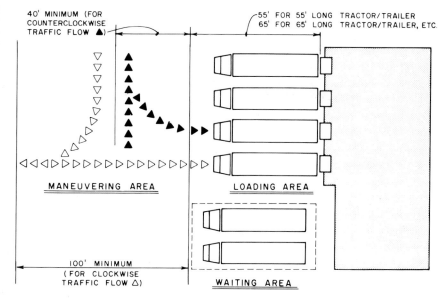

Fig. 1 Truck loading and maneuvering configuration.

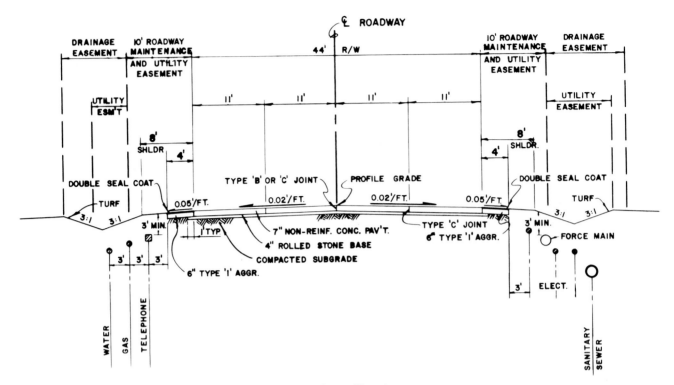

Fig. 2 Utility and pavement relationship in an industrial park in St. Louis County, Missouri.

outside reciprocal switching limits, thereby making it unattractive for industries to locate at a local station on one railroad when a significant share of their rail traffic originates or is destined on other railroads."

Assuming the desirability of rail service has been determined and the mix of land to rail served versus nonrail has been determined by market studies, several engineering and design factors must be considered—including topography, soil conditions, drainage, existing improvements, right-of-way access, building setback requirements, operational requirements, elevation and alignment of existing tracks, desire for in-plant rail service, and most suitable point(s) of intersection with existing tracks. As ULI Industrial Council member Otto Pongrace points out, "The location of rail access and the direction of that access from the main line must be discussed with the serving railroad since they may object to the point and direction of service that is most desirable for the developer."

While procedures vary, the cost of the lead track through the development is generally borne by the developer including the switch and spur track up to the property line of the individual tenant; the tenant generally pays for the remaining spur length. The railroad may participate in the costs of providing lead tracks to serve the several industrial sites within an industrial development through refunds to the developer based on car loadings. Switching tracks, sidings, and yards for storage may be necessary if required by the railroad. This additional trackage is of considerable value to the railroad since it facilitates operations. The developer should negotiate the cost of such additional trackage with the railroad.

Historically, the community has not been involved in the provision of rail service. It has been

the function of the developer to work with the railroads and share the costs based on mutual benefits. This function is in contrast to other onsite and offsite improvement such as streets and utilities. Frequently, communities have lent public powers such as improvement district financing in order to provide these facilities to further development of an employment and industrial tax base for the community [sic].

All rail service must conform to the requirements of the railroad company which will be operating over the facility. Also, rail service is subject to public service commission requirements. Many states have rules and regulations prescribed by lawful authority for clearances to or under adjacent buildings, structures, or physical obstruction of any kind.

Approval of railroad plans and construction is at the discretion of the railroad company. Close contact with railroad officials is desirable throughout all phases of planning, design, and construction. Agreements must be made between the railroad company and owner for operation and maintenance of private tracks.

The railroad company may furnish guidelines and standards for design. Every effort should be made to obtain the required information prior to any detailed layout.

For design purposes, the following information should be obtained from the railroad:

- maximum horizontal curvature and minimum tangent distances allowed for the type of layout,
- maximum grades allowed for transfer and storage,
- vertical curve requirements and maximum rate of change of grade,
- standard vertical and horizontal clearances—for lateral clearances, between centerlines of track and to fixed objects,

- turnout numbers to be used from the existing track and within the proposed layout,
- lead distances for the turnouts to be used,
- weight of rail for existing track and for proposed track,
- typical sections for roadbed width, slopes, ballast, ties, and rail configurations, and
- technical specifications.

Track design standards, such as standard rail section, turnouts, guard rails, frogs, plank crossings, signals, and others, are available from the railroad company.

Other design considerations include drainage, earthwork, slope stability analysis, crossings, rights-of-way, and special conditions required for the project. (See Figs. 3 to 8.)

Whether done by the railroad or by the developer, the construction of all tracks and appurtenances should conform to the best construction practices as prescribed by the *Manual* of the American Railway Engineering Association (AREA).

As a rule-of-thumb, when a development is rail-served: (1) the rail lead track and nearby street elevations will generally approximate one another; (2) the minimum radius of curvature of the track will be between 350 and 400 ft; (3) maximum permissible gradients along spur tracks will be about 1½ to 2 percent; and (4) the dock height should be set from 3.5 to 4.0 ft above top of rail of the spur track.

In deciding whether to provide rail service, and what portion of a development should be rail served, it is important to consider the amount of land in an industrial development which would be consumed by rail service. Admittedly, some of this land would be in required yard setbacks but this area could be used for parking, truck loading, or in some instances, structures—if not required for rail.

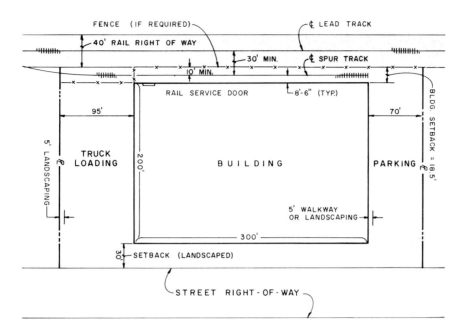

RAIL SERVED BUILDING LAYOUT
BUILDING COVERAGE = 52% OF SITE
RAIL IN RIGHT-OF-WAY, BLDG. SETBACK, SPUR ALONGSIDE BLDG.

Fig. 3

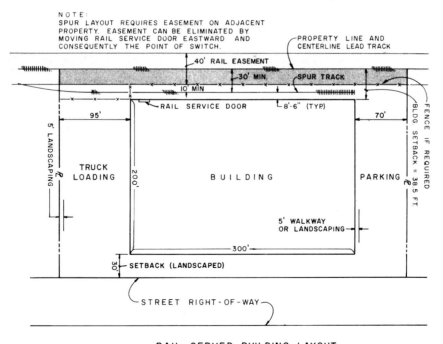

RAIL SERVED BUILDING LAYOUT
BUILDING COVERAGE = 48% OF SITE
RAIL IN EASEMENT, BLDG. SETBACK, SPUR ALONGSIDE BLDG.

Fig. 4

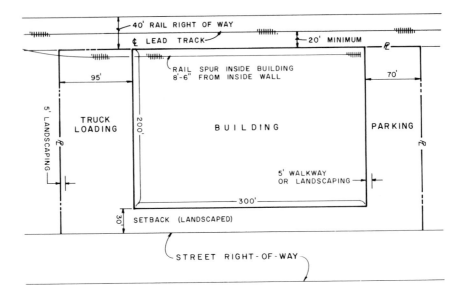

RAIL SERVED BUILDING LAYOUT
BUILDING COVERAGE = 56% OF SITE
RAIL IN RIGHT-OF-WAY, BLDG. ON PROPERTY LINE, SPUR INSIDE BLDG.

Fig. 5

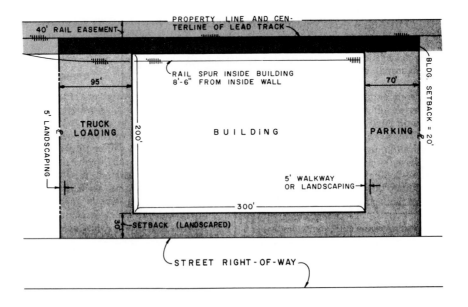

RAIL SERVED BUILDING LAYOUT
BUILDING COVERAGE = 52% OF SITE
RAIL IN EASEMENT, BLDG. SETBACK, SPUR INSIDE BLDG.

Fig. 6

TYPICAL PLANS
FOR INDUSTRIAL TRACKS
Typical Roadbed and Ballast Section

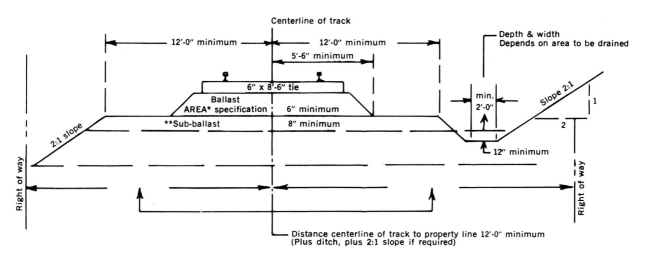

*American Railway Engineering Association

**If natural ground does not provide good drainage, 8" of porous material must be installed. Note: No draining to be diverted to railroad ditches without consent of railroad and agreement with railroad.

Fig. 7

TYPICAL CLEARANCE SECTION
INSIDE BUILDING

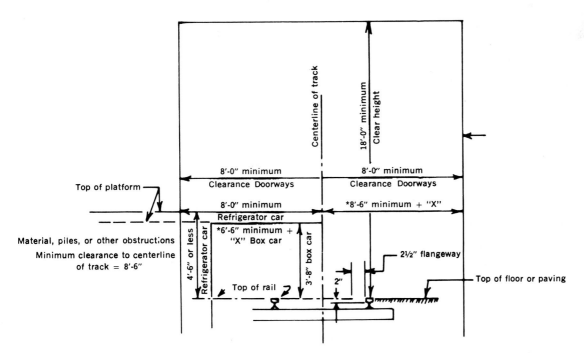

*Minimum distance can be reversed, as long as 8'-6" minimum + "X" is maintained on one side. Note: "X" = Add 1" per degree of curvature until car is totally on tangent track.

Fig. 8

INDUSTRIAL PARKS

TABLE 1 Traffic Generation Vocabulary

		Traffic Generation Rate (Vehicle Trips Per Day)			
	Density	Number/Acre		Number/1,000 Sq. Ft. Floor Area	
Land Use	(Employees/Acre)	Range	Typical	Range	Typical
Highly automated industry .... low employee density (refinery, warehouse)	5	2-8	4	0.2-1.0	0.6
Light service industry .... single-lot industry (lumber yard)	5-20	6-30	16	0.4-1.2	0.8
Industrial tract .... (5 acres) (machinery factory)	20-100	30-160	70	0.6-4.0	2.0
Office campus .... research & development (research industry)	100	150-200	170	3-8	4
Mixed central industry .... small industrial plants	Varies	10-100		1-4	

SOURCE: National Cooperative Highway Research Program, Report 121, "Protection of Highway Utility."

Traffic Generation

Understanding the nature and extent of traffic generated by various uses of land is important to the industrial land developer in providing for adequate roads. Small land developments may not in themselves generate sufficient traffic to create an overload of the existing road network. On the other hand, industrial plants often generate substantial traffic which must be accommodated by the road system. Standard values for the amount of traffic generated for various uses of land are not available; however, typical values, based upon experience, can be used. The traffic generated is generally expressed in terms of the number of trips per acre, or per 1,000 square feet of gross floor area.

In traffic generation studies for industrial areas, the principal measure of density is employees per acre. The operations with lowest employee density are highly automated industries or warehouses supporting fewer than 5 employees per acre. A second class is light service industry, generally located on small parcels and having 5 to 20 employees per acre. An industrial tract in a larger development with more intensive employment may have from 20 to 100 employees per acre. One of the most intensive industrial classes is office industry (research and development). An industrial site of this type may support more than 100 employees per acre. A fifth class is mixed industrial development which has a variable employee density. Traffic generation rates are indicated in vehicle trips per acre and in vehicle trips per thousand square feet of floor area. (See Table 1.)

As a general rule, one lane of pavement will handle from 800 to 1,200 trips per hour within the development. The actual number of cars accommodated within these limits is a function of several parameters including street layout, traffic control at intersections, and adequacy of highways serving the site. Therefore, all complex traffic movement should be analyzed by a traffic engineer to assure adequate design.

By FRANCIS W. GENCORELLI, RA, AIA

ESTABLISHING LIAISON

In most building types, the initial step is site selection. In the new-plant project, a considerable amount of time must be spent in establishing liaison with the client's organization and explaining the relevant problems to the client's planning team. The fact that most plant construction will be done by corporate clients makes it imperative that the source of responsibility be clearly established. This will make it possible to avoid misunderstandings about the relation of the proposed type of plant to its site, to its output, and to the future potential of the business.

As the first step, an organization team consisting of responsible production and engineering people should be established. Qualified outside counsel should then be selected.

The team of internal production and engineering people should be freed from all routine duties so that they may concentrate on the new construction program. This is vitally important, since no one can do the kind of creative thinking and reacting to creative thinking that a new project calls for if he is surrounded with the routine that is a necessary feature of every management procedure.

An orientation period is necessary to tune everyone in to the right point of view. A general consensus about the project should prevail. Everyone should be made to realize that decisions on site selection and plant building design will have an immense influence on operating costs and plant maintenance. It is important that the internal organizational team set itself to gather all necessary *input information* concerning the company's past growth, so as to have available necessary documentation for the future steps in the design. (See Fig. 1.)

THE SECOND STEP—SELECTION OF PLANT SITE

To a larger degree than is readily apparent, the site has a direct influence on the ultimate efficiency of the plant through the effects of site factors on plant design and construction. The consultant should be selected before a site decision is made. In many cases management selects the plant site, pays for it, and then requests the outside consultant to design the plant. The outside consultant must then design around the site conditions. The owner and his internal organization, together with the outside consultant, have many factors to consider in the survey of possible sites: physical, economic, legal, social, site size, climate, land topography, soil conditions, availability of raw materials, etc. These are too numerous to consider in detail.

THE THIRD STEP—PREPARING THE FUNDAMENTAL LAYOUT

The design of an effective plant layout is a problem of defining and responding to the analysis.

It is a system of rational three-dimensional analysis and evaluation. From the input developed by the internal organization, the outside consultant can analyze the existing flow activity space requirements, primary and secondary adjacencies, etc. It is imperative that the outside consultant be made fully aware of the idiosyncrasies of a particular product and a number of products produced in similar processes. A plant can have a layout based on *production* or on a *process*. If a company produces a large quantity of a few products, then you function on a *product layout*. If a company produces a great number of products, each with relatively small runs but similar processes, then you design on a *process layout*. In developing a new-plant project, it is obviously very unwise to consider immediate needs only. The wise management will consider its needs on a long-range plan. The entire plant site should be laid out for at least a 25-year period, with the particular building project built to serve only the needs of the next 5 years—all of which can only be projected from sales reports and anticipated markets. Expansion by growth can be a fairly accurate projection; however, expansion by acquisition cannot be easily determined. In one instance, a project increased by 300 percent during the construction period because product lines were added through company acquisitions.

The following is the initial breakdown of area allocations:

1. Administration
2. Employee facilities
3. Research and control
4. Manufacturing
5. Warehousing
6. Internal engineering
7. External engineering

Figure 2 shows area relationships.

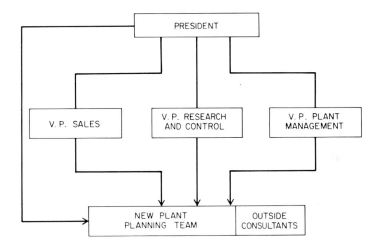

Fig. 1 Organizational chart.

TABLE 1 Rating Summary*

Site element	Rating
Labor supply and union history	20
Public utilities and water	12
Freight and transportation	10
Tax conditions	6
Site characteristics	7
Population mix, growth, and projection	6
Human transportation	4
Protection: fire, police, legal	4
Local politics and attitude	4
Local industrial mix	4
Climate	4
Local living facilities	6
Local educational facilities	6
Local recreational facilities	4
Freedom from natural disasters	3
	100

* Factors: poor, 1; fair, 2; good, 3; excellent, 4. To evaluate site, multiply point rating by factor. Site should rate 80 percent overall and rate at least "good" in those elements that are of special importance.

Industrial

INDUSTRIAL BUILDINGS, GENERAL

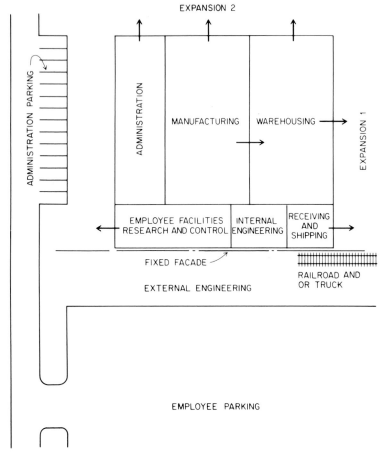

Fig. 2 Basic area relationships.

1. Administration

The following organizational relationships must be worked out before the planning of this area can be developed:

a. **Reception Room**
   Number of seats
   Receptionist—special or part of the general office, extra duties (typing, etc.), equipment

b. **Executive Area**
   Private Offices—number, occupant of each, size of each, furniture and equipment for each, closets

c. **Departments and/or Divisions**
   Accounting, bookkeeping, production, etc.

d. **Private Offices in Each Department**
   Number, occupant of each, size of each, furniture and equipment for each, closets

e. **General Work Areas in Each Department**
   Personnel in each, equipment in each, storage requirements for each

f. **Special-Purpose Rooms/Areas**

   Conference room
   Library
   Projection room
   Mail and shipping
   Reproduction room
   Secretarial pools
   Telephone equipment rooms
   Hospital areas
   PBX room—type of board
       number of positions
   IBM room
   File room
   Private toilets and showers
   Stock and storage rooms
   Rest rooms

g. **General Information**

   Interrelationship of person and department
   Clothing space
   Time clocks
   Water coolers

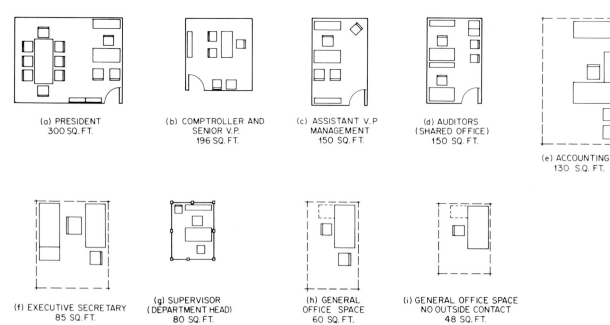

(a) PRESIDENT
300 SQ. FT.

(b) COMPTROLLER AND
SENIOR V.P.
196 SQ. FT.

(c) ASSISTANT V.P
MANAGEMENT
150 SQ. FT.

(d) AUDITORS
(SHARED OFFICE)
150 SQ. FT.

(e) ACCOUNTING
130 S.Q. FT.

(f) EXECUTIVE SECRETARY
85 SQ. FT.

(g) SUPERVISOR
(DEPARTMENT HEAD)
80 SQ. FT.

(h) GENERAL
OFFICE SPACE
60 SQ. FT.

(i) GENERAL OFFICE SPACE
NO OUTSIDE CONTACT
48 SQ. FT.

Fig. 3 Office areas.

Special lighting requirements
Plumbing requirements—special sinks, etc.
Intercom requirements

Our experience has shown that a study of the requests for space by department heads in proposed administration areas has resulted in subjective judgments based on ego-oriented requirements for space rather than objective judgments of function. The space standards shown in Fig. 3 should be used in planning the administration facilities.

In order to develop plans as accurately as possible, the following program must be initiated:

1. Survey of existing personnel, furniture, and equipment
2. Determination of approximate square footage of each department
3. Space analysis interviews with department supervisory personnel to determine existing space problems, their views on future projections, and the functional adjacencies of the departments
4. Review of factors which would have an effect on both immediate and future departmental space requirements
5. Area standards recommended
6. Determination of square footage required for all departments with an itemized breakdown by type of space, i.e., private office space, general office space, and miscellaneous areas

The projected requirements developed are based on the assumption that present policies and procedures will continue to apply in the future. Obviously, the company will initiate new policies and procedures and introduce new methods of operation. However, the extent to which any such changes would affect the projected area requirements could only be conjectured. Therefore, to minimize arbitrary judgments which would tend to dilute the validity of a study, consideration should not be given to such possible eventualities.

2. Employee Facilities

Both the quantity and the quality of the product depend not only on the sequence, precision, and efficiency of the factories, tools, and machines but on the proficiency, pride, and fitness—both mental and physical—of the personnel. The development of factory design in recent years has become more and more concerned with creature comforts for the employees.

The facilities should be near the work space, so that no time is lost getting back and forth, but they should be sufficiently insulated from the sights and sounds of the work area itself so that a real change of scene is provided. If a pleasant outside view is available, it should obviously be used. (See Fig. 4.)

A clear distinction should be made between quiet lounging places and recreation and cafeteria areas. The problems are interesting, the solutions may be various, but the reigning criteria seem to be constant—cheerfulness, comfort, and durability.

The areas in this category include the following:

Cafeteria and kitchen
Coffee lounges
Recreation areas (indoor and outdoor)
Quiet lounges
Factory men's and women's lockers and toilets
Office men's and women's lockers and toilets
Meeting rooms
First Aid and nurses station

TABLE 2 Minimum Toilet Fixture Requirements (New York State Labor Code)

No. of MEN	Water Closets	Urinals	No. of WOMEN	Water Closets	No. MEN or WOMEN	Wash Basins
1–9	1	0	1–15	1	1 20	1
10–15	1	1	16–35	2	21 40	2
16–40	2	1	36 55	3	41 60	3
41–55	2	2	56–80	4	61 80	4
56 80	3	2	81 110	5	81 100	5
81 100	4	2	111–150	6	101 125	6
101–150	4	3	151 190	7	126 150	7
151–160	5	3	191–240	8	151 175	8
161–190	5	4	241–270	9	176 200	9
191–220	6	4	271–300	10	201 225	10
221–270	6	5	301–330	11	226 250	11
271–280	7	5	331–360	12	251 275	12
281–300	7	6	361 390	13	276 300	13
301–340	8	6	391 420	14	301 325	14
341 360	8	7	421 450	15	326 350	15
361 390	9	7	451 480	16	351 375	16
391 400	10	7	481 510	17	376 400	17
401 450	10	8	511 540	18	401 425	18
451 460	11	8	541 570	19	426 450	19
461 480	11	9	571 600	20	451 475	20
481–520	12	9	601 630	21	476 500	21
521–540	12	10	631 660	22	501 525	22
541–570	13	10	661 690	23	526 550	23
571–580	14	10	691 720	24	551 575	24
581 630	14	11	721 750	25	576 600	25
631 640	15	11	751 780	26	601 625	26
641–660	15	12	781 810	27	626 650	27
661–700	16	12	811 840	28	651 675	28
701–720	16	13	841 870	29	676 700	29
721 750	17	13	871 900	30	701 725	30
751 760	18	13	901 930	31	726 750	31
761 810	18	14	931 960	32	751 775	32
811 820	19	14	961 990	33	776 800	33
821 840	19	15	991 1020	34	801 825	34
841 880	20	15			826 850	35
881–900	20	16			851 875	36
901–930	21	16			876 900	37
931–940	22	16			901 925	38
941–990	22	17			926 950	39
991–1000	23	17			951 975	40
					976 1000	41

WASH FOUNTAINS REQUIRED

Number of Fixtures	Persons Accommodated By			
	54" CIRCULAR (8 each)	54" SEMI-CIRCULAR (4 each)	36" CIRCULAR (5 each)	36" SEMI-CIRCULAR (3 each)
1	1 175	1 80	1 100	1 60
2	176 375	81 175	101 225	61 125
3	376 575	176 275	226 350	126 200
4	576 775	276 375	351 475	201 275
5	776 975	376 475	476 600	276 350
6	976 1175	476 575	601 725	351 425
7		576 675	726 850	426 500
8		676 775	851 975	501 575
9		776 875	976 1100	576 650
10		876 975		651 725
11		976–1075		726 800
12				801 875
13				876 950
14				951 1025

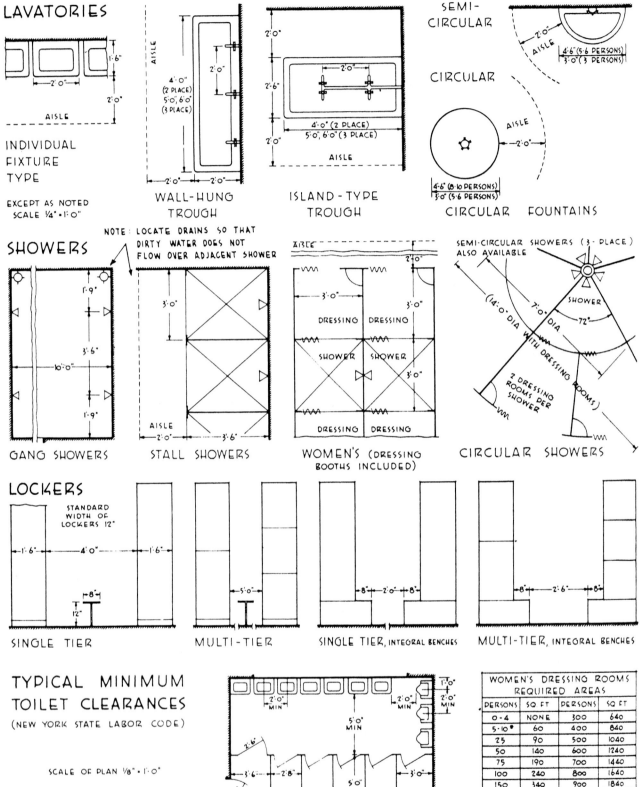

LAVATORIES

INDIVIDUAL FIXTURE TYPE

EXCEPT AS NOTED SCALE ¼"=1'-0"

WALL-HUNG TROUGH

ISLAND-TYPE TROUGH

SEMI-CIRCULAR

CIRCULAR

CIRCULAR FOUNTAINS

SHOWERS

NOTE: LOCATE DRAINS SO THAT DIRTY WATER DOES NOT FLOW OVER ADJACENT SHOWER

GANG SHOWERS

STALL SHOWERS

WOMEN'S (DRESSING BOOTHS INCLUDED)

SEMI-CIRCULAR SHOWERS (3-PLACE) ALSO AVAILABLE

CIRCULAR SHOWERS

LOCKERS

STANDARD WIDTH OF LOCKERS 12"

SINGLE TIER

MULTI-TIER

SINGLE TIER, INTEGRAL BENCHES

MULTI-TIER, INTEGRAL BENCHES

TYPICAL MINIMUM TOILET CLEARANCES

(NEW YORK STATE LABOR CODE)

SCALE OF PLAN ⅛"=1'-0"

COURTESY LOCKWOOD-GREENE ENGINEERS, INC

WOMEN'S DRESSING ROOMS REQUIRED AREAS			
PERSONS	SQ FT	PERSONS	SQ FT
0-4	NONE	300	640
5-10 *	60	400	840
25	90	500	1040
50	140	600	1240
75	190	700	1440
100	240	800	1640
150	340	900	1840
200	440	1000	2040

* BASED ON 2 SQ FT ADDITIONAL PER EACH ADDITIONAL PERSON OVER TEN (NEW YORK STATE LABOR CODE)

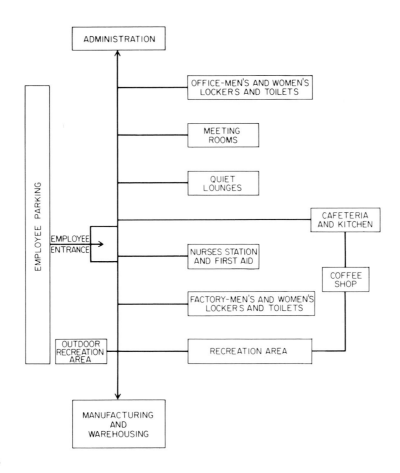

Fig. 4   Employee facilities flow.

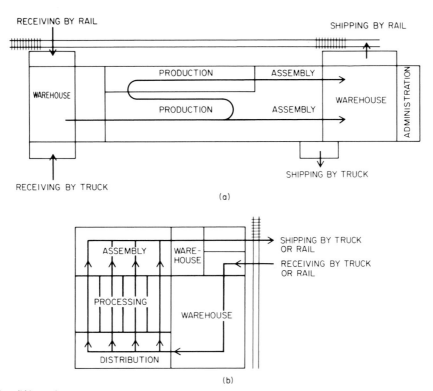

Fig. 5   (a) Layout by product. (b) Layout by process.

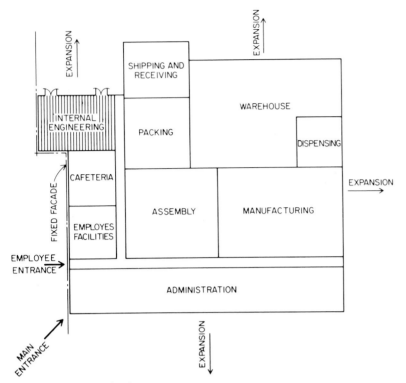

Fig. 6   Location of internal engineering.

BOILER H.P.	15-40	50-100	125-200	250-350	400-600
DIMENSION "A"	5'-9"	6'-6"	6'-10"	7'-9"	8'-6"
DIMENSION "B"	7'-5"	8'-9"	9'-7"	11'-9"	14'-3"

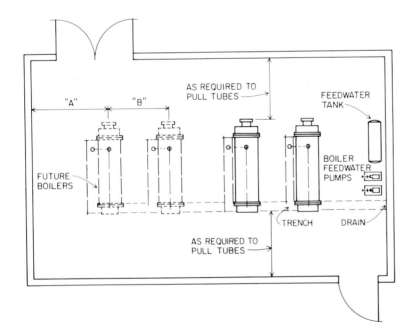

Fig. 7   Boiler room clearances.

3. Manufacturing

The trend toward automation has had a profound effect on plant design. Automation reduces employee density while increasing output. In terms of building area required, manufacturing space has diminished by some 50 percent in the last 10 years for the same process. Needless to say, productivity has increased by close to 400 percent.

As discussed previously, a plant can be designed under two different concepts, depending on the product and the number of products. *Product layout* can be said to be linear while *process layout* is parallel. This can best be decided by a flow-activity study showing number of products and the quantities of each. (See Fig. 5.)

The importance of flexibility in internal construction cannot be stated strongly enough. Except in factories producing one product (e.g., automobile assembly plants), the need is mandatory. When a manufacturer is producing several products and one succeeds far in advance of the others, his plant must be flexible enough to handle this emphasis. The other product lines must be held back until an expansion program is begun.

The following is a list of criteria for production-line evaluation:

1. Ease of flow of materials
2. Degree of flexibility
3. Ease of expansion
4. Ease of personnel movement
5. Ease of supervision
6. Least initial investment

The outside consultant, working with the organizational team, can synthesize the above criteria to produce an effective plant layout. In any plant design, it is essential that the outside consultant have available the detail for the present and projected manufacturing machinery. From this, the experience, knowledge, and imagination of the designer will yield the dividends. As used in the design of the administration spaces, templates or space standards per machine must be established, arranged, and rearranged to produce the best organization of equipment and spaces.

4. Research and Central Facilities

In the modern plant areas for research (product development) and control, laboratories are a must. As the size of the plant—and, in turn, laboratory facilities—increases, a strong case can be made for separating the two, which are basically similar installations. In the case of chemical, pharmaceutical, and dermatological plants, adjacent to each research laboratory should be a pilot plant installation which can produce, on a smaller scale, simulated manufacturing processes. In extremely large manufacturing plants, the research and product development facility should be in a separate building.

Flexibility is mandatory in the layout of research and development facilities. Any research program can be maneuvered to concentrate on a particular channel once the manufacturing advantages of a particular area of research are promising. To effect this, all or most of the research personnel will be concentrated on this product development. An inflexible laboratory layout can preclude this possibility.

It is becoming more and more prevalent in industrial research and product development installations for a large company to take research contracts from smaller companies in

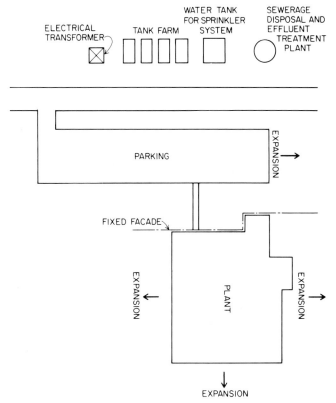

Fig. 8 Location of external engineering.

This scheme has worked, especially in a preexpansion condition. The traditional warehouse location should also permit initial expansion of manufacturing into its area. Since warehousing is the least expensive capital construction, it is reasonable to build the warehouse after manufacturing has expanded. Rarely does the structural layout differ in manufacturing and warehousing.

6. Internal Engineering

The single greatest error made in plant design is the placement of the internal engineering facilities. Invariably the inexperienced designer will centralize the heating and air-conditioning plant. But what is today centralized may, tomorrow, be right smack in the middle of your expansion direction.

The centralization concept grows from a desire to cut down the service runs of this equipment. It is a false economy. In an earlier diagram the use of a fixed facade, where no expansion takes place was pointed out. The internal engineering facility should be placed in a linear relationship to this fixed facade, and preferably at its extremity. What is extreme at first construction is centralized in your future expansion.

In many industries the development of rooftop combination air-conditioning and heating units is the answer. However these units are not developed for highly sophisticated climate control and often prove too limiting. They should only be contemplated where comfort conditions (75° to 80° dry bulb, 40 to 50 percent relative humidity) are adequate. Where a boiler plant is required for process work, its dual use for heating should be carefully analyzed. A complete engineering feasibility study is required to determine what system or systems should be utilized. (See Figs. 6 and 7.)

It is most important to build internal engineering spaces 100 percent larger than initially required. Adequate space for mechanical and electrical installation is a prime and vital consideration in industrial design.

7. External Engineering

By *external engineering* I mean all the outside utilities and storage facilities required for a plant to operate properly. Parking, truck docks, tank farms, sewerage disposal plants, electrical transformer pads, pumping stations, water storage facilities for sprinkler systems, and industrial waste disposal plants are a few of these requirements. (See Fig. 8.)

Since these are by nature permanent and expensive installations, they should not be placed in the way of any possible expansion. As in the case of the internal engineering, this external engineering facility should be placed along the fixed facade.

the same industry. With the scarcity of professionally qualified research people, this may be the only way for a relatively small industrial firm to get the necessary research work done.

Control laboratories, on the other hand, must be immediately adjacent to the manufacturing space and in many instances located in the manufacturing area. Recent federal regulations place an inspector in the manufacturing area, and he, therefore, is readily available to the control facilities.

5. Warehousing

The warehouse is the first area to feel the growing pains and therefore must be designed to signal the anticipated expansion program. It must be compressible. As the raw materials and packaging materials supplier simplifies his materials handling problem, so he creates a stocking problem for the manufacturer. Manufacturers, realizing the economies of carload or large-lot purchasing, are forced to make large capital investments in warehouse facilities in order to take advantage of these buying economies. There is, however, a point at which the law of diminishing returns steps in and no further economies can be expected.

With the increase in automation control of a warehouse, the concept of a public warehouse becomes more realistic. Where the product permits, a completely flexible warehousing operation should be used. Not all the buying is done at the same time, and it is possible that, as raw-material needs increase, the seasonal storage of finished products may be on the decline. A flexible warehousing concept would permit intermingling of raw materials and finished products and create an efficient though seemingly unordered warehouse.

INDUSTRIAL PLANTS

By RICHARD MUTHER

Features most likely to be involved in a layout problem include:
- Special or general-purpose building
- Single or multistory construction
- Shape of building
- Basement or balcony
- Windows
- Floors
- Roofs and ceilings
- Walls and columns

In addition to these, features of the site on which the building stands often affect the layout. Where this is so, the layout engineer must of course include them in his planning. These site features include:
- Rail lines and siding
- Highways and roadways
- Canals or streams
- Bridges
- Yard areas for storing, parking, lawn, gardens
- Outbuildings, such as storage tanks, water tower, well, pump house, incinerator, dump or burning area
- Platforms, docks, ramps, pits, truck or rail wells

SPECIAL OR GENERAL-PURPOSE BUILDING

The layout engineer should decide right away whether he wants a building custom-made or "bought off the shelf." Special buildings generally cost more and are less negotiable. They also have a way of becoming out of date as the product and facilities grow or shrink or change with new conditions. Yet, for many industries special buildings are essential if the plant is to operate economically.

Plants having relatively simple forming, treating, or assembly operations, as is the case with most consumers' goods industries, favor the *general-purpose building*. Here is the general type of building that can produce several different products with equal ease. Generally, this building is more permanent than its equipment or layout. The initial cost is less because of standard designs, standard building materials, and regular construction methods. These buildings can incorporate—just as well as the special plant—the "standard" good features that an industrial building should have, regardless of the type of production. In addition, general-purpose buildings can be converted readily to new products and equipment, to changing production requirements, or to new owners. This adaptability and resale potential gives the multipurpose building the edge. This means: use a special building only when necessary. But layout men can check this decision by reviewing the following list:

Use *general-purpose*, or *multipurpose, building* when these following items are important:
- Initial cost
- Possibility of selling it later for profit, a better location, foreclosure

Practical Plan Layout, McGraw-Hill Book Company, New York, 1955.

- Frequency of changes in products, materials, machinery and equipment, processes or methods
- Speed of getting the layout into production

SINGLE OR MULTISTORY CONSTRUCTION

Early factories were generally three or four stories high. Because of limited transportation facilities they had to be built in cities, where land costs were relatively high. Also, their builders who used brick had to make walls thick enough to stand up. Therefore, they reasoned, "Why not use this structure to support upper floors?"

With the coming of inexpensive and widespread transportation for employees and of steel reinforcing or supports for buildings, companies began to build out of town. Land values were lower and the plant could spread out. Today's trend toward large one-story buildings is thus a product of changing conditions.

This does not mean that every new plant should be one story high, as some industrialists advocate. Plants built around a higher-than-one-story process should certainly have upper floors. Manufacturers who decide the advertising value of a downtown plant is important will have to use several stories to utilize their land economically. And we cannot underrate gravity, even though power costs may be low. Again, when products are small and relatively valuable, as in diamond cutting or watchmaking, there is considerable saving by concentrating rather than spreading out.

Use *single-story construction*, possibly including balconies and/or a basement, when the following conditions exist:
- Product is large, heavy, or relatively inexpensive per pound
- Weight of equipment causes heavy floor loads
- Large, more or less unobstructed space is needed
- Land value is low
- Land is available for expansion

- Product is not adapted to gravity
- Erection time is limited
- Frequent changes in layout are anticipated

Perhaps the most universally economical plant today is the so-called one-and-a-half-story plant (see Fig. l). This is basically one story but may include balconies or basement.

SHAPE OF BUILDING

Early buildings were narrow because they needed natural light. They expanded by extending their ends and by adding cross buildings in a rectangular fashion. Today artificial lighting is relatively less expensive. The number and frequency of production changes are greater. Therefore, emphasis today is on plants that are relatively square and not "honeycombed" or obstructed by walls. Such plants are built in rectangular sections, and expansion is by building additional sections onto the sides or end (see Fig. 2).

Where land is limited, as in river valleys—or where property lines run at curious angles—the building must suit the limitations of the land itself. Dirty, odorous, noisy or vibration-producing operations should be segregated in separate buildings. Hazardous operations with fire or explosion possibilities also fall in this class. And service buildings used for administration, sales, personnel offices, and power plant—buildings that do not directly participate in the flow of production—can also be set apart. Use the following lists to guide your decision in the matter of *building shape*.

Use a relatively *square* building when there are:
- Frequent changes in product design
- Frequent improvements in process
- Frequent rearrangement of layout
- Restrictions on building materials or savings desired in amount of materials used (see Fig. 3)

Use *other shapes* or *separate* buildings when there are:
- Physical limitations of the land
- Property lines at curious angles

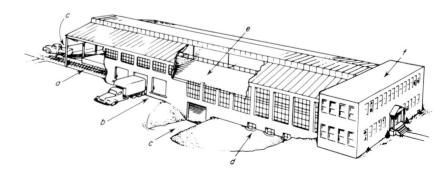

Fig. 1 Features of the one-and-a-half story building: (a) Rail siding with car floor at level of plant floor. (b) Truck tailgate level with plant floor. (c) Shallow ramp down to basement; low ramp up to floor level. (d) Windows for basement lighting. (e) Balcony or mezzanine for supporting activities and/or production. (f) Two-story office building with entrance at ground level.

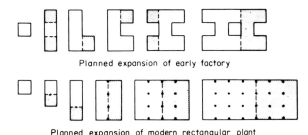

Planned expansion of early factory

Planned expansion of modern rectangular plant

Fig. 2 Planned expansion of early and modern plant buildings.

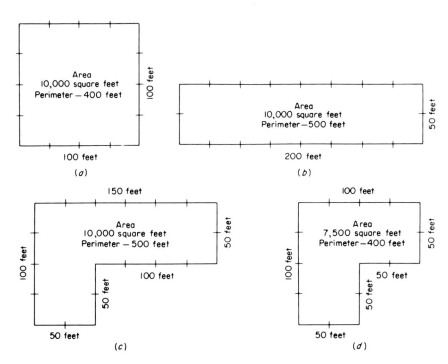

Area
10,000 square feet
Perimeter — 400 feet

100 feet

100 feet

(a)

Area
10,000 square feet
Perimeter—500 feet

50 feet

200 feet

(b)

150 feet

Area
10,000 square feet
Perimeter — 500 feet

100 feet

50 feet

100 feet

50 feet

50 feet

(c)

100 feet

Area
7,500 square feet
Perimeter—400 feet

100 feet

50 feet

50 feet

50 feet

50 feet

(d)

Fig. 3 Compare materials needed in the side walls of the four plans shown. Three plans, (a), (b), and (c), are for the same size plant, 10,000 sq ft. But of the three plans, plan (a) has the shortest perimeter wall and will use less materials than will plans (b) and (c). Plan (a) has one-third more floor space than plan (d), but the same wall area. Where material saving is of prime importance, the square plan should be advocated. (Factory Management & Maintenance.)

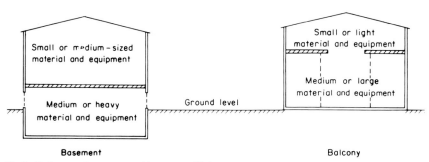

Small or medium-sized
material and equipment

Medium or heavy
material and equipment

Basement

Ground level

Small or light
material and equipment

Medium or large
material and equipment

Balcony

Fig. 4 Basic use and arrangement of basement and balcony.

• **Buildings that house operations that cause dirt, odors, noise, vibration**
• **Buildings that house operations not part of production**
• **Buildings that house operations susceptible to fire or explosion**

BASEMENT OR BALCONY

A plant can hardly avoid having a basement when it is built on land that slopes. And this has very practical advantages. Some plants are built on the side of a hill for the express purpose of having motor-vehicle entries to each floor. This offers the advantage of entry to two or more levels with a minimum of ramp construction, and it allows receiving at one level and shipping at another with flow through the plant in a U-shaped path in the vertical plane.

If you decide to have a basement, or if your new building has a basement, check to be sure it has these *desired basement features:*
• Ample headroom
• Good ventilation
• Sound foundations
• Ample lighting
• Waterproofed walls
• Floors free of groundwater seepage or flooding

Partial basements may be of real value when a basement for production purposes is not needed. Heating plant, compressors, pumps, and other auxiliary equipment are well suited to location off the production floor. This also applies to other services such as washrooms and locker rooms, toilets, transportation aisles for material handling or personnel, storage for slow-moving parts, overruns, inactive tools, dies, fixtures, patterns, and the like.

Certain processes may need a basement, as in large stamping-press work where special foundations are desirable and scrap collection is a big factor. It may be easier to excavate and build up machine foundations than to break out pits or install each foundation from floor level. Especially tall equipment may be placed in a basement so that its working level will be on the main floor. In fact, there are some plants whose main operating floor is little more than sheet-metal plates for machine tenders to stand on; all the machinery rests on a basement floor.

On the other hand, where ample headroom over equipment is required, the layout should not be confined in a basement. Extremes of this are in large equipment manufacturing or ship construction. Here cranes and large materials prohibit basement use. Yet these industries often make use of balconies for their smaller, lighter work (see Fig. 4)

Typical *cases where balconies are used* include:
• Subassembly operations with final assembly of large units on ground level
• Assembly operations with heavier forming machinery below
• Light-machine operations with heavier machines below
• Treating operations with forming operations and assembly of bulky units on ground level
• Supporting activities of all kinds to men, materials, or machinery—storage, washrooms or locker rooms, production offices, and the like—that can be kept off the production floor
• Operating or servicing upper parts of tall, high machinery
• Material storage and preparation area, including bulk material blending or packing-box making and distribution

INDUSTRIAL PLANTS

WINDOWS

Old factories had to have small windows because of the cost of construction. The introduction of large, steel-sash windows brought their cost down. Today windows are often cheaper than walls. On the other hand, windows make buildings more subject to changes in outside temperature. Plants having products or processes especially subject to changes in temperature, light or humidity find it better to have no windows at all. Chocolate factories, for instance, have to watch temperatures. Many of these plants control this condition by ventilating and air conditioning. Their light is artificial. Other plants reject windows because of the dust they let in, even with slightly pressurized air inside.

The layout man who must contend with windows recognizes that they may both help and hinder his arrangement (see Fig. 5).

The following is a list of *points to check where windows may affect the layout:*
- Brightness or glare
- Angle of light—morning and evening, winter and summer
- Heat effects to personnel and/or materials from sun on windows
- Resistance to wind, shock, fire, acids, rust
- Drafts on personnel when opened
- Access for washing or repair

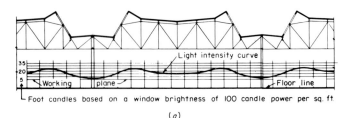

(a)

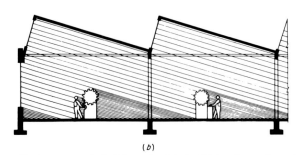

(b)

Fig. 5   Good natural lighting relates to both window and roof design. Windows in a monitor roof (a) give good uniformity and intensity. The use of roof lighting obviates the need for wall windows and is useful in large building areas and where there will be future expansion. The windows in a sawtooth roof give reasonably uniform light, especially when arched. But they cast shadows (b). At the left the worker stands in his own shadow; at the right his machine blocks the light. Nevertheless, where direct sunlight should be kept out, northerly directed windows of this type are not out of order. (From George Nelson: "Industrial Architecture of Albert Kahn, Inc.," Architectural Book Publishing Co.)

FLOORS

The levels and strengths of floors are the most important floor influence on layout. Adjoining buildings, and even those far removed that may someday be connected to the main plant, should have floors at the same level. Handling systems can then be tied in without ramps or elevators. As for floor strength, it should be checked with the architect.

Early factories had dirt or wood floors. Today, various combinations of steel and concrete give the least expensive floor. It wears well; it is strong and easy to clean. But workers who stand or walk a great deal object to the hardness of concrete floors. Also, certain materials dropped on concrete are likely to be damaged. Concrete is difficult to cut into to rearrange wiring or piping in the floor.

Workers' foot fatigue is overcome by providing wooden or rubber mats. The objections of damage to dropped parts and difficulty of rearrangement can be met by covering the concrete with wood block, wood flooring, or composition block or coating. The following list gives floor characteristics desired, though no floor will have them all:
- Various buildings at the same level
- Strong enough to carry machines and equipment
- Made from inexpensive materials
- Inexpensive to install
- Immediately ready for use
- Resistant to shock, abrasion, conducting heat, vibration
- Not slippery under any condition
- Noiseless and sound absorbing
- Attractive to the eye
- Numerous colors available
- Unaffected by changes in temperature and humidity, or by oils, acids, alkalies, salts, solvents, or water
- Odorless and sanitary
- Resilient enough to seem soft underfoot and to minimize damage to articles dropped on it

TABLE 1   Generally Recommended Ceiling Heights

Type of production	Without overhead installations *	With overhead installations †
Small-product assembly on benches; offices	9-14 ft	10-18 ft
Large-product assembly on floor or floor fixtures	Maximum height of product + 75%	Maximum height of product + 125%
Small-product forming.	Height of machinery + 100%	Height of machinery + 150%
Large-product forming	Height of machinery + 125%	Height of machinery + 125%

* Other than lighting and sprinkler.
† Air ducts, unit heaters, conveyors, etc.

- Easy to fasten machines and equipment to
- Will dissipate static electricity and is non-sparking when struck
- Easily kept clean
- Large sections easily and quickly removed and replaced

ROOFS AND CEILINGS

Roofs and ceilings affect layouts chiefly by their height above the floor. Table 1 has some generally recommended heights for use as a rule of thumb.

Roofs and ceilings are also affected in many cases by the type of construction. Figure 6 shows the several types of roof construction most commonly used.

The usefulness of overhead space may be limited by what can be attached to the roof or ceiling. Very few plants hang their machinery from the roof or ceiling. But a great many suspend material-handling equipment, service pipes or wiring, and other equipment. Such considerations as natural light, heat conduction, and dust accumulation also relate to the type and condition of the roof.

WALLS AND COLUMNS

Unlike early plants which depended on thick stonework or masonry to hold up their walls and roofs, modern buildings place their load on beams and supporting structures, generally of steel or reinforced concrete. This way, the column carries the load and no wall is needed, except to keep out the elements. This is a great help to production for it means large, unobstructed working areas.

Inner walls today are only partitions. When certain operations must be segregated, partitions that are generally built up in standard sections can easily be installed or removed. They can be made as high as necessary to shield or protect the area or can be suspended from the ceiling. This latter type of baffle keeps the floor area free but holds fumes, noise, heat, and the like from circulating throughout the building.

One feature easy to overlook is the size of openings in walls. Doors that are too low or too narrow, for example, will limit the size of material-handling equipment.

Even without interior walls, there is still the obstruction of columns used for roof sup-

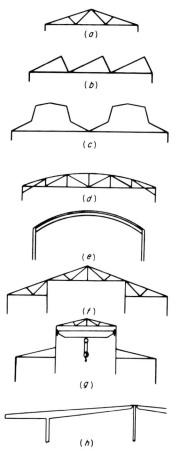

Fig. 6 Typical types of roof structures. (a) Truss. (b) Sawtooth. (c) Monitor. (d) Bowstring truss. (e) Concrete arch. (f) Three-bay, or high-low, gable. (g) High crane type. (h) Cantilever.

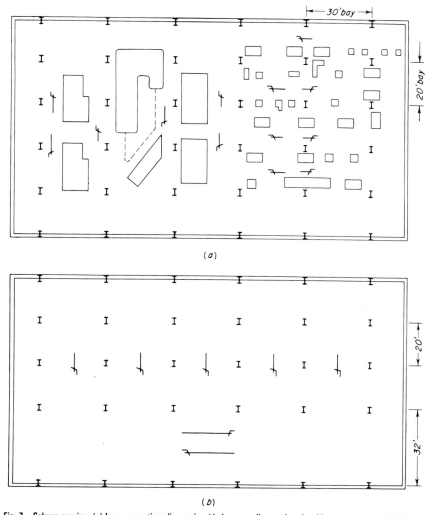

Fig. 7 Column spacing. (a) Large operations line up in wide bays; small operations in wide or narrow bays. (b) Combination of two different column spacings — to take advantage of flow lineup with wide bays.

port to plague the layout man. These columns interfere with spotting of machinery, aisles, storage areas, and overhead handling equipment. Columns cause two basic problems:

1. The way they line up tends to confine the basic flow patterns.

2. Their individual location limits the location of all facilities, especially large equipment.

The layout man will undoubtedly want to line up major aisles, stock shelves, and service lines with the columns. Large operations will lie lengthwise down through the bays with the wider spacing. Smaller materials and equipment will generally run in the narrowed spacing (see Fig. 7).

As for columns that act as obstructions to the spotting of individual machinery and equipment, the layout man must plan a column arrangement that will tie in with his layout. Yet a lot of unnecessary money can be put into a building that calls for too-wide column spacing. Some layout men admit they always consult their architect and then call for about 15 percent greater spacing than he feels is economically justified. Another layout problem is to take whatever column spacing and arrange-

ment is planned or already exists in the building and use it to best advantage. By experimenting with various alternative plans, it is often possible to juggle a neat arrangement of machinery, equipment, and supporting activities into the column layout. Then the layout man can often use the columns to advantage as follows:

- To support overhead handling equipment
- To brace up storage racks
- To fasten or fence in treating equipment
- To support balconies, catwalks, auxiliary service lines, instrument panelboards, and machinery itself

Since columns mean lost floor space, place against them and in between them other nonproductive equipment that takes floor space (drinking fountains, drains, firefighting equipment, time clocks, and the like).

SITE FEATURES

Features of the site are important in any layout that involves expansion of buildings or a layout of more than one building. Rail lines and sid-

ings, roadways, canals, and outbuildings may have to be provided, or, if they exist, may limit the layout or may have to be moved or altered. For railroad car and highway truck dimensions that may affect building features, see the data in Tables 2 to 4.

The location of an underground storage tank will limit construction or heavy outside storage in that area; dust and smoke from a foundry building should blow away from the main administration building; rail siding curves can occupy an unusually large area. These and many features of the site may be involved in any layout other than those strictly within one building (see Fig. 8).

RAILROAD CLEARANCES AND FREIGHT CAR DIMENSIONS

Normal Clearances Nominal clearances are required as a matter of safety between locomotives and cars, and structures near tracks. These are averages for straight track—some companies and states require more as noted. The clearances are based on standard 4-ft $8\frac{1}{2}$-in. track gauge. (See Figs. 9 and 10.)

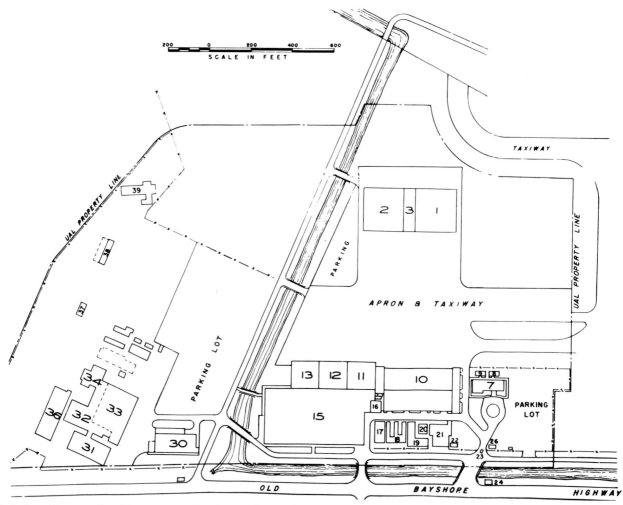

Fig. 8   External features such as highway, stream, roads, and property lines all influenced the arrangement of this site. This is the arrangement of the maintenance and repair facilities of an airline. (United Airlines.)

In planning the arrangement of buildings, they should be laid out in relation to the overall site just as the individual machine and equipment layout relate to the building. A long-range plan of development for the entire site should be obtained so that buildings can be properly integrated with each other.

TABLE 2   Freight Car Dimensions

Type of car	A Length over strikers, avg.	B Inside length Min.	Max.	C Overall width, avg.	D Inside width Min.	Max.	E Overall height, avg.	F Inside height Min.	Max.	G Floor height, avg.	Level full capacity, avg. cu ft	Tare weight, avg. lb
Flat............	53'-0"	36'-0"	60'-0"	10'-3"	8'-6"	10'-6"	....	....		3'-11"	....	48,700
Gondola.........	43'-0"	33'-6"	65'-0"	10'-4"	7'-6"	9'-6"	8'-6"	4'-8" avg.		3'-11"	1,775	42,800
Hopper..........	35'-10"	34'-10" avg.		10'-5"	10'-3" avg.		10'-8"	....			2,328	30,000
Box...........	41'-9"	40'-0"	50'-0"	10'-8"	8'-5"	9'-4"	14'-1"	7'-9"	10'-6"	3'-8"	3,468	48,200
Automobile......	52'-3"	50'-6" avg.		10'-8"	9'-2" avg.		15'-1"	10'-4" avg.		3'-7"	4,798	53,300

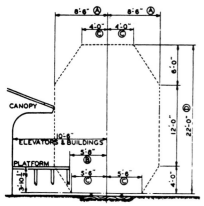

Fig. 9   Clearances are for straight trace (A) and (B). Some railroads require an 8-ft minimum (C). In some states, this clearance must be increased (D). One western railroad requires a 24-ft vertical clearance above top of ties.

TABLE 3   Average Truck-Bed Heights*

Type vehicle	Height of truck bed, in.
1- to 1½-ton panel trucks.........	40–44
1½- to 3-ton medium panel or stake body trucks..............	40–46
Large trucks and average truck-trailer units.................	48–52
Largest and heaviest tandem-wheel, dual axle, semitrailers and full trailers.................	50–56

* From Modern Materials Handling.

TABLE 4   Highway Truck Dimensions

Type vehicle	Height	Length	Width
Medium trucks......	9½ ft	34 ft	7 to 7½ ft
Large trucks and trailers........	13 ft max.	45 ft	7½ ft to 8 ft

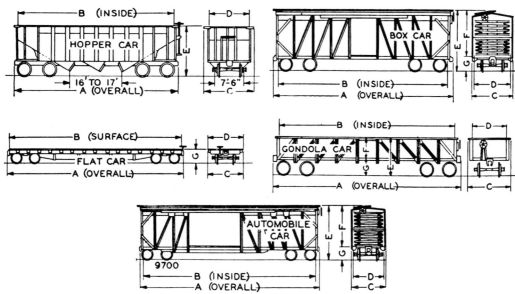

Fig. 10   Typical railroad car data.

Clearances for Curves Allowances must be made on curves, due to the increase in effective width of equipment. The increase inside curves depends on the distance between truck centers and the increase outside curves depends on length beyond trucks. Tilt of equipment toward inside of curve due to banking of rails must be included as well as any slewing action caused by tire wear and other lateral

play. As a rule, the front of a locomotive will govern effective width for a foot above top of the rail and the rear of the cab for the remainder of the height. For preliminary calculations of clearance outside curves, it will usually be ample to allow 1 in. per degree of curve plus 2 in. for all curves. For inside clearance, a general allowance of 1½ in. in addition to the middle ordinate distance for a 45-ft

chord will be sufficient.

In cases involving new construction, a sketch of clearances should be submitted to the railroad for approval.

Tracks Entering Building Some railroads permit special clearances when tracks enter coal tipples and buildings. Railroad company engineers can be contacted for requirements.

Industrial

INDUSTRIAL RAILROAD DOCKS

Current trends indicate that railcars of the future could have longer lengths and higher capacities than today's 50' cars. Railcar door openings may also increase. These trends make proper planning critical. Before planning rail docks, check with the railroad servicing your building. They can tell you about state and local codes for required centerline clearances. The accompanying diagram shows some typical dimensions for structures and platforms.

Basic Rail Dock Types

The Flush Dock Here, rail cars are spotted at doors alongside of the building. This type minimizes construction costs, maximizes space utilization inside the building and protects cargo from the elements. Building doors should be at least the same width as the largest railcar door anticipated. To meet future needs, wider openings may be considered. For protection against the elements, a shelter or inside vestibule may be needed. Also plan for outside lighting and inside aisles at least 14' wide.

Rail Platform Dock This design eliminates the need for exact spotting of railcars. Virtually any car door size can be serviced. Since cargo may be exposed to extreme weather, a canopy, at least 23' above track level, should be constructed over the platform. Due to heavy loads and heavy material handling equipment, the platform should be made of reinforced concrete. For maximum efficiency, platform depth should be at least 14'.

Inside Rail Dock This type provides the ultimate in weather protection, plus accessibility to different sized railcar openings. Railcars need not be spotted perfectly, and most states require negligible centerline clearances. This allows tracks to be close to the dock for more material handling efficiency. In cold weather areas, air curtains can be mounted over the railcar entry to reduce energy loss.

Dock Heights

Rail docks servicing dry goods box cars are typically built to a height of 42" measured from the top of the rail. Floor heights of typical box cars vary from 41" to 46". Docks servicing refrigerated rail cars are usually constructed 48" high. Older refrigerator cars have floor heights from 46" to 52", measured from the top of the rail.

Track Location

Railroad, state and local codes provide clearance for a person between the box car and the building when the train is moving. Since there is a safety consideration for material handling personnel traversing between the dock and the rail car, it's usually a good idea to minimize the legal allowable gap between the two points. Again, most often the clearance requirement is waived for inside docks. Permanent rail ramps, attached to the dock face, will increase the minimum centerline dimension by 14" to 16".

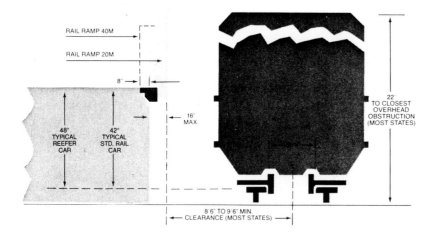

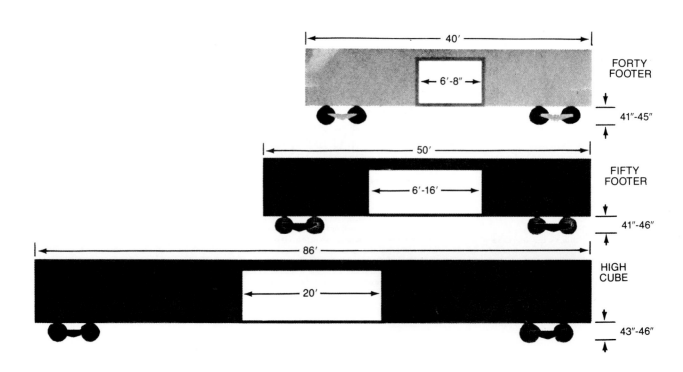

1154

Classes of Research Facilities

The Public Health Service divides research facilities into four classes: *Class A Laboratories* are designed with maximum capability for conversion from one program use to another. These are primarily intended for research in the basic scientific disciplines of biology, chemistry, and some aspects of the physical sciences. The design criteria are intended to protect the integrity of individual research programs from interference by other research within the same structure and to reduce the possibility of infection or toxic hazards to personnel in present or future research projects.

Class B Laboratories are designed with limited capabilities for conversion. This laboratory class is suited for a narrow range of activities in such disciplines as the social sciences, psychiatry, public health work, or epidemiology and could not be used for research involving the basic disciplines of chemistry and biology without major alterations in the heating, air conditioning, ventilation, plumbing, and electric power systems. The original design provides for individual room temperature control.

Class C Facilities are designed for research support, including such structures as stock barns, animal pens and runways, storage sheds, and utility structures. This class is considered functional without utility services and does not require noncombustible construction.

Class D Facilities are designed for special research functions that require a specialized environment. Their structural provisions render them inherently unsuited for conversion. The design criteria must be determined for each project. This category includes biotron or betatron buildings, hyperbaric chambers, germ free animal production facilities, biohazard control facilities, and other research buildings with specialized functions.

Planning

A health research laboratory building must have the capability to satisfy research operational needs, allowing for variation both in research projects and in occupancy, for at least 10 years. Planners and designers must recognize that the structure will have to meet a variety of functional needs, rather than the specific requirements of a single group of occupants.

The most effective administrative device for planning a health research facility that will meet both current and future requirements is a written description of the total functional needs of the program(s) expected to operate in the building. Generally called the Program of Requirements (POR), this written description lists the functions and operations that will be housed in the structure, the design criteria

Health Research Laboratory Design, National Institute of Health, U.S. Department of Health, Education, and Welfare, Washington, D.C., 1968.

for those functions, and their space needs. It also provides information on the projected staffing and the equipment which will be needed in the building. This written Program of Requirements is most valuable if it is prepared before any drawings and preferably should precede the preparation of space function relationship diagrams.

Space Blocks Where the first full occupancy staff is available to advise on the functional requirements of the structure, planning and design can be directed to smaller units of space such as individual laboratory modules, suites, or departmental laboratories. Where only a small staff is available for planning the total long-range scientific research program and its space needs, the administrator must approach planning and design with a different philosophy.

In this situation, it may be best to consider the research programs in terms of functional space blocks ranging from 3,000 to 6,000 ft each. The size of the space planning blocks can be determined by using the POR to assess the anticipated programs and staffs that will occupy the building in the first phases of its occupancy. Generally, a space block is selected that will accommodate a group of two or three of the smaller programs, satisfy the moderately-sized programs and that, in multiples, will meet the needs of the proposed major operational units.

For example, if the POR indicates that 4,000 sq ft roughly equals the special needs of each of several functions, that there are a number of smaller functions requiring 1,000 and 2,000 sq ft each, and some larger functions with space requirements of 6,000, 8,000, 10,000, 12,000, and 16,000 sq ft, it is a reasonable approach to adapt a 4,000-sq-ft space block as a planning unit. The utility systems, the circulation systems, and supporting elements are planned to make each one of the 4,000-sq-ft space blocks self-sufficient. It is then possible to assign one medium-sized program element to a space block, assign multiple smaller units to a single space block, and use several space blocks for one major component.

Space planning strategy is associated with the development of space function bubble diagrams. These diagrams can be used to relate the individual space blocks functionally and to pool several space blocks to handle one major program.

Building Shapes Planners and designers sometimes try to meet laboratory functional needs with esoteric shapes and dimensions. Although circles, hexagons, and tall slim towers may have esthetic appeal, none of them are as efficient as, or have the capability of, rectangular designs. Rectilinear laboratory equipment and office furniture and the anticipated continual interplay between rooms call for utilitarian solutions. Buildings with simple rectangular configurations, commensurate with standard laboratory equipment and furniture, and with unrestricted accessibility to mechanical utility systems, are the easiest to adapt to the changing needs of research.

Flexibility and Capability The term *flexibility* is frequently used in discussing the design characteristics of research laboratory buildings. However, *flexibility* should be interpreted with caution because most research laboratory structures should be designed with the concept of capability in mind. The structure's capability to meet varying ventilation needs for different research functions, its ability for temperature control of varying heat loads, its capability to meet the needs for fume hood, air supply, and exhaust in different concentrations with time in various areas in the building are all critical. The ability to supply electric power in high concentrations to any localized area without the need to reposition electric distribution lines within the building is a measure of the facility's capability to meet the needs of the research program that will eventually occupy the building.

Flexibility is emphasized by considering the possible location and utilization of chemical fume hoods. Saying that the building can provide for 50 chemical fume hoods is meaningless unless it is specified whether only up to a maximum of 10 can be utilized on any one floor, or whether the design capability is such that all 50 can be installed and used on one floor. A more detailed examination of the building's capability might reveal that no more than two hoods could be installed in any one laboratory module due to the limitations on supplying and exhausting air in that particular room. This approach contrasts with the method of determining the location of hoods according to requests by the initial occupants of the building. Providing supply and exhaust hoods in specific areas or rooms according to desires of the first occupant limits the capability of the building for future occupants.

THE LABORATORY BUILDING [1]

To a large extent the design of a laboratory building will be dictated by the heating, ventilating, and air-conditioning systems, and the utility distribution layout. If these factors are carefully planned first, the laboratory building design will be an efficient one, and it will still be possible to plan for structural flexibility and growth needs as well as for engineering capability.

The module plan is the most useful for the design of health research facilities. This section will briefly discuss how various groups have met some of the challenges of research laboratory design, using the module as the basis for a grid pattern. Experience with industrial and academic laboratories can prove instructive for those working with health-related facilities.

Planning for Flexibility and Growth

Architects have been trying to develop comprehensive systems which will relate the needs

[1] This section is based on an article by Jonathan Barnett in *Architectural Record,* November 1965, volume 138.

Industrial

RESEARCH LABORATORIES

of various departments and disciplines and provide ways of sharing certain facilities, such as lecture halls and teaching laboratories. In addition, such a system can provide an architectural recognition of the increasingly interdisciplinary nature of much scientific research: for example, by placing bio-physics between biology and physics, with the capability of expanding in either direction.

The system developed by Sir Leslie Martin (Fig. 1) consists of a *regular grid derived* from considerations of space, lighting, and an integrated system of structures and services. The grid forms 35-ft squares separated by 5-ft strips. Ducts and services can be introduced at any point within these strips. The system is also divided vertically, with large areas such as lecture halls, workshops, and special laboratories for heavy equipment at the lowest level, teaching laboratories above, and research areas on top. As shown in the drawings, the grid can be applied to a site, giving a rough indication of present areas and future expansion possibilities. Architectural development can go on in stages, in relation to the grid, forming segments of a larger system rather than single buildings.

Industrial Laboratories Industrial research facilities do not yet require such a comprehensive solution. Industrial laboratory space is likely to be more uniform than a university or government facility. The range of research is relatively narrow, and, as there is no strong tenure system, industry is less likely to design a laboratory around the requirements of a particular scientist. At present, therefore, industry tends to think of new laboratory space in terms of adding blocks of a set size and type. The long-range outlook, however, is probably toward the more flexible approach already employed by the universities.

University Laboratories The Chicago office of the architectural firm of Skidmore, Owings and Merrill has been working on the development of comprehensive laboratory grids for universities (Fig. 2). Such grids lend themselves to growth of almost any shape and in almost any direction.

Planning the Laboratory Complex

There are four basic areas in any laboratory complex: the area for research itself; the administrative offices; general support facilities, such as an auditorium or a cafeteria; and service facilities, such as shops and the boiler plant. The addition of teaching requirements does not change this pattern significantly. Elementary science courses are taught in special teaching laboratories and demonstration lecture halls; but more advanced students are quickly integrated into the research organization.

The chief difficulty with the nonresearch elements is to prevent them from interfering with the design of the research areas. A badly located auditorium or boiler plant can strangle expansion and interfere with efficient operation. The most comprehensive method of avoiding such difficulties is the overall planning grid.

A master plan must make provision for independent growth of all four of the basic elements of the laboratory complex, either through a campus type of development or through sufficient articulation and separation of each area.

Research Areas The research portion of the laboratory is itself divided into several basic elements. Most research areas require desk space as well as bench space; and many experiments require some sort of controlled environment, with closely regulated temperature and humidity, or the elimination of outside contamination. Controlled environment installations and other ancillary facilities frequently cannot be accommodated within the ordinary research areas. In addition, scientists frequently wish to have conference rooms directly associated with research, and there are usually some fairly extensive storage requirements.

Construction Factors Economy of construction can conflict with efficient operation. Bench areas and special installations require elaborate piping services and air conditioning; desk space, conference rooms, and storage areas do not. Bench space and special installations are usually fairly large areas; desk space, conference rooms, and storage form smaller units. In terms of economy, it makes sense to group like functions and like areas, and to separate desk space and conference rooms from research. Unfortunately, most scientists prefer desk space to be near their research, and special installations need to be associated with research as well.

The design of teaching laboratories provides an analogous situation, with less need for desk space but a requirement for preparation rooms. Resolving these contradictory requirements, while still providing for flexibility and growth, is perhaps the most difficult problem in designing a laboratory.

The possible solutions range from placing all desk space in a separate building to incorporating all offices within the laboratories. The degree of separation possible, and the ratio of one type of space to the other, varies from discipline to discipline. Figure 3 shows some of the possibilities, within a flexible space system which can be used for either purpose.

The comparative study of eight different teaching laboratory layouts (Fig. 4) assumes that all office space is located in a separate wing. Each method of organization is evaluated in terms of economy of construction and mechanical equipment, circulation, and flexibility.

A comparison of four basic types of industrial laboratories is shown in Fig. 5. The first one places the desk space within the laboratory itself. The second places the offices on one side of the corridor and the laboratories on the other. The third plan provides core laboratories and perimeter offices; the fourth provides a peripheral corridor and interior laboratories, with the desk space again incorporated in the research area. These four plans are representative of standard practice: most laboratories will be found to conform to one or another of these basic classifications.

There are, however, other possibilities. Eero Saarinen's design for the IBM Research Headquarters in Yorktown Heights places both laboratories and offices within a peripheral corridor system. If one accepts the concept that all working accommodation should be interior space, this is a highly efficient and consistent method of organization.

Some laboratories are organized as towers, rather than horizontally. Ulrich Franzen's laboratory tower at Cornell (Fig. 6) also provides interior accommodation, with laboratories that can be entered either directly from the corridor, or through the offices. Vincent G. Kling's science building at Barnard College is a tower, as are, of course, Louis I. Kahn's Richards Medical Laboratories at the University of Pennsylvania. Kahn's first towers provide completely undifferientiated space, which can be used as laboratories, offices, or corridors. The later towers have desk space around the periphery on some of the floors. The plans of both of these buildings are also illustrated in Fig. 6.

UTILITY DISTRIBUTION

General

Utility services within a research laboratory building require a great deal more emphasis than is customary in the design of the average building. Heating, ventilating, and air conditioning systems and the multiple pipes of the various laboratory services such as water, gas, vacuum, and oxygen create a demand for cubic space as well as floor space. In more recent designs, utility systems have taken a higher percentage of the gross area, with consequent reduction in net space. This special aspect of the research laboratory building sometimes comes as a surprise to architects and engineers whose experience has been mainly with commercial buildings, which need much less utility service capability. Associated with this need for additional space for utility services is the need to provide functional space for the unseen occupants of the building: maintenance and operating engineers, and the craftsmen who provide for the continual changes and adjustments in utility systems which mark an active research program.

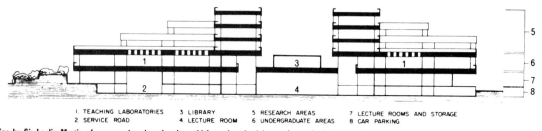

1. TEACHING LABORATORIES   3 LIBRARY   5 RESEARCH AREAS   7 LECTURE ROOMS AND STORAGE
2. SERVICE ROAD   4 LECTURE ROOM   6 UNDERGRADUATE AREAS   8 CAR PARKING

Fig. 1 Studies by Sir Leslie Martin of a comprehensive planning grid for university laboratories and of the type of development that can be based upon it.

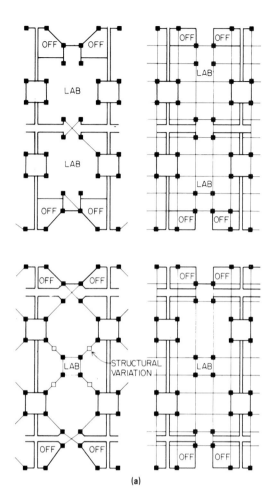

(a)

Selection of Systems

Selection of the utility distribution systems strongly influences the configuration, design, and cost of a research laboratory building. The type of utility system used should be selected as early as possible in the planning process, always before the room arrangement is fixed. Room arrangement and equipment location should follow the utility distribution pattern once this has been standardized. Arranging rooms and equipment according to the preferences of the first occupants usually results in costly, complicated utility distribution systems.

Planning a nonstandard room arrangement makes it difficult to visualize—without elaborate mockups—the configuration of space and equipment in the completed building. Then too, successive occupants are not always happy with the room arrangements selected by the first occupants. The rearrangement of plumbing and duct systems to meet preferences of successive occupants is usually costly unless these systems are installed on the standard repetitive pattern. Then a minimum of time and materials is required to rearrange the ventilation, lighting, and the plumbing and draining systems.

Standard Configuration

Utility services should be laid out with an identical configuration for every floor. This layout should be designed to meet the capability needs of the programs that will occupy the building over its life and with appropriate consideration of costs. Where it is not practical to provide an identical layout in each floor, a standard utility layout should be established for the floor which requires maximum utility services and this standard used for all the other floors, with deletions made where it is anticipated the services will not be needed for

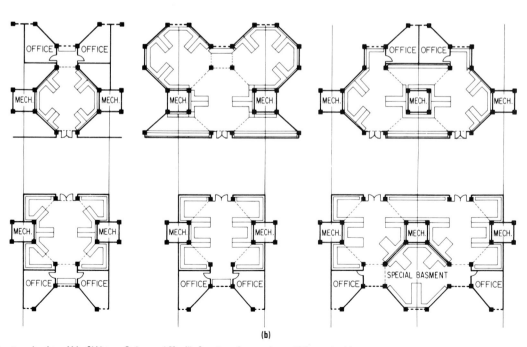

(b)

Fig. 2   (a) Laboratory planning grid by Skidmore, Owings and Merrill. A system of square bays which accepts either a diagonal or a rectilinear planning grid. Column clusters mark out circulation areas or service shafts. (b) A building unit in this system which employs a diagonal grid, and some laboratory arrangements that would be possible.

a considerable time. The arrangement of utilities should be such that installation of missing portions of the plumbing and duct systems can be made with a minimum of labor and materials.

It may be difficult for the architect and the initial user to accept an arrangement of space based on a standard utility and mechanical system distribution system rather than on the preferences of the first occupants of the space. This is somewhat similar to installing water mains, gas lines, electric power lines along the streets of the city, and then building the houses on lots in such a way that they can be connected to the public utility systems. It would be uneconomical and exceedingly difficult to maintain adequate service in the future if the building utility supply mains were installed in the streets according to the needs of each individual house.

Types of Systems

Utility services are usually provided within a research laboratory building by either a horizontal or vertical distribution system or a combination of the two. Five systems are generally used to distribute laboratory utility services:

- The utility corridor system
- The multiple interior shaft system
- The multiple exterior shaft system
- The corridor ceiling with isolated vertical shafts
- The utility floor system

Utility Corridor System In the utility corridor design all service mains and ducts are brought to the various floor levels by means of a vertical central core which distributes the utilities by vertical mains, usually from a basement, sometimes from a roof mechanical room. The horizontal distribution of utilities from the central core may be at the ceiling and downward to individual casework or it can be directly along the floor through the wall in the pipe space behind the base cabinets.

This design provides access for maintenance and service personnel to the utility piping and duct work throughout the life of the structure. It has a high degree of flexibility for meeting the needs of changes in research program and has a high capability to meet a wide range of criteria with regard to environmental control and ventilation, temperature controls, lighting, electric power, etc. Its efficiency in terms of the net assignable area and the gross area is not high. It usually runs somewhere between 50 and 60 percent.

The utility corridor design is most applicable to multistory buildings—with a square rather than rectangular shape—and it should be used with reservation for laboratories with only one or two floors. This system results in functionally efficient laboratory buildings. It is extremely useful where future expansion, either horizontal or vertical, is planned and is particularly adaptable to those arrangements where offices with window exposure are separated from the interior laboratory units. In its simplest form the system provides for a single large room on each side of the utility corridor. The first refinement of this basic plan is the horse stall arrangement, which provides for partitions separating the various work areas but provides for no doorways or divisions from the circulation area around the perimeter. The refinement continues with the installation of walls and doors to separate the circulation perimeter from the laboratories.

1. Advantages
   Excellent flexibility

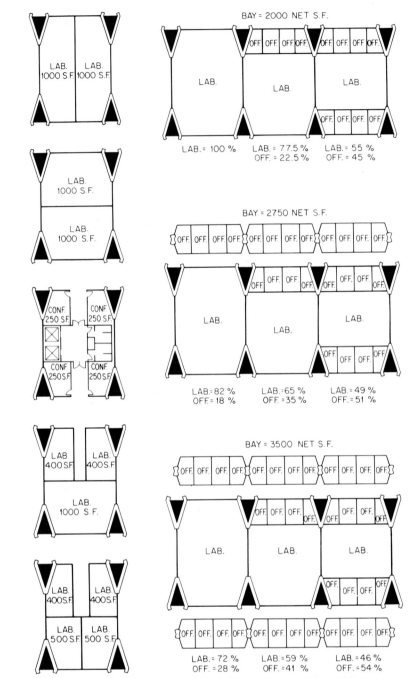

Fig. 3   A comparative study by Skidmore, Owings and Merrill of different ratios of office and laboratory space possible within a single, flexible system.

Moderately high initial cost
Low modification cost
Low replacement cost
Low cleaning (maintenance) cost
Permits full utilization of walls
Modifications do not interfere with conduct of work in adjacent modules

2. Disadvantages
   Fair net to gross area efficiency which improves when units are located in parallel, thus saving one corridor
   All rooms are "inside rooms"

Multiple Interior Shaft System This sytem provides for concealed utilities with duct work

and plumbing services in a series of regularly spaced shafts located either on both sides or on one side of a circulation corridor. All service mains and ducts are brought vertically to the various floor levels either upward or downward from the mechanical room. The shafts are located in each (or alternate) laboratory module or room on both sides of the central corridor. Distribution of utility services from the vertical shafts into the laboratory working areas is generally in the pipe space behind the laboratory benchwork. With the exception of the plumbing drains, in some designs the utility services are extended from the utility shaft below the ceiling in the laboratory and then

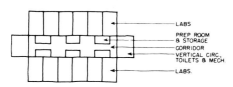

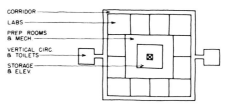

Feasibility: *Structural:* Compact plan may reduce cost. *Mechanical:* Although cores are separated, short mechanical runs reduce cost. *Circulation:* Double loaded corridors most economical. *Flexibility:* Changes may be made easily.

Feasibility: *Structural:* Economical arrangement. *Mechanical:* Very compact and economical. *Circulation:* Excessive corridors. *Flexibility:* Fair.

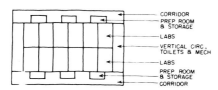

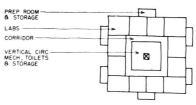

Feasibility: *Structural:* Compact plan. *Mechanical:* Separated cores and double runs of ducts, etc. may add to cost. *Circulation:* Doubling number of corridors is uneconomical. *Flexibility:* Rooms may be changed and added with ease.

Feasibility: *Structural:* Fairly economical. *Mechanical:* Very compact and economical. *Circulation:* Very economical corridor arrangement. *Flexibility:* Fair.

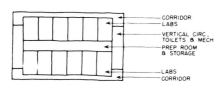

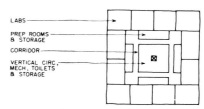

Feasibility: *Structural:* Compact plan may reduce cost. *Mechanical:* Compact system may reduce cost. *Circulation:* Double corridors uneconomical. *Flexibility:* Not as flexible as scheme above.

Feasibility: *Structural:* Economical arrangement. *Mechanical:* Very compact and economical. *Circulation:* Minimum length of corridors. *Flexibility:* Rooms changed and additions made easily.

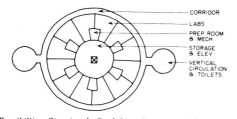

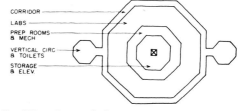

Feasibility: *Structural:* Good form for economical structure. *Mechanical:* Very compact and economical. *Circulation:* Excessive corridors. *Flexibility:* Not too flexible.

Feasibility: *Structural:* Economical structure. *Mechanical:* Very compact and economical. *Circulation:* Excessive corridors. *Flexibility:* Not too flexible.

Fig. 4 Comparative study of different teaching laboratory layouts by Hellmuth, Obata, and Kassabaum, with an evaluation of each in terms of economy and flexibility.

downward to the laboratory benches. The interior utility shaft system is not a good selection for buildings with only one or two stories; it is most efficient in multistory buildings and is frequently found in those with a long rectangular shape.

1. Advantages
   Good flexibility
   Moderate net to gross area efficiency
   Moderate initial cost
   Moderate modification cost
   Moderate replacement cost
   Easier to service than the exterior shaft system
2. Disadvantages
   More expensive and not as flexible as exposed systems
   Available space usually does not permit

individual supply and exhaust of fume hoods
Servicing interferes with traffic flow in corridors

The Multiple Exterior Shaft System This system brings service mains and ventilation duct work to the individual floor levels by a series of exterior wall vertical shafts located at each or alternate laboratory rooms or modules. Utility services are distributed from these exterior shafts into the laboratory rooms by means of the pipe space behind the base cabinets of the fixed equipment, or at the ceiling level. The multiple exterior utility shaft system generally should be considered only for multistory laboratories since its cost does not justify its use for one- or two-story buildings.

1. Advantages
   Good flexibility
   Moderate net to gross area efficiency
   Moderate initial cost
   Moderate modification cost
   Moderate replacement cost
   Low cleaning (maintenance) cost
   Permits full usage of walls
   Utilities are common with duct work and drainage systems
   Good appearance
2. Disadvantages
   More difficult to service or modify than other recommended systems
   Requires removal of one section of case work
   Modifications interfere with conduct of work in adjacent modules

Industrial
RESEARCH LABORATORIES

More expensive and not as flexible as exposed systems

Available space usually does not permit individual supply and exhaust of fume hoods

The Corridor Ceiling Distribution In this system, utilities are located in the corridor ceiling and in some cases above the ceilings of the rooms on each side of the corridor and are supplied by one or two vertical pipe shafts. Distribution from the ceiling mains to the laboratory areas may be downward to the floor and upward through the floor above in order to supply two floors from one ceiling distribution arrangement. Generally, it is preferable to provide the distribution downward within each room to avoid perforation of the floor slab and consequent leaks and flooding due to accidents in later years.

This system is commonly used in research buildings with only one or two stories or where a single research floor is inserted in a multistory building primarily designed for other than research purposes. Designs employing exposed utilities are ideal for two-story or one-story-and-basement buildings where economy of construction is a major consideration.

1. Advantages
   Excellent flexibility
   Low first cost
   Low modification cost
   Low replacement cost
   High net to gross area efficiency
   Modifications do not interfere with conduct of work in adjacent modules
2. Disadvantages
   Requires increased ceiling height for same clearance
   Limits installation of wall cabinets
   Increased cleaning (maintenance) costs
   Requires independent type of air duct installation and drainage system
   Unsightly

The Utility Floor Distribution System This system probably provides the maximum of flexibility and capability in research laboratory structures. Utilities, consisting of the duct work and the plumbing systems, are in separate floors. From the supply, the service mains and truck ventilation ducts are brought to each individual utility floor by means of a centrally located vertical shaft or tower. Then distribution is made laterally on each utility floor with final distribution made by penetrating the floor below or above to service the research laboratory areas. Although this system has almost unlimited flexibility, its cost is high and it has an extremely low net gross area of efficiency. This system is primarily suitable only to multistory buildings and is not a good selection for one or two stories.

1. Advantages
   Excellent flexibility to any portion of room
   Low modification cost
   Low replacement cost
   Modifications do not interfere with conduct of work in adjacent modules
   May be used with up-feed at every floor or may be combined with down-feed and located at every third floor
2. Disadvantages
   Very high first cost
   Low net to gross area efficiency

Plumbing Systems

A plumbing system for the health research laboratory should be suited to the type of utility distribution system selected.

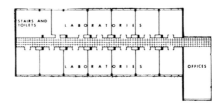

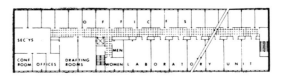

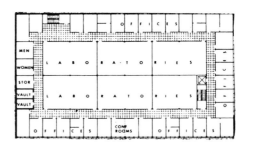

Fig. 5 Four plans by Walter Kidde Constructors, Inc. showing different basic methods of organizing an industrial laboratory.

Scope This discussion is limited to the piping systems within the laboratory building. Criteria for outside utility piping, water and sewage plants, and pumping stations are not included.

Flexibility and Capability Here again design incorporating long-term flexibility and capability is important. Focusing on the needs of individual laboratories or investigators leads to emphasis on the service piping or small services of various sinks and case work. Future revisions to such a system usually involve removal of the custom-provided service lines and either a relocation or resizing of the trunk mains in the building—a very expensive procedure.

The desirable approach is to determine plumbing service requirements either by floor or by large zones and to provide a trunk or a main distribution system that will reach all portions of the building. This should be supplemented by branch lines available to all rooms and spaces within the structure. Rooms and laboratory equipment can then be connected by small-size service piping to the nearest available branch drain bent or pressure service pipe.

As an example, plumbing stacks can be located to provide drainage capability within

10 ft of every square foot of the building, or plumbing vents and drains can be designed to provide drainage service within 20 ft of every square foot of the building.

Standardized laboratory services such as oxygen, vacuum, compressed air, hot and cold water, and gas should be designed so that the lines can be laid in parallel with a minimum of joints and elbows but appropriately equipped with valves to permit rearrangement of individual spaces without shutting off large areas of the building.

Code Requirements It is assumed that local governing codes will be followed. The following national codes may also be used for guidance: The American Insurance Association (formerly NBFU), The National Fire Protection Association, The American National Standards Association, The American Gas Association, The National Plumbing Code, and the American Water Works Association.

Functional Design Considerations

General The long-term capability and flexibility of the plumbing system requires special attention to the aspects discussed below. These considerations require that the piping follow a modular layout and, to a certain extent,

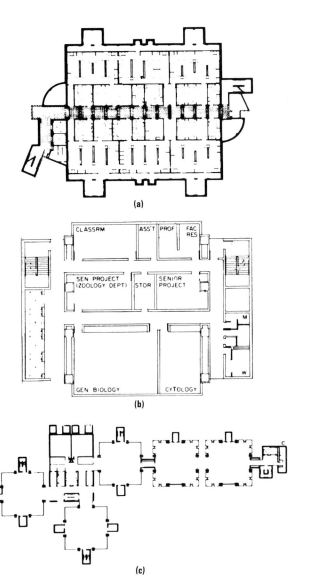

(a)

(b)

(c)

Fig. 6 Laboratory tower plans from (a) the Agronomy Building at Cornell University by Ulrich Franzen. (b) A projected science building at Barnard College by Vincent G. Kling. (c) Louis I. Kahn's Richards Laboratories.

from the partition wall. Mains and risers located near nonlaboratory space should be provided with capped or plugged tees for ease of future connection.

Pipe Sizes in Mains and Risers The selected pipe sizes should include a factor for increased future use of the various gravity and pumped systems. For sanitary waste pipe, an anticipated increase of approximately 5 to 10 percent flow may be met by initially selecting the next larger size of pipe. Pumped services may meet future increased demand flows by an increase in pump head, while staying within acceptable pipe velocities.

Central Services Required Use of utility services will vary according to the department served. To provide greater flexibility, all laboratories should have air, vacuum, water, and gas services at all work areas.

Sanitary Piping System

Venting Each fixture should be back-vented into a circuit or loop vent in a manner prescribed by code. Locating plumbing fixtures in "peninsula" casework is not recommended, because of the difficulty in getting proper back-venting of the fixture.

Pipe Materials Ordinary galvanized iron or steel should not be used in waste pipe from laboratories intended for research in biology and chemistry, where concentrated acids may be accidentally or improperly discharged into the sanitary waste system. Acid-resisting piping materials should be used in all drainage systems serving laboratories in which acids will be used. A separate acid waste system may be necessary for areas of the building where large volumes of acids are used. This system should empty into a neutralization and dilution sump prior to discharge into the sewer.

Domestic Water Supply System

Sources of Water Supply Municipal or corporation supplies are usually preferred to other sources. A private supply of water is recommended only where public water is not available or it is impracticable to extend service to the site of the laboratory building.

Water Treatment A chemical analysis should always be obtained. Treatment of cold water supply is usually not necessary when the water is obtained from a municipality or from a utility corporation. Water softeners of the Zeolite type are recommended when the water has a temporary hardness of 10 or more grains per gallon, or a total hardness of 18 or more grains per gallon. Boiler feed water softeners are recommended if the temporary hardness is 4 or more grains per gallon.

Interior Water Piping

1. *Location of Mains* The water supply system should be distributed throughout the building and the mains should generally run near the ceiling of the lowest story.

2. *No Cross Connections* Cross connections between water supply piping and waste, drain vent, or sewer piping should be strictly prohibited, whether the connection is direct or indirect.

3. *Backflow Protection of Water Piping System* Water distribution systems must be protected against backflow [the flow of water or other liquids into the distributing pipes from any other source(s) other than its intended source]. Water supply connections or out-

limits the configuration and location of individual spaces as later defined by partitions.

1. Typical central services should be provided by means of vertical risers, horizontal mains, and individual room runouts, sizing the pipes in a manner which will permit, as far as possible, independent supply and control to various floors, zones, and/or individual rooms. This design approach should result in a repetitive and standardized (grid) arrangement of the risers, mains, and major branches.

2. Piped utilities should be accessible to permit extending the systems as required by future changes in research programs. Service pipe runouts (capped off when not used initially) at regular intervals in service shafts or cores will ensure maximum accessibility for future connections with a minimum of disruption to research programs in adjacent spaces.

3. To provide for future needs, the central service systems should include space for ducts and piping not initially required, pipe size which permits increased flows to meet larger demands, and adequate space to permit normal maintenance and repair.

4. Piping material should be selected on the basis of the properties required to maintain the quality of the flow material or to withstand corrosion or erosion by the various materials to be transported.

Horizontal Mains and Vertical Stacks Pipe mains and stacks may be run exposed or concealed in pipe chases or utility corridors. Pipe chases and utility corridors should have dimensions which will ensure properly spaced pipes and provide access for maintenance personnel. The chases and utility corridors will usually include air conditioning ducts and electrical conduits. The optimal arrangement of pipe spaces would provide utility mains adjacent to each health related space, so that the service to each laboratory would not be dependent on service to other spaces. The utility corridor located between rows of laboratory spaces would meet this criteria.

Pipe Runouts to Laboratory Space Satisfactory methods of installing runouts from vertical stacks and horizontal mains are overhead on exposed ceiling or behind laboratory casework and supported

lets to plumbing fixtures, tanks, receptacles, or equipment should be protected from backflow as follows:

a. The preferred method is by means of an approved air gap, as specified in American National Standard A40.4-1942.

b. Where it is not possible to provide a minimum air gap, the supply connection should be equipped with an accessibly located backflow preventer (nonpressure type vacuum breaker) installed beyond the last control valve in compliance with American National Standard A40.6-1943.

c. An alternate approved method is the use of an industrial water system to serve all laboratory work areas. This distribution system must be independent of the potable domestic system. This can be done by connecting the industrial water main to the building service line at the point of entry into the building, beyond the point of connection for the potable water and with a suitable backflow preventer inserted between the points of potable and industrial water system connections.

Distilled and Demineralized Water

Quality of Water The quality of the water required in health related spaces will determine whether distilled or demineralized water should be distributed through a central piped system. The analysis of local water characteristics will help determine if demineralization alone will produce water of the desired quality. Where demineralization alone will not suffice, distillation is required.

Size of System Stills and storage tanks should be large enough to assure an adequate daily volume of water. Still size can be determined on the basis of a continuous 24 hour operation of the still and the provision of adequate storage tank capacity. The system should be designed so that part of it can be shut down for servicing without cutting off the entire system.

Location of Stills Stills and demineralization equipment should be located at an elevation within the building sufficient to provide gravity flow to the outlets in the piping system. Mechanically pressurized systems are not recommended, since the pump and fittings may introduce impurities into the high quality water.

Materials of Construction "Block" tin (purity in excess of 99.9 percent tin) is recommended only when ultrapure water is required. Other materials which have been successfully used alone or as lining in tanks and piping are plastics, glass, aluminum, or stainless steel. The selection of a particular distribution piping and storage tank material must be based on water purity and contamination studies, previous experiences, and cost analysis.

Fire Protection

The requirements for standpipes and/or portable fire extinguishers are set forth in applicable local or national codes. Where the fire hazard in laboratories and ancillary spaces is above normal, an automatic sprinkler system or automatic detectors should be installed. Where the application of water by usual methods would be harmful or dangerous, an automatic or manual protective system should be installed, to suit the classification of fires from which protection is needed.

Gas Piping

Design All gas piping should be designed in accordance with NFPA Standard No. 54, Installation of Gas Appliances and Gas Piping. These lines should be sized to provide for expansion of the service and to maintain adequate pressure at the workbench. In general, gas piping should not be run in trenches, tunnels, furred ceilings, or other confined spaces where leaking gas might collect and cause an explosion.

Piping Materials Gas service pipe from the street to the building should conform to the regulations of the local gas company. Gas piping inside the building should be black steel with malleable - iron - banded fittings.

Valves Gas piping should have a shutoff valve just inside the building and at other points where it would be desirable to isolate certain sections.

Compressed Air and Vacuum Systems

Air Filters and Driers Compressed air must be of high quality—substantially free of oil, impurities, and water. Centrifugal compressors are ordinarily used to provide oil-free air. If a small amount of oil is acceptable at points of use, a main oil separator with additional separators at the using equipment will be adequate.

Air driers are required when moisture will create difficulty in laboratory instruments, or where compressed air piping may be exposed to freezing temperatures. Where laboratory requirements do not dictate dew points below $40°F$, the dryness requirements can be achieved by the use of refrigerated water or direct expansion refrigeration in an aftercooler. The aftercooler may be air-cooled in the case of small compressors.

The pressure required at the workbench need not exceed 40 psig and flow requirements of 5 scfm at every station. The compressor pressure is based upon the needs of the equipment requiring the maximum pressure at point of use.

The vacuum requirements at the workbench are 5 cfm at 28 in. Hg at each service outlet. Receptor jars must be used between the equipment and the vacuum outlet, to prevent liquids and solids from entering the vacuum system. The air discharged from vacuum pumps should be exhausted outdoors, to prevent entry into the equipment room of toxic or flammable solvents.

Pipe material may be either copper or galvanized steel with threaded malleable-iron fittings.

HVAC Systems

Heating, ventilation, and air conditioning (HVAC) account for 25 percent to 50 percent of the cost of a health research facility. The design and functioning of the HVAC system should be considered very early in the planning process. Such early planning will avoid the extra expense and less satisfactory results obtained when HVAC engineering is limited to the inflexible confines of architectural design in progress.

The heating requirements of a health research facility do not differ significantly from those of a conventional commercial building, and have not been discussed here.

Electrical Supply

The power demand of laboratory instrumentation added to that of the building itself—for light, air conditioning, ventilating fans, etc.—makes the provision of electric power, and its distribution, of key importance in the planning of a health research facility.

Flexibility and capability in this case means more than planning excess capacity for future needs. When electricity stops everything in the laboratory is affected. Emergency sources of power must be provided, and a system of priorities set up to determine which functions will have first call on the emergency power supplies.

LABORATORY PLANNING

Laboratory planning is generally regarded as one of the most difficult assignments with which an architect can be confronted. It involves the development of a layout to meet an exacting set of conditions, and the integration of complicated engineering services.

It is essential that the module and layout of the individual laboratories be considered in detail before even preliminary sketch plans are prepared. This can best be done in the following sequence.

Module

A module of 10 ft is recommended; this is the distance from center to center of two peninsular benches, and it is based on a bench width of 5 ft with a space of 5 ft between. In a one-module laboratory it is the distance between the center of one partition and the center of the next; it is based on a wall thickness of 4 in, a bench 2 ft 3 in wide on one side and a table 2 ft 6 in wide on the other—to give a space between of 4 ft 11 in. Generally an entirely satisfactory and clean-cut layout can be planned with the 10-ft module, but if it is necessary to have greater flexibility (i.e. rooms 15 and 25 ft wide), then a module of 5 ft must be used. Of course, the module is dependent on the width of the benches and the space between them. The most convenient metric equivalent is a 3-m module.

Width of Bench In chemistry laboratories, the generally accepted width of benches fitted with reagent shelves is 2 ft 6 in for wall benches and 5 ft for peninsular benches. In physics laboratories, widths of 3 ft and 6 ft are sometimes preferred, with a wide shelf for electronic equipment. In some laboratories, a bench width of 2 ft or 2 ft 3 in is adequate. Where solid timber tops are used, the consideration of width in relation to cost is relatively unimportant, but where sheets of some material are being used, the width should be considered in relation to sheet size so that waste is reduced to a minimum.

Space between Benches As building costs rise, it is to be expected that the distance between benches will receive closer scrutiny. Some research laboratory planners maintain that the increasing use of mobile equipment justifies the adoption of a 6-ft space. If it is adopted, then in a building 200 ft long it means the loss of one 2-module laboratory; conversely, a decrease from 5 ft to 4 ft 6 in means a gain of one 1-module laboratory.

The distance should be determined by considerations of convenience and safety, i.e., one person should be able to pass another (working at the bench) comfortably and without risk of collision

Reproduced from *Practical Laboratory Planning*, by W. R. Ferguson (1973), by Permission of Applied Science Publishers, London, England.

if the latter should step back unexpectedly. Experience has shown that 4 ft 6 in to 5 ft is ideal; 4 ft is cramped. It must be admitted that there are laboratories in which one man works between benches separated by as little as 3 ft 3 in, but such a small space should certainly not be thought of when planning a new laboratory.

In student and routine laboratories where there is less bench space per person and often two people will be working back to back immediately opposite each other, the space between the benches should be greater than 5 ft so that there is room for others to walk down the center.

Layout of Laboratory

Having established the module, it is now necessary to settle the size and position of laboratory offices, the depth of laboratories and the position of service laboratories, fume cupboards, and service ducts. All of these are vitally important in themselves, and of course they actually determine the type of layout which is to be adopted. Let us consider each of these items.

Laboratory Offices There are many scientists still alive today who have worked in laboratories where offices were not provided; the lucky ones had tables in the laboratory and the others just shifted some equipment off the bench to make space for report writing. For a number of years now, it has been standard practice to provide every scientist with an office; it is quite usual to provide individual offices for senior technical officers also, whilst laboratory assistants are expected to share offices or have writing spaces provided for them in the laboratories.

The best location for laboratory offices is always a controversial subject. Are they to be within the laboratory, adjoining the laboratory, on the opposite side of the corridor, or grouped in a separate part of the building? Is it essential for all offices to be on an external wall?

Some senior scientists consider an 8-ft by 6-ft office within the laboratory entirely satisfactory. These people spend most of their time actually working in the laboratory and the closeness outweighs the advantages of greater privacy and silence in a larger office across the corridor. In any case, for report writing it is much more satisfactory to use a carrell in the library. The internal office shown in Fig. 1 has a 6-ft by 2-ft 6-in table with bookshelves above and a filing cabinet beneath. This layout has the advantage that the full length of the building is available for laboratories and, with an off-center corridor, the service laboratories can be conveniently located along the opposite side.

Offices which adjoin laboratories also have the advantage of closeness and they can be larger than the internal office—one dimension is fixed by the module of 10 ft—but they do have the disadvantage that they use the more expensive serviced area. The alternative is to provide offices along the unserviced area on the opposite side of the corridor, but many scientists consider this separation from the laboratory undesirable, and the further the offices are from the laboratories, the more serious this becomes. In the case of offices grouped on another floor, the scientist may even think twice before making the effort to get to his laboratory.

Some scientists consider 10 ft by 10 ft an absolute minimum for an office, and others argue strongly for 10 ft by 12 ft, or even 10 ft by 14 ft. Certainly, when the offices are along one side of a corridor, a depth of 14 ft makes it possible

to get a more satisfactory layout for stairs, toilets, etc.

For large projects, it is necessary to consider laboratories on both sides of the corridor; in this case, offices must be either in (or adjoining) laboratories or grouped in a separate wing of the building. For still larger schemes, the double-width layout provides the best solution.

Details of the various positions of offices are shown in Figs. 2, 3, 4, and 5.

Depth of Laboratories Over the last 40 years, the depth of laboratories has increased from about 16 ft to 24 or 25 ft, with some going to 27 and even 30 ft. This has resulted in a better utilization of space and, as the span is within economic limits, the additional area is obtained

at a lower cost per square foot. For the standard type of peninsular bench layout, a clear depth of 24 ft is recommended.

Service Laboratories These laboratories are either planned to be integral with the laboratory and laboratory office unit or they are provided on the opposite side of the corridor; again, the various positions are shown in Figs. 2, 3, 4, and 5. Much of the equipment housed in these rooms is expensive and therefore it must be shared; it follows that this equipment must be located so that it is convenient to the maximum number of staff.

Fume Cupboards The risk of accident is greater in a fume cupboard [hood] than elsewhere in the

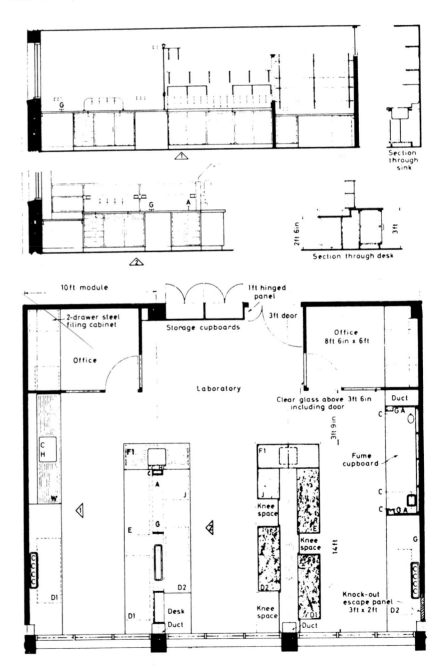

Fig. 1 Layout of a three-module, 30-ft by 24-ft laboratory.

Industrial

RESEARCH LABORATORIES

laboratory; so, for reasons of safety, one should not be located where it will block an exit. Of course, if there is an alternative exit from the laboratory, this difficulty does not arise.

Fume cupboards require an exhaust duct with a diameter of from 8 to 12 in. Preferably the duct should connect from the top center of the cupboard and rise vertically to discharge the fumes above the roof. This does not present a problem in a single-story building—except, perhaps, when the architect insists on some symmetry in the positions of the outlets on the roof. However, in a three-story building, the position of the fume cupboards and the space required for exhaust ducts become more involved; if, in the preliminary planning stage, time is spent working out these details, it will obviate later troubles such as horizontal ducts which are too long or riser shafts which are too small.

The installation can be simplified by having the laboratories requiring the most fume cupboards on the top floor; quite often the entire ground-floor space can be allotted for rooms and laboratories without any fume cupboards.

Service Ducts The mechanical services are a major feature of any laboratory and, in order to achieve good design, location, and accessibility, they must be given a lot of thought. In some laboratories the installation will involve three or four pipes, and in others there might be six or more.

For benches serviced from the external wall, there should be horizontal and vertical ducts with removable covers. For benches serviced from the corridor wall, it is necessary to have a vertical duct accessible from the corridor. In some laboratories—especially if island benches are being used—the service pipes are reticulated in the space between the floor slab and the removable ceiling. This system does have the disadvantage that it requires many holes through the floor and, in the event of floods, these will cause trouble in the room below; also, repairs and alterations seriously disrupt work in the laboratory and, what is worse, it is somebody else's laboratory! Nevertheless, this system is preferable to the use of ducts in the floor because, even at high cost, it is quite difficult to get a cover which is removable, serviceable, rigid, neat in appearance, and perfectly flush.

For large projects where the double-width layout has been adopted, a service corridor is the obvious solution because it provides excellent accessibility to horizontal and vertical pipes and, in addition, space for fume cupboard exhaust ducts and miscellaneous laboratory equipment such as pumps.

Type of Bench There are three types of bench—peninsular, island, and wall. As the names imply, the peninsular bench projects from the wall and the island bench is free-standing.

With the greater depth of laboratories, the use of peninsular benches at right angles to the windows has become almost mandatory. They are preferable to island benches because the installation of services is easier and less costly, and there is minimum shadow when they are fitted with reagent shelves. Most laboratory workers will no longer argue that the extra space required to give access to four sides of an island bench is justified.

As a general rule, wall benches under windows should be avoided; facing the sun in front of windows on the east and west elevations makes working conditions quite intolerable. For windows

facing north, screening the low-angle sun in the winter is not always satisfactory; even with south-facing windows, glare can be a problem. Wall benches between peninsular benches create inaccessible pockets on either side and, for this reason also, they are not recommended.

Whether it be a one-, two-, or three-module laboratory, the combination of peninsular and wall bench at right angles to the external wall produces the simplest layout. The one-module laboratory provides the most wall space per unit area; the three-module laboratory has the widest application because in many cases it accommodates the optimum number of staff to share equipment and facilities.

Details of a layout which has been used quite extensively are shown in Fig. 1. This layout can be adapted to meet a wide range of conditions—for example, one or both of the offices can be omitted, the number and type of bench units and service outlets can be varied, the reagent shelves can be reduced in length or omitted, or one whole bench can be omitted to leave space for equipment or a rig for setting up apparatus.

Prototype Laboratory or Bench For large projects, it is a very good idea to have a prototype laboratory, and for small schemes at least a prototype bench. If these are to achieve their real purpose, they should be complete with services and accurate to the smallest detail. Most scientists can read plans very well; however, there are always some who can't visualize the finished product, and for them, and for the builder and his subcontractors, a prototype is a great help. Invariably, after examination and discussion, some improvements or economies are effected. Also, when a prototype is available for inspection by tenders, its cost can be offset by more accurate estimating.

Windowless Laboratories and Offices Given a choice, most people would prefer to work in a laboratory which has windows; it is very pleasant to be able to look out on a garden or landscape, or even to get a glimpse of the sky. There is a prejudice against working in rooms without windows because it is thought that they create a sensation of being confined. The objection to this feeling of lack of contact with the outside world can be partially overcome if it is possible to 'look out if you want to'—for example, in some double-width laboratories, the door to the internal laboratory is opposite the door of the external office, and both are in line with the window; the doors have clear-glass top panels. In one windowless

laboratory I have visited, I was interested to see a brightly colored landscape hanging on the wall of an internal office; in another—a physics laboratory—many of the staff have worked quite happily for years in basement rooms; in yet another which has windowless laboratories and offices, the Director told me that, after 12 years' occupation, 'early apprehension that a closed-in feeling due to lack of outside windows would be a problem has not materialized.'

Laboratories without windows are shielded from the sun and external temperature variations, and it is possible to get much more accurate temperature control; another asset is more wall space. My impression is that windowless laboratories (and, to a lesser extent, windowless offices) are likely to be accepted more readily in the future.

Width of Corridors Factors which determine the width of corridors include the amount of traffic, the length of the building, and whether the doors open in or out; in overseas laboratories it is usual for doors to open into the corridors. Relevant details regarding five laboratories are:

Laboratory	Width of corridors	Length of building	Doors
Abbott	6 ft	224 ft	Single, 3 ft wide, opening out, serving rooms one side only
Battelle	7 ft 6 in	276 ft	Single, 3 ft 3 in wide, opening out
Bethlehem	7 ft	315 ft	Double, 2 ft 10 in + 1 ft wide, opening out from laboratory wall of service shaft at which point the corridor is 12 ft wide
Hoechst	6 ft 6 in	328 ft	Single, 3 ft 3 in wide, opening out from laboratory wall of service shaft at which point the corridor is 9 ft 9 in wide
National Bureau of Standards	7 ft	385 ft	Double, 3 ft + 1 ft 6 in wide, opening out from laboratory wall of service shaft at which point the corridor is 12 ft wide

There is very little traffic in the corridors of research laboratories, and in Australia, where the doors generally open into the laboratories, a width of 5 ft 6 in is adequate; furthermore, the narrower width helps to prevent the motley collection of refrigerators and cupboards which so often are lined up along one or both sides of the corridor. Nevertheless, 5 ft 6 in is an absolute minimum and assumes that there are no projecting columns; if the length of the building exceeds 200 ft, this width should be increased slightly to be visually acceptable.

Adoption of a Basic Laboratory Layout Every effort should be made to develop a basic layout which is standard throughout the building. This is not easy because on every job there is generally at least one scientist who, without any real justification, insists that his office or bench should be in a different position, and he will advance reasons why his idea of layout is necessary for some particular investigation. If he wins his argument and his laboratory layout is nonstandard, it so often happens that the project stops, or he leaves, and it is almost certain that his successor will require a different layout. On the other hand, there are some situations where it really is necessary to meet particular requirements, but these can and should be met by variations within the basic layout.

The establishment of a basic layout requires some firm decisions by the officer in charge, and these must be applied with a certain amount of ruthlessness if this proves necessary.

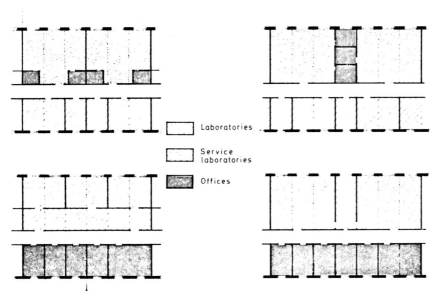

Fig. 2 Off-center corridor layouts, showing the relative positions of laboratories, service laboratories, and offices.

Layout of Building

Whilst the planning of each laboratory building has its individual problems, the range of layouts can be narrowed to a few which have been found satisfactory. Depending on the size of the project, the type of work, and the space available, any one of the following can be recommended.

Off-Center Corridor This layout has wide application for relatively small schemes—for instance, from a single-story building 100 ft long to several two- or three-story buildings about 200 ft in length. It has the great advantage that all the laboratories can have a south-facing aspect, and the two room depths provide flexibility in planning. Four variations of this layout are shown in Fig. 2.

Central Corridor This layout is more suitable for larger schemes. It has the advantage that the grouping of laboratories is more compact because they are on both sides of the corridor. Also, as the same width corridor is serving a wider building than in the case of the off-center layout, it provides a greater assignable space. However, it does mean that half the laboratories have a north-facing aspect. Two variations of this layout are shown in Fig. 3.

Double Corridor This layout provides a good interrelationship between laboratory, laboratory office, and service laboratory, and it sometimes offers the best solution when the width of the building is fixed within certain limits. It has the advantage that, as the service laboratories are windowless, it is easier to obtain accurate temperature control; in many cases, the absence of natural light is an asset. (See Fig. 4.)

Service Corridor The double-width layout shown in Fig. 5 is especially suitable for large schemes. As laboratory services become more complex, and temperature control more critical, it is likely that this type of layout will be more widely accepted. The increased area at one level contributes to more efficient operation because the scientific staff are brought closer together and the sharing of equipment is facilitated.

Assignable Area The gross area is the overall area of the building, the assignable area is the actual area of usable space, and the difference is the combined area of entrance halls, corridors, stairs, toilets, ducts, and wall thicknesses. The 'use factor' is the ratio of assignable area to gross area, and it ranges from approximately 50 to 70 percent.

The best utilization of space is obtained by having one corridor serving rooms on both sides. For example, in the simplest type of three-story building with minimum entrance hall, a 5-ft 6-in corridor with 24-ft deep laboratories along one side and 14-ft deep service laboratories along the other:

Gross area	201×47		$9447\ ft^2$
Assignable area			
Laboratories	196×24	4704	
Service laboratories (allowing five modules for stairs, toilets, elevators, and ducts)	147×14	2058	$6762\ ft^2$
Use factor $= \dfrac{6762}{9447} = 71\%$			

Obviously, a corridor serving rooms on one side only, or two corridors serving three rooms, decreases the ratio of assignable to gross area and therefore increases the cost.

Floor Space per Person The space required by scientists varies greatly. Most require a laboratory, a laboratory office, and access to several service laboratories, but quite a number need additional facilities such as glass-houses, animal pens, or large areas for pilot-plant investigations or the preparation and storage of many hundreds of specimens. Then again, some scientists use equipment which is small and commercially available, whilst others must have large equipment which often has to be specially designed and fabricated in workshops on the site.

Bench Space per Person One measure of good laboratory accommodation is adequate bench space. The layout shown in Fig. 1 provides 62 lineal feet of bench; this represents 15 lineal feet per person for four (with a maximum of five) persons. A bench length of 12 to 15 ft per person is a generally accepted standard, and an uninterrupted length is preferable to several short lengths.

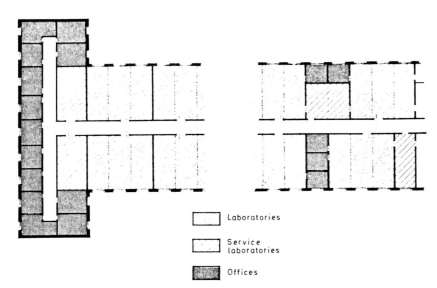

Fig. 3 Central corridor layouts, showing the relative positions of laboratories, service laboratories, and offices.

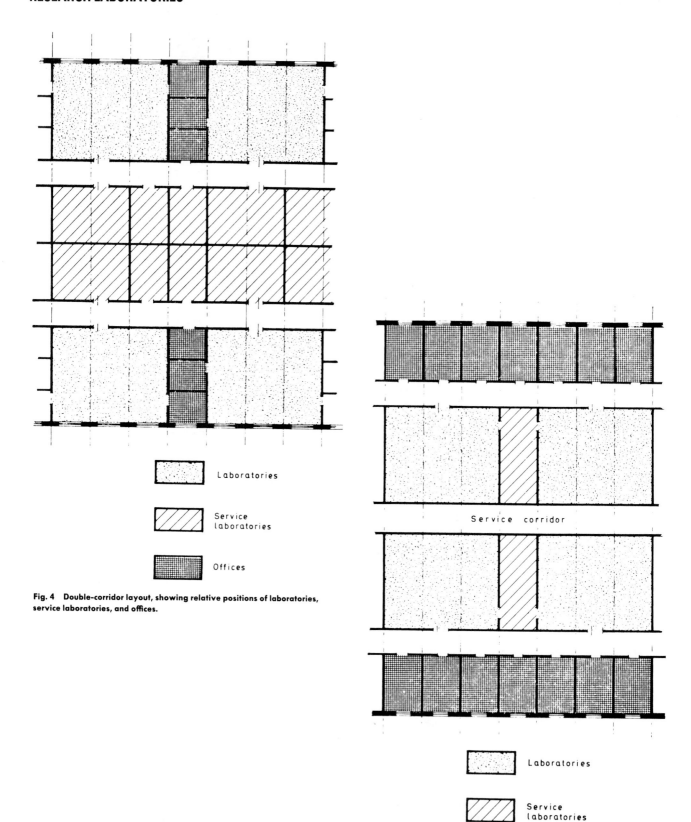

Laboratories

Service
laboratories

Offices

Fig. 4 Double-corridor layout, showing relative positions of laboratories, service laboratories, and offices.

Service corridor

Laboratories

Service
laboratories

Offices

Fig. 5 Double-width layout with service corridor, showing relative positions of laboratories, service laboratories, and offices.

WAREHOUSING AND STORAGE

Warehousing Warehousing is the receiving, storage, and delivery of goods.

Receiving Receiving is the acceptance of goods with a degree of accountability therefor.

Storage Storage is the safekeeping of goods in a warehouse or other depository.

Delivery Delivery is the transfer of goods to transportation carrier or customer.

Distribution Distribution is a function of warehousing which includes the preparation and delivery of goods according to plan or special order.

General History

Modern warehousing has progressed in recent years to a point where old warehouse structures are costly to operate. The old-type warehouse buildings usually do not have sufficient floor-load capacity in the upper floors and do not allow the adoption of economical storage methods in the receiving and shipping areas. The emphasis today is on the maximum use of the "cube" rather than the square foot of warehouse space, on distribution rather than storage, and on power handling equipment rather than hand labor.

The design of a warehouse should be based upon the most economical methods of materials handling. High stacking, with minimum use of aisles, is the keynote of maximum "cube" utilization. Modern warehouse design generally includes clear spans ranging from 60 to 100 ft, roof elevation sufficient to allow 18 to 20 ft (and higher) stacking height, and shipping and receiving areas located at box car or truck level.

Fundamentals of Modern Warehousing

One-Story-Type Building (Fig. 1) The study of multistory vs. one-story warehouses is complex and requires a complete engineering survey. The factors for consideration are partially listed herewith.
One Story:
1. Low-cost ground advisable
2. Availability of land for expansion
3. Less time for erection
4. Less area lost—sidewalls, columns, elevators, stairways, etc.
5. Adaptability to long-span construction
6. High floor loads
7. Greater flexibility for layout changes
8. Greater handling efficiency possible
9. Supervision easy and effective
10. Maximum use of daylight and natural ventilation
11. Hazardous areas easily isolated
Two (or More) Stories:

William Staniar, M.E., Editor-in-Chief, *Plant Engineering Handbook*, 2d ed., McGraw-Hill Book Company, New York, 1959.

1. High cost of ground
2. Limited area for site
3. Natural topography may permit entrance at different levels
4. Ease of expansion if foreseen
5. Floor load may be limited in upper levels
6. Product stored and handling equipment should be light in weight or small in bulk
7. Handling distances reduced with gravity flow
8. In some locations, less dirt and better ventilation on upper floors
9. Lower heat loss through roof

In general, the overall economic evaluation of the one-story warehouse indicates a lower investment per cubic foot of storage space. The low-cost types of roof construction and the reduction of steel and masonry for additional floors are the significant cost-reduction items. Another major point of concern is the demand for increased floor-load capacities to support industrial truck equipment and heavier unit loads.

Flexibility of Layout and Equipment Flexibility of storage allocations is obtained by the installation of minimum permanent storage aids. This can be accomplished by providing bolted-up types of pallet racks, bins, or shelves. The use of pallets and pallet pattern selection guides should provide the maximum cube utilization as well as stability. The large-size pallets are usually economical for warehousing operations.

Shipping and receiving areas should be designed for two-way operation over the same platform where possible. The main aisles of transportation within the warehouse should allow the passage of materials handling equipment in both directions.

Efficient material movement is best obtained by wheeled vehicles in a warehouse of peak demands. Goods can be stored or accumulated prior to shipping during off-peak periods.

The versatility of the fork truck and package conveyor is responsible for their wide acceptance. Fork trucks are made especially adaptable with a variety of attachments for special purpose handling.

Selection of Warehouse Materials Handling Equipment The proper selection and use of materials handling equipment is an important factor to initiate and maintain warehouse operation efficiency. Warehouse design is often evolved around a well-engineered handling technique.

Typical handling methods include the following:
1. Tow conveyor (dragline conveyor)
2. Pallet systems (skids, bins, racks, unit loads, etc.)
3. Tractor trailer and fork truck (wheeled vehicles)
4. Overhead systems (monorail, bridge crane, stacker crane, etc.)
5. Conveyors (vertical and horizontal movement)

Considerable emphasis has been placed on narrow-aisle handling during recent years. The narrow-aisle straddle fork truck with 100 percent selectivity of goods in stock on pallet racks has been much used. Space savings have been particularly attractive with small pallets where right-angle stacking aisles have been reduced in some cases to 6 ft. The aisle-space savings of the straddle fork truck are usually offset by increased operating cost due to the slow speeds in stacking and transporting inherent in the equipment. Increased side clearance between pallet stacks and the decreased stability of the truck chassis for high stacking heights are also items to be considered for overall evaluation.

When selectivity is not a prerequisite and bulk storage is possible, the straddle-type truck is less desirable on account of the clearance required between storage rows. A later design of the narrow-aisle type industrial truck provides forks which retract the pallet load within the wheelbase of the vehicle. Normal pallet side clearances can be maintained comparable to the standard fork truck. The front-wheel diameter has been increased to reduce floor wear experienced with the straddle fork truck with small steel wheels. The limitations of narrow-aisle equipment as listed above should not be overlooked in any warehouse operation where high turnover of inventory is required.

Tow conveyor systems have been installed in many warehouses and truck terminals where order makeup or sorting operations require maximum flexibility.

Tractor-trailer trains have been utilized to advantage where long horizontal movements are required. With a fork truck loading pallets on trailers and a second fork truck unloading pallets at the delivery point, maximum utilization of equipment is obtained. In this way, heavy tonnage can be handled in minimum time, or a tractor-train schedule can be set up for repetitive delivery to various points.

Overhead bridge cranes require no aisle space if the goods to be stored are handled with special lifting devices. Paper rolls and other large units are warehoused in this manner. Monorail systems are used as a general purpose method of handling bulky, extra long, or heavy loads in congested areas.

The stacker crane is recommended for evaluation when selectivity of pallets or unit loads is required in narrow-aisle operation. Maximum storage heights may be attained in safety for maximum vertical-height utilization. The hoisting mechanism is suspended from the overhead traveling bridge. Recent comparisons in warehouse floor-space requirements indicate that the stacker crane is more efficient than the straddle fork truck.

Fixed-route package conveyors are usually designed to handle a constant flow of material of similar products. Cases, boxes, drums, bags, etc., can be conveyed from production line, through warehouse, to shipping platform with minimum handling. Conveyors are usually engineered for a specific size and weight of product. A thorough study is required to select the most suitable and economical handling system.

Industrial
WAREHOUSES

Utilizing centrally located short-lot and bin-storage operation, coordinated by use of dragline conveyors

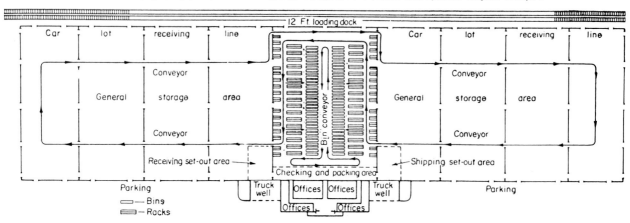

This bin layout emphasizes a direct-flow replenishment and stock selection operation

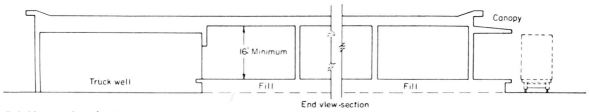

Fig. 1   Typical large warehouse layout.

Effective Warehouse and Storage Layout

The overall receiving, storage, and shipping costs can be classified generally as follows:
1. Occupancy or fixed overhead charges
2. Labor or handling expense

The principles of space utilization can be described as operating in three dimensions. The percent effectiveness (volumetric efficiency) may be calculated from the following:

Space utilization (%) = area utilization
$\times$ vertical-height utilization

$$= \frac{\text{net storage area}}{\text{gross storage area}}$$

$$\times \frac{\text{height utilized}}{\text{usable vertical height}} \times 100$$

Area utilization (Fig. 2) requires the proper analysis of alternate materials handling methods. Emphasis is placed on the study of the floor plan to provide a maximum ratio of net usable area to gross floor area. The net storage area is the floor space actually occupied by goods. The gross storage area is the usable area plus adequate operating aisles for handling facilities and traffic needs.

Additional area is usually required for miscellaneous functions. Examples are listed herewith:
1. Space for empty pallets
2. Special packaging or makeup areas
3. Irregularities due to columns, odd corners, etc.
4. Space for offices, equipment, etc.
5. Shipping and receiving areas
6. Odd lots and balances

Vertical-height utilization usually necessitates packaging evaluations plus the consideration of safety and special equipment. The maximum stack height allowable is limited by the crushing strength of the bottom package. Non-

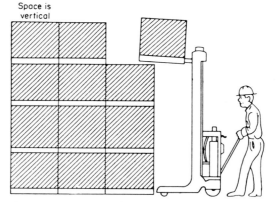

Fig. 2   Space utilization — a three-dimension operation.

stackable or fragile loads are tiered one above the other with the use of pallet racks or other storage aids. Usable vertical height (in space utilization formula) is the distance from floor to underside of sprinkler system nozzles. Fire underwriters allow a 10 percent reduction in rates when a minimum of 18 in. is left clear under the sprinkler heads (Fig. 3).

The occupancy cost of warehouse buildings includes the investment of the structure itself with corresponding fixed depreciation and maintenance expense. A vertical stacking height of 18 to 20 ft is usually found to be most economical from a cubage cost estimate review. Avoid the false concept of economy of ground-level floor construction for new buildings which in many instances results in costly "in" and "out" handling in the shipping and receiving areas. Warehouses are designed as a

rule for floor-level operation for both rail cars and trucks:
1. Rail cars—3 ft 7 in. above top of rail
2. Trucks—4 ft 4 in. (average) above ground

Doors 8 to 12 ft wide and 10 ft high are usually ample for use with high-stacking equipment. Door spacings for box cars can be set at 45 ft for standard 40-ft rail equipment. Truck delivery doors should be set at 15 ft center to center. Buildings with long-span construction are desirable to eliminate waste space and provide increased flexibility for handling operations. Spans up to 100 ft are not uncommon with little or no extra construction cost.

Effective storage layout includes careful analysis of the following:
1. Activity of item warehoused (turnover)
2. Bulk and weight of package or unit load

1168

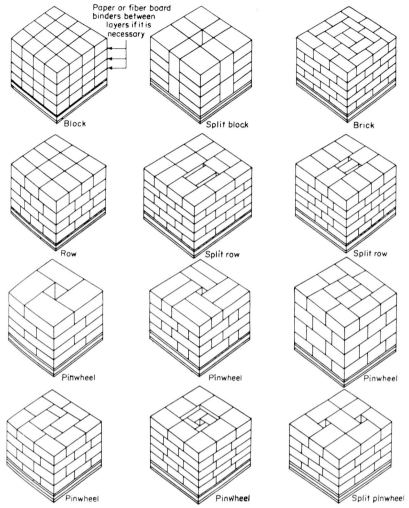

Fig. 3 Standard pallet patterns.

Block — Split block — Brick — Row — Split row — Split row — Pinwheel — Pinwheel — Pinwheel — Pinwheel — Pinwheel — Split pinwheel

Paper or fiber board binders between layers if it is necessary

Shipping and Receiving Areas The receiving area of a warehouse should be located adjacent to incoming rail or truck facilities and as convenient as possible to the storage area. The receiving dock is usually separated from the shipping area if possible to minimize cross traffic and possible confusion. The number of unloading positions required is dependent upon the volume of receipts or the maximum number of cars or trucks spotted at the same time. The light weight of portable aluminum or magnesium dockboards is desirable when power equipment is not available for positioning units of conventional steel construction.

Weather protection at the unloading positions permits continuous handling operations. Loading platforms located outside the warehouse building can be designed for one-way or two-way traffic where required.

The proper control, checking, and sorting of inbound materials is important for the prompt and efficient delivery of outbound shipments. The size of the receiving area is determined by the analysis of the temporary storage lag needed to perform the necessary inbound handling and inventory control operations.

A shipping area (or dock) receives materials for outbound shipment after selection and transfer from storage. The preassembly of orders according to plan requires sufficient room to perform packing, packaging, or preparation operations prior to shipment.

The size of the shipping area is dependent on the makeup time of filling orders and the quantity of simultaneous loading operations during peak periods.

Calculation of Storage Space (Area Utilization)

Gross
warehouse area = inside total square footage of warehouse

Net
storage area = actual area occupied by inventory, not including aisles plus space for empty pallets plus shipping and receiving areas plus allowance for "honeycombing" plus special inventory (inspection, etc.)

Interference = irregularities due to columns, odd corners, etc.

Miscellaneous = space for offices, equipment, etc.

Gross
warehouse area = net storage area plus aisles plus interference plus miscellaneous

Rule of thumb (for general package warehousing):

$$\frac{\text{gross warehouse area}}{\text{net storage area}} = \frac{3}{2}$$

or Net storage area + (50% net storage area) = gross warehouse area

This rule is accurate for average warehouses, but actual analysis of the layout is recommended.

"Honeycombing" is a warehouse term used when space is not fully occupied because of partial withdrawal of inventory. Maximum honeycombing factors are in the range of 75 to 90 percent of maximum capacity, depending upon the activity, number, and quantity of items stored.

3. Number of items and quantity of each
4. Shape, value, hazard, or other special considerations

The application of the "ton-mile" principle can serve to reduce handling costs when a floor plan is designed for the storage of a large variety of items, lots, batches, etc. The items to be stored are located within the warehouse by popularity or special groupings. Logically the most popular items are stored closest to the shipping dock to reduce the length of travel of materials handling equipment or crews. Any storage system or layout which minimizes the movement of warehouse operations reduces the ton-miles or pound-feet of work performed.

The physical characteristics of a warehouse determine the capacity factors of storage layout, namely:

1. Floor-load capacity
2. Ceiling height and allowable stack height
3. Location of doors, loading facilities, elevators, firewalls, etc.
4. Column location, size, and spacing between centers
5. Location of aisles for operating space, access to stock, and protective equipment.

The cost of handling "in" and "out" of storage is an operating expense which can never be recovered. The overall cost per unit weight or volume is thus the prime consideration of efficient warehousing and quite often is the only expense that can be reduced by improved materials handling methods.

Straight-Line Flow or Assembly-Line Principle Straight-line flow is inherently efficient and usually is adopted in warehouses adjacent to production areas. Conveyors and pallet systems illustrate typical methods of efficient handling.

Production → Warehouse → Carrier or Consignee

Order pick lines in a grocery warehouse are characterized by the assembly-line principle.

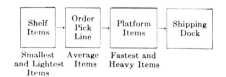

Shelf Items → Order Pick Line → Platform Items → Shipping Dock

Smallest and Lightest Items — Average Items — Fastest and Heavy Items

Industrial
WATERFRONT WAREHOUSES

Warehouses will vary considerably in different ports because of various types of cargo handled, climate, local stevedore practices, economics of various building materials, types of land transportation serving the facility, etc. The warehouse to be discussed herein is one used for the long-time storage of goods as opposed to transit sheds that receive, handle, and discharge sundry cargoes "in transit." For purposes of this study, only warehouses connected with maritime commerce, handling cargoes to and from ships will be considered.

This means a building constructed in the general vicinity of a ship berth where cargo to be shipped out or which has come in by ship can be assembled and which requires comparatively long-time storage.

For reasons of economy of operation, the distance from the operating berth should be kept to a minimum to cut down travel time for stevedore equipment and provide for the rapid loading or unloading of the ship. This distance, however, should not be so close to an operating berth that the warehouse could be used as a transit shed, thus changing its true function. Generally speaking, this would mean that a warehouse should not be closer to an operating berth than the length of the berth. Cargoes scheduled for long-time storage could then be economically transported to the warehouse.

General Dimensions

The over-all dimensions of a warehouse are quite often limited by the available space. However, where space restrictions do not occur, the size can be best established by the use to which the warehouse is to be put.

Warehouses to be used in conjunction with transit sheds should be comparable in size. This means a warehouse with a gross area of 70,000 to 90,000 square feet. The width and length can then be determined from the dimensions of the site and the space required for access roads and railroad sidings.

To maintain good fire protection, the building should be divided into compartments separated by fire walls equipped with fire doors. The type of cargo to be stored will sometimes regulate the allowable area in these compartments and also the vertical clearance under the structural framework. At least 2 ft must be provided between cargo stacks and automatic sprinklers. A clear height of 22 to 24 ft would be ample to allow for automatic sprinklers and pendant electric lights.

Service Facilities

Where space permits, it is particularly desirable to provide loading platforms at truck bed eleva-

Port Design And Construction, The American Association of Port Authorities, Washington, D.C., 1964.

tion at each side of the warehouse, and also railroad tracks for direct transfer of goods from rail car to warehouse or vice versa.

To accommodate trucks that may wish to drive into warehouses where a center aisle is provided, it is necessary to construct ramps at the ends of the building connecting the depressed areas to the regular floor level. In this way, trucks can be unloaded inside the warehouse with lift trucks.

In localities where considerable rainfall occurs, it is very desirable to have protective canopies built out over the loading platforms.

Loading platforms should be wide enough to allow for easy maneuvering of mechanized equipment during loading and unloading operations.

Column Spacing

The advisability of interior columns in warehouses is a disputed question—warehousemen contend that columns interfere with the movement of cargo. There is no doubt that a wide spacing of columns is an advantage.

Whether one row of columns along the centerline is preferable to two rows at the third points is largely a matter of opinion. One row causes less interference to cargo handling and stacking, and allows two side aisles for trucks. On the other hand, two rows allow a center truck aisle which is adequate for most conditions. The width of the building will in many cases be the deciding factor in regard to selecting the most economical span for the roof system. Clear span construction is without doubt more desirable from an operating standpoint, but the additional cost may rule it out.

The spacing of the column bays is another controversial subject. The type of roof construction in many cases will determine the economical span for roof purlins and joists. Bay spacing of 20 to 40 ft appears to be common practice.

Foundations

Foundations are either pile supported or spread footings. Careful analysis of the soil by means of borings should be made previous to design unless previously obtained data on soil characteristics is available.

When soil conditions are questionable, load tests, test pile driving and pile load tests may be required.

Where soil conditions show adequate stability, spread footings can be used. Even where areas are freshly filled, it is often possible to obtain adequate compaction with the use of mechanical compactors. The degree of compaction must be carefully measured in the field by established tests.

Structural Frame

Steel Frames Structural steel shapes are quite often used for warehouse framing because of easy availability, economy, and simplicity.

A great many steel companies are now produc-

ing "prefab" buildings of lightweight steel shapes. They come in a variety of spans and bay spacing and offer a choice of truss, arch, or rigid frame. These buildings generally require interior columns, and if the spacing of columns is such as not to interfere with the functional use of the building, they offer an economical solution to certain specific warehouse requirements.

Timber Frames Wherever timber is readily available and competitive with steel or other materials, it may be more economical to construct a warehouse using heavy mill construction. This type of structure is considered a better fire risk than unprotected steel.

The use of glued laminated wood members is also becoming quite popular. They have the decided advantage of a reduction in shrinkage and provide greater strength for a given size member.

A recent development in the Southwest is the pole-frame type of construction. Basically, it is a building with its main columns made up of treated timber poles with simple wood trusses and wood roof beams. The roof is either built up over a wood deck or of corrugated steel or aluminum supported by wood purlins. Walls are usually wood framing with corrugated metal siding. Relatively close spacing of columns is required with this type of construction which results in reduced maneuvering space for mechanical equipment.

Reinforced Concrete There are many advantages to be obtained by using reinforced concrete wall construction, such as low maintenance cost, long life, ability to withstand rough treatment by heavy stevedore equipment and high resistance to fire. Tilt-up concrete wall construction has been used considerably in recent years to great advantage. In either case, these types of wall construction are usually combined with steel or wood trusses and conventional roof decks.

An all-concrete construction method can be obtained by the use of prestressed concrete beams and columns, and in recent years thin shell barrel arches of prestressed concrete have been successfully used.

Wall Framing and Sheathing When corrugated steel or aluminum wall sheathing or one of the various new patterns of rolled metal sheathing is used, it is generally secured to steel girts and studs for steel-framed buildings and wood girts and studs for timber construction. In either case the exact spacing of girts and studs is determined largely by local building codes, wind loads, column spacing, and the gage of the metal used.

Obviously the use of reinforced or tilt-up concrete walls eliminates the need for girts and studs and provides the necessary sheathing. Concrete walls, however, do add a greater weight to foundations and increase the building cost. Offsetting this is the more permanent construction obtained

1170

and the ability to withstand rough treatment from heavy cargo-handling equipment.

As a compromise between these two systems, some warehouses are constructed with a concrete wall built up to a height of 4 or 5 ft with the lighter wall construction using girts and corrugated metal extending up to the eaves or parapet. One disadvantage of corrugated siding is its susceptibility to damage. This can be partially remedied at a moderate increase in cost by applying solid sheathing, either 1-in shiplap or the cheaper grades of plywood, secured to the girt system. This method not only protects the metal siding, but it also provides additional strength to the building to resist wind forces, and has some insulating qualities which may be desirable.

The gage of the sheet-metal siding or roofing is important. Although the standard gages are more economical and easier to procure, there are other factors which may warrant the selection of heavier gages. In areas of high winds a heavier gage than standard would be desirable, and where warehouses are located near the waterfront and subject to frequent fog and damp air conditions, heavier gage metal would be a distinct advantage to offset corrosion.

Regardless of the gage selected, it is of prime importance to use galvanized sheets to resist corrosion. The standard $1\frac{1}{4}$-oz coating is generally used, but here again the longer life obtained by using 2-oz coating may justify the additional cost. Although many warehouses are left unpainted there seems to be a trend toward more attractive buildings utilizing bright colors or contrasting panels. Prefabricated panels of aluminum or porcelain-enameled steel in various attractive colors are now available but the added cost has acted as a deterrent for most low-cost commercial projects unless offices are incorporated into the plan, in which case some distinctive design can be justified. Aluminum panels, doors, or windows used in locations that are exposed to industrial or seacoast corrosive atmospheres should be of an alloy that will resist corrosion. Alloy 6063-T5 has been successfully used in these locations.

Roof Framing, Sheathing Corrugated aluminum or galvanized steel is frequently used for roof construction. It is generally supported on steel purlins that in turn rest on steel trusses. Where the spans are not excessive, wood joists supported on steel purlins can be used. One-half-inch-thick plywood diaphragm roof sheathing is laid over the joists and a built-up composition roof applied on top. This type of construction has the advantage of providing a good bracing system in the plane of the top chord, thus taking care of wind loads and other horizontal stresses.

Two-inch-thick T & G roof sheathing is sometimes used nailed to timbers resting on the steel purlins. This type of construction also has good diaphragm qualities and, being of mill type construction, has a good fire insurance rating.

There is an endless variety of built-up composition roofs available to choose from, but a substantial watertight roof is essential and consequently nothing less than a "20-year" bonded roof should be considered.

Poured-in-place concrete and lightweight concrete, poured-in-place gypsum, and vermiculite are other materials frequently used for roof construction. The initial cost and the additional weight that must be carried by the framing system and foundation are factors that should be considered in selecting these materials, and the advantages and disadvantages carefully analyzed in relation to the overall anticipated life of the entire structure.

Floors

Floors are either portland cement concrete or asphaltic cement concrete. The final finish on portland cement concrete floors is important. Steel trowel finishes are inclined to be slippery, particularly if water or oil accumulates on the surface. A light broom finish is more desirable providing an adequate nonskid surface.

Asphaltic cement concrete makes a good wearing surface either when applied over a concrete slab or crushed-rock base. Various degrees of roughness can be obtained to provide sufficient traction for mechanized equipment. Although it is susceptible to disintegration due to oil and gasoline drippings, it is easily patched and there are various "sealers" that can be applied which alleviate this situation.

It is important that floors be given a sufficient slope to drain properly. Opinions vary as to how much this slope should be, but range between $\frac{1}{8}$-in and $\frac{1}{4}$-in per foot.

At doorways, in order to prevent rain from driving in under the doors, this slope is sometimes steepened for approximately 5 ft inside the opening. Lift trucks can negotiate this slight ramp smoothly. Another more positive method is to install a continuous drainage trough under each door equipped with a suitable grating set flush with the paved surface.

Appurtenances

Doors The finest type of door used on warehouses is the vertical rolling steel door, a door constructed of many interlocking steel slats all connected together and secured by guides on both sides of the opening. The door curtain slides vertically up the guides and is rolled up on a steel pipe barrel. The operating mechanism for this type of door is either an endless chain which turns a sprocket and train of gears connected to the pipe barrel, or by crank, bevel gears, and steel shafting. The weight of the steel curtain is counterbalanced by helical steel-spring tensioning devices. Large doors are generally motor operated, the open and closed positions being controlled by limit switches.

This type of door can also be used as a fire door, in which case the spring tension is adjusted to close the door automatically when a lever is tripped by the melting of a fusible link.

There are many "overhead" type doors on the market that are very competitive with the vertical rolling steel door. They may be metal or wood and have a large variety of operating procedures. The so-called "up and over" type is raised as a unit by means of cantilever arms and tension springs, similar to residential garage doors, and in the open position lies above and inside the door opening. A variation of this door is one in which the door folds in two leaves before assuming a horizontal position above the door opening, the advantage being that the projection into the building is reduced.

An overhead type of door composed of several horizontal sections hinged together that slides vertically in tracks at each side and above the door opening has become quite popular in recent warehouse construction. It can be constructed of wood or metal (quite often aluminum), and can be manually operated in comparatively large sizes, although it is adaptable to motor operation. In the open position, it too, lies above and inside the door opening.

All these previously described doors require a moderate amount of headroom between the door head and ceiling or roof construction, and with the exception of the vertical rolling steel door, all can be equipped with windows to provide additional day lighting.

If the eave height of the warehouse is not less than one and one-half times the door height, two-section counterbalanced vertical-lift doors can be installed, either manual or motor operated. These doors are easily and quickly opened.

The conventional one- or two-unit horizontal sliding door, although virtually foolproof, is, nevertheless, unwieldy and requires large blank wall spaces to house it in the open position. For this reason it limits the number and location of doors to the detriment of the overall design.

The spacing of doors is largely determined by the type of cargo to be stored and the frequency of loading or unloading of the stored material. Warehouses constructed for a specific commodity can have the doors located to provide the minimum travel distance for loading or unloading operations. However, most warehouses adjacent to the waterfront would accommodate a variety of cargo. It would be better to have an excess of doors rather than an insufficient number, as cargo can always be stacked in front of a closed door. It is important, however, to have doors on each side of the building opposite each other, and also to have doors on the ends so that trucks can enter or leave by means of a center aisle. Symmetrical spacing of doors allows for an efficient traffic pattern throughout the building.

The selection of door sizes should be determined by the size and type of equipment and cargo that will be used. Lift trucks, straddle carriers, and even individual cargo packages are getting larger and larger, and for safe operation require wide doorways. Doors 16 ft wide and 16 ft high are commonly used, and even doors 18 or 20 ft wide and 18 ft high. Larger size doors should preferably be motor operated for more rapid opening and closing.

Ventilators Ventilators through the roof should be provided that comply with local requirements. Ventilators are either continuous ridge type or individual round types distributed over the roof area. Some rotary types are available that are activated by the wind, and in cases where large changes of air are necessary, mechanical forced-air systems are used.

Offices and Washrooms When warehouses are located near transit sheds or other marine buildings, there is seldom any need for offices or washrooms. This is particularly true if various operators use the warehouse. In the event that one operator leases the entire facility, it may be advantageous to incorporate offices and washrooms.

Protection Devices Structural columns in the interior of the warehouse should be protected from damage caused by collision with vehicles by encasing the lower 4 to 6 ft in concrete or by setting heavy steel pipe guards around them. Likewise, main switchboards should have protective barricades, either pipe railings or concrete-filled steel posts, set about 3 ft out in front to act as a protection against motorized handling equipment.

Sprinkler risers, valves, and control mechanisms should be enclosed in a structural-steel framework covered with heavy diamond mesh screening. This will prevent any stored material from accidentally falling on the sprinkler equipment and causing it to be damaged or rendered inoperable.

WATERFRONT WAREHOUSES

Painting

Warehouses constructed of reinforced concrete need not have the enclosing walls painted. However, metal doors, windows, coping, and flashings should be painted with a good grade of exterior paint. There are several new paints on the market now that provide remarkable protection against corrosion even in the saline atmosphere of the seacoast.

Corrugated sheet-metal buildings are definitely improved in appearance by the application of paint, and the useful life of the metal is extended.

Painting the inside of warehouses improves the general lighting effect, and makes working conditions safer.

Fire-hose racks and automatic-sprinkler risers should be painted a brilliant red for ready identification. Overhead signs designating the location of electric panel boards, exit doors, and other facilities are an added convenience. Lines painted on the floor defining main aisles, cross aisles and storage areas, and "Keep Clear" areas are helpful when stacking cargo. In many warehouses smoking is prohibited, in which case "No Smoking" signs should be prominently displayed.

Fire Protection

Warehouses should be protected with a complete automatic-sprinkler system meeting the requirements of the National Board of Fire Underwriters. Wherever possible, a supervisory fire-alarm circuit connected to the local fire department alarm circuits should be provided so that in case of fire the fire department is immediately informed.

Auxiliary fire equipment such as hose racks and chemical fire extinguishers should be located at several locations in the building and be clearly designated by being painted bright red. Stacking of cargo should be so arranged that all fire equipment is easily accessible at all times.

Lighting

Natural Lighting   The best source of light for a warehouse during the daytime is natural light or sunlight. There are two methods available: (1) roof lighting and (2) sidewall lighting.

Roof lighting can be accomplished by means of (a) monitors, (b) skylights, or (c) sawtooth construction.

A combination of monitors and sawtooth construction provides very good lighting and has long been an accepted method of design. Skylights, if symmetrically spaced and a sufficient number installed, give equal distribution of light throughout the building. Skylights are sometimes a source of roof leakage and should be carefully designed and installed to insure a weathertight condition. In recent years plastic dome-type skylights have become quite popular. They come in various shapes and sizes and are readily installed on composition-type roofs and are easily made weathertight.

To maintain the desired transmission of light, all roof lighting, whether monitor or skylight, should be hosed off frequently to maintain a clean surface.

Windows can be installed in the side walls to provide additional light and in buildings using corrugated siding it is possible to obtain corrugated Fiberglas panels, either clear or translucent, that will member with the siding and provide a continuous band of light on each side of the building. All forms of side-wall lighting are subject to being blanked off by the high stacking of cargo and consequently should not be depended upon entirely to provide the desired day lighting.

Artificial Lighting   For night operation and to supplement natural light during the daytime, electric illumination should be provided. The light level should not be less than 10 foot-candles. The spacing of lights is very important and should be designed to provide adequate lighting in the aisles at all times even when cargo is stacked high. Sufficient switches should be provided to allow lights to be switched on only in certain areas where work is being done. If watchman service is maintained or when only minimum illumination is desired, separate light circuits should be installed with control switches conveniently located near entrance doors.

Type of Fixtures   The fixtures that can be used are (1) incandescent, (2) fluorescent, and (3) mercury vapor. There are advantages and disadvantages in each type.

Incandescent lamps need replacing frequently, and the convection currents set up by the hot globe cause the reflector and the light globe to become coated with dust, reducing the illumination considerably.

Fluorescent-tube lighting is becoming more popular since high-output fluorescent lamps have been developed which produce the increased illumination desired. Upkeep is still a problem with them as tubes become blackened with resultant loss of efficiency.

Mercury-vapor lighting is the most efficient, provided that sufficient mounting height can be obtained. Mercury-vapor lights require time to warm up before full illumination, so they cannot be turned on and off as readily as incandescent or fluorescent lights. In warehouses where different color codes are used on the stored cargo it is very important to use color *corrected* mercury

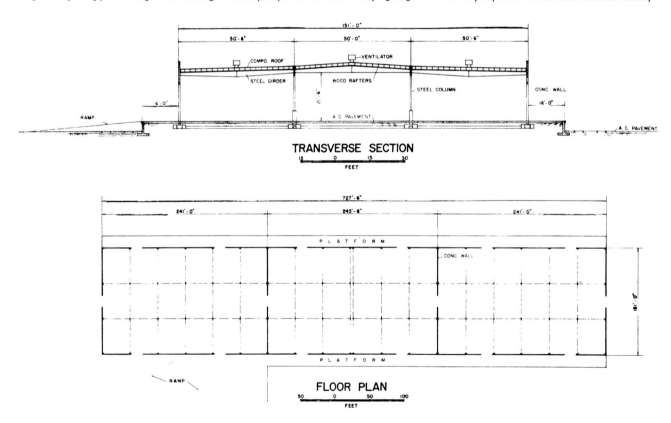

TRANSVERSE SECTION

FLOOR PLAN

Fig. 1   Typical warehouse, Port of Long Beach, California.

vapor lamps in order to be able to read the various color codes.

When any truck loading is accomplished at night, outside floodlighting of the area is essential. For safe operation, the intensity of illumination should be at least 1 foot-candle and preferably 2 foot-candles. Mercury-vapor lighting lends itself ideally for this situation as high-intensity lights can be mounted on steel poles to provide even illumination. At loading platforms lights can be mounted over doorways or on the building parapet to illuminate the platform and the trucks or railroad cars.

Wiring Before designing the electrical wiring system, the public utility company supplying the electric current should be consulted in order to determine the various systems available. The standard 120/240-volt three-wire system is adaptable to all three types of lighting. If considerable power for motors or heating is required, the 208/120-volt three-phase system would be desirable. The 480/277-volt four-wire system is adaptable to either mercury-vapor or fluorescent lighting, and considerable reductions in wire size, conduit size, and panel boards can be effected by its use. For large buildings this could mean a considerable saving in cost of the electric system. If small 120-volt single-phase loads are required, dry-type step-down transformers can be located adjacent to the sub-panel board.

Port of Long Beach, California

A plan and cross section of a warehouse at the Port of Long Beach is shown in Fig. 1.

The building is 151 ft wide and 727.5 ft long with a gross area of 109,852 sq ft. It is divided into three separate and approximately equal storage areas by 12-in-thick precast reinforced concrete transverse fire walls. Columns at the exterior walls and fire walls are reinforced concrete, poured-in-place.

Interior columns are structural steel spaced 50 ft apart, and column bays are spaced 40 ft apart.

Roof trusses and girders are of steel and support a system of 2-in by 10-in wood roof joists, $\frac{1}{2}$-in plywood diaphragm roof sheathing and a built-up composition roof.

The side and end walls contain a total of 14 vertical rolling steel doors measuring 16 ft wide by 16 ft high. Openings through the fire walls on the centerline of the building are protected by automatic self-closing vertical rolling steel fire doors 16 ft wide and 16 ft high on each side of the wall.

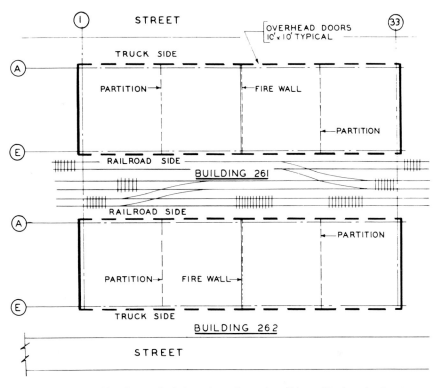

Fig. 2 Port Newark, New Jersey. Typical warehouse layout for efficient utilization of rail and truck service, cargo distribution buildings.

Truck and rail loading platforms 16 ft wide are on each side of the building with one-third of one side ramped to permit direct access into the building by vehicles.

There are no skylights or monitors on the roof or windows in the side walls. Distributed symmetrically over the roof area are 54 circular ventilators that provide the required air changes.

Artificial lighting of the interior is accomplished by 400-watt mercury vapor fixtures. All exterior loading areas are floodlighted with 400-watt mercury vapor lights.

A complete automatic sprinkler system with supervisory electric circuits is installed throughout the building, and in addition hose reels are mounted at convenient locations.

Port Newark—New Jersey

The plan in Fig. 2 illustrates typical warehouse layout utilizing modern rail and truck service. The warehouse floors are at truck and rail-car heights to facilitate easier cargo handling.

The buildings are 160 ft wide and vary from 640 ft to 960 ft long. The column spacing is 40 ft with bents every 20 ft, and the minimum interior clear height is 20 ft. The roof slope is on a 2½ on 12.

Buildings have been constructed of either structural steel or structural timber frames with aluminum roofing and siding. Plastic skylights are used to provide natural light.

Industrial

AIRPORT INDUSTRIAL PARK

PHYSICAL PLANNING

Coordination in the Preparation of the Airport Layout Plan

If the airport is considered a suitable location for an airport industrial park, the industrial park's location and land requirements should be taken into account during the preparation of the airport layout plan.

Economy of layout and operations requires that the airport industrial park be one contiguous area. In order to achieve this contiguity, careful study of the other airport land requirements must be made. It is advisable to free the maximum amount of land for industrial development consistent with retaining full expansion capability for essential airport uses such as aircraft movement areas, passenger and freight terminals, aircraft parking aprons, navigation aids, automobile parking areas, and aircraft maintenance areas.

Location on the Airport

The land available for development for an airport industrial park should be located so as to take full advantage of its airport situation.

A location which often is a good choice for the industrial park is on the side of the runway opposite the terminal. This is particularly true at airports used by air carriers, where diversion of industrial traffic from the terminal traffic boulevard is advisable. Also, in this area, airport supporting services are not competing for land to use for activities such as terminal auto parking and commercial concessions. (See Fig. 1.)

A location in the vicinity of the general aviation area has the advantage of being close to the area where the aircraft will be stored and maintained. This location keeps ground taxi time at a minimum. (See Fig. 2.)

Taxiway Access

The taxiway system connecting the aircraft movement areas with the individual units of the industrial park should be decided upon in the early stages of planning. The access routes are a determining factor in the development pattern. Proper planning of these traffic lanes will conserve land valuable for other uses — uses more productive of revenue. Determination must be made at an early stage of the proportion of the tract to be served by taxiways to the aircraft movement area of the airport. The airport owner reserves the right to establish a user charge for the privilege of access through these taxiways to the common use landing area.

Opinion is divided as to the necessity of providing taxiway access to each lot because of the relatively large amount of land this requires. In most cases a compromise can be reached by providing access to those lots

Planning the Airport Industrial Park, Federal Aviation Administration, Department of Transportation, Washington, D.C., 1965.

closest to the aircraft movement areas. A 50-ft service taxiway within a 150-ft right of way is generally sufficient for business aircraft. To minimize conflict with the street system, it is recommended that the taxiway right-of-way be located at the rear of the lots served and that the blocks be long and narrow to reduce the number of intersections between streets and taxiways. (See Fig. 1.)

Two interesting variations for providing access to the aircraft movement areas are:

1. A taxiway provided to those lots directly abutting the aircraft movement areas. (See Fig. 3.)

2. A taxiway into an aircraft parking apron which is surrounded by industrial lots. (See Fig. 4.)

In projects where no taxiway into the airport industrial park is provided, reasonable accessibility can be had by locating the industrial area in close proximity to the general aviation apron. (See Fig. 5.)

Railroad Access

If rail service is available to the site, a 20-ft right-of-way is sufficient for a single track spur. Determination should be made in advance of the proportion of the lots to receive rail service. The rail service right-of-way should be located on the opposite end of the lots from the vehicular right-of-way.

Contact with the railroad serving the area should be made to assure construction that will meet the railroad's standards. In most cases, cost of the railroad spur will have to be paid for by the management of the industrial park, but there are instances when the railroad has paid the cost of the spur track. Usually, if the railroad spur is paid for by the railroad, title to the right-of-way will have to be passed to the railroad.

Street System

The widths of the right-of-way and the pavement depend on the anticipated traffic demand. Excessive pavement width, in addition to its high cost, has the tendency to encourage on-street parking which creates traffic problems. Minimum pavement widths and strict enforcement of on-street parking prohibitions are recommended.

Curbs and gutters rather than drainage ditches are recommended in order to keep the right-of-way width to a minimum; these will facilitate drainage of the site and also assure a cleaner, more attractive site.

Airport industrial parks surveyed show considerable variation in the widths of pavements and rights of way selected. With enforcement of on-street parking prohibitions and the use of curbs and gutters, the right-of-way should be a minimum of 40 ft for a 24-ft (2-lane) pavement. These dimensions are sufficient for secondary streets. Additional lanes are required in larger developments to add capacity to meet peak hour demands. For larger developments, on streets which will have a substantial number of industrial installations, a 60-ft

right-of-way is recommended so that two additional lanes of traffic can be added when the demand warrants.

For primary feeder streets, a minimum of 48 ft of pavement within a 60-ft right-of-way is recommended.

Street intersections should have a curb radius of at least 40 ft to accommodate tractor-trailer vehicles.

It is recommended that the number of entrances into the industrial park be as few as possible to discourage use of the circulation system by traffic which is not directly related to the park. The entrances should be from a public thoroughfare with at least equivalent capacity and be separate from the airport entrance road in order to avoid traffic mix with those vehicles serving or visiting the airport.

Off-Street Parking and Loading

Off-Street Parking This should be provided for all vehicles which come into the airport industrial park. Parking spaces should be provided for employees, visitors, company vehicles and all trucks.

Employee Parking In airport industrial parks virtually all employees drive to work. Consideration should be given to overlapping requirements of successive shifts. Provision should be made for one parking space for every 1.3 employees on the combined shifts. Allowance of 300 square feet should be made for maneuvering and parking each vehicle.

Visitor Parking Parking space for visitors should be provided at the rate of one parking space for every 15 employees on the main shift.

Company Vehicles Provision of one parking space for each company vehicle is recommended.

Truck Loading Docks Loading docks should accommodate truck trailers and local pickup trucks. To accommodate truck trailers, berths should be 14 ft wide by 60 ft deep with an additional depth of 60 ft for maneuvering. For local pickup trucks, berths 10 ft wide by 20 ft deep are sufficient with a 20-ft additional depth for maneuvering. Loading docks should not be located on the street side of the building.

Entrance Driveways Entrance driveways for truck access should be offset from the truck parking ramp to prevent trucks from backing from the street into a loading dock. Curb radii of 25 ft minimum are recommended for truck access drives. Driveways for automobiles should have minimum curb radii of 15 ft.

Building Setbacks

The airport industrial parks surveyed indicate a variety of setback standards which are generally related to the size of the lots in the particular developments. Aesthetic considera-

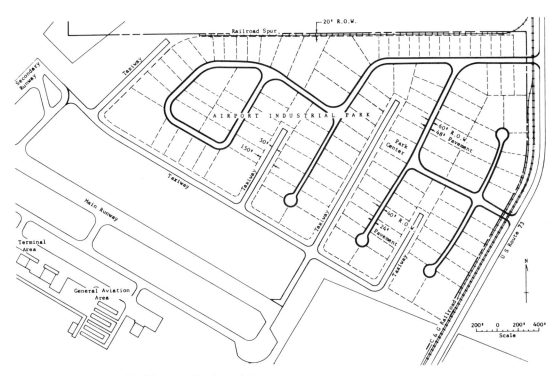

Fig. 1　Industrial park located on the opposite side of the runway from the terminal.

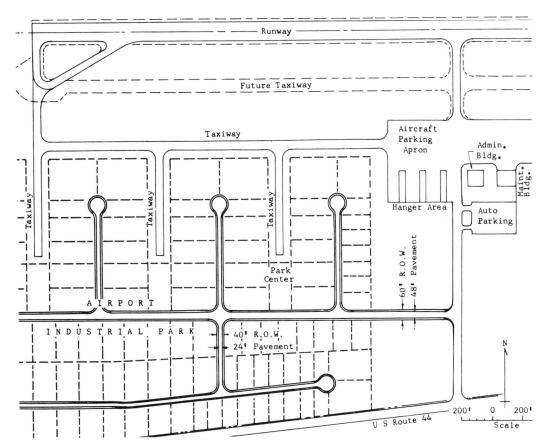

Fig. 2　Industrial park located in the vicinity of the general aviation area.

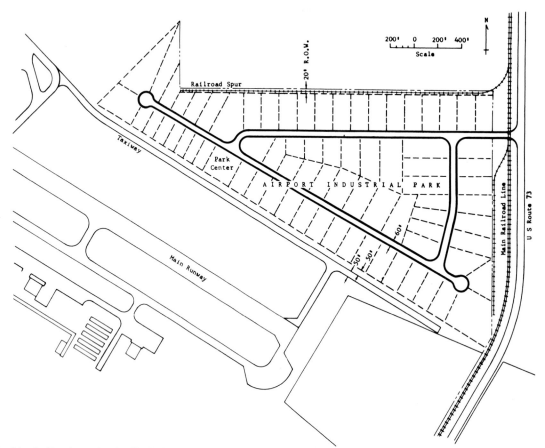

Fig. 3   Industrial park with taxiway only to lots directly abutting the aircraft movement areas.

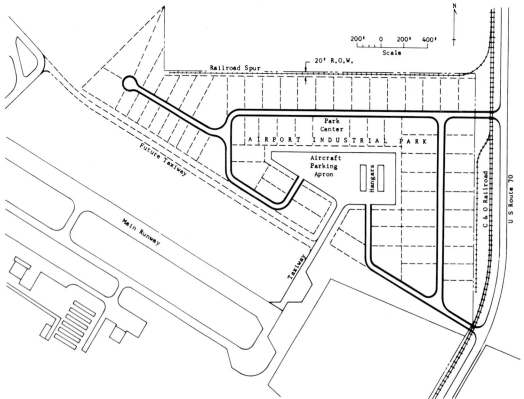

Fig. 4   Industrial park with taxiway into aircraft parking apron surrounded by industrial lots.

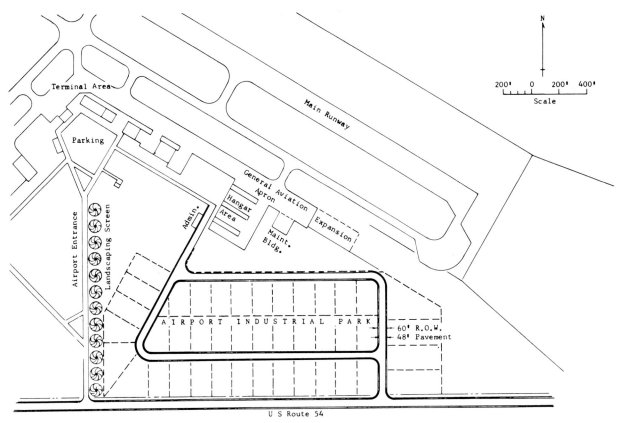

Fig. 5 Industrial park without taxiway access located adjacent to the general aviation area.

tions are significant and no single set of standards will be applicable to all airport industrial parks. The main goal is to retain a feeling of open space in the development. In addition, setbacks may be related to the topography, rougher terrain generally requiring greater setbacks to minimize the amount of site work to the developer and to neighboring tenants. On most airports, the land developed for industry will be relatively flat, which would permit setbacks to be the minimum required for aesthetic considerations, free movement of fire apparatus around structures and meeting the requirements of local ordinances.

A 30-ft front setback from the property line, using the street rights-of-way previously discussed, will allow approximately 36 to 48 ft from the edge of the street pavement. This should be sufficient in projects where the smallest lots are ½ acre or less.

Side and rear setbacks of at least 25 ft are recommended for fire safety separation, aircraft clearance and architectural harmony.

A further measure that is recommended for assuring the parklike quality of the development is to limit the amount of each site permitted to be occupied by structures. Site coverage of 60 percent should be a maximum although 50 percent is preferable.

Site Layout

An airport industrial park should be at least 50 acres to justify the management effort required for planning, promotion, and continuing operation.

Block dimensions are determined in part by the depths established for groups of lots. Within the block it is then possible to adjust lot widths to suit the needs of individual tenants.

A variety of block sizes based on lot depths of 150 ft up to 500 ft allows for inclusion in the project of sites varying from about ⅓ of an acre to 10 acres. Minimum lot width should be about 100 ft in order to provide buildable sites for small industries.

It is recommended that blocks be as long as practicable to reduce the costs incurred in the construction of cross streets. Within the industrial park, there is little need for lot-to-lot circulation because most traffic is to and from destinations outside the industrial park.

Stage construction usually is a necessity because of flexibility and cost considerations. Sections that are opened for development should be improved so that lots offered for lease or sale are developed lots rather than raw land. Streets and utilities should be provided ready for use at the sites.

Utilities

Utilities that are essential are water, sanitary sewer system, electric power, gas distribution, fire hydrants and storm sewers adequate for drainage on and off site. Utilities are provided by the sponsor through his own resources, or by arrangement with the local utility companies, so that the tenant is only required to connect his installation to existing systems.

Utility easements may be provided in the rights-of-way reserved for streets or rail spurs. Underground utilities may be provided in aircraft taxiway rights-of-way.

Park Center

Reservation of an area for a park center should be made in larger projects. This center would include the offices of the park management and maintenance functions. Facilities for the common use of park tenants could be offered, such as restaurant, banking facilities, small shops for sale of sundries and, possibly, motel facilities for the accommodation of overnight guests. Other commercial services and personal conveniences could be provided at the discretion of the park management in the park center.

DESIGN OF FACILITIES

Site Selection

Amid the many other factors influencing the choice of an industrial plant site, that of employee parking should not be overlooked. Site requirements, in some cases, may be prescribed by equal areas each for factory, storage, and parking. But parking needs frequently are affected by the type of location, since the demand for parking often may be less in locations where land costs are highest. The influences of transit service, walk-to-work trips, or drop-off trips, which are likely to be related to area type, are suggested in the table on this page.

The example shows that parking area needs for 1,600 employees may vary by as much as three acres. The total cost for employee parking may be equal or less at the rural site, however, because of lower land costs.

When land costs are high, it becomes more economical to build a second level over existing parking than to construct new surface lots. Other economic factors, such as proximity to markets or to rail service, may overcome the disadvantages of high parking costs in urban areas. Roof parking or remote parking with shuttle bus service are other solutions to meeting parking demand at confined plant sites.

Another principal traffic factor influencing site selection is the capacity of street systems to absorb peak hour loads at shift changes. While a concern primarily of public agencies, plant management is also concerned in terms of labor market accessibility as well as the ease of transporting incoming materials and outgoing products.

Design Elements

Several principles control the design of industrial plant parking facilities. First, the unique characteristics of employee parking must be taken into account. Unlike parking at shopping centers, airports and many commercial lots, industrial plant parking is characterized by long-term parking, nearly simultaneous large volumes of arrivals and departures, and brief periods of vehicle-pedestrian conflict.

Design provisions should, therefore, satisfy the following requirements:

1. Stall size that accommodates current vehicle models
2. Stall arrangements that make judicious use of the area available
3. Access to individual stalls that is safe, convenient and without delay
4. Entrances and exits that minimize delays
5. Parking locations that are close to working areas
6. Security and aesthetic treatments that meet plant and public needs

Stall Size Vehicle dimensions are the principal determinant of stall sizes. Many current models of automobiles measure 80 in. in width and 218 in. in overall length. Door-opening characteristics are another factor. As two-door models, which have larger doors than four-door models, become even more popular, there is an increasing need for wider stalls in parking facilities.

The 1959 ITE Recommended Practice on Industrial Plant Parking recommended 8-ft 6-in. stalls, which under present conditions may allow only 22 in. between vehicles for door opening. Current prevalent practice is to employ 9-ft stalls, with 10-ft stalls in some $90°$ visitor parking layouts. The effects of increasing stall width from 8 ft 6 in. to 9 ft, considering a 500-ft bay are as follows: with $90°$ parking, a reduction of from 58 to 55 spaces; with $60°$ parking, from 50 to 47 spaces.

When stall widths are less than 9 ft, double lines between stalls will assure better positioning of vehicles and minimize the possibility of wasted spaces due to improper parking.

Stall lengths must be at least 18 ft to accommodate current vehicle models. If "drive-through" parking is employed, stall length may be increased to 19 ft to allow for some clearance between vehicles.

Clearance from walls, fences, roadways or walkways can be maintained by using curbs or wheel-stops properly positioned within the stall area. A front overhang of 3 ft and a rear overhang of 5 ft are typical values to be accommodated.

Stall Arrangements Decisions about the choice of angle and the layout of aisles must be based on individual site conditions. The placement and number of entrances and exits, and the site shape and contour are the major controls. At large plants, blocks of parking by groups of three to five hundred cars are preferable to larger aggregations. Pedestrian-vehicle conflicts can be reduced, and assigned parking for different shifts and employment groups can be better controlled, through the use of such relatively small blocks.

The following general practices are desirable: use natural grades to facilitate drainage; provide for counterclockwise traffic aisle flow, since left turns are easier than right turns for drivers; have parked vehicles face downhill rather than uphill, to allow for stalled vehicles or winter weather conditions.

This report includes layout details for only one type of parking. Figure 1 illustrates a stall arrangement and an aisle design that have not been widely published—the drive-through double stall pattern, usable in either $90°$ or acute angle parking layouts.

In general, angle parking is preferred for large industrial parking facilities. First, properly designed angle parking can employ space as effectively as right-angle parking. Second, it virtually forces one-way movements, thereby simplifying control, reducing conflicts, and ensuring that daily parking practices conform to the established design. Third, it provides for easier turning movements into and out of stalls.

Drive-through angle parking design offers the further advantages of minimizing backing out of stalls and directing all aisle travel in the same direction. It conserves space more effectively than other angle parking designs. Typically, the angled drive-through layout requires 36 ft for the double stall and an 18-ft aisle (to permit passing stalled vehicles), for a unit parking depth of 54 ft. Compared with $90°$ parking, the space loss along the length of the bay—eight spaces in 500 ft according to the example—will be compensated for by the reduction in unit parking depth, from 62 or 64 ft to 54 ft, if enough bays can be used.

The disadvantage of this design of drive-through parking is that it increases the travel distance and time of a search pattern if the lot is nearly full. It also is imperative to keep the end circulation aisles two-way so that a driver will not be forced out of the lot in order to return to another parking aisle.

The drawing also gives dimensions for angle parking at $53° 8'$, an angle which has the layout convenience of being a 3-4-5 triangle. Other angles commonly used for parking are 45, 55, or $60°$. However, any angle smaller than the 3-4-5 configuration tends to be wasteful of space, without offering any significant advantage.

Where two-way aisle flow may be desirable, as in visitor parking lots, $90°$ parking is more appropriate. Site dimensions sometimes may be such that $90°$ unit parking depths are most appropriate regardless of other circumstances. The minimum $90°$ parking depth reported to Committee 6T was 61 ft, with preferences expressed for 62-64 ft as desirable dimensions. When unit parking depths are less than desirable, shortened stall lines (10–15 ft long) may encourage drivers to pull all the way into stalls.

Hypothetical Relationship of Parking Area Requirements to Location

Location	No. of employees at peak shift overlap	Percent as drivers or auto psgrs.	Number of autos to be parked*	Approx. site, sq ft	Area, acres
Urban	1,600	60	740	222	5.0
Suburban	1,600	80	990	297	6.8
Rural.	1,600	95	1,180	354	8.0

* Assuming car occupancy of 1.3 persons per car.

Parking Facilities for Industrial Plants, Institute of Traffic Engineers, Washington, D.C., 1969.

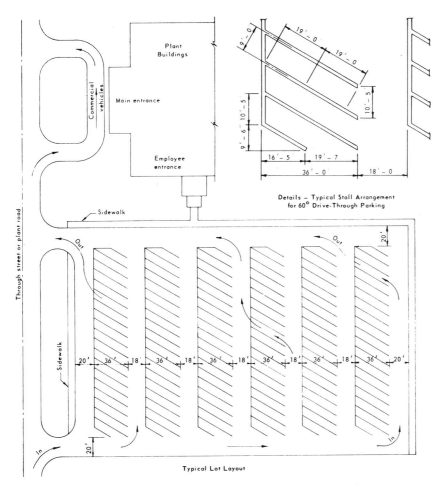

Details – Typical Stall Arrangement for 60° Drive-Through Parking

Typical Lot Layout

DESIRABLE STALL AND AISLE DIMENSIONS FOR DRIVE-THROUGH PARKING

Angle of Parking	Width of Stall	Depth of Stall Perpendicular to Aisle	Width of Aisle	Unit Parking Depth	Width of Stall Parallel to Aisle
o	W	L	A	UPD	W
90	10'	38' – 0"	24'	62' – 0	10' – 0
90	9'	38' – 0"	26'	64' – 0	9' – 0
60	9'	36' – 0"	18'	54' – 0	10' – 5
53	9'	35' – 10"	18'	53' – 10	11' – 3

Fig. 1   Drive-through lot layout.

Service Roads Many large plants require service roads between plant entrances and parking areas. Several design factors may be noted:

1. Proper control can best be achieved if service roadway lanes are clearly marked for one- or two-way operation.

2. To permit passing of a stalled vehicle, one-way, single-lane service roads must be at least 18 ft wide.

3. Incoming shift vehicles should be separated from truck deliveries and outgoing shift vehicles.

4. Service roads that permit drivers to reach those plant exits most suitable for their subsequent travel direction will minimize conflicts and capacity reduction at plant exits.

5. Pedestrian conflicts can be minimized by locating the entrances from service roads in parking areas at the end opposite to work areas.

6. Exits from parking areas to service roads will minimize conflicts if they are placed away from the main stream of pedestrians leaving work.

Plant Entrances and Exits The number and location of gates is a function of both the external roadway system and internal circulation. It may be desirable, or even necessary, to distribute peak-hour volumes among several streets to avoid overtaxing the capacity of nearby intersections. In the case of overlapping shift arrivals and departures, both internal and external conditions will dictate to a large degree the number and location of gates. Because exit peaks generally are of shorter duration, greater exit than entrance capacity usually will be required. Exit turning movements also may be less efficient, in vehicles cleared per hour, than entrance movements.

The total number of exits will be determined

by the number of lanes available at individual exits, what turns may be prohibited, and the allowable length of time for discharging peak period volumes. Observed exit rates for left- and right-turning lanes range up to 1,500 vehicles per lane per hour of green time.[1] Obviously, nearby highway intersections must provide adequate capacity to meet exit volumes in addition to nonplant traffic. A traffic engineering analysis employing the type of procedures outlined in the Highway Capacity Manual may be necessary to ensure the most effective location and design. Such an analysis certainly should be undertaken when traffic signals are contemplated, or when volumes reach magnitudes for which grade separation may need to be considered.

Where two-way flow is to be accommodated, the roadway width at gates should be at least 26 ft to facilitate turning movements to or from a major highway. The American Association of State Highway Officials design policies may be consulted for turning radii details.[2] Where guards stop incoming vehicles, checkpoints should be far enough from the highway to prevent queues forming on the highway.

Pedestrian Needs

Pedestrian-vehicle conflicts are almost inevitable, but with minimum walking distances such conflicts can be reduced. Several methods can be followed to lessen the inefficiency, congestion and safety hazards inherent in such conflicts.

1. Parking space allocations can be oriented to specific buildings.

2. Parking areas may be designed to focus on major walkways, which should be fenced or marked.

3. Where pedestrians must cross service roads or access roads to reach parking areas, crosswalks should be clearly designated by pavement markings, signs, flashing lights, or even traffic signals operated by plant security personnel. Crosswalk surfaces may be raised slightly to designate them to drivers, unless drainage problems would result.

4. Walkways may be provided under cover of buildings between parking and work areas.

5. Wherever possible, parking aisles should lead directly to the plant. This will minimize inbound problems, since close-in spaces will be taken first and later arrivals will park farther away. Pedestrians can walk past parked cars rather than crossing aisles with cars arriving and being parked.

The best means of separating pedestrians and vehicles is by constructing underpasses or overpasses at key points. Grade separation may be essential to prevent long delays and time losses, as where freight must be handled, to avoid exposure to hazardous plant operations. It may be necessary where parking facilities and plant buildings are on opposite sides of major highways. If intersection capacity problems preclude provision of a pedestrian phase in nearby traffic signals, grade-separated pedestrian crossings will be essential.

Provisions for Commercial Vehicles

Receiving and shipping needs of many industrial plants are accommodated by motor trans-

[1] Highway Research Board, "Highway Capacity Manual," Special Report #87, 1965, page 137, Washington, D.C.
[2] American Association of State Highway Officials, "A Policy on Arterial Highways in Urban Areas," Washington, D.C., 1957.

port vehicles, ranging from pickup trucks to five-axle tractor-trailer units. While the major movements involve raw materials, supplies, and finished products, a measurable amount of truck traffic is generated also by canteens, cafeterias, laboratories, or other service needs.

Unless an industrial plant is under strict security measures, motor transport vehicles normally use the same entrance and exit facilities used by employee vehicles. Where security is a question, separate truck gates may be provided with each inbound and outbound truck being checked by a guard. Gates used by trucks require two lanes, each 12 ft in width, clearly posted as to use. Controls may be required to eliminate possible conflict between trucks and other traffic, especially at periods of major employee shift arrivals and departures. The most effective control at periods of peak demand is prohibition of all commercial vehicles.

Within plant premises, it is desirable to route commercial vehicles around the periphery of the plant to loading areas and to prohibit direct access through employee parking lots. The width of driveway lanes should be not less than 10 ft nor more than 12 ft, in order to discourage illegal parking. Turning radii should be adequate for the largest vehicle anticipated, and signs and markings should conform to accepted standards.

This report does not treat the design of loading docks in detail, but the following informational comments are offered. The width of apron space or maneuvering area in front of loading docks is dependent upon the overall length of servicing vehicles, the turning radii of the equipment and the width of truck berths. Generally, the distance from the edge of the loading dock to the opposite curb, outside edge of opposite truck berths, or near edge of any physical obstruction, should equal not less than twice the overall length of the longest service vehicle. Where receiving or shipping operations necessitate an accumulation or storage of trailer units in excess of available dock apron space, a marginal area should be provided for waiting or for trailer storage separate from the apron space or any parking lot. Apron areas should be free of any passenger car parking and physically separated from any portion of the parking lots. The surface should be well paved with a dustless and durable material, graded for drainage and of sufficient bearing strength to support concentrated axle loads.

Amenities

Both employee and community relations may require that some consideration be given to parking area amenities. Much depends on location. A steel mill surrounded by steel mills will not be concerned in the same way that an electronics plant next to suburban residential areas need be.

Landscaping can be an important element in the appearance and effective use of parking areas. It can serve functionally by designating separate parking areas: aesthetically by breaking the bleakness of great expanses of asphalt.

Utilities often can be placed in landscaped areas. Some plants take landscaping amenities so seriously that preferred parking layouts may be rejected because of insufficient landscaping. There are several drawbacks to be considered, however. Improperly located shrubs may seriously reduce driver sight distances. High plantings that completely screen employee vehicles may encourage vandalism and pilferage. Deciduous trees may create trouble with sap droppings; falling leaves increase maintenance costs and also may obstruct drainage structures. In colder climates, landscaping may impede snow removal.

Noise control is sometimes an important factor. Plant noise may be materially reduced by proper location of loading docks and parking areas, although even the quietest truck is disturbing at night. Depending on terrain, noise may be buffered by fences or planting.

Lot surfacing may be an amenity factor. All lots should be properly graded for drainage and should be dust-free. Higher type surfaces, with pavement markings to designate spaces and reserved areas, may be warranted in high-landcost areas, and at activities attracting many visitors. A more efficient as well as a more attractive site will result.

Some amenities may help to reduce the total number of parking spaces required. Covered or shielded transit waiting areas, within close walking distance of buildings, may encourage a higher level of transit usage. Alternatively, shuttle buses might be operated between transit stops and plant areas. Providing turnout bays where auto passengers may be dropped off and picked up may mean that otherwise necessary parking space can be put to a more productive use.

Recreation and Entertainment

10

PLAYLOTS AND PLAYGROUNDS	1183	HAMMER THROW	1233
BADMINTON	1192	DISCUS THROW	1234
BASKETBALL (AAU)	1193	JAVELIN THROW	1235
BASKETBALL (NCAA)	1194	LONG JUMP AND TRIPLE JUMP	1236
BIDDY BASKETBALL	1195	POLE VAULT	1237
GOAL-HI BASKETBALL	1196	HIGH JUMP	1238
BOCCIE BALL	1197	ARCHERY	1239
CROQUET	1198	INTERNATIONAL SHOOTING UNION	
ONE-WALL HANDBALL	1199	AUTOMATIC TRAP	1240
THREE- AND FOUR-WALL HANDBALL	1200	FIXED NETS AND POSTS	1241
HOPSCOTCH	1201	FENCE ENCLOSURES	1242
HORSESHOES	1202	TYPICAL GRADING AND DRAINAGE DETAILS	1243
ICE HOCKEY	1203	TYPICAL PLAYING SURFACES	1244
LAWN BOWLING	1204	BASEBALL AND SOFTBALL BACKSTOPS	1245
ROQUE	1205	MOVIE THEATERS	1246
SHUFFLEBOARD	1206	Handicapped Seating	1251
DECK TENNIS	1207	500-Seat Movie Theater	1253
PLATFORM TENNIS	1208	DRIVE-IN THEATERS	1255
PADDLE TENNIS	1209	BOWLING ALLEYS	1257
TENNIS	1210	SWIMMING POOLS	1266
TETHERBALL	1211	Public Swimming Pools	1266
VOLLEYBALL	1212	Diving Pools	1269
OFFICIAL BASEBALL	1213	Residential Swimming Pools	1271
BASEBALL	1214	50-Meter Recreational Pool	1273
Bronco League (9–12 yr)	1214	25-Meter Recreational Pool	1274
Pony League (13–14 yr)	1215	25- and 50-Meter Indoor Pools	1275
Colt League (15–16 yr)	1216	HEALTH CLUBS	1277
Little League (9–12 yr)	1217	LOCKER ROOMS	1278
FIELD HOCKEY	1218	BATHHOUSES	1280
FLICKERBALL	1219	GYMNASIUM	1282
FOOTBALL (NCAA)	1220	ZOOS	1283
TOUCH AND FLAG FOOTBALL	1221	AQUARIUMS	1293
GOLF DRIVING RANGE	1222	INDOOR TENNIS BUILDING	1300
LACROSSE	1223	SPORTS ARENAS	1301
Men's	1223	GOLF COURSES AND CLUBHOUSES	1310
Women's	1224	RIFLE AND PISTOL RANGES, INDOOR	1318
SOCCER	1225	RIFLE AND CARBINE RANGES, OUTDOOR	1325
Men's and Boys'	1225	SHOOTING RANGES, OUTDOOR	1329
Women's and Girls'	1226	Trapshooting	1329
SOFTBALL, 12-INCH	1227	Skeet Shooting	1329
SOFTBALL, 16-INCH	1228	Trap Field	1330
SPEEDBALL	1229	Skeet Field	1331
TEAM HANDBALL	1230	Combination Skeet and Trap Field	1332
¼-MILE RUNNING TRACK	1231	MARINAS	1333
SHOT PUT	1232	CAMPS AND CAMP FACILITIES	1343

General

Playlots should be provided for preschool children up to 6 years of age primarily in conjunction with multifamily (townhouse and apartment) developments and in single-family neighborhoods remote from elementary schools. They are a necessary element of such developments to complement common open-space areas. Playlots may include (1) an enclosed area for play equipment and such special facilities as a sand area and a spray pool; (2) an open, turfed area for active play; and (3) a shaded area for quiet activities.

Location of Playlots

Playlots should be included as an integral part of the housing area design, and are desirably located within 300 to 400 ft of each living unit served. A playlot should be accessible without crossing any street, and the walkways thereto should have an easy gradient for pushing strollers and carriages. Playlots may be included in playgrounds close to housing areas to serve the preschool age group in the adjoining neighborhood.

Size of Playlots

The enclosed area for play equipment and special facilities should be based on a minimum of 70 sq ft per child, which is equivalent to 21 sq ft per family on the average basis of 0.3 preschool child per family. A minimum enclosed area of approximately 2,000 sq ft will serve some 30 preschool children (about 100 families). Such a size will accommodate only a limited selection of play equipment. To accommodate a full range of equipment and special facilities, including a spray pool, the minimum enclosed area should be about 4,000 sq ft, which would serve up to 50 preschool children (about 165 families). Additional space is required to accommodate the elements of the playlot outside of the enclosed area, as listed in the next paragraph. A turfed area at least 40 ft square should be provided for active games.

Playlot Activity Spaces and Elements

A playlot should comprise the following basic activity spaces and elements:
1. An enclosed area with play equipment and special facilities including
   a. Play equipment such as climbers, slides, swing sets, playwalls and playhouses, and play sculpture
   b. A sand area
   c. A spray pool
2. An open, turfed area for running and active play
3. A shaded area for quiet activities
4. Miscellaneous elements, including benches for supervising parents; walks and other paved areas wide enough for strollers, carriages, tricycles, wagons, etc.; play space dividers (fences, walks, trees, shrubs), a step-up drinking fountain, trash containers, and landscape planting.

Layout of Playlots

The specific layout and shape of each playlot will be governed by the existing site conditions and the facilities to be provided. General principles of layout are described as follows:

1. The intensively used part of the playlot with play equipment and special facilities should be surrounded by a low enclosure with supplemental planting, and provided with one entrance-exit. This design will discourage intrusion by animals or older children, provide adequate and safe control over the children, and prevent the area from becoming a thoroughfare. Adequate drainage should be provided.

2. Equipment should be selected and arranged with adequate surrounding space in small, natural play groups. Traffic flow should be planned to encourage movement throughout the playlot in a safe, orderly manner. This traffic flow may be facilitated with walks, plantings, low walls and benches.

3. Equipment which enables large numbers of children to play without taking turns (climbers, play sculpture) should be located near the entrance, yet positioned so that it will not cause congestion. With such an arrangement, children will tend to move more slowly to equipment that limits participation and requires turns (swings, slides), thereby modifying the load factor and reducing conflicts.

4. Sand areas, play walls, playhouses, and play sculpture should be located away from such pieces of equipment as swings and slides for safety and to promote a creative atmosphere for the child's world of make believe. Artificial or natural shade is desirable over the sedentary play pieces, where children will play on hot days without immediate supervision. Play sculpture may be placed in the sand area to enhance its value by providing a greater variety of play opportunities. A portion of the area should be maintained free of equipment for general sand play that is not in conflict with traffic flow.

5. Swings or other moving equipment should be located near the outside of the equipment area, and should be sufficiently separated by walls or fences to discourage children from walking into them while they are moving. Swings should be oriented toward the best view and away from the sun. Sliding equipment should preferably face north away from the summer sun. Equipment with metal surfaces should be located in available shade.

6. Spray pools should be centrally located, and step-up drinking fountains strategically placed for convenience and economy in relation to water supply and waste disposal lines.

7. The open, turfed area for running and active play, and the shaded area for such quiet activities as reading and storytelling, should be closely related to the enclosed equipment area and serve as buffer space around it.

8. Nonmovable benches should be conveniently located to assure good visibility and protection of the children at play. Durable trash containers should be provided and conveniently located to maintain a neat, orderly appearance.

Playground Characteristics

1. The playground is the chief center of outdoor play for kindergarten and school age children from 5 to 12 years of age. It also offers some opportunities for recreation for young people and adults.

2. The playground at every elementary school should be of sufficient size and design, and properly maintained, to serve both the elementary educational program and the recreational needs of all age groups in the neighborhood. Since education and recreation programs complement each other in many ways, unnecessary duplication of essential outdoor recreational facilities should be avoided. Only where this joint function is not feasible should a separate playground be developed.

3. A playground may include (a) a playlot for preschool children, (b) an enclosed playground equipment area for elementary school children, (c) an open, turfed area for active games, (d) shaded areas for quiet activities, (e) a paved, multipurpose area, (f) an area for field games, and (g) circulation and buffer space.

Location of Playground

A playground is an integral part of a complete elementary school development. School playgrounds and other playgrounds should be readily accessible from and conveniently related to the housing area served. A playground should be within $\frac{1}{4}$ to $\frac{1}{2}$ mile of every family housing unit.

Size and Number of Playgrounds

Recommended size of a playground is a minimum of 6 to 8 acres, which would serve approximately 1,000 to 1,500 families. The smallest playground that will accommodate essential activity spaces is about 3 acres, serving approximately 250 families (about 110 elementary school children). This minimum area should be increased at the rate of 0.2 to 0.4 acres for each additional 50 families. More than one playground should be provided where (1) a complete school playground is not feasible, (2) the population to be served exceeds 1,500 families, or (3) the distance from the housing units is too great.

Playground Activity Spaces and Elements

A playground should contain the following basic activity spaces and elements:

1. A playlot, as described in the preceding section, with equipment and surfacing as recommended.

2. An enclosed playground equipment area with supplemental planting for elementary school children, and with equipment as recommended.

3. An open, turfed area for informal active games for elementary school children.

4. Shaded areas for quiet activities such as reading, storytelling, quiet games, handicrafts, picnicking and horseshoe pitching for both children and adults.

5. A paved and well-lighted, multipurpose

area large enough for (a) activities such as roller skating, dancing, hopscotch, four square, and captain ball, and (b) games requiring specific courts, such as basketball, volleyball, tennis, handball, badminton, paddle tennis, and shuffleboard.

6. An area for field games, preferably well-lighted, (including softball, junior baseball, touch or flag football, soccer, track and field activities, and other games), which will also serve for informal play of field sports and kite flying, and be used occasionally for pageants, field days, and other community activities.

7. Miscellaneous elements such as public shelter, storage space, toilet facilities, drinking fountains, walks, benches, trash containers, and buffer zones with planting.

Layout of Playgrounds

The layout of a playground will vary according to size of available area, its topography, and the specific activities desired. It should fit the site with maximum preservation of the existing terrain and such natural site features as large shade trees, interesting ground forms, rock outcrops and streams. These features should be integrated into the layout to the maximum extent feasible for appropriate activity spaces, as natural divisions of various use areas, and for landscape interest. Grading should be kept to a minimum consistent with activity needs, adequate drainage and erosion control. General principles of layout are described as follows:

1. The playlot and the playground equipment area should be located adjacent to the school and to each other.

2. An open, turfed area for informal active play should be located close to the playlot and the playground equipment area for convenient use by all elementary school children.

3. Areas for quiet activities for children and adults should be somewhat removed from active play spaces and should be close to tree-shaded areas and other natural features of the site.

4. The paved multipurpose area should be set off from other areas by planting and so located near the school gymnasium that it may be used for physical education without disturbing other school classes. All posts or net supports required on the courts should be constructed with sleeves and caps which will permit removal of the posts and their supports.

5. The area for field games should be located on fairly level, well-drained land with finished grades not in excess of 2.5 percent; a minimum grade of 1 percent is acceptable on pervious soils having good percolation for proper drainage.

6. In general, the area of a playground may be divided as follows: (a) Approximately half of the area should be parklike, including the open, turfed areas for active play, the shaded areas for quiet activities, and the miscellaneous elements as described in 7 below; (b) the other half of the area should include $\frac{3}{4}$ to 1 acre for the playlot, playground equipment area, and the paved, multipurpose area, and $1\frac{3}{4}$ acres (for softball) to 4 acres (for baseball) for the field games area.

7. The playground site should be fully developed with landscape planting for activity control and traffic control, and for attractiveness. This site also should have accessible public shelter, storage for maintenance and recreation equipment, toilet facilities, drinking fountains, walks wide enough for strollers and carriages, bicycle paths, benches for adults and children, and trash containers.

General Equipment Selection Factors

The following general factors should be considered in selecting equipment for playlots and playgrounds.

Developmental and Recreational Values All equipment should contribute to the healthy growth and recreational enjoyment of the child, so that he learns to coordinate, cooperate, compete, create, enjoy, and acquire confidence. Play equipment should:

1. Develop strength, agility, coordination, balance, and courage.

2. Stimulate the child to learn social skills of sharing and playing with others, and to compete in a spirit of fair play.

3. Encourage each child to be creative and have play experiences which are meaningful to him.

4. Permit the child to have fun and a sense of complete enjoyment.

5. Assist the child in making the transition from playlot to playground.

Child Preference and Capacity Play equipment, to be selected with due regard to the child's changing preference, maturity, and capacity, should:

1. Be scaled and proportioned to meet the child's physical and emotional capacities at different age levele.

2. Permit the child to do some things alone without direct adult supervision or assistance.

3. Provide a wide variety of play opportunities to accommodate changing interests of the child.

4. Free the child's imagination.

5. Meet a variety of interests, abilities, and aptitudes.

Safety of Participants All play equipment should be designed and built for safety of the participants, and:

1. Be free of all sharp protruding surfaces caused by welds, rivets, bolts, or joints.

2. Have sufficient structural strength to withstand the expected loads.

3. Be designed to discourage incorrect use and to minimize accidents; examples are seats that discourage children from standing in swings, slides that require children to sit down before sliding, and steps or ladders that discourage more than one participant at a time.

4. Have hand or safety rails on all steps and ladders, and nonskid treads on all steps.

5. Be installed in accordance with the specific directions of the manufacturer.

6. Be placed over suitable surfaces that will reduce the danger of injury or abrasions in the event a child falls from the climbing, moving or sliding equipment. (A safe landing surface should be provided at the end of a slide chute.)

Durability of Equipment Equipment that is durable should be selected. It should be made of materials which are of sufficient strength and quality to withstand normal play wear. Wood should be used only where metal or plastics have serious disadvantages. All metal parts should be galvanized or manufactured of corrosion-resistant metals. All movable bearings should be of an oilless type. Equipment should be designed as vandal-resistant as possible (for example, wire-reinforced seats for swings).

Equipment with Eye Appeal All play equipment should be designed and selected for function, for visual appeal to stimulate the child's imagination, with pleasing proportions and

with colors in harmonious contrast to each other and the surroundings. Play equipment may have a central theme, to reflect historical significance of the area, a storybook land, a nautical motif or a space flight motif. The theme may be carried out by constructing retaining or separation walls to resemble a corral, ship, or airplane, and by appropriate design of such elements as paving, benches, and trash cans.

Ease of Maintenance Equipment should be selected which requires a minimum of maintenance. Purchased equipment should be products of established manufacturers who can provide a standard parts list. Equipment parts which are subject to wear should be replaceable. Color should be impregnated into the material, if feasible, to avoid repainting. Sand areas should be surrounded by a retaining wall and be maintained regularly to remove foreign objects and loosen the sand as a suitable play medium.

Supervision Equipment should be selected that requires a minimum of direct supervision.

Basic Play Equipment

General Play equipment may include swings, slides, and merry-go-rounds; various types of climbers; balancing equipment such as balance beams, conduit, leaping posts, and boxes; hanging equipment such as parallel bars, horizontal bars, and ladders; play walls and playhouses; and a variety of play sculpture forms. Different types of play equipment should be provided for preschool children and for elementary school children to meet the developmental and recreational needs of the two age groups.

Playlot Equipment for Preschool Children The following table indicates types, quantities, and minimum play space requirements for various types of equipment totaling about 2,800 sq ft; this area, plus additional space for circulation and play space dividers, will accommodate a full range of playlot equipment serving a neighborhood containing approximately 50 preschool children (about 165 families).

Equipment	Number of pieces	Play space requirements, ft
Climber	1	10 x 25
Junior swing set (4 swings)	1	16 x 32
Play sculpture	1	10 x 10
Play wall or playhouse	1	15 x 15
Sand area	1	15 x 15
Slide	1	10 x 25
Spray pool (including deck)	1	36 x 36

Smaller playlots may be developed to serve a neighborhood containing some 30 children (about 100 families), using a limited selection of equipment with play space requirements totaling about 1,200 sq ft; this area, plus additional space for circulation and play space dividers, should consider the following desirable priorities: (1) a sand area; (2) a climbing device such as a climber, a play wall or a piece of play sculpture; (3) a slide, and (4) a swing set. Where several playlots are provided, the equipment selections should be complementary, rather than all being the same type. For example, one playlot may include play walls or a playhouse, while another playlot may provide a piece of play sculpture. Also, such a costly but popular item as a spray pool may be justified in only one out of every two or three playlots provided.

Playground Equipment for Elementary School Children
The following table indicates types, quantities, and minimum play space requirements totaling about 6,600 sq ft; this area, plus additional space for circulation, miscellaneous elements, and buffer zones, will accommodate a full range of playground equipment serving approximately 50 children at one time.

Equipment	Number of pieces	Play space requirements, ft
Balance beam.	1	15 x 30
Climbers	3	21 x 50
Climbing poles	3	10 x 20
Horizontal bars	3	15 x 30
Horizontal ladder.	1	15 x 30
Merry-go-round	1	40 x 40
Parallel bars.	1	15 x 30
Senior swing set (6 swings)	1	30 x 45
Slide	1	12 x 35

Surfacing

General Selection of suitable surfacing materials for each type of play area and for circulation paths or walks, roads, and parking areas, should be based on the following considerations:

1. *Function* The surface should suit the purpose and the specific function of the area (such as surfaces for court games or field games, and surfaces under play equipment). The surface should also be considered from the basis of whether the area is multipurpose or single-purpose, and for seasonal or year-round usage.

2. *Economy* The factors of economy are the initial cost, replacement cost, and maintenance cost. Often an initially more expensive surfacing is the least expensive in the long run because of reduced maintenance.

3. *Durability* The durability of the surface should be evaluated in light of its resistance to the general wear caused by the participants, and resistance to extended periods of outdoor weathering such as sunlight, rain, freezing, sand, and dust.

4. *Cleanliness* The surface should be clean and attractive to participants, it should not attract or harbor insects or rodents, and it should not track into adjacent buildings or cause discoloration to children's clothing.

5. *Maintenance* Maintenance must be evaluated not only in light of the cost, but also of the time when the facility is not available for use due to repair or upkeep.

6. *Safety* The safety of the participants is a primary consideration in selecting a play surface and should not be compromised for the sake of economy.

7. *Appearance* A surface which has an attractive appearance and harmonizes with its surroundings is very desirable. Surfacing materials should encourage optimum use and enjoyment by all participants, and channel the activities in an orderly manner by providing visual contrasts.

Evaluation of Surfacing Materials

1. *Turf* This material is generally considered to be the best surface for many of the recreation activities carried on at playlots and playgrounds. Although turf is not feasible for play areas having heavy participant use, most park and recreation authorities recommend using turf wherever practicable. Underground irrigation sprinkler systems with rubber top valves should be specified in areas with inadequate seasonal rainfall to maintain a turf cover. Major reasons for using turf are that it is relatively soft, providing greater safety than other surfaces, and it has a pleasing, restful appearance with great appeal to participants. A turf surface is especially suitable for open and informal play areas for younger children, and the large field game areas for sports and general recreation use.

2. *Bituminous Concrete* This flexible paving material is the most generally used material for paving play areas. The designer should note that various asphalt grades and mixes are available, as well as color-coatings to improve appearance and maintenance. A suitable mix and careful grade control should be used to obtain a smooth, even surface, economical construction, and little or no maintenance. Bituminous concrete pavement is especially useful for paved, multipurpose areas, for tennis, basketball, and volleyball courts, roller skating and ice skating rinks, and for walks, roads, and parking areas.

3. *Portland Cement Concrete* This rigid paving material is the most favored type of surface for use in specialized areas where permanence is desired, and to provide uniformity, maximum durability, and little or no maintenance. A Portland cement concrete surface is especially useful for court games requiring a true, even surface, such as tennis and handball, for shuffleboard courts, roller skating and ice skating rinks, and for walks, curbs, roads, and parking areas.[1]

4. *Synthetic Materials* Synthetic materials that have a cushioning effect are being used by some school, park and recreation departments, primarily for safety, under play equipment. Several companies have developed successful resilient materials which provide excellent safety surfaces; these have been more expensive than the other materials discussed.

5. *Miscellaneous Materials* Materials used for specific areas include sand, sawdust, tanbark, or wood chips around and under play equipment, earth on baseball diamond infields, and brick, flagstone, or tile on walks and terraces.

[1]NOTE: Portland cement concrete and bituminous concrete surfaces are generally considered for many of the same uses. Selection of either one should include appropriateness for the purpose intended, the initial cost, and long-term cost, at each location.

PLAYLOTS AND PLAYGROUNDS

AREAS & EQUIPMENT

Desirable standards for recreation facilities have been set up by the National Recreation Association and are generally recognized. Absolute standardization is impossible because of variable factors: climatic conditions; population or institutional needs, habits or preferences; and available land or money. Information on these pages may be used in planning and space allocation.

Basic general standard for public areas is 1 acre of open space per 100 total population, of which 40 to 50 per cent should be devoted to games or other active recreation. (See also recommendations in section on "Apartments.") No set formula has been established for institutions such as churches, schools, colleges. Local conditions, such as extent of participation in organized athletics, available money, etc., should govern the choice; however, playfields for elementary and grammar schools may follow schemes outlined below.

Game areas and layouts contained in the drawings are based on practice of the New York City Department of Parks. Where games are subject to official rules, consult publications of athletic organizations or other governing bodies.

Types of public recreational areas have been set up by the National Recreation Association, based on age groups and urban or suburban needs.

Surfacing of play areas influences utility, extent and cost of upkeep, and extent of playing season. Local materials, climate, soil, intensity of use and tradition influence choice of surfacing. In general all areas require effective surface or subsurface drainage or both.

THE PLAYLOT

Playlots are intended for children of preschool age and are commonly provided in densely populated areas as a substitute for backyard play. They are also provided in interiors of large blocks in neighborhood or housing developments, often for nursery schools.

Size may vary from 6,000 to 10,000 sq ft for each 100 preschool children.

Location should be centered among population served, and accessible without crossing traffic arteries. Interior of a block is ideal if one block only is served. If available space is limited, a corner of children's playground may be used.

Plan elements include: (1) central grass plot; (2) areas with shade trees, in which apparatus and benches are set; (3) hard-surfaced walkway for wheel toys, veloci-

Table 1. Playlots

Type of Equipment or Area	Area per Unit (Sq. Ft.)	Capacity in Children	Suggested Number Included
Apparatus			
Junglegym, Jr.	180	10	1
Low Slide	170	6	1-2
Low Swing	150	1	4-8
Low See-saw	100	2	4-8
Miscellaneous			
Open Space	48-50 per child	Varies with pop. to be served	
Block Bldg. Platform	20 per child 150 per platform	7-8 per platform	1
Sand Box *	18-20 per child 300 per box	15	1-2
Benches & Tables	Optional	Varies	
Shelter for Baby Buggies	Optional	Varies	1
Flag Pole	In open area		1
Bird Bath			1
Drinking Fountain			1

*Sand boxes should be located so as to receive direct sunlight part of each day for reasons of sanitation.

pedes, etc.; (4) surrounding low fence or hedge. Distribution of area may vary with topography, apparatus included and child population served. Minimum recommendations of National Recreation Association are given in Table 1.

CHILDREN'S PLAYGROUNDS

These are intended for children 5 to 15 years old. A subdivision of this type, characterized by smaller area and fewer facilities, is called the *Junior* or *Primary Playground*, and is intended for children up to 10 or 11 years.

Size of children's playgrounds ranges from 3 acres (minimum) to 7 acres. General recommendation is 1 acre per 1,000 total population. Two small playgrounds are usually more satisfactory than one of excessive size when population served requires a large acreage.

Location is usually in an area developed for this particular use, adjoining a grade school, in a neighborhood or large park, or a portion of a neighborhood playfield. Maximum radius of area to be served should preferably not exceed one-half mile; in areas of dense population or subject to heavy traffic, one-quarter mile.

Plan elements may be subdivided into apparatus section, specialized sports area, landscaping, and miscellaneous activities. Areas required are given in Table 2. Selection and distribution of areas and equip-

Table 2. Children's playgrounds

Type of Equipment or Area	Area per Unit (Sq. Ft.)	Capacity in Children	Suggested Number Included
Apparatus			
Slide	450	6	1 (b)
Horizontal Bars	180	4	3 (b)
Horizontal Ladders	375	8	2 (b)
Traveling Rings	625	6	1
Giant Stride	1,225	6	1
Small Junglegym	180	10	1
Low Swing	150	1	4 (a)
High Swing	250	1	6 (a)
Balance Beam	100	4	1
See-saw	100	2	4
Medium Junglegym	500	20	1
Misc. Equip't & Areas			
Open Space for Games (Ages 6-10)	10,000	80	1 (a)
Wading Pool	3,000	40	1 (a)
Handcraft, Quiet Games	1,600	30	1 (a)
Outdoor Theater	2,000	30	1
Sand Box	300	15	2
Shelter House	2,500	30	1 (c)
Special Sports Areas			
Soccer Field	36,000	22	1
Playground Baseball	20,000	20	2
Volley Ball Court	2,800	20	1
Basketball Court	3,750	16	1
Jumping Pits	1,200	12	1
Paddle Tennis Courts	1,800	4	2 (d)
Handball Courts	1,050	4	2
Tether Tennis Courts	400	2	2 (d)
Horseshoe Courts	600	4	2
Tennis Courts	7,200	4	2 (d)
Straightaway Track	7,200	10	1 (d)
Landscaping	(a) 6,000		
Paths, Circulation, etc.	(a) 7,000		

(a) Minimum desirable.

(b) One or all of these units may be omitted if playground is not used in conjunction with a school.

(c) May be omitted if sanitary facilities are supplied elsewhere.

(d) May be omitted if space is limited.

ment should be based on local preference, space and money available, and topography. Guides to selection of individual game areas or equipment are included in the footnotes to Table 2 where practicable.

In addition to the usual playground equipment listed on this page, some special equipment intended to stimulate imaginative play is now widely used. The examples following were pioneering efforts in this field, developed by the New York City Housing Authority in the late 1940's. A play boat and a play airplane, included in the original line of equipment, proved to be too expensive and too hazardous and are no longer used. A wide variety of imaginative playground equipment has been developed in recent years and is available from several commercial sources.

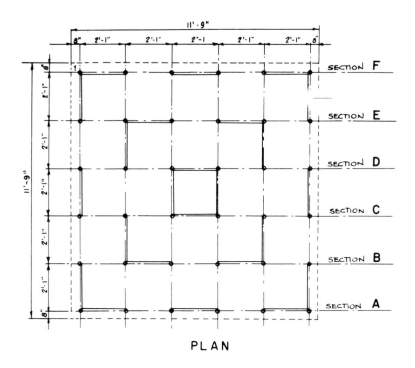

PLAN

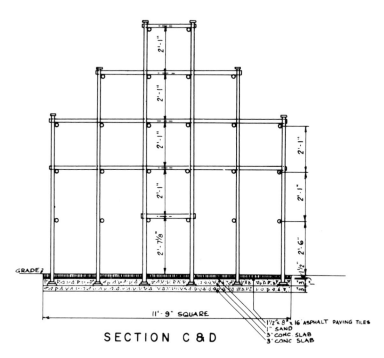

SECTION C & D

Fig. 1 Pipe-frame exercise unit.

Figures 1–4 are from *A Playground for All Children: Design Competition Program*, NYC DCP 76–13, HUD, OPDR, August 1976.

PLAYLOTS AND PLAYGROUNDS

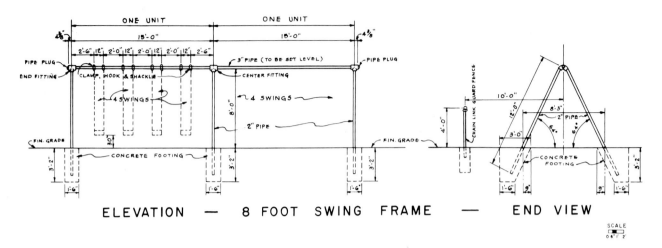

ELEVATION — 8 FOOT SWING FRAME — END VIEW

Fig. 2 Kindergarten swing (age 3 to 6).

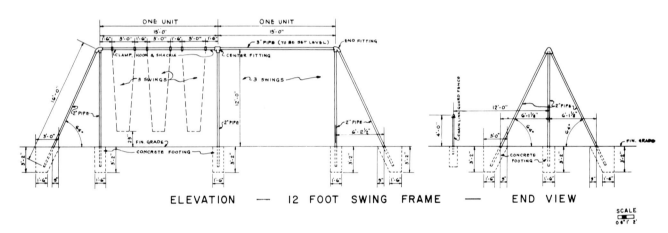

ELEVATION — 12 FOOT SWING FRAME — END VIEW

Fig. 3 Play swing (age 6 to 11).

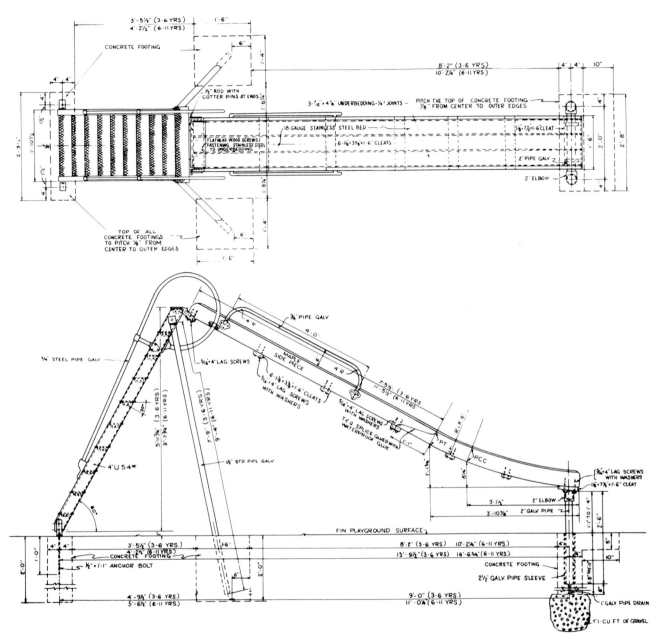

Fig. 4 Slide.

PLAYLOTS AND PLAYGROUNDS

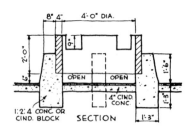

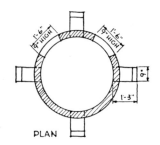

FOX HOLE

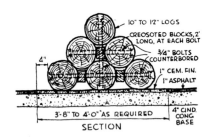

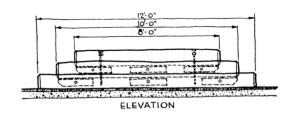

LOG PILE

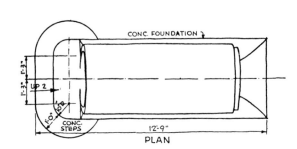

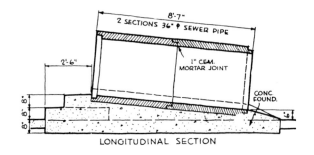

TUNNEL SLIDE

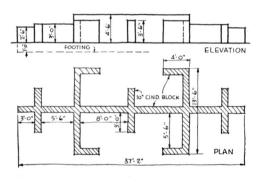

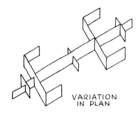

DODGER

NOTE: PROVIDE OPENINGS FOR SURFACE DRAINAGE AT FINISHED GRADE LEVEL.

Fig. 5 Special playground equipment.

PLAYLOTS AND PLAYGROUNDS

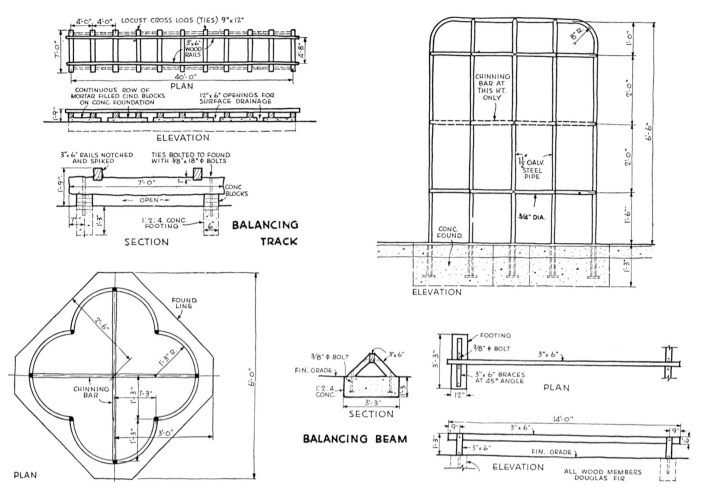

BALANCING TRACK

CIRCULAR PLAY UNIT

BALANCING BEAM

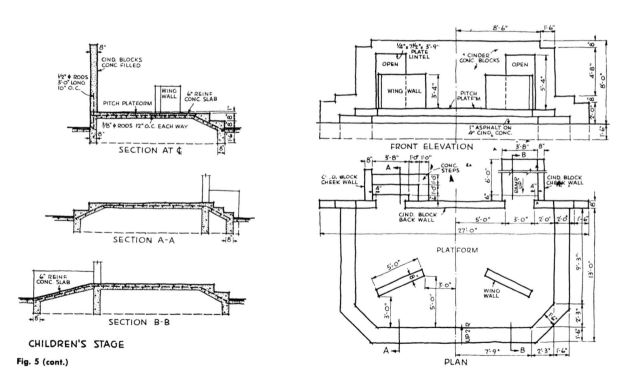

CHILDREN'S STAGE

Fig. 5 (cont.)

BADMINTON

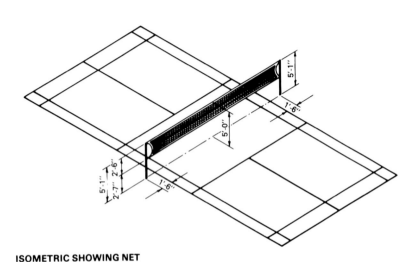

ISOMETRIC SHOWING NET

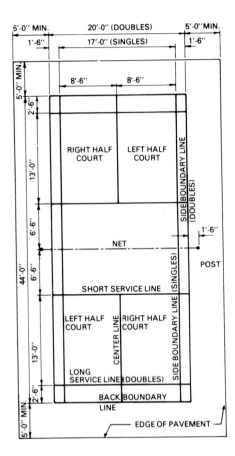

COURT LAYOUT

Fig. 1 Badminton court. All measurements for court markings are to the outside of lines except for those involving the center service line which is equally divided between right and left service courts. All court markings to be 1½" wide and preferably white or in color. Minimum distance between sides of parallel courts to be 5'-0". For net post details see Fig. 51. For surfacing details see Figs. 58 to 61.

Recommended Area Ground space is 1620 sq ft minimum to edge of pavement.

Size and Dimension Singles court is 17' × 44', doubles court is 20' × 44' with a 5'-0" minimum unobstructed area on all sides.

Orientation Preferred orientation is for the long axis to be north-south.

Surface and Drainage Surface is to be concrete or bituminous material with optional protective colorcoating for permanent installation. Drainage is to be end to end, side to side, or corner to corner diagonally at a minimum slope of 1 in. in 10 ft.

Badminton may be played on a turf court for general recreation use, with surface drainage as described above at a minimum slope of 2% and adequate underdrainage.

Material on pp. 1064–1117 from *Outdoor Sports Facilities,* Departments of the Army, Navy, and Air Force, Washington, D.C., 1975.

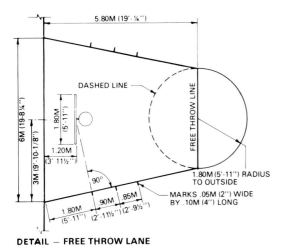

DETAIL — FREE THROW LANE

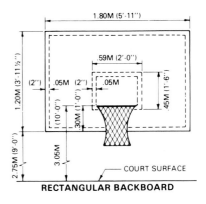

RECTANGULAR BACKBOARD

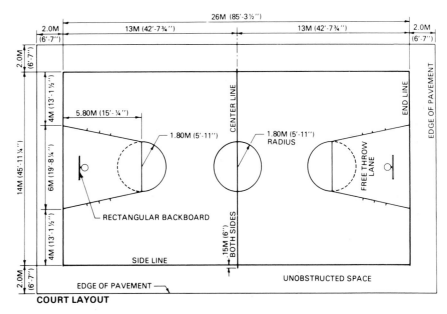

COURT LAYOUT

Fig. 2 AAU basketball court. All dimensions are to inside edge of lines except as noted. All lines to be .05 m (2") wide. Backboard shall be of any rigid weather-resistant material. The front shall be flat and painted white unless it is transparent. If the backboard is transparent, it shall be marked with a .05-m-wide white line around the border and a .45 × .59-m target area bounded with a .05-m-wide white line.

Recommended Area Ground space is 448 m^2 minimum to 540 m^2 recommended, including clear space.

Size and Dimension Playing court is 14 × 26 m with an unobstructed space of 1 m minimum to 2 m recommended on all sides.

Orientation Preferred orientation is for the long axis to be north-south.

Surface and Drainage Surface is to be concrete or bituminous material with optional protective colorcoating. Drainage is to be end to end, side to side, or corner to corner diagonally at a minimum slope of 0.02 m in 3.05 m (1 m. in 10 ft.). See Figs. 59 and 61.

Special Considerations Safety—Backboard is to be 1.65 m from support post. Post may be padded.

BASKETBALL (NCAA)

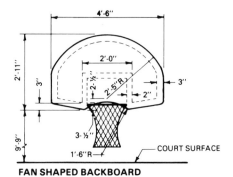

FAN SHAPED BACKBOARD

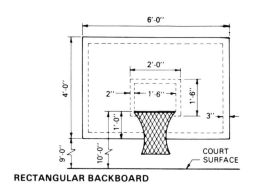

RECTANGULAR BACKBOARD

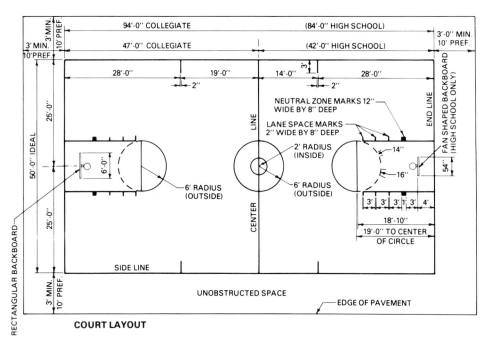

COURT LAYOUT

Fig. 3 NCAA basketball. The color of the lane space marks and neutral zone marks shall contrast with the color of the bounding lines. The midcourt marks shall be the same color as the bounding lines. All lines shall be 2 in wide (neutral zone excluded). All dimensions are to inside edge of lines except as noted. Backboard shall be of any rigid weather-resistant material. The front surface shall be flat and painted white unless it is transparent. If the backboard is transparent, it shall be marked with a 3-in wide white line around the border and an 18×24-in target area. If the backboard is transparent, it shall be marked with a 3-in wide white line around the border and an 18×24-in target area bounded with a 2-in wide white line.

Recommended Area *High School:* ground space is 5040 sq ft minimum to 7280 sq ft maximum. *Collegiate:* ground space is 5600 sq ft minimum to 7980 sq ft maximum.

Size and Dimension High school recommended court is 84×50 ft with a 10-ft unobstructed space on all sides (3 ft minimum). Collegiate recommended court is 94×50 ft with a 10-ft unobstructed space on all sides (3 ft minimum).

Orientation Preferred orientation is for the long axis to be north-south.

Surface and Drainage Surface is to be concrete or bituminous material with optional protective colorcoating. (See Figs. 59 and 61.) Drainage is to be end to end, side to side, or corner to corner diagonally at a minimum slope of 1 in. in 10 ft.

Special Considerations Safety—Backboard and goal support should have a minimum 32-in overhang and post may be padded if desired. Bottom edge and lower sides of rectangular backboard must be padded.

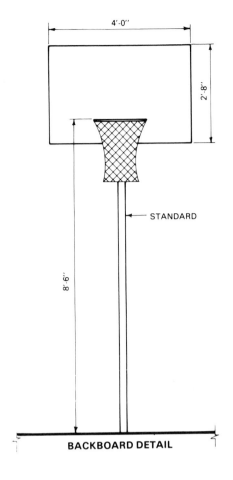

BACKBOARD DETAIL

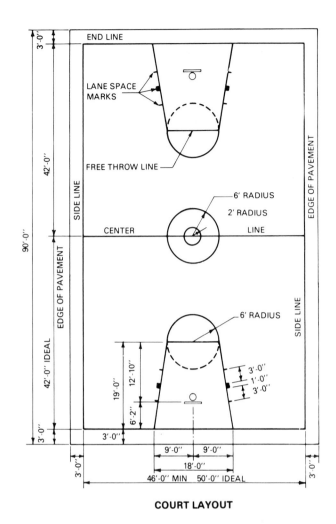

COURT LAYOUT

Fig. 4 Biddy basketball. All dimensions are to inside edge of lines except as noted. All lines shall be 2 in wide. For surfacing details see Figs. 59 and 61.

Recommended Area Ground space is 2,400 to 3,036 sq ft, including clear space.

Size and Dimension Playing court is 46'-0" to 50'-0" wide and 84'-0" long with an unobstructed space of at least 3 ft recommended on all sides.

Orientation Preferred orientation is for the long axis to be north-south.

Surface and Drainage Surface is to be concrete or bituminous material with optional protective colorcoating. Drainage is to be end to end, side to side, or corner to corner diagonally at a minimum slope of 1 in. in 10 ft.

Special Considerations Safety—Backboard support standard is to be a minimum of 2 ft, preferably 4 ft, outside of the court area. Post may be padded.

GOAL-HI BASKETBALL

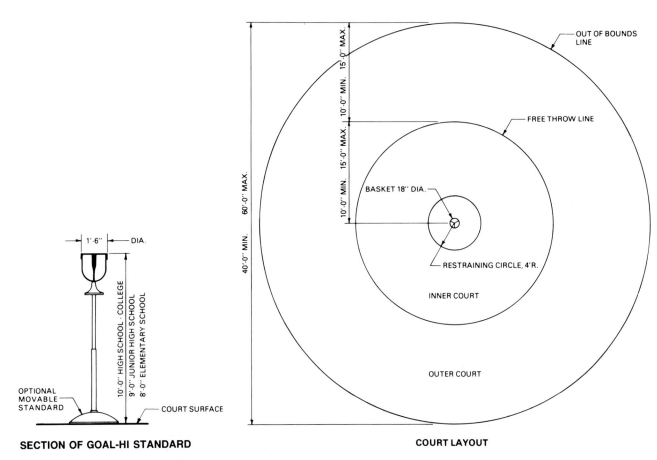

SECTION OF GOAL-HI STANDARD

COURT LAYOUT

Fig. 5 Goal-Hi basketball. All court markings to be 2 in wide. For surfacing details see Figs. 59 and 61. Goal-Hi standard may be permanently mounted, removable flush mounted, or portable as shown.

Recommended Area Ground space minimum is 1256 sq ft; maximum is 2827 sq ft.

Size and Dimension Playing court is to be an Outer Court circle with a minimum radius of 20'-0" and a maximum radius of 30'-0", surrounding an Inner Court circle with a minimum radius of 10'-0" and a maximum radius of 15'-0".

Orientation Optional.

Surface and Drainage Concrete or bituminous surface may be used for minimum maintenance, but a resilient synthetic surface is preferred for safety and comfort. Minimum slope is 1 in. in 10 ft for drainage in any direction.

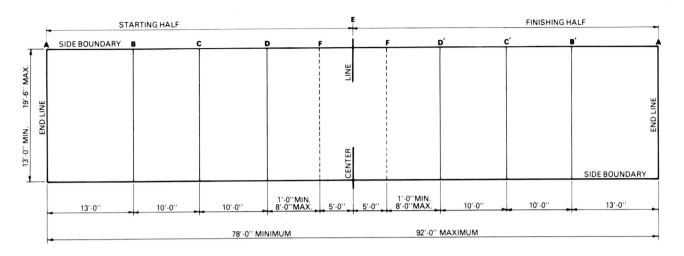

COURT LAYOUT

Fig. 6 Boccie. Court markings to be 2-in wide linen tape held in place with metal pins. For surfacing details see Figs. 58 and 60.

Recommended Area Ground space is 1,824 to 2,816 sq ft.

Size and Dimension Overall court dimensions are 13'-0" to 19'-6" wide by 78'-0" to 92'-0" long. Additional space of at least 3'-0" on each side and 9'-0" on each end is recommended.

Orientation Preferred orientation is for the long axis to be north-south although it is of minor importance.

Surface and Drainage Surface is to be preferably turf, although a mixture of sand and clay may be used. Drainage may be in any direction at a recommended slope of 1 percent for turf and level for sand-clay with underdrainage.

Special Considerations Optional low wooden barrier should be provided at each end and/or side of court.

CROQUET

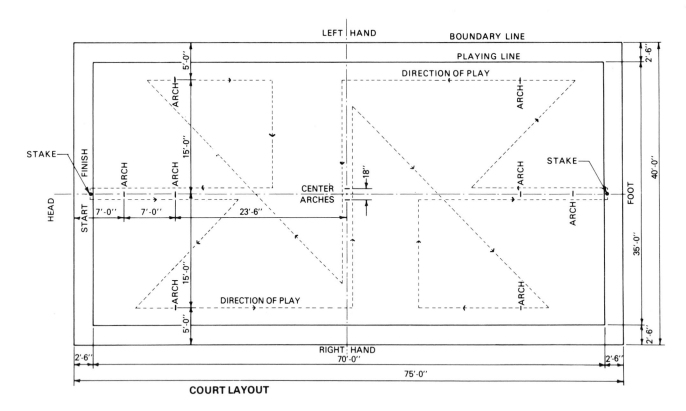

COURT LAYOUT

Fig. 7 Croquet court. Arches are ½-in dia. steel rod—3⅜ in wide and 9 in above the ground when in place. Stakes shall be made of steel and shall be firmly anchored. They shall be 11 in high and set 1½ in outside the playing line halfway between the end corners. Boundary lines are marked with strong cotton twine held by corner staples. Playing lines may be either imaginary or marked with white chalk or with smaller twine wired close to the ground. For surfacing details see Fig. 58.

Recommended Area Ground space is 3,000 sq ft.

Size and Dimension Playing area is 35×70 ft, plus minimum 2 ft-6 in on each end and side.

Orientation Orientation is not critical and may be adjusted to suit local topographic conditions.

Surface and Drainage Playing surface is to be turf closely cropped and rolled with a maximum 2 percent slope (preferably level) and adequate underdrainage.

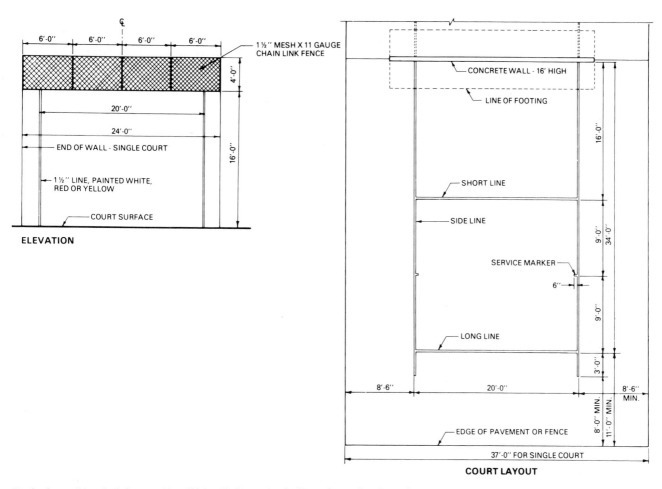

ELEVATION

COURT LAYOUT

Fig. 8   One-wall handball. Court markings 1½-in-wide lines painted white, red, or yellow. For surfacing details see Fig. 59. For fence details see Fig. 55.

Recommended Area   Ground space is 1665 sq ft plus walls and footings.

Size and Dimension   Playing court is 20'-0" wide by 34'-0" long plus a required 11'-0" minimum width of surfaced area to the rear and a recommended 8'-6" minimum width on each side. Courts in battery are to be a minimum of 6'-0" between courts.

Orientation   Preferred orientation is for the long axis to be north-south with the wall at the north end.

Surface and Drainage   Surface is to be smooth concrete with a minimum slope of 1 in. in 10 ft from the wall to the rear of the court.

Special Considerations   Fencing—Court area preferably should be fenced with a 10-ft high chain link fence.

THREE- AND FOUR-WALL HANDBALL

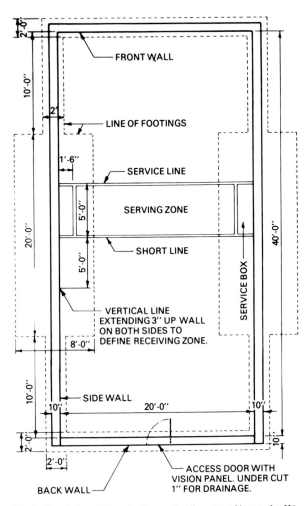

Fig. 9 Handball court layout—Four-wall. All court markings to be 1½ in wide and painted white, red, or yellow. For surfacing details see Fig. 59.

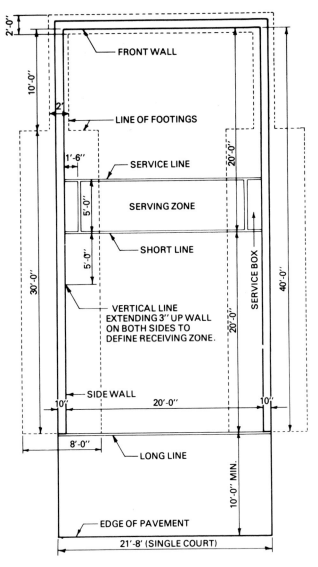

Fig. 10 Handball court layout—Three-wall. All court markings to be 1½ in wide and painted white, red, or yellow. For surfacing details see Fig. 59.

Recommended Area   Ground space for four-wall handball is 800 sq ft, plus walls and footing. Allow an additional 200 sq ft for three-wall handball.

Size and Dimension   Playing court is 20'-0" wide by 40'-0" long plus a minimum 10'-0" to the rear of the three-wall court. Overhead clearance required is 20'-0" minimum.

Orientation   Preferred orientation is for the long axis to be north-south with the front wall at north end.

Surface and Drainage   Surface is to be smooth concrete preferably with a minimum slope of 1 in. in 10 ft from front to rear of the court.

Special Considerations   Alternate four-wall court—Layout is the same as for three-wall with the exception of a minimum 12'-0" high back wall at the rear of the court (long line) and necessary wall footings. Special provisions for drainage must be made and access provided through the back wall for four-wall courts. Fencing—An optional 10-ft-high chain link fence may be provided at the rear of the pavement for three-wall courts.

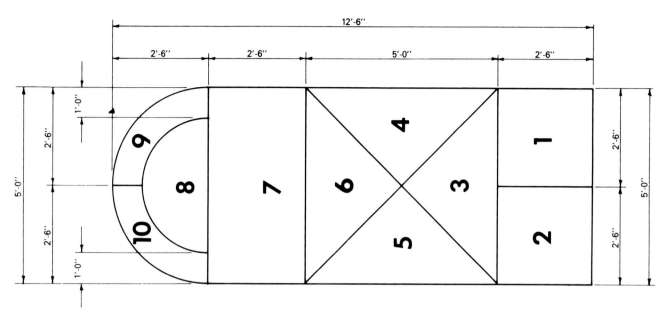

Fig. 11 Hopscotch court layout. All lines to be 1½ in wide painted with white or black acrylic paint to contrast with court surface. For surfacing details see Fig. 61.

Recommended Area Ground space is 62.5 sq ft.

Size and Dimension Playing court is 5'-0" wide by 12'-6" long.

Orientation Optional.

Surface and Drainage Surface is to be concrete or bituminous material with a lateral slope of 1 in. in 10 ft and a longitudinal slope of 1 in. in 10 ft minimum.

HORSESHOES

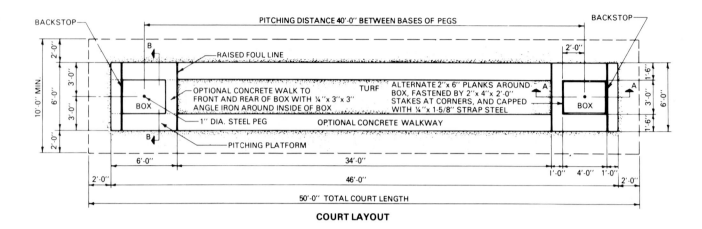

COURT LAYOUT

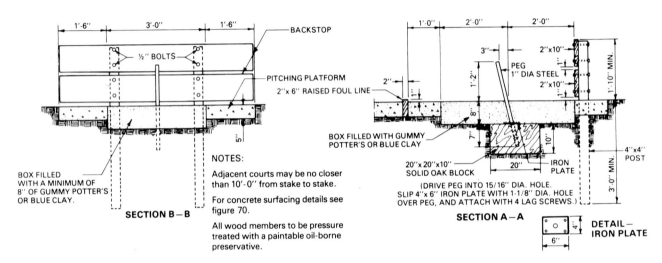

NOTES:

Adjacent courts may be no closer than 10'-0" from stake to stake.

For concrete surfacing details see figure 70.

All wood members to be pressure treated with a paintable oil-borne preservative.

Fig. 12 Horseshoe pitching court.

Recommended Area   Ground space is 1,400 sq ft, including clear space.

Size and Dimension   Playing court is 10'-0" × 50'-0" plus a recommended 10-ft minimum unobstructed area on each end and a 5-ft (minimum) wide zone on each side.

Orientation   Recommended orientation is for the long axis to be north-south.

Surface and Drainage   Surface of playing area, except for boxes and optional concrete walkways, should be turf. Area should be pitched to the side at a maximum slope of 2 percent. Elevation and slant of steel pegs should be between 2 and 3 in and equal.

Special Considerations   Boxes are to be filled with gummy potter's or blue clay. Safety—A 2'-0"-high backstop should be constructed at the end of the box to intercept overthrown or bounding shoes.

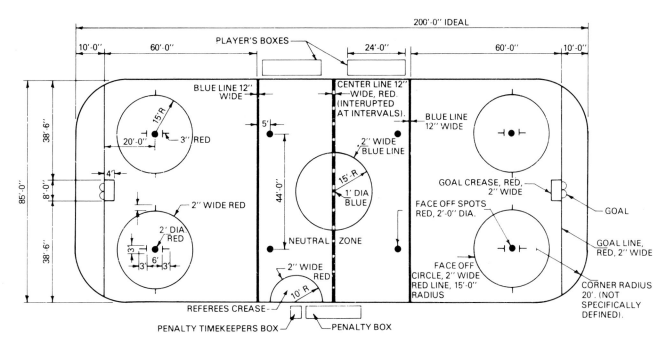

RINK LAYOUT

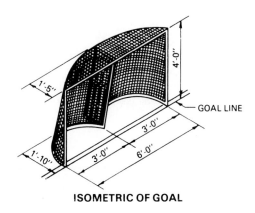

ISOMETRIC OF GOAL

Fig. 13 Ice hockey rink. The rink shall be surrounded by a wooden wall or fence known as the "boards" which shall extend not less than 40 in nor more than 48 in above the level of the ice surface. Ideal 42 in. The surface of the boards facing the ice shall be smooth and free from obstructions. All access doors to the playing surface must swing away from the ice surface. A protective screening of heavy-gauge wire or safety glass is recommended above the boards, except for the bench areas, for the protection of spectators around the rink. The centerline and the two blue lines shall extend across the rink and vertically to the top of the boards. Surface to be flooded may be sand-clay or bituminous material (see Fig. 60 or 61).

Recommended Area Ground space is 22,000 sq ft, including support area.

Size and Dimension Playing rink is 85'-0" wide by 200'-0" (minimum 185'-0") long, plus an additional 5,000 sq ft of support area.

Orientation Preferred orientation is for the long axis to be north-south.

Surface and Drainage The ice surface should be level over either sand-clay or bituminous surface. Provisions for drainage should be made on the surface beneath the ice and around the rink.

Special Considerations Ice—Unless situated in northern climates, provisions for artificial ice will be required.

LAWN BOWLING

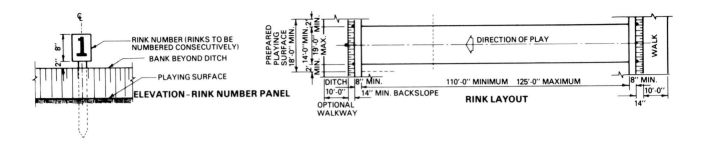

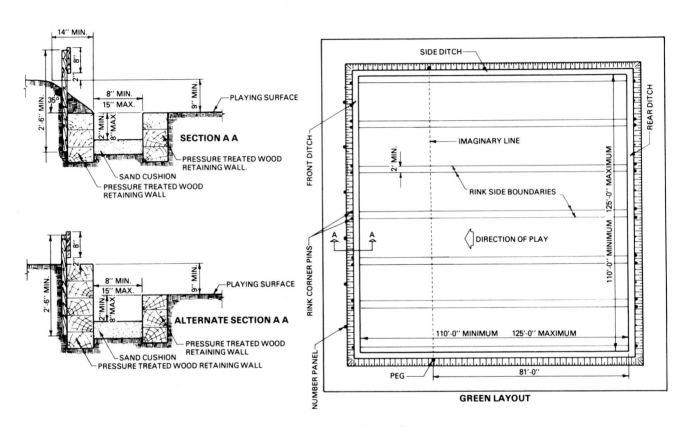

Fig. 14 Lawn bowling green. Side boundaries of rinks to be marked with a 2-in-wide green linen tape attached with pins. The four corners of the rinks shall be indicated by pins driven flush with the face of the bank on each end. Centerline of each rink shall be marked by a pin or number panel. For surfacing details see Fig. 58 or 60.

Recommended Area Square green with six rinks is 12,996 sq ft minimum to 17,424 sq ft maximum.

Size and Dimension Square green is 110 ft minimum and 125 ft maximum on each side. Additional width of 2'-0" minimum to 3'-6" maximum is required on front, rear, and sides for ditch and backslope. Rink width minimum is 14'-0", maximum 19'-0". Rink length minimum is 110'-0", maximum 125'-0".

Orientation Optional.

Surface and Drainage Surface should be of closely cropped bent grass or sand-clay. Entire green should be level, with adequate underdrainage.

Special Considerations Ditch—Depth minimum 2 in, maximum 8 in below surface of green. Width minimum 8 in, maximum 15 in.

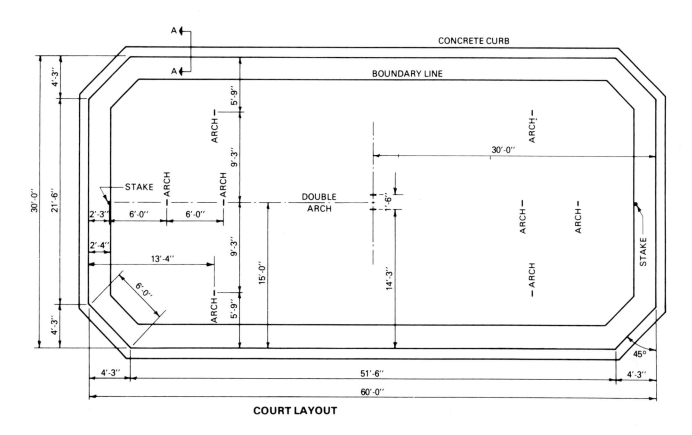

COURT LAYOUT

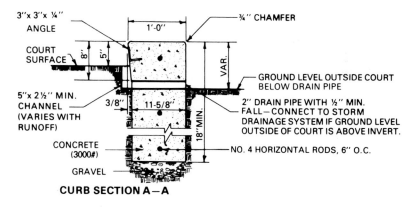

CURB SECTION A—A

Fig. 15 Roque court. Boundary lines are marked by a light depression in playing surface without raising adjacent soil. Arches are 5/8-in dia. steel rod, 3-3/8 in wide and 8 in above the surface and set in 8 in × 15 in × 6 in concrete anchors. Stakes are ¾-in dia. steel, set rigidly in the ground and extending 2 in above the surface. Playing surface should be hard, smooth and level sand-clay (see Fig. 60).

Recommended Area Ground space is 1,800 sq ft minimum, plus curb.

Size and Dimension Playing court is 30'-0" wide by 60'-0" long.

Orientation Preferred orientation is for the long axis to be north-south.

Surface and Drainage Surface is to be level and sand-clay mixture. Drainage is to be through perimeter system and/or through underdrains.

Special Considerations Concrete curb is to be provided on all sides.

SHUFFLEBOARD

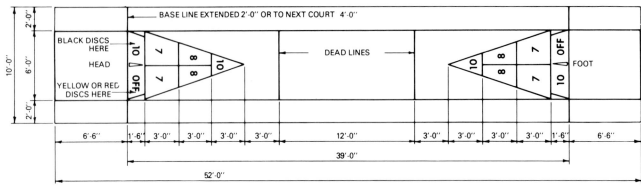

COURT LAYOUT

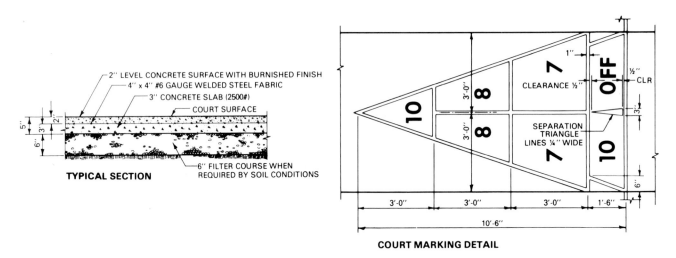

TYPICAL SECTION

COURT MARKING DETAIL

Fig. 16 Shuffleboard court. All dimensions are to centers of lines and to edge of court. Maximum line width $1\frac{1}{2}$ in, minimum $\frac{3}{4}$ in. Lines and Figures "10," "8," "7," and "10 OFF" should be marked with black shoe dye or black acrylic paint. Court to be constructed of concrete without expansion joints. A depressed alley at least 24 in wide, and not less than 4 in deep at midcourt, should be constructed between courts and on the outside of end courts. The alley should slope 1 in. in the first 6 ft of the length of the alley from each baseline, then slope to a minimum depth of 4 in at midcourt where a suitable water drain should be provided.

Recommended Area Ground space is 312 sq ft minimum.

Size and Dimension Playing court is $6'\text{-}0'' \times 52'\text{-}0''$ plus a recommended minimum of $2'\text{-}0''$ on each side or $4'\text{-}0''$ between courts in battery.

Orientation Recommended orientation is for the long axis to be north-south.

Surface and Drainage Surface is to be concrete with a burnished finish. Court surface is to be level with drainage away from the playing surface on all sides.

Special Considerations Secure covered storage for playing equipment should be provided near the court area.

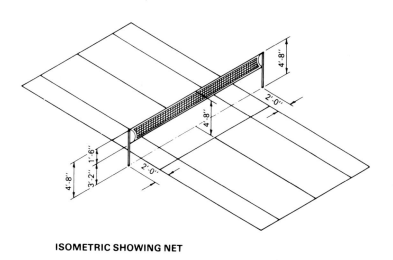

ISOMETRIC SHOWING NET

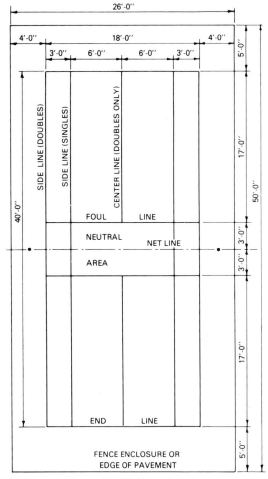

COURT LAYOUT

Fig. 17 Deck tennis court. All measurements for court markings are to the outside of lines except for those involving the center service line, which is equally divided between right and left service court. All court markings to be 1½ in wide. Fence enclosure, if provided, should be 1½-in mesh, 11 gauge chain link. For fence details, see Fig. 55. For net post details see Fig. 51 or 52. For surfacing details see Fig. 59 or 61.

Recommended Area Ground space is 1300 sq ft including clear space.

Size and Dimension Singles court is 12'-0" by 40'-0". Doubles court is 18'-0" by 40'-0". Additional paved area at least 4'-0" on sides and 5'-0" on ends is recommended.

Orientation Preferred orientation is for the long axis to be north-south.

Surface and Drainage Surface is to be concrete or bituminous material with optional protective colorcoating. Drainage is to be end to end, side to side, or corner to corner diagonally at a minimum slope of 1 in. in 10 ft.

Special Considerations Fencing—10-ft-high chain link fence is recommended on all sides of the court.

PLATFORM TENNIS

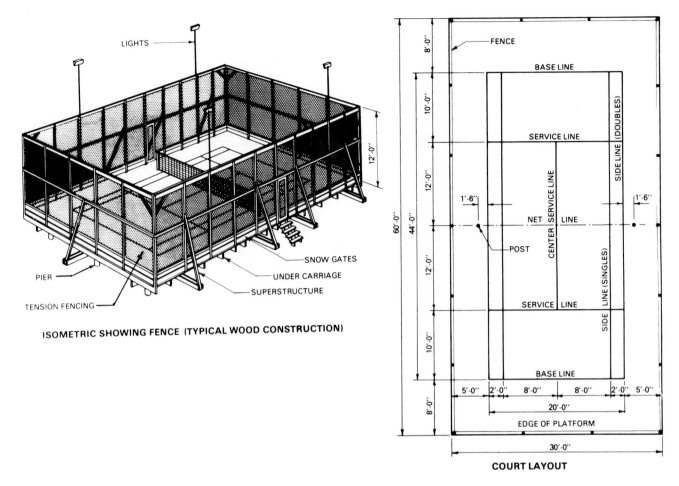

ISOMETRIC SHOWING FENCE (TYPICAL WOOD CONSTRUCTION)

COURT LAYOUT

Fig. 18 Platform tennis court. All measurements for court markings are to the outside of lines except for those involving the center service line, which is equally divided between right and left service court. All court markings to be 2 in wide. Fencing required—12'-0" high with 16-gauge hexagonal, galvanized 1-in flat wire mesh fabric. For net post details see manufacturers' literature. Net height to be 3'-1" at posts and 2'-10" at center court.

Recommended area Ground space is 1,800 sq ft to the playable perimeter fence.

Size and Dimension Playing court is 20'-0" × 44'-0" plus an 8'-0" space on each end and a 5'-0" space on each side.

Orientation Preferred orientation is for the long axis to be north-south.

Surface and Drainage Raised level platform is normally constructed of treated wood or aluminum superstructure with carriage set on concrete piers to permit construction on slopes. Drainage

is provided by ¼-in space between 6-in deck planks or channels. Snow removal is facilitated by hinged panels (snow gates) between posts around bottom of perimeter fence.

Special Considerations Tension fencing—12-ft high, 16-gauge, hexagonal, galvanized, 1-in flat wire mesh fabric must be provided on all sides of the court. Lights should be provided, since this game is played at night throughout the year. Heating units with fans under the platform are used in cold climates. Prefabricated courts are available from several manufacturers.

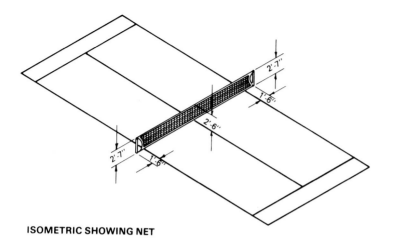

ISOMETRIC SHOWING NET

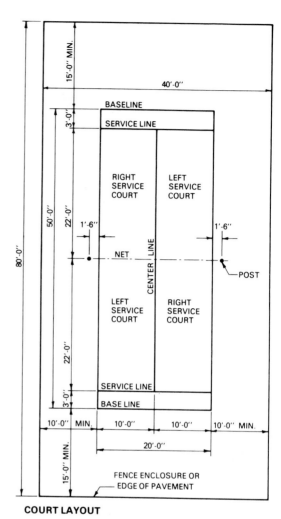

COURT LAYOUT

Fig. 19 Paddle tennis court. All measurements for court markings are to the outside of lines except for those involving the center service line, which is equally divided between right and left service court. All court markings to be 1½ in wide. Fence enclosure, if provided, should be 1½ in mesh, 11-gauge chain link. For fence details see Fig. 55. For net post details see Fig. 51. For surfacing details see Fig. 59 or 61.

Recommended Area Ground space is 3,200 sq ft minimum to edge of pavement.

Size and Dimension Playing court is 20'-0" × 50'-0" plus a 15-ft minimum space on each end and a 10-ft minimum space on each side or between courts in battery.

Orientation Preferred orientation is for the long axis to be north-south.

Surface and Drainage Surface is to be concrete or bituminous material with optional protective colorcoating. Drainage is to be end to end, side to side, or corner to corner diagonally at a minimum slope of 1 in. in 10 ft.

Special Considerations Fencing—10-ft-high chain link fence is recommended on all sides of the court.

Recreation and Entertainment

TENNIS

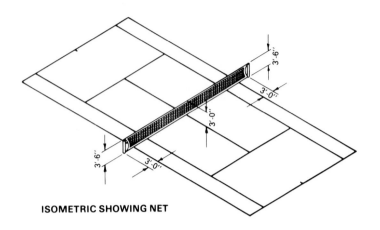

ISOMETRIC SHOWING NET

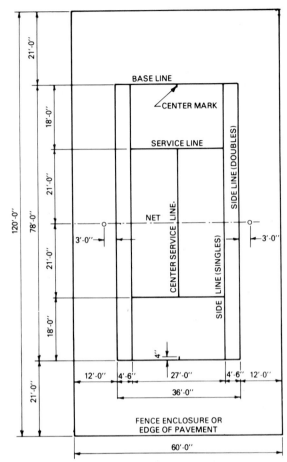

COURT LAYOUT

Fig. 20 Tennis court. All measurements for court markings are to the outside of lines except for those involving the center service line which is equally divided between the right and left service courts. All court markings to be 2 in wide. Fence enclosure, if provided, should be 10-ft-high, 11-gauge, 1¾ in mesh chain link. For fence details see Fig. 55. Minimum distance between sides of parallel courts to be 12'-0". For net post details see Fig. 52. For surfacing details see Fig. 59, 60, or 61.

Recommended Area Ground space is 7,200 sq ft minimum.

Size and Dimension Playing court is 36 × 78 ft plus at least 12 ft clearance on both sides or between courts in battery and 21 ft clearance on each end.

Orientation Orientation of long axis is to be north-south.

Surface and Drainage Surface may be concrete, or bituminous material with specialized protective colorcoating, or sand-clay. Drainage may be from end to end, side to side, or corner to corner diagonally at a minimum slope of 1 in. in 10 ft for pavement and level for sand-clay with underdrainage.

Special Considerations Fencing—Recommended 10-ft-high chain link fence on all sides.

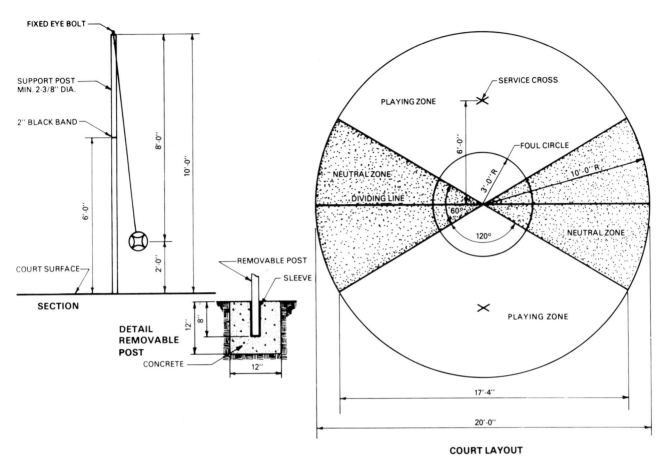

Fig. 21 Tetherball court. All measurements for court markings are to center of lines. All court markings to be 2 in wide. If colorcoating is used, the neutral zones and the playing zones should be of contrasting colors. For surfacing details see Fig. 59 or 61.

Recommended Area Ground space is 314 sq ft minimum to circumference of outer circle.

Size and Dimension Playing court is a circle 20'-0" in diameter. Pole height is 10 ft.

Orientation Recommended axis through playing zone is north-south.

Surface and Drainage Concrete or bituminous surface may be used for minimum maintenance, but a resilient synthetic surface or wood chips with adequate underdrainage is preferred for safety and comfort. Minimum slope is 1 in. in 10 ft for drainage in any direction.

VOLLEYBALL

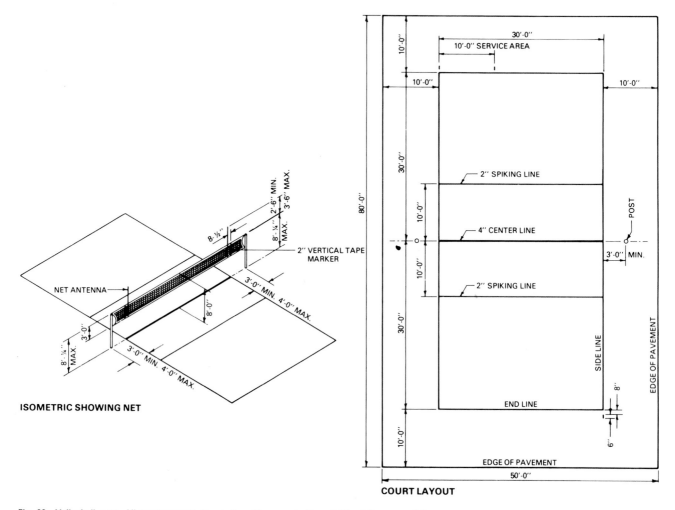

ISOMETRIC SHOWING NET

COURT LAYOUT

Fig. 22 Volleyball court. All measurements for court markings are to the outside of lines except for the centerline. All court markings to be 2 in wide except as noted. For surfacing details see Figs. 58 to 61. Net height at center to be: men 8'-0", women 7'-4¼", high school 7'-0", elementary school 6'-6". For net and post details see Fig. 53.

Recommended Area Ground space is 4000 sq ft.

Size and Dimension Playing court is 30 × 60 ft plus 6 ft minimum, 10 ft preferred, unobstructed space on all sides.

Orientation Preferred orientation is for the long axis to be north-south.

Surface and Drainage Recommended surface for intensive use is to be bituminous material or concrete, but sand-clay or turf may be used for informal play. Drainage is to be end to end, side to side or corner to corner at a minimum slope of 1 in. in 10 ft.

OFFICIAL BASEBALL
Babe Ruth Baseball (13–15 yr and 16–18 yr); Senior League Baseball (13–15 yr)

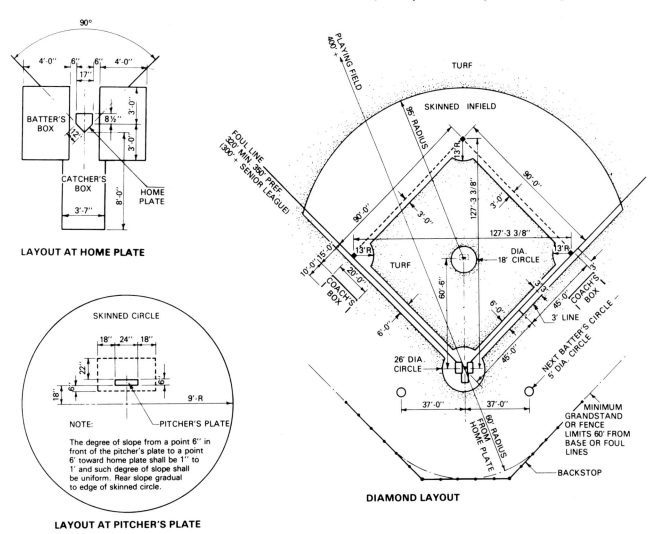

LAYOUT AT HOME PLATE

LAYOUT AT PITCHER'S PLATE

NOTE:

The degree of slope from a point 6'' in front of the pitcher's plate to a point 6' toward home plate shall be 1'' to 1' and such degree of slope shall be uniform. Rear slope gradual to edge of skinned circle.

DIAMOND LAYOUT

Fig. 23 Official baseball diamond. Foul lines, catcher's, batter's, and coach's boxes, next batter's circles, and 3-ft line shall be 2 to 3 in wide and marked with chalk or other white material. Caustic lime must not be used. Infield may be skinned. For grading and drainage details see Fig. 57. For surfacing details see Fig. 58. For backstop details see Fig. 62.

Recommended Area Ground space is 3.0 to 3.85 acres minimum.

Size and Dimension Baselines are 90'-0". Pitching distance is 60'-6". Pitcher's plate is 10 in above the level of home plate. Distance down foul lines is 320 ft minimum, 350 ft preferred. Outfield distance to center field is 400 ft +. For Senior League Baseball, recommended distance from home plate to outfield fence at all points is 300 ft +.

Orientation Optimum orientation is to locate home plate so that the pitcher is throwing across

the sun and the batter is not facing it. The line from home plate through the pitcher's mound and second base should run east-northeast.

Surface and Drainage Surface is to be turf. Infield may be skinned, and shall be graded so that the baselines and home plate are level.

Special Considerations Backstop is to be provided at a minimum distance of 40 ft or preferably 60 ft behind home plate.

Recreation and Entertainment

BASEBALL
Bronco League (9–12 yr)

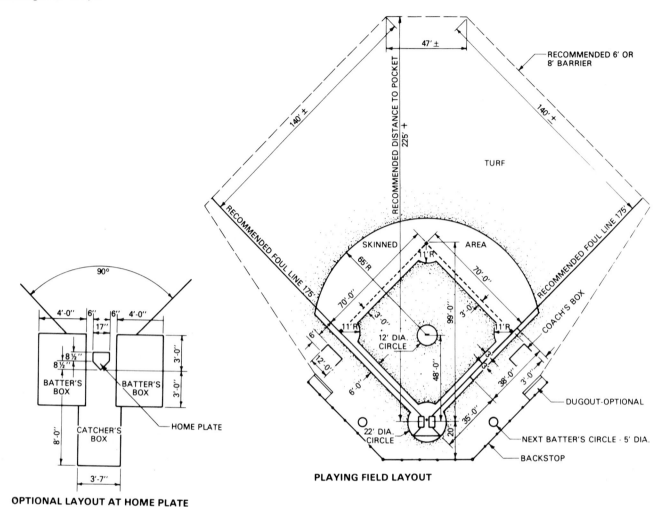

OPTIONAL LAYOUT AT HOME PLATE

PLAYING FIELD LAYOUT

Fig. 24 Bronco league baseball diamond. Foul lines, catcher's, batter's, and coach's boxes, next batter's circles, and 3-ft restraining lines shall be 2 in wide and marked with white chalk or other white material. Caustic lime must not be used. Infield may be skinned. For grading and drainage details see Fig. 57. For surfacing details see Fig. 58. For backstop details see Fig. 62.

Recommended area Ground space is 1.0 acre minimum.

Size and Dimension Baselines are 70'-0". Pitching distance is 48'-0". Pitcher's plate is 6 in above the level of home plate. Distance down foul line is 175 ft. Outfield distance to pocket in center field is 225 ft.

Orientation Optimum orientation is to locate home plate so that the pitcher is throwing across the sun and the batter is not facing it. The line from home plate through the pitcher's mound and second base should run east-northeast.

Surface and Drainage Surface is to be turf. Infield may be skinned, and shall be graded so that the baselines and home plate are level.

Special Considerations Backstop is to be provided at a recommended distance of 20 ft behind home plate.

BASEBALL
Pony League (13–14 yr)

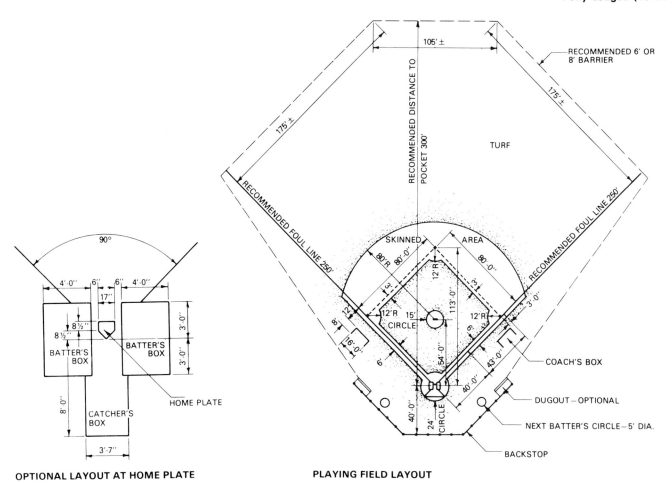

OPTIONAL LAYOUT AT HOME PLATE   PLAYING FIELD LAYOUT

Fig. 25 Pony league baseball diamond. Foul lines, catcher's, batter's, and coach's boxes, next batter's circles, and 3-ft restraining lines shall be 2 in wide and marked with white chalk or other white material. Caustic lime must not be used. Infield may be skinned. For grading and drainage details see Fig. 57. For surfacing details see Fig. 58. For backstop details see Fig. 62.

Recommended Area Ground space is 2.0 acres minimum.

Size and Dimension Baselines are 80'-0". Pitching distance is 54'-0". Pitcher's plate is 8 in above the level of home plate. Distance down foul line is 250 ft. Outfield distance to pocket in center field is 300 ft.

Orientation Optimum orientation is to locate home plate so that the pitcher is throwing across the sun and the batter is not facing it. The line from home plate through the pitcher's mound and second base should run east-northeast.

Surface and Drainage Surface is to be turf. Infield may be skinned, and shall be graded so that the baselines and home plate are level.

Special Considerations Backstop is to be provided at a recommended distance of 40 ft behind home plate.

BASEBALL
Colt League (15–16 yr)

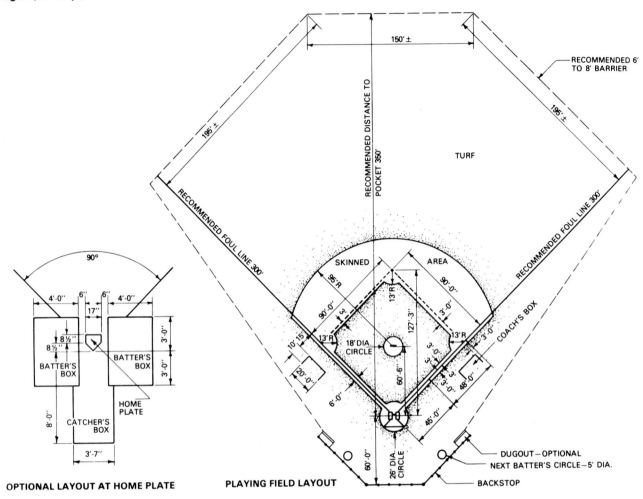

OPTIONAL LAYOUT AT HOME PLATE

PLAYING FIELD LAYOUT

Fig. 26 Colt league baseball diamond. Foul lines, catcher's, batter's, and coach's boxes, next batter's circles, and 3-ft restraining lines shall be 2 in wide and marked with white chalk or other white material. Caustic lime must not be used. Infield may be skinned. For grading and drainage details see Fig. 57. For surfacing details see Fig. 58. For backstop details see Fig. 62.

Recommended Area Ground space is 3.0 acres minimum.

Size and Dimension Baselines are 90'-0". Pitching distance is 60'-6". Pitcher's plate is 10 in above the level of home plate. Distance down foul line is 300 ft. Outfield distance to pocket in center field is 350 ft.

Orientation Optimum orientation is to locate home plate so that the pitcher is throwing across the sun and the batter is not facing it. The line from home plate through the pitcher's mound and second base should run east-northeast.

Surface and Drainage Surface is to be turf. Infield may be skinned, and shall be graded so that the baselines and home plate are level.

Special Considerations Backstop is to be provided at a recommended distance of 60 ft behind home plate.

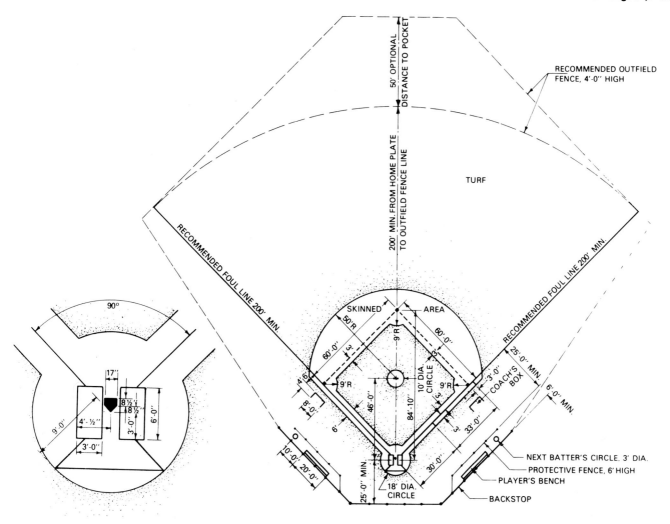

LAYOUT AT HOME PLATE

Fig. 27 Little league baseball diamond. Foul lines, catcher's, batter's, and coach's boxes, next batter's circles, and 3-ft restraining lines shall be 2 in wide and marked with white chalk or other white material. Caustic lime must not be used. Infield may be skinned. For grading and drainage details see Fig. 57. For surfacing details see Fig. 58. For backstop details see Fig. 62.

Recommended Area Ground space is 1.2 acres minimum.

Size and Dimension Baselines are 60'-0". Pitching distance is 46'-0". Pitcher's plate is 6 in above the level of home plate. Distance down foul line is 200 ft. Outfield distance to pocket in center field is 200 to 250 ft optional.

Orientation Optimum orientation is to locate home plate so that the pitcher is throwing across

the sun and the batter is not facing it. The line from home plate through the pitcher's mound and second base should run east-northeast.

Surface and Drainage Surface is to be turf. Infield may be skinned, and shall be graded so that the baselines and home plate are level.

Special Considerations Backstop is to be provided at a recommended minimum distance of 25 ft behind home plate.

FIELD HOCKEY

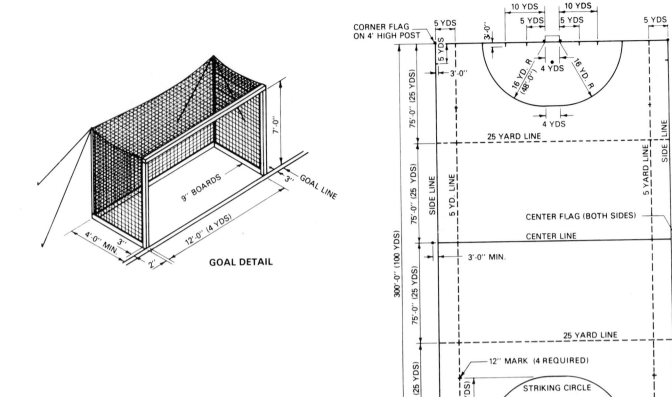

GOAL DETAIL

FIELD LAYOUT

Fig. 28 Field hockey playing field. All measurements shall be made from the inside edge of lines marking boundaries. Solid and broken lines shall be white, 3 in wide and marked with a nontoxic material which is not injurious to the eyes or skin. For grading and drainage details see Fig. 57. For surfacing details see Fig. 58.

Recommended Area Ground space is 64,000 sq ft (1.5 acres) minimum.

Size and Dimension Playing field width is 180'-0". Length is 300'-0". Additional area recommended is 10'-0" minimum unobstructed space on all sides.

Orientation Preferred orientation is for the long axis to be northwest-southeast to suit the angle of the sun in the fall playing season, or north-south for longer periods.

Surface and Drainage Surface is to be turf. Preferred grading is a longitudinal crown with a 1 percent slope from center to each side and adequate underdrainage. Grading may be from side to side or corner to corner diagonally if conditions do not permit the preferred grading.

Special Considerations Goal is to be provided at each end of the playing field.

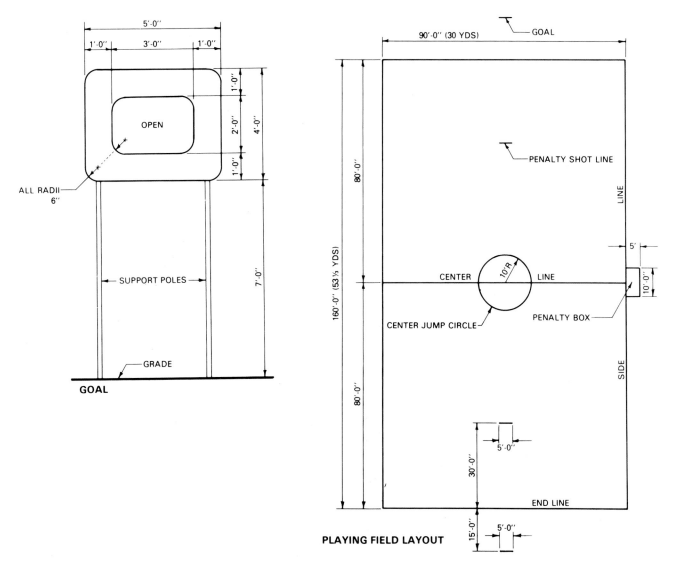

GOAL

PLAYING FIELD LAYOUT

Fig. 29 Flickerball field. All measurements should be made from the inside edge of lines marking boundaries. Lines shall be white and 3 in wide and marked with a nontoxic material which is not injurious to the eyes or skin. For grading and drainage details see Fig. 57. For surfacing details see Fig. 58.

Recommended Area Ground space is 17,600 sq ft (0.4 acre) minimum.

Size and Dimension Playing field width is 90'-0". Length is 160'-0". Goals are 15'-0" beyond each end line. Additional area recommended is 6'-0" minimum unobstructed space on all sides.

Orientation Preferred orientation is for the long axis to be northwest-southeast to suit the angle of the sun in the fall playing season, or north-south for longer periods.

Surface and Drainage Surface is to be turf. Preferred grading is a longitudinal crown with a 1 percent slope from center to each side and adequate underdrainage. Grading may be from side to side or corner to corner diagonally if conditions do not permit the preferred grading.

Special Considerations Goal is to be provided 15'-0" behind each end line.

Recreation and Entertainment

FOOTBALL (NCAA)
Pop Warner Junior League Football

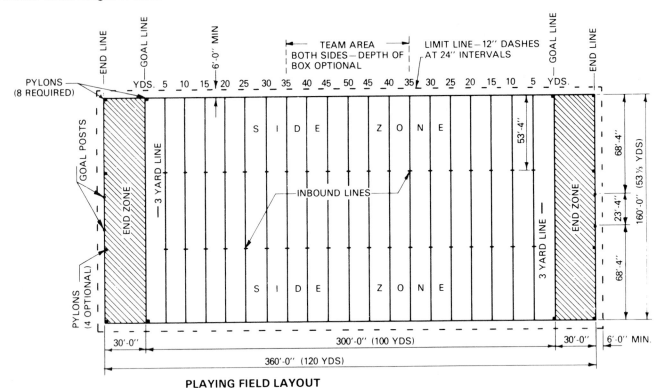

PLAYING FIELD LAYOUT

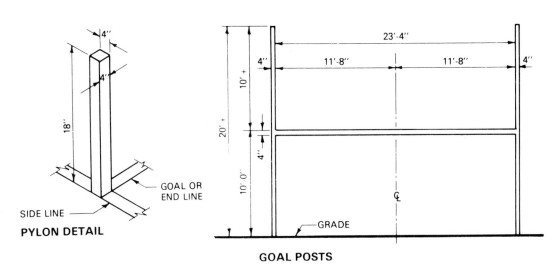

PYLON DETAIL

GOAL POSTS

Fig. 30 NCAA football field. Optional goal post may be used in the form of a single metal post set behind the end zone with a cantilevered horizontal crossbar and two uprights of the same height and spacing as for dual posts. Pylon to be constructed of soft flexible material, red or orange in color. All measurements should be made from the inside edge of lines marking boundaries. All field dimension lines shown must be marked 4 in. in width with a white, nontoxic material which is not injurious to the eyes or skin. If cross hatching in end zone is white, it shall be no closer than 2 ft to the boundary lines. For grading and drainage details see Fig. 57. For surfacing details see Fig. 58.

Recommended Area Ground space is 64,000 sq ft (1.5 acres) minimum.

Size and Dimension Playing field width is 160'-0". Length is 360'-0". Additional area required is 6'-0" minimum unobstructed space on all sides.

Orientation Preferred orientation is for the long axis to be northwest-southeast to suit the angle

of the sun in the fall playing season, or north-south for longer periods.

Surface and Drainage Surface is to be turf. Preferred grading is a longitudinal crown with a 1 percent slope from center to each side and adequate underdrainage. Grading may be from side to side or corner to corner diagonally if conditions do not permit the preferred grading.

Special Considerations Goal posts are to be provided at each end of the playing field. Pylons are to be provided as required by rules.

1220

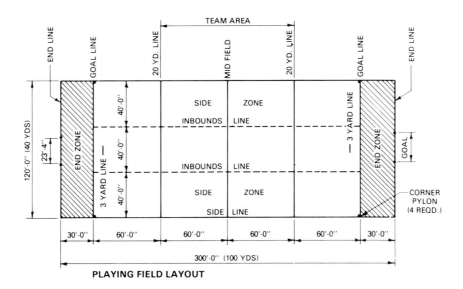

PLAYING FIELD LAYOUT

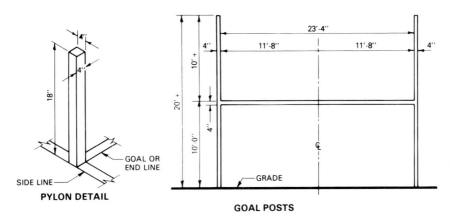

PYLON DETAIL

GOAL POSTS

Fig. 31 Touch and flag football field. Optional goal post may be used in the form of a single metal post set behind the end zone with a cantilevered horizontal crossbar and two uprights of the same height and spacing as for dual posts. Pylon to be constructed of soft flexible material, red or orange in color. All measurements should be made from the inside edge of lines marking boundaries. All field dimension lines shown must be marked 4 in. in width with a white, nontoxic material which is not injurious to the eyes or skin. If cross hatching in end zone is white, it shall be no closer than 2 ft to the boundary lines. When teams are composed of 9 or 11 players, a field 360'-0" (120-yd.) long with five 60'-0" (20-yd) zones and two 30'-0" (10-yd) end zones is recommended. For grading and drainage details see Fig. 57. For surfacing details see Fig. 58.

Recommended Area Ground space is 41,200 sq ft (0.94 acre) minimum.

Size and Dimension Playing field width is 120'-0". Length is 300'-0". Additional area recommended is 6'-0" minimum unobstructed space on all sides.

Orientation Preferred orientation is for the long axis to be northwest-southeast to suit the angle of the sun in the fall playing season, or north-south for longer periods.

Surface and Drainage Surface is to be turf. Preferred grading is a longitudinal crown with a 1 percent slope from center to each side and adequate underdrainage. Grading may be from side to side or corner to corner diagonally if conditions do not permit the preferred grading.

Special Considerations Goal posts are to be provided at each end of the playing field. Pylons are to be provided as required by rules.

GOLF DRIVING RANGE

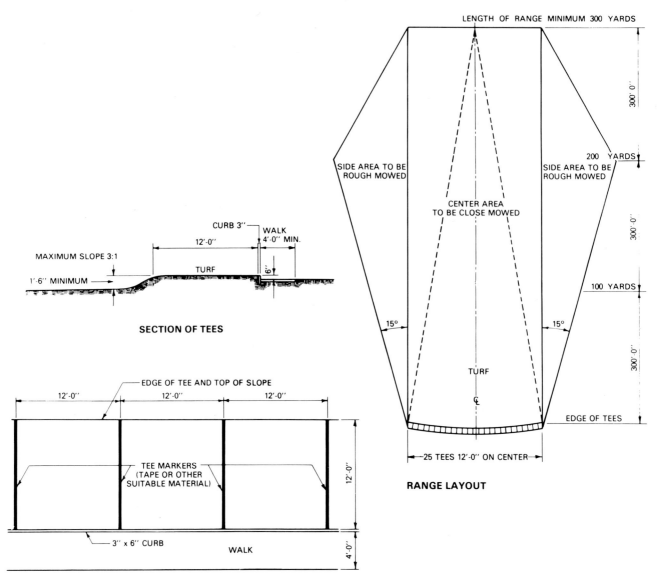

SECTION OF TEES

PLAN OF TEES

RANGE LAYOUT

Fig. 32 Driving range.

Recommended Area Ground space for minimum of 25 tees is 13.5 acres.

Size and Dimension Minimum length is 900 ft (300 yd). Minimum width, including buffer area on each side, is 690 ft (230 yd). Add 12 ft width per additional tee.

Orientation Preferred orientation is for the long axis to run southwest to northeast with the golfer driving toward the northeast.

Surface and Drainage Surface is to be turf closely mowed in center for ball collection. Side buffer areas are to be rough cut. Drainage is to be away from raised tee area and preferably across the axis of play. Side buffer areas may rise to help contain stray drives.

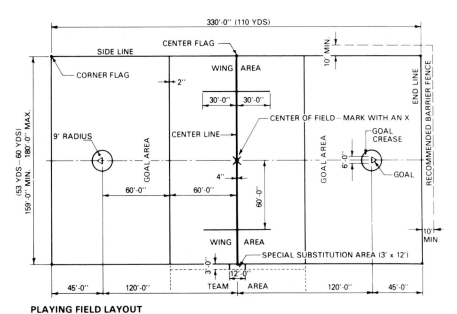

PLAYING FIELD LAYOUT

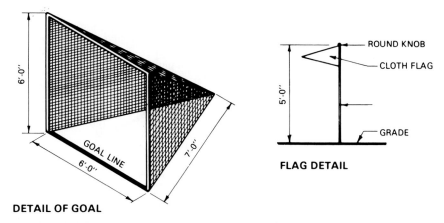

DETAIL OF GOAL

FLAG DETAIL

Fig. 33 Playing field for men's lacrosse. Goal net should be cord netting with openings of not more than 1½ in. Bottom of net must be held close to the ground with pegs or staples. Posts to be 1½-in nominal pipe painted orange and secured to the ground. Lines must be marked with a white nontoxic material which is not injurious to the eyes or skin. All lines shall be 2 in wide except the center or offside line which should be 4 in wide. All dimensions are to inside of lines except at centerline. Barrier fence, 5 or 6 ft high, should be 10'-0" minimum from end and side lines. If not used allow 20-ft space on all sides. Flexible flag markers shall be placed at the four corners of the field and at each end of the centerline. For grading and drainage details see Fig. 57. For surfacing details see Fig. 58.

Recommended Area Ground space is 62,650 sq ft (1.4 acres) to 70,000 sq ft (1.6 acres).

Size and Dimension Playing field width is 159'-0" to 180'-0". Length is 330'-0". Additional area recommended is 10'-0" minimum unobstructed space around entire perimeter of field with barrier fence, or 20'-0" without fence.

Orientation Preferred orientation is for the long axis to be northwest-southeast to suit the angle

of the sun in the fall playing season, or north-south for longer periods.

Surface and Drainage Surface is to be turf. Preferred grading is a longitudinal crown with a 1 percent slope from center to each side and adequate underdrainage. Grading may be from side to side or corner to corner diagonally if conditions do not permit the preferred grading.

Special Considerations Goal is to be provided 45'-0" in front of each end line.

LACROSSE
Women's

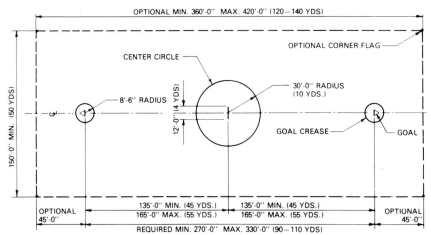

OPTIONAL MIN. 360'-0'' MAX. 420'-0'' (120—140 YDS)

OPTIONAL CORNER FLAG

CENTER CIRCLE

30'-0'' RADIUS (10 YDS.)

8'-6'' RADIUS

150'-0'' MIN. (50 YDS)

12'-0'' (4 YDS)

GOAL CREASE

GOAL

OPTIONAL 45'-0''

135'-0'' MIN. (45 YDS.)
165'-0'' MAX. (55 YDS.)

135'-0'' MIN. (45 YDS.)
165'-0'' MAX. (55 YDS.)

OPTIONAL 45'-0''

REQUIRED MIN. 270'-0'' MAX. 330'-0'' (90—110 YDS)

PLAYING FIELD LAYOUT (SHAPE VARIES)

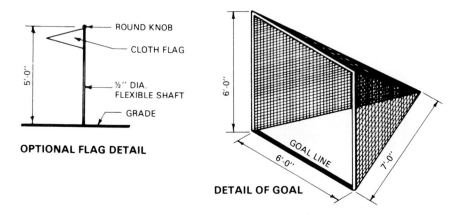

ROUND KNOB

CLOTH FLAG

5'-0''

½'' DIA. FLEXIBLE SHAFT

GRADE

OPTIONAL FLAG DETAIL

6'-0''

GOAL LINE

6'-0''

7'-0''

DETAIL OF GOAL

Fig. 34 Playing field for women's lacrosse. Goal net should be cord netting with openings of not more than 1½ in. Bottom of net must be held close to the ground with pegs or staples. Posts and crossbar shall be of wood, 2 × 2 in and shall be painted white. Goals made of pipe and painted white are considered legal but wooden goals, 2 × 2 in, are preferred. All marking lines shall be 2 in wide and marked with a white nontoxic material which is not injurious to the eyes or skin. Boundary lines are optional but should be 2 in wide if marked. Optional flag may be placed at the four corners or selected boundary points. For grading and drainage details see Fig. 57. For surfacing details see Fig. 58.

Recommended Area Ground space is optional 54,000 sq ft (1.2 acres) to 61,500 sq ft (1.4 acres).

Size and Dimension Playing field minimum width is 150'-0''. Optional length is 360'-0'' to 410'-0''. As in the original Indian game, there are no definite boundaries or shape for the field of play, but before a match the officials decide on the boundaries and declare specified obstructions out of bounds.

Orientation Preferred orientation is for the long axis to be northwest-southeast to suit the angle

of the sun in the fall playing season, or north-south for longer periods.

Surface and Drainage Surface is to be turf. Preferred grading is a longitudinal crown with a 1 percent slope from center to each side with adequate underdrainage. Grading may be from side to side or corner to corner diagonally if conditions do not permit the preferred grading.

Special Considerations Goal is to be provided 45'-0'' in front of each end line.

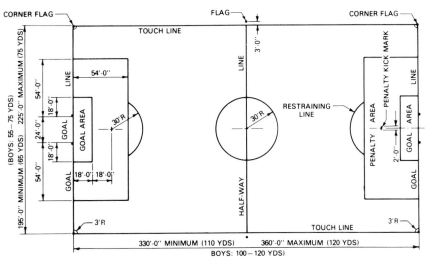

PLAYING FIELD LAYOUT

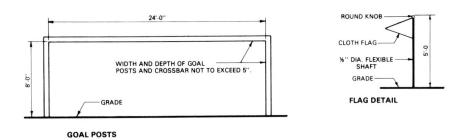

GOAL POSTS

FLAG DETAIL

Fig. 35 Playing field for men's and boys' soccer. Goal posts to be pressure treated with paintable, oil-borne preservative and painted above ground with three coats of white lead and oil. The goalposts and crossbar shall present a flat surface to the playing field, not less than 4 in nor more than 5 in. in width. Nets shall be attached to the posts, crossbar, and ground behind the goal. The top of the net must extend backward 2'-0" level with the crossbar. All dimensions are to the inside edge of lines. All lines shall be 2 in wide and marked with a white, nontoxic material which is not injurious to the eyes or skin. For grading and drainage details see Fig. 57. For surfacing details see Fig. 58.

Recommended Area Ground space is 75,250 sq ft (1.7 acres) to 93,100 sq ft (2.1 acres).

Size and Dimension Playing field width is 195'-0" to 225'-0". Length is 330'-0" to 360'-0". Additional area recommended is 10'-0" minimum unobstructed space on all sides.

Orientation Preferred orientation is for the long axis to be northwest-southeast to suit the angle of the sun in the fall playing season, or north-south for longer periods.

Surface and Drainage Surface is to be turf. Preferred grading is a longitudinal crown with a 1 percent slope from center to each side and adequate underdrainage. Grading may be from side to side or corner to corner diagonally if conditions do not permit the preferred grading.

Special Considerations Goal posts are to be provided at each end of the playing field.

SOCCER
Women's and Girls'

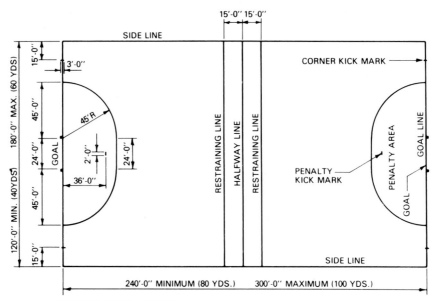

PLAYING FIELD LAYOUT

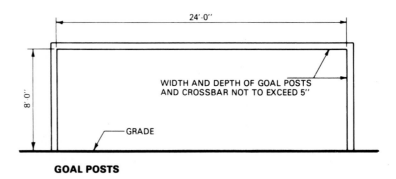

GOAL POSTS

Fig. 36 Playing field for women's and girls' soccer. Goal posts to be pressure treated with painted, oil-borne preservative and painted above ground with three coats of white lead and oil. The goal posts and crossbar shall present a flat surface to the playing field, not less than 4 in nor more than 5 in. in width. Nets shall be attached to the posts, crossbar, and ground behind the goal. The top of the net must extend backward 2'-0" level with the crossbar. All dimensions are to the inside edge of lines. All lines shall be 2 in wide and marked with a white, nontoxic material which is not injurious to the eyes or skin. For grading and drainage details see Fig. 57. For surfacing details see Fig. 58.

Recommended Area Ground space is 36,400 sq ft (0.8 acre) to 64,000 sq ft (1.4 acres).

Size and Dimension Playing field width is 120'-0" to 180'-0". Length is 240'-0" to 300'-0". Additional area recommended is 10'-0" minimum unobstructed space on all sides.

Orientation Preferred orientation is for the long axis to be northwest-southeast to suit the angle of the sun in the fall playing season, or north-south for longer periods.

Surface and Drainage Surface is to be turf. Preferred grading is a longitudinal crown with a 1 percent slope from center to each side and adequate underdrainage. Grading may be from side to side or corner to corner diagonally if conditions do not permit the preferred grading.

Special Considerations Goal posts are to be provided at each end of the playing field.

SOFTBALL, 12-INCH
Fast and Slow Pitch

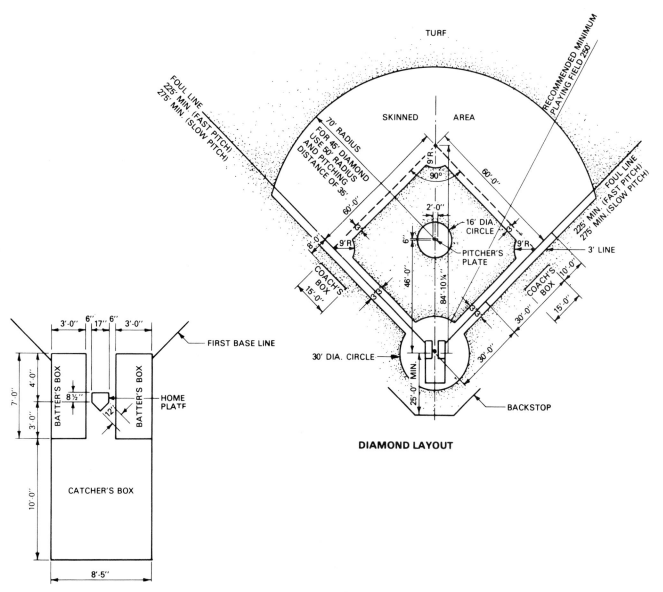

DIAMOND LAYOUT

LAYOUT AT HOME PLATE

Fig. 37 Diamond for 12-in softball. Foul lines, catcher's, batter's, and coach's boxes, and 3-ft lines are 2 to 3-in chalk lines. Pitching distance for women's softball to be 40'-0". For junior player (9–12 yr) 45-ft distance between bases, 35-ft pitching distance. For grading and drainage details see Fig. 57. For surfacing details see Fig. 58. For backstop details see Fig. 59.

Recommended Area   Ground space is 62,500 sq ft (1.5 acres) to 90,000 sq ft (2.0 acres).

Size and Dimension   Baselines are 60'-0" for men and women, 45'-0" for juniors. Pitching distances are 46'-0" for men, 40'-0" for women, 35'-0" for juniors. Fast pitch playing field is 225-ft radius from home plate between foul lines for men and women. Slow pitch is 275-ft radius for men, 250-ft radius for women.

Orientation   Optimum orientation is to locate home plate so that the pitcher is throwing across the sun and the batter is not facing it.

Surface and Drainage   Surface is to be turf. Infield may be skinned. The infield shall be graded so that the baselines and home plate are level.

Special Considerations   Backstop is to be located at a minimum distance of 25 ft behind home plate.

SOFTBALL, 16-INCH
Slow Pitch

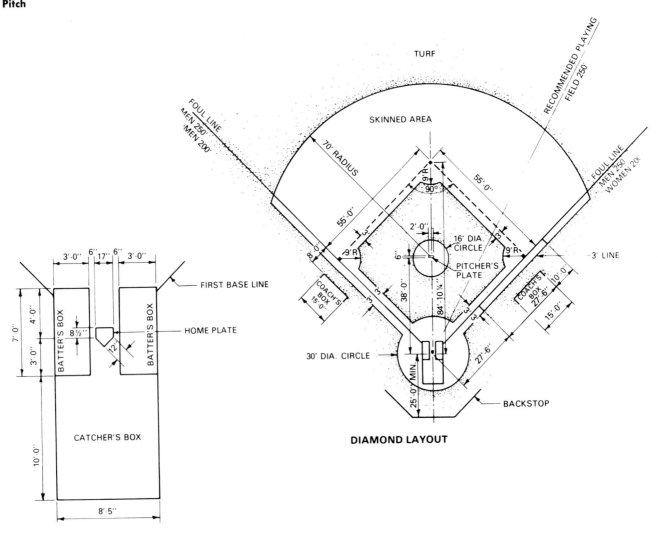

DIAMOND LAYOUT

LAYOUT AT HOME PLATE

Fig. 38 Diamond for 16-in softball. Foul lines, catcher's, batter's, and coach's boxes, and 3-ft lines are 2 to 3-in chalk lines. Baselines for women to be 50'-0". Pitching distance does not change. For grading and drainage details see Fig. 57. For surfacing details see Fig. 58. For backstop details see Fig. 63.

Recommended Area Ground space is 50,625 sq ft (1.2 acres) to 75,625 sq ft (1.7 acres).

Size and Dimension Baselines are 55'-0" for men, 50'-0" for women. Pitching distance is 38'-0" for men and women. Playing field radius from home plate between foul lines is 250 ft for men, 200 ft for women.

Orientation Optimum orientation is to locate home plate so that the pitcher is throwing across the sun and the batter is not facing it.

Surface and Drainage Surface is to be turf. Infield may be skinned. The infield shall be graded so that the baselines and home plate are level.

Special Considerations Backstop is to be located at a minimum distance of 25 ft behind home plate.

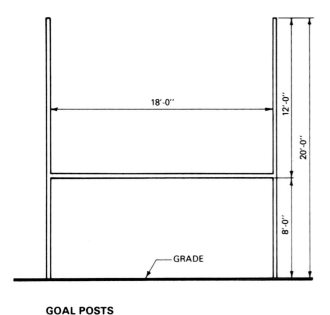

GOAL POSTS

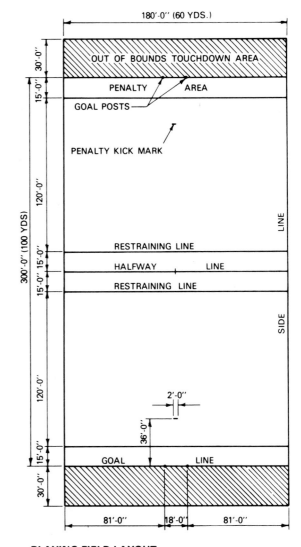

PLAYING FIELD LAYOUT

Fig. 39 Speedball field. All dimensions are to inside edge of lines. All field markings to be 2 in wide and marked with a white nontoxic material which is not injurious to the eyes or skin. For grading and drainage details see Fig. 57. For surfacing details see Fig. 58.

Recommended Area Ground space is 36,400 sq ft (.85 acre) (high school) to 76,000 sq ft (1.7 acres).

Size and Dimension Playing field width is 180'-0". Length is 300'-0". An additional 30 × 180-ft out-of-bounds touchdown area is recommended on each end and unobstructed space of 10'-0" on all sides. High school field may be 120 ft wide by 240 ft long.

Orientation Preferred orientation is for the long axis to be northwest-southeast to suit the angle

of the sun in the fall playing season, or north-south for longer periods.

Surface and Drainage Surface is to be turf. Preferred grading is a longitudinal crown with a 1 percent slope from center to each side and adequate underdrainage. Grading may be from side to side or corner to corner diagonally if conditions do not permit the preferred grading.

Special Considerations Goal posts are to be provided at each end of the playing field.

TEAM HANDBALL

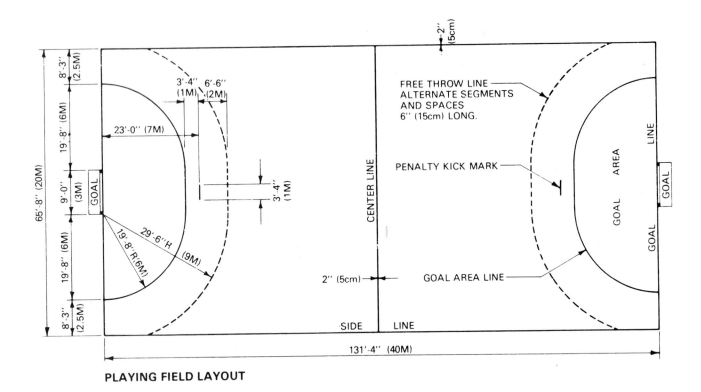

PLAYING FIELD LAYOUT

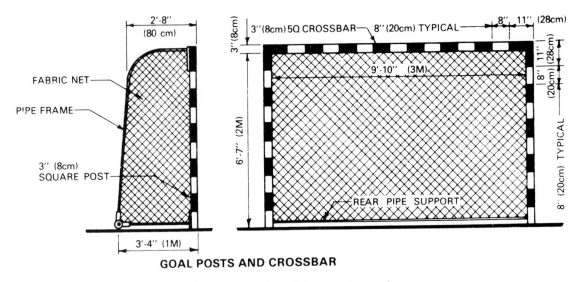

GOAL POSTS AND CROSSBAR

Fig. 40 Playing field for team handball. Team handball goal posts and crossbar are metal or wood and painted on all sides in two contrasting colors. Goals will be firmly fixed to the ground with hooked stakes. The goal line between the goal posts is the same width as the posts. All field markings are 2 in (5 cm) wide and form part of the area they enclose. Lines shall be marked with a white nontoxic material which is not injurious to eyes or skin. For grading and drainage details see Fig. 57. For surfacing details see Fig. 58.

Recommended Area Ground space is 11,230 sq ft (.25 acre) (1,066 m²).

Size and Dimension Playing field width is 65'-8" (20 m). Length is 131'-4" (40 m). Additional area recommended is 6'-0" minimum unobstructed space on all sides.

Orientation Preferred orientation is for the long axis to be northwest-southeast to suit the angle of the sun in the fall playing season, or north-south for longer periods.

Surface and Drainage Surface is to be turf. Preferred grading is a longitudinal crown with a 1 percent slope from center to each side and ade-

quate underdrainage. Grading may be from side to side or corner to corner diagonally if conditions do not permit the preferred grading.

Special Considerations Goal posts and crossbar are to be provided at each end of the playing field.

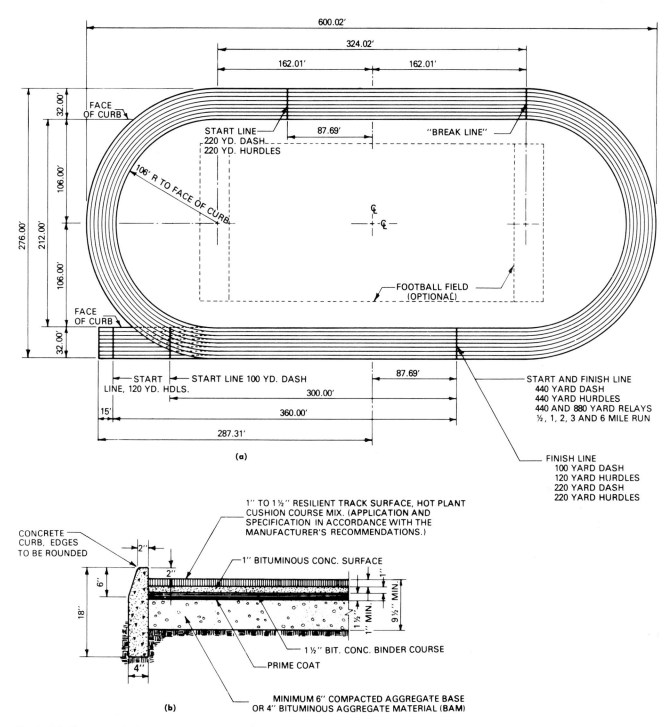

Fig. 41 *(a)* Plan-layout of a ¼-mi running track; *(b)* typical section of track. All distances in lane one shall be measured upon a line 12 in outward from the inner edge of the track. For events run in lanes around a turn, all lanes except lane one shall be measured upon a line 8 in outward from the inner line of the lane.

Recommended Area Ground space is approximately 4.3 acres.

Size and Dimension Inside radius to face of curb is 106'-0". Track width is 32'-0" for eight 4-ft-wide lanes. Overall width is 276'-0". Overall length is 600.02 ft.

Orientation The track should be oriented so that the long axis falls in a sector from north-south to northwest-southeast with the finish line at the northerly end.

Surface and Drainage Track surface is to be preferably bituminous material with a hot plant cushion course mix and optional protective colorcoat-

ing. Maximum slopes for the running track are 2 percent (1:50) inward in the center of curves, 1 percent (1:100) inward in the straightways and 0.1 percent (1:1000) in the running direction.

Special Considerations Drainage must be provided for the track surface and optional football field, but will be dependent upon site grading.

SHOT PUT

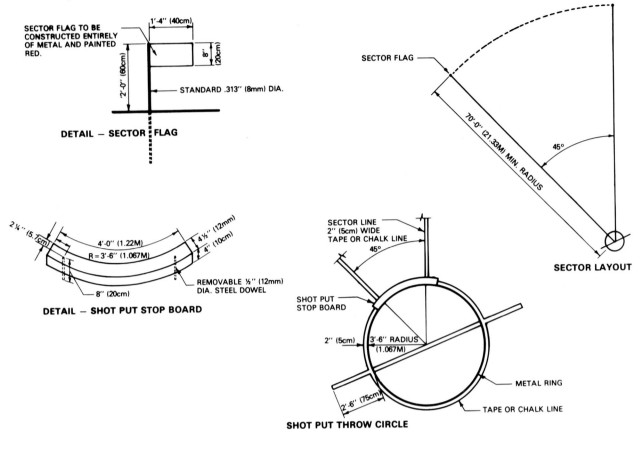

DETAIL — SECTOR FLAG

SECTOR LAYOUT

DETAIL — SHOT PUT STOP BOARD

SHOT PUT THROW CIRCLE

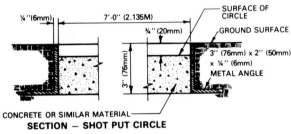

SECTION — SHOT PUT CIRCLE

Fig. 42 Shot put circle. Throwing circles to be formed of band iron or steel angle 3 in (76mm) $\times$ 2 in (50mm) $\times$ ¼ in (6mm) sunk flush with the ground outside. The surface within the circle to be ¾ in (2cm) lower than the outside level and surfaced with concrete or similar material. Sector lines to be white and marked with either cloth tape, held in place with metal pins, or chalk. Shot put stop board to be made of wood and painted white.

Recommended Area Ground space is 2100 sq ft minimum.

Size and Dimension Shot put circle is 7'-0" (2.134m) in diameter. Throwing sector is 45° angle and 70 ft (21.33m) minimum radius.

Orientation Preferred orientation is for the throwing direction to be toward the northeast quadrant.

Surface and Drainage Surface of inner circle is to be concrete or similar material. Throwing sector is to be turf at the same level as the top of the metal ring.

Special Considerations Stopboard must be firmly fixed so that its inner edge coincides with the inner edge of the shot put circle. Sector flags are required to mark end of landing zone at distance required by the competition.

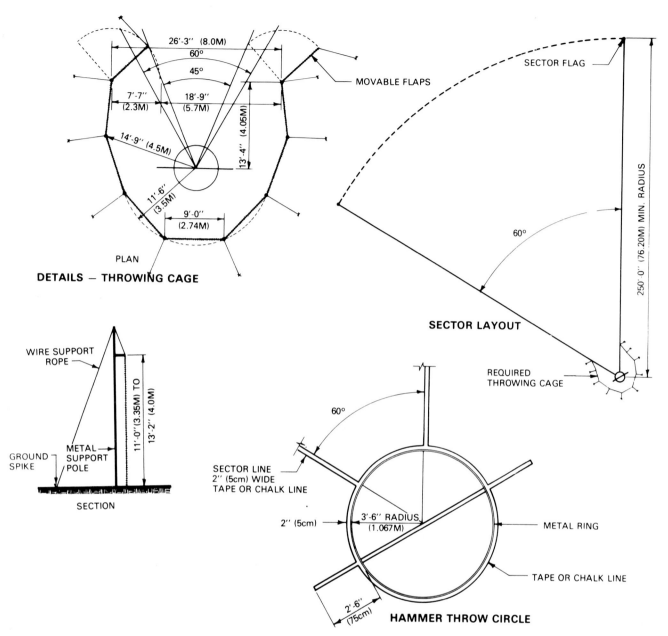

DETAILS — THROWING CAGE

SECTOR LAYOUT

SECTION

HAMMER THROW CIRCLE

Fig. 43 Hammer throw circle and throwing cage. All discus and hammer throws must be made from an enclosure or cage to insure the safety of spectators. The cage should be C-shaped in plan, the diameter being 29'-6" (9.0m) with the opening through which the throw is made 26'-3" (8.0m) wide. The height should not be less than 11 ft, but preferably 13'-2" (4.0m). A wire cable, or series of metal struts, is suspended at a height of not less than 11 ft above the ground in the shape of a letter C. The cable or series of struts, is supported in a horizontal plane by eight metal supports made in the shape of gallows, so that the C shape is formed by seven straight panels, each 9'-0" (2.74m) wide. Two movable flaps 7'-7" (2.3m) are provided at the end of the C shape to afford adjustment for different throwing sectors. The eight metal supports are set into the ground with spikes or permanent sockets sunk to a depth of approximately 1 ft (30cm) and held in position with wire ropes. A net 78'-2" (23.78m) long and 1 ft (0.3m) wider than the height of the struts, made of cord 0.5 in (12.5mm) in circumference with 2-in (50-mm) meshes is suspended from the wire or metal strut framework with the lower edge resting on the ground and turned inward. The inner edge should be weighted at intervals with sandbags. Throwing circles to be formed of continuous band iron or steel angle 3 in (76mm) $\times$ 2 in (50mm) $\times$ ¼ in (6mm) sunk flush with the ground outside. The surface within the circle to be ¾ in (2cm) lower than the outside level and surfaced with concrete or similar material. Sector lines to be white and marked with either cloth tape, held in place with metal pins, or chalk.

Recommended Area Ground space is 33,500 sq ft minimum.

Size and Dimension Hammer throw circle is 7'-0" (2.134m) in diameter. Throwing sector is 60° angle and 250 ft (76.20m) minimum radius.

Orientation Preferred orientation is for the throwing direction to be toward the northeast quadrant.

Surface and Drainage Surface of inner circle is to be concrete or similar material. Throwing sector is to be turf at the same level as the top of the metal ring.

Special Considerations For safety all throws must be made from within an approved enclosure or cage. Sector flags are required to mark end of landing zone at distance required by the competition.

DISCUS THROW

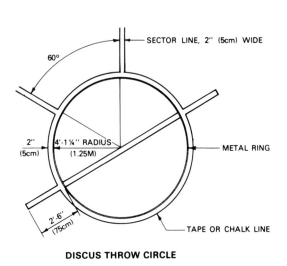

DISCUS THROW CIRCLE

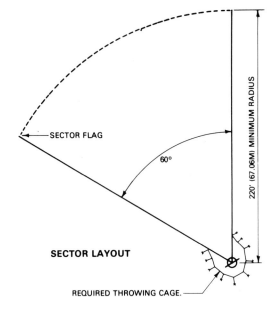

SECTOR LAYOUT

REQUIRED THROWING CAGE.

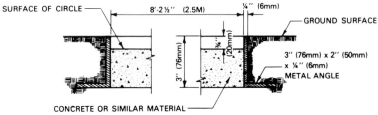

SECTION — DISCUS THROW CIRCLE

Fig. 44   Discus throw circle. Throwing circles to be formed of continuous band iron or steel angle 3 in (76mm) $\times$ 2 in (50 mm) $\times$ ¼ in (6mm) sunk flush with the ground outside. The surface within the circle to be ¾ in (2cm) lower than the outside level and surfaced with concrete or similar material. Sector lines to be white and marked with either cloth tape, held in place with metal pins, or chalk.

Recommended Area   Ground space is 25,500 sq ft minimum.

Size and Dimension   Discus throwing circle is 8'-2½ " (2.05m) in diameter. Throwing sector is 60° angle and 220 ft (67.06m) minimum radius.

Orientation   Preferred orientation is for the throwing direction to be toward the northeast quadrant.

Surface and Drainage   Surface of inner circle is to be concrete or similar material. Throwing sector is to be turf at the same level as the top of the metal ring.

Special Considerations   For safety all throws must be made from within an approved enclosure or cage. Sector flags are required to mark end of landing zone at distance required by the competition.

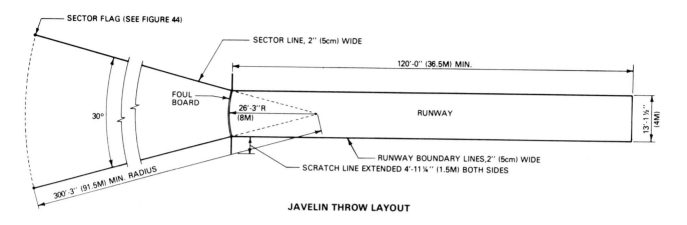

JAVELIN THROW LAYOUT

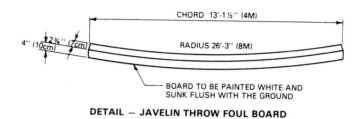

DETAIL — JAVELIN THROW FOUL BOARD

Fig. 45 Javelin throw. Sector lines to be white, 2 in (5cm) wide and marked with either cloth tape, held in place with metal pins, or chalk. Runway may be either turf or bituminous material.

Recommended Area Ground space is 24,000 sq ft minimum.

Size and Dimension Runway length is minimum 120'-0" (36.5m). Runway width is 13'-1½" (4.0m). Throwing sector is 30° angle and 300'-3" (91.5m) minimum radius.

Orientation Preferred orientation is for the throwing direction to be toward the northeast quadrant.

Surface and Drainage Runway may be turf or specialized bituminous surfacing with a maximum slope of 1 percent (1:100) laterally and 0.1 percent (1:1000) in the running direction. Throwing sector is to be turf at the same level as the runway behind the throwing arc.

Special Considerations Foul board is to be provided at end of runway. Sector flags are required to mark end of landing zone at distance required by the competition.

LONG JUMP AND TRIPLE JUMP

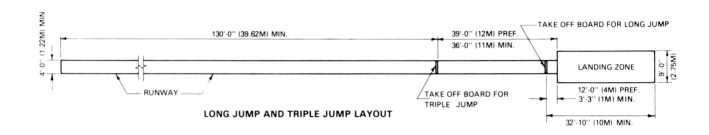

LONG JUMP AND TRIPLE JUMP LAYOUT

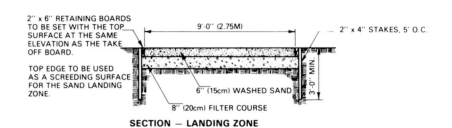

SECTION — LANDING ZONE

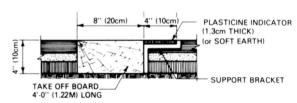

SECTION — TAKEOFF BOARD FOR LONG JUMP AND TRIPLE JUMP

Fig. 46 Long jump and triple jump. The edge of the takeoff board nearest the landing pit shall be the scratch, or foul line. The construction and material of the runway shall be extended beyond the takeoff board to the nearer edge of the landing pit.

Recommended Area Ground space is 1500 sq ft minimum.

Size and Dimension Runway length is 130'-0" (39.62m) minimum. Runway width is 4'-0" (1.22m) minimum. Landing pit width is 9'-0" (2.75m) minimum. Landing pit length is 32'-0" (10m) minimum.

Orientation Preferred orientation is for the running direction to be toward the north or northeast.

Surface and Drainage Runway preferably is to be bituminous material with a hot plant cushion course mix and optional protective colorcoating. Maximum slope is to be one percent (1 : 100) laterally and one tenth of one percent (1 : 1000) in the running direction. Landing pit is to be sand at the same elevation as the takeoff board.

Special Considerations Takeoff board is to be of wood and must be fixed immovable in the runway.

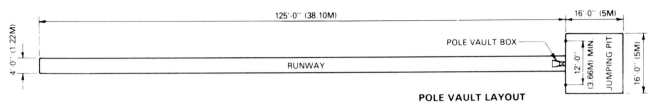

POLE VAULT LAYOUT

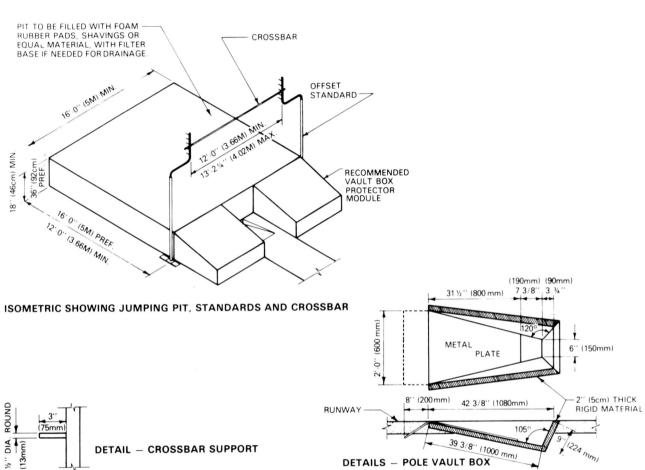

ISOMETRIC SHOWING JUMPING PIT, STANDARDS AND CROSSBAR

DETAIL — CROSSBAR SUPPORT

DETAILS — POLE VAULT BOX

Fig. 47 Pole vault. Any style of uprights or standards may be used, provided they are rigid and supported by a base not to exceed 4 in. in height above the ground. The crossbar shall rest on round pins which project not more than 3 in (75mm) at right angles from the uprights and have a maximum diameter of $\frac{1}{2}$ in (12mm). The crossbar shall be of wood or metal and triangular or circular in section with flat ends. Each side of the triangular bar shall measure 1.181 in (30mm) and the diameter of the circular bar shall be 0.984 in (25mm) minimum, 1.181 in. (30mm) maximum. Length shall be 12'-8" (3.8m) minimum, 14'-10" (4.52m) maximum.

Recommended Area Ground space is 1500 sq ft minimum.

Size and Dimension Runway length is 125'-0" (38.10m) minimum. Runway width is 4'-0" (1.22m) minimum. Vault pit width is 16'-0" (5m) minimum and depth is 12'-0" (3.66m) minimum to 16'-0" (5m) preferred. Height of material in jumping pit is 18 in (0.46m) minimum to 36 in (0.92m) preferred, with a connecting apron of the same material and decreasing height around the vaulting box.

Orientation Preferred orientation is for the running direction to be toward the north to east-northeast.

Surface and Drainage Runway preferably is to be bituminous material with a hot plant cushion course mix and optional protective colorcoating. Maximum slope is to be 1 percent (1 : 100) laterally and 0.1 percent (1 : 1000) in the running direction.

Special Considerations Pole vault box must be immovably fixed in the ground with its entire front edge flush with the front edge of the jumping pit. Jumping pit is to be filled with a resilient spongelike rubber or other synthetic material.

HIGH JUMP

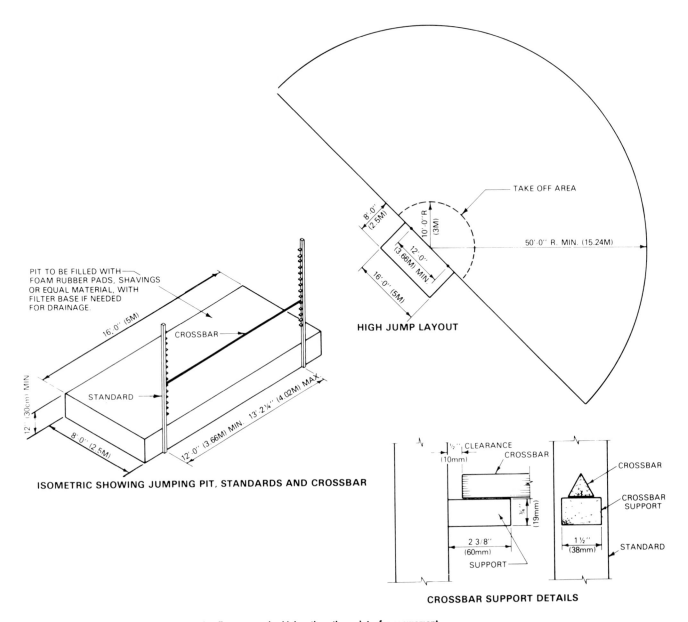

TAKE OFF AREA

8'-0" (2.5M)

10'-0" R (3M)

50'-0" R. MIN. (15.24M)

12'-0" (3.66M) MIN.

16'-0" (5M)

HIGH JUMP LAYOUT

PIT TO BE FILLED WITH FOAM RUBBER PADS, SHAVINGS OR EQUAL MATERIAL, WITH FILTER BASE IF NEEDED FOR DRAINAGE.

16'-0" (5M)

CROSSBAR

STANDARD

12" (30cm) MIN

8'-0" (2.5M)

12'-0" (3.66M) MIN. 13'-2¼" (4.02M) MAX.

ISOMETRIC SHOWING JUMPING PIT, STANDARDS AND CROSSBAR

½" CLEARANCE (10mm)

CROSSBAR

¾" (19mm)

2 3/8" (60mm)

SUPPORT

CROSSBAR

CROSSBAR SUPPORT

1½" (38mm)

STANDARD

CROSSBAR SUPPORT DETAILS

Fig. 48 High jump. No point within the takeoff area may be higher than the point of measurement. The horizontal supports of the crossbar shall be flat and rectangular, 1-½ in wide and 2-⅜ in long. The uprights shall extend at least 4 in (100mm) at all heights above the crossbar. The crossbar shall be of wood or metal and triangular or circular in section with flat ends. Each side of the triangular bar shall measure 1.181 in (30mm) and the diameter of the circular bar shall be 0.984 in (25mm) minimum or 1.181 in (30mm) maximum.

Recommended Area Ground space is 4,000 sq ft minimum.

Size and Dimension High jump runway is 50 ft (15.24m) radius semicircle. High jump pit width is 16 ft (5m) by 8 ft (2.5m) depth minimum. Height of material in jumping pit is 12 in (0.30m) minimum. Takeoff area is 10'-0" (3m) radius semicircle with centerpoint directly under center of crossbar, and no point within this area may be higher than point of measurement.

Orientation Preferred orientation is for the direction of jumping to be toward the north to east-northeast.

Surface and Drainage Runway preferably is to be constructed of bituminous material with an optional synthetic surface. Surface should be level and unvarying within its arc of 180°.

Special Considerations Jumping pit is to be filled with a resilient spongelike rubber or other synthetic material.

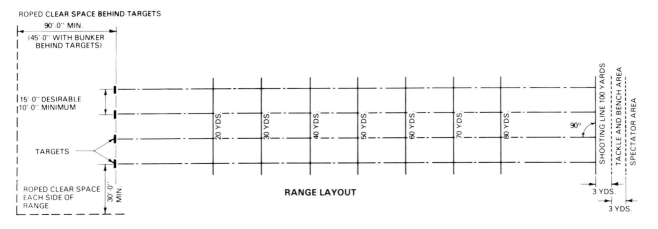

RANGE LAYOUT

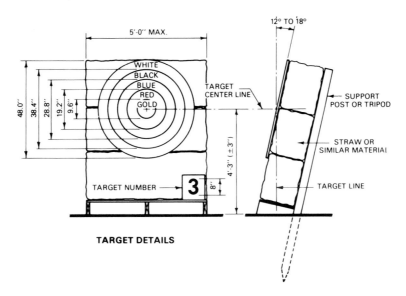

TARGET DETAILS

Fig. 49   Archery target range. Space behind and to either side of the range to be clear and free from hard objects. Background behind targets to be preferably dense trees, natural or manmade hills or protective shields. Range to be sited on fairly level land, free from obstructions, preferably sheltered from high winds and oriented to north $\pm$ 45°. Standard rounds for adults, 30–100 yd. Standard rounds for juniors, 20–50 yd. Target may be mounted on a round butt of spirally sewn straw or rush supported by a portable softwood target stand. Colors may be painted on an oilcloth cover.

Recommended Area   Ground space is 28,600 sq ft minimum (0.65 acre).

Size and Dimension   Shooting range is 300'-0" long by 10'-0" wide minimum, 15'-0" desirable, between targets. Roped clear space on each side of range is 30'-0" minimum. Roped clear space behind targets should be at least 90'-0" (45'-0" with bunker).

Orientation   Range should be located so that the archer is facing north $\pm$ 45°.

Surface and Drainage   Surface is to be turf and free from obstructions or hard objects. Drainage is to be preferably from side to side to maintain a constant, relatively level, elevation between the target and the archer at the various shooting distances.

Special Considerations   Target is to be provided as prescribed for official competition. Conspicuous signs should be provided to the side and rear to warn people of the range.

INTERNATIONAL SHOOTING UNION AUTOMATIC TRAP

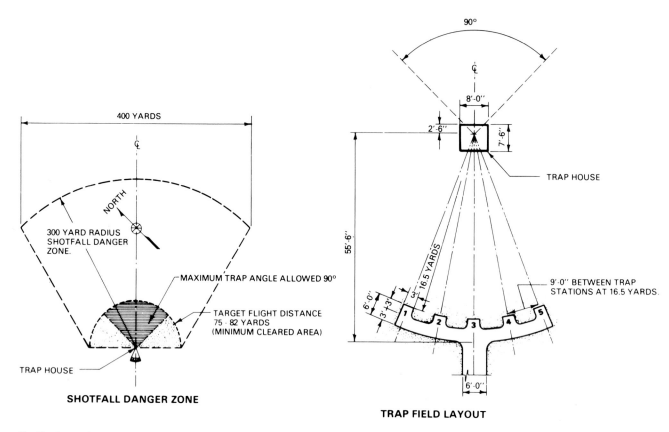

SHOTFALL DANGER ZONE

TRAP FIELD LAYOUT

Fig. 50 Automatic trap.

Recommended Area Allow 15 acres for a single field.

Size and Dimension Walks and structure occupy an overall area approximately 60 ft deep by 45 ft wide. Shooting stations may be 36 to 40 in square.

Orientation Preferred orientation is for the centerline through shooting station #3 to run northeast-southwest with the shooter facing northeast.

Surface and Drainage Shooting stations are to be portland cement concrete (PCC). Walkways may or may not be paved. Shooting area and 75- to 82-yd-radius minimum cleared area are to be turf. The 300-yd-radius shotfall danger zone

outside of the cleared area may be turf or water or left in natural condition, and the entire field should be located in a relatively flat area with an open background.

Special Considerations If shooting is entirely over land, there should be safety provisions for fencing, posting of warning signs, and clearing away of concealing brush. If shooting is over water, warnings posted on buoys or other signs are required and the trap house should be back far enough from the water's edge to permit recovery of unbroken targets. The trap-house roof must be on the same level as the shooting stations. Contact the National Rifle Association for information on trap-house construction and trap machines.

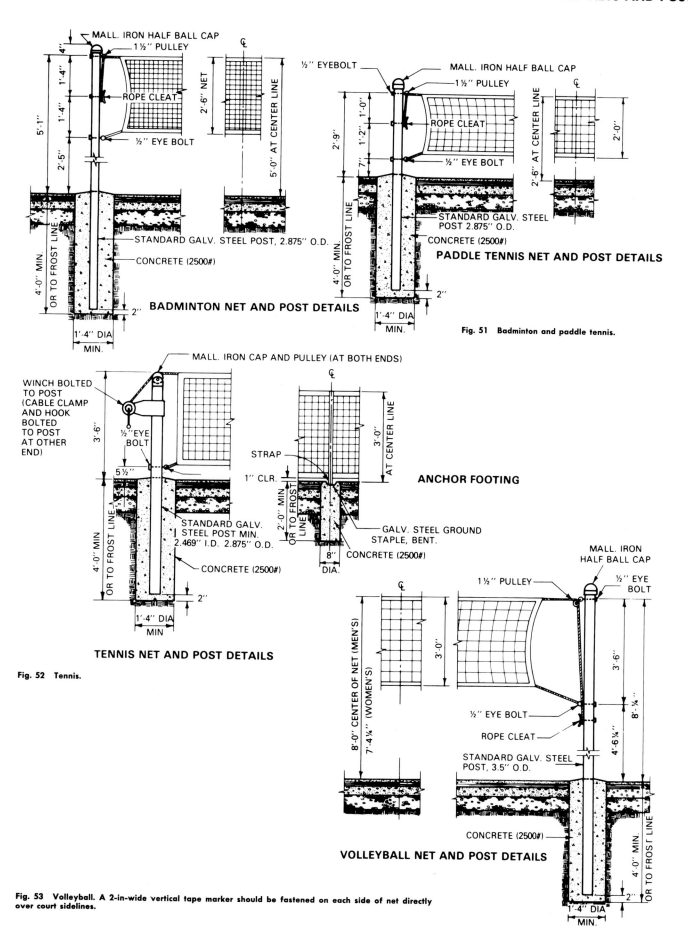

BADMINTON NET AND POST DETAILS

PADDLE TENNIS NET AND POST DETAILS

Fig. 51 Badminton and paddle tennis.

ANCHOR FOOTING

TENNIS NET AND POST DETAILS

Fig. 52 Tennis.

VOLLEYBALL NET AND POST DETAILS

Fig. 53 Volleyball. A 2-in-wide vertical tape marker should be fastened on each side of net directly over court sidelines.

FENCE ENCLOSURES

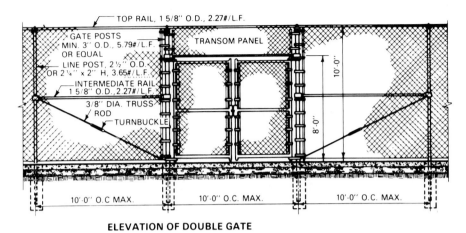

ELEVATION OF DOUBLE GATE

Fig. 54   Double gate layout shown is for information as to type and designation. In so far as possible, gate details shall be of the manufacturer's standard design. A single pedestrian gate may be used.

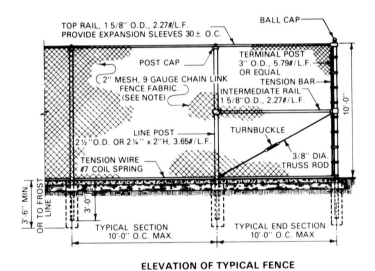

ELEVATION OF TYPICAL FENCE

Fig. 55   Typical fence. Different mesh and gauge sizes of chain link fabric are shown in notes on layout drawings for each sport.

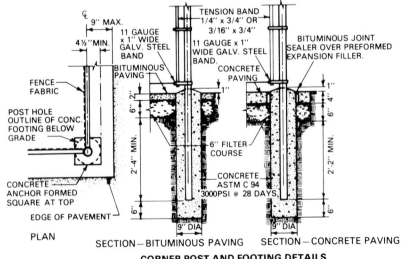

CORNER POST AND FOOTING DETAILS

Fig. 56

Layouts and details on this page are recommendations based on analysis of current construction techniques and manufacturers' equipment lines and should be utilized as a guideline in obtaining the appropriate product from local suppliers and manufacturers.

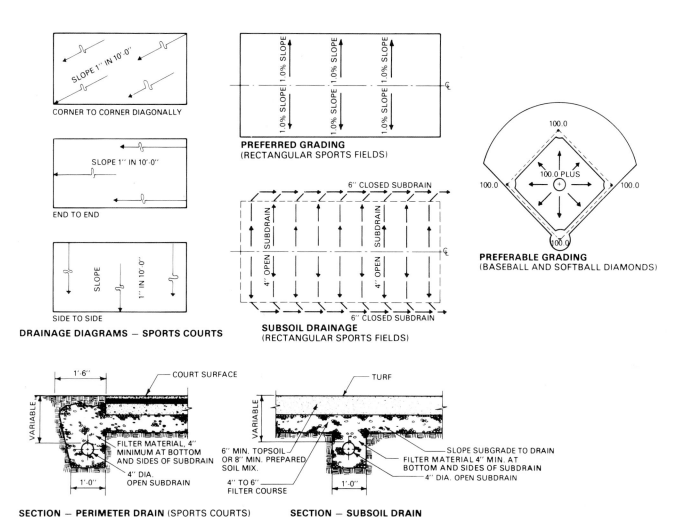

Fig. 57 Grading and drainage. See figure on individual sports for height of pitcher's plate above home plate. It is preferable that the baselines be level. If the diamond must pitch, the average slope shall be 2.0 percent from first base to third base or vice versa. The minimum slope for drainage on turf areas outside the skinned area is 1.0 percent when adequate subsoil drainage is provided. The maximum is 2.5 percent.

Court Surfaces Paved playing surfaces should be in one plane and pitched from side to side, end to end, or corner to corner diagonally, instead of in two planes pitched to or from the net. Minimum slope should be 1" in 10'-0". Subgrade should slope in the same direction as the surface. Perimeter drains may be provided for paved areas. Underdrains are not recommended beneath paved areas.

Playing fields Preferred grading for rectangular field is a longitudinal crown with 1 percent slope from center to each side. Grading may be from side to side or corner to corner diagonally if conditions do not permit the preferred grading. Subsoil drainage is to slope in the same direction as the surface. Subdrains and filter course are to be used only when subsoil conditions require. Where subsoil drainage is necessary, the spacing of subdrains is dependent on local soil conditions and rainfall. Subdrains are to have a minimum gradient of 0.15 percent. Baseball and softball fields should be graded so that the bases are level.

TYPICAL PLAYING SURFACES

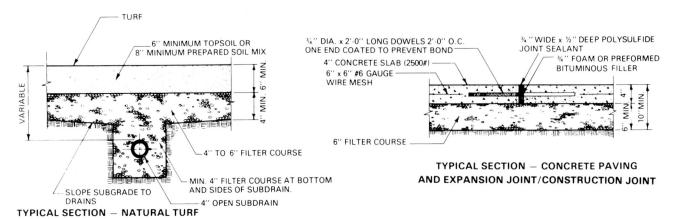

TYPICAL SECTION — NATURAL TURF

Fig. 58 Turf playing surface.

TYPICAL SECTION — CONCRETE PAVING
AND EXPANSION JOINT/CONSTRUCTION JOINT

Fig. 59 Concrete playing surface.

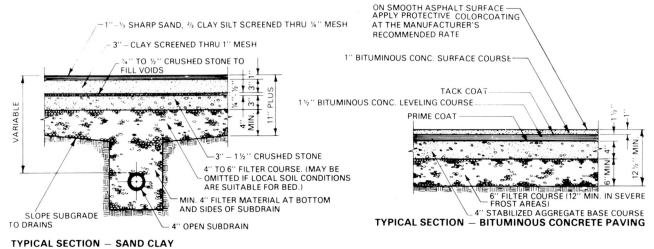

TYPICAL SECTION — SAND CLAY

Fig. 60 Sand clay playing surface.

TYPICAL SECTION — BITUMINOUS CONCRETE PAVING

Fig. 61 Bituminous playing surface.

Concrete (Fig. 59) Minimum compressive strength: 2,500 lb. Reinforcing: 6×6-in #6 gauge welded wire fabric. Minimum thickness 4 in. Expansion joints are to be provided as required and doweled 2'-0" O.C. with 3/4-in diameter $\times$ 2'-0" long dowel coated on one end to prevent bonding. Joint is to be filled with a 3/4-in foam or preformed bituminous filler and sealed with polysulfide joint sealant. Sand filter course: minimum 6-in deep required.

Bituminous Material (Fig. 61) Base: 4-in minimum stabilized aggregate base course over minimum 6-in filter course. Surface—minimum 2½ in. in two lifts: 1½-in leveling course of bituminous concrete and 1-in surface course of bituminous concrete. Sealcoat: on smooth asphalt surface apply protective colorcoating at the manufacturer's recommended rate.

Sand-Clay (Fig. 60) Filter course, 4 to 6 in, may be omitted if local soil conditions are suitable. Base course: minimum 3 in of 1½-in crushed stone choked with ¼ to ½ in of crushed fines. Surface course—minimum 4 in. in two lifts: 3-in clay screened through 1-in mesh with a 1-in surface lift of ⅓ sharp sand and ⅔ clay-silt screened through ¼-in mesh.

Natural Turf (Fig. 58) Subgrade to pitch in the same direction as the surface and slope to underdrains. Filter course, 4 to 6 in, is to be used only when subsoil conditions require. Topsoil 6 in minimum, or prepared soil mix 8 in minimum.

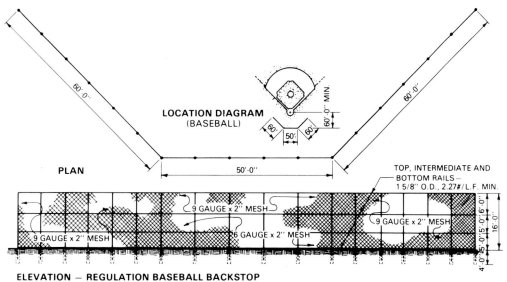

ELEVATION — REGULATION BASEBALL BACKSTOP

Fig. 62

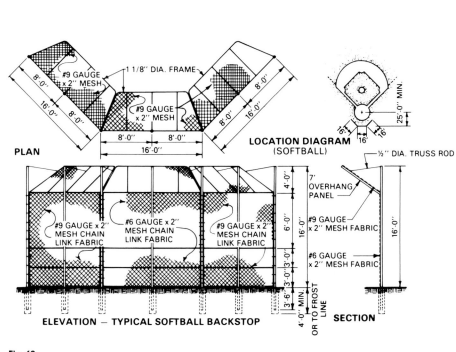

ELEVATION — TYPICAL SOFTBALL BACKSTOP

Fig. 63

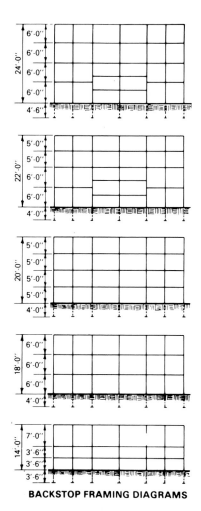

BACKSTOP FRAMING DIAGRAMS

Fig. 64

MOVIE THEATERS

By BEN SCHLANGER, *Architect*
Theater Consultant

Design requirements for cinemas, including auditory and visual considerations combined with showmanship and economy of structure, call for a type of building entirely distinct from stage theaters. The success of a commercial cinema depends on its ability to present good films in an effective manner, affording the maximum volume of patronage at admission prices that will insure an adequate profit. All patrons expect proper vision of the screen image, true reproduction of sound effects, and such comforts as will enable them to give undivided attention to the presentation.

LOCATION

The location of the cinema site is determined by its accessibility, land costs, parking facilities, and potential patronage. Big shopping centers have large parking areas that are generally unused in the evening, and may therefore be desirable locations for motion picture theaters.

SIZE

Home television and new systems of motion picture projection have brought about new criteria for determining optimum seating capacities for motion picture theaters. Home television has greatly reduced the need for the large-capacity (over 1,500 seats) "movie palaces" in urban locations, and also for the small motion picture theater in rural communities. These changes in circumstances place the cinema in somewhat the same category as the other dramatic arts of the living stage theater, where

the success of any one production depends on its quality or unusual character. The new systems of picture projection add a new dimension or an unusual character to a film, but they cannot be depended upon alone to draw the large patronage enjoyed in the era prior to home television.

Technically, the larger screens, wider films (70 mm), and new optical systems (such as Cinemascope) make possible an increase in the size of the audience that can see the film at one time. The increasing competition of home television, however, has made it almost impossible to profit from the potentially larger audience. Reduced patronage and high film-production costs have resulted in higher admission prices, which, in turn, tend to reduce further the size of the audience.

It has only recently been realized that there is a distinct advantage in having a relatively small audience with a maximum-size projected picture. The psychological effect that is thus created is that of "picture dominance," or an "at-the-scene feeling" for the viewer. Under these conditions, the picture practically fills the viewer's central range of vision (approximately 60 deg), and the distraction of the auditorium shell is greatly minimized.

Two distinct types of motion picture theaters have now developed. First is the general type of theater, catering to the more popular taste in films and requiring capacities of from 600 to 1,500 seats. The larger units must have a choice location with an adequate population to draw from and adequate parking facilities.

The second type has acquired the label "art theater." These small theaters are found mostly in the larger cities and in the university towns where there is a more sophisticated audience. Foreign films and

the better U.S. films are shown in these theaters. They usually prove profitable at capacities of from 400 to 900 seats, and often command the highest admission prices.

SHAPE AND SIZE OF PROJECTED PICTURE

Picture shape and viewing patterns are determined by fixing visual standards that enable each viewer to see the picture satisfactorily. The picture must appear undistorted, its view must be unobstructed, and its details discernible.

The average width of the projected picture, which was about 18 ft in 1938, has now approximately doubled for the 35 mm Cinemascope and 70 mm film systems, introduced in 1953. The quality of the projected picture affects the size and shape of the seating pattern. The quality of the projected picture varies with the size of the film used, however, and unfortunately most theaters still use more than one film size and projection system. Although picture widths have increased, the width of standard 35 mm film has not; consequently, when 35 mm film is used, the seats nearest the screen are less acceptable because film graininess becomes visible from these locations. When 70 mm film is used, the seats nearest the screen become desirable since film graininess is greatly reduced and these seats enable the viewers to experience the dramatic impact of "picture dominance."

A more nearly ideal motion picture theater could be designed if only one type of projection system and film width were used. For the best compromise design, to provide for all of the current systems and film widths, the following general guide may be used:

1. The first row of seats should be no closer to the screen than a position determined as follows: The angle formed with the horizontal by a line from the top of

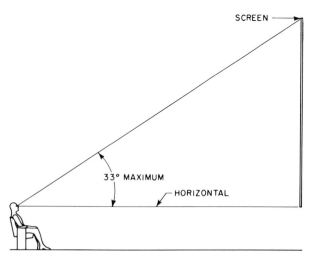

Fig. 1. Method of determining minimum distance from screen to first row of seats

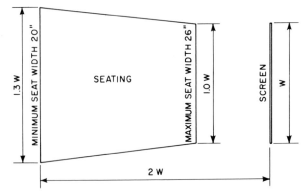

Fig. 2. Maximum viewing distance and maximum width of seating pattern

the projected picture to the eye of the viewer in a front-row seat, should not exceed 33 deg. (The top level of the projected picture should be the same for all systems of projection in a given auditorium.) See Fig. 1.

2. The maximum viewing distance should be no greater than twice the width of the widest picture to be projected (Fig. 2).

3. The width of the seating pattern should vary from 1 times the widest projected picture at the first row to 1.3 times at the row farthest from the screen (Fig. 2).

The resultant shape will be less rectangular than the long narrow theaters of the past, which are more economical to build but are unfortunately not well suited for the new systems of projection.

The seats nearest the screen will remain acceptable for use if the following general rule is followed: Projected picture widths should not exceed 35 ft for standard 35 mm film, 45 ft for Cinemascope 35 mm film, and 65 ft for 70 mm film. (See later notes regarding modification of these widths in connection with picture masking.)

In some instances in which a large seating capacity is desired, it is necessary to resort to a balcony in order to avoid the excessive viewing distance that would otherwise develop.

SCREENS AND PROJECTION OPTICS

Projection angle is the angle formed with the horizontal by a line from the projection lens to the midheight of the projected picture. Because of the increased picture width and screen curvatures recently introduced, it becomes increasingly important to have a minimum projection angle (0 deg is ideal but usually impossible). The angle should not exceed 10 deg and should be kept as low as possible in order to have a minimum distortion of picture detail.

A slight curvature in the width of the screen and semimatte screen surfaces are used to increase screen light reflection and to provide better dispersed screen illumination. This extra light is necessary for the larger screen sizes. The curvature should have a radius equal to about $1\frac{1}{4}$ times the projection distance.

PROJECTION LENSES

When a new theater is proposed it is important to determine at the outset the lens requirement for the various film systems to be projected. This information will determine the location of the projection room. The better lenses have greater focal lengths and require longer projection distances.

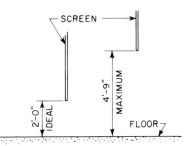

Fig. 3. Human-figure dimensions used in determining sight-line clearances

Fig. 4. Height of screen above floor at first row of seats

PICTURE MASKING

The most common method for masking the projected picture is to use a matte black surround. This is the simplest and least expensive way to absorb the fuzzy edges of the projected picture. These maskings may be in the form of a curtain that can be adjusted to mask various picture widths.

Another method is to use specially designed walls and ceiling that meet the picture edges. Instead of black trim, the masking is luminous from light reflected from the screen and blends with the projected picture. The author has designed several of these installations that have proved most satisfactory. Eye fatigue is reduced and greater dramatic impact is obtained.

If Cinemascope and 70 mm film are to be used in one theater, the luminous masking frame must be the same size for both systems, in which case a compromise is made by accepting a somewhat larger Cinemascope picture and a somewhat smaller 70 mm picture.

A compromise in the aspect ratio of the screen shape must also be made. The aspect ratio for 70 mm screen is 1 to 2.22 (height to width). For Cinemascope, the aspect ratio is 1 to 2.34. The Cinemascope frame can be cropped in the projector aperture to conform to the 1 to 2.22 aspect ratio without any meaningful loss of Cinemascope picture material.

The shape of the architectural light box in front of the screen requires special study for each seating, projection, and screen pattern.

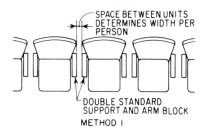

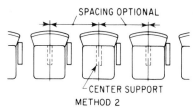

Fig. 5. Methods of obtaining wider spacing for chairs nearest screen

Maximum spacing for first row is 26 in.

FLOOR SLOPES AND SEATING

In the design of floor slopes and upper level steppings for cinema seating, it is necessary to establish the physical dimensions of the seated patron (Fig. 3) and standards for vision of the screen image. Most important is elimination of objectionable screen obstruction caused by persons seated in front of the viewer. For best dramatic impact, the bottom of the projected picture should be as close as possible to the floor under the first row of seats (Fig. 4). This in turn will require a more steeply pitched floor slope under the seats, and will eliminate the possibility of an upper tier of seats, which would have to be too steep in pitch.

The slope of the main-floor seating would also be increased for one-row vision. One-row vision provides unobstructed vision over the heads of persons in the row immediately ahead. Two-row vision is not ideal, but it is acceptable and permits milder slopes and the inclusion of an upper level of seats. Two-row vision is made more acceptable by staggering the seats to permit a view between the heads of the persons in the row immediately in front. With two-row vision the heads of all persons two or more rows in front will not obstruct any view of the screen. Two-row vision is further improved by using the widest chairs (and therefore the widest space between heads) in the rows nearest the screen. (See Fig. 5.) The view between heads is usually too narrow in the front rows where two-row vision is used. Minimum seat widths should be 20 in. for the rows farthest from screen.

MOVIE THEATERS

THEATER AUDITORIUM FLOOR SLOPES

Unit of reference in motion picture theater design is projection screen width, W. Distance from screen to first row of seats should be no less than 1 W. Best viewing distance is zone 3 W to 4 W; next in desirability are areas 2½ W to 3 W, and 4 W to 4½ W.

In theater of 22 rows, a screen 11 ft high by 15 ft wide is good for maximum viewing distance;

hence, first row of seats should be about 15 ft from screen. Recommended row spacing at least 34 in back to back.

Upward floor slope should start as far back from screen as possible, since slopes greater than 3 in between rows require risers. In diagrams shown (Figs. 6, 7, and 8), staggered seating, except in first rows of reverse-pitch schemes, reduces rear floor slope by half, and avoids dangerous

variable step heights necessary with aligned seating. When steps are used, if uniform height (fixed by rear rows) is adopted as standard, slope increases, and stadium type scheme results. *Elevated* stadium type is useful to permit space beneath for passage and services.

Drawings show all levels in relation to datum line, lowest point of floor. All pitches and rises noted in inches and decimal parts of an inch.

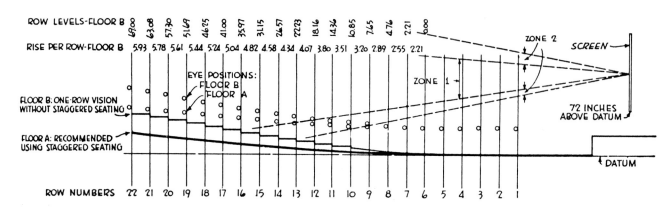

Fig. 6   Single-slope auditorium. On ground sloping 3 ft or more downward toward screen. Without staggered seats, risers required starting tenth row.

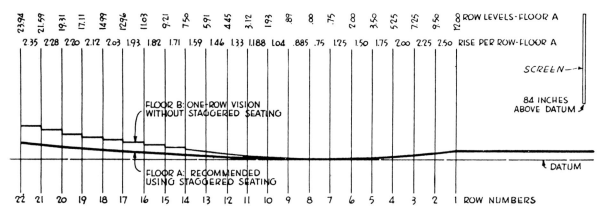

Fig. 7   Double-slope auditorium. On level ground, or on ground sloping less than 3 ft in any direction. First six rows aligned to allow view of entire screen.

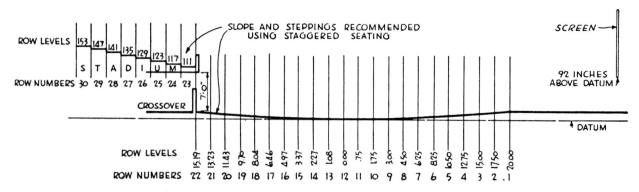

Fig. 8   Double-slope auditorium with stadium. On level ground or on ground sloping less than 3 ft in any direction. Seats in at least first six rows aligned. Crossover under first few rows of stadium saves seating area. Staggered seating and minimum clearance in crossover prevent intermediate steps.

Time-Saver Standards: A Handbook of Architectural Design, 2d ed., McGraw-Hill Book Co., New York, 1950.

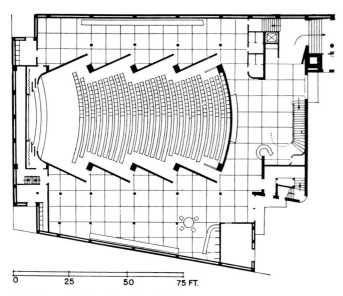

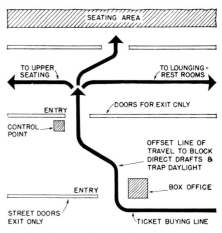

Fig. 9 Example of "continental seating."

Cinema at Turku, Finland; Erik Bryggman, architect. Minimum row spacing of 40 in. is required. More seats can be used in width to conform to larger screen requirements.

Fig. 10 Circulation diagram, showing relation of street lobby, foyer, and auditorium doors.

ROW SPACING AND AISLES

Minimum spacing between rows should be 34 in., with 1-in.-thick chair backs. Greater chair-back thickness is wasteful and unnecessary. Where 40 to 42 in. can be used for row spacing, many building-code authorities permit the elimination of all longitudinal aisles other than the aisles against the side walls. These codes, however, require frequent exit doors along the wall aisles for this type of seating. The capacity is about the same for the 34- and 40-in. spacing because of the different aisle arrangement.

The 40-in. seating scheme is sometimes termed "continental seating" because of its popularity in Europe. The extra comfort and safer egress afforded by this arrangement account for its increasing use. (See Fig. 9.)

SCREENS

All screens are perforated to allow for sound transmission from speakers placed behind the screen. (A depth of 5 ft should be provided behind the screen for the speakers.) All screens are vinyl plastic with a diffusive surface or a coated surface to increase light reflection. Lenticulated screens are also available. The screen material must be selected in accordance with the shape of the seating pattern and the strength of the projector light source.

GENERAL LIGHTING

The lighting of a cinema auditorium serves three separate functions: (1) Emergency exit and mood lighting, used during screen presentation; (2) Lighting needed during intermissions; and (3) Lighting of sufficient intensity for making announcements, clearing the house, or other rare occasions.

Types and sources of light for these needs are as follows: (1) Light reflected from the screen, of varying intensity dependent on film density; (2) Wall and ceiling surface illumination by standard lamps or tubes installed on the surface to be illuminated; and (3) Light projected on walls, ceiling, or audience from remote or concealed positions. All lighting normally required during the presentation is supplied in the front half of the auditorium by screen-reflected light. The rear portion must be illuminated by other light sources, placed so that the source is not within the spectators' normal range of vision. Placement choices are: first, at the junction of ceiling and side walls; second, on the ceiling; and third, on the side walls. The side walls rarely offer an acceptable location because, here, even low intensities are often objectionable.

Lighting during a performance should consist of a low-intensity, evenly diffused bath of light completely covering all surfaces in view, rather than either complete darkness or spotty lighting.

In considering the utilization of screen-reflected light, it is important that areas immediately surrounding the screen should not cause a lack of clarity in the projected image. Surfaces closest to the screen can be shaped, finished, and related to the screen surface so as to enhance the picture.

Emergency lighting generally must be provided separately. Where separate service lines are available, one may be used with an emergency motor generator. Alternative means of providing energy are battery systems kept charged automatically, gasoline, Diesel or gas engine generators, water turbines, and the like.

Exit signs are connected to the general emergency lighting circuit and should be legible from any point viewed. Lettering is usually a minimum of 8 in. high. All circulation areas, including foyers, lounges, and lobbies should likewise be on the emergency circuit.

TICKET BOOTHS

The location of the ticket booth depends on the space available, the character and direction of street and pedestrian traffic, and the volume and habits of patronage. The ticket booth may be isolated (as an island), centered, or included in the corner of the entrance. It should, of course, be readily identified with its function. In metropolitan areas, ticket booths are almost universally placed as close to sidewalks as building codes permit in order to attract casual passers-by. In suburban and other centers where patrons leave their homes with the express purpose of attending the cinema, ticket booths may be removed from sidewalk lobbies and placed either within secondary lobbies or in foyers. It is pos-

MOVIE THEATERS

sible to adopt a continental custom—use of an open counter located conveniently to the manager's office—in an effort to achieve an "intimate" atmosphere. When operated by only one person an area approximately 4 by 4 by 8 ft is adequate; for larger theaters, where there are generally two ticket sellers, clearances are required.

Heating is often provided from the theater heating system if the theater cellar extends under the ticket-booth space. Although electric heaters are sometimes used, they are not always satisfactory because they concentrate great amounts of heat in single spots without providing general heating. Natural ventilation is usually provided by ventilators in roofs and louvers in doors. Occasionally air-conditioning ducts are run to booths from theater systems. Space is required for change makers and electrically or manually operated ticket dispensers. It is almost universal practice to install an outside telephone for the attendant's convenience in answering calls about the program. This telephone is usually connected to another in the manager's office, with a two-way signal.

LOUNGES AND TOILETS

Lounge areas, on either level, serve to separate the toilets from the theater seating. For capacities of over 600 seats, at least two lounge areas should be provided and arranged so as to be partially or wholly visible from the lobby, foyer, or circulating areas. It is also desirable to have some part of the lounge command a view of both seating and screen in order that waiting patrons may follow seat availability as well as performance progress.

Recommended minimum toilet fixture requirements are as follows:

Theater capacity	Men	Women
Up to 400 seats	1 basin	1 basin
	1 toilet	2 toilets
	1 urinal	
400–600 seats	2 basins	2 basins
	2 toilets	3 toilets
	2 urinals	
600–1,000 seats	2 basins	2 basins
	2 toilets	4 toilets
	3 urinals	

Local codes, of course, will govern.

PROJECTION ROOMS

The usual code requirements are 48 sq ft for the first projection machine and 24 sq ft for each additional projector. Dimensions based on necessary clearances around projectors are given in Fig. 11.

Rewinding: Although at least one state law requires that film rewinding be done in the projection room, a separate rewind room adjacent to the projection room is usually considered advisable. Rewinding is done on a small table; observation ports opening to both the projection room and the auditorium permit a single operator to supervise a presentation easily while rewinding used film.

Film storage: Up to 12,000 ft of film is usually permitted to be stored in metal containers. Film safes are required for greater amounts, 24,000 ft being the usual maximum. The location should be convenient to the rewind table.

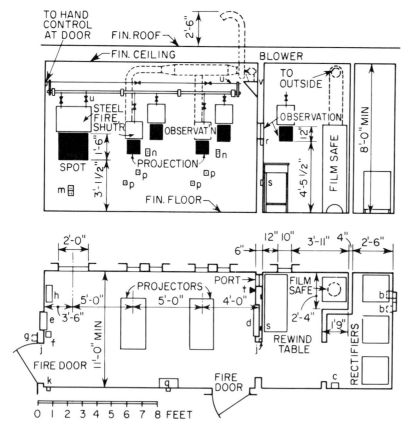

Key

a. Line fuses
b. Line switch
c. Line switch
d. Panel box (d-c)
e. Panel box (a-c)
f. Motor starter
g. Booth exhaust blower control and pilot
h. Dimmer
j. Light switch
k. Arc blower switch
m. 15A Duplex receptacle (twist lock)
n. Signal buttons
p. Sound control
q. Amplifier
r. Vaporproof fixture
s. T-L receptacle
t. Interphone
u. Fuse link support for steel fire shutter
v. Blower receptacle

Fig. 11 Plan of projection room and elevation of wall toward auditorium.

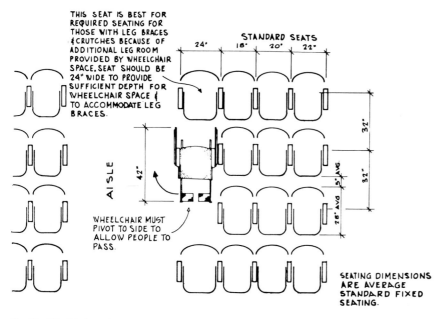

THIS SEAT IS BEST FOR REQUIRED SEATING FOR THOSE WITH LEG BRACES & CRUTCHES BECAUSE OF ADDITIONAL LEG ROOM PROVIDED BY WHEELCHAIR SPACE. SEAT SHOULD BE 24" WIDE TO PROVIDE SUFFICIENT DEPTH FOR WHEELCHAIR SPACE & TO ACCOMMODATE LEG BRACES.

WHEELCHAIR MUST PIVOT TO SIDE TO ALLOW PEOPLE TO PASS.

SEATING DIMENSIONS ARE AVERAGE STANDARD FIXED SEATING.

Fig. 12 Wheelchair seating space at aisles. Sight lines may be interrupted by wheelchair person because wheelchair seat is higher than fixed seats. This may be overcome by diagonal or other chair arrangement.

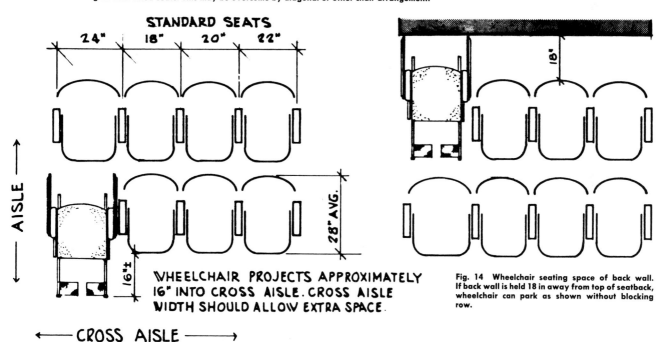

WHEELCHAIR PROJECTS APPROXIMATELY 16" INTO CROSS AISLE. CROSS AISLE WIDTH SHOULD ALLOW EXTRA SPACE.

Fig. 13 Wheelchair seating space at cross aisle.

Fig. 14 Wheelchair seating space of back wall. If back wall is held 18 in away from top of seatback, wheelchair can park as shown without blocking row.

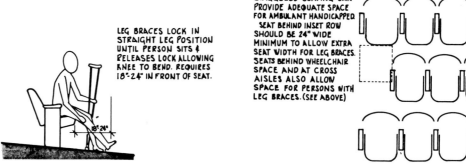

LEG BRACES LOCK IN STRAIGHT LEG POSITION UNTIL PERSON SITS & RELEASES LOCK ALLOWING KNEE TO BEND. REQUIRES 18"-24" IN FRONT OF SEAT.

STAGGERED SEATING CAN PROVIDE ADEQUATE SPACE FOR AMBULANT HANDICAPPED. SEAT BEHIND INSET ROW SHOULD BE 24" WIDE MINIMUM TO ALLOW EXTRA SEAT WIDTH FOR LEG BRACES. SEATS BEHIND WHEELCHAIR SPACE AND AT CROSS AISLES ALSO ALLOW SPACE FOR PERSONS WITH LEG BRACES. (SEE ABOVE)

Fig. 15 Seating space requirements for braces and crutches.

An Illustrated Handbook of the Handicapped, Section of the North Carolina State Building Code. 1977, Ronald Mace, AIA and Betsy Laslett, Raleigh, N.C.

MOVIE THEATERS
Handicapped Seating

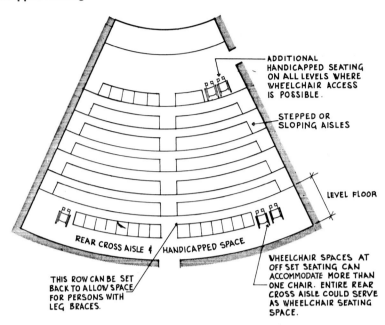

ADDITIONAL HANDICAPPED SEATING ON ALL LEVELS WHERE WHEELCHAIR ACCESS IS POSSIBLE.

STEPPED OR SLOPING AISLES

LEVEL FLOOR

REAR CROSS AISLE & HANDICAPPED SPACE

THIS ROW CAN BE SET BACK TO ALLOW SPACE FOR PERSONS WITH LEG BRACES.

WHEELCHAIR SPACES AT OFF SET SEATING CAN ACCOMMODATE MORE THAN ONE CHAIR. ENTIRE REAR CROSS AISLE COULD SERVE AS WHEELCHAIR SEATING SPACE.

Fig. 16   Example plan: small theater.

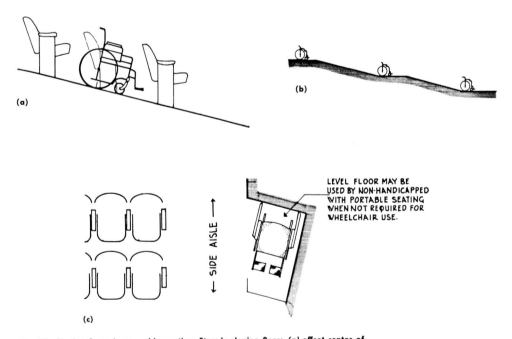

(a)

(b)

(c)

SIDE AISLE

LEVEL FLOOR MAY BE USED BY NON-HANDICAPPED WITH PORTABLE SEATING WHEN NOT REQUIRED FOR WHEELCHAIR USE.

Fig. 17   Sloping floors in assembly seating. Steeply sloping floors *(a)* offset center of gravity for wheelchairs causing discomfort during long performances. For this reason it is preferred that wheelchairs be located where floor can remain level as at cross aisles *(b)*, front and rear of theater, or in boxes to the side *(c)*.

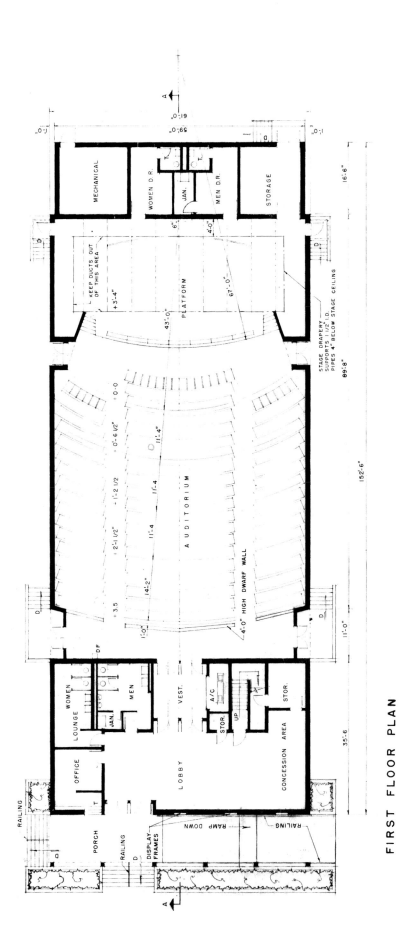

FIRST FLOOR PLAN

SECTION A-A

Fig. 18 From *Definitive Designs for Naval Shore Facilities, Department of the Navy, Washington, D.C.,* 1972.

MOVIE THEATERS
500-Seat Movie Theater

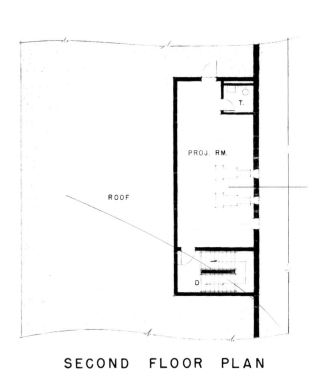

SECOND FLOOR PLAN

ELEVATION – PROJ. RM. WALL
SPLAY BOTH SIDES
OF EACH PROJ. PORT
20° ONLY WHEN WALL
IS GREATER THAN
8" THICK

SECTION
B-B

PLAN

SCHEDULE FOR DETERMINATION OF PROJECTION PORT HEIGHT

PROJECTION ANGLE	PORT HEIGHTS	
	WALLS UP TO 8" THICK	WALLS 8" TO 16" THICK
0°	4'-0"	4'-0 1/2"
2°	3'-10 1/2"	3'-11"
4°	3'-9"	3'-9 1/2"
6°	3'-7 1/2"	3'-8"
8°	3'-6"	3'-6"

PROJECTION ANGLE IS MEASURED BE-
TWEEN HORIZONTAL & LINE FROM POINT
4'-0" ABOVE PROJECTION ROOM FLOOR
TO CENTER OF SCREEN IMAGE HEIGHT

Fig. 19 From *Definitive Designs for Naval Shore Facilities,* **Department of the Navy, Washington, D.C., 1972.**

A sufficient area of inexpensive land is the prime consideration in selecting a site. Location is generally better close to town, but theaters have been successful several miles from city limits. Many states and communities are developing codes regulating location and design of drive-ins; these should be carefully investigated. Other factors to check include: proximity to other drive-ins; nature of soil; natural drainage; simple, cheap excavation and grading; nearness to railroads or other distracting noises or odors. Drive-ins are usually best located on secondary roads connecting with major highways to prevent traffic congestion. Outside city limits, septic tanks must often be used for waste disposal, wells for water supply. Theater size should be derived from potential patronage; an average of 3.28 patrons per car was reported by *Theater Catalog, 1949–50 Edition,* from a survey conducted in the Minneapolis area.

Plot Layout

Ramps The theater area is a series of ramps, laid out one behind the other in arcs. They are graded to elevate the front of each row of cars, permitting vision of screen above cars ahead. Sight lines and road grades must be established by size and terrain.

Capacity and Size Maximum capacity is limited by number of ramps possible with clear view of screen. Picture size is limited to lenses and projection equipment available. Until larger and brighter pictures are possible, about 1,000 to 1,300 cars is maximum. Smaller theaters generally average about 450 cars, larger ones near cities, 650 to 1,000 cars. *Motion Picture Herald* (Feb. 14, 1948) recommends roughly 100 ft of width for each 10 cars, and the following depths (based on full radii ramps, 38 ft o.c., and speaker posts 17 ft o.c.):

No. of cars capacity	No. of ramps	Screen to rear of ramps, ft
500	10	510
586	11	548
670	12	586
778	13	624
886	14	662
1,000	15	700

See Figs. 1 to 3.

Entrances and Exits Provide waiting space or extra wide entrance drives to get cars off highways; say for around 30 to 40 percent of capacity. An escape exit drive by ticket office gives patron a means of getting out when cars are stacked behind him. On leaving ramps, it is best to have cars drive forward for exit. Several well lighted exits will ease traffic congestion. Often front-footage is retained for commercial use.

Commercial Buildings, F. W. Dodge Corp., New York, 1954.

Surfacing Drives should minimize dust and not be slippery when wet. Crushed stone topped with gravel, oil treated or black topped, is often used.

Ticket Booths Ticket selling must get patrons in quickly to start show on time. One ticket booth can usually serve up to 300 car capacity, two up to 600, three up to 800, and four up to 1,000 cars.

Screens Screen towers should be placed so pictures cannot be seen from highway. Screen widths vary from 40 to 60 ft, depending on number of ramps and topography. Sizes often used are: 48 by 37 ft for 650 cars, 56 by 42 ft for 950 cars. It is desirable to face screen east or north; this blocks evening sun, permits earlier show. Height above ground is determined by ramp and sight angles. Tilting screen at top minimizes distortion.

The screen may be of almost any material which will take a good covering of white paint; provisions should be made for frequent and rapid repainting. Asbestos sheets, aluminum and steel decking have been used. Minimize joints to prevent distortion and streaking. The structure should withstand at least 25 lb per sq ft wind pressure and be fire-resistant. Wood frames, structural steel, reinforced concrete, even telephone poles are used. Prefabricated units are available.

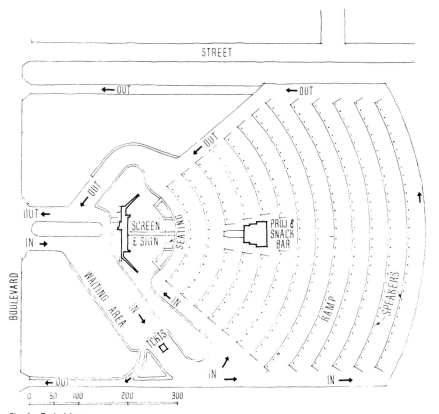

Fig. 1 Typical layout.

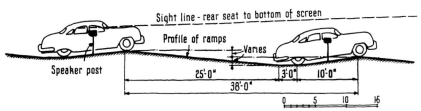

Fig. 2 Typical profile.

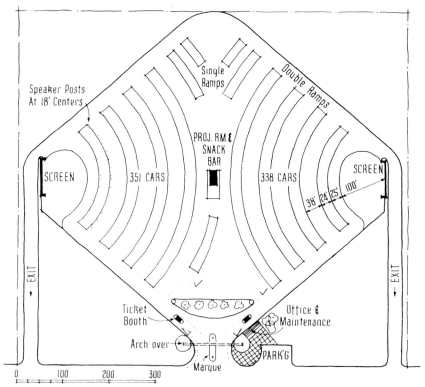

Fig. 3   Back-to-back theaters.

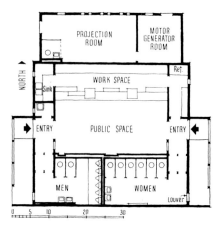

Fig. 4   Projection room/snack bar.

Seating Area   If near residential areas, provide seating for walk-in patrons, in front of screen or by concession. A children's playground is desirable.

Projection Booth   Picture size and focal length of lens control placement and design of projection booth. It is often placed about 280 ft from screen, centered in lot. Special lenses can project greater distances. Projection angle depends on ramp layout. The booth must house two operators, two projectors, a large generator, and an amplification system for speakers.

Speaker Units   Sound is best served by "in-car" speakers on posts about 16 to 18 ft o.c. Each serves two cars. Speakers may be removed from posts and hooked inside cars. Underground cables supply power. Aisle and signal lights are built into many commercial models. Electric car-heaters may be used for cool weather.

Concessions   Attractive, clean and roomy snack bars can be an important source of income. Large numbers must be served quickly during intermissions and before showings. A terrace in front of concession allows continued viewing. Illumination must not detract from screen during showing. Service carts are used for ramp service; signal lights or an intercommunication system may be used for calling carhops (Fig. 4).

Storage   Space is needed for cleanup and repair equipment, and for supplies. If speakers, junction boxes and projection equipment are removed for winter, safe, dry storage is needed on site or in a warehouse. If left in place, waterproof covers should be used. Sprays for insect control, and fire extinguishers should be on hand.

Design Notes   Illuminated signs should be placed near highway, but so as not to form a traffic hazard. The back of the screen is often used for advertising. Fencing should be high enough to cut off headlights of cars on highways. Simple, neat landscaping can help maintain desirability in the community and attract customers.

PRELIMINARY CONSIDERATIONS

The following factors dictate the plan of a bowling center:

1. The ability of an area to support the business
2. Public or private operation
3. The available capital for the immediate venture
4. Property size, location, and zoning
5. New or existing building
6. Parking requirements, required by law and for the operation of the business
7. Desired allied businesses and the local ordinances in force which govern such businesses as the following:
   a. Liquor bar or cocktail lounge
   b. Snack bar or restaurant
   c. Billiard room
   d. Meeting rooms and banquet facilities
   e. Other sport facilities
   f. Retail sale of bowling and other sporting goods
8. Automatic pinsetters or manually operated pinsetting machines
9. Selection of ball return equipment
10. Type of lane foundation
    a. 2- by 4-in. stringer foundation with 9-in.-deep pit
    b. Built up crib foundation where noise reduction is necessary or where no pit is provided
11. Automatic scorers

SITE PLANNING

Because a bowling center is a permanent building, the placement of any such structure on a parcel of property merits intensive study. The future general long-range planning for the surrounding area, contemplated zoning changes involving building lines, future road building, or anything which could alter the present character of the property should be considered at this time.

The site can be planned with relation to the following items:

1. Zoning of land restricting commercial, business, or parking.

2. Local nearby church or school building which might restrict traffic or the sale of alcoholic beverages.

3. Proposed maximum future expansion.

4. Drainage requirements, location of soil and storm sewer lines, public utilities.

5. Maximum visibility of building from street—nearby location of buildings, railroad overpasses, trees, signs, etc.

6. Availability of parking requirements for the maximum number of lanes.

7. Distance from bulk of parking related to entrance to building. This ultimately dictates location of bowling lanes and layout of public area facilities, such as control, liquor bar, snack bar, pro shop, check room, as they relate to traffic patterns within the building.

Planning Bowling Centers, Brunswick Corp., Chicago, Ill, 1968.

8. Traffic flow restrictions to entrances and exits from the property.

9. Certified soil sample test to determine if ground can support weight of a suitable building for bowling plus hydrostatic pressure.

PARKING

To accommodate the majority of bowling patrons that arrive at the lanes in cars, it is essential to provide parking facilities.

If the site allows, parking is generally preferred as close to the main entrance as possible (Fig. 1).

The parking area should be well illuminated; and, ideally, it should be paved, drained, and, in the instance of head-to-head parking, should have wheel bumpers. Blacktop is preferable to crushed stone. Blacktopping should be sealed annually.

On a national average, seven cars per lane is the general minimum requirement.

Many establishments use car jockeys during the busy hours. This speeds up the entrance of bowlers and helps conserve parking space. Usually, the tips pay for the car jockeys. Insurance is necessary.

Occasionally, music is piped into the parking areas.

It would be advisable to locate water connections throughout the parking areas. This is needed to clean the parking lot and eliminate dirt tracked into the building.

Shrubbery has frequently been used as a screening device to minimize the glare from headlights and to reduce motor noise in the parking areas, but such shrubbery should not block the view of passing traffic or exits and entrances.

Special attention should be paid to exits and entrances. It is necessary to clearly identify the entrances to the parking facilities. These entrances, as well as the exits, should be located so as not to interfere with the flow of highway traffic. Ideally, incoming and outgoing cars should not have to cross the flow of traffic.

BUILDING WIDTH

The width of the building may be determined by adding the thickness of outside walls, the width of side aisles, and the required space for columns if they exist, to the width of uninterrupted bowling lane bays. Dimensions for bowling lanes are noted in Fig. 2. Remarks concerning columns and side aisles follow.

1. Column Spacing

Naturally any designer would rather work with a clear span. However, in those establishments where supports for the structure above the lanes dictate that columns be used, it is desirable to use a minimum lateral spacing between columns of 22 ft-6¼ in.—a four lane bay plus 1 in. for clearance—to reduce transmission of noise up or down the structure of the building (Fig. 3).

Longitudinally, the fewer columns, the better. The 16 ft-1⁵⁄₁₆ in. of the approach area and

Recommended Parking Dimensions

A	DIRECTION OF PARKING	B	C	D	E	F	G	NO. OF STALLS IN LENGTH "X"	AREA PER CAR
90°	BACK IN	8'-6"	18'-0"	22'-0"	58'-0"	8'-6"	22'-0"	$\frac{X}{8.5}$	247 SQ. FT.
60°	BACK IN	8'-6"	18'-10"	18'-4"	56'-0"	9'-10"	21'-7"±	$\frac{X-11}{9.8}$	270 SQ. FT.
45°	FORWARD	8'-6"	17'-2"	12'-8"	47'-0"	12'-0"	16'-3"±	$\frac{X-17}{12}$	282 SQ. FT.

7 CARS PER LANE IS THE GENERAL NATIONAL MINIMUM PARKING REQUIRED

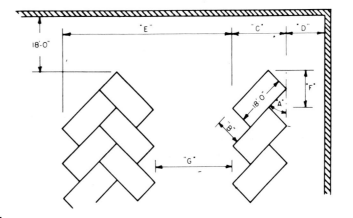

Fig. 1

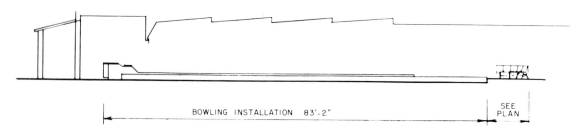

BOWLING INSTALLATION 83'-2"

SEE PLAN

Longitudinal Section

Bowling Lane Widths

THE FOLLOWING DIMENSIONS ARE NET MEASUREMENTS OF THE UNINTERRUPTED LANE WIDTHS ONLY, AND THEREFORE, ADDITIONS SHOULD BE MADE FOR COLUMNS, WALLS AND PASSAGES BETWEEN LANES OR BESIDE THEM.

NUMBER OF UNINTERRUPTED LANES	MINIMUM WIDTH 10 ½ " RETURNS
2	11'-4"
4	22'-5 ¼ "
6	33'-6 ½ "
8	44'-7¾ "
10	55'-9"
12	66'-10 ¼ "
14	77'-11 ½ "
16	89'-0¾ "
18	100'-2"
20	111'-3 ¼ "
22	122'-4 ½ "
24	133'-5 ¾ "
26	144'-7"
28	155'-8 ¼ "
30	166'-9 ½ "
32	177'-10¾ "
34	189'-0"
36	200'-1 ¼ "
38	211'-2 ½ "
40	222'-3¾ "
42	233'-5"
44	244'-6 ¼ "
46	255'-7 ½ "
48	266'-8¾ "

FOR EACH ADDITIONAL PAIR OF LANES ADD 11'-1 ¼ "

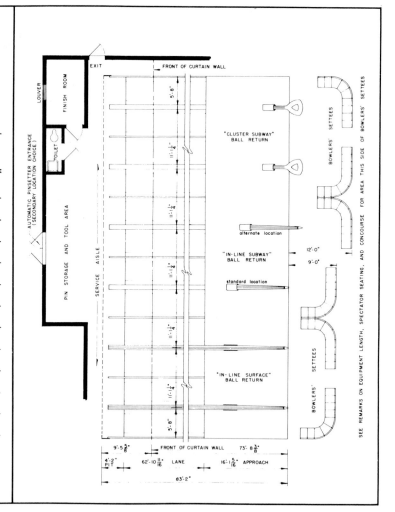

Automatic Pinsetter Entrance Requirements

FRONT ENTRANCE (FIRST CHOICE)

MINIMUM CLEAR OPENING —————————————— 6'-0" WIDE x 6'-8" HIGH.
MINIMUM CLEAR UNOBSTRUCTED PASSAGE TO PIT AREA ————— 6'-0" WIDE x 6'-8" HIGH.

REAR OR SIDE OF SERVICE AISLE (SECONDARY CHOICE)

MINIMUM CLEAR OPENING —————————————— 6'-0" WIDE x 6'-8" HIGH.
MINIMUM CLEAR UNOBSTRUCTED PASSAGE ——————— 6'-0" WIDE x 6'-8" HIGH.
IF THE OPENING IS WITHIN 6'-0" OF ANY PART OF THE KICKBACKS, THE MINIMUM UNOBSTRUCTED OPENING SHALL BE 6'-0" WIDE x 6'-8" HIGH ABOVE KICKBACKS.

Fig. 2 Key bowling lane dimensions.

at least 2 ft beyond the foul line, if possible, should be kept completely free of columns.

2. Side Aisles

The width of the side aisles is determined by the economical width of the building. The side aisle performs as a convenient indoor route for house personnel between the bowlers' area and the service aisle behind the pinsetters. It is not normally designed for use by the public or for the movement of equipment and supplies. A side aisle on each side of the building also eliminates the mental hazard of bowling "hard against the wall" on the first and last lanes.

BUILDING DEPTH

The depth of the building can be established by starting at the rear of the building. First, consider the requirements for storage and shops for equipment. Then, follow the requirements for the service aisle, the length of the bowling equipment installation, bowler and spectator seating arrangements, concourse requirements for special seating and traffic flow, and, finally, the companion accommodations. Remarks concerning each of the above follow.

1. Storage, Shops, and Service Aisle

Where the lot size affords the space, many of the larger bowling establishments erect a "lean-to" type of structure behind the rear wall of the building with entrance to this structure through fire-retarding doors, directly from the service passage. This structure can also be built against one side of the building if plot is too shallow. The purpose of this appendage to the main building is for storage of bowling supplies such as pins and spare parts, shop area (pinsetter tool room, 150-sq-ft minimum) for the fully automatic pinsetters, and toilet. Since the pit area is a noisy area, the shop should be so constructed as to be as quiet as possible, to achieve maximum working efficiency of the mechanic, although walls are not required between the storage area and the service aisle. Pay particular attention to the location of ducts and pipes which will conduct noise unless properly insulated and isolated. The depth of this structure generally varies from 8 to about 14 ft, while the width depends on the space required for the above mentioned operations. A minimum of four sets of pins per lane is usually stocked. The size of a corrugated cardboard carton of 10 pins is 9 in. deep by 16 in. by 18 in., approximately.

2. Equipment Length

The length of the bowling equipment installation is determined by using a recommended 5-ft (minimum 3-ft) clear service passage behind the lanes plus the overall length of the bowling lanes, which is 83 ft-2 in. and includes the pit, bed, and approach. To these figures, add 12 ft for bowlers' settees used with cluster subway returns or with in-line subway returns (alternate location). If in-line subway returns (standard location) or in-line surface returns are used, substitute a minimum 9-ft dimension for the 12-ft settee dimension stated above. Several examples of lane installations are provided in Figs. 4 to 7.

3. Spectator Seating

Each desired row of straight spectator seating requires a minimum of 3 ft-6 in.

If the new tables and ball racks are to be

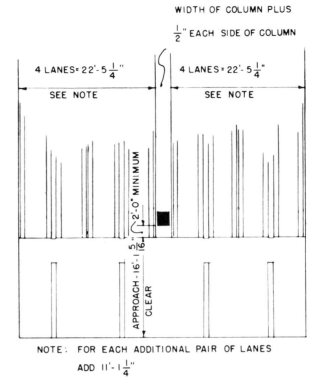

WIDTH OF COLUMN PLUS $\frac{1}{2}$" EACH SIDE OF COLUMN

4 LANES = 22'-5 $\frac{1}{4}$" SEE NOTE

4 LANES = 22'-5 $\frac{1}{4}$" SEE NOTE

2'-0" MINIMUM

APPROACH-16'-1 $\frac{5}{16}$" CLEAR

NOTE: FOR EACH ADDITIONAL PAIR OF LANES ADD 11'-1 $\frac{1}{4}$"

Fig. 3 Column spacing illustration.

incorporated behind or in place of the spectator seating, check carefully with your sales engineer regarding the suggested layouts for this equipment. Concourse tables and chairs can help convert the spectator audience into an income producing audience.

4. Concourse

The concourse or promenade, which is in back of the spectator seating, may vary in width. The clear width of the concourse should be ample to accommodate at least a peak load of 10 people per lane, and its maximum width is at the milling area, generally centered around the control counter, check rooms, and entrance lobby. The peak traffic load is usually experienced at changeover time when more than one league is in the house. Vending machines, ball cleaners, etc., are frequently located on the concourse. Adequate wall area or other provision should be considered for bulletin boards, league standing score sheets, and other announcement boards. Unless house ball storage racks are considered with spectator seating as outlined under "Spectator Seating," it will be necessary to consider this factor on the concourse.

5. Variables—Companion Accommodations

The design of the companion accommodations includes such items as the following.

Cocktail bar	Billiard room
Liquor bar	Nursery
Snack bar	Office
Precooler	Checkroom
Game room	Control
Toilets	Heating-humidity
Locker rooms	control and air-
Lounges and powder	conditioning equip-
rooms	ment
Janitor's closet	Quick service bar
Pay phones	Retail sports shop
Meeting rooms	

The control desk, the bar, snack bar, checkroom, and shoe rental must be proportioned to capacity conditions in the lanes and should be easily accessible from any part of the lanes.

Normally, a full-scale restaurant is not considered a profitable adjunct to bowling. There are exceptions, however, to disprove this rule.

All air-conditioning equipment need not be placed within the building. Often some of this equipment is placed alongside of, or on the roof of, the front end of the building in an area where space is not so valuable.

All of the foregoing are ideally placed behind the concourse, although they may be placed alongside the lanes, if necessary—provided care is taken to eliminate the hazard of distraction to the bowlers (Fig. 8).

Control The control complex is the functional heart of the entire bowling operation and sets the character of the house. Since the control is constructed by the owner or his builder, it varies with each house in size, decor, and location (Fig. 9). The following things are constant in all control counters:

1. It is the point where management greets and serves its customers. Therefore, it should be located prominently and should be well defined and lighted. From it, the operator should be able to supervise main exits and entrances, as well as the bowling lane area.

2. Since the control counter attendant assigns lanes to the public, it should contain necessary switching equipment to activate the bowling equipment and house lights over the bowling area.

3. To facilitate internal communications with patrons, the control counter also contains the public address equipment, which may be also connected with music. Intercom or phone facilities to the office, pits, or other areas of the building are also located here. A public telephone for receiving reservations or phoned messages for the house or its patrons should be included, but patrons should not be permit-

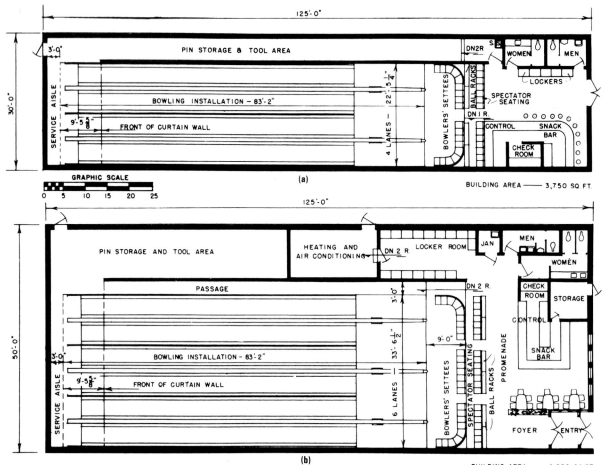

Fig. 4   (a) 4-lane installation, in-line surface ball returns. (b) 6-lane installation, in-line surface ball returns.

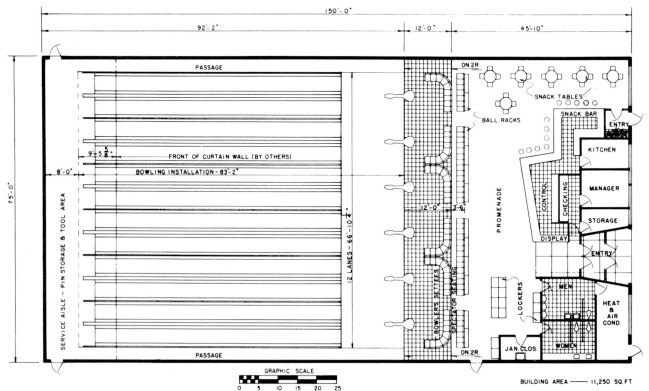

Fig. 5   12-lane installation, cluster ball returns.

ted to use this phone to conduct lengthy conversations. They are instructed to use pay phones provided for that purpose.

4. The control issues score sheets, which are collected at the end of the play. The tally of these sheets must correspond with the bowling revenue collected. For this reason, storage space for new and used bowling score sheets and a cash register are required.

5. Depending on the selected operating procedure of the installation, rental bowling shoes may be issued at the control desk directly to the customer, or a receipt may be issued to the customer at the control desk for rental shoes to be procured at the checkroom or pro shop or the house ball storage room. In the event the control counter will issue the shoes, sufficient storage space for these shoes must be provided. This space should be ventilated and so designed as to prevent the accumulation of dust and dirt. A shoe sanitizer is needed. Shoes should be kept within easy reach of the attendant.

6. Many proprietors use the control counter to help display resale items, such as balls, bags, and shoes. They also dispense such bowler's aids as ball cleaning fluid, bowling sox, grip aids, etc. These items should be displayed within sight but not within reach of the customer. In larger establishments, retail sales of bowler's equipment and supplies are often handled at a pro shop where these items, together with bowling apparel and trophies, are stocked. The merits of this decentralization must depend on each individual installation.

7. Control area should be able to observe billiard activity and have easy access to bar and/or snack restaurant area. This provides maximum utilization of personnel in slow periods of play to keep payroll at a minimum.

Billiards In many areas of the country, the companion use of billiards in bowling establishments has proved to be an extremely lucrative addition to the business. Some communities have distinct ordinances governing public billiard rooms. On an ever widening scope, the billiard room is being planned as a semi-

open area off the concourse and within easy control of the bowling control desk, which issues the playing balls (including the cue ball and chalk) in plastic racks. The customer is obliged, then, to return the full set of balls when play is completed or forfeit his deposit paid earlier (Fig. 10).

Adequate player seating is a must. Generally, a minimum of two seats per table is provided. Sand urns for cigarettes are also needed—ash trays get lost. Cocktail tables for soft drinks and sandwiches may also be provided.

Frequently, small groups of tables are sectioned off by screen-type dividers within the room. This requires considerably more space, although it affords a luxurious air of semi-privacy. Care must be taken to see that visual control is still maintained.

A small space will be required for repair of cues and general billiard storage.

Normally, three cushion or carom or snooker tables are isolated from pocket billiard tables.

A minimum of 57 in. for cue clearance is

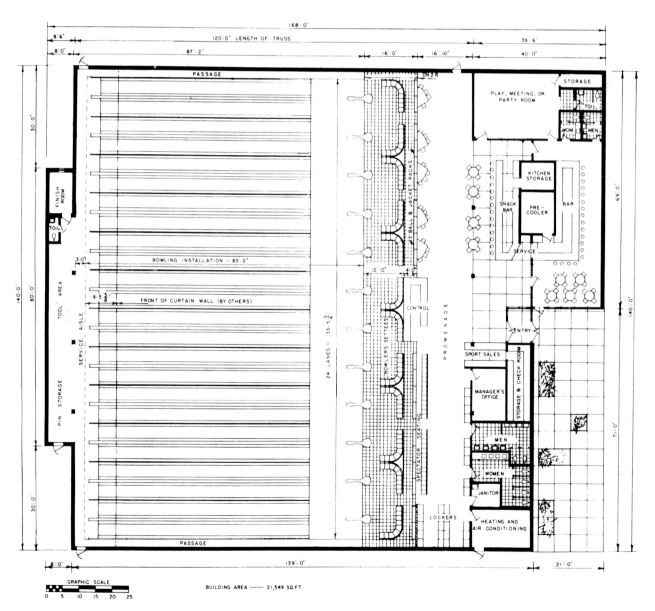

Fig. 6 24-lane installation, cluster ball returns.

BOWLING ALLEYS

needed between the table rail and any obstruction over 30 in. high.

The rooms generally have floors of vinyl asbestos tile or carpet. Carpet wears out three times as fast; vinyl tile or vinyl asbestos is *recommended*.

Lighting of 50 to 75 footcandles of even intensity on the entire playing surface, which is 30 in. above the floor, is usually accomplished with flush ceiling-mounted-type fixtures centered over each table or with a complete luminous ceiling to eliminate shadows on the tables. Light sources should be shielded with louvers.

Walls are light colored, decorative, and resistant to scuffing and soiling. Vinyl-coated products are frequently used for wall covering.

Meeting Rooms and Nurseries Meeting rooms and nurseries are often combined to perform a dual purpose. In this respect, it is necessary to survey the potential use of each function to ascertain that schedules will not coincide or overlap. Meeting rooms generally require storage closet and toilet facilities, food and beverage service, secondary egress, motion picture machine outlet and screen.

Nurseries require storage closet and toilet facilities, drinking fountain, and secondary egress (may be to an enclosed exterior play yard).

General lighting should be no less than 50 footcandles of even illumination.

In some areas, the word *nursery* implies the use of a registered or practical nurse. Therefore, the word is often changed to *children's playroom or toddlers' room*.

Locker Rooms The locker room is for ball storage cabinets only.

Normally, separate locker rooms are provided for male and female patrons. These are generally located in conjunction with the main bank of toilet facilities, and it is advantageous to plan access to the toilets through the locker rooms. This continuous traffic through a locker room is a deterrent to loiterers and malefactors. A bench for changing shoes is needed. In the case of women's locker rooms, this area often encompasses the powder bar area and lounge.

In some areas, particularly the west and southwest, the locker room is a combined area open to the concourse and accommodates both sexes. The popularity of this arrangement is growing rapidly since it conserves space and provides for family use of one facility.

The locker room usually has a vinyl asbestos tile, ceramic tile, or terrazzo floor for easy cleaning. The room should be well lighted and ventilated. Since the ball storage cabinet units stand 6 ft tall against the walls, no particular wall treatment except paint is needed. In many

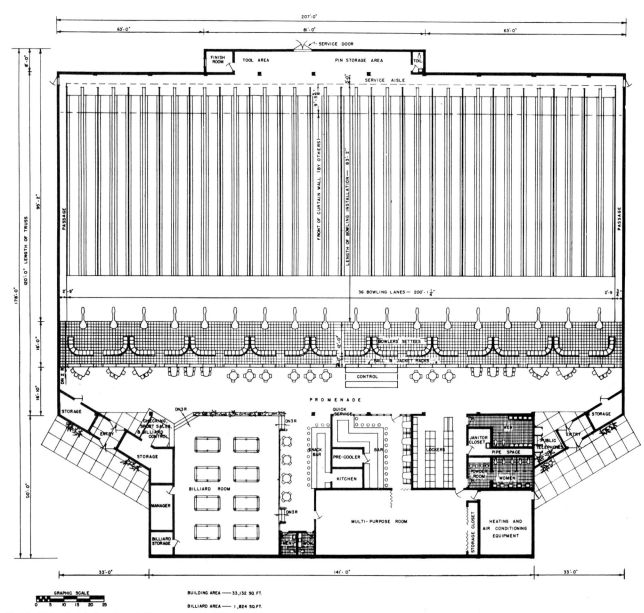

Fig. 7   36-lane installation, cluster ball returns; 8-table billiard room.

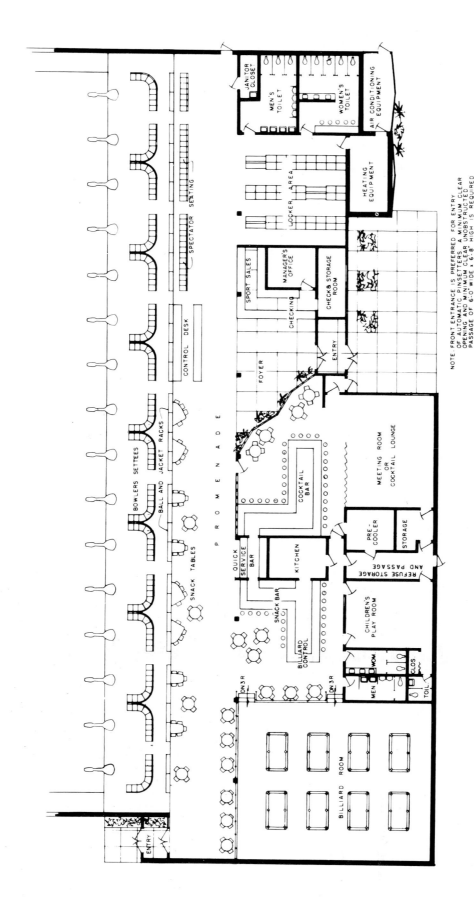

NOTE: FRONT ENTRANCE IS PREFERRED FOR ENTRY OF AUTOMATIC PINSETTERS. A MINIMUM CLEAR OPENING AND MINIMUM CLEAR UNOBSTRUCTED PASSAGE OF 6'-0 WIDE x 6'-8' HIGH IS REQUIRED

Fig. 8 Area of public occupancy.

Recreation and Entertainment

BOWLING ALLEYS

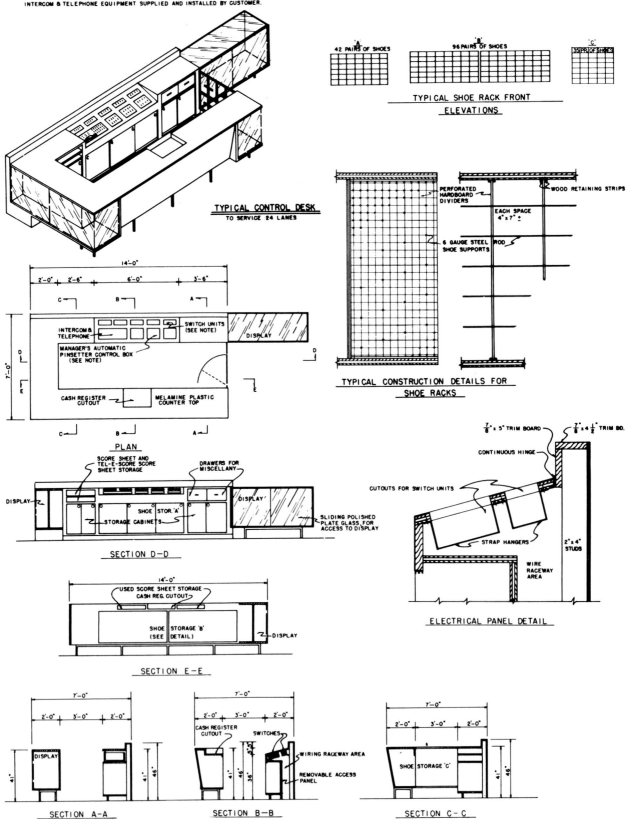

NOTE: MANAGER'S AUTOMATIC PINSETTER CONTROL BOX (LOW VOLTAGE) ONE PER EVERY EIGHT LANES. 11" WIDE x $8\frac{3}{4}$" LONG x $4\frac{3}{4}$" DEEP. SUPPLIED BY BRUNSWICK – INSTALLED BY CUSTOMER. CONTROL SWITCH UNITS FOR TEL-E-SCORE, TEL-E-FOUL, MASKING UNIT LIGHTS, APPROACH & LANE LIGHTING, EXTERIOR SIGNS ETC., TO BE SUPPLIED AND INSTALLED BY CUSTOMER. INTERCOM & TELEPHONE EQUIPMENT SUPPLIED AND INSTALLED BY CUSTOMER.

TYPICAL CONTROL DESK
TO SERVICE 24 LANES

TYPICAL SHOE RACK FRONT ELEVATIONS

TYPICAL CONSTRUCTION DETAILS FOR SHOE RACKS

PLAN

SECTION D–D

SECTION E–E

ELECTRICAL PANEL DETAIL

SECTION A–A

SECTION B–B

SECTION C–C

Fig. 9   Typical control desk.

1264

cases, open locker rooms use carpeted floors instead of tile or terrazzo.

Washrooms Public toilets are areas of heavy traffic and require constant cleaning. Since they receive constant inspection by the public, they must be kept immaculate.

The entry to any public toilet must be screened to ensure privacy.

In some areas, the law requires a couch or lounge in public rest rooms for ladies. Mirrors are required in all rest rooms.

Janitor's Closet The janitor's closet should contain a slop sink and storage area for general cleaning supplies and vacuum as well as floor polishers, lane dusters, gutter mops, lane maintenance machines, etc.

It should be located close to the front of the lanes, usually off the concourse, and should be ventilated to the outside.

An adequate size janitor's closet, minimum 4 by 6 ft; 6 by 8 ft preferred, is an asset to maintenance.

Manager's Office Most establishments of 16 lanes or over, and many smaller installations, provide an office facility. It is used by the manager and bookkeeper to perform necessary routine clerical duties such as material ordering and record keeping. The office should be under the supervision of the control, checkroom, or pro shop.

The office should be well lighted, 75 to 100 footcandles. A private toilet facility for the office is not normally provided; if public toilets are not clean enough for the manager, they are not suitable for the customer.

Snack Bars Generally, the snack bar is the only food-handling facility in the bowling establishment.

Except in circumstances that show complete justification, a complete restaurant operation is not recommended, since experience shows that a restaurant operation normally does not show profit on the same scale per square foot as the other functions in the building. The exceptions to this rule might be local areas where the restaurant is required for a

bar or liquor license, or local areas where the success of such a restaurant is assured independently of the bowling trade.

In any food-handling operation, the keynote to success is experience in the business. Such experience will point the way to efficient layout of space and equipment.

As a rule, snack bars should be brightly illuminated and decorated in lively, bright colors conducive to food consumption. Maintenance of walls and ceilings, as well as floors, counters, and equipment, is of prime importance; and the careful selection of these materials is mandatory.

Air conditioning and exhaust of cooking odors require very careful planning.

Automatic fire extinguishing systems should be installed over grills and deep-fat fryers and in hood and duct assembly. This will provide maximum safety.

Bars and Cocktail Lounges In the majority of installations, the bowling center bar (or bars) functions for the convenience of bowlers and is not intended to rely on street traffic as a normal tavern must.

The location of the bar within the bowling center is of prime importance and is related to local laws, traffic flow, and drinking habits of bowlers in the local area. If bowlers usually enjoy alcoholic beverages while bowling, a simple quick-service bar may be indicated in addition to the cocktail lounge. In bowling centers too large to be serviced by a single bar, a service bar or quickie bar on the concourse can furnish soft drinks, beer, or highballs convenient for waitress service to the lanes or for consumption at the quick-service bar. Cocktails or fancy mixed drinks would be available only at the cocktail bar. Sometimes a service bar or quickie bar requires a special license.

The decor of cocktail lounges and bars runs the gamut of interior decorating. It can be as plush or as simple as the owner decides. It may have live entertainment and it may even double as a restaurant facility. Bar size and seating capacity may be governed by local or state ordinances.

Normally in planning, consideration is given

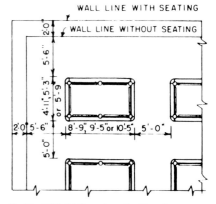

Fig. 10 Billiard table and spacing dimensions.

to some food service in the cocktail bar, if only short-order sandwiches. For this reason it is wise to locate the bar close to either the kitchen or snack bar.

Often the meeting room facility is an extension of the cocktail lounge, which can be easily screened off by use of a folding door for private functions. Toilet facilities, separate from the bowling toilets and lockers, are frequently provided for the convenience of bar patrons. Often these facilities are required by law locally.

State and municipal ordinances govern, to a large degree, the construction of walls and entrances for places where alcoholic products are sold and/or consumed.

Private "key club" operations are sometimes allowable where public bars are prohibited.

Provisions must be made for storage areas for supplies. Liquor storage should be locked. Beer requires supply storage (cases may be stacked), precooling, and an empty bottle sorting and storage area. Often a conveyor chute is used to remove empty bottles from the bar to sorting and storage areas. Easy access from the street to the storage areas is necessary for delivery of supplies.

Recreation and Entertainment

SWIMMING POOLS

Public Swimming Pools

Minimum standards prepared by the National Swimming Pool Institute

PUBLIC SWIMMING POOLS

DEFINITION AND POOL TYPES

1. All artificially constructed swimming pools other than residential pools shall be deemed to be public swimming pools. This shall not be applicable to residential pools as defined or wading or spray pools, which shall be covered under separate sections.

(a) **Private pools** which are excepted herein shall be defined as follows: "Residential swimming pools include all constructed pools which are used or intended to be used as a swimming pool in connection with a single-family residence and available only to the family of the householder and private guests."

(b) **Classifications of Pools:** For purposes of minimum standards, public swimming pools shall be defined as listed in the following categories, based upon specific characteristics of size, usage and other factors:

Type "A"—Any municipal pool, community pool, public school pool, athletic or swimming club pool.
Type "B"—Institutional pool (such as Girl Scout, Boy Scout, YMCA & YWCA, Campfire Girls and Boys' and Girls' Camps).
Type "C"—Country Club, large hotels of more than 100 units, with pools having a water surface area in excess of 1600 sq ft.
Type "D"—Motels and apartments, multiple housing units, small hotels of less than 100 units, not open to the general public and with pools having a water surface area not larger than 1600 sq ft.
Type "E"—Treatment pools, therapeutic pools and special pools for water therapy.
Type "F"—Indoor pools.
Exceptions: The above categories shall be the basis for certain specific variations from the Minimum Standards for public swimming pools as a whole.

NOTE: plans and specifications with supporting data, prepared by a professional engineer or architect holding registration in the state where pool is to be constructed, shall be, as a prerequisite, submitted to and approval obtained from said state regulator agency prior to award of any contract for equipment purchase or construction.

STRUCTURAL FEATURES, MATERIALS, MARKINGS

2. Structural Stability: All public pools shall be constructed of an inert and enduring material, designed to withstand all anticipated loading for both pool empty and pool full conditions. Working stresses shall be based upon predetermined ultimate strengths of materials used, with a factor of safety of not less than 2½.

Provision shall be made for the relief of pressures which might occur as a result of unbalanced exterior hydrostatic pressures, or means shall be provided for positive and continuous drainage from under the pool floor or around the pool walls, whether ground water is present, or might occur at some future time.

Special provisions shall be made to protect the pool structures from both internal and external stresses which may develop due to freezing in cold climates.

3. Obstructions: There shall be no obstruction extending from the wall or the floor, extending into the clear area of the diving portion of the pool. There shall be a completely unobstructed clear distance of 13 ft above the diving board.

4. Wall & Floor Finish: Wall and floor finish shall be of masonry, tile or other inert and impervious material and shall be reasonably enduring. Finish shall be moderately smooth and of a white or light color.

5. Depth Markers: Depth of water shall be plainly marked at or above the water surface on the vertical pool wall and on the edge of the deck or walk next to the pool, at maximum and minimum points

The technical data presented here gives basic requirements for public and semi-public pool design, systems and equipment. It is intended by the NSPI to serve as recommended minimum standards, and not as a model code.

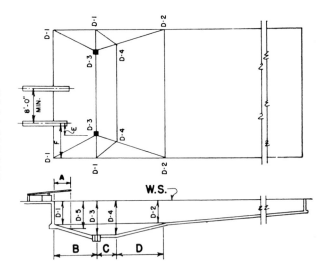

STANDS & BOARDS		Depth—Feet & Inches					Length of Section—Feet & Inches					
		D-1	D-2	D-3	D-4	D-5	A	B	C	D	E	F
3-Meter Board	Min.	5-0	4-6	10-0	9-9	8-6	5-0	*6-0	*9-0	20-0	1-0	8-0
	Max.		5-6				6-0	10-0				
1-Meter Board	Min.	5-0	4-6	8-6	8-3	7-6	5-0	*6-0	*9-0	15-0	1-0	8-0
	Max.		5-6				6-0	10-0				
Deck Level Board	Min.	5-0	4-6	8-0	7-6		2-6	†6-0	†6-0	12-0	1-0	8-0
	Max.		5-6				4-0	10-0				

As D-2 varies between min. and max., D may vary, but slope of D may not exceed 1 ft vert. to 4 ft horiz. D-1 shall be at end wall of diving area, or not more than 12 in. from it

* B & C May vary to attain 15'—0" Min.
† B & C May vary to attain total 12'—0" Min.

1266

and at the points of break between the deep and shallow portions and at intermediate increments of depth, spaced at not more than 25 ft intervals. Depth markers shall be in numerals of 4 in. min. height and of a color contrasting with background. Markers shall be on both sides and ends of the pool.

6. Lifeguard Chairs: Each public swimming pool shall have at least one elevated lifeguard chair. This shall be presumed to be adequate for 2,000 sq ft of pool surface area and one additional lifeguard chair shall be provided for each additional area of 2,000 sq ft or fraction thereof. Where a pool is provided with more than one lifeguard chair and the width is 40 ft. or more, they shall be located on each side of the pool. In Types D & E pools, lifeguard chairs need not be provided.

7. Life Line: A life line shall be provided at or near the break in grade between the shallow and deep portions of a public swimming pool, with its position marked with colored floats at not greater than 5 ft spacing. Life line shall be not less than $\frac{3}{4}$ in. min. dia.; its terminals shall be securely anchored and of corrosion-resistant material and of type which will be recessed or have no projection which will constitute a hazard.

8. Ladders: A minimum of one ladder shall be provided for each 75 ft of perimeter and not less than two ladders shall be provided at any pool. Where stairs are provided in a pool, one ladder may be deleted for each set of stairs provided. A side handrail extending up above and returning to the horizontal surface of the pool deck, curb or coping shall be provided at each side of each ladder.

All stairs entering a public pool shall be recessed. An exception to this may permit the construction of steps directly entering the pool and not recessed into the pool walls, in Types C, D, & E.

POOL DIMENSIONS, WALKS, FENCES

9. Shallow Minimum Depth: Every public swimming pool shall have a minimum depth in the shallow area of the main swimming area of not less than 3 ft, nor more than 3 ft 6 in. from the overflow level to the floor. Exceptions may be made for Types B, C, D & E pools, or in pools built principally for instruction, or in a recessed area of the main swimming pool where pool is of an irregular shape such as the leg of a T, L or Z.

10. Shallow Area: In a swimming pool with a diving area, the shallow portion of the pool shall be defined as the portion between the shallow end and the break point between the shallow area and the diving area. The slope of the floor shall be uniform from the break between the diving area and the shallow portion to the outside edge of the shallow portion and shall not be greater than 1 ft of slope in 12 ft, except in small Type B pools where the pool is less than 42 ft in overall length, in which case the rate of slope shall not exceed 1 ft in 8 ft.

11. Diving Area: The area of a public swimming pool where diving is permitted shall be, in the case of a rectangular pool, at one end, or may be in a recessed area forming one of the legs of a T, L or Z shaped pool, divorced from the main swimming area by a life line, or may be a wholly separate pool structure. Exceptions to this may be made in special-purpose type pools intended for training and instruction.

Pools of the types wherein diving is permitted shall have adequate area and depth of water for safe diving and the minimum depth and area characteristics for this area shall be as indicated in the accompanying chart.

12. Diving Towers: Diving towers in excess of 3-meters in height shall not be considered as acceptable in a public pool without special provisions, controls and definite limitations on their use.

13. Vertical Wall Depth: As a minimum, the pool walls shall be vertical at all points for a depth of not less than 2 ft 6 in.

14. Walks: Walks shall be continuous around the pool with a minimum width of 8 ft of unobstructed clear distance including a curb at the pool edge, if such a curb is used. Exceptions may be made in Types B, C, D, E, & F as follows: B—4 ft; C—4 ft; D—4 ft; E—No minimum; F—4 ft.

A minimum of a 3 ft walk width shall be provided on the sides and rear of any piece of diving equipment.

All walks, decks and terraces shall have a minimum slope of $\frac{1}{4}$ in. per foot to drains or points at which the water will have a free unobstructed flow to points of disposal at all times.

The finish texture of walks must be non-slip and such that there will be no discomfort to bare feet.

Hose bibbs shall be provided around the perimeter of the deck area at intervals such that all parts of the swimming pool deck area may be reached with a 50 ft hose.

15. Fence: A wall or other enclosure of 4 ft minimum height and with maximum 2 in. mesh, 2 in. wide vertical openings, or otherwise so constructed as to be difficult to climb, shall be provided completely enclosing the pool area, all of which shall be paved.

Exceptions may be made for Types C & D

In Types C & D where the fence is dispensed with, a hedge or other clear demarcation shall be provided, with instructions and posting clearly defining the pool area as for bathers only and from which spectators and others in street clothes are rigidly excluded.

Access to the pool by bathers shall be provided only through the bathhouse or dressing room facilities, and any other fence opening shall be for service operations only.

GUTTERS AND SKIMMERS

16. Overflow Gutters: An overflow gutter shall be installed continuous around all public swimming pools, with the exception that it may be eliminated in Types B, C, D & E. The overflow gutter may be eliminated across the top tread where steps occur.

Overflow gutter shape, wherein the outer edge of the lip is flush with the pool wall above and below and the gutter entirely recessed, shall not be permitted.

The overflow gutter depth below the overflow lip shall be a minimum of 2 in. at the high points between drains. The drains shall be spaced at a maximum of 15 ft on centers and a slope provided in the bottom of not less than $2\frac{1}{2}$ in. in 10 ft. In no sense is this intended to preclude the use of roll-out or deck level type pools where other conditions are met and satisfactory design is provided.

17. Surface Skimmers: Skimmers may be permitted in lieu of overflow gutters on swimming pools of Type B, C, D & E, providing acceptable handhold is installed. At least one skimming device shall be provided for each 800 sq ft of surface area or fraction thereof. The handhold must be no more than 9 in. above the normal water line. Skimming devices shall be built into the pool wall, and shall adequately remove floating oils and waste.

Recreation and Entertainment

SWIMMING POOLS
Public Swimming Pools

POOL POPULATION, SANITARY FACILITIES

18. Capacity of Pool in Bathers: The maximum number of persons in bathing attire within the pool enclosure or the bathing area shall be limited to one person per 20 sq ft of pool and deck area combined.

19. Bathhouse: Adequate dressing and sanitary plumbing facilities shall be provided for every public swimming pool. An exception to this may be made in Types B, C, D, E & F pools where available facilities are provided in connection with the general development for other purposes, etc., of adequate capacity and number, in close proximity to the pool.

Every bathhouse shall be provided with separate facilities for each sex with no inter-connection between the provisions for male and female. The rooms shall be well-lighted, drained, ventilated and of good construction, with impervious materials employed in general, finished in light colors and so developed and planned that good sanitation can be maintained throughout the building at all times.

(a) Minimum sanitary plumbing facilities shall be provided as follows:

Males: One water closet combination, one lavatory and one urinal shall be presumed to be adequate for the first 100 bathers.

One water closet and one urinal shall be provided for each additional 150 bathers or major fraction thereof. One lavatory shall be provided for each 200 additional bathers. A minimum of three shower heads shall be provided which shall be presumed to be adequate for the first 150 males and one shower outlet shall be provided for each additional 50 male bathers.

Females: A minimum of two water closet combinations shall be provided in each bathhouse building and this shall be presumed to be adequate for the first 100 females.

One additional water closet combination shall be provided for each additional 75 females or fraction thereof.

A minimum of two shower heads shall be provided, which shall be presumed to be adequate for the first 100 females and one shower shall be added for each 50 additional females.

One lavatory shall be provided as a minimum, which shall be considered adequate for the first 75 females. One additional

lavatory shall be provided for each additional 75 females in attendance, or major fraction thereof.

These minimum criteria for bathhouse plumbing facilities shall be based upon the anticipated maximum attendance in bathers. Facilities for either sex shall be based upon a ratio of 60% of the total number of bathers being male and 40% being female.

Shower and dressing booths shall be provided in female dressing space and dressing booths shall be provided with curtains or other means of seclusion. This condition may be subject to variation for schools and other institutional use where a pool may be open only to one sex at a time.

(b) *Drinking Fountain:* Not less than one drinking fountain shall be provided available to bathers both at the pool and in the bathhouse.

(c) *Hose Bibbs:* Hose bibbs shall be provided for flushing down the dressing rooms and bathhouse interior.

The floors of the bathhouse shall be concrete, free of joints or openings and shall be continuous throughout the area with a very slight texture to minimize slipping but which shall be relatively smooth to ensure complete cleaning. Floor drains shall be provided to ensure positive drainage of all parts of the building with a slope in the floor of not less than $\frac{1}{4}$ in. per foot, toward drains.

(d) *Hot Water:* Heated water will be provided at all shower heads. Water heater and thermostatic mixing valve shall be inaccessible to bathers and will be capable of providing 2 gpm of 90 F. water to each shower head, and no other water shall be supplied.

No differences in elevation, requiring steps, shall be provided in the interior of male and female dressing areas. No steps shall be permitted between the bathhouse and the pool deck areas adjoining and should it be necessary that the bathhouse floor be at a different elevation from the pool decks, ramps shall be provided at the access doors. Where ramps are used between the bathhouse and pool decks, the slope shall not exceed 3 in. per ft and shall be positively non-slip.

All partitions between portions of the dressing room areas, screen partitions, shower, toilet and dressing room booths shall be of durable material not subject to damage by water and shall be so designed that a water

way is provided between the partitions and floor to permit thorough cleaning of the floor area with hoses and brooms.

(e) *Soap dispensers:* Soap dispensers for providing either liquid or powdered soap shall be provided at each lavatory and between each pair of shower heads and dispensers must be of all-metal or plastic type and no glass permitted in these units.

(f) *Mirrors:* Mirrors shall be provided over each lavatory and toilet paper holders shall be provided at each water closet combination.

(g) *Water:* All water provided for drinking fountains, lavatories and showers shall be potable and meet the requirements and conform with the standards of the U. S. Public Health Service.

20. Food Service: Where provision is made for serving food and/or beverages at the pool, no containers of glass or other material which might be a hazard to bathers' feet, when broken, shall be used. The area shall be so arranged and posted to prohibit the consumption of food and beverages on the pool decks proper.

WADING POOLS

By definition, a wading pool shall normally be a small pool for non-swimming children, only, used only for wading and shall have a maximum depth at the deepest point not greater than 24 in.

Owing to the high degree of pollution likely to be present, a wading pool shall have a maximum turn-over cycle of 4 hours. The supply to the wading pool shall consist of filtered and chlorinated water from the large pool filtration and recirculation system. The circulating outlets from the wading pool may be wasted or may be returned to the circulation system of the large pool at the suction side of the pump for re-filtration. Also a waste outlet shall be provided at the deepest point of the wading pool, by means of which it shall be completely emptied to waste.

In general, standards of sanitation in circulation, surface skimming and all other details shall be equal or superior to those for swimming pools. It is considered to be very desirable to install a spray pool in lieu of a wading pool, wherein no water stands at any time but is drained away freely as it sprays over the area.

By R. JACKSON SMITH, AIA, Eggers and Higgins, Architects

DIVING POOLS

Separation of swimming and diving pools has long been common practice abroad and is an increasing trend in the United States. Diving does not require a very large pool, but it must be deep—at least 14 ft below a 10-meter platform. A swimming pool must be large in area, but it need be no more than 4 or 5 ft deep and can have a flat bottom.

Olympic requirements for diving pools are shown in the accompanying diagram and table. Minimum requirements can be met with a pool 35 by 45 ft, but a somewhat larger size, e.g., 60 by 60 ft, is usually advisable. A water-curling arrangement should be provided so that the diver can see exactly where the surface of the water is. If outdoors, the pool should be oriented so that the sun is not in the diver's eyes. Underwater observation ports are desirable.

Diving pool and platform dimensions for competitive swimming

	Board size		Ht. above water level	Distances*							
	Length	Width		A From edge of pool to end of board		B From center of board to side of pool		C From center of board to center of board		D From end of board to wall ahead	
1-meter springboard	16'	20''	3'- 3''	A-1	5'	B-1	8'	C-1	6'	D-1	25'
				7'		10'		8'		28'	
3-meter springboard	16'	20''	9'-11''	A-3	5'	B-3	12'	C-3	8'	D-3	30'
				7'		15'		10'		33'	
5-meter platform	18'	7'	16'- 5''	A-5	5'	B-5	12'	C-5	8'	D-5	35'
				7'		15'		10'		43'	
10-meter platform	20'	8'	32'-10''	A-10	5'	B-10	15'	C-10	8'	D-10	45'
	20'	10'		8'		20'		10'		52'	

Preferred dimensions appear in left-hand columns; minimum safe dimensions

SWIMMING POOLS
Diving Pools

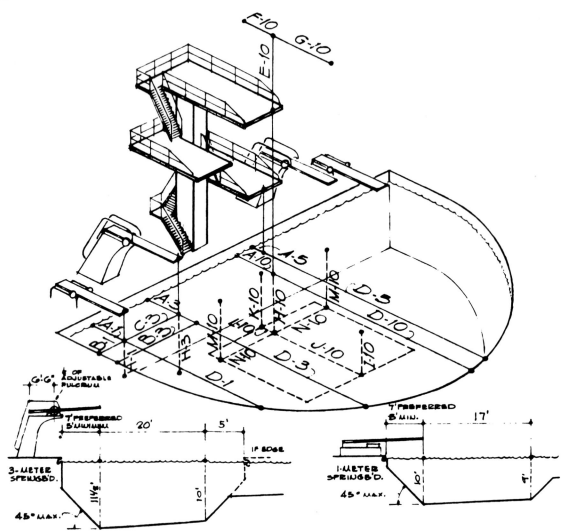

(in accordance with Olympic requirements)

	Distances*					Depths						
							In area measured from point below end of board					
E — From board to beam or ceiling above		F — Clear overhead behind board		G — Clear overhead ahead of board		H — Preferred	Min. depth	I — Depth	J — Dist. in front	K — Depth	L — Dist. in back	M — Depth	N — Dist. ba. side
E-1		F-1		G-1		H-1		I-1	J-1	K-1	L-1	M-1	N-1
	15'		5'		12'		10'						
6'				15'		11'		9'	17'	9'	3'	9'	8'
E-3		F-3		G-3		H-3		I-3	J-3	K-3	L-3	M-3	N-3
	15'		5'		12'		11½'						
6'				15'		12'		10'	20'	9'	3'	10'	10'
E-5		F-5		G-5		H-5		I-5	J-5	K-5	L-5	M-5	N-5
	15'		6'		12'		12½'						
15'		8'		15'		14'		11'	25'	9'	3'	11'	10'
E-10		F-10		G-10		H-10		I-10	J-10	K-10	L-10	M-10	N-10
	21'		6'		12'		15'						
15'		8'		15'		16'		14'	35'	10'	3'	14'	10'

appear in right-hand columns.

Minimum standards prepared by the National Swimming Pool Institute

RESIDENTIAL SWIMMING POOLS

The technical data presented here give basic requirements for residential swimming pool design, systems and equipment. It is intended by the NSPI to serve as recommended minimum standards and not as a model code.

DEFINITIONS AND NOMENCLATURE

1. Swimming Pool—Any constructed pool, used for swimming or bathing over 24 in. in depth, or with a surface area exceeding 250 sq ft.

2. Residential Swimming Pool—Any constructed pool which is used, or intended to be used, as a swimming pool in connection with a single family residence.

3. Main Outlet—The outlet(s) at the deep portion of the pool through which the main flow of water leaves the pool.

4. Main Suction—The line connecting the main outlet to the pump suction.

5. Vacuum Fitting—The fitting in the wall of the pool which is used as an outlet for connecting the underwater suction cleaning equipment.

6. Vacuum Piping—The piping which connects the vacuum fitting to the pump suction.

7. Return Piping—The piping which carries the filtered water from the filter to the pool.

8. Inlet—The fitting or opening through which water enters the pool.

9. Face Piping—The piping with all valves and fittings which is used to connect the filter system together as a unit.

10. Recirculating Piping—The piping from the pool to the filter and return to the pool, through which the water circulates.

11. Backwash Piping—The piping which extends from the backwash outlet of the filters to its terminus at the point of disposal.

12. Receptor—An approved fixture or device of such material, shape and capacity as to adequately receive the discharge from indirect waste piping, so constructed and located as to be readily cleaned.

13. Filter—Any material or apparatus by which water is clarified.

14. Underdrain—An appurtenance at the bottom of the filter to assure equal distribution of water through the filter media.

15. Filter Element—that part of a filter device which retains the filter media.

16. Recirculating Skimmer—A device connected with the pump suction used to skim the pool over a self-adjusting weir and return the water to the pool through the filter.

17. Overflow Gutter—A trough in the wall of the pool which may be used for overflow and to skim the pool surface.

18. Filter Media—The fine material which entraps the suspended particles.

19. Filter Sand—A type of filter media.

20. Filter Rock—Graded rock and gravel used to support filter sand.

21. Pool Depths—The distance between the floor of the pool and the maximum operating level when pool is in use.

22. Pool Decks—The paved area around the pool.

23. Width and Length—Shall be determined by actual water dimensions.

24. Lifeline Anchors—Rings in wall of pool at transition point between shallow and deep area.

CONSTRUCTION

The design and construction, as well as all equipment and materials, shall comply with the following requirements:

1. Structural Design—The pool structure shall be engineered and designed to withstand the expected forces to which it will be subjected.

2. Wall Slopes—To a depth of 5 ft from the top, the wall slope shall not be more than 1 ft horizontal in 5 ft vertical.

3. Floor Slopes—The slope of the floor in the shallow end shall not exceed 1 ft vertical to 7 ft horizontal. The transition point between shallow and deep water shall not be less than 4½ or more than 5 ft deep.

4. Lifeline Anchors—Provide recessed lifeline anchor in wall of pool at transition point between shallow and deep area.

5. Diving Area—Minimum depths and distances shall be as shown in table below.

DIVING AREA—MINIMUM DEPTHS AND DISTANCES

Diving Boards	Maximum Distance Above Water, in.	Minimum Depth, ft	Distance from Diving Wall, ft	Distance from Deep Point to Transition Point, ft	Minimum Overhang, ft	Minimum Width to Center of Board, ft
Deck Level	18	8	10	10	2½	7
Residential	30	8	11	11	2½	7½
1 meter	39.37	8½	12	12	3	8

SWIMMING POOLS
Residential Swimming Pools

MECHANICAL

1. Filters—Every pool shall be equipped with a recirculating system capable of filtering the entire contents of the pool in 18 hr*, or less, when the flow is calculated at a maximum of 5 gallons per minute, per square foot of filter area.

a. Filters shall be capable of maintaining the clarity of the water to permit the ready identification, through an 8 ft depth of water, of a disc 2 in. in diameter, which is divided into four quadrants in alternate colors of red and white.

b. Filter capacity shall be such that it need not be cleaned more frequently than once every four days under normal operation.

c. All filters shall be equipped with influent and offluent pressure gauges, to determine the pressure differential and frequency of cleaning.

d. All filter systems shall be equipped with an air release at the high point in the system. Each filter shall be provided with a visual means of determining when the filter has been restored to original cleanliness.

e. Operating instructions shall be posted on every filter system and all valves shall be properly designated with metal tags, indicating purpose.

2. Sand Pressure Filters—Sand filter systems shall be designed and installed to operate at a rate not to exceed 5 gallons per minute, per sq ft of filter area and to backwash at a minimum rate of 10 gallons per minute, per sq ft of surface area.

a. Filter tanks shall be fabricated to 1956 ASME Specifications for noncode pressure vessels, with the exception that standard type dished and flanged heads may be used. Tanks shall be built for a minimum of 50 pounds working pressure and tested at 150 psi. The filter underdrain shall have an effective distribution of at least 25 per cent of the cross-sectional area of the tank. Tanks placed underground shall be steel plate at least $3/16$ in. in thickness, with an approved non-corrosive exterior coating.

b. Filter tanks shall be supported in a manner to prevent tipping or settling.

3. Filter Media Specifications*
a. Filter sand shall be a hard uniformly graded, silica material with effective particle sizes, between 0.45 and 0.55 millimeters in diameter, with uniformity coefficient of 1.45 to 1.69. There shall be no limestone or clay present.

b. Filter sand shall be no less than 19 in.

Note: Standards for diatomaceous earth filters are presently being prepared by a National Committee of diatomaceous earth filter manufacturers.

in depth with a freeboard of no less than 9 in. or more than 12 in.

c. There shall be no less than four grades of rock, which shall be clean, non-crushed, rounded, non-calcareous material.

d. The total depth of the rock supporting bed shall be no less than 15 in. and each grade shall be 2 in. or greater in depth. Each layer of rock shall be leveled to prevent intermixing of adjacent grades.

e. The top layer shall vary in size between $1/8$ and $1/4$ in. The next layer shall vary in size between $1/4$ and $1/2$ in. The next layer shall vary in size between $1/2$ and $3/4$ in. The bottom layer shall vary in size between 1 and $1\frac{1}{2}$ in.

4. Recirculating Pumps—The recirculating pump shall have sufficient capacity to provide the rated flows of the filter system, without exceeding the head loss at which the pump will deliver such flows. The pump motor shall not be operated at an overload which exceeds the service factor.

a. Pool pump shall be equipped on the inlet side with an approved type hair and lint strainer. The basket of the strainer shall be non-corrosive and have an open screen surface of at least four times the cross sectional area of the inlet pipe.

5. Pool Piping—Shall be sized to permit the rated flows for filtering and cleaning without exceeding the maximum head, at which the pump will provide such flows. In general, the water velocity in the pool piping should not exceed 10 ft per second. Where velocity exceeds 10 ft per second, summary calculations should be provided to show that rated flows are possible with the pump and piping provided. The recirculating piping and fittings shall meet the following requirements:

a. The vacuum fitting(s) shall be in an accessible position(s) below water line.

b. A main outlet shall be placed at the deepest point in every pool for recirculating and emptying the pool.

c. Pool recirculation piping, passing through the pool structure, shall be copper tubing (with a minimum wall thickness of Type "L") brass or an approved equal.

d. Filtered water inlets shall be provided in sufficient quantity and shall be properly spaced to provide a maximum circulation of the main body and surface of water.

6. Valves—Fullway valves shall be installed throughout, to insure proper functioning of the filtration and piping system.

a. A valve shall be installed on the main suction line located in an accessible place outside the walls of the pool.

b. Valves up to, and including 2 in. in size

shall be brass. Sizes over 2 in. may have cast-iron or brass bodies. All working parts of valves shall be non-corrosive material.

c. Combination valves may be installed if the materials and design comply with the intent of these standards.

7. Tests—All pool piping shall be in compliance with these standards and the installation and construction of the pool piping system in accordance with the approved plans. The entire pool piping system shall be tested with a water test of 50 psi and proved tight before covering or concealing.

WATER SUPPLY AND TREATMENT

The potable water supply to any swimming pool shall be installed as required in AWWA Standards.

a. Unless an approved type of filling system is installed, such as is required by AWWA, any source of water which may be used to fill the pool shall be equipped with backflow protection.

b. No over the rim fill spout will be accepted unless located under a diving board or installed in a manner approved by local authorities so as to remove any hazard.

GENERAL

Wherever building regulations are established, generally the requirements are similar to those listed below.

a. Before commencing the installation of any swimming pool, a permit authorizing such work shall be obtained from the building department.

b. Application for permits shall be accompanied by plans and calculations in duplicate or triplicate and in sufficient detail showing the following:

1. Plot plan, elevations with dimensions all drawn to scale.
2. Pool dimensions, depths and volume in gallons.
3. Type and size of filter systems, filtration and backwash capacities.
4. Pool piping layout, with all pipe sizes and valves shown, and types of materials to be used.
5. The rated capacity and head at filtration and backwash flows of the pool pump in gpm with the size and type of motor.
6. Location and type of waste disposal system.
7. Structural, calculations and details prepared and signed by a registered engineer.

c. Set Back—Swimming pools shall be classified as accessory structures and conform to setbacks as required for such structures in local building codes.

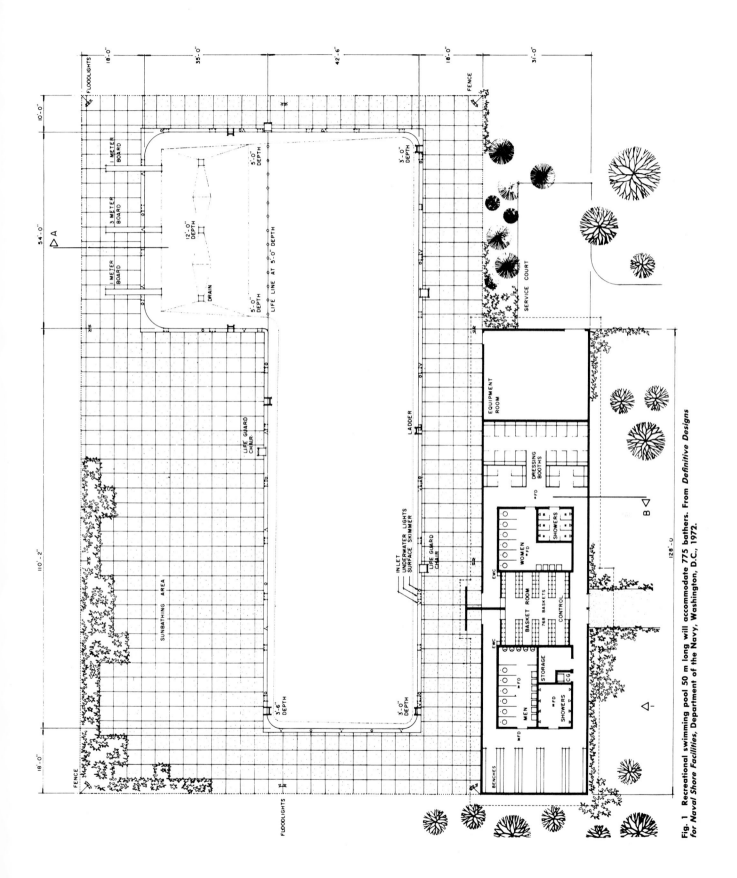

Fig. 1 Recreational swimming pool 50 m long will accommodate 775 bathers. From *Definitive Designs for Naval Shore Facilities*, Department of the Navy, Washington, D.C., 1972.

SWIMMING POOLS
25-Meter Recreational Pool

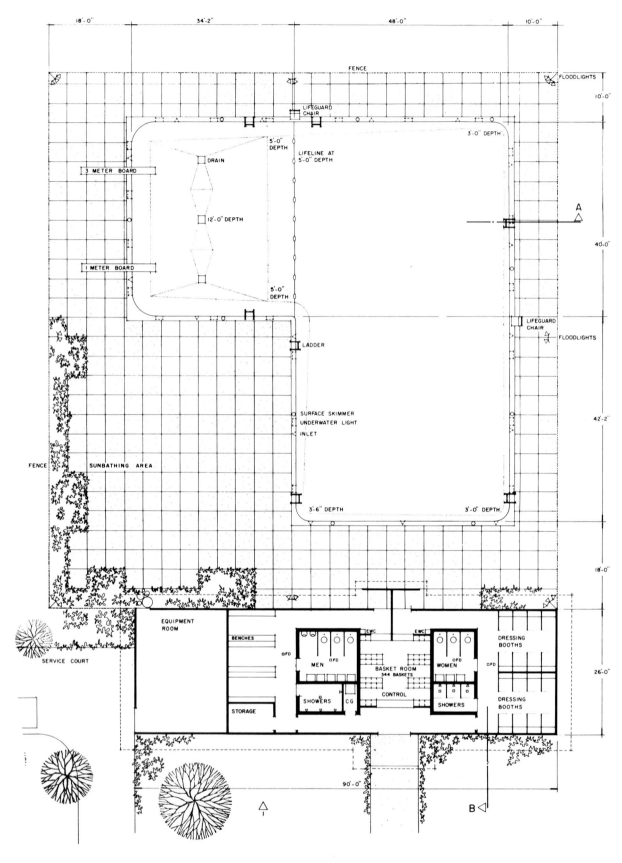

Fig. 2 Recreational swimming pool 25 m long will accommodate 340 bathers. From *Definitive Designs for Naval Shore Facilities*, Department of the Navy, Washington, D.C., 1972.

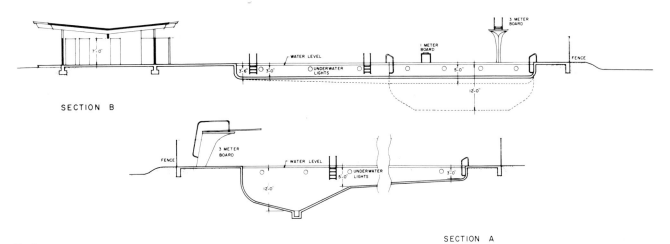

SECTION B

SECTION A
SCALE 1/8" = 1'-0"

Fig. 3

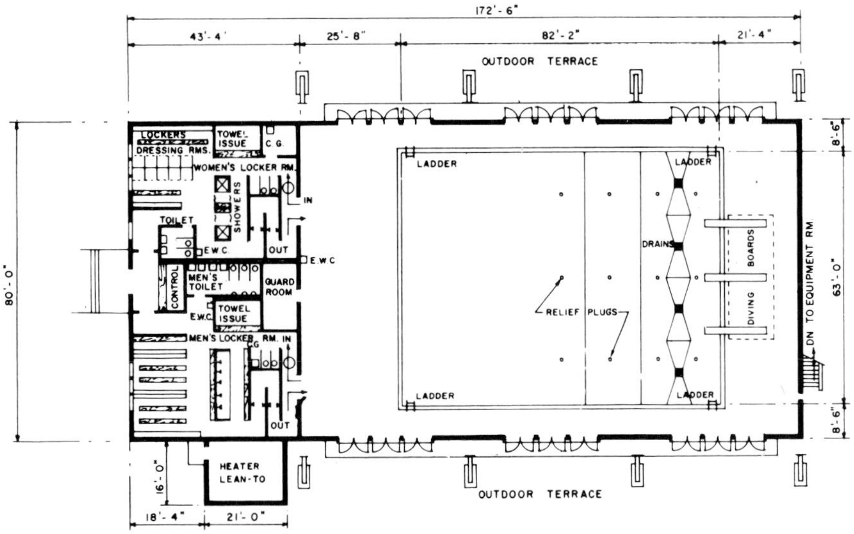

PLAN 25 METERS

Fig. 4. Twenty-five-meter pool.

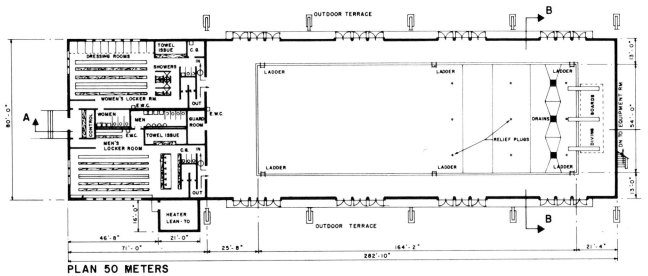

PLAN 50 METERS

Fig. 5 Fifty-meter pool.

Figures 3–9 from *Definitive Designs for Naval Shore Facilities,* Department of the Navy, Washington, D.C., 1972.

SWIMMING POOLS
25- and 50-Meter Indoor Pools

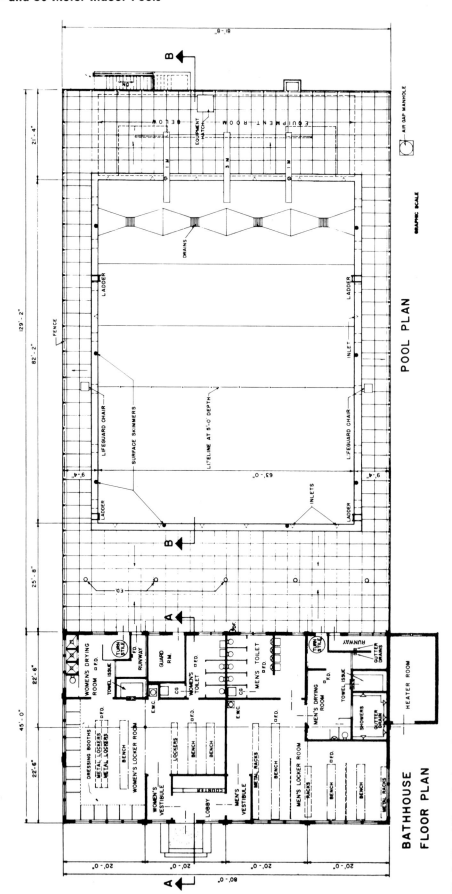

Fig. 6 Plan of 25-m swimming pool.

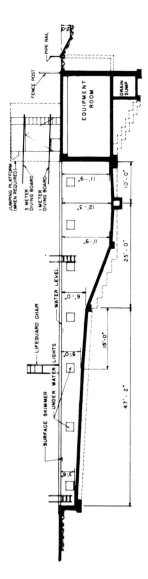

Fig. 7 Section B-B of 25-m pool in Fig. 6.

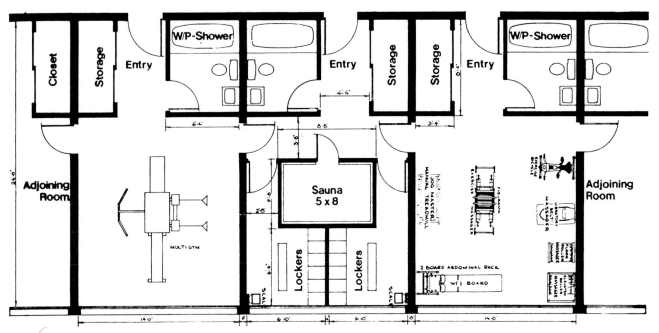

Fig. 1 Deluxe alternate facility.

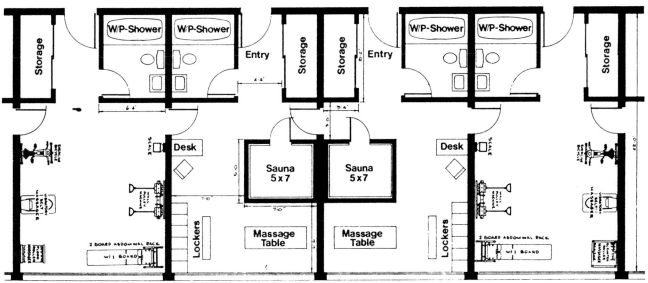

Fig. 2

Recreation and Entertainment
LOCKER ROOMS

Based on information from "A Guide for Planning Facilities for Recreation, Physical & Health Education," published by The Athletic Institute, Inc., for the National Facilities Conference.

LOCKER ROOMS

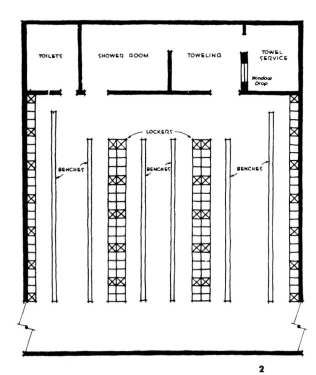

2

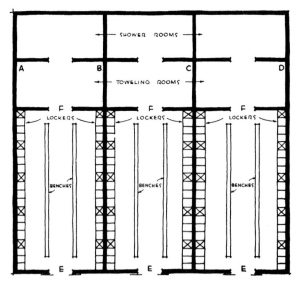

1

These plans show three dressing-locker room arrangements, each with its own particular advantages. Dressing lockers are marked with X's. Plan 1: storage lockers are grouped in small space for economy in drying uniforms with forced warm air; some congestion may result from dressing lockers being next to one another. Plan 2: distributing dressing lockers over entire area gives each participant ample dressing space. Plan 3: dressing lockers distributed over entire suite; units can be installed in any number desired and lend themselves to group dressing method for girls. By constructing walls A, B, C and D, putting a grille to ceiling above locker tiers and installing grille sliding doors at E, each unit becomes a complete dressing room for community use. Walls A, B, C and D can be omitted and gates F added to get same use and permit towel service and toilet units to be installed at points A and D

3

DESIGN NOTES

Dressing-Locker Room. An average of 14 sq. ft. per pupil in the designed peak load should be provided exclusive of the locker space so there will be adequate dressing area. Check list: sufficient mirrors, built-in drinking fountain and cuspidor in boys' dressing room, tack board.

Storage Lockers. Each pupil enrolled should have a storage locker, with an additional 10 per cent to allow for expansion. Recommended sizes, in order of preference are: $7\frac{1}{2}$ by 12 by 24 in., 6 by 12 by 36 in., $7\frac{1}{2}$ by 12 by 8 in. These were selected as being the minimum size lockers to store ordinary gym costumes and allow free hanging for ventilation.

Dressing Lockers. Lockers large enough to accommodate street clothes should be provided. The number should equal the peak load plus 10

per cent. Lockers 12 by 12 by 72 in. are recommended for secondary schools and 12 by 12 by 54 in. or 12 by 12 by 48 in. for elementary schools.

Shower Room. In the group or gang type shower, the girls should have a number of shower heads equal to

40 per cent of the designed peak load; for boys 30 per cent.

Shower heads should be at least 4 ft. apart, of a non-clogging type; height of spray should be adjustable by use of a lock. If stationary heads are installed, they should be placed

1278

so that the top of the spray will be shoulder height (usually $4\frac{1}{2}$ to 5 ft.).

One to three individual shower booths, 3 by $3\frac{1}{2}$ ft., should be provided additionally for girls.

For boys, if walk-way or walk-around shower system is desired, the number of shower heads in the shower room can be reduced by one-third. In the walk-way, spray outlets attached to the water pipe must be focused to provide coverage from shoulder height to feet. There must be a continuous spray the length of the walk-way arranged so that there will be warm, tepid and cool water as one progresses along the walk-way. The walk-way should be arranged in U shape with a total length at least 35 ft. and from 3 to 4 ft. in width. An entrance from the group shower soaping space and egress to the toweling room and swimming pool should be provided.

Both individual and master control should be provided for all groups or gang showers. The booth showers should have individual control; the walk-way only master control.

Toweling Room. The toweling room should have the same total area as the shower room and be immediately accessible to both showers and dressing room.

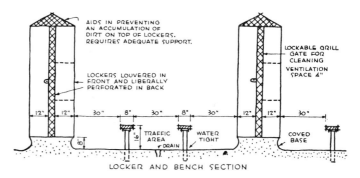

LOCKER AND BENCH SECTION

Suggested locker and bench installation

When locker height is kept down to 54 in., entire room can be supervised. Sloping locker top cannot be used, but 4 in. ventilating space should be louvered.

A ledge 18 in. high and 8 in. wide coved at wall and base, with bull nose edge, as foot drying aid is desirable.

If towel distribution is such that hanging of towels in drying room is necessary, a 1-in., non-corrosive towel bar 4 ft. from the floor and 1 to $1\frac{1}{2}$ in. from the wall is recommended.

A non-shatterable, transparent panel for supervision of toweling between the toweling and dressing room may be desired.

Towel Service and Storage Room. Adjustable shelves in sufficient number to accommodate the load are

required. A check-out window should open into or be immediately adjacent to the toweling room. If uniforms are distributed from here, a dutch door or check-out window, with counter, should open into the dressing room.

Toilet Room. Facilities should be provided in proportion to the peak load on the following basis:

Toilets	Girls	1–30	Min.	3
Toilets	Boys	1–50	Min.	2
Urinals	Boys	1–25	Min.	2
Lavatories	Girls and Boys	1–20	Min.	3

Typical combined storage-dressing locker arrangements

Area of the dressing-locker room suite required for different types of storage and dressing lockers in a typical unit for 240 girls or boys. Proportionate adjustments to be made for varying school enrollments.

Class Periods Per Day	Size of lockers and Battery Arrangement	Typical Installation	Overall height with base	Number students per day	Peak load per period	Area Required, sq. ft.	Recommendation *
six	6—storage 7½ x 12 x 24″ 1—dressing 12 x 12 x 48″ or 6—storage 7½ x 12 x 24″ 1—dressing 12 x 12 x 72″		54″ or 80″	240	40	114.80 or 90.0	1 a. grades 1–12 b. grades 9–12
six	6—storage 6 x 12 x 36″ 1—dressing 12 x 12 x 72″		80″	240	40	100.0	3 grades 10–12 only
six	6—storage 7½ x 12 x 18″ 1—dressing 12 x 12 x 54″		62″	240	40	90.0	2 grades 1–12
eight	8—storage 7½ x 12 x 18″ 1—dressing 12 x 12 x 72″		80″	240	30	67.50	2 grades 9–12
eight	8—storage 7½ x 12 x 24″ 1—dressing 12 x 12 x 48″		54″	240	30	105.0	1 grades 1–12

Numbered in order of Preference

BATHHOUSES

Information in this section was prepared by Ronald Allwork from data assembled by the Portland Cement Association; Joint Committee on Bathing Places, American Public Health Ass'n.; Conference of State Sanitary Engineers.

General. Capacity and operation of the bathhouse must be such as to avoid overcrowding at times of maximum demand; however, it is better to have an overcrowded condition a few times a year rather than to have facilities so large as to be uneconomical.

Location of bathhouse depends partly on size of pool and space available. When possible, bathhouse should be placed so as to protect pool from prevailing winds. A location at one side of the pool, or better still, at the shallow end, will reduce the danger of poor swimmers and children falling or jumping into deep water.

Size of bathhouse and selection of equipment, in relation to pool size depend on such factors as the need for: lockers, or central checking system; individual dressing rooms, or the "dormitory" system; private or group showers; and extra facilities. If patrons are permitted to use their own suits, some will come ready to swim, and dressing and check rooms may be small. But since all bathers should be required to take a cleansing shower, the number of showers needed will remain the same.

Area of bathhouse is usually 1/3 of pool area; area of dressing room approximates 1/5 pool area. It is recommended that bathhouse facilities, based on the number of bathers present at any one time (2/3 of whom may be assumed to be men), be provided as follows:

> 1 shower for each 40 bathers
> 1 lavatory for each 60 bathers
> 1 toilet for each 40 women
> 1 toilet for each 60 men
> 1 urinal for each 60 men

For rough estimate of maximum number of persons within a pool enclosure (pool and walks) assume one person for every 12 sq. ft. of pool area. Hence for a pool 30 x 75 ft., assume 190 persons.

Elements of a bathhouse vary with local requirements, but usually include: entrance lobby, ticket or cashier's booth, concessions, manager's office, public telephones, checking room, suit and towel room, dressing rooms, toilets, showers, first aid room, guard's or attendant's room, mechanical equipment, storage space, etc.

Dressing rooms. Method of checking clothes must be decided before the layout can be determined, as the method chosen affects the entire arrangement. Both individual lockers and central check rooms have been used successfully. Choice depends mainly on local conditions. A combination of the two systems may become the most desirable, since obviously requirements for a well-dressed adult and for a boy in play clothes are not the same. Lockers should be placed on a raised platform to keep them dry and to simplify floor cleaning. Lockers require most space, but tend to keep clothes in better condition. Individual dressing rooms must usually be provided for women and girls, whereas men and boys ordinarily dress in aisles between rows of lockers. A few individual dressing rooms are sometimes provided in men's dressing rooms.

Regardless of the system adopted, dressing and locker rooms should be arranged to admit a maximum of sunlight and air in order to maintain clean, sanitary conditions. Satisfactory results have been obtained from the "open-court" type, in which the roof is omitted over part of the dressing room area.

Toilets of the wall-hung type are recommended.

Showers may be either individual or group-controlled; some type of control, which eliminates any possibility of bathers being scalded, is essential.

There are many types of bathhouse equipment on the market which add to the convenience of the patrons and increase the popularity of the pool. Hair driers, comb-vending machines, exercisers and scales are frequently installed.

Planning of bathhouse elements should be such as to permit operation with minimum of personnel, particularly during slack periods.

Circulation. Arrange all facilities so patrons can pass through quickly, without confusion. The only route from dressing room to pool should be past toilets and shower rooms. Each bather should be required to take a thorough cleansing shower with soap before putting on bathing suit. By requiring each bather to pass through a group of showers before entering the pool a superficial bath will be obtained, but this must not be considered as replacing the required shower in the nude.

Toilets should be accessible directly from both dressing room and pool. Separate ones for "wet" and "dry" bathers are desirable. Disinfecting foot baths should be placed between pool and toilet.

Bathers returning from the pool should preferably pass through a separate drying room to the dressing room, and the "wet" and "dry" bathers should be separated as much as practical. Exit from bathhouse to street should be so arranged that an attendant may collect all keys, checks, suits or other supplies belonging to the establishment.

Construction. Resistance to deterioration and fire is especially important. The constant dampness which usually prevails is harmful to many materials and causes rapid deterioration. Therefore materials which are entirely satisfactory in ordinary buildings may not be desirable for bathhouses. Fire hazard must also be considered in selection of materials, particularly since the building is generally in an isolated location and without attendants a good portion of the year.

Bathhouses must be kept scrupulously clean by frequent washing. Construction should be such that washing with high pressure hose will not damage the building. Floors of bathhouses should be pitched 1/4" per ft. to frequent outlets to assure rapid drainage. Provide an ample number of hose connections to make cleaning easy. Connection should be not less than 1 in. to insure adequate water volume and pressure.

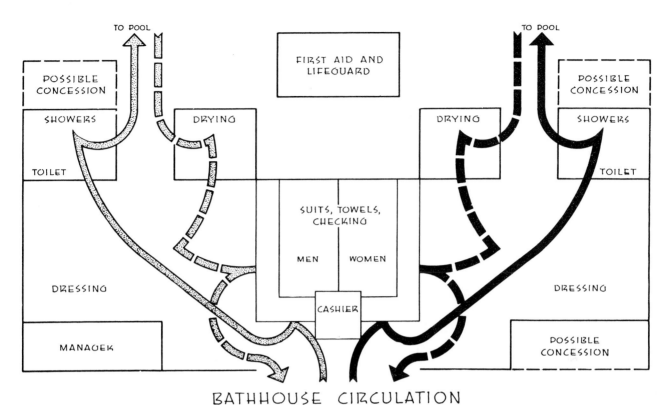

BATHHOUSE CIRCULATION

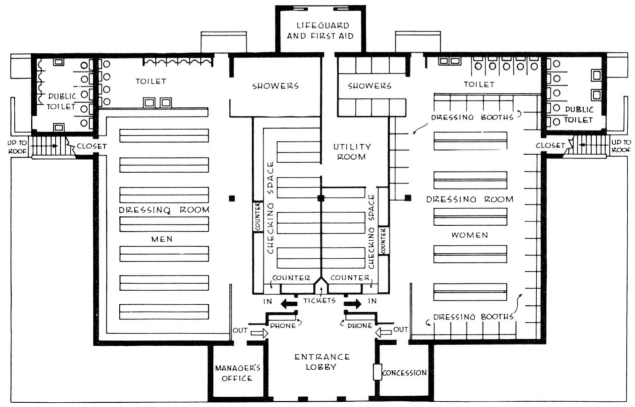

SCALE 1/16" = 1'-0"   PLAN OF TYPICAL BATHHOUSE   FOR 750 PERSON POOL

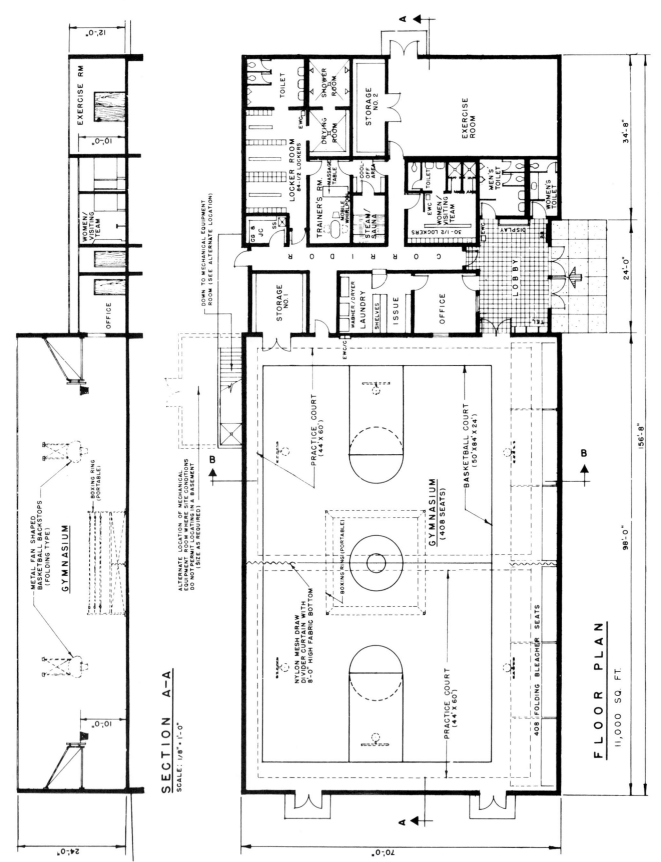

SECTION A-A
SCALE: 1/8" = 1'-0"

FLOOR PLAN
11,000 SQ. FT.

Fig. 1 Gymnasium plan and section. From *Definitive Designs for Naval Shore Facilities*, Department of the Navy, Washington, D.C., 1972.

By LAURENCE CURTIS

ZOO PLANNING

A. Display Arrangements or Themes

Introduction The categories described below are representative more of planning concepts than of existing facilities. Classification of any given zoo depends largely on its history, i.e., whether it was developed from the very beginning along a definite theme or whether it "grew like Topsy," with buildings and exhibits constructed as immediate circumstances and interests dictated. By far, the vast majority of zoos are in the latter category with very few institutions "master planned" from their inception and then built along orderly planned lines and stages of growth. It is hoped that master planning in zoos will increase.

The general present day lack of masterplanned zoos is due largely to an absence of adequate financial support at the zoo's inception. In general, most zoos attain a stage somewhat after their inception where future developmental potential is assured. It is at just such a stage that a comprehensive and overall plan for future growth and development is frequently prepared, namely a "master plan." As a result of such a history, most zoos today are in a transitional period wherein remaining elements of the "Topsy" period coexist with new stages of master-planned growth. Since a zoo is never really "finished," the typical zoo that has attained a stage of planning maturity is actually in some phase or other of its master plan development. The older a zoo, the more periods of reevaluation and master planning it generally passes through, since new ideas and new techniques of animal display are constantly being developed, altered and then discarded in response to new philosophies of zoo functions. Certainly, wherever possible and practical, a city contemplating either a new zoo or a vast remodeling of an old one should give top priority to the preparation of a master plan.

A zoo may be classified as one of the following display types according to the nature and arrangement of its exhibits; systematic, zoogeographic, habitat, behaviorial, "popular," or, most frequently, some combination of these. (See Fig. 1.)

1. Systematic Themes The arrangement of exhibits according to their taxonomic or systematic relationships; thus, all cats in one exhibit area, bears in another, hoofed animals together, etc. Historically, the earliest zoos ("menageries") were developed along this theme. From a practical standpoint of design and construction, the systematic theme allows a certain ease of daily maintenance and husbandry.

One of the distinct advantages of a systematic arrangement is the opportunity to empha-

Zoological Park Fundamentals, American Association of Zoological Parks and Aquariums, a professional branch of the National Recreation and Park Association, Washington, D.C., 1968.

size differences and similarities of related species within a single animal group. Such advantages are gained through the adjacent exhibition of related species permitting comparative viewing.

An entire zoo planned along systematic lines has been criticized as a source of "exhibit monotony." That is, when the visitor is confronted with several species in the same animal group (e.g., monkeys, bears, cats, etc.) the relative similarity in these animals tends to inhibit exhibit interest. Also, in such a display a species, which may be an outstanding exhibit by itself, may lose its attractiveness or effect when shown alongside other perhaps more spectacular members of its family group. In short, when the average visitor is confronted within a limited area with several similar animal species, he tends to be attracted to the more spectacular species often to the detriment of the others; also visitor interest declines as the number of similar animals increases until, when his saturation point is reached, he may leave an otherwise outstanding exhibit of animals for something simply "different." By breaking up such systematic exhibits (as in a zoogeographic theme) visitor interest is maintained at an optimum level with maximum exhibit diversification of similar species.

2. Zoogeographic Themes The arrangement of animal exhibits according to their geographic origin, e.g., New World, Old World, European, Asian, Eurasian, African, Australian, Australasian, Tropical American, Temperate American, Polar, Texas, etc. Thus, all of the animals in an entire zoo may be arranged zoogeographically or continentally. With such arrangements, there is practically no limit to the extent of imaginative exhibit supplements such as the use of native props from the same area as the animals, background music geographically keyed, architectural style, planting, and other exhibit features also geographically oriented. Such themes need not be worldwide in scope, but can be restricted to a given geographic area. Thus, "animals of the Southwest," "animals of Idaho," "animals of the Rocky Mountains," etc., with the concepts limited only by the imagination of the planner and available resources.

Regional zoogeographic themes would seem ideal for smaller zoos as they permit an institution with limited finances to do a small job well rather than do a big job poorly. Regional pride and expression also are important and advantageous factors in support of a regional theme.

From a practical standpoint, utilization of a local regional theme offers several inducements; ready availability of most animal species; few or no acclimational problems; generally less expensive and less complicated demands for physical structures, maintenance and operation when compared to the needs of exotic animals; and a ready availability of acclimated plants and natural exhibit props for naturalistic landscaping.

With so many apparent advantages it is diffi-

cult to understand why so few regionally oriented zoogeographic theme zoos have been built.

3 Habitat or Ecological Themes The exhibit presentation of animals selected from a given habitat has been practiced for years in public aquariums where animals (and plants) of an aquatic habitat are displayed in a single building. Thus, although an aquarium with a comprehensive exhibit may show a predominance of fishes, other representatives of the animal kingdom may also be displayed, e.g., invertebrates (sea anemones, starfish, crabs, crawfish), amphibians (frogs, toads, salamanders), aquatic reptiles (turtles, crocodilians, snakes), aquatic birds (penguins) and aquatic mammals (seals, sea lions, manatees, porpoises, walruses, and even whales). Surprisingly, although aquariums are generally associated with fish displays, the non-fish exhibits such as octopuses, seals, porpoises, large turtles, often are the most popular with the public.

The development of other habitats as theme exhibits has met with excellent public acceptance. Such habitats as "grasslands" (the popular African veldt displays, Pampas scenes, North American prairie exhibits, etc.), rain forests, subterranean exhibits (animals in burrows and cave settings), desert exhibits, etc. are forerunners of a potentially very popular and educational exhibit theme trend. In such ecologic displays naturally associated plants and animals of diverse groups (mammals, birds, reptiles, etc.) may be shown living together (or, more correctly, *apparently* together—often separated from one another by hidden barriers). Frequently, predator-prey relationships can be implied.

The educational and popularity potential of a habitat display is extremely high. It emphasizes the higher relative value of a single, large and well-executed exhibit of dozens of species and individuals as compared to a series of several dozen smaller cages each showing a single species. Depending on design, the single habitat display may involve less maintenance costs than the series of single cage units. Thus, for relatively small zoos or limited operations, adoption of a habitat theme permits maximum display for minimum budget expenditure. Due to inherent problems in such community type exhibits (competition and predation among species, plant-eaters, etc.), a small zoo should restrict itself to those designed, built and operated with a minimum of complications.

4. Behavioral Themes This relatively unexploited display area offers considerable exhibit potential. More time, research and development will undoubtedly be required before many of these display techniques are within the operational scope of the average zoo.

Typical of a behavioral exhibit theme is a nocturnal animal display where animals normally active only at night, are exhibited in darkened buildings. Special lighting is used which causes them to "reverse" their normal activity cycle, thus rendering them observable

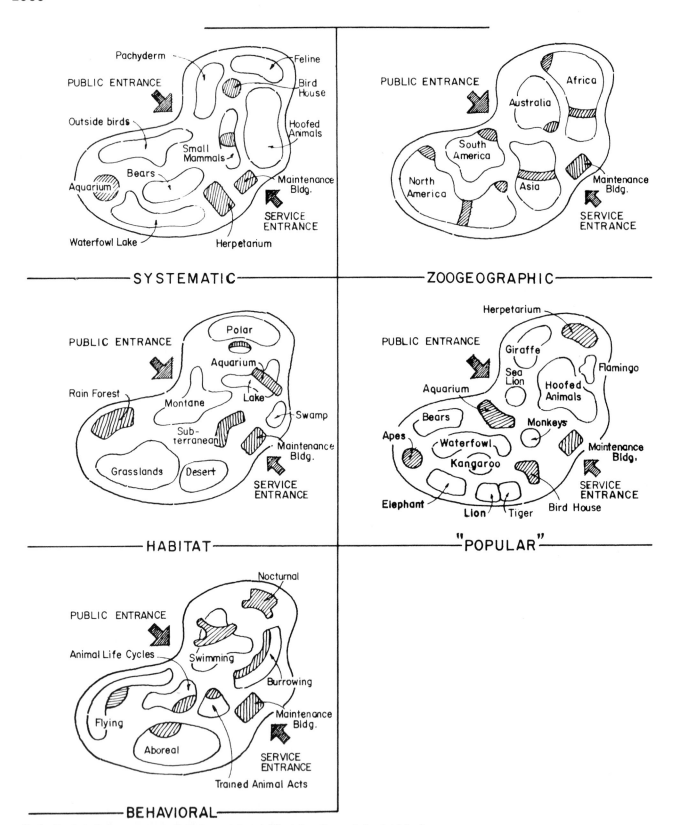

Fig. 1 Five basic display arrangements. Hatched areas indicate buildings. An entire zoo designed strictly along one display theme presents several practical problems of animal exhibit husbandry. Hence the display concept of a zoo's master plan usually involves a careful selection and combination of several themes.

by the visiting public in the daytime. In this way animals which are otherwise seen curled up asleep in the conventional "daytime" zoo exhibit are changed into active and fascinating creatures in the nocturnal display. Another example of a behavioral theme are the relatively new "automatic" trained animal acts wherein the conditioned reflex is utilized as a means of extracting certain behavior from an animal. To date these acts have been more or less limited in their application to domestic animals and a few wild species. Application of this technique to zoo exhibits holds tremendous potential for the future. Thus, in effect, zoos may exhibit not just an animal but, at the push of a button or drop of a coin, an animal going through a given sequence illustrating natural or instinctive behavior. Examples might be a raccoon removing bird eggs from a nest or a cheetah pursuing an artificial antelope.

In addition to the above, other behavioral themes which could be considered are "flying animals," "swimming animals," "burrowing animals," "climbing animals," etc. Even a comprehensive exhibit of the love life of animals—courtship, nest building, egg laying, incubation, birth, and care of offspring—has exhibit potential and stirs the imagination, perhaps in more ways than one. Depending on interpretation, the dividing line between habitat and behavioral themes may become indistinguishable.

5. "Popular" Theme Some zoos, particularly relatively small facilities, may wish simply to exhibit a limited number of animals selected and presented strictly on the basis of popular appeal rather than zoological orientation; thus the display theme would have no particular basis as regards geographic origin, systematic relationship, or such. On the basis of visitor interest, the following list might be considered a reasonably complete selection of the more popular animals generally available to zoos:

Mammals:

Giraffes	Bears
Camels	Apes
Zebras	Monkeys
Elephants	Otters
Lions	Sea lions
Tigers	Kangaroos

Birds:

Colorful, exotic, perching species	Hummingbirds
Toucans	Waterfowl (ducks, swans, and geese)
Eagles (and other birds of prey)	
Flamingos	Parrotlike birds
Penguins	Pheasants
"Giant" birds (rhea, cassowary, ostrich, emu)	

Reptiles:

Large boas and pythons	Giant tortoises
	Native snakes
Venomous snakes	Colorful reptiles
Large lizards (monitors)	Alligators and crocodiles

Exhibits and others:

Aquariums	Contact areas for children
Herpetariums (reptile and amphibian exhibits)	
	Trained sea lion shows
"Open-fronted," "walk-through," or free-flight bird displays (indoor or outdoor)	Monkey islands

Taken as a whole, selections from the above "building-block animals" would form an excellent basic collection for any small zoo. In such a plan each exhibit should be carefully selected and designed so as to achieve maximum visitor appreciation and education. Imaginativeness of display and presentation can spell the difference between a poor exhibit and an outstanding one. Compare, for example, a "caged" lion inmate in a cellblock-type enclosure to a king-of-beasts in a planted veldt and viewed across a hidden moat. Both are lions but any exhibit similarity ends there.

Also, under the heading of "popular" type themes might be included exhibits of animals that are oriented to a particular group, such as children. These exhibits are called by such names as "Children's Zoo," "Petting Zoo," "Story Book Zoo," "Mother Goose Zoo," "Junior Zoo," etc. Often nursery rhymes or children's story themes are used as the basis of such exhibits. Perhaps their main value is the presentation of an opportunity, especially to children, to hold, feed, or merely to touch an animal in safety. Thus, in these exhibits children are able to establish an especially close relationship with a live animal, a situation usually impossible in the conventional zoo. Certainly, many child-oriented zoos attract adults as well as children, and their design is frequently an adult inspiration of what children *should* be attracted to.

6. Combination Theme Obviously, unless master planned from the very beginning and along a single exhibit theme, most zoos are arranged in combinations of the above categories. Due to practical maintenance factors (animal factors as well as mechanical and architectural considerations) it is often more feasible to develop exhibits along a basic systematic theme; however, it is possible to *combine* display themes, thus gaining the multiple advantages and increasing the educational value of the displays.

For example, in a single building, a bird house (systematic theme), the individual exhibits might be grouped according to country or area of origin (zoogeographic theme). Included among the exhibits might be a rain forest or "jungle" scene consisting of birds, selected other animals and plants (habitat theme). A demonstration display of eggs incubating and hatching (a biological theme?) and a pushbutton activated trained bird demonstration of the pecking and scratching instinct (behavioral theme). Thus illustrated in a single building would be several different exhibit themes.

Utilization of various theme combinations has the further advantage of presenting the visitor with a variety of interest appeals and further reducing the possibility of exhibit monotony.

7. Zoo-Botanic Garden Combinations A most natural, logical, and financially sound arrangement is the combining of zoological and botanical gardens into a single entity. The advantages of such a combination are as follows:

a. Since zoos require landscaping, the combination operation enables the botanical aspect to serve a dual purpose.

b. In habitat and zoogeographic theme exhibits, the use of landscape materials appropriate to the animal's place of origin adds further to the educational and esthetic value of the display.

c. In nature, animals and plants are not separated systems but closely interrelated and interdependent upon one another. Such is the basis for the science of ecology. Separation of the two groups exhibitionally is thus an unnatural and generally unfortunate division.

d. Both zoological and botanical gardens have essentially the same basic purposes as reasons for their existence. Hence separate operations involve overlap of functions and subsequent fiscal overlap.

Possible disadvantages of combined zoological botanical exhibits might exist where separate facilities are desired so as to reduce visitor concentration in a single area.

GROUNDS

Specific features of the grounds, features which are not considered as part of the animal exhibits or maintenance structures, are discussed here.

A. Parking Areas

Adequate parking facilities should be planned to accommodate the average periods of maximum visitation. Various indices are available to planning engineers by which the estimated number of parking spaces needed to accommodate such periods can be determined. It is perhaps questionable to attempt to provide adequate space at a zoo to accommodate the two or three peak days of the year, which are generally the fourth of July and Labor Day.

B. Entrance

Generally, a combination entrance and exit for the public is most practical and preferable. Obviously, the fewer entrances and exits, the better the grounds security and visitor control. A single entrance-exit centrally located is optimum. Turnstiles with counters afford actual attendance checks which are always of interest in measuring the popularity of the zoo, evaluating peak loads, etc. Dogproof turnstiles are available and have special value since pet animals of any kind should be prohibited from zoos for reasons of animal health and safety. A separate entrance and exit for service vehicles should be available and as far removed from the visitor entrance as possible.

C. Landscaping

Proper horticultural treatment of the zoo grounds adds tremendously to the naturalistic and esthetic setting. Selection of plants of course is generally a function of local conditions of soil, climate, topography, as well as available irrigation facilities. As discussed above, continental plantings can be imaginatively incorporated into continentally oriented exhibits plans. Floral displays add color to the grounds and especially fragrant plantings provide a pleasant atmosphere. If plant species are labeled, then the zoo functions as a botanical exhibit as well.

D. Animal Sculpture

Zoos are ideal settings for sculpture gardens, especially animal sculpture. Many zoos locate specific pieces of animal art in association with live exhibits of the same animal. Correlation of the arts with zoo display is another example of the modern multipurpose zoo. Models and restorations of prehistoric animals also are appropriate for zoos, especially when integrated into exhibit areas of their living relatives.

E. Miscellaneous

Several items are considered here:

1. Walks Adequate sized walks of concrete, asphalt, or similar low-maintenance and permanent materials should be used. Nonskid walks should be provided wherever grades indicate. Zoo visitors frequently have their interest (and eyes) on exhibits rather than where they are walking and hence grounds planning should be especially safety oriented. Steps should be avoided wherever possible for the same reason. Low-incline ramps should be substituted wherever possible. Such planning also facilitates visitors with wheelchairs, baby carriages and especially baby strollers, the latter a frequent and useful vehicle of zoo visitors.

Use of nonstabilized materials for walkways should be avoided in zoos as any likely object can become a missile in the hands of a vandal

The width of zoo walks is an important factor since they are used for both walking as well as standing and looking. Walks fronting exhibits of high popularity require extra room to avoid traffic jams. Adequate space for future walkway enlargement should also be provided.

Some zoos have postponed initial installation of permanent walks and planting until the grounds had been used for a period of time by heavy visitor traffic. In this way, the public in effect determined their own walking routes—a habit pedestrians are often prone to do anyway unless extensive barriers are installed.

2. Visitor Transportation Systems Provisions for a visitor transportation system should be included in the initial zoo plan. Many zoos which have omitted this provision in their early planning have suffered later from cramped transport facilities as a consequence. Systems using tractor buses, miniature or narrow gauge trains, monorails and cable cars have all been successful in zoos.

3. Barriers Depending on the danger involved, barriers of one type or another are necessary to maintain the visitor at a safe distance from the animals. Guard rails, chains, cables, low fences, masonry walls, hedges (often with wires concealed in them), spiny plantings, etc., all function in this respect. In general, the least conspicuous (yet effective) barriers are to be desired.

4. Benches Since considerable walking is usually necessary in zoo visiting, rest areas for visitors should be available throughout the grounds. At the more popular attractions many spectators enjoy an opportunity to view the exhibit while seated and proper planning takes this need into account. Bird exhibits are particularly well suited for such passive recreation. Benches are best located on paved areas to simplify litter.

5. Perimeter Fence In addition to a controlled entrance and exit, the installation of a complete perimeter fence permits added visitor control and grounds security. With a complete perimeter fence, the ingress of predatory animals (such as raccoons, cats, dogs) is limited. Likewise, escaped zoo animals are more or less confined within the grounds. The addition of barbed wire at the top and a concrete footing or curb at the base adds to the effectiveness of the perimeter fence.

ANIMAL EXHIBITS

A. Introduction

In general, there are three basic and sometimes conflicting needs to be considered in planning a zoo animal exhibit, namely those of the animal, the visitor, and the attendant.

The needs of the animal take precedence over those of the other two. Since different animal species have different needs, it is important to select those species whose needs can be met without conflicting with those of the visitor and the attendant. Intelligent exhibit design, however, resolves many such conflicts and thus increases the variety of animals which may be exhibited in zoos. It therefore behooves the zoo architect to seek as much technical information and help as is available on the biological needs of the animals to be exhibited.

What has been termed the "social environment" of captive animals is as yet a poorly understood phenomenon but one which may very well exert strong influences on the health and longevity of animals in captivity. Enclosure design should reflect our knowledge of species' requirements, optimum group size, space needs, sex ratios, and facilities for exercise.

B. Design Factors to Be Considered

In order to properly design an animal exhibit which will satisfy the three basic needs cited above, the following factors should be considered:

1. Exhibit Size Largely determined by the size and activity of the animal. As a general rule, with many exceptions, however, the larger the quarters, the greater will be the husbandry success of the species.

2. Exhibit Shape Also determined largely by the specific kind of animal involved. In any case, acute corners are to be avoided since animals very often will panic when driven into a tight place.

3. Exhibit Orientation Where large areas are involved, the greatest dimension should parallel the public viewing area so as to keep the viewing distance between the visitor and the animal to a minimum. Orientation of the exhibit to the sun, especially during the summer season, should also be evaluated for special requirements or problems. Excessive glare in the viewers' eyes should be avoided, and the amount of sun which might be beneficial or detrimental to the particular animal involved should be considered. Excessive exposure to sun can be a serious health as well as maintenance problem. This is especially true of aquatic exhibits with their problems of algal control.

4. Materials Should be selected for ease of maintenance (nonporous, long wearability, low upkeep, permanence), naturalistic appearance, nontoxicity, readily available construction items in standard sizes, shapes, and specifications, etc. Due to constant exposure to weather, cleaning abrasives and detergents, acidic animal wastes, etc., the selection of exhibit construction materials used in a zoo require special investigation. Nontoxic paints should always be specified where animal contact is possible.

5. Eye Level Depending on the habitat preferences of the animal in nature (ground-living, tree-living, etc.) the visitor's eye level should be considered accordingly in planning the floor and ceiling elevations of the exhibit. In this way the animal will be within maximum viewing range of the visitor. In especially large exhibits, several visitor observation areas are often included—frequently at varied levels.

6. Step-ups Since zoo visitors occur in all sizes, from very young children on up, it behooves the designer to ensure adequate observation facilities for everyone. Where cage floors must be above floor level, the use of step-ups for children and short adults are helpful. Observation platforms of several "stepped-up" levels or ramped up decks are useful for highly popular exhibits where crowds cause visibility problems.

7. Props or Decorations Such items as are used to impart a natural setting for the exhibit in addition to fulfilling certain biological and psychological needs of the animal. Examples such as plants, trees, and rock work, termite nests (any one of which may be real or artificial), and even native artifacts (spears, shields, temple ruins, huts, etc.) all contribute to the display value of an animal exhibit. Strategically located cage props are important in providing hiding places for animals from one another, objects on which to rub, exercise, mark, sun, etc.

8. Shift Cages Enclosures should be designed so the animal may be easily shifted from the exhibit into an adjacent holding, isolation or reserve area without having to restrain or catch the animal. Viewing apertures should be designed into such facilities so that animal movements may be observed from a safe place by the attendant and, especially where flighty animals are involved, without the animal viewing the operator. Prisms used in such installations provide a wide angle of observation. The inclusion of a sliding wall of removable bars in a shift cage expands its function to that of a "squeeze cage"; another very useful item of animal husbandry. With the built-in squeeze cage an animal may be immobilized for veterinary treatment without the need of removing it from its exhibit area.

9. Barrier Depending on the kind of animal exhibited, many different types may be used to contain it within its enclosure. For esthetic reasons, those barriers which are the least visible are the most desirable. Barriers which have been used are of the following types (see Fig. 2):
a. Vertical wires held under tension
b. Bars
c. Rails
d. Moats (dry and water-filled)
e. Fencing
f. Walls (including such naturalistic features as vertical rock formations)
g. Glass (both flat and curved or "invisible")
h. Psychological (such as birds exhibited in a well-illuminated exhibit area and reluctant to fly into a darkened visitor area)
i. Electrical ("shock" fences as well as charged glass windows)
j. Thermal (refrigerated coils and hot water lines)

When structural barriers are used which interrupt the visibility of the exhibit, such restrictions may be reduced to a minimum by lowering the amount of light reflection from the barrier. With bars, fencing, etc., reflections can be reduced tremendously by painting the barrier flat black or other flat dark colors. Glass barriers, when improperly installed, become viewing barriers themselves when they pick up so many extraneous reflections that the exhibit is actually hidden from view. Tilted installations, the use of light-deflecting drop curtains and walls behind the viewer and the use of curved "invisible" glass all serve to reduce and eliminate reflections. Glass, of one design or another, is so widely used in zoos that its proper installation to avoid reflections is of paramount consideration. Glass may also serve as a viewing barrier when opaqued with condensed moisture. Frequently properly

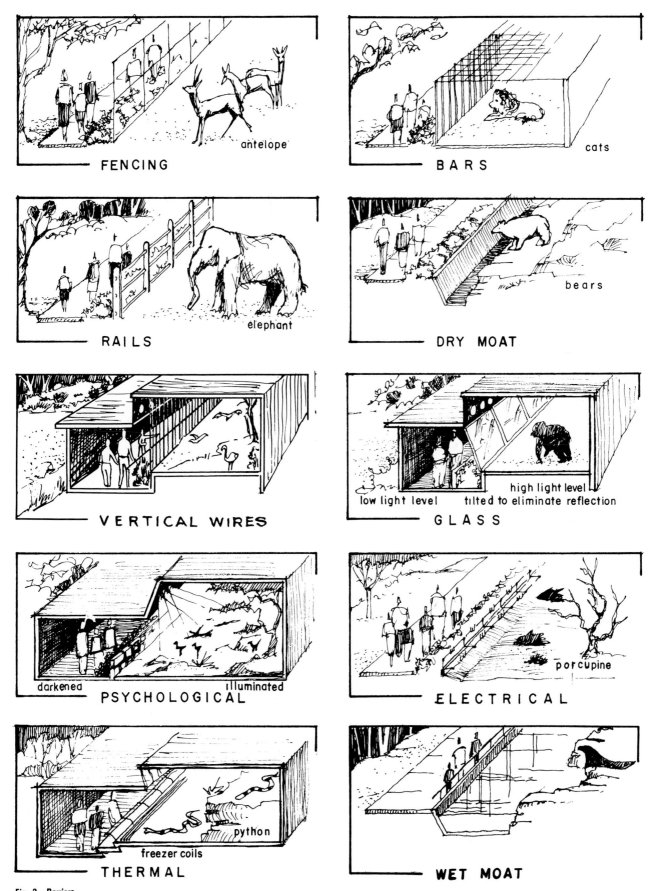

FENCING — antelope

BARS — cats

RAILS — elephant

DRY MOAT — bears

VERTICAL WIRES

GLASS — low light level / high light level / tilted to eliminate reflection

PSYCHOLOGICAL — darkened / illuminated

ELECTRICAL — porcupine

THERMAL — freezer coils / python

WET MOAT

Fig. 2 Barriers.

directed ventilation can correct this problem. So many zoos have suffered such unsatisfactory results that avoidance of these pitfalls cannot be overly stressed.

10. **Security** Adequate measures should be taken to prevent animal escapes, both by the animal breaking out through human error or because of vandalism. Exhibits in any way accessible to the public should always be key locked. Acess doors and operating levers to dangerous animal enclosures should be clearly identified.

11. **Illumination** Adequate lighting must be available for satisfactory observation of the exhibit. Daylight has the advantages of being both natural and inexpensive. However, it is not always dependable, varies seasonally, and prevents interesting lighting effects obtainable only with controlled artificial lighting. Each exhibit has its own lighting requirements which must be resolved through investigation of the animal's needs and the effects desired. Installation of infra-red, ultraviolet and germicidal lights are often of special value with certain animal species. For indoor exhibits, the use of operational skylights has several advantages where direct unhindered sunlight and ventilation are of value to the health of the animal. As has been mentioned, shade is another important planning factor and is especially important where aquatic exhibits with their attendant algal growth are concerned.

C. "Grottos," "Pens," and "Islands"

1. The term "grotto" as applied to zoo exhibits usually has reference to designs in which the animal is separated from the visitor by a moat and prevented from escape elsewhere by sheer vertical walls (often leaning slightly inward). Pigmented concrete sprayed over irregular forms lends itself well to grotto

construction resulting in interesting and naturalistic artificial rock outcrops. Natural stone for such purposes is generally not conducive to realistic outcrops. However, carved natural stone has been used effectively in some instances. Properly designed grottos can be most effectively and beautifully landscaped. Adequately drained planter "pockets," if naturalistically located, will greatly "soften" otherwise drab rockwork.

Grottos may be used effectively for many kinds of animals—reptiles, mammals and flightless or pinioned birds. The value of the grotto is in the naturalness of the setting and the lack of a barrier to interrupt the visitor's view. Designers should give careful considerations to vertical elevations so as to avoid placing the animal in a "pitlike" atmosphere. Also, excessive use of rockwork may conflict with the animal's actual habitat; therefore, a study of the animal's natural history will prevent building an unnatural "natural habitat" setting.

In northern climates where outdoor exhibition may be impractical the year round, indoor exhibit cages often are included and connected directly to the outdoor exhibit.

2. The term *pen* generally implies a yard or area enclosed by fencing, quite large spatially and without top fencing. Animals which cannot climb or fly are adaptable for display in pens. Because of the large area involved, fast-running animals (especially hoofed stock) are usually kept in pens. The section of fencing along the visitor's side of a pen may be replaced with a moat barrier for a more effective display.

3. "Island" exhibits are essentially grottos which are surrounded by a moat. Generally, the same type of animals workable in grottos will do well on islands. Where wide water moats are used, islands can successfully restrain animals capable of great leaping activity (e.g., gibbons, chimpanzees, monkeys, etc.).

Retreat quarters or "dens" must be designed into the island. With large island exhibits, access tunnels are often included for the use of attendants.

D. Outdoor Cage Units

These are structures which are completely enclosed by fencing or bars. Barriers used are generally bars or fencing and with structural floors. Functional for most any animal except those which are not psychologically adaptable to the relatively close confinement characteristic of a cage. The disadvantages of visible cage barriers can be lessened by painting the bars or fencing a flat black or similar nonreflective color. Cages grouped together should be designed with variations of size and shape so that one may avoid the monotony of a continuous series of boxes. Also, the imaginative use of naturalistic props, such as trees, driftwood, rockwork, planting, and pleasing colors helps to avoid the cellblock effect of the old menageries (Fig. 3).

E. "Walk-through" Cages

A variation of the cage concept wherein the visitor actually walks through the cage (generally through double-doored "anti-escape" entry and exit compartments). A low pedestrian barrier keeps the visitor from entering the animal area. This display concept has the advantage of permitting closer contact between the visitor and the animal without a conspicuous barrier separating them. Such displays result in a more intimate and more esthetically pleasing experience for the visitor. Walk-through cages are applicable with any relatively harmless animal species whose ability to escape can be effectively controlled with the necessary visitor entry and exit arrangement. Confinement of the animals to the exhibit area can be encouraged by supplying the proper psychological needs.

F. Animal Pools

A body of water in which aquatic or semiaquatic animals are shown, such as waterfowl, wading birds, otters, sea lions, etc. The pool may be enclosed by sheer walls, fencing, or other barriers. Underwater observation windows are extremely effective but require clear water for successful operation. Otters, seals, sea lions, penguins, and diving birds lend themselves particularly well to such display effects (Fig. 4).

G. Exhibit Buildings

Structures entered by the public in which the animals are maintained indoors, either seasonally or throughout the year. Often, outdoor cages, pens or grottos are located adjacent to a building and connect directly to exhibits inside the building. In this way, the animals may be shifted indoors, or out—according to the weather, the year around. Indoor exhibition may be desired for reasons of climate control (most animals of tropical origin) or for reasons of display effect where a darkened visitor gallery is essential (especially with glass-fronted displays).

Whenever possible it is desirable to restrict an animal display to a single exhibit area (either indoor or outdoor) for reasons of economy and to avoid practical problems of exhibition. In the latter case, the problem usually resulting from dual exhibit cages (indoor and outdoor) is that when animals have access to

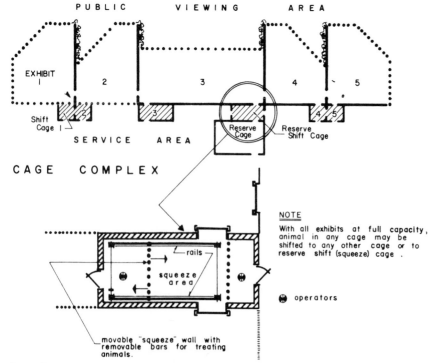

Fig. 3 A simplified plan for an outdoor animal cage complex.

both areas, the visitor must search both areas or miss the animal. Indoor cages can be designed so that the benefits of outdoor exhibition are brought indoors through the use of operational skylights, movable roofs, adequate ventilation, etc. Where adequately large indoor exhibits are impractical or too expensive, an effective compromise is to locate the indoor exhibit cage adjacent to the outdoor exhibit so that the visitor can view both from the same vantage point.

The variety of kinds of exhibit buildings is limited only by the imagination of the zoo designer. The following is a list of a few which have been either planned or built:

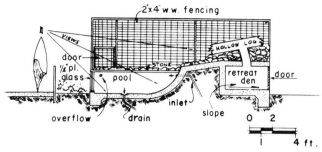

Fig. 4 The otter display shown in sectional plan here permits the observer to view these animals underwater, above the water, or on the stone deck. The exhibit design is applicable to other species of aquatic mammals, various diving birds, and aquatic reptiles. (Fort Worth Zoological Association.)

Mammals:
  Monkey house
  Ape house
  Feline house
  Small mammal
    house
  Large mammal
    house
  Nocturnal mammal
    house
  Pachyderm house
  Aquatic mammal
    house

Birds:
  Tropical bird house
  Aquatic bird house
  Penguin house

Other animals:
  Insect house
  Reptile house
  Herpetarium (reptiles and amphibians)

Habitat buildings:
  Aquarium (aquatic life)
  Underground zoo
  Rain forest
  "Habitat house" (several different habitat scenes exhibited)

Miscellaneous:
  Special exhibits buildings
  Nocturnal animal house

Combinations of several of these into one building are frequently made.

Because of the exceptionally large crowds which visit zoos, details of design and materials selection must be carefully considered in planning the public areas of zoo buildings. Floor type is important as zoo visitor traffic is generally of a "shuffling" nature. Since zoo patrons frequently consume refreshments while walking, food spillage and the resulting hazards must be anticipated. Ramps (often imbedded with nonskid materials) are much preferred to steps. Adequate ventilation is mandatory and must be separated from animal areas. Some zoos include refrigerated air conditioning for visitor comfort. Traffic flow is another important factor and with careful planning should be as well-controlled and orderly as possible, preferably one-way on busy days. Clearly marked emergency exits are generally required by law.

H. "Visitor Cages"

This concept has been used most successfully on the game plains of Africa, but has recently been adapted to zoo use. It involves allowing the animals to roam free, or apparently so, in a large enclosure and placing the visitors in a closed vehicle such as a bus or a monorail car.

SERVICE STRUCTURES

A. Administrative

Depending of course on the size of the total zoo operation, the administrative facilities will vary in both area and complexity.

1. Size Three suggested categories based on the level of administrative complexity are discussed below:

a. Minimum A single administrative office may be incorporated with other service facilities in a combined zoo service building. Or, if a zoo exhibit building is already present or planned, the administrative office can be located in such a building for reasons of economy without adversely affecting efficiency.

b. Median A separate structure for administrative offices for the zoo director, secretary and other administrative personnel.

c. Maximum Enlargement of median facilities based on additional needs of a larger operation such as additional staff members, business office(s), library, meeting room (for staff, board and other small groups) and auditorium where audiences may be assembled for pretour orientation, educational activities, etc.

2. Location It is well to have the administrative building occupy a centralized location on the zoo grounds and be near or at the main entrance, the latter being where many administrative activities occur or radiate from. Direct access of this activity to a street and parking area outside the zoo grounds facilitates the administrative operation (Fig. 5).

B. Maintenance

This facility should have top priority in any zoo construction program and certainly precedes the acquisition of any live animal collection. Included here is animal maintenance concerning the daily feeding, cleaning, and care of the animal collection in addition to animal health requirements; buildings and grounds maintenance; accession, storage, and handling of supplies; and service facilities for personnel.

1. Commissary A function directly proportional to the size of the animal collection. Size of this facility should reflect anticipated growth and its design permit future enlargement. Prevention of rodent access to stored foods and ease of pest control should be incorporated in the design (Fig. 6). Basic requirements for this activity are as follows:

a. Refrigerated Holding Facilities Both chilled and freezer storage space is needed for food holding even in the smallest of zoos. Often, however, it is more economical for a small zoo, initially at least, to rent commercial freezer locker space rather than build and operate its own expensive facility.

b. Kitchen Diet preparation area with equipment such as grinders, choppers, mixers, blenders, juicers, stoves, ovens, scales, knife sharpeners, utensils (knives, steels, spoons, etc.) and containers (pails, dish pans, trays, etc.). Thawing facilities for frozen foods are especially useful.

c. Storage Nonrefrigerated food storage

including grains, commercially prepared foods, and canned goods. Dispensing hoppers should be designed into the facility and available to either the kitchen or diet delivery vehicles. Fodder materials need to be conveniently located. The combustibility of these materials must be considered in locating this facility.

d. Location The location of the commissary ideally should be central to all operations. In large institutions, it is often more practical to develop a main and centralized commissary facility where food is stored and prepared in bulk in addition to small departmental kitchens located in the main buildings. Ease of access for the regular deliveries of foodstuffs from outside the zoo should be provided.

e. As an Exhibit? A recent trend in zoo design is to install visitor observation windows in food preparation facilities so that the public can see the complexities involved in these formerly "behind-the-scenes" activities. Valuable byproducts of such installations are neater employees and more orderly and better kept facilities. Other applications of the same principle have been made with public view windows installed for specialized equipment such as filters and pumps. Even operating, post mortem and examination rooms and laboratories have been made viewable, resulting in excellent visitor reception with consequently improved public education to the total zoo operation.

2. Hospital-Quarantine Every zoo should have facilities where newly arrived and sick animals can be isolated from the rest of the collection, preferably in a structure completely separated from animal exhibit areas. Here also may be located the headquarters for the veterinarian, whether he be a consultant or on the staff. Facilities to be provided for are as follows:
  a. Quarantine section
  b. Sick wards with "squeeze cages" and outdoor recuperating pens
  c. Operating room
  d. Pharmacy and laboratory
  e. Post-mortem room
  f. Refrigerated holding boxes for specimens to be autopsied
  g. Equipment and supplies: microscope, centrifuge, autoclave, operating table, portable cages, restraining devices, surgical and medical supplies, laboratory ware, testing equipment, pharmaceutical refrigerator, etc.

Since babies must frequently be raised without a mother for one reason or another in zoos, the establishment of animal nursery facilities should be provided for. Often such activities are placed on public view as an exhibit. A human incubator is a useful piece of equipment in this facility.

Accommodation for egg incubators and chick brooders should also be included in zoo planning. There are practical reasons for locating such in the animal health facility.

Depending on the size of the zoo operation several of the above activities can be combined into a single structure. It is desirable to either isolate this operation from direct contact with the public or locate it away from the visitor area (Fig. 7).

3. Reserve Animal Area Zoos constantly accrue animals for which exhibit space is either not presently available or when it is desired to isolate the animal from the public for purposes of breeding, holding for other zoos, etc. Also, some animal species may be exhibited seasonally outdoors and require winter holding quarters. Such animals, acclimated and healthy, invariably find their way into hospital sections or are scattered in rear service areas. A special reserve section built for the purpose is a practical and useful adjunct to the service facilities of a zoo.

4. Building and Grounds Maintenance This activity houses facilities for the conventional needs of repairs to buildings and grounds, minor construction jobs, grounds maintenance and horticulture. A shop area is a useful facility and should be included in even the smallest of

operations. Objectionable noises from the operation of power tools should be considered when locating this activity. Greenhouses to implement buildings and grounds beautification as well as planted exhibits should be included if needed. Storage facilities for tools, cleaning supplies, equipment, etc., should be located here.

Waste disposal is another important activity which should be included in maintenance planning. Incinerators are sometimes required for the disposal of dead animals.

5. Personal Facilities Employees' quarters with lockers, shower, restrooms and dining area are necessary for any operation. Not only is employee morale bolstered but personnel can be expected to be neater and more presentable when such facilities are available.

6. Combinations For a small zoo most of these maintenance functions can be efficiently designed into one central structure.

7. Location Due to the constant activities of pickup, delivery, and disposal of materials involved in the various maintenance operations, the structure or structures housing them should be located with direct access to an

"outside" or off the zoo grounds street. Service drives leading from maintenance areas to the various zoo facilities should be included in the grounds plans, preferably isolated as much as possible from public areas.

C. Public Services

Any operation which attracts the tremendous crowds which zoos engender must have adequate facilities which cater to the personal needs of visitors, as well as provisions to handle emergencies and maintain security.

1. Restrooms Inadequate and/or unclean restroom facilities do more to give a public institution an unsatisfactory reputation than any other condition—a fact which service station operators have been aware of for some time. Zoos are well advised to include the installation of toilets especially designed for children due to the large number of youthful visitors. Urinals for female visitors are also being utilized in some public restrooms.

2. Special Services Problems of crowd control are common to every zoo and proper planning must take the following factors into consideration:

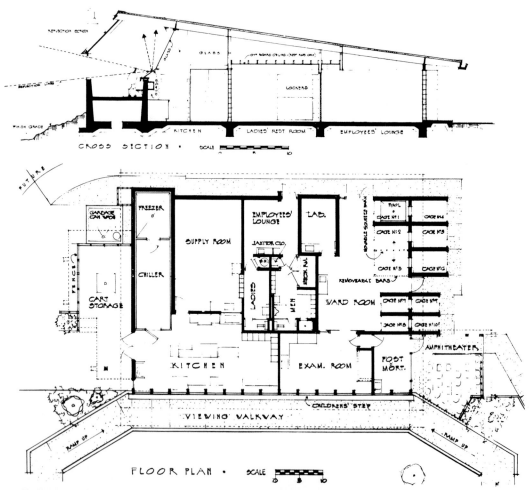

Fig. 5 The service building shown here includes commissary facilities on the left, attendants' quarters in the center rear, and animal health on the right. All activities along the building front are viewable by the public from the elevated and hooded ramp. The specially designed hood and double tilted glass eliminates reflections and yet maintains an open feeling. The kitchen area (lower left) shows the large observation windows. The amphitheater (below right) adjoins the post mortem and operating room. Here biology classes observe operations and autopsies and may take tissue specimens back to their school laboratories for further study. A two-way public address system permits question and answer interchange between the veterinarian and class. (Fort Worth Zoological Association.)

a. Public Address System For locating lost children, lost and found items, making special announcements (e.g., animal feeding times, animal demonstration and acts, etc.) and often the playing of background music.

b. Emergency Properly supplied first-aid facilities with trained personnel available should be a part of every zoo. Special instructions for the handling of intoxicated visitors, heart attack and heat victims, etc., should be available to all personnel.

c. Transportation Many zoos install vehicular systems to take visitors from one point to another or for tour or sightseeing purposes. Tractor trains, animal-drawn carts and rides, rail trains, buses, and even an overhead monorail are a few examples currently in operation in zoos. Generally, a public address system is available on such conveyances which permits lectures during tours. Availability of stroller and wheelchair rentals are also a convenience to zoo visitors.

3. Concessions Several pamphlets published by the National Recreation and Park Association are available concerning this area of design and operation. In general the following basic concessions have proven to be effective in zoos:

a. Refreshment stands for minor food and beverage items

b. Cafe and restaurant facilities

c. Vending machines for beverages, snacks and special animal foods

d. Souvenirs, gifts, and numerous educational items zoologically oriented (books, pamphlets, maps, post cards, models, etc.), jewelry, photographic film, rental cameras, etc.

e. Parking lot fees

f. Transportation systems

Profits from zoo concessions can be an important factor in subsidizing zoo budgets, thus decreasing the zoo's dependence on tax revenues.

GENERAL

A. Display

The difference between a menagerie and a zoo might be defined as follows: a menagerie is simply a collection of animals on public exhibition. A zoo is an educationally planned and oriented animal display presented to the visitor in the most esthetically pleasing, interesting and naturalistic context practical. Several display factors contribute to the qualities of a zoo and are listed as follows:

1. Signs and Labels These perform several functions and can be of the following four major varieties:

a. Natural History Common name, scientific name, habitat, geographic range and interesting natural history information. Where several species are exhibited together, these signs should be illustrated for easy identification.

b. Visitor Information Signs which advise the visitor of opening times for exhibits, acknowledgment of donations, feeding times, etc.

c. Visitor Instruction Signs for protection of animals, such as "do not feed," and warnings of potential dangers to visitors, such as crossing guard rails, entering off-limit areas, etc.

d. Directional Signs directing the visitor to exhibits, buildings, service facilities, etc.

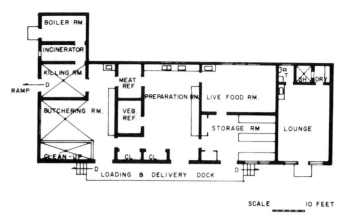

Fig. 6 The commissary shown in this plan permits an efficient operation for food storage and preparation. Facilities are provided for slaughtering food animals. (Cheyenne Mountain Zoological Park, Colorado Springs.)

Fig. 7 A combination administration and hospital building. Facilities include a library, offices, quarantine and ward rooms, laboratory, pharmacy, and winter quarters. Zoo buildings, especially service facilities, require a careful selection of construction materials, particularly those which will stand up under constant humidity and abrasion of daily cleaning. (Franklin Park Zoo, Boston.)

2. Special Technique The imagination has few limits with respect to animal exhibition. Such features as special lighting, sound effects and the like have been favorably received by the visiting public. Museum displays which supplement the live animal exhibits are extremely effective in zoos and enhance their educational value. Visitor activated pushbutton exhibits are excellent. Also, slide and film projectors which illustrate an animal activity, life cycle, or other such features, otherwise impossible to demonstrate in a live exhibit, are most effective display supplements.

3. Demonstrations With many animals it is possible to go beyond the concept of the "animal sitting in the cage." The presentation of demonstrations showing specific behavior activities may be done by a variety of techniques. Some of these demonstrations must be planned with an adequate number of animals available so that the welfare of the animal subjects is not compromised. A few examples of such exhibit supplements are as follows:

a. Electric fish demonstrations
b. Spitting (archer) fish feeding demonstration
c. Rattlesnake rattling and striking
d. Cobra hood-forming demonstration
e. Animal weighings on built-in scales
f. Conditioned-reflex demonstration
g. Otter slides
h. Porpoise and fish sounds picked up by underwater microphones
i. Observation chick incubators
j. Microprojection of invertebrates
k. Any scheduled special feeding

Demonstrations such as the above represent perhaps the greatest potential today in the development of educational zoo display.

B. Visitor Participation

Any design feature which establishes a closer relationship between the visitor and the animal is generally to be desired. Care must be taken, of course, that the welfare of neither the animal nor the visitor is endangered. For example, public animal feeding of a proper ration is a good revenue producer and, to an extent, a budget saver. Coin-operated vending machines are available which are manufactured for animal wafers. Coin-operated or pushbutton animal acts are also of interest. A number of commercially available installations have been developed for providing prerecorded information for zoo and museum visitors through "talking labels," transistorized receivers with earphones and similar devices. These devices increase the effectiveness of the zoo's educational program while also adding a personal touch to the exhibits which printed labels do not provide.

Since amateur photography is widespread, it behooves the zoo planner and operator to facilitate such activity as much as possible. Signs with meter checked camera settings for highly photographed exhibits, public dark rooms for film changing, and of course a film sales desk are facilities which zoos can make available to the photographer.

The Need and Concept

An aquarium built almost anywhere will prove to be a popular attraction. Nevertheless, to be successful, whether financially or in terms of education or recreation, it must be sited where a real need exists.

The concept of the aquarium, what it will be and do, must be determined early. Within the funds available, what usual and what special features will be included must be decided upon.

An initial simple design should be prepared which presumably will provide adequate space for the expected visitors and will also provide the necessary operating areas. These must then be considered with knowledgeable persons and be modified as required. If the aquarium is to be more than a house for living aquatic animals and plants, an exhibit specialist should be at hand to design presentations to meet the objectives of the institution.

Public aquariums are leaning more and more toward educational recreation for their visitors. It is felt that a mere lineup of tanks containing specimens identified by photographs, names, and range may be interesting, but is not sufficiently informative. Groupings of specimens may be made to illustrate environmental preferences, means of locomotion, sight, hearing, food habits, schooling, use by man, and any number of other interesting and informative themes. If these are properly presented, the visitor will unknowingly absorb and retain much knowledge of aquatic life.

Planners should, then, include in the design particular configurations of tanks, in separated groups, as a means by which a theme can be effectively carried to the audience. Contributing information can be furnished by pushbutton filmstrips, guidebooks, and by lighted legend boxes.

The Planners

We shall assume that the promoters of the aquarium have the necessary financial backing and that they realize that at least 60 per cent of the cost will be for facilities, equipment and design, most of which are peculiar to aquariums are not visible to the public.

The promoters have a site that appears to be suitable. It should be readily accessible by both public transportation and private vehicles, and should, if possible, be easily reached by tourists. Adequate vehicle parking in the area is desirable.

The most vital factor is the water supply. Usually the promoters are not competent to judge this essential ingredient, the quality of which must be known before the project can be further developed. Too often promoters assume that the water is of good quality and of sufficient, continuous volume.

At this point in the planning the promoters

Aquarium Design Criteria, Drum & Croaker, National Fisheries Center and Aquarium, U.S. Department of the Interior, Washington, D.C., 1970.

should seek professional advice, both as to the quality of the water and the volume required for the proposed facility. From here on the planning staff should include individuals competent in the aquarium field.

Designing for visitor guidance will be based upon the building and site size and an estimate of the expected visitor load. More often than not the funds available for a public aquarium will dictate the size, regardless of expected visitations. If the site is large enough, the original design may provide for future expansion.

It is desirable to have a flow pattern for visitors. Design can quite readily lead the visitor into the desired path in most situations. Upon entering, a visitor will generally turn right, provided no attractions draw him elsewhere. By placing display tanks at an angle, with the viewing glass facing the oncoming visitor, he will normally proceed in that direction. Open-floor exhibits can serve as shields and also continue to draw the visitors along the desired path (Fig. 1).

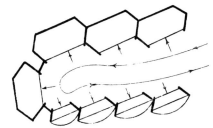

Fig. 1   Visitor's flow pattern.

Monotony is to be avoided in the placement of display tanks. They should not be lined up like railway car windows. All of them should not be set at an angle. Alcoves and jut-outs will provide variety and surprises, and can serve as dividers between special exhibits. Variety also serves to orient the visitor.

Handrails to keep the public about 3 ft from the viewing glass may be desirable. Opinion

is divided among aquarists regarding rails. When large numbers of visitors are present, a rail keeps them back from the glass and permits more people a better view. On the other hand, close inspection of small organisms is then not possible. (See Figs. 2 and 7.)

A step-up for small children is often provided. This usually is about 1 ft high and 1 ft wide, and should be part of the building structure and continuous.

The Operations Area

As previously stated, planners of aquariums often consider the facility only from the visitor's viewpoint. They do not realize that the welfare and attractiveness of the specimens and minimum costs for operation and maintenance depend upon the attention given to behind-the-scenes design.

The immediate work area behind the display tanks may be considered first. The work-area floor should be about 3 ft higher than the public area floor. This is dictated by the height of the average visitor looking into the approximate center of the viewing glass of the average large display tank. Most display tanks are placed on the floor of the work area. Obviously, very small and very large tanks will have to be placed differently. Tanks should be placed to permit ease of cleaning by aquarists.

Holding tanks to receive new specimens for quarantine and space to hold surplus or sick specimens should be placed along the rear wall of the work area or in any other convenient locations. Each of these holding tanks should have its own recirculating system. The total holding capacity should be equal to about one third of the display volume but may vary considerably, depending upon the sizes of display tanks and specimens as well as the mortality rate and replacement need (Fig. 7.)

All quarantine tanks should be provided with drain valves to permit rapid drainage after treatment procedures. All tanks should have removable pump screens.

Many aquarists feel that practically all

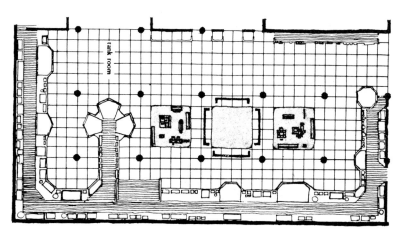

Fig. 2   Plan of tank gallery.

healthy specimens ought to be on display since they use space when held in reserve and require the same care as specimens on display. Nevertheless, too few quarantine or treatment tanks can greatly hamper operations. The exhibit/holding ratio should be carefully considered.

The various main supply pipes from the reservoirs should extend around the aquarium over the display tanks. These should be a minimum of 7 ft above the work-area floor and should have frequent tap valves from which, by flexible hose, replacement water or a continuous flow may be fed to the tanks, depending upon the system. It is important to have shutoff valves conveniently located along the major supply lines to facilitate plumbing repairs.

To reduce the possibility of accidental flooding to a minimum, automatic cut-off switches, built-in overflow drains, and failsafe devices should be planned in connection with tanks and reservoirs that are periodically drawn down and refilled.

All electrical appliances and equipment, including connector boxes, must be grounded. Outlets should not be located near the floor. Fixtures over the tanks should be protected to avoid breakage and possible danger to personnel working in water. Poles attached to brushes or other cleaning devices should be of wood or other nonmetallic material.

Natural light should be held to a minimum, unless completely controllable. Natural light promotes algae growth on interiors of tanks.

A flexible lighting system over each tank should include the capability of being lifted out of the way when cleaning tanks or feeding specimens. Sufficient waterproof outlets should be provided for auxiliary or special lighting.

A clear passageway about 6 ft wide should extend along the back of all display tanks in order to permit the easy transport of tanks, incoming specimens, etc., by fork-lift truck or four-wheel flatbed. No stairs or other obstacles should be located in this passageway.

The surface of the work-area floor should have a nonskid finish. Floor drains with sand traps are absolutely necessary and floors should be sloped to drains. Water-resistant materials should be used in all places adjacent to tanks.

Storage space for tools, nets, chemicals, and other items in frequent use should be provided. Refrigerators often are convenient for the storage of special foods, and may reduce trips to the food preparation room.

Stairs should be placed conveniently from the work area to the public area, with lock doors. Small wall desks may be provided for record keeping.

Deep washbasins with hot and cold water and towel boxes should be located conveniently in the work areas. Also, suitable containers for net sterilization should be provided.

Centrally located and convenient to the live exhibits should be the grouping of loading dock, food preparation room and freezer, offices for the biologist and chief aquarist, a room for the shipping and receiving of live specimens, and a crew room with showers and toilets. Space for the chief engineer and control and monitoring panels should be provided. The size of each of the foregoing, as well as the necessity for offices and crew room, will depend upon the size of the aquarium and the number of personnel involved in operations.

The above can be located on either the work-area level or the public-area level. If the latter is the case, a ramp should extend from the loading dock area to the work level. It is also desirable to have easy rolling access to the public area and to the administrative offices.

In any aquarium a two-way intercom system is very important.

The work area should be separated acoustically from the public area.

Interior windows may be desirable to permit visitors to view the more interesting operational features.

By JAMES W. ATZ, Associate Curator, The American Museum of Natural History

Water Quality

The chemical condition of the water in which fishes and aquatic animals without backbones (invertebrates) are kept is vital to their health. Anything suspended or dissolved in the water comes into the most intimate contact with these animals, mostly through their gills, and there is little they can do to keep harmful substances from entering their bloodstream or body. For example, only two parts of copper dissolved in a hundred million parts of water can kill some fishes within 24 hours, while acutely toxic concentrations of pesticides like Endrin need have a strength of less than one part per billion. The invertebrates are even more sensitive than fishes.

In order to keep animals as sensitive as this alive in captivity, there is only one safe rule to follow: all aquaria and other parts of water systems must be made of chemically inert materials.

The source of any water that is to be used in aquariums must be scrutinized to make certain it always has the proper chemical composition and never contains substances harmful to the exhibits. Ordinary standards of water purity are not adequate because perfectly potable fresh water or seawater, perfectly safe for bathing, may be deadly to fishes and aquatic invertebrates. As far as their water supply is concerned, these animals are much more delicate than man. Frequent troublemakers in municipal tap water are chlorine, excessive hardness, and brass or galvanized piping. A single small metallic fixture can quickly bring about the death of fish when the water running through it is soft.

As far as the aquarium's visitors are concerned, the only necessary water quality is clarity, so that they can easily see the exhibits. For large tanks (500 gal or more) the water must be very clear indeed; the water of some municipalities contains colloidal clay, and although it looks crystal clear in small tanks, its milky appearance in large ones makes viewing through it quite unsatisfactory. (Animals may live in such cloudy water without any difficulty, but water that is cloudy from the

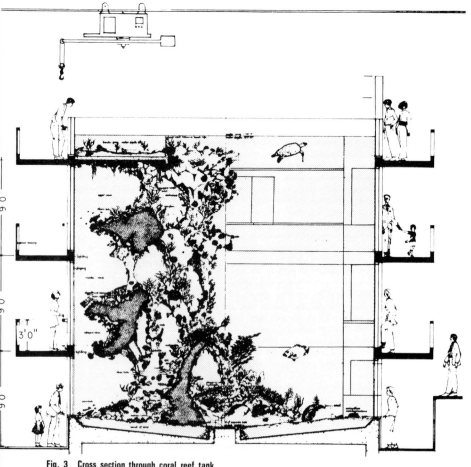

Fig. 3 Cross section through coral reef tank.

1294

presence of myriads of bacteria is unsatisfactory for both visitor and exhibit animal, although for different reasons.)

In some aquarium water systems, the water is used only once and is then discarded. These are called *open systems. Closed systems* are those in which the water is recirculated, being used over and over again.

Sometimes it is necessary to treat the water as soon as it enters the aquarium building, usually by filtering it. Natural seawater should always be filtered before being put into reservoirs or closed systems of any kind in order to remove the tiny animals and plants (plankton) that inhabit it. These floating mites cannot live under the conditions of captivity and when they die, they decompose and temporarily make the seawater toxic to larger forms of marine life. Even filtered seawater "rots" to some

extent and may have to be stored in the dark for as long as 6 weeks before becoming fit to use, particularly in small tanks.

For the great majority of exhibits, however, fresh, filtered seawater may be used without delay if it has not originated from polluted sources and if each water system contains at least 1,000 gal. On the other hand, untreated natural seawater can be used in *open* systems provided it is clear enough not to obstruct the view of the exhibits. An important advantage of this kind of arrangement is that it makes easy the exhibition of plankton-feeding animals, which subsist on the small plants and animals they strain out of the water.

Unless the aquarium can be built near a dependable source of water of the proper quality and sufficient quantity, closed water systems will be a necessity, but water that

is used over and over accumulates waste products from the animals living in it, and as time goes on, the concentration of these substances becomes intolerable. Their removal, however, presents special problems.

Aquarium animals, just like terrestrial ones, must consume oxygen to stay alive and at the same time must get rid of the carbon dioxide they produce. If the water in which they find themselves has either too little oxygen or too much carbon dioxide, they will die. Fortunately, the atmosphere provides an unlimited supply of oxygen and can take up unlimited amounts of carbon dioxide—at least the small amounts produced by aquariums. Therefore all that needs to be done is to expose enough of the aquarium water to air above the vessel so that the two gases will be exchanged at a sufficiently rapid rate. This is most easily done by

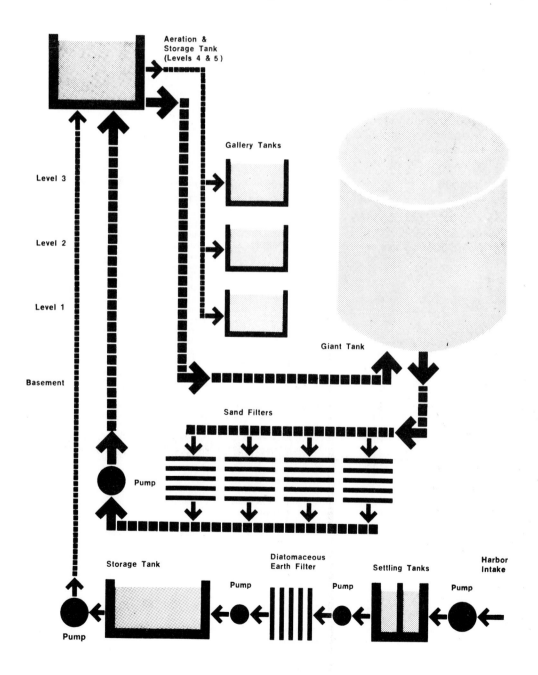

Fig. 4

the use of aerators, although circulating the water and otherwise agitating it is also very helpful. (See Fig. 4.)

The animals' other wastes are not so easily disposed of, however; in fact, no economically feasible way has yet been devised to remove them from aquarium water. Most important of all is ammonia. This is the principal waste product in the urine of fishes, and these animals excrete ammonia through their gills as well. Ammonia is also the principal excretory product of aquatic invertebrates. Other waste products, such as urea, are broken down into ammonia by bacteria in the water. In addition, ammonia is produced when bacteria bring about the decomposition of fecal fish wastes as well as any uneaten food or plants and animals that have died in the tank. It would not be far wrong to state that every bit of food put into an aquarium, except that utilized in the growth of its inhabitants, eventually turns into ammonia.

Ammonia is exceedingly toxic to almost all fishes and invertebrates. For example, trout living in water with as little as six parts per billion of ammonia show abnormal gills. Even freshwater pond fishes, which are much less sensitive to ammonia than trout or coral-reef fishes, should not be exposed to concentrations of more than one part in ten million of water.

At the present time, there is only one economical way to avoid ammonia poisoning in closed aquarium systems, and this is by taking advantage of the bacteria that change ammonia into nitrate (by oxidation), a chemical that is much less harmful to aquatic animals. These nitrifying bacteria occur naturally in all aquariums and water systems, but not in large enough numbers to quickly convert the toxic ammonia into relatively harmless nitrate. In a well-managed tank, these bacteria thrive on the walls and other surfaces, but not in the water itself, because they must be attached to some kind of solid material in order to grow and multiply. There are not enough surfaces in an aquarium to provide "homes" for sufficient numbers of nitrifying bacteria to keep the concentration of ammonia as low as it needs to be, that is, virtually zero. One of the principal functions of a filter is to provide living space for nitrifying bacteria, and countless numbers of them cover the grains of sand or gravel of the filter bed. In the future, other ways of eliminating ammonia may be found, but biological filtration is now the only practical way to do so.

In addition to the solid surface they require, nitrifying bacteria need oxygen; the water should be aerated both before and after filtration—afterwards in order to replace the oxygen used up by the filter bacteria. Nitrifying bacteria are slow multipliers (as compared with many other bacteria), and cold temperatures, acid waters, high salinity, and lack of calcium slow them down even more. Whenever an aquarium or a water system is put into operation, the number of animals put into it ought to be limited until the filter has acquired its full complement of nitrifying bacteria. A "healthy" filter is essential to a "healthy" closed aquarium water system and vice versa.

The longer the aquarium or water system is in operation, the greater the amount of nitrate that accumulates in the water. Although certain aquatic bacteria (denitrifiers) change nitrates into nitrogen gas and thus eliminate the nitrogen from the system, this process does not take place rapidly enough to prevent the buildup of nitrate in aquarium water. More-

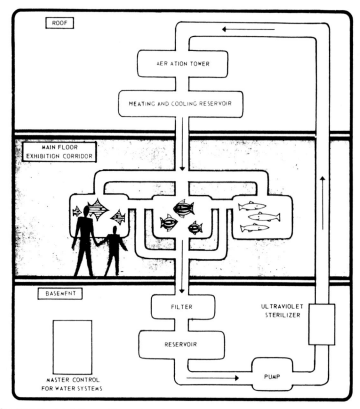

Fig. 5 Simplified diagram of the aquarium water system.

over, there are other less well-known substances that accumulate in the water in which animals are living. None of these is at all as toxic as ammonia, but they do have an inhibitory effect, especially on marine invertebrates. The only practical way to get rid of them, at the present state of aquarium technology, is by replacing part of the water at regular intervals. This is the procedure used by home aquarists who want their fishes to reproduce. By keeping the concentration of nitrates (and undoubtedly other inhibiting substances that were not measured as well) below 10 parts per million with regular replacements of fresh seawater, the London Aquarium has been able to maintain marine invertebrates it otherwise found impossible to keep alive.

Another cumulative change that takes place in aquarium water is an increase in acidity. Oxidation is a process essential to all life, and oxidation is an acid-producing process. Aquatic animals produce carbon dioxide, which becomes carbonic acid in water. All of their other waste products are eventually oxidized by bacterial action, and this, too, produces acid. In order to prevent the aquarium system from suffering from acidosis, it must be alkalized. This is absolutely essential for closed seawater systems and is usually accomplished by keeping the water in very close contact with some form of calcium carbonate (coral sand, calcite, marble chips, bivalve shells).

Proper aquarium water quality depends primarily on the following factors:
- Chemically inert material
- Suitable source of water
- Adequate circulation, aeration, and filtration
- Cleanliness, achieved mostly by avoiding overcrowding and overfeeding

- Control of waste end-products by filtration, alkalization, and dilution

Water Systems

The water system includes, in whole or part, the incoming line, a clarifying or sterilizing unit if required, storage reservoirs, the pipelines furnishing types and temperatures of water serving the display tanks, the display tanks, inflow and outflow and drainage, and filters.

Piping should be of nonmetallic materials. Water should come in contact with metal only as absolutely necessary. Metal or other piping may be used to serve cetaceans, seals, penguins, and aquatic reptiles, but expensive replacement may be necessary because of corrosion. (See Figs. 4 and 5.)

1. Open system (use and waste). This method is the least complicated and least troublesome provided an adequate source of excellent disease-free water is available. The requirement that metal not come in contact with water may not be quite so important here, as the animals are exposed to water that has passed over the metal only once and as the toxicity potential decreases due to the formation of inert oxides, etc., on the interior of metal pipes, thus forming an insulating barrier, but corrosion is a factor to be considered.

Economics must be considered when water is to be discarded after one use. As a general rule of thumb, the average display tank of specimens loaded at the rate of 1 lb. of fish per 100 gal of water should have a turnover or replacement rate of one volume each one to two hours. If the gallonage of all display tanks is 100,000 gal, a flow of 50,000 to 100,000 gal per hour would have to be maintained. Thus,

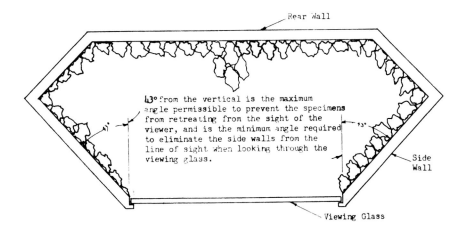

43° from the vertical is the maximum angle permissible to prevent the specimens from retreating from the sight of the viewer, and is the minimum angle required to eliminate the side walls from the line of sight when looking through the viewing glass.

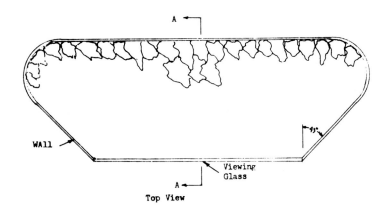

Top View

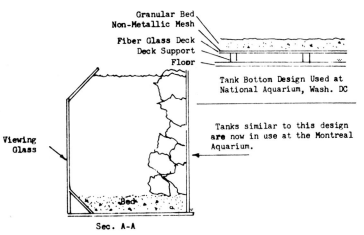

Tank Bottom Design Used at National Aquarium, Wash. DC

Tanks similar to this design are now in use at the Montreal Aquarium.

Sec. A-A

Fig. 6 Typical vanishing side wall tank installation.

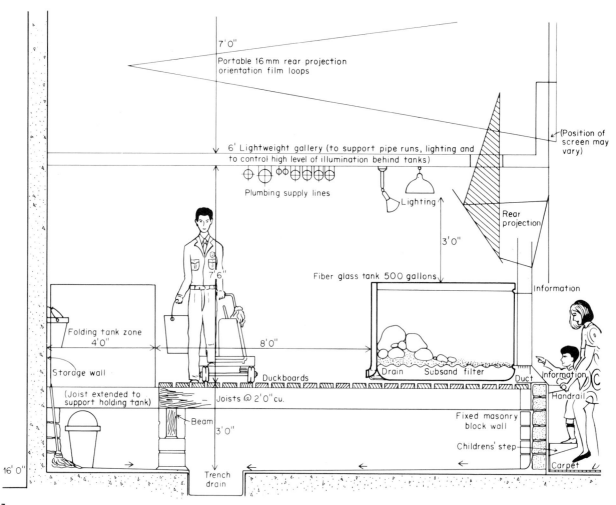

Fig. 7

1.2 to 2.4 million gal would be required each 24 hours. An added cost would arise if some waters had to be heated or cooled.

When water is used only once and discarded, the rate of turnover usually need not be as great as in closed systems, as waste products from the specimens are continually carried away.

It should be noted that the rule of thumb cited above is just that. Many species of fish can be loaded heavier, and some species, particularly invertebrates, may require a more rapid turnover of water.

2. Closed system (recirculating total system). Water continuously enters the display tanks and the overflow returns to the reservoirs after passing through filters. In theory, this method requires only the replacement of water lost by evaporation or in the process of cleaning a tank or backwashing a filter. However, seawater should be replaced at the rate of one-third of the total volume every two weeks, if possible. If this cannot be done, monitoring of nitrite, nitrate, and urea buildup becomes very important.

One serious disadvantage in a closed system is the real possibility of disease organisms from one tank being carried to all tanks. Filtration will not remove many of these. Ultraviolet radiation or passage through a reverse

osmosis process, however, is effective in removing or destroying organisms both desirable and undesirable. Reverse osmosis cannot be used with salt water.

3. Closed system (recirculating individual systems). Each display tank is provided with its own recirculating water system. Filling and minor replacement is from the main supply lines. In operation, the overflow passes through a biological filter and is pumped back to the display tank. Desired temperature range can be maintained by cooling or heating units placed in the filter or line.

In the recirculating systems, the main supply lines of water, preferably overhead, also are continually circulating at a low rate to preclude dead water and the growth of organisms in the pipes.

The plans for the National Fisheries Center include the above system (3). The city water supply contains traces of zinc and copper, detergents and chlorine. After all display and reservoir tanks are filled (approximately 3.5 million gallons) the replacement water estimated to be required is 100 gallons per minute. It is planned to pass this incoming water through the reverse osmosis process to remove the metals and detergents. The chlorine will be removed by aeration or charcoal filtering.

Display tanks of up to 2,000 gal can, for some species, be recirculated through bottom filters with water circulation controlled by air-lift pumps.

In recirculating systems it is desirable to replace at least 10 percent of fresh water and at least 40 percent of salt water each month to avoid a buildup of harmful substances. Usually a greater amount than this is replaced when the display tanks are regularly cleaned and filters backwashed.

Display Tanks

Tanks for the display of aquatic specimens are expensive. Materials in tanks for seawater must be more carefully chosen than for fresh water. Nevertheless, all tanks should be made of inert material to the greatest extent possible.

Ideal tanks are those that are least costly, light in weight, readily altered or drilled, inert in seawater, with hard and smooth interiors, among other things. No currently available materials from which tanks may be produced have quite all the foregoing desirable features. For smaller tanks (up to about 2,000 gal), fiber glass or plastic-impregnated plywood appear to be quite satisfactory.

A number of companies manufacture fiber

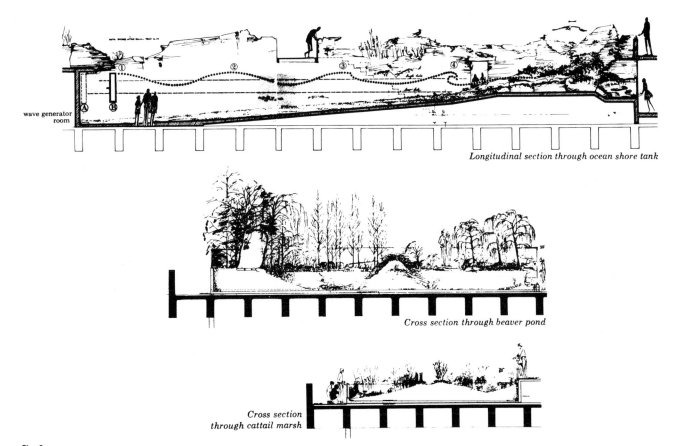

wave generator room

Longitudinal section through ocean shore tank

Cross section through beaver pond

Cross section through cattail marsh

Fig. 8

glass aquaria or holding tanks. Moreover, some of these will fabricate to specifications. It is desirable to plan to install tanks of standard sizes, preferably those that are available "off the shelf" or for which fiber glass-fabricating forms are still available.

Fiber glass is completely inert, is light in weight, and can be readily altered and drilled. Some experience by aquarium personnel will permit them to make repairs. It is quite possible, with an experienced technician, for an aquarium to fabricate its own tanks of reinforced fiber glass.

For larger tanks, reinforced concrete, steel plate, or some other substantial and suitable material will be required.

Concrete tanks should never be poured as an integral part of the building. Each such tank should be an independent unit, capable of being broken up and removed without damage to the building.

The design of tanks should consider the problems of drainage, cleaning, viewing, etc. Some tanks, because of the specimens to be held therein, may require special features, e.g., scuppers at the surface to remove oily film produced by some foods. Rapid drainage is desirable. It is preferable that gravel or sand

not touch the viewing glass. Disappearing side walls may be desired (Fig. 11.)

All concrete and metal surfaces should be coated with an epoxy sealer. This will continue to seal the inevitable hairline cracks in concrete, and thus prevent seawater (particularly) from attacking the reinforcing iron. (If possible, Monel bars should be used.) The seal also inhibits the growth of algae. Color may be added to the epoxy. Epoxy may also be used with sand to provide skidproofing for wet floors, ramps, etc. Careful application of epoxy paints over concrete will prevent blistering.

1299

INDOOR COURTS AND BUILDINGS

Number of People Per Court

An indoor facility generally has a capacity of 125–150 members per court, since the indoor court is available at least 14 hours per day, 7 days a week. There are some players who show up infrequently, while others wish to play 5 hours or more per week. Most sets played are doubles and require four people per period.

Site Selection

As previously suggested, a site should be selected which is reasonably level to avoid excessive grading problems. It should be sufficiently large to allow expansion of the number of tennis courts, the club facilities, and parking and still allow sufficient room for required setbacks of the building from the lot lines. The site should be properly zoned for tennis establishments, located as close as possible to the active tennis playing group in the community, preferably within 15 minutes driving time. Availability of utilities at low cost is highly desirable. Restrictions on height and types of construction should also be considered when choosing the site.

Clubhouse Facilities and Layout

It is generally more economical to place courts side by side if there are less than six. It then may be feasible to place three courts side by side and the additional courts end to end with the first three. Of course, the shape of the property may dictate the shape of the building to be constructed.

The person in charge should be able to see everyone who enters or leaves the building and

Community Tennis Facilities Operations, Robert M. Artz. National Recreation and Park Association, Inc., Arlington, Virginia, 1972.

goes to or from the locker rooms; it is difficult to see what is happening more than four courts away. A side-court control point is preferred. This position allows the person in charge to see all that is happening without interfering with play.

It is highly desirable to separate the teaching court from adjacent courts by a divider net to prevent balls from interfering with play in progress. The divider net can be located directly over the outside alley line of the teaching court or there should be a minimum of 10 ft on each side of the divider net to the nearest outside alley line.

Players should be able to get from locker rooms to their court out of sight of players on adjacent courts. Men's and women's locker rooms generally contain seven to eight lockers per court. Generally 1 to 1½ showers per court is sufficient in the men's locker room; ¾ to 1 shower per court (with private dressing booth) is generally sufficient for the women's locker room.

Building

The tennis court building should be 120 ft in the clear to accommodate the length of the tennis court and the space behind the end lines. The walls behind the courts should be a minimum of 16 ft high and the center of the building over the net should be a minimum of 35 ft in the clear. For safety any structural members projecting into the playing area should be padded with foam rubber or other shock-absorbent material from a point 18 in above the floor to a point 6 ft above the playing surface.

Court Surfaces

All surfaces used outdoors can be used indoors. However, certain types of porous courts require the addition of moisture on a daily basis. Adding moisture to the air will make it humid and may create condensation problems on the structure in the colder climates unless adequate precautions

are taken to insulate the outside surfaces. Because frost is not a problem indoors, the court base can probably be reduced in thickness to save money. Indoor courts should also be level.

Hard courts may be used for other purposes, and porous courts can be covered for other uses or repaired if abuse is minimal. But nonporous cushioned courts *cannot* be used for any other purposes.

Lighting

Lighting may be provided by incandescent, fluorescent, mercury vapor, or quartz lighting fixtures. Lighting intensities should be above 50-foot candles for tournament and club play and above 30 foot-candles for recreational play. It is desirable to shield the player as much as possible from a direct view of the light source, and some lighting should be directed upward to reduce the contrast between lighting above and below the lighting fixtures. When louvres are used under fluorescent lights, they can be protected by an expanded metal screen. Natural lighting may create more problems than it cures.

Other Considerations

Gas or electric radiant units, hot-water perimeter fin-tube units, and warm-air distribution duct systems provide the most uniform *heating*. Unit heaters can also be used. If air conditioning is to be considered, a duct system might be utilized for both heating and cooling.

Ventilation should meet local building codes. If no code exists, it is considered good practice to provide ½ to 1 air change per hour.

The ceiling of the court area should be a light *color*. There should be no contrasting colors for structural members. The background behind the courts should be a medium or dark color for 8 to 10 ft above the playing surface.

By ROBERT L. KNAPP, AIA, Charles Luckman Associates, New York

There are three primary sets of requirements which the sports arena designer should clearly define and then keep in proper focus during the design/planning process. They are:

1. General planning requirements
2. Spectator requirements
3. Operation/management requirements

On occasion, conflicts will develop among these criteria as the attempt is made to find the optimum solution to a particular set of problems—as for example between providing a maximum seating capacity for a large variety of events and perfect sight lines for all spectators. As these conflicts develop, the designer should be alert to them and promptly communicate alternatives to his client. In this manner a serious evaluation can be made of the alternatives at the appropriate stage of the design/planning process, thus allowing the flow of work to proceed smoothly with minimum wasted effort.

GENERAL PLANNING REQUIREMENTS

Projected Uses

Among the first program criteria to be determined regarding multipurpose arenas is the list of projected uses or events which are intended to be booked into the arena. Many events require their own unique features or support facilities which if not included in the original design and construction prove very difficult and costly to provide at a later date (e.g., inserts in playing floor surface for anchoring circus rigging). Some also have fixed dimensional or space requirements which must be accommodated and checked for sight lines. A list of the more common events currently being held in multipurpose arenas follows (Figs. 1 to 6):

Ice hockey	Horse show
Basketball	Rodeo
Boxing/wrestling	Bicycle racing
Indoor track	Rock concerts
Tennis	Stage events
Circus	Conventions
Ice show	Exhibitions
Roller derby	

Seating Capacity

The establishment of maximum seating capacity should be carefully evaluated prior to start of design. Several factors are important in making the determination including:

1. Market area
2. Professional franchises
3. Sponsor/owner
4. Budget
5. Viewing distance limitations

The market area, whether it falls within a large metropolitan region or a small college town, should have an influence on determination of optimum seating capacity. The overall size of the market area radius will depend not only upon total area population but largely on available highways and mass transit facilities. The nature of the potential audience must also be analyzed as to income levels, spending habits, and recreational preferences. The availability of competing arenas or other attractions will also be a factor.

The growing popularity of professional sports in the United States is perhaps the biggest impetus to the construction of new arenas. The professional hockey and basketball leagues require prospective new franchise owners to provide arenas of specified capacity and quality. These regulations should be checked specifically at the start of any design program, but in general terms of capacity they have specified 15,000 to 18,000 seats.

The nature of the owner or sponsor of any new arena will have some influence on the capacity decision. College or university arenas, except those with a history of top basketball teams and enthusiasm, will tend to warrant a capacity of 12,000 to 15,000 seats. A municipal arena with one or more professional teams as tenants will tend to be larger as stated above. Also arenas built privately as profit-making ventures will tend to be even larger, as well as to book a wider variety of attractions. Their economic success depends largely on creative and energetic promotion to keep "dark time" to a minimum. The operator of a municipal arena will be under somewhat less pressure to show a profit as the subsidization of operating deficits can be rationalized against the peripheral revenue an arena may bring to a locality through increased property values and business income from arena patrons.

In cases where an overall construction budget has become fixed prior to any physical planning or programming, this alone may

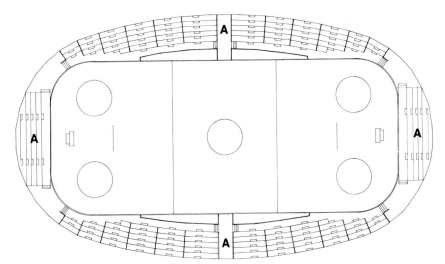

Fig. 1   Hockey.

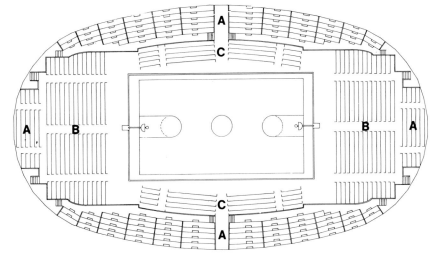

Fig. 2   Basketball.

Recreation and Entertainment
SPORTS ARENAS

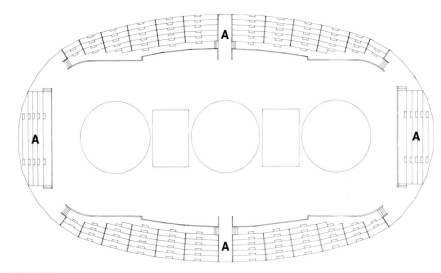

Fig. 3   Circus.

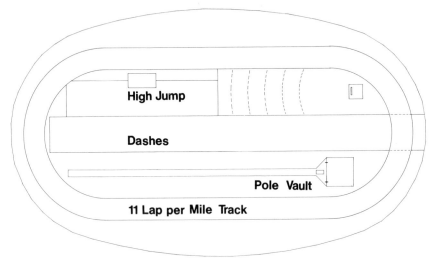

High Jump

Dashes

Pole Vault

11 Lap per Mile Track

Fig. 4   Track.

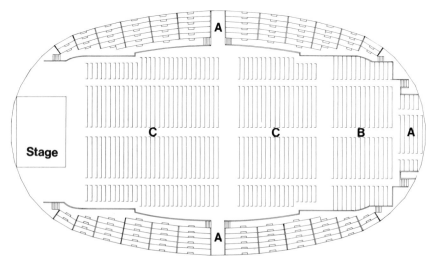

Stage

Fig. 5   Stage events.

establish the maximum capacity. Construction costs and circumstances vary too widely to attempt to quote here any cost per seat figures that would not be misleading. Estimates should be made at the completion of any schematic solution to test the scheme against the budget target. If reductions must be made, they should be balanced between capacity and quality. Too often it is a shortsighted decision to hold on to capacity at the sacrifice of material and systems quality which will have long-term penalties in operating and maintenance costs.

Possibly the most relevant factor in the determination of maximum capacity is that of optimum viewing distance. The limitations of normal visual acuity make any seating falling outside a radius of 200 ft from the center of action increasingly marginal. Although the Houston Astrodome and other planned enclosed stadiums either do hold or are promoting the inclusion of arena events, their success in terms of spectator satisfaction is less than ideal. If the 200-ft limitation is adhered to. together with a seating height limit above the floor of 65 to 70 ft (the resultant of sight-line angles and code limitations on riser heights), the maximum capacity will prove to be from 20,000 to 22,000.

Plan Configurations

One of the earliest decisions to be made in the design/planning process must be that of the basic physical form of the arena seating plan. The relative merits and problems of four plan forms in Fig. 7 will be discussed:

Straight Rows Ends and Side The straight-row arena is the simplest and most economical of all possible seating configurations. Most early gymnasiums with spectator seating took this shape, many utilizing fold-away bleachers or platforms which are readily adaptable to the straight-row plan. There is also minimum waste of seating area due to the absence of wedge-shaped sections between aisles. The seating sections are of course rectangular between pairs of parallel aisles. The aisle spacing can be set based upon the desired seat width and the maximum seats allowed between aisles, and it will remain constant for all rows. In a small arena tailored around the size of a basketball floor this shape is perfectly satisfactory. However, in a larger multiuse space where the rows would be straight for the length of ice hockey (200 ft or more) spectator viewing problems will begin to develop. As an example, a person sitting in seat X will be required to swing his line of sight laterally from left to right far enough to see both goals on the hockey ice. The view to the right requires a quite extensive movement (approximately 60° from a straight-ahead position). This will not only prove uncomfortable to the viewer (and many seats are worse than X in this regard) but visibility is additionally impaired the further the spectator must look left or right. This will be discussed at a later point dealing with sight lines and referred to as the "picket fence effect."

Straight-Row Sides and Curved-Row Ends This is perhaps the most commonly employed plan for arenas now in use. It maintains the economy and efficiency for a good portion of the seating paralleling the playing floor but takes the end seats around in a circular configuration from a radius point near each end of the floor. If the two radii are located well short of the ends of the hockey ice, thus keeping the straight rows as short as possible, a spectator in seat Y will have been relieved of much of

1302

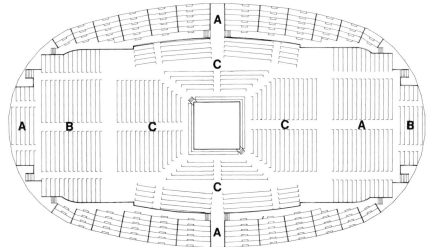

Fig. 6   Boxing.

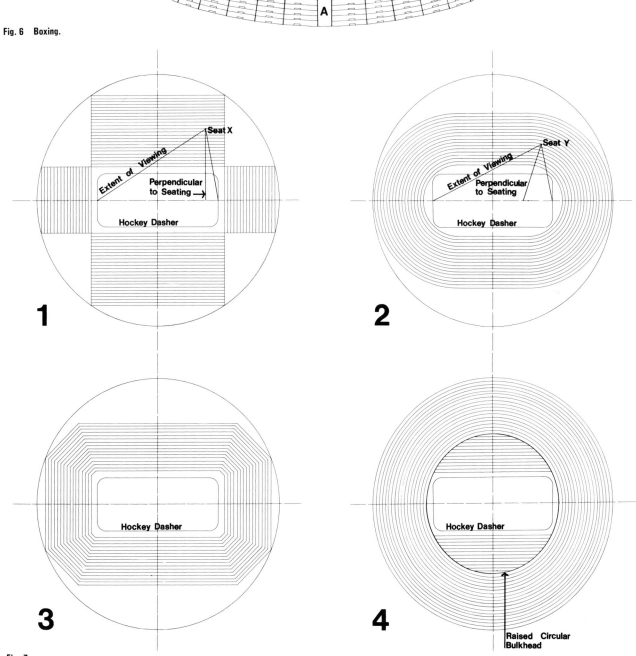

Fig. 7

the discomfort of seat X in Fig. 1. The maximum lateral movement for Y, which is now located in the curved area, is about 45°. Also, the line perpendicular to the seat falls much nearer to the center of the floor or the average center of activity for most events.

Straight Rows, and Sides with Diagonal Corners This plan configuration, also quite common, has all the advantages and disadvantages described in Fig. 1. Only those seats in the diagonal corners have relief from the lateral head-movement problem inherent in the side seats. In terms of construction economy it is the least costly of any configuration with full-perimeter seating, lending itself to precasting or other methods of repetitive trend/riser fabrication.

Circular Seating with Straight Rows at Side Lines Upon quick examination it would appear that a circular plan would be the optimum arena seating configuration. This might be true if all arena events were the size of a boxing ring and

seating could radiate outward and upward from a small central floor area. However, the introduction of an 85 $\times$ 200 ft hockey rink into the scheme brings with it almost irresolvable problems. In order to clear the ends of the hockey rink the innermost full circular row of seats must have a radius of about 110 ft. The height above the floor of this first circular row can be set no greater than 3 to 4 ft if spectators in the end seats are to see the near goal. Thus if this 4 ft height is followed around the row to the center point of the sidelines, a seat at this point will be 58 ft away from the dasher with only 4 ft of elevation. The seats along the sidelines within the space formed by the hockey dasher and the first circular row pose the dilemma. There is space for about 18 straight rows of seats, but with only 4 ft of elevation at the rear row of this group each riser could be only 2½ in. This would be too low for adequate viewing by spectators in otherwise prime seats. If the reverse approach is taken and the height of the first circular row is established at an elevation appropriate for the sideline

seats, the height will be about 10 ft (18 rows at 7 in.).

Following this 10 ft height around to the end of the rink would result in the first row end seats being 10 ft behind and 10 ft above the dasher—much too high for these spectators and those in the rows behind them to see the near goal. About the only possible way to employ this configuration is to omit the sections of straight-row seating along the sidelines and set the circular bulkhead at the low elevation. This has been done in a few arenas, the Palazzo dello Sport in Rome being one, but is not likely to be adopted in a commercial arena due to the large loss of prime revenue-producing seats. There is in addition a loss of intimacy between spectators and the game activity, which is very desirable to maintain, when such a large void exists between them.

Elliptical-Row Seating (Fig. 8) This configuration as illustrated for the Forum in Inglewood, California, and also used at Madison Square Garden in New York City has proved to be an

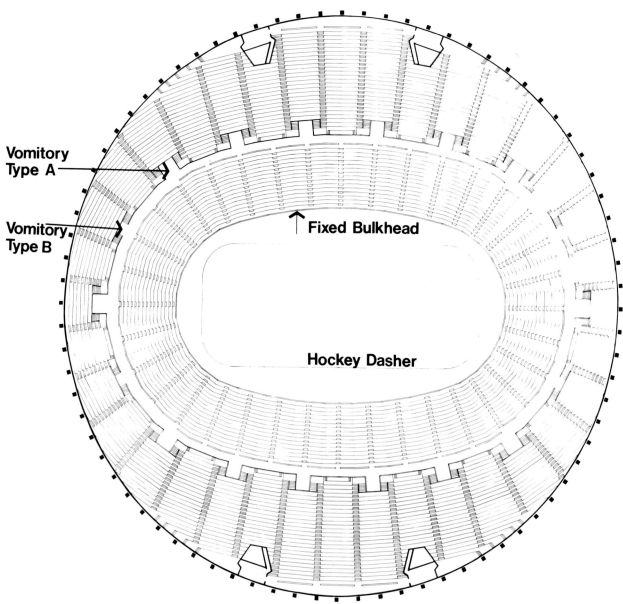

Vomitory Type A

Vomitory Type B

Fixed Bulkhead

Hockey Dasher

Fig. 8   The Forum, Inglewood, California.

optimum plan shape for this type of multiuse arena. It is the best possible adaptation of a curved-row configuration, desirable to minimize lateral head movement to the governing size of an ice hockey rink. In both examples noted above, the outer perimeter of seating was carried to a circular outer wall line. This being done primarily to take advantage of the structural economies of a cable-suspended roof system. The intersection of the elliptical seating form and the circular outer wall generate an undulating line at the perimeter. The high point of this undulation, and thus the maximum number of rows, occurs along the sidelines, and the low point with minimum seating occurs at the ends of the arena. The radius of the outer circular wall was held to approximately 200 ft to stay within the practical limits of spectator visual acuity as discussed earlier. The elliptical seating form was developed from circular arcs on a 4-center point system. Radius points for the two broader sideline curves fall 200 ft above and below the center line for the tighter end curves. They are 61 ft left and right of center.

Madison Square Garden seating differs from the Forum in one respect—the addition of a balcony (Fig. 9). As mentioned above, the main body of seating has an undulating intersection with the outer wall with a low point at the arena ends. Above these low end seats, space develops which can accommodate balcony seating. Madison Square Garden takes advantage of this option to gain maximum capacity. The balcony is given a circular configuration seven rows deep following the outer wall line. For a portion of the sideline areas the balcony blends with the main body of seating rising from below but is kept separated by a continuous circumferential bulkhead.

Seating and Sight Lines

The study of spectator sight lines in section should proceed simultaneously with development of the arena plan configuration. Sections should be developed at both the arena axis and several intermediate points in any curved plan configuration to verify the arrival point of sight for the maximum number of seats.

The "Picket Fence Effect" It is impractical to provide riser heights sufficient for spectators to see over the heads of persons in the row immediately in front. It is assumed view will be between heads of persons one row in front and over the heads of those two rows in front. Looking straight ahead, a spectator will have a reasonable wide angle of vision between two heads immediately in front. However, the further one looks to the left or right following players' action on the arena floor, the more this cone of vision between heads diminishes. It is the same effect as one gets standing a few feet in front of a picket fence. Looking straight ahead between pickets the view is little impaired, but as the eye moves left or right, the pickets gradually appear to move together until at some point they appear to form a solid surface. It is for this reason as mentioned in discussing alternate plan configurations that the curved-row plans are preferred over straight-row seating as they minimize the lateral viewing angle and thus the picket fence effect.

Two-Row Vision When plotting graphically or calculating sight-line sections, assume a spectator's seated eye level at 3 ft 11 in. above tread elevation and 5 in. from eye level to top of head. In most arena situations the hockey floor size will be the most restrictive in determining proper sight-line profiles. If sight lines can be made to work for hockey, they will be more than adequate for all other smaller floor size events.

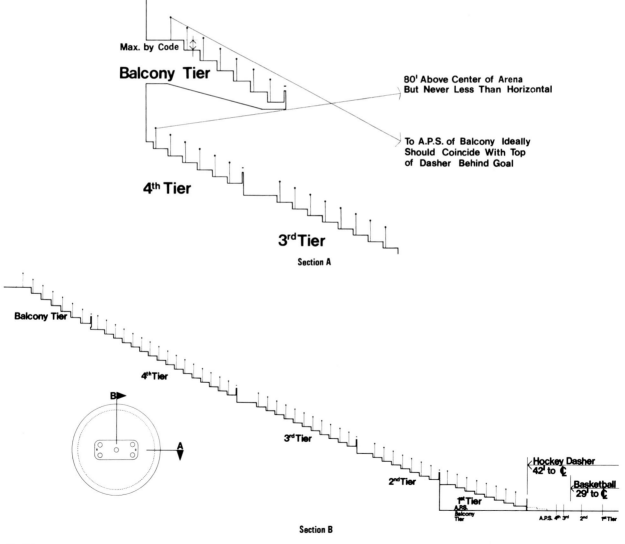

Fig. 9 Balcony.

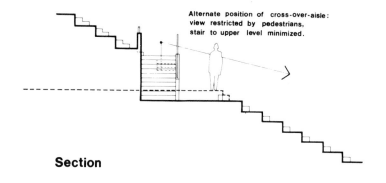

Alternate position of cross-over-aisle: view restricted by pedestrians, stair to upper level minimized.

Section

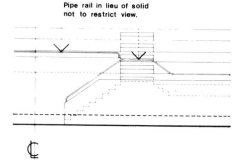

Pipe rail in lieu of solid not to restrict view.

Elevation

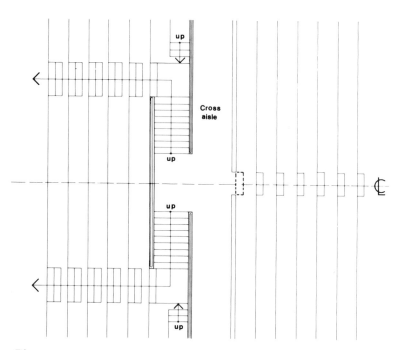

Cross aisle

Plan

Fig. 10   Vomitory – Type A.

The arrival point of sight should be made to fall at the top edge of the near hockey dasher (3 ft 6 in. above floor level). To graphically plot a series of sight lines, begin by assuming a height above the floor for the first row of fixed seats. This should be as low as possible to still accommodate temporary seating which will fall between the playing surface and the first fixed seats. Next extend a line from the arrival point of sight (APS) to the top of head of the first row spectator (tread height + 4 ft 4 in.). If you continue this line up and to the rear the distance of two rows, you will set the eye level for the third row of spectators. The trend height for this row will then be found by subtracting 3 ft 11 in. Tread heights are now established for the first and third rows; the second row will be midpoint between them. This procedure should be repeated for each successive row working from the bottom up. When a full section of seating is plotted in this manner with all sight lines meeting the same APS, the section profile will have a slightly dished or bowl effect, with each riser height being a fraction of an inch greater than the one below. For

the sake of construction economy, risers are grouped in sections of four or five of the same height before an increase is made. Several trials may need to be made to keep the overall profile within desired limits. Changes can be made in the original assumptions of first tread elevation and tread width which can alter the cross section as successive rows are plotted. For instance, if too high an elevation is selected as the lower row starting point, the upper rows may develop riser heights which exceed code limits, or the overall building height might prove too great.

Tread and Riser Dimensions   Tread width of rows should vary between 32 and 36 in. The wider dimension is generally used in the lower tiers of seats which are of shallow slope and where the extra comfort is commensurate with their premium cost. Any tread width below 32 in. should be avoided if possible especially if upholstered seats are used. In addition to sacrificing spectator comfort, narrower rows inhibit travel to concessions at intermissions and prove more time-consuming for mainte-

nance personnel to clean. Riser heights will vary from 3 or 4 in. to $22\frac{1}{2}$ in. Generally risers can go up to $7\frac{1}{2}$ in. before an additional step must be added in the aisle. Risers over 15 in. will require two steps and to accommodate the two steps the tread must be at least 36 in. wide. These tread and riser dimensions are accepted good practice but should be checked against local codes for specific situations.

Aisle Width and Spacing   Recommended aisle width is 3 ft 0 in. Spacing of aisles is usually every 14 to 15 seats. Where seating sections abut a wall or railing, the dead-end distance should not exceed 7 seats. Where aisles are radial to one another in curved configurations, each seating section cannot exceed the maximum allowable width at its upper or wide end. Thus some inefficiencies develop as at the lower end of these sections only 7 or 8 seats may separate aisles.

Crossovers – Width and Spacing   Crossover aisles will be needed at one or more locations which run horizontally parallel to the seating rows and connect the vertical aisles with vomitories leading under the seating to exits and promenades. Again local codes should be consulted for specific requirements. However, crossover width should be between 4 and 6 ft depending upon spacing of vomitories. It should be kept in mind that a bulkhead will be required at the rear side of the crossover and the tread of the first row behind it raised to a height to allow sight lines not to be interrupted by the lower seats. Where site conditions permit, it is ideal to have both a lobby/promenade and a crossover aisle at or near grade level. The seating can then be split with approximately one-half below grade and one-half above, which very much simplifies exiting problems. Crossovers at the top of balconies should generally serve not more than seven rows of seats. Aisles running up from a crossover and dead-ending at a wall or bulkhead should not serve more than 18 to 20 rows.

Vomitories   As stated earlier vomitory width and spacing will be governed by local code conditions. When they are used in connection with horizontal crossovers, stairs will be required to reach the first row to the rear of the crossover which must be elevated 4 to 5 ft. Two types of vomitories are illustrated:

Vomitory Type A (Fig. 10). Here a stair leading to the upper seating flanks either side of the vomitory passage. These stairs are entered at their lower end before reaching the crossover and thus minimize crowd congestion. Two

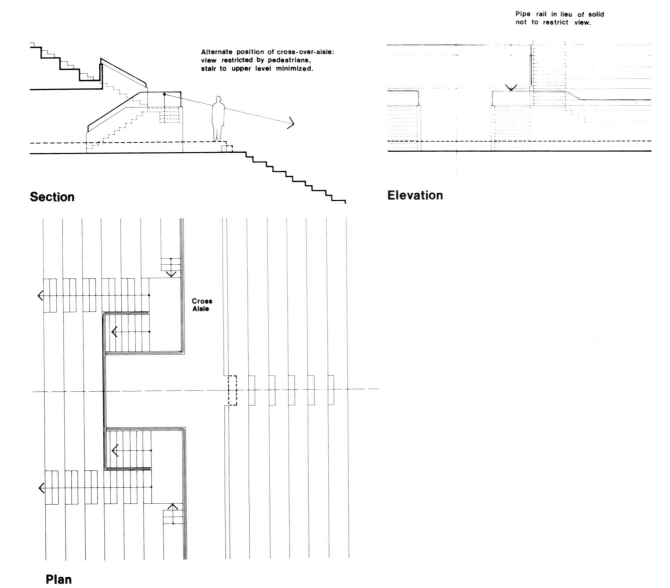

Alternate position of cross-over-aisle: view restricted by pedestrians, stair to upper level minimized.

Pipe rail in lieu of solid not to restrict view.

Section

Elevation

Cross Aisle

Plan

Fig. 11 Vomitory — Type B.

possible elevations exist for the crossover relative to the seating tread levels. It can either be flush with the last row of seats on its front side or be one riser above this last row. The crossover at the lower level minimizes visual interference for spectators in the upper seating from those walking the crossover and is the preferred alternative. The other option does reduce the height of the bulkhead and thus the number of steps required to reach the upper seating. Railings on these stairs and bulkheads should be solid for their lower portions with open pipe rail above. The total height should be kept as low as allowable to prevent sight line interference.

Vomitory Type B (Fig. 11). This detail may be used either as part of a full vomitory or as a stair access only to upper seating tiers. It is not as desirable as Type A in a vomitory situation, as the stairs empty into the traffic path between crossover and vomitory and can cause excessive congestion.

Truck Access. Access to the playing floor surface for large trucks will be required at one or more points. Vomitories at least 10 ft

wide and 14 ft high should be provided at one end of the playing floor. Two are preferred in those arenas expecting to book circus performances to allow for the promenade of animals and performers out one and in the other. Temporary treads and risers can be placed over these large vomitories to gain seating capacity when they are not in use. It also follows from the exterior to this floor level by some means as well as to the loading/receiving area of the building. Additional vomitories will be needed to give spectator access to and from the temporary floor seating setups. Also required will be an opening or vomitory at one end of the arena floor to allow for the overrun for indoor track dash events. At least 20 yards should be available past the finish line of the 60-yard dashes for this purpose.

Temporary Seating For most events some amount of temporary seating must be set up to fill in the gap between the fixed seating and the size of the playing surface or performance area. This will in some cases be flat on the floor or on shallow riser platforms.

To minimize labor cost for setups, the largest amount possible of this seating should be on platforms which telescope out from the periphery of the fixed bulkhead line. Where riser heights are sufficient to permit it, these seats can be left attached to the platforms and folded flat to allow stands to be pushed against the bulkhead wall. Where this is not practical, the seating and/or the platforms will have to be disassembled, stacked, and moved to storage areas in other parts of the building.

Crowd Movement

Great care should be taken in the design/planning process to avoid building in situations which will inhibit the smooth flow of spectators through the public circulation spaces and to and from the seating areas. This should be true for normal traffic situations or avoiding panic in emergencies. Activities which involve spectators waiting in lines must have sufficient room so that circulation is not blocked behind them. Toilet rooms must be laid out so that peak usage at intermissions is handled as fast as possible to avoid backups within the rooms and the corridors. Shallow pitch ramps should be used wherever possible in lieu of stairs at floor level changes. If escalators are used, ample room must be provided at their landings. Blockages must not occur and force dangerous situations as more spectators are forced into the space as they are delivered by the moving escalator. The general pattern of circulation must be clear, orderly, and easily comprehensible by the spectators. Graphic aids will help as discussed later, but they cannot overcome built-in planning flaws.

Building Codes

Code requirements relating to arena planning will be primarily concerned with exiting and seating circulation. It will be found that where they exist at all, regulations will vary widely from one locality to another. Many codes do not have any references to arenas at all, and interpolations must be made between specifications for theaters and outdoor stadiums. When this is the case, the designer's assumptions should be checked at an early stage with local building officials to avoid changes after final drawings are complete.

SPECTATOR REQUIREMENTS

Seating

Most arenas now being built are employing theater-type upholstered seats. The minimum recommended width is 19 in., and they should vary up to 23 in. center to center for the prime areas. In the wedge-shaped sections in curved rows, a mix of widths is usually used to make the ends of each row come out as flush as possible. Where risers are 5 in. or over, seat stanchions should be riser-mounted to facilitate cleaning. Seats should be self-rising with perforated acoustical treatment on the seat bottoms.

Concessions

Concession stands for food, beverages, souvenirs, and coat checking should be provided at convenient locations in the promenade areas. Counter areas should be as long as practical and if possible recessed in alcoves to prevent backup of patrons into circulation spaces. Storage space should be provided immediately adjacent to each counter area so that food items can be restocked to the sales area during a game or performance without a trip to the central supply point. If it is contemplated by the arena management that an outside concession firm be brought in to run the operation, it should be selected as early as possible and participate in the planning process. If the firm is an experienced national operation, it will have strong points of view on counter locations, size, visibility, and utility requirements among others. If not built into the original building, the concessionaire's desires will likely prevail at a later date and unsightly and costly additions result.

Toilet Rooms

Sets of men's and women's rest rooms should be provided at one or more locations on each public level. Their layout must provide for peak loads during the 15- to 20-minute intermission periods when hundreds of patrons will pass through each room. It is ideal if a one-way traffic flow can be developed with an in and out doorway separated by some distance. With-

in, the space should be divided with the water closets and urinals located near the entrance and the lavatories in a space near the exit. Also it is desirable if possible to design each toilet room so that half of the space can be closed off by some means during events of small attendance. This will save a good deal of operating cost for cleaning. Plumbing-line capacity should be studied carefully for peak use and generous pipe spaces with good access provided.

Graphics

A good graphics and signing control program is important not only for an attractive appearance, but for controlling and expediting crowd movement. Signing can help establish a clear pattern of movement which can easily be comprehended by the patrons. Seat colors in the arena can be keyed to ticket colors to identify the various areas or categories of seating. This can be done on a horizontal basis with rings of seats changing color as they change from one price category to another. Or the arena can be divided into quadrants each with its own color key. In cases where the arena sits within a large parking field, this color system may even extend to the exterior and guide patrons to the proper entrance as they park and approach the building. Within the seating area, signs designating sections, rows, seats, etc., should be large, clear, and located in easily read places. Signs for rest rooms, concessions, telephones, etc., should also be of good scale and clear and consistent in style. In the lobby ticketing area, space must be provided for coming attraction signs, current-event pricing, and seating plans for various event setups. It has proved successful also to have a scale model of the arena seating including colors and section identification within the ticket sales area to assist patrons with their ticket purchases.

Scoreboard

Two basic types of scoreboards are in common use. The center-hung 4-sided type is one, wall-mounted single-faced the other. The central type is usually on a drop cable system which allows it to be lowered to the floor for maintenance. The central speaker cluster can also be combined with this type scoreboard, but it should be checked early whether the same suspension height is appropriate for both scoreboard visibility and sound distribution. When the wall-mounted type is used, at least two units will be required so that all spectators will have a proper view. Very often the building management will arrange for advertising display to be incorporated into the scoreboard design as a revenue-producing device. If so, the decision should come as early as possible, as it will have obvious effect on size and detailing. The boards, of whichever type, must have provisions for the major sports that are likely to use the arena and have a portable control console that can operate from several positions depending on the sport involved.

Public/Private Clubs

Most new arenas will include a club or restaurant facility. These are often tied to the purchase of season tickets and their use restricted to these patrons. Capacity might vary from 150 to 300 people. This facility should be located within easy reach of the seating area and also be accessible to patrons at hours other than when the building is open to the general public for events. If an outside con-

cessionaire is involved for the arena, it will also likely manage this club. A typical commercial kitchen will probably be required and should be so located as to be easily serviced from the central trucking/receiving area. This kitchen may also serve to cater food to other parts of the building such as the owner's suite and press lounge.

OPERATING REQUIREMENTS

Administrative Offices

Areas for the building manager, accounting, personnel, booking, publicity, and engineer are generally provided within the building. In addition, office space may be required for the various teams who use the building, whether they are only tenants or are owned by the arena owner. Additionally, office space should be available for use by shows booked into the arena for an extended period (circus, ice shows, etc.). Also, the owner of the arena, if it is a private venture, will usually require a suite of rooms including his office, private bath, and a conference/meeting room suitable for entertaining dignitaries. Food may be catered to this area from the central club kitchen; thus it should be within easy access. It is possible in some instances that a portion of the offices mentioned could be located in other space remote from the arena. This decision and a full program of office requirements should be developed at an early stage of the design/planning process.

Ticketing Facilities

This area will vary depending upon the intended scope of events to be booked. However, in most situations, ticket booths will be required in the lobby area or an outer lobby. They should be accessible to the public during non-event periods without losing security to the remainder of the building. Madison Square Garden has 25 booths, the Forum, 20. Immediately to the rear of the booths should be a large ticket room for storage and sorting advance sale tickets. Also required will be a money room with vault, group sales office, ticket manager's office, and a work area for storing event posters and making up ticket pricing boards.

Storage

Large bulk storage areas will be needed for a variety of uses. The temporary seating setups for the arena floor will require space to store both chairs and riser platforms. These are usually stacked on metal pipe racks as high as ceilings will permit and handled with forklift trucks. Space for storing the hockey dasher boards and glass, basketball floor and goals, and indoor track must also be provided. All of these should be so located relative to the arena floor as to minimize time and cost for the setting up of each event.

Locker and Dressing Rooms

If the arena is the permanent home of two professional teams (hockey and basketball, for example), a pair of separate home team dressing rooms will be required (Fig. 12). As illustrated, the teams can share toilets, shower room, a training area, and the trainer's office. The hockey dressing area should be somewhat larger than that for the basketball dressing area because of larger team size and more cumbersome equipment. A pair of rooms for visiting teams somewhat smaller than the rooms for home

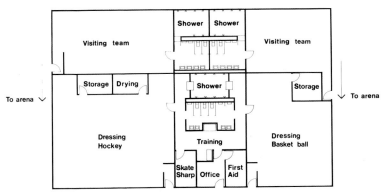

Fig. 12 Dressing rooms.

teams, can be located adjacent to or nearby with home team rooms as shown. Several smaller dressing and interview rooms should be planned in this area. Some can be for individual use, others for four to six people, and each with appropriate toilet facilities. All these spaces should be located at arena floor level with convenient vomitory access to the playing floor. Public exiting traffic should be routed away from the dressing area corridors.

Press Facilities

A press workroom with adjacent Teletype room and toilet should be located near the lower seating area. It is also desirable to include a lounge in this group with facilities to set up a small bar and food service from the main concession kitchen. A small photographer's work area and darkroom should also be provided at the arena floor level. Location of the press seating varies widely. Many arenas which have been built with elaborate press booths high above the floor have discovered them unused, reporters preferring to sit at courtside near the action. Radio and TV announcers, however, usually prefer to sit high for an overall view of the action. Booths for this purpose can be located over vomitory openings or suspended from the ceiling or balcony structure.

Concession/Vendors' Storage

Large bulk storage areas will be required for the concessionaires' supplies of dry food goods, beverages, meat, general supplies, souvenirs and programs. This may include walk-in refrigerator space and cold rooms as specified by the operator. Also needed will be a concession manager's office, a security area for counting money and a vault. Ample vendors' stations will be needed at several points around the arena. They must be located within easy reach of the seating and be laid out to allow fast refill of the seat vendor's stock. Separated inout doors are helpful.

Employee Toilets/Lockers

As seen from the following space allocation summary, several categories of employee spaces will be necessary. General cleaning and maintenance help, ushers, and concession employees each need separate toilet/locker facilities. As local conditions might warrant, space may also be needed for security guards and parking lot employees. Definitive space needs for each group will depend upon a management analysis of the numbers of staff required.

Television Broadcasting

Facilities appropriate for the telecasting of events are an important ingredient of all new arenas. Consensus as to number, location, height, and angle of camera positions is hard to find, especially if several networks or local stations are likely to be working out of the building at various times. However, an attempt should be made during the design/planning stage to meet with those broadcasting groups most likely to use the building and build in as much as possible such items as camera platforms and cable runs. Primary use of television in any arena will be for sporting events rather than stage or performance-type shows.

Camera locations for hockey and basketball should all be from the same side of the playing floor with one position high at center ice (at Madison Square Garden it is 64 ft above the floor and 120 ft back from the near dasher) and other positions at low level covering center ice and each goal. Space will also be needed for the station's remote truck, preferably at the building truck area, or a permanent TV monitor room. Any cables from the various camera positions will terminate at this point whether built-in or separately laid for each event. A built-in cable system which can be used by any station's crew is obviously desirable, as it prevents the unsightly view of large bundles of cable as well as avoids interference with circulation at the cross aisles and vomitories.

SPACE ALLOCATIONS

The following space allocations for the Forum in Inglewood, California, an arena of 18,424 seats, can serve as a planning guide and checklist of required facilities:

Area, sq ft

1. Play floor surface 26,900
2. Lobby promenade 20,000
3. Concession stands 2,500
4. Public toilets 4,800
5. Home team lockers/toilets 4,300
6. Visiting team lockers/toilets 2,100
7. Dressing/interview rooms. 1,200
8. Press work area 600
9. Darkroom 150
10. Men employee toilets/lockers 1,200
11. Women employee toilets/lockers . . . 700
12. Men ushers' toilets/lockers 400
13. Women usherettes' toilets/lockers. . . 600
14. Men concession toilets/lockers 350
15. Women concession toilets/lockers. . . 500
16. Truck dock 4,500
17. Receiving area 1,300
18. Storage — bulk 8,800
19. Storage — concessions/vendors 6,000
20. Storage — temporary seating 6,600
21. Storage — dasher glass 250
22. Ice machine 250
23. Administrative offices 9,000
24. Ticketing facilities 7,000
25. Private club dining and kitchen
26. Pay telephones — 22 booths

PUBLIC GOLF COURSES

Ideally the golf course should be designed and constructed so no major alterations ever will be required. However, even the greatest of golf courses have been revised and the organizers of a new golfing enterprise need not expect that their course will be the one in the world that will not eventually need some changes.

It always is advisable to engage the services of a competent golf course architect. Even if funds do not permit initial construction of the course so it will be completed with all the trapping of a finished course, the qualified architect's plan will provide for later installation of traps as money is available and the course will develop according to a wise plan instead of being a rather expensive and unsatisfactory exhibit of inexpert experiments.

There are many instances, particularly in rural areas, where the budget is limited. Services of a professional golf course architect may seem unnecessary. But knowhow is extremely important in planning and building a course. It is a wise investment to have someone experienced lay out the course, and especially to oversee construction.

Golf architectural authorities remind us that Nature is the best golf architect. The famed courses of Scotland which now are fundamentally as they were almost a century ago are proof that small town golf club organizers can do a great job if they are fortunate in selecting—or having available—sites that fit golf. Natural hazards make the most interesting and easiest and cheapest maintained hazards. The genius of the golf architect often shines brightest in his use of these natural features of terrain in providing shot problems.

But in many instances the ground is flat and without trees. The problem then is to provide a layout that will call for every sort of a shot that the best courses demand and that is usually done, as far as possible, simply by judicious variation in length of holes.

Such tremendous advances have been made in mechanical moving of earth that at even the flattest of sites not much money is required to move enough soil to elevate a green, taking the earth from locations where grassy hollows or areas for sand traps are left as improvements in the design of the course.

Selection of Course Site

The golf architect usually considers a number of prospective sites for a course and selects the one that, at reasonable cost of land, can be converted into a good course at minimum construction cost and maintained properly at minimum expense.

Size of property is important. For a 9-hole course, 50 acres is generally considered the minimum, and 110 acres for 18 holes. Even these areas involve risk of injury of players playing parallel holes. For the better courses,

Planning and Building the Golf Course, National Golf Foundation, Inc., Chicago.

80 acres for a 9-hole course and 160 for 18 holes is about right. Irregularly shaped plots often afford opportunities for most interesting course design.

Land shouldn't be too rugged. A gently rolling area with some trees is preferable. Land that is too hilly is tiring on players, usually necessitates too many blind shots and is more costly to keep well turfed.

The course should have practice fairway area close to the clubhouse. Some public and daily fee courses have installed practice ranges, lighted for night use, adjoining their courses or alongside the highways, and from these ranges they get considerable income and develop golfers for day play on the courses.

Accessibility

Unless absolutely unavoidable, a golf course should not be off the beaten track. This is especially important in the case of a small-town course planning on having the green fees from transients help to meet maintenance costs. Locate your course along the main highway into town. All other things being equal, design the course so one or two holes parallel the highway; it is good advertising.

Another reason for not locating the course in an out-of-the-way spot is that the club should have good transportation for the members. It should be as near to town as possible, cost of land should be taken into consideration, and the main highway from town to the club should be one that is kept in good condition and is not merely a country lane, unpaved and liable to become impassable with every heavy rain.

Soil Factors

Condition of the soil is extremely important because in the final analysis the better the stand of turf raised on fairways and greens, the more satisfactory and more popular will be the course. The ideal golf course soil is a sandy loam. It is not impossible but is expensive to grow a good stand of grass on a heavy clay. Be sure to take the character of soil into consideration when choosing the site.

Soil analysis of areas of the golf course site will be made at low cost by state agricultural departments or county agents. Considerable helpful information can be supplied by state agricultural experiment stations and county agents in determining the most desirable site from the viewpoint of good turf development and in recommending the grass seeding, growing, and maintenance program.

Past Use

Closely tied in with the above is the use to which the land has been put in the past. Is the plot a run-down farm where a large part of the plant food has been removed from the soil, or is it rich in the elements that will be necessary for successful cultivation of turf? Has the land lain idle for many years or has it been intensively cultivated by its farmer owner without his returning plant food to the soil?

The selection of property that has been well kept up as pasture land is highly advisable. Much money is saved in putting the course into excellent condition. Frequently the scenic attractions of a site are such that to the susceptible and uninformed organizers of a golf club, they totally outweigh soil conditions. A happy balance should be maintained between both factors. Pick a site which will offer no serious handicaps to the attempts of the club to grow a stand of grass and maintain it thereafter.

Power and Water Availability

Water and power are absolute necessities for any modern golf course. Even in the smallest communities, grass green courses with a clubhouse are being built. To water only greens and tees, or the whole course, and operate a clubhouse, you must have power and water.

The source of water should be close to the site, reliable and pure enough to drink and irrigate fine turf. It may be a city system, wells, lake, river or some combination. The cost of connecting to water and power supplies must be included in your plans.

How Much Clearing?

Consider next the amount of clearing that will have to be done in building the course. Will it be necessary to move many trees or grub out many stumps? Will it be an expensive proposition removing stones from the soil? Are there large swamp areas that will have to be filled in or drained? Do not misunderstand the statement above relative to clearing out trees. A golf course should, if possible, have patches of woodlands, as trees offer one of the best natural hazards if properly placed with reference to the course. However, it is an expensive matter to remove large growing trees, and the site selected should not have too many of these in those portions of the plot which will be fairways in the final picture.

Natural Golf Features

The last consideration in selecting the site is whether or not it possesses natural golf features.

This may seem to the uninitiated to be the first and most important thing to look for, but, as a matter of fact, natural golf features, while extremely desirable, are not nearly as important as the character of the soil and site location.

Rolling terrain, creek valleys, woodlands, ravines, ponds and the like, of course, make the job of designing an interesting course just so much easier, but all of these features or a substitute for them can be secured through artificial hazards. For this reason the presence or absence of natural golf features is perhaps less important than any of the factors that have been mentioned above.

Clubhouse Location

Location of the clubhouse, entrance drive, parking spaces, tennis courts, swimming pools, golf practice and lesson tees, fairways and traps and practice greens, is another job

CARD OF THE COURSE		
HOLE	YARDS	PAR
1	365	4
2	350	4
3	430	4
4	500	5
5	145	3
6	375	4
7	410	4
8	165	3
9	360	4
TOTAL	3100	35

Fig. 1   An irregular tract of ground lends itself to especially interesting architecture. Note how the architect has taken advantage of trees between fairways to demand accurate shot placement and protect players. Doglegging most of the longer holes presents a variety of problems in shot placement for the long and the short hitters. Note that only one hole — the short eighth — runs in a direct westerly direction, so watching the ball against the afternoon sun doesn't bother players on this course.

that requires a great deal of thought. The best location for the clubhouse generally is convenient to but removed from the highway. Road construction and maintenance costs must be kept in mind when locating the clubhouse.

Often the clubhouse site is a prominent hilltop, although elderly golfers may bemoan this choice because this means the finishing hole of the course must of necessity be uphill; they do not like a heavy climb at the end of a strenuous day of golf. Generally, a convenient and practical site can be found at a less elevated spot.

Mapping the Course

Authorities are well agreed on what makes the "ideal" nine-hole course in the matter of distance. All agree that such a course should measure over 3,000 yd, preferably around 3,200 yd. These authorities likewise agree that the par[1] of the course should be 35, 36, or 37, with the first mentioned most general. Just how should these 3,200 yd be apportioned among the nine holes? Most experts suggest two par-3 holes, two par-5 holes, the remaining five holes to be par-4's. Par-6 holes should be avoided. (See Fig. 1.)

Considering first the two par-3 holes, they should vary, for obvious reasons, in length; the shorter one should measure 130 to 160 yd,

[1] Par is an arbitary measure of the difficulty of a hole. It is the number of strokes an "expert golfer" would take to play the hole, always allowing him two putts after his ball is on the green. A par-3 hole, therefore, is one the "expert golfer" can reach from the tee in one shot; a par-4 hole, in two shots; a par-5, in three shots. Par figures for men and women, as established by the United States Golf Association, are as follows:
Men: Par-3, holes up to 250 yd, inclusive; par-4, 251 to 470 yds., incl.; par 5, 471 yd and over.
Women: Par-3, holes up to 210 yd, inclusive; par-4, 211 to 400 yd, incl; par-5, 401 to 575 yd; par-6, 576 yd and over.

thus requiring an exacting four-iron or five-iron from the tee; the other short hole should have the green a full long iron or wood shot away, say 180 yd or more.

The par-5 holes also should vary in length; one being on the short side for a par-5 (about 480 yd) and the other 520 to 550 yd. Both types of par-5 holes call for two full wood shots and well-hit iron approach shots.

It is advisable to provide a mixture of pars, points out architect Robert Bruce Harris. He suggests a par order of 4-5-4-3-4-5-4-3-4—36 as one that will be found highly satisfactory.

Under U.S.G.A. regulations, the minimum length of a par-4 hole is 251 yd, and throughout the country many courses contain holes of this length. Yet, only in rare instances where some physical feature redeems the lack of distance do these holes rate as even of average interest. They are too short; after the drive nothing remains but an easy chip-shot or run-up; there is no "kick" to playing so short a hole.

Indeed, this same objection attaches itself to par-4 holes even as long as 350 yd, where physical peculiarities are lacking

This distance, from 251 to 350 yd, is known among golf architects as "No Man's Land," a zone to be avoided if the course is to be genuinely popular with golfers.

Now that we have established a minimum length for the shortest of the par-4 holes, how shall we vary the length of the remaining four? It is very simple: They should be graded up by easy stages to the upper limit of par-4 (470 yd) so that after a regulation drive from the tee, the player is called upon to hit approach shots with different clubs.

Course Planning

Certain standard practices should be observed in making a course layout, among which the important ones are:

1. The distance between the green of one hole and the tee of the next should never be

more than 75 yd, and a distance of 20 to 30 yd is recommended. Tees should be not closer than 20 yd to a green because of the danger of being hit by an approaching golf ball.

2. The first tee and the ninth green of the course should be located immediately adjacent to the clubhouse. If it is practical without sacrificing other factors, bring the green of the sixth hole also near to the clubhouse. This is a feature appreciated by the golfer with only an hour to devote to his game, as six holes can be comfortably played in that time and at the finish of his available time he is once more back at the clubhouse.

3. As far as is practical, no holes should be laid out in an east-to-west direction. The reason for this is that a considerable volume of play on any golf course is in the afternoon and a player not only finds it difficult and disagreeable to follow the ball's flight into the setting sun, but it also presents a safety problem to other golfers. If an east-west hole is unavoidable, locate it among the first two or three holes of the layout so that a player will strike it as early in his round as possible. Southwest direction of holes is particularly bad.

4. The first hole of the course should be a relatively easy par-4 hole of no more than 380 to 400 yd in length. It should be comparatively free of hazards or heavy rough where a ball might be lost, and should have no features that will delay the player. This is for the obvious reason of getting the golfers started off on their game as expeditiously as possible.

5. Generally speaking, the holes should grow increasingly difficult to play as the round proceeds. It takes a golfer about three holes to get well warmed up, and asking him to execute difficult shots while he is still "cold" is not a demand that he will appreciate.

6. Whenever practical, greens should be plainly visible, and the location of sand traps and other hazards obviously apparent from the approach area, which is that portion of the fairway extending teeward for approximately 125 yd from the green.

7. Generally speaking, fairways sloping directly up or down a hillside are bad for several reasons: (a) steep sloping fairways make the playing of the shot by the majority of players a matter of luck rather than skill; (b) the up-and-down climb is fatiguing to the golfer; (c) turf is difficult to maintain on such an area.

8. If there are ravines or abrupt creek valleys on the property, a splendid short golf hole could consist of a tee located on one edge of the ravine with the green on the other, a suitable number of yards down or up the ravine. This calls for perfect control in carrying the ravine, permits the golfer to "bite off" as much of the ravine as he thinks he can carry, and does not unduly penalize the beginner, who can play straight across the ravine and then progress greenward on the other side.

9. The par-3 holes should be arranged so that the first of the two is not earlier in the round than the third hole and the other one is not later than the eighth hole. Par-3 holes should not be consecutive.

The old days of golf courses that punished the shortcomings of the dub so severely that fun was taken from the round have passed into extinction. Along with this penal design are going unnatural looking knobby bunkers, geometrically designed traps and tiny, miserably conditioned tees. Trees, slopes, creeks, lakes and other natural details will provide hazards enough for the average well-designed small-town course. If sand traps around the greens can be well maintained, their use provides the course with a feature that is of metropolitan course character. But if the construction or maintenance cost rules out such traps, turfed hollows in which the grass is allowed to grow several inches high and of a design that fits in the natural surroundings will do well (Fig. 2).

An eminent American golf architect sets forth points that are generally agreed on by members of the American Society of Golf Course Architects. He says:

The backbone holes of the modern golf course are the two-shotters, of 400 yards or over. The length of the two-shot hole offers plenty of opportunity to develop good strategy. Unfortunately, these holes are a little long for the average golfer to be able to reach in two, but this can be remedied by having sets of alternate tees.

The short holes should be kept under 200 yards in length so that every golfer has an opportunity to reach the green with a good shot and thereby obtain his par or birdie. These holes should be attractive and tantalizing in appearance with the greens designed so that they will become extremely formidable or relatively easy depending upon the position of the pin and the angle of the tee in use.

There should be as little walking as possible between greens and tees, but under certain circumstances it is more expedient to break this rule than to adhere to it. For often, where the property is rugged in type, a longer walk between the green and the tee makes it possible to obtain a good golf hole rather than a poor one.

The holes should be so different in length, character, and architectural type, that there is no feeling of duplication.

The three types of golf architecture—penal, strategic and heroic—should be used in good proportion.

In penal type construction, the traps guard the greens in bottleneck or island fashion. Here the average golfer must either hit the shot accurately or choose a club to play short in order to avoid the trouble which he would ordinarily find at his normal range. One or two holes of this type are usually sufficient in the composition of an 18-hole golf course, and should be the "short" or "drive-and-pitch" holes.

The strategic type utilizes fewer traps, adroitly placed, so that any golfer can hit with his full power but must place his shots to obtain the most favorable results. The modern golf courses are designed with about 50 per cent of the holes strategic in type. This architecture adapts itself best to holes of 400 yards or over, the par-4 holes.

The heroic is a blend of strategic and penal design. The traps or natural hazards, such as creeks, rivers, and lakes, are placed on the diagonal so that the player can bite off as much as he feels he can chew. The more he is able to carry, the more advantageous will he find his position for the next shot. This type of architecture is adaptable to all length holes, and should be utilized on 30 to 50 per cent of the holes of the course.

There should be no blind shots for ap-

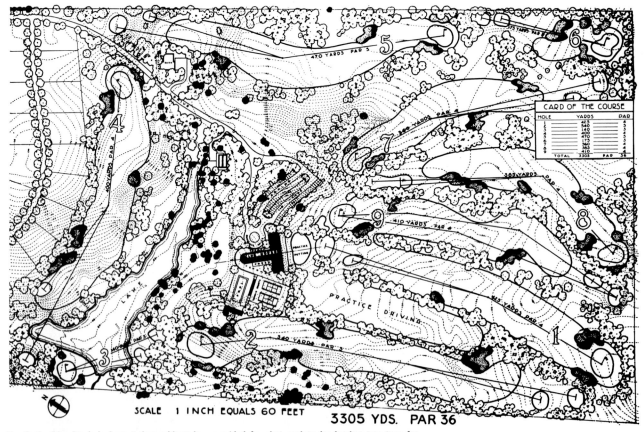

Fig. 2 In this nine-hole layout the architect has provided for shot variety by having two tees for each hole. Note too, the practice driving fairway, an important and popular course feature that many clubs have overlooked in their original planning.

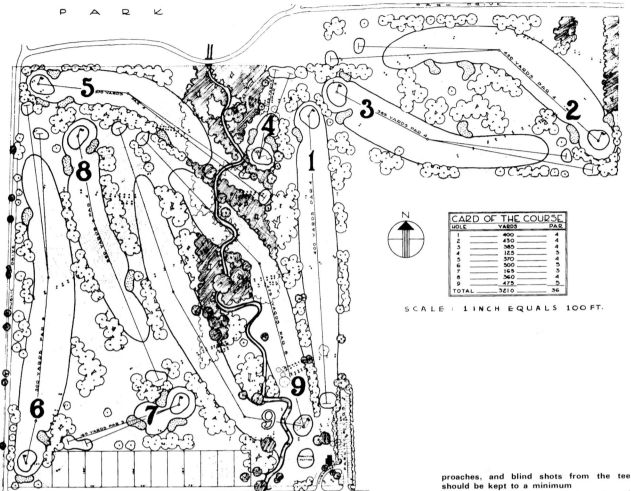

CARD OF THE COURSE

HOLE	YARDS	PAR
1	400	4
2	430	4
3	385	4
4	125	3
5	370	4
6	500	5
7	165	3
8	360	4
9	475	5
TOTAL	3210	36

SCALE : 1 INCH EQUALS 100 FT.

Fig. 3   Double tees add greatly to the variety with little expense. This plan suggests interesting use of two tees on all holes except the first and eighth, to give unusual variety to a nine-hole course. The ninth hole allows the choice of two distinctively different layouts. This sort of arrangement calls for planning that usually is beyond the capacity of any but the experienced golf architect. The 12 rectangular areas at the bottom border of the plan are prospective homesites that make especially desirable residential property when the adjacent golf hole is so laid out that golfers won't be coming into a yard for out-of-bounds balls.

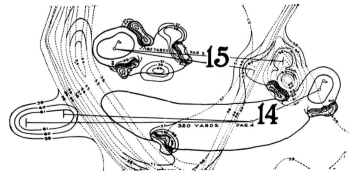

Fig. 4   Typical grading plan.

proaches, and blind shots from the tee should be kept to a minimum

There should be a sufficient number of heroic carries from the tee, but the routing should be so arranged that the player, with the loss of a stroke, should always have an alternate route to the green.

The character of the course should be so designed that during one round every club in the bag should be used.

No stereotype design can be used, but the principles of the design have to be applied in accordance with the natural terrain and the location of the proposed green.

On level or flat land a nine-hole course of 3100–3400 yards can be laid out in approximately 50 acres but it will be cramped. An 18-hole course of 6200–6500 yards or more would require at least 110 acres. This is a minimum, making the routing of the course extremely tight. Gently rolling land requires approximately 60 acres for 9 holes and 120 acres for 18. Hilly or rugged land will require considerably more because of the waste land where the contours are severe; at least 70 acres will be needed for 9 holes and 140–180 acres for 18 holes.

Before starting the routing of the course all the natural green and tee sites on the property should be examined, and as many of these as possible incorporated in the routing of the course. Natural sites should not be passed over in routing the course in order to obtain a hole of predetermined length, unless the hole would fall within the undesirable length of 250 to 350 yards.

The minimum length for a standard 18-hole golf course is 6,200 yards. A good average is 6,500 yards, and championship length is 6,700 yards and up. The short holes should range from 130–200 yards (par-3) and there

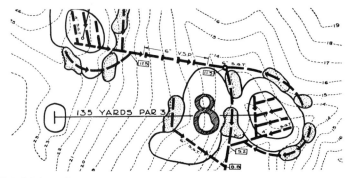

Fig. 5 Typical drainage plan.

are generally four of these holes, but there may be five. Par-4 holes should range from 350 to 470 yards, and there are generally ten of these. Par-5 holes should range from 471 to 550 yards and there are generally four of these.

The length of the hole will be determined by the slope of the terrain and the direction of play, the natural features from tee to green and at the green site, and the desire to obtain a variety of lengths throughout the 18 holes.

Fairway width generally is about 60 yards, but will vary depending upon the type of players expected to play the course, and the strategy of the play of the hole. A yardstick of fairway widths is as follows: 75–120 yards from the tee the fairway will be 40 yards wide; 120–180 yards from the tee the width will be 50 yards; 180–220 yards from the tee the width will be 60-70 yards.

The fairways can then narrow again if desired to the next landing area if the hole is long; that is in the area from 330–440 yards.

The green sizes will vary from 5,000 to 8,000 feet depending upon the length of the hole and the length of the shot called for. The shape of the green will depend upon the strategy of the design, the location and size of the traps, and the length of the shot playing to it.

Where the slope of a green is from front to back, the slope should not be more than five per cent, unless there is a break in the slope by a depression. If the depression is not too deep, the slopes of the depression can go from 10 to 15 per cent.

The slopes on the approach of a plateaued green can run as high as 20 per cent.

Mounds and slopes running from the surface of the green to the sides or back can run up to 20 per cent.

The slopes of the traps in front or on the sides playing toward the green will run from 30 to 40 per cent.

At the entrance of the traps the slopes should not be over 25 per cent so that the golfer's backswing can be taken with a full, clean stroke.

Golf Course Costs

There are four factors which determine more than anything else the wide range which one gets when trying to gather from all sources how much a golf course should cost. These are (1) the cost of land; (2) the natural assets and liabilities of the land chosen; (3) the labor and equipment costs in the area; and (4) the type of design. (See Figs. 3 to 5.)

Practice Area

In laying out the golf course it is well to have an area some 250 to 300 yds long, conveniently adjacent to the clubhouse where golfers can practice their golf shots.

Practice Putting Greens

If at all possible, there should be a practice putting green of considerable area near the clubhouse. This green should be surfaced with the same turf as the greens on the course, should be gently undulating, and is best arranged with nine or eighteen putting cups spotted about the green and numbered so that a player can putt from cup to cup in regular order.

Tennis Courts

Tennis courts get a good play at most country clubs. An area of at least 120 by 50 ft should be reserved for tennis, or larger space if survey of tennis possibilities among users of the club indicates greater need of space.

Children's Playground

Whether a club decides to operate strictly as a golfing proposition or to include the social aspects of country club life, it is a good idea to plan on a children's playground somewhere near the clubhouse.

By HAROLD J. CLIFFER, AIA

PRIVATE CLUBHOUSES

In private clubhouses functions break down as follows: social, golf and other sports, food service, storage, clerical and administrative offices, maintenance facilities, and on-site member, management and employee quarters. The individual components of these functions will vary from club to club, depending upon the size and class of operation involved. Components marked with an asterisk indicate those which are not absolutely necessary to a minimum operation.

Social Functions

In the organization of clubhouse functions the social activities are normally accommodated in the following main and supplementary areas:

Planning the Golf Clubhouse, National Golf Foundation, Inc., Chicago, 1967.

Main areas:
   Lounge
   Cocktail lounge
   Main dining room
     and ballroom
   *Private dining
     and party rooms
   *Card rooms

Supplementary areas:
   Entry
   Vestibule or
     lobby
   Men's and
     women's toilets
     and women's
     powder room
   *Porches and
     terraces
   Storage
   Checkroom

Lounge

The club lounge is really the stopping-off place for persons or groups waiting to participate in other activities as well as a passive recreation area. It is seldom occupied for long periods and should not be designed to provide seating for large groups gathering for affairs. As a matter of club economics, the space should be relatively small, not too amply furnished and accessible to the cocktail lounge. This acts as an inducement for people not able to find seating in the lounge to gather in the cocktail lounge and have a before-dinner or before-luncheon cocktail. Activity in the cocktail lounge is much more profitable from the standpoint of the management than having the lounge furniture warmed by nonpatronizing members or guests.

In addition to giving access to the cocktail lounge, the lounge should provide entrance to the dining rooms, men's and women's toilets and powder room, coat room and front desk, as well as to connecting circulation to locker rooms.

If there is a demand among the club members for provision of passive recreational activities, a library, museum, trophy room, card rooms, etc., may be provided off the lounge proper.

There has been some tendency in newer clubs to combine the lounge with the dining room. This has the unfortunate result of making the lounge into a dining room most of the time, and in creating the problem of constantly shifting furniture or in the accretion of lounge space by the dining operation, thereby reducing or eliminating the effectiveness of such a space. These spaces may well be contiguous, but some permanent full or partial division should be made between them to preserve the status of the lounge.

The provision of a fireplace in the lounge usually generates the feeling of what has been termed "a more homelike atmosphere." Whether a television set should be included in the lounge is a matter of club discretion. If a certain amount of quiet recreation is to take place in the lounge, then it would certainly be better for the television set to be placed elsewhere, preferably in the cocktail lounge or TV room, where it is an attraction and not a distraction.

Bars and Cocktail Lounge

The bar and cocktail lounge are almost consistently the profit makers for the club. The main cocktail lounge should be provided in the social end of the building. A secondary and smaller bar should be located in connection with the "Nineteenth Hole" and/or the mixed foursome's grill. Portable bars should be avail-

*Not necessary to a minimum operation.

able for large parties and receptions as the occasion warrants. As mentioned before, the main cocktail lounge should be accessible directly from the main lounge for those who wish to enjoy a before-luncheon or before-dinner cocktail. There have been some attempts made to place the bar at one end of the dining room, but this has proven unsuccessful on two counts: the drinkers feel too inhibited about imbibing freely while exposed to the scrutiny of the diners, and as a result of too little patronage, the management has complained bitterly that the bar cannot make money in such a location. Costly remodeling has been occasioned as a result of the incorrect placement of bar facilities and the lack of recognition of the traditional habits of even the most casual drinker.

Dining Rooms

The main dining room should be designed to take care of the day to day service of the membership as well as the special functions of a more regular nature. This is where the information obtained from the membership survey or from the management will come in handy in determining the scope of the dining area. Once the type and degree of patronage of the dining functions have been determined or estimated, then space can be allocated to handle the traffic. The type of menu and turnover per table are customarily used in arriving at proper space allocations for commercial operations. About 14 sq ft per seat is generally accepted as adequate in planning dining rooms for clubs.

If a dance floor is to be provided, estimates as to proper size for this function should reflect the frequency and intensity of use for a typical operating year. Normally, the dance floor may be used to accommodate tables for regular dining. However, dining space must be adequate to handle seating for those occasions on which the dance floor must remain free; otherwise a furniture moving problem is created which is both costly to the club and inconvenient to the members and guests.

In addition to a main dining room for the day to day service of members, additional private dining rooms should be provided for the private parties which are or will become a part of the club's standard operations. Most club managers at clubs with over 300 members agree that an absolute minimum of two such private dining rooms are necessary, one to handle about 20 to 25 people, and one to handle groups of about 60 to 70 people. Where two or more private dining rooms are provided, a pattern of flexibility should be considered such as using folding doors to make the spaces as adaptable as possible to a wide variation in the size of groups.

Private dining rooms should be private in the truest sense of the word. To have them open onto other dining or gathering places in any way can be a source of irritation and embarrassment to a host, who may have invited certain friends from among the membership and not others, and to the guests who have to face their uninvited friends as well. To provide privacy for the club members during outside parties or business luncheons taking place in private dining rooms, these rooms should be accessible from the lounge or the main entrance.

All dining rooms should be closely grouped around the food preparation center for the maximum speed and efficiency of service. Circulation to and from the kitchen in no case should be across public spaces. Circulation to private dining rooms should, insofar as pos-

sible, be directly from the kitchen and not through other dining spaces.

Dining porches and terraces, like other dining facilities, should be convenient to the kitchen. A dining space in or near the kitchen area should be provided for the dining room and kitchen help.

Supplementary Functions

Ordinarily, very little needs to be said about the supplementary functions of entries and vestibules, toilets, storage and check rooms. Yet, a surprising number of newer clubhouses have overlooked these features either in whole or in part. One northern club with a new clubhouse neglected to provide a vestibule to shield its members from the biting cold of the northern climate. Another club in the midwest forgot completely to include a coat checkroom. And, if any problem is common in the field of clubhouse design, it is the failure to provide adequate storage facilities. This applies to storage in all areas of the club and is discussed in more detail in a following section.

Clubhouse entrances, particularly in clubhouses located in climates which experience moderate to severe winters, should be designed with double sets of doors so that occupants of the areas immediately adjacent to the entrance are not subjected to cold blasts of air. In addition to providing more comfort, this arrangement also cuts down on heat losses and reduces fuel bills.

Provision should be made near the building entrance for a checkroom large enough to permit the storage of such items of outer apparel as are usual in the club's local climate. In addition, the checkroom should be large enough to hold a number of garments consistent with the size of the membership. Referring back to the programming in the previous section, the size of the checkroom and number of garments held should bear a direct relationship to anticipated or known patronage.

Occasionally, it is possible to make the toilet facilities of the golf section of the clubhouse available also to the lounge, dining rooms and cocktail lounge. However, it is considered better practice to keep these separate in order to be able to close off the locker room during social affairs.

The number of fixtures required in the toilet rooms normally will be dictated by local codes and ordinances. Generally accepted standards for the number of fixtures in the social end of the building are as follows:

Number of persons served	Number of water closets
75 to 100	5
101 to 125	6
126 to 150	7
151 to 175	8
More than 175	Add 1 water closet for each 30 additional persons

Where the number of men and women members is known, fixtures should be apportioned accordingly. In men's toilet rooms, 66 percent of the water closets may be replaced by urinals. Lavatories should be supplied at the rate of one for every four water closets and/or urinals. A women's powder room in connection with toilet facilities is generally provided, although it is not absolutely necessary.

Golfing and Athletic Functions

The following are the main and supplementary areas normally provided with golf and pool facilities:

Main areas:
Men's locker room, showers and toilets
Women's locker room, showers and toilets
Pro shop
  Sales and display area
  Office
  Club and cart storage
  Club cleaning room
  Stock room
  Attendant's station—
    shoe cleaning, clothes drying and
    pressing
"Nineteenth Hole" or men's bar and grill
Mixed foursome's grill
Pool locker, shower and toilet
  facilities (boys and girls)
Caddie house and caddie yard

Supplementary areas:
Entrance and vestibule from parking area
*Steam room and masseur's
  room
*Quiet rooms
*Auxiliary card room
*Electric car garage

Golf Facilities

With a little imagination, the golf facilities section of the clubhouse can be made considerably more attractive than they have been in the past. To say these accommodations often have been treated as an afterthought in clubhouse design would be an understatement. Locker rooms have been placed in dark, poorly ventilated basements, with exposed piping and ductwork overhead.

Clubhouse Circulation

The natural division of social and athletic activities in club operation is the key to clubhouse circulation patterns. One entrance should be provided to the social activities of the clubhouse, and one entrance should be provided to the athletic activities of the clubhouse from the parking area.

Within the clubhouse, circulation from the social activities entrance should proceed in the following manner from entrance to vestibule to lobby to lounge or cocktail lounge; from lounge or cocktail lounge to main dining room or private dining rooms; toilets and powder room handy to lounge, dining rooms and cocktail lounge; front office desk at lobby, offices behind; coat room at lobby; kitchen centrally located for most efficient service to all dining areas; connecting circulation to golf facilities.

Golfers should, first of all, have a separate entrance to the building and to their facilities so as not to interfere with more formal functions of the social activities end of the building. This entrance should be directly off the parking area. From the entrance, both men and women golfers should have access to their respective locker rooms. From the locker rooms, the golfers should be able to proceed to the pro shop either directly or via a corridor to check with the pro on the schedule of play, the status of foursomes, to pick up balls, tees, score cards, pencils, or some other special item of information or equipment which is needed. From the golf shop the golfer should be able to proceed directly to the first tee. From the ninth green the golfer should be able to reach the pro shop or locker room or toilets without a long hike. And, of course, the trip back to the clubhouse from the eighteenth green

*Not necessary to a minimum operation.

Recreation and Entertainment

GOLF COURSES AND CLUBHOUSES

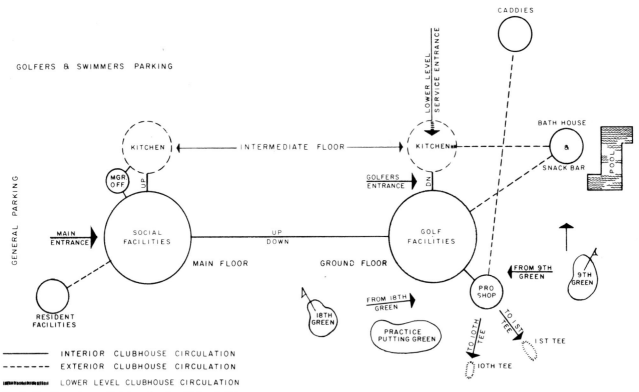

INTERIOR CLUBHOUSE CIRCULATION
EXTERIOR CLUBHOUSE CIRCULATION
LOWER LEVEL CLUBHOUSE CIRCULATION

Fig. 6 Two-floor scheme with intermediate-floor kitchen facilities.

should be as short and as easily negotiated as possible for the tired golfer. On the return trip to the clubhouse from the course, the "Nineteenth Hole," men's grill or mixed foursome's grill should be immediately accessible to the thirsty or hungry golfer. Circulation should be provided between the locker rooms and the social end of the house.

Access to teen-age facilities should be directly from the parking area without passage through the clubhouse proper.

Shown in Figs. 6 and 7, in diagrammatic form, are three basic types of clubhouse schemes. They are intended to show functional organization only. Topography, space and budgetary limitations will dictate which scheme is the most feasible in any given case. There may be times when a combination of these types is indicated. From these diagrams, the close correlation necessary between the course and site design and the building design should be apparent.

PUBLIC CLUBHOUSES

Clubhouse buildings for the municipal golf course or the privately owned public fee course are so different in operation and accommodations from the clubhouse for private clubs that they really constitute almost a separate building type. While it is true that many public course clubhouses serve as the focal point for the operation of a local golf club, it is rare that the accommodations of these structures approach the scope and quality of those of the private club.

Comparison of Private and Public Course Clubhouses

Where the private club attempts to make provision for every conceivable social and athletic need its members can afford, the

public course owner or operator, whether a municipality or a private individual, has only one objective in mind: to provide adequate and accessible golf facilities for as many persons as possible at popular prices. This means that all frills and extra services are reduced to a minimum, consistent with a profitable operation. In short, golf is a business and a means of livelihood to the private owner of a public course and a combination business and public recreation service for the municipality, where the private club is usually a cooperatively owned and subsidized social and recreational facility for the exclusive use of the owner-members. In the case of the public course, maximum turnover of play is of utmost importance from the standpoint of service to the clientele and profit to the owner, while at the private club, controlled play on the course is the objective, to assure the members available playing time without waiting or reservations. Moreover, social activities at the public course are primarily limited to socializing on the course and at the snack bar and generally little if any attempt is made, except under the rare and astute management of an occasional private entrepreneur, to provide social activities or dining facilities on or near a country-club level.

Another difference between the municipal and the privately owned public course operation is in the nature of the management. Of necessity the municipal operation must rest totally upon hired personnel or concessionaires, whereas the privately owned operation rests in the hands of the owner and his family and perhaps a minimum number of hired personnel. Fundamentally, this difference has no important implications in the design of these facilities, since it should be the objective of both types of operation to design and construct buildings which can be staffed with as few persons as possible.

Profits from public course operation are derived largely from green fees. However, most public course operators recognize the revenue producing possibilities of a snack bar, cocktail bar and golf shop. If properly designed and attended, these auxiliary operations can and do produce consistently good returns. The question facing most municipal and individual course owners is: what facilities should be provided, how big should they be and how should they be related?

Methods and Criteria for Planning the Public Course Clubhouse

Basically, the public course operator must proceed in much the same fashion as the private club to arrive at the proper size and type of building to suit his needs. The number of factors to consider are fewer but no less complex to analyze than in the case of the private club. Preliminary planning must be thorough, design must be attractive and efficient and construction must be economical.

Elements of Clubhouse Design

In a municipal course clubhouse, the essential elements of the design are the starter's booth, golf shop, food concession, lounge and public toilets. Locker and shower rooms may be incorporated into the design, although they are not necessary in all instances, and their use will depend upon local conditions. At privately owned public courses, the owner, in seeking to capitalize on his food operation, may actually increase the proportions of this accommodation to the extent that he has separate kitchen and dining facilities as well as a liquor bar or cocktail lounge.

In privately owned operations, where the owner decides to go into an extensive food

1316

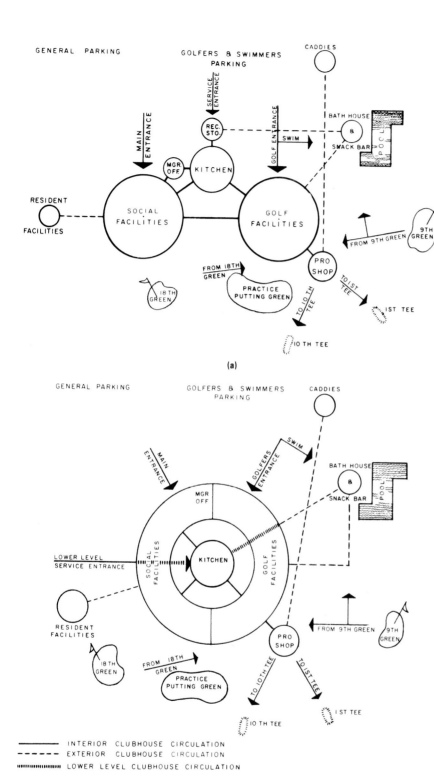

Fig. 7 One-floor scheme with (a) grade-level service entrance and (b) lower-level service entrance.

service operation, it is advisable for him, as suggested for private clubs, to call on the services of competent food service consultants as well as an architect. Before anticipating a large scale food service operation, however, the private operator would do well to assure himself that he is well acquainted with the intricacies and pitfalls of food service, or that he can obtain the service of competent personnel, concessionaire or catering service.

One of the prime considerations in the design of public clubhouse facilities is that the functions be arranged in such a way as to allow for the multi-use of employees, or so that the owner himself may attend to several operations at once.

Thus it should be possible for the starter to pinch hit in other operations, such as selling merchandise or food in slack periods. Or it should be possible for the golf professional to double as starter on slow days.

Building maintenance is handled in a number of ways in municipal operations, but the most usual manner is that city maintenance personnel handle it. The private operator, on the other hand, either has to do it himself or hire personnel to do it for him.

The more compact the facilities, the less overhead. As a general principle, the building should be designed so that as little labor as possible is required to operate and maintain the premises.

Clubhouse Functions

In the case of the public course clubhouse, the functions break down in a manner similar to those of the private clubhouse, namely into golf and social functions, in which the social function is reduced to the simple elements of a snack bar and lounge. The golf functions are mainly the golf shop, starter's room and, in some cases, locker and shower rooms.

Normally, the public course golfer will arrive at the course dressed to play with the possible exception of his shoes, which generally will be changed in his car. The question which often confronts municipalities constructing golf facilities is whether to provide shower, locker and lounge facilities, and if so, to what degree and in what manner they should be related to other activities. To establish what has been common practice along these lines, a study was conducted in which 38 communities throughout the country came up with some of the answers.

Clubhouse Relation to Other Recreational Facilities

Very often, to combine all municipal recreation facilities in one central location, municipalities will integrate the golf operation with other recreational activities.

Site Selection

Whether or not a new indoor range is to be located in an existing building or in a newly constructed one depends greatly on the legal considerations of zoning and special use permits.

Anyone planning to build an indoor range should first consult his local government for details of zoning, building codes, and special use permits. Some types of zoning will categorically exclude ranges of any kind; others will allow ranges, but require annually renewable special use permits and/or inspections by the local police or other governmental agencies. Some zoning codes will permit a recreational facility in many different zoning categories. If the proposed range is to be operated on a nonprofit basis by a civic club, fraternal order, or a group of citizens organized for that purpose, the recreational status of the facility may permit a wider range of site selections.

Once the questions or problems in zoning and permits have been resolved, the local building code should be consulted with regard to fire hazards, noise control, insurance liability, health hazards, restroom facilities, etc. This should complete the builder's responsibilities to the local authorities.

Next, the physical site selection should be considered in light of (1) accessibility—is it accessible in all weather conditions? (2) Is parking adequate? (3) Can the range be made physically secure so that there can be no unauthorized use? (4) Are water, sewerage, and electricity available? If not, what costs are involved in obtaining them?

When all of the site selection criteria are met, consideration may then be given to the decision to use an existing building or to construct a new one within the allowable geographical area.

Use of Existing Building

The use of an existing building is usually the most economical way to develop a new indoor range.

A number of factors need to be considered. First and foremost among these is space. The room in which the range is to be built should be at least 75 ft long for a 50-ft range. This allows approximately 8 ft (minimum) each for the bullet stop and firing line, plus a 9-ft assembly and spectator area. Emphasis is placed on the fact that the above dimensions are *minimum*. (See Figs. 1 to 3.)

The width of a proposed range can vary depending on how many firing points are desired. Normal points for pistol are 4 ft wide; for rifle, 6 ft. Rifle points 5 ft wide may be used if space is limited. Since most indoor ranges are used for both rifle and pistol, 6 ft should be allowed if possible.

Range Facilities Section, National Rifle Association, 1600 Rhode Island Avenue N.W., Washington, D.C.

Once it is established that there is enough space to locate the range in the existing building, the following factors must be considered:

1. Structural strength—can the floor or framework of the building support the weight of the backstop? A backstop of $\frac{1}{2}$-in. steel approximately 10 by 25 ft will weigh over 2 tons.

2. Doors and windows downrange must be permanently shut and covered with bulletproof material.

3. The walls, floors, and ceiling must either be bulletproof or be made so. This must also be a part of the structural strength survey—since adding material adds weight. A building which is built of cinder block or brick may be considered to have bulletproof walls for all practical indoor calibers. These are normally .22; .38; and .45 calibers. Wooden buildings should have wall protection of at least 2 in. of plywood. Wooden floors should be protected in the same manner, as should ceilings.

4. An air exhaust system must be supplied, and must be capable of a complete air change from 20 to 40 times per hour. The exhaust fan should be placed above the target line, with the supply to the rear of the firing line, so that combustion gases, lead dust, and other air pollutants are exhausted safely from the range area. If funds are available, a second exhaust duct should be placed just in front of the firing line so that the by-products of firing are exhausted immediately. In some states or local jurisdictions, an air filter on the exhaust may be required so that the contaminants are not exhausted into the open air.

Construction of New Range Building

A new range building may be put up as a shell, and extras added as more money becomes available, or it may be put up as a complete recreational facility. For instance, it would be entirely possible to include an indoor range as a part of a bowling alley complex which could have a restaurant and other recreational facilities.

However, regardless of the approach taken, the new building must meet all building code, zoning, and special use permit requirements as would the conversion of an existing building. In either case, it is strongly recommended that a registered architect be retained to draw up the plans.

DESIGN OF THE ACTUAL SHOOTING AREA

Once a suitable building has been converted to range use, or built specifically for that purpose, primary consideration must be given to the installation of a suitable backstop.

Since the backstop is probably the largest single expense other than the building itself, it is worth spending some time in making the decision as to which type should be purchased.

There are three basic configurations of backstops which are considered to be safe. They are:

1. $45°$ plate with either water or sand pit

2. $45°$ reverse plate with dry lead catcher
3. "Venetian blind" type backstops

According to the NRA Shooting Facilities Survey, the most common type of backstop is the $45°$ plate with a sand pit. It is also normally the least expensive to install, although maintenance may run slightly higher than for other types.

The bullet pit should cover the entire area under the backstop, and should be a minimum of 4 in. deep. The pit should be mined of accumulated lead deposits on a regular basis. The cleaning schedule depends on the amount of use, but would probably average about one mining and sifting operation per month. The sand itself should be changed about once a year, because of the unsiftable lead dust which accumulates in the sand.

The inconvenience of cleaning a sand pit may lead to the consideration of a water pit. This requires a water supply and a drain, but makes cleaning the pit an easier task. The water pit has other advantages as it creates no dust, and thereby reduces any health hazard. The lead retrieved is much cleaner than that from a sand pit, and is therefore easier to use for reloading. Lead dust which falls into the water trap is easily flushed down the drain.

Backsplatter occurs when a bullet strikes a hard surface. In the case where the surface is smooth, as a good backstop should be, relatively little backsplatter is redirected toward the firing line, and it travels only about 15 to 20 ft in small particles. Where the surface of the backstop is rough or pockmarked, the amount of backsplatter is increased greatly, and large particles can travel 25 yd or more with enough force to cause injury. This is reason enough to keep bullet traps clean, whether they use sand, water, or are of a patented variety. It should be emphasized that backsplatter is a physical phenomenon which occurs when any bullet hits any surface, and is of a much more serious nature if the bullets are made of a hard alloy than if they are of a pure lead.

Backstop Steel Specification

The type of steel which should be used for plate backstops has been a matter of discussion for many years. Different types of steel have been mentioned in reports and manuals, and it is entirely likely that most clubs have no idea what type of steel is in their present backstop.

The previous NRA recommendation for the type of steel to be used in backstops has been SAE 1020. This is too general a specification, as it deals only with the chemical content of the steel in question. In most forms it is too soft to withstand the constant impact of bullets for a long period of time.

Since this specification was inadequate, a study was undertaken to try to determine what type of steel would be satisfactory, and what type of processing treatment would be both economically feasible and have a greater durability than any type of SAE 1020.

It was found that there is a suitable steel which, when processed properly, is of greater

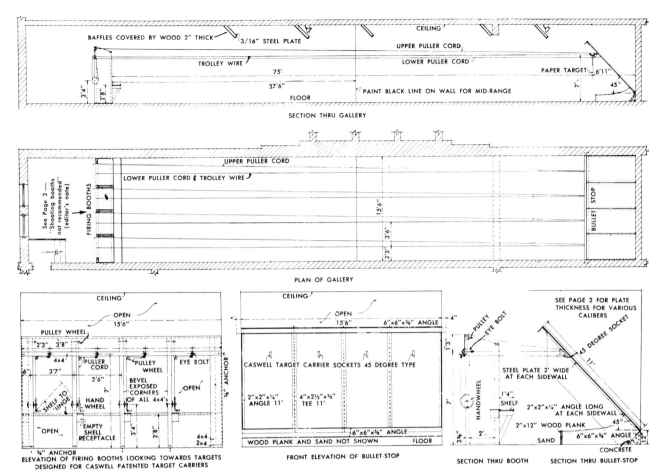

Fig. 1 Fifty-foot indoor range with club room facilities. As shown: 10 firing points each 4 ft wide. Width of building is variable depending on size of club and number of firing points. Structural details should be determined by a local architect or engineer.

durability than SAE 1020. It costs approximately twice as much, but has a much greater life expectancy.

U.S. Steel and Bethlehem Steel both have a specification which is available from warehouse stock. Other suppliers should be able to cross-reference this with little difficulty.

The U.S. Steel specification is type T1-A and the Bethlehem Steel is RQC-100-A.

These are characterized by the following specifications:

- ASTM type—A514, Grade B
- Yield strength, minimum—100,000 psi
- Tensile strength, minimum—115,000 to 135,000 psi
- Elongation in 2 in., minimum—16 to 18 percent
- Reduction of area, minimum—35 to 40 percent
- Brinnell hardness—321

This type of steel, since it is heat treated, requires low hydrogen welding practice in order to avoid impairing the performance of the material in the heat affected zone. Low heat inputs are also necessary. Further information on how to weld this material may be obtained from either U.S. Steel or Bethlehem Steel.

The General Services Administration has written a specification for target backstop

steel in their bulletin PBS: 3-1395 (INT), and the above specified steels come closest to meeting that specification in steels that are easily available in warehouse stock. The bulletin also carries the following specification for construction standards of a 45° plate backstop:

Steel plates supported by concrete or masonry should be anchored by expansion bolts or toggle bolts, as suitable for the construction, with flush countersunk heads, not more than 12 inches on center at all edges of each plate. Joints and edge lines shall be backed with a continuous $\frac{1}{2}$ inch plate not less than 4 inches wide. Bolts shall pierce both facing and back plate. Expansion bolts shall penetrate concrete not less than 2 inches.

Steel plates shall have milled edges at all joints. Joints shall be butted flush and smooth. Plates shall be free from buckle or wave after erection. Exposed edges shall be beveled at 45 degrees to a fillet approximately $\frac{1}{16}$ inch thick. There shall be no horizontal joints in any steel plate work. Welding shall be in accordance with the American Welding Society Code for Welding in Building Construction.

Steel plate jointed at and supported on structural steel supports shall be spot welded to steel supports not more than 6 inches on center.

The 45° plate backstop should be at least $\frac{1}{4}$ in. thick for standard velocity .22 caliber firing only. For .38 caliber wadcutters only, a minimum of $\frac{3}{8}$ in. thickness is suggested; and for .45 caliber pistol, including hardball, $\frac{1}{2}$ in. is recommended as the minimum. It is recommended that the above minimum figures be exceeded wherever possible. Greater thicknesses are recommended for larger calibers, not because thinner steel is penetrable by them but because the greater impact flows the steel and pocks it more easily. This requires resurfacing more often, and a $\frac{1}{4}$-in. plate, for example, would soon need replacement.

In order to avoid the unsightliness of an exposed backstop and pit, some ranges have a "curtain wall" installed. A curtain wall is simply a studded partition with $\frac{3}{4}$-in. plywood on the outer face, which in turn may be faced with acoustic tile. Removable sections are built in the wall in front of each firing point so that cleaning the pit is facilitated. A curtain wall provides a dual advantage other than neatness and the ability to use the range as a multipurpose recreation room. It stops virtually all backsplatter (which occurs from any backstop of any type), and it helps to keep dust confined to that area behind the wall.

The "venetian blind" type backstop is commercially available from several companies, and has the advantage of taking up about 40

1319

Recreation and Entertainment

RIFLE AND PISTOL RANGES, INDOOR

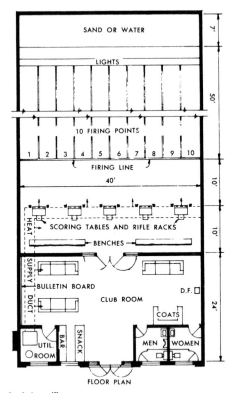
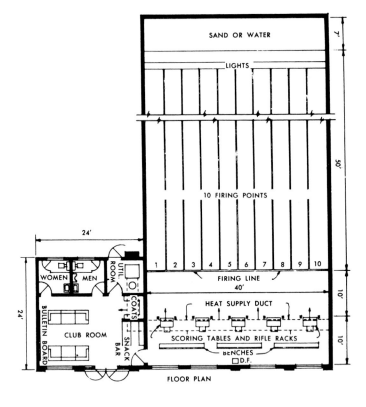

Fig. 2   Indoor rifle range.

percent of the floor space required by any of the 45° plate types. It is more expensive, however, and *should not* be installed by anyone other than the manufacturer. The reason for this is that an *improperly* installed venetian blind type backstop can be dangerous as a generator of ricochets and backsplatter. The steel plates *must* be set at precise angles and the top lip of each ground off to a knife edge so that it does not generate ricochets. (See Fig. 4.)

The so-called "reverse 45° plate" backstops are also commercially available, and because of their unconventional methods of catching bullets should also be installed only by the manufacturer.

The safety of all backstops mentioned is equal *if they are properly maintained.*

Shooting Booths Not Recommended

The NRA does not recommend the use of shooting booths for the following reasons:

They create sections of the range which are concealed from the range officer. Without visual contact with each shooter, the range officer does not have control. Without control, accident potential increases.

They may create a careless mental attitude toward the handling of firearms because they separate the individuals using the range from one another, creating the mental attitude of being relieved of the responsibility to handle firearms in a safe manner.

Booths can also increase the noise level to the individual shooter even if properly constructed because the muzzle blast tends to be reflected directly back at the shooter.

In addition, booths dilute the feeling of being in real shoulder to shoulder competition, which is an important part of tournament shooting.

A Safe Range Interior

A safe range should have walls, ceiling, and floor that are either impenetrable to the bullets of the firearms being used within it, or have internal baffling built so that the bullets cannot hit the walls or ceiling. Since the guns being fired normally on an indoor range are .22; .38; and .45 caliber, it follows that walls which are impenetrable to these calibers are adequate. If guns of higher power are to be used, additional precautions must be taken accordingly. It is not recommended that high-power rifles be fired at a conventional 45° steel backstop because of the probability of penetration rather than deflection.

Masonry walls of any type are usually safe in this case, even with the possibility of .44 magnum pistols being used. This type of wall should be relatively smooth and free of pilasters or other protrusions. If pilasters, etc., do exist, it is recommended that the surface of the wall be covered by ¾-in. plywood, at least in the area where the protrusions occur. The plywood should be laid on over standard furring strips so that in case the plywood is struck, the bullet is not likely to ricochet back out. The space behind the plywood acts as a bullet trap into which the bullet tumbles. If the plywood is flush against a wall, a bullet is more likely to ricochet back out.

Wooden or plaster type walls on an indoor range should also be smooth and free of protrusions. They should be covered completely with at least 2 in. of plywood, attached in the same manner as described for a masonry wall.

The nominal 2 in. of plywood can be two 1-in. thicknesses, or preferably three ¾-in. thicknesses of plywood. The plywood will stop any of the standard .22, .38, or .45 caliber bullets which would normally be used. If a heavier caliber is to be used, tests should

be made to determine the protection needed.

Floors which are over another room should be covered with at least 2 in. of plywood as described above for at least 8 ft in front of the firing line, and by at least 1 in. from there to the backstop, providing that .45 caliber ACP is the most powerful cartridge used in the range.

Ceilings present somewhat more of a problem. Since some buildings are constructed using precast concrete, others with steel bar joists for roof or floor supports and still others with wooden beams, measures must be taken to eliminate any possibility of ricochet or penetration. This can be accomplished by the same thickness of plywood as noted above, and at the same distance from the firing line.

Another and perhaps better way in which a high ceiling may be protected is by the use of plywood baffles, arranged vertically from the ceiling in such a way that the ceiling is not visible from the floor level of the firing line. They should not be more than 4 ft in depth. Baffles constructed in this manner will use considerably less material than covering the ceiling entirely, and have the capability of being used simultaneously as mounting for range lighting. They will also act as sound baffles, and if treated with acoustic insulating material as described later in this text, will be very effective in helping to lower the noise level within the range. (See Fig. 5.)

Any service equipment that is exposed downrange of the firing line should be protected. This may include electric wiring, lighting, water pipes, heating and ventilation ducts and exhaust fans. All of these items should be protected by two thicknesses of ¾-in. plywood backed by 12-gauge (0.1-in.) steel.

Flat metal surfaces parallel with the firing line should not exist. If such a surface exists, it should be covered with plywood as described above.

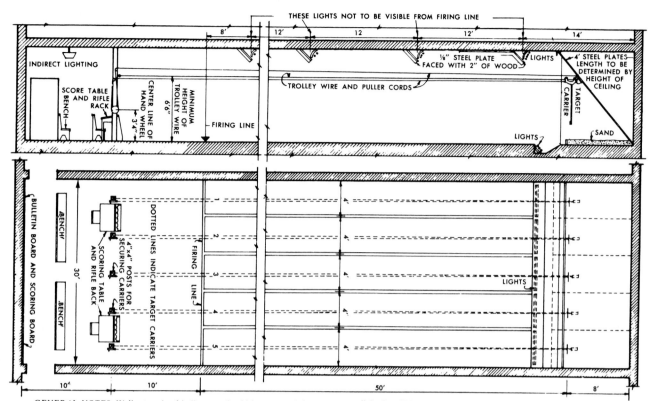

GENERAL NOTES: Walls at ends of bullet-stop should be protected from bullet splatter by ⅛″ steel plates. Doors between firing line and bullet-stop must be bolted on range side. Arrange lights to have 40 to 50 foot-candles of reflected light from the face of the targets and 5 to 10 foot-candles of indirect light at firing line. Indoor reflector flood lights furnish good light on targets if fluorescent types are not used. Paint walls, ceiling and bullet-stop a light tint of blue or green. Desirable target carriers may be purchased or made by the club "handy men". If space permits, mount target carriers behind firing line on steel pipes or 4″ x 4″ wood posts running from floor to ceiling. Provide for drinking water and toilet facilities as well as for heating and ventilation of range areas.

Fig. 3   A revolver gallery for the Minneapolis police department. (Caswell Target Carriers, Anoka, Minn.)

Range Lighting

Range lighting can be accomplished by use of either incandescent or fluorescent sources. The fluorescent type is more expensive to install, but is far more economical to operate and maintain.

Fluorescent lighting is in wide general use, although it can induce eyestrain somewhat more quickly than incandescent lighting because of the higher ultraviolet emission. Whichever type is used, it should be of the indirect or diffused type.

The intensity of the lighting should be rather high (approximately 75 footcandles), and there should be little difference in the intensity level throughout the range area. Under no circumstances should the firing line be dark or dimly lit. This can cause eyestrain. A dark firing line causes an enlargement of the pupil which results in a drop of visual acuity and a corresponding enlargement of the blur circle on the target. The lower edge of overhead lighting protective baffles should be high enough so that a shooter has no problem seeing downrange. Ideally, this would be no lower than 8 ft, so that there is as little "shut-in" feeling as possible.

Range Painting

Painting of the range should be done in light pastel tints with latex flat paint. Bland, pleasing colors such as beige or blue-greens should be selected.

Range Ventilation

One of the major hazards to health in an indoor range is the lack of proper ventilation. This condition exists on a number of ranges which are otherwise well designed.

Air should always be exhausted *away* (downrange) from the firing line. The preferred spot for a single line of exhaust ducts is over the target line, so that the lead dust generated by bullets striking the backstop is taken out of the area as quickly as possible. If possible, a second line of exhaust ducts should be placed no more than 8 ft in front of the firing line, so that the combustion gases of firing can be taken away quickly.

The combustion of smokeless powder forms carbon monoxide, carbon dioxide, nitrogen oxides, methane, and some solid organic material. All of these products are irritants and in enough concentration can make shooting unpleasant. In a poorly ventilated range, prolonged exposure can cause headaches and nausea, and can irritate eyes and respiratory passages. The major hazard of poor ventilation is the lead dust caused by the lead bullets striking the backstop. The maximum allowable concentration of lead acceptable for an 8-hour daily exposure should not exceed 0.20 milligrams per cubic meter concentration. The reason that the lead dust is considered to be the major hazard is that lead is an accumulative poison in the body and is not excreted.

The ventilation system should be designed in such a way that the total volume of air in the range is changed from 20 to 40 times per hour. A steady, positive flow of air toward the backstop at a velocity of 50 ft per minute is the acceptable minimum.

Noise Reduction

The discharge of any firearm creates a muzzle blast which has the capability of affecting hearing. Prolonged exposure to such noise levels can inflict permanent, uncorrectable hearing damage. A firearm that fires a bullet which is transonic (more than 1,140 ft per second) generates the characteristic sonic "boom" which because of its high frequency component is even more damaging to hearing.

Even .22 caliber match bullets at times exceed the speed of sound at the muzzle, and this phenomenon is accompanied by the high whiplike crack which is sometimes heard in gallery ranges. Hearing damage, therefore, can result even from the .22 rimfire cartridge.[1]

Noise Reduction on the Range

The walls, ceiling, and floors of a gallery range may be treated with effective sound absorbent materials.

The wall area next to the firing line and the ceiling directly above and for 2 or 3 ft in front

[1] Ref.—Acton & Forrest—Noise & Hearing, *Journal of the Acoustical Society of America,* April 1968

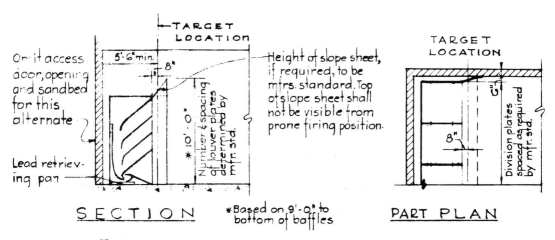

Fig. 4 "Venetian blind" type bullet trap.

General Notes on Fig. 4

1. Walls shall be 8 in thick; concrete or solid masonry units, providing minimum STC of 50.

2. Target range construction above or below occupied space shall provide minimum STC of 50.

3. Floor shall be concrete.

4. Construction above target range may be one of the following types, provided requirements for fire-resistive construction of the project are met:

 (a) concrete flat slab or concrete slab and beam
 (b) open-web steel joist
 (c) concrete ribbed slab
 (d) steel deck construction

For type (a) provide baffles at lights, beams, and other obstructions only. For types (b), (c), and (d) baffles shall be arranged so that only the baffle surface is visible from the prone firing position.

5. Information for each target range:

a. Number of firing booths required.

b. Positions required for target locations: 21'-0"; 45'-0"; 50'-0"; 75'-0"; and 100'-0". (If the 100-ft position is not required, locate the backstop at the 75-ft position and shorten the length of range accordingly.)

c. Minimum width of firing booth, if greater than shown.

d. Type of target carriers required (bullseye, silhouette, oscillating).

6. Structural fiberboard
 Flame spread: 0 to 25
 NRC: .65
 Size: 32 × 72 in (or as required)
 Color: Factory-finished white
 Installation: As shown

7. Provide waiting room, ammunition storage space, and toilets.

8. Ventilation requirements: Mechanical exhaust at plenums #1 (35 per cent) and #2 (65 per cent) necessary to maintain minimum air flow of 40 ft/min across the net open area of the firing booths. Exhaust capacity to be 110 per cent of mechanical supply ventilation.

9. Standard venetian blind trap is composed of 4 louver plates with total height = 7'-0" ±, and depth = 4'-0" ±. Manufacturers' dimensions may vary from this requirement on shop drawings for nonstandard installations. For this alternate reduce length of range, if feasible without altering overall design. Otherwise, the additional 7'-0" should be added to the space behind the firing booths.

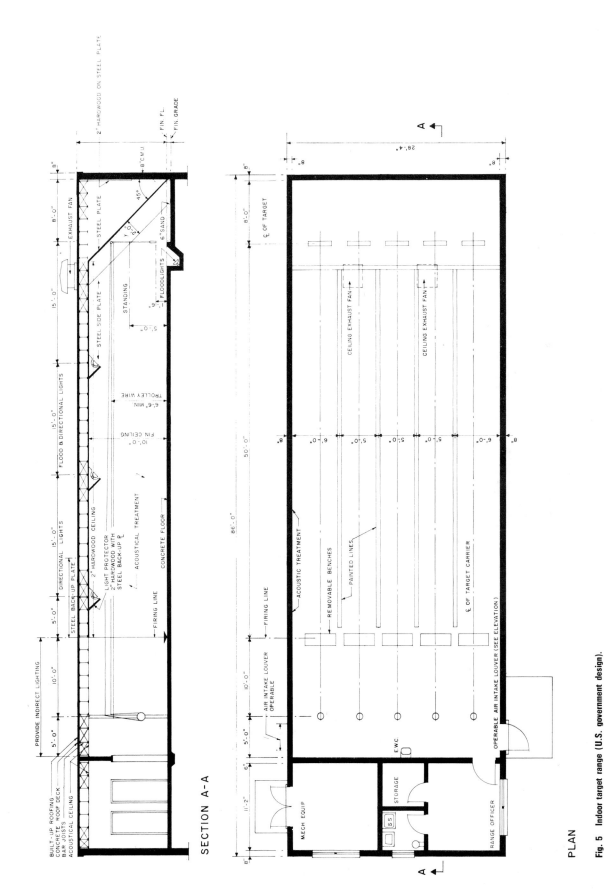

SECTION A-A

PLAN

Fig. 5   Indoor target range (U.S. government design).

Coefficients of Absorption*

Material	Coefficient of absorption			
	Frequency			
	125 Hz	500 Hz	2,000 Hz	4,000 Hz
Concrete block, coarse, unpainted	0.36	0.31	0.39	0.25
Brick wall, painted	0.01	0.02	0.02	0.03
Brick wall, unpainted	0.03	0.03	0.05	0.07
Carpet with 40-ounce felt underlay.	0.08	0.57	0.71	0.73
Heavy fabric 18 ounces per sq yd, draped	0.14	0.55	0.70	0.65
Light fabric 10 ounces per sq yd, draped	0.03	0.11	0.24	0.35
Fiber glass 2 in. thick	0.39	0.94	0.85	0.84
Wood paneling, ³⁄₈-in. plywood	0.28	0.17	0.10	0.11
Mineral fiber perforated tile, ⅝ in. thick (mounted to manufacturer's specifications in a #7 mounting) . . .	0.52	0.62	0.78	0.55
Ultraliner compressed fiber glass duct insulation, 1 in. thick	0.30	0.69	0.93	0.88

SOURCES: "Handbook of Noise Control," McGraw-Hill Book Co.; Celotex Corp.; Gustin-Bacon Corporation; Architectural Acoustical Materials Performance Data.
* Definitions of terms used in table:
Hz = frequency of the sound wave in cycles per second
Coefficient of absorption = percentage of sound absorbed by the given material

of the firing line should be treated with mineral fiber acoustical tile, which is a better material for this area since fiber glass will tend to be loosened by muzzle blast and drift down onto the shooters. It will also collect unburned powder and, eventually, may create a fire hazard.

Any maintenance painting should be done with a spray, so that the holes in the tile can be kept open. These holes are the *effective sound absorbing part of the tile.*

Carpeting the firing line and any assembly area to the rear will help considerably. Carpeting in front of the firing line can accumulate unburned powder and thereby creates a fire hazard.

The protective baffles described in the section on range interior can serve a dual purpose as sound baffles, in that they help to break up the natural resonances which are so often set up in large open spaces.

If the side of the baffles facing the firing line is faced with an acoustic insulation material, they will help to absorb some of the unwanted sound.

The breaking up of large, flat, smooth surfaces (in a range) which can reflect sound easily is one of the big factors in producing a pleasant shooting area. There is a long list of sound-absorbing materials which have been used on indoor ranges. The coefficient of absorption in the table above represents the percentage of sound energy which is absorbed by the surface described.

The table clearly shows the greater efficiency of soft, heavy materials with open-pored surfaces in the absorption of noise over materials with flat smooth surfaces. It also shows how ineffective building materials such as brick, plywood, concrete block, etc., are in the absorption of sound. The greater absorption efficiency at low frequencies (125 to 500 cycles per second) of the mineral fiber tile is readily apparent. The superiority of fiber glass in roll form at the middle and high frequencies is also clearly indicated. The discussion above pertains to noise within the range itself, and to techniques which can be used to absorb sound within the range area.

There is another field of consideration in the noise problem. This is the problem of sound transmission to the area outside the range. This noise escapes the range and annoys residents who have no interest in or connection with the range operation. Such noise will be a constant irritant to these persons, and for harmonious relationships with the community,

an effort should be made to reduce this noise to a minimum.

Since sound requires air for easiest transmission, it follows logically that the first corrective step is to block off any air leaks out of the range. It is patently impossible to seal off the range completely, but all doors can be weatherstripped, and, if necessary, a double door system may be installed (without the two doors facing each other) to form a combination entrance and sound trap.

Intake and exhaust of air should be accomplished through muffling chambers. The chambers should be maze baffled in a manner which requires the air to flow around corners. The muffling action thus achieved is very similar to that of an automobile muffler.

If the problem of sound transmission is acute, special measures may have to be taken in the layout and construction of the range. In planning and construction of an indoor range which is to be in a multipurpose building, it is strongly recommended that a competent acoustical consultant be retained.

Target Carrier Systems

An indoor range can be run much more efficiently and safely if some sort of target transport system is installed. A carrier system may be constructed of bicycle wheels and clothesline if funds are not available for anything else. On the other end of the expense spectrum, a completely automatic electrically powered system may be purchased from any one of several reputable target equipment companies.

Regardless of what target handling system is selected, targets should normally be placed with their centers approximately 5 ft off the firing-line floor level for the rifle standing and pistol position; and about 18 in. from the same level for the prone, sitting, and kneeling positions. Low target positioning is usually accomplished by the use of a detachable extension rod on the target carrier. If registered tournaments are to be held on the range, provision should be made for attaching backing targets, since they are required for all NRA Registered Smallbore Rifle competitions.

Although indoor pistol tournaments may be held without turning targets, it is strongly recommended that such targets be used. Even though this type of target holder is more difficult to construct than the simple trolley target carrier, it is still entirely feasible to construct using easily available parts.

An indoor range may be used for police firearms training. Usually the B27 target, or a reduction of that target, can be used or adapted to the standard target holder. There are special considerations for safety in police combat shooting indoors. Write NRA for further information.

Range Equipment

Ranges will normally require accessory range equipment which provides a more comfortable and pleasant place to shoot, as well as helping to increase the safety factor.

Gun racks should be placed in convenient locations, both to the rear of the firing line and in the assembly area. These racks should be constructed so as to allow the secure placement of match target rifles with scopes in them without danger of damage.

Hand-gun benches should be provided on the firing line for pistol ranges. If a range is to be used for both rifle and pistol, removable or folding pistol benches should be installed.

Trash receptacles of at least two types should also be provided—one for the spent cartridge cases, and one for other trash.

Coat racks are a necessity. They can be placed wherever convenient in the assembly area or in a special room.

Storage cabinets for target and miscellaneous items should be provided.

A bulletin board should be put up on a wall in the assembly area so that tournament scores and other pertinent information may be posted.

Shooting mats are very nearly a necessity for an indoor range. They can be purchased from one of several manufacturers, or may be cut very cheaply from used rugs, rubber matting or other suitable material.

Seating should be provided in the assembly area as well as in the area behind the firing line.

Other Space Requirements

Auxiliary rooms which should be provided for if at all possible are:

• A secure room for stowage of guns and ammunition. This room should contain space for cleaning guns and a small shop for minor repairs.

• An assembly and spectator area within the firing range room, but separated at least by a rail, should be provided. If possible, the assembly area should be cut off from the actual firing area by a waist-high partition with glass above so that firing may be observed and conversation may occur without disturbance to the shooters.

• A combination classroom and statistical office room should be completely separated from the range area. This will provide capability for statistical work during tournaments.

• Rest rooms should be provided, and undoubtedly will be required by law.

• A snack bar or restaurant is a very desirable addition to a shooting facility. In some instances, this facility augments the range income.

• An office for the range manager should be provided if not provided in the statistical office.

• A coat room or locker room is a desirable addition to any sporting facility, and shooting ranges are no exception.

• Last, but not least, a utility room containing furnace, air conditioning equipment, electrical switch panels, floor cleaning equipment, and so forth, should be provided for all indoor ranges.

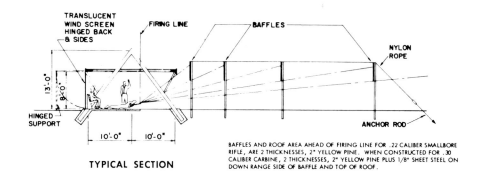

BAFFLES AND ROOF AREA AHEAD OF FIRING LINE FOR .22 CALIBER SMALLBORE RIFLE, ARE 2 THICKNESSES, 2" YELLOW PINE. WHEN CONSTRUCTED FOR .30 CALIBER CARBINE, 2 THICKNESSES, 2" YELLOW PINE PLUS 1/8" SHEET STEEL ON DOWN RANGE SIDE OF BAFFLE AND TOP OF ROOF.

TYPICAL SECTION

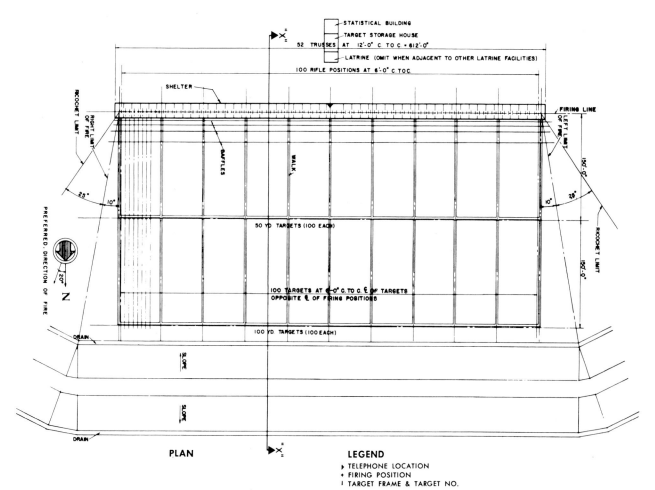

PLAN

LEGEND
- ▸ TELEPHONE LOCATION
- + FIRING POSITION
- I TARGET FRAME & TARGET NO.

Fig. 1 Small-bore rifle and carbine ranges.

Department of the Air Force. Victor B. Spector and Associates, Architects-Engineers.

RIFLE AND CARBINE RANGES, OUTDOOR

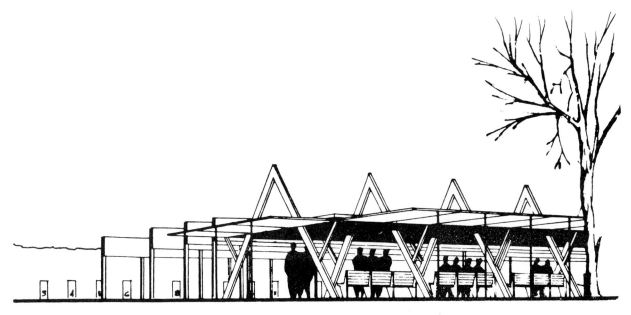

PERSPECTIVE

50 YD. TARGETS   100 YD. TARGETS

SECTION "X"–"X"

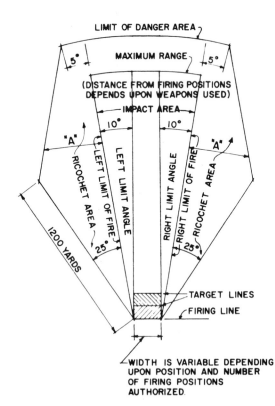

DANGER AREA PLOT PLAN

AMMUNITION	DIMENSIONS OF AREAS IN YARDS		
	A	B	MIN. RADIUS OF SECTOR [2]
CALIBER .22 LONG RIFLE	1	250	1,750
CALIBER .30 CARBINE	1	300	2,500

1. LIMIT OF SIDE RICOCHET AREA "A" IS DETERMINED BY MEASURING OUTWARD FROM THE END OF FIRING LINE (OR FIRING POSITION) AT A 25° ANGLE BEYOND THE LIMIT-OF-FIRE LINE, FOR A DISTANCE OF 1,200 YARDS, AND BY MEASURING OUTWARD 5° BEYOND THE LIMIT-OF-FIRE LINE AT THE OUTER LIMIT OF THE DANGER AREA (MAXIMUN RANGE PLUS DISTANCE "B").

2. MAXIMUM RANGE OF AMMUNITION PLUS "B".

3. SUITABLE BACKSTOP DETERMINED LOCALLY.

4. USE DANGER AREA PLOT PLAN IF LAND IS AVAILABLE, AND IF LAND IS NOT AVAILABLE USE BAFFLES, AS SHOWN IN TYPICAL SECTION.

Fig. 1 (cont.) Small-bore rifle and carbine ranges.

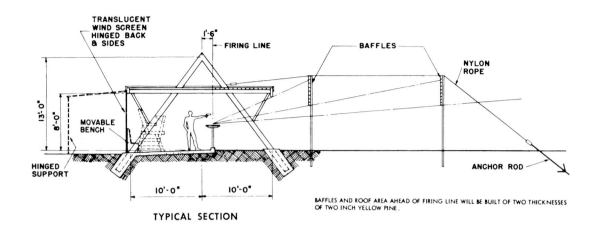

TYPICAL SECTION

BAFFLES AND ROOF AREA AHEAD OF FIRING LINE WILL BE BUILT OF TWO THICKNESSES OF TWO INCH YELLOW PINE.

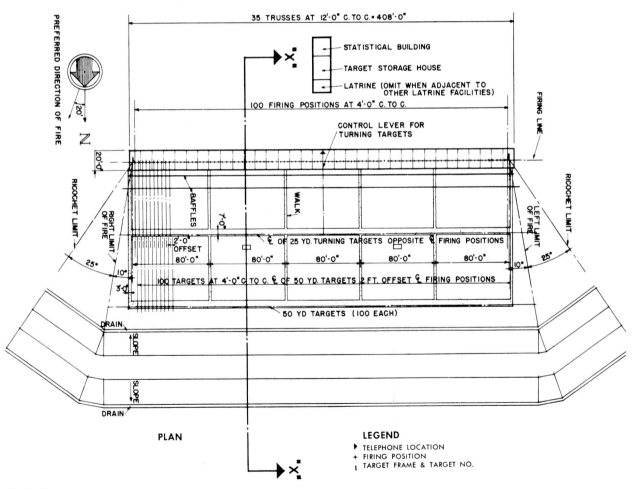

PLAN

LEGEND
- TELEPHONE LOCATION
- FIRING POSITION
- TARGET FRAME & TARGET NO.

Fig. 2 Pistol ranges.

Recreation and Entertainment

RIFLE AND CARBINE RANGES, OUTDOOR

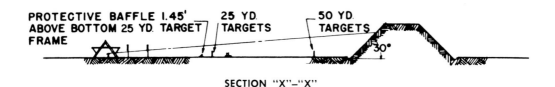

PROTECTIVE BAFFLE 1.45' ABOVE BOTTOM 25 YD. TARGET FRAME — 25 YD. TARGETS — 50 YD. TARGETS — 30°

SECTION "X"–"X"

LIMIT OF DANGER AREA

MAXIMUM RANGE

5° · · 5°

(DISTANCE FROM FIRING POSITIONS DEPENDS UPON WEPONS USED)

IMPACT AREA

10° · 10°

"A" · "A"

RICOCHET AREA

LEFT LIMIT ANGLE · LEFT LIMIT OF FIRE · RIGHT LIMIT ANGLE · RIGHT LIMIT OF FIRE

RICOCHET AREA

1200 YARDS

25° · 25°

TARGET LINES

FIRING LINE

WIDTH IS VARIABLE DEPENDING UPON POSITION AND NUMBER OF FIRING POSITIONS AUTHORIZED.

DANGER AREA PLOT PLAN

DANGER AREA LAYOUT IS USED ONLY WHEN LAND IS AVAILABLE, OTHERWISE A LAYOUT WITH BAFFLES (AS SHOWN IN SECTION "X - X") IS USED.

AMMUNITION	DIMENSIONS OF AREAS IN YARDS		
	A	B	MIN. RADIUS OF SECTOR[2]
CALIBER .22 LONG RIFLE	1	250	1,750
CENTER FIRE PISTOL	1	160	1,800
CALIBER .45	1	160	1,800

1. LIMIT OF SIDE RICOCHET AREA A IS DETERMINED BY MEASURING OUTWARD FROM THE END OF FIRING LINE (OR FIRING POSITION) AT A 25° ANGLE BEYOND THE LIMIT-OF-FIRE LINE, FOR A DISTANCE OF 1200 YARDS, AND BY MEASURING OUTWARD 5° BEYOND THE LIMIT-OF-FIRE LINE AT THE OUTER LIMIT OF DANGER AREA (MAXIMUM RANGE PLUS DISTANCE B).

2. MAXIMUM RANGE OF AMMUNITION PLUS B.

3. SUITABLE BACKSTOP DETERMINED LOCALLY.

Fig. 2 (cont.) Pistol ranges.

By WALTER L. COOK

TRAPSHOOTING

Trapshooting is the oldest of artificial clay target shooting sports. It is derived from an old live bird shooting game which originated in England in the latter part of the eighteenth century. A few years later, in the early 1800s, some English shooters formed a club called the "High Hats." The name was derived from the fact that the gentlemen in the club used their discarded high hats to "trap" live birds. A high hat with a long string attached to it would be placed out in front of the shooter, and a live pigeon would be placed under the hat. When the shooter was ready he would tip his hat and the "trap boy" would jerk the string that would pull the hat from over the pigeon; thereby, releasing the pigeon as a live target for the shooter.

In the latter part of the nineteenth century glass balls were introduced as artificial targets for trap shooters. The glass balls were filled with feathers so that when they shattered the floating feathers would make it appear as though a bird had been shot. This was the evolution of artificial targets, and it was not long thereafter that clay targets were introduced.

Layout Actual space required for trapshooting is a site 100 yd wide by 300 yd deep. The trap is located midway of the short side and throws targets at varying angles from the five shooting positions. The shooting positions are located 16 yd behind the trap and 3 yd apart. Each firing position is 16 in. wide. Additional firing positions are located at 1-yd intervals up to 27 yd from the trap. These additional firing positions are used for handicap shooting. In handicap shooting, the persons with greater shooting ability shoot from a greater distance.

When a target is thrown from the trap it rises from ground level to a height of 8 to 12 ft. It reaches its maximum height at a point about 30 ft in front of the trap, thus making it about 78 ft (16 yd plus 30 ft) from the firing positions located on the 16-yd line. The trap will carry about 48 to 52 yd from the trap. The trap can be adjusted to control the throwing distance, and usually it should be set to throw close to 48 yd since this means the target will be moving slower and better scores will result. This is particularly important where shooting is strictly recreational.

A trap-field layout is illustrated in Fig. 1. It may be observed that targets may be thrown at up to a 47° angle away from the straightaway. The usual and recommended practice is to keep targets within an angle of 22° to the left or right of the straightaway. This will make for better scores and happier shooters.

The Game A trap squad is comprised of five members. Each member of the squad fires at 25 targets to make a regulation trap "round." Each squad member shoots five shots from each of the five firing positions.

Management Aids, Bulletin No. 35, National Recreation and Park Association, Inc., Washington, D.C., 1966.

With all five members of the squad lined up on the 16-yd line, each shooter, progressing from position one on the left to position five on the right, fires at one target. This procedure is repeated four more times until each has fired five shots from each starting position. The shooters then rotate to the right one position, with the shooter on position five moving to position one. This procedure is followed until the round is completed and each member of the squad has fired five shots from each position.

While on the shooting line, only the shooter whose turn it is to fire has a loaded gun. The man to the right of the shooter may drop a shell into the chamber while the shooter is firing, but all other guns should be empty and action should be open.

The usual trap gun is 12-gauge but it may be smaller. Any conventional action type will do for singles trapshooting. The shooting distances involved cause most trapshooters to favor guns with 30- or 32-in. barrels, full choke, and raised solid or ventilated ribs. Since in the doubles game, two targets are thrown at the same time, a gun capable of firing two quick shots is required.

The American Trap Association rules specify that shot size shall not be larger than #7½. Shot shells are not to be loaded with more than 3 drams equivalent powder and not more than 1⅛ ounces of shot.

Walks The appearance of the trap field can be enhanced by having the surfaces of the shooting stations and walks made of such materials as gravel, asphalt, or concrete. The walkways for the five shooting stations, extending from the 16-yd line to the 27-yd line, should have markers or painted lines placed at 1-yd intervals, preferably with yardage numerals indicated.

SKEET SHOOTING

The short-range clay target game or skeet was originated by William Harnden Foster in 1926, at Andover, Massachusetts. It was designed to approximate field shooting at birds such as quail, grouse, dove, etc.

In its beginning it was known as "shooting around the clock." The original layout had one trap located at twelve o'clock which threw targets over six o'clock. Shooters progressed around the entire perimeter of the clock shooting at various angles. Later a second trap was located at six o'clock permitting shooters to fire at the same number of angles while going halfway around the clock. This reduced the shooting zone in half and thereby increased safety.

The skeet layout today is very similar. The targets are thrown from a high house and a low house located at opposite ends of a semicircle.

The Layout The layout for the single skeet field is shown in Fig. 2. The minimum site for the actual shooting area must be 600 yd wide by 300 yd deep. The semicircle containing the trap houses and the shooting stations is located in the middle of the long side of the site. The site should face northeast or north if it can.

The two trap houses are 120 ft 9 in. apart. The high house is located on the left of the field and the low house is located on the right. Targets shot from the high house start at a point about 10 ft above the ground. Targets shot from the low house start at a point about 3 ft above the ground. Both traps throw targets at fixed angles. The lines of flight cross each other at a point 18 ft beyond station eight and at a height of about 15 ft. The average flight distance of a skeet target is 55 yd.

There are eight stations on a skeet field. Station one is located at the base of the high house, on the left side of the semicircle. The next six stations progress around the semicircle, with station seven located at the base of the low house. Stations one through six are placed 26 ft 8⅜ in. apart. Station eight is located at the midpoint of a line perpendicular from the high house to the low house.

When electrical traps are used, the electrical control setup is located 12 ft to the rear and left of station four.

Eight-foot squad boxes are located six feet to the rear of stations one through seven.

A short gun pattern panel is desirable near the range to "sight in" a gun.

If possible four skeet fields, side by side and touching so as to use common high-low houses, are desirable for economy of construction, ease of management, and as a necessity for holding large matches.

The Game As in trapshooting, the skeet squad is normally composed of five men, and 25 shots make a round for one person. In the course of a round, a person will shoot at targets thrown one at a time from both the low house and the high house. The shooter will also fire at double targets, one target being fired from each of the trap houses simultaneously. In a round, there are sixteen singles shots, eight shots fired at four doubles, and one optional shot. The sixteen singles are shot two at each of the eight stations. The eight shots for the four doubles are fired two each at stations 1, 2, 6, and 7. The first time a target is missed, the optional shot is used as a repeat shot. If during the round of 24 shots there have been no misses, the optional shot may be taken as a single fired from any station, usually from station seven.

To begin a round, a squad moves to the squad box behind and to the right of station one. The first member of the squad moves to station one to commence shooting. Other members of the squad remain in the squad box with guns unloaded and with actions open. After the first shooter assumes the ready position with his gun at his shoulder, he calls "pull." Within one second a target appears from the high house. If the shooter is accurate or lucky he will break the target at about 20 or 25 yd from the trap house. After his first shot at the target from the high house, the shooter assumes his ready position for the target to come from the low house and then repeats the same procedure as for shot one. After the second shot from station one, the first shooter returns to the squad box and waits until the other four shooters have completed the same sequence of shots. The squad then moves as a unit to station two

SHOOTING RANGES, OUTDOOR

Skeet Shooting; Trap Field

to repeat the same procedure. After shooting singles at each of the eight stations, the squad returns to station one to commence shooting doubles. The shooters conduct themselves in the same manner as described for the singles. When the shooter calls "pull," targets are released simultaneously from the high house and the low house. The shooter fires first at the target moving away from him and then at the target moving toward him.

All gauges and types of guns may be used in skeet shooting. Since doubles are fired in each round, it is necessary to have a gun that will fire two shots in rapid succession. The short-range gunning makes short-barrelled, open-bored guns most popular.

There are four gauge classifications in skeet championship events: (1) an all-bore event in which any gauge gun may be used but in which the .12-gauge is usually favored, (2) .20-gauge

event; (3) small bore, using .28-gauge or 410 with 3-inch shells, and (4) sub-small bore, 410 with 2½-in. shells. No shot size smaller than #9 may be used in a match sanctioned by the National Skeet Shooting Association.

Trap Houses The trap house houses the target throwing equipment and can be constructed of many materials.

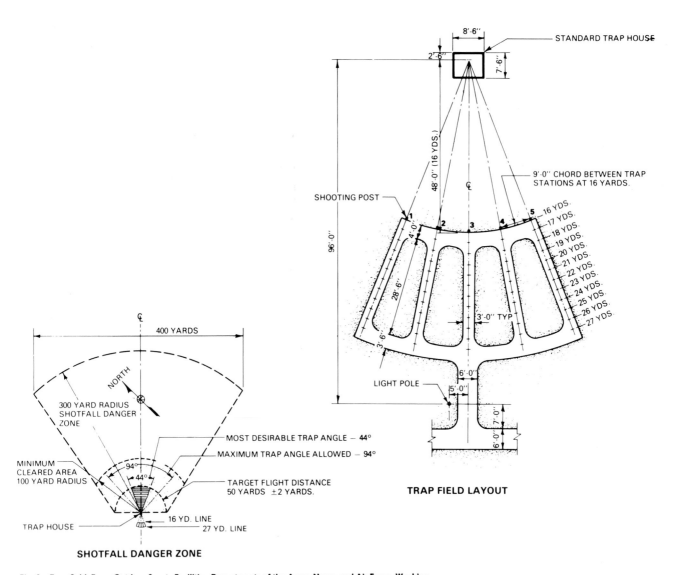

TRAP FIELD LAYOUT

SHOTFALL DANGER ZONE

Fig. 1   Trap field. From *Outdoor Sports Facilities,* Departments of the Army, Navy, and Air Force, Washington, D.C., 1975.

Specifications for Trap Field
Recommended Area Allow 16 acres for a single field. Shotfall danger zones of adjacent fields partially overlap and require only 3 acres additional land.

Size and Dimension Walks and structures occupy an overall area approximately 100 ft deep by 65 ft wide. Minimum cleared area is a section with a radius of 100 yd (1.7 acres). Shotfall danger zone is a section with a radius of 300 yd (14.8 acres).

Orientation Preferred orientation is for the centerline through shooting station #3 to run northeast-southwest with the shooter facing northeast.

Surface and Drainage Shooting stations are to be portland cement concrete (PCC). Walkways may or may not be paved. Shooting area and 100-yd-radius minimum cleared area are to be turf. The 300-yd radius shotfall danger zone may be turf or water or left in natural condition, and the entire field should be located in a relatively flat area with an open background.

Special Considerations If shooting is entirely over land, there should be safety provisions for fencing, posting of warning signs, and clearing away of concealing brush. If shooting is over water, warnings posted on buoys or other signs are required, and the trap house should be back far enough from the water's edge to permit recovery of unbroken targets. Contact the National Rifle Association for information on trap house construction and trap machines.

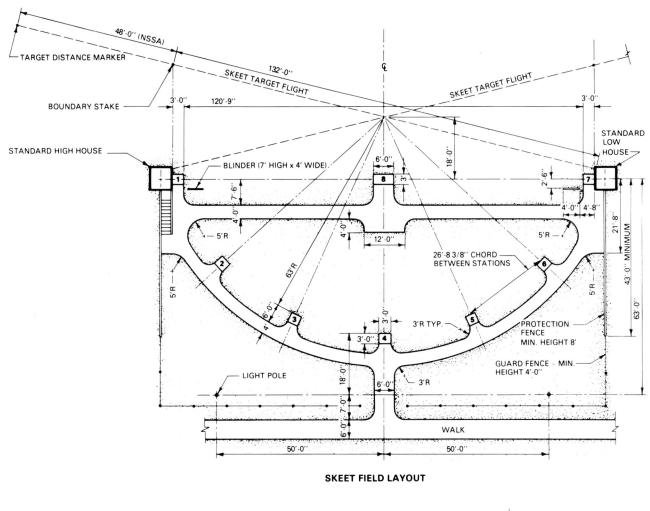

SKEET FIELD LAYOUT

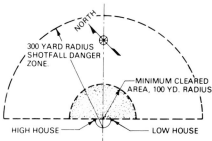

SHOTFALL DANGER ZONE

Fig. 2 Skeet field. From *Outdoor Sports Facilities*, Departments of the Army, Navy, and Air Force, Washington, D.C., 1975.

Specifications for Skeet Field

Recommended Area Allow 29 acres for a single field. Shotfall danger zones of adjacent fields partially overlap and require only 2 acres additional land.

Size and Dimension Walks and structures occupy an area approximately 130 ft wide by 80 ft deep. Minimum cleared area is a semicircle with a radius of 100 yd (3.25 acres). Shotfall danger zone is a semicircle with a radius of 300 yd (29 acres).

Orientation Preferred orientation is for the centerline from station #4 through station #8 to run northeast-southwest with the shooter facing northeast.

Surface and Drainage Shooting stations are to be portland cement concrete (PCC). Walkways may or may not be paved. Shooting area and 100-yd-radius minimum cleared area are to be turf. The 300-yd-radius shotfall danger zone may be turf or water or left in natural condition, and the entire field should be located in a relatively flat area with an open background.

Special Considerations If shooting is entirely over land, there should be safety provisions for fencing, posting of warning signs, and clearing away of concealing brush. If shooting is over water, warnings posted on buoys or other signs are required, and skeet houses should be back far enough from the water's edge to permit recovery of unbroken targets. Contact the National Rifle Association for information on skeet house construction and trap machines.

Recreation and Entertainment

SHOOTING RANGES, OUTDOOR
Combination Skeet and Trap Fields

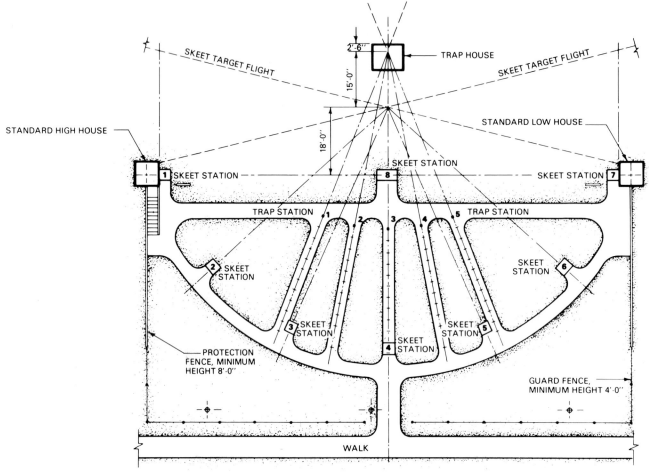

COMBINATION SKEET & TRAP FIELD LAYOUT

SHOTFALL DANGER ZONE

Fig. 3 Combination skeet and trap field. For layout dimensions and details see Fig. 2 (Skeet) and Fig. 1 (Trap). If paved, walks should be 4-in concrete reinforced with 6 × 6 in, No. 6 gauge welded wire fabric or bituminous.

Specifications
Recommended Area Allow 30 acres for a combination field.

Size and Dimension All walks and structures occur within an area approximately 130 ft wide by 115 ft deep. Minimum cleared area is contained within two superimposed segments with 100-yd radii (4 acres). Shotfall danger zone is contained within two superimposed segments with 300-yd radii (36 acres).

Orientation Preferred orientation is for the centerline from skeet station #4 through trap station #3 to skeet station #8 to run northeast-southwest with the shooter facing northeast.

Surface and Drainage Shooting stations are to be portland cement concrete (PCC). Walkways may or may not be paved. Shooting area and minimum cleared area are to be turf. Shotfall danger zone may be turf or water or left in natural condition, and the entire field should be located in a relatively flat area with an open background.

Special Consideration If shooting is entirely over land, there should be safety provisions for fencing, posting of warning signs, and clearing away of concealing brush. If shooting is over water, warnings posted on buoys or other signs are required, and the trap house should be back far enough from the water's edge to permit recovery of unbroken targets. Contact the National Rifle Association for information on skeet and trap house construction and trap machines.

SITE PLANNING

Orientation This facility should be located reasonably close to the water to expedite the dispersal of rental equipment and the performance of routine maintenance. However, careful consideration should be given to insure that the building is not located in an area subject to flooding or storm damage. The maintenance shop should have ready access to the water by overhead crane, mobile equipment, or paved launching

ramp to facilitate transporting the boats from the water to the shop for repair. The lounge should be oriented with a view of the water, but late afternoon and evening sun glare should be avoided if possible.

Launching Area It is desirable to separate this activity from normal vehicular circulation in order to avoid congestion. This is usually accomplished by locating the ramp on a separate turnaround or side road. The ramp should be related directly

to the parking area with turnaround loop between them. The access road should be sized to allow another vehicle to pass. A paved ramp capable of launching two boats simultaneously should be provided as a minimum facility. The ramp slope should be constant and range between 12 and 16 percent. This should also include a tie-up area to be used for loading and unloading the boat without interfering with the launching operations. A minimum water depth of 4 ft is required to launch a boat from a trailer. An optimum guide

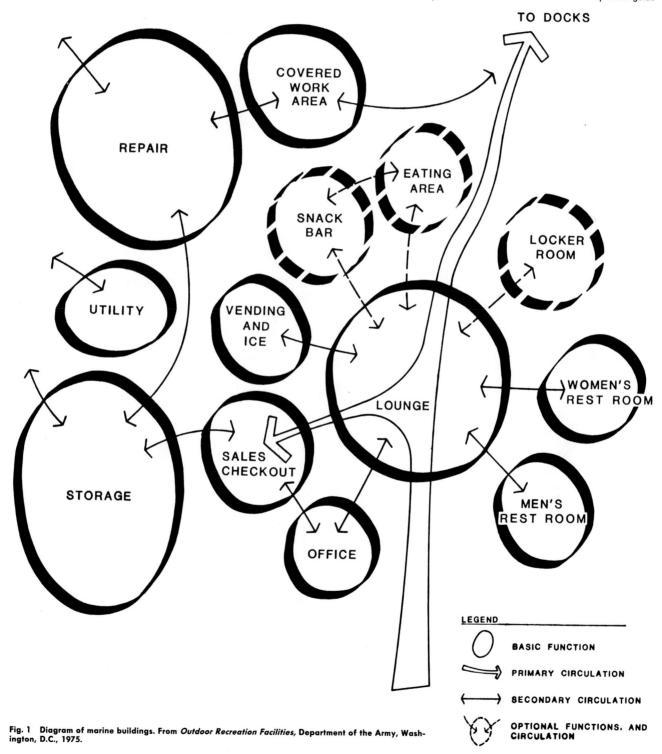

Fig. 1   Diagram of marine buildings. From *Outdoor Recreation Facilities*, Department of the Army, Washington, D.C., 1975.

1333

for calculating the number of launching ramps on small bodies of water is indicated below.

- Water skiing—One boat per five acres of water. Assume that a maximum of 10 percent of total boats in water will be involved in water skiing. However, water skiing and fishing are incompatible activities in the same area of the water body.
- Fishing or pleasure boating—One boat per two acres of water.
- Canoes or rowboats—One boat per acre of water.
- Each ramp can handle 40 launchings per day.

Docking Facilities Floating docks are preferable to stationary docks where fluctuations in water levels exceed 1½ feet. Roofed docking facilities are preferred for rental motor boats in order to reduce weather damage and the maintenance time spent in bailing the boats. A sandy area is desirable for beaching canoes, skiffs, and small sailboats. This allows the boats to be turned over when not in use. If rental dock space is to be provided, a careful projection of the numbers and sizes of boats to be docked is necessary to insure

the correct sizing of docks and provide adequate maneuvering space.

Vehicular Circulation and Parking In addition to the normal parking requirements, a parking area for combination car and boat trailer parking should be provided. Each space should be a minimum of 10 ft wide and 40 ft long. The total number of combination spaces normally should not exceed 30 percent of the total parking.

BUILDING PLANNING

Building Levels and Construction A one-level building is preferred to accommodate the required circulation and room arrangement in the marina support building. Where topography requires,

however, a modest split in level can be planned by separating the boat-repair space from the rest of the building. Heavy flooring and framing will be needed for this space to permit storage of motors and use of an overhead crane.

Functional Relationships The sales/checkout room should be located between the main entry and the access point to the docks. From this initial contact point information, tickets, and rental equipment will be dispersed. The sales/checkout room should have direct access to the general storage area, so that rental equipment can be easily removed and returned. The storage room should be related directly to the repair shop for access to equipment and spare parts. Restrooms should be easily accessible from the dock area.

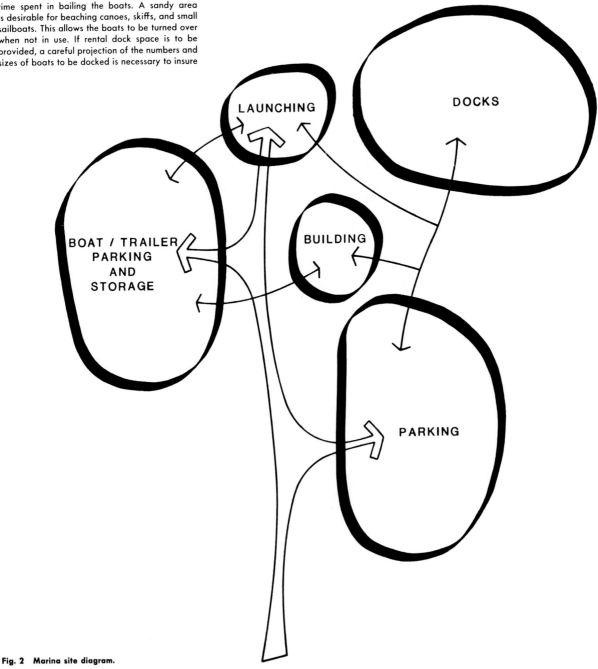

Fig. 2 Marina site diagram.

By CHARLES A. CHANEY

CLEARANCES

General

Clearances for any and all purposes within the offshore area of the marina should be considered as relative rather than as fixed values. When adequate water area is available, all clearances may be made quite liberal and limited only by the desires of the local boat owners and the financial ability of the responsible parties to pay for more extensive structures. The more serious problem of establishing proper clearances is faced when planning a marina for maximum capacity in a definitely fixed water area such as a frontage in a large municipality.

In the planning of a marina it is necessary to consider clearances that are by nature in three different classes and for three positions or operations of boats. These clearances are as follows:

1. Clearances in slips beyond the beam and length of the boat
2. Width of entrance and exit channels at the marina
3. Width of water area for maneuvering to and from slips

It is the purpose of this chapter to discuss these three items and present data from which the necessary clearances and widths of waterways may be determined together with the reasons for the recommendations so made. (See Figs. 1 and 2.)

Boatmen in various parts of the country evaluate clearances in different manners, and often a group is willing to make a larger initial investment to secure greater ease in maneuvering boats within the marina. The direction and velocity of prevailing winds and tidal variations in some localities may require larger clearance allowances to provide the desired measure of safety. Permissible clearances within slips equipped with traveler irons can be much smaller than those in slips providing cleats or rings only for the quarter lines. This is especially true when fluctuations in water level are more than about 2 ft.

Neither the establishment of the amount of clearance necessary for a typical marina, nor even proposing a set of rules whereby these may be determined, is considered as practical. It is, however, entirely reasonable and within the scope of this article to set up some clearances as suggested minima, which should not be decreased in the interest of safety and ease in maneuvering of the craft. The minimum clearances would appear to approximate those given in the following paragraphs.

Slip Clearances

The clear distances between the sides of the slip and the boats berthed therein must be sufficient to prevent the boats being tossed or

Marina Recommendations for Design, Construction, and Maintenance, 2d ed., National Association of Engine and Boat Manufacturers, Inc., Greenwich, Conn.

forced against the sturdy timber construction, thereby resulting in possible damage to both pier and boat. Clearances are required for a number of reasons such as safety of operation in moving the boat to and from the slip, compensation for the amount of slack in lines due to rise and fall of water from tides and during storms and freshets, and the prevention of damage to the superstructure of the boat when the water is rough and some rolling and tossing of the craft occurs. While it is essential that sufficient clearance be allowed in each slip, it also is advantageous to the engineers that these clearances be held to a reasonable minimum as a means of conserving space in the marina. (See Fig. 3.)

This thought can be made more impressive by the use of a simple example. Assuming that a group of 18 boats in slips are in a row along one edge of a pier, a reduction of 1 ft in the clearance on each side of each of the 18 boats would result in a gross saving in space of 36 ft. This would provide slips for two additional small-sized cruisers.

The size of the boat to be berthed will influence the side clearance in the slip. Large boats, due to their momentum, are more difficult to handle in restricted areas than the small ones. It is reasonable, then, to allow more clearance for the larger craft. The dimensions given in Fig. 4 for the minimum clear width of slips are based upon side clearances varying from 1 ft for the smallest boats to $1\frac{1}{2}$ ft for boats up to 30 ft, and to $2\frac{1}{2}$ ft for boats up to 80 ft in length. Figure 4, entitled "Dimension Diagram for Slips and Catwalks," illustrates several different arrangements of main walks, catwalks and slips and contains key letters, the values for which are given in Fig. 4. The controlling dimensions of this table assume the use of traveler irons and are typical only for the particular design of structure illustrated. No doubt other types of marina structures will be developed. In this event it is suggested that standards similar to Fig. 4 be prepared as a means of conserving the planners' time and standardizing the structures. These clearances and slip widths are considered sufficient for the sizes of boats given in the table when moderate tides up to 6 ft prevail and when the marina is in a location not subject to frequent storms with resulting high turbulent water. The engineer, in determining clearances and slip widths, should give consideration to the frequency and amount of high water in the basin together with other local conditions having a bearing on the subject. It is conceivable that these considerations will indicate the necessity for increasing the minimum slip widths and clearances recommended herein, and, as proper clearances are of primary importance for safeguarding of the vessels, the engineer should not hesitate in making any adjustments in these values he deems consistent with the conditions prevailing at the site.

Figure 4 contains suggested dimensions for all spaces that combine to make up full slip width allowances and the lengths of catwalks. Boat beams are in accordance with boat builders' catalogs and conform to Fig. 3. Slip

widths are based upon use of 2-ft-wide catwalks equipped with traveler irons. When 4-ft-wide catwalks are required, whether of the fixed or floating type, add 1 ft to the gross width of each slip. Throughout this article the figures used for beams and lengths of boats are intended to include all items such as bowsprits, fishing pulpits, tenders that project beyond the hull, etc. Slip lengths are 3 ft longer than gross boat lengths. Catwalks when not required to be full length of the slips, are usually two-thirds the length of small slips varying up to a 34-ft length for boats 50 ft or longer.

BUILDINGS

General Comment

The preceding dealt with the arrangement and construction of those parts of the marina which are along the water's edge or are built over the water for the accommodation of boats and the convenience of the boatman in performing his chores. The fixtures on shore comprise his headquarters, office, place of contact with fellow boat owners and his medium for relaxation.

The buildings constructed on the grounds of the marina constitute one of the main features of the harbor, and while they are primarily to serve a practical purpose, their importance demands that full consideration be given to the style of architecture, the design, and materials used in their construction.

Due to the prominence of these structures on the site, well planned buildings of appropriate style, located in carefully arranged and landscaped settings, will add much to the charm of the marina. The development, in every way, should become a source of pride to the community.

From the viewpoint of the management, the shore installations, including buildings, shrubbery, trees, grassy plots and even the chairs or benches provided, take on a different significance. The great majority of visitors who approach the marina from the water probably are affiliated with some distant club or organization. On the other hand, many of the visitors from the landward approach and people passing along the highway adjacent to the marina may be potential future boat owners even though they may not own boats nor have more than a layman's knowledge of boating. It is logical that the first step toward their ultimate entree would be the presentation of a well arranged building or group of buildings in a pleasingly landscaped setting with an expanse of tranquil water in the background. Most people enjoy the beauties of nature and the artistry of man's handiwork. A pleasant setting may stimulate their interest in boating and small additional investment for beautification will pay large dividends in attracting new patrons who seek recreation afloat.

Conditions controlling the uses to which buildings are devoted, their size, design, type of architecture, and even the materials of construction, will not be constant throughout the

Recreation and Entertainment
MARINAS

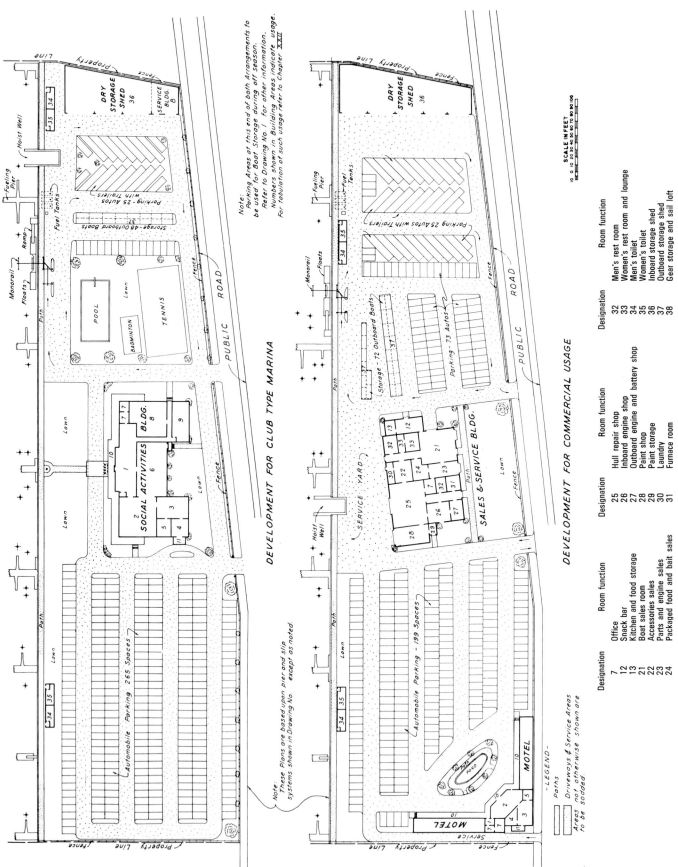

Fig. 1 Arrangement of onshore facilities.

Designation	Room function	Designation	Room function	Designation	Room function
7	Office	25	Hull repair shop	32	Men's rest room
12	Snack bar	26	Inboard engine shop	33	Women's rest room and lounge
13	Kitchen and food storage	27	Outboard engine and battery shop	34	Men's toilet
21	Boat sales room	28	Paint shop	35	Women's toilet
22	Accessories sales	29	Paint storage	36	Inboard storage shed
23	Parts and engine sales	30	Laundry	37	Outboard storage shed
24	Packaged food and bait sales	31	Furnace room	38	Gear storage and sail loft

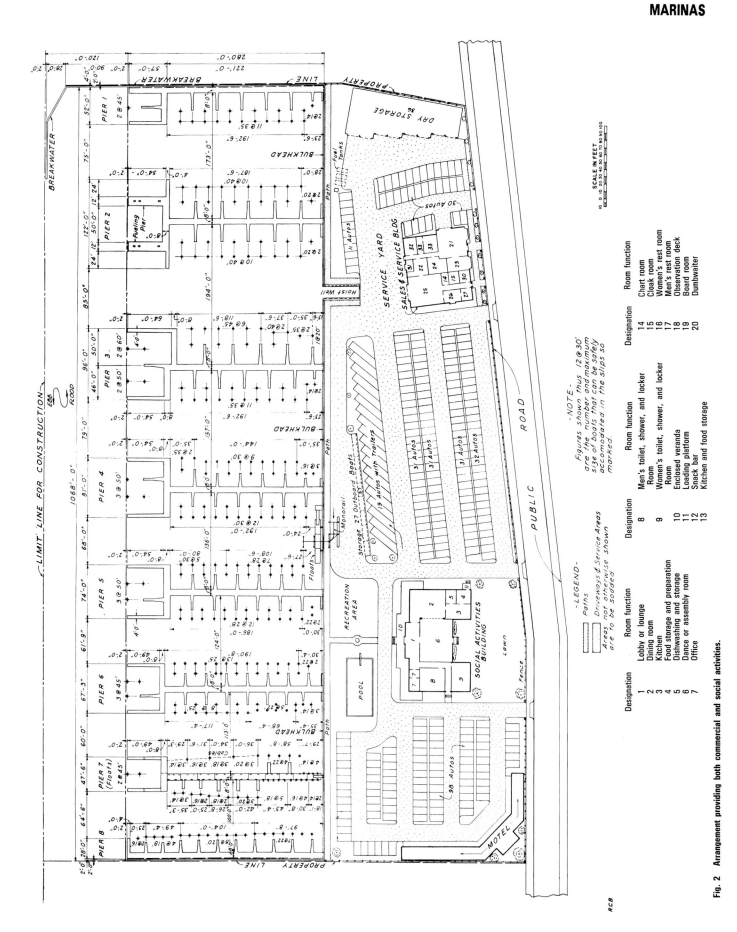

Fig. 2 Arrangement providing both commercial and social activities.

Designation	Room function	Designation	Room function	Designation	Room function
1	Lobby or lounge	8	Men's toilet, shower, and locker	14	Chart room
2	Dining room	9	Women's toilet, shower, and locker	15	Cloak room
3	Kitchen		Room	16	Women's rest room
4	Food storage and preparation	10	Enclosed veranda	17	Men's rest room
5	Dishwashing and storage	11	Loading platform	18	Observation deck
6	Dance or assembly room	12	Snack bar	19	Board room
7	Office	13	Kitchen and food storage	20	Dumbwaiter

-NOTE-

Figures shown thus 12@30' are the number and maximum size of boats that can be safely accomodated in the slips so marked.

-LEGEND-

Paths

Driveways & Service Areas

Areas not otherwise shown are to be sodded.

SCALE IN FEET
10 0 10 20 30 40 50 60 70 80 90 100

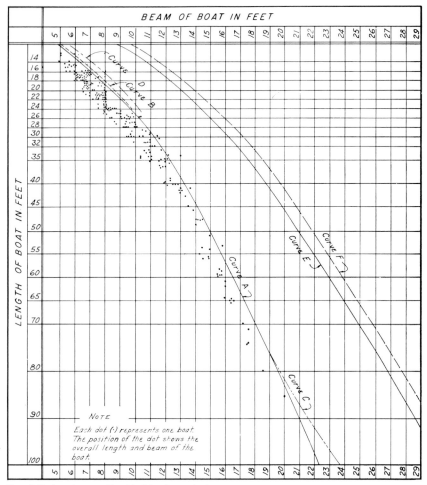

Curve A: Maximum beam considered for inboard power boats.
Curve B: Beam modification to allow for outboard boat hulls.
Curve C: Beam modification to allow for sailboat hulls.
Curve D: Distance center to center of boats when using boat holders.
Curve E: Distance center to center when using 2 foot wide catwalks with traveler irons.
Curve F: Distance center to center of 4 wide catwalks using either the floating type or fixed type equipped with traveler irons.

Fig. 3 Required slip widths for various boat lengths. (See Fig. 4 for further data and details.)

country, so a standard set of rules or recommendations cannot be suggested. An architect familiar with the local requirements should be employed to study the site and prepare plans for such buildings as are necessary in carrying on the activities of the marina.

In planning, a comprehensive scheme should be worked out covering present requirements and allowing for a reasonable amount of future expansion. When a well developed scheme based upon serious study of the problem is adhered to, future expansion becomes more practicable, less expensive to accomplish, and the ultimate development will be convenient and attractive rather than a conglomeration of poorly styled and located buildings which might otherwise result. The following paragraphs contain suggestions relative to styles of architecture, uses for buildings, designs and materials of construction.

The amount of floor space to be provided for the various activities in each of the buildings at the marina must be determined by local conditions and requirements. Several drawings in this article show plans of buildings in the onshore areas of marinas.

Floor Space Allocations

The success of any marina, whether a private club, municipal or a commercial organization, is measured to a large extent by the opinion of the patrons as to the facilities furnished for the transaction of business and for their convenience. The buildings may be judged by the same yardstick; that is, satisfaction that a reasonable or justifiable amount of floor space has been provided for each of the activities involved. It is recognized that ideas differ greatly between any two communities and that operations may vary even between two marinas in the same vicinity. It would, accordingly, be unwise to adhere to a fixed rule on space allocation in buildings at marinas. However, the following paragraphs provide some comments that may be acceptable to the planner subject to modification to meet local requirements. Figure 5 also records data regarding space allowances in some marina buildings that may serve as a guide.

Social Activities and Administration Buildings

Buildings of these two types are strictly for the purposes of establishing the relationship between the marina and its patrons, conducting the business of the facility, administering to the needs and desires of the individuals and providing for the convenience and relaxation of the boatmen and visitors. Figure 5 shows one possible arrangement for a social activities building. This may be separated from other marina commercial activities such as sales and repairs. The building should be arranged and equipped for the conduct of such social functions as are compatible with the particular region. Refer to the table accompanying Fig. 5 for space allowances used elsewhere in social activities buildings. Administration buildings, both existing and planned, vary so greatly among marina sites that a suggestion as to room arrangement is considered inadvisable. They frequently consist of only an office, toilet rooms, furnace room, watchman's headquarters and a large lobby or lounge that may be used for group assemblies as required.

Sales and Service Buildings

Very little basic information, serving as a precedent, can be offered the engineer or architect for use in determining either the arrangement or the size of the sales and service building. These buildings must be proportioned to accommodate the amount and types of work expected to be performed.

Basically, a marina is not a boat building or repair yard, although it is often necessary or desirable that a certain amount of repairing be carried on within the marina, particularly when no responsible repair yard is at hand. Boat repairing done within a municipal or club marina generally is of a minor or emergency nature. On the other hand, repairing of boats and engines is one of the usual functions of the commercial type. The repair facilities, as well as sales accommodations, are accordingly more generously proportioned for the commercial than for the other types of marinas. When repair work must be performed outdoors, rules should be enforced to maintain the area in a neat and orderly appearance. Most repair and conditioning work seems to occur in the spring and autumn, when large numbers of boats are being fitted out for the oncoming season or being laid up for the cold months.

It is very difficult to judge in advance the amount of work of this nature which may be expected at any one time, since an abrupt change in weather can result in a sudden avalanche of business. Capacity should be provided for hauling at least one large and one small boat at the same time. It is suggested that the repair shop of the municipal marina be arranged for the servicing of boats up to 36 ft in length. Facilities of the commercial marina should possibly accommodate boats up to 50 ft long. If no other repair facilities exist in the community, it might be advisable to increase these lengths. The shop space, in addition to accommodating the boats under repair, should provide for the storage of parts and for necessary power tools and adequate room for the use of special handling or other mobile equipment.

The front part of the service building can readily be partitioned off with a show window and used for the display of boats and equipment to be sold. Floor area and headroom re-

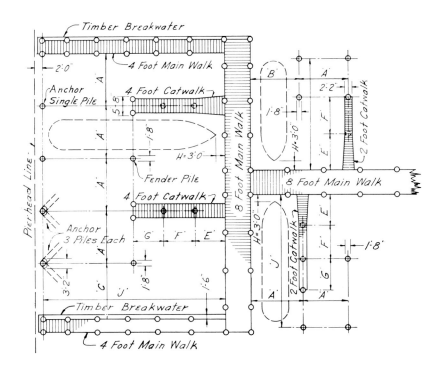

DIMENSIONS FOR SLIPS AND CATWALKS

LENGTH GROUP FOR BOATS	BEAM TO BE PROVIDED FOR	MIN. CLEARANCE FOR BEAM-TOTAL	MIN. CLEAR WIDTH OF SLIP	ALLOWANCE FOR HALF FENDER PILE	ALLOWANCE FOR HALF OF CATWALK	GROSS SLIP WIDTH TYPE "A"	GROSS SLIP WIDTH TYPE "B"	GROSS SLIP WIDTH USING 4FT FLOATS	GROSS SLIP WIDTH TYPE "C"	USABLE WIDTH OF CATWALK	1ST CATWALK SPAN LENGTH "E"	2ND CATWALK SPAN LENGTH "F"	3RD CATWALK SPAN LENGTH "G"	TOTAL LENGTH OF CATWALK	DISTANCE "J" TO ANCHOR PILE
Up to 14'	6'-7"	2'-3"	8'-10"	10"	1'-1"	10'-9"	10'-6"	11'-8"	11'-2"	2'-0"	12'-0	—	—	12'-0"	17'-0"
Over 14' to 16'	7'-4"	2'-4"	9'-8"	10"	1'-1"	11'-7	11'-4"	12'-6"	12'-0"	2'-0"	12'-0"	—	—	12'-0"	19'-0"
Over 16' to 18'	8'-0"	2'-5"	10'-5	10"	1'-1"	12'-4"	12'-1"	13'-3"	12'-9"	2'-0"	14'-0"	—	—	14'-0"	21'-0"
Over 18' to 20'	8'-7"	2'-6"	11'-1"	10"	1'-1"	13'-0	12'-9"	13'-11"	13'-5"	2'-0"	8'-0"	8'-0"	—	16'-0"	23'-0"
Over 20' to 22'	9'-3"	2'-6"	11'-9"	10"	1'-1"	13'-8"	13'-5"	14'-7"	14'-1"	2'-0"	10'-0"	8'-0"	—	18'-0"	25'-0"
Over 22' to 25'	10'-3"	2'-10"	13'-1"	10"	1'-1"	15'-0"	14'-9"	15'-11	15'-5"	2'-0"	10'-0"	8'-0"	—	18'-0"	28'-0"
Over 25' to 30'	11'-3"	3'-0	14'-3"	10"	1'-1"	16'-2"	15'-11"	17'-1"	16'-7"	2'-0"	10'-0"	10'-0"	—	20'-0"	33'-0"
Over 30' to 35'	12'-3"	3'-5"	15'-8	10"	1'-1"	17'-7	17'-4"	18'-6"	18'-0"	2'-0"	12'-0"	10'-0"	—	22'-0"	38'-0"
Over 35' to 40'	13'-3	3'-8"	16'-11"	10"	1'-1"	18'-10"	18'-7"	19'-9"	19'-3"	2'-0"	12'-0"	12'-0"	—	24'-0"	43'-0"
Over 40' to 45'	14'-1"	3'-10"	17'-11"	10"	1'-1"	19'-10"	19'-7"	20'-9"	20'-3"	2'-0"	14'-0"	12'-0"	—	26'-0"	48'-0"
Over 45' to 50'	14'-11"	4'-1"	19'-0"	10"	1'-1"	20'-11"	20'-8"	21'-10"	21'-4"	2'-0"	9'-0"	9'-0"	10'-0"	28'-0"	53'-0"
Over 50' to 60'	16'-6"	4'-6"	21'-0"	10"	1'-1"	22'-11"	22'-8"	23'-10"	23'-4	2'-0"	11'-0"	11'-0"	12'-0"	34'-0"	63'-0"
Over 60' to 70'	18'-1"	4'-11"	23'-0"	10"	2'-10"	26'-8"	24'-8"	25'-10"	25'-4"	4'-0"	11'-0"	11'-0"	12'-0"	34'-0"	73'-0"
Over 70' to 80'	19'-9	5'-2"	24'-11"	10"	2'-10"	28'-7"	26'-7"	27'-9"	26'-3"	4'-0"	11'-0"	11'-0"	12'-0"	34'-0"	83'-0"

NOTES: This tabulation is based upon use of traveler irons.
Slip widths are to be adjusted when 3 pile anchors are used.
Catwalks to be planned for full length as needed.
Refer to Diagram E for typical arrangements.

F.W.S.

Fig. 4 Dimension diagram and table for slips and catwalks. The diagram and table are to be used together to determine widths of slips, lengths of catwalks, and locations for stern anchor piles. Fixed dimensions shown in the diagram are considered sufficient for construction purposes. (See also Fig. 3.) The tabulation is based on use of traveler irons. Slip widths are to be adjusted when three pile anchors are used. Catwalks are to be planned for full length as needed. Typical arrangements are shown in the diagram.

Recreation and Entertainment
MARINAS

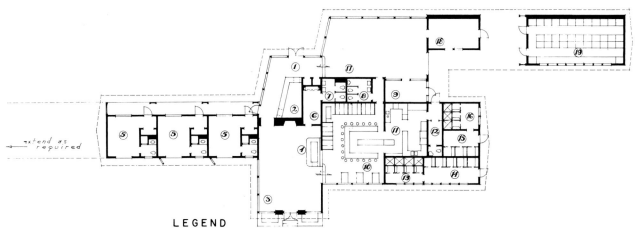

LEGEND

Main Building 141'x 61'
Locker Building 19'x37'

1. Entrance Lobby
2. Activities Office
3. Lounge 24'x31'
4. Bar
5. Bed Rooms 12'x14'

6. Ladies' Lounge
7. Ladies' Room
8. Men's Room
9. Yard & Sales Office
10. Dining Room 23'x29'
11. Kitchen 16'x20'
12. Kitchen Storage

13. Ladies' Showers
14. Ladies' Dressing Room
15. Men's Dressing Room
16. Men's Showers
17. Sales Room 21'x 40'
18. Sales Room Stock
19. Locker Room 16'x36'

FLOOR SPACE ALLOCATIONS (Sq Ft)

SOCIAL ACTIVITIES BUILDINGS

MARINA NO.	Boats in Fleet	Lounge or Lobby	Dining room	Kitchen	Food storage & preparation	Dish washing storage	Dance or assembly room	Office	Men's toilet, showers & Locker room.	Womens toilet, showers & Locker room.	Enclosed lounge	Loading platform	Snack bar	Kitchen and food storage	Chart room	Cloak room	Women's rest room	Men's rest room	Observation deck	Board room	Dumbwaiter	Furnace room	Miscellaneous
1	353	1380	1652	612	720		1380	588	616	616	2500				240		144	128	2300			300	
2	230	688	720	325	168	144	550		1050	540	760				144	96	132	300	760			96	
3	281		952	299	120	110	1122		1160	935	624		510		144	104	195	169	624				200
4	250	784	780	325	140	286	550		1050	500	740	100			140	96	286	228	740			90	
5	456	1410	3200	754	464		3200	318	556	940	900			1140	512		420	230	190			330	
6	601	1875	4900	1360	675	432	1600	264	4340	2980	1700	50			575	252	840	198	1700	468	18	420	
7	735	2260	3010	1350	625	500	3750	450	2680	1540									3180				
8	255	760	720	300	168	144	1100		980	610	740				196	100	138	276	740			100	

SALES AND SERVICE BUILDINGS

MARINA NO.	Boats in Fleet.	Office	Snack bar	Kitchen & food storage	Boat sales room	Accessories sales	Parts and engine sales	Packaged food & bait sales	Hull repairs shop	Inboard engine shop	Outboard engine shop	Paint shop	Paint storage	Laundry	Furnace room	Men's rest room	Women's rest room	Men's toilet		Gear storage
2	230	420	896	500	2000		1500	396	2350		940		1050		168	336	400			280
3	281	480			2150	780	920	520	3000	918	200			364		520	598	320		430
4	250	450		925	2200	696	1050	480	2640		1150			336		336	544	300		408
6	601	300		1460	2700	840	750	900	3600	835	484		1440	572	300	500	750	400		3200
7	735	600			2800	875	1100	625	3900	1136	280			400		500	750	320		486
8	255	300			2250	840	750	600	3000	835	485				300	500	750	300		400

Fig. 5 Marina activities buildings.

1340

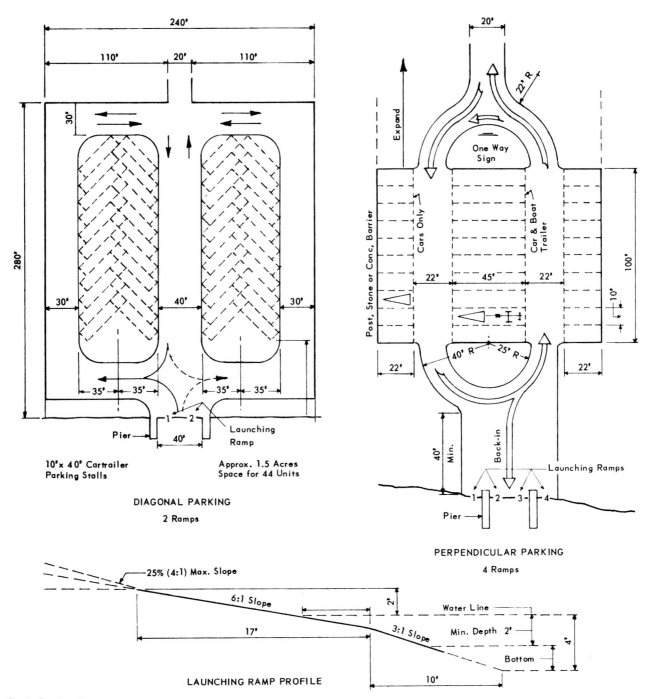

DIAGONAL PARKING

2 Ramps

10' x 40' Cartrailer Parking Stalls

Approx. 1.5 Acres Space for 44 Units

PERPENDICULAR PARKING

4 Ramps

LAUNCHING RAMP PROFILE

Fig. 6 Boat launching areas.

quirements will depend upon the number, size and types of craft to be displayed, along with space for racks, bins and counters for motors and supplies. Sailboats are best displayed under full sail, and it must be remembered that cruising craft will require additional space for boarding stairways. A ceiling height of approximately 16 ft is sufficient to accommodate most motor powered boats up to 40 ft in length, but greater heights are necessary for sailboats, again depending upon the size. Marinas using Travelift, Algonac or similar hoists to handle their display craft must also take their height into consideration.

In the event no separate administration or special activities buildings are erected, it is advisable that suitable lounge and extra toilet facilities be provided in the service building. Refer also to Fig. 5 for floor allowances that have proved satisfactory at other sites.

Pump and Engine Houses

The enclosures for fuel pumps, and the motors and engines operating boat handling equipment should be only sufficiently large to house the units with a small allowance in floor space for

their operation and maintenance. They should be of reinforced fireproof construction with lightweight roofs to lessen the horizontal force of any fuel explosions which might occur.

Covered Storage

Buildings on land for the dry storage of medium and large sized boats offer the greatest flexibility of operation, and therefore a maximum of use, when the floors are reasonably free of columns and similar obstructions. The capacity and arrangement must be determined locally from studies made of the numbers and

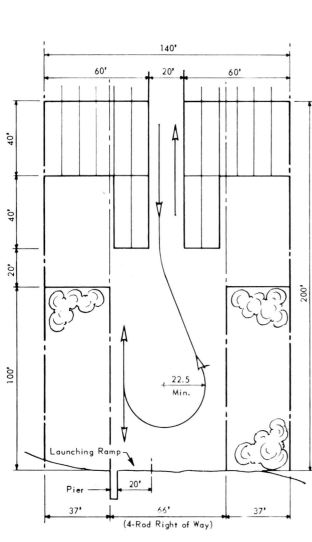

Indicating Expansion In Length & Width
From Basic 4 Rod Highway Right of Way
16-10'x 40' Car-trailer Spaces Shown

Fig. 7   Boat launching areas.

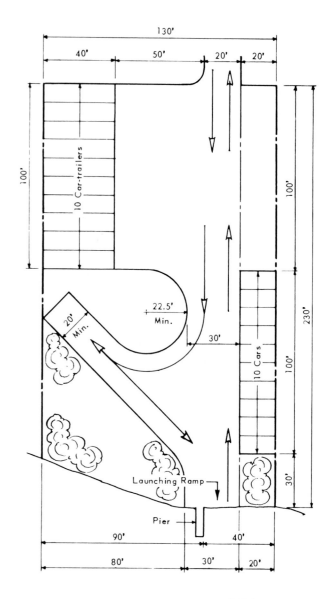

Approx. 0.60 Acres
10 Car-trailers
10 Cars Plus

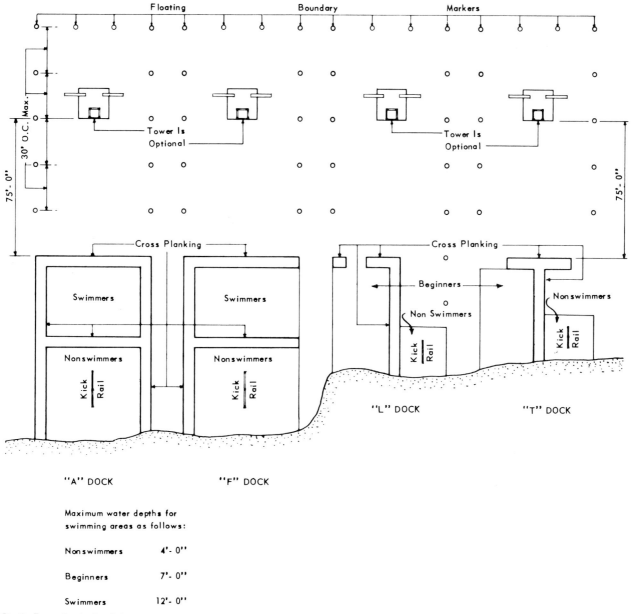

Maximum water depths for
swimming areas as follows:

Nonswimmers	4'- 0''
Beginners	7'- 0''
Swimmers	12'- 0''

Fig. 8 Types of swimming docks.

sizes of boats that are likely to be so stored in the marina. Storage buildings frequently have no doors although they are basically for winter use.

In-season dry storage of small inboard and outboard boats, usually less than 21 ft long, is rapidly expanding and is applicable to about one-third of all boats of these sizes using the marina. The owners of these boats do not desire to keep them in slips during the season and are unable to store them elsewhere on trailers. Storage sheds for the craft should be supported by a single row of columns so spaced that brackets thereon will cradle the boats. Boats may be stored on each side of the columns and usually in three tiers. One type of these sheds is provided with rolling doors on

triple tracks on each side. Another type has no doors but is provided with a roof that projects from 3 to 5 ft beyond the stored boats.

Storage lockers for boat owners should be provided to accommodate such items as outboard motors, sails and gear, cushions, flags, lights and other removable items from runabouts and other open craft. This locker space may be provided in any of the marina buildings ashore. Because of the great weight of these lockers and the stored gear, they should not be placed upon the piers or walks of the marina.

BOAT LAUNCHING AREA

Wisconsin Conservation Department supplies these two boat pier and launching sites with

car and boat trailer parking spaces for limited areas. (See Figs. 6 and 7.)

SWIMMING DOCKS

Four different types of swimming docks are here given to afford a choice depending upon the age group of the swimmer and the swimming ability of the individual. Note that all four provide a kick rail to aid in swimming instruction. The extent of the swimming docks out into the water will depend largely upon the gradient of the bottom, allowing greater or lesser area for nonswimmers. Note that a maximum water depth scale is indicated to guide in the establishment of bottom gradient. (See Fig. 8.)

CAMPS AND CAMP FACILITIES

To determine the best possible layout for a particular site, a clear understanding of established principles and standards is necessary. The application of these principles will be affected to some extent by the character of the particular site and its location, but this should not be considered sufficient reason to lay aside well-proven fundamentals.

The following principles (except statement on multiple-camp reservations) apply in the layout of a short-term camp, a single long-term camp, and each camp in a multiple-camp reservation. (See Fig. 1 and Tables 1 to 4.)

Troop Sites Give first priority to the location of the troop campsites. Consider these needs:
- Good terrain with not more than 7 percent slope.
- Approximately 3 to 4 acres of usable land to provide for 6 to 10 patrol sites (2 to 4 to be used at one time).
- Good drainage to provide runoff and to permit disposal of waste water.
- Soil to permit driving of tent stakes.
- Cover—sod and/or trees depending on the site.
- Spacing—troop sites to be at least 450 ft apart, center to center, and at least 450 ft from any program area or building.
- Distance—maximum distance from a troop site to such points as the waterfront or central lodge should be about 1,800 ft. In some instances, troop sites have been successfully located up to 2,500 ft from the central area of the camp, but travel time should be considered.

Central Area After troop sites are tentatively located and program features noted, an area of approximately 10 acres should be selected for installation of central service facilities to serve all troop sites. Most of the camp buildings will be in this area so the terrain should provide good building sites. Consider these factors:
- Entrance road will be built to this area.
- Parking area should be located so all visitors park autos prior to entering the central area.
- Picnic area for visitors should be close to the parking lot, but not in the central area.
- Administration building should be readily seen and accessible from the parking lot so people entering camp will go there first.
- Health lodge should be convenient to both the adminstration building and food service. It should also be in a reasonably quiet area.
- Central shower should be convenient to troop sites and, if it includes staff toilets, should be close to the staff tenting area.
- All buildings in the central area should be accessible by service road.
- Avoid crowding buildings. Take advantage of terrain and tree cover to screen and separate buildings.

Campsites and Facilities, Engineering Service, Boy Scouts of America.

TABLE 1 Requirements for Short-Term Camp or Reservation*

Land and troop sites	Program facilities	General service facilities
Minimum requirements		

100 to 200 acres minimum recommended
 	
10 to 14 troop sites, each with latrine, patrol tables, and fireplaces; water at each site or nearby; two-boy tents for shelter
	Scoutcraft activities areas:
	  Nature-conservation
	  Ropes, knots, and pioneering
	
	Field sports area:
	  Orienteering
		Water system—supply, storage, and distribution
		Access road
		Parking area with control gate
		Service roads
		Trails

Additional facilities as dictated by need and program		

	Picnic area
	Chapel
	Campfire circle
	Additional program areas as dictated by staff available
		Residence for camp ranger
		Maintenance facilities
		Activity shelters for severe-weather use
		First aid facilities
		Service building for use in:
		  Campmaster program (staff)
		  Meetings
		  Storage and issue of equipment
		  Training courses
		  Explorer activities
		Electricity to residence and service building

Additional requirements for camps serving large numbers of troops		
Additional acreage on the basis of 200 acres per 10 to 14 troops Troop sites as needed	Provide separate program facilities for each camp—serving 10 to 14 troops—of the reservation	Provide separate facilities for campmasters in each camp—serving 10 to 14 troops—in the reservation.

*Typical conditions: accessible (within 1 hour's drive); year-round use; maximum use—4 to 14 troops at one time.

- Consider need for access by campers, installation of utilities, health and safety measures, drainage, ventilation, sunshine, and conservation measures.
- The area will be seen and used regularly by visitors and campers, so aesthetic factors are very important.

Access, Protection, and Control Establish a single entrance to the property. It is wise to provide one or more additional points of access for emergency use only; but, whenever possible, all regular access should be at one point.

The camp entrance should be at a point on the public highway where it can be seen easily and where it will permit safe entrance and exit for vehicles.

AQUATICS

A full aquatics program is a great asset to a long-term camp. To provide facilities for swimming, diving, lifesaving, boating, canoeing, sailing, and fishing will require a fair share of the construction budget and a good deal of study and planning on the part of the camp-development committee. Obviously, it is not possible to offer all phases of the aquatic program at camps in some parts of the country.

Most states have health laws governing the construction and operation of swimming places. Ask for advice and assistance of state and local health authorities at the beginning of the project. The use and impoundment of waters is generally controlled by law and riparian rights. Check all legal aspects of plans to use, divert, and impound natural waters.

Construction of a dam or swimming pool is a complicated, technical project, and competent local engineers must always be involved.

Types of Waterfront

Types of waterfronts include natural lakes and ponds, streams and rivers, tidewater and other great bodies of water, man-made lakes and pools. (See Figs. 2 to 4.)

TABLE 2 Requirements for Small Long-Term Camp or Reservation*

Land and troop sites	Program facilities	General service facilities	

200 acres minimum recommended
 	
Six to eight troop sites, each with latrine, washstand, patrol tables, and fireplaces; two-boy tents for shelter
	Swimming area with piers or swimming pool
	Boating and canoeing facilities
	Field sports areas:
	  Rifle range
	  Archery range
	  .22 shotgun range
	  Angling
	  Orienteering
	Scoutcraft activities area:
	  Ropes, knots, and pioneering
	  Woods tools
	  Nature-conservation
	  Find your way—tracking
	  Campcraft
	  Handicraft
	Campfire circle
	Chapel
	Outpost camps
	Picnic area
		Water system—supply, storage, and distribution
		Sewage and waste-disposal facilities
		Access road and entrance gateway
		Parking area with control gate
		Service roads
		Trails
		Electric power
		Telephone
		Health lodge
		Central shower (may include staff toilets)
		Service building for camp with troops cooking by patrols:
		  Administration and program office
		  Staff dining room
		  Staff kitchen
		  Trading post
			Commissary
			Equipment storage and issue
			Service building for camp with central dining:
			  Administration and program office
			  Trading post
			  Equipment storage and issue
			Director's cabin
			Ranger's residence
			Maintenance shop
			Food-handling facilities:
			  Troops cooking by patrols
			  Commissary or store
			  Staff dining room and kitchen
			Central dining
			  Central lodge with kitchen for serving meals daily to some or all troops and staff
			  Commissary service
			  Cook's quarters

		Additional facilities which program may dictate	
	Program headquarters shelter	Activity shelters for severe-weather use Staff family cabins Facilities for leader training—adapt service building and/or	central lodge to provide meeting space. Staff family cabins may provide off-season quarters for adults.

* Typical conditions: reasonably accessible (within 2 hours' drive); some year-round use; maximum use six to either troops at one time.

TABLE 3 Requirements for Typical Long-Term Camp or Reservation*

Land and troop sites	Program facilities	General service facilities	

200 acres minimum
10 to 14 troop sites, each with latrine and wash-stand, patrol tables, and fireplaces; two-boy tents for shelter
	Swimming area with piers or swimming pool
	Boating and canoeing facilities
	Field sports areas:
	  Rifle range
	  Archery range
	  .22 shotgun range
	  Angling
	  Orienteering
	Scoutcraft activities areas:
	  Ropes, knots, and pioneering
	  Woods tools
	  Nature-conservation
	  Find your way—tracking
	  Campcraft
	  Handicraft
	  Personal fitness
	Campfire circle
	Chapel
	Outpost camps
	Picnic area
		Water system—supply, storage, distribution
		Sewage and waste-disposal facilities
		Access road and entrance gateway
		Parking area with control gate
		Service roads
		Trails
		Electric power
		Telephone
		Health lodge
		Central shower (may include staff toilets)
		Equipment storage and trading post
		Administration building:
		  Administration office
		  Program office (may be in equipment issue building)
		  Staff meeting room (where troops cook by patrols) or meeting and dining room
			(where there is central dining and patrol cooking)
			Staff kitchen (when troops cook by patrols)
			Visitors' toilets
			Staff area—tentage, platforms, toilets
			Director's cabin
			Ranger's residence
			Storage building
			Maintenance shop and yard
			Food-handling facilities:
			  Troops cooking by patrols
			  Commissary or store
			  Staff dining room and kitchen
			Central dining plus patrol cooking
			  Central lodge with kitchen for serving meals daily to some or all troops and staff
			  Commissary service
			  Cook's quarters

		Additional facilities which program may dictate	
	Program headquarters shelter	Activity shelters for severe-weather use Staff family cabins Facilities for leader training—adapt the administration	building and/or central lodge to provide meeting spaces. Staff family cabins may provide off-season quarters for adults.

* Typical conditions: reasonably accessible (within 2 hours' drive); some year-round use; maximum use—10 to 14 troops at one time.

Recreation and Entertainment

CAMPS AND CAMP FACILITIES

TABLE 4   Requirements for Multiple-Camp Reservation*

Land and troop sites	Program facilities	General service facilities	
1,000 acres — about 200 acres for each camp and the Explorer base; balance of acreage for administration area, staff family area, picnic area, and buffer lands. Each camp will provide 10 to 14 troop sites, equipped as outlined for typical long-term camp.	For each camp: Program facility requirements will be the same as outlined for typical long-term camp.	For administration area and to serve all camps: Water system — supply, storage, and distribution Sewage and waste-disposal facilities Parking area Service roads Trails Electric power Telephone Ranger's residence Assistant ranger's residence Maintenance shop Storage building Vehicle storage Food storage and handling Administration building Health lodge Staff family cabins For each Boy Scout camp: Central shower (may include staff toilets) Equipment issue and trading post Staff area — tentage, platforms, toilets First aid tent	Administration building — Program and administration office Staff meeting or dining room Visitors' toilets Food-handling facilities: Each camp may provide a different type of food service For example — Camp 1 Central lodge to serve meals to some or all troops and staff Kitchen to prepare meals for Camp 1 and to cook food to be delivered to Camp 2 Commissary to provide food for patrol cooking Camp 2 Prepared food delivered from Camp 1 for some troops Commissary to provide food for patrol cooking Camp 3 Commissary to provide food for patrol cooking

* Typical conditions: reasonably accessible (within 2 hours' drive); year-round use; three long-term camps, each serving 10 to 14 troops at one time; an Explorer base (optional).

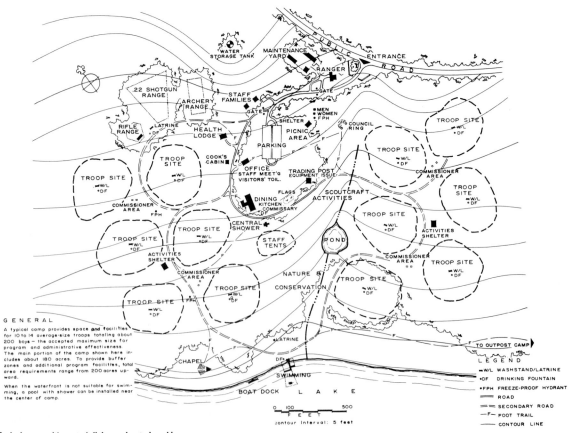

Fig. 1   Typical camp with central dining and patrol cooking.

1346

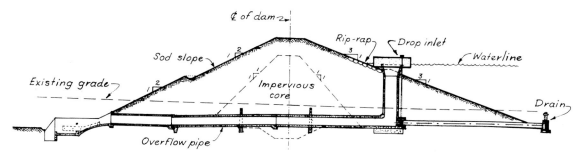

Fig. 2 Typical cross section of earth-fill dam.

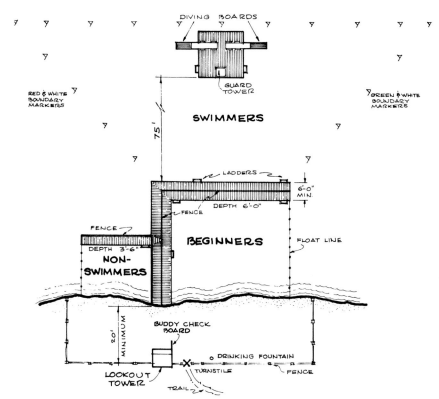

Fig. 3 Typical waterfront layout.

ling and maintaining waterfront structures, and high incidence of pollution.

Tidewater and Other Great Bodies of Water While great bodies of water offer many recreational opportunities, they are seldom well suited to the camp aquatics program. For example, tide action interferes with regular scheduling and makes instruction difficult, storms and high waves may interrupt the program for long periods of time, and waterfront structures are costly to build and maintain.

Camps located at or near tidewater should take advantage of the program possibilities offered, but should provide a pool or other body of water for instructional swimming.

Man-made Lakes Many councils have built lakes; and, when good design and construction procedures were followed, excellent results have been obtained. Even though the lake may not be suitable for swimming due to pollution or other factors, it provides for boating, canoeing, fishing, and nature study.

Selection of the site and design of the dam are not jobs for amateurs, and the best available engineer should be employed. The U.S. Soil Conservation Service has had wide experience in the design of small lakes, and their advice and help should be sought. Sound engineering experience is needed to determine the quantity and quality of water available; size of lake (consistent with the watershed and amount of water available); selection of dam site (with studies of subsoil); and type of construction for dam, spillway and other structures.

Preparation of the drawings and supervision of construction of the dam and other structures must be under the direction of the engineer.

The following are important considerations in design and construction:

• Avoid large areas of shallow water. The water tends to become warm and promote weed and alga growth.

• Provide for draining the lake. Maintenance of the beaches and waterfront structures and removal of silt will be greatly simplified. Lowering the water level in the winter may help control weeds and leeches and permit silt to wash off the beaches.

• Control silting. An upstream conservation program and silting basins may be needed.

• Grade and construct beach areas before filling the lake.

• Remove all trees and brush from the lake bed. Trees should be cut close to the ground and all debris removed. Topsoil need not be removed.

• Where flat slopes exist at the shoreline, make a vertical cut so that water will be 1 to 2 ft deep. This will minimize the growth of water plants and the breeding of mosquitoes. (This does not apply to beach areas.)

Natural Lakes and Ponds A fair-sized lake with clear and unpolluted water offers an ideal setting for development of camp aquatics facilities. Here are some of the important considerations:

• Control the whole shoreline. When the lake lies within the camp property, privacy is assured. A lake having cottages and other developments along its shores presents problems in privacy and protection.

• Control the watershed. This is a positive measure of protection against pollution. If the watershed is not owned, ask the assistance of local health authorities in making a survey of possible sources of pollution and in bringing about their elimination.

• The ideal size for a lake lies within broad limits. Thus, 15 to 20 acres might be a desirable minimum, while a desirable maximum would be 100 to 300 acres if three or four camps are to be built. Very small bodies of water are more easily polluted and are often subject to heavy weed and alga growth. On very

large lakes, it is more difficult to control the aquatics activities, and the program will often be interrupted by adverse weather conditions.

• Natural beach areas are an asset. Look for a gradually sloping bottom, preferably sandy, having a grade of 8 to 10 percent. A maximum depth of about 12 ft at a distance of 150 ft from shore is ideal. Submerged stumps, rocks, a muddy bottom, or steep slopes will require considerable work to make the area suitable for swimming.

• A nearly constant water level through the summer makes it simpler to install and maintain the various waterfront structures.

Streams and Rivers Suitable waterfronts can seldom be installed on streams or rivers, although they may offer excellent program potential for canoeing, boating, and fishing. Disadvantages, which can seldom be overcome, include flood danger and fluctuating water levels that may interrupt the daily program, strong currents that make swimming unsafe, difficulty of instal-

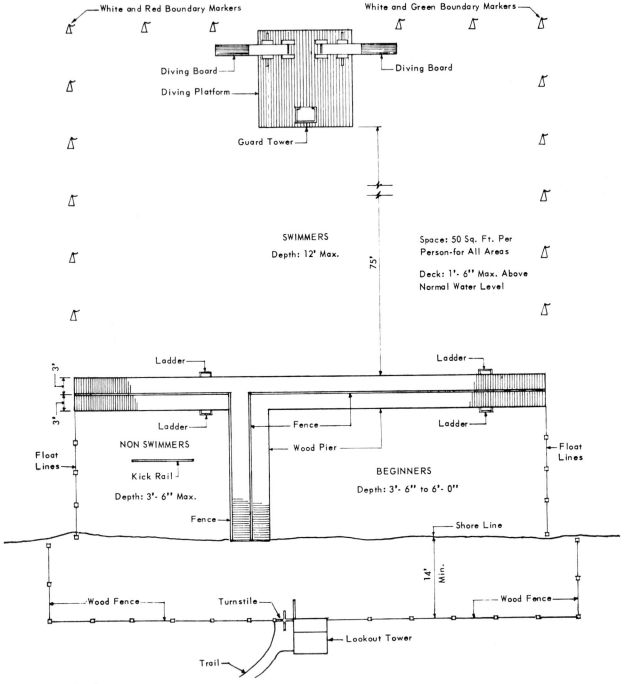

Fig. 4 Typical waterfront layout.

• Provide adequate depth. Twelve feet is a good maximum depth for the swimming area. Greater depths in other parts of the lake tend to keep the water cooler and minimize alga and plant growth.

Waterfront Layout and Facilities

Each waterfront presents a different situation, requiring specific design of the layout and structures. Such factors as bottom slope, bottom conditions, water-level fluctuation, and winter conditions will determine the most practical layout and type of structure to be installed. Whatever the situation these basic design factors apply:

• There should be one waterfront for each camp. It need not accommodate all campers at one time, but may be designed for use of one-third to one-half of the troops at one time (about 100 boys).

• Layout should include three separate areas:
1. Nonswimmers—maximum depth, 3 ft 6 in.
2. Beginners—maximum depth, 6 ft
3. Swimmers—maximum depth, 12 ft

Piers The best type of pier for the particular site depends on such factors as bottom conditions, water-level fluctuation, winter conditions, and such local considerations as the availability of materials and equipment. General types of piers include:

• *Fixed Piers* These are built to stay permanently in place and may be supported on pilings, frames, or cribs. They are most practical where ice is not destructive and where equipment is available for their construction. In a man-made lake, the pier supports may be installed before the water level is raised.

• *Removable Pier with Fixed Foundations* Where ice conditions are destructive to piers, it may be possible to install fixed supports extending within 1 or 2 ft of the water surface with deck sections attached in such a way that they may be removed in the fall.

• *Removable Piers* Prefabricated removable piers are commonly used at sites where winter conditions make fixed piers impractical.

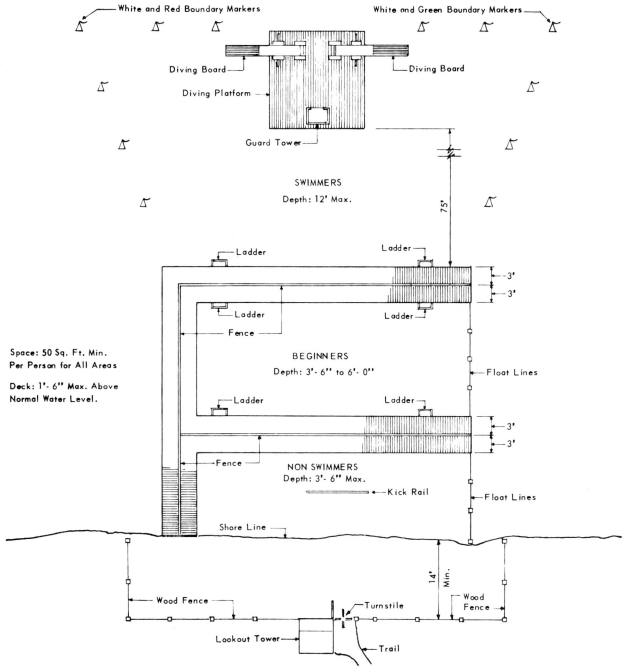

Fig. 4 (cont.) Typical waterfront layout.

These are constructed of steel or aluminum with decks of the same material or of wood. They are adjustable within limits to varying water levels. Installation and removal of these piers entail considerable work. Annual maintenance is needed (Fig. 5).

• *Floating Piers* When fluctuating water levels make it impractical to install rigid piers, floating piers may be provided. They offer such disadvantages as unsteadiness, anchorage problems, and maintenance difficulties but are practical when properly designed and installed. The flotation equipment may be steel drums or styrofoam (with wood decks), or each section may be a metal or wood air chamber. Floating aluminum piers are available from some suppliers (Fig. 6).

Anchorage may be by cable or by vertical struts passing through sleeves attached to the sections.

Watch for the following when building piers:

• *Required Widths* The minimum width of fixed piers should be 6 ft, except for special conditions as shown on the accompanying layouts. Floating piers should have a mimimum width of 8 ft.

• *Design Factors* Removable and floating piers should be designed in sections to permit easy handling on shore. Connections between sections should be sturdy and easy to secure. Piers carry heavy live loads, and supporting members must be sized accordingly An engineer should design and supervise construction of all piers.

Floats and Diving Platforms A platform or float is commonly installed at the outside limit of the swimmers' area. If diving boards are to be provided, they should be placed on a solid platform, not on a float. Diving boards should not be higher than 1 meter above the water and a maximum of two (one at each end) may be installed on one platform. A raised lifeguard platform should be installed on all floats or platforms.

Design and construction of platforms and floats are based on the same general factors outlined for piers.

Beach The beach area adjacent to the waterfront should be fenced, with a turnstile or gate providing a single entrance. If the beach is of

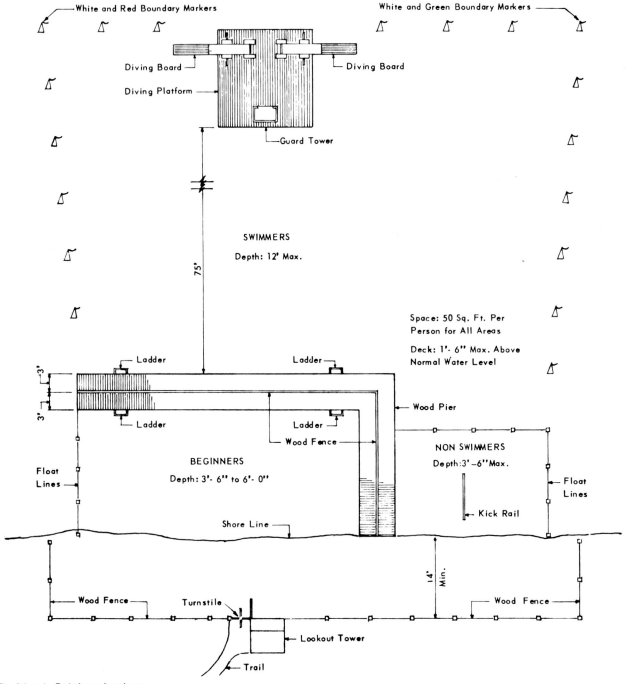

Fig. 4 (cont.) Typical waterfront layout.

sand, its slope should not exceed 3 percent or the sand will wash away rapidly. It may be necessary to build a retaining wall and diversion ditches at the back edge of the beach to maintain the proper slope and avoid excessive erosion. The beach area may be sodded, in which case a low wall is required at the water's edge.

Lookout Tower The lookout towers should be placed where the lifeguard can see every part of the swimming area without turning his head. It is usually located at least 25 ft back from the

water and halfway between the side limit markers. The tower must be high enough to allow the guard to see over all waterfront equipment and should have a roof or awning to shade his eyes and head from the sun. The base of the tower may be enclosed to provide storage for equipment.

Layout for Boating and Canoeing Boat and canoe docking and landing areas should be separate from swimming area. There may be administrative advantages in having the two areas reasonably close together. However, the boat and

canoe area should be at least 200 ft from the swimming area (Figs. 7 and 8).

A boat pier or docking facilities should be installed. Several kinds are suitable. The type and design will depend on local conditions.

Canoes are beached and racked in the shade. Canoe racks should be low so boys can use them. Provision should be made for locking up paddles and oars when not being used.

Swim Cribs When no shallow water is available for instructional swimming, it is sometimes feasible to build a crib. This is constructed of

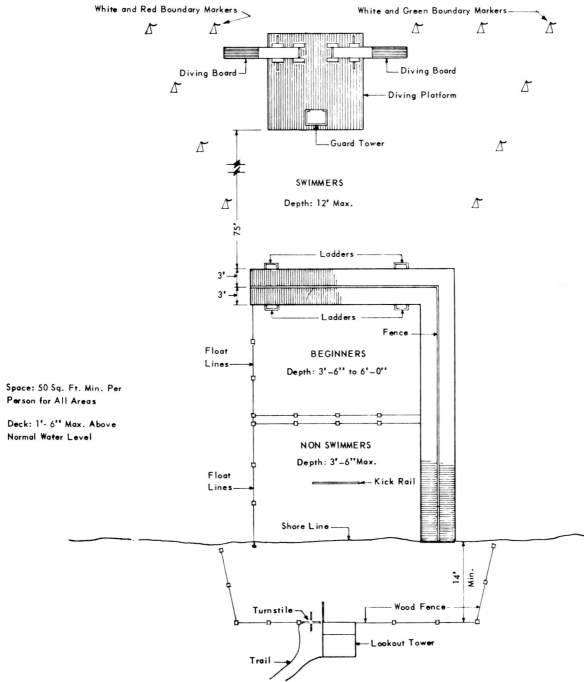

Fig. 4 (cont.) Typical waterfront layout.

wood supported on piles or rock foundations; or it may float. The depth of water in the crib should not exceed 3 ft 6 in. and a walkway and fence should extend around all sides.

Cribs are costly to build and maintain, and it is usually more practical to provide shallow water through some other means.

Swimming Pools

With increased public emphasis on health and safety, the "old swimming hole" is becoming a thing of the past. Regulations governing bathing places are in effect in most areas, and many bodies of water have been closed to swimmers. The swimming pool has replaced them for both public and private use. In areas where a lake with clear, clean water and a sandy beach is not available, the swimming pool is certainly the best alternative. Pools offer additional advantages such as easy control, assurance of pure water, and freedom from environmental interference.

Design and Layout The term *swimming pool* here refers to a pool constructed of impervious materials with the water fully recirculated and treated through filtration and chemicals.

This is known as a *recirculating swimming pool* and must be considered standard for Boy Scout camp installations. The *fill and draw* pool can seldom meet health standards and should not be installed. The *flow-through* pool requires a large continuous flow of diluting water that must meet purity standards. Such pools are not recommended.

The design and construction of a swimming pool is a complicated technical project, and competent local people should be employed to do the job. (See Fig. 9.)

The functional layout should allow for program requirements, safety, traffic flow, con-

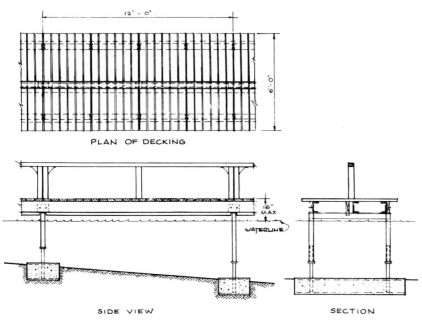

PLAN OF DECKING

SIDE VIEW

SECTION

Fig. 5 Typical details of removable pier with fixed foundation.

venience of services, and economical use of construction materials and equipment. The following elements need to be included in the swimming pool layout and design:

• *Fence* The pool should be surrounded by a fence that will fully control access to the pool both during camp operation and year round. The one entrance for swimmers should be through a gate at the shallow end of the pool.

Local conditions such as temperature, winds, and protection problems will determine the type of fence necessary. Provision should be made for spectators to see through the fence on at least one side of the pool.

• *Dressing Room and Showers* Toilets should be convenient to dressing room. Boys take a hot, cleansing shower and enter the pool

enclosure *at the shallow end.* The shower and dressing facilities should be situated far enough back from the gate to avoid crowding groups waiting to check in while others are checking out. The minimum distance is 15 ft. Double dressing and shower areas are desirable as they decrease congestion and permit more flexibility in use of the pool.

• *Walkway* A *wide* walk around the pool, sloped away from the pool edge, is required for instruction. The paved area reduces congestion when boys leave at the end of a swim period. The *minimum* widths are 12 ft at the ends and 8 ft along the sides of the pool. Concrete walkways must be finished with a lightly brushed surface to afford firm footing. *Nonswimmers, Beginners,* and *Swimmers* should

be clearly lettered at appropriate points on the edge of the pool.

• *Nonswimmers Area* The water should not be over $3\frac{1}{2}$ ft deep in this area. (Depths: 3 ft sloping to 3 ft 6 in.)

• *Beginners Area* This area should combine both shallow water and water slightly over the head of the Scout. (Depths: 3 ft 6 in. sloping to 6 ft.)

• *Swimmers Area* The remainder of the pool is for the use of more advanced swimmers. The diving board should not exceed 1 meter in height above the water, and should be located at the center of the deep end. Water depths will vary from 6 to 9 ft. Minimum depth at 7 ft beyond the diving board should be 9 ft.

• *Lookout Tower* A lookout tower should be installed. It should be high enough and so placed that the lookout can see the entire swimming area without turning his head. A roof or awning should be provided for shade.

• *Overflow Gutters* Overflow gutters must extend around the whole perimeter of the pool and must be designed in accordance with the latest standards.

• *Sidewalls* Pool sidewalls must be vertical where water is less than 6 ft deep. Sloping and curved sidewalls are dangerous and difficult to clean. Stairwells, if installed, should recess into the pool wall.

Size and Shape The size of pool for a typical camp is determined by these factors:

• Not more than four average-sized troops should use the pool at one time (60 to 65 boys).

• Since most boys are in the water throughout the swim period, allow 40 sq ft per person. Minimum pool area would therefore be about 2,600 sq ft.

• Seventy-five feet is a standard pool length, so the minimum rectangular pool would be 75 by 35 ft for a 10- to 14-troop camp.

Pools have been built in many shapes to meet special conditions. For Boy Scout camps, however, two shapes have proved to be most practical from the standpoint of use, original cost, and operating and maintenance costs. These are:

• Rectangular pool, 75 by 35 ft.

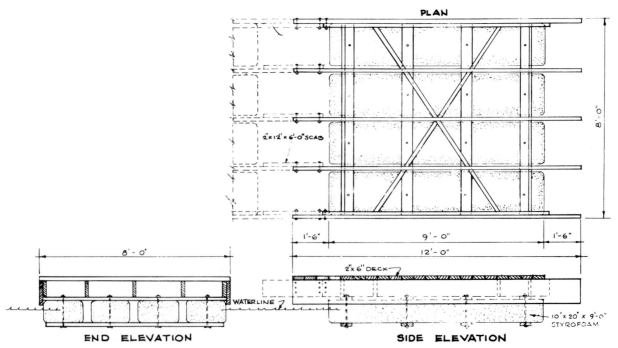

PLAN

END ELEVATION

SIDE ELEVATION

Fig. 6 Typical details of floating pier.

• Fan-shaped pool 30 ft wide at the deep end, 50 ft wide at the shallow end, and 75 ft long. This pool is only slightly larger in volume than the comparable rectangular pool, but provides considerably more shallow water. This is an important factor where the proportion of nonswimmers and beginners is large.

L-shaped pools or other variations may be entirely satisfactory when properly designed but are generally more costly than the rectangular or fan-shaped pools.

Pools smaller than 30 by 60 ft cannot adequately meet program requirements.

Site Selection The pool should be situated near the central features of the camp and approximately equidistant from the troop sites. It is best to lay out the pool on a slope with the deep end on the lower grade. This saves excavation and provides an opportunity to construct the pump room adjoining the deep end with the sidewalk above. The pool *should not* be placed in a hole.

The top grade of the pool walks should be established so that excavation will balance fill, thus saving costs and keeping the pool surface as high as possible. With the pool walls and sidewalk built above surrounding grades, there will be no likelihood of surface water getting in to contaminate the pool water. Also, groundwater and frost problems will be reduced.

Do not locate the pool under trees as leaves and bark dropping in the water will place an added burden on the filter system and may cause a stoppage in the drains.

Whenever possible, avoid facing the lookout tower or diving board toward the south or west.

Materials and Construction Features There are several types of materials used in pool construction. Experience in Boy Scout camps leads to the following conclusions about types of material:

• *Reinforced Poured Concrete* This is the most widely used and accepted material for constructing pools in Scout camps. It is long-lasting and the construction procedures and methods used are well known and can be readily supervised and inspected. This method avoids many of the variables inherent in use of other materials and has a long record of satisfactory service under varying conditions.

• *Metal* Both steel and aluminum pools have been installed and have given satisfactory service. Special consideration must be given to rust and corrosion.

• *"Gunite"* These pools have been built in great numbers, particularly for residential and other specialized uses. There are problems inherent in their design and construction that make it difficult to meet such standards as vertical sidewalls and smooth surfaces. Maintenance problems are more frequent than with other pools.

Whatever type of pool is installed, the bottom and sides must be white or light-colored and have a smooth-finish surface without cracks.

Water Supply and Treatment The recirculating pool does not require a large daily supply of water. Once filled, only 5 to 10 percent of the volume needs to be replaced daily, depending on frequency of backwashing the filters and other loss factors.

The pool water is continuously circulated by pumps through the filter system and purified by treatment with chlorine or other disinfectants. Recirculation accomplishes the dual job of removing suspended matter in the water by the straining action of the filter medium and other strainers and distributing disinfectant and other chemicals through the water to maintain proper residuals throughout.

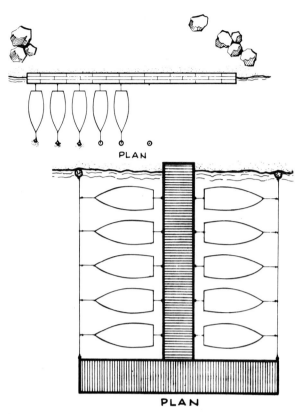

Fig. 7 Typical boat tie-up.

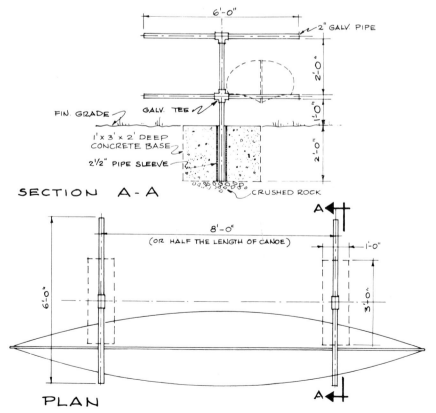

Fig. 8 Typical canoe rack.

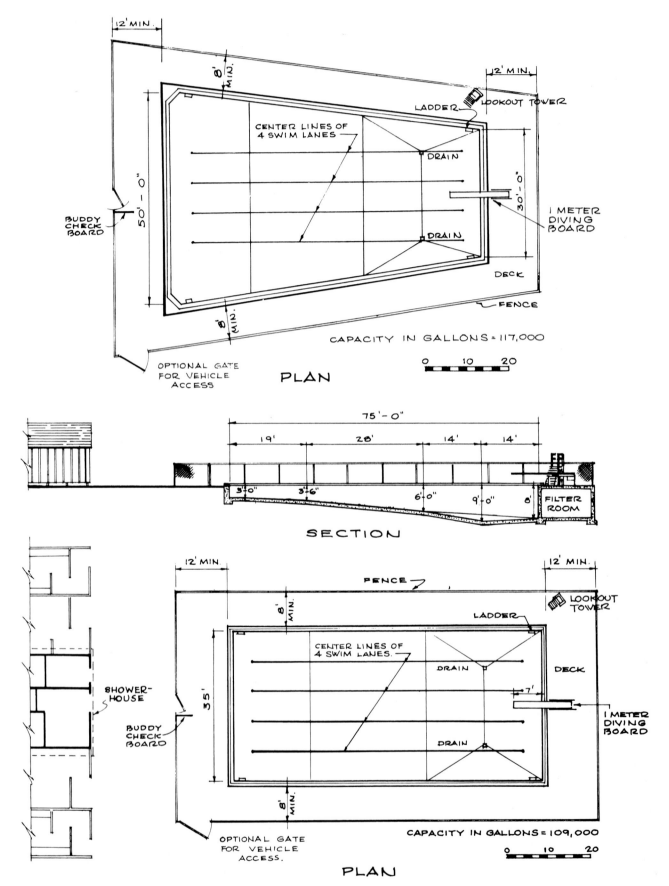

Fig. 9 Standard camp pool.

The recirculation and treatment equipment must be capable of turning over the whole pool-water volume in the period of time required by state and local ordinances—usually 8 hours. Return water inlets must be so located that there are no "dead spots" of uncirculated water in the pool.

• *Filters* There are two types of filters commonly used in pool systems: sand and gravel, and diatomaceous earth.

1. Sand and gravel filters are used extensively and have proved to be most satisfactory. They may be either of the pressure or the gravity type. The pressure type is more common, but the gravity type is preferred by many as being simpler to operate and maintain.

Because of their simplicity of operation and economy and ease of maintenance, sand and gravel filters are usually preferred for camp installations.

2. Diatomaceous earth filters are often used and offer some advantages. They may be either the pressure or vacuum type. Filters employing diatomaceous earth as a filter medium demand a more exacting operation and have caused problems in camp installations.

• *Disinfectants* Chlorine is the most commonly used disinfectant for water treatment. It not only disinfects the water as it is recirculated, but makes possible the maintenance of a residual to combat contamination as it is introduced. Chlorine may be applied as a solution of chlorine gas in water or as a hypochlorite solution. Other methods of disinfecting pool water are in limited use, but should be considered experimental at this time.

• *Suction Cleaner* Provision for a suction cleaner should be made. This is the most satisfactory method of removing dirt and other debris from the pool bottom.

SHOWER FOR POOL AND CAMP

The facilities described here are designed to serve as a pool shower, but will also serve as the central camp shower and laundry. The shower is designed for a 10- to 14-troop camp.

Functions

The functions of the shower building are to:
• Provide hot, soapy showers for all persons entering the pool
• Provide hot showers for campers anytime
• Provide minimum laundry facilities for campers and staff
• Provide storage space for first aid supplies and small equipment

Location

Shower is located at the shallow end of the pool at least 15 ft back from the pool fence. It should be on a level site, open to the sun, and with adequate space for sewage disposal.

Space Requirements

Dressing Rooms Two at about 200 sq ft each are needed.

Shower Rooms Two at about 150 sq ft each are needed.

Heater Room, Storeroom, Toilets, Laundry Totals about 400 sq ft.

Waiting Deck Provide at least 15 ft between pool fence and building; area is about 500 sq ft.

Requirement Checklist

Water Total daily demand varies but average maximum would be about 2,400 gal. Peak demand is about 50 gpm.

Hot Water A gas-fired, coil-type heater with about 100,000 Btu input and about 100 gal per hour 100° temperature rise will provide the needed hot water. Vent heater to outside and install 500-gal, insulated storage tank. Install a temperature-control valve to limit water temperature in showers to a maximum of 110°.

Sewage Disposal Disposal method depends on local conditions and ordinances. Sewage totals about 2,400 gpd. The total may be treated by installation of a 2,400-gal septic tank and disposal field. If permitted, wastes from the showers and laundry may be treated separately from those from the toilets, urinals, and lavatories. In this case, a 1,000-gal grease trap would handle the shower and laundry wastes and a 750-gal septic tank would handle the balance. Effluents would be combined and piped to the disposal field.

Light and Power Moistureproof fixtures are required. Provide outside fixtures at entrances.

Ventilation Good natural ventilation is very important. Only the storage and heater rooms should be fully enclosed, and these should be well ventilated. Dressing rooms need no roof, and shower rooms should be open to allow the sun to dry floor and walls.

Floors Concrete should have smooth finish. Provide curbs around shower room and pitch floor to drain. Also pitch dressing-room floors to drain.

Walls Install waterproof walls in shower rooms. Leave vertical space between all walls and floor to avoid rot. Walls in toilet and laundry areas should have a smooth finish for easy cleaning.

Access and Layout Provide baffled access to dressing rooms and doors with locks to storage and heater rooms. Lay out building so that camper access to the pool must be through the dressing room, the shower, and the waiting deck. Entrance to the pool is through a single gate at the shallow end.

Equipment Provision should be made for the following:
• *Dressing Rooms* Each should have benches, shelves, and hooks. There should be a toilet, urinal, and two washbasins with each dressing room.
• *Shower Rooms* Each has six to eight shower heads with individual hot and cold valves.
• *Heater Room* This contains water-heating equipment only.
• *Storage Room* Provide first aid cabinet, shelves, and hooks for equipment. If room is used as office for waterfront director, provide table and chair and install window facing pool.
• *Laundry* This room should have two laundry tubs with drainboards.

RIFLERY

All Scout camp rifle ranges and range operating practices must be certified by the Health and Safety Service of the National Council, Boy Scouts of America.

When a range site is to be selected, each property presents a different problem. A wrong selection may lead to costly construction, poor range operating conditions, or a hazard to campers or neighbors.

The range is usually located on the outskirts of camp, away from troop sites and other heavily used areas. It should be designed for use of .22 caliber rimfire rifles only. There should be 50 ft from the firing point to the face of the targets. (See Fig. 10.)

A 5- to 10-point range is adequate for the standard camp of 10 to 14 troops. Under some conditions, a larger range may be built to serve two camps at a multiple-camp reservation.

Direction of Fire A northerly direction of fire is preferred since it permits firing at any time of day without the sun shining into the eyes of the shooters or the range officer.

Backstops The purpose of the backstop is to catch and hold all bullets. It must not contain any material that will cause ricochet. Backstops may be constructed to utilize a natural slope or they may be built on level ground (Fig. 11).

• *Hillsides* A hillside that extends at least 30 ft higher than the firing point may be used. The slope must be cleared of brush to a height of 30 ft above the targets and 60 ft beyond the flanks of the target frames. Rocks must be removed or covered and a sod cover maintained to avoid ricochets. Since the firing line and target butts must be at equal elevations, it is usually necessary to excavate and grade the range site. If the exposed cut is free of rock and stones, it will make a suitable backstop.

• *Earth Embankments* When a suitable hillside is not available, an excellent backstop can be constructed of earth fill. It should be at least 10 ft high and 3 ft thick at the top with allowance for settlement. The earth must be free of stones. The embankment should extend beyond the target butts at each end, these extensions being placed as "wings" to cut off any stray bullet to the side. The embankment should be planted with grass and a sod cover maintained.

• *Earth and Timber* When suitable earth for an embankment is not available, the backstop may be constructed of heavy timber backed with sand or earth. The crib must be at least 10 ft high with wing walls. If an extra plank is added directly behind each target and so attached that it can be easily replaced, the timbers in the main structure will not need constant replacement.

Open Country In open, flat country where visibility extends for at least 3,000 ft beyond the targets and where there are no roads, trails, or grazing animals, open target butts may be used without a backstop. A body of water, navigable by canoe or larger craft, may not be used as a backstop.

Safety and Fencing Even though a suitable backstop is constructed, the range may be hazardous unless it is properly fenced and warning signs displayed. The area from the backstop to the ready line should be fenced and only one entrance provided to the area behind the firing line. Rail fencing is suitable for this purpose.

Any "blind" approaches to the range should be fenced and warning signs erected.

It is particularly important to protect areas behind the backstop.

Target Butts Targets should not be attached directly to the backstop. Erect posts and construct a frame to hold targets at the proper

1355

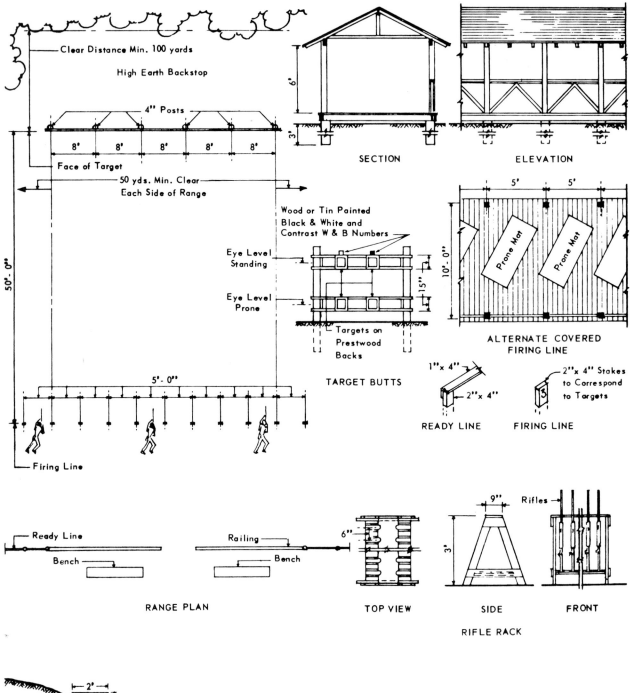

SECTION

ELEVATION

ALTERNATE COVERED
FIRING LINE

TARGET BUTTS

READY LINE   FIRING LINE

RANGE PLAN

TOP VIEW   SIDE   FRONT

RIFLE RACK

SECTION

Fig. 10   Typical rifle range.

1356

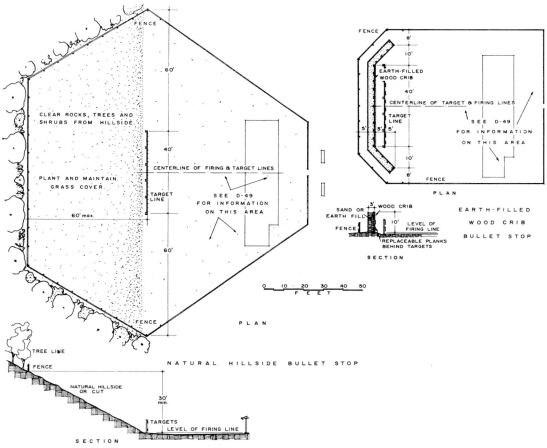

Fig. 11 Rifle range — bullet stops.

levels for prone and offhand shooting. The frames should be set 50 ft from the firing line and will need replacement periodically.

In those areas where target practice is considered to be essential to the program, every possible effort should be made to safeguard not only the shooters but others as well. If the facility is not properly designed, and the program properly conducted under the strictest regulations, this can be a very dangerous activity for any age group.

A well isolated area, with a high earthen backstop (side banks, too, if possible) should be selected. The entire area given over to this activity should be well fenced with access gained through one controlled gate. All standing vegetation should be kept cleared for at least 100 yd in back of the butts.

Firing Line The firing line should be level from end to end and well drained. A minimum of 5 ft is required between firing points. The area between firing line and the targets should be graded, drained, and have a well-maintained sod cover.

It is desirable to provide shelter over the firing line. A frame-and-canvas shelter may be constructed or a permanent shelter with a wood or concrete floor installed.

Ready Line The fence and ready line should be installed 20 ft back of the firing-line shelter. Benches should be installed for those waiting to shoot and for spectators.

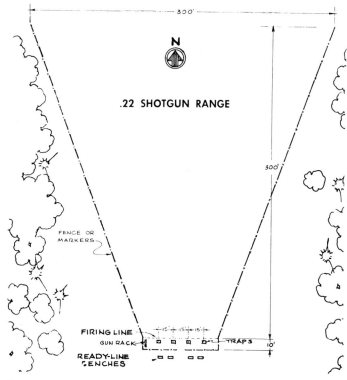

Fig. 12 .22 shotgun range.

Storage of Equipment All rifles and ammunition must be kept in locked storage when not in use on the range.

.22 Caliber Shotgun

The .22 caliber shotgun range is usually located on the outskirts of camp away from troop sites and heavily used areas. A large field makes an ideal site. The area to be protected extends 300 ft in front of the firing line, fanning out from the ends of the firing line to a width of 300 ft. The area should be cleared of brush.

The range is designed for .22 caliber smoothbore shotguns using .22 caliber shot ammunition. A four-trap range is adequate for a camp serving 10 to 14 troops (Fig. 12).

Storage of Equipment All guns and ammunition must be kept in locked storage when not in use on the range.

ARCHERY

The archery range may be located at any point in the camp where there is sufficient open area and reasonably level ground not crossed by trails. An open field is ideal. (See Fig. 13.)

An area about 150 by 250 ft will suffice for a six-target, 50-yd range adequate for a 10- to 14-troop camp. Rocks should be removed or covered to avoid breaking arrows. A sod cover is desirable. The range should be laid out so that shooters face in a northerly direction.

The range should be roped off or fenced and warning signs erected.

CAMPFIRE AREAS

The campfire is a traditional camp activity that combines fun, fellowship, and inspiration. Troop and campwide campfires are held one or more times each week. (See Figs. 14 and 15.)

WATERFRONT STORAGE BUILDING

Functions

The purpose of the waterfront storage building is to provide safe storage for boats, canoes, piers, and other waterfront equipment. It should not be used as living quarters for the waterfront staff.

Space Requirements

This will vary depending on the number of boats and canoes to be stored. A room 23 by 35 ft will store 12 canoes and 12 rowboats racked three high and will allow aisle space for moving boats in and out.

Design the building for expansion. Work space for boat repair is sometimes provided in one end of the building (Fig. 16).

CENTRAL LODGE—6-8 TROOPS—SINGLE CAMP

The central lodge is used in camps where several troops eat in one dining facility.

Function

The central lodge is used for the following purposes:
• Receiving, storage, refrigeration, and handling of food for about 125 people.
• Family-style service of meals to about 125 people at tables seating 8 each. (160 people may be seated 10 at a table for occasional meals.)

• Preparing meals for about 125 people. (Occasional meals may be served to 200 or more.)
• Commissary service for packaging and issuing raw foods to troops doing patrol cooking and to Scouts doing instructional or trail cooking. (This varies with program, but may average two troops per meal.)
• Occasional meetings or activities of large groups. (Dining hall may be used in rainy weather for some activities and religious services. Building may be used off-season for training, meetings, and other Scouting activities.)

Location

The lodge should be located in a central area convenient to troop sites. Select a good building site that is well drained, reasonably level, with adequate space for sewage disposal. Site should have a pleasant outlook, but should not be closer than 300 to 400 ft from any body of water. Orient with regard to terrain, prevailing wind, and sun. A southern exposure is usually preferred. Consider relationship to parking area and other central facilities (Fig. 17).

Space Requirements

Typical requirements for the central lodge include the following:

Kitchen Wing There should be a total of about 1,600 sq ft, including 640 sq ft for food handling and preparation, 310 sq ft for serving and dishwashing, 400 sq ft for commissary and

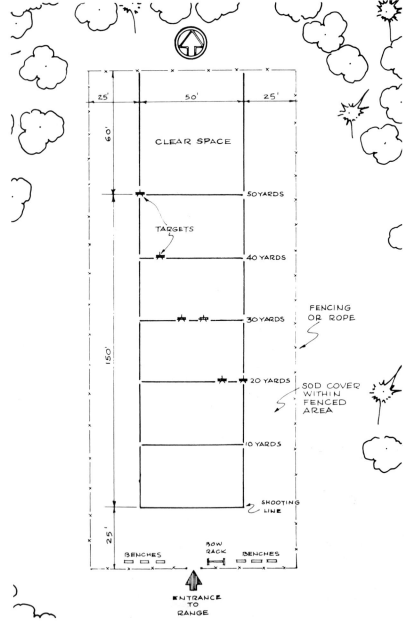

Fig. 13 Archery range.

issue porch, and 250 sq ft for storage and refrigeration. (Based on semiweekly delivery of staples and daily delivery of some perishables.) (Fig. 18)

Dining Hall About 2,000 sq ft is needed, including 1,280 sq ft for 16 tables (80 sq ft each, including seating and access space) and about 700 sq ft for aisles and circulation space, including space for setting up two more tables if necessary.

Porch This is a desirable addition in many areas. It requires an additional 850 sq ft.

Requirement Checklist

Water Daily demand (at 6 gal per person) is about 750 gal. Peak demand is about 22 gpm.

Hot Water Dishwashing (either by hand or using immersion-type dishwashing machine) and other kitchen needs require hot water. The heater should be an automatic, gas-fired, coil-type, having about 110,000 Btu rating and about 105 gal per hour 100° temperature rise. It should be vented.

Hot-Water Tank This should be galvanized, have 2-in. insulation and a 300-gal capacity.
NOTE: A sanitizing sink, for final rinse of dishes, must maintain a temperature of 180° or include an effective sanitizing agent. To establish and maintain the 180° temperature, an auxiliary heater will be required at the sink. Temperatures for dishwashing and other uses would be 110 to 120°.

Toilet Provide toilet and washbasin for cooks. Shower may be desirable. Access from cooking area to toilet must be through *two* doors.

Sewage Disposal Sewage totals about 750 gpd, usually requiring a 1,000-gal septic tank and disposal field. A grease trap will be effective for treating waste dishwater if soap (and not detergent) is used.

Light and Power Good illumination is required in all spaces. Power requirements vary with equipment used. Provide protected control panels.

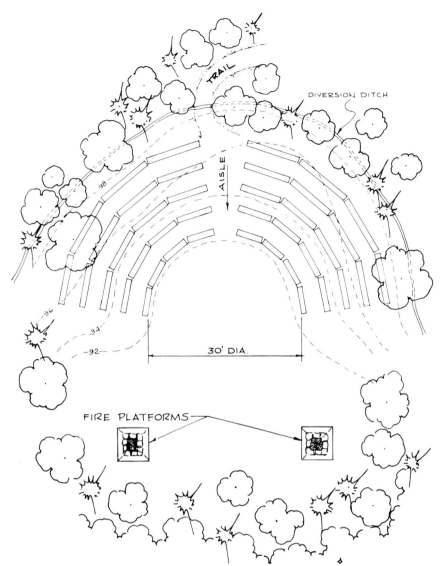

Fig. 14 Plan of council ring.

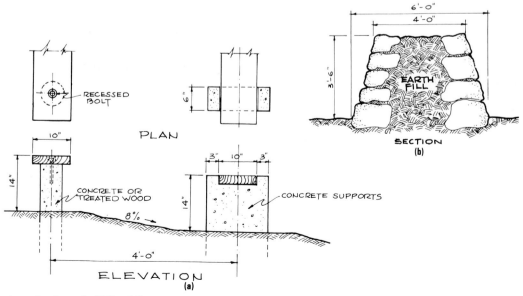

Fig. 15 (a) Two types of seat supports. (b) Fire platform.

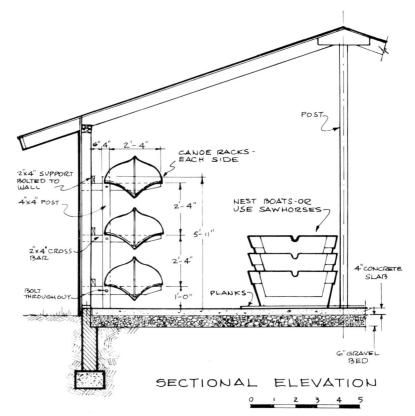

SECTIONAL ELEVATION

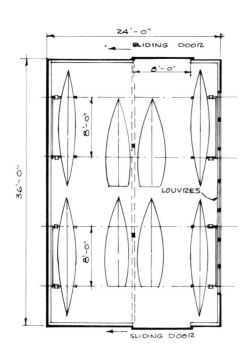

PLAN

Fig. 16 Waterfront storage building.

Refrigeration Walk-in box, having at least 64 sq ft of floor space and capable of holding a temperature of 36 to 38° is necessary. A two compartment walk-in may be installed with one compartment at 33 to 38° for meat and fowl and one compartment at 38 to 46° for other perishables.

The reach-in refrigerator should have about a 17-cu-ft capacity. A water cooler, deep freeze, and ice machine are sometimes desirable.

Heating Need will be determined by climate and use of building.

Ventilation This will also be determined by climate. Natural light and ventilation are desirable in all work and dining areas. Forced exhaust through the hood over the range is desirable for kitchen, and in some areas evaporative coolers are installed in kitchen. In most areas natural ventilation is adequate for dining hall; but large, slow-turning exhaust fans are effective and may be desirable.

Floors Smooth, impervious floors are required in all spaces. Smooth-finish concrete is most common. Provide adequate floor drains in kitchen.

Walls Interior walls of kitchen must be smooth, easily cleaned, and light color. Dining-hall walls may be unfinished.

Ceilings A ceiling may be required in kitchen area depending on type of building construction. The kitchen overhead must be clean and not a "dust-catcher." Dining halls usually have no ceiling, but the roof construction should provide a pleasing appearance.

Screening Kitchen wing and dining hall should be screened to exclude insects.

Access Provide an all-weather service road to delivery platforms at kitchen wing. Provide good walking paths to dining hall from tenting and program areas. Access trails from parking area and administration facilities should lead to the front of the dining hall—not to the kitchen wing.

Equipment and Layout – Kitchen Wing The kitchen wing should provide for the following:
• *Range* Heavy-duty, gas-fired, all hot top, about 68 by 42 in., with two ovens, double-deck high shelf, and hood with grease filters and exhaust fan.
• *Sink for Vegetable Preparation* Stainless steel, 24 by 24 by 14 in. with drainboard at one end, mounted on metal legs.
• *Sinks for Pots and Pans* Stainless steel, two compartments 30 by 30 by 14 in. with drainboards at each end, mounted on metal legs.
• *Sinks for Dishwashing* Three, stainless steel, mounted in stainless-steel counters to provide space for scraping, stacking, washing, rinsing, sanitizing, and draining dishes. (Sinks should be 24 by 24 by 14 in. Provide 10-in. splash backs on sinks and counters adjacent

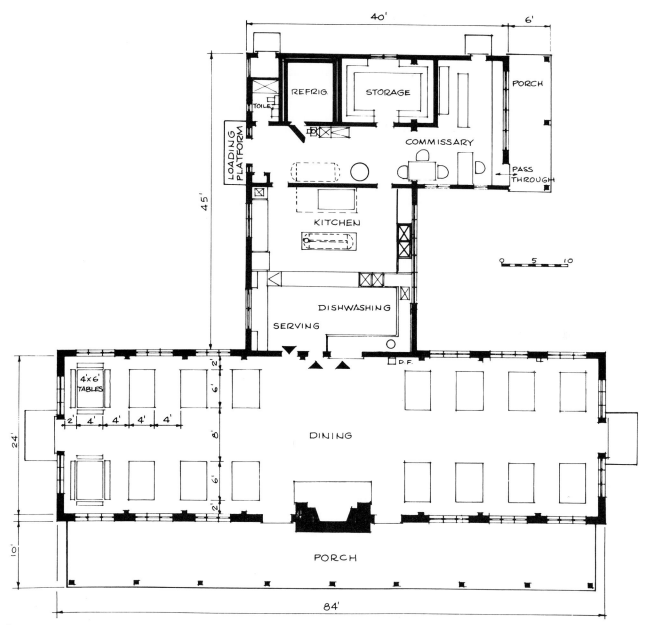

Fig. 17 Central lodge.

to wall, other edges should have raised, rolled rim. Provide overflow tubes on rinse and sanitizing sinks. Mount sinks and counters on metal legs. A three-compartment, immersion-type dishwashing machine may be substituted for the sinks. Machine should provide heating equipment to maintain required water temperature in each compartment.)

• *Mixer* Electric, table model, with 20-quart bowl, whip, and beaters.

• *Peeler* Electric, 15 lb per minute capacity.

• *Cook's Table with Utensil Rack* Maple top, about 30 by 96 in., with two stainless-steel drawers, mounted on metal legs. (Provide three-bar steel utensil rack over the table.)

• *Baker's Table* Maple top, about 30 by 72 in., with 6-in. curb at back and ends, mounted on metal legs. (Provide tier of three stainless-steel, watertight drawers and two stainless-steel, rounded-bottom tilting bins.)

• *Serving Counter* Stainless-steel, 30 in. wide, with lift-up section.

• *Clean-Dish Storage* Below serving counter. (Provide two shelves enclosed with dustproof and flytight doors, accessible from both sides; cupboards and shelving for dustproof and flytight storage of serving dishes, silver, and condiments.)

• *Pot-and-Pan Storage* Shelving under tables and work counters.

• *Wheeled Carts and Racks* Desirable for moving cartons, dirty dishes, or storing pots and pans.

• *Dry Storage* Rodentproof room for dry storage of foods, with shelf and floor space arranged for cartons and broken lots. (Space depends on frequency of deliveries.)

• *Commissary* Shelving, worktables, and counters for sorting, packaging, and setting out packaged foods for issue to patrols or individual Scouts. (Furnish desk or table for commissary man. Provide ready access to refrigeration and dry storage and to the outside. Porch is desirable at pickup counter.)

• *Traffic Flow* Provide for the following in kitchen wing:

1. Efficient flow from unloading platform to storage and refrigeration, to food preparation, and to serving counter
2. Efficient flow from soiled-dish-receiving counter to dishwashing—to clean dish storage—to dining hall
3. "In" and "out" doors from dining hall to serving counter with adequate space for circulation
4. Closing doors or shutters for all openings between kitchen and dining hall to control noise
5. Work aisles 42 in. wide between range and cook's table and between cook's table and serving counter
6. Separation of dishwashing area from food preparation area by means of counters or wall
7. Adequate counter space for return of most dirty dishes at one time

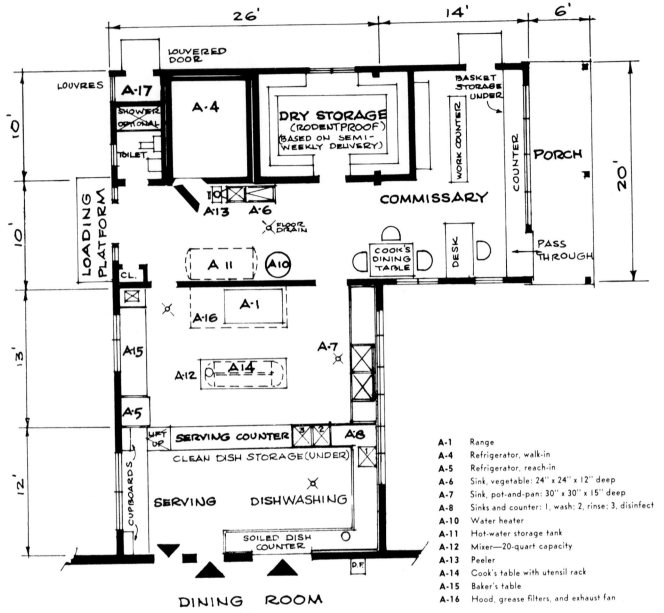

Fig. 18 Kitchen wing for central lodge. Six to eight troops, single camp.

A-1   Range
A-4   Refrigerator, walk-in
A-5   Refrigerator, reach-in
A-6   Sink, vegetable: 24'' x 24'' x 12'' deep
A-7   Sink, pot-and-pan: 30'' x 30'' x 15'' deep
A-8   Sinks and counter: 1, wash; 2, rinse; 3, disinfect
A-10   Water heater
A-11   Hot-water storage tank
A-12   Mixer—20-quart capacity
A-13   Peeler
A-14   Cook's table with utensil rack
A-15   Baker's table
A-16   Hood, grease filters, and exhaust fan

Equipment and Layout – Dining Hall The dining hall should provide for the following:

• *Tables* Smooth top, with impervious surface without cracks or raised edges 4 by 6 ft, each to seat eight for family-style dining. (Folding tables are desirable if dining hall is to be used for other activities.)

• *Chairs or Benches* Either are suitable. (Folding chairs are desirable if dining hall is to be used for other activities.)

• *Fireplace* Desirable for atmosphere, but not effective for heating whole area.

• *Drinking Fountains* Desirable. (Provide also for supplying table water.)

• *Traffic Flow* Arrange for the following in dining hall:

1. Wide doors (opening out) on at least three sides of dining hall for easy movement of campers

2. Four-foot clear aisles for waiter traffic from each table to serving and soiled-dish counters

3. Ample open area (at least 10 ft) around serving doors and soiled-dish counter

4. Clear aisles (at least 4 ft wide) to all outside doors

11

Miscellaneous

FARMSTEADS	1365	HANDICAPPED/BASIC HUMAN DIMENSIONS	1392
FARMS AND FARM BUILDINGS	1367	Wheelchair Dimensions	1393
ANIMAL FACILITY, LABORATORY	1371	Clearances	1395
GREENHOUSES	1375	HANDICAPPED/ANTHROPOMETRICS	1398
HORSE BARNS	1376	Toilets and Urinals	1398
HORSE STABLES	1379	Drinking Fountains	1399
RIDING SCHOOLS	1385	Elevators	1400
KENNELS	1387	Stairs	1401
NATURE CENTER	1389	Convenience Controls	1402
		Walkway Clearances	1403
		Ramps	1404

ZONE PLANNING

Zoning, as in Fig. 1, is a useful tool in planning new or remodeled farmsteads after the general site has been selected. Although 100-ft-wide zones are shown, wider ones are often desirable.

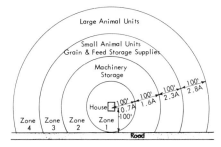

1a. Four planning zones.
If the road is busy, or if a tree windbreak is between the house and the road, set the house back further than 100'.

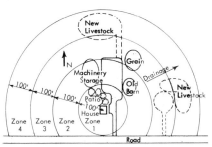

1b. Example: Livestock enterprise north of the road.
Major centers: living, livestock. Secondary centers: machinery, grain. One driveway serves all centers; a separate drive could serve a new large livestock unit.
The living area can be screened from other areas, yet it is convenient for family use, visitors, and observation. Leave space near all areas for expansion.

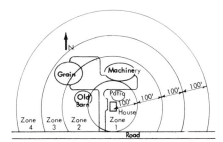

1c. Example: Grain enterprise north of the road.
Major centers: living, grain. Locate machinery and supply areas for convenience and accessibility.

Fig. 1 Farmstead planning zones. Zones help the planner organize each activity relative to all other activities, and to allow for each planning factor for each activity. Each zone is 100 ft wide—less space may lead to crowding, and wider zones are often desirable. The areas of the zones as shown are: Zone 1 = 0.7 acre; Zone 2 = 1.6 acres; Zone 3 = 2.3 acres; Zone 4 = 2.8 acres. The first three zones include most basic buildings and equipment and use about 4.6 acres.

For a farmstead with a family living area, place the house at the center of the planning zones. For a farmstead without a house, the farm court is usually the center, because vehicles, materials, and labor tend to work from the court. These 100-ft bands are activity zones, and they help locate major activity areas, help preserve a desirable family living environment, and they encourage spreading the farmstead out, leaving space for present operations and future expansion. See Figs. 1 and 2.

Zone 1—Family Living Lawns, recreation space, flower and vegetable gardens, and guest parking are close to the house. Protect Zone 1 from noise, odor, and dust as much as possible.

Farmstead Planning Handbook, Midwest Plan Service, Iowa State University, Ames, Iowa, 1974.

2a. Farmstead west of the road.
Some winter winds come from the NW. Locate the house as far west, and the livestock area as far north, as practical.

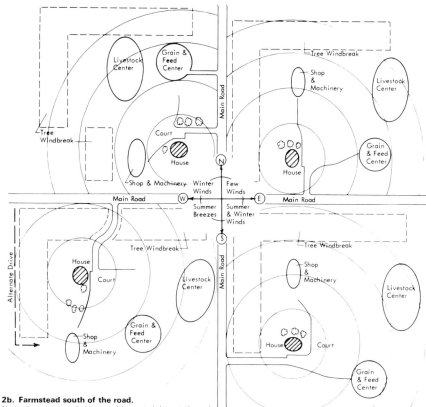

2b. Farmstead south of the road.
Note that a curved drive avoids a straight cut through the windbreak. Moving the house further south and the livestock area NE is desirable. An alternate drive location makes a good layout if the house and machine center can be reversed.

Zone 2—Machinery Center Shop, storage, and related services that are relatively quiet, dry, and odorfree are in Zone 2. Consider screening the center from family view.

Much of the driveway and farm court may be in Zone 2. Put fuel and chemical storage toward the outer edge—near the machinery, but removing odors, fire danger, and some hazard to children perhaps 200 ft from the home.

Zone 3—Grain, Feed, and Some Livestock These areas cause dust, noise, traffic and odor, and are therefore moved another zone further from the house.

Grain and feed handling and processing require electric power and good vehicle access. But, keep heavy equipment, large dryers, and fire hazard away from the house. Zone 3 is a compromise.

Small animal units may also be in Zone 3; that

2c. Farmstead north of the road.
A good relation between house, windbreak, livestock center and main road is easy with this layout.

2d. Farmstead east of the road.
As in 2c, good layout is easy, assuming drainage and other factors permit this arrangement.

Fig. 2 Farmstead and main road relationships. Only major activity centers are illustrated. Location within the farmstead area is also determined by many other factors, such as drainage, electric and water lines, sewage system, and topography.

FARMSTEADS

is, small animals or a small number of animals may not seriously degrade family living. A livestock unit close to the house is convenient for active management of maternity and nursery units or for care of pet or hobby animals.

Zone 4—Major Livestock Facilities A large unit, whether confined to a building or on drylot, creates demand for adequate space, drainage, waste management, access, loading facilities, feed distribution, and other services. It also creates noise, dust, traffic, and odors. Space for expansion is usually important. Locate major livestock production in Zone 4 or beyond.

Moving away from the old farmstead is frequently the most economical, as well as satisfactory, way to solve major expansion problems.

Zone planning applies to both cash grain and livestock farms. A grain farm can become a livestock farm and vice versa, so allow for both grain and livestock in your master design, to protect future growth, efficiency, and sale value. Adjusting to changes in health, labor supply, or economics can be difficult unless space is available for expanded and new facilities.

Farmstead and Main Road

The illustrations in Fig. 2 show some of the problems encountered in designing a farmstead plan. Prevailing winds are assumed from the NW or W in winter, and from the NW, SW, and SE in summer.

Fig. 2a shows space between buildings, an adequate court, and a good windbreak for windy climates. But, the house is SE of the livestock, so some winter winds will carry odors to the living area. If possible, plan the house further west or southwest and the livestock center further northeast.

In Fig. 2b a straight drive would permit north and northwest winds to blow directly toward the court. The layout can be improved by exchanging the house and machinery centers and using the alternate drive location shown.

In general, study prevailing wind directions. Position the house so that fewest winds blow toward it from the rest of the farmstead during the times of the year when dust, noise, odors, and insects are problems. Using the zones as described, locate the other activity areas.

All buildings should be arranged so that they can be reached by truck. The service yard and drives should allow plenty of room for traffic. Buildings can be planned so that there are large doors with plenty of head room and no interior posts. If buildings are planned this way then a tractor with a blade can clean livestock buildings and loading and unloading can be a mechanical operation instead of backbreaking labor. Figure 1 shows traffic flow.

A good farmstead plan takes advantage of natural influences. The sun's movement from east to west warms three sides of buildings if they are laid out square with the compass. Some buildings—such as corncribs, two-row central farrowing, and stanchion barns need the warmth or light of the sun on both the east and west. For that reason they should be built with the long axis north and south. Poultry laying houses and one-row farrowing houses usually face south and have most of the windows on the south side (Fig. 2).

Buildings can usually be placed so that they will shield workers and animals from winter wind without making it any harder to do the chores. Putting major openings and windows on the south and east will trap the sun's heat and, thus, give additional protection from the cold. The sun will also help to dry out livestock buildings where too much moisture is often a problem.

Service yards, barn lots, and farm structures require well-drained locations. The service area should, of course, drain away from the farmhouse. Raised ground is ideal for a farmstead setting—giving scenic advantages as well as good drainage—but a gentle slope in one direction can often be developed effectively.

Rolling land can add interest to a farmstead setting. And, if it is properly handled, it need not interfere with the efficiency of operations. An arrangement that follows the contour of the land will make maintenance easier and will improve appearance. Sometimes it may be necessary to reduce the slope or improve drainage by grading.

Living Center

The farmhouse should be fitted into its surroundings. Sunlight, direction of prevailing summer and winter winds, views (both those that already exist and those that can be developed), and location of the public road and driveway should all be considered (Fig. 3).

If the doors are on the east or the south side of the garage, you will have less trouble with snow than if they are on the north or west.

Farm Service Yard

A farm service yard makes it easy to get from one activity center of the farmstead to another. It reduces the number of gates necessary—or does away with them entirely. It provides room to maneuver farm machinery and helps make the whole farmstead look more unified. The space in the yard gives some fire protection

From *Farm Arrangements*, published by the Boy Scouts of America.

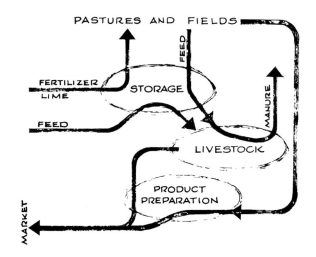

Fig. 1

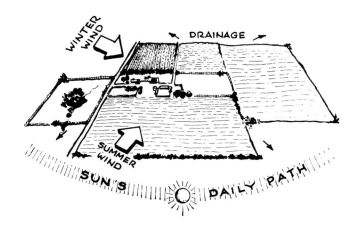

Fig. 2

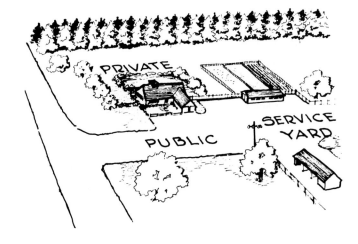

Fig. 3

Miscellaneous

FARMS AND FARM BUILDINGS

without increasing the distance that has to be traveled from one building to another. Lights near the center of the yard will illuminate the approach to all buildings and lots (Fig. 4).

The service yard should have direct access to fields and to the road. Where the service yard or lanes enter fields, cattle guards can often be used to advantage instead of gates. Notice the grate in the lane that discourages cattle from crossing, but does not prevent walking or driving a vehicle over it.

The service yard's dimensions, of course, depend on the size of the farm and the number of enterprises. Eighty feet or eight poles is the minimum width needed where vehicles are to be turned around, and a greater width is better.

The yard may be square, rectangular, L-shaped, or of any other shape—just so it remains uncluttered. Gravel or crushed rock is desirable where traffic is heaviest. Other areas should be sodded to improve the appearance.

Machinery Center

Keep farm machinery in a central storage building rather than distributed around the farmstead in driveways, small sheds, or leantos of livestock buildings. An advantage of the machinery center is that it is more convenient for making repairs and servicing equipment. If the automobile is kept there, the building should be closer to the house than would otherwise be desirable.

Sometimes the machinery center may be located along the lane to the fields. This is desirable if space in the farmstead area is limited or if all machinery traffic is confined to lanes within the farm. The warehouse type of building (with end doors) can be set just to one side of the lane. The side-opening type of structure needs to be at least 30 ft or 3 poles from the lane for convenience in getting in and out (Fig. 5).

Unless room is allowed for expansion, future shelter space may have to be separate. A location that will allow an extension on one end is desirable.

Grain Center

Usually grain is stored at the farmstead, although some grain farms have cribs in a field near a good market road. Storage at the farmstead reduces the chance of loss by theft and is also more convenient if a substantial amount of grain is fed on the farm (Fig. 6).

A spot within the service yard is best—preferably near one side where there is ample room for the use of elevators, trucks and wagons. The grain center should be accessible without opening gates. If natural drying is depended upon, a location where sunlight and air can reach the walls of cribs is important.

The grain center itself may be a crib, a combined crib and granary, or one or more grain bins. Elevating, filling, and emptying equipment can be arranged so that all grain is stored at ground level. Bins may be placed either in a circle around an elevator or in a straight line along the service yard border (on livestock farm, they may be next to the feeding area).

When the grain center is combined with a feeding center, space should be allowed for a structure to house feed-processing equipment. If the grain center has been properly related to the feeding center, the feed can be easily fed to the livestock.

Feeding Center

On livestock farms the grain storage and processing center that has been described should

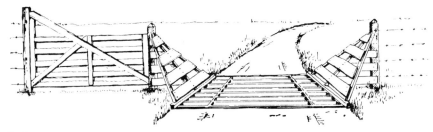

Fig. 4

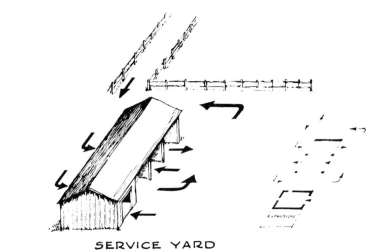

SERVICE YARD

Fig. 5

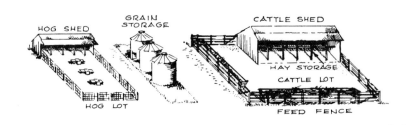

Fig. 6

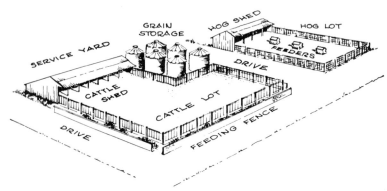

Fig. 7

1368

be one of the units making up the feeding center. Shelters for one or more classes of livestock, storage units for feed and bedding, lots, and feeding floors would also be included. Putting grain storage close to these other structures will, of course, save labor. Precautions against lightning and spontaneous combustion will help to take care of any increased fire hazard (Fig. 7).

In arranging the feeding center, take into account both sunlight direction and the direction of prevailing winds. Protection from winter wind is, of course, important—at the same time sheltered areas should get as much sunlight as possible. The center should be located so that the prevailing summer wind carries livestock odors away from the living area.

Structures for storing hay, silage, and bedding should be easy to get to from the service yard. Filling them will then be more convenient. For greater convenience, arrange the feeding area so that it does not have to be entered when grain is being unloaded for storage.

Paved feed lots are highly recommended. Feed lots for both cattle and hogs are best located near the feed storage and processing center. This is not always possible, however, when existing arrangements are being adapted for modern feeding equipment. In such a situation a mechanical conveyor or a blower-pipe arrangement might be used to move feed to bunks some distance away from the immediate feed center.

Dairy Center

Dairy structures (loose-housing or stanchion barn systems) should be on the side of the service yard closest to lanes and pastures.

The most compact system uses the stanchion barn. Usually, the long axis of the barn is north and south so that sunlight will strike both sides of the building. Exceptions, however, present no serious difficulties. The milk house or milk room is preferably located near the middle of the stanchion area and on the service yard side. Sometimes a short driveway from the service yard to the milk room may be necessary. For efficiency in feeding, the silo and feed room should also be about halfway from each end of the stanchion lines—usually on the side opposite the milk room. Where possible, the silo and feed storage should be accessible from the service yard, but this is less important than access to the milk room if a choice must be made (Figs. 8 and 9).

The loose-housing system consists of several units: a feeding area and hay storage, a bedded area and bedding storage, a milking unit with feed bin, and a milkhouse. It is less expensive to build but takes more space. These units should be arranged to allow sunlight in the bedded area while shielding the space from winter wind. An L-shape arrangement can often be formed with one side of the L made up of the bedded area and bedding storage. The other side would consist of the feeding area and hay storage. Sometimes the location of the service yard may make a straight-line arrangement desirable, although such an arrangement gives less wind protection than the L-shape. Doors to hay and bedding storage should be accessible from the service yard or from a lane leading to the yard.

The bunker silo is supplied and packed by tractor. Silage is protected by a waterproof covering that is rolled back gradually to permit feeding all across one end.

The milking unit should be located between the bedding and feeding areas. To reduce steps, the milk house should be near the milking unit. With pipeline equipment, it is important

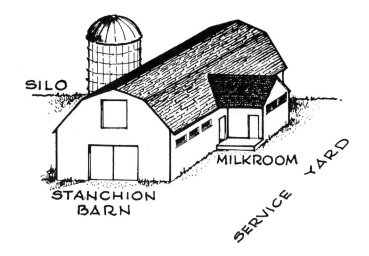

Fig. 8

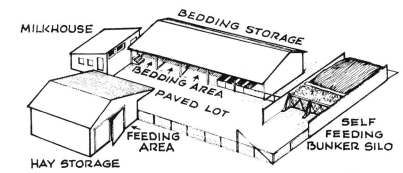

Fig. 9

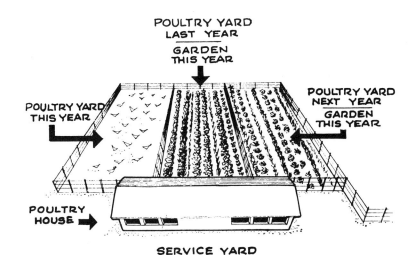

Fig. 10

Miscellaneous

FARMS AND FARM BUILDINGS

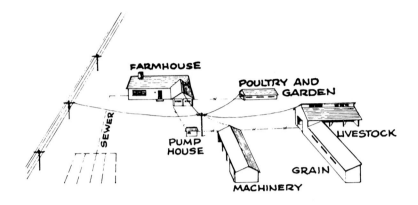

Fig. 11

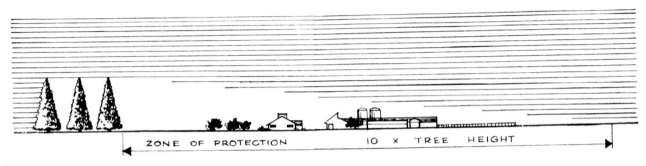

Fig. 12

to locate the milk house so that a minimum of piping is required.

Poultry Center

The following suggestions are made for typical farm poultry enterprises—not commercial poultry establishments (Fig. 10).

Provide a definite poultry center rather than allow a run-of-the-farmstead arrangement. As a general rule, it should be where the prevailing summer wind will carry odors and feathers away from the living area rather than toward it. Other than that, the location will depend on the system of handling the flock.

Adult stock should be confined to the house or at least kept in a fenced yard. If you use a poultry yard, you may wish to rotate it with the garden. This system has advantages for sanitation as well as for productive gardening. But never apply poultry manure during the gardening year.

When poultry is confined, the house should be readily accessible from the service yard. Often a good location is next to the border of the service yard, provided there is enough space to allow for future expansion of the poultry house.

Unless the operation is large enough to justify storing feed within the poultry house, the house should be fairly close to the feed center. A southern exposure that will admit the maximum amount of sunlight is also important. Water should be piped into the house.

Power, Water, and Sanitation Facilities

A well located in the living area of the farm is desirable from a sanitary standpoint, since the house should be on the best-drained area of the farmstead. You may, however, prefer a location closer to the center of water consumption or between the house and the livestock

feeding area. Direct access to the well from the service yard is desirable but not necessary.

The leader supplying electricity to the pump should come directly from the meter. In laying out the water system, it is important to keep lines as short and straight as possible. A pipeline run straight to the barn from the storage tank, with side branches to the poultry house, hog house, pastures, shop, and garden is practical in most situations (Fig. 11).

A modern sewage disposal system consists of the house sewer, septic tank, and a disposal field. The sewer line from the house to the septic tank, as well as the line to the distribution box, must be watertight and rootproof. The disposal area should be on open ground, generally out of range of tree roots.

Windbreak

Good planning guards against winter winds. Because the winter wind is normally from the northwest, the windbreak of trees should be planted on the north and west sides of the farmstead (Fig. 12).

On level or nearly level land, the ideal distance between windbreak and areas requiring the most protection such as house, livestock shelter, and feeding areas—is about 150 ft or 15 poles. The maximum distance is 300 ft or 30 poles. Since the zone of noticeable protection is equal to about ten times the height of the trees, they would have to be 30 ft high before giving protection to areas 300 ft away.

At the same time the windbreak should not be closer than 5 poles to commonly used areas, and 8 or 10 poles would be better. Snow may accumulate in the immediate lee of the windbreak, particularly during the early years of planting. Also, air movement in summer is poor as soon as the trees grow tall enough to give protection. Buildings infrequently used in winter may stand near the windbreak, provided

roofs are steep enough to keep snow from accumulating. Poultry and livestock sensitive to heat should not be kept in these buildings during the summer.

For satisfactory protection, trees should be in three rows 14 ft apart. A permanent fence around the windbreak is essential to keep out livestock and poultry. It should be at least 6 ft from the rows of trees, making the total minimum width 40 ft or 4 poles. Length of the windbreak depends largely upon the size and shape of the farmstead. It is often desirable to extend the windbreak 5 to 10 poles past the area needing protection.

While the windbreak will ordinarily follow the straight lines of field and lot boundaries, a diagonal or curved line may sometimes be desirable. For example, where the land surface slopes sharply to the northwest away from the farmstead area, planting the trees on the contour will place them higher on the slope, giving earlier protection. Or it may be possible to avoid a poorly drained area with a curve or diagonal arrangement.

For the best protection, the windbreak should be continuous and uninterrupted. So if possible, access to fields on the north and west should be at either end of the windbreak. If a lane through the windbreak is necessary, open gaps should be avoided, especially at the critical northwest corner. If the lane logically fits here, and principal traffic is to the north, the north-south strip should extend about 5 poles beyond the east-west strip. This arrangement will protect the opening from all winds of the northwest quarter except those in the north.

If it is necessary to have a gap at some point along the strip, the corner section should be farther from the farmstead than the end section. This arrangement is advantageous for a farmstead that narrows toward the east or south.

1370

The physical condition and design of animal facilities to a great extent determine the efficiency and economy of their operation and greatly influence standards for animal care. A well-designed, properly maintained facility is an essential element in good animal care.

Functional Areas

The design, scope, and size of an animal facility depend on the nature of the research activities to be conducted therein, the number of animals to be housed, the requirements for flexibility in the housing of different species, its physical relationship to the rest of the institution, and its geographical location. The following functional areas are considered essential in a modern animal facility:

1. A separate building, a separate wing, one or more floors, or separate rooms where animals can be housed apart from areas of human occupancy. A sufficient number of animal rooms or areas are required to assure separation of species when necessary, or isolation of individual projects; to provide for the receipt, quarantine, and isolation of animals; and to provide for their routine and specialized housing.

2. Specialized laboratories or areas contiguous with or near the animal housing areas for activities such as surgery; necropsy; intensive postsurgical care; radiography; preparation of special diets; and the diagnosis, treatment, and control of laboratory animal diseases. If radioisotopes, toxic substances, or pathogens are to be used, special facilities or areas must be provided.

3. Receiving and storage areas for food, bedding, supplies, and equipment.

4. An office for the administration, supervision and direction of the facility.

5. Showers, sinks, lockers, and toilets for personnel.

6. An area for washing and sterilizing equipment and supplies.

Depending upon the volume of work, a well-equipped cleaning area includes facilities such as a cage-washing machine; a bottle- or glassware-washing machine; a rack-washing machine or area; a waste can-washing machine or area; a utility sink; an autoclave for equipment, food, and bedding; and separate areas for holding soiled and clean equipment.

7. An incinerator capable of burning all animal waste and refuse, or facilities for safe and sanitary storage of such waste prior to removal.

8. An area suitable for food consumption should be provided if personnel regularly eat in the facilities that house animals.

Service Areas in Relation to the Total Size of the Animal Facilities

1. An area or areas equal in square feet to at least 25 percent of the animal housing space should be set aside for the service functions of the animal facility. The service functions in-

Guide for Laboratory Animal Facilities and Care, National Institute of Health, Department of Health, Education, and Welfare, Washington, D.C., 1968.

clude such activities as cage washing and sterilization, storage, diagnostic laboratory and office activities, receiving and quarantining of animals, and refuse disposal.

2. Where an animal facility is 1,000 sq ft or less in size, it may be possible to carry out the service functions in an area that serves other activities as well. However, a separate facility should be available for washing and sanitizing animal cages.

3. In a facility up to 10,000 sq ft in size, separate rooms or areas should be provided for the following service activities:

a. Receipt and quarantine of newly received animals

b. Receipt and storage of animal food and supplies, including refrigeration

c. Cleaning, sanitizing, and storage of cages and equipment

d. Incinerator or protected area for refuse

e. Lavatory facilities for personnel

f. Office for supervisory and administrative personnel

g. Laboratory facilities

4. In institutions having several separate animal housing facilities, or one large area, which total more than 10,000 sq ft, rooms or areas should be provided for all of the service functions listed in item 3 above. In addition, clinical laboratory facilities should be provided for the diagnosing of animal diseases.

Some duplication of service areas may be required if the animal facilities are widely dispersed.

Physical Relationship of Animal Facilities to Research or Teaching Laboratories

Animal housing areas support research and teaching laboratories. Good animal husbandry and human comfort require physical separation of animal facilities and human occupancy areas such as offices and laboratories. This can be accomplished by locating the animal quarters in a separate wing or on a separate floor in a multistory building, or by providing a separate building for animal housing. A one-story building for animal housing permits the most efficient and economical animal care operation, since vertical transport is avoided; however, this may be the least desirable choice for the research workers because of inaccessibility to their laboratories. Efficiency and economy in utilization of the research workers' time must be considered in planning animal facilities. Careful planning should make it possible to locate the animal areas adjacent to or near the laboratory areas; but they should be physically separated from the laboratories by barriers such as entry locks, separate corridors, or separate floors.

Many institutions have recently acquired and developed farm type facilities. These are useful for conditioning, isolation, quarantine, and long-term housing and maintenance of large domestic animals.

Construction Guidelines

Maintenance costs as well as initial construction costs should be considered when selecting building materials, and these materials should facilitate efficient and hygienic operation of the

animal quarters. Durable, waterproof, fire-resistant seamless materials are most desirable for interior surfaces. Paints and glazes, in addition to being highly resistant to chemical solvents, cleaning agents, and scrubbing, should be highly resistant to high-pressure sprays and impact.

1. **Corridors** Corridors should be at least 7 ft wide to permit easy flow of personnel and equipment. The floor-wall junction should be coved to facilitate cleaning. Provisions should be made for curbs or guardrails or for bumpers on equipment to protect the walls from damage. Exposed corners should be protected by reinforcing them with steel, or another durable material up to a height of 6 ft. Corridors leading to dog kennels should be provided with a noise trap such as a double-door entry lock. Wherever possible, access to utilities such as waterlines, drainpipes, and electrical connections should be through service panels or shafts located in the corridors outside the animal rooms.

2. **Animal Room Doors** Animal room doors should swing toward the corridor only if there is a recessed vestibule. They should be at least 42 in. wide and no less than 84 in. high to permit easy passage of racks and equipment. The doors should fit tightly within the frames and sills, and the frames should be completely sealed to provide a barrier against the entrance or harboring of vermin. Metal or metal-covered doors are preferable. They should be equipped with kickplates and be self-closing. Recessed handles are recommended. Viewing windows are desirable.

3. **Exterior Windows** Exterior windows and skylights are not needed in the animal rooms if adequate ventilation and lights are provided. If windows are provided, it is preferable that they be nonopening, without sills or horizontal surfaces where dust can collect, of an insulating construction (in areas of temperature extremes), and sealed with a material that will withstand repeated washing and disinfecting. If windows are opened for ventilation purposes, effective screening is essential.

4. **Floors** Floors should be smooth, waterproof, nonabsorbent, nonslip, wear resistant, acid and solvent resistant, capable of being scrubbed with detergents and disinfectants, and capable of supporting racks, equipment, and storage areas without gouging, cracking, or pitting. Depending upon the functions carried on in specific areas, the materials specified should be of a monolithic nature or should have a minimum of joints. Some materials that have proven satisfactory are terrazzo, cupric oxychloride cement, smooth hard-surfaced concrete, neoprene terrazzo, and special hardened rubber-base aggregates. A continuous waterproof membrane should be provided. Where sills are installed at the entrance to the room, they should be designed so as to allow for the passage of equipment.

5. **Walls** Walls should be monolithic, waterproof, painted, glazed or smooth, free of cracks or imperfect junctures at the door, ceiling,

ANIMAL FACILITY, LABORATORY

corners, or utility penetrations. Materials should be acid or solvent resistant, capable of withstanding scrubbing with detergents and disinfectants. The walls must be capable of withstanding water under high pressure. Provision should be made to protect walls from damage by movable equipment.

6. Ceilings Ceilings formed by the concrete floor above are satisfactory if properly smoothed, sealed, and painted. Furred ceilings of plaster or fire code plasterboard should be sealed and painted with a washable finish. Exposed pipes and fixtures at ceiling level are undesirable, especially in nonhuman primate rooms, because of the problems created by escaped animals.

7. Ventilation, Temperature, and Humidity Control

a. Effective ventilation is necessary to maintain a low concentration of atmospheric contaminants, such as odors or microorganisms, to regulate room temperature and to promote comfort. Important factors for proper ventilation are temperature, humidity, and air movement. The ability to maintain odorless facilities depends upon the number and species of animals housed, and the sanitation practices, as well as upon a properly designed ventilation system.

b. Ideally, a system should permit individual adjustments within $\pm 2^\circ$ F for any temperature within a range of 65° to 85° F. The relative humidity should be maintained year round within a range of 30 to 70 percent, according to the needs of the species being maintained. A mechanical ventilation system is necessary in most indoor facilities to meet these requirements. Air conditioning is highly recommended since it promotes environmental stability. Temperature and humidity should be controlled individually in each animal room or groups of rooms serving a common purpose. The animal facility and human occupancy areas should be ventilated separately. The system should provide frequent changes of room air without drafts. Ten to fifteen changes per hour are recommended. There should be no recirculation of room air unless it has been filtered to remove contaminants. An acceptable alternative is to provide zone control with limited recirculation of room air. Operation of the system at $74^\circ \pm 4^\circ$ F and 50 ± 20 percent relative humidity, using 100 percent fresh air during temperate weather and 50 percent fresh air during periods of temperature extremes is acceptable for situations where routine housing of animals is the primary requirement.

c. Maintenance of a given room temperature within even closer tolerances, such as $\pm 1^\circ$ F,

and of relative humidity within 5 percent, using 100 percent fresh air at all times, may be required for certain experiments. Such controls may be essential, for example, where precise environmental studies are in progress. Recording devices for temperature and humidity should be installed in such rooms, together with a failure alarm system that may control utilities and air supply. The sensing elements should be placed at approximately the average level of the animal cage floors.

d. If small animals (for example, dogs and rabbits) are housed outdoors with no access to indoor facilities, provisions to aid their natural temperature regulation are essential. When the ambient temperature falls below 50° F, some form of shelter and clean nesting materials should be provided. Materials such as shavings, straw, or paper can be used. When the ambient temperature exceeds 85° F, shade must be available and animals should be able to burrow or lie on materials several degrees cooler than the surrounding air.

8. Power and Lighting The electrical system should provide ample lighting, sufficient power outlets, safety provisions (such as explosion-proof outlets in rooms where volatile, explosive anesthetics may be used), and water-proof outlets where water is used in cleaning.

Suggested Space for the Routine Housing of Laboratory Animals

Species	Weight or age	Type of housing	Overall size (inches)			Number of animals	Housing area/animal	
			Width	Depth	Height		Sq ft	Sq in.
Dogs*	Up to 15 kg	Pen or run	48	72	...	3	8	
	15 to 30 kg	Pen or run	48	72	...	2	12	
	Over 30 kg	Pen or run	48	72	...	1	24	
	Up to 15 kg	Cage	36	32	32	1	8	
	15 to 30 kg	Cage	48	36	36	1	12	
	Over 30 kg	Cage	Refer to footnote 1					
Cats	Up to 4 kg	Cage	18	24	24	1	3	
	Over 4 kg	Cage	24	24	24	1	4	
		Group cage or pen	36	48	72	3-6	2-4	
Nonhuman primates†	Up to 1 kg	Cage	18	10	18	1-2	0.6-1.2	
	1-3 kg	Cage	24	18	24	1-2	1.5-3	
	4-6 kg	Cage	24	24	30	1-2	2-4	
	6-10 kg	Cage	30	30	36	1	6	
	Over 10 kg	Cage	36	30	48	1	7.5	
Rabbits	Up to 4 kg	Cage	18	24	16	1-2	1.5-3	
	4-5 kg	Cage	24	24	16	1	4	
Guinea pigs	Up to 350 g	Individual cage	8	12	8	1	......	96
	Over 350 g	Individual cage	12	12	8	1	......	144
	Up to 350 g	Group cage	14	20	8	2-4	......	70-140
	Over 350 g	Group cage	18	20	8	2-4	......	90-180
Hamsters		Individual cage	8	12	8	1-6	......	16-96
		Group cage	14	20	8	Up to 10	......	28 or more
Rats	150-250 g	Individual cage	8	12	8	1-3	......	32-96
		Group cage	14	20	8	4-10	......	28-70
Mice	20 g	Small group	8	12	5	5-10	......	10-20
		Large group cage	12	18	5	10-20	......	11-22
Chickens (adult)‡		Individual cage	8	18	21	1	1	
		Group cage	36	24	24	2-4	1.5-3.0	

9. Drainage All waste fixtures and equipment should be connected to soil and waste pipes through traps. If floor drains are used, the drainpipes should not be less than 4 in. in diameter. In heavy-use areas such as dog kennels, drains at least 6 in. in diameter are recommended. A flushing drain, much like an ordinary toilet bowl, set in the floor, is an effective aid in the disposal of solid waste. A porous trap bucket to screen out solid waste provides an effective alternative to removal of solid materials through the drain. All drainpipes should have short runs to the main, or they should be steeply pitched from the opening. When drains are not in use they should be capped and sealed to prevent any backflow of sewer gases. Lockable drain covers are useful in preventing use of the drains for disposal of materials which should be swept up and removed by other means.

Floor drains are not essential in animal rooms for species such as rats, mice, or hamsters. Floors in such rooms can be maintained satisfactorily by wet vacuuming, or by sweeping and mopping with appropriate disinfectants or cleaning compounds. The recommended minimum pitch of floors, where floor drains are used, is ¼ in. per foot. Proper pitching of the floor is an essential element in establishing good drainage in animal rooms;

particular attention should be paid to this detail in planning animal facilities.

10. Storage Areas: Food and Bedding, Refuse, Equipment In areas where delivery schedules are reliable, the amount of space required for food and bedding storage can be held to a minimum. The best utilization is achieved by maintaining constant turnover.

Bulk supplies of food and bedding should not be stored in animal rooms. A separate area or room should be available in which food and bedding can be stored off the floor on pallets, racks, or carts. A continuing pest control program is essential. It is most desirable for the storage areas to be verminproof.

Food storage areas should be physically separated from refuse areas. Temperatures in the storage rooms may be the ambient temperature. However, it is good practice to hold packaged animal feeds (pellet rations) at $50°$ F or less. Refrigerated storage should be available for meats, fruits, vegetables, and other perishable items.

Separate storage for animal waste and dead animals is essential. Refuse storage areas should preferably be kept below $45°$ F to reduce putrefaction of waste or animal carcasses. Obnoxious materials should be covered or packaged. The area should be constructed so

that it can be kept clean and free of vermin.

Adequate space for storing equipment is essential. This is an effective way to prevent clutter in animal rooms. All storage areas should be kept clean.

11. Noise Control Noise, both from the animals and animal-care routines, is inherent in the operation of animal facilities. Noise may be undesirable because of its effect on personnel and on the animals themselves. Inasmuch as background and "operational" noise are an environmental factor in the control of animal experiments, they should be considered in the design of animal facilities.

Ordinarily, species such as rats, mice, guinea pigs, cats, and hamsters do not create a disturbing amount of noise in animal facilities. Noise from a monkey colony can be troublesome, and, invariably, dogs are the cause of unwelcome noise. Barking is disturbing to personnel working inside and outside of the animal facilities. It may also pose important public relations problems if there are residences near the laboratory.

The physical separation of human and animal occupancy areas is the best way to minimize all disturbances to laboratory personnel from the sounds of animals and animal-care routines.

Suggested Space for the Routine Housing of Laboratory Animals (Continued)

Species	Weight or age	Type of housing	Overall size (inches)			Number of animals	Housing Area/animal	
			Width	Depth	Height		Sq ft	Sq in.
Pigeons	0.5–0.8 kg	Cage	30	30	15	5–7	. . . . .	130–180
Small birds	100–130 g	Cage	6	10	6	1–2	. . . . .	30–60
	100–130 g	Group cage	24	30	6	24	. . . . .	30
Cattle (adult)	350 kg	Stanchion	42	56	. . .	1		
	450 kg	Stanchion	45	60	. . .	1		
	550 kg	Stanchion	48	64	. . .	1		
	650 kg	Stanchion	51	68	. . .	1		
	750 kg	Stanchion	54	72	. . .	1		
	550 kg	Pen	120	144	. . .	1	120	
	650 kg	Pen	120	168	. . .	1	140	
	750 kg	Pen	120	180	. . .	1	150	
Cattle (calves)	50–75 kg	Pen	48	72	. . .	1	24	
	1½–10 mo	Group pens	. . .	. . .	. . .	Up to 10	20–25	
	Over 10 mo	Group pens	. . .	. . .	. . .	Up to 10	30–40	
Cattle (adult)		Loose housing¶	. . .	. . .	. . .	. . . . . .	50–80	
Horses	500–750 kg	Tie stall	66	96	. . .	1	44	
	500–750 kg	Pen	144	144	. . .	1	144	
Sheep and goats		Pen	. . .	. . .	. . .	. . . . . .	15–22	
Female with young		Pen	. . .	. . .	. . .	. . . . . .	20–30	
Adult male		Pen	. . .	. . .	. . .	1	20–30	
Hogs Adult sow		Pen	. . .	. . .	. . .	1	25–40	
Sow with pigs		Pen	. . .	. . .	. . .	1	48–88	
Adult boars		Pen	. . .	. . .	. . .	1	30–80	
	18–45 kg	Pen	. . .	. . .	. . .	. . . . . .	6–12	
	45–100 kg	Pen	. . .	. . .	. . .	. . . . . .	12–16	

* These recommendations may require modifications according to the body conformations of particular breeds. As a further general guide, the cage dimensions should be: (a) the height of the dog at the withers, plus at least 6 in. (height); (b) the length of the dog from the tip of the nose to the base of the tail, plus at least 6 in. (width and depth).

† These recommendations may require modifications according to the body conformations of particular species.

‡ Provide ample head room to stand erect without crouching.

¶ Loose housing is outdoor housing that includes an open shed for shelter.

12. Facilities for Washing and Sterilizing Equipment and Supplies An area for washing and sterilization is essential to keep equipment physically clean, reduce obnoxious odors, minimize the spread of infectious diseases, and provide for the comfort of experimental animals. Washing and sterilizing are best done outside of the animal rooms in an area specifically designed for the purpose and centrally located, if possible. Consideration should be given to such factors as:

a. Location with respect to animal rooms, traffic flow that separates "clean" and "dirty" areas, elevators, ease of access, and disposal of waste.

b. Soundproofing.

c. Utilities such as hot and cold water, steam, floor drains, and electric power.

d. Proximity to cage and equipment storage areas. It is essential to provide separate holding areas for soiled and clean equipment.

e. Insulation of walls and ceilings where necessary.

f. Ventilation with installation of proper vents and provisions for dissipation of steam.

g. Access doors of sufficient width to assure free movement of equipment.

Large Animals

For general purposes, large animals are defined as domestic animals, such as horses, sheep, cows, goats, and pigs.

Conventionally, these animals are housed in pens and barns. Even when ambient temperatures fall below freezing, most large animals prefer to remain outdoors if adequate feed, water, bedding, and shelter are available.

The housing of large, domestic animals in an urban research facility will parallel in many respects the housing of other laboratory animals. Because of their size, however, special consideration must be made for their restraint and confinement.

Space Recommendations for Laboratory Animals

The size of a cage, pen, or run, and the number of animals to be housed in each, are matters of professional judgment. The recommendations in the preceding table are based on the best available information concerning reasonable space allocations for the routine housing of animals in experiments. They are included here as a guide, recognizing that it is impossible to delineate cage sizes with greater precision due to varied research requirements. As has been implied the adequacy of the housing system must be under continuous review. More detailed housing standards for laboratory animals are available from the Institute of Laboratory Animal Resources, National Academy of Sciences-National Research Council.

A greenhouse must be so designed that it admits the greatest possible amount of available light.

The structural system, therefore, must be minimal in bulk, yet strong enough to support the weight of the glazing system. Site selection, building orientation, and roof pitch must all be considered with this in mind. While the glazing medium selected must be capable of high light transmission, it must also be of a weight and kind and be framed so that breakage is a minimal hazard.

A greenhouse is a transparent structure and cannot be insulated, so solar heat gain and heat loss are factors that must be considered. In spite of the difficulties inherent in the type of structure, temperature and humidity must be controlled to within a degree and a half in some cases. Then, too, plant requirements vary from dawn to dusk to dawn, and from one stage of plant growth to another.

A temperature control system specifically designed for horticultural applications (rather than conventional heating and cooling systems) must be installed in the greenhouse to create and maintain correct environmental conditions in a consistent manner.

There must be a means of introducing fresh air into the greenhouse on demand, and circulating it in an even pattern so that temperature and humidity levels are uniform throughout the house.

Instead of simple fenestration the greenhouse must be supplied with some type of ventilating sash and/or a system by which air is introduced by negative pressure and distributed through transparent ductwork, such ventilating systems being thermostatically controlled.

Greenhouses are sometimes used for other purposes than plant production alone. Some are also teaching labs, research stations, or display houses. Some must have greater degree of aesthetic appeal than others, or conform to existing architecture.

While good light exposure, unpolluted air, and free-draining soil are all basic requirements of a plant-growing environment, greenhouses often have to be sited on crowded campuses and in industrial areas.

While the greenhouse designer does not always have a free choice when it comes to site selection, some requirements are indispensable.

For instance, the greenhouse site should not be shaded by buildings or trees. Good natural exposure is preferable to a site where hills cut off late afternoon sun. A windbreak 100 or more feet away in the direction of the prevailing wind can help reduce heating costs.

Avoid sites downwind of a heating plant or incinerator stack, or where toxic fumes from chemical laboratories can be drawn into the greenhouses. Proximity to fruit or vegetable storage areas should be avoided because plants are sensitive to ethylene. If greenhouses are to be near other buildings, avoid if possible dark paved surfaces and heat-absorbing walls, which contribute to summer heat buildup. Low-lying ground has a tendency to flood during thawing out periods.

And for obvious reasons greenhouses should not be located adjacent to playgrounds or playing fields.

Greenhouse Guidelines

Greenhouse for use by	Function of greenhouse operation	Greenhouse design considerations
High school	Growing and/or maintaining small number of plant specimens for observation.	Space-10 sq ft per student enrolled in course. Requires consistent, day-to-day control of environment.
Vocational school	Providing basic experience in commercial crop production.	Space-20 sq ft per student enrolled in course. Greenhouse should be small-scale edition of commercial operation with three separate temperature zones: 50-55° min., 60° min., & 65+° min.
Liberal arts college, university	Growing and/or maintaining plant specimens. Simple research projects involving small number of plants.	Space-10 sq ft per student using dept. Often greenhouse is part of Science Building complex and must conform to other architecture or site. Many configurations possible.
Agricultural colleges	Simulating commercial production of plant materials. Propagating and finishing zones. One or more crops, such as cut flowers, pot plants, vegetables, ornamentals, etc.	Space-100+ sq ft per student in dept. Layout, facilities, equipment, controls should be designed for horticultural applications and equal to those used by commercial growers.
Scientific research	Complex research projects involving numerous plants, multiple compartments for separate climates, precise data recording. May require separate cluster of working greenhouses for major research projects.	Space-Varies from 250 sq ft up per growth chamber or compartment, depending on type of research.
Public conservatory	Display of plant collections. Usually provides three climates–tropic, temperate, arid. May require separate cluster of working greenhouses for plant production. Municipal conservatories often grow plant materials for all civic planted areas.	Space-1½ acres per million population. Provide 40,000 sq ft working greenhouses to 20,000 sq ft display area. Display buildings are enhanced by acrylic glazing, design-oriented structural systems. Criteria for working greenhouses same as for commercial.
Commercial growing operation	Actual production of plant materials. May include all stages from propagating to finishing of single or multiple crops.	Space-40,000 sq ft min for profit. Glaze with glass, fiber glass, combination, use sloping or curved roof profile. Provide 1,000 sq ft service area for 6,000 sq ft growing area. Maximum environmental control justified on basis of increased profitability. Single or multiple units, compartmentalized or open ridge and furrow.
Hobby gardening	Growing and/or maintaining small plant collections, forcing bulbs, rooting seedings, etc.	Space-100 sq ft min. Small prefabricated bldg. with environment package provides neat-appearing, horticulturally adequate unit.

The Greenhouse Design Manual, Ickes-Braun Glasshouses, Inc., Deerfield, Ill., 1971.

HORSE BARNS

Properly designed, constructed, and arranged horse buildings and equipment give increased animal comfort and performance, greater efficiency in the use of feed, and less expenditure of labor in the care of horses. Also, attractive barns add to the beauty of the landscape. In serving these purposes, barns need not be elaborate or expensive.

BUILDINGS

The primary reasons for having horse buildings are (1) to provide a place in which to confine horses and store feed and tack and (2) to modify the environment by controlling temperature, humidity, and other factors.

Types and Sizes of Horse Barns

Needs for housing horses and storage of materials vary according to the intended use of the build-

Breeding and Raising Horses, Agriculture Handbook #394, U.S. Dept. of Agriculture, Washington, D.C., 1972.

ings. Broadly speaking, horse barns are designed to serve (1) small horse establishments that have one to a few animals, (2) large horse-breeding establishments, or (3) riding, training, and boarding stables.

Various types and sizes of stalls and sheds are used in horse barns. However, in all types except the breeding shed, ceilings should be 9 ft high and doors should be 8 ft high and 4 ft wide. The breeding shed should have a ceiling 15 to 20 ft high and a door wide enough to permit entrance of vehicles.

The recommended plans for different kinds of horse barns are as follows.

Small Horse Establishments These horse barns are for housing pleasure horses or ponies or raising a few foals (Fig. 1). Box stalls should be 12 ft square and tie stalls should be 5 ft wide and 10 or 12 ft long.

Build the stalls in a row and provide a combination tack and feed room for units with one or two stalls. Use separate tack and feed rooms for units with three or more stalls. Generally, not more than a 1-month supply of feed is stored

at a time. The use of all-pelleted feed lessens storage-space requirements.

Large Horse-Breeding Establishments Large establishments need specially designed buildings for different purposes. They are as follows:

1. *Broodmare and foaling barn.* This can be a rectangular building either with a central aisle and a row of stalls along each side or with two rows of stalls back to back surrounded by an alley or runway, i.e., of the "island" type. Most broodmare stalls are 12 ft square, although they may be up to 16 ft square. A stall 16 ft square is desirable for foaling. A broodmare barn needs an office for records; toilet facilities; hot water supply; veterinary supply room; tack room; and storage space for hay, bedding, and grain.

2. *Stallion barn.* This barn provides quarters for one or more stallions. It should have a small tack and equipment room, and it may or may not have feed storage. The stalls should be 14 ft square.

Provide a paddock near the barn or, if possible, adjacent to it. The paddock can be any shape, but each side should be at least 300 ft long.

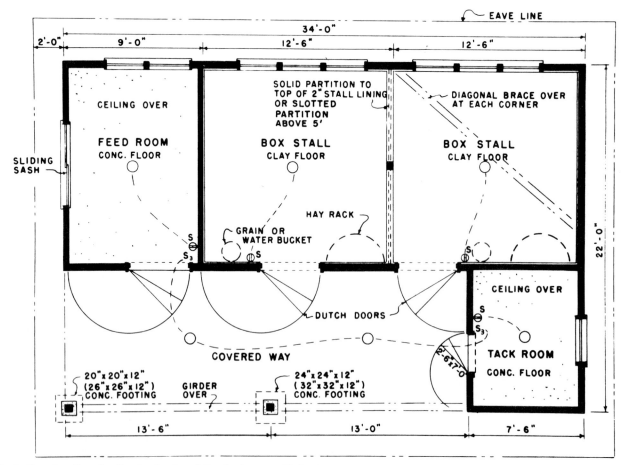

Fig. 1 Horse barn floor plan. Barn has two box stalls, a feed room, and tack room.

3. *Barren mare barn.* Use an open shed or rectangular building that has a combination rack and trough down the center or along the wall. Provide storage space for hay, grain, and bedding. Allow each animal 150 sq ft of space.

4. *Weanling and yearling quarters.* Either an open shed or a barn with stalls may be used. Both weanlings and yearlings may be kept in the same building, but different age and sex groups should be kept apart. When stalls are used, two weanlings or two yearlings may be kept together. Stalls should be 10 ft square.

5. *Breeding shed.* This should be a large, roofed enclosure that has a laboratory for the veterinarian, hot water facilities, and stalls for preparing mares for breeding and for holding foals. The shed should be 24 ft square.

6. *Isolation quarters.* These quarters are for sick animals and animals new to the farm. Use a small barn that has feed and water facilities and an adjacent paddock. Stalls should be 12 ft square.

Riding, Training, and Boarding Stables   For this purpose, the quarters may consist of (1) stalls constructed back to back in the center of the barn with an indoor ring around the stalls, (2) stalls built around the sides of the barn with the ring in the center, or (3) stalls on either side of a hallway or alleyway and the ring outdoors. Box stalls should be 10 to 12 ft square and tie stalls should be 5 ft wide and 10–12 ft long.

Environmental Control

Animals perform better and require less feed if they are raised under ideal conditions of temperature, humidity, and ventilation. Environmental control is of particular importance in horse barn construction because many horses spend most of the time in a stall. The investment in environmental control facilities must be balanced against the expected increased returns because there is a point where further expenditures for environmental control will not increase returns sufficiently to justify added cost.

Before the building is designed, it is necessary to know how much heat and moisture a horse

produces. Body heat production varies according to body weight, rate of feeding, environmental conditions, and degree of activity. Under average conditions, a 1,000-lb horse produces about 1,790 British thermal units (Btu) per hour, and a 1,500-lb horse about 2,450 Btu per hour. A horse breathes into the air approximately 17.5 lb, or 2.1 gal, of moisture per day.

Until more experimental information is available, the following environmental control recommendations, based on confinement systems used for other classes of animals, may be followed.

Temperature   A range of 45 to 75° F is satisfactory, with 55° considered best. Until a newborn foal is dry, it should be warmed to 75 to 80°. This can be done with a heat lamp.

Humidity   A range of 50 to 75 percent relative humidity is acceptable with 60 percent preferred.

Ventilation   The barn should have as little moisture and odor as possible, and it should be free from drafts. In a properly ventilated barn, the ventilation system should provide 60 cubic feet per minute (cfm) for each 1,000 lb of horse in winter and 160 cfm per 1,000 lb of horse in summer. In summer, satisfactory ventilation usually can be achieved by opening barn doors and by installing hinged walls or panels near the ceiling that swing open.

Requisites of horse barns

Whether a new horse layout is built or an old one is altered, all buildings, fences, corrals, and trees should be placed according to a master plan, for once established, they usually are difficult and expensive to move. The arrangement should make the best possible use of land and should require little walking by attendants when caring for horses.

All horse barns should meet the following requisites.

Accessibility   Barns should be on an all-weather roadway or lane to facilitate the use of horses,

delivery of feed and bedding, and removal of manure.

Dryness   Barns should be on high ground so water will drain away from them.

Expandable design   Barns should be designed so they are easy to expand if and when the time comes. Often a building can be lengthened provided no other structures or utilities interfere.

Water and electricity   Water and electricity should be available and convenient to use.

Controlled environment   Barns should be built to modify winter and summer temperatures; maintain acceptable humidity and ventilation; minimize stress on the horses' nerves; and protect horses from rain, snow, sun, and wind.

Reasonable cost   Initial cost is important but durability and maintenance should be considered, as well as such intangible values as pride and satisfaction in the buildings and advertising value.

Adequate space   Too little space may jeopardize the health and well-being of horses, but too much space means unnecessary expense.

Storage areas   Storage space for feed, bedding, and tack should be provided in the building where they are used.

Attractiveness   An attractive horse barn increases the sale value of the property. A horse barn will have aesthetic value if it has good proportions and is in harmony with the natural surroundings.

Minimum fire risk   The use of fire-resistant materials gives added protection to horses. Also, fire-retarding paints and sprays may be used.

Safety   Projections that might injure horses should be removed. Feeding and watering equipment should be arranged so attendants need not walk behind horses.

TABLE 1   Horse Fences

Post and fencing material	Post length and diameter	Size of rails, boards, or poles and gage of wire	Fence height	Number of rails, boards, or poles and mesh of wire	Distance between posts on centers
			Inches		*Feet*
Steel or aluminum posts and rails.[1]	7½ ft	10 or 20 ft. long	60	3 rails	10
	7½ ft	10 or 20 ft. long	60	4 rails	10
	8½ ft	10 or 20 ft. long	72	4 rails	10
Wooden posts and boards.	7½ ft.; 4 to 8 in	2 x 6 or 2 x 8 in. boards	60	4 boards	8
	8½ ft.; 4 to 8 in	2 x 6 or 2 x 8 in. boards	72	5 boards	8
Wooden posts and poles.	7½ ft.; 4 to 8 in	4 to 6 in. diameter	60	4 poles	8
	8½ ft.; 4 to 8 in	4 to 6 in. diameter	72	5 poles	8
Wooden posts and woven wire.[2]	7½ ft.; 4 to 8 in	9 or 11 gage staywire	55 to 58	12-in. mesh	12

[1] Because of the strength of most metal, fewer rails and posts are necessary than when wood is used.
[2] Use 1 or 2 strands of barbed wire—with barbs 3 to 4 inches apart—on top of the fence.

HORSE BARNS

Labor-saving construction This requisite is a must in any commercial horse establishment. Also, where horses are kept for pleasure, unnecessary labor should be eliminated in feeding, cleaning, and handling.

Healthful living conditions Healthy horses are better performers; therefore, barns should be easy to keep clean so they will provide healthful living conditions.

Rodent and bird control Feed and tack storage areas should be rodent- and bird-proof.

Suitable corrals and paddocks Horse barns should have well-drained, safe, fenced corrals or paddocks adjacent to them. If this is not possible, the corral or paddock should be nearby.

FEED AND WATER EQUIPMENT

The design of feed and water equipment should fill the basic need for simple and effective equipment with which to provide hay, concentrates, minerals, and water without waste or hazard to the horse. Whenever possible, for convenience and safety, feed and water equipment should be located so it can be filled without the caretaker entering the stall or corral.

Feed and water equipment may be built-in or detached. Because specialty feed and water equipment is more sanitary, flexible, and suitable, many horsemen favor it over old-style wood mangers and concrete or steel tanks. Bulk-tank feed storage may be used to advantage on large horse establishments to eliminate sacks, lessen rodent and bird problems, and make it possible to obtain feed at lower prices by ordering large amounts.

FENCES FOR HORSES

Good fences (1) maintain boundaries, (2) make horse training and other operations possible, (3) reduce losses to both animals and crops, (4) increase property values, (5) promote better relationships between neighbors, (6) lessen the likelihood of car accidents from animals getting on roads, and (7) add to the attractiveness and distinctiveness of the premises.

Large pastures in which the concentration of horses is not too great may be fenced with woven wire. The mesh of the woven wire fence should be small so horses cannot get their feet through it. Corrals, paddocks, and small pastures require stronger materials. The deficiencies of board and pole fences are: They must be kept painted; they splinter, break, and rot; and they are chewed by horses.

Until recently, conventional metal fences of steel, aluminum, wrought iron, chain link, or cable had one or more deficiencies. But metal fences have greatly improved in recent years.

Table 1 lists the materials and specifications commonly used for horse fences.

By PETER C. SMITH, Associate of the Royal Institute of British Architects

Reasons for the Provision of Stables

Before considering the planning and construction of stables in detail, a greater appreciation of the fundamental requirements might be gained by considering briefly the reasons for providing stables. A horse living out in its natural surroundings has no need of protection from the weather providing it has a sufficiency of good food. The thickness of the coat during the winter months, the natural oils in the skin and the fact that the animal may move about freely, are all adequate protection from inclement conditions. A horse living under such conditions, however, is fit only for the lightest work.

A horse in full work needs to be fit and to be kept clean. To obtain this condition requires the removal of surplus fat, a clipped coat and regular grooming. Thus not only is the coat lightened but cleaning and grooming take away a large proportion of its natural protective oils. A horse in this condition cannot satisfactorily live out and artificial methods of protection must be provided, by means of blankets and stables. Stables have, therefore, to provide to a great extent the protection to the animal which has been removed by the requirements of work and cleanliness.

Individual Requirements of Stable Buildings

It must be appreciated that the requirements of no two owners will be the same. Discounting the differences in sizes and accommodation needs of the various establishments and the purpose to which they may be put, it will be found that many owners have fixed ideas on the running of their stables which may materially affect the design. It is important therefore to discuss with the owner, not only his accommodation needs but his routine to be carried out daily. Information on the furnishing needs of each unit will also be required.

Many stables will be erected as an adjunct to an existing house and the accommodation of the buildings will depend on the ancillary accommodation for both staff and storage already available on the site. If the buildings are to be erected in conjunction with a new house, full staff and storage accommodation may be needed within the stable buildings. The provision of storage will also depend and vary on the method of running the stables; if for instance they are to be attached to a farm, the farmer might grow his own hay and leave it in the stacks to be cut as required. In such a case the provision of a hay store would not be necessary or would be of minimum size, say enough for one or at the most two weeks supply.

Staff accommodation will vary enormously. Most large establishments will have some staff living in and the provision of bed-sitting rooms or flatlets may be needed. Many small establishments are run by the client and his family, with help from local girls who will travel to and from the stables each day. Small establishments will seldom require any staff accommo-

The Design & Construction of Stables, J.A. Allen & Co., Ltd., London, 1967.

dation as the grooms will either be working in the stables or exercising the horses during the working day. When staff accommodation is required it should, preferably, be placed near to the stable buildings.

Principal Requirements of Stables

The basic needs controlling the design and construction of stable buildings may be enumerated as follows:
1. Dryness
2. Warmth
3. Adequate ventilation but with freedom from draughts
4. Good drainage
5. Good lighting, both daylight and artificial
6. Adequate and suitable water supply

Siting of Stables

Consideration must first be given to the ground upon which the stables are to be constructed. Ideally the ground should be naturally well drained, i.e. chalk or gravel, and should drain away from the buildings. Clay, which retains water, is unsuitable and if stables have to be erected on such land the water holding capacity of the site must be broken down and the water dispersed by drainage.

The buildings containing the horses must be protected from northerly or easterly winds. The doors and windows of the boxes or stalls should therefore face in a southerly direction. On a confined site this aspect may not be obtainable in which case protection must be afforded by other buildings or a belt of suitable trees.

Protection should also be made against the prevailing wind of the area blowing directly into doors and windows. Consideration of the prevailing wind, however, must be related to each individual site, as the contours of the landscape surrounding the site and the relationship of the site to woods, buildings, etc., will have a direct bearing on the effect of the wind upon that site. Therefore get to know the site conditions and plan accordingly.

Although protection from the winds is necessary, there should be a free circulation of air around the stables, so a site hemmed in by trees and buildings is quite unsuitable. Avoid siting the buildings on top of a hill or in any other very exposed position. To the opposite extreme, avoid hollows which catch the water and are invariably frost pockets during the winter months.

Stable buildings should be positioned well away from adjoining houses, and there is little doubt that most local authorities will insist on this requirement as a condition of their consent.

Ease of access to the stables is usually an important consideration with owners who look after their own animals, with only daily help. This will be appreciated by anyone who has had a sick animal in stables, requiring frequent visits during the day and night. Care must be taken, in these circumstances, to ensure that the prevailing wind does not carry the smells of the stable into any part of the house. Even

the most enthusiastic horse owner will object to the smells of his stable yard being carried into his drawing room.

Layout and the Main Requirements of the Stable Group

The units making up the whole of the stable buildings will vary not only in relationship to the size of the establishment but also to the needs of the owner. The requirements for a stable to accommodate, say, 20 horses without any existing ancillary buildings and allowing for a staff of five grooms living out or at least separately accommodated will be as follows:
1. Twenty loose boxes
*2. One sick box
3. Feed room
4. Hay store
5. Straw store or storage for alternative litter
6. Feed store
*7. Washing and cleaning room, incorporating drying facilities
8. Saddle and bridle room (tack room)
9. Utility box or boxes depending on the organization of the stable
*10. Litter drying shed
11. Manure bunkers
*12. Office, in some cases only
13. Lavatory accommodation
*14. Sitting-room for grooms
*15. Garage or covered area for motor horse box and/or trailer

In many cases this accommodation will be reduced by the omission of those items marked *, particularly in small establishments.

The relationship of the various units must be carefully considered both in respect of relationship to each other and to the site and surrounding buildings. A groom should be allowed to concentrate his energies on the horses and not be unnecessarily taxed by the necessity to carry bales of hay and straw and sacks of feed great distances. Even in these days of mechanization there are few stables, particularly small ones, which can afford to install expensive handling equipment. Care must therefore be taken to minimize the handling of heavy materials and a lot can be done in this respect by careful planning.

Layout of the Loose Boxes and Stalls

First consideration must be given to the layout of the loose boxes and stalls; but before proceeding with the design, the detailed planning requirements of the client must first be ascertained. Most clients will require loose boxes for both horses and ponies, but some may want stalls or a proportion of each. Stalls are seldom used nowadays and many existing buildings containing stalls are being converted to loose box accommodation. Stalls have many disadvantages as compared to loose boxes, their only advantages being in economy of construction and labor.

For design requirements, 12 by 12 ft may be taken as a suitable size for each loose box. This size will comfortably house a 16.0–17.0 hh. hunter. Ponies may require a lesser size, but it is felt unwise to reduce a box below 10 by 10 ft, a pony's box today may need to serve for a horse tomorrow. Stalls should be a minimum of 6 ft wide and 9 to 10 ft long.

The basic layout of the buildings containing the boxes will depend on economic considerations as well as on site conditions. It is probably true to say that most stables erected at the present time consist of a simple line of boxes, each opening directly into the open air, as shown in Figs. 1 and 2.

This is the simplest form of layout and quite practical. Depending on the number of boxes needed, they may be extended around a yard or a number of yards. The detail can be improved by extending the roof to give an overhang along the open side. This gives a covered walk and helps to protect the horses and grooms from rain and excessive sunlight.

It will thus be possible to carry out most of the work affecting the boxes under cover from the elements. This covered way should be extended to connect to the adjoining buildings of the group. Avoid supporting posts as these can form a hazard.

A more expensive layout is to have the boxes inside a building with the adjacent passage contained within the curtilage of the external walls, as shown in Fig. 3.

This layout is often found in the more elaborate layouts built during the last century. Ancillary buildings should be built so that they connect to the stables internally throughout the whole range, subject to the conditions imposed by fire precautions. The advantages of designing in this manner are that:

1. The ventilation of the building may be better controlled and draughts thus reduced to a minimum. A suitable form of mechanical ventilation may be installed.

2. Work may be carried out under better conditions and with greater comfort.

3. Easier maintenance of warmth.

4. Quieter than open stabling, which can be an important factor where stables are built near to main roads, railways, or in other areas with a high noise level.

Where site conditions are restricted, the boxes may be double banked as shown in Fig. 4 or more economically with a central passage as shown in Fig. 5.

It will be appreciated that there are many possible variations in layout which can be incorporated in the design to satisfy the needs of the client and site conditions while at all times conforming to the basic requirements of each unit.

Utility Box

In all stables, of whatever size, it is an advantage to provide, for the want of a better name, a "utility" box. Such a box may be used for a variety of purposes, clipping, grooming, shoeing, washing, and the treatment of cuts, etc. Small establishments of the type illustrated in Fig. 6 may need only one, larger establishments more. Figure 7 shows an arrangement which may be used with advantage in all establishments, irrespective of size. In this establishment the management was based on one groom to three horses and a utility box has been provided for the use of each groom. In this box all the various activities mentioned above, are carried out with greater efficiency and cleanliness.

The box, on the basis shown (ratio 1:3), need not be larger than the normal loose box. When, however, it is provided for a greater ratio it should be related to the number of horses likely to be accommodated within it at one time.

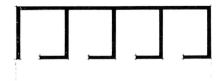

Fig. 1 Loose box.

Fig. 2 Section.

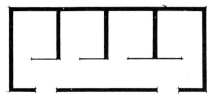

Fig. 3

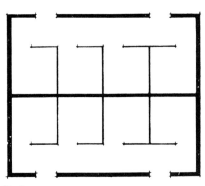

Fig. 4

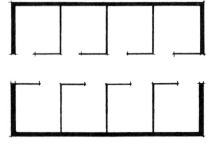

Fig. 5

The eventual size must therefore be discussed and agreed with the client. Its position should be as near as possible central to the group of loose boxes it serves.

Sick Box

At least one sick box is essential in large establishments and it is obviously of great advantage to include one in the plans of even small stables. In the main it is intended for the accommodation of an animal suffering from an infectious disease and therefore requiring to be isolated from other horses. It may in fact be used by any horse needing quiet and possibly specialized treatment.

The box should be placed well away from the stables but, as a sick animal requires to be visited more often than a healthy one, the position must be related to the convenience of those in charge of him. If possible, place it in such a position that although isolated the horse can see the other horses. Remember that horses are gregarious animals, so the patient will be happier and probably make a quicker recovery if he does not feel completely isolated from the world.

The box should be bigger than the usual box by about 50 percent. It would be wise at this planning stage to remember that the roof must be made sufficiently strong to support a sling attachment.

Feed Room

The feed room is intended to house the bins containing the feed for daily use, as opposed to the feed store which will contain the sacks of food or the containers if bulk storage is used. In small establishments it might combine with the feed store or in fact be formed as a recess out of the stable building, though this minimum arrangement is not recommended. The size will depend not only on the number of horses it serves but also on the client's arrangements for buying feed. A farmer might grow his own and, for instance, send sufficient for a week's supply across to the room from his main store, after carrying out any treatment needed. Some clients who buy from merchants will have regular weekly or fortnightly deliveries.

It is in this room that the feeds are prepared each day and it must be positioned close to and preferably directly connected with the loose boxes.

The equipment to be contained in the feed room consists of separate bins for oats, bran, barley, nuts, chaff, etc. (the bin requirements will depend on the method of feeding the horses and will often vary from one establishment to another); a sink provided with hot and cold water; a bucket filling tap to each service; and wall racks on which to hang sieves, measures, brooms, and buckets. Few small establishments will install machinery for bruising oats, chaff cutting, etc., but large establishments may require these machines, and if so allowance must be made for them in the design. Most merchants nowadays will carry out any processing required before delivery, so the need for machinery will be rare.

Feed Store

This store should open directly into the feed room and the storage areas for hay and straw should adjoin it. The necessity for this room will depend on the supply factors mentioned in the last paragraph dealing with the feed room. Many small establishments will not need

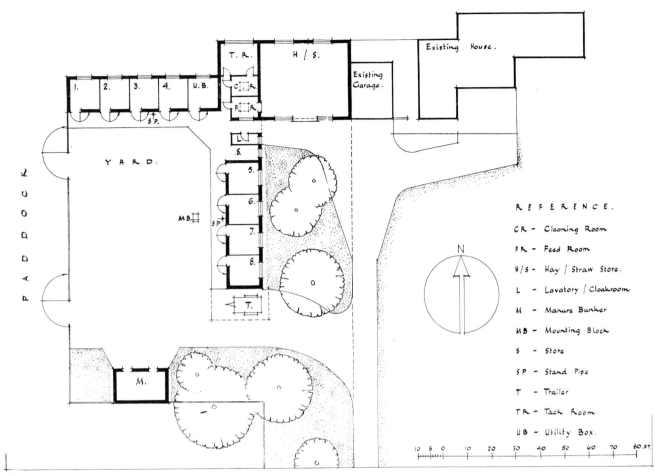

REFERENCE.

CR – Cleaning Room

FR – Feed Room

H/S – Hay / Straw Store.

L – Lavatory / Cloakroom

M – Manure Bunker

MB – Mounting Block

S – Store

SP – Stand Pipe

T – Trailer

TR – Tack Room

UB – Utility Box.

Fig. 6

a separate store and will combine the feed storage with their hay and straw storage.

Hay and Straw Stores

The stores should be situated next to the feed store, with easy access to the feed room and to the loose boxes. Hay nets will generally be filled in the hay store and then be taken direct to the boxes. If hay racks are fitted, the bales will then be taken direct to the boxes before breaking and dividing into the racks. Straw will be required at the boxes baled, and the bales are then broken before dividing between the boxes and spread to form the beds. Small quantities of hay and sometimes straw will be required in the feed room, but most will be taken direct to the loose boxes.

Storage for Other Forms of Material Used as Litter

So far only straw has been considered for use as litter. There are many other materials used, many being individual to certain parts of the country where local supplies are available. The storage of these alternative materials must be considered.

These main alternatives may be enumerated as follows:

1. Fern leaves

2. Fir needles
3. Peat
4. Sand (not sea sand)
5. Sawdust
6. Wood shavings

In some cases combinations of these materials are used, i.e., sawdust and peat.

The main essentials for the storage of any of these materials are the same as discussed for straw. They must be kept in a dry and well ventilated building. Peat is usually stored either in bales or in bulk and sawdust and wood shavings in sacks. Fern leaves and fir needles are generally stacked in bulk and require to be frequently turned.

Saddle and Bridle Room

This room, now more generally referred to as the tack room, should be positioned close to and preferably directly connected to the loose boxes under cover. In a large layout more than one room may be required (see Fig. 8).

The size will depend on the number of horses it serves and to the purposes for which those horses are used. The needs will vary from one establishment to another but the client should be able to give the necessary information to the architect for his present and possible future needs.

The layout requirements of the client will

also affect the size of the room. Some like the tack of each horse grouped together, others prefer to separate their saddles, bridles, girths, etc.

In addition to the storage of tack this room usually accommodates the medicine cabinet and poison cupboard.

In some establishments a bit case may be required, the size will be dependent on the number, types and sizes of the bits to be stored.

Chests for clean blankets, sheets and other clean clothing are usually provided in the tack room. These may be formed as built-in chests or standard chests may be obtained and space for them along the walls allowed.

This description of the requirements of the tack room has assumed throughout that a separate washing and cleaning room will be provided. In most establishments the tack room will be required to serve both purposes, in which case the fittings and services discussed below must be incorporated in the tack room.

Washing and Cleaning Room

It is of considerable advantage to provide this room in any establishment, however small. It should open directly out of the tack room and have an external door off the stable yard so that all dirty tack, etc., may be taken into it without

Miscellaneous
HORSE STABLES

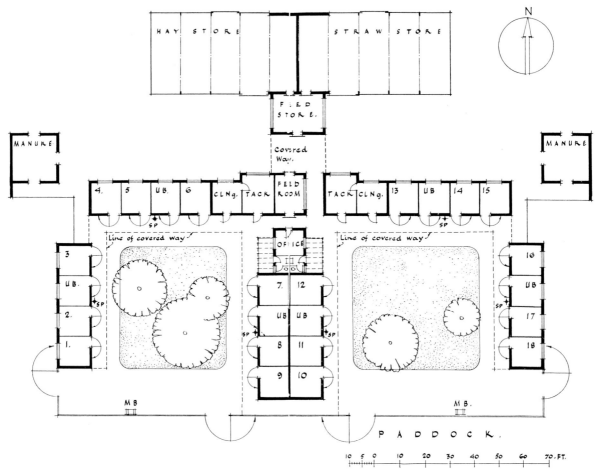

Fig. 7

the necessity of passing through the tack room.

It should be fitted with a large and deep sink or sinks, depending on size, and each sink should be provided with a constant supply of hot and cold water. Facilities may be required for washing and drying blankets, sheets, and other clothing.

Saddle room horses will also be needed. The client may have these, in which case they must be measured and due allowance made for them. If new ones are allowed for, the size required should be agreed with the client and details obtained from the proposed manufacturer.

Bridle cleaning holders will also be required. These are suspended in suitable positions from the ceiling and may be of either a fixed length or of a telescopic type. Each must be fixed in such a position that a clear area all round is allowed for cleaning purposes.

The only other items required in this room are suitable cupboards and drawers in which to store the cleaning materials.

Manure Bunkers

The storage provision for manure must be positioned well away from the area of the loose boxes but will require to be easily accessible from them. It must be adjacent to a road or drive to facilitate collection.

The usual formation is of open bunkers, and

such an arrangement is quite satisfactory. The size and cubic content of the bunkers will depend not only on the number of horses accommodated but also on the routine which each individual stable will follow regarding the disposal of the manure. Some establishments will have contracts for weekly collection or even at lesser intervals. Stables attached to farms will often deposit the manure daily at the permanent stacks or in pits so that it may be allowed to rot down and be used by the farmer on his own land when required.

Weighing Machine

A weighing platform will sometimes be required particularly in large establishments. The weighing machine should be positioned at the entrance to the stables, preferably next to the office.

Office

Large establishments and most riding schools will require an office for the manager. In most cases it will require to accommodate a desk, chairs, filing cabinets and stationery cupboard. A room of about 100 to 150 sq ft will be ample in most cases. A telephone, which should be fitted with external bells, will be required.

The office should be positioned to command

good supervision over the stable yard and over the delivery of goods. In riding schools supervision over riders passing in and out of the yard must be allowed for.

Mounting Block

Most stables will require a mounting block. This should be positioned at the side of the stable yard but should not obstruct the free use of paths or drives. A horse is mounted from the near side and there should be adequate free space to be able to lead the horse up to it in a straight line and ride off in a straight line after mounting. No horse will stand still to be mounted if its nose or tail is close to an obstruction.

Fences and Gates

Fencing and gates adjacent to or surrounding the stable yard and those surrounding paddocks should be of stout construction. The more usual type of fencing is post and rail. Gates should have a clear opening of at least 10 ft (12 ft is better) and hand gates should be 4 ft clear opening to allow the easy passage of horse and rider.

Gates will frequently be used by mounted riders so they should be fitted with hunting latches to facilitate opening.

1382

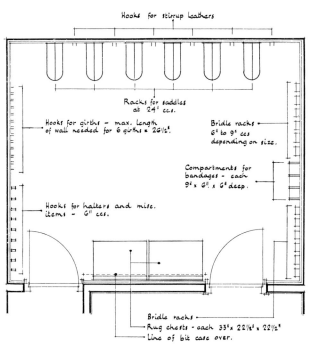

Fig. 8 Tack room.

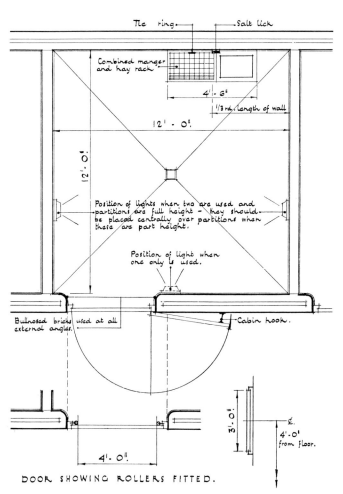

DOOR SHOWING ROLLERS FITTED.

Fig. 9 Detail of loose box.

Accommodation for Motor Boxes and Trailers

Most small stables will require accommodation for one trailer and many will own their own motor box. Provision may be required for these vehicles, either by a completely enclosed building, or by an open sided shelter. Normal garage provision should be made, though large establishments with more than one motor box may require a workshop for a mechanic and an inspection pit. Often repairs will be carried out at the local garage.

Ensure that there is adequate space for turning, for lowering ramps both side and rear, and for loading and unloading the horses. As mentioned in the case of the mounting block a horse should be brought up to the ramp in a straight line, and plenty of space should be allowed, both to ensure this and to deal with cases of horses difficult to box.

Staff Accommodation

Few small establishments will require accommodation for staff. Where the stables are close to the client's house facilities are often provided within the house itself.

In large establishments some permanent living-in staff are usually employed.

Lavatory accommodation will be required in most schemes, and if the establishment is likely to be used by the public, provision should be made for both sexes. The larger riding schools may in addition require changing and shower rooms for use by their clients.

Residential riding schools should have accommodation for both clients and staff convenient to the stables.

Loose Boxes

For the requirements of the sketch plan the size of the box was given as 12 by 12 ft. This size is adequate, but may be increased up to 16 by 16 ft. It need not be increased beyond these dimensions, except in the case of a sick box. Some clients may favor a box of rectangular shape, of say 16 by 10 ft, in which case the bedding will be positioned to cover the area well away from the external door (Fig. 9).

Stable Furniture and Services

Each box or stall will require the following items of furniture and services:
1. Manger
2. Hay rack or ring for hay net
3. Provision for water
4. Rings for tying up
5. Salt lick holder
6. Electric lighting point
7. Electric power point

Manger

The manger is a container for the horse's feed, is usually of metal, and should be fixed to the wall of the box at a height of about 3 ft from the floor. Standard mangers may be obtained constructed of galvanized steel, vitreous enamel, earthenware or stainless steel; they are designed to fit along the face of a wall or in the corner. The latter material is recommended, although expensive, but the eventual decision will depend on the clients' requirements and economic considerations. Mangers may be obtained combined with either a hay rack or a water trough. Those combined with a water trough are not recommended as they allow a horse to feed and drink at the same time. This practice is not good for the animal's digestion and at the same time usually results in fouling the water.

The usual position for the manger is on the far wall from the door. Before deciding if this position is the best it is proposed to consider the consequence of fixing the manger to alternate walls. In the first place remember that the stables are designed to accommodate horses of varying types and tempers; not only is the comfort and safety of the horse to be considered but also the safety and convenience of the staff.

Hay Rack

Hay racks may be combined with the manger or may be separate racks which should be securely fixed to the wall. Standard racks may be obtained of suitable sizes and types. The position of the rack and its height should be agreed with the client as there are essentially two schools of thought on this subject. One school maintains that it should be at low level, the horse thereby eating as near as possible

in its natural position, and the second school prefers the rack at high level, about 5 ft to the top from floor level. Five foot is recommended as a maximum height (1) to facilitate filling the rack and (2) to prevent dust and seeds getting into the horse's eyes while feeding.

Provision of Water

Horses must be provided with adequate fresh and clean water at all times. The commonest method is to provide it in a bucket. An alternative is to fit a 2-gal automatic drinking trough.

Rings

Rings will be required for both boxes and stalls for tying up and in some cases for supporting

the hay nets. Two rings per box or stall are generally considered to be adequate; if hay racks are used, one will often be sufficient.

Rings for tying up should be fixed at about 5 ft to 5 ft 6 in. high; one should be positioned close to the hay rack or hay net folder or ring. This will enable the horse to eat its hay while being cleaned or treated.

Salt Lick Holder

Many owners like to have a block of salt permanently available for each horse to lick, and suitable containers may be obtained for the special blocks which are manufactured for this purpose. The holder should be fitted over or to one side of the manger and at a height of about 5 ft.

By PETER C. SMITH, Associate of the Royal Institute of British Architects

This building is intended for use for schooling horses and riders either during inclement weather or when it is considered necessary to keep distractions to a minimum and thus allow horse or rider or both to concentrate with greater ease on the lesson in hand. This requirement is of particular importance when schooling either young horses or novice riders.

Due to the size of the building, it should be sited on level ground which should be well drained.

The size of the school will depend upon the needs of the client. A full-size military school measures 60 by 180 ft. This allows for three rides to be instructed at the same time, each working within a square of 60 by 60 ft. Although the individual clients' ideas may vary in respect of their own requirements, it is not recommended that this span be reduced, as it allows suitable space to longe a horse at the full length of a longeing rein, which measures 25 ft in length. An alternative size which may be in more demand nowadays is 66 by 132 ft (20 m by 40 m) which is the size of a dressage arena. (See Fig. 1.)

The lower parts of the walls on all four sides up to a minimum height of 4 ft should be of stout construction able to withstand rough usage and kicking. At the same time it must be sloped as shown, at an angle of about 12 to 15°, thus this splay must be formed to prevent either horse or rider from rubbing or knocking himself against the walls when using the outside track close to the walls. The splay will also prevent a horse from rubbing a rider off or damaging his knees. This lower section must therefore be lined through, clear of all posts, piers or other projections, and must be continuous and unbroken throughout the length and width of the school. This part of the wall is often constructed of stout timber or of steel framing and faced on the school side with matched boarding.

This building requires good natural lighting with an even distribution of light over the full area of the floor.

The floor may be formed by a number of methods. One method is to excavate the area within the external walls to a depth of 24 in. and fill to a depth of 18 in. with birch or hazel faggots tightly packed. The final 6 in. is then filled with tan. The tan will require to be made up from time to time as it shakes down in the interstices of the faggots. (See Fig. 2.)

An alternative to the use of tan is sawdust. This has the advantage of not "balling" in the horses feet, which is one of the disadvantages of tan. Another disadvantage of tan is that if retained and left in the horse's feet it can cause them to heat. The main disadvantage of sawdust and wood shavings is the danger of fire. Peat is probably a more satisfactory finish than either of the foregoing materials and forms a very satisfactory floor.

The floor will at times require to be damped. The most economical method of carrying out this operation is to provide a standpipe adja-

The Design & Construction of Stables, Institute of British Architects, J. A. Allen & Co., Ltd., London, 1967.

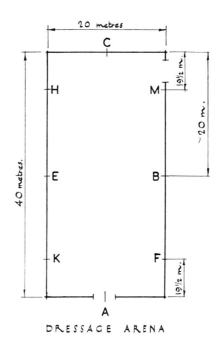

DRESSAGE ARENA

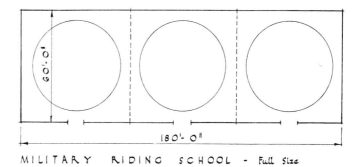

MILITARY RIDING SCHOOL - Full Size

Fig. 1

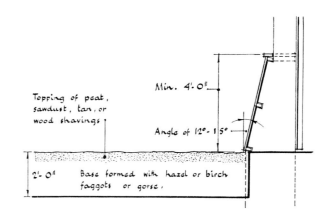

Fig. 2

1385

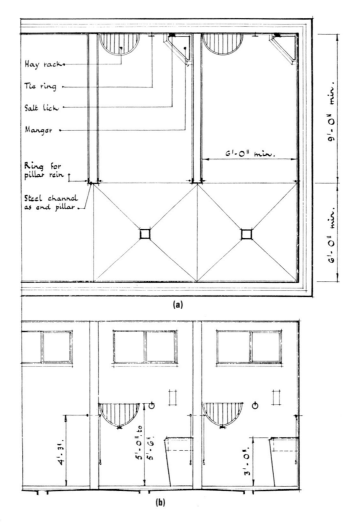

Fig. 3 Stalls. (a) Plan; (b) elevation.

cent to the building so that a hose fitted with a fine spray may be used or a lawn sprinkler fitted. If economic considerations are not too severe, a system of fine shower spray may be fitted beneath the ceiling in such a manner that the sprays give an even distribution of water over the floor. If such a system is fitted, ensure that any exposed pipes at low level are adequately protected, as detailed for low-level pipes in the boxes. It will also be necessary to provide protection against freezing to both pipes and fittings.

The entrance or entrances to the school will depend on site conditions, size, and the needs of the client. If a full-size school of 60 by 180 ft is designed for instructional purposes, three doors may be considered desirable, one to each section of the building. A school likely to be used for dressage tests will require a door in the center of one end wall and a second either at the far end or at the far side of the right-hand wall. This arrangement allows the rider to enter the arena and leave the arena at the correct points.

Entrance doors should be of adequate height to allow a rider to enter while mounted. A minimum height of 10 ft is recommended and a minimum width of 8 ft. Sliding doors are often used and these are satisfactory providing care is taken in choosing a suitable type of gearing. Handles should be fitted both externally and internally, one at about 4 ft high for operation from ground level and one at about 7 ft for use by a mounted rider.

Many schools have a gallery formed along one side of the main side walls for viewing, or along both walls. The requirements in respect of such a gallery should be discussed with the client and his full needs ascertained early in the job.

The outstanding need is that of siting in relationship to the main stable group. The building should be placed in a convenient position to the loose boxes but should be separated from them to prevent horses in the boxes from hearing the work proceeding in the school. Horses at rest very often get upset if the school is placed close to them so that they can hear either the voice of command or the horses at work. The building should also be positioned adjoining and easily accessible from schooling paddocks as it will be used as an extension of these paddocks. A road or paths should connect it to both boxes and paddocks. A school with natural lighting by means of roof lights may be oriented in any direction, but one with windows along the sides should preferably be sited due north and south longitudinally. (See Fig. 3.)

By RICHARD U. N. GAMBRILL and JAMES MACKENZIE

In general the kennel should be built on a site where the ground drains well, with proper protection from cold winter winds and with the possibility of a cooling breeze in summer. A few large shade trees around the kennel are really a necessity.

If possible a kennel should not be built where the neighbors can be annoyed by barking at night.

There are two main parts to this kind of kennel, the compartments where the dogs live, and the workroom where the food is prepared and the dogs are washed and trimmed up.

The Workroom

This should contain a stove, hot and cold water and a sink. There should also be suitable bins or closets for the feed and the bedding, and a large and well-stocked medicine closet.

It is best to have a floor that can be washed down thoroughly every day, with a drain in the middle. A large solid table is generally necessary in most kennels on which to place the dogs for trimming, stripping, etc.

There should be a washtub in the workroom with a division in the middle to wash dogs and rinse them afterwards. This is always useful in all kennels for every purpose. If raw meat is used, a refrigerator will be found invaluable, also a meat chopper to mince up the meat. Many small kennels use one of the many varieties of canned meat on the market, and these are most satisfactory and economical in the long run.

Compartments

The size of the compartments or living quarters for the dogs depends, of course, entirely on the kind of animal kept. For the sake of convenience in these plans, a compartment 5 ft square is used in every case; but this, of course, can be altered with ease and without in any way spoiling the plans. The larger the space the more comfortable for the dog, and the more room he has to exercise, but this need not be carried to excess as he is supposed to be given proper exercise outdoors. A room 5 ft square will be sufficient for any kind up to the size of setters, particularly if only one dog is to be kept in each room.

Each lodging room should lead into a small concrete yard, into which the dog can run at any time, and all these concrete yards should open into a large grass yard where the dogs can be exercised together if advisable or separately when necessary. This, of course, entails the question of fighting, and that is a matter of kennel discipline for the owner to decide himself.

Kennel Layout

The plan in Fig. 1 represents a very simple kennel with four compartments. It is useful to have a small kennel of this size near one's house in which to keep house dogs when they

Sporting Stables and Kennels, Derrydale Press, New York, 1935.

are ill, or to raise a few litters of puppies. It contains, as shown on the plan, a stove, two washtubs, a table and a bin for the feed. Each compartment opens into its own cement yard and all these yards open into a large grass yard beyond. These compartments are 5 ft square, which is large enough for any breed of dog up to a setter.

The plan in Fig. 2 represents a very useful arrangement for a private or commercial dog kennel. There is no limit to the number of compartments that can be built. If different breeds of dogs are kept, the compartments on one side can be larger than those on the other. Heat can be carried from the workroom into the living quarters. A solid partition can be put across the building below the fourth compartment. The first part would be heated and contain eight compartments for use as a hospital. The remaining compartments would have no heat. The workroom contains not only closets for bedding, feed and coal, but also a stove, sink, washtubs and table. A medicine closet

is, of course, an indispensable necessity and should be included in every kennel whether large or small.

The plan in Fig. 3 represents a somewhat different arrangement of a dog kennel. The workroom is placed at the rear with an open passageway between it and the main part of the kennels. By leaving open the doors at either end of this passageway, a free current of air is allowed to pass through at all times, which prevents smells from circulating through the kennels. Two large closets have been provided for bedding and feed. One wing of compartments should undoubtedly be heated for use as a hospital. If this cannot be done conveniently from the boiler in the workroom, a small heater can be installed in the wing itself. This plan can be limitless in size, the only disadvantage being that the compartments on the north side have not been supplied with cement yards because of the cold in wintertime. These compartments, however, can always be used for whelping pens.

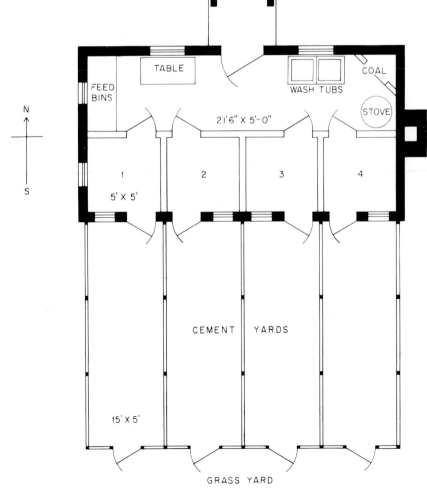

Fig. 1

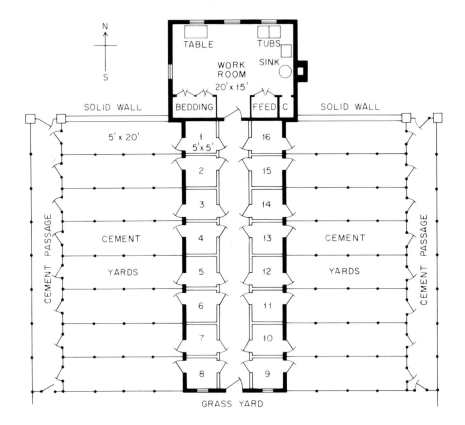

Fig. 2

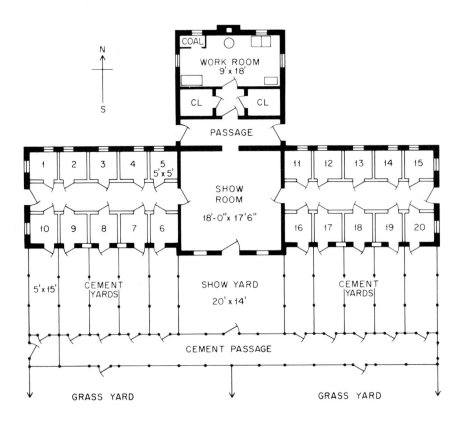

Fig. 3

The modern nature center:

- May exhibit a representative sample of such indigenous cold-blooded animals as snakes, turtles, fish, or amphibians but generally avoids warm-blooded animals because of the care they require and the excessive expense of maintaining them properly. Most centers stress the importance of observing wild creatures in their native habitats.
- Avoids large and expensive dioramas normally found in the traditional museum and favors simple, inexpensive, readily changeable displays which invite visitors to see, handle, smell, or listen—displays they can become directly involved with.
- Has areas inside its interpretive building designated as classrooms. Compared with an ordinary school classroom, they are quite informal in design and use. Basically, they are intended to orient visitors—the philosophy at most centers being that the outdoors is the primary classroom.
- Is designed for a wide variety of recreational

Guidelines for Interpretive Building Design, edited by Richard J. Manly, National Audubon Society, New York, 1977.

activities such as hiking, bird watching, and photography. But these activities are mainly passive ones and are not stressed or adequately budgeted for, although the situation may be otherwise in some public parks.
- Combines the policy elements of both park and resource management agencies. Many centers are zoned so that a percentage of the land base is left natural while other sections are designated for habitat manipulation—controlled burning, mowing, tree planting, and harvesting. Each area serves to demonstrate the responses of nature when left alone or "managed" by man.
- Is staffed by professional naturalists and highly qualified amateurs whose job it is to develop, present, and administer the various programs offered at the center.
- Extends its services to a broad cross-section of the community by scheduling activities away from the nature center proper. These may include regular radio and TV appearances, articles in newspapers, seminars for middle management business executives, workshops for teachers and natural resource managers, guest lectures, or testifying on local or regional environmental issues. The influence of the modern nature center extends beyond the nature center itself.

The Components

The Nature Center Planning Division of the National Audubon Society believes that a nature center must have four basic components to function effectively:

- *An adequate natural resource base* representing a broad diversity of natural habitats. This may require as little as twenty acres or as many as hundreds of acres.
- *Physical facilities,* including roads, trails, indoor and outdoor displays, a maintenance building, equipment, and an interpretive building.
- *Programs,* which should be varied, inspirational, instructional, and recreational in scope.
- *And people,* including a staff of professional and volunteer teacher–naturalists, administrative and maintenance personnel, and the visiting public.

THE INTERPRETIVE BUILDING

The interpretive building functions as the focal point for administrative and program activities at the nature center. A stop here will help to orient visitors and make them aware of what the center has to offer.

The design of the interpretive building should be influenced by the programs envisaged for the

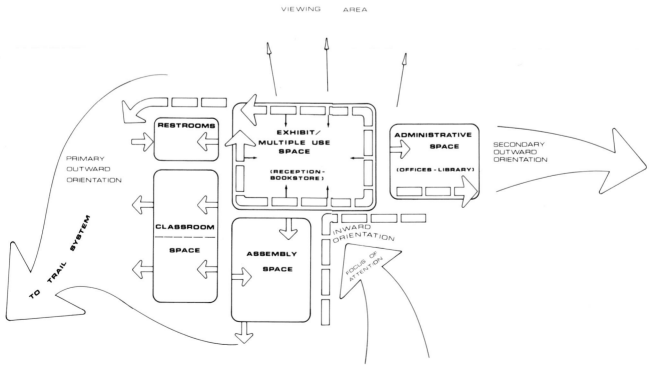

Fig. 1 Interpretive building design concept.

NATURE CENTER

nature center as well as by the physical and biological characteristics of the site.

The following are general guidelines for the siting and design of the interpretive building.

Building Site Locations

Certain basic criteria must be considered when determining the location of the interpretive building. These include:

- soil drainage and slope conditions favorable for construction
- access to the significant interpretive features at the nature center
- an esthetic setting
- avoiding biologically significant areas

- avoiding localized climatic extremes, such as frost pockets and exposure to high winds and drifting snow
- ample space to expand the building should expansion become necessary
- security from vandalism, fire, flooding, geologic faulting, and soil subsidence
- accessibility to existing roads and utilities.

Overall Building Design Considerations

- Top priority should be given to designing a functional and efficient structure. Some caution should be exercised so the interpretive building will not turn out to be an impractical architectural oddity.

- Entrances, exits, and interior spaces should be correlated with an overall traffic flow or circulation plan. Whenever possible, unsupervised groups or individuals should move through the building and over the grounds in a one-way pattern.
- The design should permit simultaneous use of the building by several groups.
- Low-profile buildings generally are less obtrusive visually than buildings with a high profile.
- The exterior of the building should be faced with wood or stone that will blend with the natural surroundings.
- Energy costs are mounting each year, and all efforts to minimize this expense should be incor-

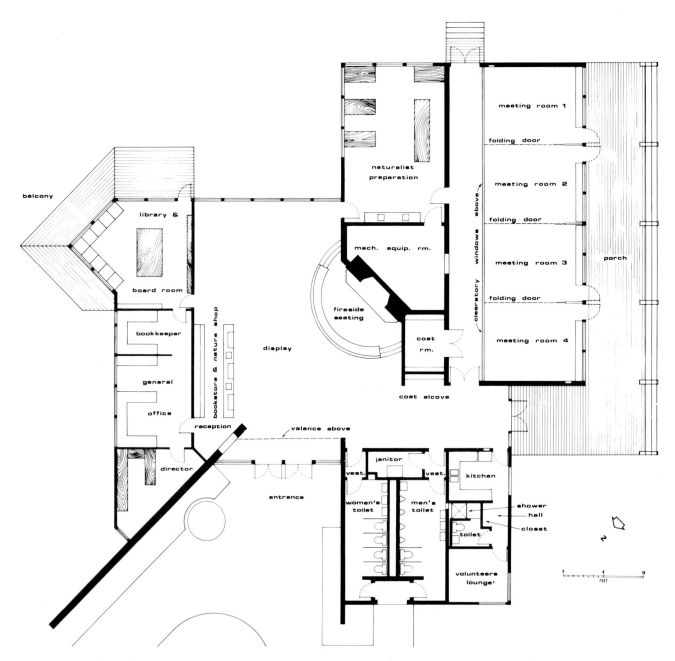

Fig. 2 Cincinnati Nature Center, *Sponsoring agency:* Cincinnati Nature Center Association; *Architect:* Harry Hake and Partners, Architects and Planners, Cincinnati, Ohio 45206.

porated in the design. The interpretive building should be a model facility for illustrating the conservation of energy. The following features should be considered:

Siting the building where it will be protected from environmental extremes— high winds, frost pockets, full sun

Thermal windows

Efficient insulation

Natural draft ventilation to minimize or eliminate the need for air conditioning

Maximizing the use of natural lighting

The development of alternative energy sources at the center by using solar, water, or wind power.

Interior Building Design Considerations

- The exhibit area in the interpretive building will be a central attraction for most of the visiting public. It should:

Have a flexible and efficient traffic flow pattern to provide easy access from the main building entrance, through the exhibits, and on to other key segments of the building or outside to the trail system.

Be provided with ample usable wall and floor space for exhibits and displays.

Be well lighted and ventilated.

Have a roomy and uncluttered appearance.

- Permanent staff members should have individual offices or work areas which afford them a reasonable degree of privacy. Additionally, many interpretive buildings have space allocated specifically for use by the volunteer staff.

- Centers that anticipate a large school attendance need several classrooms in the interpretive building. These rooms will provide space for orienting classes that arrive simultaneously before they move outdoors, and indoor activities can be held in them in case of inclement weather.

- If the nature center program will include activities for large audiences, an auditorium equipped with the necessities for lectures or audiovisual presentations will be required.

- Inadequate restroom facilities can cause undue program delays and foreshorten scheduled group activities. Therefore restrooms should be designed to accommodate peak visitor traffic to prevent such occurrences.

- Access to the restrooms from outside the interpretive building should be provided for individuals or groups visiting the nature center after normal closing hours, when interior access will be impossible.

- A reference library and reading room can be a great asset to the center's education program and, under certain situations, can serve as an auxiliary meeting room.

- An important source of income for a nature center is a bookstore and specialty shop where visitors have the opportunity to purchase natural history books, field guides, checklists, bird feeders, and other items consistent with and useful to the outdoor education program. This feature should be located where it is readily accessible to visitors, yet it should not conflict with the internal traffic flow or be an audible distraction to anyone elsewhere in the building.

- Some nature centers have wisely incorporated space for a "mud" or "wet" room in the basement of the interpretive building. There are a number of obvious advantages to this arrangement:

It provides a specific place for participants to clean up after a messy outdoor program.

It helps minimize janitorial problems.

It provides an additional storage area for program equipment, such as dip nets, snowshoes, and hip boots.

- Work space for designing and building exhibits and displays is an absolute necessity. Because of noises, noxious smells, dust, and hazards from flammable materials, it is recommended that these activities be carried out in a separate maintenance building. If this is impossible, the work area should be located in a section of the interpretive building where it will not distract from the programs in progress or pose a safety or fire hazard.

- Lack of adequate storage space seems to be a universal complaint about most interpretive buildings. Therefore, provision for plenty of storage space should be a prime concern in all planning and design phases.

- Some individuals think a photographic darkroom is an unnecessary frill in the interpretive building. Many nature centers, however, have built very exciting and successful nature photography programs around their darkrooms.

- If the interpretive building is going to successfully service a broad cross section of the community, it will have to be designed with the special requirements of small children, the aged, and the handicapped in mind. For example, ramps should be constructed in conjunction with or in lieu of stairways; special water fountains, sinks, and toilet fixtures should be installed; and exhibits should be built so they can be seen (touched, heard, and smelled, in some cases) by all visitors.

- Large windows can create a feeling of openness and intimacy with the outdoors. On the other hand, excessive and/or large windows:

Limit opportunities for wall displays.

Make darkening rooms for audiovisual programs difficult.

Raise the cost of heating and cooling if they are not thermally insulated.

Create a hazard to migrating birds, which have a tendency to crash into them and often are killed by the impact. (Attaching hawk silhouettes to individual window panes or hanging them loosely under the eaves of the roof will lessen this problem.)

- Modern carpets can withstand very heavy use, add a dimension of decorative warmth and, most importantly, muffle sounds. Carpets should be given priority as a floor covering in the exhibit area, auditorium, classrooms, and library.

- Electrical outlets and lighting fixtures often are neglected in the design of the interpretive building, only to later become a troublesome problem, particularly in the exhibit and classroom areas. Nowadays, many structures are being equipped with movable light fixtures installed on tracks mounted on the ceiling. Continuous-track electrical outlets also are available today and are preferred to standard fixtures.

HANDICAPPED/BASIC HUMAN DIMENSIONS

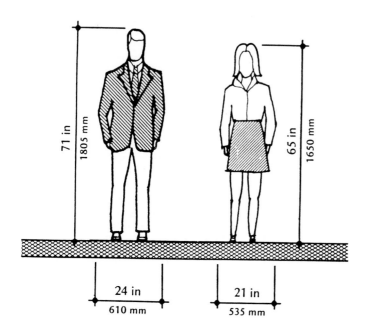

Able-Bodied Man and Woman

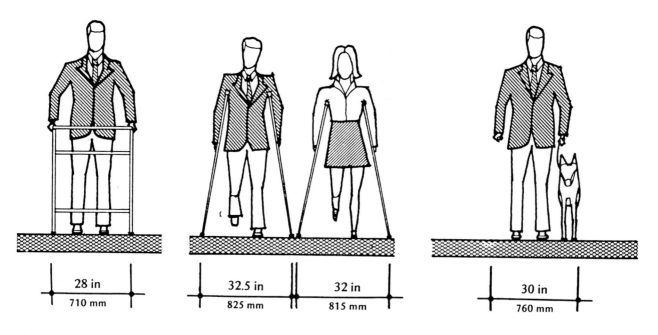

Man with Walking Aid

Fig. 1

Man and Woman on Crutches

Visually-Impaired Man with Guide Dog

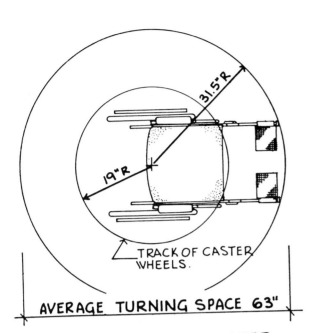

TRACK OF CASTER WHEELS.

AVERAGE TURNING SPACE 63"

PIVOT POINT AT CENTER

USUAL TURNING METHOD – MOVING ONE WHEEL FORWARD & THE OTHER BACKWARD TO PIVOT ABOUT CENTER.

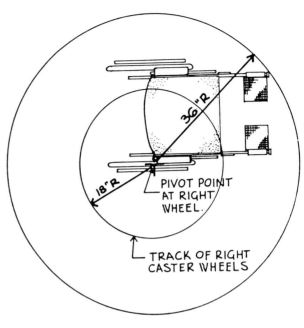

PIVOT POINT AT RIGHT WHEEL

TRACK OF RIGHT CASTER WHEELS

PIVOT POINT AT ONE WHEEL

ALTERNATE TURNING METHOD – LOCKING ONE WHEEL & TURNING THE OTHER.

Fig. 2   Turning radii of wheelchair.

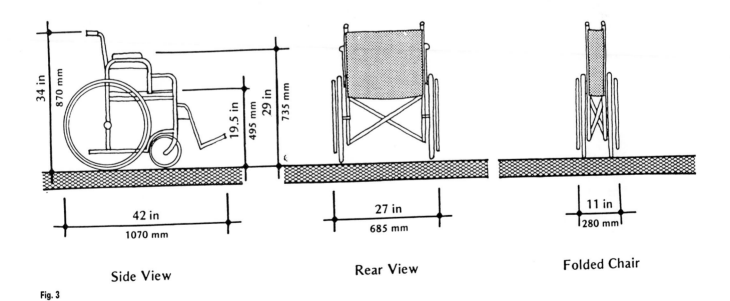

Side View

Rear View

Folded Chair

Fig. 3

Average Adult Chair Measurements (Nonmotorized)

Height: Arms from floor	29 in	(735 mm)
Height: Seat from floor	19.5 in	(495 mm)
Footrest: Min. extension	14.5 in	(365 mm)
Footrest: Max. extension	20.75 in	(525 mm)
Wheel Diameter — front	8 or 5 in	(205 or 127 mm)
Wheel Diameter — rear	24 in	(610 mm)

HANDICAPPED/BASIC HUMAN DIMENSIONS
Wheelchair Dimensions

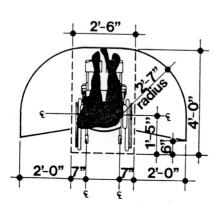

reach range
objects 4'-0" high max.

reach range
objects 4'-6" high max.

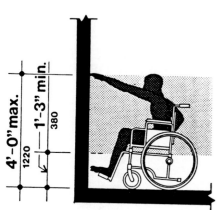

forward reach

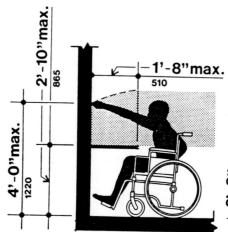

reach over obstacle
forward approach

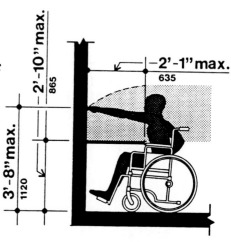

reach over obstacle
forward approach

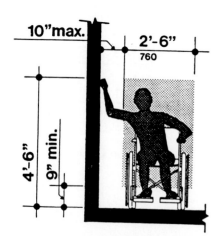

side reach
parallel approach

Fig. 4

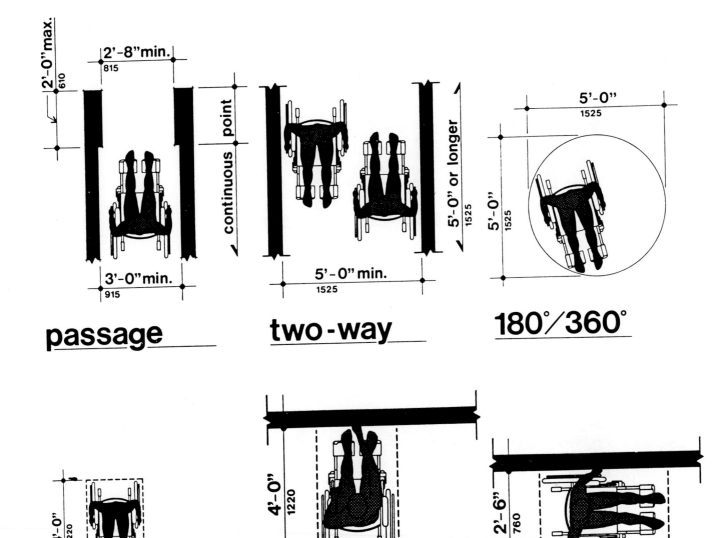

passage

2'-0" max. / 610
2'-8" min. / 815
3'-0" min. / 915

two-way

continuous point
5'-0" or longer / 1525
5'-0" min. / 1525

180°/360°

5'-0" / 1525
5'-0" / 1525

clear floor or ground space

4'-0" / 1220
2'-6" / 760

forward approach

4'-0" / 1220
2'-6" / 760

parallel approach

2'-6" / 760
4'-0" / 1220

Fig. 5

HANDICAPPED/BASIC HUMAN DIMENSIONS
Clearances

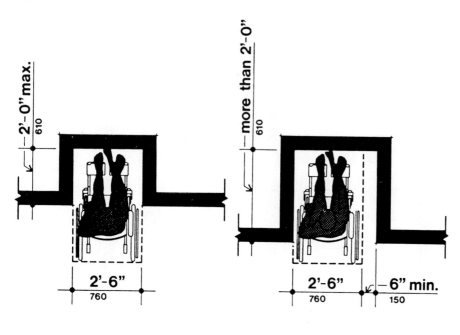

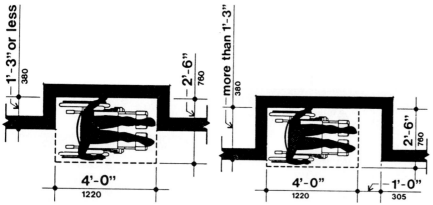

alcove

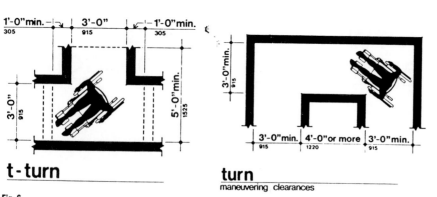

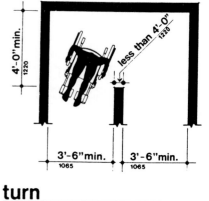

t-turn

Fig. 6

turn
maneuvering clearances

turn
maneuvering clearances

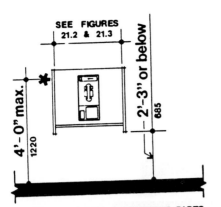

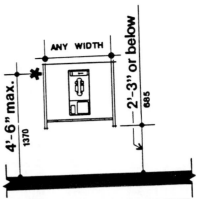

*HEIGHT TO HIGHEST OPERABLE PARTS WHICH ARE ESSENTIAL TO THE BASIC OPERATION OF THE TELEPHONE

*HEIGHT TO HIGHEST OPERABLE PARTS WHICH ARE ESSENTIAL TO THE BASIC OPERATION OF THE TELEPHONE

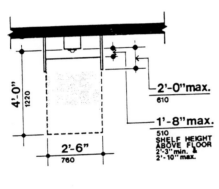

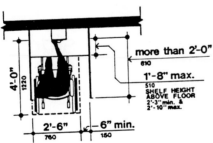

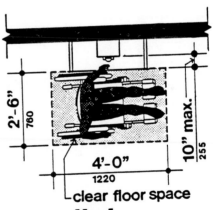

L clear floor space

forward
approach
telephone enclosures ⟨21. 2⟩

Fig. 7

parallel
approach
telephone enclosures ⟨21. 1⟩

Miscellaneous

HANDICAPPED/ANTHROPOMETRICS
Toilets and Urinals

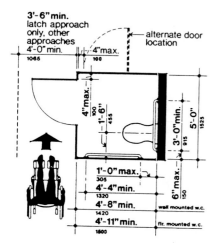

standard stall
(left-hand approach)

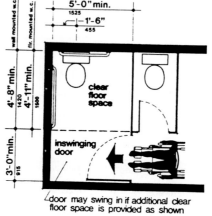

door may swing in if additional clear floor space is provided as shown

clear floor space
(right-hand approach)

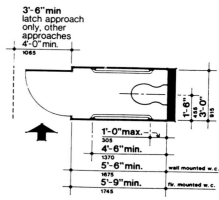

alternate stall - 3' wide

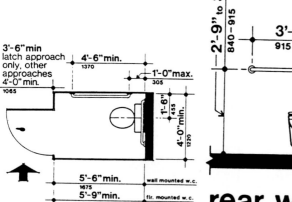

alternate stall - 4' wide (15.8)

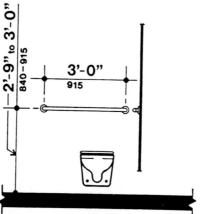

rear wall elevation
standard stall

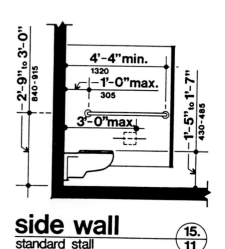

side wall
standard stall (15.11)

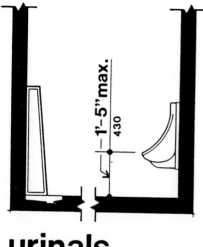

urinals

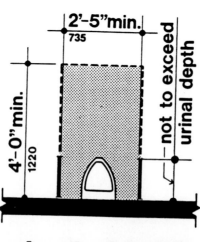

urinal shields

Fig. 8

1398

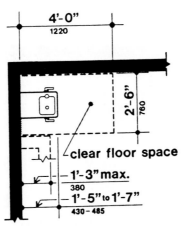

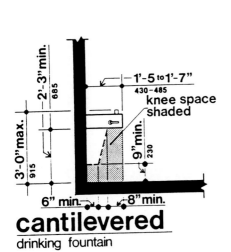

cantilevered
drinking fountain

cantilevered
drinking fountain

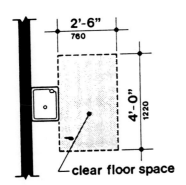

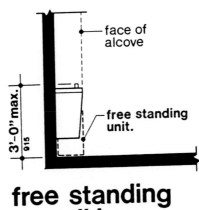

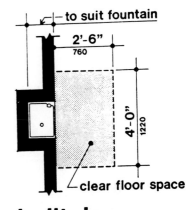

free standing or wall hung
drinking fountain

Fig. 9

free standing or wall hung
drinking fountain

built in
drinking fountain

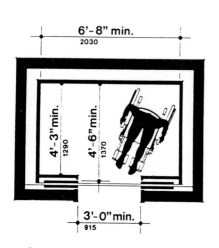

elevator car center opening

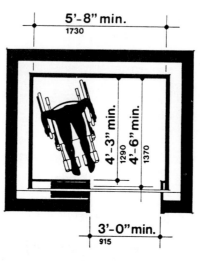

elevator car side opening

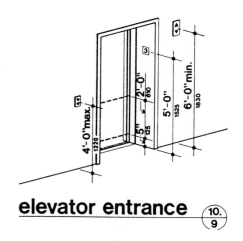

elevator entrance ⑩/⑨

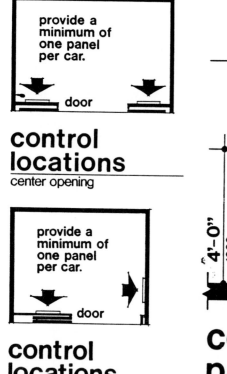

control locations
center opening

control locations
side opening

control panel

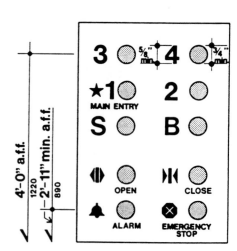

elevator control panel

Fig. 10

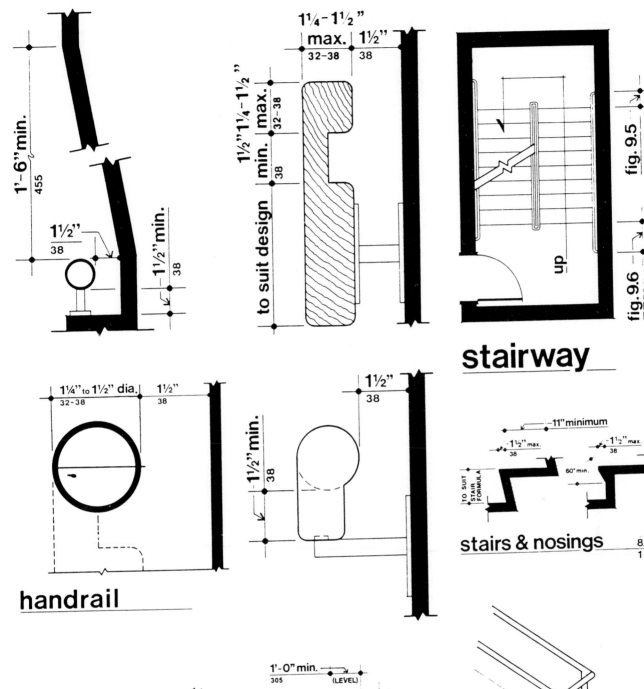

$1\frac{1}{4} - 1\frac{1}{2}$" max. $1\frac{1}{2}$"
32–38 / 38

$1'-6$" min. / 455

$1\frac{1}{2}$" / 38

$1\frac{1}{2}$" min. / 38

$1\frac{1}{2}$" $1\frac{1}{4}-1\frac{1}{2}$" to suit design / min. max. / 38 / 32–38

stairway

fig. 9.5

fig. 9.6

up

$1\frac{1}{4}$" to $1\frac{1}{2}$" dia. $1\frac{1}{2}$"
32–38 / 38

$1\frac{1}{2}$" / 38

$1\frac{1}{2}$" min. / 38

handrail

—11" minimum—

$1\frac{1}{2}$" max. / 38

$1\frac{1}{2}$" max. / 38

60° min.

TO SUIT STAIR FORMULA

stairs & nosings   8. / 1

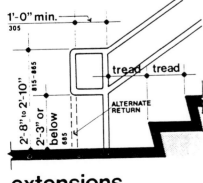

1'-0" min. / 305

2'-8" to 2'-10" / 815–865

2'-3" or below / 685

tread   tread

ALTERNATE RETURN

extensions
handrails

Fig. 11

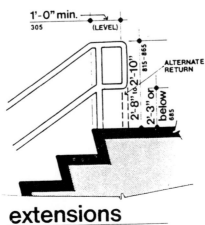

1'-0" min. / 305   (LEVEL)

2'-8" to 2'-10" / 815–865

2'-3" or below / 685

ALTERNATE RETURN

extensions
handrails

elevation of center handrail

Miscellaneous

HANDICAPPED/ANTHROPOMETRICS
Convenience Controls

Protruding Objects No protruding object should reduce the clear width of an accessible route or maneuvering space below the minimum required.

Objects mounted with their leading edge at or below 2 ft 3 in (685 mm) above the finished floor may protrude any amount (see Fig. 13).

Objects 2 ft 0 in (610 mm) long or less that are fixed to wall surfaces should not project into accessible routes more than 4 in (100 mm) if mounted with their leading edges between 2 ft 3 in and 6 ft 8 in (685 and 2030 mm) (nominal dimension) above finished floor.

Free-standing objects mounted on posts or pylons may overhang the circulation path in the direction(s) of approach a maximum of 1 ft 0 in to 6 ft 8 in (685 to 2030 mm) above ground or finished floor surface.

Objects fixed to wall surfaces may project more than 4 in (100 mm) if mounted with the lower extreme of their leading edge at or below 2 ft 3 in (685 mm) above the finished floor. These objects should not project into the required minimum clear width (see Fig. 14).

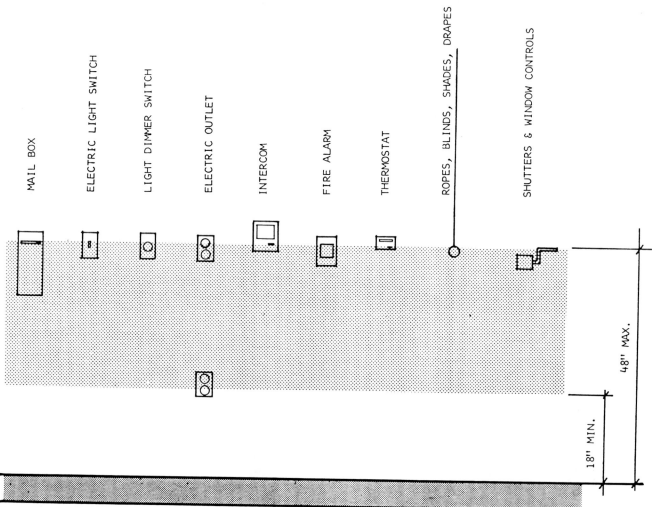

Fig. 12 Convenience controls.

1402

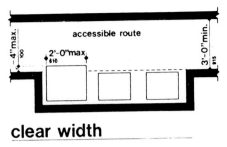

clear width

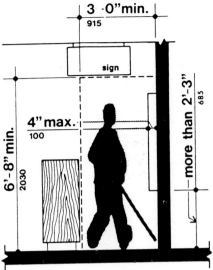

clear width
around object 24" long max.

clear width

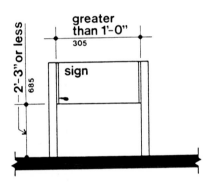

fixed obstruction
elevation

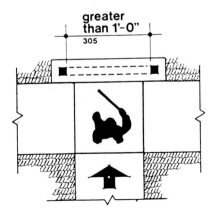

fixed obstruction
plan view

Fig. 13

NOTE: this overhang can exceed 1'-0" since object cannot be approached from this direction

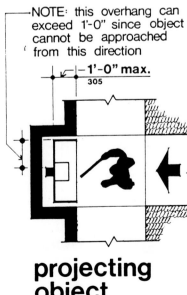

projecting object
plan view

NOTE: cane hits post or pylon before person hits object

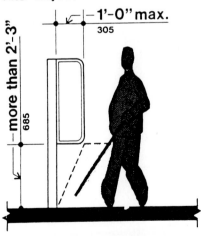

projecting object
elevation

1403

HANDICAPPED/ANTHROPOMETRICS
Ramps

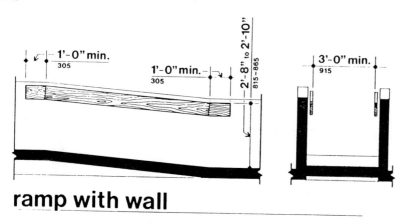

ramp with wall

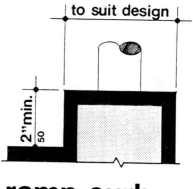

ramp curb

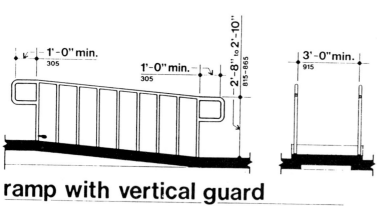

ramp with vertical guard

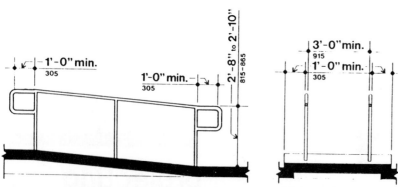

ramp with extended edge

Fig. 14

Credits

The pages listed at the end of each of the following sources refer to pages in this book on which material from the sources is found.

Adaptable Housing, Office of Policy Development and Research, U. S. Department of Housing and Urban Development, 1987. (pp. 54 [Fig. 25], 55, 57, 59, 81 [Fig. 14], 82)

Airport Fire and Rescue Equipment Building Guide, Advisory Circular Number 150/5210-10, Federal Aviation Agency, December 7, 1967. (pp. 1085, 1086)

Architects/Dock Designers Dock Lift Catalogue and Application Guide, Advance Lifts, Inc., St. Charles, Illinois, 1984. (p. 1131 [figure at bottom])

Armstrong, Leslie, A.I.A., and Roger Morgan, *Space for Dance,* edited by Mike Lipske, Publishing Center for Cultural Resources, 1984. (pp. 429–432)

Barr, Vilma and Charles E. Broudy, *Designing to Sell: A Complete Guide to Retail Store Planning and Design,* McGraw-Hill, New York, 1986. (pp. 798, 799)

Body Shop Planning Guide, 1980–81 Edition, The DeVilbiss Company, Toledo, Ohio. (pp. 944–946)

Brown, Catherine R., William B. Fleissig, and William R. Morrish, *Building for the Arts: A Guidebook for the Planning and Design of Cultural Facilities,* Western States Arts Foundation, Santa Fe, New Mexico, 1984. (pp. 377–379, 416–418, 463, 464)

Building for Storage and Maintenance of Airport Snow Removal and Ice Control Equipment: A Guide, Advisory Circular Number 150/5220-15, Federal Aviation Administration, U. S. Department of Transportation, March 25, 1983. (p. 1084)

Callender, John Hancock (editor in chief), *Time-Saver Standards for Architectural Design Data,* Sixth Edition, McGraw-Hill, New York, 1982. (p. 1144)

Carroll, Allen, *Developer's Handbook,* Coastal Area Management Program, Connecticut Department of Environmental Protection. (p. 197)

Church Buildings and Furnishings, Seabury Press, Greenwich, Connecticut. (p. 637)

De Chiara, Joseph (ed.), *Time-Saver Standards for Residential Development,* McGraw-Hill, New York, 1984. (pp. 5, 24, 25, 35–37, 43, 50, 51, 54 [Fig. 24], 56, 58, 81 [Fig. 13], 83–85, 119, 120, 1277, 1392–1404)

Design Guide: Arts and Crafts Centers, DG-1110-3-124, Engineering Division, Department of the Army, Washington, D.C., August 1976. (pp. 451–462)

Design Guide: Music and Drama Centers, DG-1110-3-120, January 1981. (pp. 411–415, 423–428)

Dock Planning for the Future, Rite-Hite Corporation, Milwaukee, Wisconsin, 1985. (pp. 1131 [text and figure at top], 1154)

Gould, Bryant Putnam, *Planning the New Corporate Headquarters,* Wiley-Interscience, New York, 1983. (pp. 880–883)

Guide for Space Planning & Layout, Federal Stock Number 7610-145-0168, Public Buildings Service, General Services Administration. (pp. 857, 858)

Heliport Design, Advisory Circular 150/5390-2, Federal Aviation Administration, U. S. Department of Transportation, January 4, 1988. (pp. 1087–1098)

The House & Home Kitchen Planning Guide, McGraw-Hill, New York, 1978. (p. 28 [Figs. 1 and 3])

Housing the Handicapped, Central Mortgage and Housing Corporation, Canada, 1977. (pp. 149, 150)

Internal Spaces of the Dwelling, Canada Mortgage and Housing Corporation, 1984. (pp. 15, 16, 18–20, 29, 31–33)

Kazarian, Edward A., *Foodservice Facilities Planning,* Second Edition, Avi Publishing Company, Inc., Westport, Connecticut, 1983. (pp. 831–834)

Macsai, John, et al., *Housing,* Wiley-Interscience, New York, 1976. (pp. 98–106)

Malkin, Jain, *The Design of Medical and Dental Facilities,* Van Nostrand Reinhold, New York, 1982. (pp. 897–901, 905–908)

Modern Dock Design, Kelley Company, Inc. (pp. 1124–1130)

Panero, Julius and Martin Zelnik, *Human Dimension and Interior Space: A Source Book of Design Reference Standards,* Watson-Guptill Publications, New York, 1979. (pp. 72, 74, 88, 800–803, 839, 840, 869, 870)

Parking Dimensions: 1989 Model Year Passenger Cars, Motor Vehicle Manufacturers Association of the United States, Inc. (pp. 916–921)

Planning and Design Guidelines for Airport Terminal Facilities, Advisory Circular 150/5360-13, Federal Aviation Administration, U. S. Department of Transportation, April 22, 1988. (pp. 1049–1065, 1069–1074)

Planning Guide for Designing Washroom Facilities for the Physically Handicapped, Bobrick Washroom Equipment, Inc., 1978. (pp. 889, 890)

Rutes, Walter A. and Richard H. Penner, *Hotel Planning and Design,* Watson-Guptill Publications, New York, 1985. (pp. 993–1003)

Tweedy, Donald B., *Office Space Planning and Management: A Manager's Guide to Techniques and Standards,* Quorum Books, New York, 1986. (pp. 859–862, 884, 885)

Uniform Federal Accessibility Standards, Architectural and Transportation Barriers Compliance Board, 1985. (pp. 53, 80, 389)

Index

Academic libraries, 297–314
Administrative suites, school, 225–227
Aged, housing for the (See Housing: for the elderly)
Agricultural buildings, 1365–1370
Airport industrial parks, 1174–1177
Airports, 1017–1074
  access roads, 1069–1074
  aircraft types and data, 1036–1041
  baggage claim, 1063
  baggage handling, 1041–1048, 1058–1060
  cargo facilities, 1069–1080
  concessionaire, 1063, 1064
  departure lounges, 1061, 1062
  food and beverage services, 1063
  gate lounge concept, 1041
  general design, 1049–1054
  industrial parks, 1174–1177
  operations, 1017–1032
  parking, 1069–1074
  roads, 1069–1074
  security inspection stations, 1061–1063
  service equipment buildings, 1081–1083
  terminal concepts, 1033, 1034, 1049–1054, 1065–1067
  ticket counters, 1055–1057
Amphitheaters, 439–441
Animal facilities and laboratories, 1371–1374
Apartment buildings, 107–120
  boiler room layout, 118
  building types, 110–112, 121–125
  community room, 117, 118
  compactor room, 118
  density for, 108
  for the elderly, 126–139, 162–168
  elevators, 113, 114
  for the handicapped, 140–142, 152–158
  laundry rooms, 119, 120
  orientation, 110
  planning, 126
  plumbing, 115
  room sizes, 100, 106, 107, 126
  site planning for, 109, 110, 121–125
  stairs, 114
  structural systems, 112
  ventilation, 110, 114
  zoning and building codes, 108, 109
Apartments, 98–106
  efficiency, 105
  for the elderly, 126–129
  planning, 98–106, 116, 121–125
  sizes, 100, 106, 126
Aquariums, 1293–1300
Archery ranges, 1239, 1358
Arenas, sports, 1301–1309
Art facilities for schools, 245, 246
Art metal shop, 456

Arts and crafts shops, 325, 441–462, 766
Audio testing area, 541
Audiovisual equipment, 351–356
Auditoriums:
  amphitheaters, 439–441
  for community theaters, 433–438
  multiuse, for theaters, 397–400, 427
  music facilities for, 246–249, 442–450
  in recreation centers, 763, 764
  school, 270
  seating, 411–422
  sight lines, 402–405, 416–418, 434
  in student unions, 327
Automobile dealer centers, 947–955
Automobile service stations, 938–943
Automobiles:
  body shop, 944, 945
  dimensions of, 916–921
  parking garages for, 913–933
  parking lots, 934–937
  ramps for, 954, 955
  service stations, 928–943
  turning radii of, 916

Backstops, baseball and softball, 1245
Badminton courts, 1192
Balconies, 101, 137
Ballet studios, 429–432
Ballrooms, 328–330
Banks, 825, 826
Barber shops, 815
Barns, horse, 1376–1378
Bars, 840
Baseball diamonds, 1213–1217, 1245
  Babe Ruth, 1213
  Bronco League, 1214
  Colt League, 1216
  Little League, 1217
  Pony League, 1215
  Senior League, 1213
Basic activities, 5
Basketball courts, 1193–1196
Bathhouses, 1280, 1281
Bathrooms, 69–85, 103, 105, 106, 115
  accessories, 70, 73, 78
  adaptable, 81–85
  clearances, 69, 70
  compartmented plans, 77–79
  dimensions, 69, 70
  for the elderly, 127, 135, 136, 139
  group homes, 160
  for the handicapped, 80–85
  planning considerations for, 69–74
  storage in, 70, 71
  three-fixture plans, 76, 103, 127
  two-fixture plans, 75
Beauty parlors, 816

Bedroom closets, 89–93, 104
Bedroom furniture, 29–37, 40, 41
Bedrooms, 29–42, 103
  for the elderly, 134, 135
  for the handicapped, 42
  in youth treatment centers, 619–621
Billiard parlors, 329, 1265
Boats:
  launching ramps, 1341–1343
  marinas, 1333–1342
  storage buildings, 1358, 1360
Boccie ball courts, 1197
Body shop, automobile, 945, 946
Boiler room layout, 118
Bookmobiles, 390, 391
Bookstacks in libraries, 383–385, 391
Bowling alleys, 1257–1265
Bowling green, lawn, 1204
Boxing platforms, 1303
Boys' clubs, 755–760
  dressing rooms, 759, 760
  educational activity in, 757
  gymnasiums, 757–759
  recreational activity in, 755, 756
  service, 760
  shower rooms, 760
  social activity in, 756
  space allocations, 755
  swimming pools, 757–760
Building codes and zoning, 108, 109
Building types, 110–112
Bus terminals, 1111–1116
  dimensions, 1114, 1115
  geometrics of, 1114
  platform types, 1115
  ramps, 1115, 1118
  space requirements, 1112, 1113
  turning radii, 1114
  types, 1111, 1113
Busing, school, 214, 215

Cafeteria, school, 236, 252–258
Camps, 1343–1362
  aquatic programs, 1344
  kitchens, 1361, 1362
  lodges, 1358, 1361, 1362
  rifle ranges, 1356–1358
  showers, 1355
  swimming docks, 1343, 1346–1351
  swimming pools, 1351–1355
  types, 1344–1346
  waterfront layout, 1344, 1348–1351
  waterfront storage, 1358, 1360
Cargo facilities, airport, 1069–1081
Carrels, library, 298–306, 314–321
Cells, jail, 731–735

Centers:
  automobile dealer, 947–955
  children's, 207, 208
  multiphasic health screening, 622–628
  nature, 1389–1391
  senior citizens', 162–168
Ceramic shop, 453
Chapels, 662–664
Child health station, 561
Children's center, 207, 208
Children's playground, 1183–1191
Church schools, 665–672
Churches:
  general, 631–637
    acoustics, 634, 635
    air-conditioning, 635
    chapels, 662–664
    choir locations, 634
    lighting, 635
    plan types, 631–634
    sites of, 631
  Lutheran, 638–642
  United Methodist, 643–654
    classrooms, 654
    fellowship halls, 646, 647–650, 654
    plan arrangements, 647–654
    site planning, 643
Cinemas, 1246–1256
Circulation:
  bedrooms, 32, 33, 36–39, 42
  dining rooms, 19–25, 101
  living/dining spaces, 27, 28
  living rooms, 6, 16
Circuses, 1302
City halls, 675–679
  building layouts, 676–679
  location, 675, 676
Classrooms, 231–235, 237, 244
  arts and crafts, 321, 451–462, 766
  church school, 665–672
  college, 273–275
  industrial education, 250, 251
  music, 246–249, 444
  synagogue school, 660, 661
  theater-arts laboratory, 357–359
Cleaner and tailor, 825
Clearances:
  bathrooms, 69, 70
  bedrooms, 31–42
  closets, 88
  dining rooms, 17, 19–26, 101, 159
  general, 5
  handicapped, 145, 154, 156, 157, 1394–1403
  home office, 43
  kitchens, 44–46, 50, 51, 102
  laundry rooms, 63, 64
  living rooms, 7, 9–14, 16
  offices, 869, 870, 887, 888
  retail shops, 800–803
Clinics, dental, 590–594
Closets, 86–97, 104
  bedroom, 89–93, 104
  cleaning equipment, 96, 97
  coat, 88, 94
  dining room, 96
  linen, 96
  planning considerations for, 86–88
  storage, 86–97, 138

Colleges and universities, 273–362
  audiovisual facilities, 351–356
  classrooms, 273–275
  communications centers, 333–335
  computation centers, 330–333
  dormitories, 282–294
    facilities, 291–294
    furniture layouts, 284, 285
    planning, 282, 283
    rooms, 286–289
    space allocation, 289
    suites, 290
    typical plans, 286–288, 293, 294
  field houses, 281, 282
  gymnasiums, 276–280
    auxiliary, 277–279
    location of, 276
  handicapped facilities, 295–297
  large-group facilities, 340–350
  lecture halls, 275, 609–612
  libraries, 297–321
    book stack capacities, 305–310
    card catalogs, 308–313
    carrels, 298–306, 314–321
    column spacing, 297, 298
    government standards for, 310, 314
    resource facilities, 337–340
    seating accommodations, 298–306
  programs and programming for, 360–362
  as regional educational centers, 335–337
  special instructional and activity areas, 279, 280
  sports facilities, 280, 281
  student unions, 322–330
  theater-arts laboratories, 357–359
Cluster development, 197
Communications centers, 333–335
Community rooms, 117, 118
Community theaters, 433–438, 463, 464
Computation centers, 330–333
Computer (EDP) facilities, 530–532, 1017–1019
Conference rooms, 473
Correctional institutions, 725–740
Courts and courthouses, 680–699
  circuit, 697–699
  customs, 698, 699
  district, 688–697
  general, 680
  hearing rooms, 696
  municipal, 712, 714, 715
  trial, 681–687
Croquet courts, 1198
Cul-de-sac streets, 190–194

Dams, earth-filled, 1347
Dance spaces, 429–432
Dead-end streets, 190–194
Deck tennis courts, 1207
Delivery suites, hospital, 509–511
Density, housing, 108, 121–125, 189
Dental clinics, 590–594
Dental offices, 902–908
Dental schools, 583–599
  administration, 598
  clinics, 590–594
  educational television, 596
  faculty facilities, 597
  graduate and postgraduate facilities, 597

Dental schools (Cont.):
  laboratories, 584–590, 597, 598
  lecture rooms, 594, 595
  libraries, 594–596
  research facilities, 585, 598
  science facilities, 584–590
  sites for, 583
  space allocations, 587, 588
  space relationships, 583, 584
  student facilities, 599
Department stores, 779–795
Desks, office, 862–871, 876, 877
Diagnostic x-ray suites, hospital, 484–489
Dimensions:
  of automobiles, 916–921
  of bars, 840
  of the human figure, 3–5, 74, 143
  of slips and catwalks, 1337–1339
  of trucks, 1123, 1124
  of wheelchairs, 143, 152
Dining areas and rooms, 17–27, 101, 128, 129, 131, 132, 159, 181, 324
Discus throw areas, 1234
Diving boards, 1269–1271
Docks:
  boat, 1337–1339
  swimming, 1343, 1346–1351
  truck loading, 1121–1124, 1126–1130
Doctors' offices, 891–901
Dog kennels, 1387, 1388
Dormitories:
  college, 282–294
  hostels, 180–185
  laundry for, 120
Drainage:
  courts and playfields, 1243
  lots, 195
Drama centers, 411–418
Drawing studio, 455
Drive-in-theaters, 1255, 1256
Drugstores, 817, 818

Eating places (See Cafeteria, school; Restaurants)
Educational centers, synogogue, 660, 661
Elderly, housing for the, 42, 126–139
Electroencephalographic suites, hospital, 496, 497
Elementary schools, 209–270
Elevators, apartment house, 113, 114
Embassies, 769–772
Entry hall, 104
Equipment, playground, 1183–1191
Exhibition spaces, 377–379

Factories (See Industrial buildings)
Farms and farm building, 1365–1370
Fellowship halls, 646–664
Fence enclosures for courts and playfields, 1242
Field hockey playing field, 1218
Field houses, college, 281, 282
Firehouses and fire stations, 700–707
Flickerball courts, 1219
Florist shop, 816
Food service facilities, school, 252–258
Football fields, 1220, 1221
Freight terminals, 1117–1130
Funeral homes, 1021, 1022

Furniture:
  bedroom, 30–37, 40, 41
  dining room, 18, 20
  home office, 43
  living room, 6–16
  office, 859–862, 876

Galleries, museum, 375–379
Garages, parking, 922–933
  mechanical elevators, 933
  ramps, 923–933
Garden apartments, 123, 188, 189
Gift shops, 812, 813
Glassblowing studio, 454
Golf clubhouses, 1314–1317
Golf courses, 1310–1317
Golf driving ranges, 1222
Grading, court, 1243
Grading, lot, 195
Grandstands, 1305–1308
Greenhouses, 1375
Group facilities, large, 340–350
Group homes, 159–161
Guidance service facilities, school, 270, 271
Gymnasiums:
  boys' club, 757–759
  college, 276–280
  public school, 236, 258–263
  recreation center, 1282
  rehabilitation center, 537

Halfway houses, 616–621
Hammer throw areas, 1233
Handball courts:
  one-wall, 1199
  team, 1210
  three- and four-wall, 1200
Handicapped, facilities for the:
  bathrooms, 42
  bedrooms, 42
  clearances, 1402
  controls, 1401
  dimensions, 1392–1403
  drinking fountains, 1398
  elevators, 1399
  housing, 126–129, 162–168
  kitchens, 42
  laundry facilities, 142
  living rooms, 42
  parking, 140, 141, 156–158
  ramps, 774, 1403
  seating in movie theaters, 1251
  stairways, 1400
  toilets, 775
Handicrafts studio, 457
Health center, mental, 548–553
Health clubs, 1277
Health stations, child, 561
Heliports, 1087–1098
  approach surfaces, 1087, 1097
  departure surfaces, 1087, 1098
  helidecks, 1088, 1092
  helipads, 1088
  hospital, 1094
  lighting, 1089, 1095
  marking symbols, 1088, 1094
  private, 1088
  public, 1090
High jump areas, 1238

High schools, 219–224
Hockey rink, ice, 1203
Hockey fields, 1218
Home arts facilities, school, 251, 252
Home office, 43
Homeowner's associations, 192–193
Homes:
  funeral, 1021, 1022
  group, 159–161
  mobile, 169–179
  nursing, 554–560
  youth treatment centers, 616–621
Hopscotch areas, 1201
Horse barns, 1376–1378
Horse riding schools, 1385, 1386
Horse stables, 1379–1384
Horseshoe pitching court, 1202
Hospitals, 467–531
  admitting department, 470, 471
  conference rooms, 473
  diagnostic x-ray suites, 484–489
  EDP units, 530–532
  electroencephalographic suites, 496, 497
  emergency activity areas, 528–530
  labor-delivery suites, 509–511
  laboratories, 503–509
  libraries, 472
  maternity suites, 509–510
  mental health centers, 503
  nurseries, 477–480
  nursing station, 474
  nursing units, 474, 475, 480–483
  occupational therapy departments, 500–503
  outpatient activity areas, 513–527
  pediatric units, 480–483
  pharmacies, 490, 491
  physical therapy departments, 497–500
  psychiatric service areas, 548–553
  radioisotope facilities, 511–513
  room sizes, 467–469
  surgical suites, 475, 476
  teletherapy units, 492–496
Hostels, youth, 180–185
Hotels, 972–1003
  back of the house, 973–977
  banquet facilities, 986–988
  bathrooms, 985, 986
  economics of, 972, 973
  food and beverage service areas, 974–977
  front of the house, 977, 978, 982
  furnishings, 998
  guestroom floors, 993–997
  guestrooms, 979–981, 983–985, 999–1003
  laundries, 974
  lobbies, 982
  plan types, 993–997
  restaurants, 982
  room sizes, 979–981, 989, 999–1003
  service areas, 973–977
  space allocations, 991, 992
  suites, 1003
Housing:
  apartment buildings, 107–120
  cluster development, 108
  density, 108, 121–125, 189
  for the elderly, 126–139
    bathrooms, 127, 135, 136, 139
    bedrooms, 134, 135
    dining areas, 128, 129, 131, 132

Housing: for the elderly (Cont.):
    kitchens, 127–131, 137, 138
    living rooms, 132–134
    neighborhood selection, 127
    planning, 130
    orientation, 110
    outdoor spaces, 136, 137, 141
    parking, 140, 141
    room sizes, 126
    senior citizens' center, 162–168
    sites, 140
    vertical circulation, 129
  for the handicapped, 140–158
    apartment layout, 150
    bathrooms, 146–149
    bedrooms, 146, 147
    community spaces, 153–155, 156
    elevators, 142
    entrances, 141
    kitchens, 144–146
    laundry facilities, 142
    living rooms, 144
    neighborhood selection, 140
    parking, 140, 141, 156–158
    ramps, 140
    storage, 152
    toilets, 154, 155
    wheelchairs, 143, 152
Human figure, dimensions for, 3, 4, 74, 143

Ice hockey rink, 1203
Indoor tennis courts, 1300
Industrial buildings:
  administration areas, 1142
  building shapes, 1148, 1149
  ceiling heights, 1150
  employee facilities, 1143, 1145
  engineering, 1147
  establishing liaisons, 1141
  manufacturing areas, 1145, 1146
  office areas, 1142
  parking, 1178–1180
  railroad tracks, 1151–1154
  research facilities, 1146
  site selection, 1151
  warehouses, 1147
Industrial parks, 1135–1140
  airport, 1174–1177
  physical planning, 1135
  rail service, 1135–1139
  site layout, 1135
  utilities, 1136
Industrial plants, 1141–1153

Jails, general, 725–740
Jails, police station, 712–717
Javelin throw areas, 1235
Jewelry shops, 808, 813–815
Jewelry studio, 456

Kennels, dog, 1387, 1388
Kitchens:
  camp, 1361, 1362
  commercial, 843–854
  hotel, 974–977
  school, 252–258
  hostel, 180–185
  residential, 44–61, 102, 105, 106
    adaptable, 54–59

Kitchens: residential (*Cont.*):
    dimensions, 44–46
    for the elderly, 127–131, 137, 138
    equipment for, 102, 137, 138
    for the handicapped, 54–59
    kitchen-laundry plans, 65
    layouts, 47–49
    plan types, 47–49, 102
    storage, 49, 50, 60, 61, 102, 138
    work areas, 44–46
    youth treatment centers, 618

Laboratories:
    animal facility, 1371–1374
    dental school, 584–590, 597, 598
    hospital, 503–509
    language, 240
    medical office, 894
    medical shcool, 568–570
    nursing school, 609, 612, 614, 615
    photographic, 1020
    research, 1155–1166
    school, 240–245
Lacrosse fields, 1223, 1224
Landscaping, office, 879, 880, 884–886
Landscaping, shopping center, 785, 786
Laundries, 62–68, 119, 120
    apartment building, 119, 120
    hotel, 974
    residential, 62–68
        equipment, 63, 64
        kitchen-laundry plans, 65
        laundry plans, 64–68
        multiuse laundry rooms, 68
        planning considerations, 62
        space requirements, 62–68
Law offices, 909–912
Lawn bowling green, 1204
Learning resource centers, 228–230
Lecture rooms:
    college, 275, 594, 595, 609–612
    dental school, 594, 595
    medical school, 565, 566
    nursing school, 609–612
Libraries:
    bookmobiles, 390, 391
    bookstacks, 383–385, 391
    branch, 380–382, 390
    carrels, 298–306, 314–321
    clearances, 385–388
    dental school, 594–596
    general, 380–391
    hospital, 472
    learning resource centers, 228–230
    location of, 357–359
    medical school, 563, 564
    nursing school, 613
    planning of, 380–387
    prison, 737, 738
    public school, 228–231
    resource facilities, 337–340
    space requirements, 383–386
Liquor stores, 818, 819
Living-dining room, 100
Living rooms, 6–16, 27, 100, 132–134
Loading docks, bus, 1111–1116
Loading docks, truck, 1121–1124, 1126–1130
Locker room, bathhouse, 1278, 1279
Locker room, school, 237–239, 261–268

Long jump area, 1236
Lot layouts, subdivision of, 191–199
Lots, parking, 934–937

Malls, shopping, 782, 783
Marinas, 1333–1342
    boat launching areas, 1341, 1342, 1343
    clearances, 1335
    layouts, 1336, 1337, 1339
    parking, 1341
    site planning, 1333, 1334
Maternity suites, hospital, 509–511
Medical offices, 891–901
    dental, 902–908
    general practice, 898
    internal medicine, 899
    laboratories, 894
    pediatrics, 899
    plastic surgery, 900
    rooms: consultation, 892, 893
        examination, 892–894
        reception, 891–893
        x-ray facilities, 895
    surgery, general, 901
    surgery, orthopedic, 901
Medical schools, 562–582
    administration areas, 563, 564
    animal quarters, 564
    laboratories, 568–570
    lecture rooms, 565, 566
    libraries, 563, 564
    research facilities, 564, 565
    science departments, 568–578
    site planning, 562, 563
Meeting rooms, student union, 326–330
Men's wear shops, 811, 812
Mental health centers, 548–553
Mobile homes and parks, 169–179
    community facilities, 171–176
    individual lots, 169, 177–179
    laundry facilities, 176
    layout, 169, 170
    utility connections, 174
Motels, 988–990, 1004–1016
    guestrooms, 988–990, 1011
    locations of, 1004–1007
    parking for, 1007–1010, 1013, 1015, 1016
    site planning, 1006–1008
    space allocations, 1011, 1013
    swimming pools, 1014
    types, 1005, 1008, 1015, 1016
Movie theaters, 1246–1254
    drive-in, 1255, 1256
    handicapped seating, 1251
    floor slopes, 1247–1249, 1252
    locations of, 1246
    lounges and toilets, 1250
    plans, 1253
    projected picture shapes and sizes, 1246, 1247
    projection rooms, 1250, 1254
    seating, 1247–1249, 1251, 1252
    sizes, 1246
    ticket booths, 1249, 1250
Multiphasic health screening centers, 622–628
Multipurpose rooms, school, 236, 237
Museum galleries, 375, 376
Museums, 365–376
Music and dance centers, 411–418

Music facilities, school, 246–249, 442–450

Nature centers, 1389–1391
Neighborhood planning, 186–199
Neighborhood recreation buildings, 765
Neighborhood service centers, 765, 767, 768
Nets, tennis, 1241
Nurseries, hospital, 477–480
Nursery schools, 203–207, 665, 667, 668
Nursing homes, 554–560
Nursing schools, 600–615
    lecture rooms, 609–612
    libraries, 613
    research laboratories, 609, 612, 614, 615
    space relationships, 602, 604, 606–608
    space requirements, 601–608, 611
Nursing units, hospital, 474, 475, 480–483

Occupational therapy facilities:
    in hospitals, 500–503
    in rehabilitation centers, 538–540, 547
Offices, 855–888
    clearances for, 869, 870, 887, 888
    chairs, 876
    computer (EDP) facilities, 1017–1019
    conference rooms, 856, 873
    dental, 902–908
    desks, 862–871, 876, 877
    furniture, 859–862, 876
    general, 855
    home, 43
    in industrial plants, 1242
    landscaping, 879, 880, 884–886
    law, 909–912
    layout, 874, 875, 878, 879
    medical, 891–901
    modular, 879, 881–883
    open area, 856
    ophthalmological, 900, 913–915
    planning of, 855, 856
    private, 856, 871, 872, 887
    radiology, 896, 897
    space allowances, 875
    toilets, 889, 890
    types, 856, 878
    washrooms, 889, 890
    work stations, 859–870
Ophthalmological offices, 900, 913–915

Paddle tennis courts, 1209
Painting studio, 455
Parking:
    automobile dimensions, 916–921
    bowling alleys, 1257
    garages, 922–933
    for the handicapped, 140, 141, 156–158
    housing, 196
    industrial plants, 1177–1180
    parking lots, 934–937
    marinas, 1341
    rehabilitation centers, 547
    schools, 214–216
    shopping centers, 782–786, 791
Parks and playgrounds, 1183–1191
Pediatric departments, hospital, 480–483
Pediatric office, 899
Performing arts center, 463, 464
Pharmacies, hospital, 490, 491
Photographic laboratories, 1020

Photography studio, 459, 460
Physical education facilities, school, 258–269
Physical therapy facilities:
 in hospitals, 497–500
 in rehabilitation centers, 534–538, 547
Pistol ranges, 1318–1328
Planetariums, 245
Plastic surgery office, 900
Planning, site (*See* Site planning)
Platform tennis courts, 1208
Playfields, 1183–1191
Playgrounds and playlots, 1183–1191
Playing surfaces, 1244
Pole vault areas, 1237
Police stations, 708–724
 administrative areas, 708–710, 720
 communications facilities, 708, 709, 721, 722
 detention facilities, 712–717
 firearms ranges, 724
 laboratories, 724
 layouts, 712, 713, 715, 719
 property rooms, 724
 site selection of, 711, 718
Pools, swimming (*See* Swimming pools)
Post offices, 773
Pottery shop, 453
Prisons, 725–740
 administrative areas, 735
 assessment of needs, 726, 727
 cells, 731–735
 correction programs at, 735–737
 recreational facilities, 739
 security: circulation and control, 730, 731,
  740
  types, 725–727
 services: commissary, 738
  food, 739
  library, 737, 738
  medical, 738
  religious, 740
 site selection of, 728
 types, 625, 626
 visitor accommodations, 739, 740
Programming in schools, 209–212
Projection systems, school, 351–356
Psychiatric facilities, 548–553

Radio stations, 960–966
Radio transmitter facilities, 965, 966
Radioisotope facilities, hospital, 511–513
Radiology office, 896, 897
Railroad docks and sidings, 1154, 1173
Railroads, industrial park, 1151–1154, 1173
Ramps:
 automobile, 954, 955
 boat launching, 1341
 bus, 1115, 1116
 drive-in theaters, 1255, 1256
 for the handicapped, 140, 297, 774
 parking garages, 923–933
Ranges:
 archery, 1239, 1358
 golf driving, 1222
 pistol, 1318–1328, 1356, 1357
 rifle, 1318–1328, 1356, 1357
 shotgun, 1357, 1358
 skeet shooting, 1319–1332
 trap shooting, 1319–1332
Recital halls, 444, 445

Recreation centers, 761–766
 community, 763–765
 gymnasiums in, 761–764
 neighborhood, 765
 planning of, 762
Recreational facilities, 215, 1183–1245
Regional educational centers, 335–337
Regional shopping centers, 779–795
 climate control, 784, 785
 landscaping, 785, 787
 and leasing satellite stores, 782, 783
 locations, 786
 malls, 782, 783
 parking and traffic control, 782, 783, 785,
  786, 791
 pedestrian areas, 783, 795
 servicing, 784
 site selection of, 780, 781, 787, 790, 791
 storefronts, 784, 795
 types, 779, 780
 zoning codes, 789
Rehabilitation centers, 533–547
 hydrotherapy, 538
 medical, 533, 534
 occupational therapy, 538–540, 547
 parking, 547
 physical therapy, 534–538, 547
 psychiatric services, 541, 542
 social services, 541, 542
 speech and hearing units, 540, 541
 vocational services, 542–547
 workshops, 542–547
Rehearsal halls, music, 443, 444
Research laboratories, 1155–1166
 medical school, 568–570
 nursing school, 609, 612, 614, 615
Research libraries (*See* Colleges and universities: libraries)
Residences:
 bathrooms, 69–85, 103–106, 115
 bedrooms, 30–42, 103, 134, 135
 closets, 86–97, 104
 dining areas, 17–27, 101, 128–131, 159, 181,
  323
 kitchens, 44–61, 102, 105, 106
 laundries, 61–68
 living rooms, 6–16
Resource facilities:
 college and university, 337–340
 learning resource centers, 228–230
Restaurants, 827–854
 booths, 835, 838, 842
 cashier's desk, 841
 dining areas, 827, 828, 831, 833–837
 employees' facilities, 841, 842
 liquor bar, 840
 lunch counter, 839
 kitchens, 843–854
 production areas, 828, 829
 receiving and storage, 829, 830
 sanitation, 830, 831
 seating, 834–838, 842
 serving, 832
 space requirements, 827, 828
 table and chair units, 834–837
Retail shops, 796–824
 barber, 815
 beauty parlor, 816
 book, 803, 812

Retail shops (*Cont.*):
 cleaners, 815
 counters in, 797–805
 displays, 797–806
 drugstores, 814, 818
 florists, 816
 gift, 812, 813
 jewelry, 808, 813–815
 liquor, 818, 819
 men's wear, 811, 812
 planning of, 794–799
 shoe, 803, 820–822
 shoe repair, 816
 shoe windows, 807
 storefronts, 784, 795
 supermarkets, 824, 825
 tailor and cleaner, 815
 women's wear, 808, 811
Riding schools, 1385, 1386
Rifle ranges, 1318–1328, 1356–1358
Roads, airport, 1069–1074
Roadways, industrial park, 1135
Room sizes:
 apartments, 100, 106, 126
 hospitals, 467, 469
 hotels, 979–981, 989, 999–1003
 housing for the elderly, 42
 motels, 988–990, 1011
Roque courts, 1205
Rowhouses, 784, 795
Running tracks, 1231

Schools:
 administrative suites, 225–227
 arts and crafts, 245, 246
 assembly hall, 236
 auditoriums, 236
 buses for, 214, 215
 cafeterias, 236, 252–258
 children's centers, 207, 208
 church, 665–672
 classrooms, 231–235, 237, 444
 colleges (*See* Colleges and universities)
 dental (*See* Dental schools)
 elementary, 209–272
 food services, 252–258
 guidance services, 271, 272
 gymnasiums, 236, 258–263
 high school, 219–224
 home arts, 251, 252
 industrial education shops, 250, 251
 junior high school, 219–224
 kinds, 218–224
 language laboratories, 240
 learning resource centers, 228–230
 libraries, 231
 lockers, 237–239, 261–268
 medical (*See* Medical schools)
 multipurpose rooms, 236, 237
 music facilities, 246–249, 444
 nursery schools, 203–206
 parking facilities, 214–216
 physical education facilities, 258–269
 planetariums, 245
 playgrounds, 215
 programming, 209–212
 recreational facilities, 215
 riding, 1385, 1386
 safety in, 216–218

Schools (*Cont.*):
science facilities, 240–245
secondary, 219–224
showers, 264, 265
site selection, 213, 214
sports facilities, 258–263, 267–269
swimming pools, 267–269
vocational education shops, 250, 251
working heights for students, 235
Science facilities, school, 240–245
dental, 584–590, 597, 598
medical, 568–578
Screens, movie theater, 1246, 1247
Sculpture studio, 454
Seaplane terminals, 1103, 1110
Seating:
auditoriums, 411–422
continental, 412, 414
conventional, 412, 414
lecture rooms, 275, 609–612
movie theaters, 1247–1249, 1251, 1252
music facilities, 246–249, 442–450
restaurants and eating places, 834–838, 842
sports arenas, 1305–1308
theaters, 411–422
Senior citizens' centers, 162–168
Service centers:
automobile, 938–943
neighborhood, 767, 768
truck, 956–959
Service equipment buildings, airport, 1081–1083
Service stations, automobile, 938–943
Sewing-laundry room, 68
Shooting ranges, 1318–1328
Shopping centers (*See* Regional shopping centers)
Shops:
automotive, 938–943
body shop, 944, 945
in rehabilitation centers, 542–547
retail, 796–824
school, 250, 251
Shot put areas, 1232
Shotgun ranges, 1357, 1358
Showrooms, automobile dealer, 947, 949
Shuffleboard courts, 1206
Sight lines, 402–405, 416, 418, 434
Site planning:
apartments, 109, 121–125
bowling alleys, 1257
churches, 643
and home owners' associations, 192, 193
and housing for the elderly, 126
libraries, 388, 390
marinas, 1333, 1334
medical schools, 562, 563
motels, 1006–1008
prisons, 728
schools, 213, 214
and subdivision layouts, 186–199
Skeet shooting ranges, 1329–1332
Slides, 1186, 1189
Soccer fields, 1225, 1226
Social centers, synogogue, 658–660
Softball fields, 1227, 1228, 1245
Space allotments:
boys' clubs, 755
bus terminals, 1112, 1113

Space allotments (*Cont.*):
dental schools, 587, 588
hotels, 991, 992
marinas, 1336–1339
motels, 1011, 1013
sports arenas, 1309
Speedball areas, 1229
Sports arenas, 1301–1309
operating requirements, 1308, 1309
plan configurations, 1302–1304
seating, 1305–1308
space allocations, 1309
Sports facilities:
colleges, 280, 281
public schools, 258–263, 267–269
Stables, 1379–1384
Stadiums, 1301–1309
Stages:
dance, 424, 428–433
drama, 424, 428
general, 408, 410, 435–437
multiuse, 427, 428
music-drama, 425
orchestral-choral, 425, 428
Stations:
automobile service, 938–943
fire, 703–707
police, 708–734
radio, 960–966
television, 967–971
STOL ports, 1099–1102
Storage facilities, residential, 66, 86–97, 104
Storefronts, retail shop, 784, 795
Stores (*See* Retail shops)
Street types, 188–194
Student unions, 322–330
Studios:
ballet, 429–432
music, 246–249, 442–450
radio, 955–960
television, 967–972
Subdivision layouts:
airport industrial parks, 1174–1177
in site planning, 186–199
Supermarkets, 823, 824
Surfaces, playfield, 215, 1244
Surgery offices:
general, 901
orthopedic, 901
plastic, 900
Surgical suites, hospital, 475, 476
Swimming, waterfront facilities, 1344, 1348–1351
Swimming docks, 1343, 1346–1351
Swimming pools, 262, 267–269, 749–751, 1266–1276
boys' club, 755–760
camp, 1344–1362
classification, 1266
dimensions, 749, 758
diving, 750, 751, 1014, 1266, 1269–1271
locker rooms, 261–267, 746, 747, 759, 760, 1278, 1279
motels, 1009, 1014
plans, 1266–1276
rehabilitation center, 537–538
sanitary facilities for, 1268
school, 267–269
wading, 537, 538

Swimming pools (*Cont.*):
YWCA building, 741, 754
Swings, play, 1184, 1185, 1188
Synagogues, 655–661
educational centers, 660, 661
social centers, 658–660
(*See also* Churches)

Table tennis areas, 329
Tailor and cleaner, 815
Team handball areas, 1230
Teletherapy units, hospital, 492–496
Television stations, 967–971
Television studios, 967–971
Temples (*See* Synagogues)
Tennis court, 1210
deck, 1207
indoor, 1300
nets, 1241
paddle, 1209
platform, 1208
table, 329
Terminals:
airport, 1038–1067
bus, 1111–1115
freight, 1117–1120
seaplane, 1103–1110
truck, 1117–1130
Testing centers, health, 622–628
Tether ball areas, 1211
Theaters, 392–410
amphitheaters, 439–441
community, 433–438, 463, 464
drive-in, 1255, 1256
house, 411–418
movie, 1246–1256
music facilities, 446–450
seating, 411–422
sight lines, 402–405, 416–418, 434
spatial requirements, 406–408, 433, 434
stage spaces, 408–410, 435–438
teaching stations, 442–444
types: arena, 395, 405
multiuse, 397–400, 427
open-thrust, 393
proscenium, 392, 393, 424, 425
Therapy facilities:
occupational, 500–503, 538–540, 547
physical, 497–500, 534–538, 547
Toilets, hotel, 182
Toilets, office, 889, 890
Toilets for the handicapped, 42, 775
Touch football area, 1221
Town halls, 675–679, 716, 717
Tracks, running, 1231
Trailers, 169–179
Trapshooting areas, 1240, 1329–1332
Treatment centers, youth, 616–621
Triple jump areas, 1236
Truck dealer facilities, 956–959
Truck dimensions, 1123, 1124
Truck docks, 1121, 1122, 1124, 1126–1130
clearances, 1122, 1123
parking 1122
service roads, 1125
Truck service facilities, 956–959
Truck terminals, 1117–1130
Turning radii:
for automobiles, 916

Turning radii (*Cont.*):
  for buses, 1114
  for trucks, 1121, 1122, 1135

Universities (*See* Colleges and universities)

Vault, pole, 1237
Vaults, bank, 825, 826
Volleyball courts, 1212
Vomitories, 1306, 1307

Wading pools, 1268
Warehouses, 1167–1173
Washroom facilities, 889, 890
Waterfront layouts, 1344, 1348–1351
Wheelchair dimensions, 143, 144, 1393
Women's wear shops, 808, 811

Woodworking shop, 461, 462, 766
Workshops:
  arts and crafts centers, 451–462
  in rehabilitation centers, 542–547
  in schools, 250, 251

X-ray suites (diagnostic), hospital, 484–489

YMCA and YWCA buildings, 741–754
  child-care facilities, 745
  design, 742, 743
  food services, 751–754
  health and recreation facilities, 745–751
  residential services, 753, 754
  sites of, 741, 742
  space areas for activities, 742–751
  swimming pools, 745–751

Youth hostels, 180–185
Youth treatment centers, 616–621
  area requirements, 616
  bedrooms, 618–621
  goals of, 616
  and halfway houses, 616
  kitchens, 617, 618
  site selection of, 617

Zoning and building codes, 108, 109
Zoos, 1283–1292
  animal exhibits, 1284–1289
  classification, 1283, 1284
  grounds, 1284, 1285
  hospital-quarantine facilities, 1289
  maintenance, 1289
  public services, 1290

ABOUT THE EDITORS

Joseph De Chiara is a practicing architect and city planner in New York City. He has taught at Columbia University, Pratt Institute, Cooper Union, the New York Institute of Technology, and the State University of New York at Farmingdale. He is the coauthor (with Lee E. Koppelman) of *Time-Saver Standards for Site Planning*, the author of *Handbook of Architectural Details for Commercial Buildings*, and the editor of *Time-Saver Standards for Residential Development*, all published by McGraw-Hill. Mr. De Chiara received a Bachelor of Architecture degree from Pratt Institute and an M.S. in city planning from Columbia University.

John Hancock Callender was formerly a professor of architecture at Pratt Institute and is now retired. He has been involved in research on new materials and methods of construction since 1932, including such subjects as industrial construction, curtain wall construction, arctic shelters, low-cost housing, and school construction. He has also taught at Columbia University and has directed research at Princeton University. Professor Callender is the editor in chief of McGraw-Hill's *Time-Saver Standards for Architectural Design Data*, currently in its sixth edition.